20

ESPN

Information Please®

Sports
Almanac

With Year in Review Commentary from ESPN anchors and analysts

Linda Cohn
*on the Top 20
Personalities*

Chris Berman
on Pro Football

Trey Wingo
*on the Top 20
Moments*

Dan Patrick
*on the Top 20
Personalities*

Stuart Scott
*on the Top 20
Moments*

Jerry Bembry *on Pro Basketball*	**Jack Edwards** *on Soccer*	**Dick Evans** *on Bowling*
Lee Corso *on College Football*	**Chris Fowler** *on College Basketball and College Football*	**Steve Levy** *on Pro Hockey*
Anne Marie Cruz *on Winter Olympics*		**Karl Ravech** *on Golf and Baseball*

D0204384

The Champions of 2002

Auto Racing
For all the statistics, see the Auto Racing section.

NASCAR Circuit
Daytona 500	Ward Burton
Coca-Cola Racing Family 600	Mark Martin
Brickyard 400	Bill Elliott
Mountain Dew Southern 500	Jeff Gordon
EA Sports 500	Dale Earnhardt Jr.
Winston Cup Points Leader	Tony Stewart, 4428 pts (through Oct. 27)

CART Circuit
CART Championship	Cristiano da Matta, 219 pts (through Oct. 27)

Indy Racing League Circuit
Indianapolis 500	Helio Castroneves
IRL Championship	Sam Hornish Jr., 531 pts

Formula One Circuit
U.S. Grand Prix	Rubens Barrichello
World Driving Champion	Michael Schumacher, 144 pts

Baseball
For all the statistics, see the Baseball section.

World Series	Anaheim def. San Francisco, 4 games to 3
MVP	Troy Glaus, Anaheim, 3B
ALCS	Anaheim def. Minnesota, 4 games to 1
NLCS	San Francisco def. St. Louis, 4 games to 1
All-Star Game	Tie, 7-7, in Milwaukee
MVP	none
College World Series	Texas 12, South Carolina 6
MVP	Huston Street, Texas, Fr., P

College Basketball
For all the statistics, see the College Basketball section.

Men's NCAA Tournament
Championship	Maryland 64, Indiana 52
MVP	Juan Dixon, Maryland, G

Women's NCAA Tournament
Championship	Connecticut 82, Oklahoma 70
MVP	Swin Cash, Connecticut, F

Pro Basketball
For all the statistics, see the Pro Basketball section.

NBA Finals	L.A. Lakers def. New Jersey, 4 games to 0
MVP	Shaquille O'Neal, L.A. Lakers, C
Eastern Final	New Jersey def. Boston, 4 games to 2
Western Final	L.A. Lakers def. Sacramento, 4 games to 3
All-Star Game	West 135, East 120 in Philadelphia
MVP	Kobe Bryant, West (L.A. Lakers), G

Bowling
For all the statistics, see the Bowling section.

Men's Major Championships
PBA World Championship	Doug Kent
ABC Masters	Brett Wolfe
BPAA U.S. Open (2001)	Mika Koivuniemi

Women's Major Championships
WIBC Queens	Kim Terrell
BPAA U.S. Open (2001)	Kim Terrell

College Football (2001)
For all the statistics, see the College Football section.

National Champions
AP	Miami-FL (12-0)
ESPN/USA Today Coaches'	Miami-FL (12-0)

Major Bowls
Rose	Miami-FL 37, Nebraska 14
Fiesta	Oregon 38, Colorado 16
Orange	Florida 56, Maryland 23
Sugar	LSU 47, Illinois 34
Heisman Trophy	Eric Crouch, Nebraska, QB

Pro Football (2001)
For all the statistics, see the Pro Football section.

Super Bowl XXXVI	New England 20, St. Louis 17
MVP	Tom Brady, New England, QB
AFC Championship	New England 24, Pittsburgh 17
NFC Championship	St. Louis 29, Philadelphia 24
Pro Bowl	AFC 38, NFC 30
MVP	Rich Gannon, Oakland, QB
CFL Grey Cup Final	Calgary 27, Winnipeg 19
MVP	Marcus Crandell, Calgary, QB

Golf
For all the statistics, see the Golf section.

Men's Major Championships
Masters	Tiger Woods
U.S. Open	Tiger Woods
British Open	Ernie Els
PGA Championship	Rich Beem

Seniors Major Championships
The Tradition	Jim Thorpe
PGA Seniors	Fuzzy Zoeller
U.S. Senior Open	Don Pooley
Senior Players Championship	Stewart Ginn

Women's Major Championships
Nabisco Championship	Annika Sorenstam
LPGA Championship	Se Ri Pak
U.S. Women's Open	Juli Inkster
Weetabix British Open	Karrie Webb

National Team Competition
Ryder Cup	Europe 15½, United States 12½
Solheim Cup	United States 15½, Europe 12½

Hockey
For all the statistics, see the Hockey section.

Stanley Cup	Detroit def. Carolina, 4 games to 1
MVP	Nicklas Lidstrom, Detroit, D
Eastern Final	Carolina def. Toronto, 4 games to 2
Western Final	Detroit def. Colorado, 4 games to 3
All-Star Game	World 8, North America 5 in Los Angeles
MVP	Eric Daze, North America (Chicago), LW

Horse Racing
For all the statistics, see the Horse Racing section.

Triple Crown Champions
Kentucky Derby	War Emblem (Victor Espinoza)
Preakness Stakes	War Emblem (Victor Espinoza)
Belmont Stakes	Sarava (Edgar Prado)

Harness Racing
Hambletonian	Chip Chip Hooray (Eric Ledford)
Little Brown Jug	Million Dollar Cam (Luc Oullette)

Soccer
For all the statistics, see the Soccer section.

World Cup Final	Brazil 2, Germany 0
MVP	Oliver Kahn, Germany, GK
MLS Cup	Los Angeles 1, New England 0 (2 OT)
MVP	Carlos Ruiz, Los Angeles, F

Tennis
For all the statistics, see the Tennis section.

Men's Grand Slam Championships
Australian Open	Thomas Johansson
French Open	Albert Costa
Wimbledon	Lleyton Hewitt
U.S. Open	Pete Sampras

Women's Grand Slam Championships
Australian Open	Jennifer Capriati
French Open	Serena Williams
Wimbledon	Serena Williams
U.S. Open	Serena Williams

Miscellaneous Champions
For more, see the Miscellaneous Sports section.

Little League World Series	Louisville, Ky.
Tour de France	Lance Armstrong (USA)
Iditarod	Martin Buser

2003

ESPN
Information Please®

Sports Almanac

Edited by

Gerry Brown

Michael Morrison

John Gettings
Associate Editor

Information Please
www.infoplease.com
Part of family EDUCATION network

HYPERION

ESPN® BOOKS

Editors
Gerry Brown, Michael Morrison

Associate Editor
John Gettings

Reporter
Chad van Dernoot

Production Editor & Graphics
Phyllis McKee

Database/Production Manager
Susan Hyde

Technical Support
Karl DeBisschop

Comments and suggestions from readers are invited. Because of the many letters received, however, it is not possible to respond personally to every correspondent. Nevertheless, all letters are welcome and each will be carefully considered. The **2003 ESPN Information Please Sports Almanac** does not rule on bets or wagers. Address all correspondence to: Sports, Information Please, 20 Park Plaza, Boston, MA 02116.
Email: ipsa@infoplease.com.

ISBN 0-7868-8715-X

FIRST EDITION

10 9 8 7 6 5 4 3 2 1

CONTENTS

6 CONTENTS

Upon picking up this book you may have said, "everybody knows and loves ESPN but what's with the Information Please in the title?" In fact you may not have even noticed it. Go ahead. Flip back and read the cover again. Information Please...this polite appellation has graced the cover of almanacs since before most of you were born. The name originates from a popular radio quiz show in the 1930s. Information Please almanacs were initially designed as a study companion to the radio show but soon took on a life of their own and have been published annually since 1947. The sports version sprang from the mind (and sweat, and broken phones) of Mike Meserole in the late 1980s and he created the very first Information Please Sports Almanac out of his bedroom back in 1989. A few of you still weren't even born yet. The book then joined forces with ESPN in the 1990s and we've been together ever since. So there you have it.

Like every year at this time, new challenges and adventures await but before we move on, we glance back briefly. Big thanks go to . . .

Production Editor Phyllis McKee for putting up with all of our last-minute changes, and to Susan Hyde for keeping the project on-time despite our best efforts. Thanks also to ESPN's John Hassan for making our lives a little easier, founding editor Mike Meserole for always remembering the Peggy Lawtons, Rick Sommers from Command Web, reporter/fact-checker and Packer backer Chad van Dernoot, the Hyperion dream team of Gretchen Young, Natalie Kaire, David Lott and Anton Markous, ESPN's Mary Moore, Jim Jenks, Craig Wachs, the entire Inside the Numbers team and all the ESPN contributors.

The book wouldn't be complete without the help of Infoplease's Borgna Brunner, Mike Rozett, Liz Kubik, Jess Brallier, Sean "Golden Goal" Dessureau, Karl DeBisschop, Boris Goldowsky, George Kane; ESPN's Russell Baxter, bowling guru Dick Evans, Russ Twoey of the PBA, Chris Murray of B.A.S.S., Doug Blodgett of the IGFA, Barbara Zidovsky of Nielsen Media Research, Rick Campbell and Gary Johnson of the NCAA, *Sports Business Daily*'s Bill Magrath, Carolyn McMahon from AP/Wide World Photos, Paul Michinard from Getty Images, Foulpole.com's Adam Polgreen, Adam Vinatieri and Christine Frantz for her World Series format.

Thanks also to our readers. We love your letters and while we don't always have time to answer each one, we do read them all. Please keep them coming.

Above all thanks to our wives: Lisa, Lori and Michele for putting up with football Sundays . . . and Saturdays for that matter. Not to mention Monday Night Football, Tuesday night golf after work, Wednesday night basketball, Thursday night poker and Friday Night Fights.

Finally, we borrow a passage used in the editor's note of the original Information Please Almanac written by founding editor John Kiernan more than 50 years ago. Some things don't change.

"There probably are some mistakes in this almanac, some errors in text and tables. We beg your indulgence for such lapses and we promise cheerfully to do better next year. In the interim, we hope you will like this almanac; it was made for you."

Gerry Brown
Michael Morrison
John Gettings

October 28, 2002
Boston

Major League Cities & Teams

As of Oct. 31, 2002, there were 131 major league teams playing or scheduled to play men's baseball, men's basketball, NFL football, hockey and men's soccer in 51 cities in the United States and Canada. Listed below are the cities and the teams that play there.

Anaheim
| AL | Angels |
| NHL | Mighty Ducks of Anaheim |

Atlanta
NL	Braves
NBA	Hawks
NFL	Falcons
NHL	Thrashers

Baltimore
| AL | Orioles |
| NFL | Ravens |

Boston
AL	Red Sox
NBA	Celtics
NFL	N.E. Patriots (Foxboro)
NHL	Bruins
MLS	N.E. Revolution (Foxboro)

Buffalo
| NFL | Bills (Orchard Park) |
| NHL | Sabres |

Calgary
| NHL | Flames |

Charlotte
| NFL | Carolina Panthers |

Chicago
AL	White Sox
NL	Cubs
NBA	Bulls
NFL	Bears
NHL	Blackhawks
MLS	Fire

Cincinnati
| NL | Reds |
| NFL | Bengals |

Cleveland
AL	Indians
NBA	Cavaliers
NFL	Browns

Columbus
| NHL | Blue Jackets |
| MLS | Crew |

Dallas
AL	Texas Rangers (Arlington)
NBA	Mavericks
NFL	Cowboys (Irving)
NHL	Stars
MLS	Burn

Denver
NL	Colorado Rockies
NBA	Nuggets
NFL	Broncos
NHL	Colorado Avalanche
MLS	Colorado Rapids

Detroit
AL	Tigers
NBA	Pistons (Auburn Hills)
NFL	Lions
NHL	Red Wings

East Rutherford
NBA	New Jersey Nets
NFL	New York Giants
NFL	New York Jets
NHL	New Jersey Devils
MLS	Metrostars

Edmonton
| NHL | Oilers |

Green Bay
| NFL | Packers |

Houston
NL	Astros
NBA	Rockets
NFL	Texans

Indianapolis
| NBA | Indiana Pacers |
| NFL | Colts |

Jacksonville
| NFL | Jaguars |

Kansas City
AL	Royals
NFL	Chiefs
MLS	Wizards

Los Angeles
NL	Dodgers
NBA	Clippers
NBA	Lakers
NHL	Kings
MLS	Galaxy

Memphis
| NBA | Grizzlies |

Miami
NL	Florida Marlins
NBA	Heat
NFL	Dolphins
NHL	Florida Panthers (Sunrise)

Milwaukee
| NL | Brewers |
| NBA | Bucks |

Minneapolis
AL	Minnesota Twins
NBA	Minnesota Timberwolves
NFL	Minnesota Vikings

Montreal
| NL | Expos |
| NHL | Canadiens |

Nashville
| NFL | Tennessee Titans |
| NHL | Predators |

New Orleans
| NBA | Hornets |
| NFL | Saints |

New York
AL	Yankees
NL	Mets (Flushing)
NBA	Knicks
NHL	Rangers
NHL	Islanders (Uniondale)

Oakland
AL	Athletics
NBA	Golden St. Warriors
NFL	Raiders

Orlando
| NBA | Magic |

Ottawa
| NHL | Senators (Kanata) |

Philadelphia
NL	Phillies
NBA	76ers
NFL	Eagles
NHL	Flyers

Phoenix
NL	Arizona Diamondbacks
NBA	Suns
NFL	Arizona Cardinals (Tempe)
NHL	Coyotes

Pittsburgh
NL	Pirates
NFL	Steelers
NHL	Penguins

Portland
| NBA | Trail Blazers |

Raleigh
| NHL | Carolina Hurricanes |

Sacramento
| NBA | Kings |

St. Louis
NL	Cardinals
NFL	Rams
NHL	Blues

St. Paul
| NHL | Minnesota Wild |

Salt Lake City
| NBA | Utah Jazz |

San Antonio
| NBA | Spurs |

San Diego
| NL | Padres |
| NFL | Chargers |

San Francisco
| NL | Giants |
| NFL | 49ers |

San Jose
| NHL | Sharks |
| MLS | Earthquakes |

Seattle
AL	Mariners
NBA	SuperSonics
NFL	Seahawks

Tampa
AL	T.B. Devil Rays (St. Petersburg)
NFL	T.B. Buccaneers
NHL	T.B. Lightning

Toronto
AL	Blue Jays
NBA	Raptors
NHL	Maple Leafs

Vancouver
| NHL | Canucks |

Washington
NBA	Wizards
NFL	Redskins (Raljon, Md.)
NHL	Capitals
MLS	D.C. United

Updates

After three failed attempts, the **Los Angeles Galaxy** finally won their first MLS Cup in 2002.

AP/Wide World Photos

AUTO RACING

Late 2002 Results
NASCAR

Date	Event	Location	Winner	Avg.mph	Earnings	Pole	Qual.mph
Oct. 20	Old Dominion 500	Martinsville	Kurt Busch	74.651	$142,175	R. Newman	92.837
Oct. 27	NAPA 500†	Atlanta	Kurt Busch	127.519	212,100	T. Stewart	–*

*Qualifying was cancelled due to inclement weather and the pole was awarded to the current Winston Cup points leader.
†Due to rain the NAPA 500 was shortened to 248 laps.
Winning Cars: FORD TAURUS (2)—Busch (2).
Remaining Races (3): Pop Secret 400 in Rockingham (Nov. 3); Checker Auto Parts 500 in Phoenix (Nov. 10); Ford 400 in Homestead-Miami (Nov. 17).

CART

Date	Event	Location	Winner	Time	Avg.mph	Pole	Qual.mph
Oct. 27	Honda Indy 300*	Queensland	Mario Dominguez	2:00:06.524	55.849	C. da Matta	111.547

Winning Cars: FORD/LOLA (1)—Dominguez.
Remaining Races (2): The 500 Presented by Toyota in Fontana, Calif. (Nov. 3); Mexico Grand Premio 2002 (Nov. 17).
*The Honda Indy 300 was shortened to 40 laps due to inclement weather.

NHRA

Date	Event		Winner	Time	MPH	2nd Place	Time	MPH
Oct. 27	ACDelco Nationals	Top Fuel	Larry Dixon	4.613	320.28	T. Schumacher	4.674	314.75
		Funny Car	John Force	4.820	305.22	T. Pedregon	4.869	301.94
		Pro Stock	Jeg Coughlin	6.969	198.55	W. Johnson	6.929	199.23

Remaining Event (1): Automobile Club of Southern California NHRA Finals in Pomona, Cal. (Nov. 7-10).

GOLF

Late 2002 Tournament Results
PGA Tour

Last Rd	Tournament	Winner	Earnings	Runner-Up
Oct. 20	The Disney Golf Classic	Bob Burns (263)	$666,000	C. DiMarco (264)
Oct. 27	Buick Challenge	Jonathan Byrd (261)	666,000	D. Toms (262)

Remaining Events (9): The Tour Championship (Oct. 31-Nov. 3); Southern Farm Bureau Classic (Oct. 31-Nov. 3); Hyundai Team Matches (Nov. 16-17); Franklin Templeton Shootout (Nov. 18-24); PGA Grand Slam of Golf (Nov. 26-27); The Skins Game (Nov. 25-Dec. 1); Target World Challenge (Dec. 2-8); World Golf Championships: EMC World Cup (Dec. 12-15); Wendy's Three-Tour Challenge (Dec. 21-22).
Note: The Tour Championship (Oct. 31-Nov. 3) is the final official PGA Tour event of 2002.

European PGA Tour

Last Rd	Tournament	Winner	Earnings	Runner-Up
Oct. 20	Cisco World Match Play Championship ..	Ernie Els (2&1)	£250,000	S. Garcia
Oct. 27	Telefonica Open de Madrid	Steen Tinning (265)	€233,330	3-way tie (266)

Remaining Events (3): Italian Open (Oct. 31-Nov. 3); Volvo Masters (Nov. 7-10); World Golf Championships: EMC World Cup (Nov. 12-15).
Second place ties (3 players or more): 3-WAY—**Madrid** (A. Coltart, B. Davis, A. Scott).

Senior PGA Tour

Last Rd	Tournament	Winner	Earnings	Runner-Up
Oct. 20	SBC Championship	Dana Quigley (201)	$217,500	B. Gilder (202)
Oct. 27	Senior Tour Championship	Tom Watson (274)	440,000	G. Morgan (276)

Remaining Events (4): Our Lucaya Senior Slam (Nov. 4-10); Hyundai Team Matches (Nov. 16-17); Office Depot Father-Son Challenge (Dec. 9-15); Wendy's Three-Tour Challenge (Dec. 21-22).

LPGA Tour

Last Rd	Tournament	Winner	Earnings	Runner-Up
Oct. 27	CJ Nine Bridges Classic ....:....	Se Ri Pak (213)	$225,000	C. Koch (219)

Remaining Events (4): Cisco World Ladies Match Play Championship (Oct. 31-Nov. 3); Mizuno Classic (Nov. 8-10); Hyundai Team Matches (Nov. 16-17); Tyco/ADT Championship (Nov. 21-24); Wendy's Three-Tour Challenge (Dec. 21-22).

TENNIS

Late 2002 Tournament Results
Men's Tour

Finals	Tournament	Winner	Earnings	Loser	Score
Oct. 6	AIG Japan Open (Tokyo)	Kenneth Carlsen	$111,600	M. Norman	76 63
Oct. 6	Kremlin Cup (Moscow)	Paul-Henri Mathieu	133,000	S. Schalken	46 62 60
Oct. 13	CA Tennis Trophy (Vienna)	Roger Federer	119,750	J. Novak	64 61 36 64
Oct. 13	Grand Prix of Tennis (Lyon)	Paul-Henri Mathieu	100,500	G. Kuerten	46 63 61
Oct. 20	TMS—Madrid	Andre Agassi	402,000	J. Novak	walkover

Finals	Tournament	Winner	Earnings	Loser	Score
Oct. 27	St. Petersburg Open ....Sebastien Grosjean		$133,000	M. Youzhny	75 64
Oct. 27	Stockholm Open.....................Paradorn Srichaphan		85,500	M. Rios	67 60 63 62
Oct. 27	Davidoff Swiss Indoors (Basel) ....David Nalbandian		133,000	F. Gonzalez	64 63 62

Remaining Events (4): Tennis Masters Series-Paris (Nov. 3); ATP Tour World Doubles Championship (Nov. 10); Tennis Masters Cup (Nov. 17); Davis Cup Final (Dec. 1).

Women's Tour

Finals	Tournament	Winner	Earnings	Loser	Score
Oct. 6	Kremlin Cup (Moscow) ....Magdalena Maleeva		$182,000	L. Davenport	57 63 76
Oct. 6	AIG Japan Open (Tokyo) ....Jill Craybas		27,000	S. Talaja	26 64 64
Oct. 13	Porsche Tennis Grand Prix (Filderstadt)...Kim Clijsters		97,000	D. Hantuchova	46 63 64
Oct. 20	Swisscom Challenge (Zurich) ....Patty Schnyder		182,000	L. Davenport	67 76 63
Oct. 20	VUB Open (Bratislava) ....Maja Matevzic		16,000	I. Benesova	60 61
Oct. 27	Generali Open (Linz)................Justine Henin		93,000	A. Stevenson	63 60
Oct. 27	Seat Open (Luxembourg) ....Kim Clijsters		35,000	M. Maleeva	61 62

Remaining Events (3): Fed Cup Final (Nov. 3); Sanex WTA Tour Championships (Nov. 10); Volvo Open (Nov. 10).

THOROUGHBRED RACING

Late 2002 Major Stakes Races

Date	Race	Location	Miles	Winner	Jockey	Purse
Sept. 28	Flower Bowl Invitational	Belmont	1 1/4 (T)	Kazzia	Jorge Chavez	$750,000
Sept. 29	Turf Classic Invitational	Belmont	1 1/2	Denon	Edgar Prado	750,000
Sept. 29	E.P. Taylor Stakes	Woodbine	1 1/4 (T)	Fraulein	Kevin Darley	750,000
Sept. 29	Canadian International*.....	Woodbine	1 1/2 (T)	Ballingarry	Michael Kinane	1,500,000
Oct. 2	Lady's Secret BC Handicap ..	Santa Anita	1 1/16	Azeri	Mike Smith	217,500
Oct. 5	Nofolk Stakes	Santa Anita	1 1/16	Kafwain	Victor Espinoza	200,000
Oct. 5	Yellow Ribbon Stakes	Santa Anita	1 1/4 (T)	Golden Apples	Patrick Valenzuela	500,000
Oct. 5	Frizette Stakes..............	Belmont	1 1/16	Storm Flag Flying	John Velazquez	500,000
Oct. 5	Champagne Stakes	Belmont	1 1/16	Toccet	Jorge Chavez	500,000
Oct. 5	Beldame Stakes	Belmont	1 1/8	Imperial Gesture	Jerry Bailey	750,000
Oct. 5	Kelso Handicap	Belmont	1 (T)	Green Fee	John Velazquez	350,000
Oct. 5	Futurity Stakes.............	Keeneland	1 1/16	Sky Mesa	Edgar Prado	434,800
Oct. 5	Ancient Title B.C. Handicap..	Santa Anita	6 F	Kalookan Queen	Alex Solis	207,875
Oct. 5	Oak Tree B.C. Mile	Santa Anita	1 (T)	Night Patrol	Jose Valdivia, Jr.	234,000
Oct. 6	Oak Leaf Stakes	Santa Anita	1 1/16	Composure	Mike Smith	200,000
Oct. 6	Goodwood B.C. Handicap ..	Santa Anita	1 1/8	Pleasantly Perfect	Alex Solis	500,000
Oct. 6	Clement L. Hirsch Turf Championship Stakes	Santa Anita	1 1/4 (T)	The Tin Man	Mike Smith	300,000
Oct. 6	Keeneland Turf Mile.........	Keeneland	1 (T)	Landseer	Edgar Prado	600,000
Oct. 6	Spinster Stakes	Keeneland	1 1/8	Take Charge Lady	Edgar Prado	546,000
Oct. 6	Prix de l'Arc de Triomphe*...	Longchamp	1 1/2 (T)	Marienbard	Frankie Dettori	€914,240
Oct. 12	My Dear Girl	Calder	1 1/16	Ivanavinalot	Manoel Cruz	400,000
Oct. 12	Calder Oaks................	Calder	1 1/8 T	Cellars Shiraz	Cornelio Velasquez	200,000
Oct. 12	In Reality Stakes...........	Calder	1 1/16	Trust N Luck	Cornelio Velasquez	400,000
Oct. 12	QE II Challenge Cup	Keeneland	1 1/8 (T)	Riskaverse	Mark Guidry	500,000
Oct. 13	Oak Tree Derby	Santa Anita	1 1/8	Johar	Alex Solis	150,000
Oct. 19	Empire Classic	Belmont	1 1/8	Gander	Richard Migliore	250,000
Oct. 20	TC of America Stakes	Keeneland	6F	French Riviera	Donnie Meche	125,000
Oct. 26	Carlton Draught Cox Plate*..	Moonee Valley	1 1/4 (T)	Northerly	Patrick Payne	2,000,000
Oct. 26	Breeders' Cup - Distaff	Arlington	1 1/8	Azeri	Mike Smith	2,161,760
Oct. 26	Breeders' Cup - Juv. Fillies....	Arlington	1 1/16	Storm Flag Flying	John Velazquez	916,000
Oct. 26	Breeders' Cup - Mile	Arlington	1 (T)	Domedriver	Thierry Thulliez	1,044,240
Oct. 26	Breeders' Cup - Sprint......	Arlington	6F	Orientate	Jerry Bailey	1,044,240
Oct. 26	Breeders' Cup - F&M Turf	Arlington	1 1/4 (T)	Starine	John Velazquez	1,172,480
Oct. 26	Breeders' Cup - Juvenile	Arlington	1 1/8	Vindication	Mike Smith	980,120
Oct. 26	Breeders' Cup - Turf*.......	Arlington	1 1/2 (T)	High Chaparral	Michael Kinane	2,216,720
Oct. 26	Breeders' Cup - Classic*.....	Arlington	1 1/4	Volponi	Jose Santos	3,664,000

*World Series Racing Championship race.

HARNESS RACING

Late 2002 Major Stakes Races

Date	Race	Raceway	Winner	Driver	Purse
Sept. 28	**Kentucky Futurity**............Lexington		Like A Prayer	Ron Pierce	$404,000
Oct. 26	**Messenger Stakes** ....The Meadows		Allamerican Ingot	David Miller	400,000

BOWLING

2002 Fall Tour Results
PBA

Final	Event	Winner	Earnings	Final	Runner-Up
Sept. 2	Dream Bowl 2002 (Yokohama)....Hugh Miller		$44,000	431-428	Yukio Yamazaki
Sept. 7	Oronamin C Japan Cup.........Robert Smith		50,000	224-222	Chris Barnes
Oct. 13	Wichita Open ....Dave D'Entremont		40,000	202-176	Chris Barnes
Oct. 20	Greater Kansas City Classic ......Pat Healey Jr.		40,000	243-227	Michael Gaither
Oct. 27	Memphis Open ....Brian Voss		40,000	253-247	Danny Wiseman

Remaining Events: See PBA 2002-03 schedule on page 763.

PWBA

Final	Event	Winner	Earnings	Final	Runner-Up
Oct. 3	Lady Ebonite Classic............Liz Johnson		$12,000	205-198	Leanne Barrette
Oct. 10	Greater Pasadena Open ....Tish Johnson		9,000	246-187	Liz Johnson
Oct. 18	Rollers and Pro Bowlers ....Tom Hein, John Handegard & Kim Terrell		15,000	668-617	Ziggy Traczenko, Hobo Boothe & Wendy Macpherson
Oct. 24	Wheelchair Awareness Classic....Tiffany Stanbrough		9,000	194-188	Kelly Kulick

Remaining Events: See PWBA fall schedule on page 764.

SOCCER

MLS Playoffs
Quarterfinals

Teams earn three points for a win and one point for a tie; first team to earn five points advances.

Date	Result
Sept. 25	at Dallas 4, Colorado 2
Sept. 28	at Colorado 1, Dallas 0
Oct. 2	Colorado 1, at Dallas 1 (Colorado advances in a series tiebreaker overtime after Game 3)

Date	Result
Sept. 25	Columbus 2, at San Jose 1
Sept. 28	at Columbus 2, San Jose 1 (Columbus wins series, 6 points to 0)

Date	Result
Sept. 26	at New England 2, Chicago 0
Sept. 29	at Chicago 2, New England 1
Oct. 2	at New England 2, Chicago 0 (New England wins series, 6 points to 3)

Date	Result
Sept. 25	at Los Angeles 3, Kansas City 2 (OT)
Sept. 28	at Kansas City 4, Los Angeles 1
Oct. 2	at Los Angeles 5, Kansas City 2 (Los Angeles wins series, 6 points to 3)

Semifinals

Date	Result
Oct. 5	at Los Angeles 4, Colorado 0
Oct. 9	Los Angeles 1, at Colorado 0 (Los Angeles wins series, 6 points to 0)

Date	Result
Oct. 6	Columbus 0, at New England 0
Oct. 9	New England 1, at Columbus 0
Oct. 17	at New England 2, Columbus 2 (OT) (New England wins series, 5 points to 2)

MLS Cup 2002

Los Angeles Galaxy def. New England Revolution, 1-0 (2OT)
Oct. 20 at Gillette Stadium, Foxboro, Mass.
Attendance: 61,316

	1	2	1OT	2OT	—F
Los Angeles	0	0	0	1	—1
New England	0	0	0	0	—0

Second Overtime: LA—Carlos Ruiz (Tyrone Marshall, Chris Albright), 113th minute.
MVP: Carlos Ruiz, Los Angeles, Forward

2002 U.S. Open Cup Final

Columbus Crew def. Los Angeles Galaxy, 1-0
Oct. 24 at Columbus Crew Stadium, Coloumbus, Ohio.
Attendance: 6,054

	1	2	—F
Columbus	1	0	—1
Los Angeles	0	0	—0

First Half: CLB-Freddy Garcia (Brian West), 30th minute.

2002 MLS Awards

Award	
Most Valuable Player ....Carlos Ruiz, LA, F
Rookie of the Year..................Kyle Martino, Clb, M
Coach of the Year ....Steve Nichol, NE
Defender of the Year ....Carlos Bocanegra, Chi
Goalkeeper of the Year ....Joe Cannon, SJ
Comeback Player of the Year ....Chris Klein, KC, M

MLS Best XI

Pos	Player	Pos	Player
F	Carlos Ruiz, Los Angeles	M	Ronnie Ekelund, San Jose
F	Taylor Twellman, New England	M	Oscar Pareja, Dallas
M	Jeff Cunningham, Columbus	D	Wade Barrett, San Jose
M	Steve Ralston, New England	D	Carlos Bocanegra, Chicago
M	Mark Chung, Colorado	D	Alexi Lalas, Los Angeles
		GK	Tim Howard, MetroStars

Personalities

Serena Williams won three Grand Slam singles titles in 2002, all over big sister Venus.

Top 20 Sports Personalities of 2002

Dan and Linda salute their top newsmakers of the year.

by **Dan Patrick** and **Linda Cohn**

Darryl Kile

The passing of the St. Louis Cardinals' spiritual leader could have divided the team. But, in a tribute to Kile's impact as a man, the loss unified the team. The Cardinals won 57 games after Kile's death, to equal his uniform number. They made the playoffs through sheer will, paying the ultimate tribute to their teammate. The team often had Kile's five-year-old son, Kannon, in the dugout for games. It must have done wonders for Kannon. And imagine what it did for the team.

The New England Patriots

Everything about their Super Bowl run was unlikely. The star quarterback, Drew Bledsoe, goes down in Game 2; the second year quarterback, Tom Brady, fills in more than capably, keeping the job even when Bledsoe returns; a head coach, Bill Belichick, who seemed best-suited as a coordinator; a defense on the small side, a virtually unknown running back; a record of 5–5 through ten games; the "Tuck Rule Game" in the snow against the Raiders; beating the Steelers soundly in Pittsburgh for the AFC Championship; and, finally, outplaying and outlasting the heavily favored Rams in the Super Bowl. By banding together so strongly, the 2001 Patriots proved that football is the ultimate team game.

Juan Dixon

The struggles he faced on the basketball court were nothing compared to what he went through in real life. Both his parents fell victim to heroin and eventually died of AIDS when he was still in high school. Basketball, even with the national spotlight shining on

Dan Patrick is a co-anchor on ESPN's SportsCenter and hosts The Dan Patrick Show from 1-4 p.m. EST, Monday through Friday on ESPN Radio.

AP/Wide World Photos

*Tragedy struck the Cardinals family in the early summer as veteran hurler, **Darryl Kile**, 33, died suddenly on June 22, just weeks after the team also lost legendary broadcaster Jack Buck.*

him, wasn't pressure. It was his escape. It was fun. So with Indiana up by two late in the national championship game, it was Dixon's time to have some fun. He calmly sank a three-pointer to put his Terrapins up by one, a lead he made sure they would never relinquish.

Oscar De La Hoya

You can call him a pretty boy or ask what a boxer is doing putting out albums, but don't ever question his guts or his willingness to suffer to stay on top. Not long ago Oscar De La Hoya was coming off the second loss of his career and could have left the punishment of boxing behind with more money than he could have ever wanted. The former lightweight didn't need to move up to junior middleweight and get tangled up with a power puncher like Fernando Vargas. But his heart got the best of his head, he got the best of Vargas, and we all got the best of De La Hoya.

Mike Bibby

He had a nondescript start in Vancouver. He still lived a bit in the

AP/Wide World Photos

*Baseball commissioner **Bud Selig** took a whole lot of heat in 2002, some of it deserved and some of it undeserved. Here he is deciding to halt the All-Star Game after 11 innings.*

shadow of his father Henry, the head coach at USC and an NCAA champion at UCLA. He was replacing the flashy and popular Jason Williams. And he wasn't even the biggest star on his own team. But in the playoffs, this David nearly slew the Goliaths from Los Angeles, taking his team one play away from the NBA Finals.

Pete Sampras

Unlike boxing, in which one punch can do the job, tennis requires two weeks of grueling effort. Because of that drawn out process, age matters in ten-nis. And we had seen Sampras labor recently through many tough losses. It seemed that the greatness that championships require had faded away. The only question was "When are you going to retire?" But now, after winning the 2002 U.S. Open over friendly rival Andre Agassi, things are different and a new question arises: Are you coming back to try and win it again?

Annika Sorenstam

Does anyone really know what kind of year this woman had? She out-Tigered Tiger in terms of sheer dominance. To recap: 20 events entered (at this writing), nine wins, 17 top tens, 15 top threes, one major victory and one missed cut. She has 17 wins in the last two years alone. Sorenstam's 2002 reminds me of Steffi Graf's 1988 when Graf won all four majors and the Olympic gold medal. The problem is that women's golf is just not in the same league as women's tennis. But Sorenstam has proven she is in a league of her own.

Michael Schumacher

While we're discussing sports that Americans don't care about, how about Michael Schumacher? In 2002 the man accomplished things in a race-car that no one ever had in the 53-year history of Formula One racing. In the 17 races on the F1 circuit, Schumacher won… eleven of them. And he was runner-up five more times. His "worst" showing of the year was a third-place finish in Malaysia. He must have stopped for coffee during the race. His naysayers claim the success is due more to the Ferrari he drives than to Schumacher himself. Just remember he won two championships in the mid-90's when he wasn't driving a Ferrari.

Bud Selig

The All-Star Game fiasco was not his fault. He can't help it if the managers are not playing to win. But that fits the year Bud had. I don't think he meant to contract any teams. But it was a scare tactic that worked. He also used the Sept. 11 anniversary and the public's take on drug testing to his advantage. He did what he had to do and kept the best interests of the game front and center. It all added up to the owners' first "win" in labor negotiations with the players' union.

Emmitt Smith

Everybody's gone. Jimmy, Troy, Michael, Moose, Deion. Only Emmitt remains. And plenty of people think he is staying around too long. But maybe he needed to outlast the other stars from his championship days for us to appreciate him. Even Emmitt admits that if Barry Sanders had kept playing, the record would be his. But Smith is now the NFL's all-time leading rusher. Considering the NFL's emphasis on the pass, Emmitt only missing five games in his whole career and the short careers of most running backs, this record may be his for a while.

* * *

AP/Wide World Photos

*Heavyweight champion **Lennox Lewis** silenced his critics, and more importantly, silenced Mike Tyson with an eighth-round knockout on June 8.*

Vonetta Flowers

All we really heard about the U.S. women's bobsled team before the Olympics was the soap opera surrounding lead driver Jean Racine and her band of brakewomen. But in the end it was "the other team" that grabbed the headlines. Jill Bakken and Vonetta Flowers steered clear of the drama, and steered their sled to U.S. gold over the favored Germans. Flowers became the first African-American, male or female, to win a Winter Olympic gold medal. When Racine came calling for her to join the "No. 1 sled" at the last minute, Flowers stayed loyal to Bakken. And the most amazing part of all? When she made her gold-medal run, she was two-months pregnant with twin boys.

Serena Williams

A tennis player hasn't been as dominant as Serena was in 2002 since

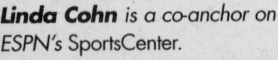

***Linda Cohn** is a co-anchor on ESPN's SportsCenter.*

Steffi Graf won everything in sight in the late 80's and early 90's. Serena won three Grand Slam titles, all over big sister Venus. The two sisters have truly turned the WTA Tour into a two-woman show, not to mention bringing fashion on the tennis court to new, eye-opening levels. If Serena hadn't hurt her ankle before the Australian Open, we could be talking about our first Grand Slam champion since Graf in 1988.

Saku Koivu

When he felt stomach pains just before the start of training camp, Canadiens captain Saku Koivu thought he just had a rough case of food poisoning. But it turned out to be so much worse. Koivu was diagnosed with a type of abdominal cancer that kills half of its victims within five years. Over the next several months, the 27-year-old went through the hell that comes with eight rounds of aggressive chemotherapy. Hockey was the last thing on his mind. In February, he was declared cancer-free. And on April 9, he made his triumphant return to the Molson Centre ice. A sold out crowd, most of which was in tears, greeted Koivu with an eight-minute standing ovation. Few things would make Canadians drown out the start of their own national anthem. This was one of them.

Mike Davis

Was there a more pressure-packed job in all of college basketball? In Indiana, basketball is more a religion than a sport. When Bobby Knight was ousted in 2000, it was up to the mild-mannered Davis to make sure the Hoosiers performed in a manner in which their fans were accustomed to. After a first-round loss to Kent State in the 2001 NCAA tournament, those fans called for his head. But at the 2002 tournament, they changed their tune, as Davis' leadership pushed the Hoosiers to a win over top-seeded Duke and an unexpected trip to the NCAA championship game.

Drew Bledsoe

Can a season that ends in a Super Bowl victory be bittersweet? It can if you're Drew Bledsoe. Forced to the sidelines in Week 2, Bledsoe had to watch someone else (Tom Brady) take the reins of his team. Where a lesser man would have whined and been a distraction, Bledsoe showed he didn't have a selfish bone in his body, keeping his mouth shut, except to give advice or encouragement to Brady. His selfless actions, and his inspiring touchdown pass in his cameo appearance in the AFC Championship Game against the Steelers were pivotal to the Patriots' Super Bowl win.

Jason Kidd

Even Michael Jordan never turned a team around this quickly. The Nets won 26 games in 2001 and had just seven winning seasons in their 25 years in the NBA! But behind Kidd's leadership and tenacity, the Nets won 52 games in 2002 and made it to the NBA Finals. Like Jordan, he makes others around him better and his presence legitimized an entire franchise.

Lennox Lewis

For years, the 6-foot-5, 250-pound heavyweight took much more abuse from critics than he ever did in the ring. Claims that he was "soft" only intensified when he was knocked out by little-known Hasim Rahman in 2001. In June 2002, however, Lewis proved them all wrong against perhaps the biggest mouth of them all, Mike Tyson. Lewis beat Tyson so thoroughly, he seemed to turn him into a nice guy. He pushed back his critics for the time being, and did his part in helping Tyson accomplish his wish to "just fade into Bolivian."

Cael Sanderson

How does a guy who doesn't lose—ever—stay so humble? Maybe his three brothers, all top-notch wrestlers, have something to do with it. Sanderson is the first wrestler in history to win four NCAA championships and go undefeated (159-0) in a four-year career. He became a living legend in the Midwest and single-handedly brought a heap of media attention to a sport that sadly doesn't get much.

George O'Leary

When it was discovered that he lied about his academic and athletic accomplishments on his resume, we all couldn't help but ask, "What in the world was he thinking?" O'Leary was forced to relinquish his title as head coach of Notre Dame, one of the most coveted jobs in college football, after just five days. And the scrutiny that followed led to even more firings and resignations throughout college sports.

Barry Bonds

Dan may have said it best in these pages last year, "Barry Bonds never asked to be loved." The accusations of him being a selfish, ego-centric player will be there no matter what he does. This year was much like his last couple of years. He fought with teammate Jeff Kent, fought off the usual steroid allegations, and once again put together one of the greatest offensive seasons ever. Unfortunately his MVP-like World Series performance wasn't quite enough to get him the first ring of his 17-year career.

Moments

Robert Horry's big buzzer-beating three-pointer against the Kings was a moment that Lakers fans won't soon forget.

AP/Wide World Photos

Top 20 Sports Moments of 2002

Stuart Scott and Trey Wingo give us their picks for the biggest moments of the year in sports.

by **Stuart Scott** and **Trey Wingo**

It's that time of year again. It's time to hand out the top 20 sports moments of the year. In 2001, it seemed like everything had a little different tone…Sept. 11 affected the sports world just as it impacted everything else.

This year, it was like a new beginning, a fresh start somehow. It's not that we *forgot* about Sept. 11. In fact I think it's quite the opposite. *Because* of Sept. 11 we realize how precious sports are and we understand their place.

The athletes aren't the real heroes. But we were also taught not to take *anything* for granted and to cherish each moment.

So in that spirit, let us cherish and remember these moments…

Stuart Scott
is an anchor/reporter on ESPN's SportsCenter.

Patriotic Super Bowl

The Rams were gonna win big, the Patriots didn't have a chance…Yeah, right. Thing is, New England didn't approve the script. They had a late rewrite and the team that started 1–3 and lost its starting quarterback beat down the high scoring Rams. They knocked the receivers silly, knocked Kurt Warner silly…and created the "non-Marshall factor." Star running back Marshall Faulk got less than 20 carries. The result? You know the ending by now. The Patriots were world champions.

Terps Take Title

They had never won a national title but had watched as three other ACC schools *had* won in the previous 20-years. But all year the Maryland Terps were convinced they were better than Duke and anybody else out there. And behind the huge heart of a 6–3 twig who could get his shot

AP/Wide World Photos

*The **New England Patriots** teamed up to shock the world in Super Bowl XXXVI, beating the Rams, 20-17, on Adam Vinatieri's momentous, game-ending field goal.*

off on anybody, they won the national title. Mad props to Juan Dixon, Gary Williams and the rest of the Terps.

Serena's Three Slams

I could put Serena Williams down three separate times, but that would be lazy. Instead I'll lump her French Open, Wimbledon and U.S. Open titles into one moment and just call her the athlete of the year...no...not the female athlete of the year...the athlete of the year. First, it became obvious that Serena and her sister Venus were the two best tennis players on Earth, just as their father had predicted. Then it became obvious

that Serena was better than Venus and everyone else. OK, sue me... I noticed her black outfit in the U.S. Open...but only a little.

St. Louis Woe

Their offense, the one that had scored 500 points three straight years, was intact. No reason to believe the Rams wouldn't be challenging for another Super Bowl in 2003. Then...*thud...pphhtt... nobody* could have guessed it: The Rams start out 0-5. Who whoulda thunk it? Probably the same people who thought the Patriots could win the Super Bowl last year.

AP/Wide World Photos

Could it be? Rain is his kryptonite? **Tiger Woods** *carded a mortal's round of 81 on the third day of the British Open at a rain-whipped Muirfield to dash his hopes of winning the Grand Slam in 2002.*

Another Green Jacket

They lengthened the course. Then they narrowed the course. So what? It didn't matter. Tiger won his second straight Masters and in the process absolutely dismantled the rest of the field or at least made them dismantle themselves. Mickelson? He imploded on Sunday. Singh? Ditto. Els? Ditto. Tiger? He's just mad he didn't hit that birdie putt on 18.

U.S. Open

No one had won the first two majors of the year since Jack Nicklaus three decades before, but no one had been this good...since Jack. In front of the most fun-filled gallery in memory at Bethpage Black on Long Island, New York. Tiger whipped the field again. The highlight of the tournament: Round one. After Tiger emerged from a porta-potty, he was greeted with a standing ovation. Then a fan said, "Hey Tiger, was that your one-iron you just used."

British Open

It would have been three-straight were it not for round three for Tiger, who was playing in the most brutal rain and wind he'd ever played in as a professional. He shot an 81. It was his worst score ever as a pro but he had no excuses. He was honest when he said,

"I played as well as I could have played." Now, we all know how long he can hit the ball. He said he caught a driver *flush*...and only hit it 200 yards. The 5-iron from 150 yards, a shot he can usually hit about 220, he hit it square...and came up short.

Tour de France

It's really very simple. We say this every year but he's the best there is. Lance Armstrong won his fourth straight Tour de France. No event is more grueling in sports and no man is more dominant. What he's been through, from almost losing his life to cancer to *this*...is phenomenal.

Home Field Disadvantage

When the world's tragedy affects the sports world everyone notices. Because of the Beltway Sniper in the Washington, D.C. area, local high school officials had to resort to holding football games at fields miles away from the schools with no one watching since times and locations for the games were only given to the teams which then played in front of empty stands.

Perfect Huskies

Oh, I almost forgot perfection. The UConn women's basketball team went undefeated on its way to winning its second national champi-

onships in the last three years. What can you say? College basketball is too tough. There are too many peaks and valleys over the course of the season. Even the best teams lose a game, right? *Aaannnggg!!* That's the wrong answer when it comes to UConn, no one person is perfect but this team sure was.

OK. That's my 10...good thing there were plenty to go around...I'm sure Trey will have no problem...

✵ ✵ ✵

Thanks, Stu. Here are my picks...

Super Introduction

Any discussion of sports events for me in 2002 deals with recovery, and the way the nation used sports to rebound in 2002 from what happened on Sept. 11, 2001. The one defining moment for me in that regard? Not the Patriots *winning* the Super Bowl, but *walking into* the Super Bowl. When the announcement came over the Superdome loudspeaker that the Patriots were going to be introduced as a team, rather than as individuals, I knew then they were going to win the game. The old saying goes that there is no "i" in team and there wasn't in the Patr*ots that night.

Trey Wingo *is a co-anchor on ESPN's SportsCenter*

Moment of Shame

The beauty of the Super Bowl of course was followed by the disaster in Salt Lake City. From a security perspective the Olympic Games were thankfully incident free, but when it came to figure skating they were also integrity free. The ridiculous judging of Canadian pairs skaters Jamie Salé and David Pelletier proved once and for all that skating judges are the farce many of us had thought they were for years anyway. My new motto is "down with Spandex and makeup in sports!"

Emmitt's Record Rush

Run, Emmitt, Run. #22 is now #1 on the NFL's all-time rushing list. Why this record doesn't get the respect it deserves is beyond me. The question that everyone seems to want answered is: Exactly how good is Emmitt Smith? Well, he's the only man with 11 1,000-yard seasons and he did it consecutively. Oh, by the way, his career yards per average? 4.3. In his 13th season...it's 4.2. The man ain't lost nuthin.

World Cup Run

America finally learns to play the world's game, putting behind them the disaster of France in 1998 when they finished 32nd out of...um...32. The American men, who nobody thought would make it out of pool play, exceeded all expectations and reached the quarterfinals in South Korea. The surprising run was much to the dismay of the rest of the globe, who clearly don't want Americans dominating yet another sport.

Mike Tyson Exposed!

Mike Tyson was exposed for what he has become: a shell of his former self. Lennox Lewis's eight-round tap dance on Iron Mike's face in Memphis ended any doubt that the only thing scary about Tyson now is his social agenda. And that's just sad. He could've been one of the greatest, instead of one of the greatest disappointments in heavyweight history.

Cards' Summer

I don't know if any team has ever had to deal with what the St. Louis Cardinals had to endure in the summer of 2002. In the span of a few weeks they lost their voice, in hall of fame announcer Jack Buck, and their soul, in starting pitcher Darryl Kile. Yet somehow, the Cards held it together, won their division and took out the defending World Series champion Diamondbacks in the playoffs before their emotional gas tank finally ran dry in October.

AP/Wide World Photos

*Goalkeeper **Brad Friedel** helped lead the United States to unprecedented success at the 2002 World Cup in South Korea. Friedel's brick-wall defense quickly cemented him as the team's starter throughout the tournament.*

Senior Moment

It was one for the ages, or the aged anyway. The surprising men's final at the U.S. Open typified the seasonal adage "fall back." Familiar foes Pete Sampras and Andre Agassi squared off one more time. As he has done before, Sampras took advantage of his killer serve to beat his old rival. This time it was for an unprecedented 14th Grand Slam singles title. The two men who simply defined Grand Slam tennis for a generation don't seem to be in a rush to concede that their generation is supposed to *be* history instead of making it.

Notre Dame is back

They say coaches don't win games, players do. That's true, unless, of course, Ty Willingham is your coach. What he did for the Fighting Irish in 2002 may be the single greatest job of motivation that college football has ever seen. Their big win over Florida State brought Notre Dame to 8–0 and inline for a major bowl game, if not a shot at a national championship. Aren't these *basically* the same players that nobody else could get to win? Willingham has my vote for national coach of the year in *every* category.

Canadian pairs skaters **Jamie Salé** *and* **David Pelletier** *couldn't believe the marks they received after skating a flawless final program at the 2002 Winter Olympics at Salt Lake City. Come to find out, they had reason to be incredulous. A judging scandal soon erupted.*

Lakers Three-peat

The Lakers' latest championship gave head coach Phil Jackson his third coaching three-peat. Think about *that* for a while. This three-peat also solidifies Shaquille O'Neal and Kobe Bryant as all-time greats. But of course, if not for a clutch Robert Horry three-pointer at the buzzer in Game 4 of the Western Conference finals, the Sacramento Kings or New Jersey Nets might now rule the roost. It seems that in every NBA postseason a role player makes an impact and for the Lakers in 2002, Horry was the guy.

Bud's Mess

Is there a commissioner in any sport less beloved or respected than baseball boss Bud Selig? From having no solid plan on how to resolve the All-Star Game when faced with a 7–7 tie in extra innings, to trying to contract a team that ended up making it to the ALCS, to barely averting a disastrous strike, Selig very nearly sunk the game of baseball single-handedly. But despite all the problems baseball faced in 2002, the game survived, which proved how great it actually is.

Calendar

Dallas Cowboys running back **Emmitt Smith** became the NFL's all-time leading rusher on Oct. 27, surpassing the late Walter Payton.

NOVEMBER 2001

Sun	Mon	Tue	Wed	Thu	Fri	Sat
					1	2	3
4	5	6	7	8	9	10
11	12	13	14	15	16	17
18	19	20	21	22	23	24
25	26	27	28	29	30	

Quote of the Month

"It makes no sense for Major League Baseball to be in markets that generate insufficient local revenues to justify the investment in the franchise."

Bud Selig, Major League Baseball commissioner, announcing on Nov. 6—less than 48 hours after one of the most exciting World Series in history—that the owners have decided to contract at least two teams before the 2002 season.

Major Downsizing

If Major League Baseball had eliminated teams before the 2002 season, it would have been the league's first reduction in more than 100 years. Here are the most recent instances of contraction in the four major men's pro leagues.

National League
1899—Baltimore Orioles, Washington Senators, Louisville Colonels and Cleveland Spiders are axed, cutting the league from 12 to eight franchises.

National Football League
1951—Baltimore Colts shut down, reducing number of teams from 13 to 12.

National Basketball Association
1954—Baltimore Bullets disband, thinning the number of teams from nine to eight.

National Hockey League
1978—Cleveland Barons and the Minnesota North Stars merge. The new franchise is located in Minnesota and leaves 17 teams remaining in the NHL.

Axis of Failure

By defeating Russia in its first Fed Cup final, Belgium joined the United States (17-8), Czechoslovakia (5-1), Spain (5-4) and France (1-0) as the only nations to claim winning records in Fed Cup finals since 1963. Here's how the rest of the world has fared.

South Africa	1-1
Australia	7-10
W. Germany/Germany	2-3
Switzerland	0-1
Netherlands	0-2
Russia	0-4
Great Britain	0-5

1 **Yankees 3B Scott Brosius** provides the ninth inning heroics and second baseman Alfonso Soriano adds a home run in the 10th, sparking New York to a 3-2 extra inning victory in Game 5 of the World Series.

Former Red Sox skipper Jimy Williams signs a three-year deal to manage the Houston Astros.

3 **Arkansas linebacker Jermaine Petty** stops Mississippi tight end Doug Zeigler short of scoring a two-point conversion, preserving the Hogs' 58-56 victory and ending the longest game in major-college football history after seven overtimes.

Junior welterweight champ Kostya Tszyu knocks out Zab Judah in the second round in Las Vegas, becoming the first boxer to unify the 140-pound titles in more than three decades.

4 **Arizona's Luis Gonzalez** flares a single over a drawn-in infield off ace closer Mariano Rivera, scoring Jay Bell and leading the Diamondbacks to a dramatic come-from-behind 3-2 victory over the N.Y. Yankees in Game 7 of the World Series.

Chicago safety Mike Brown intercepts a pass and scores the game-winning touchdown in overtime for the second straight week as the surprising Bears (6-1) beat the Browns 27-21 for their sixth victory in a row.

Ethiopia's Tesfay Jifar and Kenya's Margaret Okayo set new race records in winning the 32nd annual New York City Marathon.

6 **Baseball commissioner Bud Selig** announces plans for Major League Baseball owners to contract two teams before the 2002 season.

New Orleans lineman Kyle Turley is fined by the team and ordered to undergo counseling following his helmet-throwing tantrum late in the Saints loss to the Jets on Nov. 4.

Former Cowboys lineman Nate Newton is charged with possession with intent to distribute after police in Louisiana confiscate 213 pounds of hash from his van.

7 **Major League Baseball Players Association** officials file a grievance to block owners' plans to eliminate two teams before the 2002 season.

11 **Cardinals slugger Mark McGwire, 38,** tells ESPN he is "worn out" and retires from baseball after 16 major league seasons.

Teenagers Justine Henin and Kim Clijsters help Belgium clinch its first Fed Cup title, securing a 2-1 victory over Russia.

Winston Cup driver Ward Burton crashes into Ricky Rudd's car in pit row, striking and seriously injuring three pit crew members and a race official.

13 **Arizona ace Randy Johnson** wins his fourth Cy Young Award.

14 **Legislation geared at ending** baseball's exemption from federal antitrust laws is introduced on Capitol Hill by Sen. Paul Wellstone (D-Minn.) and U.S. Rep. John Conyers (D-Mich.) introduce.

Nine-time Olympic champion Carl Lewis is among four inductees into the National Track & Field Hall of Fame.

Duke basketball coach Mike Krzyzewski agrees to what officials call "a lifetime contract," or an extension of his current deal that will keep him at the school through at least 2011.

Former NL MVP Ken Caminiti is arrested on charges of drug possession after authorities find him in a Houston hotel room with crack cocaine.

15 **U.S. District Judge David Sam** tosses out the remaining 11 criminal fraud and conspiracy charges leveled against two former Salt Lake City Olympics organizers.

AP/Wide World Photos

Petitions bearing more than 110,000 signatures spell out "Twins" and form a baseball diamond on the Metrodome turf around representatives from Minnesota's Keep the Twins at Home organization. After this event on Nov. 26 the group delivered the papers to Major League Baseball owners in Chicago meeting to discuss the fate of their favorite team.

Yankees pitcher Roger Clemens wins his record sixth Cy Young Award.

Giants slugger Barry Bonds tells a San Francisco radio station that he received death threats during his pursuit of Mark McGwire's home run record.

16 A Minnesota judge rules that the Twins must fulfill their contractual obligation to play their 2002 home schedule at the Metrodome, apparently blocking baseball owners from contracting them before next season.

17 Heavyweight Lennox Lewis knocks out Hasim Rahman in the fourth round of their rematch in Las Vegas, becoming just the second three-time heavyweight champion in boxing history.

18 Australian tennis phenom Lleyton Hewitt, 20, defeats Sebastien Grosjean in the final of the Masters Cup and becomes the youngest male player to finish the year ranked #1.

Winston Cup driver Jeff Gordon finishes sixth in the NAPA 500 in Atlanta and clinches his fourth Winston Cup series title in nine seasons.

19 Giants slugger Barry Bonds wins a record fourth National League MVP award.

A federal judge dismisses the horse-doping case against trainer Bob Baffert, ruling that the facility in which Baffert's horse tested positive for morphine threw out the blood sample that could have proven Baffert's innocence.

Late Vikings lineman Korey Stringer is honored during a ceremony at halftime of the Vikings-Giants Monday Night Football game in Minnesota.

For the third straight Olympics the traditional torch lighting ceremony (which uses the sun's rays) is unsuccessful due to bad weather, giving the torch relay an inauspicious start to its journey to Salt Lake City.

20 Seattle outfielder Ichiro Suzuki adds the American League MVP award to the rookie of the year honors he claimed earlier in the month, joining Fred Lynn as the only players to win both awards in the same season.

Former major league manager Johnny Oates, 55, successfully undergoes surgery for a brain tumor.

24 Calgary quarterback Marcus Crandell throws for 309 yards and two touchdowns, leading the Stampeders to a 27-19 victory over Winnipeg in front of the second-largest Grey Cup audience ever (65,255).

25 Substitute Richard Morales' two goals in the game's final 20 minutes help Uruguay claim a 3-0 victory over Australia and earn the final berth in the 2002 World Cup. It will be Uruguay's first appearance in 12 years.

27 Commissioner Bud Selig has his contract extended through 2006 by baseball's owners.

Yankees third baseman Scott Brosius retires from baseball after 11 seasons and four World Series appearances.

San Francisco Judge David Garcia orders the baseball hit by Barry Bonds for his 73rd, and final, home run of 2001 be locked away until a trial answers whether it belongs to Alex Popov (who says he caught the ball but was robbed in the skirmish) or Patrick Hayashi (who says he found it loose in the pile).

DECEMBER 2001

Sun	Mon	Tue	Wed	Thu	Fri	Sat
						1
2	3	4	5	6	7	8
9	10	11	12	13	14	15
16	17	18	19	20	21	22
23	24	25	26	27	28	29
30	31					

Quote of the Month

"I don't think Cleveland will take a black eye from this. I like the fact that our fans care."

Carmen Policy, Cleveland Browns president, defending fans who endangered players, officials and other fans by hurling plastic beer bottles, cups of ice and other debris on to the field after a controversial call by officials in a Dec. 16 loss to Jacksonville. Policy apologized for the remark the next day.

Stronger Than Iron

If Cal Ripken Jr.'s consecutive games played streak makes him the Ironman, what does that make L.A. Lakers broadcaster Chick Hearn? Hearn broadcast **3,338 straight** Lakers games, dating back to Nov. 20, 1965, until emergency heart surgery on Dec. 19 caused him to miss his first game since the Johnson Administration. Here are some of the consecutive games played streaks that Hearn left in the dust.

Games	
2,362	Cal Ripken Jr. (MLB)
1,192	A.C. Green (NBA)
964	Doug Jarvis (NHL)
282	Jim Marshall (NFL)

Divide and Conquer

Division III Mt. Union College won its sixth college football championship on Dec. 15, more than any other school in its division. Here are the teams with the most football titles in each of the NCAA's four divisions.

Division	Team	Titles
I	Notre Dame	9
I-AA	Georgia Southern	6
II	North Dakota State	5
III	Mt Union (Ohio) College	6

2 **Notre Dame football coach Bob Davie** is fired just hours after his team concluded its 5-6 season.

3 **Orlando teenager Ty Tryon** becomes the youngest golfer in history to earn a spot on the PGA Tour after firing a final-round 66 to finish in the top 35 at qualifying school.

Florida Panthers coach Duane Sutter and GM Bill Torrey are fired and replaced by Mike Keenan and assistant GM Chuck Fletcher (interim).

5 **Former America's Cup skipper Peter Blake**, 53, of New Zealand, is attacked and killed by pirates during a trip to the Amazon.

Manager Joe Torre and the N.Y. Yankees announce a three-year, $16 million contract extension for the popular manager that was agreed to in October.

Indians manager Charlie Manuel, who was hospitalized twice during last season, undergoes surgery to remove his gallbladder.

Heavyweight champ Lennox Lewis files a lawsuit in Manhattan against Mike Tyson and the WBC, preventing Tyson from fighting Ray Mercer in January. The suit contends that such a fight would hurt Lewis financially.

6 **Baseball commissioner Bud Selig** testifies before the House Judiciary Committee, which is meeting to discuss baseball's antitrust exemption. Selig provides an unprecedented amount of financial data about America's national pastime, but committee members greet both his numbers and his responses with skepticism.

Penske Racing boss Roger Penske announces he's pulling his drivers (including defending champ Gil de Ferran) from CART, the open-wheel racing series he helped found, and taking them to the rival Indy Racing League in 2002.

Home Depot co-founder Arthur M. Blank agrees to buy the NFL's Atlanta Falcons for $545 million.

7 **Red Wings defenseman Nicklas Lidstrom**, 31, becomes the NHL's highest-paid defenseman, inking a two-year, $20 million deal with the team.

N.Y. Yankees outfielder David Justice is sent to the N.Y. Mets for third baseman Robin Ventura, marking just the sixth time since the Mets joined the league in 1962 that the crosstown rivals have exchanged players.

8 **LSU backup QB Matt Mauck** guides the Tigers to a 31-20 upset of Tennessee in the SEC Championship Game, knocking the Vols out of the Rose Bowl and causing an upheaval in the BCS standings.

N.Y. Knicks coach Jeff Van Gundy, 39, unexpectedly resigns as head coach of the team after a morning practice. Assistant Don Chaney replaces him and guides the Knicks to a 101-99 victory over the Pacers.

Nebraska QB Eric Crouch becomes the third Cornhusker to claim the Heisman Trophy, holding off Florida sophomore Rex Grossman by 62 points.

9 **Georgia Tech coach George O'Leary** is introduced as the new head football coach at Notre Dame.

10 **Alpine skier Bode Miller** becomes the first U.S. man to win a World Cup slalom since 1983—one day after accomplishing the same feat in the giant slalom.

N.Y. Knicks assistant Don Chaney is officially named head coach for the rest of the season.

11 **Cleveland Indians 2B Roberto Alomar** is traded to the N.Y. Mets as part of an eight-player deal.

NASCAR officials announce that starting next season all pit crew members and pit officials will be required to wear helmets and fire-resistant suits on pit row.

CART driver Dario Franchitti weds actress Ashley Judd at Skibo Castle in Franchitti's native Scotland.

AP/Wide World Photos

NFL officials at Cleveland Browns Stadium run for safety after their instant-replay-assisted call helps the visiting Jacksonville Jaguars secure a 15-10 victory on Dec. 16, causing rabid Browns fans to throw debris on to the field, halting the game for a half-hour.

12 Denver Nuggets coach Dan Issel is suspended by the team for four games after shouting profanity and ethnic remarks to a fan after a loss to the Hornets a night earlier.

Former Cowboys lineman Nate Newton is arrested on drug-possession charges for the second time in the last six weeks.

13 American League MVP Jason Giambi's seven-year, $120 million free agent deal with the N.Y. Yankees is made public after weeks of rumors.

14 Notre Dame football coach George O'Leary announces his resignation—five days after accepting the job—admitting to inaccuracies that were uncovered in his resume.

U.S. women's bobsled driver Jean Racine drops longtime pusher and friend Jen Davidson, replacing her with former track star Gea Johnson.

15 WBA heavyweight champion John Ruiz retains his title by virtue of a draw with Evander Holyfield at Foxwoods Casino in Connecticut.

Golden State coach Dave Cowens is fired and replaced on an interim basis by assistant Brian Winters.

Running back Chuck Moore rushes for 273 yards, leading Mount Union (Ohio) to a 30-27 victory over Bridgewater (Va.) and its sixth NCAA Div. III football title.

16 Rookie QB Mike McMahon leads the Detroit Lions to a 27-24 victory over Minnesota, snapping the team's season-opening losing streak at 12 games.

17 Redskins corner Darrell Green rescinds his plans to retire after the season, citing the fans reaction and an improved relationship with coach Marty Schottenheimer.

Angry Saints fans hurl beer bottles and cups onto the field after a second-half pass interference call, resulting in a brief interruption of the game and the arrest of 13 people. It's the second time in as many days that angry fans have disrupted an NFL game.

18 N.Y. Yankees free agent Tino Martinez signs a three-year deal with the St. Louis Cardinals to replace the recently retired Mark McGwire.

19 Orlando Magic forward Grant Hill will miss the remainder of the 2001-02 season after undergoing surgery today in Baltimore on his troublesome left ankle.

20 Boston Red Sox's limited partners vote unanimously to sell the team to a group led by Florida Marlins owner John Henry for a record $660 million.

L.A. Lakers broadcaster Chick Hearn misses his first game in more than 36 years after undergoing successful heart surgery which will keep him out of the broadcast booth for at least six weeks.

24 Bulls coach Tim Floyd resigns after compiling a 49-190 record in three-plus seasons with the team. Assistant Bill Berry replaces Floyd on an interim basis.

26 Nuggets coach Dan Issel is fired two weeks after his suspension for shouting profanity and making an ethnic remark to a fan. Assistant Mike Evans takes over the team.

27 Angels 1B Mo Vaughn is traded to the N.Y. Mets for pitcher Kevin Appier.

Wizards star Michael Jordan is held to six points by the Indiana Pacers, ending a streak of 866 straight NBA games in which he scored double-digit points.

JANUARY 2002

Sun	Mon	Tue	Wed	Thu	Fri	Sat
		1	2	3	4	5
6	7	8	9	10	11	12
13	14	15	16	17	18	19
20	21	22	23	24	25	26
27	28	29	30	31		

Quote of the Month

"I want DQs to continue to be as professionally managed as they are, which when combined with my love of Blizzards led me to issue my public warning to their senior management about potential employees."

Mark Cuban, Dallas Mavericks owner with tongue firmly planted in cheek, explaining his outburst after a game on Jan. 5 in which he said the NBA's head of officials, Ed Rush, may have been a great ref but he wouldn't hire him to manage a Dairy Queen restaurant.

"Coach Superior"

It didn't take long for Florida Gators coach Steve Spurrier to leave his mark on the Southeastern Conference. His 87 regular-season conference victories rank fifth all-time among SEC coaches.

Coach	School(s)	Seasons	Wins
Paul "Bear" Bryant	Kentucky/Alabama	33	159
John Vaught	Ole Miss	25	106
Vince Dooley	Georgia	25	105
Ralph "Shug" Jordan	Auburn	25	98
Steve Spurrier	Florida	12	87

Holding Court

They sure don't make home-court winning streaks in men's college basketball like they used to. When Michigan State's 53-game streak at the Breslin Center was snapped on Jan. 12 it was the longest active streak in Division I, but it was still light-years behind the all-time leader Kentucky.

Wins	Team	Seasons	Ended By
129	Kentucky	1943-45	Georgia Tech
99	St. Bonaventure	1948-61	Niagara
98	UCLA	1970-76	Oregon
86	Cincinnati	1957-64	Bradley

1 **Stanford coach Tyrone Willingham** is announced as the new head football coach at Notre Dame, becoming the first black head coach at the school in any sport. The announcement comes less than three weeks after the school's first choice, Georgia Tech's George O'Leary, resigned over inaccuracies uncovered in his resume.

Former heavyweight champ Mike Tyson rings in the new year by shouting insults in Spanish and English and throwing glass ornaments at journalists trying to interview him after arriving in Havana, Cuba.

2 **MLS Commissioner Don Garber** announces a new television deal that gives ESPN and ABC broadcasting rights for the next five seasons of Major League Soccer and the next three soccer World Cups.

4 **Florida Gators coach Steve Spurrier** shocks the football world, resigning after 12 seasons in which he led the Gators to six SEC titles and one national championship.

Minnesota Vikings coach Dennis Green is fired, ending his 10-year tenure with the team. Offensive line coach Mike Tice replaces him for the team's final game on Jan 7.

Third-base coach Ron Gardenhire is hired to replace Tom Kelly as manager of the Minnesota Twins.

The wife of Wizards president Michael Jordan, Juanita Jordan, files for divorce from her husband of 12 years, citing "irreconcilable differences."

Short-track speedskater Tommy O'Hare asks the U.S. Olympic Committee to investigate his claim that an Olympic qualifying race won by teammate Shani Davis (which knocked O'Hare out of the upcoming Winter Games) was fixed.

8 **Colts coach Jim Mora** is fired after refusing to fire defensive coordinator Vic Fangio.

Major League Soccer contracts, eliminating its two Florida franchises—the Miami Fusion and Tampa Bay Mutiny.

Former Cardinals shortstop Ozzie Smith is voted into the Baseball Hall of Fame and becomes the 37th player elected on his first ballot.

Former Gold Club owner Steve Kaplan is sentenced to 16 months in prison for his role in a racketeering case in which prosecutors claimed his strip club provided sex to pro athletes and laundered money for the Mob.

11 **Defending champion Michelle Kwan** captures her fifth consecutive U.S. figure skating title (and sixth overall) at the Staples Center in Los Angeles.

Orlando Magic owner Rich DeVos unexpectedly puts the franchise up for sale.

12 **Spartan guard Kelvin Torbert's** final-second alley-oop layup is disallowed and visiting Wisconsin captures a 64-63 victory over Michigan State, snapping the Spartan's 53-game home-court winning streak.

13 **Redskins owner Daniel Snyder** fires head coach Marty Schottenheimer, citing "philosophical differences" with his first-year coach.

14 **Buccaneers coach Tony Dungy** is fired, despite being the most successful coach in franchise history at 54-42.

Former Florida coach Steve Spurrier signs a five-year, $25 million deal to coach the Washington Redskins, making him the NFL's highest-paid coach.

15 **NCAA president Cedric Dempsey** announces his retirement effective Dec. 31, 2002 after eight years in office.

Disgruntled L.A. outfielder Gary Sheffield is dealt from the Dodgers to the Atlanta Braves for Brian Jordan, Odalis Perez and minor-league pitcher Andy Brown.

The family of deceased Vikings lineman Korey Stringer files a $100 million wrongful death suit.

AP/Wide World Photos

A brawl erupted inside New York's Hudson Theater on Jan 22 after former heavyweight champion Mike Tyson kicked off the promotional event for his much anticipated bout with Lennox Lewis by throwing a punch at one of Lewis' bodyguards.

16 **Baseball's owners approve** the $660 million sale of the Boston Red Sox to a group led by Marlins owner John Henry, hours after the Massachusetts attorney general was assured that more money in the deal will go to charity and dropped his office's investigation.

Austrian alpine star Hermann Maier officially pulls out of the Salt Lake City Olympics, ending his bid to comeback from a broken leg in time to defend his two gold medals.

Mavericks owner Mark Cuban works at a Dairy Queen in Coppell, Texas, making good on an offer he made with DQ officials after mentioning the franchise in his criticism of the head of the NBA's officials on Jan. 5.

22 **Fox broadcaster Pat Summerall** announces he will not return for a 22nd season alongside John Madden.

Former Buccaneers coach Tony Dungy signs a five-year, $13 million deal to coach the Indianapolis Colts.

Former Olympian Jack Shea, 91, the oldest living winter Olympics champion and the first of three generations of Olympians, dies of injuries sustained in a car crash a day earlier near his home in Lake Placid, N.Y.

24 **U.S. speedskater Tommy O'Hare** withdraws his request for arbitration in the case that a fixed race kept him off the U.S. Olympic team.

Teenage phenom Ty Tryon makes his professional debut on the PGA Tour, struggling to a 6-over-par 77 in the first round of the Phoenix Open.

25 **U.S. skier Picabo Street** finishes 33rd in a World Cup Super-G race in Italy, meaning she won't get a chance to defend her gold medal in the event at the Salt Lake City Games. She has already qualified for the downhill.

Dallas Stars coach Ken Hitchcock is fired less than three years after he led the team to its first Stanley Cup.

N.Y. Giants defensive coordinator John Fox is hired to coach the Carolina Panthers.

U.S. bobsleder Jen Davidson drops her grievance against driver Jean Racine after an arbitrator listened to her proposal of a race-off to determine Racine's pusher at next month's Olympics.

26 **Tennis star Jennifer Capriati** outduels Martina Hingis to win her second straight Australian Open title.

27 **Sweden's Thomas Johansson** (16th seed) beats Marat Safin in a nearly three-hour final match at the Australian Open, claiming his first ever Grand Slam title.

28 **New Jersey Devils coach Larry Robinson** is fired and replaced by Kevin Constantine.

Kentucky Derby champ Monarchos retires to stud following an ankle injury suffered last week.

29 **Ousted Redskins coach Marty Schottenheimer** inks a four-year, $10 million deal to coach the San Diego Chargers.

The Nevada Athletic Commission denies Mike Tyson a license to fight Lennox Lewis in the state, eliminating Las Vegas as a host for their heavyweight title fight.

30 **Patriots coach Bill Belichick** names Tom Brady his starting quarterback for Super Bowl XXXVI, ending three days of media speculation about whether backup Drew Bledsoe would replace the injured Brady.

31 **Sports agent William "Tank" Black** is convicted of swindling up to $14 million from pro football players he represented and faces up to 25 years in prison.

FEBRUARY 2002

Sun	Mon	Tue	Wed	Thu	Fri	Sat
					1	2
3	4	5	6	7	8	9
10	11	12	13	14	15	16
17	18	19	20	21	22	23
24	25	26	27	28		

Quote of the Month

"I have kind of mixed feelings. It's kind of fun to have a record, but it's not too much fun to get hit five times."

Carlos Quentin, Stanford right fielder, explaining how he feels about setting an NCAA record by getting hit by pitches five times in a 15-11 victory at Florida State on Feb. 11.

Still Short of the Miracle

The live broadcast of the men's ice hockey Olympic gold medal game between Canada and the United States was the highest-rated hockey game in the United States—NHL or Olympic—since the Miracle on Ice in 1980. The following is a list of the most watched hockey games in the U.S.

Rating	Game	Year
23.9	Olympics: Men's semifinal (US vs. USSR)	1980
23.2	Olympics: Men's final (US vs. Finland)	1980
10.7	Olympics: Men's final (US vs. Canada)	2002
7.2	Olympics: Men's semifinal (US vs. Russia)	2002
4.9	Olympics: Medal round (US vs. Canada)	1998
4.4	NHL: Islanders vs. Flyers (Game 7 Stanley Cup Finals)	1980

Note: With the exception of the US-USSR game, all of the above were broadcast live.

League Bowlers

Tampa Bay Buccaneers guard Randall McDaniel, who retired after 14 NFL seasons on Feb. 25, now has time to reflect on a career that will land him in the hall of fame. Take a look at the exclusive company he finds himself in after compiling 12 consecutive Pro Bowl appearances.

App.		
14	Bruce Matthews, C	1989–2002
13	Reggie White, DE	1987–99
12	Randall McDaniel, G	1990–2001
11	Anthony Munoz, OT	1982–92
11	Jerry Rice, WR	1987–97
11	Junior Seau, LB	1992–2002*

*Active streak

1 **The NCAA hands** the Alabama football program five years probation, a two-year bowl ban and heavy scholarship reductions for recruiting violations, which occurred under former coaches Mike Dubose and Gene Stallings.

U.S. keeper Kasey Keller records his fourth shutout in his last five games, leading the men's national team to a 2-0 upset of Costa Rica in the CONCACAF Gold Cup final.

3 **New England Patriots kicker Adam Vinatieri** kicks a 48-yard field goal as time expires, completing a 20-17 upset victory over the St. Louis Rams in Super Bowl XXXVI in New Orleans.

4 **The Minnesota Supreme Court** refuses to consider baseball's appeal of an injunction that forces the Twins to fulfill their Metrodome lease in 2002, effectively ending any hopes baseball had of contracting the Twins before the 2002 season.

5 **Baseball commissioner Bud Selig** tells the media that baseball won't try to eliminate teams this season but will try again in 2003.

6 **Former Orioles star Cal Ripken Jr.** buys the Utica Blue Sox of the Class A N.Y. Penn League and plans to relocate them to his hometown of Aberdeen, Md.

7 **Montreal Canadiens captain Saku Koivu** announces the stomach cancer that has sidelined him this season is in full remission and tells the media he could be back before the end of the season.

8 **Members of the 1980 Miracle on Ice team** light the Olympic cauldron, culminating the 13,500-mile torch relay and the Opening Ceremonies of the XIX Winter Games in Salt Lake City.

9 **Raiders quarterback Rich Gannon** wins his second straight Pro Bowl MVP award, leading the AFC to a 38-30 victory over the NFC in Honolulu.

10 **All-Star Game MVP Kobe Bryant** says the boos he received from the Philadelphia crowd hurt, but he still manages to lead the West to a 135-120 victory over the East.

UConn defender Chris Gbandi is selected first overall by the Dallas Burn in Major League Soccer's Super-Draft.

Russian Svetlana Feofanova sets her third world record in the women's pole vault this week, clearing 15-6¼ in Ghent, Belgium to establish a new indoor mark.

Tampa Bay Lightning GM Rick Dudley steps down and is replaced by assistant Jay Feaster.

11 **Canadians Jamie Sale and David Pelletier** find themselves in the middle of figure skating's latest controversy when rumors surface that their second-place finish in the pairs competition was fixed by judges.

Ravens defensive guru Marvin Lewis, who was passed over for the head coach job in Tampa Bay earlier this month, signs a three-year deal with the Washington Redskins that makes him the NFL's highest-paid assistant.

12 **Hall of Famer Frank Robinson** is named the new manager of the Montreal Expos after baseball owners unanimously approve the sale of the Expos to Major League Baseball and the sale of the Marlins to former Expos owner Jeffrey Loria.

13 **International Skating Union President** Ottavio Cinquanta faces an angry world press and announces that the ISU will investigate charges that figure skating judge Marie-Reine Le Gougne was pressured into voting for the Russians in the pairs competition.

14 **Limousine driver Costas Christofi**, 55, is found shot to death in the master bedroom of the New Jersey estate owned by former NBA star Jayson Williams.

AP/Wide World Photos

Canadian ice hockey fans on Saint Catherine Street in Montreal celebrate Canada's Olympic gold medal victory over the United States on Feb. 24 by spending the whole evening riding on top of city buses, instead of in them.

15 **President Jacques Rogge announces** that the executive board of the International Olympic Committee will upgrade the silver medals awarded to Canadian pairs figure skaters Jaime Sale and David Pelletier to golds.

U.S. athletes claim three medals, boosting the country's medal total to 14—a new Winter Games record.

17 **Canadians Jamie Sale and David Pelletier** share the top step of a medal podium with Russians Elena Berezhnaya and Anton Sikharulidze during a special medal ceremony where they receive gold medals.

Winston Cup driver Ward Burton avoids an 18-car wreck with 51 laps to go and claims his first Daytona 500 checkered flag.

18 **Jacksonville Jaguars tackle Tony Boselli** is the first of 19 players chosen by the Houston Texans in today's NFL's expansion draft.

Former Raiders head coach Jon Gruden agrees to a five-year deal to coach the Tampa Bay Buccaneers.

Belmont and Preakness champ Point Given receives the Eclipse Award for 2001 Horse of the Year.

19 **Pacers swingman Jalen Rose** and guard Travis Best highlight a seven-player swap with the Chicago Bulls that is completed two days before the NBA's trading deadline.

U.S. bobsledder Vonetta Flowers becomes the first African-American to win an Olympic Winter Games gold medal, pushing teammate Jill Bakken to a historic victory in the first-ever women's bobsled event.

20 **Belarus forward Vladimir Kopat's** 80-foot slapshot gets past Sweden goalie Tommy Salo, eliminating one of the tournament favorites in a shocking 4-3 upset in the Olympic men's ice hockey quarterfinals.

NBA Hall of Famer Kareem Abdul-Jabbar accepts his first coaching job, heading up the Oklahoma Storm of the U.S. Basketball League.

21 **American figure skater Sarah Hughes** skates a flawless long program, vaulting her from fourth place to first in the women's singles event at the Winter Games. Hughes' upset victory means still no Olympic gold medal for four-time world champion Michelle Kwan.

Delegations from Russia and Korea threaten to boycott the rest of the 2002 Winter Games, claiming a favorable judging bias for North American countries.

Denver Nuggets' top scorers Raef LaFrentz and Nick Van Exel plus two others are dealt to the Mavericks in return for Juwan Howard, Tim Hardaway, Donnell Harvey, a draft pick and $1 million in cash.

24 **Goalie Martin Brodeur** stops 31 shots in a 5-2 victory over the U.S. in the Olympic men's ice hockey title game, earning Canada its first hockey gold medal in 50 years.

25 **Former NBA star Jayson Williams** surrenders to New Jersey state police and is charged with manslaughter in the shooting death of his limousine driver.

Buccaneers guard Randall McDaniel retires from the NFL after 14 seasons with Minnesota and Tampa Bay.

26 **Wizards star Michael Jordan** is placed on injured reserve while he undergoes arthroscopic surgery on his right knee.

28 **Red Sox GM Dan Duquette** is fired by the team's new owners and replaced by Mike Port, vice president of baseball operations.

Fox NFL analyst John Madden agrees to join ABC for its Monday Night Football broadcasts next season.

MARCH 2002

Sun	Mon	Tue	Wed	Thu	Fri	Sat
					1	2
3	4	5	6	7	8	9
10	11	12	13	14	15	16
17	18	19	20	21	22	23
24	25	26	27	28	29	30
31						

Quote of the Month

"Judge Judy has a better understanding of the game right now than (NHL vice president of hockey operations) Colin Campbell, I bet. I got convicted and there was no murder."

Jyrki Lumme, Toronto Maple Leafs defenseman, expressing his displeasure with the two-game suspension he was given for cross-checking Buffalo's J.P. Dumont in the face during a game on March 2.

Best Ever?

The University of Connecticut women's basketball team wrapped up another undefeated season on March 31. The 2001-02 Huskies were the fourth women's team—and second UConn team—to go undefeated since women's hoops became an NCAA sport.

Season	School	Record	Margin
1985-86	Texas	34–0	26.7
1994-95	Connecticut	35–0	33.2
1997-98	Tennessee	39–0	30.1
2001-02	Connecticut	39–0	35.4

Mush Quicker Than The Rest

On March 12, Martin Buser, of Big Lake, Alaska, became the first driver to complete the Iditarod Sled Dog race in less than nine days. Buser's record pace on the race's 1,151-mile Northern Route helped two other drivers from this year's race break into the top five all-time fastest times.

Time	Driver	Year	Place
8 days, 22 hrs., 48 min.	Martin Buser	2002	1st
9 days, 49 min.	Ramy Brooks	2002	2nd
9 days, 58 min.	Doug Swingley	2000	1st
9 days, 5 hrs., 43 min.	Jeff King	1996	1st
9 days, 5 hrs., 46 min.	John Baker	2002	3rd

Note: Excluded from this table are times recorded on the race's Southern Route (odd-numbered years), which is 10-miles longer than the Northern Route. If those times were included, Doug Swingley's first-place time of 9 days, 2 hrs., 42 min. in 1995 would be in fourth place.

1 **Arkansas hoops coach Nolan Richardson** has the remainder of his $3 million contract bought out by the school, capping a week in which the coach complained he was mistreated because he is black.

2 **North Carolina midfielder Pat Jackson** scores with 21 seconds left in the sixth overtime period, giving UNC an 11-10 victory over Navy in the longest men's college lacrosse game ever.

3 **Kansas forward Nick Collison** scores 28 points, leading the Jayhawks men's basketball team to a 95-92 victory over Missouri to become the first team to sweep through the Big 12 season at 16-0.

4 **Released Ravens QB Elvis Grbac** retires from the NFL after one season with Baltimore.

Red Sox manager Joe Kerrigan is fired by the team's new management and replaced on an interim basis by third-base coach Mike Cubbage.

5 **Orlando Magic owner Rich DeVos** pulls the team off the market less than two months after revealing he wanted to sell the franchise.

6 **LPGA officials announce** that the Solheim Cup will be switched from even- to odd-numbered years beginning in 2003. The move had been anticipated since Ryder Cup officials moved their event to even-numbered years.

8 **New Orleans running back Ricky Williams** is traded to the Miami Dolphins for a pair of draft picks and a swap of fourth-round selections in next month's draft.

Patriots receiver Terry Glenn is acquired by the Green Bay Packers for a fourth-round pick in the 2002 draft plus a pick in next year's draft that is based on Glenn's performance.

11 **Cleveland bench coach Grady Little** is hired as manager of the Boston Red Sox.

Yankees outfielder Ruben Rivera is released by the team after admitting he stole teammate Derek Jeter's glove and sold it to a memorabilia agent for $2,500.

12 **Sled driver Martin Buser** crosses the finish line at the Iditarod Sled Dog Race, capturing his fourth race title and becoming the first to finish in less than nine days.

13 **LPGA Hall of Famer Nancy Lopez** announces that she'll retire from professional golf at the end of this season after 25 years on the circuit.

15 **Free agent running back Warrick Dunn** signs a six-year, $28 million contract with the Atlanta Falcons.

Referee Melanie Davis works the Illinois-San Diego State basketball game, becoming the first woman to referee a men's NCAA tournament game.

16 **Winston Cup champ Jeff Gordon's** wife, Brooke, files for divorce after seven years of marriage.

18 **Panthers forward Pavel Bure** is acquired by the N.Y. Rangers in a late-night deal signed hours before the NHL trading deadline.

Eighth-grader Brittanie Cecil of West Alexandria, Ohio dies from injuries sustained after being struck by a deflected puck while watching a Columbus Blue Jackets game at Nationwide Arena on March 16.

Commissioner Paul Tagliabue announces at NFL meetings in Orlando that late season games in the 2002-03 season may be switched from Sunday afternoon to Monday nights to provide more compelling games for ABC—much to the surprise of Fox and CBS sports television executives who had reportedly not heard of such a plan.

21 **Duke's Jason Williams misses** a last-second free throw, helping fifth-seeded Indiana knock the defending champions out of the NCAA men's basketball tournament, 74-73.

AP/Wide World Photos

Workers at the ballpark formerly known as Enron Field remove one of the stadium's exterior signs on March 26 after an agreement was worked out by the Houston Astros last month to buy back the naming rights from the bankrupt energy giant for $2.1 million.

Russian Alexei Yagudin follows his Olympic gold medal won last month with his fourth men's figure skating world championship in Nagano, Japan.

Scottish skier Alain Baxter is stripped of his Olympic slalom bronze medal by the IOC for testing positive for a banned substance he says was in a nasal inhaler.

Former men's basketball booster Ed Martin and his wife are arrested and charged with running an illegal gambling business in which Martin allegedly gave loans to University of Michigan players between 1988-99 to conceal profits.

22 Raptors star Vince Carter announces he'll undergo surgery on his left knee and miss the rest of the regular season.

Russian figure skater Irina Slutskaya holds off Michelle Kwan to win her first world championship at Nagano, Japan.

23 Iowa State senior wrestler Cael Sanderson wins his 159th straight match and becomes the first wrestler to secure an undefeated record en route to winning his fourth consecutive NCAA Division I individual championship.

24 Minnesota-Duluth's Tricia Guest scores with 4:56 remaining to earn the Bulldogs a 3-2 victory over Brown and their second consecutive NCAA Div. I women's ice hockey national championship.

25 Heavyweight champion Lennox Lewis and Mike Tyson finally find a home for their championship bout, inking a deal to fight at The Pyramid in Memphis, Tenn. on June 8.

Oklahoma guard Stacey Dales' 20 points and nine assists, leads the Sooners to a 94-60 victory over Colorado in the NCAA West Regional Championship Game, becoming the first Big 12 women's basketball team to reach the Final Four.

The Minnesota House approves a stadium plan two weeks after the state senate, setting up a compromise that could help keep the Twins in the North Star State.

28 Younger sister Serena Williams gets the best of big sister Venus, 6-2, 6-2, in the semifinals of the Nasdaq-100 in Key Biscane, Fla., defeating her elder sibling for just the second time in seven career tries.

Olympic wrestler Rulon Gardner has the middle toe on his right foot amputated because of severe frostbite he suffered while stranded outside overnight near his home in Wyoming.

Kent State coach Stan Heath, who led the men's basketball team to the Elite Eight in the NCAA tournament in his first season with the team, is hired to replace Nolan Richardson at Arkansas.

31 UConn senior Swin Cash scores 20 points and pulls down 13 rebounds, sparking the Huskies to an 82-70 victory over Oklahoma to clinch the women's basketball NCAA championship for the second time in three seasons.

Indians starter Bartolo Colon allows five hits in a 6-0 shutout of the Angels in the first game of the 2002 Major League Baseball season. It's the major league's first Opening Day shutout since 1993.

APRIL 2002

Sun	Mon	Tue	Wed	Thu	Fri	Sat
	1	2	3	4	5	6
7	8	9	10	11	12	13
14	15	16	17	18	19	20
21	22	23	24	25	26	27
28	29	30				

Quote of the Month

"Do I get the green pants for finishing second?"

Retief Goosen, PGA Tour golfer and runner up to three-time green jacket winner Tiger Woods after the final round of the Masters on April 14.

School Pride

Maryland men's basketball coach Gary Williams became the ninth coach—and first since 1974—to lead his alma mater to an NCAA Div. I national title. Here's a look at that select group. (Class) refers to their senior year and Year(s) is when they won a national title(s) with that team.

Coach	School (Class)	Year(s)
Howard Hobson	Oregon ('26)	1939
Branch McCracken	Indiana ('30)	1940
Harold "Bud" Foster	Wisconsin ('30)	1941
Vadal Peterson	Utah ('20)	1944
Phog Allen	Kansas ('09)	1952
Fred Taylor	Ohio State ('50)	1960
Ed Jucker	Cincinnati ('40)	1961-62
Norm Sloan	N.C. State ('49)	1974
Gary Williams	Maryland ('68)	2002

Draft Positions

The expansion Houston Texans made Fresno State star David Carr the 12th quarterback to be drafted first overall at the NFL draft since the American Football League merger. The following is a breakdown of number-one picks by position since 1967.

12	Quarterbacks
7	Running Backs
6	Defensive Ends
5	Defensive Tackles
2	Offensive Tackles
2	Linebackers
2	Wide Receivers

1 **Guard Juan Dixon** scores 18 points and leads Maryland to a 64-52 victory over Indiana to claim the Terrapins' first NCAA men's basketball title.

2 **Giants slugger Barry Bonds** swats two home runs in his first game of the season, his first two at-bats since last year's record-setting season.

3 **Wizards player/president Michael Jordan** announces through a written statement that he will sit out the remainder of the NBA season to rest his injured right knee.

Actress Tawny Kitaen, wife of Cleveland Indians pitcher Chuck Finley is charged with spousal abuse and battery for allegedly attacking her husband as they drove home from dinner.

4 **Boxer Oscar De La Hoya** re-injures his surgically repaired left hand in training, forcing his much anticipated May 4 junior welterweight title showdown with Fernando Vargas to be postponed.

Coral Gables, Fla. police reveal that they have no suspects in connection with an investigation into who stole copies of the football national champion Miami Hurricanes' playbook and posted them on the Internet.

5 **Atlanta Braves ace Greg Maddux** is placed on the DL for the first time in his 16-year major league career. He is battling lower back pain.

6 **Minnesota's Grant Potulny** scores in overtime, clinching a 4-3 victory over Maine and the Golden Gophers' first NCAA men's ice hockey title since 1979.

8 **Tigers manager Phil Garner** and GM Randy Smith are fired after the team's 0-6 start and replaced by bench coach Luis Pujols and team president Dave Dombrowski, respectively.

9 **Canadiens captain Saku Koivu** returns to the ice in a 4-3 victory over Ottawa, marking his first NHL game since being diagnosed with cancer seven months ago.

Indianapolis Motor Speedway officials announce that impact-absorbing "soft walls" will be added to the track in time for next month's Indy 500.

12 **Former Expos manager Felipe Alou** is hired by the Detroit Tigers to be the team's bench coach.

14 **Defending champ Tiger Woods** claims his third green jacket by firing a 1-under-par 71 in the final round of the Masters.

Distance runner Khalid Khannouchi overtakes fellow stars Haile Gebrselassie and Paul Tergat in the last two miles and breaks his own marathon record in London, crossing the finish in 2:05:38.

Drag racing legend John Force captures his 100th career funny car victory at the O'Reilly Spring Nationals in Houston.

15 **Kenyan Rodgers Rop** wins his first Boston Marathon and countrywoman Margaret Okayo sets a women's division record in her debut at the 106-year-old race.

A piece of gum supposedly chewed and spit out by Diamondbacks outfielder Luis Gonzalez is sold at an online charity auction for $10,000.

16 **Tigers pitcher Jose Lima** pitches six scoreless innings, sparking the Tigers to a 9-3 victory over Tampa Bay and ending their 0-11 start to the season—the fifth worst start in major league history dating back to 1900.

17 **Raptors center Antonio Davis** scores 21 points in a 103-85 victory over Cleveland that helps Toronto claim the seventh seed in the Eastern Conference playoffs, becoming just the third team in NBA history to reach the postseason despite losing 13-straight games at one point during the season.

Seven months after being diagnosed with non-Hodgkin's lymphoma, Montreal Canadiens captain **Saku Koivu** *returned to action April 9, much to the delight of his adoring fans.*

18 **Broadcasters Marv Albert and Mike Fratello** are injured when the limousine they are traveling in from Philadelphia to New York crashes into a truck in the early morning.

Brewers manager Davey Lopes is fired and replaced by bench coach Jerry Royster on an interim basis.

19 **Winston Cup team owner Jack Roush** is critically injured when his small plane crashes in Troy, Ala.

UConn's Sue Bird is chosen first overall by the Seattle Storm in the WNBA draft, sparking a run of four former Huskies taken in the first six picks.

20 **Fresno State QB David Carr** is selected by the expansion Houston Texans as the first pick overall in the NFL draft.

21 **Patriots coach Bill Belichick** trades one-time franchise quarterback Drew Bledsoe to the Buffalo Bills for their first-round pick in 2003.

Reds pitcher Jose Rijo completes his amazing comeback from five arm surgeries in six years, starting his first major league game since 1995 and allowing one unearned run in a 5-3 victory over the Cubs.

23 **Organizing committee president Mitt Romney** announces that the recently completed Winter Games in Salt Lake City finished with a $50.5 million profit.

Pirates third baseman Aramis Ramirez is suspended for seven games by Major League Baseball for charging the mound and throwing his batting helmet at Milwaukee pitcher Ben Sheets during a game on April 17.

25 **Masters tournament officials** announce that starting in 2003 past champions will only be able to play until age 65.

Maple Leafs captain Mats Sundin reveals to the media that he will miss the remainder of the NHL playoffs due to a broken left wrist suffered when he was hit by a puck in Toronto's first-round series against the Islanders.

26 **Colorado Rockies manager Buddy Bell** is fired after the team records a 6-16 start to the season, the worst in franchise history.

27 **Red Sox pitcher Derek Lowe throws** the first no-hitter at Fenway Park in 37 years, leading Boston to a 10-0 victory over the Devil Rays.

28 **Boston Bruins defenseman Kyle McLaren** is given a series-ending suspension for a blow to the head of Montreal forward Richard Zednick during Game 4 of the teams' first-round playoff series on April 25.

Captain Billie Jean King, who dismissed Jennifer Capriati from the U.S. Fed Cup team earlier in the week for violating team practice rules, watches Austria put the finishing touches on its 3-0 upset of the U.S. squad.

29 **Former major leaguer Darryl Strawberry** is sentenced to 18 months in prison for violating his probation for drug and solicitation of prostitution charges from 1999.

Kansas City manager Tony Muser is fired, helping set a record for major league managers fired in April (four).

30 **Former Lakers executive Jerry West** is announced as the new president of the Memphis Grizzlies.

French judge Marie-Reine Le Gougne and France's skating federation chief are suspended for three years and banned from the 2006 Winter Games by the International Skating Union for their misconduct in the Olympic pairs figure skating scandal last month.

MAY 2002

Sun	Mon	Tue	Wed	Thu	Fri	Sat
			1	2	3	4
5	6	7	8	9	10	11
12	13	14	15	16	17	18
19	20	21	22	23	24	25
26	27	28	29	30	31	

Quote of the Month

"They have been calling all morning . . . asking me not to forgive (Ferrari race team boss, Jean) Todt if he comes to make a confession."

Father Alberto Bernardoni, head of the parish in Maranello, Italy that includes Ferrari's Formula One base, explaining his parishioners' reaction to the finish of the Austrian Grand Prix on May 12 when Ferrari boss Jean Todt ordered race leader Rubens Barrichello to pull over and let teammate Michael Schumacher win.

No Horsing Around

War Emblem became the first wire-to-wire champion at the Kentucky Derby since 1988. Here is a look at the Derby winners that led from start to finish since 1960.

Year	Horse	Time
1966	Kauai King	2:02
1972	Riva Ridge	2:01⅘
1976	Bold Forbes	2:01⅗
1985	Spend a Buck	2:00⅕
1988	Winning Colors	2:02⅕
2002	War Emblem	2:01

Un-four-gettable Day

With all due respect to Seattle outfielder Mike Cameron, who hit four home runs in one game on May 2, the Dodgers' Shawn Green's four-home-run game on May 23 was one for the ages. Here is a look at his linescore and some of the records he set or tied.

AB	R	H	2B	HR	RBI
6	6	6	1	4	7

4 HRs
Tied major league record; 14th player in history to accomplish; 11th to do it in a nine-inning game.

19 Total Bases
Set a new major league record; broke Joe Adcock's (18) record set in 1954.

6 Runs Scored
Tied modern-day record held by five players; the last to do it was Edgardo Alfonzo in 1999.

2 **Seattle outfielder Mike Cameron** becomes the 13th major leaguer to hit four home runs in a game, sparking the visiting Mariners to a 15-4 victory over the White Sox.

Three more bowl games are approved by the NCAA, bringing the Division I-A total to 28.

Vanderbilt women's hoops coach Tom Collen quits less than 24 hours after accepting the job, when a Tennessee newspaper publishes part of his resume that apparently incorrectly claimed he had two master's degrees. It was later discovered that he did, in fact, earn two masters.

Anaheim coach Bryan Murray climbs out from behind the bench after one season with the Mighty Ducks to replace fired GM Pierre Gauthier and take over senior vice president duties, as well.

3 **San Francisco WR Terrell Owens** scores seven points in a U.S. Basketball League game, leading the Adirondack Wildcats over Brooklyn in Glens Falls, N.Y.

Braves rookie Damian Moss is pulled for a pinch hitter in the seventh inning despite working on a no-hitter. Moss had thrown 116 pitches, walked seven, and had only two 1-2-3 innings.

4 **Jockey Victor Espinoza** rides War Emblem to victory at the 128th Kentucky Derby, becoming the first wire-to-wire champion in 14 years.

7 **Thoroughbred Seattle Slew**, the last living Triple Crown winner, dies in his sleep at the age of 28.

10 **Washington Capitals coach Ron Wilson** is fired after five seasons with the team.

11 **Devil Rays OF Randy Winn's** home run gives Tampa Bay a 5-4 victory over Baltimore, snapping the team's losing streak at 15 games—the AL's longest since 1988.

12 **Ferrari F1 driver Michael Schumacher** scores a controversial win at the Austrian Grand Prix, passing teammate and race leader Rubens Barrichello, who was told by Ferrari officials to slow down and let Schumacher pass.

14 **Former Stars coach Ken Hitchcock** is hired by the Philadelphia Flyers, the team's fifth head coach in as many years.

15 **Former MLB catcher Tony Pena** is hired to manage the Kansas City Royals.

16 **Twelve-year-old Michelle Wie**, the youngest female golfer to appear in an LPGA event, struggles to a 9-over-par 81 in the first round of the Asahi Ryokuren International Championship in South Carolina.

Former Kings assistant Dave Tippett is hired as coach of the Dallas Stars.

18 **Kentucky Derby champ War Emblem** holds off 40-1 longshot Magic Weisner to win the 127th Preakness Stakes—the second jewel of the Triple Crown.

Junior welterweight Micky Ward wages a bloody battle with Arturo Gatti and earns a majority decision after a classic 10-rounder in Uncasville, Conn. that experts deem the odds-on-favorite for fight of the year.

19 **Mariners manager Lou Piniella** and several players are treated for smoke inhalation after the bus they were taking to the airport after a game in Boston catches fire in the Ted Williams Tunnel.

20 **Tennis star Martina Hingis** undergoes surgery in Zurich, Switzerland to repair ligaments in her left ankle.

21 **Vikings receiver Cris Carter** retires from the NFL after 15 seasons to take a job in broadcasting.

22 **Minor league coach Mike Babcock** is hired to replace Bryan Murray as coach of the Anaheim Mighty Ducks.

AP/Wide World Photos

*NASCAR driver **Elliott Sadler**, bottom, throws his helmet at Ryan Newman's car, top right, during a caution lap at The Winston, NASCAR's all-star race, at Lowe's Motor Speedway in Concord, N.C. on May 18. Sadler, who claimed a bump from Newman caused him to crash his car, was fined $5,000 for the stunt.*

23 **Dodgers outfielder Shawn Green** becomes the second major leaguer in three weeks to hit four home runs in a game, sparking the visiting Dodgers to a 16-3 victory over the Brewers.

Toronto coach Pat Quinn unexpectedly shows up behind the Maple Leafs bench before Game 4 of the team's playoff series with Carolina, 2½ hours after being released from the hospital where he was being monitored for an irregular heartbeat. He was greeted with a standing ovation, but Toronto lost 3-0.

Honda announces a deal to manufacture and supply engines for the Indy Racing League starting in 2003, meaning the 6-year-old circuit will have four engine makers next year.

Ireland's World Cup coach Mick McCarthy sends popular team captain Roy Keane home after Keane went into a tirade about McCarthy's lack of professionalism and whipped the U.K. media into a frenzy.

24 **USOC president Sandra Baldwin** resigns after admitting she falsified some of the academic credentials on her resume.

Spurs star David Robinson tells the media that the 2002-03 season—the final season in his two-year $20 million deal—will be his last in the NBA.

25 **Celtics star Paul Pierce** scores 19 of his game-high 28 points in the fourth quarter, helping Boston set an NBA playoff record for fourth-quarter comebacks by out-scoring the New Jersey Nets 41-16 in a 94-90 victory in Game 3 of the Eastern Conference finals.

26 **Defending champ Helio Castroneves** wins his second straight Indianapolis 500, but the victory is protested by Paul Tracy's team, which insists their driver passed Castroneves before the caution flag was signaled on lap 199.

Winston Cup veteran Mark Martin ends a 73-race winless streak with a victory at the Coca-Cola Racing Family 600 at Lowe's Motor Speedway.

27 **California pitcher Jocelyn Forest** tosses her second consecutive one-hitter, leading the Bears to a 6-0 victory over defending champion Arizona in the Women's College World Series. It's California's first national title in any women's sport.

28 **Carolina's Martin Gelinas** deflects in the game-winner in the Hurricanes' series-clinching 2-1 overtime victory over Toronto, sending the Hurricanes to the Stanley Cup Finals for the first time in franchise history.

29 **Former NL MVP Ken Caminiti** admits in an interview with *Sports Illustrated* that he was on steroids when he won the award in 1996, and claims at least half of current major leaguers are using them. He recants that claim two days later.

31 **Senegal's Papa Bouba Diop** scores the game's only goal in the 30th minute, leading his team to a 1-0 upset of defending champion France in the opening game of the 2002 World Cup.

Red Wings goalie Dominik Hasek sets an NHL record with his fifth shutout of the postseason, helping Detroit beat Colorado, 7-0, in Game 7 of the Western Conference finals.

JUNE 2002

Sun	Mon	Tue	Wed	Thu	Fri	Sat
						1
2	3	4	5	6	7	8
9	10	11	12	13	14	15
16	17	18	19	20	21	22
23	24	25	26	27	28	29
30						

Quote of the Month

"Tickets: $1000, hotel: $600, waiting for a meal: three hours, seeing Argentina and France go out: priceless."

Unknown fan at the Brazil-Costa Rica first round World Cup game on June 13, holding up a banner with this clever parody of a popular ad from a tournament sponsor written on it.

Crazy 8's

When Spain's Albert Costa won the French Open on June 9, it marked the first time since 1968 that there were eight different men's Grand Slam winners in the last eight Grand Slam tournaments.

2000 Wimbledon	Pete Sampras, United States
2000 U.S. Open	Marat Safin, Russia
2001 Australian Open	Andre Agassi, United States
2001 French Open	Gustavo Kuerten, Brazil
2001 Wimbledon	Goran Ivanisevic, Croatia
2001 U.S. Open	Lleyton Hewitt, Australia
2002 Australian Open	Thomas Johansson, Sweden
2002 French Open	Albert Costa, Spain

France Sings *Les Blues*

France became just third defending champion in 72 years of World Cup competition to be eliminated in the first round. The nightmare culminated with the team's 2-0 loss against Denmark on June 11. Adding insult to injury, France became the 14th team in tournament history to go scoreless. Note that (W-D-L) stands for Wins-Draws-Losses; a win is worth two points (3 pts. since 1994); and a draw one.

	W-D-L	GF	GA	Pts	Opponents
1950 Italy	1-0-1	4	3	2	Sweden, Paraguay*
1966 Brazil	1-0-2	4	6	2	Bulgaria*, Hungary, Portugal
2002 France	0-1-2	0	3	1	Senegal, Uruguay†, Denmark

*denotes a victory.
†denotes a draw.

1 **Referee Tony Orlando stops** the heavyweight fight between Evander Holyfield and Hasim Rahman in the eighth round after a huge lump swells on the left side of Rahman's head; the result of an inadvertent Holyfield head-butt.

2 **Los Angeles center Shaquille O'Neal** scores 35 points, lifting the visiting Lakers to a 112-106 overtime victory over the Kings in Game 7 of the Western Conference finals.

3 **Toronto Blue Jays manager Buck Martinez** is fired after leading the team to a 20-33 record—the team's worst start in two decades.

5 **Forward Brian McBride's** header in the 36th minute proves to be the game-winner in the U.S.'s shocking 3-2 upset of Portugal in the first round of the World Cup.

6 **Hall of Famer Bryan Trottier** is hired to be head coach of the N.Y. Rangers.

8 **Heavyweight champion Lennox Lewis** stops Mike Tyson at 2:25 of the eighth round, recording a knockout in the much-anticipated bout in Memphis, Tenn.

Triple Crown hopeful War Emblem stumbles and collides with Magic Weisner out of the gates at the Belmont Stakes, ending his bid for the Crown and opening the way for 70-1 longshot Sarava to claim horse racing's third jewel.

Tennis star Serena Williams earns her second career Grand Slam title by defeating her older sister, Venus, 7-5, 6-3, in the finals of the French Open.

9 **Spain's Albert Costa** holds off countryman Juan Carlos Ferrero in four sets to win the French Open—his first Grand Slam title.

10 **U.S. forward Clint Mathis** scores in the 24th minute, but South Korea answers in the 78th, helping the co-hosts escape with a 1-1 tie in their first round game at the World Cup.

11 **French keeper Fabien Barthez** allows two goals in a 2-0 loss to the Denmark that shockingly eliminates the World Cup's defending champion in the first round.

Cable networks HBO and Showtime announce that the Lennox Lewis-Mike Tyson fight on June 8 was the highest-grossing event in pay-per-view history, generating $103 million from 1.8 million buys in the United States.

12 **Lakers center Shaquille O'Neal** scores 34 points and wins his third consecutive Finals MVP Award, sparking Los Angeles to a 113-107 victory over the New Jersey Nets in Game 4 for an NBA Finals sweep.

13 **Detroit coach Scotty Bowman** earns his ninth NHL title after the host Red Wings defeat the Carolina Hurricanes, 3-1, in Game 5 of the Stanley Cup Finals. Bowman announces his retirement after the game.

New Jersey Devils coach Kevin Constantine is replaced by Pat Burns a little more than a month after the team's first-round exit from the playoffs.

Washington Freedom star Mia Hamm scores the game-winning goal in a victory over the Boston Breakers—her first game after missing the first two months of the WUSA season recovering from knee surgery.

14 **Poland pounds the U.S.** World Cup squad, 3-1, but the Americans manage to advance to the second round for the first time since 1930 thanks to South Korea's surprising 1-0 upset of Portugal.

15 **Mets pitcher Shawn Estes** throws a pitch behind Yankees pitcher Roger Clemens during an interleague game. It's Clemens' first at-bat against the Mets since his feud with Mets star Mike Piazza began two years ago.

16 **Masters champ Tiger Woods** completes his wire-to-wire victory at the U.S. Open, firing a final round 72 and becoming the first golfer since Jack Nicklaus (1972) to win golf's first two majors in the same year.

AP/Wide World Photos

*South Korea's **Ahn Jung-Hwan**, left, leads his teammates in celebration after scoring the game-tying goal in a draw against the United States at the World Cup on June 10. It's a crowd favorite because the co-hosts are re-enacting the controversial short-track speed skating race at the 2002 Olympics in which American Apolo Anton Ohno won the gold after South Korea's Kim Dong-Sung was disqualified.*

17 **U.S. goalie Brad Friedel** records the team's first soccer World Cup shutout since 1950 in a 2-0 victory over Mexico that sends the U.S. to the quarterfinals.

18 **Tennis legend Martina Navratilova**, 45, holds off 25-year-old Tatiana Panova 6-1, 4-6, 6-2 at Eastbourne, England to win her first pro singles match in eight years. She's now the oldest player to win a WTA match.

Michigan freshman Alan Webb, the runner who set the U.S. high school mile record in 2001, announces he's leaving school and turning pro.

19 **Former Pistons "Bad Boy" Bill Laimbeer** is hired to coach the 0-10 Detroit Shock of the WNBA.

20 **NHL commissioner Gary Bettman** announces that the league has taken over day-to-day operations of the Buffalo Sabres, at the request of owner John Rigas, who's financial difficulties are tied to the collapse of Adelphia Communications.

21 **Germany's keeper, Oliver Kahn,** stops 17 shots in a 1-0 victory over the United States, ending the Americans' unlikely run at the World Cup in the quarterfinal round.

22 **Cardinals pitcher Darryl Kile**, 33, is found dead in his Chicago hotel room by hotel officials hours before his scheduled start against the Cubs.

Marlins 2B Luis Castillo goes hitless for the first time in 36 games, ending baseball's longest hitting streak since 1987 (35 games).

23 **Doctors report that an autopsy** done on the body of Darryl Kile revealed an 80 to 90 percent blockage of two of his three coronary arteries, the likely cause of his death.

Retiring jockey Chris McCarron finishes his career with his 7,141st trip to the winner's circle, riding Came Home to victory in the Affirmed Stakes.

25 **Red Wings goalie Dominik Hasek**, 37, retires from the NHL after 12 seasons, six Vezina trophies and one Stanley Cup.

Tigers manager Luis Pujols and Royals skipper Tony Pena face off in a game at Kansas City, becoming the first Dominican-born managers to oppose each other in a major league game. (Pena's Royals win 8-6.)

Grand Rapids (Mich.) coach Bruce Cassidy, the reigning American Hockey League coach of the year, is named head coach of the NHL's Washington Capitals.

26 **Chinese center Yao Ming** is selected first overall by the Houston Rockets at the NBA draft in New York City.

27 **Cleveland ships ace Bartolo Colon** to the Montreal Expos for Lee Stevens as part of a midseason, six-player deal.

Utah Jazz center Greg Ostertag undergoes surgery that will allow him to donate one of his kidneys to his 26-year-old sister who has suffered from diabetes since she was seven.

30 **Brazilian superstar Ronaldo** scores two goals in the World Cup Final, leading Brazil past Germany, 2-0, and securing the country's fifth Cup title.

JULY 2002

Sun	Mon	Tue	Wed	Thu	Fri	Sat
	1	2	3	4	5	6
7	8	9	10	11	12	13
14	15	16	17	18	19	20
21	22	23	24	25	26	27
28	29	30	31			

Quote of the Month

"I would love to dominate the 400(-meter freestyle). I'm swimming times that no one else in the world can beat, by far, and I'm finishing second quite a lot."

Grant Hackett, Australian swimmer, describing how it feels to compete against teammate Ian Thorpe, who improved his own world record in the 400 on July 30 at the Commonwealth Games and has to date set 17 world records.

Match Made in Detroit

Will a move to Detroit earn Curtis Joseph his first NHL championship? He hopes the defending champs are the right match, after all, no active goalie without a Stanley Cup has more regular season victories.

Wins		1st Season
346	Curtis Joseph	1989-90
276	Sean Burke	1987-88
237	Felix Potvin	1991-92
206	Arturs Irbe	1991-92
196	Jocelyn Thibault	1993-94

Source: NHL

The Open's Playoff Oddities

Add this year's British Open to the list of unique endings this 142-year old tournament has witnessed:

1876—After finishing the then 36-hole tournament tied, the rules stated that leaders Bob Martin and Davie Strath play a 36-hole playoff. Before they began, however, it was reported that Strath had teed off while another group was putting on the 17th hole (an automatic disqualification). Although officials said they would delay their decision until after the playoff, Strath crumpled under the intense scrutiny and refused to participate. Martin won the title by default.

1911—The 36-hole playoff between Harry Vardon and Arnaud Massy ended abruptly. After putting out on the 35th hole Massy conceded the match. He trailed Vardon by five strokes and saw no need to play the final hole.

2002—For the first time, four golfers (Ernie Els, Stuart Appleby, Tomas Levet and Steve Elkington) finished tied for first. Also, for the first time in five occurrences a four-hole playoff didn't determine a winner. Appleby and Elkington were eliminated, but Els and Levet were forced into a sudden-death format to decide the winner. Els won on the first hole.

2 **German keeper Oliver Kahn** wins the Golden Ball Award as the World Cup tournament's most outstanding player.

Toronto goalie Curtis Joseph agrees to a three-year, $24 million deal with the Detroit Red Wings that includes a $1 million bonus if the Wings win the Stanley Cup.

Basketball legend Kareem Abdul-Jabbar leaves his job as head coach of the Oklahoma Storm of the U.S. Basketball League two days after leading them to the league championship in his first season.

3 **Indianapolis Motor Speedway president** Tony George denies Team Green's appeal to have its driver, Paul Tracy, named winner of the 2002 Indy 500, ruling that the race officials' decision was not appealable under Indy Racing League rules.

5 **Red Sox legend Ted Williams** dies in his Florida home at the age of 83.

Chicago Cubs manager Don Baylor is fired and replaced by the team's Triple A skipper Bruce Kimm.

6 **French Open champ Serena Williams** holds off her sister, Venus, 7-6, 6-3 to win the women's finals at Wimbledon. It's her second Grand Slam singles' title of the year, and her third straight defeat of Venus.

The children of Ted Williams begin to publicly feud over his remains after his oldest daughter reveals that her half-brother, John Henry Williams, has sent the body of the Red Sox legend to Arizona to be cryogenically frozen.

7 **Aussie Lleyton Hewitt** defeats David Nalbandian in straight sets in the Wimbledon men's final, becoming the tournament's first Australian-born champion in 15 years.

Major League Baseball announces it will honor the late Ted Williams by naming the All-Star Game MVP Award after him.

Brazilian driver Cristiano da Matta ties a CART series record by winning his fourth consecutive race, holding off Kenny Brack to win the Molson Indy in Toronto.

9 **Baseball Commissioner Bud Selig** is showered with a chorus of "boos" and chants of "refund" after he decides to call Major League Baseball's All-Star Game a tie, 7-7, after teams run out of pitchers after 11 innings.

10 **Winston Cup rookie Jimmie Johnson** and teammate Jeff Gordon are docked 25 points each by NASCAR, and crew chief Chad Knaus is fined $25,000 for an illegal part discovered in Johnson's car before qualifying for the Pepsi 400 on July 7.

Baseball Commissioner Bud Selig makes headlines by vowing never again to let an All-Star Game end in a tie and claiming that one major league team may not be able to meet payroll next week (he offers no specifics on either).

11 **Philadelphia police issue** an arrest warrant for 76ers star Allen Iverson, who is accused of forcing his way into an apartment with a gun displayed in his waistband and threatening two men while looking for his wife. In all, Iverson faces 14 charges, and he must remain in his home until he is scheduled to surrender to police on July 16.

Indians manager Charlie Manuel is fired after leading the Indians to their worst first-half performance since 1992.

Boxer Felix Trinidad, 29, confirms his retirement to reporters in Puerto Rico, ending a dazzling 12-year career in which he appeared in 21 title fights and won titles in three different weight classes.

15 **Titans lineman Bruce Matthews** announces his retirement from the NFL after 19 seasons in which he never missed a game due to injury and started a franchise-record 229 consecutive games.

Raiders quarterback Rich Gannon signs a six-year, $54 million contract extension with Oakland.

AP/Wide World Photos

*After claiming titles at the first two majors of the year, **Tiger Woods** saw his chances of a Grand Slam washed away by the wind-swept rain on July 20 during the third round of the British Open. Woods shot his worst score as a professional, a 10-over-par 81.*

16 **Sixers star Allen Iverson** turns himself in and is arraigned on 14 counts, including four felonies, for his alleged actions after a domestic dispute.

Fourteen former partners in the Montreal Expos file suit in Miami against baseball commissioner Bud Selig and former Expos owner Jeffrey Loria, claiming fraud involving the recent sale of the team to Major League Baseball.

Promoters for CART's German 500, scheduled for Sept. 22, call off the race, admitting that they can't host the event because the company that runs the track in Läusitz, Germany, filed for bankruptcy earlier this month.

17 **Red Wings assistant Dave Lewis** is promoted to head coach, replacing Scotty Bowman, who retired after winning his ninth Stanley Cup last month.

Seven-year-old Melvin Pompele is struck and killed by a car from the Tour de France convoy as he tried to cross the stage route. It's the second death of a Tour spectator in the last three years.

18 **Red Wings captain Steve Yzerman** announces he will undergo knee surgery that will keep him out of action for the first two months of the 2002-03 season.

Two-time Indy 500 winner Al Unser Jr. says he will seek treatment for alcohol addiction after prosecutors announce he will not face criminal charges on accusations he hit his girlfriend during an altercation on July 9.

20 **WBC Welterweight champ Vernon Forrest** (35-0) beats Shane Mosley (38-2) for the second time this year, punching his way to a unanimous 12-round decision at Conseco Fieldhouse in Indianapolis.

21 **Two-time U.S. Open champ Ernie Els** wins his third career Grand Slam title, the British Open, by fending off Thomas Levet in the first sudden death playoff in the tournament's 142-year history.

Formula One driver Michael Schumacher wins the French Grand Prix at Magny-Cours, clinching his third straight drivers' championship and joining Juan-Manuel Fangio as the only five-time champions.

25 **The family of Ted Williams** unveil a handwritten note that was signed by the Hall of Famer in November 2000, which says he wants his body frozen after death—contradicting his 1996 will, which said he wanted to be cremated.

28 **American cyclist Lance Armstrong** wins his fourth consecutive Tour de France, becoming the first American to win the world's most famous bike race four times.

29 **Sixers star Allen Iverson** has all but two of the 14 counts against him in his domestic dispute/rampage case dismissed by a Philadelphia judge after a six-hour preliminary hearing, eliminating the possibility of jail time.

NBA's board of governors approve the use of instant replay to review plays at the end of each quarter and overtime period starting next season.

Phillies third baseman Scott Rolen is traded to the St. Louis Cardinals as part of a five-player deal.

31 **Alleged Russian crime boss Alimzan Tokhtakhounov** is arrested in Italy on U.S. charges that he fixed figure skating results at the 2002 Winter Olympics.

AUGUST 2002

Sun	Mon	Tue	Wed	Thu	Fri	Sat
				1	2	3
4	5	6	7	8	9	10
11	12	13	14	15	16	17
18	19	20	21	22	23	24
25	26	27	28	29	30	31

Quote of the Month

"I need to do something to make it to where I can control my anger better. It's obvious over three-and-a-half years, I can't do it on my own."

Tony Stewart, Winston Cup driver, telling the media that he'll seek help after a post-race confrontation with a photographer on Aug. 4, earned him a $10,000 fine from NASCAR and the rest of the season on probation.

Southpaw Sluggers

On Aug. 9, San Francisco Giants slugger Barry Bonds became the fourth player to hit 600 or more home runs in a career. Of those four, however, only Bonds and Babe Ruth batted from the left side. Here is a look at the top lefty sluggers of all time.

714	Babe Ruth
600*	Barry Bonds
563	Reggie Jackson
521	Ted Williams
521	Willie McCovey
512	Eddie Mathews
511	Mel Ott

*As of Aug. 9, 2002.
Note: Switch-hitting Mickey Mantle hit 536 career home runs.

Bayou's Best

Louisiana Tech women's basketball coach Leon Barmore, who retired on Aug. 22, fell short of recording the 14th 30-win season of his career. But this year's 25-5 squad easily made the NCAA tournament, Barmore's 20th. Only Tennessee coach Pat Summitt has been invited to The Big Dance more than Barmore.

App.	Coach
21	Pat Summitt, Tennessee
20	Leon Barmore, Louisiana Tech
19	Andy Landers, Georgia
19	Debbie Ryan, Virginia
18	Jody Conradt, Texas
18	Rene Portland, Penn. St.

Source: NCAA

1 **Ravens linebacker Ray Lewis** signs a five-year contract extension worth $50 million, which includes a $19 million signing bonus.

2 **WBC President Jose Sulaiman** files a $56 million lawsuit against Mike Tyson and Lennox Lewis, saying he was knocked out, spat on and threatened during the fracas that broke out during a press conference in January.

3 **Tamp Bay's Steve Ralston** scores a goal in the 72nd minute, leading the Major League Soccer All-Stars to a 3-2 victory over the U.S. national soccer team at RFK Stadium in Washington D.C.

4 **Pole winner Tony Stewart** punches a photographer in the chest and tries to kick him as he runs towards his crew quarters after his 12th-place finish at the Brickyard 400.

6 **Philadelphia 76ers center Dikembe Mutombo** is traded to the New Jersey Nets for Keith Van Horn and Todd MacCulloch.

Mets co-owner Nelson Doubleday accuses baseball commissioner Bud Selig of conspiring with a former Arthur Andersen accountant to "manufacture phantom operating losses" for the sport.

7 **Winston Cup star Tony Stewart** tells the media he will seek anger management counseling, one day after NASCAR fined him $10,000 and put him on probation for the remainder of the season for striking a photographer after a race on Aug. 4.

CART driver Christian Fittipaldi announces he'll leave the open-wheel series after eight years and join Petty Enterprises next season, racing in a combined Busch and Winston Cup program.

8 **Utah point guard John Stockton** announces he'll return for a 19th NBA season, becoming just the third guard in league history to begin the season at age 40 or older.

9 **Giants slugger Barry Bonds** hits the 600th home run of his career off of Pittsburgh's Kip Wells at PacBell Park, joining Hank Aaron, Babe Ruth and Willie Mays in the exclusive 600+ homer club.

11 **LPGA star Karrie Webb** rallies from three strokes down to win her third British Open and her sixth major championship in the last four years.

12 **Union chief Don Fehr** announces that the players will give negotiators three days to reach an agreement before setting a strike date.

13 **Boxing promoter Bob Arum** and six others survive a fiery plane crash in Big Bear, Calif. where the small jet they were on overshot the runway.

Mets co-owner Nelson Doubleday reaches an agreement to sell his half of the team to partner Fred Wilpon, ending a dispute that culminated with a court fight over the sale of the team.

Sacramento Monarchs guard Edna Campbell appears in her first WNBA game since being diagnosed with breast cancer in February.

14 **Former Cowboys lineman Nate Newton** is sentenced to 30 months in prison after pleading guilty to marijuana possession charges in Texas. A similar case in Louisiana is still pending.

15 **Little League Baseball officials** clear the way for Harlem, N.Y. to play in the Little League World Series (which begins Aug. 16) after team officials resolve questions about the eligibility of three players. A New York newspaper had reported that the team was under investigation for using players who may have lived outside of the team's district.

Interim president Marty Mankamyer is elected U.S. Olympic Committee president, ending a three-month search to find Sandy Baldwin's replacement.

AP/Wide World Photos

Rescue workers attend to NASCAR Busch Series driver **Mike Harmon**, *who miraculously walked away from this frightening practice-run crash on Aug. 22 at Bristol Motor Speedway in which his car was sliced in half when it hit a concrete retaining wall.*

16 **The players union executive board** votes, 57-0, through a conference call to set an Aug. 31 strike date if a collective bargaining agreement is not reached with owners.

17 **Boxer Laila Ali** stops Suzy Taylor in the second round, earning the daughter of Muhammad Ali her first boxing title—the IBA super middleweight championship.

18 **Former electronics salesman Rich Beem** shoots a final-round 68, and holds off a furious charge from Tiger Woods, to claim his third pro victory at the PGA Championship at Hazeltine National GC in Chaska, Minn.

Sixth-seeded James Blake defeats Paradorn Srichaphan and becomes just the fourth African-American to win an Association of Tennis Professionals tournament title at the Legg Mason Classic at Washington D.C.

19 **Broncos running back Terrell Davis** is given a standing ovation before the team's preseason game, saluting the back who announced earlier in the week that his chronic knee injuries will force him to retire.

World Cup skiing champ Jeremy Bloom chooses to play college football at Colorado this season and sever his endorsement contracts as required by the NCAA.

21 **Denver Nuggets scout Jeff Bzdelik**, who was promoted to assistant coach last month, is named head coach of the team for the 2002-03 season.

22 **Louisiana Tech coach Leon Barmore**, who has the best winning percentage among Division I women's basketball coaches, announces his retirement after 28 seasons.

Colorado State's Cecil Sapp rushes for 178 yards in a 35-29 victory over Virginia—the first game of the longest Division I-A college football season ever (135 days).

24 **Game MVP Birgit Prinz** scores one goal and sets up another, leading Carolina to a 3-2 victory over Washington in the WUSA championship game.

NASCAR star Jeff Gordon wins the Sharpie 500 at Bristol Motor Speedway, ending a 31-race winless streak.

25 **Louisville pitcher Aaron Alvey** allows three hits and strikes out 11, sparking his team to a 1-0 victory over Japan in the finals of the Little League World Series. Alvey's first-inning home run proves to be the game-winner.

USA Wrestling President Stan Dziedzic announces that the team has pulled out of next month's world championships of freestyle wrestling in Iran, citing threats against the U.S. team.

28 **Executive director Charles Jones** announces that the 64-year-old Blue-Gray Classic college football all-star game, a Christmas Day tradition, will not be played in 2002 due to a lack of corporate sponsorship.

29 **The executive board** of the IOC postpones until November its much-anticipated decision on whether or not to cut baseball and other sports from the Olympics.

30 **Commissioner Bud Selig** and the Major League Baseball Players Association agree on a new collective bargaining agreement just hours before the Aug. 31 deadline, averting baseball's ninth work stoppage.

Club Chairman Hootie Johnson announces that Augusta National has suspended its one-year contracts with three corporate sponsors of the 2003 Masters, keeping them out of his debate with women's rights advocate Martha Burk, who wants to see the club welcome its first female member. This action would make next year's Masters the only commercial-free telecast in sports.

SEPTEMBER 2002

Sun	Mon	Tue	Wed	Thu	Fri	Sat
1	2	3	4	5	6	7
8	9	10	11	12	13	14
15	16	17	18	19	20	21
22	23	24	25	26	27	28
29	30					

Quote of the Month

"Thank you, Minnesota, for your patience and enthusiasm....and Congratulations Twins, for a most memorable season! We look forward to building our future...together."

Bud Selig, Major League Baseball commissioner, as taken from a full-page advertisement he had put in both the Twin Cities daily newspapers to congratulate the nearly contracted team for winning the AL Central Divsion title.

A's For Effort

By winning 20 consecutive games from Aug. 13 through Sept. 4, the Oakland A's set a new American League record. It was Major League Baseball's longest winning streak in 67 years and is tied for third all-time.

Year	Team	Wins
1916	New York Giants*	26
1880	Chicago Cubs*	21
1935	Chicago Cubs	21
1884	Providence Grays	20
2002	Oakland Athletics	20

*includes one tie game.

Ewing Some, You Lose Some

In announcing his retirement on Sept. 17, Patrick Ewing said he was disappointed with not winning an NBA title, but "there are other great players who never won championships." He's right. Here's a look at Ewing's teammates on the NBA's 50 Greatest Players team who never won an NBA title. Players are listed in alphabetical order with the number of pro seasons they played.

	Seasons		Seasons
Charles Barkley	16	Karl Malone†	17
Elgin Baylor	14	Pete Maravich	10
Dave Bing	12	John Stockton†	18
Patrick Ewing	17	Nate Thurmond	14
George Gervin	14*	Lenny Wilkens#	15

*includes four seasons in the ABA.

† denotes player is active.

#Wilkens did not win an NBA title as a player, but did win one as head coach of Seattle in 1979.

4   **Argentina shocks Team USA** at the World Basketball Championships in Indianapolis, holding on to an 87-80 victory and handing the U.S. its first loss in international competition since it began using NBA players in 1992 (58 consecutive wins).

5   **San Francisco kicker Jose Cortez** connects on a 36-yard field goal with six seconds left, giving the 49ers a 16-13 victory over the N.Y. Giants in the first midweek season-opening game in NFL history.

Heavyweight champion Lennox Lewis decides to give up his International Boxing Federation title rather than fight number one contender Chris Byrd.

6   **Twins starter Brad Radke** pitches a complete-game, 6-0 shutout, snapping the Oakland A's winning streak after 20 games—the third longest in baseball history.

Calgary forward Jarome Iginla, a restricted free agent, agrees to a two-year, $13 million extension with the team.

Winston Cup rookies Jimmie Johnson (pole winner) and Ryan Newman become the first rookies to sweep the front row, qualifying one-two for the Chevy Monte Carlo 400.

7   **Tennis star Serena Williams** defeats her sister, Venus, in the finals of a Grand Slam event for the third time this year, claiming her second U.S. Open women's singles title, 6-4, 6-3.

8   **ATP veterans Pete Sampras** and Andre Agassi battle in the men's singles final of the U.S. Open with Sampras ending his two-year winless drought and capturing his 14th career Grand Slam title.

Kings stars Vlade Divac and Peja Stojakovic lead Yugoslavia to a 84-77 overtime victory over Argentina to claim the title at the Men's World Basketball Championships. (U.S. finishes sixth.)

Houston QB David Carr throws two touchdown passes in a 19-10 victory over Dallas, making the Texans the first NFL expansion team to start 1-0 since the Minnesota Vikings in 1961.

9   **Sacramento Kings All-Star Chris Webber**, his father and his aunt are indicted in Detroit on charges they lied to a grand jury about gifts Webber received from former University of Michigan booster, Ed Martin, who pleaded guilty to conspiring to launder money earlier this year.

Former NBA player Bison Dele (formerly Brian Williams) is reported missing at sea somewhere between Tahiti and Honolulu under "suspicious circumstances" according to his mother.

11   **Two-time NBA All-Star Jerry Stackhouse** is traded by Detroit to Washington as part of a six-player deal between the teams.

L.A. Lakers star Shaquille O'Neal undergoes surgery to remove bone spurs from his arthritic right toe and is expected to be out six to eight weeks.

Kings forward Chris Webber pleads innocent in a Detroit courtroom to charges of lying to a jury and obstruction of justice.

14   **American sprinter Tim Montgomery** breaks Maurice Greene's record in the 100-meter race in Paris, clocking in at 9.78 and becoming the "fastest man on earth."

WBC champion Oscar De La Hoya stops Fernando Vargas with a flurry of punches in the 11th round of their junior middleweight title fight in Las Vegas.

15   **IRL driver Sam Hornish Jr.** holds off Helio Castroneves to win the Chevy 500 at Texas Motor Speedway, earning him a 20-point lead in the final driver point standings and his second straight series championship.

ROYALS BASEBALL

MLB Houston 4 ▸ Milwaukee 5 F

This image, taken from television, shows "fans" William Ligue Jr. (right) and his 15-year-old son attacking Kansas City first base coach Tom Gamboa during the ninth inning of a game against the Chicago White Sox at Comiskey Park. The jury is still out as to which institution this event brought down further: baseball or parenting.

Twins pitcher Kyle Lohse's six shutout innings paves the way for a 5-0 victory over Cleveland and clinches the once-thought-to-be-contracted Twins their first trip to the postseason since 1991.

17 Eleven-time All-Star Patrick Ewing announces his retirement after a 17-year NBA career, saying he'll join the Washington Wizards' coaching staff.

CEO Fraser Bullock announces that the Salt Lake City Organizing Committee, initially hoping to break even on a $1.3 billion budget, wound up with a $101 million profit for the 2002 Winter Games.

22 LPGA veteran Rosie Jones's 3&2 victory over Karine Icher caps the unlikely final-day comeback that helps the Americans reclaim the Solheim Cup in Edina, Minn.

France's Sebastien Grosjean defeats Andy Roddick in four sets, sparking the hosts to a 3-2 victory and eliminating the United States from the Davis Cup semifinals.

Legendary Tigers broadcaster Ernie Harwell calls his final major league game after 55 seasons, including the last 42 in Detroit.

23 L.A. Superior Court Judge Richard C. Hubbell orders a new trial in the Oakland Raiders' $1.2 billion conspiracy lawsuit against the NFL that claims the league sabotaged their plans to build a new stadium in Los Angeles. Judge Hubbell cited jury misconduct as the reason.

25 Vikings star Randy Moss is released from a Minneapolis prison and his felonious assault charge is reduced to two misdemeanors one day after being jailed for allegedly bumping a traffic control agent with his car.

WNBA stars Sheryl Swoopes (18 points) and Lisa Leslie (19) lead the U.S. women's national team to a 79-74 victory over Russia in the final of the Women's World Basketball Championships in China.

26 Wizards President Michael Jordan announces that he'll honor the second year of the two-year deal he signed (uh, with himself) to play for Washington in the 2002-03 season.

The Anaheim Angles bash three home runs in a 10-5 victory over Texas that earns them the AL wildcard and their first trip to the postseason since 1986.

27 Boston Celtics officials announce that the franchise has been sold to a group of investors for $360 million, making it the most expensive NBA team transaction in history. The deal is pending league approval.

Eagles quarterback Donovan McNabb agrees to a new 12-year contract, that could be worth a NFL-record $115 million (with incentives).

29 European Team captain Sam Torrance's gamble pays off when he sends his best players out first in the final day of the Ryder Cup and they respond by leading Europe to a three-point victory over the Americans.

Winston Cup driver Jimmie Johnson finishes 10th in the Protection One 400 in Kansas City and becomes the first rookie to top the series' points standings.

30 Ravens cornerback Chris McAlister sets an NFL record for the longest play in league history, returning a missed field goal 107 yards during a 34-23 victory over Denver on Monday Night Football.

OCTOBER 2002

Sun	Mon	Tue	Wed	Thu	Fri	Sat
		1	2	3	4	5
6	7	8	9	10	11	12
13	14	15	16	17	18	19
20	21	22	23	24	25	26
27	28	29	30	31		

Quote of the Month

"The fans needed a relay to throw it back on the field."

Mickey Hatcher, Angels hitting coach, when asked about the incredible length of Barry Bonds' home run in Game 2 of the World Series that was estimated at 485 feet.

New Sheriff in Town

Cowboys running back Emmitt Smith passed Walter Payton as the most prolific ground gainer in NFL history on Oct. 27. Here's a look at the updated top five career rushers in the NFL (through Oct. 27, 2002).

		Yrs	Car	Yards
1	Emmitt Smith	13	3929	16,743
2	Walter Payton	13	3838	16,726
3	Barry Sanders	10	3062	15,269
4	Eric Dickerson	11	2996	13,259
5	Tony Dorsett	12	2936	12,739

Note: After Emmitt Smith, Jerome Bettis is the leading rusher among active running backs with 11,202 yards through Oct. 27, 2002.

Not just some Lackey

Anaheim right-hander John Lackey, 24, became just the eighth rookie to start and only second rookie starter to win a World Series Game 7. Here's a look at the rookies to start a decisive, winner-take-all game in the World Series.

	Year	Team's Result	Pitcher's Result
John Lackey, Anaheim	2002	W, 4-1	W
Jaret Wright, Cleveland	1997	L, 2-3	ND
Joe Magrane, St. Louis	1987	L, 2-4	ND
Mel Stottlemyre, NY Yankees	1964	L, 5-7	L
Joe Black, Brooklyn	1952	L, 2-4	L
Spec Shea, NY Yankees	1947	W, 5-2	ND
Hugh Bedient, Boston Red Sox*	1912	W, 3-2	ND
Babe Adams, Pittsburgh	1909	W, 8-0	W

*Bedient got the no-decision in what was actually Game 8 of the series (Game 2 ended in a tie when the game was called at the end of the 11th due to darkness).

Note: ND stands for no decision.

1 **IBF featherweight champion Johnny Tapia** is stripped of his title because he scheduled a non-title fight against Marco Antonio Barrera, rather than defend his title as required.

The Calgary Flames acquire forwards Chris Drury and Stephane Yelle in a trade with the Colorado Avalanche for defenseman Derek Morris, Dean McAmmond and Jeff Shantz.

N.Y. Mets manager Bobby Valentine is fired two days after the team finished the season in last place in their division.

2 **Veteran point guard Mark Jackson**, 37, is signed by the Utah Jazz to backup 40-year-old starting point guard John Stockton.

4 **The New York Post reports** that Latrell Sprewell may have broken his hand when he attempted to strike the boyfriend of a woman who vomited aboard his new luxury yacht. Reportedly Sprewell missed his target and punched a wall during a party aboard the yacht in the early morning hours of Sept. 21. Sprewell surprised the Knicks when he arrived at training camp with the injured hand on Sept. 30.

5 **Angels designated hitter Shawn Wooten** and Benji Gil each have three hits in a 9-5 Game 4 victory over the Yankees, eliminating the four-time defending American League champions in the first round.

6 **Quarterback Tommy Maddox makes** his first NFL start since 1992 but his Pittsburgh Steelers fall to the New Orleans Saints, 32-29. Maddox, the only MVP in the short-lived XFL's history, started in place of the benched Kordell Stewart and went 22 of 38 for 268 yards, 3 touchdowns and one interception.

Dale Earnhardt Jr. wins the EA Sports 500 at Talladega Speedway, but Tony Stewart takes over the points lead in the Winston Cup standings supplanting rookie driver Jimmie Johnson atop the list. Johnson had entered Sunday as the only rookie to lead the Winston Cup points race in NASCAR's modern era (since 1972).

LPGA star Annika Sorenstam breaks her own record for victories in a season (eight in 2001), claiming her ninth title of the year at the Samsung World Championships in Vallejo, Calif.

7 **The Twins continue** their impressive run eliminating the Oakland A's from the postseason with a 5-4 win in Game 5 of their ALDS.

8 **The NCAA places** the University of Colorado football program on two years probation for recruiting violations.

9 **The 2002-03 NHL season** begins as the Los Angeles Kings retire Wayne Gretzky's number 99 in a seemingly redundant honor considering that the entire league retired the number when he retired in 1999. The Kings beat the Phoenix Coyotes 4-1 to close the ceremony.

10 **The NCAA names** Indiana University president Myles Brand to succeed out-going leader Cedric Dempsey as the organization's new president. San Francisco goes up 2-0 in the NLCS with a 4-1 win in Game 2 of their series with the St. Louis Cardinals.

12 **Unbeaten Miami remains so**, but just barely, as Florida State's Xaiver Beitia misses a 43-yard game-winning field goal attempt to give the No. 1 Hurricanes the 28-27 win.

13 **Packers' QB Brett Favre throws** three touchdown passes, including the 300th of his career, as Green Bay beats the defending Super Bowl champion New England Patriots, 28-10. Favre moved past John Elway on the all-time list and now trails just Dan Marino (420) and Fran Tarkenton (342). The game also saw the return to Foxboro for former Pats receiver Terry Glenn. Glenn had three catches for 19 yards.

Hockey gets the royal treatment as none-other than Her Majesty **Queen Elizabeth** *drops the puck before an exhibition game between the Canucks and Sharks in Vancouver on Oct. 7. Not pictured: The Queen drives the Zamboni at the first intermission.*

Paula Radcliffe breaks the women's world record in the marathon with her time of 2:17:18 at the Chicago Marathon in just her second 26.2-mile race.

Busch series driver Jamie McMurray wins the UAW-GM 500 at Lowe's Motor Speedway in just his second career Winston Cup start. McMurray, filling in for the injured Sterling Marlin, won earlier in his career than any racer in NASCAR's modern era.

The Anaheim Angels advance to the World Series for the first time ever with a 13-5 win over the Minnesota in Game 5 of the ALCS. The Giants take 3-1 lead in the NLCS with a 4-3 win over St. Louis in Game 4 of their series.

14 In an original, if outrageously egotistical, touchdown celebration, San Francisco receiver Terrell Owens burns Seattle's Shawn Springs then pulls a marker out of his sock and autographs the ball he just caught before handing it to a mutual friend sitting in Springs' seats as the 49ers beat the Seahawks 28-21 on Monday Night Football.

It's an all-California World Series as the San Francisco Giants close out the St. Louis Cardinals with a 2-1 win in Game 5 of the NLCS. The Giants will face inter-state rival Anaheim in the Fall Classic.

18 Hall of Famer Kirby Puckett is charged with a felony count of false imprisonment and a gross misdemeanor count of criminal sexual conduct for allegedly dragging a woman into a restaurant bathroom and grabbing her chest.

20 Carlos Ruiz scores in the second sudden death overtime period to give the Los Angeles Galaxy a 1-0 win over the New England Revolution in the 2002 MLS Cup before a championship game-record crowd of 61,316 at Gillette Stadium in Foxboro, Mass.

22 Barry Bonds becomes the first player to homer in his first three World Series games but the Anaheim Angels beat Bonds' Giants 10-4 at San Francisco's Pac Bell Park in Game 3 to take a 2-1 lead in the World Series.

23 NBA rookie Yao Ming makes his preseason debut for the Houston Rockets, the team that made him the first overall pick in the 2002 NBA draft. The 7-foot-5 Chinese center scored four points, recorded three fouls and was knocked down several times.

26 Forty three-to-1 longshot Volponi pulls a big upset in the Breeders' Cup Classic, beating some of the world's best horses including Derby and Preakness winner War Emblem. Super filly Azeri wins the Breeders' Cup Distaff to make her claim for the title of horse of the year.

27 Garret Anderson hits a three-run double and the Anaheim Angels beat the San Francisco Giants 4-1 in Game 7 of the World Series. It is the first world championship for the franchise that began play in 1961.

Emmitt Smith passes Walter Payton as the NFL's all-time leading rusher with an 11-yard run in the fourth quarter of the Cowboys' 17-14 loss to the Seattle Seahawks. Smith finishes the game with 109 yards to bring his career total to 16,743.

28 Former Mariners skipper Lou Piniella is hired by the Tampa Bay Devil Rays after 10 seasons in Seattle, agreeing to a four-year, $13 million contract that makes him the second-highest paid manager in the majors (Joe Torre). Seattle receives Devil Rays All-Star Randy Winn as compensation. Also, Oakland's Art Howe agrees to a four-year, $9.4 million deal to manage the N.Y. Mets.

Olympics
Winter Games

Year	No.	Host City	Dates
2006	XX	Turin, Italy	Feb. 4-19

Summer Games

Year	No.	Host City	Dates
2004	XXVIII	Athens, Greece	Aug. 13-29
2008	XXIX	Beijing, China	July 25-Aug. 10

All-Star Games
Baseball

Year	Site	Date
2003	Comiskey Park, Chicago	July 8
2004	Minute Maid Park, Houston	July 7

NBA Basketball

Year	Site	Date
2003	Philips Arena, Atlanta	Feb. 9
2004	Staples Center, Los Angeles	Feb. 15

NFL Pro Bowl

Year	Site	Date
2003	Aloha Stadium, Honolulu	Feb. 2
2004	Aloha Stadium, Honolulu	Feb. 8
2005	Aloha Stadium, Honolulu	Feb. 13

NHL Hockey

Year	Site	Date
2003	Office Depot Center, Sunrise, Fla.	Feb. 2
2004	XCel Energy Center, St. Paul, Minn.	Feb. 7

Auto Racing

The Daytona 500 stock car race is usually held on the Sunday before the third Monday in February, while the Indianapolis 500 is usually held on the Sunday of Memorial Day weekend in May. The following dates are tentative.

Year	Daytona 500	Indianapolis 500
2003	Feb. 16	May 25
2004	Feb. 15	May 30
2005	Feb. 20	May 29

NCAA Basketball
Men's Final Four

Year	Site	Dates
2003	Louisiana Superdome, New Orleans	April 5-7
2004	Alamodome, San Antonio	April 3-5
2005	Edward Jones Dome, St. Louis	April 2-4

Women's Final Four

Year	Site	Dates
2003	Georgia Dome, Atlanta	April 6-8
2004	New Orleans Sports Arena	April 4-6
2005	Indianapolis (RCA Dome)	April 3-5
2006	FleetCenter, Boston	April 2-4
2007	Gund Arena, Cleveland	April 1-3

Horse Racing
Triple Crown

The Kentucky Derby is always held at Churchill Downs in Louisville on the first Saturday in May, followed two weeks later by the Preakness Stakes at Pimlico Race Course in Baltimore and three weeks after that by the Belmont Stakes at Belmont Park in Elmont, N.Y.

Year	Ky Derby	Preakness	Belmont
2003	May 3	May 17	June 7
2004	May 1	May 15	June 5
2005	May 7	May 21	June 11

NFL Football
Super Bowl

No.	Site	Date
XXXVII	Qualcomm Stadium, San Diego	Jan. 26, 2003
XXXVIII	Reliant Stadium, Houston	Feb. 1, 2004
XXXIX	ALLTEL Stadium, Jacksonville	Feb. 6, 2005
XL	Ford Field, Detroit	Feb. 5, 2006

Golf
The Masters

Year	Site	Dates
2003	Augusta (Ga.) National GC	April 10-13
2004	Augusta (Ga.) National GC	April 8-11

U.S. Open

Year	Site	Dates
2003	Olympia Fields (Ill.) Country Club	June 12-15
2004	Shinnecock Hills GC, Southampton, N.Y.	June 17-20
2005	Pinehurst (N.C.) Resort & CC	June 16-19
2006	Winged Foot GC, Mamaroneck, N.Y.	June 15-18

U.S. Women's Open

Year	Site	Dates
2003	Pumpkin Ridge GC, North Plains, Ore.	July 3-6
2004	The Orchards GC, South Hadley, Mass.	TBA
2005	Cherry Hills CC, Englewood, Colo.	June 23-26

U.S. Senior Open

Year	Site	Dates
2003	Inverness Club, Toledo, Ohio	June 26-29
2004	Bellerive CC, St. Louis, Mo.	July 29-Aug. 1
2005	NCR CC, Kettering, Ohio	July 28-31

PGA Championship

Year	Site	Dates
2003	Oak Hill CC, Rochester, N.Y.	Aug. 15-17
2004	Whistling Straits GC, Kohler, Wis.	Aug. 13-15
2005	Baltusrol GC, Springfield, N.J.	TBA

British Open

Year	Site	Dates
2003	Royal St. George GC, Sandwich, England	July 17-20
2004	Royal Troon GC, Scotland	July 15-18
2005	St. Andrews, Scotland	July 14-17

Ryder Cup

Year	Site	Date
2004	Oakland Hills CC, Bloomfield Hills, Mich.	Sept. 17-19
2006	Kildare Hotel and CC, Dublin, Ireland	TBA
2008	Valhalla GC, Louisville, Ky.	TBA
2010	Celtic Manor, Wales	TBA

Soccer
World Cup

Year	Site	Dates
2006	Germany	June 9-July 9
2010	Africa	Country TBD

Women's World Cup

Year	Site	Date
2003	China	Sept. 24-Oct.11

Tennis
U.S. Open

Usually held from the last Monday in August through the second Sunday in September, with Labor Day weekend the midway point in the tournament.

Year	Site	Dates
2003	Arthur Ashe Stadium, NYC	Aug. 25-Sept. 7
2004	Arthur Ashe Stadium, NYC	Aug. 30-Sept.12

Baseball

When teams actually pitched to **Barry Bonds**, he usually made them pay. In 2002 Bonds became the fourth member of the 600-home run club.

AP/Wide World Photos

Angels Earn Their Rings

In a World Series that almost wasn't, the Angels proved that baseball is first and foremost a team game.

Karl Ravech
is an analyst for ESPN's baseball coverage.

Four years ago, in the summer of 1998, Mark McGwire and Sammy Sosa engaged in a home run hitting frenzy that broke records and rescued the game of baseball.

By 2002, the life raft they had provided had run out of air. Once again the game was sinking. Labor unrest was at hand. Terms like "competitive balance," "revenue sharing" and "luxury tax" were tossed around like hand grenades. Major League Baseball needed another work stoppage like Alex Rodriguez needed to borrow 75 cents for a soda.

Typical hardline negotiating tactics had brought the game's leaders to the edge of a cliff. With a deadline of Aug. 30, the two sides gathered in New York City one final time. I happened to be in Vancouver at the time, covering the PGA Tour. The assumption was that if a deal was to be done, it would be in the wee hours of the morning of Aug. 30. Sometime around midnight (3 a.m. EDT) I assumed I'd have the story. But constant phone calls throughout the night to the offices of the principals involved yielded the same response: "still meeting."

By the morning of Aug. 30, there was still no agreement. I had become convinced that the league was once again jumping off the cliff. At about 9:30 a.m. my cell phone rang. It was Gene Orza, the associate general counsel of the players association. "The deal is done, four years," he said. Within minutes the news was first reported on ESPN.

Uncharacteristically, baseball had avoided disaster. Not one single game was missed. For the first time in a well chronicled history of bitter battles, Commissioner Bud Selig had delivered to owners a package they not only could live with but one they could feel good about. The leadership of the players association listened to its members and

AP/Wide World Photos

*World Series MVP **Troy Glaus** celebrates the Angels' Game 7 victory over the Giants with **Jackie Autry**, the widow of former Angels owner and "Singing Cowboy" Gene Autry.*

put greed aside for the good of the game. Once the deal was done the rest of the season was gravy.

Beyond the new basic agreement, 2002 will be remembered for three things—Barry Bonds, contraction and a wild card World Series.

Coming off a season in which he hit a record 73 home runs, Bonds' numbers actually improved in 2002. His regular season on base (.582), slugging (.799) and batting (.370) averages were all off the charts. That was punctuated by a postseason virtually unmatched in the history of the game. In the World Series alone, he hit four home runs and had an on base percentage of .700, thanks in part to a record 13 walks. And yet in spite of his individual achievements, his Giants lost in seven games to fellow wild card team Anaheim, proving once again that baseball is a team game.

The Angels were picked by most experts to finish no better than third in their own division. Oakland had better pitching and Seattle was coming off a 116-win campaign. The A's did finish in first but the Angels' rush through September carried them into October.

First they beat the Yankees in the divisional series and then conquered the Twins in the ALCS. And they did it all

AP/Wide World Photos

A Minnesota Twins fan holds up this sign for Commissioner Bud Selig, sitting behind home plate, at the Metrodome during Game 1 of the ALCS.

without a "superstar." The key was their bullpen. Spearheaded by 20-year-old rookie, Francisco Rodriguez, who dazzled since his September call-up, the Angels' relief corps was eerily similar to that of the Yankees in their heyday. Rodriguez and closer Troy Percival were Anaheim's version of Mariano Rivera and John Wetteland. There is no greater compliment that can be given a team than a comparison to the Yankees. Now the Angels only need to win 25 more titles to match New York's success.

From compliments to insults. The Twins were left for dead before the season even started. Targeted for contraction by Selig, the team didn't even know if it would have a 2002 season let alone a successful one. Spared, not by an act of good but instead by the courts, the Twins plowed through the AL Central like a tornado, gathering strength and fans, who took as much pride in the team's success as they did in forcing contraction talk down the commissioner's throat. The Twins' run ended in the ALCS but their future is assured. As part of the new Collective Bargaining Agreement, contraction was mercifully put on hold until at least 2007.

The Ten Biggest Stories of the Year in Baseball

10 ▪ Florida speedster Luis Castillo slaps out hits in 35 consecutive games, the tenth-longest streak in major league history and the longest since Paul Molitor's 39-game streak in 1987.

9 ▪ No player had hit four home runs in one game since 1993. Then two players do it in a three-week span. On May 2, Seattle's Mike Cameron hits four out of Comiskey Park. Then on May 23 in Milwaukee, the Dodgers' Shawn Green goes six-for-six with four home runs, six runs and 19 total bases.

8 ▪ Rumors of steroid use and talk of random drug testing run rampant after retired slugger Ken Caminiti reveals he was on the juice during his 1996 MVP season. He also says more than half of major leaguers are currently taking steroids, a claim he later recants.

7 ▪ The owners play their own version of "musical chairs" with Bud Selig conducting the music. Marlins owner John Henry buys the Red Sox for $700 million, then Expos owner Jeffrey Loria buys the Marlins and sells the Expos to the league, presumably setting them up for contraction or relocation.

6 ▪ The Minnesota Twins, rumored to be prime candidates for contraction before the season began, win the AL Central Division by 13½ games, then beat the favored Oakland A's in the first round of the playoffs.

5 ▪ The Cardinals are dealt a tragic blow on June 22 when popular pitcher Darryl Kile, 33, is found dead in his Chicago hotel room from a blocked coronary artery.

4 ▪ Former Red Sox slugger Ted Williams, who many consider the best hitter who ever lived, dies at the age of 83. An embarrassing family battle ensues over whether his body is to be cremated or cryogenically frozen.

3 ▪ It was an interesting year for Commissioner Bud Selig, to say the least. First he threatens to contract the Twins and Expos days after the 2001 World Series. He then presides over what many consider shady sales of the Red Sox, Marlins and Expos. In July he ends the All-Star Game with the score tied, 7-7. And as all of this is happening, baseball's ninth work stoppage threatened to shut down the season. Would you want that job?

2 ▪ Barry Bonds has another season for the ages, walking an all-time record 198 times, becoming the fourth member of the 600-home run club, and leading the Giants to within one game of a World Series title.

1 ▪ Down three games to two and trailing, 5-0, in the seventh inning, the Anaheim Angels stage a ferocious rally to win Game 6, then win Game 7, 4-1, to become World Series champions.

Not so Offensive

While the offensive numbers in the World Series were huge, the same can not be said for the regular season. For the second straight year, offense has declined in the major leagues.

Category	2002	Lowest Since
Batting Avg.	.261	1992 (.256)
Runs per game	9.24	1993 (9.20)
HR per game	2.09	1998 (2.08)
ERA	4.27	1992 (4.18)

Mr. Consistency

Pitcher Greg Maddux went 16-6 for the Atlanta Braves in 2002, making it 15 consecutive seasons in which the righthander won at least 15 games, tying a major league record.

Pitcher	Streak	Seasons
Greg Maddux	1988–2002	15
Cy Young	1891–1905	15
Gaylord Perry	1966–78	13
Christy Mathewson	1903–14	12

Lidle Change

If you thought you were hot in August, look at Oakland pitcher Cory Lidle's numbers: 5-0 with a 0.20 ERA. Lidle was only 3-10 with a 5.03 ERA the rest of the season. Here's a look at the fewest earned runs allowed in a month in the last 40 years (min. 6 starts):

Month	Pitcher	ER
Sept. 1988	Orel Hershiser	0
Aug. 2002	Cory Lidle	1
May 1984	Nolan Ryan	1
Sept. 1974	Jim Kaat	2
May 1968	Joe Horlen	2

Kombination

In 2002, Randy Johnson and Curt Schilling became the first pair of team-mates to each have 300 strikeouts in the same season. Here's a look at the team-mates with the most combined strikeouts in history:

Year	Team	Ks
2001	R. Johnson/C. Schilling, Ari	665
2002	R. Johnson/C. Schilling, Ari	650
1973	N. Ryan/B. Singer, Cal	624
1965	S. Koufax/D. Drysdale, LA	592
1976	N. Ryan/F. Tanana, Cal	588

Note: In 2001, Johnson had 372 Ks to Schilling's 293.

Swingers baby!

If you could hit like Alfonso Soriano, wouldn't you swing at everything too? In 2002, the Yankees 2nd baseman had the fewest walks by anyone who also had 150 strikeouts in the same season.

	BB	K
Alfonso Soriano, '02	23	157
Butch Hobson, '77	27	162
Juan Samuel, '84	26	168
Bo Jackson, '87	30	158
Cory Snyder, '87	31	166

2002 Season in Review

Final Major League Standings

Division champions (*) and Wild Card (†) winners are noted. Number of seasons listed after each manager refers to current tenure with club.

American League

East Division

	W	L	Pct	GB	Home	Road
*New York	103	58	.640	—	52-28	51-30
Boston	93	69	.574	10½	42-39	51-30
Toronto	78	84	.481	25½	42-39	36-45
Baltimore	67	95	.414	36½	34-47	33-48
Tampa Bay	55	106	.342	48	30-51	25-55

2002 Managers: NY–Joe Torre (7th season); **Bos**–Grady Little (1st); **Tor**–Buck Martinez (2nd, 20-33) was fired on June 3 and replaced by 3rd base coach Carlos Tosca (58-51); **Bal**–Mike Hargrove (3rd); **TB**–Hal McRae (2nd).

2001 Standings: 1. New York (95-65); 2. Boston (82-79); 3. Toronto (80-82); 4. Baltimore (63-98); 5. Tampa Bay (62-100).

Central Division

	W	L	Pct	GB	Home	Road
*Minnesota	94	67	.584	—	54-27	40-40
Chicago	81	81	.500	13½	47-34	34-47
Cleveland	74	88	.457	20½	39-42	35-46
Kansas City	62	100	.383	32½	37-44	25-56
Detroit	55	106	.342	39	33-47	22-59

2002 Managers: Min–Ron Gardenhire (1st season); **Chi**–Jerry Manuel (5th); **Cle**–Charlie Manuel (3rd, 39-47) was fired on July 11 and replaced by 3rd base coach Joel Skinner (35-41); **KC**–Tony Muser (6th, 8-15) was fired on April 30 and replaced on an interim basis by bullpen coach John Mizerock (5-8) and then Tony Pena (49-77) on May 15; **Det**–Phil Garner (3rd, 0-6) was fired on April 8 and replaced by bench coach Luis Pujols (55-100).

2001 Standings: 1. Cleveland (91-71); 2. Minnesota (85-77); 3. Chicago (83-79); 4. Detroit (66-96); 5. Kansas City (65-97).

West Division

	W	L	Pct	GB	Home	Road
*Oakland	103	59	.636	—	54-27	49-32
†Anaheim	99	63	.611	4	54-27	45-36
Seattle	93	69	.574	10	48-33	45-36
Texas	72	90	.444	31	42-39	30-51

2002 Managers: Oak–Art Howe (7th season); **Ana**–Mike Scioscia (3rd); **Sea**–Lou Piniella (10th); **Tex**–Jerry Narron (2nd).

2001 Standings: 1. Seattle (116-46); 2. Oakland (102-60); 3. Anaheim (75-87); 4. Texas (73-89).

National League

East Division

	W	L	Pct	GB	Home	Road
*Atlanta	101	59	.631	—	52-28	49-31
Montreal	83	79	.512	19	49-32	34-47
Philadelphia	80	81	.497	21½	40-40	40-41
Florida	79	83	.488	23	46-35	33-48
New York	75	86	.466	26½	38-43	37-43

2002 Managers: Atl–Bobby Cox (13th season); **Mon**–Frank Robinson (1st); **Phi**–Larry Bowa (2nd); **Fla**–Jeff Torborg (1st); **NY**–Bobby Valentine (7th).

2001 Standings: 1. Atlanta (88-74); 2. Philadelphia (86-76); 3. New York (82-80); 4. Florida (76-86); 5. Montreal (68-94).

Central Division

	W	L	Pct	GB	Home	Road
*St. Louis	97	65	.599	—	52-29	45-36
Houston	84	78	.519	13	47-34	37-44
Cincinnati	78	84	.481	19	38-43	40-41
Pittsburgh	72	89	.447	24½	38-42	34-47
Chicago	67	95	.414	30	36-45	31-50
Milwaukee	56	106	.346	41	31-50	25-56

2002 Managers: St.L–Tony La Russa (7th season); **Hou**–Jimy Williams (1st); **Cin**–Bob Boone (2nd); **Pit**–Lloyd McClendon (2nd); **Chi**–Don Baylor (3rd, 34-49) was fired on July 5 and replaced by bench coach Rene Lachemann (0-1) and then Bruce Kimm (33-45); **Mil**–Dave Lopes (3rd, 3-12) was fired on April 18 and replaced by bench coach Jerry Royster (53-94).

2001 Standings: 1. Houston (93-69); 2. St. Louis (93-69); 3. Chicago (88-74); 4. Milwaukee (68-94); 5. Cincinnati (66-96); 6. Pittsburgh (62-100).

West Division

	W	L	Pct	GB	Home	Road
*Arizona	98	64	.605	—	55-26	43-38
†San Francisco	95	66	.590	2½	50-31	45-35
Los Angeles	92	70	.568	6	46-35	46-35
Colorado	73	89	.451	25	47-34	26-55
San Diego	66	96	.407	32	41-40	25-56

2002 Managers: Ari–Bob Brenly (2nd season); **SF**–Dusty Baker (10th); **LA**–Jim Tracy (2nd); **Col**–Buddy Bell (3rd, 6-16) was fired on April 26 and replaced by hitting coach Clint Hurdle (67-73); **SD**–Bruce Bochy (8th).

2001 Standings: 1. Arizona (92-70); 2. San Francisco (90-72); 3. Los Angeles (86-76); 4. San Diego (79-83); 5. Colorado (73-89).

Interleague Play Standings

American League

	W-L	Pct		W-L	Pct
Oakland	16-2	.889	Chicago	8-10	.444
Anaheim	11-7	.611	Tampa Bay	7-11	.389
New York	11-7	.611	Cleveland	6-12	.333
Seattle	11-7	.611	Detroit	6-12	.333
Minnesota	10-8	.556	Boston	5-13	.278
Baltimore	9-9	.500	Kansas City	5-13	.278
Texas	9-9	.500	**Totals**	**123-129**	**.488**
Toronto	9-9	.500			

National League

	W-L	Pct		W-L	Pct
Atlanta	15-3	.833	San Diego	8-10	.444
Los Angeles	12-6	.667	San Francisco	8-10	.444
Montreal	12-6	.667	Houston	5-7	.417
St. Louis	8-4	.667	Colorado	7-11	.389
Arizona	11-7	.611	Pittsburgh	3-9	.250
Philadelphia	10-8	.556	Cincinnati	2-10	.167
Florida	10-8	.556	Milwaukee	2-10	.167
New York	10-8	.556	**Totals**	**129-123**	**.512**
Chicago	6-6	.500			

| Boston Red Sox
Manny Ramirez
BA, OBP | Texas Rangers
Alex Rodriguez
Home Runs, RBI, Total Bases | NY Yankees
Alfonso Soriano
Hits, Runs, SB | Boston Red Sox
Pedro Martinez
ERA, Ks, Opp. BA, WHIP |

American League Leaders

(*) indicates rookie.

Batting

	Bat	Gm	AB	R	H	Avg	TB	2B	3B	HR	RBI	BB	SO	SB	Slg Pct	OBP
Manny Ramirez, Bos	R	120	436	84	152	.349	282	31	0	33	107	73	85	0	.647	.450
Mike Sweeney, KC	R	126	471	81	160	.340	265	31	1	24	86	61	46	9	.563	.417
Bernie Williams, NY	S	154	612	102	204	.333	302	37	2	19	102	83	97	8	.493	.415
Ichiro Suzuki, Sea	L	157	647	111	208	.321	275	27	8	8	51	68	62	31	.425	.388
Magglio Ordonez, Chi	R	153	590	116	189	.320	352	47	1	38	135	53	77	7	.597	.381
Jason Giambi, NY	L	155	560	120	176	.314	335	34	1	41	122	109	112	2	.598	.435
Adam Kennedy, Ana	L	144	474	65	148	.312	213	32	6	7	52	19	80	17	.449	.345
Nomar Garciaparra, Bos	R	156	635	101	197	.310	335	56	5	24	120	41	63	5	.528	.352
Miguel Tejada, Oak	R	162	662	108	204	.308	336	30	0	34	131	38	84	7	.508	.354
Garret Anderson, Ana	L	158	638	93	195	.306	344	56	3	29	123	30	80	6	.539	.332
Jim Thome, Cle	L	147	480	101	146	.304	325	19	2	52	118	122	139	1	.677	.445
Paul Konerko, Chi	R	151	570	81	173	.304	284	30	0	27	104	44	72	0	.498	.359
Shannon Stewart, Tor	R	141	577	103	175	.303	255	38	6	10	45	54	60	14	.442	.371
Ellis Burks, Cle	R	138	518	92	156	.301	280	28	0	32	91	44	108	2	.541	.362
Randall Simon, Det	L	130	482	51	145	.301	221	17	1	19	82	13	30	0	.459	.320

Note: Batters must have 3.1 plate appearances per their team's games played to qualify.

Home Runs

A. Rodriguez, Tex 57
Thome, Cle 52
Palmeiro, Tex 43
Giambi, NY 41
Soriano, NY 39
Ordonez, Chi 38
Chavez, Oak 34
Tejada, Oak 34
Delgado, Tor 33
Ramirez, Bos 33

Triples

Damon, Bos 11
Winn, TB 9
Suzuki, Sea 8
Young, Tex 8
Beltran, KC 7
Fifteen tied with 6 each.

On Base Pct.

Ramirez, Bos ..... .450
Thome, Cle ..... .445
Giambi, NY ..... .435
Sweeney, KC ..... .417
B. Williams, NY ..... .415
Delgado, Tor ..... .406
Olerud, Sea ..... .403
A. Rodriguez, Tex ..... .392
Palmeiro, Tex ..... .391

Runs Batted In

A. Rodriguez, Tex 142
Ordonez, Chi 135
Tejada, Oak 131
Anderson, Ana 123
Giambi, NY 122
Garciaparra, Bos 120
Thome, Cle 118
Glaus, Ana 111
Chavez, Oak 109
Delgado, Tor 108

Doubles

Anderson, Ana 56
Garciaparra, Bos 56
Soriano, NY 51
Ordonez, Chi 47
Beltran, KC 44
Hillenbrand, Bos 43
Posada, NY 40

Slugging Pct.

Thome, Cle ..... .677
Ramirez, Bos ..... .647
A. Rodriguez, Tex ..... .623
Giambi, NY ..... .598
Ordonez, Chi ..... .597
Palmeiro, Tex ..... .571
Sweeney, KC ..... .563

Hits

Soriano, NY 209
Suzuki, Sea 208
Tejada, Oak 204
B. Williams, NY 204
Garciaparra, Bos 197
Anderson, Ana 195
Jeter, NY 191
Ordonez, Chi 189
A. Rodriguez, Tex 187

Runs

Soriano, NY 128
A. Rodriguez, Tex 125
Jeter, NY 124
Giambi, NY 120
Damon, Bos 118
Ordonez, Chi 116
Beltran, KC 114
Durham, Chi-Oak 114

Walks

Thome, Cle 122
Giambi, NY 109
Palmeiro, Tex 104
Delgado, Tor 102
Olerud, Sea 98
Ventura, NY 90
Glaus, Ana 88
Thomas, Chi 88

Stolen Bases

	SB	CS
Soriano, NY	41	13
Beltran, KC	35	7
Jeter, NY	32	3
Damon, Bos	31	6
Cameron, Sea	31	8
Suzuki, Sea	31	15
Winn, TB	27	8

Total Bases

A. Rodriguez, Tex 389
Soriano, NY 381
Ordonez, Chi 352
Anderson, Ana 344
Tejada, Oak 336
Garciaparra, Bos 335
Giambi, NY 335
Thome, Cle 325

Strikeouts

Cameron, Sea 176
Soriano, NY 157
Glaus, Ana 144
Posada, NY 143
Thome, Cle 139
Sandberg, TB 139
Hinske*, Tor 138
Beltran, KC 135

Pitching

	Arm	W	L	ERA	Gm	GS	CG	ShO	Sv	IP	H	R	ER	HR	HB	BB	SO	WP
Pedro Martinez, Bos	R	20	4	2.26	30	30	2	0	0	199.1	144	62	50	13	15	40	239	3
Derek Lowe, Bos	R	21	8	2.58	32	32	1	1	0	219.2	166	65	63	12	12	48	127	5
Barry Zito, Oak	L	23	5	2.75	35	35	1	0	0	229.1	182	79	70	24	9	78	182	2
Tim Wakefield, Bos	R	11	5	2.81	45	15	0	0	3	163.1	121	57	51	15	9	51	134	5
Roy Halladay, Tor	R	19	7	2.93	34	34	2	1	0	239.1	223	93	78	10	7	62	168	4
Tim Hudson, Oak	R	15	9	2.98	34	34	4	2	0	238.1	237	87	79	19	8	62	152	7
Jarrod Washburn, Ana	L	18	6	3.15	32	32	1	0	0	206.0	183	75	72	19	3	59	139	5
Joel Pineiro, Sea	R	14	7	3.24	37	28	2	1	0	194.1	189	75	70	24	7	54	136	8
Jamie Moyer, Sea	L	13	8	3.32	34	34	4	2	0	230.2	198	89	85	28	9	50	147	3
Mark Mulder, Oak	L	19	7	3.47	30	30	2	1	0	207.1	182	88	80	21	11	55	159	7
Rodrigo Lopez*, Bal	R	15	9	3.57	33	28	1	0	0	196.2	172	83	78	23	5	62	136	2
Mark Buehrle, Chi	L	19	12	3.58	34	34	5	2	0	239.0	236	102	95	25	3	61	134	6
David Wells, NY	L	19	7	3.75	31	31	2	1	0	206.1	210	100	86	21	5	45	137	4
Ramon Ortiz, Ana	R	15	9	3.77	32	32	4	1	0	217.1	188	97	91	40	5	68	162	7
Rick Reed, Min	R	15	7	3.78	33	32	2	1	0	188.0	192	89	79	32	6	26	121	1

Note: Pitchers must have one inning pitched per their team's games played to qualify.

Wins

Zito, Oak	23-5
Lowe, Bos	21-8
Martinez, Bos	20-4
Halladay, Tor	19-7
Mulder, Oak	19-7
Wells, NY	19-7
Buehrle, Chi	19-12
Washburn, Ana	18-6
Mussina, NY	18-10
Byrd, KC	17-11

Losses

Sturtze, TB	4-18
Sparks, Det	8-16
Suppan, KC	9-16
Castillo, Bos	6-15
Ritchie, Chi	5-15
Redman, Det	8-15
Johnson, Bal	5-14
Seven tied with 12 each.	

Walks

Sturtze, TB	89
Sabathia, Cle	88
Garland, Chi	83
Baez, Cle	82
Park, Tex	78
Zito, Oak	78
Wright, Chi	71
Rogers, Tex	70
Lohse, Min	70

Strikeouts

Martinez, Bos	239
Clemens, NY	192
Mussina, NY	182
Zito, Oak	182
Garcia, Sea	181
Halladay, Tor	168
Ortiz, Ana	162
Mulder, Oak	159
Hudson, Oak	152
Sabathia, Cle	149

Appearances

Koch, Oak	84
Romero, Min	81
Stanton, NY	79
Karsay, NY	78
Escobar, Tor	76
Bradford, Oak	75
Rincon, Cle-Oak	71
Grimsley, KC	70
Groom, Bal	70

Innings

Halladay, Tor	239.1
Buehrle, Chi	239.0
Hudson, Oak	238.1
Moyer, Sea	230.2
Zito, Oak	229.1
Byrd, KC	228.1
Sturtze, TB	224.0
Garcia, Sea	223.2
Lowe, Bos	219.2
Ortiz, Ana	217.1

HRs Allowed

Ortiz, Ana	40
Byrd, KC	36
Sturtze, TB	33
Reed, Min	32
Suppan, KC	32
Wright, Chi	32
Garcia, Sea	30

Opp. Batting Average

Martinez, Bos	.198
Wakefield, Bos	.204
Lowe, Bos	.211
Zito, Oak	.218
Moyer, Sea	.230
Ortiz, Ana	.230
Mulder, Oak	.232
Lopez*, Bal	.234
Washburn, Ana	.235
Halladay, Tor	.244

Complete Games

Byrd, KC	7
Buehrle, Chi	5
Kennedy, TB	5
Colon, Cle	4
Hudson, Oak	4
Moyer, Sea	4
Ortiz, Ana	4
Sturtze, TB	4

Saves

	SV	BS
Guardado, Min	45	6
Koch, Oak	44	6
Percival, Ana	40	4
Urbina, Bos	40	6
Escobar, Tor	38	8
Sasaki, Sea	37	8
Acevedo, Det	28	7
Rivera, NY	28	4
Ro. Hernandez, KC	26	7
Julio*, Bal	25	6

Wild Pitches

Santana, Min	15
Clemens, NY	14
Redman, Det	11
Drese*, Cle	11
Suppan, KC	10
Ritchie, Chi	10
Wright, Chi	10
Zambrano, TB	10

WHIP
(Walks + Hits/IP)

Martinez, Bos	0.92
Lowe, Bos	0.97
Wakefield, Bos	1.05
Moyer, Sea	1.08
Zito, Oak	1.13
Mulder, Oak	1.14
Byrd, KC	1.15
Reed, Min	1.16
Washburn, Ana	1.17
Ortiz, Ana	1.18

Shutouts

Weaver, Det-NY	3
Seven tied with 2 each.	

SB Allowed

Castillo, Bos	24
Clemens, NY	23
Wakefield, Bos	21
Halladay, Tor	21
Lowe, Bos	19
Sabathia, Cle	19
Wright, Chi	19

Fielding

Put Outs

Delgado, Tor	1231
Olerud, Sea	1169
Konerko, Chi	1146
Spiezio, Ana	1093
Mientkiewicz, Min	1073
Thome, Cle	1064
Pena*, Oak-Det	1010
Posada, NY	965
Conine, Bal	956
Varitek, Bos	912

Assists

Tejada, Oak	504
A. Rodriguez, Tex	472
Garciaparra, Bos	467
Young, Tex	432
Vizquel, Cle	431
Perez, Cle	413
Soriano, NY	402
Eckstein, Ana	397
Boone, Sea	387
Bordick, Bal	372

OF Assists

Fick, Det	21
Higginson, Det	15
Winn, TB	13
Beltran, KC	12
Erstad, Ana	11
Jones, Min	11
Wells, Tor	10
Five tied with 9 each.	

Errors

Garciaparra, Bos	25
Ventura, NY	23
Hillenbrand, Bos	23
Soriano, NY	23
Halter, Det	21
Perez, KC	20
Hinske*, Tor	20
Glaus, Ana	20
Valentin, Chi	19
Tejada, Oak	19

San Francisco Giants
Barry Bonds
BA, SLG, OBP, Walks

Chicago Cubs
Sammy Sosa
Home Runs, Runs

Arizona Diamondbacks
Randy Johnson
ERA, Wins, CG, IP, Ks,
Opp. BA

Atlanta Braves
John Smoltz
Saves

National League Leaders

(*) indicates rookie.

Batting

	Bat	Gm	AB	R	H	Avg	TB	2B	3B	HR	RBI	BB	SO	SB	Slg Pct	OBP
Barry Bonds, SF	L	143	403	117	149	**.370**	322	31	2	46	110	198	47	9	.799	.582
Larry Walker, Col	L	136	477	95	161	**.338**	287	40	4	26	104	65	73	6	.602	.421
Vladimir Guerrero, Mon	R	161	614	106	206	**.336**	364	37	2	39	111	84	70	40	.593	.417
Todd Helton, Col	L	156	553	107	182	**.329**	319	39	4	30	109	99	91	5	.577	.429
Chipper Jones, Atl	S	158	548	90	179	**.327**	294	35	1	26	100	107	89	8	.536	.435
Jose Vidro, Mon	S	152	604	103	190	**.315**	296	43	3	19	96	60	70	2	.490	.378
Albert Pujols, St.L	R	157	590	118	185	**.314**	331	40	2	34	127	72	69	2	.561	.394
Jeff Kent, SF	R	152	623	102	195	**.313**	352	42	2	37	108	52	101	5	.565	.368
Jim Edmonds, St.L	L	144	476	96	148	**.311**	267	31	2	28	83	86	134	4	.561	.420
Edgardo Alfonzo, NY	R	135	490	78	151	**.308**	225	26	0	16	56	62	55	6	.459	.391
Bobby Abreu, Phi	L	157	572	102	176	**.308**	298	50	6	20	85	104	117	31	.521	.413
Gary Sheffield, Atl	R	135	492	82	151	**.307**	252	26	0	25	84	72	53	12	.512	.404
Luis Castillo, Fla	S	146	606	86	185	**.305**	219	18	5	2	39	55	76	48	.361	.364
Edgar Renteria, St.L	R	152	544	77	166	**.305**	239	36	2	11	83	49	57	22	.439	.364
Junior Spivey, Ari	R	143	538	103	162	**.301**	256	34	6	16	78	65	100	11	.476	.389

Note: Batters must have 3.1 plate appearances per their team's games played to qualify.

Home Runs

Sosa, Chi	.49
Bonds, SF	.46
Berkman, Hou	.42
Green, LA	.42
V. Guerrero, Mon	.39
Giles, Pit	.38
Burrell, Phi	.37
Kent, SF	.37
A. Jones, Atl	.35
Pujols, St.L	.34

Triples

Rollins, Phi	.10
Furcal, Atl	.8
McCracken, Ari	.8
Rolen, Phi-St.L	.8
Wilkerson*, Mon	.8
Six tied with 7 each.	

On Base Pct.

Bonds, SF	.582
Giles, Pit	.450
C. Jones, Atl	.435
Helton, Col	.429
Walker, Col	.421
Edmonds, St.L	.420
V. Guerrero, Mon	.417
Abreu, Phi	.413
Berkman, Hou	.405

Runs Batted In

Berkman, Hou	.128
Pujols, St.L	.127
Burrell, Phi	.116
Green, LA	.114
V. Guerrero, Mon	.111
Bonds, SF	.110
Rolen, Phi-St.L	.110
Helton, Col	.109
Kent, SF	.108
Sosa, Chi	.108

Doubles

Abreu, Phi	.50
Lowell, Fla	.44
Cabrera, Mon	.43
Vidro, Mon	.43
Kent, SF	.42
Walker, Cin	.42
Millar, Fla	.41

Slugging Pct.

Bonds, SF	.799
Giles, Pit	.622
Walker, Col	.602
Sosa, Chi	.594
V. Guerrero, Mon	.593
Berkman, Hou	.578
Helton, Col	.577

Hits

V. Guerrero, Mon	.206
Kent, SF	.195
Vidro, Mon	.190
Castillo, Fla	.185
Pujols, St.L	.185
Walker, Cin	.183
Helton, Col	.182
C. Jones, Atl	.179
Abreu, Phi	.176

Runs

Sosa, Chi	.122
Pujols, St.L	.118
Bonds, SF	.117
Green, LA	.110
Helton, Col	.107
Berkman, Hou	.106
V. Guerrero, Mon	.106
Spivey, Ari	.103
Vidro, Mon	.103

Walks

Bonds, SF	.198
Giles, Pit	.135
Dunn, Cin	.128
Berkman, Hou	.107
C. Jones, Atl	.107
Abreu, Phi	.104
Sosa, Chi	.103

Stolen Bases

	SB	CS
Castillo, Fla	.48	15
Pierre, Col	.47	12
Roberts, LA	.45	10
V. Guerrero, Mon	.40	20
Sanchez*, Mil	.37	14
Boone, Cin	.32	8
Four tied with 31 each.		

Total Bases

V. Guerrero, Mon	.364
Kent, SF	.352
Berkman, Hou	.334
Pujols, St.L	.331
Sosa, Chi	.330
Green, LA	.325
Bonds, SF	.322
Burrell, Phi	.319
Helton, Col	.319

Strikeouts

Hernandez, Mil	.188
Dunn, Cin	.170
Lee, Fla	.164
Wilkerson*, Mon	.161
Burrell, Phi	.153
Vaughn, NY	.145
Sosa, Chi	.144
Bellhorn, Chi	.144

Pitching

	Arm	W	L	ERA	Gm	GS	CG	ShO	Sv	IP	H	R	ER	HR	HB	BB	SO	WP
Randy Johnson, Ari	L	24	5	**2.32**	35	35	8	4	0	260.0	197	78	67	26	13	71	334	3
Greg Maddux, Atl	R	16	6	**2.62**	34	34	0	0	0	199.1	194	67	58	14	4	45	118	1
Tom Glavine, Atl	L	18	11	**2.96**	36	36	2	1	0	224.2	210	85	74	21	8	78	127	2
Odalis Perez, LA	L	15	10	**3.00**	32	32	4	2	0	222.1	182	76	74	21	4	38	155	2
Roy Oswalt, Hou	R	19	9	**3.01**	35	34	0	1	0	233.0	215	86	78	17	5	62	208	3
Elmer Dessens, Cin	R	7	8	**3.03**	30	30	0	0	0	178.0	173	70	60	24	7	49	93	3
Tomokazu Ohka, Mon	R	13	8	**3.18**	32	31	2	0	0	192.2	194	83	68	19	7	45	118	2
Randy Wolf, Phi	L	11	9	**3.20**	31	31	3	2	0	210.2	172	77	75	23	7	63	172	4
Kirk Rueter, SF	L	14	8	**3.23**	33	33	0	0	0	203.2	204	83	73	22	1	54	76	3
Curt Schilling, Ari	R	23	7	**3.23**	36	35	5	1	0	259.1	218	95	93	29	3	33	316	6
Kevin Millwood, Atl	R	18	8	**3.24**	35	34	1	1	0	217.0	186	83	78	16	8	65	178	4
Vicente Padilla, Phi	R	14	11	**3.28**	32	32	1	1	0	206.0	198	83	75	16	15	53	128	6
Wade Miller, Hou	R	15	4	**3.28**	26	26	1	1	0	164.2	151	63	60	14	6	62	144	4
A.J. Burnett, Fla	R	12	9	**3.30**	31	29	7	5	0	204.1	153	84	75	12	9	90	203	14
Steve Trachsel, NY	R	11	11	**3.37**	30	30	1	1	0	173.2	170	80	65	16	0	69	105	4

Note: Pitchers must have one inning pitched per their team's games played to qualify.

Wins

Johnson, Ari 24-5
Schilling, Ari 23-7
Oswalt, Hou 19-9
Millwood, Atl 18-8
Glavine, Atl 18-11
Morris, St.L 17-9
Maddux, Atl 16-6
Nomo, LA 16-6
Jennings*, Col 16-8

Appearances

Quantrill, LA 86
Dotel, Hou 83
Worrell, SF 80
Jones, Col 79
Looper, Fla 78
Sauerbeck, Pit 78
Stone*, Hou 78
Gagne, LA 77
V. Nunez, Fla 77

Complete Games

Johnson, Ari 8
Burnett, Fla 7
Hernandez, SF 5
Schilling, Ari 5
Five tied with 4 each.

Shutouts

Burnett, Fla 5
Johnson, Ari 4
Hernandez, SF 3
Six tied with 2 each.

Losses

Rusch, Mil 10-16
Sheets, Mil 11-16
Hernandez, SF 12-16
Hampton, Col 7-15
Thomson, NY-Col 9-14
Wells, Pit 12-14
Wright, Mil 5-13
Anderson, Pit 8-13
Ashby, LA 9-13
Vazquez, Mon 10-13
Dempster, Fla-Cin 10-13
Leiter, NY 13-13

Innings

Johnson, Ari 260.0
Schilling, Ari 259.1
Oswalt, Hou 233.0
Vazquez, Mon 230.1
Glavine, Atl 224.2
Perez, LA 222.1
Nomo, LA 220.1
Millwood, Atl 217.0
Sheets, Mil 216.2
Hernandez, SF 216.0

Saves

	SV	BS
Smoltz, Atl	55	4
Gagne, LA	52	4
M. Williams, Pit	46	4
Mesa, Phi	45	9
Nen, SF	43	8
Jimenez, Col	41	6
Hoffman, SD	38	3
Kim, Ari	36	6
Wagner, Hou	35	6
Benitez, NY	33	4

Walks

Ishii*, LA 106
Nomo, LA 101
Wood, Chi 97
Ortiz, SD 94
Dempster, Cin-Fla 93
Hampton, Col 91
Burnett, Fla 90
Moss*, Atl 89

HR Allowed

Astacio, NY 32
Helling, Ari 31
Tomko, SD 31
Rusch, Mil 30
Schilling, Ari 29
Five tied with 28 each.

Wild Pitches

Armas Jr., Mon 14
Burnett, Fla 14
Moss*, Atl 13
Schmidt, SF 12
Coggin, Phi 11
Duckworth, Phi 10
Jennings*, Col 10

SB Allowed

Leiter, NY 29
Nomo, LA 28
Maddux, Atl 24
Duckworth, Phi 24
Hernandez, SF 22
Trachsel, NY 21
Millwood, Atl 21
Anderson, Pit 21

Strikeouts

Johnson, Ari 334
Schilling, Ari 316
Wood, Chi 217
Clement, Chi 215
Oswalt, Hou 208
Burnett, Fla 203
Schmidt, SF 196
Nomo, LA 193
Vazquez, Mon 179
Millwood, Atl 178

Opp. Batting Average

Johnson, Ari 208
Burnett, Fla 209
Clement, Chi 215
Schmidt, SF 218
Moss*, Atl 221
Wood, Chi 221
Wolf, Phi 223
Schilling, Ari 224
Perez, LA 226
Millwood, Atl 230

WHIP

(Walks + Hits/IP)
Schilling, Ari 0.97
Perez, LA 0.99
Johnson, Ari 1.03
Wolf, Phi 1.12
Millwood, Atl 1.16
Oswalt, Hou 1.19
Burnett, Fla 1.19
Schmidt, SF 1.19

Fielding

Put Outs

Helton, Col 1358
Lee, Fla 1312
Young, Pit 1278
Lee, Phi 1261
Bagwell, Hou 1255
Sexson, Mil 1225
Martinez, St.L 1221
Karros, LA 1175
Vaughn, NY 1085
Lo Duca, LA 1014

Assists

Uribe, Col 505
Cabrera, Mon 498
Furcal, Atl 478
J. Wilson, Pit 463
Rollins, Phi 455
Hernandez, Mil 451
Vidro, Mon 448
Walker, Cin 438
Kent, SF 414
Renteria, St.L 410

OF Assists

V. Guerrero, Mon 14
Walker, Col 14
Giles, Pit 13
Wilkerson*, Mon 13
Sanders, SF 12
Edmonds, St.L 11
Kotsay, SD 11
Five tied with 10 each.

Errors

Cabrera, Mon 29
Furcal, Atl 27
Uribe, Col 27
Boone, Cin 22
Zeile, Col 21
Gonzalez, Chi 21
Womack, Ari 20
Beltre, LA 20
Anderson, Phi 20
Four tied with 19 each.

Team Batting Statistics

American League

Team	Avg	AB	R	H	HR	RBI	SB
Anaheim	.282	5678	851	1603	152	811	117
Boston	.277	5640	859	1560	177	810	80
New York ...	.275	5601	897	1540	223	857	100
Seattle	.275	5569	814	1531	152	771	137
Minnesota ...	.272	5582	768	1518	167	731	79
Texas	.269	5618	843	1510	230	806	62
Chicago	.268	5502	856	1475	217	819	75
Toronto......	.261	5581	813	1457	187	771	71
Oakland	.261	5558	800	1450	205	772	46
Kansas City..	.256	5535	737	1415	140	695	140
Tampa Bay ..	.253	5604	673	1418	133	640	102
Cleveland ...	.249	5423	739	1349	192	706	52
Detroit	.248	5406	575	1340	124	546	65
Baltimore....	.246	5491	667	1353	165	636	110

National League

Team	Avg	AB	R	H	HR	RBI	SB
Colorado....	.274	5512	778	1508	152	726	103
St. Louis.....	.268	5505	787	1475	175	758	86
Arizona	.267	5508	819	1471	165	783	92
San Fran. ...	.267	5497	783	1465	198	751	74
Los Angeles..	.264	5554	713	1464	155	693	96
Houston......	.262	5503	749	1441	167	719	71
Montreal	.261	5479	735	1432	162	695	118
Florida.......	.261	5496	699	1433	146	653	177
Atlanta......	.260	5495	708	1428	164	669	76
Philadelphia .	.259	5523	710	1428	165	676	104
New York ...	.256	5496	690	1409	160	650	87
Cincinnati ...	.253	5470	709	1386	169	678	116
Milwaukee ...	.253	5415	627	1369	139	597	94
San Diego...	.253	5515	662	1393	136	627	71
Chicago	.246	5496	706	1351	200	676	63
Pittsburgh....	.244	5330	641	1300	142	610	86

Team Pitching Statistics

American League

Team	ERA	W	Sv	CG	ShO	HR	BB	SO
Oakland	3.68	103	48	9	19	135	474	1021
Anaheim	3.69	99	54	7	14	169	509	999
Boston	3.75	93	51	5	17	146	430	1157
New York ...	3.87	103	53	9	11	144	403	1135
Seattle	4.07	93	43	8	12	178	441	1063
Minnesota ...	4.12	94	47	8	9	184	439	1026
Baltimore....	4.46	67	31	8	3	208	549	967
Chicago	4.53	81	35	7	7	190	528	945
Toronto......	4.80	78	41	6	6	177	590	991
Cleveland ...	4.91	74	34	9	4	142	603	1058
Detroit	4.93	55	33	11	7	163	463	794
Texas	5.15	72	33	4	4	194	669	1030
Kansas City..	5.21	62	30	12	6	212	572	909
Tampa Bay ..	5.29	55	25	12	3	215	620	925

National League

Team	ERA	W	Sv	CG	ShO	HR	BB	SO
Atlanta......	3.13	101	57	3	15	123	554	1058
San Fran. ...	3.54	95	43	10	13	116	523	992
Los Angeles .	3.69	92	56	4	15	165	555	1132
St. Louis.....	3.70	97	42	4	9	141	547	1009
New York ...	3.89	75	36	9	10	163	543	1107
Arizona	3.92	98	40	14	10	170	421	1303
Montreal	3.97	83	39	9	3	165	508	1088
Houston......	4.00	84	43	2	11	151	546	1219
Philadelphia .	4.17	80	47	5	9	153	570	1075
Pittsburgh....	4.23	72	47	2	7	163	572	920
Cincinnati ...	4.27	78	42	2	8	173	550	980
Chicago	4.29	67	23	11	9	167	606	1333
Florida......	4.36	79	36	11	12	151	631	1104
San Diego...	4.62	66	40	5	10	177	582	1108
Milwaukee ...	4.73	56	32	7	4	199	666	1026
Colorado....	5.20	73	43	1	8	225	582	920

Team Fielding Statistics

American League

Team	Pct	TC	E	PO	A	DP	TP
Minnesota ...	.987	5830	74	4334	1422	124	0
Anaheim	.986	6019	87	4357	1575	151	0
Baltimore....	.985	6163	91	4352	1720	173	0
Seattle	.985	5939	88	4336	1515	134	0
Texas	.984	6101	99	4319	1683	152	1
Chicago	.984	5961	97	4269	1595	157	0
Oakland	.984	6256	102	4356	1798	144	0
Boston	.983	6087	104	4338	1645	140	0
Toronto......	.982	6035	107	4315	1613	159	0
Cleveland ...	.981	6049	113	4274	1662	161	0
Tampa Bay ..	.979	6014	126	4321	1567	168	1
Kansas City..	.979	6155	130	4323	1702	153	0
New York ...	.979	6007	127	4356	1524	117	0
Detroit	.977	6103	142	4242	1719	148	0

National League

Team	Pct	TC	E	PO	A	DP	TP
Houston......	.986	6081	83	4335	1663	149	0
Philadelphia .	.986	6137	88	4349	1700	156	0
Los Angeles..	.985	6149	90	4373	1686	134	0
San Fran. ...	.985	6032	90	4312	1630	166	0
Arizona	.985	5935	89	4340	1506	116	0
St. Louis.....	.983	6116	103	4339	1674	168	1
Milwaukee ..	.983	6033	103	4297	1633	154	0
Florida......	.983	6111	106	4369	1636	163	1
Atlanta......	.982	6338	114	4402	1822	170	0
Colorado.....	.982	6093	112	4280	1701	158	0
Pittsburgh....	.982	6252	115	4238	1899	177	0
Cincinnati ...	.981	6254	120	4361	1773	169	0
Chicago	.981	5938	114	4324	1500	144	0
San Diego...	.979	6118	128	4309	1681	162	0
Montreal	.978	6297	139	4359	1799	160	1
New York ...	.976	6100	144	4328	1628	138	1

Pct—Fielding Percentage; **TC**—Total Chances; **E**—Errors; **PO**—Putouts; **A**—Assists; **DP**—Double Plays; **TP**—Triple Plays.

2002 All-Star Game
Tie, 7-7 (11 inn.)

73rd Baseball All-Star Game. **Date:** July 9 at Miller Park, Milwaukee, Wis.; **Managers:** Joe Torre, New York (AL) and Bob Brenly, Arizona (NL); **Ted Williams Award (MVP):** not awarded.

For just the second time in 73 years, the MLB All-Star Game ended in a tie. Due to the depletion of the American and National League rosters, Commissioner Bud Selig announced before the bottom of the 11th inning that the 11th would be the last.

American League

	AB	R	H	BI	BB	SO	Avg
Ichiro Suzuki, Sea, rf	2	0	0	0	0	0	.000
Randy Winn, TB, rf	2	1	1	0	1	1	.500
Freddy Garcia, Sea, p	1	0	0	0	0	0	.000
Shea Hillenbrand, Bos, 3b	2	0	0	0	1		.000
Robin Ventura, NY, 3b	1	0	0	0	0	1	.000
Tony Batista, Bal, ph-3b	3	1	1	0	0	1	.333
Alex Rodriguez, Tex, ss	2	0	0	0	0	2	.000
Miguel Tejada, Oak, ss	2	1	1	0	0	0	.500
Nomar Garciaparra, Bos, ss	1	0	0	0	0	0	.000
Jason Giambi, NY, 1b	2	1	1	0	0	1	.500
Paul Konerko, Chi, 1b	2	0	2	2	0	0	1.000
Mike Sweeney, KC, 1b	1	0	0	0	0	0	.000
Manny Ramirez, Bos, lf	2	0	2	1	0	0	1.000
A.J. Pierzynski, Min, ph-c	3	0	0	0	0	0	.000
Jorge Posada, NY, c	3	0	0	0	0	2	.000
Robert Fick, Det, ph-rf	2	1	1	0	0	0	.500
Torii Hunter, Min, cf	2	0	0	0	0	0	.000
Johnny Damon, Bos, cf	3	1	1	0	0	1	.333
Alfonso Soriano, NY, 2b	2	1	1	1	0	1	.500
Omar Vizquel, Cle, 2b	2	0	1	1	1	0	.500
Derek Lowe, Bos, p	0	0	0	0	0	0	—
Derek Jeter, NY, ph	1	0	0	0	0	1	.000
Garret Anderson, lf	4	0	1	0	0	0	.000
TOTALS	45	7	12	7	2	12	.267

National League

	AB	R	H	BI	BB	SO	Avg
Jose Vidro, Mon, 2b	2	0	0	0	0	0	.000
Junior Spivey, Ari, 2b	2	0	0	0	0	1	.000
Benito Santiago, SF, ph-c	2	1	0	0	0	1	.500
Todd Helton, Col, 1b	2	1	1	1	0	0	.500
Lance Berkman, Hou, 1b	3	0	1	2	0	0	.333
Barry Bonds, SF, lf	2	1	1	2	0	0	.500
Richie Sexson, Mil, 1b	1	0	0	0	0	0	.000
Adam Dunn, Cin, lf	1	0	0	0	1	0	.000
Sammy Sosa, Chi, rf	2	0	1	0	0	1	.500
Shawn Green, LA, rf	3	1	1	0	0	1	.333
Vladimir Guerrero, Mon, cf	2	1	1	0	0	1	.500
Andruw Jones, Atl, ph-cf	3	0	0	0	0	2	.000
Mike Piazza, NY, c	2	0	0	1	0	0	.000
Jose Hernandez, Mil, ss	3	0	0	0	0	2	.000
Scott Rolen, Phi, 3b	3	0	0	0	0	1	.000
Luis Castillo, Fla, 2b	2	0	0	0	0	0	.000
Jimmy Rollins, Phi, ss	2	2	2	0	0	0	1.000
Mike Lowell, Fla, ph-3b	3	1	2	0	0	0	.667
Curt Schilling, Ari, p	0	0	0	0	0	0	—
Luis Gonzalez, Ari, ph	1	0	0	0	0	0	.000
Damian Miller, Ari, c	3	1	2	1	0	0	.667
Vicente Padilla, Phi, p	1	0	0	0	1	0	1.000
TOTALS	45	7	13	7	1	11	.289

	1	2	3	4	5	6	7	8	9	10	11		R	H	E
American League	0	0	0	1	1	0	4	1	0	0	0	–	7	12	0
National League	0	1	3	0	1	0	2	0	0	0	0	–	7	13	0

LOB— American 7, National 6. **2B—** Konerko 2 and Winn (AL), Miller 2 (NL). **3B—** Vizquel (AL). **HR—** Soriano (AL, off Gagne, 0 on), Bonds (NL, off Halladay, 1 on). **SB—** Winn, Fick and Damon (AL), Berkman and Green (NL). **SF—** none. **GIDP—** none.

AL Pitching	IP	H	R	ER	BB	SO
Derek Lowe, Bos	2.0	2	1	1	0	0
Roy Halladay, Tor	1.0	3	3	3	0	1
Mark Buehrle, Chi	2.0	2	1	1	0	2
Barry Zito, Oak	0.1	0	0	0	0	0
Eddie Guardado, Min	0.2	0	0	0	0	0
Kazuhiro Sasaki, Sea	1.0	3	2	2	1	2
Ugueth Urbina, Bos	1.0	0	0	0	0	1
Mariano Rivera, NY	1.0	1	0	0	0	0
Freddy Garcia, Sea	2.0	2	0	0	0	3
TOTALS	11.0	13	7	7	1	11

NL Pitching	IP	H	R	ER	BB	SO
Curt Schilling, Ari	2.0	1	0	0	0	3
Mike Williams, Pit	1.0	0	0	0	0	2
Odalis Perez, LA	1.0	2	1	0	0	2
Eric Gagne, LA	1.0	2	1	1	0	1
Trevor Hoffman, SD	1.0	1	0	0	0	1
Mike Remlinger, Atl	0.2	1	2	2	1	0
Byung-Hyun Kim, Ari	0.1	3	2	2	0	0
Robb Nen, SF	1.0	2	1	1	0	2
John Smoltz, Atl	1.0	0	0	0	0	1
Vicente Padilla, Phi	2.0	0	0	0	1	0
TOTALS	11.0	12	7	6	2	12

PB— Piazza (NL). **WP—** Garcia (AL). **Balk—** Lowe (AL). **Umpires—** Gerry Davis (plate); Tim Tschida (1b); Chuck Meriwether (2b); Jerry Meals (3b); Marty Foster (lf); Paul Emmel (rf). **Attendance—** 41,871 (41,900 capacity). **Time—** 3:29. **TV Rating—** 9.5/17 share (FOX).

Home Run Derby
Results of the All-Star Home Run Derby at Miller Park, Milwaukee, Wis. on July 8.

First Round

	HRs	Long (feet)
Sammy Sosa, Chicago-NL	12	524
Jason Giambi, New York-AL	11	461
Paul Konerko, Chicago-AL	6	473
Richie Sexson, Milwaukee	6	480
Torii Hunter, Minnesota	3	420
Alex Rodriguez, Texas	2	492
Barry Bonds, San Francisco	2	437
Lance Berkman, Houston	1	402

Note: Top four advance to the semifinals.

Semifinals
Giambi def. Konerko, 7-6
Sosa def. Sexson, 5-4

Finals
Giambi def. Sosa, 7-1

AL Team by Team Statistics

At least 135 at bats or 40 innings pitched during the regular season, unless otherwise indicated. Players who competed for more than one AL team are listed with their final club. Players traded from the NL are listed with AL team only if they have 135 AB or 40 IP. Note that (*) indicates rookie and PTBN indicates player to be named.

Anaheim Angels

Batting (100 AB)	Avg	AB	R	H	HR	RBI	SB
Adam Kennedy	.312	474	65	148	7	52	17
Garret Anderson	.306	638	93	195	29	123	6
Orlando Palmeiro	.300	263	35	79	0	31	7
David Eckstein	.293	608	107	178	8	63	21
Shawn Wooten	.292	113	13	33	3	19	2
Brad Fullmer	.289	429	75	124	19	59	10
Tim Salmon	.286	483	84	138	22	88	6
Scott Spiezio	.285	491	80	140	12	82	6
Benji Gil	.285	130	11	37	3	20	2
Darin Erstad	.283	625	99	177	10	73	23
Troy Glaus	.250	569	99	142	30	111	10
Bengie Molina	.245	428	34	105	5	47	0

Pitching (40 IP)	ERA	W-L	Gm	IP	BB	SO
Troy Percival	1.92	4-1	58	56.1	25	68
Brendan Donnelly*	2.17	1-1	46	49.2	19	54
Scot Shields*	2.20	5-3	29	49.0	21	30
Ben Weber	2.54	7-2	63	78.0	22	43
Jarrod Washburn	3.15	18-6	32	206.0	59	139
Lou Pote	3.22	0-2	31	50.1	26	32
John Lackey*	3.66	9-4	18	108.1	33	69
Ramon Ortiz	3.77	15-9	32	217.1	68	162
Kevin Appier	3.92	14-12	32	188.1	64	132
Al Levine	4.24	4-4	52	63.2	34	40
Scott Schoeneweis	4.88	9-8	54	118.0	49	65
Aaron Sele	4.89	8-9	26	160.0	49	82

Saves: Percival (40); Weber (7); Levine (5); Donnelly and Schoeneweis (1). **Complete games:** Ortiz (4); Washburn, Lackey and Sele (1). **Shutouts:** Ortiz and Sele (1).

Baltimore Orioles

Batting (125 AB)	Avg	AB	R	H	HR	RBI	SB
Gary Matthews Jr.	.276	344	54	95	7	38	15
Jeff Conine	.273	451	44	123	15	63	8
Jerry Hairston Jr.	.268	426	55	114	5	32	21
Chris Singleton	.262	466	67	122	9	50	20
Marty Cordova	.253	458	55	116	18	64	1
Jay Gibbons	.247	490	71	121	28	69	1
Tony Batista	.244	615	90	150	31	87	5
Melvin Mora	.233	557	86	130	19	64	16
Chris Richard	.232	155	15	36	4	21	0
Geronimo Gil*	.232	422	33	98	12	45	2
Mike Bordick	.232	367	37	85	8	36	7
Brook Fordyce	.231	130	7	30	1	8	1
Brian Roberts	.227	128	18	29	1	11	9

Acquired: Matthews Jr. from NYM for P John Bale (Apr. 3).

Pitching (40 IP)	ERA	W-L	Gm	IP	BB	SO
Buddy Groom	1.60	3-2	70	62.0	12	48
Jorge Julio*	1.99	5-6	67	68.0	27	55
Willis Roberts	3.36	5-4	66	75.0	32	51
Rodrigo Lopez*	3.57	15-9	33	196.2	62	136
Rick Bauer*	3.98	6-7	56	83.2	36	45
Sidney Ponson	4.09	7-9	28	176.0	63	120
Jason Johnson	4.59	5-14	22	131.1	41	97
B.J. Ryan	4.68	2-1	67	57.2	33	56
Chris Brock	4.70	2-1	22	44.0	14	21
Travis Driskill*	4.95	8-8	29	132.2	48	78
Scott Erickson	5.55	5-12	29	160.2	68	74
Calvin Maduro	5.56	2-5	12	56.2	22	29
Sean Douglass*	6.08	0-5	15	53.1	35	44
John Stephens*	6.09	2-5	12	65.0	22	56

Saves: Julio (25); Groom (2); Roberts, Bauer, Ryan and Yorkis Perez (1). **Complete games:** Ponson and Erickson (3); Lopez and Johnson (1). **Shutouts:** Erickson (1).

Boston Red Sox

Batting (135 AB)	Avg	AB	R	H	HR	RBI	SB
Manny Ramirez	.349	436	84	152	33	107	0
Cliff Floyd	.316	171	30	54	7	18	4
Nomar Garciaparra	.310	635	101	197	24	120	5
Shea Hillenbrand	.293	634	94	186	18	83	4
Carlos Baerga	.286	182	17	52	2	19	6
Johnny Damon	.286	623	118	178	14	63	31
Rey Sanchez	.286	357	46	102	1	38	2
Brian Daubach	.266	444	62	118	20	78	2
Jason Varitek	.266	467	58	124	10	61	4
Trot Nixon	.256	532	81	136	24	94	4
Lou Merloni	.247	194	28	48	4	18	1
Doug Mirabelli	.225	151	17	34	7	25	0
Rickey Henderson	.223	179	40	40	5	16	8
Tony Clark	.207	275	25	57	3	29	0

Acquired: OF Floyd from Mon. for P Seung Jun Song, P Sun Woo Kim and PTBN (July 30); P Howry and cash from ChW for P Franklin Francisco and P Byeong An (July 31). **Waived:** P Oliver (July 2).

Pitching (40 IP)	ERA	W-L	Gm	IP	BB	SO
Pedro Martinez	2.26	20-4	30	199.1	40	239
Derek Lowe	2.58	21-8	32	219.2	48	127
Tim Wakefield	2.81	11-5	45	163.1	51	134
Ugueth Urbina	3.00	1-6	61	60.0	20	71
Casey Fossum*	3.46	5-4	43	106.2	30	101
Bob Howry	4.19	3-5	67	68.2	21	45
John Burkett	4.53	13-8	29	173.0	50	124
Darren Oliver	4.66	4-5	14	58.0	27	32
Rolando Arrojo	4.98	4-3	29	81.1	27	51
Frank Castillo	5.07	6-15	36	163.1	58	112

Saves: Urbina (40); Wakefield (3); Alan Embree (2) Fossum, Arrojo, Castillo, Wayne Gomes, Chris Haney and Willie Banks (1). **Complete games:** Martinez (2); Lowe, Burkett and Oliver (1). **Shutouts:** Lowe, Burkett and Oliver (1).

Chicago White Sox

Batting (135 AB)	Avg	AB	R	H	HR	RBI	SB
Magglio Ordonez	.320	590	116	189	38	135	7
Paul Konerko	.304	570	81	173	27	104	0
Sandy Alomar Jr.	.287	167	21	48	7	25	0
Joe Crede*	.285	200	28	57	12	35	0
Carlos Lee	.264	492	82	130	26	80	1
Tony Graffanino	.262	229	35	60	6	31	2
Kenny Lofton	.259	352	68	91	8	42	22
Aaron Rowand	.258	302	41	78	7	29	0
Frank Thomas	.252	523	77	132	28	92	3
Royce Clayton	.251	342	51	86	7	35	5
Jose Valentin	.249	474	70	118	25	75	3
Willie Harris*	.233	163	14	38	2	12	8
Jeff Liefer	.230	204	28	47	7	26	0
Mark Johnson	.209	263	31	55	4	18	0

Traded: OF Lofton to SF for P Felix Diaz and P Ryan Meaux (July 28); C Alomar Jr. to Col. for P Enemencio Pacheco (July 29).

Pitching (40 IP)	ERA	W-L	Gm	IP	BB	SO
Damaso Marte	2.83	1-1	68	60.1	18	72
Keith Foulke	2.90	2-4	65	77.2	13	58
Mark Buehrle	3.58	19-12	34	239.0	61	134
Antonio Osuna	3.86	8-2	59	67.2	28	66
Rocky Biddle	4.06	3-4	44	77.2	39	64
Matt Ginter*	4.47	1-0	33	54.1	21	37
Jon Garland	4.58	12-12	33	192.2	83	112
Mike Porzio*	4.82	2-2	32	43.0	23	33
Dan Wright	5.18	14-12	33	196.1	71	136
Gary Glover	5.20	7-8	41	138.1	52	70
Todd Ritchie	6.06	5-15	26	133.2	57	77

Saves: Foulke and Osuna (11); Marte (10); Biddle, Ginter and Glover (1). **Complete games:** Buehrle (5); Garland and Wright (1). **Shutouts:** Buehrle (2); Garland and Wright (1).

Cleveland Indians

Batting (165 AB)

	Avg	AB	R	H	HR	RBI	SB
Jim Thome	.304	480	101	146	52	118	1
Ellis Burks	.301	518	92	145	32	91	2
Karim Garcia	.297	202	30	60	16	52	0
Omar Vizquel	.275	582	85	160	14	72	18
Ricky Gutierrez	.275	353	38	97	4	38	0
John McDonald*	.250	264	35	66	1	12	3
Milton Bradley	.249	325	48	81	9	38	6
Matt Lawton	.236	416	71	98	15	57	8
Chris Magruder*	.217	258	34	56	6	29	2
Travis Fryman	.217	397	42	86	11	55	0
Einar Diaz	.206	320	34	66	2	16	0

Acquired: OF Magruder from Tex. for OF Rashad Eldridge (Apr. 4); P Mulholland, P Ricardo Rodriguez and P Francisco Cruceta from LA for P Paul Shuey (July 28).
Signed: OF Garcia (July 12); P Burba (Aug. 7).
Traded: P Colon and P Tim Drew to Mon. for IF Lee Stevens, IF Brandon Phillips, OF Grady Sizemore and P Cliff Lee (June 27); P Finley to St.L for IF Luis Garcia and OF Covelli Crisp (July 19).

Pitching (45 IP)

	ERA	W-L	Gm	IP	BB	SO
Bartolo Colon	2.55	10-4	16	116.1	31	75
C.C. Sabathia	4.37	13-11	33	210.0	88	149
Danys Baez	4.41	10-11	39	165.1	82	130
Chuck Finley	4.44	4-11	18	105.1	48	91
Terry Mulholland	4.60	3-2	16	47.0	14	21
Mark Wohlers	4.79	3-4	64	71.1	26	46
Dave Burba	5.20	5-5	35	145.1	57	95
David Riske	5.26	2-2	51	51.1	35	65
Ryan Drese*	6.55	10-9	26	137.1	62	102
Charles Nagy	8.88	1-4	19	48.2	13	22

Saves: Bob Wickman (20); Wohlers (7); Baez (6); Riske (1).
Complete games: Colon (4); Sabathia (2); Baez, Finley, Burba and Drese (1). **Shutouts:** Colon (2).

Detroit Tigers

Batting (135 AB)

	Avg	AB	R	H	HR	RBI	SB
Randall Simon	.301	482	51	145	19	82	0
Dmitri Young	.284	201	25	57	7	27	2
Bobby Higginson	.282	444	50	125	10	63	12
Wendell Magee	.271	347	34	94	6	35	2
Robert Fick	.270	556	66	150	17	63	0
Damian Jackson	.257	245	31	63	1	25	12
Ramon Santiago*	.243	222	33	54	4	20	8
Carlos Pena*	.242	397	43	96	19	52	2
George Lombard*	.241	241	34	58	5	13	13
Shane Halter	.239	410	46	98	10	39	0
Damian Easley	.224	304	29	68	8	30	1
Brandon Inge	.202	321	27	65	7	24	1
Chris Truby	.199	277	23	55	2	15	1
Craig Paquette	.194	252	20	49	4	20	1

Acquired: IF Truby from Mon. for IF Jose Macias (May 16); OF Lombard from Atl. for P Kris Keller (June 19); IF Pena, P Franklyn German and PTBN in a 3-team deal that sent P Jeff Weaver to NYY and P Ted Lilly, OF John-Ford Griffin and P Jason Arnold to Oak. (July 5).

Pitching (45 IP)

	ERA	W-L	Gm	IP	BB	SO
Juan Acevedo	2.65	1-5	65	74.2	23	43
Julio Santana	2.84	3-5	38	57.0	28	48
Mark Redman	4.21	8-15	30	203.0	51	109
Mike Maroth*	4.48	6-10	21	128.2	36	58
Brian Powell	4.84	1-5	13	57.2	21	30
Nate Cornejo	5.04	1-5	9	50.0	18	23
Steve Sparks	5.52	8-16	32	189.0	67	98
Jeff Farnsworth*	5.79	2-3	44	70.0	29	28
Adam Bernero*	6.20	4-7	28	101.2	31	69
Jose Lima	7.77	4-6	20	68.1	21	33

Saves: Acevedo (28); Oscar Henriquez (2); Walker, Paniagua and Franklyn German (1). **Complete games:** Redman and Sparks (3); Cornejo and Andy Van Hekken (1). **Shutouts:** Van Hekken (1).

Kansas City Royals

Batting (130 AB)

	Avg	AB	R	H	HR	RBI	SB
Mike Sweeney	.340	471	81	160	24	86	9
Raul Ibanez	.294	497	70	146	24	103	5
Joe Randa	.282	549	63	155	11	80	2
Carlos Beltran	.273	637	114	174	29	105	35
A.J. Hinch	.249	197	25	49	7	27	3
Michael Tucker	.248	475	65	118	12	56	23
Carlos Febles	.245	351	44	86	4	26	16
Neifi Perez	.236	554	65	131	3	37	8
Brent Mayne	.236	326	35	77	4	30	4
Aaron Guiel*	.233	240	30	56	4	38	1
Luis Alicea	.228	237	28	54	1	23	2
Chuck Knoblauch	.210	300	41	63	6	22	19
Brandon Berger*	.201	134	16	27	6	17	1

Pitching (40 IP)

	ERA	W-L	Gm	IP	BB	SO
Scott Mullen*	3.15	4-5	44	40.0	13	21
Paul Byrd	3.90	17-11	33	228.1	38	129
Jason Grimsley	3.91	4-7	70	71.1	37	59
Cory Bailey	4.11	3-4	37	46.0	31	24
Roberto Hernandez	4.33	1-3	53	52.0	12	39
Runelvys Hernandez*	4.36	4-4	12	74.1	22	45
Jeremy Affeldt*	4.64	3-4	44	77.2	37	67
Miguel Asencio*	5.11	4-7	31	123.1	64	58
Jeff Suppan	5.32	9-16	33	208.0	68	109
Darrell May	5.35	4-10	30	131.1	50	95
Shawn Sedlacek*	6.72	3-5	16	84.1	36	52
Blake Stein	7.91	0-4	27	46.2	27	42

Saves: Ro. Hernandez (26); Grimsley, Bailey, Stein and Brad Voyles (1). **Complete games:** Byrd (7); Suppan (3); May (2). **Shutouts:** Byrd (2); Suppan and May (1).

Minnesota Twins

Batting (135 AB)

	Avg	AB	R	H	HR	RBI	SB
A.J. Pierzynski	.300	440	54	132	6	49	1
Jacque Jones	.300	577	96	173	27	85	6
Bobby Kielty*	.291	289	49	84	12	46	4
Torii Hunter	.289	561	89	162	29	94	23
Cristian Guzman	.273	623	80	170	9	59	12
David Ortiz	.272	412	52	112	20	75	1
Dustin Mohr*	.269	383	55	103	12	45	6
Corey Koskie	.267	490	71	131	15	69	10
Doug Mientkiewicz	.261	467	60	122	10	64	1
Matt LeCroy	.260	181	19	47	7	27	0
Luis Rivas	.256	316	46	81	4	35	9
Brian Buchanan	.252	135	19	34	5	15	2
Denny Hocking	.250	260	28	65	2	25	0

Traded: OF Buchanan to SD for IF Jason Bartlett (July 12).

Pitching (40 IP)

	ERA	W-L	Gm	IP	BB	SO
J.C. Romero	1.89	9-2	81	81.0	36	76
LaTroy Hawkins	2.13	6-0	65	80.1	15	63
Eddie Guardado	2.93	1-3	68	67.2	18	70
Johan Santana	2.99	8-6	27	108.1	49	137
Tony Fiore*	3.16	10-3	48	91.0	43	58
Mike Jackson	3.27	2-3	58	55.0	13	29
Rick Reed	3.78	15-7	33	188.0	26	121
Kyle Lohse	4.23	13-8	32	180.2	70	124
Matt Kinney*	4.64	2-7	14	66.0	33	45
Brad Radke	4.72	9-5	21	118.1	20	62
Eric Milton	4.84	13-9	29	171.0	30	121
Joe Mays	5.38	4-8	17	95.1	25	38
Bob Wells	5.90	2-1	48	58.0	16	30

Saves: Guardado (45); Romero and Santana (1). **Complete games:** Reed, Radke and Milton (2); Lohse and Mays (1). **Shutouts:** Reed, Lohse, Radke, Milton and Mays (1).

New York Yankees

Batting (135 AB)	Avg	AB	R	H	HR	RBI	SB
Bernie Williams	.333	612	102	204	19	102	8
Jason Giambi	.314	560	120	176	41	122	2
Alfonso Soriano	.300	696	128	209	39	102	41
Derek Jeter	.297	644	124	191	18	75	32
Jorge Posada	.268	511	79	137	20	99	1
Ron Coomer	.264	148	14	39	3	17	0
John Vander Wal	.260	219	30	57	6	20	1
Robin Ventura	.247	465	68	115	27	93	3
Shane Spencer	.247	288	32	71	6	34	0
Nick Johnson*	.243	378	56	92	15	58	1
Rondell White	.240	455	59	109	14	62	1
Raul Mondesi	.232	569	90	132	26	88	15

Acquired: OF Mondesi from Tor. for P Scott Wiggins (July 1); P Weaver in a 3-team deal that sent P Ted Lilly, OF John-Ford Griffin and P Jason Arnold to Oak. and IF Carlos Pena, P Franklyn German and PTBN to Det. (July 5).

Pitching (40 IP)	ERA	W-L	Gm	IP	BB	SO
Mariano Rivera	2.74	1-4	45	46.0	11	41
Mike Stanton	3.00	7-1	79	78.0	28	44
Steve Karsay	3.26	6-4	78	88.1	30	65
Andy Pettitte	3.27	13-5	22	134.2	32	97
Ramiro Mendoza	3.44	8-4	62	91.2	16	61
Jeff Weaver	3.52	11-11	32	199.2	48	132
Orlando Hernandez	3.64	8-5	24	146.0	36	113
David Wells	3.75	19-7	31	206.1	45	137
Mike Mussina	4.05	18-10	33	215.2	48	182
Roger Clemens	4.35	13-6	29	180.0	63	192

Saves: Rivera (28); Karsay (12); Stanton (6); Mendoza (4); Weaver (3); O. Hernandez (1). **Complete games:** Pettitte and Weaver (3); Wells and Mussina (2). **Shutouts:** Weaver (3); Mussina (2); Pettitte and Wells (1).

Oakland Athletics

Batting (135 AB)	Avg	AB	R	H	HR	RBI	SB
Miguel Tejada	.308	662	108	204	34	131	7
Ray Durham	.289	564	114	163	15	70	26
Scott Hatteberg	.280	492	58	138	15	61	0
Olmedo Saenz	.276	156	15	43	6	18	1
Eric Chavez	.275	585	87	161	34	109	8
John Mabry	.275	193	27	53	11	40	1
Jeremy Giambi	.274	157	26	43	8	17	0
Mark Ellis*	.272	345	58	94	6	35	4
David Justice	.266	398	54	106	11	49	4
Jermaine Dye	.252	488	74	123	24	86	2
Terrence Long	.240	587	71	141	16	67	3
Adam Piatt	.234	137	18	32	5	18	2
Ramon Hernandez	.233	403	51	94	7	42	0
Greg Myers	.222	144	15	32	6	21	0

Acquired: IF Mabry from Phi. for OF Giambi (May 22); P Lilly, OF John-Ford Griffin and P Jason Arnold in a 3-team deal that sent to IF Carlos Pena, P Franklyn German and PTBN to Det. and P Jeff Weaver to NYY (July 5); IF Durham from ChW for P Jon Adkins (July 25); P Rincon from Cle. for IF Marshall McDougall (July 30).

Pitching (40 IP)	ERA	W-L	Gm	IP	BB	SO
Barry Zito	2.75	23-5	35	229.1	78	182
Tim Hudson	2.98	15-9	34	238.1	62	152
Chad Bradford	3.11	4-2	75	75.1	14	56
Billy Koch	3.27	11-4	84	93.2	46	93
Mark Mulder	3.47	19-7	30	207.1	55	159
Ted Lilly	3.69	5-7	22	100.0	31	77
Cory Lidle	3.89	8-10	31	192.0	39	111
Ricardo Rincon	4.18	1-4	71	56.0	11	49
Jim Mecir	4.26	6-4	61	67.2	29	53
Mike Fyhrie	4.44	2-4	16	48.2	20	29
Aaron Harang*	4.83	5-4	16	78.1	45	64
Jeff Tam	5.13	1-2	40	40.1	13	14
Erik Hiljus	6.50	3-3	9	45.2	21	29

Saves: Koch (44); Bradford (2); Rincon and Mecir (1). **Complete games:** Hudson (4); Mulder, Lilly and Lidle (2); Zito (1). **Shutouts:** Hudson and Lidle (2); Mulder and Lilly (1).

Seattle Mariners

Batting (135 AB)	Avg	AB	R	H	HR	RBI	SB
Ichiro Suzuki	.321	647	111	208	8	51	31
John Olerud	.300	553	85	166	22	102	0
Dan Wilson	.295	359	35	106	6	44	1
Bret Boone	.278	608	88	169	24	107	12
Edgar Martinez	.277	328	42	91	15	59	1
Mark McLemore	.270	337	54	91	7	41	18
Ruben Sierra	.270	419	47	113	13	60	4
Desi Relaford	.267	329	55	88	6	43	10
Carlos Guillen	.261	475	73	124	9	56	4
Ben Davis	.259	228	24	59	7	43	1
Jeff Cirillo	.249	485	51	121	6	54	8
Mike Cameron	.239	545	84	130	25	80	31
Jose Offerman	.232	284	48	66	5	31	9

Acquired: P Creek from TB for cash (Jult 24); IF Offerman from Bos. for cash (Aug. 8); P Valdes from Tex. for IF Jermaine Clark and P Derrick Van Dusen (Aug. 18).

Pitching (40 IP)	ERA	W-L	Gm	IP	BB	SO
Arthur Rhodes	2.33	10-4	66	69.2	13	81
Kazuhiro Sasaki	2.52	4-5	61	60.2	20	73
Shigetoshi Hasegawa	3.20	8-3	53	70.1	30	39
Joel Pineiro	3.24	14-7	37	194.1	54	136
Jamie Moyer	3.32	13-8	34	230.2	50	147
John Halama	3.56	6-5	31	101.0	33	70
Jeff Nelson	3.94	3-2	41	45.2	27	55
Ryan Franklin	4.02	7-5	41	118.2	22	65
Ismael Valdes	4.18	8-12	31	196.0	47	102
Freddy Garcia	4.39	16-10	34	223.2	63	181
Rafael Soriano*	4.56	0-3	10	47.1	16	32
James Baldwin	5.28	7-10	30	150.0	49	88
Doug Creek	5.82	3-2	52	55.2	35	56

Saves: Sasaki (37); Rhodes and Nelson (2); Hasegawa and Soriano (1). **Complete games:** Moyer (4); Pineiro (2); Valdes and Garcia (1). **Shutouts:** Moyer (1); Pineiro (1).

Tampa Bay Devil Rays

Batting (135 AB)	Avg	AB	R	H	HR	RBI	SB
Aubrey Huff	.313	454	67	142	23	59	4
Randy Winn	.298	607	87	181	14	75	27
Chris Gomez	.265	461	51	122	10	46	1
John Flaherty	.260	281	27	73	4	33	2
Carl Crawford*	.259	259	23	67	2	30	9
Toby Hall	.258	330	37	85	6	42	0
Jason Conti	.257	222	26	57	3	21	4
Steve Cox	.254	560	65	142	16	72	5
Ben Grieve	.251	482	62	121	19	64	8
Andy Sheets	.248	149	18	37	4	22	2
Brent Abernathy	.242	463	46	112	2	40	10
Jared Sandberg	.229	358	55	82	18	54	3
Felix Escalona*	.217	157	17	34	0	9	7
Jason Tyner	.214	168	17	36	0	9	7
Greg Vaughn	.163	251	28	41	8	29	3

Claimed: P Reichert off waivers from KC (Sept. 20).

Pitching (40 IP)	ERA	W-L	Gm	IP	BB	SO
Esteban Yan	4.30	7-8	55	69.0	29	53
Joe Kennedy	4.53	8-11	30	196.2	55	109
Paul Wilson	4.83	6-12	30	193.2	67	111
Tanyon Sturtze	5.18	4-18	33	224.0	89	137
Wilson Alvarez	5.28	2-3	29	75.0	36	56
Dan Reichert	5.32	3-5	30	66.0	25	36
Travis Harper*	5.46	5-9	37	85.2	27	60
Victor Zambrano	5.53	8-8	42	114.0	68	73
Jorge Sosa*	5.53	2-7	31	99.1	54	48
Ryan Rupe	5.60	5-10	15	90.0	25	67
Steve Kent	5.65	0-2	34	57.1	38	41
Jesus Colome	8.27	2-7	32	41.1	33	33

Saves: Yan (19); Lance Carter (2); Alvarez, Harper, Zambrano and Kent (1). **Complete games:** Kennedy (5); Sturtze (4); Rupe (2); Wilson (1). **Shutouts:** Kennedy (1).

Texas Rangers

Batting (130 AB)

	Avg	AB	R	H	HR	RBI	SB
Ivan Rodriguez	.314	408	67	128	19	60	5
Alex Rodriguez	.300	624	125	187	57	142	9
Rusty Greer	.296	199	24	59	1	17	1
Mike Lamb	.283	314	54	89	9	33	0
Juan Gonzalez	.282	277	38	78	8	35	2
Herbert Perry	.276	450	64	124	22	77	4
Rafael Palmeiro	.273	546	99	149	43	105	2
Frank Catalanotto	.269	212	42	57	3	23	9
Carl Everett	.267	374	47	100	16	62	2
Michael Young	.262	573	77	150	9	62	6
Gabe Kapler	.260	196	25	51	0	17	5
Kevin Mench*	.260	366	52	95	15	60	1
Todd Hollandsworth	.258	132	16	34	5	19	1
Bill Haselman	.246	179	16	44	3	18	0
Hank Blalock*	.211	147	16	31	3	17	0
Ruben Rivera	.209	158	17	33	4	14	4

Acquired: P Reyes and OF Hollandsworth from Col. for OF Kapler and OF Jason Romano (July 31).

Pitching (35 IP)

	ERA	W-L	Gm	IP	BB	SO
Francisco Cordero	1.79	2-0	39	45.1	13	41
Jay Powell	3.44	3-2	51	49.2	24	35
Kenny Rogers	3.84	13-8	33	210.2	70	107
Juan Alvarez*	4.76	0-4	52	39.2	21	30
Doug Davis	4.98	3-5	10	59.2	22	28
Joaquin Benoit*	5.31	4-5	17	84.2	58	59
Todd Van Poppel	5.45	3-2	50	72.2	29	85
Hideki Irabu	5.74	3-8	38	47.0	16	30
Chan Ho Park	5.75	9-8	25	145.2	78	121
Rob Bell	6.22	4-3	17	94.0	35	70
Dennys Reyes	6.38	4-3	15	42.1	21	29
Aaron Myette	10.06	2-5	15	48.1	41	48

Saves: Irabu (16); Cordero (10); Benoit, Van Poppel, Randy Flores, Danny Kolb, John Rocker, Rich Rodriguez and Anthony Telford (1). **Complete games:** Rogers (2); Davis (1). **Shutouts:** Rogers and Davis (1).

Toronto Blue Jays

Batting (135 AB)

	Avg	AB	R	H	HR	RBI	SB
Josh Phelps*	.309	265	41	82	15	58	0
Shannon Stewart	.303	577	103	175	10	45	14
Eric Hinske*	.279	566	99	158	24	84	13
Carlos Delgado	.277	505	103	140	33	108	1
Orlando Hudson*	.276	192	20	53	4	23	0
Chris Woodward	.276	312	48	86	13	45	3
Vernon Wells	.275	608	87	167	23	100	9
Dave Berg	.270	374	42	101	4	39	0
Tom Wilson*	.257	265	33	68	8	37	0
Ken Huckaby*	.245	273	29	67	3	22	0
Jose Cruz Jr.	.245	466	64	114	18	70	7
Felipe Lopez	.227	282	35	64	8	34	5
Joe Lawrence*	.180	150	16	27	2	15	2

Acquired: P Politte from Phi. for P Dan Plesac (May 26).
Claimed: P Walker off waivers from NYM (May 3).
Waived: P Eyre (Aug. 5).

Pitching (40 IP)

	ERA	W-L	Gm	IP	BB	SO
Roy Halladay	2.93	19-7	34	239.1	62	168
Cliff Politte	3.61	1-3	55	57.1	19	57
Felix Heredia	3.61	1-2	53	52.1	26	31
Kelvim Escobar	4.27	5-7	76	78.0	44	85
Pete Walker*	4.33	10-5	37	139.1	51	80
Corey Thurman*	4.37	2-3	43	68.0	45	56
Scott Eyre*	4.97	2-4	49	63.1	29	51
Chris Carpenter	5.28	4-5	13	73.1	27	45
Justin Miller*	5.54	9-5	25	102.1	66	63
Esteban Loaiza	5.71	9-10	25	151.1	38	87
Scott Cassidy*	5.73	1-4	58	66.0	32	48
Steve Parris	5.97	5-5	14	75.1	35	48
Brandon Lyon	6.53	1-4	15	62.0	19	30
Luke Prokopec	6.78	2-9	22	71.2	25	41

Saves: Escobar (38); Politte, Walker and Jason Kershner (1). **Complete games:** Loaiza (3); Halladay (2); Carpenter (1). **Shutouts:** Halladay and Loaiza (1).

Home Attendance

Overall 2002 regular season attendance in Major League Baseball was 67,941,211 in 2,412 games for an average per game crowd of 28,168, down 6.1 percent from 2001; numbers in parentheses indicate ranking in 2001; HD indicates home dates; Attendance is based on tickets sold.

American League

	Attendance	HD	Average
1 Seattle (1)	3,540,658	81	43,712
2 New York (2)	3,465,807	80	43,323
3 Baltimore (4)	2,682,917	81	33,122
4 Boston (6)	2,650,063	81	32,717
5 Cleveland (3)	2,616,940	81	32,308
6 Texas (5)	2,352,397	80	29,405
7 Anaheim (8)	2,305,557	81	28,464
8 Oakland (7)	2,169,811	81	26,788
9 Minnesota (11)	1,924,473	81	23,759
10 Chicago (12)	1,676,911	81	20,703
11 Toronto (10)	1,637,900	81	20,221
12 Detroit (9)	1,503,623	80	18,795
13 Kansas City (13)	1,323,036	77	17,182
14 Tampa Bay (14)	1,065,742	81	13,157
TOTALS	30,915,835	1127	27,432

National League

	Attendance	HD	Average
1 San Francisco (1)	3,253,203	81	40,163
2 Arizona (9)	3,198,985	81	39,494
3 Los Angeles (4)	3,131,255	81	38,657
4 St. Louis (3)	3,011,216	81	37,176
5 New York (10)	2,804,838	78	35,959
6 Chicago (6)	2,693,096	78	34,527
7 Colorado (2)	2,737,838	81	33,800
8 Atlanta (7)	2,603,484	81	32,142
9 Houston (5)	2,517,357	81	31,078
10 San Diego (12)	2,220,601	81	27,415
11 Milwaukee (8)	1,969,153	81	24,311
12 Cincinnati (13)	1,855,787	80	23,197
13 Pittsburgh (11)	1,784,670	79	22,591
14 Philadelphia (14)	1,618,230	79	20,484
15 Florida (15)	813,118	81	10,038
16 Montreal (16)	812,545	81	10,031
TOTALS	37,025,376	1285	28,814

NL Team by Team Statistics

At least 135 at bats or 40 innings pitched during the regular season unless otherwise indicated. Players who competed for more than one NL team are listed with their final club. Players traded from the AL are listed with NL team only if they have 135 AB or 40 IP. Note that (*) indicates rookie and PTBN indicates player to be named.

Arizona Diamondbacks

Batting (135 AB)	Avg	AB	R	H	HR	RBI	SB
Greg Colbrunn	.333	171	30	57	10	27	0
Danny Bautista	.325	154	22	50	6	23	4
Quinton McCracken	.309	349	60	108	3	40	5
Junior Spivey	.301	538	103	162	16	78	11
Luis Gonzalez	.288	524	90	151	28	103	9
Steve Finley	.287	505	82	145	25	89	16
Craig Counsell	.282	436	63	123	2	51	7
Tony Womack	.271	590	90	160	5	57	29
Erubiel Durazo	.261	222	46	58	16	48	0
Matt Williams	.260	215	29	56	12	40	3
Mark Grace	.252	298	43	75	7	48	2
Damian Miller	.249	297	40	74	11	42	0
David Dellucci	.245	229	34	56	7	29	2
Rod Barajas	.234	154	12	36	3	23	1

Acquired: P Fetters from Pit. for P Duaner Sanchez (July 8).

Pitching (35 IP)	ERA	W-L	Gm	IP	BB	SO
Byung-Hyun Kim	2.04	8-3	72	84.0	26	92
Randy Johnson	2.32	24-5	35	260.0	71	334
Curt Schilling	3.23	23-7	36	259.1	33	316
Mike Koplove*	3.36	6-1	55	61.2	23	46
Mike Fetters	4.09	3-3	65	55.0	37	53
Miguel Batista	4.29	8-9	36	184.2	70	112
Mike Myers	4.38	4-3	69	37.0	17	31
Rick Helling	4.51	10-12	30	175.2	48	120
Brian Anderson	4.79	6-11	35	156.0	32	81

Saves: Kim (36); Myers (4). **Complete games:** Johnson (8); Schilling (5); Batista (1). **Shutouts:** Johnson (4); Schilling (1).

Atlanta Braves

Batting (135 AB)	Avg	AB	R	H	HR	RBI	SB
Chipper Jones	.327	548	90	179	26	100	8
Matt Franco	.317	205	25	65	6	30	1
Gary Sheffield	.307	492	82	151	25	84	12
Mark DeRosa	.297	212	24	63	5	23	2
Julio Franco	.284	338	51	96	6	30	5
Rafael Furcal	.275	636	95	175	8	47	27
Darren Bragg	.269	212	34	57	3	15	5
Andruw Jones	.264	560	91	148	35	94	8
Wes Helms	.243	120	20	51	6	22	1
Javy Lopez	.233	347	31	81	11	52	0
Vinny Castilla	.232	543	56	126	12	61	4
Marcus Giles	.230	213	27	49	8	23	1
Keith Lockhart	.216	296	34	64	5	32	0
Henry Blanco	.204	221	17	45	6	22	0

Pitching (40 IP)	ERA	W-L	Gm	IP	BB	SO
Chris Hammond	0.95	7-2	63	76.0	31	63
Darren Holmes	1.81	2-2	55	54.2	12	47
Mike Remlinger	1.99	7-3	73	68.0	28	69
Greg Maddux	2.62	16-6	34	199.1	45	118
Tim Spooneybarger*	2.63	1-0	51	51.1	26	33
Tom Glavine	2.96	18-11	36	224.2	78	127
Kerry Ligtenberg	2.97	3-4	52	66.2	33	51
Kevin Millwood	3.24	18-8	35	217.0	65	178
John Smoltz	3.25	3-2	75	80.1	24	85
Damian Moss*	3.42	12-6	33	179.0	89	111
Kevin Gryboski*	3.48	2-1	57	51.2	37	33
Albie Lopez	4.37	1-4	30	55.2	18	39
Jason Marquis	5.04	8-9	22	114.1	49	84

Saves: Smoltz (55); Holmes and Spooneybarger (1). **Complete games:** Glavine (2); Millwood (1). **Shutouts:** Glavine and Millwood (1).

Chicago Cubs

Batting (150 AB)	Avg	AB	R	H	HR	RBI	SB
Sammy Sosa	.288	556	122	160	49	108	2
Moises Alou	.275	484	50	133	15	61	8
Fred McGriff	.273	523	67	143	30	103	1
Mark Bellhorn	.258	445	86	115	27	56	7
Corey Patterson	.253	592	71	150	14	54	18
Bobby Hill*	.253	190	26	48	4	20	6
Alex Gonzalez	.248	513	58	127	18	61	5
Chris Stynes	.241	195	25	47	5	26	1
Joe Girardi	.226	234	19	53	1	13	1
Roosevelt Brown	.211	204	14	43	3	23	2
Todd Hundley	.211	266	32	56	16	35	0
Chad Hermansen	.207	237	25	49	8	18	7

Acquired: OF Hermansen from Pit. for OF Darren Lewis (July 31).

Pitching (40 IP)	ERA	W-L	Gm	IP	BB	SO
Joe Borowski	2.73	4-4	73	95.2	29	97
Mark Prior*	3.32	6-6	19	116.2	38	147
Matt Clement	3.60	12-11	32	205.0	85	215
Carlos Zambrano*	3.66	4-8	32	108.1	63	93
Kerry Wood	3.66	12-11	33	213.2	97	217
Jon Lieber	3.70	6-8	21	141.0	12	87
Juan Cruz*	3.98	3-11	45	97.1	59	81
Antonio Alfonseca	4.00	2-5	66	74.1	36	61
Jason Bere	5.67	1-10	16	85.2	28	65
Kyle Farnsworth	7.33	4-6	45	46.2	24	46

Saves: Alfonseca (19); Borowski (2); Cruz and Farnsworth (1). **Complete games:** Wood (4); Clement and Lieber (3); Prior (1). **Shutouts:** Clement (2); Wood (1).

Cincinnati Reds

Batting (135 AB)	Avg	AB	R	H	HR	RBI	SB
Austin Kearns*	.315	372	66	117	13	56	6
Todd Walker	.299	612	79	183	11	64	8
Ken Griffey Jr.	.264	197	17	52	8	23	1
Sean Casey	.261	425	56	111	6	42	2
Reggie Taylor*	.254	287	41	73	9	38	11
Jason LaRue	.249	353	42	88	12	52	1
Adam Dunn	.249	535	84	133	26	71	19
Barry Larkin	.245	507	72	124	7	47	13
Aaron Boone	.241	606	83	146	26	87	32
Jose Guillen	.238	240	25	57	8	31	4

Acquired: OF Branyan from Cle. for IF Ben Broussard (June 7); P Chen from Mon. for P Jim Brower (June 14); P Dempster from Fla. for OF Juan Encarnacion (July 11); P Estes from NYM for P Pedro Feliciano, OF Elvin Andujar and 2 PTBN (Aug. 15). **Signed:** OF Guillen (Aug. 20).

Pitching (45 IP)	ERA	W-L	Gm	IP	BB	SO
John Riedling	2.70	2-4	33	46.2	26	30
Scott Williamson	2.92	3-4	65	74.0	36	84
Gabe White	2.98	6-1	62	54.1	10	41
Elmer Dessens	3.03	7-8	30	178.0	49	93
Danny Graves	3.19	7-3	68	98.2	25	58
Chris Reitsma	3.64	6-12	32	138.1	45	84
Jimmy Haynes	4.12	15-10	34	196.2	81	126
Jared Fernandez*	4.44	1-3	14	50.2	24	36
Shawn Estes	5.10	5-12	29	160.2	83	109
Jose Rijo	5.14	5-4	31	77.0	20	38
Joey Hamilton	5.27	4-10	39	124.2	50	85
Ryan Dempster	5.38	10-13	33	209.0	93	153
Bruce Chen	5.56	2-5	55	77.2	43	80
Scott Sullivan	6.06	6-5	71	78.2	31	78

Saves: Graves (32); Williamson (8); Hamilton and Sullivan (1). **Complete games:** Dempster (4); Reitsma and Estes (1). **Shutouts:** Reitsma and Estes (1).

Colorado Rockies

Batting (135 AB)

	Avg	AB	R	H	HR	RBI	SB
Larry Walker	.338	477	95	161	26	104	6
Todd Helton	.329	553	107	182	30	109	5
Jay Payton	.303	445	69	135	16	59	7
Todd Hollandsworth	.295	298	39	88	11	48	7
Juan Pierre	.287	592	90	170	1	35	47
Todd Zeile	.273	506	61	138	18	87	1
Gary Bennett	.265	291	26	77	4	26	1
Brent Butler	.259	344	55	89	9	42	2
Jose Ortiz	.250	192	22	48	1	12	2
Juan Uribe	.240	566	69	136	6	49	9
Terry Shumpert	.235	234	30	55	6	21	4
Greg Norton	.220	168	19	37	7	37	2

Acquired: OF Payton, P Mark Corey and OF Robert Stratton from NYM for P John Thomson and OF Mark Little (July 31).
Signed: P Lowe (Sept. 12).
Traded: P Reyes and OF Hollandsworth to Tex. for OF Gabe Kapler and OF Jason Romano (July 31).

Pitching (40 IP)

	ERA	W-L	Gm	IP	BB	SO
Jose Jimenez	3.56	2-10	74	73.1	11	47
Denny Stark*	4.00	11-4	32	128.1	64	64
Dennys Reyes	4.24	0-1	43	40.1	24	30
Justin Speier	4.33	5-1	63	62.1	19	47
Jason Jennings*	4.52	16-8	32	185.1	70	127
Todd Jones	4.70	1-4	79	82.1	28	73
Denny Neagle	5.26	8-11	35	164.1	63	111
Shawn Chacon	5.73	5-11	21	119.1	60	67
Sean Lowe	5.79	5-3	51	79.1	41	64
Kent Mercker	6.14	3-1	58	44.0	22	37
Mike Hampton	6.15	7-15	30	178.2	91	74

Saves: Jimenez (41); Speier and Jones (1). **Complete games:** Neagle (1). **Shutouts:** none.

Florida Marlins

Batting (135 AB)

	Avg	AB	R	H	HR	RBI	SB
Kevin Millar	.306	438	58	134	16	57	0
Luis Castillo	.305	606	86	185	2	39	48
Mike Redmond	.305	256	19	78	2	28	0
Mike Lowell	.276	597	88	165	24	92	4
Juan Encarnacion	.271	584	77	158	24	85	21
Derek Lee	.270	581	95	157	27	86	19
Eric Owens	.270	385	44	104	4	37	26
Andy Fox	.251	435	55	109	4	41	31
Mike Mordecai	.245	151	19	37	0	11	2
Preston Wilson	.243	510	80	124	23	65	20
Alex Gonzalez	.225	151	15	34	2	18	3
Charles Johnson	.217	244	18	53	6	36	0

Acquired: P Pavano, P Lloyd, IF Mordecai and P Justin Wayne from Mon. for OF Cliff Floyd, OF Wilton Guerrero and P Claudio Vargas (July 11); OF Encarnacion from Cin. for P Ryan Dempster (July 11).

Pitching (40 IP)

	ERA	W-L	Gm	IP	BB	SO
Braden Looper	3.14	2-5	78	86.0	28	55
A.J. Burnett	3.30	12-9	31	204.1	90	203
Vladimir Nunez	3.41	6-5	77	97.2	37	73
Josh Beckett*	4.10	6-7	23	107.2	44	113
Armando Almanza	4.34	3-2	51	45.2	23	57
Michael Tejera*	4.45	8-8	47	139.2	60	95
Kevin Olsen*	4.53	0-5	17	55.2	31	38
Brad Penny	4.66	8-7	24	129.1	50	93
Carl Pavano	5.16	6-10	37	136.0	45	92
Graeme Lloyd	5.21	4-5	66	57.0	19	37
Julian Tavarez	5.39	10-12	29	153.2	49	94
Vic Darensbourg	6.14	1-2	42	48.1	26	33

Saves: V. Nunez (20); Looper (13); Lloyd (5); Almanza (2); Tejera (1). **Complete games:** Burnett (7); Penny (1). **Shutouts:** Burnett (5); Penny (1).

Houston Astros

Batting (135 AB)

	Avg	AB	R	H	HR	RBI	SB
Mark Loretta	.304	283	33	86	4	27	1
Jose Vizcaino	.303	406	53	123	5	37	3
Lance Berkman	.292	578	106	169	42	128	8
Jeff Bagwell	.291	571	94	166	31	98	7
Orlando Merced	.287	251	35	72	6	30	4
Geoff Blum	.283	368	45	104	10	52	2
Daryle Ward	.276	453	41	125	12	72	1
Brian L. Hunter	.269	201	32	54	3	20	5
Julio Lugo	.261	322	45	84	8	35	9
Brad Ausmus	.257	447	57	115	6	50	2
Craig Biggio	.253	577	96	146	15	58	16
Richard Hidalgo	.235	388	54	91	15	48	6
Gregg Zaun	.222	185	18	41	3	24	1

Acquired: P Gordon from ChC for P Russ Rohlicek and 2 PTBN (Aug. 22); IF Loretta and cash from Mil. for 2 PTBN (Sept. 1).

Pitchers (40 IP)

	ERA	W-L	Gm	IP	BB	SO
Octavio Dotel	1.85	6-4	83	97.1	27	118
Billy Wagner	2.52	4-2	70	75.0	22	88
Roy Oswalt	3.01	19-9	35	233.0	62	208
Wade Miller	3.28	15-4	26	164.2	62	144
Tom Gordon	3.38	1-3	34	42.2	16	48
Peter Munro	3.57	5-5	19	80.2	23	45
Ricky Stone*	3.61	3-3	78	77.1	34	63
Carlos Hernandez*	4.38	7-5	23	111.0	61	93
Brandon Puffer*	4.43	3-3	55	69.0	38	48
Nelson Cruz	4.48	2-6	43	78.1	29	61
Shane Reynolds	4.86	3-6	13	74.0	26	47
Dave Mlicki	5.34	4-10	22	86.0	34	57
Tim Redding	5.40	3-6	18	73.1	35	63
Kirk Saarloos*	6.01	6-7	17	85.1	27	54

Saves: Wagner (35); Dotel (6); Stone and Pedro Borbon (1).
Complete games: Miller and Saarloos (1). **Shutouts:** Miller and Saarloos (1).

Los Angeles Dodgers

Batting (120 AB)

	Avg	AB	R	H	HR	RBI	SB
Dave Hansen	.292	120	15	35	2	17	1
Alex Cora	.291	258	37	75	5	28	7
Shawn Green	.285	582	110	166	42	114	8
Brian Jordan	.285	471	65	134	18	80	2
Tyler Houston	.281	320	34	90	7	40	1
Paul Lo Duca	.281	580	74	163	10	64	3
Dave Roberts	.277	422	63	117	3	34	45
Marquis Grissom	.277	343	57	95	17	60	5
Eric Karros	.271	524	52	142	13	73	4
Mark Grudzielanek	.271	536	56	145	9	50	4
Adrian Beltre	.257	587	70	151	21	75	7
Cesar Izturis	.232	439	43	102	1	31	7

Acquired: IF Houston and PTBN from Mil. for P Ben Diggins and P Shane Nance (July 23); P Shuey from Cle. for P Mulholland, P Ricardo Rodriguez and P Francisco Cruceta (July 28).

Pitching (40 IP)

	ERA	W-L	Gm	IP	BB	SO
Eric Gagne	1.97	4-1	77	82.1	16	114
Paul Quantrill	2.70	5-4	86	76.2	25	53
Odalis Perez	3.00	15-10	32	222.1	38	155
Giovanni Carrara	3.28	6-3	63	90.2	32	56
Hideo Nomo	3.39	16-6	34	220.1	101	193
Omar Daal	3.90	11-9	39	161.1	54	105
Andy Ashby	3.91	9-13	30	181.2	65	107
Guillermo Mota	4.15	1-3	43	60.2	27	49
Kazuhisa Ishii*	4.27	14-10	28	154.0	106	143
Paul Shuey	4.40	5-2	28	30.2	21	24
Kevin Brown	4.81	3-4	17	63.2	23	58
Terry Mulholland	7.31	0-0	21	32.0	7	17

Saves: Gagne (52); Quantrill, Carrara, Shuey and Jesse Orosco (1). **Complete games:** Perez (4). **Shutouts:** Perez (2).

Milwaukee Brewers

Batting (140 AB)	Avg	AB	R	H	HR	RBI	SB
Lenny Harris	.305	197	23	60	3	17	4
Alex Sanchez*	.289	394	55	114	1	33	37
Jose Hernandez	.288	525	72	151	24	73	3
Eric Young	.280	496	57	139	3	28	31
Richie Sexson	.279	570	86	159	29	102	0
Robert Machado	.261	211	19	55	3	22	0
Jeffrey Hammonds	.257	448	47	115	9	41	4
Alex Ochoa	.256	215	32	55	6	21	8
Matt Stairs	.244	270	41	66	16	41	2
Geoff Jenkins	.243	243	35	59	10	29	1
Paul Bako	.235	234	24	55	4	20	0
Ron Belliard	.211	289	30	61	3	26	2

Acquired: C Machado from ChC for OF Jackson Melian (June 9); P Matthews and OF Chris Morris from St. L for P Jamey Wright and cash (Aug. 29).
Claimed: P Figueroa off waivers from Phi. (Apr. 3).
Traded: OF Ochoa and C Sal Fasano to Ana. for C Jorge Fabregas and 2 PTBN (July 31).

Pitching (40 IP)	ERA	W-L	Gm	IP	BB	SO
Jayson Durocher*	1.88	1-1	39	48.0	21	44
Luis Vizcaino	2.99	5-3	76	81.1	30	79
Ray King	3.05	3-2	76	65.0	24	50
Mike DeJean	3.12	1-5	68	75.0	39	65
Valerio De Los Santos	3.12	2-3	51	57.2	26	38
Mike Matthews	3.94	2-1	47	45.2	29	34
Ben Sheets	4.15	11-16	34	216.2	70	170
Glendon Rusch	4.70	10-16	34	210.2	76	140
Nick Neugebauer*	4.72	1-7	12	55.1	44	47
Nelson Figueroa	5.03	1-7	30	93.0	37	51
Ruben Quevedo	5.76	6-11	26	139.0	68	93
Jose Cabrera	6.10	6-10	50	103.1	36	61

Saves: DeJean (27); Vizcaino (5). **Complete games:** Rusch (4); Sheets and Quevedo (1). **Shutouts:** Rusch and Quevedo (1).

Montreal Expos

Batting (145 AB)	Avg	AB	R	H	HR	RBI	SB
Vladimir Guerrero	.336	614	106	206	39	111	40
Jose Vidra	.315	604	103	190	19	96	2
Troy O'Leary	.286	273	27	78	3	37	1
Brian Schneider	.275	207	21	57	5	29	1
Cliff Floyd	.275	349	56	96	21	61	11
Brad Wilkerson*	.266	507	92	135	20	59	7
Michael Barrett	.263	376	41	99	12	49	0
Orlando Cabrera	.263	563	64	148	7	56	25
Andres Galarraga	.260	292	30	76	9	40	2
Jose Macias	.255	231	33	59	7	33	5
Fernando Tatis	.228	381	43	87	15	55	2
Lee Stevens	.190	205	28	39	10	31	1

Acquired: IF Macias from Det. for IF Chris Truby (May 16); P Brower from Cin. for P Bruce Chen (June 14); P Colon and P Tim Drew from Cle. for IF Stevens, IF Brandon Phillips, OF Grady Sizemore and P Cliff Lee (June 27); OF Floyd, OF Wilton Guerrero and P Claudio Vargas from Fla. for P Carl Pavano, P Graeme Lloyd, IF Mike Mordecai and P Justin Wayne (July 11).
Traded: OF Floyd to Bos. for P Seung Jun Song, P Sun Woo Kim and PTBN (July 30).

Pitching (50 IP)	ERA	W-L	Gm	IP	BB	SO
Joey Eischen	1.34	6-1	59	53.2	18	51
Scott Stewart	3.09	4-2	67	64.0	22	67
Tomokazu Ohka	3.18	13-8	32	192.2	45	118
Bartolo Colon	3.31	10-4	17	117.0	39	74
Javier Vazquez	3.91	10-13	34	230.1	49	179
Matt Herges	4.04	2-5	62	64.2	26	50
T.J. Tucker*	4.11	6-3	57	61.1	31	42
Masato Yoshii	4.11	4-9	31	131.1	32	74
Jim Brower	4.37	3-2	52	80.1	32	57
Tony Armas Jr.	4.44	12-12	29	164.1	78	131
Britt Reames	5.03	1-4	42	68.0	38	76

Saves: Stewart (17); Herges (6); Tucker (4); Eischen, Smith and Tim Drew (2); Zach Day (1). **Complete games:** Colon (4); Ohka and Vazquez (2); Yoshii (1). **Shutouts:** Colon (1).

New York Mets

Batting (135 AB)	Avg	AB	R	H	HR	RBI	SB
Edgardo Alfonzo	.308	490	78	151	16	56	6
Timo Perez	.295	444	52	131	8	47	10
Mike Piazza	.280	478	69	134	33	98	0
Roberto Alomar	.266	590	73	157	11	53	16
Roger Cedeno	.260	511	65	133	7	41	25
Mo Vaughn	.259	487	67	126	26	72	0
Rey Ordonez	.254	460	53	117	1	42	2
Vance Wilson	.245	163	19	40	5	26	0
John Valentin	.240	208	18	50	3	30	0
Jeromy Burnitz	.215	479	65	103	19	54	10
Joe McEwing	.199	196	22	39	3	26	4

Acquired: P Thomson and OF Mark Little from Col. for OF Jay Payton, P Mark Corey and OF Robert Stratton (July 31); P Reed and P Middlebrook for P Bobby M. Jones, P Josh Reynolds and OF Jay Bay (July 31); P Strickland, P Phile Seibel and OF Matt Watson from Mon. for P Bruce Chen, P Dicky Gonzalez, IF Luis Figueroa and PTBN (Apr. 5).

Pitching (40 IP)	ERA	W-L	Gm	IP	BB	SO
Steve Reed	2.01	2-5	64	67.0	14	50
Grant Roberts*	2.20	3-1	34	45.0	16	31
Armando Benitez	2.27	1-0	62	67.1	25	79
Mark Guthrie	2.44	5-3	68	48.0	19	44
Dave Weathers	2.91	6-3	71	77.1	36	61
Steve Trachsel	3.37	11-11	30	173.2	69	105
Al Leiter	3.48	13-13	33	204.1	69	172
Scott Strickland	3.54	6-9	69	68.2	33	69
Mike Bacsik*	4.37	3-2	11	55.2	19	30
John Thomson	4.71	9-14	30	181.2	44	107
Jason Middlebrook*	4.73	2-3	15	51.1	22	42
Pedro Astacio	4.79	12-11	31	191.2	63	152
Jeff D'Amico	4.94	6-10	29	145.2	37	101
Satoru Komiyama*	5.61	0-3	25	43.1	12	33

Saves: Benitez (33); Strickland (2); Reed and Guthrie (1). **Complete games:** Astacio (3); Leiter (2); Trachsel, Bacsik and D'Amico (1). **Shutouts:** Leiter (2); Trachsel, Astacio and D'Amico (1).

Philadelphia Phillies

Batting (135 AB)	Avg	AB	R	H	HR	RBI	SB
Bobby Abreu	.308	572	102	176	20	85	31
Placido Polanco	.288	548	75	158	9	49	5
Pat Burrell	.282	586	96	165	37	116	1
Mike Lieberthal	.279	476	46	133	15	52	0
Travis Lee	.265	536	55	142	13	70	5
Marlon Anderson	.258	539	64	139	8	48	5
Tomas Perez	.250	212	22	53	5	20	1
Doug Glanville	.249	422	49	105	6	29	19
Jimmy Rollins	.245	637	82	156	11	60	31
Jeremy Giambi	.244	156	32	38	12	28	0
Ricky Ledee	.227	203	33	46	8	23	1

Acquired: OF Giambi from Oak. for IF John Mabry (May 22); IF Polanco, P Timlin and P Smith from St.L for IF Scott Rolen, P Doug Nickle and cash (July 29).

Pitchers (40 IP)	ERA	W-L	Gm	IP	BB	SO
Jose Mesa	2.97	4-6	74	75.2	39	64
Mike Timlin	2.98	4-6	72	96.2	14	50
Randy Wolf	3.20	11-9	31	210.2	63	172
Carlos Silva*	3.21	5-0	68	84.0	22	41
Vicente Padilla	3.28	14-11	32	206.0	53	128
Joe Roa	4.04	4-4	14	71.1	13	35
Brett Myers*	4.25	4-5	12	72.0	29	34
Terry Adams	4.35	7-9	46	136.2	58	96
Dave Coggin	4.68	2-5	38	77.0	51	64
Rheal Cormier	5.25	5-6	54	60.0	32	49
Brandon Duckworth	5.41	8-9	30	163.0	69	167
Robert Person	5.44	4-5	16	87.2	51	61
Jose Santiago	6.70	1-3	42	47.0	15	30
Bud Smith	6.94	1-5	11	48.0	22	22

Saves: Mesa (45); Silva and Dan Plesac (1). **Complete games:** Wolf (3); Padilla and Myers (1). **Shutouts:** Wolf (2); Padilla (1).

Pittsburgh Pirates

Batting (135 AB)	Avg	AB	R	H	HR	RBI	SB
Brian Giles	.298	497	95	148	38	103	15
Jason Kendall	.283	545	59	154	3	44	15
Armando Rios	.264	208	20	55	1	24	1
Pokey Reese	.264	421	46	111	4	50	12
Craig Wilson	.264	368	48	97	16	57	2
Jack Wilson	.252	527	77	133	4	47	5
Kevin Young	.246	468	60	115	16	51	4
Rob Mackowiak	.244	385	57	94	16	48	9
Aramis Ramirez	.234	522	51	122	18	71	2
Abraham Nunez	.233	253	28	59	2	15	3
Adam Hyzdu	.232	155	24	36	11	34	0
Adrian Brown	.216	208	20	45	1	21	10

Pitching (40 IP)	ERA	W-L	Gm	IP	BB	SO
Scott Sauerbeck	2.30	5-4	78	62.2	27	70
Mike Williams	2.93	2-6	59	61.1	21	43
Mike Lincoln	3.11	2-4	55	72.1	27	50
Brian Boehringer	3.39	4-4	70	79.2	33	65
Kip Wells	3.58	12-14	33	198.1	71	134
Brian Meadows	3.88	1-6	11	62.2	14	31
Josh Fogg*	4.35	12-12	33	194.1	69	113
Joe Beimel	4.64	2-5	53	85.1	45	53
Kris Benson	4.70	9-6	25	130.1	50	79
Dave Williams	4.98	2-5	9	43.1	24	33
Jimmy Anderson	5.44	8-13	28	140.2	63	47
Ron Villone	5.81	4-6	45	93.0	34	55

Saves: M. Williams (46); Boehringer (1). **Complete games:** Wells and Anderson (1). **Shutouts:** Wells (1).

St. Louis Cardinals

Batting (135 AB)	Avg	AB	R	H	HR	RBI	SB
Albert Pujols	.314	590	118	185	34	127	2
Jim Edmonds	.311	476	96	148	28	83	4
Edgar Renteria	.305	544	77	166	11	83	22
Fernando Vina	.270	622	75	168	1	54	17
Scott Rolen	.266	580	89	154	31	110	8
Tino Martinez	.262	511	63	134	21	75	3
Eli Marrero	.262	397	63	104	18	66	14
Kerry Robinson	.260	181	27	47	1	15	7
J.D. Drew	.252	424	61	107	18	56	8
Miguel Cairo	.250	184	28	46	2	23	1
Mike Matheny	.244	315	31	77	3	35	1
Mike DeFelice	.230	174	17	40	4	19	0
Eduardo Perez	.201	154	22	31	10	26	0

Acquired: P Finley from Cle. for IF Luis Garcia and OF Covelli Crisp (July 19); IF Rolen, P Doug Nickle and cash from Phi. for IF Placido Polanco, P Mike Timlin and P Bud Smith (July 29); P Fassero from ChC for 2 PTBN (Aug. 26); P Wright and cash from Mil. for OF Chris Morris and P Mike Matthews (Aug. 29).
Signed: P White (Aug. 17).

Pitching (50 IP)	ERA	W-L	Gm	IP	BB	SO
Mike Crudale*	1.88	3-0	49	52.2	14	47
Jason Isringhausen	2.48	3-2	60	65.1	18	68
Woody Williams	2.53	9-4	17	103.1	25	76
Andy Benes	2.78	5-4	18	97.0	51	64
Steve Kline	3.39	2-1	66	58.1	21	41
Matt Morris	3.42	17-9	32	210.1	64	171
Dave Veres	3.48	5-8	71	82.2	39	68
Darryl Kile	3.72	5-4	14	84.2	28	50
Chuck Finley	3.80	7-4	14	85.1	30	83
Jason Simontacchi*	4.02	11-5	24	143.1	54	72
Luther Hackman	4.11	5-4	41	81.0	39	46
Rick White	4.31	5-7	61	62.2	21	41
Jamey Wright	5.29	7-13	23	129.1	75	77
Jeff Fassero	5.35	8-6	73	69.0	27	56
Travis Smith*	7.17	4-2	12	54.0	20	32

Saves: Isringhausen (32); Kline (6); Veres (4). **Complete games:** Williams, Benes, Morris, Finley and Wright (1). **Shutouts:** Morris, Finley and Wright (1).

San Diego Padres

Batting (135 AB)	Avg	AB	R	H	HR	RBI	SB
Ryan Klesko	.300	540	90	162	29	95	6
Mark Kotsay	.292	578	82	169	17	61	11
Phil Nevin	.285	407	53	116	12	57	4
Gene Kingsale	.278	216	27	60	2	28	9
Ramon Vazquez*	.274	423	50	116	2	32	7
Sean Burroughs*	.271	192	18	52	1	11	2
Deivi Cruz	.263	514	49	135	7	47	2
Ron Gant	.262	309	58	81	18	59	4
Bubba Trammell	.243	403	54	98	17	56	1
D'Angelo Jimenez	.240	321	39	77	3	33	4
Julius Matos*	.238	185	19	44	2	19	1
Ray Lankford	.224	205	20	46	6	26	2
Wiki Gonzalez	.220	164	16	36	1	20	0
Tom Lampkin	.217	281	32	61	10	37	4

Claimed: OF Kingsale off waivers from Sea. (June 14).
Traded: IF Jimenez to ChW for OF Alex Fernandez and C Humberto Quintero (July 12).
Released: P Jones (Sept. 4).

Pitching (40 IP)	ERA	W-L	Gm	IP	BB	SO
Trevor Hoffman	2.73	2-5	61	59.1	18	69
Oliver Perez*	3.50	4-5	16	90.0	48	94
Brian Lawrence	3.69	12-12	35	210.0	52	149
Brett Tomko	4.49	10-10	32	204.1	60	126
Jake Peavy*	4.52	6-7	17	97.2	33	90
Jeremy Fikac*	5.48	4-7	65	69.0	34	66
Bobby J. Jones	5.50	7-8	19	108.0	21	60
Brian Tollberg	6.13	1-5	12	61.2	19	33
Dennis Tankersley*	8.06	1-4	17	51.1	40	39

Saves: Hoffman (38); Brandon Villafuerte (1). **Complete games:** Tomko (3); Lawrence (2). **Shutouts:** Lawrence (2).

San Francisco Giants

Batting (135 AB)	Avg	AB	R	H	HR	RBI	SB
Barry Bonds	.370	403	117	149	46	110	9
Jeff Kent	.313	623	102	195	37	108	5
Yorvit Torrealba*	.279	136	17	38	2	14	0
Benito Santiago	.278	478	56	133	16	74	4
Ramon Martinez	.271	181	26	49	4	25	2
Kenny Lofton	.267	180	30	48	3	9	7
Bill Mueller	.262	366	51	96	7	38	0
David Bell	.261	552	82	144	20	73	1
Tom Goodwin	.260	154	23	40	1	17	16
Rich Aurilia	.257	538	76	138	15	61	1
Pedro Feliz	.253	146	14	37	2	13	0
Reggie Sanders	.250	505	75	126	23	85	18
J.T. Snow	.246	422	47	104	6	53	0
Tsuyoshi Shinjo	.238	362	42	86	9	37	5
Damon Minor*	.237	173	21	41	10	24	0
Shawon Dunston	.231	147	7	34	1	9	1

Acquired: OF Lofton from ChW for P Felix Diaz and P Ryan Meaux (July 28); IF Mueller and cash from ChC for P Jeff Verplancke (Sept. 3).

Pitching (40 IP)	ERA	W-L	Gm	IP	BB	SO
Robb Nen	2.20	6-2	68	73.2	20	81
Tim Worrell	2.25	8-2	80	72.0	30	55
Jay Witasick	2.37	1-0	44	68.1	21	54
Chad Zerbe	3.04	2-0	50	56.1	21	26
Kirk Rueter	3.23	14-8	33	203.2	54	76
Jason Schmidt	3.45	13-8	29	185.1	73	196
Russ Ortiz	3.61	14-10	33	214.1	94	137
Felix Rodriguez	4.17	8-6	71	69.0	29	58
Livan Hernandez	4.38	12-16	33	216.0	71	134
Ryan Jensen*	4.51	13-8	32	171.2	66	105
Aaron Fultz	4.79	2-2	43	41.1	19	31

Saves: Nen (43). **Complete games:** Hernandez (5); Schmidt and Ortiz (2); Jensen (1). **Shutouts:** Hernandez (3); Schmidt (2).

Players Who Played in Both Leagues in 2002

While all individual major league statistics count for career records, players cannot transfer their stats from one league to the other if they are traded during the regular season. Here are the combined stats for batters with at least 225 at bats and pitchers with at least 60 innings pitched, who played in both leagues in 2002.

Batters (225 AB)

	Avg	AB	R	H	HR	RBI	SB
Sandy Alomar Jr......	.279	283	29	79	7	37	0
CHW	.287	167	21	48	7	25	0
COL	.267	116	8	31	0	12	0
Russell Branyan	.228	378	50	86	24	56	4
CLE	.205	161	16	33	8	17	1
CIN	.244	217	34	53	16	39	3
Brian Buchanan......	.269	227	31	61	11	28	2
MIN	.252	135	19	34	5	15	2
SD	.293	92	12	27	6	13	0
Cliff Floyd	.288	520	86	150	28	79	15
FLA	.287	296	49	85	18	57	10
MON	.208	53	7	11	3	4	1
BOS	.316	171	30	54	7	18	4
Jeremy Giambi	.259	313	58	81	20	45	0
OAK	.274	157	26	43	8	17	0
PHI..............	.244	156	32	38	12	28	0
Todd Hollandsworth ..	.284	430	55	122	16	67	8
COL	.295	298	39	88	11	48	7
TEX	.258	132	16	34	5	19	1
D'Angelo Jimenez	.252	429	61	108	4	44	6
SD	.240	321	39	77	3	33	4
CHW	.287	108	22	31	1	11	2

	Avg	AB	R	H	HR	RBI	SB
Gabe Kapler.........	.279	315	37	88	2	34	11
TEX...............	.260	196	25	51	0	17	5
COL...............	.311	119	12	37	2	17	6
Kenny Lofton	.261	532	98	139	11	51	29
CHW	.259	352	68	91	8	42	22
SF	.267	180	30	48	3	9	7
Jose Macias	.249	338	43	84	7	39	8
DET...............	.234	107	10	25	0	6	3
MON..............	.255	231	33	59	7	33	5
Gary Matthews Jr.	.275	345	54	95	7	38	15
NYM..............	.000	1	0	0	0	0	0
BAL...............	.276	344	54	95	7	38	15
Alex Ochoa	.261	280	40	73	8	31	10
MIL...............	.256	215	32	55	6	21	8
ANA...............	.277	65	8	18	2	10	2
Lee Stevens	.204	358	50	73	15	57	1
MON..............	.190	205	28	39	10	31	1
CLE...............	.222	153	22	34	5	26	0
Chris Truby	.215	382	35	82	4	22	2
MON..............	.257	105	12	27	2	7	1
DET...............	.199	277	23	55	2	15	1

Pitchers (60 IP)

	ERA	W-L	Gm	IP	BB	SO
Bartolo Colon	2.93	20-8	33	233.1	70	149
CLE	2.55	10-4	16	116.1	31	75
MON	3.31	10-4	17	117.0	39	74
Alan Embree	2.03	4-6	68	62.0	20	81
SD	0.94	3-4	36	28.2	9	38
BOS	2.97	1-2	32	33.1	11	43
Scott Eyre	4.46	2-4	70	74.2	36	58
TOR	4.97	2-4	49	63.1	29	51
SF	1.59	0-0	21	11.1	7	7
Chuck Finley	4.15	11-15	32	190.2	78	174
CLE	4.44	4-11	18	105.1	48	91
ST.L	3.80	7-4	14	85.1	30	83
Brian Moehler	4.86	3-5	13	63.0	13	31
DET	2.29	1-1	3	19.2	2	13
CIN	6.02	2-4	10	43.1	11	18

	ERA	W-L	Gm	IP	BB	SO
Terry Mulholland	5.70	3-2	37	79.0	21	38
LA................	7.31	0-0	21	32.0	7	17
CLE...............	4.60	3-2	16	47.0	14	21
Cliff Politte	3.67	3-3	68	73.2	28	72
PHI	3.86	2-0	13	16.1	9	15
TOR	3.61	1-3	55	57.1	19	57
Dennys Reyes	5.33	4-4	58	82.2	45	59
COL...............	4.24	0-1	43	40.1	24	30
TEX...............	6.38	4-3	15	42.1	21	29
Paul Shuey	3.31	8-2	67	68.0	31	63
CLE...............	2.41	3-0	39	37.1	10	39
LA................	4.40	5-2	28	30.2	21	24
Pete Walker	4.36	10-5	38	140.1	51	80
NYM..............	9.00	0-0	1	1.0	0	0
TOR	4.33	10-5*	37	139.1	51	80

Baseball's Eight Work Stoppages

In 2002 the players' union and the owners narrowly avoided baseball's ninth work stoppage, coming to an agreement just hours before a proposed players' strike was set to begin. Below is a breakdown of the previous eight stoppages.

Year	Work Stoppage	Games Missed	Length	Dates	Issue
1972	Strike	86	13 days	April 1-13	Pensions
1973	Lockout	0	17 days	February 8-25	Salary arbitration
1976	Lockout	0	17 days	March 1-17	Free agency
1980	Strike	0	8 days	April 1-8	Free-agent compensation
1981	Strike	712	50 days	June 12-July 31	Free-agent compensation
1985	Strike	0	2 days	August 6-7	Salary arbitration
1990	Lockout	0	32 days	Feb. 15-March 18	Salary arbitration and salary cap
1994	Strike	920	232 days	Aug. 12-March 31	Salary cap and revenue sharing

Baseball Playoffs

DIVISIONAL SERIES | **LCS** | **LCS** | **DIVISIONAL SERIES**

WORLD SERIES 2002

| AMERICAN LEAGUE | | NATIONAL LEAGUE |

Minnesota 3
Oakland 2
— Minnesota 1
St. Louis 3
Arizona 0
— St. Louis 1
San Francisco 3
Anaheim 4
New York 1
†Anaheim 3
— Anaheim 4
Atlanta 2
†San Francisco 3
— San Francisco 4

†Wild Card Team

†Wild Card Team

Divisional Series Summaries
AMERICAN LEAGUE

Twins, 3-2

Date	Winner	Home Field
Oct. 1	Twins, 7-5	at Oakland
Oct. 2	Athletics, 9-1	at Oakland
Oct. 4	Athletics, 6-3	at Minnesota
Oct. 5	Twins, 11-2	at Minnesota
Oct. 6	Twins, 5-4	at Oakland

Game 1
Tuesday, Oct. 1, at Oakland

	1 2 3	4 5 6	7 8 9	R H E
Minnesota	0 1 2	0 0 3	1 0 0	- 7 13 3
Oakland	3 2 0	0 0 0	0 0 0	- 5 12 0

Win: Radke, Min. (1-0). **Loss:** Lilly, Oak. (0-1). **Save:** Guardado, Min. (1).
2B: Minnesota—Jones (1), Hunter (1), Cuddyer (1); Oakland—Durham 2 (2), Ellis (1). **3B:** Minnesota—Pierzynski (1). **HR:** Minnesota—Mientkiewicz (1), Koskie (1). **RBI:** Minnesota—Koskie 3 (3), Jones (1), Mientkiewicz (1), Cuddyer (1), Pierzynski (1); Oakland—Chavez 2 (2), Hatteberg (1), Justice (1). **E:** Minnesota—Guzman (1), Koskie (1), Pierzynski (1).
Attendance: 34,853 (43,662). **Time:** 3:44.

Game 2
Wednesday, Oct. 2, at Oakland

	1 2 3	4 5 6	7 8 9	R H E
Minnesota	0 0 0	0 0 1	0 0 0	- 1 7 1
Oakland	3 0 0	5 1 0	0 0 x	- 9 14 0

Win: Mulder, Oak. (1-0). **Loss:** Mays, Min. (0-1).
2B: Minnesota—Mohr (1); Oakland—Durham (3), Hatteberg (1), Tejada (1), Dye (1), Ellis (2). **3B:** Oakland—Justice (1). **HR:** Minnesota—Guzman (1); Oakland—Chavez (1). **RBI:** Minnesota—Guzman (1); Oakland—Chavez 3 (5), Justice 3 (4), Hatteberg (2), Tejada (1), Ellis (1). **E:** Minnesota—Jones (1).
Attendance: 31,953 (43,662). **Time:** 3:04.

Game 3
Friday, Oct. 4, at Minnesota

	1 2 3	4 5 6	7 8 9	R H E
Oakland	2 0 0	1 0 1	2 0 0	- 6 9 1
Minnesota	0 0 0	1 2 0	0 0 0	- 3 8 0

Win: Zito, Oak. (1-0). **Loss:** Reed, Min. (0-1). **Save:** Koch, Oak. (1).
2B: Oakland—Velarde (1); Minnesota—Jones (2), Hunter (2). **3B:** Minnesota—Koskie (1). **HR:** Oakland—Dye (1), Hatteberg (1), Durham (1). **RBI:** Oakland—Durham (1), Hatteberg (3), Long (1), Dye (1), Velarde (1), Tejada (2); Minnesota—Koskie (4), Hunter (1), Pierzynski (2). **SB:** Minnesota—Guzman (1). **E:** Oakland—Ellis (1).
Attendance: 55,932 (48,678). **Time:** 3:26.

Game 4
Saturday, Oct. 5, at Minnesota

	1 2 3	4 5 6	7 8 9	R H E
Oakland	0 0 2	0 0 0	0 0 0	- 2 7 2
Minnesota	0 0 2	7 0 0	2 0 x	-11 12 0

Win: Milton, Min. (1-0). **Loss:** Hudson, Oak. (0-1).
2B: Oakland—Hatteberg (2), Dye (2), Piatt (1); Minnesota—Jones (3), Ortiz (3), Hunter (3), Rivas (1). **HR:** Oakland—Tejada (1); Minnesota—Mientkiewicz (2). **RBI:** Oakland—Tejada 2 (4); Minnesota—Mientkiewicz 3 (4), Guzman (2), Koskie (5), Ortiz (1), Hunter (2). **E:** Oakland—Hatteberg (1), Tejada (1).
Attendance: 55,960 (48,678). **Time:** 3:20.

Game 5
Sunday, Oct. 6, at Oakland

	1 2 3	4 5 6	7 8 9	R H E
Minnesota	0 1 1	0 0 0	0 0 3	- 5 12 0
Oakland	0 0 1	0 0 0	0 0 3	- 4 11 0

Win: Radke, Min. (2-0). **Loss:** Mulder, Oak. (1-1).
2B: Minnesota—Guzman 2 (2), Ortiz (2), Hunter (4), Hocking (1); Oakland—Justice (2). **HR:** Minnesota—Pierzynski (1); Oakland—Ellis (1), Durham (2). **RBI:** Minnesota—Pierzynski 2 (4), LeCroy (1), Ortiz (2), Hocking (1); Oakland—Ellis 3 (4), Durham (2). **SB:** Minnesota—Guzman (2); Oakland—Durham (1).
Attendance: 32,146 (43,662). **Time:** 3:23.

Divisional Series Summaries (Cont.)

Angels, 3-1

Date	Winner	Home Field
Oct. 1	Yankees, 8-5	at New York
Oct. 2	Angels, 8-6	at New York
Oct. 4	Angels, 9-6	at Anaheim
Oct. 5	Angels, 9-5	at Anaheim

Game 1
Tuesday, Oct. 1, at New York

	1 2 3	4 5 6	7 8 9	R	H	E
Anaheim	0 0 1	0 2 1	0 1 0 -	5	12	0
New York	1 0 0	2 1 0	0 4 x -	8	8	1

Win: Karsay, NY (1-0). **Loss:** Weber, Ana. (0-1). **Save:** M. Rivera, NY (1).
HR: Anaheim—Glaus 2 (2); New York—Williams (1), White (1), Giambi (1), Jeter (1). **RBI:** Anaheim—Anderson 2 (2), Glaus 2 (2), Salmon (1); New York—Giambi 3 (3), Williams 3 (3), Jeter (1), White (1). **SB:** Anaheim—Eckstein (1), Erstad (1); New York—Soriano (1). **E:** New York—Posada (1).
Attendance: 56,710 (57,478). **Time:** 3:27.

Game 2
Thursday, Oct. 2, at New York

	1 2 3	4 5 6	7 8 9	R	H	E
Anaheim	1 2 1	0 0 0	0 3 1 -	8	17	1
New York	0 0 1	2 0 2	0 0 1 -	6	12	1

Win: Rodriguez, Ana. (1-0). **Loss:** O. Hernandez, NY (0-1). **Save:** Percival, Ana. (1).
2B: Anaheim—Spiezio (1). **HR:** Anaheim—Salmon (1), Spiezio (1), Anderson (1), Glaus (3); New York—Jeter (2), Soriano (1). **RBI:** Anaheim—Spiezio 3 (3), Salmon (2), Gil (1), Anderson (3), Glaus (3), Kennedy (1); New York—J. Rivera 2 (2), Soriano 2 (2), Jeter (2), Posada (1). **SB:** Anaheim—Figgins (1). **E:** Anaheim—Gil (1); New York—Jeter (1).
Attendance: 56,695 (57,478). **Time:** 4:11.

Game 3
Friday, Oct. 4, at Anaheim

	1 2 3	4 5 6	7 8 9	R	H	E
New York	3 0 3	0 0 0	0 0 0 -	6	6	0
Anaheim	0 1 2	1 0 1	1 3 x -	9	12	0

Win: Rodriguez, Ana. (2-0). **Loss:** Stanton, NY (0-1). **Save:** Percival, Ana. (2).
2B: New York—Williams (1), Ventura (1); Anaheim—Erstad (1), Salmon (1), Anderson (2), Fullmer (1), Kennedy (1). **HR:** Anaheim—Salmon (2), Kennedy (1). **RBI:** New York—Ventura 3 (3), Posada (2), Johnson (1), J. Rivera (3); Anaheim—Salmon 4 (6), Spiezio 2 (5), Kennedy 2 (3), Erstad (1). **SB:** Anaheim—Kennedy (1).
Attendance: 45,072 (45,030). **Time:** 3:52.

Game 4
Saturday, Oct. 5, at Anaheim

	1 2 3	4 5 6	7 8 9	R	H	E
New York	0 1 0	0 1 1	1 0 1 -	5	12	2
Anaheim	0 0 1	0 8 0	0 0 x -	9	15	1

Win: Washburn, Ana. (1-0). **Loss:** Wells, NY (0-1).
2B: New York—Ventura (1), Anaheim—Erstad (2), Molina (2). **HR:** New York—Posada (1); Anaheim—Wooten (1). **RBI:** New York—Jeter (3), Posada (3), Mondesi (1), Ventura (4); Anaheim—Wooten 2 (2), Molina 2 (2), Eckstein (1), Erstad (2), Salmon (7), Anderson (4), Spiezio (6). **E:** New York—Soriano (1), Wells (1); Anaheim—Glaus (1).
Attendance: 45,067 (45,030). **Time:** 3:37.

NATIONAL LEAGUE

Cardinals, 3-0

Date	Winner	Home Field
Oct. 1	Cardinals, 12-2	at Arizona
Oct. 3	Cardinals, 2-1	at Arizona
Oct. 5	Cardinals, 6-3	at St. Louis

Game 1
Tuesday, Oct. 1, at Arizona

	1 2 3	4 5 6	7 8 9	R	H	E
St. Louis	2 0 0	3 0 1	6 0 0 -	12	14	1
Arizona	1 0 1	0 0 0	0 0 0 -	2	8	2

Win: Morris, St.L (1-0). **Loss:** Johnson, Ari. (0-1).
2B: St. Louis—Matheny (1). **3B:** St. Louis—Pujols (1). **HR:** St. Louis—Rolen (1), Edmonds (1). **RBI:** St. Louis—Edmonds 2 (2), Pujols 2 (2), Rolen 2 (2), Matheny 2 (2), Morris 2 (2), Marrero (1); Arizona—Finley (1), McCracken (1). **SB:** St. Louis—Renteria (1); Arizona—Finley (1). **CS:** St. Louis—Edmonds (1). **E:** St. Louis—Renteria (1); Arizona—Womack (1), Swindell (1).
Attendance: 49,154 (49,033). **Time:** 2:55.

Game 2
Thursday, Oct. 3, at Arizona

	1 2 3	4 5 6	7 8 9	R	H	E
St. Louis	0 0 1	0 0 0	0 0 1 -	2	10	1
Arizona	0 0 0	0 0 0	0 1 0 -	1	6	0

Win: Fassero, St.L (1-0). **Loss:** Koplove, Ari. (0-1). **Save:** Isringhausen, St.L (1).
2B: Arizona—McCracken (1), Miller (1). **HR:** St. Louis—Drew (1). **RBI:** St. Louis—Drew (1), Cairo (1); Arizona—McCracken (1). **SB:** St. Louis—Renteria (1). **CS:** St. Louis—Cairo. **E:** St. Louis—Pujols (1).
Attendance: 48,856 (49,033). **Time:** 3:20.

Game 3
Saturday, Oct. 5, at St. Louis

	1 2 3	4 5 6	7 8 9	R	H	E
Arizona	0 2 0	0 1 0	0 0 0 -	3	4	0
St. Louis	0 1 1	2 0 0	0 2 x -	6	9	0

Win: Fassero, St.L (2-0). **Loss:** Batista, Ari. (0-1). **Save:** Isringhausen, St.L (2)
2B: St. Louis—Cairo (1). **HR:** Arizona—Barajas (1), Dellucci (1). **RBI:** Arizona—Dellucci 2 (2), Barajas (1); St. Louis—Cairo 2 (3), Vina (1), Pujols (3), Benes (1), Robinson (1). **CS:** St. Louis—Vina (1).
Attendance: 52,189 (49,814). **Time:** 3:14.

Giants, 3-2

Date	Winner	Home Field
Oct. 2	Giants, 8-5	at Atlanta
Oct. 3	Braves, 7-3	at Atlanta
Oct. 5	Braves, 10-2	at San Francisco
Oct. 6	Giants, 8-3	at San Francisco
Oct. 7	Giants, 3-1	at Atlanta

Game 1
Wednesday, Oct. 2, at Atlanta

	1 2 3	4 5 6	7 8 9	R	H	E
San Francisco	0 3 0	3 0 2	0 0 0 -	8	12	2
Atlanta	0 2 0	0 0 0	0 3 0 -	5	10	0

Win: Ortiz, SF (1-0). **Loss:** Glavine, Atl. (0-1). **Save:** Nen, SF (1).
2B: San Francisco—Aurilia (1), Kent (1), Santiago (1), Snow (1). **HR:** Atlanta—Lopez (1), Sheffield (1). **RBI:** San Francisco—Aurilia 2 (2), Santiago 2 (2), Snow 2 (2), Lofton (1), Bell (1); Atlanta—Lopez 2 (2), Glavine 2 (2), Sheffield (1). **E:** San Francisco—Bonds (1), Santiago (1).
Attendance: 41,903 (50,091). **Time:** 3:24.

Game 2
Thursday, Oct. 3, at Atlanta

	1 2 3	4 5 6	7 8 9	R H E
San Francisco	.0 1 0	0 0 1	0 0 1	- 3 7 0
Atlanta	.1 3 0	3 0 0	0 0 x	- 7 8 0

Win: Millwood, Atl. (1-0). **Loss:** Rueter, SF (0-1).
2B: Atlanta—DeRosa (1). **3B:** Atlanta—DeRosa (1). **HR:** San Francisco—Bonds (1), Aurilia (1), Snow (1); Atlanta—Castilla (1), Lopez (2). **RBI:** San Francisco—Aurilia (3), Bonds (1), Snow (3); Atlanta—DeRosa 2 (2), Furcal (1), C. Jones (1), Lopez (3), Castilla (1). **CS:** Atlanta—Furcal (1).
Attendance: 47,167 (50,091). **Time:** 2:58.

Game 3
Saturday, Oct. 5, at San Francisco

	1 2 3	4 5 6	7 8 9	R H E
Atlanta	.0 0 1	0 0 5	0 0 4	-10 10 0
San Francisco	.1 0 0	0 0 1	0 0 0	- 2 5 0

Win: Maddux, Atl. (1-0). **Loss:** Schmidt, SF (0-1).
2B: San Francisco—Kent (2). **3B:** Atlanta—Furcal (1). **HR:** Atlanta—Lockhart (1); San Francisco—Bonds (2). **RBI:** Atlanta—Lockhart 4 (4), A. Jones 2 (2), Castilla 2 (3), J. Franco (1), C. Jones (1); San Francisco—Kent (2), Bonds (1). **SB:** Atlanta—J. Franco (1); San Francisco—Lofton (1).
Attendance: 43,043 (41,467). **Time:** 3:23.

Game 4
Sunday, Oct. 6, at San Francisco

	1 2 3	4 5 6	7 8 9	R H E
Atlanta	.0 0 0	0 1 2	0 0 0	- 3 9 0
San Francisco	.2 2 3	0 1 0	0 0 x	- 8 11 0

Win: Hernandez, SF (1-0). **Loss:** Glavine, Atl. (0-2).
2B: Atlanta—Furcal (1), A. Jones (1), Lopez (1); San Francisco—Santiago (2), Sanders (1). **HR:** San Francisco—Aurilia (2). **RBI:** Atlanta—Furcal (2), Lopez (4), Castilla (4); San Francisco—Aurilia 4 (7), Santiago 3 (5), Bonds (3).
Attendance: 43,070 (41,467). **Time:** 3:03.

Game 5
Monday, Oct. 7, at Atlanta

	1 2 3	4 5 6	7 8 9	R H E
San Francisco	.0 1 0	1 0 0	1 0 0	- 3 6 2
Atlanta	.0 0 0	0 0 1	0 0 0	- 1 7 0

Win: Ortiz, SF (2-0). **Loss:** Millwood, Atl. (1-1). **Save:** Nen, SF (2).
2B: San Francisco—Lofton (1), Snow (2). **HR:** San Francisco—Bonds (3). **RBI:** San Francisco—Lofton (2), Bonds (4), Sanders (1); Atlanta—DeRosa (3). **SB:** Atlanta—Furcal (1). **CS:** San Francisco—Bonds (1).
Attendance: 45,203 (50,091). **Time:** 3:47.

American League Championship Series

Angels, 4-1

Date	Winner	Home Field
Oct. 8	Twins, 2-1	at Minnesota
Oct. 9	Angels, 6-3	at Minnesota
Oct. 11	Angels, 2-1	at Anaheim
Oct. 12	Angels, 7-1	at Anaheim
Oct. 13	Angels, 13-5	at Anaheim

Game 1
Tuesday, Oct. 8, at Minnesota

	1 2 3	4 5 6	7 8 9	R H E
Anaheim	.0 0 1	0 0 0	0 0 0	- 1 4 0
Minnesota	.0 1 0	0 1 0	0 0 x	- 2 5 1

Win: Mays, Min. (1-0). **Loss:** Appier, Ana. (0-1). **Save:** Guardado, Min. (2).
2B: Minnesota—Hunter (5), Koskie (1). **RBI:** Minnesota—Pierzynski (5), Koskie (6). **E:** Minnesota—Guzman (2).
Attendance: 55,562 (48,678). **Time:** 2:58.

Game 2
Wednesday, Oct. 9, at Minnesota

	1 2 3	4 5 6	7 8 9	R H E
Anaheim	.1 3 0	0 0 2	0 0 0	- 6 10 0
Minnesota	.0 0 0	0 0 3	0 0 0	- 3 11 1

Win: Ortiz, Ana. (1-0). **Loss:** Reed, Min. (0-2). **Save:** Percival, Ana. (3).
2B: Anaheim—Fullmer (2), Spiezio (2); Minnesota—Guzman (3), Hunter (6). **3B:** Anaheim—Glaus (1). **HR:** Anaheim—Erstad (1), Fullmer (1). **RBI:** Anaheim—Fullmer 2 (2), Eckstein (2), Erstad (3), Spiezio (7); Minnesota—Mientkiewicz 2 (6), Koskie (7). **CS:** Anaheim—Spiezio (1). **E:** Minnesota—Pierzynski (2).
Attendance: 55,990 (48,678). **Time:** 3:13.

Game 3
Friday, Oct. 11, at Anaheim

	1 2 3	4 5 6	7 8 9	R H E
Minnesota	.0 0 0	0 0 0	1 0 0	- 1 6 0
Anaheim	.0 1 0	0 0 0	0 1 x	- 2 7 2

Win: Rodriguez, Ana. (3-0). **Loss:** Romero, Min. (0-1). **Save:** Percival, Ana. (4).
2B: Minnesota—Jones (4); Anaheim—Anderson (3). **HR:** Anaheim—Anderson (2), Glaus (4). **RBI:** Minnesota—Jones (2); Anaheim—Anderson (4), Glaus (4). **SB:** Minnesota—Mohr (1). **E:** Anaheim—Eckstein (1), Gil (2).
Attendance: 44,234 (45,030). **Time:** 3:13.

Game 4
Saturday, Oct. 12, at Anaheim

	1 2 3	4 5 6	7 8 9	R H E
Minnesota	.0 0 0	0 0 0	0 0 1	- 1 6 2
Anaheim	.0 0 0	0 0 0	2 5 x	- 7 10 0

Win: Lackey, Ana. (1-0). **Loss:** Radke, Min. (2-1).
2B: Minnesota—Mientkiewicz (1), Koskie (2); Anaheim—Spiezio (3), Fullmer (3). **3B:** Anaheim—B. Molina (1). **RBI:** Minnesota—Ortiz (3); Anaheim—Fullmer 2 (4), B. Molina 2 (4), Glaus (5), Spiezio (8), Anderson (6). **SB:** Anaheim—Erstad (2). **CS:** Minnesota—Pierzynski (1). **E:** Minnesota—Pierzynski (3), Santana (1).
Attendance: 44,830 (45,030). **Time:** 2:49.

Game 5
Sunday, Oct. 13, at Anaheim

	1 2 3	4 5 6	7 8 9	R H E
Minnesota	.1 1 0	0 0 0	3 0 0	- 5 9 0
Anaheim	.0 0 1	0 2 0	10 0 x	-13 18 0

Win: Rodriguez, Ana. (4-0). **Loss:** Santana, Min. (0-1).
2B: Minnesota—Ortiz (3), Mohr (1). **HR:** Anaheim—Kennedy 3 (4), Spiezio (2). **RBI:** Minnesota—Jones (3), Ortiz (4), Pierzynski (6), Kielty (1); Anaheim—Kennedy 5 (8), Spiezio 3 (11), Anderson (7), Wooten (3), Eckstein (3), Erstad (4). **CS:** Anaheim—Anderson (1).
Attendance: 44,835 (45,030). **Time:** 3:30.

Most Valuable Player
Adam Kennedy, Anaheim, 2B

AVG	AB	R	H	HR	RBI	SB
.357	14	5	5	3	5	0

ALCS Composite Box Score
Anaheim Angels

Batting		LCS vs. Minnesota							Overall AL Playoffs						
	Avg	AB	R	H	HR	RBI	BB	SO	Avg	AB	R	H	HR	RBI	BB	SO
Chone Figgins	1.000	1	2	1	0	0	0	0	1.000	1	3	1	0	0	0	0
Darin Erstad	.364	22	4	8	1	2	0	3	.390	41	8	16	1	4	0	4
Adam Kennedy	.357	14	5	5	3	5	0	2	.409	22	9	9	4	8	1	4
Scott Spiezio	.353	17	5	6	1	5	2	1	.375	32	7	12	2	11	4	2
Brad Fullmer	.333	12	2	4	1	4	0	2	.316	19	3	6	1	4	1	3
Troy Glaus	.316	19	4	6	1	2	2	5	.314	35	8	11	4	5	3	8
David Eckstein	.286	21	1	6	0	2	0	0	.282	39	3	11	0	3	0	2
Garret Anderson	.250	20	3	5	1	3	1	0	.316	38	8	12	2	7	3	4
Shawn Wooten	.250	8	1	2	0	1	0	3	.471	17	5	8	1	3	0	4
Bengie Molina	.214	14	0	3	0	2	1	2	.241	29	0	7	0	4	1	3
Tim Salmon	.214	14	0	3	0	0	3	1	.242	33	3	8	2	7	4	6
Benji Gil	.000	2	0	0	0	0	0	1	.571	7	1	4	0	0	0	1
Jose Molina	.000	1	0	0	0	0	0	0	.000	1	0	0	0	0	0	0
Alex Ochoa	.000	4	2	0	0	0	0	0	.000	4	2	0	0	0	0	0
Orlando Palmeiro	.000	2	0	0	0	0	0	1	.000	2	0	0	0	0	0	3
TOTALS	.287	171	29	49	8	26	9	26	.328	320	60	105	17	66	16	44

Pitching		LCS vs. Minnesota							Overall AL Playoffs						
	ERA	W-L	Sv	Gm	IP	H	BB	SO	ERA	W-L	Sv	Gm	IP	H	BB	SO
John Lackey	0.00	1-0	0	1	7.0	3	0	7	0.00	0-0	0	2	10.0	6	1	10
Troy Percival	0.00	0-0	2	3	3.1	0	1	3	2.70	0-0	4	6	6.2	6	0	7
Francisco Rodriguez	0.00	2-0	0	4	4.1	2	2	7	1.80	4-0	0	7	10.0	4	4	15
Scott Schoeneweis	0.00	0-0	0	1	1.0	1	0	0	9.00	0-0	0	4	1.0	2	0	0
Jarrod Washburn	1.29	0-0	0	1	7.0	6	0	7	2.84	1-0	0	3	19.0	18	3	11
Ben Weber	3.38	0-0	0	3	2.2	3	0	3	8.10	0-1	0	5	3.2	5	2	3
Kevin Appier	3.48	0-1	0	2	10.1	10	4	3	4.11	0-1	0	3	15.1	15	7	6
Ramon Ortiz	5.06	1-0	0	1	5.1	10	1	3	10.13	1-0	0	2	8.0	13	5	4
Brendan Donnelly	8.10	0-0	0	3	3.1	3	0	5	10.13	0-0	0	6	5.1	6	1	7
TOTALS	2.45	4-1	2		44.0	37	7	38	4.10	7-2	4		79.0	75	23	63

Wild Pitches— LCS (Appier 2, Donnelly, Rodriguez); OVERALL (Appier 2, Rodriguez 2, Donnelly). **Hit Batters—** LCS (Donnelly); OVERALL (Appier, Donnelly, Ortiz, Percival, Washburn).

Minnesota Twins

Batting		LCS vs. Anaheim							Overall AL Playoffs						
	Avg	AB	R	H	HR	RBI	BB	SO	Avg	AB	R	H	HR	RBI	BB	SO
Dustan Mohr	.417	12	3	5	0	0	0	4	.500	14	4	7	0	0	1	4
Matthew LeCroy	.333	3	0	1	0	0	0	1	.417	12	1	5	0	1	0	4
David Ortiz	.313	16	0	5	0	2	0	5	.276	29	0	8	0	4	0	10
Corey Koskie	.278	18	3	5	0	2	2	8	.205	39	6	8	1	7	4	14
Doug Mientkiewicz	.278	18	1	5	0	2	1	4	.263	38	4	10	2	6	2	3
A.J. Pierzynski	.250	16	1	4	0	0	1	3	.344	32	5	11	1	6	2	4
Luis Rivas	.250	12	1	3	0	0	1	1	.250	24	3	6	0	0	2	5
Michael Cuddyer	.200	5	0	1	0	0	0	1	.333	18	1	6	0	1	4	4
Cristian Guzman	.167	18	3	3	0	0	0	3	.231	39	6	9	1	2	2	7
Torii Hunter	.167	18	2	3	0	0	1	3	.237	38	6	9	0	2	2	7
Jacque Jones	.100	20	0	2	0	2	0	4	.175	40	3	7	0	3	1	12
Bobby Kielty	.000	3	0	0	0	1	1	2	.000	7	0	0	0	1	1	3
Tom Prince	.000	1	0	0	0	0	0	0	.000	3	0	0	0	0	0	0
David Lamb	—	0	0	0	0	0	0	0	—	0	0	0	0	0	0	0
Denny Hocking	—	0	0	0	0	0	0	0	.500	6	0	3	0	1	0	1
TOTALS	.231	160	12	37	0	11	7	38	.263	339	39	89	5	34	21	80

Pitching		LCS vs. Anaheim							Overall AL Playoffs						
	ERA	W-L	Sv	Gm	IP	H	BB	SO	ERA	W-L	Sv	Gm	IP	H	BB	SO
Eddie Guardado	0.00	0-0	1	1	1.0	0	1	2	9.00	0-0	2	3	3.0	5	2	3
Kyle Lohse	0.00	0-0	0	1	1.0	0	0	1	0.00	0-0	0	3	5.0	2	0	6
Eric Milton	1.50	0-0	0	1	6.0	5	2	4	2.08	1-0	0	2	13.0	11	3	7
Joe Mays	2.03	1-0	0	2	13.1	12	0	3	4.76	1-1	0	3	17.0	21	2	4
Brad Radke	2.70	0-1	0	1	6.2	5	1	4	1.96	2-1	0	3	18.1	19	2	11
Bob Wells	9.00	0-0	0	2	1.0	2	0	2	9.00	0-0	0	2	1.0	2	0	2
Rick Reed	10.13	0-1	0	1	5.1	8	0	0	8.71	0-2	0	2	10.1	14	2	8
Johan Santana	10.80	0-1	0	4	3.1	4	3	4	8.53	0-1	0	6	6.1	7	2	6
LaTroy Hawkins	20.25	0-0	0	4	1.1	4	1	6	7.36	0-0	0	7	3.2	4	1	6
J.C. Romero	22.50	0-1	0	4	2.0	4	2	3	8.44	0-1	0	7	5.1	7	3	5
Mike Jackson	27.00	0-0	0	3	1.0	5	2	3	16.20	0-0	0	4	1.2	6	2	2
Tony Fiore	—								20.25	0-0	0	1	1.1	4	2	0
TOTALS	5.57	1-4	1		42.0	49	9	26	5.02	4-6	2		86.0	102	21	60

Wild Pitches— LCS (Santana 2); OVERALL (Santana 2). **Hit Batters—** LCS (Radke, Wells); OVERALL (Mays, Radke, Wells).

Score by Innings

	1	2	3		4	5	6		7	8	9		R	H	E
Anaheim	1	4	2		0	2	2		12	6	0	–	29	49	2
Minnesota	1	2	0		0	1	3		4	0	1	–	12	37	4

E: Anaheim—Eckstein, Gil; Minnesota—Pierzynski 2, Guzman, Santana. **DP:** Anaheim 4, Minnesota 4. **2B:** Anaheim—Spiezio 2, Fullmer 2, Anderson; Minnesota—Koskie 2, Hunter 2, Mohr, Ortiz, Mientkiewicz, Guzman, Jones. **3B:** Anaheim—Glaus, B. Molina. **SB:** Anaheim—Erstad; Minnesota—Mohr. **CS:** Anaheim—Spiezio, Anderson; Minnesota—Pierzynski. **S:** Anaheim—Gil, Kennedy; Minnesota—Hunter, Guzman. **SF:** Minnesota—Jones, Pierzynski. **HBP:** by Donnelly (Guzman), by Radke (B. Molina), by Wells (Eckstein). **LOB:** Anaheim—29; Minnesota—28.
Umpires: Ed Montague, Mike Everitt, Brian Gorman, Larry Young, Dana Demuth, Ed Rapuano.

National League Championship Series
Giants, 4-1

Date	Winner	Home Field
Oct. 9	Giants, 9-6	at St. Louis
Oct. 10	Giants, 4-1	at St. Louis
Oct. 12	Cardinals, 5-4	at San Francisco
Oct. 13	Giants, 4-3	at San Francisco
Oct. 14	Giants, 2-1	at San Francisco

Game 1
Wednesday, Oct. 9, at St. Louis

	1	2	3		4	5	6		7	8	9		R	H	E
San Francisco	1	4	1		0	1	2		0	0	0	-	9	11	0
St. Louis	0	1	0		0	2	2		0	1	0	-	6	11	0

Win: Rueter, SF (1-1). **Loss:** Morris, St.L (1-1). **Save:** Nen, SF (3).

2B: St. Louis—Marrero (1), Edmonds (1). **3B:** San Francisco—Bonds (1). **HR:** San Francisco—Lofton (1), Bell (1), Santiago (1); St. Louis—Pujols (1), Cairo (1), Drew (2). **RBI:** San Francisco—Santiago 4 (9), Aurilia (8), Bonds 2 (6), Lofton (3), Bell (3); St. Louis—Pujols 2 (5), Cairo 2 (5), Vina (2), Drew (2). **SB:** San Francisco—Lofton (2). **CS:** St. Louis—Robinson (1).
Attendance: 52,175 (49,814). **Time:** 3:31.

Game 2
Thursday, Oct. 10, at St. Louis

	1	2	3		4	5	6		7	8	9		R	H	E
San Francisco	1	0	0		0	2	0		0	0	1	-	4	7	0
St. Louis	0	0	0		0	0	0		0	1	0	-	1	6	0

Win: Schmidt, SF (1-1). **Loss:** Williams, St.L (0-1). **Save:** Nen, SF (4).

2B: St. Louis—Edmonds (2). **3B:** San Francisco—Snow (1). **HR:** San Francisco—Aurilia 2 (4); St. Louis—Perez (1). **RBI:** San Francisco—Aurilia 3 (11), Martinez (1); St. Louis—Perez (1).
Attendance: 52,195 (49,814). **Time:** 3:17.

Most Valuable Player

Benito Santiago, San Francisco, C

AVG	AB	R	H	HR	RBI	SB
.300	20	2	6	2	6	0

Game 3
Saturday, Oct. 12, at San Francisco

	1	2	3		4	5	6		7	8	9		R	H	E
St. Louis	0	0	2		1	1	1		0	0	0	-	5	6	1
San Francisco	0	1	0		0	3	0		0	0	0	-	4	10	0

Win: Finley, St.L (1-0). **Loss:** Witasick, SF (0-1). **Save:** Isringhausen, St.L (3).

2B: St. Louis—Pujols (1), Vina (1); San Francisco—Aurilia (2). **HR:** St. Louis—Matheny (1), Edmonds (2), Marrero (1); San Francisco—Bonds (4). **RBI:** St. Louis—Renteria (1), Edmonds 2 (4), Matheny (3), Marrero (2); San Francisco—Aurilia (12), Bonds 3 (9). **E:** St. Louis—Renteria (2).
Attendance: 42,177 (41,467). **Time:** 3:32.

Game 4
Sunday, Oct. 13, at San Francisco

	1	2	3		4	5	6		7	8	9		R	H	E
St. Louis	2	0	0		0	0	0		0	0	1	-	3	12	0
San Francisco	0	0	0		0	0	2		0	2	x	-	4	4	1

Win: Worrell, SF (1-0). **Loss:** White, St.L (0-1). **Save:** Nen, SF (5).

2B: St. Louis—Vina (2), Matheny (2); San Francisco—Snow (3). **HR:** San Francisco—Santiago (2). **RBI:** St. Louis—Edmonds 2 (6), Martinez (1); San Francisco—Snow 2 (5), Santiago 2 (11). **SB:** St. Louis—Martinez (1). **E:** San Francisco—Aurilia (1).
Attendance: 42,676 (41,467). **Time:** 3:26.

Game 5
Monday, Oct. 14, at San Francisco

	1	2	3		4	5	6		7	8	9		R	H	E
St. Louis	0	0	0		0	0	0		1	0	0	-	1	9	0
San Francisco	0	0	0		0	0	0		0	1	1	-	2	7	0

Win: Worrell, SF (2-0). **Loss:** Morris, St.L (1-2). **2B:** St. Louis—Matheny (3); San Francisco—Bell (1). **RBI:** St. Louis—Vina (3); San Francisco—Bonds (10), Lofton (4).
Attendance: 42,673 (41,467). **Time:** 3:01.

NLCS Composite Box Score
San Francisco Giants

Batting	Avg	AB	R	H	HR	RBI	BB	SO	Avg	AB	R	H	HR	RBI	BB	SO
				LCS vs. St. Louis								Overall NL Playoffs				
Russ Ortiz	1.000	1	0	1	0	0	0	0	.286	7	1	2	0	0	0	4
Shawon Dunston	.500	2	0	1	0	0	0	1	.333	3	0	1	0	0	0	2
David Bell	.412	17	4	7	1	1	2	3	.303	33	7	10	1	2	5	7
Rich Aurilia	.333	15	4	5	2	5	2	2	.278	36	8	10	4	12	3	7
Benito Santiago	.300	20	2	6	2	6	2	4	.268	41	3	11	2	11	3	9
Barry Bonds	.273	11	5	3	1	6	10	2	.286	28	10	8	4	10	14	3
Jeff Kent	.263	19	3	5	0	0	2	4	.263	38	4	10	0	1	4	11
J.T. Snow	.250	20	1	5	0	2	1	4	.282	39	4	11	1	5	2	9
Kenny Lofton	.238	21	4	5	1	2	2	4	.293	41	9	12	1	4	4	7
Reggie Sanders	.063	16	0	1	0	0	4	4	.147	34	1	5	0	1	3	9
Tom Goodwin	.000	3	0	0	0	0	0	0	.000	5	0	0	0	0	0	0
Robb Nen	.000	1	0	0	0	0	0	0	.000	1	0	0	0	0	0	1
Kirk Rueter	.000	5	0	0	0	0	0	3	.000	6	0	0	0	0	0	3
Jason Schmidt	.000	2	0	0	0	0	0	0	.000	4	0	0	0	0	0	0
Felix Rodriguez	.000	1	0	0	0	0	0	1	.000	1	0	0	0	0	0	1
Livan Hernandez	.000	1	0	0	0	0	0	1	.000	3	0	0	0	0	0	1
Ramon E. Martinez	—	1	0	0	0	0	1	0	.000	1	0	0	0	0	1	0
Pedro Feliz	—	1	0	0	0	0	0	1	.000	2	0	0	0	0	0	1
Tsuyoshi Shinjo	—	1	0	0	0	0	0	0	.000	1	0	0	0	0	0	0
TOTALS	.247	158	23	39	7	23	21	36	.247	324	47	80	13	47	39	81

Pitching	ERA	W-L	Sv	Gm	IP	H	BB	SO	ERA	W-L	Sv	Gm	IP	H	BB	SO
Scott Eyre	0.00	0-0	0	4	1.2	2	0	0	0.00	0-0	0	7	3.0	3	0	0
Aaron Fultz	0.00	0-0	0	1	0.1	0	0	0	27.00	0-0	0	3	0.1	2	0	0
Jason Schmidt	1.17	1-0	0	1	7.2	4	1	8	3.46	1-1	0	2	13.0	7	5	13
Felix Rodriguez	1.93	0-0	0	4	4.2	3	2	2	1.17	0-0	0	7	7.2	4	4	4
Tim Worrell	2.08	2-0	0	4	4.1	2	0	3	6.14	2-0	0	7	7.1	9	2	6
Robb Nen	2.70	0-0	3	3	3.1	3	1	4	1.50	0-0	5	7	6.0	7	2	5
Livan Hernandez	2.84	0-0	0	1	6.1	9	1	0	3.07	1-0	0	2	14.2	17	3	6
Kirk Rueter	4.09	1-0	0	2	11.0	15	2	3	7.07	1-1	0	3	14.0	22	4	4
Russ Ortiz	7.71	0-0	0	1	4.2	5	3	3	3.71	2-0	0	3	17.0	14	11	11
Jay Witasick	9.00	0-1	0	1	1.0	1	0	2	2.70	0-1	0	3	3.1	1	0	1
Manny Aybar	—	0-0	0	0	0.0	0	0	0	6.75	0-0	0	2	2.2	1	3	3
TOTALS	3.20	4-1	3	5	45.0	44	10	23	3.94	7-3	5	10	89.0	88	32	53

Wild Pitches—LCS (Nen, Ortiz); OVERALL (Ortiz 2, Nen). **Hit Batters**—LCS (Hernandez, Rueter); OVERALL (Hernandez 2, Rueter).

St. Louis Cardinals

Batting	Avg	AB	R	H	HR	RBI	BB	SO	Avg	AB	R	H	HR	RBI	BB	SO
				LCS vs. San Francisco								Overall NL Playoffs				
Jim Edmonds	.400	20	2	8	1	4	2	5	.355	31	3	11	2	6	4	9
Miguel Cairo	.385	13	2	5	1	2	0	2	.529	17	4	9	1	5	0	2
J.D. Drew	.385	13	1	5	1	1	1	2	.318	22	2	7	2	2	2	4
Mike Matheny	.316	19	2	6	1	1	0	2	.357	28	5	10	1	3	2	3
Albert Pujols	.263	19	2	5	1	2	2	5	.276	29	5	8	1	5	5	6
Fernando Vina	.261	23	2	6	0	0	0	0	.395	38	5	15	0	3	1	0
Eduardo Perez	.250	4	1	1	1	1	1	0	.200	5	1	1	1	1	1	0
Eli Marrero	.188	16	1	3	1	1	1	1	.136	22	1	3	1	2	1	2
Edgar Renteria	.158	19	0	3	0	1	0	2	.194	31	3	6	0	1	1	3
Tino Martinez	.143	14	1	2	0	1	2	1	.080	25	3	2	0	1	4	2
Chuck Finley	.000	2	1	0	0	0	0	0	.000	5	1	0	0	0	0	3
Andy Benes	.000	2	0	0	0	0	0	0	.000	3	0	0	0	0	1	0
Woody Williams	.000	0	0	0	0	0	0	0	.000	0	0	0	0	0	0	0
Mike DiFelice	.000	1	0	0	0	0	0	0	.000	1	0	0	0	0	0	0
Matt Morris	.000	4	0	0	0	0	0	1	.125	8	1	1	0	2	0	3
Kerry Robinson	.000	2	1	0	0	0	1	1	.250	4	1	1	0	1	1	1
Scott Rolen	—	0	0	0	0	0	0	0	.429	7	1	3	1	2	0	2
TOTALS	.257	171	16	44	7	16	10	23	.279	276	36	77	10	35	22	40

Pitching	ERA	W-L	Sv	Gm	IP	H	BB	SO	ERA	W-L	Sv	Gm	IP	H	BB	SO
Jeff Fassero	0.00	0-0	0	1	0.2	0	1	0	0.00	2-0	0	4	3.1	1	2	1
Dave Veres	0.00	0-0	0	2	3.2	2	1	5	0.00	0-0	0	2	3.2	2	1	5
Steve Kline	0.00	0-0	0	4	2.1	2	0	1	0.00	0-0	0	6	3.2	3	1	1
Andy Benes	3.38	0-0	0	1	5.1	2	4	5	4.50	0-0	0	2	10.0	4	8	10
Woody Williams	4.50	0-1	0	1	6.0	6	1	7	4.50	0-1	0	1	6.0	6	1	7
Rick White	4.50	0-1	0	3	4.0	2	2	5	3.00	0-1	0	5	6.0	4	3	6
Jason Isringhausen	4.50	0-0	1	2	2.0	1	3	3	2.25	0-0	3	4	4.0	1	3	4
Matt Morris	6.23	0-2	0	2	13.0	16	6	6	4.50	1-2	0	3	20.0	23	8	9
Chuck Finley	7.20	1-0	0	1	5.0	7	3	3	3.18	1-0	0	2	11.1	11	5	8
Mike Crudale	10.80	0-0	0	1	1.2	1	1	2	6.75	0-0	0	2	2.2	1	2	4
TOTALS	4.74	1-4	1	5	43.2	39	21	36	3.44	4-4	3	8	70.2	57	32	57

Wild Pitches—LCS (none); OVERALL (none). **Hit Batters**—LCS (Morris 3); OVERALL (Morris 3).

Score by Innings

	1	2	3	4	5	6	7	8	9		R	H	E
San Francisco	2	5	1	0	6	4	0	3	2	–	23	39	1
St. Louis	2	1	2	1	3	3	1	2	1	–	16	44	1

E: San Francisco—Aurilia; St. Louis—Renteria. **DP:** San Francisco 4, St. Louis 4. **2B:** San Francisco—Bell, Aurilia, Snow; St. Louis—Edmonds 2, Matheny 2, Vina 2, Pujols, Marrero. **3B:** San Francisco—Bonds, Snow. **SB:** San Francisco—Lofton; St. Louis—Martinez. **CS:** St. Louis—Robinson. **S:** San Francisco—Aurilia 3, Ortiz, Dunston, Schmidt, Hernandez, Martinez; St. Louis—Morris 2, Renteria, Benes, Williams. **SF:** San Francisco—Aurilia, Bonds; St. Louis—Vina, Renteria. **HBP:** by Rueter (Renteria), by Hernandez (Pujols), by Morris (Lofton, Aurilia, Kent). **LOB:** San Francisco—38; St. Louis—39.
Umpires: Randy Marsh, Jeff Nelson, Dale Scott, Jeff Kellogg, Tim Welke, Charles Reliford.

WORLD SERIES

Angels, 4-3

Date	Winner	Home Field
Oct. 19	Giants, 4-3	at Anaheim
Oct. 20	Angels, 11-10	at Anaheim
Oct. 22	Angels, 10-4	at San Francisco
Oct. 23	Giants, 4-3	at San Francisco
Oct. 24	Giants, 16-4	at San Francisco
Oct. 26	Angels, 6-5	at Anaheim
Oct. 27	Angels, 4-1	at Anaheim

Most Valuable Player
Troy Glaus, Anaheim, 3B

AVG	AB	R	H	HR	RBI	BB	TB
.385	26	7	10	3	8	4	22

Game 1
Saturday, Oct. 19, at Anaheim

San Francisco	AB	R	H	RBI	Anaheim	AB	R	H	RBI
Lofton, cf	3	0	0	0	Eckstein, ss	5	0	1	0
Aurilia, ss	4	0	0	0	Erstad, cf	5	0	1	0
Kent, 2b	4	0	0	0	Salmon, rf	4	0	1	0
Bonds, lf	3	1	1	1	Anderson, lf	4	0	1	0
Santiago, c	4	0	1	0	Glaus, 3b	4	2	2	2
Sanders, rf	3	2	1	2	Fullmer, dh	3	1	1	0
Snow, 1b	3	1	1	2	Spiezio, 1b	3	0	1	0
Bell, 3b	4	0	0	0	Figgins, pr	0	0	0	0
Shinjo, dh	3	0	1	0	Wooten, 1b	0	0	0	0
Goodwin, dh	1	0	0	0	B. Molina, c	3	0	0	0
					Palmeiro, ph	1	0	0	0
					J. Molina, c	0	0	0	0
					Kennedy, 2b	4	0	2	1
Totals	32	4	6	4	Totals	36	3	9	3

	R	H	E
San Francisco.. 020 002 000 —	4	6	0
Anaheim ...... 010 002 000 —	3	9	0

2B: Anaheim—Kennedy (1), Spiezio (1). **HR:** San Francisco—Bonds (1), Sanders (1), Snow (1); Anaheim—Glaus 2 (2). **BB:** San Francisco—Bonds, Sanders, Snow; Anaheim—Fullmer, Spiezio. **SB:** Anaheim—Fullmer (1).

San Francisco	IP	H	R	ER	BB	SO	HR	ERA
Schmidt (W, 1-0)	5⅔	9	3	3	1	6	2	4.76
Rodriguez	1⅓	0	0	0	0	1	0	0.00
Worrell	1	0	0	0	1	1	0	0.00
Nen (S, 1)	1	0	0	0	0	1	0	0.00
Anaheim								
Washburn (L, 0-1)	5⅔	6	4	4	2	5	3	6.35
Donnelly	1⅔	0	0	0	0	0	0	0.00
Schoeneweis	0	0	0	0	1	0	0	0.00
Weber	1⅔	0	0	0	0	2	0	0.00

Attendance: 44,603 (45,030). **Time:** 3:44.

Game 2
Sunday, Oct. 20, at Anaheim

San Francisco	AB	R	H	RBI	Anaheim	AB	R	H	RBI
Lofton, cf	5	0	1	0	Eckstein, ss	5	3	3	0
Aurilia, ss	5	1	1	0	Erstad, cf	5	2	2	1
Kent, 2b	5	1	1	1	Salmon, rf	4	3	4	4
Bonds, lf	2	3	1	3	Ochoa, rf	0	0	0	0
Santiago, c	5	1	1	0	Anderson, lf	5	1	2	2
Snow, 1b	4	2	2	0	Glaus, 3b	4	1	2	0
Sanders, rf	4	1	2	3	Fullmer, dh	3	0	1	0
Bell, 3b	4	1	2	0	Spiezio, 1b	3	0	1	2
Dunston, dh	4	0	1	1	B. Molina, c	4	0	0	0
					Kennedy, 2b	4	0	0	0
Totals	38	10	12	10	Totals	37	11	16	10

	R	H	E
San Francisco.. 041 040 001 —	10	12	1
Anaheim ...... 520 011 02x —	11	16	1

2B: San Francisco—Aurilia (1); Anaheim—Erstad 2 (2), Glaus (1). **HR:** San Francisco—Sanders (2), Bell (1), Kent (1), Bonds (2); Anaheim—Salmon 2 (2). **BB:** San Francisco—Bonds 3; Anaheim—Salmon, Fullmer. **SF:** Anaheim—Spiezio. **SB:** San Francisco—Sanders (1); Anaheim—Spiezio (1), Fullmer (2). **E:** San Francisco—Lofton (1); Anaheim—Anderson (1). **PB:** San Francisco—Santiago.

San Francisco	IP	H	R	ER	BB	SO	HR	ERA
Ortiz	1⅔	9	7	7	0	0	1	37.80
Zerbe	4	4	2	1	0	0	0	2.25
Witasick	0	0	0	0	1	0	0	0.00
Fultz	⅓	1	0	0	0	0	0	0.00
Rodriguez (L, 0-1)	1⅔	2	2	2	1	0	1	6.00
Worrell	⅓	0	0	0	0	0	0	0.00
Anaheim								
Appier	2	5	5	5	2	2	3	22.50
Lackey	2⅓	2	2	2	1	1	0	7.71
Weber	⅔	4	2	2	0	1	0	7.71
Rodriguez (W, 1-0)	3	0	0	0	0	4	0	0.00
Percival (S, 1)	1	1	1	1	0	0	1	9.00

Attendance: 44,584 (45,030). **Time:** 3:57.

World Series (Cont.)

Game 3
Tuesday, Oct. 22, at San Francisco

Anaheim	AB	R	H	RBI	San Francisco	AB	R	H	RBI
Eckstein, ss	5	1	2	1	Lofton, cf	4	1	0	0
Erstad, cf	6	2	3	0	Aurilia, ss	5	1	2	1
Salmon, rf	4	2	1	1	Kent, 2b	4	1	2	0
Schoenws, p	0	0	0	0	Bonds, lf	2	1	1	2
Anderson, lf	6	0	1	1	Santiago, c	4	0	0	1
Glaus, 3b	5	2	2	1	Snow, 1b	4	0	1	0
Spiezio, 1b	5	1	2	3	Sanders, rf	4	0	0	0
Kennedy, 2b	5	1	2	1	Bell, 3b	1	0	0	0
B. Molina, c	2	1	2	1	Hernandez, p	0	0	0	0
Ortiz, p	3	0	0	0	Witasick, p	0	0	0	0
Wooten, ph	1	0	0	0	Feliz, ph	1	0	0	0
Donnelly, p	0	0	0	0	Fultz, p	0	0	0	0
Gil, p	1	0	1	0	Dunston, ph	1	0	0	0
Ochoa, rf	0	0	0	0	Rodriguez, p	0	0	0	0
					Eyre, p	0	0	0	0
					Martinez, ph	1	0	0	0
Totals	**43**	**10**	**16**	**9**	**Totals**	**31**	**4**	**6**	**4**

			R	H	E
Anaheim	004	401	010 —	10	16	0
San Francisco . .	100	030	000 —	4	6	2

2B: Anaheim—Kennedy (2), Erstad (3), Salmon (1). **3B:** Anaheim—Spiezio (1). **HR:** San Francisco—Aurilia (1), Bonds (1). **BB:** Anaheim—B. Molina 3, Salmon 2, Eckstein, Glaus, Spiezio; San Francisco—Bell 3, Bonds 2, Lofton. **S:** San Francisco—Hernandez. **SB:** Anaheim—Salmon (1), Erstad (1); San Francisco—Lofton (1). **E:** San Francisco—Bell (1), Santiago (1).

Anaheim	IP	H	R	ER	BB	SO	HR	ERA
Ortiz (W, 1-0)	5	5	4	4	3	2	2	7.20
Donnelly	2	0	0	0	2	0	0	0.00
Schoeneweis	2	1	0	0	2	0	0	0.00
San Francisco								
Hernandez (L, 0-1)	3⅔	5	6	5	5	3	0	12.27
Witasick	⅓	3	2	2	1	1	0	54.00
Fultz	2	3	1	1	1	0	0	3.86
Rodriguez	1	1	0	0	0	0	0	4.50
Eyre	2	4	1	0	1	1	0	0.00

HBP: by Fultz (Kennedy).
Attendance: 42,707 (41,467). **Time:** 3:37.

Game 4
Wednesday, Oct. 23, at San Francisco

Anaheim	AB	R	H	RBI	San Francisco	AB	R	H	RBI
Eckstein, ss	3	0	0	1	Lofton, cf	4	1	3	0
Erstad, cf	4	0	0	0	Aurilia, ss	4	1	3	1
Salmon, rf	4	0	1	0	Kent, 2b	3	0	0	1
Anderson, lf	4	1	2	0	Bonds, lf	1	0	0	0
Glaus, 3b	4	1	1	2	Santiago, c	4	0	1	1
Spiezio, 1b	4	0	1	0	Snow, 1b	4	1	1	0
Gil, 2b	3	1	2	0	Sanders, rf	4	0	1	0
Kennedy, ph	1	0	1	0	Bell, 3b	4	0	2	1
B. Molina, c	3	0	1	0	Rueter, p	2	1	1	0
Fullmer, ph	1	0	0	0	Goodwin, ph	0	0	0	0
Lackey, p	2	0	1	0	Rodriguez, p	0	0	0	0
Weber, p	0	0	0	0	Worrell, p	0	0	0	0
Palmeiro, ph	1	0	0	0	Martinez, ph	1	0	0	0
Rodriguez, p	0	0	0	0	Nen, p	0	0	0	0
Totals	**34**	**3**	**10**	**3**	**Totals**		**31**	**4**	**12**	**4**

			R	H	E
Anaheim	012	000	000 —	3	10	1
San Francisco . .	000	030	01x —	4	12	1

2B: San Francisco—Aurilia (2). **HR:** Anaheim—Glaus (3). **BB:** Anaheim—Bonds 3, Goodwin. **SF:** Anaheim—Eckstein; San Francisco—Kent. **SB:** San Francisco—Goodwin (1). **CS:** San Francisco—Bell (1). **E:** Anaheim—Salmon (1); San Francisco—Bell (2). **PB:** Anaheim—B. Molina.

Anaheim	IP	H	R	ER	BB	SO	HR	ERA
Lackey	5	9	3	3	3	2	0	6.14
Weber	1	1	0	0	1	0	0	5.40
Rodriguez (L, 1-1)	2	2	1	0	0	2	0	0.00
San Francisco								
Rueter	6	9	3	3	0	2	1	4.50
Rodriguez	1	0	0	0	0	1	0	3.60
Worrell (W, 1-0)	1	0	0	0	0	0	0	0.00
Nen (S, 2)	1	1	0	0	0	0	0	0.00

Attendance: 42,703 (41,467). **Time:** 3:02.

Game 5
Thursday, Oct. 24, at San Francisco

Anaheim	AB	R	H	RBI	San Francisco	AB	R	H	RBI
Eckstein, ss	4	1	2	1	Lofton, cf	6	3	3	2
Erstad, cf	4	0	1	1	Eyre, p	0	0	0	0
Salmon, rf	4	1	1	0	Aurilia, ss	6	2	3	2
Ochoa, rf	1	0	0	0	Kent, 2b	5	4	3	4
Anderson, lf	5	0	1	0	Bonds, lf	4	2	3	1
Glaus, 3b	4	0	1	0	Santiago, c	3	0	1	3
Spiezio, 1b	2	0	0	0	Sanders, rf	1	0	0	1
Shields, p	0	0	0	0	Rodriguez, p	0	0	0	0
Kennedy, 2b	4	0	0	0	Dunston, ph	1	0	0	0
B. Molina, c	4	1	1	0	Worrell, p	0	0	0	0
J. Molina, c	0	0	0	0	Feliz, ph	1	0	0	0
Washburn, p	1	0	0	0	Goodwin, rf	0	0	0	0
Palmeiro, ph	1	1	1	0	Snow, 1b	4	2	2	0
Donnelly, p	0	0	0	0	Bell, 3b	3	2	2	1
Gil, ph	1	0	1	0	Schmidt, p	1	0	0	0
Weber, p	0	0	0	0	Zerbe, p	0	0	0	0
Wooten, 1b	1	0	1	0	Shinjo, rf-cf	2	1	0	0
Totals	**36**	**4**	**10**	**3**	**Totals**	**37**	**16**	**16**	**15**

			R	H	E
Anaheim	000	031	000 —	4	10	2
San Francisco . .	330	002	44x —	16	16	0

2B: Anaheim—Palmeiro (1), Glaus (2), Gil (1); San Francisco—Bonds 2 (2), Kent (1). **3B:** San Francisco—Lofton (1). **HR:** San Francisco—Kent 2 (3), Aurilia (2). **BB:** Anaheim—Spiezio 2, Eckstein; San Francisco—Kent, Bonds, Santiago, Sanders, Snow, Bell. **S:** San Francisco—Schmidt, Shinjo. **SF:** Anaheim—Erstad; San Francisco—Santiago, Sanders. **SB:** Anaheim—Eckstein (1). **E:** Anaheim—Erstad (1), Glaus (1).

Anaheim	IP	H	R	ER	BB	SO	HR	ERA
Washburn (L, 0-2)	4	6	6	6	5	1	0	9.31
Donnelly	1	0	0	0	0	2	0	0.00
Weber	1⅓	5	5	5	1	2	1	13.50
Shields	1⅔	5	5	1	0	1	2	5.40
San Francisco								
Schmidt	4⅔	7	3	3	3	8	0	5.23
Zerbe (W, 1-0)	1	2	1	1	0	0	0	3.60
Rodriguez	⅓	0	0	0	1	0	0	3.37
Worrell	2	1	0	0	2	0	0	0.00

HBP: by Weber (Bell). **WP:** Schmidt.
Attendance: 42,713 (41,467). **Time:** 3:53.

Game 6
Saturday, Oct. 26, at Anaheim

San Francisco	AB	R	H	RBI
Lofton, cf	5	2	2	0
Aurilia, ss	4	0	0	0
Kent, 2b	4	0	2	1
Bonds, lf	2	1	1	1
Santiago, c	3	0	0	0
Snow, 1b	4	0	1	0
Sanders, rf	4	0	0	0
Bell, 3b	4	1	1	0
Dunston, dh	3	1	1	2
Goodwin, ph	1	0	0	0
Totals	**34**	**5**	**8**	**4**

Anaheim	AB	R	H	RBI
Eckstein, ss	4	0	0	0
Erstad, cf	3	1	1	1
Salmon, rf	4	0	2	0
Figgins, pr	0	1	0	0
Ochoa, rf	0	0	0	0
Anderson, lf	4	1	1	0
Glaus, 3b	3	1	2	2
Fullmer, dh	4	1	1	0
Spiezio, 1b	3	1	1	3
B. Molina, c	2	0	0	0
Palmeiro, ph	1	0	0	0
J. Molina, c	0	0	0	0
Kennedy, 2b	4	0	2	0
Totals	**32**	**6**	**10**	**6**

					R	H	E
San Francisco..	000	031	100	—	5	8	1
Anaheim	000	000	33x	—	6	10	1

2B: San Francisco—Lofton (1); Anaheim—Glaus (3). **HR:** San Francisco—Dunston (1), Bonds (4); Anaheim—Spiezio (1); Erstad (1). **BB:** San Francisco—Bonds 2, Aurilia, Santiago; Anaheim—Erstad, Glaus, Spiezio. **S:** Anaheim—J. Molina. **SB:** San Francisco—Lofton 2 (3). **E:** San Francisco—Bonds (1); Anaheim—B. Molina (1).

San Francisco	IP	H	R	ER	BB	SO	HR	ERA
Ortiz	6⅓	4	2	2	2	2	0	10.12
Rodriguez	⅓	1	1	1	0	1	1	4.76
Eyre	0	1	0	0	0	0	0	0.00
Worrell (L, 1-1)	⅓	3	3	2	0	0	1	3.86
Nen	1	1	0	0	1	2	0	0.00

Anaheim	IP	H	R	ER	BB	SO	HR	ERA
Appier	4⅓	4	3	3	3	2	1	11.37
Rodriguez	2⅔	4	2	2	0	4	1	2.35
Donnelly (W, 1-0)	1	0	0	0	0	2	0	0.00
Percival (S, 2)	1	0	0	0	0	2	0	4.50

WP: Rodriguez (Ana.).
Attendance: 44,506 (45,030). **Time:** 3:48.

Game 7
Sunday, Oct. 27, at Anaheim

San Francisco	AB	R	H	RBI
Lofton, cf	4	0	0	0
Aurilia, ss	4	0	0	0
Kent, 2b	4	0	0	0
Bonds, lf	3	0	1	0
Santiago, c	3	1	2	0
Snow, 1b	4	0	3	0
Sanders, rf	1	0	0	1
Goodwin, rf	2	0	0	0
Bell, 3b	3	0	0	0
Feliz, dh	3	0	0	0
Shinjo, ph	1	0	0	0
Totals	**32**	**1**	**6**	**1**

Anaheim	AB	R	H	RBI
Eckstein, ss	3	1	1	0
Erstad, cf	3	1	1	0
Salmon, rf	2	1	0	0
Ochoa, rf	0	0	0	0
Anderson, lf	4	0	1	3
Glaus, 3b	2	0	0	0
Fullmer, dh	4	0	0	0
Spiezio, 1b	3	1	0	0
B. Molina, c	3	0	2	1
Kennedy, 2b	3	0	0	0
Totals	**27**	**4**	**5**	**4**

					R	H	E
San Francisco..	010	000	000	—	1	6	0
Anaheim	013	000	00x	—	4	5	0

2B: San Francisco—Snow (1); Anaheim—B. Molina 2 (2), Anderson (1). **BB:** San Francisco—Lofton, Bonds, Santiago, Bell; Anaheim—Glaus 2, Eckstein, Salmon, Spiezio. **S:** Anaheim—Erstad. **SF:** San Francisco—Sanders.

San Francisco	IP	H	R	ER	BB	SO	HR	ERA
Hernandez (L, 0-2)	2	4	4	4	4	1	0	14.29
Zerbe	1	0	0	0	0	0	0	3.00
Rueter	4	1	0	0	1	3	0	2.70
Worrell	1	0	0	0	0	1	0	3.18

Anaheim	IP	H	R	ER	BB	SO	HR	ERA
Lackey (W, 1-0)	5	4	1	1	1	4	0	4.38
Donnelly	2	1	0	0	1	2	0	0.00
Rodriguez	1	0	0	0	1	3	0	2.08
Percival (S, 3)	1	1	0	0	1	1	0	3.00

HBP: by Hernandez (Salmon).
Attendance: 44,598 (45,030). **Time:** 3:16.

World Series Composite Box Score
San Francisco Giants

	WS vs. Anaheim								Overall Playoffs							
Batting	Avg	AB	R	H	HR	RBI	BB	SO	Avg	AB	R	H	HR	RBI	BB	SO
Kirk Rueter	.500	2	1	1	0	0	0	0	.125	8	1	1	0	0	0	2
Barry Bonds	.471	17	8	8	4	6	13	3	.356	45	18	16	8	16	27	6
J.T. Snow	.407	27	6	11	1	4	2	1	.333	66	10	22	2	9	4	10
David Bell	.304	23	4	7	1	4	5	4	.304	56	11	17	2	6	10	11
Kenny Lofton	.290	31	7	9	0	2	2	2	.292	72	16	21	1	6	6	9
Jeff Kent	.276	29	6	8	3	7	1	7	.269	67	10	18	3	8	5	18
Rich Aurilia	.250	32	5	8	2	5	1	9	.265	68	13	18	6	17	4	16
Reggie Sanders	.238	21	3	5	2	6	2	9	.182	55	4	10	2	7	5	18
Benito Santiago	.231	26	2	6	0	5	3	4	.254	67	5	17	2	16	6	13
Shawon Dunston	.222	9	1	2	1	3	0	3	.250	12	1	3	1	3	0	3
Tsuyoshi Shinjo	.167	6	1	1	0	0	0	3	.143	7	1	1	0	0	0	3
Tom Goodwin	.000	4	0	0	0	0	1	2	.000	9	0	0	0	0	1	6
Jason Schmidt	.000	1	0	0	0	0	0	1	.000	5	0	0	0	0	0	4
Livan Hernandez	.000	2	0	0	0	0	0	1	.000	3	0	0	0	0	1	1
Ramon Martinez	.000	2	0	0	0	0	0	1	.000	3	0	0	0	1	1	2
Pedro Feliz	.000	5	0	0	0	0	0	2	.000	7	0	0	0	0	0	3
Russ Ortiz	—	0	0	0	0	0	0	0	.286	7	1	2	0	0	0	4
Robb Nen	—	0	0	0	0	0	0	0	—	0	0	0	0	0	0	1
Felix Rodriguez	—	0	0	0	0	0	0	0	.000	1	0	0	0	0	0	1
TOTALS	.281	235	44	66	14	42	30	50	.261	559	91	146	27	89	69	131

World Series Composite Box Score (Cont.)

Pitching	WS vs. Anaheim								Overall Playoffs							
	ERA	W-L	Sv	Gm	IP	H	BB	SO	ERA	W-L	Sv	Gm	IP	H	BB	SO
Robb Nen	0.00	0-0	2	3	3.0	2	1	3	1.00	0-0	7	10	9.0	9	3	8
Scott Eyre	0.00	0-0	0	3	3.0	5	1	2	0.00	0-0	0	10	6.0	8	1	2
Kirk Rueter	2.70	0-0	0	2	10.0	10	1	5	5.25	1-1	0	5	24.0	32	5	9
Chad Zerbe	3.00	1-0	0	3	6.0	6	0	0	3.00	1-0	0	3	6.0	6	0	0
Tim Worrell	3.18	1-1	0	6	5.2	4	1	4	4.85	3-1	0	13	13.0	13	3	10
Aaron Fultz	3.86	0-0	0	2	2.1	4	1	0	6.75	0-0	0	5	2.2	6	1	0
Felix Rodriguez	4.76	0-1	0	6	5.2	4	1	3	2.70	0-1	0	13	13.1	8	5	7
Jason Schmidt	5.23	1-0	0	2	10.1	16	4	14	4.24	2-1	0	4	23.1	23	9	27
Russ Ortiz	10.13	0-0	0	2	8.0	13	2	2	5.76	2-0	0	5	25.0	27	13	13
Livan Hernandez	14.29	0-2	0	2	5.2	9	9	4	6.20	1-2	0	4	20.1	26	12	10
Jay Witasick	54.00	0-0	0	2	0.1	3	2	1	7.36	0-1	0	5	3.2	4	2	2
Manny Aybar	—	0-0	0	0	0.0	0	0	0	6.75	0-0	0	2	2.2	2	1	3
TOTALS	5.55	3-4	2	7	60.0	76	23	38	4.59	10-7	7	17	149.0	164	55	91

Wild Pitches—WS (Schmidt); OVERALL (Ortiz 2, Nen, Schmidt). **Hit Batters**—WS (Fultz, Hernandez); OVERALL (Hernandez 3, Rueter, Fultz).

Anaheim Angels

Batting	WS vs. San Francisco								Overall Playoffs							
	Avg	AB	R	H	HR	RBI	BB	SO	Avg	AB	R	H	HR	RBI	BB	SO
Benji Gil	.800	5	1	4	0	0	0	1	.667	12	2	8	0	1	0	2
Shawn Wooten	.500	2	0	1	0	0	0	0	.474	19	5	9	1	3	0	4
John Lackey	.500	2	0	1	0	0	0	0	.500	2	0	1	0	0	0	0
Troy Glaus	.385	26	7	10	3	8	4	6	.344	61	15	21	7	13	7	14
Tim Salmon	.346	26	7	9	2	5	4	7	.288	59	10	17	4	12	8	13
David Eckstein	.310	29	6	9	0	3	0	3	.294	68	9	20	0	6	3	4
Darin Erstad	.300	30	6	9	1	3	1	4	.352	71	14	25	2	7	1	8
Bengie Molina	.286	21	2	6	0	2	3	1	.260	50	2	13	0	6	4	4
Garret Anderson	.281	32	3	9	0	3	0	3	.300	70	11	21	2	13	2	6
Adam Kennedy	.280	25	1	7	0	2	0	3	.340	47	10	16	4	10	1	11
Brad Fullmer	.267	15	3	4	0	1	2	2	.294	34	6	10	1	5	3	5
Scott Spiezio	.261	23	3	6	1	8	6	1	.327	55	10	18	3	19	10	3
Orlando Palmeiro	.250	4	1	1	0	0	0	0	.167	6	1	1	0	0	0	0
Alex Ochoa	.000	1	0	0	0	0	0	0	.000	5	2	0	0	0	0	3
Jarrod Washburn	.000	1	0	0	0	0	0	0	.000	1	0	0	0	0	0	0
Ramon Ortiz	.000	3	0	0	0	0	0	2	.000	3	0	0	0	0	0	2
Jose Molina	.000	0	0	0	0	0	0	0	.000	1	0	0	0	0	0	0
Chone Figgins	.000	0	1	0	0	0	0	0	1.000	1	4	1	0	0	0	0
TOTALS	.310	245	41	76	7	38	23	38	.320	565	101	181	24	95	39	82

Pitching	ERA	W-L	Sv	Gm	IP	H	BB	SO	ERA	W-L	Sv	Gm	IP	H	BB	SO
Scott Schoeneweis	0.00	0-0	0	2	2.0	1	1	2	3.00	0-0	0	6	3.0	3	1	2
Brendan Donnelly	0.00	1-0	0	5	7.2	1	4	6	4.15	1-0	0	11	13.0	7	5	13
Francisco Rodriguez	2.08	1-1	0	4	8.2	6	1	13	1.93	5-1	0	11	18.2	10	5	28
Troy Percival	3.00	0-0	3	3	3.0	2	1	3	2.79	0-0	7	9	9.2	8	1	10
John Lackey	4.38	1-0	0	3	12.1	15	5	7	2.42	2-0	0	5	22.1	21	6	17
Scot Shields	5.40	0-0	0	1	1.2	5	0	1	5.40	0-0	0	1	1.2	5	0	1
Ramon Ortiz	7.20	1-0	0	2	5.0	5	4	3	9.00	2-0	0	3	13.0	18	9	7
Jarrod Washburn	9.31	0-2	0	2	9.2	12	7	6	5.02	1-2	0	5	28.2	30	10	17
Kevin Appier	11.37	0-0	0	2	6.1	9	5	4	6.23	0-1	0	5	21.2	24	12	10
Ben Weber	13.50	0-0	0	4	4.2	10	2	5	10.80	0-1	0	9	8.1	15	4	8
TOTALS	5.75	4-3	3	7	61.0	66	30	50	4.82	11-5	7	16	140.0	141	53	113

Wild Pitches—WS (Rodriguez); OVERALL (Rodriguez 3, Appier 2, Donnelly). **Hit Batters**—WS (Weber); OVERALL (Appier, Donnelly, Ortiz, Percival, Washburn, Weber).

Score by Innings

	1	2	3	4	5	6	7	8	9		R	H	E
San Francisco	4	10	1	0	13	5	5	5	1	-	44	66	5
Anaheim	5	5	9	4	4	5	3	6	0	-	41	76	5

E: San Francisco—Bell 2, Bonds, Lofton, Santiago; Anaheim—Anderson, Erstad, Glaus, B. Molina, Salmon. **DP:** San Francisco 7, Anaheim 6. **2B:** San Francisco—Bonds 2, Aurilia 2, Snow, Lofton, Kent; Anaheim—Glaus 3, Erstad 3, B. Molina 2, Kennedy 2, Gil, Salmon, Anderson, Spiezio, Palmeiro. **3B:** San Francisco—Lofton; Anaheim—Spiezio. **SB:** San Francisco—Lofton 3, Sanders, Goodwin; Anaheim—Fullmer 2, Salmon, Eckstein, Erstad, Spiezio. **CS:** San Francisco—Bell. **S:** San Francisco—Lofton, Shinjo, Schmidt, Hernandez; Anaheim—Eckstein, Erstad, Spiezio. **SF:** San Francisco—Sanders 2, Kent, Santiago; Anaheim—Eckstein, Erstad, J. Molina. **PB:** San Francisco—Santiago; Anaheim—B. Molina. **HBP:** by Fultz (Kennedy), by Hernandez (Salmon), by Weber (Bell). **LOB:** San Francisco—47; Anaheim—54.
Umpires: Jerry Crawford, Angel Hernandez, Tim Tschida, Mike Winters, Mike Reilly, Tim McClelland.

COLLEGE

Final *Baseball America* Top 25

Final 2002 Division I Top 25, voted on by the editors of *Baseball America* and released after the NCAA College World Series. Given are final records (excluding ties) and winning percentage (including all postseason games); records in College World Series and team eliminated by (DNP indicates team did not play in tourney); head coach (career years and four-year college record including 2002 postseason); preseason ranking and rank before start of CWS.

		Record	Pct	CWS Recap	Head Coach	Preseason Rank	Rank before CWS
1	Texas	57-15	.792	4-0	Augie Garrido (34 yrs: 1380-666-8)	9	2
2	South Carolina	57-18	.760	4-2 (Texas)	Ray Tanner (15 yrs: 669-286-3)	14	3
3	Clemson	54-17	.761	2-2 (S. Carolina)	Jack Leggett (23 yrs: 811-462)	2	4
4	Stanford	47-18	.723	2-2 (Texas)	Mark Marquess (26 yrs: 1093-535-5)	1	5
5	Rice	52-14	.788	0-2 (Notre Dame)	Wayne Graham (11 yrs: 478-212)	11	1
6	Notre Dame	50-18	.735	1-2 (Stanford)	Paul Mainieri (14 yrs: 506-300-1)	5	6
7	Florida State	60-14	.811	DNP	Mike Martin (23 yrs: 1239-416-3)	6	7
8	Georgia Tech	52-16	.754	1-2 (S. Carolina)	Danny Hall (15 yrs: 604-289)	13	8
9	Nebraska	47-21	.691	0-2 (S. Carolina)	Dave Van Horn (9 yrs: 371-168)	8	9
10	Houston	48-17	.738	DNP	Rayner Noble (8 yrs: 294-194)	NR	10
11	Louisiana St.	44-22	.667	DNP	Smoke Laval (8 yrs: 285-181)	7	11
12	Wake Forest	47-13	.783	DNP	George Greer (21 yrs: 668-447-7)	21	12
13	Alabama	51-15	.773	DNP	Jim Wells (13 yrs: 563-241)	NR	13
14	USC	37-24	.607	DNP	Mike Gillespie (16 yrs: 645-356-2)	4	14
15	Florida	46-19	.708	DNP	Pat McMahon (10 yrs: 399-193)	NR	15
16	Richmond	53-13	.803	DNP	Ron Atkins (18 yrs: 560-405-4)	NR	16
17	North Carolina	43-21	.672	DNP	Mike Fox (4 yrs: 161-82)	19	17
18	CS-Northridge	41-17	.707	DNP	Mike Batesole (7 yrs: 256-158-1)	22	18
19	Florida Atlantic	46-21	.687	DNP	Kevin Cooney (19 yrs: 657-396-9)	NR	19
20	Miami-FL	34-29	.540	DNP	Jim Morris (21 yrs: 931-392-2)	3	20
21	Long Beach St.	39-21	.650	DNP	Mike Weathers (3 yrs: 79-60)	NR	21
22	Arizona St.	37-21	.638	DNP	Pat Murphy (18 yrs: 677-337-3)	18	22
23	Wichita St.	47-16	.746	DNP	Gene Stephenson (25 yrs: 1357-421-3)	12	23
24	San Jose St.	45-17	.726	DNP	Sam Piraro (16 yrs: 536-384-4)	NR	24
25	Arkansas	35-28	.556	DNP	Norm DeBriyn (33 yrs: 1161-650-6)	NR	25

College World Series

CWS Seeds: 1. Notre Dame (49-16); **2.** Clemson (52-15); **3.** Georgia Tech (51-14); **4.** Rice (52-12); **5.** Texas (53-15); **6.** South Carolina (53-16); **7.** Nebraska (47-19); **8.** Stanford (45-16).

Bracket One

June 14—Georgia Tech 11 . . . . .South Carolina 0
June 14—Clemson 11 .Nebraska 10
June 16—South Carolina 10 . . . . .Nebraska 8 (out)
June 16—Clemson 9 . . . . .Georgia Tech 7
June 18—South Carolina 9 . . . . .Georgia Tech 5 (out)
June 19—South Carolina 12 . . . . .Clemson 4
June 21—South Carolina 10 . . . . .Clemson 2 (out)

Bracket Two

June 15—Stanford 4 .Notre Dame 3
June 15—Texas 2 . . . . .Rice 1
June 17—Notre Dame 5 . . . . .Rice 3 (out)
June 17—Texas 8 . . . . .Stanford 7
June 18—Stanford 5 . . . . .Notre Dame 3 (out)
June 20—Texas 6 . . . . .Stanford 5 (out)

CWS Championship Game

Saturday, June 22, at Rosenblatt Stadium in Omaha, Neb.

	1	2	3	4	5	6	7	8	9	R	H	E
South Carolina	1	1	0	0	0	0	2	2	0	— 6	10	3
Texas	3	1	0	0	3	1	0	4	x	—12	13	2

Win: TEX—Justin Simmons (16-1). **Loss:** SC—Aaron Rawl (7-2). **Save:** Huston Street (14). **Strikeouts:** SC—Rawl and Matt Campbell 2; TEX—Simmons 4, Alan Bomer and Street 1. **2B:** SC—Yaron Peters, Trey Dyson and Landon Powell; TEX—Omar Quintanilla 2, Dustin Majewski and Brandon Fahey. **HR:** TEX—Chris Carmichael (2). **SB:** TEX—Fahey (9). **Attendance:** 24,089. **Time** 3:19.

Most Outstanding Player

Huston Street, Texas, RP

IP	H	ER	BB	K	W-L	Svs
6.1	2	1	3	5	0-0	4

All-Tournament Team

C—Landon Powell, South Carolina; **1B**—Michael Johnson, Clemson; **2B**—Tim Moss, Texas; **3B**—Omar Quintanilla, Texas; **SS**—Victor Menocal, Georgia Tech; **OF**—Sam Fuld, Stanford; Justin Harris, South Carolina; Dustin Majewski, Texas; **DH**—Steve Stanley, Notre Dame; **P**—Justin Simmons, Texas; Huston Street, Texas.

Annual Awards

Chosen by *Baseball America*, *Collegiate Baseball*, National Collegiate Baseball Writers Association, American Baseball Coaches Association and USA Baseball. The Rotary Smith award is chosen by college sports information directors.

Player of the Year

Khalil Greene, SS, Clemson . . . .*BA*, *CB*, Dick Howser (NCBWA), ABCA, Smith, Golden Spikes (USA Baseball)

Coach of the Year

Augie Garrido, Texas . . . .*BA*, *CB*, ABCA

Consensus All-America Team

NCAA Division I players cited most frequently by the following four selectors: the American Baseball Coaches Assn. (ABCA), *Baseball America*, *Collegiate Baseball* and the National Collegiate Baseball Writers Assn. (NCBWA).

First Team

Pos		Cl	Avg	HR	RBI
C	Jed Morris, Nebraska	Jr.	.382	23	90
1B	Yaron Peters, S. Carolina	Sr.	.377	29	95
2B	Rickie Weeks, Southern	So.	.495	20	96
SS	Khalil Greene, Clemson	Sr.	.470	27	91
3B	Ryan Barthelemy, Florida St.	Sr.	.357	17	94
OF	Steve Stanley, Notre Dame	Sr.	.439	1	36
OF	Bobby Malek, Michigan St.	Jr.	.402	16	66
OF	Sam Fuld, Stanford	So.	.375	8	47
UT	Jesse Crain, Houston	Jr.	.310	11	47

Pos		Cl	W-L	Sv	ERA
P	Brad Sullivan, Houston	Cl	13-1	0	1.82
P	Bryan Bullington, Ball St.	Jr.	11-3	0	2.84
P	Jeremy Guthrie, Stanford	Jr.	13-2	0	2.51
P	Justin Simmons, Texas	So.	16-1	0	2.52
P	Tim Stauffer, Richmond	So.	15-3	0	1.54
P	Blake Taylor, S. Carolina	Sr.	6-1	21	2.63

Second Team

Pos		Cl	Avg	HR	RBI
C	Tony Richie, Florida St.	So.	.353	13	75
1B	Nate Gold, Gonzaga	Sr.	.333	33	76
2B	James Jurries, Tulane	Sr.	.400	20	74
SS	Drew Meyer, S. Carolina	Jr.	.359	6	40
3B	Jeff Baker, Clemson	Jr.	.325	25	87
OF	Brian Wright, N.C. State	Sr.	.418	14	73
OF	Joey Gomes, Santa Clara	Sr.	.408	10	51
OF	Chris Maples, N. Carolina	Sr.	.347	23	79
UT	John McCurdy, Maryland	Jr.	.443	19	77

Pos		Cl	W-L	Sv	ERA
P	Kyle Sleeth, Wake Forest	So.	14-0	0	2.97
P	Alex Hart, Florida	Jr.	13-3	0	3.24
P	Philip Humber, Rice	Fr.	11-1	0	2.77
P	Shane Komine, Nebraska	Jr.	10-0	0	2.33
P	Dave Bush, Wake Forest	Sr.	8-1	13	1.64
P	Royce Ring, San Diego St.	Jr.	5-1	17	1.85

NCAA Division I Leaders

Batting

Average

(At least 75 AB & 2.5/Gm)		Gm	AB	H	Avg
Rickie Weeks, Southern	So.	54	198	98	.495
Curtis Granderson, Ill.-Chicago	Jr.	55	207	100	.483
Khalil Greene, Clemson	Sr.	71	285	134	.470
Antoin Gray, Southern	Jr.	54	205	92	.449
Anthony Bocchino, Marist	Sr.	55	207	92	.444
John McCurdy, Maryland	Jr.	54	221	98	.443
Terry Trofholz, TCU	So.	57	213	94	.441
Steve Stanley, Notre Dame	Sr.	68	271	119	.439
Joe Wickman, UNLV	Fr.	46	142	62	.437
Tom Merkle, NY Tech	Sr.	52	186	80	.430

Home Runs (per game)

(At least 15 HR)		Cl	Gm	HR	Avg
Nate Gold, Gonzaga	Sr.		56	33	0.59
Bradley Eldred, Florida Int'l	Sr.		61	29	0.48
Cary Page, Morehead St.	Jr.		55	26	0.47
Bubba Lavender, Morehead St.	Sr.		56	24	0.43
Kelly Hunt, Bowling Green	Jr.		54	22	0.41
Yaron Peters, South Carolina	Sr.		72	29	0.40
Ryan Kenning, New Mexico St.	Sr.		61	24	0.39
Mike Arbinger, Ohio	Sr.		51	20	0.39
Tom Merkle, NY Tech	Sr.		52	20	0.38
Kevin Matuszek, Morehead St.	Jr.		55	21	0.38

Runs Batted In (per game)

(At least 50 RBI)		Cl	Gm	RBI	Avg
Rickie Weeks, Southern	So.		54	96	1.78
Ryan Kenning, New Mexico St.	Sr.		61	96	1.57
Kelly Hunt, Bowling Green	Jr.		54	84	1.56
Gabe Veloz, New Mexico St.	Sr.		61	92	1.51
Jamie D'antona, Wake Forest	So.		57	83	1.46
Antoin Gray, Southern	Jr.		54	77	1.43
John McCurdy, Maryland	Jr.		54	77	1.43
Chris Alexander, New Mexico	Jr.		56	78	1.39
Scott Martin, Delaware St.	Jr.		49	68	1.39
Kevin Matuszek, Morehead St.	Jr.		55	76	1.38

Stolen Bases (per game)

(At least 25)		Cl	Gm	SB	SBA	Avg
Bartowski Cowan, Alabama St.	So.		50	54	58	1.08
Ryan McGraw, Coastal Carolina	So.		60	63	63	1.05
Matt Lemanczyk, Sacred Heart	Sr.		47	41	41	0.87
Ashley Allen, Alabama St.	Jr.		47	40	47	0.85
Chris Walker, Ga. Southern	Sr.		64	48	54	0.75
Christopher Graziano, Villanova	Jr.		53	38	45	0.72
Russ Adams, North Carolina	Jr.		63	45	57	0.71
Casey Fahy, Delaware	Sr.		56	40	40	0.71
Micah Simmons, Bethune-Cook.	Sr.		61	43	46	0.70
Aulston Taylor, Texas Southern	Sr.		40	28	31	0.70

Pitching

Earned Run Avg.

(At least 50 inn.)		Cl	Gm	IP	ERA
Justin Cerbone, Central Conn. St.	Sr.		17	60.0	1.35
Randy Corn, The Citadel	Sr.		39	59.0	1.37
Steve Obenchain, Evansville	Jr.		25	78.1	1.38
Jeff Stovall, Furman	Sr.		23	86.1	1.46
Matt Hamer, The Citadel	Jr.		35	77.1	1.51
Tim Stauffer, Richmond	So.		20	146.0	1.54
John Tetuan, Wichita St.	Jr.		16	89.0	1.72
Devin Monds, Northeastern	Fr.		11	65.0	1.80
Von Stertzbach, Central Fla.	Jr.		21	64.2	1.81
Brad Sullivan, Houston	So.		18	128.2	1.82

Wins

		Cl	Gm	IP	W-L
Justin Simmons, Texas	So.		20	128.1	16-1
Tim Stauffer, Richmond	So.		20	146.0	15-3
Kyle Sleeth, Wake Forest	So.		18	118.1	14-0
Brad Sullivan, Houston	So.		18	128.2	13-1
Kyle Bakker, Georgia Tech	So.		19	134.2	13-2
Jeremy Guthrie, Stanford	Jr.		20	157.2	13-2
Matt Lynch, Florida St.	Jr.		20	130.1	13-2
Alex Hart, Florida	Jr.		17	111.0	13-3
Steven Herce, Rice	Jr.		17	119.1	13-3
Steve Reba, Clemson	Sr.		20	112.2	13-4
Matt Henrie, Clemson	Jr.		21	112.2	13-5

Strikeouts (per 9 inn.)

(At least 50 inn.)	Cl	IP	SO	Avg
Chad Pleiness, Central Mich.	Sr.	68.0	100	13.2
Jared Thomas, Oakland	Jr.	71.0	103	13.1
Ben Crockett, Harvard	Sr.	84.0	117	12.5
Rich Hill, Michigan	Jr.	76.1	104	12.3
Joseph Blanton, Kentucky	Jr.	100.0	133	12.0
Bryan Bullington, Ball St.	Jr.	104.2	139	11.9
Randy Corn, The Citadel	Sr.	59.0	76	11.6
Clay Hensley, Lamar	Sr.	100.0	127	11.4
Rene Recio, Oral Roberts	So.	84.2	106	11.3
Anthony Pearson, Jackson St.	Jr.	76.2	95	11.1

Saves

	Cl	IP	ERA	Saves
Blake Taylor, South Carolina	Sr.	85.2	2.63	21
Royce Ring, San Diego St.	Jr.	39.0	1.85	17
James Russell, Villanova	Jr.	27.0	2.33	15
Matt Freisleben, WI-Milw.	Sr.	45.1	4.17	15
Kyle Edens, Baylor	Sr.	52.1	3.44	14
Huston Street, Texas	Fr.	47.0	0.96	14
Randy Corn, The Citadel	Sr.	59.0	1.37	13
Dave Bush, Wake Forest	Sr.	60.1	1.64	13
Five tied with 12 each.				

Other College World Series

Participants' final records in parentheses.

NCAA Div. II

at Montgomery, Ala. (May 25-June 1)

Participants: Ashland, Ohio (47-11); Cal State Chico (52-9), Central Missouri St. (52-6); Columbus St., Ga. (43-14); Delta State, Miss. (50-6); Florida Southern (43-14); Kutztown, Penn. (35-22); Massachusetts-Lowell (33-16).

Championship: Columbus St. def. Cal State Chico, 5-3.

NCAA Div. III

at Appleton, Wis. (May 24-28)

Participants: Carthage, Wis. (34-9); Christopher Newport, Va. (35-14); College of New Jersey (34-12); Concordia-Austin, Texas (35-11); Eastern Connecticut St. (35-10-1); Lakeland, Wis. (33-14-1); Marietta, Ohio (37-7-1); Rensselaer, N.Y. (32-9).

Championship: Eastern Connecticut St. def. Marietta, 8-0.

NAIA

at Lewiston, Idaho (May 24-31)

Participants: Albertson, Idaho (39-18-1); Bellevue, Neb. (44-15-1); Embry-Riddle, Fla. (49-10); Indiana Tech (47-15-1); Lewis-Clark State, Idaho (36-15); Mayville State, ND (31-13); Ohio Dominican (41-11); Oklahoma City (54-13); Olivet Nazarene, Ill. (40-14); Spalding, Ky. (55-21).

Championship: Lewis-Clark def. Oklahoma City, 12-8.

NJCAA Div. I

at Grand Junction, Colo. (May 26-June 1)

Participants: Central Arizona (45-17); Cowley County CC, Kan. (43-14); Jefferson, Mo. (42-15); John A. Logan, Ill. (37-19); Lamar CC, Colo. (57-3); Louisburg, N.C. (49-9); Manatee CC, Fla. (38-18); Middle Georgia (49-16); San Jacinto-North, Texas (51-9); Wallace State CC, Ala. (39-10).

Championship: Central Arizona def. Manatee CC, 18-8.

2002 MLB First-Year Player Draft

First round selections at the 38th First-Year Player Draft held June 4-5, 2002 in New York. Clubs select in reverse order of their standing from the preceding season. The worst National League team selects first in even years and the worst American League team goes first in odd years. Leagues then alternate picks throughout the rounds.

First Round

No		Pos
1	Pittsburgh ....Bryan Bullington, Ball St.	RHP
2	Tampa Bay..........B.J. Upton, Greenbriar Christian HS, Chesapeake, Va.	SS
3	Cincinnati..........Chris Gruler, Liberty HS Brentwood, Calif.	RHP
4	Baltimore ....Adam Loewen, Fraser Valley Christian HS, Surrey, B.C.	LHP
5	Montreal.......Clint Everts, Cypress Falls HS Houston, Texas	RHP
6	Kansas City..Zack Greinke, Apopka (Fla.) HS	RHP
7	Milwaukee .....Prince Fielder, Eau Gallie HS Melbourne, Fla.	1B
8	Detroit......Scott Moore, Cypress (Calif.) HS	SS
9	Colorado......Jeff Francis, British Columbia	LHP
10	Texas ....Drew Meyer, South Carolina	SS
11	Florida.......Jeremy Hermida, Wheeler HS Marietta, Ga.	OF
12	Anaheim ....Joe Saunders, Virginia Tech	LHP
13	San Diego ....Khalil Greene, Clemson	SS
14	Toronto.........Russ Adams, North Carolina	SS
15	New York-NL ..Scott Kazmir, Cypress Falls HS Houston, Texas	LHP

No		Pos
16	**a**-Oakland ....Nick Swisher, Ohio St.	1B
17	Philadelphia............Cole Hamels, Rancho Bernardo HS, San Diego, Calif.	LHP
18	Chicago-AL ....Roger Ring, San Diego St.	LHP
19	Los Angeles .James Loney, Lawrence Elkins HS Missouri City, Texas	1B
20	Minnesota ....Denard Span, Catholic HS Tampa, Fla.	OF
21	Chicago-NL.........Bobby Brownlie, Rutgers	RHP
22	Cleveland ....Jeremy Guthrie, Stanford	RHP
23	Atlanta..........Jeff Francoeur, Parkview HS Lilburn, Ga.	OF
24	**b**-Oakland ....Joseph Blanton, Kentucky	RHP
25	San Francisco.........Matt Cain, Houston HS Germantown, Tenn.	RHP
26	Oakland ....John McCurdy, Maryland	SS
27	Arizona ....Sergio Santos, Mater Dei HS Hacienda Heights, Calif.	SS
28	Seattle ......John Mayberry Jr., Rockhurst HS Kansas City, Mo.	1B
29	Houston...Derick Grigsby, Northeast Texas CC	RHP
30	**c**-Oakland ....Ben Fritz, Fresno St.	RHP

Acquired picks: **a**-from Boston for signing Johnny Damon; **b**-from NY Yankees for signing Jason Giambi; **c**-from St. Louis for signing Jason Isringhausen.

Minor League Triple-A Final Standings
Division champions (*) and Wild Card (†) winners are noted.

International League

North Division

	W	L	Pct	GB
*Scranton-WB (Phillies)	91	53	.632	—
†Buffalo (Indians)	87	57	.604	4
Ottawa (Expos)	80	61	.567	9½
Syracuse (Blue Jays)	64	80	.444	27
Pawtucket (Red Sox)	60	84	.417	31
Rochester (Orioles)	55	89	.382	36

South Division

	W	L	Pct	GB
*Durham (Devil Rays)	80	64	.556	—
Richmond (Braves)	75	67	.528	4
Norfolk (Mets)	70	73	.490	9½
Charlotte (White Sox)	55	88	.385	24½

West Division

	W	L	Pct	GB
*Toledo (Tigers)	81	63	.563	—
Louisville (Reds)	79	65	.549	2
Indianapolis (Brewers)	67	76	.469	13½
Columbus (Yankees)	59	83	.415	21

Playoffs
First Round (Best-of-Five)

Durham 3 ....Toledo 0
Buffalo 3 ....Scranton-WB 0

Championship (Best-of-Five)
Durham vs. Buffalo

Sept. 10	Durham, 6-4 (10 inn.)	at Buffalo
Sept. 11	Durham, 8-1	at Buffalo
Sept. 12	Durham, 2-0	at Durham

Durham wins Governors' Cup, 3-0

Pacific Coast League

American Conference

Eastern Division

	W	L	Pct	GB
*Oklahoma (Rangers)	75	69	.521	—
New Orleans (Astros)	75	69	.521	—
Nashville (Pirates)	72	71	.503	2½
Memphis (Cardinals)	71	71	.500	3

Note: Oklahoma won the division over New Orleans by virtue of a better head-to-head record (10-6).

Central Division

	W	L	Pct	GB
*Salt Lake (Angels)	78	66	.542	—
Omaha (Royals)	76	68	.528	2
Iowa (Cubs)	71	73	.493	7
Colorado Springs (Rockies)	58	86	.403	20

Pacific Conference

Northern Division

	W	L	Pct	GB
*Edmonton (Twins)	81	59	.579	—
Portland (Padres)	72	71	.503	10½
Calgary (Marlins)	67	71	.486	13
Tacoma (Mariners)	65	76	.461	16½

Southern Division

	W	L	Pct	GB
*Las Vegas (Dodgers)	85	59	.590	—
Tucson (D'Backs)	73	68	.518	10½
Sacramento (A's)	66	78	.458	19
Fresno (Giants)	57	87	.396	28

Playoffs
Conference Finals (Best-of-Five)

Salt Lake 3 ....Oklahoma 0
Edmonton 3 ....Las Vegas 1

Championship (Best-of-Five)
Salt Lake vs. Edmonton

Sept. 10	Salt Lake, 7-5	at Edmonton
Sept. 11	Edmonton, 7-4	at Edmonton
Sept. 13	Edmonton, 6-4	at Salt Lake
Sept. 14	Edmonton, 10-7	at Salt Lake

Edmonton wins PCL Championship, 3-1

2002 International League All-Star Team

As selected by the league's managers, coaches, media and club representatives.

Pos. Name, Team (Affiliate)

C	Johnny Estrada, Scranton-WB (Phillies)
1B	Joe Vitiello, Ottawa (Expos)
2B	Marco Scutaro, Norfolk (Mets)
3B	Joe Crede, Charlotte (White Sox)
SS	Nick Punto, Scranton-WB (Phillies)
OF	Marlon Byrd, Scranton-WB (Phillies)
OF	Endy Chavez, Ottawa (Expos)
OF	Raul Gonzalez, Louisville (Reds)
DH	Kevin Witt, Louisville (Reds)
UT	David Doster, Scranton-WB (Phillies)
SP	Joe Roa, Scranton-WB (Phillies)
RP	Lee Gardner, Durham (Devil Rays)

Awards

MVP ....Raul Gonzalez, OF, Louisville
Pitcher of the Year ....Joe Roa, Scranton-WB
Rookie of the Year ....Carl Crawford, Durham
Manager of the Year ....Marc Bombard, Scranton-WB

2002 Pacific Coast League All-Star Team

As selected by the league's managers and media representatives.

Pos. Name, Team (Affiliate)

C	Javier Valentin, Edmonton (Twins)
1B	Lyle Overbay, Tucson (Diamondbacks)
2B	Joe Thurston, Las Vegas (Dodgers)
3B	Jason Wood, Calgary (Marlins)
SS	Aaron Holbert, Tacoma (Mariners)
OF	Robb Quinlan, Salt Lake (Angels)
OF	Michael Restovich, Edmonton (Twins)
OF	Michael Ryan, Edmonton (Twins)
DH	Ivan Cruz, Memphis (Cardinals)
SP	Scott Randall, Edmonton (Twins)
SP	Jeriome Robertson, New Orleans (Astros)
RP	Jeff Williams, Las Vegas (Dodgers)

Awards

MVP ....Robb Quinlan, OF, Salt Lake
Pitcher of the Year ... Jeriome Robertson, New Orleans
Rookie of the Year ....Robb Quinlan, OF, Salt Lake
Manager of the Year ....Brad Mills, Las Vegas

1876-2002
Through the Years

ESPN
Information Please®
SPORTS ALMANAC

The World Series

The World Series began in 1903 when Pittsburgh of the older National League (founded in 1876) invited Boston of the American League (founded in 1901) to play a best-of-9 game series to determine which of the two league champions was the best. Boston was the surprise winner, 5 games to 3. The 1904 NL champion New York Giants refused to play Boston the following year, so there was no Series. Giants' owner John T. Brush and his manager John McGraw both despised AL president Ban Johnson and considered the junior circuit to be a minor league. By the following year, however, Brush and Johnson had smoothed out their differences and the Giants agreed to play Philadelphia in a best-of-7 game series. Since then the World Series has been a best-of-7 format, except from 1919-21 when it returned to best-of-9.

After surviving two world wars and an earthquake in 1989, the World Series was cancelled for only the second time in 1994 due to the players' strike.

In the chart below, the National League teams are listed in CAPITAL letters. Also, each World Series champion's wins and losses are noted in parentheses after the Series score in games.

Multiple champions: New York Yankees (26); Philadelphia-Oakland A's and St. Louis Cardinals (9); Brooklyn-Los Angeles Dodgers (6); Boston Red Sox, Cincinnati Reds, New York-San Francisco Giants and Pittsburgh Pirates (5); Detroit Tigers (4); Baltimore Orioles, Boston-Milwaukee-Atlanta Braves and Washington Senators-Minnesota Twins (3); Chicago Cubs, Chicago White Sox, Cleveland Indians, New York Mets and Toronto Blue Jays (2).

Year	Winner	Manager	Series	Loser	Manager
1903	Boston Red Sox	Jimmy Collins	5-3 (LWLLWWWW)	PITTSBURGH	Fred Clarke
1904	Not held				
1905	NY GIANTS	John McGraw	4-1 (WLWWW)	Philadelphia A's	Connie Mack
1906	Chicago White Sox	Fielder Jones	4-2 (WLWLWW)	CHICAGO CUBS	Frank Chance
1907	CHICAGO CUBS	Frank Chance	4-0-1 (TWWWW)	Detroit	Hughie Jennings
1908	CHICAGO CUBS	Frank Chance	4-1 (WWLWW)	Detroit	Hughie Jennings
1909	PITTSBURGH	Fred Clarke	4-3 (WLWLWLW)	Detroit	Hughie Jennings
1910	Philadelphia A's	Connie Mack	4-1 (WWWLW)	CHICAGO CUBS	Frank Chance
1911	Philadelphia A's	Connie Mack	4-2 (LWWWLW)	NY GIANTS	John McGraw
1912	Boston Red Sox	Jake Stahl	4-3-1 (WTLWWLLW)	NY GIANTS	John McGraw
1913	Philadelphia A's	Connie Mack	4-1 (WLWVW)	NY GIANTS	John McGraw
1914	BOSTON BRAVES	George Stallings	4-0	Philadelphia A's	Connie Mack
1915	Boston Red Sox	Bill Carrigan	4-1 (LWWWW)	PHILA. PHILLIES	Pat Moran
1916	Boston Red Sox	Bill Carrigan	4-1 (WWLWW)	BROOKLYN	Wilbert Robinson
1917	Chicago White Sox	Pants Rowland	4-2 (WWLLWW)	NY GIANTS	John McGraw
1918	Boston Red Sox	Ed Barrow	4-2 (WLWLW)	CHICAGO CUBS	Fred Mitchell
1919	CINCINNATI	Pat Moran	5-3 (WWLWWLLW)	Chicago White Sox	Kid Gleason
1920	Cleveland	Tris Speaker	5-2 (WLLWWWW)	BROOKLYN	Wilbert Robinson
1921	NY GIANTS	John McGraw	5-3 (LLWWLWWW)	NY Yankees	Miller Huggins
1922	NY GIANTS	John McGraw	4-0-1 (WTWWW)	NY Yankees	Miller Huggins
1923	NY Yankees	Miller Huggins	4-2 (LWLWWW)	NY GIANTS	John McGraw
1924	Washington	Bucky Harris	4-3 (LWLWLWW)	NY GIANTS	John McGraw
1925	PITTSBURGH	Bill McKechnie	4-3 (LWLLWWW)	Washington	Bucky Harris
1926	ST.L. CARDINALS	Rogers Hornsby	4-3 (LWWLLWW)	NY Yankees	Miller Huggins
1927	NY Yankees	Miller Huggins	4-0	PITTSBURGH	Donie Bush
1928	NY Yankees	Miller Huggins	4-0	ST.L. CARDINALS	Bill McKechnie
1929	Philadelphia A's	Connie Mack	4-1 (WWLWW)	CHICAGO CUBS	Joe McCarthy
1930	Philadelphia A's	Connie Mack	4-2 (WWLLWW)	ST.L. CARDINALS	Gabby Street
1931	ST.L. CARDINALS	Gabby Street	4-3 (LWWLWLW)	Philadelphia A's	Connie Mack
1932	NY Yankees	Joe McCarthy	4-0	CHICAGO CUBS	Charlie Grimm
1933	NY GIANTS	Bill Terry	4-1 (WWLWW)	Washington	Joe Cronin
1934	ST.L. CARDINALS	Frankie Frisch	4-3 (WLWLLWW)	Detroit	Mickey Cochrane
1935	Detroit	Mickey Cochrane	4-2 (LWWWLW)	CHICAGO CUBS	Charlie Grimm
1936	NY Yankees	Joe McCarthy	4-2 (LWWWLW)	NY GIANTS	Bill Terry
1937	NY Yankees	Joe McCarthy	4-1 (WWWLW)	NY GIANTS	Bill Terry
1938	NY Yankees	Joe McCarthy	4-0	CHICAGO CUBS	Gabby Hartnett
1939	NY Yankees	Joe McCarthy	4-0	CINCINNATI	Bill McKechnie
1940	CINCINNATI	Bill McKechnie	4-3 (LWLWLWW)	Detroit	Del Baker
1941	NY Yankees	Joe McCarthy	4-1 (WLWWW)	BKLN. DODGERS	Leo Durocher
1942	ST.L. CARDINALS	Billy Southworth	4-1 (LWWWW)	NY Yankees	Joe McCarthy
1943	NY Yankees	Joe McCarthy	4-1 (WLWWW)	ST.L. CARDINALS	Billy Southworth
1944	ST.L. CARDINALS	Billy Southworth	4-2 (LWWLWW)	St. Louis Browns	Luke Sewell
1945	Detroit	Steve O'Neill	4-3 (LWLWWLW)	CHICAGO CUBS	Charlie Grimm
1946	ST.L. CARDINALS	Eddie Dyer	4-3 (LWLWLWW)	Boston Red Sox	Joe Cronin
1947	NY Yankees	Bucky Harris	4-3 (WWLLWLW)	BKLN. DODGERS	Burt Shotton

Year	Winner	Manager	Series	Loser	Manager
1948	Cleveland	Lou Boudreau	4-2 (LWWWLW)	BOSTON BRAVES	Billy Southworth
1949	NY Yankees	Casey Stengel	4-1 (WLWWW)	BKLN. DODGERS	Burt Shotton
1950	NY Yankees	Casey Stengel	4-0	PHILA. PHILLIES	Eddie Sawyer
1951	NY Yankees	Casey Stengel	4-2 (LWLWWW)	NY GIANTS	Leo Durocher
1952	NY Yankees	Casey Stengel	4-3 (LWLWLWW)	BKLN. DODGERS	Charlie Dressen
1953	NY Yankees	Casey Stengel	4-2 (WWLLWW)	BKLN. DODGERS	Charlie Dressen
1954	NY GIANTS	Leo Durocher	4-0	Cleveland	Al Lopez
1955	BKLN. DODGERS	Walter Alston	4-3 (LLWWWLW)	NY Yankees	Casey Stengel
1956	NY Yankees	Casey Stengel	4-3 (LLWWWLW)	BKLN. DODGERS	Walter Alston
1957	MILW. BRAVES	Fred Haney	4-3 (LLWWLWW)	NY Yankees	Casey Stengel
1958	NY Yankees	Casey Stengel	4-3 (LLWLWWW)	MILW. BRAVES	Fred Haney
1959	LA DODGERS	Walter Alston	4-2 (LWWLWW)	Chicago White Sox	Al Lopez
1960	PITTSBURGH	Danny Murtaugh	4-3 (WLLWWLW)	NY Yankees	Casey Stengel
1961	NY Yankees	Ralph Houk	4-1 (WLWWW)	CINCINNATI	Fred Hutchinson
1962	NY Yankees	Ralph Houk	4-3 (WLWLWLW)	SF GIANTS	Alvin Dark
1963	LA DODGERS	Walter Alston	4-0	NY Yankees	Ralph Houk
1964	ST.L. CARDINALS	Johnny Keane	4-3 (WLLWWLW)	NY Yankees	Yogi Berra
1965	LA DODGERS	Walter Alston	4-3 (LLWWWLW)	Minnesota	Sam Mele
1966	Baltimore	Hank Bauer	4-0	LA DODGERS	Walter Alston
1967	ST.L. CARDINALS	Red Schoendienst	4-3 (WLWWLLW)	Boston Red Sox	Dick Williams
1968	Detroit	Mayo Smith	4-3 (LWLLWWW)	ST.L. CARDINALS	Red Schoendienst
1969	NY METS	Gil Hodges	4-1 (LWWWW)	Baltimore	Earl Weaver
1970	Baltimore	Earl Weaver	4-1 (WWWLW)	CINCINNATI	Sparky Anderson
1971	PITTSBURGH	Danny Murtaugh	4-3 (LLWWWLW)	Baltimore	Earl Weaver
1972	Oakland A's	Dick Williams	4-3 (WWLWLLW)	CINCINNATI	Sparky Anderson
1973	Oakland A's	Dick Williams	4-3 (WLWLLWW)	NY METS	Yogi Berra
1974	Oakland A's	Alvin Dark	4-1 (LWWWW)	LA DODGERS	Walter Alston
1975	CINCINNATI	Sparky Anderson	4-3 (LWWLWLW)	Boston Red Sox	Darrell Johnson
1976	CINCINNATI	Sparky Anderson	4-0	NY Yankees	Billy Martin
1977	NY Yankees	Billy Martin	4-2 (WLWWLW)	LA DODGERS	Tommy Lasorda
1978	NY Yankees	Bob Lemon	4-2 (LLWWWW)	LA DODGERS	Tommy Lasorda
1979	PITTSBURGH	Chuck Tanner	4-3 (LWLLWWW)	Baltimore	Earl Weaver
1980	PHILA. PHILLIES	Dallas Green	4-2 (WWLLWW)	Kansas City	Jim Frey
1981	LA DODGERS	Tommy Lasorda	4-2 (LLWWWW)	NY Yankees	Bob Lemon
1982	ST.L. CARDINALS	Whitey Herzog	4-3 (LWWLLWW)	Milwaukee Brewers	Harvey Kuenn
1983	Baltimore	Joe Altobelli	4-1 (LWWWW)	PHILA. PHILLIES	Paul Owens
1984	Detroit	Sparky Anderson	4-1 (WLWWW)	SAN DIEGO	Dick Williams
1985	Kansas City	Dick Howser	4-3 (LLWLWWW)	ST.L. CARDINALS	Whitey Herzog
1986	NY METS	Davey Johnson	4-3 (LLWWLWW)	Boston Red Sox	John McNamara
1987	Minnesota	Tom Kelly	4-3 (WWLLLWW)	ST.L. CARDINALS	Whitey Herzog
1988	LA DODGERS	Tommy Lasorda	4-1 (WWLWW)	Oakland A's	Tony La Russa
1989	Oakland A's	Tony La Russa	4-0	SF GIANTS	Roger Craig
1990	CINCINNATI	Lou Piniella	4-0	Oakland A's	Tony La Russa
1991	Minnesota	Tom Kelly	4-3 (WWLLLWW)	ATLANTA BRAVES	Bobby Cox
1992	Toronto	Cito Gaston	4-2 (LWWWLW)	ATLANTA BRAVES	Bobby Cox
1993	Toronto	Cito Gaston	4-2 (WLWWLW)	PHILA. PHILLIES	Jim Fregosi
1994	Not held				
1995	ATLANTA BRAVES	Bobby Cox	4-2 (WWLWLW)	Cleveland	Mike Hargrove
1996	NY Yankees	Joe Torre	4-2 (LLWWWW)	ATLANTA BRAVES	Bobby Cox
1997	FLORIDA	Jim Leyland	4-3 (WLWLWLW)	Cleveland	Mike Hargrove
1998	NY Yankees	Joe Torre	4-0	SAN DIEGO	Bruce Bochy
1999	NY Yankees	Joe Torre	4-0	ATLANTA BRAVES	Bobby Cox
2000	NY Yankees	Joe Torre	4-1 (WWLWW)	NY METS	Bobby Valentine
2001	ARIZONA	Bob Brenly	4-3 (WLLWLWW)	NY Yankees	Joe Torre
2002	Anaheim	Mike Scioscia	4-3 (LWWLLWW)	SF GIANTS	Dusty Baker

Most Valuable Players

Currently selected by media panel and World Series official scorers. Presented by *Sport* magazine from 1955-88 and by Major League Baseball since 1989. Winner who did not play for World Series champions is in **bold** type.

Multiple winners: Bob Gibson, Reggie Jackson and Sandy Koufax (2).

Year		Year		Year	
1955	Johnny Podres, Bklyn, P	1965	Sandy Koufax, LA, P	1975	Pete Rose, Cin., 3B
1956	Don Larsen, NY, P	1966	Frank Robinson, Bal., OF	1976	Johnny Bench, Cin., C
1957	Lew Burdette, Mil., P	1967	Bob Gibson, St.L., P	1977	Reggie Jackson, NY, OF
1958	Bob Turley, NY, P	1968	Mickey Lolich, Det., P	1978	Bucky Dent, NY, SS
1959	Larry Sherry, LA, P	1969	Donn Clendenon, NY, 1B	1979	Willie Stargell, Pit., 1B
1960	**Bobby Richardson**, NY, 2B	1970	Brooks Robinson, Bal., 3B	1980	Mike Schmidt, Phi., 3B
1961	Whitey Ford, NY, P	1971	Roberto Clemente, Pit., OF	1981	Pedro Guerrero, LA, OF;
1962	Ralph Terry, NY, P	1972	Gene Tenace, Oak., C		Ron Cey, LA, 3B;
1963	Sandy Koufax, LA, P	1973	Reggie Jackson, Oak.; OF		& Steve Yeager, LA, C
1964	Bob Gibson, St.L., P	1974	Rollie Fingers, Oak., P	1982	Darrell Porter, St.L., C

Year		Year		Year	
1983	Rick Dempsey, Bal., C	1990	Jose Rijo, Cin., P	1997	Livan Hernandez, Fla., P
1984	Alan Trammell, Det., SS	1991	Jack Morris, Min., P	1998	Scott Brosius, NY, 3B
1985	Bret Saberhagen, KC, P	1992	Pat Borders, Tor., C	1999	Mariano Rivera, NY, P
1986	Ray Knight, NY, 3B	1993	Paul Molitor, Tor., DH/1B/3B	2000	Derek Jeter, NY, SS
1987	Frank Viola, Min., P	1994	Series not held.	2001	Curt Schilling, Ari., P
1988	Orel Hershiser, LA, P	1995	Tom Glavine, Atl., P		& Randy Johnson, Ari., P
1989	Dave Stewart, Oak., P	1996	John Wetteland, NY, P	2002	Troy Glaus, Ana., 3B

All-Time World Series Leaders
CAREER
World Series leaders through 2002. Years listed indicate number of World Series appearances.

Hitting

Games
	Yrs	Gm
Yogi Berra, NY Yankees	14	75
Mickey Mantle, NY Yankees	12	65
Elston Howard, NY Yankees—Boston	10	54
Hank Bauer, NY Yankees	9	53
Gil McDougald, NY Yankees	8	53

At Bats
	Yrs	AB
Yogi Berra, NY Yankees	14	259
Mickey Mantle, NY Yankees	12	230
Joe DiMaggio, NY Yankees	10	199
Frankie Frisch, NY Giants-St.L. Cards	8	197
Gil McDougald, NY Yankees	8	190

Batting Avg. (minimum 50 AB)
	AB	H	Avg
Pepper Martin, St.L. Cards	55	23	.418
Paul Molitor, Mil. Brewers-Tor. Blue Jays	55	23	.418
Lou Brock, St. Louis	87	34	.391
Marquis Grissom, Atl-Cle.	77	30	.390
Thurman Munson, NY Yankees	67	25	.373
George Brett, Kansas City	51	19	.373
Hank Aaron, Milw. Braves	55	20	.364

Hits
	AB	H	Avg
Yogi Berra, NY Yankees	259	71	.274
Mickey Mantle, NY Yankees	230	59	.257
Frankie Frisch, NYG-St.L. Cards	197	58	.294
Joe DiMaggio, NY Yankees	199	54	.271
Hank Bauer, NY Yankees	188	46	.245
Pee Wee Reese, Brooklyn	169	46	.272

Runs
	Gm	R
Mickey Mantle, NY Yankees	65	42
Yogi Berra, NY Yankees	75	41
Babe Ruth, Boston Red Sox-NY Yankees	41	37
Lou Gehrig, NY Yankees	34	30
Joe DiMaggio, NY Yankees	51	27

Home Runs
	AB	HR
Mickey Mantle, NY Yankees	230	18
Babe Ruth, Boston Red Sox-NY Yankees	129	15
Yogi Berra, NY Yankees	259	12
Duke Snider, Brooklyn-LA	133	11
Lou Gehrig, NY Yankees	119	10
Reggie Jackson, Oakland-NY Yankees	98	10

Runs Batted In
	Gm	RBI
Mickey Mantle, NY Yankees	65	40
Yogi Berra, NY Yankees	75	39
Lou Gehrig, NY Yankees	34	35
Babe Ruth, Boston Red Sox-NY Yankees	41	33
Joe DiMaggio, NY Yankees	51	30

World Series Appearances
In the 98 years that the World Series has been contested, American League teams have won 58 championships while National League teams have won 40.

The following teams are ranked by number of appearances through the 2002 World Series; (*) indicates AL teams.

	App	W	L	Pct.	Last Series	Last Title
NY Yankees*	38	26	12	.684	2001	2000
Bklyn/LA Dodgers	18	6	12	.333	1988	1988
NY/SF Giants	17	5	12	.294	2002	1954
St.L. Cardinals	15	9	6	.600	1987	1982
Phi/KC/Oak.A's*	14	9	5	.643	1990	1989
Chicago Cubs	10	2	8	.200	1945	1908
Boston Red Sox*	9	5	4	.556	1986	1918
Cincinnati Reds	9	5	4	.556	1990	1990
Detroit Tigers*	9	4	5	.444	1984	1984
Bos/Mil/Atl.Braves	9	3	6	.333	1999	1995
Pittsburgh Pirates	7	5	2	.714	1979	1979
St.L/Bal.Orioles*	7	3	4	.429	1983	1983
Wash/Min.Twins*	6	3	3	.500	1991	1991
Cle. Indians*	5	2	3	.400	1997	1948
Phi. Phillies	5	1	4	.200	1993	1980
Chi. White Sox*	4	2	2	.500	1959	1917
NY Mets	4	2	2	.500	2000	1986
Tor. Blue Jays*	2	2	0	1.000	1993	1993
KC Royals*	2	1	1	.500	1985	1985
SD Padres	2	0	2	.000	1998	—
Anaheim Angels*	1	1	0	1.000	2002	2002
Ari. Diamondbacks	1	1	0	1.000	2001	2001
Fla. Marlins	1	1	0	1.000	1997	1997
Sea/Mil.Brewers*	1	0	1	.000	1982	—

Stolen Bases
	Gm	SB
Lou Brock, St. Louis	21	14
Eddie Collins, Phi. A's-Chisox	34	14
Frank Chance, Chi. Cubs	20	10
Davey Lopes, Los Angeles	23	10
Phil Rizzuto, NY Yankees	52	10

Total Bases
	Gm	TB
Mickey Mantle, NY Yankees	65	123
Yogi Berra, NY Yankees	75	117
Babe Ruth, Boston Red Sox-NY Yankees	41	96
Lou Gehrig, NY Yankees	34	87
Joe DiMaggio, NY Yankees	51	84

Slugging Pct. (minimum 50 AB)
	AB	Pct
Reggie Jackson, Oakland-NY Yankees	98	.755
Babe Ruth, Boston Red Sox-NY Yankees	129	.744
Lou Gehrig, NY Yankees	119	.731
Al Simmons, Phi. A's-Cincinnati	73	.658
Lou Brock, St. Louis	87	.655

Pitching

Games

	Yrs	Gm
Whitey Ford, NY Yankees	11	22
Mike Stanton, Atlanta-NY Yankees	6	20
Mariano Rivera, NY Yankees	5	18
Rollie Fingers, Oakland	3	16
Allie Reynolds, NY Yankees	6	15
Bob Turley, NY Yankees	5	15
Clay Carroll, Cincinnati	3	14

Wins

	Gm	W-L
Whitey Ford, NY Yankees	22	10-8
Bob Gibson, St. Louis	9	7-2
Allie Reynolds, NY Yankees	15	7-2
Red Ruffing, NY Yankees	10	7-2
Lefty Gomez, NY Yankees	7	6-0
Chief Bender, Philadelphia A's	10	6-4
Waite Hoyt, NY Yankees-Phi. A's	12	6-4

ERA (minimum 25 IP)

	Gm	IP	ERA
Jack Billingham, Cincinnati	7	25.1	0.36
Harry Brecheen, St. Louis	7	32.2	0.83
Babe Ruth, Boston Red Sox	3	31.0	0.87
Sherry Smith, Brooklyn	3	30.1	0.89
Sandy Koufax, Los Angeles	8	57.0	0.95

Saves

	Gm	IP	Sv
Mariano Rivera, NY Yankees	18	27.0	8
Rollie Fingers, Oakland	16	33.1	6
Allie Reynolds, NY Yankees	15	77.1	4
Johnny Murphy, NY Yankees	8	16.1	4
John Wetteland, NY Yankees	5	4.1	4
Robb Nen, Florida-SF	7	7.2	4

Nine pitchers tied with 3 each.

Shutouts

	GS	CG	ShO
Christy Mathewson, NY Giants	11	10	4
Three Finger Brown, Chi. Cubs	7	5	3
Whitey Ford, NY Yankees	22	7	3

Seven pitchers tied with 2 each.

Innings Pitched

	Gm	IP
Whitey Ford, NY Yankees	22	146.0
Christy Mathewson, NY Giants	11	101.2
Red Ruffing, NY Yankees	10	85.2
Chief Bender, Philadelphia A's	10	85.0
Waite Hoyt, NY Yankees-Phi. A's	12	83.2

Complete Games

	GS	CG	W-L
Christy Mathewson, NY Giants	11	10	5-5
Chief Bender, Philadelphia A's	10	9	6-4
Bob Gibson, St. Louis	9	8	7-2
Whitey Ford, NY Yankees	22	7	10-8
Red Ruffing, NY Yankees	10	7	7-2

Strikeouts

	Gm	IP	SO
Whitey Ford, NY Yankees	22	146.0	94
Bob Gibson, St. Louis	9	81.0	92
Allie Reynolds, NY Yankees	15	77.1	62
Sandy Koufax, Los Angeles	8	57.0	61
Red Ruffing, NY Yankees	10	85.2	61

Losses

	Gm	W-L
Whitey Ford, NY Yankees	22	10-8
Christy Mathewson, NY Giants	11	5-5
Joe Bush, Phi. A's-Bosox-NY Yankees	9	2-5
Rube Marquard, NY Giants-Brooklyn	11	2-5
Eddie Plank, Philadelphia A's	7	2-5
Schoolboy Rowe, Detroit	8	2-5

League Championship Series

Division play came to the major leagues in 1969 when both the American and National Leagues expanded to 12 teams. With an East and West Division in each league, League Championship Series (LCS) became necessary to determine the NL and AL pennant winners. In 1994, teams were realigned into three divisions, the East, Central, and West with division winners and one wildcard team playing a best-of-5 League Divisional Series (see following pages for LDS results) to determine the LCS competitors. In the tables below, the East Division champions are noted by the letter E, the Central division champions by C and the West Division champions by W. Wildcard winners are noted by WC. Also, each playoff winner's wins and losses are noted in parentheses after the series score. The LCS changed from best-of-5 to best-of-7 in 1985. Each league's LCS was cancelled in 1994 due to the players' strike.

National League

Multiple champions: Atlanta, Cincinnati and LA Dodgers (5); NY Mets (4); Philadelphia and St. Louis (3); Pittsburgh, San Diego and San Francisco (2).

Year	Winner	Manager	Series	Loser	Manager
1969	E—New York	Gil Hodges	3-0	W—Atlanta	Lum Harris
1970	W—Cincinnati	Sparky Anderson	3-0	E—Pittsburgh	Danny Murtaugh
1971	E—Pittsburgh	Danny Murtaugh	3-1 (LWWW)	W—San Francisco	Charlie Fox
1972	W—Cincinnati	Sparky Anderson	3-2 (LWLWW)	E—Pittsburgh	Bill Virdon
1973	E—New York	Yogi Berra	3-2 (LWLWW)	W—Cincinnati	Sparky Anderson
1974	W—Los Angeles	Walter Alston	3-1 (WWLW)	E—Pittsburgh	Danny Murtaugh
1975	W—Cincinnati	Sparky Anderson	3-0	E—Pittsburgh	Danny Murtaugh
1976	W—Cincinnati	Sparky Anderson	3-0	E—Philadelphia	Danny Ozark
1977	W—Los Angeles	Tommy Lasorda	3-1 (LWWW)	E—Philadelphia	Danny Ozark
1978	W—Los Angeles	Tommy Lasorda	3-1 (WWLW)	E—Philadelphia	Danny Ozark
1979	E—Pittsburgh	Chuck Tanner	3-0	W—Cincinnati	John McNamara
1980	E—Philadelphia	Dallas Green	3-2 (WLLWW)	W—Houston	Bill Virdon
1981	W—Los Angeles	Tommy Lasorda	3-2 (WLLWW)	E—Montreal	Jim Fanning
1982	E—St. Louis	Whitey Herzog	3-0	W—Atlanta	Joe Torre
1983	E—Philadelphia	Paul Owens	3-1 (WLWW)	W—Los Angeles	Tommy Lasorda
1984	W—San Diego	Dick Williams	3-2 (LLWWW)	E—Chicago	Jim Frey
1985	E—St. Louis	Whitey Herzog	4-2 (LLWWWW)	W—Los Angeles	Tommy Lasorda
1986	E—New York	Davey Johnson	4-2 (LWWLWW)	W—Houston	Hal Lanier
1987	E—St. Louis	Whitey Herzog	4-3 (WLWLLWW)	W—San Francisco	Roger Craig
1988	W—Los Angeles	Tommy Lasorda	4-3 (LWWLWLW)	E—New York	Davey Johnson
1989	W—San Francisco	Roger Craig	4-1 (WLWWW)	E—Chicago	Don Zimmer

Year	Winner	Manager	Series	Loser	Manager
1990	W–Cincinnati	Lou Piniella	4-2 (LWWWLW)	E–Pittsburgh	Jim Leyland
1991	W–Atlanta	Bobby Cox	4-3 (LWWLLWW)	E–Pittsburgh	Jim Leyland
1992	W–Atlanta	Bobby Cox	4-3 (WWLWLLW)	E–Pittsburgh	Jim Leyland
1993	E–Philadelphia	Jim Fregosi	4-2 (WLLWWW)	W–Atlanta	Bobby Cox
1994	Not held				
1995	E–Atlanta	Bobby Cox	4-0	C–Cincinnati	Davey Johnson
1996	E–Atlanta	Bobby Cox	4-3 (WLLLWWW)	C–St. Louis	Tony La Russa
1997	WC–Florida	Jim Leyland	4-2 (WLWLWW)	E–Atlanta	Bobby Cox
1998	W–San Diego	Bruce Bochy	4-2 (WWWLLW)	E–Atlanta	Bobby Cox
1999	E–Atlanta	Bobby Cox	4-2 (WWWLLW)	WC–New York	Bobby Valentine
2000	WC–New York	Bobby Valentine	4-1 (WWLWW)	C–St. Louis	Tony La Russa
2001	W–Arizona	Bob Brenly	4-1 (WLWWW)	E–Atlanta	Bobby Cox
2002	WC–San Francisco	Dusty Baker	4-1 (WWLWW)	C–St. Louis	Tony La Russa

NLCS Most Valuable Players

Winners who did not play for NLCS champions are in **bold** type.

Multiple winner: Steve Garvey (2).

Year		Year		Year	
1977	Dusty Baker, LA, OF	1986	**Mike Scott,** Hou., P	1994	LCS not held.
1978	Steve Garvey, LA, 1B	1987	**Jeff Leonard,** SF, OF	1995	Mike Devereaux, Atl., OF
1979	Willie Stargell, Pit., 1B	1988	Orel Hershiser, LA, P	1996	Javy Lopez, Atl., C
1980	Manny Trillo, Phi., 2B	1989	Will Clark, SF, 1B	1997	Livan Hernandez, Fla., P
1981	Burt Hooton, LA, P	1990	Rob Dibble, Cin., P	1998	Sterling Hitchcock, SD, P
1982	Darrell Porter, St.L., C		& Randy Myers, Cin., P	1999	Eddie Perez, Atl., C
1983	Gary Matthews, Phi., OF	1991	Steve Avery, Atl., P	2000	Mike Hampton, NY, P
1984	Steve Garvey, SD, 1B	1992	John Smoltz, Atl., P	2001	Craig Counsell, Ari., 2B
1985	Ozzie Smith, St.L., SS	1993	Curt Schilling, Phi., P	2002	Benito Santiago, SF, C

American League

Multiple champions: NY Yankees (9); Oakland (6); Baltimore (5); Boston, Cleveland, Kansas City, Minnesota and Toronto (2).

Year	Winner	Manager	Series	Loser	Manager
1969	E–Baltimore	Earl Weaver	3-0	W–Minnesota	Billy Martin
1970	E–Baltimore	Earl Weaver	3-0	W–Minnesota	Bill Rigney
1971	E–Baltimore	Earl Weaver	3-0	W–Oakland	Dick Williams
1972	W–Oakland	Dick Williams	3-2 (WWLLW)	E–Detroit	Billy Martin
1973	W–Oakland	Dick Williams	3-2 (LWWLW)	E–Baltimore	Earl Weaver
1974	W–Oakland	Alvin Dark	3-1 (LWWW)	E–Baltimore	Earl Weaver
1975	E–Boston	Darrell Johnson	3-0	W–Oakland	Alvin Dark
1976	E–New York	Billy Martin	3-2 (WLWLW)	W–Kansas City	Whitey Herzog
1977	E–New York	Billy Martin	3-2 (LWLWW)	W–Kansas City	Whitey Herzog
1978	E–New York	Bob Lemon	3-1 (WLWW)	W–Kansas City	Whitey Herzog
1979	E–Baltimore	Earl Weaver	3-1 (WWLW)	W–California	Jim Fregosi
1980	W–Kansas City	Jim Frey	3-0	E–New York	Dick Howser
1981	E–New York	Bob Lemon	3-0	W–Oakland	Billy Martin
1982	E–Milwaukee	Harvey Kuenn	3-2 (LLWWW)	W–California	Gene Mauch
1983	E–Baltimore	Joe Altobelli	3-1 (LWWW)	W–Chicago	Tony La Russa
1984	E–Detroit	Sparky Anderson	3-0	W–Kansas City	Dick Howser
1985	W–Kansas City	Dick Howser	4-3 (LLWLWWW)	E–Toronto	Bobby Cox
1986	E–Boston	John McNamara	4-3 (LWLLWWW)	W–California	Gene Mauch
1987	W–Minnesota	Tom Kelly	4-1 (WWLWW)	E–Detroit	Sparky Anderson
1988	W–Oakland	Tony La Russa	4-0	E–Boston	Joe Morgan
1989	W–Oakland	Tony La Russa	4-1 (WWLWW)	E–Toronto	Cito Gaston
1990	W–Oakland	Tony La Russa	4-0	E–Boston	Joe Morgan
1991	W–Minnesota	Tom Kelly	4-1 (WLWWW)	E–Toronto	Cito Gaston
1992	E–Toronto	Cito Gaston	4-2 (LWWWLW)	W–Oakland	Tony La Russa
1993	E–Toronto	Cito Gaston	4-2 (WWLLWW)	W–Chicago	Gene Lamont
1994	Not held				
1995	C–Cleveland	Mike Hargrove	4-2 (LWLWWW)	W–Seattle	Lou Piniella
1996	E–New York	Joe Torre	4-1 (WLWWW)	WC–Baltimore	Davey Johnson
1997	C–Cleveland	Mike Hargrove	4-2 (WLWWLW)	E–Baltimore	Davey Johnson
1998	E–New York	Joe Torre	4-2 (WLLWWW)	C–Cleveland	Mike Hargrove
1999	E–New York	Joe Torre	4-1 (WWLWW)	WC–Boston	Jimy Williams
2000	E–New York	Joe Torre	4-2 (LWWLWW)	WC–Seattle	Lou Piniella
2001	E–New York	Joe Torre	4-1 (WWWLW)	W–Seattle	Lou Piniella
2002	WC–Anaheim	Mike Scioscia	4-1 (LWWWW)	C–Minnesota	Ron Gardenhire

ALCS Most Valuable Players

Winner who did not play for ALCS champions is in **bold** type.

Multiple winner: Dave Stewart (2).

Year		Year		Year	
1980	Frank White, KC, 2B	1988	Dennis Eckersley, Oak., P	1996	Bernie Williams, NY, OF
1981	Graig Nettles, NY, 3B	1989	Rickey Henderson, Oak., OF	1997	Marquis Grissom, Cle., OF
1982	**Fred Lynn**, Cal., OF	1990	Dave Stewart, Oak., P	1998	David Wells, NY, P
1983	Mike Boddicker, Bal., P	1991	Kirby Puckett, Min., OF	1999	Orlando Hernandez, NY, P
1984	Kirk Gibson, Det., OF	1992	Roberto Alomar, Tor., 2B	2000	Dave Justice, NY, OF
1985	George Brett, KC, 3B	1993	Dave Stewart, Tor., P	2001	Andy Pettitte, NY, P
1986	Marty Barrett, Bos., 2B	1994	LCS not held.	2002	Adam Kennedy, Ana., 2B
1987	Gary Gaetti, Min., 3B	1995	Orel Hershiser, Cle., P		

League Divisional Series

In 1994, leagues were realigned into three divisions, the East, Central, and West with division winners and one wildcard team playing a best-of-5 League Divisional Series to determine the LCS competitors. In the tables below, the East Division champions are noted by the letter E, the Central division champions by C and the West Division champions by W. Wildcard winners are noted by WC. Also, each playoff winner's wins and losses are noted in parentheses after the series score. Each league's LDS was cancelled in 1994 due to the players' strike.

National League

Multiple champions: Atlanta (6); St. Louis (3); NY Mets (2).

Year	Winner	Manager	Series	Loser	Manager
1995	E–Atlanta	Bobby Cox	3-1 (WWLW)	WC–Colorado	Don Baylor
	C–Cincinnati	Davey Johnson	3-0	W–Los Angeles	Tommy Lasorda
1996	E–Atlanta	Bobby Cox	3-0	WC–Los Angeles	Bill Russell
	C–St. Louis	Tony La Russa	3-0	W–San Diego	Bruce Bochy
1997	E–Atlanta	Bobby Cox	3-0	C–Houston	Larry Dierker
	WC–Florida	Jim Leyland	3-0	W–San Francisco	Dusty Baker
1998	E–Atlanta	Bobby Cox	3-0	WC–Chicago	Jim Riggleman
	W–San Diego	Bruce Bochy	3-1 (WLWW)	C–Houston	Larry Dierker
1999	E–Atlanta	Bobby Cox	3-1 (WLWW)	C–Houston	Larry Dierker
	WC–New York	Bobby Valentine	3-1 (WLWW)	W–Arizona	Buck Showalter
2000	C–St. Louis	Tony La Russa	3-0	E–Atlanta	Bobby Cox
	WC–New York	Bobby Valentine	3-1 (LWWW)	W–San Francisco	Dusty Baker
2001	E–Atlanta	Bobby Cox	3-0	C–Houston	Larry Dierker
	W–Arizona	Bob Brenly	3-2 (WLWLW)	WC–St. Louis	Tony La Russa
2002	WC–San Francisco	Dusty Baker	3-2 (WLLWW)	E–Atlanta	Bobby Cox
	C–St. Louis	Tony La Russa	3-0	W–Arizona	Bob Brenly

American League

Multiple champions: NY Yankees (5); Cleveland and Seattle (3); Baltimore (2).

Year	Winner	Manager	Series	Loser	Manager
1995	C–Cleveland	Mike Hargrove	3-0	E–Boston	Kevin Kennedy
	W–Seattle	Lou Piniella	3-2 (LLWWW)	WC–New York	Buck Showalter
1996	E–New York	Joe Torre	3-1 (LWWW)	W–Texas	Johnny Oates
	WC–Baltimore	Davey Johnson	3-1 (WWLW)	C–Cleveland	Mike Hargrove
1997	E–Baltimore	Davey Johnson	3-1 (WWLW)	W–Seattle	Lou Piniella
	C–Cleveland	Mike Hargrove	3-2 (LWLWW)	WC–New York	Joe Torre
1998	E–New York	Joe Torre	3-0	W–Texas	Johnny Oates
	C–Cleveland	Mike Hargrove	3-1 (LWWW)	WC–Boston	Jimy Williams
1999	E–New York	Joe Torre	3-0	W–Texas	Johnny Oates
	WC–Boston	Jimy Williams	3-2 (LLWWW)	C–Cleveland	Mike Hargrove
2000	E–New York	Joe Torre	3-2 (LWWLW)	W–Oakland	Art Howe
	WC–Seattle	Lou Piniella	3-0	C–Chicago	Jerry Manuel
2001	E–New York	Joe Torre	3-2 (LLWWW)	WC–Oakland	Art Howe
	W–Seattle	Lou Piniella	3-2 (LWLWW)	C–Cleveland	Charlie Manuel
2002	WC–Anaheim	Mike Scioscia	3-1 (LWWW)	E–New York	Joe Torre
	C–Minnesota	Ron Gardenhire	3-2 (WLLWW)	W–Oakland	Art Howe

Other Playoffs

Ten times since 1946, playoffs have been necessary to decide league or division championships or wild card berths when two teams were tied at the end of the regular season. Additionally, in the strike year of 1981 there were playoffs between the first and second half-season champions in both leagues.

National League

Year	NL	W	L	Manager	Year	NL	W	L	Manager
1946	Brooklyn	96	58	Leo Durocher	1959	Milwaukee	86	68	Fred Haney
	St. Louis	96	58	Eddie Dyer		Los Angeles	86	68	Walter Alston
	Playoff: (Best-of-3) St. Louis, 2-0					Playoff: (Best-of-3) Los Angeles, 2-0			
	NL	**W**	**L**	**Manager**		**NL**	**W**	**L**	**Manager**
1951	Brooklyn	96	58	Charlie Dressen	1962	Los Angeles	101	61	Walter Alston
	New York	96	58	Leo Durocher		San Francisco	101	61	Alvin Dark
	Playoff: (Best-of-3) New York, 2-1 (WLW)					Playoff: (Best-of-3) San Francisco, 2-1 (WLW)			

Year	NL West	W	L	Manager
1980	Houston	92	70	Bill Virdon
	Los Angeles	92	70	Tommy Lasorda

Playoff: (1 game) Houston, 7-1 (at LA)

Year	NL East	W	L	Manager
1981	(1st Half) Philadelphia	34	21	Dallas Green
	(2nd Half) Montreal	30	23	Jim Fanning

Playoff: (Best-of-5) Montreal, 3-2 (WWLLW)

Year	NL West	W	L	Manager
1981	(1st Half) Los Angeles	36	21	Tommy Lasorda
	(2nd Half) Houston	33	20	Bill Virdon

Playoff: (Best-of-5) Los Angeles, 3-2 (LLWWW)

Year	NL Wild Card	W	L	Manager
1998	Chicago	89	73	Jim Riggleman
	San Francisco	89	73	Dusty Baker

Playoff: (1 game) Chicago, 5-3 (at Chicago)

Year	NL Wild Card	W	L	Manager
1999	Cincinnati	96	66	Jack McKeon
	New York	96	66	Bobby Valentine

Playoff: (1 game) New York, 5-0 (at Cincinnati)

American League

Year	AL	W	L	Manager
1948	Boston	96	58	Joe McCarthy
	Cleveland	96	58	Lou Boudreau

Playoff: (1 game) Cleveland, 8-3 (at Boston)

Year	AL East	W	L	Manager
1978	Boston	99	63	Don Zimmer
	New York	99	63	Bob Lemon

Playoff: (1 game) New York, 5-4 (at Boston)

Year	AL East	W	L	Manager
1981	(1st Half) N.Y.	34	22	Bob Lemon
	(2nd Half) Milw.	31	22	Buck Rodgers

Playoff: (Best-of-5) New York, 3-2 (WWLLW)

Year	AL West	W	L	Manager
1981	(1st Half) Oakland	37	23	Billy Martin
	(2nd Half) Kan. City	30	23	Jim Frey

Playoff: (Best-of-5), Oakland, 3-0

Year	AL West	W	L	Manager
1995	Seattle	78	66	Lou Piniella
	California	78	66	M. Lachemann

Playoff: (1 game) Seattle, 9-1 (at Seattle)

Regular Season League & Division Winners

Regular season National and American League pennant winners from 1900-68, as well as West and East divisional champions from 1969-93. In 1994, both leagues went to three divisions, West, Central and East, and each league also sent a wild card (WC) team to the playoffs. Note that (*) indicates 1994 divisional champion is unofficial (due to the players' strike). Note that **GA** column indicates games ahead of the second place club.

National League

Year	Team	W	L	Pct	GA	Year	Team	W	L	Pct	GA
1900	Brooklyn	82	54	.603	4½	1937	New York	95	57	.625	3
1901	Pittsburgh	90	49	.647	7½	1938	Chicago	89	63	.586	2
1902	Pittsburgh	103	36	.741	27½	1939	Cincinnati	97	57	.630	4½
1903	Pittsburgh	91	49	.650	6½	1940	Cincinnati	100	53	.654	12
1904	New York	106	47	.693	13	1941	Brooklyn	100	54	.649	2½
1905	New York	105	48	.686	9	1942	St. Louis	106	48	.688	2
1906	Chicago	116	36	.763	20	1943	St. Louis	105	49	.682	18
1907	Chicago	107	45	.704	17	1944	St. Louis	105	49	.682	14½
1908	Chicago	99	55	.643	1	1945	Chicago	98	56	.636	3
1909	Pittsburgh	110	42	.724	6½	1946	St. Louis†	98	58	.628	2
1910	Chicago	104	50	.675	13	1947	Brooklyn	94	60	.610	5
1911	New York	99	54	.647	7½	1948	Boston	91	62	.595	6½
1912	New York	103	48	.682	10	1949	Brooklyn	97	57	.630	1
1913	New York	101	51	.664	12½	1950	Philadelphia	91	63	.591	2
1914	Boston	94	59	.614	10½	1951	New York†	98	59	.624	1
1915	Philadelphia	90	62	.592	7	1952	Brooklyn	96	57	.627	4½
1916	Brooklyn	94	60	.610	2½	1953	Brooklyn	105	49	.682	13
1917	New York	98	56	.636	10	1954	New York	97	57	.630	5
1918	Chicago	84	45	.651	10½	1955	Brooklyn	98	55	.641	13½
1919	Cincinnati	96	44	.686	9	1956	Brooklyn	93	61	.604	1
1920	Brooklyn	93	61	.604	7	1957	Milwaukee	95	59	.617	8
1921	New York	94	59	.614	4	1958	Milwaukee	92	62	.597	8
1922	New York	93	61	.604	7	1959	Los Angeles†	88	68	.564	2
1923	New York	95	58	.621	4½	1960	Pittsburgh	95	59	.617	7
1924	New York	93	60	.608	1½	1961	Cincinnati	93	61	.604	4
1925	Pittsburgh	95	58	.621	8½	1962	San Francisco†	103	62	.624	1
1926	St. Louis	89	65	.578	2	1963	Los Angeles	99	63	.611	6
1927	Pittsburgh	94	60	.610	1½	1964	St. Louis	93	69	.574	1
1928	St. Louis	95	59	.617	2	1965	Los Angeles	97	65	.599	2
1929	Chicago	98	54	.645	10½	1966	Los Angeles	95	67	.586	1½
1930	St. Louis	92	62	.597	2	1967	St. Louis	101	60	.627	10½
1931	St. Louis	101	53	.656	13	1968	St. Louis	97	65	.599	9
1932	Chicago	90	64	.584	4	1969	West—Atlanta	93	69	.574	3
1933	New York	91	61	.599	5		East—N.Y. Mets	100	62	.617	8
1934	St. Louis	95	58	.621	2	1970	West—Cincinnati	102	60	.630	14½
1935	Chicago	100	54	.649	4		East—Pittsburgh	89	73	.549	5
1936	New York	92	62	.597	5						

Year		W	L	Pct	GA
1971	West—San Francisco	90	72	.556	1
	East—Pittsburgh	97	65	.599	7
1972	West—Cincinnati	95	59	.617	10½
	East—Pittsburgh	96	59	.619	11
1973	West—Cincinnati	99	63	.611	3½
	East—N.Y. Mets	82	79	.509	1½
1974	West—Los Angeles	102	60	.630	4
	East—Pittsburgh	88	74	.543	1½
1975	West—Cincinnati	108	54	.667	20
	East—Pittsburgh	92	69	.571	6½
1976	West—Cincinnati	102	60	.630	10
	East—Philadelphia	101	61	.623	9
1977	West—Los Angeles	98	64	.605	10
	East—Philadelphia	101	61	.623	5
1978	West—Los Angeles	95	67	.586	2½
	East—Philadelphia	90	72	.556	1½
1979	West—Cincinnati	90	71	.559	1½
	East—Pittsburgh	98	64	.605	2
1980	West—Houston †	93	70	.571	1
	East—Philadelphia	91	71	.562	1
1981	West—Los Angeles$	63	47	.573	—
	East—Montreal$	60	48	.556	—
1982	West—Atlanta	89	73	.549	1
	East—St. Louis	92	70	.568	3
1983	West—Los Angeles	91	71	.562	3
	East—Philadelphia	90	72	.556	6
1984	West—San Diego	92	70	.568	12
	East—Chicago	96	65	.596	6½
1985	West—Los Angeles	95	67	.586	5½
	East—St. Louis	101	61	.623	3
1986	West—Houston	96	66	.593	10
	East—N.Y. Mets	108	54	.667	21½
1987	West—San Francisco	90	72	.556	6
	East—St. Louis	95	67	.586	3
1988	West—Los Angeles	94	67	.584	7
	East—N.Y. Mets	100	60	.625	15
1989	West—San Francisco	92	70	.568	3
	East—Chicago	93	69	.574	6
1990	West—Cincinnati	91	71	.562	5
	East—Pittsburgh	95	67	.586	4

Year		W	L	Pct	GA
1991	West—Atlanta	94	68	.580	1
	East—Pittsburgh	98	64	.605	14
1992	West—Atlanta	98	64	.605	8
	East—Pittsburgh	96	66	.593	9
1993	West—Atlanta	104	58	.642	1
	East—Philadelphia	97	65	.599	3
1994	West—Los Angeles*	58	56	.509	3½
	Central—Cincinnati*	66	48	.579	½
	East—Montreal*	74	40	.649	6
1995	West—Los Angeles	78	66	.542	1
	Central—Cincinnati	85	59	.590	9
	East—Atlanta	90	54	.625	21
	WC—Colorado	77	67	.535	—
1996	West—San Diego	91	71	.562	1
	Central—St. Louis	88	74	.543	6
	East—Atlanta	96	66	.593	8
	WC—Los Angeles	90	72	.556	—
1997	West—San Francisco	90	72	.556	2
	Central—Houston	84	78	.519	5
	East—Atlanta	101	61	.623	9
	WC—Florida	92	70	.568	—
1998	West—San Diego	98	64	.605	9½
	Central—Houston	102	60	.630	12½
	East—Atlanta	106	56	.654	18
	WC—Chicago†	90	73	.552	—
1999	West—Arizona	100	62	.617	14
	Central—Houston	97	65	.599	1½
	East—Atlanta	103	59	.636	6½
	WC—N.Y. Mets†	97	66	.595	—
2000	West—San Francisco	97	65	.599	11
	Central—St. Louis	95	67	.586	10
	East—Atlanta	95	67	.586	1
	WC—N.Y. Mets	94	68	.580	—
2001	West—Arizona	92	70	.568	2
	Central—Houston@	93	69	.574	—
	East—Atlanta	88	74	.543	2
	WC—St. Louis	93	69	.574	—
2002	West—Arizona	98	64	.605	2½
	Central—St. Louis	97	65	.599	13
	East—Atlanta	101	59	.631	19
	WC—San Francisco	95	66	.590	—

†**Regular season playoffs:** See "Other Playoffs" on pages 96-97 for details.
$**Divisional playoffs:** See "Other Playoffs" on pages 96-97 for details.
@Houston (93-69) won the division over St. Louis (93-69) due to a better head-to-head record.

American League

Year		W	L	Pct	GA
1901	Chicago	83	53	.610	4
1902	Philadelphia	83	53	.610	5
1903	Boston	91	47	.659	14½
1904	Boston	95	59	.617	1½
1905	Philadelphia	92	56	.622	2
1906	Chicago	93	58	.616	3
1907	Detroit	92	58	.613	1½
1908	Detroit	90	63	.588	½
1909	Detroit	98	54	.645	3½
1910	Philadelphia	102	48	.680	14½
1911	Philadelphia	101	50	.669	13½
1912	Boston	105	47	.691	14
1913	Philadelphia	96	57	.627	6½
1914	Philadelphia	99	53	.651	8½
1915	Boston	101	50	.669	2½
1916	Boston	91	63	.591	2
1917	Chicago	100	54	.649	9
1918	Boston	75	51	.595	2½
1919	Chicago	88	52	.629	3½
1920	Cleveland	98	56	.636	2
1921	New York	98	55	.641	4½
1922	New York	94	60	.610	1
1923	New York	98	54	.645	16
1924	Washington	92	62	.597	2
1925	Washington	96	55	.636	8½

Year		W	L	Pct	GA
1926	New York	91	63	.591	3
1927	New York	110	44	.714	19
1928	New York	101	53	.656	2½
1929	Philadelphia	104	46	.693	18
1930	Philadelphia	102	52	.662	8
1931	Philadelphia	107	45	.704	13½
1932	New York	107	47	.695	13
1933	Washington	99	53	.651	7
1934	Detroit	101	53	.656	7
1935	Detroit	93	58	.616	3
1936	New York	102	51	.667	19½
1937	New York	102	52	.662	13
1938	New York	99	53	.651	9½
1939	New York	106	45	.702	17
1940	Detroit	90	64	.584	1
1941	New York	101	53	.656	17
1942	New York	103	51	.669	9
1943	New York	98	56	.636	13½
1944	St. Louis	89	65	.578	1
1945	Detroit	88	65	.575	1½
1946	Boston	104	50	.675	12
1947	New York	97	57	.630	12
1948	Cleveland†	97	58	.626	1
1949	New York	97	57	.630	1
1950	New York	98	56	.636	3

Year		W	L	Pct	GA		Year		W	L	Pct	GA
1951	New York	98	56	.636	5		1986	West—California	92	70	.568	5
1952	New York	95	59	.617	2			East—Boston	95	66	.590	5½
1953	New York	99	52	.656	8½		1987	West—Minnesota	85	77	.525	2
1954	Cleveland	111	43	.721	8			East—Detroit	98	64	.605	2
1955	New York	96	58	.623	3		1988	West—Oakland	104	58	.642	13
1956	New York	97	57	.630	9			East—Boston	89	73	.549	1
1957	New York	98	56	.636	8		1989	West—Oakland	99	63	.611	7
1958	New York	92	62	.597	10			East—Toronto	89	73	.549	2
1959	Chicago	94	60	.610	5		1990	West—Oakland	103	59	.636	9
								East—Boston	88	74	.543	2
1960	New York	97	57	.630	8		1991	West—Minnesota	95	67	.586	8
1961	New York	109	53	.673	8			East—Toronto	91	71	.562	7
1962	New York	96	66	.593	5		1992	West—Oakland	96	66	.593	6
1963	New York	104	57	.646	10½			East—Toronto	96	66	.593	4
1964	New York	99	63	.611	1		1993	West—Chicago	94	68	.580	8
1965	Minnesota	102	60	.630	7			East—Toronto	95	67	.586	7
1966	Baltimore	97	63	.606	9		1994	West—Texas*	52	62	.456	1
1967	Boston	92	70	.568	1			Central—Chicago*	67	46	.593	1
1968	Detroit	103	59	.636	12			East—New York*	70	43	.619	6½
1969	West—Minnesota	97	65	.599	9		1995	West—Seattle†	79	66	.545	1
	East—Baltimore	109	53	.673	19			Central—Cleveland	100	44	.694	30
								East—Boston	86	58	.597	7
1970	West—Minnesota	98	64	.605	9			WC—New York	79	65	.549	—
	East—Baltimore	108	54	.667	15		1996	West—Texas	90	72	.556	4½
1971	West—Oakland	101	60	.627	16			Central—Cleveland	99	62	.615	14½
	East—Baltimore	101	57	.639	12			East—New York	92	70	.568	4
1972	West—Oakland	93	62	.600	5½			WC—Baltimore	88	74	.543	—
	East—Detroit	86	70	.551	½		1997	West—Seattle	90	72	.556	6
1973	West—Oakland	94	68	.580	6			Central—Cleveland	86	75	.534	6
	East—Baltimore	97	65	.599	8			East—Baltimore	98	64	.605	2
1974	West—Oakland	90	72	.556	5			WC—New York	96	66	.593	—
	East—Baltimore	91	71	.562	2		1998	West—Texas	88	74	.543	3
1975	West—Oakland	98	64	.605	7			Central—Cleveland	89	73	.549	9
	East—Boston	95	65	.594	4½			East—New York	114	48	.704	22
1976	West—Kansas City	90	72	.556	2½			WC—Boston	92	70	.568	—
	East—New York	97	62	.610	10½		1999	West—Texas	95	67	.586	8
1977	West—Kansas City	102	60	.630	8			Central—Cleveland	97	65	.599	21½
	East—New York	100	62	.617	2½			East—New York	98	64	.605	4
1978	West—Kansas City	92	70	.568	5			WC—Boston	94	68	.580	—
	East—New York†	100	63	.613	1		2000	West—Oakland	91	70	.565	½
1979	West—California	88	74	.543	3			Central—Chicago	95	67	.586	5
	East—Baltimore	102	57	.642	8			East—New York	87	74	.540	2½
1980	West—Kansas City	97	65	.599	14			WC—Seattle	91	71	.562	—
	East—New York	103	59	.636	3		2001	West—Seattle	116	46	.716	14
1981	West—Oakland$	64	45	.587	—			Central—Cleveland	91	71	.562	6
	East—New York$	59	48	.551	—			East—New York	95	65	.594	13½
1982	West—California	93	69	.574	3			WC—Oakland	102	60	.630	—
	East—Milwaukee	95	67	.586	1		2002	West—Oakland	103	59	.636	4
1983	West—Chicago	99	63	.611	20			Central—Minnesota	94	67	.584	13½
	East—Baltimore	98	64	.605	6			East—New York	103	58	.640	10½
1984	West—Kansas City	84	78	.519	3			WC—Anaheim	99	63	.611	—
	East—Detroit	104	58	.642	15							
1985	West—Kansas City	91	71	.562	1							
	East—Toronto	99	62	.615	2							

†**Regular season playoffs:** See "Other Playoffs" on pages 96-97 for details.
$**Divisional playoffs:** See "Other Playoffs" on pages 96-97 for details.

The All-Star Game

Baseball's first All-Star Game was held on July 6, 1933, before 47,595 at Comiskey Park in Chicago. From that year on, the All-Star Game has matched the best players in the American League against the best in the National. From 1959-62, two All-Star Games were played. The only year an All-Star Game wasn't played was 1945, when World War II travel restrictions made it necessary to cancel the meeting. The NL leads the series, 40-31-2. In the chart below, the American League is listed in **bold** type.

In 2002 Major League Baseball announced that the game's MVP award will be known as the Ted Williams Award, named after the Red Sox Hall of Famer.

MVP Multiple winners: Gary Carter, Steve Garvey, Willie Mays and Cal Ripken Jr. (2).

Year	Host		AL Manager	NL Manager	MVP
1933	**American,** 4-2	Chicago (AL)	Connie Mack	John McGraw	No award
1934	**American,** 9-7	New York (NL)	Joe Cronin	Bill Terry	No award
1935	**American,** 4-1	Cleveland	Mickey Cochrane	Frankie Frisch	No award
1936	National, 4-3	Boston (NL)	Joe McCarthy	Charlie Grimm	No award
1937	**American,** 8-3	Washington	Joe McCarthy	Bill Terry	No award
1938	National, 4-1	Cincinnati	Joe McCarthy	Bill Terry	No award
1939	**American,** 3-1	New York (AL)	Joe McCarthy	Gabby Hartnett	No award

The All-Star Game (Cont.)

Year		Host	AL Manager	NL Manager	MVP
1940	National, 4-0	St. Louis (NL)	Joe Cronin	Bill McKechnie	No award
1941	**American,** 7-5	Detroit	Del Baker	Bill McKechnie	No award
1942	**American,** 3-1	New York (NL)	Joe McCarthy	Leo Durocher	No award
1943	**American,** 5-3	Philadelphia (AL)	Joe McCarthy	Billy Southworth	No award
1944	National, 7-1	Pittsburgh	Joe McCarthy	Billy Southworth	No award
1945	Not held				
1946	**American,** 12-0	Boston (AL)	Steve O'Neill	Charlie Grimm	No award
1947	**American,** 2-1	Chicago (NL)	Joe Cronin	Eddie Dyer	No award
1948	**American,** 5-2	St. Louis (AL)	Bucky Harris	Leo Durocher	No award
1949	**American,** 11-7	Brooklyn	Lou Boudreau	Billy Southworth	No award
1950	National, 4-3 (14)	Chicago (AL)	Casey Stengel	Burt Shotton	No award
1951	National, 8-3	Detroit	Casey Stengel	Eddie Sawyer	No award
1952	National, 3-2 (5, rain)	Philadelphia (NL)	Casey Stengel	Leo Durocher	No award
1953	National, 5-1	Cincinnati	Casey Stengel	Charlie Dressen	No award
1954	**American,** 11-9	Cleveland	Casey Stengel	Walter Alston	No award
1955	National, 6-5 (12)	Milwaukee	Al Lopez	Leo Durocher	No award
1956	National, 7-3	Washington	Casey Stengel	Walter Alston	No award
1957	**American,** 6-5	St. Louis	Casey Stengel	Walter Alston	No award
1958	**American,** 4-3	Baltimore	Casey Stengel	Fred Haney	No award
1959-a	National, 5-4	Pittsburgh	Casey Stengel	Fred Haney	No award
1959-b	**American,** 5-3	Los Angeles	Casey Stengel	Fred Haney	No award
1960-a	National, 5-3	Kansas City	Al Lopez	Walter Alston	No award
1960-b	National, 6-0	New York	Al Lopez	Walter Alston	No award
1961-a	National, 5-4 (10)	San Francisco	Paul Richards	Danny Murtaugh	No award
1961-b	TIE, 1-1 (9, rain)	Boston	Paul Richards	Danny Murtaugh	No award
1962-a	National, 3-1	Washington	Ralph Houk	Fred Hutchinson	Maury Wills, LA (NL), SS
1962-b	**American,** 9-4	Chicago (NL)	Ralph Houk	Fred Hutchinson	Leon Wagner, LA (AL), OF
1963	National, 5-3	Cleveland	Ralph Houk	Alvin Dark	Willie Mays, SF, OF
1964	National, 7-4	New York (NL)	Al Lopez	Walter Alston	Johnny Callison, Phi., OF
1965	National, 6-5	Minnesota	Al Lopez	Gene Mauch	Juan Marichal, SF, P
1966	National, 2-1 (10)	St. Louis	Sam Mele	Walter Alston	Brooks Robinson, Bal., 3B
1967	National, 2-1 (15)	California	Hank Bauer	Walter Alston	Tony Perez, Cin., 3B
1968	National, 1-0	Houston	Dick Williams	Red Schoendienst	Willie Mays, SF, OF
1969	National, 9-3	Washington	Mayo Smith	Red Schoendienst	Willie McCovey, SF, 1B
1970	National, 5-4 (12)	Cincinnati	Earl Weaver	Gil Hodges	Carl Yastrzemski, Bos., OF-1B
1971	**American,** 6-4	Detroit	Earl Weaver	Sparky Anderson	Frank Robinson, Bal., OF
1972	National, 4-3 (10)	Atlanta	Earl Weaver	Danny Murtaugh	Joe Morgan, Con., 2B
1973	National, 7-1	Kansas	Dick Williams	Sparky Anderson	Bobby Bonds, SF, OF
1974	National, 7-2	Pittsburgh	Dick Williams	Yogi Berra	Steve Garvey, LA, 1B
1975	National, 6-3	Milwaukee	Alvin Dark	Walter Alston	Bill Madlock, Chi. (NL), 3B & Jon Matlack, NY (NL), P
1976	National, 7-1	Philadelphia	Darrell Johnson	Sparky Anderson	George Foster, Cin., OF
1977	National, 7-5	New York (AL)	Billy Martin	Sparky Anderson	Don Sutton, LA, P
1978	National, 7-3	San Diego	Billy Martin	Tommy Lasorda	Steve Garvey, LA, 1B
1979	National, 7-6	Seattle	Bob Lemon	Tommy Lasorda	Dave Parker, Pit, OF
1980	National, 4-2	Los Angeles	Earl Weaver	Chuck Tanner	Ken Griffey, Cin., OF
1981	National, 5-4	Cleveland	Jim Frey	Dallas Green	Gary Carter, Mon., C
1982	National, 4-1	Montreal	Billy Martin	Tommy Lasorda	Dave Concepcion, Cin., SS
1983	**American,** 13-3	Chicago (AL)	Harvey Kuenn	Whitey Herzog	Fred Lynn, Cal., OF
1984	National, 3-1	San Francisco	Joe Altobelli	Paul Owens	Gary Carter, Mon., C
1985	National, 6-1	Minnesota	Sparky Anderson	Dick Williams	LaMarr Hoyt, SD, P
1986	**American,** 3-2	Houston	Dick Howser	Whitey Herzog	Roger Clemens, Bos., P
1987	National, 2-0 (13)	Oakland	John McNamara	Davey Johnson	Tim Raines, Mon., OF
1988	**American,** 2-1	Cincinnati	Tom Kelly	Whitey Herzog	Terry Steinbach, Oak., C
1989	**American,** 5-3	California	Tony La Russa	Tommy Lasorda	Bo Jackson, KC, OF
1990	**American,** 2-0	Chicago (NL)	Tony La Russa	Roger Craig	Julio Franco, Tex., 2B
1991	**American,** 4-2	Toronto	Tony La Russa	Lou Piniella	Cal Ripken Jr., Bal., SS
1992	**American,** 13-6	San Diego	Tom Kelly	Bobby Cox	Ken Griffey Jr., Sea., OF
1993	**American,** 9-3	Baltimore	Cito Gaston	Bobby Cox	Kirby Puckett, Min., OF
1994	National, 8-7 (10)	Pittsburgh	Cito Gaston	Jim Fregosi	Fred McGriff, Atl., 1B
1995	National, 3-2	Texas	Buck Showalter	Felipe Alou	Jeff Conine, Fla., PH
1996	National, 6-0	Philadelphia	Mike Hargrove	Bobby Cox	Mike Piazza, LA, C
1997	**American,** 3-1	Cleveland	Joe Torre	Bobby Cox	Sandy Alomar Jr., Cle., C
1998	**American,** 13-8	Colorado	Mike Hargrove	Jim Leyland	Roberto Alomar, Bal., 2B
1999	**American,** 4-1	Boston	Joe Torre	Bruce Bochy	Pedro Martinez, Bos., P
2000	**American,** 6-3	Atlanta	Joe Torre	Bobby Cox	Derek Jeter, NY (AL), SS
2001	**American,** 4-1	Seattle	Joe Torre	Bobby Valentine	Cal Ripken Jr., Bal., SS-3B
2002	TIE, 7-7 (11 inn.) *	Milwaukee	Joe Torre	Bob Brenly	No award

* Due to the depletion of both the AL and NL rosters, Commissioner Bud Selig announced before the bottom of the 11th inning that the 11th would be the final inning.

Major League Franchise Origins

Here is what the current 30 teams in Major League Baseball have to show for the years they have put in as members of the National League (NL) and American League (AL). Pennants and World Series championships are since 1901.

National League

	1st Year	Pennants & World Series	Franchise Stops
Arizona Diamondbacks	1998	1 NL (2001) 1 WS (2001)	• Phoenix (1998–)

Atlanta Braves	1876	9 NL (1914,48,57-58,91-92,95,96,99)
		3 WS (1914,57,95)
			• Boston (1876–1952)
			   Milwaukee (1953–65)
			   Atlanta (1966–)

Chicago Cubs	1876	10 NL (1906-08,10,18,29,32,35,38,45) 2 WS (1907-08)	• Chicago (1876–)
Cincinnati Reds	1876	9 NL (1919,39-40,61,70,72,75-76,90) 5 WS (1919,40,75-76,90)	• Cincinnati (1876–80) Cincinnati (1890–)
Colorado Rockies	1993	None	• Denver (1993–)
Florida Marlins	1993	1 NL (1997) 1 WS (1997)	• Miami (1993–)
Houston Astros	1962	None	• Houston (1962–)
Los Angeles Dodgers	1890	18 NL (1916,20,41,47,49,52-53,55-56, 59,63, 65-66,74,77-78, 81,88) 6 WS (1955,59,63,65,81,88)	• Brooklyn (1890-1957) Los Angeles (1958–)
Milwaukee Brewers	1969	1 AL (1982)	• Seattle (1969) Milwaukee (1970–)
Montreal Expos	1969	None	• Montreal (1969–)
New York Mets	1962	4 NL (1969,73,86,00) 2 WS (1969,86)	• New York (1962–)
Philadelphia Phillies	1883	5 NL (1915,50,80,83,93) 1 WS (1980)	• Philadelphia (1883–)
Pittsburgh Pirates	1887	7 NL (1903,09,25,27,60,71,79) 5 WS (1909,25,60,71,79)	• Pittsburgh (1887–)
St. Louis Cardinals	1892	15 NL (1926,28,30-31,34,42-44,46,64, 67-68,82,85,87) 9 WS (1926,31,34,42,44,46,64,67,82)	• St. Louis (1892–)
San Diego Padres	1969	2 NL (1984,98)	• San Diego (1969–)
San Francisco Giants	1883	17 NL (1905,11-13,17,21-24,33,36-37,51, 54,62,89,2002) 5 WS (1905,21-22,33,54)	• New York (1883–1957) San Francisco (1958–)

American League

	1st Year	Pennants & World Series	Franchise Stops
Anaheim Angels	1961	1 AL (2002) 1 WS (2002)	• Los Angeles (1961–65) Anaheim, CA (1966–)

Baltimore Orioles	1901	7 AL (1944,66,69-71,79,83)
		3 WS (1966,70,83)
			• Milwaukee (1901)
			   St. Louis (1902–53)
			   Baltimore (1954–)

Boston Red Sox	1901	9 AL (1903,12,15-16,18,46,67,75,86) 5 WS (1903,12,15-16,18)	• Boston (1901–)
Chicago White Sox	1901	4 AL (1906,17,19,59) 2 WS (1906,17)	• Chicago (1901–)
Cleveland Indians	1901	5 AL (1920,48,54,95,97) 2 WS (1920,48)	• Cleveland (1901–)
Detroit Tigers	1901	9 AL (1907-09,34-35,40,45,68,84) 4 WS (1935,45,68,84)	• Detroit (1901–)
Kansas City Royals	1969	2 AL (1980,85) 1 WS (1985)	• Kansas City (1969–)

Minnesota Twins	1901	6 AL (1924-25,33,65,87,91)
		3 WS (1924,87,91)
			• Washington, DC (1901–60)
			   Bloomington, MN (1961–81)
			   Minneapolis (1982–)

New York Yankees	1901	38 AL (1921-23,26-28,32,36-39,41-43,47, 49-53,55-58,60-64,76-78,81,96,98-01) 26 WS (1923,27-28,32,36-39,41,43,47, 49-53,56,58,61-62,77-78,96,98-00)	• Baltimore (1901–02) New York (1903–)

Oakland Athletics	1901	14 AL (1905,10-11,13-14,29-31,72-74,
		88-90)
		9 WS (1910-11,13,29-30,72-74,89)
			• Philadelphia (1901-54)
			   Kansas City (1955–67)
			   Oakland (1968–)

Seattle Mariners	1977	None	• Seattle (1977–)
Tampa Bay Devil Rays	1998	None	• Tampa Bay (1998–)
Texas Rangers	1961	None	• Washington, DC (1961–71) Arlington, TX (1972–)
Toronto Blue Jays	1977	2 AL (1992-93) 2 WS (1992-93)	• Toronto (1977–)

The Growth of Major League Baseball

The National League (founded in 1876) and the American League (founded in 1901) were both eight-team circuits at the turn of the century and remained that way until expansion finally came to Major League Baseball in the 1960s. The AL added two teams in 1961 and the NL did the same a year later. Both leagues went to 12 teams and split into two divisions in 1969. The AL then grew by two more teams to 14 in 1977, but the NL didn't follow suit until adding its 13th and 14th clubs in 1993. The NL added two teams (making it 16) in 1998 when the expansion Arizona Diamondbacks entered the league and the Milwaukee Brewers moved over from the AL. The Tampa Bay Devil Rays joined the AL in 1998, keeping the AL at 14 teams.

Expansion Timetable (Since 1901)

1961—Los Angeles Angels (now Anaheim) and Washington Senators (now Texas Rangers) join AL; **1962**—Houston Colt .45s (now Astros) and New York Mets join NL; **1969**—Kansas City Royals and Seattle Pilots (now Milwaukee Brewers) join AL, while Montreal Expos and San Diego Padres join NL; **1977**—Seattle Mariners and Toronto Blue Jays join AL; **1993**—Colorado Rockies and Florida Marlins join NL; **1998**—Arizona Diamondbacks join NL and Tampa Bay Devil Rays join AL.

City and Nickname Changes

National League

1953—Boston Braves move to Milwaukee; **1958**—Brooklyn Dodgers move to Los Angeles and New York Giants move to San Francisco; **1965**—Houston Colt .45s renamed Astros; **1966**—Milwaukee Braves move to Atlanta.

Other nicknames: Boston (Beaneaters and Doves through 1908, and Bees from 1936-40); **Brooklyn** (Superbas through 1926, then Robins from 1927-31; then Dodgers from 1932-57); **Cincinnati** (Red Legs from 1944-45, then Redlegs from 1954-60, then Reds since 1961); **Philadelphia** (Blue Jays from 1943-44).

American League

1902—Milwaukee Brewers move to St. Louis and become Browns; **1903**—Baltimore Orioles move to New York and become Highlanders; **1913**—NY Highlanders renamed Yankees; **1954**—St. Louis Browns move to Baltimore and become Orioles; **1955**—Philadelphia Athletics move to Kansas City; **1961**—Washington Senators move to Bloomington, Minn., and become Minnesota Twins; **1965**—LA Angels renamed California Angels; **1966**—California Angels move to Anaheim; **1968**—KC Athletics move to Oakland and become A's; **1970**—Seattle Pilots move to Milwaukee and become Brewers; **1972**—Washington Senators move to Arlington, Texas, and become Rangers; **1982**—Minnesota Twins move to Minneapolis; **1987**—Oakland A's renamed Athletics; **1997**—California Angels renamed Anaheim Angels.

Other nicknames: Boston (Pilgrims, Puritans, Plymouth Rocks and Somersets through 1906); **Cleveland** (Broncos, Blues, Naps and Molly McGuires through 1914); **Washington** (Senators through 1904, then Nationals from 1905-44, then Senators again from 1945-60).

National League Pennant Winners from 1876-99

Founded in 1876, the National League played 24 seasons before the turn of the century and its eventual rivalry with the younger American League.

Multiple winners: Boston (8); Chicago (6); Baltimore (3); Brooklyn, New York and Providence (2).

Year		Year		Year		Year	
1876	Chicago	1882	Chicago	1888	New York	1894	Baltimore
1877	Boston	1883	Boston	1889	New York	1895	Baltimore
1878	Boston	1884	Providence	1890	Brooklyn	1896	Baltimore
1879	Providence	1885	Chicago	1891	Boston	1897	Boston
1880	Chicago	1886	Chicago	1892	Boston	1898	Boston
1881	Chicago	1887	Detroit	1893	Boston	1899	Brooklyn

Champions of Leagues That No Longer Exist

A Special Baseball Records Committee appointed by the commissioner in 1968 that four extinct leagues qualified for major league status—the American Association (1882-91), the Union Association (1884), the Players' League (1890) and the Federal League (1914-15). The first years of the American League (1900) and Federal League (1913) were not recognized.

American Association

Year	Champion	Manager	Year	Champion	Manager	Year	Champion	Manager
1882	Cincinnati	Pop Snyder	1886	St. Louis	Charlie Comiskey	1890	Louisville	Jack Chapman
1883	Philadelphia	Lew Simmons	1887	St. Louis	Charlie Comiskey	1891	Boston	Arthur Irwin
1884	New York	Jim Mutrie	1888	St. Louis	Charlie Comiskey			
1885	St. Louis	Charlie Comiskey	1889	Brooklyn	Bill McGunnigle			

Union Association

Year	Champion	Manager
1884	St. Louis	Henry Lucas

Players' League

Year	Champion	Manager
1890	Boston	King Kelly

Federal League

Year	Champion	Manager
1914	Indianapolis	Bill Phillips
1915	Chicago	Joe Tinker

Annual Batting Leaders (since 1900)
Batting Average
National League

Multiple winners: Tony Gwynn and Honus Wagner (8); Rogers Hornsby and Stan Musial (7); Roberto Clemente and Bill Madlock (4); Pete Rose, Larry Walker and Paul Waner (3); Hank Aaron, Richie Ashburn, Jake Daubert, Tommy Davis, Ernie Lombardi, Willie McGee, Lefty O'Doul, Dave Parker and Edd Roush (2).

Year		Avg	Year		Avg	Year		Avg
1900	Honus Wagner, Pit	.381	1935	Arky Vaughan, Pit	.385	1970	Rico Carty, Atl	.366
1901	Jesse Burkett, St.L	.382	1936	Paul Waner, Pit	.373	1971	Joe Torre, St.L	.363
1902	Ginger Beaumont, Pit	.357	1937	Joe Medwick, St.L	.374	1972	Billy Williams, Chi	.333
1903	Honus Wagner, Pit	.355	1938	Ernie Lombardi, Cin	.342	1973	Pete Rose, Cin	.338
1904	Honus Wagner, Pit	.349	1939	Johnny Mize, St.L	.349	1974	Ralph Garr, Atl	.353
1905	Cy Seymour, Cin	.377				1975	Bill Madlock, Chi	.354
1906	Honus Wagner, Pit	.339	1940	Debs Garms, Pit	.355	1976	Bill Madlock, Chi	.339
1907	Honus Wagner, Pit	.350	1941	Pete Reiser, Bklyn	.343	1977	Dave Parker, Pit	.338
1908	Honus Wagner, Pit	.354	1942	Ernie Lombardi, Bos	.330	1978	Dave Parker, Pit	.334
1909	Honus Wagner, Pit	.339	1943	Stan Musial, St.L	.357	1979	Keith Hernandez, St.L	.344
			1944	Dixie Walker, Bklyn	.357			
1910	Sherry Magee, Phi	.331	1945	Phil Cavarretta, Chi	.355	1980	Bill Buckner, Chi	.324
1911	Honus Wagner, Pit	.334	1946	Stan Musial, St.L	.365	1981	Bill Madlock, Pit	.341
1912	Heinie Zimmerman, Chi	.372	1947	Harry Walker, St.L-Phi	.363	1982	Al Oliver, Mon	.331
1913	Jake Daubert, Bklyn	.350	1948	Stan Musial, St.L	.376	1983	Bill Madlock, Pit	.323
1914	Jake Daubert, Bklyn	.329	1949	Jackie Robinson, Bklyn	.342	1984	Tony Gwynn, SD	.351
1915	Larry Doyle, NY	.320				1985	Willie McGee, St.L	.353
1916	Hal Chase, Cin	.339	1950	Stan Musial, St.L	.346	1986	Tim Raines, Mon	.334
1917	Edd Roush, Cin	.341	1951	Stan Musial, St.L	.355	1987	Tony Gwynn, SD	.370
1918	Zack Wheat, Bklyn	.335	1952	Stan Musial, St.L	.336	1988	Tony Gwynn, SD	.313
1919	Edd Roush, Cin	.321	1953	Carl Furillo, Bklyn	.344	1989	Tony Gwynn, SD	.336
			1954	Willie Mays, NY	.345			
1920	Rogers Hornsby, St.L	.370	1955	Richie Ashburn, Phi	.338	1990	Willie McGee, St.L	.335
1921	Rogers Hornsby, St.L	.397	1956	Hank Aaron, Mil	.328	1991	Terry Pendleton, Atl	.319
1922	Rogers Hornsby, St.L	.401	1957	Stan Musial, St.L	.351	1992	Gary Sheffield, SD	.330
1923	Rogers Hornsby, St.L	.384	1958	Richie Ashburn, Phi	.350	1993	Andres Galarraga, Col	.370
1924	Rogers Hornsby, St.L	.424	1959	Hank Aaron, Mil	.355	1994	Tony Gwynn, SD	.394
1925	Rogers Hornsby, St.L	.403				1995	Tony Gwynn, SD	.368
1926	Bubbles Hargrave, Cin	.353	1960	Dick Groat, Pit	.325	1996	Tony Gwynn, SD	.353
1927	Paul Waner, Pit	.380	1961	Roberto Clemente, Pit	.351	1997	Tony Gwynn, SD	.372
1928	Rogers Hornsby, Bos	.387	1962	Tommy Davis, LA	.346	1998	Larry Walker, Col	.363
1929	Lefty O'Doul, Phi	.398	1963	Tommy Davis, LA	.326	1999	Larry Walker, Col	.379
			1964	Roberto Clemente, Pit	.339			
1930	Bill Terry, NY	.401	1965	Roberto Clemente, Pit	.329	2000	Todd Helton, Col	.372
1931	Chick Hafey, St.L	.349	1966	Matty Alou, Pit	.342	2001	Larry Walker, Col	.350
1932	Lefty O'Doul, Bklyn	.368	1967	Roberto Clemente, Pit	.357	2002	Barry Bonds, SF	.370
1933	Chuck Klein, Phi	.368	1968	Pete Rose, Cin	.335			
1934	Paul Waner, Pit	.362	1969	Pete Rose, Cin	.348			

American League

Multiple winners: Ty Cobb (12); Rod Carew (7); Ted Williams (6); Wade Boggs (5); Harry Heilmann (4); George Brett, Nap Lajoie, Tony Oliva and Carl Yastrzemski (3); Luke Appling, Joe DiMaggio, Ferris Fain, Jimmie Foxx, Nomar Garciaparra, Edgar Martinez, Pete Runnels, Al Simmons, George Sisler and Mickey Vernon (2).

Year		Avg	Year		Avg	Year		Avg
1901	Nap Lajoie, Phi	.422	1924	Babe Ruth, NY	.378	1947	Ted Williams, Bos	.343
1902	Ed Delahanty, Wash	.376	1925	Harry Heilmann, Det	.393	1948	Ted Williams, Bos	.369
1903	Nap Lajoie, Cle	.355	1926	Heinie Manush, Det	.378	1949	George Kell, Det	.343
1904	Nap Lajoie, Cle	.381	1927	Harry Heilmann, Det	.398			
1905	Elmer Flick, Cle	.306	1928	Goose Goslin, Wash	.379	1950	Billy Goodman, Bos	.354
1906	George Stone, St.L	.358	1929	Lew Fonseca, Cle	.369	1951	Ferris Fain, Phi	.344
1907	Ty Cobb, Det	.350				1952	Ferris Fain, Phi	.327
1908	Ty Cobb, Det	.324	1930	Al Simmons, Phi	.381	1953	Mickey Vernon, Wash	.337
1909	Ty Cobb, Det	.377	1931	Al Simmons, Phi	.390	1954	Bobby Avila, Clev	.341
			1932	Dale Alexander, Det-Bos	.367	1955	Al Kaline, Det	.340
1910	Ty Cobb, Det	.385	1933	Jimmie Foxx, Phi	.356	1956	Mickey Mantle, NY	.353
1911	Ty Cobb, Det	.420	1934	Lou Gehrig, NY	.363	1957	Ted Williams, Bos	.388
1912	Ty Cobb, Det	.410	1935	Buddy Myer, Wash	.349	1958	Ted Williams, Bos	.328
1913	Ty Cobb, Det	.390	1936	Luke Appling, Chi	.388	1959	Harvey Kuenn, Det	.353
1914	Ty Cobb, Det	.368	1937	Charlie Gehringer, Det	.371			
1915	Ty Cobb, Det	.369	1938	Jimmie Foxx, Bos	.349	1960	Pete Runnels, Bos	.320
1916	Tris Speaker, Cle	.386	1939	Joe DiMaggio, NY	.381	1961	Norm Cash, Det	.361*
1917	Ty Cobb, Det	.383				1962	Pete Runnels, Bos	.326
1918	Ty Cobb, Det	.382	1940	Joe DiMaggio, NY	.352	1963	Carl Yastrzemski, Bos	.321
1919	Ty Cobb, Det	.384	1941	Ted Williams, Bos	.406	1964	Tony Oliva, Min	.323
			1942	Ted Williams, Bos	.356	1965	Tony Oliva, Min	.321
1920	George Sisler, St.L	.407	1943	Luke Appling, Chi	.328	1966	Frank Robinson, Bal	.316
1921	Harry Heilmann, Det	.394	1944	Lou Boudreau, Clev	.327	1967	Carl Yastrzemski, Bos	.326
1922	George Sisler, St.L	.420	1945	Snuffy Stirnweiss, NY	.309	1968	Carl Yastrzemski, Bos	.301
1923	Harry Heilmann, Det	.403	1946	Mickey Vernon, Wash	.353	1969	Rod Carew, Min	.332

Batting Average (Cont.)

Year	Avg	Year	Avg	Year	Avg
1970 Alex Johnson, Cal.	.329	1982 Willie Wilson, KC.	.332	1994 Paul O'Neill, NY	.359
1971 Tony Oliva, Min	.337	1983 Wade Boggs, Bos.	.361	1995 Edgar Martinez, Sea	.356
1972 Rod Carew, Min	.318	1984 Don Mattingly, NY	.343	1996 Alex Rodriguez, Sea	.358
1973 Rod Carew, Min	.350	1985 Wade Boggs, Bos.	.368	1997 Frank Thomas, Chi	.347
1974 Rod Carew, Min	.364	1986 Wade Boggs, Bos.	.357	1998 Bernie Williams, NY.	.339
1975 Rod Carew, Min	.359	1987 Wade Boggs, Bos.	.363	1999 Nomar Garciaparra, Bos.	.357
1976 George Brett, KC	.333	1988 Wade Boggs, Bos.	.366		
1977 Rod Carew, Min	.388	1989 Kirby Puckett, Min.	.339	2000 Nomar Garciaparra, Bos.	.372
1978 Rod Carew, Min	.333			2001 Ichiro Suzuki, Sea.	.350
1979 Fred Lynn, Bos	.333	1990 George Brett, KC	.329	2002 Manny Ramirez, Bos	.349
		1991 Julio Franco, Tex	.341	*Norm Cash later admitted to using a	
1980 George Brett, KC	.390	1992 Edgar Martinez, Sea	.343	corked bat the entire season. He	
1981 Carney Lansford, Bos.	.336	1993 John Olerud, Tor	.363	played 16 other seasons and never hit better than .286.	

Home Runs
National League

Multiple winners: Mike Schmidt (8); Ralph Kiner (7); Gavvy Cravath and Mel Ott (6); Hank Aaron, Chuck Klein, Willie Mays, Johnny Mize, Cy Williams and Hack Wilson (4); Willie McCovey (3); Ernie Banks, Johnny Bench, Barry Bonds, George Foster, Rogers Hornsby, Tim Jordan, Dave Kingman, Eddie Mathews, Mark McGwire, Dale Murphy, Bill Nicholson, Dave Robertson, Wildfire Schulte, Sammy Sosa and Willie Stargell (2).

Year	HR	Year	HR	Year	HR
1900 Herman Long, Bos	.12	1933 Chuck Klein, Phi	.28	1966 Hank Aaron, Atl	.44
1901 Sam Crawford, Cin	.16	1934 Rip Collins, St.L	.35	1967 Hank Aaron, Atl	.39
1902 Tommy Leach, Pit	.6	& Mel Ott, NY	.35	1968 Willie McCovey, SF	.36
1903 Jimmy Sheckard, Bklyn	.9	1935 Wally Berger, Bos	.34	1969 Willie McCovey, SF	.45
1904 Harry Lumley, Bklyn	.9	1936 Mel Ott, NY.	.33		
1905 Fred Odwell, Cin.	.9	1937 Joe Medwick, St.L	.31	1970 Johnny Bench, Cin	.45
1906 Tim Jordan, Bklyn	.12	& Mel Ott, NY	.31	1971 Willie Stargell, Pit	.48
1907 Dave Brain, Bos	.10	1938 Mel Ott, NY.	.36	1972 Johnny Bench, Cin	.40
1908 Tim Jordan, Bklyn	.12	1939 Johnny Mize, St.L	.28	1973 Willie Stargell, Pit	.44
1909 Red Murray, NY	.7			1974 Mike Schmidt, Phi	.36
		1940 Johnny Mize, St.L	.43	1975 Mike Schmidt, Phi	.38
1910 Fred Beck, Bos.	.10	1941 Dolph Camilli, Bklyn	.34	1976 Mike Schmidt, Phi	.38
& Wildfire Schulte, Chi	.10	1942 Mel Ott, NY.	.30	1977 George Foster, Cin	.52
1911 Wildfire Schulte, Chi	.21	1943 Bill Nicholson, Chi	.29	1978 George Foster, Cin	.40
1912 Heinie Zimmerman, Chi.	.14	1944 Bill Nicholson, Chi	.33	1979 Dave Kingman, NY	.48
1913 Gavvy Cravath, Phi	.19	1945 Tommy Holmes, Bos	.28		
1914 Gavvy Cravath, Phi	.19	1946 Ralph Kiner, Pit	.23	1980 Mike Schmidt, Phi	.48
1915 Gavvy Cravath, Phi	.24	1947 Ralph Kiner, Pit	.51	1981 Mike Schmidt, Phi	.31
1916 Cy Williams, Chi	.12	& Johnny Mize, NY	.51	1982 Dave Kingman, NY	.37
& Dave Robertson, NY.	.12	1948 Ralph Kiner, Pit	.40	1983 Mike Schmidt, Phi	.40
1917 Gavvy Cravath, Phi	.12	& Johnny Mize, NY	.40	1984 Dale Murphy, Atl.	.36
& Dave Robertson, NY	.12	1949 Ralph Kiner, Pit	.54	& Mike Schmidt, Phi	.36
1918 Gavvy Cravath, Phi.	.8			1985 Dale Murphy, Atl.	.37
1919 Gavvy Cravath, Phi	.12	1950 Ralph Kiner, Pit	.47	1986 Mike Schmidt, Phi	.37
		1951 Ralph Kiner, Pit	.42	1987 Andre Dawson, Chi	.49
1920 Cy Williams, Phi	.15	1952 Ralph Kiner, Pit	.37	1988 Darryl Strawberry, NY	.39
1921 George Kelly, NY	.23	& Hank Sauer, Chi	.37	1989 Kevin Mitchell, SF	.47
1922 Rogers Hornsby, St.L.	.42	1953 Eddie Mathews, Mil	.47		
1923 Cy Williams, Phi	.41	1954 Ted Kluszewski, Cin	.49	1990 Ryne Sandberg, Chi	.40
1924 Jack Fournier, Bklyn	.27	1955 Willie Mays, NY	.51	1991 Howard Johnson, NY	.38
1925 Rogers Hornsby, St.L.	.39	1956 Duke Snider, Bklyn	.43	1992 Fred McGriff, SD	.35
1926 Hack Wilson, Chi	.21	1957 Hank Aaron, Mil	.44	1993 Barry Bonds, SF	.46
1927 Cy Williams, Phi	.30	1958 Ernie Banks, Chi	.47	1994 Matt Williams, SF	.43
& Hack Wilson, Chi	.30	1959 Eddie Mathews, Mil	.46	1995 Dante Bichette, Col	.40
1928 Jim Bottomley, St.L.	.31			1996 Andres Galarraga, Col	.47
& Hack Wilson, Chi	.31	1960 Ernie Banks, Chi	.41	1997 Larry Walker, Col	.49
1929 Chuck Klein, Phi	.43	1961 Orlando Cepeda, SF	.46	1998 Mark McGwire, St.L	.70
		1962 Willie Mays, SF	.49	1999 Mark McGwire, St.L	.65
1930 Hack Wilson, Chi	.56	1963 Hank Aaron, Mil	.44		
1931 Chuck Klein, Phi	.31	& Willie McCovey, SF	.44	2000 Sammy Sosa, Chi	.50
1932 Chuck Klein, Phi	.38	1964 Willie Mays, SF	.47	2001 Barry Bonds, SF	.73
& Mel Ott, NY	.38	1965 Willie Mays, SF	.52	2002 Sammy Sosa, Chi	.49

American League

Multiple winners: Babe Ruth (12); Harmon Killebrew (6); Home Run Baker, Harry Davis, Jimmie Foxx, Hank Greenberg, Ken Griffey Jr., Reggie Jackson, Mickey Mantle and Ted Williams (4); Lou Gehrig and Jim Rice (3); Dick Allen, Tony Armas, Jose Canseco, Joe DiMaggio, Larry Doby, Cecil Fielder, Juan Gonzalez, Mark McGwire, Wally Pipp, Alex Rodriguez, Al Rosen and Gorman Thomas (2).

Year	HR	Year	HR	Year	HR
1901 Nap Lajoie, Phi	.14	1905 Harry Davis, Phi	.8	1909 Ty Cobb, Det	.9
1902 Socks Seybold, Phi	.16	1906 Harry Davis, Phi	.12	1910 Jake Stahl, Bos	.10
1903 Buck Freeman, Bos	.13	1907 Harry Davis, Phi	.8	1911 Home Run Baker, Phi	.11
1904 Harry Davis, Phi	.10	1908 Sam Crawford, Det	.7		

Year	HR
1912 Home Run Baker, Phi	.10
& Tris Speaker, Bos	.10
1913 Home Run Baker, Phi	.12
1914 Home Run Baker, Phi	.9
1915 Braggo Roth, Chi-Cle	.7
1916 Wally Pipp, NY	.12
1917 Wally Pipp, NY	.9
1918 Babe Ruth, Bos	.11
& Tilly Walker, Phi	.11
1919 Babe Ruth, Bos	.29
1920 Babe Ruth, NY	.54
1921 Babe Ruth, NY	.59
1922 Ken Williams, St.L	.39
1923 Babe Ruth, NY	.41
1924 Babe Ruth, NY	.46
1925 Bob Meusel, NY	.33
1926 Babe Ruth, NY	.47
1927 Babe Ruth, NY	.60
1928 Babe Ruth, NY	.54
1929 Babe Ruth, NY	.46
1930 Babe Ruth, NY	.49
1931 Lou Gehrig, NY	.46
& Babe Ruth, NY	.46
1932 Jimmie Foxx, Phi	.58
1933 Jimmie Foxx, Phi	.48
1934 Lou Gehrig, NY	.49
1935 Jimmie Foxx, Phi	.36
& Hank Greenberg, Det	.36
1936 Lou Gehrig, NY	.49
1937 Joe DiMaggio, NY	.46
1938 Hank Greenberg, Det	.58
1939 Jimmie Foxx, Bos	.35
1940 Hank Greenberg, Det	.41
1941 Ted Williams, Bos	.37
1942 Ted Williams, Bos	.36

Year	HR
1943 Rudy York, Det	.34
1944 Nick Etten, NY	.22
1945 Vern Stephens, St.L	.24
1946 Hank Greenberg, Det	.44
1947 Ted Williams, Bos	.32
1948 Joe DiMaggio, NY	.39
1949 Ted Williams, Bos	.43
1950 Al Rosen, Cle	.37
1951 Gus Zernial, Chi-Phi	.33
1952 Larry Doby, Cle	.32
1953 Al Rosen, Cle	.43
1954 Larry Doby, Cle	.32
1955 Mickey Mantle, NY	.37
1956 Mickey Mantle, NY	.52
1957 Roy Sievers, Wash	.42
1958 Mickey Mantle, NY	.42
1959 Rocky Colavito, Cle	.42
& Harmon Killebrew, Wash	.42
1960 Mickey Mantle, NY	.40
1961 Roger Maris, NY	.61
1962 Harmon Killebrew, Min	.48
1963 Harmon Killebrew, Min	.45
1964 Harmon Killebrew, Min	.49
1965 Tony Conigliaro, Bos	.32
1966 Frank Robinson, Bal	.49
1967 Harmon Killebrew, Min	.44
& Carl Yastrzemski, Bos	.44
1968 Frank Howard, Wash	.44
1969 Harmon Killebrew, Min	.49
1970 Frank Howard, Wash	.44
1971 Bill Melton, Chi	.33
1972 Dick Allen, Chi	.37
1973 Reggie Jackson, Oak	.32
1974 Dick Allen, Chi	.32

Year	HR
1975 Reggie Jackson, Oak	.36
& George Scott, Mil	.36
1976 Graig Nettles, NY	.32
1977 Jim Rice, Bos	.39
1978 Jim Rice, Bos	.46
1979 Gorman Thomas, Mil	.45
1980 Reggie Jackson, NY	.41
& Ben Oglivie, Mil	.41
1981 Tony Armas, Oak	.22
Dwight Evans, Bos	.22
Bobby Grich, Cal	.22
& Eddie Murray, Bal	.22
1982 Reggie Jackson, Cal	.39
& Gorman Thomas, Mil	.39
1983 Jim Rice, Bos	.39
1984 Tony Armas, Bos	.43
1985 Darrell Evans, Det	.40
1986 Jesse Barfield, Tor	.40
1987 Mark McGwire, Oak	.49
1988 Jose Canseco, Oak	.42
1989 Fred McGriff, Tor	.36
1990 Cecil Fielder, Det	.51
1991 Jose Canseco, Oak	.44
& Cecil Fielder, Det	.44
1992 Juan Gonzalez, Tex	.43
1993 Juan Gonzalez, Tex	.46
1994 Ken Griffey Jr., Sea	.40
1995 Albert Belle, Cle	.50
1996 Mark McGwire, Oak	.52
1997 Ken Griffey Jr., Sea	.56
1998 Ken Griffey Jr., Sea	.56
1999 Ken Griffey Jr., Sea	.48
2000 Troy Glaus, Ana	.47
2001 Alex Rodriguez, Tex	.52
2002 Alex Rodriguez, Tex	.57

Runs Batted In
National League

Multiple winners: Hank Aaron, Rogers Hornsby, Sherry Magee, Mike Schmidt and Honus Wagner (4); Johnny Bench, George Foster, Joe Medwick, Johnny Mize and Heinie Zimmerman (3); Ernie Banks, Jim Bottomley, Orlando Cepeda, Gavvy Cravath, Andres Galarraga, George Kelly, Chuck Klein, Willie McCovey, Dale Murphy, Stan Musial, Bill Nicholson, Sammy Sosa and Hack Wilson (2).

Year	RBI
1900 Elmer Flick, Phi	.110
1901 Honus Wagner, Pit	.126
1902 Honus Wagner, Pit	.91
1903 Sam Mertes, NY	.104
1904 Bill Dahlen, NY	.80
1905 Cy Seymour, Cin	.121
1906 Jim Nealon, Pit	.83
& Harry Steinfeldt, Chi	.83
1907 Sherry Magee, Phi	.85
1908 Honus Wagner, Pit	.109
1909 Honus Wagner, Pit	.100
1910 Sherry Magee, Phi	.123
1911 Wildfire Schulte, Chi	.121
1912 Heinie Zimmerman, Chi	.103
1913 Gavvy Cravath, Phi	.128
1914 Sherry Magee, Phi	.103
1915 Gavvy Cravath, Phi	.115
1916 Heinie Zimmerman, Chi-NY	.83
1917 Heinie Zimmerman, NY	.102
1918 Sherry Magee, Cin	.76
1919 Hy Myers, Bklyn	.73
1920 Rogers Hornsby, St.L	.94
& George Kelly, NY	.94
1921 Rogers Hornsby, St.L	.126
1922 Rogers Hornsby, St.L	.152
1923 Irish Meusel, NY	.125
1924 George Kelly, NY	.136

Year	RBI
1925 Rogers Hornsby, St.L	.143
1926 Jim Bottomley, St.L	.120
1927 Paul Waner, Pit	.131
1928 Jim Bottomley, St.L	.136
1929 Hack Wilson, Chi	.159
1930 Hack Wilson, Chi	.191
1931 Chuck Klein, Phi	.121
1932 Don Hurst, Phi	.143
1933 Chuck Klein, Phi	.120
1934 Mel Ott, NY	.135
1935 Wally Berger, Bos	.130
1936 Joe Medwick, St.L	.138
1937 Joe Medwick, St.L	.154
1938 Joe Medwick, St.L	.122
1939 Frank McCormick, Cin	.128
1940 Johnny Mize, St.L	.137
1941 Dolph Camilli, Bklyn	.120
1942 Johnny Mize, NY	.110
1943 Bill Nicholson, Chi	.128
1944 Bill Nicholson, Chi	.122
1945 Dixie Walker, Bklyn	.124
1946 Enos Slaughter, St.L	.130
1947 Johnny Mize, NY	.138
1948 Stan Musial, St.L	.131
1949 Ralph Kiner, Pit	.127
1950 Del Ennis, Phi	.126
1951 Monte Irvin, NY	.121

Year	RBI
1952 Hank Sauer, Chi	.121
1953 Roy Campanella, Bklyn	.142
1954 Ted Kluszewski, Cin	.141
1955 Duke Snider, Bklyn	.136
1956 Stan Musial, St.L	.109
1957 Hank Aaron, Mil	.132
1958 Ernie Banks, Chi	.129
1959 Ernie Banks, Chi	.143
1960 Hank Aaron, Mil	.126
1961 Orlando Cepeda, SF	.142
1962 Tommy Davis, LA	.153
1963 Hank Aaron, Mil	.130
1964 Ken Boyer, St.L	.119
1965 Deron Johnson, Cin	.130
1966 Hank Aaron, Atl	.127
1967 Orlando Cepeda, St.L	.111
1968 Willie McCovey, SF	.105
1969 Willie McCovey, SF	.126
1970 Johnny Bench, Cin	.148
1971 Joe Torre, St.L	.137
1972 Johnny Bench, Cin	.125
1973 Willie Stargell, Pit	.119
1974 Johnny Bench, Cin	.129
1975 Greg Luzinski, Phi	.120
1976 George Foster, Cin	.121
1977 George Foster, Cin	.149
1978 George Foster, Cin	.120

Runs Batted In (Cont.)

Year		RBI	Year		RBI	Year		RBI
1979	Dave Winfield, SD	118	1986	Mike Schmidt, Phi	119	1995	Dante Bichette, Col	128
1980	Mike Schmidt, Phi	121	1987	Andre Dawson, Chi	137	1996	Andres Galarraga, Col	150
1981	Mike Schmidt, Phi	91	1988	Will Clark, SF	109	1997	Andres Galarraga, Col	140
1982	Dale Murphy, Atl	109	1989	Kevin Mitchell, SF	125	1998	Sammy Sosa, Chi	158
	& Al Oliver, Mon	109				1999	Mark McGwire, St.L	147
1983	Dale Murphy, Atl	121	1990	Matt Williams, SF	122			
1984	Gary Carter, Mon	106	1991	Howard Johnson, NY	117	2000	Todd Helton, Col	147
	& Mike Schmidt, Phi	106	1992	Darren Daulton, Phi	109	2001	Sammy Sosa, Chi	160
1985	Dave Parker, Cin	125	1993	Barry Bonds, SF	123	2002	Lance Berkman, Hou	128
			1994	Jeff Bagwell, Hou	116			

American League

Multiple winners: Babe Ruth (6); Lou Gehrig (5); Ty Cobb, Hank Greenberg and Ted Williams (4); Albert Belle, Sam Crawford, Cecil Fielder, Jimmie Foxx, Jackie Jensen, Harmon Killebrew, Vern Stephens and Bobby Veach (3); Home Run Baker, Cecil Cooper, Harry Davis, Joe DiMaggio, Buck Freeman, Nap Lajoie, Roger Maris, Jim Rice, Al Rosen, and Bobby Veach (2).

Year		RBI	Year		RBI	Year		RBI
1901	Nap Lajoie, Phi	125	1936	Hal Trosky, Cle	162	1970	Frank Howard, Wash	126
1902	Buck Freeman, Bos	121	1937	Hank Greenberg, Det	183	1971	Harmon Killebrew, Min	119
1903	Buck Freeman, Bos	104	1938	Jimmie Foxx, Bos	175	1972	Dick Allen, Chi	113
1904	Nap Lajoie, Cle	102	1939	Ted Williams, Bos	145	1973	Reggie Jackson, Oak	117
1905	Harry Davis, Phi	83				1974	Jeff Burroughs, Tex	118
1906	Harry Davis, Phi	96	1940	Hank Greenberg, Det	150	1975	George Scott, Mil	109
1907	Ty Cobb, Det	116	1941	Joe DiMaggio, NY	125	1976	Lee May, Bal	109
1908	Ty Cobb, Det	108	1942	Ted Williams, Bos	137	1977	Larry Hisle, Min	119
1909	Ty Cobb, Det	107	1943	Rudy York, Det	118	1978	Jim Rice, Bos	139
			1944	Vern Stephens, St.L	109	1979	Don Baylor, Cal	139
1910	Sam Crawford, Det	120	1945	Nick Etten, NY	111			
1911	Ty Cobb, Det	144	1946	Hank Greenberg, Det	127	1980	Cecil Cooper, Mil	122
1912	Home Run Baker, Phi	133	1947	Ted Williams, Bos	114	1981	Eddie Murray, Bal	78
1913	Home Run Baker, Phi	126	1948	Joe DiMaggio, NY	155	1982	Hal McRae, KC	133
1914	Sam Crawford, Det	104	1949	Ted Williams, Bos	159	1983	Cecil Cooper, Mil	126
1915	Sam Crawford, Det	112		& Vern Stephens, Bos	159		& Jim Rice, Bos	126
	& Bobby Veach, Det	112	1950	Walt Dropo, Bos	144	1984	Tony Armas, Bos	123
1916	Del Pratt, St.L	103		& Vern Stephens, Bos	144	1985	Don Mattingly, NY	145
1917	Bobby Veach, Det	103	1951	Gus Zernial, Chi-Phi	129	1986	Joe Carter, Cle	121
1918	Bobby Veach, Det	78	1952	Al Rosen, Cle	105	1987	George Bell, Tor	134
1919	Babe Ruth, Bos	114	1953	Al Rosen, Cle	145	1988	Jose Canseco, Oak	124
			1954	Larry Doby, Cle	126	1989	Ruben Sierra, Tex	119
1920	Babe Ruth, NY	137	1955	Ray Boone, Det	116			
1921	Babe Ruth, NY	171		& Jackie Jensen, Bos	116	1990	Cecil Fielder, Det	132
1922	Ken Williams, St.L	155	1956	Mickey Mantle, NY	130	1991	Cecil Fielder, Det	133
1923	Babe Ruth, NY	131	1957	Roy Sievers, Wash	114	1992	Cecil Fielder, Det	124
1924	Goose Goslin, Wash	129	1958	Jackie Jensen, Bos	122	1993	Albert Belle, Cle	129
1925	Bob Meusel, NY	138	1959	Jackie Jensen, Bos	112	1994	Kirby Puckett, Min	112
1926	Babe Ruth, NY	145				1995	Albert Belle, Cle	126
1927	Lou Gehrig, NY	175	1960	Roger Maris, NY	112		& Mo Vaughn, Bos	126
1928	Lou Gehrig, NY	142	1961	Roger Maris, NY	142	1996	Albert Belle, Cle	148
	& Babe Ruth, NY	142	1962	Harmon Killebrew, Min	126	1997	Ken Griffey Jr., Sea	147
1929	Al Simmons, Phi	157	1963	Dick Stuart, Bos	118	1998	Juan Gonzalez, Tex	157
			1964	Brooks Robinson, Bal	118	1999	Manny Ramirez, Cle	165
1930	Lou Gehrig, NY	174	1965	Rocky Colavito, Cle	108			
1931	Lou Gehrig, NY	184	1966	Frank Robinson, Bal	122	2000	Edgar Martinez, Sea	145
1932	Jimmie Foxx, Phi	169	1967	Carl Yastrzemski, Bos	121	2001	Bret Boone, Sea	141
1933	Jimmie Foxx, Phi	163	1968	Ken Harrelson, Bos	109	2002	Alex Rodriguez, Tex	142
1934	Lou Gehrig, NY	165	1969	Harmon Killebrew, Min	140			
1935	Hank Greenberg, Det	170						

Batting Triple Crown Winners

Players who led either league in Batting Average, Home Runs and Runs Batted In over a single season.

National League

	Year	Avg	HR	RBI
Paul Hines, Providence	1878	.358	4	50
Hugh Duffy, Boston	1894	.438	18	145
Heinie Zimmerman, Chicago	1912	.372	14	103
Rogers Hornsby, St. Louis	1922	.401	42	152
Rogers Hornsby, St. Louis	1925	.403	39	143
Chuck Klein, Philadelphia	1933	.368	28	120
Joe Medwick, St. Louis	1937	.374	31*	154

*Tied for league lead in HRs with Mel Ott, NY.

American League

	Year	Avg	HR	RBI
Nap Lajoie, Philadelphia	1901	.422	14	125
Ty Cobb, Detroit	1909	.377	9	115
Jimmie Foxx, Philadelphia	1933	.356	48	163
Lou Gehrig, New York	1934	.363	49	165
Ted Williams, Boston	1942	.356	36	137
Ted Williams, Boston	1947	.343	32	114
Mickey Mantle, New York	1956	.353	52	130
Frank Robinson, Baltimore	1966	.316	49	122
Carl Yastrzemski, Boston	1967	.326	44*	121

*Tied for league lead in HRs with Harmon Killebrew, Min.

Stolen Bases
National League

Multiple winners: Max Carey (10); Lou Brock (8); Vince Coleman and Maury Wills (6); Honus Wagner (5); Bob Bescher, Kiki Cuyler, Willie Mays and Tim Raines (4); Bill Bruton, Frankie Frisch, Pepper Martin and Tony Womack (3); George Burns, Luis Castillo, Frank Chance, Augie Galan, Marquis Grissom, Stan Hack, Sam Jethroe, Davey Lopes, Omar Moreno, Pete Reiser and Jackie Robinson (2).

Year	SB	Year	SB	Year	SB
1900 Patsy Donovan, St.L	.45	1933 Pepper Martin, St.L	.26	1968 Lou Brock, St.L	.62
& George Van Haltren, NY	.45	1934 Pepper Martin, St.L	.23	1969 Lou Brock, St.L	.53
1901 Honus Wagner, Pit	.49	1935 Augie Galan, Chi	.22		
1902 Honus Wagner, Pit	.42	1936 Pepper Martin, St.L	.23	1970 Bobby Tolan, Cin	.57
1903 Frank Chance, Chi	.67	1937 Augie Galan, Chi	.23	1971 Lou Brock, St.L	.64
& Jimmy Sheckard, Bklyn	.67	1938 Stan Hack, Chi	.16	1972 Lou Brock, St.L	.63
1904 Honus Wagner, Pit	.53	1939 Stan Hack, Chi	.17	1973 Lou Brock, St.L	.70
1905 Art Devlin, NY	.59	& Lee Handley, Pit	.17	1974 Lou Brock, St.L	.118
& Billy Maloney, Chi	.59			1975 Davey Lopes, LA	.77
1906 Frank Chance, Chi	.57	1940 Lonny Frey, Cin	.22	1976 Davey Lopes, LA	.63
1907 Honus Wagner, Pit	.61	1941 Danny Murtaugh, Phi	.18	1977 Frank Taveras, Pit	.70
1908 Honus Wagner, Pit	.53	1942 Pete Reiser, Bklyn	.20	1978 Omar Moreno, Pit.	.71
1909 Bob Bescher, Cin	.54	1943 Arky Vaughan, Bklyn	.20	1979 Omar Moreno, Pit.	.77
		1944 Johnny Barrett, Pit	.28		
1910 Bob Bescher, Cin	.70	1945 Red Schoendienst, St.L	.26	1980 Ron LeFlore, Mon	.97
1911 Bob Bescher, Cin	.81	1946 Pete Reiser, Bklyn	.34	1981 Tim Raines, Mon	.71
1912 Bob Bescher, Cin	.67	1947 Jackie Robinson, Bklyn.	.29	1982 Tim Raines, Mon	.78
1913 Max Carey, Pit	.61	1948 Richie Ashburn, Phi.	.32	1983 Tim Raines, Mon	.90
1914 George Burns, NY	.62	1949 Jackie Robinson, Bklyn	.37	1984 Tim Raines, Mon	.75
1915 Max Carey, Pit	.36			1985 Vince Coleman, St.L.	.110
1916 Max Carey, Pit	.63	1950 Sam Jethroe, Bos.	.35	1986 Vince Coleman, St.L.	.107
1917 Max Carey, Pit	.46	1951 Sam Jethroe, Bos.	.35	1987 Vince Coleman, St.L.	.109
1918 Max Carey, Pit	.58	1952 Pee Wee Reese, Bklyn	.30	1988 Vince Coleman, St.L.	.81
1919 George Burns, NY	.40	1953 Bill Bruton, Mil.	.26	1989 Vince Coleman, St.L.	.65
		1954 Bill Bruton, Mil.	.34		
1920 Max Carey, Pit	.52	1955 Bill Bruton, Mil.	.25	1990 Vince Coleman, St.L.	.77
1921 Frankie Frisch, NY	.49	1956 Willie Mays, NY	.40	1991 Marquis Grissom, Mon	.76
1922 Max Carey, Pit	.51	1957 Willie Mays, NY	.38	1992 Marquis Grissom, Mon	.78
1923 Max Carey, Pit	.51	1958 Willie Mays, SF	.31	1993 Chuck Carr, Fla.	.58
1924 Max Carey, Pit	.49	1959 Willie Mays, SF	.27	1994 Craig Biggio, Hou	.39
1925 Max Carey, Pit	.46			1995 Quilvio Veras, Fla	.56
1926 Kiki Cuyler, Pit	.35	1960 Maury Wills, LA	.50	1996 Eric Young, Col	.53
1927 Frankie Frisch, St.L	.48	1961 Maury Wills, LA	.35	1997 Tony Womack, Pit	.60
1928 Kiki Cuyler, Chi	.37	1962 Maury Wills, LA	.104	1998 Tony Womack, Pit	.58
1929 Kiki Cuyler, Chi	.43	1963 Maury Wills, LA	.40	1999 Tony Womack, Ari	.72
		1964 Maury Wills, LA	.53		
1930 Kiki Cuyler, Chi	.37	1965 Maury Wills, LA	.94	2000 Luis Castillo, Fla	.62
1931 Frankie Frisch, St.L	.28	1966 Lou Brock, St.L	.74	2001 Juan Pierre, Col	.46
1932 Chuck Klein, Phi	.20	1967 Lou Brock, St.L	.52	& Jimmy Rollins, Phi	.46
				2002 Luis Castillo, Fla	.48

30 Homers & 30 Stolen Bases in One Season

National League

	Year	Gm	HR	SB
Willie Mays, NY Giants	1956	152	36	40
Willie Mays, NY Giants	1957	152	35	38
Hank Aaron, Milwaukee	1963	161	44	31
Bobby Bonds, San Francisco	1969	158	32	45
Bobby Bonds, San Francisco	1973	160	39	43
Dale Murphy, Atlanta	1983	162	36	30
Eric Davis, Cincinnati	1987	129	37	50
Howard Johnson, NY Mets	1987	157	36	32
Darryl Strawberry, NY Mets	1987	154	39	36
Howard Johnson, NY Mets	1989	153	36	41
Ron Gant, Atlanta	1990	152	32	33
Barry Bonds, Pittsburgh	1990	151	33	52
Ron Gant, Atlanta	1991	154	32	34
Howard Johnson, NY Mets	1991	156	38	30
Barry Bonds, Pittsburgh	1992	140	34	39
Sammy Sosa, Chicago	1993	159	33	36
Barry Bonds, San Francisco	1995	144	33	31
Sammy Sosa, Chicago	1995	144	36	34
Barry Bonds, San Francisco	1996	158	42	40
Ellis Burks, Colorado	1996	156	40	32
Dante Bichette, Colorado	1996	159	31	31
Barry Larkin, Cincinnati	1996	152	33	36

	Year	Gm	HR	SB
Larry Walker, Colorado	1997	153	49	33
Barry Bonds, San Francisco	1997	159	40	37
Raul Mondesi, Los Angeles	1997	159	30	32
Jeff Bagwell, Houston	1997	162	43	31
Jeff Bagwell, Houston	1999	162	42	30
Raul Mondesi, Los Angeles	1999	159	33	36
Preston Wilson, Florida	2000	161	31	36
Vladimir Guerrero, Montreal	2001	159	34	37
Bobby Abreu, Philadelphia	2001	162	31	36
Vladimir Guerrero, Montreal	2002	161	39	40

American League

	Year	Gm	HR	SB
Kenny Williams, St. Louis	1922	153	39	37
Tommy Harper, Milwaukee	1970	154	31	38
Bobby Bonds, New York	1975	145	32	30
Bobby Bonds, California	1977	158	37	41
Bobby Bonds, Chicago-Texas	1978	156	31	43
Joe Carter, Cleveland	1987	149	32	31
Jose Canseco, Oakland	1988	158	42	40
Alex Rodriguez, Seattle	1998	161	42	46
Shawn Green, Toronto	1998	158	35	35
Jose Cruz Jr., Toronto	2001	146	34	32
Alfonso Soriano, New York	2002	156	39	41

Stolen Bases (Cont.)
American League

Multiple winners: Rickey Henderson (12); Luis Aparicio (9); Bert Campaneris, George Case and Ty Cobb (6); Kenny Lofton (5); Ben Chapman, Eddie Collins and George Sisler (4); Bob Dillinger, Minnie Minoso and Bill Werber (3); Elmer Flick, Tommy Harper, Brian Hunter, Clyde Milan, Johnny Mostil, Bill North and Snuffy Stirnweiss (2).

Year		SB	Year		SB	Year		SB
1901	Frank Isbell, Chi	.52	1935	Bill Werber, Bos	.29	1969	Tommy Harper, Sea	.73
1902	Topsy Hartsel, Phi	.47	1936	Lyn Lary, St.L	.37			
1903	Harry Bay, Cle	.45	1937	Ben Chapman, Wash-Bos	..35	1970	Bert Campaneris, Oak	.42
1904	Elmer Flick, Cle	.42		& Bill Werber, Bos	.35	1971	Amos Otis, KC	.52
1905	Danny Hoffman, Phi	.46	1938	Frank Crosetti, NY	.27	1972	Bert Campaneris, Oak	.52
1906	John Anderson, Wash	.39	1939	George Case, Wash	.51	1973	Tommy Harper, Bos	.54
	& Elmer Flick, Cle	.39				1974	Bill North, Oak	.54
1907	Ty Cobb, Det	.49	1940	George Case, Wash	.35	1975	Mickey Rivers, CA	.70
1908	Patsy Dougherty, Chi	.47	1941	George Case, Wash	.33	1976	Bill North, Oak	.75
1909	Ty Cobb, Det	.76	1942	George Case, Wash	.44	1977	Freddie Patek, KC	.53
			1943	George Case, Wash	.61	1978	Ron LeFlore, Det	.68
1910	Eddie Collins, Phi	.81	1944	Snuffy Stirnweiss, NY	.55	1979	Willie Wilson, KC	.83
1911	Ty Cobb, Det	.83	1945	Snuffy Stirnweiss, NY	.33			
1912	Clyde Milan, Wash	.88	1946	George Case, Cle	.28	1980	Rickey Henderson, Oak	.100
1913	Clyde Milan, Wash	.75	1947	Bob Dillinger, St.L	.34	1981	Rickey Henderson, Oak	.56
1914	Fritz Maisel, NY	.74	1948	Bob Dillinger, St.L	.28	1982	Rickey Henderson, Oak	.130
1915	Ty Cobb, Det	.96	1949	Bob Dillinger, St.L	.20	1983	Rickey Henderson, Oak	.108
1916	Ty Cobb, Det	.68				1984	Rickey Henderson, Oak	.66
1917	Ty Cobb, Det	.55	1950	Dom DiMaggio, Bos	.15	1985	Rickey Henderson, NY	.80
1918	George Sisler, St.L	.45	1951	Minnie Minoso, Cle-Chi	.31	1986	Rickey Henderson, NY	.87
1919	Eddie Collins, Chi	.33	1952	Minnie Minoso, Chi	.22	1987	Harold Reynolds, Sea	.60
			1953	Minnie Minoso, Chi	.25	1988	Rickey Henderson, NY	.93
1920	Sam Rice, Wash	.63	1954	Jackie Jensen, Bos	.22	1989	R. Henderson, NY-Oak	.77
1921	George Sisler, St.L	.35	1955	Jim Rivera, Chi	.25			
1922	George Sisler, St.L	.51	1956	Luis Aparicio, Chi	.21	1990	Rickey Henderson, Oak	.65
1923	Eddie Collins, Chi	.47	1957	Luis Aparicio, Chi	.28	1991	Rickey Henderson, Oak	.58
1924	Eddie Collins, Chi	.42	1958	Luis Aparicio, Chi	.29	1992	Kenny Lofton, Cle	.66
1925	Johnny Mostil, Chi	.43	1959	Luis Aparicio, Chi	.56	1993	Kenny Lofton, Cle	.70
1926	Johnny Mostil, Chi	.35				1994	Kenny Lofton, Cle	.60
1927	George Sisler, St.L	.27	1960	Luis Aparicio, Chi	.51	1995	Kenny Lofton, Cle	.54
1928	Buddy Myer, Bos	.30	1961	Luis Aparicio, Chi	.53	1996	Kenny Lofton, Cle	.75
1929	Charlie Gehringer, Det	..28	1962	Luis Aparicio, Chi	.31	1997	Brian Hunter, Det	.74
			1963	Luis Aparicio, Bal	.40	1998	Rickey Henderson, Oak	.66
1930	Marty McManus, Det	.23	1964	Luis Aparicio, Bal	.57	1999	Brian Hunter, Det-Sea	.44
1931	Ben Chapman, NY	.61	1965	Bert Campaneris, KC	.51			
1932	Ben Chapman, NY	.38	1966	Bert Campaneris, KC	.52	2000	Johnny Damon, KC	.46
1933	Ben Chapman, NY	.27	1967	Bert Campaneris, KC	.55	2001	Ichiro Suzuki, Sea	.56
1934	Bill Werber, Bos	.40	1968	Bert Campaneris, Oak	.62	2002	Alfonso Soriano, NY	.41

Consecutive Game Streaks
Regular season games through 2002.

Games Played

Gm		Dates of Streak
2632	Cal Ripken Jr., Bal	.5/30/82 to 9/19/98
2130	Lou Gehrig, NY	.6/1/25 to 4/30/39
1307	Everett Scott, Bos-NY	.6/20/16 to 5/5/25
1207	Steve Garvey, LA-SD	.9/3/75 to 7/29/83
1117	Billy Williams, Cubs	.9/22/63 to 9/2/70
1103	Joe Sewell, Cle	.9/13/22 to 4/30/30
895	Stan Musial, St.L	.4/15/52 to 8/23/57
829	Eddie Yost, Wash	.4/30/49 to 5/11/55
822	Gus Suhr, Pit	.9/11/31 to 6/4/37
798	Nellie Fox, Chisox	.8/8/55 to 9/3/60
745	Pete Rose, Cin-Phi	.9/2/78 to 8/23/83
740	Dale Murphy, Atl	.9/26/81 to 7/8/86
730	Richie Ashburn, Phi	.6/7/50 to 4/13/55
717	Ernie Banks, Cubs	.8/28/56 to 6/22/61
678	Pete Rose, Cin	.9/28/73 to 5/7/78

Others

Gm			Gm	
673	Earl Averill		565	Aaron Ward
652	Frank McCormick		540	Candy LaChance
648	Sandy Alomar Sr.		535	Buck Freeman
618	Eddie Brown		533	Fred Luderus
585	Roy McMillan		511	Clyde Milan
577	George Pinckney		511	Charlie Gehringer
574	Steve Brodie		508	Vada Pinson

Hitting

	Gm	Year
Joe DiMaggio, New York (AL)	.56	1941
Willie Keeler, Baltimore (NL)	.44	1897
Pete Rose, Cincinnati (NL)	.44	1978
Bill Dahlen, Chicago (NL)	.42	1894
George Sisler, St. Louis (AL)	.41	1922
Ty Cobb, Detroit (AL)	.40	1911
Paul Molitor, Milwaukee (AL)	.39	1987
Tommy Holmes, Boston (NL)	.37	1945
Billy Hamilton, Philadelphia (NL)	.36	1894
Fred Clarke, Louisville (NL)	.35	1895
Ty Cobb, Detroit (AL)	.35	1917
Luis Castillo, Florida (NL)	.35	2002
Ty Cobb, Detroit (AL)	.34	1912
George Sisler, St. Louis (AL)	.34	1925
George McQuinn, St. Louis (AL)	.34	1938
Dom DiMaggio, Boston (AL)	.34	1949
Benito Santiago, San Diego (NL)	.34	1987
George Davis, New York (NL)	.33	1893
Hal Chase, New York (AL)	.33	1907
Rogers Hornsby, St. Louis (NL)	.33	1922
Heinie Manush, Washington (AL)	.33	1933
Ed Delahanty, Philadelphia (NL)	.31	1899
Nap Lajoie, Cleveland (AL)	.31	1906
Sam Rice, Washington (AL)	.31	1924
Willie Davis, Los Angeles (NL)	.31	1969
Rico Carty, Atlanta (NL)	.31	1970
Ken Landreaux, Minnesota (AL)	.31	1980
Vladimir Guerrero, Montreal (NL)	.31	1999

Annual Pitching Leaders (since 1900)

Winning Percentage

At least 15 wins, except in strike years of 1981 and 1994 (when the minimum was 10).

National League

Multiple winners: Ed Reulbach and Tom Seaver (3); Larry Benton, Harry Brecheen, Jack Chesbro, Paul Derringer, Freddie Fitzsimmons, Don Gullett, Claude Hendrix, Carl Hubbell, Randy Johnson, Sandy Koufax, Bill Lee, Greg Maddux, Christy Mathewson, Don Newcombe, Preacher Roe and John Smoltz (2).

Year		W-L	Pct	Year		W-L	Pct
1900	Jesse Tannehill, Pittsburgh	20-6	.769	1953	Carl Erskine, Brooklyn	20-6	.769
1901	Jack Chesbro, Pittsburgh	21-10	.677	1954	Johnny Antonelli, New York	21-7	.750
1902	Jack Chesbro, Pittsburgh	28-6	.824	1955	Don Newcombe, Brooklyn	20-5	.800
1903	Sam Leever, Pittsburgh	25-7	.781	1956	Don Newcombe, Brooklyn	27-7	.794
1904	Joe McGinnity, New York	35-8	.814	1957	Bob Buhl, Milwaukee	18-7	.720
1905	Christy Mathewson, New York	31-8	.795	1958	Warren Spahn, Milwaukee	22-11	.667
1906	Ed Reulbach, Chicago	19-4	.826		& Lew Burdette, Milwaukee	20-10	.667
1907	Ed Reulbach, Chicago	17-4	.810	1959	Roy Face, Pittsburgh	18-1	.947
1908	Ed Reulbach, Chicago	24-7	.774				
1909	Howie Camnitz, Pittsburgh	25-6	.806	1960	Ernie Broglio, St. Louis	21-9	.700
	& Christy Mathewson, New York	25-6	.806	1961	Johnny Podres, Los Angeles	18-5	.783
				1962	Bob Purkey, Cincinnati	23-5	.821
1910	King Cole, Chicago	20-4	.833	1963	Ron Perranoski, Los Angeles	16-3	.842
1911	Rube Marquard, New York	24-7	.774	1964	Sandy Koufax, Los Angeles	19-5	.792
1912	Claude Hendrix, Pittsburgh	24-9	.727	1965	Sandy Koufax, Los Angeles	26-8	.765
1913	Bert Humphries, Chicago	16-4	.800	1966	Juan Marichal, San Francisco	25-6	.806
1914	Bill James, Boston	26-7	.788	1967	Dick Hughes, St. Louis	16-6	.727
1915	Grover Alexander, Phila.	31-10	.756	1968	Steve Blass, Pittsburgh	18-6	.750
1916	Tom Hughes, Boston	16-3	.842	1969	Tom Seaver, New York	25-7	.781
1917	Ferdie Schupp, New York	21-7	.750				
1918	Claude Hendrix, Chicago	19-7	.731	1970	Bob Gibson, St. Louis	23-7	.767
1919	Dutch Ruether, Cincinnati	19-6	.760	1971	Don Gullett, Cincinnati	16-6	.727
				1972	Gary Nolan, Cincinnati	15-5	.750
1920	Burleigh Grimes, Brooklyn	23-11	.676	1973	Tommy John, Los Angeles	16-7	.696
1921	Bill Doak, St. Louis	15-6	.714	1974	Andy Messersmith, Los Angeles	20-6	.769
1922	Pete Donohue, Cincinnati	18-9	.667	1975	Don Gullett, Cincinnati	15-4	.789
1923	Dolf Luque, Cincinnati	27-8	.771	1976	Steve Carlton, Philadelphia	20-7	.741
1924	Emil Yde, Pittsburgh	16-3	.842	1977	John Candelaria, Pittsburgh	20-5	.800
1925	Bill Sherdel, St. Louis	15-6	.714	1978	Gaylord Perry, San Diego	21-6	.778
1926	Ray Kremer, Pittsburgh	20-6	.769	1979	Tom Seaver, Cincinnati	16-6	.727
1927	Larry Benton, Boston-NY	17-7	.708				
1928	Larry Benton, New York	25-9	.735	1980	Jim Bibby, Pittsburgh	19-6	.760
1929	Charlie Root, Chicago	19-6	.760	1981	Tom Seaver, Cincinnati	14-2	.875
				1982	Phil Niekro, Atlanta	17-4	.810
1930	Freddie Fitzsimmons, NY	19-7	.731	1983	John Denny, Philadelphia	19-6	.760
1931	Paul Derringer, St. Louis	18-8	.692	1984	Rick Sutcliffe, Chicago	16-1	.941
1932	Lon Warneke, Chicago	22-6	.786	1985	Orel Hershiser, Los Angeles	19-3	.864
1933	Ben Cantwell, Boston	20-10	.667	1986	Bob Ojeda, New York	18-5	.783
1934	Dizzy Dean, St. Louis	30-7	.811	1987	Dwight Gooden, New York	15-7	.682
1935	Bill Lee, Chicago	20-6	.769	1988	David Cone, New York	20-3	.870
1936	Carl Hubbell, New York	26-6	.813	1989	Mike Bielecki, Chicago	18-7	.720
1937	Carl Hubbell, New York	22-8	.733				
1938	Bill Lee, Chicago	22-9	.710	1990	Doug Drabek, Pittsburgh	22-6	.786
1939	Paul Derringer, Cincinnati	25-7	.781	1991	John Smiley, Pittsburgh	20-8	.714
					& Jose Rijo, Cincinnati	15-6	.714
1940	Freddie Fitzsimmons, Bklyn	16-2	.889	1992	Bob Tewksbury, St. Louis	16-5	.762
1941	Elmer Riddle, Cincinnati	19-4	.826	1993	Mark Portugal, Houston	18-4	.818
1942	Larry French, Brooklyn	15-4	.789	1994	Marvin Freeman, Colorado	10-2	.833
1943	Mort Cooper, St. Louis	21-8	.724	1995	Greg Maddux, Atlanta	19-2	.905
1944	Ted Wilks, St. Louis	17-4	.810	1996	John Smoltz, Atlanta	24-8	.750
1945	Harry Brecheen, St. Louis	14-4	.778	1997	Greg Maddux, Atlanta	19-4	.826
1946	Murray Dickson, St. Louis	15-6	.714	1998	John Smoltz, Atlanta	17-3	.850
1947	Larry Jansen, New York	21-5	.808	1999	Mike Hampton, Houston	22-4	.846
1948	Harry Brecheen, St. Louis	20-7	.741				
1949	Preacher Roe, Brooklyn	15-6	.714	2000	Randy Johnson, Arizona	19-7	.731
				2001	Curt Schilling, Arizona	22-6	.786
1950	Sal Maglie, New York	18-4	.818	2002	Randy Johnson, Arizona	24-5	.828
1951	Preacher Roe, Brooklyn	22-3	.880				
1952	Hoyt Wilhelm, New York	15-3	.833				

Note: In 1984, Sutcliffe was also 4-5 with Cleveland for a combined AL-NL record of 20-6 (.769).

Winning Percentage (Cont.)
American League

Multiple winners: Lefty Grove (5); Chief Bender, Roger Clemens and Whitey Ford (3); Johnny Allen, Eddie Cicotte, Mike Cuellar, Lefty Gomez, Ron Guidry, Catfish Hunter, Randy Johnson, Walter Johnson, Pedro Martinez, Jim Palmer, Pete Vuckovich and Smokey Joe Wood (2).

Year		W-L	Pct	Year		W-L	Pct
1901	Clark Griffith, Chicago	24-7	.774	1954	Sandy Consuegra, Chicago	16-3	.842
1902	Bill Bernhard, Phila-Cleve	18-5	.783	1955	Tommy Byrne, New York	16-5	.762
1903	Cy Young, Boston	28-9	.757	1956	Whitey Ford, New York	19-6	.760
1904	Jack Chesbro, New York	41-12	.774	1957	Dick Donovan, Chicago	16-6	.727
1905	Andy Coakley, Philadelphia	20-7	.741		& Tom Sturdivant, New York	16-6	.727
1906	Eddie Plank, Philadelphia	19-6	.760	1958	Bob Turley, New York	21-7	.750
1907	Wild Bill Donovan, Detroit	25-4	.862	1959	Bob Shaw, Chicago	18-6	.750
1908	Ed Walsh, Chicago	40-15	.727	1960	Jim Perry, Cleveland	18-10	.643
1909	George Mullin, Detroit	29-8	.784	1961	Whitey Ford, New York	25-4	.862
1910	Chief Bender, Philadelphia	23-5	.821	1962	Ray Herbert, Chicago	20-9	.690
1911	Chief Bender, Philadelphia	17-5	.773	1963	Whitey Ford, New York	24-7	.774
1912	Smokey Joe Wood, Boston	34-5	.872	1964	Wally Bunker, Baltimore	19-5	.792
1913	Walter Johnson, Washington	36-7	.837	1965	Mudcat Grant, Minnesota	21-7	.750
1914	Chief Bender, Philadelphia	17-3	.850	1966	Sonny Siebert, Cleveland	16-8	.667
1915	Smokey Joe Wood, Boston	15-5	.750	1967	Joe Horlen, Chicago	19-7	.731
1916	Eddie Cicotte, Chicago	15-7	.682	1968	Denny McLain, Detroit	31-6	.838
1917	Reb Russell, Chicago	15-5	.750	1969	Jim Palmer, Baltimore	16-4	.800
1918	Sad Sam Jones, Boston	16-5	.762	1970	Mike Cuellar, Baltimore	24-8	.750
1919	Eddie Cicotte, Chicago	29-7	.806	1971	Dave McNally, Baltimore	21-5	.808
1920	Jim Bagby, Cleveland	31-12	.721	1972	Catfish Hunter, Oakland	21-7	.750
1921	Carl Mays, New York	27-9	.750	1973	Catfish Hunter, Oakland	21-5	.808
1922	Joe Bush, New York	26-7	.788	1974	Mike Cuellar, Baltimore	22-10	.688
1923	Herb Pennock, New York	19-6	.760	1975	Mike Torrez, Baltimore	20-9	.690
1924	Walter Johnson, Washington	23-7	.767	1976	Bill Campbell, Minnesota	17-5	.773
1925	Stan Coveleski, Washington	20-5	.800	1977	Paul Splittorff, Kansas City	16-6	.727
1926	George Uhle, Cleveland	27-11	.711	1978	Ron Guidry, New York	25-3	.893
1927	Waite Hoyt, New York	22-7	.759	1979	Mike Caldwell, Milwaukee	16-6	.727
1928	General Crowder, St. Louis	21-5	.808	1980	Steve Stone, Baltimore	25-7	.781
1929	Lefty Grove, Philadelphia	20-6	.769	1981	Pete Vuckovich, Milwaukee	14-4	.778
1930	Lefty Grove, Philadelphia	28-5	.848	1982	Pete Vuckovich, Milwaukee	18-6	.750
1931	Lefty Grove, Philadelphia	31-4	.886		& Jim Palmer, Baltimore	15-5	.750
1932	Johnny Allen, New York	17-4	.810	1983	Rich Dotson, Chicago	22-7	.759
1933	Lefty Grove, Philadelphia	24-8	.750	1984	Doyle Alexander, Toronto	17-6	.739
1934	Lefty Gomez, New York	26-5	.839	1985	Ron Guidry, New York	22-6	.786
1935	Eldon Auker, Detroit	18-7	.720	1986	Roger Clemens, Boston	24-4	.857
1936	Monte Pearson, New York	19-7	.731	1987	Roger Clemens, Boston	20-9	.690
1937	Johnny Allen, Cleveland	15-1	.938	1988	Frank Viola, Minnesota	24-7	.774
1938	Red Ruffing, New York	21-7	.750	1989	Bret Saberhagen, Kansas City	23-6	.793
1939	Lefty Grove, Boston	15-4	.789	1990	Bob Welch, Oakland	27-6	.818
1940	Schoolboy Rowe, Detroit	16-3	.842	1991	Scott Erickson, Minnesota	20-8	.714
1941	Lefty Gomez, New York	15-5	.750	1992	Mike Mussina, Baltimore	18-5	.783
1942	Ernie Bonham, New York	21-5	.808	1993	Jimmy Key, New York	18-6	.750
1943	Spud Chandler, New York	20-4	.833	1994	Jason Bere, Chicago	12-2	.857
1944	Tex Hughson, Boston	18-5	.783	1995	Randy Johnson, Seattle	18-2	.900
1945	Hal Newhouser, Detroit	25-9	.735	1996	Charles Nagy, Cleveland	17-5	.773
1946	Boo Ferriss, Boston	25-6	.806	1997	Randy Johnson, Seattle	20-4	.833
1947	Allie Reynolds, New York	19-8	.704	1998	David Wells, New York	18-4	.818
1948	Jack Kramer, Boston	18-5	.783	1999	Pedro Martinez, Boston	23-4	.852
1949	Ellis Kinder, Boston	23-6	.793	2000	Tim Hudson, Oakland	20-6	.769
1950	Vic Raschi, New York	21-8	.724	2001	Roger Clemens, New York	20-3	.870
1951	Bob Feller, Cleveland	22-8	.733	2002	Pedro Martinez, Boston	20-4	.833
1952	Bobby Shantz, Philadelphia	24-7	.774				
1953	Ed Lopat, New York	16-4	.800				

Earned Run Average

Earned Run Averages were based on at least 10 complete games pitched (1900-49), at least 154 innings pitched (1950-60), and at least 162 innings pitched since 1961 in the AL and 1962 in the NL. In the strike years of 1981, '94 and '95, qualifiers had to pitch at least as many innings as the total number of games their team played that season.

National League

Multiple winners: Grover Alexander, Sandy Koufax and Christy Mathewson (5); Greg Maddux (4); Carl Hubbell, Randy Johnson, Tom Seaver, Warren Spahn and Dazzy Vance (3); Kevin Brown, Bill Doak, Ray Kremer, Dolf Luque, Howie Pollet, Nolan Ryan, Bill Walker and Bucky Walters (2).

Year		ERA	Year		ERA	Year		ERA
1900	Rube Waddell, Pit	2.37	1935	Cy Blanton, Pit	2.58	1970	Tom Seaver, NY	2.81
1901	Jesse Tannehill, Pit	2.18	1936	Carl Hubbell, NY	2.31	1971	Tom Seaver, NY	1.76
1902	Jack Taylor, Chi	1.33	1937	Jim Turner, Bos	2.38	1972	Steve Carlton, Phi	1.97
1903	Sam Leever, Pit	2.06	1938	Bill Lee, Chi	2.66	1973	Tom Seaver, NY	2.08
1904	Joe McGinnity, NY	1.61	1939	Bucky Walters, Cin	2.29	1974	Buzz Capra, Atl	2.28
1905	Christy Mathewson, NY	1.27	1940	Bucky Walters, Cin	2.48	1975	Randy Jones, SD	2.24
1906	Three Finger Brown, Chi	1.04	1941	Elmer Riddle, Cin	2.24	1976	John Denny, St.L	2.52
1907	Jack Pfiester, Chi	1.15	1942	Mort Cooper, St.L	1.78	1977	John Candelaria, Pit	2.34
1908	Christy Mathewson, NY	1.43	1943	Howie Pollet, St.L	1.75	1978	Craig Swan, NY	2.43
1909	Christy Mathewson, NY	1.14	1944	Ed Heusser, Cin	2.38	1979	J.R. Richard, Hou	2.71
1910	George McQuillan, Phi	1.60	1945	Hank Borowy, Chi	2.13	1980	Don Sutton, LA	2.21
1911	Christy Mathewson, NY	1.99	1946	Howie Pollet, St.L	2.10	1981	Nolan Ryan, Hou	1.69
1912	Jeff Tesreau, NY	1.96	1947	Warren Spahn, Bos	2.33	1982	Steve Rogers, Mon	2.40
1913	Christy Mathewson, NY	2.06	1948	Harry Brecheen, St.L	2.24	1983	Atlee Hammaker, SF	2.25
1914	Bill Doak, St.L	1.72	1949	Dave Koslo, NY	2.50	1984	Alejandro Peña, LA	2.48
1915	Grover Alexander, Phi	1.22	1950	Jim Hearn, St.L-NY	2.49	1985	Dwight Gooden, NY	1.53
1916	Grover Alexander, Phi	1.55	1951	Chet Nichols, Bos	2.88	1986	Mike Scott, Hou	2.22
1917	Grover Alexander, Phi	1.86	1952	Hoyt Wilhelm, NY	2.43	1987	Nolan Ryan, Hou	2.76
1918	Hippo Vaughn, Chi	1.74	1953	Warren Spahn, Mil	2.10	1988	Joe Magrane, St.L	2.18
1919	Grover Alexander, Chi	1.72	1954	Johnny Antonelli, NY	2.30	1989	Scott Garrelts, SF	2.28
1920	Grover Alexander, Chi	1.91	1955	Bob Friend, Pit	2.83	1990	Danny Darwin, Hou	2.21
1921	Bill Doak, St.L	2.59	1956	Lew Burdette, Mil	2.70	1991	Dennis Martinez, Mon	2.39
1922	Rosy Ryan, NY	3.01	1957	Johnny Podres, Bklyn	2.66	1992	Bill Swift, SF	2.08
1923	Dolf Luque, Cin	1.93	1958	Stu Miller, SF	2.47	1993	Greg Maddux, Atl	2.36
1924	Dazzy Vance, Bklyn	2.16	1959	Sam Jones, SF	2.83	1994	Greg Maddux, Atl	1.56
1925	Dolf Luque, Cin	2.63	1960	Mike McCormick, SF	2.70	1995	Greg Maddux, Atl	1.63
1926	Ray Kremer, Pit	2.61	1961	Warren Spahn, Mil	3.02	1996	Kevin Brown, Fla	1.89
1927	Ray Kremer, Pit	2.47	1962	Sandy Koufax, LA	2.54	1997	Pedro Martinez, Mon	1.90
1928	Dazzy Vance, Bklyn	2.09	1963	Sandy Koufax, LA	1.88	1998	Greg Maddux, Atl	2.22
1929	Bill Walker, NY	3.09	1964	Sandy Koufax, LA	1.74	1999	Randy Johnson, Ari	2.48
1930	Dazzy Vance, Bklyn	2.61	1965	Sandy Koufax, LA	2.04	2000	Kevin Brown, LA	2.58
1931	Bill Walker, NY	2.26	1966	Sandy Koufax, LA	1.73	2001	Randy Johnson, Ari	2.49
1932	Lon Warneke, Chi	2.37	1967	Phil Niekro, Atl	1.87	2002	Randy Johnson, Ari	2.32
1933	Carl Hubbell, NY	1.66	1968	Bob Gibson, St.L	1.12			
1934	Carl Hubbell, NY	2.30	1969	Juan Marichal, SF	2.10			

Note: In 1945, Borowy had a 3.13 ERA in 18 games with New York (AL) for a combined ERA of 2.65.

American League

Multiple winners: Lefty Grove (9); Roger Clemens (6); Walter Johnson (5); Pedro Martinez (3); Spud Chandler, Stan Coveleski, Red Faber, Whitey Ford, Lefty Gomez, Ron Guidry, Addie Joss, Hal Newhouser, Jim Palmer, Gary Peters, Luis Tiant and Ed Walsh (2).

Year		ERA	Year		ERA	Year		ERA
1901	Cy Young, Bos	1.62	1919	Walter Johnson, Wash	1.49	1937	Lefty Gomez, NY	2.33
1902	Ed Siever, Det	1.91	1920	Bob Shawkey, NY	2.45	1938	Lefty Grove, Bos	3.08
1903	Earl Moore, Cle	1.77	1921	Red Faber, Chi	2.48	1939	Lefty Grove, Bos	2.54
1904	Addie Joss, Cle	1.59	1922	Red Faber, Chi	2.80	1940	Ernie Bonham, NY	1.90
1905	Rube Waddell, Phi	1.48	1923	Stan Coveleski, Cle	2.76	1941	Thornton Lee, Chi	2.37
1906	Doc White, Chi	1.52	1924	Walter Johnson, Wash	2.72	1942	Ted Lyons, Chi	2.10
1907	Ed Walsh, Chi	1.60	1925	Stan Coveleski, Wash	2.84	1943	Spud Chandler, NY	1.64
1908	Addie Joss, Cle	1.16	1926	Lefty Grove, Phi	2.51	1944	Dizzy Trout, Det	2.12
1909	Harry Krause, Phi	1.39	1927	Wilcy Moore, NY	2.28	1945	Hal Newhouser, Det	1.81
1910	Ed Walsh, Chi	1.27	1928	Garland Braxton, Wash	2.51	1946	Hal Newhouser, Det	1.94
1911	Vean Gregg, Cle	1.81	1929	Lefty Grove, Phi	2.81	1947	Spud Chandler, NY	2.46
1912	Walter Johnson, Wash	1.39	1930	Lefty Grove, Phi	2.54	1948	Gene Bearden, Cle	2.43
1913	Walter Johnson, Wash	1.09	1931	Lefty Grove, Phi	2.06	1949	Mel Parnell, Bos	2.77
1914	Dutch Leonard, Bos	1.01	1932	Lefty Grove, Phi	2.84	1950	Early Wynn, Cle	3.20
1915	Smokey Joe Wood, Bos	1.49	1933	Monte Pearson, Cle	2.33	1951	Saul Rogovin, Det-Chi	2.78
1916	Babe Ruth, Bos	1.75	1934	Lefty Gomez, NY	2.33	1952	Allie Reynolds, NY	2.06
1917	Eddie Cicotte, Chi	1.53	1935	Lefty Grove, Bos	2.70	1953	Ed Lopat, NY	2.42
1918	Walter Johnson, Wash	1.27	1936	Lefty Grove, Bos	2.81	1954	Mike Garcia, Cle	2.64

Earned Run Average (Cont.)

Year	ERA	Year	ERA	Year	ERA
1955 Billy Pierce, Chi	1.97	1971 Vida Blue, Oak	1.82	1987 Jimmy Key, Tor	2.76
1956 Whitey Ford, NY	2.47	1972 Luis Tiant, Bos	1.91	1988 Allan Anderson, Min	2.45
1957 Bobby Shantz, NY	2.45	1973 Jim Palmer, Bal	2.40	1989 Bret Saberhagen, KC	2.16
1958 Whitey Ford, NY	2.01	1974 Catfish Hunter, Oak	2.49		
1959 Hoyt Wilhelm, Bal	2.19	1975 Jim Palmer, Bal	2.09	1990 Roger Clemens, Bos	1.93
		1976 Mark Fidrych, Det	2.34	1991 Roger Clemens, Bos	2.62
1960 Frank Baumann, Chi	2.67	1977 Frank Tanana, Cal	2.54	1992 Roger Clemens, Bos	2.41
1961 Dick Donovan, Wash	2.40	1978 Ron Guidry, NY	1.74	1993 Kevin Appier, KC	2.56
1962 Hank Aguirre, Det	2.21	1979 Ron Guidry, NY	2.78	1994 Steve Ontiveros, Oak	2.65
1963 Gary Peters, Chi	2.33			1995 Randy Johnson, Sea	2.48
1964 Dean Chance, LA	1.65	1980 Rudy May, NY	2.47	1996 Juan Guzman, Tor	2.93
1965 Sam McDowell, Cle	2.18	1981 Steve McCatty, Oak	2.32	1997 Roger Clemens, Tor	2.05
1966 Gary Peters, Chi	1.98	1982 Rick Sutcliffe, Cle	2.96	1998 Roger Clemens, Tor	2.65
1967 Joe Horlen, Chi	2.06	1983 Rick Honeycutt, Tex	2.42	1999 Pedro Martinez, Bos	2.07
1968 Luis Tiant, Cle	1.60	1984 Mike Boddicker, Bal	2.79		
1969 Dick Bosman, Wash	2.19	1985 Dave Stieb, Tor	2.48	2000 Pedro Martinez, Bos	1.74
		1986 Roger Clemens, Bos	2.48	2001 Freddy Garcia, Sea	3.05
1970 Diego Segui, Oak	2.56			2002 Pedro Martinez, Bos	2.26

Strikeouts

National League

Multiple winners: Dazzy Vance (7); Grover Alexander (6); Steve Carlton, Christy Mathewson and Tom Seaver (5); Dizzy Dean, Randy Johnson, Sandy Koufax and Warren Spahn (4); Don Drysdale, Sam Jones and Johnny Vander Meer (3); David Cone, Dwight Gooden, Bill Hallahan, J.R. Richard, Robin Roberts, Nolan Ryan, Curt Schilling, John Smoltz and Hippo Vaughn (2).

Year	SO	Year	SO	Year	SO
1900 Rube Waddell, Pit	130	1936 Van Lingle Mungo, Bklyn	238	1970 Tom Seaver, NY	283
1901 Noodles Hahn, Cin	239	1937 Carl Hubbell, NY	159	1971 Tom Seaver, NY	289
1902 Vic Willis, Bos	225	1938 Clay Bryant, Chi	135	1972 Steve Carlton, Phi	310
1903 Christy Mathewson, NY	267	1939 Claude Passeau, Phi-Chi	137	1973 Tom Seaver, NY	251
1904 Christy Mathewson, NY	212	& Bucky Walters, Cin	137	1974 Steve Carlton, Phi	240
1905 Christy Mathewson, NY	206			1975 Tom Seaver, NY	243
1906 Fred Beebe, Chi-St.L	171	1940 Kirby Higbe, Phi	137	1976 Tom Seaver, NY	235
1907 Christy Mathewson, NY	178	1941 John Vander Meer, Cin	202	1977 Phil Niekro, Atl	262
1908 Christy Mathewson, NY	259	1942 John Vander Meer, Cin	186	1978 J.R. Richard, Hou	303
1909 Orval Overall, Chi	205	1943 John Vander Meer, Cin	174	1979 J.R. Richard, Hou	313
		1944 Bill Voiselle, NY	161		
1910 Earl Moore, Phi	185	1945 Preacher Roe, Pit	148	1980 Steve Carlton, Phi	286
1911 Rube Marquard, NY	237	1946 Johnny Schmitz, Chi	135	1981 F. Valenzuela, LA	180
1912 Grover Alexander, Phi	195	1947 Ewell Blackwell, Cin	193	1982 Steve Carlton, Phi	286
1913 Tom Seaton, Phi	168	1948 Harry Brecheen, St.L	149	1983 Steve Carlton, Phi	275
1914 Grover Alexander, Phi	214	1949 Warren Spahn, Bos	151	1984 Dwight Gooden, NY	276
1915 Grover Alexander, Phi	241			1985 Dwight Gooden, NY	268
1916 Grover Alexander, Phi	167	1950 Warren Spahn, Bos	191	1986 Mike Scott, Hou	306
1917 Grover Alexander, Phi	201	1951 Don Newcombe, Bklyn	164	1987 Nolan Ryan, Hou	270
1918 Hippo Vaughn, Chi	148	& Warren Spahn, Bos	164	1988 Nolan Ryan, Hou	228
1919 Hippo Vaughn, Chi	141	1952 Warren Spahn, Bos	183	1989 Jose DeLeon, St.L	201
		1953 Robin Roberts, Phi	198		
1920 Grover Alexander, Chi	173	1954 Robin Roberts, Phi	185	1990 David Cone, NY	233
1921 Burleigh Grimes, Bklyn	136	1955 Sam Jones, Chi	198	1991 David Cone, NY	241
1922 Dazzy Vance, Bklyn	134	1956 Sam Jones, Chi	176	1992 John Smoltz, Atl	215
1923 Dazzy Vance, Bklyn	197	1957 Jack Sanford, Phi	188	1993 Jose Rijo, Cin	227
1924 Dazzy Vance, Bklyn	262	1958 Sam Jones, St.L	225	1994 Andy Benes, SD	189
1925 Dazzy Vance, Bklyn	221	1959 Don Drysdale, LA	242	1995 Hideo Nomo, LA	236
1926 Dazzy Vance, Bklyn	140			1996 John Smoltz, Atl	276
1927 Dazzy Vance, Bklyn	184	1960 Don Drysdale, LA	246	1997 Curt Schilling, Phi	319
1928 Dazzy Vance, Bklyn	200	1961 Sandy Koufax, LA	269	1998 Curt Schilling, Phi	300
1929 Pat Malone, Chi	166	1962 Don Drysdale, LA	232	1999 Randy Johnson, Ari	364
		1963 Sandy Koufax, LA	306		
1930 Bill Hallahan, St.L	177	1964 Bob Veale, Pit	250	2000 Randy Johnson, Ari	347
1931 Bill Hallahan, St.L	159	1965 Sandy Koufax, LA	382	2001 Randy Johnson, Ari	372
1932 Dizzy Dean, St.L	191	1966 Sandy Koufax, LA	317	2002 Randy Johnson, Ari	334
1933 Dizzy Dean, St.L	199	1967 Jim Bunning, Phi	253		
1934 Dizzy Dean, St.L	195	1968 Bob Gibson, St.L	268		
1935 Dizzy Dean, St.L	190	1969 Ferguson Jenkins, Chi	273		

American League

Multiple winners: Walter Johnson (12); Nolan Ryan (9); Bob Feller and Lefty Grove (7); Rube Waddell (6); Roger Clemens and Sam McDowell (5); Randy Johnson (4); Lefty Gomez, Mark Langston, Pedro Martinez and Camilo Pascual (3); Len Barker, Tommy Bridges, Jim Bunning, Hal Newhouser, Allie Reynolds, Herb Score, Ed Walsh and Early Wynn (2).

Year	SO	Year	SO	Year	SO
1901 Cy Young, Bos	158	1937 Lefty Gomez, NY	194	1971 Mickey Lolich, Det	308
1902 Rube Waddell, Phi	210	1938 Bob Feller, Cle	240	1972 Nolan Ryan, Cal	329
1903 Rube Waddell, Phi	302	1939 Bob Feller, Cle	246	1973 Nolan Ryan, Cal	383
1904 Rube Waddell, Phi	349			1974 Nolan Ryan, Cal	367
1905 Rube Waddell, Phi	287	1940 Bob Feller, Cle	261	1975 Frank Tanana, Cal	269
1906 Rube Waddell, Phi	196	1941 Bob Feller, Cle	260	1976 Nolan Ryan, Cal	327
1907 Rube Waddell, Phi	232	1942 Tex Hughson, Bos	113	1977 Nolan Ryan, Cal	341
1908 Ed Walsh, Chi	269	& Bobo Newsom, Wash	113	1978 Nolan Ryan, Cal	260
1909 Frank Smith, Chi	177	1943 Allie Reynolds, Cle	151	1979 Nolan Ryan, Cal	223
		1944 Hal Newhouser, Det	187		
1910 Walter Johnson, Wash	313	1945 Hal Newhouser, Det	212	1980 Len Barker, Cle	187
1911 Ed Walsh, Chi	255	1946 Bob Feller, Cle	348	1981 Len Barker, Cle	127
1912 Walter Johnson, Wash	303	1947 Bob Feller, Cle	196	1982 Floyd Bannister, Sea	209
1913 Walter Johnson, Wash	243	1948 Bob Feller, Cle	164	1983 Jack Morris, Det	232
1914 Walter Johnson, Wash	225	1949 Virgil Trucks, Det	153	1984 Mark Langston, Sea	204
1915 Walter Johnson, Wash	203			1985 Bert Blyleven, Cle-Min	206
1916 Walter Johnson, Wash	228	1950 Bob Lemon, Cle	170	1986 Mark Langston, Sea	245
1917 Walter Johnson, Wash	188	1951 Vic Raschi, NY	164	1987 Mark Langston, Sea	262
1918 Walter Johnson, Wash	162	1952 Allie Reynolds, NY	160	1988 Roger Clemens, Bos	291
1919 Walter Johnson, Wash	147	1953 Billy Pierce, Chi	186	1989 Nolan Ryan, Tex	301
		1954 Bob Turley, Bal	185		
1920 Stan Coveleski, Cle	133	1955 Herb Score, Cle	245	1990 Nolan Ryan, Tex	232
1921 Walter Johnson, Wash	143	1956 Herb Score, Cle	263	1991 Roger Clemens, Bos	241
1922 Urban Shocker, St.L	149	1957 Early Wynn, Cle	184	1992 Randy Johnson, Sea	241
1923 Walter Johnson, Wash	130	1958 Early Wynn, Chi	179	1993 Randy Johnson, Sea	308
1924 Walter Johnson, Wash	158	1959 Jim Bunning, Det	201	1994 Randy Johnson, Sea	204
1925 Lefty Grove, Phi	116			1995 Randy Johnson, Sea	294
1926 Lefty Grove, Phi	194	1960 Jim Bunning, Det	201	1996 Roger Clemens, Bos	257
1927 Lefty Grove, Phi	174	1961 Camilo Pascual, Min	221	1997 Roger Clemens, Tor	292
1928 Lefty Grove, Phi	183	1962 Camilo Pascual, Min	206	1998 Roger Clemens, Tor	271
1929 Lefty Grove, Phi	170	1963 Camilo Pascual, Min	202	1999 Pedro Martinez, Bos	313
		1964 Al Downing, NY	217		
1930 Lefty Grove, Phi	209	1965 Sam McDowell, Cle	325	2000 Pedro Martinez, Bos	284
1931 Lefty Grove, Phi	175	1966 Sam McDowell, Cle	225	2001 Hideo Nomo, Bos	220
1932 Red Ruffing, NY	190	1967 Jim Lonborg, Bos	246	2002 Pedro Martinez, Bos	239
1933 Lefty Gomez, NY	163	1968 Sam McDowell, Cle	283		
1934 Lefty Gomez, NY	158				
1935 Tommy Bridges, Det	163	1969 Sam McDowell, Cle	279		
1936 Tommy Bridges, Det	175	1970 Sam McDowell, Cle	304		

Pitching Triple Crown Winners

Pitchers who led either league in Earned Run Average, Wins and Strikeouts over a single season.

National League

	Year	ERA	W-L	SO
Tommy Bond, Bos	1877	2.11	40-17	170
Hoss Radbourn, Prov	1884	1.38	60-12	441
Tim Keefe, NY	1888	1.74	35-12	333
John Clarkson, Bos	1889	2.73	49-19	284
Amos Rusie, NY	1894	2.78	36-13	195
Christy Mathewson, NY	1905	1.27	31-8	206
Christy Mathewson, NY	1908	1.43	37-11	259
Grover Alexander, Phi	1915	1.22	31-10	241
Grover Alexander, Phi	1916	1.55	33-12	167
Grover Alexander, Phi	1917	1.86	30-13	201
Hippo Vaughn, Chi	1918	1.74	22-10	148
Grover Alexander, Chi	1920	1.91	27-14	173
Dazzy Vance, Bklyn	1924	2.16	28-6	262
Bucky Walters, Cin	1939	2.29	27-11	137
Sandy Koufax, LA	1963	1.88	25-5	306
Sandy Koufax, LA	1965	2.04	26-8	382
Sandy Koufax, LA	1966	1.73	27-9	317
Steve Carlton, Phi	1972	1.97	27-10	310
Dwight Gooden, NY	1985	1.53	24-4	268
Randy Johnson, Ari	2002	2.32	24-5	334

Ties: In 1894, Rusie tied for league lead in wins with Jouett Meekin, NY (36-10); in 1939, Walters tied for league lead in strikeouts with Claude Passeau, Phi-Chi; in 1963, Koufax tied for the league lead in wins with Juan Marichal, SF.

American League

	Year	ERA	W-L	SO
Cy Young, Bos	1901	1.62	33-10	158
Rube Waddell, Phi	1905	1.48	26-11	287
Walter Johnson, Wash	1913	1.09	36-7	243
Walter Johnson, Wash	1918	1.27	23-13	162
Walter Johnson, Wash	1924	2.72	23-7	158
Lefty Grove, Phi	1930	2.54	28-5	209
Lefty Grove, Phi	1931	2.06	31-4	175
Lefty Gomez, NY	1934	2.33	26-5	158
Lefty Gomez, NY	1937	2.33	21-11	194
Hal Newhouser, Det	1945	1.81	25-9	212
Roger Clemens, Tor	1997	2.05	21-7	292
Roger Clemens, Tor	1998	2.65	20-6	271
Pedro Martinez, Bos	1999	2.07	23-4	313

Ties: In 1998, Clemens tied for league lead in wins with David Cone, NY (20-7) and Rick Helling, Tex (20-7).

Saves

The "save" was created by Chicago baseball writer Jerome Holtzman in the 1960's and accepted as an official statistic by the Official Rules Committee of Major League Baseball in 1969. From 1973-74, a save was credited to a pitcher who finished a game his team won. From 1973-74, a save was credited to a pitcher who finished a game his team won with the tying or winning run on base or at bat. Since 1975 a pitcher has been credited with a save when he meets all three of the following conditions:

(1) He is the finishing pitcher in a game won by his club; (2) He is not the winning pitcher; (3) He qualifies under one of the following conditions: (a) He enters the game with a lead of no more than three runs and pitches for at least one inning; (b) He enters the game, regardless of the count, with the potential tying run either on base, or at bat, or on deck (that is, the potential tying run is either already on base or is one of the first two batsmen he faces); (c) He pitches effectively for at least three innings. No more than one save may be credited in each game.

National League

Multiple winners: Bruce Sutter (5); John Franco and Lee Smith (3); Rawly Eastwick, Rollie Fingers, Mike Marshall, Randy Myers and Todd Worrell (2).

Year		Svs	Year		Svs	Year		Svs
1969	Fred Gladding, Hou	29	1980	Bruce Sutter, Chi	28	1992	Lee Smith, St.L	43
			1981	Bruce Sutter, St.L	25	1993	Randy Myers, Chi	53
1970	Wayne Granger, Cin	35	1982	Bruce Sutter, St.L	36	1994	John Franco, NY	30
1971	Dave Giusti, Pit	30	1983	Lee Smith, Chi	29	1995	Randy Myers, Chi	38
1972	Clay Carroll, Cin	37	1984	Bruce Sutter, St.L	45	1996	Jeff Brantley, Cin	44
1973	Mike Marshall, Mon	31	1985	Jeff Reardon, Mon	41		& Todd Worrell, LA	44
1974	Mike Marshall, LA	21	1986	Todd Worrell, St.L	36	1997	Jeff Shaw, Cin	42
1975	Rawly Eastwick, Cin	22	1987	Steve Bedrosian, Phi	40	1998	Trevor Hoffman, SD	53
	& Al Hrabosky, St.L	22	1988	John Franco, Cin	39	1999	Ugueth Urbina, Mon	41
1976	Rawly Eastwick, Cin	26	1989	Mark Davis, SD	44			
1977	Rollie Fingers, SD	35				2000	Antonio Alfonseca, Fla	45
1978	Rollie Fingers, SD	37	1990	John Franco, NY	33	2001	Robb Nen, SF	45
1979	Bruce Sutter, Chi	37	1991	Lee Smith, St.L	47	2002	John Smoltz, Atl	55

American League

Multiple winners: Dan Quisenberry (5); Rich Gossage (3); Dennis Eckersley, Sparky Lyle, Ron Perranoski and Mariano Rivera (2).

Year		Svs	Year		Svs	Year		Svs
1969	Ron Perranoski, Min	31	1981	Rollie Fingers, Mil	28	1993	Jeff Montgomery, KC	45
			1982	Dan Quisenberry, KC	35		& Duane Ward, Tor	45
1970	Ron Perranoski, Min	34	1983	Dan Quisenberry, KC	45	1994	Lee Smith, Bal	33
1971	Ken Sanders, Mil	31	1984	Dan Quisenberry, KC	44	1995	Jose Mesa, Cle	46
1972	Sparky Lyle, NY	35	1985	Dan Quisenberry, KC	37	1996	John Wetteland, NY	43
1973	John Hiller, Det	38	1986	Dave Righetti, NY	46	1997	Randy Myers, Bal	45
1974	Terry Forster, Chi	24	1987	Tom Henke, Tor	34	1998	Tom Gordon, Bos	46
1975	Rich Gossage, Chi	26	1988	Dennis Eckersley, Oak	45	1999	Mariano Rivera, NY	45
1976	Sparky Lyle, NY	23	1989	Jeff Russell, Tex	38			
1977	Bill Campbell, Bos	31				2000	Todd Jones, Det	42
1978	Rich Gossage, NY	27	1990	Bobby Thigpen, Chi	57		& Derek Lowe, Bos	42
1979	Mike Marshall, Min	32	1991	Bryan Harvey, Cal	46	2001	Mariano Rivera, NY	50
			1992	Dennis Eckersley, Oak	51	2002	Eddie Guardado, Min	45
1980	Rich Gossage, NY	33						
	& Dan Quisenberry, KC	33						

Perfect Games

Seventeen pitchers have thrown perfect games (27 up, 27 down) in major league history. However, the game pitched by Ernie Shore is not considered to be official.

National League

	Game	Date	Score
Lee Richmond	Wor. vs Cle.	6/12/1880	1-0
Monte Ward	Prov. vs Bos.	6/17/1880	5-0
Jim Bunning	Phi. at NY	6/21/1964	6-0
Sandy Koufax	LA vs Chi.	9/9/1965	1-0
Tom Browning	Cin. vs LA	9/16/1988	1-0
Dennis Martinez	Mon. at LA	7/28/1991	2-0

Note: Pittsburgh's Harvey Haddix pitched 12 perfect innings against the Milwaukee Braves on May 26, 1959 before losing, 1-0, in the 13th. Braves' lead-off batter Felix Mantilla reached on a throwing error by Pirates 3B Don Hoak, Eddie Mathews sacrificed Mantilla to 2nd, Hank Aaron was walked intentionally, and Joe Adcock hit a 3-run HR. Adcock, however, passed Aaron on the bases and was only credited with a 1-run double.

Note: Montreal's Pedro Martinez pitched nine perfect innings against the San Diego Padres on June 3, 1995 before surrendering a leadoff double to Bip Roberts in the 10th. He was then relieved by Mel Rojas, who finished the game, which Montreal won, 1-0.

American League

	Game	Date	Score
Cy Young	Bos. vs Phi.	5/5/1904	3-0
Addie Joss	Cle. vs Chi.	10/2/1908	1-0
Ernie Shore	Bos. vs Wash.	6/23/1917	4-0*
Charlie Robertson	Chi. at Det.	4/30/1922	2-0
Catfish Hunter	Oak. vs Min.	5/8/1968	4-0
Len Barker	Cle. vs Tor.	5/15/1981	3-0
Mike Witt	Cal. at Tex.	9/30/1984	1-0
Kenny Rogers	Tex. vs Cal.	7/28/1994	4-0
David Wells	NY vs Min.	5/17/1998	4-0
David Cone	NY vs Mon.	7/18/1999	6-0

*Babe Ruth started for Boston, walking Senators' lead-off batter Ray Morgan, then was thrown out of game by umpire Brick Owens for arguing the call. Shore came on in relief. Morgan was caught stealing and Shore retired the next 26 batters in a row. While technically not a perfect game—since he didn't start—Shore gets credit anyway.

World Series

Pitcher	Game	Date	Score
Don Larsen	NY vs Bklyn	10/8/1956	2-0

No-Hit Games

Nine innings or more, including perfect games, since 1876. Losing pitchers in **bold** type. **Multiple no-hitters:** Nolan Ryan (7); Sandy Koufax (4); Larry Cocoran, Bob Feller and Cy Young (3); Jim Bunning, Steve Busby, Carl Erskine, Bob Forsch, Pud Galvin, Ken Holtzman, Addie Joss, Hub Leonard, Jim Maloney, Christy Mathewson, Hideo Nomo, Allie Reynolds, Warren Spahn, Bill Stoneham, Virgil Trucks, Johnny Vander Meer and Don Wilson (2).

National League

Year	Date	Pitcher	Result	Year	Date	Pitcher	Result
1876	7/15	George Bradley	St.L vs Har, 2-0	1960	5/15	Don Cardwell	Chi vs St.L, 4-0
1880	6/12	Lee Richmond	Wor vs Cle, 1-0 (perfect game)		8/18	Lew Burdette	Mil vs Phi, 1-0
					9/16	Warren Spahn	Mil vs Phi, 4-0
	6/17	Monte Ward	Prov vs Buf, 5-0 (perfect game)	1961	4/28	Warren Spahn	Mil vs SF, 1-0
				1962	6/30	Sandy Koufax	LA vs NY, 5-0
	8/19	Larry Corcoran	Chi vs Bos, 6-0	1963	5/11	Sandy Koufax	LA vs SF, 1-0
	8/20	Pud Galvin	Buf at Wor, 1-0		5/17	Don Nottebart	Hou vs Phi, 4-1
1882	9/20	Larry Corcoran	Chi vs Wor, 1-0		6/15	Juan Marichal	SF vs Hou, 1-0
1883	7/25	Old Hoss Radbourn	Prov at Cle, 8-0	1964	4/23	**Ken Johnson**	Hou vs Cin, 0-1
	9/13	Hugh Daily	Cle at Phi, 1-0		6/4	Sandy Koufax	LA at Phi, 3-0
1884	6/27	Larry Cocoran	Chi vs Prov, 6-0		6/21	Jim Bunning	Phi at NY, 6-0 (perfect game)
	8/4	Pud Galvin	Buf at Det, 18-0				
1885	7/27	John Clarkson	Chi vs Prov, 6-0	1965	8/19	Jim Maloney	Cin at Chi, 1-0 (10)
	8/29	Charlie Ferguson	Phi vs Prov, 1-0		9/9	Sandy Koufax	LA vs Chi, 1-0 (perfect game)
1891	6/22	Tom Lovett	Bklyn vs NY, 4-0				
	7/31	Amos Rusie	NY vs Bklyn, 11-0	1967	6/18	Don Wilson	Hou vs Atl, 2-0
1892	8/6	John Stivetts	Bos vs Bklyn, 11-0	1968	7/29	George Culver	Cin at Phi, 6-1
	8/22	Ben Sanders	Lou vs Bal, 6-2		9/17	Gaylord Perry	SF vs St.L, 1-0
	10/22	Bumpus Jones	Cin vs Pit, 7-1 (1st major league game)		9/18	Ray Washburn	St.L at SF, 2-0 (next day, same park)
1893	8/16	Bill Hawke	Bal vs Wash, 5-0	1969	4/17	Bill Stoneman	Mon at Phi, 7-0
1897	9/18	Cy Young	Cle vs Cin, 6-0		4/30	Jim Maloney	Cin vs Hou, 10-0
1898	4/22	Ted Breitenstein	Cin vs Pit, 11-0		5/1	Don Wilson	Hou at Cin, 4-0
	4/22	Jim Hughes	Bal vs Bos, 8-0		8/19	Ken Holtzman	Chi vs Atl, 3-0
	7/8	Frank Donahue	Phi vs Bos, 5-0		9/20	Bob Moose	Pit at NY, 4-0
	8/21	Walter Thornton	Chi vs Bklyn, 2-0	1970	6/12	Dock Ellis	Pit at SD, 2-0
1899	5/25	Deacon Phillippe	Lou vs NY, 7-0		7/20	Bill Singer	LA vs Phi, 5-0
1900	7/12	Noodles Hahn	Cin vs Phi, 4-0	1971	6/3	Ken Holtzman	Chi at Cin, 1-0
1901	7/15	Christy Mathewson	NY vs St.L, 5-0		6/23	Rick Wise	Phi at Cin, 4-0
1903	9/18	Chick Fraser	Phi at Chi, 10-0		8/14	Bob Gibson	St.L at Pit, 11-0
1905	6/13	Christy Mathewson	NY at Chi, 1-0	1972	4/16	Burt Hooton	Chi vs Phi, 4-0
1906	5/1	John Lush	Phi at Bklyn, 1-0		9/2	Milt Pappas	Chi vs SD, 8-0
	7/20	Mal Eason	Bklyn at St.L, 2-0		10/2	Bill Stoneman	Mon vs NY, 7-0
1907	5/8	Frank Pfeffer	Bos vs Cin, 6-0	1973	8/5	Phil Niekro	Atl vs SD, 9-0
	9/20	Nick Maddox	Pit vs Bkn, 2-1	1975	8/24	Ed Halicki	SF vs NY, 6-0
1908	7/4	Hooks Wiltse	NY vs Phi, 1-0 (10)	1976	7/9	Larry Dierker	Hou vs Mon, 6-0
	9/5	Nap Rucker	Bklyn vs Bos, 6-0		8/9	John Candelaria	Pit vs LA, 2-0
1912	9/6	Jeff Tesreau	NY at Phi, 3-0		9/29	John Montefusco	SF vs Atl, 9-0
1914	9/9	George Davis	Bos vs Phi, 7-0	1978	4/16	Bob Forsch	St.L vs Phi, 5-0
1915	4/15	Rube Marquard	NY vs Bklyn, 2-0		6/16	Tom Seaver	Cin vs St.L, 4-0
	8/31	Jimmy Lavender	Chi at N.Y, 2-0	1979	4/7	Ken Forsch	Hou vs Atl, 6-0
1916	6/16	Tom Hughes	Bos vs. Pit, 2-0	1980	6/27	Jerry Reuss	LA at SF, 4-0
1917	5/2	Fred Toney	Cin at Chi, 1-0 (10)	1981	5/10	Charlie Lea	Mon vs SF, 4-0
1919	5/11	Hod Eller	Cin at St.L, 6-0		9/26	Nolan Ryan	Hou vs LA, 5-0
1922	5/7	Jesse Barnes	NY vs Phi, 6-0	1983	9/26	Bob Forsch	St.L vs Mon, 3-0
1924	7/17	Jesse Haines	St.L vs Bos, 5-0	1986	9/25	Mike Scott	Hou vs SF, 2-0
1925	9/17	Dazzy Vance	Bklyn vs Phi, 10-1	1988	9/16	Tom Browning	Cin vs LA, 1-0 (perfect game)
1929	5/8	Carl Hubbell	NY vs Pit, 2-0				
1934	9/21	Paul Dean	St.L vs Bklyn, 3-0	1990	6/29	Fernando Valenzuela	LA vs St.L, 6-0
1938	6/11	Johnny Vander Meer	Cin vs Bos, 3-0		8/15	Terry Mulholland	Phi vs SF, 6-0
	6/15	Johnny Vander Meer	Cin vs Bklyn, 6-0 (consecutive starts)	1991	5/23	Tommy Greene	Phi at Mon, 2-0
					7/28	Dennis Martinez	Mon at LA, 2-0 (perfect game)
1940	4/30	Tex Carleton	Bklyn at Cin, 3-0				
1941	8/30	Lon Warneke	St.L at Cin, 2-0		9/11	Kent Mercker (6), Mark Wohlers (2) & Alejandro Peña (1)	Atl vs SD, 1-0 (combined no-hitter)
1944	4/27	Jim Tobin	Bos vs Bklyn, 2-0				
	5/15	Clyde Shoun	Cin vs Bos, 1-0				
1946	4/23	Ed Head	Bklyn at NY, 2-0	1992	8/17	Kevin Gross	LA vs SF, 2-0
1947	6/18	Ewell Blackwell	Cin vs Bos, 6-0	1993	9/8	Darryl Kile	Hou vs NY, 7-1
1948	9/9	Rex Barney	Bklyn at NY, 2-0	1994	4/8	Kent Mercker	Atl at LA, 6-0
1950	8/11	Vern Bickford	Bos vs Bklyn, 7-0	1995	7/14	Ramon Martinez	LA vs Fla, 7-0
1951	5/6	Cliff Chambers	Pit at Bos, 3-0	1996	5/11	Al Leiter	Fla vs Col, 11-0
1952	6/19	Carl Erskine	Bklyn vs Chi, 5-0		9/17	Hideo Nomo	LA at Col, 9-0
1954	6/12	Jim Wilson	Mil vs Phi, 2-0	1997	6/10	Kevin Brown	Fla at SF, 9-0
1955	5/12	Sam Jones	Chi vs Pit, 4-0		7/12	Francisco Cordova (9) Ricardo Rincon (1)	Pit vs. Hou, 3-0 (10 inn.) (combined no-hitter)
1956	5/12	Carl Erskine	Bklyn vs NY, 3-0				
	9/25	Sal Maglie	Bklyn vs Phi, 5-0	1999	6/25	Jose Jimenez	St.L vs Ari, 1-0
				2001	5/12	A.J. Burnett	Fla vs SD, 3-0
					9/3	Bud Smith	St.L vs SD, 4-0

No-Hit Games (Cont.)
American League

Year	Date	Pitcher	Result
1902	9/20	Jimmy Callahan	Chi vs Det, 3-0
1904	5/5	Cy Young	Bos vs Phi, 3-0 (perfect game)
	8/17	Jesse Tannehill	Bos vs Chi, 6-0
1905	7/22	Weldon Henley	Phi at St. L, 6-0
	9/6	Frank Smith	Chi at Det, 15-0
	9/27	Bill Dinneen	Bos vs Chi, 2-0
1908	6/30	Cy Young	Bos at NY, 8-0
	9/18	Dusty Rhoades	Cle vs Bos, 2-0
	9/20	Frank Smith	Chi vs Phi, 1-0
	10/2	Addie Joss	Cle vs Chi, 1-0 (perfect game)
1910	4/20	Addie Joss	Cle at Chi, 1-0
	5/12	Chief Bender	Phi vs Cle, 4-0
1911	7/19	Smokey Joe Wood	Bos vs St. L, 5-0
	8/27	Ed Walsh	Chi vs Bos, 5-0
1912	7/4	George Mullin	Det vs St. L, 7-0
	8/30	Earl Hamilton	St. L at Det, 5-1
1914	5/31	Joe Benz	Chi vs Cle, 6-1
1916	6/16	Rube Foster	Bos vs NY, 2-0
	8/26	Joe Bush	Phi vs Cle, 5-0
	8/30	Hub Leonard	Bos vs St. L, 4-0
1917	4/14	Ed Cicotte	Chi at St. L, 11-0
	4/24	George Mogridge	NY at Bos, 2-1
	5/5	Ernie Koob	St. L vs Chi, 1-0
	5/6	Bob Groom	St. L vs Chi, 3-0
	6/23	Babe Ruth (0) & Ernie Shore (9)	Bos vs Wash, 4-0 (combined no-hitter)
1918	6/3	Hub Leonard	Bos at Det, 5-0
1919	9/10	Ray Caldwell	Cle at NY, 3-0
1920	7/1	Walter Johnson	Wash at Bos, 1-0
1922	4/30	Charlie Robertson	Chi at Det, 2-0 (perfect game)
1923	9/4	Sam Jones	NY at Phi, 2-0
	9/7	Howard Ehmke	Bos at Phi, 4-0
1926	8/21	Ted Lyons	Chi at Bos, 6-0
1931	4/29	Wes Ferrell	Cle vs St. L, 9-0
	8/8	Bob Burke	Wash vs Bos, 5-0
1935	8/31	Vern Kennedy	Chi vs Cle, 5-0
1937	6/1	Bill Dietrich	Chi vs St. L, 8-0
1938	8/27	Monte Pearson	NY vs Cle, 13-0
1940	4/16	Bob Feller	Cle at Chi, 1-0 (Opening Day)
1945	9/9	Dick Fowler	Phi vs St. L, 1-0
1946	4/30	Bob Feller	Cle vs NY, 1-0
1947	7/10	Don Black	Cle vs Phi, 3-0
	9/3	Bill McCahan	Phi vs Wash, 3-0
1948	6/30	Bob Lemon	Cle at Det, 2-0
1951	7/1	Bob Feller	Cle vs Det, 2-1
	7/12	Allie Reynolds	NY vs Cle, 1-0
	9/28	Allie Reynolds	NY vs Bos, 8-0
1952	5/15	Virgil Trucks	Det vs Wash, 1-0
	8/25	Virgil Trucks	Det at NY, 1-0
1953	5/6	Bobo Holloman	St. L vs Phi, 6-0 (first major league start)
1956	7/14	Mel Parnell	Bos vs Chi, 4-0
	10/8	Don Larsen	NY vs Bklyn, 2-0 (perfect W. Series game)
1957	8/20	Bob Keegan	Chi vs Wash, 6-0
1958	7/20	Jim Bunning	Det at Bos, 3-0
	9/20	Hoyt Wilhelm	Bal vs NY, 1-0
1962	5/5	Bo Belinsky	LA vs Bal, 2-0
	6/26	Earl Wilson	Bos vs LA, 2-0
	8/1	Bill Monbouquette	Bos at Chi, 1-0
	8/26	Jack Kralick	Min vs KC, 1-0

Year	Date	Pitcher	Result
1965	9/16	Dave Morehead	Bos vs Cle, 2-0
1966	6/10	Sonny Siebert	Cle vs Wash, 2-0
1967	4/30	**Steve Barber** (8⅔) & **Stu Miller** (⅓)	Bal vs Det, 1-2 (combined no-hitter)
	8/25	Dean Chance	Min vs Cle, 2-1
	9/10	Joel Horlen	Chi vs Det, 6-0
1968	4/27	Tom Phoebus	Bal vs Bos, 6-0
	5/8	Catfish Hunter	Oak vs Min, 4-0 (perfect game)
1969	8/13	Jim Palmer	Bal vs Oak, 8-0
1970	7/3	Clyde Wright	Cal vs Oak, 4-0
	9/21	Vida Blue	Oak vs Min, 6-0
1973	4/27	Steve Busby	KC at Det, 3-0
	5/15	Nolan Ryan	Cal vs KC, 3-0
	7/15	Nolan Ryan	Cal at Det, 6-0
	7/30	Jim Bibby	Tex at Oak, 6-0
1974	6/19	Steve Busby	KC at Mil, 2-0
	7/19	Dick Bosman	Cle at Oak, 4-0
	9/28	Nolan Ryan	Cal at Min, 4-0
1975	6/1	Nolan Ryan	Cal vs Bal, 1-0
	9/28	Vida Blue (5), Glenn Abbott (1), Paul Lindblad (1), & Rollie Fingers (2)	Oak vs Cal, 5-0 (combined no-hitter)
1976	7/28	John Odom (5) & Francisco Barrios (4)	Chi at Oak, 2-1 (combined no-hitter)
1977	5/14	Jim Colborn	KC vs Tex, 6-0
	5/30	Dennis Eckersley	Cle vs Cal, 1-0
	9/22	Bert Blyleven	Tex at Cal, 6-0
1981	5/15	Len Barker	Cle vs Tor, 3-0 (perfect game)
1983	7/4	Dave Righetti	NY vs Bos, 4-0
	9/29	Mike Warren	Oak vs Chi, 3-0
1984	4/7	Jack Morris	Det at Chi, 4-0
	9/30	Mike Witt	Cal at Tex, 1-0 (perfect game)
1986	9/19	Joe Cowley	Chi at Cal, 7-1
1987	4/15	Juan Nieves	Mil at Bal, 7-0
1990	4/11	Mark Langston (7) & Mike Witt (2)	Cal vs Sea, 1-0 (combined no-hitter)
	6/2	Randy Johnson	Sea vs Det, 2-0
	6/11	Nolan Ryan	Tex at Oak, 5-0
	6/29	Dave Stewart	Oak at Tor, 5-0
	9/2	Dave Stieb	Tor at Cle, 3-0
1991	5/1	Nolan Ryan	Tex vs Tor, 3-0
	7/13	Bob Milacki (6), Mike Flanagan (1), Mark Williamson (1) & Gregg Olson (1)	Bal at Oak, 2-0 (combined no-hitter)
	8/11	Wilson Alvarez	Chi at Bal, 7-0
	8/26	Bret Saberhagen	KC vs Chi, 7-0
1993	4/22	Chris Bosio	Sea vs Bos, 7-0
	9/4	Jim Abbott	NY vs Cle, 4-0
1994	4/27	Scott Erickson	Min vs Mil, 6-0
	7/28	Kenny Rogers	Tex vs Cal, 4-0 (perfect game)
1996	5/14	Dwight Gooden	NY vs Sea, 2-0
1998	5/17	David Wells	NY vs Min, 4-0 (perfect game)
1999	7/18	David Cone	NY vs Mon, 6-0 (perfect game)
	9/11	Eric Milton	Min vs Ana, 7-0
2001	4/4	Hideo Nomo	Bos at Bal, 3-0
2002	4/27	Derek Lowe	Bos vs TB, 10-0

All-Time Major League Leaders

Based on statistics compiled by *The Baseball Encyclopedia* (9th ed.); through 2002 regular season.

CAREER

Players active in 2002 in **bold** type.

Batting

Note that (*) indicates left-handed hitter and (†) indicates switch-hitter.

Batting Average

(Minimum 3,000 AB)

		Yrs	AB	H	Avg
1	Ty Cobb*	.24	11,434	4189	.366
2	Rogers Hornsby	.23	8,173	2930	.358
3	Joe Jackson*	.13	4,981	1772	.356
4	Ed Delahanty	.16	7,505	2596	.346
5	Tris Speaker*	.22	10,195	3514	.345
6	Ted Williams*	.19	7,706	2654	.344
7	Billy Hamilton*	.14	6,269	2159	.344
8	Dan Brouthers*	.19	6,711	2296	.342
9	Babe Ruth*	.22	8,399	2873	.342
10	Harry Heilmann	.17	7,787	2660	.342
11	Pete Browning	.13	4,820	1646	.341
12	Willie Keeler*	.19	8,591	2932	.341
13	Bill Terry*	.14	6,428	2193	.341
14	George Sisler*	.15	8,267	2812	.340
15	Lou Gehrig*	.17	8,001	2721	.340
16	Jesse Burkett*	.16	8,421	2850	.338
17	Tony Gwynn*	.20	9,288	3141	.338
18	Nap Lajoie	.21	9,589	3242	.338
19	Riggs Stephenson	.14	4,508	1515	.336
20	Al Simmons	.20	8,759	2927	.334
21	Paul Waner*	.20	9,459	3152	.333
22	Eddie Collins*	.25	9,949	3315	.333
23	Stan Musial*	.22	10,972	3630	.331
24	Sam Thompson*	.14	5,984	1979	.331
25	Heinie Manush*	.17	7,654	2524	.330

Hits

		Yrs	AB	H	Avg
1	Pete Rose†	.24	14,053	**4256**	.303
2	Ty Cobb*	.24	11,434	**4189**	.366
3	Hank Aaron	.23	12,364	**3771**	.305
4	Stan Musial*	.22	10,972	**3630**	.331
5	Tris Speaker*	.22	10,195	**3514**	.345
6	Carl Yastrzemski*	.23	11,988	**3419**	.285
7	Honus Wagner	.21	10,430	**3415**	.327
8	Paul Molitor	.21	10,835	**3319**	.306
9	Eddie Collins*	.25	9,949	**3315**	.333
10	Willie Mays	.22	10,881	**3283**	.302
11	Eddie Murray†	.21	11,336	**3255**	.287
12	Nap Lajoie	.21	9,589	**3242**	.338
13	Cal Ripken Jr.	.21	11,551	**3184**	.276
14	George Brett*	.21	10,349	**3154**	.305
15	Paul Waner*	.20	9,459	**3152**	.333
16	Robin Yount	.20	11,008	**3142**	.285
17	Tony Gwynn*	.20	9,288	**3141**	.338
18	Dave Winfield	.22	11,003	**3110**	.283
19	Rod Carew*	.19	9,315	**3053**	.328
20	**Rickey Henderson**	.24	10,889	**3040**	.279
21	Lou Brock*	.19	10,332	**3023**	.293
22	Wade Boggs*	.18	9,180	**3010**	.328
23	Al Kaline	.22	10,116	**3007**	.297
24	Cap Anson	.22	9,108	**3000**	.329
	Roberto Clemente	.18	9,454	**3000**	.317

Players Active in 2002

		Yrs	AB	H	Avg
1	Nomar Garciaparra	.7	3,154	1033	.328
2	Vladimir Guerrero	.7	3,369	1085	.322
3	Mike Piazza	.11	5,116	1641	.321
4	Larry Walker*	.14	5,880	1863	.317
5	Derek Jeter	.8	4,388	1390	.317
6	Edgar Martinez	.16	6,230	1973	.317
7	Manny Ramirez	.10	4,435	1400	.316
8	Frank Thomas	.13	6,065	1902	.314
9	Jason Giambi*	.8	3,958	1224	.309
10	Chipper Jones†	.9	4,589	1419	.309
11	Alex Rodriguez	.9	4,382	1354	.309
12	Bernie Williams†	.12	5,958	1833	.308
13	Mark Grace*	.15	7,930	2418	.305

Players Active in 2002

		Yrs	AB	H	Avg
1	Rickey Henderson	.24	10,889	**3040**	.279
2	Rafael Palmeiro*	.17	8,992	**2634**	.293
3	Tim Raines†	.23	8,872	**2605**	.294
4	Roberto Alomar†	.15	8,386	**2546**	.304
5	Barry Bonds*	.17	8,335	**2462**	.295
6	Mark Grace*	.15	7,930	**2418**	.305
7	Fred McGriff*	.17	8,388	**2403**	.287
8	Julio Franco	.18	7,672	**2300**	.300
9	Craig Biggio	.15	7,960	**2295**	.288
10	Andres Galarraga	.17	7,814	**2248**	.288
11	Barry Larkin	.17	7,350	**2172**	.293
12	Ellis Burks	.16	7,001	**2049**	.293
13	B.J. Surhoff	.16	7,293	**2048**	.281

Games Played

1	Pete Rose	3562
2	Carl Yastrzemski	3308
3	Hank Aaron	3298
4	**Rickey Henderson**	3051
5	Ty Cobb	3035
6	Stan Musial	3026
	Eddie Murray	3026
8	Cal Ripken Jr.	3001
9	Willie Mays	2992
10	Dave Winfield	2973
11	Rusty Staub	2951
12	Brooks Robinson	2896
13	Robin Yount	2856
14	Al Kaline	2834
15	Harold Baines	2830
16	Eddie Collins	2826
17	Reggie Jackson	2820
18	Frank Robinson	2808
19	Honus Wagner	2792
20	Tris Speaker	2789

At Bats

1	Pete Rose	14,053
2	Hank Aaron	12,364
3	Carl Yastrzemski	11,988
4	Cal Ripken Jr.	11,551
5	Ty Cobb	11,434
6	Eddie Murray	11,336
7	Robin Yount	11,008
8	Dave Winfield	11,003
9	Stan Musial	10,972
10	**Rickey Henderson**	10,889
11	Willie Mays	10,881
12	Paul Molitor	10,835
13	Brooks Robinson	10,654
14	Honus Wagner	10,430
15	George Brett	10,349
16	Lou Brock	10,332
17	Luis Aparicio	10,230
18	Tris Speaker	10,195
19	Al Kaline	10,116
20	Rabbit Maranville	10,078

Total Bases

1	Hank Aaron	6856
2	Stan Musial	6134
3	Willie Mays	6066
4	Ty Cobb	5854
5	Babe Ruth	5793
6	Pete Rose	5752
7	Carl Yastrzemski	5539
8	Eddie Murray	5397
9	Frank Robinson	5373
10	Dave Winfield	5221
11	Cal Ripken Jr.	5168
12	Tris Speaker	5101
13	Lou Gehrig	5060
14	George Brett	5044
15	Mel Ott	5041
16	**Barry Bonds**	4961
17	Jimmie Foxx	4956
18	Ted Williams	4884
19	Honus Wagner	4862
20	Paul Molitor	4854

Home Runs

		Yrs	AB	HR	AB/HR
1	Hank Aaron	23	12,364	755	16.4
2	Babe Ruth*	22	8,399	714	11.8
3	Willie Mays	22	10,881	660	16.5
4	**Barry Bonds***	17	8,335	613	13.6
5	Frank Robinson	21	10,006	586	17.1
6	Mark McGwire	16	6,187	583	10.6
7	Harmon Killebrew	22	8,147	573	14.2
8	Reggie Jackson*	21	9,864	563	17.5
9	Mike Schmidt	18	8,352	548	15.2
10	Mickey Mantle†	18	8,102	536	15.1
11	Jimmie Foxx	20	8,134	534	15.2
12	Ted Williams*	19	7,706	521	14.8
	Willie McCovey*	22	8,197	521	15.7
14	Eddie Mathews*	17	8,537	512	16.7
	Ernie Banks	19	9,421	512	18.4
16	Mel Ott*	22	9,456	511	18.5
17	Eddie Murray†	21	11,336	504	22.5
18	**Sammy Sosa**	14	7,026	499	14.1
19	Lou Gehrig*	17	8,001	493	16.2
20	**Rafael Palmeiro***	17	8,992	490	18.4
21	**Fred McGriff***	17	8,388	478	17.5
22	Willie Stargell*	21	7,927	475	16.7
	Stan Musial*	22	10,972	475	23.1
24	**Ken Griffey Jr.***	14	6,913	468	14.8
25	Dave Winfield	22	11,003	465	23.7

Runs Batted In

		Yrs	Gm	RBI	P/G
1	Hank Aaron	23	3298	2297	.70
2	Babe Ruth*	22	2503	2213	.88
3	Lou Gehrig*	17	2164	1995	.92
4	Stan Musial*	22	3026	1951	.64
5	Ty Cobb*	24	3034	1938	.64
6	Jimmie Foxx	20	2317	1922	.83
7	Eddie Murray†	21	2980	1917	.64
8	Willie Mays	22	2992	1903	.64
9	Mel Ott*	22	2730	1860	.68
10	Carl Yastrzemski*	23	3308	1844	.56
11	Ted Williams*	19	2292	1839	.80
12	Dave Winfield	22	2973	1833	.62
13	Al Simmons	20	2215	1827	.82
14	Frank Robinson	21	2808	1812	.65
15	Honus Wagner	21	2792	1732	.62
16	Cap Anson	22	2276	1715	.75
17	Reggie Jackson*	21	2820	1702	.60
18	Cal Ripken Jr.	21	3001	1695	.56
19	Tony Perez	23	2777	1652	.59
	Barry Bonds*	17	2439	1652	.68
21	Ernie Banks	19	2528	1636	.65
22	Harold Baines*	22	2830	1628	.58
23	Goose Goslin*	18	2287	1609	.70
24	Nap Lajoie	21	2480	1599	.64
25	Mike Schmidt	18	2404	1595	.66
	George Brett*	21	2707	1595	.59

Players Active in 2002

		Yrs	AB	HR	AB/HR
1	Barry Bonds*	17	8,335	613	13.6
2	Sammy Sosa	14	7,026	499	14.1
3	Rafael Palmeiro*	17	8,992	490	18.4
4	Fred McGriff*	17	8,388	478	17.5
5	Ken Griffey Jr.*	14	6,913	468	14.8
6	Juan Gonzalez	14	6,101	405	15.1
7	Andres Galarraga	17	7,814	386	20.2
8	Jeff Bagwell	12	6,520	380	17.2
9	Frank Thomas	13	6,065	376	16.1
10	Matt Williams	16	6,866	374	18.4
11	Greg Vaughn	14	6,066	352	17.2
12	Mike Piazza	11	5,116	347	14.7
13	Ellis Burks	16	7,001	345	20.3
14	Gary Sheffield	15	6,153	340	18.1
15	Larry Walker*	14	5,880	335	17.6

Players Active in 2002

		Yrs	Gm	RBI	P/G
1	Barry Bonds*	17	2439	1652	.68
2	Rafael Palmeiro*	17	2413	1575	.65
3	Fred McGriff*	17	2347	1503	.64
4	Andres Galarraga	17	2140	1381	.65
5	Ken Griffey Jr.*	14	1861	1358	.73
6	Sammy Sosa	14	1875	1347	.72
7	Jeff Bagwell	12	1795	1321	.74
8	Juan Gonzalez	14	1573	1317	.84
9	Frank Thomas	13	1698	1285	.76
10	Matt Williams	16	1822	1202	.66
11	Ruben Sierra†	16	1898	1181	.62
12	Ellis Burks	16	1934	1177	.61
13	Larry Walker*	14	1663	1133	.68
14	Mark Grace*	15	2179	1130	.52
15	Rickey Henderson	24	3051	1110	.36

Runs

1	**Rickey Henderson**	2288
2	Ty Cobb	2246
3	Babe Ruth	2174
	Hank Aaron	2174
5	Pete Rose	2165
6	Willie Mays	2062
7	Stan Musial	1949
8	Lou Gehrig	1888
9	Tris Speaker	1882
10	Mel Ott	1859
11	**Barry Bonds**	1830
12	Frank Robinson	1829
13	Eddie Collins	1821
14	Carl Yastrzemski	1816
15	Ted Williams	1798
16	Paul Molitor	1782
17	Charlie Gehringer	1774
18	Jimmie Foxx	1751
19	Honus Wagner	1736
20	Willie Keeler	1727

Extra Base Hits

1	Hank Aaron	1477
2	Stan Musial	1377
3	Babe Ruth	1356
4	Willie Mays	1323
5	**Barry Bonds**	1200
6	Lou Gehrig	1190
7	Frank Robinson	1186
8	Carl Yastrzemski	1157
9	Ty Cobb	1136
10	Tris Speaker	1131
11	George Brett	1119
12	Ted Williams	1117
	Jimmie Foxx	1117
14	Eddie Murray	1099
15	Dave Winfield	1093
16	Cal Ripken Jr.	1078
17	Reggie Jackson	1075
18	Mel Ott	1071
19	**Rafael Palmeiro**	1048
20	Pete Rose	1041

Slugging Percentage
(Minimum 3,000 AB)

1	Babe Ruth	.690
2	Ted Williams	.634
3	Lou Gehrig	.632
4	Jimmie Foxx	.609
5	Hank Greenberg	.605
6	**Manny Ramirez**	.599
7	**Barry Bonds**	.595
8	Mark McGwire	.588
9	**Vladimir Guerrero**	.588
10	Joe DiMaggio	.579
11	**Alex Rodriguez**	.579
12	Rogers Hornsby	.577
13	**Mike Piazza**	.576
14	**Larry Walker**	.574
15	Brian Giles	.570
16	**Frank Thomas**	.568
17	**Jim Thome**	.567
18	Albert Belle	.564
19	**Juan Gonzalez**	.563
20	Johnny Mize	.562

Stolen Bases

1	**Rickey Henderson**	1403
2	Lou Brock	938
3	Billy Hamilton	912
4	Ty Cobb	892
5	**Tim Raines**	808
6	Vince Coleman	752
7	Eddie Collins	745
8	Max Carey	738
9	Honus Wagner	722
10	Joe Morgan	689
11	Arlie Latham	679
12	Willie Wilson	668
13	Bert Campaneris	649
14	Tom Brown	627
15	Otis Nixon	620
16	George Davis	616
17	Dummy Hoy	594
18	Maury Wills	586
19	George Van Haltren	583
20	Ozzie Smith	580

Walks

1	**Rickey Henderson**	2179
2	Babe Ruth	2062
3	Ted Williams	2019
4	**Barry Bonds**	1922
5	Joe Morgan	1865
6	Carl Yastrzemski	1845
7	Mickey Mantle	1733
8	Mel Ott	1708
9	Eddie Yost	1614
10	Darrell Evans	1605
11	Stan Musial	1599
12	Pete Rose	1566
13	Harmon Killebrew	1559
14	Lou Gehrig	1508
15	Mike Schmidt	1507
16	Eddie Collins	1499
17	Willie Mays	1464
18	Jimmie Foxx	1452
19	Eddie Mathews	1444
20	Frank Robinson	1420

Strikeouts

1	Reggie Jackson	2597
2	Jose Canseco	1942
3	**Andres Galarraga**	1939
4	Willie Stargell	1936
5	Mike Schmidt	1883
6	Tony Perez	1867
7	**Sammy Sosa**	1834
8	Dave Kingman	1816
9	**Fred McGriff**	1797
10	Bobby Bonds	1757
11	Dale Murphy	1748
12	Lou Brock	1730
13	Mickey Mantle	1710
14	Harmon Killebrew	1699
15	Chili Davis	1698
16	Dwight Evans	1697
17	Dave Winfield	1686
18	**Rickey Henderson**	1678
19	Gary Gaetti	1602
20	Mark McGwire	1596

Pitching

Note that (*) indicates left-handed pitcher. Active pitching leaders are listed for wins and strikeouts.

Wins

		Yrs	GS	W	L	Pct
1	Cy Young	22	815	**511**	316	.618
2	Walter Johnson	21	666	**417**	279	.599
3	Christy Mathewson	17	551	**373**	188	.665
	Grover Alexander	20	598	**373**	208	.642
5	Pud Galvin	15	688	**365**	310	.541
6	Warren Spahn*	21	665	**363**	245	.597
7	Kid Nichols	15	561	**361**	208	.634
8	Tim Keefe	14	594	**342**	225	.603
9	Steve Carlton*	24	709	**329**	244	.574
10	John Clarkson	12	518	**328**	178	.648
11	Eddie Plank*	17	529	**326**	194	.627
12	Don Sutton	23	756	**324**	256	.559
	Nolan Ryan	27	773	**324**	292	.526
14	Phil Niekro	24	716	**318**	274	.537
15	Gaylord Perry	22	690	**314**	265	.542
16	Tom Seaver	20	647	**311**	205	.603
17	Old Hoss Radbourn	12	503	**309**	195	.613
18	Mickey Welch	13	549	**307**	210	.594
19	Lefty Grove*	17	456	**300**	141	.680
	Early Wynn	23	612	**300**	244	.551
21	Bobby Mathews	15	568	**297**	248	.545
22	**Roger Clemens**	19	573	**293**	151	.660
23	Tommy John*	26	700	**288**	231	.555
24	Bert Blyleven	22	685	**287**	250	.534
25	Robin Roberts	19	609	**286**	245	.539
26	Tony Mullane	13	504	**284**	220	.563
	Ferguson Jenkins	19	594	**284**	226	.557
28	Jim Kaat*	25	625	**283**	237	.544
29	**Greg Maddux**	17	535	**273**	152	.642
	Red Ruffing	22	536	**273**	225	.548

Strikeouts

		Yrs	IP	SO	P/9
1	Nolan Ryan	27	5386.0	**5714**	9.55
2	Steve Carlton*	24	5217.1	**4136**	7.13
3	**Roger Clemens**	19	4067.0	**3909**	8.65
4	**Randy Johnson***	15	3008.1	**3746**	11.21
5	Bert Blyleven	22	4970.0	**3701**	6.70
6	Tom Seaver	20	4782.2	**3640**	6.85
7	Don Sutton	23	5282.1	**3574**	6.09
8	Gaylord Perry	22	5350.1	**3534**	5.94
9	Walter Johnson	21	5914.1	**3508**	5.34
10	Phil Niekro	24	5404.1	**3342**	5.57
11	Ferguson Jenkins	19	4500.2	**3192**	6.38
12	Bob Gibson	17	3884.1	**3117**	7.22
13	Jim Bunning	17	3760.1	**2855**	6.83
14	Mickey Lolich*	16	3638.1	**2832**	7.01
15	Cy Young	22	7356.0	**2803**	3.43
16	Frank Tanana*	21	4186.2	**2773**	5.96
17	David Cone	16	2880.2	**2655**	8.29
18	**Greg Maddux**	17	3750.1	**2641**	6.34
19	**Chuck Finley***	17	3197.1	**2610**	7.35
20	Warren Spahn*	21	5243.2	**2583**	4.43
21	Bob Feller	18	3827.0	**2581**	6.07
22	Tim Keefe	14	5049.2	**2564**	4.57
23	Jerry Koosman*	19	3839.1	**2556**	5.99
24	Christy Mathewson*	17	4781.0	**2502**	4.71
25	Don Drysdale	14	3432.0	**2486**	6.52
26	Jack Morris	18	3824.2	**2478**	5.83
27	Mark Langston*	16	2962.2	**2464**	7.49
28	Jim Kaat*	25	4530.1	**2461**	4.89
29	Sam McDowell*	15	2492.1	**2453**	8.86
30	Luis Tiant	19	3486.1	**2416**	6.24

Pitchers Active in 2002

		Yrs	GS	W	L	Pct
1	Roger Clemens	19	573	**293**	151	.660
2	Greg Maddux	17	535	**273**	152	.642
3	Tom Glavine*	16	505	**242**	143	.629
4	Randy Johnson*	15	426	**224**	106	.679
5	Chuck Finley*	17	467	**200**	173	.536
6	David Wells*	16	356	**185**	121	.605
7	Kevin Brown	16	409	**183**	122	.600
8	Mike Mussina	12	355	**182**	102	.641
9	Jamie Moyer*	16	387	**164**	125	.567
10	John Smoltz	14	361	**163**	118	.580

Pitchers Active in 2002

		Yrs	IP	SO	P/9
1	Roger Clemens	19	4067.0	**3909**	8.65
2	Randy Johnson*	15	3008.1	**3746**	11.21
3	Greg Maddux	17	3750.1	**2641**	6.34
4	Chuck Finley*	17	3197.1	**2610**	7.35
5	Curt Schilling	15	2418.0	**2348**	8.74
6	John Smoltz	15	2553.2	**2240**	7.89
7	Pedro Martinez	11	1892.1	**2220**	10.56
8	Kevin Brown	16	2840.0	**2079**	6.59
9	Tom Glavine*	16	3344.2	**2054**	5.53
10	Andy Benes	14	2505.1	**2000**	7.18

Winning Pct.
(Minimum 100 wins)

		Yrs	W-L	Pct
1	Al Spalding	.7	252-65	.795
2	Spud Chandler	11	109-43	.717
3	**Pedro Martinez**	11	152-63	.707
4	Dave Foutz	11	147-66	.690
5	Whitey Ford*	16	236-106	.690
6	Bob Caruthers	.9	218-99	.688
7	Don Gullett*	.9	109-50	.686
8	Lefty Grove*	17	300-141	.680
9	**Randy Johnson***	15	224-106	.679
10	Joe Wood	11	117-57	.672
11	Vic Raschi	10	132-66	.667
12	Larry Corcoran	.8	177-89	.665
13	Christy Mathewson	17	373-188	.665
14	**Roger Clemens**	19	293-151	.660
15	Sam Leever	13	194-100	.660

Losses

		Yrs	GS	W	L	Pct
1	Cy Young	22	815	511	**316**	.618
2	Pud Galvin	15	688	365	**310**	.541
3	Nolan Ryan	27	773	324	**292**	.526
4	Walter Johnson	21	666	417	**279**	.599
5	Phil Niekro	24	716	318	**274**	.537
6	Gaylord Perry	22	690	314	**265**	.542
7	Don Sutton	23	756	324	**256**	.559
8	Jack Powell	16	516	245	**254**	.491
9	Eppa Rixey*	21	552	266	**251**	.515
10	Bert Blyleven	22	685	287	**250**	.534
11	Bobby Mathews	15	568	297	**248**	.545
12	Robin Roberts	19	609	286	**245**	.539
	Warren Spahn*	21	665	363	**245**	.597
14	Early Wynn	23	612	300	**244**	.551
	Steve Carlton*	24	709	329	**244**	.574

Appearances

1	**Jesse Orosco**	1186
2	Dennis Eckersley	1071
3	Hoyt Wilhelm	1070
4	Kent Tekulve	1050
5	Lee Smith	1022
6	**Dan Plesac**	1006
7	Rich Gossage	1002
8	John Franco	998
9	Lindy McDaniel	987
10	**Mike Jackson**	960
11	Rollie Fingers	944
12	Gene Garber	931
13	Cy Young	906
14	Sparky Lyle	899
15	Jim Kaat	898

Innings Pitched

1	Cy Young	7356.0
2	Pud Galvin	6003.1
3	Walter Johnson	5914.1
4	Phil Niekro	5404.1
5	Nolan Ryan	5386.0
6	Gaylord Perry	5350.1
7	Don Sutton	5282.1
8	Warren Spahn	5243.2
9	Steve Carlton	5217.1
10	Grover Alexander	5190.0
11	Kid Nichols	5056.1
12	Tim Keefe	5049.2
13	Bert Blyleven	4970.0
14	Bobby Mathews	4956.0
15	Mickey Welch	4802.0

Earned Run Avg.
(Minimum 1500 IP)

1	Ed Walsh	1.82
2	Addie Joss	1.89
3	Al Spalding	2.04
4	Three Finger Brown	2.06
5	Monte Ward	2.10
6	Christy Mathewson	2.13
7	Rube Waddell	2.16
8	Walter Johnson	2.17
9	Orval Overall	2.23
10	Tommy Bond	2.25
11	Will White	2.28
12	Ed Reulbach	2.28
13	Jim Scott	2.30
14	Eddie Plank	2.35
15	Larry Corcoran	2.36

Shutouts

1	Walter Johnson	110
2	Grover Alexander	90
3	Christy Mathewson	79
4	Cy Young	76
5	Eddie Plank	69
6	Warren Spahn	63
7	Nolan Ryan	61
	Tom Seaver	61
8	Bert Blyleven	60
10	Don Sutton	58
11	Pud Galvin	57
	Ed Walsh	57
13	Bob Gibson	56
14	Three Finger Brown	55
	Steve Carlton	55

Walks Allowed

1	Nolan Ryan	2795
2	Steve Carlton	1833
3	Phil Niekro	1809
4	Early Wynn	1775
5	Bob Feller	1764
6	Bobo Newsom	1732
7	Amos Rusie	1704
8	Charlie Hough	1665
9	Gus Weyhing	1566
10	Red Ruffing	1541
11	Bump Hadley	1442
12	Warren Spahn	1434
13	Earl Whitehill	1431
14	Tony Mullane	1408
15	Sad Sam Jones	1396

HRs Allowed

1	Robin Roberts	505
2	Ferguson Jenkins	484
3	Phil Niekro	482
4	Don Sutton	472
5	Frank Tanana	448
6	Warren Spahn	434
7	Bert Blyleven	430
8	Steve Carlton	414
9	Gaylord Perry	399
10	Jim Kaat	395
11	Jack Morris	389
12	Charlie Hough	383
13	Tom Seaver	380
14	Catfish Hunter	374
15	Jim Bunning	372
	Dennis Martinez	372

Saves

1	Lee Smith	478
2	John Franco	422
3	Dennis Eckersley	390
4	Jeff Reardon	367
5	**Trevor Hoffman**	352
6	Randy Myers	347
7	Rollie Fingers	341
8	John Wetteland	330
9	**Roberto Hernandez**	320
10	Rick Aguilera	318
11	**Robb Nen**	314
12	Tom Henke	311
13	Rich Gossage	310
14	Jeff Montgomery	304
15	Doug Jones	303
16	Bruce Sutter	300
17	Rod Beck	266
18	Todd Worrell	256
19	Dave Righetti	252
20	**Troy Percival**	250
21	Dan Quisenberry	244
22	**Mariano Rivera**	243
23	Sparky Lyle	238
24	Hoyt Wilhelm	227
25	**Jose Mesa**	225
26	Gene Garber	218
27	Gregg Olson	217
28	Dave Smith	216
29	Jeff Shaw	203
30	Bobby Thigpen	201

SINGLE SEASON
Through 2002 regular season.

Batting

Home Runs

		Year	Gm	AB	HR
1	Barry Bonds, SF	2001	153	476	73
2	Mark McGwire, St.L	1998	155	509	70
3	Sammy Sosa, Chi-NL	1998	159	643	66
4	Mark McGwire, St.L	1999	153	521	65
5	Sammy Sosa, Chi-NL	2001	160	577	64
6	Sammy Sosa, Chi-NL	1999	162	625	63
7	Roger Maris, NY-AL	1961	162	590	61
8	Babe Ruth, NY-AL	1927	151	540	60
9	Babe Ruth, NY-AL	1921	152	540	59
10	Mark McGwire, Oak-St.L	1997	156	540	58
	Hank Greenberg, Det	1938	155	556	58
	Jimmie Foxx, Phi-AL	1932	154	585	58
13	**Alex Rodriguez**, Tex	2002	162	624	57
	Luis Gonzalez, Ari	2001	162	609	57
15	Hack Wilson, Chi-NL	1930	155	585	56
	Ken Griffey Jr., Sea	1997	157	608	56
	Ken Griffey Jr., Sea	1998	161	633	56
18	Babe Ruth, NY-AL	1920	142	458	54
	Mickey Mantle, NY-AL	1961	153	514	54
	Babe Ruth, NY-AL	1928	154	536	54
	Ralph Kiner, Pit	1949	152	549	54

Hits

		Year	AB	H	Avg
1	George Sisler, StL-AL	1920	631	**257**	.407
2	Bill Terry, NY-NL	1930	633	**254**	.401
	Lefty O'Doul, Phi-NL	1929	638	**254**	.398
4	Al Simmons, Phi-AL	1925	658	**253**	.384
5	Rogers Hornsby, StL-NL	1922	623	**250**	.401
	Chuck Klein, Phi-NL	1930	648	**250**	.386
7	Ty Cobb, Det	1911	591	**248**	.420
8	George Sisler, StL-AL	1922	586	**246**	.420
9	Ichiro Suzuki, Sea	2001	692	**242**	.350
10	Babe Herman, Bklyn	1930	614	**241**	.393
	Heinie Manush, StL-AL	1928	638	**241**	.378
12	Wade Boggs, Bos	1985	653	**240**	.368
	Darin Erstad, Ana	2000	676	**240**	.355
14	Rod Carew, Min.	1977	616	**239**	.388
15	Don Mattingly, NY-AL	1986	677	**238**	.352
16	Harry Heilmann, Det	1921	602	**237**	.394
	Paul Waner, Pit.	1927	623	**237**	.380
	Joe Medwick, StL-NL	1937	633	**237**	.374
19	Jack Tobin, StL-AL	1921	671	**236**	.352
20	Rogers Hornsby, StL-NL	1921	592	**235**	.397

Batting Average

From 1900-49

		Year	AB	H	Avg
1	Rogers Hornsby, StL-NL	1924	536	227	.424
2	Nap Lajoie, Phi-AL	1901	543	229	.422
3	George Sisler, StL-AL	1922	586	246	.420
4	Ty Cobb, Det	1911	591	248	.420
5	Ty Cobb, Det	1912	533	227	.410
6	Joe Jackson, Cle	1911	571	233	.408
7	George Sisler, StL-AL	1920	631	257	.407
8	Ted Williams, Bos-AL	1941	456	185	.406
9	Rogers Hornsby, StL-NL	1925	504	203	.403
10	Harry Heilmann, Det	1923	524	211	.403

Since 1950

		Year	AB	H	Avg
1	Tony Gwynn, SD	1994	419	175	.394
2	George Brett, KC	1980	449	175	.390
3	Ted Williams, Bos	1957	420	163	.388
4	Rod Carew, Min.	1977	616	239	.388
5	Larry Walker, Col	1999	438	166	.379
6	Todd Helton, Col	2000	580	216	.372
7	Nomar Garciaparra, Bos	2000	529	197	.372
8	Tony Gwynn, SD	1997	592	220	.372
9	Andres Galarraga, Col	1993	470	174	.370
10	Tony Gwynn, SD	1987	589	218	.370

Total Bases

From 1900-49

		Year	TB
1	Babe Ruth, New York-AL	1921	457
2	Rogers Hornsby, St. Louis-NL	1922	450
3	Lou Gehrig, New York-AL	1927	447
4	Chuck Klein, Philadelphia-NL	1930	445
5	Jimmie Foxx, Philadelphia-AL	1932	438
6	Stan Musial, St. Louis-NL	1948	429
7	Hack Wilson, Chicago-NL	1930	423
8	Chuck Klein, Philadelphia-NL	1932	420
9	Lou Gehrig, New York-AL	1930	419
10	Joe DiMaggio, New York-AL	1937	418

Since 1950

		Year	TB
1	Sammy Sosa, Chicago-NL	2001	425
2	Luis Gonzalez, Arizona	2001	419
3	Sammy Sosa, Chicago-NL	1998	416
4	Barry Bonds, San Francisco	2001	411
5	Larry Walker, Colorado	1997	409
6	Jim Rice, Boston	1978	406
7	Todd Helton, Colorado	2000	405
8	Todd Helton, Colorado	2001	402
9	Hank Aaron, Milwaukee	1959	400
10	Albert Belle, Chicago-AL	1998	399

Runs Batted In

From 1900-49

		Year	Avg	HR	RBI
1	Hack Wilson, Chi-NL	1930	.356	56	191
2	Lou Gehrig, NY-AL	1931	.341	46	184
3	Hank Greenberg, Det	1937	.337	40	183
4	Lou Gehrig, NY-AL	1927	.373	47	175
	Jimmie Foxx, Bos-AL	1938	.349	50	175
6	Lou Gehrig, NY-AL	1930	.379	41	174
7	Babe Ruth, NY-AL	1921	.378	59	171
8	Chuck Klein, Phi-NL	1930	.386	40	170
	Hank Greenberg, Det	1935	.328	36	170
10	Jimmie Foxx, Phi-AL	1932	.364	58	169

Since 1950

		Year	Avg	HR	RBI
1	Manny Ramirez, Cle	1999	.333	44	165
2	Sammy Sosa, Chi-NL	2001	.328	64	160
3	Sammy Sosa, Chi-NL	1998	.308	66	158
4	Juan Gonzalez, Tex	1998	.318	45	157
5	Tommy Davis, LA-NL	1962	.346	27	153
6	Albert Belle, Chi-AL	1998	.328	49	152
7	Andres Galarraga, Col	1996	.304	47	150
8	George Foster, Cin	1977	.320	52	149
9	Rafael Palmeiro, Tex	1999	.324	47	148
	Johnny Bench, Cin	1970	.293	45	148
	Albert Belle, Cle	1996	.311	48	148

Runs

		Year	Runs
1	Babe Ruth, New York-AL	1921	177
2	Lou Gehrig, New York-AL	1936	167
3	Babe Ruth, New York-AL	1928	163
	Lou Gehrig, New York-AL	1931	163
5	Babe Ruth, New York-AL	1920	158
	Babe Ruth, New York-AL	1927	158
	Chuck Klein, Philadelphia-NL	1930	158
8	Rogers Hornsby, Chicago-NL	1929	156
9	Kiki Cuyler, Chicago-NL	1930	155
10	Lefty O'Doul, Philadelphia-NL	1929	152
	Woody English, Chicago-NL	1930	152
	Al Simmons, Philadelphia-AL	1930	152
	Chuck Klein, Philadelphia-NL	1932	152
	Jeff Bagwell, Houston	2000	152
15	Babe Ruth, New York-AL	1923	151
	Jimmie Foxx, Philadelphia-AL	1932	151
	Joe DiMaggio, New York-AL	1937	151
18	Babe Ruth, New York-AL	1930	150
	Ted Williams, Boston-AL	1949	150
20	Lou Gehrig, New York-AL	1927	149
	Babe Ruth, New York-AL	1931	149

Walks

		Year	BB
1	**Barry Bonds**, San Francisco	2002	198
2	Barry Bonds, San Francisco	2001	177
3	Babe Ruth, New York-AL	1923	170
4	Ted Williams, Boston-AL	1947	162
	Ted Williams, Boston-AL	1949	162
	Mark McGwire, St. Louis	1998	162
7	Ted Williams, Boston-AL	1946	156
8	Barry Bonds, San Francisco	1996	151
	Eddie Yost, Washington	1956	151
10	Jeff Bagwell, Houston	1999	149
	Eddie Joost, Philadelphia-AL	1949	149

Extra Base Hits

		Year	EBH
1	Babe Ruth, New York-AL	1921	119
2	Lou Gehrig, New York-AL	1927	117
3	Chuck Klein, Philadelphia-NL	1930	107
	Barry Bonds, San Francisco	2001	107
5	Todd Helton, Colorado	2001	105
6	Chuck Klein, Philadelphia-NL	1932	103
	Hank Greenberg, Detroit	1937	103
	Stan Musial, St. Louis-NL	1948	103
	Albert Belle, Cleveland	1995	103
	Todd Helton, Colorado	2000	103
	Sammy Sosa, Chicago-NL	2001	103

Slugging Percentage
From 1900-49

		Year	Pct
1	Babe Ruth, New York-AL	1920	.847
2	Babe Ruth, New York-AL	1921	.846
3	Babe Ruth, New York-AL	1927	.772
4	Lou Gehrig, New York-AL	1927	.765
5	Babe Ruth, New York-AL	1923	.764
6	Rogers Hornsby, St. Louis-NL	1925	.756
7	Jimmie Foxx, Philadelphia-AL	1932	.749
8	Babe Ruth, New York-AL	1924	.739
9	Babe Ruth, New York-AL	1926	.737
10	Ted Williams, Boston-AL	1941	.735

Since 1950

		Year	Pct
1	Barry Bonds, San Francisco	2001	.863
2	**Barry Bonds**, San Francisco	2002	.799
3	Mark McGwire, St. Louis	1998	.752
4	Jeff Bagwell, Houston	1994	.750
5	Sammy Sosa, Chicago-NL	2001	.737
6	Ted Williams, Boston	1957	.731
7	Mark McGwire, Oakland	1996	.730
8	Frank Thomas, Chicago-AL	1994	.729
9	Larry Walker, Colorado	1997	.720

Doubles

		Year	2B
1	Earl Webb, Boston-AL	1931	67
2	George Burns, Cleveland	1926	64
	Joe Medwick, St. Louis-NL	1936	64
4	Hank Greenberg, Detroit	1934	63
5	Paul Waner, Pittsburgh	1932	62
6	Charlie Gehringer, Detroit	1936	60
7	Tris Speaker, Cleveland	1923	59
	Chuck Klein, Philadelphia-NL	1930	59
	Todd Helton, Colorado	2000	59
10	Three tied with 57 each.		

Triples
From 1900-49

		Year	3B
1	Chief Wilson, Pittsburgh	1912	36
2	Joe Jackson, Cleveland	1912	26
3	Sam Crawford, Detroit	1914	26
4	Kiki Cuyler, Pittsburgh	1925	26
5	Three tied with 25 each.		

Since 1950

		Year	3B
1	Willie Wilson, Kansas City	1985	21
	Lance Johnson, New York-NL	1996	21
3	Willie Mays, New York-NL	1957	20
	George Brett, Kansas City	1979	20
	Cristian Guzman, Minnesota	2000	20

Stolen Bases

		Year	SB
1	Rickey Henderson, Oakland	1982	130
2	Lou Brock, St. Louis	1974	118
3	Vince Coleman, St. Louis	1985	110
4	Vince Coleman, St. Louis	1987	109
5	Rickey Henderson, Oakland	1983	108
6	Vince Coleman, St. Louis	1986	107
7	Maury Wills, Los Angeles-NL	1962	104
8	Rickey Henderson, Oakland	1980	100
9	Ron LeFlore, Montreal	1980	97
10	Ty Cobb, Detroit	1915	96
	Omar Moreno, Pittsburgh	1980	96
12	Maury Wills, Los Angeles	1965	94
13	Rickey Henderson, New York-AL	1988	93
14	Tim Raines, Montreal	1983	90
15	Clyde Milan, Washington	1912	88

Strikeouts

		Year	SO
1	Bobby Bonds, San Francisco	1970	189
2	**Jose Hernandez**, Milwaukee	2002	188
3	Bobby Bonds, San Francisco	1969	187
	Preston Wilson, Florida	2000	187
5	Rob Deer, Milwaukee	1987	186
6	Pete Incaviglia, Texas	1986	185
	Jose Hernandez, Milwaukee	2001	185
	Jim Thome, Cleveland	2001	185
9	Cecil Fielder, Detroit	1990	182
10	Mo Vaughn, Anaheim	2000	181

Pinch Hits
Career pinch hits in parentheses.

		Year	PH	
1	John Vander Wal, Colorado	1995	28	(117)
2	Lenny Harris, Col-Ari	1999	26	(173)
3	Jose Morales, Montreal	1976	25	(123)
4	Dave Philley, Baltimore	1961	24	(93)
	Vic Davalillo, St. Louis	1970	24	(95)
	Rusty Staub, New York-NL	1983	24	(100)
	Gerald Perry, St. Louis	1993	24	(95)

Note: Harris (173) is the career leader.

Pitching
Wins

From 1900-49

		Year	W	L	Pct
1	Jack Chesbro, NY-AL	1904	41	12	.774
2	Ed Walsh, Chi-AL	1908	40	15	.727
3	Christy Mathewson, NY-NL	1908	37	11	.771
4	Walter Johnson, Wash	1913	36	7	.837
5	Joe McGinnity, NY-NL	1904	35	8	.814
6	Smokey Joe Wood, Bos-AL	1912	34	5	.872
7	Cy Young, Bos-AL	1901	33	10	.767
	Grover Alexander, Phi-NL	1916	33	12	.733
	Christy Mathewson, NY-NL	1904	33	12	.733
10	Cy Young, Bos-AL	1902	32	11	.744

Since 1950

		Year	W	L	Pct
1	Denny McLain, Det	1968	31	6	.838
2	Robin Roberts, Phi-NL	1952	28	7	.800
3	Bob Welch, Oak	1990	27	6	.818
	Don Newcombe, Bklyn	1956	27	7	.794
	Sandy Koufax, LA	1966	27	9	.750
	Steve Carlton, Phi.	1972	27	10	.730
7	Sandy Koufax, LA	1965	26	8	.765
	Juan Marichal, SF	1968	26	9	.743

Note: 11 pitchers tied with 25 wins, including Marichal twice.

Earned Run Average

From 1900-49

		Year	ShO	ERA
1	Dutch Leonard, Bos-AL	1914	7	1.01
2	Three Finger Brown, Chi-NL	1906	10	1.04
3	Walter Johnson, Wash	1913	11	1.09
4	Christy Mathewson, NY-NL	1909	8	1.14
5	Jack Pfiester, Chi-NL	1907	3	1.15
6	Addie Joss, Cle.	1908	9	1.16
7	Carl Lundgren, Chi-NL	1907	7	1.17
8	Grover Alexander, Phi-NL	1915	12	1.22
9	Cy Young, Bos-AL	1908	3	1.26
10	Three pitchers tied at 1.27			

Since 1950

		Year	ShO	ERA
1	Bob Gibson, St.L	1968	13	1.12
2	Dwight Gooden, NY-NL	1985	8	1.53
3	Greg Maddux, Atl.	1994	3	1.56
4	Luis Tiant, Cle	1968	9	1.60
5	Greg Maddux, Atl	1995	3	1.63
6	Dean Chance, LA-AL	1964	11	1.65
7	Nolan Ryan, Cal	1981	3	1.69
8	Sandy Koufax, LA	1966	5	1.73
9	Sandy Koufax, LA	1964	7	1.74
10	Pedro Martinez, Bos	2000	4	1.74

Note: Koufax's ERA in 1964 was 1.735. Martinez' ERA in 2000 was 1.742. The Yankees' Ron Guidry narrowly missed the top 10 list with an ERA of 1.743 in 1978.

Winning Pct.

		Year	W-L	Pct
1	Roy Face, Pit	1959	18-1	.947
2	Rick Sutcliffe, Chi-NL*	1984	16-1	.941
3	Johnny Allen, Cle	1937	15-1	.938
4	Greg Maddux, Atl	1995	19-2	.904
5	Randy Johnson, Sea.	1995	18-2	.900
6	Ron Guidry, NY-AL	1978	25-3	.893
7	Freddie Fitzsimmons, Bklyn.	1940	16-2	.889
8	Lefty Grove, Phi-AL	1931	31-4	.886
9	Bob Stanley, Bos.	1978	15-2	.882
10	Preacher Roe, Bklyn	1951	22-3	.880

*Sutcliffe began 1984 with Cleveland and was 4-5 before being traded to the Cubs; his overall winning pct. was .769 (20-6).

Appearances

		Year	App	Sv
1	Mike Marshall, LA	1974	106	21
2	Kent Tekulve, Pit	1979	94	31
3	Mike Marshall, LA	1973	92	31
4	Kent Tekulve, Pit	1978	91	31
5	Wayne Granger, Cin.	1969	90	27
	Mike Marshall, Min	1979	90	32
	Kent Tekulve, Phi.	1987	90	3

Innings Pitched (since 1920)

		Year	IP	W-L
1	Wilbur Wood, Chi-AL	1972	376.2	24-17
2	Mickey Lolich, Det	1971	376.0	25-14
3	Bob Feller, Cle	1946	371.1	26-15
4	Grover Alexander, Chi-NL	1920	363.1	27-14
5	Wilbur Wood, Chi-AL	1973	359.1	24-20

Walks Allowed (since 1920)

		Year	BB	SO
1	Bob Feller, Cle	1938	208	240
2	Nolan Ryan, Cal	1977	204	341
3	Nolan Ryan, Cal	1974	202	367
4	Bob Feller, Cle	1941	194	260
5	Bobo Newsom, St.L-AL	1938	192	226

Strikeouts

		Year	SO	P/9
1	Nolan Ryan, Cal	1973	383	10.57
2	Sandy Koufax, LA	1965	382	10.24
3	Randy Johnson, Ari	2001	372	13.41
4	Nolan Ryan, Cal	1974	367	9.93
5	Randy Johnson, Ari	1999	364	12.06
6	Rube Waddell, Phi-AL	1904	349	8.20
7	Bob Feller, Cle	1946	348	8.43
8	Randy Johnson, Ari	2000	347	12.56
9	Nolan Ryan, Cal	1977	341	10.26
10	**Randy Johnson**, Ari	2002	334	11.56

Saves

		Year	App	Sv
1	Bobby Thigpen, Chi-AL	1990	77	57
2	**John Smoltz**, Atl	2002	75	55
3	Randy Myers, Chi-NL	1993	73	53
	Trevor Hoffman, SD	1998	66	53
5	**Eric Gagne**, LA	2002	77	52
6	Dennis Eckersley, Oak	1992	69	51
	Rod Beck, Chi-NL	1998	81	51
8	Mariano Rivera, NY-AL	2001	71	50
9	Dennis Eckersley, Oak	1990	63	48
	Rod Beck, SF	1993	76	48
	Jeff Shaw, Cin-LA	1998	73	48

Shutouts

		Year	ShO	ERA
1	Grover Alexander, Phi-NL	1916	16	1.55
2	Jack Coombs, Phi-AL	1910	13	1.30
	Bob Gibson, St.L	1968	13	1.12
4	Christy Mathewson, NY-NL	1908	12	1.43
	Grover Alexander, Phi-NL	1915	12	1.22

Home Runs Allowed

		Year	HRs
1	Bert Blyleven, Minnesota	1986	50
2	Jose Lima, Houston	2000	48
3	Robin Roberts, Philadelphia	1956	46
	Bert Blyleven, Minnesota	1987	46
5	Pedro Ramos, Washington	1957	43

SINGLE GAME
Through 2002 regular season.

Batting

Home Runs

No		Date	Inn
4	Bobby Lowe, Boston-NL	5/30/1894	9
	Ed Delahanty, Philadelphia-NL	7/13/1896	9
	Lou Gehrig, New York-AL	6/3/1932	9
	Chuck Klein, Philadelphia-NL	7/10/1936	10
	Pat Seerey, Chicago-AL	7/18/1948	11
	Gil Hodges, Brooklyn	8/31/1950	9
	Joe Adcock, Milwaukee	7/31/1954	9
	Rocky Colavito, Cleveland	6/10/1959	9
	Willie Mays, San Francisco	4/30/1961	9
	Mike Schmidt, Philadelphia	4/17/1976	10
	Bob Horner, Atlanta	7/6/1986	9
	Mark Whiten, St. Louis	9/7/1993	9
	Mike Cameron, Seattle	5/2/2002	9
	Shawn Green, Los Angeles	5/23/2002	9

Hits

No		Date	Inn
9	Johnny Burnett, Cleveland (9-for-11)	7/10/1932	18
7	Wilbert Robinson, Baltimore (7-for-7)	6/10/1892	9
	Rennie Stennett, Pittsburgh (7-for-7)	9/16/1975	9
	Cesar Gutierrez, Detroit (7-for-7)	6/21/1970	12
	Rocky Colavito, Detroit (7-for-10)	6/24/1962	22

Runs Batted In

No		Date	Inn
12	Jim Bottomley, St. Louis-NL	9/16/1924	9
	Mark Whiten, St. Louis	9/7/1993	9

Runs

No		Date	Inn
7	Guy Hecker, Louisville	8/15/1886	9

Pitching

Strikeouts

No		Date	Inn
21	Tom Cheney, Washington	9/12/1962	16
20	Roger Clemens, Boston	4/29/1986	9
	Roger Clemens, Boston	9/18/1996	9
	Kerry Wood, Chicago-NL	5/6/1998	9
	Randy Johnson, Arizona	5/8/2001	9*

Innings Pitched

No		Date
26	Leon Cadore, Brooklyn (tie, 1-1)	5/1/1920
	Joe Oeschger, Boston-NL (tie, 1-1)	5/1/1920

*Johnson struck out 20 in nine innings and was removed with the game tied, 1-1. Arizona beat Cincinnati, 4-3, in 11 innings.

Unassisted Triple Plays

One of the rarest feats in baseball, the unassisted triple play has been accomplished only 12 times in major league history. Ironically, in what can only be described as a statistic anomaly, the trick was turned twice in two days in May of 1927.

Player, Position, Team	Date	Opponent
Paul Hines, OF, Providence	May 8, 1878	Boston-NL
Neal Ball, SS, Cleveland	July 19, 1909	Boston-AL
Bill Wambganss, 2B, Cleveland*	Oct. 10, 1920	Brooklyn
George Burns, 1B, Boston-AL	Sept. 14, 1923	Cleveland
Ernie Padgett, SS, Boston-NL	Oct. 6, 1923	Philadelphia
Glenn Wright, SS, Pittsburgh	May 7, 1925	St.Louis-NL
Jimmy Cooney, SS, Chicago-NL	May 30, 1927	Pittsburgh
Johnny Neun, 1B, Detroit	May 31, 1927	Cleveland
Ron Hansen, SS, Washington	July 30, 1968	Cleveland
Mickey Morandini, 2B, Philadelphia	Sept. 20, 1992	Pittsburgh
John Valentin, SS, Boston	July 8, 1994	Seattle
Randy Velarde, 2B, Oakland	May 29, 2000	NY Yankees

*World Series game

Most Gold Gloves (by position)

Gold Gloves have been awarded since the 1957 season by Rawlings Sporting Goods to superior major league fielders at each position in both leagues. Voting has been conducted by a panel of sportswriters appointed by The Sporting News publisher J.G. Taylor Spink (1957), major league players (1958-1964) and managers and coaches (1965-present). Top 5 in each position are listed, through the 2001 season.

Pitchers	No
1 Jim Kaat	16
2 Greg Maddux	12
3 Bob Gibson	9
4 Bobby Shantz	8
5 Mark Langston	7

Catchers	No
1 Johnny Bench	10
Ivan Rodriguez	10
3 Bob Boone	7
4 Jim Sundberg	6
5 Bill Freehan	5

First Basemen	No
1 Keith Hernandez	11
2 Don Mattingly	9
3 George Scott	8
4 Vic Power	7
Bill White	7

Second Basemen	No
1 Roberto Alomar	10
2 Ryne Sandberg	9
3 Bill Mazeroski	8
Frank White	8
5 Joe Morgan	5
Bobby Richardson	5

Third Basemen	No
1 Brooks Robinson	16
2 Mike Schmidt	10
3 Buddy Bell	6
4 Robin Ventura	6
5 Three tied with 5 each.	

Shortstops	No
1 Ozzie Smith	13
2 Luis Aparicio	9
Omar Vizquel	9
4 Mark Belanger	8
5 Dave Concepcion	5

Outfielders	No
1 Roberto Clemente	12
Willie Mays	12
3 Ken Griffey Jr.	10
Al Kaline	10
5 Five tied with 8 each.	

All-Time Winningest Managers

Top 20 Major League career victories through the 2002 season. Career, regular season and postseason (playoffs and World Series) records are noted along with AL and NL pennants and World Series titles won. Managers active during 2002 season in **bold** type.

		Career				Regular Season			Postseason			
		Yrs	W	L	Pct	W	L	Pct	W	L	Pct	Titles
1	Connie Mack	53	**3755**	3967	.486	3731	3948	.486	24	19	.558	9 AL, 5 WS
2	John McGraw	33	**2866**	2012	.588	2840	1984	.589	26	28	.482	10 NL, 3 WS
3	Sparky Anderson	26	**2228**	1855	.547	2194	1834	.545	34	21	.618	4 NL, 1 AL, 3 WS
4	Bucky Harris	29	**2168**	2228	.493	2157	2218	.493	11	10	.524	3 AL, 2 WS
5	Joe McCarthy	24	**2155**	1346	.616	2125	1333	.615	30	13	.698	1 NL, 8 AL, 7 WS
6	Walter Alston	23	**2063**	1634	.558	2040	1613	.558	23	21	.523	7 NL, 4 WS
7	Leo Durocher	24	**2015**	1717	.540	2008	1709	.540	7	8	.467	3 NL, 1 WS
8	**Tony La Russa**	24	**1960**	1743	.529	1924	1712	.529	36	31	.537	3 AL, 1 WS
9	Casey Stengel	25	**1942**	1868	.510	1905	1842	.508	37	26	.587	10 AL, 7 WS
10	Gene Mauch	26	**1907**	2044	.483	1902	2037	.483	5	7	.417	—None—
11	Bill McKechnie	25	**1904**	1737	.523	1896	1723	.524	8	14	.364	4 NL, 2 WS
12	**Bobby Cox**	21	**1866**	1460	.561	1805	1404	.562	61	56	.521	5 NL, 1 WS
13	**Joe Torre**	21	**1636**	1476	.526	1579	1448	.522	57	28	.671	5 AL, 4 WS
14	Tommy Lasorda	21	**1630**	1469	.526	1599	1439	.526	31	30	.508	4 NL, 2 WS
15	Ralph Houk	20	**1627**	1539	.514	1619	1531	.514	8	8	.500	3 AL, 2 WS
16	Fred Clarke	19	**1609**	1189	.575	1602	1181	.576	7	8	.467	4 NL, 1 WS
17	Dick Williams	21	**1592**	1474	.519	1571	1451	.520	21	23	.477	3 AL, 1 NL, 2 WS
18	Earl Weaver	17	**1506**	1080	.582	1480	1060	.583	26	20	.565	4 AL, 1 WS
19	Clark Griffith	20	**1491**	1367	.522	1491	1367	.522	0	0	.000	1 AL (1901)
20	Miller Huggins	17	**1431**	1149	.555	1413	1134	.555	18	15	.545	6 AL, 3 WS

Notes: John McGraw's postseason record also includes two World Series tie games (1912,'22); Miller Huggins postseason record also includes one World Series tie game (1922).

Where They Managed

Alston—Brooklyn/Los Angeles NL (1954-76); **Anderson**—Cincinnati NL (1970-78), Detroit AL (1979-95); **Clarke**—Louisville NL (1897-99), Pittsburgh NL (1900-15); **Cox**—Atlanta (1978-81, 1990–), Toronto (1982-85); **Durocher**—Brooklyn NL (1939-46,48), New York NL (1948-55), Chicago NL (1966-72), Houston NL (1972-73); **Griffith**—Chicago AL (1901-02), New York NL (1903-08), Cincinnati NL (1909-11), Washington AL (1912-20); **Harris**—Washington AL (1924-28,35-42,50-54), Detroit AL (1929-33,55-56), Boston AL (1934), Philadelphia NL (1943), New York AL (1947-48); **Houk**—New York AL (1961-63,66-73), Detroit AL (1974-78), Boston AL (1981-84); **Huggins**—St. Louis NL (1913-17), New York AL (1918-29); **La Russa**—Chicago AL (1979-86), Oakland (1986-95), St. Louis (1996–); **Lasorda**—Los Angeles NL (1976-96); **Mack**—Pittsburgh NL (1894-96), Philadelphia AL (1901-50).

Mauch—Philadelphia NL (1960-68), Montreal NL (1969-75), Minnesota AL (1976-80), California AL (1981-82,85-87); **McCarthy**—Chicago NL (1926-30), New York AL (1931-46), Boston AL (1948-50); **McGraw**—Baltimore NL (1899), Baltimore AL (1901-02), New York NL (1902-32); **McKechnie**—Newark FL (1915), Pittsburgh NL (1922-26), St. Louis NL (1928-29), Boston NL (1930-37), Cincinnati NL (1938-46); **Stengel**—Brooklyn NL (1934-36), Boston NL (1938-43), New York AL (1949-60), New York NL (1962-65); **Torre**—New York NL (1977-81), Atlanta (1982-84), St. Louis (1990-95), New York AL (1996–); **Weaver**—Baltimore AL (1968-82,85-86); **Williams**—Boston AL (1967-69), Oakland AL (1971-73), California AL (1974-76), Montreal NL (1977-81), San Diego NL (1982-85), Seattle AL (1986-88).

Regular Season Winning Pct.

Minimum of 750 victories.

		Yrs	W	L	Pct	Pen
1	Joe McCarthy	24	2125	1333	**.615**	9
2	Charlie Comiskey	12	838	541	**.608**	4
3	Frank Selee	16	1284	862	**.598**	5
4	Billy Southworth	13	1044	704	**.597**	4
5	Frank Chance	11	946	648	**.593**	4
6	John McGraw	33	2840	1984	**.589**	10
7	Al Lopez	17	1410	1004	**.584**	2
8	Earl Weaver	17	1480	1060	**.583**	4
9	Cap Anson	20	1296	947	**.578**	5
10	Fred Clarke	19	1602	1181	**.576**	4
11	Davey Johnson	14	1148	888	**.564**	1
12	**Bobby Cox**	21	1805	1404	**.562**	5
13	Steve O'Neill	14	1040	821	**.559**	1
14	Walter Alston	23	2040	1613	**.558**	7
15	Bill Terry	10	823	661	**.555**	3
16	Miller Huggins	17	1413	1134	**.555**	6
17	Billy Martin	16	1253	1013	**.553**	2
18	Harry Wright	18	1000	825	**.548**	3
19	Charlie Grimm	19	1287	1067	**.547**	3
20	Sparky Anderson	26	2194	1834	**.545**	5

World Series Victories

		App	W	L	T	Pct	WS
1	Casey Stengel	10	**37**	26	0	.587	7
2	Joe McCarthy	9	**30**	13	0	.698	7
3	John McGraw	9	**26**	28	2	.482	3
4	Connie Mack	8	**24**	19	0	.558	5
5	Walter Alston	7	**20**	20	0	.500	4
6	**Joe Torre**	5	**19**	7	0	.731	4
7	Miller Huggins	6	**18**	15	1	.544	3
8	Sparky Anderson	5	**16**	12	0	.571	3
9	Tommy Lasorda	4	**12**	11	0	.522	2
	Dick Williams	4	**12**	14	0	.462	2
11	Frank Chance	4	**11**	9	1	.548	2
	Bucky Harris	3	**11**	10	0	.524	2
	Billy Southworth	4	**11**	11	0	.500	2
	Earl Weaver	4	**11**	13	0	.458	1
	Bobby Cox	5	**11**	18	0	.379	1
16	Whitey Herzog	3	**10**	11	0	.476	1
17	Bill Carrigan	2	**8**	2	0	.800	2
	Danny Murtaugh	2	**8**	6	0	.571	2
	Cito Gaston	2	**8**	6	0	.571	2
	Tom Kelly	2	**8**	6	0	.571	2
	Ralph Houk	3	**8**	8	0	.500	2
	Bill McKechnie	4	**8**	14	0	.364	2

Active Managers' Records

Regular season games only; through 2002 (updated as of Oct. 28).

National League

		Yrs	W	L	Pct
1	Tony La Russa, St.L.....24		**1924**	1712	.529
2	Bobby Cox, Atl........21		**1805**	1404	.562
3	Art Howe, NY 11		**992**	951	.511
4	Dusty Baker, SF 10		**840**	715	.540
5	Jimy Williams, Hou.....10		**779**	671	.537
6	Frank Robinson, Mon...12		**763**	830	.479
7	Bruce Bochy, SD 8		**630**	648	.493
8	Jeff Torborg, Fla.......10		**618**	696	.470
9	Bob Boone, Cin. 5		**325**	386	.457
10	Larry Bowa, Phi. 4		**247**	284	.465
11	Bob Brenly, Ari.........2		**190**	134	.586
12	Jim Tracy, LA.........2		**178**	146	.549
13	Lloyd McClendon, Pit.....2		**134**	189	.415
14	Clint Hurdle, Col. 1		**67**	73	.479
	Chicago				
	Milwaukee				

American League

		Yrs	W	L	Pct
1	Joe Torre, NY.........21		**1579**	1448	.522
2	Lou Piniella, TB 16		**1319**	1135	.537
3	Mike Hargrove, Bal....12		**925**	872	.515
4	Buck Showalter, Tex.....7		**563**	504	.528
5	Jerry Manuel, Chi........5		**414**	395	.512
6	Mike Scioscia, Ana. 3		**256**	230	.527
7	Ron Gardenhire, Min.....1		**94**	67	.584
8	Grady Little, Bos........1		**93**	69	.574
9	Carlos Tosca, Tor. 1		**58**	51	.532
10	Tony Pena, KC 1		**49**	77	.389
11	Alan Trammell, Det.......0		**0**	0	.000
	Eric Wedge, Cle.........0		**0**	0	.000
	Oakland				
	Seattle				

Annual Awards

MOST VALUABLE PLAYER

There have been three different Most Valuable Player awards in baseball since 1911—the Chalmers Award (1911-14), presented by the Detroit-based automobile company; the League Award (1922-29), presented by the National and American Leagues; and the Baseball Writers' Award (since 1931), presented by the Baseball Writers' Association of America. Statistics for winning players are provided below. Stats for winning pitchers before advent of Cy Young Award are in MVP Pitchers' Statistics table.

Multiple winners: NL—Barry Bonds (4); Roy Campanella, Stan Musial and Mike Schmidt (3); Ernie Banks, Johnny Bench, Rogers Hornsby, Carl Hubbell, Willie Mays, Joe Morgan and Dale Murphy (2). **AL**—Yogi Berra, Joe DiMaggio, Jimmie Foxx and Mickey Mantle (3); Mickey Cochrane, Lou Gehrig, Juan Gonzalez, Hank Greenberg, Walter Johnson, Roger Maris, Hal Newhouser, Cal Ripken Jr., Frank Thomas, Ted Williams and Robin Yount (2). **NL & AL**—Frank Robinson (2, one in each).

Chalmers Award

National League

Year		Pos	HR	RBI	Avg
1911	Wildfire Schulte, Chi ....OF		21	121	.300
1912	Larry Doyle, NY 2B		10	90	.330
1913	Jake Daubert, Bklyn 1B		2	52	.350
1914	Johnny Evers, Bos 2B		1	40	.279

American League

Year		Pos	HR	RBI	Avg
1911	Ty Cobb, Det..............OF		8	144	.420
1912	Tris Speaker, Bos..........OF		10	98	.383
1913	Walter Johnson, Wash .....P		—	—	—
1914	Eddie Collins, Phi 2B		2	85	.344

League Award

National League

Year		Pos	HR	RBI	Avg
1922	No selection				
1923	No selection				
1924	Dazzy Vance, Bklyn ....P		—	—	—
1925	Rogers Hornsby, St.L.....2B-Mgr		39	143	.403
1926	Bob O'Farrell, St.L C		7	68	.293
1927	Paul Waner, Pit............OF		9	131	.380
1928	Jim Bottomley, St.L.........1B		31	136	.325
1929	Rogers Hornsby, Chi........2B		39	149	.380

American League

Year		Pos	HR	RBI	Avg
1922	George Sisler, St.L 1B		8	105	.420
1923	Babe Ruth, NY ....OF		41	131	.393
1924	Walter Johnson, Wash ....P		—	—	—
1925	Roger Peckinpaugh, Wash...SS		4	64	.294
1926	George Burns, Cle 1B		4	114	.358
1927	Lou Gehrig, NY............1B		47	175	.373
1928	Mickey Cochrane, Phi C		10	57	.293
1929	No selection				

Most Valuable Player
National League

Year		Pos	HR	RBI	Avg
1931	Frankie Frisch, St.L 2B		4	82	.311
1932	Chuck Klein, Phi ....OF		38	137	.348
1933	Carl Hubbell, NY............P		—	—	—
1934	Dizzy Dean, St.L ....P		—	—	—
1935	Gabby Hartnett, Chi.........C		13	91	.344
1936	Carl Hubbell, NY............P		—	—	—
1937	Joe Medwick, St.L..........OF		31	154	.374
1938	Ernie Lombardi, Cin C		19	95	.342
1939	Bucky Walters, Cin ....P		—	—	—
1940	Frank McCormick, Cin 1B		19	127	.309
1941	Dolf Camilli, Bklyn 1B		34	120	.285
1942	Mort Cooper, St.L ....P		—	—	—
1943	Stan Musial, St.L...........OF		13	81	.357
1944	Marty Marion, St.L ....SS		6	63	.267
1945	Phil Cavarretta, Chi 1B		6	97	.355
1946	Stan Musial, St.L.......1B-OF		16	103	.365
1947	Bob Elliott, Bos 3B		22	113	.317
1948	Stan Musial, St.L...........OF		39	131	.376
1949	Jackie Robinson, Bklyn......2B		16	124	.342
1950	Jim Konstanty, Phi ....P		—	—	—
1951	Roy Campanella, Bklyn C		33	108	.325
1952	Hank Sauer, Chi...........OF		37	121	.270
1953	Roy Campanella, Bklyn C		41	142	.312
1954	Willie Mays, NY ....OF		41	110	.345
1955	Roy Campanella, Bklyn C		32	107	.318
1956	Don Newcombe, Bklyn.......P		—	—	—
1957	Hank Aaron, Mil ....OF		44	132	.322
1958	Ernie Banks, Chi ....SS		47	129	.313
1959	Ernie Banks, Chi ....SS		45	143	.304
1960	Dick Groat, Pit.............SS		2	50	.325
1961	Frank Robinson, Cin ....OF		37	124	.323
1962	Maury Wills, LA ....SS		6	48	.299
1963	Sandy Koufax, LA ....P		—	—	—
1964	Ken Boyer, St.L 3B		24	119	.295
1965	Willie Mays, SF ....OF		52	112	.317
1966	Roberto Clemente, Pit ......OF		29	119	.317
1967	Orlando Cepeda, St.L 1B		25	111	.325
1968	Bob Gibson, St.L ....P		—	—	—

Year		Pos	HR	RBI	Avg
1969	Willie McCovey, SF	1B	45	126	.320
1970	Johnny Bench, Cin	C	45	148	.293
1971	Joe Torre, St.L.	3B	24	137	.363
1972	Johnny Bench, Cin	C	40	125	.270
1973	Pete Rose, Cin.	OF	5	64	.338
1974	Steve Garvey, LA	1B	21	111	.312
1975	Joe Morgan, Cin	2B	17	94	.327
1976	Joe Morgan, Cin	2B	27	111	.320
1977	George Foster, Cin.	OF	52	149	.320
1978	Dave Parker, Pit	OF	30	117	.334
1979	Keith Hernandez, St.L.	1B	11	105	.344
	Willie Stargell, Pit	1B	32	82	.281
1980	Mike Schmidt, Phi	3B	48	121	.286
1981	Mike Schmidt, Phi	3B	31	91	.316
1982	Dale Murphy, Atl	OF	36	109	.281
1983	Dale Murphy, Atl	OF	36	121	.302
1984	Ryne Sandberg, Chi	2B	19	84	.314
1985	Willie McGee, St.L.	OF	10	82	.353
1986	Mike Schmidt, Phi	3B	37	119	.290
1987	Andre Dawson, Chi	OF	49	137	.287
1988	Kirk Gibson, LA	OF	25	76	.290
1989	Kevin Mitchell, SF	OF	47	125	.291
1990	Barry Bonds, Pit	OF	33	114	.301
1991	Terry Pendleton, Atl.	3B	22	86	.319
1992	Barry Bonds, Pit	OF	34	103	.311
1993	Barry Bonds, SF	OF	46	123	.336
1994	Jeff Bagwell, Hou	1B	39	116	.368
1995	Barry Larkin, Cin	SS	15	66	.319
1996	Ken Caminiti, SD	3B	40	130	.326
1997	Larry Walker, Col.	OF	49	130	.366
1998	Sammy Sosa, Chi	OF	66	158	.308
1999	Chipper Jones, Atl	3B	45	110	.319
2000	Jeff Kent, SF	2B	33	125	.334
2001	Barry Bonds, SF	OF	73	137	.328

American League

Year		Pos	HR	RBI	Avg
1931	Lefty Grove, Phi	P	—	—	—
1932	Jimmie Foxx, Phi	1B	58	169	.364
1933	Jimmie Foxx, Phi	1B	48	163	.356
1934	Mickey Cochrane, Det	C-Mgr	2	76	.320
1935	Hank Greenberg, Det	1B	36	170	.328
1936	Lou Gehrig, NY	1B	49	152	.354
1937	Charlie Gehringer, Det	2B	14	96	.371
1938	Jimmie Foxx, Bos	1B	50	175	.349
1939	Joe DiMaggio, NY	OF	30	126	.381
1940	Hank Greenberg, Det	OF	41	150	.340
1941	Joe DiMaggio, NY	OF	30	125	.357
1942	Joe Gordon, NY	2B	18	103	.322°
1943	Spud Chandler, NY	P	—	—	—
1944	Hal Hewhouser, Det	P	—	—	—
1945	Hal Hewhouser, Det	P	—	—	—
1946	Ted Williams, Bos.	OF	38	123	.342
1947	Joe DiMaggio, NY	OF	20	97	.315
1948	Lou Boudreau, Cle	SS-Mgr	18	106	.355
1949	Ted Williams, Bos.	OF	43	159	.343
1950	Phil Rizzuto, NY	SS	7	66	.324
1951	Yogi Berra, NY	C	27	88	.294
1952	Bobby Shantz, Phi	P	—	—	—
1953	Al Rosen, Cle.	3B	43	145	.336
1954	Yogi Berra, NY	C	22	125	.307
1955	Yogi Berra, NY	C	27	108	.272
1956	Mickey Mantle, NY	OF	52	130	.353
1957	Mickey Mantle, NY	OF	34	94	.365
1958	Jackie Jensen, Bos	OF	35	122	.286
1959	Nellie Fox, Chi	2B	2	70	.306
1960	Roger Maris, NY	OF	39	112	.283
1961	Roger Maris, NY	OF	61	142	.269
1962	Mickey Mantle, NY	OF	30	89	.321
1963	Elston Howard, NY	C	28	85	.287
1964	Brooks Robinson, Bal	3B	28	118	.317
1965	Zoilo Versalles, Min	SS	19	77	.273
1966	Frank Robinson, Bal	OF	49	122	.316
1967	Carl Yastrzemski, Bos	OF	44	121	.326
1968	Denny McLain, Det	P	—	—	—
1969	Harmon Killebrew, Min	3B-1B	49	140	.276
1970	Boog Powell, Bal.	1B	35	114	.297
1971	Vida Blue, Oak	P	—	—	—
1972	Dick Allen, Chi	1B	37	113	.308
1973	Reggie Jackson, Oak.	OF	32	117	.293
1974	Jeff Burroughs, Tex	OF	25	118	.301
1975	Fred Lynn, Bos.	OF	21	105	.331
1976	Thurman Munson, NY	C	17	105	.302
1977	Rod Carew, Min	1B	14	100	.388
1978	Jim Rice, Bos.	OF-DH	46	139	.315
1979	Don Baylor, Cal	OF-DH	36	139	.296
1980	George Brett, KC	3B	24	118	.390
1981	Rollie Fingers, Mil	P	—	—	—
1982	Robin Yount, Mil	SS	29	114	.331
1983	Cal Ripken Jr., Bal.	SS	27	102	.318
1984	Willie Hernandez, Det	P	—	—	—
1985	Don Mattingly, NY	1B	35	145	.324
1986	Roger Clemens, Bos	P	—	—	—
1987	George Bell, Tor	OF	47	134	.308
1988	Jose Canseco, Oak	OF	42	124	.307
1989	Robin Yount, Mil	OF	21	103	.318
1990	Rickey Henderson, Oak	OF	28	61	.325
1991	Cal Ripken Jr., Bal.	SS	34	114	.323
1992	Dennis Eckersley, Oak	P	—	—	—
1993	Frank Thomas, Chi	1B	41	128	.317
1994	Frank Thomas, Chi	1B	38	101	.353
1995	Mo Vaughn, Bos	1B	39	126	.300
1996	Juan Gonzalez, Tex	OF-DH	47	144	.314
1997	Ken Griffey Jr., Sea	OF	56	147	.304
1998	Juan Gonzalez, Tex	OF	45	157	.318
1999	Ivan Rodriguez, Tex	C	35	113	.332
2000	Jason Giambi, Oak	1B	43	137	.333
2001	Ichiro Suzuki, Sea	OF	8	69	.350

MVP Pitchers' Statistics

Pitchers have been named Most Valuable Player on 23 occasions, 10 times in the NL and 13 in the AL. Four have been relief pitchers—Jim Konstanty, Rollie Fingers, Willie Hernandez and Dennis Eckersley. For statistics of MVP pitchers since 1956, see Cy Young Award tables on following page.

National League

Year		Gm	W-L	SV	ERA
1924	Dazzy Vance, Bklyn	35	28-6	0	2.16
1933	Carl Hubbell, NY	45	23-12	5	1.66
1934	Dizzy Dean, St.L.	50	30-7	7	2.66
1936	Carl Hubbell, NY	42	26-6	3	2.31
1939	Bucky Walters, Cin	39	27-11	0	2.29
1942	Mort Cooper, St.L.	37	22-7	0	1.78
1950	Jim Konstanty, Phi	74	16-7	22	2.66

American League

Year		Gm	W-L	SV	ERA
1913	Walter Johnson, Wash	47	36-7	2	1.09
1924	Walter Johnson, Wash	38	23-7	0	2.72
1931	Lefty Grove, Phi	41	31-4	5	2.06
1943	Spud Chandler, NY	30	20-4	0	1.64
1944	Hal Newhouser, Det	47	29-9	2	2.22
1945	Hal Newhouser, Det	40	25-9	2	1.81
1952	Bobby Shantz, Phi	33	24-7	0	2.48

CY YOUNG AWARD

Voted on by the Baseball Writers Association of America. One award was presented from 1956-66, two since 1967. Pitchers who won the MVP and Cy Young awards in the same season are in **bold** type.

Multiple winners: NL—Steve Carlton and Greg Maddux (4); Randy Johnson, Sandy Koufax and Tom Seaver (3); Bob Gibson and Tom Glavine (2). **AL**—Roger Clemens (6); Jim Palmer (3); Pedro Martinez and Denny McLain (2). **NL & AL**—Randy Johnson (4, three in NL, one in AL), Pedro Martinez (3, two in AL, one in NL) and Gaylord Perry (2, one in each).

NL and AL Combined

Year	National League	Gm	W-L	SV	ERA	Year	American League	Gm	W-L	SV	ERA
1956	**Don Newcombe**, Bklyn	38	27-7	0	3.06	1958	Bob Turley, NY	33	21-7	1	2.97
1957	Warren Spahn, Mil.	39	21-11	3	2.69	1959	Early Wynn, Chi	37	22-10	0	3.17
1960	Vernon Law, Pit	35	20-9	0	3.08	1961	Whitey Ford, NY	39	25-4	0	3.21
1962	Don Drysdale, LA	43	25-9	1	2.83	1964	Dean Chance, LA	46	20-9	4	1.65
1963	**Sandy Koufax**, LA	40	25-5	0	1.88						
1965	Sandy Koufax, LA	43	26-8	2	2.04						
1966	Sandy Koufax, LA	41	27-9	0	1.73						

Separate League Awards

	National League						American League				
Year		Gm	W-L	SV	ERA	Year		Gm	W-L	SV	ERA
1967	Mike McCormick, SF	40	22-10	0	2.85	1967	Jim Lonborg, Bos	39	22-9	0	3.16
1968	**Bob Gibson**, St.L	34	22-9	0	1.12	1968	**Denny McLain**, Det	41	31-6	0	1.96
1969	Tom Seaver, NY	36	25-7	0	2.21	1969	Denny McLain, Det	42	24-9	0	2.80
							Mike Cuellar, Bal	39	23-11	0	2.38
1970	Bob Gibson, St.L	34	23-7	0	3.12	1970	Jim Perry, Min	40	24-12	0	3.03
1971	Ferguson Jenkins, Chi	39	24-13	0	2.77	1971	Vida Blue, Oak	39	24-8	0	1.82
1972	Steve Carlton, Phi	41	27-10	0	1.97	1972	Gaylord Perry, Cle	41	24-16	1	1.92
1973	Tom Seaver, NY	36	19-10	0	2.08	1973	Jim Palmer, Bal	38	22-9	1	2.40
1974	Mike Marshall, LA	106	15-12	21	2.42	1974	Catfish Hunter, Oak	41	25-12	0	2.49
1975	Tom Seaver, NY	36	22-9	0	2.38	1975	Jim Palmer, Bal	39	23-11	1	2.09
1976	Randy Jones, SD	40	22-14	0	2.74	1976	Jim Palmer, Bal	40	22-13	0	2.51
1977	Steve Carlton, Phi	36	23-10	0	2.64	1977	Sparky Lyle, NY	72	13-5	26	2.17
1978	Gaylord Perry, SD	37	21-6	0	2.72	1978	Ron Guidry, NY	35	25-3	0	1.74
1979	Bruce Sutter, Chi	62	6-6	37	2.23	1979	Mike Flanagan, Bal	39	23-9	0	3.08
1980	Steve Carlton, Phi	38	24-9	0	2.34	1980	Steve Stone, Bal	37	25-7	0	3.23
1981	Fernando Valenzuela, LA	25	13-7	0	2.48	1981	**Rollie Fingers**, Mil	47	6-3	28	1.04
1982	Steve Carlton, Phi	38	23-11	0	3.10	1982	Pete Vuckovich, Mil	30	18-6	0	3.34
1983	John Denny, Phi	36	19-6	0	2.37	1983	LaMarr Hoyt, Chi	36	24-10	0	3.66
1984	Rick Sutcliffe, Chi	20*	16-1	0	2.69	1984	**Willie Hernandez**, Det	80	9-3	32	1.92
1985	Dwight Gooden, NY	35	24-4	0	1.53	1985	Bret Saberhagen, KC	32	20-6	0	2.87
1986	Mike Scott, Hou	37	18-10	0	2.22	1986	**Roger Clemens**, Bos	33	24-4	0	2.48
1987	Steve Bedrosian, Phi	65	5-3	40	2.83	1987	Roger Clemens, Bos	36	20-9	0	2.97
1988	Orel Hershiser, LA	35	23-8	1	2.26	1988	Frank Viola, Min	35	24-7	0	2.64
1989	Mark Davis, SD	70	4-3	44	1.85	1989	Bret Saberhagen, KC	36	23-6	0	2.16
1990	Doug Drabek, Pit	33	22-6	0	2.76	1990	Bob Welch, Oak	35	27-6	0	2.95
1991	Tom Glavine, Atl	34	20-11	0	2.55	1991	Roger Clemens, Bos	35	18-10	0	2.62
1992	Greg Maddux, Chi	35	20-11	0	2.18	1992	**Dennis Eckersley**, Oak	69	7-1	51	1.91
1993	Greg Maddux, Atl	36	20-10	0	2.36	1993	Jack McDowell, Chi	34	22-10	0	3.37
1994	Greg Maddux, Atl	25	16-6	0	1.56	1994	David Cone, KC	23	16-5	0	2.94
1995	Greg Maddux, Atl	28	19-2	0	1.63	1995	Randy Johnson, Sea	30	18-2	0	2.48
1996	John Smoltz, Atl	35	24-8	0	2.94	1996	Pat Hentgen, Tor	35	20-10	0	3.22
1997	Pedro Martinez, Mon	31	17-8	0	1.90	1997	Roger Clemens, Tor	34	21-7	0	2.05
1998	Tom Glavine, Atl	33	20-6	0	2.47	1998	Roger Clemens, Tor	33	20-6	0	2.65
1999	Randy Johnson, Ari	35	17-9	0	2.48	1999	Pedro Martinez, Bos	31	23-4	0	2.07
2000	Randy Johnson, Ari	35	19-7	0	2.64	2000	Pedro Martinez, Bos	29	18-6	0	1.74
2001	Randy Johnson, Ari	35	21-6	0	2.49	2001	Roger Clemens, NY	33	20-3	0	3.51

*NL games only, Sutcliffe pitched 15 games with Cleveland before being traded to the Cubs.

ROOKIE OF THE YEAR

Voted on by the Baseball Writers Assn. of America. One award was presented from 1947-48. Two awards (one for each league) have been presented since 1949. Winners who were also named MVP in the same season are in **bold** type.

NL and AL Combined

Year		Pos	Year		Pos
1947	Jackie Robinson, Brooklyn	1B	1948	Alvin Dark, Boston-NL	SS

National League

Year		Pos	Year		Pos	Year		Pos
1949	Don Newcombe, Bklyn	P	1952	Joe Black, Bklyn	P	1955	Bill Virdon, St.L	OF
1950	Sam Jethroe, Bos	OF	1953	Jim Gilliam, Bklyn	2B	1956	Frank Robinson, Cin	OF
1951	Willie Mays, NY	OF	1954	Wally Moon, St.L	OF	1957	Jack Sanford, Phi	P

Year		Pos
1958	Orlando Cepeda, SF	1B
1959	Willie McCovey, SF	1B
1960	Frank Howard, LA	OF
1961	Billy Williams, Chi	OF
1962	Ken Hubbs, Chi	2B
1963	Pete Rose, Cin	2B
1964	Richie Allen, Phi	3B
1965	Jim Lefebvre, LA	2B
1966	Tommy Helms, Cin	3B
1967	Tom Seaver, NY	P
1968	Johnny Bench, Cin	C
1969	Ted Sizemore, LA	2B
1970	Carl Morton, Mon	P
1971	Earl Williams, Atl	C
1972	Jon Matlack, NY	P

Year		Pos
1973	Gary Matthews, SF	OF
1974	Bake McBride, St.L	OF
1975	John Montefusco, SF	P
1976	Butch Metzger, SD & Pat Zachry, Cin	P P
1977	Andre Dawson, Mon	OF
1978	Bob Horner, Atl	3B
1979	Rick Sutcliffe, LA	P
1980	Steve Howe, LA	P
1981	Fernando Valenzuela, LA	P
1982	Steve Sax, LA	2B
1983	Darryl Strawberry, NY	OF
1984	Dwight Gooden, NY	P
1985	Vince Coleman, St.L	OF
1986	Todd Worrell, St.L	P

Year		Pos
1987	Benito Santiago, SD	C
1988	Chris Sabo, Cin	3B
1989	Jerome Walton, Chi	OF
1990	David Justice, Atl	OF
1991	Jeff Bagwell, Hou	1B
1992	Eric Karros, LA.	1B
1993	Mike Piazza, LA	C
1994	Raul Mondesi, LA	OF
1995	Hideo Nomo, LA	P
1996	Todd Hollandsworth, LA	OF
1997	Scott Rolen, Phi	3B
1998	Kerry Wood, Chi	P
1999	Scott Williamson, Cin	P
2000	Rafael Furcal, Atl	SS
2001	Albert Pujols, St.L	OF-3B

American League

Year		Pos
1949	Roy Sievers, St.L	OF
1950	Walt Dropo, Bos	1B
1951	Gil McDougald, NY	3B
1952	Harry Byrd, Phi	P
1953	Harvey Kuenn, Det	SS
1954	Bob Grim, NY	P
1955	Herb Score, Cle	P
1956	Luis Aparicio, Chi	SS
1957	Tony Kubek, NY	INF-OF
1958	Albie Pearson, Wash	OF
1959	Bob Allison, Wash	OF
1960	Ron Hansen, Bal	SS
1961	Don Schwall, Bos	P
1962	Tom Tresh, NY	SS-OF
1963	Gary Peters, Chi	P
1964	Tony Oliva, Min	OF
1965	Curt Blefary, Bal	OF
1966	Tommie Agee, Chi	OF

Year		Pos
1967	Rod Carew, Min	2B
1968	Stan Bahnsen, NY	P
1969	Lou Piniella, KC	OF
1970	Thurman Munson, NY	C
1971	Chris Chambliss, Cle	1B
1972	Carlton Fisk, Bos	C
1973	Al Bumbry, Bal	OF
1974	Mike Hargrove, Tex	1B
1975	**Fred Lynn**, Bos	OF
1976	Mark Fidrych, Det	P
1977	Eddie Murray, Bal	DH-1B
1978	Lou Whitaker, Det	2B
1979	John Castino, Min & Alfredo Griffin, Tor	3B SS
1980	Joe Charboneau, Cle	OF-DH
1981	Dave Righetti, NY	P
1982	Cal Ripken Jr., Bal	SS-3B
1983	Ron Kittle, Chi	OF

Year		Pos
1984	Alvin Davis, Sea	1B
1985	Ozzie Guillen, Chi	SS
1986	Jose Canseco, Oak	OF
1987	Mark McGwire, Oak	1B
1988	Walt Weiss, Oak.	SS
1989	Gregg Olson, Bal	P
1990	Sandy Alomar Jr., Cle	C
1991	Chuck Knoblauch, Min	2B
1992	Pat Listach, Mil	SS
1993	Tim Salmon, Cal	OF
1994	Bob Hamelin, KC	DH
1995	Marty Cordova, Min	OF
1996	Derek Jeter, NY	SS
1997	Nomar Garciaparra, Bos	SS
1998	Ben Grieve, Oak	OF
1999	Carlos Beltran, KC	OF
2000	Kazuhiro Sasaki, Sea	P
2001	**Ichiro Suzuki**, Sea	OF

MANAGER OF THE YEAR

Voted on by the Baseball Writers Association of America. Two awards (one for each league) presented since 1983. Note that (*) indicates manager's team won division championship and (†) indicates unofficial division won in 1994.

Multiple winners: Dusty Baker and Tony La Russa (3); Sparky Anderson, Bobby Cox, Tommy Lasorda, Jim Leyland, Lou Piniella and Joe Torre (2).

National League

Year		Improvement		
1983	Tommy Lasorda, LA	88-74	to	91-71*
1984	Jim Frey, Chi	71-91	to	96-75*
1985	Whitey Herzog, St. L	84-78	to	101-61*
1986	Hal Lanier, Hou	83-79	to	96-66*
1987	Buck Rodgers, Mon	78-83	to	91-71
1988	Tommy Lasorda, LA	73-89	to	94-67*
1989	Don Zimmer, Chi	77-85	to	93-69*
1990	Jim Leyland, Pit	74-88	to	95-67*
1991	Bobby Cox, Atl.	65-97	to	94-68*
1992	Jim Leyland, Pit	98-64*	to	96-66*
1993	Dusty Baker, SF	72-90	to	103-59
1994	Felipe Alou, Mon	94-68	to	74-40†
1995	Don Baylor, Col	53-64	to	77-67
1996	Bruce Bochy, SD	70-74	to	91-71
1997	Dusty Baker, SF	68-94	to	90-72
1998	Larry Dierker, Hou	84-78	to	102-60*
1999	Jack McKeon, Cin	77-85	to	96-67
2000	Dusty Baker, SF	86-76	to	97-65*
2001	Larry Bowa, Phi	65-97	to	86-76

American League

Year		Improvement		
1983	Tony La Russa, Chi	87-75	to	99-63*
1984	Sparky Anderson, Det	92-70	to	104-58*
1985	Bobby Cox, Tor	89-73	to	99-62*
1986	John McNamara, Bos	81-81	to	95-66*
1987	Sparky Anderson, Det	87-75	to	98-64*
1988	Tony La Russa, Oak	81-81	to	104-58*
1989	Frank Robinson, Bal	54-107	to	87-75
1990	Jeff Torborg, Chi	69-92	to	94-68
1991	Tom Kelly, Min	74-88	to	95-67*
1992	Tony La Russa, Oak	84-78	to	96-66*
1993	Gene Lamont, Chi	86-76	to	94-68*
1994	Buck Showalter, NY	88-74	to	70-43†
1995	Lou Piniella, Sea	49-63	to	79-66*
1996	Joe Torre, NY & Johnny Oates, Tex	79-65 74-70	to to	92-70 90-72
1997	Davey Johnson, Bal	88-74	to	98-64
1998	Joe Torre, NY	96-66	to	114-48*
1999	Jimy Williams, Bos	92-70	to	94-68
2000	Jerry Manuel, Chi	75-86	to	95-67*
2001	Lou Piniella, Sea	91-71	to	116-46*

COLLEGE BASEBALL

College World Series

The NCAA Division I College World Series has been held in Kalamazoo, Mich. (1947-48), Wichita, Kan. (1949) and Omaha, Neb. (since 1950).

Multiple winners: USC (12); Arizona St., LSU and Texas (5); Miami-FL (4); Arizona, CS-Fullerton and Minnesota (3); California, Michigan, Oklahoma and Stanford (2).

Year	Winner	Coach	Score	Runner-up	Year	Winner	Coach	Score	Runner-up
1947	California	Clint Evans	8-7	Yale	1975	Texas	Cliff Gustafson	5-1	S. Carolina
1948	USC	Sam Barry	9-2	Yale	1976	Arizona	Jerry Kindall	7-1	E. Michigan
1949	Texas	Bibb Falk	10-3	W. Forest	1977	Arizona St.	Jim Brock	2-1	S. Carolina
1950	Texas	Bibb Falk	3-0	Wash. St.	1978	USC	Rod Dedeaux	10-3	Ariz. St.
1951	Oklahoma	Jack Baer	3-2	Tennessee	1979	CS-Fullerton	Augie Garrido	2-1	Arkansas
1952	Holy Cross	Jack Barry	8-4	Missouri	1980	Arizona	Jerry Kindall	5-3	Hawaii
1953	Michigan	Ray Fisher	7-5	Texas	1981	Arizona St.	Jim Brock	7-4	Okla. St.
1954	Missouri	Hi Simmons	4-1	Rollins	1982	Miami-FL	Ron Fraser	9-3	Wichita St.
1955	Wake Forest	Taylor Sanford	7-6	W. Mich.	1983	Texas	Cliff Gustafson	4-3	Alabama
1956	Minnesota	Dick Siebert	12-1	Arizona	1984	CS-Fullerton	Augie Garrido	3-1	Texas
1957	California	Geo. Wolfman	1-0	Penn St.	1985	Miami-FL	Ron Fraser	10-6	Texas
1958	USC	Rod Dedeaux	8-7	Missouri	1986	Arizona	Jerry Kindall	10-2	Fla. St.
1959	Oklahoma St.	Toby Greene	5-3	Arizona	1987	Stanford	M. Marquess	9-5	Okla. St.
1960	Minnesota	Dick Siebert	2-1	USC	1988	Stanford	M. Marquess	9-4	Ariz. St.
1961	USC	Rod Dedeaux	1-0	Okla. St.	1989	Wichita St.	G. Stephenson	5-3	Texas
1962	Michigan	Don Lund	5-4	S. Clara	1990	Georgia	Steve Webber	2-1	Okla. St.
1963	USC	Rod Dedeaux	5-2	Arizona	1991	LSU	Skip Bertman	6-3	Wichita St.
1964	Minnesota	Dick Siebert	5-1	Missouri	1992	Pepperdine	Andy Lopez	3-2	CS-Fullerton
1965	Arizona St.	Bobby Winkles	2-1	Ohio St.	1993	LSU	Skip Bertman	8-0	Wichita St.
1966	Ohio St.	Marty Karow	8-2	Okla. St.	1994	Oklahoma	Larry Cochell	13-5	Ga. Tech
1967	Arizona St.	Bobby Winkles	11-2	Houston	1995	CS-Fullerton	Augie Garrido	11-5	USC
1968	USC	Rod Dedeaux	4-3	So. Ill.	1996	LSU	Skip Bertman	9-8	Miami-FL
1969	Arizona St.	Bobby Winkles	10-1	Tulsa	1997	LSU	Skip Bertman	13-6	Alabama
1970	USC	Rod Dedeaux	2-1	Fla. St.	1998	USC	Mike Gillespie	21-14	Arizona St.
1971	USC	Rod Dedeaux	7-2	So. Ill.	1999	Miami-FL	Jim Morris	6-5	Fla. St.
1972	USC	Rod Dedeaux	1-0	Ariz. St.	2000	LSU	Skip Bertman	6-5	Stanford
1973	USC	Rod Dedeaux	4-3	Ariz. St.	2001	Miami-FL	Jim Morris	12-1	Stanford
1974	USC	Rod Dedeaux	7-3	Miami-FL	2002	Texas	Augie Garrido	12-6	S. Carolina

Most Outstanding Player

The Most Outstanding Player has been selected every year of the College World Series since 1949. Winners who did not play for the CWS champion are listed in **bold** type. No player has won the award more than once.

Year	Year	Year
1949 **Charles Teague,** W. Forest, 2B	1967 Ron Davini, Ariz. St., C	1985 Greg Ellena, Miami-FL, LF
1950 **Ray VanCleef,** Rutgers, CF	1968 Bill Seinsoth, USC, 1B	1986 Mike Senne, Arizona, DH
1951 **Sidney Hatfield,** Tenn., P-1B	1969 John Dolinsek, Ariz. St., LF	1987 Paul Carey, Stanford, RF
1952 James O'Neill, Holy Cross, P	1970 **Gene Ammann,** Fla. St., P	1988 Lee Plemel, Stanford, P
1953 **J.L. Smith,** Texas, P	1971 **Jerry Tabb,** Tulsa, 1B	1989 Greg Brummett, Wich. St., P
1954 **Tom Yewcic,** Mich. St., C	1972 Russ McQueen, USC, P	1990 Mike Rebhan, Georgia, P
1955 **Tom Borland,** Okla. St., P	1973 **Dave Winfield,** Minn., P-OF	1991 Gary Hymel, LSU, C
1956 Jerry Thomas, Minn., P	1974 George Milke, USC, P	1992 **Phil Nevin,** CS-Fullerton, 3B
1957 **Cal Emery,** Penn St., P-1B	1975 Mickey Reichenbach, Texas, 1B	1993 Todd Walker, LSU, 2B
1958 Bill Thom, USC, P	1976 Steve Powers, Arizona, P-DH	1994 Chip Glass, Oklahoma, OF
1959 Jim Dobson, Okla. St., 3B	1977 Bob Horner, Ariz. St., 3B	1995 Mark Kotsay, CS-Fullerton, OF
1960 John Erickson, Minn., 2B	1978 Rod Boxberger, USC, P	1996 **Pat Burrell,** Miami-FL, 3B
1961 **Littleton Fowler,** Okla. St., P	1979 Tony Hudson, CS-Fullerton, P	1997 Brandon Larson, LSU, SS
1962 **Bob Garibaldi,** Santa Clara, P	1980 Terry Francona, Arizona, LF	1998 Wes Rachels, USC, 2B
1963 Bud Hollowell, USC, C	1981 Stan Holmes, Ariz. St., LF	1999 **Marshall McDougall,** Fla. St., 2B
1964 **Joe Ferris,** Maine, P	1982 Dan Smith, Miami-FL, P	2000 Trey Hodges, LSU, P
1965 Sal Bando, Ariz. St., 3B	1983 Calvin Schiraldi, Texas, P	2001 Charlton Jimerson, Miami-FL, CF
1966 Steve Arlin, Ohio St., P	1984 John Fishel, CS-Fullerton, OF	2002 Huston Street, Texas, P

Annual Awards
Golden Spikes Award

First presented in 1978 by USA Baseball, honoring the nation's best amateur player; sponsored by the Major League Baseball Players Association. Alex Fernandez, the 1990 winner, has been the only junior college player chosen.

Year	Year	Year
1978 Bob Horner, Ariz. St, 2B	1987 Jim Abbott, Michigan, P	1996 Travis Lee, San Diego St., 1B
1979 Tim Wallach, CS-Fullerton, 1B	1988 Robin Ventura, Okla. St., 3B	1997 J.D. Drew, Florida St., OF
1980 Terry Francona, Arizona, OF	1989 Ben McDonald, LSU, P	1998 Pat Burrell, Miami-FL, 3B
1981 Mike Fuentes, Fla. St., OF	1990 Alex Fernandez, Miami-Dade, P	1999 Jason Jennings, Baylor, DH/P
1982 Augie Schmidt, N. Orleans, SS	1991 Mike Kelly, Ariz. St., OF	2000 Kip Bouknight, South Carolina, P
1983 Dave Magadan, Alabama, 1B	1992 Phil Nevin, CS-Fullerton, 3B	2001 Mark Prior, USC, P
1984 Oddibe McDowell, Ariz. St., OF	1993 Darren Dreifort, Wichita St., P	2002 Khalil Greene, Clemson, SS
1985 Will Clark, Miss. St., 1B	1994 Jason Varitek, Ga. Tech, C	
1986 Mike Loynd, Fla. St., P	1995 Mark Kotsay, CS-Fullerton, OF	

Baseball America Player of the Year

Presented to the College Player of the Year since 1981 by *Baseball America*.

Year	Year	Year
1981 Mike Sodders, Ariz. St., 3B	1989 Ben McDonald, LSU, P	1997 J.D. Drew, Florida St., OF
1982 Jeff Ledbetter, Fla. St., OF/P	1990 Mike Kelly, Ariz. St., OF	1998 Jeff Austin, Stanford, P
1983 Dave Magadan, Alabama, 1B	1991 David McCarty, Stanford, 1B	1999 Jason Jennings, Baylor, DH/P
1984 Oddibe McDowell, Ariz. St., OF	1992 Phil Nevin, CS-Fullerton, 3B	2000 Mark Teixeira, Ga. Tech, 3B
1985 Pete Incaviglia, Okla. St., OF	1993 Brooks Kieschnick, Texas, DH/P	2001 Mark Prior, USC, P
1986 Casey Close, Michigan, OF	1994 Jason Varitek, Ga. Tech, C	2002 Khalil Greene, Clemson, SS
1987 Robin Ventura, Okla. St., 3B	1995 Todd Helton, Tenn., 1B/P	
1988 John Olerud, Wash. St., 1B/P	1996 Kris Benson, Clemson, P	

Dick Howser Trophy

Presented to the College Player of the Year since 1987, by the American Baseball Coaches Association (ABCA) from 1987-98 and the National Collegiate Baseball Writers Association (NCBWA) beginning in 1999. Sponsored by Verizon and the St. Petersburg Area Chamber of Commerce. Named after the late two-time All-America shortstop and college coach at Florida State. Howser was also a major league manager with Kansas City and the New York Yankees.

Multiple winner: Brooks Kieschnick (2).

Year	Year	Year
1987 Mike Fiore, Miami-FL, OF	1993 Brooks Kieschnick, Texas, DH/P	1999 Jason Jennings, Baylor, DH/P
1988 Robin Ventura, Okla. St., 3B	1994 Jason Varitek, Ga. Tech, C	2000 Mark Teixeira, Ga. Tech, 3B
1989 Scott Bryant, Texas, DH	1995 Todd Helton, Tenn., 1B/P	2001 Mark Prior, USC, P
1990 Paul Ellis, UCLA, C	1996 Kris Benson, Clemson, P	2002 Khalil Greene, Clemson, SS
1991 Bobby Jones, Fresno St., P	1997 J.D. Drew, Florida St., OF	
1992 Brooks Kieschnick, Texas, DH/P	1998 Eddie Furniss, LSU, 1B	

Baseball America Coach of the Year

Presented to the College Coach of the Year since 1981 by *Baseball America*.

Multiple winners: Skip Bertman, Augie Garrido, Dave Snow and Gene Stephenson (2).

Year	Year	Year
1981 Ron Fraser, Miami-FL	1988 Jim Brock, Arizona St.	1996 Skip Bertman, LSU
1982 Gene Stephenson, Wichita St.	1989 Dave Snow, Long Beach St.	1997 Jim Wells, Alabama
1983 Barry Shollenberger, Alabama	1990 Steve Webber, Georgia	1998 Pat Murphy, Arizona St.
1984 Augie Garrido, CS-Fullerton	1991 Jim Hendry, Creighton	1999 Wayne Graham, Rice
1985 Ron Polk, Mississippi St.	1992 Andy Lopez, Pepperdine	2000 Ray Tanner, S. Carolina
1986 Skip Bertman, LSU	1993 Gene Stephenson, Wichita St.	2001 Dave Van Horn, Nebraska
& Dave Snow, Loyola-CA	1994 Jim Morris, Miami-FL	2002 Augie Garrido, Texas
1987 Mark Marquess, Stanford	1995 Rod Delmonico, Tennessee	

All-Time Winningest Coaches

Coaches active in 2002 are in **bold** type. Records given are for four-year colleges only. For winning percentage, a minimum 10 years in Division I is required.

Top 25 Winning Percentage

		Yrs	W	L	T	Pct
1	John Barry	40	619	147	6	.806
2	W.J. Disch	29	465	115	0	.802
3	Cliff Gustafson	29	1427	373	2	.792
4	Harry Carlson	17	143	41	0	.777
5	**Gene Stephenson**	25	1357	421	3	.763
6	George Jacobs	11	76	25	0	.752
7	Bobby Winkles	13	524	173	0	.752
8	**Mike Martin**	23	1239	416	3	.748
9	Frank Sancet	23	831	283	8	.744
10	Ron Fraser	30	1271	438	9	.742
11	Bob Wren	28	464	160	4	.742
12	Bibb Falk	25	435	152	0	.741
13	**Gary Ward**	21	1022	361	1	.739
14	Skip Bertman	18	870	330	3	.724
15	Bud Middaugh	22	821	319	1	.720
16	J.F. "Pop" McKale	30	302	118	7	.715
17	Jim Brock	23	1100	440	0	.714
18	Toby Green	21	318	132	0	.707
19	Joe Arnold	18	750	313	2	.705
20	**Jim Morris**	21	931	392	2	.703
21	Joe Bedenk	32	380	159	3	.701
22	**Jim Wells**	13	563	241	0	.700
23	**Ray Tanner**	15	669	286	3	.700
24	Rod Dedeaux	45	1332	571	11	.699
25	Enos Semore	22	851	370	1	.697

Top 25 Victories

		Yrs	W	L	T	Pct
1	Cliff Gustafson	29	**1427**	373	2	.792
2	**Augie Garrido**	33	**1380**	666	8	.674
3	**Gene Stephenson**	25	**1357**	421	3	.763
4	**Chuck Hartman**	43	**1338**	705	8	.654
5	Rod Dedeaux	45	**1332**	571	11	.699
6	**Larry Hays**	32	**1320**	706	2	.651
7	**Bob Bennett**	34	**1300**	757	8	.631
8	Ron Fraser	30	**1271**	438	9	.742
9	Jack Stallings	39	**1258**	796	5	.612
10	**Larry Cochell**	36	**1246**	739	3	.628
11	**Mike Martin**	23	**1239**	416	3	.748
12	**Jim Dietz**	31	**1230**	751	18	.620
13	Al Ogletree	41	**1217**	713	1	.631
14	Chuck Brayton	33	**1162**	523	8	.689
15	Bill Wilhelm	36	**1161**	536	10	.683
	Norm DeBriyn	33	**1161**	650	6	.641
17	**Richard Jones**	36	**1160**	670	5	.634
18	**Ron Polk**	29	**1157**	558	1	.675
19	**Gary Adams**	33	**1109**	832	12	.571
20	Jim Brock	23	**1100**	440	0	.714
21	**Mark Marquess**	26	**1093**	533	5	.673
22	Les Murakami	30	**1077**	570	4	.654
23	Bob Hannah	36	**1054**	463	6	.694
24	**Gary Ward**	21	**1022**	361	1	.739
25	**Jay Bergman**	26	**1013**	562	3	.643

Other NCAA Champions
Division II

Multiple winners: Florida Southern (8); Cal Poly Pomona and Tampa (3); CS-Chico, CS-Northridge, Jacksonville St., Troy St., UC-Irvine and UC-Riverside (2).

Year		Year		Year		Year	
1968	Chapman, CA	1977	UC-Riverside	1986	Troy St., AL	1995	Florida Southern
1969	Illinois St.	1978	Florida Southern	1987	Troy St., AL	1996	Kennesaw St., GA
1970	CS-Northridge	1979	Valdosta St., GA	1988	Florida Southern	1997	CS-Chico
1971	Florida Southern	1980	Cal Poly Pomona	1989	Cal Poly SLO	1998	Tampa
1972	Florida Southern	1981	Florida Southern	1990	Jacksonville St., AL	1999	CS-Chico
1973	UC-Irvine	1982	UC-Riverside	1991	Jacksonville St., AL	2000	Southeastern Okla.
1974	UC-Irvine	1983	Cal Poly Pomona	1992	Tampa	2001	St. Mary's, TX
1975	Florida Southern	1984	CS-Northridge	1993	Tampa	2002	Columbus St., GA
1976	Cal Poly Pomona	1985	Florida Southern	1994	Central Missouri St.		

Division III

Multiple winners: Eastern Conn. St. (4); Marietta and Montclair St. (3); CS-Stanislaus, Glassboro St., Ithaca, NC-Wesleyan, Southern Maine and Wm. Paterson, NJ (2).

Year		Year		Year		Year	
1976	CS-Stanislaus	1983	Marietta, OH	1990	Eastern Conn. St.	1997	Southern Maine
1977	CS-Stanislaus	1984	Ramapo, NJ	1991	Southern Maine	1998	Eastern Conn. St.
1978	Glassboro St., NJ	1985	Wisconsin-Oshkosh	1992	Wm. Paterson, NJ	1999	NC-Wesleyan
1979	Glassboro St., NJ	1986	Marietta, OH	1993	Montclair St., NJ	2000	Montclair St., NJ
1980	Ithaca, NY	1987	Monclair St., NJ	1994	Wisconsin-Oshkosh	2001	St. Thomas, MN
1981	Marietta, OH	1988	Ithaca, NY	1995	La Verne, CA	2002	Eastern Conn. St.
1982	Eastern Conn. St.	1989	NC-Wesleyan	1996	Wm. Paterson, NJ		

Major League Number One Draft Picks

The Major League First-Year Player Draft has been held every year since 1965. Clubs select in reverse order of their won-loss records from the previous regular season with National League and American League teams alternating. AL teams select first in odd-numbered years while NL teams go first in even-numbered years. The pool of draftees consists of graduated high school players, junior or senior college players, Junior college players and anyone over the age of 21. Listed are the top selections from each draft.

Year		Pos	Team	Year		Pos	Team
1965	Rick Monday	OF	Kansas City Athletics	1984	Shawn Abner	OF	New York Mets
1966	Steve Chilcott	C	New York Mets	1985	B.J. Surhoff	C	Milwaukee Brewers
1967	Rom Blomberg	1B	New York Yankees	1986	Jeff King	IF	Pittsburgh Pirates
1968	Tim Foli	IF	New York Mets	1987	Ken Griffey Jr.	OF	Seattle Mariners
1969	Jeff Burroughs	OF	Washington Senators	1988	Andy Benes	P	San Diego Padres
1970	Mike Ivie	C	San Diego Padres	1989	Ben McDonald	P	Baltimore Orioles
1971	Danny Goodwin	C	Chicago White Sox	1990	Chipper Jones	SS	Atlanta Braves
1972	Dave Roberts	IF	San Diego Padres	1991	Brien Taylor	P	New York Yankees
1973	David Clyde	P	Texas Rangers	1992	Phil Nevin	3B	Houston Astros
1974	Bill Almon	IF	San Diego Padres	1993	Alex Rodriguez	SS	Seattle Mariners
1975	Danny Goodwin	C	California Angels	1994	Paul Wilson	P	New York Mets
1976	Floyd Bannister	P	Houston Astros	1995	Darin Erstad	OF/P	California Angels
1977	Harold Baines	OF	Chicago White Sox	1996	Kris Benson	P	Pittsburgh Pirates
1978	Bob Horner	3B	Atlanta Braves	1997	Matt Anderson	P	Detroit Tigers
1979	Al Chambers	OF	Seattle Mariners	1998	Pat Burrell	3B	Philadelphia Phillies
1980	Darryl Strawberry	OF	New York Mets	1999	Josh Hamilton	OF	T.B. Devil Rays
1981	Mike Moore	P	Seattle Mariners	2000	Adrian Gonzalez	1B	Florida Marlins
1982	Shawon Dunston	SS	Chicago Cubs	2001	Joe Mauer	C	Minnesota Twins
1983	Tim Belcher	P	Minnesota Twins	2002	Bryan Bullington	P	Pittsburgh Pirates

Straight to the Majors

Since Major League baseball began its First-Year Player Draft in 1965, 19 selections have advanced directly to the major leagues without first playing in the minors

Draft		Pos	Team	Draft		Pos	Team
1967	Mike Adamson, USC	P	Baltimore	1978	Tim Conroy, Gateway HS (Pa.)	P	Oakland
1969	Steve Dunning, Stanford	P	Cleveland		Bob Horner, Arizona St.	3B	Atlanta
1971	Pete Broberg, Dartmouth	P	Washington		Brian Milner, Southwest HS (Tex.)	C	Toronto
	Rob Ellis, Michigan St.	OF	Milwaukee		Mike Morgan, Valley HS (Nev.)	P	Oakland
	Burt Hooton, Texas	P	Chicago-NL	1985	Pete Incaviglia, Oklahoma St.	OF	Montreal
1972	Dave Roberts, Oregon	3B	San Diego	1988	Jim Abbott, Michigan	P	California
1973	Dick Ruthven, Fresno St.	P	Philadelphia	1989	John Olerud, Washington St.	1B	Toronto
	David Clyde, Westchester HS (Tex.)	P	Texas	1995	Ariel Prieto, Fajardo U (Cuba)	P	Oakland
	Dave Winfield, Minnesota	OF	San Diego	2000	Xavier Nady, California	3B	San Diego
	Eddie Bane, Arizona St.	P	Minnesota				

College Football

Penn State's **Joe Paterno** is carried off the field after winning his 324th game on Oct. 27, 2001 to break Paul "Bear" Bryant's long-standing record.

AP/Wide World Photos

The Perfect Storm

The Miami Hurricanes blew through the Rose Bowl, capping a perfect season in an imperfect world.

Chris Fowler
is the host of ESPN's College GameDay

On the sidelines of the Rose Bowl, a big question was circulating: Were we watching the University of Miami's best football team ever? Twenty minutes into the game, easier questions had already been answered.

Would Miami simply run right past a much slower Nebraska squad? Would Oregon have put up a better fight? Would the BCS system that sent the Huskers to this "title game" look sillier than ever? The answers: yes, yep, and you betcha.

The Hurricanes were unleashing on the poor Huskers a stockpile of frustration several seasons old, punctuating a triumphant 2001 campaign of payback. They'd been bullied as underclassmen, their program weakened by probation. A BCS-snubbing the previous year, which sent hated Florida State to the title game provided further fuel.

Taking much of the punishment was Eric Crouch, whose brilliant Heisman-crowned career came to a painful ending. Only the toughness that let Crouch absorb more than a thousand career body blows kept him in one piece.

Crouch or Harrington...Huskers, Ducks or Buffaloes...the Rose Bowl opponent would not have mattered. Or as Miami's Jerome McDougle eloquently stated afterward, "We'd whup the crap out of Oregon." Who could argue?

So back to that bigger argument. Would this team (which included five of the first 27 NFL draft picks last April, plus junior quarterback Ken Dorsey and sophomore stud receiver Andre Johnson) have whupped the Hurricanes of 1983, '87, '89 or '91, Miami's previous national champions?

They believe so. And many stars of the glory days agree. That was the

AP/Wide World Photos

*Miami defensive end **Andrew Williams** celebrates the Hurricanes' Rose Bowl win over Nebraska giving them an undefeated season and the school's fifth national championship.*

motivational message several of them sent as the Canes left for Pasadena: "You dominate this title game, you can call yourselves Miami's best ever."

That title is the most coveted of all for players kept keenly aware of their program's past, thanks to Miami's omnipresent network of visible and vocal ex-players. To get the ultimate compliment from greats who'd been thoroughly embarrassed by the mess Ed Reed, Ken Dorsey, Joaquin Gonzalez, and other veterans had inherited was priceless.

As the time slowly drained that chilly night in Pasadena, the tears of triumph and tragedy caused by a col-lege football season unlike any other seemed, already, so far away.

It was a season christened by Adam Taliaferro, recovered enough from paralysis to lead his Penn State team-mates through the tunnel. Joe Paterno shed more tears a month later, his wife Sue there for an on-field embrace when he finally surpassed Bear Bryant's win total.

It was a season energized by the improbable heroics of Maryland, Illinois and LSU, all of which muscled onto the BCS main stage.

It was also an autumn when college football games seemed, for a time, completely irrelevant.

AP/Wide World Photos

George O'Leary stepped down as Notre Dame football coach just five days after leaving Georgia Tech for the position when details included on his resume came into question.

On Sept. 13 I drove through Lincoln, Neb., a city that had been frenzied a few days earlier by Big Red's rout of Notre Dame. That day it was silent. Memorial Stadium resembled a huge concrete relic from a happier, more frivolous era. The blue skies overhead were eerily empty of jet streams.

This September day in Nebraska, no one was talking college football. How could anyone get excited about a game? America needed to heal, and the overheated controversy about whether to play or postpone that week's schedule was in itself trivial talk.

After pausing to mourn, our passion for football slowly returned, of course. The traditions of Saturday were comforting. The difference: stadiums were, for a time, filled with folks who felt less like rivals divided than Americans united. Pausing for the national anthem never before seemed so meaningful.

These games became gatherings, forums for tens of thousands to honor victims, show patriotism and display the collective will to carry on. Where else but a big stadium could so many share so much?

Ultimately, it was an autumn when college football games seemed worth cherishing, more than ever.

Lee Corso's Ten Biggest Stories of the Year in College Football

10 ■ Maryland (ACC), LSU (SEC), Illinois (Big Ten) and Louisiana Tech (WAC) are the surprise winners of conference titles.

9 ■ Nebraska quarterback Eric Crouch wins the Heisman Trophy.

8 ■ Arkansas and Mississippi play the longest game in college football history. The Razorbacks win it, 58–56, after seven overtimes.

7 ■ Florida State fails to win the ACC championship after having won or shared every title since it joined the conference in 1992. The Seminoles (8–4) also fail to win 10 games and are not ranked in the top five for the first time in 15 years.

6 ■ Steve Spurrier resigns after 12 brilliant seasons as the University of Florida's head coach and winds up with the NFL's Washington Redskins. Spurrier's successor at Florida is New Orleans Saints' defensive coordinator Ron Zook, a former defensive coordinator at Florida.

5 ■ Joe Paterno finally passes Bear Bryant as the winningest coach in major-college history, but Penn State finishes 5-6, the first time in Paterno's 36-year career he has suffered consecutive losing seasons. Meanwhile, Eastern Kentucky's Roy Kidd and Delaware's Tubby Raymond become the eighth and ninth coaches to win 300 games.

4 ■ Miami ties a record by winning its fifth national championship in 19 years, and Larry Coker becomes the second coach to capture a national championship in his rookie season, when it crushes Nebraska, 37-14, in the Rose Bowl. Take that, BCS!

3 ■ The Bowl Championship Series keeps tweaking its formula, and the more it tweaks, the more people get upset. Colorado, which crushed Nebraska, 62–36, and Texas in the Big 12 Championship Game, and 10-1 Oregon were bypassed in favor of Nebraska.

2 ■ Notre Dame fires coach Bob Davie after a 5-6 season, then hires George O'Leary away from Georgia Tech. O'Leary lasts only five days and resigns when it is discovered that he fibbed on a job application to Syracuse University two decades earlier. O'Leary gave false information about his college playing career and his postgraduate degrees. Notre Dame finally hires Tyrone Willingham from Stanford, who becomes the first black head coach in any sport at Notre Dame.

1 ■ Sept. 11 was the top story everywhere for the year 2001. All Division I-A games scheduled for the following Saturday, Sept. 15 are postponed. When the games resumed, many teams wore American flag decals on their helmets and uniforms.

Rushing Into It

Eric Crouch ran his way to the Heisman Trophy in 2002, in fact he ran his whole career at Nebraska. But as impressive as his rushing numbers were, he's not even in the top three running quarterbacks in Division I-A history. Here's a look at the college passers with the most success calling their own numbers.

Quarterback	Rush Yds
Antwaan Randle El, Indiana	3895
Dee Dowis, Air Force	3612
Kareem Wilson, Ohio	3597
Eric Crouch, Nebraska	3434
Chris McCoy, Navy	3401

Straight to the Top

Miami's Larry Coker became just the third head coach in Division I-A history to win a national championship in his first year as the team's coach. Interestingly, the last two to do it were at Miami. Coker joined Bennie Oosterbaan as the only men to win national titles in their rookie seasons as head coaches.

Year	Coach, School
2001	Larry Coker, Miami-FL
1989	Dennis Erickson, Miami-FL
1948	Bennie Oosterbaan, Michigan

Tenacious D

Miami can, in large part, attribute its national championship in 2001 to its smothering defense. The Hurricanes allowed a total of just 33 first-half points all season long. Here's a look at the fewest points allowed by quarter in Division I-A college football in 2001.

Team	Points	Quarter
Miami-FL	13	2nd
Oklahoma	16	3rd
Nebraska	17	3rd
Miami-FL	20	1st

Cardiac Quacks

Oregon may have been squeezed out of the BCS title game because of margin of victory, but those familiar with the Ducks have seen them win many a close game. During the 1997-2001 seasons, no team in the nation won more games by a touchdown or less than Oregon. Here is the list of teams with the most wins by seven points or less over the last five seasons.

Team	Wins
Oregon	22
Washington	20
Michigan	19
Georgia Tech	17
Wisconsin	17

2001-2002
Season in Review

Information Please®
ESPN
SPORTS ALMANAC

Final AP Top 25 Poll

Voted on by panel of 72 sportswriters & broadcasters and released on Jan. 4, 2002, following the Rose Bowl: winning team receives the Bear Bryant Trophy, given since 1983; first place votes in parentheses, records, total points (based on 25 for 1st, 24 for 2nd, etc.) bowl game result, head coach and career record, preseason rank (released Aug. 11, 2001) and final regular season rank (released Dec. 9, 2001).

		Final Record	Points	Bowl Game	Head Coach	Aug. 11 Rank	Dec. 9 Rank
1	Miami-FL (72)	12-0	1,800	won Rose	Larry Coker (1 yr: 12-0)	2	1
2	Oregon	11-1	1,726	won Fiesta	Mike Bellotti (11 yrs: 81-48-2)	7	2
3	Florida	10-2	1,611	won Orange	Steve Spurrier (15 yrs: 142-40-2)	1	5
4	Tennessee	11-2	1,581	won Citrus	Phillip Fulmer (10 yrs: 95-20)	8	8
5	Texas	11-2	1,374	won Holiday	Mack Brown (18 yrs: 124-87-1)	5	9
6	Oklahoma	11-2	1,373	won Cotton	Bob Stoops (3 yrs: 31-7)	3	10
7	LSU	10-3	1,350	won Sugar	Nick Saban (8 yrs: 61-33-1)	14	12
8	Nebraska	11-2	1,348	lost Rose	Frank Solich (4 yrs: 42-9)	4	4
9	Colorado	10-3	1,335	lost Fiesta	Gary Barnett (12 yrs: 63-72-2)	NR	3
10	Washington St.	10-2	1,074	won Sun	Mike Price (21 yrs: 119-119)	NR	13
11	Maryland	10-2	1,065	lost Orange	Ralph Friedgen (1 yr: 10-2)	NR	6
12	Illinois	10-2	1,045	lost Sugar	Ron Turner (5 yrs: 26-31)	NR	7
13	South Carolina	9-3	975	won Outback	Lou Holtz (30 yrs: 233-113-7)	21	14
14	Syracuse	10-3	856	won Insight.com	Paul Pasqualoni (16 yrs: 125-56-1)	NR	18
15	Florida St.	8-4	686	won Gator	Bobby Bowden (36 yrs: 323-91-4)	6	24
16	Stanford	9-3	673	lost Seattle	Tyrone Willingham (7 yrs: 44-36-1)	NR	11
17	Louisville	11-2	621	won Liberty	John L. Smith (13 yrs: 103-54)	NR	23
18	Virginia Tech	8-4	437	lost Gator	Frank Beamer (21 yrs: 149-88-4)	9	15
19	Washington	8-4	414	lost Holiday	Rick Neuheisel (9 yrs: 52-19)	15	21
20	Michigan	8-4	325	lost Citrus	Lloyd Carr (7 yrs: 66-20)	12	17
21	Boston College	8-4	318	won Music City	Tom O'Brien (5 yrs: 31-27)	NR	NR
22	Georgia	8-4	277	lost Music City	Mark Richt (1 yr: 8-4)	NR	16
23	Toledo	10-2	237	won Motor City	Tom Amstutz (1 yr: 10-2)	NR	25
24	Georgia Tech	8-5	178	won Seattle	George O'Leary (8 yrs: 52-33) & Mac McWhorter (1 yr: 1-0)	10	NR
25	BYU	12-2	144	lost Liberty	Gary Crowton (4 yrs: 33-15)	NR	19

Other teams receiving votes: 26. **Marshall** (11-2, won GMAC Bowl, 117 points); 27. **Fresno State** (11-3, lost Silicon Valley Classic, 104 pts); 28. **Hawaii** (9-3, no bowl, 95 pts); 29. **Ohio State** (7-5, lost Outback Bowl, 59 pts); 30. **North Carolina** (8-5, won Peach Bowl, 56 pts); 31. **Texas A&M** (8-4, won GalleryFurniture.com Bowl, 41 pts); 32. **Michigan State** (7-5, won Silicon Valley Classic, 37 pts); 34. **Clemson** (7-5, won Humanitarian Bowl) and **Utah** (8-4, won Las Vegas Bowl, 9 pts); 36. **Mississippi** (7-4, no bowl, 6 pts); 37. **Alabama** (7-5, won Independence Bowl), **Pittsburgh** (7-5, won Tangerine Bowl) and **UCLA** (7-4, no bowl, 4 pts), 40. **Iowa** (7-5, won Alamo Bowl, 1 pt).

AP Preseason and Final Regular Season Polls

First place votes in parentheses.

Top 25
(Aug. 11, 2001)

	Pts		Pts
1 Florida (20)	1,716	14 LSU	763
2 Miami-FL (33)	1,700	15 Washington	683
3 Oklahoma (10)	1,588	16 Northwestern	667
4 Nebraska (4)	1,525	17 UCLA	639
5 Texas (5)	1,461	18 Notre Dame	599
6 Florida St.	1,441	19 Clemson	569
7 Oregon	1,354	20 Mississippi St.	521
8 Tennessee	1,344	21 South Carolina	350
9 Virginia Tech	1,169	22 Wisconsin	237
10 Georgia Tech	1,005	23 Ohio St.	181
11 Oregon St.	974	24 Colorado St.	179
12 Michigan	919	25 Alabama	136
13 Kansas St.	902		

Top 25
(Dec. 9, 2001)

	Pts		Pts
1 Miami-FL (72)	1,800	14 South Carolina	742
2 Oregon	1,698	15 Virginia Tech	732
3 Colorado	1,649	16 Georgia	672
4 Nebraska	1,556	17 Michigan	620
5 Florida	1,396	18 Syracuse	523
6 Maryland	1,384	19 BYU	522
7 Illinois	1,381	20 Fresno St.	518
8 Tennessee	1,309	21 Washington	502
9 Texas	1,226	22 Ohio St.	268
10 Oklahoma	1,222	23 Louisville	225
11 Stanford	1,088	24 Florida St.	160
12 LSU	1,006	25 Toledo	85
13 Washington St.	897		

2001-2002 Bowl Games

Listed by bowls matching highest-ranked teams as of final regular season AP poll (released Dec. 9, 2001). Attendance figures indicate tickets sold.

Bowl	Winner	Regular Season	Loser	Regular Season	Score	Date	Attendance
Rose . . . . #1	Miami-FL	11-0	#4 Nebraska	11-1	37-14	Jan. 3	93,781
Fiesta . . . . #2	Oregon	10-1	#3 Colorado	10-2	38-16	Jan. 1	74,118
Orange . . . . #5	Florida	9-2	#6 Maryland	10-1	56-23	Jan. 2	73,640
Sugar . . . . #12	LSU	9-3	#7 Illinois	10-1	47-34	Jan. 1	77,688
Citrus . . . . #8	Tennessee	10-2	#17 Michigan	8-3	45-17	Jan. 1	59,693
Holiday . . . . #9	Texas	10-2	#21 Washington	8-3	47-43	Dec. 28	60,548
Cotton . . . . #10	Oklahoma	10-2	Arkansas	7-4	10-3	Jan. 1	72,955
Seattle	Georgia Tech	7-5	#11 Stanford	9-2	24-14	Dec. 27	30,144
Sun . . . . #13	Washington St.	9-2	Purdue	6-5	33-27	Dec. 31	47,812
Outback . . . . #14	South Carolina	8-3	#22 Ohio St.	7-4	31-28	Jan. 1	66,249
Gator . . . . #24	Florida St.	7-4	#15 Virginia Tech	8-3	30-17	Jan. 1	72,202
Music City	Boston College	7-4	#16 Georgia	8-3	20-16	Dec. 28	46,125
Insight.com . . . . #18	Syracuse	9-3	Kansas St.	6-5	26-3	Dec. 29	40,028
Liberty . . . . #23	Louisville	10-2	#19 BYU	12-1	28-10	Dec. 31	58,968
Silicon Valley Classic	Michigan St.	6-5	#20 Fresno St.	11-2	44-35	Dec. 31	30,456
Motor City . . . . #25	Toledo	9-2	Cincinnati	7-4	23-16	Dec. 29	44,164
Alamo	Iowa	6-5	Texas Tech	7-4	19-16	Dec. 29	65,232
GMAC	Marshall	10-2	East Carolina	6-5	64-61 (2 OT)	Dec. 19	40,139
GalleryFurniture.com	Texas A&M	7-4	TCU	6-5	28-9	Dec. 28	53,480
Peach	North Carolina	7-5	Auburn	7-4	16-10	Dec. 31	71,827
Independence	Alabama	6-5	Iowa St.	7-4	14-13	Dec. 27	45,627
Las Vegas	Utah	7-4	USC	6-5	10-6	Dec. 25	30,894
Tangerine	Pittsburgh	6-5	N.C. State	8-4	34-19	Dec. 20	28,562
Humanitarian	Clemson	6-5	Louisiana Tech	7-4	49-24	Dec. 31	23,472
New Orleans	Colorado St.	6-5	North Texas	5-6	45-20	Dec. 18	27,004

FAVORITES:

Rose (Miami by 8); **Fiesta** (Colorado by 2½); **Orange** (Florida by 14); **Sugar** (LSU by 2½); **Citrus** (Tennessee by 3½); **Holiday** (Texas by 12½); **Cotton** (Oklahoma by 13½); **Seattle** (Stanford by 5); **Sun** (Washington St. by 8); **Outback** (South Carolina by 2); **Gator** (Virginia Tech by 2½); **Music City** (Georgia by 4); **Insight.com** (Kansas St. by 5½); **Liberty** (Louisville by 3); **Silicon Valley** (Fresno St. by 5½); **Motor City** (Toledo by 3½); **Alamo** (Texas Tech by 1); **GMAC** (East Carolina by 2); **GalleryFurniture.com** (Texas A&M by 6); **Peach** (North Carolina by 2); **Independence** (Alabama by 6½); **Las Vegas** (USC by 3½); **Tangerine** (Even); **Humanitarian** (Clemson by 6½); **New Orleans** (Colorado by 12½).

PER TEAM PAYOUTS:

Nokia Sugar, **Tostitos Fiesta**, **FedEx Orange** and **Rose** ($11-13 million); **Capital One Florida Citrus** ($4.25 million); **Outback** ($2.2 million); **SBC Cotton** and **Culligan Holiday** ($2 million); **Chick-fil-A Peach** ($1.8 million); **Toyota Gator** ($1.4 million); **AXA Liberty** ($1.3 million); **Sylvania Alamo** ($1.2 million); **MainStay Independence** and **Wells Fargo Sun** ($1 million); **Sega Sports Las Vegas**, ($800,000); **Silicon Valley**, **Insight.com**, **New Orleans**, **GMAC**, **989 Sports Seattle**, **Visit Florida Tangerine**, **Motor City**, **GalleryFurniture.com**, **Music City** and **Crucial.com Humanitarian** ($750,000).

Final BCS Rankings

The Bowl Championship Series rankings were used for the first time during the 1998 season to determine BCS bowl match-ups and revised slightly for the 1999 and 2001 seasons. The final rankings were released Dec. 9, 2001. Note that S-rank refers to schedule rank and L refers to games lost.

	— Polls —		Computer Rankings										Sub	Quality	
	AP	ESPN	A&H	A/C	R.B.	K.M.	D.R.	Sag.	S-H	P.W.	Sched.	S-rank	L	Total	wins	Total
1 Miami-FL 1	1	1	1	1	1	1	1	1	1	1	18	0.72	0	2.72	0.1	2.62
2 Nebraska 4	4	2	2	2	3	2	3	2	2	14		0.56	1	7.73	0.5	7.23
3 Colorado 3	3	4	5	4	4	5	5	5	3	2	0.08		2	9.58	2.3	7.28
4 Oregon 2	2	3	3	3	2	8	7	6	7	31		1.24		1	9.07	0.4	8.67
5 Florida 5	5	9	8	7	8	4	2	3	5	19		0.76	2	13.59	0.5	13.09
6 Tennessee 8	8	5	4	8	6	7	8	7	4	3	0.12		2	16.29	1.6	14.69
7 Texas 9	9	8	9	10	9	3	4	4	6	33		1.32	2	18.99	1.2	17.79
8 Illinois 7	7	7	6	12	5	12	10	12	37		1.48		1	19.31	0.0	19.31
9 Stanford 11	11	6	7	11	5	9	9	8	8	22		0.88	2	21.71	1.3	20.41
10 Maryland 6	6	14	10	5	10	11	11	14	11	78		3.12	1	21.29	0.0	21.29
11 Oklahoma 10	10	10	11	9	13	6	6	9	9	36		1.44	2	22.44	0.9	21.54
12 Washington St. . .13	13	12	12	12	7	10	13	10	13	42		1.68	2	27.51	0.6	26.91
13 LSU 12	12	11	13	14	14	12	18	15	14	10	0.40		3	28.73	1.0	27.73
14 South Carolina .14	14	20	19	19	17	17	23	23	17	40		1.60	3	37.77	0.0	37.77
15 Washington . . .20	21	13	15	15	11	16	15	17	13	21		0.84	3	39.17	1.0	38.17

Explanation Key

Schedule Rank—Rank of schedule strength compared to other Division I-A teams divided by 25. This component is calculated by determining the cumulative won/loss records of the team's opponents (66.6 percent) and the cumulative won/loss record of the team's opponents' opponents (33.3 percent).

Losses—One point for each loss during the season.

National Championship Game

Miami and Nebraska were ranked first and second, respectively, in the final Bowl Championship Series rankings (released Dec. 9, 2001) and according to the BCS plan met in the so-called National Championship Game at the Rose Bowl on Jan. 3. Opponents' records and AP rank listed below are day of game.

Miami Hurricanes (11-0)

Date	AP Rank	Opponent	Result
Sept. 1	#2	at Penn St. (0-0)	W, 33-7
Sept. 8	#1	Rutgers (1-0)	W, 61-0
Sept. 27	#1	at Pittsburgh (1-1)	W, 43-21
Oct. 6	#1	Troy St. (1-2)	W, 38-7
Oct. 13	#2	at #14 Florida St. (3-1)	W, 49-27
Oct. 25	#1	West Virginia (2-4)	W, 45-3
Nov. 3	#1	Temple (2-5)	W, 38-0
Nov. 10	#1	at Boston College (6-2)	W, 18-7
Nov. 17	#1	#14 Syracuse (8-2)	W, 59-0
Nov. 24	#1	#12 Washington (8-2)	W, 65-7
Dec. 1	#1	#14 Virginia Tech (8-2)	W, 26-24

Final Statistics

Passing (5 Att)	Att	Cmp	Pct.	Yds	TD	Rate
Ken Dorsey	.318	184	57.9	2652	23	146.1
Derrick Crudup	.22	10	45.5	100	1	98.6

Interceptions: Dorsey 9.

Top Receivers	No	Yds	Avg	Long	TD
Jeremy Shockey	.40	519	13.0	56	7
Andre Johnson	.37	682	18.4	64	10
Ethenic Sands	.26	385	14.8	37	1
Kevin Beard	.25	409	16.4	47	2
Daryl Jones	.19	240	12.6	34	0
Najeh Davenport	.14	190	13.6	32	2
Clinton Portis	.12	125	10.4	21	1
Jason Geathers	.9	112	12.4	30	1

Top Rushers	Car	Yds	Avg	Long	TD
Clinton Portis	.220	1200	5.5	45	10
Frank Gore	.62	562	9.1	77	5
Willis McGahee	.67	314	4.7	21	3
Najeh Davenport	.23	54	2.3	7	3
Derrick Crudup	.7	35	5.0	24	1
Jarrett Payton	.14	26	1.9	6	2

Most Touchdowns	TD	Run	Rec	Ret	Pts
Clinton Portis	.11	10	1	0	66
Andre Johnson	.10	0	10	0	60
Jeremy Shockey	.7	0	7	0	42
Frank Gore	.5	5	0	0	30
Najeh Davenport	.5	3	2	0	30
Phil Buchanon	.3	0	0	3	18
Willis McGahee	.3	3	0	0	18

2-Pt. Conversions: (0-1).

Kicking	FG/Att	Lg	PAT/Att	Pts
Todd Sievers	.21/26	48	56/58	119

Punting	No	Yds	Long	Blkd	Avg
Freddie Capshaw	.36	1503	59	2	41.8

Most Interceptions		Most Sacks	
Edward Reed	.9	William Joseph	10.0
Phil Buchanon	.5	Jamaal Green	6.0
James Lewis	.3	Jerome McDougle	6.0

Nebraska Cornhuskers (11-1)

Date	AP Rank	Opponent	Result
Aug. 25	#4	TCU (0-0)	W, 21-7
Sept. 1	#4	Troy St. (0-0)	W, 42-14
Sept. 8	#5	#17 Notre Dame (0-0)	W, 27-10
Sept. 20	#4	Rice (2-0)	W, 48-3
Sept. 29	#4	at Missouri (1-1)	W, 36-3
Oct. 6	#4	Iowa St. (3-0)	W, 48-14
Oct. 13	#4	at Baylor (2-2)	W, 48-7
Oct. 20	#3	Texas Tech (3-2)	W, 41-31
Oct. 27	#3	#2 Oklahoma (7-0)	W, 20-10
Nov. 3	#2	at Kansas (2-5)	W, 51-7
Nov. 10	#2	Kansas St. (4-4)	W, 31-21
Nov. 23	#2	at #14 Colorado (8-2)	L, 36-62

Final Statistics

Passing (5 Att)	Att	Cmp	Pct.	Yds	TD	Rate
Eric Crouch	.189	105	55.6	1510	7	124.3
Jammal Lord	.8	5	62.5	65	0	105.8

Interceptions: Crouch 10, Lord 1.

Top Receivers	No	Yds	Avg	Long	TD
Wilson Thomas	.37	616	16.6	78	3
Tracey Wistrom	.21	323	15.4	37	2
Thunder Collins	.19	189	9.9	45	0
John Gibson	.18	266	14.8	41	1
Jon Bowling	.4	75	18.8	27	1
Kyle Ringenberg	.3	49	16.3	20	0
Judd Davies	.2	9	4.5	11	0
Eric Crouch	.1	63	63.0	63	1
Paul Kastl	.1	19	19.0	19	0
Ben Cornelsen	.1	18	18.0	18	0
John Klem	.1	9	9.0	9	0

Top Rushers	Car	Yds	Avg	Long	TD
Dahrran Diedrick	.233	1299	5.6	38	15
Eric Crouch	.203	1115	5.5	95	18
Thunder Collins	.94	647	6.9	50	5
Judd Davies	.40	238	5.9	42	4
DeAntae Grixby	.25	104	4.2	13	0
Steve Kriewald	.18	95	5.3	24	1
Jammal Lord	.22	83	3.8	33	2
Josh Davis	.8	61	7.6	13	1
Ben Cornelsen	.2	33	16.5	36	0

Most Touchdowns	TD	Run	Rec	Ret	Pts
Eric Crouch	.19	18	1	0	116
Dahrran Diedrick	.15	15	0	0	92
Thunder Collins	.5	5	0	0	30
Judd Davies	.4	4	0	0	24
Wilson Thomas	.3	0	3	0	18
Jammal Lord	.2	2	0	0	12
Tracey Wistrom	.2	0	2	0	12

2-Pt. Conversions: (2-7), Crouch, Diedrick.

Kicking	FG/Att	Lg	PAT/Att	Pts
Josh Brown	.10/14	43	34/37	64
Sandro DeAngelis	.2/3	21	15/16	21

Punting	No	Yds	Long	Blk	Avg
Kyle Larson	.56	2381	68	0	42.5

Most Interceptions		Most Sacks	
Willie Amos	.4	Demoine Adams	.5.5
		Chris Kelsay	.5.0
		Justin Smith	.4.0
		Jamie Burrow	.3.5

Rose Bowl

Thursday, Jan. 3, 2002 at Rose Bowl, Pasadena, Calif.

#4 Nebraska (Big 12).........0   0   7   7 **—14**
#1 Miami-FL (Big East).........7   27   0   3 **—37**

1st; 6:51; **Miami**— Andre Johnson 49-yd pass from Ken Dorsey (Todd Sievers kick).

2nd; 14:33; **Miami**— Clinton Portis 39-yd run (Sievers kick).

2nd; 12:52; **Miami**— James Lewis 47-yd INT return (Sievers kick).

2nd; 10:40; **Miami**— Jeremy Shockey 21-yd pass from Dorsey (kick failed).

2nd; 3:35; **Miami**— Johnson 8-yd pass from Dorsey (Sievers kick).

3rd; 2:39; **Nebraska**— Judd Davies 16-yd run (Josh Brown kick).

4th; 14:28; **Nebraska**— DeJuan Groce 71-yd punt return (Brown kick).

4th; 10:04; **Miami**— Sievers 37-yd FG.

Favorite: Miami by 8   **Attendance:** 93,781
Field: Grass   **Weather:** High clouds
Time: 3:10   **TV Rating:** 13.8/22 (ABC)
Co-MVPs: Ken Dorsey and Andre Johnson, Miami-FL

Team Statistics

	Neb	Mia
Touchdowns	2	5
Rushing	1	1
Passing	0	3
Kick/Punt returns	1	0
Interception returns	0	1
Safeties	0	0
Time of possession	34:16	25:44
First downs	16	18
Rushing	14	6
Passing	2	12
Penalty	0	0
Total Plays	67	61
Carries/yards (includ. sacks)	49/197	26/110
Passing yards	62	362
Completions/attempts	5/15	22/35
Return yardage	85	84
Fumbles/lost	4/2	2/0
Penalties/yards	4/26	12/85
Punts/average	5/40.6	4/35.8
3rd down conversions	5/15	6/13
4th down conversions	1/4	0/0

INDIVIDUAL STATISTICS

Nebraska Cornhuskers

Passing (5 Att)	Att	Cmp	Pct.	Yds	TD	Int
Eric Crouch	15	5	33.3	62	0	1

Rushing	Car	Yds	Avg	Long	TD
Eric Crouch	22	114	5.2	37	0
Dahrran Diedrick	15	47	3.1	20	0
Judd Davies	5	16	3.2	16	1
Thunder Collins	6	10	1.7	6	0
Ben Zajicek	1	10	10.0	10	0
TOTAL	49	197	4.1	37	1

Receiving	No	Yds	Avg	Long	TD
Wilson Thomas	3	36	12.0	21	0
Tracey Wistrom	2	26	13.0	18	0
TOTAL	5	62	12.4	21	0

Field Goals	20-29	30-39	40-49	50-59	Total
none					

Punting	No	Yds	Long	Blk	Avg
Kyle Larson	5	203	55	0	40.6

Punt Returns	No	Yds	Long	Avg	TD
DeJuan Groce	3	85	71	28.3	1

Kickoff Returns	No	Yds	Long	Avg	TD
Josh Davis	5	119	38	23.8	0

Sacks
none

Interceptions
Keyuo Craver 1

Miami Hurricanes

Passing (5 Att)	Att	Cmp	Pct.	Yds	TD	Int
Ken Dorsey	35	22	62.9	362	3	1

Rushing	Car	Yds	Avg	Long	TD
Clinton Portis	20	104	5.2	39	1
Willis McGahee	2	7	3.5	7	0
Frank Gore	2	3	1.5	4	0
Team	2	-4	-2.0	-2	0
TOTAL	26	110	4.2	39	1

Receiving	No	Yds	Avg	Long	TD
Andre Johnson	7	199	28.4	49	2
Jeremy Shockey	5	85	17.0	22	1
Kevin Beard	4	41	10.3	22	0
Clinton Portis	4	26	6.5	9	0
Daryl Jones	1	7	7.0	7	0
Robert Williams	1	4	4.0	4	0
TOTAL	22	362	16.5	49	3

Field Goals	20-29	30-39	40-49	50-59	Total
Todd Sievers	0-0	1-1	0-1	0-0	1-2

Punting	No	Yds	Long	Blk	Avg
Freddie Capshaw	4	143	45	0	35.8

Punt Returns	No	Yds	Long	Avg	TD
Phillip Buchanon	4	37	23	9.3	0

Kickoff Returns	No	Yds	Long	Avg	TD
Andre Johnson	2	27	21	13.5	0

Sacks
Jonathan Vilma 1.0
D.J. Williams 1.0
Phillip Buchanon 1.0

Interceptions
James Lewis 1

Other Final Division I-A Polls
USA Today/ESPN Coaches' Poll

Voted on by panel of 60 Division I-A head coaches; winning team receives the Sears Trophy (originally the McDonald's Trophy, 1991-93); first place votes in parentheses with total points (based on 25 for 1st, 24 for 2nd, etc.).

	Pts		Pts		Pts		Pts
1 Miami-FL (60)	1,500	8 LSU	1,099	15 Florida St.	556	22 Toledo	188
2 Oregon	1,434	9 Colorado	1,031	16 Louisville	524	23 Boston College	174
3 Florida	1,351	10 Maryland	885	17 Stanford	502	24 BYU	172
4 Tennessee	1,284	11 Washington St.	879	18 Virginia Tech	394	25 Georgia	163
5 Texas	1,207	12 Illinois	846	19 Washington	369		
6 Oklahoma	1,141	13 South Carolina	837	20 Michigan	363		
7 Nebraska	1,101	14 Syracuse	736	21 Marshall	223		

Other teams receiving votes: 26. Georgia Tech (112 points), 27. North Carolina (84), 28. Fresno State (81), 29. Ohio St. (66), 30. Texas A&M (57), 31. Michigan St. (45), 32. Hawaii (36), 33. Arkansas (13), 34. Alabama (12), 35. Utah (9), 36. Pittsburgh (8), 37. Auburn and Iowa (5), 39. Clemson (4), 40. Iowa St. (2), 41. Texas Tech and UCLA (1).

AP Weekly Ratings

The Associated Press Top 25 college football polls on a weekly basis are listed below. The table starts with the preseason and progresses through the season. There was no poll released the week of Sept. 16, 2001 because games were not played in the wake of the Sept. 11 terrorist attacks.

	Pre	Aug 27	Sep 2	Sep 9	Sep 23	Sep 30	Oct 7	Oct 14	Oct 21	Oct 28	Nov 4	Nov 11	Nov 18	Nov 25	Dec 2	Dec 9	Jan 4
Florida	1	1	2	2	2	2	1	7	6	4	4	4	3	2	6	5	3
Miami-FL	2	2	1	1	1	1	2	1	1	1	1	1	1	1	1	1	1
Oklahoma	3	3	3	3	3	3	3	2	2	3	3	3	4	11	11	10	6
Nebraska	4	4	5	4	4	4	4	3	3	2	2	2	2	6	5	4	8
Texas	5	5	4	5	5	5	11	9	7	5	5	5	5	3	10	9	5
Florida St.	6	6	6	6	18	16	14	21	19	14	10	21	NR	NR	24	24	15
Oregon	7	7	7	7	6	7	5	5	11	8	7	7	6	4	3	2	2
Tennessee	8	8	8	8	7	6	13	11	9	7	6	6	7	5	2	8	4
Virginia Tech	9	9	9	9	8	8	6	6	5	12	23	18	16	14	15	15	18
Georgia Tech	10	11	10	10	9	17	15	23	21	23	20	NR	21	NR	NR	NR	24
Oregon St.	11	10	22	22	19	NR	NR	NR	NR	NR	NR	NR	NR	NR	NR	NR	NR
Michigan	12	12	11	20	17	15	12	10	8	6	12	11	11	17	17	17	20
Kansas St.	13	13	12	12	11	12	24	NR	NR	NR	NR	NR	NR	NR	NR	NR	NR
LSU	14	14	13	15	14	13	NR	NR	NR	NR	NR	NR	NR	22	21	12	7
Washington	15	15	15	13	13	11	10	15	13	11	8	16	12	19	20	21	19
Northwestern	16	16	16	16	16	14	NR	22	NR	NR	NR	NR	NR	NR	NR	NR	NR
UCLA	17	17	14	12	9	7	4	4	9	17	20	NR	NR	NR	NR	NR	NR
Notre Dame	18	18	17	23	NR	NR	NR	NR	NR	NR	NR	NR	NR	NR	NR	NR	NR
Clemson	19	19	20	19	NR	19	16	13	NR	NR	NR	NR	NR	NR	NR	NR	NR
Mississippi St.	20	20	18	17	21	NR	NR	NR	NR	NR	NR	NR	NR	NR	NR	NR	NR
South Carolina	21	21	21	18	15	13	9	16	12	17	14	22	18	15	14	14	13
Wisconsin	22	22	23	NR	NR	NR	NR	NR	NR	NR	NR	NR	NR	NR	NR	NR	NR
Ohio St.	23	23	24	21	NR	NR	21	NR	NR	NR	NR	NR	25	NR	23	22	NR
Colorado St.	24	24	NR	NR	NR	NR	NR	NR	NR	NR	NR	NR	NR	NR	NR	NR	NR
Alabama	25	25	NR	NR	NR	NR	NR	NR	NR	NR	NR	NR	NR	NR	NR	NR	NR
Fresno St.	NR	NR	19	11	10	10	8	8	18	NR	NR	NR	23	21	19	20	NR
Georgia	NR	NR	25	NR	NR	NR	19	17	15	18	19	23	19	16	16	16	22
BYU	NR	NR	NR	24	20	20	18	18	16	13	9	8	9	10	9	19	25
Louisville	NR	NR	NR	25	NR	NR	NR	NR	NR	25	19	17	24	23	23	17	17
Illinois	NR	NR	NR	NR	22	NR	NR	22	21	15	12	10	8	8	7	7	12
Michigan St.	NR	NR	NR	NR	23	NR	NR	NR	NR	22	NR	NR	NR	NR	NR	NR	NR
Purdue	NR	NR	NR	NR	24	21	17	24	24	20	NR	NR	NR	NR	NR	NR	NR
Toledo	NR	NR	NR	NR	25	23	NR	25	NR	NR	NR	NR	NR	25	25	23	23
Stanford	NR	NR	NR	NR	NR	22	23	NR	20	10	16	13	13	12	12	11	16
Texas A&M	NR	NR	NR	NR	NR	24	25	NR	24	NR	24	NR	NR	NR	NR	NR	NR
Maryland	NR	NR	NR	NR	NR	25	22	12	10	15	13	10	8	7	7	6	11
Colorado	NR	NR	NR	NR	NR	NR	20	14	25	25	21	15	14	9	4	3	9
Washington St.	NR	NR	NR	NR	NR	NR	19	14	16	17	9	15	13	13	13	10	10
Auburn	NR	NR	NR	NR	NR	NR	20	17	NR	24	17	NR	25	NR	NR	NR	NR
North Carolina	NR	NR	NR	NR	NR	NR	NR	23	22	NR	NR	NR	NR	NR	NR	NR	NR
Syracuse	NR	NR	NR	NR	NR	NR	NR	NR	19	18	14	22	18	18	18	18	14
Marshall	NR	NR	NR	NR	NR	NR	NR	NR	NR	18	NR	24	20	20	NR	NR	NR
Arkansas	NR	NR	NR	NR	NR	NR	NR	NR	NR	NR	NR	NR	24	NR	NR	NR	NR
Boston College	NR	NR	NR	NR	NR	NR	NR	NR	NR	NR	NR	NR	25	NR	NR	NR	21

NCAA Division I-A Final Standings

Standings based on conference games only; overall records include postseason games.

Atlantic Coast Conference

	Conference				Overall			
	W	L	PF	PA	W	L	PF	PA
*Maryland	7	1	261	173	10	2	413	266
*Florida St.	6	2	304	194	8	4	403	304
*North Carolina	5	3	237	145	8	5	337	271
*N.C. State	4	4	212	185	7	5	319	257
*Georgia Tech	4	4	246	215	8	5	405	281
*Clemson	4	4	246	268	7	5	369	339
Wake Forest	3	5	213	247	6	5	292	311
Virginia	3	5	178	244	5	7	249	331
Duke	0	8	164	390	0	11	212	491

*Bowls (4-2): Maryland (lost Orange); Florida St. (won Gator); North Carolina (won Peach); N.C. State (lost Tangerine); Georgia Tech (won Seattle), Clemson (won Humanitarian).

Big East Conference

	Conference				Overall			
	W	L	PF	PA	W	L	PF	PA
*Miami-FL	7	0	290	55	12	0	512	117
*Syracuse	6	1	196	144	10	3	334	247
*Virginia Tech	4	3	199	106	8	4	376	177
*Boston College	4	3	205	125	8	4	337	227
*Pittsburgh	4	3	174	161	7	5	296	245
Temple	2	5	67	203	4	7	198	311
West Virginia	1	6	137	185	3	8	235	268
Rutgers	0	7	36	325	2	9	119	397

*Bowls (4-1): Miami-FL (lost Rose); Syracuse (won Insight.com); Virginia Tech (lost Gator); Boston College (won Music City); Pittsburgh (won Tangerine).

Big Ten Conference

	Conference				Overall			
	W	L	PF	PA	W	L	PF	PA
*Illinois	7	1	261	199	10	2	390	285
*Michigan	6	2	216	135	8	4	320	237
*Ohio St.	5	3	223	174	7	5	312	244
*Iowa	4	4	263	206	7	5	391	258
*Purdue	4	4	153	193	6	6	250	278
Indiana	4	4	239	220	5	6	305	298
Penn St.	4	4	189	208	5	6	248	281
*Michigan St.	3	5	223	238	7	5	374	311
Wisconsin	3	5	215	260	5	7	313	346
Northwestern	2	6	197	300	4	7	320	378
Minnesota	2	6	191	237	4	7	308	299

*Bowls (2-4): Illinois (lost Sugar); Michigan (lost Citrus); Ohio St. (lost Outback); Iowa (won Alamo); Purdue (lost Sun); Michigan St. (won Silicon Valley Classic).

I-A Independents

	W	L	PF	PA
South Florida	8	3	387	231
Troy State	7	4	246	269
Central Florida	6	5	333	204
Notre Dame	5	6	214	215
Utah State	4	7	316	421
Connecticut	2	9	192	370
Navy	0	10	183	344

Big 12 Conference

North	Conference				Overall			
	W	L	PF	PA	W	L	PF	PA
*Colorado	8	1	282	227	10	3	412	318
*Nebraska	7	1	311	155	11	2	463	226
*Iowa St.	4	4	203	189	7	5	309	245
*Kansas St.	3	5	213	166	6	6	330	205
Missouri	3	5	180	249	4	7	240	330
Kansas	1	7	114	333	3	8	182	398

South	Conference				Overall			
	W	L	PF	PA	W	L	PF	PA
*Texas	7	2	332	117	11	2	517	207
*Oklahoma	6	2	207	126	11	2	397	169
*Texas A&M	4	4	130	157	8	4	248	213
*Texas Tech	4	4	244	215	7	5	402	281
Oklahoma St.	2	6	179	241	4	7	242	281
Baylor	0	8	109	329	3	8	205	357

Big 12 championship game: Colorado 39, Texas 37 (Dec. 1).

*Bowls (3-5): Colorado (lost Fiesta); Nebraska (lost Rose); Texas (won Holiday); Oklahoma (won Cotton); Texas A&M (won GalleryFurniture.com); Texas Tech (lost Alamo); Iowa St. (lost Independence); Kansas St. (lost Insight.com).

Conference USA

	Conference				Overall			
	W	L	PF	PA	W	L	PF	PA
*Louisville	6	1	237	136	11	2	394	223
*Cincinnati	5	2	205	189	7	5	336	290
UAB	5	2	204	116	6	5	265	206
*East Carolina	5	2	252	184	6	6	421	360
Southern Miss.	4	3	191	101	6	5	278	186
*TCU	4	3	192	194	6	6	289	285
Memphis	3	4	196	183	5	6	294	281
Army	2	5	150	257	3	8	229	365
Tulane	1	6	180	306	3	9	344	495
Houston	0	7	137	278	0	11	190	432

*Bowls (1-3): Louisville (won Liberty); Cincinnati (lost Motor City); East Carolina (lost GMAC); TCU (lost GalleryFurniture.com).

Mid-American Conference

Eastern	Conference				Overall			
	W	L	PF	PA	W	L	PF	PA
*Marshall	8	1	347	215	11	2	512	369
Miami-OH	6	2	215	168	7	5	319	309
Bowling Green	5	3	228	137	8	3	333	215
Kent St.	5	3	196	179	6	5	248	281
Akron	4	4	236	242	4	7	281	360
Buffalo	1	7	216	263	3	8	205	286
Ohio	1—	7	160	245	1	10	198	323

Western	Conference				Overall			
	W	L	PF	PA	W	L	PF	PA
*Toledo	6	2	292	247	10	2	407	297
Northern Illinois	4	3	195	204	6	5	303	292
Ball St.	4	3	199	191	5	6	268	296
Western Michigan	4	4	208	190	5	6	277	266
Central Michigan	2	6	178	257	3	8	251	368
Eastern Michigan	1	6	164	254	2	9	197	356

MAC championship game: Toledo 41, Marshall 36 (Nov. 30).

*Bowl (2-0): Marshall (won GMAC); Toledo (won Motor City).

Mountain West Conference

	Conference				Overall			
	W	L	PF	PA	W	L	PF	PA
*BYU	.7	0	302	194	12	2	618	424
*Colorado State	..5	2	180	163	7	5	298	274
*Utah	.4	3	206	114	8	4	329	210
New Mexico	..4	3	182	179	6	5	304	243
Air Force	..3	4	204	248	6	6	337	386
UNLV	.3	4	198	169	4	7	284	270
San Diego St.	..2	5	115	195	3	8	184	290
Wyoming	..0	7	132	257	2	9	229	368

*Bowls (2-1): BYU (lost Liberty); Colorado St. (won New Orleans); Utah (won Las Vegas).

Pacific 10 Conference

	Conference				Overall			
	W	L	PF	PA	W	L	PF	PA
*Oregon	.7	1	281	181	11	1	412	256
*Stanford	.6	2	312	266	9	3	422	339
*Washington St.	.6	2	257	187	10	2	420	269
*Washington	.6	2	227	237	8	4	353	370
*USC	.5	3	249	150	6	6	298	207
UCLA	.4	4	243	185	7	4	317	225
Oregon St.	.3	5	191	183	6	6	287	259
Arizona	.2	6	223	317	5	6	320	377
Arizona St.	.1	7	220	312	4	7	374	361
California	.0	8	148	333	1	10	201	431

*Bowls (2-3): Oregon (won Fiesta); Washington (lost Holiday); Washington St. (won Sun); Stanford (lost Seattle); USC (lost Las Vegas).

Southeastern Conference

	Conference				Overall			
Eastern	W	L	PF	PA	W	L	PF	PA
*Tennessee	.7	1	225	148	11	2	400	251
*Florida	.6	2	341	122	10	2	538	178
*South Carolina	.5	3	189	160	9	3	310	230
*Georgia	.5	3	204	167	8	4	331	228
Kentucky	.1	7	206	285	2	9	259	367
Vanderbilt	.0	8	128	315	2	9	226	402

	Conference				Overall			
Western	W	L	PF	PA	W	L	PF	PA
*LSU	.5	3	231	203	10	3	418	302
*Auburn	.5	3	152	193	7	5	254	281
*Alabama	.4	4	203	177	7	5	318	232
*Arkansas	.4	4	208	220	7	5	294	279
Mississippi	.4	4	262	262	7	4	391	310
Mississippi St.	.2	6	119	216	3	8	196	288

SEC championship game: LSU 31, Tennessee 20 (Dec. 8).

*Bowls (5-3): Tennessee (won Citrus); Florida (won Orange); LSU (won Sugar); Auburn (lost Peach); Alabama (won Independence); South Carolina (won Outback); Georgia (lost Music City); Arkansas (lost Cotton).

Sun Belt Conference

	Conference				Overall			
	W	L	PF	PA	W	L	PF	PA
Middle Tenn. St.	.5	1	248	152	8	3	408	286
*North Texas	..5	1	200	104	5	7	275	293
New Mexico St.	..4	2	209	163	5	7	286	400
LA-Lafayette	.2	4	163	192	3	8	234	365
Arkansas St.	.2	4	90	194	2	9	177	357
LA-Monroe	.2	4	105	152	2	9	148	351
Idaho	.1	5	234	292	1	10	313	495

*Bowls (0-1): North Texas (lost New Orleans).

Western Athletic Conference

	Conference				Overall			
	W	L	PF	PA	W	L	PF	PA
*La. Tech	.7	1	311	223	7	5	406	390
*Fresno St.	.6	2	330	191	11	3	560	344
Boise St.	.6	2	307	184	8	4	411	280
Hawaii	.5	3	277	180	9	3	483	318
Rice	.5	3	273	247	8	4	333	335
SMU	.4	4	189	212	4	7	226	295
Nevada	.3	5	249	317	3	8	286	431
San Jose St.	.3	5	241	295	3	9	295	461
UTEP	.1	7	170	326	2	9	235	414
Tulsa	.0	8	133	305	1	10	191	387

*Bowls (0-2): Louisiana Tech (lost Humanitarian); Fresno St. (lost Silicon Valley Classic).

NCAA Division I-A Individual Leaders

REGULAR SEASON

Total Offense

		Rushing				Passing		Total Offense			
	Cl	Car	Gain	Loss	Net	Att	Yds	Plays	Yds	YdsPP	YdsPG
Rex Grossman, Florida	So.	34	95	87	8	395	3896	429	3904	9.10	354.9
Byron Leftwich, Marshall	Jr.	64	241	149	92	470	4132	534	4224	7.91	352.0
David Carr, Fresno St.	Sr.	88	259	162	97	476	4299	564	4396	7.79	338.2
Nick Rolovich, Hawaii	Sr.	49	157	153	4	405	3361	454	3365	7.41	336.5
Luke McCown, La. Tech	So.	87	317	173	144	470	3337	557	3481	6.25	316.5
Kliff Kingsbury, Texas Tech	Jr.	66	152	200	-48	528	3502	594	3454	5.81	314.0
Brandon Doman, BYU	Sr.	142	745	289	456	408	3542	550	3998	7.27	307.5
Woodrow Dantzler, Clemson	Sr.	206	1244	*240	1004	311	2360	517	3364	6.51	305.8
Zak Kustok, Northwestern	Sr.	175	745	165	580	404	2692	579	3272	5.65	297.5
Ryan Dinwiddie, Boise St.	So.	71	256	159	97	322	3043	393	3140	7.99	285.5

All-Purpose Yards

	Cl	Gm	Rush	Rec	PR	KOR	Total Yds	YdsPG
Levron Williams, Indiana	Sr.	11	1401	289	0	511	2201	200.09
Bernard Berrian, Fresno St.	Jr.	13	101	1270	552	668	2591	199.31
Mewelde Moore, Tulane	So.	12	1421	756	0	82	2259	188.25
Luke Staley, BYU	Jr.	11	1582	334	0	102	2018	183.45
Emmett White, Utah St.	Sr.	11	1361	408	125	120	2014	183.09
William Green, Boston College	Jr.	10	1559	260	0	0	1819	181.90
Chris Douglas, Duke	So.	11	841	233	0	775	1849	168.09
Chance Kretschmer, Nevada	Fr.	11	1732	55	0	0	1787	162.45
Brock Forsey, Boise St.	Jr.	12	1207	369	0	362	1938	161.50
Bruce Perry, Maryland	So.	11	1242	359	0	117	1718	156.18

Florida
Rex Grossman
Total Offense and Passing
Efficiency

Nevada
Chance Kretschmer
Rushing

Utah St.
Kevin Curtis
Receptions

Miami
Edward Reed
Interceptions

Passing Efficiency

(Minimum 15 attempts per game)

	Cl	Gm	Att	Cmp	Cmp Pct	Int	Int Pct	Yds	Yds/Att	TD	TD Pct	Rating Points
Rex Grossman, Florida	So.	11	395	259	65.57	12	3.04	3896	9.86	34	8.61	170.8
David Carr, Fresno St.	Sr.	13	476	308	64.71	7	1.47	4299	9.03	42	8.82	166.7
Wes Counts, Middle Tenn. St.	Sr.	11	259	188	72.59	4	1.54	2327	8.98	17	6.56	166.6
Ryan Dinwiddie, Boise St.	So.	11	322	201	62.42	11	3.42	3043	9.45	29	9.01	164.7
Byron Leftwich, Marshall	Jr.	12	470	315	67.02	7	1.49	4132	8.79	38	8.09	164.6
Jeff Smoker, Michigan St.	So.	10	230	144	62.61	7	3.04	2203	9.58	18	7.83	162.8
Brandon Doman, BYU	Sr.	13	408	261	63.97	8	1.96	3542	8.68	33	8.09	159.7
Chris Rix, Florida St.	Fr.	11	286	165	57.69	13	4.55	2734	9.56	24	8.39	156.6
Jeff Krohn, Arizona St.	So.	10	213	115	53.99	7	3.29	1942	9.12	19	8.92	153.4
Nick Rolovich, Hawaii	Sr.	10	405	233	57.53	9	2.22	3361	8.30	34	8.40	150.5
Casey Clausen, Tennessee	So.	12	354	227	64.12	9	2.54	2969	8.39	22	6.21	150.0
Jeff Welsh, W. Michigan	Sr.	8	213	134	62.91	4	1.88	1702	7.99	15	7.04	149.5
Darian Durant, N. Carolina	Fr.	12	223	142	63.68	10	4.48	1843	8.26	17	7.62	149.3
Bobby Pesavento, Colorado	Sr.	9	139	85	61.15	4	2.88	1234	8.88	8	5.76	149.0
Kyle McCann, Iowa	Sr.	11	226	148	65.49	11	4.87	1867	8.26	16	7.08	148.5

Rushing

	Cl	Car	Yds	TD	YdsPG
Chance Kretschmer, Nevada	Fr.	302	1732	15	157.45
William Green, Boston College	Jr.	265	1559	15	155.90
Luke Staley, BYU	Jr.	196	1582	24	143.82
Larry Ned, San Diego St.	Sr.	311	1549	15	140.82
Anthony Davis, Wisconsin	Fr.	291	1466	11	133.27
Leonard Henry, E. Carolina	Jr.	184	1432	16	130.18
Chester Taylor, Toledo	Jr.	268	1430	20	130.00
Levron Williams, Indiana	Sr.	212	1401	17	127.36
Dameon Hunter, Utah	Sr.	257	1396	9	126.91
Marcus Merriweather, Ball St.	Sr.	268	1244	12	124.40
Emmett White, Utah St.	Sr.	250	1361	13	123.73
Travis Stephens, Tennessee	Sr.	291	1464	10	122.00

Games: All played 11, except Green and Merriweather (10) and Stephens (12).

Field Goals

	Cl	FG/Att	Pct	P/Gm
Todd Sievers, Miami-FL	Jr.	21/26	.808	1.91
Jeff Chandler, Florida	Sr.	19/22	.864	1.90
Steve Azar, N. Illinois	So.	20/26	.769	1.82
Jarvis Wallum, Wyoming	Jr.	20/23	.870	1.82
Travis Dorsch, Purdue	Sr.	20/25	.800	1.82
Asen Asparuhov, Fresno St.	Jr.	23/30	.767	1.77
Tim Duncan, Oklahoma	Jr.	20/28	.714	1.67
Jeremy Flores, Colorado	Sr.	18/24	.750	1.64
Josh Scobee, La. Tech	So.	18/22	.818	1.64

Games: All played 11, except Chandler (10), Asparuhov (13) and Duncan (12).
Longest FG of season: 58 yds by Damon Fine, Nevada vs. UNLV (Oct. 6, 2001)

Receptions

	Cl	No	Yds	TD	P/Gm
Kevin Curtis, Utah St.	Jr.	100	1531	10	9.09
Ricky Williams, Texas Tech	Sr.	92	617	4	8.36
Josh Reed, LSU	Jr.	94	1740	7	7.83
Darius Watts, Marshall	So.	91	1417	18	7.58
Don Shoals, Tulsa	Sr.	75	908	4	7.50
Marquise Walker, Michigan	Sr.	81	1043	11	7.36
Rashaun Woods, Oklahoma St.	So.	80	1023	10	7.27
Ryan McGuffey, Wyoming	So.	65	751	1	7.22
Reno Mahe, BYU	Jr.	91	1211	9	7.00
Rodney Wright, Fresno St.	Sr.	91	1331	10	7.00
Ashley Lelie, Hawaii	Jr.	84	1713	19	7.00
Edell Shepherd, San Jose St.	Sr.	83	1500	14	6.92
Billy McMullen, Virginia	Jr.	83	1060	12	6.92

Games: All played 12, except Curtis, Williams, Walker, Woods (11), Shoals (10), McGuffey (9), Mahe and Wright (13).

Interceptions

	Cl	No	Yds	TD	P/Gm
Edward Reed, Miami-FL	Sr.	9	206	2	.82
Lamont Thompson, Wash. St.	Sr.	8	96	1	.73
Kevin Thomas, UNLV	Sr.	7	213	3	.64
Derek Ross, Ohio St.	Sr.	7	194	1	.64
Nathan Vasher, Texas	So.	7	17	0	.58

Games: All played 11 except Vasher (12)

Scoring

Non-Kickers

	Cl	TD	Pts	P/Gm
Luke Staley, BYU..............	Jr.	28	170*	15.45
Dwone Hicks, Mid. Tenn. St.	Jr.	24	148†	13.45
Chester Taylor, Toledo	Jr.	23	138	12.55
Levron Williams, Indiana	Sr.	19	114	10.36
William Green, Boston Coll.	Jr.	17	102	10.20
Leonard Henry, E. Carolina ...	Sr.	18	108	9.82
Ricky Williams, Texas Tech	Sr.	18	108	9.82
Eric Crouch, Nebraska	Sr.	19	116	9.67
Ashley Lelie, Hawaii	Jr.	19	114	9.50
LaBrandon Toefield, LSU	So.	19	114	9.50

Games: All played 11, except Green (10), Crouch, Lelie and Toefield (12).
*includes one 2-pt conversion.
†includes two 2-pt conversions.

Kickers

	FG/Att	PAT/Att	Pts	P/Gm
Todd Sievers, Miami-FL	21/26	56/58	119	10.82
Jeff Chandler, Florida	19/22	46/48	103	10.30
Asen Asparuhov, Fresno St. ...	23/30	55/57	124	9.54
Tim Duncan, Oklahoma	20/28	45/47	111	9.25
Justin Ayat, Hawaii	19/29	54/57	111	9.25
Josh Scobee, La. Tech	18/22	44/45	98	8.91
Jeremy Flores, Colorado.....	18/24	40/42	94	8.55
Dusty Mangum, Texas.......	16/23	54/55	102	8.50
Matt Payne, BYU	12/17	73/76	109	8.38
Steve Azar, N. Illinois	20/26	31/32	91	8.27

Games: All played 11, except Chandler (10), Duncan, Ayat, Mangum (12), Asparuhov and Payne (13).

Punting
(Minimum of 3.6 per game)

	Cl	No	Yds	Avg
Travis Dorsch, Purdue	Sr.	49	2370	48.37
Dave Zastudil, Ohio	Sr.	50	2280	45.60
Andy Groom, Ohio St.	Sr.	44	1981	45.02
Steve Mullins, Utah St.	Jr.	50	2241	44.82
John Skaggs, Navy	So.	48	2151	44.81
Glenn Pakulak, Kentucky	Jr.	56	2492	44.50
Brooks Barnard, Maryland.......	Jr.	54	2401	44.46

Punt Returns
(Minimum of 1.2 per game)

	Cl	No	Yds	TD	Avg
Roman Hollowell, Colorado.......	Sr.	29	522	2	18.00
Luke Powell, Stanford	Jr.	19	304	0	16.00
DeAndrew Rubin, S. Florida......	Jr.	26	406	1	15.62
Ronnie Hamilton, Duke	Sr.	20	311	1	15.55
Dexter Wynn, Colorado St.	So.	14	214	0	15.29
Nathan Vasher, Texas..........	So.	37	554	1	14.97
Phillip Buchanon, Miami-FL......	Jr.	31	464	2	14.97
Keenan Howry, Oregon	Jr.	32	465	2	14.53
DeJuan Groce, Nebraska........	Jr.	33	469	1	14.21
Bernard Berrian, Fresno St.	Jr.	39	552	1	14.15

Kickoff Returns
(Minimum of 1.2 per game)

	Cl	No	Yds	TD	Avg
Chris Massey, Oklahoma St.	Jr.	15	522	1	34.80
Chad Owens, Hawaii............	Fr.	24	807	2	33.63
Derrick Hamilton, Clemson........	Fr.	15	476	1	31.73
Tom Pace, Arizona St............	Sr.	17	537	1	31.59
Corey Parchman, Ball St.	Sr.	15	465	2	31.00
Roc Alexander, Washington.......	So.	19	555	1	29.21
David Mikell, Boise St.	So.	25	709	1	28.36
Aaron Lockett, Kansas St.	Sr.	14	397	1	28.36
Herb Haygood, Michigan St........	Sr.	19	524	2	27.58
Jason Armstead, Mississippi.......	Jr.	19	524	1	27.58

NCAA Division I-A Team Leaders
REGULAR SEASON

Scoring Offense

	Gm	Record	Pts	Avg
BYU.....................	13	12-1	608	46.77
Florida	11	9-2	482	43.82
Miami-FL.................	11	11-0	475	43.18
Fresno St.................	13	11-2	525	40.38
Hawaii	12	9-3	483	40.25
Texas	12	10-2	470	39.17
Nebraska	12	11-1	449	37.42
Marshall.................	12	10-2	448	37.33
Mid. Tenn St..............	11	8-3	408	37.09
Stanford	11	9-2	408	37.09

Scoring Defense

	Gm	Record	Pts	Avg
Miami-FL..................	11	11-0	103	9.4
Va. Tech	11	8-3	147	13.4
Texas....................	12	10-2	164	13.7
Oklahoma	12	10-2	166	13.8
Florida	11	9-2	155	14.1
Nebraska	12	11-1	189	15.8
Kansas St.	11	6-5	179	16.3
So. Miss.	11	6-5	186	16.9
Michigan	11	8-3	192	17.5
Louisville.................	12	10-2	213	17.8

Total Offense

	Gm	Plays	Yds	Avg	TD	YdsPG
BYU..............	13	991	7057	7.12	82	542.85
Florida	11	788	5803	7.36	61	527.55
Marshall..........	12	880	6060	6.89	61	505.00
Fresno St..........	13	983	6464	6.58	65	497.23
Mid. Tenn. St.	11	781	5296	6.78	56	481.45
Idaho	11	872	5113	5.86	42	464.82
Hawaii	12	855	5552	6.49	61	462.67
Miami-FL..........	11	762	5003	6.57	59	454.82
Nevada	11	871	4993	5.73	35	453.91
Stanford	11	840	4967	5.91	54	451.55

Note: Touchdowns scored by rushing and passing only.

Total Defense

	Gm	Plays	Yds	Avg	TD	YdsPG
Texas..............	12	754	2834	3.76	22	236.17
Va. Tech	11	725	2617	3.61	17	237.91
Kansas St.	11	684	2886	4.22	21	262.36
Oklahoma	12	813	3154	3.88	18	262.83
UAB..............	11	719	2925	4.07	24	265.91
Miami-FL..........	11	759	2980	3.93	14	270.91
Pittsburgh	11	786	3131	3.98	29	284.64
Nebraska	12	813	3446	4.24	24	287.17
Florida	11	712	3192	4.48	19	290.18
Texas A&M........	11	798	3234	4.05	24	294.00

Note: Opponents' TDs scored by rushing and passing only.

Single Game Highs

INDIVIDUAL

Rushing Yards

Yds	
327	Chance Kretschmer, Nevada vs. UTEP (Nov. 24)
301	DeShaun Foster, UCLA vs. Washington (Oct. 13)
285	Larry Ned, San Diego St. vs. Eastern Ill. (Oct. 6)
285	Onterrio Smith, Oregon vs. Wash. St. (Oct. 27)

Total Offense

Yds	
657	Brian Lindgren, Idaho vs. Mid. Tenn. St. (Oct. 6)
558	Nick Rolovichm, Hawaii vs. BYU (Dec. 8)
540	Rohan Davey, LSU vs. Alabama (Nov. 3)

Receptions

Att	
19	Josh Reed, LSU vs. Alabama (Nov. 3)
15	Four tied, including twice by Marquise Walker, Mich.

Receiving Yards

Yds	
326	Nate Burleson, Nevada vs. San Jose St. (Nov. 10)
293	Josh Reed, LSU vs. Alabama (Nov. 3)
285	Ashley Lelie, Hawaii vs. Air Force (Nov. 24)

Passing Yards

Yds	
637	Brian Lindgren, Idaho vs. Mid. Tenn. St. (Oct. 6)
543	Nick Rolovich, Hawaii vs. BYU (Dec. 8)
528	Rohan Davey, LSU vs. Alabama (Nov. 3)

Passes Completed

No	
49	Brian Lindgren, Idaho vs. Mid. Tenn. St. (Oct. 6)
44	Kliff Kingsbury, Tex. Tech vs. Okla. St. (Nov. 10)
40	Kliff Kingsbury, Tex. Tech vs. Texas (Sept. 29)
40	Ben Roethlisberger, Miami-OH vs. Hawaii (Nov. 17)

TEAM

Total Offense Yards Gained

Yds	
849	San Jose St. vs. Nevada (Nov. 10)
791	Nevada vs. San Jose St. (Nov. 10)

Total Defense Yards Allowed

Yds	
57	LA-Lafayette vs. Nicholls St. (Sept. 1)
67	Texas vs. Kansas (Nov. 10)

Annual Awards

Player of the Year

Eric Crouch, Nebraska . . . . .Heisman, Camp
Rex Grossman, Florida . . . . .AP
Ken Dorsey, Miami-FL . . . . .Maxwell

Position Players of the Year

O'Brien Award (Quarterback) . . . . .Eric Crouch, Nebraska
Walker Award (Running Back) . . . . .Lucas Staley, BYU
Biletnikoff Award (Receiver) . . . . Josh Reed, LSU
Outland Trophy (Interior Lineman) . .Bryant McKinnie, Miami-FL
Lombardi Award (Lineman) . . . . . . Julius Peppers, N. Carolina
Butkus Award (Linebacker) . . . . .Rocky Calmus, Oklahoma
Thorpe Award (Defensive Back) . . . . .Roy Williams, Oklahoma
Nagurski Award (Defensive Player) . .Roy Williams, Oklahoma
Groza Award (Kicker) . . . . .Seth Marler, Tulane
Payton Award (IAA Player of the Year) . . . . . .Brian Westbrook,
    Villanova, RB
Hill Trophy (Div. II Player of the Year) . . .Dusty Bonner, Valdosta
    St., QB
Melberger Award (Div. III Player of the Year) . . . .Chuck Moore,
    Mt. Union, RB

Coach of the Year

Ralph Friedgen, Maryland .AFCA, AP, Camp, Dodd, FWAA
Larry Coker, Miami-FL . . . . .AFCA

Heisman Trophy Vote

Presented since 1935 by the Downtown Athletic Club of New York City and named after former college coach and DAC athletic director John W. Heisman. Voting done by national media and former Heisman winners. Each ballot allows for three names (points based on 3 for 1st, 2 for 2nd and 1 for 3rd).

Top 10 Vote-Getters

	Pos	1st	2nd	3rd	Pts
Eric Crouch, Nebraska	QB	162	98	88	770
Rex Grossman, Florida	QB	137	105	87	708
Ken Dorsey, Miami-FL	QB	109	122	67	638
Joey Harrington, Oregon . . .	QB	54	68	66	364
David Carr, Frenso St.	QB	34	60	58	280
Antwaan Randle El, Indiana .QB		46	39	51	267
Roy Williams, Oklahoma . . . . .S		13	36	35	146
Bryant McKinnie, Miami-FL . .OT		26	12	14	116
Dwight Freeney, Syracuse . . .DE		2	6	24	42
Julius Peppers, N. Carolina . .DE		2	10	15	41

Consensus All-America Team

NCAA Division I-A players cited most frequently by the following selectors: AFCA, AP, and Walter Camp Foundation. (*) indicates unanimous selection.

Offense

	Player	Class	Ht	Wt
WR	Jabar Gaffney*, Florida . . . . .So.	6-1	197
WR	Josh Reed, LSU . . . . .Jr.	5-11	200
TE	Dan Graham*, Colorado. . . . . .Sr.	6-3	245
C	LeCharles Bentley*, Ohio St. . . . . .Sr.	6-2	300
OL	Bryant McKinnie*, Miami-FL . . . . .Sr.	6-9	336
OL	Terrence Metcalf, Mississippi . . . . .Sr.	6-4	315
OL	Mike Williams, Texas . . . . .Sr.	6-6	345
OL	Toniu Fonoti, Nebraska . . . . .Jr.	6-4	340
QB	Rex Grossman, Florida . . . . .So.	6-1	218
RB	Lucas Staley*, BYU . . . . .Jr.	6-1	218
RB	William Green, Boston College . . . . . .Sr.	6-1	215
K	Damon Duval*, Auburn. . . . . .Jr.	6-1	186

Defense

	Player	Class	Ht	Wt
DL	Julius Peppers*, N. Carolina . . . . .Jr.	6-6	290
DL	Dwight Freeney*, Syracuse . . . . .Sr.	6-2	250
DL	Alex Brown, Florida . . . . .Sr.	6-3	264
DL	John Henderson*, Tennessee . . . . .Sr.	6-7	290
LB	Rocky Calmus*, Oklahoma . . . . .Sr.	6-3	238
LB	Robert Thomas, UCLA . . . . .Sr.	6-2	237
LB	LeVar Fisher, N.C. State . . . . .Sr.	6-2	233
LB	E.J. Henderson, Maryland . . . . .Jr.	6-2	243
DB	Quentin Jammer*, Texas . . . . .Sr.	6-1	200
DB	Edward Reed*, Miami-FL . . . . .Sr.	6-0	198
DB	Roy Williams*, Oklahoma . . . . .Jr.	6-1	221
P	Travis Dorsch*, Purdue . . . . .Sr.	6-6	222

Underclassmen who declared for the 2002 draft

Thirty-nine players forfeited the remainder of their college eligibility and declared for the NFL draft in 2002. NFL teams drafted 27 underclassmen. Players listed in alphabetical order; first round selections in **bold** type.

	Pos	Drafted by	Overall pick
Terreal Bierria, Georgia	S	Seattle	120
Antonio Bryant, Pittsburgh	WR	Dallas	63
Phillip Buchanon, Miami-FL	CB	Oakland	17
Joe Burns, Ga. Tech	RB	Not Drafted	—
Reche Caldwell, Florida	WR	San Diego	48
T.J. Duckett, Mich. St.	RB	Atlanta	29
Trev Faulk, LSU	LB	Not Drafted	—
Toniu Fonoti, Nebraska	G	San Diego	39
Jabar Gaffney, Florida	WR	Houston	33
Charles Grant, Georgia	DE	New Orleans	25
William Green, Boston Coll.	RB	Cleveland	16
Albert Haynesworth, Tenn.	DT	Tennessee	15
Gary Hobbs, Arkansas	OT	Not Drafted	—
Dennis Johnson, Kentucky	DE	Arizona	98
Ryan Johnson, Memphis	WR	Not Drafted	—
Michael Josiah, Louisville	DE	Not Drafted	—
Ashley Lelie, Hawaii	WR	Denver	19
Tavon Mason, Virginia	WR	Not Drafted	—
Randy McMichael, Georgia	TE	Miami	114
Michael Pearson, Florida	OT	Jacksonville	40
Julius Peppers, N. Carolina	DE	Carolina	2
Clinton Portis, Miami-FL	RB	Denver	51
Saleem Rasheed, Alabama	LB	San Fran.	69
Tellis Redmon, Minnesota	RB	Not Drafted	—
Josh Reed, LSU	WR	Buffalo	36
Derek Ross, Ohio St.	CB	Dallas	75
Darnell Sanders, Ohio St.	TE	Cleveland	122
Lito Sheppard, Florida	CB	Philadelphia	26
Jeremy Shockey, Miami-FL	TE	NY Giants	14
Bobby Sippio, Western Ky.	DB	Not Drafted	—
Akil Smith, Clemson	OT	Not Drafted	—
Derek Smith, Kentucky	TE	Not Drafted	—
Bo Springfield, TCU	DB	Not Drafted	—
Luke Staley, BYU	RB	Detroit	214
Donte Stallworth, Tenn.	WR	New Orleans	13
Jerramy Stevens, Washington	TE	Seattle	28
Glenn Sumter, Memphis	DB	Not Drafted	—
Ramon Walker, Pittsburgh	S	Houston	153
Roy Williams, Oklahoma	S	Dallas	8

NCAA Division I-AA Final Standings

Standings based on conference games only; overall records include postseason games.

Atlantic 10 Conference

	Conference				Overall			
	W	L	PF	PA	W	L	PF	PA
*Hofstra	7	2	335	243	9	3	441	294
*Maine	7	2	276	193	9	3	352	269
Villanova	7	2	349	275	8	3	401	306
*Wm. & Mary	7	2	278	217	8	4	362	295
Rhode Island	6	3	174	207	8	3	272	252
Northeastern	5	165	176	5	6	225	224	
Delaware	4	5	181	161	4	6	188	199
Richmond	3	6	163	144	3	8	201	189
Massachusetts	3	6	158	293	3	8	178	342
New Hampshire	2	7	242	325	4	7	329	392
James Madison	0	9	145	232	2	9	201	260

*Playoffs (1-3): Maine (1-1), Hofstra (0-1), William & Mary (0-1).

Big Sky Conference

	Conference				Overall			
	W	L	PF	PA	W	L	PF	PA
*Montana	7	0	250	151	15	1	533	293
*Northern Arizona	5	2	277	230	8	4	399	341
Portland St.	5	2	250	205	7	4	365	314
Montana St.	4	3	228	174	6	6	309	329
Eastern Wash.	3	4	259	262	7	4	461	349
Weber St.	2	5	221	275	3	8	347	441
Idaho St.	1	6	179	275	4	7	331	333
Sacramento St.	1	6	179	271	2	9	249	424

*Playoffs (4-1): Montana (4-0), Northern Arizona (0-1).

Gateway Athletic Conference

	Conference				Overall			
	W	L	PF	PA	W	L	PF	PA
*Northern Iowa	6	1	165	120	11	3	377	340
Youngstown St.	5	2	217	139	8	3	368	191
*Western Ky.	2	199	91	8	4	318	146	
Western Ill.	4	3	189	173	5	5	257	290
SW Missouri St.	3	4	165	199	6	5	297	271
Indiana St.	2	5	120	207	3	8	168	347
Illinois St.	2	5	188	237	2	9	258	375
Southern Ill.	1	6	109	186	1	10	167	339

*Playoffs (2-2): Northern Iowa (2-1), Western Kentucky (0-1).

Ivy League

	Conference				Overall			
	W	L	PF	PA	W	L	PF	PA
Harvard	7	0	220	150	9	0	293	184
Pennsylvania	6	1	184	96	8	1	264	103
Brown	5	2	241	170	6	3	319	235
Princeton	3	4	180	133	3	6	200	202
Columbia	3	4	162	231	3	7	206	326
Cornell	2	5	120	219	2	7	187	292
Yale	1	6	155	200	1	6	214	249
Dartmouth	1	6	147	210	1	8	202	301

Playoffs: League does not play postseason games.

Metro Atlantic Athletic Conference

	Conference				Overall			
	W	L	PF	PA	W	L	PF	PA
Duquesne	6	0	252	54	8	3	370	183
St. Peter's	6	1	192	56	10	1	288	90
Fairfield	5	2	211	152	5	5	273	256
Iona	2	3	94	121	3	5	151	232
La Salle	2	4	64	145	5	4	154	206
Marist	2	4	76	106	3	6	146	197
Canisius	1	5	127	251	1	8	151	377
Siena	1	6	76	207	1	8	93	276

Playoffs: No teams invited.

Mid-Eastern Athletic Conference

	Conference				Overall			
	W	L	PF	PA	W	L	PF	PA
*Florida A&M	7	1	290	196	7	4	346	300
Hampton	6	2	243	200	7	4	334	315
N. Carolina A&T	5	3	289	187	8	3	376	229
Bethune-Cookman	5	3	245	174	6	4	303	205
South Carolina St.	5	3	193	189	6	5	231	241
Delaware St.	3	5	236	249	5	6	315	324
Norfolk St.	3	5	107	228	5	6	161	278
Morgan St.	1	7	188	274	2	8	239	295
Howard	1	7	193	287	2	9	232	374

*Playoffs (0-1): Florida A&M (0-1).

NCAA Division I-AA Final Standings (Cont.)

Northeast Conference

	Conference				Overall			
	W	L	PF	PA	W	L	PF	PA
Sacred Heart 8	0	336	145	11	0	450	167
Robert Morris.......6	1	274	149	6	3	310	219
Albany 5	2	185	152	7	3	236	195
Monmouth (N.J.) ...5	2	162	106	7	3	240	154
Stony Brook 3	5	191	209	3	6	211	238
Wagner............3	5	225	235	3	6	249	276
Central Conn. 2	5	116	153	2	7	146	233
St. John's..........1	6	50	182	1	9	85	268
St. Francis (Pa.) 0	7	34	242	0	10	78	381

Playoffs: No teams invited.

Ohio Valley Conference

	Conference				Overall			
	W	L	PF	PA	W	L	PF	PA
*Eastern Ill........6	1	222	121	9	2	403	255
Eastern Ky. 5	1	169	88	8	2	320	155
Tennessee Tech 4	2	203	131	7	3	313	213
Tennessee St.......3	3	185	174	8	3	389	223
Murray St..........2	4	136	163	4	6	216	315
SE Missouri St......2	5	177	196	4	7	279	281
Tenn.-Martin.......0	6	87	274	1	10	198	422

Playoffs (0-1): Eastern Illinois (0-1).

Patriot League

	Conference				Overall			
	W	L	PF	PA	W	L	PF	PA
*Lehigh............7	0	253	103	11	1	427	216
Colgate...........5	1	150	75	7	3	244	189
Fordham 5	2	192	145	7	4	329	245
Bucknell 4	3	162	93	6	4	240	157
Holy Cross 3	4	169	196	4	6	247	279
Towson 2	5	102	203	3	7	149	257
Lafayette..........1	6	165	219	2	8	210	308
Georgetown.......0	6	60	220	3	7	160	316

Playoffs (1-1): Lehigh (1-1).

Pioneer League

	Conference				Overall			
North	W	L	PF	PA	W	L	PF	PA
Dayton 4	0	153	47	10	1	453	167
Butler 2	2	103	123	5	5	278	328
San Diego.........2	2	81	95	6	3	236	203
Drake 1	3	95	111	5	5	276	278
Valparaiso 1	3	58	114	3	8	149	282

	Conference				Overall			
South	W	L	PF	PA	W	L	PF	PA
Jacksonville........3	0	122	37	6	5	268	268
Morehead St.......1	1	84	80	6	5	298	246
Davidson..........1	2	37	85	5	4	199	208
Austin Peay........0	3	43	84	3	7	236	265

Playoffs: No teams invited.

Best Conference Playoff Records

Postseason records for 2001 season.

	W-L	Pct
Big Sky 4-1	.800
Southern 6-3	.667
Gateway Athletic 2-2	.500
Patriot 1-1	.500
Atlantic 10 1-3	.250
Southland 1-3	.250
Ohio Valley 0-1	.000
Mid-Eastern Athletic................0-1	.000

Southern Conference

	Conference				Overall			
	W	L	PF	PA	W	L	PF	PA
*Ga. Southern 7	1	276	98	12	2	525	215
*Furman 7	1	282	99	12	3	477	221
*Appalachian St. ...6	2	227	153	9	4	411	278
W. Carolina.......5	3	195	194	7	4	280	231
E. Tenn St. 4	4	137	178	6	5	193	226
Wofford 3	5	197	204	4	7	260	290
The Citadel........2	6	134	140	3	7	172	183
Tenn.-Chatt. 1	7	106	281	3	8	217	338
VMI 1	7	118	325	1	10	164	446

*Playoffs (6-3): Furman (3-1), Ga. Southern (2-1), Appalachian St. (1-1).

Southland Conference

	Conference				Overall			
	W	L	PF	PA	W	L	PF	PA
*Sam Houston St. ...5	1	198	145	10	3	470	322
*McNeese St. 5	1	152	110	8	4	347	206
*Northwestern St...4	2	164	112	8	4	319	232
Stephen F. Austin...2	4	166	140	6	5	246	264
Jacksonville St......2	4	177	204	5	6	349	305
Nicholls St..........1	5	142	187	3	8	218	308
SW Texas St. 0	6	77	178	4	7	188	258

*Playoffs (1-3): Sam Houston St. (1-1), Northwestern St. (0-1), McNeese St. (0-1).

Southwestern Athletic Conference

	Conference				Overall			
Eastern	W	L	PF	PA	W	L	PF	PA
Jackson St. 6	2	294	219	7	4	389	342
Alcorn St...........5	2	210	199	6	5	269	312
Alabama St..........6	3	303	251	8	4	444	298
Alabama A&M 3	6	188	202	4	7	215	246
Miss. Valley St.......0	8	157	338	0	11	176	472

	Conference				Overall			
Western	W	L	PF	PA	W	L	PF	PA
Grambling 8	1	346	157	10	1	413	214
Southern 6	2	230	129	7	4	275	214
Prairie View 2	5	143	219	3	7	194	302
Texas Southern......2	6	144	181	3	7	191	245
Ark.-Pine Bluff......2	7	120	250	4	7	154	270

Playoffs: No teams invited.

NCAA I-AA Independents

	W	L	PF	PA
Gardner Webb 5	4	268	227
Cal Poly-SLO 6	5	292	248
St. Mary's (Ca.)....................6	5	249	242
Samford 5	5	269	274
Charleston Southern 5	6	262	253
Morris Brown 5	6	215	277
Florida Atlantic....................4	6	177	245
Cal St.-Northridge..................3	7	342	390
Liberty 3	8	225	404
Savannah St.......................2	7	105	283
Elon 2	9	199	346
Southern Utah 2	9	219	296

Eastern Illinois
Tony Romo
Passing Efficiency

CS-Northridge
Drew Amerson
Receptions

St. Peter's
John Ambrose
Interceptions

Northeastern
L.J. McKanas
Rushing

NCAA Division I-AA Regular Season Leaders
INDIVIDUAL

Passing Efficiency
(Minimum 15 attempts per game)

	Cl	Gm	Att	Cmp	Cmp Pct	Int	Int Pct	Yds	Yds/ Att	TD	TD Pct	Rating Points
Tony Romo, Eastern Ill.	Jr.	10	207	138	66.67	6	2.90	2068	9.99	21	10.14	178.3
Rocky Butler, Hofstra	Sr.	11	335	206	61.49	4	1.19	3311	9.88	30	8.96	171.7
Brant Hall, Lehigh	Sr.	8	176	106	60.23	3	1.70	1684	9.57	16	9.09	167.2
Neil Rose, Harvard	Sr.	8	198	127	64.14	5	2.53	1830	9.24	15	7.58	161.7
Darnell Kennedy, Alabama St.	Sr.	12	347	202	58.21	12	3.46	3158	9.10	33	9.51	159.1
Grant Swallows, Tennessee Tech	Sr.	10	253	161	63.64	11	4.35	2361	9.33	19	7.51	158.1
Josh McCown, Sam Houston St.	Sr.	11	341	210	61.58	8	2.35	2884	8.46	29	8.50	156.0
Dave Corley, William & Mary	Jr.	11	283	167	59.01	9	3.18	2584	9.13	19	6.71	151.5
Justin Holtfreter, Sacred Heart	Sr.	10	272	153	56.25	8	2.94	2371	8.72	23	8.46	151.5
Juston Wood, Portland St.	Jr.	11	366	218	59.56	5	1.37	3200	8.74	23	6.28	151.0

Total Offense

	Cl	Rush	Pass	Yds	YdsPG
Marcus Brady, CS-Northridge	Sr.	277	3355	3632	363.2
Robert Kent, Jackson St.	So.	170	3615	3785	344.1
Rocky Butler, Hofstra	Sr.	453	3311	3764	342.2
Darnell Kennedy, Alabama St.	Sr.	511	3158	3669	305.8
Josh McCown, Sam Houston St.	Sr.	354	2884	3238	294.4
Juston Wood, Portland St.	Jr.	11	3200	3211	291.9
Fred Salanoa, E. Washington	Sr.	100	3057	3157	287.0
Shannon Harris, Tenn. St.	Sr.	129	3008	3137	285.2
Ryan Day, N. Hampshire	Sr.	480	2605	3085	280.5
Sam Clemons, Western Ill.	Sr.	138	2615	2753	275.3

Games: All played 11, except Kent and Clemons (10) and Kennedy (12).

Receptions

	Cl	No	Yds	TD	P/Gm
Drew Amerson, CS-Northridge	Jr.	97	1244	5	9.70
Chas Gessner, Brown	Jr.	83	1182	12	9.22
Carl Morris, Harvard	Jr.	71	943	12	7.89
Billy Brown, Yale	Sr.	71	946	6	7.89
T.C. Taylor, Jackson St.	Sr.	84	1234	11	7.64
Josh Snyder, Lehigh	Sr.	74	1241	12	7.40
Aryvia Holmes, Samford	Sr.	74	1042	8	7.40
Jonathon Cooper, Sam Houston St.	Sr.	78	1301	17	7.09
Jim Horan, Bucknell	Jr.	59	714	3	6.56
Terry Charles, Portland St.	Sr.	71	1096	12	6.45

Games: All played 9, except Amerson, Snyder, Holmes (10) Taylor and Cooper (11).

Rushing

	Cl	Car	Yds	TD	YdsPG
Jesse Chatman, E. Washington	Sr.	285	2096	24	190.55
LJ. McKanas, Northeastern	Sr.	342	1756	14	159.64
Brian Westbrook, Villanova	Sr.	249	1603	22	145.73
Kris Ryan, Pennsylvania	Sr.	267	1304	15	144.89
Ryan Fuqua, Portland St.	Fr.	210	1586	15	144.18
Johnnie Gray, Weber St.	Sr.	305	1571	15	142.82
Ryan Johnson, Montana St.	Jr.	303	1537	14	139.73
Yohance Humphrey, Montana	Sr.	303	1658	17	138.17
C.J. Hudson, Eastern Ky.	Fr.	217	1221	12	135.67
Louis Ivory, Furman	Sr.	251	1492	19	135.64

Games: All played 11, except Ryan, Hudson (9) and Humphery (12).

Interceptions

	Cl	No	Yds	TD	Int/Gm
Jon Ambrose, St. Peter's	Jr.	11	222	2	1.00
Mark Kasmer, Dayton	Jr.	9	212	3	.90
Leigh Bodden, Duquesne	Jr.	9	51	1	.90
Jamar Williams, Morgan St.	Jr.	8	-4	1	.73
Tony Tiller, E. Tenn. St.	So.	7	102	0	.64
Terrence Arnold, Southern U.	Sr.	7	50	0	.64
Chuck Wesley, Rhode Island	Sr.	7	138	1	.64
Art Smith, Northeastern	Sr.	7	143	1	.64
LaVar Greene, Youngstown St.	Sr.	7	73	1	.64

Games: All played 11, except Kasmer and Bodden (10).

NCAA Division I-AA Regular Season Leaders (Cont.)

Scoring
Non-Kickers

	Cl	TD	XPt	Pts	P/Gm
Brian Westbrook, Villanova	Sr.	29	1	176	16.00
Jesse Chatman, E. Washington	Sr.	28	2	172	15.64
J.R. Taylor, Eastern Ill.	Jr.	20	0	120	12.00
P.J. Mays, Youngstown St.	Jr.	22	0	132	12.00
Stephan Lewis, UNH	Jr.	19	3	120	10.91

Games: All played 11, except Taylor (10).

Kickers

	Cl	FG/Att	PAT/Att	Pts
Troy Griggs, E. Washington	Sr.	14/20	51/53	93
Brian Morgan, Grambling	Fr.	18/25	39/51	93
Chris Snyder, Montana	So.	13/22	46/47	85
Brian Kelley, Lehigh	Jr.	12/17	44/47	80
Scott Shelton, Ga. Southern	Jr.	12/19	44/46	80

Games: All played 11, except Kelley (10) and Snyder (12).

Field Goals

	Cl	FG/Att	Pct	P/Gm
Brian Morgan, Grambling	Fr.	18/25	.720	1.64
Shane Andrus, Murray St.	So.	15/22	.682	1.50
Taylor Northrop, Princeton	Sr.	13/18	.722	1.44
Four tied with 1.27 per game.				

Games: All played 11, except Andrus (10) and Northrop (9).

Longest FG of season: 54 yds by Javier Garcia, Idaho St. vs. Northern Arizona (Oct. 6)

Punt/Kickoff Leaders

Punting	Cl	No	Yds	Avg
Eddie Johnson, Idaho St.	Jr.	49	2270	46.33

Punt Returns	Cl	No	Yds	TD	Avg
Curtis DeLoatch, N.C. A&T	So.	20	530	5	26.50

Kickoff Returns	Cl	No	Yds	TD	Avg
Brian Bratton, Furman	Fr.	14	521	3	37.21

TEAM
REGULAR SEASON
Scoring Offense

	Gm	Record	Pts	Avg		Gm	Record	Pts	Avg
Eastern Washington	11	7-4	461	41.91	Alabama St.	12	8-4	444	37.00
Sacred Heart	10	10-0	419	41.90	Villanova	11	8-3	401	36.45
Dayton	11	10-1	453	41.18	E. Illinois	10	9-1	360	36.00
Lehigh	10	10-0	383	38.30	Duquesne	10	8-2	355	35.50
Hofstra	11	9-2	417	37.91	Brown	9	6-3	319	35.44
Grambling	11	10-1	413	37.55	Furman	11	9-2	389	35.36
Sam Houston St.	11	9-2	412	37.45	Jackson St.	11	7-4	389	35.36
Ga. Southern	11	10-1	410	37.27	Tennessee St.	11	8-3	389	35.36

Scoring Defense

	Gm	Record	Pts	Avg		Gm	Record	Pts	Avg
St. Peter's	11	10-1	90	8.2	Monmouth	10	7-3	154	15.4
Western Ky.	11	8-3	122	11.1	Eastern Ky.	10	8-2	155	15.5
Pennsylvania	9	8-1	103	11.4	Bucknell	10	6-4	157	15.7
Ga. Southern	11	10-1	132	12.0	Lehigh	10	10-0	158	15.8
Furman	11	9-2	154	14.0	Richmond	11	3-8	189	17.2
Dayton	11	10-1	167	15.2	Youngstown St.	11	8-3	191	17.4
Duquesne	10	8-2	152	15.2	McNeese St.	11	8-3	192	17.5
Sacred Heart	10	10-0	152	15.2	The Citadel	10	3-7	183	18.3

Total Offense

	Record	Plays	Yds	Avg		Record	Plays	Yds	Avg
E. Washington	7-4	784	5659	514.45	St. Peter's	10-1	627	1735	157.73
Hofstra	9-2	790	5408	491.64	Western Ky.	8-3	668	2565	233.18
Alabama St.	8-4	817	5752	479.33	McNeese St.	8-3	722	2790	253.64
Portland St.	7-4	729	5255	477.73	Sacred Heart	10-0	626	2573	257.30
CS-Northridge	3-7	788	4687	468.70	Bucknell	6-4	671	2601	260.10
Tennessee St.	8-3	856	5112	464.73	Ga. Southern	10-1	722	2875	261.36
Jackson St.	7-4	897	4993	453.91	Eastern Ky.	8-2	649	2635	263.50
Villanova	8-3	768	4970	451.82	Duquesne	8-2	668	2676	267.60
New Hampshire	4-7	874	4941	449.18	Appalachian St.	8-3	695	2973	270.27
Brown	6-3	628	4024	447.11	Furman	9-2	740	3010	273.64
Harvard	9-0	656	4005	445.00	Richmond	3-8	627	3078	279.82
Weber St.	3-8	846	4894	444.91	Bethune-Cookman	6-4	649	2803	280.30
Sam Houston St.	9-2	770	4811	437.36	Pennsylvania	8-1	625	2554	283.78
Jacksonville St.	5-6	729	4705	427.73	Norfolk St.	5-6	751	3199	290.82
William & Mary	8-3	757	4688	426.18	Dayton	10-1	718	3203	291.18
Eastern Ill.	9-1	600	4246	424.60	Northwestern St.	8-3	728	3211	291.91

Total Defense

NCAA Playoffs

Division I-AA

First Round (Dec. 1)

at Montana 28 ....Northwestern St. 19
at Sam Houston St. 34 ....N. Arizona 31
at Maine 14.............................McNeese St. 10
Northern Iowa 49.......................at Eastern Ill. 43
at Ga. Southern 60......................Florida A&M 35
at Appalachian St. 40 ....William & Mary 27
at Lehigh 27 ....OT..............Hofstra 24
at Furman 24..........................Western Ky. 20

Quarterfinals (Dec. 8)

at Montana 49 ....Sam Houston St. 28
at Northern Iowa 56 ....Maine 28
at Ga. Southern 38.................Appalachian St. 24
at Furman 34 ....Lehigh 17

Semifinals (Dec. 15)

at Montana 38 ....Northern Iowa 0
Furman 24 ....at Ga. Southern 17

Championship Game
Dec. 21 at Chattanooga, Tenn. (Att: 12,698)

Montana 13..................................Furman 6
(15-1)   (12-3)

Division II

First Round (Nov. 17)

at North Dakota 42......................Winona St. 28
at Pittsburg St. 20 ....Nebraska-Omaha 7
Tarleton St. 28 ....at Chadron St. 24
UC-Davis 37 ....at Tex A&M-Kingsville 32
at Valdosta St. 40 ....Fort Valley St. 24
at Catawba 35.......................Central Arkansas 34
at Grand Valley St. 42 ....Bloomsburg 14
at Saginaw Valley St. 33 ....Indiana (Pa.) 32

Quarterfinals (Nov. 24)

at North Dakota 38......................Pittsburg St. 0
at UC-Davis 42 ....Tarleton St. 25
Catawba 37 ....OT............at Valdosta St. 34
at Grand Valley St. 33 ....Saginaw Valley St. 30

Semifinals (Dec. 1)

at North Dakota 14.......................UC-Davis 25
at Grand Valley St. 34 ....Catawba 16

Championship Game
Dec. 8 at Florence, Ala. (Att: 6,113)

North Dakota 17....................Grand Valley St. 14
(14-1)   (13-1)

Division I-AA, II and III Awards
Coaches of the Year

AFCA (NCAA Div. I-AA) ....Bobby Johnson, Furman
AFCA (College Div. II) ....Dale Lennon, North Dakota
AFCA (College Div. III) ....Larry Kehres, Mt. Union

Division III

First Round (Nov. 17)

at Augustana 54..........................Defiance 14
Wittenberg 38 ....OT .....at Hardin-Simmons 35
at Thomas More 34 ....MacMurray 30
Pacific Lutheran 27........OT ....at Whitworth 26
at WI-Stevens Point 37.......................Bethel 27
at St. John's (Minn.) 27 ....St. Norbert 20
Ithaca 35 ....at Montclair St. 23
at Rowan 40 ....SUNY Brockport 17
W. Connecticut St. 8 ....at Westfield St. 7
at Trinity 30 ....Mary Hardin-Baylor 6
at Wash. & Jeff. 24................Western Maryland 21
at Widener 56...................Christopher Newport 7

Second Round (Nov. 24)

at Mount Union 32 ....Augustana 7
Wittenberg 41 ....at Thomas More 0
Pacific Lutheran 27........OT ....at Central (Iowa) 21
at St. John's 9....................WI-Stevens Point 7
Ithaca 27 ....at Rensselaer 14
at Rowan 43 ....W. Connecticut St. 14
at Bridgewater (Va.) 41 ....Trinity 37
at Widener 46...................Wash. & Jeff. 30

Quarterfinals (Dec. 1)

at Mount Union 49.....................Wittenberg 21
at St. John's 31 ....Pacific Lutheran 6
at Rowan 48.................................Ithaca 0
at Bridgewater 57 ....Widener 32

Semifinals (Dec. 8)

at Mount Union 35 ....St. John's 14
at Bridgewater 29 ....Rowan 24

Amos Alonzo Stagg Bowl
Dec. 15 at Salem, Va. (Att: 7,992)

Mount Union 30......................Bridgewater 27
(14-0)   (12-1)

NAIA Playoffs
Division I
First Round (Nov. 17)

at Georgetown (Ky.) 42 ....Tri-State (Ind.) 21
Sioux Falls (S.D.) 27 ......OT.........at Mary (N.D.) 21
at Evangel (Mo.) 48 ....Kansas Wesleyan 0
at Carroll (Mont.) 45..........Valley City State (N.D.) 27
at Benedictine (Kan.) 29 ....NW Oklahoma St. 27
at Southern Oregon 54...............McKendree (Ill.) 10
at Concordia (Neb.) 31 ....St. Ambrose (Iowa) 26
at Campbellsville (Ky.) 42 ....St. Francis (Ind.) 21

Quarterfinals (Nov. 24)

at Carroll 16...................Southern Oregon 13
Benedictine 34.........................at Evangel 30
at Georgetown 76 ....Campbellsville 0
at Sioux Falls 34 ....Concordia 0

Semifinals (Dec. 1)

at Georgetown 31...........................Carroll 22
at Sioux Falls 40...........................Benedictine 6

Championship
Dec. 15 at Savannah, Tenn.

Georgetown 49.........................Sioux Falls 27
(14-0)   (12-2)

National Champions

Over the last 132 years, there have been 25 major selectors of national champions by way of polls (11), mathematical rating systems (10) and historical research (4). The best-known and most widely circulated of these surveys, the Associated Press poll of sportswriters and broadcasters, first appeared during the 1936 season. Champions prior to 1936 have been determined by retro polls, ratings and historical research.

The Early Years (1869-1935)

National champions based on the Dickinson mathematical system (DS) and three historical retro polls taken by the College Football Researchers Association (CFRA), the National Championship Foundation (NCF) and the Helms Athletic Foundation (HF). The CFRA and NCF polls start in 1869, college football's inaugural year, while the Helms poll begins in 1883, the first season the game adopted a point system for scoring. Frank Dickinson, an economics professor at Illinois, introduced his system in 1926 and retro-picked winners in 1924 and '25. Bowl game results were counted in the Helms selections, but not in the other three.

Multiple champions: Yale (18); Princeton (17); Harvard (9); Michigan (7); Notre Dame and Penn (4); Alabama, California, Cornell, Illinois, Pittsburgh and USC (3); Georgia Tech, Minnesota and Penn St. (2).

Year		Record	Year		Record	Year		Record
1869	**Princeton**	1-1-0	1880	**Yale** (CFRA)	4-0-1	1891	**Yale**	13-0-0
1870	**Princeton**	1-0-0		**& Princeton** (NCF)	4-0-1	1892	**Yale**	13-0-0
1871	No games played		1881	**Yale**	5-0-1	1893	**Princeton**	11-0-0
1872	**Princeton**	1-0-0	1882	**Yale**	8-0-0	1894	**Yale**	16-0-0
1873	**Princeton**	1-0-0	1883	**Yale**	8-0-0	1895	**Penn**	14-0-0
1874	**Yale**	3-0-0	1884	**Yale**	8-0-1	1896	**Princeton** (CFRA)	10-0-1
1875	**Princeton** (CFRA)	2-0-0	1885	**Princeton**	9-0-0		**& Lafayette** (NCF)	11-0-1
	& Harvard (NCF)	4-0-0	1886	**Yale**	9-0-1	1897	**Penn**	15-0-0
1876	**Yale**	3-0-0	1887	**Yale**	9-0-0	1898	**Harvard**	11-0-0
1877	**Yale**	3-0-1	1888	**Yale**	13-0-0	1899	**Princeton** (CFRA)	12-1-0
1878	**Princeton**	6-0-0	1889	**Princeton**	10-0-0		**& Harvard** (NCF, HF)	10-0-1
1879	**Princeton**	4-0-1	1890	**Harvard**	11-0-0			

Year		Record	Bowl Game	Head Coach	Outstanding Player
1900	**Yale**	12-0-0	No bowl	Malcolm McBride	Perry Hale, HB
1901	**Harvard** (CFRA)	12-0-0	No bowl	Bill Reid	Bob Kernan, HB
	& Michigan (NCF, HF)	11-0-0	Won Rose	Hurry Up Yost	Neil Snow, E
1902	**Michigan**	11-0-0	No bowl	Hurry Up Yost	Boss Weeks, QB
1903	**Princeton**	11-0-0	No bowl	Art Hillebrand	John DeWitt, G
1904	**Penn** (CFRA, HF)	12-0-0	No bowl	Carl Williams	Andy Smith, FB
	& Michigan (NCF)	10-0-0	No bowl	Hurry Up Yost	Willie Heston, HB
1905	**Chicago**	10-0-0	No bowl	Amos Alonzo Stagg	Walter Eckersall, QB
1906	**Princeton**	9-0-1	No bowl	Bill Roper	Cap Wister, E
1907	**Yale**	9-0-1	No bowl	Bill Knox	Tad Jones, HB
1908	**Penn** (CFRA, HF)	11-0-1	No bowl	Sol Metzger	Hunter Scarlett, E
	& LSU (NCF)	10-0-0	No bowl	Edgar Wingard	Doc Fenton, QB
1909	**Yale**	12-1-0	No bowl	Howard Jones	Ted Coy, FB
1910	**Harvard** (CFRA, HF)	8-0-1	No bowl	Percy Haughton	Percy Wendell, HB
	& Pittsburgh (NCF)	9-0-0	No bowl	Joe Thompson	Ralph Galvin, C
1911	**Princeton** (CFRA, HF)	8-0-2	No bowl	Bill Roper	Sam White, E
	& Penn St. (NCF)	8-0-1	No bowl	Bill Hollenback	Dexter Very, E
1912	**Harvard** (CFRA, HF)	9-0-0	No bowl	Percy Haughton	Charley Brickley, HB
	& Penn St. (NCF)	8-0-0	No bowl	Bill Hollenback	Dexter Very, E
1913	**Harvard**	9-0-0	No bowl	Percy Haughton	Eddie Mahan, FB
1914	**Army**	9-0-0	No bowl	Charley Daly	John McEwan, C
1915	**Cornell**	9-0-0	No bowl	Al Sharpe	Charley Barrett, QB
1916	**Pittsburgh**	8-0-0	No bowl	Pop Warner	Bob Peck, C
1917	**Georgia Tech**	9-0-0	No bowl	John Heisman	Ev Strupper, HB
1918	**Pittsburgh** (CFRA, HF)	4-1-0	No bowl	Pop Warner	Tom Davies, HB
	& Michigan (NCF)	5-0-0	No bowl	Hurry Up Yost	Frank Steketee, FB
1919	**Harvard** (CFRA-tie, HF)	9-0-1	Won Rose	Bob Fisher	Eddie Casey, HB
	Illinois (CFRA-tie)	6-1-0	No bowl	Bob Zuppke	Chuck Carney, E
	& Notre Dame (NCF)	9-0-0	No bowl	Knute Rockne	George Gipp, HB
1920	**California**	9-0-0	Won Rose	Andy Smith	Dan McMillan, T
1921	**California** (CFRA)	9-0-1	Tied Rose	Andy Smith	Brick Muller, E
	& Cornell (NCF, HF)	8-0-0	No bowl	Gil Dobie	Eddie Kaw, HB
1922	**Princeton** (CFRA)	8-0-0	No bowl	Bill Roper	Herb Treat, T
	California (NCF)	9-0-0	No bowl	Andy Smith	Brick Muller, E
	& Cornell (HF)	8-0-0	No bowl	Gil Dobie	Eddie Kaw, HB

Year		Record	Bowl Game	Head Coach	Outstanding Player
1923	**Illinois** (CFRA, HF)	8-0-0	No bowl	Bob Zuppke	Red Grange, HB
	& **Michigan** (NCF)	8-0-0	No bowl	Hurry Up Yost	Jack Blott, C
1924	**Notre Dame**	10-0-0	Won Rose	Knute Rockne	"The Four Horsemen"*
1925	**Alabama** (CFRA, HF)	10-0-0	Won Rose	Wallace Wade	Johnny Mack Brown, HB
	& **Dartmouth** (DS)	8-0-0	No bowl	Jesse Hawley	Swede Oberlander, HB
1926	**Alabama** (CFRA, HF)	9-0-1	Tied Rose	Wallace Wade	Hoyt Winslett, E
	& **Stanford** (DS)	10-0-1	Tied Rose	Pop Warner	Ted Shipkey, E
1927	**Yale** (CFRA)	7-1-0	No bowl	Tad Jones	Bill Webster, G
	& **Illinois** (NCF, HF, DS)	7-0-1	No bowl	Bob Zuppke	Bob Reitsch, C
1928	**Georgia Tech** (CFRA, NCF, HF)	10-0-0	Won Rose	Bill Alexander	Pete Pund, C
	& **USC** (DS)	9-0-1	No bowl	Howard Jones	Jesse Hibbs, T
1929	**Notre Dame**	9-0-0	No bowl	Knute Rockne	Frank Carideo, QB
1930	**Alabama** (CFRA)	10-0-0	Won Rose	Wallace Wade	Fred Sington, T
	& **Notre Dame** (NCF, HF, DS)	10-0-0	No bowl	Knute Rockne	Marchy Schwartz, HB
1931	**USC**	10-1-0	Won Rose	Howard Jones	John Baker, G
1932	**USC** (CFRA, NCF, HF)	10-0-0	Won Rose	Howard Jones	Ernie Smith, T
	& **Michigan** (DS)	8-0-0	No bowl	Harry Kipke	Harry Newman, QB
1933	**Michigan**	8-0-0	No bowl	Harry Kipke	Chuck Bernard, C
1934	**Minnesota**	8-0-0	No bowl	Bernie Bierman	Pug Lund, HB
1935	**Minnesota** (CFRA, NCF, HF)	8-0-0	No bowl	Bernie Bierman	Dick Smith, T
	& **SMU** (DS)	12-1-0	Lost Rose	Matty Bell	Bobby Wilson, HB

*Notre Dame's Four Horsemen were Harry Stuhldreher (QB), Jim Crowley (HB), Don Miller (HB-P) and Elmer Layden (FB).

The Media Poll Years (since 1936)

National champions according to seven media and coaches' polls: Associated Press (since 1936), United Press (1950-57), International News Service (1952-57), United Press International (1958-92), Football Writers Association of America (since 1954), National Football Foundation and Hall of Fame (since 1959) and USA Today/CNN (since 1991). In 1991, the American Football Coaches Association switched outlets for its poll from UPI to USA Today/CNN and then to USA Today/ESPN in 1997.

After 29 years of releasing its final Top 20 poll in early December, AP named its 1965 national champion following that season's bowl games. AP returned to a pre-bowls final vote in 1966 and '67, but has polled its writers and broadcasters after the bowl games since the 1968 season. The FWAA has selected its champion after the bowl games since the 1955 season, the NFF-Hall of Fame since 1971, UPI after 1974, USA Today/CNN 1991-96, and USA Today/ESPN since 1997.

The Associated Press changed the name of its national championship award from the AP trophy to the Bear Bryant Trophy after the legendary Alabama coach's death in 1983. The Football Writers' trophy is called the Grantland Rice Award (after the celebrated sportswriter) and the NFF-Hall of Fame trophy is called the MacArthur Bowl (in honor of Gen. Douglas MacArthur).

Multiple champions: Notre Dame (9); Alabama and Oklahoma (7); Ohio St. (6); Miami-FL, Nebraska and USC (5); Minnesota (4); Michigan St. and Texas (3); Army, Florida St., Georgia Tech, Michigan, Penn St., Pittsburgh and Tennessee (2).

Year		Record	Bowl Game	Head Coach	Outstanding Player
1936	**Minnesota**	7-1-0	No bowl	Bernie Bierman	Ed Widseth, T
1937	**Pittsburgh**	9-0-1	No bowl	Jock Sutherland	Marshall Goldberg, HB
1938	**TCU**	11-0-0	Won Sugar	Dutch Meyer	Davey O'Brien, QB
1939	**Texas A&M**	11-0-0	Won Sugar	Homer Norton	John Kimbrough, FB
1940	**Minnesota**	8-0-0	No bowl	Bernie Bierman	George Franck, HB
1941	**Minnesota**	8-0-0	No bowl	Bernie Bierman	Bruce Smith, HB
1942	**Ohio St.**	9-1-0	No bowl	Paul Brown	Gene Fekete, FB
1943	**Notre Dame**	9-1-0	No bowl	Frank Leahy	Angelo Bertelli, QB
1944	**Army**	9-0-0	No bowl	Red Blaik	Glenn Davis, HB
1945	**Army**	9-0-0	No bowl	Red Blaik	Doc Blanchard, FB
1946	**Notre Dame**	8-0-1	No bowl	Frank Leahy	Johnny Lujack, QB
1947	**Notre Dame**	9-0-0	No bowl	Frank Leahy	Johnny Lujack, QB
1948	**Michigan**	9-0-0	No bowl	Bennie Oosterbaan	Dick Rifenburg, E
1949	**Notre Dame**	10-0-0	No bowl	Frank Leahy	Leon Hart, E
1950	**Oklahoma**	10-1-0	Lost Sugar	Bud Wilkinson	Leon Heath, FB
1951	**Tennessee**	10-0-0	Lost Sugar	Bob Neyland	Hank Lauricella, TB
1952	**Michigan St.** (AP, UP)	9-0-0	No bowl	Biggie Munn	Don McAuliffe, HB
	& **Georgia Tech** (INS)	12-0-0	Won Sugar	Bobby Dodd	Hal Miller, T
1953	**Maryland**	10-1-0	Lost Orange	Jim Tatum	Bernie Faloney, QB
1954	**Ohio St.** (AP, INS)	10-0-0	Won Rose	Woody Hayes	Howard Cassady, HB
	& **UCLA** (UP, FW)	9-0-0	No bowl	Red Sanders	Jack Ellena, T
1955	**Oklahoma**	11-0-0	Won Orange	Bud Wilkinson	Jerry Tubbs, C
1956	**Oklahoma**	10-0-0	No bowl	Bud Wilkinson	Tommy McDonald, HB
1957	**Auburn** (AP)	10-0-0	No bowl	Shug Jordan	Jimmy Phillips, E
	& **Ohio St.** (UP, FW, INS)	9-1-0	Won Rose	Woody Hayes	Bob White, FB
1958	**LSU** (AP, UPI)	11-0-0	Won Sugar	Paul Dietzel	Billy Cannon, HB
	& **Iowa** (FW)	8-1-1	Won Rose	Forest Evashevski	Randy Duncan, QB
1959	**Syracuse**	11-0-0	Won Cotton	Ben Schwartzwalder	Ernie Davis, HB
1960	**Minnesota** (AP, UPI, NFF)	8-2-0	Lost Rose	Murray Warmath	Tom Brown, G
	& **Mississippi** (FW)	10-0-1	Won Sugar	Johnny Vaught	Jake Gibbs, QB
1961	**Alabama** (AP, UPI, NFF)	11-0-0	Won Sugar	Bear Bryant	Billy Neighbors, T
	& **Ohio St.** (FW)	8-0-1	No bowl	Woody Hayes	Bob Ferguson, HB
1962	**USC**	11-0-0	Won Rose	John McKay	Hal Bedsole, E
1963	**Texas**	11-0-0	Won Cotton	Darrell Royal	Scott Appleton, T

National Champions (Cont.)

Year		Record	Bowl Game	Head Coach	Outstanding Player
1964	**Alabama** (AP, UPI),	10-1-0	Lost Orange	Bear Bryant	Joe Namath, QB
	Arkansas (FW)	11-0-0	Won Cotton	Frank Broyles	Ronnie Caveness, LB
	& **Notre Dame** (NFF)	9-1-0	No bowl	Ara Parseghian	John Huarte, QB
1965	**Alabama** (AP, FW-tie)	9-1-1	Won Orange	Bear Bryant	Paul Crane, C
	& **Michigan St.** (UPI, NFF, FW-tie)	10-1-0	Lost Rose	Duffy Daugherty	George Webster, LB
1966	**Notre Dame** (AP, UPI, FW, NFF-tie)	9-0-1	No bowl	Ara Parseghian	Jim Lynch, LB
	& **Michigan St.** (NFF-tie)	9-0-1	No bowl	Duffy Daugherty	Bubba Smith, DE
1967	**USC**	10-1-0	Won Rose	John McKay	O.J. Simpson, HB
1968	**Ohio St.**	10-0-0	Won Rose	Woody Hayes	Rex Kern, QB
1969	**Texas**	11-0-0	Won Cotton	Darrell Royal	James Street, QB
1970	**Nebraska** (AP, FW)	11-0-1	Won Orange	Bob Devaney	Jerry Tagge, QB
	Texas (UPI, NFF-tie)	10-1-0	Lost Cotton	Darrell Royal	Steve Worster, RB
	& **Ohio St.** (NFF-tie)	9-1-0	Lost Rose	Woody Hayes	Jim Stillwagon, MG
1971	**Nebraska**	13-0-0	Won Orange	Bob Devaney	Johnny Rodgers, WR
1972	**USC**	12-0-0	Won Rose	John McKay	Charles Young, TE
1973	**Notre Dame** (AP, FW, NFF)	11-0-0	Won Sugar	Ara Parseghian	Mike Townsend, DB
	& **Alabama** (UPI)	11-1-0	Lost Sugar	Bear Bryant	Buddy Brown, OT
1974	**Oklahoma** (AP)	11-0-0	No bowl	Barry Switzer	Joe Washington, RB
	& **USC** (UPI, FW, NFF)	10-1-1	Won Rose	John McKay	Anthony Davis, RB
1975	**Oklahoma**	11-1-0	Won Orange	Barry Switzer	Lee Roy Selmon, DT
1976	**Pittsburgh**	12-0-0	Won Sugar	Johnny Majors	Tony Dorsett, RB
1977	**Notre Dame**	11-1-0	Won Cotton	Dan Devine	Ross Browner, DE
1978	**Alabama** (AP, FW, NFF)	11-1-0	Won Sugar	Bear Bryant	Marty Lyons, DT
	& **USC** (UPI)	12-1-0	Won Rose	John Robinson	Charles White, RB
1979	**Alabama**	12-0-0	Won Sugar	Bear Bryant	Jim Bunch, OT
1980	**Georgia**	12-0-0	Won Sugar	Vince Dooley	Herschel Walker, RB
1981	**Clemson**	12-0-0	Won Orange	Danny Ford	Jeff Davis, LB
1982	**Penn St.**	11-1-0	Won Sugar	Joe Paterno	Todd Blackledge, QB
1983	**Miami-FL**	11-1-0	Won Orange	H. Schnellenberger	Bernie Kosar, QB
1984	**BYU**	13-0-0	Won Holiday	LaVell Edwards	Robbie Bosco, QB
1985	**Oklahoma**	11-1-0	Won Orange	Barry Switzer	Brian Bosworth, LB
1986	**Penn St.**	12-0-0	Won Fiesta	Joe Paterno	D.J. Dozier, RB
1987	**Miami-FL**	12-0-0	Won Orange	Jimmy Johnson	Steve Walsh, QB
1988	**Notre Dame**	12-0-0	Won Fiesta	Lou Holtz	Tony Rice, QB
1989	**Miami-FL**	11-1-0	Won Sugar	Dennis Erickson	Craig Erickson, QB
1990	**Colorado** (AP, FW, NFF)	11-1-1	Won Orange	Bill McCartney	Eric Bieniemy, RB
	& **Georgia Tech** (UPI)	11-0-1	Won Citrus	Bobby Ross	Shawn Jones, QB
1991	**Miami-FL** (AP)	12-0-0	Won Orange	Dennis Erickson	Gino Torretta, QB
	& **Washington** (USA, FW, NFF)	12-0-0	Won Rose	Don James	Steve Emtman, DT
1992	**Alabama**	13-0-0	Won Sugar	Gene Stallings	Eric Curry, DE
1993	**Florida St.**	12-1-0	Won Orange	Bobby Bowden	Charlie Ward, QB
1994	**Nebraska**	13-0-0	Won Orange	Tom Osborne	Zach Wiegert, OT
1995	**Nebraska**	12-0-0	Won Fiesta	Tom Osborne	Tommie Frazier, QB
1996	**Florida**	12-1*	Won Sugar	Steve Spurrier	Danny Wuerffel, QB
1997	**Michigan** (AP, FW, NFF)	12-0	Won Rose	Lloyd Carr	Charles Woodson, DB
	& **Nebraska** (ESPN/USA)	13-0	Won Orange	Tom Osborne	Ahman Green, RB
1998	**Tennessee**	13-0	Won Fiesta	Phillip Fulmer	Peerless Price, WR
1999	**Florida St.**	12-0	Won Sugar	Bobby Bowden	Peter Warrick, WR
2000	**Oklahoma**	13-0	Won Orange	Bob Stoops	Josh Heupel, QB
2001	**Miami-FL**	12-0	Won Rose	Larry Coker	Ken Dorsey, QB

*The NCAA instituted overtime for regular season games in 1996.

Number 1 vs. Number 2

Since the Associated Press writers poll started keeping track of such things in 1936, the No. 1 and No. 2 ranked teams in the country have met 33 times; 20 during the regular season and 13 in bowl games. Since the first showdown in 1943, the No. 1 team has beaten the No. 2 team 21 times, lost 10 and there have been two ties. Each showdown is listed below with the date, the match-up, each team's record going into the game, the final score, the stadium and site.

Date		Match-up		Stadium	Date		Match-up		Stadium
Oct. 9	#1	Notre Dame (2-0)	35	Michigan	Nov. 9	#1	Army (7-0)	0	Yankee
1943	#2	Michigan (3-0)	12	(Ann Arbor)	1946	#2	Notre Dame (5-0)	0	(New York)
Nov. 20	#1	Notre Dame (8-0)	14	Notre Dame	Jan. 1	#1	USC (10-0)	42	ROSE BOWL
1943	#2	Iowa Pre-Flight (8-0)	13	(South Bend)	1963	#2	Wisconsin (8-1)	37	(Pasadena)
Dec. 2	#1	Army (8-0)	23	Municipal	Oct. 12	#1	Texas (3-0)	28	Cotton Bowl
1944	#2	Navy (6-2)	7	(Baltimore)	1963	#2	Oklahoma (2-0)	7	(Dallas)
Nov. 10	#1	Army (6-0)	48	Yankee	Jan. 1	#1	Texas (10-0)	28	COTTON BOWL
1945	#2	Notre Dame (5-0-1)	0	(New York)	1964	#2	Navy (9-1)	6	(Dallas)
Dec. 1	#1	Army (8-0)	32	Municipal	Nov. 19	#1	Notre Dame (8-0)	10	Spartan
1945	#2	Navy (7-0-1)	13	(Philadelphia)	1966	#2	Michigan St. (9-0)	10	(East Lansing)

Date	Match-up	Stadium
Sept. 28 1968	#1 Purdue (1-0) .... 37 #2 Notre Dame (1-0) 22	Notre Dame (South Bend)
Jan. 1 1969	#1 Ohio St. (9-0) .... 27 #2 USC (9-0-1) 16	ROSE BOWL (Pasadena)
Dec. 6 1969	#1 Texas (9-0) .... 15 #2 Arkansas (9-0) 14	Razorback (Fayetteville)
Nov. 25 1971	#1 Nebraska (10-0) .... 35 #2 Oklahoma (9-0) 31	Owen Field (Norman)
Jan. 1 1972	#1 Nebraska (12-0) .... 38 #2 Alabama (11-0) 6	ORANGE BOWL (Miami)
Jan. 1 1979	#2 Alabama (10-1) .... 14 #1 Penn St. (11-0) 7	SUGAR BOWL (New Orleans)
Sept. 26 1981	#1 USC (2-0) .... 28 #1 Oklahoma (1-0) 24	Coliseum (Los Angeles)
Jan. 1 1983	#2 Penn St. (10-1) .... 27 #1 Georgia (11-0) 23	SUGAR BOWL (New Orleans)
Oct. 19 1985	#1 Iowa (5-0) .... 12 #2 Michigan (5-0) 10	Kinnick (Iowa City)
Sept. 27 1986	#1 Miami-FL (3-0) .... 28 #1 Oklahoma (2-0) 16	Orange Bowl (Miami)
Jan. 2 1987	#2 Penn St. (11-0) .... 14 #1 Miami-FL (11-0) 10	FIESTA BOWL (Tempe)
Nov. 21 1987	#2 Oklahoma (10-0) ...... 17 #1 Nebraska (10-0) 7	Memorial (Lincoln)

Date	Match-up	Stadium
Jan. 1 1988	#2 Miami-FL (11-0) .... 20 #1 Oklahoma (11-0) 14	ORANGE BOWL (Miami)
Nov. 26 1988	#1 Notre Dame (10-0) .... 27 #2 USC (10-0) 10	Coliseum (Los Angeles)
Sept. 16 1989	#1 Notre Dame (1-0) ..... 24 #2 Michigan (0-0) 19	Michigan (Ann Arbor)
Nov. 16 1991	#2 Miami-FL (8-0) .... 17 #1 Florida St. (10-0) 16	Doak Campbell (Tallahassee)
Jan. 1 1993	#2 Alabama (12-0) .... 34 #1 Miami-FL (11-0) 13	SUGAR BOWL (New Orleans)
Nov. 13 1993	#2 Notre Dame (9-0) ..... 31 #1 Florida St. (9-0) 24	Notre Dame (South Bend)
Jan. 1 1994	#1 Florida St. (11-1) ...... 18 #2 Nebraska (11-0) 16	ORANGE BOWL (Miami)
Jan. 2 1996	#1 Nebraska (11-0) .... 62 #2 Florida (12-0) 24	FIESTA BOWL (Tempe)
Nov. 30 1996	#2 Florida St. (10-0) ...... 24 #1 Florida (10-1) 21	Doak Campbell (Tallahassee)
Jan. 4 1999	#1 Tennessee (12-0) ...... 23 #2 Florida St. (11-1) 16	FIESTA BOWL (Tempe)
Jan. 4 2000	#1 Florida St. (11-0) ...... 46 #2 Virginia Tech (11-0) ... 29	SUGAR BOWL (New Orleans)

Note: Bowl games are listed in CAPITAL letters.

Top 50 Rivalries

Top Division I-A and I-AA series records, including games through the 2001 season. All rivalries listed below are renewed annually with the following exceptions. **Nebraska-Oklahoma** now play only when matched up as part of the rotating Big 12 schedule.

RECENTLY DISCONTINUED SERIES: **Penn State vs Pitt** in 2001 after 96 games (Penn State ahead 50-42-4), **Baylor vs TCU** in 1995 after 102 games (Baylor ahead 48-47-7); **Florida vs Miami-FL** in 1991 after 49 games (Florida ahead, 25-24); **Miami-FL vs Notre Dame** in 1990 after 23 games (ND ahead, 15-7-1). Note that Miami beat Florida in the 2000 Sugar Bowl.

	Gm	Series Leader		Gm	Series Leader
Air Force-Army	.36	Air Force (23-12-1)	**Michigan-Michigan St.**	.94	Michigan (61-28-5)
Air Force-Navy	.34	Air Force (24-10-0)	**Michigan-Notre Dame**	.29	Michigan (17-11-1)
Alabama-Auburn	.66	Alabama (38-27-1)	**Michigan-Ohio St.**	.98	Michigan (56-36-6)
Alabama-Tennessee	.84	Alabama (42-35-7)	**Minnesota-Wisconsin**	.111	Minnesota (58-45-8)
Arizona-Arizona St.	.75	Arizona (43-31-1)	**Mississippi-Miss. St.**	.98	Ole Miss (55-37-6)
Army-Navy	.102	Army (49-46-7)	**Missouri-Kansas**	.110	Missouri (51-50-9)
Auburn-Georgia	.105	Auburn (51-46-8)	**Nebraska-Oklahoma**	.80	Oklahoma (40-37-3)
California-Stanford	.104	Stanford (54-39-11)	**N. Mexico-N. Mexico St.**	.91	New Mexico (59-27-5)
The Citadel-VMI	.61	The Citadel (30-29-2)	**N. Carolina-N.C. State**	.91	N. Carolina (60-25-6)
Clemson-S. Carolina	.99	Clemson (59-36-4)	**Notre Dame-Purdue**	.73	Notre Dame (48-23-2)
Colorado-Nebraska	.60	Nebraska (43-15-2)	**Notre Dame-USC**	.73	Notre Dame (42-26-5)
Colo. St.-Wyoming	.91	Colorado St. (48-38-5)	**Oklahoma-Okla. St.**	.96	Oklahoma (74-15-7)
Duke-N. Carolina	.87	N. Carolina (48-36-4)*	**Oregon-Oregon St.**	.105	Oregon (53-42-10)
Florida-Florida St.	.46	Florida (27-17-2)	**Penn-Cornell**	.108	Penn (62-41-5)
Florida-Georgia	.80	Georgia (46-32-2)	**Pittsburgh-West Va**	.94	Pitt (57-34-3)
Florida St.-Miami,FL	.45	Miami (25-20-0)	**Princeton-Yale**	.124	Yale (66-48-10)
Georgia-Georgia Tech	.96	Georgia (53-38-5)*	**Purdue-Indiana**	.104	Purdue (63-35-6)
Grambling-Southern	.50	Southern (26-24-0)	**Richmond-Wm. & Mary**	.111	Wm. & Mary (57-49-5)
Harvard-Yale	.118	Yale (64-46-8)	**Tennessee-Vanderbilt**	.95	Tennessee (64-26-5)
Iowa-Iowa St.	.49	Iowa (33-16-0)	**Texas-Oklahoma**	.96	Texas (56-35-5)
Kansas-Kansas St.	.99	Kansas (61-33-5)	**Texas-Texas A&M**	.108	Texas (69-34-5)
Kentucky-Tennessee	.97	Tennessee (65-23-9)	**UCLA-USC**	.71	USC (37-27-7)
Lafayette-Lehigh	.137	Lafayette (71-61-5)	**Utah-BYU**	.77	Utah (45-28-4)*
LSU-Tulane	.94	LSU (65-22-7)*	**Utah-Utah St.**	.99	Utah (66-29-4)
Miami,OH-Cincinnati	.106	Miami (56-43-7)	**Washington-Wash. St.**	.94	Washington (62-26-6)

*Disputed series records: UNC claims lead of 49-35-4; Georgia claims lead of 53-36-5; Tulane claims LSU leads 62-23-7; Utah claims lead of 48-31-4

Associated Press Final Polls

The Associated Press introduced its weekly college football poll of sportswriters (later, sportswriters and broadcasters) in 1936. The final AP poll was released at the end of the regular season until 1965, when bowl results were included for one year. After a two-year return to regular season games only, the final poll has come out after the bowls since 1968. Starting in 1989, the AP Poll has ranked 25 teams.

1936

Final poll released Nov. 30. Top 20 regular season results after that: **Dec. 5**–#8 Notre Dame tied USC, 13-13; #17 Tennessee tied Ole Miss, 0-0; #18 Arkansas over Texas, 6-0. **Dec. 12**–#16 TCU over #6 Santa Clara, 9-0.

		As of Nov. 30	Head Coach	After Bowls
1	Minnesota	7-1-0	Bernie Bierman	same
2	LSU	9-0-1	Bernie Moore	9-1-1
3	Pittsburgh	7-1-1	Jock Sutherland	8-1-1
4	Alabama	8-0-1	Frank Thomas	same
5	Washington	7-1-1	Jimmy Phelan	7-2-1
6	Santa Clara	7-0-0	Buck Shaw	8-1-0
7	Northwestern	7-1-0	Pappy Waldorf	same
8	Notre Dame	6-2-0	Elmer Layden	6-2-1
9	Nebraska	7-2-0	Dana X. Bible	same
10	Penn	7-1-0	Harvey Harman	same
11	Duke	9-1-0	Wallace Wade	same
12	Yale	7-1-0	Ducky Pond	same
13	Dartmouth	7-1-1	Red Blaik	same
14	Duquesne	7-2-0	John Smith	8-2-0
15	Fordham	5-1-2	Jim Crowley	same
16	TCU	7-2-2	Dutch Meyer	9-2-2
17	Tennessee	6-2-1	Bob Neyland	6-2-2
18	Arkansas	6-3-0	Fred Thomsen	7-3-0
	Navy	6-3-0	Tom Hamilton	same
20	Marquette	7-1-0	Frank Murray	7-2-0

Key Bowl Games

Sugar–#6 Santa Clara over #2 LSU, 21-14; **Rose**–#3 Pitt over #5 Washington, 21-0; **Orange**–#14 Duquesne over Mississippi St., 13-12; **Cotton**–#16 TCU over #20 Marquette, 16-6.

1937

Final poll released Nov. 29. Top 20 regular season results after that: **Dec. 4**–#18 Rice over SMU, 15-7.

		As of Nov. 29	Head Coach	After Bowls
1	Pittsburgh	9-0-1	Jock Sutherland	same
2	California	9-0-1	Stub Allison	10-0-1
3	Fordham	7-0-1	Jim Crowley	same
4	Alabama	9-0-0	Frank Thomas	9-1-0
5	Minnesota	6-2-0	Bernie Bierman	same
6	Villanova	8-0-1	Clipper Smith	same
7	Dartmouth	7-0-2	Red Blaik	same
8	LSU	9-1-0	Bernie Moore	9-2-0
9	Notre Dame	6-2-1	Elmer Layden	same
	Santa Clara	8-0-0	Buck Shaw	9-0-0
11	Nebraska	6-1-2	Biff Jones	same
12	Yale	6-1-1	Ducky Pond	same
13	Ohio St.	6-2-0	Francis Schmidt	same
14	Holy Cross	8-0-2	Eddie Anderson	same
	Arkansas	6-2-2	Fred Thomsen	same
16	TCU	4-2-2	Dutch Meyer	same
17	Colorado	8-0-0	Bunnie Oakes	8-1-0
18	Rice	4-3-2	Jimmy Kitts	6-3-2
19	North Carolina	7-1-1	Ray Wolf	same
20	Duke	7-2-1	Wallace Wade	same

Key Bowl Games

Rose–#2 Cal over #4 Alabama, 13-0; **Sugar**–#9 Santa Clara over #8 LSU, 6-0; **Cotton**–#18 Rice over #17 Colorado, 28-14; **Orange**–Auburn over Michigan St., 6-0.

1938

Final poll released Dec. 5. Top 20 regular season results after that: **Dec. 26**–#14 Cal over Georgia Tech, 13-7.

		As of Dec. 5	Head Coach	After Bowls
1	TCU	10-0-0	Dutch Meyer	11-0-0
2	Tennessee	10-0-0	Bob Neyland	11-0-0
3	Duke	9-0-0	Wallace Wade	9-1-0
4	Oklahoma	10-0-0	Tom Stidham	10-1-0
5	Notre Dame	8-1-0	Elmer Layden	same
6	Carnegie Tech	7-1-0	Bill Kern	7-2-0
7	USC	8-2-0	Howard Jones	9-2-0
8	Pittsburgh	8-2-0	Jock Sutherland	same
9	Holy Cross	8-1-0	Eddie Anderson	same
10	Minnesota	6-2-0	Bernie Bierman	same
11	Texas Tech	10-0-0	Pete Cawthon	10-1-0
12	Cornell	5-1-1	Carl Snavely	same
13	Alabama	7-1-1	Frank Thomas	same
14	California	9-1-0	Stub Allison	10-1-0
15	Fordham	6-1-2	Jim Crowley	same
16	Michigan	6-1-1	Fritz Crisler	same
17	Northwestern	4-2-2	Pappy Waldorf	same
18	Villanova	8-0-1	Clipper Smith	same
19	Tulane	7-2-1	Red Dawson	same
20	Dartmouth	7-2-0	Red Blaik	same

Key Bowl Games

Sugar–#1 TCU over #6 Carnegie Tech, 15-7; **Orange**–#2 Tennessee over #4 Oklahoma, 17-0; **Rose**–#7 USC over #3 Duke, 7-3; **Cotton**–St. Mary's over #11 Texas Tech 20-13.

1939

Final poll released Dec. 11. Top 20 regular season results after that: None.

		As of Dec. 11	Head Coach	After Bowls
1	Texas A&M	10-0-0	Homer Norton	11-0-0
2	Tennessee	10-0-0	Bob Neyland	10-1-0
3	USC	7-0-2	Howard Jones	8-0-2
4	Cornell	8-0-0	Carl Snavely	same
5	Tulane	8-0-1	Red Dawson	8-1-1
6	Missouri	8-1-0	Don Faurot	8-2-0
7	UCLA	6-0-4	Babe Horrell	same
8	Duke	8-1-0	Wallace Wade	same
9	Iowa	6-1-1	Eddie Anderson	same
10	Duquesne	8-0-1	Buff Donelli	same
11	Boston College	9-1-0	Frank Leahy	9-2-0
12	Clemson	8-1-0	Jess Neely	9-1-0
13	Notre Dame	7-2-0	Elmer Layden	same
14	Santa Clara	5-1-3	Buck Shaw	same
15	Ohio St.	6-2-0	Francis Schmidt	same
16	Georgia Tech	7-2-0	Bill Alexander	8-2-0
17	Fordham	6-2-0	Jim Crowley	same
18	Nebraska	7-1-1	Biff Jones	same
19	Oklahoma	6-2-1	Tom Stidham	same
20	Michigan	6-2-0	Fritz Crisler	same

Key Bowl Games

Sugar–#1 Texas A&M over #5 Tulane, 14-13; **Rose**–#3 USC over #2 Tennessee, 14-0; **Orange**–#16 Georgia Tech over #6 Missouri, 21-7; **Cotton**–#12 Clemson over #11 Boston College, 6-3.

1940

Final poll released Dec. 2. Top 20 regular season results after that: **Dec. 7**–#16 SMU over Rice, 7-6.

		As of Dec. 2	Head Coach	After Bowls
1	Minnesota	8-0-0	Bernie Bierman	same
2	Stanford	9-0-0	Clark Shaughnessy	10-0-0
3	Michigan	7-1-0	Fritz Crisler	same
4	Tennessee	10-0-0	Bob Neyland	10-1-0
5	Boston College	10-0-0	Frank Leahy	11-0-0
6	Texas A&M	8-1-0	Homer Norton	9-1-0
7	Nebraska	8-1-0	Biff Jones	8-2-0
8	Northwestern	6-2-0	Pappy Waldorf	same
9	Mississippi St.	9-0-1	Allyn McKeen	10-0-1
10	Washington	7-2-0	Jimmy Phelan	same
11	Santa Clara	6-1-1	Buck Shaw	same
12	Fordham	7-1-0	Jim Crowley	7-2-0
13	Georgetown	8-1-0	Jack Hagerty	8-2-0
14	Penn	6-1-1	George Munger	same
15	Cornell	6-2-0	Carl Snavely	same
16	SMU	7-1-1	Matty Bell	8-1-1
17	Hardin-Simmons	9-0-0	Warren Woodson	same
18	Duke	7-2-0	Wallace Wade	same
19	Lafayette	9-0-0	Hooks Mylin	same
20	–			

Note: Only 19 teams ranked.

Key Bowl Games

Rose–#2 Stanford over #7 Nebraska, 21-13; **Sugar**– #5 Boston College over #4 Tennessee, 19-13; **Cotton**–#6 Texas A&M over #12 Fordham, 13-12; **Orange**–#9 Mississippi St. over #13 Georgetown, 14-7.

1941

Final poll released Dec. 1. Top 20 regular season results after that: **Dec. 6**–#4 Texas over Oregon, 71-7; #9 Texas A&M over #19 Washington St., 7-0; #16 Mississippi St. over San Francisco, 26-13.

		As of Dec. 1	Head Coach	After Bowls
1	Minnesota	8-0-0	Bernie Bierman	same
2	Duke	9-0-0	Wallace Wade	9-1-0
3	Notre Dame	8-0-1	Frank Leahy	same
4	Texas	7-1-1	Dana X. Bible	8-1-1
5	Michigan	6-1-1	Fritz Crisler	same
6	Fordham	7-1-0	Jim Crowley	8-1-0
7	Missouri	8-1-0	Don Faurot	8-2-0
8	Duquesne	8-0-0	Buff Donelli	same
9	Texas A&M	8-1-0	Homer Norton	9-2-0
10	Navy	7-1-1	Swede Larson	same
11	Northwestern	5-3-0	Pappy Waldorf	same
12	Oregon St.	7-2-0	Lon Stiner	8-2-0
13	Ohio St.	6-1-1	Paul Brown	same
14	Georgia	8-1-1	Wally Butts	9-1-1
15	Penn	7-1-1	George Munger	same
16	Mississippi St.	7-1-1	Allyn McKeen	8-1-1
17	Mississippi	6-2-1	Harry Mehre	same
18	Tennessee	8-2-0	John Barnhill	same
19	Washington St.	6-3-0	Babe Hollingbery	6-4-0
20	Alabama	8-2-0	Frank Thomas	9-2-0

Note: 1942 Rose Bowl moved to Durham, N.C., for one year after outbreak of World War II.

Key Bowl Games

Rose–#12 Oregon St. over #2 Duke, 20-16; **Sugar**–#6 Fordham over #7 Missouri, 2-0; **Cotton**–#20 Alabama over #9 Texas A&M, 29-21; **Orange**–#14 Georgia over TCU, 40-26.

1942

Final poll released Nov. 30. Top 20 regular season results after that: **Dec. 5**–#6 Notre Dame tied Great Lakes Naval Station, 13-13; #13 UCLA over Idaho, 40-13; #14 William & Mary over Oklahoma, 14-7; #17 Washington St. lost to Texas A&M, 21-0; #18 Mississippi St. over San Francisco, 19-7. **Dec. 12**–#13 UCLA over USC, 14-7.

		As of Nov. 30	Head Coach	After Bowls
1	Ohio St.	9-1-0	Paul Brown	same
2	Georgia	10-1-0	Wally Butts	11-1-0
3	Wisconsin	8-1-1	Harry Stuhldreher	same
4	Tulsa	10-0-0	Henry Frnka	10-1-0
5	Georgia Tech	9-1-0	Bill Alexander	9-2-0
6	Notre Dame	7-2-1	Frank Leahy	7-2-2
7	Tennessee	8-1-1	John Barnhill	9-1-1
8	Boston College	8-1-0	Denny Myers	8-2-0
9	Michigan	7-3-0	Fritz Crisler	same
10	Alabama	7-3-0	Frank Thomas	8-3-0
11	Texas	8-2-0	Dana X. Bible	9-2-0
12	Stanford	6-4-0	Marchy Schwartz	same
13	UCLA	5-3-0	Babe Horrell	7-4-0
14	William & Mary	8-1-1	Carl Voyles	9-1-1
15	Santa Clara	7-2-0	Buck Shaw	same
16	Auburn	6-4-1	Jack Meagher	same
17	Washington St.	6-1-2	Babe Hollingbery	6-2-2
18	Mississippi St.	7-2-0	Allyn McKeen	8-2-0
19	Minnesota	5-4-0	George Hauser	same
	Holy Cross	5-4-1	Ank Scanlon	same
	Penn St.	6-1-1	Bob Higgins	same

Key Bowl Games

Rose–#2 Georgia over #13 UCLA, 9-0; **Sugar**–#7 Tennessee over #4 Tulsa, 14-7; **Cotton**–#11 Texas over #5 Georgia Tech, 14-7; **Orange**–#10 Alabama over #8 Boston College, 37-21.

1943

Final poll released Nov. 29. Top 20 regular season results after that: **Dec. 11**–#10 March Field over #19 Pacific, 19-0.

		As of Nov. 29	Head Coach	After Bowls
1	Notre Dame	9-1-0	Frank Leahy	same
2	Iowa Pre-Flight	9-1-0	Don Faurot	same
3	Michigan	8-1-0	Fritz Crisler	same
4	Navy	8-1-0	Billick Whelchel	same
5	Purdue	9-0-0	Elmer Burnham	same
6	Great Lakes Naval Station	10-2-0	Tony Hinkle	same
7	Duke	8-1-0	Eddie Cameron	same
8	DelMonte Pre-Flight	7-1-0	Bill Kern	same
9	Northwestern	6-2-0	Pappy Waldorf	same
10	March Field	8-1-0	Paul Schissler	9-1-0
11	Army	7-2-1	Red Blaik	same
12	Washington	4-0-0	Ralph Welch	4-1-0
13	Georgia Tech	7-3-0	Bill Alexander	8-3-0
14	Texas	7-1-0	Dana X. Bible	7-1-1
15	Tulsa	6-0-1	Henry Frnka	6-1-1
16	Dartmouth	6-1-0	Earl Brown	same
17	Bainbridge Navy Training School	7-0-0	Joe Maniaci	same
18	Colorado College	7-0-0	Hal White	same
19	Pacific	7-1-0	Amos A. Stagg	7-2-0
20	Penn	6-2-1	George Munger	same

Key Bowl Games

Rose–USC over #12 Washington, 29-0; **Sugar**–#13 Georgia Tech over #15 Tulsa, 20-18; **Cotton**–#14 Texas tied Randolph Field, 7-7; **Orange**–LSU over Texas A&M, 19-14.

Associated Press Final Polls (Cont.)

1944

Final poll released Dec. 4. Top 20 regular season results after that: **Dec. 10**–#3 Randolph Field over #10 March Field, 20-7; #18 Fort Pierce over Kessler Field, 34-7; Morris Field over #20 Second Air Force, 14-7.

	As of Dec. 4	Head Coach	After Bowls
1	Army.............9-0-0	Red Blaik	same
2	Ohio St............9-0-0	Carroll Widdoes	same
3	Randolph Field 10-0-0	Frank Tritico	12-0-0
4	Navy.............6-3-0	Oscar Hagberg	same
5	Bainbridge Navy Training School....10-0-0	Joe Maniaci	same
6	Iowa Pre-Flight 10-1-0	Jack Meagher	same
7	USC..............7-0-2	Jeff Cravath	8-0-2
8	Michigan 8-2-0	Fritz Crisler	same
9	Notre Dame........8-2-0	Ed McKeever	same
10	March Field 7-0-2	Paul Schissler	7-1-2
11	Duke 5-4-0	Eddie Cameron	6-4-0
12	Tennessee........7-0-1	John Barnhill	7-1-1
13	Georgia Tech......8-2-0	Bill Alexander	8-3-0
14	Norman Pre-Flight...6-0-0	John Gregg	same
15	Illinois...........5-4-1	Ray Eliot	same
16	El Toro Marines....8-1-0	Dick Hanley	same
17	Great Lakes Naval Station 9-2-1	Paul Brown	same
18	Fort Pierce 8-0-0	Hamp Pool	9-0-0
19	St. Mary's Pre-Flight ..4-4-0	Jules Sikes	same
20	Second Air Force ...10-2-1	Bill Reese	10-4-1

Key Bowl Games
Treasury–#3 Randolph Field over #20 Second Air Force, 13-6; **Rose**–#7 USC over #12 Tennessee, 25-0; **Sugar**–#11 Duke over Alabama, 29-26; **Orange**–Tulsa over #13 Georgia Tech, 26-12; **Cotton**–Oklahoma A&M over TCU, 34-0.

1945

Final poll released Dec. 3. Top 20 regular season results after that: None.

	As of Dec. 3	Head Coach	After Bowls
1	Army.............9-0-0	Red Blaik	same
2	Alabama 9-0-0	Frank Thomas	10-0-0
3	Navy.............7-1-1	Oscar Hagberg	same
4	Indiana..........9-0-1	Bo McMillan	same
5	Oklahoma A&M 8-0-0	Jim Lookabaugh	9-0-0
6	Michigan 7-3-0	Fritz Crisler	same
7	St. Mary's-CA 7-1-0	Jimmy Phelan	7-2-0
8	Penn 6-2-0	George Munger	same
9	Notre Dame.......7-2-1	Hugh Devore	same
10	Texas............9-1-0	Dana X. Bible	10-1-0
11	USC 7-3-0	Jeff Cravath	7-4-0
12	Ohio St. 7-2-0	Carroll Widdoes	same
13	Duke 6-2-0	Eddie Cameron	same
14	Tennessee........8-1-0	John Barnhill	same
15	LSU 7-2-0	Bernie Moore	same
16	Holy Cross 8-1-0	John DeGrosa	8-2-0
17	Tulsa 8-2-0	Henry Frnka	8-3-0
18	Georgia 8-2-0	Wally Butts	9-2-0
19	Wake Forest.......4-3-1	Peahead Walker	5-3-1
20	Columbia 8-1-0	Lou Little	same

Key Bowl Games
Rose–#2 Alabama over #11 USC, 34-14; **Sugar**–#5 Oklahoma A&M over #7 St. Mary's, 33-13; **Cotton**–#10 Texas over Missouri, 40-27; **Orange**–Miami-FL over #16 Holy Cross, 13-6.

1946

Final poll released Dec. 2. Top 20 regular season results after that: None.

	As of Dec. 2	Head Coach	After Bowls
1	Notre Dame.......8-0-1	Frank Leahy	same
2	Army.............9-0-1	Red Blaik	same
3	Georgia 10-0-0	Wally Butts	11-0-0
4	UCLA 10-0-0	Bert LaBrucherie	10-1-0
5	Illinois 7-2-0	Ray Eliot	8-2-0
6	Michigan 6-2-1	Fritz Crisler	same
7	Tennessee........9-1-0	Bob Neyland	9-2-0
8	LSU 9-1-0	Bernie Moore	9-1-1
9	North Carolina 8-1-1	Carl Snavely	8-2-1
10	Rice 8-2-0	Jess Neely	9-2-0
11	Georgia Tech......8-2-0	Bobby Dodd	9-2-0
12	Yale 7-1-1	Howard Odell	same
13	Penn 6-2-0	George Munger	same
14	Oklahoma 7-3-0	Jim Tatum	8-3-0
15	Texas............8-2-0	Dana X. Bible	same
16	Arkansas 6-3-1	John Barnhill	6-3-2
17	Tulsa 9-1-0	J.O. Brothers	same
18	N.C. State 8-2-0	Beattie Feathers	8-3-0
19	Delaware 9-0-0	Bill Murray	10-0-0
20	Indiana...........6-3-0	Bo McMillan	same

Key Bowl Games
Sugar–#3 Georgia over #9 N. Carolina, 20-10; **Rose**–#5 Illinois over #4 UCLA, 45-14; **Orange**–#10 Rice over #7 Tennessee, 8-0; **Cotton**–#8 LSU tied #16 Arkansas, 0-0.

1947

Final poll released Dec. 8. Top 20 regular season results after that: None.

	As of Dec. 8	Head Coach	After Bowls
1	Notre Dame.......9-0-0	Frank Leahy	same
2	Michigan 9-0-0	Fritz Crisler	10-0-0
3	SMU 9-0-1	Matty Bell	9-0-2
4	Penn St. 9-0-0	Bob Higgins	9-0-1
5	Texas............9-1-0	Blair Cherry	10-1-0
6	Alabama 8-2-0	Red Drew	8-3-0
7	Penn 7-0-1	George Munger	same
8	USC 7-1-1	Jeff Cravath	7-2-1
9	North Carolina 8-2-0	Carl Snavely	same
10	Georgia Tech......9-1-0	Bobby Dodd	10-1-0
11	Army.............5-2-2	Red Blaik	same
12	Kansas 8-0-2	George Sauer	8-1-2
13	Mississippi 8-2-0	Johnny Vaught	9-2-0
14	William & Mary ...9-1-0	Rube McCray	9-2-0
15	California.........9-1-0	Pappy Waldorf	same
16	Oklahoma 7-2-1	Bud Wilkinson	same
17	N.C. State 5-3-1	Beattie Feathers	same
18	Rice 6-3-1	Jess Neely	same
19	Duke 4-3-2	Wallace Wade	same
20	Columbia 7-2-0	Lou Little	same

Key Bowl Games
Rose–#2 Michigan over #8 USC, 49-0; **Cotton**–#3 SMU tied #4 Penn St., 13-13; **Sugar**–#5 Texas over #6 Alabama, 27-7; **Orange**–#10 Georgia Tech over #12 Kansas, 20-14.
Note: An unprecedented "Who's No. 1?" poll was conducted by AP after the Rose Bowl game, pitting Notre Dame against Michigan. The Wolverines won the vote, 226-119, but AP ruled that the Irish would be the No. 1 team of record.

1948

Final poll released Nov. 29. Top 20 regular season results after that: **Dec. 3**–#12 Vanderbilt over Miami-FL, 33-6: **Dec. 4**–#2 Notre Dame tied USC, 14-14; #11 Clemson over The Citadel, 20-0.

		As of Nov. 29	Head Coach	After Bowls
1	Michigan	9-0-0	Bennie Oosterbaan	same
2	Notre Dame	9-0-0	Frank Leahy	9-0-1
3	North Carolina	9-0-1	Carl Snavely	9-1-1
4	California	10-0-0	Pappy Waldorf	10-1-0
5	Oklahoma	9-1-0	Bud Wilkinson	10-1-0
6	Army	8-0-1	Red Blaik	same
7	Northwestern	7-2-0	Bob Voigts	8-2-0
8	Georgia	9-1-0	Wally Butts	9-2-0
9	Oregon	9-1-0	Jim Aiken	9-2-0
10	SMU	8-1-1	Matty Bell	9-1-1
11	Clemson	9-0-0	Frank Howard	11-0-0
12	Vanderbilt	7-2-1	Red Sanders	8-2-1
13	Tulane	9-1-0	Henry Frnka	same
14	Michigan St.	6-2-2	Biggie Munn	same
15	Mississippi	8-1-0	Johnny Vaught	same
16	Minnesota	7-2-0	Bernie Bierman	same
17	William & Mary	6-2-2	Rube McCray	7-2-2
18	Penn St.	7-1-1	Bob Higgins	same
19	Cornell	8-1-0	Lefty James	same
20	Wake Forest	6-3-0	Peahead Walker	6-4-0

Note: Big Nine "no-repeat" rule kept Michigan from Rose Bowl.

Key Bowl Games

Sugar–#5 Oklahoma over #3 North Carolina, 14-6; **Rose**–#7 Northwestern over #4 Cal, 20-14; **Orange**–Texas over #8 Georgia, 41-28; **Cotton**–#10 SMU over #9 Oregon, 21-13.

1949

Final poll released Nov. 28. Top 20 regular season results after that: **Dec. 2**–#14 Maryland over Miami-FL, 13-0. **Dec. 3**–#1 Notre Dame over SMU, 27-20; #10 Pacific over Hawaii, 75-0.

		As of Nov. 28	Head Coach	After Bowls
1	Notre Dame	9-0-0	Frank Leahy	10-0-0
2	Oklahoma	10-0-0	Bud Wilkinson	11-0-0
3	California	10-0-0	Pappy Waldorf	10-1-0
4	Army	9-0-0	Red Blaik	same
5	Rice	9-1-0	Jess Neely	10-1-0
6	Ohio St.	6-1-2	Wes Fesler	7-1-2
7	Michigan	6-2-1	Bennie Oosterbaan	same
8	Minnesota	7-2-0	Bernie Bierman	same
9	LSU	8-2-0	Gaynell Tinsley	8-3-0
10	Pacific	10-0-0	Larry Siemering	11-0-0
11	Kentucky	9-2-0	Bear Bryant	9-3-0
12	Cornell	8-1-0	Lefty James	same
13	Villanova	8-1-0	Jim Leonard	same
14	Maryland	7-1-0	Jim Tatum	9-1-0
15	Santa Clara	7-2-1	Len Casanova	8-2-1
16	North Carolina	7-3-0	Carl Snavely	7-4-0
17	Tennessee	7-2-1	Bob Neyland	same
18	Princeton	6-3-0	Charlie Caldwell	same
19	Michigan St.	6-3-0	Biggie Munn	same
20	Missouri	7-3-0	Don Faurot	7-4-0
	Baylor	8-2-0	Bob Woodruff	same

Key Bowl Games

Sugar–#2 Oklahoma over #9 LSU, 35-0; **Rose**–#6 Ohio St. over #3 Cal, 17-14; **Cotton**–#5 Rice over #16 North Carolina, 27-13; **Orange**–#15 Santa Clara over #11 Kentucky, 21-13.

1950

Final poll released Nov. 27. Top 20 regular season results after that: **Nov. 30**–#3 Texas over Texas A&M, 17-0. **Dec. 1**–#15 Miami-FL over Missouri, 27–9. **Dec. 2**–#1 Oklahoma over Okla. A&M, 41-14; Navy over #2 Army, 14-2; #4 Tennessee over Vanderbilt, 43-0; #16 Alabama over Auburn, 34-0; #19 Tulsa over Houston, 28-21; #20 Tulane tied LSU, 14-14. **Dec. 9**–#3 Texas over LSU, 21-6.

		As of Nov. 27	Head Coach	After Bowls
1	Oklahoma	9-0-0	Bud Wilkinson	10-1-0
2	Army	8-0-0	Red Blaik	8-1-0
3	Texas	7-1-0	Blair Cherry	9-2-0
4	Tennessee	9-1-0	Bob Neyland	11-1-0
5	California	9-0-1	Pappy Waldorf	9-1-1
6	Princeton	9-0-0	Charlie Caldwell	same
7	Kentucky	10-1-0	Bear Bryant	11-1-0
8	Michigan St.	8-1-0	Biggie Munn	same
9	Michigan	5-3-1	Bennie Oosterbaan	6-3-1
10	Clemson	8-0-1	Frank Howard	9-0-1
11	Washington	8-2-0	Howard Odell	same
12	Wyoming	9-0-0	Bowden Wyatt	10-0-0
13	Illinois	7-2-0	Ray Eliot	same
14	Ohio St.	6-3-0	Wes Fesler	same
15	Miami-FL	8-0-1	Andy Gustafson	9-1-1
16	Alabama	8-2-0	Red Drew	9-2-0
17	Nebraska	6-2-1	Bill Glassford	same
18	Wash. & Lee	8-2-0	George Barclay	8-3-0
19	Tulsa	8-1-1	J.O. Brothers	9-1-1
20	Tulane	6-2-0	Henry Frnka	6-2-1

Key Bowl Games

Sugar–#7 Kentucky over #1 Oklahoma, 13-7; **Cotton**–#4 Tennessee over #3 Texas, 20-14; **Rose**–#9 Michigan over #5 Cal, 14-6; **Orange**–#10 Clemson over #15 Miami-FL, 15-14.

1951

Final poll released Dec. 3. Top 20 regular season results after that: None.

		As of Dec. 3	Head Coach	After Bowls
1	Tennessee	10-0-0	Bob Neyland	10-1-0
2	Michigan St.	9-0-0	Biggie Munn	same
3	Maryland	9-0-0	Jim Tatum	10-0-0
4	Illinois	8-0-1	Ray Eliot	9-0-1
5	Georgia Tech	10-0-1	Bobby Dodd	11-0-1
6	Princeton	9-0-0	Charlie Caldwell	same
7	Stanford	9-1-0	Chuck Taylor	9-2-0
8	Wisconsin	7-1-1	Ivy Williamson	same
9	Baylor	8-1-1	George Sauer	8-2-1
10	Oklahoma	8-2-0	Bud Wilkinson	same
11	TCU	6-4-0	Dutch Meyer	6-5-0
12	California	8-2-0	Pappy Waldorf	same
13	Virginia	8-1-0	Art Guepe	same
14	San Francisco	9-0-0	Joe Kuharich	same
15	Kentucky	7-4-0	Bear Bryant	8-4-0
16	Boston Univ.	6-4-0	Buff Donelli	same
17	UCLA	5-3-1	Red Sanders	same
18	Washington St.	7-3-0	Forest Evashevski	same
19	Holy Cross	8-2-0	Eddie Anderson	same
20	Clemson	7-2-0	Frank Howard	7-3-0

Key Bowl Games

Sugar–#3 Maryland over #1 Tennessee, 28-13; **Rose**–#4 Illinois over #7 Stanford, 40-7; **Orange**–#5 Georgia Tech over #9 Baylor, 17-14; **Cotton**–#15 Kentucky over #11 TCU, 20-7.

Associated Press Final Polls (Cont.)

1952

Final poll released Dec. 1. Top 20 regular season results after that: **Dec. 6**–#15 Florida over #20 Kentucky, 27-20.

			As of Dec. 1	Head Coach	After Bowls
1	Michigan St.	9-0-0		Biggie Munn	same
2	Georgia Tech	...11-0-0		Bobby Dodd	12-0-0
3	Notre Dame	7-2-1		Frank Leahy	same
4	Oklahoma	8-1-1		Bud Wilkinson	same
5	USC	9-1-0		Jess Hill	10-1-0
6	UCLA	8-1-0		Red Sanders	same
7	Mississippi	8-0-2		Johnny Vaught	8-1-2
8	Tennessee	8-1-1		Bob Neyland	8-2-1
9	Alabama	9-2-0		Red Drew	10-2-0
10	Texas	8-2-0		Ed Price	9-2-0
11	Wisconsin	6-2-1		Ivy Williamson	6-3-1
12	Tulsa	8-1-1		J.O. Brothers	8-2-1
13	Maryland	7-2-0		Jim Tatum	same
14	Syracuse	7-2-0		Ben Schwartzwalder	7-3-0
15	Florida	6-3-0		Bob Woodruff	8-3-0
16	Duke	8-2-0		Bill Murray	same
17	Ohio St.	6-3-0		Woody Hayes	same
18	Purdue	4-3-2		Stu Holcomb	same
19	Princeton	8-1-0		Charlie Caldwell	same
20	Kentucky	5-3-2		Bear Bryant	5-4-2

Note: Michigan St. would officially join Big Ten in 1953.

Key Bowl Games

Sugar–#2 Georgia Tech over #7 Ole Miss, 24-7; **Rose**–#5 USC over #11 Wisconsin, 7-0; **Cotton**–#10 Texas over #8 Tennessee, 16-0; **Orange**–#9 Alabama over #14 Syracuse, 61-6.

1953

Final poll released Nov. 30. Top 20 regular season results after that: **Dec. 5**–#2 Notre Dame over SMU, 40-14.

			As of Nov. 30	Head Coach	After Bowls
1	Maryland	10-0-0		Jim Tatum	10-1-0
2	Notre Dame	8-0-1		Frank Leahy	9-0-1
3	Michigan St.	8-1-0		Biggie Munn	9-1-0
4	Oklahoma	8-1-1		Bud Wilkinson	9-1-1
5	UCLA	8-1-0		Red Sanders	8-2-0
6	Rice	8-2-0		Jess Neely	9-2-0
7	Illinois	7-1-1		Ray Eliot	same
8	Georgia Tech	8-2-1		Bobby Dodd	9-2-1
9	Iowa	5-3-1		Forest Evashevski	same
10	West Virginia	8-1-0		Art Lewis	8-2-0
11	Texas	7-3-0		Ed Price	same
12	Texas Tech	10-1-0		DeWitt Weaver	11-1-0
13	Alabama	6-2-3		Red Drew	6-3-3
14	Army	7-1-1		Red Blaik	same
15	Wisconsin	6-2-1		Ivy Williamson	same
16	Kentucky	7-2-1		Bear Bryant	same
17	Auburn	7-2-1		Shug Jordan	7-3-1
18	Duke	7-2-1		Bill Murray	same
19	Stanford	6-3-1		Chuck Taylor	same
20	Michigan	6-3-0		Bennie Oosterbaan	same

Key Bowl Games

Orange–#4 Oklahoma over #1 Maryland, 7-0; **Rose**–#3 Michigan St. over #5 UCLA, 28-20; **Cotton**–#6 Rice over #13 Alabama, 28-6; **Sugar**–#8 Georgia Tech over #10 West Virginia, 42-19.

1954

Final poll released Nov. 29. Top 20 regular season results after that: **Dec. 4**–#4 Notre Dame over SMU, 26-14.

			As of Nov. 29	Head Coach	After Bowls
1	Ohio St.	9-0-0		Woody Hayes	10-0-0
2	UCLA	9-0-0		Red Sanders	same
3	Oklahoma	10-0-0		Bud Wilkinson	same
4	Notre Dame	8-1-0		Terry Brennan	9-1-0
5	Navy	7-2-0		Eddie Erdelatz	8-2-0
6	Mississippi	9-1-0		Johnny Vaught	9-2-0
7	Army	7-2-0		Red Blaik	same
8	Maryland	7-2-1		Jim Tatum	same
9	Wisconsin	7-2-0		Ivy Williamson	same
10	Arkansas	8-2-0		Bowden Wyatt	8-3-0
11	Miami-FL	8-1-0		Andy Gustafson	same
12	West Virginia	8-1-0		Art Lewis	same
13	Auburn	7-3-0		Shug Jordan	8-3-0
14	Duke	7-2-1		Bill Murray	8-2-1
15	Michigan	6-3-0		Bennie Oosterbaan	same
16	Virginia Tech	8-0-1		Frank Moseley	same
17	USC	8-3-0		Jess Hill	8-4-0
18	Baylor	7-3-0		George Sauer	7-4-0
19	Rice	7-3-0		Jess Neely	same
20	Penn St.	7-2-0		Rip Engle	same

Note: PCC and Big Seven "no-repeat" rules kept UCLA and Oklahoma from Rose and Orange bowls, respectively.

Key Bowl Games

Rose–#1 Ohio St. over #17 USC, 20-7; **Sugar**–#5 Navy over #6 Ole Miss, 21-0; **Cotton**–Georgia Tech over #10 Arkansas, 14-6; **Orange**–#14 Duke over Nebraska, 34-7.

1955

Final poll released Nov. 28. Top 20 regular season results after that: None.

			As of Nov. 28	Head Coach	After Bowls
1	Oklahoma	10-0-0		Bud Wilkinson	11-0-0
2	Michigan St.	8-1-0		Duffy Daugherty	9-1-0
3	Maryland	10-0-0		Jim Tatum	10-1-0
4	UCLA	9-1-0		Red Sanders	9-2-0
5	Ohio St.	7-2-0		Woody Hayes	same
6	TCU	9-1-0		Abe Martin	9-2-0
7	Georgia Tech	8-1-1		Bobby Dodd	9-1-1
8	Auburn	8-1-1		Shug Jordan	8-2-1
9	Notre Dame	8-2-0		Terry Brennan	same
10	Mississippi	9-1-0		Johnny Vaught	10-1-0
11	Pittsburgh	7-3-0		John Michelosen	7-4-0
12	Michigan	7-2-0		Bennie Oosterbaan	same
13	USC	6-4-0		Jess Hill	same
14	Miami-FL	6-3-0		Andy Gustafson	same
15	Miami-OH	9-0-0		Ara Parseghian	same
16	Stanford	6-3-1		Chuck Taylor	same
17	Texas A&M	7-2-1		Bear Bryant	same
18	Navy	6-2-1		Eddie Erdelatz	same
19	West Virginia	8-2-0		Art Lewis	same
20	Army	6-3-0		Red Blaik	same

Note: Big Ten "no-repeat" rule kept Ohio St. from Rose Bowl.

Key Bowl Games

Orange–#1 Oklahoma over #3 Maryland, 20-6; **Rose**–#2 Michigan St. over #4 UCLA, 17-14; **Cotton**–#10 Ole Miss over #6 TCU, 14-13; **Sugar**–#7 Georgia Tech over #11 Pitt, 7-0; **Gator**–Vanderbilt over #8 Auburn, 25-13.

1956

Final poll released Dec. 3. Top 20 regular season results after that: **Dec. 8**–#13 Pitt over #6 Miami-FL, 14-7.

		As of Dec. 3	Head Coach	After Bowls
1	Oklahoma	10-0-0	Bud Wilkinson	same
2	Tennessee	10-0-0	Bowden Wyatt	10-1-0
3	Iowa	8-1-0	Forest Evashevski	9-1-0
4	Georgia Tech	9-1-0	Bobby Dodd	10-1-0
5	Texas A&M	9-0-1	Bear Bryant	same
6	Miami-FL	8-0-1	Andy Gustafson	8-1-1
7	Michigan	7-2-0	Bennie Oosterbaan	same
8	Syracuse	7-1-0	Ben Schwartzwalder	7-2-0
9	Michigan St.	7-2-0	Duffy Daugherty	same
10	Oregon St.	7-2-1	Tommy Prothro	7-3-1
11	Baylor	8-2-0	Sam Boyd	9-2-0
12	Minnesota	6-1-2	Murray Warmath	same
13	Pittsburgh	6-2-1	John Michelosen	7-3-1
14	TCU	7-3-0	Abe Martin	8-3-0
15	Ohio St.	6-3-0	Woody Hayes	same
16	Navy	6-1-2	Eddie Erdelatz	same
17	G. Washington	7-1-1	Gene Sherman	8-1-1
18	USC	8-2-0	Jess Hill	same
19	Clemson	7-1-2	Frank Howard	7-2-2
20	Colorado	7-2-1	Dallas Ward	8-2-1

Note: Big Seven "no-repeat" rule kept Oklahoma from Orange Bowl and Texas A&M was on probation.

Key Bowl Games

Sugar–#11 Baylor over #2 Tennessee, 13-7; **Rose**–#3 Iowa over #10 Oregon St., 35-19; **Gator**–#4 Georgia Tech over #13 Pitt, 21-14; **Cotton**–#14 TCU over #8 Syracuse, 28-27; **Orange**–#20 Colorado over #19 Clemson, 27-21.

1957

Final poll released Dec. 2. Top 20 regular season results after that: **Dec. 7**–#10 Notre Dame over SMU, 54-21.

		As of Dec. 2	Head Coach	After Bowls
1	Auburn	10-0-0	Shug Jordan	same
2	Ohio St.	8-1-0	Woody Hayes	9-1-0
3	Michigan St.	8-1-0	Duffy Daugherty	same
4	Oklahoma	9-1-0	Bud Wilkinson	10-1-0
5	Navy	8-1-1	Eddie Erdelatz	9-1-1
6	Iowa	7-1-1	Forest Evashevski	same
7	Mississippi	8-1-1	Johnny Vaught	9-1-1
8	Rice	7-3-0	Jess Neely	7-4-0
9	Texas A&M	8-2-0	Bear Bryant	8-3-0
10	Notre Dame	6-3-0	Terry Brennan	7-3-0
11	Texas	6-3-1	Darrell Royal	6-4-1
12	Arizona St.	10-0-0	Dan Devine	same
13	Tennessee	7-3-0	Bowden Wyatt	8-3-0
14	Mississippi St.	6-2-1	Wade Walker	same
15	N.C. State	7-1-2	Earle Edwards	same
16	Duke	6-2-2	Bill Murray	6-3-2
17	Florida	6-2-1	Bob Woodruff	same
18	Army	7-2-0	Red Blaik	same
19	Wisconsin	6-3-0	Milt Bruhn	same
20	VMI	9-0-1	John McKenna	same

Note: Auburn on probation, ineligible for bowl game.

Key Bowl Games

Rose–#2 Ohio St. over Oregon, 10-7; **Orange**–#4 Oklahoma over #16 Duke, 48-21; **Cotton**–#5 Navy over #8 Rice, 20-7; **Sugar**–#7 Ole Miss over #11 Texas, 39-7; **Gator**–#13 Tennessee over #9 Texas A&M, 3-0.

1958

Final poll released Dec. 1. Top 20 regular season results after that: None.

		As of Dec. 1	Head Coach	After Bowls
1	LSU	10-0-0	Paul Dietzel	11-0-0
2	Iowa	7-1-1	Forest Evashevski	8-1-1
3	Army	8-0-1	Red Blaik	same
4	Auburn	9-0-1	Shug Jordan	same
5	Oklahoma	9-1-0	Bud Wilkinson	10-1-0
6	Air Force	9-0-1	Ben Martin	9-0-2
7	Wisconsin	7-1-1	Milt Bruhn	same
8	Ohio St.	6-1-2	Woody Hayes	same
9	Syracuse	8-1-0	Ben Schwartzwalder	8-2-0
10	TCU	8-2-0	Abe Martin	8-2-1
11	Mississippi	8-2-0	Johnny Vaught	9-2-0
12	Clemson	8-2-0	Frank Howard	8-3-0
13	Purdue	6-1-2	Jack Mollenkopf	same
14	Florida	6-3-1	Bob Woodruff	6-4-1
15	South Carolina	7-3-0	Warren Giese	same
16	California	7-3-0	Pete Elliott	7-4-0
17	Notre Dame	6-4-0	Terry Brennan	same
18	SMU	6-4-0	Bill Meek	same
19	Oklahoma St.	7-3-0	Cliff Speegle	8-3-0
20	Rutgers	8-1-0	John Stiegman	same

Key Bowl Games

Sugar–#1 LSU over #12 Clemson, 7-0; **Rose**–#2 Iowa over #16 Cal, 38-12; **Orange**–#5 Oklahoma over #9 Syracuse, 21-6; **Cotton**–#6 Air Force tied #10 TCU, 0-0.

1959

Final poll released Dec. 7. Top 20 regular season results after that: None.

		As of Dec. 7	Head Coach	After Bowls
1	Syracuse	10-0-0	Ben Schwartzwalder	11-0-0
2	Mississippi	9-1-0	Johnny Vaught	10-1-0
3	LSU	9-1-0	Paul Dietzel	9-2-0
4	Texas	9-1-0	Darrell Royal	9-2-0
5	Georgia	9-1-0	Wally Butts	10-1-0
6	Wisconsin	7-2-0	Milt Bruhn	7-3-0
7	TCU	8-2-0	Abe Martin	8-3-0
8	Washington	9-1-0	Jim Owens	10-1-0
9	Arkansas	8-2-0	Frank Broyles	9-2-0
10	Alabama	7-1-2	Bear Bryant	7-2-2
11	Clemson	8-2-0	Frank Howard	9-2-0
12	Penn St.	8-2-0	Rip Engle	9-2-0
13	Illinois	5-3-1	Ray Eliot	same
14	USC	8-2-0	Don Clark	same
15	Oklahoma	7-3-0	Bud Wilkinson	same
16	Wyoming	9-1-0	Bob Devaney	same
17	Notre Dame	5-5-0	Joe Kuharich	same
18	Missouri	6-4-0	Dan Devine	6-5-0
19	Florida	5-4-1	Bob Woodruff	same
20	Pittsburgh	6-4-0	John Michelosen	same

Note: Big Seven "no-repeat" rule kept Oklahoma from Orange Bowl.

Key Bowl Games

Cotton–#1 Syracuse over #4 Texas, 23-14; **Sugar**–#2 Ole Miss over #3 LSU, 21-0; **Orange**–#5 Georgia over #18 Missouri, 14-0; **Rose**–#8 Washington over #6 Wisconsin, 44-8; **Bluebonnet**–#11 Clemson over #7 TCU, 23-7; **Gator**–#9 Arkansas over Georgia Tech, 14-7; **Liberty**–#12 Penn St. over #10 Alabama, 7-0.

Associated Press Final Polls (Cont.)

1960

Final poll released Nov. 28. Top 20 regular season results after that: **Dec. 3**—UCLA over #10 Duke, 27-6.

		As of Nov. 28	Head Coach	After Bowls
1	Minnesota	8-1-0	Murray Warmath	8-2-0
2	Mississippi	9-0-1	Johnny Vaught	10-0-1
3	Iowa	8-1-0	Forest Evashevski	same
4	Navy	9-1-0	Wayne Hardin	9-2-0
5	Missouri	9-1-0	Dan Devine	10-1-0
6	Washington	9-1-0	Jim Owens	10-1-0
7	Arkansas	8-2-0	Frank Broyles	8-3-0
8	Ohio St.	7-2-0	Woody Hayes	same
9	Alabama	8-1-1	Bear Bryant	8-1-2
10	Duke	7-2-0	Bill Murray	8-3-0
11	Kansas	7-2-1	Jack Mitchell	same
12	Baylor	8-2-0	John Bridgers	8-3-0
13	Auburn	8-2-0	Shug Jordan	same
14	Yale	9-0-0	Jordan Olivar	same
15	Michigan St.	6-2-1	Duffy Daugherty	same
16	Penn St.	6-3-0	Rip Engle	7-3-0
17	New Mexico St.	10-0-0	Warren Woodson	11-0-0
18	Florida	8-2-0	Ray Graves	9-2-0
19	Syracuse	7-2-0	Ben Schwartzwalder	same
	Purdue	4-4-1	Jack Mollenkopf	same

Key Bowl Games

Rose—#6 Washington over #1 Minnesota, 17-7; **Sugar**—#2 Ole Miss over Rice, 14-6; **Orange**—#5 Missouri over #4 Navy, 21-14; **Cotton**—#10 Duke over #7 Arkansas, 7-6; **Bluebonnet**—#9 Alabama tied Texas, 3-3.

1961

Final poll released Dec. 4. Top 20 regular season results after that: None.

		As of Dec. 4	Head Coach	After Bowls
1	Alabama	10-0-0	Bear Bryant	11-0-0
2	Ohio St.	8-0-1	Woody Hayes	same
3	Texas	9-1-0	Darrell Royal	10-1-0
4	LSU	9-1-0	Paul Dietzel	10-1-0
5	Mississippi	9-1-0	Johnny Vaught	9-2-0
6	Minnesota	7-2-0	Murray Warmath	8-2-0
7	Colorado	9-1-0	Sonny Grandelius	9-2-0
8	Michigan St.	7-2-0	Duffy Daugherty	same
9	Arkansas	8-2-0	Frank Broyles	8-3-0
10	Utah St.	9-0-1	John Ralston	9-1-1
11	Missouri	7-2-1	Dan Devine	same
12	Purdue	6-3-0	Jack Mollenkopf	same
13	Georgia Tech	7-3-0	Bobby Dodd	7-4-0
14	Syracuse	7-3-0	Ben Schwartzwalder	8-3-0
15	Rutgers	9-0-0	John Bateman	same
16	UCLA	7-3-0	Bill Barnes	7-4-0
17	Rice	7-3-0	Jess Neely	7-4-0
	Penn St.	7-3-0	Rip Engle	8-3-0
	Arizona	8-1-1	Jim LaRue	same
20	Duke	7-3-0	Bill Murray	same

Note: Ohio St. faculty council turned down Rose Bowl invitation citing concern with OSU's overemphasis on sports.

Key Bowl Games

Sugar—#1 Alabama over #9 Arkansas, 10-3; **Cotton**—#3 Texas over #5 Ole Miss, 12-7; **Orange**—#4 LSU over #7 Colorado, 25-7; **Rose**—#6 Minnesota over #16 UCLA, 21-3; **Gotham**—Baylor over #10 Utah St., 24-9.

1962

Final poll released Dec. 3. Top 10 regular season results after that: None.

		As of Dec. 3	Head Coach	After Bowls
1	USC	10-0-0	John McKay	11-0-0
2	Wisconsin	8-1-0	Milt Bruhn	8-2-0
3	Mississippi	9-0-0	Johnny Vaught	10-0-0
4	Texas	9-0-1	Darrell Royal	9-1-1
5	Alabama	9-1-0	Bear Bryant	10-1-0
6	Arkansas	9-1-0	Frank Broyles	9-2-0
7	LSU	8-1-1	Charlie McClendon	9-1-1
8	Oklahoma	8-2-0	Bud Wilkinson	8-3-0
9	Penn St.	9-1-0	Rip Engle	9-2-0
10	Minnesota	6-2-1	Murray Warmath	same

Key Bowl Games

Rose—#1 USC over #2 Wisconsin, 42-37; **Sugar**—#3 Ole Miss over #6 Arkansas, 17-13; **Cotton**—#7 LSU over #4 Texas, 13-0; **Orange**—#5 Alabama over #8 Oklahoma, 17-0; **Gator**—Florida over #9 Penn St., 17-7.

1963

Final poll released Dec. 9. Top 10 regular season results after that: **Dec. 14**—#8 Alabama over Miami-FL, 17-12.

		As of Dec. 9	Head Coach	After Bowls
1	Texas	10-0-0	Darrell Royal	11-0-0
2	Navy	9-1-0	Wayne Hardin	9-2-0
3	Illinois	7-1-1	Pete Elliott	8-1-1
4	Pittsburgh	9-1-0	John Michelosen	same
5	Auburn	9-1-0	Shug Jordan	9-2-0
6	Nebraska	9-1-0	Bob Devaney	10-1-0
7	Mississippi	7-0-2	Johnny Vaught	7-1-2
8	Alabama	7-2-0	Bear Bryant	9-2-0
9	Michigan St.	6-2-1	Duffy Daugherty	same
10	Oklahoma	8-2-0	Bud Wilkinson	same

Key Bowl Games

Cotton—#1 Texas over #2 Navy, 28-6; **Rose**—#3 Illinois over Washington, 17-7; **Orange**—#6 Nebraska over #5 Auburn, 13-7; **Sugar**—#8 Alabama over #7 Ole Miss, 12-7.

1964

Final poll released Nov. 30. Top 10 regular season results after that: **Dec. 5**—Florida over #7 LSU, 20-6.

		As of Nov. 30	Head Coach	After Bowls
1	Alabama	10-0-0	Bear Bryant	10-1-0
2	Arkansas	10-0-0	Frank Broyles	11-0-0
3	Notre Dame	9-1-0	Ara Parseghian	same
4	Michigan	8-1-0	Bump Elliott	9-1-0
5	Texas	9-1-0	Darrell Royal	10-1-0
6	Nebraska	9-1-0	Bob Devaney	9-2-0
7	LSU	7-1-1	Charlie McClendon	8-2-1
8	Oregon St.	8-2-0	Tommy Prothro	8-3-0
9	Ohio St.	7-2-0	Woody Hayes	same
10	USC	7-3-0	John McKay	same

Key Bowl Games

Orange—#5 Texas over #1 Alabama, 21-17; **Cotton**—#2 Arkansas over #6 Nebraska, 10-7; **Rose**—#4 Michigan over #8 Oregon St., 34-7; **Sugar**—#7 LSU over Syracuse, 13-10.

1965

Final poll taken after bowl games for the first time.

		Head Coach	Regular Season
		After Bowls	
1	Alabama 9-1-1	Bear Bryant	8-1-1
2	Michigan St. 10-1-0	Duffy Daugherty	10-0-0
3	Arkansas 10-1-0	Frank Broyles	10-0-0
4	UCLA 8-2-1	Tommy Prothro	7-1-1
5	Nebraska........10-1-0	Bob Devaney	10-0-0
6	Missouri 8-2-1	Dan Devine	7-2-1
7	Tennessee.......8-1-2	Doug Dickey	6-1-2
8	LSU 8-3-0	Charlie McClendon	7-3-0
9	Notre Dame......7-2-1	Ara Parseghian	same
10	USC 7-2-1	John McKay	same

Key Bowl Games

Rankings below reflect final regular season poll, released Nov. 29. No bowls for then #8 USC or #9 Notre Dame. **Rose**–#5 UCLA over #1 Michigan St., 14-12; **Cotton**–LSU over #2 Arkansas, 14-7; **Orange**–#4 Alabama over #3 Nebraska, 39-28; **Sugar**–#6 Missouri over Florida, 20-18; **Bluebonnet**–#7 Tennessee over Tulsa, 27-6; **Gator**–Georgia Tech over #10 Texas Tech, 31-21.

1966

Final poll released Dec. 5, returning to pre-bowl status. Top 10 regular season results after that: None.

		Head Coach	After Bowls
		As of Dec. 5	
1	Notre Dame.......9-0-1	Ara Parseghian	same
2	Michigan St. 9-0-1	Duffy Daugherty	same
3	Alabama 10-0-0	Bear Bryant	11-0-0
4	Georgia 9-1-0	Vince Dooley	10-1-0
5	UCLA 9-1-0	Tommy Prothro	same
6	Nebraska.........9-1-0	Bob Devaney	9-2-0
7	Purdue 8-2-0	Jack Mollenkopf	9-2-0
8	Georgia Tech......9-1-0	Bobby Dodd	9-2-0
9	Miami-FL.........7-2-1	Charlie Tate	8-2-1
10	SMU 8-2-0	Hayden Fry	8-3-0

Key Bowl Games

Sugar–#3 Alabama over #6 Nebraska, 34-7; **Cotton**–#4 Georgia over #10 SMU, 24-9; **Rose**–#7 Purdue over USC, 14-13; **Orange**–Florida over #8 Georgia Tech, 27-12; **Liberty**–#9 Miami-FL over Virginia Tech, 14-7.

1967

Final poll released Nov. 27. Top 10 regular season results after that: **Dec. 2**–#2 Tennessee over Vanderbilt, 41-14; #3 Oklahoma over Oklahoma St., 38-14; #8 Alabama over Auburn, 7-3.

		Head Coach	After Bowls
		As of Nov. 27	
1	USC 9-1-0	John McKay	10-1-0
2	Tennessee........8-1-0	Doug Dickey	9-2-0
3	Oklahoma 8-1-0	Chuck Fairbanks	10-1-0
4	Indiana...........9-1-0	John Pont	9-2-0
5	Notre Dame......8-2-0	Ara Parseghian	same
6	Wyoming.........10-0-0	Lloyd Eaton	10-1-0
7	Oregon St........7-2-1	Dee Andros	same
8	Alabama 7-1-1	Bear Bryant	8-2-1
9	Purdue 8-2-0	Jack Mollenkopf	same
10	Penn St..........8-2-0	Joe Paterno	8-2-1

Key Bowl Games

Rose–#1 USC over #4 Indiana, 14-3; **Orange**–#3 Oklahoma over #2 Tennessee, 26-24; **Sugar**–LSU over #6 Wyoming, 20-13; **Cotton**–Texas A&M over #8 Alabama, 20-16; **Gator**–#10 Penn St. tied Florida St. 17-17.

1968

Final poll taken after bowl games for first time since close of 1965 season.

		Head Coach	Regular Season
		After Bowls	
1	Ohio St..........10-0-0	Woody Hayes	9-0-0
2	Penn St. 11-0-0	Joe Paterno	10-0-0
3	Texas............9-1-1	Darrell Royal	8-1-1
4	USC 9-1-1	John McKay	9-0-1
5	Notre Dame......7-2-1	Ara Parseghian	same
6	Arkansas 10-1-0	Frank Broyles	9-1-0
7	Kansas 9-2-0	Pepper Rodgers	9-1-0
8	Georgia 8-1-2	Vince Dooley	8-0-2
9	Missouri 8-3-0	Dan Devine	7-3-0
10	Purdue 8-2-0	Jack Mollenkopf	same
11	Oklahoma 7-4-0	Chuck Fairbanks	7-3-0
12	Michigan 8-2-0	Bump Elliott	same
13	Tennessee.......8-2-1	Doug Dickey	8-1-1
14	SMU 8-3-0	Hayden Fry	7-3-0
15	Oregon St........7-3-0	Dee Andros	same
16	Auburn 7-4-0	Shug Jordan	6-4-0
17	Alabama 8-3-0	Bear Bryant	8-2-0
18	Houston 6-2-2	Bill Yeoman	same
19	LSU 8-3-0	Charlie McClendon	7-3-0
20	Ohio Univ.......10-1-0	Bill Hess	10-0-0

Key Bowl Games

Rankings below reflect final regular season poll, released Dec. 2. No bowls for then #7 Notre Dame and #11 Purdue. **Rose**–#1 Ohio St. over #2 USC, 27-16; **Orange**–#3 Penn St. over #6 Kansas, 15-14; **Sugar**–#9 Arkansas over #4 Georgia, 16-2; **Cotton**–#5 Texas over #8 Tennessee, 36-13; **Bluebonnet**–#20 SMU over #10 Oklahoma, 28-27; **Gator**–#16 Missouri over #12 Alabama, 35-10.

1969

Final poll taken after bowl games.

		Head Coach	Regular Season
		After Bowls	
1	Texas 11-0-0	Darrell Royal	10-0-0
2	Penn St. 11-0-0	Joe Paterno	10-0-0
3	USC 10-0-1	John McKay	9-0-1
4	Ohio St. 8-1-0	Woody Hayes	same
5	Notre Dame......8-2-1	Ara Parseghian	8-1-1
6	Missouri 9-2-0	Dan Devine	9-1-0
7	Arkansas 9-2-0	Frank Broyles	9-1-0
8	Mississippi 8-3-0	Johnny Vaught	7-3-0
9	Michigan 8-3-0	Bo Schembechler	8-2-0
10	LSU 9-1-0	Charlie McClendon	same
11	Nebraska........9-2-0	Bob Devaney	8-2-0
12	Houston 9-2-0	Bill Yeoman	8-2-0
13	UCLA 8-1-1	Tommy Prothro	same
14	Florida 9-1-1	Ray Graves	8-1-1
15	Tennessee.......9-2-0	Doug Dickey	9-1-0
16	Colorado 8-3-0	Eddie Crowder	7-3-0
17	West Virginia ...10-1-0	Jim Carlen	9-1-0
18	Purdue 8-2-0	Jack Mollenkopf	same
19	Stanford 7-2-1	John Ralston	same
20	Auburn 8-3-0	Shug Jordan	8-2-0

Key Bowl Games

Rankings below reflect final regular season poll, released Dec. 8. No bowls for then #4 Ohio St., #8 LSU and #10 UCLA.

Cotton–#1 Texas over #9 Notre Dame, 21-17; **Orange**–#2 Penn St. over #6 Missouri, 10-3; **Sugar**–#13 Ole Miss over #3 Arkansas, 27-22; **Rose**–#5 USC over #7 Michigan, 10-3.

Associated Press Final Polls (Cont.)

1970

	After Bowls	Head Coach	Regular Season
1 Nebraska	11-0-1	Bob Devaney	10-0-1
2 Notre Dame	10-1-0	Ara Parseghian	9-0-1
3 Texas	10-1-0	Darrell Royal	10-0-0
4 Tennessee	11-1-0	Bill Battle	10-1-0
5 Ohio St.	9-1-0	Woody Hayes	9-0-0
6 Arizona St.	11-0-0	Frank Kush	10-0-0
7 LSU	9-3-0	Charlie McClendon	9-2-0
8 Stanford	9-3-0	John Ralston	8-3-0
9 Michigan	9-1-0	Bo Schembechler	same
10 Auburn	9-2-0	Shug Jordan	8-2-0
11 Arkansas	9-2-0	Frank Broyles	same
12 Toledo	12-0-0	Frank Lauterbur	11-0-0
13 Georgia Tech	9-3-0	Bud Carson	8-3-0
14 Dartmouth	9-0-0	Bob Blackman	same
15 USC	6-4-1	John McKay	same
16 Air Force	9-3-0	Ben Martin	9-2-0
17 Tulane	8-4-0	Jim Pittman	7-4-0
18 Penn St.	7-3-0	Joe Paterno	same
19 Houston	8-3-0	Bill Yeoman	same
20 Oklahoma	7-4-1	Chuck Fairbanks	7-4-0
Mississippi	7-4-0	Johnny Vaught	7-3-0

Key Bowl Games

Rankings below reflect final regular season poll, released Dec. 7. No bowls for then #4 Arkansas and #7 Michigan.

Cotton—#6 Notre Dame over #1 Texas, 24-11; **Rose**—#12 Stanford over #2 Ohio St., 27-17; **Orange**—#3 Nebraska over #8 LSU, 17-12; **Sugar**—#5 Tennessee over #11 Air Force, 34-13; **Peach**—#9 Ariz. St. over N. Carolina, 48-26.

1971

	After Bowls	Head Coach	Regular Season
1 Nebraska	13-0-0	Bob Devaney	12-0-0
2 Oklahoma	11-1-0	Chuck Fairbanks	10-1-0
3 Colorado	10-2-0	Eddie Crowder	9-2-0
4 Alabama	11-1-0	Bear Bryant	11-0-0
5 Penn St.	11-1-0	Joe Paterno	10-1-0
6 Michigan	11-1-0	Bo Schembechler	11-0-0
7 Georgia	11-1-0	Vince Dooley	10-1-0
8 Arizona St.	11-1-0	Frank Kush	10-1-0
9 Tennessee	10-2-0	Bill Battle	9-2-0
10 Stanford	9-3-0	John Ralston	8-3-0
11 LSU	9-3-0	Charlie McClendon	8-3-0
12 Auburn	9-2-0	Shug Jordan	9-1-0
13 Notre Dame	8-2-0	Ara Parseghian	same
14 Toledo	12-0-0	John Murphy	11-0-0
15 Mississippi	10-2-0	Billy Kinard	9-2-0
16 Arkansas	8-3-1	Frank Broyles	8-2-1
17 Houston	9-3-0	Bill Yeoman	9-2-0
18 Texas	8-3-0	Darrell Royal	8-2-0
19 Washington	8-3-0	Jim Owens	same
20 USC	6-4-1	John McKay	same

Key Bowl Games

Rankings below reflect final regular season poll, released Dec. 6.

Orange—#1 Nebraska over #2 Alabama, 38-6; **Sugar**—#3 Oklahoma over #5 Auburn, 40-22; **Rose**—#16 Stanford over #4 Michigan, 13-12; **Gator**—#6 Georgia over N. Carolina, 7-3; **Bluebonnet**—#7 Colorado over #15 Houston, 29-17; **Fiesta**—#8 Ariz. St. over Florida St., 45-38; **Cotton**—#10 Penn St. over #12 Texas, 30-6.

1972

	After Bowls	Head Coach	Regular Season
1 USC	12-0-0	John McKay	11-0-0
2 Oklahoma	11-1-0	Chuck Fairbanks	10-1-0
3 Texas	10-1-0	Darrell Royal	9-1-0
4 Nebraska	9-2-1	Bob Devaney	8-2-1
5 Auburn	10-1-0	Shug Jordan	9-1-0
6 Michigan	10-1-0	Bo Schembechler	same
7 Alabama	10-2-0	Bear Bryant	10-1-0
8 Tennessee	10-2-0	Bill Battle	9-2-0
9 Ohio St.	9-2-0	Woody Hayes	9-1-0
10 Penn St.	10-2-0	Joe Paterno	10-1-0
11 LSU	9-2-1	Charlie McClendon	9-1-1
12 North Carolina	11-1-0	Bill Dooley	10-1-0
13 Arizona St.	10-2-0	Frank Kush	9-2-0
14 Notre Dame	8-3-0	Ara Parseghian	8-2-0
15 UCLA	8-3-0	Pepper Rodgers	same
16 Colorado	8-4-0	Eddie Crowder	8-3-0
17 N.C. State	8-3-1	Lou Holtz	7-3-1
18 Louisville	9-1-0	Lee Corso	same
19 Washington St.	7-4-0	Jim Sweeney	same
20 Georgia Tech	7-4-1	Bill Fulcher	6-4-1

Key Bowl Games

Rankings below reflect final regular season poll, released Dec. 4. No bowl for then #8 Michigan.

Rose—#1 USC over #3 Ohio St., 42-17; **Sugar**—#2 Oklahoma over #5 Penn St., 14-0; **Cotton**—#7 Texas over #4 Alabama, 17-13; **Orange**—#9 Nebraska over #12 Notre Dame, 40-6; **Gator**—#6 Auburn over #13 Colorado, 24-3; **Bluebonnet**—#11 Tennessee over #10 LSU, 24-17.

1973

	After Bowls	Head Coach	Regular Season
1 Notre Dame	11-0-0	Ara Parseghian	10-0-0
2 Ohio St.	10-0-1	Woody Hayes	9-0-1
3 Oklahoma	10-0-1	Barry Switzer	same
4 Alabama	11-1-0	Bear Bryant	11-0-0
5 Penn St.	12-0-0	Joe Paterno	11-0-0
6 Michigan	10-0-1	Bo Schembechler	same
7 Nebraska	9-2-1	Tom Osborne	8-2-1
8 USC	9-2-1	John McKay	9-1-1
9 Arizona St.	11-1-0	Frank Kush	10-1-0
Houston	11-1-0	Bill Yeoman	10-1-0
11 Texas Tech	11-1-0	Jim Carlen	10-1-0
12 UCLA	9-2-0	Pepper Rodgers	same
13 LSU	9-3-0	Charlie McClendon	9-2-0
14 Texas	8-3-0	Darrell Royal	8-2-0
15 Miami-OH	11-0-0	Bill Mallory	10-0-0
16 N.C. State	9-3-0	Lou Holtz	8-3-0
17 Missouri	8-4-0	Al Onofrio	7-4-0
18 Kansas	7-4-1	Don Fambrough	7-3-1
19 Tennessee	8-4-0	Bill Battle	8-3-0
20 Maryland	8-4-0	Jerry Claiborne	8-3-0
Tulane	9-3-0	Bennie Ellender	9-2-0

Key Bowl Games

Rankings below reflect final regular season poll, released Dec. 3. No bowls for then #2 Oklahoma (probation), #5 Michigan and #9 UCLA.

Sugar—#3 Notre Dame over #1 Alabama, 24-23; **Rose**—#4 Ohio St. over #7 USC, 42-21; **Orange**—#6 Penn St. over #13 LSU, 16-9; **Cotton**—#12 Nebraska over #8 Texas, 19-3; **Fiesta**—#10 Ariz. St. over Pitt, 28-7; **Bluebonnet**—#14 Houston over #17 Tulane, 47-7.

1974

	After Bowls	Head Coach	Regular Season
1 Oklahoma	11-0-0	Barry Switzer	same
2 USC	10-1-1	John McKay	9-1-1
3 Michigan	10-1-0	Bo Schembechler	same
4 Ohio St.	10-2-0	Woody Hayes	10-1-0
5 Alabama	11-1-0	Bear Bryant	11-0-0
6 Notre Dame	10-2-0	Ara Parseghian	9-2-0
7 Penn St.	10-2-0	Joe Paterno	9-2-0
8 Auburn	10-2-0	Shug Jordan	9-2-0
9 Nebraska	9-3-0	Tom Osborne	8-3-0
10 Miami-OH	10-0-1	Dick Crum	9-0-1
11 N.C. State	9-2-1	Lou Holtz	9-2-0
12 Michigan St.	7-3-1	Denny Stolz	same
13 Maryland	8-4-0	Jerry Claiborne	8-3-0
14 Baylor	8-4-0	Grant Teaff	8-3-0
15 Florida	8-4-0	Doug Dickey	8-3-0
16 Texas A&M	8-3-0	Emory Ballard	same
17 Mississippi St.	9-3-0	Bob Tyler	8-3-0
Texas	8-4-0	Darrell Royal	8-3-0
19 Houston	8-3-1	Bill Yeoman	8-3-0
20 Tennessee	7-3-2	Bill Battle	6-3-2

Key Bowl Games

Rankings below reflect final regular season poll, released Dec. 2. No bowls for #1 Oklahoma (probation) and then #4 Michigan.

Orange–#9 Notre Dame over #2 Alabama, 13-11; **Rose**–#5 USC over #3 Ohio St., 18-17; **Gator**–#6 Auburn over #11 Texas, 27-3; **Cotton**–#7 Penn St. over #12 Baylor, 41-20; **Sugar**–#8 Nebraska over #18 Florida, 13-10; **Liberty**–Tennessee over #10 Maryland, 7-3.

1975

	After Bowls	Head Coach	Regular Season
1 Oklahoma	11-1-0	Barry Switzer	10-1-0
2 Arizona St.	12-0-0	Frank Kush	11-0-0
3 Alabama	11-1-0	Bear Bryant	10-1-0
4 Ohio St.	11-1-0	Woody Hayes	11-0-0
5 UCLA	9-2-1	Dick Vermeil	8-2-1
6 Texas	10-2-0	Darrell Royal	9-2-0
7 Arkansas	10-2-0	Frank Broyles	9-2-0
8 Michigan	8-2-2	Bo Schembechler	8-1-2
9 Nebraska	10-2-0	Tom Osborne	10-1-0
10 Penn St.	9-3-0	Joe Paterno	9-2-0
11 Texas A&M	10-2-0	Emory Bellard	10-1-0
12 Miami-OH	11-1-0	Dick Crum	10-1-0
13 Maryland	9-2-1	Jerry Claiborne	8-2-1
14 California	8-3-0	Mike White	same
15 Pittsburgh	8-4-0	Johnny Majors	7-4-0
16 Colorado	9-3-0	Bill Mallory	9-2-0
17 USC	8-4-0	John McKay	7-4-0
18 Arizona	9-2-0	Jim Young	same
19 Georgia	9-3-0	Vince Dooley	9-2-0
20 West Virginia	9-3-0	Bobby Bowden	8-3-0

Key Bowl Games

Rankings below reflect final regular season poll, released Dec. 1. Texas A&M was unbeaten and ranked 2nd in that poll, but lost to #18 Arkansas, 31-6, in its final regular season game on Dec.6.

Rose–#11 UCLA over #1 Ohio St., 23-10; **Liberty**–#17 USC over #2 Texas A&M, 20-0; **Orange**–#3 Oklahoma over #5 Michigan, 14-6; **Sugar**–#4 Alabama over #8 Penn St., 13-6; **Fiesta**–#7 Ariz. St. over #6 Nebraska, 17-14; **Bluebonnet**–#9 Texas over #10 Colorado, 38-21; **Cotton**–#18 Arkansas over #12 Georgia, 31-10.

1976

	After Bowls	Head Coach	Regular Season
1 Pittsburgh	12-0-0	Johnny Majors	11-0-0
2 USC	11-1-0	John Robinson	10-1-0
3 Michigan	10-2-0	Bo Schembechler	10-1-0
4 Houston	10-2-0	Bill Yeoman	9-2-0
5 Oklahoma	9-2-1	Barry Switzer	8-2-1
6 Ohio St.	9-2-1	Woody Hayes	8-2-1
7 Texas A&M	10-2-0	Emory Bellard	9-2-0
8 Maryland	11-1-0	Jerry Claiborne	11-0-0
9 Nebraska	9-3-1	Tom Osborne	8-3-1
10 Georgia	10-2-0	Vince Dooley	10-1-0
11 Alabama	9-3-0	Bear Bryant	8-3-0
12 Notre Dame	9-3-0	Dan Devine	8-3-0
13 Texas Tech	10-2-0	Steve Sloan	10-1-0
14 Oklahoma St.	9-3-0	Jim Stanley	8-3-0
15 UCLA	9-2-1	Terry Donahue	9-1-1
16 Colorado	8-4-0	Bill Mallory	8-3-0
17 Rutgers	11-0-0	Frank Burns	same
18 Kentucky	8-4-0	Fran Curci	7-4-0
19 Iowa St.	8-3-0	Earle Bruce	same
20 Mississippi St.	9-2-0	Bob Tyler	same

Key Bowl Games

Rankings below reflect final regular season poll, released Nov. 29. No bowl for then #20 Miss. St. (probation).

Sugar–#1 Pitt over #5 Georgia, 27-3; **Rose**–#3 USC over #2 Michigan, 14-6; **Cotton**–#6 Houston over #4 Maryland, 30-21; **Liberty**–#16 Alabama over #7 UCLA, 36-6; **Fiesta**–#8 Oklahoma over Wyoming, 41-7; **Bluebonnet**–#13 Nebraska over #9 Texas Tech, 27-24; **Sun**–#10 Texas A&M over Florida, 37-14; **Orange**–#11 Ohio St. over #12 Colorado, 27-10.

1977

	After Bowls	Head Coach	Regular Season
1 Notre Dame	11-1-0	Dan Devine	10-1-0
2 Alabama	11-1-0	Bear Bryant	10-1-0
3 Arkansas	11-1-0	Lou Holtz	10-1-0
4 Texas	11-1-0	Fred Akers	11-0-0
5 Penn St.	11-1-0	Joe Paterno	10-1-0
6 Kentucky	10-1-0	Fran Curci	same
7 Oklahoma	10-2-0	Barry Switzer	10-1-0
8 Pittsburgh	9-2-1	Jackie Sherrill	8-2-1
9 Michigan	10-2-0	Bo Schembechler	10-1-0
10 Washington	8-4-0	Don James	7-4-0
11 Ohio St.	9-3-0	Woody Hayes	9-2-0
12 Nebraska	9-3-0	Tom Osborne	8-3-0
13 USC	8-4-0	John Robinson	7-4-0
14 Florida St.	10-2-0	Bobby Bowden	9-2-0
15 Stanford	9-3-0	Bill Walsh	8-3-0
16 San Diego St.	10-1-0	Claude Gilbert	same
17 North Carolina	8-3-1	Bill Dooley	8-2-1
18 Arizona St.	9-3-0	Frank Kush	9-2-0
19 Clemson	8-3-1	Charley Pell	8-2-1
20 BYU	9-2-0	LaVell Edwards	same

Key Bowl Games

Rankings below reflect final regular season poll, released Nov. 28. No bowl for then #7 Kentucky (probation).

Cotton–#5 Notre Dame over #1 Texas, 38-10; **Orange**–#6 Arkansas over #2 Oklahoma, 31-6; **Sugar**–#3 Alabama over #9 Ohio St., 35-6; **Rose**–#13 Washington over #4 Michigan, 27-20; **Fiesta**–#8 Penn St. over #15 Ariz. St., 42-30; **Gator**–#10 Pitt over #11 Clemson, 34-3.

Associated Press Final Polls (Cont.)

1978

		After Bowls	Head Coach	Regular Season
1	Alabama	11-1-0	Bear Bryant	10-1-0
2	USC	12-1-0	John Robinson	11-1-0
3	Oklahoma	11-1-0	Barry Switzer	10-1-0
4	Penn St.	11-1-0	Joe Paterno	11-0-0
5	Michigan	10-2-0	Bo Schembechler	10-1-0
6	Clemson	11-1-0	Charley Pell	10-1-0
7	Notre Dame	9-3-0	Dan Devine	8-3-0
8	Nebraska	9-3-0	Tom Osborne	9-2-0
9	Texas	9-3-0	Fred Akers	8-3-0
10	Houston	9-3-0	Bill Yeoman	9-2-0
11	Arkansas	9-2-1	Lou Holtz	9-2-0
12	Michigan St.	8-3-0	Darryl Rogers	same
13	Purdue	9-2-1	Jim Young	8-2-1
14	UCLA	8-3-1	Terry Donahue	8-3-0
15	Missouri	8-4-0	Warren Powers	7-4-0
16	Georgia	9-2-1	Vince Dooley	9-1-1
17	Stanford	8-4-0	Bill Walsh	7-4-0
18	N.C. State	9-3-0	Bo Rein	8-3-0
19	Texas A&M	8-4-0	Emory Bellard (4-2) & Tom Wilson (4-2)	7-4-0
20	Maryland	9-3-0	Jerry Claiborne	9-2-0

Key Bowl Games

Rankings below reflect final regular season poll, released Dec. 4. No bowl for then #12 Michigan St. (probation).

Sugar—#2 Alabama over #1 Penn St., 14-7; **Rose**—#3 USC over #5 Michigan, 17-10; **Orange**—#4 Oklahoma over #6 Nebraska, 31-24; **Gator**—#7 Clemson over #20 Ohio St., 17-15; **Fiesta**—#8 Arkansas tied #15 UCLA, 10-10; **Cotton**—#10 Notre Dame over #9 Houston, 35-34.

1980

		After Bowls	Head Coach	Regular Season
1	Georgia	12-0-0	Vince Dooley	11-0-0
2	Pittsburgh	11-1-0	Jackie Sherrill	10-1-0
3	Oklahoma	10-2-0	Barry Switzer	9-2-0
4	Michigan	10-2-0	Bo Schembechler	9-2-0
5	Florida St.	10-2-0	Bobby Bowden	10-1-0
6	Alabama	10-2-0	Bear Bryant	9-2-0
7	Nebraska	10-2-0	Tom Osborne	9-2-0
8	Penn St.	10-2-0	Joe Paterno	9-2-0
9	Notre Dame	9-2-1	Dan Devine	9-1-1
10	North Carolina	11-1-0	Dick Crum	10-1-0
11	USC	8-2-1	John Robinson	same
12	BYU	12-1-0	LaVell Edwards	11-1-0
13	UCLA	9-2-0	Terry Donahue	same
14	Baylor	10-2-0	Grant Teaff	10-1-0
15	Ohio St.	9-3-0	Earle Bruce	9-2-0
16	Washington	9-3-0	Don James	9-2-0
17	Purdue	9-3-0	Jim Young	8-3-0
18	Miami-FL	9-3-0	H. Schnellenberger	8-3-0
19	Mississippi St.	9-3-0	Emory Bellard	9-2-0
20	SMU	8-4-0	Ron Meyer	8-3-0

Key Bowl Games

Rankings below reflect final regular season poll, released Dec. 8.

Sugar—#1 Georgia over #7 Notre Dame, 17-10; **Orange**—#4 Oklahoma over #2 Florida St., 18-17; **Gator**—#3 Pitt over #18 S. Carolina, 37-9; **Rose**—#5 Michigan over #16 Washington, 23-6; **Cotton**—#9 Alabama over #6 Baylor, 30-2; **Sun**—#8 Nebraska over #17 Miss. St., 31-17; **Fiesta**—#10 Penn St. over #11 Ohio St., 31-19; **Bluebonnet**—#13 N. Carolina over Texas, 16-7.

1979

		After Bowls	Head Coach	Regular Season
1	Alabama	12-0-0	Bear Bryant	11-0-0
2	USC	11-0-1	John Robinson	10-0-1
3	Oklahoma	11-1-0	Barry Switzer	10-1-0
4	Ohio St.	11-1-0	Earle Bruce	11-0-0
5	Houston	11-1-0	Bill Yeoman	10-1-0
6	Florida St.	11-1-0	Bobby Bowden	11-0-0
7	Pittsburgh	11-1-0	Jackie Sherrill	10-1-0
8	Arkansas	10-2-0	Lou Holtz	10-1-0
9	Nebraska	10-2-0	Tom Osborne	10-1-0
10	Purdue	10-2-0	Jim Young	9-2-0
11	Washington	9-3-0	Don James	8-3-0
12	Texas	9-3-0	Fred Akers	9-2-0
13	BYU	11-1-0	LaVell Edwards	11-0-0
14	Baylor	8-4-0	Grant Teaff	7-4-0
15	North Carolina	8-3-1	Dick Crum	7-3-1
16	Auburn	8-3-0	Doug Barfield	same
17	Temple	10-2-0	Wayne Hardin	9-2-0
18	Michigan	8-4-0	Bo Schembechler	8-3-0
19	Indiana	8-4-0	Lee Corso	7-4-0
20	Penn St.	8-4-0	Joe Paterno	7-4-0

Key Bowl Games

Rankings below reflect final regular season poll, released Dec. 3. No bowl for then #17 Auburn (probation).

Sugar—#2 Alabama over #6 Arkansas, 24-9; **Rose**—#3 USC over #1 Ohio St., 17-16; **Orange**—#5 Oklahoma over #4 Florida St., 24-7; **Sun**—#13 Washington over #11 Texas, 14-7; **Cotton**—#8 Houston over #7 Nebraska, 17-14; **Fiesta**—#10 Pitt over Arizona, 16-10.

1981

		After Bowls	Head Coach	Regular Season
1	Clemson	12-0-0	Danny Ford	11-0-0
2	Texas	10-1-1	Fred Akers	9-1-1
3	Penn St.	10-2-0	Joe Paterno	9-2-0
4	Pittsburgh	11-1-0	Jackie Sherrill	10-1-0
5	SMU	10-1-0	Ron Meyer	same
6	Georgia	10-2-0	Vince Dooley	10-1-0
7	Alabama	9-2-1	Bear Bryant	9-1-1
8	Miami-FL	9-2-0	H. Schnellenberger	same
9	North Carolina	10-2-0	Dick Crum	9-2-0
10	Washington	10-2-0	Don James	9-2-0
11	Nebraska	9-3-0	Tom Osborne	9-2-0
12	Michigan	9-3-0	Bo Schembechler	8-3-0
13	BYU	11-2-0	LaVell Edwards	10-2-0
14	USC	9-3-0	John Robinson	9-2-0
15	Ohio St.	9-3-0	Earle Bruce	8-3-0
16	Arizona St.	9-2-0	Darryl Rogers	same
17	West Virginia	9-3-0	Don Nehlen	8-3-0
18	Iowa	8-4-0	Hayden Fry	8-3-0
19	Missouri	8-4-0	Warren Powers	7-4-0
20	Oklahoma	7-4-1	Barry Switzer	6-4-1

Key Bowl Games

Rankings below reflect final regular season poll, released Nov. 30. No bowl for then #5 SMU (probation), #9 Miami-FL (probation), and #17 Ariz. St. (probation).

Orange—#1 Clemson over #4 Nebraska, 22-15; **Sugar**—#10 Pitt over #2 Georgia, 24-20; **Cotton**—#6 Texas over #3 Alabama, 14-12; **Fiesta**—#7 Penn St. over #8 USC, 26-10; **Gator**—#11 N. Carolina over Arkansas, 31-27; **Rose**—#12 Washington over #13 Iowa, 28-0.

1982

		After Bowls	Head Coach	Regular Season
1	Penn St.	11-1-0	Joe Paterno	10-1-0
2	SMU	11-0-1	Bobby Collins	10-0-1
3	Nebraska	12-1-0	Tom Osborne	11-1-0
4	Georgia	11-1-0	Vince Dooley	11-0-0
5	UCLA	10-1-1	Terry Donahue	9-1-1
6	Arizona St.	10-2-0	Darryl Rogers	9-2-0
7	Washington	10-2-0	Don James	9-2-0
8	Clemson	9-1-1	Danny Ford	same
9	Arkansas	9-2-1	Lou Holtz	8-2-1
10	Pittsburgh	9-3-0	Foge Fazio	9-2-0
11	LSU	8-3-1	Jerry Stovall	8-2-1
12	Ohio St.	9-3-0	Earle Bruce	8-3-0
13	Florida St.	9-3-0	Bobby Bowden	8-3-0
14	Auburn	9-3-0	Pat Dye	8-3-0
15	USC	8-3-0	John Robinson	same
16	Oklahoma	8-4-0	Barry Switzer	8-3-0
17	Texas	9-3-0	Fred Akers	9-2-0
18	North Carolina	8-4-0	Dick Crum	7-4-0
19	West Virginia	9-3-0	Don Nehlen	9-2-0
20	Maryland	8-4-0	Bobby Ross	8-3-0

Key Bowl Games

Rankings below reflect final regular season poll, released Dec. 6. No bowl for then #7 Clemson (probation) and #15 USC (probation).

Sugar–#2 Penn St. over #1 Georgia, 27-23; **Orange**–#3 Nebraska over #13 LSU, 21-20; **Cotton**–#4 SMU over #6 Pitt, 7-3; **Rose**–#5 UCLA over #19 Michigan, 24-14; **Aloha**–#9 Washington over #16 Maryland, 21-20; **Fiesta**–#11 Ariz. St. over #12 Oklahoma, 32-21; **Bluebonnet**–#14 Arkansas over Florida, 28-24.

1984

		After Bowls	Head Coach	Regular Season
1	BYU	13-0-0	LaVell Edwards	12-0-0
2	Washington	11-1-0	Don James	10-1-0
3	Florida	9-1-1	Charley Pell (0-1-1) & Galen Hall (9-0)	same
4	Nebraska	10-2-0	Tom Osborne	9-2-0
5	Boston College	10-2-0	Jack Bicknell	9-2-0
6	Oklahoma	9-2-1	Barry Switzer	9-1-1
7	Oklahoma St.	10-2-0	Pat Jones	9-2-0
8	SMU	10-2-0	Bobby Collins	9-2-0
9	UCLA	9-3-0	Terry Donahue	8-3-0
10	USC	9-3-0	Ted Tollner	8-3-0
11	South Carolina	10-2-0	Joe Morrison	10-1-0
12	Maryland	9-3-0	Bobby Ross	8-3-0
13	Ohio St.	9-3-0	Earle Bruce	9-2-0
14	Auburn	9-4-0	Pat Dye	8-4-0
15	LSU	8-3-1	Bill Arnsparger	8-2-1
16	Iowa	8-4-1	Hayden Fry	7-4-1
17	Florida St.	7-3-2	Bobby Bowden	7-3-1
18	Miami-FL	8-5-0	Jimmy Johnson	8-4-0
19	Kentucky	9-3-0	Jerry Claiborne	8-3-0
20	Virginia	8-2-2	George Welsh	7-2-2

Key Bowl Games

Rankings below reflect final regular season poll, released Dec. 3. No bowl for then #3 Florida (probation).

Holiday–#1 BYU over Michigan, 24-17; **Orange**–#4 Washington over #2 Oklahoma, 28-17; **Sugar**–#5 Nebraska over #11 LSU, 28-10; **Rose**–#18 USC over #6 Ohio St., 20-17; **Gator**–#9 Okla. St. over #7 S. Carolina, 21-14; **Cotton**–#8 BC over Houston, 45-28; **Aloha**–#10 SMU over #17 Notre Dame, 27-20.

1983

		After Bowls	Head Coach	Regular Season
1	Miami-FL	11-1-0	H. Schnellenberger	10-1-0
2	Nebraska	12-1-0	Tom Osborne	12-0-0
3	Auburn	11-1-0	Pat Dye	10-1-0
4	Georgia	10-1-1	Vince Dooley	9-1-1
5	Texas	11-1-0	Fred Akers	11-0-0
6	Florida	9-2-1	Charley Pell	8-2-1
7	BYU	11-1-0	LaVell Edwards	10-1-0
8	Michigan	9-3-0	Bo Schembechler	9-2-0
9	Ohio St.	9-3-0	Earle Bruce	8-3-0
10	Illinois	10-2-0	Mike White	10-1-0
11	Clemson	9-1-1	Danny Ford	same
12	SMU	10-2-0	Bobby Collins	10-1-0
13	Air Force	10-2-0	Ken Hatfield	9-2-0
14	Iowa	9-3-0	Hayden Fry	9-2-0
15	Alabama	8-4-0	Ray Perkins	7-4-0
16	West Virginia	9-3-0	Don Nehlen	8-3-0
17	UCLA	7-4-1	Terry Donahue	6-4-1
18	Pittsburgh	8-3-1	Foge Fazio	8-2-1
19	Boston College	9-3-0	Jack Bicknell	9-2-0
20	East Carolina	8-3-0	Ed Emory	same

Key Bowl Games

Rankings below reflect final regular season poll, released Dec. 5. No bowl for then #12 Clemson (probation).

Orange–#5 Miami-FL over #1 Nebraska, 31-30; **Cotton**–#7 Georgia over #2 Texas, 10-9; **Sugar**–#3 Auburn over #8 Michigan, 9-7; **Rose**–UCLA over #4 Illinois, 45-9; **Holiday**–#9 BYU over Missouri, 21-17; **Gator**–#11 Florida over #10 Iowa, 14-6; **Fiesta**–#14 Ohio St. over #15 Pitt, 28-23.

1985

		After Bowls	Head Coach	Regular Season
1	Oklahoma	11-1-0	Barry Switzer	10-1-0
2	Michigan	10-1-1	Bo Schembechler	9-1-1
3	Penn St.	11-1-0	Joe Paterno	11-0-0
4	Tennessee	9-1-2	Johnny Majors	8-1-2
5	Florida	9-1-1	Galen Hall	same
6	Texas A&M	10-2-0	Jackie Sherrill	9-2-0
7	UCLA	9-2-1	Terry Donahue	8-2-1
8	Air Force	12-1-0	Fisher DeBerry	11-1-0
9	Miami-FL	10-2-0	Jimmy Johnson	10-1-0
10	Iowa	10-2-0	Hayden Fry	10-1-0
11	Nebraska	9-3-0	Tom Osborne	9-2-0
12	Arkansas	10-2-0	Ken Hatfield	9-2-0
13	Alabama	9-2-1	Ray Perkins	8-2-1
14	Ohio St.	9-3-0	Earle Bruce	8-3-0
15	Florida St.	9-3-0	Bobby Bowden	8-3-0
16	BYU	11-3-0	LaVell Edwards	11-2-0
17	Baylor	9-3-0	Grant Teaff	8-3-0
18	Maryland	9-3-0	Bobby Ross	8-3-0
19	Georgia Tech	9-2-1	Bill Curry	8-2-1
20	LSU	9-2-1	Bill Arnsparger	9-1-1

Key Bowl Games

Rankings below reflect final regular season poll, released Dec. 9. No bowl for then #6 Florida (probation).

Orange–#3 Oklahoma over #1 Penn St., 25-10; **Sugar**–#8 Tennessee over #2 Miami-FL, 35-7; **Rose**–UCLA over #4 Iowa, 45-28; **Fiesta**–#5 Michigan over #7 Nebraska, 27-23; **Bluebonnet**–#10 Air Force over Texas, 24-16; **Cotton**–#11 Texas A&M over #16 Auburn, 36-16.

Associated Press Final Polls (Cont.)

1986

		After Bowls	Head Coach	Regular Season
1	Penn St.	12-0-0	Joe Paterno	11-0-0
2	Miami-FL	11-1-0	Jimmy Johnson	11-0-0
3	Oklahoma	11-1-0	Barry Switzer	10-1-0
4	Arizona St.	10-1-1	John Cooper	9-1-1
5	Nebraska	10-2-0	Tom Osborne	9-2-0
6	Auburn	10-2-0	Pat Dye	9-2-0
7	Ohio St.	10-3-0	Earle Bruce	9-3-0
8	Michigan	11-2-0	Bo Schembechler	11-1-0
9	Alabama	10-3-0	Ray Perkins	9-3-0
10	LSU	9-3-0	Bill Arnsparger	9-2-0
11	Arizona	9-3-0	Larry Smith	8-3-0
12	Baylor	9-3-0	Grant Teaff	8-3-0
13	Texas A&M	9-3-0	Jackie Sherrill	9-2-0
14	UCLA	8-3-1	Terry Donahue	7-3-1
15	Arkansas	9-3-0	Ken Hatfield	9-2-0
16	Iowa	9-3-0	Hayden Fry	8-3-0
17	Clemson	8-2-2	Danny Ford	7-2-2
18	Washington	8-3-1	Don James	8-2-1
19	Boston College	9-3-0	Jack Bicknell	8-3-0
20	Virginia Tech	9-2-1	Bill Dooley	8-2-1

Key Bowl Games

Rankings below reflect final regular season poll, released Dec. 1.

Fiesta—#2 Penn St. over #1 Miami-FL, 14-10; **Orange**—#3 Oklahoma over #9 Arkansas, 42-8; **Rose**—#7 Ariz. St. over #4 Michigan, 22-15; **Sugar**—#6 Nebraska over #5 LSU, 30-15; **Cotton**—#11 Ohio St. over #8 Texas A&M, 28-12; **Citrus**—#10 Auburn over USC, 16-7; **Sun**—#13 Alabama over #12 Washington, 28-6.

1987

		After Bowls	Head Coach	Regular Season
1	Miami-FL	12-0-0	Jimmy Johnson	11-0-0
2	Florida St.	11-1-0	Bobby Bowden	10-1-0
3	Oklahoma	11-1-0	Barry Switzer	11-0-0
4	Syracuse	11-0-1	Dick MacPherson	11-0-0
5	LSU	10-1-1	Mike Archer	9-1-1
6	Nebraska	10-2-0	Tom Osborne	10-1-0
7	Auburn	9-1-2	Pat Dye	9-1-1
8	Michigan St.	9-2-1	George Perles	8-2-1
9	UCLA	10-2-0	Terry Donahue	9-2-0
10	Texas A&M	10-2-0	Jackie Sherrill	9-2-0
11	Oklahoma St.	10-2-0	Pat Jones	9-2-0
12	Clemson	10-2-0	Danny Ford	9-2-0
13	Georgia	9-3-0	Vince Dooley	8-3-0
14	Tennessee	10-2-1	Johnny Majors	9-2-1
15	South Carolina	8-4-0	Joe Morrison	8-3-0
16	Iowa	10-3-0	Hayden Fry	9-3-0
17	Notre Dame	8-4-0	Lou Holtz	8-3-0
18	USC	8-4-0	Larry Smith	8-3-0
19	Michigan	8-4-0	Bo Schembechler	7-4-0
20	Arizona St.	7-4-1	John Cooper	6-4-1

Key Bowl Games

Rankings below reflect final regular season poll, released Dec. 7.

Orange—#2 Miami-FL over #1 Oklahoma, 20-14; **Fiesta**—#3 Florida St. over #5 Nebraska, 31-28; **Sugar**—#4 Syracuse tied #6 Auburn, 16-16; **Gator**—#7 LSU over #9 S. Carolina, 30-13; **Rose**—#8 Mich. St. over #16 USC, 20-17; **Aloha**—#10 UCLA over Florida, 20-16; **Cotton**—#13 Texas A&M over #12 Notre Dame, 35-10.

1988

		After Bowls	Head Coach	Regular Season
1	Notre Dame	12-0-0	Lou Holtz	11-0-0
2	Miami-FL	11-1-0	Jimmy Johnson	10-1-0
3	Florida St.	11-1-0	Bobby Bowden	10-1-0
4	Michigan	9-2-1	Bo Schembechler	8-2-1
5	West Virginia	11-1-0	Don Nehlen	11-0-0
6	UCLA	10-2-0	Terry Donahue	9-2-0
7	USC	10-2-0	Larry Smith	10-1-0
8	Auburn	10-2-0	Pat Dye	10-1-0
9	Clemson	10-2-0	Danny Ford	9-2-0
10	Nebraska	11-2-0	Tom Osborne	11-1-0
11	Oklahoma St.	10-2-0	Pat Jones	9-2-0
12	Arkansas	10-2-0	Ken Hatfield	10-1-0
13	Syracuse	10-2-0	Dick MacPherson	9-2-0
14	Oklahoma	9-3-0	Barry Switzer	9-2-0
15	Georgia	9-3-0	Vince Dooley	8-3-0
16	Washington St.	9-3-0	Dennis Erickson	8-3-0
17	Alabama	9-3-0	Bill Curry	8-3-0
18	Houston	9-3-0	Jack Pardee	9-2-0
19	LSU	8-4-0	Mike Archer	8-3-0
20	Indiana	8-3-1	Bill Mallory	7-3-1

Key Bowl Games

Rankings below reflect final regular season poll, released Dec. 5.

Fiesta—#1 Notre Dame over #3 West Va., 34-21; **Orange**—#2 Miami-FL over #6 Nebraska, 23-3; **Sugar**—#4 Florida St. over #7 Auburn, 13-7; **Rose**—#11 Michigan over #5 USC, 22-14; **Cotton**—#9 UCLA over #8 Arkansas, 17-3; **Citrus**—#13 Clemson over #10 Oklahoma, 13-6.

1989

		After Bowls	Head Coach	Regular Season
1	Miami-FL	11-1-0	Dennis Erickson	10-1-0
2	Notre Dame	12-1-0	Lou Holtz	11-1-0
3	Florida St.	10-2-0	Bobby Bowden	9-2-0
4	Colorado	11-1-0	Bill McCartney	11-0-0
5	Tennessee	11-1-0	Johnny Majors	10-1-0
6	Auburn	10-2-0	Pat Dye	9-2-0
7	Michigan	10-2-0	Bo Schembechler	10-1-0
8	USC	9-2-1	Larry Smith	8-2-1
9	Alabama	10-2-0	Bill Curry	10-1-0
10	Illinois	10-2-0	John Mackovic	9-2-0
11	Nebraska	10-2-0	Tom Osborne	10-1-0
12	Clemson	10-2-0	Danny Ford	9-2-0
13	Arkansas	10-2-0	Ken Hatfield	10-1-0
14	Houston	9-2-0	Jack Pardee	same
15	Penn St.	8-3-1	Joe Paterno	7-3-1
16	Michigan St.	8-4-0	George Perles	7-4-0
17	Pittsburgh	8-3-1	Mike Gottfried (7-3-1) & Paul Hackett (1-0)	7-3-1
18	Virginia	10-3-0	George Welsh	10-2-0
19	Texas Tech	9-3-0	Spike Dykes	8-3-0
20	Texas A&M	8-4-0	R.C. Slocum	8-3-0
21	West Virginia	8-3-1	Don Nehlen	8-2-1
22	BYU	10-3-0	LaVell Edwards	10-2-0
23	Washington	8-4-0	Don James	7-4-0
24	Ohio St.	8-4-0	John Cooper	8-3-0
25	Arizona	8-4-0	Dick Tomey	7-4-0

Key Bowl Games

Rankings below reflect final regular season poll, released Dec. 11. No bowl for then #13 Houston (probation).

Orange—#4 Notre Dame over #1 Colorado, 21-6; **Sugar**—#2 Miami-FL over #7 Alabama, 33-25; **Rose**—#12 USC over #3 Michigan, 17-10; **Fiesta**—#5 Florida St. over #6 Nebraska, 41-17; **Cotton**—#8 Tennessee over #10 Arkansas, 31-27; **Hall of Fame**—#9 Auburn over #21 Ohio St., 31-14; **Citrus**—#11 Illinois over #15 Virginia, 31-21.

1990

		Head Coach	Regular Season
	After Bowls	**Head Coach**	**Regular Season**
1	Colorado 11-1-1	Bill McCartney	10-1-1
2	Georgia Tech . . .11-0-1	Bobby Ross	10-0-1
3	Miami-FL 10-2-0	Dennis Erickson	9-2-0
4	Florida St. 10-2-0	Bobby Bowden	9-2-0
5	Washington 10-2-0	Don James	9-2-0
6	Notre Dame 9-3-0	Lou Holtz	9-2-0
7	Michigan 9-3-0	Gary Moeller	8-3-0
8	Tennessee 9-2-2	Johnny Majors	8-2-2
9	Clemson 10-2-0	Ken Hatfield	9-2-0
10	Houston 10-1-0	John Jenkins	same
11	Penn St. 9-3-0	Joe Paterno	9-2-0
12	Texas 10-2-0	David McWilliams	10-1-0
13	Florida 9-2-0	Steve Spurrier	same
14	Louisville 10-1-1	H. Schnellenberger	9-1-1
15	Texas A&M 9-3-1	R.C. Slocum	8-3-1
16	Michigan St. 8-3-1	George Perles	7-3-1
17	Oklahoma 8-3-0	Gary Gibbs	same
18	Iowa 8-4-0	Hayden Fry	8-3-0
19	Auburn 8-3-1	Pat Dye	7-3-1
20	USC 8-4-1	Larry Smith	8-3-1
21	Mississippi 9-3-0	Billy Brewer	9-2-0
22	BYU 10-3-0	LaVell Edwards	10-2-0
23	Virginia 8-4-0	George Welsh	8-3-0
24	Nebraska 9-3-0	Tom Osborne	9-2-0
25	Illinois 8-4-0	John Mackovic	8-3-0

Key Bowl Games

Rankings below reflect final regular season poll, released Dec. 3. No bowl for then #9 Houston (probation), #11 Florida (probation) and #20 Oklahoma (probation).

Orange–#1 Colorado over #5 Notre Dame, 10-9; **Citrus**–#2 Ga. Tech over #19 Nebraska, 45-21; **Cotton**–#4 Miami-FL over #3 Texas, 46-3; **Blockbuster**–#6 Florida St. over #7 Penn St., 24-17; **Rose**–#8 Washington over #17 Iowa, 46-34; **Sugar**–#10 Tennessee over Virginia, 23-22; **Gator**–#12 Michigan over #15 Ole Miss, 35-3.

1991

		Head Coach	Regular Season
	After Bowls	**Head Coach**	**Regular Season**
1	Miami-FL 12-0-0	Dennis Erickson	11-0-0
2	Washington 12-0-0	Don James	11-0-0
3	Penn St. 11-2-0	Joe Paterno	10-2-0
4	Florida St. 11-2-0	Bobby Bowden	10-2-0
5	Alabama 11-1-0	Gene Stallings	10-1-0
6	Michigan 10-2-0	Gary Moeller	10-1-0
7	Florida 10-2-0	Steve Spurrier	10-1-0
8	California 10-2-0	Bruce Snyder	9-2-0
9	East Carolina 11-1-0	Bill Lewis	10-1-0
10	Iowa 10-1-1	Hayden Fry	10-1-0
11	Syracuse 10-2-0	Paul Pasqualoni	9-2-0
12	Texas A&M 10-2-0	R.C. Slocum	10-1-0
13	Notre Dame 10-3-0	Lou Holtz	9-3-0
14	Tennessee 9-3-0	Johnny Majors	9-2-0
15	Nebraska 9-2-1	Tom Osborne	9-1-1
16	Oklahoma 9-3-0	Gary Gibbs	8-3-0
17	Georgia 9-3-0	Ray Goff	8-3-0
18	Clemson 9-2-1	Ken Hatfield	9-1-1
19	UCLA 9-3-0	Terry Donahue	8-3-0
20	Colorado 8-3-1	Bill McCartney	8-2-1
21	Tulsa 10-2-0	David Rader	9-2-0
22	Stanford 8-4-0	Dennis Green	8-3-0
23	BYU 8-3-2	LaVell Edwards	8-3-1
24	N.C. State 9-3-0	Dick Sheridan	9-2-0
25	Air Force 10-3-0	Fisher DeBerry	9-3-0

Key Bowl Games

Rankings below reflect final regular season poll, taken Dec. 2.

Orange–#1 Miami-FL over #11 Nebraska, 22-0; **Rose**–#2 Washington over #4 Michigan, 34-14; **Sugar**–#18 Notre Dame over #3 Florida, 39-28; **Cotton**–#5 Florida St. over #9 Texas A&M, 10-2; **Fiesta**–#6 Penn St. over #10 Tennessee, 42-17; **Holiday**–#7 Iowa tied BYU, 13-13; **Blockbuster**–#8 Alabama over #15 Colorado, 30-25; **Citrus**–#14 California over #13 Clemson, 37-13; **Peach**–#12 East Carolina over #21 N.C. State, 37-34.

1992

		Head Coach	Regular Season
	After Bowls	**Head Coach**	**Regular Season**
1	Alabama 13-0-0	Gene Stallings	12-0-0
2	Florida St. 11-1-0	Bobby Bowden	10-1-0
3	Miami-FL 11-1-0	Dennis Erickson	11-0-0
4	Notre Dame 10-1-1	Lou Holtz	9-1-1
5	Michigan 9-0-3	Gary Moeller	8-0-3
6	Syracuse 10-2-0	Paul Pasqualoni	9-2-0
7	Texas A&M 12-1-0	R.C. Slocum	12-0-0
8	Georgia 10-2-0	Ray Goff	9-2-0
9	Stanford 10-3-0	Bill Walsh	9-3-0
10	Florida 9-4-0	Steve Spurrier	8-4-0
11	Washington 9-3-0	Don James	9-2-0
12	Tennessee 9-3-0	Johnny Majors (5-3) & Phillip Fulmer (4-0)	8-3-0
13	Colorado 9-2-1	Bill McCartney	9-1-1
14	Nebraska 9-3-0	Tom Osborne	9-2-0
15	Washington St. 9-3-0	Mike Price	8-3-0
16	Mississippi 9-3-0	Billy Brewer	8-3-0
17	N.C. State 9-3-1	Dick Sheridan	9-2-1
18	Ohio St. 8-3-1	John Cooper	8-2-1
19	North Carolina 9-3-0	Mack Brown	8-3-0
20	Hawaii 11-2-0	Bob Wagner	10-2-0
21	Boston College 8-3-1	Tom Coughlin	8-2-1
22	Kansas 8-4-0	Glen Mason	7-4-0
23	Mississippi St. 7-5-0	Jackie Sherrill	7-4-0
24	Fresno St. 9-4-0	Jim Sweeney	9-3-0
25	Wake Forest 8-4-0	Bill Dooley	7-4-0

Key Bowl Games

Rankings below reflect final regular season poll, taken Dec. 5.

Sugar–#2 Alabama over #1. Miami-FL, 34-13; **Orange**–#3 Florida St. over #11 Nebraska, 27-14; **Cotton**–#5 Notre Dame over #4 Texas A&M, 28-3; **Fiesta**–#6 Syracuse over #10 Colorado, 26-22; **Rose**–#7 Michigan over #9 Washington, 38-31; **Citrus**–#8 Georgia over #15 Ohio St., 21-14.

All-Time AP Top 20

The composite AP Top 20 from the 1936 season through the 2001 season, based on the final rankings of each year. The final AP poll has been taken after the bowl games in 1965 and since 1968. Team point totals are based on 20 points for all 1st place finishes, 19 for each 2nd, etc. Also listed are the number of times each team has been named national champion by AP and times ranked in the final Top 10 and Top 20.

		Pts	No.1	Top 10	Top 20
1	Notre Dame 632		8	34	45
2	Michigan 602		2	34	49
3	Oklahoma 593		7	31	43
4	Alabama 564		6	31	42
5	Nebraska 546		4	29	41
6	Ohio St. 518		3	24	41
7	Tennessee 450		2	22	37
8	Texas 431		2	20	34
9	USC 414		3	20	36
10	Penn St. 403		2	21	35
11	UCLA 322		0	16	29
12	Florida St. 320		2	16	21
13	Miami-FL 310		5	15	25
14	LSU 291		1	15	26
15	Auburn 284		1	14	27
16	Arkansas 267		0	13	25
17	Georgia 262		1	14	24
18	Florida 257		1	13	21
19	Michigan St. 252		1	13	20
20	Washington 222		0	11	21

Associated Press Final Polls (Cont.)

1993

		After Bowls	Head Coach	Regular Season
1	Florida St	12-1-0	Bobby Bowden	11-1-0
2	Notre Dame	11-1-0	Lou Holtz	10-1-0
3	Nebraska	11-1-0	Tom Osborne	11-0-0
4	Auburn	11-0-0	Terry Bowden	11-0-0
5	Florida	11-2-0	Steve Spurrier	10-2-0
6	Wisconsin	10-1-1	Barry Alvarez	9-1-1
7	West Virginia	11-1-0	Don Nehlen	11-0-0
8	Penn St	10-2-0	Joe Paterno	9-2-0
9	Texas A&M	10-2-0	R.C. Slocum	10-1-0
10	Arizona	10-2-0	Dick Tomey	9-2-0
11	Ohio St	10-1-1	John Cooper	9-1-1
12	Tennessee	9-2-1	Phillip Fulmer	9-1-1
13	Boston College	9-3-0	Tom Coughlin	8-3-0
14	Alabama	9-3-1	Gene Stallings	8-3-1
15	Miami-FL	9-3-0	Dennis Erickson	9-2-0
16	Colorado	8-3-1	Bill McCartney	7-3-1
17	Oklahoma	9-3-0	Gary Gibbs	8-3-0
18	UCLA	8-4-0	Terry Donahue	8-3-0
19	North Carolina	10-3-0	Mack Brown	10-2-0
20	Kansas St	9-2-1	Bill Snyder	8-2-1
21	Michigan	8-4-0	Gary Moeller	7-4-0
22	Va. Tech	9-3-0	Frank Beamer	9-2-0
23	Clemson	9-3-0	Ken Hatfield (8-3) & Tommy West (1-0)	8-3-0
24	Louisville	9-3-0	H. Schnellenberger	8-3-0
25	California	9-4-0	Keith Gilbertson	8-4-0

Key Bowl Games

Rankings below reflect final regular season poll, taken Dec. 5. No bowl for then #5 Auburn (probation).
Orange–#1 Florida St. over #2 Nebraska, 18-16; **Sugar**–#8 Florida over #3 West Virginia, 41-7; **Cotton**–#4 Notre Dame over #7 Texas A&M, 24-21; **Citrus**–#13 Penn St. over #6 Tennessee, 31-13; **Rose**–#9 Wisconsin over #14 UCLA, 21-16; **Fiesta**–#11 Arizona over #10 Miami-FL, 29-0; **Holiday**–#11 Ohio St. over BYU, 28-21; **Gator**–#18 Alabama over #12 North Carolina, 24-10; **Carquest**–#15 Boston College over Virginia, 31-13.

1994

		After Bowls	Head Coach	Regular Season
1	Nebraska	13-0-0	Tom Osborne	12-0-0
2	Penn St	12-0-0	Joe Paterno	11-0-0
3	Colorado	11-1-0	Bill McCartney	10-1-0
4	Florida St	10-1-1	Bobby Bowden	9-1-1
5	Alabama	12-1-0	Gene Stallings	11-1-0
6	Miami-FL	10-2-0	Dennis Erickson	10-1-0
7	Florida	10-2-1	Steve Spurrier	10-1-1
8	Texas A&M	10-0-1	R.C. Slocum	same
9	Auburn	9-1-1	Terry Bowden	same
10	Utah	10-2-0	Ron McBride	9-2-0
11	Oregon	9-4-0	Rich Brooks	9-3-0
12	Michigan	8-4-0	Gary Moeller	7-4-0
13	USC	8-3-1	John Robinson	7-3-1
14	Ohio St	9-4-0	John Cooper	9-3-0
15	Virginia	9-3-0	George Welsh	8-3-0
16	Colorado St	10-2-0	Sonny Lubick	10-1-0
17	N.C. State	9-3-0	Mike O'Cain	8-3-0
18	BYU	10-3-0	LaVell Edwards	9-3-0
19	Kansas St	9-3-0	Bill Snyder	9-2-0
20	Arizona	8-4-0	Dick Tomey	8-3-0
21	Washington St	8-4-0	Mike Price	7-4-0
22	Tennessee	8-4-0	Phillip Fulmer	7-4-0
23	Boston College	7-4-1	Dan Henning	6-4-1
24	Mississippi St	8-4-0	Jackie Sherrill	8-3-0
25	Texas	8-4-0	John Mackovic	7-4-0

Key Bowl Games

Rankings below reflect final regular season poll, taken Dec. 4. No bowls for then #8 Texas A&M (probation) and #9 Auburn (probation).
Orange–#1 Nebraska over #3 Miami-FL, 24-17; **Rose**–#2 Penn St. over #12 Oregon, 38-20; **Fiesta**–#4 Colorado over Notre Dame, 41-24; **Sugar**–#7 Florida St. over #5 Florida, 23-17; **Citrus**–#6 Alabama over #13 Ohio St., 24-17; **Freedom**–#14 Utah over #15 Arizona, 16-13.

1995

		After Bowls	Head Coach	Regular Season
1	Nebraska	12-0-0	Tom Osborne	11-0-0
2	Florida	12-1-0	Steve Spurrier	12-0-0
3	Tennessee	11-1-0	Phillip Fulmer	10-1-0
4	Florida St	10-2-0	Bobby Bowden	9-2-0
5	Colorado	10-2-0	Rick Neuheisel	9-2-0
6	Ohio St	11-2-0	John Cooper	11-1-0
7	Kansas St	10-2-0	Bill Snyder	9-2-0
8	Northwestern	10-2-0	Gary Barnett	10-1-0
9	Kansas	10-2-0	Glen Mason	9-2-0
10	Va. Tech	10-2-0	Frank Beamer	9-2-0
11	Notre Dame	9-3-0	Lou Holtz	9-2-0
12	USC	9-2-1	John Robinson	8-2-1
13	Penn St	9-3-0	Joe Paterno	8-3-0
14	Texas	10-2-1	John Mackovic	10-1-1
15	Texas A&M	9-3-0	R.C. Slocum	8-3-0
16	Virginia	9-4-0	George Welsh	8-4-0
17	Michigan	9-4-0	Lloyd Carr	9-3-0
18	Oregon	9-3-0	Mike Bellotti	9-2-0
19	Syracuse	9-3-0	Paul Pasqualoni	8-3-0
20	Miami-FL	8-3-0	Butch Davis	same
21	Alabama	8-3-0	Gene Stallings	same
22	Auburn	8-4-0	Terry Bowden	8-3-0
23	Texas Tech	9-3-0	Spike Dykes	8-3-0
24	Toledo	11-0-1	Gary Pinkel	10-0-1
25	Iowa	8-4-0	Hayden Fry	7-4-0

Key Bowl Games

Rankings below reflect final regular season poll, taken Dec. 3. No bowl for then #21 Alabama (probation) and #22 Miami-FL (probation).
Fiesta–#1 Nebraska over #2 Florida, 62-24; **Rose**–#17 USC over #3 Northwestern, 41-32; **Citrus**–#4 (tie) Tennessee over #4 (tie) Ohio St., 20-14; **Orange**–#8 Florida St. over #6 Notre Dame, 31-26; **Cotton**–#7 Colorado over #12 Oregon, 38-6; **Sugar**–#13 Va. Tech over #9 Texas, 28-10; **Holiday**–#10 Kansas St. over Colo. St., 54-21; **Aloha**–#11 Kansas over UCLA, 51-30; **Alamo**–#19 Texas A&M over #14 Michigan, 22-20; **Outback**–#15 Penn St. over #16 Auburn, 43-14; **Peach**–#18 Virginia over Georgia, 34-27; **Gator**–Syracuse over #23 Clemson, 41-0.

1996

	After Bowls	Head Coach	Regular Season
1	Florida............12-1	Steve Spurrier	11-1
2	Ohio St.............11-1	John Cooper	10-1
3	Florida St 11-1	Bobby Bowden	11-0
4	Arizona St. 11-1	Bruce Snyder	11-0
5	BYU 14-1	LaVell Edwards	13-1
6	Nebraska..........11-2	Tom Osborne	10-2
7	Penn St.............11-2	Joe Paterno	10-2
8	Colorado..........10-2	Rick Neuheisel	9-2
9	Tennessee 10-2	Phillip Fulmer	9-2
10	North Carolina.....10-2	Mack Brown	9-2
11	Alabama..........10-3	Gene Stallings	9-3
12	LSU...............10-2	Gerry DiNardo	9-2
13	Virginia Tech.......10-2	Frank Beamer	10-1
14	Miami-FL 9-3	Butch Davis	8-3
15	Northwestern 9-3	Gary Barnett	9-2
16	Washington.........9-3	Jim Lambright	9-2
17	Kansas St. 9-3	Bill Snyder	9-2
18	Iowa 9-3	Hayden Fry	8-3
19	Notre Dame 8-3	Lou Holtz	same
20	Michigan...........8-4	Lloyd Carr	8-3
21	Syracuse 9-3	Paul Pasqualoni	8-3
22	Wyoming 10-2	Joe Tiller	same
23	Texas 8-5	John Mackovic	8-4
24	Auburn............8-4	Terry Bowden	7-4
25	Army 10-2	Bob Sutton	10-1

Key Bowl Games

Rankings below reflect final regular season poll, taken Dec. 8. No bowl for then #18 Notre Dame and #22 Wyoming. **Sugar**–#3 Florida over #1 Florida St., 52-20; **Rose**–#4 Ohio St. over #2 Arizona St., 20-17; **Fiesta**–#7 Penn St. over #20 Texas, 38-15; **Cotton**–#5 BYU over #14 Kansas St., 19-15; **Citrus**–#9 Tennessee over #11 Northwestern, 48-28; **Orange**–#6 Nebraska over #10 Virginia Tech, 41-21; **Gator**–#12 North Carolina over #25 West Virginia, 20-13; **Outback**–#16 Alabama over #15 Michigan, 17-14. **Carquest**–#19 Miami over Virginia, 31-21.

1997

	After Bowls	Head Coach	Regular Season
1	Michigan..........12-0	Lloyd Carr	11-0
2	Nebraska 13-0	Tom Osborne	12-0
3	Florida St 11-1	Bobby Bowden	10-1
4	Florida............10-2	Steve Spurrier	9-2
5	UCLA.............10-2	Bob Toledo	9-2
6	North Carolina....11-1	Mack Brown (10-1) & Carl Torbush (1-0)	10-1
7	Tennessee 11-2	Phillip Fulmer	11-1
8	Kansas St...........11-1	Bill Snyder	10-1
9	Washington St......10-2	Mike Price	10-1
10	Georgia 10-2	Jim Donnan	9-2
11	Auburn 10-3	Terry Bowden	9-3
12	Ohio St.............10-3	John Cooper	10-2
13	LSU...............9-3	Gerry DiNardo	8-3
14	Arizona St..........8-3	Bruce Snyder	7-3
15	Purdue 9-3	Joe Tiller	8-3
16	Penn St. 9-3	Joe Paterno	9-2
17	Colorado St........11-2	Sonny Lubick	10-2
18	Washington.........8-4	Jim Lambright	7-4
19	So. Mississippi......9-3	Jeff Bower	8-3
20	Texas A&M 9-4	R.C. Slocum	9-3
21	Syracuse 9-4	Paul Pasqualoni	9-3
22	Mississippi.........8-4	Tommy Tuberville	7-4
23	Missouri 7-5	Larry Smith	6-5
24	Oklahoma St........8-4	Bobby Simmons	8-3
25	Georgia Tech 7-5	George O'Leary	6-5

Key Bowl Games

Rankings below reflect final regular season poll, taken Dec. 7. **Rose**–#1 Michigan over #7 Washington St., 21-16; **Orange**–#2 Nebraska over #3 Tennessee, 42-17; **Sugar**–#4 Florida St. over #10 Ohio St., 31-14; **Gator**–#5 North Carolina over Virginia Tech, 42-3; **Cotton**–#6 UCLA over #19 Texas A&M, 29-23; **Citrus**–#8 Florida over #12 Penn St., 21-6; **Fiesta**–#9 Kansas St. over #14 Syracuse, 35-18; **Outback**–#11 Georgia over Wisconsin, 33-6; **Peach**–#13 Auburn over Clemson, 21-17; **Independence**–#15 LSU over Notre Dame, 27-9; **Alamo**–#16 Purdue over #24 Oklahoma St., 33-20; **Holiday**–#17 Colorado St. over #20 Missouri, 35-24.

1998

	After Bowls	Head Coach	Regular Season
1	Tennessee 13-0	Phillip Fulmer	12-0
2	Ohio St.............11-1	John Cooper	10-1
3	Florida St..........11-2	Bobby Bowden	11-1
4	Arizona............12-1	Dick Tomey	11-1
5	Florida............10-2	Steve Spurrier	9-2
6	Wisconsin..........11-1	Barry Alvarez	10-1
7	Tulane 12-0	Tommy Bowden	11-0
8	UCLA.............10-2	Bob Toledo	10-1
9	Georgia Tech 10-2	George O'Leary	9-2
10	Kansas St..........11-2	Bill Snyder	11-1
11	Texas A&M 11-3	R.C. Slocum	11-2
12	Michigan..........10-3	Lloyd Carr	9-3
13	Air Force..........12-1	Fisher DeBerry	11-1
14	Georgia 9-3	Jim Donnan	8-3
15	Texas 9-3	Mack Brown	8-3
16	Arkansas 9-3	Houston Nutt	9-2
17	Penn St. 9-3	Joe Paterno	8-3
18	Virginia 9-3	George Welsh	9-2
19	Nebraska...........9-4	Frank Solich	9-3
20	Miami-FL 9-3	Butch Davis	8-3
21	Missouri 8-4	Larry Smith	7-4
22	Notre Dame 9-3	Bob Davie	9-2
23	Va. Tech 9-3	Frank Beamer	8-3
24	Purdue 9-4	Joe Tiller	8-4
25	Syracuse 8-4	Paul Pasqualoni	8-3

Key Bowl Games

Rankings below reflect final regular season poll, taken Dec. 6. **Fiesta**– #1 Tennessee over #2 Florida St., 23-16; **Sugar**–#3 Ohio St. over #8 Texas A&M, 24-14; **Orange**–#7 Florida over #18 Syracuse, 31-10; **Rose**–#9 Wisconsin over #6 UCLA, 38-31; **Holiday**–#5 Arizona over #14 Nebraska, 23-20; **Citrus**–#15 Michigan over #11 Arkansas, 45-31; **Gator**–#12 Georgia Tech over #17 Notre Dame, 35-28; **Cotton**–#20 Texas over #25 Mississippi St., 38-11; **Peach**–#19 Georgia over #13 Virginia, 35-33; **Alamo**–Purdue over #4 Kansas St., 37-34; **Outback**–#22 Penn St. over Kentucky, 26-14.

Associated Press Final Polls (Cont.)

1999

		After Bowls	Head Coach	Regular Season
1	Florida St.	12-0	Bobby Bowden	11-0
2	Va. Tech	11-1	Frank Beamer	11-0
3	Nebraska	12-1	Frank Solich	11-1
4	Wisconsin	10-2	Barry Alvarez	9-2
5	Michigan	10-2	Lloyd Carr	9-2
6	Kansas St.	11-1	Bill Snyder	10-1
7	Michigan St.	10-2	Nick Saban (9-2) & B. Williams (1-0)	9-2
8	Alabama	10-3	Mike DuBose	10-2
9	Tennessee	9-3	Phillip Fulmer	8-3
10	Marshall	13-0	Bob Pruett	12-0
11	Penn St.	10-3	Joe Paterno	9-3
12	Florida	9-4	Steve Spurrier	9-3
13	Mississippi St.	10-2	Jackie Sherrill	9-2
14	Southern Miss.	9-3	Jeff Bower	8-3
15	Miami-FL	9-4	Butch Davis	8-4
16	Georgia	8-4	Jim Donnan	7-4
17	Arkansas	8-4	Houston Nutt	7-4
18	Minnesota	8-4	Glen Mason	8-3
19	Oregon	9-3	Mike Bellotti	8-3
20	Georgia Tech	8-4	George O'Leary	8-3
21	Texas	9-5	Mack Brown	9-4
22	Mississippi	8-4	David Cutcliffe	7-4
23	Texas A&M	8-4	R.C. Slocum	8-3
24	Illinois	8-4	Ron Turner	7-4
25	Purdue	7-5	Joe Tiller	7-4

Key Bowl Games

Rankings below reflect final regular season poll, taken Dec. 5. **Sugar**–#1 Florida St. over #2 Va. Tech, 46-29; **Fiesta**–#3 Nebraska over #6 Tennessee, 31-21; **Rose**–#4 Wisconsin over #22 Stanford, 17-9; **Orange**–#8 Michigan over #5 Alabama, 35-34; **Holiday**–#7 Kansas St. over Washington, 24-20; **Citrus**–#9 Michigan St. over #10 Florida, 37-34; **Motor City**–#11 Marshall over BYU, 21-3; **Sun**–Oregon over #12 Minnesota, 24-20; **Alamo**–#13 Penn St. over #18 Texas A&M, 24-0; **Cotton**–#24 Arkansas over #14 Texas, 27-6; **Peach**–#15 Mississippi St. over Clemson, 17-7; **Liberty**–#16 Southern Miss. over Colorado St., 23-17; **Gator**–#23 Miami-FL over #17 Georgia Tech, 28-13; **Outback**–#21 Georgia over #19 Purdue, 28-25.

2000

		After Bowls	Head Coach	Regular Season
1	Oklahoma	13-0	Bob Stoops	12-0
2	Miami-FL	11-1	Butch Davis	10-1
3	Washington	11-1	Rick Neuheisel	10-1
4	Oregon St.	11-1	Dennis Erickson	10-1
5	Florida St.	11-2	Bobby Bowden	11-1
6	Va. Tech	11-1	Frank Beamer	10-1
7	Oregon	10-2	Mike Bellotti	9-2
8	Nebraska	10-2	Frank Solich	9-2
9	Kansas St.	11-3	Bill Snyder	10-3
10	Florida	10-3	Steve Spurrier	10-2
11	Michigan	9-3	Lloyd Carr	8-3
12	Texas	9-3	Mack Brown	9-2
13	Purdue	8-4	Joe Tiller	8-3
14	Colorado St.	10-2	Sonny Lubick	9-2
15	Notre Dame	9-3	Bob Davie	9-2
16	Clemson	9-3	Tommy Bowden	9-2
17	Georgia Tech	9-3	George O'Leary	9-2
18	Auburn	9-4	Tommy Tuberville	9-3
19	South Carolina	8-4	Lou Holtz	7-4
20	Georgia	8-4	Jim Donnan	7-4
21	TCU	10-2	D. Franchione (10-1) & G. Patterson (0-1)	10-1
22	LSU	8-4	Nick Saban	7-4
23	Wisconsin	9-4	Barry Alvarez	8-4
24	Mississippi St.	8-4	Jackie Sherrill	7-4
25	Iowa St.	9-3	Dan McCarney	8-3

Key Bowl Games

Rankings below reflect final regular season poll, taken Dec. 4. **Orange**–#1 Oklahoma over #3 Florida St., 13-2; **Sugar**–#2 Miami-FL over #7 Florida, 37-20; **Rose**–#4 Washington over #14 Purdue, 34-24; **Fiesta**–#5 Oregon St. over #10 Notre Dame, 41-9; **Gator**–#6 Virginia Tech over #16 Clemson, 41-20; **Holiday**–#8 Oregon over #12 Texas, 35-30; **Alamo**–#9 Nebraska over #18 Northwestern, 66-17; **Cotton**–#11 Kansas St. over #21 Tennessee, 35-21; **Mobile**–Southern Miss. over #13 TCU, 28-21; **Peach**–LSU over #15 Georgia Tech, 28-14; **Citrus**–#17 Michigan over #20 Auburn, 31-28; **Outback**–South Carolina over #19 Ohio St., 24-7; **Liberty**–#23 Colorado St. over #22 Louisville, 22-17; **Oahu**–#24 Georgia over Virginia, 37-14.

2001

		After Bowls	Head Coach	Regular Season
1	Miami-FL	12-0	Larry Coker	11-0
2	Oregon	11-1	Mike Bellotti	10-1
3	Florida	10-2	Steve Spurrier	9-2
4	Tennessee	11-2	Phillip Fulmer	10-2
5	Texas	11-2	Mack Brown	10-2
6	Oklahoma	11-2	Bob Stoops	10-2
7	LSU	10-3	Nick Saban	9-3
8	Nebraska	11-2	Frank Solich	11-1
9	Colorado	10-3	Gary Barnett	10-2
10	Washington St.	10-2	Mike Price	9-2
11	Maryland	10-2	Ralph Friedgen	10-1
12	Illinois	10-2	Ron Turner	10-1
13	South Carolina	9-3	Lou Holtz	8-3
14	Syracuse	10-3	Paul Pasqualoni	9-3
15	Florida St.	8-4	Bobby Bowden	7-4
16	Stanford	9-3	Tyrone Willingham	9-2
17	Louisville	11-2	John L. Smith	10-2
18	Va. Tech	8-4	Frank Beamer	8-3
19	Washington	8-4	Rick Neuheisel	8-3
20	Michigan	8-4	Lloyd Carr	8-3
21	Boston College	8-4	Tom O'Brien	7-4
22	Georgia	8-4	Mark Richt	8-3
23	Toledo	10-2	Tom Amstutz	9-2
24	Georgia Tech	8-5	George O'Leary (7-5) & Mac McWhorter (1-0)	7-5
25	BYU	12-2	Gary Crowton	12-1

Key Bowl Games

Rankings below reflect final regular season poll, taken Dec. 9. **Rose**–#1 Miami-FL over #4 Nebraska, 37-14; **Fiesta**–#2 Oregon over #3 Colorado, 38-16; **Orange**–#5 Florida over #6 Maryland, 56-23; **Sugar**–#12 LSU over #7 Illinois 47-34; **Citrus**–#8 Tennessee over #17 Michigan, 45-17; **Holiday**–#9 Texas over #21 Washington, 47-43; **Cotton**–#10 Oklahoma over Arkansas, 10-3; **Seattle**–Georgia Tech over #11 Stanford, 24-14; **Sun**–#13 Washington St. over Purdue, 33-27; **Outback**–#14 South Carolina over #22 Ohio St., 31-28; **Gator**–#24 Florida St. over #15 Virginia Tech, 30-17; **Music City**–Boston College over #16 Georgia 20-16; **Liberty**–#23 Louisville over #19 BYU, 28-10; **Insight.com**–#18 Syracuse over Kansas St., 26-3.

Bowl Games

From Jan. 1, 1902 through Jan. 3, 2002. Please note that the Bowl selection process is now dominated by the Bowl Championship Series (which includes the Fiesta, Orange, Rose and Sugar bowls) and the following non-BCS bowls' so called "automatic berths" are contingent upon several factors, including the leftovers from the BCS, Notre Dame's record and the record of their designated choices.

Rose Bowl

City: Pasadena, Calif. **Stadium:** Rose Bowl. **Capacity:** 102,083. **Playing surface:** Grass. **First game:** Jan. 1, 1902. **Playing sites:** Tournament Park (1902, 1916-22), Rose Bowl (1923-41 and since 1943) and Duke Stadium in Durham, N.C. (1942, due to wartime restrictions following Japan's attack at Pearl Harbor on Dec. 7, 1941). **Corporate sponsor:** AT&T (since 1998).

Automatic berths: Pacific Coast Conference champion vs. opponent selected by PCC (1924-45 seasons); Big Ten champion vs. Pac-10 champion (1946-97); Bowl Championship Series: Big Ten champion vs. Pac-10 champion, if available (1998-2000, 2002-05 seasons) and #1 vs. #2 in Jan. 2002 and Jan. 2006.

Multiple wins: USC (20); Michigan (8); Washington (7); Ohio St. (6); Stanford and UCLA (5); Alabama (4); Illinois, Michigan St. and Wisconsin (3); California and Iowa (2).

Year		Year		Year	
1902*	Michigan 49, Stanford 0	1945	USC 25, Tennessee 0	1975	USC 18, Ohio St. 17
1916	Washington St. 14, Brown 0	1946	Alabama 34, USC 14	1976	UCLA 23, Ohio St. 10
1917	Oregon 14, Penn 0	1947	Illinois 45, UCLA 14	1977	USC 14, Michigan 6
1918	Mare Island 19, Camp Lewis 7	1948	Michigan 49, USC 0	1978	Washington 27, Michigan 20
1919	Great Lakes 17, Mare Island 0	1949	Northwestern 20, California 14	1979	USC 17, Michigan 10
1920	Harvard 7, Oregon 6	1950	Ohio St. 17, California 14	1980	USC 17, Ohio St. 16
1921	California 28, Ohio St. 0	1951	Michigan 14, California 6	1981	Michigan 23, Washington 6
1922	0-0, California vs Wash. & Jeff.	1952	Illinois 40, Stanford 7	1982	Washington 28, Iowa 0
1923	USC 14, Penn St. 0	1953	USC 7, Wisconsin 0	1983	UCLA 24, Michigan 14
1924	14-14, Navy vs Washington	1954	Michigan St. 28, UCLA 20	1984	UCLA 45, Illinois 9
1925	Notre Dame 27, Stanford 10	1955	Ohio St. 20, USC 7	1985	USC 20, Ohio St. 17
1926	Alabama 20, Washington 19	1956	Michigan St. 17, UCLA 14	1986	UCLA 45, Iowa 28
1927	7-7, Alabama vs Stanford	1957	Iowa 35, Oregon St. 19	1987	Arizona St. 22, Michigan 15
1928	Stanford 7, Pittsburgh 6	1958	Ohio St. 10, Oregon 7	1988	Michigan St. 20, USC 17
1929	Georgia Tech 8, California 7	1959	Iowa 38, California 12	1989	Michigan 22, USC 14
1930	USC 47, Pittsburgh 14	1960	Washington 44, Wisconsin 8	1990	USC 17, Michigan 10
1931	Alabama 24, Washington St. 0	1961	Washington 17, Minnesota 7	1991	Washington 46, Iowa 34
1932	USC 21, Tulane 12	1962	Minnesota 21, UCLA 3	1992	Washington 34, Michigan 14
1933	USC 35, Pittsburgh 0	1963	USC 42, Wisconsin 37	1993	Michigan 38, Washington 31
1934	Columbia 7, Stanford 0	1964	Illinois 17, Washington 7	1994	Wisconsin 21, UCLA 16
1935	Alabama 29, Stanford 13	1965	Michigan 34, Oregon St. 7	1995	Penn St. 38, Oregon 20
1936	Stanford 7, SMU 0	1966	UCLA 14, Michigan St. 12	1996	USC 41, Northwestern 32
1937	Pittsburgh 21, Washington 0	1967	Purdue 14, USC 13	1997	Ohio St. 20, Arizona St. 17
1938	California 13, Alabama 0	1968	USC 14, Indiana 3	1998	Michigan 21, Washington St. 16
1939	USC 7, Duke 3	1969	Ohio St. 27, USC 16	1999	Wisconsin 38, UCLA 31
1940	USC 14, Tennessee 0	1970	USC 10, Michigan 3	2000	Wisconsin 17, Stanford 9
1941	Stanford 21, Nebraska 13	1971	Stanford 27, Ohio St. 17	2001	Washington 34, Purdue 24
1942	Oregon St. 20, Duke 16	1972	Stanford 13, Michigan 12	2002	Miami-FL 37, Nebraska 14
T943	Georgia 9, UCLA 0	1973	USC 42, Ohio St. 17		
1944	USC 29, Washington 0	1974	Ohio St. 42, USC 21	*January game since 1902.	

Fiesta Bowl

City: Tempe, Ariz. **Stadium:** Sun Devil. **Capacity:** 73,656. **Playing surface:** Grass. **First game:** Dec. 27, 1971. **Playing site:** Sun Devil Stadium (since 1971). **Corporate title sponsors:** Sunkist Citrus Growers (1986-91), IBM OS/2 (1993-95) and Frito-Lay Tostitos chips (since 1996).

Automatic berths: Western Athletic Conference champion vs. at-large opponent (1971-79 seasons); Two of first five picks from 8-team Bowl Coalition pool (1992-94). Bowl Alliance (#1 vs. #2 on Jan. 2, 1996; #3 vs. #5 on Jan. 1, 1997; and #4 vs. #6 on Dec. 31, 1997); Big 12 champion vs. next best team in pool (New Bowl Alliance 1995-1997 seasons); Bowl Championship Series: #1 vs. #2 on Jan. 4, 1999 and Jan., 2003 and Big 12 champion, if available, vs. at-large (1999-2001 and 2003-05 seasons).

Multiple wins: Penn St. (6); Arizona St. (5); Florida St. and Nebraska (2).

Year		Year		Year	
1971†	Arizona St. 45, Florida St. 38	1984	Ohio St. 28, Pittsburgh 23	1996	Nebraska 62, Florida 24
1972	Arizona St. 49, Missouri 35	1985	UCLA 39, Miami-FL 37	1997	Penn St. 38, Texas 15
1973	Arizona St. 28, Pittsburgh 7	1986	Michigan 27, Nebraska 23	1997†	Kansas St. 35, Syracuse 18
1974	Oklahoma St. 16, BYU 6	1987	Penn St. 14, Miami-FL 10	1999	Tennessee 23, Florida St. 16
1975	Arizona St. 17, Nebraska 14	1988	Florida St. 31, Nebraska 28		
1976	Oklahoma 41, Wyoming 7	1989	Notre Dame 34, West Va. 21	2000	Nebraska 31, Tennessee 21
1977	Penn St. 42, Arizona St. 30			2001	Oregon St. 41, Notre Dame 9
1978	10-10, Arkansas vs UCLA	1990	Florida St. 41, Nebraska 17	2002	Oregon 38, Colorado 16
1979	Pittsburgh 16, Arizona 10	1991	Louisville 34, Alabama 7		
		1992	Penn St. 42, Tennessee 17	†December game from 1971-80 and	
1980	Penn St. 31, Ohio St. 19	1993	Syracuse 26, Colorado 22	in '97.	
1982*	Penn St. 26, USC 10	1994	Arizona 29, Miami-FL 0	* January game since 1982.	
1983	Arizona St. 32, Oklahoma 21	1995	Colorado 41, Notre Dame 24		

Bowl Games (Cont.)
Sugar Bowl

City: New Orleans, La. **Stadium:** Louisiana Superdome. **Capacity:** 77,446. **Playing surface:** AstroTurf. **First game:** Jan. 1, 1935. **Playing sites:** Tulane Stadium (1935-74) and Superdome (since 1975). **Corporate title sponsors:** USF&G Financial Services (1987-95) and Nokia cellular telephones of Finland (starting in 1995).

Automatic berths: SEC champion vs. at-large opponent (1976-91 seasons); SEC champion vs. one of first five picks from 8-team Bowl Coalition pool (1992-94 seasons); #4 vs. #6 on Dec. 31, 1995; #1 vs. #2 on Jan. 2, 1997; and #3 vs. #5 on Jan. 1, 1998; Bowl Championship Series: SEC champion, if available, vs. at-large (1998-99, 2000-02, 2004-05 seasons) and #1 vs. #2 on Jan. 4, 2000 and 2004.

Multiple wins: Alabama (8); Mississippi (5); Florida St., Georgia Tech, LSU, Oklahoma and Tennessee (4); Nebraska (3); Florida, Georgia, Miami-FL, Notre Dame, Pittsburgh, Santa Clara and TCU (2).

Year		Year		Year	
1935*	Tulane 20, Temple 14	1959	LSU 7, Clemson 0	1983	Penn St. 27, Georgia 23
1936	TCU 3, LSU 2			1984	Auburn 9, Michigan 7
1937	Santa Clara 21, LSU 14	1960	Mississippi 21, LSU 0	1985	Nebraska 28, LSU 10
1938	Santa Clara 6, LSU 0	1961	Mississippi 14, Rice 6	1986	Tennessee 35, Miami-FL 7
1939	TCU 15, Carnegie Tech 7	1962	Alabama 10, Arkansas 3	1987	Nebraska 30, LSU 15
		1963	Mississippi 17, Arkansas 13	1988	16-16, Syracuse vs Auburn
1940	Texas A&M 14, Tulane 13	1964	Alabama 12, Mississippi 7	1989	Florida St. 13, Auburn 7
1941	Boston College 19, Tennessee 13	1965	LSU 13, Syracuse 10		
1942	Fordham 2, Missouri 0	1966	Missouri 20, Florida 18	1990	Miami-FL 33, Alabama 25
1943	Tennessee 14, Tulsa 7	1967	Alabama 34, Nebraska 7	1991	Tennessee 23, Virginia 22
1944	Georgia Tech 20, Tulsa 18	1968	LSU 20, Wyoming 13	1992	Notre Dame 39, Florida 28
1945	Duke 29, Alabama 26	1969	Arkansas 16, Georgia 2	1993	Alabama 34, Miami-FL 13
1946	Okla. A&M 33, St.Mary's 13			1994	Florida 41, West Va. 7
1947	Georgia 20, N. Carolina 10	1970	Mississippi 27, Arkansas 22	1995	Florida St. 23, Florida 17
1948	Texas 27, Alabama 7	1971	Tennessee 34, Air Force 13	1995†	Va. Tech 28, Texas 10
1949	Oklahoma 14, N. Carolina 6	1972	Oklahoma 40, Auburn 22	1997	Florida 52, Florida St. 20
		1972†	Oklahoma 14, Penn St. 0	1998	Florida St. 31, Ohio St. 14
1950	Oklahoma 35, LSU 0	1973	Notre Dame 24, Alabama 23	1999	Ohio St. 24, Texas A&M 14
1951	Kentucky 13, Oklahoma 7	1974	Nebraska 13, Florida 10		
1952	Maryland 28, Tennessee 13	1975	Alabama 13, Penn St. 6	2000	Florida St. 46, Va. Tech 29
1953	Georgia Tech 24, Mississippi 7	1977*	Pittsburgh 27, Georgia 3	2001	Miami-FL 37, Florida 20
1954	Georgia Tech 42, West Va. 19	1978	Alabama 35, Ohio St. 6	2002	LSU 47, Illinois 34
1955	Navy 21, Mississippi 0	1979	Alabama 14, Penn St. 7		
1956	Georgia Tech 7, Pittsburgh 0			*January game from 1935-72 and	
1957	Baylor 13, Tennessee 7	1980	Alabama 24, Arkansas 9	since 1977 (except in 1995).	
1958	Mississippi 39, Texas 7	1981	Georgia 17, Notre Dame 10	†Game played on Dec. 31 from	
		1982	Pittsburgh 24, Georgia 20	1972-75 and in 1995.	

Orange Bowl

City: Miami, Fla. **Stadium:** Pro Player. **Capacity:** 74,916. **Playing surface:** Grass. **First game:** Jan. 1, 1935. **Playing sites:** Orange Bowl (1935-95); Pro Player Stadium (since 1996). **Corporate title sponsor:** Federal Express (since 1989).

Automatic berths: Big 8 champion vs. Atlantic Coast Conference champion (1953-57 seasons); Big 8 champion vs. at-large opponent (1958-63 seasons and 1975-91 seasons); Big 8 champion vs. one of first five picks from 8-team Bowl Coalition pool (1992-94 seasons); #3 vs. #5 on Jan. 1, 1996; #4 vs. #6 on Dec. 31, 1996; and #1 vs. #2 on Jan. 2, 1998 (New Bowl Alliance 1995-97 seasons); Bowl Championship Series: Big East or ACC champion, if available, vs. at-large (1998-99, 2001-03, 2005 seasons) and #1 vs. #2 Jan. 3, 2001 and Jan. 2005.

Multiple wins: Oklahoma (12); Nebraska (8); Miami-FL (5); Alabama (4); Florida, Florida State, Georgia Tech and Penn St. (3); Clemson, Colorado, Georgia, LSU, Notre Dame and Texas (2).

Year		Year		Year	
1935*	Bucknell 26, Miami-FL 0	1955	Duke 34, Nebraska 7	1975	Notre Dame 13, Alabama 11
1936	Catholic U. 20, Mississippi 19	1956	Oklahoma 20, Maryland 6	1976	Oklahoma 14, Michigan 6
1937	Duquesne 13, Mississippi St. 12	1957	Colorado 27, Clemson 21	1977	Ohio St. 27, Colorado 10
1938	Auburn 6, Michigan St. 0	1958	Oklahoma 48, Duke 21	1978	Arkansas 31, Oklahoma 6
1939	Tennessee 17, Oklahoma 0	1959	Oklahoma 21, Syracuse 6	1979	Oklahoma 31, Nebraska 24
1940	Georgia Tech 21, Missouri 7	1960	Georgia 14, Missouri 0	1980	Oklahoma 24, Florida St. 7
1941	Mississippi St. 14, Georgetown 7	1961	Missouri 21, Navy 14	1981	Oklahoma 18, Florida St. 17
1942	Georgia 40, TCU 26	1962	LSU 25, Colorado 7	1982	Clemson 22, Nebraska 15
1943	Alabama 37, Boston College 21	1963	Alabama 17, Oklahoma 0	1983	Nebraska 21, LSU 20
1944	LSU 19, Texas A&M 14	1964	Nebraska 13, Auburn 7	1984	Miami-FL 31, Nebraska 30
1945	Tulsa 26, Georgia Tech 12	1965†	Texas 21, Alabama 17	1985	Washington 28, Oklahoma 17
1946	Miami-FL 13, Holy Cross 6	1966	Alabama 39, Nebraska 28	1986	Oklahoma 25, Penn St. 10
1947	Rice 8, Tennessee 0	1967	Florida 27, Georgia Tech 12	1987	Oklahoma 42, Arkansas 8
1948	Georgia Tech 20, Kansas 14	1968	Oklahoma 26, Tennessee 24	1988	Miami-FL 20, Oklahoma 14
1949	Texas 41, Georgia 28	1969	Penn St. 15, Kansas 14	1989	Miami-FL 23, Nebraska 3
1950	Santa Clara 21, Kentucky 13	1970	Penn St. 10, Missouri 3	1990	Notre Dame, 21, Colorado 6
1951	Clemson 15, Miami-FL 14	1971	Nebraska 17, LSU 12	1991	Colorado 10, Notre Dame 9
1952	Georgia Tech 17, Baylor 14	1972	Nebraska 38, Alabama 6	1992	Miami-FL 22, Nebraska 0
1953	Alabama 61, Syracuse 6	1973	Nebraska 40, Notre Dame 6	1993	Florida St. 27, Nebraska 14
1954	Oklahoma 7, Maryland 0	1974	Penn St. 16, LSU 9	1994	Florida St. 18, Nebraska 16

Year		Year		
1995	Nebraska 24, Miami-FL 17	1999	Florida 31, Syracuse 10	*January game 1935-1996 and since
1996	Florida St. 31, Notre Dame 26			'98.
1996**Nebraska 41, Virginia Tech 21		2000	Michigan 35, Alabama 34	**December game in 1996
1998*	Nebraska 42, Tennessee 17	2001	Oklahoma 13, Florida St. 2	†Night game since 1965.
		2002	Florida 56, Maryland 23	

Cotton Bowl

City: Dallas, Tex. **Stadium:** Cotton Bowl. **Capacity:** 68,252. **Playing surface:** Grass. **First game:** Jan 1, 1937. **Playing sites:** Fair Park Stadium (1937) and Cotton Bowl (since 1938). **Corporate title sponsor:** Mobil Corporation (1988-95), SBC Communications Inc., previously Southwestern Bell, (since 1997).

Automatic berths: SWC champion vs. at-large opponent (1941-91 seasons); SWC champion vs. one of first five picks from 8-team Bowl Coalition pool (1992-1994 seasons); second pick from Big 12 vs. first choice of WAC champion or second pick from Pac-10 (1995-97 seasons); Big 12 vs. SEC (since 1998).

Multiple wins: Texas (10); Notre Dame (5); Texas A&M (4); Arkansas and Rice (3); Alabama, Georgia, Houston, LSU, Penn St., SMU, Tennessee, TCU and UCLA (2).

Year		Year		Year	
1937*	TCU 16, Marquette 6	1960	Syracuse 23, Texas 14	1983	SMU 7, Pittsburgh 3
1938	Rice 28, Colorado 14	1961	Duke 7, Arkansas 6	1984	Georgia 10, Texas 9
1939	St. Mary's 20, Texas Tech 13	1962	Texas 12, Mississippi 7	1985	Boston College 45, Houston 28
1940	Clemson 6, Boston College 3	1963	LSU 13, Texas 0	1986	Texas A&M 36, Auburn 16
1941	Texas A&M 13, Fordham 12	1964	Texas 28, Navy 6	1987	Ohio St. 28, Texas A&M 12
1942	Alabama 29, Texas A&M 21	1965	Arkansas 10, Nebraska 7	1988	Texas A&M 35, Notre Dame 10
1943	Texas 14, Georgia Tech 7	1966	LSU 14, Arkansas 7	1989	UCLA 17, Arkansas 3
1944	7-7, Texas vs Randolph Field	1966†	Georgia 24, SMU 9	1990	Tennessee 31, Arkansas 27
1945	Oklahoma A&M 34, TCU 0	1968*	Texas A&M 20, Alabama 16	1991	Miami-FL 46, Texas 3
1946	Texas 40, Missouri 27	1969	Texas 36, Tennessee 13	1992	Florida St. 10, Texas A&M 2
1947	0-0, Arkansas vs LSU	1970	Texas 21, Notre Dame 17	1993	Notre Dame 28, Texas A&M 3
1948	13-13, SMU vs Penn St.	1971	Notre Dame 24, Texas 11	1994	Notre Dame 24, Texas A&M 21
1949	SMU 21, Oregon 13	1972	Penn St. 30, Texas 6	1995	USC 55, Texas Tech 14
1950	Rice 27, N. Carolina 13	1973	Texas 17, Alabama 13	1996	Colorado 38, Oregon 6
1951	Tennessee 20, Texas 14	1974	Nebraska 19, Texas 3	1997	BYU 19, Kansas St. 15
1952	Kentucky 20, TCU 7	1975	Penn St. 41, Baylor 20	1998	UCLA 29, Texas A&M 23
1953	Texas 16, Tennessee 0	1976	Arkansas 31, Georgia 10	1999	Texas 38, Mississippi St. 11
1954	Rice 28, Alabama 6	1977	Houston 30, Maryland 21	2000	Arkansas 27, Texas 6
1955	Georgia Tech 14, Arkansas 6	1978	Notre Dame 38, Texas 10	2001	Kansas St. 35, Tennessee 21
1956	Mississippi 14, TCU 13	1979	Notre Dame 35, Houston 34	2002	Oklahoma 10, Arkansas 3
1957	TCU 28, Syracuse 27	1980	Houston 17, Nebraska 14	*January game from 1937-66 and
1958	Navy 20, Rice 7	1981	Alabama 30, Baylor 2	since 1968.
1959	0-0, TCU vs Air Force	1982	Texas 14, Alabama 12	†Game played on Dec. 31, 1966.

Florida Citrus Bowl

City: Orlando, Fla. **Stadium:** Florida Citrus Bowl. **Capacity:** 70,188. **Playing surface:** Grass. **First game:** Jan. 1, 1947. **Name change:** Tangerine Bowl (1947-82) and Florida Citrus Bowl (since 1983). **Playing sites:** Tangerine Bowl (1947-72, 1974-82), Florida Field in Gainesville (1973), Orlando Stadium (1983-85) and Florida Citrus Bowl (since 1986). The Tangerine Bowl, Orlando Stadium and Florida Citrus Bowl are all the same stadium. **Corporate title sponsors:** Florida Department of Citrus (1983-2002), CompUSA (1992-99), Ourhouse.com (2000) and Capital One (since 2001).

Automatic berths: Championship game of Atlantic Coast Regional Conference (1964-67 seasons); Mid-American Conference champion vs. Southern Conference champion (1968-71 seasons); ACC champion vs. at-large opponent (1988-91 seasons); second pick from SEC, if available, vs. second pick from Big 10, if available (since 1992 season).

Multiple wins: Tennessee (4); East Texas St., Miami-OH and Toledo (3); Auburn, Catawba, Clemson, East Carolina, Florida and Michigan (2).

Year		Year		Year	
1947*	Catawba 31, Maryville 6	1966	Morgan St. 14, West Chester 6	1987*	Auburn 16, USC 7
1948	Catawba 7, Marshall 0	1967	Tenn-Martin 25, West Chester 8	1988	Clemson 35, Penn St. 10
1949	21-21, Murray St. vs Sul Ross St.	1968	Richmond 49, Ohio U. 42	1989	Clemson 13, Oklahoma 6
1950	St. Vincent 7, Emory & Henry 6	1969	Toledo 56, Davidson 33	1990	Illinois 31, Virginia 21
1951	M. Harvey 35, Emory & Henry 14	1970	Toledo 40, Wm. & Mary 12	1991	Georgia Tech 45, Nebraska 21
1952	Stetson 35, Arkansas St. 20	1971	Toledo 28, Richmond 3	1992	California 37, Clemson 13
1953	E. Texas St. 33, Tenn. Tech 0	1972	Tampa 21, Kent St. 18	1993	Georgia 21, Ohio St. 14
1954	7-7, E. Texas St. vs Arkansas St.	1973	Miami-OH 16, Florida 7	1994	Penn St. 31, Tennessee 13
1955	Neb.-Omaha 7, Eastern Ky. 6	1974	Miami-OH 21, Georgia 10	1995	Alabama 24, Ohio St. 17
1956	6-6, Juniata vs Missouri Valley	1975	Miami-OH 20, S. Carolina 7	1996	Tennessee 20, Ohio St. 14
1957	W. Texas St. 20, So. Miss. 13	1976	Oklahoma 49, BYU 21	1997	Tennessee 48, Northwestern 28
1958	E. Texas St. 10, So. Miss. 9	1977	Florida St. 40, Texas Tech 17	1998	Florida 21, Penn St. 6
1958†	E. Texas St. 26, Mo. Valley 7	1978	N.C. State 30, Pittsburgh 17	1999	Michigan 45, Arkansas 31
1960*	Mid. Tenn. 21, Presbyterian 12	1979	LSU 34, Wake Forest 10	2000	Michigan St. 37, Florida 34
1960†	Citadel 27, Tenn. Tech 0	1980	Florida 35, Maryland 20	2001	Michigan 31, Auburn 28
1961	Lamar 21, Middle Tenn. 14	1981	Missouri 19, Southern Miss. 17	2002	Tennessee 45, Michigan 17
1962	Houston 49, Miami-OH 21	1982	Auburn 33, Boston College 26	*January game from 1947-58, in
1963	Western Ky. 27, Coast Guard 9	1983	Tennessee 30, Maryland 23	1960 and since 1987.
1964	E. Carolina 14, Massachusetts 13	1984	17-17, Florida St. vs Georgia	†December game in 1958 and 1960-
1965	E. Carolina 31, Maine 0	1985	Ohio St. 7, BYU 7	85.

Bowl Games (Cont.)
Gator Bowl

City: Jacksonville, Fla. **Stadium:** ALLTEL Stadium. **Capacity:** 73,000. **Playing surface:** Grass. **First game:** Jan. 1, 1946. **Playing sites:** Gator Bowl (1946-93), Florida Field in Gainesville (1994) and New Gator Bowl (since 1995). Name was changed to ALLTEL Stadium in 1997. **Corporate title sponsors:** Mazda Motors of America, Inc. (1986-91), Outback Steakhouse, Inc. (1992-94) and Toyota Motor Co. (since 1995).

Automatic berths: Third pick from SEC vs. sixth pick from 8-team Bowl Coalition pool (1992-94 seasons); second pick from ACC, if available, vs. second pick from Big East or Notre Dame, if available (since 1995 season).

Multiple wins: Florida (6); North Carolina (5); Auburn, Clemson and Florida St. (4); Georgia Tech and Tennessee (3); Georgia, Maryland, Miami-FL, Oklahoma, Pittsburgh, and Texas Tech (2).

Year		Year		Year	
1946*	Wake Forest 26, S. Carolina 14	1966	Tennessee 18, Syracuse 12	1987	LSU 30, S. Carolina 13
1947	Oklahoma 34, N.C. State 13	1967	17-17, Florida St. vs Penn St.	1989*	Georgia 34, Michigan St. 27
1948	20-20, Maryland vs Georgia	1968	Missouri 35, Alabama 10	1989†	Clemson 27, West Va. 7
1949	Clemson 24, Missouri 23	1969	Florida 14, Tennessee 13	1991*	Michigan 35, Mississippi 3
1950	Maryland 20, Missouri 7	1971*	Auburn 35, Mississippi 28	1991†	Oklahoma 48, Virginia 14
1951	Wyoming 20, Wash. & Lee 7	1971†	Georgia 7, N. Carolina 3	1992	Florida 27, N.C. State 10
1952	Miami-FL 14, Clemson 0	1972	Auburn 24, Colorado 3	1993	Alabama 24, N. Carolina 10
1953	Florida 14, Tulsa 13	1973	Texas Tech 28, Tennessee 19	1994	Tennessee 45, Va. Tech 23
1954	Texas Tech 35, Auburn 13	1974	Auburn 27, Texas 3	1996*	Syracuse 41, Clemson 0
1954†	Auburn 33, Baylor 13	1975	Maryland 13, Florida 0	1997	N. Carolina 20, West Va. 13
1955	Vanderbilt 25, Auburn 13	1976	Notre Dame 20, Penn St. 9	1998	N. Carolina 42, Va. Tech 3
1956	Georgia Tech 21, Pittsburgh 14	1977	Pittsburgh 34, Clemson 3	1999	Ga. Tech 35, Notre Dame 28
1957	Tennessee 3, Texas A&M 0	1978	Clemson 17, Ohio St. 15	2000	Miami-FL 28, Ga. Tech 13
1958	Mississippi 7, Florida 3	1979	N. Carolina 17, Michigan 15	2001	Va. Tech 41, Clemson 20
1960*	Arkansas 14, Georgia Tech 7	1980	Pittsburgh 37, S. Carolina 9	2002	Florida St. 30, Va. Tech 17
1960†	Florida 13, Baylor 12	1981	N. Carolina 31, Arkansas 27		
1961	Penn St. 30, Georgia Tech 15	1982	Florida St. 31, West Va. 12	*January game from 1946-54, 1960, 1965, 1971, 1989, 1991 and since 1996.	
1962	Florida 17, Penn St. 7	1983	Florida 14, Iowa 6		
1963	N. Carolina 35, Air Force 0	1984	Oklahoma St. 21, S. Carolina 14	†December game from 1954-58, 1960-63, 1965-69, 1971-87, 1989 and 1991-94.	
1965*	Florida St. 36, Oklahoma 19	1985	Florida St. 34, Oklahoma St. 23		
1965†	Georgia Tech 31, Texas Tech 21	1986	Clemson 27, Stanford 21		

Bowl Championship Series

Division I-A football remains the only NCAA sport on any level that does not have a sanctioned national champion. To that end, the Bowl Coalition was formed in 1992 and was updated and renamed the Bowl Alliance in 1995 in an attempt to keep the bowl system intact while forcing an annual championship game between the regular season's two top-ranked teams.

The Bowl Championship Series is the organizers' latest attempt to finally guarantee that the teams ranked #1 and #2 will play each other in a "national title game" come January. The key difference from the 1992-97 Bowl Coalition/Bowl Alliance is that the Bowl Championship Series includes the Big 10 and Pac-10 champions. These teams, which were originally locked into playing in the Rose Bowl, are allowed under the new system to move to another bowl game in order to create a match-up featuring the #1 and #2 teams.

The bowls (the Fiesta, Orange, and Sugar) which made up the old Bowl Alliance kept their spots when the Rose Bowl joined this new four-bowl alliance. The Fiesta Bowl held the first national championship (#1 vs. #2) game under the Bowl Championship Series contract (Jan. 4, 1999), it was followed by the Sugar (Jan. 4, 2000) the Orange (Jan. 3, 2001) and the Rose Bowl (Jan. 3, 2002). The BCS has successfully matched the top two teams in the country (according to the AP Poll) in two of the last four years.

Oklahoma played Florida St. in the BCS title game on Jan. 3, 2001 despite the fact that Miami-FL was #2 in the AP poll. FSU was the second-ranked team in the BCS rankings and therefore met Oklahoma, the top-ranked team, even though the Seminoles lost to Miami during the regular season. Controversy was averted when Oklahoma beat FSU 13-2 in the Orange Bowl. The following season, top-ranked Miami met BCS #2 Nebraska instead of Oregon, which was ranked second in both polls, at the Rose Bowl. Once again, total anarchy was avoided when Miami beat the Cornhuskers in the BCS title game to remain unbeaten.

Originally, ABC paid the BCS members $525 million over seven years in rights fees for the four "title" games, with a three year option clause. The option was exercised in January 2000 and ABC and the BCS agreed on an additional eighth year as well. The future schedule for the BCS championship game: Fiesta (2003), Sugar (2004), Orange (2005) and Rose (2006).

The 1992 Coalition, which lasted three seasons, consolidated the resources of four major bowl games (the Cotton, Fiesta, Orange and Sugar), the champions of five major conferences (the ACC, Big East, Big Eight, Southeastern and Southwest) and the national following of independent Notre Dame. It worked two out of three years with #1 vs. #2 showdowns in the 1993 Sugar Bowl (#2 Alabama over #1 Miami-FL) and 1994 Orange Bowl (#1 Florida St. over #2 Nebraska). The 1995 Orange Bowl had to settle for #1 Nebraska beating #3 Miami-FL because #2 Penn St., the Big Ten champion, was obligated to play in the Rose Bowl.

The Bowl Alliance, which ended a three-year run after the 1997 season, was an updated version of the Coalition.

Holiday Bowl

City: San Diego, Calif. **Stadium:** Qualcomm. **Capacity:** 71,000. **Playing surface:** Grass. **First game:** Dec. 22, 1978. **Playing site:** San Diego/Jack Murphy Stadium (since 1978). Name changed to Qualcomm Stadium in 1997. **Corporate title sponsors:** Sea World (1986-90), Thrifty Car Rental (1991-94), Chrysler-Plymouth Division of Chrysler Corp. (1995-97), U.S. Filter/Culligan Water Tech. (1998-2001) and Pacific Life Insurance Co. (since 2002).

Automatic berths: WAC champion vs. at-large opponent (1978-84, 1986-90 seasons); WAC champ vs. second pick from Big 10 (1991 season); WAC champ vs. third pick from Big 10 (1992-94 seasons); choice of WAC champion, if available, or second pick from Pac-10, if available vs. third pick from Big 12, if available (1995-99); second pick from Pac-10 vs. third pick from Big 12 (since 2000).

Multiple wins: BYU (4); Iowa, Kansas St. and Ohio St. (2).

Year		Year		Year	
1978†	Navy 23, BYU 16	1987	Iowa 20, Wyoming 19	1996	Colorado 33, Washington 21
1979	Indiana 38, BYU 37	1988	Oklahoma St. 62, Wyoming 14	1997	Colorado St. 35, Missouri 24
1980	BYU 46, SMU 45	1989	Penn St. 50, BYU 39	1998	Arizona 23, Nebraska 20
1981	BYU 38, Washington St. 36	1990	Texas A&M 65, BYU 14	1999	Kansas St. 24, Washington 20
1982	Ohio St. 47, BYU 17	1991	13-13, Iowa vs BYU	2000	Oregon 35, Texas 30
1983	BYU 21, Missouri 17	1992	Hawaii 27, Illinois 17	2001	Texas 47, Washington 43
1984	BYU 24, Michigan 17	1993	Ohio St. 28, BYU 21	†December game since 1978.
1985	Arkansas 18, Arizona St. 17	1994	Michigan 24, Colo. St. 14		
1986	Iowa 39, San Diego St. 38	1995	Kansas St. 54, Colorado St. 21		

Outback Bowl

City: Tampa, Fla. **Stadium:** Raymond James. **Capacity:** 66,005. **Playing surface:** Grass. **First game:** Dec. 23, 1986. **Name change:** Hall of Fame Bowl (1986-95) and Outback Bowl (since 1995). **Playing sites:** Tampa/Houlihan's Stadium (1986-98) and Raymond James Stadium (since 1999). **Corporate title sponsor:** Outback Steakhouse, Inc. (since 1995).

Automatic berths: Fourth pick from ACC vs. fourth pick from Big 10 (1993-94 seasons); third pick from Big 10, if available, vs. third pick from SEC, if available (1995-99); fourth pick from Big 10 vs. third pick from SEC (2000 season).

Multiple wins: Georgia, Michigan, Penn St., South Carolina and Syracuse (2).

Year		Year		Year	
1986†	Boston College 27, Georgia 24	1993	Tennessee 38, Boston Col. 23	1999	Penn St. 26, Kentucky 14
1988*	Michigan 28, Alabama 24	1994	Michigan 42, N.C. State 7	2000	Georgia 28, Purdue 25
1989	Syracuse 23, LSU 10	1995	Wisconsin 34, Duke 20	2001	S. Carolina 24, Ohio St. 7
1990	Auburn 31, Ohio St. 14	1996	Penn St. 43, Auburn 14	2002	S. Carolina 31, Ohio St. 28
1991	Clemson 30, Illinois 0	1997	Alabama 17, Michigan 14	†December game in 1986.
1992	Syracuse 24, Ohio St. 17	1998	Georgia 33, Wisconsin 6	*January game since 1988.

Peach Bowl

City: Atlanta, Ga. **Stadium:** Georgia Dome. **Capacity:** 71,228. **Playing surface:** AstroTurf. **First game:** Dec. 30, 1968. **Playing sites:** Grant Field (1968-70), Atlanta-Fulton County Stadium (1971-92) and Georgia Dome (since 1993). **Corporate title sponsor:** Chick-fil-A (since 1998).

Automatic berths: Third pick from ACC vs. at-large opponent (1992 season); third pick from ACC vs. fourth pick from SEC (1993-94 seasons); third pick from ACC, if available, vs. fourth pick from SEC, if available (since 1995 season).

Multiple wins: N.C. State (4); LSU and West Virginia (3); Auburn, Georgia, North Carolina and Virginia (2).

Year		Year		Year	
1968†	LSU 31, Florida St. 27	1981†	West Va. 26, Florida 6	1995*	N.C. State 24, Miss. St. 24
1969	West Va. 14, S. Carolina 3	1982	Iowa 28, Tennessee 22	1995†	Virginia 34, Georgia 27
1970	Arizona St. 48, N. Carolina 26	1983	Florida St. 28, N. Carolina 3	1996	LSU 10, Clemson 7
1971	Mississippi 41, Georgia Tech 18	1984	Virginia 27, Purdue 24	1998*	Auburn 21, Clemson 17
1972	N.C. State 49, West Va. 13	1985	Army 31, Illinois 29	1998†	Georgia 35, Virginia 33
1973	Georgia 17, Maryland 16	1986	Va. Tech 25, N.C. State 24	1999	Mississippi St. 17, Clemson 7
1974	6-6, Vanderbilt vs Texas Tech	1988*	Tennessee 27, Indiana 22	2000	LSU 28, Ga. Tech 14
1975	West Va. 13, N.C. State 10	1988†	N.C. State 28, Iowa 23	2001	N. Carolina 16, Auburn 10
1976	Kentucky 21, N. Carolina 0	1989	Syracuse 19, Georgia 18	†December game from 1968-79,
1977	N.C. State 24, Iowa St. 14	1990	Auburn 27, Indiana 23	1981-86, 1988-90, 1993, 1995,
1978	Purdue 41, Georgia Tech 21	1992*	E. Carolina 37, N.C. State 34	1996, 1998 and since 1999.
1979	Baylor 24, Clemson 18	1993	N. Carolina 21, Miss. St. 17	*January game in 1981, 1988, 1992-
1981*	Miami-FL 20, Va. Tech 10	1993†	Clemson 14, Kentucky 13	93, 1995 and 1998.

Alamo Bowl

City: San Antonio, Tex. **Stadium:** Alamodome. **Capacity:** 65,000. **Playing surface:** AstroTurf. **First game:** Dec. 31, 1993. **Playing site:** Alamodome (since 1993). **Corporate title sponsors:** Builders Square (1993-98) and Sylvania (1999-2001).

Automatic berths: third pick from SWC vs. fourth pick from Pac-10 (1993-94 seasons); fourth pick from Big 10, if available vs. fourth pick from Big 12, if available (1995-99 seasons); fourth pick from Big 12 vs. third pick from Big 10 (2000 season).

Multiple wins: Iowa and Purdue (2).

Year		Year		Year	
1993†	California 37, Iowa 3	1997	Purdue 33, Oklahoma St. 20	2001	Iowa 19, Texas Tech 16
1994	Washington St. 10, Baylor 3	1998	Purdue 37, Kansas St. 34	†December game since 1993.
1995	Texas A&M 22, Michigan 20	1999	Penn St. 24, Texas A&M 0		
1996	Iowa 27, Texas Tech 0	2000	Nebraska 66, Northwestern 17		

Bowl Games (Cont.)
Sun Bowl

City: El Paso, Tex. **Stadium:** Sun Bowl. **Capacity:** 52,000. **Playing surface:** AstroTurf. **First game:** Jan. 1, 1936. **Name changes:** Sun Bowl (1936-85), John Hancock Sun Bowl (1986-88), John Hancock Bowl (1989-93) and Sun Bowl (since 1994). **Playing sites:** Kidd Field (1936-62) and Sun Bowl (since 1963). **Corporate title sponsors:** John Hancock Financial Services (1986-93), Norwest Bank (1996-98), Wells Fargo (since 1999).

Automatic berths: Eighth pick from 8-team Bowl Coalition pool vs. at-large opponent (1992); Seventh and eighth picks from 8-team Bowl Coalition pool (1993-94 seasons); third pick from Pac-10, if available, vs. fifth pick from Big 10, if available (since 1995 season).

Multiple wins: Texas Western/UTEP (5); Alabama and Wyoming (3); Nebraska, New Mexico St., North Carolina, Oklahoma, Oregon, Pittsburgh, Southwestern, Stanford, Texas, West Texas St. and West Virginia (2).

Year		Year		Year	
1936*	14-14, Hardin-Simmons vs New Mexico St.	1958*	Louisville 34, Drake 20	1981	Oklahoma 40, Houston 14
		1958†	Wyoming 14, Hardin-Simmons 6	1982	N. Carolina 26, Texas 10
1937	Hardin-Simmons 34, Texas Mines 6	1959	New Mexico St. 28, N. Texas 8	1983	Alabama 28, SMU 7
1938	West Va. 7, Texas Tech 6			1984	Maryland 28, Tennessee 27
1939	Utah 26, New Mexico 0	1960	New Mexico St. 20, Utah St. 13	1985	13-13, Georgia vs Arizona
		1961	Villanova 17, Wichita 9	1986	Alabama 28, Washington 6
1940	0-0, Catholic U. vs Arizona St.	1962	West Texas 15, Ohio U. 14	1987	Oklahoma St. 35, West Va. 33
1941	W. Reserve 26, Arizona St. 13	1963	Oregon 21, SMU 14	1988	Alabama 29, Army 28
1942	Tulsa 6, Texas Tech 0	1964	Georgia 7, Texas Tech 0	1989	Pittsburgh 31, Texas A&M 28
1943	Second Air Force 13, Hardin-Simmons 7	1965	Texas Western 13, TCU 12		
		1966	Wyoming 28, Florida St. 20	1990	Michigan St. 17, USC 16
1944	Southwestern 7, New Mexico 0	1967	UTEP 14, Mississippi 7	1991	UCLA 6, Illinois 3
1945	Southwestern 35, U. of Mexico 0	1968	Auburn 34, Arizona 10	1992	Baylor 20, Arizona 15
1946	New Mexico 34, Denver 24	1969	Nebraska 45, Georgia 6	1993	Oklahoma 41, Texas Tech 10
1947	Cincinnati 18, Va. Tech 6			1994	Texas 35, N. Carolina 31
1948	Miami-OH 13, Texas Tech 12	1970	Georgia Tech 17, Texas Tech 9	1995	Iowa 38, Washington 18
1949	West Va. 21, Texas Mines 12	1971	LSU 33, Iowa St. 15	1996	Stanford 38, Michigan St. 0
		1972	N. Carolina 32, Texas Tech 28	1997	Arizona St. 17, Iowa 7
1950	Tex. Western 33, Georgetown 20	1973	Missouri 34, Auburn 17	1998	TCU 28, USC 19
1951	West Texas 14, Cincinnati 13	1974	Miss. St. 26, N. Carolina 24	1999	Oregon 24, Minnesota 20
1952	Texas Tech 25, Pacific 14	1975	Pittsburgh 33, Kansas 19	2000	Wisconsin 21, UCLA 20
1953	Pacific 26, Southern Miss. 7	1977*	Texas A&M 37, Florida 14	2001	Washington St. 33, Purdue 27
1954	Tex. Western 37, So. Miss. 14	1977†	Stanford 24, LSU 14		
1955	Tex. Western 47, Florida St. 20	1978	Texas 42, Maryland 0	*January game from 1936-58 and in 1977.
1956	Wyoming 21, Texas Tech 14	1979	Washington 14, Texas 7	
1957	Geo. Wash. 13, Tex. Western 0	1980	Nebraska 31, Miss. St. 17	†December game from 1958-75 and since 1977.

Insight.com Bowl

City: Tucson, Ariz. **Stadium:** Arizona. **Capacity:** 57,803. **Playing surface:** Grass. **First game:** Dec. 31, 1989. **Name change:** Copper Bowl (1989-1996), Insight.com Bowl (since 1997). **Playing site:** Arizona Stadium (since 1989). **Corporate title sponsors:** Domino's Pizza (1990-91), Weiser Lock (1992-1996) and Insight Enterprises (since 1997).

Automatic berths: Third pick from WAC vs. at-large opponent (1992 season); third pick from WAC vs. fourth pick from Big Eight (1993-94 seasons); second pick from WAC vs. sixth pick from Big 12 (1995-97); third pick from Big East or Notre Dame, if available vs. fifth pick from Big 12, if available (since 1998 season).

Multiple wins: Arizona (2).

Year		Year		Year	
1989†	Arizona 17, N.C. State 10	1994	BYU 31, Oklahoma 6	1999	Colorado 62, Boston College 28
1990	California 17, Wyoming 15	1995	Texas Tech 55, Air Force 41	2000	Iowa St. 37, Pittsburgh 29
1991	Indiana 24, Baylor 0	1996	Wisconsin 38, Utah 10	2001	Syracuse 26, Kansas St. 3
1992	Washington St. 31, Utah 28	1997	Arizona 20, New Mexico 14		
1993	Kansas St. 52, Wyoming 17	1998	Missouri 34, W. Virginia 31	†December game since 1989.

Liberty Bowl

City: Memphis, Tenn. **Stadium:** Liberty Bowl Memorial. **Capacity:** 62,380. **Playing surface:** Grass. **First game:** Dec. 19, 1959. **Playing sites:** Municipal Stadium in Philadelphia (1959-63), Convention Hall in Atlantic City, N.J. (1964), Memphis Memorial Stadium (1965-75) and Liberty Bowl Memorial Stadium (since 1976). Memphis Memorial Stadium renamed Liberty Bowl Memorial in 1976. **Corporate title sponsors:** St. Jude's Hospital (since 1993), AXA/Equitable (since 1997).

Automatic berths: Commander-in-Chief's Trophy winner (Army, Navy or Air Force) vs. at-large opponent (1989-92 seasons); none (1993 season); first pick from independent group of Cincinnati, East Carolina, Memphis, Southern Miss. and Tulane vs. at-large opponent (for 1994 and '95 seasons); Conference USA champion vs. fourth pick from the Big East (1996-97 seasons); Conference USA champion, if available, vs. fifth, sixth or seventh pick or at-large from SEC (1998-99 seasons); Mountain West champion vs. Conference USA champion, if available (2000 season).

Multiple wins: Mississippi (4); Penn St. and Tennessee (3); Air Force, Alabama, Louisville, N.C. State, Southern Miss., Syracuse and Tulane (2).

Year		Year		Year	
1959†	Penn St. 7, Alabama 0	1966	Miami-FL 14, Virginia Tech 7	1973	N.C. State 31, Kansas 18
1960	Penn St. 41, Oregon 12	1967	N.C. State 14, Georgia 7	1974	Tennessee 7, Maryland 3
1961	Syracuse 15, Miami-FL 14	1968	Mississippi 34, Virginia Tech 17	1975	USC 20, Texas A&M 0
1962	Oregon St. 6, Villanova 0	1969	Colorado 47, Alabama 33	1976	Alabama 36, UCLA 6
1963	Mississippi St. 16, N.C. State 12	1970	Tulane 17, Colorado 3	1977	Nebraska 21, N. Carolina 17
1964	Utah 32, West Virginia 6	1971	Tennessee 14, Arkansas 13	1978	Missouri 20, LSU 15
1965	Mississippi 13, Auburn 7	1972	Georgia Tech 31, Iowa St. 30	1979	Penn St. 9, Tulane 6

Year		Year		Year	
1980	Purdue 28, Missouri 25	1988	Indiana 34, S. Carolina 10	1996	Syracuse 30, Houston 17
1981	Ohio St. 31, Navy 28	1989	Mississippi 42, Air Force 29	1997	Southern Miss. 41, Pittsburgh 7
1982	Alabama 21, Illinois 15	1990	Air Force 23, Ohio St. 11	1998	Tulane 41, BYU 27
1983	Notre Dame 19, Boston Col. 18	1991	Air Force 38, Mississippi St. 15	1999	Southern Miss. 23, Colorado St. 17
1984	Auburn 21, Arkansas 15	1992	Mississippi 13, Air Force 0	2000	Colorado St. 22, Louisville 17
1985	Baylor 21, LSU 7	1993	Louisville 18, Michigan St. 7	2001	Louisville 28, BYU 10
1986	Tennessee 21, Minnesota 14	1994	Illinois 30, E. Carolina 0		†December game since 1959.
1987	Georgia 20, Arkansas 17	1995	E. Carolina 19, Stanford 13		

Tangerine Bowl

City: Orlando, Fla. **Stadium:** Florida Citrus. **Capacity:** 65,525. **Playing surface:** Grass. **First game:** Dec. 28, 1990. **Name change:** Blockbuster Bowl (1990-93), Carquest Bowl (1994-97), Micron PC Bowl (1998), MicronPC.com Bowl (1999-2000) and Tangerine Bowl (since 2001). The game was called the Sunshine Football Classic for a short time in the off-season after Carquest Auto Parts dropped its sponsorship and before Micron signed on. Also, this game should not be confused with the Tangerine Bowl that became the Citrus Bowl in 1982. **Playing sites:** Joe Robbie Stadium (1990-2000). Name changed to Pro Player Stadium in 1996. **Corporate title sponsors:** Blockbuster Video (1990-93), Carquest Auto Parts (1993-97) and Micron Electronics (1998-2000).

Automatic berths: Penn St. vs. seventh pick from 8-team Bowl Coalition pool (1992 season); third pick from Big East vs. fifth pick from SEC (1993-94 seasons); third pick from Big East vs. fifth pick from SEC (1995 season); third pick from Big East vs. fourth pick from ACC (1996-97 seasons); sixth pick from Big Ten, if available, vs. fourth pick from ACC, if available (1998-2000 seasons); fifth pick from ACC vs. fifth pick from Big East (2001).

Multiple wins: Miami-FL (2).

Year		Year		Year	
1990†	Florida St. 24, Penn St. 17	1995†	N. Carolina 20, Arkansas 10	2000	N.C. State 38, Minnesota 30
1991	Alabama 30, Colorado 25	1996	Miami-FL 31, Virginia 21	2001	Pittsburgh 34, N.C. State 19
1993*	Stanford 24, Penn St. 3	1997	Ga. Tech 35, W. Virginia 30		†December game from 1990-91 and
1994	Boston College 31, Virginia 13	1998	Miami-FL 46, N.C. State 23		since 1995.
1995	S. Carolina 24, West Va. 21	1999	Illinois 63, Virginia 21		*January game 1993-95.

Seattle Bowl

City: Seattle, Wash. **Stadium:** Safeco Field. **Capacity:** 47,116 (for baseball). **Playing surface:** Grass. **First game:** Dec. 25, 1998. **Name change:** Oahu Bowl (1998-2000); Seattle Bowl (since 2001). **Playing sites:** Aloha Stadium (1998-2000), Safeco Field (2001), new Seahawks stadium (2002–). **Corporate title sponsor:** Jeep Eagle Division of Chrysler (1998-2000), 989 Sports (since 2001).

Automatic berths: second or third pick from WAC, if available, vs. fifth pick from Pac-10, if available (1998-99 seasons); fourth or fifth pick from Pac-10 vs. fourth or fifth pick from Big East or fourth pick from ACC (2000 season).

Year		Year			
1998†	Air Force 45, Washington 25	2000	Georgia 37, Virginia 14		†December game since 1998.
1999	Hawaii 23, Oregon St. 17	2001	Georgia Tech 24, Stanford 14		

Humanitarian Bowl

City: Boise, Idaho. **Stadium:** Bronco. **Capacity:** 30,000. **Playing surface:** AstroTurf. **First game:** Dec. 29, 1997. **Playing sites:** Bronco Stadium (since 1997). **Corporate title sponsor:** World Sports Humanitarian Hall of Fame (since 1997) and Crucial.com (since 1999).

Automatic berths: Big West champion, if available, vs. at-large (since 1997 season).

Multiple wins: Boise St. (2).

Year		Year		Year	
1997†	Cincinnati 35, Utah St. 19	1999	Boise St. 34, Louisville 31	2001	Clemson 49, La. Tech 24
1998	Idaho 42, Southern Miss. 35	2000	Boise St. 38, UTEP 23		†December game since 1997.

Las Vegas Bowl

City: Las Vegas, Nev. **Stadium:** Sam Boyd. **Capacity:** 40,000. **Playing surface:** AstroTurf. **First game:** Dec. 18, 1992. **Playing site:** Sam Boyd Stadium (since 1992). **Corporate title sponsor:** EA Sports (1999-2000) Sega Sports (since 2001).

Automatic berths: Mid-American champion vs. Big West champion (1992-96 season); none (1997 season); second or third pick from WAC, if available vs. at-large (since 1998 season).

Multiple wins: Fresno St. (4); UNLV (3); Bowling Green, San Jose St., Toledo and Utah (2).

Year		Year		Year	
1981†	Toledo 27, San Jose St. 25	1990	San Jose St. 48, C. Michigan 24	1999	Utah 17, Fresno St. 16
1982	Fresno St. 29, Bowling Green 28	1991	Bowling Green 28, Fresno St. 21	2000	UNLV 31, Arkansas 14
1983	Northern Ill. 20, CS-Fullerton 15	1992	Bowling Green 35, Nevada 34	2001	Utah 10, USC 6
1984*	UNLV 30, Toledo 13	1993	Utah St. 42, Ball St. 33		†December game since 1981.
1985	Fresno St. 51, Bowling Green 7	1994	UNLV 52, C. Michigan 24		* Toledo later ruled winner of 1984
1986	San Jose St. 37, Miami-OH 7	1995	Toledo 40, Nevada 37 (OT)		game by forfeit because UNLV used
1987	E. Michigan 30, San Jose St. 27	1996	Nevada 18, Ball St. 15		ineligible players.
1988	Fresno St. 35, W. Michigan 30	1997	Oregon 41, Air Force 13		
1989	Fresno St. 27, Ball St. 6	1998	N. Carolina 20, San Diego St. 13		

Note: The MAC and Big West champs met in a bowl game from 1981 to 1996, originally in Fresno at the California Bowl (1981-88, 1992) and California Raisin Bowl (1989-91). The results from 1981-91 are included below.

Bowl Games (Cont.)

Independence Bowl

City: Shreveport, La. **Stadium:** Independence. **Capacity:** 50,832. **Playing surface:** Grass. **First game:** Dec. 13, 1976. **Playing site:** Independence Stadium (since 1976). **Corporate title sponsors:** Poulan/Weed Eater (1990-97), Sanford (1998-2000) and Mainstay (since 2001). **Automatic berths:** Southland Conference champion vs. at-large opponent (1976-81 seasons); none (1982-95 seasons); fifth pick from SEC, if available, vs. at-large (1995-97 season); fifth, sixth or seventh pick from SEC, if available, vs. at-large (1998-99 season); sixth pick from Big 12 vs. SEC (2000 season).

Multiple wins: Mississippi (3); Air Force, LSU and Southern Miss (2).

Year		Year		Year	
1976†	McNeese St. 20, Tulsa 16	1985	Minnesota 20, Clemson 13	1994	Virginia 20, TCU 10
1977	La. Tech 24, Louisville 14	1986	Mississippi 20, Texas Tech 17	1995	LSU 45, Michigan St. 26
1978	E. Carolina 35, La. Tech 13	1987	Washington 24, Tulane 12	1996	Auburn 32, Army 29
1979	Syracuse 31, McNeese St. 7	1988	Southern Miss 38, UTEP 18	1997	LSU 27, Notre Dame 9
1980	Southern Miss 16, McNeese St. 14	1989	Oregon 27, Tulsa 24	1998	Mississippi 35, Texas Tech 18
1981	Texas A&M 33, Oklahoma St. 16			1999	Mississippi 27, Oklahoma 25
1982	Wisconsin 14, Kansas St. 3	1990	34-34, La. Tech vs Maryland	2000	Mississippi St. 43, Texas A&M 41
1983	Air Force 9, Mississippi 3	1991	Georgia 24, Arkansas 15	2001	Alabama 14, Iowa St. 13
1984	Air Force 23, Va. Tech 7	1992	Wake Forest 39, Oregon 35	†December game since 1976.	
		1993	Va. Tech 45, Indiana 20		

Motor City Bowl

City: Pontiac, Mich. **Stadium:** Pontiac Silverdome. **Capacity:** 80,368. **Playing surface:** Turf. **First game:** Dec. 26, 1997. **Playing site:** Pontiac Silverdome (since 1997). **Corporate title sponsor:** Ford Division of Ford Motor Company (since 1997), Daimler Chrysler and General Motors (since 2002). **Automatic berths:** Mid-American champions vs at-large (1997-99 season); Mid-American champions vs. fourth pick from Conference USA (2000 season).

Multiple wins: Marshall (3).

Year		Year		Year	
1997†	Mississippi 34, Marshall 31	1999	Marshall 21, BYU 3	2001	Toledo 23, Cincinnati 16
1998	Marshall 48, Louisville 29	2000	Marshall 25, Cincinnati 14	†December game since 1997.	

Music City Bowl

City: Nashville, Tenn. **Stadium:** Adelphia Coliseum. **Capacity:** 67,000. **Playing surface:** Grass. **First game:** Dec. 29, 1998. **Playing sites:** Vanderbilt Stadium (1998) and Adelphia Coliseum (since 1999). **Corporate title sponsors:** American General (1998), HomePoint.com (1999-2000) and Gaylord Hotels (since 2002). **Automatic berths:** sixth choice from the SEC, if available, vs. at-large (1998-99 season); fourth pick from Big East, if available vs. SEC (2000 season).

Year		Year			
1998†	Va. Tech 38, Alabama 7	2000	West Va. 49, Mississippi 38	†December game since 1998.	
1999	Syracuse 20, Kentucky 13	2001	Boston Col. 20, Georgia 16		

GMAC Bowl

City: Mobile, Ala. **Stadium:** Ladd-Peebles. **Capacity:** 40,646. **Playing surface:** Grass. **First game:** Dec. 22, 1999. **Name change:** Mobile Bowl (1999-2000), GMAC Bowl (since 2001). **Playing sites:** Ladd-Peebles Stadium (since 1999). **Corporate title sponsors:** GMAC Financial Services (since 2001). **Automatic berths:** WAC champions (if team is from the east) or second pick from WAC vs. second pick from Conference USA, if available (2000 season).

Year		Year		
1999†	TCU 28, E. Carolina 14	2001	Marshall 64, East Carolina 61	
2000	So. Miss 28, TCU 21			†December game since 1999.

GalleryFurniture.com Bowl

City: Houston, Tex. **Stadium:** Astrodome. **Capacity:** 59,969. **Playing surface:** Turf. **First game:** Dec. 27, 2000. **Playing sites:** Astrodome (since 2000). **Corporate title sponsors:** GalleryFurniture.com (since 2000). **Automatic berths:** Big 12 vs. Conference USA.

Year		
2000†	E. Carolina 40, Tex. Tech 27	†December game since 2000.
2001	Texas A&M 28, TCU 9	

Silicon Valley Classic

City: San Jose, Calif. **Stadium:** Spartan. **Capacity:** 30,578. **Playing surface:** Grass. **First game:** Dec. 31, 2000. **Playing sites:** Spartan Stadium (since 2000). **Corporate title sponsors:** none. **Automatic berths:** WAC vs. at-large

Year		Year		
2000†	Air Force 37, Fresno St. 34	2001	Michigan St. 44, Fresno St. 35	†December game since 2000.

New Orleans Bowl

City: New Orleans, La. **Stadium:** Louisiana Superdome. **Capacity:** 70,200. **Playing surface:** Turf. **First game:** Dec. 18, 2001. **Playing sites:** Louisiana Superdome (since 2001). **Corporate title sponsors:** none. **Automatic berths:** Sun Belt champion vs. Conference USA (since 2002).

Year	
2001†	Colorado St. 45, North Texas 20

†December game since 2001.

All-Time Winningest Division I-A Teams

Schools classified as Division I-A for at least 10 years; through 2001 season (including bowl games).

Top 25 Winning Percentage

		Yrs	Gm	W	L	T	Pct	Bowls App	Record	2001 Season Bowl	Record
1	Notre Dame	113	1070	781	247	42	.750	24	13-11-0	none	5-6
2	Michigan	122	1115	813	266	36	.745	33	17-16-0	lost Citrus	8-4
3	Alabama*	107	1068	744	281	43	.717	51	29-19-3	won Independence	7-5
4	Nebraska	112	1105	764	301	40	.710	40	20-20-0	lost Rose	11-2
5	Oklahoma	107	1046	713	280	53	.707	35	22-12-1	won Cotton	11-2
6	Texas	109	1092	755	304	33	.707	41	19-20-2	won Holiday	11-2
7	Ohio St.	112	1076	731	292	53	.704	33	14-19-0	lost Outback	7-5
8	Tennessee*	105	1064	718	294	52	.699	42	23-19-0	won Citrus	11-2
9	Penn St.	115	1104	744	319	41	.692	36	23-11-2	none	5-6
10	USC	109	1032	684	294	54	.689	40	25-15-0	lost Las Vegas	6-6
11	Florida St.*	55	606	400	189	17	.674	30	18-10-2	won Gator	8-4
12	Washington*	112	1016	625	341	50	.640	28	14-13-1	lost Holiday	8-4
13	Miami-OH*	113	985	604	337	44	.636	7	5-2-0	none	7-5
14	Georgia	108	1069	649	366	54	.632	37	19-15-3	lost Music City	8-4
15	Miami-FL	75	785	484	282	19	.629	26	15-11-0	won Rose	12-0
16	LSU*	108	1038	628	363	47	.628	33	16-16-1	won Sugar	10-3
17	Arizona St.	89	815	494	297	24	.621	19	10-8-1	none	4-7
18	Auburn*	109	1034	617	370	47	.619	28	14-12-2	lost Peach	7-5
19	Central Michigan	101	860	515	309	36	.618	2	0-2-0	none	3-8
20	Florida	95	963	574	349	40	.617	29	14-15-0	won Orange	10-2
21	Colorado*	112	1036	621	379	36	.617	24	11-13-0	lost Fiesta	10-3
22	Army	112	1054	621	382	51	.613	4	2-2-0	none	3-8
23	Texas A&M	107	1055	617	390	48	.608	27	13-14-0	won Gallery Furniture	8-4
24	Syracuse	112	1111	648	414	49	.605	21	12-8-1	won Insight.com	10-3
25	UCLA	83	846	491	318	37	.602	23	11-11-1	none	7-4

*Includes games forfeited following rulings by the NCAA Executive Council and/or the Committee on Infractions.

Top 50 Victories

		Wins			Wins			Wins
1	Michigan	813		Texas A&M	617	35	Maryland	545
2	Notre Dame	781	19	Georgia Tech	609	36	Missouri	544
3	Nebraska	764	20	North Carolina	608		Boston College	544
4	Texas	755	21	West Virginia	606	38	Wisconsin	541
5	Penn St.	744	22	Miami-OH	604	39	Illinois	536
	Alabama	744	23	Pittsburgh	603	40	Utah	532
7	Ohio St.	731	24	Arkansas	601	41	Vanderbilt	527
8	Tennessee	718	25	Minnesota	591		Stanford	527
9	Oklahoma	713	26	Virginia Tech	587	43	Purdue	522
10	USC	684	27	Navy	579	44	Kentucky	521
11	Georgia	649	28	Clemson	578	45	Kansas	518
12	Syracuse	648	29	Florida	574	46	Central Michigan	515
13	LSU	628	30	Michigan St.	568	47	Arizona	513
14	Washington	625	31	Mississippi	566	48	Iowa	508
15	Army	621	32	Virginia	561	49	Oregon	502
	Colorado	621	33	California	559	50	Louisiana Tech	501
17	Auburn	617	34	Rutgers	552			

Top 30 Bowl Appearances

		App	Record			App	Record			App	Record
1	Alabama	51	29-19-3	12	Arkansas	32	10-19-3	23	Notre Dame	24	13-11-0
2	Tennessee	42	23-19-0	13	Georgia Tech	30	20-10-0		North Carolina	24	12-12-0
3	Texas	41	19-20-2		Florida St	30	18-10-2		Colorado	24	11-13-0
4	USC	40	25-15-0	15	Mississippi	29	17-12-0	26	UCLA	23	11-11-1
	Nebraska	40	20-20-0		Florida	29	14-15-0		BYU	23	7-15-1
6	Georgia	37	19-15-3	17	Auburn	28	14-12-2	28	Missouri	21	9-12-0
7	Penn St	36	23-11-2		Washington	28	14-13-1		West Virginia	21	9-12-0
8	Oklahoma	35	22-12-1	19	Texas A&M	27	13-14-0		Syracuse	21	12-8-1
9	LSU	33	16-16-1	20	Miami-FL	26	15-11-0		Pittsburgh	21	9-12-0
	Ohio St.	33	14-19-0	21	Texas Tech	25	5-19-1				
	Michigan	33	17-16-0		Clemson	25	13-12-0				

Note: Alabama, Georgia, Georgia Tech, Miami-FL, Notre Dame, Ohio State and Penn State are the only schools that have won all four of the traditional major bowl games—the Rose, Orange, Sugar and Cotton. Ohio State, Penn State and Notre Dame are the only schools to have won those four and the recently prestigious Fiesta bowl.

Major Conference Champions
Atlantic Coast Conference

Founded in 1953 when charter members all left Southern Conference to form ACC. **Charter members** (7): Clemson, Duke, Maryland, North Carolina, N.C. State, South Carolina and Wake Forest. **Admitted later** (3): Virginia in 1953 (began play in '54), Georgia Tech in 1979 (began play in '83); Florida St. in 1990 (began play in '92). **Withdrew later** (1): South Carolina in 1971 (became an independent after '70 season).

2002 playing membership (9): Clemson, Duke, Florida St., Georgia Tech, Maryland, North Carolina, N.C. State, Virginia and Wake Forest.

Multiple titles: Clemson (13); Florida St. and Maryland (9); Duke and N.C. State (7); North Carolina (5); Georgia Tech & Virginia (2).

Year		Year		Year		Year	
1953	Duke (4-0) & Maryland (3-0)	1965	Clemson (5-2) & N.C. State (5-2)	1979	N.C. State (5-1)	1991	Clemson (6-0-1)
1954	Duke (4-0)	1966	Clemson (6-1)	1980	North Carolina (6-0)	1992	Florida St. (8-0)
1955	Maryland (4-0) & Duke (4-0)	1967	Clemson (6-0)	1981	Clemson (6-0)	1993	Florida St. (8-0)
1956	Clemson (4-0-1)	1968	N.C. State (6-1)	1982	Clemson (6-0)	1994	Florida St. (8-0)
1957	N.C. State (5-0-1)	1969	South Carolina (6-0)	1983	Clemson (7-0) † & Maryland (5-0)	1995	Virginia (7-1) & Florida St. (7-1)
1958	Clemson (5-1)	1970	Wake Forest (5-1)	1984	Maryland (5-0)	1996	Florida St. (8-0)
1959	Clemson (6-1)	1971	North Carolina (6-0)	1985	Maryland (6-0)	1997	Florida St. (8-0)
1960	Duke (5-1)	1972	North Carolina (6-0)	1986	Clemson (5-1-1)	1998	Florida St. (7-1) & Georgia Tech (7-1)
1961	Duke (5-1)	1973	N.C. State (6-0)	1987	Clemson (6-1)	1999	Florida St. (8-0)
1962	Duke (6-0)	1974	Maryland (6-0)	1988	Clemson (6-1)		
1963	North Carolina (6-1) & N.C. State (6-1)	1975	Maryland (5-0)	1989	Virginia (6-1) & Duke (6-1)	2000	Florida St. (8-0)
1964	N.C. State (5-2)	1976	Maryland (5-0)			2001	Maryland (7-1)
		1977	North Carolina (5-0-1)	1990	Georgia Tech (6-0-1)	†On probation, ineligible for championship.	
		1978	Clemson (6-0)				

Big East Conference

Founded in 1991 when charter members gave up independent football status to form Big East. **Charter members** (8): Boston College, Miami-FL, Pittsburgh, Rutgers, Syracuse, Temple, Virginia Tech and West Virginia. **Note:** Temple and Virginia Tech are Big East members in football only.

2002 playing membership (8): Boston College, Miami-FL, Pittsburgh, Rutgers, Syracuse, Temple, Virginia Tech and West Virginia.

Conference champion: Member schools needed two years to adjust their regular season schedules in order to begin round-robin conference play in 1993. In the meantime, the 1991 and '92 Big East titles went to the highest-ranked member in the final regular season *USA Today*/CNN coaches' poll.

Multiple titles: Miami-FL (7); Syracuse (4); Virginia Tech (3).

Year		Year		Year		Year	
1991	Miami-FL (2-0, #1) & Syracuse (5-0, #16)	1994	Miami-FL (7-0)	1996	Virginia Tech (6-1), Miami-FL (6-1) & Syracuse (6-1)	1998	Syracuse (6-1)
1992	Miami-FL (4-0, #1)	1995	Virginia Tech (6-1) & Miami-FL (6-1)	1997	Syracuse (6-1)	1999	Virginia Tech (7-0)
1993	West Virginia (7-0)					2000	Miami-FL (7-0)
						2001	Miami-FL (7-0)

Big Ten Conference

Originally founded in 1895 as the Intercollegiate Conference of Faculty Representatives, better known as the Western Conference. **Charter members** (7): Chicago, Illinois, Michigan, Minnesota, Northwestern, Purdue and Wisconsin. **Admitted later** (5): Indiana and Iowa in 1899; Ohio St. in 1912; Michigan St. in 1950 (began play in '53); Penn St. in 1990 (began play in '93). **Withdrew later** (2): Michigan in 1907 (rejoined in '17); Chicago in 1940 (dropped football after '39 season). **Note:** Iowa belonged to both the Western and Missouri Valley conferences from 1907-10.

Unofficially called the **Big Ten** from 1912 until Chicago's withdrawal in 1939, then the **Big Nine** from 1940 until Michigan St. began conference play in 1953. Formally named the **Big Ten** in 1984 and has kept the name even after adding Penn St. as its 11th member in 1990.

2002 playing membership (11): Illinois, Indiana, Iowa, Michigan, Michigan St., Minnesota, Northwestern, Ohio St., Penn St., Purdue and Wisconsin.

Multiple titles: Michigan (40); Ohio St. (28); Minnesota (18); Illinois (15); Wisconsin (11); Iowa (9); Purdue and Northwestern (8); Chicago and Michigan St. (6); Indiana (2).

Year		Year		Year		Year	
1896	Wisconsin (2-0-1)	1906	Wisconsin (3-0), Minnesota (2-0) & Michigan (1-0)	1918	Illinois (4-0), Michigan (2-0) & Purdue (1-0)	1928	Illinois (4-1)
1897	Wisconsin (3-0)					1929	Purdue (5-0)
1898	Michigan (3-0)	1907	Chicago (4-0)	1919	Illinois (6-1)	1930	Michigan (5-0) & Northwestern (5-0)
1899	Chicago (4-0)	1908	Chicago (5-0)	1920	Ohio St. (5-0)		
1900	Iowa (3-0-1) & Minnesota (3-0-1)	1909	Minnesota (3-0)	1921	Iowa (5-0)	1931	Purdue (5-1), Michigan (5-1) & Northwestern (5-1)
		1910	Illinois (4-0) & Minnesota (2-0)	1922	Iowa (5-0) & Michigan (4-0)		
1901	Michigan (4-0) & Wisconsin (2-0)					1932	Michigan (6-0) & Purdue (5-0-1)
1902	Michigan (5-0)	1911	Minnesota (3-0-1)	1923	Illinois (5-0) & Michigan (4-0)		
1903	Michigan (3-0-1), Minnesota (3-0-1) & Northwestern (1-0-2)	1912	Wisconsin (6-0)	1924	Chicago (3-0-3)	1933	Michigan (5-0-1) & Minnesota (2-0-4)
		1913	Chicago (7-0)	1925	Michigan (5-1)		
		1914	Illinois (6-0)	1926	Michigan (5-0) & Northwestern (5-0)	1934	Minnesota (5-0)
1904	Minnesota (3-0) & Michigan (2-0)	1915	Minnesota (3-0-1) & Illinois (3-0-2)	1927	Illinois (5-0) & Minnesota (3-0-1)	1935	Minnesota (5-0) & Ohio St. (5-0)
1905	Chicago (7-0)	1916	Ohio St. (4-0)			1936	Northwestern (6-0)
		1917	Ohio St. (4-0)			1937	Minnesota (5-0)

Year		Year		Year		Year	
1938	Minnesota (4-1)	1956	Iowa (5-1)	1973	Ohio St. (7-0-1) & Michigan (7-0-1)	1989	Michigan (8-0)
1939	Ohio St. (5-1)	1957	Ohio St. (7-0)			1990	Iowa (6-2),
1940	Minnesota (6-0)	1958	Iowa (5-1)	1974	Ohio St. (7-1) & Michigan (7-1)		Michigan (6-2), Michigan St. (6-2)
1941	Minnesota (5-0)	1959	Wisconsin (5-2)	1975	Ohio St. (8-0)		& Illinois (6-2)
1942	Ohio St. (5-1)	1960	Minnesota (5-1) & Iowa (5-1)	1976	Michigan (7-1) & Ohio St. (7-1)	1991	Michigan (8-.90)
1943	Purdue (6-0) & Michigan (6-0)	1961	Ohio St. (6-0)	1977	Michigan (7-1) & Ohio St. (7-1)	1992	Michigan (6-0-2)
1944	Ohio St. (6-0)	1962	Wisconsin (6-1)	1978	Michigan (7-1) & Michigan St. (7-1)	1993	Wisconsin (6-1-1) & Ohio St. (6-1-1)
1945	Indiana (5-0-1)	1963	Illinois (5-1-1)	1979	Ohio St. (8-0)	1994	Penn St. (8-0)
1946	Illinois (6-1)	1964	Michigan (6-1)	1980	Michigan (8-0)	1995	Northwestern (8-0)
1947	Michigan (6-0)	1965	Michigan St. (7-0)	1981	Iowa (6-2) & Ohio St. (6-2)	1996	Ohio St. (7-1) & Northwestern (7-1)
1948	Michigan (6-0)	1966	Michigan St. (7-0)	1982	Michigan (8-1)	1997	Michigan (8-0)
1949	Ohio St. (4-1-1) & Michigan (4-1-1)	1967	Indiana (6-1), Purdue (6-1) & Minnesota (6-1)	1983	Illinois (9-0)	1998	Ohio St. (7-1), Wisconsin (7-1)
1950	Michigan (4-1-1)	1968	Ohio St. (7-0)	1984	Ohio St. (7-2)		& Michigan (7-1)
1951	Illinois (5-0-1)	1969	Ohio St. (6-1) & Michigan (6-1)	1985	Iowa (7-1)	1999	Wisconsin (7-1)
1952	Wisconsin (4-1-1) & Purdue (4-1-1)	1970	Ohio St. (7-0)	1986	Michigan (7-1) & Ohio St. (7-1)	2000	Purdue (6-2), Michigan (6-2)
1953	Michigan St. (5-1) & Illinois (5-1)	1971	Michigan (8-0)	1987	Michigan St. (7-0-1)		& Northwestern (6-2)
1954	Ohio St. (7-0)	1972	Ohio St. (7-1) & Michigan (7-1)	1988	Michigan (7-0-1)	2001	Illinois (7-1)
1955	Ohio St. (6-0)						

Big Eight Conference (1907-1996)

Originally founded in 1907 as the Missouri Valley Intercollegiate Athletic Assn. **Charter members** (5): Iowa, Kansas, Missouri, Nebraska and Washington University of St. Louis. **Admitted later** (11): Drake and Iowa St. (then Ames College) in 1908; Kansas St. (then Kansas College of Applied Science and Agriculture) in 1913; Grinnell (Iowa) College in 1919; Oklahoma in 1920; Oklahoma A&M (now Oklahoma St.) in 1925; Colorado in 1947 (began play in '48).

Withdrew later (9): Iowa in 1911 (left for Big Ten after 1910 season), Colorado, Iowa St., Kansas, Kansas St. Missouri, Nebraska, Oklahoma and Oklahoma St. in 1996 (left for Big 12 after 1995 season); **Excluded later** (4): Drake, Grinnell, Oklahoma A&M and Washington-MO (left out when MVIAA cut membership to six teams in 1928).

Streamlined MVIAA unofficially called **Big Six** from 1928-47 with surviving members Iowa St., Kansas, Kansas St., Missouri, Nebraska and Oklahoma. Became the **Big Seven** after 1947 season when Colorado came over from the Skyline Conference, and then the **Big Eight** with the return of Oklahoma A&M in 1957. A&M, which resumed conference play in '60, became Oklahoma St. on July 10, 1957. The MVIAA was officially renamed the Big Eight in 1964. The league folded in 1996 when the existing members formed the newly created Big 12 along with four schools from the Southwest Conference.

Multiple titles: Nebraska (43); Oklahoma (34); Missouri (12); Colorado and Kansas (5); Iowa St. and Oklahoma St. (2).

Year		Year		Year		Year	
1907	Iowa (1-0) & Nebraska (1-0)	1928	Nebraska (4-0)	1952	Oklahoma (5-0-1)	1976	Colorado (5-2), Oklahoma (5-2)
1908	Kansas (4-0)	1929	Nebraska (3-0-2)	1953	Oklahoma (6-0)		& Oklahoma St.
1909	Missouri (4-0-1)	1930	Kansas (4-1)	1954	Oklahoma (6-0)		(5-2)
1910	Nebraska (2-0)	1931	Nebraska (5-0)	1955	Oklahoma (6-0)	1977	Oklahoma (7-0)
1911	Iowa St. (2-0) & Nebraska (2-0-1)	1932	Nebraska (5-0)	1956	Oklahoma (6-0)	1978	Nebraska (6-1) & Oklahoma (6-1)
1912	Iowa St. (2-0) & Nebraska (2-0)	1933	Nebraska (5-0)	1957	Oklahoma (6-0)		
		1934	Kansas St. (5-0)	1958	Oklahoma (6-0)	1979	Oklahoma (7-0)
1913	Missouri (4-0) & Nebraska (3-0)	1935	Nebraska (4-0-1)	1959	Oklahoma (5-1)		
		1936	Nebraska (5-0)	1960	Missouri (7-0)	1980	Oklahoma (7-0)
1914	Nebraska (3-0)	1937	Nebraska (3-0-2)	1961	Colorado (7-0)	1981	Nebraska (7-0)
1915	Nebraska (4-0)	1938	Oklahoma (5-0)	1962	Oklahoma (7-0)	1982	Nebraska (7-0)
1916	Nebraska (3-1)	1939	Missouri (5-0)	1963	Nebraska (7-0)	1983	Nebraska (7-0)
1917	Nebraska (2-0)	1940	Nebraska (5-0)	1964	Nebraska (6-1)	1984	Oklahoma (6-1) & Nebraska (6-1)
1918	Vacant (WW I)	1941	Missouri (5-0)	1965	Nebraska (7-0)		
1919	Missouri (4-0-1)	1942	Missouri (4-0-1)	1966	Nebraska (6-1)	1985	Oklahoma (7-0)
1920	Oklahoma (4-0-1)	1943	Oklahoma (5-0)	1967	Oklahoma (7-0)	1986	Oklahoma (7-0)
1921	Nebraska (3-0)	1944	Oklahoma (4-0-1)	1968	Kansas (6-1) & Oklahoma (6-1)	1987	Oklahoma (7-0)
1922	Nebraska (5-0)	1945	Missouri (5-0)			1988	Nebraska (7-0)
1923	Nebraska (3-0-2) & Kansas (3-0-3)	1946	Oklahoma (4-1) & Kansas (4-1)	1969	Missouri (6-1) & Nebraska (6-1)	1989	Colorado (7-0)
1924	Missouri (5-1)	1947	Kansas (4-0-1) & Oklahoma (4-0-1)	1970	Nebraska (7-0)	1990	Colorado (7-0)
1925	Missouri (5-1)	1948	Oklahoma (5-0)	1971	Nebraska (7-0)	1991	Nebraska (6-0-1) & Colorado (6-0-1)
1926	Okla. A&M (3-0-1)	1949	Oklahoma (5-0)	1972	Nebraska (5-1-1)*		
1927	Missouri (5-1)	1950	Oklahoma (6-0)	1973	Oklahoma (7-0)	1992	Nebraska (6-1)
		1951	Oklahoma (6-0)	1974	Oklahoma (7-0)	1993	Nebraska (7-0)
				1975	Nebraska (6-1) & Oklahoma (6-1)	1994	Nebraska (7-0)
						1995	Nebraska (7-0)

*Oklahoma (6-1) forfeited title in 1972 after a player was ruled ineligible.

Major Conference Champions (Cont.)

Big 12 Conference

Originally founded in 1996 by the former teams of the Big Eight and four schools from the Southwest Conference. The league stages a conference championship game between the two division winners on the first Saturday in December. **Playing sites:** Trans World Dome in St. Louis (1996, 1998), the Alamodome in San Antonio (1997, 1999), Arrowhead Stadium in Kansas City, Mo. (2000) and Texas Stadium in Irving, Texas (2001). The 2002 game is set for Houston's Reliant Stadium and the game returns to Arrowhead Stadium in 2003.

2002 playing membership: (12) NORTH—Colorado, Iowa St., Kansas, Kansas St., Missouri and Nebraska; SOUTH—Baylor, Oklahoma, Oklahoma St., Texas, Texas A&M and Texas Tech.

Multiple titles: Nebraska (2).

Year	Year	Year
1996 Texas 37, Nebraska 27	1998 Texas A&M 36, Kansas St. 33	2000 Oklahoma 27, Kansas St. 24
1997 Nebraska 54, Texas A&M 15	1999 Nebraska 22, Texas 6	2001 Colorado 39, Texas 37

Big West Conference (1969-2000)

Originally founded in 1969 as Pacific Coast Athletic Assn. **Charter members** (7): CS-Los Angeles, Fresno St., Long Beach St., Pacific, San Diego St., San Jose St. and UC-Santa Barbara. **Admitted later** (12): CS-Fullerton in 1974; Utah St. in 1977 (began play in '78); UNLV in 1982; New Mexico St. in 1983 (began play in '84); Nevada in 1991 (began play in '92); Arkansas St., Louisiana Tech, Northern Illinois and SW Louisiana in 1992 (all four began play in football only in '93); Boise St., Idaho and North Texas in 1994 (all three began play in '96); Arkansas St. rejoined in 1999 (in football only). **Withdrew later** (14): CS-Los Angeles and UC-Santa Barbara in 1972 (both dropped football after '71 season; San Diego St. in 1975 (became an independent after '75 season); Fresno St. in 1991 (left for WAC after '91 season); Long Beach St. in 1991 (dropped football after '91 season); CS-Fullerton in 1992 (dropped football after '92 season); San Jose St. and UNLV in 1994 (left for WAC after '95 season); Pacific in 1995 (dropped football after '95 season); Arkansas St., Louisiana Tech, Northern Illinois and SW Louisiana in 1995 (all four returned to independent football status after '95 season); Nevada in 2000 (left for WAC after '99 season). **Conference renamed** Big West in 1988.

Multiple titles: San Jose St. (8); Fresno St. (6); Nevada, San Diego St. and Utah St. (5); Long Beach St. (3); Boise St., CS-Fullerton and SW Louisiana (2).

Year		Year		Year	
1969	San Diego St. (6-0)	1981	San Jose St. (5-0)	1993	Utah St. (5-1)
1970	Long Beach St. (5-1)	1982	Fresno St. (6-0)		& SW Louisiana (5-1)
	& San Diego St. (5-1)	1983	CS-Fullerton (5-1)	1994	UNLV (5-1),
1971	Long Beach St. (5-1)	1984	CS-Fullerton (6-1)†		Nevada (5-1),
1972	San Diego St. (4-0)	1985	Fresno St. (7-0)		& SW Louisiana (5-1)
1973	San Diego St. (3-0-1)	1986	San Jose St. (7-0)	1995	Nevada (6-0)
1974	San Diego St. (4-0)	1987	San Jose St. (7-0)	1996	Nevada (4-1)
1975	San Jose St. (5-0)	1988	Fresno St. (7-0)		& Utah St. (4-1)
1976	San Jose St. (4-0)	1989	Fresno St. (7-0)	1997	Utah St. (4-1)
1977	Fresno St. (4-0)	1990	San Jose St. (7-0)		& Nevada (4-1)
1978	San Jose St. (4-1)	1991	Fresno St. (6-1)	1998	Idaho (4-1)
	& Utah St. (4-1)		& San Jose St. (6-1)	1999	Boise St. (5-1)
1979	Utah St. (4-0-1)*	1992	Nevada (5-1)	2000	Boise St. (5-0)
1980	Long Beach St. (5-0)				

*San Jose St. (4-0-1) forfeited share of title in 1979 for use of an ineligible player.
†UNLV (7-0) forfeited title in 1984 for use of ineligible players.

Conference USA

Founded in 1994 by six independent football schools which began play as a conference in 1996. **Charter members** (6): Cincinnati, Houston, Louisville, Memphis, Southern Mississippi and Tulane. **Admitted later** (4): East Carolina in 1997, Army in 1998, Univ. of Alabama-Birmingham in 1999, Texas Christian Univ. in 2001; **2002 playing members** (10): Alabama-Birmingham, Army, Cincinnati, East Carolina, Houston, Louisville, Memphis, Southern Mississippi, TCU and Tulane.

Multiple titles: Southern Mississippi (3), Louisville (2).

Year	Year	Year
1996 Southern Mississippi (4-1)	1998 Tulane (6-0)	2000 Louisville (6-1)
& Houston (4-1)	1999 Southern Mississippi (6-0)	2001 Louisville (6-1)
1997 Southern Mississippi (6-0)		

Mid-American Conference

Founded in 1946. **Charter members** (6): Butler, Cincinnati, Miami-OH, Ohio University, Western Michigan and Western Reserve (Miami and WMU began play in '48). **Admitted later** (12): Kent St. (now Kent) and Toledo in 1951 (Toledo began play in '52); Bowling Green in 1952; Marshall in 1954; Central Michigan and Eastern Michigan in 1972 (CMU began play in '75 and EMU in '76); Ball St. and Northern Illinois in 1973 (both began play in '75); Akron in 1991 (began play in '92); Marshall and Northern Illinois in 1995 (both resumed play in '97); Buffalo in 1995 (resumed play in '99); Central Florida in 2002. **Withdrew later** (5): Butler in 1950 (left for the Indiana Collegiate Conference); Cincinnati in 1953 (went independent); Western Reserve (now Case Western) in 1955 (left for President's Athletic Conference); Marshall in 1969 (went independent); and Northern Illinois in 1986 (went independent).

2002 playing membership (14): EAST—Akron, Buffalo, Central Florida, Kent St., Marshall, Miami-OH and Ohio University; WEST—Ball St., Bowling Green, Central Michigan, Eastern Michigan, Northern Illinois, Toledo and Western Michigan.

Multiple titles: Miami-OH (13); Bowling Green (10); Toledo (8); Ball St. and Ohio University (5); Central Michigan, Cincinnati and Marshall (4); Western Michigan (2).

Year		Year		Year		Year	
1947	Cincinnati (3-1)	1960	Ohio Univ. (6-0)	1972	Kent St. (4-1)	1987	Eastern Mich. (7-1)
1948	Miami-OH (4-0)	1961	Bowling Green (5-1)	1973	Miami-OH (5-0)	1988	Western Mich. (7-1)
1949	Cincinnati (4-0)	1962	Bowling Green (5-0-1)	1974	Miami-OH (5-0)	1989	Ball St. (6-1-1)
1950	Miami-OH (4-0)	1963	Ohio Univ. (5-1)	1975	Miami-OH (6-0)	1990	Central Mich. (7-1)
1951	Cincinnati (3-0)	1964	Bowling Green (5-1)	1976	Ball St. (4-1)		& Toledo (7-1)
1952	Cincinnati (3-0)	1965	Bowling Green (5-1)	1977	Miami-OH (5-0)	1991	Bowling Green (8-0)
1953	Ohio Univ. (5-0-1)		& Miami-OH (5-1)	1978	Ball St. (8-0)	1992	Bowling Green (8-0)
	& Miami-OH (3-0-1)	1966	Miami-OH (5-1)	1979	Central Mich. (8-0-1)	1993	Ball St. (7-0-1)
1954	Miami-OH (4-0)		& Western Mich. (5-1)			1994	Central Mich. (8-1)
1955	Miami-OH (5-0)	1967	Toledo (5-1)	1980	Central Mich. (7-2)	1995	Toledo (7-0-1)
1956	Bowling Green (5-0-1)		& Ohio Univ. (5-1)	1981	Toledo (8-1)	1996	Ball St. (7-1)
	& Miami-OH (4-0-1)	1968	Ohio Univ. (6-0)	1982	Bowling Green (7-2)		
1957	Miami-OH (5-0)	1969	Toledo (5-0)	1983	Northern Ill. (8-1)		
1958	Miami-OH (5-0)	1970	Toledo (5-0)	1984	Toledo (7-1-1)		
1959	Bowling Green (6-0)	1971	Toledo (5-0)	1985	Bowling Green (9-0)		
				1986	Miami-OH (6-2)		

MAC Championship Game

After expanding to 12 teams (and then 13 in 1999 with the addition of Buffalo) and splitting into two divisions in 1997, the MAC now stages a conference championship game between the two division winners on the first Saturday in December. The game was played at Marshall Stadium in Huntington, W.V. (1997-2000) and Glass Bowl Stadium in Toledo, Ohio (2001).

Year		Year		Year	
1997	Marshall 34, Toledo 13	1999	Marshall 34, W. Michigan 30	2000	Marshall 19, W. Michigan 14
1998	Marshall 23, Toledo 17			2001	Toledo 41, Marshall 36

Mountain West Conference

Founded in 1999. **Charter members** (8): Air Force, Brigham Young, Colorado St., New Mexico, Nevada-Las Vegas, San Diego St., Utah and Wyoming.

2002 playing membership (8): Air Force, Brigham Young, Colorado St., New Mexico, Nevada-Las Vegas, San Diego St., Utah and Wyoming.

Multiple titles: BYU and Colorado St. (2).

Year		Year		Year	
1999	BYU (5-2), Colorado St. (5-2) & Utah (5-2)	2000	Colorado St. (6-1)	2001	BYU (7-0)

Pacific-10 Conference

Originally founded in 1915 as Pacific Coast Conference. **Charter members** (4): California, Oregon, Oregon St. and Washington. **Admitted later** (6): Washington St. in 1917; Stanford in 1918; Idaho and USC (Southern Cal) in 1922; Montana in 1924; and UCLA in 1928. **Withdrew later** (1): Montana in 1950 (left for the Mountain States Conf.).

The **PCC** dissolved in 1959 and the **AAWU** (Athletic Assn. of Western Universities) was founded. **Charter members** (5): California, Stanford, UCLA, USC and Washington. **Admitted later** (5): Washington St. in 1962; Oregon and Oregon St. in 1964; Arizona and Arizona St. in 1978. **Conference renamed** Pacific-8 in 1968 and Pacific-10 in 1978.

2002 playing membership (10): Arizona, Arizona St., California, Oregon, Oregon St., Stanford, UCLA, USC, Washington and Washington St.

Multiple titles: USC (31); UCLA (17); Washington (15); California (13); Stanford (12); Oregon (7); Oregon St. (5); Washington St. (3); Arizona St. (2).

Year		Year		Year		Year	
1916	Washington (3-0-1)	1938	USC (6-1)	1959	Washington (3-1),	1982	UCLA (5-1-1)
1917	Washington St. (3-0)		& California (6-1)		USC (3-1)	1983	UCLA (6-1-1)
1918	California (3-0)	1939	USC (5-0-2)		& UCLA (3-1)	1984	USC (7-1)
1919	Oregon (2-1)		& UCLA (5-0-3)	1960	Washington (4-0)	1985	UCLA (6-2)
	& Washington (2-1)	1940	Stanford (7-0)	1961	UCLA (3-1)	1986	Arizona St. (5-1-1)
1920	California (3-0)	1941	Oregon St. (7-2)	1962	USC (4-0)	1987	USC (7-1)
1921	California (5-0)	1942	UCLA (6-1)	1963	Washington (4-1)		& UCLA (7-1)
1922	California (5-0)	1943	USC (4-0)	1964	Oregon St. (3-1)	1988	USC (8-0)
1923	California (5-0)	1944	USC (3-0-2)		& USC (3-1)	1989	USC (6-0-1)
1924	Stanford (3-0-1)	1945	USC (5-1)	1965	UCLA (4-0)	1990	Washington (7-1)
1925	Washington (5-0)	1946	UCLA (7-0)	1966	USC (4-1)	1991	Washington (8-0)
1926	Stanford (4-0)	1947	USC (6-0)	1967	USC (6-1)	1992	Washington (6-2)
1927	USC (4-0-1)	1948	California (6-0)	1968	USC (6-0)		& Stanford (6-2)
	& Stanford (4-0-1)		& Oregon (6-0)	1969	USC (6-0)	1993	UCLA (6-2),
1928	USC (4-0-1)	1949	California (7-0)	1970	Stanford (6-1)		Arizona (6-2)
1929	USC (6-1)	1950	California (5-0-1)	1971	Stanford (6-1)		& USC (6-2)
1930	Washington St. (6-0)	1951	Stanford (6-1)	1972	USC (7-0)	1994	Oregon (7-1)
1931	USC (7-0)	1952	USC (6-0)	1973	USC (7-0)	1995	USC (6-1-1)
1932	USC (6-0)	1953	UCLA (6-0)	1974	USC (6-0-1)		& Washington (6-1-1)
1933	Oregon (4-1)	1954	UCLA (6-0)	1975	UCLA (6-1)	1996	Arizona St. (8-0)
	& Stanford (4-1)	1955	UCLA (6-0)		& California (6-1)	1997	Washington St. (7-1)
1934	Stanford (5-0)	1956	Oregon St. (6-1-1)	1976	USC (7-0)		& UCLA (7-1)
1935	California (4-1),	1957	Oregon (6-2)	1977	Washington (6-1)	1998	UCLA (8-0)
	Stanford (4-1)		& Oregon St. (6-2)	1978	USC (6-1)	1999	Stanford (7-1)
	& UCLA (4-1)	1958	California (6-1)	1979	USC (6-0-1)	2000	Washington (7-1),
1936	Washington (6-0-1)			1980	Washington (6-1)		Oregon St. (7-1)
1937	California (6-0-1)			1981	Washington (6-2)		& Oregon (7-1)
						2001	Oregon (7-1)

Major Conference Champions (Cont.)
Southeastern Conference

Founded in 1933 when charter members all left Southern Conference to form SEC. **Charter members** (13): Alabama, Auburn, Florida, Georgia, Georgia Tech, Kentucky, LSU (Louisiana St.), Mississippi, Mississippi St., Sewanee, Tennessee, Tulane and Vanderbilt. **Admitted later** (2): Arkansas and South Carolina in 1990 (both began play in '92). **Withdrew later** (3): Sewanee in 1940; Georgia Tech in 1964; and Tulane in 1966.

   2002 playing membership (12): Alabama, Arkansas, Auburn, Florida, Georgia, Kentucky, LSU, Mississippi, Mississippi St., South Carolina, Tennessee and Vanderbilt. **Note:** Conference title decided by championship game between Western and Eastern division winners since 1992.

   Multiple titles: Alabama (21); Tennessee (13); Georgia (10); Florida (9); LSU (8); Mississippi (6); Auburn and Georgia Tech (5); Kentucky and Tulane (3).

Year		Year		Year		Year	
1933	Alabama (5-0-1)	1949	Tulane (5-1)	1966	Alabama (6-0)	1982	Georgia (6-0)
1934	Tulane (8-0)	1950	Kentucky (5-1)		& Georgia (6-0)	1983	Auburn (6-0)
	& Alabama (7-0)	1951	Georgia Tech (7-0)	1967	Tennessee (6-0)	1984	Florida (5-0-1)*
1935	LSU (5-0)		& Tennessee (5-0)	1968	Georgia (5-0-1)	1985	Florida (5-1)†
1936	LSU (6-0)	1952	Georgia Tech (6-0)	1969	Tennessee (5-1)		& Tennessee (5-1)
1937	Alabama (6-0)	1953	Alabama (4-0-3)	1970	LSU (5-0)	1986	LSU (5-1)
1938	Tennessee (7-0)	1954	Mississippi (5-1)	1971	Alabama (7-0)	1987	Auburn (5-0-1)
1939	Tennessee (6-0),	1955	Mississippi (5-1)	1972	Alabama (7-1)	1988	Auburn (6-1)
	Georgia Tech (6-0)	1956	Tennessee (6-0)	1973	Alabama (8-0)		& LSU (6-1)
	& Tulane (5-0)	1957	Auburn (7-0)	1974	Alabama (6-0)	1989	Alabama (6-1),
1940	Tennessee (5-0)	1958	LSU (6-0)	1975	Alabama (6-0)		Tennessee (6-1)
1941	Mississippi St. (4-0-1)	1959	Georgia (7-0)	1976	Georgia (5-1)		& Auburn (6-1)
1942	Georgia (6-1)	1960	Mississippi (5-0-1)		& Kentucky (5-1)	1990	Florida (6-1)†
1943	Georgia Tech (3-0)	1961	Alabama (7-0)	1977	Alabama (7-0)		& Tennessee (5-1-1)
1944	Georgia Tech (4-0)		& LSU (6-0)		& Kentucky (6-0)	1991	Florida (7-0)
1945	Alabama (6-0)	1962	Mississippi (6-0)	1978	Alabama (6-0)		
1946	Georgia (5-0)	1963	Mississippi (5-0-1)	1979	Alabama (6-0)	*Title vacated.	
	& Tennessee (5-0)	1964	Alabama (8-0)	1980	Georgia (6-0)	†On probation, ineligible	
1947	Mississippi (6-1)	1965	Alabama (6-1-1)	1981	Georgia (6-0)	for championship.	
1948	Georgia (6-0)				& Alabama (6-0)		

Southwest Conference (1914-95)

Founded in 1914 as Southwest Intercollegiate Athletic Conference. **Charter members** (8): Arkansas, Baylor, Oklahoma, Oklahoma A&M (now Oklahoma St.), Rice, Southwestern, Texas and Texas A&M. **Admitted later** (5): SMU (Southern Methodist) in 1918; Phillips University in 1920; TCU (Texas Christian) in 1923; Texas Tech in 1956 (began play in '60); Houston in 1971 (began play in '76). **Withdrew later** (13): Southwestern in 1917 (went independent); Oklahoma in 1920 (left for Missouri Valley after '19 season); Phillips in 1921; Oklahoma A&M (now Oklahoma St.) in 1925 (left for Big Six); Arkansas in 1990 (left for SEC after '91 season); Baylor, Texas, Texas A&M and Texas Tech in 1994 (all four left for Big 12 after '95 season); Rice, SMU and TCU in 1994 (all three left for WAC after '95 season); Houston in 1994 (left for Conference USA after '95 season). Conference folded on June 30, 1996.

   Multiple titles: Texas (25); Texas A&M (17); Arkansas (13); SMU (9); TCU (9); Rice (7); Baylor (5); Houston (4); Texas Tech (2).

Year		Year		Year		Year	
1914	No champion	1940	Texas A&M (5-1)	1961	Texas (6-1)	1981	SMU (7-1)
1915	Oklahoma (3-0)	1941	Texas A&M (5-1)		& Arkansas (6-1)	1982	SMU (7-0-1)
1916	No champion	1942	Texas (5-0)	1962	Texas (6-0-1)	1983	Texas (8-0)
1917	Texas A&M (2-0)	1943	Texas (5-0)	1963	Texas (7-0)	1984	SMU (6-2)
1918	No champion	1944	TCU (3-1-1)	1964	Arkansas (7-0)		& Houston (6-2)
1919	Texas A&M (4-0)	1945	Texas (5-1)	1965	Arkansas (7-0)	1985	Texas A&M (7-1)
1920	Texas (5-0)	1946	Rice (5-1)	1966	SMU (6-1)	1986	Texas A&M (7-1)
1921	Texas A&M (3-0-2)		& Arkansas (5-1)	1967	Texas A&M (6-1)	1987	Texas A&M (6-1)
1922	Baylor (5-0)	1947	SMU (5-0-1)	1968	Arkansas (6-1)	1988	Arkansas (7-0)
1923	SMU (5-0)	1948	SMU (5-0-1)		& Texas (6-1)	1989	Arkansas (7-1)
1924	Baylor (4-0-1)	1949	Rice (6-0)	1969	Texas (7-0)	1990	Texas (8-0)
1925	Texas A&M (4-1)	1950	Texas (6-0)	1970	Texas (7-0)	1991	Texas A&M (8-0)
1926	SMU (5-0)	1951	TCU (5-1)	1971	Texas (6-1)	1992	Texas A&M (7-0)
1927	Texas A&M (4-0-1)	1952	Texas (6-0)	1972	Texas (7-0)	1993	Texas A&M (7-0)
1928	Texas (5-1)	1953	Rice (5-1)	1973	Texas (7-0)	1994	Baylor, Rice, TCU,
1929	TCU (4-0-1)		& Texas (5-1)	1974	Baylor (6-1)		Texas and Texas Tech†
1930	Texas (4-1)	1954	Arkansas (5-1)	1975	Arkansas (6-1),		(4-3)
1931	SMU (5-0-1)	1955	TCU (5-1)		Texas (6-1)	1995	Texas (7-0)
1932	TCU (5-0)	1956	Texas A&M (6-0)		& Texas A&M (6-1)		
1933	Arkansas (4-1)*	1957	Rice (5-1)	1976	Houston (7-1)	*Arkansas (4-1) forced to	
1934	Rice (5-1)	1958	TCU (5-1)		& Texas Tech (7-1)	vacate 1933 title for use of	
1935	SMU (6-0)	1959	Texas (5-1),	1977	Texas (8-0)	ineligible player.	
1936	Arkansas (5-1)		TCU (5-1)	1978	Houston (7-1)	†Texas A&M had the best	
1937	Rice (4-1-1)		& Arkansas (5-1)	1979	Houston (7-1)	record (6-0-1) in 1994 but	
1938	TCU (6-0)	1960	Arkansas (6-1)		& Arkansas (7-1)	was on probation and there-	
1939	Texas A&M (6-0)			1980	Baylor (8-0)	fore ineligible for the South-	
						west championship.	

SEC Championship Game

Since expanding to 12 teams and splitting into two divisions in 1992, the SEC has staged a conference championship game between the two division winners on the first Saturday in December. The game has been played at Legion Field in Birmingham, Ala., (1992-93) and the Georgia Dome in Atlanta (since 1994). The divisions: EAST— Florida, Georgia, Kentucky, South Carolina, Tennessee and Vanderbilt; WEST— Alabama, Arkansas, Auburn, LSU, Mississippi and Mississippi St.

Year	Year	Year
1992 Alabama 28, Florida 21	1996 Florida 45, Alabama 30	2000 Florida 28, Auburn 6
1993 Florida 28, Alabama 23	1997 Tennessee 30, Auburn 29	2001 LSU 31, Tennessee 20
1994 Florida 24, Alabama 23	1998 Tennessee 24, Miss. St. 14	
1995 Florida 34, Arkansas 3	1999 Alabama 34, Florida 7	

Sun Belt Conference

Founded in 2001 when the Sun Belt Conference sponsored football for the first time. **Charter members** (7): Arkansas State, Idaho, Louisiana-Lafayette, Louisiana-Monroe, Middle Tennessee State, New Mexico State and North Texas.

2002 playing members: same.

Year	
2001	North Texas (5-1) & Mid. Tenn. St. (5-1)

Western Athletic Conference

Founded in 1962 when charter members left the Skyline and Border conferences to form the WAC. **Charter members** (6): Arizona and Arizona St. from Border; BYU (Brigham Young), New Mexico, Utah and Wyoming from Skyline. **Admitted later** (15): Colorado St. and UTEP (Texas-El Paso) in 1967 (both began play in '68); San Diego St. in 1978; Hawaii in 1979; Air Force in 1980; Fresno St. in 1991 (began play in '92); Rice, San Jose St., SMU , TCU , Tulsa and UNLV in 1994 (all began play in '96); Nevada in 2000; Boise St. and Louisiana Tech in 2001. **Withdrew later** (11): Arizona and Arizona St. in 1978 (left for Pac-10 after '77 season); Air Force, BYU, Colorado St., New Mexico, San Diego St., UNLV, Utah and Wyoming (left to form Mountain West conference in '99); TCU in 2000 (left for Conference USA after 2000 season).

2002 playing membership (10): Boise St., Fresno St., Hawaii, Louisiana Tech, Nevada, Rice, San Jose St., SMU, Tulsa and UTEP.

Multiple titles: BYU (19); Arizona St. and Wyoming (7); Air Force, Fresno St., New Mexico and Colorado St. (3); Arizona, Hawaii, TCU and Utah (2).

Year		Year		Year		Year	
1962	New Mexico (2-1-1)	1973	Arizona St. (6-1) & Arizona (6-1)	1983	BYU (7-0)	1993	BYU (6-2), Fresno St. (6-2) & Wyoming (6-2)
1963	New Mexico (3-1)	1974	BYU (6-0-1)	1984	BYU (8-0)	1994	Colorado St. (7-1)
1964	Utah (3-1), New Mexico (3-1) & Arizona (3-1)	1975	Arizona St. (7-0)	1985	Air Force (7-1) & BYU (7-1)	1995	Colorado St. (6-2), Air Force (6-2), BYU (6-2) & Utah (6-2)
1965	BYU (4-1)	1976	BYU (6-1) & Wyoming (6-1)	1986	San Diego St. (7-1)	1999	Fresno St. (5-2), Hawaii (7-2) & TCU (7-2)
1966	Wyoming (5-0)	1977	Arizona St. (6-1) & BYU (6-1)	1987	Wyoming (8-0)	2000	TCU (7-1) & UTEP (7-1)
1967	Wyoming (5-0)	1978	BYU (5-1)	1988	Wyoming (8-0)	2001	La. Tech (7-1)
1968	Wyoming (6-1)	1979	BYU (7-0)	1989	BYU (7-1)		
1969	Arizona St. (6-1)	1980	BYU (6-1)	1990	BYU (7-1)		
1970	Arizona St. (7-0)	1981	BYU (7-1)	1991	BYU (7-0-1)		
1971	Arizona St. (7-0)	1982	BYU (7-1)	1992	Hawaii (6-2), BYU (6-2) & Fresno St. (6-2)		
1972	Arizona St. (5-1)						

Longest Division I Streaks

Winning Streaks

(Including bowl games)

No		Seasons	Spoiler	Score
47	Oklahoma	1953-57	Notre Dame	7-0
39	Washington	1908-14	Oregon St.	0-0
37	Yale	1890-93	Princeton	6-0
37	Yale	1887-89	Princeton	10-0
35	Toledo	1969-71	Tampa	21-0
34	Penn	1894-96	Lafayette	6-4
31	Oklahoma	1948-50	Kentucky	13-7*
31	Pittsburgh	1914-18	Cleve. Naval	10-9
31	Penn	1896-98	Harvard	10-0
30	Texas	1968-70	Notre Dame	24-11*
29	Miami-FL	1990-93	Alabama	34-13
29	Michigan	1901-03	Minnesota	6-6
28	Alabama†	1991-93	Tennessee	17-17
28	Alabama	1978-80	Mississippi St.	6-3
28	Oklahoma	1973-75	Kansas	23-3
28	Michigan St.	1950-53	Purdue	6-0
27	Nebraska	1901-04	Colorado	6-0
26	Nebraska	1994-96	Arizona St.	19-0
26	Cornell	1921-24	Williams	14-7
26	Michigan	1903-05	Chicago	2-0

*Kentucky beat Oklahoma in 1951 Sugar Bowl and Notre Dame beat Texas in 1971 Cotton Bowl.

†Alabama was forced to forfeit eight victories and one tie in 1993 by the NCAA Committee on Infractions.

Unbeaten Streaks

(Including bowl games)

No	W-T		Seasons	Spoiler	Score
63	59-4	Washington	1907-17	California	27-0
56	55-1	Michigan	1901-05	Chicago	2-0
50	46-4	California	1920-25	Olympic Club	15-0
48	47-1	Oklahoma	1953-57	N. Dame	7-0
48	47-1	Yale	1885-89	Princeton	10-0
47	42-5	Yale	1879-85	Princeton	6-5
44	42-2	Yale	1894-96	Princeton	24-6
42	39-3	Yale	1904-08	Harvard	4-0
39	37-2	N. Dame	1946-50	Purdue	28-14
37	36-1	Oklahoma	1972-75	Kansas	23-3
37	37-0	Yale	1890-93	Princeton	6-0
35	35-0	Toledo	1967-71	Tampa	21-0
35	34-1	Minnesota	1903-05	Wisconsin	16-12

Losing Streaks

No		Seasons	Victim	Score
80	Prairie View	1989-98	Langston	14-12
44	Columbia	1983-88	Princeton	16-14
34	Northwestern	1979-82	No. Illinois	31-6
28	Virginia	1958-60	Wm. & Mary	21-6
28	Kansas St.	1944-48	Arkansas St.	37-6

Note: Virginia ended its losing streak in the opening game of the 1961 season.

Major Conference Champions (Cont.)
WAC Championship Game

In addition to expanding to 16 teams and splitting into two divisions in 1996, the WAC staged a conference championship game between the two division winners on the first Saturday in December at Sam Boyd Stadium in Las Vegas until eight teams split off and formed the Mountain West Conference in 1999. The divisions: PACIFIC—BYU, Fresno St., Hawaii, New Mexico, San Diego St., San Jose St., UTEP, Utah; MOUNTAIN—Air Force, Colorado St., Rice, SMU, TCU, Tulsa, UNLV, Wyoming.

Year		Year		Year	
1996	BYU 28, Wyoming 25 (OT)	1997	Colorado St. 41, New Mexico 13	1998	Air Force 20, BYU 13

Annual NCAA Division I-A Leaders
Note that Oklahoma A&M is now Oklahoma St. and Texas Mines is now UTEP.

Rushing
Individual championship decided on Rushing Yards (1937-69), and on Yards Per Game (since 1970).

Multiple winners: Troy Davis, Marshall Faulk, Art Luppino, Ed Marinaro, Rudy Mobley, Jim Pilot, O.J. Simpson, LaDainian Tomlinson and Ricky Williams (2).

Year		Car	Yards	Year		Car	Yards	P/Gm
1937	Byron (Whizzer) White, Colorado	181	1121	1970	Ed Marinaro, Cornell	285	1425	158.3
1938	Len Eshmont, Fordham	132	831	1971	Ed Marinaro, Cornell	356	1881	209.0
1939	John Polanski, Wake Forest	137	882	1972	Pete VanValkenburg, BYU	232	1386	138.6
1940	Al Ghesquiere, Detroit	146	957	1973	Mark Kellar, Northern Ill	291	1719	156.3
1941	Frank Sinkwich, Georgia	209	1103	1974	Louie Giammona, Utah St.	329	1534	153.4
1942	Rudy Mobley, Hardin-Simmons	187	1281	1975	Ricky Bell, USC	357	1875	170.5
1943	Creighton Miller, Notre Dame	151	911	1976	Tony Dorsett, Pittsburgh	338	1948	177.1
1944	Red Williams, Minnesota	136	911	1977	Earl Campbell, Texas	267	1744	158.5
1945	Bob Fenimore, Oklahoma A&M	142	1048	1978	Billy Sims, Oklahoma	231	1762	160.2
1946	Rudy Mobley, Hardin-Simmons	227	1262					
1947	Wilton Davis, Hardin-Simmons	193	1173	1979	Charles White, USC	293	1803	180.3
1948	Fred Wendt, Texas Mines	184	1570	1980	George Rogers, S. Carolina	297	1781	161.9
1949	John Dottley, Ole Miss	208	1312	1981	Marcus Allen, USC	403	2342	212.9
1950	Wilford White, Arizona St	199	1502	1982	Ernest Anderson, Okla. St.	353	1877	170.6
1951	Ollie Matson, San Francisco	245	1566	1983	Mike Rozier, Nebraska	275	2148	179.0
1952	Howie Waugh, Tulsa	164	1372	1984	Keith Byars, Ohio St.	313	1655	150.5
1953	J.C. Caroline, Illinois	194	1256	1985	Lorenzo White, Mich. St.	386	1908	173.5
1954	Art Luppino, Arizona	179	1359	1986	Paul Palmer, Temple	346	1866	169.6
1955	Art Luppino, Arizona	209	1313	1987	Ickey Woods, UNLV	259	1658	150.7
1956	Jim Crawford, Wyoming	200	1104	1988	Barry Sanders, Okla. St.	344	2628	238.9
1957	Leon Burton, Arizona St	117	1126	1989	Anthony Thompson, Ind	358	1793	163.0
1958	Dick Bass, Pacific	205	1361	1990	Gerald Hudson, Okla. St.	279	1642	149.3
1959	Pervis Atkins, New Mexico St.	130	971	1991	Marshall Faulk, S. Diego St.	201	1429	158.8
1960	Bob Gaiters, New Mexico St	197	1338	1992	Marshall Faulk, S. Diego St.	265	1630	163.0
1961	Jim Pilot, New Mexico St.	191	1278	1993	LeShon Johnson, No. Ill.	327	1976	179.6
1962	Jim Pilot, New Mexico St.	208	1247	1994	Rashaan Salaam, Colorado	298	2055	186.8
1963	Dave Casinelli, Memphis St	219	1016	1995	Troy Davis, Iowa St.	345	2010	182.7
1964	Brian Piccolo, Wake Forest	252	1044	1996	Troy Davis, Iowa St.	402	2185	198.6
1965	Mike Garrett, USC	267	1440	1997	Ricky Williams, Texas	279	1893	172.1
1966	Ray McDonald, Idaho	259	1329	1998	Ricky Williams, Texas	361	2124	193.1
1967	O.J. Simpson, USC	266	1415	1999	LaDainian Tomlinson, TCU	268	1850	168.2
1968	O.J. Simpson, USC	355	1709	2000	LaDainian Tomlinson, TCU	369	2158	196.2
1969	Steve Owens, Oklahoma	358	1523	2001	Chance Kretschmer, Nevada	302	1732	157.5

All-Purpose Yardage
Multiple winners: Marcus Allen, Pervis Atkins, Ryan Benjamin, Troy Davis, Troy Edwards, Louie Giammona, Tom Harmon, Art Luppino, Napolean McCallum, O.J. Simpson, Charles White and Gary Wood (2).

Year		Yards	P/Gm	Year		Yards	P/Gm
1937	Byron (Whizzer) White, Colorado	1970	246.3	1953	J.C. Caroline, Illinois	1470	163.3
1938	Parker Hall, Ole Miss	1420	129.1	1954	Art Luppino, Arizona	2193	219.3
1939	Tom Harmon, Michigan	1208	151.0	1955	Jim Swink, TCU	1702	170.2
1940	Tom Harmon, Michigan	1312	164.0		& Art Luppino, Arizona	1702	170.2
1941	Bill Dudley, Virginia	1674	186.0	1956	Jack Hill, Utah St.	1691	169.1
1942	Complete records not available			1957	Overton Curtis, Utah St	1608	160.8
1943	Stan Koslowski, Holy Cross	1411	176.4	1958	Dick Bass, Pacific	1878	187.8
1944	Red Williams, Minnesota	1467	163.0	1959	Pervis Atkins, New Mexico St	1800	180.0
1945	Bob Fenimore, Oklahoma A&M	1577	197.1	1960	Pervis Atkins, New Mexico St	1613	161.3
1946	Rudy Mobley, Hardin-Simmons	1765	176.5	1961	Jim Pilot, New Mexico St	1606	160.6
1947	Wilton Davis, Hardin-Simmons	1798	179.8	1962	Gary Wood, Cornell	1395	155.0
1948	Lou Kusserow, Columbia	1737	193.0	1963	Gary Wood, Cornell	1508	167.6
1949	Johnny Papit, Virginia	1611	179.0	1964	Donny Anderson, Texas Tech	1710	171.0
1950	Wilford White, Arizona St.	2065	206.5	1965	Floyd Little, Syracuse	1990	199.0
1951	Ollie Matson, San Francisco	2037	226.3	1966	Frank Quayle, Virginia	1616	161.6
1952	Billy Vessels, Oklahoma	1512	151.2	1967	O.J. Simpson, USC	1700	188.9

Year		Yards	P/Gm	Year		Yards	P/Gm
1968	O.J. Simpson, USC	1966	196.6	1985	Napoleon McCallum, Navy	2330	211.8
1969	Lynn Moore, Army	1795	179.5	1986	Paul Palmer, Temple	2633	239.4
1970	Don McCauley, North Carolina	2021	183.7	1987	Eric Wilkerson, Kent St.	2074	188.6
1971	Ed Marinaro, Cornell	1932	214.7	1988	Barry Sanders, Oklahoma St.	3250	295.5
1972	Howard Stevens, Louisville	2132	213.2	1989	Mike Pringle, CS-Fullerton	2690	244.6
1973	Willard Harrell, Pacific	1777	177.7	1990	Glyn Milburn, Stanford	2222	202.0
1974	Louie Giammona, Utah St	1984	198.4	1991	Ryan Benjamin, Pacific	2995	249.6
1975	Louie Giammona, Utah St.	2045	185.9	1992	Ryan Benjamin, Pacific	2597	236.1
1976	Tony Dorsett, Pittsburgh	2021	183.7	1993	LeShon Johnson, Northern Ill.	2082	189.3
1977	Earl Campbell, Texas	1855	168.6	1994	Rashaan Salaam, Colorado	2349	213.5
1978	Charles White, USC	2096	174.7	1995	Troy Davis, Iowa St.	2466	224.2
1979	Charles White, USC	1941	194.1	1996	Troy Davis, Iowa St.	2364	214.9
1980	Marcus Allen, USC	1794	179.4	1997	Troy Edwards, La. Tech	2144	194.9
1981	Marcus Allen, USC	2559	232.6	1998	Troy Edwards, La. Tech	2784	232.0
1982	Carl Monroe, Utah	2036	185.1	1999	Trevor Insley, Nevada	2176	197.8
1983	Napoleon McCallum, Navy	2385	216.8	2000	Emmett White, Utah St.	2628	238.9
1984	Keith Byars, Ohio St.	2284	207.6	2001	Levron Williams, Indiana	2201	200.1

Total Offense

Individual championship decided on Total Yards (1937-69) and on Yards Per Game (since 1970).

Multiple winners: Tim Rattay (3); Johnny Bright, Bob Fenimore, Mike Maxwell and Jim McMahon (2).

Year		Plays	Yards	Year		Plays	Yards	P/Gm
1937	Byron (Whizzer) White, Colorado	224	1596	1970	Pat Sullivan, Auburn	333	2856	285.6
1938	Davey O'Brien, TCU	291	1847	1971	Gary Huff, Florida St	386	2653	241.2
1939	Kenny Washington, UCLA	259	1370	1972	Don Strock, Va. Tech	480	3170	288.2
1940	Johnny Knolla, Creighton	298	1420	1973	Jesse Freitas, San Diego St.	4]0	2901	263.7
1941	Bud Schwenk, Washington-MO	354	1928	1974	Steve Joachim, Temple	331	2227	222.7
1942	Frank Sinkwich, Georgia	341	2187	1975	Gene Swick, Toledo	490	2706	246.0
1943	Bob Hoernschemeyer, Indiana	355	1648	1976	Tommy Kramer, Rice	562	3272	297.5
1944	Bob Fenimore, Oklahoma A&M	241	1758	1977	Doug Williams, Gambling	377	3229	293.5
1945	Bob Fenimore, Oklahoma A&M	203	1641	1978	Mike Ford, SMU	459	2957	268.8
1946	Travis Bidwell, Auburn	339	1715	1979	Marc Wilson, BYU	488	3580	325.5
1947	Fred Enke, Arizona	329	1941	1980	Jim McMahon, BYU	540	4627	385.6
1948	Stan Heath, Nevada-Reno	233	1992	·1981	Jim McMahon, BYU	487	3458	345.8
1949	Johnny Bright, Drake	275	1950	1982	Todd Dillon, Long Beach St	585	3587	326.1
1950	Johnny Bright, Drake	320	2400	1983	Steve Young, BYU	531	4346	395.1
1951	Dick Kazmaier, Princeton	272	1827	1984	Robbie Bosco, BYU	543	3932	327.7
1952	Ted Marchibroda, Detroit	305	1813	1985	Jim Everett, Purdue	518	3589	326.3
1953	Paul Larson, California	262	1572	1986	Mike Perez, San Jose St.	425	2969	329.9
1954	George Shaw, Oregon	276	1536	1987	Todd Santos, San Diego St.	562	3688	307.3
1955	George Welsh, Navy	203	1348	1988	Scott Mitchell, Utah	589	4299	390.8
1956	John Brodie, Stanford	295	1642	1989	Andre Ware, Houston	628	4661	423.7
1957	Bob Newman, Washington St	263	1444	1990	David Klingler, Houston	704	5221	474.6
1958	Dick Bass, Pacific	218	1440	1991	Ty Detmer, BYU	478	4001	333.4
1959	Dick Norman, Stanford	319	2018	1992	Jimmy Klingler, Houston	544	3768	342.6
1960	Billy Kilmer, UCLA	292	1889	1993	Chris Vargas, Nevada	535	4332	393.8
1961	Dave Hoppmann, Iowa St.	320	1638	1994	Mike Maxwell, Nevada	477	3498	318.0
1962	Terry Baker, Oregon St	318	2276	1995	Mike Maxwell, Nevada	443	3623	402.6
1963	George Mira, Miami-FL	394	2318	1996	Josh Wallwork, Wyoming	525	4209	350.8
1964	Jerry Rhome, Tulsa	470	3128	1997	Tim Rattay, La. Tech	541	3968	360.7
1965	Bill Anderson, Tulsa	580	3343	1998	Tim Rattay, La. Tech	602	4840	403.3
1966	Virgil Carter, BYU	388	2545	1999	Tim Rattay, La. Tech	562	3810	381.0
1967	Sal Olivas, New Mexico St.	368	2184	2000	Drew Brees, Purdue	564	3939	358.1
1968	Greg Cook Cincinnati	507	3210	2001	Rex Grossman, Florida	429	3904	354.9
1969	Dennis Shaw, San Diego St	388	3197					

Passing

Individual championship decided on Completions (1937-69), on Completions Per Game (1970-78) and on Passing Efficiency rating points (since 1979).

Multiple winners: Elvis Grbac, Don Heinrich, Jim McMahon, Davey O'Brien and Don Trull (2).

Year		Cmp	Pct	TD	Yds	Year		Cmp	Pct	TD	Yds
1937	Davey O'Brien, TCU	94	.402	–	969	1946	Travis Tidwell, Auburn	79	.500	5	943
1938	Davey O'Brien, TCU	93	.557	–	1457	1947	Charlie Conerly, Ole Miss	133	.571	18	1367
1939	Kay Eakin, Arkansas	78	.404	–	962	1948	Stan Heath, Nev-Reno	126	.568	22	2005
1940	Billy Sewell, Wash. St.	86	.494	–	1023	1949	Adrian Burk, Baylor	110	.576	14	1428
1941	Bud Schwenk, Wash.-MO	114	.487	–	1457	1950	Don Heinrich, Washington	134	.606	14	1846
1942	Ray Evans, Kansas	101	.505	–	1117	1951	Don Klosterman, Loyola-CA	159	.505	9	1843
1943	Johnny Cook, Georgia	73	.465	–	1007	1952	Don Heinrich, Washington	137	.507	13	1647
1944	Paul Rickards, Pittsburgh	84	.472	–	997	1953	Bob Garrett, Stanford	118	.576	17	1637
1945	Al Dekdebrun, Cornell	90	.464	–	1227	1954	Paul Larson, California	125	.641	10	1537

Annual NCAA Division I-A Leaders (Cont.)

Year		Cmp	Pct	TD	Yds
1955	George Welsh, Navy	94	.627	8	1319
1956	John Brodie, Stanford	139	.579	12	1633
1957	Ken Ford, H-Simmons	115	.561	14	1254
1958	Buddy Humphrey, Baylor	112	.574	7	1316
1959	Dick Norman, Stanford	152	.578	11	1963
1960	Harold Stephens, H-Simm.	145	.566	3	1254
1961	Chon Gallegos, S. Jose St	117	.594	14	1480
1962	Don Trull, Baylor	125	.546	11	1627
1963	Don Trull, Baylor	174	.565	12	2157
1964	Jerry Rhome, Tulsa	224	.687	32	2870
1965	Bill Anderson, Tulsa	296	.582	30	3464
1966	John Eckman, Wichita St	195	.426	7	2339
1967	Terry Stone, N. Mexico	160	.476	9	1946
1968	Chuck Hixson, SMU	265	.566	21	3103
1969	John Reaves, Florida	222	.561	24	2896

Year		Cmp	P/Gm	TD	Yds
1970	Sonny Sixkiller, Wash	186	18.6	15	2303
1971	Brian Sipe, S. Diego St.	196	17.8	17	2532
1972	Don Strock, Va. Tech	228	20.7	16	3243
1973	Jesse Freitas, S. Diego St.	227	20.6	21	2993
1974	Steve Bartkowski, Cal	182	16.5	12	2580
1975	Craig Penrose, S. Diego St.	198	18.0	15	2660
1976	Tommy Kramer, Rice	269	24.5	21	3317
1977	Guy Benjamin, Stanford	208	20.8	19	2521
1978	Steve Dils, Stanford	247	22.5	22	2943

Year		Cmp	TD	Yds	Rating
1979	Turk Schonert, Stanford	148	19	1922	163.0
1980	Jim McMahon, BYU	284	47	4571	176.9
1981	Jim McMahon, BYU	272	30	3555	155.0
1982	Tom Ramsey, UCLA	191	21	2824	153.5
1983	Steve Young, BYU	306	33	3902	168.5
1984	Doug Flutie, BC	233	27	3454	152.9
1985	Jim Harbaugh, Michigan	139	18	1913	163.7
1986	Vinny Testaverde, Miami-FL	175	26	2557	165.8
1987	Don McPherson, Syracuse	129	22	2341	164.3
1988	Timm Rosenbach, Wash. St.	199	23	2791	162.0
1989	Ty Detmer, BYU	265	32	4560	175.6
1990	Shawn Moore, Virginia	144	21	2262	160.7
1991	Elvis Grbac, Michigan	152	24	1955	169.0
1992	Elvis Grbac, Michigan	112	15	1465	154.2
1993	Trent Dilfer, Fresno St.	217	28	3276	173.1
1994	Kerry Collins, Penn St.	176	21	2679	172.9
1995	Danny Wuerffel, Florida	210	35	3266	178.4
1996	Steve Sarkisian, BYU	278	33	4027	173.6
1997	Cade McNown, UCLA	173	22	2877	168.6
1998	Shaun King, Tulane	223	36	3232	183.3
1999	Michael Vick, Va. Tech	90	12	1840	180.4
2000	Bart Hendricks, Boise St.	210	35	3364	170.6
2001	Rex Grossman, Florida	259	34	3896	170.8

Receptions

Championship decided on Passes Caught (1937-69) and on Catches Per Game (since 1970). Touchdown totals unavailable in 1939 and 1941-45.

Multiple winners: Neil Armstrong, Hugh Campbell, Manny Hazard, Reid Moseley, Jason Phillips, Howard Twilley and Alex Van Dyke (2).

Year		No	TD	Yds
1937	Jim Benton, Arkansas	47	7	754
1938	Sam Boyd, Baylor	32	5	537
1939	Ken Kavanaugh, LSU	30	–	467
1940	Eddie Bryant, Virginia	30	2	222
1941	Hank Stanton, Arizona	50	–	820
1942	Bill Rogers, Texas A&M	39	–	432
1943	Neil Armstrong, Okla. A&M	39	–	317
1944	Reid Moseley, Georgia	32	–	506
1945	Reid Moseley, Georgia	31	–	662
1946	Neil Armstrong, Okla. A&M	32	1	479
1947	Barney Poole, Ole Miss	52	8	513
1948	Red O'Quinn, Wake Forest	39	7	605
1949	Art Weiner, N. Carolina	52	7	762
1950	Gordon Cooper, Denver	46	8	569
1951	Dewey McConnell, Wyoming	47	9	725
1952	Ed Brown, Fordham	57	6	774
1953	John Carson, Georgia	45	4	663
1954	Jim Hanifan, California	44	7	569
1955	Hank Burnine, Missouri	44	2	594
1956	Art Powell, San Jose St.	40	5	583
1957	Stuart Vaughan, Utah	53	5	756
1958	Dave Hibbert, Arizona	61	4	606
1959	Chris Burford, Stanford	61	6	756
1960	Hugh Campbell, Wash. St.	66	10	881
1961	Hugh Campbell, Wash. St.	53	5	723
1962	Vern Burke, Oregon St	69	10	1007
1963	Lawrence Elkins, Baylor	70	8	873
1964	Howard Twilley, Tulsa	95	13	1178
1965	Howard Twilley, Tulsa	134	16	1779
1966	Glenn Meltzer, Wichita St	91	4	1115
1967	Bob Goodridge, Vanderbilt	79	6	1114
1968	Ron Sellers, Florida St.	86	12	1496
1969	Jerry Hendren, Idaho	95	12	1452

Year		No	P/Gm	TD	Yds
1970	Mike Mikolayunas, Davidson	87	8.7	8	1128
1971	Tom Reynolds, San Diego St	67	6.7	7	1070
1972	Tom Forzani, Utah St	85	7.7	8	1169
1973	Jay Miller, BYU	100	9.1	8	1181
1974	D. McDonald, San Diego St	86	7.8	7	1157
1975	Bob Farnham, Brown	56	6.2	2	701
1976	Billy Ryckman, La. Tech	77	7.0	10	1382
1977	W. Tolleson, W. Carolina	73	6.6	7	1101
1978	Dave Petzke, Northern Ill	91	8.3	11	1217
1979	Rick Beasley, Appalach. St	74	6.7	12	1205
1980	Dave Young, Purdue	67	6.1	8	917
1981	Pete Harvey, N. Texas St	57	6.3	3	743
1982	Vincent White, Stanford	68	6.8	6	677
1983	Keith Edwards, Vanderbilt	97	8.8	8	909
1984	David Williams, Illinois	101	9.2	8	1278
1985	Rodney Carter, Purdue	98	8.9	4	1099
1986	Mark Templeton, L. Beach St	99	9.0	2	688
1987	Jason Phillips, Houston	99	9.0	3	875
1988	Jason Phillips, Houston	108	9.8	15	1444
1989	Manny Hazard, Houston	142	12.9	22	1689
1990	Manny Hazard, Houston	78	7.8	9	946
1991	Fred Gilbert, Houston	106	9.6	7	957
1992	Sherman Smith, Houston	103	9.4	6	923
1993	Chris Penn, Tulsa	105	9.6	12	1578
1994	Alex Van Dyke, Nevada	98	8.9	8	1246
1995	Alex Van Dyke, Nevada	129	11.7	16	1854
1996	Damond Wilkins, Nevada	114	10.4	4	1121
1997	Eugene Baker, Kent	103	9.4	18	1549
1998	Troy Edwards, La. Tech	140	11.7	27	1996
1999	Trevor Insley, Nevada	134	12.2	13	2060
2000	James Jordan, La. Tech	109	9.1	4	1003
2001	Kevin Curtis, Utah St.	100	9.1	10	1531

Scoring

Championship decided on Total Points (1937-69) and on Points Per Game (since 1970).

Multiple winners: Tom Harmon and Billy Sims (2).

Year		TD	XP	FG	Pts	Year		TD	XP	FG	Pts	P/Gm
1937	Byron (Whizzer) White, Colo.	16	23	1	122	1970	Brian Bream, Air Force	20	0	0	120	12.0
1938	Parker Hall, Ole Miss	11	7	0	73		& Gary Kosins, Dayton	18	0	0	108	12.0
1939	Tom Harmon, Michigan	14	15	1	102	1971	Ed Marinaro, Cornell	24	4	0	148	16.4
1940	Tom Harmon, Michigan	16	18	1	117	1972	Harold Henson, Ohio St	20	0	0	120	12.0
1941	Bill Dudley, Virginia	18	23	1	134	1973	Jim Jennings, Rutgers	21	2	0	128	11.6
1942	Bob Steuber, Missouri	18	13	0	121	1974	Bill Marek, Wisconsin	19	0	0	114	12.7
1943	Steve Van Buren, LSU	14	14	0	98	1975	Pete Johnson, Ohio St	25	0	0	150	13.6
1944	Glenn Davis, Army	20	0	0	120	1976	Tony Dorsett, Pitt	22	2	0	134	12.2
1945	Doc Blanchard, Army	19	1	0	115	1977	Earl Campbell, Texas	19	0	0	114	10.4
1946	Gene Roberts, Tenn-Chatt.	18	9	0	117	1978	Billy Sims, Oklahoma	20	0	0	120	10.9
1947	Lou Gambino, Maryland	16	0	0	96	1979	Billy Sims, Oklahoma	22	0	0	132	12.0
1948	Fred Wendt, Texas Mines	20	32	0	152	1980	Sammy Winder, So. Miss	20	0	0	120	10.9
1949	George Thomas, Oklahoma	19	3	0	117	1981	Marcus Allen, USC	23	0	0	138	12.5
1950	Bobby Reynolds, Nebraska	22	25	0	157	1982	Greg Allen, Fla. St	21	0	0	126	11.5
1951	Ollie Matson, San Francisco	21	0	0	126	1983	Mike Rozier, Nebraska	29	0	0	174	14.5
1952	Jackie Parker, Miss. St.	16	24	0	120	1984	Keith Byars, Ohio St	24	0	0	144	13.1
1953	Earl Lindley, Utah St.	13	3	0	81	1985	Bernard White, B. Green.	19	0	0	114	10.4
1954	Art Luppino, Arizona	24	22	0	166	1986	Steve Bartalo, Colo. St	19	0	0	114	10.4
1955	Jim Swink, TCU	20	5	0	125	1987	Paul Hewitt, S. Diego St.	24	0	0	144	12.0
1956	Clendon Thomas, Oklahoma	18	0	0	108	1988	Barry Sanders, Okla.St.	39	0	0	234	21.3
1957	Leon Burton, Ariz. St.	16	0	0	96	1989	Anthony Thompson, Ind	25	4	0	154	14.0
1958	Dick Bass, Pacific	18	8	0	116	1990	Stacey Robinson, No. Ill.	19	6	0	120	10.9
1959	Pervis Atkins, N. Mexico St.	17	5	0	107	1991	Marshall Faulk, S.D. St.	23	2	0	140	15.6
1960	Bob Gaiters, N. Mexico St.	23	7	0	145	1992	Garrison Hearst, Georgia	21	0	0	126	11.5
1961	Jim Pilot, N. Mexico St.	21	12	0	138	1993	Bam Morris, Texas Tech	22	2	0	134	12.2
1962	Jerry Logan, W. Texas St.	13	32	0	110	1994	Rashaan Salaam, Colo	24	0	0	144	13.1
1963	Cosmo Iacavazzi, Princeton	14	0	0	84	1995	Eddie George, Ohio St.	24	0	0	144	12.0
	& Dave Casinelli, Memphis St.	14	0	0	84	1996	Corey Dillon, Washington	23	0	0	138	12.6
1964	Brian Piccolo, Wake Forest	17	9	0	111	1997	Ricky Williams, Texas	25	2	0	152	13.8
1965	Howard Twilley, Tulsa	16	31	0	127	1998	Troy Edwards, La. Tech	31	2	0	188	15.7
1966	Ken Hebert, Houston	11	41	2	113	1999	Shaun Alexander, Alabama	24	0	0	144	13.1
1967	Leroy Keyes, Purdue	19	0	0	114	2000	Lee Suggs, Va. Tech	28	0	0	168	15.3
1968	Jim O'Brien, Cincinnati	12	31	13	142	2001	Luke Staley, BYU	28	2	0	170	15.5
1969	Steve Owens, Oklahoma	23	0	0	138							

All-Time NCAA Division I-A Leaders

Through the 2001 regular season. The NCAA does not recognize active players among career Per Game leaders.

CAREER

Passing

(Minimum 500 Completions)

	Passing Efficiency	Years	Rating
1	Danny Wuerffel, Florida	1993-96	163.6
2	Ty Detmer, BYU	1988-91	162.7
3	Steve Sarkisian, BYU	1995-96	162.0
4	Billy Blanton, San Diego St.	1993-96	157.1
5	Jim McMahon, BYU	1977-78, 80-81	156.9

	Yards Gained	Years	Yards
1	Ty Detmer, BYU	1988-91	15,031
2	Tim Rattay, La. Tech	1997-99	12,746
3	Chris Redman, Louisville	1996-99	12,541
4	Todd Santos, San Diego St	1984-87	11,425
5	Tim Lester, W. Michigan	1996-99	11,299

	Completions	Years	No
1	Chris Redman, Louisville	1996-99	1031
2	Tim Rattay, La. Tech	1997-99	1015
3	Ty Detmer, BYU	1988-91	958
4	Drew Brees, Purdue	1997-00	942
5	Todd Santos, San Diego St	1984-87	910

Rushing

	Yards Gained	Years	Yards
1	Ron Dayne, Wisconsin	1996-99	6397
2	Ricky Williams, Texas	1995-98	6279
3	Tony Dorsett, Pittsburgh	1973-76	6082
4	Charles White, USC	1976-79	5598
5	Travis Prentice, Miami-OH	1996-99	5596

Receptions

	Catches	Years	No
1	Arnold Jackson, Louisville	1997-00	300
2	Trevor Insley, Nevada	1996-99	298
3	Geoff Noisy, Nevada	1995-98	295
4	Troy Edwards, La. Tech	1996-98	280
5	Aaron Turner, Pacific	1989-92	266

	Catches Per Game	Years	No	P/Gm
1	Manny Hazard, Houston	1989-90	220	10.5
2	Alex Van Dyke, Nevada	1994-95	227	10.3
3	Howard Twilley, Tulsa	1963-65	261	10.0
4	Jason Phillips, Houston	1987-88	207	9.4
5	Troy Edwards, La. Tech	1996-98	280	8.2

	Yards Gained	Years	No	Yards
1	Trevor Insley, Nevada	1996-99	298	5005
2	Marcus Harris, Wyoming	1993-96	259	4518
3	Ryan Yarborough, Wyoming	1990-93	229	4357
4	Troy Edwards, La. Tech	1996-98	280	4352
5	Aaron Turner, Pacific	1989-92	266	4345

	Yards Per Game	Years	Yards	P/Gm
1	Ed Marinaro, Cornell	1969-71	4715	174.6
2	O.J. Simpson, USC	1967-68	3124	164.4
3	Herschel Walker, Georgia	1980-82	5259	159.4
4	LeShon Johnson, No. Ill.	1992-93	3314	150.6
5	Ron Dayne, Wisconsin	1996-99	6397	148.8

All-Time NCAA Division I-A Leaders (Cont.)

Total Offense

	Yards Gained	Years	Yards
1	Ty Detmer, BYU	1988-91	14,665
2	Tim Rattay, La. Tech	1997-99	12,689
3	Chris Redman, Louisville	1996-99	12,129
4	Drew Brees, Purdue	1997-00	11,815
5	David Neill, Nevada	1998-01	11,664

*Culpepper played I-AA with Central Florida in 1995.

	Yards Per Game	Years	Yards	P/Gm
1	Tim Rattay, La. Tech	1997-99	12,689	382.4
2	Chris Vargas, Nevada	1992-93	6,417	320.9
3	Ty Detmer, BYU	1988-91	14,665	318.8
4	Daunte Culpepper*, C. Fla.	1996-98	10,344	313.5
5	Mike Perez, San Jose St	1986-87	6,182	309.1

All-Purpose Yardage

	Yards Gained	Years	Yards
1	Ricky Williams, Texas	1995-98	7206
2	Napoleon McCallum, Navy	1981-85	7172
3	Darrin Nelson, Stanford	1977-78, 80-81	6885
4	Kevin Faulk, LSU	1995-98	6833
5	Ron Dayne, Wisconsin	1996-99	6701

	Yards Per Game	Years	Yards	P/Gm
1	Ryan Benjamin, Pacific	1990-92	5706	237.8
2	Sheldon Canley, S. Jose St.	1988-90	5146	205.8
3	Howard Stevens, Louisville	1971-72	3873	193.7
4	O.J. Simpson, USC	1967-68	3666	192.9
5	Alex Van Dyke, Nevada	1994-95	4146	188.5

Miscellaneous

	Interceptions	Years	No
1	Al Brosky, Illinois	1950-52	29
2	John Provost, Holy Cross	1972-74	27
	Martin Bayless, Bowling Green	1980-83	27
4	Tom Curtis, Michigan	1967-69	25
	Tony Thurman, Boston College	1981-84	25
	Tracy Saul, Texas Tech.	1989-92	25

	Punt Return Average*	Years	Avg
1	Jack Mitchell, Oklahoma	1946-48	23.6
2	Gene Gibson, Cincinnati	1949-50	20.5
3	Eddie Macon, Pacific	1949-51	18.9
4	Jackie Robinson, UCLA	1939-40	18.8
5	Mike Fuller, Auburn	1972-74	17.7

*Minimum 1.2 punt returns per game and 30 career returns.

	Punting Average*	Years	Avg
1	Todd Sauerbrun, West Va.	1991-94	46.3
2	Reggie Roby, Iowa	1979-82	45.6
3	Greg Montgomery, Mich. St.	1985-87	45.4
4	Tom Tupa, Ohio St.	1984-87	45.2
5	Barry Helton, Colorado	1984-87	44.9

*At least 150 punts.

	Kickoff Return Average*	Years	Avg
1	Anthony Davis, USC	1972-74	35.1
2	Eric Booth, So. Miss.	1994-97	32.4
3	Overton Curtis, Utah St.	1957-58	31.0
4	Fred Montgomery, New Mexico St.	1991-92	30.5
5	Allie Taylor, Utah St.	1966-68	29.3

*Minimum 1.2 kickoff returns per game and 30 career returns.

Scoring
Non-kickers

	Points	Years	TD	Xpt	FG	Pts
1	Travis Prentice, Miami-OH	1996-99	78	0	0	468
2	Ricky Williams, Texas	1995-98	75	2	0	452
3	Anthony Thompson, Ind.	1986-89	65	4	0	394
4	Ron Dayne, Wisconsin	1996-99	63	0	0	378
5	Marshall Faulk, S.D. St.	1991-93	62	4	0	376

	Touchdown Catches	Years	No
1	Troy Edwards, La. Tech	1996-98	50
2	Aaron Turner, Pacific	1989-92	43
3	Ryan Yarborough, Wyoming	1990-93	42
4	Clarkston Hines, Duke	1986-89	38
	Marcus Harris, Wyoming	1993-96	38

	Points Per Game	Years	Pts	P/Gm
1	Marshall Faulk, S. Diego St.	1991-93	376	12.1
2	Ed Marinaro, Cornell	1969-71	318	11.8
3	Bill Burnett, Arkansas	1968-70	294	11.3
4	Steve Owens, Oklahoma	1967-69	336	11.2
5	Eddie Talboom, Wyoming	1948-50	303	10.8

	Touchdowns Rushing	Years	No
1	Travis Prentice, Miami-OH	1996-99	73
2	Ricky Williams, Texas	1995-98	72
3	Anthony Thompson, Indiana	1986-89	64
4	Ron Dayne, Wisconsin	1996-99	63
5	Eric Crouch, Nebraska	1998-01	59

Kickers

	Points	Years	FG	XP	Pts
1	Roman Anderson, Hou	1988-91	70	213	423
2	Carlos Huerta, Mia-FL	1988-91	73	178	397
3	Jason Elam, Hawaii	1988-89, 91-92	79	158	395
4	Derek Schmidt, Fla. St	1984-87	73	174	393
5	Kris Brown, Nebraska	1995-98	57	217	388

	Field Goals	Years	No
1	Jeff Jaeger, Washington	1983-86	80
2	John Lee, UCLA	1982-85	79
	Jason Elam, Hawaii	1988-89, 91-92	79
4	Philip Doyle, Alabama	1987-90	78
	Luis Zendejas, Arizona St	1981-84	78

	Touchdowns Passing	Years	No
1	Ty Detmer, BYU	1988-91	121
2	Tim Rattay, La. Tech	1997-99	115
3	Danny Wuerffel, Florida	1993-96	114
4	Chad Pennington, Marshall	1997-99	100
5	David Klingler, Houston	1988-91	91

SINGLE SEASON
Rushing

	Yards Gained	Year	Gm	Car	Yards
	Barry Sanders, Okla. St	1988	11	344	2628
	Marcus Allen, USC	1981	11	403	2342
	Troy Davis, Iowa St.	1996	11	402	2185
	LaDainian Tomlinson, TCU	2000	11	369	2158
	Mike Rozier, Nebraska	1983	12	275	2148

	Yards Per Game	Year	Gm	Yards	P/Gm
	Barry Sanders, Okla. St	1988	11	2628	238.9
	Marcus Allen, USC	1981	11	2342	212.9
	Ed Marinaro, Cornell	1971	9	1881	209.0
	Troy Davis, Iowa St.	1996	11	2185	198.6
	LaDainian Tomlinson, TCU	2000	11	2158	196.2

Passing
(Minimum 15 Attempts Per Game)

Passing Efficiency	Year	Rating
Shaun King, Tulane	1998	183.3
Michael Vick, Va. Tech	1999	180.4
Danny Wuerffel, Florida	1995	178.4
Jim McMahon, BYU	1980	176.9
Ty Detmer, BYU	1989	175.6

Yards Gained	Year	Yards
Ty Detmer, BYU	1990	5188
David Klingler, Houston	1990	5140
Tim Rattay, La. Tech	1998	4943
Andre Ware, Houston	1989	4699
Jim McMahon, BYU	1980	4571

Completions	Year	Att	No
Tim Rattay, La. Tech	1998	559	380
David Klingler, Houston	1990	643	374
Andre Ware, Houston	1989	578	365
Kliff Kingsbury, Texas Tech	2001	528	364
Tim Couch, Kentucky	1997	547	363

Receptions

Catches	Year	Gm	No
Manny Hazard, Houston	1989	11	142
Troy Edwards, La. Tech	1998	12	140
Howard Twilley, Tulsa	1965	10	134
Trevor Insley, Nevada	1999	11	134
Alex Van Dyke, Nevada	1995	11	129

Catches Per Game	Year	No	P/Gm
Howard Twilley, Tulsa	1965	134	13.4
Manny Hazard, Houston	1989	142	12.9
Trevor Insley, Nevada	1999	134	12.2
Alex Van Dyke, Nevada	1995	129	11.7
Troy Edwards, La. Tech	1998	140	11.7

Yards Gained	Year	No	Yards
Trevor Insley, Nevada	1999	134	2060
Troy Edwards, La. Tech	1998	140	1996
Alex Van Dyke, Nevada	1995	129	1854
Howard Twilley, Tulsa	1965	134	1779
Josh Reed, LSU	2001	94	1740

Total Offense

Yards Gained	Year	Gm	Plays	Yards
David Klingler, Houston	1990	11	704	5221
Ty Detmer, BYU	1990	12	635	5022
Tim Rattay, La. Tech	1998	12	602	4840
Andre Ware, Houston	1989	11	628	4661
Jim McMahon, BYU	1980	12	540	4627

Yards Per Game	Year	Gm	Yards	P/Gm
David Klingler, Houston	1990	11	5221	474.6
Andre Ware, Houston	1989	11	4661	423.7
Ty Detmer, BYU	1990	12	5022	418.5
Tim Rattay, La. Tech	1998	12	4840	403.3
Mike Maxwell, Nevada	1995	9	3623	402.6

All-Purpose Yardage

Yards Gained	Year	Yards
Barry Sanders, Okla. St	1988	3250
Ryan Benjamin, Pacific	1991	2995
Troy Edwards, La. Tech	1998	2784
Mike Pringle, CS-Fullerton	1989	2690
Paul Palmer, Temple	1986	2633

Yards Per Game	Year	Yards	P/Gm
Barry Sanders, Okla. St	1988	3250	295.5
Ryan Benjamin, Pacific	1991	2995	249.6
Byron (Whizzer) White, Colo	1937	1970	246.3
Mike Pringle, CS-Fullerton	1989	2690	244.6
Paul Palmer, Temple	1986	2633	239.4

Scoring

Points	Year	TD	Xpt	FG	Pts
Barry Sanders, Okla. St	1988	39	0	0	234
Troy Edwards, La. Tech	1998	31	2	0	188
Mike Rozier, Nebraska	1983	29	0	0	174
Lydell Mitchell, Penn St	1971	29	0	0	174
Luke Staley, BYU	2001	28	2	0	170

Points Per Game	Year	Pts	P/Gm
Barry Sanders, Okla. St	1988	234	21.3
Bobby Reynolds, Nebraska	1950	157	17.4
Art Luppino, Arizona	1954	166	16.6
Ed Marinaro, Cornell	1971	148	16.4
Lydell Mitchell, Penn St	1971	174	15.8

Touchdowns Rushing	Year	No
Barry Sanders, Okla. St	1988	37
Mike Rozier, Nebraska	1983	29
Ricky Williams, Texas	1998	27
Lee Suggs, Va. Tech	2000	27
Ricky Williams, Texas	1997	25
Travis Prentice, Miami-OH	1997	25

Touchdowns Passing	Year	No
David Klingler, Houston	1990	54
Jim McMahon, BYU	1980	47
Andre Ware, Houston	1989	46
Tim Rattay, La. Tech	1998	46
David Carr, Fresno St.	2001	42

Touchdown Catches	Year	No
Troy Edwards, La. Tech	1998	27
Randy Moss, Marshall	1997	25
Manny Hazard, Houston	1989	22
Desmond Howard, Michigan	1991	19
Ashley Lelie, Hawaii	2001	19

Field Goals	Year	No
John Lee, UCLA	1984	29
Paul Woodside, West Virginia	1982	28
Luis Zendejas, Arizona St	1983	28
Fuad Reveiz, Tennessee	1982	27
Sebastian Janikowski, FSU	1998	27

Miscellaneous

Interceptions	Year	No
Al Worley, Washington	1968	14
George Shaw, Oregon	1951	13

Eight tied with 12 each.

Punting Average*	Year	Avg
Chad Kessler, LSU	1997	50.3
Reggie Roby, Iowa	1981	49.8
Kirk Wilson, UCLA	1956	49.3
Todd Sauerbrun, West Virginia	1994	48.4
Travis Dorsch, Purdue	2001	48.4

*Qualifiers for championship.

Punt Return Average*	Year	Avg
Bill Blackstock, Tennessee	1951	25.9
George Sims, Baylor	1948	25.0
Gene Derricotte, Michigan	1947	24.8

*At least 1.2 returns per game.

Kickoff Return Average*	Year	Avg
Paul Allen, BYU	1961	40.1
Tremain Mack, Miami-FL	1996	39.5
Leeland McElroy, Texas A&M	1993	39.3
Forrest Hall, San Francisco	1946	38.2
Tony Ball, Tenn-Chattanooga	1977	36.4

*At least 1.2 kickoff returns per game.

All-Time NCAA Division I-A Leaders (Cont.)
SINGLE GAME

Rushing				Total Offense			
Yards Gained	**Opponent**	**Year**	**Yds**	**Yards Gained**	**Opponent**	**Year**	**Yds**
LaDainian Tomlinson, TCU	UTEP	1999	406	David Klingler, Houston	Arizona St.	1990	732
Tony Sands, Kansas	Missouri	1991	396	Matt Vogler, TCU	Houston	1990	696
Marshall Faulk, San Diego St	Pacific	1991	386	David Klingler, Houston	TCU	1990	625
Troy Davis, Iowa St.	Missouri	1996	378	Scott Mitchell, Utah	Air Force	1988	625
Anthony Thompson, Indiana	Wisconsin	1989	377	Jimmy Klingler, Houston	Rice	1992	612

Passing				Receiving			
Yards Gained	**Opponent**	**Year**	**Yds**	**Catches**	**Opponent**	**Year**	**No**
David Klingler, Houston	Arizona St.	1990	716	Randy Gatewood, UNLV	Idaho	1994	23
Matt Vogler, TCU	Houston	1990	690	Jay Miller, BYU	New Mexico	1973	22
Brian Lindgren, Idaho	Mid. Tenn. St.	2001	637	Troy Edwards, La. Tech	Nebraska	1998	21
Scott Mitchell, Utah	Air Force	1988	631	Chris Daniels, Purdue	Mich. St.	1999	21
Jeremy Leach, New Mexico	Utah	1989	622	Two tied with 20 each.			

Completions				Yards Gained			
	Opponent	**Year**	**No**		**Opponent**	**Year**	**Yds**
Drew Brees, Purdue	Wisconsin	1998	55	Troy Edwards, La. Tech	Nebraska	1998	405
Rusty LaRue, Wake Forest	Duke	1995	55	Randy Gatewood, UNLV	Idaho	1994	363
Rusty LaRue, Wake Forest	N.C. St.	1995	50	Chuck Hughes, UTEP*	N. Texas St.	1965	349
Brian Lindgren, Idaho	Mid. Tenn. St.	2001	49	Nate Burleson, Nevada	San Jose St.	2001	326
David Klingler, Houston	SMU	1990	48	Rick Eber, Tulsa	Idaho St.	1967	322
				*UTEP was Texas Western in 1965.			

Scoring

Points				Touchdown Catches			
	Opponent	**Year**	**Pts**		**Opponent**	**Year**	**No**
Howard Griffith, Illinois	So. Ill.	1990	48	Tim Delaney, S. Diego St	N. Mex. St.	1969	6
Marshall Faulk, S. Diego St.	Pacific	1991	44	**Note:** Delaney's TD catches (2-22-34-31-30-9).			
Jim Brown, Syracuse	Colgate	1956	43				
Showboat Boykin, Ole Miss	Miss. St.	1951	42	**Field Goals**	**Opponent**	**Year**	**No**
Fred Wendt, UTEP*	N. Mex. St.	1948	42	Dale Klein, Nebraska	Missouri	1985	7
*UTEP was Texas Mines in 1948.				Mike Prindle, W. Mich.	Marshall	1984	7

Note: Klein's FGs (32-22-43-44-29-43-43); Prindle's FGs (32-44-42-23-48-41-27).

Touchdowns Rushing				Extra Points (Kick)			
	Opponent	**Year**	**No**		**Opponent**	**Year**	**No**
Howard Griffith, Illinois	So. Ill	1990	8	Terry Leiweke, Houston	Tulsa	1968	13
Showboat Boykin, Ole Miss	Miss. St.	1951	7	Derek Mahoney, Fresno St	New Mexico	1991	13

Note: Griffith's TD runs (5-51-7-41-5-18-5-3).

Touchdowns Passing			
	Opponent	**Year**	**No**
David Klingler, Houston	E. Wash.	1990	11
Dennis Shaw, San Diego St	N. Mex. St.	1969	9

Note: Klinger's TD passes (5-48-29-7-3-7-40-8-7-8-51).

Longest Plays (since 1941)

Rushing				Passing			
	Opponent	**Year**	**Yds**		**Opponent**	**Year**	**Yds**
Gale Sayers, Kansas	Nebraska	1963	99	Scott Ankrom to James Maness, TCU	Rice	1984	99
Max Anderson, Ariz. St	Wyoming	1967	99	Gino Torretta to Horace Copeland,			
Ralph Thompson, W. Texas St	Wich. St.	1970	99	Miami-FL	Ark.	1991	99
Kelsey Finch, Tennessee	Florida	1977	99	John Paci to Thomas Lewis, Indiana	Penn St.	1993	99
Eric Vann, Kansas	Oklahoma	1997	99	Drew Brees to Vinny Sutherland, Purdue	North-		
Eleven tied at 98 each.					western	1999	99

Passing				Field Goals			
	Opponent	**Year**	**Yds**		**Opponent**	**Year**	**Yds**
Fred Owens to Jack Ford, Portland	St. Mary's	1947	99	Steve Little, Arkansas	Texas	1977	67
Bo Burris to Warren McVea, Houston	Wash. St.	1966	99	Russell Erxleben, Texas	Rice	1977	67
Colin Clapton to Eddie Jenkins,				Joe Williams, Wichita St	So. Ill.	1978	67
Holy Cross	Boston U.	1970	99	Tony Franklin, Tex. A&M	Baylor	1976	65
Terry Peel to Robert Ford, Houston	Syracuse	1970	99	Martin Gramatica, Kan. St.	No. Ill.	1998	65
Terry Peel to Robert Ford, Houston	S. Diego St.	1972	99				
Cris Collinsworth to							
Derrick Gaffney, Florida	Rice	1977	99				

Annual Awards
Heisman Trophy

Originally presented in 1935 as the DAC Trophy by the Downtown Athletic Club of New York City to the best college football player east of the Mississippi. In 1936, players across the country were eligible and the award was renamed the Heisman Trophy following the death of former college coach and DAC athletic director John W. Heisman.

Multiple winner: Archie Griffin (2).

Winners in junior year (13): Doc Blanchard (1945), Ty Detmer (1990); Archie Griffin (1974), Desmond Howard (1991), Vic Janowicz (1950), Rashaan Salaam (1994), Barry Sanders (1988), Billy Sims (1978), Roger Staubach (1963), Doak Walker (1948), Herschel Walker (1982), Andre Ware (1989) and Charles Woodson (1997).

Winners on AP national champions (10): Angelo Bertelli (Notre Dame, 1943); Doc Blanchard (Army, 1945); Tony Dorsett (Pittsburgh, 1976); Leon Hart (Notre Dame, 1949); Johnny Lujack (Notre Dame, 1947); Davey O'Brien (TCU, 1938); Bruce Smith (Minnesota, 1941); Charlie Ward (Florida St., 1993); Danny Wuerffel (Florida, 1996); and Charles Woodson (Michigan, 1997).

Year		Points
1935	**Jay Berwanger,** Chicago, HB	84
	2nd–Monk Meyer, Army, HB	29
	3rd–Bill Shakespeare, Notre Dame, HB	23
	4th–Pepper Constable, Princeton, FB	20
1936	**Larry Kelley,** Yale, E	219
	2nd–Sam Francis, Nebraska, FB	47
	3rd–Ray Buivid, Marquette, HB	43
	4th–Sammy Baugh, TCU, HB	39
1937	**Clint Frank,** Yale, HB	524
	2nd–Byron (Whizzer) White, Colo., HB	264
	3rd–Marshall Goldberg, Pitt, HB	211
	4th–Alex Wojciechowicz, Fordham, C	85
1938	**Davey O'Brien,** TCU, QB	519
	2nd–Marshall Goldberg, Pitt, HB	294
	3rd–Sid Luckman, Columbia, QB	154
	4th–Bob MacLeod, Dartmouth, HB	78
1939	**Nile Kinnick,** Iowa, HB	651
	2nd–Tom Harmon, Michigan, HB	405
	3rd–Paul Christman, Missouri, QB	391
	4th–George Cafego, Tennessee, QB	296
1940	**Tom Harmon,** Michigan, HB	1303
	2nd–John Kimbrough, Texas A&M, FB	841
	3rd–George Franck, Minnesota, HB	102
	4th–Frankie Albert, Stanford, QB	90
1941	**Bruce Smith,** Minnesota, HB	554
	2nd–Angelo Bertelli, Notre Dame, QB	345
	3rd–Frankie Albert, Stanford, QB	336
	4th–Frank Sinkwich, Georgia, HB	249
1942	**Frank Sinkwich,** Georgia, TB	1059
	2nd–Paul Governali, Columbia, QB	218
	3rd–Clint Castleberry, Ga. Tech, HB	99
	4th–Mike Holovak, Boston College, FB	95
1943	**Angelo Bertelli,** Notre Dame, QB	648
	2nd–Bob Odell, Penn, HB	177
	3rd–Otto Graham, Northwestern, QB	140
	4th–Creighton Miller, Notre Dame, HB	134
1944	**Les Horvath,** Ohio St., TB-QB	412
	2nd–Glenn Davis, Army, HB	287
	3rd–Doc Blanchard, Army, FB	237
	4th–Don Whitmire, Navy, T	115
1945	**Doc Blanchard,** Army, FB	860
	2nd–Glenn Davis, Army, HB	638
	3rd–Bob Fenimore, Oklahoma A&M, HB	187
	4th–Herman Wedemeyer, St. Mary's, HB	152
1946	**Glenn Davis,** Army, HB	792
	2nd–Charlie Trippi, Georgia, HB	435
	3rd–Johnny Lujack, Notre Dame, QB	379
	4th–Doc Blanchard, Army, FB	267
1947	**Johnny Lujack,** Notre Dame, QB	742
	2nd–Bob Chappuis, Michigan, HB	555
	3rd–Doak Walker, SMU, HB	196
	4th–Charlie Conerly, Mississippi, QB	186
1948	**Doak Walker,** SMU, HB	778
	2nd–Charlie Justice, N. Carolina, HB	443
	3rd–Chuck Bednarik, Penn, C	336
	4th–Jackie Jensen, California, HB	143
1949	**Leon Hart,** Notre Dame, E	995
	2nd–Charlie Justice, N. Carolina, HB	272
	3rd–Doak Walker, SMU, HB	229
	4th–Arnold Galiffa, Army QB	196
1950	**Vic Janowicz,** Ohio St., HB	633
	2nd–Kyle Rote, SMU, HB	280
	3rd–Reds Bagnell, Penn, HB	231
	4th–Babe Parilli, Kentucky, QB	214
1951	**Dick Kazmaier,** Princeton, TB	1777
	2nd–Hank Lauricella, Tennessee, HB	424
	3rd–Babe Parilli, Kentucky, HB	344
	4th–Bill McColl, Stanford, E	313
1952	**Billy Vessels,** Oklahoma, HB	525
	2nd–Jack Scarbath, Maryland, QB	367
	3rd–Paul Giel, Minnesota, HB	329
	4th–Donn Moomaw, UCLA, C	257
1953	**Johnny Lattner,** Notre Dame, HB	1850
	2nd–Paul Giel, Minnesota, HB	1794
	3rd–Paul Cameron, UCLA, HB	444
	4th–Bernie Faloney, Maryland, QB	258
1954	**Alan Ameche,** Wisconsin, FB	1068
	2nd–Kurt Burris, Oklahoma, C	838
	3rd–Howard Cassady, Ohio St., HB	810
	4th–Ralph Guglielmi, Notre Dame, QB	691
1955	**Howard Cassady,** Ohio St., HB	2219
	2nd–Jim Swink, TCU, HB	742
	3rd–George Welsh, Navy, QB	383
	4th–Earl Morrall, Michigan St., QB	323
1956	**Paul Hornung,** Notre Dame, QB	1066
	2nd–Johnny Majors, Tennessee, HB	994
	3rd–Tommy McDonald, Oklahoma, HB	973
	4th–Jerry Tubbs, Oklahoma, C	724
1957	**John David Crow,** Texas A&M, HB	1183
	2nd–Alex Karras, Iowa, T	693
	3rd–Walt Kowalczyk, Mich. St., HB	630
	4th–Lou Michaels, Kentucky, T	330
1958	**Pete Dawkins,** Army, HB	1394
	2nd–Randy Duncan, Iowa, QB	1021
	3rd–Billy Cannon, LSU, HB	975
	4th–Bob White, Ohio St., FB	365
1959	**Billy Cannon,** LSU, HB	1929
	2nd–Richie Lucas, Penn St., QB	613
	3rd–Don Meredith, SMU, QB	286
	4th–Bill Burrell, Illinois, G	196
1960	**Joe Bellino,** Navy, HB	1793
	2nd–Tom Brown, Minnesota, G	731
	3rd–Jake Gibbs, Mississippi, QB	453
	4th–Ed Dyas, Auburn, HB	319
1961	**Ernie Davis,** Syracuse, HB	824
	2nd–Bob Ferguson, Ohio St., HB	771
	3rd–Jimmy Saxton, Texas, HB	551
	4th–Sandy Stephens, Minnesota, QB	543
1962	**Terry Baker,** Oregon St., QB	707
	2nd–Jerry Stovall, LSU, HB	618
	3rd–Bobby Bell, Minnesota, T	429
	4th–Lee Roy Jordan, Alabama, C	321
1963	**Roger Staubach,** Navy, QB	1860
	2nd–Billy Lothridge, Ga. Tech, QB	504
	3rd–Sherman Lewis, Mich. St., HB	369
	4th–Don Trull, Baylor, QB	253
1964	**John Huarte,** Notre Dame, QB	1026
	2nd–Jerry Rhome, Tulsa, QB	952
	3rd–Dick Butkus, Illinois, C	505
	4th–Bob Timberlake, Michigan, QB	361
1965	**Mike Garrett,** USC, HB	926
	2nd–Howard Twilley, Tulsa, E	528
	3rd–Jim Grabowski, Illinois, FB	481
	4th–Donny Anderson, Texas Tech, HB	408
1966	**Steve Spurrier,** Florida, QB	1679
	2nd–Bob Griese, Purdue, QB	816
	3rd–Nick Eddy, Notre Dame, HB	456
	4th–Gary Beban, UCLA, QB	318
1967	**Gary Beban,** UCLA, QB	1968
	2nd–O.J. Simpson, USC, HB	1722
	3rd–Leroy Keyes, Purdue, HB	1366
	4th–Larry Csonka, Syracuse, FB	136
1968	**O.J. Simpson,** USC, HB	2853
	2nd–Leroy Keyes, Purdue, HB	1103
	3rd–Terry Hanratty, Notre Dame, QB	387
	4th–Ted Kwalick, Penn St., TE	254
1969	**Steve Owens,** Oklahoma, HB	1488
	2nd–Mike Phipps, Purdue, QB	1344
	3rd–Rex Kern, Ohio St., QB	856
	4th–Archie Manning, Mississippi, QB	582
1970	**Jim Plunkett,** Stanford, QB	2229
	2nd–Joe Theismann, Notre Dame, QB	1410
	3rd–Archie Manning, Mississippi, QB	849
	4th–Steve Worster, Texas, RB	398

Annual Awards (Cont.)

Year		Points
1971	**Pat Sullivan,** Auburn, QB	1597
	2nd–Ed Marinaro, Cornell, RB	1445
	3rd–Greg Pruitt, Oklahoma, RB	586
	4th–Johnny Musso, Alabama, RB	365
1972	**Johnny Rodgers,** Nebraska, FL	1310
	2nd–Greg Pruitt, Oklahoma, RB	966
	3rd–Rich Glover, Nebraska, MG	652
	4th–Bert Jones, LSU, QB	351
1973	**John Cappelletti,** Penn St., RB	1057
	2nd–John Hicks, Ohio St., OT	524
	3rd–Roosevelt Leaks, Texas, RB	482
	4th–David Jaynes, Kansas, QB	394
1974	**Archie Griffin,** Ohio St., RB	1920
	2nd–Anthony Davis, USC, RB	819
	3rd–Joe Washington, Oklahoma, RB	661
	4th–Tom Clements, Notre Dame, QB	244
1975	**Archie Griffin,** Ohio St., RB	1800
	2nd–Chuck Muncie, California, RB	730
	3rd–Ricky Bell, USC, RB	708
	4th–Tony Dorsett, Pitt, RB	616
1976	**Tony Dorsett,** Pittsburgh, RB	2357
	2nd–Ricky Bell, USC, RB	1346
	3rd–Rob Lytle, Michigan, RB	413
	4th–Terry Miller, Oklahoma St., RB	197
1977	**Earl Campbell,** Texas, RB	1547
	2nd–Terry Miller, Oklahoma St., RB	812
	3rd–Ken MacAfee, Notre Dame, TE	343
	4th–Doug Williams, Grambling, QB	266
1978	**Billy Sims,** Oklahoma, RB	827
	2nd–Chuck Fusina, Penn St., QB	750
	3rd–Rick Leach, Michigan, QB	435
	4th–Charles White, USC, RB	354
1979	**Charles White,** USC, RB	1695
	2nd–Billy Sims, Oklahoma, RB	773
	3rd–Marc Wilson, BYU, QB	589
	4th–Art Schlichter, Ohio St., QB	251
1980	**George Rogers,** South Carolina, RB	1128
	2nd–Hugh Green, Pittsburgh, DE	861
	3rd–Herschel Walker, Georgia, RB	683
	4th–Mark Herrmann, Purdue, QB	405
1981	**Marcus Allen,** USC, RB	1797
	2nd–Herschel Walker, Georgia, RB	1199
	3rd–Jim McMahon, BYU, QB	706
	4th–Dan Marino, Pitt, QB	256
1982	**Herschel Walker,** Georgia, RB	1926
	2nd–John Elway, Stanford, QB	1231
	3rd–Eric Dickerson, SMU, RB	465
	4th–Anthony Carter, Michigan, WR	142
1983	**Mike Rozier,** Nebraska, RB	1801
	2nd–Steve Young, BYU, QB	1172
	3rd–Doug Flutie, Boston College, QB	253
	4th–Turner Gill, Nebraska, QB	190
1984	**Doug Flutie,** Boston College, QB	2240
	2nd–Keith Byars, Ohio St., RB	1251
	3rd–Robbie Bosco, BYU, QB	443
	4th–Bernie Kosar, Miami-FL, QB	320
1985	**Bo Jackson,** Auburn, RB	1509
	2nd–Chuck Long, Iowa, QB	1464
	3rd–Robbie Bosco, BYU, QB	459
	4th–Lorenzo White, Michigan St., RB	391
1986	**Vinny Testaverde,** Miami-FL, QB	2213
	2nd–Paul Palmer, Temple, RB	672
	3rd–Jim Harbaugh, Michigan, QB	458
	4th–Brian Bosworth, Oklahoma, LB	395

Year		Points
1987	**Tim Brown**, Notre Dame, WR	1442
	2nd–Don McPherson, Syracuse, QB	831
	3rd–Gordie Lockbaum, Holy Cross, WR-DB	657
	4th–Lorenzo White, Michigan St., RB	632
1988	**Barry Sanders,** Oklahoma St., RB	1878
	2nd–Rodney Peete, USC, QB	912
	3rd–Troy Aikman, UCLA, QB	582
	4th–Steve Walsh, Miami-FL, QB	341
1989	**Andre Ware,** Houston, QB	1073
	2nd–Anthony Thompson, Ind., RB	1003
	3rd–Major Harris, West Va., QB	709
	4th–Tony Rice, Notre Dame, QB	523
1990	**Ty Detmer,** BYU, QB	1482
	2nd–Rocket Ismail, Notre Dame, FL	1177
	3rd–Eric Bieniemy, Colorado, RB	798
	4th–Shawn Moore, Virginia, QB	465
1991	**Desmond Howard,** Michigan, WR	2077
	2nd–Casey Weldon, Florida St., QB	503
	3rd–Ty Detmer, BYU, QB	445
	4th–Steve Emtman, Washington, DT	357
1992	**Gino Torretta,** Miami-FL, QB	1400
	2nd–Marshall Faulk, San Diego St., RB	1080
	3rd–Garrison Hearst, Georgia, RB	982
	4th–Marvin Jones, Florida St., LB	392
1993	**Charlie Ward,** Florida St., QB	2310
	2nd–Heath Shuler, Tennessee, QB	688
	3rd–David Palmer, Alabama, RB	292
	4th–Marshall Faulk, S. Diego St., RB	250
1994	**Rashaan Salaam,** Colorado, RB	1743
	2nd–Ki-Jana Carter, Penn St., RB	901
	3rd–Steve McNair, Alcorn St., QB	655
	4th–Kerry Collins, Penn St., QB	639
1995	**Eddie George,** Ohio St., RB	1460
	2nd–Tommie Frazier, Nebraska, QB	1196
	3rd–Danny Wuerffel, Florida, QB	987
	4th–Darnell Autry, Northwestern, RB	535
1996	**Danny Wuerffel,** Florida, QB	1363
	2nd–Troy Davis, Iowa St., RB	1174
	3rd–Jake Plummer, Arizona St., QB	685
	4th–Orlando Pace, Ohio St., OT	599
1997	**Charles Woodson,** Michigan, DB-WR	1815
	2nd–Peyton Manning, Tennessee, QB	1543
	3rd–Ryan Leaf, Washington St., QB	861
	4th–Randy Moss, Marshall, WR	253
1998	**Ricky Williams,** Texas, RB	2355
	2nd–Michael Bishop, Kansas St., QB	792
	3rd–Cade McNown, UCLA, QB	696
	4th–Tim Couch, Kentucky, QB	527
1999	**Ron Dayne,** Wisconsin, RB	2042
	2nd–Joe Hamilton, Ga. Tech, QB	994
	3rd–Michael Vick, Va. Tech, QB	319
	4th–Drew Brees, Purdue, QB	308
2000	**Chris Weinke,** Florida St., QB	1628
	2nd–Josh Heupel, Oklahoma, QB	1552
	3rd–Drew Brees, Purdue, QB	619
	4th–LaDainian Tomlinson, TCU, RB	566
2001	**Eric Crouch,** Nebraska, QB	770
	2nd–Rex Grossman, Florida, QB	708
	3rd–Ken Dorsey, Miami-FL, QB	638
	4th–Joey Harrington, Oregon, QB	364

Maxwell Award

First presented in 1937 by the Maxwell Memorial Football Club of Philadelphia, the award is named after Robert (Tiny) Maxwell, a Philadelphia native who was a standout lineman at the University of Chicago at the turn of the century. Like the Heisman, the Maxwell is given to the outstanding college player in the nation. Both awards have gone to the same player in the same season 34 times. Those players are preceded by (#). Glenn Davis of Army and Doak Walker of SMU won both but in different years.

Multiple winner: Johnny Lattner (2).

Year	Year	Year
1937 #Clint Frank, Yale, HB	1959 Rich Lucas, Penn St., QB	1980 Hugh Green, Pitt, DE
1938 #Davey O'Brien, TCU, QB		1981 #Marcus Allen, USC, RB
1939 #Nile Kinnick, Iowa, HB	1960 #Joe Bellino, Navy, HB	1982 #Herschel Walker, Georgia, RB
	1961 Bob Ferguson, Ohio St., HB	1983 #Mike Rozier, Nebraska, RB
1940 #Tom Harmon, Michigan, HB	1962 #Terry Baker, Oregon St., QB	1984 #Doug Flutie, Boston Col., QB
1941 Bill Dudley, Virginia, HB	1963 #Roger Staubach, Navy, QB	1985 Chuck Long, Iowa, QB
1942 Paul Governali, Columbia, QB	1964 Glenn Ressler, Penn St., G	1986 #V. Testaverde, Miami-FL, QB
1943 Bob Odell, Penn, HB	1965 Tommy Nobis, Texas, LB	1987 Don McPherson, Syracuse, QB
1944 Glenn Davis, Army, HB	1966 Jim Lynch, Notre Dame, LB	1988 #Barry Sanders, Okla. St., RB
1945 #Doc Blanchard, Army, FB	1967 #Gary Beban, UCLA, QB	1989 Anthony Thompson, Indiana, RB
1946 Charley Trippi, Georgia, HB	1968 #O.J. Simpson, USC, HB	
1947 Doak Walker, SMU, HB	1969 Mike Reid, Penn St., DT	1990 #Ty Detmer, BYU, QB
1948 Chuck Bednarik, Penn, C		1991 #Desmond Howard, Mich., WR
1949 #Leon Hart, Notre Dame, E	1970 #Jim Plunkett, Stanford, QB	1992 #Gino Torretta, Miami-FL, QB
	1971 Ed Marinaro, Cornell, RB	1993 #Charlie Ward, Florida St., QB
1950 Reds Bagnell, Penn, HB	1972 Brad Van Pelt, Michigan St., DB	1994 Kerry Collins, Penn St., QB
1951 #Dick Kazmaier, Princeton, TB	1973 #John Cappelletti, Penn St., RB	1995 #Eddie George, Ohio St., RB
1952 Johnny Lattner, Notre Dame, HB	1974 Steve Joachim, Temple, QB	1996 #Danny Wuerffel, Florida, QB
1953 #Johnny Lattner, N. Dame, HB	1975 #Archie Griffin, Ohio St., RB	1997 Peyton Manning, Tennessee, QB
1954 Ron Beagle, Navy, E	1976 #Tony Dorsett, Pitt, RB	1998 #Ricky Williams, Texas, RB
1955 #Howard Cassady, Ohio St., HB	1977 Ross Browner, Notre Dame, DE	1999 #Ron Dayne, Wisconsin, RB
1956 Tommy McDonald, Okla., HB	1978 Chuck Fusina, Penn St., QB	
1957 Bob Reifsnyder, Navy, T	1979 #Charles White, USC, RB	2000 Drew Brees, Purdue, QB
1958 #Pete Dawkins, Army, HB		2001 Ken Dorsey, Miami-FL, QB

Outland Trophy

First presented in 1946 by the Football Writers Association of America, honoring the nation's outstanding interior lineman. The award is named after its benefactor, Dr. John H. Outland (Kansas, Class of 1898). Players listed in **bold** type helped lead their team to a national championship (according to AP).

Multiple winner: Dave Rimington (2). **Winners in junior year:** Ross Browner (1976), Steve Emtman (1991), Orlando Pace (1996) and Rimington (1981).

Year	Year	Year
1946 **George Connor**, N. Dame, T	1965 Tommy Nobis, Texas, G	1984 Bruce Smith, Virginia Tech, DT
1947 Joe Steffy, Army, G	1966 Loyd Phillips, Arkansas, T	1985 Mike Ruth, Boston College, NG
1948 Bill Fischer, Notre Dame, G	1967 **Ron Yary**, USC, T	1986 Jason Buck, BYU, DT
1949 Ed Bagdon, Michigan St., G	1968 Bill Stanfill, Georgia, T	1987 Chad Hennings, Air Force, DT
	1969 Mike Reid, Penn St., DT	1988 Tracy Rocker, Auburn, DT
1950 Bob Gain, Kentucky, T		1989 Mohammed Elewonibi, BYU, G
1951 Jim Weatherall, Oklahoma, T	1970 Jim Stillwagon, Ohio St., MG	
1952 Dick Modzelewski, Maryland, T	1971 **Larry Jacobson**, Neb., DT	1990 Russell Maryland, Miami-FL, NT
1953 J.D. Roberts, Oklahoma, G	1972 Rich Glover, Nebraska, MG	1991 Steve Emtman, Washington, DT
1954 Bill Brooks, Arkansas, G	1973 John Hicks, Ohio St., OT	1992 Will Shields, Nebraska, G
1955 Calvin Jones, Iowa, G	1974 Randy White, Maryland, DT	1993 Rob Waldrop, Arizona, NG
1956 Jim Parker, Ohio St., G	1975 **Lee Roy Selmon**, Okla., DT	1994 **Zach Wiegert**, Nebraska, OT
1957 Alex Karras, Iowa, T	1976 Ross Browner, Notre Dame, DE	1995 Jonathan Ogden, UCLA, OT
1958 Zeke Smith, Auburn, G	1977 Brad Shearer, Texas, DT	1996 Orlando Pace, Ohio St., OT
1959 Mike McGee, Duke, T	1978 Greg Roberts, Oklahoma, G	1997 Aaron Taylor, Nebraska, G
	1979 Jim Richter, N.C. State, C	1998 Kris Farris, UCLA, OT
1960 **Tom Brown**, Minnesota, G		1999 Chris Samuels, Alabama, OT
1961 Merlin Olsen, Utah St., T	1980 Mark May, Pittsburgh, OT	
1962 Bobby Bell, Minnesota, T	1981 Dave Rimington, Nebraska, C	2000 John Henderson, Tennessee, DT
1963 **Scott Appleton**, Texas, T	1982 Dave Rimington, Nebraska, C	2001 **Bryant McKinnie**, Miami-FL, OT
1964 Steve DeLong, Tennessee, T	1983 Dean Steinkuhler, Nebraska, C	

Butkus Award

First presented in 1985 by the Downtown Athletic Club of Orlando, Fla., to honor the nation's outstanding linebacker. The award is named after Dick Butkus, two-time consensus All-America at Illinois and six-time All-Pro with the Chicago Bears.

Multiple winner: Brian Bosworth (2).

Year	Year	Year
1985 Brian Bosworth, Oklahoma	1991 Erick Anderson, Michigan	1997 Andy Katzenmoyer, Ohio St.
1986 Brian Bosworth, Oklahoma	1992 Marvin Jones, Florida St.	1998 Chris Claiborne, USC
1987 Paul McGowan, Florida St.	1993 Trev Alberts, Nebraska	1999 LaVar Arrington, Penn St.
1988 Derrick Thomas, Alabama	1994 Dana Howard, Illinois	2000 Dan Morgan, Miami-FL
1989 Percy Snow, Michigan St.	1995 Kevin Hardy, Illinois	2001 Rocky Calmus, Oklahoma
1990 Alfred Williams, Colorado	1996 Matt Russell, Colorado	

Lombardi Award

First presented in 1970 by the Rotary Club of Houston, honoring the nation's best lineman. The award is named after pro football coach Vince Lombardi who, as a guard, was a member of the famous "Seven Blocks of Granite" at Fordham in the 1930s. The Lombardi and Outland awards have gone to the same player in the same year ten times. Those players are preceded by (#). Ross Browner of Notre Dame won both, but in different years.

Multiple winner: Orlando Pace (2).

Year	Year	Year
1970 #Jim Stillwagon, Ohio St., MG	1972 #Rich Glover, Nebraska, MG	1974 #Randy White, Maryland, DT
1971 Walt Patulski, Notre Dame, DE	1973 #John Hicks, Ohio St., OT	1975 #Lee Roy Selmon, Okla., DT

Annual Awards (Cont.)

Year		Year		Year	
1976	Wilson Whitley, Houston, DT	1985	Tony Casillas, Oklahoma, NG	1994	Warren Sapp, Miami-FL, DT
1977	Ross Browner, Notre Dame, DE	1986	Cornelius Bennett, Alabama, LB	1995	Orlando Pace, Ohio St., OT
1978	Bruce Clark, Penn St., DT	1987	Chris Spielman, Ohio St., LB	1996	#Orlando Pace, Ohio St., OT
1979	Brad Budde, USC, G	1988	#Tracy Rocker, Auburn, DT	1997	Grant Wistrom, Nebraska, DE
1980	Hugh Green, Pitt, DE	1989	Percy Snow, Michigan St., LB	1998	Dat Nguyen, Tex. A&M, LB
1981	Kenneth Sims, Texas, DT	1990	Chris Zorich, Notre Dame, NT	1999	Corey Moore, Va. Tech, DE
1982	#Dave Rimington, Neb., C	1991	#Steve Emtman, Wash., DT	2000	Jamal Reynolds, Florida St., DE
1983	#Dean Steinkuhler, Neb., G	1992	Marvin Jones, Florida St., LB	2001	Julius Peppers, North Carolina, DE
1984	Tony Degrate, Texas, DT	1993	Aaron Taylor, Notre Dame, OT		

O'Brien Quarterback Award

First presented in 1977 as the O'Brien Memorial Trophy, the award went to the outstanding player in the Southwest. In 1981, however, the Davey O'Brien Educational and Charitable Trust of Ft. Worth renamed the prize the O'Brien National Quarterback Award and now honors the nation's best quarterback. The award is named after 1938 Heisman Trophy-winning QB Davey O'Brien of Texas Christian.

Multiple winners: Ty Detmer, Mike Singletary and Danny Wuerffel (2).

Memorial Trophy

Year		Year	
1977	Earl Campbell, Texas, RB	1979	Mike Singletary, Baylor, LB
1978	Billy Sims, Oklahoma, RB	1980	Mike Singletary, Baylor, LB

National QB Award

Year		Year		Year	
1981	Jim McMahon, BYU	1988	Troy Aikman, UCLA	1995	Danny Wuerffel, Florida
1982	Todd Blackledge, Penn St.	1989	Andre Ware, Houston	1996	Danny Wuerffel, Florida
1983	Steve Young, BYU	1990	Ty Detmer, BYU	1997	Peyton Manning, Tennessee
1984	Doug Flutie, Boston College	1991	Ty Detmer, BYU	1998	Michael Bishop, Kansas St.
1985	Chuck Long, Iowa	1992	Gino Torretta, Miami-FL	1999	Joe Hamilton, Ga. Tech
1986	Vinny Testaverde, Miami, FL	1993	Charlie Ward, Florida St.	2000	Chris Weinke, Florida St.
1987	Don McPherson, Syracuse	1994	Kerry Collins, Penn St.	2001	Eric Crouch, Nebraska

Thorpe Award

First presented in 1986 by the Jim Thorpe Athletic Club of Oklahoma City to honor the nation's outstanding defensive back. The award is named after Jim Thorpe–Olympic champion and two-time consensus All-America halfback at Carlisle.

Year		Year		Year	
1986	Thomas Everett, Baylor	1991	Terrell Buckley, Florida St.	1997	Charles Woodson, Michigan
1987	Bennie Blades, Miami-FL & Rickey Dixon, Oklahoma	1992	Deon Figures, Colorado	1998	Antoine Winfield, Ohio St.
		1993	Antonio Langham, Alabama	1999	Tyrone Carter, Minnesota
1988	Deion Sanders, Florida St.	1994	Chris Hudson, Colorado	2000	Jamar Fletcher, Wisconsin
1989	Mike Carrier, USC	1995	Greg Myers, Colorado St.	2001	Roy Williams, Oklahoma
1990	Darryl Lewis, Arizona	1996	Lawrence Wright, Florida		

Payton Award

First presented in 1987 by the Sports Network and Division I-AA sports information directors to honor the nation's outstanding Division I-AA player. The award is named after Walter Payton, the NFL's all-time leading rusher who was an All-America running back at Jackson St.

Year		Year		Year	
1987	Kenny Gamble, Colgate, RB	1993	Doug Nussmeier, Idaho, QB	1999	Adrian Peterson, Ga. Southern, RB
1988	Dave Meggett, Towson St., RB	1994	Steve McNair, Alcorn St., QB	2000	Louis Ivory, Furman, RB
1989	John Friesz, Idaho, QB	1995	Dave Dickenson, Montana, QB	2001	Brian Westbrook, Villanova, RB
1990	Walter Dean, Grambling, RB	1996	Archie Amerson, N. Arizona, RB		
1991	Jamie Martin, Weber St., QB	1997	Brian Finneran, Villanova, WR		
1992	Michael Payton, Marshall, QB	1998	Jerry Azumah, N. Hampshire, RB		

Hill Trophy

First presented in 1986 by the Harlon Hill Awards Committee in Florence, Ala., to honor the nation's outstanding Division II player. The award is named after three-time NFL All-Pro Harlon Hill, who played college ball at North Alabama.

Multiple winners: Johnny Bailey (3), Dusty Bonner (2).

Year		Year		Year	
1986	Jeff Bentrim, N. Dakota St., QB	1992	Ronald Moore, Pittsburg St., RB	1998	Brian Shay, Emporia St., RB
1987	Johnny Bailey, Texas A&I, RB	1993	Roger Graham, New Haven, RB	1999	Corte McGuffet, N. Colo., RB
1988	Johnny Bailey, Texas A&I, RB	1994	Chris Hatcher, Valdosta St., QB	2000	Dusty Bonner, Valdosta St., QB
1989	Johnny Bailey, Texas A&I, RB	1995	Ronald McKinnon, N. Alabama, LB	2001	Dusty Bonner, Valdosta St., QB
1990	Chris Simdorn, N. Dakota St., QB	1996	Jarrett Anderson, Truman St., RB		
1991	Ronnie West, Pittsburg St., WR	1997	Irv Sigler, Bloomsburg, RB		

All-Time Winningest Division I-A Coaches

Minimum of 10 years in Division I-A through 2001 season. Regular season and bowl games included. Coaches active in 2001 in **bold** type.

Top 25 Winning Percentage

		Yrs	W	L	T	Pct
1	Knute Rockne	13	105	12	5	.881
2	Frank Leahy	13	107	13	9	.864
3	George Woodruff	12	142	25	2	.846
4	Barry Switzer	16	157	29	4	.837
5	Tom Osborne	25	255	49	3	.836
6	Percy Haughton	13	96	17	6	.832
7	Bob Neyland	21	173	31	12	.829
8	Hurry Up Yost	29	196	36	12	.828
9	**Phillip Fulmer**	10	95	20	0	.826
10	Bud Wilkinson	17	145	29	4	.826
11	Jock Sutherland	20	144	28	14	.812
12	Bob Devaney	16	136	30	7	.806
13	Frank Thomas	19	141	33	9	.795
14	Henry Williams	23	141	34	12	.786
15	Gil Dobie	33	180	45	15	.781
16	Bear Bryant	38	323	85	17	.780
17	Fred Folsom	19	106	28	6	.779
18	**Bobby Bowden**	36	323	91	4	.778
19	**Steve Spurrier**	15	142	40	2	.777
20	Bo Schembechler	27	234	65	8	.775
21	**Joe Paterno**	36	327	97	3	.769
22	Fritz Crisler	18	116	32	9	.768
23	Charley Moran	18	122	33	12	.766
24	Wallace Wade	24	171	49	10	.765
25	Frank Kush	22	176	54	1	.764

Top 25 Victories

		Yrs	W	L	T	Pct
1	**Joe Paterno**	36	327	97	3	.769
2	**Bobby Bowden**	36	323	91	4	.778
	Bear Bryant	38	323	85	17	.780
4	Pop Warner	44	319	106	32	.733
5	Amos Alonzo Stagg	57	314	199	35	.605
6	LaVell Edwards	29	257	101	3	.722
7	Tom Osborne	25	255	49	3	.836
8	Woody Hayes	33	238	72	10	.759
9	Bo Schembechler	27	234	65	8	.775
10	**Lou Holtz**	30	233	113	7	.670
11	Hayden Fry	37	232	178	10	.564
12	Jess Neely	40	207	176	19	.539
13	Warren Woodson	31	203	95	14	.673
14	Don Nehlen	30	202	128	8	.609
15	Vince Dooley	25	201	77	10	.715
	Eddie Anderson	39	201	128	15	.606
17	Jim Sweeney	32	200	154	4	.564
18	Dana X. Bible	33	198	72	23	.715
19	Dan McGugin	30	197	55	19	.762
20	Hurry Up Yost	29	196	36	12	.828
21	Howard Jones	29	194	64	21	.733
22	John Cooper	24	192	84	6	.691
23	Johnny Vaught	25	190	61	12	.745
24	George Welsh	28	189	132	4	.588
25	John Heisman	36	185	70	17	.711
	Johnny Majors	29	185	137	10	.572

Note: Eddie Robinson of Division I-AA Grambling St. (1941-42, 1945-97) is the all-time NCAA leader in coaching wins with a 408-165-15 record and .708 winning pct. over 55 seasons.

Where They Coached

Anderson–Loras (1922-24), DePaul (1925-31), Holy Cross (1933-38), Iowa (1939-42), Holy Cross (1950-64); **Bible**–Mississippi College (1913-15), LSU (1916), Texas A&M (1917,1919-28), Nebraska (1929-36), Texas (1937-46); **Bowden**–Samford (1959-62), West Virginia (1970-75), Florida St. (1976–); **Bryant**–Maryland (1945), Kentucky (1946-53), Texas A&M (1954-57), Alabama (1958-82); **Cooper**–Tulsa (1977-84), Arizona St. (1985-87), Ohio St. (1988-2000); **Crisler**–Minnesota (1930-31), Princeton (1932-37), Michigan (1938-47); **Devaney**–Wyoming (1957-61), Nebraska (1962-72); **Dobie**–North Dakota St. (1906-07), Washington (1908-16), Navy (1917-19), Cornell (1920-35), Boston College (1936-38); **V. Dooley**–Georgia (1964-88); **Edwards**–BYU (1972-2000); **Folsom**–Colorado (1895-99, 1901-02), Dartmouth (1903-06), Colorado (1908-15); **Fry**–SMU (1962-72), North Texas (1973-78), Iowa (1979-98); **Fulmer**–Tennessee (1992–).

Haughton–Cornell (1899-1900), Harvard (1908-16), Columbia (1923-24); **Hayes**–Denison (1946-48), Miami-OH (1949-50), Ohio St. (1951-78); **Heisman**–Oberlin (1892), Akron (1893), Oberlin (1894), Auburn (1895-99), Clemson (1900-03), Georgia Tech (1904-19), Penn (1920-22), Washington & Jefferson (1923), Rice (1924-27); **Holtz**–William & Mary (1969-71), N.C. State (1972-75), Arkansas (1977-83), Minnesota (1984-85), Notre Dame (1986-96), South Carolina (1999–); **Jones**–Syracuse (1908), Yale (1909), Ohio St. (1910), Yale (1913), Iowa (1916-23), Duke (1924), USC (1925-40); **Kush**–Arizona St. (1958-79); **Leahy**–Boston College (1939-40), Notre Dame (1941-43, 1946-53); **Majors**–Iowa St. (1968-72), Pittsburgh (1973-76, 93-96), Tennessee (1977-92); **Moran**–Texas A&M (1909-14), Centre (1919-23), Bucknell (1924-26), Catawba (1930-33).

Neely–Rhodes (1924-27), Clemson (1931-39), Rice (1940-66); **Nehlen**–Bowling Green (1968-76), West Virginia (1980-2000); **Neyland**–Tennessee (1926-34, 1936-40, 1946-52); **Osborne**–Nebraska (1973-97); **Paterno**–Penn St. (1966–); **Rockne**–Notre Dame (1918-30); **Schembechler**–Miami-OH (1963-68), Michigan (1969-89); **Spurrier**–Duke (1987-89), Florida (1990-2001); **Stagg**–Springfield College (1890-91), Chicago (1892-1932), Pacific (1933-46); **Sutherland**–Lafayette (1919-23), Pittsburgh (1924-38); **Sweeney**–Montana St. (1963-67), Washington St. (1968-75), Fresno St. (1976-96); **Switzer**–Oklahoma (1973-88).

Thomas–Chattanooga (1925-28), Alabama (1931-42, 1944-46); **Vaught**–Mississippi (1947-70); **Wade**–Alabama (1923-30), Duke (1931-41, 1946-50); **Warner**–Georgia (1895-96), Cornell (1897-98), Carlisle (1899-1903), Cornell (1904-06), Carlisle (1907-13), Pittsburgh (1915-23), Stanford (1924-32), Temple (1933-38); **Welsh**–Navy (1973-81), Virginia (1982-2000); **Wilkinson**–Oklahoma (1947-63); **Williams**–Army (1891), Minnesota (1900-21); **Woodruff**–Penn (1892-1901), Illinois (1903), Carlisle (1905); **Woodson**–Central Arkansas (1935-39), Hardin-Simmons (1941-42, 1946-51), Arizona (1952-56), New Mexico St. (1958-67), Trinity-TX (1972-73); **Yost**–Ohio Wesleyan (1897), Nebraska (1898), Kansas (1899), Stanford (1900), Michigan (1901-23, 1925-26).

All-Time Winningest Division I-A Coaches (Cont.)

All-Time Bowl Appearances
Coaches active in 2001 in **bold** type.

		Overall		
		App	W	L	T
1	**Joe Paterno**	.30	20	9	1
2	Bear Bryant	.29	15	12	2
3	Tom Osborne	.25	12	13	0
4	**Bobby Bowden**	.25	18	6	1
5	LaVell Edwards	.22	7	14	1
6	**Lou Holtz**	.21	11	8	2
7	Vince Dooley	.20	8	10	2
8	Johnny Vaught	.18	10	8	0
9	Hayden Fry	.17	7	9	1
	Bo Schembechler	.17	5	12	0
11	Johnny Majors	.16	9	7	0
	Darrell Royal	.16	8	7	1
13	Don James	.15	10	5	0
	George Welsh	.15	5	10	0
15	John Cooper	.14	5	9	0
16	Bobby Dodd	.13	9	4	0
	Terry Donahue	.13	8	4	1
	Barry Switzer	.13	8	5	0
	Charlie McClendon	.13	7	6	0
	Jackie Sherrill	.13	7	6	0

Active Coaches' Victories
(Minimum 5 years in Division I-A.)

		Yrs	W	L	T	Pct
1	Joe Paterno, Penn St.	.36	**327**	97	3	.769
2	Bobby Bowden, Fla. St.	.36	**323**	91	4	.778
3	Lou Holtz, South Carolina	.30	**233**	113	7	.670
4	Jackie Sherrill, Miss. St.	.23	**175**	101	4	.632
5	Ken Hatfield, Rice	.22	**155**	108	4	.588
6	Frank Beamer, Va. Tech	.21	**149**	88	4	.627
7	Dennis Franchione, Alabama	.18	**145**	71	2	.670
8	Fisher DeBerry, Air Force	.18	**141**	78	1	.643
9	Dennis Erickson, Oregon St.	.16	**136**	52	1	.722
10	Paul Pasqualoni, Syracuse	.16	**125**	56	1	.690
11	Mack Brown, Texas	.18	**124**	87	1	.587
12	John Robinson, UNLV	.15	**119**	56	4	.676
	Mike Price, Wash. St.	.21	**119**	119	0	.500
14	R.C. Slocum, Texas A&M	.13	**117**	41	2	.738
15	Bill Snyder, Kansas St.	.13	**105**	49	1	.681
16	John L. Smith, Louisville	.13	**103**	54	0	.656
17	Sonny Lubick, Colorado St.	.13	**95**	53	0	.642
	Phillip Fulmer, Tennessee	.10	**95**	20	0	.826
19	John Mackovic, Arizona	.14	**90**	70	3	.561
20	Glen Mason, Minnesota	.16	**85**	96	1	.470

Note: Only four coaches— **Bill Alexander** of Georgia Tech (1920-44); **Bob Neyland** of Tennessee (1926-34, 36-40, 46-52); **Frank Thomas** of Alabama (1931-42, 44-46) and **Joe Paterno** of Penn State (1966–)— have taken teams to the Rose, Orange, Sugar and Cotton Bowls. Paterno has won all four, while Alexander and Thomas won three and Neyland two.

AFCA Coach of the Year
First presented in 1935 by the American Football Coaches Association.

Multiple winners: Joe Paterno (4), Bear Bryant (3), John McKay and Darrell Royal (2).

Years

1935 Pappy Waldorf, Northwestern
1936 Dick Harlow, Harvard
1937 Hooks Mylin, Lafayette
1938 Bill Kern, Carnegie Tech
1939 Eddie Anderson, Iowa
1940 Clark Shaughnessy, Stanford
1941 Frank Leahy, Notre Dame
1942 Bill Alexander, Georgia Tech
1943 Amos Alonzo Stagg, Pacific
1944 Carroll Widdoes, Ohio St.
1945 Bo McMillin, Indiana
1946 Red Blaik, Army
1947 Fritz Crisler, Michigan
1948 Bennie Oosterbaan, Michigan
1949 Bud Wilkinson, Oklahoma
1950 Charlie Caldwell, Princeton
1951 Chuck Taylor, Stanford
1952 Biggie Munn, Michigan St.
1953 Jim Tatum, Maryland
1954 Red Sanders, UCLA
1955 Duffy Daugherty, Michigan St.
1956 Bowden Wyatt, Tennessee
1957 Woody Hayes, Ohio St.

Years

1958 Paul Dietzel, LSU
1959 Ben Schwartzwalder, Syracuse
1960 Murray Warmath, Minnesota
1961 Bear Bryant, Alabama
1962 John McKay, USC
1963 Darrell Royal, Texas
1964 Frank Broyles, Arkansas
   & Ara Parseghian, Notre Dame
1965 Tommy Prothro, UCLA
1966 Tom Cahill, Army
1967 John Pont, Indiana
1968 Joe Paterno, Penn St.
1969 Bo Schembechler, Michigan
1970 Charlie McClendon, LSU
   & Darrell Royal, Texas
1971 Bear Bryant, Alabama
1972 John McKay, USC
1973 Bear Bryant, Alabama
1974 Grant Teaff, Baylor
1975 Frank Kush, Arizona St.
1976 Johnny Majors, Pittsburgh
1977 Don James, Washington
1978 Joe Paterno, Penn St.

Years

1979 Earle Bruce, Ohio St.
1980 Vince Dooley, Georgia
1981 Danny Ford, Clemson
1982 Joe Paterno, Penn St.
1983 Ken Hatfield, Air Force
1984 LaVell Edwards, BYU
1985 Fisher DeBerry, Air Force
1986 Joe Paterno, Penn St.
1987 Dick MacPherson, Syracuse
1988 Don Nehlen, West Virginia
1989 Bill McCartney, Colorado
1990 Bobby Ross, Georgia Tech
1991 Bill Lewis, East Carolina
1992 Gene Stallings, Alabama
1993 Barry Alvarez, Wisconsin
1994 Tom Osborne, Nebraska
1995 Gary Barnett, Northwestern
1996 Bruce Snyder, Arizona St.
1997 Lloyd Carr, Michigan
1998 Phillip Fulmer, Tennessee
1999 Frank Beamer, Va. Tech
2000 Bob Stoops, Oklahoma
2001 Ralph Friedgen, Maryland
   & Larry Coker, Miami-FL

FWAA Coach of the Year
First presented in 1957 by the Football Writers Association of America. The FWAA and AFCA awards have both gone to the same coach in the same season 31 times. Those double winners are preceded by (#).

Multiple winners: Woody Hayes and Joe Paterno (3); Lou Holtz, Johnny Majors and John McKay (2).

Year

1957 #Woody Hayes, Ohio St.
1958 #Paul Dietzel, LSU
1959 #Ben Schwartzwalder, Syracuse
1960 #Murray Warmath, Minnesota
1961 Darrell Royal, Texas
1962 #John McKay, USC
1963 #Darrell Royal, Texas

Year

1964 #Ara Parseghian, Notre Dame
1965 Duffy Daugherty, Michigan St.
1966 #Tom Cahill, Army
1967 #John Pont, Indiana
1968 Woody Hayes, Ohio St.
1969 #Bo Schembechler, Michigan
1970 Alex Agase, Northwestern

Year

1971 Bob Devaney, Nebraska
1972 #John McKay, USC
1973 Johnny Majors, Pitt
1974 #Grant Teaff, Baylor
1975 Woody Hayes, Ohio St.
1976 #Johnny Majors, Pitt
1977 Lou Holtz, Arkansas

Year	Year	Year
1978 #Joe Paterno, Penn St.	1986 #Joe Paterno, Penn St.	1994 Rich Brooks, Oregon
1979 #Earle Bruce, Ohio St.	1987 #Dick MacPherson, Syracuse	1995 #Gary Barnett, Northwestern
1980 #Vince Dooley, Georgia	1988 Lou Holtz, Notre Dame	1996 #Bruce Snyder, Arizona St.
1981 #Danny Ford, Clemson	1989 #Bill McCartney, Colorado	1997 Mike Price, Washington St.
1982 #Joe Paterno, Penn St.	1990 #Bobby Ross, Georgia Tech	1998 #Phillip Fulmer, Tennessee
1983 Howard Schnellenberger, Miami-FL	1991 Don James, Washington	1999 #Frank Beamer, Va. Tech
1984 #LaVell Edwards, BYU	1992 #Gene Stallings, Alabama	2000 #Bob Stoops, Oklahoma
1985 #Fisher DeBerry, Air Force	1993 Terry Bowden, Auburn	2001 #Ralph Friedgen, Maryland

All-Time NCAA Division I-AA Leaders
CAREER

Total Offense

	Yards Gained	Years	Yards
1	Steve McNair, Alcorn St.	1991-94	16,823
2	Marcus Brady, CS-Northridge	1998-01	13,095
3	Willie Totten, Miss. Valley	1982-85	13,007
4	Jamie Martin, Weber St.	1989-92	12,287
5	Doug Nussmeier, Idaho	1990-93	12,054

	Yards per Game	Years	Yards	P/Gm
1	Steve McNair, Alcorn St.	1991-94	16,823	400.5
2	Neil Lomax, Portland St.	1978-80	11,647	352.9
3	Aaron Flowers, CS-N'ridge	1996-97	6,754	337.7
4	Chris Sanders, Chatt.	1999-00	7,247	329.4
5	Dave Dickenson, Montana	1992-95	11,523	329.2

Passing
(Minimum 500 Completions)

	Passing Efficiency	Years	Rating
1	Shawn Knight, William & Mary	1991-94	170.8
2	Dave Dickenson, Montana	1992-95	166.3
3	Drew Miller, Montana	1999-00	160.5
4	Doug Nussmeier, Idaho	1990-93	154.4
5	Mark Washington, Jackson St.	1996-99	153.5

	Yards Gained	Years	Yards
1	Steve McNair, Alcorn St.	1991-94	14,496
2	Willie Totten, Miss. Valley	1982-85	12,711
3	Marcus Brady, CS-Northridge	1998-01	12,479
4	Jamie Martin, Weber St.	1989-92	12,207
5	Neil Lomax, Portland St.	1978-80	11,550

Receiving

	Catches	Years	No
1	Jacquay Nunnally, Fla. A&M	1997-00	317
2	Stephen Campbell, Brown	1997-00	305
3	Jerry Rice, Miss. Valley	1981-84	301
4	Kasey Dunn, Idaho	1988-91	268
5	Sean Morey, Brown	1995-98	251

	Yards Gained	Years	No	Yards
1	Jerry Rice, Miss. Valley	1981-84	301	4693
2	Jacquay Nunnally, Fla. A&M	1997-00	317	4239
3	Cedric Ward, N. Iowa	1993-96	176	3876
4	Sean Morey, Brown	1995-98	251	3850
5	Kasey Dunn, Idaho	1988-91	268	3847

Rushing

	Yards Gained	Years	Yards
1	Adrian Peterson, Ga. So.	1998-01	6559
2	Charles Roberts, CS-Sac.	1997-00	6553
3	Jerry Azumah, N. Hampshire	1995-98	6193
4	Matt Cannon, S. Utah	1997-00	5489
5	Reggie Green, Siena	1994-97	5415

	Yards per Game	Years	Yards	P/Gm
1	Arnold Mickens, Butler	1994-95	3813	190.7
2	Adrian Peterson, Ga. So.	1998-01	6559	156.2
3	Aaron Stecker, W. Ill.	1997-98	3081	154.1
4	Tim Hall, Robert Morris	1994-95	2908	153.1
5	Jerry Azumah, N. Hampshire	1995-98	6193	151.0

Miscellaneous

	Interceptions	Years	No
1	Dave Murphy, Holy Cross	1986-89	28
2	Cedric Walker, S.F. Austin	1990-93	25
3	Issiac Holt, Alcorn St.	1981-84	24
	Bill McGovern, Holy Cross	1981-84	24
	Darren Sharper, Wm. & Mary	1993-96	24

	Punting Average	Years	Avg
1	Pumpy Tudors, Tenn.-Chatt.	1989-91	44.4
2	Case de Brujin, Idaho St.	1978-81	43.7
3	Terry Belden, Northern Ariz.	1990-93	43.4
4	Chad Stanley, SF Austin	1996-98	43.3
5	George Cimadevilla, East Tenn. St.	1983-86	43.0

	Punt Return Average*	Years	Avg
1	Willie Ware, Miss. Valley	1982-85	16.4
2	Buck Phillips, Western Ill.	1994-95	16.4
3	Tim Egerton, Delaware St.	1986-89	16.1
4	Mark Orlando, Towson St.	1991-94	15.7
5	Joseph Jefferson, Western Ky.	1998-01	15.3

	Kickoff Return Average*	Years	Avg
1	Lamont Brightful, E. Wash.	1998-01	30.0
2	Troy Brown, Marshall	1991-92	29.7
3	Charles Swann, Indiana St.	1989-91	29.3
4	Craig Richardson, Eastern Wash.	1983-86	28.5
5	Ramondo North, N.C. A&T	1998-00	28.3

*(Minimum 1.2 returns per game)

Scoring
NON-KICKERS

	Points	Years	TD	XP	Pts
1	Adrian Peterson, Ga. Southern	1998-01	89	10	544
2	Brian Westbrook, Villanova	1997-98, 00-01	87	2	524
3	Matt Cannon, S. Utah	1997-00	69	6	420
4	Jerry Azumah, N. Hampshire	1995-98	69	4	418
5	Sherriden May, Idaho	1991-94	61	0	366

	Touchdowns Passing	Years	No
1	Willie Totten, Miss. Valley	1982-85	139
2	Steve McNair, Alcorn St.	1991-94	119
3	Marcus Brady, CS-Northridge	1998-01	109
4	Dave Dickenson, Montana	1992-95	96
5	Chris Boden, Villanova	1996-99	93

	Touchdowns Rushing	Years	No
1	Adrian Peterson, Ga. Southern	1998-01	84
2	Matt Cannon, S. Utah	1997-00	69
3	David Dinkins, Morehead St.	1997-00	63
4	Jerry Azumah, N. Hampshire	1995-98	60
5	Charles Roberts, CS-Sacramento	1997-00	56

	Touchdown Catches	Years	No
1	Jerry Rice, Miss. Valley	1981-84	50
2	Rennie Benn, Lehigh	1982-85	44
3	Dedric Ward, N. Iowa	1993-96	41
4	Sean Morey, Brown	1995-98	39
	Gharun Hester, Georgetown	1997-00	39

All-Time NCAA Division I-AA Leaders (Cont.)

KICKERS

	Points	Years	FG	XP	Pts		Field Goals	Years	No
1	Marty Zendejas, Nevada	1984-87	72	169	385	1	Marty Zendejas, Nevada	1984-87	72
2	Dave Ettinger, Hofstra	1994-97	62	140	326	2	Kirk Roach, Western Carolina	1984-87	71
3	B. Mitchell, Marshall/					3	Tony Zendejas, Nevada	1981-83	70
	N. Iowa	1987, 89-91	64	130	322	4	Scott Shields, Weber St.	1995-98	67
4	Scott Shields, Weber St.	1995-98	67	109	310	5	B. Mitchell, Marshall/N. Iowa	1987,89-91	64
5	Thayne Doyle, Idaho	1988-91	49	160	307				

All-Time Winningest Division I-AA Teams

Includes record at a senior college only, minimum of 20 seasons of competition. Bowl and playoff games are included.

Top 20 Winning Percentage

		Yrs	Gm	W	L	T	Pct.	Playoffs W-L-T
1	Yale	129	1171	809	307	55	.714	0-0-0
2	Florida A&M	69	703	490	195	18	.710	5-8-0
3	Grambling St.	59	633	440	178	15	.707	9-7-0
4	Tennessee St.	74	694	469	195	30	.697	8-4-1
5	Princeton	132	1123	743	330	50	.684	0-0-0
6	Harvard	127	1152	743	359	50	.667	1-0-0
7	Georgia Southern	33	377	244	126	7	.656	36-7-0
8	Jackson St.	56	577	369	195	13	.651	1-11-1
9	Southern	80	781	482	274	25	.633	6-1-0
10	Eastern Kentucky	78	777	478	272	27	.633	17-17-0
11	Pennsylvania	125	1223	749	432	42	.630	0-1-0
12	Fordham	103	1148	696	399	53	.629	2-3-0
13	Hofstra	61	591	365	215	11	.627	4-12-0
14	Dartmouth	120	1039	627	366	46	.626	6-1-0
15	Dayton	94	892	543	323	26	.623	16-11-0
16	Appalachian St.	72	761	457	275	29	.620	9-15-0
17	McNeese St.	51	553	304	205	14	.617	11-12-0
18	S. Carolina St.	74	688	407	254	27	.611	6-5-0
19	Youngstown St.	61	624	369	238	17	.605	26-9-0
20	Delaware	110	992	575	374	43	.601	24-14-0

Top 50 Victories

		Wins			Wins			Wins
1	Yale	809	18	Drake	501	35	Montana	439
2	Pennsylvania	749	19	Villanova	496	36	Maine	436
3	Princeton	743	20	Furman	494	37	Western Ill.	434
	Harvard	743	21	Florida A&M	490	38	Howard	433
5	Fordham	696	22	Southern	482	39	VMI	431
6	Dartmouth	627		William & Mary	482		Richmond	431
7	Lafayette	592	24	Massachusetts	478	41	SW Texas St.	429
8	Cornell	588		E. Kentucky	478	42	The Citadel	419
9	Lehigh	576	26	Tennessee St.	469	43	Eastern Ill.	413
10	Delaware	575	27	Hampton	461	44	Idaho St.	412
11	Holy Cross	548	28	W. Kentucky	459	45	Murray St.	409
12	Dayton	543	29	Appalachian St.	457	46	S. Carolina St.	407
13	N. Iowa	531	30	Tenn-Chat	451	47	SW Missouri St.	402
14	Bucknell	529	31	Northwestern St.	449		E. Washington	402
15	Colgate	528	32	New Hampshire	446	49	N.C. A&T	401
16	Brown	527	33	Georgetown	441	50	Wofford	400
17	Butler	507	34	Grambling St.	440			

Top 10 Playoff Game Appearances

Ranked by NCAA Division I-AA playoff games played from 1978-2001. CH refers to championships won.

		Years	Games	Record	CH			Years	Games	Record	CH
1	Georgia Southern	13	43	36-7	6	6	Furman	11	24	14-10	1
2	Eastern Ky.	17	31	16-15	2	7	Delaware	11	22	11-11	0
3	Marshall*	8	29	23-6	2	8	Northern Iowa	10	21	11-10	0
	Youngstown St.	10	29	23-6	4	9	Appalachian St.	11	19	8-11	0
5	Montana	12	28	18-10	2	10	Idaho*	11	17	6-11	0
							McNeese St.	9	17	8-9	0

*Marshall (1997) and Idaho (1996) have moved up to I-A.

Active Division I-AA Coaches

Minimum of 5 years as a Division I-A and/or Division I-AA through 2001 season.

Top 10 Winning Percentage

	Yrs	W	L	T	Pct
1 Mike Kelly, Dayton	21	195	40	1	.828
2 Al Bagnoli, Pennsylvania	20	153	50	0	.754
3 Pete Richardson, Southern	14	120	41	1	.744
4 Greg Gattuso, Duquesne	9	71	25	0	.740
5 Joe Walton, Robert Morris	8	58	21	1	.731
6 Joe Gardi, Hofstra	12	99	36	2	.730
7 Roy Kidd, Eastern Ky.	38	307	119	8	.717
8 Billy Joe, Florida A&M	28	221	89	4	.709
9 Joe Taylor, Hampton	19	146	59	4	.708
10 Walt Hameline, Wagner	21	150	68	2	.686

Top 10 Victories

	Yrs	W	L	T	Pct
1 Roy Kidd, Eastern Ky.	38	307	119	8	.717
2 Billy Joe, Florida A&M	28	221	89	4	.709
3 Ron Randleman, Sam Houston St.	33	201	148	6	.575
4 Mike Kelly, Dayton	21	195	40	1	.828
5 Bill Hayes, N. Carolina A&T	26	191	96	2	.664
6 Al Bagnoli, Pennsylvania	20	153	50	0	.754
7 Walt Hameline, Wagner	21	150	68	2	.686
8 Bob Ricca, St. John's	24	146	100	1	.593
Joe Taylor, Hampton	19	146	59	4	.708
10 Jimmye Laycock, Wm. & Mary	22	145	102	2	.586

Note: Eddie Robinson of Grambling St. (1941-42, 1945-97) retired following the 1997 season as the all-time NCAA leader in coaching wins with a 408-165-15 record and a .707 winning pct. over 55 seasons.

Division I-AA Coach of the Year

First presented in 1983 by the American Football Coaches Association.

Multiple winners: Mark Duffner, Paul Johnson and Erk Russell (2).

Year
1983 Rey Dempsey, Southern Ill.
1984 Dave Arnold, Montana St.
1985 Dick Sheridan, Furman
1986 Erk Russell, Ga. Southern
1987 Mark Duffner, Holy Cross
1988 Jimmy Satterfield, Furman
1989 Erk Russell, Ga. Southern

Year
1990 Tim Stowers, Ga. Southern
1991 Mark Duffner, Holy Cross
1992 Charlie Taafe, Citadel
1993 Dan Allen, Boston Univ.
1994 Jim Tressel, Youngstown St.
1995 Don Read, Montana
1996 Ray Tellier, Columbia

Year
1997 Andy Talley, Villanova
1998 Mark Whipple, Massachusetts
1999 Paul Johnson, Ga. Southern
2000 Paul Johnson, Ga. Southern
2001 Bobby Johnson, Furman

NCAA Playoffs

Division I-AA

Established in 1978 as a four-team playoff. Tournament field increased to eight teams in 1981, 12 teams in 1982 and 16 teams in 1986. Automatic berths are awarded to champions of the Big Sky, Gateway, Mid-Eastern Athletic, Ohio Valley, Patriot, Southern, Southland and Atlantic 10 (formerly Yankee) conferences.

Multiple winners: Georgia Southern (6); Youngstown St. (4); Eastern Kentucky, Marshall and Montana (2).

Year	Winner	Score	Loser	Year	Winner	Score	Loser
1978	Florida A&M	35-28	Massachusetts	1990	Georgia Southern	36-13	Nevada-Reno
1979	Eastern Kentucky	30-7	Lehigh, PA	1991	Youngstown St., OH	25-17	Marshall
1980	Boise St., ID	31-29	Eastern Kentucky	1992	Marshall	31-28	Youngstown St.
1981	Idaho St.	34-23	Eastern Kentucky	1993	Youngstown St.	17-5	Marshall
1982	Eastern Kentucky	17-14	Delaware	1994	Youngstown St.	28-14	Boise St.
1983	Southern Illinois	43-7	Western Carolina	1995	Montana	22-20	Marshall
1984	Montana St.	19-6	Louisiana Tech	1996	Marshall	49-29	Montana
1985	Georgia Southern	44-42	Furman, SC	1997	Youngstown St.	10-9	McNeese St.
1986	Georgia Southern	48-21	Arkansas St.	1998	Massachusetts	55-43	Georgia Southern
1987	NE Louisiana	43-42	Marshall, WV	1999	Georgia Southern	59-24	Youngstown St.
1988	Furman, SC	17-12	Georgia Southern	2000	Georgia Southern	27-25	Montana
1989	Georgia Southern	37-34	S.F. Austin St.	2001	Montana	13-6	Furman

Division II

Established in 1973 as an eight-team playoff. Tournament field increased to 16 teams in 1988. From 1964-72, eight qualifying NCAA College Division member institutions competed in four regional bowl games, but there was no tournament and no national championship until 1973.

Multiple winners: North Dakota St. (5); North Alabama (3); Northern Colorado, Northwest Missouri St., Southwest Texas St. and Troy St. (2).

Year	Winner	Score	Loser	Year	Winner	Score	Loser
1973	Louisiana Tech	34-0	Western Kentucky	1988	North Dakota St.	35-21	Portland St., OR
1974	Central Michigan	54-14	Delaware	1989	Mississippi Col.	3-0	Jacksonville St., AL
1975	Northern Michigan	16-14	Western Kentucky	1990	North Dakota St.	51-11	Indiana, PA
1976	Montana St.	24-13	Akron, OH	1991	Pittsburg St., KS	23-6	Jacksonville St., AL
1977	Lehigh, PA	33-0	Jacksonville St., AL	1992	Jacksonville St., AL	17-13	Pittsburg St., KS
1978	Eastern Illinois	10-9	Delaware	1993	North Alabama	41-34	Indiana, PA
1979	Delaware	38-21	Youngstown St., OH	1994	North Alabama	16-10	Tex. A&M (Kings.)
				1995	North Alabama	22-7	Pittsburg St., KS
1980	Cal Poly-SLO	21-13	Eastern Illinois	1996	Northern Colorado	23-14	Carson-Newman
1981	SW Texas St.	42-13	North Dakota St.	1997	Northern Colorado	51-0	New Haven
1982	SW Texas St.	34-9	UC-Davis	1998	NW Missouri St.	24-6	Carson-Newman
1983	North Dakota St.	41-21	Central St., OH	1999	NW Missouri St.	58-52*	Carson-Newman
1984	Troy St., AL	18-17	North Dakota St.	2000	Delta St., MS	63-34	Bloomsburg, PA
1985	North Dakota St.	35-7	North Alabama	2001	North Dakota	17-14	Grand Valley St.
1986	North Dakota St.	27-7	South Dakota				
1987	Troy St., AL	31-17	Portland St., OR	*Four overtimes			

Division III

Established in 1973 as a four-team playoff. Tournament field increased to eight teams in 1975, 16 teams in 1985 and 28 teams in 1999. From 1969-72, four qualifying NCAA College Division member institutions competed in two regional bowl games, but there was no tournament and no national championship until 1973. (*) denotes overtime.

Multiple winners: Mt. Union (6); Augustana (4); Ithaca (3); Dayton, Widener, WI-La Crosse and Wittenberg (2).

Year	Winner	Score	Loser	Year	Winner	Score	Loser
1973	Wittenberg, OH	41-0	Juniata, PA	1988	Ithaca	39-24	Central, IA
1974	Central, IA	10-8	Ithaca, NY	1989	Dayton	17-7	Union
1975	Wittenberg	28-0	Ithaca	1990	Allegheny, PA	21-14*	Lycoming, PA
1976	St. John's, MN	31-28	Towson St., MD	1991	Ithaca	34-20	Dayton
1977	Widener, PA	39-36	Wabash, IN	1992	WI-La Crosse	16-12	Wash. & Jeff., PA
1978	Baldwin-Wallace	24-10	Wittenberg	1993	Mt. Union, OH	34-24	Rowan, NJ
1979	Ithaca, NY	14-10	Wittenberg	1994	Albion, MI	38-15	Wash. & Jeff.
1980	Dayton, OH	63-0	Ithaca	1995	WI-La Crosse	36-7	Rowan
1981	Widener, PA	17-10	Dayton, OH	1996	Mt. Union	56-24	Rowan
1982	West Georgia	14-0	Augustana, IL	1997	Mt. Union	61-12	Lycoming
1983	Augustana	21-17	Union, NY	1998	Mt. Union	44-24	Rowan
1984	Augustana	21-12	Central, IA	1999	Pacific Lutheran	42-13	Rowan
1985	Augustana	20-7	Ithaca	2000	Mt. Union	10-7	St. John's, MN
1986	Augustana	31-3	Salisbury St., MD	2001	Mt. Union	30-27	Bridgewater, VA
1987	Wagner, NY	19-3	Dayton				

NAIA Playoffs

Division I

Established in 1956 as two-team playoff. Tournament field increased to four teams in 1958, eight teams in 1978 and 16 teams in 1987 before cutting back to eight teams in 1989. NAIA went back to a single division 16-team playoff in 1997. The title game has ended in a tie four times (1956, '64, '84 and '85). Note that Northeastern St., OK was called NE Oklahoma in 1958.

Multiple winners: Texas A&I (7); Carson-Newman (5); Central Arkansas and Central St-OH (3); Abilene Christian, Central St-OK, Elon, Georgetown-KY, Northeastern St-OK, Pittsburg St. and St. John's-MN (2).

Year	Winner	Score	Loser	Year	Winner	Score	Loser
1956	Montana St.	0-0	St. Joseph's, IN	1979	Texas A&I	20-14	Central St., OK
1957	Pittsburg St., KS	27-26	Hillsdale, MI	1980	Elon, NC	17-10	NE Oklahoma
1958	NE Oklahoma	19-13	Northern Arizona	1981	Elon, NC	3-0	Pittsburg St., KS
1959	Texas A&I	20-7	Lenoir-Rhyne, NC	1982	Central St., OK	14-11	Mesa, CO
1960	Lenoir-Rhyne, NC	15-14	Humboldt St., CA	1983	Car-Newman, TN	36-28	Mesa, CO
1961	Pittsburg St., KS	12-7	Linfield, OR	1984	Car-Newman, TN	19-19	Central Arkansas
1962	Central St., OK	28-13	Lenoir-Rhyne, NC	1985	Hillsdale, MI	10-10	Central Arkansas
1963	St. John's, MN	33-27	Prairie View, TX	1986	Car-Newman, TN	17-0	Cameron, OK
1964	Concordia, MN	7-7	Sam Houston, TX	1987	Cameron, OK	30-2	Car-Newman, TN
1965	St. John's, MN	33-0	Linfield, OR	1988	Car-Newman, TN	56-21	Adams St., CO
1966	Waynesburg, PA	42-21	WI-Whitewater	1989	Car-Newman, TN	34-20	Emporia St., KS
1967	Fairmont St., WV	28-21	Eastern Wash.	1990	Central St., OH	38-16	Mesa, CO
1968	Troy St., AL	43-35	Texas A&I	1991	Central Arkansas	19-16	Central St., OH
1969	Texas A&I	32-7	Concordia, MN	1992	Central St., OH	19-16	Gardner-Webb, NC
1970	Texas A&I	48-7	Wofford, SC	1993	E. Central, OK	49-35	Glenville St., WV
1971	Livingston, AL	14-12	Arkansas Tech	1994	N'eastern St., OK	13-12	Ark-Pine Bluff
1972	East Texas St.	21-18	Car-Newman, TN	1995	Central St., OK	37-7	N'eastern St., OK
1973	Abilene Christian	42-14	Elon, NC	1996	SW Oklahoma St.	33-31	Montana Tech
1974	Texas A&I	34-23	Henderson, AR	1997	Findlay, OH	14-7	Willamette, ORE
1975	Texas A&I	37-0	Salem, WV	1998	Azusa Pacific, CA	17-14	Olivet Nazarene, IL
1976	Texas A&I	26-0	Central Arkansas	1999	NW Oklahoma St.	34-26	Georgetown, KY
1977	Abilene Christian	24-7	SW Oklahoma	2000	Georgetown, KY	20-0	NW Oklahoma St.
1978	Angelo St., TX	34-14	Elon, NC	2001	Georgetown, KY	49-27	Sioux Falls, S.D.

Division II

Established in 1970 as four-team playoff. Tournament field increased to eight teams in 1978 and 16 teams in 1987. NAIA went back to a single division playoff in 1997. The title game has ended in a tie twice (1981 and '87).

Multiple winners: Westminster (6); Findlay, Linfield and Pacific Lutheran (3); Concordia-MN, Northwestern-IA and Texas Lutheran (2).

Year	Winner	Score	Loser	Year	Winner	Score	Loser
1970	Westminster, PA	21-16	Anderson, IN	1984	Linfield, OR	33-22	Northwestern, IA
1971	Calif. Lutheran	20-14	Westminster, PA	1985	WI-La Crosse	24-7	Pacific Lutheran
1972	Missouri Southern	21-14	Northwestern, IA	1986	Linfield, OR	17-0	Baker, KS
1973	Northwestern, IA	10-3	Glenville St., WV	1987	Pacific Lutheran	16-16	WI-Stevens Pt.*
1974	Texas Lutheran	42-0	Missouri Valley	1988	Westminster, PA	21-14	WI-La Crosse
1975	Texas Lutheran	34-8	Calif. Lutheran	1989	Westminster, PA	51-30	WI-La Crosse
1976	Westminster, PA	20-13	Redlands, CA	1990	Peru St., NE	17-7	Westminster, PA
1977	Westminster, PA	17-9	Calif. Lutheran	1991	Georgetown, KY	28-20	Pacific Lutheran
1978	Concordia, MN	7-0	Findlay, OH	1992	Findlay, OH	26-13	Linfield, OR
1979	Findlay, OH	51-6	Northwestern, IA	1993	Pacific Lutheran	50-20	Westminster, PA
1980	Pacific Lutheran	38-10	Wilmington, OH	1994	Westminster, PA	27-7	Pacific Lutheran
1981	Austin College, TX	24-24	Concordia, MN	1995	Findlay, OH	21-21	Central Wash.
1982	Linfield, OR	33-15	Wm. Jewell, MO	1996	Sioux Falls, S.D.	47-25	W. Washington
1983	Northwestern, IA	25-21	Pacific Lutheran				

*Wisconsin-Stevens Point forfeited its entire 1987 schedule due to its use of an ineligible player.

Professional Football

Patriots kicker **Adam Vinatieri** celebrates after nailing his Super Bowl-winning 48-yard field goal.

AP/Wide World Photos

A Victory for All

Three cheers for the red, white and blue. Brady, Vinatieri and a stingy defense lead the Pats to the title.

Chris Berman
is the host of ESPN's NFL Prime Time.

Perhaps The Swami hasn't lost his touch after all. Note this final paragraph in last year's seasonal review in the ESPN Sports Almanac:

"The Rams won it all with offense in 1999. The Ravens got it done with defense in 2000. Different formulas, but identical results. Perhaps it will be a kicking game that leads a team to victory in Super Bowl XXXVI."

As Adam Vinatieri's 48-yard field goal on the final play of the game gave the New England Patriots a stunning 20–17 victory over the heavily favored St. Louis Rams at New Orleans in Super Bowl XXXVI, you couldn't help but smile.

The Patriots' championship run was even more incredible when you consider that the team's offensive unit scored just one touchdown in each of their postseason wins over the Raiders, Steelers and Rams. That overtime victory over Oakland in a steady snowstorm (in the final game at Foxboro Stadium) featured another amazing moment by Vinatieri, whose game-tying 45-yard field goal with only 27 seconds to play (aided by a non-fumble by quarterback Tom Brady following a sack by Raiders cornerback Charles Woodson) was perhaps the greatest kick in NFL history.

So for the third year in a row, a team that failed to post a winning record the previous season rebounded to capture the Vince Lombardi Trophy. And for the second time in three years, the game to decide it all came down to the final play. This "super" Super Bowl capped off a magnificent and memorable season, not only for Patriots owner Robert Kraft and all of the long-suffering New England fans, but for all of us who love sports and use it as a diversion during difficult times.

We will never forget how the 2001 season began. Less than 24 hours after

AP/Wide World Photos

*With the score knotted, 17-17, little time left on the clock and no timeouts, Patriots quarterback **Tom Brady** directed the Patriots downfield to set up the game-winning field goal.*

Week 1 ended, our world changed forever with the events in New York City, Washington D.C. and Shanksville, Penn. But after the NFL and the world of sports took an appropriate back seat (and a week off) out of respect for our nation's losses, the season resumed.

It was only fitting that the Patriots would come away winners despite major adversity. Coming off a 5–11 showing in 2000 and losers of their first two games, things were made more complex for the Pats with the loss of quarterback Drew Bledsoe, injured in a loss to the Jets. But enter Brady, the former sixth-round draft choice, who displayed maturity not often associated with a second-year player who had thrown only a handful of passes as a rookie.

Still, while Brady became the youngest quarterback to win the Super Bowl, it was really the foresight of head coach Bill Belichick that turned Beantown into Titletown. In what proved to be a Super Bowl warmup and a 24–17 loss to the Rams on Nov.18, Brady was constantly looking to the sidelines at a healthy Bledsoe to see if he would be replaced. Belichick declared Brady his starter for the remainder of the season, and the Patriots never looked back—winning their final nine games.

*Green Bay's Brett Favre slides under the waiting arms of Giants defensive end **Michael Strahan**, giving him a new NFL single-season sack record.*

Speaking of looking back, there were other great stories as well. We saw the resurgence of the once-proud Bears, Steelers, Packers and 49ers, all of whom parlayed strong finishes in 2000 into playoff appearances in '01. Of the four, 13–3 Chicago was the biggest surprise. Led by NFL Coach of the Year Dick Jauron and inspiring middle linebacker Brian Urlacher, the new Monsters of the Midway more than doubled their win total from the previous season (5–11), won their first division title since 1990 and made their first trip to the playoffs since 1994.

Elsewhere, quarterback Donovan McNabb and the Philadelphia Eagles continued their ascent and came within a game of the Super Bowl, Jerry Rice showed that despite a change of address (Oakland), he can still get it done and St. Louis running back Marshall Faulk proved weekly why he's clearly the best player on the planet.

But when it was all said and done, this Hollywood script of a season had its happy ending. An underdog had prevailed and the red, white and blue had come out on top.

The Ten Biggest Stories of the Year in Pro Football

10 Rams running back Marshall Faulk is once again unstoppable in the regular season, following up his record-breaking 26-TD season with 21 more in 2001. He joins Hall of Famer Earl Campbell as the only three-time AP Offensive Players of the Year.

9 The Indianapolis Colts, who were preseason favorites to take the AFC East, fall to fourth place in a nightmarish season. Star back Edgerrin James tears an ACL in Week 7 and Peyton Manning gets the interception bug, leading to a 6–10 record and the firing of coach Jim Mora.

8 On consecutive days in December in Cleveland and New Orleans, irate fans hurl beer bottles, ice and other assorted items at referees after calls go against their teams. Browns president Carmen Policy infuriates many by saying, "I like the fact that our fans care." He later apologizes.

7 After a forgetful 2000-01 season, Green Bay quarterback Brett Favre returns with a vengeance, throwing 32 touchdowns and leading the Packers to a 12–4 mark and a playoff berth.

6 Patriots quarterback Drew Bledsoe is hammered by Jets linebacker Moe Lewis in Week 2, causing a partially torn rib cage and internal bleeding. Backup Tom Brady replaces him and goes 11–3 the rest of the season.

5 The Chicago Bears, last-place finishers in the NFC Central in each of the past four years, go 13–3 and win the division. Two of those wins come on overtime touchdowns by safety Mike Brown in consecutive weeks.

4 N.Y. Giants defensive lineman Michael Strahan records 22.5 sacks to break Mark Gastineau's 16-year-old single-season record (22). The record-breaking sack is a controversial one, however, as many accuse his friend Brett Favre of taking a dive under Strahan just to get him the record.

3 Vikings Pro Bowl offensive tackle Korey Stringer collapses of heatstroke and dies 15 hours later, after a preseason practice in Minnesota in brutally hot and humid conditions.

2 In the driving snow at Foxboro, Patriots kicker Adam Vinatieri boots a 45-yarder to force overtime and then a 23-yarder to give the Pats a 16–13 win in the AFC divisional semifinals against the Raiders. The Raiders cry foul over the controversial "tuck rule" that keeps a late Patriots drive alive.

1 Vinatieri does it again, kicking a 48-yard field goal with no time left to give the Patriots a 20–17 win over the heavily favored Rams in Super Bowl XXXVI. Tom Brady directs his offense on a gutsy last-minute drive to set up the winning FG and is named MVP.

A Man Named Brady

With the Patriots stunning 20–17 win over the Rams in Super Bowl XXXVI, Tom Brady became the youngest starting quarterback in NFL history to win a Super Bowl, passing two legendary hall of famers.

	Super Bowl	Age
Tom Brady	XXXVI	24 years, 6 mos
Joe Montana	XVI	25 years, 7 mos
Joe Namath	III	25 years, 7 mos

Note: Montana and Namath were each exactly 9,358 days old at the time of their Super Bowl wins.

Back Yards

The Patriots won Super Bowl XXXVI despite the Rams outgaining them on offense by 160 yards, by far the largest deficit in total yards for a winning team in Super Bowl history (the Rams gained 427 yards to the Patriots' 267). It's just the fourth time a winner has been outgained in the Super Bowl.

	Score	Yardage Deficit
XXXVI	Patriots 20, Rams 17	−160
XVI	49ers 26, Bengals 21	−81
XXX	Cowboys 27, Steelers 17	−56
XXXII	Broncos 31, Packers 24	−48

History Repeats Itself

New England now has three Super Bowl appearances since 1986, and all three were held at the Superdome in New Orleans. As the table below shows, the last two Patriot runs to the Super Bowl were remarkably similar.

	1996	2001
Began Season	0-2	0-2
Finished Season	11-5	11-5
Def. in Playoffs	Steelers	Steelers
S. B. Site	Superdome	Superdome

Double Trouble

St. Louis running back Marshall Faulk set an NFL single-season record with 26 touchdowns in 2000, then followed that up with 21 more in 2001. His two-year total of 47 is tied for the most in NFL history. Listed below are the most touchdowns in consecutive seasons in NFL history.

Season		TD
2000-01	Marshall Faulk, St. Louis	47
1994-95	Emmitt Smith, Dallas	47
1995-96	Emmitt Smith, Dallas	40
1986-87	Jerry Rice, San Fran.	39

Note: TD Totals—Faulk '00-01 (26-21); Smith '94-95 (22-25); Smith '95-96 (25-15); Rice '86-87 (16-23).

2001-2002
Season in Review

Information Please®
SPORTS ALMANAC

Final NFL Standings

Division champions (*) and wild card playoff qualifiers (†) are noted; division champions with two best records received first round byes. Number of seasons listed after each head coach refers to latest tenure with club through 2001 season.

American Football Conference
Eastern Division

	W	L	T	PF	PA	vs Div	vs AFC
*New England	11	5	0	371	272	6-2	8-4
†Miami	11	5	0	344	290	5-3	9-3
†NY Jets	10	6	0	308	295	5-3	8-4
Indianapolis	6	10	0	413	486	3-5	5-7
Buffalo	3	13	0	265	420	1-7	2-10

Note: New England (11-5) won the division over Miami (11-5) due to a better record within the division.
2001 Head Coaches: NE—Bill Belichick (2nd season); **Mia**—Dave Wannstedt (2nd); **NY**—Herman Edwards (1st); **Ind**—Jim Mora (4th); **Buf**—Gregg Williams (1st).
2000 Standings: 1. Miami (11-5); 2. Indianapolis (10-6); 3. NY Jets (9-7); 4. Buffalo (8-8); 5. New England (5-11).

Central Division

	W	L	T	PF	PA	vs Div	vs AFC
*Pittsburgh	13	3	0	352	212	7-3	10-3
†Baltimore	10	6	0	303	265	6-4	8-4
Cleveland	7	9	0	285	319	5-5	6-7
Tennessee	7	9	0	336	388	3-7	4-8
Jacksonville	6	10	0	294	286	5-5	5-8
Cincinnati	6	10	0	226	309	4-6	5-8

2001 Head Coaches: Pit—Bill Cowher (10th season); **Bal**—Brian Billick (3rd); **Cle**—Butch Davis (1st); **Ten**—Jeff Fisher (8th); **Jax**—Tom Coughlin (7th); **Cin**—Dick LeBeau (2nd).
2000 Standings: 1. Tennessee (13-3); 2. Baltimore (12-4); 3. Pittsburgh (9-7); 4. Jacksonville (7-9); 5. Cincinnati (4-12); 6. Cleveland (3-13).

Western Division

	W	L	T	PF	PA	vs Div	vs AFC
*Oakland	10	6	0	399	327	6-2	7-5
Seattle	9	7	0	301	324	5-3	8-4
Denver	8	8	0	340	339	4-4	5-7
Kansas City	6	10	0	320	344	4-4	5-7
San Diego	5	11	0	332	321	1-7	3-9

2001 Head Coaches: Oak—Jon Gruden (4th season); **Sea**—Mike Holmgren (3rd); **Den**—Mike Shanahan (7th); **KC**—Dick Vermeil (1st); **SD**—Mike Riley (3rd).
2000 Standings: 1. Oakland (12-4); 2. Denver (11-5); 3. Kansas City (7-9); 4. Seattle (6-10); 5. San Diego (1-15).

National Football Conference
Eastern Division

	W	L	T	PF	PA	vs Div	vs NFC
*Philadelphia	11	5	0	343	208	6-2	8-4
Washington	8	8	0	256	303	4-4	6-6
NY Giants	7	9	0	294	321	4-4	5-7
Arizona	7	9	0	295	343	2-6	4-8
Dallas	5	11	0	246	338	4-4	5-7

2001 Head Coaches: Phi—Andy Reid (3rd season); **Wash**—Marty Schottenheimer (1st); **NY**—Jim Fassel (5th); **Ariz**—Dave McGinnis (2nd); **Dal**—Dave Campo (2nd).
2000 Standings: 1. NY Giants (12-4); 2. Philadelphia (11-5); 3. Washington (8-8); 4. Dallas (5-11); 5. Arizona (3-13).

Central Division

	W	L	T	PF	PA	vs Div	vs NFC
*Chicago	13	3	0	338	203	6-2	10-2
†Green Bay	12	4	0	390	266	6-2	9-3
†Tampa Bay	9	7	0	324	280	4-4	7-5
Minnesota	5	11	0	290	390	3-5	4-8
Detroit	2	14	0	270	424	1-7	2-10

2001 Head Coaches: Chi—Dick Jauron (3rd season); **GB**—Mike Sherman (2nd); **TB**—Tony Dungy (6th); **Min**—Dennis Green (10th, 5-10) was replaced on Jan. 4, 2002 by asst. Mike Tice (0-1); **Det**—Marty Mornhinweg (1st).
2000 Standings: 1. Minnesota (11-5); 2. Tampa Bay (10-6); 3. Green Bay (9-7); 4. Detroit (9-7); 5. Chicago (5-11).

Western Division

	W	L	T	PF	PA	vs Div	vs NFC
*St. Louis	14	2	0	503	273	7-1	10-2
†San Francisco	12	4	0	409	282	6-2	8-4
New Orleans	7	9	0	333	409	4-4	5-7
Atlanta	7	9	0	291	377	3-5	6-6
Carolina	1	15	0	253	410	0-8	1-11

2001 Head Coaches: St.L—Mike Martz (2nd season); **SF**—Steve Mariucci (5th); **NO**—Jim Haslett (2nd); **Atl**—Dan Reeves (5th); **Car**—George Seifert (3rd).
2000 Standings: 1. New Orleans (10-6); 2. St. Louis (10-6); 3. Carolina (7-9); 4. San Francisco (6-10); 5. Atlanta (4-12).

2002 NFL Realignment

With the addition of the Houston Texans in the 2002 season, the NFL's 32 teams were realigned into eight divisions of four teams each.

AFC
East: Buffalo, Miami, New England, NY Jets
South: Houston, Indianapolis, Jacksonville, Tennessee
North: Baltimore, Cincinnati, Cleveland, Pittsburgh
West: Denver, Kansas City, Oakland, San Diego

NFC
East: Dallas, NY Giants, Philadelphia, Washington
South: Atlanta, Carolina, New Orleans, Tampa Bay
North: Chicago, Detroit, Green Bay, Minnesota
West: Arizona, St. Louis, San Francisco, Seattle

NFL Regular Season Individual Leaders

(* indicates rookies)

Passing Efficiency

(Minimum of 224 attempts)

AFC	Att	Cmp	Cmp Pct	Yds	Yds/ Att	TD	Long	Int	Sack/Lost	Rating Points
Rich Gannon, Oak.	549	361	65.8	3828	6.97	27	49	9	27/155	95.5
Steve McNair, Ten.	431	264	61.3	3350	7.77	21	71-td	12	37/251	90.2
Tom Brady, NE	413	264	63.9	2843	6.88	18	91-td	12	41/216	86.5
Peyton Manning, Ind.	547	343	62.7	4131	7.55	26	86-td	23	29/232	84.1
Mark Brunell, Jax	473	289	61.1	3309	7.00	19	44	13	57/387	84.1
Kordell Stewart, Pit.	442	266	60.2	3109	7.03	14	90-td	11	29/175	81.7
Jay Fiedler, Mia.	450	273	60.7	3290	7.31	20	74-td	19	27/178	80.3
Brian Griese, Den.	451	275	61.0	2827	6.27	23	65-td	19	38/241	78.5
Alex Van Pelt, Buf.	307	178	58.0	2056	6.70	12	80-td	11	14/73	76.4
Vinny Testaverde, NYJ	441	260	59.0	2752	6.24	15	40-td	14	18/122	75.3
Tim Couch, Cle.	454	272	59.9	3040	6.70	17	78	21	51/353	73.1
Doug Flutie, SD.	521	294	56.4	3464	6.65	15	78	18	25/168	72.0
Trent Green, KC	523	296	56.6	3783	7.23	17	67-td	24	39/198	71.1
Elvis Grbac, Bal.	467	265	56.7	3033	6.49	15	77-td	18	28/215	71.1
Matt Hasselbeck, Sea.	321	176	54.8	2023	6.30	7	64	8	38/251	70.9

NFC	Att	Cmp	Cmp Pct	Yds	Yds/ Att	TD	Long	Int	Sack/Lost	Rating Points
Kurt Warner, St.L	546	375	68.7	4830	8.85	36	65-td	22	38/233	101.4
Jeff Garcia, SF	504	316	62.7	3538	7.02	32	61-td	12	26/114	94.8
Brett Favre, GB	510	314	61.6	3921	7.69	32	67-td	15	22/151	94.1
Donovan McNabb, Phi.	493	285	57.8	3233	6.56	25	64-td	12	39/273	84.3
Chris Chandler, Atl.	365	223	61.1	2847	7.80	16	94-td	14	41/261	84.1
Daunte Culpepper, Min.	366	235	64.2	2612	7.14	14	57-td	13	33/186	83.3
Jake Plummer, Ari.	525	304	57.9	3653	6.96	18	68-td	14	29/204	79.6
Brad Johnson, TB	559	340	60.8	3406	6.09	13	47	11	44/269	77.7
Kerry Collins, NYG	568	327	57.6	3764	6.63	19	76	16	36/206	77.1
Charlie Batch, Det.	341	198	58.1	2392	7.01	12	76	12	33/176	76.8
Aaron Brooks, NO.	558	312	55.9	3832	6.87	26	63	22	50/330	76.4
Jim Miller, Chi.	395	228	57.7	2299	5.82	13	66-td	10	11/72	74.9
Tony Banks, Wash.	370	198	53.5	2386	6.45	10	85-td	10	29/173	71.3
Chris Weinke*, Car.	540	293	54.3	2931	5.43	11	48	19	26/177	62.0

Receptions

AFC	No	Yds	Avg	Long	TD
Rod Smith, Den.	113	1343	11.9	65-td	11
Jimmy Smith, Jax.	112	1373	12.3	35-td	8
Marvin Harrison, Ind.	109	1524	14.0	68	15
Troy Brown, NE	101	1199	11.9	60-td	5
Hines Ward, Pit.	94	1003	10.7	34	4
Keenan McCardell, Jax	93	1110	11.9	45	6
Tim Brown, Oak.	91	1165	12.8	46-td	9
Kevin Johnson, Cle.	84	1097	13.1	55-td	9
Jerry Rice, Oak.	83	1139	13.7	40-td	9
Larry Centers, Buf.	80	620	7.8	26	2
Qadry Ismail, Bal.	74	1059	14.3	77-td	7
Derrick Mason, Ten.	73	1128	15.5	71-td	9
Tony Gonzalez, KC	73	917	12.6	36	6
Shannon Sharpe, Bal.	73	811	11.1	37	2
Charlie Garner, Oak.	72	578	8.0	27	2

NFC	No	Yds	Avg	Long	TD
Keyshawn Johnson, TB.	106	1266	11.9	47	1
Marty Booker, Chi.	100	1071	10.7	66-td	8
David Boston, Ari.	98	1598	16.3	61-td	8
Terrell Owens, SF	93	1412	15.2	60-td	16
Joe Horn, NO.	83	1265	15.2	56	9
Marshall Faulk, St.L.	83	765	9.2	65-td	9
Randy Moss, Min.	82	1233	15.0	73-td	10
Torry Holt, St.L.	81	1363	16.8	51	7
Willie Jackson, NO	81	1046	12.9	63	5
Johnnie Morton, Det.	77	1154	15.0	76	4
Cris Carter, Min.	73	871	11.9	52	6
Amani Toomer, NYG	72	1054	14.6	60-td	5
Tiki Barber, NYG.	72	577	8.0	44	0
Warrick Dunn, TB	68	557	8.2	31	3
Isaac Bruce, St.L	64	1106	17.3	51-td	6

Rushing

AFC	Att	Yds	Avg	Long	TD
Priest Holmes, KC	327	1555	4.8	41	8
Curtis Martin, NYJ	333	1513	4.5	47	10
Shaun Alexander, Sea.	309	1318	4.3	88-td	14
Corey Dillon, Cin.	340	1315	3.9	96-td	10
LaDainian Tomlinson*, SD.	339	1236	3.6	54	10
Antowain Smith, NE.	287	1157	4.0	44	12
Dominic Rhodes*, Ind.	233	1104	4.7	77-td	9
Jerome Bettis, Pit.	225	1072	4.8	48	4
Lamar Smith, Mia.	313	968	3.1	25	6
Eddie George, Ten.	315	939	3.0	27	5
Stacey Mack, Jax	213	877	4.1	54	9
Charlie Garner, Oak.	211	839	4.0	38	1
Travis Henry*, Buf.	213	729	3.4	25	4
Terrell Davis, Den.	167	701	4.2	57	0
Mike Anderson, Den.	175	678	3.9	62-td	4

NFC	Att	Yds	Avg	Long	TD
Stephen Davis, Wash.	356	1432	4.0	32	5
Ahman Green, GB	304	1387	4.6	83-td	9
Marshall Faulk, St.L.	260	1382	5.3	71-td	12
Ricky Williams, NO.	313	1245	4.0	46	6
Garrison Hearst, SF	252	1206	4.8	43-td	4
Anthony Thomas*, Chi.	278	1183	4.3	46	7
Emmitt Smith, Dal.	261	1021	3.9	44	3
Tiki Barber, NYG	166	865	5.2	36	4
Michael Pittman, Ari.	241	846	3.5	42	5
Maurice Smith, Atl.	237	760	3.2	58	5
Ron Dayne, NYG	180	690	3.8	61	7
James Stewart, Det.	143	685	4.8	38	1
Michael Bennett*, Min.	172	682	4.0	31-td	2
Mike Alstott, TB	165	680	4.1	39-td	10
Richard Huntley, Car.	166	665	4.0	25	2

St. Louis Rams
Kurt Warner
Passing Efficiency

Kansas City Chiefs
Priest Holmes
Rushing and All-Purpose

St. Louis Rams
Marshall Faulk
Scoring

New York Giants
Michael Strahan
Sacks

All-Purpose Yardage

AFC	Rush	Rec	Ret	Total
Priest Holmes, KC	1555	614	0	2169
Derrick Mason, Ten.	0	1128	876	2004
Curtis Martin, NYJ	1513	320	0	1833
Troy Brown, NE	91	1199	426	1716
Dominic Rhodes*, Ind.	1104	224	356	1684
Chris Chambers*, Mia.	-11	883	811	1683
Shaun Alexander, Sea.	1318	343	0	1661
Jermaine Lewis, Bal.	33	32	1558	1623
LaDainian Tomlinson*, SD	1236	367	0	1603
Terrence Wilkins, Ind.	0	332	1226	1558
Corey Dillon, Cin.	1315	228	0	1543
Ronney Jenkins, SD.	-1	0	1541	1540
Marvin Harrison, Ind.	3	1524	0	1527
Charlie Garner, Oak.	839	578	0	1417
Charlie Rogers, Sea.	0	7	1364	1371

NFC	Rush	Rec	Ret	Total
Marshall Faulk, St.L	1382	765	0	2147
Steve Smith*, Car.	43	154	1795	1992
Ahman Green, GB	1387	594	0	1981
Reggie Swinton*, Dal.	-4	117	1741	1854
Desmond Howard, Det.	25	133	1647	1805
Tiki Barber, NYG	865	577	338	1780
Ricky Williams, NO.	1245	511	0	1756
MarTay Jenkins, Ari.	4	518	1120	1642
Stephen Davis, Wash.	1432	205	0	1637
David Boston, Ari.	35	1598	0	1633
Brian Mitchell, Phi.	9	122	1492	1623
Garrison Hearst, SF	1206	347	0	1553
Darrick Vaughn, Atl.	0	0	1491	1491
Terrell Owens, SF	21	1412	0	1433
Deuce McAllister*, NO	91	166	1115	1372

Ret column indicates all kickoff, punt, fumble and interception returns.

Touchdowns

AFC	TD	Rush	Rec	Ret	Pts
Shaun Alexander, Sea.	16	14	2	0	96
Marvin Harrison, Ind.	15	0	15	0	90
Corey Dillon, Cin.	13	10	3	0	78
Antowain Smith, NE	13	12	1	0	78
Rod Smith, Den.	11	0	11	0	68†
Derrick Mason, Ten.	10	0	9	1	62†
Tim Brown, Oak.	10	0	9	1	60
Priest Holmes, KC	10	8	2	0	60
Stacey Mack, Jax	10	9	1	0	60
Curtis Martin, NYJ	10	10	0	0	60
Dominic Rhodes*, Ind.	10	9	0	1	60
LaDainian Tomlinson*, SD	10	10	0	0	60

NFC	TD	Rush	Rec	Ret	Pts
Marshall Faulk, St.L.	21	12	9	0	128†
Terrell Owens, SF	16	0	16	0	96
Mike Alstott, TB	11	10	1	0	70&
Ahman Green, GB	11	9	2	0	66
Randy Moss, Min.	10	0	10	0	60
Bubba Franks, GB	9	0	9	0	54
Joe Horn, NO	9	0	9	0	54
Bill Schroeder, GB	9	0	9	0	54
Marty Booker, Chi.	8	0	8	0	48
David Boston, Ari.	8	0	8	0	48
James Thrash, Phi.	8	0	8	0	48

† Includes one 2-point conversion.
& Includes two 2-point conversions.

Scoring

Kickers

AFC	PAT	FG	Long	Pts
Mike Vanderjagt, Ind.	41/42	28/34	52	125
Kris Brown, Pit.	34/37	30/44	55	124
Jason Elam, Den.	31/31	31/36	50	124
Matt Stover, Bal.	25/25	30/35	49	115
Adam Vinatieri, NE.	41/42	24/30	54	113
Sebastien Janikowski, Oak.	42/42	23/28	52	111
Todd Peterson, KC	27/28	27/35	51	108
John Hall, NYJ	32/32	24/31	53	104
Olindo Mare, Mia.	39/40	19/21	46	96
Phil Dawson, Cle.	29/30	22/25	48	95
Joe Nedney, Ten.	34/35	20/28	51	94
Rian Lindell, Sea.	33/33	20/32	54	93
Wade Richey, SD	26/26	21/32	51	89

NFC	PAT	FG	Long	Pts
Jeff Wilkins, St.L.	58/58	23/29	54	127
David Akers, Phi.	37/38	26/31	50	115
Jay Feely*, Atl.	28/28	29/37	55	115
John Carney, NO.	32/32	27/31	50	113
Paul Edinger, Chi.	34/34	26/31	48	112
Ryan Longwell, GB	44/45	20/31	54	104
Jose Cortez*, SF	47/47	18/25	52	101
Brett Conway, Wash.	22/22	26/33	55	100
Morten Andersen, NYG	29/30	23/28	51	98
Martin Gramatica, TB	28/28	23/29	49	97
John Kasay, Car.	22/23	23/28	52	91
Jason Hanson, Det.	23/23	21/30	54	86
Gary Anderson, Min.	29/30	15/18	44	74
Bill Gramatica*, Ari.	25/25	16/20	50	73

NFL Regular Season Individual Leaders (Cont.)

Interceptions

AFC	No	Yds	Long	TD
Anthony Henry*, Cle.	10	177	97-td	1
Deltha O'Neal, Den.	9	115	42	0
Ryan McNeil, SD.	8	55	33	0
Six tied with 5 int's each.				

NFC	No	Yds	Long	TD
Ronde Barber, TB	10	86	36-td	1
Kwamie Lassiter, Ari.	9	80	25	0
Doug Evans, Car.	8	126	49	1
Zack Bronson, SF.	7	165	97-td	2
Ahmed Plummer, SF	7	45	24	0
Four tied with 6 int's each.				

Sacks

AFC	No
Peter Boulware, Bal.	15.0
John Abraham, NYJ	13.0
Jamir Miller, Cle.	13.0
Marcellus Wiley, SD	13.0
Jason Gildon, Pit.	12.0

NFC	No
Michael Strahan, NYG.	22.5
Leonard Little, St.L	14.5
Charlie Clemons, NO.	13.5
Kabeer Gbaja-Biamila, GB	13.5
Patrick Kerney, Atl.	12.0

Punting

AFC	No	Yds	Lg	Avg	In20
Shane Lechler, Oak.	73	3375	65	46.2	23
Tom Rouen, Den.	81	3668	64	45.3	25
Hunter Smith, Ind.	68	3023	65	44.5	12
Jeff Feagles, Sea.	85	3730	68	43.9	26
Chris Hanson, Jax.	82	3577	59	43.6	24

NFC	No	Yds	Lg	Avg	In20
Todd Sauerbrun, Car.	93	4419	73	47.5	35
Mitch Berger, Min.	47	2046	67	43.5	10
Sean Landeta, Phi.	97	4221	64	43.5	26
John Jett, Det.	58	2512	62	43.3	16
Rodney Williams*, NYG	91	3905	90	42.9	25

Punt Returns

(Minimum of 20 returns)

AFC	No	Yds	Avg	Long	TD
Troy Brown, NE	29	413	14.2	85-td	2
Deltha O'Neal, Den.	31	405	13.1	86-td	1
Jermaine Lewis, Bal.	42	519	12.4	62	0
Jeff Ogden, Mia.	32	377	11.8	48	0
Tim Dwight, SD	24	271	11.3	84-td	1

NFC	No	Yds	Avg	Long	TD
Darrien Gordon, Atl.	31	437	14.1	74	0
Reggie Swinton*, Dal.	31	414	13.4	65-td	1
Eric Metcalf, Wash.	33	412	12.5	89-td	1
Brian Mitchell, Phi.	39	467	12.0	54	0
Arnold Jackson*, Ari.	40	461	11.5	55	0

Kickoff Returns

(Minimum of 20 returns)

AFC	No	Yds	Avg	Long	TD
Ronney Jenkins, SD.	58	1541	26.6	93-td	2
Jermaine Lewis, Bal.	42	1039	24.7	76	0
Chris Cole, Den.	48	1127	23.5	52	0
Terry Kirby, Oak.	46	1066	23.2	90-td	1
Troy Edwards, Pit.	20	462	23.1	81	0

NFC	No	Yds	Avg	Long	TD
Steve Smith*, Car.	56	1431	25.6	99-td	2
Desmond Howard, Det.	57	1446	25.4	91	0
Brian Mitchell, Phi.	41	1025	25.0	94-td	1
Darrick Vaughn, Atl.	61	1491	24.4	96-td	1
Deuce McAllister*, NO	45	1091	24.2	63	0

Single Game Highs

Passing Yards

AFC	Cmp/Att	Yds	TD
Peyton Manning, Ind. vs. Buf. (9/23)	23/29	421	4
Jon Kitna, Cin. vs. Pit. (12/30, OT)	35/68	411	2
Doug Flutie, SD vs. Sea. (12/30)	34/53	377	1
Peyton Manning, Ind. vs. SF (11/25)	31/51	370	1
Tom Brady, NE vs. SD (10/14, OT)	33/54	364	2

NFC	Cmp/Att	Yds	TD
Charlie Batch, Det. vs. Ari. (11/18)	36/62	436	3
Chris Chandler, Atl. vs. Buf. (12/23)	28/40	431	2
Kurt Warner, St.L vs. NE (11/18)	30/42	401	3
Brad Johnson, TB vs. Chi. (11/18)	40/56	399	0
Kerry Collins, NYG vs. GB (1/6)	36/59	386	1

Rushing Yards

AFC	Car	Yds	TD
Shaun Alexander, Sea. vs. Oak. (11/11)	35	266	3
Corey Dillon, Cin. vs. Det. (10/28)	27	184	2
Priest Holmes, KC vs. SD (11/4)	30	181	0
Dominic Rhodes*, Ind. vs Atl. (12/16)	29	177	2
Shaun Alexander, Sea. vs. Jax (10/7)	31	176	2

NFC	Car	Yds	TD
Marshall Faulk, St.L vs. Car. (12/23)	30	202	2
Trung Canidate, St.L vs. NYJ (10/21)	23	195	2
Anthony Thomas*, Chi. vs. Cin. (10/21)	22	188	1
Marshall Faulk, St.L vs. Car. (11/11)	15	183	2
Anthony Thomas*, Chi. vs. TB (12/16)	31	173	1

Receiving Yards

AFC	Ct	Yds	TD
Eric Moulds, Buf. vs. Mia. (11/25)	6	196	2
Derrick Mason, Ten. vs. Cin. (1/6)	9	186	2
Marvin Harrison, Ind. vs. Mia. (11/11)	9	174	3
Jerome Pathon, Ind. vs. Buf. (9/23)	9	168	1
Plaxico Burress, Pit. vs. Bal. (12/16)	8	164	1

NFC	Ct	Yds	TD
Rod Gardner*, Wash. vs. Car. (10/21, OT)	6	208	1
Torry Holt, St.L vs. Ind. (12/30)	7	203	2
Terrell Owens, SF vs. Atl. (10/14, OT)	9	183	3
Isaac Bruce, St.L vs. NO (10/28)	7	179	1
Randy Moss, Min. vs. NYG (11/19)	10	171	3

NFL Bests

Longest Field Goal
55 yds. . . . . .by three players

Longest Run from Scrimmage
96 yds. . . . . .Corey Dillon, Cin. vs. Det. (10/28) TD

Longest Pass Play
94 yds . . . .Chris Chandler to Jamal Anderson, Atl. vs. Car.
(9/23) TD

Longest Interception Return
100 yds . . . . .Brock Marion, Mia. vs. Buf. (1/6) TD

Longest Punt Return
89 yds. . . . . .Eric Metcalf, Wash. vs. NYG (10/28) TD

Longest Kickoff Return
101 yds . . . . .Derrick Mason, Ten. vs. Cin. (11/18) TD

NFL Regular Season Team Leaders

Offense

AFC	For	Avg	Rush	Pass	Total	Avg
Indianapolis	413	25.8	1966	3989	5955	372.2
Pittsburgh	352	22.0	2774	3113	5887	367.9
Kansas City	320	20.0	2008	3665	5673	354.6
Oakland	399	24.9	1654	3707	5361	335.1
Tennessee	336	21.0	1794	3558	5352	334.5
San Diego	332	20.8	1695	3505	5200	325.0
Buffalo	265	16.6	1686	3451	5137	321.1
Baltimore	303	18.9	1810	3314	5124	320.3
New England	371	23.2	1793	3089	4882	305.1
Jacksonville	294	18.4	1600	3240	4840	302.5
Miami	344	21.5	1664	3157	4821	301.3
Denver	340	21.3	1877	2940	4817	301.1
Cincinnati	226	14.1	1712	3088	4800	300.0
NY Jets	308	19.3	2054	2741	4795	299.7
Seattle	301	18.8	1936	2836	4772	298.3
Cleveland	285	17.8	1351	2801	4152	259.5

NFC	For	Avg	Rush	Pass	Total	Avg
St. Louis	503	31.4	2027	4663	6690	418.1
San Francisco	409	25.6	2244	3445	5689	355.6
Green Bay	390	24.4	1693	3770	5463	341.4
NY Giants	294	18.4	1777	3558	5335	333.4
New Orleans	333	20.8	1712	3514	5226	326.6
Minnesota	290	18.1	1609	3576	5185	324.1
Atlanta	291	18.2	1773	3297	5070	316.9
Detroit	270	16.9	1398	3596	4994	312.1
Philadelphia	343	21.4	1778	3145	4923	307.7
Arizona	295	18.4	1449	3449	4898	306.1
Chicago	338	21.1	1742	2952	4694	293.4
Tampa Bay	324	20.3	1371	3323	4694	293.4
Washington	256	16.0	1948	2487	4435	277.2
Dallas	246	15.4	2184	2218	4402	275.1
Carolina	253	15.8	1372	2882	4254	265.9

Defense

AFC	Opp	Avg	Rush	Pass	Total	Avg
Pittsburgh	212	13.3	1195	2942	4137	258.6
Baltimore	265	16.6	1411	3035	4446	277.9
Miami	290	18.1	1779	2829	4608	288.0
Denver	339	21.2	1492	3282	4774	298.4
Cincinnati	309	19.3	1675	3157	4832	302.0
San Diego	321	20.1	1504	3400	4904	306.5
Jacksonville	286	17.9	1611	3459	5070	316.9
Oakland	327	20.4	1988	3083	5071	316.9
NY Jets	295	18.4	2154	2999	5153	322.1
Seattle	324	20.3	1721	3485	5206	325.4
Buffalo	420	26.3	2133	3159	5292	330.8
Cleveland	319	19.9	2208	3089	5297	331.1
Kansas City	344	21.5	2140	3164	5304	331.5
New England	272	17.0	1855	3497	5352	334.5
Tennessee	388	24.3	1431	4084	5515	344.7
Indianapolis	486	30.4	2115	3600	5715	357.2

NFC	Opp	Avg	Rush	Pass	Total	Avg
St. Louis	273	17.1	1385	3086	4471	279.4
Dallas	338	21.1	1710	2889	4599	287.4
Tampa Bay	280	17.5	1702	2951	4653	290.8
Philadelphia	208	13.0	1837	2864	4701	293.8
Washington	303	18.9	1869	2977	4846	302.9
Green Bay	266	16.6	1769	3168	4937	308.6
San Francisco	282	17.6	1571	3383	4954	309.6
NY Giants	321	20.1	1545	3430	4975	310.9
Chicago	203	12.7	1313	3665	4978	311.1
New Orleans	409	25.6	1715	3355	5070	316.9
Detroit	424	26.5	1993	3528	5521	345.1
Minnesota	390	24.4	2299	3367	5666	354.1
Arizona	343	21.4	2087	3598	5685	355.3
Atlanta	377	23.6	1943	3902	5845	365.3
Carolina	410	25.6	2301	3642	5943	371.4

Offensive Downs

AFC	Tot	First Downs Rush	Pass	Pen	3rd Downs Made	Att	Pct	4th Downs Made	Att	Pct
Indianapolis	343	110	206	27	85	205	41.5	5	8	62.5
Kansas City	324	119	178	27	70	195	35.9	5	16	31.3
Oakland	316	102	195	19	81	209	38.8	8	13	61.5
Pittsburgh	314	148	150	16	106	232	45.7	6	12	50.0
Denver	304	106	174	24	83	219	37.9	4	10	40.0
Baltimore	299	92	180	27	82	230	35.7	3	13	23.1
Cincinnati	294	96	176	22	93	243	38.3	6	23	26.1
New England	292	101	163	28	91	221	41.2	7	17	41.2
San Diego	290	92	177	21	79	221	35.7	3	4	75.0
Jacksonville	289	85	181	23	70	198	35.4	3	12	25.0
Tennessee	288	87	179	22	98	233	42.1	2	15	13.3
Buffalo	287	75	180	32	75	217	34.6	12	24	50.0
NY Jets	274	105	151	18	76	200	38.0	6	12	50.0
Seattle	274	107	141	26	77	213	36.2	8	17	47.1
Miami	263	95	154	14	89	215	41.4	9	14	64.3
Cleveland	238	78	139	21	68	210	32.4	6	12	50.0

NFC	Tot	First Downs Rush	Pass	Pen	3rd Downs Made	Att	Pct	4th Downs Made	Att	Pct
St. Louis	357	104	236	17	96	192	50.0	8	11	72.7
San Francisco	328	121	184	23	95	213	44.6	9	17	52.9
Tampa Bay	298	84	189	25	80	228	35.1	11	17	64.7
NY Giants	295	93	189	13	78	220	35.5	6	13	46.2
New Orleans	294	87	184	23	89	227	39.2	6	18	33.3
Detroit	289	74	184	31	76	222	34.2	12	25	48.0
Minnesota	288	88	179	21	88	210	41.9	8	18	44.4
Green Bay	282	72	187	23	72	197	36.5	3	6	50.0
Atlanta	280	85	165	30	89	217	41.0	5	17	29.4
Chicago	277	100	153	24	74	225	32.9	10	21	47.6
Arizona	277	77	177	23	57	196	29.1	10	20	50.0
Philadelphia	256	90	146	20	68	220	30.9	9	13	69.2
Dallas	247	114	110	23	71	215	33.1	4	16	25.0
Washington	241	104	122	15	79	223	35.4	4	13	30.8
Carolina	236	68	144	24	67	219	30.6	5	21	23.8

AFC Team by Team Results

(*) indicates overtime game. Please note that due to the events of Sept. 11, 2001, all Week 2 games (originally scheduled for Sept. 16-17) were postponed and rescheduled for the final week of the season (Jan. 6-7, 2002).

Baltimore Ravens (10-6)

Chicago	W, 17-6
at Cincinnati	L, 10-21
at Denver	W, 20-13
Tennessee	W, 26-7
at Green Bay	L, 23-31
at Cleveland	L, 14-24
Jacksonville	W, 18-17
at Pittsburgh	W, 13-10
at Tennessee	W, 16-10
Cleveland	L, 17-27
at Jacksonville	W, 24-21
Indianapolis	W, 39-27
OPEN	—
Pittsburgh	L, 21-26
Cincinnati	W, 16-0
at Tampa Bay	L, 10-22
Minnesota	W, 19-3

Buffalo Bills (3-13)

New Orleans	L, 6-24
at Indianapolis	L, 26-42
Pittsburgh	L, 3-20
NY Jets	L, 36-42
OPEN	—
at Jacksonville	W, 13-10
at San Diego	L, 24-27
Indianapolis	L, 14-30
at N. England	L, 11-21
Seattle	L, 20-23
Miami	L, 27-34
at San Fran.	L, 0-35
Carolina	W, 25-24
N. England	L, 9-12*
at Atlanta	L, 30-33
at NY Jets	W, 14-9
at Miami	L, 7-34

Cincinnati Bengals (6-10)

N. England	W, 23-17
Baltimore	W, 21-10
at San Diego	L, 14-28
at Pittsburgh	L, 7-16
Cleveland	W, 24-14
Chicago	L, 0-24
at Detroit	W, 31-27
OPEN	—
at Jacksonville	L, 13-30
Tennessee	L, 7-20
at Cleveland	L, 0-18
Tampa Bay	L, 13-16*
Jacksonville	L, 10-14
at NY Jets	L, 14-15
at Baltimore	L, 0-16
Pittsburgh	W, 26-23*
at Tennessee	W, 23-21

Cleveland Browns (7-9)

Seattle	L, 6-9
Detroit	W, 24-14
at Jacksonville	W, 23-14
San Diego	W, 20-16
at Cincinnati	L, 14-24
Baltimore	W, 24-14
OPEN	—
at Chicago	L, 21-27*
Pittsburgh	L, 12-15*
at Baltimore	W, 27-17
Cincinnati	W, 18-0
Tennessee	L, 15-31
at N. England	L, 16-27
Jacksonville	L, 10-15
at Green Bay	L, 7-30
at Tennessee	W, 41-38
at Pittsburgh	L, 7-28

Denver Broncos (8-8)

NY Giants	W, 31-20
at Arizona	W, 38-17
Baltimore	L, 13-20
Kansas City	W, 20-6
at Seattle	L, 21-34
at San Diego	L, 10-27
N. England	W, 31-20
at Oakland	L, 28-38
San Diego	W, 26-16
Washington	L, 10-17
at Dallas	W, 26-24
at Miami	L, 10-21
Seattle	W, 20-7
at Kansas City	L, 23-26*
OPEN	—
Oakland	W, 23-17
at Indianapolis	L, 10-29

Indianapolis Colts (6-10)

at NY Jets	W, 45-24
Buffalo	W, 42-26
at N. England	L, 13-44
OPEN	—
Oakland	L, 18-23
N. England	L, 17-38
at Kansas City	W, 35-28
at Buffalo	W, 30-14
Miami	L, 24-27
at New Orleans	L, 20-34
San Fran.	L, 21-40
at Baltimore	L, 27-39
at Miami	L, 6-41
Atlanta	W, 41-27
NY Jets	L, 28-29
at St. Louis	L, 17-42
Denver	W, 29-10

Jacksonville Jaguars (6-10)

Pittsburgh	W, 21-3
Tennessee	W, 13-6
Cleveland	L, 14-23
at Seattle	L, 15-24
OPEN	—
Buffalo	L, 10-13
at Baltimore	L, 17-18
at Tennessee	L, 24-28
Cincinnati	W, 30-13
at Pittsburgh	L, 7-20
Baltimore	L, 21-24
Green Bay	L, 21-28
at Cincinnati	W, 14-10
at Cleveland	W, 15-10
at Minnesota	W, 33-3
Kansas City	L, 26-30
at Chicago	L, 13-33

Kansas City Chiefs (6-10)

Oakland	L, 24-27
NY Giants	L, 3-13
at Washington	W, 45-13
at Denver	L, 6-20
Pittsburgh	L, 17-20
at Arizona	L, 16-24
Indianapolis	L, 28-35
at San Diego	W, 25-20
at NY Jets	L, 7-27
OPEN	—
Seattle	W, 19-7
Philadelphia	L, 10-23
at Oakland	L, 26-28
Denver	W, 26-23*
San Diego	W, 20-17
at Jacksonville	W, 30-26
at Seattle	L, 18-21

Miami Dolphins (11-5)

at Tennessee	W, 31-23
Oakland	W, 18-15
at St. Louis	L, 10-42
N. England	W, 30-10
at NY Jets	L, 17-21
OPEN	—
at Seattle	W, 24-20
Carolina	W, 23-6
at Indianapolis	W, 27-24
NY Jets	L, 0-24
at Buffalo	W, 34-27
Denver	W, 21-10
Indianapolis	W, 41-6
at San Fran.	L, 0-21
at N. England	L, 13-20
Atlanta	W, 21-14
Buffalo	W, 34-7

New England Patriots (11-5)

at Cincinnati	L, 17-23
NY Jets	L, 3-10
Indianapolis	W, 44-13
at Miami	L, 10-30
San Diego	W, 29-26*
at Indianapolis	W, 38-17
at Denver	L, 20-31
at Atlanta	W, 24-10
Buffalo	W, 21-11
St. Louis	L, 17-24
New Orleans	W, 34-17
at NY Jets	W, 17-16
Cleveland	W, 27-16
at Buffalo	W, 12-9*
Miami	W, 20-13
OPEN	—
at Carolina	W, 38-6

New York Jets (10-6)

Indianapolis	L, 24-45
at N. England	W, 10-3
San Fran.	L, 17-19
at Buffalo	W, 42-36
Miami	W, 21-17
St. Louis	L, 14-34
at Carolina	W, 13-12
at New Orleans	W, 16-9
Kansas City	W, 27-7
at Miami	W, 24-0
OPEN	—
N. England	L, 16-17
at Pittsburgh	L, 7-18
Cincinnati	W, 15-14
at Indianapolis	W, 29-28
Buffalo	L, 9-14
at Oakland	W, 24-22

Oakland Raiders (10-6)

at Kansas City	W, 27-24
at Miami	L, 15-18
Seattle	W, 38-14
Dallas	W, 28-21
at Indianapolis	W, 23-18
OPEN	—
at Philadelphia	W, 20-10
Denver	W, 38-28
at Seattle	L, 27-34
San Diego	W, 34-24
at NY Giants	W, 28-10
Arizona	L, 31-34*
Kansas City	W, 28-26
at San Diego	W, 13-6
Tennessee	L, 10-13
at Denver	L, 17-23
NY Jets	L, 22-24

Pittsburgh Steelers (13-3)

at Jacksonville	L, 3-21
OPEN	—
at Buffalo	W, 20-3
Cincinnati	W, 16-7
at Kansas City	W, 20-17
at Tampa Bay	W, 17-10
Tennessee	W, 34-7
Baltimore	L, 10-13
at Cleveland	W, 15-12*
Jacksonville	W, 20-7
at Tennessee	W, 34-24
Minnesota	W, 21-16
NY Jets	W, 18-7
at Baltimore	W, 26-21
Detroit	W, 47-14
at Cincinnati	L, 23-26*
Cleveland	W, 28-7

San Diego Chargers (5-11)

Washington	W, 30-3
at Dallas	W, 32-21
Cincinnati	W, 28-14
at Cleveland	L, 16-20
at N. England	L, 26-29*
Denver	W, 27-10
Buffalo	W, 27-24
Kansas City	L, 20-25
at Denver	L, 16-26
at Oakland	L, 24-34
Arizona	L, 17-20
at Seattle	L, 10-13*
at Philadelphia	L, 14-24
Oakland	L, 6-13
at Kansas City	L, 17-20
Seattle	L, 22-25
OPEN	—

Seattle Seahawks (9-7)

at Cleveland	W, 9-6
Philadelphia	L, 3-27
at Oakland	L, 14-38
Jacksonville	W, 24-15
Denver	W, 34-21
OPEN	—
Miami	L, 20-24
at Washington	L, 14-27
Oakland	W, 34-27
at Buffalo	W, 23-20
at Kansas City	L, 7-19
San Diego	W, 13-10*
at Denver	L, 7-20
Dallas	W, 29-3
at NY Giants	L, 24-27
at San Diego	W, 25-22
Kansas City	W, 21-18

Tennessee Titans (7-9)

Miami	L, 23-31
at Jacksonville	L, 6-13
OPEN	—
at Baltimore	L, 7-26
Tampa Bay	W, 31-28*
at Detroit	W, 27-24
at Pittsburgh	L, 7-34
Jacksonville	W, 28-24
Baltimore	L, 10-16
at Cincinnati	W, 20-7
Pittsburgh	L, 24-34
at Cleveland	W, 31-15
at Minnesota	L, 24-42
Green Bay	W, 26-20
at Oakland	W, 13-10
Cleveland	L, 38-41
Cincinnati	L, 21-23

NFC Team by Team Results

(*) indicates overtime game

Arizona Cardinals (7-9)

OPEN	—
Denver	L, 17-38
Atlanta	L, 14-34
at Philadelphia	W, 21-20
at Chicago	L, 13-20
Kansas City	W, 24-16
at Dallas	L, 3-17
Philadelphia	L, 7-21
NY Giants	L, 10-17
Detroit	W, 45-38
at San Diego	W, 20-17
at Oakland	W, 34-31*
Washington	L, 10-20
at NY Giants	L, 13-17
Dallas	W, 17-10
at Carolina	W, 30-7
at Washington	L, 17-20

Atlanta Falcons (7-9)

at San Fran.	L, 13-16*
Carolina	W, 24-16
at Arizona	W, 34-14
Chicago	L, 3-31
San Fran.	L, 31-37*
at New Orleans	W, 20-13
OPEN	—
N. England	L, 10-24
Dallas	W, 20-13
at Green Bay	W, 23-20
at Carolina	W, 10-7
St. Louis	L, 6-35
New Orleans	L, 10-28
at Indianapolis	L, 27-41
Buffalo	W, 33-30
at Miami	L, 14-21
at St. Louis	L, 13-31

Carolina Panthers (1-15)

at Minnesota	W, 24-13
at Atlanta	L, 16-24
Green Bay	L, 7-28
at San Fran.	L, 14-24
New Orleans	L, 25-27
at Washington	L, 14-17*
NY Jets	L, 12-13
at Miami	L, 6-23
at St. Louis	L, 14-48
San Fran.	L, 22-25*
Atlanta	L, 7-10
at New Orleans	L, 23-27
at Buffalo	L, 24-25
OPEN	—
St. Louis	L, 32-38
Arizona	L, 7-30
N. England	L, 6-38

Chicago Bears (13-3)

at Baltimore	L, 6-17
Minnesota	W, 17-10
OPEN	—
at Atlanta	W, 31-3
Arizona	W, 20-13
at Cincinnati	W, 24-0
San Fran.	W, 37-31*
Cleveland	W, 27-21*
Green Bay	L, 12-20
at Tampa Bay	W, 27-24
at Minnesota	W, 13-6
Detroit	W, 13-10
at Green Bay	L, 7-17
Tampa Bay	W, 27-3
at Washington	W, 20-15
at Detroit	W, 24-0
Jacksonville	W, 33-13

Dallas Cowboys (5-11)

Tampa Bay	L, 6-10
San Diego	L, 21-32
at Philadelphia	L, 18-40
at Oakland	L, 21-28
Washington	W, 9-7
OPEN	—
Arizona	W, 17-3
at NY Giants	L, 24-27*
at Atlanta	L, 13-20
Philadelphia	L, 3-36
Denver	L, 24-26
at Washington	W, 20-14
NY Giants	W, 20-13
at Seattle	L, 3-29
at Arizona	L, 10-17
San Fran.	W, 27-21
at Detroit	L, 10-15

Detroit Lions (2-14)

at Green Bay	L, 6-28
at Cleveland	L, 14-24
OPEN	—
St. Louis	L, 0-35
at Minnesota	L, 26-31
Tennessee	L, 24-27
Cincinnati	L, 27-31
at San Fran.	L, 13-21
Tampa Bay	L, 17-20
at Arizona	L, 38-45
Green Bay	L, 27-29
at Chicago	L, 10-13
at Tampa Bay	L, 12-15
Minnesota	W, 27-24
at Pittsburgh	L, 14-47
Chicago	L, 0-24
Dallas	W, 15-10

Green Bay Packers (12-4)

Detroit	W, 28-6
Washington	W, 37-0
at Carolina	W, 28-7
at Tampa Bay	L, 10-14
Baltimore	W, 31-23
at Minnesota	L, 13-35
OPEN	—
Tampa Bay	W, 21-20
at Chicago	W, 20-12
Atlanta	L, 20-23
at Detroit	W, 29-27
at Jacksonville	W, 28-21
Chicago	W, 17-7
at Tennessee	L, 20-26
Cleveland	W, 30-7
Minnesota	W, 24-13
at NY Giants	W, 34-25

Minnesota Vikings (5-11)

Carolina	L, 13-24
at Chicago	L, 10-17
Tampa Bay	W, 20-16
at New Orleans	L, 15-28
Detroit	W, 31-26
Green Bay	W, 35-13
at Tampa Bay	L, 14-41
OPEN	—
at Philadelphia	L, 17-48
NY Giants	W, 28-16
Chicago	L, 6-13
at Pittsburgh	L, 16-21
Tennessee	W, 42-24
at Detroit	L, 24-27
Jacksonville	L, 3-33
at Green Bay	L, 13-24
at Baltimore	L, 3-19

NFC Team by Team Results (Cont.)

New Orleans Saints (7-9)

at Buffalo	W, 24-6
OPEN	—
at NY Giants	L, 13-21
Minnesota	W, 28-15
at Carolina	W, 27-25
Atlanta	L, 13-20
at St. Louis	W, 34-31
NY Jets	L, 9-16
at San Fran.	L, 27-28
Indianapolis	W, 34-20
at N. England	L, 17-34
Carolina	W, 27-23
at Atlanta	W, 28-10
St. Louis	L, 21-34
at Tampa Bay	L, 21-48
Washington	L, 10-40
San Fran.	L, 0-38

New York Giants (7-9)

at Denver	L, 20-31
at Kansas City	W, 13-3
New Orleans	W, 21-13
Washington	W, 23-9
at St. Louis	L, 14-15
Philadelphia	L, 9-10
at Washington	L, 21-35
Dallas	W, 27-24*
at Arizona	W, 17-10
at Minnesota	L, 16-28
Oakland	L, 10-28
OPEN	—
at Dallas	L, 13-20
Arizona	W, 17-13
Seattle	W, 27-24
at Philadelphia	L, 21-24
Green Bay	L, 25-34

Philadelphia Eagles (11-5)

St. Louis	L, 17-20*
at Seattle	W, 27-3
Dallas	W, 40-18
Arizona	L, 20-21
OPEN	—
at NY Giants	W, 10-9
Oakland	L, 10-20
at Arizona	W, 21-7
Minnesota	W, 48-17
at Dallas	W, 36-3
Washington	L, 3-13
at Kansas City	W, 23-10
San Diego	W, 24-14
at Washington	W, 20-6
at San Fran.	L, 3-13
NY Giants	W, 24-21
at Tampa Bay	W, 17-13

St. Louis Rams (14-2)

at Philadelphia	W, 20-17*
at San Fran.	W, 30-26
Miami	W, 42-10
at Detroit	W, 35-0
NY Giants	W, 15-14
at NY Jets	W, 34-14
New Orleans	L, 31-34
OPEN	—
Carolina	W, 35-10
at N. England	W, 24-17
Tampa Bay	L, 17-24
at Atlanta	W, 35-6
San Fran.	W, 27-14
at New Orleans	W, 34-21
at Carolina	W, 38-32
Indianapolis	W, 42-17
Atlanta	W, 31-13

San Francisco 49ers (12-4)

Atlanta	W, 16-13*
St. Louis	L, 26-30
at NY Jets	W, 19-17
Carolina	W, 24-14
at Atlanta	W, 37-31*
OPEN	—
at Chicago	L, 31-37*
Detroit	W, 21-13
New Orleans	W, 28-22
at Carolina	W, 25-22*
at Indianapolis	W, 40-21
Buffalo	W, 35-0
at St. Louis	L, 14-27
Miami	W, 21-0
Philadelphia	W, 13-3
at Dallas	L, 21-27
at New Orleans	W, 38-0

Tampa Bay Buccaneers (9-7)

at Dallas	W, 10-6
OPEN	—
at Minnesota	L, 16-20
Green Bay	W, 14-10
at Tennessee	L, 28-31*
Pittsburgh	L, 10-17
Minnesota	W, 41-14
at Green Bay	L, 20-21
at Detroit	W, 20-17
Chicago	L, 24-27
at St. Louis	W, 24-17
at Cincinnati	W, 16-13*
Detroit	W, 15-12
at Chicago	L, 3-27
New Orleans	W, 48-21
Baltimore	W, 22-10
Philadelphia	L, 13-17

Washington Redskins (8-8)

at San Diego	L, 3-30
at Green Bay	L, 0-37
Kansas City	L, 13-45
at NY Giants	L, 9-23
at Dallas	L, 7-9
Carolina	W, 17-14*
NY Giants	W, 35-21
Seattle	W, 27-14
OPEN	—
at Denver	W, 17-10
at Philadelphia	W, 13-3
Dallas	L, 14-20
at Arizona	W, 20-10
Philadelphia	L, 6-20
Chicago	L, 15-20
at New Orleans	W, 40-10
Arizona	W, 20-17

Takeaways/Giveaways

AFC	Takeaways			Giveaways			Net Diff	NFC	Takeaways			Giveaways			Net Diff
	Int	Fum	Total	Int	Fum	Total			Int	Fum	Total	Int	Fum	Total	
NY Jets	20	19	39	14	7	21	+18	Tampa Bay	28	11	39	12	10	22	+17
Denver	22	15	37	19	8	27	+10	San Francisco	24	10	34	12	7	19	+15
Cleveland	33	9	42	21	12	33	+9	Chicago	20	17	37	16	8	24	+13
New England	22	13	35	15	13	28	+7	Green Bay	20	19	39	15	12	27	+12
Pittsburgh	16	12	28	12	9	21	+7	Philadelphia	14	19	33	14	10	24	+9
Seattle	14	13	27	12	9	21	+6	Washington	23	11	34	13	15	28	+6
San Diego	19	12	31	18	11	29	+2	Atlanta	18	12	30	17	11	28	+2
Oakland	17	7	24	9	16	25	-1	Carolina	24	12	36	22	13	35	+1
Jacksonville	12	12	24	14	13	27	-3	NY Giants	15	13	28	16	13	29	-1
Tennessee	13	11	24	17	11	28	-4	Arizona	17	7	24	14	13	27	-3
Kansas City	13	13	26	24	9	33	-7	New Orleans	15	15	30	22	13	35	-5
Baltimore	16	12	28	20	16	36	-8	Dallas	9	16	25	20	14	34	-9
Cincinnati	13	15	28	26	11	37	-9	St. Louis	21	13	34	22	22	44	-10
Miami	17	11	28	19	19	38	-10	Detroit	16	6	22	24	14	38	-16
Indianapolis	15	10	25	23	15	38	-13	Minnesota	8	10	18	23	16	39	-21
Buffalo	11	8	19	20	13	33	-14	TOTALS	272	191	463	262	191	453	+10
TOTALS	273	192	465	283	192	475	-10								

AFC Team by Team Statistics

Players with more than one team during the regular season are listed with club they ended season with; (*) indicates rookies.

Baltimore Ravens

Passing (5 Att)	Att	Cmp	Pct	Yds	TD	Rate
Elvis Grbac	.467	265	56.7	3033	15	71.1
Randall Cunningham	.89	54	60.7	573	3	81.3

Interceptions: Grbac 18, Cunningham 2.

Top Receivers	No	Yds	Avg	Long	TD
Qadry Ismail	.74	1059	14.3	77-td	7
Shannon Sharpe	.73	811	11.1	37	2
Travis Taylor	.42	560	13.3	63	3
Brandon Stokley	.24	344	14.3	46	2
Obafemi Ayanbadejo	.24	121	5.0	18	1
Moe Williams	.23	210	9.1	46	0

Top Rushers	Car	Yds	Avg	Long	TD
Terry Allen	.168	658	3.9	26	3
Jason Brookins*	.151	551	3.6	25	5
Moe Williams	.65	291	4.5	55	0
Obafemi Ayanbadejo	.46	173	3.8	17	1
Travis Taylor	.5	46	9.2	16	0

Most Touchdowns	TD	Run	Rec	Ret	Pts
Qadry Ismail	.7	0	7	0	44
Jason Brookins*	.5	5	0	0	30
Terry Allen	.3	3	0	0	18
Travis Taylor	.3	0	3	0	18
Three tied at 2 each.					

2-Pt. Conversions: (1-6) Ismail.

Kicking	PAT/Att	FG/Att	Lg	Pts
Matt Stover	.25/25	30/35	49	115

Punts (10 or more)	No	Yds	Long	Avg	In20
Kyle Richardson	.85	3309	65	38.9	29

Most Interceptions	Most Sacks
Duane Starks 4	Peter Boulware 15

Buffalo Bills

Passing (5 Att)	Att	Cmp	Pct	Yds	TD	Rate
Alex Van Pelt	.307	178	58.0	2056	12	76.4
Rob Johnson	.216	134	62.0	1465	5	76.3
Travis Brown	.33	15	45.5	201	1	50.2

Interceptions: Van Pelt 11, Johnson 7, Brown 2.

Top Receivers	No	Yds	Avg	Long	TD
Larry Centers	.80	620	7.8	26	2
Eric Moulds	.67	904	13.5	80-td	5
Peerless Price	.55	895	16.3	70-td	7
Jay Riemersma	.53	590	11.1	36	3
Travis Henry*	.22	179	8.1	40	0
Reggie Germany*	.12	203	16.9	39	0
Jeremy McDaniel	.11	129	11.7	22	0

Top Rushers	Car	Yds	Avg	Long	TD
Travis Henry*	.213	729	3.4	25	4
Shawn Bryson	.80	341	4.3	68-td	2
Rob Johnson	.36	241	6.7	23	1
Larry Centers	.34	160	4.7	50	2

Most Touchdowns	TD	Run	Rec	Ret	Pts
Peerless Price	.7	0	7	0	42
Eric Moulds	.5	0	5	0	32
Larry Centers	.4	2	2	0	24
Travis Henry*	.4	4	0	0	24
Jay Riemersma	.3	0	3	0	18

2-Pt. Conversions: (1-7) Moulds.

Kicking	PAT/Att	FG/Att	Lg	Pts
Jake Arians*	.16/17	12/21	49	52
Shayne Graham*	.7/7	6/8	41	25

Punts (10 or more)	No	Yds	Long	Avg	In20
Brian Moorman*	.80	3262	66	40.8	16

Most Interceptions	Most Sacks
Nate Clements* 3	Aaron Schobel* 6.5

Cincinnati Bengals

Passing (5 Att)	Att	Cmp	Pct	Yds	TD	Rate
Jon Kitna	.581	313	53.9	3216	12	61.1
Scott Mitchell	.12	4	33.3	38	0	3.5
Akili Smith	.8	5	62.5	37	0	73.4

Interceptions: Kitna 22, Mitchell 3.

Top Receivers	No	Yds	Avg	Long	TD
Peter Warrick	.70	667	9.5	33	1
Darnay Scott	.57	819	14.4	49	2
Corey Dillon	.34	228	6.7	17	3
Chad Johnson*	.28	329	11.8	28	1
Ron Dugans	.28	251	9.0	31	2
T.J. Houshmandzadeh*	.21	228	10.9	23	0
Brandon Bennett	.20	150	7.5	15	0

Top Rushers	Car	Yds	Avg	Long	TD
Corey Dillon	.340	1315	3.9	96-td	10
Brandon Bennett	.50	232	4.6	36	0
Jon Kitna	.27	73	2.7	20	1

Most Touchdowns	TD	Run	Rec	Ret	Pts
Corey Dillon	.13	10	3	0	78
Ron Dugans	.2	0	2	0	14
Darnay Scott	.2	0	2	0	12
Eight tied with 1 each for 6 pts.					

2-Pt. Conversions: (1-1) Dugans.

Kicking	PAT/Att	FG/Att	Lg	Pts
Neil Rackers	.23/24	17/28	52	74

Punts (10 or more)	No	Yds	Long	Avg	In20
Nick Harris*	.84	3372	57	40.1	21

Most Interceptions	Most Sacks
Kevin Kaesviharn* 3	Reinard Wilson 9
Artrell Hawkins 3	

Cleveland Browns

Passing (5 Att)	Att	Cmp	Pct	Yds	TD	Rate
Tim Couch	.454	272	59.9	3040	17	73.1
Kelly Holcomb	.12	7	58.3	114	1	118.1

Interceptions: Couch 21.

Top Receivers	No	Yds	Avg	Long	TD
Kevin Johnson	.84	1097	13.1	55-td	9
Jamel White	.44	418	9.5	45	1
Quincy Morgan*	.30	432	14.4	78	2
JaJuan Dawson	.22	281	12.8	44	1
Dennis Northcutt	.18	211	11.7	26	0
O.J. Santiago	.17	153	9.0	27	2

Top Rushers	Car	Yds	Avg	Long	TD
James Jackson*	.195	554	2.8	22	2
Jamel White	.126	443	3.5	51	5
Ben Gay*	.51	172	3.4	40	1
Tim Couch	.38	128	3.4	15	0

Most Touchdowns	TD	Run	Rec	Ret	Pts
Kevin Johnson	.9	0	9	0	54
Jamel White	.6	5	1	0	38
James Jackson*	.2	2	0	0	12
Quincy Morgan*	.2	0	2	0	12
O.J. Santiago	.2	0	2	0	12
Mike Sellers	.2	2	0	0	12

2-Pt. Conversions: (1-1) White.

Kicking	PAT/Att	FG/Att	Lg	Pts
Phil Dawson	.29/30	22/25	48	95

Punts (10 or more)	No	Yds	Long	Avg	In20
Chris Gardocki	.99	4249	69	42.9	25

Most Interceptions	Most Sacks
Anthony Henry* 10	Jamir Miller 13

Denver Broncos

Passing (5 Att)	Att	Cmp	Pct	Yds	TD	Rate
Brian Griese	.451	275	61.0	2827	23	78.5
Gus Frerotte	.48	30	62.5	308	3	101.7
Jarious Jackson*	.12	7	58.3	73	0	76.0

Interceptions: Griese 19.

Top Receivers	No	Yds	Avg	Long	TD
Rod Smith	.113	1343	11.9	65-td	11
Desmond Clark	.51	566	11.1	39	6
Dwayne Carswell	.34	299	8.8	25	4
Patrick Hape	.15	96	6.4	25	3
Terrell Davis	.12	69	5.8	16	0

Top Rushers	Car	Yds	Avg	Long	TD
Terrell Davis	.167	701	4.2	57	0
Mike Anderson	.175	678	3.9	62-td	4
Olandis Gary	.57	228	4.0	29	1
Brian Griese	.50	173	3.5	24	1

Most Touchdowns	TD	Run	Rec	Ret	Pts
Rod Smith	.11	0	11	0	68
Desmond Clark	.6	0	6	0	36
Mike Anderson	.4	4	0	0	26
Dwayne Carswell	.4	0	4	0	26
Patrick Hape	.3	0	3	0	18

2-Pt. Conversions: (3-4) Anderson, Carswell, R. Smith.

Kicking	PAT/Att	FG/Att	Lg	Pts
Jason Elam	.31/31	31/36	50	124

Punts (10 or more)	No	Yds	Long	Avg	In20
Tom Rouen	.81	3668	64	45.3	25

Most Interceptions		Most Sacks	
Deltha O'Neal	.9	Trevor Pryce	.7
		Bill Romanowski	.7

Indianapolis Colts

Passing (5 Att)	Att	Cmp	Pct	Yds	TD	Rate
Peyton Manning	..547	343	62.7	4131	26	84.1
Mark Rypien	.9	5	55.6	57	0	74.8

Interceptions: Manning 23.

Top Receivers	No	Yds	Avg	Long	TD
Marvin Harrison	.109	1524	14.0	68	15
Marcus Pollard	.47	739	15.7	86-td	8
Terrence Wilkins	.34	332	9.8	28	0
Dominic Rhodes*	.34	224	6.6	19	0
Ken Dilger	.32	343	10.7	44	1
Reggie Wayne*	.27	345	12.8	43	0

Top Rushers	Car	Yds	Avg	Long	TD
Dominic Rhodes*	.233	1104	4.7	77-td	9
Edgerrin James	.151	662	4.4	29-td	3
Peyton Manning	.35	157	4.5	33-td	4
Kevin McDougal	.17	48	2.8	12	0

Most Touchdowns	TD	Run	Rec	Ret	Pts
Marvin Harrison	.15	0	15	0	90
Dominic Rhodes*	.10	9	0	1	60
Marcus Pollard	.8	0	8	0	48
Peyton Manning	.4	4	0	0	24
Edgerrin James	.3	3	0	0	20
Jerome Pathon	.2	0	2	0	12

2-Pt. Conversions: (3-5) Dilger, James, McDougal.

Kicking	PAT/Att	FG/Att	Lg	Pts
Mike Vanderjagt	.41/42	28/34	52	125

Punts (10 or more)	No	Yds	Long	Avg	In20
Hunter Smith	.68	3023	65	44.5	12

Most Interceptions		Most Sacks	
Jeff Burris	.3	Chad Bratzke	.8.5
David Macklin	.3		

Jacksonville Jaguars

Passing (5 Att)	Att	Cmp	Pct	Yds	TD	Rate
Mark Brunell	.473	289	61.1	3309	19	84.1
Jonathan Quinn*	.22	12	52.5	361	1	69.1

Interceptions: Brunell 13, Quinn 1.

Top Receivers	No	Yds	Avg	Long	TD
Jimmy Smith	.112	1373	12.3	35-td	8
Keenan McCardell	.93	1110	11.9	45	6
Kyle Brady	.36	386	10.7	20-td	2
Stacey Mack	.23	165	7.2	25	1
Sean Dawkins	.20	234	11.7	28	0
Elvis Joseph*	.18	183	10.2	29-td	2

Top Rushers	Car	Yds	Avg	Long	TD
Stacey Mack*	.213	877	4.1	54	9
Elvis Joseph*	.68	294	4.3	27	0
Mark Brunell	.39	224	5.7	38	1
Fred Taylor	.30	116	3.9	24	0

Most Touchdowns	TD	Run	Rec	Ret	Pts
Stacey Mack	.10	9	1	0	60
Jimmy Smith	.8	0	8	0	48
Keenan McCardell	.6	0	6	0	38
Elvis Joseph*	.3	0	2	1	18
Kyle Brady	.2	0	2	0	12

2-Pt. Conversions: (1-2) McCardell.

Kicking	PAT/Att	FG/Att	Lg	Pts
Mike Hollis	.29/31	18/28	48	83
Jaret Holmes	.1/1	0/0	0	1

Punts (10 or more)	No	Yds	Long	Avg	In20
Chris Hanson	.82	3577	59	43.6	24

Most Interceptions		Most Sacks	
Hardy Nickerson	.3	Tony Brackens	.11
Aaron Beasley	.3		

Kansas City Chiefs

Passing (5 Att)	Att	Cmp	Pct	Yds	TD	Rate
Trent Green	.523	296	56.6	3783	17	71.1

Interceptions: Green 24.

Top Receivers	No	Yds	Avg	Long	TD
Tony Gonzalez	.73	917	12.6	36	6
Priest Holmes	.62	614	9.9	67-td	2
Marvin Minnis*	.33	511	15.5	56	1
Eddie Kennison	.31	491	15.8	65	1
DEN	.15	169	11.3	36	1
KC	.16	322	20.1	65	0
Tony Richardson	.30	265	8.8	47	0
Derrick Alexander	.27	470	17.4	46	3

Top Rushers	Car	Yds	Avg	Long	TD
Priest Holmes	.327	1555	4.8	41	8
Tony Richardson	.66	191	2.9	19	7
Trent Green	.35	158	4.5	16	0
Mike Cloud	.7	54	7.7	16	1

Most Touchdowns	TD	Run	Rec	Ret	Pts
Priest Holmes	.10	8	2	0	60
Tony Richardson	.7	7	0	0	42
Tony Gonzalez	.6	0	6	0	38
Derrick Alexander	.3	0	3	0	18
Larry Parker	.2	0	2	0	12

2-Pt. Conversions: (3-6) Gonzalez, Green, Kennison.

Kicking	PAT/Att	FG/Att	Lg	Pts
Todd Peterson	.27/28	27/35	51	108

Punts (10 or more)	No	Yds	Long	Avg	In20
Dan Stryzinski	.73	2976	76	40.8	27

Most Interceptions		Most Sacks	
Eric Warfield	.4	Duane Clemons	.7

Miami Dolphins

Passing (5 Att)	Att	Cmp	Pct	Yds	TD	Rate
Jay Fiedler	.450	273	60.7	3290	20	80.3

Interceptions: Fiedler 19.

Top Receivers	No	Yds	Avg	Long	TD
James McKnight	.55	684	12.4	40	3
Oronde Gadsden	.55	674	12.3	61	3
Chris Chambers*	.48	883	18.4	74-td	7
Lamar Smith	.30	234	7.8	65-td	2
Travis Minor*	.29	263	9.1	29	1
Dedric Ward	.21	209	10.0	20	0
Jed Weaver	.18	215	11.9	27	2

Top Rushers	Car	Yds	Avg	Long	TD
Lamar Smith	.313	968	3.1	25	6
Jay Fiedler	.73	321	4.4	26	4
Travis Minor*	.59	281	4.8	56-td	2

Most Touchdowns	TD	Run	Rec	Ret	Pts
Lamar Smith	.8	6	2	0	48
Chris Chambers*	.7	0	7	0	42
Jay Fiedler	.4	4	0	0	24
Travis Minor*	.4	2	1	1	24
James McKnight	.3	0	3	0	20
Oronde Gadsden	.3	0	3	0	18

2-Pt. Conversions: (1-1) McKnight.

Kicking	PAT/Att	FG/Att	Lg	Pts
Olindo Mare	.39/40	19/21	46	96

Punts (10 or more)	No	Yds	Long	Avg	In20
Matt Turk	.81	3321	77	41.0	28

Most Interceptions		Most Sacks	
Brock Marion	.5	Jason Taylor	.8.5

New England Patriots

Passing (5 Att)	Att	Cmp	Pct	Yds	TD	Rate
Tom Brady	.413	264	63.9	2843	18	86.5
Drew Bledsoe	.66	40	60.6	400	2	75.3

Interceptions: Brady 12, Bledsoe 2.

Top Receivers	No	Yds	Avg	Long	TD
Troy Brown	.101	1199	11.9	60-td	5
David Patten	.51	749	14.7	91-td	4
Kevin Faulk	.30	189	6.3	28	2
Marc Edwards	.25	166	6.6	17	2
Antowain Smith	.19	192	10.1	41-td	1
Terry Glenn	.14	204	14.6	23	1
Jermaine Wiggins	.14	133	9.5	31	4
Charles Johnson	.14	111	7.9	24-td	1

Top Rushers	Car	Yds	Avg	Long	TD
Antowain Smith	.287	1157	4.0	44	12
Kevin Faulk	.41	169	4.1	24	1
Marc Edwards	.51	141	2.8	14	1
J.R. Redmond	.35	119	3.4	16	0

Most Touchdowns	TD	Run	Rec	Ret	Pts
Antowain Smith	.13	12	1	0	78
Troy Brown	.7	0	5	2	42
David Patten	.5	1	4	0	30
Jermaine Wiggins	.4	0	4	0	24

2-Pt. Conversions: (0-1).

Kicking	PAT/Att	FG/Att	Lg	Pts
Adam Vinatieri	.41/42	24/30	54	113

Punts (10 or more)	No	Yds	Long	Avg	In20
Ken Walter	.49	1964	58	40.1	24

Released: Lee Johnson on Oct. 15 (see Min.). **Signed:** Walter on Oct. 17.

Most Interceptions		Most Sacks	
Otis Smith	.5	Bobby Hamilton	.7

New York Jets

Passing (5 Att)	Att	Cmp	Pct	Yds	TD	Rate
Vinny Testaverde	.441	260	59.0	2752	15	75.3
Chad Pennington	.20	10	50.0	92	1	79.6

Interceptions: Testaverde 14.

Top Receivers	No	Yds	Avg	Long	TD
Laveranues Coles	.59	868	14.7	40-td	7
Wayne Chrebet	.56	750	13.4	36	1
Curtis Martin	.53	320	6.0	27	0
Richie Anderson	.40	252	6.3	22	2
Anthony Becht	.36	321	8.9	24	5
Kevin Swayne*	.13	203	15.6	27	0

Top Rushers	No	Yds	Avg	Long	TD
Curtis Martin	.333	1513	4.5	47	10
LaMont Jordan*	.39	292	7.5	46-td	1
Laveranues Coles	.10	108	10.8	20	0
Richie Anderson	.26	102	3.9	12	0

Most Touchdowns	TD	Run	Rec	Ret	Pts
Curtis Martin	.10	10	0	0	60
Laveranues Coles	.7	0	7	0	42
Anthony Becht	.5	0	5	0	30
Richie Anderson	.2	0	2	0	12
LaMont Jordan*	.2	1	1	0	12

2-Pt. Conversions: (0-2).

Kicking	PAT/Att	FG/Att	Lg	Pts
John Hall	.32/32	24/31	53	104

Punts (10 or more)	No	Yds	Long	Avg	In20
Tom Tupa	.67	2575	59	38.4	21

Most Interceptions		Most Sacks	
Aaron Glenn	.5	John Abraham	.13

Oakland Raiders

Passing (5 Att)	Att	Cmp	Pct	Yds	TD	Rate
Rich Gannon	.549	361	65.8	3828	27	95.5

Interceptions: Gannon 9.

Top Receivers	No	Yds	Avg	Long	TD
Tim Brown	.91	1165	12.8	46-td	9
Jerry Rice	.83	1139	13.7	40-td	9
Charlie Garner	.72	578	8.0	27	2
Roland Williams	.33	298	9.0	49	3
Jerry Porter	.19	220	11.6	21	0
Jon Ritchie	.19	154	8.1	17	2
Jeremy Brigham	.12	85	7.1	17	1
Randy Jordan	.12	61	5.1	11	1

Top Rushers	Car	Yds	Avg	Long	TD
Charlie Garner	.211	839	4.0	38	1
Tyrone Wheatley	.88	276	3.1	22	5
Rich Gannon	.63	231	3.7	17	2
Zack Crockett	.57	145	2.5	10	6

Most Touchdowns	TD	Run	Rec	Ret	Pts
Tim Brown	.10	0	9	1	60
Jerry Rice	.9	0	9	0	54
Zack Crockett	.6	6	0	0	36
Tyrone Wheatley	.6	5	1	0	36

2-Pt. Conversions: (1-2) Gannon.

Kicking	PAT/Att	FG/Att	Lg	Pts
Sebastian Janikowski	.42/42	23/28	52	111
Brad Daluiso	.1/2	3/4	44	10

Signed: Daluiso (Jan. 3). **Released:** Daluiso (Jan. 9).

Punts (10 or more)	No	Yds	Long	Avg	In20
Shane Lechler	.73	3375	65	46.2	23

Most Interceptions		Most Sacks	
Tory James	.5	Regan Upshaw	.7

Pittsburgh Steelers

Passing (5 Att)	Att	Cmp	Pct	Yds	TD	Rate
Kordell Stewart	442	266	60.2	3109	14	81.7
Tommy Maddox	9	7	77.8	154	1	116.2

Interceptions: Stewart 11, Maddox 1.

Top Receivers	No	Yds	Avg	Long	TD
Hines Ward	94	1003	10.7	34	4
Plaxico Burress	66	1008	15.3	43	6
Bobby Shaw	24	409	17.0	90-td	2
Troy Edwards	19	283	14.9	57	0
Chris Fuamatu-Ma'afala	16	127	7.9	54	1
Amos Zereoue	13	154	11.8	62	1
Mark Bruener	12	98	8.2	21	0

Top Rushers	Car	Yds	Avg	Long	TD
Jerome Bettis	225	1072	4.8	48	4
Kordell Stewart	96	537	5.6	48-td	5
C. Fuamatu-Ma'afala	120	453	3.8	46	3
Amos Zereoue	85	441	5.2	32	1

Most Touchdowns	TD	Run	Rec	Ret	Pts
Plaxico Burress	6	0	6	0	36
Kordell Stewart	5	5	0	0	30
Jerome Bettis	4	4	0	0	24
Chris Fuamatu-Ma'afala	4	3	1	0	24
Hines Ward	4	0	4	0	24

Four tied with 2 each for 12 pts.

2-Pt. Conversions: (0-1).

Kicking	PAT/Att	FG/Att	Lg	Pts
Kris Brown	34/37	30/44	55	124

Punts (10 or more)	No	Yds	Long	Avg	In20
Josh Miller	59	2505	64	42.5	23

Most Interceptions		Most Sacks	
Chad Scott	5	Jason Gildon	12

San Diego Chargers

Passing (5 Att)	Att	Cmp	Pct	Yds	TD	Rate
Doug Flutie	521	294	56.4	3464	15	72.0
Drew Brees*	27	15	55.6	221	1	94.8

Interceptions: Flutie 18.

Top Receivers	No	Yds	Avg	Long	TD
Curtis Conway	71	1125	15.8	72-td	6
LaDainian Tomlinson*	59	367	6.2	27	0
Jeff Graham	52	811	15.6	61-td	5
Freddie Jones	35	388	11.1	34	4
Tim Dwight	25	406	16.2	78	0
Terrell Fletcher	23	184	8.0	27	0

Top Rushers	No	Yds	Avg	Long	TD
LaDainian Tomlinson*	339	1236	3.6	54	10
Doug Flutie	53	192	3.6	16	1
Curtis Conway	7	116	16.6	67-td	1
Terrell Fletcher	29	107	3.7	16	0

Most Touchdowns	TD	Run	Rec	Ret	Pts
LaDainian Tomlinson*	10	10	0	0	60
Curtis Conway	7	1	6	0	42
Jeff Graham	5	0	5	0	30
Freddie Jones	4	0	4	0	24

2-Pt. Conversions: (0-3).

Kicking	PAT/Att	FG/Att	Lg	Pts
Wade Richey	26/26	21/32	51	89
Steve Christie	6/6	9/11	41	33

Signed: Christie (Nov. 28).

Punts (10 or more)	No	Yds	Long	Avg	In20
Darren Bennett	78	3308	62	42.4	25

Most Interceptions		Most Sacks	
Ryan McNeil	8	Marcellus Wiley	13

Seattle Seahawks

Passing (5 Att)	Att	Cmp	Pct	Yds	TD	Rate
Matt Hasselbeck	321	176	54.8	2023	7	70.9
Trent Dilfer	122	73	59.8	1014	7	92.0
Brock Huard	17	9	52.9	127	1	96.9

Interceptions: Hasselbeck 8, Dilfer 4.

Top Receivers	No	Yds	Avg	Long	TD
Darrell Jackson	70	1081	15.4	64	8
Shaun Alexander	44	343	7.8	28-td	2
Koren Robinson*	39	536	13.7	42	1
Bobby Engram	29	400	13.8	31	0
Christian Fauria	21	188	9.0	30	1
Mack Strong	17	141	8.3	35	0
James Williams	12	212	17.7	49	1

Top Rushers	Car	Yds	Avg	Long	TD
Shaun Alexander	309	1318	4.3	88-td	14
Ricky Watters	72	318	4.4	40	1
Matt Hasselbeck	40	141	3.5	17	0
Mack Strong	17	55	3.2	12	0

Most Touchdowns	TD	Run	Rec	Ret	Pts
Shaun Alexander	16	14	2	0	96
Darrell Jackson	8	0	8	0	48
Itula Mili	2	0	2	0	12

2-Pt. Conversions: (1-1) Fauria.

Kicking	PAT/Att	FG/Att	Lg	Pts
Rian Lindell	33/33	20/32	54	93

Punts (10 or more)	No	Yds	Lg	Avg	In20
Jeff Feagles	85	3730	68	43.9	26

Most Interceptions		Most Sacks	
Willie Williams	4	John Randle	11

Tennessee Titans

Passing (5 Att)	Att	Cmp	Pct	Yds	TD	Rate
Steve McNair	431	264	61.3	3350	21	90.2
Neil O'Donnell	76	42	55.3	496	2	73.1

Interceptions: McNair 12, O'Donnell 2.

Top Receivers	No	Yds	Avg	Long	TD
Derrick Mason	73	1128	15.5	71-td	9
Frank Wycheck	60	672	11.2	30	4
Kevin Dyson	54	825	15.3	68-td	7
Eddie George	37	279	7.5	25	0
Erron Kinney	25	263	10.5	24	1
Drew Bennett*	24	329	13.7	50	1
Mike Green	12	64	5.3	10	1

Top Rushers	Car	Yds	Avg	Long	TD
Eddie George	315	939	3.0	27	5
Steve McNair	75	414	5.5	24	5
Skip Hicks	56	341	6.1	51	1
Mike Green	15	71	4.7	21	1

Most Touchdowns	TD	Run	Rec	Ret	Pts
Derrick Mason	10	0	9	1	62
Kevin Dyson	7	0	7	0	44
Eddie George	5	5	0	0	30
Steve McNair	5	5	0	0	30
Frank Wycheck	4	0	4	0	24

2-Pt. Conversions: (3-4) Bennett, K. Dyson, Mason.

Kicking	PAT/Att	FG/Att	Lg	Pts
Joe Nedney	34/35	20/28	51	94

Punts (10 or more)	No	Yds	Long	Avg	In20
Craig Hentrich	85	3567	70	42.0	28

Most Interceptions		Most Sacks	
Samari Rolle	3	Jevon Kearse	10
Andre Dyson*	3		

NFC Team by Team Statistics

Players with more than one team during the regular season are listed with club they ended season with; (*) indicates rookies.

Arizona Cardinals

Passing (5 Att)

Passing (5 Att)	Att	Cmp	Pct	Yds	TD	Rate
Jake Plummer	.525	304	57.9	3653	18	79.6

Interceptions: Plummer 14.

Top Receivers	No	Yds	Avg	Long	TD
David Boston	.98	1598	16.3	61-td	8
Michael Pittman	.42	264	6.3	27	0
Frank Sanders	.41	618	15.1	68-td	2
MarTay Jenkins	.32	518	16.2	53	3
Tywan Mitchell	.25	196	7.8	24-td	2
Thomas Jones	.21	151	7.2	18	0

Top Rushers	Car	Yds	Avg	Long	TD
Michael Pittman	.241	846	3.5	42	5
Thomas Jones	.112	380	3.4	21	5
Jake Plummer	.35	163	4.7	21	0

Most Touchdowns	TD	Run	Rec	Ret	Pts
David Boston	.8	0	8	0	48
Thomas Jones	.5	5	0	0	30
Michael Pittman	.5	5	0	0	30
MarTay Jenkins	.3	0	3	0	18

2-Pt. Conversions: (1-1) Plummer.

Kicking	PAT/Att	FG/Att	Lg	Pts
Bill Gramatica*	.25/25	16/20	50	73
Cedric Oglesby*	.7/7	5/6	41	22

Signed: Oglesby (Dec. 18).

Punts (10 or more)	No	Yds	Long	Avg	In20
Scott Player	.67	2779	58	41.5	17
Chad Stanley	.19	751	54	39.5	4

Signed: Stanley off waivers from SF (Nov. 6). **Released:** Stanley (Dec. 4).

Most Interceptions		Most Sacks	
Kwamie Lassiter	.9	Rob Fredrickson	.4

Atlanta Falcons

Passing (5 Att)	Att	Cmp	Pct	Yds	TD	Rate
Chris Chandler	.365	223	61.1	2847	16	84.1
Michael Vick*	.113	50	44.2	785	2	62.7

Interceptions: Chandler 14, Vick 3.

Top Receivers	No	Yds	Avg	Long	TD
Terance Mathis	.51	564	11.1	34	2
Bob Christian	.45	392	8.7	42	2
Tony Martin	.37	548	14.8	63-td	3
Shawn Jefferson	.37	539	14.6	48	2
Alge Crumpler*	.25	330	13.2	57-td	3
Brian Finneran	.23	491	21.3	52	3
Maurice Smith	.19	230	12.1	79-td	1

Top Rushers	Car	Yds	Avg	Long	TD
Maurice Smith	.237	760	3.2	58	5
Michael Vick*	.31	289	9.3	35	1
Bob Christian	.44	284	6.5	53	2
Jamal Anderson	.55	190	3.5	14	1

Most Touchdowns	TD	Run	Rec	Ret	Pts
Maurice Smith	.6	5	1	0	36
Bob Christian	.4	2	2	0	24
Alge Crumpler*	.3	0	3	0	18
Brian Finneran	.3	0	3	0	18
Tony Martin	.3	0	3	0	18

2-Pt. Conversions: (1-1) Jefferson.

Kicking	PAT/Att	FG/Att	Lg	Pts
Jay Feely*	.28/28	29/37	55	115

Punts (10 or more)	No	Yds	Long	Avg	In20
Chris Mohr	.69	2680	55	38.8	25

Most Interceptions		Most Sacks	
Ray Buchanan	.5	Patrick Kerney	.12
Ashley Ambrose	.5		

Carolina Panthers

Passing (5 Att)	Att	Cmp	Pct	Yds	TD	Rate
Chris Weinke*	.540	293	54.3	2931	11	62.0
Matt Lytle	.30	17	56.7	133	1	39.3
Dameyune Craig	.8	4	50.0	34	0	61.5

Interceptions: Weinke 19, Lytle 3.

Top Receivers	No	Yds	Avg	Long	TD
Donald Hayes	.52	597	11.5	48	2
Muhsin Muhammad	.50	585	11.7	43	1
Wesley Walls	.43	452	10.5	25	5
Isaac Byrd	.37	492	13.3	42	1
Brad Hoover	.26	185	7.1	19	0
Chris Hetherington	.23	124	5.4	15	0

Top Rushers	Car	Yds	Avg	Long	TD
Richard Huntley	.165	665	4.0	25	2
Tim Biakabutuka	.53	230	4.3	27	1
Nick Goings*	.66	197	3.0	16	0
Chris Weinke	.37	128	3.5	23	6

Most Touchdowns	TD	Run	Rec	Ret	Pts
Chris Weinke*	.6	6	0	0	36
Wesley Walls	.5	0	5	0	30
Richard Huntley	.3	2	1	0	18
Steve Smith*	.3	0	0	3	18

2-Pt. Conversions: (0-4).

Kicking	PAT/Att	FG/Att	Lg	Pts
John Kasay	.22/23	23/28	52	91

Punts (10 or more)	No	Yds	Long	Avg	In20
Todd Sauerbrun	.93	4419	73	47.5	35

Most Interceptions		Most Sacks	
Doug Evans	.8	Mike Rucker	.9

Chicago Bears

Passing (5 Att)	Att	Cmp	Pct	Yds	TD	Rate
Jim Miller	.395	228	57.7	2299	13	74.9
Shane Matthews	.129	84	65.1	694	5	72.3

Interceptions: Miller 10, Matthews 6.

Top Receivers	No	Yds	Avg	Long	TD
Marty Booker	.100	1071	10.7	66-td	8
Dez White	.45	428	9.5	32	0
David Terrell*	.34	415	12.2	62	4
James Allen	.30	203	6.8	34-td	1
Marcus Robinson	.23	269	11.7	34-td	2
Anthony Thomas*	.22	178	8.1	23	0
Fred Baxter	.22	148	6.7	19	2

Top Rushers	Car	Yds	Avg	Long	TD
Anthony Thomas*	.278	1183	4.3	46	7
James Allen	.135	469	3.5	19	1
Leon Johnson	.20	99	5.0	34	4

Most Touchdowns	TD	Run	Rec	Ret	Pts
Marty Booker	.8	0	8	0	48
Anthony Thomas*	.7	7	0	0	44
Leon Johnson	.4	4	0	0	24
David Terrell*	.4	0	4	0	24

Five tied with 2 each for 12 pts.

2-Pt. Conversions: (1-1) Thomas.

Kicking	PAT/Att	FG/Att	Lg	Pts
Paul Edinger	.34/34	26/31	48	112

Punts (10 or more)	No	Yds	Lg	Avg	In20
Brad Maynard	.87	3709	60	42.6	36

Most Interceptions		Most Sacks	
Mike Brown	.5	Rosevelt Colvin	.10.5

Dallas Cowboys

Passing (10 Att)	Att	Cmp	Pct	Yds	TD	Rate
Quincy Carter*	176	90	51.1	1072	5	63.0
Anthony Wright	98	48	49.0	529	5	61.1
Ryan Leaf	88	45	51.1	494	1	57.7
Clint Stoerner	49	26	53.1	314	3	53.8

Interceptions: Carter 7, Wright and Stoerner 5, Leaf 3.
Signed: Leaf (Oct. 12).

Top Receivers	No	Yds	Avg	Long	TD
Raghib Ismail	53	834	15.7	80-td	2
Joey Galloway	52	699	13.4	47-td	3
Emmitt Smith	17	116	6.8	22	0
Michael Wiley	16	99	6.2	17	1
Jackie Harris	15	141	9.4	28	2

Top Rushers	Car	Yds	Avg	Long	TD
Emmitt Smith	261	1021	3.9	44	3
Troy Hambrick	113	579	5.1	80	2
Michael Wiley	34	247	7.3	58	0
Quincy Carter	45	150	3.3	17	1

Most Touchdowns	TD	Run	Rec	Ret	Pts
Joey Galloway	3	0	3	0	18
Emmitt Smith	3	3	0	0	18

Six tied with 2 each for 12 pts.

2-Pt. Conversions: (0-2).

Kicking	PAT/Att	FG/Att	Lg	Pts
Tim Seder	12/12	11/17	46	51
Jon Hilbert*	12/12	11/16	43	45

Signed: Hilbert (Nov. 13).

Punts (10 or more)	No	Yds	Long	Avg	In20
Micah Knorr	78	3135	57	40.2	25

Most Interceptions		Most Sacks	
Darren Woodson	3	Greg Ellis	6

Detroit Lions

Passing (5 Att)	Att	Cmp	Pct	Yds	TD	Rate
Charlie Batch	341	198	58.1	2392	12	76.8
Ty Detmer	151	92	60.9	906	3	56.9
Mike McMahon*	115	53	46.1	671	3	69.9

Interceptions: Batch 12, Detmer 10, McMahon 1.

Top Receivers	No	Yds	Avg	Long	TD
Johnnie Morton	77	1154	15.0	76	4
Cory Schlesinger	60	466	7.8	38	0
Lamont Warren	40	336	8.4	36	1
David Sloan	37	409	11.1	27	7
James Stewart	23	242	10.5	56	1
Germane Crowell	22	289	13.1	46-td	2
Larry Foster	22	283	12.9	36	0

Top Rushers	Car	Yds	Avg	Long	TD
James Stewart	143	685	4.8	38	1
Lamont Warren	61	191	3.1	34	3
Cory Schlesinger	47	154	3.3	26	3
Mike McMahon*	27	145	5.4	22	1

Most Touchdowns	TD	Run	Rec	Ret	Pts
David Sloan	7	0	7	0	42
Lamont Warren	4	3	1	0	26
Johnnie Morton	4	0	4	0	24
Cory Schlesinger	3	3	0	0	18

2-Pt. Conversions: (2-7) McMahon, Warren.

Kicking	PAT/Att	FG/Att	Lg	Pts
Jason Hanson	23/23	21/30	54	86

Punts (10 or more)	No	Yds	Long	Avg	In20
John Jett	58	2512	62	43.3	16
Leo Araguz	17	713	55	41.9	6

Signed: Araguz (Nov. 27). **Waived:** Araguz (Dec. 18).

Most Interceptions		Most Sacks	
Todd Lyght	4	Robert Porcher	11

Green Bay Packers

Passing (5 Att)	Att	Cmp	Pct	Yds	TD	Rate
Brett Favre	510	314	61.6	3921	32	94.1

Interceptions: Favre 15.

Top Receivers	No	Yds	Avg	Long	TD
Ahman Green	62	594	9.6	42	2
Bill Schroeder	53	918	17.3	67-td	9
Antonio Freeman	52	818	15.7	63	6
Bubba Franks	36	322	8.9	31	9
Corey Bradford	31	526	17.0	56	2
Dorsey Levens	24	159	6.6	19	1
William Henderson	21	193	9.2	26	0

Top Rushers	Car	Yds	Avg	Long	TD
Ahman Green	304	1387	4.6	83-td	9
Dorsey Levens	44	165	3.8	40	0
Brett Favre	38	56	1.5	14	1

Most Touchdowns	TD	Run	Rec	Ret	Pts
Ahman Green	11	9	2	0	66
Bubba Franks	9	0	0	0	54
Bill Schroeder	9	0	9	0	54
Antonio Freeman	6	0	6	0	38

Two tied with 2 each for 12 pts.

2-Pt. Conversions: (1-2) Freeman.

Kicking	PAT/Att	FG/Att	Lg	Pts
Ryan Longwell	44/45	20/31	54	104

Punts (10 or more)	No	Yds	Long	Avg	In20
Josh Bidwell	82	3485	68	42.5	21

Most Interceptions		Most Sacks	
Darren Sharper	6	Kabeer Gbaja-Biamila	13.5

Minnesota Vikings

Passing (5 Att)	Att	Cmp	Pct	Yds	TD	Rate
Daunte Culpepper	366	235	64.2	2612	14	83.3
Spergeon Wynn	98	48	49.0	418	1	38.6
Todd Bouman	89	51	57.3	795	8	98.3

Interceptions: Culpepper 13, Wynn 6, Bouman 4.

Top Receivers	No	Yds	Avg	Long	TD
Randy Moss	82	1233	15.0	73-td	10
Cris Carter	73	871	11.9	52	6
Byron Chamberlain	57	666	11.7	47-td	3
Michael Bennett*	29	226	7.8	80-td	1
Jake Reed	27	309	11.4	27	1

Top Rushers	Car	Yds	Avg	Long	TD
Michael Bennett*	172	682	4.0	31-td	2
Daunte Culpepper	71	416	5.9	34	5
Doug Chapman	63	195	3.1	19	0
Jimmy Kleinsasser	23	72	3.1	11	1

Most Touchdowns	TD	Run	Rec	Ret	Pts
Randy Moss	10	0	10	0	60
Cris Carter	6	0	6	0	36
Daunte Culpepper	5	5	0	0	34
Michael Bennett*	3	2	1	0	18
Byron Chamberlain	3	0	3	0	18

2-Pt. Conversions: (3-5) Culpepper 2, Reed.

Kicking	PAT/Att	FG/Att	Lg	Pts
Gary Anderson	29/30	15/18	44	74

Punts (10 or more)	No	Yds	Long	Avg	In20
Lee Johnson	49	2028	76	41.4	12
NE.	24	1045	76	43.5	3
MIN.	25	983	59	39.3	9
Mitch Berger	47	2046	67	43.5	10

Most Interceptions		Most Sacks	
Robert Griffith	2	Chris Hovan	6
Eric Kelly*	2		

New Orleans Saints

Passing (5 Att)	Att	Cmp	Pct	Yds	TD	Rate
Aaron Brooks	.558	312	55.9	3832	26	76.4

Interceptions: Brooks 22.

Top Receivers	No	Yds	Avg	Long	TD
Joe Horn	.83	1265	15.2	56	9
Willie Jackson	.81	1046	12.9	63	5
Ricky Williams	.60	511	8.5	42	1
Robert Wilson	.21	277	13.2	44	0
Boo Williams*	.20	202	10.1	26	3
Deuce McAllister*	.15	166	11.1	22-td	1
Cam Cleeland	.13	138	10.6	19-td	4

Top Rushers	Car	Yds	Avg	Long	TD
Ricky Williams	.313	1245	4.0	46	6
Aaron Brooks	.80	358	4.5	26	1
Deuce McAllister*	.16	91	5.7	54-td	1

Most Touchdowns	TD	Run	Rec	Ret	Pts
Joe Horn	.9	0	9	0	54
Ricky Williams	.7	6	1	0	42
Willie Jackson	.5	0	5	0	32
Cam Cleeland	.4	0	4	0	24
Boo Williams*	.3	0	3	0	18

2-Pt. Conversions: (1-4) Jackson.

Kicking	PAT/Att	FG/Att	Lg	Pts
John Carney	.32/32	27/31	50	113

Punts (10 or more)	No	Yds	Long	Avg	In20
Toby Gowin	.76	3180	62	41.8	24

Most Interceptions		Most Sacks	
Sammy Knight	.6	Charlie Clemons	.13.5

Philadelphia Eagles

Passing (5 Att)	Att	Cmp	Pct	Yds	TD	Rate
Donovan McNabb	.493	285	57.8	3233	25	84.3
Koy Detmer	.14	5	35.7	51	0	17.3
A.J. Feeley*	.14	10	71.4	143	2	114.0

Interceptions: McNabb 12, Detmer and Feeley 1.

Top Receivers	No	Yds	Avg	Long	TD
James Thrash	.63	833	13.2	64-td	8
Duce Staley	.63	626	9.9	46-td	2
Todd Pinkston	.42	586	14.0	62-td	4
Chad Lewis	.41	422	10.3	33	6
Cecil Martin	.24	124	5.2	17	2
Freddie Mitchell*	.21	283	13.5	29	1

Top Rushers	Car	Yds	Avg	Long	TD
Duce Staley	.166	604	3.6	44-td	2
Correll Buckhalter*	.129	586	4.5	48	2
Donovan McNabb	.82	482	5.9	33	2

Most Touchdowns	TD	Run	Rec	Ret	Pts
James Thrash	.8	0	8	0	48
Chad Lewis	.6	0	6	0	36
Todd Pinkston	.4	0	4	0	24
Duce Staley	.4	2	2	0	24

2-Pt. Conversions: (0-0).

Kicking	PAT/Att	FG/Att	Lg	Pts
David Akers	.37/38	26/31	50	115

Punts (10 or more)	No	Yds	Long	Avg	In20
Sean Landeta	.97	4221	64	43.5	26

Most Interceptions		Most Sacks	
Troy Vincent	.3	Hugh Douglas	.9.5

New York Giants

Passing (5 Att)	Att	Cmp	Pct	Yds	TD	Rate
Kerry Collins	.568	327	57.6	3764	19	77.1

Interceptions: Collins 16.

Top Receivers	No	Yds	Avg	Long	TD
Amani Toomer	.72	1054	14.6	60-td	5
Tiki Barber	.72	577	8.0	44	0
Ike Hilliard	.52	659	12.7	38	6
Joe Jurevicius	.51	706	13.8	46-td	3
Greg Comella	.39	253	6.5	26	1
Dan Campbell	.13	148	11.4	25	1
Ron Dixon	.8	227	28.4	62	1

Top Rushers	Car	Yds	Avg	Long	TD
Tiki Barber	.166	865	5.2	36	4
Ron Dayne	.180	690	3.8	61	7
Damon Washington	.28	89	3.2	22	0
Kerry Collins	.39	73	1.9	11	0

Most Touchdowns	TD	Run	Rec	Ret	Pts
Ron Dayne	.7	7	0	0	44
Ike Hilliard	.6	0	6	0	36
Amani Toomer	.5	0	5	0	30
Tiki Barber	.4	4	0	0	26
Joe Jurevicius	.3	0	3	0	18
Marcellus Rivers*	.2	0	2	0	12

2-Pt. Conversions: (2-2) Barber, Dayne.

Kicking	PAT/Att	FG/Att	Lg	Pts
Morten Andersen	.29/30	23/28	51	98
Owen Pochman*	.0/0	0/2	—	0

Punts (10 or more)	No	Yds	Long	Avg	In20
Rodney Williams*	.91	3905	90	42.9	25

Most Interceptions		Most Sacks	
Will Allen*	.4	Michael Strahan	.22.5

St. Louis Rams

Passing (5 Att)	Att	Cmp	Pct	Yds	TD	Rate
Kurt Warner	.546	375	68.7	4830	36	101.4

Interceptions: Warner 22.

Top Receivers	No	Yds	Avg	Long	TD
Marshall Faulk	.83	765	9.2	65-td	9
Torry Holt	.81	1363	16.8	51	7
Isaac Bruce	.64	1106	17.3	51-td	6
Ricky Proehl	.40	563	14.1	37	5
Az-zahir Hakim	.39	374	9.6	33	3
Ernie Conwell	.38	431	11.3	47	4
Trung Canidate	.17	154	9.1	29	0

Top Rushers	Car	Yds	Avg	Long	TD
Marshall Faulk	.260	1382	5.3	71-td	12
Trung Canidate	.78	441	5.7	45	6
Kurt Warner	.28	60	2.1	23	0

Most Touchdowns	TD	Run	Rec	Ret	PTS
Marshall Faulk	.21	12	9	0	128
Torry Holt	.7	0	7	0	42
Isaac Bruce	.6	0	6	0	36
Trung Canidate	.6	6	0	0	36
Ricky Proehl	.5	0	5	0	32
Ernie Conwell	.5	1	4	0	30
Az-zahir Hakim	.3	0	3	0	18

2-Pt. Conversions: (2-4) Faulk, Proehl.

Kicking	PAT/Att	FG/Att	Lg	Pts
Jeff Wilkins	.58/58	23/29	54	127

Punts (10 or more)	No	Yds	Long	Avg	In20
John Baker	.43	1809	58	42.1	9

Most Interceptions		Most Sacks	
Dre' Bly	.6	Leonard Little	.14.5

San Francisco 49ers

Passing (5 Att)	Att	Cmp	Pct	Yds	TD	Rate
Jeff Garcia	504	316	62.7	3538	32	94.8

Interceptions: Garcia 12.

Top Receivers	No	Yds	Avg	Long	TD
Terrell Owens	93	1412	15.2	60-td	16
J.J. Stokes	54	585	10.8	47	7
Garrison Hearst	41	347	8.5	60-td	1
Eric Johnson*	40	362	9.1	24	3
Tai Streets	28	345	12.3	52	1
Kevan Barlow*	22	247	11.2	61-td	1

Top Rushers	Car	Yds	Avg	Long	TD
Garrison Hearst	252	1206	4.8	43-td	4
Kevan Barlow*	125	512	4.1	25	4
Jeff Garcia	72	254	3.5	25	5
Terry Jackson	22	138	6.3	15	1

Most Touchdowns	TD	Run	Rec	Ret	Pts
Terrell Owens	16	0	16	0	96
J.J. Stokes	7	0	7	0	42
Kevan Barlow*	5	4	1	0	30
Jeff Garcia	5	5	0	0	30
Garrison Hearst	5	4	1	0	30

2-Pt. Conversions: (1-3) Johnson.

Kicking	PAT/Att	FG/Att	Lg	Pts
Jose Cortez*	47/47	18/25	52	101

Punts (10 or more)	No	Yds	Long	Avg	In20
Jason Baker	69	2813	64	40.8	21

Most Interceptions		Most Sacks	
Zack Bronson	7	Andre Carter*	6.5
Ahmed Plummer	7		

Washington Redskins

Passing (5 Att)	Att	Cmp	Pct	Yds	TD	Rate
Tony Banks	370	198	53.5	2386	10	71.3
Jeff George	42	23	54.8	168	0	34.6
Kent Graham	19	13	68.4	131	2	122.9

Interceptions: Banks 10, George 3.

Top Receivers	No	Yds	Avg	Long	TD
Michael Westbrook	57	664	11.6	76-td	4
Rod Gardner*	46	741	16.1	85-td	4
Stephen Davis	28	205	7.3	29	0
Kevin Lockett	22	293	13.3	34	0
Zeron Flemister	18	196	10.9	33	2

Top Rushers	Car	Yds	Avg	Long	TD
Stephen Davis	356	1432	4.0	32	5
Ki-Jana Carter	63	308	4.9	30	3
Tony Banks	47	152	3.2	17	2
Donnell Bennett	10	39	3.9	8	0

Most Touchdowns	TD	Run	Rec	Ret	Pts
Stephen Davis	5	5	0	0	32
Rod Gardner*	4	0	4	0	24
Michael Westbrook	4	0	4	0	24
Ki-Jana Carter	3	3	0	0	18

2-Pt. Conversions: (2-3) Bennett, Davis.

Top Kickers	PAT/Att	FG/Att	Lg	Pts
Brett Conway	22/22	26/33	55	100

Punts (10 or more)	No	Yds	Long	Avg	In20
Bryan Barker	90	3747	59	41.6	27

Most Interceptions		Most Sacks	
Fred Smoot*	5	Bruce Smith	5

Tampa Bay Buccaneers

Passing (5 Att)	Att	Cmp	Pct	Yds	TD	Rate
Brad Johnson	559	340	60.8	3406	13	77.7
Shaun King	31	21	67.7	210	0	73.3

Interceptions: Johnson 11, King 1.

Top Receivers	No	Yds	Avg	Long	TD
Keyshawn Johnson	106	1266	11.9	47	1
Warrick Dunn	68	557	8.2	31	3
Jacquez Green	36	402	11.2	35	1
Dave Moore	35	285	8.1	29	4
Mike Alstott	35	231	6.6	19-td	1
Karl Williams	24	314	13.1	42	1
Jameel Cook*	17	89	5.2	16	0

Top Rushers	Car	Yds	Avg	Long	TD
Mike Alstott	165	680	4.1	39-td	10
Warrick Dunn	158	447	2.8	21-td	3
Brad Johnson	39	120	3.1	21	3
Aaron Stecker	24	72	3.0	17	1

Most Touchdowns	TD	Run	Rec	Ret	Pts
Mike Alstott	11	10	1	0	70
Warrick Dunn	6	3	3	0	36
Dave Moore	4	0	4	0	24
Brad Johnson	3	3	0	0	18
Aaron Stecker	2	1	1	0	12
Karl Williams	2	0	1	1	12

2-Pt. Conversions: (3-4) Alstott 2, King.

Kicking	PAT/Att	FG/Att	Lg	Pts
Martin Gramatica	28/28	23/29	49	97
Doug Brien	2/2	5/6	42	17

Signed: Brien (Dec. 27).

Punts (10 or more)	No	Yds	Long	Avg	In20
Mark Royals	83	3382	61	40.7	26

Most Interceptions		Most Sacks	
Ronde Barber	10	Simeon Rice	11

Overall Club Rankings

Combined AFC and NFC rankings by yards gained on offense and yards given up on defense. Teams are ranked by offense with AFC teams in *italics*.

	Offense			Defense		
	Rush	Pass	Rank	Rush	Pass	Rank
St. Louis	5	1	1	3	10	3
Indianapolis	7	2	2	25	27	29
Pittsburgh	1	21	3	1	4	1
San Francisco	2	14	4	9	19	13
Kansas City	6	5	5	27	14	23
Green Bay	21	3	6	16	15	12
Oakland	24	4	7	22	9	18
Tennessee	12	8t	8	5	31	25
NY Giants	15	8t	9	8	21	14
New Orleans	18t	10	10	14	17	16t
San Diego	20	11	11	7	20	11
Minnesota	25	7	12	30	18	27
Buffalo	22	12	13	26	13	21
Baltimore	11	16	14	4	8	2
Atlanta	16	17	15	21	30	30
Detroit	28	6	16	23	25	26
Philadelphia	14	20	17	18	2	7
Arizona	27	13	18	24	26	28
New England	13	22	19	19	24	24
Jacksonville	26	18	20	10	22	16t
Miami	23	19	21	17	1	5
Denver	10	25	22	6	16	8
Cincinnati	18t	23	23	11	12	9
NY Jets	4	29	24	28	7	19
Seattle	9	27	25	15	23	20
Tampa Bay	30	15	26t	12	5	6
Chicago	17	24	26t	2	29	15
Washington	8	30	28	20	6	10
Dallas	3	31	29	13	3	4
Carolina	29	26	30	31	28	31
Cleveland	31	28	31	29	11	22

NFL Playoffs

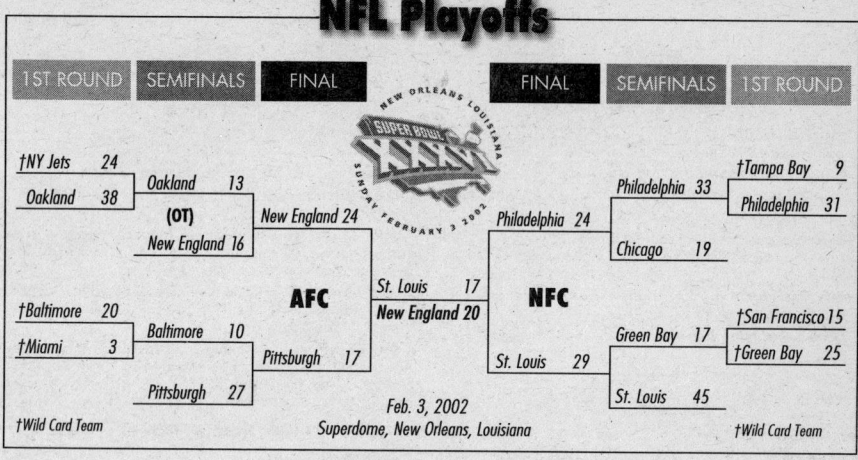

| 1ST ROUND | SEMIFINALS | FINAL | | FINAL | SEMIFINALS | 1ST ROUND |

†NY Jets 24
Oakland 38
Oakland 13
(OT)
New England 16
New England 24

†Baltimore 20
†Miami 3
Baltimore 10
Pittsburgh 17
Pittsburgh 27

AFC

St. Louis 17
New England 20

Feb. 3, 2002
Superdome, New Orleans, Louisiana

†Wild Card Team

Philadelphia 24
St. Louis 29

NFC

Philadelphia 33
Chicago 19
Green Bay 17
St. Louis 45

†Tampa Bay 9
Philadelphia 31
†San Francisco 15
†Green Bay 25

†Wild Card Team

Playoff Game Summaries

Team records listed in parentheses indicate records before game.

WILD CARD ROUND

AFC

Raiders, 38-24

NY Jets (10-6)	0	3	7	14—	**24**
Oakland (10-6)	6	10	0	22—	**38**

Date—Jan. 12. **Att**—61,503. **Time**—2:56.

1st Quarter: OAK—Sebastian Janikowski 21-yd FG, 8:26; OAK—Janikowski 41-yd FG, 0:44.

2nd Quarter: NYJ—John Hall 45-yd FG, 12:45; OAK—Janikowski 45-yd FG, 6:45; OAK—Tim Brown 2-yd pass from Rich Gannon (Janikowski kick), 0:22.

3rd Quarter: NYJ—Wayne Chrebet 17-yd pass from Vinny Testaverde (Hall kick), 11:36.

4th Quarter: OAK—Zack Crockett 2-yd run (Charlie Garner run), 14:57; NYJ—Richie Anderson 3-yd pass from Testaverde (Hall kick), 10:18; OAK—Jerry Rice 21-yd pass from Gannon (Janikowski kick), 5:53; NYJ—Chrebet 4-yd pass from Testaverde (Hall kick), 1:52; OAK—Garner 80-yd run (Janikowski kick), 1:27.

Ravens, 20-3

Baltimore (10-6)	0	7	7	6—	**20**
Miami (11-5)	3	0	0	0—	**3**

Date—Jan. 13. **Att**—72,251. **Time**—2:51.

1st Quarter: MIA—Olindo Mare 33-yd FG, 12:46.

2nd Quarter: BAL—Terry Allen 4-yd run (Matt Stover kick), 13:34.

3rd Quarter: BAL—Travis Taylor 4-yd pass from Elvis Grbac (Stover kick), 1:20.

4th Quarter: BAL—Stover 35-yd FG, 11:05; BAL—Stover 40-yd FG, 2:01.

NFC

Eagles, 31-9

Tampa Bay (9-7)	3	6	0	0—	**9**
Philadelphia (11-5)	3	14	7	7—	**31**

Date—Jan. 12. **Att**—65,847. **Time**—2:59.

1st Quarter: TB—Martin Gramatica 36-yd FG, 10:48; PHI—David Akers 26-yd FG, 6:18.

2nd Quarter: PHI—Chad Lewis 16-yd pass from Donovan McNabb (Akers kick), 12:17; TB—Gramatica 32-yd FG, 6:13; PHI—Duce Staley 23-yd pass from McNabb (Akers kick), 0:35; TB—Gramatica 27-yd FG, 0:00.

3rd Quarter: PHI—Correll Buckhalter 25-yd run (Akers kick), 6:57.

4th Quarter: PHI—Damon Moore 59-yd interception return (Akers kick), 2:08.

Packers, 25-15

San Francisco (12-4)	0	7	0	8—	**15**
Green Bay (12-4)	6	0	9	10—	**25**

Date—Jan. 13. **Att**—59,825. **Time**—2:49.

1st Quarter: GB—Antonio Freeman 5-yd pass from Brett Favre (Ryan Longwell kick failed), 4:02.

2nd Quarter: SF—Garrison Hearst 2-yd run (Jose Cortez kick), 0:11.

3rd Quarter: GB—Longwell 26-yd FG, 8:52; GB—Bubba Franks 19-yd pass from Brett Favre (2-pt attempt failed), 3:26.

4th Quarter: SF—Tai Streets 14-yd pass from Jeff Garcia (Streets pass from Garcia), 12:00; GB—Longwell 45-yd FG, 7:02; GB—Ahman Green 9-yd run (Longwell kick), 1:55.

NFL Playoffs (Cont.)
DIVISIONAL SEMIFINALS

AFC

🏈 Patriots, 16-13 (OT)

Oakland (11-6)................0 7 6 0 0— **13**
New England (11-5)..........0 0 3 10 3— **16**

Date—Jan. 19. **Att**—60,292. **Time**—3:32.

2nd Quarter: OAK—James Jett 13-yd pass from Rich Gannon (Sebastian Janikowski kick), 12:14.

3rd Quarter: NE—Adam Vinatieri 23-yd FG, 8:39; OAK—Janikowski 38-yd FG, 4:14; OAK—Janikowski 45-yd FG, 1:41.

4th Quarter: NE—Tom Brady 6-yd run (Vinatieri kick), 7:52; NE—Vinatieri 45-yd FG, 0:27.

Overtime: NE—Vinatieri 23-yd FG, 6:31.

🏈 Steelers, 27-10

Baltimore (11-6)..............0 3 7 0— **10**
Pittsburgh (13-3)............10 10 0 7— **27**

Date—Jan. 20. **Att**—63,976. **Time**—3:10.

1st Quarter: PIT—Kris Brown 21-yd FG, 9:07; PIT—Amos Zereoue 1-yd run (Brown kick), 3:49.

2nd Quarter: PIT—Zereoue 1-yd run (Brown kick), 5:43; PIT—Brown 46-yd FG, 3:46; BAL—Matt Stover 26-yd FG, 0:51.

3rd Quarter: BAL—Jermaine Lewis 88-yd punt return (Stover kick), 7:18.

4th Quarter: PIT—Plaxico Burress 32-yd pass from Kordell Stewart (Brown kick), 14:11.

NFC

🏈 Eagles, 33-19

Philadelphia (12-5)...........6 7 7 13— **33**
Chicago (13-3)................0 7 7 5— **19**

Date—Jan. 19. **Att**—66,944. **Time**—2:58.

1st Quarter: PHI—David Akers 34-yd FG, 9:04; PHI—Akers 23-yd FG, 3:22.

2nd Quarter: CHI—Ahmad Merritt 47-yd run (Paul Edinger kick), 5:29; PHI—Cecil Martin 13-yd pass from Donovan McNabb (Akers kick), 0:14.

3rd Quarter: CHI—Jerry Azumah 39-yd interception return (Edinger kick), 12:25; PHI—Duce Staley 6-yd pass from McNabb (Akers kick), 5:55.

4th Quarter: CHI—Edinger 38-yd FG, (14:16); PHI—Akers 40-yd FG, 8:48; PHI—Akers 46-yd FG, 6:28; PHI—McNabb 5-yd run (Akers kick), 3:21; CHI—Safety, Sean Landeta runs out of end zone, 0:00.

🏈 Rams, 45-17

Green Bay (13-4).............7 3 0 7— **17**
St. Louis (14-2)..............7 17 14 7— **45**

Date—Jan. 20. **Att**—66,338. **Time**—3:05.

1st Quarter: ST.L—Aeneas Williams 29-yd interception return (Jeff Wilkins kick), 9:11; GB—Antonio Freeman 22-yd pass from Brett Favre (Ryan Longwell kick), 2:35.

2nd Quarter: ST.L—Torry Holt 4-yd pass from Kurt Warner (Wilkins kick), 14:58; ST.L—James Hodgins 4-yd pass from Warner (Wilkins kick), 12:36; GB—Longwell 28-yd FG, 4:18; ST.L—Wilkins 27-yd FG, 0:21.

3rd Quarter: ST.L—Marshall Faulk 7-yd run (Wilkins kick), 9:44; ST.L—Tommy Polley 34-yd interception return (Wilkins kick), 8:12.

4th Quarter: ST.L—Williams 32-yd interception return (Wilkins kick), 7:50; GB—Freeman 8-yd pass from Favre (Longwell kick), 5:46.

CONFERENCE CHAMPIONSHIPS

AFC

🏈 Patriots, 24-17

New England (12-5)..........7 7 7 3— **24**
Pittsburgh (14-3)............0 3 14 0— **17**

Date—Jan. 27. **Att**—64,704. **Time**—3:46.

1st Quarter: NE—Troy Brown 55-yd punt return (Adam Vinatieri kick), 3:42.

2nd Quarter: PIT—Kris Brown 30-yd FG, 13:33; NE—David Patten 11-yd pass from Drew Bledsoe (Vinatieri kick), 0:58.

3rd Quarter: NE—Antwan Harris 49-yd blocked FG return, lateral from Brown (Vinatieri kick), 8:51; PIT—Jerome Bettis 1-yd run (Brown kick), 5:11; PIT—Amos Zereoue 11-yd run (Brown kick), 1:29.

4th Quarter: NE—Vinatieri 44-yd FG, 11:12.

NFC

🏈 Rams, 29-24

Philadelphia (13-5)...........3 14 0 7— **24**
St. Louis (15-2)..............10 3 9 7— **29**

Date—Jan. 27. **Att**—66,502. **Time**—3:09.

1st Quarter: ST.L—Isaac Bruce 5-yd pass from Kurt Warner (Jeff Wilkins kick), 12:00; PHI—David Akers 46-yd FG, 5:44; ST.L—Wilkins 27-yd FG, 1:06.

2nd Quarter: PHI—Duce Staley 1-yd run (Akers kick), 6:56; ST.L—Wilkins 39-yd FG, 3:52; PHI—Todd Pinkston 12-yd pass from Donovan McNabb (Akers kick), 0:46.

3rd Quarter: ST.L—Wilkins 41-yd FG, 8:01; ST.L—Marshall Faulk 1-yd run (Wilkins kick), 1:18.

4th Quarter: ST.L—Faulk 1-yd run (Wilkins kick), 6:55; PHI—McNabb 3-yd run (Akers kick), 2:56.

Super Bowl XXXVI

Sunday, Feb. 3, 2002 at the Superdome in New Orleans, Louisiana

St. Louis (16-2) 3	0	0	14—	**17**
New England (13-5)..........0	14	3	3—	**20**

1st: ST.L—Jeff Wilkins 50-yd FG, 3:10. Drive: 48 yards in 10 plays. Key play: Marshall Faulk 14-yd pass from Kurt Warner to NE 39.

2nd: NE—Ty Law 47-yd interception return (Adam Vinatieri kick), 8:49. **NE**—David Patten 8-yd pass from Tom Brady (Vinatieri kick), 0:31. Drive: 40 yards in 5 plays. Key play: Terrell Buckley 15-yd return of Ricky Proehl fumble to St.L 40.

3rd: NE—Vinatieri 37-yd FG, 1:18. Drive: 14 yards in 5 plays. Key play: Otis Smith 30-yd interception return to St.L 33.

4th: St.L—Warner 2-yd run (Wilkins kick), 9:31. Drive: 77 yards in 12 plays. Key plays: Faulk 22-yd pass from Warner to NE 9. **St.L**—Proehl 26-yd pass from Warner (Wilkins kick), 1:30. Drive: 55 yards in 3 plays. Key play: Az-zahir Hakim 18-yd pass from Warner to NE 37. **NE**—Vinatieri 48-yd FG, 0:00. Drive: 53 yards in 9 plays. Key play: Troy Brown 23-yd pass from Brady to St.L 36.

Favorite: Rams by 14   **Attendance:** 72,922
Field: Artificial Turf   **Time:** 3:24
Start time: 5:40 CST   **TV Rating:** 40.4/61 share (FOX)
MVP—Tom Brady, New England QB (16-27 for 145 yds, 1 TD, 0 INT)

Officials: Bernie Kukar (referee); Jeff Rice (umpire); Ron Phares (LJ); Laird Hayes (SJ); Mark Hittner (HL); Scott Green (BJ); Pete Morelli (FJ).

Team Statistics

	Rams	Patriots
First downs...........................26		15
Rushing 7		6
Passing 16		8
Penalty 3		1
3rd down efficiency.................5/13		2/11
4th down efficiency 0/0		0/0
Total offense (net yards)..............427		267
Plays 69		54
Average gain 6.2		4.9
Rushes/yards 22/90		25/133
Passing yards (net) 337		134
Times sacked/yards lost 3/28		2/11
Passing yards (gross) 365		145
Completions/attempts................28/44		16/27
Yards per pass 7.2		4.6
Times intercepted 2		0
Return yardage 88		181
Punt returns/yards 3/6		1/4
Kickoff returns/yards 4/82		4/100
Interceptions/yards...................0/0		2/77
Fumbles/lost 2/1		0/0
Penalties/yards.....................6/39		5/31
Punts/average 4/39.8		8/43.1
Field Goals made/attempted 1/2		2/2
Time of possession 33:30		26:30

Individual Statistics

St. Louis Rams

Passing	Att	Cmp	Pct.	Yds	TD	Int
Kurt Warner.........44	28	63.6	365	1	2

Receiving	No	Yds	Avg	Long	TD
Az-zahir Hakim 5	90	18.0	29	0
Isaac Bruce 5	56	11.2	22	0
Torry Holt 5	49	9.8	18	0
Marshall Faulk 4	54	13.5	22	0
Ricky Proehl 3	71	23.7	30	1
Jeff Robinson 2	18	9.0	12	0
Ernie Conwell 2	8	4.0	9	0
Yo Murphy 1	11	11.0	11	0
James Hodgins 1	8	8.0	8	0
TOTAL....................28	365	13.0	30	1

Rushing	Car	Yds	Avg	Long	TD
Marshall Faulk 17	76	4.5	15	0
Kurt Warner 3	6	2.0	5	1
Az-zahir Hakim 1	5	5.0	5	0
James Hodgins 1	3	3.0	3	0
TOTAL....................22	90	4.1	15	1

Field Goals	20-29	30-39	40-49	50-59	Total
Jeff Wilkins 0-0	0-0	0-0	1-2	1-2

Punting	No	Yds	Avg	Long	In 20	TB
John Baker 4	159	39.8	49	3	1

Punt Returns	Ret	Yds	Long	Avg	FC	TD
Dre' Bly 3	6	7	2.0	2	0

Kickoff Returns	Ret	Yds	Long	Avg	FC	TD
Yo Murphy 3	81	38	27.0	0	0
Marshall Faulk 1	1	1	1.0	0	0
TOTAL....................4	82	38	20.5	0	0

Interceptions	No	Yds	Long	Avg	TD
none

Sacks
Grant Wistrom 1
Leonard Little 1

Most Tackles (solo)
Tommy Polley 6

New England Patriots

Passing	Att	Cmp	Pct.	Yds	TD	Int
Tom Brady 27	16	59.3	145	1	0

Receiving	No	Yds	Avg	Long	TD
Troy Brown 6	89	14.8	23	0
J.R. Redmond 3	24	8.0	11	0
Jermaine Wiggins 2	14	7.0	8	0
Marc Edwards 2	7	3.5	5	0
David Patten 1	8	8.0	8	1
Antowan Smith 1	4	4.0	4	0
Kevin Faulk 1	-1	-1.0	-1	0
TOTAL...................16	145	9.1	23	1

Rushing	Car	Yds	Avg	Long	TD
Antowain Smith 18	92	5.1	17	0
David Patten 1	22	22.0	22	0
Kevin Faulk 2	15	7.5	8	0
Marc Edwards 2	5	2.5	3	0
Tom Brady 1	3	3.0	3	0
J.R. Redmond 1	-4	-4.0	-4	0
TOTAL...................25	133	5.3	22	0

Field Goals	20-29	30-39	40-49	50-59	Total
Adam Vinatieri 0-0	1-1	1-1	0-0	2-2

Punting	No	Yds	Avg	Long	In 20	TB
Ken Walter 8	345	43.1	53	4	2

Punt Returns	Ret	Yds	Long	Avg	FC	TD
Troy Brown 1	4	4	4.0	1	0

Kickoff Returns	Ret	Yds	Long	Avg	FC	TD
Patrick Pass...............3	85	35	28.3	0	0
Troy Brown 1	15	15	15.0	0	0
TOTAL....................4	100	35	25.0	0	0

Interceptions	No	Yds	Long	Avg	TD
Ty Law 1	47	47	47.0	1
Otis Smith 1	30	30	30.0	0
TOTAL....................2	77	47	38.5	1

Sacks
Three tied at 1.

Most Tackles (solo)
Ty Law 7

Super Bowl Finalists' Playoff Statistics

St. Louis Rams (2-1)

Passing	Att	Cmp	Pct.	Yds	TD	Rating
Kurt Warner	107	68	63.6	793	4	86.7

Interceptions: Warner 3.

Top Receivers	No	Yds	Avg	Long	TD
Torry Holt	15	191	12.7	50	1
Isaac Bruce	14	159	11.4	22	1
Marshall Faulk	14	114	8.1	23	0
Az-zahir Hakim	11	149	13.5	29	0
Ernie Conwell	5	41	8.2	19	0

Top Rushers	Car	Yds	Avg	Long	TD
Marshall Faulk	64	317	5.0	38	3
Az-zahir Hakim	2	14	7.0	9	0
Kurt Warner	9	8	0.9	5	1
James Hodgins	1	3	3.0	3	0

Touchdowns	TD	Run	Rec	Ret	Pts
Marshall Faulk	3	3	0	0	18
Aeneas Williams	2	0	0	2	12

Six tied with 1 each for 6 pts.

Kicking		PAT/Att	FG/Att	Lg	Pts
Jeff Wilkins		10/10	5/7	50	25

Punts	No	Yds	Avg	Long	In20
John Baker	12	504	42.0	53	6

Most Interceptions		Most Sacks	
Aeneas Williams	3	Leonard Little	3
Tommy Polley	2	Grant Wistrom	2

New England Patriots (3-0)

Passing	Att	Cmp	Pct.	Yds	TD	Rate
Tom Brady	97	60	61.9	572	1	77.3
Drew Bledsoe	21	10	47.6	102	1	77.9

Interceptions: Brady 1.

Top Receivers	No	Yds	Avg	Long	TD
Troy Brown	18	253	14.1	29	0
Jermaine Wiggins	14	89	6.4	22	0
David Patten	13	154	11.8	25	2
J.R. Redmond	9	69	7.7	20	0
Marc Edwards	9	62	6.9	13	0

Top Rushers	Car	Yds	Avg	Long	TD
Antowain Smith	53	204	3.8	19	0
David Patten	1	22	22.0	22	0
Tom Brady	8	22	2.8	6-td	1
Kevin Faulk	3	14	4.7	8	0

Touchdowns	TD	Run	Rec	Ret	Pts
David Patten	2	0	2	0	12
Antwan Harris	1	0	0	1	6
Ty Law	1	0	0	1	6
Troy Brown	1	0	0	1	6
Tom Brady	1	1	0	0	6

Kicking		PAT/Att	FG/Att	Lg	Pts
Adam Vinatieri		6/6	6/7	48	24

Punts	No	Yds	Avg	Long	In20
Ken Walter	23	899	39.1	53	7

Most Interceptions	Most Sacks	
Five tied with 1 each.	Willie McGinest	2
	Tedy Bruschi	1.5

NFL Playoff Leaders

Passing Efficiency
(Minimum of 25 attempts)

	Gm	Att	Cmp	Cmp%	Yards	Avg Gain	TD	TD%	Int	Int%	Rating
Vinny Testaverde, NYJ	1	41	27	65.9	277	6.76	3	7.3	0	0.0	109.5
Rich Gannon, Oak	2	60	40	66.7	453	7.55	3	5.0	0	0.0	105.8
Jeff Garcia, SF	1	32	22	68.8	233	7.28	1	3.1	1	3.1	87.1
Kurt Warner, St.L	3	107	68	63.6	793	7.41	4	3.7	3	2.8	86.7
Donovan McNabb, Phi	3	95	60	63.2	627	6.60	5	5.3	3	3.2	86.6

Receptions

	No	Yds	Avg	Long	TD
Troy Brown, NE	18	253	14.1	29	0
Duce Staley, Phi	17	139	8.2	23-td	2
Torry Holt, St.L	15	191	12.7	50	1
Isaac Bruce, St.L	14	159	11.4	22	1
Marshall Faulk, St.L	14	114	8.1	23	0
Jermaine Wiggins, NE	14	89	6.4	22	0

Rushing

	No	Yds	Avg	Long	TD
Marshall Faulk, St.L	64	317	5.0	38	3
Charlie Garner, Oak	32	222	6.9	80-td	1
Antowain Smith, NE	53	204	3.8	19	0
Ahman Green, GB	37	180	4.9	49	1
Duce Staley, Phi	44	139	3.2	20	1

Touchdowns

	TD	Rush	Rec	Ret	Pts
Antonio Freeman, GB	3	0	3	0	18
Marshall Faulk, St.L	3	3	0	0	18
Duce Staley, Phi	3	1	2	0	18
Amos Zereoue, Pit	3	3	0	0	18
Aeneas Williams, St.L	2	0	0	2	12
Wayne Chrebet, NYJ	2	0	2	0	12
Donovan McNabb, Phi	2	2	0	0	12
David Patten, NE	2	0	2	0	12

Kicking

	PAT	FG	Long	Pts
David Akers, Phi	10/10	6/6	46	28
Jeff Wilkins, St.L	10/10	5/7	50	25
Adam Vinatieri, NE	6/6	6/7	48	24
Sebastian Janikowski, Oak	4/4	5/5	45	19
Kris Brown, Pit	5/5	3/5	46	14

Interceptions

	No	Yds	Long	TD
Damon Moore, Phi	3	77	59-td	1
Aeneas Williams, St.L	3	61	32-td	2
Tommy Polley, St.L	2	35	34-td	1
Brent Alexander, Pit	2	32	32	0
Twenty tied with 1 each.				

Sacks

	No
Jason Gildon, Pit	3
Leonard Little, St.L	3
Grant Wistrom, St.L	2
Willie McGinest, NE	2
Hugh Douglas, Phi	2
Simeon Rice, TB	2

NFL Pro Bowl

52nd NFL Pro Bowl Game and 32nd AFC-NFC contest (series is tied, 16-16). **Date:** Feb. 9, 2002 at Aloha Stadium in Honolulu. **Coaches:** Bill Cowher, Pit. (AFC) and Andy Reid, Phi. (NFC). **Most Valuable Player:** QB Rich Gannon, Oak. (8 for 10, 137 yds, 2 TD).

AFC	21	7	0	10—	**38**
NFC	13	3	0	14—	**30**

1st: NFC—Ahman Green 2-yd run (David Akers kick), 14:33; NFC—Akers 29-yd FG, 11:30; AFC—Marvin Harrison 55-yd pass from Rich Gannon (Jason Elam kick), 10:32; AFC—Curtis Martin 4-yd run (Elam kick), 8:36; AFC—Priest Holmes 39-yd run (Elam kick), 4:43; NFC—Akers 41-yd FG, 0:00.

2nd: AFC—Ken Dilger 18-yd pass from Gannon (Elam kick), 12:03; NFC—Akers 49-yd FG, 0:06.

4th: NFC—Terrell Owens 8-yd pass from Donovan McNabb (Akers kick), 8:12; AFC—Elam 38-yd FG, 3:41; AFC—Ray Lewis 13-yd interception return (Elam kick), 2:49; NFC—Garrison Hearst 15-yd pass from McNabb (Akers kick), 1:32.

Attendance— 50,301. **TV Rating**— 4.3/9 share (ABC). **Time**— 3:26.

STARTING LINEUPS

As voted on by NFL players, coaches, and fans. (*) denotes injured and unable to play.

American Conference

Pos	Offense	Pos	Defense
WR	Marvin Harrison, Ind.	E	John Abraham, NYJ
WR	Rod Smith*, Den.	E	Marcellus Wiley, SD
TE	Tony Gonzalez*, KC	T	Trevor Pryce*, Den.
T	Lincoln Kennedy, Oak.	T	John Randle, Sea.
T	Jonathan Ogden, Bal.	LB	Jason Gildon, Pit.
G	Alan Faneca, Pit.	LB	Jamir Miller, Cle.
G	Will Shields, KC	LB	Ray Lewis, Bal.
C	Kevin Mawae, NYJ	CB	Sam Madison*, Mia.
QB	Rich Gannon, Oak.	CB	Charles Woodson*, Oak.
RB	Curtis Martin, NYJ	SS	Rodney Harrison, SD
FB	Larry Centers, Buf.	FS	Rod Woodson, Bal.
K	Jason Elam, Den.	P	Shane Lechler, Oak.
KR	Jermaine Lewis, Bal.	ST	Ian Gold, Den.

Reserves

Offense: WR—Tim Brown, Oak. and Jimmy Smith*, Jax.; **TE**—Shannon Sharpe, Bal. and Dwayne Carswell, Den.; **T**—Walter Jones, Sea.; **G**—Ruben Brown, Buf.; **C**—Bruce Matthews, Ten.; **QB**—Tom Brady, NE and Kordell Stewart, Pit.; **RB**—Priest Holmes, KC and Jerome Bettis*, Pit.

Defense: E—Jevon Kearse, Ten.; **T**—Sam Adams, Bal.; **LB**—Junior Seau, SD and Zach Thomas*, Mia.; **CB**—Deltha O'Neal, Den.; **SS**—Lawyer Milloy, NE.

Replacements: OFFENSE—WR Troy Brown, NE for R. Smith; WR Hines Ward, Pit. for J. Smith; TE Ken Dilger, Ind. for Gonzalez; RB Corey Dillon, Cin. for Bettis. DEFENSE—T Gary Walker, Ten. for Pryce; LB Al Wilson, Den. for Thomas; CB Ryan McNeil, SD for Madison; CB Ty Law, NE for Woodson. NEED PLAYER—LB Kendrell Bell, Pit.

National Conference

Pos	Offense	Pos	Defense
WR	David Boston, Ari.	E	Hugh Douglas, Phi.
WR	Terrell Owens, SF	E	Michael Strahan, NYG
TE	Bubba Franks, GB	T	La'Roi Glover, NO
T	Orlando Pace*, St.L	T	Warren Sapp*, TB
T	Chris Samuels, Wash.	LB	LaVar Arrington, Wash.
G	Larry Allen*, Dal.	LB	Derrick Brooks*, TB
G	Ron Stone, NYG	LB	Brian Urlacher, Chi.
C	Olin Kreutz, Chi.	CB	Ronde Barber, TB
QB	Brett Favre*, GB	CB	Aeneas Williams, St.L
RB	Marshall Faulk, St.L	SS	Sammy Knight, NO
FB	Mike Alstott, TB	FS	Brian Dawkins, Phi.
K	David Akers, Phi.	P	Todd Sauerbrun, Car.
KR	Steve Smith, Car.	ST	Larry Whigham, Chi.

Reserves

Offense: WR—Isaac Bruce*, St.L and Keyshawn Johnson, TB; **TE**—Wesley Walls*, Car. and Chad Lewis, Phi.; **T**—James Williams, Chi.; **G**—Ray Brown, SF; **C**—Matt Birk*, Min.; **QB**—Jeff Garcia, SF and Kurt Warner, St.L; **RB**—Ahman Green, GB and Garrison Hearst, SF.

Defense: E—Robert Porcher, Det.; **T**—Bryant Young, SF; **LB**—Jessie Armstead, NYG and Jeremiah Trotter, Phi.; **CB**—Troy Vincent*, Phi.; **SS**—John Lynch, TB.

Replacements: OFFENSE—WR Torry Holt, St.L for Bruce; T Tra Thomas, Phi. for Pace; G Adam Timmerman, St.L for Allen; C Jeremy Newberry, SF for Birk; TE Byron Chamberlain, Min. for Walls; QB Donovan McNabb, Phi. for Favre. DEFENSE—T Ted Washington, Chi. for Sapp; LB Dexter Coakley, Dal. for Brooks; CB Champ Bailey, Wash. for Vincent. NEED PLAYER—LB Keith Brooking, Atl.

Annual Awards

The NFL does not sanction any of the major postseason awards for players and coaches, but many are given out. Among the presenters for the 2001 regular season were AP, The Maxwell Football Club of Philadelphia (Bert Bell Award for player; Greasy Neale Award for coach), *The Sporting News* and the Pro Football Writers of America/*Pro Football Weekly*.

Most Valuable Player

Kurt Warner, St. Louis, QB..........................AP
Marshall Faulk, St. Louis, RB.............*TSN*, Bell, PFWA

Offensive Players of the Year

Marshall Faulk, St. Louis, RB...................AP, PFWA

Defensive Player of the Year

Michael Strahan, NY Giants, DE...............AP, PFWA

Rookies of the Year

NFL	Kendrell Bell, Pittsburgh, LB	..........*TSN*, PFWA
Offense	Anthony Thomas, Chicago, RB	........AP, PFWA
Defense	Kendrell Bell, Pittsburgh, LB	...........AP, PFWA

Coach of the Year

Dick Jauron, Chicago.............AP, *TSN*, Neale, PFWA

2001 All-NFL Team

The 2001 All-NFL team combining the All-Pro selections of the Associated Press, *The Sporting News (TSN)* and the Pro Football Writers of America/*Pro Football Weekly* (PFWA). Holdovers from the 2000 All-NFL Team in **bold** type.

Offense

Pos		Selectors
WR—	David Boston, Arizona	AP, *TSN*, PFWA
WR—	**Terrell Owens**, San Francisco	AP, *TSN*, PFWA
TE—	**Tony Gonzalez**, Kansas City	AP, *TSN*, PFWA
T—	**Orlando Pace**, St. Louis	AP, *TSN*, PFWA
T—	Walter Jones, Seattle	AP
T—	**Jonathan Ogden**, Baltimore	*TSN*, PFWA
G—	Alan Faneca, Pittsburgh	AP, *TSN*, PFWA
G—	**Larry Allen**, Dallas	AP, *TSN*, PFWA
C—	**Kevin Mawae**, NY Jets	AP, *TSN*, PFWA
QB—	Kurt Warner, St. Louis	AP, *TSN*, PFWA
RB—	**Marshall Faulk**, St. Louis	AP, *TSN*, PFWA
RB—	Priest Holmes, Kansas City	AP
RB—	Curtis Martin, NY Jets	*TSN*, PFWA

Defense

Pos		Selectors
DE—	Michael Strahan, NY Giants	AP, *TSN*, PFWA
DE—	John Abraham, NY Jets	AP, *TSN*, PFWA
DT—	Ted Washington, Chicago	AP, *TSN*
DT—	**Warren Sapp**, Tampa Bay	AP, *TSN*, PFWA
DT—	Sam Adams, Baltimore	PFWA
LB—	Brian Urlacher, Chicago	AP, *TSN*, PFWA
LB—	**Ray Lewis**, Baltimore	AP, *TSN*
LB—	Jason Gildon, Pittsburgh	AP, PFWA
LB—	Jamir Miller, Cleveland	AP, *TSN*, PFWA
CB—	Aeneas Williams, St. Louis	AP, *TSN*, PFWA
CB—	Ronde Barber, Tampa Bay	AP, PFWA
CB—	Charles Woodson, Oakland	*TSN*
S—	Brian Dawkins, Philadelphia	AP, *TSN*, PFWA
S—	Mike Brown, Chicago	AP
S—	Rodney Harrison, San Diego	*TSN*
S—	**John Lynch**, Tampa Bay	PFWA

Specialists

Pos		Selectors
PK—	David Akers, Philadelphia	AP, *TSN*, PFWA
P—	Todd Sauerbrun, Carolina	AP, *TSN*, PFWA
KR—	Steve Smith, Carolina	AP, *TSN*, PFWA

Pos		Selectors
PR—	Jermaine Lewis, Baltimore	*TSN*
PR—	Troy Brown, New England	PFWA
ST—	Larry Whigham, Chicago	PFWA

2002 College Draft

First and second round selections at the 67th annual NFL College Draft held April 20-21, 2002, in New York City. Nineteen underclassmen were among the first 65 players chosen and are listed in capital LETTERS. (*) indicates supplemental pick.

First Round

No	Team		Pos
1	Houston	David Carr, Fresno St.	QB
2	Carolina	JULIUS PEPPERS, North Carolina	DE
3	Detroit	Joey Harrington, Oregon	QB
4	Buffalo	Mike Williams, Texas	OT
5	San Diego	Quentin Jammer, Texas	CB
6	Kansas City	Ryan Sims, North Carolina	DT
7	Minnesota	Bryant McKinnie, Miami-FL	OT
8	Dallas	ROY WILLIAMS, Oklahoma	SS
9	Jacksonville	John Henderson, Tennessee	DT
10	Cincinnati	Levi Jones, Arizona St.	OT
11	Indianapolis	Dwight Freeney, Syracuse	DE
12	Arizona	Wendell Bryant, Wisconsin	DT
13	New Orleans	DONTE' STALLWORTH, Tennessee	WR
14	NY Giants	JEREMY SHOCKEY, Miami-FL	TE
15	Tennessee	ALBERT HAYNESWORTH, Tennessee	DT
16	Cleveland	WILLIAM GREEN, Boston College	RB
17	Oakland	PHILLIP BUCHANON, Miami-FL	CB
18	Atlanta	T.J. DUCKETT, Michigan St.	RB
19	Denver	ASHLEY LELIE, Hawaii	WR
20	Green Bay	Javon Walker, Florida St.	WR
21	New England	Daniel Graham, Colorado	TE
22	NY Jets	Bryan Thomas, UAB	DE
23	Oakland	Napoleon Harris, Northwestern	LB
24	Baltimore	Edward Reed, Miami-FL	FS
25	New Orleans	CHARLES GRANT, Georgia	DE
26	Philadelphia	LITO SHEPPARD, Florida	CB
27	San Francisco	Mike Rumph, Miami-FL	CB
28	Seattle	JERRAMY STEVENS, Washington	TE
29	Chicago	Marc Colombo, Boston College	OT
30	Pittsburgh	Kendall Simmons, Auburn	OT
31	St. Louis	Robert Thomas, UCLA	LB
32	Washington	Patrick Ramsey, Tulane	QB

Second Round

No	Team		Pos
33	Houston	JABAR GAFFNEY, Florida	WR
34	Carolina	DeShaun Foster, UCLA	RB
35	Detroit	Kalimba Edwards, South Carolina	DE
36	Buffalo	JOSH REED, LSU	WR
37	Dallas	Andre Gurode, Colorado	C
38	Minnesota	Raonall Smith, Washington St.	LB
39	San Diego	TONIU FONOTI, Nebraska	OT
40	Jacksonville	MIKE PEARSON, Florida	OT
41	Cincinnati	Lamont Thompson, Washington St.	FS
42	Indianapolis	Larry Tripplett, Washington	DT
43	Kansas City	Eddie Freeman, UAB	DT
44	New Orleans	LeCharles Bentley, Ohio St.	C
45	Tennessee	Clevan Williams, Stanford	FS
46	NY Giants	Tim Carter, Auburn	WR
47	Cleveland	Andre Davis, Virginia Tech	WR
48	San Diego	RECHE CALDWELL, Florida	WR
49	Arizona	Levar Fisher, N.C. State	LB
50	Houston*	Chester Pitts, San Diego St.	OT
51	Denver	CLINTON PORTIS, Miami-FL	RB
52	Baltimore	Anthony Weaver, Notre Dame	DT
53	Oakland	Langston Walker, California	OT
54	Seattle	Maurice Morris, Oregon	RB
55	Oakland	Doug Jolley, BYU	TE
56	Washington	Ladell Betts, Iowa	RB
57	NY Jets	Jon McGraw, Kansas St.	FS
58	Philadelphia	Michael Lewis, Colorado	SS
59	Philadelphia	Sheldon Brown, South Carolina	CB
60	San Diego	Anton Palepoi, UNLV	DE
61	Buffalo	Ryan Denney, BYU	DE
62	Pittsburgh	Antwaan Randle El, Indiana	WR
63	Dallas	ANTONIO BRYANT, Pittsburgh	WR
64	St. Louis	Travis Fisher, Central Florida	CB
65	New England	Deion Branch, Louisville	WR

NFL Europe

Final 2002 Standings

	W	L	T	Pct.	PF	PA
*Rhein	7	3	0	.700	166	156
*Berlin	6	4	0	.600	231	188
Frankfurt	6	4	0	.600	189	174
Scotland	5	5	0	.500	197	172
Amsterdam	4	6	0	.400	218	202
Barcelona	2	8	0	.200	202	311

*World Bowl participants

Note: The teams with the top two records after the regular season play in the World Bowl. Berlin (6-4) advanced over Frankfurt (6-4) due to a better points differential in head-to-head games.

World Bowl X

June 22, 2002 at Rheinstadion, Dusseldorf, Germany (Att: 53,109)

Berlin (6-4)	13	7	3	3 —	**26**
Rhein (7-3)	0	0	7	13 —	**20**

MVP: Dane Looker, Berlin, WR (11 catches for 111 yards and 2 TDs)

Regular Season Individual Leaders

Passing Efficiency
(Min. 140 pass attempts)

	Att	Cmp	Cmp Pct	Yds	Yds/ Att	TD	TD Pct	Long	Int	Int Pct	Rating
Ted White, Bar	171	96	56.1	1165	6.81	13	7.6	69	5	2.9	90.4
Kevin Daft, Ams	301	178	59.1	1981	6.58	15	5.0	59	9	3.0	83.0
Todd Husak, Ber	356	208	58.4	2386	6.70	14	3.9	66	14	3.9	75.4
Joe Hamilton, Fra	193	99	51.3	1301	6.74	8	4.1	68	8	4.1	69.5
Tee Martin, Rhe	203	101	49.8	1017	5.01	5	2.5	35	6	3.0	60.3

Scoring

Touchdowns

	TD	Rus	Rec	Ret	Pts
Rafael Cooper, Ams	10	8	1	1	60
Jamal Robertson, Rhe	8	8	0	0	48
Richmond Flowers, Bar	6	0	6	0	36
Curtis Alexander, Fra	6	6	0	0	36
Herbert Goodman, Sco	6	6	0	0	36
Anthony White, Ber	6	6	0	0	36

Kicking

	PAT	FG/FGA	Lg	Pts
Ola Kimrin, Fra	20/22	12/24	52	57
Jesus Angoy, Bar	24/24	10/12	47	54
Rob Hart, Sco	20/20	10/10	32	50
Manfred Burgsmuller, Rhe	19/19	9/10	36	46
Danny Boyd, Ber	9/9	10/19	47	39

Rushing

	Car	Yards	Avg	Long	TD
Herbert Goodman, Sco	206	877	4.3	36-td	6
Curtis Alexander, Fra	152	831	5.5	36-td	6
Jamal Robertson, Rhe	151	792	5.2	90-td	8
Rafael Cooper, Ams	155	751	4.8	77-td	8
Anthony White, Ber	113	525	4.6	62	6

Receptions

	No	Yards	Avg	Long	TD
Dane Looker, Ber	54	661	12.2	55-td	5
Marcus Knight, Ams	40	546	13.7	51	5
Anthony White, Ber	38	370	9.7	41	0
DeRonnie Pitts, Bar	36	393	10.9	40-td	5
Richmond Flowers, Bar	34	508	14.9	61-td	6
Ryan Collins, Ams	34	280	8.2	31-td	2

Punting

	No	Yards	Avg	Long	In20
Andrew Bayes, Ams	53	2338	44.1	63	12
Gabe Lindstrom, Fra	47	2008	42.7	66	14
Dirk Johnson, Rhe	56	2391	42.7	67	23
Aron Langley, Sco	41	1722	42.0	61	13
Brian Morton, Ber	30	1197	39.9	54	6

Sacks

	No
Ron Warner, Bar	6.0
Jerome Davis, Fra	5.5
Dwayne Missouri, Ber	5.5
Keith Washington, Bar	5.0
Mike Sutton, Ams	4.5
DeAngelo Lloyd, Fra	4.5

Interceptions

	No	Yds	Long	TD
Deke Cooper, Rhe	5	27	26	0
Ahmad Hawkins, Ber	4	42	37-td	

Seven tied with 3 each.

All-NFL Europe League Team

The All-NFL Europe League Team as selected by NFL Europe coaches, media and fans.

Offense
QB	Todd Husak, Ber
WR	Marcus Knight, Ams
WR	Dane Looker, Ber
WR	Jimi Redmond, Fra
RB	Jamal Robertson, Rhe
TE	Ryan Collins, Ams
T	Jarvis Borum, Sco
G	Al Jackson, Rhe
C	Ben Hamilton, Ber
G	Josh Lovelady, Sco
T	Patrick Venzke, Rhe

Defense
DE	Mike Sutton, Ams
DT	Norris McCleary, Fra
DT	Brandon Miller, Rhe
DE	Jerome Davis, Fra
LB	Tim Johnson, Rhe
LB	June Waddy, Ber
LB	Maugaula Tuitele, Rhe
CB	Earthwind Moreland, Rhe
S	Deke Cooper, Rhe
S	Scott Shields, Sco
CB	Corey Ivy, Fra

Special Teams
K	Jesus Angoy, Bar
P	Dirk Johnson, Rhe
Spec.	J.J. Moses, Sco

Annual Awards

Offensive MVP	Jamal Robertson, Rhein, RB
Defensive MVP	Deke Cooper, Rhein, S
Coach of the Year	Peter Vaas, Berlin

Canadian Football League
Final 2001 Standings

Division champions (*) and playoff qualifiers (†) are noted. Ties and overtime losses (OTL) are each worth one point in the standings.

East Division

	W	L	T	OTL	Pts	PF	PA
*Winnipeg	14	4	0	0	28	509	383
†Hamilton	11	7	0	0	22	440	420
†Montreal	9	9	0	0	18	454	419
Toronto	7	11	0	1	15	432	455

West Division

	W	L	T	OTL	Pts	PF	PA
*Edmonton	9	9	0	1	19	439	463
†Calgary	8	10	0	1	17	478	476
†Brit. Columbia	8	10	0	0	16	417	445
Saskatchewan	6	12	0	0	12	308	416

Playoffs
Division Semifinals (Nov. 11)

East: at Hamilton 24 .... Montreal 12
West: at Calgary 28 .... B.C. 19

Division Finals (Nov. 18)

East: at Winnipeg 27 .... Hamilton 13
West: Calgary 34 .... at Edmonton 16

89th Grey Cup Championship
November 25, 2001 at Olympic Stadium in Montreal, Quebec

(Att: 65,255)

Winnipeg	4	0	8	7 — 19
Calgary	0	17	0	10 — 27

MVP: Marcus Crandell, Calgary, QB (18-35 for 309 yards, 2 TD, 0 INT)

Regular Season Individual Leaders
Passing Yards

	Att	Cmp	Cmp Pct	Yds	Yds/ Att	TD	TD Pct	Int	Int Pct	Rating
Khari Jones, Win.	546	329	60.3	4545	8.3	30	5.5	23	4.2	87.8
Danny McManus, Ham.	571	326	57.1	4465	7.8	19	3.3	9	1.6	86.7
Anthony Calvillo, Mon.	412	250	60.7	3671	8.9	16	3.9	9	2.2	93.7
Jason Maas, Edm.	391	232	59.3	3646	9.3	21	5.4	12	3.1	95.4
Damon Allen, B.C.	471	251	53.3	3631	7.7	18	3.8	14	3.0	78.8

Scoring

Touchdowns	TD	Rus	Rec	Ret	Pts
Mike Pringle, Mon.	17	16	1	0	102
Milt Stegall, Win.	14	0	14	0	84
Mike Jenkins, Toronto	13	8	5	0	78
Sean Millington, B.C.	12	11	1	0	72
Edward Hervey, Edm.	12	0	12	0	72

Kicking	PAT	FG	S*	Pts
Sean Fleming, Edm.	37/37	45/57	11	183
Paul Osbaldiston, Ham.	34/34	47/58	8	183
Terry Baker, Mon.	43/43	42/53	12	181
Mark McLoughlin, Calg.	44/44	42/57	10	180
Troy Westwood, Win.	54/54	31/51	12	159

*Singles (or Rouges)

Rushing

	Car	Yards	Avg	TD
Mike Jenkins, Tor.	271	1484	5.5	8
Kelvin Anderson, Calg.	262	1383	5.3	6
Mike Pringle, Mon.	262	1323	5.0	16
Darren Davis, Sask.	217	1243	5.7	4
Ronald Williams, Ham.	243	1200	4.9	8

Receptions

	No	Yards	Avg	TD
Terry Vaughn, Edm.	98	1497	15.3	5
Milt Stegall, Win.	81	1214	15.0	14
Darren Flutie, Ham.	80	1206	15.1	6
Derrell Mitchell, Tor.	78	1376	17.6	6
Edward Hervey, Edm.	77	1447	18.8	12
Andrew Grigg, Ham.	77	1150	14.9	3

All-CFL Team

Offense	Defense
WR Travis Moore, Calg.	E Joe Montford, Ham.
WR Edward Hervey, Edm.	E Elfrid Payton, Tor.
T Bruce Beaton, Edm.	T Doug Brown, Win.
T Dave Mudge, Win.	T Joe Fleming, Calg.
G Jay McNeil, Calg.	LB Chris Shelling, Ham.
G Brett MacNeil, Win.	LB Barrin Simpson, B.C.
C Brian Chiu, Mon.	LB Terry Ray, Edm.
QB Khari Jones, Win.	DB Juran Bolden, Win.
RB Kelvin Anderson, Calg.	DB Harold Nash, Win.
RB Mike Jenkins, Tor.	DB Wayne Shaw, Tor.
SB Terry Vaughn, Edm.	DB Eric Carter, B.C.
SB Milt Stegall, Win.	S Rob Hitchcock, Ham.

Specialists
K—Paul Osbaldiston, Ham.
P—Terry Baker, Mon.
Special Teams—Charles Roberts, Win.

Most Outstanding Awards

Player .... Khari Jones, Winnipeg, QB	Rookie .... Barrin Simpson, British Columbia, LB
Canadian .... Doug Brown, Winnipeg, DT	Tom Pate Award (Sportsmanship) .... Rick Walters, Edmonton, SB
Offensive Lineman .... Dave Mudge, Winnipeg, T	
Defensive Player .... Joe Montford, Hamilton, DE	Coach .... Dave Ritchie, Winnipeg

Arena Football
Final 2002 Standings

Division champions (*) and playoff qualifiers (†) are noted; top twelve teams advance to the playoffs, with top four receiving first-round byes.

American Conference
Central Division

	W	L	T	Pct.	PF	PA
*Chicago	9	5	0	.643	747	671
†Grand Rapids	8	6	0	.571	756	759
†Indiana	7	7	0	.500	669	640
Detroit	1	13	0	.071	544	740

Western Division

	W	L	T	Pct.	PF	PA
*San Jose	13	1	0	.929	878	660
†Arizona	11	3	0	.786	729	624
†Los Angeles	8	6	0	.571	731	694
†Dallas	7	7	0	.500	742	755

National Conference
Eastern Division

	W	L	T	Pct.	PF	PA
*New Jersey	9	5	0	.643	714	662
†Buffalo	6	8	0	.429	627	675
Toronto	5	9	0	.357	644	656
New York	3	11	0	.214	666	804

Southern Division

	W	L	T	Pct.	PF	PA
*Orlando	7	7	0	.500	637	669
†Carolina	6	8	0	.429	624	665
†Tampa Bay	6	8	0	.429	666	715
Georgia	6	8	0	.429	703	688

Annual Awards

Tinactin Ironman of the Year . . . . Greg Hopkins, Los Angeles
Offensive Player of the Year . . . . Mark Grieb, San Jose
Defensive Player of the Year . . . . . . Clevan Thomas, San Jose
Rookie of the Year . . . . Clevan Thomas, San Jose
Coach of the Year . . . . Darren Arbet, San Jose

ArenaBowl XVI

August 18, 2002 at the Compaq Center at San Jose, Calif.

(Att: 16,945)

Arizona	0	0	0	14 —	**14**
San Jose	7	17	14	14 —	**52**

MVP: John Dutton, San Jose, QB (20-26 for 236 yards, 5 TD, 0 INT.)

arenafootball2
Final 2002 Standings

Division champions (*) and playoff qualifiers (†) are noted; top two teams from each division advance to the playoffs.

American Conference
Northeast Division

	W	L	T	Pct.	PF	PA
*Albany	13	3	0	.813	684	567
†Rochester	7	9	0	.438	687	718
Wilkes-Barre/Scranton	6	10	0	.375	663	741
New Haven	6	10	0	.375	649	739
Mohegan	3	13	0	.188	556	734

Southern Division

	W	L	T	Pct.	PF	PA
*Tallahassee	9	7	0	.563	793	740
†Florida	9	7	0	.563	647	609
Jacksonville	8	8	0	.500	727	736
Charleston	7	9	0	.438	701	771

Atlantic Division

	W	L	T	Pct.	PF	PA
*Cape Fear	13	3	0	.813	743	476
†Richmond	12	4	0	.750	869	563
Norfolk	8	8	0	.500	653	753
Roanoke	8	8	0	.500	602	658
Greensboro	3	13	0	.188	677	833

Eastern Division

	W	L	T	Pct.	PF	PA
*Macon	13	3	0	.813	885	719
†Augusta	13	3	0	.813	847	684
Carolina	5	11	0	.313	624	739
Columbus	4	12	0	.250	620	776

National Conference
Midwest Division

	W	L	T	Pct.	PF	PA
*Peoria	11	5	0	.688	819	597
Quad City	10	6	0	.625	817	736
†Wichita	6	10	0	.375	595	721
Louisville	2	14	0	.125	514	820

Note: Quad City was ruled ineligible for the 2002 playoffs due to various violations of league policy.

Southern Division

	W	L	T	Pct.	PF	PA
*Tennessee Valley	13	3	0	.813	803	619
†Birmingham	11	5	0	.688	814	634
Pensacola	8	8	0	.500	775	727
Mobile	0	16	0	.000	458	901

Central Division

	W	L	T	Pct.	PF	PA
*Tulsa	14	2	0	.875	913	670
†Arkansas	11	5	0	.688	876	716
Bossier City	9	7	0	.563	772	688
Memphis	5	11	0	.313	684	817

Western Division

	W	L	T	Pct.	PF	PA
*Bakersfield	9	7	0	.563	736	625
†San Diego	7	9	0	.438	726	728
Hawaii	5	11	0	.313	745	856
Fresno	4	12	0	.250	639	902

Annual Awards

Ironman of the Year . . . . . . Kevin Harvey, Richmond, WR/DB
Offensive Player of the Year . . . . Mitch Allner, Tulsa, OS
Defensive Player of the Year . . . . Kelly Snell, Tenn. Valley, DS
Rookie of the Year . . . . Lincoln Dupree, Peoria, DS/KR
Coach of the Year . . . . Ron Selesky, Albany

ArenaCup 2002

August 23, 2002 at the Peoria (Ill.) Civic Center.

(Att: 7,552)

Florida	7	6	12	22 —	**47**
Peoria	6	17	13	29 —	**65**

MVP: Cornell Craig, Peoria, OS (5 catches for 62 yards, 3 TD)

ESPN Information Please® SPORTS ALMANAC

1920-2002 Through the Years

The Super Bowl

The first AFL-NFL World Championship Game, as it was originally called, was played seven months after the two leagues agreed to merge in June of 1966. It became the Super Bowl (complete with roman numerals) by the third game in 1969. The Super Bowl winner has been presented the Vince Lombardi Trophy since 1971. Lombardi, whose Green Bay teams won the first two title games, died in 1970. NFL champions (1966-69) and NFC champions (since 1970) are listed in CAPITAL letters.

Multiple winners: Dallas and San Francisco (5); Pittsburgh (4); Green Bay, Oakland-LA Raiders and Washington (3); Denver, Miami and NY Giants (2).

Bowl	Date	Winner	Head Coach	Score	Loser	Head Coach	Site
I	1/15/67	GREEN BAY	Vince Lombardi	35-10	Kansas City	Hank Stram	Los Angeles
II	1/14/68	GREEN BAY	Vince Lombardi	33-14	Oakland	John Rauch	Miami
III	1/12/69	NY Jets	Weeb Ewbank	16-7	BALT. COLTS	Don Shula	Miami
IV	1/11/70	Kansas City	Hank Stram	23-7	MINNESOTA	Bud Grant	New Orleans
V	1/17/71	Balt. Colts	Don McCafferty	16-13	DALLAS	Tom Landry	Miami
VI	1/16/72	DALLAS	Tom Landry	24-3	Miami	Don Shula	New Orleans
VII	1/14/73	Miami	Don Shula	14-7	WASHINGTON	George Allen	Los Angeles
VIII	1/13/74	Miami	Don Shula	24-7	MINNESOTA	Bud Grant	Houston
IX	1/12/75	Pittsburgh	Chuck Noll	16-6	MINNESOTA	Bud Grant	New Orleans
X	1/18/76	Pittsburgh	Chuck Noll	21-17	DALLAS	Tom Landry	Miami
XI	1/9/77	Oakland	John Madden	32-14	MINNESOTA	Bud Grant	Pasadena
XII	1/15/78	DALLAS	Tom Landry	27-10	Denver	Red Miller	New Orleans
XIII	1/21/79	Pittsburgh	Chuck Noll	35-31	DALLAS	Tom Landry	Miami
XIV	1/20/80	Pittsburgh	Chuck Noll	31-19	LA RAMS	Ray Malavasi	Pasadena
XV	1/25/81	Oakland	Tom Flores	27-10	PHILADELPHIA	Dick Vermeil	New Orleans
XVI	1/24/82	SAN FRANCISCO	Bill Walsh	26-21	Cincinnati	Forrest Gregg	Pontiac, MI
XVII	1/30/83	WASHINGTON	Joe Gibbs	27-17	Miami	Don Shula	Pasadena
XVIII	1/22/84	LA Raiders	Tom Flores	38-9	WASHINGTON	Joe Gibbs	Tampa
XIX	1/20/85	SAN FRANCISCO	Bill Walsh	38-16	Miami	Don Shula	Stanford
XX	1/26/86	CHICAGO	Mike Ditka	46-10	New England	Raymond Berry	New Orleans
XXI	1/25/87	NY GIANTS	Bill Parcells	39-20	Denver	Dan Reeves	Pasadena
XXII	1/31/88	WASHINGTON	Joe Gibbs	42-10	Denver	Dan Reeves	San Diego
XXIII	1/22/89	SAN FRANCISCO	Bill Walsh	20-16	Cincinnati	Sam Wyche	Miami
XXIV	1/28/90	SAN FRANCISCO	George Seifert	55-10	Denver	Dan Reeves	New Orleans
XXV	1/27/91	NY GIANTS	Bill Parcells	20-19	Buffalo	Marv Levy	Tampa
XXVI	1/26/92	WASHINGTON	Joe Gibbs	37-24	Buffalo	Marv Levy	Minneapolis
XXVII	1/31/93	DALLAS	Jimmy Johnson	52-17	Buffalo	Marv Levy	Pasadena
XXVIII	1/30/94	DALLAS	Jimmy Johnson	30-13	Buffalo	Marv Levy	Atlanta
XXIX	1/29/95	SAN FRANCISCO	George Seifert	49-26	San Diego	Bobby Ross	Miami
XXX	1/28/96	DALLAS	Barry Switzer	27-17	Pittsburgh	Bill Cowher	Tempe, AZ
XXXI	1/26/97	GREEN BAY	Mike Holmgren	35-21	New England	Bill Parcells	New Orleans
XXXII	1/25/98	Denver	Mike Shanahan	31-24	GREEN BAY	Mike Holmgren	San Diego
XXXIII	1/31/99	Denver	Mike Shanahan	34-19	ATLANTA	Dan Reeves	Miami
XXXIV	1/30/00	ST.L RAMS	Dick Vermeil	23-16	Tennessee	Jeff Fisher	Atlanta
XXXV	1/28/01	Balt. Ravens	Brian Billick	34-7	NY GIANTS	Jim Fassel	Tampa
XXXVI	2/3/02	New England	Bill Belichick	20-17	ST.L RAMS	Mike Martz	New Orleans

Super Bowl Appearances

App		W	L	Pct	PF	PA	App		W	L	Pct	PF	PA
8	Dallas	5	3	.625	221	132	3	New England	1	2	.333	51	98
6	Denver	2	4	.333	115	206	2	Baltimore Colts	1	1	.500	23	29
5	San Francisco	5	0	1.000	188	89	2	Kansas City	1	1	.500	33	42
5	Pittsburgh	4	1	.800	120	100	2	Cincinnati	0	2	.000	37	46
5	Washington	3	2	.600	122	103	1	Baltimore Ravens	1	0	1.000	34	7
5	Miami	2	3	.400	74	103	1	Chicago	1	0	1.000	46	10
4	Green Bay	3	1	.750	127	76	1	NY Jets	1	0	1.000	16	7
4	Oak/LA Raiders	3	1	.750	111	66	1	Atlanta	0	1	.000	19	34
4	Buffalo	0	4	.000	73	139	1	Philadelphia	0	1	.000	10	27
4	Minnesota	0	4	.000	34	95	1	San Diego	0	1	.000	26	49
3	NY Giants	2	1	.667	66	73	1	Tennessee	0	1	.000	16	23
3	LA/St.L Rams	1	2	.333	59	67							

Pete Rozelle Award (MVP)

The Most Valuable Player in the Super Bowl. Currently selected by a 15-member panel made up of national pro football writers and broadcasters chosen by the NFL (80 percent) and fans voting via the internet (20 percent). Presented by *Sport* magazine from 1967-89 and by the NFL since 1990. Named after former NFL commissioner Pete Rozelle in 1990. Winner who did not play for Super Bowl champion is in **bold** type.

Multiple winners: Joe Montana (3); Terry Bradshaw and Bart Starr (2).

Bowl		Bowl		Bowl	
I	Bart Starr, Green Bay, QB	XIII	Terry Bradshaw, Pittsburgh, QB	XXVI	Mark Rypien, Washington, QB
II	Bart Starr, Green Bay, QB	XIV	Terry Bradshaw, Pittsburgh, QB	XXVII	Troy Aikman, Dallas, QB
III	Joe Namath, NY Jets, QB	XV	Jim Plunkett, Oakland, QB	XXVIII	Emmitt Smith, Dallas, RB
IV	Len Dawson, Kansas City, QB	XVI	Joe Montana, San Francisco, QB	XXIX	Steve Young, San Francisco, QB
V	**Chuck Howley**, Dallas, LB	XVII	John Riggins, Washington, RB	XXX	Larry Brown, Dallas, CB
VI	Roger Staubach, Dallas, QB	XVIII	Marcus Allen, LA Raiders, RB	XXXI	Desmond Howard, Green Bay, KR
VII	Jake Scott, Miami, S	XIX	Joe Montana, San Francisco, QB	XXXII	Terrell Davis, Denver, RB
VIII	Larry Csonka, Miami, RB	XX	Richard Dent, Chicago, DE	XXXIII	John Elway, Denver, QB
IX	Franco Harris, Pittsburgh, RB	XXI	Phil Simms, NY Giants, QB	XXXIV	Kurt Warner, St. Louis, QB
X	Lynn Swann, Pittsburgh, WR	XXII	Doug Williams, Washington, QB	XXXV	Ray Lewis, Baltimore, LB
XI	Fred Biletnikoff, Oakland, WR	XXIII	Jerry Rice, San Francisco, WR	XXXVI	Tom Brady, New England, QB
XII	Harvey Martin, Dallas, DE & Randy White, Dallas, DT	XXIV	Joe Montana, San Francisco, QB		
		XXV	Ottis Anderson, NY Giants, RB		

All-Time Super Bowl Leaders

Through 2002; participants in Super Bowl XXXVI in **bold** type.

CAREER

Passing Efficiency

		Gm	Att	Cmp	Cmp%	Yards	Avg Gain	TD	TD%	Int	Int%	Rating
1	Phil Simms, NYG	1	25	22	88.0	268	10.72	3	12.0	0	0.0	150.9
2	Steve Young, SF	2	39	26	66.7	345	8.85	6	15.4	0	0.0	134.1
3	Doug Williams, Wash.	1	29	18	62.1	340	11.72	4	13.8	1	3.4	128.1
4	Joe Montana, SF	4	122	83	68.0	1142	9.36	11	9.0	0	0.0	127.8
5	Jim Plunkett, Raiders	2	46	29	63.0	433	9.41	4	8.7	0	0.0	122.8
6	Terry Bradshaw, Pit	4	84	49	58.3	932	11.10	9	10.7	4	4.8	112.8
7	Troy Aikman, Dal.	3	80	56	70.0	689	8.61	5	6.3	1	1.3	111.9
8	Bart Starr, GB.	2	47	29	61.7	452	9.62	3	6.4	1	2.1	106.0
9	Brett Favre, GB	2	69	39	56.5	502	7.28	5	7.2	1	1.4	97.6
10	Roger Staubach, Dal.	4	98	61	62.2	734	7.49	8	8.2	4	4.1	95.4

Ratings based on performance standards established for completion percentage, average gain, touchdown percentage and interception percentage. Quarterbacks are allocated points according to how their statistics measure up to those standards. Minimum 25 passing attempts.

Passing Yards

		Gm	Att	Cmp	Pct	Yds
1	Joe Montana, SF	4	122	83	68.0	1142
2	John Elway, Den	5	152	76	50.0	1128
3	Terry Bradshaw, Pit	4	84	49	58.3	932
4	Jim Kelly, Buf	4	145	81	55.9	829
5	**Kurt Warner**, St.L	2	89	52	58.4	779
6	Roger Staubach, Dal.	4	98	61	62.2	734
7	Troy Aikman, Dal.	3	80	56	70.0	689
8	Brett Favre, GB	2	69	39	56.5	502
9	Fran Tarkenton, Min	3	89	46	51.7	489
10	Bart Starr, GB.	2	47	29	61.7	452
11	Jim Plunkett, Raiders	2	46	29	63.0	433
12	Joe Theismann, Wash.	2	58	31	53.4	386
13	Len Dawson, KC	2	44	28	63.6	353
14	Steve Young, SF	2	39	26	66.7	345
15	Doug Williams, Wash.	1	29	18	62.1	340

Receptions

		Gm	No	Yds	Avg	TD
1	Jerry Rice, SF	3	28	512	18.3	7
2	Andre Reed, Buf	4	27	323	12.0	0
3	Roger Craig, SF	3	20	212	10.6	2
	Thurman Thomas, Buf	4	20	144	7.2	0
5	Jay Novacek, Dal	3	17	148	8.7	2
6	Lynn Swann, Pit	4	16	364	22.8	3
7	Michael Irvin, Dal	3	16	256	16.0	2
8	Chuck Foreman, Min.	3	15	139	9.3	0
9	Cliff Branch, Raiders	3	14	181	12.9	3
10	Don Beebe, Buf	3	12	171	14.3	2
	Torry Holt, St.L	2	12	158	13.2	1
	Preston Pearson, Bal-Pit-Dal	5	12	105	8.8	0
	Kenneth Davis, Buf	4	12	72	6.0	0
	Antonio Freeman, GB	2	12	231	19.3	3
15	John Stallworth, Pit	4	11	268	24.4	3
	Isaac Bruce, St.L	2	11	218	19.8	1
	Dan Ross, Cin	1	11	104	9.5	2

Rushing

		Gm	Car	Yds	Avg	TD
1	Franco Harris, Pit.	4	101	354	3.5	4
2	Larry Csonka, Mia.	3	57	297	5.2	2
3	Emmitt Smith, Dal.	3	70	289	4.1	5
4	Terrell Davis, Den.	2	55	259	4.7	3
5	John Riggins, Wash.	2	64	230	3.6	2
6	Timmy Smith, Wash.	1	22	204	9.3	2
	Thurman Thomas, Buf	4	52	204	3.9	4
8	Roger Craig, SF	3	52	201	3.9	2
9	Marcus Allen, Raiders	1	20	191	9.5	2
10	Tony Dorsett, Dal	2	31	162	5.2	1

All-Purpose Yards

		Gm	Rush	Rec	Ret	Total
1	Jerry Rice, SF	3	15	512	0	527
2	Franco Harris, Pit.	4	354	114	0	468
3	Roger Craig, SF	3	201	212	0	413
4	Lynn Swann, Pit	4	-7	364	34	391
5	Thurman Thomas, Buf	4	204	144	0	348
6	Emmitt Smith, Dal.	3	289	56	0	345
7	Antonio Freeman, GB	2	0	231	104	335
8	Andre Reed, Buf	4	0	323	0	323
9	Terrell Davis, Den.	2	259	58	0	317
10	Larry Csonka, Mia.	3	297	17	0	314

All-Time Super Bowl Leaders (Cont.)
Scoring

Points

		Gm	TD	FG	PAT	Pts
1	Jerry Rice, SF	3	7	0	0	42
2	Emmitt Smith, Dal	3	5	0	0	30
3	Roger Craig, SF	3	4	0	0	24
	Franco Harris, Pit	4	4	0	0	24
	Thurman Thomas, Buf	4	4	0	0	24
	John Elway, Den	5	4	0	0	24
7	Ray Wersching, SF	2	0	5	7	22
8	Don Chandler, GB	2	0	4	8	20
9	Cliff Branch, Raiders	3	3	0	0	18
	John Stallworth, Pit	4	3	0	0	18
	Lynn Swann, Pit	4	3	0	0	18
	Ricky Watters, SF	1	3	0	0	18
	Terrell Davis, Den	2	3	0	0	18
	Antonio Freeman, GB	2	3	0	0	18
15	Chris Bahr, Raiders	2	0	3	8	17
	Jason Elam, Den	2	0	3	8	17

Punting
(Minimum 10 Punts)

		Gm	No	Yds	Avg.
1	Jerrel Wilson, KC	2	11	511	46.5
2	Kyle Richardson, Bal	1	10	430	43.0
3	Ray Guy, Raiders	3	14	587	41.9
4	Larry Seiple, Mia	3	15	620	41.3
5	Mike Eischeid, Raiders-Min	3	17	698	41.1

Punt Returns
(Minimum 4 returns)

		Gm	No	Yds	Avg.	TD
1	John Taylor, SF	3	6	94	15.7	0
2	Desmond Howard, GB	1	6	90	15.0	0
3	Neal Colzie, Raiders	1	4	43	10.8	0
4	Dana McLemore, SF	1	5	51	10.2	0
5	Mike Fuller, Cin	1	4	35	8.8	0

Kickoff Returns
(Minimum 4 returns)

		Gm	No	Yds	Avg.	TD
1	Tim Dwight, Atl	1	5	210	42.0	1
2	Desmond Howard, GB	1	4	154	38.5	1
3	Fulton Walker, Mia	2	8	283	35.4	1
4	Andre Coleman, SD	1	8	242	30.3	1
5	Larry Anderson, Pit	2	8	207	25.9	0

Touchdowns

		Gm	Rush	Rec	Ret	TD
1	Jerry Rice, SF	3	0	7	0	7
2	Emmitt Smith, Dal	3	5	0	0	5
3	Roger Craig, SF	3	2	2	0	4
	Franco Harris, Pit	4	4	0	0	4
	John Elway, Den	5	4	0	0	4
	Thurman Thomas, Buf	4	4	0	0	4
7	Cliff Branch, Raiders	3	0	3	0	3
	John Stallworth, Pit	4	0	3	0	3
	Lynn Swann, Pit	4	0	3	0	3
	Ricky Watters, SF	1	1	2	0	3
	Terrell Davis, Den	2	3	0	0	3
	Antonio Freeman, GB	2	0	3	0	3
13	Twenty-four tied with 2 TDs each:					

Marcus Allen, Raiders; Ottis Anderson, NYG; Pete Banaszak, Raiders; Don Beebe, Buf.; Gary Clark, Wash.; Larry Csonka, Mia.; Eddie George, Ten.; Howard Griffith, Den.; Michael Irvin, Dal.; Butch Johnson, Dal.; Jim Kiick, Mia.; Max McGee, GB; Jim McMahon, Chi.; Bill Miller, Raiders; Joe Montana, SF; Elijah Pitts, GB; Tom Rathman, SF; John Riggins, Wash.; Gerald Riggs, Wash.; Dan Ross, Cin.; Ricky Sanders, Wash.; Timmy Smith, Wash.; John Taylor, SF and Duane Thomas, Dal.

Interceptions

		Gm	No	Yds	TD
1	Larry Brown, Dal	3	3	77	0
	Chuck Howley, Dal	2	3	63	0
	Rod Martin, Raiders	2	3	44	0
4	Randy Beverly, NYJ	1	2	0	0
	Mel Blount, Pit	4	2	23	0
	Brad Edwards, Wash	1	2	56	0
	Thomas Everett, Dal.	2	2	22	0
	Darrien Gordon, SD-Den	3	2	108	0
	Jake Scott, Mia	3	2	63	0
	Mike Wagner, Pit.	4	2	45	0
	James Washington, Dal	2	2	25	0
	Barry Wilburn, Wash	1	2	11	0
	Eric Wright, SF	4	2	25	0

Sacks

		Gm	No
1	Charles Haley, SF-Dal	5	4.5
2	Reggie White, GB	2	3
	Leonard Marshall, NYG	2	3
	Danny Stubbs, SF	2	3
	Jeff Wright, Buf	4	3

Four or More Super Bowl Wins

Dallas Cowboys (5)

Year	Bowl	Head Coach	Quarterback	MVP	Opponent	Score	Site
1972	VI	Tom Landry	Roger Staubach	Staubach	Miami	24-3	New Orleans
1978	XII	Tom Landry	Roger Staubach	Harvey Martin & Randy White	Denver	27-10	New Orleans
1993	XXVII	Jimmy Johnson	Troy Aikman	Aikman	Buffalo	52-17	Pasadena
1994	XXVIII	Jimmy Johnson	Troy Aikman	Emmitt Smith	Buffalo	30-13	Atlanta
1996	XXX	Barry Switzer	Troy Aikman	Larry Brown	Pittsburgh	27-17	Tempe

San Francisco 49ers (5)

Year	Bowl	Head Coach	Quarterback	MVP	Opponent	Score	Site
1982	XVI	Bill Walsh	Joe Montana	Montana	Cincinnati	26-21	Pontiac
1985	XIX	Bill Walsh	Joe Montana	Montana	Miami	38-16	Stanford
1989	XXIII	Bill Walsh	Joe Montana	Jerry Rice	Cincinnati	20-16	Miami
1990	XXIV	George Seifert	Joe Montana	Montana	Denver	55-10	New Orleans
1995	XXIX	George Seifert	Steve Young	Young	San Diego	49-26	Miami

Pittsburgh Steelers (4)

Year	Bowl	Head Coach	Quarterback	MVP	Opponent	Score	Site
1975	IX	Chuck Noll	Terry Bradshaw	Franco Harris	Minnesota	16-6	New Orleans
1976	X	Chuck Noll	Terry Bradshaw	Lynn Swann	Dallas	21-17	Miami
1979	XIII	Chuck Noll	Terry Bradshaw	Bradshaw	Dallas	35-31	Miami
1980	XIV	Chuck Noll	Terry Bradshaw	Bradshaw	LA Rams	31-19	Pasadena

SINGLE GAME

Passing

Yards Gained

		Year	Att/Cmp	Yds
1	Kurt Warner, St.L vs Ten	2000	45/24	414
2	**Kurt Warner**, St.L vs NE	2002	44/28	365
3	Joe Montana, SF vs Cin	1989	36/23	357
4	Doug Williams, Wash vs Den	1988	29/18	340
5	John Elway, Den vs Atl	1999	29/18	336
6	Joe Montana, SF vs Mia	1985	35/24	331
7	Steve Young, SF vs SD	1995	36/24	325
8	Terry Bradshaw, Pit vs Dal	1979	30/17	318
	Dan Marino, Mia vs SF	1985	50/29	318
10	Terry Bradshaw, Pit vs Rams	1980	21/14	309

Touchdown Passes

		Year	TD	Int
1	Steve Young, SF vs SD	1995	6	0
2	Joe Montana, SF vs Den	1990	5	0
3	Terry Bradshaw, Pit vs Dal	1979	4	1
	Doug Williams, Wash vs Den	1988	4	1
	Troy Aikman, Dal vs Buf	1993	4	0
6	Roger Staubach, Dal vs Pit	1979	3	1
	Jim Plunkett, Raiders vs Phi	1981	3	0
	Joe Montana, SF vs Mia	1985	3	0
	Phil Simms, NYG vs Den	1987	3	0
	Brett Favre, GB vs Den	1998	3	1

Receiving

Catches

		Year	No	Yds	TD
1	Dan Ross, Cin vs SF	1982	11	104	2
	Jerry Rice, SF vs Cin	1989	11	215	1
3	Tony Nathan, Mia vs SF	1985	10	83	0
	Jerry Rice, SF vs SD	1995	10	149	3
	Andre Hastings, Pit vs Dal	1996	10	98	0
6	Ricky Sanders, Wash vs Den	1988	9	193	2
	Antonio Freeman, GB vs Den	1998	9	126	2

Five tied with 8 each, including twice by Andre Reed.

Yards Gained

		Year	No	Yds	TD
1	Jerry Rice, SF vs Cin	1989	11	215	1
2	Ricky Sanders, Wash vs Den	1988	9	193	2
3	Isaac Bruce, St.L vs Ten	2000	6	162	1
4	Lynn Swann, Pit vs Dal	1976	4	161	1
5	Andre Reed, Buf vs Dal	1993	8	152	0
	Rod Smith, Den vs Atl	1999	5	152	1
7	Jerry Rice, SF vs SD	1995	10	149	3
8	Jerry Rice, SF vs Den	1990	7	148	3
9	Max McGee, GB vs KC	1967	7	138	2
10	George Sauer, NYJ vs Bal	1969	8	133	0

Rushing

Yards Gained

		Year	Car	Yds	TD
1	Timmy Smith, Wash vs Den	1988	22	204	2
2	Marcus Allen, Raiders vs Wash	1984	20	191	2
3	John Riggins, Wash vs Mia	1983	38	166	1
4	Franco Harris, Pit vs Min	1975	34	158	1
5	Terrell Davis, Den vs GB	1998	30	157	3
6	Larry Csonka, Mia vs Min	1974	33	145	2
7	Clarence Davis, Raiders vs Min	1977	16	137	0
8	Thurman Thomas, Buf vs NYG	1991	15	135	1
9	Emmitt Smith, Dal vs Buf	1994	30	132	2
10	Matt Snell, NYJ vs Bal	1969	30	121	1
11	Tom Matte, Bal vs NYJ	1969	11	116	0
12	Larry Csonka, Mia vs Wash	1973	15	112	1
13	Emmitt Smith, Dal vs Buf	1993	22	108	1
14	Ottis Anderson, NYG vs Buf	1991	21	102	1
	Terrell Davis, Den vs Atl	1999	25	102	0
	Jamal Lewis, Bal vs NYG	2001	27	102	0

Scoring

Points

		Year	TD	FG	PAT	Pts
1	Roger Craig, SF vs Mia	1985	3	0	0	18
	Jerry Rice, SF vs Den	1990	3	0	0	18
	Jerry Rice, SF vs SD	1995	3	0	0	18
	Ricky Watters, SF vs SD	1995	3	0	0	18
	Terrell Davis, Den vs GB	1998	3	0	0	18
6	Don Chandler, GB vs Raiders	1968	0	4	3	15

Touchdowns

		Year	TD	Rush	Rec
1	Roger Craig, SF vs Mia	1985	3	1	2
	Jerry Rice, SF vs Den	1990	3	0	3
	Jerry Rice, SF vs SD	1995	3	0	3
	Ricky Watters, SF vs SD	1995	3	1	2
	Terrell Davis, Den vs GB	1998	3	3	0

Punt Returns

(Minimum 3 returns)

		Year	No	Yds	Avg
1	John Taylor, SF vs Cin	1989	3	56	18.7
2	Desmond Howard, GB vs NE	1997	6	90	15.0
3	John Taylor, SF vs Den	1990	3	38	12.7
4	Kelvin Martin, Dal vs Buf	1993	3	35	11.7

All-Purpose Yards

Yards Gained

		Year	Run	Rec	Tot
1	Desmond Howard, GB vs NE	1997	0	0	244
2	Andre Coleman, SD vs SF	1995	0	0	242
3	Ricky Sanders, Wash vs Den	1988	193	-4	235
4	Antonio Freeman, GB vs Den	1998	0	126	230
5	Jerry Rice, SF vs Cin	1989	5	215	220
6	Tim Dwight, Atl vs Den	1999	5	0	215
7	Timmy Smith, Wash vs Den	1988	204	9	213
8	Marcus Allen, Raiders vs Wash	1984	191	18	209
9	Stephen Starring, NE vs Chi	1986	0	39	192
10	Fulton Walker, Mia vs Wash	1983	0	0	190
	Thurman Thomas, Buf vs NYG	1991	135	55	190

Return Yardage: Howard 244, Coleman 242, Sanders 46, Freeman 104, Dwight 210, Starring 153, Walker 190.

Interceptions

		Year	No	Yds	TD
1	Rod Martin, Raiders vs Phi	1981	3	44	0

Eight tied with 2 each.

Punting

(Minimum 4 punts)

		Year	No	Yds	Avg
1	Bryan Wagner, SD vs SF	1995	4	195	48.8
2	Jerrel Wilson, KC vs Min	1970	4	194	48.5
3	Jim Miller, SF vs Cin	1982	4	185	46.3

Kickoff Returns

(Minimum 3 returns)

		Year	No	Yds	Avg
1	Fulton Walker, Mia vs Wash	1983	4	190	47.5
2	Tim Dwight, Atl vs Den	1999	5	210	42.0
3	Desmond Howard, GB vs NE	1997	4	154	38.5
4	Larry Anderson, Pit vs Rams	1980	5	162	32.4
5	Rick Upchurch, Den vs Dal	1978	3	94	31.3

Super Bowl Playoffs

The Super Bowl forced the NFL to set up pro football's first guaranteed multiple-game playoff format. Over the years, the NFL-AFL merger, the creation of two conferences comprised of four divisions each and the proliferation of wild card entries has seen the postseason field grow from four teams (1966), to six (1967-68), to eight (1969-77), to 10 (1978-81, 1983-89), to the present 12 (since 1990).

In 1968, there was a special playoff between Oakland and Kansas City which were both 12-2 and tied for first in the AFL's Western Division. In 1982, when a 57-day players' strike shortened the regular season to just nine games, playoff berths were extended to 16 teams (eight from each conference) and a 15-game tournament was played.

Note that in the following year-by-year summary, records of finalists include all games leading up to the Super Bowl; (*) indicates non-division winners or wild card teams.

1966 SEASON

AFL Playoffs

Championship . . . . Kansas City 31, at Buffalo 7

NFL Playoffs

Championship . . . . Green Bay 34, at Dallas 27

Super Bowl I

Jan. 15, 1967
Memorial Coliseum, Los Angeles
Favorite: Packers by 14   Attendance: 61,946

Kansas City (12-2-1) 0   10   0   0 **—10**
Green Bay (13-2) 7   7   14   7 **—35**
MVP: Green Bay QB Bart Starr (16 for 23, 250 yds, 2 TD, 1 Int)

1967 SEASON

AFL Playoffs

Championship . . . . at Oakland 40, Houston 7

NFL Playoffs

Eastern Conference . . . . at Dallas 52, Cleveland 14
Western Conference . . . . at Green Bay 28, LA Rams 7
Championship . . . . at Green Bay 21, Dallas 17

Super Bowl II

Jan. 14, 1968
Orange Bowl, Miami
Favorite: Packers by 13½   Attendance: 75,546

Green Bay (11-4-1) 3   13   10   7 **—33**
Oakland (14-1) 0   7   0   7 **—14**
MVP: Green Bay QB Bart Starr (13 for 24, 202 yds, 1 TD)

1968 SEASON

AFL Playoffs

Western Div. Playoff . . . . at Oakland 41, Kansas City 6
AFL Championship . . . . at NY Jets 27, Oakland 23

NFL Playoffs

Eastern Conference . . . . at Cleveland 31, Dallas 20
Western Conference . . . . at Baltimore 24, Minnesota 14
NFL Championship . . . . Baltimore 34, at Cleveland 0

Super Bowl III

Jan. 12, 1969
Orange Bowl, Miami
Favorite: Colts by 18   Attendance: 75,389

NY Jets (12-3) 0   7   6   3 **—16**
Baltimore (15-1) 0   0   0   7 **—7**
MVP: NY Jets QB Joe Namath (17 for 28, 206 yds)

1969 SEASON

AFL Playoffs

Inter-Division . . . . *Kansas City 13, at NY Jets 6
                   at Oakland 56, *Houston 7
AFL Championship . . . . Kansas City 17, at Oakland 7

NFL Playoffs

Eastern Conference . . . . Cleveland 38, at Dallas 14
Western Conference . . . . at Minnesota 23, LA Rams 20
NFL Championship . . . . at Minnesota 27, Cleveland 7

Super Bowl IV

Jan. 11, 1970
Tulane Stadium, New Orleans
Favorite: Vikings by 12   Attendance: 80,562

Minnesota (14-2) 0   0   7   0 **— 7**
Kansas City (13-3) 3   13   7   0 **—23**
MVP: KC QB Len Dawson (12 for 17, 142 yds, 1 TD, 1 Int)

1970 SEASON

AFC Playoffs

First Round . . . . at Baltimore 17, Cincinnati 0
                   at Oakland 21, *Miami 14
Championship . . . . at Baltimore 27, Oakland 17

NFC Playoffs

First Round. . . . . at Dallas 5, *Detroit 0
              San Francisco 17, at Minnesota 14
Championship . . . . Dallas 17, at San Francisco 10

Super Bowl V

Jan. 17, 1971
Orange Bowl, Miami
Favorite: Cowboys by 2½   Attendance: 79,204

Baltimore (13-2-1) 0   6   0   10 **—16**
Dallas (12-4) 3   10   0   0 **—13**
MVP: Dallas LB Chuck Howley (2 interceptions for 22 yds)

1971 SEASON

AFC Playoffs

First Round. . . . . Miami 27, at Kansas City 24 (OT)
                 *Baltimore 20, at Cleveland 3
Championship . . . . at Miami 21, Baltimore 0

NFC Playoffs

First Round . . . . Dallas 20, at Minnesota 12
          at San Francisco 24, *Washington 20
Championship . . . . at Dallas 14, San Francisco 3

Super Bowl VI

Jan. 16, 1972
Tulane Stadium, New Orleans
Favorite: Cowboys by 6   Attendance: 81,023

Dallas (13-3) 3   7   7   7 **—24**
Miami (12-3-1) 0   3   0   0 **—3**
MVP: Dallas QB Roger Staubach (12 for 19, 119 yds, 2 TD)

1972 SEASON

AFC Playoffs

First Round . . . . .at Pittsburgh 13, Oakland 7
at Miami 20, *Cleveland 14
Championship . . . . .Miami 21, at Pittsburgh 17

NFC Playoffs

First Round . . . .*Dallas 30, at San Francisco 28
at Washington 16, Green Bay 3
Championship . . . . .at Washington 26, Dallas 3

Super Bowl VII

Jan. 14, 1973
Memorial Coliseum, Los Angeles
Favorite: Redskins by 1½   Attendance: 90,182

Miami (16-0) 7   7   0   0 **—14**
Washington (13-3) 0   0   0   7 **—7**
MVP: Miami safety Jake Scott (2 Interceptions for 63 yds)

1973 SEASON

AFC Playoffs

First Round . . . . .at Oakland 33, *Pittsburgh 14
at Miami 34, Cincinnati 16
Championship . . . . .at Miami 27, Oakland 10

NFC Playoffs

First Round . . . . .at Minnesota 27, *Washington 20
at Dallas 27, LA Rams 16
Championship . . . . .Minnesota 27, at Dallas 10

Super Bowl VIII

Jan. 13, 1974
Rice Stadium, Houston
Favorite: Dolphins by 6½   Attendance: 71,882

Minnesota (14-2) 0   0   0   7 **—7**
Miami (12-4) 14   3   7   0 **—24**
MVP: Miami FB Larry Csonka (33 carries, 145 yds, 2 TD)

1974 SEASON

AFC Playoffs

First Round . . . . .at Oakland 28, Miami 26
at Pittsburgh 32, *Buffalo 14
Championship . . . . .Pittsburgh 24, at Oakland 13

NFC Playoffs

First Round . . . . .at Minnesota 30, St. Louis 14
at LA Rams 19, *Washington 10
Championship . . . . .at Minnesota 14, LA Rams 10

Super Bowl IX

Jan. 12, 1975
Tulane Stadium, New Orleans
Favorite: Steelers by 3   Attendance: 80,997

Pittsburgh (12-3-1) 0   2   7   7 **—16**
Minnesota (12-4) 0   0   0   6 **—6**
MVP: Pittsburgh RB Franco Harris (34 carries, 158 yds, 1 TD)

1975 SEASON

AFC Playoffs

First Round . . . . .at Pittsburgh 28, Baltimore 10
at Oakland 31, *Cincinnati 28
Championship . . . . .at Pittsburgh 16, Oakland 10

NFC Playoffs

First Round . . . . .at LA Rams 35, St. Louis 23
*Dallas 17, at Minnesota 14
Championship . . . . .Dallas 37, at LA Rams 7

Super Bowl X

Jan. 18, 1976
Orange Bowl, Miami
Favorite: Steelers by 6½   Attendance: 80,187

Dallas (12-4) 7   3   0   7 **—17**
Pittsburgh (14-2) 7   0   0   14 **—21**
MVP: Pittsburgh WR Lynn Swann (4 catches, 161 yds, 1 TD)

1976 SEASON

AFC Playoffs

First Round . . . . .at Oakland 24, *New England 21
Pittsburgh 40, at Baltimore 14
Championship . . . . .at Oakland 24, Pittsburgh 7

NFC Playoffs

First Round . . . . .at Minnesota 35, *Washington 20
LA Rams 14, at Dallas 12
Championship . . . . .at Minnesota 24, LA Rams 13

Super Bowl XI

Jan. 9, 1977
Rose Bowl, Pasadena
Favorite: Raiders by 4½   Attendance: 103,438

Oakland (15-1) 0   16   3   13 **—32**
Minnesota (13-2-1) 0   0   7   7 **—14**
MVP: Oakland WR Fred Biletnikoff (4 catches, 79 yds)

1977 SEASON

AFC Playoffs

First Round . . . . .at Denver 34, Pittsburgh 21
*Oakland 37, at Baltimore 31 (OT)
Championship . . . . .at Denver 20, Oakland 17

NFC Playoffs

First Round . . . . .at Dallas 37, *Chicago 7
Minnesota 14, at LA Rams 7
Championship . . . . .at Dallas 23, Minnesota 6

Super Bowl XII

Jan. 15, 1978
Louisiana Superdome, New Orleans
Favorite: Cowboys by 6   Attendance: 75,583

Dallas (14-2) 10   3   7   7 **—27**
Denver (14-2) 0   0   10   0 **—10**
MVPs: Dallas DE Harvey Martin and DT Randy White (Cowboys' defense forced 8 turnovers)

1978 SEASON

AFC Playoffs

First Round . . . .*Houston 17, at *Miami 9
Second Round . . . . .Houston 31, at New England 14
at Pittsburgh 33, Denver 10
Championship . . . . .at Pittsburgh 34, Houston 5

NFC Playoffs

First Round . . . . .at *Atlanta 14, *Philadelphia 13
Second Round . . . . .at Dallas 27, Atlanta 20
at LA Rams 34, Minnesota 10
Championship . . . . .Dallas 28, at LA Rams 0

Super Bowl XIII

Jan. 21, 1979
Orange Bowl, Miami
Favorite: Steelers by 4   Attendance: 79,484

Pittsburgh (16-2) 7   14   0   14 **—35**
Dallas (14-4) 7   7   3   14 **—31**
MVP: Pittsburgh QB Terry Bradshaw (17 for 30, 318 yds, 4 TD, 1 Int)

Super Bowl Playoffs (Cont.)

1979 SEASON

AFC Playoffs

First Round..................at *Houston 13, *Denver 7
Second Round.............Houston 17, at San Diego 14
 at Pittsburgh 34, Miami 14
Championship ....at Pittsburgh 27, Houston 13

NFC Playoffs

First Round ....at *Philadelphia 27, *Chicago 17
Second Round ....at Tampa Bay 24, Philadelphia 17
 LA Rams 21, at Dallas 19
Championship ....LA Rams 9, at Tampa Bay 0

Super Bowl XIV

Jan. 20, 1980
Rose Bowl, Pasadena
Favorite: Steelers by 10½ Attendance: 103,985

LA Rams (11-7)........7	6	6	0	**—19**
Pittsburgh (14-4).............3	7	7	14	**—31**

MVP: Pittsburgh QB Terry Bradshaw (14 for 21, 309 yds, 2 TD, 3 Int)

1980 SEASON

AFC Playoffs

First Round ....at *Oakland 27, *Houston 7
Second Round..............at San Diego 20, Buffalo 14
 Oakland 14, at Cleveland 12
Championship ....Oakland 34, at San Diego 27

NFC Playoffs

First Round ....at *Dallas 34, *LA Rams 13
Second Round ....at Philadelphia 31, Minnesota 16
 Dallas 30, at Atlanta 27
Championship ....at Philadelphia 20, Dallas 7

Super Bowl XV

Jan. 25, 1981
Louisiana Superdome, New Orleans
Favorite: Eagles by 3 Attendance: 76,135

Oakland (14-5) 14	0	10	3	**—27**
Philadelphia (14-4)...........0	3	0	7	**—10**

MVP: Oakland QB Jim Plunkett (13 for 21, 261 yds, 3 TD)

1981 SEASON

AFC Playoffs

First Round ....*Buffalo 31, at *NY Jets 27
Second Round..........San Diego 41, at Miami 38 (OT)
 at Cincinnati 28, Buffalo 21
Championship ....at Cincinnati 27, San Diego 7

NFC Playoffs

First Round...........*NY Giants 27, at *Philadelphia 21
Second Round ....at Dallas 38, Tampa Bay 0
 at San Francisco 38, NY Giants 24
Championship ....at San Francisco 28, Dallas 27

Super Bowl XVI

Jan. 24, 1982
Pontiac Silverdome, Pontiac, Mich.
Favorite: Pick'em Attendance: 81,270

San Francisco (15-3)..........7	13	0	6	**—26**
Cincinnati (14-4)...............0	0	7	14	**—21**

MVP: San Francisco QB Joe Montana (14 for 22, 157 yds, 1 TD; 6 carries, 18 yds, 1 TD)

1982 SEASON

A 57-day players' strike shortened the regular season from 16 games to nine. The playoff format was changed to a 16-team tournament open to the top eight teams in each conference.

AFC Playoffs

First Round ....at LA Raiders 27, Cleveland 10
 at Miami 28, New England 13
 NY Jets 44, at Cincinnati 17
 San Diego 31, at Pittsburgh 28
Second Round ....NY Jets 17, at LA Raiders 14
 at Miami 34, San Diego 13
Championship ....at Miami 14, NY Jets 0

NFC Playoffs

First Round ....at Washington 31, Detroit 7
 at Dallas 30, Tampa Bay 17
 at Green Bay 41, St. Louis 16
 at Minnesota 30, Atlanta 24
Second Round...........at Washington 21, Minnesota 7
 at Dallas 37, Green Bay 26
Championship ....at Washington 31, Dallas 17

Super Bowl XVII

Jan. 30, 1983
Rose Bowl, Pasadena
Favorite: Dolphins by 3 Attendance: 103,667

Miami (10-2) 7	10	0	0	**—17**
Washington (11-1) 0	10	3	14	**—27**

MVP: Washington RB John Riggins (38 carries, 166 yds, 1 TD; 1 catch, 15 yds)

1983 SEASON

AFC Playoffs

First Round ....at *Seattle 31, *Denver 7
Second Round ....Seattle 27, at Miami 20
 at LA Raiders 38, Pittsburgh 10
Championship ....at LA Raiders 30, Seattle 14

NFC Playoffs

First Round.................*LA Rams 24, at *Dallas 17
Second Round...........at San Francisco 24, Detroit 23
 at Washington 51, LA Rams 7
Championship ....at Washington 24, San Francisco 21

Super Bowl XVIII

Jan. 22, 1984
Tampa Stadium, Tampa
Favorite: Redskins by 3 Attendance: 72,920

Washington (16-2) 0	3	6	0	**—9**
LA Raiders (14-4)..........7	14	14	3	**—38**

MVP: LA Raiders RB Marcus Allen (20 carries, 191 yds, 2 TD; 2 catches, 18 yds)

Most Popular Playing Sites

Stadiums hosting more than one Super Bowl.

No		Years
6	Superdome (N. Orleans)	1978, 81, 86, 90, 97, 2002
5	Orange Bowl (Miami)	1968-69, 71, 76, 79
5	Rose Bowl (Pasadena)	1977, 80, 83, 87, 93
3	Tulane Stadium (N. Orleans)	1970, 72, 75
3	Joe Robbie/Pro Player Stadium (Miami)	1989, 95, 99
2	LA Memorial Coliseum	1967, 73
2	Tampa Stadium	1984, 91
2	Jack Murphy/Qualcomm Stadium (San Diego)	1988, 98
2	Georgia Dome (Atlanta)	1994, 2000

1984 SEASON

AFC Playoffs

First Round.................at *Seattle 13, *LA Raiders 7
Second Round ....at Miami 31, Seattle 10
Pittsburgh 24, at Denver 17
Championship...............at Miami 45, Pittsburgh 28

NFC Playoffs

First Round..............*NY Giants 16, at *LA Rams 13
Second Round........at San Francisco 21, NY Giants 10
Chicago 23, at Washington 19
Championship ....at San Francisco 23, Chicago 0

Super Bowl XIX

Jan. 20, 1985
Stanford Stadium, Stanford, Calif.
Favorite: 49ers by 3   Attendance: 84,059

Miami (16-2) 10	6	0	0	**—16**
San Francisco (17-1)..........7	21	10	0	**—38**

MVP: San Francisco QB Joe Montana (24 for 35, 331 yds, 2 TD; 5 carries, 59 yards, 1 TD)

1985 SEASON

AFC Playoffs

First Round ....*New England 26, at *NY Jets 14
Second Round...............at Miami 24, Cleveland 21
New England 27, at LA Raiders 20
Championship ....New England 31, at Miami 14

NFC Playoffs

First Round ....at *NY Giants 17, *San Francisco 3
Second Round ....at LA Rams 20, Dallas 0
at Chicago 21, NY Giants 0
Championship ....at Chicago 24, LA Rams 0

Super Bowl XX

Jan. 26, 1986
Louisiana Superdome, New Orleans
Favorite: Bears by 10   Attendance: 73,818

Chicago Bears (17-1).........13	10	21	2	**—46**
New England (14-5)...........3	0	0	7	**—10**

MVP: Chicago DE Richard Dent (Bears defense: 7 sacks, 6 turnovers, 1 safety and gave up just 123 total yards)

1986 SEASON

AFC Playoffs

First Round..............at *NY Jets 35, *Kansas City 15
Second Round ....at Cleveland 23, NY Jets 20 (OT)
at Denver 22, New England 17
Championship ....Denver 23, at Cleveland 20 (OT)

NFC Playoffs

First Round..............at *Washington 19, *LA Rams 7
Second Round ....Washington 27, at Chicago 13
at NY Giants 49, San Francisco 3
Championship ....at NY Giants 17, Washington 0

Super Bowl XXI

Jan. 25, 1987
Rose Bowl, Pasadena
Favorite: Giants by 9½   Attendance: 101,063

Denver (13-5) 10	0	0	10	**—20**
NY Giants (16-2)...............7	2	17	13	**—39**

MVP: NY Giants QB Phil Simms (22 for 25, 268 yds, 3 TD; 3 carries, 25 yds)

1987 SEASON

A 24-day players' strike shortened the regular season to 15 games with replacement teams playing for three weeks.

AFC Playoffs

First Round ....at *Houston 23, *Seattle 20 (OT)
Second Round ....at Cleveland 38, Indianapolis 21
at Denver 34, Houston 10
Championship ....at Denver 38, Cleveland 33

NFC Playoffs

First Round..........*Minnesota 44, at *New Orleans 10
Second Round........Minnesota 36, at San Francisco 24
Washington 21, at Chicago 17
Championship ....at Washington 17, Minnesota 10

Super Bowl XXII

Jan. 31, 1988
San Diego/Jack Murphy Stadium
Favorite: Broncos by 3½   Attendance: 73,302

Washington (13-4) 0	35	0	7	**—42**
Denver (12-4-1)...............10	0	0	0	**—10**

MVP: Washington QB Doug Williams (18 for 29, 340 yds, 4 TD, 1 Int)

1988 SEASON

AFC Playoffs

First Round...............*Houston 24, at *Cleveland 23
Second Round.................at Buffalo 17, Houston 10
at Cincinnati 21, Seattle 13
Championship ....at Cincinnati 21, Buffalo 10

NFC Playoffs

First Round...........at *Minnesota 28, *LA Rams 17
Second Round..........at San Francisco 34, Minnesota 9
at Chicago 20, Philadelphia 12
Championship ....San Francisco 28, at Chicago 3

Super Bowl XXIII

Jan. 22, 1989
Joe Robbie Stadium, Miami
Favorite: 49ers by 7   Attendance: 75,129

Cincinnati (14-4)...............0	3	10	3	**—16.**
San Francisco (12-6).........3	0	3	14	**—20**

MVP: San Francisco WR Jerry Rice (11 catches, 215 yds, 1 TD; 1 carry, 5 yds)

1989 SEASON

AFC Playoffs

First Round ....*Pittsburgh 26, at *Houston 23
Second Round ....at Cleveland 34, Buffalo 30
at Denver 24, Pittsburgh 23
Championship ....at Denver 37, Cleveland 21

NFC Playoffs

First Round...............*LA Rams 21, at *Philadelphia 7
Second Round ....LA Rams 19, NY Giants 13 (OT)
at San Francisco 41, Minnesota 13
Championship ....at San Francisco 30, LA Rams 3

Super Bowl XXIV

Jan. 28, 1990
Louisiana Superdome, New Orleans
Favorite: 49ers by 12½   Attendance: 72,919

San Francisco (17-2) 13	14	14	14	**—55**
Denver (13-6) 3	0	7	0	**—10**

MVP: San Francisco QB Joe Montana (22 for 29, 297 yds, 5 TD)

Super Bowl Playoffs (Cont.)

1990 SEASON

AFC Playoffs
First Round..............at *Miami 17, *Kansas City 16
at Cincinnati 41, *Houston 14
Second Round................at Buffalo 44, Miami 34
at LA Raiders 20, Cincinnati 10
Championship...............at Buffalo 51, LA Raiders 3

NFC Playoffs
First Round ....*Washington 20, at *Philadelphia 6
at Chicago 16, *New Orleans 6
Second Round ....at San Francisco 28, Washington 10
at NY Giants 31, Chicago 3
Championship ....NY Giants 15, at San Francisco 13

Super Bowl XXV
Jan. 27, 1991
Tampa Stadium, Tampa
Favorite: Bills by 7   Attendance: 73,813

Buffalo (15-4)	3	9	0	7	**—19**
NY Giants (16-3)	3	7	7	3	**—20**

MVP: NY Giants RB Ottis Anderson (21 carries, 102 yds, 1 TD; 1 catch, 7 yds)

1991 SEASON

AFC Playoffs
First Round ....at *Kansas City 10, *LA Raiders 6
at Houston 17, *NY Jets 10
Second Round.................at Denver 26, Houston 24
at Buffalo 37, Kansas City 14
Championship.................at Buffalo 10, Denver 7

NFC Playoffs
First Round ....*Atlanta 27, at New Orleans 20
+*Dallas 17, at *Chicago 13
Second Round ....at Washington 24, Atlanta 7
at Detroit 38, Dallas 6
Championship.............at Washington 41, Detroit 10

Super Bowl XXVI
Jan. 26, 1992
Hubert Humphrey Metrodome, Minneapolis
Favorite: Redskins by 7   Attendance: 63,130

Washington (16-2)	0	17	14	6	**—37**
Buffalo (15-3)	0	0	10	14	**—24**

MVP: Washington QB Mark Rypien (18 for 33, 292 yds, 2 TD, 1 Int)

1992 SEASON

AFC Playoffs
First Round ....at *Buffalo 41, *Houston 38 (OT)
at San Diego 17, *Kansas City 0
Second Round.................Buffalo 24, at Pittsburgh 3
at Miami 31, San Diego 0
Championship ....Buffalo 29, at Miami 10

NFC Playoffs
First Round ....*Washington 24, at Minnesota 7
*Philadelphia 36, at *New Orleans 20
Second Round ....at San Francisco 20, Washington 13
at Dallas 34, Philadelphia 10
Championship ....Dallas 30, at San Francisco 20

Super Bowl XXVII
Jan. 31, 1993
Rose Bowl, Pasadena
Favorite: Cowboys by 7   Attendance: 98,374

Buffalo (14-5)	7	3	7	0	**—17**
Dallas (15-3)	14	14	3	21	**—52**

MVP: Dallas QB Troy Aikman (22 for 30, 273 yds, 4 TD)

1993 SEASON

AFC Playoffs
First Round........at Kansas City 27, *Pittsburgh 24 (OT)
at *LA Raiders 42, *Denver 24
Second Round..............at Buffalo 29, LA Raiders 23
Kansas City 28, at Houston 20
Championship ....at Buffalo 30, Kansas City 13

NFC Playoffs
First Round................*Green Bay 28, at Detroit 24
at *NY Giants 17, *Minnesota 10
Second Round.........at San Francisco 44, NY Giants 3
at Dallas 27, Green Bay 17
Championship ....at Dallas 38, San Francisco 21

Super Bowl XXVIII
Jan. 30, 1994
Georgia Dome, Atlanta
Favorite: Cowboys by 10½   Attendance: 72,817

Dallas (15-4)	6	0	14	10	**—30**
Buffalo (14-5)	3	10	0	0	**—13**

MVP: Dallas RB Emmitt Smith (30 carries, 132 yds, 2 TDs; 4 catches, 26 yds)

1994 SEASON

AFC Playoffs
First Round................at Miami 27, *Kansas City 17
at *Cleveland 20, *New England 13
Second Round..............at Pittsburgh 29, Cleveland 9
San Diego 22, Miami 21
Championship ....San Diego 17, at Pittsburgh 13

NFC Playoffs
First Round ....at *Green Bay 16, *Detroit 12
*Chicago 25, at Minnesota 18
Second Round ....at San Francisco 44, Chicago 15
at Dallas 35, Green Bay 9
Championship ....at San Francisco 38, Dallas 28

Super Bowl XXIX
Jan. 29, 1995
Joe Robbie Stadium, Miami
Favorite: 49ers by 18   Attendance: 74,107

San Diego (13-5)	7	3	8	8	**—26**
San Francisco (15-3)	14	14	14	7	**—49**

MVP: San Francisco QB Steve Young (24 for 36, 325 yds, 6 TD)

1995 SEASON

AFC Playoffs
First Round.....................at Buffalo 37, *Miami 22
*Indianapolis 35, at San Diego 20
Second Round ....at Pittsburgh 40, Buffalo 21
Indianapolis 10, at Kansas City 7
Championship...........at Pittsburgh 20, Indianapolis 16

NFC Playoffs
First Round ....at *Philadelphia 58, *Detroit 37
at Green Bay 37, *Atlanta 20
Second Round........Green Bay 27, at San Francisco 17
at Dallas 30, Philadelphia 11
Championship ....at Dallas 38, Green Bay 27

Super Bowl XXX
Jan. 28, 1996
Sun Devil Stadium, Tempe, Ariz.
Favorite: Cowboys by 13½   Attendance: 76,347

Dallas (14-4)	10	3	7	7	**—27**
Pittsburgh (13-5)	0	7	0	10	**—17**

MVP: Dallas CB Larry Brown (2 interceptions for 77 yds)

1996 SEASON

AFC Playoffs

First Round ....*Jacksonville 30, at *Buffalo 27
at Pittsburgh 42, *Indianapolis 14
Second Round ....Jacksonville 30, at Denver 27
at New England 28, Pittsburgh 3
Championship ....at New England 20, Jacksonville 6

NFC Playoffs

First Round...............at Dallas 40, *Minnesota 15
at *San Francisco 14, *Philadelphia 0
Second Round.......at Green Bay 35, San Francisco 14
at Carolina 26, Dallas 17
Championship ....at Green Bay 30, Carolina 13

Super Bowl XXXI

Jan. 26, 1997
Louisiana Superdome, New Orleans
Favorite: Packers by 14   Attendance: 72,301

New England (13-5)..........14   0   7   0 —**21**
Green Bay (15-3)............10   17   8   0 —**35**
MVP: Green Bay KR Desmond Howard (4 kickoff returns for 154 yds and 1 TD, also 6 punt returns for 90 yds)

1997 SEASON

AFC Playoffs

First Round ....at *Denver 42, *Jacksonville 17
at New England 17, *Miami 3
Second Round ....at Pittsburgh 7, New England 6
Denver 14, at Kansas City 10
Championship................Denver 24, at Pittsburgh 21

NFC Playoffs

First Round ....*Minnesota 23, at NY Giants 22
at *Tampa Bay 20, *Detroit 10
Second Round.........at San Francisco 38, Minnesota 22
at Green Bay 21, Tampa Bay 7
Championship ....Green Bay 23, at San Francisco 10

Super Bowl XXXII

Jan. 25, 1998
Qualcomm Stadium, San Diego
Favorite: Packers by 11½   Attendance: 68,912

Green Bay (15-3)............7   7   3   7 —**24**
Denver (15-4)..............7   10   7   7 —**31**
MVP: Denver RB Terrell Davis (30 carries, 157 yds, 3 TDs; 2 catches, 8 yds)

1998 SEASON

AFC Playoffs

First Round..................at *Miami 24, *Buffalo 17
at Jacksonville 25, *New England 10
Second Round ....at NY Jets 34, Jacksonville 24
at Denver 38, Miami 3
Championship................at Denver 23, NY Jets 10

NFC Playoffs

First Round.........at *San Francisco 30, *Green Bay 27
*Arizona 20, at Dallas 7
Second Round ....at Atlanta 20, San Francisco 18
at Minnesota 41, Arizona 21
Championship ....Atlanta 30, at Minnesota 27 (OT)

Super Bowl XXXIII

Jan. 31, 1999
Pro Player Stadium, Miami
Favorite: Broncos by 7½   Attendance: 74,803

Denver (16-2) 7   10   0   17 —**34**
Atlanta (16-2) 3   3   0   13 —**19**
MVP: Denver QB John Elway (18 for 29, 336 yds, 1 TD, 1 Int and 1 rushing TD)

1999 SEASON

AFC Playoffs

First Round................at *Tennessee 22, *Buffalo 16
*Miami 20, at Seattle 17
Second Round ....at Jacksonville 62, Miami 7
Tennessee 19, at Indianapolis 16
Championship ....Tennessee 33, at Jacksonville 14

NFC Playoffs

First Round ....at Washington 27, *Detroit 13
at *Minnesota 27, *Dallas 10
Second Round.........at Tampa Bay 14, Washington 13
at St. Louis 49, Minnesota 37
Championship ....at St. Louis 11, Tampa Bay 6

Super Bowl XXXIV

Jan. 30, 2000
Georgia Dome, Atlanta
Favorite: Rams by 7   Attendance: 72,625

St. Louis (15-3) 3   6   7   7 —**23**
Tennessee (16-3) 0   0   6   10 —**16**
MVP: St. Louis QB Kurt Warner (24 for 45, 414 yds, 2 TD)

2000 SEASON

AFC Playoffs

First Round ....at Miami 23, *Indianapolis 17 (OT)
at *Baltimore 21, *Denver 3
Second Round ....at Oakland 27, Miami 0
Baltimore 24, at Tennessee 10
Championship ....Baltimore 16, at Oakland 3

NFC Playoffs

First Round............at New Orleans 31, *St. Louis 28
at *Philadelphia 21, *Tampa Bay 3
Second Round ....at Minnesota 34, New Orleans 16
at NY Giants 20, Philadelphia 10
Championship............at NY Giants 41, Minnesota 0

Super Bowl XXXV

Jan. 28, 2001
Raymond James Stadium, Tampa
Favorite: Ravens by 3   Attendance: 71,921

Baltimore (15-4)..............7   3   14   10 —**34**
NY Giants (14-4) 0   0   7   0 —**7**
MVP: Baltimore LB Ray Lewis (5 tackles, 4 passes defended)

2001 SEASON

AFC Playoffs

First Round...............at Oakland 38, *NY Jets 24
*Baltimore 20, at *Miami 3
Second Round......at New England 16, Oakland 13 (OT)
at Pittsburgh 27, Baltimore 10
Championship......... New England 24, at Pittsburgh 17

NFC Playoffs

First Round ....at Philadelphia 31, *Tampa Bay 9
at *Green Bay 25, *San Francisco 15
Second Round...........Philadelphia 33, at Chicago 19
at St. Louis 45, Green Bay 17
Championship............at St. Louis 29, Philadelphia 24

Super Bowl XXXVI

Feb. 3, 2002
Louisiana Superdome, New Orleans
Favorite: Rams by 14   Attendance: 72,922

St. Louis (16-2) 3   0   0   14 —**17**
New England (13-5)...........0   14   3   3 —**20**
MVP: New England QB Tom Brady (16 for 27, 145 yds, 1 TD)

Before the Super Bowl

The first NFL champion was the Akron Pros in 1920, when the league was called the American Professional Football Association (APFA) and the title went to the team with the best regular season record. The APFA changed its name to the National Football League in 1922.

The first playoff game with the championship at stake came in 1932, when the Chicago Bears (6-1-6) and Portsmouth (Ohio) Spartans (6-1-4) ended the regular season tied for first place. The Bears won the subsequent playoff, 9-0. Due to a snowstorm and cold weather, the game was moved from Wrigley Field to an improvised 80-yard dirt field at Chicago Stadium, making it the first indoor title game as well.

The NFL Championship Game decided the league title until the NFL merged with the AFL and the first Super Bowl was played following the 1966 season.

NFL Champions, 1920-32

Winning player-coaches noted by position.

Multiple winners: Canton-Cleveland Bulldogs and Green Bay (3); Chicago Staleys/Bears (2).

Year	Champion	Head Coach	Year	Champion	Head Coach
1920	Akron Pros	Fritz Pollard, HB & Elgie Tobin, QB	1927	New York Giants	Earl Potteiger, QB
			1928	Providence Steam Roller	Jimmy Conzelman, HB
1921	Chicago Staleys	George Halas, E	1929	Green Bay Packers	Curly Lambeau, QB
1922	Canton Bulldogs	Guy Chamberlin, E	1930	Green Bay Packers	Curly Lambeau
1923	Canton Bulldogs	Guy Chamberlin, E	1931	Green Bay Packers	Curly Lambeau
1924	Cleveland Bulldogs	Guy Chamberlin, E	1932	Chicago Bears	Ralph Jones
1925	Chicago Cardinals	Norm Barry		(Bears beat Portsmouth-OH in playoff, 9-0)	
1926	Frankford Yellow Jackets	Guy Chamberlin, E			

NFL-NFC Championship Game

NFL Championship games from 1933-69 and NFC Championship games since the completion of the NFL-AFL merger following the 1969 season.

Multiple winners: Green Bay (10); Dallas (8); Chicago Bears and Washington (7); NY Giants (6); San Francisco and Cle-LA-St.L Rams (5); Cleveland Browns, Detroit, Minnesota, and Philadelphia (4); Baltimore Colts (3).

Season	Winner	Head Coach	Score	Loser	Head Coach	Site
1933	Chicago Bears	George Halas	23-21	New York	Steve Owen	Chicago
1934	New York	Steve Owen	30-13	Chicago Bears	George Halas	New York
1935	Detroit	Potsy Clark	26-7	New York	Steve Owen	Detroit
1936	Green Bay	Curly Lambeau	21-6	Boston Redskins	Ray Flaherty	New York
1937	Washington Redskins	Ray Flaherty	28-21	Chicago Bears	George Halas	Chicago
1938	New York	Steve Owen	23-17	Green Bay	Curly Lambeau	New York
1939	Green Bay	Curly Lambeau	27-0	New York	Steve Owen	Milwaukee
1940	Chicago Bears	George Halas	73-0	Washington	Ray Flaherty	Washington
1941	Chicago Bears	George Halas	37-9	New York	Steve Owen	Chicago
1942	Washington	Ray Flaherty	14-6	Chicago Bears	Hunk Anderson & Luke Johnsos	Washington
1943	Chicago Bears	Hunk Anderson & Luke Johnsos	41-21	Washington	Arthur Bergman	Chicago
1944	Green Bay	Curly Lambeau	14-7	New York	Steve Owen	New York
1945	Cleveland Rams	Adam Walsh	15-14	Washington	Dudley DeGroot	Cleveland
1946	Chicago Bears	George Halas	24-14	New York	Steve Owen	New York
1947	Chicago Cardinals	Jimmy Conzelman	28-21	Philadelphia	Greasy Neale	Chicago
1948	Philadelphia	Greasy Neale	7-0	Chicago Cardinals	Jimmy Conzelman	Philadelphia
1949	Philadelphia	Greasy Neale	14-0	Los Angeles Rams	Clark Shaughnessy	Los Angeles
1950	Cleveland Browns	Paul Brown	30-28	Los Angeles	Joe Stydahar	Cleveland
1951	Los Angeles	Joe Stydahar	24-17	Cleveland	Paul Brown	Los Angeles
1952	Detroit	Buddy Parker	17-7	Cleveland	Paul Brown	Cleveland
1953	Detroit	Buddy Parker	17-16	Cleveland	Paul Brown	Detroit
1954	Cleveland	Paul Brown	56-10	Detroit	Buddy Parker	Cleveland
1955	Cleveland	Paul Brown	38-14	Los Angeles	Sid Gillman	Los Angeles
1956	New York	Jim Lee Howell	47-7	Chicago Bears	Paddy Driscoll	New York
1957	Detroit	George Wilson	59-14	Cleveland	Paul Brown	Detroit
1958	Balt. Colts	Weeb Ewbank	23-17*	New York	Jim Lee Howell	New York
1959	Balt. Colts	Weeb Ewbank	31-16	New York	Jim Lee Howell	Baltimore
1960	Philadelphia	Buck Shaw	17-13	Green Bay	Vince Lombardi	Philadelphia
1961	Green Bay	Vince Lombardi	37-0	New York	Allie Sherman	Green Bay
1962	Green Bay	Vince Lombardi	16-7	New York	Allie Sherman	New York
1963	Chicago	George Halas	14-10	New York	Allie Sherman	Chicago
1964	Cleveland	Blanton Collier	27-0	Balt. Colts	Don Shula	Cleveland
1965	Green Bay	Vince Lombardi	23-12	Cleveland	Blanton Collier	Green Bay
1966	Green Bay	Vince Lombardi	34-27	Dallas	Tom Landry	Dallas
1967	Green Bay	Vince Lombardi	21-17	Dallas	Tom Landry	Green Bay
1968	Balt. Colts	Don Shula	34-0	Cleveland	Blanton Collier	Cleveland
1969	Minnesota	Bud Grant	27-7	Cleveland	Blanton Collier	Minnesota
1970	Dallas	Tom Landry	17-10	San Francisco	Dick Nolan	San Francisco
1971	Dallas	Tom Landry	14-3	San Francisco	Dick Nolan	Dallas
1972	Washington	George Allen	26-3	Dallas	Tom Landry	Washington

Season	Winner	Head Coach	Score	Loser	Head Coach	Site
1973	Minnesota	Bud Grant	27-10	Dallas	Tom Landry	Dallas
1974	Minnesota	Bud Grant	14-10	Los Angeles	Chuck Knox	Minnesota
1975	Dallas	Tom Landry	37-7	Los Angeles	Chuck Knox	Los Angeles
1976	Minnesota	Bud Grant	24-13	Los Angeles	Chuck Knox	Minnesota
1977	Dallas	Tom Landry	23-6	Minnesota	Bud Grant	Dallas
1978	Dallas	Tom Landry	28-0	Los Angeles	Ray Malavasi	Los Angeles
1979	Los Angeles	Ray Malavasi	9-0	Tampa Bay	John McKay	Tampa Bay
1980	Philadelphia	Dick Vermeil	20-7	Dallas	Tom Landry	Philadelphia
1981	San Francisco	Bill Walsh	28-27	Dallas	Tom Landry	San Francisco
1982	Washington	Joe Gibbs	31-17	Dallas	Tom Landry	Washington
1983	Washington	Joe Gibbs	24-21	San Francisco	Bill Walsh	Washington
1984	San Francisco	Bill Walsh	23-0	Chicago	Mike Ditka	San Francisco
1985	Chicago	Mike Ditka	24-0	Los Angeles	John Robinson	Chicago
1986	New York	Bill Parcells	17-0	Washington	Joe Gibbs	New York
1987	Washington	Joe Gibbs	17-10	Minnesota	Jerry Burns	Washington
1988	San Francisco	Bill Walsh	28-3	Chicago	Mike Ditka	Chicago
1989	San Francisco	George Seifert	30-3	Los Angeles	John Robinson	San Francisco
1990	New York	Bill Parcells	15-13	San Francisco	George Seifert	San Francisco
1991	Washington	Joe Gibbs	41-10	Detroit	Wayne Fontes	Washington
1992	Dallas	Jimmy Johnson	30-20	San Francisco	George Seifert	San Francisco
1993	Dallas	Jimmy Johnson	38-21	San Francisco	George Seifert	Dallas
1994	San Francisco	George Seifert	38-28	Dallas	Barry Switzer	San Francisco
1995	Dallas	Barry Switzer	38-27	Green Bay	Mike Holmgren	Dallas
1996	Green Bay	Mike Holmgren	30-13	Carolina	Dom Capers	Green Bay
1997	Green Bay	Mike Holmgren	23-10	San Francisco	Steve Mariucci	San Francisco
1998	Atlanta	Dan Reeves	30-27*	Minnesota	Dennis Green	Minnesota
1999	St. Louis	Dick Vermeil	11-6	Tampa Bay	Tony Dungy	St. Louis
2000	New York	Jim Fassel	41-0	Minnesota	Dennis Green	New York
2001	St. Louis	Mike Martz	29-24	Philadelphia	Andy Reid	St. Louis

*Sudden death overtime

NFL-NFC Championship Game Appearances

App		W	L	Pct	PF	PA	App		W	L	Pct	PF	PA
17	NY Giants	6	11	.353	281	322	8	Minnesota	4	4	.500	135	151
16	Dallas Cowboys	8	8	.500	361	319	6	Detroit	4	2	.667	139	141
14	Cle-LA-St.L Rams	5	9	.357	163	300	6	Philadelphia	4	2	.667	103	77
13	Green Bay Packers	10	3	.769	303	177	4	Baltimore Colts	3	1	.750	88	60
13	Chicago Bears	7	6	.538	286	245	2	Chicago Cardinals	1	1	.500	28	28
12	Boston-Wash. Redskins	7	5	.583	222	255	2	Tampa Bay	0	2	.000	6	20
12	San Francisco	5	7	.417	245	222	1	Atlanta	1	0	1.000	30	27
11	Cleveland Browns	4	7	.364	224	253	1	Carolina	0	1	.000	13	30

AFL-AFC Championship Game

AFL Championship games from 1960-69 and AFC Championship games since the completion of the NFL-AFL merger following the 1969 season.

Multiple winners: Buffalo and Denver (6); Miami and Pittsburgh (5); Oakland-LA Raiders (4); Dallas Texans-KC Chiefs, Houston Oilers-Tennessee Titans and New England (3); Cincinnati, Jacksonville and San Diego (2).

Season	Winner	Head Coach	Score	Loser	Head Coach	Site
1960	Houston	Lou Rymkus	24-16	LA Chargers	Sid Gillman	Houston
1961	Houston	Wally Lemm	10-3	SD Chargers	Sid Gillman	San Diego
1962	Dallas	Hank Stram	20-17*	Houston	Pop Ivy	Houston
1963	San Diego	Sid Gillman	51-10	Boston Patriots	Mike Holovak	San Diego
1964	Buffalo	Lou Saban	20-7	San Diego	Sid Gillman	Buffalo
1965	Buffalo	Lou Saban	23-0	San Diego	Sid Gillman	San Diego
1966	Kansas City	Hank Stram	31-7	Buffalo	Joel Collier	Buffalo
1967	Oakland	John Rauch	40-7	Houston	Wally Lemm	Oakland
1968	NY Jets	Weeb Ewbank	27-23	Oakland	John Rauch	New York
1969	Kansas City	Hank Stram	17-7	Oakland	John Madden	Oakland
1970	Balt. Colts	Don McCafferty	27-17	Oakland	John Madden	Baltimore
1971	Miami	Don Shula	21-0	Balt. Colts	Don McCafferty	Miami
1972	Miami	Don Shula	21-17	Pittsburgh	Chuck Noll	Pittsburgh
1973	Miami	Don Shula	27-10	Oakland	John Madden	Miami
1974	Pittsburgh	Chuck Noll	24-13	Oakland	John Madden	Oakland
1975	Pittsburgh	Chuck Noll	16-10	Oakland	John Madden	Pittsburgh
1976	Oakland	John Madden	24-7	Pittsburgh	Chuck Noll	Oakland
1977	Denver	Red Miller	20-17	Oakland	John Madden	Denver
1978	Pittsburgh	Chuck Noll	34-5	Houston	Bum Phillips	Pittsburgh
1979	Pittsburgh	Chuck Noll	27-13	Houston	Bum Phillips	Pittsburgh
1980	Oakland	Tom Flores	34-27	San Diego	Don Coryell	San Diego
1981	Cincinnati	Forrest Gregg	27-7	San Diego	Don Coryell	Cincinnati
1982	Miami	Don Shula	14-0	NY Jets	Walt Michaels	Miami
1983	LA Raiders	Tom Flores	30-14	Seattle	Chuck Knox	Los Angeles
1984	Miami	Don Shula	45-28	Pittsburgh	Chuck Noll	Miami

AFL-AFC Championship Game (Cont.)

Season	Winner	Head Coach	Score	Loser	Head Coach	Site
1985	New England	Raymond Berry	31-14	Miami	Don Shula	Miami
1986	Denver	Dan Reeves	23-20*	Cleveland	Marty Schottenheimer	Cleveland
1987	Denver	Dan Reeves	38-33	Cleveland	Marty Schottenheimer	Denver
1988	Cincinnati	Sam Wyche	21-10	Buffalo	Marv Levy	Cincinnati
1989	Denver	Dan Reeves	37-21	Cleveland	Bud Carson	Denver
1990	Buffalo	Marv Levy	51-3	LA Raiders	Art Shell	Buffalo
1991	Buffalo	Marv Levy	10-7	Denver	Dan Reeves	Buffalo
1992	Buffalo	Marv Levy	29-10	Miami	Don Shula	Miami
1993	Buffalo	Marv Levy	30-13	Kansas City	Marty Schottenheimer	Buffalo
1994	San Diego	Bobby Ross	17-13	Pittsburgh	Bill Cowher	Pittsburgh
1995	Pittsburgh	Bill Cowher	20-16	Indianapolis	Ted Marchibroda	Pittsburgh
1996	New England	Bill Parcells	20-6	Jacksonville	Tom Coughlin	New England
1997	Denver	Mike Shanahan	24-21	Pittsburgh	Bill Cowher	Pittsburgh
1998	Denver	Mike Shanahan	23-10	NY Jets	Bill Parcells	Denver
1999	Tennessee	Jeff Fisher	33-14	Jacksonville	Tom Coughlin	Jacksonville
2000	Balt. Ravens	Brian Billick	16-3	Oakland	Jon Gruden	Oakland
2001	New England	Bill Belichick	24-17	Pittsburgh	Bill Cowher	Pittsburgh

*Sudden death overtime

AFL-AFC Championship Game Appearances

App		W	L	Pct	PF	PA	App		W	L	Pct	PF	PA
13	Oakland-LA Raiders	4	9	.308	231	280	4	Boston-NE Patriots	3	1	.750	85	88
11	Pittsburgh	5	6	.455	224	212	3	Baltimore-Indy Colts	1	2	.333	43	58
8	Buffalo	6	2	.750	180	92	3	NY Jets	1	2	.333	37	60
8	LA-San Diego Chargers	2	6	.250	128	161	3	Cleveland	0	3	.000	74	98
7	Denver	6	1	.857	172	132	2	Cincinnati	2	0	1.000	48	17
7	Miami	5	2	.714	152	115	2	Jacksonville	0	2	.000	20	53
7	Houston Oilers/Ten. Titans	3	4	.429	109	154	1	Baltimore Ravens	1	0	1.000	16	3
4	Dallas Texans/KC Chiefs	3	1	.750	81	61	1	Seattle	0	1	.000	14	30

NFL Divisional Champions

The NFL adopted divisional play for the first time in 1967, splitting both conferences into two four-team divisions—the Capitol and Century divisions in the East and the Central and Coastal divisions in the West. A merger with the AFL in 1970 increased NFL membership to 26 teams and made it necessary for realignment. Two 13-team conferences—the AFC and NFC—were formed by moving established NFL clubs in Baltimore, Cleveland and Pittsburgh to the AFC and rearranging both conferences into Eastern, Central and Western divisions. Expansion has since increased the league to 32 teams (beginning in 2002) with four NFC divisions and four AFC divisions, all with four teams each.

Division champions are listed below; teams that went on to win the Super Bowl are in **bold** type. Note that in the 1980 season, Oakland won the Super Bowl as a wild card team, as did Denver in 1997 and Baltimore in 2000; and in 1982, the players' strike shortened the regular season to nine games and eliminated divisional play for one season.

Multiple champions (since 1970): **AFC**—Pittsburgh (14); Miami (12); Oakland-LA Raiders (11); Denver (9); Buffalo (7); Baltimore-Indianapolis Colts and Cleveland (6); Cincinnati, New England and San Diego (5); Kansas City (4); Houston Oilers-Tennessee Titans (3); Jacksonville and Seattle (2). **NFC**—San Francisco (16); Dallas (15); Minnesota (14); LA-St. Louis Rams (10); Chicago (7); Washington (6); NY Giants (5); Green Bay (4); Detroit, Philadelphia and Tampa Bay (3); Atlanta, New Orleans and St. Louis Cardinals (2).

American Football League

Season	East	West
1966	Buffalo	Kansas City

Season	East	West
1967	Houston	Oakland
1968	**NY Jets**	Oakland
1969	NY Jets	Oakland

National Football League

Season	East	West
1966	Dallas	**Green Bay**

Season	East	Century	Central	Coastal
1967	Dallas	Cleveland	**Green Bay**	LA Rams
1968	Dallas	Cleveland	Minnesota	Baltimore
1969	Dallas	Cleveland	Minnesota	LA Rams

Note: Kansas City, an AFL second-place team, won the Super Bowl in the 1969 season.

American Football Conference

Season	East	Central	West
1970	**Balt. Colts**	Cincinnati	Oakland
1971	Miami	Cleveland	Kansas City
1972	**Miami**	Pittsburgh	Oakland
1973	**Miami**	Cincinnati	Oakland
1974	Miami	**Pittsburgh**	Oakland
1975	Balt. Colts	**Pittsburgh**	Oakland
1976	Balt. Colts	Pittsburgh	**Oakland**
1977	Balt. Colts	Pittsburgh	Denver
1978	New England	**Pittsburgh**	Denver
1979	Miami	**Pittsburgh**	San Diego
1980	Buffalo	Cleveland	San Diego
1981	Miami	Cincinnati	San Diego
1982	—		
1983	Miami	Pittsburgh	**LA Raiders**
1984	Miami	Pittsburgh	Denver
1985	Miami	Cleveland	LA Raiders
1986	New England	Cleveland	Denver
1987	Indianapolis	Cleveland	Denver

National Football Conference

Season	East	Central	West
1970	Dallas	Minnesota	San Francisco
1971	**Dallas**	Minnesota	San Francisco
1972	Washington	Green Bay	San Francisco
1973	Dallas	Minnesota	LA Rams
1974	St. Louis	Minnesota	LA Rams
1975	St. Louis	Minnesota	LA Rams
1976	Dallas	Minnesota	LA Rams
1977	**Dallas**	Minnesota	LA Rams
1978	Dallas	Minnesota	LA Rams
1979	Dallas	Tampa Bay	LA Rams
1980	Philadelphia	Minnesota	Atlanta
1981	Dallas	Tampa Bay	**San Francisco**
1982	—		
1983	Washington	Detroit	San Francisco
1984	Washington	Chicago	**San Francisco**
1985	Dallas	**Chicago**	LA Rams
1986	**NY Giants**	Chicago	San Francisco
1987	**Washington**	Chicago	San Francisco

American Football Conference

Season	East	Central	West	Season	East	Central	West
1988	Buffalo	Cincinnati	Seattle	1988	Philadelphia	Chicago	**San Francisco**
1989	Buffalo	Cleveland	Denver	1989	NY Giants	Minnesota	**San Francisco**
1990	Buffalo	Cincinnati	LA Raiders	1990	**NY Giants**	Chicago	San Francisco
1991	Buffalo	Houston	Denver	1991	**Washington**	Detroit	New Orleans
1992	Miami	Pittsburgh	San Diego	1992	**Dallas**	Minnesota	San Francisco
1993	Buffalo	Houston	Kansas City	1993	**Dallas**	Detroit	San Francisco
1994	Miami	Pittsburgh	San Diego	1994	Dallas	Minnesota	**San Francisco**
1995	Buffalo	Pittsburgh	Kansas City	1995	**Dallas**	Green Bay	San Francisco
1996	New England	Pittsburgh	Denver	1996	Dallas	**Green Bay**	Carolina
1997	New England	Pittsburgh	Kansas City	1997	NY Giants	Green Bay	San Francisco
1998	NY Jets	Jacksonville	**Denver**	1998	Dallas	Minnesota	Atlanta
1999	Indianapolis	Jacksonville	Seattle	1999	Washington	Tampa Bay	**St. Louis**
2000	Miami	Tennessee	Oakland	2000	NY Giants	Minnesota	New Orleans
2001	**New England**	Pittsburgh	Oakland	2001	Philadelphia	Chicago	St. Louis

Overall Postseason Games

The postseason records of all NFL teams, ranked by number of playoff games participated in from 1933–2001.

Gm		W	L	Pct	PF	PA	Gm		W	L	Pct	PF	PA
53	Dallas Cowboys	32	21	.604	1271	979	22	Balt-Indianapolis Colts	10	12	.455	393	431
40	San Francisco 49ers	24	16	.600	999	784	20	Boston-NE Patriots	10	10	.500	370	404
40	Oakland-LA Raiders	23	17	.575	936	715	19	Dallas Texans/KC Chiefs	8	11	.421	301	384
40	Cle-LA-St.L Rams	18	22	.450	703	848	18	LA-San Diego Chargers	7	11	.389	332	428
40	Minnesota Vikings	17	23	.425	779	913	17	Detroit Lions	7	10	.412	365	404
39	Miami Dolphins	20	19	.513	780	848	14	New York Jets	6	8	.429	284	285
38	Pittsburgh Steelers	22	16	.579	845	741	12	Cincinnati Bengals	5	7	.417	246	257
37	Boston-Wash. Redskins	22	15	.595	778	642	10	Atlanta Falcons	4	6	.400	208	260
36	New York Giants	16	20	.444	609	660	10	Tampa Bay Buccaneers	3	7	.300	100	201
34	Green Bay Packers	23	11	.676	814	618	8	Jacksonville Jaguars	4	4	.500	208	200
30	Cleveland Browns	11	19	.367	596	692	8	Seattle Seahawks	3	5	.375	145	159
29	Buffalo Bills	14	15	.483	681	658	7	Chi-St.L-Ari. Cardinals	2	5	.286	122	182
29	Chicago Bears	14	15	.483	598	585	6	Baltimore Ravens	5	1	.833	125	53
28	Denver Broncos	16	12	.571	616	657	6	New Orleans Saints	1	5	.167	103	185
27	Houston Oilers/Ten. Titans	12	15	.444	471	626	2	Carolina Panthers	1	1	.500	39	47
25	Philadelphia Eagles	12	13	.480	478	449							

All-Time Postseason Leaders

Through Super Bowl XXXVI in 2002; participants in 2001 season playoffs in **bold** type.

CAREER

Passing Efficiency

Ratings based on performance standards established for completion percentage, average gain, touchdown percentage and interception percentage. Minimum 150 passing attempts.

		Gm	Cmp%	Yds	TD	Int	Rtg
1	Bart Starr	10	61.0	1753	15	3	104.8
2	Joe Montana	23	62.7	5772	45	21	95.6
3	Kenny Anderson	6	66.3	1321	9	6	93.5
4	**Kurt Warner**	7	63.1	2221	15	10	92.3
5	Joe Theismann	10	60.7	1782	11	7	91.4

Passing

Completions		Gm	Cmp
1	Joe Montana, SF-KC	23	460
2	Dan Marino, Miami	18	385
3	John Elway, Denver	22	355

Yards Gained		Gm	Yds
1	Joe Montana, SF-KC	23	5772
2	John Elway, Denver	22	4964
3	Dan Marino, Miami	18	4510

Games

Played		Gm
1	D.D. Lewis, Dallas	27
2	Larry Cole, Dallas	26
3	Charlie Waters, Dallas	25
	Jerry Rice, SF-Oak	25

Coached		Gm
1	Tom Landry, Dallas	36
	Don Shula, Balt. Colts-Miami	36
3	Chuck Noll, Pittsburgh	24

Rushing

	Yards Gained	Gm	Car	Yds	Avg
1	Emmitt Smith, Dallas	17	349	1586	4.54
2	Franco Harris, Pittsburgh	19	400	1556	3.89
3	Thurman Thomas, Buffalo	21	339	1442	4.25

Receiving

	Catches	Gm	No	Yds	Avg
1	**Jerry Rice**, SF-Oak	25	137	2042	14.9
2	Michael Irvin, Dallas	16	87	1315	15.1
3	Andre Reed, Buffalo	21	85	1229	14.5

	Yards Gained	Gm	Yds
1	**Jerry Rice**, SF-Oak	25	2042
2	Michael Irvin, Dallas	16	1315
3	Cliff Branch, Oakland-LA	22	1289

Scoring

	Points	Gm	TD	FG	PAT	Pts
1	Gary Anderson, Pit-Phi-SF-Min	21	0	30	53	143
2	Thurman Thomas, Buffalo	21	21	0	0	126
	Emmitt Smith, Dallas	17	21	0	0	126

	Touchdowns	Gm	Run	Rec	Ret	No
1	Thurman Thomas, Buffalo	21	16	5	0	21
	Emmitt Smith, Dallas	17	19	2	0	21
3	**Jerry Rice**, SF-Oak	25	0	20	0	20

	Field Goals	Gm	Att	FG	Pct
1	Gary Anderson, Pit-Phi-SF-Min	21	37	30	.811
2	George Blanda, Chi-Hou-Oak	19	39	22	.564
3	Steve Christie, Buffalo	12	25	22	.880

Champions of Leagues That No Longer Exist

No professional league in American sports has had to contend with more pretenders to the throne than the NFL. Eight times in nine decades, a rival league has risen up to challenge the NFL and seven of them (including the XFL) went under in less than five seasons. Only the fourth American Football League (1960-69) succeeded, forcing the older league to sue for peace and a full partnership in 1966.

Of the seven leagues that didn't make it, only the All-America Football Conference (1946-49) lives on—the Cleveland Browns and San Francisco 49ers joined the NFL after the AAFC folded in 1949. The champions of leagues past are listed below.

American Football League I

Year		Head Coach
1926	Philadelphia Quakers (8-2)	Bob Folwell

Note: Philadelphia was challenged to a postseason game by the 7th place New York Giants (8-4-1) of the NFL. The Giants won, 31-0, in a snowstorm.

American Football League II

Year		Head Coach
1936	Boston Shamrocks (8-3)	George Kenneally
1937	Los Angeles Bulldogs (9-0)	Gus Henderson

Note: Boston was scheduled to play 2nd place Cleveland (5-2-2) in the '36 championship game, but the Shamrock players refused to participate because they were owed pay for past games.

American Football League III

Year		Head Coach
1940	Columbus Bullies (8-1-1)	Phil Bucklew
1941	Columbus Bullies (5-1-2)	Phil Bucklew

All-America Football Conference

Year	Winner	Head Coach	Score	Loser	Head Coach	Site
1946	Cleveland Browns	Paul Brown	14-9	NY Yankees	Ray Flaherty	Cleveland
1947	Cleveland Browns	Paul Brown	14-3	NY Yankees	Ray Flaherty	New York
1948	Cleveland Browns	Paul Brown	49-7	Buffalo Bills	Red Dawson	Cleveland
1949	Cleveland Browns	Paul Brown	21-7	S.F. 49ers	Buck Shaw	Cleveland

World Football League

Year	Winner	Head Coach	Score	Loser	Head Coach	Site
1974	Birmingham Americans	Jack Gotta	22-21	Florida Blazers	Jack Pardee	Birmingham

United States Football League

Year	Winner	Head Coach	Score	Loser	Head Coach	Site
1983	Michigan Panthers	Jim Stanley	24-22	Philadelphia Stars	Jim Mora	Denver
1984	Philadelphia Stars	Jim Mora	23-3	Arizona Wranglers	George Allen	Tampa
1985	Baltimore Stars	Jim Mora	28-24	Oakland Invaders	Charlie Sumner	E. Rutherford

XFL

Year	Winner	Head Coach	Score	Loser	Head Coach	Site
2001	Los Angeles Xtreme	Al Luginbill	38-6	San Fran. Demons	Jim Skipper	Los Angeles

Defunct Leagues

AFL I (1926): Boston Bulldogs, Brooklyn Horseman, Chicago Bulls, Cleveland Panthers, Los Angeles Wildcats, New York Yankees, Newark Bears, Philadelphia Quakers, Rock Island Independents.

AFL II (1936-37): Boston Shamrocks (1936-37); Brooklyn Tigers (1936); Cincinnati Bengals (1937); Cleveland Rams (1936); Los Angeles Bulldogs (1937); New York Yankees (1936-37); Pittsburgh Americans (1936-37); Rochester Tigers (1936-37).

AFL III (1940-41): Boston Bears (1940); Buffalo Indians (1940-41); Cincinnati Bengals (1940-41); Columbus Bullies (1940-41); Milwaukee Chiefs (1940-41); New York Yankees (1940) renamed Americans (1941).

AAFC (1946-49): Brooklyn Dodgers (1946-48) merged to become Brooklyn-New York Yankees (1949); Buffalo Bisons (1946) renamed Bills (1947-49); Chicago Rockets (1946-48) renamed Hornets (1949); Cleveland Browns (1946-49); Los Angeles Dons (1946-49); Miami Seahawks (1946) became Baltimore Colts (1947-49); New York Yankees (1946-48) merged to become Brooklyn-New York Yankees (1949); San Francisco 49ers (1946-49).

WFL (1974-75): Birmingham Americans (1974) renamed Vulcans (1975); Chicago Fire (1974) renamed Winds (1975); Detroit Wheels (1974); Florida Blazers (1974) became San Antonio Wings (1975); The Hawaiians (1974-75); Houston Texans (1974) also known as Grizzlies (1975); New York Stars (1974) became Charlotte Hornets (1974-75); Philadelphia Bell (1974-75); Portland Storm (1974) renamed Thunder (1975); Southern California Sun (1974-75).

USFL (1983-85): Arizona Wranglers (1983-84) merged with Oklahoma to become Arizona Outlaws (1985); Birmingham Stallions (1983-85); Boston Breakers (1983) became New Orleans Breakers (1984) and then Portland Breakers (1985); Chicago Blitz (1983-84); Denver Gold (1983-85); Houston Gamblers (1984-85); Jacksonville Bulls (1984-85); Los Angeles Express (1983-85); Memphis Showboats (1984-85); Michigan Panthers (1983-84) merged with Oakland (1985); New Jersey Generals (1983-85); Oakland Invaders (1983-85); Oklahoma Outlaws (1984) merged with Arizona to become Arizona Outlaws (1985); Philadelphia Stars (1983-84) became Baltimore Stars (1985); Pittsburgh Maulers (1984); San Antonio Gunslingers (1984-85); Tampa Bay Bandits (1983-85); Washington Federals (1983-84) became Orlando Renegades (1985).

XFL (2001): Birmingham Thunderbolts, Chicago Enforcers, Las Vegas Outlaws, Los Angeles Xtreme, Memphis Maniax, New York/New Jersey Hitmen, Orlando Rage, San Francisco Demons.

NFL Pro Bowl

A postseason All-Star game between the new league champion and a team of professional all-stars was added to the NFL schedule in 1939. In the first game at Wrigley Field in Los Angeles, the NY Giants beat a team made up of players from NFL teams and two independent clubs in Los Angeles (the LA Bulldogs and Hollywood Stars). An all-NFL All-Star team provided the opposition over the next four seasons, but the game was cancelled in 1943.

The Pro Bowl was revived in 1951 as a contest between conference all-star teams: American vs National (1951-53), Eastern vs Western (1954-70), and AFC vs NFC (since 1971). The current series is tied, 16-16.

The MVP trophy was named the Dan McGuire Award in 1984 after the late SF 49ers publicist and *Honolulu Advertiser* sports columnist.

Year	Winner	Score	Loser
1939	NY Giants	13-10	All-Stars
1940	Green Bay	16-7	All-Stars
1940	Chicago Bears	28-14	All-Stars
1942	Chicago Bears	35-24	All-Stars
1942	All-Stars	17-14	Washington
1943-50		No game	

Year	Winner	MVP
1951	American, 28-27	Otto Graham, Cle., QB
1952	National, 30-13	Dan Towler, LA Rams, HB
1953	National, 27-7	Don Doll, Det., DB
1954	East, 20-9	Chuck Bednarik, Phi., LB
1955	West, 26-19	Billy Wilson, SF, E
1956	East, 31-30	Ollie Matson, Cards, HB
1957	West, 19-10	Back—Bert Rechichar, Bal.
		Line—Ernie Stautner, Pit.
1958	West, 26-7	Back—Hugh McElhenny, SF
		Line—Gene Brito, Wash.
1959	East, 28-21	Back—Frank Gifford, NY
		Line—Doug Atkins, Chi.
1960	West, 38-21	Back—Johnny Unitas, Bal.
		Line—Big Daddy Lipscomb, Pit.
1961	West, 35-31	Back—Johnny Unitas, Bal.
		Line—Sam Huff, NY
1962	West, 31-30	Back—Jim Brown, Cle.
		Line—Henry Jordan, GB
1963	East, 30-20	Back—Jim Brown, Cle.
		Line—Big Daddy Lipscomb, Pit.
1964	West, 31-17	Back—Johnny Unitas, Bal.
		Line—Gino Marchetti, Bal.
1965	West, 34-14	Back—Fran Tarkenton, Min.
		Line—Terry Barr, Det.
1966	East, 36-7	Back—Jim Brown, Cle.
		Line—Dale Meinhart, St. L.
1967	East, 20-10	Back—Gale Sayers, Chi.
		Line—Floyd Peters, Phi.
1968	West, 38-20	Back—Gale Sayers, Chi.
		Line—Dave Robinson, GB
1969	West, 10-7	Back—Roman Gabriel, LA Rams
		Line—Merlin Olsen, LA Rams

Year	Winner	MVP
1970	West, 16-13	Back—Gale Sayers, Chi.
		Line—George Andrie, Dal.
1971	NFC, 27-6	Back—Mel Renfro, Dal.
		Line—Fred Carr, GB
1972	AFC, 26-13	Off—Jan Stenerud, KC
		Def—Willie Lanier, KC
1973	AFC, 33-28	O.J. Simpson, Buf., RB
1974	AFC, 15-13	Garo Yepremian, Mia., PK
1975	NFC, 17-10	James Harris, LA Rams, QB
1976	NFC, 23-20	Billy Johnson, Hou., KR
1977	AFC, 24-14	Mel Blount, Pit., CB
1978	NFC, 14-13	Walter Payton, Chi., RB
1979	NFC, 13-7	Ahmad Rashad, Min., WR
1980	NFC, 37-27	Chuck Muncie, NO, RB
1981	NFC, 21-7	Eddie Murray, Det., PK
1982	AFC, 16-13	Kellen Winslow, SD, WR
		& Lee Roy Selmon, TB, DE
1983	NFC, 20-19	Dan Fouts, SD, QB
		& John Jefferson, GB, WR
1984	NFC, 45-3	Joe Theismann, Wash., QB
1985	AFC, 22-14	Mark Gastineau, NYJ, DE
1986	NFC, 28-24	Phil Simms, NYG, QB
1987	AFC, 10-6	Reggie White, Phi., DE
1988	AFC, 15-6	Bruce Smith, Buf., DE
1989	NFC, 34-3	Randall Cunningham, Phi., QB
1990	NFC, 27-21	Jerry Gray, LA Rams, CB
1991	AFC, 23-21	Jim Kelly, Buf., QB
1992	NFC, 21-15	Michael Irvin, Dal., WR
1993	AFC, 23-20 (OT)	Steve Tasker, Buf., Sp. Teams
1994	NFC, 17-3	Andre Rison, Atl., WR
1995	AFC, 41-13	Marshall Faulk, Ind., RB
1996	NFC, 20-13	Jerry Rice, SF, WR
1997	AFC, 26-23 (OT)	Mark Brunell, Jax, QB
1998	AFC, 29-24	Warren Moon, Sea., QB
1999	AFC, 23-10	Ty Law, NE, CB
		& Keyshawn Johnson, NYJ, WR
2000	NFC, 51-31	Randy Moss, Min., WR
2001	AFC, 38-17	Rich Gannon, Oak., QB
2002	AFC, 38-30	Rich Gannon, Oak., QB

Playing sites: Wrigley Field in Los Angeles (1939); Gilmore Stadium in Los Angeles (1940–both games); Polo Grounds in New York (Jan., 1942); Shibe Park in Philadelphia (Dec., 1942); Memorial Coliseum in Los Angeles (1951-72 and 1979); Texas Stadium in Irving, TX (1973); Arrowhead Stadium in Kansas City (1974); Orange Bowl in Miami (1975); Superdome in New Orleans (1976); Kingdome in Seattle (1977); Tampa Stadium in Tampa (1978) and Aloha Stadium in Honolulu (since 1980).

AFL All-Star Game

The AFL did not play an All-Star game after its first season in 1960 but did stage All-Star games from 1962-70. All-Star teams from the Eastern and Western divisions played each other every year except 1966 with the West winning the series, 6-2. In 1966, the league champion Buffalo Bills met an elite squad made up of the best players from the league's other eight clubs and lost, 30-19.

Year	Winner	MVP
1962	West, 47-27	Cotton Davidson, Oak., QB
1963	West, 21-14	Off—Curtis McClinton, Dal.
		Def—Earl Faison, SD
1964	West, 27-24	Off—Keith Lincoln, SD
		Def—Archie Matsos, Oak.
1965	West, 38-14	Off—Keith Lincoln, SD
		Def—Willie Brown, Den.
1966	All-Stars 30	Off—Joe Namath, NY
	Buffalo 19	Def—Frank Buncom, SD

Year	Winner	MVP
1967	East, 30-23	Off—Babe Parilli, Bos.
		Def—Verlon Biggs, NY
1968	East, 25-24	Off—Joe Namath, NY
		& Don Maynard, NY
		Def—Speedy Duncan, SD
1969	West, 38-25	Off—Len Dawson, KC
		Def—George Webster, Hou.
1970	West, 26-3	John Hadl, SD, QB

Playing sites: Balboa Stadium in San Diego (1962-64); Jeppesen Stadium in Houston (1965); Rice Stadium in Houston (1966); Oakland Coliseum (1967); Gator Bowl in Jacksonville (1968-69) and Astrodome in Houston (1970).

NFL Franchise Origins

Here is what the current 32 teams in the National Football League have to show for the years they have put in as members of the American Professional Football Association (APFA), the NFL, the All-America Football Conference (AAFC) and the American Football League (AFL). Years given for league titles indicate seasons championships were won.

American Football Conference

	First Season	League Titles	Franchise Stops
Baltimore Ravens	1996 (NFL)	1 Super Bowl (2000)	• Baltimore (1996—)
Buffalo Bills	1960 (AFL)	2 AFL (1964-65)	• Buffalo (1960-72) Orchard Park, NY (1973—)
Cincinnati Bengals	1968 (AFL)	None	• Cincinnati (1968—)
Cleveland Browns	1946 (AAFC)	4 AAFC (1946-49) 4 NFL (1950,54-55,64)	• Cleveland (1946-95, 99—)
Denver Broncos	1960 (AFL)	2 Super Bowls (1997-98)	• Denver (1960—)
Houston Texans	2002 (NFL)	None	• Houston (2002—)
Indianapolis Colts	1953 (NFL)	3 NFL (1958-59,68) 1 Super Bowl (1970)	• Baltimore (1953-83) Indianapolis (1984—)
Jacksonville Jaguars	1995 (NFL)	None	• Jacksonville, FL (1995—)
Kansas City Chiefs	1960 (AFL)	3 AFL (1962,66,69) 1 Super Bowl (1969)	• Dallas (1960-62) Kansas City (1963—)
Miami Dolphins	1966 (AFL)	2 Super Bowls (1972-73)	• Miami (1966—)
New England Patriots	1960 (AFL)	1 Super Bowl (2001)	• Boston (1960-70) Foxboro, MA (1971—)
New York Jets	1960 (AFL)	1 AFL (1968) 1 Super Bowl (1968)	• New York (1960-83) E. Rutherford, NJ (1984—)
Oakland Raiders	1960 (AFL)	1 AFL (1967) 3 Super Bowls (1976,80,83)	• Oakland (1960-81, 1995—) Los Angeles (1982-94)
Pittsburgh Steelers	1933 (NFL)	4 Super Bowls (1974-75,78-79)	• Pittsburgh (1933—)
San Diego Chargers	1960 (AFL)	1 AFL (1963)	• Los Angeles (1960) San Diego (1961—)
Tennessee Titans	1960 (AFL)	2 AFL (1960-61)	• Houston (1960-96) Memphis (1997) Nashville (1998—)

National Football Conference

	First Season	League Titles	Franchise Stops
Arizona Cardinals	1920 (APFA)	2 NFL (1925,47)	• Chicago (1920-59) St. Louis (1960-87) Tempe, AZ (1988—)
Atlanta Falcons	1966 (NFL)	None	• Atlanta (1966—)
Carolina Panthers	1995 (NFL)	None	• Clemson, SC (1995) Charlotte, NC (1996—)
Chicago Bears	1920 (APFA)	8 NFL (1921, 32-33,40-41,43,46,63) 1 Super Bowl (1985)	• Decatur, IL (1920) Chicago (1921—)
Dallas Cowboys	1960 (NFL)	5 Super Bowls (1971,77,92-93,95)	• Dallas (1960-70) Irving, TX (1971—)
Detroit Lions	1930 (NFL)	4 NFL (1935,52-53,57)	• Portsmouth, OH (1930-33) Detroit (1934-74, 2002—) Pontiac, MI (1975-2001)
Green Bay Packers	1921 (APFA)	11 NFL (1929-31,36,39,44,61-62,65-67) 3 Super Bowls (1966-67,96)	• Green Bay (1921—)
Minnesota Vikings	1961 (NFL)	1 NFL (1969)	• Bloomington, MN (1961-81) Minneapolis, MN (1982—)
New Orleans Saints	1967 (NFL)	None	• New Orleans (1967—)
New York Giants	1925 (NFL)	4 NFL (1927,34,38,56) 2 Super Bowls (1986,90)	• New York (1925-73,75) New Haven, CT (1973-74) E. Rutherford, NJ (1976—)
Philadelphia Eagles	1933 (NFL)	3 NFL (1948-49,60)	• Philadelphia (1933—)
St. Louis Rams	1937 (NFL)	2 NFL (1945,51) 1 Super Bowl (1999)	• Cleveland (1937-45) Los Angeles (1946-79) Anaheim (1980-94) St. Louis (1995—)
San Francisco 49ers	1946 (AAFC)	5 Super Bowls (1981,84,88-89,94)	• San Francisco (1946—)
Seattle Seahawks	1976 (NFL)	None	• Seattle (1976—)
Tampa Bay Buccaneers	1976 (NFL)	None	• Tampa, FL (1976—)
Washington Redskins	1932 (NFL)	2 NFL (1937,42) 3 Super Bowls (1982,87,91)	• Boston (1932-36) Washington, DC (1937-96) Raljon, MD (1997—)

The Growth of the NFL

Of the 14 franchises that comprised the American Professional Football Association in 1920, only two remain—the Arizona Cardinals (then the Chicago Cardinals) and the Chicago Bears (originally the Decatur-IL Staleys). Green Bay joined the APFC in 1921 and the league changed its name to the NFL in 1922. Since then, 54 NFL clubs have come and gone, six rival leagues have expired and two other leagues have been swallowed up.

The NFL merged with the **All-America Football Conference** (1946-49) following the 1949 season and adopted three of its seven clubs—the Baltimore Colts, Cleveland Browns and San Francisco 49ers. The four remaining AAFC teams—the Brooklyn/NY Yankees, Buffalo Bills, Chicago Hornets and Los Angeles Dons—did not survive. After the 1950 season, the financially troubled Colts were sold back to the NFL. The league folded the team and added its players to the 1951 college draft pool. A new Baltimore franchise, also named the Colts, joined the NFL in 1953.

The formation of the **American Football League** (1960-69) was announced in 1959 with ownership lined up in eight cities—Boston, Buffalo, Dallas, Denver, Houston, Los Angeles, Minneapolis and New York. Set to begin play in the autumn of 1960, the AFL was stunned early that year when Minneapolis withdrew to accept an offer to join the NFL as an expansion team in 1961. The new league responded by choosing Oakland to replace Minneapolis and inherit the departed team's draft picks. Since no AFL team actually played in Minneapolis, it is not considered the original home of the Oakland Raiders.

In 1966, the NFL and AFL agreed to a merger that resulted in the first Super Bowl (originally called the AFL-NFL World Championship Game) following the '66 league playoffs. In 1970, the now 10-member AFL officially joined the NFL, forming a 26-team league made up of two conferences of three divisions each. In 2002, the 32-team league was realigned into two conferences of four divisions each.

Expansion/Merger Timetable
For teams currently in NFL.

1921–Green Bay Packers; **1925**–New York Giants; **1930**–Portsmouth-OH Spartans (now Detroit Lions); **1932**–Boston Braves (now Washington Redskins); **1933**–Philadelphia Eagles and Pittsburgh Pirates (now Steelers); **1937**–Cleveland Rams (now St. Louis); **1950**–added AAFC's Cleveland Browns and San Francisco 49ers; **1953**–Baltimore Colts (now Indianapolis).

1960–Dallas Cowboys; **1961**–Minnesota Vikings; **1966**–Atlanta Falcons; **1967**–New Orleans Saints; **1970**–added AFL's Boston Patriots (now New England), Buffalo Bills, Cincinnati Bengals (1968 expansion team), Denver Broncos, Houston Oilers (now Tennessee Titans), Kansas City Chiefs, Miami Dolphins (1966 expansion team), New York Jets, Oakland Raiders and San Diego Chargers (the AFL-NFL merger divided the league into two 13-team conferences with old-line NFL clubs Baltimore, Cleveland and Pittsburgh moving to the AFC); **1976**–Seattle Seahawks and Tampa Bay Buccaneers (Seattle was originally in the NFC West and Tampa Bay in the AFC West, but were switched to AFC West and NFC Central, respectively, in 1977); **1995**–Carolina Panthers and Jacksonville Jaguars; **1996**–Cleveland Browns move to Baltimore and become Ravens. City of Cleveland retains rights to team name, colors and all memorabilia; **1999**–Cleveland Browns return to the NFL. **2002**–Houston Texans. Seattle moves back to the NFC West.

City and Nickname Changes

1921—Decatur Staleys move to Chicago; **1922**—Chicago Staleys renamed Bears; **1933**—Boston Braves renamed Redskins; **1937**—Boston Redskins move to Washington; **1934**—Portsmouth (Ohio) Spartans move to Detroit and become Lions; **1941**—Pittsburgh Pirates renamed Steelers; **1943**—Philadelphia and Pittsburgh merge for one season and become Phil-Pitt, or the "Steagles"; **1944**—Chicago Cardinals and Pittsburgh merge for one season and become Card-Pitt; **1946**—Cleveland Rams move to Los Angeles.

1960—Chicago Cardinals move to St. Louis; **1961**—Los Angeles Chargers (AFL) move to San Diego; **1963**—New York Titans (AFL) renamed Jets and Dallas Texans (AFL) move to Kansas City and become Chiefs; **1971**—Boston Patriots become New England Patriots; **1982**—Oakland Raiders move to Los Angeles; **1984**—Baltimore Colts move to Indianapolis; **1988**—St. Louis Cardinals move to Phoenix; **1994**—Phoenix Cardinals become Arizona Cardinals; **1995**—L.A. Rams move to St. Louis and L.A. Raiders move back to Oakland; **1996**—Cleveland Browns move to Baltimore and become Ravens. City of Cleveland retains rights to team name, colors and all memorabilia; **1997**—Houston Oilers move to Memphis and become Tennessee Oilers; **1998**—Tennessee Oilers move to Nashville; **1999**—Tennessee Oilers renamed Titans.

Defunct NFL Teams

Teams that once played in the APFA and NFL, but no longer exist.

Akron-OH–Pros (1920-25) and Indians (1926); **Baltimore**–Colts (1950); **Boston**–Bulldogs (1926) and Yanks (1944-48); **Brooklyn**–Lions (1926), Dodgers (1930-43) and Tigers (1944); **Buffalo**–All-Americans (1920-23), Bisons (1924-25), Rangers (1926), Bisons (1927,1929); **Canton-OH**–Bulldogs (1920-23,1925-26); **Chicago**–Tigers (1920); **Cincinnati**–Celts (1921) and Reds (1933-34); **Cleveland**–Tigers (1920), Indians (1921), Indians (1923), Bulldogs (1924-25,1927) and Indians (1931); **Columbus-OH**–Panhandles (1920-22) and Tigers (1923-26); **Dallas**–Texans (1952); **Dayton-OH**–Triangles (1920-29).

Detroit–Heralds (1920-21), Panthers (1925-26) and Wolverines (1928); **Duluth-MN**–Kelleys (1923-25) and Eskimos (1926-27); **Evansville-IN**–Crimson Giants (1921-22); **Frankford-PA**–Yellow Jackets (1924-31); **Hammond-IN**–Pros (1920-26); **Hartford**–Blues (1926); **Kansas City**–Blues (1924) and Cowboys (1925-26); **Kenosha-WI**–Maroons (1924); **Los Angeles**–Buccaneers (1926); **Louisville**–Brecks (1921-23) and Colonels (1926); **Marion-OH**–Oorang Indians (1922-23); **Milwaukee**–Badgers (1922-26); **Minneapolis**–Marines (1922-24) and Red Jackets (1929-30); **Muncie-IN**–Flyers (1920-21).

New York–Giants (1921), Yankees (1927-28), Bulldogs (1949) and Yankees (1950-51); **Newark-NJ**–Tornadoes (1930); **Orange-NJ**–Tornadoes (1929); **Pottsville-PA**–Maroons (1925-28); **Providence-RI**–Steam Roller (1925-31); **Racine-WI**–Legion (1922-24) and Tornadoes (1926); **Rochester-NY**–Jeffersons (1920-25); **Rock Island-IL**–Independents (1920-26); **Staten Island-NY**–Stapletons (1929-32); **St. Louis**–All-Stars (1923) and Gunners (1934); **Toledo-OH**–Maroons (1922-23); **Tonawanda-NY**–Kardex (1921), also called Lumbermen; **Washington**–Senators (1921).

Annual NFL Leaders

Individual leaders in NFL (1932-69), NFC (since 1970), AFL (1960-69) and AFC (since 1970).

Passing

Since 1932, the NFL has used several formulas to determine passing leadership, from Total Yards alone (1932-37), to the current rating system—adopted in 1973—that takes Completions, Completion Percentage, Yards Gained, TD Passes, Interceptions, Interception Percentage and other factors into account. The quarterbacks listed below all led the league according to the system in use at the time.

Multiple winners: Sammy Baugh and Steve Young (6); Joe Montana and Roger Staubach (5); Arnie Herber, Sonny Jurgensen, Bart Starr and Norm Van Brocklin (3); Ed Danowski, Otto Graham, Cecil Isbell, Milt Plum, Kurt Warner and Bob Waterfield (2).

NFL-NFC

Year		Att	Cmp	Yds	TD	Year		Att	Cmp	Yds	TD
1932	Arnie Herber, GB	101	37	639	9	1967	Sonny Jurgensen, Wash	508	288	3747	31
1933	Harry Newman, NY	136	53	973	11	1968	Earl Morrall, Bal	317	182	2909	26
1934	Arnie Herber, GB	115	42	799	8	1969	Sonny Jurgensen, Wash	442	274	3102	22
1935	Ed Danowski, NY	113	57	794	10	1970	John Brodie, SF	378	223	2941	24
1936	Arnie Herber, GB	173	77	1239	11	1971	Roger Staubach, Dal	211	126	1882	15
1937	Sammy Baugh, Wash	171	81	1127	8	1972	Norm Snead, NY	325	196	2307	17
1938	Ed Danowski, NY	129	70	848	7	1973	Roger Staubach, Dal	286	179	2428	23
1939	Parker Hall, Cle. Rams	208	106	1227	9	1974	Sonny Jurgensen, Wash	167	107	1185	11
1940	Sammy Baugh, Wash	177	111	1367	12	1975	Fran Tarkenton, Min	425	273	2994	25
1941	Cecil Isbell, GB	206	117	1479	15	1976	James Harris, LA	158	91	1460	8
1942	Cecil Isbell, GB	268	146	2021	24	1977	Roger Staubach, Dal	361	210	2620	18
1943	Sammy Baugh, Wash	239	133	1754	23	1978	Roger Staubach, Dal	413	231	3190	25
1944	Frank Filchock, Wash	147	84	1139	13	1979	Roger Staubach, Dal	461	267	3586	27
1945	Sammy Baugh, Wash	182	128	1669	11	1980	Ron Jaworski, Phi	451	257	3529	27
	& Sid Luckman, Chi. Bears	217	117	1725	14	1981	Joe Montana, SF	488	311	3565	19
1946	Bob Waterfield, LA	251	127	1747	18	1982	Joe Theismann, Wash	252	161	2033	13
1947	Sammy Baugh, Wash	354	210	2938	25	1983	Steve Bartkowski, Atl	432	274	3167	22
1948	Tommy Thompson, Phi	246	141	1965	25	1984	Joe Montana, SF	432	279	3630	28
1949	Sammy Baugh, Wash	255	145	1903	18	1985	Joe Montana, SF	494	303	3653	27
1950	Norm Van Brocklin, LA	233	127	2061	18	1986	Tommy Kramer, Min	372	208	3000	24
1951	Bob Waterfield, LA	176	88	1566	13	1987	Joe Montana, SF	398	266	3054	31
1952	Norm Van Brocklin, LA	205	113	1736	14	1988	Wade Wilson, Min	332	204	2746	15
1953	Otto Graham, Cle	258	167	2722	11	1989	Don Majkowski, GB	599	353	4318	27
1954	Norm Van Brocklin, LA	260	139	2637	13	1990	Joe Montana, SF	520	321	3944	26
1955	Otto Graham, Cle	185	98	1721	15	1991	Steve Young, SF	279	180	2517	17
1956	Ed Brown, Chi. Bears	168	96	1667	11	1992	Steve Young, SF	402	268	3465	25
1957	Tommy O'Connell, Cle	110	63	1229	9	1993	Steve Young, SF	462	314	4023	29
1958	Eddie LeBaron, Wash	145	79	1365	11	1994	Steve Young, SF	461	324	3969	35
1959	Charlie Conerly, NY	194	113	1706	14	1995	Brett Favre, GB	570	359	4413	38
1960	Milt Plum, Cle	250	151	2297	21	1996	Steve Young, SF	316	214	2410	14
1961	Milt Plum, Cle	302	177	2416	16	1997	Steve Young, SF	356	241	3029	19
1962	Bart Starr, GB	285	178	2438	12	1998	Randall Cunningham, Min	425	259	3704	34
1963	Y.A. Tittle, NY	367	221	3145	36	1999	Kurt Warner, St.L	499	325	4353	41
1964	Bart Starr, GB	272	163	2144	15	2000	Trent Green, St.L	240	145	2063	16
1965	Rudy Bukich, Chi	312	176	2641	20	2001	Kurt Warner, St.L	546	375	4830	36
1966	Bart Starr, GB	251	156	2257	14						

Note: In 1945, Sammy Baugh and Sid Luckman tied with 8 points on an inverse rating system.

AFL-AFC

Multiple winners: Dan Marino (5); Ken Anderson and Len Dawson (4); Bob Griese, Daryle Lamonica, Warren Moon and Ken Stabler (2).

Year		Att	Cmp	Yds	TD	Year		Att	Cmp	Yds	TD
1960	Jack Kemp, LA	406	211	3018	20	1981	Ken Anderson, Cin	479	300	3753	29
1961	George Blanda, Hou	362	187	3330	36	1982	Ken Anderson, Cin	309	218	2495	12
1962	Len Dawson, Dal	310	189	2759	29	1983	Dan Marino, Mia	296	173	2210	20
1963	Tobin Rote, SD	286	170	2510	20	1984	Dan Marino, Mia	564	362	5084	48
1964	Len Dawson, KC	354	199	2879	30	1985	Ken O'Brien, NY	488	297	3888	25
1965	John Hadl, SD	348	174	2798	20	1986	Dan Marino, Mia	623	378	4746	44
1966	Len Dawson, KC	284	159	2527	26	1987	Bernie Kosar, Cle	389	241	3033	22
1967	Daryle Lamonica, Oak	425	220	3228	30	1988	Boomer Esiason, Cin	388	223	3572	28
1968	Len Dawson, KC	224	131	2109	17	1989	Dan Marino, Mia	550	308	3997	24
1969	Greg Cook, Cin	197	106	1854	15	1990	Warren Moon, Hou	584	362	4689	33
1970	Daryle Lamonica, Oak	356	179	2516	22	1991	Jim Kelly, Buf	474	304	3844	33
1971	Bob Griese, Mia	263	145	2089	19	1992	Warren Moon, Hou	346	224	2521	18
1972	Earl Morrall, Mia	150	83	1360	11	1993	John Elway, Den	551	348	4030	25
1973	Ken Stabler, Oak	260	163	1997	14	1994	Dan Marino, Mia	615	385	4453	30
1974	Ken Anderson, Cin	328	213	2667	18	1995	Jim Harbaugh, Ind	314	200	2575	17
1975	Ken Anderson, Cin	377	228	3169	21	1996	John Elway, Den	466	287	3328	26
1976	Ken Stabler, Oak	291	194	2737	27	1997	Mark Brunell, Jax	435	264	3281	18
1977	Bob Griese, Mia	307	180	2252	22	1998	Vinny Testaverde, NYJ	421	259	3256	29
1978	Terry Bradshaw, Pit	368	207	2915	28	1999	Peyton Manning, Ind	533	331	4135	26
1979	Dan Fouts, SD	530	332	4082	24	2000	Brian Griese, Den	336	216	2688	19
1980	Brian Sipe, Cle	554	337	4132	30	2001	Rich Gannon, Oak	549	361	3828	27

Receptions
NFL-NFC

Multiple winners: Don Hutson (8); Raymond Berry, Tom Fears, Pete Pihos, Jerry Rice, Sterling Sharpe and Billy Wilson (3); Dwight Clark, Herman Moore, Muhsin Muhammad, Ahmad Rashad and Charley Taylor (2).

Year		No	Yds	Avg	TD	Year		No	Yds	Avg	TD
1932	Ray Flaherty, NY	21	350	16.7	3	1967	Charley Taylor, Wash	70	990	14.1	9
1933	Shipwreck Kelly, Bklyn	22	246	11.2	3	1968	Clifton McNeil, SF	71	994	14.0	7
1934	Joe Carter, Phi	16	238	14.9	4	1969	Dan Abramowicz, NO	73	1015	13.9	7
	& Red Badgro, NY	16	206	12.9	1	1970	Dick Gordon, Chi	71	1026	14.5	13
1935	Tod Goodwin, NY	26	432	16.6	4	1971	Bob Tucker, NY	59	791	13.4	4
1936	Don Hutson, GB	34	536	15.8	8	1972	Harold Jackson, Phi	62	1048	16.9	4
1937	Don Hutson, GB	41	552	13.5	7	1973	Harold Carmichael, Phi	67	1116	16.7	9
1938	Gaynell Tinsley, Chi. Cards	41	516	12.6	1	1974	Charles Young, Phi	63	696	11.0	3
1939	Don Hutson, GB	34	846	24.9	6	1975	Chuck Foreman, Min	73	691	9.5	9
1940	Don Looney, Phi	58	707	12.2	4	1976	Drew Pearson, Dal	58	806	13.9	6
1941	Don Hutson, GB	58	739	12.7	10	1977	Ahmad Rashad, Min	51	681	13.4	2
1942	Don Hutson, GB	74	1211	16.4	17	1978	Rickey Young, Min	88	704	8.0	5
1943	Don Hutson, GB	47	776	16.5	11	1979	Ahmad Rashad, Min	80	1156	14.5	9
1944	Don Hutson, GB	58	866	14.9	9	1980	Earl Cooper, SF	83	567	6.8	4
1945	Don Hutson, GB	47	834	17.7	9	1981	Dwight Clark, SF	85	1105	13.0	4
1946	Jim Benton, LA	63	981	15.6	6	1982	Dwight Clark, SF	60	913	12.2	5
1947	Jim Keane, Chi. Bears	64	910	14.2	10	1983	Roy Green, St. L	78	1227	15.7	14
1948	Tom Fears, LA	51	698	13.7	4		Charlie Brown, Wash	78	1225	15.7	8
1949	Tom Fears, LA	77	1013	13.2	9		& Earnest Gray, NY	78	1139	14.6	5
1950	Tom Fears, LA	84	1116	13.3	7	1984	Art Monk, Wash	106	1372	12.9	7
1951	Elroy Hirsch, LA	66	1495	22.7	17	1985	Roger Craig, SF	92	1016	11.0	6
1952	Mac Speedie, Cle	62	911	14.7	5	1986	Jerry Rice, SF	86	1570	18.3	15
1953	Pete Pihos, Phi	63	1049	16.7	10	1987	J.T. Smith, St. L	91	1117	12.3	8
1954	Pete Pihos, Phi	60	872	14.5	10	1988	Henry Ellard, LA	86	1414	16.4	10
	& Billy Wilson, SF	60	830	13.8	5	1989	Sterling Sharpe, GB	90	1423	15.8	12
1955	Pete Pihos, Phi	62	864	13.9	7	1990	Jerry Rice, SF	100	1502	15.0	13
1956	Billy Wilson, SF	60	889	14.8	5	1991	Michael Irvin, Dal	93	1523	16.4	8
1957	Billy Wilson, SF	52	757	14.6	6	1992	Sterling Sharpe, GB	108	1461	13.5	13
1958	Raymond Berry, Bal	56	794	14.2	9	1993	Sterling Sharpe, GB	112	1274	11.4	11
	& Pete Retzlaff, Phi	56	766	13.7	2	1994	Cris Carter, Min	122	1256	10.3	7
1959	Raymond Berry, Bal	66	959	14.5	14	1995	Herman Moore, Det	123	1686	13.7	14
1960	Raymond Berry, Bal	74	1298	17.5	10	1996	Jerry Rice, SF	108	1254	11.6	8
1961	Red Phillips, LA	78	1092	14.0	5	1997	Herman Moore, Det	104	1293	12.4	8
1962	Bobby Mitchell, Wash	72	1384	19.2	11	1998	Frank Sanders, Ari	89	1145	12.9	3
1963	Bobby Joe Conrad, St. L	73	967	13.2	10	1999	Muhsin Muhammad, Car	96	1253	13.1	8
1964	Johnny Morris, Chi. Bears	93	1200	12.9	10	2000	Muhsin Muhammad, Car	102	1183	11.6	6
1965	Dave Parks, SF	80	1344	16.8	12	2001	Keyshawn Johnson, TB	106	1266	11.9	1
1966	Charley Taylor, Wash	72	1119	15.5	12						

AFL-AFC

Multiple winners: Lionel Taylor (5); Lance Alworth, Haywood Jeffires, Lydell Mitchell and Kellen Winslow (3); Fred Biletnikoff, Todd Christensen, Carl Pickens and Al Toon (2).

Year		No	Yds	Avg	TD	Year		No	Yds	Avg	TD
1960	Lionel Taylor, Den	92	1235	13.4	12	1981	Kellen Winslow, SD	88	1075	12.2	10
1961	Lionel Taylor, Den	100	1176	11.8	4	1982	Kellen Winslow, SD	54	721	13.4	6
1962	Lionel Taylor, Den	77	908	11.8	4	1983	Todd Christensen, LA	92	1247	13.6	12
1963	Lionel Taylor, Den	78	1101	14.1	10	1984	Ozzie Newsome, Cle	89	1001	11.2	5
1964	Charley Hennigan, Hou	101	1546	15.3	8	1985	Lionel James, SD	86	1027	11.9	6
1965	Lionel Taylor, Den	85	1131	13.3	6	1986	Todd Christensen, LA	95	1153	12.1	8
1966	Lance Alworth, SD	73	1383	18.9	13	1987	Al Toon, NY	68	976	14.4	5
1967	George Sauer, NY	75	1189	15.9	6	1988	Al Toon, NY	93	1067	11.5	5
1968	Lance Alworth, SD	68	1312	19.3	10	1989	Andre Reed, Buf	88	1312	14.9	9
1969	Lance Alworth, SD	64	1003	15.7	4	1990	Haywood Jeffires, Hou	74	1048	14.2	8
1970	Marlin Briscoe, Buf	57	1036	18.2	8		& Drew Hill, Hou	74	1019	13.8	5
1971	Fred Biletnikoff, Oak	61	929	15.2	9	1991	Haywood Jeffires, Hou	100	1181	11.8	7
1972	Fred Biletnikoff, Oak	58	802	13.8	7	1992	Haywood Jeffires, Hou	90	913	10.1	9
1973	Fred Willis, Hou	57	371	6.5	1	1993	Reggie Langhorne, Ind	85	1038	12.2	3
1974	Lydell Mitchell, Bal	72	544	7.6	2	1994	Ben Coates, NE	96	1174	12.2	7
1975	Reggie Rucker, Cle	60	770	12.8	3	1995	Carl Pickens, Cin	99	1234	12.5	17
	& Lydell Mitchell, Bal	60	544	9.1	4	1996	Carl Pickens, Cin	100	1180	11.8	12
1976	MacArthur Lane, KC	66	686	10.4	1	1997	Tim Brown, Oak	104	1408	13.5	5
1977	Lydell Mitchell, Bal	71	620	8.7	4	1998	O.J. McDuffie, Mia	90	1050	11.7	7
1978	Steve Largent, Sea	71	1168	16.5	8	1999	Jimmy Smith, Jax	116	1636	14.1	6
1979	Joe Washington, Bal	82	750	9.1	3	2000	Marvin Harrison, Ind	102	1413	13.9	14
1980	Kellen Winslow, SD	89	1290	14.5	9	2001	Rod Smith, Den	113	1343	11.9	11

Annual NFL Leaders (Cont.)
Rushing

NFL-NFC

Multiple winners: Jim Brown (8); Walter Payton and Barry Sanders (5); Emmitt Smith and Steve Van Buren (4); Eric Dickerson (3); Cliff Battles, John Brockington, Larry Brown, Bill Dudley, Leroy Kelly, Bill Paschal, Joe Perry, Gale Sayers, Stephen Davis and Whizzer White (2).

Year		Car	Yds	Avg	TD	Year		Car	Yds	Avg	TD
1932	Cliff Battles, Bos	148	576	3.9	3	1967	Leroy Kelly, Cle	235	1205	5.1	11
1933	Jim Musick, Bos	173	809	4.7	5	1968	Leroy Kelly, Cle	248	1239	5.0	16
1934	Beattie Feathers, Chi. Bears	119	1004	8.4	8	1969	Gale Sayers, Chi	236	1032	4.4	8
1935	Doug Russell, Chi. Cards	140	499	3.6	0	1970	Larry Brown, Wash	237	1125	4.7	5
1936	Tuffy Leemans, NY	206	830	4.0	2	1971	John Brockington, GB	216	1105	5.1	4
1937	Cliff Battles, Wash	216	874	4.0	5	1972	Larry Brown, Wash	285	1216	4.3	8
1938	Whizzer White, Pit.	152	567	3.7	4	1973	John Brockington, GB	265	1144	4.3	3
1939	Bill Osmanski, Chi. Bears	121	699	5.8	7	1974	Lawrence McCutcheon, LA	236	1109	4.7	3
1940	Whizzer White, Det.	146	514	3.5	5	1975	Jim Otis, St.l.	269	1076	4.0	5
1941	Pug Manders, Bklyn	111	486	4.4	5	1976	Walter Payton, Chi	311	1390	4.5	13
1942	Bill Dudley, Pit.	162	696	4.3	5	1977	Walter Payton, Chi	339	1852	5.5	14
1943	Bill Paschal, NY	147	572	3.9	10	1978	Walter Payton, Chi	333	1395	4.2	11
1944	Bill Paschal, NY	196	737	3.8	9	1979	Walter Payton, Chi	369	1610	4.4	14
1945	Steve Van Buren, Phi	143	832	5.8	15	1980	Walter Payton, Chi	317	1460	4.6	6
1946	Bill Dudley, Pit	146	604	4.1	3	1981	George Rogers, NO	378	1674	4.4	13
1947	Steve Van Buren, Phi	217	1008	4.6	13	1982	Tony Dorsett, Dal	177	745	4.2	5
1948	Steve Van Buren, Phi	201	945	4.7	10	1983	Eric Dickerson, LA	390	1808	4.6	18
1949	Steve Van Buren, Phi	263	1146	4.4	11	1984	Eric Dickerson, LA	379	2105	5.6	14
1950	Marion Motley, Cle	140	810	5.8	3	1985	Gerald Riggs, Atl	397	1719	4.3	10
1951	Eddie Price, NY Giants	271	971	3.6	7	1986	Eric Dickerson, LA	404	1821	4.5	11
1952	Dan Towler, LA	156	894	5.7	10	1987	Charles White, LA	324	1374	4.2	11
1953	Joe Perry, SF	192	1018	5.3	10	1988	Herschel Walker, Dal	361	1514	4.2	5
1954	Joe Perry, SF	173	1049	6.1	8	1989	Barry Sanders, Det	280	1470	5.3	14
1955	Alan Ameche, Bal.	213	961	4.5	9	1990	Barry Sanders, Det	255	1304	5.1	13
1956	Rick Casares, Chi. Bears	234	1126	4.8	12	1991	Emmitt Smith, Dal	365	1563	4.3	12
1957	Jim Brown, Cle	202	942	4.7	9	1992	Emmitt Smith, Dal	373	1713	4.6	18
1958	Jim Brown, Cle	257	1527	5.9	17	1993	Emmitt Smith, Dal	283	1486	5.3	9
1959	Jim Brown, Cle	290	1329	4.6	14	1994	Barry Sanders, Det	331	1883	5.7	7
1960	Jim Brown, Cle	215	1257	5.8	9	1995	Emmitt Smith, Dal	377	1773	4.7	25
1961	Jim Brown, Cle	305	1408	4.6	8	1996	Barry Sanders, Det	307	1553	5.1	11
1962	Jim Taylor, GB	272	1474	5.4	19	1997	Barry Sanders, Det	335	2053	6.1	11
1963	Jim Brown, Cle	291	1863	6.4	12	1998	Jamal Anderson, Atl	410	1846	4.5	14
1964	Jim Brown, Cle	280	1446	5.2	7	1999	Stephen Davis, Wash	290	1405	4.8	17
1965	Jim Brown, Cle	289	1544	5.3	17	2000	Robert Smith, Min	295	1521	5.2	7
1966	Gale Sayers, Chi	229	1231	5.4	8	2001	Stephen Davis, Wash	356	1432	4.0	5

Note: Jim Brown led the NFL in rushing eight of his nine years in the league. The one season he didn't win (1962) he finished fourth (996 yds) behind Jim Taylor, John Henry Johnson of Pittsburgh (1,141 yds) and Dick Bass of the LA Rams (1,033 yds).

AFL-AFC

Multiple winners: Earl Campbell and O.J. Simpson (4); Terrell Davis and Thurman Thomas (3); Eric Dickerson, Cookie Gilchrist, Edgerrin James, Floyd Little, Jim Nance and Curt Warner (2).

Year		Car	Yds	Avg	TD	Year		Car	Yds	Avg	TD
1960	Abner Haynes, Dal.	157	875	5.6	9	1981	Earl Campbell, Hou	361	1376	3.8	10
1961	Billy Cannon, Hou	200	948	4.7	6	1982	Freeman McNeil, NY	151	786	5.2	6
1962	Cookie Gilchrist, Buf	214	1096	5.1	13	1983	Curt Warner, Sea.	335	1449	4.3	13
1963	Clem Daniels, Oak	215	1099	5.1	3	1984	Earnest Jackson, SD	296	1179	4.0	8
1964	Cookie Gilchrist, Buf	230	981	4.3	6	1985	Marcus Allen, LA	380	1759	4.6	11
1965	Paul Lowe, SD	222	1121	5.0	7	1986	Curt Warner, Sea	319	1481	4.6	13
1966	Jim Nance, Bos	299	1458	4.9	11	1987	Eric Dickerson, Ind	223	1011	4.5	5
1967	Jim Nance, Bos	269	1216	4.5	7	1988	Eric Dickerson, Ind	388	1659	4.3	14
1968	Paul Robinson, Cin	238	1023	4.3	8	1989	Christian Okoye, KC	370	1480	4.0	12
1969	Dickie Post, SD	182	873	4.8	6	1990	Thurman Thomas, Buf	271	1297	4.8	11
1970	Floyd Little, Den	209	901	4.3	3	1991	Thurman Thomas, Buf	288	1407	4.9	7
1971	Floyd Little, Den	284	1133	4.0	6	1992	Barry Foster, Pit	390	1690	4.3	11
1972	O.J. Simpson, Buf.	292	1251	4.3	6	1993	Thurman Thomas, Buf	355	1315	3.7	6
1973	O.J. Simpson, Buf.	332	2003	6.0	12	1994	Chris Warren, Sea.	333	1545	4.6	9
1974	Otis Armstrong, Den	263	1407	5.3	9	1995	Curtis Martin, NE.	368	1487	4.0	14
1975	O.J. Simpson, Buf.	329	1817	5.5	16	1996	Terrell Davis, Den	345	1538	4.5	13
1976	O.J. Simpson, Buf.	290	1503	5.2	8	1997	Terrell Davis, Den	369	1750	4.7	15
1977	Mark van Eeghen, Oak	324	1273	3.9	7	1998	Terrell Davis, Den	392	2008	5.1	21
1978	Earl Campbell, Hou	302	1450	4.8	13	1999	Edgerrin James, Ind	369	1553	4.2	13
1979	Earl Campbell, Hou	368	1697	4.6	19	2000	Edgerrin James, Ind	387	1709	4.4	13
1980	Earl Campbell, Hou	373	1934	5.2	13	2001	Priest Holmes, KC	327	1555	4.8	8

Note: Eric Dickerson was traded to Indianapolis from the NFC's LA Rams during the 1987 season. In three games with the Rams, he carried the ball 60 times for 277 yds, a 4.6 avg and 1 TD. His official AFC statistics above came in nine games with the Colts.

Scoring

NFL-NFC

Multiple winners: Don Hutson (5); Dutch Clark, Pat Harder, Paul Hornung, Chip Lohmiller and Mark Moseley (3); Kevin Butler, Mike Cofer, Fred Cox, Marshall Faulk, Jack Manders, Chester Marcol, Eddie Murray, Emmitt Smith, Gordy Soltau and Doak Walker (2).

Year		TD	FG	PAT	Pts	Year		TD	FG	PAT	Pts
1932	Dutch Clark, Portsmouth	6	3	10	55	1968	Leroy Kelly, Cle	20	0	0	120
1933	Glenn Presnell, Portsmouth	6	6	10	64	1969	Fred Cox, Min	0	26	43	121
	& Ken Strong, NY	6	5	13	64	1970	Fred Cox, Min	0	30	35	125
1934	Jack Manders, Chi. Bears	3	10	31	79	1971	Curt Knight, Wash.	0	29	27	114
1935	Dutch Clark, Det	6	1	16	55	1972	Chester Marcol, GB	0	33	29	128
1936	Dutch Clark, Det	7	4	19	73	1973	David Ray, LA	0	30	40	130
1937	Jack Manders, Chi. Bears	5	8	15	69	1974	Chester Marcol, GB	0	25	19	94
1938	Clarke Hinkle, GB	7	3	7	58	1975	Chuck Foreman, Min	22	0	0	132
1939	Andy Farkas, Wash	11	0	2	68	1976	Mark Moseley, Wash	0	22	31	97
1940	Don Hutson, GB	7	0	15	57	1977	Walter Payton, Chi	16	0	0	96
1941	Don Hutson, GB	12	1	20	95	1978	Frank Corral, LA	0	29	31	118
1942	Don Hutson, GB	17	1	33	138	1979	Mark Moseley, Wash	0	25	39	114
1943	Don Hutson, GB	12	3	26	117	1980	Eddie Murray, Det.	0	27	35	116
1944	Don Hutson, GB	9	0	31	85	1981	Rafael Septien, Dal	0	27	40	121
1945	Steve Van Buren, Phi	18	0	2	110		& Eddie Murray, Det.	0	25	46	121
1946	Ted Fritsch, GB	10	9	13	100	1982	Wendell Tyler, LA	13	0	0	78
1947	Pat Harder, Chi. Cards	7	7	39	102	1983	Mark Moseley, Wash	0	33	62	161
1948	Pat Harder, Chi. Cards	6	7	53	110	1984	Ray Wersching, SF	0	25	56	131
1949	Gene Roberts, NY Giants	17	0	0	102	1985	Kevin Butler, Chi	0	31	51	144
	& Pat Harder, Chi. Cards	8	3	45	102	1986	Kevin Butler, Chi	0	28	36	120
1950	Doak Walker, Det	11	8	38	128	1987	Jerry Rice, SF	23	0	0	138
1951	Elroy Hirsch, LA	17	0	0	102	1988	Mike Cofer, SF	0	27	40	121
1952	Gordy Soltau, SF	7	6	34	94	1989	Mike Cofer, SF	0	29	49	136
1953	Gordy Soltau, SF	6	10	48	114	1990	Chip Lohmiller, Wash.	0	30	41	131
1954	Bobby Walston, Phi	11	4	36	114	1991	Chip Lohmiller, Wash.	0	31	56	149
1955	Doak Walker, Det	7	9	27	96	1992	Chip Lohmiller, Wash.	0	30	30	120
1956	Bobby Layne, Det	5	12	33	99		& Morten Andersen, NO	0	29	33	120
1957	Sam Baker, Wash	1	14	29	77	1993	Jason Hanson, Det	0	34	28	130
	& Lou Groza, Cle	0	15	32	77	1994	Emmitt Smith, Dal	22	0	0	132
1958	Jim Brown, Cle	18	0	0	108		& Fuad Reveiz, Min	0	34	30	132
1959	Paul Hornung, GB	7	7	31	94	1995	Emmitt Smith, Dal	25	0	0	150
1960	Paul Hornung, GB	15	15	41	176	1996	John Kasay, Car.	0	37	34	145
1961	Paul Hornung, GB	10	15	41	146	1997	Richie Cunningham, Dal.	0	34	24	126
1962	Jim Taylor, GB	19	0	0	114	1998	Gary Anderson, Min.	0	35	59	164
1963	Don Chandler, NY.	0	18	52	106	1999	Jeff Wilkins, St.L.	0	20	64	124
1964	Lenny Moore, Bal	20	0	0	120	2000	Marshall Faulk, St.L	26	0	4	160
1965	Gale Sayers, Chi.	22	0	0	132	2001	Marshall Faulk, St.L	21	0	2	128
1966	Bruce Gossett, LA	0	28	29	113						
1967	Jim Bakken, St.L	0	27	36	117						

AFL-AFC

Multiple winners: Gino Cappelletti (5); Gary Anderson (3); Jim Breech, Roy Gerela, Gene Mingo, Nick Lowery, John Smith, Pete Stoyanovich, Jim Turner and Mike Vanderjagt (2).

Year		TD	FG	PAT	Pts	Year		TD	FG	PAT	Pts
1960	Gene Mingo, Den	6	18	33	123		& Jim Breech, Cin	0	22	49	115
1961	Gino Cappelletti, Bos	8	17	48	147	1982	Marcus Allen, LA.	14	0	0	84
1962	Gene Mingo, Den	4	27	32	137	1983	Gary Anderson, Pit.	0	27	38	119
1963	Gino Cappelletti, Bos	2	22	35	113	1984	Gary Anderson, Pit.	0	24	45	117
1964	Gino Cappelletti, Bos	7	25	36	155	1985	Gary Anderson, Pit.	0	33	40	139
1965	Gino Cappelletti, Bos	9	17	27	132	1986	Tony Franklin, NE	0	32	44	140
1966	Gino Cappelletti, Bos	6	16	35	119	1987	Jim Breech, Cin	0	24	25	97
1967	George Blanda, Oak	0	20	56	116	1988	Scott Norwood, Buf	0	32	33	129
1968	Jim Turner, NY	0	34	43	145	1989	David Treadwell, Den	0	27	39	120
1969	Jim Turner, NY	0	32	33	129	1990	Nick Lowery, KC	0	34	37	139
1970	Jan Stenerud, KC	0	30	26	116	1991	Pete Stoyanovich, Mia	0	31	28	121
1971	Garo Yepremian, Mia.	0	28	33	117	1992	Pete Stoyanovich, Mia	0	30	34	124
1972	Bobby Howfield, NY.	0	27	40	121	1993	Jeff Jaeger, LA	0	35	27	132
1973	Roy Gerela, Pit.	0	29	36	123	1994	John Carney, SD	0	34	33	135
1974	Roy Gerela, Pit.	0	20	33	93	1995	Norm Johnson, Pit.	0	34	39	141
1975	O.J. Simpson, Buf	23	0	0	138	1996	Cary Blanchard, Ind	0	36	27	135
1976	Toni Linhart, Bal	0	20	49	109	1997	Mike Hollis, Jax	0	31	41	134
1977	Errol Mann, Oak	0	20	39	99	1998	Steve Christie, Buf.	0	33	41	140
1978	Pat Leahy, NY	0	22	41	107	1999	Mike Vanderjagt, Ind	0	34	43	145
1979	John Smith, NE	0	23	46	115	2000	Matt Stover, Bal	0	35	30	135
1980	John Smith, NE	0	26	51	129	2001	Mike Vanderjagt, Ind	0	28	41	125
1981	Nick Lowery, KC	0	26	37	115						

All-Time NFL Leaders
Through 2001 regular season.
CAREER
Players active in 2001 in **bold** type.
Passing Efficiency

Ratings based on performance standards established for completion percentage, average gain, touchdown percentage and interception percentage. Quarterbacks are allocated points according to how their statistics measure up to those standards. Minimum 1500 passing attempts.

		Yrs	Att	Cmp	Cmp%	Yards	Avg Gain	TD	TD%	Int	Int%	Rating
1	Steve Young	15	4149	2667	64.3	33,124	7.98	232	5.6	107	2.6	96.8
2	Joe Montana	15	5391	3409	63.2	40,551	7.52	273	5.1	139	2.6	92.3
3	**Brett Favre**	11	5442	3311	60.8	38,627	7.10	287	5.3	172	3.2	86.8
4	Dan Marino	17	8358	4967	59.4	61,361	7.34	420	5.0	252	3.0	86.4
5	**Peyton Manning**	4	2226	1357	61.0	16,418	7.38	111	5.0	81	3.6	85.1
6	**Mark Brunell**	8	3145	1897	60.3	22,521	7.16	125	4.0	79	2.5	85.0
7	Jim Kelly	11	4779	2874	60.1	35,467	7.42	237	5.0	175	3.7	84.4
8	Roger Staubach	11	2958	1685	57.0	22,700	7.67	153	5.2	109	3.7	83.4
9	**Brad Johnson**	10	2380	1466	61.6	16,379	6.88	92	3.9	68	2.9	83.069
10	**Rich Gannon**	14	3295	1949	59.2	22,256	6.75	145	4.4	88	2.7	83.060
11	Neil Lomax	8	3153	1817	57.6	22,771	7.22	136	4.3	90	2.9	82.7
12	Sonny Jurgensen	18	4262	2433	57.1	32,224	7.56	255	6.0	189	4.4	82.625
13	Len Dawson	19	3741	2136	57.1	28,711	7.67	239	6.4	183	4.9	82.555
14	Ken Anderson	16	4475	2654	59.3	32,838	7.34	197	4.4	160	3.6	81.858
15	Bernie Kosar	12	3365	1994	59.3	23,301	6.92	124	3.7	87	2.6	81.8
16	Danny White	13	2950	1761	59.7	21,959	7.44	155	5.3	132	4.5	81.715
17	**Neil O'Donnell**	12	3197	1844	57.7	21,434	6.70	118	3.7	67	2.1	81.655
18	Troy Aikman	12	4715	2898	61.5	32,942	6.99	165	3.5	141	3.0	81.6
19	Dave Krieg	19	5311	3105	58.5	38,147	7.18	261	4.9	199	3.7	81.499
20	**Randall Cunningham**	17	4289	2429	56.6	29,979	6.99	207	4.8	134	3.1	81.471
21	**Steve McNair**	7	2288	1333	58.3	16,035	7.01	86	3.8	61	2.7	81.3
22	Boomer Esiason	14	5205	2969	57.0	37,920	7.29	247	4.7	184	3.5	81.1
23	Warren Moon	17	6823	3988	58.5	49,325	7.23	291	4.3	233	3.4	80.901
24	Steve Beuerlein	12	3148	1793	57.0	22,732	7.22	139	4.4	102	3.2	80.853
25	**Chris Chandler**	14	3590	2083	58.0	25,948	7.23	161	4.5	127	3.5	80.8

Note: The NFL does not recognize records from the All-American Football Conference (1946-49). If it did, **Otto Graham** would rank 4th (after Favre) with the following stats: 10 Yrs; 2,626 Att; 1,464 Comp; 55.8 Comp Pct; 23,584 Yards; 8.98 Avg Gain; 174 TD; 6.6 TD Pct; 135 Int; 5.1 Int.Pct; and 86.6 Rating Pts.

Touchdown Passes

	No
1 Dan Marino	420
2 Fran Tarkenton	342
3 John Elway	300
4 Warren Moon	291
5 Johnny Unitas	290
6 **Brett Favre**	287
7 Joe Montana	273
8 Dave Krieg	261
9 Sonny Jurgensen	255
10 Dan Fouts	254
11 Boomer Esiason	247
12 John Hadl	244
13 **Vinny Testaverde**	241
14 Len Dawson	239
15 Jim Kelly	237
16 George Blanda	236
17 Steve Young	232
18 John Brodie	214
19 Terry Bradshaw	212
Y.A. Tittle	212
21 Jim Hart	209
22 **Randall Cunningham**	207
23 Jim Everett	203
24 Roman Gabriel	201
25 Phil Simms	199
26 Ken Anderson	197
27 Joe Ferguson	196
Bobby Layne	196
Steve DeBerg	196
Norm Snead	196
31 Ken Stabler	194
32 Bob Griese	192
33 Sammy Baugh	187
34 Craig Morton	183
35 Steve Grogan	182
36 Ron Jaworski	179
37 Babe Parilli	178
38 Charlie Conerly	173
Joe Namath	173
Norm Van Brocklin	173
41 Charley Johnson	170
42 **Drew Bledsoe**	166
43 Troy Aikman	165
44 Daryle Lamonica	164
Jim Plunkett	164

Note: The NFL does not recognize records from the All-American Football Conference (1946-49). If it did, **Y.A. Tittle** would move up from 19th to 13th (after Hadl) with 242 TDs and **Otto Graham** would rank 38th (after Parilli) with 174 TDs.

Passes Intercepted

	No
1 George Blanda	277
2 John Hadl	268
3 Fran Tarkenton	266
4 Norm Snead	257
5 Johnny Unitas	253
6 Dan Marino	252
7 Jim Hart	247
8 Bobby Layne	245
9 Dan Fouts	242
10 Warren Moon	233
11 **Vinny Testaverde**	230
12 John Elway	226
13 John Brodie	224
14 Ken Stabler	222
15 Y.A. Tittle	221
16 Joe Namath	220
Babe Parilli	220
18 Terry Bradshaw	210
19 Joe Ferguson	209
20 Steve Grogan	208
21 Steve DeBerg	204
22 Sammy Baugh	203
23 Dave Krieg	199
24 Jim Plunkett	198
25 Tobin Rote	191

Passing Yards

		Yrs	Att	Comp	Pct	Yards
1	Dan Marino	17	8358	4967	59.4	61,361
2	John Elway	16	7250	4123	56.9	51,475
3	Warren Moon	17	6823	3988	58.5	49,325
4	Fran Tarkenton	18	6467	3686	57.0	47,003
5	Dan Fouts	15	5604	3297	58.8	43,040
6	Joe Montana	15	5391	3409	63.2	40,551
7	Johnny Unitas	18	5186	2830	54.6	40,239
8	Vinny Testaverde	15	5644	3157	55.9	39,059
9	Brett Favre	11	5442	3311	60.8	38,627
10	Dave Krieg	19	5311	3105	58.5	38,147
11	Boomer Esiason	14	5205	2969	57.0	37,920
12	Jim Kelly	11	4779	2874	60.1	35,467
13	Jim Everett	12	4923	2841	57.7	34,837
14	Jim Hart	19	5076	2593	51.1	34,665
15	Steve DeBerg	17	5024	2874	57.2	34,241
16	John Hadl	16	4687	2363	50.4	33,503
17	Phil Simms	14	4647	2576	55.4	33,462
18	Steve Young	15	4149	2667	64.3	33,124
19	Troy Aikman	12	4715	2898	61.5	32,942
20	Ken Anderson	16	4475	2654	59.3	32,838
21	Sonny Jurgensen	18	4262	2433	57.1	32,224
22	John Brodie	17	4491	2469	55.0	31,548
23	Norm Snead	15	4353	2276	52.3	30,797
24	R. Cunningham	17	4289	2429	56.6	29,979
25	Joe Ferguson	18	4519	2369	52.4	29,817

Note: The NFL does not recognize records from the All-American Football Conference (1946-49). If it did, **Y.A. Tittle** would rank 19th (after Young) with the following stats: 17 Yrs; 4,395 Att; 2,427 Comp; 55.2 Pct; and 33,070 Yards.

Receptions

		Yrs	No	Yards	Avg	TD
1	Jerry Rice	17	1364	20,386	14.9	185
2	Cris Carter	15	1093	13,833	12.7	129
3	Andre Reed	16	951	13,198	13.9	87
4	Art Monk	16	940	12,721	13.5	68
5	Tim Brown	14	937	13,237	14.1	95
6	Irving Fryar	17	851	12,785	15.0	84
7	Steve Largent	14	819	13,089	16.0	100
8	Henry Ellard	16	814	13,777	16.9	65
9	Larry Centers	12	765	6,303	8.2	27
10	James Lofton	16	764	14,004	18.3	75
11	Charlie Joiner	18	750	12,146	16.2	65
	Michael Irvin	12	750	11,904	15.9	65
13	Andre Rison	12	743	10,205	13.7	84
14	Gary Clark	11	699	10,856	15.5	65
15	Shannon Sharpe	12	692	8,604	12.4	51
16	Herman Moore	11	670	9,174	13.7	62
17	Terance Mathis	12	666	8,591	12.9	61
18	Ozzie Newsome	13	662	7,980	12.1	47
19	Charley Taylor	13	649	9,110	14.0	79
20	Drew Hill	15	634	9,831	15.5	60
21	Don Maynard	15	633	11,834	18.7	88
22	Raymond Berry	13	631	9,275	14.7	68
23	Rob Moore	10	628	9,368	14.9	49
24	Keith Byars	13	610	5,661	9.3	31
25	Sterling Sharpe	7	595	8,134	13.7	65
	Anthony Miller	10	595	9,148	15.4	63

Rushing

		Yrs	Car	Yards	Avg	TD
1	Walter Payton	13	3838	16,726	4.4	110
2	Emmitt Smith	12	3798	16,187	4.3	148
3	Barry Sanders	10	3062	15,269	5.0	99
4	Eric Dickerson	11	2996	13,259	4.4	90
5	Tony Dorsett	12	2936	12,739	4.3	77
6	Jim Brown	9	2359	12,312	5.2	106
7	Marcus Allen	16	3022	12,243	4.1	123
8	Franco Harris	13	2949	12,120	4.1	91
9	Thurman Thomas	13	2877	12,074	4.2	65
10	John Riggins	14	2916	11,352	3.9	104
11	O.J. Simpson	11	2404	11,236	4.7	61
12	Jerome Bettis	9	2686	10,876	4.0	53
13	Ricky Watters	10	2622	10,643	4.1	78
14	Ottis Anderson	14	2562	10,273	4.0	81
15	Marshall Faulk	8	2155	9,442	4.4	79
16	Earl Campbell	8	2187	9,407	4.3	74
17	Curtis Martin	7	2343	9,267	4.0	64
18	Terry Allen	10	2152	8,614	4.0	73
19	Jim Taylor	10	1941	8,597	4.4	83
20	Joe Perry	14	1737	8,378	4.8	53
21	Ernest Byner	14	2095	8,261	3.9	56
22	Herschel Walker	12	1954	8,225	4.2	61
23	Roger Craig	11	1991	8,189	4.1	56
24	Gerald Riggs	10	1989	8,188	4.1	69
25	Larry Csonka	11	1891	8,081	4.3	64

Note: The NFL does not recognize records from the All-American Football Conference (1946-49). If it did, **Joe Perry** would move up from 20th to 15th (after Anderson) with the following stats: 16 Yrs; 1,929 Att; 9,723 Yards; 5.0 Avg; and 71 TD.

All-Purpose Yards

		Rush	Rec	Ret	Total
1	Walter Payton	16,726	4,538	539	21,803
2	Jerry Rice	625	20,386	6	21,017
3	Brian Mitchell	1,947	2,298	16,018	20,263
4	Emmitt Smith	16,187	2,923	0	19,110
5	Barry Sanders	15,269	2,921	118	18,308
6	Herschel Walker	8,225	4,859	5,084	18,168
7	Tim Brown	171	13,237	4,455	17,863
8	Marcus Allen	12,243	5,411	-6	17,648
9	Eric Metcalf	2,385	5,572	9,226	17,183
10	Thurman Thomas	12,074	4,458	0	16,532
11	Tony Dorsett	12,739	3,554	33	16,326
12	Henry Ellard	50	13,777	1,891	15,718
13	Irving Fryar	242	12,785	2,567	15,594
14	Jim Brown	12,312	2,499	648	15,459
15	Eric Dickerson	13,259	2,137	15	15,411
16	Marshall Faulk	9,442	5,447	31	14,920
17	Glyn Milburn	817	1,322	12,772	14,911
18	James Brooks	7,962	3,621	3,327	14,910
19	Ricky Watters	10,643	4,248	0	14,891
20	Franco Harris	12,120	2,287	215	14,622
21	O.J. Simpson	11,236	2,142	990	14,368
22	James Lofton	246	14,004	27	14,277
23	Cris Carter	41	13,833	244	14,118
24	Bobby Mitchell	2,735	7,954	3,389	14,078
25	Dave Meggett	1,684	3,038	9,274	13,996

Years played: Allen (16), Brooks (12), J. Brown (9), T. Brown (14), Carter (15), Dickerson (11), Dorsett (12), Ellard (16), Faulk (8), Fryar (17), Harris (13), Lofton (16), Meggett (10), Metcalf (12), Milburn (9), Bri. Mitchell (12), Bo. Mitchell (11), Payton (13), Rice (17), Sanders (10), Simpson (11), Smith (12), Thomas (13), Walker (12) and Watters (10).

All-Time NFL Leaders (Cont.)
Scoring

Points

		Yrs	TD	FG	PAT	Total
1	**Gary Anderson**	20	0	476	705	2133
2	**Morten Andersen**	20	0	464	644	2036
3	George Blanda	26	9	335	943	2002
4	Norm Johnson	18	0	366	638	1736
5	Nick Lowery	18	0	383	562	1711
6	Jan Stenerud	19	0	373	580	1699
7	Eddie Murray	19	0	352	538	1594
8	Al Del Greco	17	0	347	543	1584
9	Pat Leahy	18	0	304	558	1470
10	Jim Turner	16	1	304	521	1439
11	Matt Bahr	17	0	300	522	1422
12	Mark Moseley	16	0	300	482	1382
13	Jim Bakken	17	0	282	534	1380
14	Fred Cox	15	0	282	519	1365
15	Lou Groza	17	1	234	641	1349
16	Jim Breech	14	0	243	517	1246
17	Pete Stoyanovich	12	0	272	420	1236
18	Chris Bahr	14	0	241	490	1213
19	Kevin Butler	13	0	265	413	1208
20	**Steve Christie**	12	0	281	364	1207
21	**John Carney**	14	0	290	331	1201
22	Jerry Rice	17	196	0	0	1184†
23	**Matt Stover**	11	0	267	333	1134
24	Gino Cappelletti	11	42	176	350	1130†
25	Ray Wersching	15	0	222	456	1122

† Cappelletti's total and Rice's total both include four 2-point conversions.

Note: The NFL does not recognize records from the All-American Football Conference (1946-49). If it did, **Lou Groza** would move up from 15th to 7th (after Stenerud) with the following stats: 21 Yrs; 1 TD; 264 FG, 810 PAT; 1,608 Pts.

Touchdowns

		Yrs	Rush	Rec	Ret	Total
1	**Jerry Rice**	17	10	185	1	196
2	**Emmitt Smith**	12	148	11	0	159
3	Marcus Allen	16	123	21	1	145
4	**Cris Carter**	15	0	129	1	130
5	Jim Brown	9	106	20	0	126
6	Walter Payton	13	110	15	0	125
7	John Riggins	14	104	12	0	116
8	Lenny Moore	12	63	48	2	113
9	**Marshall Faulk**	8	79	31	0	110
10	Barry Sanders	10	99	10	0	109
11	Don Hutson	11	3	99	3	105
12	Steve Largent	14	1	100	0	101
13	Franco Harris	13	91	9	0	100
	Tim Brown	14	1	95	4	100
15	Eric Dickerson	11	90	6	0	96
16	Jim Taylor	10	83	10	0	93
17	Tony Dorsett	12	77	13	1	91
	Bobby Mitchell	11	18	65	8	91
	Ricky Watters	10	78	13	0	91
20	Leroy Kelly	10	74	13	3	90
	Charley Taylor	13	11	79	0	90
22	Irving Fryar	17	1	84	3	88
	Don Maynard	15	0	88	0	88
	Andre Reed	16	1	87	0	88
	Thurman Thomas	13	65	23	0	88

Interceptions

		Yrs	No	Yards	TD
1	Paul Krause	16	81	1185	3
2	Emlen Tunnell	14	79	1282	4
3	Dick (Night Train) Lane	14	68	1207	5
4	Ken Riley	15	65	596	5
5	Ronnie Lott	14	63	730	5

Sacks

		Yrs	No
1	Reggie White	15	198
2	**Bruce Smith**	17	186
3	Kevin Greene	15	160
4	Chris Doleman	15	150.5
5	Richard Dent	15	137.5

Note: The NFL did not begin officially compiling sacks until 1982. Deacon Jones, who played with the Rams, Chargers and Redskins from 1961-74, is often credited with 173½ sacks. Jack Youngblood and Alan Page are unofficially credited with 150½ and 148, respectively. Also, Lawrence Taylor has 142 career sacks if you count his rookie year of 1981, the year before sacks became an official stat.

Safeties

		Yrs	No
1	Ted Hendricks	15	4
	Doug English	10	4
3	Seventeen players tied with 3 each.		

Kickoff Returns
Minimum 75 returns.

		Yrs	No	Yards	Avg	TD
1	Gale Sayers	7	91	2781	30.6	6
2	Lynn Chandnois	7	92	2720	29.6	3
3	Abe Woodson	9	193	5538	28.7	5
4	Buddy Young	6	90	2514	27.9	2
5	Travis Williams	5	102	2801	27.5	6

Punting
Minimum 300 punts.

		Yrs	No	Yards	Avg
1	Sammy Baugh	16	338	15,245	45.1
2	Tommy Davis	11	511	22,833	44.7
3	**Darren Bennett**	7	602	26,800	44.5
4	Yale Lary	11	503	22,279	44.3
5	**Tom Rouen**	9	612	26,907	44.0

Punt Returns
Minimum 75 returns.

		Yrs	No	Yards	Avg	TD
1	George McAfee	8	112	1431	12.8	2
2	Jack Christiansen	8	85	1084	12.8	8
3	Claude Gibson	5	110	1381	12.6	3
4	**Darrien Gordon**	8	279	3421	12.3	6
5	Bill Dudley	9	124	1515	12.2	3

Long-Playing Records

Seasons

		No
1	George Blanda, QB-K	26
2	Earl Morrall, QB	21
3	Jim Marshall, DE	20
	Jackie Slater, OL	20
	Gary Anderson, K	20
	Morten Andersen, K	20

Games

		No
1	George Blanda, QB-K	340
2	**Gary Anderson**, K	309
3	**Morten Andersen**, K	308
4	**Bruce Matthews**, OL	296
5	Jim Marshall, DE	282

Consecutive Games

		No
1	Jim Marshall, DE	282
2	Mick Tingelhoff, C	240
3	Jim Bakken, K	234
	Gary Anderson, K	234
	Morten Andersen, K	234

SINGLE SEASON
Passing

Yards Gained	Year	Att	Cmp	Pct	Yds
Dan Marino, Mia	1984	564	362	64.2	5084
Kurt Warner, St.L	2001	546	375	68.7	4830
Dan Fouts, SD	1981	609	360	59.1	4802
Dan Marino, Mia	1986	623	378	60.7	4746
Dan Fouts, SD	1980	589	348	59.1	4715
Warren Moon, Hou	1991	655	404	61.7	4690
Warren Moon, Hou	1990	584	362	62.0	4689
Neil Lomax, St.L	1984	560	345	61.6	4614
Drew Bledsoe, NE	1994	691	400	57.9	4555
Lynn Dickey, GB	1983	484	286	59.7	4458

Efficiency	Year	Att/Cmp	TD	Rtg
Steve Young, SF	1994	461/324	35	112.8
Joe Montana, SF	1989	386/271	26	112.4
Milt Plum, Cle	1960	250/151	21	110.4
Sammy Baugh, Wash	1945	182/128	11	109.9
Kurt Warner, St.L	1999	499/325	41	109.2
Dan Marino, Mia	1984	564/362	48	108.9
Sid Luckman, Bears	1943	202/110	28	107.5
Steve Young, SF	1992	402/268	25	107.0
Randall Cunningham, Min	1998	425/259	34	106.0
Bart Starr, GB	1966	251/156	14	105.0

Receptions

Catches	Year	No	Yds
Herman Moore, Det	1995	123	1686
Jerry Rice, SF	1995	122	1848
Cris Carter, Min	1995	122	1371
Cris Carter, Min	1994	122	1256
Isaac Bruce, St.L	1995	119	1781
Jimmy Smith, Jax	1999	116	1636
Marvin Harrison, Ind	1999	115	1663
Rod Smith, Den	2001	113	1343
Jimmy Smith, Jax	2001	112	1373
Jerry Rice, SF	1994	112	1499
Sterling Sharpe, GB	1993	112	1274
Michael Irvin, Dal	1995	111	1603
Terance Mathis, Atl	1994	111	1342

Rushing

Yards Gained	Year	Car	Yds	Avg
Eric Dickerson, LA Rams	1984	379	2105	5.6
Barry Sanders, Det	1997	335	2053	6.1
Terrell Davis, Den	1998	392	2008	5.1
O.J. Simpson, Buf	1973	332	2003	6.0
Earl Campbell, Hou	1980	373	1934	5.2
Barry Sanders, Det	1994	331	1883	5.7
Jim Brown, Cle	1963	291	1863	6.4
Walter Payton, Chi	1977	339	1852	5.5
Jamal Anderson, Atl	1998	410	1846	4.5
Eric Dickerson, LA Rams	1986	404	1821	4.5
O.J. Simpson, Buf	1975	329	1817	5.5
Eric Dickerson, LA Rams	1983	390	1808	4.6

Scoring

Points	Year	TD	PAT	FG	Pts
Paul Hornung, GB	1960	15	41	15	176
Gary Anderson, Min	1998	0	59	35	164
Mark Moseley, Wash	1983	0	62	33	161
Marshall Faulk, St.L	2000	26	4	0	160
Gino Cappelletti, Bos	1964	7	38	25	155
Emmitt Smith, Dal	1995	25	0	0	150
Chip Lohmiller, Wash	1991	0	56	31	149
Gino Cappelletti, Bos	1961	8	48	17	147
Paul Hornung, GB	1961	10	41	15	146
Jim Turner, Jets	1968	0	43	34	145
John Kasay, Car.	1996	0	34	37	145
Mike Vanderjagt, Ind.	1999	0	43	34	145
John Riggins, Wash	1983	24	0	0	144
Kevin Butler, Chi	1985	0	51	31	144
Olindo Mare, Mia	1999	0	27	39	144
Norm Johnson, Pit	1995	0	39	34	141

Touchdowns	Year	Rush	Rec	Ret	Total
Marshall Faulk, St.L	2000	18	8	0	26
Emmitt Smith, Dal	1995	25	0	0	25
John Riggins, Wash	1983	24	0	0	24
Terrell Davis, Den	1998	21	2	0	23
O.J. Simpson, Buf.	1975	16	7	0	23
Jerry Rice, SF	1987	1	22	0	23
Gale Sayers, Chi	1966	14	6	2	22
Chuck Foreman, Min	1975	13	9	0	22
Emmitt Smith, Dal	1994	21	1	0	22
Jim Brown, Cle	1965	17	4	0	21
Joe Morris, NY Giants	1985	21	0	0	21
Terry Allen, Wash	1996	21	0	0	21
Marshall Faulk, St.L	2001	12	9	0	21
Lenny Moore, Bal	1964	16	3	1	20
Leroy Kelly, Cle	1968	16	4	0	20
Eric Dickerson, LA Rams	1983	18	2	0	20

Note: The NFL regular season schedule grew from 12 games (1947-60) to 14 (1961-77) to 16 (1978-present). The AFL regular season schedule was always 14 games (1960-69).

Touchdowns Passing

	Year	No
Dan Marino, Miami	1984	48
Dan Marino, Miami	1986	44
Kurt Warner, St. Louis	1999	41
Brett Favre, Green Bay	1996	39
Brett Favre, Green Bay	1995	38
George Blanda, Houston	1961	36
Y.A. Tittle, NY Giants	1963	36
Steve Young, San Francisco	1998	36
Steve Beuerlein, Carolina	1999	36
Kurt Warner, St. Louis	2001	36
Brett Favre, Green Bay	1997	35
Steve Young, San Francisco	1994	35
Randall Cunningham, Minnesota	1998	34

Nine tied with 33 each, incl. Warren Moon twice.

Touchdowns Receiving

	Year	No
Jerry Rice, San Francisco	1987	22
Mark Clayton, Miami	1984	18
Sterling Sharpe, Green Bay	1994	18
Don Hutson, Green Bay	1942	17
Elroy (Crazylegs) Hirsch, LA Rams	1951	17
Bill Groman, Houston	1961	17
Jerry Rice, San Francisco	1989	17
Cris Carter, Minnesota	1995	17
Carl Pickens, Cincinnati	1995	17
Randy Moss, Minnesota	1998	17
Art Powell, Oakland	1963	16
Terrell Owens, SF	2001	16

Eight tied with 15 each, incl. Rice three times.

All-Time NFL Leaders (Cont.)

Touchdowns Rushing

	Year	No
Emmitt Smith, Dallas	1995	25
John Riggins, Washington	1983	24
Joe Morris, NY Giants	1985	21
Emmitt Smith, Dallas	1994	21
Terry Allen, Washington	1996	21
Terrell Davis, Denver	1998	21
Jim Taylor, Green Bay	1962	19'
Earl Campbell, Houston	1979	19
Chuck Muncie, San Diego	1981	19
Eric Dickerson, LA Rams	1983	18
George Rogers, Washington	1986	18
Emmitt Smith, Dallas	1992	18
Marshall Faulk, St. Louis	2000	18
Jim Brown, Cleveland	1958	17
Jim Brown, Cleveland	1965	17
Stephen Davis, Washington	1999	17

Field Goals

	Year	Att	No
Olindo Mare, Miami	1999	46	39
John Kasay, Carolina	1996	45	37
Cary Blanchard, Indianapolis	1996	40	36
Al Del Greco, Tennessee	1998	39	36
Ali Haji-Sheikh, NY Giants	1983	42	35
Jeff Jaeger, LA Raiders	1993	44	35
Gary Anderson, Minnesota	1998	35	35
Matt Stover, Baltimore	2000	39	35
Jim Turner, NY Jets	1968	46	34
Nick Lowery, Kansas City	1990	37	34
Jason Hanson, Detroit	1993	43	34
John Carney, San Diego	1994	38	34
Fuad Reveiz, Minnesota	1994	39	34
Norm Johnson, Pittsburgh	1995	41	34
Richie Cunningham, Dallas	1997	37	34
Mike Vanderjagt, Indianapolis	1999	38	34
Todd Peterson, Seattle	1999	40	34
Joe Nedney, Den.-Car.	2000	38	34

Interceptions

	Year	No
Dick (Night Train) Lane, Detroit	1952	14
Dan Sandifer, Washington	1948	13
Spec Sanders, NY Yanks	1950	13
Lester Hayes, Oakland	1980	13

Punting

Qualifiers	Year	Avg
Sammy Baugh, Washington	1940	51.4
Yale Lary, Detroit	1963	48.9
Sammy Baugh, Washington	1941	48.7
Yale Lary, Detroit	1961	48.4

Kickoff Returns

	Year	Avg
Travis Williams, Green Bay	1967	41.1
Gale Sayers, Chicago Bears	1967	37.7
Ollie Matson, Chicago Cards	1958	35.5

Punt Returns

	Year	Avg
Herb Rich, Baltimore	1950	23.0
Jack Christiansen, Detroit	1952	21.5
Dick Christy, NY Titans	1961	21.3
Bob Hayes, Dallas	1968	20.8

Sacks

	Year	No		Year	No
Michael Strahan, NY Giants	2001	22.5	Chris Doleman, Minnesota	1989	21
Mark Gastineau, NY Jets	1984	22	Lawrence Taylor, NY Giants	1986	20.5
Reggie White, Philadelphia	1987	21	Derrick Thomas, Kansas City	1990	20

Note: The NFL did not begin officially compiling sacks until 1982. Cincinnati's Coy Bacon is widely, although not officially, credited with 26 sacks during the 1976 season.

SINGLE GAME

Passing

Yards Gained	Date	Yds
Norm Van Brocklin, LA vs NY Yanks	9/28/51	554
Warren Moon, Hou vs KC	12/16/90	527
Boomer Esiason, Ariz vs Wash.	11/10/96	522
Dan Marino, Mia vs NYJ	10/23/88	521
Phil Simms, NYG vs Cin	10/13/85	513

Completions	Date	No
Drew Bledsoe, NE vs Min	11/13/94	45
Richard Todd, NYJ vs SF	9/21/80	42
Vinny Testaverde, NYJ vs Sea	12/6/98	42
Warren Moon, Hou vs Dal	11/10/91	41
Ken Anderson, Cin vs SD	12/20/82	40
Phil Simms, NYG vs Cin	10/13/85	40
Brad Johnson, TB vs Chi	11/18/01	40

Receiving

Catches	Date	No
Terrell Owens, SF vs Chi	12/17/00	20
Tom Fears, LA vs GB	12/3/50	18
Clark Gaines, NYJ vs SF	9/21/80	17
Sonny Randle, St.L vs NYG	11/4/62	16
Keenan McCardell, Jax vs St.L.	10/20/96	16
Jerry Rice, SF vs LA Rams	11/20/94	16

Yards Gained	Date	Yds
Flipper Anderson, LA Rams vs NO	11/26/89	336
Stephone Paige, KC vs SD	12/22/85	309
Jim Benton, Cle vs Det	11/22/45	303
Cloyce Box, Det vs Bal	12/3/50	302
Jimmy Smith, Jax vs Bal	9/10/00	291
Jerry Rice, SF vs Det	9/25/95	289

Rushing

Yards Gained	Date	Yds
Corey Dillon, Cin vs Den	10/22/00	278
Walter Payton, Chi vs Min	11/20/77	275
O.J. Simpson, Buf vs Det	11/25/76	273
Shaun Alexander, Sea vs Oak	11/11/01	266
Mike Anderson, Den vs NO	12/3/00	251
O.J. Simpson, Buf vs NE	9/16/73	250
Willie Ellison, LA Rams vs NO	12/5/71	247
Corey Dillon, Cin vs Ten	12/4/97	246

All-Purpose Yards

	Date	Yds
Glyn Milburn, Den vs Sea	12/10/95	404
Billy Cannon, Hou vs NY Titans	12/10/61	373
Tyrone Hughes, NO vs LA Rams	10/23/94	347
Lionel James, SD vs Raiders	11/10/85	345
Timmy Brown, Phi vs St.L	12/16/62	341
Gale Sayers, Chi vs Min	12/18/66	339
Gale Sayers, Chi vs SF	12/12/65	336
Flipper Anderson, LA Rams vs NO	11/26/89	336

Scoring

Points

	Date	Pts
Ernie Nevers, Chi. Cards vs Chi. Bears	11/28/29	40
Dub Jones, Cle vs Chi. Bears	11/25/51	36
Gale Sayers, Chi vs SF	12/12/65	36
Paul Hornung, GB vs Bal	10/8/61	33
Bob Shaw, Chi. Cards vs Bal	10/2/50	30
Jim Brown, Cle vs Bal	11/1/59	30
Abner Haynes, Dal. Texans vs Oak	11/26/61	30
Billy Cannon, Hou vs NY Titans	12/10/61	30
Cookie Gilchrist, Buf vs NY Jets	12/8/63	30
Kellen Winslow, SD vs Oak	11/22/81	30
Jerry Rice, SF vs Atl	10/14/90	30
James Stewart, Jax vs Phi	10/12/97	30

Note: Nevers celebrated Thanksgiving, 1929, by scoring all of the Chicago Cardinals' points on six rushing TDs and four PATs. The Cards beat Red Grange and the Chicago Bears, 40-6.

Touchdowns Passing

	Date	No
Sid Luckman, Chi. Bears vs NYG	11/14/43	7
Adrian Burk, Phi vs Wash	10/17/54	7
George Blanda, Hou vs NY Titans	11/19/61	7
Y.A. Tittle, NYG vs Wash	10/28/62	7
Joe Kapp, Min vs Bal	9/28/69	7

Touchdowns Receiving

	Date	No
Bob Shaw, Chi. Cards vs Bal	10/2/50	5
Kellen Winslow, SD vs Oak	11/22/81	5
Jerry Rice, SF vs Atl	10/14/90	5

Touchdowns Rushing

	Date	No
Ernie Nevers, Chi. Cards vs Chi. Bears	11/28/29	6
Jim Brown, Cle vs Bal	11/1/59	5
Cookie Gilchrist, Buf vs NY Jets	12/8/63	5
James Stewart, Jax vs Phi	10/12/97	5

Field Goals

	Date	No
Jim Bakken, St.L vs Pit	9/24/67	7
Chris Boniol, Dal vs GB	11/18/96	7
Rich Karlis, Min vs LA Rams	11/5/89	7

Fourteen players tied with 6 FGs.

Note: Bakken was 7-for-9, Boniol and Karlis 7-for-7.

Extra Point Kicks

	Date	No
Pat Harder, Cards vs NYG	10/17/48	9
Bob Waterfield, LA Rams vs Bal	10/22/50	9
Charlie Gogolak, Wash vs NYG	11/27/66	9

Interceptions

	No
By 18 players	4

Sacks

	Date	No
Derrick Thomas, KC vs Sea	11/11/90	7
Fred Dean, SF vs NO	11/13/83	6
Derrick Thomas, KC vs Oak	9/6/98	6
William Gay, Det vs TB	9/4/83	5.5

Longest Plays

Passing (all for TDs)

	Date	Yds
Frank Filchock to Andy Farkas, Wash vs Pit	10/15/39	99
George Izo to Bobby Mitchell, Wash vs Cle	9/15/63	99
Karl Sweetan to Pat Studstill, Det vs Bal	10/16/66	99
Sonny Jurgensen to Gerry Allen, Wash vs Chi	9/15/68	99
Jim Plunkett to Cliff Branch, LA Raiders vs Wash	10/2/83	99
Ron Jaworski to Mike Quick, Phi vs Atl	11/10/85	99
Stan Humphries to Tony Martin, SD vs Sea	9/18/94	99
Brett Favre to Robert Brooks, GB vs Chi	9/11/95	99

Runs from Scrimmage (all for TDs)

	Date	Yds
Tony Dorsett, Dal vs Min	1/3/83	99
Andy Uram, GB vs Chi. Cards	10/8/39	97
Bob Gage, Pit vs Bears	12/4/49	97
Jim Spavital, Balt. Colts vs GB	11/5/50	96
Bob Hoernschemeyer, Det vs NY Yanks	11/23/50	96
Garrison Hearst, SF vs NYJ	9/6/98	96
Corey Dillon, Cin vs Det	10/28/01	96

Punts

	Date	Yds
Steve O'Neal, NYJ vs Den	9/21/69	98
Joe Lintzenich, Chi. Bears vs NYG	11/15/31	94
Shawn McCarthy, NE vs Buf	11/3/91	93

Field Goals

	Date	Yds
Tom Dempsey, NO vs Det	11/8/70	63
Jason Elam, Den vs Jax	10/25/98	63
Steve Cox, Cle vs Cin	10/21/84	60
Morten Andersen, NO vs Chi	10/27/91	60
Tony Franklin, Phi vs Dal	11/12/79	59
Pete Stoyanovich, Mia vs NYJ	11/12/89	59
Steve Christie, Buf vs Mia	9/26/93	59
Morten Andersen, Atl vs SF	12/24/95	59

Punt Returns (all for TDs)

	Date	Yds
Robert Bailey, Rams vs NO	10/23/94	103
Gil LeFebvre, Cin vs Bklyn	12/3/33	98
Charlie West, Min vs Wash	11/3/68	98
Dennis Morgan, Dal vs St.L	10/13/74	98
Terance Mathis, NYJ vs Dal	11/4/90	98
Greg Pruitt, LA Raiders vs Wash	10/2/83	97

Kickoff Returns (all for TDs)

	Date	Yds
Al Carmichael, GB vs Chi. Bears	10/7/56	106
Noland Smith, KC vs Den	12/17/67	106
Roy Green, St.L vs Dal	10/21/79	106

Interception Returns (all for TDs)

	Date	Yds
James Willis (14 yds) lateral to Troy Vincent (90 yds), Phi vs Dal	11/3/96	104
Vencie Glenn, SD vs Den	11/29/87	103
Louis Oliver, Mia vs Buf	10/4/92	103

Six players tied with 102-yd returns.

Chicago College All-Star Game

On Aug. 31, 1934, a year after sponsoring Major League Baseball's first All-Star Game, *Chicago Tribune* sports editor Arch Ward presented the first Chicago College All-Star Game at Soldier Field. A crowd of 79,432 turned out to see an all-star team of graduated college seniors battle the 1933 NFL champion Chicago Bears to a scoreless tie. The preseason game was played at Soldier Field and pitted the College All-Stars against the defending NFL champions (1933-1966) or Super Bowl champions (1967-75) every year except 1935 until it was cancelled in 1977. The NFL champs won the series, 31-9-1.

Year	Year	Year
1934 Chi. Bears 0, All-Stars 0	1949 Philadelphia 38, All-Stars 0	1964 Chi. Bears 28, All-Stars 17
1935 Chi. Bears 5, All-Stars 0	1950 All-Stars 17, Philadelphia 7	1965 Cleveland 24, All-Stars 16
1936 Detroit 7, All-Stars 0	1951 Cleveland 33, All-Stars 0	1966 Green Bay 38, All-Stars 0
1937 All-Stars 6, Green Bay 0	1952 LA Rams 10, All-Stars 7	1967 Green Bay 27, All-Stars 0
1938 All-Stars 28, Washington 16	1953 Detroit 24, All-Stars 10	1968 Green Bay 34, All-Stars 17
1939 NY Giants 9, All-Stars 0	1954 Detroit 31, All-Stars 6	1969 NY Jets 26, All-Stars 24
1940 Green Bay 45, All-Stars 28	1955 All-Stars 30, Cleveland 27	
1941 Chi. Bears 37, All-Stars 13	1956 Cleveland 26, All-Stars 0	1970 Kansas City 24, All-Stars 3
1942 Chi. Bears 21, All-Stars 0	1957 NY Giants 22, All-Stars 12	1971 Baltimore 24, All-Stars 17
1943 All-Stars 27, Washington 7	1958 All-Stars 35, Detroit 19	1972 Dallas 20, All-Stars 7
1944 Chi. Bears 24, All-Stars 21	1959 Baltimore 29, All-Stars 0	1973 Miami 14, All-Stars 3
1945 Green Bay 19, All-Stars 7		1974 No Game (NFLPA Strike)
1946 All-Stars 16, LA Rams 0	1960 Baltimore 32, All-Stars 7	1975 Pittsburgh 21, All-Stars 14
1947 All-Stars 16, Chi. Bears 0	1961 Philadelphia 28, All-Stars 14	1976 Pittsburgh 24, All-Stars 0*
1948 Chi. Cards 28, All-Stars 0	1962 Green Bay 42, All-Stars 20	*Downpour flooded field, game called
	1963 All-Stars 20, Green Bay 17	with 1:22 left in 3rd quarter.

Number One Draft Choices

In an effort to blunt the dominance of the Chicago Bears and New York Giants in the 1930s and distribute talent more evenly throughout the league, the NFL established the college draft in 1936. The first player chosen in the first draft was Jay Berwanger, who was also college football's first Heisman Trophy winner. In all, 16 Heisman winners have also been the NFL's No. 1 draft choice. They are noted in **bold** type. The American Football League (formed in 1960) held its own draft for six years before agreeing to merge with the NFL and select players in a common draft starting in 1967.

Year	Team		Year	Team	
1936	Philadelphia	**Jay Berwanger**, HB, Chicago	1967	Baltimore	Bubba Smith, DT, Michigan St.
1937	Philadelphia	Sam Francis, FB, Nebraska	1968	Minnesota	Ron Yary, T, USC
1938	Cleveland Rams	Corbett Davis, FB, Indiana	1969	Buffalo	**O.J. Simpson**, RB, USC
1939	Chicago Cards	Ki Aldrich, C, TCU			
1940	Chicago Cards	George Cafego, HB, Tennessee	1970	Pittsburgh	Terry Bradshaw, QB, La.Tech
1941	Chicago Bears	**Tom Harmon**, HB, Michigan	1971	New England	**Jim Plunkett**, QB, Stanford
1942	Pittsburgh	Bill Dudley, HB, Virginia	1972	Buffalo	Walt Patulski, DE, Notre Dame
1943	Detroit	**Frank Sinkwich**, HB, Georgia	1973	Houston	John Matuszak, DE, Tampa
1944	Boston Yanks	**Angelo Bertelli**, QB, N. Dame	1974	Dallas	Ed (Too Tall) Jones, DE, Tenn. St.
1945	Chicago Cards	Charley Trippi, HB, Georgia	1975	Atlanta	Steve Bartkowski, QB, Calif.
1946	Boston Yanks	Frank Dancewicz, QB, N. Dame	1976	Tampa Bay	Lee Roy Selmon, DE, Oklahoma
1947	Chicago Bears	Bob Fenimore, HB, Okla. A&M	1977	Tampa Bay	Ricky Bell, RB, USC
1948	Washington	Harry Gilmer, QB, Alabama	1978	Houston	**Earl Campbell**, RB, Texas
1949	Philadelphia	Chuck Bednarik, C, Penn	1979	Buffalo	Tom Cousineau, LB, Ohio St.
1950	Detroit	**Leon Hart**, E, Notre Dame	1980	Detroit	**Billy Sims**, RB, Oklahoma
1951	NY Giants	Kyle Rote, HB, SMU	1981	New Orleans	**George Rogers**, RB, S. Carolina
1952	LA Rams	Bill Wade, QB, Vanderbilt	1982	New England	Kenneth Sims, DT, Texas
1953	San Francisco	Harry Babcock, E, Georgia	1983	Baltimore	John Elway, QB, Stanford
1954	Cleveland	Bobby Garrett, QB, Stanford	1984	New England	Irving Fryar, WR, Nebraska
1955	Baltimore	George Shaw, QB, Oregon	1985	Buffalo	Bruce Smith, DE, Va. Tech
1956	Pittsburgh	Gary Glick, DB, Colo. A&M	1986	Tampa Bay	**Bo Jackson**, RB, Auburn
1957	Green Bay	**Paul Hornung**, QB, N. Dame	1987	Tampa Bay	**V. Testaverde**, QB, Miami-FL
1958	Chicago Cards	King Hill, QB, Rice	1988	Atlanta	Aundray Bruce, LB, Auburn
1959	Green Bay	Randy Duncan, QB, Iowa	1989	Dallas	Troy Aikman, QB, UCLA
1960	NFL–LA Rams	**Billy Cannon**, HB, LSU	1990	Indianapolis	Jeff George, QB, Illinois
	AFL–No choice		1991	Dallas	Russell Maryland, DT, Miami-FL
1961	NFL–Minnesota	Tommy Mason, HB, Tulane	1992	Indianapolis	Steve Emtman, DT, Washington
	AFL–Buffalo	Ken Rice, G, Auburn	1993	New England	Drew Bledsoe, QB, Washington St.
1962	NFL–Washington	**Ernie Davis**, HB, Syracuse	1994	Cincinnati	Dan Wilkinson, DT, Ohio St.
	AFL–Oakland	Roman Gabriel, QB, N.C. State	1995	Cincinnati	Ki-Jana Carter, RB, Penn St.
1963	NFL–LA Rams	**Terry Baker**, QB, Oregon St.	1996	NY Jets	Keyshawn Johnson, WR, USC
	AFL–Kan.City	Buck Buchanan, DT, Grambling	1997	St. Louis	Orlando Pace, OT, Ohio St.
1964	NFL–San Fran	Dave Parks, E, Texas Tech	1998	Indianapolis	Peyton Manning, QB, Tennessee
	AFL–Boston	Jack Concannon, QB, Boston Col.	1999	Cleveland	Tim Couch, QB, Kentucky
1965	NFL–NY Giants	Tucker Frederickson, FB, Auburn	2000	Cleveland	Courtney Brown, DE, Penn St.
	AFL–Houston	Lawrence Elkins, E, Baylor	2001	Atlanta	Michael Vick, QB, Va. Tech
1966	NFL–Atlanta	Tommy Nobis, LB, Texas	2002	Houston	David Carr, QB, Fresno St.
	AFL–Miami	Jim Grabowski, FB, Illinois			

AP/Wide World Photos
Don Shula

NFL Media
Marty Schottenheimer

AP/Wide World Photos
Bill Parcells

NFL Media
Mike Holmgren

All-Time Winningest NFL Coaches

NFL career victories through the 2001 season. Career, regular season and playoff records are noted along with NFL, AFL and Super Bowl titles won. Coaches active during 2001 season in **bold** type.

		Career				Regular Season				Playoffs			
		Yrs	W	L	T	Pct	W	L	T	Pct	W	L	Pct.	League Titles
1	Don Shula	33	**347**	173	6	.665	328	156	6	.676	19	17	.528	2 Super Bowls and 1 NFL
2	George Halas	40	**324**	151	31	.671	318	148	31	.671	6	3	.667	5 NFL
3	Tom Landry	29	**270**	178	6	.601	250	162	6	.605	20	16	.556	2 Super Bowls
4	Curly Lambeau	33	**229**	134	22	.623	226	132	22	.624	3	2	.600	6 NFL
5	Chuck Noll	23	**209**	156	1	.572	193	148	1	.566	16	8	.667	4 Super Bowls
6	Chuck Knox	22	**193**	158	1	.550	186	147	1	.558	7	11	.389	—None—
7	**Dan Reeves**	21	**188**	157	1	.545	178	149	1	.544	10	8	.556	—None—
8	Paul Brown	21	**170**	108	6	.609	166	100	6	.621	4	8	.333	3 NFL
9	Bud Grant	18	**168**	108	5	.607	158	96	5	.620	10	12	.455	1 NFL
10	**M. Schottenheimer**	16	**158**	104	1	.603	153	93	1	.621	5	11	.313	—None—
11	Marv Levy	17	**154**	120	1	.562	143	112	0	.561	11	8	.579	—None—
12	Steve Owen	23	**153**	108	17	.581	151	100	17	.595	2	8	.200	2 NFL
13	Bill Parcells	15	**149**	106	1	.584	138	100	1	.579	11	6	.647	2 Super Bowls
14	Joe Gibbs	12	**140**	65	0	.683	124	60	0	.674	16	5	.762	3 Super Bowls
15	Hank Stram	17	**136**	100	10	.573	131	97	10	.571	5	3	.625	1 Super Bowl and 3 AFL
16	Weeb Ewbank	20	**134**	130	7	.507	130	129	7	.502	4	1	.800	1 Super Bowl, 2 NFL, and 1 AFL
17	Mike Ditka	14	**127**	101	0	.557	121	95	0	.560	6	6	.500	1 Super Bowl
18	**Jim Mora**	15	**125**	112	0	.527	125	106	0	.541	0	6	.000	—None—
19	**George Seifert**	11	**124**	67	0	.649	114	62	0	.648	10	5	.667	2 Super Bowls
20	Sid Gillman	18	**123**	104	7	.541	122	99	7	.550	1	5	.167	1 AFL
21	George Allen	12	**118**	54	5	.681	116	47	5	.705	2	7	.222	—None—
22	Don Coryell	14	**114**	89	1	.561	111	83	1	.572	3	6	.333	—None—
23	John Madden	10	**112**	39	7	.731	103	32	7	.750	9	7	.563	1 Super Bowl
24	**Mike Holmgren**	10	**108**	67	0	.617	99	61	0	.619	9	6	.600	1 Super Bowl
25	Buddy Parker	15	**107**	76	9	.581	104	75	9	.577	3	1	.750	2 NFL

Notes: The NFL does not recognize records from the All-American Football Conference (1946-49). If it did, **Paul Brown** (52-4-3 in four AAFC seasons) would move up from 8th to 5th on the all-time list with the following career stats— 25 Yrs; 222 Wins; 112 Losses; 9 Ties; .660 Pct; 9-8 playoff record; and 4 AAFC titles.

The NFL also considers the Playoff Bowl or "Runner-up Bowl" (officially: the Bert Bell Benefit Bowl) as a postseason exhibition game. The Playoff Bowl was contested every year from 1960-69 in Miami between Eastern and Western Conference second place teams. While the games did not count, six of the coaches above went to the Playoff Bowl at least once and came away with the following records— Allen (2-0), Brown (0-1), Grant (0-1), Landry (1-2), Lombardi (1-1) and Shula (2-0).

Where They Coached

Allen—LA Rams (1966-70), Washington (1971-77); **Brown**—Cleveland (1950-62), Cincinnati (1968-75); **Coryell**—St. Louis (1973-77), San Diego (1978-86); **Ditka**— Chicago (1982-92), New Orleans (1997-99); **Ewbank**— Baltimore (1954-62), NY Jets (1963-73); **Gibbs**—Washington (1981-92); **Gillman**—LA Rams (1955-59), LA-San Diego Chargers (1960-69), Houston (1973-74).

Grant—Minnesota (1967-83,1985); **Halas**—Chicago Bears (1920-29,33-42,46-55,58-67); **Holmgren**—Green Bay (1992-98), Seattle (1999—); **Knox**— LA Rams (1973-77, 1992-94); Buffalo (1978-82), Seattle (1983-91); **Lambeau**—Green Bay (1921-49), Chicago Cards (1950-51), Washington (1952-53); **Landry**—Dallas (1960-88); **Levy**— Kansas City (1978-82), Buffalo (1986-97); **Madden**—Oakland (1969-78); **Mora**—New Orleans (1986-1995), Indianapolis (1998-2001).

Noll—Pittsburgh (1969-91); **Owen**—NY Giants (1931-53); **Parcells**— NY Giants (1983-90), New England (1993-97), NY Jets (1997-99); **Parker**—Chicago Cards (1949), Detroit (1951-56), Pittsburgh (1957-64); **Reeves**— Denver (1981-92), NY Giants (1993-96), Atlanta (1997—); **Schottenheimer**— Cleveland (1984-88), Kansas City (1989-98), Washington (2001), San Diego (2002—); **Seifert**—San Francisco (1989-96), Carolina (1999-2001); **Shula**—Baltimore (1963-69), Miami (1970-95); **Stram**—Dallas-Kansas City (1960-74), New Orleans (1976-77).

Top Winning Percentages

Minimum of 85 NFL victories, including playoffs.

		Yrs	W	L	T	Pct
1	Vince Lombardi	10	105	35	6	.740
2	John Madden	10	112	39	7	.731
3	Joe Gibbs	12	140	65	0	.683
4	George Allen	12	118	54.	5	.681
5	George Halas	40	324	151	31	.671
6	Don Shula	33	347	173	6	.665
7	**George Seifert**	11	124	67	0	.649
8	Curly Lambeau	33	229	134	22	.623
9	Bill Walsh	10	102	63	1	.617
10	**Mike Holmgren**	10	108	67	0	.617
11	**Mike Shanahan**	9	87	54	0	.617
12	Paul Brown	21	170	108	6	.609
13	**Bill Cowher**	10	105	68	0	.607
14	Bud Grant	18	168	108	5	.607
15	**Marty Schottenheimer**	16	158	104	1	.603
16	Tom Landry	29	270	178	6	.601
17	**Dennis Green**	10	101	70	0	.591
18	Bill Parcells	15	149	106	1	.584
19	Steve Owen	23	153	108	17	.581
20	Buddy Parker	15	107	76	9	.581
21	Hank Stram	17	136	100	10	.573
22	Chuck Noll	23	209	156	1	.572
23	Jimmy Johnson	9	89	68	0	.567
24	Marv Levy	17	154	120	0	.562
25	Don Coryell	14	114	89	1	.561

Note: If AAFC records are included, **Paul Brown** moves from 12th to 7th with a percentage of .660 (25 yrs, 222-112-9) and **Buck Shaw** would be 11th at .619 (8 yrs, 91-55-5).

Active Coaches' Victories

Through 2001 season, including playoffs.

		Yrs	W	L	T	Pct
1	Dan Reeves, Atlanta	21	**188**	157	1	.545
2	Marty Schottenheimer, SD	16	**158**	104	1	.603
3	Mike Holmgren, Seattle	10	**108**	67	0	.617
4	Bill Cowher, Pittsburgh	10	**105**	68	0	.607
5	Dick Vermeil, KC	11	**88**	87	0	.503
6	Mike Shanahan, Denver	9	**87**	54	0	.617
7	Jeff Fisher, Tennessee	8	**68**	55	0	.553
8	Tom Coughlin, Jacksonville	7	**66**	54	0	.550
9	Dave Wannstedt, Miami	8	**64**	69	0	.481
10	Tony Dungy, Indianapolis	6	**56**	46	0	.549
	Bill Belichick, New England	7	**56**	61	0	.479
12	Steve Mariucci, San Fran	5	**49**	36	0	.576
13	Jim Fassel, NY Giants	5	**46**	37	1	.554
14	Jon Gruden, Tampa Bay	4	**40**	28	0	.588
15	Brian Billick, Baltimore	3	**35**	19	0	.648
16	Dom Capers, Houston	4	**31**	35	0	.470
17	Andy Reid, Philadelphia	3	**30**	23	0	.566
18	Mike Martz, St. Louis	2	**26**	10	0	.722
19	Dick Jauron, Chicago	3	**24**	25	0	.490
20	Mike Sherman, Green Bay	2	**22**	12	0	.647
21	Jim Haslett, New Orleans	2	**18**	16	0	.529
22	Herman Edwards, NY Jets	1	**10**	7	0	.588
	Dick LeBeau, Cincinnati	2	**10**	19	0	.345
	Dave Campo, Dallas	2	**10**	22	0	.313
25	Dave McGinnis, Arizona	2	**8**	17	0	.320
26	Butch Davis, Cleveland	1	**7**	9	0	.438
27	Gregg Williams, Buffalo	1	**3**	13	0	.188
28	Marty Mornhinweg, Detroit	1	**2**	14	0	.125
29	John Fox, Carolina	0	**0**	0	0	.000
	Steve Spurrier, Washington	0	**0**	0	0	.000
	Bill Callahan, Oakland	0	**0**	0	0	.000
	Mike Tice, Minnesota	1	**0**	1	0	.000

Annual Awards
Most Valuable Player

Currently, the NFL does not sanction an official MVP award. It awarded the Joe F. Carr Trophy (Carr was NFL president from 1921-39) to the league MVP from 1938 to 1946. Since then, four principal MVP awards have been given out throughout the years and are noted below: UPI (1953-69), AP (since 1957), the Maxwell Club of Philadelphia's Bert Bell Trophy (since 1959) and the Pro Football Writers Assn. (since 1976). UPI switched to AFC and NFC Player of the Year awards in 1970 and then discontinued its awards in 1997.

Multiple winners (more than one season): Jim Brown (4); Randall Cunningham, Brett Favre, Johnny Unitas and Y.A. Tittle (3); Earl Campbell, Marshall Faulk, Otto Graham, Don Hutson, Joe Montana, Walter Payton, Barry Sanders, Ken Stabler, Joe Theismann, Kurt Warner and Steve Young (2).

Year	Awards
1938 Mel Hein, NY Giants, C	Carr
1939 Parker Hall, Cleveland Rams, HB	Carr
1940 Ace Parker, Brooklyn, HB	Carr
1941 Don Hutson, Green Bay, E	Carr
1942 Don Hutson, Green Bay, E	Carr
1943 Sid Luckman, Chicago Bears, QB	Carr
1944 Frank Sinkwich, Detroit, HB	Carr
1945 Bob Waterfield, Cleveland Rams, QB	Carr
1946 Bill Dudley, Pittsburgh, HB	Carr
1947-52 No award	
1953 Otto Graham, Cleveland Browns, QB	UPI
1954 Joe Perry, San Francisco, FB	UPI
1955 Otto Graham, Cleveland, QB	UPI
1956 Frank Gifford, NY Giants, HB	UPI
1957 Y.A. Tittle, San Francisco, QB	UPI
& Jim Brown, Cleveland, FB	AP
1958 Jim Brown, Cleveland, FB	UPI
& Gino Marchetti, Baltimore, DE	AP
1959 Johnny Unitas, Baltimore, QB	UPI, Bell
& Charley Conerly, NY Giants, QB	AP
1960 Norm Van Brocklin, Phi., QB	UPI, AP (tie), Bell
& Joe Schmidt, Detroit, LB	AP (tie)
1961 Paul Hornung, Green Bay, HB	UPI, AP, Bell
1962 Y.A. Tittle, NY Giants, QB	UPI
Jim Taylor, Green Bay, FB	AP
& Andy Robustelli, NY Giants, DE	Bell
1963 Jim Brown, Cleveland, FB	UPI, Bell
& Y.A. Tittle, NY Giants, QB	AP

Year	Awards
1964 Johnny Unitas, Baltimore, QB	UPI, AP, Bell
1965 Jim Brown, Cleveland, FB	UPI, AP
& Pete Retzlaff, Philadelphia, TE	Bell
1966 Bart Starr, Green Bay, QB	UPI, AP
& Don Meredith, Dallas, QB	Bell
1967 Johnny Unitas, Baltimore, QB	UPI, AP, Bell
1968 Earl Morrall, Baltimore, QB	UPI, AP
& Leroy Kelly, Cleveland, RB	Bell
1969 Roman Gabriel, LA Rams, QB	UPI, AP, Bell
1970 John Brodie, San Francisco, QB	AP
& George Blanda, Oakland, QB-PK	Bell
1971 Alan Page, Minnesota, DT	AP
& Roger Staubach, Dallas, QB	Bell
1972 Larry Brown, Washington, RB	AP, Bell
1973 O.J. Simpson, Buffalo, RB	AP, Bell
1974 Ken Stabler, Oakland, QB	AP
& Merlin Olsen, LA Rams, DT	Bell
1975 Fran Tarkenton, Minnesota, QB	AP, Bell
1976 Bert Jones, Baltimore, QB	AP, PFWA
& Ken Stabler, Oakland, QB	Bell
1977 Walter Payton, Chicago, RB	AP, PFWA
& Bob Griese, Miami, QB	Bell
1978 Terry Bradshaw, Pittsburgh, QB	AP, Bell
& Earl Campbell, Houston, RB	PFWA
1979 Earl Campbell, Houston, RB	AP, Bell, PFWA
1980 Brian Sipe, Cleveland, QB	AP, Bell, PFWA
& Ron Jaworski, Philadelphia, QB	Bell
1981 Ken Anderson, Cincinnati, QB	AP, Bell, PFWA

Year	Awards
1982 Mark Moseley, Washington, PK	AP
Joe Theismann, Washington, QB	Bell
& Dan Fouts, San Diego, QB	PFWA
1983 Joe Theismann, Washington, QB	AP, PFWA
& John Riggins, Washington, RB	Bell
1984 Dan Marino, Miami, QB	AP, Bell, PFWA
1985 Marcus Allen, LA Raiders, RB	AP, PFWA
& Walter Payton, Chicago, RB	Bell
1986 Lawrence Taylor, NY Giants, LB	AP, Bell, PFWA
1987 Jerry Rice, San Francisco, WR	Bell, PFWA
& John Elway, Denver, QB	AP
1988 Boomer Esiason, Cincinnati, QB	AP, PFWA
& Randall Cunningham, Phila., QB	Bell
1989 Joe Montana, San Francisco, QB	AP, Bell, PFWA
1990 Randall Cunningham, Phila., QB	Bell, PFWA
& Joe Montana, San Francisco, QB	AP

Year	Awards
1991 Thurman Thomas, Buffalo, RB	AP, PFWA
& Barry Sanders, Detroit, RB	Bell
1992 Steve Young, San Francisco, QB	AP, Bell, PFWA
1993 Emmitt Smith, Dallas, RB	AP, Bell, PFWA
1994 Steve Young, San Francisco, QB	AP, Bell, PFWA
1995 Brett Favre, Green Bay, QB	AP, Bell, PFWA
1996 Brett Favre, Green Bay, QB	AP, Bell, PFWA
1997 Barry Sanders, Detroit, RB	AP*, Bell, PFWA
& Brett Favre, Green Bay, QB	AP*
1998 Terrell Davis, Denver, RB	AP, PFWA
& Randall Cunningham, Minnesota, QB	Bell
1999 Kurt Warner, St. Louis, QB	AP, Bell, PFWA
2000 Marshall Faulk, St. Louis, RB	AP, PFWA
& Rich Gannon, Oakland, QB	Bell
2001 Kurt Warner, St. Louis, QB	AP
& Marshall Faulk, St. Louis, RB	Bell, PFWA

*In 1997 for the first time in history, two players tied for the AP MVP award.

AP Offensive Player of the Year

Selected by The Associated Press in balloting by a nationwide media panel. Given out since 1972. Rookie winners are in **bold** type.

Multiple winners: Earl Campbell and Marshall Faulk (3); Terrell Davis, Jerry Rice and Barry Sanders (2).

Year	Pos	Year	Pos	Year	Pos
1972 Larry Brown, Was	RB	1982 Dan Fouts, SD	QB	1992 Steve Young, SF	QB
1973 O.J. Simpson, Buf	RB	1983 Joe Theismann, Was	QB	1993 Jerry Rice, SF	WR
1974 Ken Stabler, Oak	QB	1984 Dan Marino, Mia	QB	1994 Barry Sanders, Det	RB
1975 Fran Tarkenton, Min	QB	1985 Marcus Allen, Raiders	RB	1995 Brett Favre, GB	QB
1976 Bert Jones, Bal	QB	1986 Eric Dickerson, Rams	RB	1996 Terrell Davis, Den	RB
1977 Walter Payton, Chi	RB	1987 Jerry Rice, SF	WR	1997 Barry Sanders, Det	RB
1978 **Earl Campbell**, Hou	RB	1988 Roger Craig, SF	RB	1998 Terrell Davis, Den	RB
1979 Earl Campbell, Hou	RB	1989 Joe Montana, SF	QB	1999 Marshall Faulk, St.L	RB
1980 Earl Campbell, Hou	RB	1990 Warren Moon, Hou	QB	2000 Marshall Faulk, St.L	RB
1981 Ken Anderson, Cin	QB	1991 Thurman Thomas, Buf	RB	2001 Marshall Faulk, St.L	RB

AP Defensive Player of the Year

Selected by The Associated Press in balloting by a nationwide media panel. Given out since 1971. Rookie winners are in **bold** type.

Multiple winners: Lawrence Taylor (3); Joe Greene, Mike Singletary, Bruce Smith and Reggie White (2).

Year	Pos	Year	Pos	Year	Pos
1971 Alan Page, Min	DT	1982 Lawrence Taylor, NYG	LB	1993 Rod Woodson, Pit	CB
1972 Joe Greene, Pit	DT	1983 Doug Betters, Mia	DE	1994 Deion Sanders, SF	CB
1973 Dick Anderson, Mia	S	1984 Kenny Easley, Sea	S	1995 Bryce Paup, Buf	LB
1974 Joe Greene, Pit	DT	1985 Mike Singletary, Chi	LB	1996 Bruce Smith, Buf	DE
1975 Mel Blount, Pit	CB	1986 Lawrence Taylor, NYG	LB	1997 Dana Stubblefield, SF	DT
1976 Jack Lambert, Pit	LB	1987 Reggie White, Phi	DE	1998 Reggie White, GB	DE
1977 Harvey Martin, Dal	DE	1988 Mike Singletary, Chi	LB	1999 Warren Sapp, TB	DT
1978 Randy Gradishar, Den	LB	1989 Keith Millard, Min	DT	2000 Ray Lewis, Bal	LB
1979 Lee Roy Selmon, TB	DE	1990 Bruce Smith, Buf	DE	2001 Michael Strahan, NYG	DE
1980 Lester Hayes, Oak	CB	1991 Pat Swilling, NO	LB		
1981 **Lawrence Taylor**, NYG	LB	1992 Cortez Kennedy, Sea	DT		

UPI NFC Player of the Year

Given out by UPI from 1970-96. Offensive and defensive players honored since 1983. Rookie winners are in **bold** type.

Multiple winners: Eric Dickerson, Reggie White and Mike Singletary (3); Brett Favre, Charles Haley, Walter Payton, Lawrence Taylor and Steve Young (2).

Year	Pos	Year	Pos	Year	Pos
1970 John Brodie, SF	QB	1984 Off–Eric Dickerson, Rams	RB	1991 Off–Mark Rypien, Was	QB
1971 Alan Page, Min	DT	Def–Mike Singletary, Chi	LB	Def–Reggie White, Phi	DE
1972 Larry Brown, Was	RB	1985 Off–Walter Payton, Chi	RB	1992 Off–Steve Young, SF	QB
1973 John Hadl, Rams	QB	Def–Mike Singletary, Chi	LB	Def–Chris Doleman, Min	DE
1974 Jim Hart, St.L	QB	1986 Off–Eric Dickerson, Rams	RB	1993 Off–Emmitt Smith, Dal	RB
1975 Fran Tarkenton, Min	QB	Def–Lawrence Taylor, NYG	LB	Def–Eric Allen, Phi	CB
1976 Chuck Foreman, Min	RB	1987 Off–Jerry Rice, SF	WR	1994 Off–Steve Young, SF	QB
1977 Walter Payton, Chi	RB	Def–Reggie White, Phi	DE	Def–Charles Haley, Dal	DE
1978 Archie Manning, NO	QB	1988 Off–Roger Craig, SF	RB	1995 Off–Brett Favre, GB	QB
1979 Ottis Anderson, St.L	RB	Def–Mike Singletary, Chi	LB	Def–Reggie White, GB	DE
1980 Ron Jaworski, Phi	QB	1989 Off–Joe Montana, SF	QB	1996 Off–Brett Favre, GB	QB
1981 Tony Dorsett, Dal	RB	Def–Keith Millard, Min	DT	Def–Kevin Greene, Car	LB
1982 Mark Moseley, Was	PK	1990 Off–Randall Cunningham, Phi	QB	1997 Award discontinued.	
1983 Off–Eric Dickerson, Rams	RB	Def–Charles Haley, SF	LB		
Def–Lawrence Taylor, NYG	LB				

Annual Awards (Cont.)
UPI AFL-AFC Player of the Year

Presented by UPI to the top player in the AFL (1960-69) and AFC (1970-96). Offensive and defensive players have been honored since 1983. Rookie winners are in **bold** type.

Multiple winners: Bruce Smith (4); O.J. Simpson (3); Cornelius Bennett, George Blanda, John Elway, Dan Fouts, Daryle Lamonica, Dan Marino and Curt Warner (2).

Year		Pos	Year		Pos	Year		Pos
1960	**Abner Haynes**, Dal	HB	1978	**Earl Campbell**, Hou	RB	1989	Off–Christian Okoye, KC	RB
1961	George Blanda, Hou	QB	1979	Dan Fouts, SD	QB		Def–Michael Dean Perry, Cle	NT
1962	Cookie Gilchrist, Buf	FB	1980	Brian Sipe, Cle	QB	1990	Off–Warren Moon, Hou	QB
1963	Lance Alworth, SD	FL	1981	Ken Anderson, Cin	QB		Def–Bruce Smith, Buf	DE
1964	Gino Cappelletti, Bos	FL-PK	1982	Dan Fouts, SD	QB	1991	Off–Thurman Thomas, Buf	RB
1965	Paul Lowe, SD	HB	1983	Off–**Curt Warner**, Sea	RB		Def–Cornelius Bennett, Buf	LB
1966	Jim Nance, Bos	FB		Def–Rod Martin, Raiders	LB	1992	Off–Barry Foster, Pit	RB
1967	Daryle Lamonica, Raiders	QB	1984	Off–Dan Marino, Mia	QB		Def–Junior Seau, SD	LB
1968	Joe Namath, NYJ	QB		Def–Mark Gastineau, NYJ	DE	1993	Off–John Elway, Den	QB
1969	Daryle Lamonica, Raiders	QB	1985	Off–Marcus Allen, Raiders	RB		Def–Rod Woodson, Pit	CB
1970	George Blanda, Raiders	QB-PK		Def–Andre Tippett, NE	LB	1994	Off–Dan Marino, Mia	QB
1971	Otis Taylor, KC	WR	1986	Off–Curt Warner, Sea	RB		Def–Greg Lloyd, Pit	LB
1972	O.J. Simpson, Buf	RB		Def–Rulon Jones, Den	DE	1995	Off–Jim Harbaugh, Ind	QB
1973	O.J. Simpson, Buf	RB	1987	Off–John Elway, Den	QB		Def–Bryce Paup, Buf	LB
1974	Ken Stabler, Raiders	QB		Def–Bruce Smith, Buf	DE	1996	Off–Terrell Davis, Den	RB
1975	O.J. Simpson, Buf	RB	1988	Off–Boomer Esiason, Cin	QB		Def–Bruce Smith, Buf	DE
1976	Bert Jones, Bal	QB		Def–Bruce Smith, Buf	DE	1997	Award discontinued.	
1977	Craig Morton, Den	QB		& Cornelius Bennett, Buf	LB			

UPI NFL-NFC Rookie of the Year

Presented by UPI to the top rookie in the NFL (1955-69) and NFC (1970-96). Players who were the overall first pick in the NFL draft are in **bold** type.

Year		Pos	Year		Pos	Year		Pos
1955	Alan Ameche, Bal	FB	1970	Bruce Taylor, SF	DB	1985	Jerry Rice, SF	WR
1956	Lenny Moore, Bal	HB	1971	John Brockington, GB	RB	1986	Reuben Mayes, NO	RB
1957	Jim Brown, Cle	FB	1972	Chester Marcol, GB	PK	1987	Robert Awalt, St.L	TE
1958	Jimmy Orr, Pit	FL	1973	Charle Young, Phi	TE	1988	Keith Jackson, Phi	TE
1959	Boyd Dowler, GB	FL	1974	John Hicks, NY	G	1989	Barry Sanders, Det	RB
1960	Gail Cogdill, Det	FL	1975	Mike Thomas, Wash	RB	1990	Mark Carrier, Chi	S
1961	Mike Ditka, Chi	TE	1976	Sammy White, Min	WR	1991	Lawrence Dawsey, TB	WR
1962	Ronnie Bull, Chi	RB	1977	Tony Dorsett, Dal	RB	1992	Robert Jones, Dal	LB
1963	Paul Flatley, Min	FL	1978	Bubba Baker, Det	DE	1993	Jerome Bettis, LA	RB
1964	Charley Taylor, Wash	HB	1979	Ottis Anderson, St.L	RB	1994	Bryant Young, SF	DT
1965	Gale Sayers, Chi	HB	1980	**Billy Sims**, Det	RB	1995	Rashaan Salaam, Chi	RB
1966	Johnny Roland, St.L	HB	1981	**George Rogers**, NO	RB	1996	Simeon Rice, Ari	DE
1967	Mel Farr, Det	RB	1982	Jim McMahon, Chi	QB	1997	Award discontinued.	
1968	Earl McCullough, Det	FL	1983	Eric Dickerson, LA	RB			
1969	Calvin Hill, Dal	RB	1984	Paul McFadden, Phi	PK			

UPI AFL-AFC Rookie of the Year

Presented by UPI to the top rookie in the AFL (1960-69) and AFC (1970-96). Players who were the overall first pick in the AFL or NFL draft are in **bold** type.

Year		Pos	Year		Pos	Year		Pos
1960	Abner Haynes, Dal	HB	1973	Bobbie Clark, Cin	RB	1986	Leslie O'Neal, SD	DE
1961	Earl Faison, SD	DE	1974	Don Woods, SD	RB	1987	Shane Conlan, Buf	LB
1962	Curtis McClinton, Dal	FB	1975	Robert Brazile, Hou	LB	1988	John Stephens, NE	RB
1963	Billy Joe, Den	FB	1976	Mike Haynes, NE	DB	1989	Derrick Thomas, KC	LB
1964	Matt Snell, NY	FB	1977	A.J. Duhe, Mia	DE	1990	Richmond Webb, Mia	OT
1965	Joe Namath, NY	QB	1978	**Earl Campbell**, Hou	RB	1991	Mike Croel, Den	LB
1966	Bobby Burnett, Buf	HB	1979	Jerry Butler, Buf	WR	1992	Dale Carter, KC	CB
1967	George Webster, Hou	LB	1980	Joe Cribbs, Buf	RB	1993	Rick Mirer, Sea	QB
1968	Paul Robinson, Cin	RB	1981	Joe Delaney, KC	RB	1994	Marshall Faulk, Ind	RB
1969	Greg Cook, Cin	QB	1982	Marcus Allen, LA	RB	1995	Curtis Martin, NE	RB
1970	Dennis Shaw, Buf	QB	1983	Curt Warner, Sea	RB	1996	Terry Glenn, NE	WR
1971	**Jim Plunkett**, NE	QB	1984	Louis Lipps, Pit	WR	1997	Award discontinued.	
1972	Franco Harris, Pit	RB	1985	Kevin Mack, Cle	RB			

AP Offensive Rookie of the Year

Selected by The Associated Press in balloting by a nationwide media panel. Given out since 1967.

Year		Pos	Year		Pos	Year		Pos
1967	Mel Farr, Det	RB	1979	Ottis Anderson, St.L.	RB	1991	Leonard Russell, NE	RB
1968	Earl McCullouch, Det	OE	1980	Billy Sims, Det	RB	1992	Carl Pickens, Cin	WR
1969	Calvin Hill, Dal	RB	1981	George Rogers, NO	RB	1993	Jerome Bettis, Rams	RB
1970	Dennis Shaw, Buf	QB	1982	Marcus Allen, Raiders	RB	1994	Marshall Faulk, Ind	RB
1971	John Brockington, GB	RB	1983	Eric Dickerson, Rams	RB	1995	Curtis Martin, NE	RB
1972	Franco Harris, Pit	RB	1984	Louis Lipps, Pit	WR	1996	Eddie George, Hou	RB
1973	Chuck Foreman, Min	RB	1985	Eddie Brown, Cin	WR	1997	Warrick Dunn, TB	RB
1974	Don Woods, SD	RB	1986	Reuben Mayes, NO	RB	1998	Randy Moss, Min	WR
1975	Mike Thomas, Was	RB	1987	Troy Stradford, Mia	RB	1999	Edgerrin James, Ind	RB
1976	Sammy White, Min	WR	1988	John Stephens, NE	RB	2000	Mike Anderson, Den	RB
1977	Tony Dorsett, Dal	RB	1989	Barry Sanders, Det	RB	2001	Anthony Thomas, Chi	RB
1978	Earl Campbell, Hou	RB	1990	Emmitt Smith, Dal	RB			

AP Defensive Rookie of the Year

Selected by The Associated Press in balloting by a nationwide media panel. Given out since 1967.

Year		Pos	Year		Pos	Year		Pos
1967	Lem Barney, Det	CB	1979	Jim Haslett, Buf	LB	1990	Mark Carrier, Chi	S
1968	Claude Humphrey, Atl	DE	1980	Buddy Curry, Atl	LB	1991	Mike Croel, Den	LB
1969	Joe Greene, Pit	DT		& Al Richardson, Atl	LB	1992	Dale Carter, KC	CB
1970	Bruce Taylor, SF	CB	1981	Lawrence Taylor, NYG	LB	1993	Dana Stubblefield, SF	DT
1971	Isiah Robertson, Rams	LB	1982	Chip Banks, Cle	LB	1994	Tim Bowens, Mia	DT
1972	Willie Buchanon, GB	CB	1983	Vernon Maxwell, Bal	LB	1995	Hugh Douglas, NYJ	DE
1973	Wally Chambers, Chi	DT	1984	Bill Maas, KC	DT	1996	Simeon Rice, Ari	DE
1974	Jack Lambert, Pit	LB	1985	Duane Bickett, Ind	LB	1997	Peter Boulware, Bal	LB
1975	Robert Brazile, Hou	LB	1986	Leslie O'Neal, SD	DE	1998	Charles Woodson, Raiders	CB
1976	Mike Haynes, NE	CB	1987	Shane Conlan, Buf	LB	1999	Jevon Kearse, Ten	DE
1977	A.J. Duhe, Mia	DE	1988	Erik McMillan, NYJ	S	2000	Brian Urlacher, Chi	LB
1978	Al Baker, Det	DE	1989	Derrick Thomas, KC	LB	2001	Kendrell Bell, Pit	LB

Coach of the Year

Presented by UPI to the top coach in the AFL-NFL (1955-69) and AFC-NFC (1970-96). In 1997, the UPI awards were discontinued. Awards beginning in 1997 are the consensus selections from presenters such as AP, The Maxwell Football Club of Philadelphia, *The Sporting News* and the Pro Football Writers Association. Records indicate the team's change in record from the previous season.

Multiple winners: Dan Reeves (4); Paul Brown, Chuck Knox and Don Shula (3); George Allen, Leeman Bennett, Mike Ditka, George Halas, Tom Landry, Marv Levy, Bill Parcells, Jack Pardee, Sam Rutigliano, Lou Saban, Allie Sherman, Marty Schottenheimer, Dick Vermeil and Bill Walsh (2).

Year		Improvement	Year		Improvement
1955	NFL–Joe Kuharich, Washington	3-9 to 8-4	1974	NFC–Don Coryell, St. Louis	4-9-1 to 10-4
1956	NFL–Buddy Parker, Detroit	3-9 to 9-3		AFC–Sid Gillman, Houston	1-13 to 7-7
1957	NFL–Paul Brown, Cleveland	5-7 to 9-2-1	1975	NFC–Tom Landry, Dallas	8-6 to 10-4
1958	NFL–Weeb Ewbank, Baltimore	7-5 to 9-3		AFC–Ted Marchibroda, Baltimore	2-12 to 10-4
1959	NFL–Vince Lombardi, Green Bay	1-10-1 to 7-5	1976	NFC–Jack Pardee, Chicago	4-10 to 7-7
1960	NFL–Buck Shaw, Philadelphia	7-5 to 10-2		AFC–Chuck Fairbanks, New England	3-11 to 11-3
	AFL–Lou Rymkus, Houston	10-4	1977	NFC–Leeman Bennett, Atlanta	4-10 to 7-7
1961	NFL–Allie Sherman, New York	6-4-2 to 10-3-1		AFC–Red Miller, Denver	9-5 to 12-2
	AFL–Wally Lemm, Houston	10-4 to 10-3-1	1978	NFC–Dick Vermeil, Philadelphia	5-9 to 9-7
1962	NFL–Allie Sherman, New York	10-3-1 to 12-2		AFC–Walt Michaels, New York	3-11 to 8-8
	AFL–Jack Faulkner, Denver	3-11 to 7-7	1979	NFC–Jack Pardee, Washington	8-8 to 10-6
1963	NFL–George Halas, Chicago	9-5 to 11-1-2		AFC–Sam Rutigliano, Cleveland	8-8 to 9-7
	AFL–Al Davis, Oakland	1-13 to 10-4	1980	NFC–Leeman Bennett, Atlanta	6-10 to 12-4
1964	NFL–Don Shula, Baltimore	8-6 to 12-2		AFC–Sam Rutigliano, Cleveland	9-7 to 11-5
	AFL–Lou Saban, Buffalo	7-6-1 to 12-2	1981	NFC–Bill Walsh, San Francisco	6-10 to 13-3
1965	NFL–George Halas, Chicago	5-9 to 9-5		AFC–Forrest Gregg, Cincinnati	6-10 to 12-4
	AFL–Lou Saban, Buffalo	12-2 to 10-3-1	1982	NFC–Joe Gibbs, Washington	8-8 to 8-1
1966	NFL–Tom Landry, Dallas	7-7 to 10-3-1		AFC–Tom Flores, Los Angeles	7-9 to 8-1
	AFL–Mike Holovak, Boston	4-8-2 to 8-4-2	1983	NFC–John Robinson, Los Angeles	2-7 to 9-7
1967	NFL–George Allen, Los Angeles	8-6 to 11-1-2		AFC–Chuck Knox, Seattle	4-5 to 9-7
	AFL–John Rauch, Oakland	8-5-1 to 13-1	1984	NFC–Bill Walsh, San Francisco	10-6 to 15-1
1968	NFL–Don Shula, Baltimore	11-1-2 to 13-1		AFC–Chuck Knox, Seattle	9-7 to 12-4
	AFL–Hank Stram, Kansas City	9-5 to 12-2	1985	NFC–Mike Ditka, Chicago	10-6 to 15-1
1969	NFL–Bud Grant, Minnesota	8-6 to 12-2		AFC–Raymond Berry, New England	9-7 to 11-5
	AFL–Paul Brown, Cincinnati	3-11 to 4-9-1	1986	NFC–Bill Parcells, New York	10-6 to 14-2
1970	NFC–Alex Webster, New York	6-8 to 9-5		AFC–Marty Schottenheimer, Cleveland	8-8 to 12-4
	AFC–Paul Brown, Cincinnati	4-9-1 to 8-6	1987	NFC–Jim Mora, New Orleans	7-9 to 12-3
1971	NFC–George Allen, Washington	6-8 to 9-4-1		AFC–Ron Meyer, Indianapolis	3-13 to 9-6
	AFC–Don Shula, Miami	10-4 to 10-3-1	1988	NFC–Mike Ditka, Chicago	11-4 to 12-4
1972	NFC–Dan Devine, Green Bay	4-8-2 to 10-4		AFC–Marv Levy, Buffalo	7-8 to 12-4
1973	NFC–Chuck Knox, Los Angeles	6-7-1 to 12-2	1989	NFC–Lindy Infante, Green Bay	4-12 to 10-6
	AFC–John Ralston, Denver	5-9 to 7-5-2		AFC–Dan Reeves, Denver	8-8 to 11-5

Annual Awards (Cont.)

Year		Improvement
1990	NFC–Jimmy Johnson, Dallas	1-15 to 7-9
	AFC–Art Shell, Los Angeles	8-8 to 12-4
1991	NFC–Wayne Fontes, Detroit	6-10 to 12-4
	AFC–Dan Reeves, Denver	5-11 to 12-4
1992	NFC–Dennis Green, Minnesota	8-8 to 11-5
	AFC–Bobby Ross, San Diego	4-12 to 11-5
1993	NFC–Dan Reeves, New York	6-10 to 11-5
	AFC–Marv Levy, Buffalo	11-5 to 12-4
1994	NFC–Dave Wannstedt, Chicago	7-9 to 9-7
	AFC–Bill Parcells, New England	5-11 to 10-6

Year		Improvement
1995	NFC–Ray Rhodes, Philadelphia	7-9 to 10-6
	AFC–Marty Schottenheimer, Kansas City	9-7 to 13-3
1996	NFC–Dom Capers, Carolina	7-9 to 12-4
	AFC–Tom Coughlin, Jacksonville	4-12 to 9-7
1997	NFL–Jim Fassel, NY Giants	6-10 to 10-5-1
1998	NFL–Dan Reeves, Atlanta	7-9 to 14-2
1999	NFL–Dick Vermeil, St. Louis	4-12 to 13-3
2000	NFL–Jim Haslett, New Orleans	3-13 to 10-6
2001	NFL–Dick Jauron, Chicago	5-11 to 13-3

CANADIAN FOOTBALL

The Grey Cup

Earl Grey, the Governor-General of Canada (1904-11), donated a trophy in 1909 for the Rugby Football Championship of Canada. The trophy, which later became known as the Grey Cup, was originally open to competition for teams registered with the Canada Rugby Union. Since 1954, the Cup has gone to the champion of the Canadian Football League (CFL).

Overall multiple winners: Toronto Argonauts (14); Edmonton Eskimos (11); Winnipeg Blue Bombers (9); Hamilton Tiger-Cats (8); Ottawa Rough Riders (7); Calgary Stampeders and Hamilton Tigers (5); B.C. Lions, Montreal Alouettes and University of Toronto (4); Queen's University (3); Ottawa Senators, Sarnia Imperials, Saskatchewan Roughriders and Toronto Balmy Beach (2).

CFL multiple winners (since 1954): Edmonton (11); Hamilton and Winnipeg (7); Ottawa (5); B.C. Lions, Calgary and Toronto (4); Montreal (3); Saskatchewan (2).

Year	Cup Final
1909	Univ. of Toronto 26, Toronto Parkdale 6
1910	Univ. of Toronto 16, Hamilton Tigers 7
1911	Univ. of Toronto 14, Toronto Argonauts 7
1912	Hamilton Alerts 11, Toronto Argonauts 4
1913	Hamilton Tigers 44, Toronto Parkdale 2
1914	Toronto Argonauts 14, Univ. of Toronto 2
1915	Hamilton Tigers 13, Toronto Rowing 7
1916-19	Not held (WWI)
1920	Univ. of Toronto 16, Toronto Argonauts 3
1921	Toronto Argonauts 23, Edmonton Eskimos 0
1922	Queens Univ. 13, Edmonton Elks 1
1923	Queens Univ. 54, Regina Roughriders 0
1924	Queens Univ. 11, Toronto Balmy Beach 3
1925	Ottawa Senators 24, Winnipeg Tigers 1
1926	Ottawa Senators 10, Univ. of Toronto 7
1927	Toronto Balmy Beach 9, Hamilton Tigers 6
1928	Hamilton Tigers 30, Regina Roughriders 0
1929	Hamilton Tigers 14, Regina Roughriders 3
1930	Toronto Balmy Beach 11, Regina Roughriders 6
1931	Montreal AAA 22, Regina Roughriders 0
1932	Hamilton Tigers 25, Regina Roughriders 6
1933	Toronto Argonauts 4, Sarnia Imperials 3

Year	Cup Final
1934	Sarnia Imperials 20, Regina Roughriders 12
1935	Winnipeg 'Pegs 18, Hamilton Tigers 12
1936	Sarnia Imperials 26, Ottawa Rough Riders 20
1937	Toronto Argonauts 4, Winnipeg Blue Bombers 3
1938	Toronto Argonauts 30, Winnipeg Blue Bombers 7
1939	Winnipeg Blue Bombers 8, Ottawa Rough Riders 7
1940	Gm 1: Ottawa Rough Riders 8, Toronto B-Beach 2
	Gm 2: Ottawa Rough Riders 12, Toronto B-Beach 5
1941	Winnipeg Blue Bombers 18, Ottawa Rough Riders 16
1942	Toronto RACF 8, Winnipeg RACF 5
1943	Hamilton Wildcats 23, Winnipeg RACF 14
1944	Montreal HMCS 7, Hamilton Wildcats 6
1945	Toronto Argonauts 35, Winnipeg Blue Bombers 0
1946	Toronto Argonauts 28, Winnipeg Blue Bombers 6
1947	Toronto Argonauts 10, Winnipeg Blue Bombers 9
1948	Calgary Stampeders 12, Ottawa Rough Riders 7
1949	Montreal Alouettes 28, Calgary Stampeders 15
1950	Toronto Argonauts 13, Winnipeg Blue Bombers 0
1951	Ottawa Rough Riders 21, Saskatch. Roughriders 14
1952	Toronto Argonauts 21, Edmonton Eskimos 11
1953	Hamilton Tiger-Cats 12, Winnipeg Blue Bombers 6

Year	Winner	Head Coach	Score	Loser	Head Coach	Site
1954	Edmonton	Frank (Pop) Ivy	26-25	Montreal	Doug Walker	Toronto
1955	Edmonton	Frank (Pop) Ivy	34-19	Montreal	Doug Walker	Vancouver
1956	Edmonton	Frank (Pop) Ivy	50-27	Montreal	Doug Walker	Toronto
1957	Hamilton	Jim Trimble	32-7	Winnipeg	Bud Grant	Toronto
1958	Winnipeg	Bud Grant	35-28	Hamilton	Jim Trimble	Vancouver
1959	Winnipeg	Bud Grant	21-7	Hamilton	Jim Trimble	Toronto
1960	Ottawa	Frank Clair	16-6	Edmonton	Eagle Keys	Vancouver
1961	Winnipeg	Bud Grant	21-14(OT)	Hamilton	Jim Trimble	Toronto
1962	Winnipeg	Bud Grant	28-27*	Hamilton	Jim Trimble	Toronto
1963	Hamilton	Ralph Sazio	21-10	B.C. Lions	Dave Skrien	Vancouver
1964	B.C. Lions	Dave Skrien	34-24	Hamilton	Ralph Sazio	Toronto
1965	Hamilton	Ralph Sazio	22-16	Winnipeg	Bud Grant	Toronto
1966	Saskatchewan	Eagle Keys	29-14	Ottawa	Frank Clair	Vancouver
1967	Hamilton	Ralph Sazio	24-1	Saskatchewan	Eagle Keys	Ottawa
1968	Ottawa	Frank Clair	24-21	Calgary	Jerry Williams	Toronto
1969	Ottawa	Frank Clair	29-11	Saskatchewan	Eagle Keys	Montreal
1970	Montreal	Sam Etcheverry	23-10	Calgary	Jim Duncan	Toronto
1971	Calgary	Jim Duncan	14-11	Toronto	Leo Cahill	Vancouver
1972	Hamilton	Jerry Williams	13-10	Saskatchewan	Dave Skrien	Hamilton
1973	Ottawa	Jack Gotta	22-18	Edmonton	Ray Jauch	Toronto
1974	Montreal	Marv Levy	20-7	Edmonton	Ray Jauch	Vancouver

Year	Winner	Head Coach	Score	Loser	Head Coach	Site
1975	Edmonton	Ray Jauch	9-8	Montreal	Marv Levy	Calgary
1976	Ottawa	George Brancato	23-20	Saskatchewan	John Payne	Toronto
1977	Montreal	Marv Levy	41-6	Edmonton	Hugh Campbell	Montreal
1978	Edmonton	Hugh Campbell	20-13	Montreal	Joe Scannella	Toronto
1979	Edmonton	Hugh Campbell	17-9	Montreal	Joe Scannella	Montreal
1980	Edmonton	Hugh Campbell	48-10	Hamilton	John Payne	Toronto
1981	Edmonton	Hugh Campbell	26-23	Ottawa	George Brancato	Montreal
1982	Edmonton	Hugh Campbell	32-16	Toronto	Bob O'Billovich	Toronto
1983	Toronto	Bob O'Billovich	18-17	B.C. Lions	Don Matthews	Vancouver
1984	Winnipeg	Cal Murphy	47-17	Hamilton	Al Bruno	Edmonton
1985	B.C. Lions	Don Matthews	37-24	Hamilton	Al Bruno	Montreal
1986	Hamilton	Al Bruno	39-15	Edmonton	Jack Parker	Vancouver
1987	Edmonton	Joe Faragalli	38-36	Toronto	Bob O'Billovich	Vancouver
1988	Winnipeg	Mike Riley	22-21	B.C. Lions	Larry Donovan	Ottawa
1989	Saskatchewan	John Gregory	43-40	Hamilton	Al Bruno	Toronto
1990	Winnipeg	Mike Riley	50-11	Edmonton	Joe Faragalli	Vancouver
1991	Toronto	Adam Rita	36-21	Calgary	Wally Buono	Winnipeg
1992	Calgary	Wally Buono	24-10	Winnipeg	Urban Bowman	Toronto
1993	Edmonton	Ron Lancaster	33-23	Winnipeg	Cal Murphy	Calgary
1994	B.C. Lions	Dave Ritchie	26-23	Baltimore	Don Matthews	Vancouver
1995	Baltimore	Don Matthews	37-20	Calgary	Wally Buono	Regina
1996	Toronto	Don Matthews	43-37	Edmonton	Ron Lancaster	Hamilton
1997	Toronto	Don Matthews	47-23	Saskatchewan	Jim Daley	Edmonton
1998	Calgary	Wally Buono	26-24	Hamilton	Ron Lancaster	Winnipeg
1999	Hamilton	Ron Lancaster	32-21	Calgary	Wally Buono	Vancouver
2000	B.C. Lions	Steve Buratto	28-26	Montreal	Charlie Taaffe	Calgary
2001	Calgary	Wally Buono	27-19	Winnipeg	Dave Ritchie	Montreal

*Halted by fog in 4th quarter, final 9:29 played the following day.

CFL Most Outstanding Player

Regular season Player of the Year as selected by The Football Reporters of Canada since 1953.

Multiple winners: Doug Flutie (6); Russ Jackson and Jackie Parker (3); Dieter Brock, Ron Lancaster and Mike Pringle (2).

Year	Year	Year
1953 Billy Vessels, Edmonton, RB	1970 Ron Lancaster, Saskatch., QB	1987 Tom Clements, Winnipeg, QB
1954 Sam Etcheverry, Montreal, QB	1971 Don Jonas, Winnipeg, QB	1988 David Williams, B.C. Lions, WR
1955 Pat Abbruzzi, Montreal, RB	1972 Garney Henley, Hamilton, WR	1989 Tracy Ham, Edmonton, QB
1956 Hal Patterson, Montreal, E-DB	1973 Geo. McGowan, Edmonton, WR	1990 Mike Clemons, Toronto, RB
1957 Jackie Parker, Edmonton, RB	1974 Tom Wilkinson, Edmonton, QB	1991 Doug Flutie, B.C. Lions, QB
1958 Jackie Parker, Edmonton, QB	1975 Willie Burden, Calgary, RB	1992 Doug Flutie, Calgary, QB
1959 Johnny Bright, Edmonton, RB	1976 Ron Lancaster, Saskatch., QB	1993 Doug Flutie, Calgary, QB
1960 Jackie Parker, Edmonton, QB	1977 Jimmy Edwards, Hamilton, RB	1994 Doug Flutie, Calgary, QB
1961 Bernie Faloney, Hamilton, QB	1978 Tony Gabriel, Ottawa, TE	1995 Mike Pringle, Baltimore, RB
1962 George Dixon, Montreal, RB	1979 David Green, Montreal, RB	1996 Doug Flutie, Toronto, QB
1963 Russ Jackson, Ottawa, QB	1980 Dieter Brock, Winnipeg, QB	1997 Doug Flutie, Toronto, QB
1964 Lovell Coleman, Calgary, RB	1981 Dieter Brock, Winnipeg, QB	1998 Mike Pringle, Montreal, RB
1965 George Reed, Saskatchewan, RB	1982 Condredge Holloway, Tor., QB	1999 Danny McManus, Hamilton, QB
1966 Russ Jackson, Ottawa, QB	1983 Warren Moon, Edmonton, QB	2000 Dave Dickenson, Calgary, QB
1967 Peter Liske, Calgary, QB	1984 Willard Reaves, Winnipeg, RB	2001 Khari Jones, Winnipeg, QB
1968 Bill Symons, Toronto, RB	1985 Merv Fernandez, B.C. Lions, WR	
1969 Russ Jackson, Ottawa, QB	1986 James Murphy, Winnipeg, WR	

All-Time CFL Leaders

Through the 2001 season. Players active in 2001 are in **bold** type.

Passing Yards

		Yrs	Att	Cmp	Yards	Cmp Pct	Avg Gain	TD	Int	Rating
1	**Damon Allen**	17	6951	3839	54,420	55.2	14.2	295	228	81.2
2	Ron Lancaster	19	6233	3384	50,535	54.3	14.9	333	396	72.4
3	Matt Dunigan	14	5476	3057	43,857	55.8	14.3	306	211	84.5
4	Doug Flutie	8	4854	2975	41,355	61.3	13.9	270	155	93.9
5	Tracy Ham	12	4945	2670	40,534	53.9	15.2	284	164	86.4

Rushing Yards

		Yrs	Car	Yards	Avg	TD
1	George Reed	13	3243	16,116	5.0	134
2	**Mike Pringle**	10	2391	13,680	5.7	104
3	Johnny Bright	13	1969	10,909	5.5	69
4	**Damon Allen**	17	1466	9,989	6.8	78
5	Normie Kwong	13	1745	9,022	5.2	78

Receiving Yards

		Yrs	Ct	Yards	Avg	TD
1	Allen Pitts	11	966	14,891	15.4	117
2	**Darren Flutie**	11	908	13,430	14.8	62
3	Ray Elgaard	14	830	13,198	15.9	78
4	Don Narcisse	13	919	12,366	13.5	75
5	Brian Kelly	9	575	11,169	19.4	97

NFL EUROPE

The World League of American Football was formed in 1991 with hopes of expanding the popularity of the NFL to overseas markets. Funded by the NFL, the inaugural league in 1991 consisted of three European teams (London, Barcelona and Frankfurt), and seven North American teams (New York/New Jersey, Orlando, Montreal, Raleigh-Durham, Birmingham, Sacramento and San Antonio). The second season used the same format with Columbus, Ohio, replacing Raleigh-Durham.

In the fall of 1992, the NFL and WLAF Board of Directors voted to restructure the league to include more European teams. Play was subsequently suspended. In 1993, NFL clubs approved a six-team European-only league to resume play in 1995 with teams in Amsterdam, Barcelona, Frankfurt, London, Rhein and Scotland. In January 1998, the name of the league was changed to NFL Europe. Berlin was added for the 1999 season and London was disbanded.

The World Bowl

The first World Bowl was held in 1991 in front of 61,108 fans at London's Wembley Stadium. In 1991 and 1992, when the league consisted of three divisions, the top team from each division and one wild-card team advanced to the playoffs, with the winners of each game advancing to the World Bowl. There was no game played in 1993 or 1994. Since 1995, the top two regular season teams advance directly to the World Bowl.

Multiple Winners: Berlin, Frankfurt and Rhein (2).

Year	Winner	Head Coach	Score	Loser	Head Coach	Site
1991	London	Larry Kennan	21-0	Barcelona	Jack Bicknell	London
1992	Sacramento	Kay Stephenson	21-17	Orlando	Galen Hall	Montreal
1995	Frankfurt	Ernie Stautner	26-22	Amsterdam	Al Luginbill	Amsterdam
1996	Scotland	Jim Criner	32-27	Frankfurt	Ernie Stautner	Edinburgh, Scot.
1997	Barcelona	Jack Bicknell	38-24	Rhein	Galen Hall	Barcelona
1998	Rhein	Galen Hall	34-10	Frankfurt	Dick Curl	Frankfurt
1999	Frankfurt	Dick Curl	38-24	Barcelona	Jack Bicknell	Dusseldorf
2000	Rhein	Galen Hall	13-10	Scotland	Jim Criner	Frankfurt
2001	Berlin	Peter Vaas	24-17	Barcelona	Jack Bicknell	Amsterdam
2002	Berlin	Peter Vaas	26-20	Rhein	Pete Kuharchek	Dusseldorf

World Bowl MVP

Year	Year	Year
1991 Dan Crossman, London, S	1997 Jon Kitna, Barcelona, QB	2001 Jonathan Quinn, Berlin, QB
1992 Davis Archer, Sacramento, QB	1998 Jim Arellanes, Rhein, QB	2002 Dane Looker, Berlin, WR
1995 Paul Justin, Frankfurt, QB	1999 Andy McCullough, Frankfurt, WR	
1996 Yo Murphy, Scotland, WR	2000 Aaron Stecker, Scotland, RB	

ARENA FOOTBALL

The Arena Football League debuted in June of 1987 with four teams in Chicago, Denver, Pittsburgh and Washington D.C. Currently there are 16 teams in the league, divided into two conferences and four divisions.

ArenaBowl

Multiple Winners: Detroit and Tampa Bay (4); Arizona and Orlando (2).

Bowl	Year	Winner	Head Coach	Score	Loser	Head Coach	Site
I	1987	Denver	Tim Marcum	45-16	Pittsburgh	Joe Haering	Pittsburgh
II	1988	Detroit	Tim Marcum	24-13	Chicago	Perry Moss	Chicago
III	1989	Detroit	Tim Marcum	39-26	Pittsburgh	Joe Haering	Detroit
IV	1990	Detroit	Perry Moss	51-27	Dallas	Ernie Stautner	Detroit
V	1991	Tampa Bay	Fran Curci	48-42	Detroit	Tim Marcum	Detroit
VI	1992	Detroit	Tim Marcum	56-38	Orlando	Perry Moss	Orlando
VII	1993	Tampa Bay	Lary Kuharich	51-31	Detroit	Tim Marcum	Detroit
VIII	1994	Arizona	Danny White	36-31	Orlando	Perry Moss	Orlando
IX	1995	Tampa Bay	Tim Marcum	48-35	Orlando	Perry Moss	St. Petersburg
X	1996	Tampa Bay	Tim Marcum	42-38	Iowa	John Gregory	Des Moines
XI	1997	Arizona	Danny White	55-33	Iowa	John Gregory	Phoenix
XII	1998	Orlando	Jay Gruden	62-31	Tampa Bay	Tim Marcum	Tampa
XIII	1999	Albany	Mike Dailey	59-48	Orlando	Jay Gruden	Albany
XIV	2000	Orlando	Jay Gruden	41-38	Nashville	Pat Sperduto	Orlando
XV	2001	Grand Rapids	Michael Trigg	64-42	Nashville	Pat Sperduto	Grand Rapids
XVI	2002	San Jose	Darren Arbet	52-14	Arizona	Danny White	San Jose

ArenaBowl MVP

Multiple Winners: George LaFrance (3); Jay Gruden (2).

Year	Year	Year
1987 Gary Mullen, Denver, WR	1992 George LaFrance, Detroit, OS	1997 Donnie Davis, Arizona, QB
1988 Steve Griffin, Detroit, WR/DB	1993 Jay Gruden, Tampa Bay, QB	1998 Rick Hamilton, Orlando, FB/LB
1989 George LaFrance, Detroit, WR/DB	1994 Sherdrick Bonner, Arizona, QB	1999 Eddie Brown, Albany, OS
1990 Art Schlichter, Detroit, QB	1995 George LaFrance, Tampa Bay, OS	2000 Connell Maynor, Orlando, QB
1991 Jay Gruden, Tampa Bay, QB	1996 Stevie Thomas, Tampa Bay, WR/LB	2001 Terrill Shaw, Grand Rapids, OS
		2002 John Dutton, San Jose, QB

College Basketball

Mike Davis stepped out of Bob Knight's shadow as he led surprising Indiana to the Final Four.

AP/Wide World Photos

Terps Take Juan Way

Juan Dixon, the rare senior star in today's college basketball, leads Maryland to its first national title.

Chris Fowler
is the host of ESPN's College GameDay

As time ticks down on each Final Four, fairy tales are fulfilled. For the lucky dozen, personal journeys end in collective triumph.

In the final hour of April 1, 2002, Juan Dixon lived his dream. With an underhand heave, he sent the championship game ball soaring toward the high ceiling of Atlanta's Georgia Dome. Then he was buried near the baseline under a beefy avalanche: 500-plus pounds of Maryland Terrapin teammates, Lonny Baxter and Tahj Holden. The skinny senior emerged undamaged and undeniably delirious.

The depth of Dixon's joy is not easily explained. Perhaps his brother Phil, with whom he shared a postgame hug, is the only one able to appreciate Juan's journey.

Sure, most fairy tales feature sad chapters. But the pain Dixon endured no kid deserves. Both his parents were destroyed by heroin addiction and died of AIDS from sharing infected needles. All around him, peers made the wrong choices and were swallowed by the streets of Baltimore.

But Dixon's drive to make it couldn't be stopped. As a 150-pound high school senior, he was labeled too frail for the ACC wars, but Gary Williams took a flyer on the gritty local kid few programs coveted.

At the end of his sophomore year, Dixon still hadn't started a game. He sat deep in the shadows of former teammate Steve Francis and other ACC guards.

Patience was rewarded. By the time he arrived in Atlanta for the 2002 Final Four, Dixon was Maryland's all-time leading scorer. No small feat, but in truth, his career to that point had been overshadowed by conference rival Jason Williams of Duke. By the

AP/Wide World Photos

*Maryland's leader **Juan Dixon** cut down the nets at the Final Four after taking the Terrapins to their first national championship. Dixon won the Tournament Most Outstanding Player Award.*

end of *his* sophomore year, Williams had collected countless All-America honors, a couple of conference crowns and a national title. Much of that had been at the expense of Dixon and his Terps, including an agonizing collapse from 22 points up in the 2001 national semifinals. By Championship Monday a year later, Williams' college career was over, ending on a sour note with a missed free throw that would have tied Indiana in the final seconds of a regional semi.

Finally, the national stage was Dixon's to seize. He started fast, per-fect on four field goals and two free throws in the first 10 minutes. But when Indiana adjusted its defense and clamped down on Dixon, he shrank into the background scenery. With Dixon scoreless for more than 20 minutes, the Terps' 12-point lead vanished, as the Hoosiers edged in front with 9:53 remaining. Was this another Maryland meltdown, an even more painful reprise of the debacles with Duke?

The answer came exactly 13 sec-onds later, the moment Dixon chose to re-appear. His three-pointer reclaimed the lead and steadied his teammates.

AP/Wide World Photos

Connecticut's women's program returned to the top of the heap with a national title and an undefeated season, the second of head coach Geno Auriemma's career.

Next time down, Dixon floated a fadeaway over his defensive protagonist, Dane Fife. The two had been chirping at each other all night, but it was Dixon who delivered the last word.

The Terps were ahead to stay, as the perimeter gas that had fueled the Hoosiers' NCAA drive finally ran dry. Mike Davis' bunch was symbolized by guard Tom Coverdale, who fought for 32 minutes on a heavily taped ankle—showing heart and winning respect. The coach and program had finally emerged from the cloud of a certain ex-coach's blustery departure.

But this was Dixon's fairy tale. The Final Four's most outstanding player (18 points and five steals in his college finale) was quick to share it with his posse, notably senior stalwarts Baxter and Byron Mounton, and with the coach who believed in him.

The reward was sweet, considering the sweat and toil Williams had poured into the resurrection of his alma mater's hoops program, and the faith he had shown four years earlier in the bean-pole Baltimore point guard who would never give in or give up.

Dick Vitale's Ten Biggest Stories of the Year in College Basketball

10 ▪ Jason Williams returns to Duke for his junior year, rejecting the advances of the NBA, for the time being anyway. The talented point guard captures national player of the year honors despite the Blue Devils' upset loss to surprising Indiana in the Sweet 16.

9 ▪ Rick Pitino returns to the college coaching ranks with the University of Louisville, the archrival of the University of Kentucky, where he garnered national attention in guiding the Wildcats to the 1996 NCAA title.

8 ▪ Longtime college coach Jerry Tarkanian retires after rebuilding the basketball program at his alma mater Fresno State. Tarkanian built an amazing career record of 778-202 in 31 seasons as a Division I coach.

7 ▪ Veteran coaches Mike Krzyzewski of Duke and John Chaney of Temple are inducted into the National Basketball Hall of Fame in Springfield, Mass.

6 ▪ The Soap Opera in Fayetteville. Head coach Nolan Richardson, who won a national title with the Razorbacks in 1994, cuts ties with the University of Arkansas in an abrupt and controversial departure as the school's head coach.

5 ▪ Mike Davis, in just his second year as head coach at Indiana University, stuns fans across the country when he leads the Hoosiers all the way to the finals of the NCAA tournament.

4 ▪ The sudden and total collapse of the University of North Carolina Basketball. The Tar Heels fail to gain an NCAA tournament bid for the first time in 28 years.

3 ▪ Bob Knight, the General, revitalizes Texas Tech basketball in his return to college basketball following his departure from Indiana and guides the Red Raiders into the NCAA tourney.

2 ▪ Head Coach Geno Auriemma and the University of Connecticut's Lady Huskies dominate women's college basketball going undefeated in 39 games and capturing the NCAA championship.

1 ▪ Gary Williams cuts down the nets as senior star Juan Dixon, the tournament's most outstanding player, leads the University of Maryland to the school's first NCAA title.

It's About Time

Maryland won its first national championship after 19 NCAA tournament appearances, only Connecticut and Arkansas made more tournaments before winning a title. Trip number 19 was the charm for the Terps, who beat Indiana for the crown.

Team	Appearances	Year Won
Connecticut	21	1999
Arkansas	20	1994
Maryland	19	2002
Villanova	17	1985
Arizona	16	1997
Duke	15	1991

Frigid Finals

The Indiana Hoosiers, who had shot so hot during their tournament run, turned ice cold in the national title game with Maryland. In fact, the 2002 Hoosiers lead the list of lowest field goal percentages in an NCAA title game since 1979.

Team (Year)	FG Pct
Indiana (2002)	34.5
UCLA (1980)	36.5
Arizona* (1997)	37.9
Michigan (1992)	37.9
Houston (1983)	38.2
Kentucky* (1996)	38.4

*won game.

Upsetting Habit

Arizona is the biggest giant-killer in the NCAA tournament. Often a giant itself, Arizona nonetheless leads the nation with seven upset wins over one-seeds at the tourney when seeded two or lower.

Team	Wins
Arizona	7
Duke	6
Kansas	4
Indiana	4
North Carolina	3
N.C. State	3

Terra-Pinned!

Maryland took control late in the national championship game with Indiana. Here's a look at some key numbers that show how Maryland took it home over the game's final nine minutes and 52 seconds.

Stat	Maryland	Indiana
Points	22	8
FG-FGA	4-7	3-16
FT-FTA	13-17	0-0
Rebounds	14	6
Steals	2	0

2001-2002
Season in Review

ESPN
Information Please®
SPORTS ALMANAC

Final Regular Season AP Men's Top 25 Poll
Taken **before** start of NCAA tournament.

The sportswriters & broadcasters poll: first place votes in parentheses; records through Monday, March 11, 2002; total points (based on 25 for 1st, 24 for 2nd, etc.); record in NCAA tourney and team lost to; head coach (career years and record including 2002 postseason), and preseason ranking. Teams in **bold** type went on to reach NCAA Final Four. Indiana, which did not make the final regular-season Top 25, was the other Final Four team.

		Mar. 11 Record	Points	NCAA Recap	Head Coach	Preseason Rank
1	Duke (58)	29-3	1759	2-1 (Indiana)	Mike Krzyzewski (27 yrs: 637-226)	1
2	**Kansas** (10)	29-3	1667	4-1 (Maryland)	Roy Williams (14 yrs: 388-93)	7
3	**Oklahoma** (2)	27-4	1630	4-1 (Indiana)	Kelvin Sampson (18 yrs: 363-222)	25
4	**Maryland** (1)	26-4	1572	6-0	Gary Williams (24 yrs: 481-271)	2
5	Cincinnati	30-3	1529	1-1 (UCLA)	Bob Huggins (21 yrs: 500-172)	NR
6	Gonzaga	29-3	1356	0-1 (Wyoming)	Mark Few (3 yrs: 81-20)	NR
7	Arizona	22-9	1196	2-1 (Oklahoma)	Lute Olson (29 yrs: 662-236)	NR
8	Alabama	26-7	1192	1-1 (Kent St.)	Mark Gottfried (7 yrs: 104-51)	24
9	Pittsburgh	27-5	1191	2-1 (Kent St.)	Ben Howland (8 yrs: 140-94)	NR
10	Connecticut	24-6	1048	3-1 (Maryland)	Jim Calhoun (30 yrs: 623-286)	NR
11	Oregon	23-8	1033	3-1 (Kansas)	Ernie Kent (9 yrs: 184-138)	NR
12	Marquette	25-7	887	0-1 (Tulsa)	Tom Crean (3 yrs: 56-35)	NR
13	Illinois	24-8	848	2-1 (Kansas)	Bill Self (9 yrs: 183-97)	3
14	Ohio St.	23-7	830	1-1 (Missouri)	Jim O'Brien (20 yrs: 337-274)	NR
15	Florida	22-8	735	0-1 (Creighton)	Billy Donovan (8 yrs: 159-85)	6
16	Kentucky	20-9	629	2-1 (Kentucky)	Tubby Smith (12 yrs: 256-105)	4
17	Mississippi St.	26-7	587	1-1 (Texas)	Rick Stansbury (4 yrs: 79-50)	NR
18	USC	22-9	531	0-1 (NC-Wilmington)	Henry Bibby (7 yrs: 104-85)	20
19	Western Ky.	28-3	510	0-1 (Stanford)	Dennis Felton (4 yrs: 76-45)	NR
20	Oklahoma St.	23-8	423	0-1 (Kent St.)	Eddie Sutton (32 yrs: 702-278)	18
21	Miami-FL	24-7	349	0-1 (Missouri)	Perry Clarke (13 yrs: 225-162)	NR
22	Xavier	25-5	308	1-1 (Oklahoma)	Thad Matta (2 yrs: 50-14)	NR
23	Georgia	21-9	296	1-1 (S. Illinois)	Jim Harrick (22 yrs: 452-226)	NR
24	Stanford	19-9	268	1-1 (Kansas)	Mike Montgomery (24 yrs: 493-233)	13
25	Hawaii	27-5	130	0-1 (Xavier)	Riley Wallace (15 yrs: 258-231)	NR

Others receiving votes: 26. **Indiana** (20-11) 128 points; 27. **N.C. State** (22-10) 108; 28. **California** (22-8) 92; 29. Kent State (27-5) 74; 30. Texas Tech (23-8) 49; 31. Pepperdine (22-8) 44; 32. Wake Forest (20-12) 24; 33. **Texas** (20-11) and **UCLA** (19-11) 12; 35. **Michigan St.** (19-11) 7; 36. Central Connecticut (28-4) and Pennsylvania (25-6) 5; 38. Wisconsin (18-12) 4; 39. Notre Dame (21-10) 3; 40. Butler (25-5), Creighton (22-8), Southern Illinois (26-7), **Tulsa** (26-6).

NCAA Men's Division I Tournament Seeds

	WEST		MIDWEST		SOUTH		EAST
1	Cincinnati (30-3)	1	Kansas (29-3)	1	Duke (29-3)	1	Maryland (26-4)
2	Oklahoma (27-4)	2	Oregon (23-8)	2	Alabama (26-7)	2	Connecticut (24-6)
3	Arizona (22-9)	3	Mississippi St. (26-7)	3	Pittsburgh (27-5)	3	Georgia (21-9)
4	Ohio State (23-7)	4	Illinois (24-8)	4	USC (22-9)	4	Kentucky (20-9)
5	Miami-FL (24-7)	5	Florida (22-8)	5	Indiana (20-11)	5	Marquette (26-6)
6	Gonzaga (29-3)	6	Texas (20-11)	6	California (22-8)	6	Texas Tech (23-8)
7	Xavier (22-9)	7	Wake Forest (20-12)	7	Oklahoma St. (23-8)	7	N.C. State (22-10)
8	UCLA (19-11)	8	Stanford (19-9)	8	Notre Dame (21-10)	8	Wisconsin (18-12)
9	Mississippi (20-10)	9	Western Ky. (28-3)	9	Charlotte (18-11)	9	St. John's (20-11)
10	Hawaii (27-5)	10	Pepperdine (22-8)	10	Kent St. (27-5)	10	Michigan St. (19-11)
11	Wyoming (21-8)	11	Boston Coll. (20-11)	11	Pennsylvania (25-6)	11	So. Illinois (26-7)
12	Missouri (21-11)	12	Creighton (22-8)	12	Utah (21-8)	12	Tulsa (26-6)
13	Davidson (21-9)	13	San Diego St. (21-11)	13	NC-Wilmington (22-9)	13	Valparaiso (25-7)
14	UCSB (20-10)	14	McNeese St. (21-8)	14	Central Conn. St. (27-4)	14	Murray St. (19-12)
15	Ill-Chicago (20-13)	15	Montana (16-14)	15	Florida Atlantic (19-11)	15	Hampton (26-6)
16	Boston Univ. (22-9)	16	Holy Cross (18-14)	16	Winthrop (19-11)	16	Siena* (17-18)

*Siena defeated Alcorn St., 81-77, in the NCAA Tournament play-in game for a berth in the field of 64.

2002 NCAA Basketball Men's Division

1st ROUND March 14 | **2nd ROUND** March 16 | **SWEET 16** March 21 | **ELITE EIGHT** March 23 | **FINAL FOUR** March 30 | **NATIONAL CHAMPIONSHIP** | **FINAL FOUR** March 30 | **ELITE EIGHT** March 24 | **SWEET 16** March 22 | **2nd ROUND** March 17 | **1st ROUND** March 15

SOUTH

(1) Duke 84
(16) Winthrop 37
(1) Duke 84
(8) Notre Dame 77
(9) Charlotte 63
(1) Duke 73
(5) Indiana 75
(5) Indiana 76
(4) Southern Cal 89
(13) UNC Wilm. 93
(13) UNC Wilm. 67
(5) Indiana 74
(6) California 82
(11) Pennsylvania 75
(6) California 50
(3) Pittsburgh 71
(3) Pittsburgh 73
(3) Pittsburgh 63
(14) Cht.Conn.St 54
(11) Oklahoma St 61
(10) Kent St 69
(10) Kent St 71
(10) Kent St 78
(2) Alabama 86
(15) Fla. Atlantic 78
(2) Alabama 58

(5) Indiana 81
(10) Kent St 69
(5) Indiana 73

WEST

(1) Cincinnati 90
(16) Boston U 52
(1) Cincinnati 101
(8) UCLA 105
(9) Mississippi 58
(8) UCLA 73
(12) Missouri 93
(4) Ohio St 69
(4) Ohio St 64
(13) Davidson 64
(11) Wyoming 73
(11) Wyoming 60
(3) Arizona 86
(14) UC Santa Barbara 81
(3) Arizona 68
(7) Xavier 70
(2) Oklahoma 71
(2) Oklahoma 78
(15) Ill Chicago 63

(12) Missouri 82
(3) Arizona 67
(12) Missouri 75

(8) UCLA 73
(12) Missouri 83

(3) Arizona 67
(2) Oklahoma 88

(2) Oklahoma 81

FINAL FOUR Atlanta 2002

(5) Indiana 73
(2) Oklahoma 64

(1) Maryland **64**
(5) Indiana 52

Georgia Dome
Atlanta, Georgia
Monday, April 1, 2002

EAST

(1) Maryland 85
(16) Siena 70
(1) Maryland 87
(8) Wisconsin 57
(8) Wisconsin 80
(9) St. John's 70
(1) Maryland 78
(5) Marquette 69
(5) Tulsa 71
(5) Tulsa 82
(4) Kentucky 83
(13) Valparaiso 68
(4) Kentucky 87
(4) Kentucky 68
(6) Texas Tech 68
(11) So. Illinois 76
(11) So. Illinois 77
(11) So. Illinois 59
(3) Georgia 85
(14) Murray St 68
(3) Georgia 75
(7) N.C. State 69
(2) N.C. State 74
(10) Michigan St 58
(2) Connecticut 77
(15) Hampton 67

Play-in Game to East (16) seed
(15) Siena 81
(16) Alcorn St 77

(1) Maryland 90
(2) Connecticut 82

(1) Maryland 97

MIDWEST

(1) Kansas 70
(16) Holy Cross 59
(1) Kansas 86
(8) Stanford 84
(8) Stanford 63
(9) W. Kentucky 68
(1) Kansas 73
(5) Florida 82
(12) Creighton 83
(12) Creighton 60
(4) Illinois 93
(13) San Diego St 64
(4) Illinois 72
(4) Illinois 69
(6) Texas 70
(11) Boston Col. 57
(6) Texas 68
(6) Texas 70
(3) Mississippi St 70
(14) McNeese St 58
(11) Mississippi St 64
(7) Wake Forest 83
(2) Oregon 74
(7) Wake Forest 87
(2) Oregon 81
(10) Pepperdine 74
(15) Montana 62
(2) Oregon 92

(1) Kansas 73
(4) Illinois 69

(6) Texas 70
(2) Oregon 72

(1) Kansas 104
(2) Oregon 86

(1) Kansas 88

NCAA Men's Championship Game

64th NCAA Division I Championship Game. **Date:** Monday, April 1, at the Georgia Dome in Atlanta. **Coaches:** Gary Williams of Maryland and Mike Davis of Indiana. **Favorite:** Maryland by 8.
Attendance: 53,406; **Officials:** Dick Cartmell, Jim Burr, Tony Greene; **TV Rating:** 15.0/24 share (CBS).

Indiana 52

	Min	FG M-A	FT M-A	Pts	Reb O-T	A	PF
Jared Jeffries	32	4-11	0-1	8	1-7	3	4
Kyle Hornsby	35	5-12	0-1	14	2-5	0	4
Jarrad Odle	18	0-4	0-3	0	1-4	1	2
Tom Coverdale	32	3-11	0-0	8	0-4	2	2
Dane Fife	36	4-9	0-0	11	2-5	1	3
A.J. Moye	7	1-1	0-0	2	0-0	0	1
George Leach	2	0-0	0-0	0	0-0	0	0
Donald Perry	10	1-3	0-0	3	0-1	0	1
Jeff Newton	28	2-7	2-2	6	3-5	2	3
TOTALS	200	20-58	2-7	52	9-31	9	20

Three-point FG: 10-23 (Jeffries 0-1, Hornsby 4-8, Coverdale 2-7, Fife 3-6, Perry 1-1); **Team Rebounds:** 0; **Blocked Shots:** 3 (Jeffries, Leach, Newton); **Turnovers:** 16 (Coverdale 4, Jeffries 4, Fife 2, Moye 2, Hornsby, Newton, Odle, Perry); **Steals:** 10 (Coverdale 4, Fife 2, Hornsby 2, Jeffries, Moye, Newton, Odle); **Percentages:** 2-Pt FG (.286), 3-Pt FG (.435), Total FG (.345), Free Throws (.286).

Maryland 64

	Min	FG M-A	FT M-A	Pts	Reb O-T	A	PF
Byron Mouton	27	1-5	2-2	4	2-4	1	2
Chris Wilcox	24	4-8	2-4	10	2-7	0	3
Lonny Baxter	32	6-15	3-8	15	2-14	0	1
Juan Dixon	38	6-9	4-4	18	1-5	3	1
Steven Blake	33	2-6	2-2	6	0-6	3	2
Drew Nicholas	22	1-2	5-6	7	1-3	0	0
Ryan Randle	4	1-1	0-0	2	0-0	0	1
Tahj Holden	20	0-2	2-2	2	1-3	4	3
TOTALS	200	21-48	20-28	64	9-42	11	13

Three-point FG: 2-9 (Dixon 2-4, Blake 0-3, Nicholas 0-1, Holden 0-1); **Team Rebounds:** 0; **Blocked Shots:** 6 (Baxter 3, Holden, Mouton, Wilcox); **Turnovers:** 16 (Dixon 7, Blake 4, Baxter, Holden, Mouton, Nicholas, Wilcox); **Steals:** 12 (Dixon 5, Blake 2, Mouton 2, Baxter, Nicholas, Wilcox). **Percentages:** 2-Pt FG (.487), 3-Pt FG (.222), Total FG (.438), Free Throws (.714).

Indiana (Big Ten)	25	27	—	52
Maryland (ACC)	31	33	—	64

Final ESPN/USA Today Coaches' Poll

Taken **after** NCAA Tournament.

Voted on by a panel of 31 Division I head coaches following the NCAA tournament; first place votes in parentheses with total points (based on 25 for 1st, 24 for 2nd, etc.). Schools on major probation are ineligible to be ranked.

		W-L	Pts	Before NCAAs W-L	Rank
1	Maryland (31)	32-4	775	26-4	4
2	Kansas	33-4	720	29-3	2
3	Indiana	25-12	701	19-10	NR
4	Oklahoma	31-5	692	27-4	3
5	Duke	31-4	606	29-3	1
6	Connecticut	27-7	586	24-6	13
7	Oregon	26-9	586	23-8	11
8	Cincinnati	31-4	489	30-3	5
9	Pittsburgh	29-6	482	27-5	7
10	Arizona	24-10	458	22-9	8
11	Illinois	26-9	410	24-8	NR
12	Kent State	30-6	402	27-5	NR
13	Kentucky	22-10	394	20-9	15
14	Alabama	27-8	281	26-7	1
15	Missouri	24-12	272	21-11	NR
16	Gonzaga	29-4	264	29-3	6
17	Ohio State	24-8	237	23-7	12
18	Texas	22-12	186	20-11	NR
	Marquette	26-7	186	26-6	10
20	UCLA	21-12	170	19-11	NR
21	Mississippi St.	27-8	162	26-7	18
22	So. Illinois	28-8	157	26-7	NR
23	Florida	22-9	140	22-8	14
24	Xavier	26-6	116	25-5	19
25	N.C. State	23-11	86	22-10	25

Others receiving votes: 26. USC (80 pts); 27. **Miami-FL** (66); 28. **Wake Forest** (54); 29. **Notre Dame, Georgia** and **Western Kentucky** (44); 32. **California** (35); 33. **Oklahoma St.** (31); 34. **Stanford** (30); 35. **Tulsa** (20); 37. **Wisconsin** (17); 38. **Hawaii** (15); 39. **Hawaii** (15); 40. **Wyoming** (11); 41. **Texas Tech** (8); 42. **Memphis** (6); 43. **Creighton** and **NC-Wilmington** (5); 45. **Butler** (2).

THE FINAL FOUR

at the Georgia Dome in Atlanta.
(Mar. 30-April 1).

Semifinal—Game One

South Regional champ Indiana vs. West Regional champ Oklahoma; Saturday, Mar. 30 (5:31 p.m. tipoff). **Coaches:** Mike Davis, Indiana and Kelvin Sampson, Oklahoma. **Favorite:** Oklahoma by 7.

Indiana (Big Ten)	30	43	—	73
Oklahoma (Big 12)	34	30	—	64

High scorers— Jeff Newton, Indiana (19) and Aaron McGhee, Oklahoma (22); **Att—** 53,378; **TV rating—** 9.4/20 share (CBS).

Semifinal—Game Two

East Regional champion Maryland vs. Midwest Regional champ Kansas; Saturday, Mar. 30 (8:12 p.m. tipoff). **Coaches:** Gary Williams, Maryland and Roy Williams, Kansas. **Favorite:** Kansas by 1½.

Maryland (ACC)	44	53	—	97
Kansas (Big 12)	37	51	—	88

High scorers— Juan Dixon, Maryland (33) and Nick Collison, Kansas (21); **Att—** 53,378; **TV rating—** 11.3/21 share (CBS).

Most Outstanding Player

Juan Dixon, senior guard Maryland. SEMIFINAL—37 minutes, 33 points, 3 rebounds, 2 assists, 2 steals; FINAL—38 minutes, 18 points, 5 rebounds, 3 assists, 5 steals.

All-Final Four Team

Dixon, senior forward/center Lonny Baxter and sophomore forward/center Chris Wilcox of Maryland; junior forward Kyle Hornsby and senior guard Dane Fife of Indiana.

NCAA Finalists' Tournament and Season Statistics

At least 10 games played during the overall season.

Indiana (25-12)

| | NCAA Tournament | | | | | | Overall Season | | | | | |
| | | | −Per Game− | | | | | | −Per Game− | | |
	Gm	FG%	TPts	Pts	Reb	Ast	Gm	FG%	TPts	Pts	Reb	Ast
Jared Jeffries	6	.463	84	14.0	8.2	1.8	36	.457	539	15.0	7.6	2.1
Jeff Newton	6	.694	63	10.5	5.5	1.2	37	.496	298	8.1	5.1	0.8
Tom Coverdale	6	.390	57	9.5	3.8	4.8	37	.417	439	11.9	3.2	4.8
Kyle Hornsby	6	.476	56	9.3	2.8	2.7	37	.429	286	7.7	2.6	1.9
A.J. Moye	6	.700	48	8.0	1.8	0.5	37	.479	218	5.9	3.1	0.6
Dane Fife	6	.483	44	7.3	2.0	2.7	37	.461	321	8.7	2.6	2.5
Jarrad Odle	6	.526	43	7.2	3.5	0.7	35	.540	309	8.8	5.0	0.7
Donald Perry	6	.500	33	5.5	2.2	0.8	37	.378	95	2.6	1.4	1.1
George Leach	5	.500	3	0.6	0.6	0.0	32	.500	90	2.8	2.5	0.3
Mark Johnson	1	.000	0	0.0	0.0	0.0	12	.167	3	0.3	0.3	0.0
INDIANA	6	.510	431	71.8	30.3	15.2	37	.460	2607	70.5	35.2	14.8
OPPONENTS	6	.408	393	65.5	33.3	9.8	37	.408	2316	62.6	33.5	11.1

Three-pointers: NCAA TOURNAMENT—Hornsby (13-27), Fife (11-19), Coverdale (10-25), Moye (4-6), Perry (4-5), Jeffries (3-9), Odle (2-3), Team (47-94 for .500 pct.); OVERALL—Hornsby (72-161), Coverdale (70-189), Fife (66-138), Jeffries (27-71), Moye (20-50), Perry (7-31), Odle (4-9), Tapak (2-4), Johnson (1-2), Newton (1-2), Team (270-657 for .411 pct.).

Maryland (32-4)

| | NCAA Tournament | | | | | | Overall Season | | | | | |
| | | | −Per Game− | | | | | | −Per Game− | | |
	Gm	FG%	TPts	Pts	Reb	Ast	Gm	FG%	TPts	Pts	Reb	Ast
Juan Dixon	6	.542	155	25.8	3.8	3.2	36	.469	735	20.4	4.6	2.9
Lonny Baxter	6	.561	94	15.7	8.5	0.7	36	.545	533	15.2	8.2	0.8
Chris Wilcox	6	.516	81	13.5	5.5	1.0	36	.504	432	12.0	7.1	1.5
Byron Mouton	6	.351	42	7.0	5.0	1.7	36	.469	401	11.1	5.0	2.1
Drew Nicholas	6	.387	41	6.8	2.3	2.3	36	.477	255	7.1	2.3	2.4
Steve Blake	6	.289	37	6.2	3.8	6.7	36	.382	287	8.0	3.8	7.9
Tahj Holden	6	.563	35	5.8	3.2	1.0	36	.453	202	5.6	2.7	1.2
Ryan Randle	6	.467	14	2.3	3.1	0.1	34	.524	129	3.8	3.1	0.1
Andre Collins	2	.500	2	1.0	0.0	0.0	22	.667	48	2.2	0.5	0.9
Calvin McCall	3	—	0	0.0	0.0	0.0	19	.526	27	1.4	0.8	0.1
Earl Badu	1	—	0	0.0	0.0	2.0	12	.500	4	0.3	0.3	0.4
MARYLAND	6	.476	501	83.5	38.5	17.0	36	.482	3060	85.0	41.1	19.8
OPPONENTS	6	.400	417	69.5	35.0	14.2	36	.399	2552	70.9	37.4	13.6

Three-pointers: NCAA TOURNAMENT— Dixon (22-43), Nicholas (7-19), Blake (6-21), Holden (2-6), Team (37-93 for .398 pct.); OVERALL— Dixon (92-232), Blake (44-128), Nicholas (38-96), Holden (17-40), Mouton (15-55), Collins (5-10), McCall (5-10), Grinnon (1-4), Randle (1-1), Wilcox (0-2), Baxter (0-1), Badu (0-1), Team (217-580 for .374 pct.).

Indiana's Schedule

Reg. Season
(19-10)

W at Charlotte 65-61
W at AK-Anchorage ...101-66
L Marquette 49-50
W Texas 77-71
W at N. Carolina 79-66
L at So. Illinois 60-72
W Notre Dame 76-75
W Ball State 74-61
L Miami 53-58
L Kentucky 52-66
W E. Washington 87-60
L Butler 64-66
W at Northwestern 59-44
W Penn State 61-54
W Michigan St........83-65
W at Iowa 77-66
L at Ohio St. 67-73
W at Penn St. 85-51
W Illinois 88-57
W Purdue 66-52
L at Minnesota 74-88

W Iowa 79-51
W Louisville 77-62
L Wisconsin 63-64
W at Michigan 75-55
W Ohio St. 63-57
L at Michigan St. ..54-57
L at Illinois 62-70
W Northwestern 79-67

Big Ten Tourney
(1-1)

W Michigan St.......67-56
L Iowa 60-62

NCAA Tourney
(5-1)

W Utah 75-56
W NC-Wilmington ..76-67
W Duke 74-73
W Kent St. 81-69
W Oklahoma 73-64
L Maryland 52-64

Maryland's Schedule

Reg. Season
(25-3)

L Arizona 67-71
W Temple..........82-74
W American 83-53
W Delaware St. 77-53
W Illinois 76-63
W Princeton 61-53
W Connecticut 77-65
W Detroit..........79-54
W Monmouth 91-55
L at Oklahoma 56-72
W William & Mary .103-75
W at N.C. State 72-65
W Norfolk St........92-69
W North Carolina ..112-79
W at Georgia Tech..92-87
L at Duke 78-99
W Clemson 99-90
W at Wake Forest ..85-63
W Florida St. 84-63
W at Virginia 91-87

W N.C. State 89-73
W at North Carolina .92-77
W Georgia Tech.....85-65
W Duke.............87-73
W at Clemson 84-68
W Wake Forest.....90-89
W at Florida St.....85-59
W Virginia 112-92

ACC Tourney
(1-1)

W Florida St........85-59
L N.C. State 82-86

NCAA Tourney
(6-0)

W Siena 85-70
W Wisconsin 87-57
W Kentucky........78-68
W Connecticut 90-82
W Kansas 97-88
W Indiana 64-52

Final NCAA Men's Division I Standings

Conference records include regular season games only. Overall records include all postseason tournament games.

America East Conference

Team	Conference			Overall		
	W	L	Pct	W	L	Pct
Vermont	13	3	.812	21	8	.724
*Boston University	13	3	.812	22	10	.688
Hartford	10	6	.625	14	18	.438
New Hampshire	8	8	.500	11	17	.393
Maine	7	9	.438	12	18	.400
Binghamton	6	10	.375	9	19	.321
Albany	5	11	.312	8	20	.286
Northeastern	5	11	.312	7	21	.250
Stony Brook	5	11	.312	6	22	.214

Conf. Tourney Final: Boston University 66, Maine 40.
***NCAA Tourney (0-1):** Boston University (0-1).

Atlantic Coast Conference

Team	Conference			Overall		
	W	L	Pct	W	L	Pct
*Maryland	15	1	.938	32	4	.889
*Duke	13	3	.813	31	4	.886
*Wake Forest	9	7	.562	21	13	.617
*N.C. State	9	7	.562	23	11	.676
Virginia	7	9	.438	17	12	.567
Georgia Tech	7	9	.438	15	16	.484
North Carolina	4	12	.250	8	20	.286
Florida St	4	12	.250	12	17	.414
Clemson	4	12	.250	13	17	.433

Conf. Tourney Final: Duke 91, N.C. State 61.
***NCAA Tourney (10-3):** Maryland (6-0), Duke (2-1), Wake Forest (1-1), N.C. State (1-1).

Atlantic Sun Conference

Team	Conference			Overall		
	W	L	Pct	W	L	Pct
*Georgia St.	14	6	.700	20	11	.645
Troy St.	14	6	.700	18	10	.643
*Florida Atlantic	13	7	.650	19	12	.613
Samford	12	8	.600	15	14	.517
Central Florida	12	8	.600	17	12	.586
Jacksonville	12	8	.600	18	12	.600
Jacksonville St.	8	12	.421	13	16	.448
Belmont	8	12	.421	11	17	.393
Stetson	7	13	.350	10	16	.385
Campbell	6	14	.300	8	19	.296
Mercer	4	16	.200	6	23	.207

Conf. Tourney Final: Florida Atlantic 76, Georgia St. 75.
***NCAA Tourney (0-1):** Florida Atlantic (0-1).
†NIT (0-1): Georgia St. (0-1).

Atlantic 10 Conference

East	Conference			Overall		
	W	L	Pct	W	L	Pct
†Temple	12	4	.750	19	15	.559
†St. Joseph's	12	4	.750	19	12	.613
†St. Bonaventure	8	8	.500	17	13	.567
Massachusetts	6	10	.375	13	16	.448
Fordham	4	12	.250	8	20	.286
Rhode Island	4	12	.250	8	20	.286

West	Conference			Overall		
	W	L	Pct	W	L	Pct
*Xavier	14	2	.875	26	6	.813
†Richmond	11	5	.688	22	14	.611
†Dayton	10	6	.625	21	11	.656
La Salle	6	10	.375	15	17	.469
Geo. Washington	5	11	.313	12	16	.429
Duquesne	4	12	.250	9	19	.321

Note: There are 12 teams in the Atlantic 10.
Conf. Tourney Final: Xavier 73, Richmond 60.
***NCAA Tourney (1-1):** Xavier (1-1).
†NIT (9-5): Temple (4-1), Richmond (3-1), St. Joseph's (1-1), Dayton (1-1), St. Bonaventure (0-1).

Big East Conference

East	Conference			Overall		
	W	L	Pct	W	L	Pct
*Connecticut	13	3	.813	27	7	.794
*Miami-FL	10	6	.625	24	8	.750
*St. John's	9	7	.563	20	12	.625
*Boston College	8	8	.500	20	12	.625
†Villanova	7	9	.438	19	13	.594
Providence	6	10	.375	15	16	.484
Virginia Tech	4	12	.250	10	18	.357

West	Conference			Overall		
	W	L	Pct	W	L	Pct
*Pittsburgh	13	3	.813	29	6	.829
*Notre Dame	10	6	.625	22	11	.667
Georgetown	9	7	.563	19	11	.633
†Syracuse	9	7	.563	23	13	.639
†Rutgers	8	8	.500	18	13	.581
Seton Hall	5	11	.313	12	18	.400
West Virginia	1	15	.063	8	20	.286

Conf. Tourney Final: Connecticut 74, Pittsburgh 65.
***NCAA Tourney (6-5):** Connecticut (3-1), Pittsburgh (2-1), Notre Dame (1-1), Boston College (0-1), St. John's (0-1).
†NIT (5-3): Syracuse (3-1), Villanova (2-1), Rutgers (0-1).

Big Sky Conference

Team	Conference			Overall		
	W	L	Pct	W	L	Pct
†Montana St	12	2	.857	20	10	.667
Eastern Washington	10	4	.714	17	13	.567
Weber St	8	6	.571	18	11	.621
Northern Arizona	7	7	.500	14	14	.500
*Montana	7	7	.500	16	15	.516
Portland St.	6	8	.429	12	16	.429
Sacramento St.	3	11	.214	9	19	.321
Idaho St	3	11	.214	10	17	.370

Conf. Tourney Final: Montana 70, Eastern Washington 66.
***NCAA Tourney (0-1):** Montana (0-1).
†NIT (1-1): Montana St. (1-1).

Big South Conference

Team	Conference			Overall		
	W	L	Pct	W	L	Pct
*Winthrop	10	4	.714	19	11	.613
NC-Asheville	10	4	.714	13	15	.464
Radford	9	5	.643	15	16	.484
Charleston Southern	8	6	.571	12	17	.414
Elon	7	7	.500	13	16	.433
High Point	5	9	.357	11	19	.367
Coastal Carolina	5	9	.357	8	20	.286
Liberty	2	12	.143	5	25	.167

Conf. Tourney Final: Winthrop 70, High Point 48.
***NCAA Tourney (0-1):** Winthrop (0-1).

Big Ten Conference

Team	Conference			Overall		
	W	L	Pct	W	L	Pct
*Ohio St.	11	5	.688	24	8	.750
*Illinois	11	5	.688	26	9	.743
*Indiana	11	5	.688	25	12	.676
*Wisconsin	11	5	.688	19	13	.594
*Michigan St	10	6	.625	19	12	.613
†Minnesota	9	7	.563	18	13	.581
Northwestern	7	9	.438	16	13	.552
†Iowa	5	11	.313	19	16	.543
Purdue	5	11	.313	13	18	.419
Michigan	5	11	.313	11	18	.379
Penn St	3	13	.188	7	21	.250

Note: There are 11 teams in the Big Ten.
Conf. Tourney Final: Ohio State 81, Iowa 64.
***NCAA Tourney (9-5):** Indiana (5-1), Illinois (2-1), Ohio State (1-1), Wisconsin (1-1), Michigan State (0-1).
†NIT (1-2): Minnesota (1-1), Iowa (0-1).

Final NCAA Men's Division I Standings (Cont.)

Big 12 Conference

Team	Conference			Overall		
	W	L	Pct	W	L	Pct
*Kansas	16	0	1.000	33	4	.892
*Oklahoma	13	3	.813	31	5	.861
*Oklahoma St.	10	6	.625	23	9	.719
*Texas Tech	10	6	.625	23	9	.719
*Texas	10	6	.625	22	12	.647
*Missouri	9	7	.563	24	12	.667
Nebraska	6	10	.375	13	15	.464
Kansas St	6	10	.375	13	16	.448
Colorado	5	11	.313	15	14	.517
Baylor	4	12	.250	16	16	.467
Iowa St.	4	12	.250	12	19	.387
Texas A&M	3	13	.188	9	22	.290

Conf. Tourney Final: Oklahoma 64, Kansas 55.
***NCAA Tourney (13-6):** Kansas (4-1), Oklahoma (4-1), Oklahoma St. (0-1), Texas Tech (0-1), Texas (2-1), Missouri (3-1).

Big West Conference

Team	Conference			Overall		
	W	L	Pct	W	L	Pct
†Utah St	13	5	.722	23	8	.742
†UC-Irvine	13	5	.722	21	11	.656
*UC-Santa Barbara	11	7	.611	20	11	.645
Pacific	11	7	.611	20	10	.667
Cal St.-Northridge	11	7	.611	12	18	.429
Cal Poly-SLO	9	9	.500	15	12	.556
Long Beach St	9	9	.500	13	17	.433
Idaho	6	12	.333	9	19	.321
UC-Riverside	5	13	.278	8	18	.308
Cal St.-Fullerton	2	16	.111	5	22	.185

Conf. Tourney Final: UC-Santa Barbara 60, Utah St. 56.
***NCAA Tourney (0-1):** UC-Santa Barbara (0-1).
†**NIT (0-2):** Utah State (0-1), UC-Irvine (0-1).

Colonial Athletic Association

Team	Conference			Overall		
	W	L	Pct	W	L	Pct
*NC-Wilmington	14	4	.778	23	10	.697
†George Mason	13	5	.722	19	10	.655
Va. Commonwealth	11	7	.611	21	11	.656
Drexel	11	7	.611	14	14	.500
Delaware	9	9	.500	14	16	.467
Old Dominion	7	11	.389	13	16	.448
Towson	7	11	.389	11	18	.379
William & Mary	7	11	.389	10	19	.345
James Madison	6	12	.333	14	15	.483
Hofstra	5	13	.278	12	20	.375

Conf. Tourney Final: NC-Wilmington 66, Virginia Commonwealth 51.
***NCAA Tourney (1-1):** NC-Wilmington (1-1).
†**NIT (0-1):** George Mason (0-1).

Conference USA

Team	Conference			Overall		
American Division	W	L	Pct	W	L	Pct
*Cincinnati	14	2	.875	31	4	.886
*Marquette	13	3	.813	26	7	.788
Charlotte	11	5	.688	18	12	.600
Saint Louis	9	7	.563	15	16	.484
Louisville	8	8	.500	19	13	.594
East Carolina	5	11	.313	12	18	.400
DePaul	2	14	.125	9	19	.321

	Conference			Overall		
National Division	W	L	Pct	W	L	Pct
†Memphis	12	4	.750	27	9	.750
†Houston	9	7	.563	18	15	.545
†So. Florida	8	8	.500	19	13	.594
Ala-Birmingham	6	10	.375	13	17	.433
Texas Christian	6	10	.375	16	15	.516
Tulane	5	11	.313	14	15	.483
So. Mississippi	4	12	.250	10	17	.370

Conf. Tourney Final: Cincinnati 77, Marquette 63.
***NCAA Tourney (1-2):** Cincinnati (1-1), Marquette (0-1).
†**NIT (5-2):** Memphis (5-0), Houston (0-1), So. Florida (0-1).

Horizon League

Team	Conference			Overall		
	W	L	Pct	W	L	Pct
†Butler	12	4	.750	26	6	.812
†Detroit	11	5	.688	18	13	.581
WI-Milwaukee	11	5	.688	16	13	.552
Wright St	9	7	.562	17	11	.607
Loyola-IL	9	7	.567	17	13	.567
*Illinois-Chicago	8	8	.500	20	14	.588
Cleveland St	6	10	.375	12	16	.429
WI-Green Bay	4	12	.250	9	21	.300
Youngstown St.	2	14	.125	5	23	.179

Conf. Tourney Final: Illinois-Chicago 76, Loyola-IL 75 (OT).
***NCAA Tourney (0-1):** Illinois-Chicago (0-1).
†**NIT Tourney (1-2):** Butler (1-1), Detroit (0-1).

Ivy League

Team	Conference			Overall		
	W	L	Pct	W	L	Pct
*Pennsylvania	11	3	.786	25	7	.781
†Yale	11	3	.786	21	11	.656
†Princeton	11	3	.786	16	12	.571
Brown	8	6	.571	17	10	.630
Harvard	7	7	.500	14	12	.538
Columbia	4	10	.286	11	17	.393
Dartmouth	2	12	.143	9	18	.333
Cornell	2	12	.143	5	22	.185

Conf. Tourney Final: Ivy League has no tournament.
Three-way tie-breaker: Yale 76, Princeton 60 (Mar. 7); Pennsylvania 77, Yale 58 (Mar. 9).
***NCAA Tourney (0-1):** Pennsylvania (0-1).
†**NIT (1-2):** Yale (1-1), Princeton (0-1).

Metro Atlantic Athletic Conference

Team	Conference			Overall		
	W	L	Pct	W	L	Pct
Rider	13	5	.722	17	11	.607
Marist	13	5	.722	19	9	.679
Manhattan	12	6	.667	20	9	.690
Niagara	12	6	.667	18	14	.563
Iona	10	8	.556	13	17	.433
Fairfield	9	9	.500	12	17	.414
*Siena	9	9	.500	19	11	.486
Canisius	5	13	.278	10	20	.333
Loyola	4	14	.222	5	23	.179
St. Peter's	3	15	.167	4	24	.143

Conf. Tourney Final: Siena 92, Niagara 77.
***NCAA Tourney (1-1):** Siena (1-1).

Mid-American Conference

East	Conference			Overall		
	W	L	Pct	W	L	Pct
*Kent St.	17	1	.944	30	6	.833
†Bowling Green	12	6	.667	24	9	.727
Ohio	11	7	.611	17	11	.607
Miami-OH	9	9	.500	13	18	.419
Marshall	8	10	.444	15	15	.500
Buffalo	7	11	.389	12	18	.400
Akron	5	13	.278	10	21	.323

West	Conference			Overall		
	W	L	Pct	W	L	Pct
†Ball St.	12	6	.667	23	12	.657
Toledo	11	7	.611	16	14	.533
Western Mich	10	8	.556	17	13	.567
N. Illinois	8	10	.444	12	16	.429
Central Mich	5	13	.278	9	19	.321
Eastern Mich	2	16	.111	6	24	.200

Conf. Tourney Final: Kent State 70, Bowling Green 59.
***NCAA Tourney (3-1):** Kent State (3-1).
†**NIT (3-2):** Ball St. (3-1), Bowling Green (0-1).

Mid-Continent Conference

Team	Conference			Overall		
	W	L	Pct	W	L	Pct
*Valparaiso	12	2	.857	25	8	.758
Oral Roberts	10	4	.714	17	14	.548
Oakland	10	4	.714	17	13	.567
Southern Utah	8	6	.571	11	16	.407
Missouri-KC	7	7	.500	18	11	.621
Indiana-Purdue	6	8	.429	15	15	.500
Western Illinois	3	11	.214	12	16	.429
Chicago St.	0	14	.000	2	26	.071

Conf. Tourney Final: Valparaiso 88, Indiana-Purdue 55.
***NCAA Tourney (0-1):** Valparaiso (0-1).

Mid-Eastern Athletic Conference

Team	Conference			Overall		
	W	L	Pct	W	L	Pct
*Hampton	17	1	.944	26	6	.813
Delaware St.	12	6	.667	16	13	.552
Howard	11	7	.611	18	13	.581
S.C. State	10	7	.588	14	16	.467
N. Carolina A&T	10	7	.588	11	16	.407
Norfolk St.	9	9	.500	10	19	.345
Florida A&M	9	9	.500	9	19	.321
Bethune-Cookman	8	10	.444	12	17	.414
MD-Eastern Shore	7	11	.389	11	18	.379
Coppin St.	3	15	.167	6	25	.194
Morgan St.	2	16	.111	3	25	.107

Conf. Tourney Final: Hampton 80, Howard 62.
***NCAA Tourney (0-1):** Hampton (0-1).

Missouri Valley Conference

Team	Conference			Overall		
	W	L	Pct	W	L	Pct
*Southern Illinois	14	4	.778	28	8	.778
*Creighton	14	4	.778	23	9	.719
Illinois St.	12	6	.667	17	14	.548
SW Missouri St.	11	7	.611	17	15	.531
Wichita St.	9	9	.500	15	15	.500
Drake	9	9	.500	14	15	.483
Northern Iowa	8	10	.444	14	15	.483
Bradley	5	13	.278	9	20	.310
Evansville	4	14	.222	7	21	.250
Indiana St.	4	14	.222	6	24	.200

Conf. Tourney Final: Creighton 84, Southern Illinois 76.
***NCAA Tourney (3-2):** Southern Illinois (2-1), Creighton (1-1).

Mountain West Conference

Team	Conference			Overall		
	W	L	Pct	W	L	Pct
*Wyoming	11	3	.786	22	9	.710
*Utah	10	4	.714	21	9	.700
†UNLV	9	5	.643	21	11	.656
*San Diego St.	7	7	.500	21	12	.636
†Brigham Young	7	7	.500	18	12	.600
†New Mexico	6	8	.429	16	14	.533
Colorado St.	3	11	.214	12	18	.400
Air Force	3	11	.214	9	19	.321

Conf. Tourney Final: San Diego St. 78, UNLV 75.
***NCAA Tourney (1-3):** Wyoming (1-1), Utah (0-1), San Diego St. (0-1).
†**NIT (2-3):** UNLV (1-1), Brigham Young (1-1), New Mexico (0-1).

Northeast Conference

Team	Conference			Overall		
	W	L	Pct	W	L	Pct
*Central Connecticut St.	19	1	.950	27	5	.844
MD-Baltimore County	15	5	.750	20	9	.690
†Wagner	15	5	.750	19	10	.655
Monmouth	14	6	.700	18	12	.600
St. Francis-NY	13	7	.650	18	11	.621
Robert Morris	11	9	.550	12	18	.400
Quinnipiac	10	10	.500	14	16	.467
Sacred Heart	7	13	.350	8	20	.286
LIU Brooklyn	5	15	.250	5	22	.185
St. Francis-PA	5	15	.250	6	21	.222
Fairleigh Dickinson	4	16	.200	4	25	.138
Mt. St. Mary's	2	18	.100	3	24	.111

Conf. Tourney Final: Central Connecticut St. 78, Quinnipiac 71.
***NCAA Tourney (0-1):** Central Connecticut St. (0-1).
†**NIT (0-1):** Wagner (0-1).

Ohio Valley Conference

Team	Conference			Overall		
	W	L	Pct	W	L	Pct
†Tennessee Tech	15	1	.938	27	7	.794
Morehead St	11	5	.688	18	11	.621
*Murray St.	10	6	.625	19	13	.613
Austin Peay	8	8	.500	14	18	.438
Tennessee-Martin	7	9	.438	15	14	.517
Eastern Illinois	7	9	.438	15	16	.484
Tennessee St.	7	9	.438	11	16	.407
SE Missouri St	4	12	.250	6	22	.214
Eastern Kentucky	3	13	.188	7	20	.259

Conf. Tourney Final: Murray State 70, Tennessee Tech 69.
***NCAA Tourney (0-1):** Murray St. (0-1).
†**NIT (3-1):** Tennessee Tech (3-1).

Pacific-10 Conference

Team	Conference			Overall		
	W	L	Pct	W	L	Pct
*Oregon	14	4	.778	26	9	.743
*California	12	6	.667	23	9	.719
*Arizona	12	6	.667	24	10	.706
*USC	12	6	.667	22	10	.688
*Stanford	12	6	.667	20	10	.667
*UCLA	11	7	.611	21	12	.636
†Arizona St	7	11	.389	14	15	.483
Washington	5	13	.278	11	18	.379
Oregon St	4	14	.222	12	17	.414
Washington St	1	17	.056	6	21	.222

Conf. Tourney Final: Arizona 81, USC 71.
***NCAA Tourney (9-6):** Oregon (3-1), Arizona (2-1), UCLA (2-1), Stanford (1-1), California (1-1), USC (0-1).
†**NIT (0-1):** Arizona St. (0-1).

Final NCAA Men's Division I Standings (Cont.)

Patriot League

Team	Conference W	L	Pct	Overall W	L	Pct
American	10	4	.714	18	12	.600
*Holy Cross	9	5	.643	18	15	.545
Bucknell	8	6	.571	13	16	.448
Colgate	8	6	.571	17	11	.607
Lafayette	8	6	.571	15	14	.517
Army	6	8	.429	12	16	.429
Navy	5	9	.357	10	20	.333
Lehigh	2	12	.143	5	23	.179

Conf. Tourney Final: Holy Cross 58, American 54.

***NCAA Tourney (0-1):** Holy Cross (0-1).

Southeastern Conference

Eastern Div.	Conference W	L	Pct	Overall W	L	Pct
*Georgia	10	6	.625	22	10	.688
*Kentucky	10	6	.625	22	10	.688
*Florida	10	6	.625	22	9	.710
Tennessee	7	9	.438	15	16	.484
†Vanderbilt	6	10	.375	17	15	.531
†South Carolina	6	10	.375	22	15	.595

Western Div.	Conference W	L	Pct	Overall W	L	Pct
*Alabama	12	4	.750	27	8	.771
*Mississippi St.	10	6	.625	27	8	.771
*Mississippi	9	7	.563	20	11	.645
†LSU	6	10	.375	19	15	.559
Arkansas	6	10	.375	14	15	.483
Auburn	4	12	.250	12	16	.429

Conf. Tourney Final: Mississippi St. 61, Alabama 58.

***NCAA Tourney (5-6):** Kentucky (2-1), Georgia (1-1), Alabama (1-1), Mississippi St. (1-1), Mississippi (0-1), Florida (0-1).

†NIT (6-3): South Carolina (4-1), Vanderbilt (1-1), LSU (1-1).

Southern Conference

North Div.	Conference W	L	Pct	Overall W	L	Pct
*Davidson	11	5	.688	21	10	.677
†NC-Greensboro	11	5	.688	20	11	.645
East Tennessee St	11	5	.688	18	10	.643
W. Carolina	6	10	.375	12	16	.429
Virginia Military	5	11	.312	10	18	.357
Appalachian St	5	11	.312	10	18	.357

South Div.	Conference W	L	Pct	Overall W	L	Pct
College of Charleston	9	7	.562	21	9	.700
Georgia Southern	9	7	.562	16	12	.571
Chattanooga	9	7	.562	16	14	.533
The Citadel	8	8	.500	17	12	.586
Furman	7	9	.438	17	14	.548
Wofford	5	11	.312	11	18	.379

Conf. Tourney Final: Davidson 62, Furman 57.

***NCAA Tourney (0-1):** Davidson (0-1).

Southland Conference

Team	Conference W	L	Pct	Overall W	L	Pct
*McNeese St.	17	3	.850	21	9	.700
Louisiana-Monroe	15	5	.750	20	12	.625
Texas-San Antonio	13	7	.650	19	10	.655
Lamar	11	9	.550	15	14	.517
Stephen F. Austin	10	10	.500	13	15	.464
SW Texas St.	10	10	.500	12	16	.429
Sam Houston St.	9	11	.450	14	14	.500
Texas-Arlington	9	11	.450	12	15	.444
Northwestern St.	9	11	.450	13	18	.419
SE Louisiana	6	14	.300	7	20	.259
Nicholls St	1	19	.050	2	25	.074

Conf. Tourney Final: McNeese St. 65, Louisiana-Monroe 43.

***NCAA Tourney (0-1):** McNeese St. (0-1).

Southwestern Athletic Conference

Team	Conference W	L	Pct	Overall W	L	Pct
Alcorn St.	16	2	.889	21	10	.677
Alabama A&M	12	6	.667	19	10	.655
Alabama St.	12	6	.667	19	13	.594
Texas Southern	10	8	.556	11	17	.393
Miss. Valley St	9	9	.500	12	17	.414
Prairie View A&M	8	10	.444	10	20	.333
Jackson St	8	10	.444	9	19	.321
Grambling	7	11	.389	9	19	.321
Southern	6	12	.333	7	20	.259
Ark-Pine Bluff	2	16	.111	2	26	.071

Conf. Tourney Final: Alcorn St. 70, Alabama St. 67.

***NCAA Tourney (0-1):** Alcorn St. (0-1).

Sun Belt Conference

East	Conference W	L	Pct	Overall W	L	Pct
*Western Kentucky	13	1	.929	28	4	.875
Ark-Little Rock	8	6	.571	18	11	.621
Middle Tennessee	6	8	.429	14	15	.483
Arkansas St	5	9	.357	15	16	.484
Florida International	4	10	.286	10	20	.333

West	Conference W	L	Pct	Overall W	L	Pct
†Louisiana-Lafayette	11	4	.733	20	11	.645
New Mexico St.	11	4	.433	20	12	.625
New Orleans	9	6	.600	15	14	.517
North Texas	8	7	.533	15	14	.517
Denver	3	12	.200	8	20	.286
South Alabama	2	13	.133	7	21	.250

Conf. Tourney Final: Western Kentucky 76, Louisiana-Lafayette 70.

***NCAA Tourney (0-1):** Western Kentucky (0-1).

†NIT (0-1): Louisiana-Lafayette (0-1).

West Coast Conference

Team	Conference W	L	Pct	Overall W	L	Pct
*Gonzaga	13	1	.929	29	4	.879
*Pepperdine	13	1	.929	22	9	.710
San Francisco	8	6	.571	13	15	.464
Santa Clara	8	6	.571	13	15	.464
San Diego	7	7	.500	16	13	.552
St. Mary's-CA	3	11	.214	9	20	.310
Loyola Marymount	2	12	.143	9	20	.310
Portland	2	12	.143	6	24	.200

Conf. Tourney Final: Gonzaga 96, Pepperdine 90.

***NCAA Tourney (0-2):** Gonzaga (0-1), Pepperdine (0-1).

Western Athletic Conference

Team	Conference			Overall		
	W	L	Pct	W	L	Pct
*Hawaii	15	3	.833	27	6	.818
*Tulsa	15	3	.833	27	7	.794
†Louisiana Tech	14	4	.778	22	10	.688
SMU	10	8	.556	15	14	.517
Nevada	9	9	.500	17	13	.567
†Fresno St.	9	9	.500	19	15	.559
Boise St.	6	12	.333	13	17	.433
Rice	5	13	.278	10	19	.345
San Jose St.	4	14	.222	10	22	.313
UTEP	3	15	.167	10	22	.313

Conf. Tourney Final: Hawaii 73, Tulsa 59.
*NCAA Tourney (1-2): Tulsa (1-1), Hawaii (0-1).
†NIT (2-2): La. Tech (2-1), Fresno St. (0-1).

Division I Independents

Team	W	L	Pct
Gardner Webb	19	8	.679
Texas-Pan American	20	10	.667
Centenary	14	13	.519
Birmingham Southern	13	14	.481
Texas A&M-Corpus Christi	12	15	.444
IPFW	7	21	.250
David Lipscomb	6	21	.214
Morris Brown	4	25	.138

Best in Show

Conferences with at least two wins in the 2002 NCAA's; number of tournament teams in parentheses.

	W-L	Pct		W-L	Pct
ACC (4)	10-3	.769	Pac-10 (6)	9-6	.600
Mid-Am (1)	3-1	.750	MVC (2)	3-2	.600
Big 12 (6)	13-6	.684	Big East (5)	6-5	.545
Big Ten (5)	9-5	.643	SEC (6)	5-6	.455

Annual Awards

Player of the Year

Jason Williams, Duke.....AP, USBWA, Naismith, Wooden, NABC
Drew Gooden, Kansas.....NABC

Wooden Award Voting

Presented since 1977 by the Los Angeles Athletic Club and named after the former Purdue All-America and UCLA coach John Wooden. Voting done by 1,047-member panel of national media; candidates must have a cumulative college grade point average of 2.0 (out of 4.0) and be making progress toward graduation.

		Cl	Pos	Pts
1	Jason Williams, Duke	Jr.	G	5,223
2	Drew Gooden, Kansas	Jr.	F	4,323
3	Juan Dixon, Maryland	Sr.	G	3,845
4	Steve Logan, Cincinnati	Sr.	G	2,887
5	Dan Dickau, Gonzaga	Sr.	G	2,886

Div. II and III Annual Awards

Awarded by the National Association of Basketball Coaches.

Players of the Year
Div. II .... Ronald Murray, Shaw
Div. III .... Jeff Gibbs, Otterbein

Coaches of the Year
Div. II .... Mike Dunlap, Metropolitan St.
Div. III .... Dick Reynolds, Otterbein
NAIA .... Harry Statham, McKendree
JuCo .... Jeff Kidder, Dixie St.

Coaches of the Year

Ben Howland, Pittsburgh .... AP, USBWA, Naismith
Kelvin Sampson, Oklahoma .... NABC

Consensus All-America Team

The NCAA Division I players cited most frequently by the following All-America selectors: AP, U.S. Basketball Writers, National Assn. of Basketball Coaches and Wooden Award Committee. (*) indicates unanimous first team selection. Holdover from 2001-02 first team in **bold** type.

First Team

	Class	Hgt	Pos
Jason Williams*, Duke	Jr.	6-2	G
Dan Dickau, Gonzaga	Sr.	6-0	G
Drew Gooden*, Kansas	Jr.	6-10	F
Juan Dixon*, Maryland	Sr.	6-3	G
Steve Logan*, Cincinnati	Sr.	6-1	G

Second Team

	Class	Hgt	Pos
Mike Dunleavy, Duke	Jr.	6-9	F
Casey Jacobsen, Stanford	Jr.	6-6	F
Jared Jeffries, Indiana	So.	6-10	F
Sam Clancy, USC	Sr.	6-7	F
David West, Xavier	Jr.	6-9	F

Third Team

	Class	Hgt	Pos
Carlos Boozer, Duke	Jr.	6-9	C
Udonis Haslem, Florida	Sr.	6-8	C
Tayshaun Prince, Kentucky	Sr.	6-9	G
Jason Gardner, Arizona	Jr.	5-10	G
Caron Butler, Connecticut	So.	6-7	F

NCAA Men's Division I Leaders

Includes games through NCAA and NIT tourneys.

INDIVIDUAL

Scoring

	Cl	Gm	FG%	3FG/Att	FT%	Reb	Ast	Stl	Blk	Pts	Avg	Hi
Jason Conley, VMI	Fr.	28	46.7	79/237	81.8	224	67	82	11	820	29.3	42
Henry Domercant, E. Illinois	Jr.	31	43.7	104/269	89.2	223	67	36	21	817	26.4	40
Mire Chatman, TX-Pan Am.	Sr.	29	48.4	65/186	69.9	158	112	105	14	760	26.2	46
Ernest Bremer, St. Bonaventure	Sr.	30	41.3	88/266	80.3	140	92	56	2	738	24.6	35
Melvin Ely, Fresno St.	Sr.	28	56.3	0/1	73.5	254	50	19	89	653	23.3	35
Lynn Greer, Temple	Sr.	31	40.4	95/246	87.3	97	130	52	5	719	23.2	47
Nick Stapleton, Austin Peay	Sr.	32	44.9	72/215	73.9	74	85	43	3	742	23.2	37
Keith McLeod, Bowling Green	Sr.	33	45.2	89/216	80.7	137	90	65	2	755	22.9	42
Chris Davis, N. Texas	Jr.	29	47.9	46/137	75.9	187	74	24	5	653	22.5	32
Ricky Minard, Morehead St.	So.	29	49.6	65/167	78.4	201	96	73	29	646	22.3	38
Kevin Martin, W. Carolina	Fr.	28	48.4	73/191	82.8	133	43	51	10	619	22.1	39
Steve Logan, Cincinnati	Sr.	35	45.7	86/230	87.3	107	187	32	0	770	22.0	41
Damon Hancock, SMU	Sr.	26	42.8	48/136	66.1	114	94	23	0	572	22.0	30
Casey Jacobsen, Stanford	Jr.	30	44.1	64/172	77.6	135	106	18	3	658	21.9	49
Michael Watson, UMKC	So.	29	35.3	95/276	78.9	91	82	54	5	635	21.9	34
David Bailey, Loyola-IL.	Jr.	30	43.2	54/180	74.5	109	138	54	2	651	21.7	42
Troy Bell, Boston College	Jr.	32	40.7	32/216	88.3	130	123	72	8	691	21.6	42
Richard Toussaint, Bet.-Cook.	Jr.	29	46.2	2/15	79.5	124	21	39	9	625	21.6	46
Jason Williams, Duke	Jr.	35	45.7	108/282	67.6	124	187	76	3	746	21.3	38
Leon Rodgers, N. Illinois	Sr.	28	50.8	33/74	79.7	239	62	19	17	596	21.3	31

Rebounding

	Cl	Gm	No	Avg
Jeremy Bishop, Quinnipiac	Jr.	29	347	12.0
Bruce Jenkins, N.C. A&T	Sr.	28	329	11.8
Curtis Borchardt, Stanford	Jr.	29	332	11.4
Drew Gooden, Kansas	Jr.	37	423	11.4
Corey Jackson, Nevada	Sr.	29	323	11.1
Reggie Evans, Iowa	Sr.	34	378	11.1
Trevor Gaines, Vermont	Sr.	29	320	11.0
Theron Smith, Ball St.	Jr.	35	381	10.9
Ryan Humphrey, Notre Dame	Sr.	31	337	10.9
Stephane Pelle, Colorado	Jr.	29	314	10.8
Hector Romero, New Orleans	Jr.	28	302	10.8
J.R. Vanhoose, Marshall	Sr.	30	319	10.6
Kelly Wise, Memphis	Sr.	32	330	10.3
Donald Cole, Sam Houston St.	Jr.	28	287	10.3
Rashod Kent, Rutgers	Sr.	31	317	10.2

Assists

	Cl	Gm	No	Avg
T.J. Ford, Texas	Fr.	33	273	8.3
Steve Blake, Maryland	Jr.	36	286	7.9
Edward Scott, Clemson	Jr.	30	238	7.9
Sean Kennedy, Marist	Sr.	28	222	7.9
Chris Thomas, Notre Dame	Fr.	33	252	7.6
Matt Montague, BYU	Sr.	30	217	7.2
Brandin Knight, Pittsburgh	Jr.	35	251	7.2
Mychal Covington, Oakland	Sr.	28	198	7.1
Reggie Kohn, S. Florida	Jr.	32	220	6.9
Aaron Miles, Kansas	Fr.	37	252	6.8
Guilherme Da Luz, Furman	Jr.	31	206	6.6
Sean Peterson, Ga. Southern	Sr.	28	186	6.6
Marquis Sykes, Morehead St.	Jr.	29	189	6.5
Brandon Pardon, Bowling Green	Sr.	33	209	6.3
Delvon Arrington, Florida St.	Sr.	29	182	6.3

Field Goal Percentage

Minimum 5 Field Goals made per game.

	Cl	Gm	FG	FGA	Pct
Adam Mark, Belmont	So.	26	150	212	70.8
Carlos Boozer, Duke	Jr.	35	230	346	66.5
David Harrison, Colorado	Fr.	27	139	218	63.8
Rolan Roberts, S. Illinois	Sr.	36	209	346	60.4
Jermaine Hall, Wagner	Jr.	29	240	400	60.0
Chris Stockwell, St. Francis-NY	Jr.	29	155	260	59.6
Len Matela, Bowling Green	Sr.	33	192	323	59.4
Justin Rowe, Maine	Jr.	30	158	266	59.4
James Moore, N. Mexico St.	So.	32	184	310	59.4
Nick Collison, Kansas	Jr.	37	245	414	59.2
Damien Kinloch, Tenn. Tech	Jr.	34	186	316	58.9
Henry Williams, S. Alabama	Jr.	28	141	241	58.5
Travis Reed, Long Beach St.	Sr.	30	177	303	58.4
Patrick Doctor, America	Sr.	30	166	286	58.0
Omar Barlett, Jacksonville St.	Jr.	29	155	269	57.6

Free Throw Percentage

Minimum 2.5 Free Throws made per game.

	Cl	Gm	FT	FTA	Pct
Cary Cochran, Nebraska	Sr.	28	71	77	92.2
Gary Buchanan, Villanova	Jr.	32	112	123	91.1
Cain Doliboa, Wright St.	Sr.	28	80	88	90.9
Salim Stoudamire, Arizona	Fr.	34	103	114	90.4
Jake Sullivan, Iowa St.	So.	28	117	130	90.0
Jobey Thomas, Charlotte	Sr.	30	98	109	89.9
Juan Dixon, Maryland	Sr.	36	141	157	89.8
Chris Spatola, Army	Sr.	28	113	126	89.7
Eric Channing, New Mexico St.	Sr.	31	93	104	89.4
Travis Cantrell, Citadel	Sr.	29	92	103	89.3
Henry Domercant, Eastern Ill.	Jr.	31	189	212	89.2
Kyle Korver, Creighton	Jr.	29	97	109	89.0
Donta Richardson, Wyoming	Jr.	31	113	127	89.0
Chris Thomas, Notre Dame	Fr.	33	120	135	88.9
Greg Lakey, Loyola Marymount	Sr.	29	79	89	88.8

Texas
T.J. Ford
Assists

Nebraska
Cary Cochran
Free Throw Pct.

Louisiana-Monroe
Wojciech Myrda
Blocks

Alabama A&M
Desmond Cambridge
Steals

3-Pt Field Goal Percentage

Minimum 1.5 Three-Point FGs made per game.

	Cl	Gm	FG	FGA	Pct
Dante Swanson, Tulsa	Jr.	33	73	149	49.0
Cain Doliboa, Wright St.	Sr.	28	104	217	47.9
Jake Sullivan, Iowa St.	So.	28	60	127	47.2
Jeff Boschee, Kansas	Sr.	37	110	237	46.4
Ray Abellard, C. Florida	Jr.	29	80	173	46.2
Cameron Crisp, Tenn.Tech	So.	37	72	156	46.2
John Hamilton, Weber St.	So.	29	76	165	46.1
Eric Channing, New Mexico St.	Sr.	31	81	176	46.0
Jordan Kardos, Ill-Chicago	Sr.	34	69	150	46.0
Dan Dickau, Gonzaga	Sr.	32	117	256	45.7

3-Pt Field Goals Per Game

	Cl	Gm	No	Avg
Cain Doliboa, Wright St.	Sr.	28	104	3.7
Jobey Thomas, Charlotte	Sr.	30	110	3.7
Dan Dickau, Gonzaga	Sr.	32	117	3.7
Wes Burtner, Belmont	Sr.	28	100	3.6
Jason Morgan, St. Francis-NY	Sr.	28	100	3.6
Sharif Chambliss, Penn St.	So.	28	99	3.5
Travis Cantrell, Citadel	Sr.	29	102	3.5
Bryan Buchanan, IUPUI	Jr.	25	84	3.4
Henry Domercant, Eastern Ill.	Jr.	31	104	3.4
Nick Zachery, Arkansas-LR	So.	28	93	3.3
Clarence Gilbert, Missouri	Sr.	36	118	3.3

Blocked Shots

	Cl	Gm	No	Avg
Wojciech Myrda, La-Monroe	Sr.	32	172	5.4
D'or Fischer, Northwestern St.	So.	30	133	4.4
Emeka Okafor, Connecticut	Fr.	34	138	4.1
Justin Rowe, Maine	Jr.	30	121	4.0
Deng Gai, Fairfield	Fr.	29	115	4.0
Nick Billings, Binghamton	Fr.	21	80	3.8
Moussa Badiane, E. Carolina	Fr.	24	87	3.6
Jason Jennings, Arkansas St.	Sr.	30	101	3.4
Kendrick Moore, Oral Roberts	Jr.	31	103	3.3
Robert Battle, Drexel	Jr.	28	91	3.3
Kyle Davis, Auburn	So.	24	77	3.2
Vili Morton, UC-Riverside	So.	26	83	3.2

Steals

	Cl	Gm	No	Avg
Desmond Cambridge, Alabama A&M	Sr.	29	160	5.5
John Linehan, Providence	Sr.	31	139	4.5
Mire Chatman, TX-Pan Am	Sr.	29	105	3.6
Marques Green, St. Bonaventure	So.	30	102	3.4
Marcus Hatten, St. John's	Jr.	32	105	3.3
Carlos Morban, Fla. Int'l.	Fr.	29	87	3.0
Jason Conley, VMI	Fr.	28	82	2.9
James Thues, Syracuse	So.	36	101	2.8
Markus Carr, CS-Northridge	Sr.	28	78	2.8
Kevin Braswell, Georgetown	Sr.	30	81	2.7
Alexis McMillan, Stetson	Jr.	26	69	2.7

Single Game Highs

Points

No		Opponent	Date
50	D. Cambridge, Ala. A&M	TX Southern	Feb. 25
49	Casey Jacobsen, Stanford	Ariz. St.	Jan. 31
47	Lynn Greer, Temple	Wisconsin	Dec. 3

Rebounds

No		Opponent	Date
27	Andre Brown, DePaul	TCU	Feb. 6
	Amien Hicks, Morris Brown	Clark Atlanta	Jan. 14
26	Jamal Brown TCU	N. Texas	Dec. 23

Assists

No		Opponent	Date
17	Brad Boyd, La.-Lafayette	North Texas	Jan. 24
	Sean Peterson, Ga. So.	W. Carolina	Jan. 21
	Imari Sawyer, DePaul	Youngstown St.	Nov. 25

Blocks

No		Opponent	Date
13	W. Myrda, La.-Monroe	TX-San Antonio	Jan. 17
12	D'or Fischer, N'western St.	Siena	Nov. 21
11	W. Myrda, La.-Monroe	Nicholls St.	Feb. 16

Steals

No		Opponent	Date
12	Jehiel Lewis, Navy	Bucknell	Jan. 12
11	Four tied		

3-point FGs

No		Opponent	Date
14	Ronald Blackshear, Marshall	Akron	Mar. 1
12	Clarence Gilbert, Missouri	Colorado	Feb. 23
11	T.J. Sorrentine, UVM	Northeastern	Jan. 17

NCAA Men's Division I Leaders (Cont.)
TEAM

Scoring Offense

	Gm	W-L	Pts	Avg
Kansas	37	33-4	3365	90.9
Duke	35	31-4	3112	88.9
Oregon	35	26-9	2994	85.5
TCU	31	16-15	2645	85.3
Maryland	36	32-4	3060	85.0
Arizona	34	24-10	2793	82.1
Wake Forest	34	21-13	2789	82.0
E. Tennessee St.	28	18-10	2281	81.5
Wagner	29	19-10	2362	81.4
Pepperdine	31	22-9	2519	81.3
Gonzaga	33	29-4	2677	81.1
Georgetown	30	19-11	2433	81.1
Stanford	30	20-10	2420	80.7
St. Bonaventure	30	17-13	2416	80.5
Florida	31	22-9	2495	80.5

Won-Lost Percentage

	W	L	Pct
Kansas	33	4	89.2
Maryland	32	4	88.9
Cincinnati	31	4	88.6
Duke	31	4	88.6
Gonzaga	29	4	87.9
Western Ky.	28	4	87.5
Oklahoma	31	5	86.1
Central Conn. St.	27	5	84.4
Kent St.	30	6	83.3
Pittsburgh	29	6	82.9
Hawaii	27	6	81.8
Butler	26	6	81.3
Xavier	26	6	81.3
Connecticut	27	7	79.4
Tennessee Tech	27	7	79.4
Tulsa	27	7	79.4

Scoring Defense

	Gm	W-L	Pts	Avg
Columbia	28	11-17	1596	57.0
Princeton	28	16-12	1606	57.4
Butler	32	26-6	1849	57.8
Utah St.	31	23-8	1800	58.1
Northwestern	29	16-13	1715	59.1
Holy Cross	33	18-15	1968	59.6
Samford	29	15-14	1748	60.3
Cincinnati	35	31-4	2115	60.4
Marquette	33	26-7	2004	60.7
Col. of Charleston	30	21-9	1824	60.8
UC-Santa Barbara	31	20-11	1889	60.9
Pittsburgh	35	29-6	2133	60.9
Utah	30	21-9	1839	61.3
Richmond	36	22-14	2213	61.5
Air Force	28	9-19	1722	61.5

Field Goal Percentage

	FG	FGA	Pct
Kansas	1259	2487	50.6
Duke	1093	2209	49.5
Bowling Green	834	1709	48.8
Oregon	1014	2082	48.7
Ohio St.	825	1702	48.5
Ohio	741	1531	48.4
Morehead St.	796	1647	48.3
Connecticut	972	2012	48.3
Maryland	1083	2248	48.2
Hampton	933	1940	48.1
Tennessee Tech	915	1906	48.0
Mississippi St.	943	1965	48.0
Wright St.	698	1455	48.0
Pennsylvania	815	1701	47.9
Wake Forest	1001	2094	47.8
Portland St.	723	1513	47.8

Scoring Margin

	Off	Def	Mar
Duke	88.9	69.2	19.7
Cincinnati	78.2	60.4	17.8
Kansas	90.9	74.7	16.2
Gonzaga	81.1	66.6	14.5
Maryland	85.0	70.9	14.1
Florida	80.5	66.6	13.9
Oklahoma	78.0	64.6	13.3
Western Ky.	77.8	64.7	13.2
Oregon	85.5	72.5	13.0
Butler	70.3	57.8	12.6
Marquette	73.1	60.7	12.4
Kent St.	75.9	64.0	11.9
Valparaiso	77.7	66.1	11.6
Pittsburgh	72.3	60.9	11.3
Memphis	80.0	68.8	11.2

Field Goal Percentage Defense

	FG	FGA	Pct
Va. Commonwealth	767	2052	37.4
Cincinnati	761	2035	37.4
Col. of Charleston	663	1762	37.6
Davidson	692	1822	38.0
Connecticut	830	2182	38.0
UC-Santa Barbara	623	1625	38.3
Gonzaga	773	2006	38.5
Boston Univ.	687	1760	39.0
Villanova	739	1883	39.2
La-Lafayette	709	1803	39.3
Utah St.	655	1665	39.3
Siena	817	2076	39.4
Memphis	864	2190	39.5
Pittsburgh	765	1937	39.5
Rutgers	713	1805	39.5
Georgetown	759	1920	39.5

Rebound Margin

	Off	Def	Mar
Gonzaga	41.5	32.6	8.9
La. Tech	40.9	32.2	8.8
Kansas	44.3	35.5	8.7
Stanford	41.8	33.3	8.5
Dayton	39.9	31.7	8.3
Michigan St.	37.5	29.6	7.9
Wyoming	40.2	32.4	7.7
Tennessee Tech	38.5	31.3	7.2
Central Conn. St.	39.0	32.0	7.0
Virginia Tech	39.8	33.1	6.8
Memphis	42.8	36.2	6.6
Utah St.	36.0	29.5	6.5
Mississippi St.	38.8	32.4	6.5
Colorado	43.1	36.6	6.4
Western Ky.	38.4	32.0	6.4

Free Throw Percentage

	FT	FTA	Pct
Morehead St.	485	619	78.4
Loyola Marymount	466	600	77.7
Illinois St.	427	551	77.5
Miami-FL	523	678	77.1
Michigan St.	442	573	77.1
Oregon	662	861	76.9
Oklahoma	549	716	76.7
SE Missouri St.	428	560	76.4
BYU	523	688	76.0
UMKC	361	475	76.0
St. Bonaventure	514	677	75.9
Akron	554	731	75.8
UC-Santa Barbara	479	634	75.6
N.C. State	561	743	75.5
Belmont	360	477	75.5

3-point FG Percentage

	3PT	3PTA	Pct
Marshall	252	595	42.4
Oregon	304	721	42.2
Kansas	224	536	41.8
Indiana	270	659	41.0
Portland St.	233	570	40.9
Central Florida	200	492	40.7
SW Missouri St.	201	495	40.6
Utah	236	582	40.5
Ill-Chicago	251	619	40.5
Tulsa	259	369	40.5
Wright St.	222	548	40.5
UC-Santa Barbara	201	499	40.3
Pennsylvania	266	668	39.8
SW Texas St.	215	541	39.7
BYU	170	428	39.7

3-point FG Made Per Game

	Gm	No	Avg
St. Bonaventure	30	314	10.5
Dartmouth	27	263	9.7
Nebraska	28	267	9.5
Belmont	28	264	9.4
Troy St.	28	258	9.2
Baylor	30	273	9.1
Missouri	36	326	9.1
Mississippi Valley St.	29	258	8.9
WI-Milwaukee	29	257	8.9
Ball St.	35	310	8.9
Vanderbilt	32	282	8.8
Temple	34	298	8.8
Butler	32	280	8.8
Western Ky.	32	279	8.7
Oregon	35	304	8.7

Underclassmen in NBA Draft

Forty-two division I players (19 juniors, 10 sophomores and 8 freshmen), 1 junior college player, and 4 high school seniors forfeited the remainder of their college eligibility and declared for the 2002 NBA Draft which took place at Madison Square Garden in New York City on June 26.

Players are listed in alphabetical order; first round selections in **bold** type, high school players in *italics*.

	Cl	Drafted by	Overall Pick
Lee Benson Jr., Brown Mackie	Fr.	not drafted	—
Rodney Bias, Shelton St.	So.	not drafted	—
Cordell Billups, Pierce College	So.	not drafted	—
Carlos Boozer, Duke	Jr.	Cleveland	35
Curtis Borchardt, Stanford	Jr.	Orlando	18
Caron Butler, Connecticut	So.	Miami	10
DeAngelo Collins, Inglewood HS (CA)	HS	not drafted	—
Lenny Cooke, Central Flint HS (MI)	HS	not drafted	—
Mike Dunleavy, Duke	Jr.	Golden St.	3
Drew Gooden, Kansas	Jr.	Memphis	4
Rod Grizzard, Alabama	Jr.	Washington	39
Marcus Haislip, Tennessee	Jr.	Milwaukee	13
Rashid Hardwick, E. Okla. St.	Fr.	not drafted	—
Adam Harrington, Auburn	Jr.	not drafted	—
Casey Jacobsen, Stanford	Jr.	Phoenix	22
Chris Jefferies, Fresno St.	Jr.	L.A. Lakers	27
Jared Jeffries, Indiana	So.	Washington	12
Muhammed Lasege, Louisville	Fr.	not drafted	—
Tito Maddox, Fresno St.	Fr.	Houston	38
Kei Madison, Okaloosa-Walton JC	So.	not drafted	—
Roger Mason Jr., Virginia	Jr.	Chicago	31
"Smush" Parker, Fordham	So.	not drafted	—
Giedrius Rinkevicius, Bridgton Acad. (ME)	HS	not drafted	—
Kareem Rush, Missouri	Jr.	Toronto	20
Jamal Sampson, California	Fr.	Utah	47
Jerry Sanders, N. Illinois	So.	not drafted	—
Eddie Shelby, Dixie St. (UT)	So.	not drafted	—
Bobby Smith, Robert Morris	Jr.	not drafted	—
Melvin Steward, E. New Mexico	Jr.	not drafted	—
Amare Stoudemire, Cypress Creek HS (FL)	HS	Phoenix	9
Marcus Taylor, Michigan St.	So.	Minnesota	52
Terrell Taylor, Creighton	Jr.	not drafted	—
Dajuan Wagner, Memphis	Fr.	Cleveland	6
Adrian Walton, Fordham	Fr.	not drafted	—
Joseph Ward, Fort Hays St. (KS)	Jr.	not drafted	—
Omar Weaver, Riverside CC (CA)	Fr.	not drafted	—
Chris Wilcox, Maryland	So	L.A. Clippers	8
Troy Wiley, Rhode Island	Jr.	not drafted	—
Frank Williams, Illinois	Jr.	Denver	25
George Williams, Houston	Jr.	not drafted	—
Jay Williams, Duke	Jr.	Chicago	2
Qyntel Woods, NE Miss.	So.	Portland	21

Note: Twenty-four players who initially declared themselves eligible for the 2002 NBA Draft withdrew their names before the June 19 deadline.

Other 2002 Men's Tournaments

NIT Tournament

The 65th annual National Invitation Tournament had a 40-team field. First three rounds played on home courts of higher seeded teams. Semifinal, Third Place and Championship games played March 26-28 at Madison Square Garden in New York City.

Opening Round

at Richmond 74 ....OT.................Wagner 67
Montana St. 77 ....at Utah St. 69
at Ball St. 98 ....South Florida 92
St. Joseph's 73 ....at George Mason 64
at Louisiana Tech 83 ....La-Lafayette 63
at Vanderbilt 59..............................Houston 50
at Dayton 80.................................Detroit 69
at Tennessee Tech 64 ....Georgia St. 62

1st Round

at Syracuse 76 ....St. Bonaventure 66
at Butler 81..........................Bowling Green 69
at Minnesota 95 ....New Mexico 62
at Richmond 63 ....Montana St. 48
Ball St. 76 ....at St. Joseph's 54
LSU 63 ....at Iowa 61
at UNLV 96...............................Arizona St. 91
South Carolina 74......................at Virginia 67
Temple 81 ....at Fresno St. 75
at Louisville 66 ....Princeton 65
at Villanova 84 ....Manhattan 80
at Louisiana Tech 83 ....Vanderbilt 69
Tennessee Tech 68 ....at Dayton 59
Yale 67..................................at Rutgers 65
at BYU 78 ....UC-Irvine 55
at Memphis 82..................NC-Greensboro 62

2nd Round

at Syracuse 66 ....Butler 65
Richmond 67 ....at Minnesota 66
Ball St. 75 ....at LSU 65
at South Carolina 75........................UNLV 65
Temple 65 ....at Louisville 64
at Villanova 67...........................La. Tech 64
Tennessee Tech 80 ....at Yale 61
at Memphis 80.............................BYU 69

Quarterfinals

Syracuse 66 ....at Richmond 46
at South Carolina 82 ....Ball St. 47
at Temple 63 ....Villanova 57
at Memphis 79.....................Tennessee Tech 73

Semifinals

South Carolina 66........................Syracuse 59
Memphis 78 ....Temple 77

Third Place

Temple 65 ....Syracuse 54

Championship

Memphis 72.........................South Carolina 62

Most Valuable Players

NIT
Dajuan Wagner, Memphis guard

NCAA Division II
Patrick Mutombo, Metropolitan St. forward

NCAA Division III
Jeff Gibbs, Otterbein center

NAIA Division I
Michael Williamson, U. of Sci. & Arts (Okla.) guard

NAIA Division II
Daniel Cutbirth, Evangel (Mo.) guard

NCAA Division II

The eight regional winners of the 48-team field: NORTHEAST—Adelphi (28-2); EAST—Indiana-Pa. (27-4); SOUTH ATLANTIC—Shaw (27-4); SOUTH—West Georgia (24-8); SOUTH CENTRAL—NW Missouri St. (29-2); GREAT LAKES—Kentucky Wesleyan (29-2); NORTH CENTRAL—Metropolitan St. (28-6); WEST—CS-San Bernadino (28-1).

The Elite Eight was played March 20-23, at Evansville, Ind. There was no Third Place game.

Quarterfinals

Ky. Wesleyan 71 ....Adelphi 46
Metro St. 65 ....CS-San Bernadino 48
Shaw 102 ....West Georgia 84
Indiana (Pa.) 78 ....NW Missouri St. 72

Semifinals

Ky. Wesleyan 101 ....Shaw 92
Metro St. 82..........................Indiana (Pa.) 52

Championship

Metro St. 80.......................Ky. Wesleyan 72

NCAA Division III

Sixty-four teams played into the 32-team Division III field. The four sectional winners: ATLANTIC—Elizabethtown (28-2); EAST/NORTHEAST—Rochester (24-4); NORTH—Carthage (27-1); MIDWEST—Otterbein (28-3).

The Final Four was played March 15-16, at Salem Civic Center in Salem, Va.

Semifinals

Elizabethtown 93........2 OT.............Rochester 83
Otterbein 70 ....Carthage 66

Third Place

Carthage 72 ....Rochester 51

Championship

Otterbein 102 ....Elizabethtown 83

NAIA Division I

The quarterfinalists, in alphabetical order, after two rounds of the 32-team NAIA tournament: Azusa Pacific, Calif. (28-7); Barat (33-5); Huston-Tillotson (25-7); Oklahoma Baptist (31-4); Oklahoma City (26-7); Olivet Nazarene (27-9); Science and Arts, Okla. (22-7); Westmont (23-10).

All tournament games played, March 13-19, at the Municipal Auditorium, Kansas City, Mo. There was no Third Place game.

Quarterfinals: Azusa Pacific def. Oklahoma City, 80-72; Oklahoma Baptist def. Olivet Nazarene, 89-69; Science and Arts def. Huston-Tillotson, 92-77; Barat def. Westmont, 91-79.

Semifinals: Oklahoma Baptist def. Azusa Pacific, 93-81; Science and Arts def. Barat, 111-106 (OT).

Championship: Science and Arts def. Oklahoma Baptist, 96-79.

NAIA Division II

The semifinalists, in alphabetical order, after three rounds of the 32-team NAIA tournament: Cornerstone, Mich. (34-4); Evangel, Mo. (34-1); Northwestern, Iowa (30-5); Robert Morris, Ill. (33-5).

All tournament games played, March 6-12, at Point Lookout, Missouri. There was no Third Place game.

Semifinals: Evangel def. Nortwestern, 81-79; Robert Morris def. Cornerstone, 82-75.

Championship: Evangel def. Robert Morris, 84-61.

Final Regular Season AP Women's Top 25 Poll

Taken **before** start of NCAA tournament.

The sportswriters & broadcasters poll: first place votes in parentheses; records through Sunday, March 10, 2001; total points (based on 25 for 1st, 24 for 2nd, etc.); record in NCAA tourney and team lost to; head coach (career years and career record including 2002 postseason), and preseason ranking. Teams in **bold** type went on to reach the NCAA Final Four.

		Mar. 10 Record	Points	NCAA Recap	Head Coach	Preseason Rank
1	**Connecticut** (44)	33-0	1,100	6-0	Geno Auriemma (17 yrs: 455-98)	1
2	**Oklahoma**	27-3	1,031	5-1 (Connecticut)	Sherri Coale (6 yrs: 113-73)	4
3	**Duke**	27-3	1,020	4-1 (Oklahoma)	Gail Goestenkors (10 yrs: 237-82)	5
4	Vanderbilt	27-6	935	3-1 (Tennessee)	Jim Foster (24 yrs: 504-225)	3
5	Stanford	30-2	931	2-1 (Colorado)	Tara VanDerveer (20 yrs: 490-124)	9
6	**Tennessee**	25-4	907	4-1 (Connecticut)	Pat Summitt (28 yrs: 788-158)	2
7	Baylor	26-5	826	1-1 (Drake)	Kim Mulkey-Robinson (2 yrs: 48-15)	14
8	Louisiana Tech	25-4	769	0-1 (UC Santa Barbara)	Leon Barmore (19 yrs: 576-87)	6
9	Purdue	23-5	734	1-1 (Old Dominion)	Kristy Curry (3 yrs: 78-21)	11
10	Iowa St.	23-8	658	1-1 (BYU)	Bill Fennelly (13 yrs: 328-112)	8
11	Kansas St.	24-7	640	2-1 (Old Dominion)	Deb Patterson (6 yrs: 97-84)	NR
12	Colorado	21-9	589	3-1 (Oklahoma)	Ceal Barry (23 yrs: 455-249)	12
13	South Carolina	22-6	535	3-1 (Duke)	Susan Walvius (12 yrs: 171-171)	NR
14	Texas	20-9	524	2-1 (Duke)	Jody Conradt (33 yrs: 788-258)	NR
15	Old Dominion	25-5	438	3-1 (Connecticut)	Wendy Larry (18 yrs: 405-146)	18
16	North Carolina	24-8	418	2-1 (Vanderbilt)	Sylvia Hatchell (27 yrs: 602-249)	NR
17	Texas Tech	18-11	314	2-1 (Oklahoma)	Marsha Sharp (19 yrs: 459-141)	7
18	Minnesota	21-7	293	1-1 (North Carolina)	Brenda Oldfield (3 yrs: 57-30)	NR
19	Cincinnati	26-4	263	1-1 (South Carolina)	Laurie Pirtle (20 yrs: 314-248)	NR
20	Colorado St.	24-6	239	0-1 (Tulane)	Tom Collen (5 yrs: 129-33)	24
21	Boston College	23-7	232	0-1 (Mississippi)	Cathy Inglese (16 yrs: 269-187)	NR
22	LSU	17-11	192	1-1 (Colorado)	Sue Gunter (32 yrs: 651-296)	NR
23	Florida Int'l	26-5	141	1-1 (Penn St.)	Cindy Russo (25 yrs: 526-201)	NR
24	Florida	18-10	112	0-1 (BYU)	Carol Ross (12 yrs: 247-121)	13
	Penn St.	21-11	112	2-1 (Connecticut)	Rene Portland (26 yrs: 595-207)	21

Others receiving votes: 26. **Arizona St.** (24-8, 105 points); 27. **Arkansas** (19-11, 44); 28. **Notre Dame** (19-9, 39); 29. **Indiana** (17-13, 35); 30. **UNLV** (23-7, 23); 31. **Georgia** (19-10, 17); 32. **Villanova** (19-10, 16); 33. **TCU** (23-6, 13); 34. **BYU** (22-8, 11); 35. **Wisconsin** (19-11, 9); 36. **Santa Barbara** (25-5, 8); 37. **Creighton** (24-9) and **Drake** (23-7, 5); 39. **Mississippi St.** (18-11), **New Mexico** (22-8) and **Virginia Tech** (19-10, 24); 42. **Kent St.** (20-10), **Pepperdine** (23-7) and **Temple** (20-10, 1).

NCAA Women's Division I Tournament Seeds

	WEST		MIDWEST		MIDEAST		EAST
1	Oklahoma (27-3)	1	Vanderbilt (27-6)	1	Connecticut (33-0)	1	Duke (27-3)
2	Stanford (30-2)	2	Tennessee (25-4)	2	Purdue (23-5)	2	Baylor (26-5)
3	Colorado (21-9)	3	Iowa St. (23-8)	3	Kansas St. (24-7)	3	South Carolina (22-6)
4	Texas Tech (18-11)	4	North Carolina (25-7)	4	Penn St. (21-11)	4	Texas (20-9)
5	Boston College (23-7)	5	Minnesota (21-7)	5	Florida Int'l (26-5)	5	La. Tech (25-4)
6	LSU (17-11)	6	Florida (18-10)	6	Arkansas (19-11)	6	Cincinnati (26-4)
7	Colorado St. (24-6)	7	Notre Dame (19-9)	7	Old Dominion (25-5)	7	Drake (23-7)
8	Pepperdine (23-7)	8	Wisconsin (19-11)	8	Virginia (17-12)	8	TCU (23-6)
9	Villanova (19-10)	9	Arizona St. (24-8)	9	Iowa (17-10)	9	Indiana (17-13)
10	Tulane (23-10)	10	New Mexico (22-8)	10	Georgia (19-10)	10	Syracuse (18-12)
11	Santa Clara (21-9)	11	BYU (22-8)	11	Clemson (17-11)	11	St. Peter's (25-5)
12	Mississippi St. (18-11)	12	UNLV (23-7)	12	Creighton (24-9)	12	UC-Santa Barbara (25-5)
13	S.F. Austin (24-5)	13	Harvard (21-5)	13	Chattanooga (23-7)	13	WI-Green Bay (24-6)
14	Southern (26-4)	14	Temple (20-10)	14	Kent St. (20-10)	14	Liberty (23-7)
15	Weber St. (22-8)	15	Georgia St. (21-9)	15	Austin Peay (19-11)	15	Bucknell (21-9)
16	Hartford (16-14)	16	Oakland (17-13)	16	St. Francis-PA (18-11)	16	Norfolk St. (22-8)

2002 NCAA Basketball Women's Division

1st ROUND March 15-16	2nd ROUND March 17-18	SWEET 16 March 23 & 25	ELITE EIGHT March 29	FINAL FOUR March 31	NATIONAL CHAMPIONSHIP	FINAL FOUR March 31	ELITE EIGHT March 29	SWEET 16 March 23 & 25	2nd ROUND March 17-18	1st ROUND March 15-16

MIDEAST

(1) Connecticut 86	
(16) St. Francis 37	(1) Connecticut 86
(8) Virginia 62	
(9) Iowa 69	(9) Iowa 48
(5) Florida Int'l 73	
(12) Creighton 58	(5) Florida Int'l 79
(4) Penn St 82	
(13) Chattanooga 67	(4) Penn St 96
(6) Arkansas 78	
(11) Clemson 68	(6) Arkansas 68
(3) Kansas St 93	
(14) Kent St 65	(3) Kansas St 82
(7) Old Dominion 68	
(10) Georgia 54	(7) Old Dominion 74
(2) Purdue 80	
(15) Austin Peay 49	(2) Purdue 70

(1) Connecticut 82
(4) Penn St 64
(3) Kansas St 62
(7) Old Dominion 88

(1) Connecticut 85
(7) Old Dominion 64

(1) Connecticut 79

MIDWEST

(1) Vanderbilt 63	
(16) Oakland 38	(1) Vanderbilt 61
(8) Wisconsin 70	
(9) Arizona 73	(9) Arizona 35
(5) Minnesota 71	
(12) UNLV 54	(5) Minnesota 69
(4) North Carolina 85	
(13) Harvard 58	(4) North Carolina 72
(6) Florida 52	
(11) Brigham Young 90	(11) Brigham Young 75
(3) Iowa St 72	
(14) Temple 57	(3) Iowa St 69
(10) Notre Dame 58	
(10) New Mexico 44	(10) Notre Dame 50
(2) Tennessee 98	
(15) Georgia St 68	(2) Tennessee 89

(1) Vanderbilt 70
(4) North Carolina 61
(11) Brigham Young 57
(2) Tennessee 68

(1) Vanderbilt 63
(2) Tennessee 56

WEST

(1) Oklahoma 84	
(16) Hartford 52	(1) Oklahoma 66
(8) Pepperdine 46	
(9) Villanova 67	(9) Villanova 53
(12) Boston College 59	
(12) Mississippi St 65	(12) Mississippi St 55
(4) Texas Tech 84	
(13) S.F. Austin 65	(4) Texas Tech 77
(6) LSU 84	
(11) Santa Clara 78	(6) LSU 58
(3) Colorado 88	
(14) Southern U 61	(3) Colorado 69
(10) Colorado St 69	
(10) Tulane 73	(10) Tulane 55
(2) Stanford 76	
(15) Weber St 51	(2) Stanford 77

(1) Oklahoma 72
(4) Texas Tech 62
(3) Colorado 62
(2) Stanford 59

(1) Oklahoma 94
(3) Colorado 60

(1) Oklahoma 86

EAST

(1) Duke 95	
(16) Norfolk St 48	(1) Duke 76
(8) TCU 55	
(9) Indiana 45	(8) TCU 66
(5) Louisiana Tech 56	
(12) UC Santa Barb 57	(12) UC Santa Barb 60
(4) Texas 60	
(13) Wis-Green Bay 55	(4) Texas 76
(6) Cincinnati 76	
(11) St. Peter's 63	(6) Cincinnati 56
(3) South Carolina 69	
(14) Liberty 61	(3) South Carolina 75
(7) Drake 87	
(10) Syracuse 69	(7) Drake 76
(2) Baylor 80	
(15) Bucknell 56	(2) Baylor 72

(1) Duke 62
(4) Texas 46
(3) South Carolina 79
(7) Drake 65

(1) Duke 77
(3) South Carolina 68

(1) Duke 71

NATIONAL CHAMPIONSHIP

(1) **Connecticut 82**
(1) Oklahoma 70

**Alamodome
University of Texas, San Antonio, Texas
Monday April 1, 2002**

NCAA Championship Game

Oklahoma 70

	Min	FG M-A	FT M-A	Pts	Reb O-T	A	PF
Caton Hill	32	3-10	1-2	9	3-8	4	4
Rosalind Ross	35	6-13	1-2	17	3-4	1	1
Jamie Talbert	26	2-6	2-2	6	2-4	0	2
Laneishea Caufield	40	3-10	8-9	14	1-3	4	3
Stacey Dales	34	7-15	2-3	18	0-3	1	5
Dionnah Jackson	28	3-8	0-2	6	0-0	2	1
Shannon Selmon	5	0-0	0-0	0	0-0	0	1
TOTALS	200	24-62	14-20	70	9-22	12	17

Three-point FG: 8-20 (Hill 2-3, Ross 4-10, Caufield 0-1, Dales 2-4, Jackson 0-2); **Team Rebounds:** 3; **Blocked Shots:** 2 (Dales, Talbert); **Turnovers:** 15 (Caufield 4, Dales 3, Jackson 3, Hill 2, Ross 2, Talbert); **Steals:** 12 (Caufield, Talbert, Hill 2, Jackson 2, Ross); **Percentages:** 2-Pt FG (.381); 3-Pt FG (.400); Total FG (.387); Free Throws (.700).

Connecticut 82

	Min	FG M-A	FT M-A	Pts	Reb O-T	A	PF
Swin Cash	39	5-9	10-12	20	6-13	4	2
Tamika Williams	36	6-7	0-0	12	5-9	2	2
Asjha Jones	30	9-14	1-2	19	1-9	0	4
Diana Taurasi	3	5-16	3-3	13	1-3	4	3
Sue Bird	36	3-9	8-8	14	0-3	4	3
Ashley Battle	4	1-1	0-0	2	0-0	0	1
Jessica Moore	11	1-1	0-0	2	0-1	0	0
Maria Conlon	5	0-0	0-0	0	0-2	1	1
TOTALS	200	30-57	22-25	82	13-40	15	16

Three-point FG: 0-9 (Taurasi 0-6, Bird 0-3); **Team Rebounds:** 4; **Blocked Shots:** 8 (Jones 5, Cash, Moore, Williams); **Turnovers:** 21 (Cash 6, Jones 5, Bird 4, Taurasi 2, Williams 2, Battle, Conlon); **Steals:** 7 (Cash 2, Taurasi 2, Bird, Williams, Jones); **Percentages:** 2-Pt FG (.625); 3-Pt FG (.000); Total FG (.526); Free Throws (.880).

Oklahoma (Big 12)	30	40— **70**
Connecticut (Big East)	42	40— **82**

Technical Fouls: None. **Officials:** Scott Yarbrough, Lisa Mattingly, Melissa Barlow. **Attendance:** 29,619. **TV Rating:** 4.1/7 share (ESPN).

Final ESPN/USA Today Coaches' Poll

Taken **after** NCAA tournament.

Voted on by panel of 40 women's coaches and media following the NCAA tournament: first place votes in parentheses.

		Pts			Pts
1	Connecticut (40)	1,000	13	Texas	473
2	Oklahoma	960	14	Purdue	445
3	Tennessee	898	15	Baylor	421
4	Duke	875	16	Iowa St.	385
5	Vanderbilt	835	17	BYU	347
6	South Carolina	737	18	Penn St.	325
7	Old Dominion	716	19	La. Tech.	264
8	Stanford	689	20	Drake	244
9	Colorado	647	21	Minnesota	204
10	Kansas St.	560	22	LSU	148
11	North Carolina	512	23	Cincinnati	107
12	Texas Tech	503	24	Colorado St.	83
			25	TCU	79

WOMEN'S FINAL FOUR

at San Antonio, Texas (March 29-31).

Semifinals

Connecticut 79 . . . . Tennessee 56
Oklahoma 86 . . . . Duke 71

Championship

Connecticut 82 . . . . Oklahoma 70

Final Records: Connecticut (36-0), Oklahoma (30-3), Duke (30-3), Tennessee (28-4).

Most Outstanding Player: Swin Cash, Connecticut forward. SEMIFINAL—34 minutes, 13 points, 4 rebounds, 4 blocks; FINAL—39 minutes, 20 points, 13 rebounds, 4 assists, 1 block.

All-Tournament Team: Cash, forward/center Asjha Jones and guard Sue Bird of Connecticut and Stacey Dales and Rosalind Ross of Oklahoma.

Annual Awards

Player of the Year

Sue Bird, Connecticut . . . . . . AP, Broderick, Wade, USBWA, Naismith

Coach of the Year

Brenda Oldfield, Minnesota . . . . AP, USBWA
Geno Auriemma, Connecticut . . . . WBCA, Naismith

Consensus All-America Team

The NCAA Division I players cited most frequently by the Associated Press, US Basketball Writers Assn., the Women's Basketball Coaches Assn. and the Women's Basketball News Service. Holdover from 2000-01 All-America first team in **bold** type; (*) indicates unanimous first team selection.

First Team

	Class	Hgt	Pos
Sue Bird, Connecticut*	Sr.	5-9	G
Stacey Dales, Oklahoma*	Jr.	6-0	G
Alana Beard, Duke*	So.	5-11	G/F
Chantelle Anderson, Vanderbilt	Jr.	6-6	C
LaToya Thomas, Miss. St.*	Jr.	6-2	F

Second Team

	Class	Hgt	Pos
Swin Cash, Connecticut	Sr.	6-2	F
Nicole Powell, Stanford	So.	6-2	F
Kelly Mazzante, Penn St.	So.	6-0	G
Diana Taurasi, Connecticut	So.	6-0	G/F
Angie Welle, Iowa St.	Sr.	6-4	F/C

Other Women's Tournaments

WNIT (Mar. 27 at Eugene, Oregon): Final—Oregon def. Houston, 54-52.
NCAA Division II (Mar. 23 at Rochester, Minn.): Final—Cal Poly-Pomona def. SE Oklahoma St., 73-62.
NCAA Division III (Mar. 16 at Terre Haute, Ind.): Final—UW-Stevens Point def. St. Lawrence, 67-65.
NAIA Division I (Mar. 19 at Jackson, Tenn.): Final—Oklahoma City def. Southern Nazarene (Okla.), 82-73.
NAIA Division II (Mar. 12 at Sioux City, Iowa): Final—Hastings (Neb.) def. Cornerstone (Mich.), 73-69.

NCAA Women's Division I Leaders

Includes games through NCAA and NIT tourneys.

INDIVIDUAL

Scoring

	Cl	Gm	Pts	Avg
Kelly Mazzante, Penn St.	So.	35	872	24.9
LaToya Thomas, Miss. St.	Jr.	31	763	24.6
Janet Holt, Tenn. Tech	Sr.	30	714	23.8
Susan Moran, St. Joseph's	Sr.	32	744	23.3
Chandi Jones, Houston	So.	34	766	22.5
Lenae Williams, DePaul	Sr.	29	653	22.5
Molly Creamer, Bucknell	Jr.	31	695	22.4
Lindsay Whalen, Minnesota	So.	30	667	22.2
Brooke Armistead, Austin Peay	Sr.	31	687	22.2
Jacklyn Winfield, Southern	Sr.	31	666	21.5
Nikki Reddick, Coastal Carolina	So.	29	621	21.4
Jenny Nett, Wofford	Sr.	29	613	21.1
Katharine Hanks, Dartmouth	Jr.	25	517	20.7
Chantelle Anderson, Vanderbilt	Jr.	37	765	20.7
Shameka Jackson, Alabama St.	Jr.	29	599	20.7
Krista Ragan, Oral Roberts	Sr.	29	598	20.6
Angie Welle, Iowa St.	Sr.	33	676	20.5
Linda Frölich, UNLV	Sr.	29	594	20.5
Shauna Geronzin, Canisius	Sr.	28	570	20.4
Sarah Judd, Oakland	Sr.	31	623	20.1

Rebounding

	Cl	Gm	No	Avg
Mandi Carver, Idaho St.	Sr.	27	336	12.4
Jermisha Dosty, St. Mary's	Sr.	29	344	11.9
Rosalee Mason, Manhattan	So.	29	344	11.9
Vanessa Hayden, Florida	So.	29	343	11.8
Jennifer Butler, Massachusetts	Jr.	30	353	11.8
Andrea Gardner, Howard	Sr.	28	325	11.6
Cheryl Moody, Florida Int'l	Sr.	33	378	11.5
Natasha Thomas, UAB	So.	28	319	11.4
Angela Buckner, Wichita St.	So.	24	272	11.3
Sheena Johnson, TX-Arlington	So.	24	271	11.3
Angie Welle, Iowa St.	Sr.	33	372	11.3
Lauren Forsthoff, Bethune-Cook.	Sr.	27	283	10.5
Kat Sungy, Jacksonville	Jr.	27	283	10.5
Gunta Basko, Siena	Jr.	30	314	10.5
Vershaun Jones, Central Mich.	Sr.	28	291	10.4

Assists

	Cl	Gm	No	Avg
La'Terrica Dobin, Northwestern St.	Jr.	29	250	8.6
Sara Nord, Louisville	So.	30	235	7.8
Temeka Johnson, LSU	So.	24	179	7.5
Michele Koclanes, Richmond	Sr.	30	221	7.4
Becki Ashbaugh, Santa Clara	Sr.	31	227	7.3
Erica Vicente, SW Missouri St.	Sr.	29	208	7.2
Krisey Sanders, Chicago St.	Jr.	29	197	6.8
Jess Strom, Penn St.	Fr.	35	235	6.7
Jayme Chikos, Elon	Jr.	27	181	6.7
Shiri Sharon, Duquesne	So.	28	184	6.6
Sheila Lambert, Baylor	Sr.	33	216	6.5
Toccara Williams, Texas A&M	So.	29	187	6.4
Kristen Sharp, Cincinnati	Jr.	32	205	6.4
Jennifer Monti, Harvard	Sr.	28	178	6.4
Amy Wright, Arkansas	Sr.	32	203	6.3
Nicole Powell, Stanford	So.	35	220	6.3
Nina Vecchio, Marist	So.	28	176	6.3
Lindsey Wilson, Iowa St.	Jr.	33	207	6.3
Amy Waugh, Xavier	Jr.	31	194	6.3
Laura Ingham, Nevada	Jr.	28	173	6.2
Cristina Ciocan, South Carolina	So.	30	185	6.2

Blocked Shots

	Cl	Gm	No	Avg
Vanessa Hayden, Florida	So.	29	126	4.3
Sonja Brown, Southern Miss.	Jr.	28	101	3.6
Sarah Richey, La-Lafayette	Jr.	28	86	3.1
Amanda Barksdale, Notre Dame.	Jr.	26	78	3.0
Jordan Adams, New Mexico	Jr.	31	92	3.0

Steals

	Cl	Gm	No	Avg
Shrieka Evans, Grambling	Jr.	28	137	4.9
Latesha Lee, Jackson St.	So.	29	129	4.4
Chanel Spriggs, American	So.	26	110	4.2
Toccara Williams, Texas A&M	So.	29	117	4.0
Kelly Komara, Purdue	Sr.	30	120	4.0

TEAM

Scoring Offense

	Gm	W-L	Pts	Avg
Connecticut	39	39-0	3394	87.0
Duke	35	31-4	2922	83.5
Eastern Ky.	31	23-8	2507	80.9
Stanford	35	32-3	2809	80.3
North Carolina	35	26-9	2797	79.9
Tennessee	34	29-5	2715	79.9
Minnesota	30	22-8	2390	79.7
Morehead St.	29	21-8	2303	79.4
Canisius	28	12-16	2199	78.5

Scoring Defense

	Gm	W-L	Pts	Avg
Connecticut	39	39-0	2012	51.6
TX-San Antonio	28	16-12	1477	52.8
Southern U.	31	26-5	1643	53.0
Louisiana Tech	30	25-5	1605	53.5
Old Dominion	34	28-6	1880	55.3
South Alabama	28	17-11	1564	55.9
Hawaii	31	23-8	1738	56.1
Jackson St.	29	16-13	1626	56.1
Villanova	31	20-11	1756	56.6
New Mexico	31	22-9	1768	57.0
Virginia Tech	32	21-11	1831	57.2

High-Point Games

Individual

No		Opponent	Date
49	Kelly Mazzante, Penn St.	Minnesota	Dec. 28
43	Molly Creamer, Bucknell	Army	Jan. 16
	LaToya Thomas, Mississippi St.	Georgia	Jan. 13
41	Lindsay Whalen, Minnesota	Purdue	Feb. 14
	Laura Kooij, George Mason	Chatt.	Nov. 24
	Lenae Williams, DePaul	Iowa St.	Nov. 21
	Janet Holt, Tennessee Tech	Mississippi	Nov. 15

Scoring Margin

	Off	Def	Mar
Connecticut	87.0	51.6	35.4
Louisiana Tech	76.3	53.5	22.8
Old Dominion	75.3	55.3	20.0
Duke	83.5	64.3	19.2
Stanford	80.3	61.4	18.9
Oklahoma	78.2	61.9	16.3
Cincinnati	74.5	58.9	15.6
Southern U.	68.3	53.0	15.3
Vanderbilt	72.5	57.3	15.2

1901-2002
Through the Years

ESPN
Information Please®
SPORTS ALMANAC

National Champions and NCAA Final Four

The Helms Foundation of Los Angeles, under the direction of founder Bill Schroeder, selected national college basketball champions from 1942-82 and researched retroactive picks from 1901-41. The first NIT tournament and then the NCAA tournament have settled the national championship since 1938, but there are four years (1939, '40, '44 and '54) where the Helms selections differ. In 1939, Helms picked undefeated LIU-Brooklyn (24-0), winners of the NIT. In 1940, Helms picked USC (20-3) although they were beaten by Kansas in the West Regionals of the NCAA tourney. In 1944, Helms picked unbeaten Army (15-0). Army did not lift its policy barring postseason play until the 1961 NIT. In 1954, Helms chose unbeaten Kentucky (25-0), even though Kentucky refused its NCAA bid after seniors Cliff Hagan, Frank Ramsey and Lou Tsioropoulos were declared ineligible.

Multiple champions (1901-37): Chicago, Columbia and Wisconsin (3); Kansas, Minnesota, Notre Dame, Penn, Pittsburgh, Syracuse and Yale (2). **Multiple champions (since 1938):** UCLA (11); Kentucky (7); Indiana (5); Duke and North Carolina (3); Cincinnati, Kansas, Louisville, Michigan St., N.C. State, Oklahoma A&M (now Oklahoma St.) and San Francisco (2).

Year		Record	Head Coach	Outstanding Player
1901	**Yale**	10-4	No coach	G.M. Clark, F
1902	**Minnesota**	11-0	Louis Cooke	W.C. Deering, F
1903	**Yale**	15-1	W.H. Murphy	R.B. Hyatt, F
1904	**Columbia**	17-1	No coach	Harry Fisher, F
1905	**Columbia**	19-1	No coach	Harry Fisher, F
1906	**Dartmouth**	16-2	No coach	George Grebenstein, F
1907	**Chicago**	22-2	Joseph Raycroft	John Schommer, C
1908	**Chicago**	21-2	Joseph Raycroft	John Schommer, C
1909	**Chicago**	12-0	Joseph Raycroft	John Schommer, C
1910	**Columbia**	11-1	Harry Fisher	Ted Kiendl, F
1911	**St. John's-NY**	14-0	Claude Allen	John Keenan, F/C
1912	**Wisconsin**	15-0	Doc Meanwell	Otto Stangel, F
1913	**Navy**	9-0	Louis Wenzell	Laurence Wild, F
1914	**Wisconsin**	15-0	Doc Meanwell	Gene Van Gent, C
1915	**Illinois**	16-0	Ralph Jones	Ray Woods, G
1916	**Wisconsin**	20-1	Doc Meanwell	George Levis, F
1917	**Washington St.**	25-1	Doc Bohler	Roy Bohler, G
1918	**Syracuse**	16-1	Edmund Dollard	Joe Schwarzer, G
1919	**Minnesota**	13-0	Louis Cooke	Arnold Oss, F
1920	**Penn**	22-1	Lon Jourdet	George Sweeney, F
1921	**Penn**	21-2	Edward McNichol	Danny McNichol, G
1922	**Kansas**	16-2	Phog Allen	Paul Endacott, G
1923	**Kansas**	17-1	Phog Allen	Paul Endacott, G
1924	**North Carolina**	25-0	Bo Shepard	Jack Cobb, F
1925	**Princeton**	21-2	Al Wittmer	Art Loeb, G
1926	**Syracuse**	19-1	Lew Andreas	Vic Hanson, F
1927	**Notre Dame**	19-1	George Keogan	John Nyikos, C
1928	**Pittsburgh**	21-0	Doc Carlson	Chuck Hyatt, F
1929	**Montana St.**	36-2	Schubert Dyche	John (Cat) Thompson, F
1930	**Pittsburgh**	23-2	Doc Carlson	Chuck Hyatt, F
1931	**Northwestern**	16-1	Dutch Lonborg	Joe Reiff, C
1932	**Purdue**	17-1	Piggy Lambert	John Wooden, G
1933	**Kentucky**	20-3	Adolph Rupp	Forest Sale, F
1934	**Wyoming**	26-3	Willard Witte	Les Witte, G
1935	**NYU**	19-1	Howard Cann	Sid Gross, F
1936	**Notre Dame**	22-2-1	George Keogan	John Moir, F
1937	**Stanford**	25-2	John Bunn	Hank Luisetti, F

Year		Record	Winner	Head Coach	Outstanding Player
1938	**Temple**	23-2	NIT	James Usilton	Meyer Bloom, G

Year	Champion	Runner-up	Score	Final Two		Third Place
1939	Oregon	Ohio St.	46-33	@ Evanston, IL	Oklahoma	Villanova
1940	Indiana	Kansas	60-42	@ Kansas City	Duquesne	USC
1941	Wisconsin	Washington St.	39-34	@ Kansas City	Arkansas	Pittsburgh
1942	Stanford	Dartmouth	53-38	@ Kansas City	Colorado	Kentucky
1943	Wyoming	Georgetown	46-34	@ New York	DePaul	Texas
1944	Utah	Dartmouth	42-40 (OT)	@ New York	Iowa St.	Ohio St.
1945	Oklahoma A&M	NYU	49-45	@ New York	Arkansas	Ohio St.

Year	Champion	Runner-up	Score	Final Two	Third Place	Fourth Place
1946	Oklahoma A&M	North Carolina	43-40	@ New York	Ohio St.	California
1947	Holy Cross	Oklahoma	58-47	@ New York	Texas	CCNY
1948	Kentucky	Baylor	58-42	@ New York	Holy Cross	Kansas St.
1949	Kentucky	Oklahoma A&M	46-36	@ Seattle	Illinois	Oregon St.
1950	CCNY	Bradley	71-68	@ New York	N.C. State	Baylor
1951	Kentucky	Kansas St.	68-58	@ Minneapolis	Illinois	Oklahoma A&M

Year	Champion	Runner-up	Score	Third Place	Fourth Place	Final Four
1952	Kansas	St. John's	80-63	Illinois	Santa Clara	@ Seattle
1953	Indiana	Kansas	69-68	Washington	LSU	@ Kansas City
1954	La Salle	Bradley	92-76	Penn St.	USC	@ Kansas City
1955	San Francisco	La Salle	77-63	Colorado	Iowa	@ Kansas City
1956	San Francisco	Iowa	83-71	Temple	SMU	@ Evanston, IL
1957	North Carolina	Kansas	54-53 (3OT)	San Francisco	Michigan St.	@ Kansas City
1958	Kentucky	Seattle	84-72	Temple	Kansas St.	@ Louisville
1959	California	West Virginia	71-70	Cincinnati	Louisville	@ Louisville
1960	Ohio St.	California	75-55	Cincinnati	NYU	@ San Francisco
1961	Cincinnati	Ohio St.	70-65 (OT)	St. Joseph's-PA	Utah	@ Kansas City
1962	Cincinnati	Ohio St.	71-59	Wake Forest	UCLA	@ Louisville
1963	Loyola-IL	Cincinnati	60-58 (OT)	Duke	Oregon St.	@ Louisville
1964	UCLA	Duke	98-83	Michigan	Kansas St.	@ Kansas City
1965	UCLA	Michigan	91-80	Princeton	Wichita St.	@ Portland, OR
1966	Texas Western	Kentucky	72-65	Duke	Utah	@ College Park, MD
1967	UCLA	Dayton	79-64	Houston	North Carolina	@ Louisville
1968	UCLA	North Carolina	78-55	Ohio St.	Houston	@ Los Angeles
1969	UCLA	Purdue	92-72	Drake	North Carolina	@ Louisville
1970	UCLA	Jacksonville	80-69	New Mexico St.	St. Bonaventure	@ College Park, MD
1971	UCLA	Villanova	68-62	Western Ky.	Kansas	@ Houston
1972	UCLA	Florida St.	81-76	North Carolina	Louisville	@ Los Angeles
1973	UCLA	Memphis St.	87-66	Indiana	Providence	@ St. Louis
1974	N.C. State	Marquette	76-64	UCLA	Kansas	@ Greensboro, NC
1975	UCLA	Kentucky	92-85	Louisville	Syracuse	@ San Diego
1976	Indiana	Michigan	86-68	UCLA	Rutgers	@ Philadelphia
1977	Marquette	North Carolina	67-59	UNLV	NC-Charlotte	@ Atlanta
1978	Kentucky	Duke	94-88	Arkansas	Notre Dame	@ St. Louis
1979	Michigan St.	Indiana St.	75-64	DePaul	Penn	@ Salt Lake City
1980	Louisville	UCLA	59-54	Purdue	Iowa	@ Indianapolis
1981	Indiana	North Carolina	63-50	Virginia	LSU	@ Philadelphia

Year	Champion	Runner-up	Score	Third Place		Final Four
1982	North Carolina	Georgetown	63-62	Houston	Louisville	@ New Orleans
1983	N.C. State	Houston	54-52	Georgia	Louisville	@ Albuquerque
1984	Georgetown	Houston	84-75	Kentucky	Virginia	@ Seattle
1985	Villanova	Georgetown	66-64	Memphis St.	St. John's	@ Lexington
1986	Louisville	Duke	72-69	Kansas	LSU	@ Dallas
1987	Indiana	Syracuse	74-73	Providence	UNLV	@ New Orleans
1988	Kansas	Oklahoma	83-79	Arizona	Duke	@ Kansas City
1989	Michigan	Seton Hall	80-79 (OT)	Duke	Illinois	@ Seattle
1990	UNLV	Duke	103-73	Arkansas	Georgia Tech	@ Denver
1991	Duke	Kansas	72-65	North Carolina	UNLV	@ Indianapolis
1992	Duke	Michigan	71-51	Cincinnati	Indiana	@ Minneapolis
1993	North Carolina	Michigan	77-71	Kansas	Kentucky	@ New Orleans
1994	Arkansas	Duke	76-72	Arizona	Florida	@ Charlotte
1995	UCLA	Arkansas	89-78	North Carolina	Oklahoma St.	@ Seattle
1996	Kentucky	Syracuse	76-67	UMass	Mississippi St.	@ E. Rutherford, NJ
1997	Arizona	Kentucky	84-79 (OT)	Minnesota	North Carolina	@ Indianapolis
1998	Kentucky	Utah	78-69	Stanford	North Carolina	@ San Antonio
1999	Connecticut	Duke	77-74	Michigan St.	Ohio St.	@ St. Petersburg, FL
2000	Michigan St.	Florida	89-76	Wisconsin	North Carolina	@ Indianapolis
2001	Duke	Arizona	82-72	Michigan St.	Maryland	@ Minneapolis
2002	Maryland	Indiana	64-52	Oklahoma	Kansas	@ Atlanta

Note: Six teams have had their standing in the Final Four vacated for using ineligible players: 1961–St. Joseph's-PA (3rd place); 1971–Villanova (Runner-up) and Western Kentucky (3rd); 1980–UCLA (Runner-up); 1985–Memphis St. (3rd); 1996–UMass (3rd)

The Red Cross Benefit Games, 1943-45

For three seasons during World War II, the NCAA and NIT champions met in a benefit game at Madison Square Garden in New York to raise money for the Red Cross. The NCAA champs won all three games.

Year	Winner	Score	Loser
1943	Wyoming (NCAA)	52-47	St. John's (NIT)
1944	Utah (NCAA)	43-36	St. John's (NIT)
1945	Oklahoma A&M (NCAA)	52-44	DePaul (NIT)

Most Outstanding Player

A Most Outstanding Player has been selected every year of the NCAA tournament. Winners who did not play for the tournament champion are listed in **bold** type. The 1939 and 1951 winners are unofficial and not recognized by the NCAA. Statistics listed are for Final Four games only.

Multiple winners: Lew Alcindor (3); Alex Groza, Bob Kurland, Jerry Lucas and Bill Walton (2).

Year		Gm	FGM	Pct	3PTM	3PTA	FTM	Pct	Reb	Ast	Blk	Stl	PPG
1939	**Jimmy Hull**, Ohio St............	2	15	—	—	—	10	.833	—	—	—	—	20.0
1940	Marv Huffman, Indiana	2	7	—	—	—	4	—	—	—	—	—	9.0
1941	John Kotz, Wisconsin	2	8	—	—	—	6	—	—	—	—	—	11.0
1942	Howie Dallmar, Stanford	2	8	—	—	—	4	.667	—	—	—	—	10.0
1943	Kenny Sailors, Wyoming	2	10	—	—	—	8	.727	—	—	—	—	14.0
1944	Arnie Ferrin, Utah	2	11	—	—	—	6	—	—	—	—	—	14.0
1945	Bob Kurland, Okla. A&M........	2	16	—	—	—	5	—	—	—	—	—	18.5
1946	Bob Kurland, Okla. A&M........	2	21	—	—	—	10	.667	—	—	—	—	26.0
1947	George Kaftan, Holy Cross	2	18	—	—	—	12	.706	—	—	—	—	24.0
1948	Alex Groza, Kentucky...........	2	16	—	—	—	5	—	—	—	—	—	18.5
1949	Alex Groza, Kentucky...........	2	19	—	—	—	14	—	—	—	—	—	26.0
1950	Irwin Dambrot, CCNY	2	12	.429	—	—	4	.500	—	—	—	—	14.0
1951	Bill Spivey, Kentucky...........	2	20	.400	—	—	10	.625	37	—	—	—	25.0
1952	Clyde Lovellette, Kansas........	2	24	—	—	—	18	—	—	—	—	—	33.0
1953	**B.H. Born**, Kansas	2	17	—	—	—	17	—	—	—	—	—	25.5
1954	Tom Gola, La Salle	2	12	—	—	—	14	—	—	—	—	—	19.0
1955	Bill Russell, San Francisco	2	19	—	—	—	9	—	—	—	—	—	23.5
1956	**Hal Lear**, Temple	2	32	—	—	—	16	—	—	—	—	—	40.0
1957	**Wilt Chamberlain**, Kansas	2	18	.514	—	—	19	.704	25	—	—	—	32.5
1958	**Elgin Baylor**, Seattle	2	18	.340	—	—	12	.750	41	—	—	—	24.0
1959	**Jerry West**, West Virginia.......	2	22	.667	—	—	22	.688	25	—	—	—	33.0
1960	Jerry Lucas, Ohio St............	2	16	.667	—	—	3	1.000	23	—	—	—	17.5
1961	**Jerry Lucas**, Ohio St...........	2	20	.714	—	—	16	.941	25	—	—	—	28.0
1962	Paul Hogue, Cincinnati	2	23	.639	—	—	12	.632	38	—	—	—	29.0
1963	**Art Heyman**, Duke	2	18	.409	—	—	15	.682	19	—	—	—	25.5
1964	Walt Hazzard, UCLA	2	11	.550	—	—	8	.667	10	—	—	—	15.0
1965	**Bill Bradley**, Princeton..........	2	34	.630	—	—	19	.950	24	—	—	—	43.5
1966	**Jerry Chambers**, Utah..........	2	25	.532	—	—	20	.833	35	—	—	—	35.0
1967	Lew Alcindor, UCLA	2	14	.609	—	—	11	.458	38	—	—	—	19.5
1968	Lew Alcindor, UCLA	2	22	.629	—	—	9	.900	34	—	—	—	26.5
1969	Lew Alcindor, UCLA	2	23	.676	—	—	16	.640	41	—	—	—	31.0
1970	Sidney Wicks, UCLA............	2	15	.714	—	—	9	.600	34	—	—	—	19.5
1971	**Howard Porter**, Villanova.....	2	20	.488	—	—	7	.778	24	—	—	—	23.5
1972	Bill Walton, UCLA	2	20	.690	—	—	17	.739	41	—	—	—	28.5
1973	Bill Walton, UCLA	2	28	.824	—	—	2	.400	30	—	—	—	29.0
1974	David Thompson, N.C. State......	2	19	.514	—	—	11	.786	17	—	—	—	24.5
1975	Richard Washington, UCLA.......	2	23	.548	—	—	8	.727	20	—	—	—	27.0
1976	Kent Benson, Indiana	2	17	.500	—	—	7	.636	18	—	—	—	20.5
1977	Butch Lee, Marquette...........	2	11	.344	—	—	8	1.000	6	2	1	1	15.0
1978	Jack Givens, Kentucky..........	2	28	.651	—	—	8	.667	17	4	1	3	32.0
1979	Magic Johnson, Michigan St.	2	17	.680	—	—	19	.864	17	3	0	2	26.5
1980	Darrell Griffith, Louisville	2	23	.622	—	—	11	.688	7	15	0	2	28.5
1981	Isiah Thomas, Indiana............	2	14	.560	—	—	9	.818	4	9	3	4	18.5
1982	James Worthy, N. Carolina......	2	20	.741	—	—	2	.286	8	9	0	4	21.0
1983	**Akeem Olajuwon**, Houston ...2	2	16	.552	—	—	9	.643	40	3	2	5	20.5
1984	Patrick Ewing, Georgetown	2	8	.571	—	—	2	1.000	18	1	15	1	9.0
1985	Ed Pinckney, Villanova	2	8	.571	—	—	12	.750	15	6	3	0	14.0
1986	Pervis Ellison, Louisville..........	2	15	.600	—	—	6	.750	24	2	3	1	18.0
1987	Keith Smart, Indiana	2	14	.636	0	1	7	.778	7	7	0	2	17.5
1988	Danny Manning, Kansas	2	25	.556	0	1	6	.667	17	4	8	9	28.0
1989	Glen Rice, Michigan.............	2	24	.490	7	16	4	1.000	16	1	0	3	29.5
1990	Anderson Hunt, UNLV...........	2	19	.613	9	16	2	.500	4	9	1	1	24.5
1991	Christian Laettner, Duke	2	12	.545	1	1	21	.913	17	2	1	2	23.0
1992	Bobby Hurley, Duke	2	10	.417	7	12	8	.800	3	11	0	3	17.5
1993	Donald Williams, N. Carolina 2	2	15	.652	10	14	10	1.000	4	1	0	2	25.0
1994	Corliss Williamson, Arkansas 2	2	21	.500	0	0	10	.714	21	8	3	4	26.0
1995	Ed O'Bannon, UCLA...........	2	16	.457	3	8	10	.769	25	3	1	7	22.5
1996	Tony Delk, Kentucky	2	15	.417	8	16	6	.546	9	2	3	2	22.0
1997	Miles Simon, Arizona	2	17	.459	3	10	17	.773	8	6	0	1	24.0
1998	Jeff Sheppard, Kentucky.........	2	16	.552	4	10	7	.778	10	7	0	4	21.5
1999	Richard Hamilton, Connecticut 2	2	20	.513	3	7	8	.727	12	4	1	2	25.5
2000	Mateen Cleaves, Michigan St. 2	2	8	.444	3	4	10	.833	6	5	0	2	14.5
2001	Shane Battier, Duke.............	2	13	.464	5	12	12	.706	19	8	6	2	21.5
2002	Juan Dixon, Maryland	2	16	.593	7	15	12	.800	8	5	0	7	25.5

Final Four All-Decade Teams

To celebrate the 50th anniversary of the NCAA tournament in 1989, five All-Decade teams were selected by a blue ribbon panel of coaches and administrators. An All-Time Final Four team was also chosen. Selections were actually made prior to the 1988 tournament.

Selection panel: Vic Bubas, Denny Crum, Wayne Duke, Dave Gavitt, Joe B. Hall, Jud Heathcote, Hank Iba, Pete Newell, Dean Smith, John Thompson and John Wooden.

All-Time Team

	Years
Lew Alcindor, UCLA	1967-69
Larry Bird, Indiana St.	1979
Wilt Chamberlain, Kansas	1957
Magic Johnson, Mich. St.	1979
Michael Jordan, N. Carolina	1982

All-1950s

	Years
Elgin Baylor, Seattle	1958
Wilt Chamberlain, Kansas	1957
Tom Gola, La Salle	1954
K.C. Jones, San Francisco	1955
Clyde Lovellette, Kansas	1952
Oscar Robertson, Cinn.	1959-60
Guy Rodgers, Temple	1958
Lennie Rosenbluth, N. Carolina	1957
Bill Russell, San Francisco	1955-56
Jerry West, West Virginia	1959

All-1970s

	Years
Kent Benson, Indiana	1976
Larry Bird, Indiana St.	1979
Jack Givens, Kentucky	1978
Magic Johnson, Mich. St.	1979
Marques Johnson, UCLA	1975-76
Scott May, Indiana	1976
David Thompson, N.C. State	1974
Bill Walton, UCLA	1972-74
Sidney Wicks, UCLA	1969-71
Keith Wilkes, UCLA	1972-74

All-1940s

	Years
Ralph Beard, Kentucky	1948-49
Howie Dallmar, Stanford	1942
Dwight Eddleman, Illinois	1949
Arnie Ferrin, Utah	1944
Alex Groza, Kentucky	1948-49
George Kaftan, Holy Cross	1947
Bob Kurland, Okla. A&M	1945-46
Jim Pollard, Stanford	1942
Kenny Sailors, Wyoming	1943
Gerry Tucker, Oklahoma	1947

All-1960s

	Years
Lew Alcindor, UCLA	1967-69
Bill Bradley, Princeton	1965
Gail Goodrich, UCLA	1964-65
John Havlicek, Ohio St.	1961-62
Elvin Hayes, Houston	1967
Walt Hazzard, UCLA	1964
Jerry Lucas, Ohio St	1960-61
Jeff Mullins, Duke	1964
Cazzie Russell, Michigan	1965
Charlie Scott, N. Carolina	1968-69

All-1980s

	Years
Steve Alford, Indiana	1987
Johnny Dawkins, Duke	1986
Patrick Ewing, Georgetown	1982-84
Darrell Griffith, Louisville	1980
Michael Jordan, N. Carolina	1982
Rodney McCray, Louisville	1980
Akeem Olajuwon, Houston	1983-84
Ed Pinckney, Villanova	1985
Isiah Thomas, Indiana	1981
James Worthy, N. Carolina	1982

Note: Lew Alcindor later changed his name to Kareem Abdul-Jabbar; Keith Wilkes later changed his first name to Jamaal; and Akeem Olajuwon later changed the spelling of his first name to Hakeem.

Seeds at the Final Four

Year	Seeds (Total)	Teams
1979	1,2,2,9 (14)	Indiana St., **Michigan St.**, DePaul, Pennsylvania
1980	2,5,6,8 (21)	**Louisville**, Iowa, Purdue, UCLA
1981	1,1,2,3 (7)	Virginia, LSU, N. Carolina, **Indiana**
1982	1,1,3,6 (11)	**N. Carolina**, Georgetown, Louisville, Houston
1983	1,1,4,6 (12)	Houston, Louisville, Georgia, **N.C. State**
1984	1,1,2,7 (11)	Kentucky, **Georgetown**, Houston, Virginia
1985	1,1,2,8 (12)	St. John's, Georgetown, Memphis, **Villanova**
1986	1,1,2,11 (15)	Duke, Kansas, **Louisville**, LSU
1987	1,1,2,6 (10)	UNLV, **Indiana**, Syracuse, Providence
1988	1,1,2,6 (10)	Arizona, Oklahoma, Duke, **Kansas**
1989	1,2,3,3 (9)	Illinois, Duke, Seton Hall, **Michigan**
1990	1,3,4,4 (12)	**UNLV**, Duke, Ga. Tech, Arkansas
1991	1,1,2,3 (7)	UNLV, N. Carolina, **Duke**, Kansas
1992	1,2,4,6 (13)	**Duke**, Indiana, Cincinnati, Michigan
1993	1,1,1,2 (5)	**N. Carolina**, Kentucky, Michigan, Kansas
1994	1,2,2,3 (8)	**Arkansas**, Arizona, Duke, Florida
1995	1,2,2,4 (9)	**UCLA**, Arkansas, N. Carolina, Okla. St.
1996	1,1,4,5 (11)	**Kentucky**, UMass, Syracuse, Miss. St.
1997	1,1,1,4 (7)	Kentucky, N. Carolina, Minnesota, **Arizona**
1998	1,2,3,3 (9)	N. Carolina, **Kentucky**, Stanford, Utah
1999	1,1,1,4 (7)	**Connecticut**, Duke, Michigan St., Ohio St.
2000	1,5,8,8 (22)	**Michigan St.**, Florida, Wisconsin, N. Carolina
2001	1,1,2,3 (7)	**Duke**, Michigan St., Arizona, Maryland
2002	1,1,2,5 (9)	**Maryland**, Kansas, Oklahoma, Indiana

All-Time Seeds Records

All-time records of NCAA tournament seeds since tourney began seeding teams in 1979. Records are through the 2002 NCAA Tournament. Note that 1st refers to championships. 2nd refers to runners-up and FF refers to Final Four appearances not including 1st and 2nd place finishes.

Seed	W	L	Pct.	1st	2nd	FF
1	293	84	.777	13	9	19
2	211	91	.699	5	6	9
3	144	94	.605	2	4	4
4	133	95	.583	1	1	6
5	109	97	.529	0	2	2
6	130	94	.580	2	1	3
7	77	96	.445	0	0	1
8	75	95	.441	1	1	2
9	55	97	.362	0	0	1
10	67	96	.411	0	0	0
11	42	92	.313	0	0	1
12	39	92	.298	0	0	0
13	18	72	.200	0	0	0
14	15	72	.172	0	0	0
15	4	72	.053	0	0	0
16	0	72	.000	0	0	0

Collegiate Commissioners Association Tournament

The Collegiate Commissioners Association staged an eight-team tournament for teams that didn't make the NCAA tournament in 1974 and '75.

Most Valuable Players: 1974–Kent Benson, Indiana; 1975–Bob Elliot, Arizona.

Year	Winner	Score	Loser	Site
1974	Indiana	85-60	USC	St. Louis
1975	Drake	83-76	Arizona	Louisville

NCAA Tournament Appearances

App		W-L	F4	Championships	App		W-L	F4	Championships
44	Kentucky	91-39	13	7 (1948-49,51,58,78,96,98)	22	Ohio St.	37-21	9	1 (1960)
38	UCLA	85-31	15	11 (1964-65,67-73,75,95)	22	Illinois	29-23	4	None
35	N. Carolina	81-35	15	3 (1957,82,93)	21	DePaul	20-24	2	None
31	Indiana	57-26	8	5 (1940,53,76,81,87)	21	Arizona	34-20	3	1 (1997)
31	Kansas	65-31	11	2 (1952,88)	21	Cincinnati	38-20	6	2 (1961-62)
29	Louisville	48-31	7	2 (1980,86)	21	Oklahoma	27-21	4	None
27	Syracuse	40-28	3	None	20	Michigan	41-19	6	1 (1989)
27	St. John's	27-29	2	None	20	Iowa	27-22	3	None
26	Arkansas	39-26	6	1 (1994)	20	Texas	19-23	2	None
26	Duke	75-23	13	3 (1991-92, 2001)	20	Missouri	17-20	0	None
26	Notre Dame	27-30	1	None	19	Purdue	26-19	2	None
25	Villanova	37-25	3	1 (1985)	19	BYU	11-22	0	None
25	Temple	31-25	2	None	19	Oklahoma St.	30-18	5	2 (1945-46)
23	Connecticut	30-23	1	1 (1999)	19	Maryland	32-18	2	1 (2002)
23	Utah	32-26	4	1 (1944)	19	Pennsylvania	13-21	1	None
22	Kansas St.	27-26	4	None	18	Houston	26-23	5	None
22	Georgetown	38-21	4	1 (1984)	18	West Virginia	13-18	1	None
22	Princeton	13-26	1	None	18	N.C. State	28-17	3	2 (1974,83)
22	Marquette	28-23	2	1 (1977)	18	Western Ky.	15-19	1	None

Note: Although all NCAA tournament appearances are included above, the NCAA has officially voided the records of Villanova (4-1) and Western Ky. (4-1) in 1971; UCLA (5-1) in 1980 and again (0-1) in 1999; Oregon St. (2-3) from 1980-82; Memphis (9-5) from 1982-86; DePaul (6-4) from 1986-89; N.C. State (0-2) from 1987-88; Kentucky (2-1) and Maryland (1-1) in 1988; Missouri (3-1) in 1994; Connecticut (2-1) and Purdue (1-1) in 1996; Arizona (0-1) in 1999.

All-Time NCAA Division I Tournament Leaders

Through 2002; minimum of six games; **Last** column indicates final year played.

CAREER

Scoring

	Points	Yrs	Last	Gm	Pts
1	Christian Laettner, Duke	4	1992	23	407
2	Elvin Hayes, Houston	3	1968	13	358
3	Danny Manning, Kansas	4	1988	16	328
4	Oscar Robertson, Cincinnati	3	1960	10	324
5	Glen Rice, Michigan	4	1989	13	308
6	Lew Alcindor, UCLA	3	1969	12	304
7	Bill Bradley, Princeton	3	1965	9	303
	Corliss Williamson, Arkansas	3	1995	15	303
	Juan Dixon, Maryland	4	2002	16	294
10	Austin Carr, Notre Dame	3	1971	7	289

	Average	Yrs	Last	Pts	Avg
1	Austin Carr, Notre Dame	3	1971	289	41.3
2	Bill Bradley, Princeton	3	1965	303	33.7
3	Oscar Robertson, Cincinnati	3	1960	324	32.4
4	Jerry West, West Virginia	3	1960	275	30.6
5	Bob Pettit, LSU	2	1954	183	30.5
6	Dan Issel, Kentucky	3	1970	176	29.3
	Jim McDaniels, Western Ky.	2	1971	176	29.3
8	Dwight Lamar, SW Louisiana	2	1973	175	29.2
9	Bo Kimble, Loyola-CA	3	1990	204	29.1
10	David Robinson, Navy	3	1987	200	28.6

Rebounds

	Total	Yrs	Last	Gm	No
1	Elvin Hayes, Houston	3	1968	13	222
2	Lew Alcindor, UCLA	3	1969	12	201
3	Jerry Lucas, Ohio St.	3	1962	12	197
4	Bill Walton, UCLA	3	1974	12	176
5	Christian Laettner, Duke	4	1992	23	169
6	Tim Duncan, Wake Forest	4	1997	11	165
7	Paul Hogue, Cincinnati	3	1962	12	160
8	Sam Lacey, New Mexico St.	3	1970	11	157
9	Derrick Coleman, Syracuse	4	1990	14	155
10	Akeem Olajuwon, Houston	3	1984	15	153

	Average	Yrs	Last	Reb	Avg
1	Johnny Green, Michigan St.	2	1959	118	19.7
2	Artis Gilmore, Jacksonville	2	1971	115	19.2
3	Paul Silas, Creighton	3	1964	111	18.5
4	Len Chappell, Wake Forest	2	1962	137	17.1
5	Elvin Hayes, Houston	3	1968	222	17.1
6	Lew Alcindor, UCLA	3	1969	201	16.8
7	Jerry Lucas, Ohio St.	3	1962	197	16.4
8	Tim Duncan, Wake Forest	4	1997	165	15.0
9	Bill Walton, UCLA	3	1974	176	14.7
10	Sam Lacey, New Mexico St.	3	1970	157	14.3

3-Pt Field Goals

	Total	Yrs	Last	Gm	No
1	Bobby Hurley, Duke	4	1993	20	42
2	Tony Delk, Kentucky	4	1996	17	40
3	Jeff Fryer, Loyola-CA	3	1990	7	38
	Donald Williams, North Carolina	4	1995	15	38
	Juan Dixon, Maryland	4	2002	16	38

Assists

	Total	Yrs	Last	Gm	No
1	Bobby Hurley, Duke	4	1993	20	145
2	Sherman Douglas, Syracuse	4	1989	14	106
3	Greg Anthony, UNLV	3	1991	15	100
4	Mark Wade, UNLV	2	1987	8	93
	Rumeal Robinson, Michigan	3	1990	11	93
	Jacque Vaughn, Kansas	4	1997	13	93
	Anthony Epps, Kentucky	4	1997	18	93

SINGLE TOURNAMENT

Scoring

	Points	Year	Gm	Pts
1	Glen Rice, Michigan	1989	6	184
2	Bill Bradley, Princeton	1965	5	177
3	Elvin Hayes, Houston	1968	5	167
4	Danny Manning, Kansas	1988	6	163
5	Hal Lear, Temple	1956	5	160
	Jerry West, West Virginia	1959	5	160

	Average	Year	Gm	Pts	Avg
1	Austin Carr, Notre Dame	1970	3	158	52.7
2	Austin Carr, Notre Dame	1971	3	125	41.7
3	Jerry Chambers, Utah	1966	4	143	35.8
	Bo Kimble, Loyola-CA	1990	4	143	35.8
5	Bill Bradley, Princeton	1965	5	177	35.4
6	Clyde Lovellette, Kansas	1952	4	141	35.3

Rebounds

	Total	Year	Gm	No	Avg
1	Elvin Hayes, Houston	1968	5	97	19.4
2	Artis Gilmore, Jacksonville	1970	5	93	18.6
3	Elgin Baylor, Seattle	1958	5	91	18.2
4	Sam Lacey, New Mexico St.	1970	5	90	18.0
5	Clarence Glover, Western Ky.	1971	5	89	17.8

Assists

	Total	Year	Gm	No	Avg
1	Mark Wade, UNLV	1987	5	61	12.2
2	Rumeal Robinson, Michigan	1989	6	56	9.3
3	Sherman Douglas, Syracuse	1987	6	49	8.2
4	Bobby Hurley, Duke	1992	6	47	7.8
5	Lazarus Sims, Syracuse	1996	6	46	7.7

SINGLE GAME

Scoring

	Points	Year	Pts
1	Austin Carr, Notre Dame vs Ohio Univ	1970	61
2	Bill Bradley, Princeton vs Wichita St.	1965	58
3	Oscar Robertson, Cincinnati vs Arkansas	1958	56
4	Austin Carr, Notre Dame vs Kentucky	1970	52
	Austin Carr, Notre Dame vs TCU	1971	52
6	David Robinson, Navy vs Michigan	1987	50
7	Elvin Hayes, Houston vs Loyola-IL	1968	49
8	Hal Lear, Temple vs SMU	1956	48
9	Austin Carr, Notre Dame vs Houston	1971	47
10	Dave Corzine, DePaul vs Louisville	1978	46
11	Bob Houbregs, Washington vs Seattle	1953	45
	Austin Carr, Notre Dame vs Iowa	1970	45
	Bo Kimble, Loyola-CA vs New Mexico St.	1990	45
14	Seven players tied with 44 each.		

Rebounds

	Total	Year	No
1	Fred Cohen, Temple vs UConn	1956	34
2	Nate Thurmond, Bowl. Green vs Miss. St.	1963	31
3	Jerry Lucas, Ohio St. vs Kentucky	1961	30
4	Toby Kimball, UConn vs St. Joseph's-PA	1965	29
5	Elvin Hayes, Houston vs Pacific	1966	28

Assists

	Total	Year	No
1	Mark Wade, UNLV vs Indiana	1987	18
2	Sam Crawford, N. Mexico St. vs Nebraska	1993	16
3	Kenny Patterson, DePaul vs Syracuse	1985	15
	Keith Smart, Indiana vs Auburn	1987	15
5	Six players tied with 14 each.		

SINGLE FINAL FOUR GAME

Letters in the **Year** column indicate the following: C for Consolation Game, F for Final and S for Semifinal.

Scoring

	Points	Year	Pts
1	Bill Bradley, Princeton vs Wichita St	1965-C	58
2	Hal Lear, Temple vs SMU	1956-C	48
3	Bill Walton, UCLA vs Memphis St	1973-F	44
4	Bob Houbregs, Washington vs LSU	1953-C	42
	Jack Egan, St. Joseph's-PA vs Utah	1961-C	42*
	Gail Goodrich, UCLA vs Michigan	1965-C	42
7	Jack Givens, Kentucky vs Duke	1978-F	41
8	Oscar Robertson, Cincinnati vs L'ville	1959-C	39
	Al Wood, N. Carolina vs Virginia	1981-S	39
10	Jerry West, West Va. vs Louisville	1959-S	38
	Jerry Chambers, Utah vs Texas Western	1966-S	38
	Freddie Banks, UNLV vs Indiana	1987-S	38

*Four overtimes.

Rebounds

	Total	Year	No
1	Bill Russell, San Francisco vs Iowa	1956-F	27
2	Elvin Hayes, Houston vs UCLA	1967-S	24
3	Bill Russell, San Francisco vs SMU	1956-S	23
4	Four players tied with 22 each.		

Assists

	Total	Year	No
1	Mark Wade, UNLV vs Indiana	1987-S	18
2	Rumeal Robinson, Michigan vs Illinois	1989-S	12
	Edgar Padilla, UMass vs Ky.	1996-S	12
4	Michael Jackson, G'town vs St. John's	1985-S	11
	Milt Wagner, Louisville vs LSU	1986-S	11
	Rumeal Robinson, Mich. vs Seton Hall	1989-F	11*

*Overtime.

Teams in Both NCAA and NIT

Fourteen teams played in both the NCAA and NIT tournaments from 1940-52. Colorado (1940), Utah (1944), Kentucky (1949) and BYU (1951) won one of the titles, while CCNY won two in 1950, beating Bradley in both championship games.

Year		NIT	NCAA
1940	Colorado	**Won Final**	Lost 1st Rd
	Duquesne	Lost Final	Lost 2nd Rd
1944	Utah	Lost 1st Rd	**Won Final**
1949	Kentucky	Lost 2nd Rd	**Won Final**
1950	CCNY	**Won Final**	**Won Final**
	Bradley	Lost Final	Lost Final
1951	BYU	**Won Final**	Lost 2nd Rd
	St. John's	Lost 3rd Rd	Lost 2nd Rd
	N.C. State	Lost 2nd Rd	Lost 2nd Rd
	Arizona	Lost 2nd Rd	Lost 1st Rd
1952	St. John's	Lost 2nd Rd	Lost Final
	Dayton	Lost Final	Lost 1st Rd
	Duquesne	Lost 3rd Rd	Lost 2nd Rd
	Saint Louis	Lost 2nd Rd	Lost 2nd Rd

Most Popular Final Four Sites

The NCAA has staged its Men's Division I championship—the Final Two (1939-51) and Final Four (since 1952)—at 32 different arenas and indoor stadiums in 27 different cities. The following facilities have all hosted the event more than once.

No	Arena	Years
9	Municipal Auditorium (KC)	1940-42, 53-55, 57, 61, 64
7	Madison Sq. Garden (NYC)	1943-48, 50
6	Freedom Hall (Louisville)	1958-59, 62-63, 67, 69
3	Kingdome (Seattle)	1984, 89, 95
	RCA Dome (Indianapolis)	1991, 97, 2000
	Superdome (New Orleans)	1982, 87, 93
2	Cole Field House (College Park, Md.)	1966, 70
	Edmundson Pavilion (Seattle)	1949, 52
	HHH Metrodome (Minneapolis)	1992, 2001
	LA Sports Arena	1968, 72
	St. Louis Arena	1973, 78
	Spectrum (Philadelphia)	1976, 81

NIT Championship

The National Invitation Tournament began under the sponsorship of the Metropolitan New York Basketball Writers Association in 1938. The NIT is now administered by the Metropolitan Intercollegiate Basketball Association. All championship games have been played at Madison Square Garden.

Multiple winners: St. John's (5); Bradley (4); BYU, Dayton, Kentucky, LIU-Brooklyn, Michigan, Minnesota, Providence, Temple, Tulsa, Virginia and Virginia Tech (2).

Year	Winner	Score	Loser	Year	Winner	Score	Loser
1938	Temple	60-36	Colorado	1971	North Carolina	84-66	Georgia Tech
1939	LIU-Brooklyn	44-32	Loyola-IL	1972	Maryland	100-69	Niagara
1940	Colorado	51-40	Duquesne	1973	Virginia Tech	92-91 (OT)	Notre Dame
1941	LIU-Brooklyn	56-42	Ohio Univ.	1974	Purdue	97-81	Utah
1942	West Virginia	47-45	Western Ky.	1975	Princeton	80-69	Providence
1943	St. John's	48-27	Toledo	1976	Kentucky	71-67	NC-Charlotte
1944	St. John's	47-39	DePaul	1977	St. Bonaventure	94-91	Houston
1945	DePaul	71-54	Bowling Green	1978	Texas	101-93	N.C. State
1946	Kentucky	46-45	Rhode Island	1979	Indiana	53-52	Purdue
1947	Utah	49-45	Kentucky	1980	Virginia	58-55	Minnesota
1948	Saint Louis	65-52	NYU	1981	Tulsa	86-84 (OT)	Syracuse
1949	San Francisco	48-47	Loyola-IL	1982	Bradley	67-58	Purdue
1950	CCNY	69-61	Bradley	1983	Fresno St.	69-60	DePaul
1951	BYU	62-43	Dayton	1984	Michigan	83-63	Notre Dame
1952	La Salle	75-64	Dayton	1985	UCLA	65-62	Indiana
1953	Seton Hall	58-46	St. John's	1986	Ohio St.	73-63	Wyoming
1954	Holy Cross	71-62	Duquesne	1987	Southern Miss.	84-80	La Salle
1955	Duquesne	70-58	Dayton	1988	Connecticut	72-67	Ohio St.
1956	Louisville	93-80	Dayton	1989	St. John's	73-65	Saint Louis
1957	Bradley	84-83	Memphis St.	1990	Vanderbilt	74-72	Saint Louis
1958	Xavier-OH	78-74 (OT)	Dayton	1991	Stanford	78-72	Oklahoma
1959	St. John's	76-71 (OT)	Bradley	1992	Virginia	81-76 (OT)	Notre Dame
1960	Bradley	88-72	Providence	1993	Minnesota	62-61	Georgetown
1961	Providence	62-59	Saint Louis	1994	Villanova	80-73	Vanderbilt
1962	Dayton	73-67	St. John's	1995	Virginia Tech	65-64 (OT)	Marquette
1963	Providence	81-66	Canisius	1996	Nebraska	60-56	St. Joseph's
1964	Bradley	86-54	New Mexico	1997	Michigan	82-72	Florida St.
1965	St. John's	55-51	Villanova	1998	Minnesota	79-72	Penn St.
1966	BYU	97-84	NYU	1999	California	61-60	Clemson
1967	Southern Illinois	71-56	Marquette	2000	Wake Forest	71-61	Notre Dame
1968	Dayton	61-48	Kansas	2001	Tulsa	79-60	Alabama
1969	Temple	89-76	Boston Coll.	2002	Memphis	72-62	South Carolina
1970	Marquette	65-53	St. John's				

Most Valuable Player

A Most Valuable Player has been selected every year of the NIT tournament. Winners who did not play for the tournament champion are listed in **bold** type.

Multiple winners: None. However, Tom Gola of La Salle is the only player to be named MVP in the NIT (1952) and Most Outstanding Player of the NCAA tournament (1954).

Year
1938 Don Shields, Temple
1939 **Bill Lloyd**, St. John's
1940 Bob Doll, Colorado
1941 **Frank Baumholtz**, Ohio U.
1942 Rudy Baric, West Virginia
1943 Harry Boykoff, St. John's
1944 Bill Kotsores, St. John's
1945 George Mikan, DePaul
1946 **Ernie Calverley**, Rhode Island
1947 Vern Gardner, Utah
1948 Ed Macauley, Saint Louis
1949 Don Lofgan, San Francisco
1950 Ed Warner, CCNY
1951 Roland Minson, BYU
1952 Tom Gola, La Salle
    & Norm Grekin, La Salle
1953 Walter Dukes, Seton Hall
1954 Togo Palazzi, Holy Cross
1955 **Maurice Stokes**, St. Francis-PA
1956 Charlie Tyra, Louisville
1957 **Win Wilfong**, Memphis St.
1958 Hank Stein, Xavier-OH
1959 Tony Jackson, St. John's
1960 **Lenny Wilkens**, Providence
1961 Vinny Ernst, Providence
1962 Bill Chmielewski, Dayton
1963 Ray Flynn, Providence

Year
1964 Lavern Tart, Bradley
1965 Ken McIntyre, St. John's
1966 **Bill Melchionni**, Villanova
1967 Walt Frazier, So. Illinois
1968 Don May, Dayton
1969 **Terry Driscoll**, Boston College
1970 Dean Meminger, Marquette
1971 Bill Chamberlain, N. Carolina
1972 Tom McMillen, Maryland
1973 **John Shumate**, Notre Dame
1974 **Mike Sojourner**, Utah
1975 **Ron Lee**, Oregon
1976 **Cedric Maxwell**, NC-Charlotte
1977 Greg Sanders, St. Bonaventure
1978 Ron Baxter, Texas
    & Jim Krivacs, Texas
1979 Clarence Carter, Indiana
    & Ray Tolbert, Indiana
1980 Ralph Sampson, Virginia
1981 Greg Stewart, Tulsa
1982 Mitchell Anderson, Bradley
1983 Ron Anderson, Fresno St.
1984 Tim McCormick, Michigan
1985 Reggie Miller, UCLA
1986 Brad Sellers, Ohio St.
1987 Randolph Keys, So. Miss.
1988 Phil Gamble, Connecticut

Year
1989 Jayson Williams, St. John's
1990 Scott Draud, Vanderbilt
1991 Adam Keefe, Stanford
1992 Bryant Stith, Virginia
1993 Voshon Lenard, Minnesota
1994 **Doremus Bennerman**, Siena
1995 Shawn Smith, Va. Tech
1996 Erick Strickland, Nebraska
1997 Robert Traylor, Michigan
1998 Kevin Clark, Minnesota
1999 Sean Lampley, California
2000 Robert O'Kelley, Wake Forest
2001 Marcus Hill, Tulsa
2002 Dajuan Wagner, Memphis

All-Time NIT Team

As selected by a media panel (Mar. 15, 1997).

Walt Frazier, S. Illinois
George Mikan, DePaul
Tom Gola, La Salle
Maurice Stokes, St. Francis-PA
Ralph Beard, Kentucky

All-Time Winningest Division I Teams
Top 25 Winning Percentage

Division I schools with best winning percentages through 2001-02 season (including tournament games). Years in Division I only; minimum 20 years. NCAA tournament columns indicate years in tournament, record and number of championships.

		First Year	Yrs	Games	Won	Lost	Tied	Pct	NCAA Tourney Yrs	W-L	Titles
1	Kentucky	1903	99	2386	1817	568	1	.762	44	91-39	7
2	North Carolina	1911	92	2439	1789	650	0	.733	35	81-35	3
3	UNLV	1959	44	1256	904	352	0	.720	14	30-13	1
4	Kansas	1899	104	2516	1771	745	0	.704	31	65-31	2
5	UCLA	1920	83	2165	1510	655	0	.697	38	85-31	11
6	St. John's	1908	95	2391	1641	750	0	.686	27	27-29	0
7	Duke	1906	97	2448	1680	768	0	.686	26	75-23	3
8	Syracuse	1901	101	2304	1572	732	0	.682	27	40-28	0
9	Western Kentucky	1915	83	2153	1439	714	0	.668	18	15-19	0
10	Utah	1909	94	2234	1467	767	0	.657	23	32-26	1
11	Arkansas	1924	79	2091	1368	723	0	.654	26	39-26	1
12	Indiana	1901	102	2331	1519	812	0	.652	31	57-26	5
13	Temple	1895	106	2448	1590	858	0	.650	25	31-25	0
14	Louisville	1912	88	2177	1406	771	0	.646	29	48-31	2
15	Notre Dame	1898	97	2334	1505	828	1	.645	26	27-30	0
16	Illinois	1906	97	2224	1433	791	0	.644	22	29-23	0
17	Arizona	1905	97	2194	1410	784	0	.643	21	34-20	1
18	Weber St.	1963	40	1136	729	407	0	.642	12	6-13	0
19	DePaul	1924	79	1943	1240	703	0	.638	21	20-24	0
20	Pennsylvania	1897	102	2405	1533	870	2	.638	19	13-21	0
21	Villanova	1921	82	2118	1346	772	0	.636	25	37-25	1
22	Purdue	1897	104	2262	1434	838	0	.634	19	26-19	0
23	Cincinnati	1902	101	2246	1423	823	0	.634	21	38-20	2
24	Murray St.	1926	77	1988	1256	732	0	.632	11	1-11	0
25	Connecticut	1901	99	2101	1318	783	0	.627	23	30-23	1

Top 35 All-Time Victories

Division I schools with most victories through 2001-02 (including postseason tournaments). Minimum 20 years in Division I.

	Wins		Wins		Wins		Wins
1 Kentucky	1817	10 UCLA	1510	19 Cincinnati	1423	28 Ohio St.	1358
2 North Carolina	1789	11 Notre Dame	1505	20 Arizona	1410	29 Montana St.	1348
3 Kansas	1771	12 Oregon St.	1503	21 Louisville	1406	Alabama	1348
4 Duke	1680	13 Utah	1467	22 N.C. State	1401	31 Villanova	1346
5 St. John's	1641	14 Princeton	1459	23 West Virginia	1398	32 Washington St.	1345
6 Temple	1590	15 Western Ky.	1439	24 Bradley	1396	33 Iowa	1341
7 Syracuse	1572	16 Purdue	1434	25 Texas	1386	34 Oklahoma	1337
8 Penn	1533	17 Washington	1433	26 Arkansas	1368	35 USC	1335
9 Indiana	1519	Illinois	1433	27 Fordham	1365		

Top 30 Single-Season Victories

Division I schools with most victories in a season through 2001-02 (including postseason tournaments). NCAA champions in **bold** type.

		Year	Record			Year	Record			Year	Record
1	UNLV	1987	37-2		Kentucky	1947	34-3		Duke	1998	32-4
	Duke	1999	37-2		**Georgetown**	1984	34-3		Louisville	1983	32-4
	Duke	1986	37-3		Arkansas	1991	34-4		Kentucky	1986	32-4
4	**Kentucky**	1948	36-3		**N. Carolina**	1993	34-4		N. Carolina	1987	32-4
5	Massachusetts*	1996	35-2		N. Carolina	1998	34-4		Temple	1987	32-4
	Georgetown	1985	35-3	25	Indiana St.	1979	33-1		**Maryland**	2002	32-4
	Arizona	1988	35-3		**Louisville**	1980	33-3		Bradley	1950	32-5
	Duke	2001	35-4		Kansas	2002	33-4		Connecticut	1998	32-5
	Kansas	1986	35-4		Michigan St.	1999	33-5		Tulsa	2000	32-5
	Kansas	1998	35-4		UNLV	1986	33-5		Iowa St.	2000	32-5
	Kentucky	1998	35-4	30	**N. Carolina**	1957	32-0		Marshall	1947	32-5
	Oklahoma	1988	35-4		**Indiana**	1976	32-0		Houston	1984	32-5
	UNLV	1990	35-5		**Kentucky**	1949	32-2		Bradley	1951	32-6
	Kentucky	1997	35-5		**Kentucky**	1951	32-2		**Louisville**	1986	32-7
15	UNLV	1991	34-1		**N. Carolina**	1982	32-2		Duke	1991	32-7
	Connecticut	1999	34-2		Temple	1988	32-2		Arkansas	1995	32-7
	Duke	1992	34-2		Arkansas	1978	32-3		**Michigan St.**	2000	32-7
	Kentucky	1996	34-2		Bradley	1986	32-3				
	Kansas	1997	34-2		Connecticut*	1996	32-3				

*NCAA later stripped UMass of its four 1996 tournament victories after learning that center Marcus Camby accepted gifts from an agent. UConn was stripped of its two 1996 tournament victories because two players illegally accepted plane tickets.

Associated Press Final Polls

Taken before NCAA, NIT and Collegiate Commissioner's Association (1974-75) tournaments.

The Associated Press introduced its weekly college basketball poll of sportswriters (later, sportswriters and broadcasters) during the 1948-49 season.

Since the NCAA Division I tournament has determined the national champion since 1939, the final AP poll ranks the nation's best teams through the regular season and conference tournaments.

Except for four seasons (see AP Post-Tournament Final Polls), the final AP poll has been released prior to the NCAA and NIT tournaments and has gone from a Top 10 (1949 and 1963-67) to a Top 20 (1950-62 and 1968-89) to a Top 25 (since 1990). Tournament champions are in **bold** type.

1949

		Before Tourns	Head Coach	Final Record
1	**Kentucky**	.29-1	Adolph Rupp	32-2
2	Oklahoma A&M	.21-4	Hank Iba	23-5
3	Saint Louis	.22-3	Eddie Hickey	22-4
4	Illinois	.19-3	Harry Combes	21-4
5	Western Ky.	.25-3	Ed Diddle	25-4
6	Minnesota	.18-3	Ozzie Cowles	same
7	Bradley	.25-6	Forddy Anderson	27-8
8	**San Francisco**	.21-5	Pete Newell	25-5
9	Tulane	.24-4	Cliff Wells	same
10	Bowling Green	.21-6	Harold Anderson	24-7

NCAA Final Four (at Edmundson Pavilion, Seattle): **Third Place**–Illinois 57, Oregon St. 53. **Championship**–Kentucky 46, Oklahoma A&M 36.

NIT Final Four (at Madison Square Garden): **Semifinals**–San Francisco 49, Bowling Green 39; Loyola-IL 55, Bradley 50. **Third Place**–Bowling Green 82, Bradley 77. **Championship**–San Francisco 48, Loyola-IL 47.

1950

		Before Tourns	Head Coach	Final Record
1	Bradley	.28-3	Forddy Anderson	32-5
2	Ohio St.	.21-3	Tippy Dye	22-4
3	Kentucky	.25-4	Adolph Rupp	25-5
4	Holy Cross	.27-2	Buster Sheary	27-4
5	N.C. State	.25-5	Everett Case	27-6
6	Duquesne	.22-5	Dudey Moore	23-6
7	UCLA	.24-5	John Wooden	24-7
8	Western Ky.	.24-5	Ed Diddle	25-6
9	St. John's	.23-4	Frank McGuire	24-5
10	La Salle	.20-3	Ken Loeffler	21-4
11	Villanova	.25-4	Al Severance	same
12	San Francisco	.19-6	Pete Newell	19-7
13	LIU-Brooklyn	.20-4	Clair Bee	20-5
14	Kansas St.	.17-7	Jack Gardner	same
15	Arizona	.26-4	Fred Enke	26-5
16	Wisconsin	.17-5	Bud Foster	same
17	San Jose St.	.21-7	Walter McPherson	same
18	Washington St.	.19-13	Jack Friel	same
19	Kansas	.14-11	Phog Allen	same
20	Indiana	.17-5	Branch McCracken	same

Note: Unranked **CCNY**, coached by Nat Holman, won both the NCAAs and NIT. The Beavers entered the postseason at 17-5 and had a final record of 24-5.

NCAA Final Four (at Madison Square Garden): **Third Place**–N. Carolina St. 53, Baylor 41. **Championship**–CCNY 71, Bradley 68.

NIT Final Four (at Madison Square Garden): **Semifinals**–Bradley 83, St. John's 72; CCNY 62, Duquesne 52. **Third Place**–St. John's 69, Duquesne 67 (OT). **Championship**–CCNY 69, Bradley 61.

1951

		Before Tourns	Head Coach	Final Record
1	**Kentucky**	.28-2	Adolph Rupp	32-2
2	Oklahoma A&M	.27-4	Hank Iba	29-6
3	Columbia	.22-0	Lou Rossini	22-1
4	Kansas St.	.22-3	Jack Gardner	25-4
5	Illinois	.19-4	Harry Combes	22-5
6	Bradley	.32-6	Forddy Anderson	same
7	Indiana	.19-3	Branch McCracken	same
8	N.C. State	.29-4	Everett Case	30-7
9	St. John's	.22-3	Frank McGuire	26-5
10	Saint Louis	.21-7	Eddie Hickey	22-8
11	**BYU**	.22-8	Stan Watts	26-10
12	Arizona	.24-4	Fred Enke	24-6
13	Dayton	.24-4	Tom Blackburn	27-5
14	Toledo	.23-8	Jerry Bush	same
15	Washington	.22-5	Tippy Dye	24-6
16	Murray St.	.21-6	Harlan Hodges	same
17	Cincinnati	.18-3	John Wiethe	18-4
18	Siena	.19-8	Dan Cunha	same
19	USC	.21-6	Forrest Twogood	same
20	Villanova	.25-6	Al Severance	25-7

NCAA Final Four (at Williams Arena, Minneapolis): **Third Place**–Illinois 61, Oklahoma St. 46. **Championship**–Kentucky 68, Kansas St. 58.

NIT Final Four (at Madison Sq. Garden): **Semifinals**–Dayton 69, St. John's 62 (OT); BYU 69, Seton Hall 59. **Third Place**–St. John's 70, Seton Hall 68 (2 OT). **Championship**–BYU 62, Dayton 43.

1952

		Before Tourns	Head Coach	Final Record
1	Kentucky	.28-2	Adolph Rupp	29-3
2	Illinois	.19-3	Harry Combes	22-4
3	Kansas St.	.19-5	Jack Gardner	same
4	Duquesne	.21-1	Dudey Moore	23-4
5	Saint Louis	.22-6	Eddie Hickey	23-8
6	Washington	.25-6	Tippy Dye	same
7	Iowa	.19-3	Bucky O'Connor	same
8	**Kansas**	.24-3	Phog Allen	28-3
9	West Virginia	.23-4	Red Brown	same
10	St. John's	.22-3	Frank McGuire	25-5
11	Dayton	.24-3	Tom Blackburn	28-5
12	Duke	.24-6	Harold Bradley	same
13	Holy Cross	.23-3	Buster Sheary	24-4
14	Seton Hall	.25-2	Honey Russell	25-3
15	St. Bonaventure	.19-5	Ed Melvin	21-6
16	Wyoming	.27-6	Everett Shelton	28-7
17	Louisville	.20-5	Peck Hickman	20-6
18	Seattle	.29-7	Al Brightman	29-8
19	UCLA	.19-10	John Wooden	19-12
20	SW Texas St.	.30-1	Milton Jowers	same

Note: Unranked La Salle, coached by Ken Loeffler, won the NIT. The Explorers entered the postseason at 21-7 and had a final record of 25-7.

NCAA Final Four (at Edmundson Pavillion, Seattle): **Semifinals**–St. John's 61, Illinois 59; Kansas 74, Santa Clara 59. **Third Place**–Illinois 67, Santa Clara 64. **Championship**–Kansas 80, St. John's 63.

NIT Final Four (at Madison Sq. Garden): **Semifinals**–La Salle 59, Duquesne 46; Dayton 69, St. Bonaventure 54. **Third Place**–St. Bonaventure 48, Duquesne 34. **Championship**–La Salle 75, Dayton 64.

Associated Press Final Polls (Cont.)

1953

		Head Coach	Final Record
1	**Indiana** 18-3	Branch McCracken	23-3
2	La Salle 25-2	Ken Loeffler	25-3
3	**Seton Hall** 28-2	Honey Russell	31-2
4	Washington 27-2	Tippy Dye	30-3
5	LSU............22-1	Harry Rabenhorst	24-3
6	Kansas.........16-5	Phog Allen	19-6
7	Oklahoma A&M .22-6	Hank Iba	23-7
	Kansas St......17-4	Jack Gardner	same
9	Western Ky. 25-5	Ed Diddle	25-6
10	Illinois 18-4	Harry Combes	same
11	Oklahoma City...18-4	Doyle Parrick	18-6
12	N.C. State.......26-6	Everett Case	same
13	Notre Dame 17-4	John Jordan	19-5
14	Louisville 21-5	Peck Hickman	22-6
	Seattle 27-3	Al Brightman	29-4
16	Miami-OH.......17-5	Bill Rohr	17-6
17	Eastern Ky. 16-8	Paul McBrayer	16-9
18	Duquesne 18-7	Dudey Moore	21-8
	Navy...........16-4	Ben Carnevale	16-5
20	Holy Cross 18-5	Buster Sheary	20-6

NCAA Final Four (at Municipal Auditorium, Kansas City): **Semifinals**–Indiana 80, LSU 67; Kansas 79, Washington 53. **Third Place**–Washington 88, LSU 69. **Championship**–Indiana 69, Kansas 68.

NIT Final Four (at Madison Sq. Garden): **Semifinals**–Seton Hall 74, Manhattan 56; St. John's 64, Duquesne 55. **Third Place**–Duquesne 81, Manhattan 67. **Championship**–Seton Hall 58, St. John's 46.

1955

		Head Coach	Final Record
1	**San Francisco**..23-1	Phil Woolpert	28-1
2	Kentucky 22-2	Adolph Rupp	23-3
3	La Salle 22-4	Ken Loeffler	26-5
4	N.C. State.......28-4	Everett Case	same
5	Iowa...........17-5	Bucky O'Connor	19-7
6	**Duquesne** 19-4	Dudey Moore	22-4
7	Utah............23-3	Jack Gardner	24-4
8	Marquette 22-2	Jack Nagle	24-3
9	Dayton 23-3	Tom Blackburn	25-4
10	Oregon St. 21-7	Slats Gill	22-8
11	Minnesota 15-7	Ozzie Cowles	same
12	Alabama........19-5	Johnny Dee	same
13	UCLA...........21-5	John Wooden	same
14	G. Washington ..24-6	Bill Reinhart	same
15	Colorado........16-5	Bebe Lee	19-6
16	Tulsa...........20-6	Clarence Iba	21-7
17	Vanderbilt 16-6	Bob Polk	same
18	Illinois 17-5	Harry Combes	same
19	West Virginia ...19-10	Fred Schaus	19-11
20	Saint Louis......19-7	Eddie Hickey	20-8

NCAA Final Four (at Municipal Auditorium, Kansas City): **Semifinals**–La Salle 76, Iowa 73; San Francisco 62, Colorado 50. **Third Place**–Colorado 75, Iowa 74. **Championship**–San Francisco 77, La Salle 63.

NIT Final Four (at Madison Square Garden): **Semifinals**–Dayton 79, St. Francis-PA 73 (OT); Duquesne 65, Cincinnati 51. **Third Place**–Cincinnati 96, St. Francis-PA 91 (OT). **Championship**–Duquesne 70, Dayton 58.

1954

		Head Coach	Final Record
1	Kentucky 25-0	Adolph Rupp	same*
2	Indiana 19-3	Branch McCracken	20-4
3	Duquesne 24-2	Dudey Moore	26-3
4	Western Ky. 28-1	Ed Diddle	29-3
5	Oklahoma A&M .23-4	Hank Iba	24-5
6	Notre Dame 20-2	John Jordan	22-3
7	Kansas.........16-5	Phog Allen	same
8	**Holy Cross**.....23-2	Buster Sheary	26-2
9	LSU............21-3	Harry Rabenhorst	21-5
10	**La Salle** 21-4	Ken Loeffler	26-4
11	Iowa...........17-5	Bucky O'Connor	same
12	Duke 22-6	Harold Bradley	same
13	Colorado A&M ..22-5	Bill Strannigan	22-7
14	Illinois 17-5	Harry Combes	same
15	Wichita 27-3	Ralph Miller	27-4
16	Seattle 26-1	Al Brightman	26-2
17	N.C. State.......26-6	Everett Case	28-7
18	Dayton 24-6	Tom Blackburn	25-7
	Minnesota 17-5	Ozzie Cowles	same
20	Oregon St. 19-10	Slats Gill	same
	UCLA...........18-7	John Wooden	same
	USC............17-12	Forrest Twogood	19-14

*Kentucky turned down invitation to NCAA tournament after NCAA declared seniors Cliff Hagan, Frank Ramsey and Lou Tsioropoulos ineligible for postseason play.

NCAA Final Four (at Municipal Auditorium, Kansas City): **Semifinals**–La Salle 69, Penn St. 54; Bradley 74, USC 72. **Third Place**–Penn St. 70, USC 61. **Championship**–La Salle 92, Bradley 76.

NIT Final Four (at Madison Square Garden): **Semifinals**–Duquesne 66, Niagara 51; Holy Cross 75, Western Ky. 69. **Third Place**–Niagara 71, Western Ky. 65. **Championship**–Holy Cross 71, Duquesne 62.

1956

		Head Coach	Final Record
1	**San Francisco**..25-0	Phil Woolpert	29-0
2	N.C. State.......24-3	Everett Case	24-4
3	Dayton 23-3	Tom Blackburn	25-4
4	Iowa...........17-5	Bucky O'Connor	20-6
5	Alabama........21-3	Johnny Dee	same
6	**Louisville** 23-3	Peck Hickman	26-3
7	SMU 22-2	Doc Hayes	25-4
8	UCLA...........21-5	John Wooden	22-6
9	Kentucky 19-5	Adolph Rupp	20-6
10	Illinois 18-4	Harry Combes	same
11	Oklahoma City...18-6	Abe Lemons	20-7
12	Vanderbilt 19-4	Bob Polk	same
13	North Carolina ..18-5	Frank McGuire	same
14	Holy Cross 22-4	Roy Leenig	22-5
15	Temple 23-3	Harry Litwack	27-4
16	Wake Forest 19-9	Murray Greason	same
17	Duke 19-7	Harold Bradley	same
18	Utah............21-5	Jack Gardner	22-6
19	Oklahoma A&M .18-8	Hank Iba	18-9
20	West Virginia ...21-8	Fred Schaus	21-9

NCAA Final Four (at McGaw Hall, Evanston, IL): **Semifinals**–Iowa 83, Temple 76; San Francisco 76, SMU 68. **Third Place**–Temple 90, SMU 81. **Championship**–San Francisco 83, Iowa 71.

NIT Final Four (at Madison Square Garden): **Semifinals**–Dayton 89, St. Francis-NY 58; Louisville 89, St. Joseph's-PA 79. **Third Place**–St. Joseph's-PA 93, St. Francis-NY 82. **Championship**–Louisville 93, Dayton 80.

1957

		Before Tourns	Head Coach	Final Record
1	**N. Carolina**	.27-0	Frank McGuire	32-0
2	Kansas	.21-2	Dick Harp	24-3
3	Kentucky	.22-4	Adolph Rupp	23-5
4	SMU	.21-3	Doc Hayes	22-4
5	Seattle	.24-2	John Castellani	24-3
6	Louisville	.21-5	Peck Hickman	same
7	West Va.	.25-4	Fred Schaus	25-5
8	Vanderbilt	.17-5	Bob Polk	same
9	Oklahoma City	.17-8	Abe Lemons	19-9
10	Saint Louis	.19-7	Eddie Hickey	19-9
11	Michigan St.	.14-8	Forddy Anderson	16-10
12	Memphis St.	.21-5	Bob Vanatta	24-6
13	California	.20-4	Pete Newell	21-5
14	UCLA	.22-4	John Wooden	same
15	Mississippi St.	.17-8	Babe McCarthy	same
16	Idaho St.	.24-2	John Grayson	25-4
17	Notre Dame	.18-7	John Jordan	20-8
18	Wake Forest	.19-9	Murray Greason	same
19	Canisius	.20-5	Joe Curran	22-6
20	Oklahoma A&M	.17-9	Hank Iba	same

Note: Unranked **Bradley**, coached by Chuck Orsborn, won the NIT. The Braves entered the tourney at 19-7 and had a final record of 22-7.

NCAA Final Four (at Municipal Auditorium, Kansas City): **Semifinals**–North Carolina 74, Michigan St. 70 (3 OT); Kansas 80, San Francisco 56. **Third Place**–San Francisco 67, Michigan St. 60. **Championship**–North Carolina 54, Kansas 53 (3 OT).

NIT Final Four (at Madison Square Garden): **Semifinals**–Memphis St. 80, St. Bonaventure 78; Bradley 78, Temple 66. **Third Place**–Temple 67, St. Bonaventure 50. **Championship**–Bradley 84, Memphis St. 83.

1958

		Before Tourns	Head Coach	Final Record
1	West Virginia	.26-1	Fred Schaus	26-2
2	Cincinnati	.24-2	George Smith	25-3
3	Kansas St.	.20-3	Tex Winter	22-5
4	San Francisco	.24-1	Phil Woolpert	25-2
5	Temple	.24-2	Harry Litwack	27-3
6	Maryland	.20-6	Bud Millikan	22-7
7	Kansas	.18-5	Dick Harp	same
8	Notre Dame	.22-4	John Jordan	24-5
9	**Kentucky**	.19-6	Adolph Rupp	23-6
10	Duke	.18-7	Harold Bradley	same
11	Dayton	.23-3	Tom Blackburn	25-4
12	Indiana	.12-10	Branch McCracken	13-11
13	North Carolina	.19-7	Frank McGuire	same
14	Bradley	.20-6	Chuck Orsborn	20-7
15	Mississippi St.	.20-5	Babe McCarthy	same
16	Auburn	.16-6	Joel Eaves	same
17	Michigan St.	.16-6	Forddy Anderson	same
18	Seattle	.20-6	John Castellani	24-7
19	Oklahoma St.	.19-7	Hank Iba	21-8
20	N.C. State	.18-6	Everett Case	same

Note: Unranked **Xavier-OH**, coached by Jim McCafferty, won the NIT. The Musketeers entered the tourney at 15-11 and had a final record of 19-11.

NCAA Final Four (at Freedom Hall, Louisville): **Semifinals**–Kentucky 61, Temple 60; Seattle 73, Kansas St. 51. **Third Place**–Temple 67, Kansas St. 57. **Championship**–Kentucky 84, Seattle 72.

NIT Final Four (at Madison Square Garden): **Semifinals**–Dayton 80, St. John's 56; Xavier-OH 72, St. Bonaventure 53. **Third Place**–St. Bonaventure 84, St. John's 69. **Championship**–Xavier-OH 78, Dayton 74 (OT).

1959

		Before Tourns	Head Coach	Final Record
1	Kansas St.	.24-1	Tex Winter	25-2
2	Kentucky	.23-2	Adolph Rupp	24-3
3	Mississippi St.	.24-1	Babe McCarthy	same*
4	Bradley	.23-3	Chuck Orsborn	25-4
5	Cincinnati	.23-3	George Smith	26-4
6	N.C. State	.22-4	Everett Case	same
7	Michigan St.	.18-3	Forddy Anderson	19-4
8	Auburn	.20-2	Joel Eaves	same
9	North Carolina	.20-4	Frank McGuire	20-5
10	West Virginia	.24-5	Fred Schaus	29-5
11	**California**	.21-4	Pete Newell	25-4
12	Saint Louis	.20-5	John Benington	20-6
13	Seattle	.23-6	Vince Cazzetta	same
14	St. Joseph's-PA	.22-3	Jack Ramsay	22-5
15	St. Mary's-CA	.18-5	Jim Weaver	19-6
16	TCU	.19-5	Buster Brannon	20-6
17	Oklahoma City	.20-6	Abe Lemons	20-7
18	Utah	.21-5	Jack Gardner	21-7
19	St. Bonaventure	.20-2	Eddie Donovan	20-3
20	Marquette	.21-3	Eddie Hickey	23-6

*Mississippi St. turned down invitation to NCAA tournament because it was an integrated event.

Note: Unranked **St. John's**, coached by Joe Lapchick, won the NIT. The Redmen entered the tourney at 16-6 and had a final record of 20-6.

NCAA Final Four (at Freedom Hall, Louisville): **Semifinals**–West Virginia 94, Louisville 79; California 64, Cincinnati 58. **Third Place**–Cincinnati 98, Louisville 85. **Championship**–California 71, West Virginia 70.

NIT Final Four (at Madison Square Garden): **Semifinals**–Bradley 59, NYU 57; St. John's 76, Providence 55. **Third Place**–NYU 71, Providence 57. **Championship**–St. John's 76, Bradley 71 (OT).

1960

		Before Tourns	Head Coach	Final Record
1	Cincinnati	.25-1	George Smith	28-2
2	California	.24-1	Pete Newell	28-2
3	**Ohio St.**	.21-3	Fred Taylor	25-3
4	**Bradley**	.24-2	Chuck Orsborn	27-2
5	West Virginia	.24-4	Fred Schaus	26-5
6	Utah	.24-2	Jack Gardner	26-3
7	Indiana	.20-4	Branch McCracken	same
8	Utah St.	.22-4	Cecil Baker	24-5
9	St. Bonaventure	.19-3	Eddie Donovan	21-5
10	Miami-FL	.23-3	Bruce Hale	23-4
11	Auburn	.19-3	Joel Eaves	same
12	NYU	.19-4	Lou Rossini	22-5
13	Georgia Tech	.21-5	Whack Hyder	22-6
14	Providence	.21-4	Joe Mullaney	24-5
15	Saint Louis	.19-7	John Benington	19-8
16	Holy Cross	.20-5	Roy Leenig	20-6
17	Villanova	.19-5	Al Severance	20-6
18	Duke	.15-10	Vic Bubas	17-11
19	Wake Forest	.21-7	Bones McKinney	same
20	St. John's	.17-7	Joe Lapchick	17-8

NCAA Final Four (at the Cow Palace, San Fran.): **Semifinals**–Ohio St. 76, NYU 54; California 77, Cincinnati 69. **Third Place**–Cincinnati 95, NYU 71. **Championship**–Ohio St. 75, California 55.

NIT Final Four (at Madison Square Garden): **Semifinals**–Bradley 82, St. Bonaventure 71; Providence 68, Utah St. 62. **Third Place**–Utah St. 99, St. Bonaventure 93. **Championship**–Bradley 88, Providence 72.

Associated Press Final Polls (Cont.)

1961

		Before Tourns	Head Coach	Final Record
1	Ohio St.	24-0	Fred Taylor	27-1
2	**Cincinnati**	23-3	Ed Jucker	27-3
3	St. Bonaventure	22-3	Eddie Donovan	24-4
4	Kansas St.	22-3	Tex Winter	23-4
5	North Carolina	19-4	Frank McGuire	same
6	Bradley	21-5	Chuck Orsborn	same
7	USC	20-6	Forrest Twogood	21-8
8	Iowa	18-6	S. Scheuerman	same
9	West Virginia	23-4	George King	same
10	Duke	22-6	Vic Bubas	same
11	Utah	21-6	Jack Gardner	23-8
12	Texas Tech	14-9	Polk Robison	15-10
13	Niagara	16-4	Taps Gallagher	16-5
14	Memphis St.	20-2	Bob Vanatta	20-3
15	Wake Forest	17-10	Bones McKinney	19-11
16	St. John's	20-4	Joe Lapchick	20-5
17	St. Joseph's-PA	22-4	Jack Ramsay	25-5
18	Drake	19-7	Maury John	same
19	Holy Cross	19-4	Roy Leenig	22-5
20	Kentucky	18-8	Adolph Rupp	19-9

Note: Unranked **Providence**, coached by Joe Mullaney, won the NIT. The Friars entered the tourney at 20-5 and had a final record of 24-5.

NCAA Final Four (at Municipal Auditorium, Kansas City): **Semifinals**—Ohio St. 95, St. Joseph's-PA 69; Cincinnati 82, Utah 67. **Third Place**—St. Joseph's-PA 127, Utah 120 (4 OT). **Championship**—Cincinnati 70, Ohio St. 65 (OT).

NIT Final Four (at Madison Square Garden) **Semifinals**—St. Louis 67, Dayton 60; Providence 90, Holy Cross 83 (OT). **Third Place**—Holy Cross 85, Dayton 67. **Championship**—Providence 62, St. Louis 59.

1962

		Before Tourns	Head Coach	Final Record
1	Ohio St.	23-1	Fred Taylor	26-2
2	**Cincinnati**	25-2	Ed Jucker	29-2
3	Kentucky	22-2	Adolph Rupp	23-3
4	Mississippi St.	19-6	Babe McCarthy	same
5	Bradley	21-6	Chuck Orsborn	21-7
6	Kansas St.	22-3	Tex Winter	same
7	Utah	23-3	Jack Gardner	same
8	Bowling Green	21-3	Harold Anderson	same
9	Colorado	18-6	Sox Walseth	19-7
10	Duke	20-5	Vic Bubas	same
11	Loyola-IL	21-3	George Ireland	23-4
12	St. John's	19-4	Joe Lapchick	21-5
13	Wake Forest	18-8	Bones McKinney	22-9
14	Oregon St.	22-4	Slats Gill	24-5
15	West Virginia	24-5	George King	24-6
16	Arizona St.	23-3	Ned Wulk	23-4
17	Duquesne	20-5	Red Manning	22-7
18	Utah St.	21-5	Ladell Andersen	22-7
19	UCLA	16-9	John Wooden	18-11
20	Villanova	19-6	Jack Kraft	21-7

Note: Unranked **Dayton**, coached by Tom Blackburn, won the NIT. The Flyers entered the tourney at 20-6 and had a final record of 24-6.

NCAA Final Four (at Freedom Hall, Louisville): **Semifinals**—Ohio St. 84, Wake Forest 68; Cincinnati 72, UCLA 70. **Third Place**—Wake Forest 82, UCLA 80. **Championship**—Cincinnati 71, Ohio St. 59.

NIT Final Four (at Madison Square Garden): **Semifinals**—Dayton 98, Loyola-IL 82; St. John's 76, Duquesne 65. **Third Place**—Loyola-IL 95, Duquesne 84. **Championship**—Dayton 73, St. John's 67.

1963

AP ranked only 10 teams from the 1962-63 season through 1967-68.

		Before Tourns	Head Coach	Final Record
1	Cincinnati	23-1	Ed Jucker	26-2
2	Duke	24-2	Vic Bubas	27-3
3	**Loyola-IL**	24-2	George Ireland	29-2
4	Arizona St.	24-2	Ned Wulk	26-3
5	Wichita	19-7	Ralph Miller	19-8
6	Mississippi St.	21-5	Babe McCarthy	22-6
7	Ohio St.	20-4	Fred Taylor	same
8	Illinois	19-5	Harry Combes	20-6
9	NYU	17-3	Lou Rossini	18-5
10	Colorado	18-6	Sox Walseth	19-7

Note: Unranked **Providence**, coached by Joe Mullaney, won the NIT. The Friars entered the tourney at 21-4 and had a final record of 24-4.

NCAA Final Four (at Freedom Hall, Louisville): **Semifinals**—Loyola-IL 94, Duke 75; Cincinnati 80, Oregon St. 46. **Third Place**—Duke 85, Oregon St. 63. **Championship**—Loyola-IL 60, Cincinnati 58 (OT).

NIT Final Four (at Madison Square Garden): **Semifinals**—Providence 70, Marquette 64; Canisius 61, Villanova 46. **Third Place**—Marquette 66, Villanova 58. **Championship**—Providence 81, Canisius 66.

1964

AP ranked only 10 teams from the 1962-63 season through 1967-68.

		Before Tourns	Head Coach	Final Record
1	**UCLA**	26-0	John Wooden	30-0
2	Michigan	20-4	Dave Strack	23-5
3	Duke	23-4	Vic Bubas	26-5
4	Kentucky	21-4	Adolph Rupp	21-6
5	Wichita St.	22-5	Ralph Miller	23-6
6	Oregon St.	25-3	Slats Gill	25-4
7	Villanova	22-3	Jack Kraft	24-4
8	Loyola-IL	20-5	George Ireland	22-6
9	DePaul	21-3	Ray Meyer	21-4
10	Davidson	22-4	Lefty Driesell	same

Note: Unranked **Bradley**, coached by Chuck Orsborn, won the NIT. The Braves entered the tourney at 20-6 and finished with a record of 23-6.

NCAA Final Four (at Municipal Auditorium, Kansas City): **Semifinals**—Duke 91, Michigan 80; UCLA 90, Kansas St. 84. **Third Place**—Michigan 100, Kansas St. 90. **Championship**—UCLA 98, Duke 83.

NIT Final Four (at Madison Square Garden): **Semifinals**—New Mexico 72, NYU 65; Bradley 67, Army 52. **Third Place**—Army 60, NYU 59. **Championship**—Bradley 86, New Mexico 54.

Undefeated National Champions

Seven NCAA seasons have ended with an undefeated national champion. UCLA has accomplished the feat four times.

Year		W-L
1956	San Francisco	29-0
1957	North Carolina	32-0
1964	UCLA	30-0
1967	UCLA	30-0
1972	UCLA	30-0
1973	UCLA	30-0
1976	Indiana	32-0

1965

AP ranked only 10 teams from the 1962-63 season through 1967-68.

		Before Tourns	Head Coach	Final Record
1	Michigan	21-3	Dave Strack	24-4
2	UCLA	24-2	John Wooden	28-2
3	St. Joseph's-PA	25-1	Jack Ramsay	26-3
4	Providence	22-1	Joe Mullaney	24-2
5	Vanderbilt	23-3	Roy Skinner	24-4
6	Davidson	24-2	Lefty Driesell	same
7	Minnesota	19-5	John Kundla	same
8	Villanova	21-4	Jack Kraft	23-5
9	BYU	21-5	Stan Watts	21-7
10	Duke	20-5	Vic Bubas	same

Note: Unranked **St. John's**, coached by Joe Lapchick, won the NIT. The Redmen entered the tourney at 17-8 and finished with a record of 21-8.
NCAA Final Four (at Memorial Coliseum, Portland, OR): **Semifinals**–Michigan 93, Princeton 76; UCLA 108, Wichita St. 89. **Third Place**–Princeton 118, Wichita St. 82. **Championship**–UCLA 91, Michigan 80.
NIT Final Four (at Madison Square Garden): **Semifinals**–Villanova 91, NYU 69; St. John's 67, Army 60. **Third Place**–Army 75, NYU 74. **Championship**– St. John's 55, Villanova 51.

1966

AP ranked only 10 teams from the 1962-63 season through 1967-68.

		Before Tourns	Head Coach	Final Record
1	Kentucky	24-1	Adolph Rupp	27-2
2	Duke	23-3	Vic Bubas	26-4
3	Texas Western	23-1	Don Haskins	28-1
4	Kansas	22-3	Ted Owens	23-4
5	St. Joseph's-PA	22-4	Jack Ramsay	24-5
6	Loyola-IL	22-2	George Ireland	22-3
7	Cincinnati	21-5	Tay Baker	21-7
8	Vanderbilt	22-4	Roy Skinner	same
9	Michigan	17-7	Dave Strack	18-8
10	Western Ky.	23-2	Johnny Oldham	25-3

Note: Unranked **BYU**, coached by Stan Watts, won the NIT. The Cougars entered the tourney at 17-5 and had a final record of 20-5.
NCAA Final Four (at Cole Fieldhouse, College Park, MD): **Semifinals**–Kentucky 83, Duke 79; Texas Western 85, Utah 78. **Third Place**–Duke 79, Utah 77. **Championship**–Texas Western 72, Kentucky 65.
NIT Final Four (at Madison Square Garden): **Semifinals**–BYU 66, Army 60; NYU 69, Villanova 63. **Third Place**–Villanova 76, Army 65. **Championship**–BYU 97, NYU 84.

1967

AP ranked only 10 teams from the 1962-63 season through 1967-68.

		Before Tourns	Head Coach	Final Record
1	UCLA	26-0	John Wooden	30-0
2	Louisville	23-3	Peck Hickman	23-5
3	Kansas	22-3	Ted Owens	23-4
4	North Carolina	24-4	Dean Smith	26-6
5	Princeton	23-2	B. van Breda Kolff	25-3
6	Western Ky.	23-2	Johnny Oldham	23-3
7	Houston	23-3	Guy Lewis	27-4
8	Tennessee	21-5	Ray Mears	21-7
9	Boston College	19-2	Bob Cousy	21-3
10	Texas Western	20-5	Don Haskins	22-6

Note: Unranked **Southern Illinois**, coached by Jack Hartman, won the NIT. The Salukis entered the tourney at 20-2 and had a final record of 24-2.
NCAA Final Four (at Freedom Hall, Louisville): **Semifinals**–Dayton 76, N. Carolina 62; UCLA 73, Houston 58. **Third Place**–Houston 84, N. Carolina 62. **Championship**–UCLA 79, Dayton 64.
NIT Final Four (at Madison Square Garden): **Semifinals**–Marquette 83, Marshall 78; Southern Ill. 79, Rutgers 70. **Third Place**–Rutgers 93, Marshall 76. **Championship**–Southern Ill. 71, Marquette 56.

1968

AP ranked only 10 teams from the 1962-63 season through 1967-68.

		Before Tourns	Head Coach	Final Record
1	Houston	28-0	Guy Lewis	31-2
2	UCLA	25-1	John Wooden	29-1
3	St. Bonaventure	22-0	Larry Weise	23-2
4	North Carolina	25-3	Dean Smith	28-4
5	Kentucky	21-4	Adolph Rupp	22-5
6	New Mexico	23-3	Bob King	23-5
7	Columbia	21-4	Jack Rohan	23-5
8	Davidson	22-4	Lefty Driesell	24-5
9	Louisville	20-6	John Dromo	21-7
10	Duke	21-5	Vic Bubas	22-6

Note: Unranked **Dayton**, coached by Don Donoher, won the NIT. The Flyers entered the tourney at 17-9 and had a final record of 21-9.
NCAA Final Four (at the Sports Arena, Los Angeles): **Semifinals**–N. Carolina 80, Ohio St. 66; UCLA 101, Houston 69. **Third Place**–Ohio St. 89, Houston 85. **Championship**–UCLA 78, N. Carolina 55.
NIT Final Four (at Madison Square Garden): **Semifinals**–Dayton 76, Notre Dame 74 (OT); Kansas 58, St. Peter's 46. **Third Place**–Notre Dame 81, St.Peter's 78. **Championship**–Dayton 61, Kansas 48.

All-Time AP Top 20

The composite AP Top 20 from the 1948-49 season through 2001-02, based on the final regular season rankings of each year. The AP poll has been taken before the NCAA and NIT tournaments each season since 1949 except in 1953 and '54 and again in 1974 and '75 when the final poll came out after the postseason. Team point totals are based on 20 points for all 1st place finishes, 19 for each 2nd, etc. Also listed are the number of times ranked No.1 by AP going into the tournaments, and times ranked in the pre-tournament Top 10 and Top 20.

		Pts	No.1	Top 10	Top 20			Pts	No.1	Top 10	Top 20
1	Kentucky	619	7	35	42	11	Notre Dame	190	0	12	18
2	North Carolina	510	5	28	36	12	Illinois	189	0	9	20
3	UCLA	449	7	22	35	13	N.C. State	176	1	9	16
4	Duke	415	6	23	32		Ohio St.	176	2	10	13
5	Kansas	340	1	18	26	15	Marquette	175	0	11	16
6	Indiana	293	4	16	24	16	UNLV	173	2	8	13
7	Cincinnati	249	2	13	18	17	Arkansas	166	0	9	15
8	Louisville	233	0	11	22	18	Syracuse	160	0	9	17
9	Arizona	214	1	10	18	19	Maryland	154	0	8	15
10	Michigan	200	2	10	15	20	Utah	152	0	7	16

Associated Press Final Polls (Cont.)

1969

		Before Tourns	Head Coach	Final Record
1	**UCLA**	25-1	John Wooden	29-1
2	La Salle	23-1	Tom Gola	same*
3	Santa Clara	26-1	Dick Garibaldi	27-2
4	North Carolina	25-3	Dean Smith	27-5
5	Davidson	24-2	Lefty Driesell	26-3
6	Purdue	20-4	George King	23-5
7	Kentucky	22-4	Adolph Rupp	23-5
8	St. John's	22-4	Lou Carnesecca	23-6
9	Duquesne	19-4	Red Manning	21-5
10	Villanova	21-4	Jack Kraft	21-5
11	Drake	24-4	Maury John	26-5
12	New Mexico St.	23-3	Lou Henson	24-5
13	South Carolina	20-6	Frank McGuire	21-7
14	Marquette	22-4	Al McGuire	24-5
15	Louisville	20-5	John Dromo	21-6
16	Boston College	21-3	Bob Cousy	24-4
17	Notre Dame	20-6	Johnny Dee	20-7
18	Colorado	20-6	Sox Walseth	21-7
19	Kansas	20-6	Ted Owens	20-7
20	Illinois	19-5	Harvey Schmidt	same

*On probation

Note: Unranked **Temple**, coached by Harry Litwack, won the NIT. The Owls entered the tourney at 18-8 and finished with a record of 22-8.

NCAA Final Four (at Freedom Hall, Louisville): **Semifinals**—Purdue 92, N. Carolina 65; UCLA 85, Drake 82. **Third Place**—Drake 104, N. Carolina 84. **Championship**—UCLA 92, Purdue 72.

NIT Final Four (at Madison Square Garden): **Semifinals**—Temple 63, Tennessee 58; Boston College 73, Army 61. **Third Place**—Tennessee 64, Army 52. **Championship**—Temple 89, Boston College 76.

1971

		Before Tourns	Head Coach	Final Record
1	UCLA	25-1	John Wooden	29-1
2	Marquette	26-0	Al McGuire	28-1
3	Penn	26-0	Dick Harter	28-1
4	Kansas	25-1	Ted Owens	27-3
5	USC	24-2	Bob Boyd	24-2
6	South Carolina	23-4	Frank McGuire	23-6
7	Western Ky.	20-5	John Oldham	24-6
8	Kentucky	22-4	Adolph Rupp	22-6
9	Fordham	25-1	Digger Phelps	26-3
10	Ohio St.	19-5	Fred Taylor	20-6
11	Jacksonville	22-3	Tom Wasdin	22-4
12	Notre Dame	19-7	Johnny Dee	20-9
13	**N. Carolina**	22-6	Dean Smith	26-6
14	Houston	20-6	Guy Lewis	22-7
15	Duquesne	21-3	Red Manning	21-4
16	Long Beach St.	21-4	Jerry Tarkanian	23-5
17	Tennessee	20-6	Ray Mears	21-7
18	Villanova	19-5	Jack Kraft	23-6
19	Drake	20-7	Maury John	21-8
20	BYU	18-9	Stan Watts	18-11

NCAA Final Four (at the Astrodome, Houston): **Semifinals**—Villanova 92, Western Ky. 89 (2 OT); UCLA 68, Kansas 60. **Third Place**—Western Ky. 77, Kansas 75. **Championship**—UCLA 68, Villanova 62.

NIT Final Four (at Madison Square Garden): **Semifinals**—N. Carolina 73, Duke 69; Ga.Tech 76, St. Bonaventure 71 (2 OT). **Third Place**—St. Bonaventure 92, Duke 88 (OT). **Championship**—N. Carolina 84, Ga.Tech 66.

1970

		Before Tourns	Head Coach	Final Record
1	Kentucky	25-1	Adolph Rupp	26-2
2	**UCLA**	24-2	John Wooden	28-2
3	St. Bonaventure	22-1	Larry Weise	25-3
4	Jacksonville	23-1	Joe Williams	27-2
5	New Mexico St.	23-2	Lou Henson	27-3
6	South Carolina	25-3	Frank McGuire	25-3
7	Iowa	19-4	Ralph Miller	20-5
8	**Marquette**	22-3	Al McGuire	26-3
9	Notre Dame	20-6	Johnny Dee	21-8
10	N.C. State	22-6	Norm Sloan	23-7
11	Florida St.	23-3	Hugh Durham	23-3
12	Houston	24-3	Guy Lewis	25-5
13	Penn	25-1	Dick Harter	25-2
14	Drake	21-6	Maury John	22-7
15	Davidson	22-4	Terry Holland	22-5
16	Utah St.	20-6	Ladell Andersen	22-7
17	Niagara	21-5	Frank Layden	22-7
18	Western Ky.	22-2	John Oldham	22-3
19	Long Beach St.	23-3	Jerry Tarkanian	24-5
20	USC	18-8	Bob Boyd	18-8

NCAA Final Four (at Cole Fieldhouse, College Park, MD): **Semifinals**—Jacksonville 91, St. Bonaventure 83; UCLA 93, New Mexico St. 77. **Third Place**—N. Mexico St. 79, St. Bonaventure 73. **Championship**—UCLA 80, Jacksonville 69.

NIT Final Four (at Madison Square Garden): **Semifinals**—St. John's 60, Army 59; Marquette 101, LSU 79. **Third Place**—Army 75, LSU 68. **Championship**—Marquette 65, St. John's 53.

1972

		Before Tourns	Head Coach	Final Record
1	**UCLA**	26-0	John Wooden	30-0
2	North Carolina	23-4	Dean Smith	26-5
3	Penn	23-2	Chuck Daly	25-3
4	Louisville	23-4	Denny Crum	26-5
5	Long Beach St.	23-3	Jerry Tarkanian	25-4
6	South Carolina	22-4	Frank McGuire	24-5
7	Marquette	24-2	Al McGuire	25-4
8	SW Louisiana	23-3	Beryl Shipley	25-4
9	BYU	21-4	Stan Watts	21-5
10	Florida St.	23-5	Hugh Durham	27-6
11	Minnesota	17-6	Bill Musselman	18-7
12	Marshall	23-3	Carl Tacy	23-4
13	Memphis St.	21-6	Gene Bartow	21-7
14	**Maryland**	23-5	Lefty Driesell	27-5
15	Villanova	19-6	Jack Kraft	20-8
16	Oral Roberts	25-1	Ken Trickey	26-2
17	Indiana	17-7	Bob Knight	17-8
18	Kentucky	20-6	Adolph Rupp	21-7
19	Ohio St.	18-6	Fred Taylor	same
20	Virginia	21-6	Bill Gibson	21-7

NCAA Final Four (at the Sports Arena, Los Angeles): **Semifinals**—Florida St. 79, N. Carolina 75; UCLA 96, Louisville 77. **Third Place**—N. Carolina 105, Louisville 91. **Championship**—UCLA 81, Florida St. 76.

NIT Final Four (at Madison Square Garden): **Semifinals**—Maryland 91, Jacksonville 77; Niagara 69, St. John's 67. **Third Place**—Jacksonville 83, St. John's 80. **Championship**—Maryland 100, Niagara 69.

1973

		Before Tourns	Head Coach	Final Record
1	**UCLA**	26-0	John Wooden	30-0
2	N.C. State	27-0	Norm Sloan	same*
3	Long Beach St.	24-2	Jerry Tarkanian	26-3
4	Providence	24-2	Dave Gavitt	27-4
5	Marquette	23-3	Al McGuire	25-4
6	Indiana	19-5	Bob Knight	22-6
7	SW Louisiana	23-2	Beryl Shipley	24-5
8	Maryland	22-6	Lefty Driesell	23-7
9	Kansas St.	22-4	Jack Hartman	23-5
10	Minnesota	20-4	Bill Musselman	21-5
11	North Carolina	22-7	Dean Smith	25-8
12	Memphis St.	21-5	Gene Bartow	24-6
13	Houston	23-3	Guy Lewis	23-4
14	Syracuse	22-4	Roy Danforth	24-5
15	Missouri	21-5	Norm Stewart	21-6
16	Arizona St.	18-7	Ned Wulk	19-9
17	Kentucky	19-7	Joe B. Hall	20-8
18	Penn	20-5	Chuck Daly	21-7
19	Austin Peay	21-5	Lake Kelly	22-7
20	San Francisco	22-4	Bob Gaillard	23-5

*N.C. State was ineligible for NCAA tournament for using improper methods to recruit David Thompson.

Note: Unranked **Virginia Tech**, coached by Don DeVoe, won the NIT. The Hokies entered the tourney at 18-5 and finished with a record of 22-5.

NCAA Final Four (at The Arena, St. Louis): **Semifinals**—Memphis St. 98, Providence 85; UCLA 70, Indiana 59. **Third Place**—Indiana 97, Providence 79. **Championship**—UCLA 87, Memphis St. 66.

NIT Final Four (at Madison Square Garden): **Semifinals**—Va. Tech 74, Alabama 73; Notre Dame 78, N. Carolina 71. **Third Place**—N. Carolina 88, Alabama 69. **Championship**—Va. Tech 92, Notre Dame 91 (OT).

1974

		Before Tourns	Head Coach	Final Record
1	**N.C. State**	26-1	Norm Sloan	30-1
2	UCLA	23-3	John Wooden	26-4
3	Notre Dame	24-2	Digger Phelps	26-3
4	Maryland	23-5	Lefty Driesell	same
5	Providence	26-3	Dave Gavitt	28-4
6	Vanderbilt	23-3	Roy Skinner	23-5
7	Marquette	22-4	Al McGuire	26-5
8	North Carolina	22-5	Dean Smith	22-6
9	Long Beach St.	24-2	Lute Olson	same
10	**Indiana**	20-5	Bob Knight	23-5
11	Alabama	22-4	C.M. Newton	same
12	Michigan	21-4	Johnny Orr	22-5
13	Pittsburgh	23-3	Buzz Ridl	25-4
14	Kansas	21-5	Ted Owens	23-7
15	USC	22-4	Bob Boyd	24-5
16	Louisville	21-6	Denny Crum	21-7
17	New Mexico	21-6	Norm Ellenberger	22-7
18	South Carolina	22-4	Frank McGuire	22-5
19	Creighton	22-6	Eddie Sutton	23-7
20	Dayton	19-7	Don Donoher	20-9

NCAA Final Four (at Greensboro, NC, Coliseum): **Semifinals**—N.C. State 80, UCLA 77 (2 OT); Marquette 64, Kansas 51. **Third Place**—UCLA 78, Kansas 61. **Championship**—N.C. State 76, Marquette 64.

NIT Final Four (at Madison Square Garden): **Semifinals**—Purdue 78, Jacksonville 63; Utah 117, Boston Col. 93. **Third Place**—Boston Col. 87, Jacksonville 77. **Championship**—Purdue 87, Utah 81.

CCA Final Four (at The Arena, St. Louis): **Semifinals**—Indiana 73, Toledo 72; USC 74, Bradley 73. **Championship**—Indiana 85, USC 60.

1975

		Before Tourns	Head Coach	Final Record
1	Indiana	29-0	Bob Knight	31-1
2	**UCLA**	23-3	John Wooden	28-3
3	Louisville	24-2	Denny Crum	28-3
4	Maryland	22-4	Lefty Driesell	24-5
5	Kentucky	22-4	Joe B. Hall	26-5
6	North Carolina	21-7	Dean Smith	23-8
7	Arizona St.	23-3	Ned Wulk	25-4
8	N.C. State	22-6	Norm Sloan	22-6
9	Notre Dame	18-8	Digger Phelps	19-10
10	Marquette	23-3	Al McGuire	23-4
11	Alabama	22-4	C.M. Newton	22-5
12	Cincinnati	21-5	Gale Catlett	23-6
13	Oregon St.	18-10	Ralph Miller	19-12
14	**Drake**	16-10	Bob Ortegel	19-10
15	Penn	23-4	Chuck Daly	23-5
16	UNLV	22-4	Jerry Tarkanian	24-5
17	Kansas St.	18-8	Jack Hartman	20-9
18	USC	18-7	Bob Boyd	18-8
19	Centenary	25-4	Larry Little	same
20	Syracuse	20-7	Roy Danforth	23-9

NCAA Final Four (at San Diego Sports Arena): **Semifinals**—Kentucky 95, Syracuse 79; UCLA 75, Louisville 74 (OT). **Third Place**—Louisville 96, Syracuse 88 (OT). **Championship**—UCLA 92, Kentucky 85.

NIT Championship (at Madison Sq. Garden): Princeton 80, Providence 69. No Top 20 teams played in NIT.

CCA Championship (at Freedom Hall, Louisville): Drake 83, Arizona 76. No.14 Drake and No.18 USC were only Top 20 teams in CCA.

1976

		Before Tourns	Head Coach	Final Record
1	**Indiana**	27-0	Bob Knight	32-0
2	Marquette	25-1	Al McGuire	27-2
3	UNLV	28-1	Jerry Tarkanian	29-2
4	Rutgers	28-0	Tom Young	31-2
5	UCLA	24-3	Gene Bartow	28-4
6	Alabama	22-4	C.M. Newton	23-5
7	Notre Dame	22-5	Digger Phelps	23-6
8	North Carolina	25-3	Dean Smith	25-4
9	Michigan	21-6	Johnny Orr	25-7
10	Western Mich.	24-2	Eldon Miller	25-3
11	Maryland	22-6	Lefty Driesell	same
12	Cincinnati	25-5	Gale Catlett	25-6
13	Tennessee	21-5	Ray Mears	21-6
14	Missouri	24-4	Norm Stewart	26-5
15	Arizona	22-8	Fred Snowden	24-9
16	Texas Tech	24-5	Gerald Myers	25-6
17	DePaul	19-8	Ray Meyer	20-9
18	Virginia	18-11	Terry Holland	18-12
19	Centenary	22-5	Larry Little	same
20	Pepperdine	21-5	Gary Colson	22-6

NCAA Final Four (at the Spectrum, Phila.); **Semifinals**—Michigan 86, Rutgers 70; Indiana 65, UCLA 51. **Third Place**—UCLA 106, Rutgers 92. **Championship**—Indiana 86, Michigan 68.

NIT Championship (at Madison Square Garden): Kentucky 71, NC-Charlotte 67. No Top 20 teams played in NIT.

Associated Press Final Polls (Cont.)

1977

		Before Tourns	Head Coach	Final Record
1	Michigan	24-3	Johnny Orr	26-4
2	UCLA	24-3	Gene Bartow	25-4
3	Kentucky	24-3	Joe B. Hall	26-4
4	UNLV	25-2	Jerry Tarkanian	29-3
5	North Carolina	24-4	Dean Smith	28-5
6	Syracuse	25-3	Jim Boeheim	26-4
7	**Marquette**	20-7	Al McGuire	25-7
8	San Francisco	29-1	Bob Gaillard	29-2
9	Wake Forest	20-7	Carl Tacy	22-8
10	Notre Dame	21-6	Digger Phelps	22-7
11	Alabama	23-4	C.M. Newton	25-6
12	Detroit	24-3	Dick Vitale	25-4
13	Minnesota	24-3	Jim Dutcher	same*
14	Utah	22-6	Jerry Pimm	23-7
15	Tennessee	22-5	Ray Mears	22-6
16	Kansas St.	23-6	Jack Hartman	24-7
17	NC-Charlotte	25-3	Lee Rose	28-5
18	Arkansas	26-1	Eddie Sutton	26-2
19	Louisville	21-6	Denny Crum	21-7
20	VMI	25-3	Charlie Schmaus	26-4

*On probation

NCAA Final Four (at the Omni, Atlanta): **Semifinals**—Marquette 51, NC-Charlotte 49; N. Carolina 84, UNLV 83. **Third Place**—UNLV 106, NC-Charlotte 94. **Championship**—Marquette 67, N. Carolina 59.

NIT Championship (at Madison Square Garden): St. Bonaventure 94, Houston 91. No. 11 Alabama was only Top 20 team in NIT.

1978

		Before Tourns	Head Coach	Final Record
1	**Kentucky**	25-2	Joe B. Hall	30-2
2	UCLA	24-2	Gary Cunningham	25-3
3	DePaul	25-2	Ray Meyer	27-3
4	Michigan St.	23-4	Jud Heathcote	25-5
5	Arkansas	28-3	Eddie Sutton	32-3
6	Notre Dame	20-6	Digger Phelps	23-8
7	Duke	23-6	Bill Foster	27-7
8	Marquette	24-3	Hank Raymonds	24-4
9	Louisville	22-6	Denny Crum	23-7
10	Kansas	24-4	Ted Owens	24-5
11	San Francisco	22-5	Bob Gaillard	23-6
12	New Mexico	24-3	Norm Ellenberger	24-4
13	Indiana	20-7	Bob Knight	21-8
14	Utah	22-5	Jerry Pimm	23-6
15	Florida St.	23-5	Hugh Durham	23-6
16	North Carolina	23-7	Dean Smith	23-8
17	**Texas**	22-5	Abe Lemons	26-5
18	Detroit	24-3	Dave Gaines	25-4
19	Miami-OH	18-8	Darrell Hedric	19-9
20	Penn	19-7	Bob Weinhauer	20-8

NCAA Final Four (at the Checkerdome, St. Louis): **Semifinals**—Kentucky 64, Arkansas 59; Duke 90, Notre Dame 86. **Third Place**—Arkansas 71, Notre Dame 69. **Championship**—Kentucky 94, Duke 88.

NIT Championship (at Madison Square Garden): Texas 101, N.C. State 93. No. 17 Texas and No. 18 Detroit were only Top 20 teams in NIT.

1979

		Before Tourns	Head Coach	Final Record
1	Indiana St.	29-0	Bill Hodges	33-1
2	UCLA	23-4	Gary Cunningham	25-5
3	**Michigan St.**	21-6	Jud Heathcote	26-6
4	Notre Dame	22-5	Digger Phelps	24-6
5	Arkansas	23-4	Eddie Sutton	25-5
6	DePaul	22-5	Ray Meyer	26-6
7	LSU	22-5	Dale Brown	23-6
8	Syracuse	25-3	Jim Boeheim	26-4
9	North Carolina	23-5	Dean Smith	23-6
10	Marquette	21-6	Hank Raymonds	22-7
11	Duke	22-7	Bill Foster	22-8
12	San Francisco	21-6	Dan Belluomini	22-7
13	Louisville	23-7	Denny Crum	24-8
14	Penn	21-5	Bob Weinhauer	25-7
15	Purdue	23-7	Lee Rose	27-8
16	Oklahoma	20-9	Dave Bliss	21-11
17	St. John's	18-10	Lou Carnesecca	21-11
18	Rutgers	21-8	Tom Young	22-9
19	Toledo	21-6	Bob Nichols	22-7
20	Iowa	20-7	Lute Olson	20-8

NCAA Final Four (at Special Events Center, Salt Lake City): **Semifinals**—Michigan St. 101, Penn 67; Indiana St. 76, DePaul 74; **Third Place**—DePaul 96, Penn 93; **Championship**—Michigan St. 75, Indiana St. 64.

NIT Championship (at Madison Square Garden): Indiana 53, Purdue 52. No. 15 Purdue was the only Top 20 team in NIT.

1980

		Before Tourns	Head Coach	Final Record
1	DePaul	26-1	Ray Meyer	26-2
2	**Louisville**	28-3	Denny Crum	33-3
3	LSU	24-5	Dale Brown	26-6
4	Kentucky	28-5	Joe B. Hall	29-6
5	Oregon St.	26-3	Ralph Miller	26-4
6	Syracuse	25-3	Jim Boeheim	26-4
7	Indiana	20-7	Bob Knight	21-8
8	Maryland	23-6	Lefty Driesell	24-7
9	Notre Dame	20-7	Digger Phelps	20-8
10	Ohio St.	24-5	Eldon Miller	21-8
11	Georgetown	24-5	John Thompson	26-6
12	BYU	24-4	Frank Arnold	24-5
13	St. John's	24-4	Lou Carnesecca	24-5
14	Duke	22-8	Bill Foster	24-9
15	North Carolina	21-7	Dean Smith	21-8
16	Missouri	23-5	Norm Stewart	25-6
17	Weber St.	26-2	Neil McCarthy	26-3
18	Arizona St.	21-6	Ned Wulk	22-7
19	Iona	28-4	Jim Valvano	29-5
20	Purdue	19-9	Lee Rose	23-10

NCAA Final Four (at Market Square Arena, Indianapolis): **Semifinals**—Louisville 80, Iowa 72; UCLA 67, Purdue 62; **Championship**—Louisville 59, UCLA 54.

NIT Championship (at Madison Square Garden): Virginia 58, Minnesota 55. No Top 20 teams played in NIT.

1981

		Before Tourns	Head Coach	Final Record
1	DePaul	27-1	Ray Meyer	27-2
2	Oregon St.	26-1	Ralph Miller	26-2
3	Arizona St.	24-3	Ned Wulk	24-4
4	LSU	28-3	Dale Brown	31-5
5	Virginia	25-3	Terry Holland	29-4
6	North Carolina	25-7	Dean Smith	29-8
7	Notre Dame	22-5	Digger Phelps	23-6
8	Kentucky	22-5	Joe B. Hall	22-6
9	**Indiana**	21-9	Bob Knight	26-9
10	UCLA	20-6	Larry Brown	20-7
11	Wake Forest	22-6	Carl Tacy	22-7
12	Louisville	21-8	Denny Crum	21-9
13	Iowa	21-6	Lute Olson	21-7
14	Utah	24-4	Jerry Pimm	25-5
15	Tennessee	20-7	Don DeVoe	21-8
16	BYU	22-6	Frank Arnold	25-7
17	Wyoming	23-5	Jim Brandenburg	24-6
18	Maryland	20-9	Lefty Driesell	21-10
19	Illinois	20-7	Lou Henson	21-8
20	Arkansas	22-7	Eddie Sutton	24-8

NCAA Final Four (at the Spectrum, Phila.): **Semifinals**–N. Carolina 78, Virginia 65; Indiana 67, LSU 49. **Third Place**–Virginia 78, LSU 74. **Championship**–Indiana 63, N. Carolina 50.

NIT Championship (at Madison Square Garden): Tulsa 86, Syracuse 84. No Top 20 teams played in NIT.

1982

		Before Tourns	Head Coach	Final Record
1	N. Carolina	27-2	Dean Smith	32-2
2	DePaul	26-1	Ray Meyer	26-2
3	Virginia	29-3	Terry Holland	30-4
4	Oregon St.	23-4	Ralph Miller	25-5
5	Missouri	26-3	Norm Stewart	27-4
6	Georgetown	26-6	John Thompson	30-7
7	Minnesota	22-5	Jim Dutcher	23-6
8	Idaho	26-2	Don Monson	27-3
9	Memphis St.	23-4	Dana Kirk	24-5
10	Tulsa	24-5	Nolan Richardson	24-6
11	Fresno St.	26-2	Boyd Grant	27-3
12	Arkansas	23-5	Eddie Sutton	23-6
13	Alabama	23-6	Wimp Sanderson	24-7
14	West Virginia	26-3	Gale Catlett	27-4
15	Kentucky	22-7	Joe B. Hall	22-8
16	Iowa	20-7	Lute Olson	21-8
17	Ala-Birmingham	23-5	Gene Bartow	25-6
18	Wake Forest	20-8	Carl Tacy	21-9
19	UCLA	21-6	Larry Farmer	21-6
20	Louisville	20-9	Denny Crum	23-10

NCAA Final Four (at the Superdome, New Orleans): **Semifinals**–N. Carolina 68, Houston 63; Georgetown 50, Louisville 46. **Championship**–N. Carolina 63, Georgetown 62.

NIT Championship (at Madison Square Garden): Bradley 67, Purdue 58. No Top 20 teams played in NIT.

1983

		Before Tourns	Head Coach	Final Record
1	Houston	27-2	Guy Lewis	31-3
2	Louisville	29-3	Denny Crum	32-4
3	St. John's	27-4	Lou Carnesecca	28-5
4	Virginia	27-4	Terry Holland	29-5
5	Indiana	23-5	Bob Knight	24-6
6	UNLV	28-2	Jerry Tarkanian	28-3
7	UCLA	23-5	Larry Farmer	23-6
8	North Carolina	26-7	Dean Smith	28-8
9	Arkansas	25-3	Eddie Sutton	26-4
10	Missouri	26-7	Norm Stewart	26-8
11	Boston College	24-6	Gary Williams	25-7
12	Kentucky	22-7	Joe B. Hall	23-8
13	Villanova	22-7	Rollie Massimino	24-8
14	Wichita St.	25-3	Gene Smithson	same*
15	Tenn-Chatt.	26-3	Murray Arnold	26-4
16	**N.C. State**	20-10	Jim Valvano	26-10
17	Memphis St.	22-7	Dana Kirk	23-8
18	Georgia	21-9	Hugh Durham	24-10
19	Oklahoma St.	24-6	Paul Hansen	24-7
20	Georgetown	21-9	John Thompson	22-10

*On probation

NCAA Final Four (at The Pit, Albuquerque, NM): **Semifinals**–N.C. State 67, Georgia 60; Houston 94, Louisville 81. **Championship**–N.C. State 54, Houston 52.

NIT Championship (at Madison Square Garden): Fresno St. 69, DePaul 60. No Top 20 teams played in NIT.

1984

		Before Tourns	Head Coach	Final Record
1	North Carolina	27-2	Dean Smith	28-3
2	**Georgetown**	29-3	John Thompson	34-3
3	Kentucky	26-4	Joe B. Hall	29-5
4	DePaul	26-2	Ray Meyer	27-3
5	Houston	28-4	Guy Lewis	32-5
6	Illinois	24-4	Lou Henson	26-5
7	Oklahoma	29-4	Billy Tubbs	29-5
8	Arkansas	25-6	Eddie Sutton	25-7
9	UTEP	27-3	Don Haskins	27-4
10	Purdue	22-6	Gene Keady	22-7
11	Maryland	23-7	Lefty Driesell	24-8
12	Tulsa	27-3	Nolan Richardson	27-4
13	UNLV	27-5	Jerry Tarkanian	29-6
14	Duke	24-9	Mike Krzyzewski	24-10
15	Washington	22-6	Marv Harshman	24-7
16	Memphis St.	24-6	Dana Kirk	26-7
17	Oregon St.	22-6	Ralph Miller	22-7
18	Syracuse	22-8	Jim Boeheim	23-9
19	Wake Forest	21-8	Carl Tacy	23-9
20	Temple	25-4	John Chaney	26-5

NCAA Final Four (at the Kingdome, Seattle): **Semifinals**–Houston 49, Virginia 47 (OT); Georgetown 53, Kentucky 40. **Championship**–Georgetown 84, Houston 75.

NIT Championship (at Madison Square Garden): Michigan 83, Notre Dame 63. No Top 20 teams played in NIT.

Highest-Rated College Games on TV

The dozen highest-rated college basketball games seen on U.S. television have been NCAA tournament championship games, led by the 1979 Michigan State-Indiana State final that featured Magic Johnson and Larry Bird.

Listed below are the finalists (winning team first), date of game, TV network, and TV rating and audience share (according to Nielson Media Research).

		Date	Net	Rtg/Sh			Date	Net	Rtg/Sh
1	Michigan St.-Indiana St.	3/26/79	NBC	24.1/38	7	N. Carolina-Georgetown	3/29/82	CBS	21.6/31
2	Villanova-Georgetown	4/1/85	CBS	23.3/33	8	UCLA-Kentucky	3/31/75	NBC	21.3/33
3	Duke-Michigan	4/6/92	CBS	22.7/35	9	Michigan-Seton Hall	4/3/89	CBS	21.3/33
4	N.C. State-Houston	4/4/83	CBS	22.3/32	10	Louisville-Duke	3/31/86	CBS	20.7/31
5	N. Carolina-Michigan	4/5/93	CBS	22.2/34	11	Indiana-N. Carolina	3/30/81	NBC	20.7/29
6	Arkansas-Duke	4/4/94	CBS	21.6/33	12	UCLA-Memphis St.	3/26/73	NBC	20.5/32

Associated Press Final Polls (Cont.)

1985

			Before Tourns	Head Coach	Final Record
1	Georgetown		30-2	John Thompson	35-3
2	Michigan		25-3	Bill Frieder	26-4
3	St. John's		27-3	Lou Carnesecca	31-4
4	Oklahoma		28-5	Billy Tubbs	31-6
5	Memphis St.		27-3	Dana Kirk	31-4
6	Georgia Tech		24-7	Bobby Cremins	27-8
7	North Carolina		24-8	Dean Smith	27-9
8	Louisiana Tech		27-2	Andy Russo	29-3
9	UNLV		27-3	Jerry Tarkanian	28-4
10	Duke		22-7	Mike Krzyzewski	23-8
11	VCU		25-5	J.D. Barnett	26-6
12	Illinois		24-8	Lou Henson	26-9
13	Kansas		25-7	Larry Brown	26-8
14	Loyola-IL		25-5	Gene Sullivan	27-6
15	Syracuse		21-8	Jim Boeheim	22-9
16	N.C. State		20-9	Jim Valvano	23-10
17	Texas Tech		23-7	Gerald Myers	23-8
18	Tulsa		23-7	Nolan Richardson	23-8
19	Georgia		21-8	Hugh Durham	22-9
20	LSU		19-9	Dale Brown	19-10

Note: Unranked **Villanova**, coached by Rollie Massimino, won the NCAAs. The Wildcats entered the tourney at 19-10 and had a final record of 25-10.

NCAA Final Four (at Rupp Arena, Lexington, KY): **Semifinals**– Georgetown 77, St. John's 59; Villanova 52, Memphis St. 45. **Championship**–Villanova 66, Georgetown 64.

NIT Championship (at Madison Square Garden): UCLA 65, Indiana 62. No Top 20 teams played in NIT.

1987

			Before Tourns	Head Coach	Final Record
1	UNLV		33-1	Jerry Tarkanian	37-2
2	North Carolina		29-3	Dean Smith	32-4
3	**Indiana**		24-4	Bob Knight	30-4
4	Georgetown		26-4	John Thompson	29-5
5	DePaul		26-2	Joey Meyer	28-3
6	Iowa		27-4	Tom Davis	30-5
7	Purdue		24-4	Gene Keady	25-5
8	Temple		31-3	John Chaney	32-4
9	Alabama		26-4	Wimp Sanderson	28-5
10	Syracuse		26-6	Jim Boeheim	31-7
11	Illinois		23-7	Lou Henson	23-8
12	Pittsburgh		24-7	Paul Evans	25-8
13	Clemson		25-5	Cliff Ellis	25-6
14	Missouri		24-9	Norm Stewart	24-10
15	UCLA		24-6	Walt Hazzard	25-7
16	New Orleans		25-3	Benny Dees	26-4
17	Duke		22-8	Mike Krzyzewski	24-9
18	Notre Dame		22-7	Digger Phelps	24-8
19	TCU		23-6	Jim Killingsworth	24-7
20	Kansas		23-10	Larry Brown	25-11

NCAA Final Four (at the Superdome, New Orleans): **Semifinals**–Syracuse 77, Providence 63; Indiana 97, UNLV 93. **Championship**–Indiana 74, Syracuse 73.

NIT Championship (at Madison Square Garden): Southern Miss. 84, La Salle 80. No Top 20 teams played in NIT.

1986

			Before Tourns	Head Coach	Final Record
1	Duke		32-2	Mike Krzyzewski	37-3
2	Kansas		31-3	Larry Brown	35-4
3	Kentucky		29-3	Eddie Sutton	32-4
4	St. John's		30-4	Lou Carnesecca	31-5
5	Michigan		27-4	Bill Frieder	28-5
6	Georgia Tech		25-6	Bobby Cremins	27-7
7	**Louisville**		26-7	Denny Crum	32-7
8	North Carolina		26-5	Dean Smith	28-6
9	Syracuse		25-5	Jim Boeheim	26-6
10	Notre Dame		23-5	Digger Phelps	23-6
11	UNLV		31-4	Jerry Tarkanian	33-5
12	Memphis St.		27-5	Dana Kirk	28-6
13	Georgetown		23-7	John Thompson	24-8
14	Bradley		31-2	Dick Versace	32-3
15	Oklahoma		25-8	Billy Tubbs	26-9
16	Indiana		21-7	Bob Knight	21-8
17	Navy		27-4	Paul Evans	30-5
18	Michigan St.		21-7	Jud Heathcote	23-8
19	Illinois		21-9	Lou Henson	22-10
20	UTEP		27-5	Don Haskins	27-6

NCAA Final Four (at Reunion Arena, Dallas): **Semifinals**–Duke 71, Kansas 67; Louisville 88, LSU 77. **Championship**–Louisville 72, Duke 69.

NIT Championship (at Madison Square Garden): Ohio St. 73, Wyoming 63. No Top 20 teams played in NIT.

1988

			Before Tourns	Head Coach	Final Record
1	Temple		29-1	John Chaney	32-2
2	Arizona		31-2	Lute Olson	35-3
3	Purdue		27-3	Gene Keady	29-4
4	Oklahoma		30-3	Billy Tubbs	35-4
5	Duke		24-6	Mike Krzyzewski	28-7
6	Kentucky		25-5	Eddie Sutton	27-6
7	North Carolina		24-6	Dean Smith	27-7
8	Pittsburgh		23-6	Paul Evans	24-7
9	Syracuse		25-8	Jim Boeheim	26-9
10	Michigan		24-7	Bill Frieder	26-8
11	Bradley		26-4	Stan Albeck	26-5
12	UNLV		27-5	Jerry Tarkanian	28-6
13	Wyoming		26-5	Benny Dees	26-6
14	N.C. State		24-7	Jim Valvano	24-8
15	Loyola-CA		27-3	Paul Westhead	28-4
16	Illinois		22-9	Lou Henson	23-10
17	Iowa		22-9	Tom Davis	24-10
18	Xavier-OH		26-3	Pete Gillen	26-4
19	BYU		25-5	Ladell Andersen	26-6
20	Kansas St.		22-8	Lon Kruger	25-9

Note: Unranked **Kansas**, coached by Larry Brown, won the NCAAs. The Jayhawks entered the tourney at 21-11 and had a final record of 27-11.

NCAA Final Four (at Kemper Arena, Kansas City): **Semifinals**–Kansas 66, Duke 59; Oklahoma 86, Arizona 78. **Championship**–Kansas 83, Oklahoma 79.

NIT Championship (at Madison Square Garden): Connecticut 72, Ohio St. 67. No Top 20 teams played in NIT.

1989

		Head Coach	Before Tourns	Final Record
1	Arizona	Lute Olson	27-3	29-4
2	Georgetown	John Thompson	26-4	29-5
3	Illinois	Lou Henson	27-4	31-5
4	Oklahoma	Billy Tubbs	28-5	30-6
5	North Carolina	Dean Smith	27-7	29-8
6	Missouri	Norm Stewart & Rich Daly*	27-7	29-8
7	Syracuse	Jim Boeheim	27-7	30-8
8	Indiana	Bob Knight	25-7	27-8
9	Duke	Mike Krzyzewski	24-7	28-8
10	**Michigan**	Bill Frieder (24-7) & Steve Fisher (6-0)	24-7	30-7
11	Seton Hall	P.J. Carlesimo	26-6	31-7
12	Louisville	Denny Crum	22-8	24-9
13	Stanford	Mike Montgomery	26-6	26-7
14	Iowa	Tom Davis	22-9	23-10
15	UNLV	Jerry Tarkanian	26-7	29-8
16	Florida St.	Pat Kennedy	22-7	22-8
17	West Virginia	Gale Catlett	25-4	26-5
18	Ball State	Rick Majerus	28-2	29-3
19	N.C. State	Jim Valvano	20-8	22-9
20	Alabama	Wimp Sanderson	23-7	23-8

NCAA Final Four (at The Kingdome, Seattle): **Semifinals**—Seton Hall 95, Duke 78; Michigan 83, Illinois 81. **Championship**—Michigan 80, Seton Hall 79 (OT).

NIT Championship (at Madison Square Garden): St. John's 73, St. Louis 65. No Top 20 teams played in NIT.

*Norm Stewart's assistant Rich Daly temporarily took over for his ailing boss (Daly coached the final 14 games of the season) but returned to his role as an assistant when Stewart recovered before the start of the following season.

1990

		Head Coach	Before Tourns	Final Record
1	Oklahoma	Billy Tubbs	26-4	27-5
2	**UNLV**	Jerry Tarkanian	29-5	35-5
3	Connecticut	Jim Calhoun	28-5	31-6
4	Michigan St.	Jud Heathcote	26-5	28-6
5	Kansas	Roy Williams	29-4	30-5
6	Syracuse	Jim Boeheim	24-6	26-7
7	Arkansas	Nolan Richardson	26-4	30-5
8	Georgetown	John Thompson	23-6	24-7
9	Georgia Tech	Bobby Cremins	24-6	28-7
10	Purdue	Gene Keady	21-7	22-8
11	Missouri	Norm Stewart	26-5	26-6
12	La Salle	Speedy Morris	29-1	30-2
13	Michigan	Steve Fisher	22-7	23-8
14	Arizona	Lute Olson	24-6	25-7
15	Duke	Mike Krzyzewski	24-8	29-9
16	Louisville	Denny Crum	26-7	27-8
17	Clemson	Cliff Ellis	24-8	26-9
18	Illinois	Lou Henson	21-7	21-8
19	LSU	Dale Brown	22-8	23-9
20	Minnesota	Clem Haskins	20-8	23-9
21	Loyola-CA	Paul Westhead	23-5	26-6
22	Oregon St.	Jim Anderson	22-6	22-7
23	Alabama	Wimp Sanderson	24-8	26-9
24	New Mexico St.	Neil McCarthy	26-4	26-5
25	Xavier-OH	Pete Gillen	26-4	28-5

NCAA Final Four (at McNichols Sports Arena, Denver): **Semifinals**—Duke 97, Arkansas 83; UNLV 90, Georgia Tech 81. **Championship**—UNLV 103, Duke 73.

NIT Championship (at Madison Square Garden): Vanderbilt 74, St. Louis 72. No Top 25 teams played in NIT.

1991

		Head Coach	Before Tourns	Final Record
1	UNLV	Jerry Tarkanian	30-0	34-1
2	Arkansas	Nolan Richardson	31-3	34-4
3	Indiana	Bob Knight	27-4	29-5
4	North Carolina	Dean Smith	25-5	29-6
5	Ohio St.	Randy Ayers	25-3	27-4
6	**Duke**	Mike Krzyzewski	26-7	32-7
7	Syracuse	Jim Boeheim	26-5	26-6
8	Arizona	Lute Olson	26-6	28-7
9	Kentucky	Rick Pitino	22-6	same*
10	Utah	Rick Majerus	28-3	30-4
11	Nebraska	Danny Nee	26-7	26-8
12	Kansas	Roy Williams	22-7	27-8
13	Seton Hall	P.J. Carlesimo	22-8	25-9
14	Oklahoma St.	Eddie Sutton	22-7	24-8
15	New Mexico St.	Neil McCarthy	23-5	23-6
16	UCLA	Jim Harrick	23-8	23-9
17	E. Tennessee St.	Alan LaForce	28-4	28-5
18	Princeton	Pete Carril	24-2	24-3
19	Alabama	Wimp Sanderson	21-9	23-10
20	St. John's	Lou Carnesecca	20-8	23-9
21	Mississippi St.	Richard Williams	20-8	20-9
22	LSU	Dale Brown	20-9	20-10
23	Texas	Tom Penders	22-8	23-9
24	DePaul	Joey Meyer	20-8	20-9
25	Southern Miss.	M.K. Turk	21-7	21-8

*On probation

NCAA Final Four (at the Hoosier Dome, Indianapolis): **Semifinals**—Kansas 79, North Carolina 73; Duke 79, UNLV 77. **Championship**—Duke 72, Kansas 65.

NIT Championship (at Madison Square Garden): Stanford 78, Oklahoma 72. No Top 25 teams played in NIT.

1992

		Head Coach	Before Tourns	Final Record
1	**Duke**	Mike Krzyzewski	28-2	34-2
2	Kansas	Roy Williams	26-4	27-5
3	Ohio St.	Randy Ayers	23-5	26-6
4	UCLA	Jim Harrick	25-4	28-5
5	Indiana	Bob Knight	23-6	27-7
6	Kentucky	Rick Pitino	26-6	29-7
7	UNLV	Jerry Tarkanian	26-2	same*
8	USC	George Raveling	23-5	24-6
9	Arkansas	Nolan Richardson	25-7	26-8
10	Arizona	Lute Olson	24-6	24-7
11	Oklahoma St.	Eddie Sutton	26-7	28-8
12	Cincinnati	Bob Huggins	25-4	29-5
13	Alabama	Wimp Sanderson	25-8	26-9
14	Michigan St.	Jud Heathcote	21-7	22-8
15	Michigan	Steve Fisher	20-8	25-9
16	Missouri	Norm Stewart	20-8	21-9
17	Massachusetts	John Calipari	28-4	30-5
18	North Carolina	Dean Smith	21-9	23-10
19	Seton Hall	P.J. Carlesimo	21-8	23-9
20	Florida St.	Pat Kennedy	20-9	22-10
21	Syracuse	Jim Boeheim	21-9	22-10
22	Georgetown	John Thompson	21-9	22-10
23	Oklahoma	Billy Tubbs	21-8	21-9
24	DePaul	Joey Meyer	20-8	20-9
25	LSU	Dale Brown	20-9	21-10

*On probation

NCAA Final Four (at the Metrodome, Minneapolis): **Semifinals**—Michigan 76, Cincinnati 72; Duke 81, Indiana 78. **Championship**—Duke 71, Michigan 51.

NIT Championship (at Madison Square Garden): Virginia 81, Notre Dame 76 (OT). No Top 25 teams played in NIT.

Associated Press Final Polls (Cont.)

1993

		Before Tourns	Head Coach	Final Record
1	Indiana	28-3	Bob Knight	31-4
2	Kentucky	26-3	Rick Pitino	30-4
3	Michigan	26-4	Steve Fisher	31-5
4	**N. Carolina**	28-4	Dean Smith	34-4
5	Arizona	24-3	Lute Olson	24-4
6	Seton Hall	27-6	P.J. Carlesimo	28-7
7	Cincinnati	24-4	Bob Huggins	27-5
8	Vanderbilt	26-5	Eddie Fogler	28-6
9	Kansas	25-6	Roy Williams	29-7
10	Duke	23-7	Mike Krzyzewski	24-8
11	Florida St.	22-9	Pat Kennedy	25-10
12	Arkansas	20-8	Nolan Richardson	22-9
13	Iowa	22-8	Tom Davis	23-9
14	Massachusetts	23-6	John Calipari	24-7
15	Louisville	20-8	Denny Crum	22-9
16	Wake Forest	19-8	Dave Odom	21-9
17	New Orleans	26-3	Tim Floyd	26-4
18	Georgia Tech	19-10	Bobby Cremins	19-11
19	Utah	23-6	Rick Majerus	24-7
20	Western Ky.	24-5	Ralph Willard	26-6
21	New Mexico	24-6	Dave Bliss	24-7
22	Purdue	18-9	Gene Keady	18-10
23	Oklahoma St.	19-8	Eddie Sutton	20-9
24	New Mexico St.	25-7	Neil McCarthy	26-8
25	UNLV	21-7	Rollie Massimino	21-8

NCAA Final Four (at the Superdome, New Orleans). **Semifinals**—North Carolina 78, Kansas 68; Michigan 81, Kentucky 78 (OT). **Championship**—North Carolina 77, Michigan 71.

NIT Championship (at Madison Square Garden): Minnesota 62, Georgetown 61. No. 25 UNLV was the only Top 25 team that played in the NIT.

1994

		Before Tourns	Head Coach	Final Record
1	North Carolina	27-6	Dean Smith	28-7
2	**Arkansas**	25-3	Nolan Richardson	31-3
3	Purdue	26-4	Gene Keady	29-5
4	Connecticut	27-4	Jim Calhoun	29-5
5	Missouri	25-3	Norm Stewart	28-4
6	Duke	23-5	Mike Krzyzewski	28-6
7	Kentucky	26-6	Rick Pitino	27-7
8	Massachusetts	27-6	John Calipari	28-7
9	Arizona	25-5	Lute Olson	29-6
10	Louisville	26-5	Denny Crum	28-6
11	Michigan	21-7	Steve Fisher	24-8
12	Temple	22-7	John Chaney	23-8
13	Kansas	25-7	Roy Williams	27-8
14	Florida	25-7	Lon Kruger	29-8
15	Syracuse	21-6	Jim Boeheim	23-7
16	California	22-7	Todd Bozeman	22-8
17	UCLA	21-6	Jim Harrick	21-7
18	Indiana	19-8	Bob Knight	21-9
19	Oklahoma St.	23-9	Eddie Sutton	24-10
20	Texas	25-7	Tom Penders	26-8
21	Marquette	22-8	Kevin O'Neill	24-9
22	Nebraska	20-9	Danny Nee	20-10
23	Minnesota	20-11	Clem Haskins	21-12
24	Saint Louis	23-5	Charlie Spoonhour	23-6
25	Cincinnati	22-9	Bob Huggins	22-10

NCAA Final Four (at the Charlotte Coliseum). **Semifinals**—Arkansas 91, Arizona 82; Duke 70, Florida 65. **Championship**—Arkansas 76, Duke 72.

NIT Championship (at Madison Square Garden): Villanova 80, Vanderbilt 73. No top 25 teams played in NIT.

1995

		Before Tourns	Head Coach	Final Record
1	**UCLA**	25-2	Jim Harrick	31-2
2	Kentucky	25-4	Rick Pitino	28-5
3	Wake Forest	24-5	Dave Odom	26-6
4	North Carolina	24-5	Dean Smith	28-6
5	Kansas	23-5	Roy Williams	25-6
6	Arkansas	27-6	Nolan Richardson	32-7
7	Massachusetts	26-4	John Calipari	26-5
8	Connecticut	25-4	Jim Calhoun	28-5
9	Villanova	25-7	Steve Lappas	25-8
10	Maryland	24-7	Gary Williams	26-8
11	Michigan St.	22-5	Jud Heathcote	22-6
12	Purdue	24-6	Gene Keady	25-7
13	Virginia	22-8	Jeff Jones	25-9
14	Oklahoma St.	23-9	Eddie Sutton	27-10
15	Arizona	23-7	Lute Olson	23-8
16	Arizona St.	22-8	Bill Frieder	24-9
17	Oklahoma	23-8	Kelvin Sampson	23-9
18	Mississippi St.	20-7	Richard Williams	22-8
19	Utah	27-5	Rick Majerus	28-6
20	Alabama	22-9	David Hobbs	23-10
21	Western Ky.	26-3	Matt Kilcullen	27-4
22	Georgetown	19-9	John Thompson	21-10
23	Missouri	19-8	Norm Stewart	20-9
24	Iowa St.	22-10	Tim Floyd	23-11
25	Syracuse	19-9	Jim Boeheim	20-10

NCAA Final Four (at the Kingdome, Seattle). **Semifinals**— UCLA 74, Oklahoma St. 61; Arkansas 75, North Carolina 68. **Championship**— UCLA 89, Arkansas 78.

NIT Championship (at Madison Square Garden): Virginia Tech 65, Marquette 64 (OT). No top 25 teams played in NIT.

1996

		Before Tourns	Head Coach	Final Record
1	Massachusetts	31-1	John Calipari	35-2
2	**Kentucky**	28-2	Rick Pitino	34-2
3	Connecticut	30-2	Jim Calhoun	32-3
4	Georgetown	26-7	John Thompson	29-8
5	Kansas	26-4	Roy Williams	29-5
6	Purdue	25-5	Gene Keady	26-6
7	Cincinnati	25-4	Bob Huggins	28-5
8	Texas Tech	28-1	James Dickey	30-2
9	Wake Forest	23-5	Dave Odom	26-6
10	Villanova	25-6	Steve Lappas	26-7
11	Arizona	24-6	Lute Olson	26-7
12	Utah	25-6	Rick Majerus	27-7
13	Georgia Tech	22-11	Bobby Cremins	24-12
14	UCLA	23-7	Jim Harrick	23-8
15	Syracuse	24-8	Jim Boeheim	29-9
16	Memphis	22-7	Larry Finch	22-8
17	Iowa St.	23-8	Tim Floyd	24-9
18	Penn St.	21-6	Jerry Dunn	21-7
19	Mississippi St.	22-7	Richard Williams	26-8
20	Marquette	22-7	Mike Deane	23-8
21	Iowa	22-8	Tom Davis	23-9
22	Virginia Tech	22-5	Bill Foster	23-6
23	New Mexico	27-4	Dave Bliss	28-5
24	Louisville	20-11	Denny Crum	22-12
25	North Carolina	20-10	Dean Smith	21-11

NCAA Final Four (at the Meadowlands, E. Rutherford, N.J.): **Semifinals**— Kentucky 81, Massachusetts 74; Syracuse 77, Mississippi St. 69. **Championship**— Kentucky 76, Syracuse 54.

NIT Championship (at Madison Square Garden): Nebraska 60, St. Joseph's 56. No top 25 teams played in NIT.

1997

		Before Tourns	Head Coach	Final Record
1	Kansas	32-1	Roy Williams	34-2
2	Utah	26-3	Rick Majerus	29-4
3	Minnesota	27-3	Clem Haskins	31-4
4	North Carolina	24-6	Dean Smith	28-7
5	Kentucky	30-4	Rick Pitino	35-5
6	South Carolina	24-7	Eddie Fogler	24-8
7	UCLA	21-7	Steve Lavin	24-8
8	Duke	23-8	Mike Krzyzewski	24-9
9	Wake Forest	23-6	Dave Odom	24-7
10	Cincinnati	25-7	Bob Huggins	26-8
11	New Mexico	24-7	Dave Bliss	25-8
12	St. Joseph's	24-6	Phil Martelli	26-7
13	Xavier	22-5	Skip Prosser	23-6
14	Clemson	21-9	Rick Barnes	23-10
15	**Arizona**	19-9	Lute Olson	25-9
16	Charleston	28-2	John Kresse	29-3
17	Georgia	24-8	Tubby Smith	24-9
18	Iowa St.	20-8	Tim Floyd	22-9
19	Illinois	21-9	Lon Kruger	22-10
20	Villanova	23-9	Steve Lappas	24-10
21	Stanford	20-7	Mike Montgomery	22-8
22	Maryland	21-10	Gary Williams	21-11
23	Boston College	21-8	Jim O'Brien	22-9
24	Colorado	21-9	Ricardo Patton	22-10
25	Louisville	23-8	Denny Crum	26-9

NCAA Final Four (at the RCA Dome, Indianapolis): **Semifinals**– Kentucky 78, Minnesota 69; Arizona 66, North Carolina 58. **Championship**– Arizona 84, Kentucky 79 (OT).

NIT Championship (at Madison Square Garden): Michigan 82, Florida St. 72. No top 25 teams played in NIT.

1998

		Before Tourns	Head Coach	Final Record
1	North Carolina	30-3	Bill Guthridge	34-4
2	Kansas	34-3	Roy Williams	35-4
3	Duke	29-3	Mike Krzyzewski	32-4
4	Arizona	27-4	Lute Olson	30-5
5	**Kentucky**	29-4	Tubby Smith	35-4
6	Connecticut	29-4	Jim Calhoun	32-5
7	Utah	25-3	Rick Majerus	30-4
8	Princeton	26-1	Bill Carmody	27-2
9	Cincinnati	26-5	Bob Huggins	27-6
10	Stanford	26-4	Mike Montgomery	30-5
11	Purdue	26-7	Gene Keady	28-8
12	Michigan	24-8	Brian Ellerbe	25-9
13	Mississippi	22-6	Rob Evans	22-7
14	South Carolina	23-7	Eddie Fogler	23-8
15	TCU	27-5	Billy Tubbs	27-6
16	Michigan St.	20-7	Tom Izzo	22-8
17	Arkansas	23-8	Nolan Richardson	24-9
18	New Mexico	23-7	Dave Bliss	24-8
19	UCLA	22-8	Steve Lavin	24-9
20	Maryland	19-10	Gary Williams	21-11
21	Syracuse	24-8	Jim Boeheim	26-9
22	Illinois	22-9	Lon Kruger	23-10
23	Xavier	22-7	Skip Prosser	22-8
24	Temple	21-8	John Chaney	21-9
25	Murray St.	29-3	Mark Gottfried	29-4

NCAA Final Four (at the Alamodome, San Antonio): **Semifinals**– Kentucky 86, Stanford 85 (OT); Utah 65, North Carolina 59. **Championship**– Kentucky 78, Utah 69.

NIT Championship (at Madison Square Garden): Minnesota 79, Penn St. 72. No top 25 teams played in NIT.

AP Post-Tournament Final Polls

The final AP Top 20 poll has been released after the NCAA tournament and NIT four times– in 1953 and '54 and again in 1974 and '75. Those four polls are listed below; teams that were not included in the last regular season polls are in *CAPITAL* italic letters.

1953

		Final Record
1	Indiana	23-3
2	Seton Hall	31-2
3	Kansas	19-6
4	Washington	30-3
5	LSU	24-3
6	La Salle	25-3
7	*ST. JOHN'S*	17-6
8	Okla. A&M	23-7
9	Duquesne	21-8
10	Notre Dame	19-5
11	Illinois	18-4
12	Kansas St.	17-4
13	Holy Cross	20-6
14	Seattle	29-4
15	*WAKE FOREST*	22-7
16	*SANTA CLARA*	20-7
17	Western Ky.	25-6
18	N.C. State	26-6
19	*DEPAUL*	19-9
20	*SW MISSOURI*	24-4

1954

		Final Record
1	Kentucky	25-0
2	La Salle	26-4
3	Holy Cross	26-2
4	Indiana	20-4
5	Duquesne	26-3
6	Notre Dame	22-3
7	*BRADLEY*	19-13
8	Western Ky.	29-3
9	*PENN ST.*	18-6
10	Okla. A&M	24-5
11	USC	19-14
12	*GEO. WASH.*	23-3
13	Iowa	17-5
14	LSU	21-5
15	Duke	22-6
16	*NIAGARA*	24-6
17	Seattle	26-2
18	Kansas	16-5
19	Illinois	17-5
20	*MARYLAND*	23-7

1974

		Final Record
1	N.C. State	30-1
2	UCLA	26-4
3	Marquette	26-5
4	Maryland	23-5
5	Notre Dame	26-3
6	Michigan	22-5
7	Kansas	23-7
8	Providence	28-4
9	Indiana	23-5
10	Long Beach St.	24-2
11	*PURDUE*	22-8
12	North Carolina	22-6
13	Vanderbilt	23-5
14	Alabama	22-4
15	*UTAH*	22-8
16	Pittsburgh	25-4
17	USC	24-5
18	*ORAL ROBERTS*	23-6
19	South Carolina	22-5
20	Dayton	20-9

1975

		Final Record
1	UCLA	28-3
2	Kentucky	26-5
3	Indiana	31-1
4	Louisville	28-3
5	Maryland	24-5
6	Syracuse	23-9
7	N.C. State	22-6
8	Arizona St.	25-4
9	North Carolina	23-8
10	Alabama	22-5
11	Marquette	23-4
12	*PRINCETON*	22-8
13	Cincinnati	23-6
14	Notre Dame	19-10
15	Kansas St.	20-9
16	Drake	19-10
17	UNLV	24-5
18	Oregon St.	19-12
19	*MICHIGAN*	19-8
20	Penn	23-5

Pre-Tournament Records

1953– St. John's (Al DeStefano, 14-5); Wake Forest (Murray Greason, 21-6); Santa Clara (Bob Feerick, 18-6); DePaul (Ray Meyer, 18-7); SW Missouri St. (Bob Vanatta, 19-4 before NAIA tourney). **1954**– Bradley (Forddy Anderson, 15-12); Penn St. (Elmer Gross, 14-5); George Washington (Bill Reinhart, 23-2); Niagara (Taps Gallagher, 22-5); Maryland (Bud Millikan, 23-7). **1974**– Purdue (Fred Schaus, 18-8); Utah (Bill Foster, 19-7); Oral Roberts (Ken Trickey, 21-5). **1975**– Princeton (Pete Carril, 18-8); Michigan (Johnny Orr, 19-7).

Associated Press Final Polls (Cont.)

1999

	Before Tourns	Head Coach	Final Record
1 Duke	32-1	Mike Krzyzewski	37-2
2 Michigan St.	29-4	Tom Izzo	33-5
3 **Connecticut**	28-2	Jim Calhoun	34-2
4 Auburn	27-3	Cliff Ellis	29-4
5 Maryland	26-5	Gary Williams	28-6
6 Utah	27-4	Rick Majerus	28-5
7 Stanford	25-6	Mike Montgomery	26-7
8 Kentucky	25-8	Tubby Smith	28-9
9 St. John's	25-8	Mike Jarvis	28-9
10 Miami-FL	22-6	Leonard Hamilton	23-7
11 Cincinnati	26-5	Bob Huggins	27-6
12 Arizona	22-6	Lute Olson	22-7
13 North Carolina	24-9	Bill Guthridge	24-10
14 Ohio St.	23-8	Jim O'Brien	27-9
15 UCLA	22-8	Steve Lavin	22-9
16 College of Charleston	28-2	John Kresse	28-3
17 Arkansas	22-10	Nolan Richardson	23-11
18 Wisconsin	22-9	Dick Bennett	22-10
19 Indiana	22-10	Bobby Knight	23-11
20 Tennessee	20-8	Jerry Green	21-9
21 Iowa	18-9	Tom Davis	20-10
22 Kansas	22-9	Roy Williams	23-10
23 Florida	20-8	Billy Donovan	22-9
24 NC-Charlotte	22-10	Bob Lutz	23-11
25 New Mexico	24-8	Dave Bliss	25-9

NCAA Final Four (at the Tropicana Field, St. Petersburg):
Semifinals– Duke 68, Michigan St. 62; Connecticut 64, Ohio St. 58. **Championship–** Connecticut 77, Duke 74.

NIT Championship (at Madison Square Garden): California 61, Clemson 60. No top 25 teams played in NIT.

2000

	Before Tourns	Head Coach	Final Record
1 Duke	27-4	Mike Krzyzewski	29-5
2 **Michigan St.**	26-7	Tom Izzo	32-7
3 Stanford	26-3	Mike Montgomery	27-4
4 Arizona	26-6	Lute Olson	27-7
5 Temple	26-5	John Chaney	27-6
6 Iowa St.	29-4	Larry Eustachy	32-5
7 Cincinnati	28-3	Bob Huggins	29-4
8 Ohio St.	22-6	Jim O'Brien	23-7
9 St. John's	24-7	Mike Jarvis	25-8
10 LSU	26-5	John Brady	28-6
11 Tennessee	24-6	Jerry Green	26-7
12 Oklahoma	26-6	Kelvin Sampson	27-7
13 Florida	24-7	Billy Donovan	29-8
14 Oklahoma St.	24-6	Eddie Sutton	27-7
15 Texas	23-8	Rick Barnes	24-9
16 Syracuse	26-6	Jim Boeheim	26-6
17 Maryland	24-9	Gary Williams	25-10
18 Tulsa	29-4	Bill Self	32-5
19 Kentucky	22-9	Tubby Smith	23-10
20 Connecticut	24-9	Jim Calhoun	25-10
21 Illinois	21-9	Lon Kruger	22-10
22 Indiana	20-8	Bobby Knight	20-9
23 Miami-FL	21-10	Leonard Hamilton	23-11
24 Auburn	23-9	Cliff Ellis	24-10
25 Purdue	21-9	Gene Keady	24-10

NCAA Final Four (at the RCA Dome, Indianapolis):
Semifinals– Michigan St. 53, Wisconsin 41; Florida 71, North Carolina 59. **Championship–** Michigan St. 89, Florida 76.

NIT Championship (at Madison Square Garden): Wake Forest 71, Notre Dame 61. No top 25 teams played in NIT.

2001

	Before Tourns	Head Coach	Final Record
1 **Duke**	29-4	Mike Krzyzewski	35-4
2 Stanford	28-2	Mike Montgomery	31-3
3 Michigan St.	24-4	Tom Izzo	28-5
4 Illinois	24-7	Bill Self	27-8
5 Arizona	23-7	Lute Olson	28-8
6 North Carolina	25-6	Matt Doherty	26-7
7 Boston College	26-4	Al Skinner	27-5
8 Florida	23-6	Billy Donovan	24-7
9 Kentucky	22-9	Tubby Smith	24-10
10 Iowa St.	25-5	Larry Eustachy	25-6
11 Maryland	21-10	Gary Williams	25-11
12 Kansas	24-6	Roy Williams	26-7
13 Oklahoma	26-6	Kelvin Sampson	26-7
14 Mississippi	25-7	Rod Barnes	27-8
15 UCLA	21-8	Steve Lavin	23-9
16 Virginia	20-8	Pete Gillen	20-9
17 Syracuse	24-8	Jim Boeheim	25-9
18 Texas	25-8	Rick Barnes	25-9
19 Notre Dame	19-9	Mike Brey	20-10
20 Indiana	21-12	Mike Davis	21-13
21 Georgetown	23-7	Craig Esherick	25-8
22 St. Joseph's	25-6	Phil Martelli	26-7
23 Wake Forest	19-10	Dave Odom	19-11
24 Iowa	22-11	Steve Alford	23-12
25 Wisconsin	18-10	Dick Bennett (2-1) & Brad Soderberg (16-10)	18-11

NCAA Final Four (at the HHH Metrodome, Minneapolis):
Semifinals–Duke 95, Maryland 84; Arizona 80, Michigan St. 61. **Championship–**Duke 82, Arizona 72.

NIT Championship (at Madison Square Garden): Tulsa 79, Alabama 60. No top 25 teams played in NIT.

2002

	Before Tourns	Head Coach	Final Record
1 Duke	29-3	Mike Krzyzewski	32-4
2 Kansas	29-3	Roy Williams	33-4
3 Oklahoma	27-4	Kelvin Sampson	31-5
4 **Maryland**	26-4	Gary Williams	32-4
5 Cincinnati	30-3	Bob Huggins	31-4
6 Gonzaga	29-3	Mark Few	29-4
7 Arizona	22-9	Lute Olson	24-10
8 Alabama	26-7	Mark Gottfried	27-8
9 Pittsburgh	27-5	Ben Howland	29-6
10 Connecticut	24-6	Jim Calhoun	27-7
11 Oregon	23-8	Ernie Kent	26-9
12 Marquette	25-7	Tom Crean	25-8
13 Illinois	24-8	Bill Self	26-9
14 Ohio St.	23-7	Jim O'Brien	24-8
15 Florida	22-8	Billy Donovan	22-9
16 Kentucky	22-9	Tubby Smith	22-10
17 Mississippi St.	26-7	Rick Stansbury	27-8
18 USC	22-9	Henry Bibby	22-10
19 Western Ky.	26-7	Dennis Felton	28-4
20 Oklahoma St.	23-8	Eddie Sutton	23-9
21 Miami-FL	24-7	Perry Clark	24-8
22 Xavier	25-5	Thad Matta	26-6
23 Georgia	21-9	Jim Harrick	22-10
24 Stanford	19-9	Mike Montgomery	20-10
25 Hawaii	27-5	Riley Wallace	27-6

NCAA Final Four (at the Georgia Dome, Atlanta):
Semifinals–Maryland 97, Kansas 88; Indiana 73, Oklahoma 64. **Championship–**Maryland 64, Indiana 52.

NIT Championship (at Madison Square Garden): Memphis 72, South Carolina 62. No top 25 teams played in NIT.

Division I Winning Streaks

Full Season
(Including tournaments)

No		Seasons	Broken by	Score
88	UCLA	1971-74	Notre Dame	71-70
60	San Francisco	1955-57	Illinois	62-33
47	UCLA	1966-68	Houston	71-69
45	UNLV	1990-91	Duke	79-77
44	Texas	1913-17	Rice	24-18
43	Seton Hall	1939-41	LIU-Bklyn	49-26
43	LIU-Brooklyn	1935-37	Stanford	45-31
41	UCLA	1968-69	USC	46-44
39	Marquette	1970-71	Ohio St.	60-59
37	Cincinnati	1962-63	Wichita St.	65-64
37	North Carolina	1957-58	West Virginia	75-64
36	N.C. State	1974-75	Wake Forest	83-78
35	Arkansas	1927-29	Texas	26-25

Regular Season
(Not including tournaments)

No		Seasons	Broken by	Score
76	UCLA	1971-74	Notre Dame	71-70
57	Indiana	1975-77	Toledo	59-57
56	Marquette	1970-72	Detroit	70-49
54	Kentucky	1952-55	Georgia Tech	59-58
51	San Francisco	1955-57	Illinois	62-33
48	Penn	1970-72	Temple	57-52
47	Ohio St	1960-62	Wisconsin	86-67
44	Texas	1913-17	Rice	24-18
43	UCLA	1966-68	Houston	71-69
43	LIU-Brooklyn	1935-37	Stanford	45-31
42	Seton Hall	1939-41	LIU-Bklyn	49-26

Home Court

No		Seasons	Broken By	Score
129	Kentucky	1943-55	Georgia Tech	59-58
99	St. Bonaventure	1948-61	Detroit	77-70
98	UCLA	1970-76	Oregon	65-45
86	Cincinnati	1957-64	Kansas	51-47
81	Arizona	1945-51	Kansas St.	76-57

No		Seasons	Broken By	Score
81	Marquette	1967-73	Notre Dame	71-69
80	Lamar	1978-84	Louisiana Tech	68-65
75	Long Beach St.	1968-74	San Francisco	94-84
72	UNLV	1974-78	New Mexico	102-98
71	Arizona	1987-92	UCLA	89-87

Annual NCAA Division I Leaders
Scoring

The NCAA did not begin keeping individual scoring records until the 1947-48 season. All averages include postseason games where applicable.

Multiple winners: Pete Maravich and Oscar Robertson (3); Darrell Floyd, Charles Jones, Harry Kelly, Frank Selvy and Freeman Williams (2).

Year		Gm	Pts	Avg	Year		Gm	Pts	Avg
1948	Murray Wier, Iowa	19	399	21.0	1976	Marshall Rodgers, Texas-Pan Am	25	919	36.8
1949	Tony Lavelli, Yale	30	671	22.4	1977	Freeman Williams, Portland St.	26	1010	38.8
1950	Paul Arizin, Villanova	29	735	25.3	1978	Freeman Williams, Portland St.	27	969	35.9
1951	Bill Mlkvy, Temple	25	731	29.2	1979	Lawrence Butler, Idaho St.	27	812	30.1
1952	Clyde Lovellette, Kansas	28	795	28.4	1980	Tony Murphy, Southern-BR	29	932	32.1
1953	Frank Selvy, Furman	25	738	29.5	1981	Zam Fredrick, S. Carolina	27	781	28.9
1954	Frank Selvy, Furman	29	1209	41.7	1982	Harry Kelly, Texas Southern	29	862	29.7
1955	Darrell Floyd, Furman	25	897	35.9	1983	Harry Kelly, Texas Southern	29	835	28.8
1956	Darrell Floyd, Furman	28	946	33.8	1984	Joe Jakubick, Akron	27	814	30.1
1957	Grady Wallace, S. Carolina	29	906	31.2	1985	Xavier McDaniel, Wichita St	31	844	27.2
1958	Oscar Robertson, Cincinnati	28	984	35.1	1986	Terrance Bailey, Wagner	29	854	29.4
1959	Oscar Robertson, Cincinnati	30	978	32.6	1987	Kevin Houston, Army	29	953	32.9
1960	Oscar Robertson, Cincinnati	30	1011	33.7	1988	Hersey Hawkins, Bradley	31	1125	36.3
1961	Frank Burgess, Gonzaga	26	842	32.4	1989	Hank Gathers, Loyola-CA	31	1015	32.7
1962	Billy McGill, Utah	26	1009	38.8	1990	Bo Kimble, Loyola-CA	32	1131	35.3
1963	Nick Werkman, Seton Hall	22	650	29.5	1991	Kevin Bradshaw, US Int'l	28	1054	37.6
1964	Howie Komives, Bowling Green	23	844	36.7	1992	Brett Roberts, Morehead St	29	815	28.1
1965	Rick Barry, Miami-FL	26	973	37.4	1993	Greg Guy, Texas-Pan Am	19	556	29.3
1966	Dave Schellhase, Purdue	24	781	32.5	1994	Glenn Robinson, Purdue	34	1030	30.3
1967	Jimmy Walker, Providence	28	851	30.4	1995	Kurt Thomas, TCU	27	781	28.9
1968	Pete Maravich, LSU	26	1138	43.8	1996	Kevin Granger, Texas Southern	24	648	27.0
1969	Pete Maravich, LSU	26	1148	44.2	1997	Charles Jones, LIU-Brooklyn	30	903	30.1
1970	Pete Maravich, LSU	31	1381	44.5	1998	Charles Jones, LIU-Brooklyn	30	869	29.0
1971	Johnny Neumann, Ole Miss	23	923	40.1	1999	Alvin Young, Niagara	29	728	25.1
1972	Dwight Lamar, SW La.	29	1054	36.3	2000	Courtney Alexander, Fresno St.	27	669	24.8
1973	Bird Averitt, Pepperdine	25	848	33.9	2001	Ronnie McCollum, Centenary	27	787	29.1
1974	Larry Fogle, Canisius	25	835	33.4	2002	Jason Conley, VMI	28	820	29.3
1975	Bob McCurdy, Richmond	26	855	32.9					

Note: Eighteen underclassmen have won the title. **Freshmen** (1)–Conley (2002); **Sophomores** (4)–Robertson (1958), Maravich (1968), Neumann (1971) and Fogle (1974); **Juniors** (13)–Selvy (1953), Floyd (1955), Robertson (1959), Werkman (1963), Maravich (1969), Lamar (1972), Williams (1977), Kelly (1982), Bailey (1986), Gathers (1989), Guy (1993), Robinson (1994) and Jones (1997).

Rebounds

The NCAA did not begin keeping individual rebounding records until the 1950-51 season. From 1956-62, the championship was decided on highest percentage of recoveries out of all rebounds made by both teams in all games. All averages include postseason games where applicable.

Multiple winners: Artis Gilmore, Jerry Lucas, Xavier McDaniel, Kermit Washington and Leroy Wright (2).

Year		Gm	No	Avg	Year		Gm	No	Avg
1951	Ernie Beck, Penn	27	556	20.6	1977	Glenn Mosley, Seton Hall	29	473	16.3
1952	Bill Hannon, Army	17	355	20.9	1978	Ken Williams, N. Texas	28	411	14.7
1953	Ed Conlin, Fordham	26	612	23.5	1979	Monti Davis, Tennessee St.	26	421	16.2
1954	Art Quimby, Connecticut	26	588	22.6	1980	Larry Smith, Alcorn State	26	392	15.1
1955	Charlie Slack, Marshall	21	538	25.6	1981	Darryl Watson, Miss. Valley St.	27	379	14.0
1956	Joe Holup, G. Washington	26	604	25.6	1982	LaSalle Thompson, Texas	27	365	13.5
1957	Elgin Baylor, Seattle	25	508	23.5	1983	Xavier McDaniel, Wichita St.	28	403	14.4
1958	Alex Ellis, Niagara	25	536	26.2	1984	Akeem Olajuwon, Houston	37	500	13.5
1959	Leroy Wright, Pacific	26	652	23.8	1985	Xavier McDaniel, Wichita St.	31	460	14.8
1960	Leroy Wright, Pacific	17	380	23.4	1986	David Robinson, Navy	35	455	13.0
1961	Jerry Lucas, Ohio St.	27	470	19.8	1987	Jerome Lane, Pittsburgh	33	444	13.5
1962	Jerry Lucas, Ohio St.	28	499	21.1	1988	Kenny Miller, Loyola-IL	29	395	13.6
1963	Paul Silas, Creighton	27	557	20.6	1989	Hank Gathers, Loyola-CA	31	426	13.7
1964	Bob Pelkington, Xavier-OH	26	567	21.8	1990	Anthony Bonner, St. Louis	33	456	13.8
1965	Toby Kimball, Connecticut	23	483	21.0	1991	Shaquille O'Neal, LSU	28	411	14.7
1966	Jim Ware, Oklahoma City	29	607	20.9	1992	Popeye Jones, Murray St.	30	431	14.4
1967	Dick Cunningham, Murray St.	22	479	21.8	1993	Warren Kidd, Mid. Tenn. St.	26	386	14.8
1968	Neal Walk, Florida	25	494	19.8	1994	Jerome Lambert, Baylor	24	355	14.8
1969	Spencer Haywood, Detroit	22	472	21.5	1995	Kurt Thomas, TCU	27	393	14.6
1970	Artis Gilmore, Jacksonville	28	621	22.2	1996	Marcus Mann, Miss. Valley St.	29	394	13.6
1971	Artis Gilmore, Jacksonville	26	603	23.2	1997	Tim Duncan, Wake Forest	31	457	14.7
1972	Kermit Washington, American	23	455	19.8	1998	Ryan Perryman, Dayton	33	412	12.5
1973	Kermit Washington, American	22	439	20.0	1999	Ian McGinnis, Dartmouth	26	317	12.2
1974	Marvin Barnes, Providence	32	597	18.7	2000	Darren Phillip, Fairfield	29	405	14.0
1975	John Irving, Hofstra	21	323	15.4	2001	Chris Marcus, Western Ky.	31	374	12.1
1976	Sam Pellom, Buffalo	26	420	16.2	2002	Jeremy Bishop, Quinnipiac	29	347	12.0

Note: Only three players have ever led the NCAA in scoring and rebounding in the same season: Xavier McDaniel of Wichita St. (1985), Hank Gathers of Loyola-Marymount (1989) and Kurt Thomas of TCU (1995).

Assists

The NCAA did not begin keeping individual assist records until the 1983-84 season. All averages include postseason games where applicable.

Multiple winner: Avery Johnson (2).

Year		Gm	No	Avg
1984	Craig Lathen, IL-Chicago	29	274	9.45
1985	Rob Weingard, Hofstra	24	228	9.50
1986	Mark Jackson, St. John's	36	328	9.11
1987	Avery Johnson, Southern-BR	31	333	10.74
1988	Avery Johnson, Southern-BR	30	399	13.30
1989	Glenn Williams, Holy Cross	28	278	9.93
1990	Todd Lehmann, Drexel	28	260	9.29
1991	Chris Corchiani, N.C. State	31	299	9.65
1992	Van Usher, Tennessee Tech	29	254	8.76
1993	Sam Crawford, N. Mexico St	34	310	9.12
1994	Jason Kidd, California	30	272	9.06
1995	Nelson Haggerty, Baylor	28	284	10.14
1996	Raimonds Miglinieks, UC-Irvine	27	230	8.52
1997	Kenny Mitchell, Dartmouth	26	203	7.81
1998	Ahlon Lewis, Arizona St.	32	294	9.19
1999	Doug Gottlieb, Oklahoma St.	34	299	8.79
2000	Mark Dickel, UNLV	31	280	9.03
2001	Markus Carr, CS-Northridge	32	286	8.94
2002	T.J. Ford, Texas	33	273	8.27

Blocked Shots

The NCAA did not begin keeping individual blocked shots records until the 1985-86 season. All averages include postseason games where applicable.

Multiple winners: Keith Closs, David Robinson and Tarvis Williams (2).

Year		Gm	No	Avg
1986	David Robinson, Navy	35	207	5.91
1987	David Robinson, Navy	32	144	4.50
1988	Rodney Blake, St. Joe's-PA	29	116	4.00
1989	Alonzo Mourning, G'town	34	169	4.97
1990	Kenny Green, Rhode Island	26	124	4.77
1991	Shawn Bradley, BYU	34	177	5.21
1992	Shaquille O'Neal, LSU	30	157	5.23
1993	Theo Ratliff, Wyoming	28	124	4.43
1994	Grady Livingston, Howard	26	115	4.42
1995	Keith Closs, Cen. Conn. St.	26	139	5.35
1996	Keith Closs, Cen. Conn. St.	28	178	6.36
1997	Adonal Foyle, Colgate	28	180	6.43
1998	Jerome James, Florida A&M	27	125	4.63
1999	Tarvis Williams, Hampton	27	135	5.00
2000	Ken Johnson, Ohio St.	30	161	5.37
2001	Tarvis Williams, Hampton	32	147	4.59
2002	Wojciech Myrda, La-Monroe	32	172	5.38

All-Time NCAA Division I Individual Leaders

Through 2001-02; includes regular season and tournament games; **Last** column indicates final year played.

CAREER

Scoring

	Points	Yrs	Last	Gm	Pts
1	Pete Maravich, LSU	3	1970	83	3667
2	Freeman Williams, Port. St.	4	1978	106	3249
3	Lionel Simmons, La Salle	4	1990	131	3217
4	Alphonso Ford, Miss. Val. St.	4	1993	109	3165
5	Harry Kelly, Texas Southern	4	1983	110	3066
6	Hersey Hawkins, Bradley	4	1988	125	3008
7	Oscar Robertson, Cincinnati	3	1960	88	2973
8	Danny Manning, Kansas	4	1988	147	2951
9	Alfredrick Hughes, Loyola-IL	4	1985	120	2914
10	Elvin Hayes, Houston	3	1968	93	2884
11	Larry Bird, Indiana St.	3	1979	94	2850
12	Otis Birdsong, Houston	4	1977	116	2832
13	Kevin Bradshaw, Beth-Cook/US Int'l	4	1991	111	2804
14	Allan Houston, Tennessee	4	1993	128	2801
15	Hank Gathers, USC/Loyola-CA	4	1990	117	2723
16	Reggie Lewis, Northeastern	4	1987	122	2708
17	Daren Queenan, Lehigh	4	1988	118	2703
18	Byron Larkin, Xavier-OH	4	1988	121	2696
19	David Robinson, Navy	4	1987	127	2669
20	Wayman Tisdale, Oklahoma	3	1985	104	2661

	Average	Yrs	Last	Pts	Avg
1	Pete Maravich, LSU	3	1970	3667	44.2
2	Austin Carr, Notre Dame	3	1971	2560	34.6
3	Oscar Robertson, Cinn	3	1960	2973	33.8
4	Calvin Murphy, Niagara	3	1970	2548	33.1
5	Dwight Lamar, SW La	2	1973	1862	32.7
6	Frank Selvy, Furman	3	1954	2538	32.5
7	Rick Mount, Purdue	3	1970	2323	32.3
8	Darrell Floyd, Furman	3	1956	2281	32.1
9	Nick Werkman, Seton Hall	3	1964	2273	32.0
10	Willie Humes, Idaho St.	2	1971	1510	31.5
11	William Averitt, Pepperdine	2	1973	1541	31.4
12	Elgin Baylor, Idaho/Seattle	3	1958	2500	31.3
13	Elvin Hayes, Houston	3	1968	2884	31.0
14	Freeman Williams, Port. St.	4	1978	3249	30.7
15	Larry Bird, Indiana St.	3	1979	2850	30.3
16	Bill Bradley, Princeton	3	1965	2503	30.2
17	Rich Fuqua, Oral Roberts	2	1973	1617	29.9
18	Wilt Chamberlain, Kansas	2	1958	1433	29.9
19	Rick Barry, Miami-FL	3	1965	2298	29.8
20	Doug Collins, Illinois St.	3	1973	2240	29.1

	Field Goal Pct.	Yrs	Last	FG	FGA	Pct
1	Steve Johnson, Ore. St.	4	1981	828	1222	.678
2	Michael Bradley, Ky./Villanova	3	2001	441	651	.677
3	Murray Brown, Fla. St.	4	1980	566	847	.668
4	Lee Campbell, M.Tenn St./SW Mo.St.	3	1990	411	618	.665
5	Warren Kidd, M.Tenn.St.	3	1993	496	747	.664
6	Todd MacCulloch, Wash.	4	1999	702	1058	.664
7	Joe Senser, West Chester	4	1979	476	719	.662
8	Kevin McGee, UC-Irvine	2	1982	552	841	.656
9	O. Phillips, Pepperdine	2	1983	404	618	.654
10	Bill Walton, UCLA	3	1974	747	1147	.651

Note: minimum 400 FGs made and an average of four per game.

	Free Throw Pct.	Yrs	Last	FT	FTA	Pct
1	Greg Starrick, Ky/So.Ill	4	1972	341	375	.909
2	Jack Moore, Nebraska	4	1982	446	495	.901
3	Steve Henson, Kansas St.	4	1990	361	401	.900
4	Steve Alford, Indiana	4	1987	535	596	.898
5	Bob Lloyd, Rutgers	3	1967	543	605	.898
6	Jim Barton, Dartmouth	4	1989	394	440	.895
7	Tommy Boyer, Arkansas	3	1963	315	353	.892
8	Rob Robbins, N. Mexico	4	1991	309	348	.888
9	Marcus Wilson, Evansville	4	1999	455	513	.887
10	Sean Miller, Pitt	4	1992	317	358	.885

Note: minimum 300 FTs made and an average of two per game.

	3-Pt Field Goals	Yrs	Last	Gm	3FG
1	Curtis Staples, Virginia	4	1998	122	413
2	Keith Veney, Lamar/Marshall	4	1997	111	409
3	Doug Day, Radford	4	1993	117	401
4	Ronnie Schmitz, Missouri-KC	4	1993	112	378
5	Mark Alberts, Akron	4	1993	107	375

	3-Pt Field Goal Pct.	Yrs	Last	3FG	Att	Pct
1	Tony Bennett, Wisc-GB	4	1992	290	584	.497
2	Keith Jennings, E.Tenn.St.	4	1991	223	452	.493
3	Kirk Manns, Michigan St.	4	1990	212	446	.475
4	Tim Locum, Wisconsin	4	1991	227	481	.472
5	David Olson, Eastern Ill.	4	1992	262	562	.466

Note: minimum 200 3FGs made.

All-Time Highest Scoring Teams
SINGLE SEASON
Scoring Offense

Team	Season	Gm	Pts	Avg
Loyola-CA	1990	32	3918	122.4
Loyola-CA	1989	31	3486	112.5
UNLV	1976	31	3426	110.5
Loyola-CA	1988	32	3528	110.3
UNLV	1977	32	3426	107.1
Oral Roberts	1972	28	2943	105.1
Southern-BR	1991	28	2924	104.4
Loyola-CA	1991	31	3211	103.6
Oklahoma	1988	39	4012	102.9
Oklahoma	1989	36	3680	102.2

All-Time NCAA Division I Individual Leaders (Cont.)

Rebounds

Total (before 1973)	Yrs	Last	Gm	No
1 Tom Gola, La Salle	4	1955	118	2201
2 Joe Holup, G. Washington	4	1956	104	2030
3 Charlie Slack, Marshall	4	1956	88	1916
4 Ed Conlin, Fordham	4	1955	102	1884
5 Dickie Hemric, Wake Forest	4	1955	104	1802
6 Paul Silas, Creighton.............	3	1964	81	1751
7 Art Quimby, Connecticut	4	1955	80	1716
8 Jerry Harper, Alabama	4	1956	93	1688
9 Jeff Cohen, Wm. & Mary	4	1961	103	1679
10 Steve Hamilton, Morehead St.....	4	1958	102	1675

Total (since 1973)	Yrs	Last	Gm	No
1 Tim Duncan, Wake Forest	4	1997	128	1570
2 Derrick Coleman, Syracuse	4	1990	143	1537
3 Malik Rose, Drexel	4	1996	120	1514
4 Ralph Sampson, Virginia	4	1983	132	1511
5 Pete Padgett, Nevada-Reno	4	1976	104	1464
6 Lionel Simmons, La Salle	4	1990	131	1429
7 Anthony Bonner, St. Louis.......	4	1990	133	1424
8 Tyrone Hill, Xavier-OH .:.......	4	1990	126	1380
9 Popeye Jones, Murray St.	4	1992	123	1374
10 Michael Brooks, La Salle	4	1980	114	1372

Average (before 1973)	Yrs	Last	No	Avg
1 Artis Gilmore, Jacksonville	2	1971	1224	22.7
2 Charlie Slack, Marshall	4	1956	1916	21.8
3 Paul Silas, Creighton........	3	1964	1751	21.6
4 Leroy Wright, Pacific.............	3	1960	1442	21.5
5 Art Quimby, Connecticut	4	1955	1716	21.5

Note: minimum 800 rebounds.

Average (since 1973)	Yrs	Last	No	Avg
1 Glenn Mosley, Seton Hall........	4	1977	1263	15.2
2 Bill Campion, Manhattan	3	1975	1070	14.2
3 Pete Padgett, Nevada-Reno	4	1976	1464	14.1
4 Bob Warner, Maine	4	1976	1304	13.6
5 Shaquille O'Neal, LSU	3	1992	1217	13.5

Note: minimum 650 rebounds.

Assists

Total	Yrs	Last	Gm	No
1 Bobby Hurley, Duke	4	1993	140	1076
2 Chris Corchiani, N.C. State.......	4	1991	124	1038
3 Ed Cota, N. Carolina	4	2000	138	1030
4 Keith Jennings, E. Tenn. St.......	4	1991	127	983
5 Sherman Douglas, Syracuse	4	1989	138	960
6 Tony Miller, Marquette	4	1995	123	956
7 Greg Anthony, Portland/UNLV	4	1991	138	950
8 Doug Gottlieb, ND/Okla St.......	4	2000	124	947
9 Gary Payton, Oregon St..........	4	1990	120	938
10 Orlando Smart, San Fran	4	1994	116	902
11 Andre LaFleur, Northeastern	4	1987	128	894

Average	Yrs	Last	No	Avg
1 A. Johnson, Cameron/Southern ...	3	1988	838	8.91
2 Sam Crawford, N. Mexico St......	2	1993	592	8.84
3 Mark Wade, Okla/UNLV	3	1987	693	8.77
4 Chris Corchiani, N.C. State......	4	1991	1038	8.37
5 Taurence Chisholm, Delaware....	4	1988	877	7.97
6 Van Usher, Tennessee Tech.......	3	1992	676	7.95
7 Anthony Manuel, Bradley.......	3	1989	855	7.92
8 Chico Fletcher, Ark. St...........	4	2000	893	7.83
9 Gary Payton, Oregon St..........	4	1990	938	7.82
10 Orlando Smart, San Fran	4	1994	902	7.78

Note: minimum 550 assists.

Blocked Shots

Average	Yrs	Last	No	Avg
1 Keith Closs, Cen. Conn. St.......	2	1996	317	5.87
2 Adonal Foyle, Colgate	3	1997	492	5.66
3 David Robinson, Navy	2	1987	351	5.24
4 Shaquille O'Neal, LSU	3	1992	412	4.58
5 Troy Murphy, Notre Dame	3	2001	425	4.52

Note: minimum 225 blocked shots.

Steals

Average	Yrs	Last	No	Avg
1 Mookie Blaylock, Oklahoma	2	1989	281	3.80
2 Ronn McMahon, Eastern Wash...	3	1990	225	3.52
3 Eric Murdock, Providence	4	1991	376	3.21
4 Van Usher, Tennessee Tech.......	3	1992	270	3.18
5 Pepe Sanchez, Temple	4	2000	365	3.15

Note: minimum 225 steals.

2000 Points/1000 Rebounds

For a combined total of 4000 or more.

	Gm	Pts	Reb	Total
1 Tom Gola, La Salle........	118	2462	2201	4663
2 Lionel Simmons, La Salle ...	131	3217	1429	4646
3 Elvin Hayes, Houston	93	2884	1602	4486
4 Dickie Hemric, W. Forest ...	104	2587	1802	4389
5 Oscar Robertson, Cinn....	88	2973	1338	4311
6 Joe Holup, G. Wash	104	2226	2030	4256
7 Harry Kelly, TX-Southern	110	3066	1085	4151
8 Danny Manning, Kansas....	147	2951	1187	4138
9 Larry Bird, Indiana St........	94	2850	1247	4097
10 Elgin Baylor, Col. Idaho/ Seattle	80	2500	1559	4059
11 Michael Brooks, La Salle....	114	2628	1372	4000

Years Played–Baylor (1956-58); **Bird** (1977-79); **Brooks** (1977-80); **Gola** (1952-55); **Hayes** (1966-68); **Hemric** (1952-55); **Holup** (1953-56); **Kelly** (1980-83); **Manning** (1985-88); **Robertson** (1958-60); **Simmons** (1987-90).

SINGLE SEASON

Scoring

Points	Year	Gm	Pts
1 Pete Maravich, LSU	1970	31	1381
2 Elvin Hayes, Houston............	1968	33	1214
3 Frank Selvy, Furman..........	1954	29	1209
4 Pete Maravich, LSU	1969	26	1148
5 Pete Maravich, LSU	1968	26	1138
6 Bo Kimble, Loyola-CA	1990	32	1131
7 Hersey Hawkins, Bradley.......	1988	31	1125
8 Austin Carr, Notre Dame	1970	29	1106
9 Austin Carr, Notre Dame	1971	29	1101
10 Otis Birdsong, Houston	1977	36	1090

Average	Year	Gm	Pts	Avg
1 Pete Maravich, LSU	1970	31	1381	44.5
2 Pete Maravich, LSU	1969	26	1148	44.2
3 Pete Maravich, LSU	1968	26	1138	43.8
4 Frank Selvy, Furman.............	1954	29	1209	41.7
5 Johnny Neumann, Ole Miss	1971	23	923	40.1
6 Freeman Williams, Port. St.	1977	26	1010	38.8
7 Billy McGill, Utah..............	1962	26	1009	38.8
8 Calvin Murphy, Niagara.........	1968	24	916	38.2
9 Austin Carr, Notre Dame	1970	29	1106	38.1
10 Austin Carr, Notre Dame	1971	29	1101	38.0

Field Goal Pct.

	Field Goal Pct.	Year	FG	FGA	Pct
1	Steve Johnson, Oregon St.	1981	235	315	.746
2	Dwayne Davis, Florida	1989	179	248	.722
3	Keith Walker, Utica	1985	154	216	.713
4	Steve Johnson, Oregon St.	1980	211	297	.710
5	Adam Mark, Belmont	2002	150	212	.708

Free Throw Pct.

	Free Throw Pct.	Year	FT	FTA	Pct
1	Craig Collins, Penn St.	1985	94	98	.959
2	Rod Foster, UCLA	1982	95	100	.950
3	Clay McKnight, Pacific	2000	74	78	.949
4	Carlos Gibson, Marshall	1978	84	89	.944
5	Danny Basile, Marist	1994	84	89	.944

3-Pt Field Goal Pct.

	3-Pt Field Goal Pct.	Year	3FG	Att	Pct
1	Glenn Tropf, Holy Cross	1988	52	82	.634
2	Sean Wightman, W. Mich	1992	48	76	.632
3	Keith Jennings, E. Tenn. St.	1991	84	142	.592
4	Dave Calloway, Monmouth	1989	48	82	.585
5	Steve Kerr, Arizona	1988	114	199	.573

Assists

	Average	Year	Gm	No	Avg
1	Avery Johnson, Southern-BR	1988	30	399	13.3
2	Anthony Manuel, Bradley	1988	31	373	12.0
3	Avery Johnson, Southern-BR	1987	31	333	10.7
4	Mark Wade, UNLV	1987	38	406	10.7
5	Glenn Williams, Holy Cross	1989	28	278	9.9

Rebounds

	Average (before 1973)	Year	Gm	No	Avg
1	Charlie Slack, Marshall	1955	21	538	25.6
2	Leroy Wright, Pacific	1959	26	652	25.1
3	Art Quimby, Connecticut	1955	25	611	24.4
4	Charlie Slack, Marshall	1956	22	520	23.6
5	Ed Conlin, Fordham	1953	26	612	23.5

	Average (since 1973)	Year	Gm	No	Avg
1	Kermit Washington, American	1973	25	511	20.4
2	Marvin Barnes, Providence	1973	30	571	19.0
3	Marvin Barnes, Providence	1974	32	597	18.7
4	Pete Padgett, Nevada	1973	26	462	17.8
5	Jim Bradley, Northern Ill	1973	24	426	17.8

Blocked Shots

	Average	Year	Gm	No	Avg
1	Adonal Foyle, Colgate	1997	28	180	6.42
2	Keith Closs, Cen. Conn. St.	1996	28	178	6.36
3	David Robinson, Navy	1986	35	207	5.91
4	Wojciech Myrda, La-Monroe	2002	32	172	5.38
5	Ken Johnson, Ohio St.	2000	30	161	5.37

Steals

	Average	Year	Gm	No	Avg
1	Desmond Cambridge, Ala. A&M.	2002	29	160	5.52
2	Darron Brittman, Chicago St.	1986	28	139	4.96
3	Aldwin Ware, Florida A&M	1988	29	142	4.90
4	John Linehan, Providence	2002	31	139	4.48
5	Ronn McMahon, East Wash	1990	29	130	4.48

SINGLE GAME

Scoring

	Points vs Div. I Team	Year	Pts
1	Kevin Bradshaw, US Int'l vs Loyola-CA	1991	72
2	Pete Maravich, LSU vs Alabama	1970	69
3	Calvin Murphy, Niagara vs Syracuse	1969	68
4	Jay Handlan, Wash. & Lee vs Furman	1951	66
	Pete Maravich, LSU vs Tulane	1969	66
	Anthony Roberts, Oral Rbts vs N.C. A&T	1977	66
7	Anthony Roberts, Oral Rbts vs Ore	1977	65
	Scott Haffner, Evansville vs Dayton	1989	65
9	Pete Maravich, LSU vs Kentucky	1970	64
10	Johnny Neumann, Ole Miss vs LSU	1971	63
	Hersey Hawkins, Bradley vs Detroit	1988	63

	Points vs Non-Div. I Team	Year	Pts
1	Frank Selvy, Furman vs Newberry	1954	100
2	Paul Arizin, Villanova vs Phi. NAMC	1949	85
3	Freeman Williams, Port. St. vs Rocky Mt	1978	81
4	Bill Mlkvy, Temple vs Wilkes	1951	73
5	Freeman Williams, Port. St. vs So. Ore	1977	71

Note: Bevo Francis of Division II Rio Grande (Ohio) scored an overall collegiate record 113 points against Hillsdale in 1954. He also scored 84 against Alliance and 82 against Bluffton that same season.

Assists

		Year	No
1	Tony Fairley, Baptist vs Armstrong St.	1987	22
	Avery Johnson, Southern-BR vs TX-South	1988	22
	Sherman Douglas, Syracuse vs Providence	1989	22
4	Mark Wade, UNLV vs Navy	1986	21
	Kelvin Scarborough, N. Mexico vs Hawaii	1987	21
	Anthony Manuel, Bradley vs UC-Irvine	1987	21
	Avery Johnson, Southern-BR vs Ala. St.	1988	21

3-Pt Field Goals

		Year	No
1	Keith Veney, Marshall vs Morehead St.	1996	15
2	Dave Jamerson, Ohio U. vs Charleston	1989	14
	Askia Jones, Kansas St. vs Fresno St.	1994	14
4	Ronald Blackshear, Marshall vs. Akron	2002	13
5	Gary Bosserd, Niagara vs Siena	1987	12
	Darrin Fitzgerald, Butler vs Detroit	1987	12
	Al Dillard, Arkansas vs Delaware St.	1993	12
	Mitch Taylor, South-BR vs La. Christian	1995	12
	David McMahan, Winthrop vs C. Carolina	1996	12

Rebounds

	Total (before 1973)	Year	No
1	Bill Chambers, Wm. & Mary vs Virginia	1953	51
2	Charlie Slack, Marshall vs M. Harvey	1954	43
3	Tom Heinsohn, Holy Cross vs BC	1955	42
4	Art Quimby, UConn vs BU	1955	40
5	Three players tied with 39 each.		

	Total (since 1973)	Year	No
1	Larry Abney, Fresno St. vs SMU	2000	35
2	David Vaughn, Oral Roberts vs Brandeis	1973	34
3	Robert Parish, Centenary vs So. Miss	1973	33
4	Durand Macklin, LSU vs Tulane	1976	32
	Jervaughn Scales, South-BR vs Grambling	1994	32

Blocked Shots

		Year	No
1	David Robinson, Navy vs NC-Wilmington	1986	14
	Shawn Bradley, BYU vs Eastern Ky	1990	14
	Roy Rogers, Alabama vs Georgia	1996	14
	Loren Woods, Arizona vs Oregon	2000	14
5	Kevin Roberson, Vermont vs UNH	1992	13
	Jim McIlvaine, Marquette vs No. Ill	1993	13
	Keith Closs, C. Conn. St. vs St. Fran-PA	1994	13
	D'or Fischer, N'Western St. vs SW Tex. St.	2001	13
	Wojciech Myrda, La-Monroe vs. Tx-SA	2002	13

All-Time NCAA Division I Individual Leaders (Cont.)

Steals

		Year	No		Year	No
1	Mookie Blaylock, Oklahoma vs Centenary	1987	13	Richard Duncan, Mid. Tenn St. vs E. Ky.	1999	12
	Mookie Blaylock, Oklahoma vs Loyola-CA	1988	13	Greedy Daniels, TCU vs Ark-Pine Bluff	2001	12
3	Kenny Robertson, Cleve. St. vs Wagner	1988	12	Jehiel Lewis, Navy vs Bucknell	2002	12
	Terry Evans, Oklahoma vs Florida A&M	1993	12			

Players of the Year and Top Draft Picks

Consensus College Players of the Year and first overall selections in NBA draft since the abolition of the NBA's territorial draft in 1966. Top draft picks who became Rookie of the Year are in **bold** type; (*) indicates top draft pick chosen as junior, (**) indicates top draft pick chosen as sophomore, (†) indicates top draft pick chosen as a high school senior.

Year	Player of the Year	Top Draft Pick
1966	Cazzie Russell, Mich.	Cazzie Russell, NY
1967	Lew Alcindor, UCLA	Jimmy Walker, Det.
1968	Elvin Hayes, Houston	Elvin Hayes, SD
1969	Lew Alcindor, UCLA	**Lew Alcindor**, Mil.
1970	Pete Maravich, LSU	Bob Lanier, Det.
1971	Sidney Wicks, UCLA	Austin Carr, Cle.
1972	Bill Walton, UCLA	LaRue Martin, Por.
1973	Bill Walton, UCLA	Doug Collins, Phi.
1974	Bill Walton, UCLA	Bill Walton, Por.
1975	David Thompson, N.C. St.	David Thompson, Atl.
1976	Scott May, Indiana	John Lucas, Hou.
1977	Marques Johnson, UCLA	Kent Benson, Ind.
1978	Butch Lee, Marquette	
	& Phil Ford, N. Caro.	Mychal Thompson, Por.
1979	Larry Bird, Indiana St.	Magic Johnson, LAL**
1980	Mark Aguirre, DePaul	Joe Barry Carroll, G. St.
1981	Ralph Sampson, Va.	
	& Danny Ainge, BYU	Mark Aguirre, Dal.
1982	Ralph Sampson, Va.	James Worthy, LAL*
1983	Ralph Sampson, Va.	**Ralph Sampson**, Hou.
1984	Michael Jordan, N. Caro.	Akeem Olajuwon, Hou.
1985	Patrick Ewing, G'town	
	& Chris Mullin, St. John's	**Patrick Ewing**, NY
1986	Walter Berry, St. John's	Brad Daugherty, Cle.

Year	Player of the Year	Top Draft Pick
1987	David Robinson, Navy	**David Robinson**, SA
1988	Hersey Hawkins, Bradley	
	& Danny Manning, Kan.	Danny Manning, LAC
1989	Sean Elliott, Arizona	
	& Danny Ferry, Duke	Pervis Ellison, Sac.
1990	Lionel Simmons, La Salle	**Derrick Coleman**, NJ
1991	Larry Johnson, UNLV	
	& Shaquille O'Neal, LSU	**Larry Johnson**, Cha.
1992	Christian Laettner, Duke	**Shaquille O'Neal**, Orl.*
1993	Calbert Cheaney, Ind.	**Chris Webber**, Orl.**
1994	Glenn Robinson, Purdue	Glenn Robinson, Mil.*
1995	Ed O'Bannon, UCLA	
	& Joe Smith, Maryland	Joe Smith, G. St.**
1996	Marcus Camby, UMass	**Allen Iverson**, Phi.**
1997	Tim Duncan, Wake Forest	**Tim Duncan**, SA
1998	Antawn Jamison, N. Caro.	M. Olowokandi, LAC
1999	Elton Brand, Duke	**Elton Brand**, Chi.**
2000	Kenyon Martin, Cincinnati	Kenyon Martin, NJ
2001	Shane Battier, Duke	
	& Jason Williams, Duke	Kwame Brown, Wash.†
2002	Jason Williams, Duke	
	& Drew Gooden, Kansas	Yao Ming, Hou.

Annual Awards

UPI picked the first national Division I Player of the Year in 1955. Since then, the U.S. Basketball Writers Assn. (1959), the Commonwealth Athletic Club of Kentucky's Adolph Rupp Trophy (1961), the Atlanta Tip-Off Club (1969), the National Assn. of Basketball Coaches (1975), and the LA Athletic Club's John Wooden Award (1977) have joined in. UPI discontinued its award in 1997.

Since 1977, the first year all the following awards were given out, the same player has won all of them in the same season 13 times: Marques Johnson in 1977, Larry Bird in 1979, Ralph Sampson in both 1982 and '83, Michael Jordan in 1984, David Robinson in 1987, Lionel Simmons in 1990, Calbert Cheaney in 1993, Glenn Robinson in 1994, Tim Duncan in 1997, Antawn Jamison in 1998, Elton Brand in 1999 and Kenyon Martin in 2000.

United Press International

Voted on by a panel of UPI college basketball writers and first presented in 1955.
Multiple winners: Oscar Robertson, Ralph Sampson and Bill Walton (3); Lew Alcindor and Jerry Lucas (2).

Year	Year	Year
1955 Tom Gola, La Salle	1970 Pete Maravich, LSU	1985 Chris Mullin, St. John's
1956 Bill Russell, San Francisco	1971 Austin Carr, Notre Dame	1986 Walter Berry, St. John's
1957 Chet Forte, Columbia	1972 Bill Walton, UCLA	1987 David Robinson, Navy
1958 Oscar Robertson, Cincinnati	1973 Bill Walton, UCLA	1988 Hersey Hawkins, Bradley
1959 Oscar Robertson, Cincinnati	1974 Bill Walton, UCLA	1989 Danny Ferry, Duke
1960 Oscar Robertson, Cincinnati	1975 David Thompson, N.C. State	1990 Lionel Simmons, La Salle
1961 Jerry Lucas, Ohio St.	1976 Scott May, Indiana	1991 Shaquille O'Neal, LSU
1962 Jerry Lucas, Ohio St.	1977 Marques Johnson, UCLA	1992 Jim Jackson, Ohio St.
1963 Art Heyman, Duke	1978 Butch Lee, Marquette	1993 Calbert Cheaney, Indiana
1964 Gary Bradds, Ohio St.	1979 Larry Bird, Indiana St.	1994 Glenn Robinson, Purdue
1965 Bill Bradley, Princeton	1980 Mark Aguirre, DePaul	1995 Joe Smith, Maryland
1966 Cazzie Russell, Michigan	1981 Ralph Sampson, Virginia	1996 Ray Allen, UConn
1967 Lew Alcindor, UCLA	1982 Ralph Sampson, Virginia	1997 award discontinued
1968 Elvin Hayes, Houston	1983 Ralph Sampson, Virginia	
1969 Lew Alcindor, UCLA	1984 Michael Jordan, N. Carolina	

U.S. Basketball Writers Association

Voted on by the USBWA and first presented in 1959.
Multiple winners: Ralph Sampson and Bill Walton (3); Lew Alcindor, Jerry Lucas and Oscar Robertson (2).

Year	Year	Year
1959 Oscar Robertson, Cincinnati	1961 Jerry Lucas, Ohio St.	1963 Art Heyman, Duke
1960 Oscar Robertson, Cincinnati	1962 Jerry Lucas, Ohio St.	1964 Walt Hazzard, UCLA

Year	Year	Year
1965 Bill Bradley, Princeton	1978 Phil Ford, North Carolina	1991 Larry Johnson, UNLV
1966 Cazzie Russell, Michigan	1979 Larry Bird, Indiana St.	1992 Christian Laettner, Duke
1967 Lew Alcindor, UCLA	1980 Mark Aguirre, DePaul	1993 Calbert Cheaney, Indiana
1968 Elvin Hayes, Houston	1981 Ralph Sampson, Virginia	1994 Glenn Robinson, Purdue
1969 Lew Alcindor, UCLA	1982 Ralph Sampson, Virginia	1995 Ed O'Bannon, UCLA
1970 Pete Maravich, LSU	1983 Ralph Sampson, Virginia	1996 Marcus Camby, UMass
1971 Sidney Wicks, UCLA	1984 Michael Jordan, N. Carolina	1997 Tim Duncan, Wake Forest
1972 Bill Walton, UCLA	1985 Chris Mullin, St. John's	1998 Antawn Jamison, N. Carolina
1973 Bill Walton, UCLA	1986 Walter Berry, St. John's	1999 Elton Brand, Duke
1974 Bill Walton, UCLA	1987 David Robinson, Navy	2000 Kenyon Martin, Cincinnati
1975 David Thompson, N.C. State	1988 Hersey Hawkins, Bradley	2001 Shane Battier, Duke
1976 Adrian Dantley, Notre Dame	1989 Danny Ferry, Duke	2002 Jason Williams, Duke
1977 Marques Johnson, UCLA	1990 Lionel Simmons, La Salle	

Rupp Trophy

Voted on by AP sportswriters and broadcasters and first presented in 1961 by the Commonwealth Athletic Club of Kentucky in the name of former University of Kentucky coach Adolph Rupp.

Multiple winners: Ralph Sampson (3); Lew Alcindor, Jerry Lucas, David Thompson and Bill Walton (2).

Year	Year	Year
1961 Jerry Lucas, Ohio St.	1975 David Thompson, N.C. State	1989 Sean Elliott, Arizona
1962 Jerry Lucas, Ohio St.	1976 Scott May, Indiana	1990 Lionel Simmons, La Salle
1963 Art Heyman, Duke	1977 Marques Johnson, UCLA	1991 Shaquille O'Neal, LSU
1964 Gary Bradds, Ohio St.	1978 Butch Lee, Marquette	1992 Christian Laettner, Duke
1965 Bill Bradley, Princeton	1979 Larry Bird, Indiana St.	1993 Calbert Cheaney, Indiana
1966 Cazzie Russell, Michigan	1980 Mark Aguirre, DePaul	1994 Glenn Robinson, Purdue
1967 Lew Alcindor, UCLA	1981 Ralph Sampson, Virginia	1995 Joe Smith, Maryland
1968 Elvin Hayes, Houston	1982 Ralph Sampson, Virginia	1996 Marcus Camby, UMass
1969 Lew Alcindor, UCLA	1983 Ralph Sampson, Virginia	1997 Tim Duncan, Wake Forest
1970 Pete Maravich, LSU	1984 Michael Jordan, N. Carolina	1998 Antawn Jamison, N. Carolina
1971 Austin Carr, Notre Dame	1985 Patrick Ewing, Georgetown	1999 Elton Brand, Duke
1972 Bill Walton, UCLA	1986 Walter Berry, St. John's	2000 Kenyon Martin, Cincinnati
1973 Bill Walton, UCLA	1987 David Robinson, Navy	2001 Shane Battier, Duke
1974 David Thompson, N.C. State	1988 Hersey Hawkins, Bradley	2002 Jason Williams, Duke

Naismith Award

Voted on by a panel of coaches, sportswriters and broadcasters and first presented in 1969 by the Atlanta Tip-Off Club in 1969 in the name of the inventor of basketball, Dr. James Naismith.

Multiple winners: Ralph Sampson and Bill Walton (3).

Year	Year	Year
1969 Lew Alcindor, UCLA	1981 Ralph Sampson, Virginia	1993 Calbert Cheaney, Indiana
1970 Pete Maravich, LSU	1982 Ralph Sampson, Virginia	1994 Glenn Robinson, Purdue
1971 Austin Carr, Notre Dame	1983 Ralph Sampson, Virginia	1995 Joe Smith, Maryland
1972 Bill Walton, UCLA	1984 Michael Jordan, N. Carolina	1996 Marcus Camby, UMass
1973 Bill Walton, UCLA	1985 Patrick Ewing, Georgetown	1997 Tim Duncan, Wake Forest
1974 Bill Walton, UCLA	1986 Johnny Dawkins, Duke	1998 Antawn Jamison, N. Carolina
1975 David Thompson, N.C. State	1987 David Robinson, Navy	1999 Elton Brand, Duke
1976 Scott May, Indiana	1988 Danny Manning, Kansas	2000 Kenyon Martin, Cincinnati
1977 Marques Johnson, UCLA	1989 Danny Ferry, Duke	2001 Shane Battier, Duke
1978 Butch Lee, Marquette	1990 Lionel Simmons, La Salle	2002 Jason Williams, Duke
1979 Larry Bird, Indiana St.	1991 Larry Johnson, UNLV	
1980 Mark Aguirre, DePaul	1992 Christian Laettner, Duke	

National Association of Basketball Coaches

Voted on by the National Assn. of Basketball Coaches and presented by the Eastman Kodak Co. from 1975-94.

Multiple winners: Ralph Sampson and Jason Williams (2).

Year	Year	Year
1975 David Thompson, N.C. State	1985 Patrick Ewing, Georgetown	1995 Shawn Respert, Mich. St.
1976 Scott May, Indiana	1986 Walter Berry, St. John's	1996 Marcus Camby, UMass
1977 Marques Johnson, UCLA	1987 David Robinson, Navy	1997 Tim Duncan, Wake Forest
1978 Phil Ford, North Carolina	1988 Danny Manning, Kansas	1998 Antawn Jamison, N. Carolina
1979 Larry Bird, Indiana St.	1989 Sean Elliott, Arizona	1999 Elton Brand, Duke
1980 Michael Brooks, La Salle	1990 Lionel Simmons, La Salle	2000 Kenyon Martin, Cincinnati
1981 Danny Ainge, BYU	1991 Larry Johnson, UNLV	2001 Jason Williams, Duke
1982 Ralph Sampson, Virginia	1992 Christian Laettner, Duke	2002 Jason Williams, Duke
1983 Ralph Sampson, Virginia	1993 Calbert Cheaney, Indiana	& Drew Gooden, Kansas
1984 Michael Jordan, N. Carolina	1994 Glenn Robinson, Purdue	

Wooden Award

Voted on by a panel of coaches, sportswriters and broadcasters and first presented in 1977 by the Los Angeles Athletic Club in the name of former Purdue All-American and UCLA coach John Wooden. Unlike the other five player of the year awards, candidates for the Wooden must have a minimum grade point average of 2.00 (out of 4.00).

Multiple winner: Ralph Sampson (2).

Year	Year	Year
1977 Marques Johnson, UCLA	1986 Walter Berry St. John's	1995 Ed O'Bannon, UCLA
1978 Phil Ford, North Carolina	1987 David Robinson, Navy	1996 Marcus Camby, UMass
1979 Larry Bird, Indiana St.	1988 Danny Manning, Kansas	1997 Tim Duncan, Wake Forest
1980 Darrell Griffith, Louisville	1989 Sean Elliott, Arizona	1998 Antawn Jamison, N. Carolina
1981 Danny Ainge, BYU	1990 Lionel Simmons, La Salle	1999 Elton Brand, Duke
1982 Ralph Sampson, Virginia	1991 Larry Johnson, UNLV	2000 Kenyon Martin, Cincinnati
1983 Ralph Sampson, Virginia	1992 Christian Laettner, Duke	2001 Shane Battier, Duke
1984 Michael Jordan, N. Carolina	1993 Calbert Cheaney, Indiana	2002 Jason Williams, Duke
1985 Chris Mullin, St. John's	1994 Glenn Robinson, Purdue	

All-Time Winningest Division I Coaches

Minimum of 10 seasons as Division I head coach; regular season and tournament games included; coaches active during 2001-02 in **bold** type.

Top 30 Winning Percentage

		Yrs	W	L	Pct
1	Clair Bee	21	412	87	**.826**
2	Adolph Rupp	41	876	190	**.822**
3	**Roy Williams**	14	388	93	**.807**
4	John Wooden	29	664	162	**.804**
5	**John Kresse**	23	560	143	**.797**
6	**Jerry Tarkanian**	31	778	202	**.794**
7	Dean Smith	36	879	254	**.776**
8	Harry Fisher	13	147	44	**.770**
9	Frank Keaney	27	387	117	**.768**
10	George Keogan	24	385	117	**.767**
11	Jack Ramsay	11	231	71	**.765**
12	Vic Bubas	10	213	67	**.761**
13	Chick Davies	21	314	106	**.748**
14	Ray Mears	21	399	135	**.747**
15	**Bob Huggins**	21	500	172	**.744**
16	Al McGuire	20	405	143	**.739**
17	Everett Case	18	376	133	**.739**
18	Phog Allen	48	746	264	**.739**
19	**Jim Boeheim**	26	623	221	**.738**
20	**Mike Krzyzewski**	27	637	226	**.738**
21	**Lute Olson**	29	662	236	**.737**
22	Walter Meanwell	22	280	101	**.735**
23	Bill Musselman	12	232	85	**.732**
24	**Rick Majerus**	18	397	146	**.731**
25	**Rick Pitino**	16	371	137	**.730**
26	**John Chaney**	30	675	253	**.727**
27	Lew Andreas	25	355	134	**.726**
28	**Bob Knight**	36	787	298	**.725**
29	Lou Carnesecca	24	526	200	**.725**
30	Fred Schaus	12	251	96	**.723**

Top 30 Victories

		Yrs	W	L	Pct
1	Dean Smith	36	**879**	254	.776
2	Adolph Rupp	41	**876**	190	.822
3	**Jim Phelan**	48	**819**	508	.617
4	**Bob Knight**	36	**787**	298	.725
5	**Lefty Driesell**	40	**782**	388	.668
6	**Jerry Tarkanian**	31	**778**	202	.794
7	Hank Iba	41	**767**	338	.694
8	Ed Diddle	42	**759**	302	.715
	Lou Henson	39	**759**	389	.662
10	Phog Allen	48	**746**	264	.739
11	Norm Stewart	38	**731**	375	.661
12	Ray Meyer	42	**724**	354	.672
13	Don Haskins	38	**719**	353	.671
14	**Eddie Sutton**	32	**702**	278	.716
15	Denny Crum	30	**675**	295	.696
	John Chaney	30	**675**	253	.727
17	John Wooden	29	**664**	162	.804
18	**Lute Olson**	29	**662**	236	.737
19	Ralph Miller	38	**657**	382	.632
20	Marv Harshman	40	**654**	449	.593
21	Gene Bartow	34	**647**	353	.647
22	**Mike Krzyzewski**	27	**637**	226	.738
23	Cam Henderson	35	**630**	243	.722
24	Norm Sloan	37	**624**	393	.614
25	**Jim Boeheim**	26	**623**	221	.738
	Jim Calhoun	30	**623**	286	.685
27	Slats Gill	36	**599**	392	.604
28	Abe Lemons	34	**597**	344	.634
29	John Thompson	27	**596**	239	.714
30	**Billy Tubbs**	28	**595**	297	.667

Note: Clarence (Bighouse) Gaines of Division II Winston-Salem St. (1947-93) retired after the 1992-93 season to finish his 47-year career ranked No. 3 on the all-time NCAA list of all coaches regardless of division. His record is 828-446 with a .650 winning percentage.

Where They Coached

Allen—Baker (1906-08), Kansas (1908-09), Haskell (1909), Central Mo. St. (1913-19), Kansas (1920-56); **Andreas**—Syracuse (1925-43; 45-50); **Bartow**—Central Mo. St. (1962-64), Valparaiso (1965-70), Memphis St. (1971-74), Illinois (1975), UCLA (1976-77), UAB (1979-96); **Bee**—Rider (1929-31), LIU-Brooklyn (1932-45, 46-51); **Boeheim**—Syracuse (1977–); **Bubas**—Duke (1960-69); **Calhoun**—Northeastern (1973-86), Connecticut (1987–); **Carnesecca**—St. John's (1966-70, 74-92); **Case**—N.C. State (1947-64); **Chaney**—Cheyney St. (1973-82), Temple (1983–); **Crum**—Louisville (1972-01); **Davies**—Duquesne (1925-43, 47-48); **Diddle**—Western Ky. (1923-64); **Driesell**—Davidson (1961-69), Maryland (1970-86), J. Madison (1989-97), Georgia St. (1997–); **Fisher**—Columbia (1907-16), Army (1922-23, 25).

Gill—Oregon St. (1929-64); **Harshman**—Pacific Lutheran (1946-58), Wash. St. (1959-71), Washington (1972-85); **Haskins**—UTEP (1962-99); **Henderson**—Muskingum (1920-22), Davis & Elkins (1923-35), Marshall (1936-55); **Henson**—Hardin-Simmons (1963-66), N. Mexico St. (1967-75), Illinois (1976-96), N. Mexico St. (1997–); **Huggins**—Walsh (1981-83), Akron (1985-89), Cincinnati (1990–); **Iba**—NW Missouri St. (1930-33), Colorado (1934), Oklahoma St. (1935-70); **Keaney**—Rhode Island (1921-48); **Keogan**—St. Louis (1916), Allegheny (1919), Valparaiso (1920-21), Notre Dame (1924-43); **Knight**—Army (1966-71), Indiana (1972-00), Texas Tech (2001–); **Kresse**—Charleston (1979–); **Krzyzewski**—Army (1976-80), Duke (1981–).

Lemons—Okla. City (1956-73), Pan American (1974-76), Texas (1977-82), Okla. City (1984-90); **Majerus**—Marquette (1984-86), Ball St. (1988-89), Utah (1991–); **McGuire**—Belmont Abbey (1958-64), Marquette (1965-77); **Meanwell**

Wisconsin (1912-17, 21-34), Missouri (1918-20); **Mears**–Wittenberg (1957-62), Tennessee (1963-77); **Meyer**–DePaul (1943-84); **R. Miller**–Wichita St. (1952-64), Iowa (1965-70), Oregon St. (1971-89); **Musselman**–Ashland (1966-71), Minnesota (1972-75), S. Alabama (1996-97); **Olson**–Long Beach St. (1974), Iowa (1975-83), Arizona (1984–); **Phelan**–Mount St. Mary's (1955–); **Pitino**–Boston Univ. (1979-83), Providence (1986-87), Kentucky (1989-97), Louisville (2001–).

Ramsay–St. Joseph's-PA (1956-66); **Rupp**–Kentucky (1931-72); **Schaus**–West Va. (1955-60), Purdue (1973-78); **Sloan**–Presbyterian (1952-55), Citadel (1957-60), Florida (1961-66), N.C. State (1967-80), Florida (1981-89); **Smith**–North Carolina (1962-97); **Stewart**–No. Iowa (1962-67), Missouri (1968-99); **Sutton**–Creighton (1970-74), Arkansas (1975-85), Kentucky (1986-89), Oklahoma St. (1991–); **Tarkanian**–Long Beach St. (1969-73), UNLV (1974-92), Fresno St. (1995-2002); **Thompson**–Georgetown (1973-99); **Tubbs**–Southwestern (1971-73), Lamar (1976-80), Oklahoma (1981-93), TCU (1994-2002); **Williams**– Kansas (1989–); **Wooden**–Indiana St. (1947-48), UCLA (1949-75).

Most NCAA Tournaments

Through 2002; listed are number of appearances, overall tournament record, times reaching Final Four, and number of NCAA championships. (*) denotes that actual records are different from official NCAA records.

App		W-L	F4	Championships
27	Dean Smith	65-27	11	2 (1982, 93)
24	**Bob Knight**	42-21	5	3 (1976, 81, 87)
23	Denny Crum	42-23	6	2 (1980, 86)
23	Lute Olson*	39-23	5	1 (1997)
23	**Eddie Sutton***	32-23	2	None
21	**Jim Boeheim**	32-21	2	None
20	Adolph Rupp	30-18	6	4 (1948-49, 51, 58)
20	John Thompson	34-19	3	1 (1984)
19	**Lou Henson**	19-20	2	None
18	Lou Carnesecca	17-20	1	None
18	**Jerry Tarkanian**	38-18	4	1 (1990)
18	**Mike Krzyzewski**	58-15	9	3 (1991-92, 2001)
17	**John Chaney**	23-17	0	None
17	**Gene Keady***	18-17	0	None
16	John Wooden	47-10	12	10 (1964-65, 67-73, 75)
16	Norm Stewart*	12-16	0	None
16	Nolan Richardson	26-15	3	1 (1994)
16	**Jim Harrick**	18-15	1	1 (1995)
15	**Jim Calhoun***	29-14	1	1 (1999)
15	Digger Phelps	17-17	1	None
14	Don Haskins	14-13	1	1 (1966)
14	Guy Lewis	26-18	5	None
13	Dale Brown	15-14	2	None
13	Ray Meyer	14-16	2	None
13	**Lefty Driesell**	16-14	0	None

Active Coaches' Victories

Minimum five seasons in Division I.

		Yrs	W	L	Pct
1	Jim Phelan, Mt. St. Mary's	48	819	508	.617
2	Bob Knight, Texas Tech	36	787	298	.725
3	Lefty Driesell, Georgia St.	40	782	388	.668
4	Lou Henson, N. Mexico St.	39	759	389	.662
5	Eddie Sutton, Okla. St.	32	702	278	.716
6	John Chaney, Temple	30	675	253	.727
7	Lute Olson, Arizona	29	662	236	.737
8	Mike Krzyzewski, Duke	27	637	226	.738
9	Jim Boeheim, Syracuse	26	623	221	.738
	Jim Calhoun, UConn	30	623	286	.685
11	Hugh Durham, Jacksonville	34	591	385	.606
12	Dave Bliss, Baylor	27	510	314	.619
13	Rollie Massimino, Cleveland St.	28	507	369	.579
	Gene Keady, Purdue	24	507	243	.676
15	Bob Huggins, Cincinnati	21	500	172	.744
16	Don DeVoe, Navy	29	499	346	.591
17	Cliff Ellis, Auburn	27	498	311	.616
18	Mike Montgomery, Stanford	24	493	233	.679
19	Gary Williams, Maryland	24	481	271	.640
20	Jim Harrick, Georgia	22	452	226	.667
21	Ben Braun, California	25	451	305	.597
22	Rick Majerus, Utah	18	397	146	.731
23	Roy Williams, Kansas	14	388	93	.807
24	Danny Nee, Duquesne	22	377	298	.558
25	John Beilein, Richmond	20	372	215	.634

Annual Awards

UPI picked the first national Division I Coach of the Year in 1955. Since then, the U.S. Basketball Writers Assn. (1959), AP (1967), the National Assn. of Basketball Coaches (1969), and the Atlanta Tip-Off Club (1987) have joined in. Since 1987, the first year all five awards were given out, no coach has won all of them in the same season.

United Press International

Voted on by a panel of UPI college basketball writers and first presented in 1955.

Multiple winners: John Wooden (6); Bob Knight, Ray Meyer, Adolph Rupp, Norm Stewart, Fred Taylor and Phil Woolpert (2).

Year		Year		Year	
1955	Phil Woolpert, San Francisco	1970	John Wooden, UCLA	1985	Lou Carnesecca, St. John's
1956	Phil Woolpert, San Francisco	1971	Al McGuire, Marquette	1986	Mike Krzyzewski, Duke
1957	Frank McGuire, North Carolina	1972	John Wooden, UCLA	1987	John Thompson, Georgetown
1958	Tex Winter, Kansas St.	1973	John Wooden, UCLA	1988	John Chaney, Temple
1959	Adolph Rupp, Kentucky	1974	Digger Phelps, Notre Dame	1989	Bob Knight, Indiana
1960	Pete Newell, California	1975	Bob Knight, Indiana	1990	Jim Calhoun, Connecticut
1961	Fred Taylor, Ohio St.	1976	Tom Young, Rutgers	1991	Rick Majerus, Utah
1962	Fred Taylor, Ohio St.	1977	Bob Gaillard, San Francisco	1992	Perry Clark, Tulane
1963	Ed Jucker, Cincinnati	1978	Eddie Sutton, Arkansas	1993	Eddie Fogler, Vanderbilt
1964	John Wooden, UCLA	1979	Bill Hodges, Indiana St.	1994	Norm Stewart, Missouri
1965	Dave Strack, Michigan	1980	Ray Meyer, DePaul	1995	Leonard Hamilton, Miami-FL
1966	Adolph Rupp, Kentucky	1981	Ralph Miller, Oregon St.	1996	Gene Keady, Purdue
1967	John Wooden, UCLA	1982	Norm Stewart, Missouri	1997	award discontinued
1968	Guy Lewis, Houston	1983	Jerry Tarkanian, UNLV		
1969	John Wooden, UCLA	1984	Ray Meyer, DePaul		

Annual Awards (Cont.)
U.S. Basketball Writers Association
Voted on by the USBWA and first presented in 1959.

Multiple winners: John Wooden (5); Bob Knight (3); Lou Carnesecca, John Chaney, Ray Meyer and Fred Taylor (2).

Year	Year	Year
1959 Eddie Hickey, Marquette	1974 Norm Sloan, N.C. State	1989 Bob Knight, Indiana
1960 Pete Newell, California	1975 Bob Knight, Indiana	1990 Roy Williams, Kansas
1961 Fred Taylor, Ohio St.	1976 Bob Knight, Indiana	1991 Randy Ayers, Ohio St.
1962 Fred Taylor, Ohio St.	1977 Eddie Sutton, Arkansas	1992 Perry Clark, Tulane
1963 Ed Jucker, Cincinnati	1978 Ray Meyer, DePaul	1993 Eddie Fogler, Vanderbilt
1964 John Wooden, UCLA	1979 Dean Smith, North Carolina	1994 Charlie Spoonhour, St. Louis
1965 Butch van Breda Kolff, Princeton	1980 Ray Meyer, DePaul	1995 Kelvin Sampson, Oklahoma
1966 Adolph Rupp, Kentucky	1981 Ralph Miller, Oregon St.	1996 Gene Keady, Purdue
1967 John Wooden, UCLA	1982 John Thompson, Georgetown	1997 Clem Haskins, Minnesota
1968 Guy Lewis, Houston	1983 Lou Carnesecca, St. John's	1998 Tom Izzo, Michigan St.
1969 Maury John, Drake	1984 Gene Keady, Purdue	1999 Cliff Ellis, Auburn
1970 John Wooden, UCLA	1985 Lou Carnesecca, St. John's	2000 Larry Eustachy, Iowa St.
1971 Al McGuire, Marquette	1986 Dick Versace, Bradley	2001 Al Skinner, Boston College
1972 John Wooden, UCLA	1987 John Chaney, Temple	2002 Ben Howland, Pittsburgh
1973 John Wooden, UCLA	1988 John Chaney, Temple	

Associated Press
Voted on by AP sportswriters and broadcasters and first presented in 1967.

Multiple winners: John Wooden (5); Bob Knight (3); Guy Lewis, Ray Meyer, Ralph Miller and Eddie Sutton (2).

Year	Year	Year
1967 John Wooden, UCLA	1979 Bill Hodges, Indiana St.	1991 Randy Ayers, Ohio St.
1968 Guy Lewis, Houston	1980 Ray Meyer, DePaul	1992 Roy Williams, Kansas
1969 John Wooden, UCLA	1981 Ralph Miller, Oregon St.	1993 Eddie Fogler, Vanderbilt
1970 John Wooden, UCLA	1982 Ralph Miller, Oregon St.	1994 Norm Stewart, Missouri
1971 Al McGuire, Marquette	1983 Guy Lewis, Houston	1995 Kelvin Sampson, Oklahoma
1972 John Wooden, UCLA	1984 Ray Meyer, DePaul	1996 Gene Keady, Purdue
1973 John Wooden, UCLA	1985 Bill Frieder, Michigan	1997 Clem Haskins, Minnesota
1974 Norm Sloan, N.C. State	1986 Eddie Sutton, Kentucky	1998 Tom Izzo, Michigan St.
1975 Bob Knight, Indiana	1987 Tom Davis, Iowa	1999 Cliff Ellis, Auburn
1976 Bob Knight, Indiana	1988 John Chaney, Temple	2000 Larry Eustachy, Iowa St.
1977 Bob Gaillard, San Francisco	1989 Bob Knight, Indiana	2001 Matt Doherty, North Carolina
1978 Eddie Sutton, Arkansas	1990 Jim Calhoun, Connecticut	2002 Ben Howland, Pittsburgh

National Association of Basketball Coaches
Voted on by NABC membership and first presented in 1969.

Multiple winners: John Wooden (3); Gene Keady and Mike Krzyzewski (2).

Year	Year	Year
1969 John Wooden, UCLA	1981 Ralph Miller, Oregon St.	1993 Eddie Fogler, Vanderbilt
1970 John Wooden, UCLA	& Jack Hartman, Kansas St.	1994 Nolan Richardson, Arkansas
1971 Jack Kraft, Villanova	1982 Don Monson, Idaho	& Gene Keady, Purdue
1972 John Wooden, UCLA	1983 Lou Carnesecca, St. John's	1995 Jim Harrick, UCLA
1973 Gene Bartow, Memphis St.	1984 Marv Harshman, Washington	1996 John Calipari, UMass
1974 Al McGuire, Marquette	1985 John Thompson, Georgetown	1997 Clem Haskins, Minnesota
1975 Bob Knight, Indiana	1986 Eddie Sutton, Kentucky	1998 Bill Guthridge, N. Carolina
1976 Johnny Orr, Michigan	1987 Rick Pitino, Providence	1999 Mike Krzyzewski, Duke
1977 Dean Smith, North Carolina	1988 John Chaney, Temple	& Jim O'Brien, Ohio St.
1978 Bill Foster, Duke	1989 P.J. Carlesimo, Seton Hall	2000 Gene Keady, Purdue
& Abe Lemons, Texas	1990 Jud Heathcote, Michigan St.	2001 Tom Izzo, Michigan St.
1979 Ray Meyer, DePaul	1991 Mike Krzyzewski, Duke	2002 Kelvin Sampson, Oklahoma
1980 Lute Olson, Iowa	1992 George Raveling, USC	

Naismith Award
Voted on by a panel of coaches, sportswriters and broadcasters and first presented by the Atlanta Tip-Off Club in 1987 in the name of the inventor of basketball, Dr. James Naismith.

Multiple winner: Mike Krzyzewski (3).

Year	Year	Year
1987 Bob Knight, Indiana	1993 Dean Smith, North Carolina	1999 Mike Krzyzewski, Duke
1988 Larry Brown, Kansas	1994 Nolan Richardson, Arkansas	2000 Mike Montgomery, Stanford
1989 Mike Krzyzewski, Duke	1995 Jim Harrick, UCLA	2001 Rod Barnes, Mississippi
1990 Bobby Cremins, Georgia Tech	1996 John Calipari, UMass	2002 Ben Howland, Pittsburgh
1991 Randy Ayers, Ohio St.	1997 Roy Williams, Kansas	
1992 Mike Krzyzewski, Duke	1998 Bill Guthridge, N. Carolina	

Player of the Year and NBA MVP

College Players of the Year who have gone on to win the NBA's Most Valuable Player award:

Bill Russell COLLEGE–San Francisco (1956); PROS–Boston Celtics (1958, 1961, 1962, 1963 and 1965).
Oscar Robertson COLLEGE–Cincinnati (1958, 1959 and 1960); PROS–Cincinnati Royals (1964).
Kareem Abdul-Jabbar COLLEGE–UCLA (1967 and 1969); PROS–Milwaukee Bucks (1971, 1972 and 1974) and LA Lakers (1976, 1977 and 1980).
Bill Walton COLLEGE–UCLA (1972, 1973 and 1974); PROS–Portland Trail Blazers (1978).
Larry Bird COLLEGE–Indiana St. (1979); PROS–Boston Celtics (1984, 1985, and 1986).
Michael Jordan COLLEGE–North Carolina (1984); PROS–Chicago Bulls (1988, 1991, 1992, 1996 and 1998).
David Robinson COLLEGE–Navy (1987); PROS–San Antonio Spurs (1995).
Shaquille O'Neal COLLEGE–LSU (1991); PROS–LA Lakers (2000).
Tim Duncan COLLEGE–Wake Forest (1997); PROS–San Antonio Spurs (2002).

Other Men's Champions

The NCAA has sanctioned national championship tournaments for Division II since 1957 and Division III since 1975. The NAIA sanctioned a single tournament from 1937-91, then split into two divisions in 1992.

NCAA Div. II Finals

Multiple winners: Kentucky Wesleyan (8); Evansville (5); CS-Bakersfield (3); Metropolitan State, North Alabama and Virginia Union (2).

Year	Winner	Score	Loser	Year	Winner	Score	Loser
1957	Wheaton, IL	89-65	Ky. Wesleyan	1981	Florida Southern	73-68	Mt. St. Mary's, MD
1958	South Dakota	75-53	St. Michael's, VT	1982	Dist. of Columbia	73-63	Florida Southern
1959	Evansville, IN	83-67	SW Missouri St.	1983	Wright St., OH	92-73	Dist. of Columbia
1960	Evansville	90-69	Chapman, CA	1984	Central Mo. St.	81-77	St. Augustine's, NC
1961	Wittenberg, OH	42-38	SE Missouri St.	1985	Jacksonville St.	74-73	South Dakota St.
1962	Mt. St. Mary's, MD	58-57*	CS-Sacramento	1986	Sacred Heart, CT	93-87	SE Missouri St.
1963	South Dakota St.	42-40	Wittenberg, OH	1987	Ky. Wesleyan	92-74	Gannon, PA
1964	Evansville	72-59	Akron, OH	1988	Lowell, MA	75-72	AK-Anchorage
1965	Evansville	85-82*	Southern Illinois	1989	N.C. Central	73-46	SE Missouri St.
1966	Ky. Wesleyan	54-51	Southern Illinois	1990	Ky. Wesleyan	93-79	CS-Bakersfield
1967	Winston-Salem, NC	77-74	SW Missouri St.	1991	North Alabama	79-72	Bridgeport, CT
1968	Ky. Wesleyan	63-52	Indiana St.	1992	Virginia Union	100-75	Bridgeport
1969	Ky. Wesleyan	75-71	SW Missouri St.	1993	CS-Bakersfield	85-72	Troy St., AL
1970	Phila. Textile	76-65	Tennessee St.	1994	CS-Bakersfield	92-86	Southern Ind.
1971	Evansville	97-82	Old Dominion, VA	1995	Southern Indiana	71-63	UC-Riverside
1972	Roanoke, VA	84-72	Akron, OH	1996	Fort Hays St.	70-63	N. Kentucky
1973	Ky. Wesleyan	78-76*	Tennessee St.	1997	CS-Bakersfield	57-56	N. Kentucky
1974	Morgan St., MD	67-52	SW Missouri St.	1998	UC-Davis	83-77	Ky. Wesleyan
1975	Old Dominion	76-74	New Orleans	1999	Ky. Wesleyan	75-60	Metropolitan St.
1976	Puget Sound, WA	83-74	Tennessee-Chatt.	2000	Metropolitan St.	97-79	Ky. Wesleyan
1977	Tennessee-Chatt.	71-62	Randolph-Macon	2001	Ky. Wesleyan	72-63	Washburn, KS
1978	Cheyney, PA	47-40	WI-Green Bay	2002	Metropolitan St.	80-72	Ky. Wesleyan
1979	North Alabama	64-50	WI-Green Bay	*Overtime			
1980	Virginia Union	80-74	New York Tech				

NCAA Div. III Finals

Multiple winners: North Park (5); WI-Platteville (4); Calvin, Potsdam St., Scranton and WI-Whitewater (2).

Year	Winner	Score	Loser	Year	Winner	Score	Loser
1975	LeMoyne-Owen, TN	57-54	Glassboro St., NJ	1991	WI-Platteville	81-74	Franklin Marshall
1976	Scranton, PA	60-57	Wittenberg, OH	1992	Calvin, MI	62-49	Rochester, NY
1977	Wittenberg, OH	79-66	Oneonta St., NY	1993	Ohio Northern	71-68	Augustana, IL
1978	North Park, IL	69-57	Widener, PA	1994	Lebanon Valley, PA	66-59*	NYU
1979	North Park, IL	66-62	Potsdam St., NY	1995	WI-Platteville	69-55	Manchester, IN
1980	North Park, IL	83-76	Upsala, NJ	1996	Rowan, NJ	100-93	Hope, MI
1981	Potsdam St., NY	67-65*	Augustana, IL	1997	Illinois Wesleyan	89-86	Neb-Wesleyan
1982	Wabash, IN	83-62	Potsdam St., NY	1998	WI-Platteville	69-56	Hope, MI
1983	Scranton, PA	64-63	Wittenberg, OH	1999	WI-Platteville	76-75**	Hampden-Sydney
1984	WI-Whitewater	103-86	Clark, MA	2000	Calvin, MI	79-74	WI-Eau Claire
1985	North Park, IL	72-71	Potsdam St., NY	2001	Catholic, DC	76-62	Wm. Paterson
1986	Potsdam St., NY	76-73	LeMoyne-Owen, TN	2002	Otterbein	102-83	Elizabethtown
1987	North Park, IL	106-100	Clark, MA	*Overtime			
1988	Ohio Wesleyan	92-70	Scranton, PA	**Double overtime			
1989	WI-Whitewater	94-86	Trenton St., NJ				
1990	Rochester, NY	43-42	DePauw, IN				

NAIA Finals, 1937-91

Multiple winners: Grand Canyon, Hamline, Kentucky St. and Tennessee St. (3); Central Missouri, Central St., Fort Hays St. and SW Missouri St. (2).

Year	Winner	Score	Loser
1937	Central Missouri	35-24	Morningside, IA
1938	Central Missouri	45-30	Roanoke, VA
1939	Southwestern, KS	32-31	San Diego St.
1940	Tarkio, MO	52-31	San Diego St.
1941	San Diego St.	36-32	Murray St., KY
1942	Hamline, MN	33-31	SE Oklahoma
1943	SE Missouri St.	34-32	NW Missouri St.
1944	Not held		
1945	Loyola-LA	49-36	Pepperdine, CA
1946	Southern Illinois	49-40	Indiana St.
1947	Marshall, WV	73-59	Mankato St., MN
1948	Louisville, KY	82-70	Indiana St.
1949	Hamline, MN	57-46	Regis, CO
1950	Indiana St.	61-47	East Central, OK
1951	Hamline, MN	69-61	Millikin, IL
1952	SW Missouri St.	73-64	Murray St., KY
1953	SW Missouri St.	79-71	Hamline, MN
1954	St.Benedict's, KS	62-56	Western Illinois
1955	East Texas St.	71-54	SE Oklahoma
1956	McNeese St., LA	60-55	Texas Southern
1957	Tennessee St.	92-73	SE Oklahoma
1958	Tennessee St.	85-73	Western Illinois
1959	Tennessee St.	97-87	Pacific-Luth., WA
1960	SW Texas St.	66-44	Westminster, PA
1961	Grambling, LA	95-75	Georgetown, KY
1962	Prairie View, TX	62-53	Westminster, PA
1963	Pan American, TX	73-62	Western Carolina
1964	Rockhurst, MO	66-56	Pan American, TX
1965	Central St., OH	85-51	Oklahoma Baptist
1966	Oklahoma Baptist	88-59	Georgia Southern
1967	St.Benedict's, KS	71-65	Oklahoma Baptist
1968	Central St., OH	51-48	Fairmont St., WV
1969	Eastern N. Mex	99-76	MD-Eastern Shore
1970	Kentucky St.	79-71	Central Wash.
1971	Kentucky St.	102-82	Eastern Michigan
1972	Kentucky St.	71-62	WI-Eau Claire
1973	Guilford, NC	99-96	MD-Eastern Shore
1974	West Georgia	97-79	Alcorn St., MS

Year	Winner	Score	Loser
1975	Grand Canyon, AZ	65-54	M'western St., TX
1976	Coppin St., MD	96-91	Henderson St., AR
1977	Texas Southern	71-44	Campbell, NC
1978	Grand Canyon	79-75	Kearney St., NE
1979	Drury, MO	60-54	Henderson St., AR
1980	Cameron, OK	84-77	Alabama St.
1981	Beth. Nazarene, OK	86-85*	AL-Huntsville
1982	SC-Spartanburg	51-38	Biola, CA
1983	Charleston, SC	57-53	WV-Wesleyan
1984	Fort Hays St., KS	48-46*	WI-Stevens Pt.
1985	Fort Hays St.	82-80*	Wayland Bapt., TX
1986	David Lipscomb, TN	67-54	AR-Monticello
1987	Washburn, KS	79-77	West Virginia St.
1988	Grand Canyon	88-86*	Auburn-Montg, AL
1989	St.Mary's, TX	61-58	East Central, OK
1990	Birm-Southern, AL	88-80	WI-Eau Claire
1991	Oklahoma City	77-74	Central Arkansas

*Overtime

NAIA Div. I Finals

NAIA split tournament into two divisions in 1992.

Multiple winners: Life, GA and Oklahoma City (3).

Year	Winner	Score	Loser
1992	Oklahoma City	82-73*	Central Arkansas
1993	Hawaii Pacific	88-83	Okla. Baptist
1994	Oklahoma City	99-81	Life, GA
1995	Birm-Southern	92-76	Pfeiffer, NC
1996	Oklahoma City	86-80	Georgetown, KY
1997	Life, GA	73-64	Okla. Baptist
1998	Georgetown, KY	83-69	So. Nazarene
1999	Life, GA	63-60	Mobile, AL
2000	Life, GA	61-59	Georgetown, KY
2001	Faulkner, AL	63-59	Science & Arts, OK
2002	Science & Arts, OK	96-79	Okla. Baptist

*Overtime

NAIA Div. II Finals

NAIA split tournament into two divisions in 1992.

Multiple winner: Bethel, IN (3).

Year	Winner	Score	Loser
1992	Grace, IN	85-79*	Northwestern-IA
1993	Williamette, OR	63-56	Northern St., SD
1994	Eureka, IL	98-95*	Northern St.
1995	Bethel, IN	103-95*	NW Nazarene, ID
1996	Albertson, ID	81-72*	Whitworth, WA
1997	Bethel	95-94	Siena Heights, MI
1998	Bethel	89-87	Oregon Tech

Year	Winner	Score	Loser
1999	Cornerstone, MI	113-109	Bethel
2000	Embry-Riddle, FL	75-63	Ozarks, MO
2001	Northwestern, IA	82-78	Mid. Am. Nazarene, KS
2002	Evangel, MO	84-61	Robert Morris, IL

*Overtime

WOMEN

NCAA Final Four

Replaced the Association of Intercollegiate Athletics for Women (AIAW) tournament in 1982 as the official playoff for the national championship.

Multiple winners: Tennessee (6); Connecticut (3); Louisiana Tech, Stanford and USC (2).

Year	Champion	Head Coach	Score	Runner-up	Third Place	
1982	Louisiana Tech	Sonya Hogg	76-62	Cheyney	Maryland	Tennessee
1983	USC	Linda Sharp	69-67	Louisiana Tech	Georgia	Old Dominion
1984	USC	Linda Sharp	72-61	Tennessee	Cheyney	Louisiana Tech
1985	Old Dominion	Marianne Stanley	70-65	Georgia	NE Louisiana	Western Ky.
1986	Texas	Jody Conradt	97-81	USC	Tennessee	Western Ky.
1987	Tennessee	Pat Summitt	67-44	Louisiana Tech	Long Beach St.	Texas
1988	Louisiana Tech	Leon Barmore	56-54	Auburn	Long Beach St.	Tennessee
1989	Tennessee	Pat Summitt	76-60	Auburn	Louisiana Tech	Maryland
1990	Stanford	Tara VanDerveer	88-81	Auburn	Louisiana Tech	Virginia
1991	Tennessee	Pat Summitt	70-67(OT)	Virginia	Connecticut	Stanford
1992	Stanford	Tara VanDerveer	78-62	Western Kentucky	SW Missouri St.	Virginia

Year	Champion	Head Coach	Score	Runner-up		Third Place	
1993	Texas Tech	Marsha Sharp	84-82	Ohio St.	Iowa	Vanderbilt	
1994	N. Carolina	Sylvia Hatchell	60-59	Louisiana Tech	Alabama	Purdue	
1995	Connecticut	Geno Auriemma	70-64	Tennessee	Georgia	Stanford	
1996	Tennessee	Pat Summitt	83-65	Georgia	Connecticut	Stanford	
1997	Tennessee	Pat Summitt	68-59	Old Dominion	Stanford	Notre Dame	
1998	Tennessee	Pat Summitt	93-75	Louisiana Tech	Arkansas	N.C. State	
1999	Purdue	Carolyn Peck	62-45	Duke	Louisiana Tech	Georgia	
2000	Connecticut	Geno Auriemma	71-52	Tennessee	Penn St.	Rutgers	
2001	Notre Dame	Muffet McGraw	68-66	Purdue	Connecticut	SW Missouri St.	
2002	Connecticut	Geno Auriemma	82-70	Oklahoma	Tennessee	Duke	

Final Four sites: 1982 (Norfolk, Va.), **1983** (Norfolk, Va.), **1984** (Los Angeles), **1985** (Austin), **1986** (Lexington), **1987** (Austin), **1988** (Tacoma), **1989** (Tacoma), **1990** (Knoxville), **1991** (New Orleans), **1992** (Los Angeles), **1993** (Atlanta), **1994** (Richmond), **1995** (Minneapolis), **1996** (Charlotte), **1997** (Cincinnati), **1998** (Kansas City), **1999** (San Jose), **2000** (Philadelphia), **2001** (St. Louis), **2002** (San Antonio).

Most Outstanding Player

A Most Outstanding Player has been selected every year of the NCAA tournament. Winner who did not play for the tournament champion is listed in **bold,** type.
Multiple winners: Chamique Holdsclaw and Cheryl Miller (2).

Year		Year		Year	
1982	Janice Lawrence, La. Tech	1989	Bridgette Gordon, Tennessee	1996	Michelle Marciniak, Tennessee
1983	Cheryl Miller, USC	1990	Jennifer Azzi, Stanford	1997	Chamique Holdsclaw, Tenn.
1984	Cheryl Miller, USC	1991	**Dawn Staley,** Virginia	1998	Chamique Holdsclaw, Tenn.
1985	Tracy Claxton, Old Dominion	1992	Molly Goodenbour, Stanford	1999	Ukari Figgs, Purdue
1986	Clarissa Davis, Texas	1993	Sheryl Swoopes, Texas Tech	2000	Shea Ralph, Connecticut
1987	Tonya Edwards, Tennessee	1994	Charlotte Smith, N. Carolina	2001	Ruth Riley, Notre Dame
1988	Erica Westbrooks, La. Tech	1995	Rebecca Lobo, Connecticut	2002	Swin Cash, Connecticut

All-Time NCAA Division I Tournament Leaders

Through 2001-02; minimum of six games; **Last** column indicates final year played.

CAREER

Scoring

	Total Points	Yrs	Last	Pts	Avg
1	Chamique Holdsclaw, Tenn	4	1999	**479**	21.8
2	Bridgette Gordon, Tenn	4	1989	**388**	21.6
3	Cheryl Miller, USC	4	1986	**333**	20.8
4	Janice Lawrence, La. Tech	3	1984	**312**	22.3
5	Penny Toler, Long Beach St.	4	1989	**291**	22.4
6	Dawn Staley, Virginia	4	1992	**274**	18.3
7	Cindy Brown, Long Beach St.	4	1987	**263**	21.9
	Venus Lacy, La. Tech	3	1990	**263**	18.8
9	Clarissa Davis, Texas	3	1989	**261**	21.8
10	Janet Harris, Georgia	4	1985	**254**	19.5

Rebounds

	Total Rebounds	Yrs	Last	No	Avg
1	Chamique Holdsclaw, Tenn	4	1999	**188**	8.5
2	Cheryl Miller, USC	4	1986	**170**	10.6
3	Sheila Frost, Tennessee	4	1989	**162**	9.0
4	Val Whiting, Stanford	4	1993	**161**	10.1
5	Venus Lacy, La. Tech	3	1990	**148**	10.6
6	Bridgette Gordon, Tenn	4	1989	**142**	7.9
7	Kirsten Cummings, Long Beach St.	4	1985	**136**	10.5
8	Nora Lewis, La. Tech	3	1989	**130**	9.3
9	Pam McGee, USC	4	1984	**127**	9.8
10	Daedra Charles, Tenn.	3	1991	**125**	9.6
	Paula McGee, USC	3	1984	**125**	9.6

SINGLE GAME

Scoring

		Year	Pts
1	Lorri Bauman, Drake vs Maryland	1982	50
2	Sheryl Swoopes, Texas Tech vs Ohio St	1993	47
3	Barbara Kennedy, Clemson vs Penn St	1982	43
4	Jackie Stiles, SW Mo. St. vs. Duke	2001	41
5	LaTaunya Pollard, L. Beach St. vs Howard	1982	40
	Cindy Brown, L. Beach St. vs Ohio St	1987	40
	Tamika Whitmore, Memphis vs. YSU	1998	40
	Tara Mitchem, SW Mo. St. vs. Toledo	2001	40

Rebounds

		Year	No
1	Cheryl Taylor, Tenn. Tech vs Georgia	1985	23
	Charlotte Smith, N. Car. vs La. Tech	1994	23
3	Daedra Charles, Tenn. vs SW Missouri	1991	22
4	Cherie Nelson, USC vs Western Ky	1987	21
5	Alison Lang, Oregon vs Missouri	1982	20
	Shelda Arceneaux, S.D. St. vs L. Beach St.	1984	20
	Tracy Claxton, ODU vs Georgia	1985	20
	Brigette Combs, West. Ky. vs West Va	1989	20
	Tandreia Green, West. Ky. vs West Va	1989	20

Associated Press Final Top 10 Polls

The Associated Press weekly women's college basketball poll was begun by Mel Greenberg of *The Philadelphia Inquirer* during the 1976-77 season. Although the poll was started as a Top 20 in 1977 and was expanded to a Top 25 in 1990, only the Top 10 from each poll are listed below due to space constraints. The Association of Intercollegiate Athletics for Women (AIAW) Tournament determined the Division I national champion from 1972-81. The NCAA began its women's Division I tournament in 1982. The final AP Polls were taken before the NCAA tournament. Eventual national champions are in **bold** type.

#	1977	1982	1987	1992	1997	2002
1	**Delta St.**	**Louisiana Tech**	Texas	Virginia	Connecticut	**Connecticut**
2	Immaculata	Cheyney	Auburn	Tennessee	Old Dominion	Oklahoma
3	St. Joseph's-PA	Maryland	Louisiana Tech	**Stanford**	Stanford	Duke
4	CS-Fullerton	Tennessee	Long Beach St.	S.F. Austin St.	North Carolina	Vanderbilt
5	Tennessee	Texas	Rutgers	Mississippi	Louisiana Tech	Stanford
6	Tennessee Tech	USC	Georgia	Miami-FL	Georgia	Tennessee
7	Wayland Baptist	Old Dominion	**Tennessee**	Iowa	Florida	Baylor
8	Montclair St.	Rutgers	Mississippi	Maryland	Alabama	Louisiana Tech
9	S.F. Austin St.	Long Beach St.	Iowa	Penn St.	LSU	Purdue
10	N.C. State	Penn St.	Ohio St.	SW Missouri St.	**Tennessee**	Iowa St.

#	1978	1983	1988	1993	1998
1	Tennessee	**USC**	Tennessee	Vanderbilt	**Tennessee**
2	Wayland Baptist	Louisiana Tech	Iowa	Tennessee	Old Dominion
3	N.C. State	Texas	Auburn	Ohio St.	Connecticut
4	Montclair St.	Old Dominion	Texas	Iowa	Louisiana Tech
5	**UCLA**	Cheyney	**Louisiana Tech**	**Texas Tech**	Stanford
6	Maryland	Long Beach St.	Ohio St.	Stanford	Texas Tech
7	Queens-NY	Maryland	Long Beach St.	Auburn	North Carolina
8	Valdosta St.	Penn St.	Rutgers	Penn St.	Duke
9	Delta St.	Georgia	Maryland	Virginia	Arizona
10	LSU	Tennessee	Virginia	Colorado	N.C. State

#	1979	1984	1989	1994	1999
1	**Old Dominion**	Texas	**Tennessee**	Tennessee	**Purdue**
2	Louisiana Tech	Louisiana Tech	Auburn	Penn St.	Tennessee
3	Tennessee	Georgia	Louisiana Tech	Connecticut	Louisiana Tech
4	Texas	Old Dominion	Stanford	**North Carolina**	Colorado St.
5	S.F. Austin St.	**USC**	Maryland	Colorado	Old Dominion
6	UCLA	Long Beach St.	Texas	Louisiana Tech	Connecticut
7	Rutgers	Kansas St.	Long Beach St.	USC	Rutgers
8	Maryland	LSU	Iowa	Purdue	Notre Dame
9	Cheyney	Cheyney	Colorado	Texas Tech	Texas Tech
10	Wayland Baptist	Mississippi	Georgia	Virginia	Duke

#	1980	1985	1990	1995	2000
1	**Old Dominion**	Texas	Louisiana Tech	**Connecticut**	**Connecticut**
2	Tennessee	NE Louisiana	**Stanford**	Colorado	Tennessee
3	Louisiana Tech	Long Beach St.	Washington	Tennessee	Louisiana Tech
4	South Carolina	Louisiana Tech	Tennessee	Stanford	Georgia
5	S.F. Austin St.	**Old Dominion**	UNLV	Texas Tech	Notre Dame
6	Maryland	Mississippi	S.F. Austin St.	Vanderbilt	Penn St.
7	Texas	Ohio St.	Georgia	Penn St.	Iowa St.
8	Rutgers	Georgia	Texas	Louisiana Tech	Rutgers
9	Long Beach St.	Penn St.	Auburn	Western Ky.	UC-Santa Barbara
10	N.C. State	Auburn	Iowa	Virginia	Duke

#	1981	1986	1991	1996	2001
1	**Louisiana Tech**	**Texas**	Penn St.	Louisiana Tech	Connecticut
2	Tennessee	Georgia	Virginia	Connecticut	**Notre Dame**
3	Old Dominion	USC	Georgia	Stanford	Tennessee
4	USC	Louisiana Tech	**Tennessee**	**Tennessee**	Georgia
5	Cheyney	Western Ky.	Purdue	Georgia	Duke
6	Long Beach St.	Virginia	Auburn	Old Dominion	Louisiana Tech
7	UCLA	Auburn	N.C. State	Iowa	Oklahoma
8	Maryland	Long Beach St.	LSU	Penn St.	Iowa St.
9	Rutgers	LSU	Arkansas	Texas Tech	Purdue
10	Kansas	Rutgers	Western Ky.	Alabama	Vanderbilt

All-Time AP Top 10

The composite AP Top 10 from the 1976-77 season through 2001-02, based on the final regular season rankings of each year. Team points are based on 10 points for all 1st place finishes, 9 for each 2nd, etc. Also listed are the number of times ranked No. 1 by AP going into the tournaments, and times ranked in the pre-tournament Top 10.

		Pts	No. 1	Top 10			Pts	No. 1	Top 10
1	Tennessee	182	5	24	6	Georgia	72	0	13
2	Louisiana Tech	164	4	22	7	Stanford	64	0	9
3	Old Dominion	81	2	11	8	Penn St.	46	1	10
4	Connecticut	80	5	9	9	Long Beach St.	45	0	10
	Texas	80	4	17	10	Auburn	42	0	8

All-Time Winningest Division I Teams

Division I schools with best winning percentages and most victories through 2001-02 (including postseason tournaments). Although official NCAA women's basketball records didn't begin until the 1981-82 season, results from previous seasons are included below.

Top 10 Winning Percentage

		Yrs	W	L	Pct
1	Louisiana Tech	28	793	133	.856
2	Tennessee	57	881	215	.804
3	Montana	24	554	158	.778
4	Texas	28	709	215	.767
5	Old Dominion	33	735	232	.760
6	S. F. Austin St.	30	714	228	.758
7	Mount St. Mary's*	28	546	212	.720
8	Utah	28	574	227	.717
9	Virginia	29	607	241	.716
10	St. Peter's	35	612	243	.716

*Includes records prior to Division I.

Top 10 Victories

		Yrs	W	L	Pct
1	Tennessee	57	881	215	.804
2	Louisiana Tech	28	793	133	.856
3	Old Dominion	33	735	232	.760
4	S.F. Austin St.	30	714	228	.758
5	Texas	28	709	215	.767
6	James Madison	80	704	398	.639
7	Tennessee Tech	32	696	284	.710
8	Long Beach St.	40	692	297	.700
9	Richmond	82	643	447	.590
10	Penn St.	38	639	254	.716

Annual NCAA Division I Leaders

All averages include postseason games

Scoring

Multiple winners: Cindy Blodgett, Andrea Congreaves and Jackie Stiles (2).

Year		Gm	Pts	Avg
1982	Barbara Kennedy, Clemson	31	908	29.3
1983	LaTaunya Pollard, L. Beach St	31	907	29.3
1984	Deborah Temple, Delta St	28	873	31.2
1985	Anucha Browne, Northwestern	28	855	30.5
1986	Wanda Ford, Drake	30	919	30.6
1987	Tresa Spaulding, BYU	28	810	28.9
1988	LeChandra LeDay, Grambling	28	850	30.4
1989	Patricia Hoskins, Miss. Valley	27	908	33.6
1990	Kim Perrot, SW Louisiana	28	839	30.0
1991	Jan Jensen, Drake	30	888	29.6
1992	Andrea Congreaves, Mercer	28	925	33.0
1993	Andrea Congreaves, Mercer	26	805	31.0
1994	Kristy Ryan, CS-Sacramento	26	727	28.0
1995	Koko Lahanas, CS-Fullerton	29	778	26.8
1996	Cindy Blodgett, Maine	32	889	27.8
1997	Cindy Blodgett, Maine	30	810	27.0
1998	Allison Feaster, Harvard	28	797	28.5
1999	Tamika Whitmore, Memphis	32	843	26.3
2000	Jackie Stiles, SW Missouri St.	32	890	27.8
2001	Jackie Stiles, SW Missouri St.	35	1062	30.3
2002	Kelly Mazzante, Penn St.	35	872	24.9

Rebounds

Multiple winner: Patricia Hoskins (2).

Year		Gm	No	Avg
1982	Anne Donovan, Old Dominion	28	412	14.7
1983	Deborah Mitchell, Miss. Col	28	447	16.0
1984	Joy Kellog, Oklahoma City	23	373	16.2
1985	Rosina Pearson, Beth-Cookman	26	480	18.5
1986	Wanda Ford, Drake	30	506	16.9
1987	Patricia Hoskins, Miss. Valley St.	28	476	17.0
1988	Katie Beck, East Tenn. St.	25	441	17.6
1989	Patricia Hoskins, Miss. Valley St.	27	440	16.3
1990	Pam Hudson, Northwestern St	29	438	15.1
1991	Tarcha Hollis, Grambling	29	443	15.3
1992	Christy Greis, Evansville	28	383	13.7
1993	Ann Barry, Nevada	25	355	14.2
1994	DeShawne Blocker, E. Tenn. St.	26	450	17.3
1995	Tera Sheriff, Jackson St.	29	401	13.8
1996	Dana Wynne, Seton Hall	29	372	12.8
1997	Etolia Mitchell, Georgia St.	25	330	13.2
1998	Alisha Hill, Howard	30	397	13.2
1999	Monica Logan, UMBC	27	364	13.5
2000	Malveata Johnson, N.C. A&T	27	363	13.4
2001	Andrea Gardner, Howard	31	439	14.2
2002	Mandi Carver, Idaho St.	27	336	12.4

Note: Wanda Ford (1986) and Patricia Hoskins (1989) each led the country in scoring and rebounds in the same year.

All-Time NCAA Division I Individual Leaders

Through 2001-02; includes regular season and tournament games; Official NCAA women's basketball records began with 1981-82 season. Players who competed earlier than that are not included below; **Last** column indicates final year played.

CAREER

Scoring

Average	Yrs	Last	Pts	Avg
1 Patricia Hoskins, Miss. Valley St.	4	1989	3122	28.4
2 Sandra Hodge, New Orleans	4	1984	2860	26.7
3 Jackie Stiles, SW Mo. St.	4	2001	3206	26.1
4 Lorri Bauman, Drake	4	1984	3115	26.0
5 Andrea Congreaves, Mercer	4	1993	2796	25.9
6 Cindy Blodgett, Maine	4	1998	3005	25.5
7 Valorie Whiteside, Aplach St.	4	1988	2944	25.4
8 Joyce Walker, LSU	4	1984	2906	24.8
9 Tarcha Hollis, Grambling	4	1991	2058	24.2
10 Korie Hlede, Duquesne	4	1998	2631	24.1

Rebounds

Average	Yrs	Last	Reb	Avg
1 Wanda Ford, Drake	4	1986	1887	16.1
2 Patricia Hoskins, Miss. Valley St.	4	1989	1662	15.1
3 Tarcha Hollis, Grambling	4	1991	1185	13.9
4 Katie Beck, East Tenn. St.	4	1988	1404	13.4
5 Marilyn Stephens, Temple	4	1984	1519	13.0
6 Natalie Williams, UCLA	4	1994	1137	12.8
7 Cheryl Taylor, Tenn. Tech	4	1987	1532	12.8
8 DeShawne Blocker, E. Tenn. St.	4	1995	1361	12.7
9 Olivia Bradley, West Virginia	4	1985	1484	12.7
10 Judy Mosley, Hawaii	4	1990	1441	12.6

SINGLE SEASON

Scoring

Average	Year	Gm	Pts	Avg
1 Patricia Hoskins, Miss.Valley St.	1989	27	908	33.6
2 Andrea Congreaves, Mercer	1992	28	925	33.0
3 Deborah Temple, Delta St.	1984	28	873	31.2
4 Andrea Congreaves, Mercer	1993	26	805	31.0
5 Wanda Ford, Drake	1986	30	919	30.6
6 Anucha Browne, Northwestern	1985	28	855	30.5
7 LeChandra LeDay, Grambling	1988	28	850	30.4
8 Jackie Stiles, SW Mo. St.	2001	35	1062	30.3
9 Kim Perrot, SW Louisiana	1990	28	841	30.0
10 Tina Hutchinson, San Diego St.	1984	30	898	29.9

Scoring (Single Game)

Average	Year	Pts
1 Cindy Brown, Long Beach St. vs San Jose St.	1987	60
2 Lorri Bauman, Drake vs SW Missouri St.	1984	58
Kim Perrot, SW La. vs SE La.	1990	58
4 Jackie Stiles, SW Mo. St. vs Evansville	2000	56
5 Patricia Hoskins, Miss.Valley St. vs South-BR	1989	55
Patricia Hoskins, Miss.Valley St. vs Ala. St.	1989	55
7 Wanda Ford, Drake vs SW Missouri St.	1986	54
Anjinea Hopson, Grambling vs Jackson St.	1994	54
Mary Lowry, Baylor vs Texas	1994	54
10 Chris Starr, Nevada vs CS-Sacramento	1983	53
Felisha Edwards, NE La. vs Southern Miss.	1991	53
Sheryl Swoopes, Texas Tech vs Texas	1993	53

Winningest Active Division I Coaches

Minimum of five seasons as Division I head coach; regular season and tournament games included.

Top 10 Winning Percentage

	Yrs	W	L	Pct
1 Leon Barmore, La. Tech	20	576	87	.869
2 Pat Summitt, Tennessee	28	788	158	.833
3 Geno Auriemma, Connecticut	17	464	98	.826
4 Tara VanDerveer, Stanford	23	548	156	.778
5 Robin Selvig, Montana	24	555	158	.778
6 Andy Landers, Georgia	23	564	170	.768
7 Marsha Sharp, Texas Tech	20	478	153	.758
8 Jody Conradt, Texas	33	788	258	.753
9 Vivian Stringer, Rutgers	30	652	219	.749
10 Bill Fennelly, Iowa St.	14	328	112	.745

Top 10 Victories

	Yrs	W	L	Pct
1 Jody Conradt, Texas	33	788	258	.753
Pat Summitt, Tennessee	28	788	158	.833
3 Vivian Stringer, Rutgers	30	652	219	.749
4 Sue Gunter, LSU	32	651	296	.688
5 Kay Yow, N.C. State	31	625	268	.700
6 Sylvia Hatchell, N. Carolina	27	602	249	.707
7 Rene Portland, Penn St.	26	595	207	.742
8 Theresa Grentz, Illinois	28	591	241	.710
9 Mike Granelli, St. Peter's	30	578	220	.724
10 Leon Barmore, La. Tech	20	576	87	.869

Annual Awards

The Broderick Award was first given out to the Women's Division I or Large School Player of the Year in 1977. Since then, the National Assn. for Girls and Women in Sports (1978), the Women's Basketball Coaches Assn. (1983), the Atlanta Tip-Off Club (1983) and the Associated Press (1995) have joined in.

Since 1983, the first year as many as four awards were given out, the same player has won all of them in the same season twice: Cheryl Miller of USC in 1985 and Rebecca Lobo of Connecticut in 1995.

Associated Press

Voted on by AP sportswriters and broadcasters and first presented in 1995.

Multiple winner: Chamique Holdsclaw (2).

Year	Year	Year
1995 Rebecca Lobo, Connecticut	1998 Chamique Holdsclaw, Tennessee	2001 Ruth Riley, Notre Dame
1996 Jennifer Rizzotti, Connecticut	1999 Chamique Holdsclaw, Tennessee	2002 Sue Bird, Connecticut
1997 Kara Wolters, Connecticut	2000 Tamika Catchings, Tennessee	

Broderick Award

Voted on by a national panel of women's collegiate athletic directors and first presented by the late Thomas Broderick, an athletic outfitter, in 1977. Honda has presented the award since 1987. Basketball Player of the Year is one of 10 nominated for Collegiate Woman Athlete of the Year; (*) indicates player also won Athlete of the Year.

Multiple winners: Chamique Holdsclaw, Nancy Lieberman, Cheryl Miller and Dawn Staley (2).

Year	Year	Year
1977 Lucy Harris, Delta St.*	1979 Nancy Lieberman, Old Dominion*	1981 Lynette Woodard, Kansas
1978 Ann Meyers, UCLA*	1980 Nancy Lieberman, Old Dominion*	1982 Pam Kelly, La. Tech

Year	Year	Year
1983 Anne Donovan, Old Dominion	1990 Jennifer Azzi, Stanford	1997 Chamique Holdsclaw, Tennessee
1984 Cheryl Miller, USC*	1991 Dawn Staley, Virginia	1998 Chamique Holdsclaw, Tennessee*
1985 Cheryl Miller, USC	1992 Dawn Staley, Virginia	1999 Stephanie White-McCarty, Purdue
1986 Kamie Ethridge, Texas*	1993 Sheryl Swoopes, Texas Tech	2000 Shea Ralph, Connecticut
1987 Katrina McClain, Georgia	1994 Lisa Leslie, USC	2001 Jackie Stiles, SW Missouri St.*
1988 Teresa Weatherspoon, La. Tech*	1995 Rebecca Lobo, Connecticut	
1989 Bridgette Gordon, Tennessee	1996 Jennifer Rizzotti, Connecticut	

Wade Trophy

Voted on by the National Assn. for Girls and Women in Sports (NAGWS) and awarded for academics and community service as well as player performance. First presented in 1978 in the name of former Delta St. coach Lily Margaret Wade.

Multiple winner: Nancy Lieberman (2).

Year	Year	Year
1978 Carol Blazejowski, Montclair St.	1987 Shelly Pennefather, Villanova	1996 Jennifer Rizzotti, Connecticut
1979 Nancy Lieberman, Old Dominion	1988 Teresa Weatherspoon, La. Tech	1997 DeLisha Milton, Florida
1980 Nancy Lieberman, Old Dominion	1989 Clarissa Davis, Texas	1998 Ticha Penicheiro, Old Dominion
1981 Lynette Woodard, Kansas	1990 Jennifer Azzi, Stanford	1999 Stephanie White-McCarty, Purdue
1982 Pam Kelly, La. Tech	1991 Daedra Charles, Tennessee	2000 Edwina Brown, Texas
1983 LaTaunya Pollard, L. Beach St.	1992 Susan Robinson, Penn St.	2001 Jackie Stiles, SW Missouri St.
1984 Janice Lawrence, La. Tech	1993 Karen Jennings, Nebraska	2002 Sue Bird, Connecticut
1985 Cheryl Miller, USC	1994 Carol Ann Shudlick, Minnesota	
1986 Kamie Ethridge, Texas	1995 Rebecca Lobo, Connecticut	

Naismith Trophy

Voted on by a panel of coaches, sportswriters and broadcasters and first presented in 1983 by the Atlanta Tip-Off Club in the name of the inventor of basketball, Dr. James Naismith.

Multiple winners: Cheryl Miller (3); Clarissa Davis, Chamique Holdsclaw and Dawn Staley (2).

Year	Year	Year
1983 Anne Donovan, Old Dominion	1990 Jennifer Azzi, Stanford	1997 Kate Starbird, Stanford
1984 Cheryl Miller, USC	1991 Dawn Staley, Virginia	1998 Chamique Holdsclaw, Tennessee
1985 Cheryl Miller, USC	1992 Dawn Staley, Virginia	1999 Chamique Holdsclaw, Tennessee
1986 Cheryl Miller, USC	1993 Sheryl Swoopes, Texas Tech	2000 Tamika Catchings, Tennessee
1987 Clarissa Davis, Texas	1994 Lisa Leslie, USC	2001 Ruth Riley, Notre Dame
1988 Sue Wicks, Rutgers	1995 Rebecca Lobo, Connecticut	2002 Sue Bird, Connecticut
1989 Clarissa Davis, Texas	1996 Saudia Roundtree, Georgia	

Women's Basketball Coaches Association

Voted on by the WBCA and first presented by Champion athletic outfitters in 1983.

Multiple winners: Chamique Holdsclaw, Cheryl Miller and Dawn Staley (2).

Year	Year	Year
1983 Anne Donovan, Old Dominion	1990 Venus Lacy, La. Tech	1997 Kate Starbird, Stanford
1984 Janice Lawrence, La. Tech	1991 Dawn Staley, Virgina	1998 Chamique Holdsclaw, Tennessee
1985 Cheryl Miller, USC	1992 Dawn Staley, Virginia	1999 Chamique Holdsclaw, Tennessee
1986 Cheryl Miller, USC	1993 Sheryl Swoopes, Texas Tech	2000 Tamika Catchings, Tennessee
1987 Katrina McClain, Georgia	1994 Lisa Leslie, USC	2001 Ruth Riley, Notre Dame
1988 Michelle Edwards, Iowa	1995 Rebecca Lobo, Connecticut	2002 discontinued
1989 Clarissa Davis, Texas	1996 Saudia Roundtree, Georgia	

Coach of the Year Award

Voted on by the Women's Basketball Coaches Assn. and first presented by Converse athletic outfitters in 1983.

Multiple winners: Geno Auriemma and Pat Summitt (3), Jody Conradt and Vivian Stringer (2).

Year	Year	Year
1983 Pat Summitt, Tennessee	1990 Kay Yow, N.C. State	1997 Geno Auriemma, Connecticut
1984 Jody Conradt, Texas	1991 Rene Portland, Penn St.	1998 Pat Summitt, Tennessee
1985 Jim Foster, St. Joseph's-PA	1992 Ferne Labati, Miami-FL	1999 Carolyn Peck, Purdue
1986 Jody Conradt, Texas	1993 Vivian Stringer, Iowa	2000 Geno Auriemma, Connecticut
1987 Theresa Grentz, Rutgers	1994 Marsha Sharp, Texas Tech	2001 Muffet McGraw, Notre Dame
1988 Vivian Stringer, Iowa	1995 Pat Summitt, Tennessee	2002 Geno Auriemma, Connecticut
1989 Tara VanDerveer, Stanford	1996 Leon Barmore, La. Tech	

Other Women's Champions

The NCAA has sanctioned national championship tournaments for Division II and Division III since 1982. The NAIA sanctioned a single tournament from 1981-91, then split in to two divisions in 1992.

NCAA Div. II Finals

Multiple winners: North Dakota St. and Cal Poly Pomona (5); Delta St. and North Dakota (3).

Year	Winner	Score	Loser
1982	Cal Poly Pomona	93-74	Tuskegee, AL
1983	Virginia Union	73-60	Cal Poly Pomona
1984	Central Mo.St.	80-73	Virginia Union
1985	Cal Poly Pomona	80-69	Central Mo.St.
1986	Cal Poly Pomona	70-63	North Dakota St.
1987	New Haven, CT	77-75	Cal Poly Pomona
1988	Hampton, VA	65-48	West Texas St.
1989	Delta St., MS	88-58	Cal Poly Pomona
1990	Delta St., MS	77-43	Bentley, MA
1991	North Dakota St.	81-74	SE Missouri St.
1992	Delta St., MS	65-63	North Dakota St.
1993	North Dakota St.	95-63	Delta St.
1994	North Dakota St.	89-56	CS-San Bernardino
1995	North Dakota St.	98-85	Portland St.
1996	North Dakota St.	104-78	Shippensburg, PA
1997	North Dakota	94-78	S. Indiana
1998	North Dakota	92-76	Emporia St.
1999	North Dakota	80-63	Arkansas Tech
2000	Northern Kentucky	71-62	North Dakota St.
2001	Cal Poly Pomona	87-80*	North Dakota
2002	Cal Poly Pomona	74-62	SE Oklahoma St.

*Overtime

NCAA Div. III Finals

Multiple winners: Washington (4); Capital, Elizabethtown and WI-Stevens Point (2).

Year	Winner	Score	Loser
1982	Elizabethtown, PA	67-66*	NC-Greensboro
1983	North Central, IL	83-71	Elizabethtown, PA
1984	Rust College, MS	51-49	Elizabethtown, PA
1985	Scranton, PA	68-59	New Rochelle, NY
1986	Salem St., MA	89-85	Bishop, TX
1987	WI-Stevens Pt.	81-74	Concordia, MN
1988	Concordia, MN	65-57	St. John Fisher, NY
1989	Elizabethtown, PA	66-65	CS-Stanislaus
1990	Hope, MI	65-63	St. John Fisher
1991	St. Thomas, MN	73-55	Muskingum, OH
1992	Alma, MI	79-75	Moravian, PA
1993	Central Iowa	71-63	Capital, OH
1994	Capital, OH	82-63	Washington, MO
1995	Capital, OH	59-55	WI-Oshkosh
1996	WI-Oshkosh	66-50	Mt. Union, OH
1997	NYU	72-70	WI-Eau Claire
1998	Washington, MO	77-69	So. Maine
1999	Washington, MO	74-65	College of St. Benedict, MN
2000	Washington, MO	79-33	So. Maine
2001	Washington, MO	67-45	Messiah, PA
2002	WI-Stevens Pt.	67-65	St. Lawrence, NY

*Overtime

NAIA Finals

Multiple winners: One tournament–SW Oklahoma (4); Div. I tourney–Southern Nazarene and Oklahoma City (4); Arkansas Tech (2); Div. II tourney–Northern St. and Western Oregon (2).

Year	Winner	Score	Loser
1981	Kentucky St.	73-67	Texas Southern
1982	SW Oklahoma	80-45	Mo. Southern
1983	SW Oklahoma	80-68	AL-Huntsville
1984	NC-Asheville	72-70*	Portland, OR
1985	SW Oklahoma	55-54	Saginaw Val., MI
1986	Francis Marion, SC	75-65	Wayland Baptist, TX
1987	SW Oklahoma	60-58	North Georgia
1988	Oklahoma City	113-95	Claflin, SC
1989	So. Nazarene, OK	98-96	Claflin, SC
1990	SW Oklahoma	82-75	AR-Monticello
1991	Ft. Hays St., KS	57-53	SW Oklahoma
1992	I– Arkansas Tech	84-68	Wayland Baptist, TX
	II– Northern St., SD	73-56	Tarleton St., TX
1993	I– Arkansas Tech	76-75	Union, TN
	II– No. Montana	71-68	Northern St., SD
1994	I– So. Nazarene	97-74	David Lipscomb, TN
	II– Northern St., SD	48-45	Western Oregon
1995	I– So. Nazarene	78-77	SE Oklahoma
	II– Western Oregon	75-67	NW Nazarene, ID
1996	I– So. Nazarene	80-79	SE Oklahoma
	II– Western Oregon	80-77	Huron, SD
1997	I– So. Nazarene	78-73	Union, TN
	II– NW Nazarene	64-46	Black Hills St., SD
1998	I– Union, TN	73-70	So. Nazarene
	II– Walsh, OH	73-66	Mary Hardin-Baylor
1999	I– Oklahoma City	72-55	Simon Fraser, B.C.
	II– Shawnee St., OH	80-65	St. Francis, IN
2000	I– Oklahoma City	64-55	Simon Fraser, B.C.
	II– Mary, N.D.	59-49	Northwestern, IA
2001	I– Oklahoma City	69-52	Auburn Montgomery, AL
	II– Northwestern, IA	77-50	Albertson, ID
2002	I– Oklahoma City	82-73	So. Nazarene
	II– Hastings, NE	73-69	Cornerstone, MI

*Overtime

AIAW Finals

The Association of Intercollegiate Athletics for Women Large College tournament determined the women's national champion for 10 years until supplanted by the NCAA.

In 1982, most Division I teams entered the first NCAA tournament rather than the last one staged by the AIAW.

Year	Winner	Score	Loser
1972	Immaculata, PA	52-48	West Chester, PA
1973	Immaculata, PA	59-52	Queens College, NY
1974	Immaculata, PA	68-53	Mississippi College
1975	Delta St., MS	90-81	Immaculata, PA
1976	Delta St., MS	69-64	Immaculata, PA
1977	Delta St., MS	68-55	LSU
1978	UCLA	90-74	Maryland
1979	Old Dominion	75-65	Louisiana Tech
1980	Old Dominion	68-53	Tennessee
1981	Louisiana Tech	79-59	Tennessee
1982	Rutgers	83-77	Texas

Professional Basketball

Michael Jordan *couldn't lift the Wizards into the playoffs but his return didn't go unnoticed.*

Lakers Net Three-peat

Even the return of Michael Jordan and the rise of the Nets couldn't keep Shaq and Kobe from another title.

Jerry Bembry
is the NBA Editor for ESPN The Magazine.

It was going to be MJ's year, at least according to the die-hard Michael Jordan fans who assumed his return after three years would somehow elevate the Washington Wizards to elite status.

It was suppose to be the Mavericks' year, at least that's what many fans assumed after Dallas acquired Nick Van Exel and Raef LaFrentz in a trade that bolstered the offense of a team that would go on to average a league-high 105.2 points per game.

It was supposed to be Sacramento's year, at least according to a handful of so-called basketball experts—this one included—who assumed their talent, depth and maturity would lead to the NBA paying homage to the Kings.

Yet the 2001-02 NBA season turned out to be the Lakers' year, thanks to the game's best coach (Phil Jackson), best all-around player (Kobe Bryant) and most dominant force (Shaquille O'Neal). In sweeping through the Finals (where Shaq won his third straight Finals MVP award), the Lakers earned a three-peat and drew comparisons to the MJ-led Bulls dynasty that twice won three consecutive titles in the 1990's.

That the Lakers were the league's best team was no real surprise in a season that was nonetheless full of astonishing results. Want proof? How about the Nets, a team that in 25 NBA seasons had never won more than 47 games and had advanced past the first round of the playoffs just once. Newcomer Jason Kidd's impact was immediate and implausible as he took a team that had won 26 games during the 2000-01 season to 52 wins during the 2001-02 season and brought them to the Finals.

New Jersey's success? Chalk it up to the sudden shift of power in the Eastern Conference. New Jersey, Detroit and Boston failed to make the playoffs during the 2000-01 season, but this year earned

AP/Wide World Photos

*The **Lakers** three-peated with a sweep of the Nets and unless something changes, Kobe Bryant, Shaquille O'Neal and friends look to be in the midst of a long title run.*

the top three seeds. In the process New Jersey's Kidd emerged as an MVP candidate; Detroit's Ben Wallace became the fourth player in history to lead the NBA in rebounds and blocked shots while his coach Rick Carlisle was named coach of the year; and Boston's Antoine Walker and Paul Pierce matured quickly to become all-star teammates.

How did the perennial Eastern Conference powers fair? The Sixers followed their trip to the 2001 Finals with a first-round exit in 2002. The Bucks, after coming within a shot of the 2001 Eastern Conference Finals, were ripped by dissension and didn't even make the playoffs.

Neither did the Heat nor the Knicks. Miami was the league's lowest scoring team (87.2 ppg) and never recovered from a 5-23 start as Pat Riley endured his first losing season in 20 years of coaching. The Knicks kept announcing sellouts at the World's Most Famous Arena, even as fans by the thousands abandoned a team that won just 30 times.

No, the true power was out west where owner Mark Cuban was fined $500,000 for saying he wouldn't hire head of officials Ed Rush to run a Dairy Queen (Cuban wound up working at a DQ for a day), but made deals to provide the Mavs help for Dirk Nowitzki, Steve Nash and Michael Finley.

*New Jersey point guard **Jason Kidd** led the Nets past the surprising Celtics and into the NBA Finals before suffering a four-game sweep at the hands of the defending-champion Lakers.*

Dallas was eventually derailed in the postseason by the Kings, who with Mike Bibby making an impact in his first playoff appearance, were on the verge of taking a 3-1 playoff lead on the Lakers in the Western Conference Finals.

Enter Robert "Big Shot" Horry, whose buzzer beating three-pointer gave the Lakers a Game 4 victory and saved the season. And by the end of the playoffs Shaq—who spent the entire season battling zone defenses designed to control him (they didn't) and bad feet that were somewhat successful in slowing him— was dominant, averaging 36.3 points, 12.3 rebounds and shooting 66.2 per-cent from the free-throw line during the sweep in the Finals.

Surely, as Shaq dominated during the 113-107 win in Game 4 of the Finals, Lakers' radio announcer Chick Hearn told fans the game was "in the refrigerator."

Hearn, whose streak of 3,338 straight Laker game broadcasts ended during the 2001-02 season after having a heart valve replaced, died during the offseason.

Even if the Lakers manage to win their fourth straight title next season, somehow it won't feel the same without "the Jell-O jigglin."

Jerry Bembry's Ten Biggest Stories of the Year in Pro Basketball

10 ▪ **Play it Again**—Baron Davis is robbed of a game-winning shot that comes before the horn; the Kings missed their best shot at a title when a Samaki Walker shot was ruled after the horn. Embarrassed by those playoff blunders, the NBA announces it is going to give instant replay a try to deal with questionable buzzer-beaters. Now that's the right call.

9 ▪ **Phil 'Er Up**—Sure, Red Auerbach's not impressed with Phil Jackson as a coach and calls the teams that the Zen Master has taken over "ready-made." Still, the numbers don't lie: Jackson's coached nine of the last 12 NBA champions, tying Auerbach for most championships as coach. Ready-made or not, that's impressive.

8 ▪ **Charlotte Stung**—Charlotte fans once cared. The Hornets led the NBA in attendance in eight of their 14 seasons. They just got fed up with an owner who let his best players get away, refused to sell to Michael Jordan and lived an off-the-court soap-opera life. After five straight seasons of falling attendance the Hornets move to New Orleans—leaving Charlotte a prime place for relocation or expansion.

7 ▪ **A.I. Unplugged**—Tired of the trade rumors and criticism, Allen Iverson sits down to meet the press. The 30 minutes that followed on that May afternoon was emotional, compelling and raw. If the Osbournes deliver big ratings for MTV, why not the Iversons on ESPN?

6 ▪ **Foreign Affairs**—Pau Gasol (Spain), is the top rookie, Yao Ming (China) is the top pick and guys named Hilario (Brazil), Nachbar (Italy) and Welsch (Slovenia) are selected in the first round. Six foreign-born players are taken in the first round in 2002, and 62 over the last six years—proof of the globalization of the NBA.

5 ▪ **King Of Kings**—Mike Bibby averages 13.7 ppg during the regular season, quiet support to All-Stars Chris Webber and Peja Stojakovic. During the 2002 playoffs—his first—Bibby emerges as a go-to guy, averaging 20.2 ppg and nearly takes Sacramento to the Finals. Bibby's coming out party probably earned him an extra $30 million. Talk about perfect timing.

4 ▪ **Big Shot Rob**—Shaq and Kobe owe their third ring to Robert Horry and his heroics in Game 4 of the conference finals against Sacramento. The Kings thought they had a 3-1 series lead when Vlade Divac smacked the ball away after a missed shot by Shaq. Perhaps instinctually, Horry was planted just beyond the arc and launched the shot that changed the series.

3 ▪ **Trading Places**—Jason Kidd pledged his new team would reach .500, and make the New York-area a two-team town. And Kidd accomplishes what Stephon Marbury couldn't: he transforms the New Jersey Nets, taking a team from 26 wins to 52 and a trip to the Finals. Not a bad prediction—except for that part about New York being a two-team town.

2 ▪ **Like Mike**—Slight paunch, achy knees, and no lift going to the basket, Michael Jordan, in his highly anticipated return after a three-year absence, seems more like us. While MJ scores 45 and 51 in back-to-back games, and has the Wizards thinking

playoffs at midseason, his knees take him from Air Jordan to Floor Jordan—crushing all postseason hopes.

1 ▪ **Three The Hard Way**—Four regular season loses to last place teams? Shaq's sore big toe? A second place division finish, and lack of home court advantage throughout the playoffs? Winning championships are rarely easy. But Shaq gets healthy in the nick of time, and even hits his free throws in leading the Lakers to a three-peat and establishing himself as one of the most dominant players in history.

Two Much

Shaquille O'Neal and Kobe Bryant scored a collective 252 points in their sweep of the Nets. Their average of 63.0 ppg is the third most by a pair of teammates who both averaged at least 25.0 ppg in NBA Finals history. The record is held by Elgin Baylor and Jerry West, but they lost the series all three times they appear on this list.

Year	Duo	PPG
1962	Baylor/West, LAL	71.7
1963	Baylor/West, LAL	63.3
2002	O'Neal/Bryant, LAL	63.0
1966	West/Baylor, LAL	58.9
1961	Hagan/Pettit, St.L	57.8

Rookie of the Year

Detroit Pistons' coach Rick Carlisle became just the sixth man in history to win the NBA's Coach of the Year Award in his rookie year as a head coach. Here's a look at the list of coaches to earn the accolade in their first season in charge.

Year	Coach	W-L
2002	Rick Carlisle, Det.	50-32
2000	Doc Rivers, Orl.	41-41
1998	Larry Bird, Ind.	58-24
1987	Mike Schuler, Port.	49-33
1967	Johnny Kerr, Chi.	33-48
1963	Harry Gallatin, St.L.	48-32

2001-2002
Season in Review

ESPN
Information Please®
SPORTS ALMANAC

Final NBA Standings

Division champions (*) and playoff qualifiers (†) are noted. Number of seasons listed after each head coach refers to current tenure with club.

Western Conference
Midwest Division

	W	L	Pct	GB	Per Game For	Opp
*San Antonio	58	24	.707	—	96.7	90.5
†Dallas	57	25	.695	1	105.2	101.0
†Minnesota	50	32	.610	8	99.3	96.0
†Utah	44	38	.537	14	96.0	95.1
Houston	28	54	.341	30	92.3	97.2
Denver	27	55	.329	31	92.2	98.0
Memphis	23	59	.280	35	89.9	97.3

Head Coaches: SA—Gregg Popovich (6th season); **Dal**—Don Nelson (5th); **Min**—Phil Saunders (7th); **Utah**—Jerry Sloan (14th); **Hou**—Rudy Tomjanovich (11th); **Den**—Dan Issel (3rd, 9-17) resigned Dec. 26, 2001 and was replaced by assistant Mike Evans (18-38); **Mem**—Sidney Lowe (2nd).

2000-01 Standings: 1. San Antonio (58-24); 2. Utah (53-29); 3. Dallas (53-29); 4. Minnesota (47-35); 5. Houston (45-37); 6. Denver (40-42); 7. Vancouver (23-59).

Pacific Division

	W	L	Pct	GB	Per Game For	Opp
*Sacramento	61	21	.744	—	104.6	97.0
†LA Lakers	58	24	.707	3	101.3	94.1
†Portland	49	33	.598	12	96.6	93.7
†Seattle	45	37	.549	16	97.7	94.7
LA Clippers	39	43	.476	22	95.7	96.1
Phoenix	36	46	.439	25	95.1	95.8
Golden St.	21	61	.256	40	97.7	103.1

Head Coaches: Sac—Rick Adelman (4th season); **LAL**—Phil Jackson (3rd); **Port**—Maurice Cheeks (1st); **Sea**—Nate McMillan (2nd); **LAC**—Alvin Gentry (2nd); **Pho**—Scott Skiles (3rd, 25-26) resigned on Feb. 17, 2002 and was replaced by assistant Frank Johnson (11-20); **G.St.**—Dave Cowens (2nd, 8-15) was fired on Dec. 16, 2001 and replaced by assistant Brian Winters (13-46).

2000-01 Standings: 1. LA Lakers (56-26); 2. Sacramento (55-27); 3. Phoenix (51-31); 4. Portland (50-32); 5. Seattle (44-38); 6. LA Clippers (31-51); 7. Golden St. (17-65).

Eastern Conference
Atlantic Division

	W	L	Pct	GB	Per Game For	Opp
*New Jersey	52	30	.634	—	96.2	92.0
†Boston	49	33	.598	3	96.4	94.1
†Orlando	44	38	.537	8	100.5	98.9
†Philadelphia	43	39	.524	9	91.0	89.4
Washington	37	45	.451	15	92.8	94.2
Miami	36	46	.439	16	87.2	88.7
New York	30	52	.366	22	91.6	95.6

Head Coaches: NJ—Byron Scott (2nd season); **Bos**—Jim O'Brien (2nd); **Orl**—Doc Rivers (3rd); **Phi**—Larry Brown (5th); **Wash**—Doug Collins (1st); **Mia**—Pat Riley (7th); **NY**—Jeff Van Gundy (7th, 10-9) resigned Dec. 8, 2001 and was replaced by assistant Don Chaney (20-43).

2000-01 Standings: 1. Philadelphia (56-26); 2. Miami (50-32); 3. New York (48-34); 4. Orlando (43-39); 5. Boston (36-46); 6. New Jersey (26-56); 7. Washington (19-63).

Central Division

	W	L	Pct	GB	Per Game For	Opp
*Detroit	50	32	.610	—	94.3	92.2
†Charlotte	44	38	.537	6	93.9	92.9
†Toronto	42	40	.512	8	91.4	91.8
†Indiana	42	40	.512	8	96.8	96.5
Milwaukee	41	41	.500	9	97.5	97.7
Atlanta	33	49	.402	17	94.0	98.3
Cleveland	29	53	.354	21	95.3	98.6
Chicago	21	61	.256	29	89.5	98.0

Head Coaches: Det—Rick Carlisle (1st season); **Char**—Paul Silas (4th); **Tor**—Lenny Wilkens (2nd); **Ind**—Isiah Thomas (2nd); **Mil**—George Karl (4th); **Atl**—Lon Kruger (2nd); **Cle**—John Lucas (1st); **Chi**—Tim Floyd (4th, 4-23) resigned on Dec. 28, 2001 and was replaced by assistant Bill Cartwright (17-38).

2000-01 Standings: 1. Milwaukee (52-30); 2. Toronto (47-35); 3. Charlotte (46-36); 4. Indiana (41-41); 5. Detroit (32-50); 6. Cleveland (30-52); 7. Atlanta (25-57); 8. Chicago (15-67).

Overall Conference Standings

Sixteen teams—eight from each conference—qualify for the NBA Playoffs; (*) indicates division champions.

Western Conference

		W	L	Home	Away	Div	Conf
1	Sacramento*	.61	21	36-5	25-16	15-9	37-15
2	San Antonio*	.58	24	32-9	26-15	21-3	38-14
3	LA Lakers	.58	24	34-7	24-17	16-8	37-15
4	Dallas	.57	25	30-11	27-14	16-8	34-18
5	Minnesota	.50	32	29-12	21-20	15-9	29-23
6	Portland	.49	33	30-11	19-22	14-10	27-25
7	Seattle	.45	37	26-15	19-22	13-11	26-26
8	Utah	.44	38	25-16	19-22	8-16	25-27
	LA Clippers	.39	43	25-16	14-27	9-15	23-29
	Phoenix	.36	46	23-18	13-28	12-12	24-28
	Houston	.28	54	18-23	10-31	9-15	18-34
	Denver	.27	55	20-21	7-34	8-16	19-33
	Memphis	.23	59	15-26	8-33	7-17	14-38
	Golden St.	.21	61	14-27	7-34	5-19	13-39

Eastern Conference

		W	L	Home	Away	Div	Conf
1	New Jersey*	.52	30	33-8	19-22	16-8	35-19
2	Detroit*	.50	32	26-15	24-17	20-8	38-16
3	Boston	.49	33	27-14	22-19	17-7	35-19
4	Charlotte	.44	38	21-20	23-18	17-11	31-23
5	Orlando	.44	38	27-14	17-24	12-12	29-25
6	Philadelphia	.43	39	22-19	21-20	14-11	31-23
7	Toronto	.42	40	24-17	18-23	17-11	29-25
8	Indiana	.42	40	25-16	17-24	13-15	27-27
	Milwaukee	.41	41	25-16	16-25	17-11	29-25
	Washington	.37	45	22-19	15-26	12-13	25-29
	Miami	.36	46	23-18	18-23	10-14	22-32
	Atlanta	.33	49	23-18	10-31	11-17	21-33
	New York	.30	52	19-22	11-30	4-20	20-34
	Cleveland	.29	53	20-21	9-32	12-16	20-34
	Chicago	.21	61	14-27	7-34	5-23	13-41

2002 NBA All-Star Game
West, 135-120

51st NBA All-Star Game. **Date:** Feb. 10, at The First Union Center in Philadelphia; **Coaches:** Byron Scott, New Jersey (East) and Don Nelson, Dallas (West); **MVP:** Kobe Bryant, LA Lakers (31 points, 5 rebounds, 5 assists); Starters chosen by fan vote, (Toronto's Vince Carter was the leading vote-getter for the third consecutive year, receiving 1,470,176); bench chosen by conference coaches' vote.

Western Conference

Pos	Starters	Min	FG M-A	Pts	Reb	A
G	Kobe Bryant, LAL	30	12-25	31	5	5
G	Steve Francis, Hou	18	1-8	3	2	3
F	Kevin Garnett, Min	24	7-15	14	12	2
F	Chris Webber, Sac	20	3-7	8	3	4
C	Tim Duncan, SA	29	7-11	14	14	2
Bench						
G	Steve Nash, Dal	24	3-9	8	3	9
F	Dirk Nowitzki, Dal	24	5-11	12	8	3
G	Gary Payton, Sea	22	7-13	18	1	6
C	Elton Brand, Chi	19	3-5	6	10	1
G	Predrag Stojakovic, Sac.	18	4-10	11	2	1
F	Wally Szczerbiak, Min	12	4-6	10	3	3
	TOTALS	240	56-120	135	63	39

Three-Point FG: 13-30 (Payton 4-6, Stojakovic 3-5, Szczerbiak 2-3, Nash 2-4, Webber 1-2, Nowitzki 1-4, Bryant 0-4, Francis 0-1, Garnett 0-1); **Free Throws:** 10-14 (Bryant 7-7, Nowitzki 1-1, Francis 1-2, Webber 1-4); **Percentages:** FG (.467), Three-Pt. FG (.433), Free Throws (.714); **Turnovers:** 14 (Duncan 3, Payton 3, Francis 2, Webber 2, Nowitzki 2, Brand 2); **Steals:** 11 (Payton 3, Francis 2, Garnett 2, Bryant, Webber, Nash, Szczerbiak); **Blocked Shots:** 3 (Duncan 2, Brand); **Fouls:** 12 (Bryant 2, Webber 2, Brand 2, Francis, Garnett, Duncan, Nash, Nowitzki, Payton); **Team Rebounds:** 9.

Eastern Conference

Pos	Starters	Min	FG M-A	Pts	Reb	A
G	Allen Iverson, Phi	25	2-9	5	4	3
G	Jason Kidd, Pho	18	1-2	2	1	3
F	Michael Jordan, Wash.	22	4-13	8	4	1
F	Antoine Walker, Bos	16	3-8	8	2	1
C	Dikembe Mutombo, Phi.	21	3-5	8	10	0
Bench						
G	Ray Allen, Mil	25	6-17	15	3	5
G	Paul Pierce, Bos	23	9-18	19	7	3
G	Tracy McGrady, Orl	23	9-15	24	3	4
F	S. Abdur-Rahim, Atl	21	4-4	9	6	0
F	Jermaine O'Neal, Ind	17	2-5	7	7	0
C	Alonzo Mourning, Mia	16	6-7	13	3	2
C	Baron Davis, Cha	13	1-5	2	1	5
	TOTALS	240	50-108	120	51	29

Three-Point FG: 9-29 (Allen 3-10, Walker 2-4, McGrady 2-4, Abdur-Rahim 1-1, Pierce 1-6, Kidd 0-1, Davis 0-3); **Free Throws:** 11-13 (McGrady 4-4, O'Neal 3-4, Mutombo 2-2, Mourning 1-1, Iverson 1-2); **Percentages:** FG (.463), Three-Pt. FG (.310), Free Throws (.846); **Turnovers:** 15 (Davis 2, Iverson 2, Walker 2, Mutombo 2, Kidd, Jordan, Allen, McGrady, O'Neal, Mourning); **Steals:** 11 (Allen 3, McGrady 3, Jordan 2, Kidd, Walker, Pierce); **Blocked Shots:** 3 (Mourning 2, Mutombo); **Fouls:** 12 (Allen 3, Abdur-Rahim 2, Jordan, Walker, Pierce, McGrady, O'Neal, Mourning, Davis); **Team Rebounds:** 5.

	1	2	3	4	F
West	32	40	28	35	—135
East	24	31	22	43	—120

Halftime— West, 72-55; **Third Quarter—** West, 100-77; **Technical Fouls—** none; **Officials—** Bennett Salvatore, Derrick Stafford, Jess Kersey; **Attendance—** 19,581; **Time—** 2:07; **TV Rating—** 8.2/15 share (NBC).

NBA 3-point Shootout

Eight players are invited to compete in the annual three-point shooting contest held during All-Star Weekend, since 1986. Each shooter has 60 seconds to shoot the 25 balls in five racks outside the three-point line. Each ball is worth one point, except the last ball in each rack, which is worth two points. Highest scores advance. First prize: $25,000.

First Round	Pts
Wesley Person, Cle	21
Predrag Stojakovic, Sac	20
Steve Nash, Dal	15
Failed to advance	**Pts**
Quentin Richardson, LAC	14
Ray Allen, Mil	14
Mike Miller, Orl	10
Paul Pierce, Bos	8
Steve Smith, SA	8
Finals	**Pts**
Predrag Stojakovic	19*
Wesley Person	19
Steve Nash	18

*Stojakovic beat Person, 9-5, in a 24-second overtime.

Slam Dunk Contest

Four players competed at the 2002 NBA Slam Dunk contest. In the past six years players were invited to compete in the slam dunk contest that was held annually from 1984-97 before being replaced by the 2Ball competition. The slam dunk contest made its return in 2000. The four competitors are selected based on "the creativity and artistry they have displayed in dunking" over the course of the season. The first round consists of two slam dunk matches. Everyone attempts three dunks, one of which must involve a teammate and another of which involved having to spin a "wheel of fortune" that has them imitate great dunkers of the past. The lowest score is thrown out and the combined total of the remaining two dunks decides the winner. The dunks are judged by five judges on a scale from six to ten. The two first round winners advance to the final round and attempt two dunks. The combined score of the two dunks determines the winner.

The 2002 Slam Dunk contests competitors were Steve Francis of the Houston Rockets, defending champion Desmond Mason of the Seattle SuperSonics, Jason Richardson of the Golden State Warriors, and Gerald Wallace of the Sacramento Kings. First prize: $25,000.

First Round
Jason Richardson def. Desmond Mason 98-84
Gerald Wallace def. Steve Francis................84-77
Finals
Jason Richardson def. Gerald Wallace 85-80

Philadelphia 76ers
Allen Iverson
Scoring & Steals

Detroit Pistons
Ben Wallace
Rebounds & Blocked Shots

Cleveland Cavaliers
Andre Miller
Assists

San Antonio Spurs
Steve Smith
3-Pt. FG Pct.

NBA Regular Season Individual Leaders

Scoring

(*indicates rookie)

	Gm	Min	FG	FG%	3pt/Att	FT	FT%	Reb	Ast	Stl	Blk	Pts	Avg	Hi
Allen Iverson, Phi.	60	2622	665	.398	78/268	475	.812	269	331	168	13	1883	**31.4**	58
Shaquille O'Neal, LAL	67	2422	712	.579	0/1	398	.555	715	200	41	137	1822	**27.2**	46
Paul Pierce, Bos.	82	3302	707	.442	210/520	520	.809	566	261	154	86	2144	**26.1**	48
Tracy McGrady, Orl	76	2912	715	.451	103/283	415	.748	596	400	119	73	1948	**25.6**	50
Tim Duncan, SA.	82	3329	764	.508	1/10	560	.799	1042	307	61	203	2089	**25.5**	53
Kobe Bryant, LAL.	80	3063	749	.469	33/132	488	.829	441	438	118	35	2019	**25.2**	56
Vince Carter, Tor	60	2385	559	.428	121/313	245	.798	313	239	94	43	1484	**24.7**	43
Dirk Nowitzki, Dal	76	2891	600	.477	139/350	440	.853	755	186	83	77	1779	**23.4**	40
Karl Malone, Utah	80	3040	635	.454	9/25	509	.797	686	341	152	59	1788	**22.4**	39
Antoine Walker, Bos.	81	3406	666	.394	222/645	240	.741	714	407	122	38	1794	**22.1**	42
Gary Payton, Sea	82	3301	737	.467	74/236	267	.797	396	737	131	26	1815	**22.1**	43
Ray Allen, Mil	69	2525	530	.462	229/528	214	.873	312	271	88	18	1503	**21.8**	47
Cuttino Mobley, Hou	74	3116	595	.438	149/377	267	.850	300	187	109	37	1606	**21.7**	41
Jerry Stackhouse, Det	76	2685	524	.397	86/300	495	.858	315	403	77	37	1629	**21.4**	40
Shareef Abdur-Rahim, Atl.	77	2980	598	.461	21/70	419	.801	696	239	98	81	1636	**21.2**	50
Predrag Stojakovic, Sac.	71	2649	547	.484	129/310	283	.876	373	175	81	14	1506	**21.2**	36
Kevin Garnett, Min	81	3175	659	.470	37/116	359	.801	981	422	96	126	1714	**21.2**	37
Michael Finley, Dal	69	2754	569	.463	76/224	210	.837	360	230	65	25	1424	**20.6**	39
Jalen Rose, Chi	83	3153	663	.455	89/246	281	.839	373	355	78	45	1696	**20.4**	44
Stephon Marbury, Pho	82	3187	625	.442	71/248	353	.781	266	666	77	13	1674	**20.4**	36
Allan Houston, NY	77	2914	568	.437	136/346	295	.870	252	190	54	10	1567	**20.4**	44
Antawn Jamison, G. St.	82	3033	614	.447	68/210	323	.734	556	161	70	45	1619	**19.7**	35
Sam Cassell, Mil	74	2605	554	.463	71/204	282	.860	312	493	90	12	1461	**19.7**	33
Latrell Sprewell, NY	81	3326	573	.404	145/403	284	.821	298	313	94	14	1575	**19.4**	49
Jason Terry, Atl	78	2967	524	.430	172/444	284	.835	270	444	144	13	1504	**19.3**	46

Rebounds

	Gm	Off	Def	Tot	Avg
Ben Wallace, Det	80	318	721	1039	13.0
Tim Duncan, SA.	82	268	774	1042	12.7
Kevin Garnett, Min	81	243	738	981	12.1
Danny Fortson, G.St.	77	290	609	899	11.7
Elton Brand, LAC	80	396	529	925	11.6
Dikembe Mutombo, Phi	80	254	609	863	10.8
Jermaine O'Neal, Ind.	72	188	569	757	10.5
Dirk Nowitzki, Dal	76	120	635	755	9.9
Shawn Marion, Pho	81	211	593	804	9.9
P.J. Brown, Cha	80	273	513	786	9.8
Antonio Davis, Tor.	77	254	486	740	9.6
Kurt Thomas, NY	82	814	533	747	9.1
Shareef Abdur-Rahim, Atl.	77	198	498	696	9.0
Pau Gasol*, Mem	82	238	492	730	8.9
Michael Olowokandi, LAC	80	164	547	711	8.9

Assists

	Gm	Ast	Avg
Andre Miller, Cle.	81	882	10.9
Jason Kidd, NJ	82	808	9.9
Gary Payton, Sea	82	737	9.0
Baron Davis, Cha	82	698	8.5
John Stockton, Utah	82	674	8.2
Stephon Marbury, Pho	82	666	8.1
Jamaal Tinsley*, Ind	80	647	8.1
Jason Williams, Mem	65	519	8.0
Steve Nash, Dal	82	634	7.7
Mark Jackson, NY.	82	605	7.4
Sam Cassell, Mil	74	493	6.7
Nick Van Exel, Dal	72	478	6.6
Eric Snow, Phi	61	400	6.6
Damon Stoudamire, Por	75	490	6.5
Jeff McInnis, LAC.	81	500	6.2

Field Goal Pct.

	Gm	FG	Att	Pct
Shaquille O'Neal, LAL	.67	712	1229	.579
Elton Brand, LAC	.80	532	1010	.527
Donyell Marshall, Utah	.58	343	661	.519
Pau Gasol*, Mem	.82	551	1064	.518
John Stockton, Utah	.82	401	775	.517
Alonzo Mourning, Mia	.75	447	866	.516
Ruben Patterson, Por	.75	319	619	.515
Corliss Williamson, Det	.78	411	806	.510
Tim Duncan, SA	.82	764	1504	.508
Brent Barry, Sea	.81	401	790	.508
Wally Szczerbiak, Min.	.82	609	1200	.508

Free Throw Pct.

	Gm	FT	Att	Pct
Reggie Miller, Ind	.79	296	325	.911
Richard Hamilton, Wash	.63	300	337	.890
Darrell Armstrong, Orl	.82	182	205	.888
Damon Stoudamire, Por	.75	174	196	.888
Steve Nash, Dal	.82	260	293	.887
Chauncey Billups, Min	.82	207	234	.885
Chris Whitney, Wash	.82	154	175	.880
Steve Smith, SA	.77	159	181	.878
Predrag Stojakovic, Sac	.71	283	323	.876
Troy Hudson, Orl	.81	176	201	.876
Jamal Mashburn, Cha	.40	211	241	.876

3-Point Field Goal Pct.

	Gm	3FG	Att	Pct
Steve Smith, SA	.77	116	246	.472
Jon Barry, Det	.82	121	258	.469
Eric Piatkowski, LAC	.71	111	238	.466
Wally Szczerbiak, Min.	.82	87	191	.455
Steve Nash, Dal	.82	156	343	.455
Hubert Davis, Wash	.51	57	126	.452
Tyronn Lue, Wash	.71	63	141	.447
Michael Redd, Mil	.67	88	198	.444

High-Point Games

	Opp	Date	FG–FT–Pts
Allen Iverson, Phi	vs. Hou	1/15/2002	21–14–58
Kobe Bryant, LAL	vs. Mem	1/14/2002	21–11–56
Tim Duncan, SA	vs. Dal	12/26/2001	19–15–53
Michael Jordan, Wash	vs. Cha	12/29/2001	21–9–51
S. Abdur-Rahim, Atl	vs. Det	11/23/2001	21–8–50
Tracy McGrady, Orl	vs. Was	3/8/2002	18–10–50
Latrell Sprewell, NY	vs. Bos	12/11/2001	18–7–49
Paul Pierce, Bos	@ NJ	12/1/2001	13–17–48
Tracy McGrady, Orl	vs. Mil	3/19/2002	18–6–48
Latrell Sprewell, NY	@ Mil	12/26/2002	17–5–48

Blocked Shots

	Gm	Blk	Avg
Ben Wallace, Det	.80	278	3.48
Raef LaFrentz, Den	.78	213	2.73
Alonzo Mourning, Mia	.75	186	2.48
Tim Duncan, SA	.82	203	2.48
Dikembe Mutombo, Phi	.80	190	2.38
Jermaine O'Neal, Ind	.72	166	2.31
Erick Dampier, G. St.	.73	167	2.29
Adonal Foyle, G. St	.79	168	2.13
Pau Gasol*, Mem	.82	169	2.06
Shaquille O'Neal, LAL	.67	137	2.04

Steals

	Gm	Stl	Avg
Allen Iverson, Phi	.60	168	2.80
Ron Artest, Chi	.55	141	2.56
Jason Kidd, NJ	.82	175	2.13
Baron Davis, Cha	.82	172	2.10
Doug Christie, Sac	.81	160	1.98
Darrell Armstrong, Orl	.82	157	1.91
Karl Malone, Utah	.80	152	1.90
Paul Pierce, Bos	.82	154	1.88
Kenny Anderson, Bos	.76	141	1.86
John Stockton, Utah	.82	152	1.85

Rookie Leaders

Scoring

	Gm	FG	FT	Pts	Avg
Pau Gasol, Mem	.82	551	338	1441	17.6
Shane Battier, Mem	.78	412	198	1125	14.4
Jason Richardson, G. St.	.80	464	141	1151	14.4
Gilbert Arenas, G. St.	.47	174	124	511	10.9
Andrei Kirilenko, Utah	.82	285	285	880	10.7

Field Goal Pct.

	Gm	FG	Att	Pct
Pau Gasol, Mem	.82	551	1064	.518
Zeljko Rebraca, Det	.74	189	374	.505
Eddy Curry, Chi	.72	189	377	.501
Tyson Chandler, Chi	.71	151	304	.497
Predrag Drobnjak, Sea	.64	191	414	.461

Rebounds

	Gm	Off	Def	Tot	Avg
Pau Gasol, Mem	.82	238	492	730	8.9
Eddie Griffin, Hou	.73	117	299	416	5.7
Shane Battier, Mem	.78	180	238	418	5.4
Brendan Haywood, Wash	.62	143	179	322	5.2
Andrei Kirilenko, Utah	.82	149	253	402	4.9

Assists

	Gm	No	Avg
Jamaal Tinsley, Ind	.80	647	8.1
Tony Parker, SA	.77	334	4.3
Gilbert Arenas, G. St.	.47	174	3.7
Kenny Satterfield, Den	.36	108	3.0
Speedy Claxton, Phi	.67	198	3.0

Personal Fouls

Kurt Thomas, NY	.341
Raef LaFrentz, Dal	.281
Jermaine O'Neal, Ind	.269
Juwan Howard, Den	.265
Elden Campbell, Cha	.264
Radoslav Nesterovic, Min	.262

Disqualifications

Raef LaFrentz, Dal	.11
Ron Artest, Ind	.10
Jamaal Tinsley*, Ind	.9
Kenyon Martin, NJ	.8
Kurt Thomas, NY	.8
Alonzo Mourning, Mia	.7
Chris Mihm, Cle	.7

Turnovers

Jason Kidd, NJ	.286
Stephon Marbury, Pho	.284
Jamaal Tinsley*, Ind	.270
Jerry Stackhouse, Det	.266
Karl Malone, Utah	.263
Tim Duncan, SA	.263

Triple Doubles

Jason Kidd, NJ	.8
Andre Miller, Cle	.3
Steve Francis, Hou	.2
Gary Payton, Sea	.2
Jamaal Tinsley*, Ind	.2
Antoine Walker, Bos	.2

Minutes Played

Antoine Walker, Bos	.3406
Tim Duncan, SA	.3329
Latrell Sprewell, NY	.3326
Baron Davis, Cha	.3318
Paul Pierce, Bos	.3302

Technical Fouls

Rasheed Wallace, Port	.27
Karl Malone, Utah	.20
Bonzi Wells, Port	.19
Alonzo Mourning, Mia	.18
Anthony Mason, Mil	.17
Antoine Walker, Bos	.17
Shareef Abdur-Rahim, Atl	.17

Team by Team Statistics

Players who competed for more than one team during the regular season are listed with their final club; (*) indicates rookies.

Atlanta Hawks

	Gm	FG%	Tpts	PPG	RPG	APG
Shareef Abdur-Rahim	.77	.461	1636	21.2	9.0	3.1
Jason Terry	.78	.430	1504	19.3	3.5	5.7
Toni Kukoc	.59	.419	584	9.9	3.7	3.6
Nazr Mohammed	.82	.461	795	9.7	7.9	0.4
Dion Glover	.55	.421	492	8.9	3.1	1.5
Theo Ratliff	.3	.500	26	8.7	5.3	0.3
DerMarr Johnson	.72	.396	602	8.4	3.4	1.1
Ira Newble	.42	.498	338	8.0	5.3	1.1
Chris Crawford	.7	.467	53	7.6	3.6	0.7
Emanual Davis	.28	.354	185	6.6	2.6	2.4
Jacque Vaughn	.82	.470	540	6.6	2.0	4.3
Alan Henderson	.26	.509	143	5.5	3.7	0.4
Hanno Mottola	.82	.440	396	4.8	3.3	0.6
Mark Strickland	.46	.446	208	4.5	2.8	0.4
Reggie Slater	.4	.385	16	4.0	1.8	0.3
Cal Bowdler	.52	.351	162	3.1	2.1	0.2
Leon Smith	.14	.385	31	2.2	2.2	0.2
Dickey Simpkins	.1	.000	0	0.0	0.0	1.0

Triple Doubles: none. **3-pt FG leader:** Terry (172).
Steals leader: Terry (144). **Blocks leader:** Abdur-Rahim (81).
Signed: F Strickland (Nov. 14), C/F Smith (Jan. 15).

Boston Celtics

	Gm	FG%	Tpts	PPG	RPG	APG
Paul Pierce	.82	.442	2144	26.1	6.9	3.2
Antoine Walker	.81	.394	1794	22.1	8.8	5.0
Rodney Rogers	.77	.471	917	11.9	4.5	1.5
Kenny Anderson	.76	.436	731	9.6	3.6	5.3
Tony Delk	.63	.384	597	9.5	3.2	2.1
Erick Strickland	.79	.389	606	7.7	2.7	2.3
Tony Battie	.74	.541	510	6.9	6.5	0.5
Eric Williams	.74	.374	472	6.4	3.0	1.5
Vitaly Potapenko	.79	.455	363	4.6	4.4	0.4
Walter McCarty	.56	.444	212	3.8	2.3	0.7
Milt Palacio	.41	.385	152	3.7	1.2	1.3
Kedrick Brown*	.29	.329	63	2.2	1.7	0.5
Mark Blount	.44	.421	94	2.1	1.9	0.2
Joseph Forte*	.8	.083	6	0.8	0.8	0.8
Randy Brown	.1	.000	0	0.0	0.0	2.0

Triple Doubles: Walker (2). **3-pt FG leader:** Walker (222).
Steals leaders: Pierce (154). **Blocks leader:** Pierce (86).
Signed: G Strickland (Nov. 2).
Acquired: F Rogers and G Delk from Phoenix for F Joe Johnson, G Randy Brown, G Milt Palacio and a 2002 first-round pick. (Feb. 20).

Charlotte Hornets

	Gm	FG%	Tpts	PPG	RPG	APG
Jamal Mashburn	.40	.407	858	21.5	6.1	4.3
Baron Davis	.82	.417	1484	18.1	4.3	8.5
David Wesley	.67	.400	951	14.2	2.1	3.5
Elden Campbell	.77	.484	1074	13.9	6.9	1.3
Lee Nailon	.79	.483	851	10.8	3.7	1.2
Jamaal Magloire	.82	.551	699	8.5	5.6	0.4
P.J. Brown	.80	.474	669	8.4	9.8	1.3
Stacey Augmon	.77	.427	357	4.6	2.9	1.3
George Lynch	.45	.369	172	3.8	4.1	1.2
Robert Traylor	.61	.426	228	3.7	3.1	0.6
Matt Bullard	.31	.339	105	3.4	1.5	0.5
Bryce Drew	.61	.429	210	3.4	1.2	1.7
Kirk Haston*	.15	.282	26	1.7	1.3	0.3
Jerome Moiso	.15	.400	16	1.1	1.7	0.3
Eldridge Recasner	.1	.000	0	0.0	0.0	0.0

Triple Doubles: Davis (1). **3-pt FG leader:** Davis (170).
Steals leader: Davis (172). **Blocks leader:** Campbell (137).

Chicago Bulls

	Gm	FG%	Tpts	PPG	RPG	APG
Jalen Rose	.83	.455	1696	20.4	4.5	4.3
Marcus Fizer	.76	.438	938	12.3	5.6	1.6
Travis Best	.74	.440	581	7.9	2.0	4.4
Jamal Crawford	.23	.476	214	9.3	1.5	2.4
Eddie Robinson	.29	.453	262	9.0	2.7	1.3
Trenton Hassell*	.78	.425	681	8.7	3.3	2.2
Eddy Curry*	.72	.501	483	6.7	3.8	0.3
Tyson Chandler*	.71	.497	436	6.1	4.8	0.8
A.J. Guyton	.45	.361	244	5.4	1.0	1.8
Fred Hoiberg	.79	.416	345	4.4	2.7	1.7
Charles Oakley	.57	.369	216	3.8	6.0	2.0
Dalibor Bagaric	50	.404	185	3.7	3.2	0.5
Norm Richardson	.11	.385	30	2.7	0.7	0.2

Triple Doubles: none. **3-pt FG leader:** Hassell (60).
Steals leader: Hoiberg (61). **Blocks leader:** Chandler (93).
Acquired: F Rose, G Best and G Richardson and a conditional second-round pick from Indiana for G Ron Mercer, G Kevin Ollie, F Ron Artest and C Brad Miller (Feb. 20).

Cleveland Cavaliers

	Gm	FG%	Tpts	PPG	RPG	APG
Lamond Murray	.71	.436	1176	16.6	5.2	2.2
Andre Miller	.81	.454	1335	16.5	4.7	10.9
Wesley Person	.78	.495	1176	15.1	3.8	2.2
Ricky Davis	.82	.481	959	11.7	3.0	2.2
Zydrunas Ilgauskas	.62	.425	690	11.1	5.4	1.1
Jumaine Jones	.81	.448	671	8.3	6.0	1.4
Tyrone Hill	.26	.390	209	8.0	10.5	0.9
Chris Mihm	.74	.420	569	7.7	5.3	0.3
Trajan Langdon	.44	.398	209	4.8	1.3	1.4
Michael Doleac	.42	.417	194	4.6	4.0	0.6
Bryant Stith	.50	.372	208	4.2	1.7	0.8
Brian Skinner	.65	.543	224	3.4	4.3	0.3
Bimbo Coles	.47	.384	149	3.2	1.2	2.3
Jeff Trepagnier*	.12	.304	18	1.5	1.0	1.0
DeSagana Diop*	.18	.414	25	1.4	0.9	0.3

Triple Doubles: Miller (3). **3-pt FG leader:** Person (143).
Steals leader: Miller (126). **Blocks leader:** Mihm (89).

Dallas Mavericks

	Gm	FG%	Tpts	PPG	RPG	APG
Dirk Nowitzki	.76	.477	1779	23.4	9.9	2.4
Michael Finley	.69	.463	1424	20.6	5.2	3.3
Nick Van Exel	.72	.409	1322	18.4	5.7	6.6
Steve Nash	.82	.483	1466	17.9	3.1	7.7
Raef LaFrentz	.78	.458	1051	13.5	7.4	1.1
Avery Johnson	.68	.479	535	7.9	1.0	4.2
Adrian Griffin	.58	.499	415	7.2	3.9	1.8
Eduardo Najera	.62	.500	400	6.5	5.5	0.6
Greg Buckner	.44	.525	253	5.8	3.9	1.1
Wang Zhizhi	.55	.440	308	5.6	2.0	0.4
Tariq Abdul-Wahad	.24	.374	135	5.6	3.5	1.0
Johnny Newman	.47	.453	198	4.2	1.0	0.3
Shawn Bradley	.53	.479	215	4.1	3.3	0.4
Danny Manning	.41	.477	165	4.0	2.6	0.7
Evan Eschmeyer	.31	.420	62	2.0	3.2	0.3
Darrick Martin	.3	.000	1	0.3	0.3	1.0
Charlie Bell	.2	.000	0	0.0	0.5	0.0

Triple Doubles: none. **3-pt FG leader:** Nash (156).
Steals leader: Nowitzki (83). **Blocks leader:** LaFrentz (213).
Signed: F Newman (Nov. 28).
Acquired: G Van Exel, G Johnson, G Abdul-Wahad and C LaFrentz from Denver for F Juwan Howard, G Tim Hardaway and a 2002 first-round pick (Feb. 22).

Denver Nuggets

	Gm	FG%	Tpts	PPG	RPG	APG
Juwan Howard 81		.460	1185	14.6	7.6	2.1
Voshon Leonard 71		.410	813	11.5	2.6	1.8
Antonio McDyess 10		.573	113	11.3	5.5	1.8
James Posey 73		.376	782	10.7	5.9	2.5
Tim Hardaway 68		.365	652	9.6	1.8	4.1
Isaiah Rider 10		.457	93	9.3	3.3	1.2
George McCloud 69		.358	604	8.8	3.6	3.0
Calbert Cheaney 68		.481	494	7.3	3.5	1.6
Zendon Hamilton 54		.420	324	6.0	4.7	0.3
Donnell Harvey 47		.498	270	5.7	4.8	0.8
Kenny Satterfield* 36		.367	189	5.3	1.4	3.0
Mengke Bateer 27		.402	139	5.1	3.6	0.8
Scott Williams 41		.396	202	4.9	5.1	0.3
Ryan Bowen 75		.479	364	4.9	4.0	0.7
Carlos Arroyo* 37		.441	111	3.0	1.1	1.9
Shawnelle Scott 21		.493	82	3.9	4.9	0.4
Chris Andersen 24		.338	72	3.0	3.2	0.3

Triple Doubles: none. **3-pt FG leader:** Leonard (89).
Steals leader: Posey (114). **Blocks leader:** Posey (39).
Signed: F Anderson (Nov. 22).
Acquired: F Howard, G Hardaway and a 2002 first-round pick for G Nick Van Exel, G Avery Johnson, G Tariq Abdul-Wahad and C Raef LaFrentz from Dallas (Feb. 22).

Detroit Pistons

	Gm	FG%	Tpts	PPG	RPG	APG
Jerry Stackhouse 76		.397	1629	21.4	4.1	5.3
Clifford Robinson 80		.425	1166	14.6	4.8	2.5
Corliss Williamson . . .78		.510	1063	13.6	4.1	1.2
Chucky Atkins 79		.466	957	12.1	2.0	3.3
Jon Barry 82		.489	739	9.0	2.9	3.3
Ben Wallace 80		.531	609	7.6	13.0	1.4
Zeljko Rebraca* 74		.505	513	6.9	3.9	0.5
Dana Barros 29		.385	193	6.7	2.0	2.7
Damon Jones 67		.401	340	5.1	1.5	2.1
Ratko Varda 1		.667	5	5.0	1.0	0.0
Michael Curry 82		.453	329	4.0	2.0	1.5
Rodney White* 16		.350	56	3.5	1.1	0.8
Victor Alexander 15		.353	40	2.7	1.9	0.4
Mikki Moore 30		.475	79	2.6	1.8	0.4
Brian Cardinal 8		.462	17	2.1	0.8	0.3

Triple Doubles: Wallace (1). **3-pt FG leader:** Atkins (138).
Steals leader: Wallace (138). **Blocks leader:** Wallace (278).

Golden St. Warriors

	Gm	FG%	Tpts	PPG	RPG	APG
Antawn Jamison 82		.447	1619	19.7	6.8	2.0
Jason Richardson* 80		.426	1151	14.4	4.3	3.0
Larry Hughes 73		.423	895	12.3	3.4	4.3
Danny Fortson 77		.428	864	11.2	11.7	1.6
Gilbert Arenas* 47		.453	511	10.9	2.8	3.7
Bob Sura 78		.424	778	10.0	3.3	3.5
Erick Dampier 73		.435	554	7.6	5.3	1.2
Chris Mills 66		.417	489	7.4	2.9	1.1
Troy Murphy* 82		.421	480	5.9	3.9	0.9
Adonal Foyle 79		.444	379	4.8	4.9	0.5
Mookie Blaylock 35		.342	119	3.4	1.5	3.3
Cedric Henderson 12		.484	36	3.0	0.3	0.3
Dean Oliver 20		.370	42	2.1	0.4	1.1
Dean Garrett 34		.327	36	1.1	1.7	0.1

Triple Doubles: none. **3-pt FG leader:** Richardson (82).
Steals leader: Hughes (113). **Blocks leader:** Foyle (168).
Acquired: F Garrett and a second-round pick from Minnesota for C Marc Jackson (Feb. 22).

Houston Rockets

	Gm	FG%	Tpts	PPG	RPG	APG
Cuttino Mobley 74		.438	1606	21.7	4.1	2.5
Steve Francis 57		.417	1234	21.6	7.0	6.4
Kenny Thomas 72		.478	1015	14.1	7.2	1.9
Walt Williams 48		.419	450	9.4	3.4	1.4
Eddie Griffin* 73		.366	642	8.8	5.7	0.7
Glen Rice 20		.389	172	8.6	2.4	1.6
Moochie Norris 82		.398	665	8.1	3.0	4.9
Kelvin Cato 75		.583	493	6.6	7.0	0.4
Kevin Willis 52		.440	315	6.1	5.8	0.3
Oscar Torres* 65		.396	389	6.0	1.9	0.6
Jason Collier 25		.432	106	4.2	3.3	0.4
Terence Morris* 68		.384	255	3.8	3.1	0.9
Tierre Brown* 40		.426	123	3.1	1.1	1.8
Dan Langhi 34		.392	107	3.1	2.0	0.4

Triple Doubles: Francis (2). **3-pt FG leader:** Mobley (149).
Steals leader: Mobley (109). **Blocks leader:** Griffin (134).

Indiana Pacers

	Gm	FG%	Tpts	PPG	RPG	APG
Jermaine O'Neal 72		.479	1371	19.0	10.5	1.6
Reggie Miller 79		.453	1304	16.5	2.8	3.2
Ron Mercer 53		.397	735	13.9	3.4	2.4
Brad Miller 76		.499	1032	13.6	8.2	2.0
Ron Artest 55		.423	727	13.2	4.9	2.3
Al Harrington 44		.475	576	13.1	6.3	1.2
Jamaal Tinsley* 80		.380	751	9.4	3.7	8.1
Jonathan Bender 78		.430	581	7.4	3.1	0.8
Travis Best 44		.439	302	6.9	1.6	4.0
Austin Croshere 76		.413	516	6.8	3.9	1.0
Jeff Foster 82		.449	467	5.7	6.8	0.9
Kevin Ollie 81		.388	462	5.7	2.3	3.6
Carlos Rogers 22		.558	59	2.7	1.7	0.1
Primoz Brezec* 22		.483	43	2.0	1.3	0.3
Bruno Sundov 22		.400	32	1.5	1.0	0.1
Jamison Brewer* 13		.400	4	0.3	0.6	0.7
Norm Richardson 3		.000	0	0.0	0.3	0.3

Triple Doubles: Tinsley (2). **3-pt FG leader:** Miller (180).
Steals leader: Tinsley (138). **Blocks leader:** O'Neal (166).
Acquired: G Mercer, G Ollie, F Artest and C Miller from Chicago for F Jalen Rose, G Travis Best and G Norm Richardson and a conditional second-round pick (Feb. 20).

Los Angeles Clippers

	Gm	FG%	Tpts	PPG	RPG	APG
Elton Brand 80		.527	1453	18.2	11.6	2.4
Jeff McInnis 81		.413	1184	14.6	2.6	6.2
Quentin Richardson . .81		.432	1076	13.3	4.1	1.6
Lamar Odom 29		.419	379	13.1	6.1	5.9
Corey Maggette 63		.443	717	11.4	3.7	1.8
Michael Olowokandi . .80		.433	885	11.1	8.9	1.1
Darius Miles 82		.481	779	9.5	5.5	2.2
Eric Piatkowski 71		.439	626	8.8	2.6	1.6
Keyon Dooling 14		.386	58	4.1	0.2	0.9
Earl Boykins 80		.400	280	4.1	0.8	2.1
Tremaine Fowlkes* 22		.391	74	3.4	2.9	0.8
Sean Rooks 61		.418	183	3.0	2.0	0.4
Harold Jamison 25		.512	54	2.2	1.6	0.2
Doug Overton 18		.318	39	2.2	0.7	0.7
Obinna Ekezie 29		.333	54	1.9	1.2	0.1
Eldridge Recasner 5		.333	5	1.0	0.0	1.0

Triple Doubles: none. **3-pt FG leader:** Richardson (133).
Steals leader: Brand (80). **Blocks leader:** Brand (163).
Signed: G Recasner (Dec. 21), G Overton (Feb. 14), F Fowlkes (Feb. 24).

Los Angeles Lakers

	Gm	FG%	Tpts	PPG	RPG	APG
Shaquille O'Neal	.67	.579	1822	27.2	10.7	3.0
Kobe Bryant	.80	.469	2019	25.2	5.5	5.5
Derek Fisher	.70	.411	786	11.2	2.1	2.6
Rick Fox	.82	.421	645	7.9	4.7	3.5
Devean George	.82	.411	581	7.1	3.7	1.4
Robert Horry	.81	.398	550	6.8	5.9	2.9
Samaki Walker	.69	.512	460	6.7	7.0	0.9
Lindsey Hunter	.82	.382	473	5.8	1.5	1.6
S. Medvedenko	.71	.477	331	4.7	2.2	0.6
Mitch Richmond	.64	.405	260	4.1	1.5	0.9
Brian Shaw	.58	.353	169	2.9	1.9	1.5
Mark Madsen	.59	.452	167	2.8	2.7	0.7
Mike Penberthy	.3	.500	5	1.7	0.7	0.7
Joseph Crispin	.2	.250	10	1.7	0.2	0.3
Jelani McCoy	.21	.571	26	1.2	1.2	0.3

Triple Doubles: Bryant (1). **3-pt FG leader:** Fisher (144).
Steals leader: Bryant (118). **Blocks leader:** O'Neal (137).

Memphis Grizzlies

	Gm	FG%	Tpts	PPG	RPG	APG
Pau Gasol*	.82	.518	1441	17.6	8.9	2.7
Jason Williams	.65	.382	959	14.8	3.0	8.0
Shane Battier*	.78	.429	1125	14.4	5.4	2.8
Lorenzen Wright	.43	.459	516	12.0	9.4	1.0
Stromile Swift	.68	.480	803	11.8	6.3	0.7
Michael Dickerson	.4	.313	43	10.8	3.0	2.3
Rodney Buford	.63	.435	591	9.4	4.3	1.1
Brevin Knight	.53	.422	371	7.0	2.1	5.7
Grant Long	.66	.426	417	6.3	3.5	2.1
Tony Massenburg	.73	.456	403	5.5	4.4	0.4
Elliot Perry	.2	.500	11	5.5	2.0	3.5
Willie Solomon*	.62	.341	321	5.2	1.1	1.5
Eddie Gill	.23	.424	116	5.0	1.2	2.1
Nick Anderson	.15	.276	60	4.0	2.2	0.9
Antonis Fotsis	.28	.404	108	3.9	2.2	0.4
Isaac Austin	.21	.391	76	3.6	3.4	0.6
Isaac Fontaine	.6	.214	11	1.8	0.8	0.7

Triple Doubles: none. **3-pt FG leader:** Williams (127).
Steals leader: Battier (121). **Blocks leader:** Gasol (169).
Signed: G Gill (Feb. 24), G Fontaine (Mar. 3).

Miami Heat

	Gm	FG%	Tpts	PPG	RPG	APG
Eddie Jones	.81	.432	1480	18.3	4.7	3.2
Alonzo Mourning	.75	.516	1178	15.7	8.4	1.2
Jim Jackson	.55	.442	589	10.7	5.3	2.5
Rod Strickland	.76	.443	794	10.4	3.1	6.1
Brian Grant	.72	.469	673	9.3	8.0	1.9
Eddie House	.64	.399	514	8.0	1.7	1.9
LaPhonso Ellis	.66	.418	469	7.1	4.3	0.8
Chris Gatling	.54	.447	345	6.4	3.8	0.5
Kendall Gill	.65	.384	372	5.7	2.8	1.5
Sean Marks	.21	.432	96	4.6	3.6	0.4
Anthony Carter	.46	.342	198	4.3	2.5	4.7
Malik Allen*	.12	.431	52	4.3	3.2	0.4
Vladimir Stepania	.67	.470	285	4.3	4.0	0.2
Sam Mack	.12	.286	40	3.3	1.2	0.3
Mike James*	.15	.349	42	2.8	0.9	1.3
Tang Hamilton	.9	.526	20	2.2	2.0	0.6
Ernest Brown*	.3	.167	3	1.0	2.0	0.0

Triple Doubles: none. **3-pt FG leader:** Jones (149).
Steals leader: Jones (117). **Blocks leader:** Mourning (186).
Signed: G James (Dec. 19).

Milwaukee Bucks

	Gm	FG%	Tpts	PPG	RPG	APG
Ray Allen	.69	.462	1503	21.8	4.5	3.9
Glenn Robinson	.66	.467	1366	20.7	6.2	2.5
Sam Cassell	.74	.463	1461	19.7	4.2	6.7
Tim Thomas	.74	.420	869	11.7	4.1	1.4
Michael Redd	.67	.483	767	11.4	3.3	1.4
Anthony Mason	.82	.505	787	9.6	7.9	4.2
Greg Anthony	.60	.403	474	7.9	2.2	4.7
Jason Caffey	.23	.500	99	4.3	2.2	0.5
Darvin Ham	.70	.569	303	4.3	2.9	1.0
Rafer Alston	.50	.346	177	3.5	1.4	2.9
Joel Przybilla	.71	.535	190	2.7	4.0	0.3
Ervin Johnson	.81	.461	208	2.6	5.8	0.3
Mark Pope	.45	.396	87	1.9	1.6	0.4
Greg Foster	.6	.222	7	1.2	1.3	0.2

Triple Doubles: none. **3-pt FG leader:** Allen (229).
Steals leader: Robinson (97). **Blocks leader:** Przybilla (118).
Signed: G Anthony (Mar. 7).

Minnesota Timberwolves

	Gm	FG%	Tpts	PPG	RPG	APG
Kevin Garnett	.81	.470	1714	21.2	12.1	5.2
Wally Szczerbiak	.82	.508	1531	18.7	4.8	3.1
Chauncey Billups	.82	.423	1027	12.5	2.8	5.5
Terrell Brandon	.32	.425	397	12.4	2.9	8.3
Joe Smith	.72	.511	767	10.7	6.3	1.1
Anthony Peeler	.82	.421	737	9.0	2.5	2.2
Radoslav Nesterovic	.82	.493	687	8.4	6.5	0.9
Gary Trent	.64	.507	478	7.5	4.2	0.9
Marc Jackson	.39	.366	186	4.8	3.3	0.4
Robert Pack	.16	.368	62	3.9	1.4	3.1
Sam Mitchell	.74	.432	244	3.3	1.1	0.6
Felipe Lopez	.67	.378	169	2.5	1.2	0.6
William Avery	.28	.289	71	2.5	0.9	1.3
Maurice Evans*	.10	.474	21	2.1	0.4	0.4
Loren Woods*	.60	.344	110	1.8	2.0	0.4

Triple Doubles: Billups (1). **3-pt FG leader:** Billups (124).
Steals leader: Garnett (96). **Blocks leader:** Garnett (126).
Signed: G Pack (Mar. 19).
Acquired: C Jackson from Golden State for F Dean Garrett and a second-round pick (Feb. 22).

New Jersey Nets

	Gm	FG%	Tpts	PPG	RPG	APG
Kenyon Martin	.73	.463	1086	14.9	5.3	2.6
Keith Van Horn	.81	.433	1199	14.8	7.5	2.0
Jason Kidd	.82	.391	1208	14.7	7.3	9.9
Kerry Kittles	.82	.466	1102	13.4	3.4	2.6
Todd MacCulloch	.62	.531	604	9.7	6.1	1.3
Richard Jefferson*	.79	.457	742	9.4	3.7	1.8
Lucious Harris	.74	.464	675	9.1	2.8	1.6
Aaron Williams	.82	.526	592	7.2	4.1	0.9
Jason Collins*	.77	.421	350	4.5	3.9	1.1
Derrick Dial	.25	.319	73	2.9	1.8	1.2
Anthony Johnson	.34	.411	94	2.8	0.9	1.4
Brian Scalabrine	.28	.343	60	2.1	1.8	0.8
Brandon Armstrong*	.35	.318	64	1.8	0.5	0.2
Donny Marshall	.20	.276	30	1.5	1.1	0.3
Reggie Slater	.4	1.000	5	1.3	0.5	0.0
Steve Goodrich	.9	.200	5	0.6	0.6	0.0

Triple Doubles: Kidd (8). **3-pt FG leader:** Kidd (117).
Steals leader: Kidd (175). **Blocks leaders:** Martin (121).
Signed: G Johnson and G Marshall (Jan. 30).

New York Knicks

	Gm	FG%	Tpts	PPG	RPG	APG
Allan Houston	.77	.437	1567	20.4	3.3	2.5
Latrell Sprewell	.81	.404	1575	19.4	3.7	3.9
Kurt Thomas	.82	.494	1143	13.9	9.1	1.1
Marcus Camby	.29	.448	322	11.1	11.1	1.1
C. Weatherspoon	.56	.418	494	8.8	8.2	1.1
Mark Jackson	.82	.439	686	8.4	3.8	7.4
Charlie Ward	.63	.373	326	5.2	2.0	3.2
Shandon Anderson	.82	.399	411	5.0	3.0	0.9
Howard Eisley	.39	.337	171	4.4	1.3	2.6
Lavor Postell	.23	.333	93	4.0	0.7	0.2
Travis Knight	.49	.363	98	2.0	2.1	0.2
Larry Robinson	.2	.250	3	1.5	1.0	0.0
Felton Spencer	.32	.231	29	0.9	1.6	0.1

Triple Doubles: Jackson (1). **3-pt FG leader:** Sprewell (145).
Steals leader: Sprewell (94). **Blocks leader:** Thomas (79).

Orlando Magic

	Gm	FG%	Tpts	PPG	RPG	APG
Tracy McGrady	.76	.451	1948	25.6	7.9	5.3
Grant Hill	.14	.426	235	16.8	8.9	4.6
Mike Miller	.63	.438	956	15.2	4.3	3.1
Darrell Armstrong	.82	.419	1015	12.4	3.9	5.5
Troy Hudson	.81	.434	950	11.7	1.8	3.1
Pat Garrity	.80	.426	884	11.1	4.2	1.2
Horace Grant	.76	.513	608	8.0	6.3	1.4
Monty Williams	.68	.547	484	7.1	3.5	1.4
Patrick Ewing	.65	.444	390	6.0	4.0	0.5
Jaren Jackson	.9	.405	39	4.3	1.9	0.9
Steven Hunter*	.53	.456	189	3.6	1.8	0.1
Don Reid	.68	.474	224	3.3	2.6	0.4
Andrew DeClercq	.61	.450	162	2.7	2.7	0.4
Jud Buechler	.66	.373	111	1.7	1.8	0.5
Jeryl Sasser*	.7	.214	10	1.4	1.0	0.3
Dee Brown	.7	.150	7	1.0	1.3	0.3

Triple Doubles: McGrady (1). **3-pt FG leader:** Garrity (169).
Steals leader: Armstrong (157). **Blocks leader:** McGrady (73).
Signed: G Brown (Mar. 13); G Jackson (Apr. 3).
Acquired: G/F Buechler from Phoenix and an option to swap second-round picks in 2005 with the L.A. Clippers and sent F Bo Outlaw, a first-round pick in 2002 and cash to Phoenix in a three-team trade (Nov. 17).

Philadelphia 76ers

	Gm	FG%	Tpts	PPG	RPG	APG
Allen Iverson	.60	.398	1883	31.4	4.5	5.5
Derrick Coleman	.58	.450	875	15.1	8.8	1.7
Aaron McKie	.48	.449	587	12.2	4.0	3.7
Eric Snow	.61	.442	738	12.1	3.5	6.6
Matt Harpring	.81	.461	958	11.8	7.1	1.3
Dikembe Mutombo	.80	.501	920	11.5	10.8	1.0
Speedy Claxton*	.67	.400	480	7.2	2.4	3.0
Jabari Smith	.11	.476	55	5.0	1.3	0.5
Corie Blount	.72	.458	259	3.6	5.1	0.6
Raja Bell	.74	.429	254	3.4	1.5	1.0
Ira Bowman	.3	.714	10	3.3	0.3	0.3
Vonteego Cummings	.58	.417	192	3.3	0.9	1.0
Derrick McKey	.41	.426	119	2.9	3.1	1.1
Samuel Dalembert*	.34	.440	51	1.5	2.0	0.1
Damone Brown*	.17	.381	23	1.4	0.2	0.1
Tim James	.9	.385	12	1.3	0.8	0.1
Alvin Jones*	.23	.400	26	1.1	1.6	0.1
Michael Ruffin	.15	.269	16	1.1	3.4	0.3
Matt Geiger	.4	.125	3	0.8	1.5	0.0

Triple Doubles: Iverson & Mutombo (1). **3-pt FG leader:** Iverson (78).
Steals leader: Iverson (168). **Blocks leader:** Mutombo (190).
Signed: F James (Nov. 7); F Ruffin (Nov. 23); F McKey (Jan. 15).

Phoenix Suns

	Gm	FG%	Tpts	PPG	RPG	APG
Stephon Marbury	.82	.442	1674	20.4	3.2	8.1
Shawn Marion	.81	.469	1547	19.1	9.9	2.0
Anfernee Hardaway	.80	.418	959	12.0	4.4	4.1
Joe Johnson*	.77	.430	581	7.5	3.3	2.3
Jake Tsakalidis	.67	.475	491	7.3	5.6	0.3
Tom Gugliotta	.44	.422	285	6.5	5.0	1.8
Jake Voskuhl	.59	.554	296	5.0	4.2	0.3
John Wallace	.46	.435	231	5.0	1.8	0.6
Dan Majerle	.65	.343	300	4.6	2.7	1.4
Joseph Crispin	.15	.411	69	4.6	0.7	1.6
Bo Outlaw	.83	.555	376	4.5	4.4	1.5
Alton Ford*	.53	.517	164	3.1	2.0	0.1
Milt Palacio	.69	.383	231	3.3	1.1	1.2
Daniel Santiago	.3	.500	8	2.7	2.3	0.7
Charlie Bell	.5	.273	8	1.6	0.8	0.4

Triple Doubles: Hardaway (1). **3-pt FG leader:** Majerle (79).
Steals leader: Marion (149). **Blocks leader:** Marion (86).
Acquired: F Outlaw, a first-round pick in 2002 and cash from Orlando for G/F Jud Buechler to the Magic and guard Vinny Del Negro to the Los Angeles Clippers in a three-team trade (Nov. 17); F Johnson, G Brown, G Palacio and a 2002 first-round pick from Boston for F Rodney Rogers and G Tony Delk (Feb. 20).

Portland Trailblazers

	Gm	FG%	Tpts	PPG	RPG	APG
Rasheed Wallace	.79	.469	1521	19.3	8.2	1.9
Bonzi Wells	.74	.469	1255	17.0	6.0	2.8
Damon Stoudamire	.75	.402	1016	13.5	3.9	6.5
Rúben Patterson	.75	.515	839	11.2	4.0	1.4
Derek Anderson	.70	.404	757	10.8	2.7	3.1
Scottie Pippen	.62	.411	659	10.6	5.2	5.9
Dale Davis	.78	.510	742	9.5	8.8	1.2
Shawn Kemp	.75	.430	454	6.1	3.8	0.7
Steve Kerr	.65	.470	269	4.1	0.9	1.0
Erick Barkley	.19	.353	58	3.1	0.9	1.8
Zach Randolph*	.41	.449	114	2.8	1.7	0.3
Mitchell Butler	.11	.435	29	2.6	1.3	0.5
Rick Brunson	.59	.398	125	2.1	1.2	1.9
R. Boumtje Boumtje*	.33	.406	39	1.2	1.7	0.1
Chris Dudley	.43	.400	48	1.1	1.9	0.3

Triple Doubles: none. **3-pt FG leader:** Wallace (114).
Steals leader: Wells (113). **Blocks leader:** Wallace (101).

Sacramento Kings

	Gm	FG%	Tpts	PPG	RPG	APG
Chris Webber	.54	.495	1322	24.5	10.1	4.8
Predrag Stojakovic	.71	.484	1506	21.2	5.3	2.5
Mike Bibby	.80	.453	1098	13.7	2.8	5.0
Doug Christie	.81	.460	972	12.0	4.6	4.2
Vlade Divac	.80	.472	888	11.1	8.4	3.7
Bobby Jackson	.81	.443	896	11.1	3.1	2.0
Hidayet Turkoglu	.80	.422	810	10.1	4.5	2.0
Scot Pollard	.80	.550	509	6.4	7.1	0.7
Lawrence Funderburke	.56	.469	264	4.7	3.5	0.6
Gerald Wallace*	.54	.429	173	3.2	1.6	0.5
Mateen Cleaves	.32	.441	70	2.2	0.3	0.8
Brent Price	.20	.333	31	1.6	0.4	0.5
Jabari Smith	.12	.286	18	1.5	1.2	0.5
Chucky Brown	.18	.370	21	1.2	1.8	0.3

Triple Doubles: Divac (1). **3-pt FG leader:** Stojakovic (129).
Steals leader: Christie (160). **Blocks leader:** Divac (94).
Signed: F Brown (Feb. 27).

San Antonio Spurs

	Gm	FG%	Tpts	PPG	RPG	APG
Tim Duncan	82	.508	2089	25.5	12.7	3.7
David Robinson	78	.507	951	12.2	8.3	1.2
Steve Smith	77	.455	895	11.6	2.5	2.0
Malik Rose	82	.463	772	9.4	6.0	0.7
Antonio Daniels	82	.440	753	9.2	2.1	2.8
Tony Parker*	77	.419	705	9.2	2.6	4.3
Charles Smith	60	.425	441	7.4	2.2	1.3
Bruce Bowen	59	.389	412	7.0	2.7	1.5
Terry Porter	72	.424	399	5.5	2.3	2.8
Danny Ferry	50	.429	229	4.6	1.8	1.0
Stephen Jackson	23	.374	89	3.9	1.1	0.5
Jason Hart	10	.526	26	2.6	1.3	1.2
Amal McCaskill	27	.408	52	1.9	1.3	1.0
Mark Bryant	30	.455	56	1.9	1.5	0.3
Cherokee Parks	42	.361	63	1.5	1.4	0.2

Triple Doubles: none. **3-pt FG leader:** Smith (116).
Steals leader: Parker (89). **Blocks leader:** Duncan (203).
Signed: G Hart (Dec. 20).

Utah Jazz

	Gm	FG%	Tpts	PPG	RPG	APG
Karl Malone	80	.454	1788	22.4	8.6	4.3
Donyell Marshall	58	.519	859	14.8	7.6	1.7
John Stockton	82	.517	1102	13.4	3.2	8.2
Andrei Kirilenko*	82	.450	880	10.7	4.9	1.1
Bryon Russell	66	.380	636	9.6	4.5	2.1
John Crotty	41	.471	284	6.9	1.8	3.4
Scott Padgett	75	.476	500	6.7	3.8	1.1
Jarron Collins*	70	.461	450	6.4	4.2	0.8
Rusty LaRue	33	.395	193	5.8	1.5	2.2
DeShawn Stevenson	67	.385	325	4.9	2.0	1.7
John Starks	66	.368	290	4.4	1.0	1.1
Quincy Lewis	36	.448	144	4.0	1.2	1.0
Greg Ostertag	74	.453	245	3.3	4.2	0.7
John Amaechi	54	.325	175	3.2	2.0	0.5

Triple Doubles: none. **3-pt FG leader:** Russell (77).
Steals leader: Stockton, Malone (152). **Blocks leader:** Kirilenko (159).
Signed: G LaRue (Jan. 28).

Seattle Supersonics

	Gm	FG%	Tpts	PPG	RPG	APG
Gary Payton	82	.467	1815	22.1	4.8	9.0
Rashard Lewis	71	.468	1195	16.8	7.0	1.7
Brent Barry	81	.508	1164	14.4	5.4	5.3
Vin Baker	55	.485	774	14.1	6.4	1.3
Desmond Mason	75	.464	931	12.4	4.7	1.4
Predrag Drobnjak*	64	.461	437	6.8	3.4	0.8
V. Radmanovic*	61	.412	407	6.7	3.8	1.3
Ansu Sesay	9	.500	58	6.4	2.2	0.9
Calvin Booth	15	.427	93	6.2	3.6	1.1
Jerome James	56	.491	298	5.3	4.1	0.4
Art Long	63	.492	285	4.5	4.0	0.7
Shammond Williams	50	.420	221	4.4	1.3	1.7
Earl Watson*	64	.453	231	3.6	1.3	2.0
Randy Livingston	13	.278	41	3.2	1.9	2.0
Antonio Harvey	3	.333	9	1.8	1.8	1.0
Olumide Oyedeji	36	.537	55	1.5	2.2	0.1

Triple Doubles: Payton (2). **3-pt FG leader:** Barry (164).
Steals leader: Barry (147). **Blocks leader:** James (86).
Signed: G Livingston (Mar. 9).

Washington Wizards

	Gm	FG%	Tpts	PPG	RPG	APG
Michael Jordan	60	.416	1375	22.9	5.7	5.2
Richard Hamilton	63	.435	1260	20.0	3.4	2.7
Chris Whitney	82	.418	833	10.2	1.9	3.8
Courtney Alexander	56	.470	549	9.8	2.6	1.5
Tyronn Lue	71	.427	555	7.8	1.7	3.5
Hubert Davis	51	.448	365	7.2	1.5	2.1
Christian Laettner	57	.464	404	7.1	5.3	2.6
Popeye Jones	79	.437	554	7.0	7.3	1.6
Tyrone Nesby	70	.435	443	6.3	4.5	1.3
Jahidi White	71	.538	383	5.4	6.3	0.2
Brendan Haywood*	62	.493	315	5.1	5.2	0.5
Kwame Brown*	57	.387	258	4.5	3.5	0.8
Etan Thomas*	44	.536	203	4.3	3.9	0.1
Bobby Simmons*	30	.453	112	3.7	1.7	0.6

Triple Doubles: none. **3-pt FG leader:** Whitney (131).
Steals leader: Jordan (85). **Blocks leader:** Haywood (91).
Signed: G Vanterpool (Mar. 5). **Claimed:** F Obinna Ekezie (Dec. 1).

Toronto Raptors

	Gm	FG%	Tpts	PPG	RPG	APG
Vince Carter	60	.428	1484	24.7	5.2	4.0
Antonio Davis	77	.426	1113	14.5	9.6	2.0
Morris Peterson	63	.438	883	14.0	3.5	2.4
Alvin Williams	82	.415	971	11.8	3.4	5.7
Keon Clark	81	.490	915	11.3	7.4	1.1
Jerome Williams	68	.490	518	7.6	5.7	1.1
Hakeem Olajuwon	61	.464	435	7.1	6.0	1.1
Dell Curry	56	.406	360	6.4	1.4	1.1
Tracy Murray	40	.411	227	5.7	1.3	0.5
Chris Childs	69	.328	285	4.1	2.2	5.1
Mamadou N'diaye	5	.600	20	4.0	2.2	0.0
Derrick Dial	7	.423	28	4.0	1.6	0.6
Eric Montross	49	.402	116	2.4	2.9	0.3
Jermaine Jackson	24	.476	57	2.4	1.1	2.4
Michael Stewart	11	.348	22	2.0	2.3	0.3
Michael Bradley*	26	.520	30	1.2	0.9	0.1

Triple Doubles: none. **3-pt FG leader:** Carter (121).
Steals leader: A. Williams (135). **Blocks leader:** Clark (122).
Signed: G Jackson (Jan. 11); G Dial (Mar. 29).

Individual Single Game Highs
Most Field Goals Made

21 . . . . Allen Iverson, Phi. vs. Hou. (1/15)
Kobe Bryant, LAL vs. Mem. (1/14)
Michael Jordan, Wash. vs. Cha. (12/29)
Shareef Abdur-Rahim, Atl. vs. Det. (11/23)

Most Field Goals Attempted

42 . . . . Allen Iverson, Phi. vs. Hou. (1/15)

Most Assists

23 . . Jamaal Tinsley, Ind.
vs Wash. (11/22)

Most Rebounds

28 . . . . Ben Wallace, Det.
vs. Bos. (3/24)

NBA Regular Season Team Leaders
Offense

—Per Game—

WEST	Pts	Reb	Ast	FGM-FGA	FG%	3PM-3PA	3Pt%	FTM-FTA	FT%	OFF-DEF	TRB	TO	BLKS
Dallas	105.2	42.5	22.1	3200-6930	.462	621-1645	.378	1608-1994	.806	918-2568	3486	992	392
Sacramento	104.6	45.3	23.9	3267-7003	.467	426-1160	.367	1618-2154	.751	1013-2702	3715	1128	375
LA Lakers	101.3	44.3	23.0	3150-6840	.461	510-1439	.354	1494-2138	.699	1022-2607	3629	1040	478
Minnesota	99.3	44.2	24.3	3175-6887	.461	396-1047	.378	1399-1754	.798	1059-2562	3621	1097	427
Seattle	97.7	40.3	23.5	3131-6681	.469	489-1292	.378	1263-1672	.755	968-2333	3301	1124	364
Golden State	97.7	46.7	20.8	2998-6989	.429	320-994	.322	1693-2344	.722	1334-2493	3827	1378	523
San Antonio	96.7	42.4	20.0	2913-6363	.458	438-1211	.362	1668-2449	.742	907-2566	3473	1180	537
Portland	96.6	43.0	23.5	3004-6671	.450	466-1318	.354	1451-1901	.763	1085-2444	3529	1172	368
Utah	96.0	42.2	24.4	2869-6374	.450	280-842	.333	1853-2430	.763	1109-2349	3458	1353	523
LA Clippers	95.7	43.4	20.9	2970-6668	.445	408-1147	.356	1498-2026	.739	1083-2474	3557	1214	540
Phoenix	95.1	42.7	22.4	3097-6934	.447	358-1096	.327	1250-1630	.767	1072-2430	3502	1205	401
Houston	92.3	41.9	18.1	2837-6629	.428	496-1480	.335	1402-1893	.741	1025-2411	3436	1156	445
Denver	92.2	41.8	22.2	2915-6870	.424	423-1285	.329	1306-1756	.744	1117-2310	3427	1205	462
Memphis	89.9	41.4	21.8	2851-6535	.436	336-1096	.307	1334-1883	.708	984-2413	3397	1344	488

—Per Game—

EAST	Pts	Reb	Ast	FGM-FGA	FG%	3PM-3PA	3Pt%	FTM-FTA	FT%	OFF-DEF	TRB	TO	BLKS
Orlando	100.5	41.2	22.0	3087-6893	.448	620-1660	.373	1446-1917	.754	942-2440	3382	1119	384
Milwaukee	97.5	41.4	22.5	3041-6577	.462	593-1583	.375	1321-1767	.748	841-2557	3398	1157	388
Indiana	96.8	42.7	23.0	2935-6580	.446	405-1195	.339	1663-2155	.772	930-2568	3498	1249	436
Boston	96.4	42.2	21.0	2852-6731	.424	699-1946	.359	1498-1960	.764	891-2570	3461	1114	292
New Jersey	96.2	43.3	24.3	3042-6816	.446	403-1194	.338	1402-1907	.735	1039-2515	3554	1189	490
Cleveland	95.3	42.1	23.1	2948-6582	.448	387-1026	.377	1529-1980	.772	968-2483	3451	1196	470
Detroit	94.3	38.7	21.5	2845-6300	.452	567-1509	.376	1478-1954	.756	810-2366	3176	1193	565
Atlanta	94.0	41.5	20.2	2901-6610	.439	423-1194	.354	1486-1942	.765	955-2445	3400	1275	350
Charlotte	93.9	43.5	21.5	2893-6580	.440	346-994	.348	1568-2105	.745	1059-2505	3564	1150	470
Washington	92.8	42.0	20.9	2938-6664	.441	305-786	.388	1428-1866	.765	1055-2393	3448	1068	354
New York	91.6	40.7	21.0	2817-6520	.432	474-1344	.353	1406-1786	.787	876-2458	3334	1192	288
Toronto	91.4	42.1	21.7	2919-6727	.434	387-1109	.349	1269-1717	.739	1114-2336	3450	1174	454
Philadelphia	91.0	44.2	20.0	2804-6436	.436	214-715	.299	1639-2104	.779	1092-2534	3626	1256	363
Chicago	89.5	40.0	22.2	2811-6491	.433	300-868	.346	1413-1958	.722	924-2359	3283	1252	361
Miami	87.2	42.0	20.3	2801-6382	.439	312-899	.347	1236-1708	.724	902-2544	3446	1217	448

Defense

—Per Game—

WEST	Pts	Reb	Ast	FGM-FGA	FG%	3PM-3PA	3Pt%	FTM-FTA	FT%	OFF-DEF	TRB	TO	BLKS
San Antonio	90.5	43.3	18.8	2883-6775	.426	374-1108	.338	1283-1651	.777	1003-2429	3432	1128	428
Portland	93.7	39.2	23.7	2951-6508	.453	466-1285	.363	1312-1771	.741	890-2328	3218	1147	410
LA Lakers	94.1	43.2	20.0	2872-6777	.424	399-1259	.317	1577-2072	.761	1016-2526	3542	1100	354
Seattle	94.7	41.7	22.3	2966-6605	.449	472-1374	.344	1362-1844	.739	1091-2326	3417	1205	400
Utah	95.1	38.2	19.3	2777-6218	.447	465-1215	.383	1779-2308	.771	928-2204	3132	1328	548
Phoenix	95.8	43.0	22.2	2957-6663	.444	433-1208	.358	1511-2013	.751	1029-2493	3522	1200	475
Minnesota	96.0	39.5	22.6	2962-6654	.445	492-1321	.372	1452-1958	.742	912-2326	3238	1037	409
LA Clippers	96.1	42.0	22.7	3074-6866	.448	407-1145	.355	1329-1783	.745	1064-2379	3443	1009	439
Sacramento	97.0	44.9	22.4	3218-7108	.440	386-1145	.337	1312-1764	.744	1065-2617	3682	1197	387
Houston	97.2	43.3	22.4	3191-6875	.464	370-1028	.360	1221-1623	.752	1045-2507	3552	949	415
Memphis	97.3	45.1	23.9	3119-6829	.457	398-1112	.358	1346-1788	.753	1135-2560	3695	1164	457
Denver	98.0	43.0	24.0	3005-6540	.459	424-1173	.361	1602-2144	.747	995-2529	3524	1122	560
Dallas	101.0	44.7	22.7	3094-6851	.452	452-1293	.350	1640-2184	.751	1065-2600	3665	1121	377
Golden State	103.1	43.3	24.4	3213-6993	.459	404-1162	.348	1622-2125	.763	1100-2450	3550	1132	512

—Per Game—

EAST	Pts	Reb	Ast	FGM-FGA	FG%	3PM-3PA	3Pt%	FTM-FTA	FT%	OFF-DEF	TRB	TO	BLKS
Miami	88.7	41.2	17.8	2666-6279	.425	379-1109	.342	1565-2127	.736	894-2484	3378	1073	353
Philadelphia	89.4	40.6	21.6	2771-6500	.426	438-1322	.331	1350-1798	.751	981-2348	3329	1147	458
Toronto	91.8	41.8	19.9	2820-6390	.441	377-1089	.346	1513-2011	.752	995-2436	3431	1191	393
New Jersey	92.0	42.9	19.1	2858-6668	.429	409-1175	.348	1423-1890	.753	999-2517	3516	1244	439
Detroit	92.2	42.7	20.0	2926-6546	.447	359-993	.362	1349-1787	.755	991-2511	3502	1206	335
Charlotte	92.9	41.0	20.0	2850-6594	.432	433-1156	.375	1488-1938	.768	963-2399	3362	1074	422
Boston	94.1	45.9	22.0	2797-6579	.425	514-1511	.340	1612-2091	.771	954-2807	3761	1285	476
Washington	94.2	40.7	22.2	2953-6534	.452	422-1191	.354	1396-1849	.755	960-2376	3336	1062	414
New York	95.6	42.7	21.5	2924-6570	.445	443-1256	.353	1550-2047	.757	959-2540	3499	1059	385
Indiana	96.5	43.4	21.6	2977-6800	.438	418-1200	.348	1544-2062	.749	1048-2514	3562	1120	466
Milwaukee	97.7	42.5	23.0	3016-6846	.441	493-1377	.358	1489-1967	.757	1050-3488	2438	992	361
Chicago	98.0	42.6	25.2	3027-6514	.465	421-1177	.358	1560-2090	.746	944-2553	3497	1122	399
Atlanta	98.3	43.0	22.6	3065-6674	.459	472-1329	.355	1456-1957	.744	1003-2522	3525	1177	508
Cleveland	98.6	40.4	24.3	3053-6678	.457	473-1200	.394	1506-2014	.748	928-2381	3310	1018	459
Orlando	98.9	45.4	23.5	3116-6828	.456	409-1161	.352	1470-1994	.737	1086-2633	3719	1241	383

2002 NBA Playoffs

| 1ST ROUND | SEMIFINALS | FINAL | | FINAL | SEMIFINALS | 1ST ROUND |

(1) New Jersey 3
(8) Indiana 2
→ **(1) New Jersey 4**
→ **(1) New Jersey 4**

(4) Charlotte 3
(5) Orlando 1
→ **(4) Charlotte 1**

EASTERN CONFERENCE
→ **(1) New Jersey 0** / **(3) LA Lakers 4**

(3) Boston 3
(6) Philadelphia 2
→ **(3) Boston 4**
→ **(3) Boston 2**

(2) Detroit 3
(7) Toronto 2
→ **(2) Detroit 1**

(1) Sacramento 3
WESTERN CONFERENCE
→ **(3) LA Lakers 4**

(1) Sacramento 4
(4) Dallas 1

(1) Sacramento 3
(8) Utah 1
(4) Dallas 3
(5) Minnesota 0

(3) LA Lakers 4
(2) San Antonio 1

(3) LA Lakers 3
(6) Portland 0
(2) San Antonio 3
(7) Seattle 2

Series Summaries

WESTERN CONFERENCE

FIRST ROUND (Best of 5)

	W-L	Avg.	Leading Scorer
Utah	1-3	88.0	Malone (20.0)
Sacramento	3-1	89.0	Webber (20.8)

Date	Winner	Home Court
Apr. 20	Kings, 89-86	at Sacramento
Apr. 23	Jazz, 93-86	at Sacramento
Apr. 27	Kings, 90-87	at Utah
Apr. 29	Kings, 91-86	at Utah

	W-L	Avg.	Leading Scorer
San Antonio	3-2	96.4	Duncan (20.6)
Seattle	2-3	86.2	Payton (22.2)

Date	Winner	Home Court
Apr. 20	Spurs, 110-89	at San Antonio
Apr. 22	Sonics, 98-90	at San Antonio
Apr. 27	Spurs, 102-75	at Seattle
May 1	Sonics, 91-79	at Seattle
May 3	Spurs, 101-78	at San Antonio

	W-L	Avg.	Leading Scorer
LA Lakers	3-0	96.7	Bryant (26.0)
Portland	0-3	91.3	Wallace (25.3)

Date	Winner	Home Court
Apr. 21	Lakers, 95-87	at Los Angeles
Apr. 25	Lakers, 103-96	at Los Angeles
Apr. 28	Lakers, 92-91	at Portland

	W-L	Avg.	Leading Scorer
Dallas	3-0	112.7	Nowitzki (33.3)
Minnesota	0-3	102.0	Garnett (24.0)

Date	Winner	Home Court
Apr. 21	Mavericks, 101-94	at Dallas
Apr. 24	Mavericks, 122-110	at Dallas
Apr. 28	Mavericks, 115-102	at Minnesota

SEMIFINALS (Best of 7)

	W-L	Avg.	Leading Scorer
Dallas	4-1	106.8	Nowitzki (25.4 ppg)
Sacramento	1-4	112.8	Webber (25.28 ppg)

Date	Winner	Home Court
May 4	Kings, 108-91	at Sacramento
May 6	Mavericks, 110-102	at Sacramento
May 9	Kings, 125-119	at Dallas
May 11	Kings, 115-113	at Dallas
May 13	Kings, 114-101	at Sacramento

	W-L	Avg.	Leading Scorer
San Antonio	1-4	85.8	Duncan (29.0)
LA Lakers	4-1	90.0	Bryant (26.2)

Date	Winner	Home Court
May 5	Lakers, 86-80	at Los Angeles
May 7	Spurs, 88-85	at Los Angeles
May 10	Lakers, 99-89	at San Antonio
May 12	Lakers, 87-85	at San Antonio
May 14	Lakers, 93-87	at Los Angeles

CHAMPIONSHIP (Best of 7)

	W-L	Avg.	Leading Scorer
Sacramento	3-4	99.6	Webber (24.3)
LA Lakers	4-3	99.3	O'Neal (30.3)

Date	Winner	Home Court
May 18	Lakers, 106-99	at Sacramento
May 20	Kings, 96-90	at Sacramento
May 24	Kings, 103-90	at Los Angeles
May 26	Lakers, 100-99	at Los Angeles
May 28	Kings, 92-91	at Sacramento
May 31	Lakers, 106-102	at Los Angeles
June 2	Lakers, 112-106 (OT)	at Sacramento

EASTERN CONFERENCE

FIRST ROUND (Best of 5)

	W-L	Avg.	Leading Scorer
Indiana	2-3	91.6	R. Miller (23.6)
New Jersey	3-2	91.4	Kidd (22.2)

Date	Winner	Home Court
Apr. 20	Pacers, 89-83	at New Jersey
Apr. 22	Nets, 95-79	at New Jersey
Apr. 26	Nets, 85-84	at Indiana
Apr. 30	Pacers, 97-74	at Indiana
May 2	Nets, 120-109 (2 OT)	at New Jersey

	W-L	Avg.	Leading Scorer
Toronto	2-3	83.8	Davis (17.0)
Detroit	3-2	86.6	Stackhouse (16.4)

Date	Winner	Home Court
Apr. 21	Pistons, 85-63	at Detroit
Apr. 24	Pistons, 96-91	at Detroit
Apr. 27	Raptors, 94-84	at Toronto
Apr. 29	Raptors, 89-83	at Toronto
May 2	Pistons, 85-82	at Detroit

	W-L	Avg.	Leading Scorer
Philadelphia	2-3	88.4	Iverson (30.0)
Boston	3-2	91.3	Pierce (24.6)

Date	Winner	Home Court
Apr. 21	Celtics, 92-82	at Boston
Apr. 25	Celtics, 93-85	at Boston
Apr. 28	76ers, 108-103	at Philadelphia
May 1	76ers, 83-81	at Philadelphia
May 3	Celtics, 120-87	at Boston

	W-L	Avg.	Leading Scorer
Orlando	1-3	93.8	McGrady (30.8)
Charlotte	3-1	98.8	Davis (25.0)

Date	Winner	Home Court
Apr. 20	Hornets, 80-79	at Charlotte
Apr. 23	Magic, 111-103	at Charlotte
Apr. 27	Hornets, 110-100 (OT)	at Orlando
Apr. 30	Hornets 102-85	at Orlando

SEMIFINALS (Best of 7)

	W-L	Avg.	Leading Scorer
Charlotte	1-4	94.0	Davis (20.6)
New Jersey	4-1	98.0	Kidd (18.4)

Date	Winner	Home Court
May 5	Nets, 99-93	at New Jersey
May 7	Nets, 102-88	at New Jersey
May 9	Hornets, 115-97	at Charlotte
May 12	Nets, 89-79	at Charlotte
May 15	Nets, 103-95	at New Jersey

	W-L	Avg.	Leading Scorer
Detroit	1-4	79.4	Stackhouse (18.8)
Boston	4-1	83.0	Pierce (20.2)

Date	Winner	Home Court
May 5	Pistons, 94-86	at Detroit
May 8	Celtics, 85-77	at Detroit
May 10	Celtics, 66-64	at Boston
May 12	Celtics, 90-79	at Boston
May 14	Celtics, 90-81	at Detroit

CHAMPIONSHIP (Best of 7)

	W-L	Avg.	Leading Scorer
Boston	2-4	92.7	Pierce (23.7)
New Jersey	4-2	95.5	Kidd (17.5)

Date	Winner	Home Court
May 19	Nets, 104-97	at New Jersey
May 21	Celtics, 93-86	at New Jersey
May 25	Celtics, 94-90	at Boston
May 27	Nets, 94-92	at Boston
May 29	Nets, 103-92	at New Jersey
May 31	Nets, 96-88	at Boston

Final Playoff Standings

(Ranked by victories)

	Gm	W	L	Pct	Per Game For	Per Game Opp
LA Lakers	19	15	4	.789	97.8	94.1
New Jersey	20	11	9	.550	95.4	95.4
Sacramento	16	10	6	.625	101.1	98.8
Boston	16	9	7	.563	91.3	88.4
Dallas	8	4	4	.500	109.0	108.8
Charlotte	9	4	5	.444	96.1	96.1
San Antonio	10	4	6	.400	91.1	88.1
Detroit	10	4	6	.500	83.0	83.4
Indiana	5	2	3	.400	91.6	91.4
Toronto	5	2	3	.400	83.8	86.6
Philadelphia	5	2	3	.400	89.0	97.8
Seattle	5	2	3	.400	86.2	96.4
Orlando	4	1	3	.250	93.8	98.8
Utah	4	1	3	.250	88.0	89.0
Minnesota	3	0	3	.000	102.0	112.7
Portland	3	0	3	.000	91.3	96.7

NBA FINALS (Best of 7)

	W-L	Avg.	Leading Scorer
New Jersey	0-4	96.8	Kidd (19.6)
LA Lakers	4-0	106.0	O'Neal (36.3)

Date	Winner	Home Court
June 5	Lakers, 99-94	at Los Angeles
June 7	Lakers, 106-83	at Los Angeles
June 9	Lakers, 106-103	at New Jersey
June 12	Lakers, 113-107	at New Jersey

Most Valuable Player
Shaquille O'Neal, Lakers, C
36.3 ppg, 12.3 rpg, 2.75 bpg

Off-season Coaching Changes in 2002

Team	Old Coach	Why left?	New Coach	Old Job
Denver	Mike Evans	interim	Jeff Bzdelik	Asst., Nuggets
Golden St.	Brian Winters	interim	Eric Musselman	Asst., Hawks

NBA Finals Box Scores

Game 1

Date: June 5, 2002; **Attendance:** 18,997; **Time:** 2:40.
Officials: Joe Crawford, Ron Garretson, Jack Nies.

	1	2	3	4	F
New Jersey	14	22	27	31	—94
LA Lakers	29	19	24	27	—99

New Jersey	Min	FG M-A	FT M-A	Pts	Reb O-T	A	PF
Jason Kidd	43	11-26	0-1	23	6-10	10	1
Kerry Kittles	25	3-7	2-2	9	0-0	1	1
Kenyon Martin	37	7-22	6-9	21	3-6	2	3
Keith Van Horn	35	5-14	0-0	12	2-6	1	6
Todd MacCulloch	25	5-9	0-2	10	6-8	0	3
Lucious Harris	25	1-5	3-4	5	1-3	2	3
Richard Jefferson	22	2-4	0-2	4	0-6	1	3
Aaron Williams	15	2-5	0-0	4	1-4	1	4
Jason Collins	8	1-1	3-4	5	2-2	1	5
Anthony Johnson	5	0-1	1-2	1	0-0	0	0
TOTALS	240	37-94	15-26	94	21-45	19	29

Three-point FG: 5-16 (Van Horn 2-6, Kittles 1-2, Kidd 1-3, Martin 1-3, Harris 0-2); **Team Rebounds:** 15; **Blocked Shots:** 4 (Kittles, Martin, MacCulloch, Williams); **Turnovers:** 11 (Van Horn 4, Martin 3, MacCulloch 2, Kittles, Kidd); **Steals:** 9 (Kidd 3, Williams 3, MacCulloch 2, Jefferson); **Percentages:** Total FG (.394), 3-Pt FG (.313), Free Throws (.577) **Technical:** 1 (Martin).

LA Lakers	Min	FG M-A	FT M-A	Pts	Reb O-T	A	PF
Kobe Bryant	43	6-16	10-11	22	1-3	6	2
Derek Fisher	36	4-7	4-4	13	0-1	2	1
Robert Horry	41	2-6	1-2	5	1-8	4	2
Rick Fox	39	5-8	4-6	14	5-8	3	5
Shaquille O'Neal	40	12-22	12-21	36	2-16	1	2
Brian Shaw	11	0-2	0-0	0	2-2	5	2
Devean George	11	1-5	1-1	3	1-3	0	2
Samaki Walker	8	1-2	0-0	2	3-7	0	1
Lindsey Hunter	6	1-3	0-0	2	1-1	0	2
Stanislav Medvedenko	5	1-1	0-0	2	1-1	0	1
TOTALS	240	33-72	32-45	99	17-50	21	20

Three-point FG: 1-10 (Fisher 1-2, Bryant 0-2, Horry 0-2, Fox 0-1, Shaw 0-1, George 0-1, Hunter 0-1); **Team Rebounds:** 10; **Blocked Shots:** 8 (O'Neal 4, Horry 2, Shaw, Walker); **Turnovers:** 16 (O'Neal 5, Bryant 4, Fisher 2, Fox 2, Walker, George); **Steals:** 8 (Horry 3, Fox 3, O'Neal, Bryant, Fisher); **Percentages:** Total FG (.458), 3-Pt FG (.100), Free Throws (.711); **Technical:** 1 (Shaw).

Game 2

Date: June 7, 2002; **Attendance:** 18,997; **Time:** 2:29.
Officials: Steve Javie, Bennett Salvatore, Don Vaden.

	1	2	3	4	F
New Jersey	21	22	18	22	—83
LA Lakers	27	22	28	29	—106

New Jersey	Min	FG M-A	FT M-A	Pts	Reb O-T	A	PF
Jason Kidd	39	3-8	2-3	17	4-9	7	3
Kerry Kittles	29	9-19	2-4	23	1-3	3	4
Kenyon Martin	35	2-8	2-4	6	2-5	2	5
Keith Van Horn	24	3-9	3-4	9	4-8	1	2
Todd MacCulloch	15	1-3	0-0	2	2-5	0	4
Richard Jefferson	32	3-6	4-8	10	2-5	3	2
Jason Collins	21	2-2	2-2	6	0-1	0	4
Lucious Harris	18	0-9	2-2	2	2-2	2	1
Aaron Williams	15	2-7	0-0	4	2-3	0	2
Anthony Johnson	10	2-5	0-0	4	1-2	0	0
Donny Marshall	1	0-1	0-0	0	0-0	0	0
Brian Scalabrine	1	0-0	0-0	0	0-0	0	0
TOTALS	240	30-86	17-27	83	20-43	18	27

Three-point FG: 6-22 (Kidd 3-8, Kittles 3-9, Harris 0-2, Martin 0-1, Van Horn 0-1, Marshall 0-1); **Team Rebounds:** 11; **Blocked Shots:** 5 (Kidd, Kittles, MacCulloch, Collins, Williams); **Turnovers:** 13 (Kidd 5, Martin 4, Kittles, MacCulloch, Jefferson, Collins); **Steals:** 11 (Martin 3, Kidd 2, Kittles 2, Van Horn 2, MacCulloch, Harris); **Percentages:** Total FG (.349), 3-Pt FG (.273), Free Throws (.630).

LA Lakers	Min	FG M-A	FT M-A	Pts	Reb O-T	A	PF
Kobe Bryant	42	9-15	3-4	24	1-8	3	2
Derek Fisher	29	4-9	2-4	12	2-5	3	5
Robert Horry	43	4-9	0-0	9	4-10	4	2
Rick Fox	36	3-6	2-2	10	1-8	6	5
Shaquille O'Neal	41	14-23	12-14	40	3-12	5	4
Brian Shaw	22	2-6	0-0	5	0-2	2	2
Devean George	17	3-7	0-0	6	1-2	0	1
Samaki Walker	5	0-1	0-0	0	0-0	0	0
Lindsey Hunter	3	0-2	0-0	0	0-0	0	0
Mark Madsen	2	0-0	0-0	0	0-0	0	0
TOTALS	240	39-78	19-24	106	12-47	26	21

Three-point FG: 9-16 (Bryant 3-3, Fisher 2-3, Fox 2-4, Shaw 1-2, Horry 1-3, Hunter 0-1); **Team Rebounds:** 9; **Blocked Shots:** 7 (Horry 3, Bryant, Fox, O'Neal, Shaw); **Turnovers:** 16 (Bryant 4, O'Neal 4, Fisher 2, Horry 2, Fox 2, Shaw, Walker); **Steals:** 6 (Horry 3, Bryant 2, Fox); **Percentages:** Total FG (.500), 3-Pt FG (.563), Free Throws (.792).

Game 3

Date: June 9, 2002; **Attendance:** 19,215; **Time:** 2:38; **Officials:** Dick Bavetta, Dan Crawford, Bob Delaney.

	1	2	3	4	F
LA Lakers	31	21	26	28	—106
New Jersey	23	23	32	25	—103

LA Lakers	Min	FG M-A	FT M-A	Pts	Reb O-T	A	PF
Kobe Bryant	46	14-23	7-10	36	1-6	4	3
Derek Fisher	31	4-7	2-4	13	0-3	6	3
Rick Fox	37	2-6	2-2	7	0-4	2	2
Robert Horry	31	2-4	0-0	6	0-7	3	5
Shaquille O'Neal	42	12-19	11-17	35	5-11	2	1
Devean George	24	2-4	2-2	6	1-8	0	3
Brian Shaw	19	1-4	0-0	3	0-1	0	0
Samaki Walker	6	0-1	0-0	0	0-0	0	1
Stanislav Medvedenko	4	0-0	0-0	0	0-0	0	2
Lindsey Hunter	2	0-0	0-0	0	0-0	0	2
TOTALS	240	37-68	24-35	106	7-40	17	22

Three-point FG: 8-16 (Fisher 3-3, Horry 2-3, Fox 1-2, Shaw 1-4); **Team Rebounds:** 11; **Blocked Shots:** 10 (O'Neal 4, Bryant 2, George 2, Fox, Horry); **Turnovers:** 19 (Bryant 6, Fisher 3, Fox 3, Horry 3, O'Neal 2, George, Shaw); **Steals:** 7 (Horry 3, Bryant, Fox, George, Shaw); **Percentages:** Total FG (.544), 3-Pt FG (.500), Free Throws (.686) **Technical** 1 (Horry).

New Jersey	Min	FG M-A	FT M-A	Pts	Reb O-T	A	PF
Jason Kidd	43	13-23	3-5	30	1-5	10	3
Kerry Kittles	29	3-6	1-2	7	1-3	3	1
Kenyon Martin	43	11-17	4-6	26	1-4	4	3
Keith Van Horn	31	6-14	0-0	14	0-5	3	5
Todd MacCulloch	14	4-8	2-2	10	0-1	0	3
Jason Collins	27	0-4	2-2	2	2-3	0	4
Richard Jefferson	22	4-5	0-0	8	0-3	0	1
Lucious Harris	19	1-5	0-0	2	0-3	2	1
Aaron Williams	7	1-1	2-2	4	0-0	0	6
Anthony Johnson	5	0-0	0-0	0	0-0	0	0
TOTALS	240	43-83	14-19	103	5-27	22	27

Three-point FG: 3-12 (Van Horn 2-4, Kidd 1-5, Kittles 0-2, Martin 0-1); **Team Rebounds:** 9; **Blocked Shots:** 5 (Martin 2, Kidd, Van Horn, MacCulloch); **Turnovers:** 13 (Martin 5, Kidd 2, MacCulloch 2, Collins 2, Jefferson 2); **Steals:** 13 (Kidd 3, Kittles 3, Harris 3, Martin 2, Jefferson 2); **Percentages:** Total FG (.518), 3-Pt FG (.250), Free Throws (.737).

Game 4

Date: June 12, 2002; **Attendance:** 19,296; **Time:** 2:24; **Officials:** Ted Bernhardt, Bernie Fryer, Eddie F. Rush.

	1	2	3	4	F
LA Lakers	27	31	26	29	—113
New Jersey	34	23	23	27	—107

LA Lakers	Min	FG M-A	FT M-A	Pts	Reb O-T	A	PF
Kobe Bryant	44	7-16	9-11	25	0-6	8	4
Derek Fisher	36	5-10	1-2	13	0-5	4	1
Robert Horry	44	3-5	4-4	12	1-4	6	4
Rick Fox	32	2-3	2-2	8	0-5	3	2
Shaquille O'Neal	43	12-20	10-16	34	3-10	4	2
Devean George	20	4-7	0-0	11	2-6	0	1
Brian Shaw	15	3-9	0-0	6	1-2	3	0
Samaki Walker	5	0-0	2-2	2	0-1	0	1
Mitch Richmond	1	1-1	0-0	2	0-0	0	0
TOTALS	240	37-71	28-37	113	7-39	28	15

Three-point FG: 11–19 (George 3–4, Bryant 2–3, Horry 2–3, Fox 2–3, Fisher 2–4, Shaw 0–2); **Team Rebounds:** 5; **Blocked Shots:** 3 (O'Neal 2, Horry); **Turnovers:** 9 (Fox 4, O'Neal 3, Bryant, Horry); **Steals:** 7 (Bryant 2, Horry 2, Fox 2, O'Neal); **Percentages:** Total FG (.521), 3-Pt FG (.579), Free Throws (.757); **Technical:** 1 (Assistant Coach Cleamons).

New Jersey	Min	FG M-A	FT M-A	Pts	Reb O-T	A	PF
Jason Kidd	43	5-14	2-2	13	1-5	12	1
Kerry Kittles	23	4-10	2-2	11	2-2	3	1
Kenyon Martin	43	15-28	5-7	35	2-11	2	4
Keith Van Horn	31	3-7	0-0	7	1-4	4	2
Todd MacCulloch	20	4-8	0-0	8	4-6	2	4
Lucious Harris	29	9-13	3-4	22	2-3	2	1
Richard Jefferson	21	2-6	1-1	5	0-4	1	1
Jason Collins	19	2-3	0-0	4	1-4	0	6
Aaron Williams	9	1-3	0-0	2	1-2	0	2
Donny Marshall	1	0-0	0-0	0	0-0	0	0
Anthony Johnson	1	0-0	0-0	0	0-0	1	0
TOTALS	240	45-92	13-16	107	14-41	27	22

Three-point FG: 4–9 (Van Horn 1–1, Harris 1–1, Kittles 1–3, Kidd 1–4); **Team Rebounds:** 8; **Blocked Shots:** 4 (Kidd, Martin, MacCulloch, Collins); **Turnovers:** 8 (Kidd 4, Martin 2, Kittles, Van Horn); **Steals:** 5 (Kidd, Kittles, Martin, Jefferson, Collins); **Percentages:** Total FG (.489), 3-Pt FG (.444), Free Throws (.813) **Technical:** 1 (Martin).

NBA Playoff Leaders

Scoring

	Gm	FG	FT	Pts	Avg
Tracy McGrady, Orlando	4	42	34	123	30.8
Allen Iverson, Philadelphia	5	45	51	150	30.0
Shaquille O'Neal, LA Lakers	19	203	135	541	28.5
Dirk Nowitzki, Dallas	8	73	65	227	28.4
Tim Duncan, San Antonio	9	82	83	248	27.6
Kobe Bryant, LA Lakers	19	187	110	506	26.6
Michael Finley, Dallas	8	69	45	197	24.6
Paul Pierce, Boston	16	122	120	394	24.6
Chris Webber, Sacramento	16	160	59	379	23.7
Reggie Miller, Indiana	5	42	21	118	23.6
Baron Davis, Charlotte	9	71	40	203	22.6
Gary Payton, Seattle	5	45	17	111	22.2
Antoine Walker, Boston	16	131	50	354	22.1
Mike Bibby, Sacramento	16	114	71	324	20.2
Jason Kidd, New Jersey	20	147	80	391	19.5
Jerry Stackhouse, Detroit	10	53	52	176	17.6
Jermaine O'Neal, Indiana	5	34	18	86	17.2
Antonio Davis, Toronto	5	34	17	85	17.0
Kenyon Martin, New Jersey	20	129	76	336	16.8
David Wesley, Charlotte	9	52	21	142	15.8

High Point Games

	Date	FG-FT—Pts
Paul Pierce, Bos. vs. Phi.	May 3	16-6–46
Allen Iverson, Phi. vs. Bos.	Apr. 28	10-19–42
Shaquille O'Neal, LAL vs. Sac.	May 31	14-13–41
Shaquille O'Neal, LAL vs. NJ	June 7	14-12–40
Dirk Nowitzki, Dal. at Min.	Apr. 28	11-14–39

Rebounds

	Gm	Off	Def	Tot	Avg
Kevin Garnett, Minnesota	3	16	40	56	18.7
Ben Wallace, Detroit	10	48	113	161	16.1
Tim Duncan, San Antonio	9	28	102	130	14.4
Dirk Nowitzki, Dallas	8	17	88	105	13.1
Shaquille O'Neal, LA Lakers	19	67	172	239	12.6

Assists

	Gm	No	Avg
John Stockton, Utah	4	40	10.0
Jason Kidd, Phoenix	20	182	9.1
Steve Nash, Dallas	8	70	8.8
Baron Davis, Charlotte	9	71	7.9
Chris Childs, Toronto	5	37	7.4

NBA Finalists' Composite Box Scores

New Jersey Nets (11-9)

		Overall Playoffs						Finals vs. Los Angeles				
			—Per Game—						—Per Game—			
	Gm	FG%	TPts	Pts	Reb	Ast	Gm	FG%	TPts	Pts	Reb	Ast
Jason Kidd	20	.415	391	19.6	8.2	9.1	4	.438	83	20.8	7.3	9.8
Kenyon Martin	20	.424	336	16.8	5.8	2.9	4	.467	88	22.0	6.5	2.5
Keith Van Horn	20	.402	266	13.3	6.7	2.1	4	.386	42	10.5	5.8	2.3
Kerry Kittles	20	.435	241	12.1	3.2	2.3	4	.452	50	12.5	2.0	2.5
Lucious Harris	20	.489	177	8.9	2.7	0.9	4	.344	31	7.8	2.8	2.0
Richard Jefferson	20	.465	139	7.0	4.6	1.3	4	.524	27	6.8	4.5	1.3
Aaron Williams	20	.479	130	6.5	3.5	0.8	4	.375	14	3.5	2.3	0.3
Todd MacCulloch	20	.491	123	6.2	5.2	0.7	4	.500	30	7.5	5.0	0.5
Jason Collins	17	.364	49	2.9	2.4	0.4	4	.500	17	4.3	2.5	0.3
Anthony Johnson	19	.377	50	2.6	0.7	1.1	4	.333	5	1.3	0.5	0.3
Donny Marshall	7	.200	3	0.4	0.0	0.0	2	.000	0	0.0	0.0	0.0
Brian Scalabrine	6	.333	2	0.3	0.5	0.0	1	.000	0	0.0	0.0	0.0
NETS	20	.432	1907	95.4	42.7	21.3	4	.437	387	96.8	39.0	21.5
OPPONENTS	20	.435	1908	95.4	44.1	20.4	4	.505	424	106.0	44.0	23.0

Three-pointers: PLAYOFFS—Van Horn (37-for-84), Kittles (18-68), Kidd (17-90), Harris (8-22), Martin (2-9), Johnson (1-10), Jefferson (0-2), Williams (0-1), Marshall (0-4), Scalabrine (0-1), Team (83-291, .285); FINALS—Kidd (6-for-20), Van Horn (5-12), Kittles (5-16), Martin (1-5), Harris (1-5), Marshall (0-1), Team (17-59, .305).

Los Angeles Lakers (15-4)

| | Overall Playoffs | | | | | | Finals vs. New Jersey | | | | | |
| | Gm | FG% | TPts | —Per Game— | | | Gm | FG% | TPts | —Per Game— | | |
				Pts	Reb	Ast				Pts	Reb	Ast
Shaquille O'Neal	19	.529	541	28.5	12.6	2.8	4	.595	145	36.3	12.3	3.8
Kobe Bryant	19	.434	506	26.6	5.8	4.6	4	.514	107	26.8	5.8	5.3
Derek Fisher	19	.357	193	10.2	3.3	2.7	4	.515	51	12.8	3.5	3.8
Rick Fox	19	.482	186	9.8	5.4	3.4	4	.522	39	9.8	6.3	3.5
Robert Horry	19	.449	176	9.3	8.1	3.2	4	.458	32	8.0	7.3	4.3
Devean George	19	.365	95	5.0	3.6	0.6	4	.435	26	6.5	4.8	0.0
Samaki Walker	19	.462	62	3.3	4.1	0.2	4	.250	4	1.0	2.0	0.0
Brian Shaw	19	.333	55	2.9	1.8	1.6	4	.286	14	3.5	7.8	2.5
Lindsey Hunter	18	.311	36	2.0	0.4	0.6	3	.200	2	0.7	0.3	0.0
Mitch Richmond	2	1.000	3	1.5	0.5	0.0	1	1.000	3	2.0	0.0	0.0
Stanislav Medvedenko	7	.600	6	0.9	0.6	0.0	2	1.000	2	1.0	0.5	0.0
Mark Madsen	7	.000	0	0.0	0.3	0.0	1	.000	0	0.0	0.0	0.0
LAKERS	19	.444	1859	97.8	45.4	19.6	4	.505	424	106.0	44.0	23.0
OPPONENTS	19	.426	1787	94.1	42.2	20.1	4	.437	387	96.8	39.0	21.5

Three-pointers: PLAYOFFS—Fisher (19-for-81), Horry (24-62), Bryant (22-58), Fox (15-43), Shaw (9-32), Hunter (8-29), George (8-35), Walker (1-1), Madsen (0-1), Team (116-342, .339); FINALS—Fisher (8-for-12), Bryant (6-11), Fox (5-11), Horry (5-11), George (3-5), Shaw (2-9), Hunter (0-2), Team (29-61, .475).

Annual Awards

Most Valuable Player

The Maurice Podoloff Trophy; voting by 126-member panel of local and national pro basketball writers and broadcasters. Each ballot has five entries; points awarded on 10-7-5-3-1 basis.

	1st	2nd	3rd	4th	5th	Pts
Tim Duncan, San Antonio	57	38	20	5	3	954
Jason Kidd, New Jersey	45	41	26	9	3	897
Shaquille O'Neal, LA Lakers	15	38	40	25	5	696
Tracy McGrady, Orlando	7	5	28	45	10	390
Kobe Bryant, LA Lakers	1	1	4	15	16	98
Gary Payton, Seattle	1	1	1	5	17	54
Chris Webber, Sacramento	0	1	1	5	10	37
Dirk Nowitzki, Dallas	0	0	1	4	14	31
Allen Iverson, Philadelphia	0	0	1	4	12	29
Ben Wallace, Detroit	0	0	2	8	8	24
Paul Pierce, Boston	0	0	1	1	14	22
Kevin Garnett, Minnesota	0	0	0	3	8	17
Michael Jordan, Wash	0	1	1	1	1	16
Steve Nash, Dallas	0	0	0	1	2	5
Jerry Stackhouse, Detroit	0	0	0	1	0	3
Elton Brand, LA Clippers	0	0	0	0	1	1
Mike Bibby, Sacramento	0	0	0	0	1	1
Predrag Stojakovic, Sac	0	0	0	0	1	1

All-NBA Teams

Voting by a 126-member panel of local and national pro basketball writers and broadcasters. Each ballot has entries for three teams; points awarded on 5-3-1 basis. First Team repeaters from 2000-01 are in **bold** type.

Pos	First Team	1st	Pts
F	Tracy McGrady, Orlando	80	513
F	**Tim Duncan**, San Antonio	124	626
C	**Shaquille O'Neal**, LA Lakers	125	626
G	Kobe Bryant, LA Lakers	72	507
G	**Jason Kidd**, New Jersey	115	601

Pos	Second Team	1st	Pts
F	Kevin Garnett, Minnesota	31	391
F	Chris Webber, Sacramento	21	339
F	Dirk Nowitzki, Dallas	22	358
G	Gary Payton, Seattle	11	284
G	Allen Iverson, Philadelphia	12	272

Pos	Third Team	1st	Pts
F	Ben Wallace, Detroit	3	195
F	Jermaine O'Neal, Indiana	0	78
C	Dikembe Mutombo, Philadelphia	0	105
G	Paul Pierce, Boston	9	230
G	Steve Nash, Dallas	1	96

All-Defensive Teams

Voting by NBA head coaches. Each ballot has entries for two teams; two points given for 1st team, one for 2nd. Coaches cannot vote for own players. First Team repeaters from 2000-01 are in **bold** type.

Pos	First Team	1st	Pts
F	**Tim Duncan**, San Antonio	17	40
F	**Kevin Garnett**, Minnesota	10	27
C	Ben Wallace, Detroit	24	51
G	**Gary Payton**, Seattle	20	47
G	**Jason Kidd**, New Jersey	15	37

Pos	Second Team	1st	Pts
F	Bruce Bowen, San Antonio	6	21
F	Clifford Robinson, Detroit	5	14
C	Dikembe Mutombo, Philadelphia	9	27
G	Kobe Bryant, LA Lakers	12	32
G	Doug Christie, Sacramento	7	25

Coach of the Year

The Red Auerbach Trophy; voting by 126-member panel of local and national pro basketball writers and broadcasters. Each ballot has one entry.

	Votes	Improvement
Rick Carlisle, Detroit	73	32-50 to 50-32
Rick Adelman, Sacramento	21	55-27 to 61-21
Byron Scott, New Jersey	15	26-56 to 52-30
Nate McMillan, Seattle	7	44-38 to 45-37
Maurice Cheeks, Portland	4	50-32 to 49-33
Jim O'Brien, Boston	2	36-46 to 49-33
Doug Collins, Washington	1	19-63 to 37-45
Alvin Gentry, LA Clippers	1	31-51 to 39-43
Don Nelson, Dallas	1	53-29 to 57-25
Isiah Thomas, Indiana	1	41-41 to 42-40

Annual Awards (Cont.)

Rookie of the Year

The Eddie Gottlieb Trophy; voting by 126-member panel of local and national pro basketball writers and broadcasters. Each ballot has one entry.

	Pos	Votes
Pau Gasol, Memphis	F	117
Richard Jefferson, New Jersey	F	3
Jason Richardson, Golden State	G/F	2
Jamaal Tinsley, Indiana	G	2
Andrei Kirilenko, Utah	F	2

All-Rookie Team

Voting by NBA's 29 head coaches, who cannot vote for players on their team. Each ballot has entries for two five-man teams, regardless of position; two points given for 1st team, one for 2nd. First team votes in parentheses.

First Team	College	Pts
Pau Gasol, Memphis (28)	—	56
Shane Battier, Memphis (26)	Duke	54
Jason Richardson, Golden St. (25)	Mich. St.	53
Tony Parker, San Antonio (20)	—	48
Andrei Kirilenko, Utah (18)	—	45

Second Team	College	Pts
Jamaal Tinsley, Indiana (15)	Iowa St.	43
Richard Jefferson, New Jersey (8)	Arizona	35
Eddie Griffin, Houston (2)	Seton Hall	21
Zeljko Rebraca, Detroit (2)	—	15
Vladimir Radmanovic, Seattle (1)	—	11
Joe Johnson, Phoenix	Arkansas	11

IBM Award

Created prior to the 1983-84 season to honor the player who contributes most to his team's overall success and utilizes a computer evaluation of key offensive and defensive statistics to determine an overall leader. The formula is as follows: (Player points-FGA+REB+AST+STL+BLK-PF-TO+(team wins x 10) x 250)/(team points-FGA+REB+AST+STL+BLK-PF-TO).

	Pos	Pts
Tim Duncan, San Antonio	C	112.82
Ben Wallace, Detroit	C	103.75
Kevin Garnett, Minnesota	F	101.51
Elton Brand, LA Clippers	C	94.67
Shaquille O'Neal, LA Lakers	C	90.89
Jason Kidd, New Jersey	G	90.10
Paul Pierce, Boston	G	89.32
Dirk Nowitzki, Dallas	F	88.85
Tracy McGrady, Orlando	F	87.29
Gary Payton, Seattle	G	83.35

Sixth-Man Award

Voted on by a 126-member panel of local and national pro basketball writers and broadcasters.

	Pos	Votes
Corliss Williamson, Detroit	F	56
Bobby Jackson, Sacramento	G	30
Quentin Richardson, LA Clippers	G	20
Malik Rose, San Antonio	F	8
Desmond Mason, Seattle	F/G	3
Troy Hudson, Orlando	G	3
Hidayet Turkoglu, Sacramento	F	2
Ricky Davis, Cleveland	F	1
Robert Horry, LA Lakers	F	1
Jacque Vaughn, Atlanta	G	1

Most Improved Player Award

Voted on by a 126-member panel of local and national pro basketball writers and broadcasters.

	Pos	Votes
Jermaine O'Neal, Indiana	F	52
Ben Wallace, Detroit	C	16
Steve Nash, Dallas	G	9
Jerry Stackhouse, Detroit	G	7
Brent Barry, Seattle	G	6
Wally Szczerbiak, Minnesota	F	5
Troy Hudson, Orlando	G	4
Michael Olowokandi, LA Clippers	C	4
Kenyon Martin, New Jersey	F	3
Andre Miller, Cleveland	G	3
Michael Redd, Milwaukee	G	3
Desmond Mason, Seattle	F/G	2
Gary Payton, Seattle	G	2
Kenny Thomas, Houston	F	2
Hidayet Turkoglu, Sacramento	F	2
Ricky Davis, Cleveland	F	1
Todd MacCulloch, New Jersey	C	1
Bobby Jackson, Sacramento	G	1
Lee Nailon, Charlotte	F	1
Wesley Person, Cleveland	G	1
Jason Terry, Atlanta	G	1

Defensive Player of the Year Award

Voted on by a 120-member panel of local and national pro basketball writers and broadcasters.

	Pos	Votes
Ben Wallace, Detroit	C	116
Kevin Garnett, Minnesota	F	2
Kobe Bryant, LA Lakers	G	1
Dikembe Mutombo, Philadelphia	C	1

Sportsmanship Award

Each of the NBA's 29 teams nominated one player from their roster "who best represents the ideals of sportsmanship on the court," then a panel made up of former NBA players Tommy Heinsohn, Eddie Johnson, Gil McGregor, Ed Pinckney and Kenny Smith selected the four divisional winners from the pool of nominees. The award winner is chosen from the four divisional winners in vote by a 126-member panel of local and national pro basketball writers and broadcasters. The winner receives the Joe Dumars Trophy, named for the Detroit Pistons guard who won the inaugural sportsmanship award in 1996.

	Div	Pos	Votes
Steve Smith, San Antonio	Midwest	G/F	65
P.J. Brown, Charlotte	Central	F	28
LaPhonso Ellis, Miami	Atlantic	C/F	22
Shawn Marion, Phoenix	Pacific	F	11

J. Walter Kennedy Citizenship Award

The award, named for the NBA's second commissioner, is presented annually by the Professional Basketball Writers Association to an NBA player or coach for exemplary community service. Other nominees for this season's J. Walter Kennedy Citizenship Award included Portland's Steve Kerr (runner-up), Philadelphia's Eric Snow, Toronto's Jerome Williams and Dallas' Steve Nash.

Alonzo Mourning, Miami

2002 College Draft

First and second round picks at the 56th annual NBA College Draft held June 26, 2002 held in New York City at the Theatre at Madison Square Garden. The order of the first 13 positions were determined by a Draft Lottery held May 19, in Secaucus, N.J. Positions 14 through 28 reflect regular season records in reverse order. The NBA stripped Minnesota of their first-round draft picks through 2004 for signing Joe Smith to an illegal contract. Underclassmen selected are noted in CAPITAL letters.

First Round

Team	Pos
1 Houston .Yao Ming, China	C
2 Chicago . . . . JAY WILLIAMS, Duke	PG
3 Golden State . . . . .MIKE DUNLEAVY, Duke	G/F
4 Memphis . . . . .DREW GOODEN, Kansas	F
5 Denver . . . . .Nikoloz Tskitishvili, Italy	F
6 Cleveland . . . . DAJUAN WAGNER, Memphis	G
7 New York . . . . . .a-Maybyner "Nene" Hilario, Brazil	F/C
8 b-L.A. Clippers . . . . . . .CHRIS WILCOX, Maryland	F
9 Phoenix .AMARE STOUDEMIRE, Cypress Creek HS	F
10 Miami . . . . .CARON BUTLER, Connecticut	F
11 Washington . . . . .JARED JEFFRIES, Indiana	F
12 L.A. Clippers . . . . .Melvin Ely, Fresno St.	F/C
13 Milwaukee . . . . .MARCUS HASLIP, Tennessee	F
14 Indiana .Fred Jones, Oregon	G
15 c-Houston . . . . .Bostjan Nachbar, Italy	F
16 Philadelphia . . . . .d-Jiri Welsch, Slovenia	G
17 e-Washington . . . . .Juan Dixon, Maryland	G
18 Orlando . . . . .f-CURTIS BORCHARDT, Stanford	C
19 Utah . . . . .f-Ryan Humphrey, Notre Dame	F
20 g-Toronto . . . . .h-KAREEM RUSH, Missouri	G
21 Portland . . .QYNTEL WOODS, NE Mississippi CC	G/F
22 i-Phoenix . . . . .CASEY JACOBSEN, Stanford	G/F
23 Detroit . . . . .Tayshaun Prince, Kentucky	F
24 New Jersey . . . . .Nenad Krstic, Yugoslavia	F/C
25 j-Denver . . . . .a-FRANK WILLIAMS, Illinois	G
26 San Antonio . . . . .k-John Salmons, Miami	G/F
27 L.A. Lakers . . . . .h-CHRIS JEFFRIES, Fresno St.	F
28 Sacramento . . . . .l-Dan Dickau, Gonzaga	G

Second Round

Team	Pos
30 Golden State . . . . .Steve Logan, Cincinnati	G
31 Chicago . . . . .ROGER MASON JR., Virginia	G
32 Memphis . . . . .Robert Archibald, Illinois	F
33 Denver . . . . .Vincent Yarbrough, Tennessee	F
34 m-Milwaukee . . . . .Dan Gadzuric, UCLA	C
35 Cleveland . . . . .CARLOS BOOZER, Duke	F/C
36 New York . . . . .Milos Vujanic, Yugoslavia	G
37 Atlanta . . . . .David Andersen, Australia	F/C
38 Houston . . . . .TITO MADDOX, Fresno St.	G
39 n-Washington . . . . .ROD GRIZZARD, Alabama	G
40 Washington . . . . .Juan Carlos Navarro, Spain	G
41 L.A. Clippers . . . . .Mario Kasun, Croatia	C
42 Milwaukee . . . . .Ronald Murray, Shaw	G
43 o-Portland . . . . .Jason Jennings, Arkansas St.	C
44 p-Chicago . . . . .Lonny Baxter, Maryland	F/C
45 Philadelphia . . . . .Sam Clancy, USC	F
46 q-Memphis . . . . .r-Matt Barnes, UCLA	F
47 Utah . . . . .f-JAMAL SAMPSON, California	F/C
48 s-Milwaukee . . . . .t-Chris Owens, Texas	F
49 Seattle . . . . .Peter Fehse, Germany	F
50 Boston . . . . .Darius Songaila, Wake Forest	F
51 Portland . . . . .Federico Kammerichs, Argentina	F
52 Minnesota . . . . . . .MARCUS TAYLOR, Michigan St.	G
53 Miami . . . . .Rasual Butler, LaSalle	F
54 New Jersey . . . . .Tamar Slay, Marshall	G
55 Dallas . . . . .Mladen Sekularac, Yugoslavia	G/F
56 u-San Antonio . . . . .Luis Scola, Argentina	F
57 San Antonio . . . .k-Randy Holcomb, San Diego St.	F
58 Sacramento . .Corsley Edwards, C. Connecticut St.	F

Acquired Picks

FIRST ROUND: **a**-New York traded F "Nene" Hilario, C Marcus Camby and G Mark Jackson to Denver for F Antonio McDyess, G Frank Williams, and a 2003 second-round pick; **b**-from Toronto; **c**-from Toronto; **d**-Philadelphia traded G Jiri Welsch to Golden State for two future picks; **e**-from New Orleans; **f**-Orlando traded rights to C Curtis Borchardt to Utah for F Ryan Humphrey and F Jamal Sampson. The Magic later traded the rights to Sampson to Milwaukee for C Rashard Griffith; **g**-from Seattle via New York; **h**-Toronto traded rights to G Kareem Rush and F Tracy Murray to L.A. Lakers for G Lindsey Hunter and the rights to F Chris Jeffries; **i**-from Boston; **j**-from Dallas; **k**-San Antonio traded F Mark Bryant, rights to G/F John Salmons and rights to F Randy Holcomb to Philadelphia for G Speedy Claxton; **l**-Sacramento traded rights to G Dan Dickau to Atlanta for a future first-round pick; **m**-from Houston; **n**-from Phoenix via Denver; **o**-from Toronto via Chicago; **p**-from Indiana; **q**-from Orlando; **r**-Memphis traded F Nick Anderson and rights to F Matt Barnes to Cleveland for G Wesley Person; **s**-from New Orleans; **t**-Milwaukee traded the rights to F Chris Owens to Memphis for a future second-round pick; **u**-from L.A. Lakers.

2002 FIBA World Championships

Fourteenth World Basketball Championship held Aug. 29-Sept. 8, 2002 at Indianapolis, Ind.

Second Round

(*) indicated team advanced to quarterfinals. Other teams relegated to classification games.

Group E	W	L	Pts
*Spain 5		1	10
*Puerto Rico 5		1	10
*Brazil 4		2	8
*Yugoslavia 4		2	8
Turkey 2		4	4
Angola 1		5	2

Group F	W	L	Pts
*Argentina 6		0	12
*United States 5		1	10
*Germany .4		2	8
*New Zealand 3		3	6
Russia 2		4	4
China 1		5	2

Quarterfinals

Germany 70 . . . . .Spain 62
Yugoslavia 81 . . . . .United States 78
Argentina 78 . . . . .Brazil 67
New Zealand 65 . . . . .Puerto Rico 63

Semifinals

Argentina 86 . . . . .Germany 80
Yugoslavia 89 . . . . .New Zealand 78

Bronze Medal Game

Germany 117 . . . . .New Zealand 94

Gold Medal Game

Held Sept. 8, 2002 at Conseco Fieldhouse. Attendance: 17,079.

Yugoslavia 84 . . . . .OT . . . . .Argentina 77

Continental Basketball Association
Final Standings

QW refers to quarters won. Teams get 3 points for a win, 1 point for each quarter won and ½ point for any quarters tied. (*) denotes playoff qualifiers.

American Conference

	W	L	QW	Pts	Home	Road
*Sioux Falls	33	23	114.5	213.5	19-9	14-14
*Rockford	31	25	120.5	213.5	15-13	16-12
Grand Rapids	30	26	114.0	204.0	16-12	14-14
Gary	22	34	100.0	166.0	13-15	9-19

National Conference

	W	L	QW	Pts	Home	Road
*Dakota	26	14	95.0	173.0	17-3	9-11
*Fargo-Moorhead	25	15	80.5	155.5	15-5	10-10
Flint	17	23	77.5	128.5	14-6	3-17
Saskatchewan	8	32	66.0	90.0	7-13	1-19

Playoffs
Semifinals

Mar. 26   Dakota 99 . . . . OT . . . at Fargo-Moorhead 98
Mar. 27   at Dakota 108 . . . . Fargo-Moorhead 107
Mar. 29   at Dakota 113 . . . . Fargo-Moorhead 101
      Dakota wins series, 3 games to 0

Mar. 28   Sioux Falls 95 . . . . at Rockford 87
Mar. 30   at Rockford 110 . . . . Sioux Falls 106
Mar. 31   Rockford 92 . . . . at Sioux Falls 89
Apr. 2   Rockford 104 . . . . at Sioux Falls 93
      Rockford wins series, 3 games to 1

CBA Annual Awards

Most Valuable Player . . . . Miles Simon, Dakota
Newcomer of the Year . . . . . . Miles Simon, Dakota
Rookie of the Year . . . . Kenneth Inge, Rockford
Def. Player of the Year . . . . Willie Murdaugh, Sask.
Coach of the Year . . . . Dave Joerger, Dakota

Final

Saturday, April 6 at Rockford MetroCentre, Rockford, Ill.
Attendance: 7,201. **Time:** 2:20.

	1	2	3	4	F
Dakota Wizards	33	26	25	32	—116
Rockford Lightning	33	26	22	28	—109

Playoff MVP: Miles Simon, Dakota, G (19.5 ppg, 6.5 apg)

CBA Regular Season Individual Leaders
Scoring

	Gm	Pts	Avg
Sean Colson, Grand Rapids	50	1183	23.7
Miles Simon, Dakota	38	873	23.0
Ruben Nembhard, F-M	40	882	22.1
Damian Owens, Gary	21	452	21.5
James Collins, Grand Rapids	52	1071	20.6
Dickey Simpkins, Rockford	26	532	20.5
Gerald Brown, Gary	22	446	20.3
Willie Murdaugh, Saskatchewan	27	505	18.7

Field Goal Pct.

	FGM	FGA	Pct
Shawn Daniels, Dakota	103	168	.613
Chianti Roberts, Fargo-Moorhead	113	188	.601
Antwon Hall, Gary	94	170	.553
Jeff Sanders, Rockford	435	817	.532
Courtney James, Dakota	208	398	.523
Willie Simms, Grand Rapids	360	694	.519
Ken Johnson, Dakota	109	211	.517
Terrance Shannon, Rockford	110	213	.516

Rebounding

	Gm	Reb	Avg
Dickey Simpkins, Rockford	26	309	11.9
Antonio Smith, Grand Rapids	56	638	11.4
Terquin Mott, Grand Rapids	40	401	10.0
Jeff Sanders, Rockford	56	561	10.0
Courtney James, Dakota	40	374	9.4
Sean Lampley, Saskatchewan	20	178	8.9
Damian Owens, Gary	21	179	8.5
Simeon Haley, Flint	36	268	7.4

Assists

	Gm	Ast	Avg
Sean Colson, Grand Rapids	50	396	7.9
Gerald Brown, Gary	22	170	7.7
Tim Winn, Saskatchewan	39	267	6.8
Ruben Nembhard, Fargo-Moorhead	40	264	6.6
Willie Murdaugh, Saskatchewan	27	166	6.1
Lazarus Sims, Rockford	41	248	6.0
Billy Keys, Fargo-Moorhead	39	220	5.6
Miles Simon, Dakota	38	194	5.1

National Basketball Development League

The NBDL is a feeder league founded by the NBA in 2001. The individual teams do not have direct relationships with NBA clubs but players (and coaches) are called-up to the NBA occasionally. (*) denotes playoff qualifiers.

Final Standings

	W	L	Pct	GB
*North Charleston Lowgators	36	20	.640	—
*Greenville Groove	36	20	.640	—
*Columbus Riverdragons	31	25	.550	5
*Mobile Revelers	30	26	.540	6
Huntsville Flight	26	30	.460	10
Asheville Altitude	26	30	.460	10
Fayetteville Patriots	21	35	.380	15
Roanoke Dazzle	18	38	.320	18

Playoffs
Semifinals (Best of 3)

Mar. 28   Columbus 81 . . . . at Greenville 78
Mar. 29   Greenville 96 . . . . at Columbus 78
Apr. 6   at Greenville 79 . . . . Columbus 78
      Greenville wins series, 2 games to 1

Mar. 24   Mobile 78 . . . . at N. Charleston 75
Apr. 3   N. Charleston 77 . . . . at Mobile 70
Apr. 6   at N. Charleston 80 . . . . Mobile 78
      N. Charleston wins series, 2 games to 1

Finals (Best of 3)

Apr. 8   at Greenville 81 . . . .   N. Charleston 63
Apr. 10 Greenville 75 . . . .   at N. Charleston 68
Greenville wins series, 2 games to 0

Annual Awards

Most Valuable Player . . . . .Ansu Sesay, Greenville
Rookie of the Year . . . . .Fred House, N. Charleston
Def. Player of the Year . . . . .Jeff Myers, Greenville
Sportsmanship . . . . .Michael Wilks, Huntsville

Scoring

	Gm	Pts	Avg
Isaac Fontaine, Mobile. 52	906	17.4
Gabe Muoneke, Columbus 47	804	17.1
Tremaine Fowlkes, Columbus 42	701	16.7
Greg Stempin, Fayetteville. 48	752	15.7
Terrell McIntyre, Fayetteville. 39	598	15.3

All-NBDL Team

Pos		Team
F	Tremaine Fowlkes . . . . .Columbus
F	Ansu Sesay . . . . .Greenville
C	Thomas Hamilton . . . . .Greenville
G	Isaac Fontaine . . . . .Mobile
G	Billy Thomas . . . . .Greenville

Assists

	Gm	Ast	Avg
Omar Cook, Fayetteville 35	272	7.8
Scoonie Penn, Asheville 28	141	5.0
Terrell McIntyre, Fayetteville. 39	190	4.9
Nate Green, N. Charleston. 35	143	4.1
Chris Garner, Columbus 48	195	4.1

Rebounds

	Gm	Reb	Avg
Thomas Hamilton, Greenville 50	468	9.4
Shelly Clark, Huntsville. 28	247	8.8
Derek Hood, Mobile. 54	468	8.7
Kareem Poole, Columbus. 55	420	7.6
Antwain Smith, Fayetteville 36	259	7.2

Women's National Basketball Association
Final WNBA Standings

Conference champions (*) and playoff qualifiers (†) are noted. GB refers to Games Behind leader. Number of seasons listed after each head coach refers to current tenure with club.

Eastern Conference

	W	L	Pct	GB	Home	Road
*New York. 18	14	.562	—	10-6	8-8
†Charlotte 18	14	.562	—	11-5	7-9
†Washington 17	15	.531	1	9-7	8-8
†Indiana. 16	16	.500	2	10-6	6-10
Orlando 16	16	.500	2	10-6	6-10
Miami. 15	17	.469	3	9-7	6-10
Cleveland. 10	22	.312	8	4-12	6-10
Detroit 9	23	.281	9	7-9	2-14

Head Coaches: NY–Richie Adubato (4th season); **Cha**–Anne Donovan (2nd); **Wash**– Marianne Stanley (1st); **Ind**–Nell Fortner (2nd); **Orl**–Dee Brown (1st); **Mia**–Ron Rothstein (3rd); **Cle**–Dan Hughes (3rd); **Det**–Greg Williams (2nd, 0-10) replaced on June 19 by Bill Laimbeer (9-13).
2001 Standings: 1. Cleveland (22-10); 2. New York (21-11); 3. Miami (20-12); 4. Charlotte (18-14); 5. Orlando (13-19); 6. Indiana (10-22); 7. Detroit (10-22); 8. Washington (10-22).

Western Conference

	W	L	Pct	GB	Home	Road
*Los Angeles 25	7	.781	—	12-4	13-3
†Houston 24	8	.750	1	14-2	10-6
†Utah 20	12	.625	5	12-4	8-8
†Seattle 17	15	.531	8	10-6	7-9
Portland 16	16	.500	9	9-7	7-9
Sacramento 14	18	.438	11	10-6	4-12
Phoenix 11	21	.344	14	10-6	1-15
Minnesota 10	22	.312	15	7-9	3-13

Head Coaches: LA–Michael Cooper (3rd season); **Hou**–Van Chancellor (6th); **Utah**–Candi Harvey (2nd); **Sea**–Lin Dunn (3rd); **Port**–Linda Hargrove (3rd); **Sac**–Maura McHugh (2nd); **Pho**–Cynthia Cooper (2nd, 6-4) resigned on June 26 was replaced by Linda Sharp (5-17); **Min**–Brian Agler (4th, 6-13) replaced on July 16 by assistant Heidi VanDerveer (1st, 4-9).
2001 Standings: 1. Los Angeles (28-4); 2. Sacramento (20-12); 3. Utah (19-13); 4. Houston (19-13); 5. Phoenix (13-19); 5. Minnesota (12-20); 6. Portland (11-21); 8. Seattle (10-22).

WNBA Regular Season Individual Leaders

Scoring

	Gm	Pts	Avg
Chamique Holdsclaw, Washington . . .20	397	19.9
Tamika Catchings, Indiana 32	594	18.6
Sheryl Swoopes, Houston 32	592	18.5
Lauren Jackson, Seattle 28	482	17.2
Lisa Leslie, Los Angeles. 31	523	16.9
Mwadi Mabika, Los Angeles 32	539	16.8
Tina Thompson, Houston 29	485	16.7
Katie Smith, Minnesota 31	512	16.5
Shannon Johnson, Orlando. 31	499	16.1
Adrienne Goodson, Utah. 32	503	15.7

Rebounding

	Gm	Reb	Avg
Chamique Holdsclaw, Washington . . .20	232	11.6
Lisa Leslie, Los Angeles. 31	322	10.4
Margo Dydek, Utah. 30	262	8.7
Tamika Catchings, Indiana 32	276	8.6
Natalie Williams, Utah 31	255	8.2
Tina Thompson, Houston 29	217	7.5
Tamika Williams, Minnesota 31	229	7.4
Tari Phillips, New York 32	223	7.0
Swin Cash, Detroit 32	222	6.9
Adrain Williams, Phoenix 32	220	6.9

Field Goal Pct.

	FGM	FGA	Pct
Alisa Burras, Portland	117	186	.629
Tamika Williams, Minnesota	124	221	.561
Ann Wauters, Cleveland	120	217	.553
Tammy Sutton-Brown, Charlotte	129	243	.531
Yolanda Griffith, Sacramento	93	179	.520
Lisa Harrison, Phoenix	120	242	.496
Tari Phillips, New York	183	373	.491
DeLisha Milton, Los Angeles	132	271	:487
Olympia Scott-Richardson, Indiana	113	232	.487
DeMya Walker, Portland	139	287	.484

Assists

	Gm	Ast	Avg
Ticha Penicheiro, Sacramento	24	192	8.0
Sue Bird, Seattle	32	191	6.0
Teresa Weatherspoon, New York	32	181	5.7
Shannon Johnson, Orlando	31	163	5.3
Dawn Staley, Charlotte	32	164	5.1
Jennifer Azzi, Utah	32	158	4.9
Nikki Teasley, Los Angeles	32	140	4.4
Debbi Black, Miami	32	137	4.3
Tamecka Dixon, Los Angeles	30	119	4.0
Tamika Catchings, Indiana	32	118	3.7

WNBA Annual Awards

Most Valuable Player.....Sheryl Swoopes, Houston
Rookie of the Year.......Tamika Catchings, Indiana
Most Improved............Coco Miller, Washington

Def. Player of the Year....Sheryl Swoopes, Houston
Coach of the Year.....Marianne Stanley, Washington
Sportsmanship Award.....Jennifer Gillom, Phoenix

WNBA Playoffs
First Round (Best of 3)

East
Aug. 16 at Indiana 73 ....New York 55
Aug. 18 at New York 84 ....Indiana 65
Aug. 20 at New York 75 ....Indiana 60
New York Liberty wins series, 2-1

Aug. 15 at Washington 74 ....Charlotte 62
Aug. 17 Washington 62 ....at Charlotte 59
Washington Mystics win series, 2-0

West
Aug. 15 Los Angeles 78 ....at Seattle 61
Aug. 17 at Los Angeles 69 ....Seattle 59
Los Angeles Sparks win series, 2-0

Aug. 17 at Utah 66 ....Houston 59
Aug. 18 at Houston 83.... 2 OT ....Utah 77
Aug. 20 Utah 75 ....at Houston 72
Utah Starzz wins series, 2-1

Conference Finals (Best of 3)

East
Aug. 22 at Washington 79 ....New York 74
Aug. 24 at New York 96 ....Washington 79
Aug. 25 at New York 64 ....Washington 57
New York Liberty wins series, 2-1

West
Aug. 22 Los Angeles 75 ....at Utah 67
Aug. 24 at Los Angeles 103 ....Utah 77
Los Angeles Sparks win series, 2-0

Championship Series (Best of 3)
Los Angeles wins series, 2 games to 0

	W-L	Avg	Leading Scorer
Los Angeles	2-0	70.0	Mabika & Leslie (16.0)
New York	0-2	64.5	Hammon (13.5)

Date	Winner	Home Court
Aug. 29	Sparks, 71-63	at New York
Aug. 31	Sparks, 69-66	at Los Angeles

Finals MVP: Lisa Leslie, Los Angeles, C, (16.0 ppg, 8.0 rpg, 2.0 bpg)

WNBA 2002 Attendance
Attendance figures below are for the regular season and teams are listed in alphabetical order.

Team	Home Games	Total Attendance	Average Attendance
Charlotte Sting	16	106,670	6,667
Cleveland Rockers	16	149,084	9,318
Detroit Shock	16	94,171	5,886
Houston Comets	16	173,852	10,866
Indiana Fever	16	134,945	8,434
Los Angeles Sparks	16	186,410	11,651
Miami Sol	16	141,252	8,828
Minnesota Lynx	16	125,110	7,819
New York Liberty	16	234,717	14,670
Orlando Miracle	16	113,837	7,115
Phoenix Mercury	16	139,798	8,737
Portland Fire	16	128,656	8,041
Sacramento Monarchs	16	144,179	9,011
Seattle Storm	16	111,774	6,986
Utah Starzz	16	118,720	7,420
Washington Mystics	16	259,237	16,202
WNBA TOTALS	256	2,362,412	9,228

1938-2002
Through the Years

Information Please®
SPORTS ALMANAC

The NBA Finals

Although the National Basketball Association traces its first championship back to the 1946-47 season, the league was then called the Basketball Association of America (BAA). It did not become the NBA until after the 1948-49 season when the BAA and the National Basketball League (NBL) agreed to merge.

In the chart below, the Eastern finalists (representing the NBA Eastern Division from 1947-70, and the NBA Eastern Conference since 1971) are listed in CAPITAL letters. Also, each NBA champion's wins and losses are noted in parentheses after the series score.

Multiple winners: Boston (16); Minneapolis-LA Lakers (14); Chicago Bulls (6); Phi-SF-Golden St. Warriors and Syracuse Nationals-Phi. 76ers (3); Detroit, Houston and New York (2).

Year	Winner	Head Coach	Series	Loser	Head Coach
1947	PHILADELPHIA WARRIORS	Eddie Gottlieb	4-1 (WWWLW)	Chicago Stags	Harold Olsen
1948	Baltimore Bullets	Buddy Jeannette	4-2 (LWWWLW)	PHILA. WARRIORS	Eddie Gottlieb
1949	Minneapolis Lakers	John Kundla	4-2 (WWWLLW)	WASH. CAPITOLS	Red Auerbach
1950	Minneapolis Lakers	John Kundla	4-2 (WLWWLW)	SYRACUSE	Al Cervi
1951	Rochester	Les Harrison	4-3 (WWWLLLW)	NEW YORK	Joe Lapchick
1952	Minneapolis Lakers	John Kundla	4-3 (WLWLWLW)	NEW YORK	Joe Lapchick
1953	Minneapolis Lakers	John Kundla	4-1 (LWWWW)	NEW YORK	Joe Lapchick
1954	Minneapolis Lakers	John Kundla	4-3 (WLWLWLW)	SYRACUSE	Al Cervi
1955	SYRACUSE	Al Cervi	4-3 (WWLLLWW)	Ft. Wayne Pistons	Charley Eckman
1956	PHILADELPHIA WARRIORS	George Senesky	4-1 (LWWWW)	Ft. Wayne Pistons	Charley Eckman
1957	BOSTON	Red Auerbach	4-3 (LWLWWLW)	St. Louis Hawks	Alex Hannum
1958	St. Louis Hawks	Alex Hannum	4-2 (WLWLWW)	BOSTON	Red Auerbach
1959	BOSTON	Red Auerbach	4-0	Mpls. Lakers	John Kundla
1960	BOSTON	Red Auerbach	4-3 (WLWLWLW)	St. Louis Hawks	Ed Macauley
1961	BOSTON	Red Auerbach	4-1 (WWLWW)	St. Louis Hawks	Paul Seymour
1962	BOSTON	Red Auerbach	4-3 (WLLWLWW)	LA Lakers	Fred Schaus
1963	BOSTON	Red Auerbach	4-2 (WLWLWW)	LA Lakers	Fred Schaus
1964	BOSTON	Red Auerbach	4-1 (WWLWW)	SF Warriors	Alex Hannum
1965	BOSTON	Red Auerbach	4-1 (WWLWW)	LA Lakers	Fred Schaus
1966	BOSTON	Red Auerbach	4-3 (LWWWLLW)	LA Lakers	Fred Schaus
1967	PHILADELPHIA 76ERS	Alex Hannum	4-2 (WWLWLW)	SF Warriors	Bill Sharman
1968	BOSTON	Bill Russell	4-2 (WLWLWW)	LA Lakers	B.van Breda Kolff
1969	BOSTON	Bill Russell	4-3 (LLWWLWW)	LA Lakers	B.van Breda Kolff
1970	NEW YORK	Red Holzman	4-3 (WLWLWLW)	LA Lakers	Joe Mullaney
1971	Milwaukee	Larry Costello	4-0	BALT. BULLETS	Gene Shue
1972	LA Lakers	Bill Sharman	4-1 (LWWWW)	NEW YORK	Red Holzman
1973	NEW YORK	Red Holzman	4-1 (LWWWW)	LA Lakers	Bill Sharman
1974	BOSTON	Tommy Heinsohn	4-3 (WLWLWLW)	Milwaukee	Larry Costello
1975	Golden St. Warriors	Al Attles	4-0	WASH. BULLETS	K.C. Jones
1976	BOSTON	Tommy Heinsohn	4-2 (WWLLWW)	Phoenix	John MacLeod
1977	Portland	Jack Ramsay	4-2 (LLWWWW)	PHILA. 76ERS	Gene Shue
1978	WASHINGTON BULLETS	Dick Motta	4-3 (LWLWLWW)	Seattle	Lenny Wilkens
1979	Seattle	Lenny Wilkens	4-1 (LWWWW)	WASH. BULLETS	Dick Motta
1980	LA Lakers	Paul Westhead	4-2 (WLWLWW)	PHILA. 76ERS	Billy Cunningham
1981	BOSTON	Bill Fitch	4-2 (WLWLWW)	Houston	Del Harris
1982	LA Lakers	Pat Riley	4-2 (WLWWLW)	PHILA. 76ERS	Billy Cunningham
1983	PHILADELPHIA 76ERS	Billy Cunningham	4-0	LA Lakers	Pat Riley
1984	BOSTON	K.C. Jones	4-3 (LWLWWLW)	LA Lakers	Pat Riley
1985	LA Lakers	Pat Riley	4-2 (LWWWLW)	BOSTON	K.C. Jones
1986	BOSTON	K.C. Jones	4-2 (WWLWLW)	Houston	Bill Fitch
1987	LA Lakers	Pat Riley	4-2 (WWLWLW)	BOSTON	K.C. Jones
1988	LA Lakers	Pat Riley	4-3 (LWWLLWW)	DETROIT PISTONS	Chuck Daly
1989	DETROIT PISTONS	Chuck Daly	4-0	LA Lakers	Pat Riley
1990	DETROIT	Chuck Daly	4-1 (WLWWW)	Portland	Rick Adelman
1991	CHICAGO	Phil Jackson	4-1 (LWWWW)	LA Lakers	Mike Dunleavy
1992	CHICAGO	Phil Jackson	4-2 (WLWLWW)	Portland	Rick Adelman
1993	CHICAGO	Phil Jackson	4-2 (WWLWLW)	Phoenix	Paul Westphal
1994	Houston	Rudy Tomjanovich	4-3 (WLWLLWW)	NEW YORK	Pat Riley
1995	Houston	Rudy Tomjanovich	4-0	ORLANDO	Brian Hill

Year	Winner	Head Coach	Series	Loser	Head Coach
1996	CHICAGO	Phil Jackson	4-2 (WWWLLW)	Seattle	George Karl
1997	CHICAGO	Phil Jackson	4-2 (WWLLWW)	Utah	Jerry Sloan
1998	CHICAGO	Phil Jackson	4-2 (LWWWLW)	Utah	Jerry Sloan
1999	San Antonio	Gregg Popovich	4-1 (WWLWW)	NEW YORK	Jeff Van Gundy
2000	LA Lakers	Phil Jackson	4-2 (WWLWLW)	INDIANA	Larry Bird
2001	LA Lakers	Phil Jackson	4-1 (LWWWW)	PHILA. 76ERS	Larry Brown
2002	LA Lakers	Phil Jackson	4-0	NEW JERSEY	Byron Scott

Note: Four finalists were led by player-coaches: **1948**—Buddy Jeannette (guard) of Baltimore; **1950**—Al Cervi (guard) of Syracuse; **1968**—Bill Russell (center) of Boston; **1969**—Bill Russell (center) of Boston.

Most Valuable Player

Selected by an 11-member media panel. Winner who did not play for the NBA champion is in **bold** type.

Multiple winners: Michael Jordan (6); Magic Johnson and Shaquille O'Neal (3); Kareem Abdul-Jabbar, Larry Bird, Hakeem Olajuwon and Willis Reed (2).

Year		Year		Year	
1969	**Jerry West**, LA Lakers, G	1981	Cedric Maxwell, Boston, F	1993	Michael Jordan, Chicago, G
1970	Willis Reed, New York, C	1982	Magic Johnson, LA Lakers, G	1994	Hakeem Olajuwon, Houston, C
1971	Lew Alcindor, Milwaukee, C	1983	Moses Malone, Philadelphia, C	1995	Hakeem Olajuwon, Houston, C
1972	Wilt Chamberlain, LA Lakers, C	1984	Larry Bird, Boston, F	1996	Michael Jordan, Chicago, G
1973	Willis Reed, New York, C	1985	K. Abdul-Jabbar, LA Lakers, C	1997	Michael Jordan, Chicago, G
1974	John Havlicek, Boston, F	1986	Larry Bird, Boston, F	1998	Michael Jordan, Chicago, G
1975	Rick Barry, Golden State, G	1987	Magic Johnson, LA Lakers, G	1999	Tim Duncan, San Antonio, F/C
1976	Jo Jo White, Boston, G	1988	James Worthy, LA Lakers, F	2000	Shaquille O'Neal, LA Lakers, C
1977	Bill Walton, Portland, C	1989	Joe Dumars, Detroit, G	2001	Shaquille O'Neal, LA Lakers, C
1978	Wes Unseld, Washington, C	1990	Isiah Thomas, Detroit, G	2002	Shaquille O'Neal, LA Lakers, C
1979	Dennis Johnson, Seattle, G	1991	Michael Jordan, Chicago, G		
1980	Magic Johnson, LA Lakers, G/C	1992	Michael Jordan, Chicago, G		

Note: Lew Alcindor changed his name to Kareem Abdul-Jabbar after the 1970-71 season.

All-Time NBA Playoff Leaders

Through the 2002 playoffs.

CAREER

Years listed indicate number of playoff appearances. Players active in 2002 in **bold** type. DNP indicates player that was active in 2002 but did not participate in playoffs.

Points

		Yrs	Gm	Pts	Avg
1	**Michael Jordan** (DNP)	13	179	5987	33.4
2	Kareem Abdul-Jabbar	18	237	5762	24.3
3	Jerry West	13	153	4457	29.1
4	**Karl Malone**	17	167	4421	26.5
5	Larry Bird	12	164	3897	23.8
6	John Havlicek	13	172	3776	22.0
7	**Hakeem Olajuwon**	15	145	3755	25.9
8	Magic Johnson	13	190	3701	19.5
9	Elgin Baylor	12	134	3623	27.0
10	**Scottie Pippen**	15	204	3619	17.7
11	Wilt Chamberlain	13	160	3607	22.5
12	**Shaquille O'Neal**	9	124	3497	28.2
13	Kevin McHale	13	169	3182	18.8
14	Dennis Johnson	13	180	3116	17.3
15	Julius Erving	11	141	3088	21.9
16	James Worthy	9	143	3022	21.1
17	Clyde Drexler	15	145	2963	20.4
18	Sam Jones	12	154	2909	18.9
19	Charles Barkley	13	123	2833	23.0
20	Robert Parish	16	184	2820	15.3

Scoring Average

Minimum of 25 games or 700 points.

		Yrs	Gm	Pts	Avg
1	**Michael Jordan** (DNP)	13	179	5987	33.4
2	**Allen Iverson**	4	45	1363	30.3
3	Jerry West	13	153	4457	29.1
4	**Shaquille O'Neal**	9	124	3497	28.2
5	Elgin Baylor	12	134	3623	27.0
6	George Gervin	9	59	1592	27.0
7	**Karl Malone**	17	167	4421	26.5
8	**Hakeem Olajuwon**	15	145	3755	25.9
9	Dominique Wilkins	9	55	1421	25.8
10	Bob Pettit	9	88	2240	25.5
11	Rick Barry	7	74	1833	24.8
12	Bernard King	5	28	687	24.5
13	Alex English	10	68	1661	24.4
14	Kareem Abdul-Jabbar	18	237	5762	24.3
15	Paul Arizin	8	49	1186	24.2
16	**Tim Duncan**	4	48	1146	23.9
17	Larry Bird	12	164	3897	23.8
18	George Mikan	9	91	2141	23.5
19	**Reggie Miller**	12	109	2563	23.5
20	Charles Barkley	13	123	2833	23.0

Field Goals

		Yrs	FG	Att	Pct
1	Kareem Abdul-Jabbar	18	2356	4422	.533
2	**Michael Jordan** (DNP)	13	2188	4497	.487
3	Jerry West	13	1622	3460	.469
4	**Karl Malone**	17	1611	3466	.465
5	**Hakeem Olajuwon**	15	1504	2847	.528
6	Larry Bird	12	1458	3090	.472
7	John Havlicek	13	1451	3329	.436
8	Wilt Chamberlain	13	1425	2728	.522
9	Elgin Baylor	12	1388	3161	.439
10	**Scottie Pippen**	15	1326	2987	.444

Free Throws

		Yrs	FT	Att	Pct
1	**Michael Jordan** (DNP)	13	1463	1766	.828
2	Jerry West	13	1213	1507	.805
3	**Karl Malone**	17	1193	1611	.741
4	Kareem Abdul-Jabbar	18	1050	1419	.740
5	Magic Johnson	12	1040	1241	.838
6	Larry Bird	12	901	1012	.891
7	John Havlicek	13	874	1046	.836
8	Elgin Baylor	12	847	1101	.769
9	**Shaquille O'Neal**	9	787	1503	.524
10	**Scottie Pippen**	15	770	1065	.723

Assists

		Yrs	Gm	No	Avg
1	Magic Johnson	13	190	2346	12.3
2	**John Stockton**	18	177	1813	10.2
3	Larry Bird	12	164	1062	6.5
4	**Scottie Pippen**	15	204	1035	5.1
5	**Michael Jordan** (DNP)	13	179	1022	5.7

Rebounds

		Yrs	Gm	No	Avg
1	Bill Russell	13	165	4104	24.9
2	Wilt Chamberlain	13	160	3913	24.5
3	Kareem Abdul-Jabbar	18	237	2481	10.5
4	**Karl Malone**	17	167	1843	11.1
5	Wes Unseld	12	119	1777	14.9

Appearances

	No
Kareem Abdul-Jabbar	18
John Stockton	18
Robert Parish	16
Karl Malone	17
Jerome Kersey	15
Dolph Schayes	15
Hakeem Olajuwon	15
Paul Silas	14

Games Played

	No		No
K. Abdul-Jabbar	237	**John Stockton**	177
Scottie Pippen	204	John Havlicek	170
Danny Ainge	193	Kevin McHale	169
Magic Johnson	190	Michael Cooper	168
Robert Parish	184	**Karl Malone**	167
Byron Scott	183	Bill Russell	165
Dennis Johnson	180	Larry Bird	164
Michael Jordan (DNP)	179	Paul Silas	163

SINGLE GAME

Points

	Date	FG-FT-Pts
Michael Jordan, Chi at Bos*	4/20/86	22-19-63
Elgin Baylor, LA at Bos	4/14/62	22-17-61
Wilt Chamberlain, Phi vs Syr	3/22/62	22-12-56
Michael Jordan, Chi at Mia	4/29/92	20-16-56
Charles Barkley, Pho vs G.St.	5/4/94	23-7-56
Rick Barry, SF vs Phi	4/18/67	22-11-55
Michael Jordan, Chi vs Cle	5/1/88	24-7-55
Michael Jordan, Chi vs Pho	4/16/93	21-13-55
Michael Jordan, Chi vs. Wash	4/27/97	22-10-55

*Double overtime.

Field Goals

	Date	FG	Att
Wilt Chamberlain, Phi vs Syr	3/14/60	24	42
John Havlicek, Bos vs Atl	4/1/73	24	36
Michael Jordan, Chi vs Cle	5/1/88	24	45

Eight tied with 22 each.

Miscellaneous

3-Pt Field Goals

	Date	No
Rex Chapman, Pho at Sea	4/25/97	9
Dan Majerle, Pho vs Sea	6/1/93	8
Allen Iverson, Phi vs Tor	5/16/01	8

Eight tied with 7 each.

Assists

	Date	No
Magic Johnson, LA vs Pho	5/15/84	24
John Stockton, Utah vs LA Lakers	5/17/88	24
Magic Johnson, LA Lakers at Port	5/3/85	23
John Stockton, Utah vs Port	4/25/96	23
Doc Rivers, Atl vs Bos	5/16/88	22

Four tied with 21 each.

Rebounds

	Date	No
Wilt Chamberlain, Phi vs Bos	4/5/67	41
Bill Russell, Bos vs Phi	3/23/58	40
Bill Russell, Bos vs St.L	3/29/60	40
Bill Russell, Bos vs LA*	4/18/62	40

Three tied with 39 each.

*Overtime.

Appearances in NBA Finals

Standings of all NBA teams that have reached the NBA Finals since 1947.

App		Titles	Last Won
27	Minneapolis-LA Lakers	14	2002
19	Boston Celtics	16	1986
9	Syracuse Nats-Phila. 76ers	3	1983
8	New York Knicks	2	1973
6	Chicago Bulls	6	1998
6	Phila-SF-Golden St. Warriors	3	1975
5	Ft. Wayne-Detroit Pistons	2	1990
4	Houston Rockets	2	1995
4	St. Louis Hawks	1	1958
4	Baltimore-Washington Bullets	1	1978
3	Portland Trail Blazers	1	1977
3	Seattle SuperSonics	1	1979
2	Milwaukee Bucks	1	1971
2	Phoenix Suns	0	—
2	Utah Jazz	0	—
1	Baltimore Bullets	1	1948
1	Rochester Royals	1	1951
1	San Antonio Spurs	1	1999
1	Chicago Stags	0	—
1	Orlando Magic	0	—
1	Washington Capitols	0	—
1	Indiana Pacers	0	—
1	New Jersey Nets	0	—

Change of address: The St. Louis Hawks now play in Atlanta and the Rochester Royals are now the Sacramento Kings.

Teams now defunct: Baltimore Bullets (1947-55), Chicago Stags (1946-50) and Washington Capitols (1946-51).

NBA FINALS

Points

Series		Year	Pts
4-Gm	Shaquille O'Neal, LAL vs NJ	2002	145
5-Gm	Allen Iverson, Phi vs LAL	2001	178
6-Gm	Michael Jordan, Chi vs Pho	1993	246
7-Gm	Elgin Baylor, LA vs Bos	1962	284

Field Goals

Series		Year	No
4-Gm	Hakeem Olajuwon, Hou vs Orl	1995	56
5-Gm	Allen Iverson, Phi vs LAL	2001	66
6-Gm	Michael Jordan, Chi vs Pho	1993	101
7-Gm	Elgin Baylor, LA vs Bos	1962	101

Assists

Series		Year	No
4-Gm	Bob Cousy, Bos vs Mpls	1959	51
5-Gm	Magic Johnson, LAL vs Chi	1991	62
6-Gm	Magic Johnson, LAL vs Bos	1985	84
7-Gm	Magic Johnson, LA vs Bos	1984	95

Rebounds

Series		Year	No
4-Gm	Bill Russell, Bos vs Mpls	1959	118
5-Gm	Bill Russell, Bos vs St.L	1961	144
6-Gm	Wilt Chamberlain, Phi vs SF	1967	171
7-Gm	Bill Russell, Bos vs LA	1962	189

The National Basketball League

The NBL started with 13 previously independent teams in 1937-38 and although GE, Firestone and Goodyear were gone by late 1942, ran 12 years before merging with the three-year-old Basketball Association of America in 1949 to form the NBA.

Multiple champions: Akron Firestone Non-Skids, Fort Wayne Zollner Pistons, Oshkosh All-Stars (2).

Year	Winner	Series	Loser	Year	Winner	Series	Loser
1938	Goodyear Wingfoots	2-1	Oshkosh All-Stars	1944	Ft. Wayne Pistons	3-0	Sheboygan Redskins
1939	Firestone Non-Skids	3-2	Oshkosh All-Stars	1945	Ft. Wayne Pistons	3-2	Sheboygan Redskins
1940	Firestone Non-Skids	3-2	Oshkosh All-Stars	1946	Rochester Royals	3-0	Sheboygan Redskins
1941	Oshkosh All-Stars	3-0	Sheboygan Redskins	1947	Chicago Gears	3-2	Rochester Royals
1942	Oshkosh All-Stars	2-1	Ft. Wayne Pistons	1948	Minneapolis Lakers	3-1	Rochester Royals
1943	Sheboygan Redskins	2-1	Ft. Wayne Pistons	1949	Anderson Packers	3-0	Oshkosh All-Stars

NBA All-Star Game

The NBA staged its first All-Star Game before 10,094 at Boston Garden on March 2, 1951. From that year on, the game has matched the best players in the East against the best in the West. Winning coaches are listed first. East leads series, 32-18.

Multiple MVP winners: Bob Pettit (4); Michael Jordan and Oscar Robertson (3); Bob Cousy, Julius Erving, Magic Johnson, Karl Malone and Isiah Thomas (2).

Year		Host	Coaches	Most Valuable Player
1951	East 111, West 94	Boston	Joe Lapchick, John Kundla	Ed Macauley, Boston
1952	East 108, West 91	Boston	Al Cervi, John Kundla	Paul Arizin, Philadelphia
1953	West 79, East 75	Ft. Wayne	John Kundla, Joe Lapchick	George Mikan, Minneapolis
1954	East 98, West 93 (OT)	New York	Joe Lapchick, John Kundla	Bob Cousy, Boston
1955	East 100, West 91	New York	Al Cervi, Charley Eckman	Bill Sharman, Boston
1956	West 108, East 94	Rochester	Charley Eckman, George Senesky	Bob Pettit, St. Louis
1957	East 109, West 97	Boston	Red Auerbach, Bobby Wanzer	Bob Cousy, Boston
1958	East 130, West 118	St. Louis	Red Auerbach, Alex Hannum	Bob Pettit, St. Louis
1959	West 124, East 108	Detroit	Ed Macauley, Red Auerbach	Bob Pettit, St. Louis & Elgin Baylor, Minneapolis
1960	East 125, West 115	Philadelphia	Red Auerbach, Ed Macauley	Wilt Chamberlain, Philadelphia
1961	West 153, East 131	Syracuse	Paul Seymour, Red Auerbach	Oscar Robertson, Cincinnati
1962	West 150, East 130	St. Louis	Fred Schaus, Red Auerbach	Bob Pettit, St. Louis
1963	East 115, West 108	Los Angeles	Red Auerbach, Fred Schaus	Bill Russell, Boston
1964	East 111, West 107	Boston	Red Auerbach, Fred Schaus	Oscar Robertson, Cincinnati
1965	East 124, West 123	St. Louis	Red Auerbach, Alex Hannum	Jerry Lucas, Cincinnati
1966	East 137, West 94	Cincinnati	Red Auerbach, Fred Schaus	Adrian Smith, Cincinnati
1967	West 135, East 120	San Francisco	Fred Schaus, Red Auerbach	Rick Barry, San Francisco
1968	East 144, West 124	New York	Alex Hannum, Red Auerbach	Hal Greer, Philadelphia
1969	East 123, West 112	Baltimore	Gene Shue, Richie Guerin	Oscar Robertson, Cincinnati
1970	East 142, West 135	Philadelphia	Red Holzman, Richie Guerin	Willis Reed, New York
1971	West 108, East 107	San Diego	Larry Costello, Red Holzman	Lenny Wilkens, Seattle
1972	West 112, East 110	Los Angeles	Bill Sharman, Tom Heinsohn	Jerry West, Los Angeles
1973	East 104, West 84	Chicago	Tom Heinsohn, Bill Sharman	Dave Cowens, Boston
1974	West 134, East 123	Seattle	Larry Costello, Tom Heinsohn	Bob Lanier, Detroit
1975	East 108, West 102	Phoenix	K.C. Jones, Al Attles	Walt Frazier, New York
1976	East 123, West 109	Philadelphia	Tom Heinsohn, Al Attles	Dave Bing, Washington
1977	West 125, East 124	Milwaukee	Larry Brown, Gene Shue	Julius Erving, Philadelphia
1978	East 133, West 125	Atlanta	Billy Cunningham, Jack Ramsay	Randy Smith, Buffalo
1979	West 134, East 129	Detroit	Lenny Wilkens, Dick Motta	David Thompson, Denver
1980	East 144, West 136 (OT)	Washington	Billy Cunningham, Lenny Wilkens	George Gervin, San Antonio
1981	East 123, West 120	Cleveland	Billy Cunningham, John MacLeod	Nate Archibald, Boston
1982	East 120, West 118	New Jersey	Bill Fitch, Pat Riley	Larry Bird, Boston
1983	East 132, West 123	Los Angeles	Billy Cunningham, Pat Riley	Julius Erving, Philadelphia
1984	East 154, West 145 (OT)	Denver	K.C. Jones, Frank Layden	Isiah Thomas, Detroit
1985	West 140, East 129	Indiana	Pat Riley, K.C. Jones	Ralph Sampson, Houston
1986	East 139, West 132	Dallas	K.C. Jones, Pat Riley	Isiah Thomas, Detroit
1987	West 154, East 149 (OT)	Seattle	Pat Riley, K.C. Jones	Tom Chambers, Seattle
1988	East 138, West 133	Chicago	Mike Fratello, Pat Riley	Michael Jordan, Chicago
1989	West 143, East 134	Houston	Pat Riley, Lenny Wilkens	Karl Malone, Utah
1990	East 130, West 113	Miami	Chuck Daly, Pat Riley	Magic Johnson, LA Lakers
1991	East 116, West 114	Charlotte	Chris Ford, Rick Adelman	Charles Barkley, Philadelphia
1992	West 153, East 113	Orlando	Don Nelson, Phil Jackson	Magic Johnson, LA Lakers
1993	West 135, East 132 (OT)	Salt Lake City	Paul Westphal, Pat Riley	Karl Malone, Utah & John Stockton, Utah
1994	East 127, West 118	Minneapolis	Lenny Wilkens, George Karl	Scottie Pippen, Chicago
1995	West 139, East 112	Phoenix	Paul Westphal, Brian Hill	Mitch Richmond, Sacramento
1996	East 129, West 118	San Antonio	Phil Jackson, George Karl	Michael Jordan, Chicago
1997	East 132, West 120	Cleveland	Doug Collins, Rudy Tomjanovich	Glen Rice, Charlotte
1998	East 135, West 114	New York	Larry Bird, George Karl	Michael Jordan, Chicago
1999	Not held—due to lockout			
2000	West 137, East 126	Oakland	Jeff Van Gundy, Phil Jackson	Tim Duncan, San Antonio & Shaquille O'Neal, LA Lakers
2001	East 111, West 110	Washington	Larry Brown, Rick Adelman	Allen Iverson, Philadelphia
2002	West 135, East 120	Philadelphia	Don Nelson, Byron Scott	Kobe Bryant, LA Lakers

NBA Franchise Origins

Here is what the current 29 teams in the National Basketball Association have to show for the years they have put in as members of the National Basketball League (NBL), Basketball Association of America (BAA), the NBA, and the American Basketball Association (ABA). League titles are noted by year won.

Western Conference

	First Season	League Titles	Franchise Stops
Dallas Mavericks	1980-81 (NBA)	None	•Dallas (1980–)
Denver Nuggets	1967-68 (ABA)	None	•Denver (1967–)
Golden St. Warriors	1946-47 (BAA)	1 BAA (1947)	•Philadelphia (1946-62)
		2 NBA (1956,75)	San Francisco (1962-71)
			Oakland (1971–)
Houston Rockets	1967-68 (NBA)	2 NBA (1994-95)	•San Diego (1967-71)
			Houston (1971–)
Los Angeles Clippers	1970-71 (NBA)	None	•Buffalo (1970-78)
			San Diego (1978-84)
			Los Angeles (1984–)
Los Angeles Lakers	1947-48 (NBL)	1 NBL (1948)	•Minneapolis (1947-60)
		1 BAA (1949)	Los Angeles (1960-67)
		14 NBA (1950,52-54,72,	Inglewood, CA (1967-99)
		80,82,85,87-88,00-02)	Los Angeles (1999–)
Memphis Grizzlies	1995-96 (NBA)	None	•Vancouver (1995-01)
			Memphis, TN (2001–)
Minnesota Timberwolves	1989-90 (NBA)	None	•Minneapolis (1989–)
Phoenix Suns	1968-69 (NBA)	None	•Phoenix (1968–)
Portland Trail Blazers	1970-71 (NBA)	1 NBA (1977)	•Portland (1970–)
Sacramento Kings	1945-46 (NBL)	1 NBL (1946)	•Rochester, NY (1945-58)
		1 NBA (1951)	Cincinnati (1958-72)
			KC-Omaha (1972-75)
			Kansas City (1975-85)
			Sacramento (1985–)
San Antonio Spurs	1967-68 (ABA)	1 NBA (1999)	•Dallas (1967-73)
			San Antonio (1973–)
Seattle SuperSonics	1967-68 (NBA)	1 NBA (1979)	•Seattle (1967–)
Utah Jazz	1974-75 (NBA)	None	•New Orleans (1974-79)
			Salt Lake City (1979–)

Eastern Conference

	First Season	League Titles	Franchise Stops
Atlanta Hawks	1946-47 (NBL)	1 NBA (1958)	•Tri-Cities (1946-51)
			Milwaukee (1951-55)
			St. Louis (1955-68)
			Atlanta (1968–)
Boston Celtics	1946-47 (BAA)	16 NBA (1957,59-66,68-69	•Boston (1946–)
		74,76,81,84,86)	
Chicago Bulls	1966-67 (NBA)	6 NBA (1991-93,96-98)	•Chicago (1966–)
Cleveland Cavaliers	1970-71 (NBA)	None	•Cleveland (1970-74)
			Richfield, OH (1974-94)
			Cleveland (1994–)
Detroit Pistons	1941-42 (NBL)	2 NBL (1944-45)	•Ft. Wayne, IN (1941-57)
		2 NBA (1989-90)	Detroit (1957-78)
			Pontiac, MI (1978-88)
			Auburn Hills, MI (1988–)
Indiana Pacers	1967-68 (ABA)	3 ABA (1970,72-73)	•Indianapolis (1967–)
Miami Heat	1988-89 (NBA)	None	•Miami (1988–)
Milwaukee Bucks	1968-69 (NBA)	1 NBA (1971)	•Milwaukee (1968–)
New Jersey Nets	1967-68 (ABA)	2 ABA (1974,76)	•Teaneck, NJ (1967-68)
			Commack, NY (1968-69)
			W. Hempstead, NY (1969-71)
			Uniondale, NY (1971-77)
			Piscataway, NJ (1977-81)
			E. Rutherford, NJ (1981–)
New Orleans Hornets	1988-89 (NBA)	None	•Charlotte (1988-2002)
			New Orleans (2002–)
New York Knicks	1946-47 (BAA)	2 NBA (1970,73)	•New York (1946–)
Orlando Magic	1989-90 (NBA)	None	•Orlando, FL (1989–)
Philadelphia 76ers	1949-50 (NBA)	3 NBA (1955,67,83)	•Syracuse (1949-63)
			Philadelphia (1963–)
Toronto Raptors	1995-96 (NBA)	None	•Toronto (1995–)
Washington Wizards	1961-62 (NBA)	1 NBA (1978)	•Chicago (1961-63)
			Baltimore (1963-73)
			Landover, MD (1973–)

Note: The Tri-Cities Blackhawks represented Moline and Rock Island, Ill., and Davenport, Iowa.

The Growth of the NBA

Of the 11 franchises that comprised the Basketball Association of America (BAA) at the start of the 1946-47 season, only three remain—the Boston Celtics, New York Knickerbockers and Golden State Warriors (originally Philadelphia Warriors).

Just before the start of the 1948-49 season, four teams from the more established **National Basketball League** (NBL)—the Ft. Wayne Pistons (now Detroit), Indianapolis Jets, Minneapolis Lakers (now Los Angeles) and Rochester Royals (now Sacramento Kings)—joined the BAA.

A year later, the six remaining NBL franchises—Anderson (Ind.), Denver, Sheboygan (Wisc.), the Syracuse Nationals (now Philadelphia 76ers), Tri-Cities Blackhawks (now Atlanta Hawks) and Waterloo (Iowa)—joined along with the new Indianapolis Olympians and the BAA became the 17-team **National Basketball Association**.

The NBA was down to 10 teams by the 1950-51 season and slipped to eight by 1954-55 with Boston, New York, Philadelphia and Syracuse in the Eastern Division, and Ft. Wayne, Milwaukee (formerly Tri-Cities), Minneapolis and Rochester in the West.

By 1960, five of those surviving eight teams had moved to other cities but by the end of the decade the NBA was a 14-team league. It also had a rival, the **American Basketball Association**, which began play in 1967 with a red, white and blue ball, a three-point line and 11 teams. After a nine-year run, the ABA merged four clubs—the Denver Nuggets, Indiana Pacers, New York Nets and San Antonio Spurs—with the NBA following the 1975-76 season. The NBA adopted the three-point shot in 1979-80.

Expansion/Merger Timetable

For teams currently in NBA.

1948—Added NBL's Ft. Wayne Pistons (now Detroit), Minneapolis Lakers (now Los Angeles) and Rochester Royals (now Sacramento Kings); **1949**—Syracuse Nationals (now Philadelphia 76ers) and Tri-Cities Blackhawks (now Atlanta Hawks).

1961—Chicago Packers (now Washington Wizards); **1966**—Chicago Bulls; **1967**—San Diego Rockets (now Houston) and Seattle SuperSonics; **1968**—Milwaukee Bucks and Phoenix Suns.

1970—Buffalo Braves (now Los Angeles Clippers), Cleveland Cavaliers and Portland Trail Blazers; **1974**—New Orleans Jazz (now Utah); **1976**—added ABA's Denver Nuggets, Indiana Pacers, New York Nets (now New Jersey) and San Antonio Spurs.

1980—Dallas Mavericks; **1988**—Charlotte Hornets and Miami Heat; **1989**—Minnesota Timberwolves and Orlando Magic.

1995—Toronto Raptors and Vancouver Grizzlies (Now Memphis).

City and Nickname Changes

1951—Tri-Cities Blackhawks, who divided home games between Moline and Rock Island, Ill., and Davenport, Iowa, move to Milwaukee and become the Hawks; **1955**—Milwaukee Hawks move to St. Louis; **1957**—Ft. Wayne Pistons move to Detroit, while Rochester Royals move to Cincinnati.

1960—Minneapolis Lakers move to Los Angeles; **1962**—Chicago Packers renamed Zephyrs, while Philadelphia Warriors move to San Francisco; **1963**—Chicago Zephyrs move to Baltimore and become Bullets, while Syracuse Nationals move to Philadelphia and become 76ers; **1968**—St. Louis Hawks move to Atlanta.

1971—San Diego Rockets move to Houston, while San Francisco Warriors move to Oakland and become Golden State Warriors; **1972**—Cincinnati Royals move to Midwest, divide home games between Kansas City, Mo., and Omaha, Neb., and become Kings; **1973**—Baltimore Bullets move to Landover, Md., outside Washington and become Capital Bullets; **1974**—Capital Bullets renamed Washington Bullets; **1975**—KC-Omaha Kings settle in Kansas City; **1977**—New York Nets move from Uniondale, N.Y., to Piscataway, N.J. (later East Rutherford) and become New Jersey Nets; **1978**—Buffalo Braves move to San Diego and become Clippers; **1979**—New Orleans Jazz move to Salt Lake City and become Utah Jazz.

1984—San Diego Clippers move to Los Angeles; **1985**—Kansas City Kings move to Sacramento.

1997—Washington Bullets become Washington Wizards.

2001—Vancouver Grizzlies move to Memphis, Tenn.; **2002**—Charlotte Hornets move to New Orleans.

Defunct NBA Teams

Teams that once played in the BAA and NBA, but no longer exist.

Anderson (Ind.)—Packers (1949-50); **Baltimore**—Bullets (1947-55); **Chicago**—Stags (1946-50); **Cleveland**—Rebels (1946-47); **Denver**—Nuggets (1949-50); **Detroit**—Falcons (1946-47); **Indianapolis**—Jets (1948-49) and Olympians (1949-53); **Pittsburgh**—Ironmen (1946-47); **Providence**—Steamrollers (1946-49); **St. Louis**—Bombers (1946-50); **Sheboygan (Wisc.)**—Redskins (1949-50); **Toronto**—Huskies (1946-47); **Washington**—Capitols (1946-51); **Waterloo (Iowa)**—Hawks (1949-50).

ABA Teams (1967-76)

Anaheim—Amigos (1967-68, moved to LA); **Baltimore**—Claws (1975, never played); **Carolina**—Cougars (1969-74, moved to St. Louis); **Dallas**—Chaparrals (1967-73, called Texas Chaparrals in 1970-71, moved to San Antonio); **Denver**—Rockets (1967-76, renamed Nuggets in 1974-76); **Miami**—Floridians (1968-72, called simply Floridians from 1970-72).

Houston—Mavericks (1967-69, moved to North Carolina); **Indiana**—Pacers (1967-76); **Kentucky**—Colonels (1967-76); **Los Angeles**—Stars (1968-70, moved to Utah); **Memphis**—Pros (1970-75, renamed Tams in 1972 and Sounds in 1974, moved to Baltimore); **Minnesota**—Muskies (1967-68, moved to Miami) and Pipers (1968-69, moved back to Pittsburgh); **New Jersey**—Americans (1967-68, moved to New York).

New Orleans—Buccaneers (1967-70, moved to Memphis); **New York**—Nets (1968-76); **Oakland**—Oaks (1967-69, moved to Washington); **Pittsburgh**—Pipers (1967-68, moved to Minnesota), Pipers (1969-72, renamed Condors in 1970); **St. Louis**—Spirits of St. Louis (1974-76); **San Antonio**—Spurs (1973-76); **San Diego**—Conquistadors (1972-75, renamed Sails in 1975); **Utah**—Stars (1970-75); **Virginia**—Squires (1970-76); **Washington**—Caps (1969-70, moved to Virginia).

Annual NBA Leaders
Scoring

Decided by total points from 1947-69, and per game average since 1970. A lockout in 1999 shortened the regular season to 50 games.

Multiple winners: Michael Jordan (10); Wilt Chamberlain (7); George Gervin (4); Allen Iverson, Neil Johnston, Bob McAdoo and George Mikan (3); Kareem Abdul-Jabbar, Paul Arizin, Adrian Dantley, Shaquille O'Neal and Bob Pettit (2).

Year		Gm	Pts	Avg	Year		Gm	Pts	Avg
1947	Joe Fulks, Phi	60	1389	23.2	1975	Bob McAdoo, Buf	82	2831	34.5
1948	Max Zaslofsky, Chi	48	1007	21.0	1976	Bob McAdoo, Buf	78	2427	31.1
1949	George Mikan, Mpls	60	1698	28.3	1977	Pete Maravich, NO	73	2273	31.1
					1978	George Gervin, SA	82	2232	27.2
1950	George Mikan, Mpls	68	1865	27.4	1979	George Gervin, SA	80	2365	29.6
1951	George Mikan, Mpls	68	1932	28.4					
1952	Paul Arizin, Phi	66	1674	25.4	1980	George Gervin, SA	78	2585	33.1
1953	Neil Johnston, Phi	70	1564	22.3	1981	Adrian Dantley, Utah	80	2452	30.7
1954	Neil Johnston, Phi	72	1759	24.4	1982	George Gervin, SA	79	2551	32.3
1955	Neil Johnston, Phi	72	1631	22.7	1983	Alex English, Den	82	2326	28.4
1956	Bob Pettit, St.L	72	1849	25.7	1984	Adrian Dantley, Utah	79	2418	30.6
1957	Paul Arizin, Phi	71	1817	25.6	1985	Bernard King, NY	55	1809	32.9
1958	George Yardley, Det	72	2001	27.8	1986	Dominique Wilkins, Atl	78	2366	30.3
1959	Bob Pettit, St.L	72	2105	29.2	1987	Michael Jordan, Chi	82	3041	37.1
					1988	Michael Jordan, Chi	82	2868	35.0
1960	Wilt Chamberlain, Phi	72	2707	37.6	1989	Michael Jordan, Chi	81	2633	32.5
1961	Wilt Chamberlain, Phi	79	3033	38.4					
1962	Wilt Chamberlain, Phi	80	4029	50.4	1990	Michael Jordan, Chi	82	2753	33.6
1963	Wilt Chamberlain, SF	80	3586	44.8	1991	Michael Jordan, Chi	82	2580	31.5
1964	Wilt Chamberlain, SF	80	2948	36.9	1992	Michael Jordan, Chi	80	2404	30.1
1965	Wilt Chamberlain, SF-Phi	73	2534	34.7	1993	Michael Jordan, Chi	78	2541	32.6
1966	Wilt Chamberlain, Phi	79	2649	33.5	1994	David Robinson, SA	80	2383	29.8
1967	Rick Barry, SF	78	2775	35.6	1995	Shaquille O'Neal, Orl	79	2315	29.3
1968	Dave Bing, Det	79	2142	27.1	1996	Michael Jordan, Chi	82	2491	30.4
1969	Elvin Hayes, SD	82	2327	28.4	1997	Michael Jordan, Chi	82	2431	29.7
					1998	Michael Jordan, Chi	82	2357	28.7
1970	Jerry West, LA	74	2309	31.2	1999	Allen Iverson, Phi	48	1284	26.8
1971	Lew Alcindor, Mil	82	2596	31.7					
1972	Kareem Abdul-Jabbar, Mil	81	2822	34.8	2000	Shaquille O'Neal, LAL	79	2344	29.7
1973	Nate Archibald, KC-Omaha	80	2719	34.0	2001	Allen Iverson, Phi	71	2207	31.1
1974	Bob McAdoo, Buf	74	2261	30.6	2002	Allen Iverson, Phi	60	1883	31.4

Note: Lew Alcindor changed his name to Kareem Abdul-Jabbar after the 1970-71 season.

Rebounds

Decided by total rebounds from 1951-69 and per game average since 1970.

Multiple winners: Wilt Chamberlain (11); Dennis Rodman (7); Moses Malone (6); Bill Russell (4); Elvin Hayes, Dikembe Mutombo and Hakeem Olajuwon (2).

Year		Gm	No	Avg	Year		Gm	No	Avg
1951	Dolph Schayes, Syr	66	1080	16.4	1978	Len Robinson, NO	82	1288	15.7
1952	Larry Foust, Ft. Wayne	66	880	13.3	1979	Moses Malone, Hou	82	1444	17.6
	& Mel Hutchins, Mil	66	880	13.3					
1953	George Mikan, Mpls	70	1007	14.4	1980	Swen Nater, SD	81	1216	15.0
1954	Harry Gallatin, NY	72	1098	15.3	1981	Moses Malone, Hou	80	1180	14.8
1955	Neil Johnston, Phi	72	1085	15.1	1982	Moses Malone, Hou	81	1188	14.7
1956	Bob Pettit, St.L	72	1164	16.2	1983	Moses Malone, Phi	78	1194	15.3
1957	Maurice Stokes, Roch	72	1256	17.4	1984	Moses Malone, Phi	71	950	13.4
1958	Bill Russell, Bos	69	1564	22.7	1985	Moses Malone, Phi	79	1031	13.1
1959	Bill Russell, Bos	70	1612	23.0	1986	Bill Laimbeer, Det	82	1075	13.1
					1987	Charles Barkley, Phi	68	994	14.6
1960	Wilt Chamberlain, Phi	72	1941	27.0	1988	Michael Cage, LAC	72	938	13.0
1961	Wilt Chamberlain, Phi	79	2149	27.2	1989	Hakeem Olajuwon, Hou	82	1105	13.5
1962	Wilt Chamberlain, Phi	80	2052	25.7					
1963	Wilt Chamberlain, SF	80	1946	24.3	1990	Hakeem Olajuwon, Hou	82	1149	14.0
1964	Bill Russell, Bos	78	1930	24.7	1991	David Robinson, SA	82	1063	13.0
1965	Bill Russell, Bos	78	1878	24.1	1992	Dennis Rodman, Det	82	1530	18.7
1966	Wilt Chamberlain, Phi	79	1943	24.6	1993	Dennis Rodman, Det	62	1232	18.3
1967	Wilt Chamberlain, Phi	81	1957	24.2	1994	Dennis Rodman, SA	79	1132	17.3
1968	Wilt Chamberlain, Phi	82	1952	23.8	1995	Dennis Rodman, SA	49	823	16.8
1969	Wilt Chamberlain, LA	81	1712	21.1	1996	Dennis Rodman, Chi	64	952	14.9
					1997	Dennis Rodman, Chi	55	883	16.1
1970	Elvin Hayes, SD	82	1386	16.9	1998	Dennis Rodman, Chi	80	1201	15.0
1971	Wilt Chamberlain, LA	82	1493	18.2	1999	Chris Webber, Sac	42	545	13.0
1972	Wilt Chamberlain, LA	82	1572	19.2					
1973	Wilt Chamberlain, LA	82	1526	18.6	2000	Dikembe Mutombo, Atl	82	1157	14.1
1974	Elvin Hayes, Cap*	81	1463	18.1	2001	Dikembe Mutombo, Atl-Phi	75	1015	13.5
1975	Wes Unseld, Wash	73	1077	14.8	2002	Ben Wallace, Det	80	1039	13.0
1976	Kareem Abdul-Jabbar, LA	82	1383	16.9					
1977	Bill Walton, Port	65	934	14.4					

*The Baltimore Bullets moved to Landover, Md. in 1973-74 and became first the Capital Bullets, then the Washington Bullets in 1974-75.

Annual NBA Leaders (Cont.)
Assists

Decided by total assists from 1952-69 and per game average since 1970.

Multiple winners: John Stockton (9); Bob Cousy (8); Oscar Robertson (6); Magic Johnson and Kevin Porter (4); Jason Kidd (3); Andy Phillip and Guy Rodgers (2).

Year		No	Year		No	Year		No
1947	Ernie Calverly, Prov	.202	1966	Oscar Robertson, Cin	.847	1985	Isiah Thomas, Det	13.9
1948	Howie Dallmar, Phi	.120	1967	Guy Rodgers, Chi	.908	1986	Magic Johnson, LAL	12.6
1949	Bob Davies, Roch	.321	1968	Wilt Chamberlain, Phi	.702	1987	Magic Johnson, LAL	12.2
1950	Dick McGuire, NY	.386	1969	Oscar Robertson, Cin	.772	1988	John Stockton, Utah	13.8
1951	Andy Phillip, Phi	.414	1970	Lenny Wilkens, Sea	9.1	1989	John Stockton, Utah	13.6
1952	Andy Phillip, Phi	.539	1971	Norm Van Lier, Chi	10.1	1990	John Stockton, Utah	14.5
1953	Bob Cousy, Bos	.547	1972	Jerry West, LA	9.7	1991	John Stockton, Utah	14.2
1954	Bob Cousy, Bos	.518	1973	Nate Archibald, KC-O	11.4	1992	John Stockton, Utah	13.7
1955	Bob Cousy, Bos	.557	1974	Ernie DiGregorio, Buf	8.2	1993	John Stockton, Utah	12.0
1956	Bob Cousy, Bos	.642	1975	Kevin Porter, Wash	8.0	1994	John Stockton, Utah	12.6
1957	Bob Cousy, Bos	.478	1976	Slick Watts, Sea	8.1	1995	John Stockton, Utah	12.3
1958	Bob Cousy, Bos	.463	1977	Don Buse, Ind	8.5	1996	John Stockton, Utah	11.2
1959	Bob Cousy, Bos	.557	1978	Kevin Porter, Det-NJ	10.2	1997	Mark Jackson, Den-Ind	11.4
1960	Bob Cousy, Bos	.715	1979	Kevin Porter, Det	13.4	1998	Rod Strickland, Wash	10.5
1961	Oscar Robertson, Cin	.690	1980	M.R. Richardson, NY	10.1	1999	Jason Kidd, Pho	10.8
1962	Oscar Robertson, Cin	.899	1981	Kevin Porter, Wash	9.1	2000	Jason Kidd, Pho	10.1
1963	Guy Rodgers, SF	.825	1982	Johnny Moore, SA	9.6	2001	Jason Kidd, Pho	9.8
1964	Oscar Robertson, Cin	.868	1983	Magic Johnson, LA	10.5	2002	Andre Miller, Cle	10.9
1965	Oscar Robertson, Cin	.861	1984	Magic Johnson, LA	13.1			

Field Goal Percentage

Multiple winners: Wilt Chamberlain (9); Shaquille O'Neal (6); Artis Gilmore (4); Neil Johnston (3); Bob Feerick, Johnny Green, Alex Groza, Cedric Maxwell, Kevin McHale, Gheorghe Muresan, Kenny Sears and Buck Williams (2).

Year		Pct	Year		Pct	Year		Pct
1947	Bob Feerick, Wash	.401	1966	Wilt Chamberlain, Phi	.540	1985	James Donaldson, LAC	.637
1948	Bob Feerick, Wash	.340	1967	Wilt Chamberlain, Phi	.683	1986	Steve Johnson, SA	.632
1949	Arnie Risen, Roch	.423	1968	Wilt Chamberlain, Phi	.595	1987	Kevin McHale, Bos	.604
1950	Alex Groza, Indpls	.478	1969	Wilt Chamberlain, LA	.583	1988	Kevin McHale, Bos	.604
1951	Alex Groza, Indpls	.470	1970	Johnny Green, Cin	.559	1989	Dennis Rodman, Det.	.595
1952	Paul Arizin, Phi	.448	1971	Johnny Green, Cin	.587	1990	Mark West, Pho.	.625
1953	Neil Johnston, Phi	.452	1972	Wilt Chamberlain, LA	.649	1991	Buck Williams, Port	.602
1954	Ed Macauley, Bos	.486	1973	Wilt Chamberlain, LA	.727	1992	Buck Williams, Port	.604
1955	Larry Foust, Ft.W	.487	1974	Bob McAdoo, Buf	.547	1993	Cedric Ceballos, Pho	.576
1956	Neil Johnston, Phi.	.457	1975	Don Nelson, Bos	.539	1994	Shaquille O'Neal, Orl	.599
1957	Neil Johnston, Phi.	.447	1976	Wes Unseld, Wash	.561	1995	Chris Gatling, G.St	.633
1958	Jack Twyman, Cin	.452	1977	K. Abdul-Jabbar, LA	.579	1996	Gheorghe Muresan, Wash.	.584
1959	Kenny Sears, NY	.490	1978	Bobby Jones, Den	.578	1997	Gheorghe Muresan, Wash.	.604
1960	Kenny Sears, NY	.477	1979	Cedric Maxwell, Bos	.584	1998	Shaquille O'Neal, LAL	.584
1961	Wilt Chamberlain, Phi	.509	1980	Cedric Maxwell, Bos	.609	1999	Shaquille O'Neal, LAL	.576
1962	Walt Bellamy, Chi	.519	1981	Artis Gilmore, Chi.	.670	2000	Shaquille O'Neal, LAL	.574
1963	Wilt Chamberlain, SF	.528	1982	Artis Gilmore, Chi.	.652	2001	Shaquille O'Neal, LAL	.572
1964	Jerry Lucas, Cin	.527	1983	Artis Gilmore, SA	.626	2002	Shaquille O'Neal, LAL	.579
1965	W. Chamberlain, SF-Phi	.510	1984	Artis Gilmore, SA	.631			

Free Throw Percentage

Multiple winners: Bill Sharman (7); Rick Barry (6); Larry Bird and Reggie Miller (4); Mark Price and Dolph Schayes (3); Mahmoud Abdul-Rauf, Larry Costello, Ernie DiGregorio, Bob Feerick, Kyle Macy, Calvin Murphy, Oscar Robertson and Larry Siegfried (2).

Year		Pct	Year		Pct	Year		Pct
1947	Fred Scolari, Wash	.811	1966	Larry Siegfried, Bos	.881	1985	Kyle Macy, Pho	.907
1948	Bob Feerick, Wash	.788	1967	Adrian Smith, Cin	.903	1986	Larry Bird, Bos	.896
1949	Bob Feerick, Wash	.859	1968	Oscar Robertson, Cin	.873	1987	Larry Bird, Bos	.910
1950	Max Zaslofsky, Chi	.843	1969	Larry Siegfried, NY	.864	1988	Jack Sikma, Mil	.922
1951	Joe Fulks, Phi	.855	1970	Flynn Robinson, Mil	.898	1989	Magic Johnson, LAL	.911
1952	Bob Wanzer, Roch	.904	1971	Chet Walker, Chi	.859	1990	Larry Bird, Bos	.930
1953	Bill Sharman, Bos	.850	1972	Jack Marin, Bal	.894	1991	Reggie Miller, Ind	.918
1954	Bill Sharman, Bos	.844	1973	Rick Barry, G.St.	.902	1992	Mark Price, Cle	.947
1955	Bill Sharman, Bos	.897	1974	Ernie DiGregorio, Buf	.902	1993	Mark Price, Cle	.948
1956	Bill Sharman, Bos	.867	1975	Rick Barry, G.St.	.904	1994	M. Abdul-Rauf, Den	.956
1957	Bill Sharman, Bos	.905	1976	Rick Barry, G.St.	.923	1995	Spud Webb, Sac	.934
1958	Dolph Schayes, Syr	.904	1977	Ernie DiGregorio, Buf	.945	1996	M. Abdul-Rauf, Den	.930
1959	Bill Sharman, Bos	.932	1978	Rick Barry, G.St.	.924	1997	Mark Price, G.St.	.906
1960	Dolph Schayes, Syr	.892	1979	Rick Barry, Hou	.947	1998	Chris Mullin, Ind.	.939
1961	Bill Sharman, Bos	.921	1980	Rick Barry, Hou	.935	1999	Reggie Miller, Ind	.915
1962	Dolph Schayes, Syr	.896	1981	Calvin Murphy, Hou	.958	2000	Jeff Hornacek, Utah	.950
1963	Larry Costello, Syr	.881	1982	Kyle Macy, Pho	.899	2001	Reggie Miller, Ind	.928
1964	Oscar Robertson, Cin	.853	1983	Calvin Murphy, Hou	.920	2002	Reggie Miller, Ind	.911
1965	Larry Costello, Phi	.877	1984	Larry Bird, Bos	.888			

Blocked Shots

Decided by per game average since 1973-74 season.

Multiple winners: Kareem Abdul-Jabbar and Mark Eaton (4); George Johnson, Dikembe Mutombo and Hakeem Olajuwon (3); Manute Bol and Alonzo Mourning (2).

Year		Gm	No	Avg
1974	Elmore Smith, LA	81	393	4.85
1975	Kareem Abdul-Jabbar, Mil	65	212	3.26
1976	Kareem Abdul-Jabbar, LA	82	338	4.12
1977	Bill Walton, Port	65	211	3.25
1978	George Johnson, NJ	81	274	3.38
1979	Kareem Abdul-Jabbar, LA	80	316	3.95
1980	Kareem Abdul-Jabbar, LA	82	280	3.41
1981	George Johnson, SA	82	278	3.39
1982	George Johnson, SA	75	234	3.12
1983	Tree Rollins, Atl	80	343	4.29
1984	Mark Eaton, Utah	82	351	4.28
1985	Mark Eaton, Utah	82	456	5.56
1986	Manute Bol, Wash	80	397	4.96
1987	Mark Eaton, Utah	79	321	4.06
1988	Mark Eaton, Utah	82	304	3.71
1989	Manute Bol, G.St.	80	345	4.31
1990	Akeem Olajuwon, Hou	82	376	4.59
1991	Hakeem Olajuwon, Hou	56	221	3.95
1992	David Robinson, SA	68	305	4.49
1993	Hakeem Olajuwon, Hou	82	342	4.17
1994	Dikembe Mutombo, Den	82	336	4.10
1995	Dikembe Mutombo, Den	82	321	3.91
1996	Dikembe Mutombo, Den	74	332	4.49
1997	Shawn Bradley, Dal-NJ	73	248	3.40
1998	Marcus Camby, Tor	63	230	3.65
1999	Alonzo Mourning, Mia	46	180	3.91
2000	Alonzo Mourning, Mia	79	294	3.72
2001	Theo Ratliff, Phi-Atl	50	187	3.74
2002	Ben Wallace, Det	80	278	3.48

Note: Akeem Olajuwon changed the spelling of his first name to Hakeem during the 1990-91 season.

Steals

Decided by per game average since 1973-74 season.

Multiple winners: Michael Jordan, Micheal Ray Richardson and Alvin Robertson (3); Mookie Blaylock, Allen Iverson, Magic Johnson and John Stockton (2).

Year		Gm	No	Avg
1974	Larry Steele, Port	81	217	2.68
1975	Rick Barry, G.St.	80	228	2.85
1976	Slick Watts, Sea	82	261	3.18
1977	Don Buse, Ind	81	281	3.47
1978	Ron Lee, Pho	82	225	2.74
1979	M.L. Carr, Det	80	197	2.46
1980	Micheal Ray Richardson, NY	82	265	3.23
1981	Magic Johnson, LA	37	127	3.43
1982	Magic Johnson, LA	78	208	2.67
1983	Micheal Ray Richardson, G. ST-NJ	64	182	2.84
1984	Rickey Green, Utah	81	215	2.65
1985	Micheal Ray Richardson, NJ	82	243	2.96
1986	Alvin Robertson, SA	82	301	3.67
1987	Alvin Robertson, SA	81	260	3.21
1988	Michael Jordan, Chi	82	259	3.16
1989	John Stockton, Utah	82	263	3.21
1990	Michael Jordan, Chi	82	227	2.77
1991	Alvin Robertson, SA	81	246	3.04
1992	John Stockton, Utah	82	244	2.98
1993	Michael Jordan, Chi	78	221	2.83
1994	Nate McMillan, Sea	73	216	2.96
1995	Scottie Pippen, Chi	79	232	2.94
1996	Gary Payton, Sea	81	231	2.85
1997	Mookie Blaylock, Atl	78	212	2.72
1998	Mookie Blaylock, Atl	70	183	2.61
1999	Kendall Gill, NJ	50	134	2.68
2000	Eddie Jones, Cha	72	192	2.67
2001	Allen Iverson, Phi	71	178	2.51
2002	Allen Iverson, Phi	60	168	2.80

All-Time NBA Regular Season Leaders

Through the 2001-02 regular season.

CAREER

Players active in 2001-02 in **bold** type.

Points

		Yrs	Gm	Pts	Avg
1	Kareem Abdul-Jabbar	20	1560	38,387	24.6
2	**Karl Malone**	17	1353	34,707	25.7
3	Wilt Chamberlain	14	1045	31,419	30.1
4	**Michael Jordan**	14	990	30,652	31.0
5	Moses Malone	19	1329	27,409	20.6
6	Elvin Hayes	16	1303	27,313	21.0
7	**Hakeem Olajuwon**	18	1238	26,946	21.8
8	Oscar Robertson	14	1040	26,710	25.7
9	Dominique Wilkins	15	1074	26,668	24.8
10	John Havlicek	16	1270	26,395	20.8
11	Alex English	15	1193	25,613	21.5
12	Jerry West	14	932	25,192	27.0
13	**Patrick Ewing**	17	1183	24,815	21.0
14	Charles Barkley	16	1073	23,757	22.1
15	Robert Parish	21	1611	23,334	14.5
16	Adrian Dantley	15	955	23,177	24.3
17	Elgin Baylor	14	846	23,149	27.4
18	**Reggie Miller**	15	1173	22,623	19.3
19	Clyde Drexler	15	1086	22,195	20.4
20	Larry Bird	13	897	21,791	24.3
21	Hal Greer	15	1122	21,586	19.2
22	Walt Bellamy	14	1043	20,941	20.1
23	Bob Pettit	11	792	20,880	26.4
24	George Gervin	14	791	20,708	26.2
25	**Mitch Richmond**	14	976	20,497	21.0
26	**David Robinson**	13	923	20,244	21.9
27	Tom Chambers	16	1107	20,049	18.1
28	Bernard King	14	874	19,655	22.5
29	Walter Davis	15	1033	19,521	18.9
30	Terry Cummings	18	1183	19,460	16.4

Scoring Average

Minimum of 400 games or 10,000 points.

		Yrs	Gm	Pts	Avg
1	**Michael Jordan**	14	990	30,652	31.0
2	Wilt Chamberlain	14	1045	31,419	30.1
3	**Shaquille O'Neal**	10	675	18,634	27.6
4	Elgin Baylor	14	846	23,149	27.4
5	Jerry West	14	932	25,192	27.0
6	**Allen Iverson**	6	405	10,908	26.9
7	Bob Pettit	11	792	20,880	26.4
8	George Gervin	14	791	20,708	26.2
9	Oscar Robertson	14	1040	26,710	25.7
10	**Karl Malone**	17	1353	34,707	25.7
11	Dominique Wilkins	15	1074	26,668	24.8
12	Kareem Abdul-Jabbar	20	1560	38,387	24.6
13	Larry Bird	13	897	21,791	24.3
14	Adrian Dantley	15	955	23,177	24.3
15	Pete Maravich	10	658	15,948	24.2
16	Rick Barry	10	794	18,395	23.2
17	Paul Arizin	10	713	16,266	22.8
18	George Mikan	9	520	11,764	22.6
19	Bernard King	14	874	19,655	22.5
20	David Thompson	8	509	11,264	22.1
21	Charles Barkley	16	1073	23,757	22.1
22	**Chris Webber**	9	529	11,667	22.1
23	Bob McAdoo	14	852	18,787	22.1
24	Julius Erving	11	836	18,364	22.0
25	**David Robinson**	13	923	20,244	21.9
26	**Hakeem Olajuwon**	18	1238	26,946	21.8
27	Alex English	15	1193	25,613	21.5
28	**Jerry Stackhouse**	8	512	10,867	21.2
29	**Glenn Robinson**	8	568	12,010	21.1
30	**Mitch Richmond**	14	976	20,497	21.0

All-Time NBA Regular Season Leaders (Cont.)

NBA-ABA Top 20

Points

All-Time combined regular season scoring leaders, including ABA service (1968-76). NBA players with ABA experience are listed in CAPITAL letters. Players active during 2001-02 are in **bold** type.

		Yrs	Pts	Avg
1	Kareem Abdul-Jabbar	20	38,387	24.6
2	**Karl Malone**	17	34,707	25.7
3	Wilt Chamberlain	14	31,419	30.1
4	**Michael Jordan**	14	30,652	31.0
5	JULIUS ERVING	16	30,026	24.2
6	MOSES MALONE	21	29,580	20.3
7	DAN ISSEL	15	27,482	22.6
8	Elvin Hayes	16	27,313	21.0
9	**Hakeem Olajuwon**	18	26,946	21.8
10	Oscar Robertson	14	26,710	25.7
11	Dominique Wilkins	15	26,668	24.8
12	GEORGE GERVIN	14	26,595	25.1
13	John Havlicek	16	26,395	20.8
14	Alex English	15	25,613	21.5
15	RICK BARRY	14	25,279	24.8
16	Jerry West	14	25,192	27.0
17	ARTIS GILMORE	17	24,941	18.8
18	**Patrick Ewing**	17	24,815	21.0
19	Charles Barkley	16	23,757	22.1
20	Robert Parish	21	23,334	14.5

ABA Totals: BARRY (4 yrs, 226 gm, 6884 pts, 30.5 avg); ERVING (5 yrs, 407 gm, 11,662 pts, 28.7 avg); GERVIN (4 yrs, 269 gm, 5887 pts, 21.9 avg); GILMORE (5 yrs, 420 gm, 9362 pts, 22.3 avg); ISSEL (6 yrs, 500 gm, 12,823 pts, 25.6 avg); MALONE (2 yrs, 126 gm, 2171 pts, 17.2 avg).

Field Goals

		Yrs	FG	Att	Pct
1	Kareem Abdul-Jabbar	20	15,837	28,307	.559
2	**Karl Malone**	17	12,737	24,521	.519
3	Wilt Chamberlain	14	12,681	23,497	.540
4	**Michael Jordan**	14	11,513	23,010	.500
5	Elvin Hayes	16	10,976	24,272	.452
6	**Hakeem Olajuwon**	18	10,749	20,991	.512
7	Alex English	15	10,659	21,036	.507
8	John Havlicek	16	10,513	23,930	.439
9	Dominique Wilkins	15	9,963	21,589	.461
10	Robert Parish	21	9,614	17,914	.537

Note: If field goals made in the ABA are included, consider these NBA-ABA totals: Julius Erving (11,818), Dan Issel (10,431), George Gervin (10,368), Moses Malone (10,277) and Rick Barry (9,695).

Free Throws

		Yrs	FT	Att	Pct
1	**Karl Malone**	17	9145	12,342	.741
2	Moses Malone	19	8531	11,090	.769
3	Oscar Robertson	14	7694	9,185	.838
4	Jerry West	14	7160	8,801	.814
5	**Michael Jordan**	14	7061	8,448	.836
6	Dolph Schayes	16	6979	8,273	.844
7	Adrian Dantley	15	6832	8,351	.818
8	Kareem Abdul-Jabbar	20	6712	9,304	.721
9	Charles Barkley	16	6349	8,643	.734
10	Bob Pettit	11	6182	8,119	.761

Note: If free throws made in the ABA are included, consider these totals: Moses Malone (9,018), Dan Issel (6,591), and Julius Erving (6,256).

Assists

		Yrs	Gm	No	Avg
1	**John Stockton**	18	1422	15,177	10.7
2	Magic Johnson	13	906	10,141	11.2
3	Oscar Robertson	14	1040	9,887	9.5
4	**Mark Jackson**	15	1172	9,840	8.4
5	Isiah Thomas	13	979	9,061	9.3
6	**Rod Strickton**	14	970	7,490	7.7
7	Maurice Cheeks	15	1101	7,392	6.7
8	Lenny Wilkens	15	1077	7,211	6.7
9	Bob Cousy	14	924	6,955	7.5
10	**Gary Payton**	12	947	6,927	7.3

Rebounds

		Yrs	Gm	No	Avg
1	Wilt Chamberlain	14	1045	23,924	22.9
2	Bill Russell	13	963	21,620	22.5
3	Kareem Abdul-Jabbar	20	1560	17,440	11.2
4	Elvin Hayes	16	1303	16,279	12.5
5	Moses Malone	19	1329	16,212	12.2
6	Robert Parish	21	1611	14,715	9.1
7	Nate Thurmond	14	964	14,464	15.0
8	Walt Bellamy	14	1043	14,241	13.7
9	**Karl Malone**	17	1353	13,973	10.3
10	Wes Unseld	13	984	13,769	14.0

Note: If rebounds accumulated in the ABA are included, consider the following totals: Moses Malone (17,834) and Artis Gilmore (16,330).

Steals

		Yrs	Gm	No
1	**John Stockton**	18	1422	3128
2	**Michael Jordan**	14	990	2391
3	Maurice Cheeks	15	1101	2310
4	Clyde Drexler	15	1086	2207
5	**Scottie Pippen**	15	1091	2181

Note: Steals have only been an official stat since the 1973-74 season.

Blocked Shots

		Yrs	Gm	No
1	**Hakeem Olajuwon**	18	1238	3830
2	Kareem Abdul-Jabbar	20	1560	3189
3	Mark Eaton	11	875	3064
4	**Patrick Ewing**	17	1183	2894
5	**David Robinson**	13	923	2843

Note: Blocked shots have only been an official stat since the 1973-74 season. Also, note that if ABA records are included, consider the following block totals: Artis Gilmore (3,178).

Games Played

		Yrs	Career	Gm
1	Robert Parish	21	1976-97	1611
2	Kareem Abdul-Jabbar	20	1970-89	1560
3	**John Stockton**	18	1984–	1422
4	**Karl Malone**	17	1985–	1353
5	Moses Malone	19	1976-95	1329

Note: If ABA records are included, consider the following game totals: Moses Malone (1,455) and Artis Gilmore (1,329).

Personal Fouls

		Yrs	Gm	Fouls	DQ
1	Kareem Abdul-Jabbar	20	1560	4657	48
2	Robert Parish	21	1611	4443	86
3	**Hakeem Olajuwon**	18	1238	4383	80
4	Charles Oakley	17	1183	4323	63
5	Buck Williams	17	1307	4267	58

Note: If ABA records are included, consider the following personal foul totals: Artis Gilmore (4,529) and Caldwell Jones (4,436).

SINGLE SEASON

Scoring Average

		Season	Avg
1	Wilt Chamberlain, Phi	1961-62	50.4
2	Wilt Chamberlain, SF	1962-63	44.8
3	Wilt Chamberlain, Phi	1960-61	38.4
4	Elgin Baylor, LA	1961-62	38.3
5	Wilt Chamberlain, Phi	1959-60	37.6
6	Michael Jordan, Chi	1986-87	37.1
7	Wilt Chamberlain, SF	1963-64	36.9
8	Rick Barry, SF	1966-67	35.6
9	Michael Jordan, Chi	1987-88	35.0
10	Elgin Baylor, LA	1960-61	34.8
	Kareem Abdul-Jabbar, Mil	1971-72	34.8

Field Goal Pct.

		Season	Pct
1	Wilt Chamberlain, LA	1972-73	.727
2	Wilt Chamberlain, SF	1966-67	.683
3	Artis Gilmore, Chi	1980-81	.670
4	Artis Gilmore, Chi	1981-82	.652
5	Wilt Chamberlain, LA	1971-72	.649

Free Throw Pct.

		Season	Pct
1	Calvin Murphy, Hou	1980-81	.958
2	Mahmoud Abdul-Rauf, Den	1993-94	.956
3	Mark Price, Cle	1992-93	.948
4	Mark Price, Cle	1991-92	.947
	Rick Barry, Hou	1978-79	.947

3-Pt Field Goal Pct.

		Season	Pct
1	Steve Kerr, Chi	1994-95	.524
2	Jon Sundvold, Mia	1988-89	.522
3	Tim Legler, Wash	1995-96	.522
4	Steve Kerr, Chi	1995-96	.515
5	Detlef Schrempf, Sea	1994-95	.514

Assists

		Season	Avg
1	John Stockton, Utah	1989-90	14.5
2	John Stockton, Utah	1990-91	14.2
3	Isiah Thomas, Det	1984-85	13.9
4	John Stockton, Utah	1987-88	13.8
5	John Stockton, Utah	1991-92	13.7
6	John Stockton, Utah	1988-89	13.6
7	Kevin Porter, Det	1978-79	13.4
8	Magic Johnson, LAL	1983-84	13.1
9	Magic Johnson, LAL	1988-89	12.8
10	Magic Johnson, LAL	1984-85	12.6
	John Stockton, Utah	1993-94	12.6

Rebounds

		Season	Avg
1	Wilt Chamberlain, Phi	1960-61	27.2
2	Wilt Chamberlain, Phi	1959-60	27.0
3	Wilt Chamberlain, Phi	1961-62	25.7
4	Bill Russell, Bos	1963-64	24.7
5	Wilt Chamberlain, Phi	1965-66	24.6

Blocked Shots

		Season	Avg
1	Mark Eaton, Utah	1984-85	5.56
2	Manute Bol, Wash	1985-86	4.96
3	Elmore Smith, LA	1973-74	4.85
4	Mark Eaton, Utah	1985-86	4.61
5	Hakeem Olajuwon, Hou	1989-90	4.59

Steals

		Season	Avg
1	Alvin Robertson, SA	1985-86	3.67
2	Don Buse, Ind	1976-77	3.47
3	Magic Johnson, LAL	1980-81	3.43
4	Micheal Ray Richardson, NY	1979-80	3.23
5	Alvin Robertson, SA	1986-87	3.21

SINGLE GAME

Points

	Date	FG-FT	Pts
Wilt Chamberlain, Phi vs NY	3/2/62	36-28-	100
Wilt Chamberlain, Phi vs LA***	12/8/61	31-16-	78
Wilt Chamberlain, Phi vs Chi	1/13/62	29-15-	73
Wilt Chamberlain, SF at NY	11/16/62	29-15-	73
David Thompson, Den at Det	4/9/78	28-17-	73
Wilt Chamberlain, SF at LA	11/3/62	29-14-	72
Elgin Baylor, LA at NY	11/15/60	28-15-	71
David Robinson, SA at LAC	4/24/94	26-18-	71
Wilt Chamberlain, SF at Syr	3/10/63	27-16-	70
Michael Jordan, Chi at Cle*	3/28/90	23-21-	69
Wilt Chamberlain, Phi at Chi	12/16/67	30- 8-	68
Pete Maravich, NO vs NYK	2/25/77	26-16-	68
Wilt Chamberlain, Phi vs NY	3/9/61	27-13-	67
Wilt Chamberlain, Phi at St. L	2/17/62	26-15-	67
Wilt Chamberlain, Phi vs NY	2/25/62	25-17-	67
Wilt Chamberlain, SF vs LA	1/11/63	28-11-	67
Wilt Chamberlain, LA vs Pho	2/9/69	29- 8-	66
Wilt Chamberlain, Phi at Cin	2/13/62	24-17-	65
Wilt Chamberlain, Phi at St. L	2/27/62	25-15-	65
Wilt Chamberlain, Phi vs LA	2/7/66	28- 9-	65
Elgin Baylor, Mpls vs Bos	11/8/59	25-14-	64
Rick Barry, G.St. vs Port	3/26/74	30- 4-	64
Michael Jordan, Chi vs Orl	1/16/93	27- 9-	64

*Overtime
***Triple overtime.

Note: Wilt Chamberlain's 100-point game vs New York was played at Hershey, Penn.

Field Goals

	Date	FG	Att
Wilt Chamberlain, Phi vs NY	3/2/62	36	63
Wilt Chamberlain, Phi vs LA***	12/8/61	31	62
Wilt Chamberlain, Phi at Chi	12/16/67	30	40
Rick Barry, G.St. vs Port	2/26/74	30	45

Wilt Chamberlain made 29 four times.

***Triple overtime.

Free Throws

	Date	FT	Att
Wilt Chamberlain, Phi vs NY	3/2/62	28	32
Adrian Dantley, Utah vs Hou	1/4/84	28	29
Adrian Dantley, Utah vs Den	11/25/83	27	31
Adrian Dantley, Utah vs Dal	10/31/80	26	29
Michael Jordan, Chi vs NJ	2/26/87	26	27

3-Pt Field Goals

	Date	No
Dennis Scott, Orl vs Atl	4/18/96	11
Brian Shaw, Mia at Mil	4/8/93	10
Joe Dumars, Det vs Min	11/8/94	10
George McCloud, Dal vs Pho	12/16/95	10*

Many tied with 9 each

* Overtime

All-Time NBA Regular Season Leaders (Cont.)

Assists

	Date	No
Scott Skiles, Orl vs Den	12/30/90	30
Kevin Porter, NJ vs Hou	2/24/78	29
Bob Cousy, Bos vs Mpls	2/27/59	28
Guy Rodgers, SF vs St.L	3/14/63	28
John Stockton, Utah vs SA	1/15/91	28

Rebounds

	Date	No
Wilt Chamberlain, Phi vs Bos	11/24/60	55
Bill Russell, Bos vs Syr	2/5/60	51
Bill Russell, Bos vs Phi	11/16/57	49
Bill Russell, Bos vs Det	3/11/65	49
Wilt Chamberlain, Phi vs Syr	2/6/60	45
Wilt Chamberlain, Phi vs LA	1/21/61	45

Blocked Shots

	Date	No
Elmore Smith, LA vs Port	10/28/73	17
Manute Bol, Wash vs Atl	1/25/86	15
Manute Bol, Wash vs Ind	2/26/87	15
Shaquille O'Neal, Orl at NJ	11/20/93	15

Steals

	Date	No
Larry Kenon, San Antonio at KC	12/26/76	11
Kendall Gill, NJ vs Mia	4/3/99	11

14 different players tied with 10 each, including Alvin Robertson, who had 10 steals in a game four times.

All-Time Winningest NBA Coaches

Top 25 NBA career victories through the 2001-02 season. Career, regular season and playoff records are noted along with NBA titles won. Coaches active during 2001-02 season in **bold** type.

		Career			Regular Season			Playoffs			
		Yrs	W	L	Pct	W	L	Pct	W	L	Pct	NBA Titles
1	**Lenny Wilkens**	29	**1348**	1150	.540	1268	1056	.546	80	94	.460	1 (1979)
2	**Pat Riley**	20	**1240**	612	.670	1085	512	.679	155	100	.608	4 (1982,85,87-88)
3	**Don Nelson**	24	**1095**	877	.555	1036	806	.562	59	71	.454	None
4	Red Auerbach	20	**1037**	548	.654	938	479	.662	99	69	.589	9 (1957, 59-66)
5	Bill Fitch	25	**999**	1160	.463	944	1106	.460	55	54	.505	1 (1981)
6	Dick Motta	25	**991**	1087	.477	935	1017	.479	56	70	.444	1 (1978)
7	Jack Ramsay	21	**908**	841	.519	864	783	.525	44	58	.431	1 (1977)
8	**Jerry Sloan**	17	**905**	562	.617	828	486	.630	77	76	.503	None
9	Larry Brown	19	**894**	717	.555	831	651	.561	63	66	.488	None
10	**Phil Jackson**	12	**882**	312	.739	726	258	.738	156	54	.743	9 (1991-93,96-98,00-02)
11	Cotton Fitzsimmons	21	**867**	824	.513	832	775	.518	35	49	.417	None
12	Gene Shue	22	**814**	908	.473	784	861	.477	30	47	.390	None
13	Red Holzman	18	**754**	652	.536	696	604	.535	58	48	.547	2 (1970, 73)
	John MacLeod	18	**754**	711	.515	707	657	.518	47	54	.465	None
15	George Karl	15	**723**	522	.581	666	459	.592	57	63	.475	None
16	Chuck Daly	14	**713**	488	.594	638	437	.593	75	51	.595	2 (1989-90)
17	Doug Moe	15	**661**	579	.533	628	529	.543	33	50	.398	None
18	K.C. Jones	10	**603**	309	.661	522	252	.674	81	57	.587	2 (1984,86)
19	**Rick Adelman**	12	**597**	411	.592	544	361	.601	50	50	.515	None
20	Del Harris	14	**594**	507	.540	556	457	.549	38	50	.432	None
21	Mike Fratello	14	**592**	499	.543	572	465	.552	20	34	.370	None
22	Al Attles	14	**588**	548	.518	557	518	.518	31	30	.508	1 (1975)
23	Billy Cunningham	8	**520**	235	.689	454	196	.698	66	39	.629	1 (1983)
24	Alex Hannum	12	**508**	446	.537	471	412	.533	47	34	.580	2 (1958, 67)
25	Rudy Tomjanovich	11	**511**	397	.563	460	358	.562	51	39	.567	2 (1994-95)

Note: The NBA does not recognize records from the National Basketball League (1937-49), the American Basketball League (1961-62) or the American Basketball Assn. (1968-76), so the following NBL, ABL and ABA overall coaching records are not included above: NBL–**John Kundla** (51-19 and a title in 1 year). ABA–**Larry Brown** (249-129 in 4 yrs), **Alex Hannum** (194-164 and one title in 4 yrs), **K.C. Jones** (30-58 in 1 yr); **Kevin Loughery** (189-95 and one title in 3 yrs).

Where They Coached

Adelman—Portland (1988-94), Golden State (1995-97), Sacramento (1998–); **Attles**—Golden St. (1970-80,80-83); **Auerbach**—Washington (1946-49), Tri-Cities (1949-50), Boston (1950-66); **Brown**—Denver (1976-79), New Jersey (1981-83), San Antonio (1988-92), LA Clippers (1992-93), Indiana (1993-97), Philadelphia (1997–); **Cunningham**—Philadelphia (1977-85); **Daly**—Cleveland (1981-82), Detroit (1983-92), New Jersey (1992-94), Orlando (1997-99); **Fitch**—Cleveland (1970-79), Boston (1979-83), Houston (1983-88), New Jersey (1989-92), LA Clippers (1994-98); **Fitzsimmons**—Phoenix (1970-72), Atlanta (1972-76), Buffalo (1977-78), Kansas City (1978-84), San Antonio (1984-86), Phoenix (1988-92, 95-96); **Fratello**—Atlanta (1980-90), Cleveland (1993-99).

Hannum—St. Louis (1957-58), Syracuse (1960-63), San Francisco (1963-66), Phila. 76ers (1966-68), Houston (1970-71); **Harris**—Houston (1979-83), Milwaukee (1987-92), LA Lakers (1994-99); **Holzman**—Milwaukee-St. Louis Hawks (1954-57), NY Knicks (1968-77,78-82); **Jackson**—Chicago (1989-98), LA Lakers (1999–); **Jones**—Washington (1973-76), Boston (1983-88), Seattle (1990-92); **Karl**—Cleveland (1984-86); Golden St. (1986-88), Seattle (1991-98), Milwaukee (1999–); **MacLeod**—Phoenix (1973-87), Dallas (1987-89), NY Knicks (1990-91); **Moe**—San Antonio (1976-80), Denver (1981-90), Philadelphia (1992-93).

Motta—Chicago (1968-76), Washington (1976-80), Dallas (1980-87), Sacramento (1990-91), Dallas (1994-96), Denver (1997); **Nelson**—Milwaukee (1976-87), Golden St. (1988-95), New York (1995-96), Dallas (1997–); **Ramsay**—Philadelphia (1968-72), Buffalo (1972-76), Portland (1976-86), Indiana (1986-89); **Riley**—LA Lakers (1981-90), New York (1991-95), Miami (1995–); **Shue**—Baltimore (1967-73), Philadelphia (1973-77), San Diego Clippers (1978-80), Washington (1980-86), LA Clippers (1987-89); **Sloan**—Chicago (1979-82), Utah (1988–); **Tomjanovich**—Houston (1991–); **Wilkens**—Seattle (1969-72), Portland (1974-76), Seattle (1977-85), Cleveland (1986-93), Atlanta (1993-00), Toronto (2000–).

Top Winning Percentages

Minimum of 350 victories, including playoffs; coaches active during 2001-02 season in **bold** type.

		Yrs	W	L	Pct
1	**Phil Jackson**	12	882	312	**.739**
2	Billy Cunningham	8	520	235	**.689**
3	**Pat Riley**	20	1240	612	**.670**
4	K.C. Jones	10	603	309	**.661**
5	Red Auerbach	20	1037	548	**.654**
6	**Jerry Sloan**	17	905	562	**.617**
7	Tommy Heinsohn	9	474	296	**.616**
8	Chuck Daly	14	713	488	**.594**
9	**Rick Adelman**	12	597	411	**.592**
10	Larry Costello	10	467	323	**.591**
11	John Kundla	11	485	338	**.589**
12	**George Karl**	15	723	522	**.581**
13	Bill Sharman	7	368	267	**.580**
14	Al Cervi	9	359	267	**.573**
15	**Rudy Tomjanovich**	11	511	397	**.563**
16	Joe Lapchick	9	356	277	**.562**
17	**Don Nelson**	24	1095	877	**.555**
18	**Larry Brown**	19	894	717	**.555**
19	Mike Fratello	14	592	499	**.543**
20	Bill Russell	8	375	317	**.542**
21	**Lenny Wilkens**	29	1348	1150	**.540**
22	Del Harris	14	594	507	**.540**
23	Alex Hannum	12	518	446	**.537**
24	Red Holzman	18	754	652	**.536**
25	Doug Moe	15	661	579	**.533**

Active Coaches' Victories

Through 2001-02 season, including playoffs.

		Yrs	W	L	Pct
1	Lenny Wilkens, Toronto	29	1348	1150	.540
2	Pat Riley, Miami	20	1240	612	.670
3	Don Nelson, Dallas	24	1095	877	.555
4	Jerry Sloan, Utah	17	905	562	.617
5	Larry Brown, Philadelphia	19	894	717	.555
6	Phil Jackson, LA Lakers	12	882	312	.739
7	George Karl, Milwaukee	15	723	522	.581
8	Rick Adelman, Sacramento	12	597	411	.592
9	Rudy Tomjanovich, Houston	11	511	397	.563
10	Doug Collins, Washington	7	310	265	.539
	Gregg Popovich, San Antonio	6	310	185	.626
12	Don Chaney, New York	10	285	425	.401
13	Phil Saunders, Minnesota	7	282	263	.517
14	Paul Silas, New Orleans	4	250	300	.455
15	John Lucas, Cleveland	5	171	232	.424
16	Alvin Gentry, LA Clippers	6	160	190	.457
17	Doc Rivers, Orlando	3	130	124	.512
18	Byron Scott, New Jersey	2	89	95	.484
19	Isiah Thomas, Indiana	2	86	87	.497
20	Nate McMillan, Seattle	2	85	69	.552
21	Jim O'Brien, Boston	2	82	64	.564
22	Sidney Lowe, Memphis	4	79	220	.264
23	Lon Kruger, Atlanta	2	58	106	.354
24	Rick Carlisle, Detroit	1	54	38	.587
25	Maurice Cheeks, Portland	1	49	36	.576
26	Bill Cartwright, Chicago	1	17	38	.309
27	Frank Johnson, Phoenix	1	11	20	.355
28	Jeff Bzdelik, Denver	0	0	0	—
	Eric Musselman, Golden St.	0	0	0	—

Annual Awards
Most Valuable Player

The Maurice Podoloff Trophy for regular season MVP. Named after the first commissioner (then president) of the NBA. Winners first selected by the NBA players (1956-80) then a national panel of pro basketball writers and broadcasters (since 1981). Winners' scoring averages are provided; (*) indicates led league.

Multiple winners: Kareem Abdul-Jabbar (6); Michael Jordan and Bill Russell (5); Wilt Chamberlain (4); Larry Bird, Magic Johnson and Moses Malone (3); Karl Malone and Bob Pettit (2).

Year		Avg
1956	Bob Pettit, St. Louis, F	25.7*
1957	Bob Cousy, Boston, G	20.6
1958	Bill Russell, Boston, C	16.6
1959	Bob Pettit, St. Louis, F	29.2*
1960	Wilt Chamberlain, Philadelphia, C	37.6*
1961	Bill Russell, Boston, C	16.9
1962	Bill Russell, Boston, C	18.9
1963	Bill Russell, Boston, C	16.8
1964	Oscar Robertson, Cincinnati, G	31.4
1965	Bill Russell, Boston, C	14.1
1966	Wilt Chamberlain, Philadelphia, C	33.5*
1967	Wilt Chamberlain, Philadelphia, C	24.1
1968	Wilt Chamberlain, Philadelphia, C	24.3
1969	Wes Unseld, Baltimore, C	13.8
1970	Willis Reed, New York, C	21.7
1971	Lew Alcindor, Milwaukee, C	31.7*
1972	Kareem Abdul-Jabbar, Milwaukee, C	34.8*
1973	Dave Cowens, Boston, C	20.5
1974	Kareem Abdul-Jabbar, Milwaukee, C	27.0
1975	Bob McAdoo, Buffalo, F	34.5*
1976	Kareem Abdul-Jabbar, LA, C	27.7
1977	Kareem Abdul-Jabbar, LA, C	26.2
1978	Bill Walton, Portland, C	18.9
1979	Moses Malone, Houston, C	24.8
1980	Kareem Abdul-Jabbar, LA, C	24.8
1981	Julius Erving, Philadelphia, F	24.6
1982	Moses Malone, Houston, C	31.1
1983	Moses Malone, Philadelphia, C	24.5
1984	Larry Bird, Boston, F	24.2
1985	Larry Bird, Boston, F	28.7
1986	Larry Bird, Boston, F	25.8
1987	Magic Johnson, LAL, G	23.9
1988	Michael Jordan, Chicago, G	35.0*
1989	Magic Johnson, LAL, G	22.5
1990	Magic Johnson, LAL, G	22.3
1991	Michael Jordan, Chicago, G	31.5*
1992	Michael Jordan, Chicago, G	30.1*
1993	Charles Barkley, Phoenix, F	25.6
1994	Hakeem Olajuwon, Houston, C	27.3
1995	David Robinson, San Antonio, C	27.6
1996	Michael Jordan, Chicago, G	30.4*
1997	Karl Malone, Utah, F	27.4
1998	Michael Jordan, Chicago, G	28.7*
1999	Karl Malone, Utah, F	23.8
2000	Shaquille O'Neal, LAL, C	29.7*
2001	Allen Iverson, Philadelphia, G	31.1*
2002	Tim Duncan, San Antonio, C	25.5

Note: Lew Alcindor changed his name to Kareem Abdul-Jabbar after the 1970-71 season.

Annual Awards (Cont.)
Rookie of the Year

The Eddie Gottlieb Trophy for outstanding rookie of the regular season. Named after the pro basketball pioneer and owner-coach of the first NBA champion Philadelphia Warriors. Winners selected by a national panel of pro basketball writers and broadcasters. Winners' scoring averages provided; (*) indicates led league; winners who were also named MVP are in **bold** type.

Year		Avg	Year		Avg
1953	Don Meineke, Ft. Wayne, F	10.8	1979	Phil Ford, Kansas City, G	15.9
1954	Ray Felix, Baltimore, C	17.6	1980	Larry Bird, Boston, F	21.3
1955	Bob Pettit, Milwaukee Hawks, F.	20.4	1981	Darrell Griffith, Utah, G	20.6
1956	Maurice Stokes, Rochester, F/C	16.8	1982	Buck Williams, New Jersey, F	15.5
1957	Tommy Heinsohn, Boston, F	16.2	1983	Terry Cummings, San Diego, F	23.7
1958	Woody Sauldsberry, Philadelphia, F/C	12.8	1984	Ralph Sampson, Houston, C	21.0
1959	Elgin Baylor, Minneapolis, F	24.9	1985	Michael Jordan, Chicago, G	28.2
1960	**Wilt Chamberlain**, Philadelphia, C	37.6*	1986	Patrick Ewing, New York, C	20.0
1961	Oscar Robertson, Cincinnati, G	30.5	1987	Chuck Person, Indiana, F	18.8
1962	Walt Bellamy, Chicago Packers, C	31.6	1988	Mark Jackson, New York, G	13.6
1963	Terry Dischinger, Chicago Zephyrs, F	25.5	1989	Mitch Richmond, Golden St., G	22.0
1964	Jerry Lucas, Cincinnati, F/C	17.7	1990	David Robinson, San Antonio, C	24.3
1965	Willis Reed, New York, C	19.5	1991	Derrick Coleman, New Jersey, F	18.4
1966	Rick Barry, San Francisco, F	25.7	1992	Larry Johnson, Charlotte, F	19.2
1967	Dave Bing, Detroit, G	20.0	1993	Shaquille O'Neal, Orlando,C	23.4
1968	Earl Monroe, Baltimore, G	24.3	1994	Chris Webber, Golden St., F	17.5
1969	**Wes Unseld**, Baltimore, C	13.8	1995	Grant Hill, Detroit, F	19.9
1970	Lew Alcindor, Milwaukee Bucks, C	28.8		& Jason Kidd, Dallas, G	11.7
1971	Dave Cowens, Boston, C	17.0	1996	Damon Stoudamire, Toronto, G	19.0
	& Geoff Petrie, Portland, G	24.8	1997	Allen Iverson, Philadelphia, G	23.5
1972	Sidney Wicks, Portland, F	24.5	1998	Tim Duncan, San Antonio, F/C	21.6
1973	Bob McAdoo, Buffalo, C/F	18.0	1999	Vince Carter, Toronto, F	18.3
1974	Ernie DiGregorio, Buffalo, G	15.2	2000	Elton Brand, Chicago, F	20.1
1975	Keith Wilkes, Golden St., F	14.2		& Steve Francis, Houston, G	18.0
1976	Alvan Adams, Phoenix, C	19.0	2001	Mike Miller, Orlando, G/F	11.9
1977	Adrian Dantley, Buffalo, F	20.3	2002	Pau Gasol, Memphis, F	17.6
1978	Walter Davis, Phoenix, G	24.2			

Note: The Chicago Packers changed their name to the Zephyrs after 1961-62 season. Also, Lew Alcindor changed his name to Kareem Abdul-Jabbar after the 1970-71 season.

Sixth Man Award

Awarded to the Best Player Off the Bench for the regular season. Winners selected by a national panel of pro basketball writers and broadcasters. **Multiple winners:** Kevin McHale, Ricky Pierce and Detlef Schrempf (2).

Year		Year		Year	
1983	Bobby Jones, Phi., F	1990	Ricky Pierce, Mil., G/F	1997	John Starks, NY, G
1984	Kevin McHale, Bos., F	1991	Detlef Schrempf, Ind., F	1998	Danny Manning, Pho., F
1985	Kevin McHale, Bos., F	1992	Detlef Schrempf, Ind., F	1999	Darrell Armstrong, Orl., G
1986	Bill Walton, Bos., F/C	1993	Cliff Robinson, Port., F	2000	Rodney Rogers, Pho., F
1987	Ricky Pierce, Mil., G/F	1994	Dell Curry, Char., G	2001	Aaron McKie, Phi., G
1988	Roy Tarpley, Dal., F	1995	Anthony Mason, NY, F	2002	Corliss Williamson, Det., F
1989	Eddie Johnson, Pho., F	1996	Toni Kukoc, Chi., F		

Number One Draft Choices

Overall first choices in the NBA draft since the abolition of the territorial draft in 1966. Players who became Rookie of the Year are in **bold** type. The draft lottery began in 1985.

Year		Overall 1st Pick	Year		Overall 1st Pick
1966	New York	Cazzie Russell, Michigan	1985	New York	**Patrick Ewing**, Georgetown
1967	Detroit	Jimmy Walker, Providence	1986	Cleveland	Brad Daugherty, N. Carolina
1968	San Diego	Elvin Hayes, Houston	1987	San Antonio	**David Robinson**, Navy
1969	Milwaukee	**Lew Alcindor**, UCLA	1988	LA Clippers	Danny Manning, Kansas
1970	Detroit	Bob Lanier, St. Bonaventure	1989	Sacramento	Pervis Ellison, Louisville
1971	Cleveland	Austin Carr, Notre Dame	1990	New Jersey	**Derrick Coleman**, Syracuse
1972	Portland	LaRue Martin, Loyola-Chicago	1991	Charlotte	**Larry Johnson**, UNLV
1973	Philadelphia	Doug Collins, Illinois St.	1992	Orlando	**Shaquille O'Neal**, LSU
1974	Portland	Bill Walton, UCLA	1993	Orlando	**Chris Webber**, Michigan
1975	Atlanta	David Thompson, N.C. State	1994	Milwaukee	Glenn Robinson, Purdue
1976	Houston	John Lucas, Maryland	1995	Golden St.	Joe Smith, Maryland
1977	Milwaukee	Kent Benson, Indiana	1996	Philadelphia	**Allen Iverson**, Georgetown
1978	Portland	Mychal Thompson, Minnesota	1997	San Antonio	**Tim Duncan**, Wake Forest
1979	LA Lakers	Magic Johnson, Michigan St.	1998	LA Clippers	Michael Olowokandi, Pacific
1980	Golden St.	Joe Barry Carroll, Purdue	1999	Chicago	**Elton Brand**, Duke
1981	Dallas	Mark Aguirre, DePaul	2000	New Jersey	Kenyon Martin, Cincinnati
1982	LA Lakers	James Worthy, N. Carolina	2001	Washington	Kwame Brown, Glynn Acad.
1983	Houston	**Ralph Sampson**, Virginia	2002	Houston	Yao Ming, China
1984	Houston	Akeem Olajuwon, Houston			

Note: Lew Alcindor changed his name to Kareem Abdul-Jabbar after the 1970-71 season; Akeem Olajuwon changed his first name to Hakeem in 1991; in 1975 David Thompson signed with Denver of the ABA and did not play for Atlanta; David Robinson joined NBA for 1989-90 season after fulfilling military obligation.

Defensive Player of the Year

Awarded to the Best Defensive Player for the regular season. Winners selected by a national panel of pro basketball writers and broadcasters.

Multiple winners: Dikembe Mutombo (4); Mark Eaton, Sidney Moncrief, Alonzo Mourning, Hakeem Olajuwon and Dennis Rodman (2).

Year	Year	Year
1983 Sidney Moncrief, Mil., G	1990 Dennis Rodman, Det., F	1996 Gary Payton, Sea., G
1984 Sidney Moncrief, Mil., G	1991 Dennis Rodman, Det., F	1997 Dikembe Mutombo, Atl., C
1985 Mark Eaton, Utah, C	1992 David Robinson, SA, C	1998 Dikembe Mutombo, Atl., C
1986 Alvin Robertson, SA, G	1993 Hakeem Olajuwon, Hou., C	1999 Alonzo Mourning, Mia., C
1987 Michael Cooper, LAL, F	1994 Hakeem Olajuwon, Hou., C	2000 Alonzo Mourning, Mia., C
1988 Michael Jordan, Chi., G	1995 Dikembe Mutombo, Den., C	2001 Dikembe Mutombo, Atl.-Phi., C
1989 Mark Eaton, Utah, C		2002 Ben Wallace, Det., C/F

Most Improved Player

Awarded to the Most Improved Player for the regular season. Winners selected by a national panel of pro basketball writers and broadcasters.

Year	Year	Year
1986 Alvin Robertson, SA, G	1992 Pervis Ellison, Wash., C	1997 Isaac Austin, Miami, C
1987 Dale Ellis, Sea., G	1993 Mahmoud Abdul-Rauf, Den., G	1998 Alan Henderson, Atl., F
1988 Kevin Duckworth, Port., C	1994 Don MacLean, Wash., F	1999 Darrell Armstrong, Orl., G
1989 Kevin Johnson, Pho., G	1995 Dana Barros, Phi., G	2000 Jalen Rose, Ind., G
1990 Rony Seikaly, Mia., C	1996 Gheorghe Muresan, Wash., C	2001 Tracy McGrady, Orl., F
1991 Scott Skiles, Orl., G		2002 Jermaine O'Neal, Ind., F

Coach of the Year

The Red Auerbach Trophy for outstanding coach of the year. Renamed in 1967 for the former Boston coach who led the Celtics to nine NBA titles. Winners selected by a national panel of pro basketball writers and broadcasters. Previous season and winning season records are provided; (*) indicates division title.

Multiple winners: Don Nelson and Pat Riley (3); Bill Fitch, Cotton Fitzsimmons and Gene Shue (2).

Year		Improvement		Year		Improvement	
1963	Harry Gallatin, St. L	.29-51	to 48-32	1983	Don Nelson, Mil	.55-27*	to 51-31*
1964	Alex Hannum, SF	.31-49	to 48-32*	1984	Frank Layden, Utah	.30-52	to 45-37*
1965	Red Auerbach, Bos	.59-21*	to 61-18*	1985	Don Nelson, Mil	.50-32*	to 59-23*
1966	Dolph Schayes, Phi	.40-40	to 55-25*	1986	Mike Fratello, Atl	.34-48	to 50-32
1967	Johnny Kerr, Chi	.Expan.	to 33-48	1987	Mike Schuler, Port	.40-42	to 49-33
1968	Richie Guerin, St. L	.39-42	to 56-26*	1988	Doug Moe, Den	.37-45	to 54-28*
1969	Gene Shue, Balt	.36-46	to 57-25*	1989	Cotton Fitzsimmons, Pho	.28-54	to 55-27
1970	Red Holzman, NY	.54-28	to 60-22*	1990	Pat Riley, LA Lakers	.57-25*	to 63-19*
1971	Dick Motta, Chi	.39-43	to 51-31	1991	Don Chaney, Hou	.41-41	to 52-30
1972	Bill Sharman, LA	.48-34*	to 69-13*	1992	Don Nelson, GS	.44-38	to 55-27
1973	Tommy Heinsohn, Bos	.56-26*	to 68-14*	1993	Pat Riley, NY	.51-31	to 60-22
1974	Ray Scott, Det	.40-42	to 52-30	1994	Lenny Wilkens, Atl	.43-39	to 57-25*
1975	Phil Johnson, KC-Omaha	.33-49	to 44-38	1995	Del Harris, LA Lakers	.33-49	to 48-34
1976	Bill Fitch, Cle	.40-42	to 49-33*	1996	Phil Jackson, Chi	.47-35	to 72-10*
1977	Tom Nissalke, Hou	.40-42	to 49-33*	1997	Pat Riley, Mia	.42-40	to 61-21
1978	Hubie Brown, Atl	.31-51	to 41-41	1998	Larry Bird, Ind	.39-43	to 58-24
1979	Cotton Fitzsimmons, KC	.31-51	to 48-34*	1999	Mike Dunleavy, Port	.46-36	to 35-15*
1980	Bill Fitch, Bos	.29-53	to 61-21*	2000	Doc Rivers, Orlando	.33-17	to 41-41
1981	Jack McKinney, Ind	.37-45	to 44-38	2001	Larry Brown, Phila	.49-33	to 56-26*
1982	Gene Shue, Wash	.39-43	to 43-39	2002	Rick Carlisle, Det	.32-50	to 50-32*

World Championships

The World Basketball Championships for men and women have been played regularly at four-year intervals (give or take a year) since 1970. The men's tournament began in 1950 and the women's in 1953. The Federation Internationale de Basketball Amateur (FIBA), which governs the World and Olympic tournaments, was founded in 1932. FIBA first allowed professional players from the NBA to participate in 1994. A team of collegians represented the USA in 1998.

Men

Multiple wins: Yugoslavia (5); Soviet Union and USA (3); Brazil (2).

Year	
1950	**Argentina**, United States, Chile
1954	**United States**, Brazil, Philippines
1959	**Brazil**, United States, Chile
1963	**Brazil**, Yugoslavia, Soviet Union
1967	**Soviet Union**, Yugoslavia, Brazil
1970	**Yugoslavia**, Brazil, Soviet Union
1974	**Soviet Union**, Yugoslavia, United States
1978	**Yugoslavia**, Soviet Union, Brazil
1982	**Soviet Union**, United States, Yugoslavia
1986	**United States**, Soviet Union, Yugoslavia
1990	**Yugoslavia**, Soviet Union, United States
1994	**United States**, Russia, Croatia
1998	**Yugoslavia**, Russia, United States
2002	**Yugoslavia**, Argentina, Germany

Women

Multiple wins: USA (7); Soviet Union (6).

Year	
1953	**United States**, Chile, France
1957	**United States**, Soviet Union, Czechoslovakia
1959	**Soviet Union**, Bulgaria, Czechoslovakia
1964	**Soviet Union**, Czechoslovakia, Bulgaria
1967	**Soviet Union**, South Korea, Czechoslovakia
1971	**Soviet Union**, Czechoslovakia, Brazil
1975	**Soviet Union**, Japan, Czechoslovakia
1979	**United States**, South Korea, Canada
1983	**Soviet Union**, United States, China
1986	**United States**, Soviet Union, Canada
1990	**United States**, Yugoslavia, Cuba
1994	**Brazil**, China, United States
1998	**United States**, Russia, Australia
2002	**United States**, Russia, Australia

NBA Photos

NBA's 50 Greatest Players

In October 1996, as part of its 50th anniversary celebration, the NBA named the 50 greatest players in league history. The voting was done by a league-approved panel of media, former players and coaches, current and former general managers and team executives. The players are listed alphabetically along with the dates of their professional careers and positions. Active players are in **bold** type.

Player	Pos	Player	Pos	Player	Pos
Kareem Abdul-Jabbar, 1969-89	C	George Gervin, 1972-86	G	Robert Parish, 1976-97	C
Nate Archibald, 1970-84	G	Hal Greer, 1958-73	G	Bob Pettit, 1954-65	F/C
Paul Arizin, 1950-61	F/G	John Havlicek, 1962-78	F/G	**Scottie Pippen**, 1987—	F
Charles Barkley, 1984-00	F	Elvin Hayes, 1968-84	F/C	Willis Reed, 1964-74	C
Rick Barry, 1965-80	F	Magic Johnson, 1979-91, 96	G	Oscar Robertson, 1960-74	G
Elgin Baylor, 1958-72	F	Sam Jones, 1957-69	G	**David Robinson**, 1989—	C
Dave Bing, 1966-78	G	**Michael Jordan**, 1984-93, 95-98, 01—	G	Dolph Schayes, 1948-64	F/C
Larry Bird, 1979-92	F			Bill Russell, 1956-69	C
Wilt Chamberlain, 1959-73	C	Jerry Lucas, 1963-74	F/C	Bill Sharman, 1950-61	G
Bob Cousy, 1950-63, 69-70	G	**Karl Malone**, 1985—	F	**John Stockton**, 1984—	G
Dave Cowens, 1970-80, 1982-83	C	Moses Malone, 1974-95	C	Isiah Thomas, 1981-94	G
Billy Cunningham, 1965-76	G	Pete Maravich, 1970-80	G	Nate Thurmond, 1963-77	C/F
Dave DeBusschere, 1962-74	F	Kevin McHale, 1980-93	F	Wes Unseld, 1968-81	C/F
Clyde Drexler, 1983-98	G	George Mikan, 1946-54, 55-56	C	Bill Walton, 1974-88	C
Julius Erving, 1971-87	F	Earl Monroe, 1967-80	G	Jerry West, 1960-74	G
Patrick Ewing, 1985-2002	C	**Hakeem Olajuwon**, 1984—	C	Lenny Wilkens, 1960-75	G
Walt Frazier, 1967-80	G	**Shaquille O'Neal**, 1992—	C	James Worthy, 1982-94	F

Note: Rick Barry, Billy Cunningham, Julius Erving, George Gervin and Moses Malone all played part of their pro careers in the ABA.

NBA's 10 Greatest Coaches

In December 1996, as part of its 50th anniversary celebration, the NBA named the 10 greatest coaches in league history. The voting was done by a league-approved panel of media. The coaches are listed alphabetically along with the dates of their professional coaching careers and overall records, including playoff games, and number of NBA titles won. Active coaches are in **bold** type.

Coach	W	L	Pct.	Titles	Coach	W	L	Pct.	Titles
Red Auerbach, 1946-66	1037	548	.654	9	**Don Nelson**, 1976-96, 97—	1095	877	.555	0
Chuck Daly, 1981-94, 97-99	713	488	.594	2	Jack Ramsay, 1968-89	908	841	.519	1
Bill Fitch, 1970-98	999	1160	.463	1	**Pat Riley**, 1981—	1240	612	.670	4
Red Holzman, 1953-82	754	652	.536	2	**Lenny Wilkens**, 1969—	1348	1150	.540	1
Phil Jackson, 1989-98, 99—	882	312	.739	9	TOTALS	9461	6978	.576	34
John Kundla, 1947-59	485	338	.589	5					

American Basketball Association
ABA Finals

The American Basketball Assn. began play in 1967-68 as a 10-team rival of the 21-year-old NBA. The ABA, which introduced the three-point basket, a multi-colored ball and the All-Star Game Slam Dunk Contest, lasted nine seasons before folding following the 1975-76 season. Four ABA teams—Denver, Indiana, New York and San Antonio—survived to enter the NBA in 1976-77. The NBA also adopted the three-point basket (in 1979-80) and the All-Star Game Slam Dunk Contest. The older league, however, refused to take in the ABA ball.

Multiple winners: Indiana (3); New York (2).

Year	Winner	Head Coach	Series	Loser	Head Coach
1968	Pittsburgh Pipers	Vince Cazzetta	4-3 (WLLWLWW)	New Orleans Bucs	Babe McCarthy
1969	Oakland Oaks	Alex Hannum	4-1 (WLWWW)	Indiana Pacers	Bob Leonard
1970	Indiana Pacers	Bob Leonard	4-2 (WWLWLW)	Los Angeles Stars	Bill Sharman
1971	Utah Stars	Bill Sharman	4-3 (WWLLWLW)	Kentucky Colonels	Frank Ramsey
1972	Indiana Pacers	Bob Leonard	4-2 (WLWLWW)	New York Nets	Lou Carnesecca
1973	Indiana Pacers	Bob Leonard	4-3 (WLLWWLW)	Kentucky Colonels	Joe Mullaney
1974	New York Nets	Kevin Loughery	4-1 (WWWLW)	Utah Stars	Joe Mullaney
1975	Kentucky Colonels	Hubie Brown	4-1 (WWWLW)	Indiana Pacers	Bob Leonard
1976	New York Nets	Kevin Loughery	4-2 (WLWWLW)	Denver Nuggets	Larry Brown

Most Valuable Player

Winners' scoring averages provided; (*) indicates led league.

Multiple winners: Julius Erving (3); Mel Daniels (2).

Year		Avg
1968	Connie Hawkins, Pittsburgh, C	26.8*
1969	Mel Daniels, Indiana, C	24.0
1970	Spencer Haywood, Denver, C	30.0*
1971	Mel Daniels, Indiana, C	21.0
1972	Artis Gilmore, Kentucky, C	23.8
1973	Billy Cunningham, Carolina, F	24.1
1974	Julius Erving, New York, F	27.4*
1975	George McGinnis, Indiana, F	29.8*
	& Julius Erving, New York, F	27.9
1976	Julius Erving, New York, F	29.3*

Rookie of the Year

Winners' scoring averages provided; (*) indicates led league. Rookies who were also named Most Valuable Player are in **bold** type.

Year		Avg
1968	Mel Daniels, Minnesota, C	22.2
1969	Warren Armstrong, Oakland, G	21.5
1970	**Spencer Haywood**, Denver, C	30.0*
1971	Dan Issel, Kentucky, C	29.8*
	& Charlie Scott, Virginia, G	27.1
1972	**Artis Gilmore**, Kentucky, C	23.8
1973	Brian Taylor, New York, G	15.3
1974	Swen Nater, Virginia-SA, C	14.1
1975	Marvin Barnes, St. Louis, C	24.0
1976	David Thompson, Denver, F	26.0

Note: Warren Armstrong changed his name to Warren Jabali after the 1970-71 season.

Coach of the Year

Previous season and winning season records are provided; (*) indicates division title.

Multiple winner: Larry Brown (3).

Year		Improvement	
1968	Vince Cazzetta, Pittsburgh		54-24*
1969	Alex Hannum, Oakland	22-56	to 60-18*
1970	Joe Belmont, Denver	44-34	to 51-33*
	& Bill Sharman, LA Stars	33-45	to 43-41
1971	Al Bianchi, Virginia	44-40	to 55-29*
1972	Tom Nissalke, Dallas	30-54	to 42-42
1973	Larry Brown, Carolina	35-49	to 57-27*
1974	Babe McCarthy, Kentucky	56-28	to 53-31
	& Joe Mullaney, Utah	55-29*	to 51-33*
1975	Larry Brown, Denver	37-47	to 65-19*
1976	Larry Brown, Denver	65-19*	to 60-24*

Scoring Leaders

Scoring championship decided by per game point average every season.

Multiple winner: Julius Erving (3).

Year		Gm	Avg	Pts
1968	Connie Hawkins, Pittsburgh	70	1875	26.8
1969	Rick Barry, Oakland	35	1190	34.0
1970	Spencer Haywood, Denver	84	2519	30.0
1971	Dan Issel, Kentucky	83	2480	29.8
1972	Charlie Scott, Virginia	73	2524	34.6
1973	Julius Erving, Virginia	71	2268	31.9
1974	Julius Erving, New York	84	2299	27.4
1975	George McGinnis, Indiana	79	2353	29.8
1976	Julius Erving, New York	84	2462	29.3

ABA All-Star Game

The ABA All-Star Game was an Eastern Division vs. Western Division contest from 1968-75. League membership had dropped to seven teams by 1976, the ABA's last season, so the team in first place at the break (Denver) played an All-Star team made up from the other six clubs.

Series: East won 5, West 3 and Denver 1.

Year	Result	Host	Coaches	Most Valuable Player
1968	East 126, West 120	Indiana	Jim Pollard, Babe McCarthy	Larry Brown, New Orleans
1969	West 133, East 127	Louisville	Alex Hannum, Gene Rhodes	John Beasley, Dallas
1970	West 128, East 98	Indiana	Babe McCarthy, Bob Leonard	Spencer Haywood, Denver
1971	East 126, West 122	Carolina	Al Bianchi, Bill Sharman	Mel Daniels, Indiana
1972	East 142, West 115	Louisville	Joe Mullaney, Ladell Andersen	Dan Issel, Kentucky
1973	West 123, East 111	Utah	Ladell Andersen, Larry Brown	Warren Jabali, Denver
1974	East 128, West 112	Virginia	Babe McCarthy, Joe Mullaney	Artis Gilmore, Kentucky
1975	East 151, West 124	San Antonio	Kevin Loughery, Larry Brown	Freddie Lewis, St. Louis
1976	Denver 144, ABA 138	Denver	Larry Brown, Kevin Loughery	David Thompson, Denver

Continental Basketball Association

Originally named the Eastern Pennsylvania Basketball League when it formed on April 23, 1946, the league changed names several times before becoming known as the Eastern Basketball Association. In 1978, the EBA was redubbed the CBA. The CBA suspended operations following the 2000 season but reorganized for the 2001-02 season.

Multiple champions: Allentown and Wilkes-Barre (8); Scranton, Tampa Bay and Williamsport (3); Albany, La Crosse, Pottsville, Rochester, Wilmington and Yakima (2).

Year		Year		Year		Year	
1947	Wilkes-Barre Barons	1963	Allentown Jets	1977	Scranton Apollos	1992	La Crosse Catbirds
1948	Reading Keys	1964	Camden Bullets	1978	Wilkes-Barre Barons	1993	Omaha Racers
1949	Pottsville Packers	1965	Allentown Jets	1979	Rochester Zeniths	1994	Quad City Thunder
1950	Williamsport Billies	1966	Wilmington Blue	1980	Anchorage Northern	1995	Yakima Sun Kings
1951	Sunbury Mercuries		Bombers		Knights	1996	Sioux Falls Skyforce
1952	Pottsville Packers	1967	Wilmington Blue	1981	Rochester Zeniths	1997	Oklahoma City
1953	Williamsport Billies		Bombers	1982	Lancaster Lightning		Calvary
1954	Williamsport Billies	1968	Allentown Jets	1983	Detroit Spirits	1998	Quad City Thunder
1955	Wilkes-Barre Barons	1969	Wilkes-Barre Barons	1984	Albany Patroons	1999	Connecticut Pride
1956	Wilkes-Barre Barons	1970	Allentown Jets	1985	Tampa Bay Thrillers	2000	Yakima Sun Kings
1957	Scranton Miners	1971	Scranton Apollos	1986	Tampa Bay Thrillers	2002	Dakota Wizards
1958	Wilkes-Barre Barons	1972	Allentown Jets	1987	Rapid City Thrillers*		
1959	Wilkes-Barre Barons	1973	Wilkes-Barre Barons	1988	Albany Patroons	*The Tampa Bay Thrillers	
1960	Easton Madisons	1974	Hartford Capitols	1989	Tulsa Fast Breakers	moved to Rapid City, S.D.	
1961	Baltimore Bullets	1975	Allentown Jets	1990	La Crosse Catbirds	at the end of the 1987 regu-	
1962	Allentown Jets	1976	Allentown Jets	1991	Wichita Falls Texans	lar season.	

WOMEN

Women's National Basketball Association
League Champions

The WNBA, owned and operated by the NBA, began play in 1997 as an eight-team summer league. The league added two teams prior to its second season (1998) and again expanded by two teams before its third season in 1999. Four more teams were added before the 2000 season, bringing the total number of teams to 16. The WNBA champion was determined by a single-game playoff between the winners of the semifinals in the league's 1997 inaugural season, before going to a best-of-three championship series in 1998.

Multiple winner: Houston (4); Los Angeles (2).

Year	Champions	Head Coach	Score	Runners-up	Head Coach
1997	Houston Comets	Van Chancellor	65-51	New York Liberty	Nancy Darsch
1998	Houston Comets	Van Chancellor	2-1 (LWW)	Phoenix Mercury	Cheryl Miller
1999	Houston Comets	Van Chancellor	2-1 (WLW)	New York Liberty	Richie Adubato
2000	Houston Comets	Van Chancellor	2-0	New York Liberty	Richie Adubato
2001	Los Angeles Sparks	Michael Cooper	2-0	Charlotte Sting	Anne Donovan
2002	Los Angeles Sparks	Michael Cooper	2-0	New York Liberty	Richie Adubato

Most Valuable Player

Winner's scoring averages provided; (*) indicates led league.

Multiple winner: Cynthia Cooper and Sheryl Swoopes (2).

Year		Avg
1997	Cynthia Cooper, Houston	22.2*
1998	Cynthia Cooper, Houston	22.7*
1999	Yolanda Griffith, Sacramento	18.8
2000	Sheryl Swoopes, Houston	20.7*
2001	Lisa Leslie, Los Angeles	19.5
2002	Sheryl Swoopes, Houston	18.5

Coach of the Year

Previous season and winning season's record are provided; (*) indicates division title.

Multiple winner: Van Chancellor (3).

Year		Improvement
1997	Van Chancellor, Houston	18-10*
1998	Van Chancellor, Houston	18-10 to 27-3*
1999	Van Chancellor, Houston	27-3 to 26-6*
2000	Michael Cooper, Los Angeles	20-12 to 28-4*
2001	Dan Hughes, Cleveland	17-15 to 22-10*
2002	Marianne Stanley, Washington	10-22 to 17-15

American Basketball League (1997–98)
League Champions

The American Basketball League began play in 1996 as an eight-team league. Before the 1997-98 season the league added an expansion franchise in Long Beach, Calif. while the Richmond Rage was relocated to Philadelphia. In the spring of 1998, the league announced plans to dissolve an original franchise, the Atlanta Glory, and expand to Chicago and Nashville before the 1998-99 season, increasing the league's size to 10 teams. The ABL finals was a best of five series. Each ABL champion's wins and losses are noted in parentheses after the series score. The ABL folded before the 1999 season.

Multiple winner: Columbus (2).

Year	Champions	Head Coach	Series	Runners-up	Head Coach
1997	Columbus Quest	Brian Agler	3-2 (WLLWW)	Richmond Rage	Lisa Boyer
1998	Columbus Quest	Brian Agler	3-2 (LLWWW)	Long Beach StingRays	Maura McHugh

Most Valuable Player

Winner's scoring averages provided; (*) indicates led league.

Year		Avg
1997	Nikki McCray, Columbus	19.9
1998	Natalie Williams, Portland	21.9*

Coach of the Year

Previous season and winning season's record are provided; (*) indicates division title.

Year		Improvement
1997	Brian Agler, Columbus	31-9*
1998	Lin Dunn, Portland	14-26 to 27-17

Hockey

Scotty Bowman walks off the ice with his
record-breaking ninth, and last, Stanley Cup.

AP/Wide World Photos

Aged to Perfection

With half the team headed for the hall of fame, there was just no stopping the Red Wings in 2001–02.

Steve Levy *is a hockey play-by-play announcer and host of ESPN's National Hockey Night.*

The most important goal of the 2001–02 NHL season was not scored in Game 5 of the Stanley Cup Finals, or in any game of the Finals for that matter. It wasn't scored in the conference finals, or even in the conference semifinals.

Without a doubt, it was scored in the Western Conference Quarterfinals. It was scored in Game 3 at General Motors Place in Vancouver with the Canucks and Red Wings tied, 1–1, midway through the second period. That's when Wings defenseman Nicklas Lidstrom beat Canucks goalie Daniel Cloutier, the Canucks and the rest of the NHL to win the Stanley Cup.

The goal was not exactly a beauty, merely a soft floater from the red line. But it will look like a 100-mph blast in the box score for years to come.

Vancouver had shocked the hockey world by winning the first two games of the series in Detroit. But looking back, the aging Red Wings probably can't even remember being down 0–2 in the series (memory loss in sports can be a beautiful thing).

In my opinion, that Lidstrom goal was the turning point of the entire playoffs, the wakeup call for Detroit and the announcement to the rest of the NHL that the team that was supposed to win it all would do just that.

Sure, Colorado took them to seven games in the Western Conference Finals. But when the Wings were up against the wall, down three games to two, they outscored the Avalanche 9–0 over the final two games, including a 7–0 pasting in Game 7. Patrick Roy and the Avs are probably hoping they can lose some of their memory too.

As predictable as it was that Detroit was one team in the Cup Finals, it was equally *un*predictable that Carolina was its dance partner. I called the Hurricanes' Eastern Conference Finals-

AP/Wide World Photos

*Veteran goalie **Dominik Hasek** finally had his name etched on Lord Stanley's Cup in 2002. He gave up a measly seven goals in the Cup Finals against Carolina. This wasn't one of them.*

clinching game in Toronto, and I remember my last line from the telecast.

"Strange but true, say it with me folks, the Carolina Hurricanes are going to the Stanley Cup Finals."

If it sounded like I was trying to convince myself along with our viewers, I was. The common thought around the hockey world was, "Great story but they're going out in four." Much like the NBA Finals, the sports world—not just the hockey world—reached for the brooms. Detroit vs. Carolina? This series had sweep written all over it.

So what happens? Ron Francis scores in overtime and the Hurricanes

win Game 1 in Detroit, making everyone that made fun of the fact that Raleigh even has a pro hockey club look silly.

As it turned out, Detroit won the next four games. But it certainly wasn't easy. And while it doesn't show up on the scoreboard, the home of the Hurricanes provided as fine a hockey atmosphere as I've ever experienced. It was really quite similar to the early success of the Florida Panthers, who advanced to the Cup Finals in 1996. Like Raleigh, Miami wasn't supposed to be a hockey town, but those fans rocked their building in similar fashion.

Kellie Landis/Getty Images

*Calgary right wing **Jarome Iginla**, the league's Art Ross Trophy winner and only 50-goal scorer, took another huge step towards stardom in 2001–02.*

Carolina's challenge now is to hang around the upper echelon of the league, something the Panthers couldn't do.

The Hurricanes are a good club, they just had the misfortune of facing these Red Wings. Hopefully you had a chance to see this team in person at least once. Hasek, Hull, Yzerman, Lidstrom, Shanahan, Chelios. We may never see anything like that again. When you purchased a ticket for them, home or away, you were assured of seeing something special, possibly the greatest collection of hockey names ever assembled on one team.

Half the team will likely wind up in the hall of fame, and the other half would've been the top half on most of the other teams in the league. Just listening to the public address announcer list its starting lineup might've been worth the price of admission by itself.

Can they repeat? Coach Scotty Bowman and goaltender Dominik Hasek both retired after the Finals,

continued on page 388 ▶

Steve Levy's Ten Biggest Stories of the Year in Hockey

10 ▪ The Rangers and Stars, with their bloated payrolls, fail to make the playoffs. And the Flyers can't make it out of the first round. As always, these things are subject to change, but I might just pick the Rangers and Stars to meet in the 2003 Stanley Cup Finals.

9 ▪ Be careful what you wish for, or what you say you wish for. Just ask Jaromir Jagr how he enjoyed his first season in Washington.

8 ▪ Scotty Bowman and Dominik Hasek go out on top and on their own terms. There's really nothing left for either to accomplish. Hasek already had the individual accolades and needed only a Cup to complete the puzzle. And with the way coaches are getting fired these days, some of Bowman's records are likely to stand forever.

7 ▪ Hooray for Jarome Iginla and Jose Theodore. The winners of the Art Ross Trophy (Iginla) and Hart Trophy (Theodore) give the NHL two young stars to promote and fans in Calgary and Montreal something to cheer about, a rare occurrence in recent years.

6 ▪ Along those same lines, it's great to see the Canadiens, Blackhawks and Bruins bring their franchises back to life. All three made the postseason in 2002, along with the Wings and Leafs, making the Rangers the only Original Six team to be shut out.

5 ▪ We already knew how good Avs center Peter Forsberg was, but to miss an entire regular season and then display the form he did during the playoffs (leading all scorers) is simply astounding.

4 ▪ As amazing as Forsberg's accomplishment was, coming back from foot surgery, let's face it, his life wasn't really in jeopardy. But Saku Koivu's was. The popular Canadiens captain returns from non-Hodgkin's lymphoma and energizes the Habs to a first-round upset of top-seeded Boston.

3 ▪ The Olympic hockey tournament at Salt Lake City is the way the game was meant to be played. The two best teams make it to the gold medal game. The only thing better than having Canada beat the U.S. would've been if the outcome was in doubt in the final seconds.

2 ▪ Sure the Red Wings are the No. 1 team in the world, but in my opinion they're only the No. 2 story. They were supposed to win...and they did. But I still can't help staring at their roster.

1 ▪ The Hurricanes didn't have low expectations, they had *no* expectations. But they're the reason we become sports fans, because you just never know what can happen. As Chris Berman says, "that's why they play the games."

electing to go out on top. But that can actually work in the Red Wings' favor. Replacing them will re-energize this franchise, as their absence will give the rest of the club something to prove.

They say the Stanley Cup is the hardest trophy to win in all of sports. So imagine how difficult it is to win two of them in a row. In the last ten years, only one team has done it—the Red Wings of course, in 1997–98.

Season of Milestones

In 2001–02, Brendan Shanahan became the seventh player in NHL history to record his 500th goal, 500th assist and 1,000th point in the same season. The last three are Red Wings.

	Season
Brendan Shanahan, Detroit	2001-02
Pat Verbeek, Detroit	1999-2000
Dino Ciccarelli, Detroit	1993-94
Mike Gartner, NY Rangers	1991-92
Lanny McDonald, Calgary	1988-89
Mike Bossy, NY Islanders	1985-86
Frank Mahovlich, Montreal	1972-73

Old Timers

With his ninth Stanley Cup title in 2002, Detroit coach Scotty Bowman tied the record for the oldest head coach in major pro sports history to win a championship.

	Title	Age
S. Bowman, '02	Stanley Cup	68
G. Halas, '63	NFL Champ.	68
C. Stengel, '58	World Series	68

Two Timers

Brett Hull became the sixth player in history to reach the Stanley Cup Finals with two different teams, and score at least 10 goals in both postseasons.

	1st Team	2nd Team
Brett Hull	'00 DAL	'02 DET
Wayne Gretzky	EDM*	'93 LA
Claude Lemieux	'86 MON	'95 NJ
Ken Linseman	'84 EDM	'88 BOS
Mark Messier	EDM*	'94 NYR
Joe Nieuwendyk	'89 CALG	'99 DAL

*Gretzky and Messier reached the Finals with Edmonton multiple times.

Kids in the Hall

Many believe the 2001–02 Red Wings have at least nine players headed for the hall of fame. Below are the most hall of famers from a major pro team.

	League	No.
1961 Packers	NFL	11
1962 Packers	NFL	10
1972-73 Canadiens	NHL	10
1966-67 Maple Leafs	NHL	10
1955-56 Canadiens	NHL	10

ESPN Information Please® SPORTS ALMANAC

2001-2002 Season in Review

Final NHL Standings

Division champions (*) and playoff qualifiers (†) are noted. OL signifies any game that was tied after regulation play but lost in overtime. Number of seasons listed after each head coach refers to current tenure with club through 2001-02 season.

Western Conference
Central Division

	W	L	T	OL	Pts	GF	GA
*Detroit	51	17	10	4	116	251	187
†St. Louis	43	27	8	4	98	227	188
†Chicago	41	27	13	1	96	216	207
Nashville	28	41	13	0	69	196	230
Columbus	22	47	8	5	57	164	255

Head Coaches: Det—Scotty Bowman (9th season); **St.L**—Joel Quenneville (6th); **Chi**—Brian Sutter (1st); **Nash**—Barry Trotz (4th); **Clb**—Dave King (2nd).

Northwest Division

	W	L	T	OL	Pts	GF	GA
*Colorado	45	28	8	1	99	212	169
†Vancouver	42	30	7	3	94	254	211
Edmonton	38	28	12	4	92	205	182
Calgary	32	35	12	3	79	201	220
Minnesota	26	35	12	9	73	195	238

Head Coaches: Col—Bob Hartley (4th season); **Van**—Marc Crawford (4th); **Edm**—Craig MacTavish (2nd); **Calg**—Greg Gilbert (2nd); **Min**—Jacques Lemaire (2nd).

Pacific Division

	W	L	T	OL	Pts	GF	GA
*San Jose	44	27	8	3	99	248	199
†Phoenix	40	27	9	6	95	228	210
†Los Angeles	40	27	11	4	95	214	190
Dallas	36	28	13	5	90	215	213
Anaheim	29	42	8	3	69	175	198

Head Coaches: SJ—Darryl Sutter (5th season); **Pho**—Bob Francis (3rd); **LA**—Andy Murray (3rd); **Dal**—Ken Hitchcock (7th; 23-17-6-4) was fired and replaced by asst. Rick Wilson (13-11-7-1) on Jan. 25; **Ana**—Bryan Murray (1st).

Eastern Conference
Northeast Division

	W	L	T	OL	Pts	GF	GA
*Boston	43	24	6	9	101	236	201
†Toronto	43	25	10	4	100	249	207
†Ottawa	39	27	9	7	94	243	208
†Montreal	36	31	12	3	87	207	209
Buffalo	35	35	11	1	82	213	200

Head Coaches: Bos—Robbie Ftorek (1st season); **Tor**—Pat Quinn (4th); **Ott**—Jacques Martin (7th, 38-26-9-7) and Roger Neilson (1-1-0-0); **Mon**—Michel Therrien (2nd); **Buf**—Lindy Ruff (5th).
Note: Ottawa asst. coach Roger Neilson was the team's head coach for the final two games of the season, his 999th and 1000th career games as a head coach.

Atlantic Division

	W	L	T	OL	Pts	GF	GA
*Philadelphia	42	27	10	3	97	234	192
†NY Islanders	42	28	8	4	96	239	220
†New Jersey	41	28	9	4	95	205	187
NY Rangers	36	38	4	4	80	227	258
Pittsburgh	28	41	8	5	69	198	249

Head Coaches: Phi—Bill Barber (2nd season); **NYI**—Peter Laviolette (1st); **NJ**—Larry Robinson (3rd, 21-20-7-3) was fired and replaced by Kevin Constantine (20-8-2-1) on Jan. 28; **NYR**—Ron Low (2nd); **Pit**—Ivan Hlinka (2nd, 0-4-0-0) was fired and replaced by asst. Rick Kehoe (28-37-8-5) on Oct. 15, 2001.

Southeast Division

	W	L	T	OL	Pts	GF	GA
*Carolina	35	26	16	5	91	217	217
Washington	36	33	11	2	85	228	240
Tampa Bay	27	40	11	4	69	178	219
Florida	22	44	10	6	60	180	250
Atlanta	19	47	11	5	54	187	288

Head Coaches: Car—Paul Maurice (7th season); **Wash**—Ron Wilson (5th); **TB**—John Tortorella (2nd); **Fla**—Duane Sutter (2nd, 6-15-2-3) was fired and replaced by Mike Keenan (16-29-8-3) on Dec. 3, 2001; **Atl**—Curt Fraser (3rd).

Home & Away, Division, Conference Records

Sixteen teams—eight from each conference—qualify for the Stanley Cup Playoffs; (*) indicates division champions.

Western Conference

		Pts	Home	Away	Div
1	Detroit*	116	28-7-5-1	23-10-5-3	10-6-4-2
2	Colorado*	99	24-12-4-1	21-16-4-0	10-6-4-0
3	San Jose*	99	25-11-3-2	19-16-5-1	10-9-1-1
4	St. Louis	98	27-12-1-1	16-15-7-3	10-7-3-2
5	Chicago	96	28-7-5-1	13-20-8-0	9-6-5-0
6	Phoenix	95	27-8-3-3	13-19-6-3	7-10-3-2
7	Los Angeles	95	22-12-6-1	18-15-5-3	10-6-4-2
8	Vancouver	94	23-11-5-2	19-19-2-1	10-8-2-0
	Edmonton	92	23-14-4-0	15-14-8-4	10-5-5-0
	Dallas	90	18-13-6-4	18-15-7-1	9-9-2-0
	Calgary	79	14-14-8-5	12-21-7-1	8-8-4-0
	Minnesota	73	14-14-8-5	12-21-4-4	4-15-1-4
	Anaheim	69	15-19-5-2	14-23-3-1	8-10-2-1
	Nashville	69	17-16-8-0	11-25-5-0	7-10-3-0
	Columbus	57	14-18-5-4	8-29-3-1	5-12-3-3

Eastern Conference

		Pts	Home	Away	Div
1	Boston*	101	23-11-2-5	20-13-4-4	9-10-1-1
2	Philadelphia*	97	24-12-4-3	22-14-5-0	10-8-2-1
3	Carolina*	91	15-13-11-2	20-13-5-3	11-4-5-1
4	Toronto	100	24-11-6-0	19-14-4-4	10-5-5-2
5	NY Islanders	96	21-13-5-2	21-15-3-2	11-8-1-2
6	New Jersey	95	22-13-4-2	19-15-5-2	10-8-2-1
7	Ottawa	94	21-13-3-4	18-14-6-3	8-11-1-2
8	Montreal	87	21-13-6-1	15-18-6-2	6-10-4-1
	Washington	85	21-12-6-2	15-21-5-0	12-4-4-0
	Buffalo	82	20-16-5-0	15-19-6-1	10-7-3-0
	NY Rangers	80	19-19-2-1	17-19-2-3	7-12-1-2
	Pittsburgh	69	16-20-4-1	12-21-4-4	8-10-2-2
	Tampa Bay	69	16-17-5-3	11-23-6-1	7-10-3-0
	Florida	60	11-23-3-4	11-21-7-2	5-12-3-2
	Atlanta	54	11-21-9-0	8-26-2-5	4-9-7-2

2002 NHL All-Star Game

World 8, North America 5

52nd NHL All-Star Game. **Date:** Feb. 2 at the Staples Center in Los Angeles; **Coaches:** Scotty Bowman, Detroit (World) and Pat Quinn, Toronto (North America); **MVP:** Eric Daze, Chicago left wing (North America)—two goals, one assist.

Starters were chosen by fan vote while reserves were selected by the NHL's Hockey Operations Department, after consultation with NHL general managers. Head coaches whose teams had the best winning percentage in the Western Conference (World) and Eastern Conference (North America) on Jan. 2 and 4, respectively, were named all-star head coaches.

Center Espen Knutsen was added to the **World** team as an injury replacement for Jere Lehtinen.

Defenseman Chris Chelios and center Mike York were added to the **North American** team as injury replacements for Brian Rafalski and Eric Lindros, respectively.

World

Pos	Starters	G	A	Pts	PM
W	Teemu Selanne, San Jose	2	0	2	0
C	Sergei Fedorov, Detroit	1	0	1	0
D	Sandis Ozolinsh, Florida	0	1	1	0
W	Jaromir Jagr, Washington	0	0	0	0
D	Nicklas Lidstrom, Detroit	0	0	0	0
	Reserves				
W	Markus Naslund, Vancouver	2	1	3	0
W	Sami Kapanen, Carolina	1	1	2	0
C	Espen Knutsen, Columbus	1	1	2	0
C	Mats Sundin, Toronto	0	2	2	0
C	Alexei Zhamnov, Chicago	1	1	2	0
W	Patrik Elias, New Jersey	0	1	1	0
D	Sergei Gonchar, Washington	0	1	1	0
D	Tomas Kaberle, Toronto	0	1	1	0
C	Alexei Yashin, NY Islanders	0	1	1	0
C	Pavol Demitra, St. Louis	0	0	0	0
D	Jaroslav Modry, Los Angeles	0	0	0	0
W	Zigmund Palffy, Los Angeles	0	0	0	0
D	Alexei Zhitnik, Buffalo	0	0	0	0
	TOTALS	8	11	19	0

Goaltenders	Mins	Shots	Saves	GA
Dominik Hasek, Det.	20:00	13	10	3
Tommy Salo, Edm.	20:00	17	15	2
Nikolai Khabibulin, TB	20:00	20	20	0
TOTALS	60:00	50	45	5

North America

Pos	Starters	G	A	Pts	PM
C	Vincent Damphousse, San Jose	1	2	3	0
D	Rob Blake, Colorado	0	1	1	0
D	Chris Pronger, St. Louis	0	1	1	0
W	Brendan Shanahan, Detroit	0	0	0	0
W	Owen Nolan, San Jose	0	0	0	0
	Reserves				
W	Eric Daze, Chicago	2	1	3	0
D	Ed Jovanovski, Vancouver	1	0	1	0
C	Mario Lemieux, Pittsburgh	1	0	1	0
C	Paul Kariya, Anaheim	0	1	1	0
D	Chris Chelios, Detroit	0	0	0	0
W	Jarome Iginla, Calgary	0	0	0	0
D	Brian Leetch, NY Rangers	0	0	0	0
W	Mark Parrish, NY Islanders	0	0	0	0
D	Wade Redden, Ottawa	0	0	0	0
C	Jeremy Roenick, Philadelphia	0	0	0	0
C	Joe Sakic, Colorado	0	0	0	0
C	Joe Thornton, Boston	0	0	0	0
C	Mike York, NY Rangers	0	0	0	0
	TOTALS	5	6	11	0

Goaltenders	Mins	Shots	Saves	GA
Patrick Roy, Col.	20:00	14	12	2
Jose Theodore, Mon.	20:00	9	8	1
Sean Burke, Pho.	19:06	14	11	3
TOTALS	59:06	37	31	6

Note: The World team scored two empty net goals.

Score by Periods

	1	2	3	Final
World	2	1	5	— 8
North America	3	2	0	— 5

Power plays: World—0/0; North America—0/0. **Officials:** Dave Jackson and Don Van Massenhoven (referees), Andy McElman and Mark Pare (linesmen). **Attendance:** 18,118. **TV Rating:** 2.0/5 share (ABC).

2002 NHL Skills Competition

World, 12-11

Puck Control Relay
Team:	World (Sundin, Ozolinsh, Selanne)
Individual:	Paul Kariya (North America)

Fastest Skater
Team:	World (Avg.14.484 sec.: Demitra, Fedorov, Kapanen)
Individual:	Sami Kapanen, World (14.039 sec.)

Hardest Shot
Team:	North America (Avg. 95.0 mph: Iginla, Thornton, Chelios, Blake)
Individual:	Sergei Fedorov, World (101.5 mph)

Shooting Accuracy (targets/shots)
Team:	North America (14/28: Iginla, Daze, Roenick, Shanahan)
Individual:	Jarome Iginla, North America & Markus Naslund, World (4/6)

Pass and Score
Team:	North America wins, 1-0

Breakaway Relay
Team:	World wins, 7-6

Goaltender Competition
(combined Pass and Score + Breakaway Relay)
Individual:	Patrick Roy, North America & Dominik Hasek, World

Calgary Flames
Jarome Iginla
Scoring, Goals

Washington Capitals
Adam Oates
Assists

Detroit Red Wings
Chris Chelios
Plus/Minus

Colorado Avalanche
Patrick Roy
GAA, ShO

NHL Regular Season Individual Leaders

(*) indicates rookie eligible for Calder Trophy.

Scoring

	Pos	Gm	G	A	Pts	+/-	PM	PP	SH	GW	GT	Shots	Pct
Jarome Iginla, Calgary	R	82	52	44	96	27	77	16	1	7	2	311	16.7
Markus Naslund, Vancouver	L	81	40	50	90	22	50	8	0	6	1	302	13.2
Todd Bertuzzi, Vancouver	R	72	36	49	85	21	110	14	0	3	0	203	17.7
Mats Sundin, Toronto	C	82	41	39	80	6	94	10	2	9	2	262	15.6
Jaromir Jagr, Washington	R	69	31	48	79	0	30	10	0	3	0	197	15.7
Joe Sakic, Colorado	C	82	26	53	79	12	18	9	1	4	1	260	10.0
Pavol Demitra, St. Louis	C	82	35	43	78	14	46	11	0	10	0	212	16.5
Adam Oates, Wash.-Phi.	C	80	14	64	78	-4	28	3	0	0	0	102	13.7
Mike Modano, Dallas	C	78	34	43	77	14	38	6	2	5	0	219	15.5
Ron Francis, Carolina	C	80	27	50	77	4	18	14	0	5	2	165	16.4
Alexei Kovalev, Pittsburgh	R	67	32	44	76	2	80	8	1	3	2	266	12.0
Keith Tkachuk, St. Louis	L	73	38	37	75	21	117	13	0	7	1	244	15.6
Brendan Shanahan, Detroit	L	80	37	38	75	23	118	12	3	7	3	277	13.4
Alexei Yashin, NY Islanders	C	78	32	43	75	-3	25	15	0	5	0	239	13.4
Craig Conroy, Calgary	C	81	27	48	75	24	32	7	2	4	1	146	18.5
Jason Allison, Los Angeles	C	72	19	55	74	2	68	5	0	2	2	139	13.7
Eric Lindros, NY Rangers	C	72	37	36	73	19	138	12	1	4	0	196	18.9
Miroslav Satan, Buffalo	R	82	37	36	73	14	33	15	5	5	0	267	13.9
Glen Murray, LA-Bos.	R	82	41	30	71	31	40	9	0	9	0	246	16.7
Daniel Alfredsson, Ottawa	R	78	37	34	71	3	45	9	1	4	2	243	15.2

Goals

Iginla, Calg.	52
Guerin, Bos.	41
Murray, LA-Bos.	41
Sundin, Tor.	41
Naslund, Van.	40
Bondra, Wash.	39
Daze, Chi.	38
Tkachuk, St.L	38
Satan, Buf.	37
Shanahan, Det.	37
Lindros, NYR	37
Alfredsson, Ott.	37

Assists

Oates, Wash.-Phi.	64
Allison, LA	55
Sakic, Col.	53
Francis, Car.	50
Lidstrom, Det.	50
Naslund, Van.	50
Stumpel, LA-Bos.	50
Bertuzzi, Van.	49
Conroy, Calg.	48
Brunette, Min.	48
Jagr, Wash.	48

Defensemen Points

Gonchar, Wash.	59
Lidstrom, Det.	59
Blake, Col.	56
Leetch, NYR	55
Ozolinsh, Car.-Fla.	52
Jovanovski, Van.	48
Numminen, Pho.	48
Rafalski, NJ	47
Pronger, St.L	47
MacInnis, St.L	46

Rookie Points

Heatley, Atl.	67
Kovalchuk, Atl.	51
Huselius, Fla.	45
Cole, Car.	40
Datsyuk, Det.	35
Erat, Nash.	33
Vrbata, Col.	30
McDonald, Ana.	28
Bell, Chi.	28
Hagman, Fla.	28
Dupuis, Min.	27
Beech, Pit.	25

Plus/Minus

Chelios, Det.	40
Roenick, Phi.	32
Gagne, Phi.	31
Murray, LA-Bos.	31
Chara, Ott.	30
Nylander, Chi.	28
O'Donnell, Bos.	27
Iginla, Calg.	27
Lehtinen, Dal.	27
Arvedson, Ott.	27
Weinrich, Phi.	27

Penalty Minutes

Worrell, Fla.	354
Ference, Fla.	254
Neil*, Ott.	231
Sawyer, Ana.	221
Fleury, NYR	216
Nazarov, Bos.-Pho.	215
Barnaby, TB-NYR	214
Lambert, Ana.	213
Roy, Ott.-TB	211
Shelley*, Clb.	206

Power Play Goals

Bondra, Wash.	17
Iginla, Calg.	16
Palffy, LA.	15
Satan, Buf.	15
Yashin, NYI	15
Bertuzzi, Van.	14
Francis, Car.	14
Robitaille, Det.	13
Tkachuk, St.L	13
Seven tied with 12 each.	

Short-Handed Goals

Rolston, Bos	9
Peca, NYI	6
Satan, Buf.	5
Bates, NYI	4
Roest, Min.	4
Ten tied with 3 each.	

Shots

Guerin, Bos.	.355
Bondra, Wash.	.333
Rolston, Bos.	.331
Iginla, Calg.	.311
Naslund, Van.	.302
Kariya, Ana.	.289
Bure, Fla.-NYR	.287
Hossa, Ott.	.278
Shanahan, Det.	.277
O'Neill, Car.	.272

Shooting Pct.
(Min. 70 shots)

Briere, Pho.	.21.5
Hrdina, Pit.	.20.9
Deadmarsh, LA	.20.9
H. Sedin, Van.	.20.5
Palffy, LA	.19.9
Brunette, Min.	.19.8
Comrie, Edm.	.19.4
Tucker, Tor.	.19.4
Lindros, NYR	.18.9
Parrish, NYI	.18.5

Hits

Svehla, Fla.	.386
Kasparaitis, Pit.-Col.	.373
Hatcher, Dal.	.330
Chara, Ott.	.299
Cole*, Car.	.257
Doan, Pho.	.254
McCabe, Tor.	.250
McGillis, Phi.	.246
Klemm, Chi.	.243
Boughner, Calg.	.239

Minutes/Game
(Min. 50 Games)

Pronger, St.L.	.29:28
Aucoin, NYI	.28:53
Lidstrom, Det.	.28:48
Blake, Col.	.27:34
MacInnis, St.L	.26:55
Zubov, Dal.	.26:46
Hatcher, Dal.	.26:40
Niinimaa, Edm.	.26:01
Foote, Col.	.25:59
Leetch, NYR	.25:51

Goaltending
(Minimum 26 games)

	Gm	Min	GAA	GA	Shots	Sv%	EN	ShO	Record	Offense G	A	Pts	PM
Patrick Roy, Colorado	63	3773	1.94	122	1629	.925	6	9	32-23-8	0	3	3	26
Roman Cechmanek, Philadelphia	46	2603	2.05	89	1131	.921	2	4	24-13-6	0	0	0	10
Marty Turco, Dallas	31	1519	2.09	53	670	.921	4	2	15-6-2	0	0	0	10
Jose Theodore, Montreal	67	3864	2.11	136	1972	.931	9	7	30-24-10	0	2	2	2
Jean-Sebastien Giguere, Anaheim	53	3127	2.13	111	1384	.920	3	4	20-25-6	0	0	0	28
Martin Brodeur, New Jersey	73	4347	2.15	156	1655	.906	5	4	38-26-9	0	4	4	8
Dominik Hasek, Detroit	65	3872	2.17	140	1654	.915	2	5	41-15-8	0	1	1	8
Brent Johnson, St. Louis	58	3491	2.18	127	1293	.902	5	5	34-20-4	0	4	4	2
Byron Dafoe, Boston	64	3827	2.21	141	1520	.907	5	4	35-26-3	0	1	1	27
Martin Biron, Buffalo	72	4085	2.22	151	1781	.915	5	4	31-28-10	0	1	1	8
Tommy Salo, Edmonton	69	4035	2.22	149	1713	.913	5	6	30-28-10	0	1	1	10
Curtis Joseph, Toronto	51	3065	2.23	114	1210	.906	4	4	29-17-5	0	1	1	10
Sean Burke, Phoenix	60	3587	2.29	137	1711	.920	3	5	33-21-6	0	1	1	14
Evgeni Nabokov, San Jose	67	3901	2.29	149	1818	.918	5	7	37-24-5	1	3	4	14
Felix Potvin, Los Angeles	71	4071	2.31	157	1686	.907	3	6	31-27-8	0	1	1	19

Wins

Hasek, Det.	.41
Brodeur, NJ	.38
Nabokov, SJ.	.37
Dafoe, Bos.	.35
Johnson, St.L	.34
Burke, Pho.	.33
Thibault, Chi.	.33
Osgood, NYI	.32
Roy, Colo.	.32
Four tied with 31 each.	

Shutouts

Roy, Col.	.9
Cloutier, Van.	.7
Khabibulin, TB	.7
Lalime, Ott.	.7
Nabokov, SJ	.7
Theodore, Mon.	.7
Salo, Edm.	.6
Potvin, LA	.6
Thibault, Chi.	.6
Kolzig, Wash.	.6
Hedberg, Pit.	.6

Save Pct.

Theodore, Mon.	.931
Roy, Col.	.925
Cechmanek, Phi.	.921
Turco, Dal.	.921
Khabibulin, TB	.920
Burke, Pho.	.920
Giguere, Ana.	.920
Nabokov, SJ	.918
Hasek, Det.	.915
Luongo, Fla.	.915
Biron, Buf.	.915

Losses

Hedberg, Pit.	.34
Hnilicka, Atl.	.33
Luongo, Fla.	.33
Khabibulin, TB	.32
Kolzig, Wash.	.29
Salo, Edm.	.28
Biron, Buf.	.28
Turek, Calg.	.28
Tugnutt, Clb.	.27
Belfour, Dal.	.27
Potvin, LA	.27

Team Goaltending

WESTERN	GAA	Mins	GA	Shots	Sv%	EN	SO	EASTERN	GAA	Mins	GA	Shots	Sv%	EN	SO
Colorado	2.04	4979	169	2177	.922	10	11	New Jersey	2.25	4988	187	1900	.902	8	4
Edmonton	2.19	4996	182	2120	.914	5	8	Philadelphia	2.31	4986	192	2139	.910	7	7
Detroit	2.24	5008	187	2159	.913	2	7	Buffalo	2.41	4986	200	2120	.906	9	4
St. Louis	2.26	4990	188	1847	.898	7	7	Boston	2.42	4993	201	2057	.902	5	6
Los Angeles	2.29	4989	190	2051	.907	5	8	Toronto	2.49	4986	207	2044	.899	5	5
Anaheim	2.39	4976	198	2253	.912	7	5	Ottawa	2.50	4991	208	2126	.902	3	10
San Jose	2.40	4973	199	2335	.915	7	9	Montreal	2.51	4989	209	2597	.920	9	7
Chicago	2.49	4996	207	2077	.900	5	6	Carolina	2.59	5021	217	2214	.902	5	5
Phoenix	2.52	4993	210	2349	.911	6	6	Tampa Bay	2.63	4997	219	2523	.913	10	9
Vancouver	2.54	4978	211	2079	.899	5	8	NY Islanders	2.65	4987	220	2285	.904	9	6
Dallas	2.55	5008	213	2135	.900	7	3	Washington	2.89	4987	240	2357	.898	7	6
Calgary	2.65	4990	220	2242	.902	7	7	Pittsburgh	2.99	4994	249	2394	.896	6	6
Nashville	2.76	4995	230	2314	.901	7	5	Florida	3.01	4987	250	2666	.906	8	5
Minnesota	2.85	5004	238	2297	.896	1	6	NY Rangers	3.12	4963	258	2618	.901	6	2
Columbus	3.07	4979	255	2469	.897	9	3	Atlanta	3.46	4994	288	2911	.901	14	3

Power Play/Penalty Killing

Power play and penalty killing conversions. Power play: No—number of opportunities; GF—goals for; Pct—percentage. Penalty killing: No—number of times shorthanded; GA—goals against; Pct—percentage of penalties killed; SH—shorthanded goals for.

	—Power Play—			—Penalty Killing—					—Power Play—			—Penalty Killing—			
WESTERN	No	GF	Pct	No	GA	Pct	SH	EASTERN	No	GF	Pct	No	GA	Pct	SH
Los Angeles	353	73	20.7	366	49	86.6	5	Washington	299	58	19.4	325	58	82.2	2
Detroit	359	73	20.3	343	48	86.0	9	New Jersey	261	44	16.9	264	43	83.7	2
Vancouver	372	69	18.5	379	57	85.0	3	Ottawa	331	55	16.6	307	48	84.4	11
Colorado	344	62	18.0	315	41	87.0	7	NY Islanders	363	59	16.3	366	52	85.8	17
Chicago	302	54	17.9	340	63	81.5	4	Carolina	390	63	16.2	332	54	83.7	4
St. Louis	356	62	17.4	379	56	85.2	5	Toronto	349	54	15.5	328	51	84.5	9
Dallas	350	60	17.1	319	59	81.5	7	Montreal	301	45	15.0	276	38	86.2	7
San Jose	368	59	16.0	380	54	85.8	15	Tampa Bay	311	46	14.8	273	40	85.3	6
Phoenix	341	53	15.5	356	60	83.1	8	NY Rangers	326	48	14.7	398	80	79.9	8
Edmonton	333	51	15.3	348	50	85.6	12	Florida	341	50	14.7	393	76	80.7	8
Calgary	364	55	15.1	356	66	81.5	10	Pittsburgh	335	47	14.0	352	57	83.8	5
Minnesota	373	55	14.7	362	62	82.9	11	Boston	283	39	13.8	348	45	87.1	14
Nashville	337	48	14.2	354	50	85.9	6	Buffalo	374	50	13.4	304	41	86.5	7
Columbus	356	50	14.0	306	52	83.0	3	Philadelphia	299	39	13.0	293	40	86.3	8
Anaheim	373	43	11.5	330	46	86.1	4	Atlanta	306	37	12.1	358	65	81.8	3

Single Game Highs
INDIVIDUAL

Goals		Opponent	Date	Points			
4	Jiri Dopita, Philadelphia	Atlanta	Jan. 8	5	14 tied.		
4	Pascal Rheaume, Atlanta	Florida	Jan. 19				
3	55 tied.			**Saves**		**Opponent**	**Date**
				57	Roberto Luongo, Florida	Detroit	Feb. 27
Assists		**Opponent**	**Date**	53	Dwayne Roloson, Minnesota	Boston	Nov. 8
5	Joe Thornton, Boston	Florida	Dec. 28	53	Milan Hnilicka, Atlanta	Boston	Dec. 18
4	16 tied.			50	Frederic Cassivi, Atlanta	Ottawa	March 23

Team by Team Statistics

High scorers and goaltenders with at least ten games played. Players who competed for more than one team during the regular season are listed with their final club; (*) indicates rookies eligible for Calder Trophy.

Mighty Ducks of Anaheim

Top Scorers	Gm	G	A	Pts	+/-	PM	PP
Paul Kariya	82	32	25	57	-15	28	11
Matt Cullen	79	18	30	48	-1	24	3
Mike Leclerc	82	20	24	44	-12	107	8
Jeff Friesen	81	17	26	43	-1	44	1
Oleg Tverdovsky	73	6	26	32	0	31	2
Andy McDonald*	53	7	21	28	2	10	2
German Titov	66	13	14	27	4	36	1
Jason York	74	5	20	25	-11	60	3
Steve Rucchin	38	7	16	23	-3	6	4
Samuel Pahlsson	80	6	14	20	-16	26	1
Patric Kjellberg	77	8	11	19	-12	16	4
NASH	12	1	3	4	-3	6	0
ANA	65	7	8	15	-9	10	4
Dan Bylsma	77	8	9	17	5	28	0
Keith Carney	60	5	9	14	14	30	0
Pavel Trnka	71	2	11	13	-5	66	1
Ruslan Salei	82	4	7	11	-10	97	0
Marc Chouinard	45	4	5	9	2	10	0
Denny Lambert	73	2	5	7	1	213	0
Sergei Krivokrasov	26	2	3	5	-2	36	0
MIN	9	1	1	2	-1	17	0
ANA	17	1	2	3	-1	19	0

Acquired: LW Kjellberg from Nash. for RW Petr Tenkrat (Nov. 1); RW Krivokrasov from Min. for a '02 7th-round pick and future considerations (Nov. 1).

Goalies (10 Gm)	Gm	Min	GAA	Record	SV%
J-S Giguere	53	3127	2.13	20-25-6	.920
Steve Shields	33	1777	2.67	9-20-2	.907
ANAHEIM	82	4976	2.39	29-45-8	.912

Shutouts: Giguere (4). **Assists:** none. **PM:** Giguere (28), Shields (4).

Atlanta Thrashers

Top Scorers	Gm	G	A	Pts	+/-	PM	PP
Dany Heatley*	82	26	41	67	-19	56	7
Ilya Kovalchuk*	65	29	22	51	-19	28	7
Tony Hrkac	80	18	26	44	-12	12	5
Lubos Bartecko	71	13	14	27	-15	30	1
Frantisek Kaberle	61	5	20	25	-11	24	1
Yannick Tremblay	66	9	15	24	-15	47	1
Patrik Stefan	59	7	16	23	-4	22	0
Pascal Rheaume	61	11	11	22	-4	29	6
CHI	19	0	2	2	-1	4	0
ATL	42	11	9	20	-3	25	6
Tomi Kallio	60	8	14	22	-8	12	1
Daniel Tjarnqvist*	75	2	16	18	-22	14	1
Per Svartvadet	78	3	12	15	-12	24	0
Andy Sutton	43	2	8	10	-4	81	1
MIN	19	2	4	6	-4	35	1
ATL	24	0	4	4	0	46	0
Brian Pothier*	33	3	6	9	-19	22	1
Jeff Odgers	46	4	4	8	-3	135	0
Todd Reirden	65	3	5	8	-25	82	1
Andreas Karlsson	42	1	7	8	-8	20	0

Three tied with 6 points each.

Acquired: D Sutton from Min. for RW Hnat Domenichelli (Jan. 22). **Claimed:** C Rheaume off waivers from Chi. (Nov. 14).

Goalies (10 Gm)	Gm	Min	GAA	Record	SV%
Milan Hnilicka	60	3367	3.19	13-33-10	.908
Damian Rhodes	15	769	3.67	2-10-1	.893
ATLANTA	82	4994	3.46	19-52-11	.901

Shutouts: Hnilicka (3). **Assists:** Hnilicka (2). **PM:** Hnilicka (8).

Boston Bruins

Top Scorers	Gm	G	A	Pts	+/-	PM	PP
Glen Murray	82	41	30	71	31	40	9
LA	9	6	5	11	5	0	4
BOS	73	35	25	60	26	40	5
Sergei Samsonov	74	29	41	70	21	27	3
Joe Thornton	66	22	46	68	7	127	6
Bill Guerin	78	41	25	66	-1	91	10
Brian Rolston	82	31	31	62	11	30	6
Jozef Stumpel	81	8	50	58	22	18	1
LA	9	1	3	4	1	4	0
BOS	72	7	47	54	21	14	1
Martin Lapointe	68	17	23	40	12	101	4
Marty McInnis	79	11	17	28	-15	33	2
ANA	60	9	14	23	-14	25	2
BOS	19	2	3	5	-1	8	0
Rob Zamuner	66	12	13	25	6	24	1
Sean O'Donnell	80	3	22	25	27	89	1
P.J. Axelsson	78	7	17	24	6	16	0
Hal Gill	79	4	18	22	16	77	0
Nick Boynton*	80	4	14	18	18	107	0
Don Sweeney	81	3	15	18	22	35	1
Mike Knuble	54	8	6	14	9	42	0
Sean Brown	73	6	5	11	7	174	3
EDM	61	6	4	10	8	127	3
BOS	12	0	1	1	-1	47	0

Acquired: RW Murray and C Stumpel from LA for C Jason Allison and LW Mikko Eloranta (Oct. 24); RW McInnis from Ana. for a '02 3rd-round pick (Mar. 5); D Brown from Edm. for D Bobby Allen (Mar. 19).

Goalies (10 Gm)	Gm	Min	GAA	Record	SV%
Byron Dafoe	64	3827	2.21	35-26-3	.907
John Grahame	19	1079	2.89	8-7-2	.897
BOSTON	82	4993	2.42	43-33-6	.902

Shutouts: Dafoe (4), Grahame (1). **Assists:** Dafoe and Grahame (1). **PM:** Dafoe (27), Grahame (6).

Buffalo Sabres

Top Scorers	Gm	G	A	Pts	+/-	PM	PP
Miroslav Satan	82	37	36	73	14	33	15
Stu Barnes	68	17	31	48	6	26	5
Tim Connolly	82	10	35	45	4	34	3
J.P. Dumont	76	23	21	44	-10	42	7
Maxim Afinogenov	81	21	19	40	-9	69	3
Chris Gratton	82	15	24	39	0	75	1
Curtis Brown	82	20	17	37	-4	32	4
Alexei Zhitnik	82	1	33	34	-1	80	1
Jason Woolley	59	8	20	28	-6	34	6
Vaclav Varada	76	7	16	23	-7	82	1
Vyacheslav Kozlov	38	9	13	22	0	16	3
Taylor Pyatt	48	10	10	20	4	35	0
Erik Rasmussen	69	8	11	19	-1	34	0
James Patrick	56	5	8	13	3	16	1
Dmitri Kalinin	58	2	11	13	-6	26	0
Jay McKee	81	2	11	13	18	43	0
Rhett Warrener	65	5	5	10	15	113	0
Richard Smehlik	60	3	6	9	-9	22	0
Bob Corkum	75	3	5	8	-32	20	0
ATL	65	3	4	7	-30	16	0
BUF	10	0	1	1	-2	4	0
Denis Hamel	61	2	6	8	-1	28	0
Brian Campbell	29	3	3	6	0	12	0
Eric Boulton	35	2	3	5	-1	129	0
Rob Ray	71	2	3	5	-3	200	0

Acquired: C Corkum from Atl. for a '02 5th-round pick (Mar. 19).

Goalies (10 Gm)	Gm	Min	GAA	Record	Sv%
Martin Biron	72	4085	2.22	31-28-10	.915
Mika Noronen*	10	518	2.66	4-3-1	.894
BUFFALO	82	4986	2.41	35-36-11	.906

Shutouts: Biron (4). **Assists:** Biron (1). **PM:** Biron (8), Noronen (2).

Calgary Flames

Top Scorers	Gm	G	A	Pts	+/-	PM	PP
Jarome Iginla	82	52	44	96	27	77	16
Craig Conroy	81	27	48	75	24	32	7
Dean McAmmond	73	21	30	51	2	60	7
Derek Morris	61	4	30	34	-4	88	2
Marc Savard	56	14	19	33	-18	48	7
Toni Lydman	79	6	22	28	-8	52	1
Igor Kravchuk	78	4	22	26	3	19	1
Rob Niedermayer	57	6	14	20	-15	49	1
Clarke Wilm	66	4	14	18	-1	61	0
Chris Clark	64	10	7	17	-12	79	2
Scott Nichol	60	8	9	17	-9	107	2
Jamie Wright	44	4	12	16	6	20	0
Dave Lowry	62	7	6	13	-20	51	2
Denis Gauthier	66	5	8	13	9	91	0
Steve Begin*	51	7	5	12	-3	79	1
Ronald Petrovicky	77	5	7	12	0	85	1
Blake Sloan	67	2	9	11	-17	50	0
CLB	60	2	7	9	-18	46	0
CALG	7	0	2	2	1	4	0
Robyn Regehr	78	2	6	8	-24	93	0
Jeff Shantz	40	3	3	6	-3	23	2
Bob Boughner	79	2	4	6	9	170	0

Two tied with 4 points each.

Acquired: LW Sloan from Clb. for D Jamie Allison (Mar. 19).

Goalies (10 Gm)	Gm	Min	GAA	Record	SV%
Roman Turek	69	4081	2.53	30-28-11	.906
Mike Vernon	18	825	2.76	2-9-1	.899
CALGARY	82	4990	2.65	32-38-12	.902

Shutouts: Turek (5), Vernon (1). **Assists:** Turek (5), Vernon (3). **PM:** Turek (4).

Carolina Hurricanes

Top Scorers	Gm	G	A	Pts	+/-	PM	PP
Ron Francis	80	27	50	77	4	18	14
Sami Kapanen	77	27	42	69	9	23	11
Jeff O'Neill	76	31	33	64	-5	63	11
Rod Brind'Amour	81	23	32	55	3	40	5
Bates Battaglia	82	21	25	46	-6	44	5
Erik Cole*	81	16	24	40	-10	35	3
Sean Hill	72	7	26	33	0	89	4
ST.L	23	0	3	3	1	28	0
CAR	49	7	23	30	-1	61	4
Josef Vasicek	78	14	17	31	-7	53	3
Martin Gelinas	72	13	16	29	-1	30	3
Marek Malik	82	4	19	23	8	88	0
Glen Wesley	77	5	13	18	-8	56	1
Kevyn Adams	77	6	11	17	-5	43	0
FLA	44	4	8	12	-3	28	0
CAR	33	2	3	5	-2	15	0
Bret Hedican	57	5	11	16	-1	22	0
FLA	31	3	7	10	-4	12	0
CAR	26	2	4	6	3	10	0
David Tanabe	78	1	15	16	-13	35	0
Aaron Ward	79	3	11	14	0	74	0
Jeff Daniels	65	4	1	5	-6	12	0
Jaroslav Svoboda*	10	2	2	4	0	2	0

Acquired: D Hill from St.L for D Steven Halko and a '02 4th-round pick (Dec. 5); C Adams, D Hedican, D Tomas Malec and a conditional 2nd-round pick from Fla. for D Sandis Ozolinsh and C Byron Ritchie (Jan. 16); G Weekes from TB for RW Shane Willis and LW Chris Dingman (Mar. 5).

Goalies (10 Gm)	Gm	Min	GAA	Record	Sv%
Arturs Irbe	51	2974	2.54	20-19-11	.902
Kevin Weekes	21	950	2.72	5-9-0	.916
TB	19	830	2.89	3-9-0	.915
CAR	2	120	1.50	2-0-0	.927
CAROLINA	82	5021	2.59	35-31-16	.902

Shutouts: Irbe (3), Weekes (2 with TB). **Assists:** Irbe (1). **PM:** Irbe (10).

Chicago Blackhawks

Top Scorers	Gm	G	A	Pts	+/-	PM	PP
Eric Daze	.82	38	32	70	17	36	12
Alexei Zhamnov	.77	22	45	67	8	67	6
Tony Amonte	.82	27	39	66	11	67	6
Michael Nylander	.82	15	46	61	28	50	6
Steve Sullivan	.78	21	39	60	23	67	3
Kyle Calder	.81	17	36	53	8	47	6
Phil Housley	.80	15	24	39	-3	34	8
Igor Korolev	.82	9	20	29	-5	20	0
Mark Bell*	.80	12	16	28	-6	124	1
Tom Fitzgerald	.78	8	12	20	-7	39	0
NASH	.63	7	9	16	-4	33	0
CHI	.15	1	3	4	-3	6	0
Jon Klemm	.82	4	16	20	-3	42	2
Boris Mironov	.64	4	14	18	15	68	0
Lyle Odelein	.77	2	16	18	-28	93	0
CLB	.65	2	14	16	-28	89	0
CHI	.12	0	2	2	0	4	0
Steve Thomas	.34	11	4	15	0	17	3
Alexander Karpovtsev	.65	1	9	10	10	40	0
Joe Reekie	.55	2	6	8	-5	69	0
WASH	.38	2	4	6	-7	41	0
CHI	.17	0	2	2	2	28	0
Steve Poapst	.56	1	7	8	6	30	0

Acquired: D Reekie from Wash. for a '02 4th-round pick (Jan. 17); RW Fitzgerald from Nash. for a '03 4th-round pick and future considerations (Mar. 13); D Odelein from Clb. for D Jaroslav Spacek and a '03 2nd-round pick (Mar. 19).

Goalies (10 Gm)	Gm	Min	GAA	Record	SV%
Steve Passmore	.23	1142	2.26	8-5-4	.904
Jocelyn Thibault	.67	3838	2.49	33-23-9	.902
CHICAGO	.82	4996	2.49	41-28-13	.900

Shutouts: Thibault (6). **Assists:** Passmore (1). **PM:** Passmore (2), Thibault (1).

Colorado Avalanche

Top Scorers	Gm	G	A	Pts	+/-	PM	PP
Joe Sakic	.82	26	53	79	12	18	9
Rob Blake	.75	16	40	56	16	58	10
Alex Tanguay	.70	13	35	48	8	36	7
Chris Drury	.82	21	25	46	1	38	5
Steve Reinprecht	.67	19	27	46	14	18	4
Milan Hejduk	.62	21	23	44	0	24	7
Martin Skoula	.82	10	21	31	-3	42	5
Radim Vrbata*	.52	18	12	30	7	14	6
Adam Foote	.55	5	22	27	7	55	1
Greg de Vries	.82	8	12	20	18	57	1
Mike Keane	.78	6	11	17	-4	38	1
ST.L	.56	4	6	10	-2	22	1
COL	.22	2	5	7	-2	16	0
Stephane Yelle	.73	5	12	17	1	48	0
Eric Messier	.74	5	10	15	-5	26	0
Brian Willsie*	.56	7	7	14	4	14	2
Darius Kasparaitis	.80	2	12	14	0	142	0
PIT	.69	2	12	14	-1	123	0
COL	.11	0	0	0	1	19	0
Pascal Trepanier	.74	4	9	13	4	59	2
Dan Hinote	.58	6	6	12	8	39	0
Brad Larsen*	.50	2	7	9	4	47	1
Riku Hahl*	.22	2	3	5	1	14	0
Scott Parker	.63	1	4	5	0	154	0

Acquired: RW Keane from St.L for RW Shjon Podein (Feb. 11); D Kasparaitis from Pit. for D Rick Berry and LW Ville Nieminen (Mar. 19).

Goalies (10 Gm)	Gm	Min	GAA	Record	SV%
David Aebischer	.21	1184	1.88	13-6-0	.931
Patrick Roy	.63	3773	1.94	32-23-8	.925
COLORADO	.82	4979	2.04	45-29-8	.922

Shutouts: Roy (9), Aebischer (2). **Assists:** Roy (3). **PM:** Roy (26), Aebischer (4).

Columbus Blue Jackets

Top Scorers	Gm	G	A	Pts	+/-	PM	PP
Ray Whitney	.67	21	40	61	-22	12	6
Mike Sillinger	.80	20	23	43	-35	54	8
Espen Knutsen	.77	11	31	42	-28	47	5
Grant Marshall	.81	15	18	33	-20	86	6
David Vyborny	.75	13	18	31	-14	6	6
Deron Quint	.75	7	18	25	-34	26	3
Tyler Wright	.77	13	11	24	-40	100	4
Jaroslav Spacek	.74	5	13	18	-4	53	1
CHI	.60	3	10	13	5	29	0
CLB	.14	2	3	5	-9	24	1
Geoff Sanderson	.42	11	5	16	-15	12	5
Serge Aubin	.71	8	8	16	-20	32	1
Rostislav Klesla*	.75	8	8	16	-6	74	1
Robert Kron	.59	4	11	15	-14	4	1
Brett Harkins	.25	2	12	14	-5	8	2
Kevin Dineen	.59	5	8	13	-6	62	0
Mattias Timander	.78	4	7	11	-34	44	1
Jean-Luc Grand-Pierre	.81	2	6	8	-28	90	0
Jody Shelley*	.52	3	3	6	1	206	0
Radim Bicanek	.60	1	5	6	-15	34	0
Chris Nielsen	.23	2	3	5	-3	4	0
Sean Pronger	.26	3	1	4	-4	4	0

Acquired: D Spacek and a '03 2nd-round pick from Chi. for D Lyle Odelein (Mar. 19).

Goalies (10 Gm)	Gm	Min	GAA	Record	SV%
Ron Tugnutt	.44	2502	2.85	12-27-3	.900
Marc Denis	.42	2335	3.11	9-24-5	.899
COLUMBUS	.82	4979	3.07	22-52-8	.897

Shutouts: Tugnutt (2), Denis (1). **Assists:** Tugnutt and Denis (1). **PM:** Denis (2).

Dallas Stars

Top Scorers	Gm	G	A	Pts	+/-	PM	PP
Mike Modano	.78	34	43	77	14	38	6
Jere Lehtinen	.73	25	24	49	27	14	7
Pierre Turgeon	.66	15	32	47	-4	16	7
Jason Arnott	.73	25	20	45	2	65	10
NJ	.63	22	19	41	3	59	8
DAL	.10	3	1	4	-1	6	2
Sergei Zubov	.80	12	32	44	-4	22	8
Brenden Morrow	.72	17	18	35	12	109	4
Darryl Sydor	.78	4	29	33	3	50	2
Kirk Muller	.78	10	20	30	-12	28	4
Derian Hatcher	.80	4	21	25	12	87	1
Richard Matvichuk	.82	9	12	21	11	52	4
Pat Verbeek	.64	7	13	20	-4	72	3
Randy McKay	.69	7	11	18	4	72	3
NJ	.55	6	7	13	2	65	3
DAL	.14	1	4	5	2	7	0
Manny Malhotra	.72	8	6	14	-4	47	0
NYR	.56	7	6	13	-1	42	0
DAL	.16	1	0	1	-3	5	0
Scott Pellerin	.68	4	10	14	-11	21	0
BOS	.35	1	5	6	-6	6	0
DAL	.33	3	5	8	-5	15	0
Rob DiMaio	.61	6	6	12	-2	25	0
Brent Gilchrist	.45	3	6	9	-9	14	0
DET	.19	1	1	2	-3	8	0
DAL	.26	2	5	7	-6	6	0

Acquired: C Malhotra and LW Barrett Heisten from NYR for LW Martin Rucinsky and C Roman Lyashenko (Mar. 12); C Arnott and RW McKay from NJ for C Joe Nieuwendyk and RW Jamie Langenbrunner (Mar. 19). **Claimed:** LW Pellerin off waivers from Bos. (Jan. 12); C Gilchrist off waivers from Det. (Feb. 13).

Goalies (10 Gm)	Gm	Min	GAA	Record	SV%
Marty Turco	.31	1519	2.09	15-6-2	.921
Ed Belfour	.60	3467	2.65	21-27-11	.895
DALLAS	.82	5008	2.55	36-33-13	.900

Shutouts: Turco (2), Belfour (1). **Assists:** Belfour (5). **PM:** Belfour (12), Turco (10).

Detroit Red Wings

Top Scorers	Gm	G	A	Pts	+/-	PM	PP
Brendan Shanahan	.80	37	38	75	23	118	12
Sergei Fedorov	.81	31	37	68	20	36	10
Brett Hull	.82	30	33	63	18	35	7
Nicklas Lidstrom	.78	9	50	59	13	20	6
Luc Robitaille	.81	30	20	50	-2	38	13
Steve Yzerman	.52	13	35	48	11	18	5
Igor Larionov	.70	11	32	43	-5	50	4
Chris Chelios	.79	6	33	39	40	126	1
Pavel Datsyuk*	.70	11	24	35	4	4	2
Kris Draper	.82	15	15	30	26	56	0
Tomas Holmstrom	.69	8	18	26	-12	58	6
Boyd Devereaux	.79	9	16	25	9	24	0
Kirk Maltby	.82	9	15	24	15	40	0
Mathieu Dandenault	.81	8	12	20	-5	44	2
Steve Duchesne	.64	3	15	18	3	28	1
Fredrik Olausson	.47	2	13	15	9	22	0
Darren McCarty	.62	5	7	12	2	98	0
Jason Williams*	.25	8	2	10	2	4	4
Jiri Fischer	.80	2	8	10	17	67	0
Jiri Slegr	.46	3	6	9	-20	59	1
ATL	.38	3	5	8	-21	51	1
DET	.8	0	1	1	1	8	0
Sean Avery*	.36	2	2	4	1	68	0
Maxim Kuznetsov*	.39	1	2	3	0	40	0
Uwe Krupp	.8	0	1	1	-1	8	0
Jesse Wallin*	.15	0	1	1	-1	13	0

Acquired: D Slegr from Atl. for C Yuri Butsayev and a '02 3rd-round pick (Mar. 19).

Goalies (10 Gm)	Gm	Min	GAA	Record	Sv%
Dominik Hasek	.65	3872	2.17	41-15-8	.915
Manny Legace	.20	1117	2.42	10-6-2	.911
DETROIT	.82	5008	2.24	51-21-10	.913

Shutouts: Hasek (5), Legace (1). **Assists:** Hasek and Legace (1). **PM:** Hasek (8).

Edmonton Oilers

Top Scorers	Gm	G	A	Pts	+/-	PM	PP
Mike York	.81	20	41	61	7	16	3
NYR	.69	18	39	57	8	16	2
EDM	.12	2	2	4	-1	0	1
Mike Comrie	.82	33	27	60	16	45	8
Anson Carter	.82	28	32	60	3	25	12
Ryan Smyth	.61	15	35	50	7	48	7
Janne Niinimaa	.81	5	39	44	13	80	1
Jochen Hecht	.82	16	24	40	4	60	5
Todd Marchant	.82	12	22	34	7	41	0
Dan Cleary	.65	10	19	29	-1	51	2
Mike Grier	.82	8	17	25	1	32	0
Eric Brewer	.81	7	18	25	-5	45	6
Shawn Horcoff	.61	8	14	22	3	18	0
Georges Laraque	.80	5	14	19	6	157	1
Jason Smith	.74	5	13	18	14	103	0
Ethan Moreau	.80	11	5	16	4	81	0
Josh Green	.80	10	5	15	9	52	1
Marty Reasoner	.52	6	5	11	0	41	3
Steve Staios	.73	5	5	10	10	108	0
Domenic Pittis	.22	0	6	6	-2	8	0
Scott Ferguson	.50	3	2	5	11	75	0
Brian Swanson*	.8	1	1	2	-1	0	0

Acquired: C York and a '02 4th-round pick from NYR for LW Rem Murray and D Tom Poti (Mar. 19).

Goalies (10 Gm)	Gm	Min	GAA	Record	Sv%
Jussi Markkanen	.14	784	1.84	6-4-2	.929
Tommy Salo	.69	4035	2.22	30-28-10	.913
EDMONTON	.82	4996	2.19	38-32-12	.914

Shutouts: Salo (6), Markkanen (2). **Assists:** Salo (1). **PM:** Salo (2).

Florida Panthers

Top Scorers	Gm	G	A	Pts	+/-	PM	PP
Sandis Ozolinsh	.83	14	38	52	-7	58	3
CAR	.46	4	19	23	-4	34	1
FLA	.37	10	19	29	-3	24	2
Kristian Huselius*	.79	23	22	45	-4	14	6
Marcus Nilson	.81	14	19	33	-14	55	6
Jason Wiemer	.70	11	20	31	-4	178	5
Ivan Novoseltsev	.70	13	16	29	-10	44	1
Olli Jokinen	.80	9	20	29	-16	98	3
Robert Svehla	.82	7	22	29	-19	87	3
Niklas Hagman*	.78	10	18	28	-6	8	0
Viktor Kozlov	.50	9	18	27	-16	20	6
Valeri Bure	.31	8	10	18	-3	12	2
Brad Ference	.80	2	15	17	-13	254	0
Pierre Dagenais*	.42	10	4	14	-10	8	3
NJ	.16	3	3	6	-5	4	1
FLA	.26	7	1	8	-5	4	2
Byron Ritchie	.35	5	6	11	-2	36	2
CAR	.4	0	0	0	0	2	0
FLA	.31	5	6	11	-2	34	2
Igor Ulanov	.53	0	10	10	-7	64	0
NYR	.39	0	6	6	-4	53	0
FLA	.14	0	4	4	-3	11	0
Peter Worrell	.79	4	5	9	-15	354	0

Acquired: D Ozolinsh and C Ritchie from Car. for D Bret Hedican, D Tomas Malec, C Kevyn Adams and a conditional 2nd-round pick (Jan. 16); D Ulanov, D Filip Novak, a '02 1st-round pick and switch of '03 2nd-round picks from NYR for RW Pavel Bure (Mar. 18). **Claimed:** RW Dagenais off waivers from NJ (Jan. 12).

Goalies (10 Gm)	Gm	Min	GAA	Record	Sv%
Roberto Luongo	.58	3030	2.77	16-33-4	.915
Trevor Kidd	.33	1683	3.21	4-16-5	.895
FLORIDA	.82	4987	3.01	22-50-10	.906

Shutouts: Luongo (4), Kidd (1). **Assists:** Luongo and Kidd (1). **PM:** Luongo (6).

Los Angeles Kings

Top Scorers	Gm	G	A	Pts	+/-	PM	PP
Jason Allison	.73	19	55	74	2	68	5
Adam Deadmarsh	.76	29	33	62	8	71	12
Zigmund Palffy	.63	32	27	59	5	26	15
Cliff Ronning	.81	19	35	54	0	32	5
NASH	.67	18	31	49	0	24	4
LA	.14	1	4	5	0	8	1
Jaroslav Modry	.80	4	38	42	-4	65	4
Bryan Smolinski	.80	13	25	38	7	56	4
Steve Heinze	.73	15	16	31	-15	46	0
Mathieu Schneider	.55	7	23	30	3	68	4
Philippe Boucher	.80	7	23	30	0	94	4
Craig Johnson	.72	13	14	27	14	24	0
Eric Belanger	.53	8	16	24	2	21	2
Ian Laperriere	.81	8	14	22	5	125	0
Lubomir Visnovsky	.72	4	17	21	-5	14	1
Mikko Eloranta	.77	9	9	18	-1	56	1
BOS	.6	0	0	0	-1	2	0
LA	.71	9	9	18	0	54	1
Aaron Miller	.74	5	12	17	14	54	0
Brad Chartrand	.46	7	9	16	5	40	0
Kelly Buchberger	.74	6	7	13	-13	105	0
Mattias Norstrom	.79	2	9	11	-2	38	0

Acquired: C Allison and LW Eloranta from Bos. for RW Glen Murray and C Jozef Stumpel (Oct. 24); LW Ronning from Nash. for D Jari Karalahti and a cond. '03 pick (Mar. 19).

Goalies (10 Gm)	Gm	Min	GAA	Record	Sv%
Jamie Storr	.19	886	1.90	9-4-3	.922
Felix Potvin	.71	4071	2.31	31-27-8	.907
LOS ANGELES	.82	4989	2.29	40-31-11	.907

Shutouts: Potvin (6), Storr (2). **Assists:** Potvin (1). **PM:** Potvin (19), Storr (4).

Minnesota Wild

Top Scorers	Gm	G	A	Pts	+/-	PM	PP
Andrew Brunette	.81	21	48	69	-4	18	10
Marian Gaborik	.78	30	37	67	0	34	10
Jim Dowd	.82	13	30	43	-14	54	5
Sergei Zholtok	.73	19	20	39	-10	28	10
Antti Laaksonen	.82	16	17	33	-5	22	0
Wes Walz	.64	10	20	30	0	43	0
Pascal Dupuis*	.76	15	12	27	-10	16	3
Richard Park	.63	10	15	25	-1	10	2
Hnat Domenichelli	.67	9	16	25	-23	44	1
ATL	.40	8	11	19	-18	34	1
MIN	.27	1	5	6	-5	10	0
Darby Hendrickson	.68	9	15	24	-22	50	2
Filip Kuba	.62	5	19	24	-6	32	3
Lubomir Sekeras	.69	4	20	24	-7	34	4
Stacy Roest	.58	10	11	21	-3	8	1
Aaron Gavey	.71	6	11	17	-21	38	1
Willie Mitchell	.68	3	10	13	-16	68	0
Jason Marshall	.80	5	6	11	-8	148	1
Nick Schultz*	.52	4	6	10	0	14	1
Ladislav Benysek	.74	1	7	8	-12	28	0
Tony Virta	.8	2	3	5	0	0	0
Matt Johnson	.60	4	0	4	-13	183	0
Brad Brown	.51	0	4	4	-11	123	0

Acquired: RW Domenichelli from Atl. for D Andy Sutton (Jan. 22).

Goalies (10 Gm)	Gm	Min	GAA	Record	Sv%
Dwayne Roloson	.45	2506	2.68	14-20-7	.901
Manny Fernandez	.44	2463	3.05	12-24-5	.892
MINNESOTA	.82	5004	2.85	26-44-12	.896

Shutouts: Roloson (5), Fernandez (1). **Assists:** none. **PM:** Roloson (8), Fernandez (4).

Montreal Canadiens

Top Scorers	Gm	G	A	Pts	+/-	PM	PP
Yanic Perreault	.82	27	29	56	-3	40	6
Richard Zednik	.82	22	22	44	-3	59	4
Oleg Petrov	.75	24	17	41	-4	12	3
Doug Gilmour	.70	10	31	41	-7	48	5
Joe Juneau	.70	8	28	36	-3	10	1
Andreas Dackell	.79	15	18	33	-3	24	2
Patrice Brisebois	.71	4	29	33	9	25	2
Sergei Berezin	.70	11	15	26	2	8	4
PHO	.41	7	9	16	-1	4	1
MON	.29	4	6	10	3	4	3
Craig Rivet	.82	8	17	25	1	76	0
Andrei Markov	.56	5	19	24	-1	24	2
Chad Kilger	.75	8	15	23	-7	27	0
Shaun Van Allen	.73	8	13	21	0	26	0
DAL	.19	2	4	6	-5	6	0
MON	.54	6	9	15	5	20	0
Jan Bulis	.53	9	10	19	-2	8	1
Mike Ribeiro	.43	8	10	18	-11	12	3
Donald Audette	.33	5	13	18	3	20	3
DAL	.20	4	8	12	2	12	3
MON	.13	1	5	6	1	8	0
Stephane Quintal	.75	6	10	16	-7	87	1
Bill Lindsay	.76	5	10	15	-11	140	0
FLA	.63	4	7	11	-11	117	0
MON	.13	1	3	4	0	23	0

Acquired: C Van Allen and RW Audette from Dal. for LW Martin Rucinsky and LW Benoit Brunet (Nov. 21); LW Berezin from Pho. for LW Brian Savage, a '02 or '03 3rd-round pick and future considerations (Jan. 25). **Claimed:** LW Lindsay off waivers from Fla. (Mar. 19). **Signed:** free agent C Gilmour (Oct. 6).

Goalies (10 Gm)	Gm	Min	GAA	Record	Sv%
Jose Theodore	.67	3864	2.11	30-24-10	.931
Jeff Hackett	.15	717	3.18	5-5-2	.904
MONTREAL	.82	4989	2.51	36-34-12	.920

Shutouts: Theodore (7). **Assists:** Theodore (2). **PM:** Theodore and Hackett (2).

Nashville Predators

Top Scorers	Gm	G	A	Pts	+/-	PM	PP
Greg Johnson	.82	18	26	44	-14	38	3
Denis Arkhipov	.82	20	22	42	-18	16	7
Kimmo Timonen	.82	13	29	42	2	28	5
Scott Hartnell	.75	14	27	41	5	111	3
Andy Delmore	.73	16	22	38	-13	22	11
Vladimir Orszagh	.79	15	21	36	-15	56	5
Martin Erat*	.80	9	24	33	-11	32	2
David Legwand	.63	11	19	30	1	54	1
Vitali Yachmenev	.75	11	16	27	-16	14	1
Petr Tenkrat	.67	8	16	24	-10	34	0
ANA	.9	0	0	0	-6	6	0
NASH	.58	8	16	24	-4	28	0
Karlis Skrastins	.82	4	13	17	-12	36	0
Greg Classen	.55	5	6	11	1	30	0
Bubba Berenzweig*	.26	3	7	10	-3	14	0
Scott Walker	.28	4	5	9	-13	18	1
Jukka Hentunen	.38	4	5	9	-9	4	1
CALG	.28	2	3	5	-9	4	1
NASH	.10	2	2	4	0	0	0

Three tied with 8 points each.

Acquired: RW Tenkrat from Ana. for LW Patric Kjellberg (Nov. 1); RW Hentunen from Calg. for a conditional '03 pick (Mar. 17).

Goalies (10 Gm)	Gm	Min	GAA	Record	Sv%
Mike Dunham	.58	3316	2.61	23-24-9	.906
Tomas Vokoun	.29	1471	2.69	5-14-4	.903
NASHVILLE	.82	4995	2.76	28-41-13	.901

Shutouts: Dunham (3), Vokoun (2). **Assists:** Dunham (2). **PM:** Dunham, Vokoun and Jan Lasak (2).

New Jersey Devils

Top Scorers	Gm	G	A	Pts	+/-	PM	PP
Patrik Elias	.75	29	32	61	4	36	8
Joe Nieuwendyk	.81	25	33	58	0	22	6
DAL	.67	23	24	47	-2	18	6
NJ	.14	2	9	11	2	4	0
Bobby Holik	.81	25	29	54	7	97	6
Petr Sykora	.73	21	27	48	12	44	4
Scott Gomez	.76	10	38	48	-4	36	1
Brian Rafalski	.76	7	40	47	15	18	2
Sergei Brylin	.76	16	28	44	21	10	5
Scott Niedermayer	.76	11	22	33	12	30	2
Jamie Langenbrunner	.82	13	19	32	-9	77	0
DAL	.68	10	16	26	-11	54	0
NJ	.14	3	3	6	2	23	0
Stephane Richer	.68	14	14	28	-9	14	1
PIT	.58	13	12	25	-8	14	1
NJ	.10	1	2	3	-1	0	0
John Madden	.82	15	8	23	6	25	0
Valeri Kamensky	.54	7	14	21	1	20	0
DAL	.24	3	9	12	3	2	0
NJ	.30	4	8	12	-2	18	-0
Scott Stevens	.82	1	16	17	15	44	0
Jay Pandolfo	.65	4	10	14	12	15	0
Brian Gionta*	.33	4	7	11	10	8	0
Sergei Nemchinov	.68	5	5	10	-9	10	0
Andreas Salomonsson	.39	4	5	9	-12	22	1
Christian Berglund*	.15	2	7	9	-3	8	0
Jim McKenzie	.67	3	5	8	0	123	1

Acquired: LW Kamensky from Dal. for D Andre Lakos and future considerations (Jan. 16); C Nieuwendyk and RW Langenbrunner from Dal. for C Jason Arnott and RW Randy McKay (Mar. 19); RW Richer from Pit. for a '02 conditional pick (Mar. 19).

Goalies (10 Gm)	Gm	Min	GAA	Record	Sv%
Martin Brodeur	.73	4347	2.15	38-26-9	.906
NEW JERSEY	.82	4988	2.25	41-32-9	.902

Shutouts: Brodeur (4). **Assists:** Brodeur (4). **PM:** Brodeur (8), John Vanbiesbrouck (4).

New York Islanders

Top Scorers	Gm	G	A	Pts	+/-	PM	PP
Alexei Yashin	.78	32	43	75	-3	25	15
Mark Parrish	.78	30	30	60	10	32	9
Michael Peca	.80	25	35	60	19	62	3
Shawn Bates	.71	17	35	52	18	30	1
Mariusz Czerkawski	.82	22	29	51	-8	48	6
Brad Isbister	.79	17	21	38	1	113	4
Oleg Kvasha	.71	13	25	38	-4	80	2
Roman Hamrlik	.70	11	26	37	7	78	4
Adrian Aucoin	.81	12	22	34	23	62	7
Kenny Jonsson	.76	10	22	32	15	26	2
Dave Scatchard	.80	12	15	27	-4	111	3
Kip Miller	.37	17	7	24	2	6	2
Claude Lapointe	.80	9	12	21	-9	60	0
Dick Tarnstrom	.62	3	16	19	-12	38	0
Jason Blake	.82	8	10	18	-11	36	0
Mats Lindgren	.59	3	12	15	0	16	0
Darren Van Impe	.67	3	8	11	12	59	2
NYR	.17	1	0	1	3	12	1
FLA	.36	1	6	7	3	31	1
NYI	.14	1	2	3	6	16	0
Eric Cairns	.74	2	5	7	-2	176	0

Acquired: D Van Impe from Fla. for a '03 5th-round pick (Mar. 19).

Goalies (10 Gm)	Gm	Min	GAA	Record	Sv%
Chris Osgood	.66	3743	2.50	32-25-6	.910
Garth Snow	.25	1217	2.71	10-7-2	.900
NY ISLANDERS	.82	4987	2.65	42-32-8	.904

Shutouts: Osgood (4), Snow (2). **Assists:** Osgood (4). **PM:** Snow (14), Osgood (10).

New York Rangers

Top Scorers	Gm	G	A	Pts	+/-	PM	PP
Eric Lindros	.72	37	36	73	19	138	12
Pavel Bure	.68	34	35	69	-5	62	12
FLA	.56	22	27	49	-14	56	9
NYR	.12	12	8	20	9	6	3
Theo Fleury	.82	24	39	63	0	216	7
Brian Leetch	.82	10	45	55	14	28	1
Petr Nedved	.78	21	25	46	-8	36	6
Martin Rucinsky	.75	11	27	38	8	42	3
MON	.18	2	6	8	-1	12	1
DAL	.42	6	11	17	3	24	2
NYR	.15	3	10	13	6	6	0
Radek Dvorak	.65	17	20	37	-20	14	3
Vladimir Malakhov	.81	6	22	28	10	83	1
Rem Murray	.80	8	19	27	-4	18	0
EDM	.69	7	17	24	5	14	0
NYR	.11	1	2	3	-9	4	0
Tom Poti	.66	2	23	25	-10	44	2
EDM	.55	1	16	17	-6	42	1
NYR	.11	1	7	8	-4	2	1
Andreas Johansson	.70	14	10	24	6	46	3
Sandy McCarthy	.82	10	13	23	-8	171	1
Mark Messier	.41	7	16	23	-1	32	2
Bryan Berard	.82	2	21	23	-1	60	0
Matthew Barnaby	.77	8	13	21	-10	214	0
TB	.29	0	0	0	3	70	0
NYR	.48	8	13	21	-3	144	0

Acquired: RW Barnaby from TB for LW Zdeno Ciger (Dec. 12); LW Rucinsky and C Roman Lyashenko from Dal. for C Manny Malhotra and LW Barrett Heisten (Mar. 12); RW Bure from Fla. for D Igor Ulanov, D Filip Novak, a '02 1st-round pick and switch of '03 2nd-round picks (Mar. 18); LW Murray and D Poti from Edm. for C Mike York and a '02 4th-round pick (Mar. 19).

Goalies (10 Gm)	Gm	Min	GAA	Record	Sv%
Mike Richter	.55	3195	2.95	24-26-4	.906
Dan Blackburn*	.31	1737	3.28	12-16-0	.898
NY RANGERS	.82	4963	3.12	36-42-4	.901

Shutouts: Richter (2). **Assists:** none. **PM:** Blackburn (10), Richter (4).

Ottawa Senators

Top Scorers	Gm	G	A	Pts	+/-	PM	PP
Daniel Alfredsson	.78	37	34	71	3	45	9
Radek Bonk	.82	25	45	70	3	52	6
Marian Hossa	.80	31	35	66	11	50	9
Martin Havlat	.72	22	28	50	-7	66	9
Todd White	.81	20	30	50	12	24	4
Shawn McEachern	.80	15	31	46	9	52	5
Magnus Arvedson	.74	12	27	39	27	35	0
Wade Redden	.79	9	25	34	22	48	4
Mike Fisher	.58	15	9	24	8	55	0
Zdeno Chara	.75	10	13	23	30	156	1
Benoit Brunet	.61	9	14	23	-3	12	1
MON	.16	0	2	2	-4	4	0
DAL	.32	4	9	13	5	8	0
OTT	.13	5	3	8	-4	0	1
Chris Phillips	.63	6	16	22	5	29	1
Sami Salo	.66	4	14	18	1	14	1
Karel Rachunek	.51	3	15	18	7	24	1
Chris Neil*	.72	10	7	17	5	231	1
Juha Ylonen	.80	4	11	15	-11	10	0
TB	.65	3	10	13	-10	8	0
OTT	.15	1	1	2	-1	2	0
Chris Herperger	.72	4	9	13	4	43	0
Curtis Leschyshyn	.79	1	9	10	-5	44	0

Acquired: LW Ylonen from TB for LW Andre Roy and a '02 6th-round pick (Mar. 15); LW Brunet from Dal. for a conditional '03 pick (Mar. 16).

Goalies (10 Gm)	Gm	Min	GAA	Record	Sv%
Jani Hurme	.25	1039	2.48	12-9-1	.907
Patrick Lalime	.61	3583	2.48	27-24-8	.903
OTTAWA	.82	4991	2.50	39-34-9	.902

Shutouts: Lalime (7), Hurme (3). **Assists:** Lalime (1). **PM:** Lalime (19), Hurme (17).

Philadelphia Flyers

Top Scorers	Gm	G	A	Pts	+/-	PM	PP
Adam Oates	.80	14	64	78	-4	28	3
WASH	.66	11	57	68	-2	22	3
PHI	.14	3	7	10	-2	6	0
Jeremy Roenick	.75	21	46	67	32	74	5
Simon Gagne	.79	33	33	66	31	32	4
Mark Recchi	.80	22	42	64	5	46	7
John LeClair	.82	25	26	51	5	30	4
Keith Primeau	.75	19	29	48	-3	128	5
Kim Johnsson	.82	11	30	41	12	42	5
Justin Williams	.75	17	23	40	11	32	0
Donald Brashear	.81	9	23	32	-8	199	1
VAN	.31	5	8	13	-8	90	1
PHI	.50	4	15	19	0	109	0
Marty Murray	.74	12	15	27	10	10	1
Jiri Dopita	.52	11	16	27	9	8	3
Ruslan Fedotenko	.78	17	9	26	15	43	0
Eric Desjardins	.65	6	19	25	-1	24	2
Eric Weinrich	.80	4	20	24	27	26	0
Dan McGillis	.75	5	14	19	17	46	2
Chris Therien	.77	4	10	14	16	30	0
Paul Ranheim	.79	5	4	9	5	36	1
Luke Richardson	.72	1	8	9	18	102	0
Todd Fedoruk	.55	3	4	7	-2	141	0
Billy Tibbetts	.42	1	6	7	-16	178	0
PIT	.33	1	5	6	-13	109	0
PHI	.9	0	1	1	-3	69	0

Acquired: LW Brashear from Van. for LW Jan Hlavac and TB's '02 3rd-round pick (Dec. 17); C Tibbetts from Pit. for C Kent Manderville and '02 1st, 2nd and 3rd-round picks (Mar. 19); C Oates from Wash. for G Maxime Ouellet and '02 1st, 2nd and 3rd-round picks (Mar. 19).

Goalies (10 Gm)	Gm	Min	GAA	Record	Sv%
Roman Cechmanek	.46	2603	2.05	24-13-6	.921
Brian Boucher	.41	2295	2.41	18-16-4	.905
PHILADELPHIA	.82	4998	2.31	42-30-10	.910

Shutouts: Cechmanek (4), Boucher (2). **Assists:** PM: Cechmanek and Neil Little (10), Boucher (4).

Phoenix Coyotes

Top Scorers	Gm	G	A	Pts	+/-	PM	PP
Daymond Langkow	80	27	35	62	18	36	6
Daniel Briere	78	32	28	60	6	52	12
Shane Doan	81	20	29	49	11	61	6
Teppo Numminen	76	13	35	48	13	20	4
Michal Handzus	79	14	30	44	-8	34	3
Ladislav Nagy	74	23	19	42	6	50	5
Brian Savage	77	20	21	41	-13	38	9
MON	47	14	15	29	-14	30	7
PHO	30	6	6	12	1	8	2
Claude Lemieux	82	16	25	41	-5	70	4
Danny Markov	72	6	30	36	-7	67	4
Mike Johnson	57	5	22	27	14	28	1
Paul Mara	75	7	17	24	-6	58	2
Krys Kolanos*	57	11	11	22	6	48	0
Brad May	72	10	12	22	11	95	1
Landon Wilson	47	7	12	19	4	46	1
Radoslav Suchy	81	5	12	17	25	10	1
Todd Simpson	67	2	13	15	20	152	0
Ossi Vaananen	76	2	12	14	6	74	0
Andrei Nazarov	77	6	5	11	-5	215	0
BOS	47	0	2	2	-2	164	0
PHO	30	6	3	9	7	51	0
Denis Pederson	48	2	6	8	-4	51	0
VAN	29	1	5	6	-2	31	0
PHO	19	1	1	2	-2	20	0
Drake Berehowsky	57	2	6	8	0	60	0
VAN	25	1	3	4	-5	18	0
PHO	32	1	4	5	5	42	0

Acquired: C Pederson and D Berehowsky from Van. for RW Trevor Letowski, LW Todd Warriner, RW Tyler Bouck and a '03 3rd-round pick (Dec. 28); LW Savage, a '02 or '03 3rd-round pick and future considerations from Mon. for LW Sergei Berezin (Jan. 25); LW Nazarov from Bos. for a '02 5th-round pick (Jan. 25).

Goalies (10 Gm)	Gm	Min	GAA	Record	Sv%
Sean Burke	60	3587	2.29	33-21-6	.920
Robert Esche	22	1145	2.72	6-10-2	.902
PHOENIX	82	4993	2.52	40-33-9	.911

Shutouts: Burke (5), Esche (1). **Assists:** Burke (1). **PM:** Esche (16), Burke (14), Patrick DesRochers (2).

Pittsburgh Penguins

Top Scorers	Gm	G	A	Pts	+/-	PM	PP
Alexei Kovalev	67	32	44	76	2	80	8
Jan Hrdina	79	24	33	57	-7	50	6
Robert Lang	62	18	32	50	9	16	5
Aleksey Morozov	72	20	29	49	-7	16	7
Randy Robitaille	58	14	23	37	-23	33	5
LA	18	4	3	7	-9	17	2
PIT	40	10	20	30	-14	16	3
Mario Lemieux	24	6	25	31	0	14	2
Michal Rozsival	79	9	20	29	-6	47	4
Ville Nieminen	66	11	16	27	-1	38	1
COL	53	10	14	24	1	30	1
PIT	13	1	2	3	-2	8	0
Kris Beech*	79	10	15	25	-25	45	2
Toby Petersen*	79	8	10	18	-15	4	1
Dan LaCouture	82	6	11	17	-19	71	0
Milan Kraft	68	8	8	16	-9	16	1
Shean Donovan	61	8	7	15	-21	44	1
ATL	48	6	6	12	-16	40	1
PIT	13	2	1	3	-5	4	0
Jeff Toms	52	9	5	14	-9	14	2
NYR	38	7	4	11	-4	10	2
PIT	14	2	1	3	-5	4	0

Acquired: LW Nieminen and D Rick Berry from Col. for D Darius Kasparaitis (Mar. 19). **Claimed:** RW Robitaille off waivers from LA (Jan. 4); RW Donovan off waivers from Atl. (Mar. 15); C Toms off waivers from NYR (Mar. 16).

Goalies (10 Gm)	Gm	Min	GAA	Record	Sv%
Johan Hedberg	66	3877	2.75	25-34-7	.904
J-S Aubin	21	1094	3.56	3-12-1	.879
PITTSBURGH	82	4994	2.99	28-46-8	.896

Shutouts: Hedberg (6). **Assists:** Hedberg (1). **PM:** Hedberg (22).

St. Louis Blues

Top Scorers	Gm	G	A	Pts	+/-	PM	PP
Pavol Demitra	82	35	43	78	14	46	11
Keith Tkachuk	73	38	37	75	21	117	13
Doug Weight	61	15	34	49	20	40	3
Chris Pronger	78	7	40	47	23	120	4
Al MacInnis	71	11	35	46	2	52	6
Cory Stillman	80	23	22	45	8	36	6
Scott Mellanby	64	15	26	41	-5	93	8
Scott Young	67	19	21	40	11	26	5
Ray Ferraro	76	14	23	37	-30	74	4
ATL	61	8	19	27	-32	66	2
ST.L	15	6	4	10	2	8	2
Dallas Drake	80	11	15	26	8	87	1
Alexander Khavanov	81	3	21	24	9	55	0
Shjon Podein	64	8	10	18	2	41	0
COL	41	6	6	12	0	39	0
ST.L	23	2	4	6	2	2	0
Jamal Mayers	77	9	8	17	9	99	0
Mike Eastwood	71	7	10	17	-3	41	0
Tyson Nash	64	6	7	13	2	100	0
Sergei Varlamov*	52	5	7	12	4	26	0
Bryce Salvador	66	5	7	12	3	78	1
Daniel Corso	41	5	6	11	3	6	1
Mike Van Ryn*	48	2	8	10	10	18	0
Jeff Finley	78	0	6	6	12	30	0
Reed Low	58	0	5	5	-3	160	0
Mark Rycroft*	9	0	3	3	0	6	0
Marc Bergevin	30	0	3	3	6	2	0

Acquired: RW Podein from Col. for RW Mike Keane (Feb. 11); C Ferraro from Atl. for a '02 4th-round pick (Mar. 18).

Goalies (10 Gm)	Gm	Min	GAA	Record	Sv%
Brent Johnson	58	3491	2.18	34-20-4	.902
Fred Brathwaite	25	1446	2.24	9-11-4	.901
ST. LOUIS	82	4990	2.26	43-31-8	.898

Shutouts: Johnson (5), Brathwaite (2). **Assists:** Johnson (4). **PM:** Johnson (2).

San Jose Sharks

Top Scorers	Gm	G	A	Pts	+/-	PM	PP
Owen Nolan	75	23	43	66	7	93	8
Vincent Damphousse	82	20	38	58	8	60	7
Teemu Selanne	82	29	25	54	-11	40	9
Mike Ricci	79	19	34	53	9	44	5
Patrick Marleau	79	21	23	44	9	40	3
Scott Thornton	77	26	16	42	11	116	6
Marco Sturm	77	21	20	41	23	32	4
Niklas Sundstrom	73	9	30	39	7	50	0
Gary Suter	82	6	27	33	13	57	3
Adam Graves	81	17	14	31	11	51	5
Brad Stuart	82	6	23	29	13	39	2
Matt Bradley*	54	9	13	22	22	43	0
Todd Harvey	69	9	13	22	16	73	0
Bryan Marchment	72	2	20	22	22	178	0
Marcus Ragnarsson	70	5	15	20	4	44	2
Jeff Jillson	48	5	13	18	2	29	3
Mike Rathje	52	5	12	17	23	48	4
Scott Hannan	75	2	12	14	10	57	0
Stephane Matteau	55	7	4	11	4	15	1
Alex Korolyuk	32	3	7	10	2	14	0
Mark Smith	49	3	3	6	-1	72	0
Shawn Heins	17	0	2	2	1	24	0
Steve Bancroft	5	0	1	1	-2	2	0

Goalies (10 Gm)	Gm	Min	GAA	Record	Sv%
Evgeni Nabokov	67	3901	2.29	37-24-5	.918
Miikka Kiprusoff*	20	1041	2.48	7-6-3	.915
SAN JOSE	82	4973	2.40	44-30-8	.915

Shutouts: Nabokov (7), Kiprusoff (2). **Assists:** Nabokov (3). **PM:** Nabokov (14), Kiprusoff (4).

Tampa Bay Lightning

Top Scorers	Gm	G	A	Pts	+/-	PM	PP
Brad Richards	82	20	42	62	-18	13	5
Vaclav Prospal	81	18	37	55	-11	38	7
Dave Andreychuk	82	21	17	38	-12	109	9
Vincent Lecavalier	76	20	17	37	-18	61	5
Martin St. Louis	53	16	19	35	4	20	6
Ben Clymer	81	14	20	34	-10	36	4
Pavel Kubina	82	11	23	34	-22	106	5
Fredrik Modin	54	14	17	31	0	27	2
Dan Boyle	66	8	18	26	-16	39	3
FLA	25	3	3	6	-1	12	1
TB	41	5	15	20	-15	27	2
Zdeno Ciger	56	12	13	25	-15	26	1
NYR	29	6	7	13	-3	16	1
TB	27	6	6	12	-12	10	0
Shane Willis	80	11	13	24	-8	30	2
CAR	59	7	10	17	-8	24	2
TB	21	4	3	7	0	6	0
Andre Roy	65	7	9	16	-2	211	0
OTT	56	6	8	14	3	148	0
TB	9	1	1	2	-5	63	0
Jimmie Olvestad*	74	3	11	14	3	24	0
Sheldon Keefe	39	6	7	13	-11	16	0
Jassen Cullimore	78	4	9	13	-1	58	0
Cory Sarich	72	0	11	11	-4	105	0

Acquired: LW Ciger from NYR for RW Matthew Barnaby (Dec. 12); D Boyle from Fla. for a '03 5th-round pick (Jan. 7); RW Willis and LW Chris Dingman from Car. for G Kevin Weekes (Mar. 5); LW Roy and a '02 6th-round pick from Ott. for LW Juha Ylonen (Mar. 15).

Goalies (10 Gm)	Gm	Min	GAA	Record	Sv%
Nikolai Khabibulin	70	3896	2.36	24-32-10	.920
TAMPA BAY	82	4997	2.63	27-44-11	.913

Shutouts: Khabibulin (7). **Assists:** Khabibulin (2). **PM:** Khabibulin.

Toronto Maple Leafs

Top Scorers	Gm	G	A	Pts	+/-	PM	PP
Mats Sundin	82	41	39	80	6	94	10
Darcy Tucker	77	24	35	59	24	92	7
Alexander Mogilny	66	24	33	57	1	8	5
Mikael Renberg	71	14	38	52	11	36	4
Robert Reichel	78	20	31	51	7	26	1
Gary Roberts	69	21	27	48	-4	63	6
Jonas Hoglund	82	13	34	47	11	26	1
Bryan McCabe	82	17	26	43	16	129	8
Tomas Kaberle	69	10	29	39	5	2	5
Travis Green	82	11	23	34	13	61	3
Shayne Corson	74	12	21	33	11	120	0
Tie Domi	74	9	10	19	3	157	0
Dimitri Yushkevich	55	6	13	19	14	26	3
Alyn McCauley	82	6	10	16	10	18	0
Garry Valk	63	5	10	15	2	28	0
Jyrki Lumme	66	4	9	13	8	22	1
DAL	15	0	1	1	-5	4	0
TOR	51	4	8	12	13	18	1
Cory Cross	50	3	9	12	11	54	0
Aki Berg	81	1	10	11	14	46	0
Paul Healey	21	3	7	10	7	2	0

Acquired: D Lumme from Dal. for D Dave Manson (Nov. 21); G Barrasso from Car. for a '03 4th-round pick (Mar. 15).

Goalies (10 Gm)	Gm	Min	GAA	Record	Sv%
Curtis Joseph	51	3065	2.23	29-17-5	.906
Tom Barrasso	38	2127	2.62	15-14-5	.907
CAR	34	1908	2.61	13-12-5	.906
TOR	4	219	2.74	2-2-0	.909
Corey Schwab	30	1646	2.73	12-10-5	.894
TORONTO	82	4986	2.49	43-29-10	.899

Shutouts: Joseph (4), Barrasso (2 with Car.), Schwab (1). **Assists:** Joseph (1). **PM:** Joseph (10), Barrasso (4 with Car.), Schwab (2).

Vancouver Canucks

Top Scorers	Gm	G	A	Pts	+/-	PM	PP
Markus Naslund	81	40	50	90	22	50	8
Todd Bertuzzi	72	36	49	85	21	110	14
Brendan Morrison	82	23	44	67	18	26	6
Andrew Cassels	53	11	39	50	5	22	7
Ed Jovanovski	82	17	31	48	-7	101	7
Trevor Linden	80	13	24	37	-5	71	3
WASH	16	1	2	3	-2	6	1
VAN	64	12	22	34	-3	65	2
Henrik Sedin	82	16	20	36	9	36	3
Mattias Ohlund	81	10	26	36	16	56	4
Matt Cooke	82	13	20	33	4	111	1
Daniel Sedin	79	9	23	32	1	32	4
Jan Hlavac	77	16	15	31	9	18	1
PHI	31	7	3	10	5	8	0
VAN	46	9	12	21	4	10	1
Trevor Letowski	75	9	16	25	4	19	1
PHO	33	2	6	8	2	4	0
VAN	42	7	10	17	2	15	1
Brent Sopel	66	8	17	25	21	44	1
Trent Klatt	34	7	15	22	9	10	2
Scott Lachance	81	1	10	11	15	50	0
Bryan Helmer	40	5	5	10	10	53	2
Artem Chubarov	51	5	5	10	-3	10	0

Acquired: C Linden and a conditional 2nd-round pick from Wash. for a '02 1st-round pick (Nov. 10); LW Hlavac and TB's '02 3rd-round pick from Phi. for LW Donald Brashear (Dec. 17); RW Letowski, LW Todd Warriner, RW Tyler Bouck and a '03 3rd-round pick from Pho. for D Drake Berehowsky and C Denis Pederson (Dec. 28). **Signed:** free agent G Skudra (Nov. 7).

Goalies (10 Gm)	Gm	Min	GAA	Record	Sv%
Peter Skudra	23	1166	2.42	10-8-2	.907
Dan Cloutier	62	3502	2.43	31-22-5	.901
VANCOUVER	82	4978	2.54	42-33-7	.899

Shutouts: Cloutier (7), Skudra (1). **Assists:** Alexander Auld (1). **PM:** Cloutier (20), Skudra (2).

Washington Capitals

Top Scorers	Gm	G	A	Pts	+/-	PM	PP
Jaromir Jagr	69	31	48	79	0	30	10
Peter Bondra	77	39	31	70	-2	80	17
Sergei Gonchar	76	26	33	59	-1	58	7
Ulf Dahlen	69	23	29	52	-5	8	7
Dainius Zubrus	71	17	26	43	5	38	4
Andrei Nikolishin	80	13	23	36	-1	40	1
Chris Simon	82	14	17	31	-8	137	1
Dmitri Khristich	61	9	12	21	2	12	3
Jeff Halpern	48	5	14	19	-9	29	0
Glen Metropolit	35	1	16	17	1	6	0
TB	2	0	0	0	-2	0	0
WASH	33	1	16	17	3	6	0
Ken Klee	68	8	8	16	4	38	2
Benoit Hogue	58	7	8	15	-5	37	0
DAL	32	3	3	6	-4	24	0
BOS	17	4	4	8	-3	9	0
WASH	9	0	1	1	2	4	0
Sylvain Cote	70	3	11	14	-15	26	1
Steve Konowalchuk	28	2	12	14	-2	23	0
Frantisek Kucera	56	1	13	14	7	12	0
Matt Pettinger*	61	3	7	10	-8	44	1
Brendan Witt	68	3	7	10	-1	78	0
Colin Forbes	38	5	3	8	-2	15	0
Joe Sacco	65	0	7	7	-13	51	0
Rob Zettler	49	1	4	5	3	56	0

Claimed: RW Metropolit off waivers from TB (Oct. 20); RW Hogue off waivers from Bos. (Mar. 19). **Signed:** free agent LW Forbes (Jan. 8).

Goalies (10 Gm)	Gm	Min	GAA	Record	Sv%
Olaf Kolzig	71	4131	2.79	31-29-8	.908
Craig Billington	17	710	3.04	4-5-3	.878
WASHINGTON	82	4987	2.89	36-35-11	.898

Shutouts: Kolzig (6). **Assists:** Kolzig (1). **PM:** Kolzig (8).

Stanley Cup Playoffs

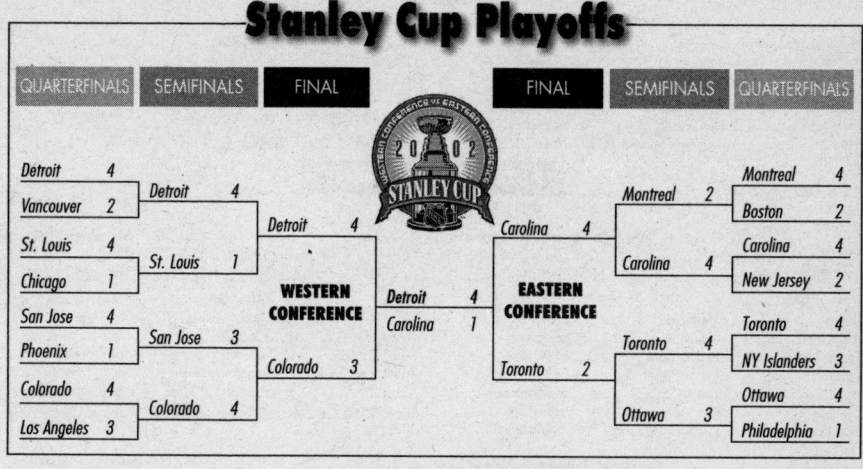

Stanley Cup Playoffs
Series Summaries

WESTERN CONFERENCE

FIRST ROUND (Best of 7)

	W-L	GF	Leading Scorers
Detroit	4-2	22	Yzerman (3-5–8)
			& Shanahan (1-7–8)
Vancouver	2-4	16	Three tied with 5 pts.

Date	Winner	Home Ice
April 17	Canucks, 4-3 (OT)	at Detroit
April 19	Canucks, 5-2	at Detroit
April 21	Red Wings, 3-1	at Vancouver
April 23	Red Wings, 4-2	at Vancouver
April 25	Red Wings, 4-0	at Detroit
April 27	Red Wings, 6-4	at Vancouver

Shutouts: Hasek, Detroit (1).

	W-L	GF	Leading Scorers
San Jose	4-1	13	Marleau (3-3–6)
Phoenix	1-4	7	Doan (2-2–4)

Date	Winner	Home Ice
April 17	Sharks, 2-1	at San Jose
April 20	Coyotes, 3-1	at San Jose
April 22	Sharks, 4-1	at Phoenix
April 24	Sharks, 2-1	at Phoenix
April 26	Sharks, 4-1	at San Jose

	W-L	GF	Leading Scorers
Colorado	4-3	16	Forsberg (1-6–7)
Los Angeles	3-4	13	Palffy (4-5–9)

Date	Winner	Home Ice
April 18	Avalanche, 4-3	at Colorado
April 20	Avalanche, 5-3	at Colorado
April 22	Kings, 3-1	at Los Angeles
April 23	Avalanche, 1-0	at Los Angeles
April 25	Kings, 1-0 (OT)	at Colorado
April 27	Kings, 3-1	at Los Angeles
April 29	Avalanche, 4-0	at Colorado

Shutouts: Roy, Colorado (2); Potvin, Los Angeles (1).

	W-L	GF	Leading Scorers
St. Louis	4-1	13	Demitra (3-4–7)
Chicago	1-4	5	Nylander (0-3–3)

Date	Winner	Home Ice
April 18	Blackhawks, 2-1	at St. Louis
April 20	Blues, 2-0	at St. Louis
April 21	Blues, 4-0	at Chicago
April 23	Blues, 1-0	at Chicago
April 25	Blues, 5-3	at St. Louis

Shutouts: Johnson, St. Louis (3).

SEMIFINALS (Best of 7)

	W-L	GF	Leading Scorers
Detroit	4-1	14	Yzerman (2-3–5)
			& Shanahan (3-2–5)
St. Louis	1-4	11	Tkachuk (4-2–6)

Date	Winner	Home Ice
May 2	Red Wings, 2-0	at Detroit
May 4	Red Wings, 3-2	at Detroit
May 7	Blues, 6-1	at St. Louis
May 9	Red Wings, 4-3	at St. Louis
May 11	Red Wings, 4-0	at Detroit

Shutouts: Hasek, Detroit (2).

	W-L	GF	Leading Scorers
Colorado	4-3	25	Forsberg (6-6–12)
San Jose	3-4	21	Nolan (4-3–7)
			& Ricci (2-5–7)

Date	Winner	Home Ice
May 1	Sharks, 6-3	at Colorado
May 4	Avalanche, 8-2	at Colorado
May 6	Sharks, 6-4	at San Jose
May 8	Avalanche, 4-1	at San Jose
May 11	Sharks, 5-3	at Colorado
May 13	Avalanche, 2-1 (OT)	at San Jose
May 15	Avalanche, 1-0	at Colorado

Shutouts: Roy, Colorado (1).

CHAMPIONSHIP (Best of 7)

	W-L	GF	Leading Scorers
Detroit	4-3	22	Hull (3-3–6)
			& Yzerman (1-5–6)
Colorado	3-4	13	Forsberg (2-6–8)

Date	Winner	Home Ice
May 18	Red Wings, 5-3	at Detroit
May 20	Avalanche, 4-3 (OT)	at Detroit
May 22	Red Wings, 2-1 (OT)	at Colorado
May 25	Avalanche, 3-2	at Colorado
May 27	Avalanche, 2-1 (OT)	at Detroit
May 29	Red Wings, 2-0	at Colorado
May 31	Red Wings, 7-0	at Detroit

Shutouts: Hasek, Detroit (2).

EASTERN CONFERENCE

FIRST ROUND (Best of 7)

	W-L	GF	Leading Scorers
Montreal	4-2	20	Zednik (4-4–8)
Boston	2-4	18	Guerin (4-2–6)
			& Thornton (2-4–6)

Date	Winner	Home Ice
April 18	Canadiens, 5-2	at Boston
April 21	Bruins, 6-4	at Boston
April 23	Canadiens, 5-3	at Montreal
April 25	Bruins, 5-2	at Montreal
April 27	Canadiens, 2-1	at Boston
April 29	Canadiens, 2-1	at Montreal

	W-L	GF	Leading Scorers
Ottawa	4-1	11	Alfredsson (3-3–6)
Philadelphia	1-4	2	Oates (0-2–2)

Date	Winner	Home Ice
April 17	Flyers, 1-0 (OT)	at Philadelphia
April 20	Senators, 3-0	at Philadelphia
April 22	Senators, 3-0	at Ottawa
April 24	Senators, 3-0	at Ottawa
April 26	Senators, 2-1 (OT)	at Philadelphia

Shutouts: Cechmanek, Philadelphia (1); Lalime, Ottawa (3).

	W-L	GF	Leading Scorers
Carolina	4-2	9	Three tied with 3 pts.
New Jersey	2-4	11	Elias (2-4–6)

Date	Winner	Home Ice
April 17	Hurricanes, 2-1	at Carolina
April 19	Hurricanes, 2-1 (OT)	at Carolina
April 21	Devils, 4-0	at New Jersey
April 23	Devils, 3-1	at New Jersey
April 24	Hurricanes, 3-2 (OT)	at Carolina
April 27	Hurricanes, 1-0	at New Jersey

Shutouts: Brodeur, New Jersey (1); Weekes, Carolina (1).

	W-L	GF	Leading Scorers
Toronto	4-3	22	Roberts (2-5–7)
			& McCauley (1-6–7)
NY Islanders	3-4	21	Three tied with 7 pts.

Date	Winner	Home Ice
April 18	Maple Leafs, 3-1	at Toronto
April 20	Maple Leafs, 2-0	at Toronto
April 23	Islanders, 6-1	at New York
April 24	Islanders, 4-3	at New York
April 26	Maple Leafs, 6-3	at Toronto
April 28	Islanders, 5-3	at New York
April 30	Maple Leafs, 4-2	at Toronto

Shutouts: Joseph, Toronto (1).

SEMIFINALS (Best of 7)

	W-L	GF	Leading Scorers
Carolina	4-2	21	Battaglia (4-6–10)
Montreal	2-4	12	Audette (2-2–4)
			& Quintal (1-3–4)

Date	Winner	Home Ice
May 3	Hurricanes, 2-0	at Carolina
May 5	Canadiens, 4-1	at Carolina
May 7	Canadiens, 2-1 (OT)	at Montreal
May 9	Hurricanes, 4-3 (OT)	at Montreal
May 12	Hurricanes, 5-1	at Carolina
May 13	Hurricanes, 8-2	at Montreal

Shutouts: Weekes, Carolina (1).

	W-L	GF	Leading Scorers
Toronto	4-3	16	Roberts (5-5–10)
Ottawa	3-4	18	Alfredsson (4-3–7)

Date	Winner	Home Ice
May 2	Senators, 5-0	at Toronto
May 4	Maple Leafs, 3-2 (3OT)	at Toronto
May 6	Senators, 3-2	at Ottawa
May 8	Maple Leafs, 2-1	at Ottawa
May 10	Senators, 4-2	at Toronto
May 12	Maple Leafs, 4-3	at Ottawa
May 14	Maple Leafs, 3-0	at Toronto

Shutouts: Lalime, Ottawa (1); Joseph, Toronto (1).

CHAMPIONSHIP (Best of 7)

	W-L	GF	Leading Scorers
Carolina	4-2	10	Francis (2-2–4)
Toronto	2-4	6	Sundin (1-3–4)

Date	Winner	Home Ice
May 16	Maple Leafs, 2-1	at Carolina
May 19	Hurricanes, 2-1 (OT)	at Carolina
May 21	Hurricanes, 2-1 (OT)	at Toronto
May 23	Hurricanes, 3-0	at Toronto
May 25	Maple Leafs, 1-0	at Carolina
May 28	Hurricanes, 2-1 (OT)	at Toronto

Shutouts: Irbe, Carolina (1); Joseph, Toronto (1).

STANLEY CUP FINAL (Best of 7)

	W-L	GF	Leading Scorers
Detroit	4-1	14	Fedorov (1-4–5)
Carolina	1-4	7	O'Neill (3-1–4)

Date	Winner	Home Ice
June 4	Hurricanes, 3-2 (OT)	at Detroit
June 6	Red Wings, 3-1	at Detroit
June 8	Red Wings, 3-2 (3OT)	at Carolina
June 10	Red Wings, 3-0	at Carolina
June 13	Red Wings, 3-1	at Detroit

Shutouts: Hasek, Detroit (1).

Conn Smythe Trophy (Playoff MVP)
Nicklas Lidstrom, Detroit, D
23 games, 5 goals, 11 assists, 16 points, plus-6

Stanley Cup Final Box Scores

Game 1

Tuesday, June 4, at Detroit

Carolina.............................0 2 0 1 — 3
Detroit...............................1 1 0 0 — 2

1st Period: DET—Fedorov 5 (Yzerman), 15:21 (pp).

2nd Period: CAR—Hill 4 (Kapanen, Francis), 3:30 (pp); DET—Maltby 2 (McCarty), 10:39; CAR—O'Neill 6 (Ward), 19:10.

Overtime: CAR—Francis 6 (O'Neill, Kapanen), 0:58.

Shots on Goal: Carolina—7-13-5-1—26; Detroit—8-12-5-0—25. **Power plays:** Carolina 1-6; Detroit 1-7. **Goalies:** Carolina, Irbe (25 shots, 23 saves); Detroit, Hasek (26 shots, 23 saves). **Attendance:** 20,058.

Game 2

Thursday, June 6, at Detroit

Carolina................................1 0 0 — 1
Detroit.................................1 0 2 — 3

1st Period: DET—Maltby 3 (Draper, Chelios), 6:33 (sh); CAR—Brind'Amour 4 (unassisted), 14:47 (sh).

3rd Period: DET—Lidstrom 5 (Fedorov, Yzerman), 14:52 (pp); DET—Draper 2 (Lidstrom, Olausson), 15:05.

Shots on Goal: Carolina—7-4-6—17; Detroit—9-8-13-30.

Power plays: Carolina 0-8; Detroit 1-8. **Goalies:** Carolina, Irbe (30 shots, 27 saves); Detroit, Hasek (17 shots, 16 saves). **Attendance:** 20,058.

Game 3

Saturday, June 8, at Carolina

Detroit......................0 1 1 0 0 1 — 3
Carolina....................1 0 1 0 0 0 — 2

1st Period: CAR—Vasicek 3 (Gelinas, Wesley), 14:49.

2nd Period: DET—Larionov 3 (Hull), 5:33.

3rd Period: CAR—O'Neill 7 (Francis), 7:34; DET—Hull 9 (Lidstrom, Fedorov), 18:46.

3rd Overtime: DET—Larionov 4 (Holmstrom, Duchesne), 14:47.

Shots on Goal: Detroit—6-7-16-11-6-6—52; Carolina—8-6-7-5-8-9—43. **Power plays:** Detroit 0-4; Carolina 0-5. **Goalies:** Detroit, Hasek (43 shots, 41 saves); Carolina, Irbe (52 shots, 49 saves). **Attendance:** 18,982.

Game 4

Monday, June 10, at Carolina

Detroit................................0 1 2 — 3
Carolina...............................0 0 0 — 0

2nd Period: DET—Hull 10 (Devereaux, Olausson), 6:32.

3rd Period: DET—Larionov 5 (Fischer, Holmstrom), 3:43; DET—Shanahan 6 (Fedorov, Chelios), 14:43.

Shots on Goal: Detroit—10-6-11-27; Carolina—6-7-4-17. **Power plays:** Detroit 0-2; Carolina 0-2. **Goalies:** Detroit, Hasek (17 shots, 17 saves); Carolina, Irbe (27 shots, 24 saves). **Attendance:** 18,986.

Game 5

Thursday, June 13, at Detroit

Carolina...............................0 1 0 — 1
Detroit.................................0 2 1 — 3

2nd period: DET—Holmstrom 8 (Larionov, Chelios), 4:07; DET—Shanahan 7 (Fedorov, Yzerman), 14:04 (pp); CAR—O'Neill 8 (Hill, Wesley), 18:50 (pp).

3rd period: DET—Shanahan 8 (Yzerman), 19:15 (en).

Shots on Goal: Carolina—5-7-5—17; Detroit—12-8-6-26. **Power plays:** Carolina 1-3; Detroit 1-4. **Goalies:** Carolina, Irbe (25 shots, 23 saves); Detroit, Hasek (17 shots, 16 saves). **Attendance:** 20,058.

Final Stanley Cup Standings

	Gm	W	L	For	Opp	Dif
Detroit	.23	16	7	72	47	+25
Carolina	.23	13	10	47	43	+4
Colorado	.21	11	10	54	56	-2
Toronto	.20	10	10	44	49	-5
Ottawa	.12	7	5	29	18	+11
San Jose	.12	7	5	34	32	+2
Montreal	.12	6	6	32	39	-7
St. Louis	.10	5	5	24	19	+5
NY Islanders	.7	3	4	21	22	-1
Los Angeles	.7	3	4	13	16	-3
New Jersey	.6	2	4	11	9	+2
Boston	.6	2	4	18	20	-2
Vancouver	.6	2	4	16	22	-6
Phoenix	.5	1	4	7	13	-6
Chicago	.5	1	4	5	13	-8
Philadelphia	.5	1	4	2	11	-9

Stanley Cup Leaders

Scoring

	Gm	G	A	Pts	+/-	PM	PP
Peter Forsberg, Col	.20	9	18	27	8	20	0
Steve Yzerman, Det	.23	6	17	23	4	10	4
Joe Sakic, Col	.21	9	10	19	-2	4	4
Brendan Shanahan, Det	.23	8	11	19	5	20	1
Gary Roberts, Tor	.19	7	12	19	6	56	3
Sergei Fedorov, Det	.23	5	14	19	4	20	2
Brett Hull, Det	.23	10	8	18	1	4	3
Ron Francis, Car	.23	6	10	16	-2	6	4
Nicklas Lidstrom, Det	.23	5	11	16	6	2	2
Alyn McCauley, Tor	.20	5	10	15	3	4	1
Bates Battaglia, Car	.23	5	9	14	2	14	1
Chris Chelios, Det	.23	1	13	14	15	44	1

Goaltending

(Minimum 390 minutes)

	Gm	Min	W-L	ShO	GAA
Patrick Lalime, Ott	.12	778	7-5	4	1.39
Kevin Weekes, Car	.8	408	3-2	2	1.62
Arturs Irbe, Car	.18	1078	10-8	1	1.67
Brent Johnson, St.L	.10	590	5-5	3	1.83
Dominik Hasek, Det	.23	1455	16-7	6	1.86
Felix Potvin, LA	.7	417	3-4	1	2.16
Curtis Joseph, Tor	.20	1253	10-10	3	2.30
Patrick Roy, Col	.21	1241	11-10	3	2.51
Chris Osgood, NYI	.7	392	3-4	0	2.60
Evgeni Nabokov, SJ	.12	712	7-5	0	2.61
Jose Theodore, Mon	.12	686	6-6	0	3.06

Goals

Hull, Det	.10
Forsberg, Col	.9
Sakic, Col	.9
Mogilny, Tor	.8
O'Neill, Car	.8
Holmstrom, Det	.8
Shanahan, Det	.8

Assists

Forsberg, Col	.18
Yzerman, Det	.17
Fedorov, Det	.14
Chelios, Det	.13
Roberts, Tor	.12
Lidstrom, Det	.11
Shanahan, Det	.11

Wins

Hasek, Det	.16-7
Roy, Col	.11-10
Irbe, Car	.10-8
Joseph, Tor	.10-10
Lalime, Ott	.7-5
Nabokov, SJ	.7-5
Theodore, Mon	.6-6

Save Pct.

Lalime, Ott	.946
Weekes, Car	.939
Irbe, Car	.938
Johnson, St.L	.929
Potvin, LA	.925
Hasek, Det	.920
Theodore, Mon	.915

Finalists' Composite Box Scores

Detroit Red Wings (16-7)

Top Scorers	Pos	Overall Playoffs								Finals vs Carolina							
		Gm	G	A	Pts	+/-	PM	PP	S	Gm	G	A	Pts	+/-	PM	PP	S
Steve Yzerman	C	23	6	17	23	4	10	4	52	5	0	4	4	0	0	0	13
Brendan Shanahan	L	23	8	11	19	5	20	1	78	5	3	0	3	-1	6	1	16
Sergei Fedorov	C	23	5	14	19	4	20	2	88	5	1	4	5	0	6	1	21
Brett Hull	R	23	10	8	18	1	4	3	61	5	2	1	3	0	2	0	10
Nicklas Lidstrom	D	23	5	11	16	6	2	2	41	5	1	2	3	1	2	1	16
Chris Chelios	D	23	1	13	14	15	44	1	28	5	0	3	3	7	4	0	5
Tomas Holmstrom	R	23	8	3	11	7	8	3	34	5	1	1	2	3	0	0	8
Igor Larionov	C	18	5	6	11	5	4	0	24	5	3	1	4	4	0	0	8
Luc Robitaille	L	23	4	5	9	4	10	1	43	5	0	1	1	2	4	0	6
Darren McCarty	R	23	4	4	8	5	34	0	26	5	0	1	1	2	0	0	9
Pavel Datsyuk*	C	21	3	3	6	1	2	1	20	5	0	0	0	0	0	0	5
Jiri Fischer	D	22	3	3	6	6	30	0	24	4	0	1	1	3	4	0	5
Kirk Maltby	L	23	3	3	6	7	32	0	36	5	2	0	2	3	4	0	10
Boyd Devereaux	L	21	2	4	6	5	4	0	29	5	0	1	1	1	4	0	8
Fredrik Olausson	D	21	2	4	6	3	10	1	23	5	0	2	2	-1	2	0	4
Steve Duchesne	D	23	0	6	6	6	24	0	15	5	0	1	1	0	10	0	3
Kris Draper	R	23	2	3	5	4	20	0	44	5	1	1	2	3	4	0	12
Mathieu Dandenault	D	23	1	2	3	7	8	0	11	5	0	0	0	-1	2	0	1
Jiri Slegr	D	1	0	0	0	2	2	0	2	1	0	0	0	2	2	0	2
Uwe Krupp	D	2	0	0	0	-5	2	0	1	0	0	0	0	0	0	0	0
Jason Williams*	R	9	0	0	0	-1	2	0	7	0	0	0	0	0	0	0	0

Overtime goals—OVERALL (Larionov, Olausson); FINALS (Larionov). **Shorthanded goals**—OVERALL (Hull 2, Maltby 2, Fedorov, Lidstrom, Dandenault); FINALS (Maltby). **Power Play conversions**—OVERALL (19 for 99, 19.2%); FINALS (3 for 25, 12.0%).

Goaltending	Gm	Min	GAA	GA	SA	Sv%	W-L	Gm	Min	GAA	GA	SA	Sv%	W-L
Dominik Hasek	23	1455	1.86	45	562	.920	16-7	5	355	1.18	7	120	.942	4-1
Manny Legace	1	11	5.45	1	2	.500	0-0	0	0	0	0	0	—	0-0
TOTAL	23	1471	1.92	47	565	.917	16-7	5	355	1.18	7	120	.942	4-1

Empty Net Goals—OVERALL (1), FINALS (none). **Shutouts**—OVERALL (Hasek 6), FINALS (Hasek). **Assists**—OVERALL (Hasek), FINALS (none). **Penalty Minutes**—OVERALL (Hasek 8), FINALS (none).

Carolina Hurricanes (13-10)

Top Scorers	Pos	Overall Playoffs								Finals vs Detroit							
		Gm	G	A	Pts	+/-	PM	PP	S	Gm	G	A	Pts	+/-	PM	PP	S
Ron Francis	C	23	6	10	16	-2	6	4	51	5	1	2	3	-2	0	0	9
Bates Battaglia	L	23	9	5	14	2	14	1	44	5	0	0	0	-4	4	0	6
Jeff O'Neill	L	23	8	5	13	2	27	3	72	5	3	1	4	-2	2	1	15
Rod Brind'Amour	C	23	4	8	12	-3	16	2	48	5	1	0	1	-3	4	0	10
Erik Cole*	R	23	6	3	9	-2	30	1	68	5	0	0	0	-6	10	0	14
Sami Kapanen	R	23	1	8	9	-2	6	0	50	5	0	2	2	-3	0	0	10
Sean Hill	D	23	4	4	8	0	20	4	57	5	1	1	2	-6	12	1	9
Martin Gelinas	L	23	3	4	7	6	10	0	33	5	0	1	1	2	4	0	8
Josef Vasicek	C	23	3	2	5	6	12	0	32	5	1	0	1	0	4	0	10
Bret Hedican	D	23	1	4	5	0	20	0	39	5	0	0	0	1	4	0	9
Jaroslav Svoboda*	L	23	1	4	5	2	28	1	26	5	0	0	0	-1	8	0	1
Niclas Wallin	D	23	2	1	3	-2	12	0	17	5	0	0	0	-1	2	0	4
Marek Malik	D	23	0	3	3	3	18	0	24	5	0	0	0	-3	4	0	6
Aaron Ward	D	23	1	1	2	0	22	0	23	5	0	0	0	1	0	0	5
Glen Wesley	D	22	0	2	2	0	12	0	21	5	0	0	0	-2	3	0	4
Tommy Westlund	R	19	1	0	1	2	0	0	6	5	0	0	0	1	0	0	0
Kevyn Adams	C	23	1	0	1	-1	4	0	23	5	0	0	0	-1	0	0	1
David Tanabe	D	1	0	1	1	0	0	0	3	0	0	0	0	0	0	0	0
Jeff Daniels	C	23	0	1	1	-1	0	0	7	5	0	0	0	-1	0	0	1
Craig Adams	R	1	0	0	0	0	0	0	0	0	0	0	0	0	0	0	0
Craig MacDonald*	C	4	0	0	0	-1	2	0	1	0	0	0	0	0	0	0	0

Overtime goals—OVERALL (Wallin 2, Francis, Battaglia, O'Neill, Gelinas, Vasicek); FINALS (Francis). **Shorthanded goals**—OVERALL (Brind'Amour); FINALS (Brind'Amour). **Power Play conversions**—OVERALL (16 for 103, 15.5%); FINALS (2 for 24, 8.3%).

Goaltending	Gm	Min	GAA	GA	SA	Sv%	W-L	Gm	Min	GAA	GA	SA	Sv%	W-L
Kevin Weekes	8	408	1.62	11	180	.939	3-2	0	0	0	0	—	—	0-0
Arturs Irbe	18	1078	1.67	30	480	.938	10-8	5	354	2.20	13	161	.919	1-4
TOTAL	23	1493	1.73	43	662	.935	13-10	5	354	2.80	14	162	.914	1-4

Empty Net Goals—OVERALL (2); FINALS (1). **Shutouts**—OVERALL (Weekes 2, Irbe); FINALS (none). **Assists**—OVERALL (none); FINALS (none). **Penalty Minutes**—OVERALL (none), FINALS (none).

Annual Awards

Voting for the Hart, Calder, Norris, Lady Byng, Selke, and Masterton Trophies is conducted after the regular season by the Professional Hockey Writers' Association. The Vezina Trophy is selected by the NHL general managers, while the Jack Adams Award is selected by NHL broadcasters. Points are awarded on 10–7–5–3–1 basis except for the Vezina Trophy and the Adams Award which are awarded 5–3–1.

Hart Trophy
For Most Valuable Player

	Pos	1st	2nd	3rd	4th	5th	Pts
Jose Theodore, Mon	G	26	16	9	5	2—	434†
Jarome Iginla, Calg	R	23	18	12	5	3—	434
Patrick Roy, Col	G	8	15	12	11	5—	283
Sean Burke, Pho	G	2	5	16	10	7—	172
Markus Naslund, Van	L	0	0	4	10	14—	64

†Theodore won on the first tie breaker (first-place votes).

Calder Trophy
For Rookie of the Year

	Pos	1st	2nd	3rd	4th	5th	Pts
Dany Heatley, Atl	R	48	11	2	0	1—	568
Ilya Kovalchuk, Atl	L	14	45	1	2	0—	466
Kristian Huselius, Fla	L	0	2	31	12	9—	214
Pavel Datsyuk, Det	C	0	1	5	12	11—	79
Erik Cole, Car	R	0	1	4	12	11—	74

Norris Trophy
For Best Defenseman

	1st	2nd	3rd	4th	5th	Pts
Nicklas Lidstrom, Det	29	20	7	2	1—	472
Chris Chelios, Det	28	10	13	4	4—	431
Rob Blake, Col	4	19	22	12	2—	321
Sergei Gonchar, Wash	0	6	6	22	9—	147
Chris Pronger, St.L	0	4	1	8	5—	62

Vezina Trophy
For Outstanding Goaltender

	1st	2nd	3rd	Pts
Jose Theodore, Mon	15	9	3—	105†
Patrick Roy, Col	12	15	0—	105
Sean Burke, Pho	2	1	14—	27
Evgeni Nabokov, SJ	0	3	1—	10
Martin Brodeur, NJ	1	0	2—	7

†Theodore won on the first tie breaker (first-place votes).

Lady Byng Trophy
For Sportsmanship and Gentlemanly Play

	Pos	1st	2nd	3rd	4th	5th	Pts
Ron Francis, Car	C	28	13	7	6	3—	427
Joe Sakic, Col	C	12	19	10	6	4—	325
Nicklas Lidstrom, Det	D	10	10	11	5	3—	243
Adam Oates, Wash-Phi	C	1	4	4	11	2—	93
Paul Kariya, Ana	R	3	6	1	1	2—	82

Selke Trophy
For Best Defensive Forward

	Pos	1st	2nd	3rd	4th	5th	Pts
Michael Peca, NYI	C	25	10	10	7	3—	394
Craig Conroy, Calg	C	7	9	4	7	4—	178
Jere Lehtinen, Dal	R	2	10	11	9	3—	175
Mike Ricci, SJ	C	8	5	2	3	4—	138
Brian Rolston, Bos	C	3	8	6	5	6—	137

Adams Award
For Coach of the Year

	1st	2nd	3rd	Pts
Bob Francis, Pho	27	16	7—	190
Brian Sutter, Chi	15	21	13—	151
Robbie Ftorek, Bos	10	14	16—	108
Scotty Bowman, Det	8	7	7—	68
Michel Therrien, Mon	5	1	6—	34

AP/Wide World Photos

Jose Theodore took home the Hart (r) and the Vezina, and led the Canadiens to their first playoff berth since 1998.

Other Awards

Lester B. Pearson Award (NHL Players Assn. MVP)—Jarome Iginla, Calgary; **Jennings Trophy** (goaltenders with a minimum of 25 games played for team with fewest goals against)—Patrick Roy, Colorado; **Maurice "Rocket" Richard Trophy** (regular season goal-scoring leader)—Jarome Iginla, Calgary; **Art Ross Trophy** (regular season points leader)—Jarome Iginla, Calgary; **Masterton Trophy** (perseverance, sportsmanship, and dedication to hockey)—Saku Koivu, Montreal; **King Clancy Trophy** (leadership and humanitarian contributions to community)—Ron Francis, Carolina; **Lester Patrick Trophy** (outstanding service to hockey in the U.S.)—Olympic and NHL head coach Herb Brooks, St. Louis Blues GM Larry Pleau, and the 1960 U.S. Olympic hockey team.

All-NHL Team

Voting by Pro Hockey Writers' Association (PHWA). Holdovers from 2000-01 All-NHL first team in **bold** type.

	First Team		Second Team
G	Patrick Roy, Col	G	Jose Theodore, Mon
D	Chris Chelios, Det	D	Rob Blake, Col
D	**Nicklas Lidstrom**, Det	D	Sergei Gonchar, Wash
C	**Joe Sakic**, Col	C	Mats Sundin, Tor
R	Jarome Iginla, Calg	R	Bill Guerin, Bos
L	Markus Naslund, Van	L	Brendan Shanahan, Det

All-Rookie Team

Voting by PHWA. Vote totals not released.

Pos		Pos	
G	Dan Blackburn, NYR	F	Dany Heatley, Atl
D	Nick Boynton, Bos	F	Ilya Kovalchuk, Atl
D	Rostislav Klesla, Clb	F	Kristian Huselius, Fla

2002 NHL Draft

First and second round selections at the 40th annual NHL Entry Draft held June 22-23, 2002, at Air Canada Centre in Toronto. The order of the first 14 positions were determined by a draft lottery of non-playoff teams held April 16 in New York City. Only the worst five teams from the 2001-02 regular season had the chance to win the first overall pick. No team could move up more than four spots in the draft order or drop more than one position. Positions 15 through 30 reflect regular season records in reverse order.

First Round

	Team	Player, Last Team	Pos
1	**a**-Columbus	Rick Nash, London (OHL)	L
2	Atlanta	Kari Lehtonen, Jokerit (Fin)	G
3	**b**-Florida	Jay Bouwmeester, Medicine Hat (WHL)	D
4	**c**-Philadelphia	Joni Pitkanen, Karpat (Fin)	D
5	Pittsburgh	Ryan Whitney, Boston Univ. (HE)	D
6	Nashville	Scottie Upshall, Kamloops (WHL)	R
7	Anaheim	Joffrey Lupul, Medicine Hat (WHL)	R
8	Minnesota	Pierre-Marc Bouchard, Chicoutimi (QMJHL)	C
9	**d**-Florida	Petr Taticek, Sault-Ste-Marie (OHL)	C
10	**e**-Calgary	Eric Nystrom, Michigan (CCHA)	L
11	Buffalo	Keith Ballard, Minnesota (WCHA)	D
12	Washington	Steve Eminger, Kitchener (OHL)	D
13	**f**-Washington	Alexander Syemin, Chelyabinsk (Rus)	L
14	**g**-Montreal	Christopher Higgins, Yale (ECAC)	C
15	Edmonton	Jesse Niinimaki, Ilves (Fin)	C
16	Ottawa	Jakub Klepis, Portland (WHL)	C
17	**i**-Washington	Boyd Gordon, Red Deer (WHL)	R
18	Los Angeles	Denis Grebeshkov, Yaroslavl (Rus)	D
19	Phoenix	Jakub Koreis, Plzen (Cze)	C
20	**j**-Buffalo	Daniel Paille, Guelph (OHL)	L
21	Chicago	Anton Babchuk, Elektrostal (Rus)	D
22	NY Islanders	Sean Bergenheim, Jokerit (Fin)	L
23	**k**-Phoenix	Ben Eager, Oshawa (OHL)	L
24	Toronto	Alexander Steen, Frolunda (Swe)	C
25	Carolina	Cam Ward, Red Deer (WHL)	G
26	**l**-Dallas	Martin Vagner, Hull (QMJHL)	D
27	San Jose	Mike Morris, St. Sebastian's, Mass. (HS)	R
28	Colorado	Jonas Johansson, Jönköping (Swe)	L
29	Boston	Hannu Toivonen, Hameenlinna (Fin)	G
30	**m**-Atlanta	Jim Slater, Michigan St. (CCHA)	C

Second Round

	Team	Player, Last Team	Pos
31	**n**-Edmonton	Jeff Deslauriers, Chicoutimi (QMJHL)	G
32	**o**-Dallas	Janos Vas, Malmo Jr. (Sweden)	L
33	**p**-NY Rangers	Lee Falardeau, Michigan St. (CCHA)	C
34	**q**-Dallas	Tobias Stephan, Chur (Swi)	G
35	Pittsburgh	Ondrej Nemec, Vsetin (Cze)	D
36	**r**-Edmonton	Jarret Stoll, Kootenay (WHL)	C
37	Anaheim	Tim Brent, St. Michael's (OHL)	C
38	Minnesota	Josh Harding, Regina (WHL)	G
39	Calgary	Brian McConnell, Boston Univ. (HE)	C
40	**s**-Florida	Rob Globke, Notre Dame (CCHA)	R
41	**t**-Columbus	Joakim Lindström, MoDo (Swe)	R
42	**u**-Dallas	Marius Hollet, Farjestad (Swe)	C
43	Dallas	Trevor Daley, Sault-Ste-Marie (OHL)	D
44	Edmonton	Matt Greene, Green Bay (USHL)	D
45	Montreal	Tomas Linhart, Pardubice (Cze)	D
46	**v**-Phoenix	David LeNeveu, Cornell (ECAC)	G
47	Ottawa	Alexei Kaigorodov, Magnitogorsk (Rus)	C
48	**w**-St. Louis	Alexei Shkotov, Elektrostal (Rus)	R
49	Vancouver	Kiril Koltsov, Omsk (Rus)	D
50	Los Angeles	Sergei Anshakov, HC CKSA (Rus)	L
51	**x**-New Jersey	Anton Kadeykin, Elektrostal (Rus)	D
52	**y**-San Jose	Dan Spang, Winchester, Mass. (HS)	D
53	New Jersey	Barry Tallackson, Minnesota (WCHA)	R
54	Chicago	Duncan Keith, Michigan St. (CCHA)	D
55	**z**-Vancouver	Denis Grot, Elektrostal (Rus)	D
56	**aa**-Boston	Vladislav Evseev, HC CKSA (Rus)	D
57	Toronto	Matthew Stajan, Belleville (OHL)	C
58	**bb**-Detroit	Jiri Hudler, Liberec (Cze)	C
59	**cc**-Washington	Maxime Daigneault, Val d'Or (QMJHL)	G
60	**dd**-Tampa Bay	Adam Henrich, Brampton (OHL)	L
61	Colorado	Johnny Boychuk, Calgary (WHL)	D
62	**ee**-St. Louis	Andrei Mikhnov, Sudbury (OHL)	L
63	Detroit	Tomas Fleischmann, Vitkovice (Cze)	L

Acquired picks: a—from Florida; **b**—from Columbus; **c**—from Tampa Bay; **d**—from Calgary; **e**—from NY Rangers via Florida; **f**—from Dallas; **g**—from Edmonton; **h**—from Montreal; **i**—from Vancouver; **j**—from New Jersey via Dallas and Columbus; **k**—from St. Louis; **l**—from Philadelphia via Washington; **m**—from Detroit via Buffalo and Columbus; **n**—from Atlanta via Buffalo; **o**—from Columbus; **p**—from Florida; **q**—from Tampa Bay via Ottawa and Philadelphia; **r**—from Nashville via Buffalo; **s**—from NY Rangers; **t**—from Buffalo via Atlanta; **u**—from Washington; **v**—compensatory pick for the loss of Jeremy Roenick; **w**—compensatory pick for the loss of Pierre Turgeon; **x**—compensatory pick for the loss of Alexander Mogilny; **y**—from Phoenix via Philadelphia and Tampa Bay; **z**—from NY Islanders via Tampa Bay and Washington; **aa**—from St. Louis; **bb**—from Carolina; **cc**—from Philadelphia; **dd**—from San Jose; **ee**—from Boston.

U.S. Division I College Hockey

Final regular season standings; overall records, including all postseason tournament games, in parentheses.

Central Collegiate Hockey Assn.

	W	L	T	Pts	GF	GA
*Michigan (28-11-5)	19	5	4	42	97	56
*Michigan St. (27-9-5)	18	6	4	40	84	47
N. Michigan (26-12-2)	16	10	2	34	86	69
Alaska-Fairbanks (22-12-3)	15	10	3	33	91	85
Nebraska-Omaha (21-16-4)	13	11	4	30	72	64
W. Michigan (19-15-4)	13	12	3	29	92	92
Notre Dame (16-17-5)	12	12	4	28	95	86
Ohio St. (20-16-4)	12	13	4	28	71	81
Ferris St. (15-20-1)	12	15	1	25	86	83
Miami-OH (12-22-2)	9	17	2	20	68	88
Bowling Green (9-25-6)	7	18	3	17	78	104
Lake Superior St. (8-27-2)	4	22	2	10	38	106

Conf. Tourney Final: Michigan 3, Michigan St. 2.

*NCAA Tourney (2-2): Michigan (2-1), Michigan St. (0-1).

College Hockey America

	W	L	T	Pts	GF	GA
Wayne State (21-11-4)	15	2	3	33	84	48
Bemidji State (12-18-5)	8	7	4	22	65	61
Alab.-Huntsville (18-18-1)	10	9	1	21	75	77
Niagara (17-17-1)	8	10	1	19	61	65
Air Force (16-16-2)	6	10	2	14	53	63
Findlay (11-22-2)	5	14	1	11	57	81

Conf. Tourney Final: Wayne State 5, Alab.-Huntsville 4 (OT).

NCAA Tourney: No teams invited.

Note: Two conference games were worth four points in the standings, as opposed to the usual two. They were Bemidji State's 4-2 win over Air Force on Jan. 19, and Niagara's 4-0 win over Air Force on Jan. 27.

Eastern Collegiate Athletic Conf.

	W	L	T	Pts	GF	GA
*Cornell (25-8-2)	17	3	2	36	74	34
Clarkson (17-15-6)	11	6	5	27	62	51
*Harvard (15-15-4)	10	9	3	23	67	62
Rensselaer (20-13-4)	10	9	3	23	64	59
Dartmouth (14-13-5)	9	8	5	23	66	59
Brown (14-15-2)	10	10	2	22	52	53
Colgate (13-19-2)	10	10	2	22	53	59
Princeton (11-18-2)	10	10	2	22	51	63
St. Lawrence (11-21-2)	9	11	2	20	62	64
Yale (10-19-2)	9	11	2	20	70	65
Union (13-13-6)	8	11	3	19	53	58
Vermont (3-26-2)	3	18	1	7	46	93

Conf. Tourney Final: Harvard 4, Cornell 3 (2OT).
*NCAA Tourney (1-2): Cornell (1-1), Harvard (0-1).

Hockey East Association

	W	L	T	Pts	GF	GA
*New Hampshire (30-7-3)	17	4	3	37	103	49
*Boston University (25-10-3)	15	6	3	33	80	65
*Maine (26-11-7)	14	5	5	33	99	62
UMass-Lowell (22-13-3)	12	9	3	27	70	67
Northeastern (19-17-3)	11	11	2	24	69	74
Boston College (18-18-2)	10	13	1	21	73	81
Providence (13-20-5)	8	13	3	19	68	82
Merrimack (11-23-2)	6	16	2	14	54	87
UMass-Amherst (8-24-2)	3	19	2	8	45	94

Conf. Tourney Final: New Hampshire 3, Maine 1.
*NCAA Tourney (4-3): Maine (3-1), New Hampshire (1-1), Boston University (0-1).

Metro Atlantic Athletic Conf.

	W	L	T	Pts	GF	GA
Mercyhurst (24-10-3)	21	2	3	45	103	48
*Quinnipiac (20-13-5)	15	6	5	35	89	57
Sacred Heart (16-14-4)	15	8	3	33	92	72
Holy Cross (17-12-5)	14	7	5	33	95	69
Canisius (14-17-4)	13	9	4	30	94	71
Connecticut (13-16-7)	11	10	5	27	86	89
Iona (13-18-2)	12	12	2	26	92	91
Army (9-17-6)	9	11	6	24	87	86
American Int'l (7-21-0)	6	20	0	12	59	112
Fairfield (6-23-3)	4	19	3	11	53	91
Bentley (4-26-2)	4	20	2	10	57	121

Conf. Tourney Final: Quinnipiac 6, Mercyhurst 4.
NCAA Tourney (0-1): Quinnipiac (0-1).

Western Collegiate Hockey Assn.

	W	L	T	Pts	GF	GA
*Denver (32-8-1)	21	6	1	43	108	63
*St. Cloud St. (29-11-2)	19	7	2	40	117	65
*Minnesota (32-8-4)	18	7	3	39	113	84
*Colorado College (27-13-3)	16	10	2	34	95	74
Wisconsin (16-19-4)	12	13	3	27	88	90
MSU-Mankato (16-20-2)	11	15	2	24	84	107
North Dakota (16-19-2)	11	15	2	24	103	100
Alaska-Anchorage (12-19-5)	10	14	4	24	79	96
Minnesota-Duluth (13-24-3)	6	19	3	15	72	112
Michigan Tech (8-28-2)	4	22	2	10	66	134

Conf. Tourney Final: Denver 5, Minnesota 2.
*NCAA Tourney (4-3): Minnesota (3-0), Colorado College (1-1), Denver (0-1), St. Cloud St. (0-1).

Hobey Baker Award

For College Hockey Player of the Year. Voting is done by a 24-member panel of national media, college coaches, pro scouts, and officials.

	Cl	Pos
Winner: Jordan Leopold, Minnesota	Sr.	D

USA Today/American Hockey Magazine Coaches Poll

Taken April 8, 2002 after the NCAA Tournament. First place votes are in parentheses.

	League	W	L	T	Pts
1 Minnesota (19)	WCHA	32	8	4	285
2 Maine	HE	26	11	7	266
3 New Hampshire	HE	30	7	3	240
4 Michigan	CCHA	28	11	5	230
5 Denver	WCHA	32	8	1	212
6 Boston University	HE	25	10	3	174
7 Colorado College	WCHA	27	13	3	149
8 Michigan St.	CCHA	27	9	5	148
9 Cornell	ECAC	25	8	2	144
10 St. Cloud St.	WCHA	29	11	2	138

Scoring Leaders

Including postseason games; minimum 20 games.

	Cl	Gm	G	A	Pts	Avg
Darren Haydar, UNH	Sr.	40	31	45	76	**1.90**
John Pohl, Minnesota	Sr.	44	27	52	79	**1.80**
Mark Hartigan, St. Cloud St.	Jr.	42	37	38	75	**1.79**
Colin Hemingway, UNH	Jr.	40	33	33	66	**1.65**
Matt Murley, Rensselaer	Sr.	32	24	23	47	**1.47**

Goaltending Leaders

Including postseason games; minimum 15 games.

	Cl	Record	Sv%	GAA
Wade Dubielewicz, Denver	Jr.	20-4-0	.943	**1.72**
Ryan Miller, Michigan St.	Jr.	26-9-5	.936	**1.77**
Matt Underhill, Cornell	Sr.	14-6-1	.922	**1.80**
Yann Danis, Brown	So.	11-10-2	.938	**1.86**
Cam McCormick, UMass-Lowell	Sr.	13-6-3	.920	**1.88**

NCAA Division I Tournament Regional Seeds

Frozen Four teams in **bold**.

West
1 Denver (32-7-1)
2 **Minnesota** (29-8-4)
3 Michigan St. (27-8-5)
4 **Michigan** (26-10-5)
5 St. Cloud St. (29-10-2)
6 Colorado College (26-12-3)

East
1 **New Hampshire** (29-6-3)
2 Boston University (25-9-3)
3 **Maine** (23-10-7)
4 Cornell (24-7-2)
5 Quinnipiac (20-12-5)
6 Harvard (15-14-4)

West Regional

Held at Yost Arena in Ann Arbor, Mich., March 22-23. Single elimination, two second round winners advance to Frozen Four.

First Round

Colorado College 2........................Michigan St. 0
Michigan 4.............................St. Cloud St. 2
(Byes: Minnesota and Denver)

Second Round

Minnesota 4........................Colorado College 2
Michigan 5.................................Denver 3

East Regional

Held at the Worcester (Mass.) Centrum, March 23-24. Single elimination, two second round winners advance to Frozen Four.

First Round

Maine 4..................OT.............Harvard 3
Cornell 6................................Quinnipiac 1
(Byes: New Hampshire and Boston University)

Second Round

Maine 4..........................Boston University 3
New Hampshire 4..............................Cornell 3

THE FROZEN FOUR

Held at Xcel Energy Center in St. Paul, Minn, April 4 and April 6. Single elimination; no consolation game.

Semifinals

Maine 7 . . . . .New Hampshire 2
Minnesota 3 . . . . .Michigan 2

Championship Game

Minnesota, 4-3 (OT)

Maine (HE) . . . . .0 1 2 0 — **3**
Minnesota (WCHA) . . . . .1 1 1 1 — **4**

1st Period: MIN—Keith Ballard 10 (Troy Riddle, Nick Angell), 7:18 (pp).
2nd Period: ME—Michael Schutte 12 (Peter Metcalf, Niko Dimitrakos), 4:47 (pp); MIN—John Pohl 27 (Nick Anthony, Angell), 5:38.
3rd Period: ME—Schutte 13 (Prestin Ryan, Todd Jackson), 1:17; ME—Robert Liscak 17 (Dimitrakos), 15:27; MIN—Matt Koalska 10 (Riddle, Pohl), 19:07.
Overtime: MIN—Grant Potulny 15 (Pohl, Jordan Leopold), 16:58 (pp).
Goalies: ME—Matt Yeats (35 shots, 31 saves); MIN—Adam Hauser (45 shots, 42 saves). **Attendance:** 19,324.
Most Outstanding Player: Grant Potulny, sophomore forward; 2 goals in semifinal game; game-winning goal in championship game.
All-Tournament Team: Potulny, forward John Pohl, and goalie Adam Hauser of Minnesota; forward Robert Liscak and defensemen Peter Metcalf and Michael Schutte of Maine.

Division I All-America

First team JOFA Division I All-Americans as chosen by the American Hockey Coaches Association. Holdovers from 2000-01 All-America first team in **bold** type.

West Team

Pos		Yr	Hgt	Wgt
G	**Ryan Miller**, Michigan St.	Jr	6-2	160
D	**Jordan Leopold**, Minnesota	Sr	6-0	210
D	Mike Komisarek, Michigan	So	6-4	225
F	John Pohl, Minnesota	Sr	6-0	187
F	Mike Cammalleri, Michigan	Jr	5-10	185
F	Mark Hartigan, St. Cloud St.	Jr	6-0	200

East Team

Pos		Yr	Hgt	Wgt
G	Matt Underhill, Cornell	Sr	6-2	210
D	Jim Fahey, Northeastern	Sr	6-0	196
D	Doug Murray, Cornell	Jr	6-3	230
F	Mark Cavosie, Rensselaer	Jr	6-0	180
F	Darren Haydar, New Hampshire	Sr	5-9	170
F	Colin Hemingway, New Hampshire	Jr	6-1	190

Division III
Frozen Four

March 15-16 in Middlebury, Vt.

Semifinals

Wisconsin-Superior 5 . . . . .Plattsburgh St. (N.Y.) 0
Norwich (Vt.) 5 .Middlebury (Vt.) 2

Championship

Championship:
Wisc.-Superior 3 . . . . .OT . . . . .Norwich 2
Final records: Wisc.-Superior (24-5-5); Norwich (27-5-0); Plattsburgh St. (21-9-4); Middlebury (26-2-1).

Women's College Hockey

NCAA Division I Frozen Four

Held March 22 and 24 at the Whittemore Center in Durham, N.H.

Semifinals

Minnesota-Duluth 3 . . . . .Niagara 2
Brown 2 . . . . .Minnesota 1

Third Place

Niagara 2 . . . . .Minnesota 2 (tie)

Championship

Minnesota-Duluth 3 . . . . .Brown 2
Final records: Minnesota-Duluth (24-6-4); Brown (25-8-2); Minnesota (28-4-6); Niagara (26-8-2).
Most Outstanding Player: Kristy Zamora; Brown, senior forward; 1 goal in semifinal game, 2 goals in championship game.
All-Tournament Team: Zamora and defenseman Meredith Ostrander, Brown; forward Joanne Eustace and defenseman Larissa Luther, Minnesota-Duluth; forward Kelly Stephens, Minnesota; goalie Tania Pinelli, Niagara.

NCAA Division III Championship

Held March 5-9 at the Murray Athletic Center in Elmira, N.Y.

Semifinals

Manhattanville, N.Y. 2 . . . . .OT . . . . . . .Bowdoin (Maine) 1
Elmira, N.Y. 8 . . . . .Gust. Adolphus (Minn.) 5

Third Place

Gustavus Adolphus 2 . . . . .Bowdoin 1

Championship

Elmira 2 . . . . .Manhattanville 1
Final records: Elmira (26-1-1); Manhattanville (23-2-2); Gustavus Adolphus (23-5-2); Bowdoin (24-5-1).
Note: In 2001-02, women's college hockey was sanctioned as an official NCAA sport at the Division III level. Championships were previously sponsored by the American Women's College Hockey Alliance (AWCHA).

Patty Kazmaier Award

For Women's Division I College Hockey Player of the Year. Voting is done by a 12-member panel of national media, Division I college coaches, and one USA Hockey member.

		Cl	Pos
Winner: Brooke Whitney, Northeastern		Sr	F

MINOR LEAGUE HOCKEY

American Hockey League

Division champions (*) and playoff qualifiers (†) are noted. T denotes any game that was tied after regulation play and a five-minute overtime period. OL signifies any game that was tied after regulation play but lost in overtime. They are each worth one point in the standings.

Eastern Conference
East Division

Team (Affiliate)	W	L	T	OL	Pts	GF	GA
*Bridgeport (NYI)	43	25	8	4	98	240	192
†Hartford (NYR)	41	26	10	3	95	249	243
†Providence (Bos)	35	33	8	4	82	190	223
Springfield (Pho/TB)	35	41	2	2	74	213	237
Albany (NJ)	14	42	12	12	52	172	271

North Division

Team (Affiliate)	W	L	T	OL	Pts	GF	GA
*Lowell (Car)	41	25	11	3	96	229	209
†Manchester (LA)	38	28	11	3	90	236	225
†Worcester (St.L)	39	33	7	1	86	245	218
Portland (Wash)	30	31	15	4	79	220	225

Canadian Division

Team (Affiliate)	W	L	T	OL	Pts	GF	GA
*Quebec (Mon)	35	27	15	3	88	257	254
†Hamilton (Edm)	37	30	10	3	87	247	205
†St. John's (Tor)	34	27	17	2	87	256	240
†Manitoba (Van)	39	33	4	4	86	270	260
Saint John (Calg)	29	34	13	4	75	182	202

Scoring Leaders

	Gm	G	A	Pts	PM
Donald MacLean, St.J's	75	33	54	87	49
Eric Boguniecki, Wor	63	38	46	84	181
Rob Brown, Chi	80	29	54	83	103
Brad Smyth, Har	79	34	48	82	90
Jason Chimera, Ham	77	26	51	77	158

Goaltending Leaders

(At least 1590 minutes)	GP	GAA	Sv%	Record
Martin Prusek, GR	33	1.83	.930	18-8-5
Neil Little, Phi	33	2.02	.926	13-15-7
Philippe Sauve	55	2.13	.928	25-20-6

Western Conference
West Division

Team (Affiliate)	W	L	T	OL	Pts	GF	GA
*Grand Rapids (Ott)	42	27	11	0	95	217	178
†Houston (Min)	39	26	10	5	93	234	232
†Utah (Dal)	40	29	6	5	91	240	225
†Chicago (Atl)	37	31	7	5	86	250	236
Milwaukee (Nash)	30	35	TO	5	75	198	207

Central Division

Team (Affiliate)	W	L	T	OL	Pts	GF	GA
*Syracuse (Clb)	39	23	13	5	96	228	193
†Rochester (Buf)	32	30	15	3	82	206	211
†Cincinnati (Ana)	33	33	11	3	80	216	211
Cleveland (SJ)	29	40	7	4	69	223	268

South Division

Team (Affiliate)	W	L	T	OL	Pts	GF	GA
*Norfolk (Chi)	38	26	12	4	92	222	205
†Hershey (Col)	36	27	11	6	89	200	193
†Philadelphia (Phi)	33	27	15	5	86	206	210
Wilkes-Barre (Pit)	20	44	13	3	56	201	274

Calder Cup Finals

	W-L	GF	Leading Scorers
Bridgeport	4-1	11	Four tied with 4 each.
Chicago	1-4	18	Brown (3-9–12)

Date	Winner	Home Ice
May 24	Chicago, 5-4 (OT)	at Bridgeport
May 25	Bridgeport, 2-1	at Bridgeport
May 30	Chicago, 4-0	at Chicago
May 31	Chicago, 4-2	at Chicago
June 3	Chicago, 4-3 (2OT)	at Chicago

East Coast Hockey League

Division champions (*) and playoff qualifiers (†) are noted. GF and GA refer to goals for and against.

Northern Conference
Northeast Division

Team (Affiliate)	W	L	T	Pts	GF	GA
*Trenton (Phi./NYI)	46	16	10	102	238	178
†Charlotte (NYR)	41	20	11	93	256	207
†Atlantic City (Indep.)	42	22	8	92	233	209
†Roanoke (Indep.)	35	26	11	81	242	223
Richmond (SJ/Wash.)	32	30	10	74	191	225
Reading (LA)	27	36	9	63	182	215
Greensboro (Car)	23	41	8	54	188	278

Northwest Division

Team (Affiliate)	W	L	T	Pts	GF	GA
*Dayton (Clb)	40	20	12	92	222	196
†Peoria (St.L)	41	23	8	90	206	179
†Johnstown (Calg)	39	31	2	80	220	232
Cincinnati (Nash)	36	30	6	78	210	207
Wheeling (Pit)	36	32	4	76	213	208
Toledo (Det)	28	34	10	66	225	265

Southern Conference
Southeast Division

Team (Affiliate)	W	L	T	Pts	GF	GA
*Greenville (Atl/Bos)	43	23	6	92	231	198
†Pee Dee (Indep.)	41	25	6	88	236	218
†Columbia (Van)	36	22	14	86	211	197
†South Carolina (Buf)	39	26	7	85	235	225
Florida (Car)	37	27	8	82	207	221
Augusta (Indep.)	36	26	10	82	218	224
Macon (Fla)	29	31	12	70	194	242
Columbus (Edm)	24	37	11	59	197	242

Southwest Division

Team (Affiliate)	W	L	T	Pts	GF	GA
*Louisiana (Min)	56	12	4	116	261	156
†Mississippi (Mon/Pho)	41	26	5	87	251	222
†Pensacola (TB)	38	28	6	82	247	242
†Jackson (Chi)	34	29	9	77	187	202
†New Orleans (Indep.)	36	32	4	76	211	209
Mobile (Ott)	28	26	18	74	215	237
Arkansas (Indep.)	31	31	10	72	189	206
Baton Rouge (Indep.)	29	35	8	66	187	244

MINOR LEAGUE HOCKEY (Cont.)

Scoring Leaders

	Gm	G	A	Pts	PM
Louis Dumont, Pens	72	32	70	102	139
Dave Seitz, SC	72	44	54	98	116
Steffon Walby, Miss	63	42	51	93	52
Francois Fortier, Miss	71	36	55	91	55
Dany Bousquet, PD	72	35	56	91	87

Goaltending Leaders

(At least 1440 minutes)	GP	GAA	Sv%	Record
Frederic Cloutier, Lou	36	1.84	.945	28-5-3
Dan Murphy, Tren	45	2.12	.921	30-10-4
Marc Magliarditi, Lou	37	2.26	.924	28-7-1

Kelly Cup Finals

	W-L	GF	Leading Scorers
Greenville	4-0	18	Pepperall (2-5–7)
Dayton	0-4	7	Ling (1-3–4)

Date	Winner	Home Ice
May 3	Greenville, 6-2	at Greenville
May 5	Greenville, 4-1	at Greenville
May 8	Greenville, 3-2 (OT)	at Dayton
May 10	Greenville, 5-2	at Dayton

World Hockey Championships

MEN

The World Hockey Championships, held in Göteborg, Karlstad and Jönköping, Sweden from April 26-May 11, 2002. Top three teams (*) in each group after preliminary round-robin advance to the second round. Fourth-place teams play in a consolation round. Top four teams from each group of the second round advance to the quarterfinals.

Final Round Robin Standings

GROUP A	W-L-T	Pts	GF	GA
*Czech Republic	3-0-0	6	17	8
*Germany	2-1-0	4	17	9
*Switzerland	1-2-0	2	5	9
Japan	0-3-0	0	6	19

GROUP B	W-L-T	Pts	GF	GA
*Finland	3-0-0	6	14	1
*Slovakia	2-1-0	4	13	7
*Ukraine	1-2-0	2	7	8
Poland	0-3-0	0	0	18

GROUP C	W-L-T	Pts	GF	GA
*Sweden	3-0-0	6	15	5
*Russia	2-1-0	4	14	6
*Austria	1-2-0	2	11	14
Slovenia	0-3-0	0	6	21

GROUP D	W-L-T	Pts	GF	GA
*Canada	3-0-0	6	11	2
*United States	2-1-0	4	9	6
*Latvia	1-2-0	2	7	8
Italy	0-3-0	0	3	14

Second Round

GROUP E	W-L-T	Pts	GF	GA
*Czech Republic	5-0-0	10	25	11
*Canada	4-1-0	8	13	10
*United States	2-2-1	5	13	11
*Germany	2-2-1	5	14	14
Switzerland	1-4-0	2	8	18
Latvia	0-5-0	0	10	19

GROUP F	W-L-T	Pts	GF	GA
*Sweden	4-1-0	8	19	7
*Finland	4-1-0	8	12	6
*Slovakia	4-1-0	8	20	15
*Russia	1-3-1	3	13	15
Ukraine	1-3-1	3	10	20
Austria	0-5-0	0	12	23

Note: Although they each finished the second round with three points, Russia advanced to the playoff round over Ukraine due to a better goal differential.

Quarterfinals

Finland 3		United States 1
Sweden 6		Germany 2
Russia 3		Czech Republic 1
Slovakia 3		Canada 2

Semifinals

Russia 3	OT*	Finland 2
Slovakia 3	OT*	Sweden 2

* After a scoreless overtime, Russia and Slovakia each won their game in a penalty shootout.

Bronze Medal Game

Sweden 5 .... Finland 3

Gold Medal Game

Slovakia 4 .... Russia 3

Scoring Leaders

	Gm	G	A	Pts	PM
Miroslav Satan, Slovakia	9	5	8	13	2
Kristian Huselius, Sweden	9	5	6	11	0
Peter Bondra, Slovakia	9	7	2	9	20
Jaromir Jagr, Czech Republic	7	4	4	8	2
Richard Lintner, Slovakia	9	4	4	8	22
Timo Parssinen, Finland	9	3	5	8	4
Jan Benda, Germany	7	1	7	8	14

Goaltending Leaders

(At least 200 minutes)	Gm	Min	Sv%	GAA
Jussi Markkanen, Finland	7	429	.937	1.40
Ryan Miller, United States	4	238	.950	1.76
Milan Hnilicka, Czech Republic	5	298	.917	1.81
J-S Giguere, Canada	5	253	.921	1.89
Tommy Salo, Sweden	7	429	.921	1.96

Tournament All-Star Team

(Selected by media)

First team: G—Maxim Sokolov, Russia; **D**—Richard Lintner, Slovakia; Thomas Rhodin, Sweden; **F**—Miroslav Satan, Slovakia (MVP); Niklas Hagman, Finland; Peter Bondra, Slovakia.

Note: Due to the 2002 Winter Olympics in Salt Lake City, no IIHF Women's World Hockey Championships were held in 2002. For men's and women's Olympic hockey coverage, see pages 672-673.

1893-2002
Through the Years

Information Please®
SPORTS ALMANAC

The Stanley Cup

The Stanley Cup was originally donated to the Canadian Amateur Hockey Association by Sir Frederick Arthur Stanley, Lord Stanley of Preston and 16th Earl of Derby, who had become interested in the sport while Governor General of Canada from 1888 to 1893. Stanley wanted the trophy to be a challenge cup, contested for each year by the best amateur hockey teams in Canada.

In 1893, the Cup was presented without a challenge to the AHA champion Montreal Amateur Athletic Association team. Every year since, however, there has been a playoff. In 1914, Cup trustees limited the field challenging for the trophy to the champion of the eastern professional National Hockey Association (NHA, organized in 1910) and the western professional Pacific Coast Hockey Association (PCHA, organized in 1912).

The NHA disbanded in 1917 and the National Hockey League (NHL) was formed. From 1918 to 1926, the NHL and PCHA champions played for the Cup with the Western Canada Hockey League (WCHL) champion joining in a three-way challenge in 1923 and '24. The PCHA disbanded in 1924, while the WCHL became the Western Hockey League (WHL) for the 1925-26 season and folded the following year. The NHL playoffs have decided the winner of the Stanley Cup ever since.

Champions, 1893-1917

Multiple winners: Montreal Victorias and Montreal Wanderers (4); Montreal Amateur Athletic Association and Ottawa Silver Seven (3); Montreal Shamrocks, Ottawa Senators, Quebec Bulldogs and Winnipeg Victorias (2).

Year		Year		Year	
1893	Montreal AAA	1901	Winnipeg Victorias	1909	Ottawa Senators
1894	Montreal AAA	1902	Montreal AAA	1910	Montreal Wanderers
1895	Montreal Victorias	1903	Ottawa Silver Seven	1911	Ottawa Senators
1896	(Feb.) Winnipeg Victorias	1904	Ottawa Silver Seven	1912	Quebec Bulldogs
	(Dec.) Montreal Victorias	1905	Ottawa Silver Seven	1913	Quebec Bulldogs
1897	Montreal Victorias	1906	Montreal Wanderers	1914	Toronto Blueshirts (NHA)
1898	Montreal Victorias	1907	(Jan.) Kenora Thistles	1915	Vancouver Millionaires (PCHA)
1899	Montreal Shamrocks		(Mar.) Montreal Wanderers	1916	Montreal Canadiens (NHA)
1900	Montreal Shamrocks	1908	Montreal Wanderers	1917	Seattle Metropolitans (PCHA)

Champions Since 1918

Multiple winners: Montreal Canadiens (23); Toronto Arenas-St. Pats-Maple Leafs (13); Detroit Red Wings (10); Boston Bruins and Edmonton Oilers (5); NY Islanders, NY Rangers and Ottawa Senators (4); Chicago Blackhawks (3); Colorado Avalanche, Montreal Maroons, New Jersey Devils, Philadelphia Flyers and Pittsburgh Penguins (2).

Year	Winner	Head Coach	Series	Loser	Head Coach
1918	Toronto Arenas	Dick Carroll	3-2 (WLWLW)	Vancouver (PCHA)	Frank Patrick
1919	No Decision*				
1920	Ottawa	Pete Green	3-2 (WWLLW)	Seattle (PCHA)	Pete Muldoon
1921	Ottawa	Pete Green	3-2 (LWWLW)	Vancouver (PCHA)	Frank Patrick
1922	Toronto St. Pats	Eddie Powers	3-2 (LWLWW)	Vancouver (PCHA)	Frank Patrick
1923	Ottawa	Pete Green	3-1 (WLWW)	Vancouver (PCHA)	Frank Patrick
			2-0	Edmonton (WCHL)	K.C. McKenzie
1924	Montreal	Leo Dandurand	2-0	Vancouver (PCHA)	Frank Patrick
			2-0	Calgary (WCHL)	Eddie Oatman
1925	Victoria (WCHL)	Lester Patrick	3-1 (WWLW)	Montreal	Leo Dandurand
1926	Montreal Maroons	Eddie Gerard	3-1 (WWLW)	Victoria (WHL)	Lester Patrick
1927	Ottawa	Dave Gill	2-0-2 (TWTW)	Boston	Art Ross
1928	NY Rangers	Lester Patrick	3-2 (LWLWW)	Montreal Maroons	Eddie Gerard
1929	Boston	Cy Denneny	2-0	NY Rangers	Lester Patrick
1930	Montreal	Cecil Hart	2-0	Boston	Art Ross
1931	Montreal	Cecil Hart	3-2 (WLLWW)	Chicago	Art Duncan
1932	Toronto	Dick Irvin	3-0	NY Rangers	Lester Patrick
1933	NY Rangers	Lester Patrick	3-1 (WWLW)	Toronto	Dick Irvin
1934	Chicago	Tommy Gorman	3-1 (WWLW)	Detroit	Jack Adams
1935	Montreal Maroons	Tommy Gorman	3-0	Toronto	Dick Irvin
1936	Detroit	Jack Adams	3-1 (WWLW)	Toronto	Dick Irvin
1937	Detroit	Jack Adams	3-2 (LWLWW)	NY Rangers	Lester Patrick
1938	Chicago	Bill Stewart	3-1 (WLWW)	Toronto	Dick Irvin
1939	Boston	Art Ross	4-1 (WLWWW)	Toronto	Dick Irvin

* The 1919 finals were cancelled after five games due to an influenza epidemic with Montreal and Seattle (PCHA) tied at 2-2-1.

The Stanley Cup (Cont.)

Year	Winner	Head Coach	Series	Loser	Head Coach
1940	NY Rangers	Frank Boucher	4-2 (WWLLWW)	Toronto	Dick Irvin
1941	Boston	Cooney Weiland	4-0	Detroit	Jack Adams
1942	Toronto	Hap Day	4-3 (LLLWWWW)	Detroit	Jack Adams
1943	Detroit	Ebbie Goodfellow	4-0	Boston	Art Ross
1944	Montreal	Dick Irvin	4-0	Chicago	Paul Thompson
1945	Toronto	Hap Day	4-3 (WWWLLLW)	Detroit	Jack Adams
1946	Montreal	Dick Irvin	4-1 (WWWLW)	Boston	Dit Clapper
1947	Toronto	Hap Day	4-2 (LWWWLW)	Montreal	Dick Irvin
1948	Toronto	Hap Day	4-0	Detroit	Tommy Ivan
1949	Toronto	Hap Day	4-0	Detroit	Tommy Ivan
1950	Detroit	Tommy Ivan	4-3 (WLWLLWW)	NY Rangers	Lynn Patrick
1951	Toronto	Joe Primeau	4-1 (WLWWW)	Montreal	Dick Irvin
1952	Detroit	Tommy Ivan	4-0	Montreal	Dick Irvin
1953	Montreal	Dick Irvin	4-1 (WLWWW)	Boston	Lynn Patrick
1954	Detroit	Tommy Ivan	4-3 (WLWWLLW)	Montreal	Dick Irvin
1955	Detroit	Jimmy Skinner	4-3 (WWLLWLW)	Montreal	Dick Irvin
1956	Montreal	Toe Blake	4-1 (WWLWW)	Detroit	Jimmy Skinner
1957	Montreal	Toe Blake	4-1 (WWWLW)	Boston	Milt Schmidt
1958	Montreal	Toe Blake	4-2 (WLWLWW)	Boston	Milt Schmidt
1959	Montreal	Toe Blake	4-1 (WWLWW)	Toronto	Punch Imlach
1960	Montreal	Toe Blake	4-0	Toronto	Punch Imlach
1961	Chicago	Rudy Pilous	4-2 (WLWLWW)	Detroit	Sid Abel
1962	Toronto	Punch Imlach	4-2 (WWLLWW)	Chicago	Rudy Pilous
1963	Toronto	Punch Imlach	4-1 (WWLWW)	Detroit	Sid Abel
1964	Toronto	Punch Imlach	4-3 (WLWLLWW)	Detroit	Sid Abel
1965	Montreal	Toe Blake	4-3 (WWLLWLW)	Chicago	Billy Reay
1966	Montreal	Toe Blake	4-2 (LLWWWW)	Detroit	Sid Abel
1967	Toronto	Punch Imlach	4-2 (LWWLWW)	Montreal	Toe Blake
1968	Montreal	Toe Blake	4-0	St. Louis	Scotty Bowman
1969	Montreal	Claude Ruel	4-0	St. Louis	Scotty Bowman
1970	Boston	Harry Sinden	4-0	St. Louis	Scotty Bowman
1971	Montreal	Al MacNeil	4-3 (LLWWLWW)	Chicago	Billy Reay
1972	Boston	Tom Johnson	4-2 (WWLWLW)	NY Rangers	Emile Francis
1973	Montreal	Scotty Bowman	4-2 (WWLWLW)	Chicago	Billy Reay
1974	Philadelphia	Fred Shero	4-2 (WLWLWW)	Boston	Bep Guidolin
1975	Philadelphia	Fred Shero	4-2 (WWLLWW)	Buffalo	Floyd Smith
1976	Montreal	Scotty Bowman	4-0	Philadelphia	Fred Shero
1977	Montreal	Scotty Bowman	4-0	Boston	Don Cherry
1978	Montreal	Scotty Bowman	4-2 (WWLLWW)	Boston	Don Cherry
1979	Montreal	Scotty Bowman	4-1 (LWWWW)	NY Rangers	Fred Shero
1980	NY Islanders	Al Arbour	4-2 (WLWWLW)	Philadelphia	Pat Quinn
1981	NY Islanders	Al Arbour	4-1 (WWWLW)	Minnesota	Glen Sonmor
1982	NY Islanders	Al Arbour	4-0	Vancouver	Roger Neilson
1983	NY Islanders	Al Arbour	4-0	Edmonton	Glen Sather
1984	Edmonton	Glen Sather	4-1 (WLWWW)	NY Islanders	Al Arbour
1985	Edmonton	Glen Sather	4-1 (LWWWW)	Philadelphia	Mike Keenan
1986	Montreal	Jean Perron	4-1 (LWWWW)	Calgary	Bob Johnson
1987	Edmonton	Glen Sather	4-3 (WWLWLLW)	Philadelphia	Mike Keenan
1988	Edmonton	Glen Sather	4-0	Boston	Terry O'Reilly
1989	Calgary	Terry Crisp	4-2 (WLLWWW)	Montreal	Pat Burns
1990	Edmonton	John Muckler	4-1 (WWLWW)	Boston	Mike Milbury
1991	Pittsburgh	Bob Johnson	4-2 (LWLWWW)	Minnesota	Bob Gainey
1992	Pittsburgh	Scotty Bowman	4-0	Chicago	Mike Keenan
1993	Montreal	Jacques Demers	4-1 (LWWWW)	Los Angeles	Barry Melrose
1994	NY Rangers	Mike Keenan	4-3 (LWWWLLW)	Vancouver	Pat Quinn
1995	New Jersey	Jacques Lemaire	4-0	Detroit	Scotty Bowman
1996	Colorado	Marc Crawford	4-0	Florida	Doug MacLean
1997	Detroit	Scotty Bowman	4-0	Philadelphia	Terry Murray
1998	Detroit	Scotty Bowman	4-0	Washington	Ron Wilson
1999	Dallas	Ken Hitchcock	4-2 (LWWLWW)	Buffalo	Lindy Ruff
2000	New Jersey	Larry Robinson	4-2 (WLWLWW)	Dallas	Ken Hitchcock
2001	Colorado	Bob Hartley	4-3 (WLWLWWW)	New Jersey	Larry Robinson
2002	Detroit	Scotty Bowman	4-1 (LWWWW)	Carolina	Paul Maurice

M.J. O'Brien Trophy

Donated by Canadian mining magnate M.J. O'Brien, whose son Ambrose founded the National Hockey Association in 1910. Originally presented to the NHA champion until the league's demise in 1917, the trophy then passed to the NHL champion through 1927. It was awarded to the NHL's Canadian Division winner from 1927-38 and the Stanley Cup runner-up from 1939-50 before being retired in 1950.

NHA winners included the Montreal Wanderers (1910), original Ottawa Senators (1911 and '15), Quebec Bulldogs (1912 and '13), Toronto Blueshirts (1914) and Montreal Canadiens (1916 and '17).

Conn Smythe Trophy

The Most Valuable Player of the Stanley Cup Playoffs, as selected by the Pro Hockey Writers Association. Presented since 1965 by Maple Leaf Gardens Limited in the name of the former Toronto coach, GM and owner, Conn Smythe. Winners who did not play for the Cup champion are in **bold** type.

Multiple winners: Patrick Roy (3); Wayne Gretzky, Mario Lemieux, Bobby Orr and Bernie Parent (2).

Year	Year	Year
1965 Jean Beliveau, Mon., C	1978 Larry Robinson, Mon., D	1991 Mario Lemieux, Pit., C
1966 **Roger Crozier**, Det., G	1979 Bob Gainey, Mon., LW	1992 Mario Lemieux, Pit., C
1967 Dave Keon, Tor., C	1980 Bryan Trottier, NYI, C	1993 Patrick Roy, Mon., G
1968 **Glenn Hall**, St.L., G	1981 Butch Goring, NYI, C	1994 Brian Leetch, NYR, D
1969 Serge Savard, Mon., D	1982 Mike Bossy, NYI, RW	1995 Claude Lemieux, NJ, RW
1970 Bobby Orr, Bos., D	1983 Billy Smith, NYI, G	1996 Joe Sakic, Col., C
1971 Ken Dryden, Mon., G	1984 Mark Messier, Edm., LW	1997 Mike Vernon, Det., G
1972 Bobby Orr, Bos., D	1985 Wayne Gretzky, Edm., C	1998 Steve Yzerman, Det., C
1973 Yvan Cournoyer, Mon., RW	1986 Patrick Roy, Mon., G	1999 Joe Nieuwendyk, Dal., C
1974 Bernie Parent, Phi., G	1987 **Ron Hextall**, Phi., G	2000 Scott Stevens, NJ, D
1975 Bernie Parent, Phi., G	1988 Wayne Gretzky, Edm., C	2001 Patrick Roy, Col., G
1976 **Reggie Leach**, Phi., RW	1989 Al MacInnis, Calg., D	2002 Nicklas Lidstrom, Det., D
1977 Guy Lafleur, Mon., RW	1990 Bill Ranford, Edm., G	

Note: Ken Dryden (1971) and Patrick Roy (1986) are the only players to win as rookies.

All-Time Stanley Cup Playoff Leaders
CAREER

Stanley Cup Playoff leaders through 2002. Years listed indicate number of playoff appearances. Players active in 2002 are in **bold** type; (DNP) indicates player that was active in 2002 but did not participate in playoffs.

Scoring

Points

		Yrs	Gm	G	A	Pts
1	Wayne Gretzky	16	208	122	260	382
2	**Mark Messier** (DNP)	17	236	109	186	295
3	Jari Kurri	14	200	106	127	233
4	Glenn Anderson	15	225	93	121	214
5	Paul Coffey	16	194	59	137	196
6	**Doug Gilmour**	17	182	60	128	188
7	**Brett Hull**	17	186	100	84	184
	Bryan Trottier	17	221	71	113	184
9	Ray Bourque	21	214	41	139	180
10	Jean Beliveau	17	162	79	97	176
11	**Steve Yzerman**	17	177	67	108	175
	Denis Savard	16	169	66	109	175
13	**Mario Lemieux** (DNP)	8	107	76	96	172
14	Denis Potvin	14	185	56	108	164
15	Mike Bossy	10	129	85	75	160
	Gordie Howe	20	157	68	92	160
	Bobby Smith	13	184	64	96	160
	Sergei Fedorov	12	158	49	111	160
19	**Al MacInnis**	18	174	39	120	159
20	**Claude Lemieux**	16	226	80	77	157
21	Larry Murphy	20	215	37	115	152
22	Stan Mikita	18	155	59	91	150
23	**Joe Sakic**	9	135	65	83	148
	Brian Propp	13	160	64	84	148
25	**Jaromir Jagr** (DNP)	11	140	65	82	147

Goals

		Yrs	Gm	G
1	Wayne Gretzky	16	208	122
2	**Mark Messier** (DNP)	17	236	109
3	Jari Kurri	15	200	106
4	**Brett Hull**	17	186	100
5	Glenn Anderson	15	225	93
6	Mike Bossy	10	129	85
7	Maurice Richard	15	133	82
8	**Claude Lemieux**	16	226	80
9	Jean Beliveau	17	162	79
10	**Mario Lemieux** (DNP)	8	107	76

Assists

		Yrs	Gm	A
1	Wayne Gretzky	16	208	260
2	**Mark Messier** (DNP)	17	236	186
3	Ray Bourque	21	214	139
4	Paul Coffey	16	194	137
5	**Doug Gilmour**	17	182	128
6	Jari Kurri	15	200	127
7	Glenn Anderson	15	225	121
8	**Al MacInnis**	18	174	120
9	Larry Robinson	20	227	116
10	Larry Murphy	20	215	115

The Stanley Cup (Cont.)

Goaltending
Wins

		Gm	W-L	Pct	GAA
1	**Patrick Roy**	240	148-90	.622	2.30
2	Grant Fuhr	150	92-50	.648	2.92
3	Billy Smith	132	88-36	.710	2.73
4	Ken Dryden	112	80-32	.714	2.40
5	**Ed Belfour** (DNP)	141	79-57	.581	2.14
6	**Mike Vernon** (DNP)	138	77-56	.579	2.68
7	Jacques Plante	112	71-37	.657	2.17
8	Andy Moog	132	68-57	.544	3.04
9	**Martin Brodeur**	115	67-48	.583	1.88
10	**Tom Barrasso** (DNP)	119	61-54	.530	3.01

Shutouts

		Gm	GAA	No
1	**Patrick Roy**	240	2.30	22
2	Clint Benedict	48	1.80	15
	Jacques Plante	112	2.17	15
	Curtis Joseph	118	2.53	15
5	Turk Broda	102	1.98	13
	Martin Brodeur	115	1.88	13

Goals Against Average
Minimum of 50 games played

		Gm	Min	GA	GAA
1	**Martin Brodeur**	115	7211	226	1.88
2	George Hainsworth	52	3486	112	1.93
3	Turk Broda	101	6389	211	1.98
4	**Dominik Hasek**	97	5972	202	2.03
5	**Ed Belfour** (DNP)	141	8639	308	2.14
6	Jacques Plante	112	6652	240	2.16
7	**Chris Osgood**	75	4381	161	2.21
8	**Patrick Roy**	240	14786	568	2.30
9	Ken Dryden	112	6846	274	2.40
10	Bernie Parent	71	4302	174	2.43

Note: Clint Benedict had an average of 1.80 but played in only 48 games.

Games Played

		Yrs	Gm
1	**Patrick Roy**, Mon-Col	16	240
2	Grant Fuhr, Edm-Buf-St.L	14	150
3	**Ed Belfour**, Chi-Dal (DNP)	11	141
4	**Mike Vernon**, Calg-Det-SJ-Fla (DNP)	14	138
5	Billy Smith, NY Islanders	13	132
	Andy Moog, Edm-Bos-Dal-Mon	16	132

Miscellaneous
Championships

		Yrs	Cups
1	Henri Richard, Montreal	18	11
2	Yvan Cournoyer, Montreal	15	10
	Jean Beliveau, Montreal	17	10
4	Claude Provost, Montreal	14	9
5	Jacques Lemaire, Montreal	11	8
	Maurice Richard, Montreal	15	8
	Red Kelly, Detroit-Toronto	19	8

Years in Playoffs

		Yrs	Gm
1	Ray Bourque, Boston-Colorado	21	214
2	Gordie Howe, Detroit-Hartford	20	157
	Larry Robinson, Montreal-Los Angeles	20	227
	Larry Murphy, LA-Wash-Min-Pit-Tor-Det	20	215
5	**Scott Stevens**, Wash-St.L-NJ	19	209
	Red Kelly, Detroit-Toronto	19	164

Games Played

		Yrs	Gm
1	**Mark Messier**, Edm-NYR-Van (DNP)	17	236
2	Guy Carbonneau, Mon-St.L-Dal	17	231
3	Larry Robinson, Montreal-Los Angeles	20	227
4	**Claude Lemieux**, Mon-NJ-Col-Pho	16	226
5	Glenn Anderson, Edm-Tor-NYR-St.L	15	225

Penalty Minutes

		Yrs	Gm	Min
1	Dale Hunter, Que-Wash-Col	18	186	729
2	Chris Nilan, Mon-NYR-Bos-Mon	12	111	541
3	**Claude Lemieux**, Mon-NJ-Col-Pho	16	226	519
4	**Rick Tocchet**, Phi-Pit-Bos-Pho (DNP)	13	145	471
5	Willi Plett, Atl-Calg-Min-Bos	10	83	466

Appearances in Cup Finals

Standings of all teams that have reached the Stanley Cup championship round, since 1918.

App		Cups	Last Won
32	Montreal Canadiens	23*	1993
22	Detroit Red Wings	10	2002
21	Toronto Maple Leafs	13†	1967
17	Boston Bruins	5	1972
10	New York Rangers	4	1994
10	Chicago Blackhawks	3	1961
7	Philadelphia Flyers	2	1975
6	Edmonton Oilers	5	1990
5	New York Islanders	4	1983
5	Vancouver Millionaires (PCHA)	0	—
4	(original) Ottawa Senators	4	1927
4	Minnesota/Dallas (North) Stars	1	1999
3	New Jersey Devils	2	2000
3	Montreal Maroons	2	1935
3	St. Louis Blues	0	—
2	Colorado Avalanche	2	2001
2	Pittsburgh Penguins	2	1992
2	Calgary Flames	1	1989
2	Victoria Cougars (WCHL-WHL)	1	1925
2	Buffalo Sabres	0	—
2	Seattle Metropolitans (PCHA)	0	—
2	Vancouver Canucks	0	—
1	Calgary Tigers (WCHL)	0	—
1	Carolina Hurricanes	0	—
1	Edmonton Eskimos (WCHL)	0	—
1	Florida Panthers	0	—
1	Los Angeles Kings	0	—
1	Washington Capitals	0	—

*Les Canadiens also won the Cup in 1916 for a total of 24. Also, their final with Seattle in 1919 was cancelled due to an influenza epidemic that claimed the life of the Habs' Joe Hall.

†Toronto has won the Cup under three nicknames—Arenas (1918), St. Pats (1922) and Maple Leafs (1932,42,45,47-49,51,62-64,67).

Teams now defunct (7): Calgary Tigers, Edmonton Eskimos, Montreal Maroons, (original) Ottawa Senators, Seattle, Vancouver Millionaires and Victoria. Edmonton (1923) and Calgary (1924) represented the WCHL and later the WHL, while Vancouver (1918,1921-23) and Seattle (1919-20) played out of the PCHA.

SINGLE SEASON
Scoring
Points

		Year	Gm	G	A	Pts
1	Wayne Gretzky, Edm	1985	18	17	30	47
2	Mario Lemieux, Pit	1991	23	16	28	44
3	Wayne Gretzky, Edm	1988	19	12	31	43
4	Wayne Gretzky, LA	1993	24	15	25	40
5	Wayne Gretzky, Edm	1983	16	12	26	38
6	Paul Coffey, Edm	1985	18	12	25	37
7	Mike Bossy, NYI	1981	18	17	18	35
	Wayne Gretzky, Edm	1984	19	13	22	35
	Doug Gilmour, Tor	1993	21	10	25	35
10	Six tied with 34 each.					

Goals

		Year	Gm	No
1	Reggie Leach, Philadelphia	1976	16	19
	Jari Kurri, Edmonton	1985	18	19
3	Joe Sakic, Colorado	1996	22	18
4	Seven tied with 17 each, including three times by Mike Bossy.			

Assists

		Year	Gm	No
1	Wayne Gretzky, Edmonton	1988	19	31
2	Wayne Gretzky, Edmonton	1985	18	30
3	Wayne Gretzky, Edmonton	1987	21	29
4	Mario Lemieux, Pittsburgh	1991	23	28
5	Wayne Gretzky, Edmonton	1983	16	26

Goaltending
Wins

1 14 tied with 16 each.

Shutouts

		Year	Gm	No
1	**Dominik Hasek**, Detroit	2002	23	6
2	14 tied with 4 each.			

Goals Against Average

	(Min. 8 games played)	Year	Gm	Min	GA	GAA
1	Terry Sawchuk, Det	1952	8	480	5	0.63
2	Clint Benedict, Mon-M	1928	9	555	8	0.89
3	Turk Broda, Tor	1951	9	509	9	1.06
4	Dave Kerr, NYR	1937	9	553	10	1.11
5	Jacques Plante, Mon	1960	8	489	11	1.35

Note: Average determined by games played through 1942-43 season and by minutes played since then.

SINGLE SERIES
Points

	Year	Rd	G-A—Pts
Rick Middleton, Bos vs Buf	1983	DF	5-14—19
Wayne Gretzky, Edm vs Chi	1985	CF	4-14—18
Mario Lemieux, Pit vs Wash	1992	DSF	7-10—17
Barry Pedersen, Bos vs Buf	1983	DF	7-9—16
Doug Gilmour, Tor vs SJ	1994	CSF	3-13—16

Goals

	Year	Rd	No
Jari Kurri, Edm vs Chi	1985	CF	12
Newsy Lalonde, Mon vs Ott	1919	SF*	11
Tim Kerr, Phi vs Pit	1989	DF	10
Five tied with 9 each.			

*NHL final prior to Stanley Cup series with Seattle (PCHA).

Assists

	Year	Rd	No
Rick Middleton, Bos vs Buf	1983	DF	14
Wayne Gretzky, Edm vs Chi	1985	CF	14
Wayne Gretzky, Edm vs LA	1987	DSF	13
Doug Gilmour, Tor vs SJ	1994	CSF	13
Four tied with 11 each.			

SINGLE GAME
Points

	Date	G	A	Pts
Patrik Sundstrom, NJ vs Wash	4/22/88	3	5	8
Mario Lemieux, Pit vs Phi	4/25/89	3	5	8
Wayne Gretzky, Edm at Calg	4/17/83	4	3	7
Wayne Gretzky, Edm at Win	4/25/85	3	4	7
Wayne Gretzky, Edm vs LA	4/9/87	1	6	7

Goals

	Date	No
Newsy Lalonde, Mon vs Ott	3/1/19	5
Maurice Richard, Mon vs Tor	3/23/44	5
Darryl Sittler, Tor vs Phi	4/22/76	5
Reggie Leach, Phi vs Bos	5/6/76	5
Mario Lemieux, Pit vs Phi	4/25/89	5

Assists

	Date	No
Mikko Leinonen, NYR vs Phi	4/8/82	6
Wayne Gretzky, Edm vs LA	4/9/87	6
10 tied with 5 each.		

Five Longest Playoff Overtime Games

The 5 longest overtime games in Stanley Cup history. Note the following Series initials: SF (semifinals), CQF (conference quarterfinal), CSF (conference semifinal), DSF (division semifinal), QF (quarterfinal) and Final (Cup final). Series winners are in **bold** type; (*) indicates deciding game of series.

		OTs	Elapsed Time	Goal Scorer	Date	Series	Location
1	**Detroit** 1, Montreal Maroons 0	6	176:30	Mud Bruneteau	3/24/36	SF, Gm 1	Montreal
2	**Toronto** 1, Boston 0	6	164:46	Ken Doraty	4/3/33	SF, Gm 5	Toronto
3	**Philadelphia** 2, Pittsburgh 1	5	152:01	Keith Primeau	5/4/00	CSF, Gm 4	Pittsburgh
4	**Pittsburgh** 3 Washington 2	4	139:15	Petr Nedved	4/24/96	CQF, Gm 4	Washington
5	Toronto 3, **Detroit** 2	4	130:18	Jack McLean	3/23/43	SF, Gm 2	Detroit

NHL All-Star Game

Three benefit NHL All-Star Games were staged in the 1930s for forward Ace Bailey and the families of Howie Morenz and Babe Siebert. Bailey, of Toronto, suffered a fractured skull on a career-ending check by Boston's Eddie Shore. Morenz, the Montreal Canadiens' legend, died of a heart attack at 35 after a severely broken leg ended his career. Siebert, who played with both Montreal teams, drowned at age 35.

The All-Star Game was revived at the start of the 1947-48 season as an annual exhibition match between the defending Stanley Cup champion and all-stars from the league's other five teams. The format has changed several times since then. The game was moved to midseason in 1966-67 and became an East vs. West contest in 1968-69. The Eastern (East, 1968-1974; Wales, 1975-93) Conference leads the series 18-7-1. In 1998, the East-West format was abandoned for one pitting North American all-stars against all-stars from the rest of the world. North America leads that series 3-2.

NHL All-Star Game (Cont.)
Benefit Games

Date	Occasion		Host	Coaches
2/14/34	Ace Bailey Benefit	Toronto 7, All-Stars 3	Toronto	Dick Irvin, Lester Patrick
11/3/37	Howie Morenz Memorial	All-Stars 6, Montreals* 5	Montreal	Jack Adams, Ceil Hart
10/29/39	Babe Seibert Memorial	All-Stars 5, Canadiens 3	Montreal	Art Ross, Pit Lepine

*Combined squad of Montreal Canadiens and Montreal Maroons.

All-Star Games

Multiple MVP winners: Wayne Gretzky and Mario Lemieux (3); Bobby Hull and Frank Mahovlich (2).

Year		Host	Coaches	Most Valuable Player
1947	All-Stars 4, Toronto 3	Toronto	Dick Irvin, Hap Day	No award
1948	All-Stars 3, Toronto 1	Chicago	Tommy Ivan, Hap Day	No award
1949	All-Stars 3, Toronto 1	Toronto	Tommy Ivan, Hap Day	No award
1950	Detroit 7, All-Stars 1	Detroit	Tommy Ivan, Lynn Patrick	No award
1951	1st Team 2, 2nd Team 2	Toronto	Joe Primeau, Hap Day	No award
1952	1st Team 1, 2nd Team 1	Detroit	Tommy Ivan, Dick Irvin	No award
1953	All-Stars 3, Montreal 1	Montreal	Lynn Patrick, Dick Irvin	No award
1954	All-Stars 2, Detroit 2	Detroit	King Clancy, Jim Skinner	No award
1955	Detroit 3, All-Stars 1	Detroit	Jim Skinner, Dick Irvin	No award
1956	All-Stars 1, Montreal 1	Montreal	Jim Skinner, Toe Blake	No award
1957	All-Stars 5, Montreal 3	Montreal	Milt Schmidt, Toe Blake	No award
1958	Montreal 6, All-Stars 3	Montreal	Toe Blake, Milt Schmidt	No award
1959	Montreal 6, All-Stars 3	Montreal	Toe Blake, Punch Imlach	No award
1960	All-Stars 2, Montreal 1	Montreal	Punch Imlach, Toe Blake	No award
1961	All-Stars 3, Chicago 1	Chicago	Sid Abel, Rudy Pilous	No award
1962	Toronto 4, All-Stars 1	Toronto	Punch Imlach, Rudy Pilous	Eddie Shack, Tor., RW
1963	All-Stars 3, Toronto 3	Toronto	Sid Abel, Punch Imlach	Frank Mahovlich, Tor., LW
1964	All-Stars 3, Toronto 2	Toronto	Sid Abel, Punch Imlach	Jean Beliveau, Mon., C
1965	All-Stars 5, Montreal 2	Montreal	Billy Reay, Toe Blake	Gordie Howe, Det., RW
1966	No game (see below)			
1967	Montreal 3, All-Stars 0	Montreal	Toe Blake, Sid Abel	Henri Richard, Mon., C
1968	Toronto 4, All-Stars 3	Toronto	Punch Imlach, Toe Blake	Bruce Gamble, Tor., G
1969	West 3, East 3	Montreal	Scotty Bowman, Toe Blake	Frank Mahovlich, Det., LW
1970	East 4, West 1	St. Louis	Claude Ruel, Scotty Bowman	Bobby Hull, Chi., LW
1971	West 2, East 1	Boston	Scotty Bowman, Harry Sinden	Bobby Hull, Chi., LW
1972	East 3, West 2	Minnesota	Al MacNeil, Billy Reay	Bobby Orr, Bos., D
1973	East 5, West 4	NY Rangers	Tom Johnson, Billy Reay	Greg Polis, Pit., LW
1974	West 6, East 4	Chicago	Billy Reay, Scotty Bowman	Garry Unger, St.L., C
1975	Wales 7, Campbell 1	Montreal	Bep Guidolin, Fred Shero	Syl Apps Jr., Pit., C
1976	Wales 7, Campbell 5	Philadelphia	Floyd Smith, Fred Shero	Peter Mahovlich, Mon., C
1977	Wales 4, Campbell 3	Vancouver	Scotty Bowman, Fred Shero	Rick Martin, Buf., LW
1978	Wales 3, Campbell 2 (OT)	Buffalo	Scotty Bowman, Fred Shero	Billy Smith, NYI, G
1979	No game (see below)			
1980	Wales 6, Campbell 3	Detroit	Scotty Bowman, Al Arbour	Reggie Leach, Phi., RW
1981	Campbell 4, Wales 1	Los Angeles	Pat Quinn, Scotty Bowman	Mike Liut, St.L., G
1982	Wales 4, Campbell 2	Washington	Al Arbour, Glen Sonmor	Mike Bossy, NYI, RW
1983	Campbell 9, Wales 3	NY Islanders	Roger Neilson, Al Arbour	Wayne Gretzky, Edm., C
1984	Wales 7, Campbell 6	New Jersey	Al Arbour, Glen Sather	Don Maloney, NYR, LW
1985	Wales 6, Campbell 4	Calgary	Al Arbour, Glen Sather	Mario Lemieux, Pit., C
1986	Wales 4, Campbell 3 (OT)	Hartford	Mike Keenan, Glen Sather	Grant Fuhr, Edm., G
1987	No game (see below)			
1988	Wales 6, Campbell 5 (OT)	St. Louis	Mike Keenan, Glen Sather	Mario Lemieux, Pit., C
1989	Campbell 9, Wales 5	Edmonton	Glen Sather, Terry O'Reilly	Wayne Gretzky, LA, C
1990	Wales 12, Campbell 7	Pittsburgh	Pat Burns, Terry Crisp	Mario Lemieux, Pit., C
1991	Campbell 11, Wales 5	Chicago	John Muckler, Mike Milbury	Vincent Damphousse, Tor., LW
1992	Campbell 10, Wales 6	Philadelphia	Bob Gainey, Scotty Bowman	Brett Hull, St.L., RW
1993	Wales 16, Campbell 6	Montreal	Scotty Bowman, Mike Keenan	Mike Gartner, NYR, RW
1994	East 9, West 8	NY Rangers	Jacques Demers, Barry Melrose	Mike Richter, NYR, G
1995	No game (see below)			
1996	East 5, West 4	Boston	Doug MacLean, Scotty Bowman	Ray Bourque, Bos., D
1997	East 11, West 7	San Jose	Doug MacLean, Ken Hitchcock	Mark Recchi, Mon., RW
1998	North America 8, World 7	Vancouver	Jacques Lemaire, Ken Hitchcock	Teemu Selanne, Ana., RW
1999	North America 8, World 6	Tampa	Ken Hitchcock, Lindy Ruff	Wayne Gretzky, NYR, C
2000	World 9, North America 4	Toronto	Scotty Bowman, Pat Quinn	Pavel Bure, Fla., RW
2001	North America 14, World 12	Denver	Joel Quenneville, Jacques Martin	Bill Guerin, Bos., RW
2002	World 8, North America 5	Los Angeles	Scotty Bowman, Pat Quinn	Eric Daze, Chi., LW

No All-Star Game: in 1966 (moved from start of season to mid-season); in 1979 (replaced by Challenge Cup series with USSR); in 1987 (replaced by Rendez-Vous '87 series with USSR); and in 1995 (cancelled when NHL lockout shortened season to 48 games).

NHL Franchise Origins

Here is what the current 30 teams in the National Hockey League have to show for the years they have put in as members of the NHL, the early National Hockey Association (NHA) and the more recent World Hockey Association (WHA). League titles and Stanley Cup championships are noted by year won. The Stanley Cup has automatically gone to the NHL champion since the 1926-27 season. Following the 1992-93 season, the NHL renamed the Clarence Campbell Conference the Western Conference, while the Prince of Wales Conference became the Eastern Conference.

Western Conference

	First Season	League Titles	Franchise Stops
Anaheim, Mighty Ducks of	1993-94 (NHL)	None	•Anaheim, CA (1993—)
Calgary Flames	1972-73 (NHL)	1 Cup (1989)	•Atlanta (1972-80)
			Calgary (1980—)
Chicago Blackhawks	1926-27 (NHL)	3 Cups (1934,38,61)	•Chicago (1926—)
Colorado Avalanche	1972-73 (WHA)	1 WHA (1977)	•Quebec City (1972-95)
		2 Cups (1996, 2001)	Denver (1995—)
Columbus Blue Jackets	2000-01 (NHL)	None	•Columbus, OH (2000—)
Dallas Stars	1967-68 (NHL)	1 Cup (1999)	•Bloomington, MN (1967-93)
			Dallas (1993—)
Detroit Red Wings	1926-27 (NHL)	10 Cups (1936-37,43,50,52,54-55,97,98, 2002)	•Detroit (1926—)
Edmonton Oilers	1972-73 (WHA)	5 Cups (1984-85,87-88,90)	•Edmonton (1972—)
Los Angeles Kings	1967-68 (NHL)	None	•Inglewood, CA (1967-99)
			Los Angeles (1999—)
Minnesota Wild	2000-01 (NHL)	None	•St. Paul, MN (2000—)
Nashville Predators	1998-99 (NHL)	None	•Nashville, TN (1998—)
Phoenix Coyotes	1972-73 (WHA)	3 WHA (1976, 78-79)	•Winnipeg (1972-96)
			Phoenix (1996—)
St. Louis Blues	1967-68 (NHL)	None	•St. Louis (1967—)
San Jose Sharks	1991-92 (NHL)	None	•San Francisco (1991-93)
			San Jose (1993—)
Vancouver Canucks	1970-71 (NHL)	None	•Vancouver (1970—)

Eastern Conference

	First Season	League Titles	Franchise Stops
Atlanta Thrashers	1999-00 (NHL)	None	•Atlanta (1999—)
Boston Bruins	1924-25 (NHL)	5 Cups (1929,39,41,70,72)	•Boston (1924—)
Buffalo Sabres	1970-71 (NHL)	None	•Buffalo (1970—)
Carolina Hurricanes	1972-73 (WHA)	1 WHA (1973)	•Boston (1972-74)
			W. Springfield, MA (1974-75)
			Hartford, CT (1975-78)
			Springfield, MA (1978-80)
			Hartford (1980-97)
			Greensboro, NC (1997-99)
			Raleigh, NC (1999—)
Florida Panthers	1993-94 (NHL)	None	•Miami (1993-98)
			Sunrise, FL (1998—)
Montreal Canadiens	1909-10 (NHA)	2 NHA (1916-17)	•Montreal (1909—)
		2 NHL (1924-25)	
		24 Cups (1916,24,30-31,44,46,53,56-60,65-66,68-69,71,73,76-79,86,93)	
New Jersey Devils	1974-75 (NHL)	2 Cups (1995, 2000)	•Kansas City (1974-76)
			Denver (1976-82)
			E. Rutherford, NJ (1982—)
New York Islanders	1972-73 (NHL)	4 Cups (1980-83)	•Uniondale, NY (1972—)
New York Rangers	1926-27 (NHL)	4 Cups (1928,33,40,94)	•New York (1926—)
Ottawa Senators	1992-93 (NHL)	None	•Ottawa (1992-1996)
			Kanata, Ont. (1996—)
Philadelphia Flyers	1967-68 (NHL)	2 Cups (1974-75)	•Philadelphia (1967—)
Pittsburgh Penguins	1967-68 (NHL)	2 Cups (1991-92)	•Pittsburgh (1967—)
Tampa Bay Lightning	1992-93 (NHL)	None	•Tampa, FL (1992-93)
			St. Petersburg, FL (1993-96)
			Tampa, FL (1996—)
Toronto Maple Leafs	1916-17 (NHA)	2 NHL (1918,22)	•Toronto (1916—)
		13 Cups (1918,22,32,42,45,47-49,51,62-64,67)	
Washington Capitals	1974-75 (NHL)	None	•Landover, MD (1974-97)
			Washington, D.C. (1997—)

Note: The Hartford Civic Center roof collapsed after a snowstorm in January 1978, forcing the Whalers to move their home games to Springfield, Mass., for two years.

The Growth of the NHL

Of the four franchises that comprised the National Hockey League (NHL) at the start of the 1917-18 season, only two remain—the Montreal Canadiens and the Toronto Maple Leafs (originally the Toronto Arenas). From 1919-26, eight new teams joined the league, but only four—the Boston Bruins, Chicago Blackhawks (originally Black Hawks), Detroit Red Wings (originally Cougars) and New York Rangers—survived.

It was 41 years before the NHL expanded again, doubling in size for the 1967-68 season with new teams in Bloomington (Minn.), Los Angeles, Oakland, Philadelphia, Pittsburgh and St. Louis. The league had 16 clubs by the start of the 1972-73 season, but it also had a rival in the **World Hockey Association,** which debuted that year with 12 teams.

The NHL added two more teams in 1974 and merged the struggling Cleveland Barons (originally the Oakland Seals) and Minnesota North Stars in 1978, before absorbing four WHA clubs—the Edmonton Oilers, Hartford Whalers, Quebec Nordiques and Winnipeg Jets—in time for the 1979-80 season. Seven expansion teams joined the league in the 1990s, with two more being added in 2000 to make it an even 30.

Expansion/Merger Timetable

For teams currently in NHL.

1919—Quebec Bulldogs finally take the ice after sitting out NHL's first two seasons; **1924**—Boston Bruins and Montreal Maroons; **1925**—New York Americans and Pittsburgh Pirates; **1926**—Chicago Black Hawks (now Blackhawks), Detroit Cougars (now Red Wings) and New York Rangers; **1932**—Ottawa Senators return after sitting out 1931-32 season.

1967—California-Oakland Seals (later Cleveland Barons), Los Angeles Kings, Minnesota North Stars, Philadelphia Flyers, Pittsburgh Penguins and St. Louis Blues.

1970—Buffalo Sabres and Vancouver Canucks; **1972**—Atlanta Flames (now Calgary) and New York Islanders; **1974**—Kansas City Scouts (now New Jersey Devils) and Washington Capitals; **1978**—Cleveland Barons merge with Minnesota North Stars (now Dallas Stars) and team remains in Minnesota; **1979**—added WHA's Edmonton Oilers, Hartford Whalers (now Carolina Hurricanes), Quebec Nordiques (now Colorado Avalanche) and Winnipeg Jets (now Phoenix Coyotes).

1991—San Jose Sharks; **1992**—Ottawa Senators and Tampa Bay Lightning; **1993**—Mighty Ducks of Anaheim and Florida Panthers; **1998**—Nashville Predators; **1999**—Atlanta Thrashers.

2000—Columbus Blue Jackets and Minnesota Wild.

City and Nickname Changes

1919—Toronto Arenas renamed St. Pats; **1920**—Quebec Bulldogs move to Hamilton and becomes Tigers (will fold in 1925); **1926**—Toronto St. Pats renamed Maple Leafs; **1929**—Detroit Cougars renamed Falcons.

1930—Pittsburgh Pirates move to Philadelphia and become Quakers (will fold in 1931); **1932**—Detroit Falcons renamed Red Wings; **1934**—Ottawa Senators move to St. Louis and become Eagles (will fold in 1935); **1941**—New York Americans renamed Brooklyn Americans (will fold in 1942).

1967—California renamed Oakland Seals three months into first season; **1970**—Oakland Seals renamed California Golden Seals; **1975**—California Golden Seals renamed Seals; **1976**—California Seals move to Cleveland and become Barons, while Kansas City Scouts move to Denver and become Colorado Rockies; **1978**—Cleveland Barons merge with Minnesota North Stars and become Minnesota North Stars.

1980—Atlanta Flames move to Calgary; **1982**—Colorado Rockies move to East Rutherford, N.J., and become New Jersey Devils; **1986**—Chicago Black Hawks renamed Blackhawks; **1993**—Minnesota North Stars move to Dallas and become Stars. **1995**—Quebec Nordiques move to Denver and become Colorado Avalanche; **1996**—Winnipeg Jets move to Phoenix and become Coyotes; **1997**—Hartford Whalers move to Greensboro, N.C. and become Carolina Hurricanes; **1999**—Carolina Hurricanes move to Raleigh, N.C.

Defunct NHL Teams

Teams that once played in the NHL, but no longer exist.

Brooklyn—Americans (1941-42, formerly NY Americans from 1925-41); **Cleveland**—Barons (1976-78, originally California-Oakland Seals from 1967-76); **Hamilton (Ont.)**—Tigers (1920-25, originally Quebec Bulldogs from 1919-20); **Montreal**—Maroons (1924-38) and Wanderers (1917-18); **New York**—Americans (1925-41, later Brooklyn Americans for 1941-42); **Oakland**—Seals (1967-76, also known as California Seals and Golden Seals and later Cleveland Barons from 1976-78); **Ottawa**—Senators (1917-31 and 1932-34, later St. Louis Eagles for 1934-35); **Philadelphia**—Quakers (1930-31, originally Pittsburgh Pirates from 1925-30); **Pittsburgh**—Pirates (1925-30, later Philadelphia Quakers for 1930-31); **Quebec**—Bulldogs (1919-20, later Hamilton Tigers from 1920-25); **St. Louis**—Eagles (1934-35), originally Ottawa Senators (1917-31 and 1932-34).

WHA Teams (1972-79)

Baltimore—Blades (1975); **Birmingham**—Bulls (1976-78); **Calgary**—Cowboys (1975-77); **Chicago**—Cougars (1972-75); **Cincinnati**—Stingers (1975-79); **Cleveland**—Crusaders (1972-76, moved to Minnesota); **Denver**—Spurs (1975-76, moved to Ottawa); **Edmonton**—Oilers (1972-79, originally called Alberta Oilers in 1972-73); **Houston**—Aeros (1972-78); **Indianapolis**—Racers (1974-78).

Los Angeles—Sharks (1972-74, moved to Michigan); **Michigan**—Stags (1974-75, moved to Baltimore); **Minnesota**—Fighting Saints (1972-76) and New Fighting Saints (1976-77); **New England**—Whalers (1972-79, played in Boston from 1972-74, West Springfield, MA from 1974-75, Hartford from 1975-78 and Springfield, MA in 1979); **New Jersey**—Knights (1973-74, moved to San Diego); **New York**—Raiders (1972-73, renamed Golden Blades in 1973, moved to New Jersey).

Ottawa—Nationals (1972-73, moved to Toronto) and Civics (1976); **Philadelphia**—Blazers (1972-73, moved to Vancouver); **Phoenix**—Roadrunners (1974-77); **Quebec**—Nordiques (1972-79); **San Diego**—Mariners (1974-77); **Toronto**—Toros (1973-76, moved to Birmingham, AL); **Vancouver**—Blazers (1973-75, moved to Calgary); **Winnipeg**—Jets (1972-79).

Annual NHL Leaders

Art Ross Trophy (Scoring)

Given to the player who leads the league in points scored and named after the former Boston Bruins general manager-coach. First presented in 1948, names of prior leading scorers have been added retroactively. A tie for the scoring championship is broken three ways: 1. total goals; 2. fewest games played; 3. first goal scored.

Multiple Winners: Wayne Gretzky (10); Gordie Howe and Mario Lemieux (6); Phil Esposito and Jaromir Jagr (5); Stan Mikita (4); Bobby Hull and Guy Lafleur (3); Max Bentley, Charlie Conacher, Bill Cook, Babe Dye, Bernie Geoffrion, Elmer Lach, Newsy Lalonde, Joe Malone, Dickie Moore, Howie Morenz, Bobby Orr and Sweeney Schriner (2).

Year		Gm	G	A	Pts	Year		Gm	G	A	Pts
1918	Joe Malone, Mon	20	44	0	44	1961	Bernie Geoffrion, Mon	64	50	45	95
1919	Newsy Lalonde, Mon	17	23	9	32	1962	Bobby Hull, Chi	70	50	34	84
1920	Joe Malone, Que	24	39	6	45	1963	Gordie Howe, Det	70	38	48	86
1921	Newsy Lalonde, Mon	24	33	8	41	1964	Stan Mikita, Chi	70	39	50	89
1922	Punch Broadbent, Ott	24	32	14	46	1965	Stan Mikita, Chi	70	28	59	87
1923	Babe Dye, Tor	22	26	11	37	1966	Bobby Hull, Chi	65	54	43	97
1924	Cy Denneny, Ott	21	22	1	23	1967	Stan Mikita, Chi	70	35	62	97
1925	Babe Dye, Tor	29	38	6	44	1968	Stan Mikita, Chi	72	40	47	87
1926	Nels Stewart, Maroons	36	34	8	42	1969	Phil Esposito, Bos	74	49	77	126
1927	Bill Cook, NYR	44	33	4	37	1970	Bobby Orr, Bos	76	33	87	120
1928	Howie Morenz, Mon	43	33	18	51	1971	Phil Esposito, Bos	78	76	76	152
1929	Ace Bailey, Tor	44	22	10	32	1972	Phil Esposito, Bos	76	66	67	133
1930	Cooney Weiland, Bos	44	43	30	73	1973	Phil Esposito, Bos	78	55	75	130
1931	Howie Morenz, Mon	39	28	23	51	1974	Phil Esposito, Bos	78	68	77	145
1932	Busher Jackson, Tor	48	28	25	53	1975	Bobby Orr, Bos	80	46	89	135
1933	Bill Cook, NYR	48	28	22	50	1976	Guy Lafleur, Mon	80	56	69	125
1934	Charlie Conacher, Tor	42	32	20	52	1977	Guy Lafleur, Mon	80	56	80	136
1935	Charlie Conacher, Tor	47	36	21	57	1978	Guy Lafleur, Mon	79	60	72	132
1936	Sweeney Schriner, NYA	48	19	26	45	1979	Bryan Trottier, NYI	76	47	87	134
1937	Sweeney Schriner, NYA	48	21	25	46	1980	Marcel Dionne, LA	80	53	84	137
1938	Gordie Drillon, Tor	48	26	26	52	1981	Wayne Gretzky, Edm	80	55	109	164
1939	Toe Blake, Mon	48	24	23	47	1982	Wayne Gretzky, Edm	80	92	120	212
1940	Milt Schmidt, Bos	48	22	30	52	1983	Wayne Gretzky, Edm	80	71	125	196
1941	Bill Cowley, Bos	46	17	45	62	1984	Wayne Gretzky, Edm	74	87	118	205
1942	Bryan Hextall, NYR	48	24	32	56	1985	Wayne Gretzky, Edm	80	73	135	208
1943	Doug Bentley, Chi	50	33	40	73	1986	Wayne Gretzky, Edm	80	52	163	215
1944	Herbie Cain, Bos	48	36	46	82	1987	Wayne Gretzky, Edm	79	62	121	183
1945	Elmer Lach, Mon	50	26	54	80	1988	Mario Lemieux, Pit	77	70	98	168
1946	Max Bentley, Chi	47	31	30	61	1989	Mario Lemieux, Pit	76	85	114	199
1947	Max Bentley, Chi	60	29	43	72	1990	Wayne Gretzky, LA	73	40	102	142
1948	Elmer Lach, Mon	60	30	31	61	1991	Wayne Gretzky, LA	78	41	122	163
1949	Roy Conacher, Chi	60	26	42	68	1992	Mario Lemieux, Pit	64	44	87	131
1950	Ted Lindsay, Det	69	23	55	78	1993	Mario Lemieux, Pit	60	69	91	160
1951	Gordie Howe, Det	70	43	43	86	1994	Wayne Gretzky, LA	81	38	92	130
1952	Gordie Howe, Det	70	47	39	86	1995	Jaromir Jagr, Pit	48	32	38	70
1953	Gordie Howe, Det	70	49	46	95	1996	Mario Lemieux, Pit	70	69	92	161
1954	Gordie Howe, Det	70	33	48	81	1997	Mario Lemieux, Pit	76	50	72	122
1955	Bernie Geoffrion, Mon	70	38	37	75	1998	Jaromir Jagr, Pit	77	35	67	102
1956	Jean Beliveau, Mon	70	47	41	88	1999	Jaromir Jagr, Pit	81	44	83	127
1957	Gordie Howe, Det	70	44	45	89	2000	Jaromir Jagr, Pit	63	42	54	96
1958	Dickie Moore, Mon	70	36	48	84	2001	Jaromir Jagr, Pit	81	52	69	121
1959	Dickie Moore, Mon	70	41	55	96	2002	Jarome Iginla, Calg	82	52	44	96
1960	Bobby Hull, Chi	70	39	42	81						

Note: The three times players have tied for total points in one season the player with more goals has won the trophy. In 1961-62, Hull outscored Andy Bathgate of NY Rangers, 50 goals to 28. In 1979-80, Dionne outscored Wayne Gretzky of Edmonton, 53-51. In 1995, Jagr outscored Eric Lindros of Philadelphia, 32-29.

Goals

Multiple Winners: Bobby Hull (7); Phil Esposito (6); Charlie Conacher, Wayne Gretzky, Gordie Howe and Maurice Richard (5); Bill Cooke, Babe Dye, Brett Hull, Mario Lemieux, Pavel Bure and Teemu Selanne (3); Jean Beliveau, Doug Bentley, Peter Bondra, Mike Bossy, Bernie Geoffrion, Bryan Hextall, Joe Malone and Nels Stewart (2).

Year		No	Year		No	Year		No
1918	Joe Malone, Mon	44	1927	Bill Cook, NYR	33	1936	Charlie Conacher, Tor	23
1919	Odie Cleghorn, Mon	23	1928	Howie Morenz, Mon	33		& Bill Thoms, Tor	23
	& Newsy Lalonde, Mon	23	1929	Ace Bailey, Tor	22	1937	Larry Aurie, Det	23
1920	Joe Malone, Que	39	1930	Cooney Weiland, Bos	43		& Nels Stewart, Bos-NYA	23
1921	Babe Dye, Ham-Tor	35	1931	Charlie Conacher, Tor	31	1938	Gordie Drillon, Tor	26
1922	Punch Broadbent, Ott	32	1932	Charlie Conacher, Tor	34	1939	Roy Conacher, Bos	26
1923	Babe Dye, Tor	26		& Bill Cook, NYR	34	1940	Bryan Hextall, NYR	24
1924	Cy Denneny, Ott	22	1933	Bill Cook, NYR	28	1941	Bryan Hextall, NYR	26
1925	Babe Dye, Tor	38	1934	Charlie Conacher, Tor	32	1942	Lynn Patrick, NYR	32
1926	Nels Stewart, Maroons	34	1935	Charlie Conacher, Tor	36	1943	Doug Bentley, Chi	33

Annual NHL Leaders (Cont.)

Year	No	Year	No	Year	No
1944 Doug Bentley, Chi	.38	1964 Bobby Hull, Chi	.43	1984 Wayne Gretzky, Edm	.87
1945 Maurice Richard, Mon	.50	1965 Norm Ullman, Tor	.42	1985 Wayne Gretzky, Edm	.73
1946 Gaye Stewart, Tor	.37	1966 Bobby Hull, Chi	.54	1986 Jari Kurri, Edm	.68
1947 Maurice Richard, Mon	.45	1967 Bobby Hull, Chi	.52	1987 Wayne Gretzky, Edm	.62
1948 Ted Lindsay, Det	.33	1968 Bobby Hull, Chi	.44	1988 Mario Lemieux, Pit	.70
1949 Sid Abel, Det	.28	1969 Bobby Hull, Chi	.58	1989 Mario Lemieux, Pit	.85
1950 Maurice Richard, Mon	.43	1970 Phil Esposito, Bos	.43	1990 Brett Hull, St.L	.72
1951 Gordie Howe, Det	.43	1971 Phil Esposito, Bos	.76	1991 Brett Hull, St.L	.86
1952 Gordie Howe, Det	.47	1972 Phil Esposito, Bos	.66	1992 Brett Hull, St.L	.70
1953 Gordie Howe, Det	.49	1973 Phil Esposito, Bos	.55	1993 Alexander Mogilny, Buf	.76
1954 Maurice Richard, Mon	.37	1974 Phil Esposito, Bos	.68	& Teemu Selanne, Win	.76
1955 Bernie Geoffrion, Mon	.38	1975 Phil Esposito, Bos	.61	1994 Pavel Bure, Van	.60
& Maurice Richard, Mon	.38	1976 Reggie Leach, Phi	.61	1995 Peter Bondra, Wash	.34
1956 Jean Beliveau, Mon	.47	1977 Steve Shutt, Mon	.60	1996 Mario Lemieux, Pit	.69
1957 Gordie Howe, Det	.44	1978 Guy Lafleur, Mon	.60	1997 Keith Tkachuk, Pho	.52
1958 Dickie Moore, Mon	.36	1979 Mike Bossy, NYI	.69	1998 Teemu Selanne, Ana	.52
1959 Jean Beliveau, Mon	.45	1980 Danny Gare, Buf	.56	& Peter Bondra, Wash	.52
		Charlie Simmer, LA	.56	1999 Teemu Selanne, Ana	.47
1960 Bronco Horvath, Bos	.39	& Blaine Stoughton, Hart	.56	
& Bobby Hull, Chi	.39	1981 Mike Bossy, NYI	.68	2000 Pavel Bure, Fla	.58
1961 Bernie Geoffrion, Mon	.50	1982 Wayne Gretzky, Edm	.92	2001 Pavel Bure, Fla	.59
1962 Bobby Hull, Chi	.50	1983 Wayne Gretzky, Edm	.71	2002 Jarome Iginla, Calg	.52
1963 Gordie Howe, Det	.38				

Assists

Multiple Winners: Wayne Gretzky (16); Bobby Orr (5); Adam Oates, Frank Boucher, Bill Cowley, Phil Esposito, Gordie Howe, Jaromir Jagr, Elmer Lach, Mario Lemieux, Stan Mikita and Joe Primeau (3); Syl Apps, Andy Bathgate, Jean Beliveau, Doug Bentley, Art Chapman, Bobby Clarke, Ron Francis, Ted Lindsay, Bert Olmstead, Henri Richard and Bryan Trottier (2).

Year	No	Year	No	Year	No
1918 No official records kept.		1948 Doug Bentley, Chi	.37	1977 Guy Lafleur, Mon	.80
1919 Newsy Lalonde, Mon	.9	1949 Doug Bentley, Chi	.43	1978 Bryan Trottier, NYI	.77
1920 Corbett Denneny, Tor	.12	1950 Ted Lindsay, Det	.55	1979 Bryan Trottier, NYI	.87
1921 Louis Berlinquette, Mon	.9	1951 Gordie Howe, Det	.43	1980 Wayne Gretzky, Edm	.86
Harry Cameron, Tor	.9	& Teeder Kennedy, Tor	.43	1981 Wayne Gretzky, Edm	.109
& Joe Matte, Ham	.9	1952 Elmer Lach, Mon	.50	1982 Wayne Gretzky, Edm	.120
1922 Punch Broadbent, Ott	.14	1953 Gordie Howe, Det	.46	1983 Wayne Gretzky, Edm	.125
& Leo Reise, Ham	.14	1954 Gordie Howe, Det	.48	1984 Wayne Gretzky, Edm	.118
1923 Ed Bouchard, Ham	.12	1955 Bert Olmstead, Mon	.48	1985 Wayne Gretzky, Edm	.135
1924 King Clancy, Ott	.8	1956 Bert Olmstead, Mon	.56	1986 Wayne Gretzky, Edm	.163
1925 Cy Denneny, Ott	.15	1957 Ted Lindsay, Det	.55	1987 Wayne Gretzky, Edm	.121
1926 Frank Nighbor, Ott	.13	1958 Henri Richard, Mon	.52	1988 Wayne Gretzky, Edm	.109
1927 Dick Irvin, Chi	.18	1959 Dickie Moore, Mon	.55	1989 Wayne Gretzky, LA	.114
1928 Howie Morenz, Mon	.18	1960 Don McKenney, Bos	.49	& Mario Lemieux, Pit	.114
1929 Frank Boucher, NYR	.16	1961 Jean Beliveau, Mon	.58	1990 Wayne Gretzky, LA	.102
1930 Frank Boucher, NYR	.36	1962 Andy Bathgate, NYR	.56	1991 Wayne Gretzky, LA	.122
1931 Joe Primeau, Tor	.32	1963 Henri Richard, Mon	.50	1992 Wayne Gretzky, LA	.90
1932 Joe Primeau, Tor	.37	1964 Andy Bathgate, NYR-Tor	.58	1993 Adam Oates, Bos	.97
1933 Frank Boucher, NYR	.28	1965 Stan Mikita, Chi	.59	1994 Wayne Gretzky, LA	.92
1934 Joe Primeau, Tor	.32	1966 Jean Beliveau, Mon	.48	1995 Ron Francis, Pit	.48
1935 Art Chapman, NYA	.34	Stan Mikita, Chi	.48	1996 Ron Francis, Pit	.92
1936 Art Chapman, NYA	.28	& Bobby Rousseau, Mon	.48	& Mario Lemieux, Pit	.92
1937 Syl Apps, Tor	.29	1967 Stan Mikita, Chi	.62	1997 Mario Lemieux, Pit	.72
1938 Syl Apps, Tor	.29	1968 Phil Esposito, Bos	.49	& Wayne Gretzky, NYR	.72
1939 Bill Cowley, Bos	.34	1969 Phil Esposito, Bos	.77	1998 Jaromir Jagr, Pit	.67
1940 Milt Schmidt, Bos	.30	1970 Bobby Orr, Bos	.87	& Wayne Gretzky, NYR	.67
1941 Bill Cowley, Bos	.45	1971 Bobby Orr, Bos	.102	1999 Jaromir Jagr, Pit	.83
1942 Phil Watson, NYR	.37	1972 Bobby Orr, Bos	.80	2000 Mark Recchi, Phi	.63
1943 Bill Cowley, Bos	.45	1973 Phil Esposito, Bos	.75	2001 Jaromir Jagr, Pit	.69
1944 Clint Smith, Chi	.49	1974 Bobby Orr, Bos	.90	& Adam Oates, Wash	.69
1945 Elmer Lach, Mon	.54	1975 Bobby Clarke, Phi	.89	2002 Adam Oates, Wash-Phi	.64
1946 Elmer Lach, Mon	.34	& Bobby Orr, Bos	.89	
1947 Billy Taylor, Det	.46	1976 Bobby Clarke, Phi	.89	

Goals Against Average

Average determined by games played through 1942-43 season and by minutes played since then. Minimum of 15 games from 1917-18 season through 1925-26; minimum of 25 games since 1926-27 season. Not to be confused with the Vezina Trophy. Goaltenders who posted the season's lowest goals against average, but did not win the Vezina are in **bold** type.

Multiple Winners: Jacques Plante (9); Clint Benedict and Bill Durnan (6); Johnny Bower, Ken Dryden and Tiny Thompson (4); Patrick Roy and Georges Vezina (3); Ed Belfour, Frankie Brimsek, Turk Broda, George Hainsworth, Dominik Hasek, Harry Lumley, Bernie Parent, Pete Peeters and Terry Sawchuk (2).

Year	GAA	Year	GAA	Year	GAA
1918 Georges Vezina, Mon	3.82	1947 Bill Durnan, Mon	2.30	1976 Ken Dryden, Mon	2.03
1919 Clint Benedict, Ott	2.94	1948 Turk Broda, Tor	2.38	1977 Bunny Larocque, Mon	2.09
		1949 Bill Durnan, Mon	2.10	1978 Ken Dryden, Mon	2.05
1920 Clint Benedict, Ott	2.67			1979 Ken Dryden, Mon	2.30
1921 Clint Benedict, Ott	3.13	1950 Bill Durnan, Mon	2.20		
1922 Clint Benedict, Ott	3.50	1951 Al Rollins, Tor	1.77	1980 Bob Sauve, Buf	2.36
1923 Clint Benedict, Ott	2.25	1952 Terry Sawchuk, Det	1.90	1981 Richard Sevigny, Mon	2.40
1924 Georges Vezina, Mon	2.00	1953 Terry Sawchuk, Det	1.90	1982 **Denis Herron,** Mon	2.64
1925 Georges Vezina, Mon	1.87	1954 Harry Lumley, Tor	1.86	1983 Pete Peeters, Bos	2.36
1926 Alex Connell, Ott	1.17	1955 **Harry Lumley,** Tor	1.94	1984 **Pat Riggin,** Wash	2.66
1927 **Clint Benedict,** Mon-M	1.51	1956 Jacques Plante, Mon	1.86	1985 **Tom Barrasso,** Buf	2.66
1928 Geo. Hainsworth, Mon	1.09	1957 Jacques Plante, Mon	2.02	1986 **Bob Froese,** Phi	2.55
1929 Geo. Hainsworth, Mon	0.98	1958 Jacques Plante, Mon	2.11	1987 **Brian Hayward,** Mon	2.81
		1959 Jacques Plante, Mon	2.16	1988 **Pete Peeters,** Wash	2.78
1930 Tiny Thompson, Bos	2.23			1989 Patrick Roy, Mon	2.47
1931 Roy Worters, NYA	1.68	1960 Jacques Plante, Mon	2.54		
1932 Chuck Gardiner, Chi	1.92	1961 Johnny Bower, Tor	2.50	1990 **Mike Liut,** Hart-Wash	2.53
1933 Tiny Thompson, Bos	1.83	1962 Jacques Plante, Mon	2.37	1991 Ed.Belfour, Chi	2.47
1934 **Wilf Cude,** Det-Mon	1.57	1963 **Jacques Plante,** Mon	2.49	1992 Patrick Roy, Mon	2.36
1935 Lorne Chabot, Chi	1.83	1964 **Johnny Bower,** Tor	2.11	1993 **Felix Potvin,** Tor	2.50
1936 Tiny Thompson, Bos	1.71	1965 Johnny Bower, Tor	2.38	1994 Dominik Hasek, Buf	1.95
1937 Norm Smith, Det	2.13	1966 **Johnny Bower,** Tor	2.25	1995 Dominik Hasek, Buf	2.11
1938 Tiny Thompson, Bos	1.85	1967 Glenn Hall, Chi	2.38	1996 **Ron Hextall,** Phi	2.17
1939 Frankie Brimsek, Bos	1.58	1968 Gump Worsley, Mon	1.98	1997 **Martin Brodeur,** NJ	1.88
		1969 **Jacques Plante,** St.L	1.96	1998 **Ed Belfour,** Dal	1.88
1940 Dave Kerr, NYR	1.60			1999 **Ron Tugnutt,** Ott	1.79
1941 Turk Broda, Tor	2.06	1970 **Ernie Wakely,** St.L	2.11		
1942 Frankie Brimsek, Bos	2.45	1971 **Jacques Plante,** Tor	1.88	2000 **Brian Boucher,** Phi	1.91
1943 John Mowers, Det	2.47	1972 Tony Esposito, Chi	1.77	2001 **Marty Turco,** Dal	1.90
1944 Bill Durnan, Mon	2.18	1973 Ken Dryden, Mon	2.26	2002 **Patrick Roy,** Col	1.94
1945 Bill Durnan, Mon	2.42	1974 Bernie Parent, Phi	1.89		
1946 Bill Durnan, Mon	2.60	1975 Bernie Parent, Phi	2.03		

Penalty Minutes

Multiple Winners: Red Horner (8); Gus Mortson and Dave Schultz (4); Bert Corbeau, Lou Fontinato and Tiger Williams (3); Matthew Barnaby, Billy Boucher, Carl Brewer, Red Dutton, Pat Egan, Bill Ezinicki, Joe Hall, Tim Hunter, Keith Magnuson, Chris Nilan, Jimmy Orlando and Rob Ray (2).

Year	Min	Year	Min	Year	Min
1918 Joe Hall, Mon	60	1947 Gus Mortson, Tor	133	1976 Steve Durbano, Pit-KC	370
1919 Joe Hall, Mon	85	1948 Bill Barilko, Tor	147	1977 Tiger Williams, Tor	338
		1949 Bill Ezinicki, Tor	145	1978 Dave Schultz, LA-Pit	405
1920 Cully Wilson, Tor	79			1979 Tiger Williams, Tor	298
1921 Bert Corbeau, Mon	86	1950 Bill Ezinicki, Tor	144		
1922 Sprague Cleghorn, Mon	63	1951 Gus Mortson, Tor	142	1980 Jimmy Mann, Win	287
1923 Billy Boucher, Mon	52	1952 Gus Kyle, Bos	127	1981 Tiger Williams, Van	343
1924 Bert Corbeau, Tor	55	1953 Maurice Richard, Mon	112	1982 Paul Baxter, Pit	409
1925 Billy Boucher, Mon	92	1954 Gus Mortson, Chi	132	1983 Randy Holt, Wash	275
1926 Bert Corbeau, Tor	121	1955 Fern Flaman, Bos	150	1984 Chris Nilan, Mon	338
1927 Nels Stewart, Mon-M	133	1956 Lou Fontinato, NYR	202	1985 Chris Nilan, Mon	358
1928 Eddie Shore, Bos	165	1957 Gus Mortson, Chi	147	1986 Joey Kocur, Det	377
1929 Red Dutton, Mon-M	139	1958 Lou Fontinato, NYR	152	1987 Tim Hunter, Calg	361
		1959 Ted Lindsay, Chi	184	1988 Bob Probert, Det	398
1930 Joe Lamb, Ott	119			1989 Tim Hunter, Calg	375
1931 Harvey Rockburn, Det	118	1960 Carl Brewer, Tor	150		
1932 Red Dutton, NYA	107	1961 Pierre Pilote, Chi	165	1990 Basil McRae, Min	351
1933 Red Horner, Tor	144	1962 Lou Fontinato, Mon	167	1991 Rob Ray, Buf	350
1934 Red Horner, Tor	146	1963 Howie Young, Det	273	1992 Mike Peluso, Chi	408
1935 Red Horner, Tor	125	1964 Vic Hadfield, NYR	151	1993 Marty McSorley, LA	399
1936 Red Horner, Tor	167	1965 Carl Brewer, Tor	177	1994 Tie Domi, Win	347
1937 Red Horner, Tor	124	1966 Reg Fleming, Bos-NYR	166	1995 Enrico Ciccone, TB	225
1938 Red Horner, Tor	82	1967 John Ferguson, Mon	177	1996 Matthew Barnaby, Buf	335
1939 Red Horner, Tor	85	1968 Barclay Plager, St.L	153	1997 Gino Odjick, Van	371
		1969 Forbes Kennedy, Phi-Tor	219	1998 Donald Brashear, Van	372
1940 Red Horner, Tor	87			1999 Rob Ray, Buf	261
1941 Jimmy Orlando, Det	99	1970 Keith Magnuson, Chi	213		
1942 Pat Egan, NYA	124	1971 Keith Magnuson, Chi	291	2000 Denny Lambert, Atl	219
1943 Jimmy Orlando, Det	99	1972 Bryan Watson, Pit	212	2001 Matthew Barnaby, Pit-TB	265
1944 Mike McMahon, Mon	98	1973 Dave Schultz, Phi	259	2002 Peter Worrell, Fla	354
1945 Pat Egan, Bos	86	1974 Dave Schultz, Phi	348		
1946 Jack Stewart, Det	73	1975 Dave Schultz, Phi	472		

All-Time NHL Regular Season Leaders

Through 2002 regular season.

CAREER

Players active during 2002 season in **bold** type.

Points

		Yrs	Gm	G	A	Pts
1	Wayne Gretzky	20	1487	894	1963	2857
2	Gordie Howe	26	1767	801	1049	1850
3	**Mark Messier**	23	1602	658	1146	1804
4	Marcel Dionne	18	1348	731	1040	1771
5	**Ron Francis**	21	1569	514	1187	1701
6	**Steve Yzerman**	19	1362	658	1004	1662
7	**Mario Lemieux**	14	812	654	947	1601
8	Phil Esposito	18	1282	717	873	1590
9	Ray Bourque	22	1612	410	1169	1579
10	Paul Coffey	21	1409	396	1135	1531
11	Stan Mikita	22	1394	541	926	1467
12	Bryan Trottier	18	1279	524	901	1425
13	Dale Hawerchuk	16	1188	518	891	1409
14	Jari Kurri	17	1251	601	797	1398
15	**Doug Gilmour**	19	1412	439	945	1384
16	John Bucyk	23	1540	556	813	1369
17	**Adam Oates**	17	1210	330	1027	1357
18	Guy Lafleur	17	1126	560	793	1353
19	Denis Savard	17	1196	473	865	1338
20	Mike Gartner	19	1432	708	627	1335
21	Gilbert Perreault	17	1191	512	814	1326
22	**Luc Robitaille**	16	1205	620	668	1288
23	Alex Delvecchio	24	1549	456	825	1281
24	Jean Ratelle	21	1281	491	776	1267
25	**Joe Sakic**	14	1016	483	774	1257
26	**Dave Andreychuk**	20	1443	593	654	1247
27	**Brett Hull**	17	1101	679	567	1246
28	Peter Stastny	15	977	450	789	1239
29	Norm Ullman	20	1410	490	739	1229
30	Jean Beliveau	20	1125	507	712	1219

Goals

		Yrs	Gm	No
1	Wayne Gretzky	20	1487	894
2	Gordie Howe	26	1767	801
3	Marcel Dionne	18	1348	731
4	Phil Esposito	18	1282	717
5	Mike Gartner	19	1432	708
6	**Brett Hull**	17	1101	679
7	**Steve Yzerman**	19	1362	658
	Mark Messier	23	1602	658
9	**Mario Lemieux**	14	812	654
10	**Luc Robitaille**	16	1205	620
11	Bobby Hull	16	1063	610
12	Dino Ciccarelli	19	1232	608
13	Jari Kurri	17	1251	601
14	**Dave Andreychuk**	20	1443	593
15	Mike Bossy	10	752	573
16	Guy Lafleur	17	1126	560
17	John Bucyk	23	1540	556
18	Michel Goulet	15	1089	548
19	Maurice Richard	18	978	544
20	Stan Mikita	22	1394	541
21	Frank Mahovlich	18	1181	533
22	Bryan Trottier	18	1279	524
23	**Pat Verbeek**	20	1424	522
24	Dale Hawerchuk	16	1188	518
25	**Ron Francis**	21	1569	514
26	Gilbert Perreault	17	1191	512
27	Jean Beliveau	20	1125	507
28	**Brendan Shanahan**	15	1108	503
29	Joe Mullen	17	1062	502
30	Lanny McDonald	16	1111	500

Assists

		Yrs	Gm	No
1	Wayne Gretzky	20	1487	1963
2	**Ron Francis**	21	1569	1187
3	Ray Bourque	22	1612	1169
4	**Mark Messier**	23	1602	1146
5	Paul Coffey	21	1409	1135
6	Gordie Howe	26	1767	1049
7	Marcel Dionne	18	1348	1040
8	**Adam Oates**	17	1210	1027
9	**Steve Yzerman**	19	1362	1004
10	**Mario Lemieux**	14	812	947
11	**Doug Gilmour**	19	1412	945
12	Larry Murphy	21	1615	929
13	Stan Mikita	22	1394	926
14	Bryan Trottier	18	1279	901
15	Dale Hawerchuk	16	1188	891
16	**Al MacInnis**	21	1333	880
17	Phil Esposito	18	1281	873
18	**Phil Housley**	20	1437	871
19	Denis Savard	17	1196	865
20	Bobby Clarke	15	1144	852

Penalty Minutes

		Yrs	Gm	Min
1	Tiger Williams	14	962	3966
2	Dale Hunter	19	1407	3565
3	Marty McSorley	17	961	3381
4	**Bob Probert**	16	935	3300
5	Tim Hunter	16	815	3146
6	**Rob Ray**	13	848	3097
7	**Craig Berube**	16	999	3049
8	Chris Nilan	13	688	3043
9	**Tie Domi**	13	784	3027
10	**Rick Tocchet**	18	1144	2974
11	**Pat Verbeek**	20	1424	2905
12	**Dave Manson**	16	1103	2792
13	Scott Stevens	20	1516	2722
14	Willi Plett	12	834	2572
15	**Gino Odjick**	12	605	2567

NHL-WHA Top 15

All-time regular season scoring leaders, including games played in World Hockey Association (1972-79). NHL players with WHA experience are listed in CAPITAL letters. Players active during 2002 are in **bold** type.

Points

		Yrs	G	A	Pts
1	WAYNE GRETZKY	21	940	2027	2967
2	GORDIE HOWE	32	975	1383	2358
3	**MARK MESSIER**	24	659	1156	1815
4	BOBBY HULL	23	913	895	1808
5	Marcel Dionne	18	731	1040	1771
6	**Ron Francis**	21	514	1187	1701
7	**Steve Yzerman**	19	658	1004	1662
8	**Mario Lemieux**	14	654	947	1601
9	Phil Esposito	18	717	873	1590
10	Ray Bourque	22	410	1169	1579
11	Paul Coffey	21	396	1135	1531
12	Stan Mikita	22	541	926	1467
13	Bryan Trottier	18	524	901	1425
14	Dale Hawerchuk	16	518	891	1409
15	Jari Kurri	17	601	797	1398

WHA Totals: GRETZKY (1 yr, 80 gm, 46-64—110); HOWE (6 yrs, 419 gm, 174-334—508); MESSIER (1 yr, 52 gm, 1-10—11); HULL (7 yrs, 411 gm, 303-335—638).

Years Played

		Yrs	Career	Gm
1	Gordie Howe	26	1946-71, 79-80	1767
2	Alex Delvecchio	24	1950-74	1549
	Tim Horton	24	1949-50, 51-74	1446
4	**Mark Messier**	23	1979-	1602
	John Bucyk	23	1955-78	1540
6	Ray Bourque	22	1979-2001	1612
	Stan Mikita	22	1958-80	1394
	Doug Mohns	22	1953-75	1390
	Dean Prentice	22	1952-74	1378
10	Larry Murphy	21	1980-2001	1615
	Ron Francis	21	1981-	1569
	Harry Howell	21	1952-73	1411
	Paul Coffey	21	1980-2001	1409
	Ron Stewart	21	1952-73	1353
	Al MacInnis	21	1982-	1333
	Jean Ratelle	21	1960-81	1281
	Allan Stanley	21	1948-69	1244
	Eric Nesterenko	21	1951-72	1219
	Marcel Pronovost	21	1950-70	1206
	George Armstrong	21	1949-50, 51-71	1187
	Terry Sawchuk	21	1949-70	971
	Gump Worsley	21	1952-53, 54-74	862

Note: Combined NHL-WHA years played: Howe (32); Howell and Messier (24); Bobby Hull (23); Norm Ullman, Nesterenko, Frank Mahovlich and Dave Keon (22); Wayne Gretzky (21).

Games Played

		Yrs	Career	Gm
1	Gordie Howe	26	1946-71, 79-80	1767
2	Larry Murphy	21	1980-2001	1615
3	Ray Bourque	22	1979-2001	1612
4	**Mark Messier**	23	1979-	1602
5	**Ron Francis**	21	1981-	1569
6	Alex Delvecchio	24	1950-74	1549
7	John Bucyk	23	1955-78	1540
8	**Scott Stevens**	20	1982-	1516
9	Wayne Gretzky	20	1979-99	1487
10	Tim Horton	24	1949-50, 51-74	1446
11	**Dave Andreychuk**	20	1982-	1443
12	**Phil Housley**	20	1982-	1437
13	Mike Gartner	19	1979-98	1432
14	**Pat Verbeek**	20	1982-	1424
15	**Doug Gilmour**	19	1983-	1412

Note: Combined NHL-WHA games played: Howe (2,186), Messier (1,654), Dave Keon (1,597), Howell (1,581), Gretzky (1,567), Ullman (1,554), Gartner (1,510), Bobby Hull (1,474) and Frank Mahovlich (1,418).

Goaltending

Wins

		Yrs	Gm	W	L	T	Pct
1	**Patrick Roy**	18	966	**516**	300	118	.616
2	Terry Sawchuk	21	971	**447**	330	172	.562
3	Jacques Plante	18	837	**434**	247	146	.614
4	Tony Esposito	16	886	**423**	306	152	.566
5	Glenn Hall	18	906	**407**	326	163	.545
6	Grant Fuhr	19	868	**403**	295	114	.567
7	**Mike Vernon**	19	781	**385**	273	92	.575
8	**J. Vanbiesbrouck**	20	882	**374**	346	119	.517
9	Andy Moog	18	713	**372**	209	88	.622
10	**Tom Barrasso**	18	771	**368**	273	86	.565
11	**Ed Belfour**	14	735	**364**	242	100	.586
12	Rogie Vachon	16	795	**355**	291	127	.541
13	**Curtis Joseph**	13	706	**346**	260	81	.563
14	Gump Worsley	21	861	**335**	352	150	.490
15	Harry Lumley	16	804	**330**	329	143	.501
16	**Martin Brodeur**	10	592	**324**	168	85	.635
17	Billy Smith	18	680	**305**	233	105	.556
18	Turk Broda	12	629	**302**	224	101	.562
19	Ron Hextall	13	608	**296**	214	69	.571
	Mike Richter	14	653	**296**	252	72	.535

Losses

		Yrs	Gm	W	L	T	Pct
1	Gump Worsley	21	861	335	**352**	150	.490
2	Gilles Meloche	18	788	270	**351**	131	.446
3	**J. Vanbiesbrouck**	20	882	374	**346**	119	.517
4	Terry Sawchuk	21	971	447	**330**	172	.562
5	Harry Lumley	16	804	330	**329**	143	.501

Goals Against Average
Minimum of 300 games played.

Before 1950

		Gm	Min	GA	GAA
1	George Hainsworth	465	29,415	937	1.91
2	Alex Connell	417	26,050	830	1.91
3	Chuck Gardiner	316	19,687	664	2.02
4	Lorne Chabot	411	25,307	860	2.04
5	Tiny Thompson	553	34,175	1183	2.08

Since 1950

		Gm	Min	GA	GAA
1	**Martin Brodeur**	592	34,583	1272	2.21
2	**Dominik Hasek**	581	33,745	1254	2.23
3	Ken Dryden	397	23,352	870	2.24
4	Jacques Plante	837	49,533	1965	2.38
5	**Chris Osgood**	455	26,217	1056	2.42

Shutouts

		Yrs	Games	No
1	Terry Sawchuk	21	971	103
2	George Hainsworth	11	465	94
3	Glenn Hall	18	906	84
4	Jacques Plante	18	837	82
5	Alex Connell	12	417	81
	Tiny Thompson	12	553	81
7	Tony Esposito	16	886	76
8	Lorne Chabot	11	411	73
9	Harry Lumley	16	804	71
10	Roy Worters	12	484	66
11	Turk Broda	12	629	62
12	**Dominik Hasek**	12	581	61
	Patrick Roy	18	966	61
14	John Roach	14	491	58
	Ed Belfour	14	735	58

NHL-WHA Top 15

All-time regular season wins leaders, including games played in World Hockey Association (1972-79). NHL goaltenders with WHA experience are listed in CAPITAL LETTERS. Players active during 2002 are in **bold** type.

Wins

		Yrs	W	L	T	Pct
1	**Patrick Roy**	18	**516**	300	118	.616
2	JACQUES PLANTE	19	**449**	261	147	.610
3	Terry Sawchuk	21	**447**	330	172	.562
4	Tony Esposito	16	**423**	306	152	.566
5	Glenn Hall	18	**407**	326	163	.545
6	Grant Fuhr	19	**403**	295	114	.567
7	**Mike Vernon**	19	**385**	273	92	.575
8	**J. Vanbiesbrouck**	20	**374**	346	119	.517
9	Andy Moog	18	**372**	209	88	.622
10	**Tom Barrasso**	18	**368**	273	86	.565
11	**Ed Belfour**	14	**364**	242	100	.586
12	Rogie Vachon	16	**355**	291	127	.541
13	**Curtis Joseph**	13	**346**	260	81	.563
14	Gump Worsley	21	**335**	352	150	.490
15	Harry Lumley	16	**330**	329	143	.501

WHA Totals: PLANTE (1 yr, 31 gm, 15-14-1).

All-Time NHL Regular Season Leaders (Cont.)
SINGLE SEASON

Scoring
Points

		Season	G	A	Pts
1	Wayne Gretzky, Edm	1985-86	52	163	215
2	Wayne Gretzky, Edm	1981-82	92	120	212
3	Wayne Gretzky, Edm	1984-85	73	135	208
4	Wayne Gretzky, Edm	1983-84	87	118	205
5	Mario Lemieux, Pit	1988-89	85	114	199
6	Wayne Gretzky, Edm	1982-83	71	125	196
7	Wayne Gretzky, Edm	1986-87	62	121	183
8	Mario Lemieux, Pit	1987-88	70	98	168
	Wayne Gretzky, LA	1988-89	54	114	168
10	Wayne Gretzky, Edm	1980-81	55	109	164\
11	Wayne Gretzky, LA	1990-91	41	122	163
12	Mario Lemieux, Pit	1995-96	69	92	161
13	Mario Lemieux, Pit	1992-93	69	91	160
14	Steve Yzerman, Det	1988-89	65	90	155
15	Phil Esposito, Bos	1970-71	76	76	152
16	Bernie Nicholls, LA	1988-89	70	80	150
17	Jaromir Jagr, Pit	1995-96	62	87	149
	Wayne Gretzky, Edm	1987-88	40	109	149
19	Pat LaFontaine, Buf	1992-93	53	95	148
20	Mike Bossy, NYI	1981-82	64	83	147

WHA 150 points or more: 154—Marc Tardif, Que. (1977-78).

Goals

		Season	Gm	No
1	Wayne Gretzky, Edm	1981-82	80	92
2	Wayne Gretzky, Edm	1983-84	74	87
3	Brett Hull, St.L	1990-91	78	86
4	Mario Lemieux, Pit	1988-89	76	85
5	Alexander Mogilny, Buf	1992-93	77	76
	Phil Esposito, Bos	1970-71	78	76
	Teemu Selanne, Win	1992-93	84	76
8	Wayne Gretzky, Edm	1984-85	80	73
9	Brett Hull, St.L	1989-90	80	72
10	Jari Kurri, Edm	1984-85	73	71
	Wayne Gretzky, Edm	1982-83	80	71
12	Brett Hull, St.L	1991-92	73	70
	Mario Lemieux, Pit	1987-88	77	70
	Bernie Nicholls, LA	1988-89	79	70
15	Mario Lemieux, Pit	1992-93	60	69
	Mario Lemieux, Pit	1995-96	70	69
	Mike Bossy, NYI	1978-79	80	69
18	Phil Esposito, Bos	1973-74	78	68
	Jari Kurri, Edm	1985-86	78	68
	Mike Bossy, NYI	1980-81	79	68

WHA 70 goals or more: 77—Bobby Hull, Win. (1974-75); 75—Real Cloutier, Que. (1978-79); 71—Marc Tardif, Que. (1975-76); 70—Anders Hedberg, Win. (1976-77).

Assists

		Season	Gm	No
1	Wayne Gretzky, Edm	1985-86	80	163
2	Wayne Gretzky, Edm	1984-85	80	135
3	Wayne Gretzky, Edm	1982-83	80	125
4	Wayne Gretzky, LA	1990-91	78	122
5	Wayne Gretzky, Edm	1986-87	79	121
6	Wayne Gretzky, Edm	1981-82	80	120
7	Wayne Gretzky, Edm	1983-84	74	118
8	Mario Lemieux, Pit	1988-89	76	114
	Wayne Gretzky, LA	1988-89	78	114
10	Wayne Gretzky, Edm	1987-88	64	109
	Wayne Gretzky, Edm	1980-81	80	109
12	Wayne Gretzky, LA	1989-90	73	102
	Bobby Orr, Bos	1970-71	78	102
14	Mario Lemieux, Pit	1987-88	77	98
15	Adam Oates, Bos	1992-93	84	97

WHA 95 assists or more: 106—Andre Lacroix, San Diego (1974-75).

Goaltending
Wins

		Season	Record
1	Bernie Parent, Phi	1973-74	47-13-12
2	Bernie Parent, Phi	1974-75	44-14- 9
	Terry Sawchuk, Det	1950-51	44-13-13
	Terry Sawchuk, Det	1951-52	44-14-12
5	Martin Brodeur, NJ	1999-00	43-20- 8
	Martin Brodeur, NJ	1997-98	43-17- 8
	Tom Barrasso, Pit	1992-93	43-14- 5
	Ed Belfour, Chi	1990-91	43-19- 7
9	Jacques Plante, Mon	1955-56	42-12-10
	Jacques Plante, Mon	1961-62	42-14-14
	Ken Dryden, Mon	1975-76	42-10- 8
	Mike Richter, NYR	1993-94	42-12- 6
	Roman Turek, St.L	1999-00	42-15- 9
	Martin Brodeur, NJ	2000-01	42-17-11

Most WHA wins in one season: 44—Richard Brodeur, Que. (1975-76).

Losses

		Season	Record
1	Gary Smith, Cal	1970-71	19-48- 4
2	Al Rollins, Chi	1953-54	12-47- 7
3	Peter Sidorkiewicz, Ott	1992-93	8-46- 3
4	Harry Lumley, Chi	1951-52	17-44- 9
5	Harry Lumley, Chi	1950-51	12-41-10
	Craig Billington, Ott	1993-94	11-41- 4

Most WHA losses in one season: 36—Don McLeod, Van. (1974-75) and Andy Brown, Ind. (1974-75).

Shutouts

		Season	Gm	No
1	George Hainsworth, Mon	1928-29	44	22
2	Alex Connell, Ottawa	1925-26	36	15
	Alex Connell, Ottawa	1927-28	44	15
	Hal Winkler, Bos	1927-28	44	15
	Tony Esposito, Chi	1969-70	63	15

Most WHA shutouts in one season: 5—Gerry Cheevers, Cle. (1972-73) and Joe Daly, Win. (1975-76).

Goals Against Average
Before 1950

		Season	Gm	GAA
1	George Hainsworth, Mon	1928-29	44	0.98
2	George Hainsworth, Mon	1927-28	44	1.09
3	Alex Connell, Ottawa	1925-26	36	1.17
4	Tiny Thompson, Bos	1928-29	44	1.18
5	Roy Worters, NY Americans	1928-29	38	1.21

Since 1950

		Season	Gm	GAA
1	Tony Esposito, Chi	1971-72	48	1.77
2	Al Rollins, Tor	1950-51	40	1.77
3	Ron Tugnutt, Ott	1998-99	43	1.79
4	Harry Lumley, Tor	1953-54	69	1.86
5	Jacques Plante, Mon	1955-56	64	1.86

Penalty Minutes

		Season	PM
1	Dave Schultz, Phi	1974-75	472
2	Paul Baxter, Pit	1981-82	409
3	Mike Peluso, Chi	1991-92	408
4	Dave Schultz, LA-Pit	1977-78	405
5	Marty McSorley, LA	1992-93	399
6	Bob Probert, Det	1987-88	398
7	Basil McRae, Min	1987-88	382
8	Joey Kocur, Det	1985-86	377
9	Tim Hunter, Calg	1988-89	375
10	Donald Brashear, Van	1997-98	372

WHA 355 minutes or more: 365—Curt Brackenbury, Min-Que. (1975-76).

SINGLE GAME
Scoring

Points

	Date	G-A—Pts
Darryl Sittler, Tor vs Bos	2/7/76	6-4—10
Maurice Richard, Mon vs Det	12/28/44	5-3— 8
Bert Olmstead, Mon vs Chi	1/9/54	4-4— 8
Tom Bladon, Phi vs Cle	12/11/77	4-4— 8
Bryan Trottier, NYI vs NYR	12/23/78	5-3— 8
Peter Stastny, Que at Wash	2/22/81	4-4— 8
Anton Stastny, Que at Wash	2/22/81	3-5— 8
Wayne Gretzky, Edm vs NJ	11/19/83	3-5— 8
Wayne Gretzky, Edm vs Min	1/4/84	4-4— 8
Paul Coffey, Edm vs Det	3/14/86	2-6— 8
Mario Lemieux, Pit vs St.L	10/15/88	2-6— 8
Bernie Nicholls, LA vs Tor	12/1/88	2-6— 8
Mario Lemieux, Pit vs NJ	12/31/88	5-3— 8

Goals

	Date	No
Joe Malone, Que vs Tor	1/31/20	7
Newsy Lalonde, Mon vs Tor	1/10/20	6
Joe Malone, Que vs Ott	3/10/20	6
Corb Denneny, Tor vs Ham	1/26/21	6
Cy Denneny, Ott vs Ham	3/7/21	6
Syd Howe, Det vs NYR	2/3/44	6
Red Berenson, St.L at Phi	11/7/68	6
Darryl Sittler, Tor vs Bos	2/7/76	6

Assists

	Date	No
Billy Taylor, Det at Chi	3/16/47	7
Wayne Gretzky, Edm vs Wash	2/15/80	7
Wayne Gretzky, Edm at Chi	12/11/85	7
Wayne Gretzky, Edm vs Que	2/14/86	7
24 players tied with 6 each.		

Penalty Minutes

	Date	Min
Randy Holt, LA at Phi	3/11/79	67
Frank Bathe, Phi vs LA	3/11/79	55
Russ Anderson, Pit vs Edm	1/19/80	51

Penalties

	Date	No
Chris Nilan, Bos vs Har	3/31/91	10*
Eight tied with 9 each.		

* Nilan accumulated six minors, two majors, one 10-minute misconduct and one game misconduct.

All-Time Winningest NHL Coaches

Top 20 NHL career victories through the 2001-02 season. Career, regular season and playoff records are noted along with NHL titles won. Coaches active during 2001-02 season in **bold** type. **Note:** In the following tables, overtime losses are considered losses.

		Career				Regular Season				Playoffs				
		Yrs	W	L	T	Pct	W	L	T	Pct	W	L	T	Pct	Stanley Cups
1	**Scotty Bowman**	.30	1467	713	314	.651	1244	583	314	.654	223	130	0	.632	9 (1973, 76-79, 92, 97-98, 2002)
2	Al Arbour	.22	904	663	248	.566	781	577	248	.564	123	86	0	.589	4 (1980-83)
3	Dick Irvin	.26	790	609	228	.556	690	521	226	.559	100	88	2	.532	4 (1932,44,46,53)
4	**Mike Keenan**	.16	646	507	132	.554	555	438	132	.552	91	69	0	.569	1 (1994)
5	**Pat Quinn**	.16	612	486	137	.551	527	408	137	.556	85	78	0	.524	None
6	Billy Reay	.16	599	445	175	.563	542	385	175	.571	57	60	0	.487	None
7	Toe Blake	.13	582	292	159	.640	500	255	159	.634	82	37	0	.689	8 (1956-60,65-66,68)
8	Glen Sather	.11	553	305	110	.628	464	268	110	.616	89	37	0	.706	4 (1984-85,87-88)
9	**Bryan Murray**	.14	547	457	131	.540	513	413	131	.547	34	44	0	.436	None
10	**Roger Neilson**	.16	511	436	159	.534	460	381	159	.540	51	55	0	.481	None
11	Pat Burns	.12	473	373	129	.551	412	314	129	.557	61	59	0	.508	None
12	Jack Adams	.21	465	442	162	.511	413	390	161	.512	52	52	1	.500	3 (1936-37, 43)
13	Jacques Demers	.13	464	510	130	.479	409	467	130	.471	55	43	0	.561	1 (1993)
14	Fred Shero	.10	451	272	119	.606	390	225	119	.612	61	47	0	.565	2 (1974-75)
15	Punch Imlach	.15	439	384	148	.528	395	336	148	.534	44	48	0	.478	4 (1962-64,67)
16	Emile Francis	.13	433	326	112	.561	393	273	112	.577	40	53	0	.430	None
17	**Brian Sutter**	.11	429	387	116	.523	401	347	116	.531	28	40	0	.412	None
18	Sid Abel	.16	414	470	155	.473	382	426	155	.477	32	44	0	.421	None
19	Terry Murray	.11	406	331	89	.545	360	288	89	.549	46	43	0	.517	None
20	Bob Berry	.11	395	377	121	.510	384	355	121	.517	11	22	0	.333	None

Where They Coached

Abel—Chicago (1952-54), Detroit (1957-68,69-70), St. Louis (1971-72), Kansas City (1975-76); **Adams**—Toronto (1922-23), Detroit (1927-47); **Arbour**—St. Louis (1970-73), NY Islanders (1973-86,88-94); **Berry**—Los Angeles (1978-81), Montreal (1981-84), Pittsburgh (1984-87), St. Louis (1992-94); **Blake**—Montreal (1955-68); **Bowman**—St. Louis (1967-71), Montreal (1971-79), Buffalo (1979-87), Pittsburgh (1991-93), Detroit (1993-2002); **Burns**—Montreal (1988-92), Toronto (1992-96), Boston (1997-2000), New Jersey (2002-).

Demers—Quebec (1979-80), St. Louis (1983-86), Detroit (1986-90), Montreal (1992-95), Tampa Bay (1997-99); **Francis**—NY Rangers (1965-75), St. Louis (1976-77,81-83); **Imlach**—Toronto (1958-69), Buffalo (1970-72), Toronto (1979-81); **Irvin**—Chicago (1930-31,55-56), Toronto (1931-40), Montreal (1940-55); **Keenan**—Philadelphia (1984-88), Chicago (1988-92), NY Rangers (1993-94), St. Louis (1994-96), Vancouver (1997-99), Boston (2000-01), Florida (2001-); **B. Murray**—Washington (1982-90), Detroit (1990-93), Florida (1997-98), Anaheim (2001-02); **T. Murray**—Washington (1990-94), Philadelphia (1994-97), Florida (1998-2000).

Neilson—Toronto (1977-79), Buffalo (1979-81), Vancouver (1982-83), Los Angeles (1984), NY Rangers (1989-93), Florida (1993-95), Philadelphia (1998-00), Ottawa (2002); **Quinn**—Philadelphia (1978-82), Los Angeles (1984-87), Vancouver (1990-94, 96), Toronto (1998—); **Reay**—Toronto (1957-59), Chicago (1963-77); **Sather**—Edmonton (1979-89, 93-94); **Shero**—Philadelphia (1971-78), NY Rangers (1978-81); **Sutter**—St. Louis (1988-92), Boston (1992-95), Calgary (1997-2000), Chicago (2001-).

Top Winning Percentages

Minimum of 275 victories, including playoffs.

		Yrs	W	L	T	Pct.
1	**Scotty Bowman**	30	1467	713	314	**.651**
2	Toe Blake	13	582	292	159	**.640**
3	Glen Sather	11	553	305	110	**.628**
4	**Ken Hitchcock**	7	324	199	60	**.607**
5	Fred Shero	10	451	272	119	**.606**
6	Don Cherry	6	281	177	77	**.597**
7	Tommy Ivan	9	324	205	111	**.593**
8	Al Arbour	22	904	663	248	**.566**
9	Billy Reay	16	599	445	175	**.563**
10	Emile Francis	13	433	326	112	**.561**
11	Hap Day	10	308	237	81	**.557**
12	Dick Irvin	26	790	609	228	**.556**
13	**Mike Keenan**	16	646	507	132	**.554**
14	**Marc Crawford**	8	314	245	80	**.554**
15	Lester Patrick	13	312	242	115	**.552**
16	Art Ross	18	393	310	95	**.552**
17	Pat Burns	12	473	373	129	**.551**
18	**Pat Quinn**	16	612	486	137	**.551**
19	Bob Johnson	6	275	223	58	**.547**
20	**Jacques Lemaire**	9	347	281	94	**.546**
21	Terry Murray	11	406	331	89	**.545**
22	**Bryan Murray**	14	547	457	131	**.540**
23	**Roger Neilson**	16	511	436	159	**.534**
24	Punch Imlach	15	439	384	148	**.528**
25	**Darryl Sutter**	8	323	287	84	**.526**
26	**Brian Sutter**	11	429	387	116	**.523**
27	Terry Crisp	9	310	286	78	**.518**
28	**Jacques Martin**	9	336	311	101	**.517**
29	Jack Adams	21	465	442	162	**.511**
30	Bob Berry	11	395	377	121	**.510**

Active Coaches' Victories

Through 2001-02 season, including playoffs.

		Yrs	W	L	T	Pct.
1	Mike Keenan, Fla.	16	**646**	507	132	.554
2	Pat Quinn, Tor.	16	**612**	486	137	.551
3	Pat Burns, NJ	12	**473**	373	129	.551
4	Brian Sutter, Chi.	11	**429**	387	116	.523
5	Jacques Lemaire, Min.	9	**347**	281	94	.546
6	Jacques Martin, Ott.	9	**336**	311	101	.517
7	Ken Hitchcock, Phi.	7	**324**	199	60	.607
8	Darryl Sutter, SJ	8	**323**	287	84	.526
9	Marc Crawford, Van.	8	**314**	245	80	.554
10	Joel Quenneville, St.L	6	**268**	183	59	.583
11	Paul Maurice, Car.	7	**255**	262	80	.494
12	Bob Hartley, Col.	4	**232**	137	39	.616
13	Lindy Ruff, Buf.	5	**221**	182	61	.542
14	Robbie Ftorek, Bos.	5	**206**	157	36	.561
15	Dave King, Clb.	5	**167**	185	48	.478
16	Andy Murray, LA	3	**127**	107	36	.537
17	Barry Trotz, Nash.	4	**118**	174	36	.415
18	Bob Francis, Pho.	3	**116**	106	34	.520
19	Craig MacTavish, Edm.	2	**79**	67	24	.535
20	Michel Therrien, Mon.	2	**65**	73	18	.474
21	Curt Fraser, Atl.	3	**56**	160	30	.289
22	Peter Laviolette, NYI	1	**45**	36	8	.551
23	John Tortorella, TB	3	**39**	78	12	.349
24	Greg Gilbert, Calg.	2	**36**	46	14	.448
25	Rick Kehoe, Pit.	1	**28**	42	8	.410
26	Mike Babcock, Ana.	0	**0**	0	0	.000
	Dave Lewis, Det.	0	**0**	0	0	.000
	Dave Tippett, Dal.	0	**0**	0	0	.000
	Brian Trottier, NYR.	0	**0**	0	0	.000
	Bruce Cassidy, Wash.	0	**0**	0	0	.000

Annual Awards

Hart Memorial Trophy

Awarded to the player "adjudged to be the most valuable to his team" and named after Cecil Hart, the former manager-coach of the Montreal Canadiens. Winners selected by Pro Hockey Writers Assn. (PHWA). Winners' scoring statistics or goaltender W-L records and goals against average are provided; (*) indicates led or tied for league lead.

Multiple Winners: Wayne Gretzky (9); Gordie Howe (6); Eddie Shore (4); Bobby Clarke, Mario Lemieux, Howie Morenz and Bobby Orr (3); Jean Beliveau, Bill Cowley, Phil Esposito, Dominik Hasek, Bobby Hull, Guy Lafleur, Mark Messier, Stan Mikita and Nels Stewart (2).

Year		G	A	Pts
1924	Frank Nighbor, Ottawa, C	10	3	13
1925	Billy Burch, Hamilton, C	20	4	24
1926	Nels Stewart, Maroons, C	34	8	42*
1927	Herb Gardiner, Mon., D	6	6	12
1928	Howie Morenz, Mon., C	33	18	51
1929	Roy Worters, NYA, G	16-13-9;		1.21
1930	Nels Stewart, Maroons, C	39	16	55
1931	Howie Morenz, Mon., C	28	23	51*
1932	Howie Morenz, Mon., C	24	25	49
1933	Eddie Shore, Bos., D	8	27	35
1934	Aurel Joliat, Mon., LW	22	15	37
1935	Eddie Shore, Bos., D	7	26	33
1936	Eddie Shore, Bos., D	3	16	19
1937	Babe Siebert, Mon., D	8	20	28
1938	Eddie Shore, Bos., D	3	14	17
1939	Toe Blake, Mon., LW	24	23	47*
1940	Ebbie Goodfellow, Det., D	11	17	28
1941	Bill Cowley, Bos., C	17	45	62*
1942	Tommy Anderson, NYA, D	12	29	41
1943	Bill Cowley, Bos., C	27	45	72
1944	Babe Pratt, Tor., D	17	40	57
1945	Elmer Lach, Mon., C	26	54	80*
1946	Max Bentley, Chi., C	31	30	61*
1947	Maurice Richard, Mon., RW	45	26	71
1948	Buddy O'Connor, NYR, C	24	36	60
1949	Sid Abel, Det., C	28	26	54
1950	Chuck Rayner, NYR, G	28-30-11;		2.62
1951	Milt Schmidt, Bos., C	22	39	61
1952	Gordie Howe, Det., RW	47	39	86*
1953	Gordie Howe, Det., RW	49	46	95*
1954	Al Rollins, Chi., G	12-47-7;		3.23
1955	Ted Kennedy, Tor., C	10	42	52
1956	Jean Beliveau, Mon., C	47	41	88
1957	Gordie Howe, Det., RW	44	45	89*
1958	Gordie Howe, Det., RW	33	44	77
1959	Andy Bathgate, NYR, RW	40	48	88
1960	Gordie Howe, Det., RW	28	45	73
1961	Bernie Geoffrion, Mon., RW	50	45	95*
1962	Jacques Plante, Mon., G	42-14-14;		2.37*
1963	Gordie Howe, Det., RW	38	48	86*
1964	Jean Beliveau, Mon., C	28	50	78
1965	Bobby Hull, Chi., LW	39	32	71
1966	Bobby Hull, Chi., LW	54	43	97*
1967	Stan Mikita, Chi., C	35	62	97*
1968	Stan Mikita, Chi., C	40	47	87*
1969	Phil Esposito, Bos., C	49	77	126*
1970	Bobby Orr, Bos., D	33	87	120*
1971	Bobby Orr, Bos., D	37	102	139
1972	Bobby Orr, Bos., D	37	80	117
1973	Bobby Clarke, Phi., C	37	67	104
1974	Phil Esposito, Bos., C	68	77	145*
1975	Bobby Clarke, Phi., C	27	89	116

Year		G	A	Pts	Year		G	A	Pts
1976	Bobby Clarke, Phi., C	30	89	119	1990	Mark Messier, Edm., C	45	84	129
1977	Guy Lafleur, Mon., RW	56	80	136*	1991	Brett Hull, St. L., RW	86	45	131
1978	Guy Lafleur, Mon., RW	60	72	132*	1992	Mark Messier, NYR, C	35	72	107
1979	Bryan Trottier, NYI., C	47	87	134*	1993	Mario Lemieux, Pit., C	69	91	160*
1980	Wayne Gretzky, Edm., C	51	86	137*	1994	Sergei Fedorov, Det., C	56	64	120
1981	Wayne Gretzky, Edm., C	55	109	164*	1995	Eric Lindros, Phi., C	29	41	70*
1982	Wayne Gretzky, Edm., C	92	120	212*	1996	Mario Lemieux, Pit., C	69	92	161*
1983	Wayne Gretzky, Edm., C	71	125	196*	1997	Dominik Hasek, Buf., G	37-20-10;		2.27
1984	Wayne Gretzky, Edm., C	87	118	205*	1998	Dominik Hasek, Buf., G	33-23-13;		2.09
1985	Wayne Gretzky, Edm., C	73	135	208*	1999	Jaromir Jagr, Pit., RW	44	83	127*
1986	Wayne Gretzky, Edm., C	52	163	215*	2000	Chris Pronger, St.L, D	14	48	62
1987	Wayne Gretzky, Edm., C	62	121	183*	2001	Joe Sakic, Col., C	54	64	118
1988	Mario Lemieux, Pit., C	70	98	168*	2002	Jose Theodore, Mon., G	30-24-10;		2.11
1989	Wayne Gretzky, LA, C	54	114	168					

Calder Memorial Trophy

Awarded to the most outstanding rookie of the year and named after Frank Calder, the late NHL president (1917-43). Since the 1990-91 season, all eligible candidates must not have attained their 26th birthday by Sept. 15 of their rookie year. Winners selected by PHWA. Winners' scoring statistics or goaltender W-L record & goals against average are provided.

Year		G	A	Pts	Year		G	A	Pts
1933	Carl Voss, NYR-Det., C	8	15	23	1968	Derek Sanderson, Bos., C	24	25	49
1934	Russ Blinco, Maroons, C	14	9	23	1969	Danny Grant, Min., LW	34	31	65
1935	Sweeney Schriner, NYA, LW	18	22	40	1970	Tony Esposito, Chi., G	38-17-8;		2.17
1936	Mike Karakas, Chi., G	21-19-8;		1.92	1971	Gilbert Perreault, Buf., C	38	34	72
1937	Syl Apps, Tor., C	16	29	45	1972	Ken Dryden, Mon., G	39-8-15;		2.24
1938	Cully Dahlstrom, Chi., C	10	9	19	1973	Steve Vickers, NYR, LW	30	23	53
1939	Frankie Brimsek, Bos., G	33-9-1;		1.58	1974	Denis Potvin, NYI, D	17	37	54
1940	Kilby McDonald, NYR, LW	15	13	28	1975	Eric Vail, Atl., LW	39	21	60
1941	John Quilty, Mon., C	18	16	34	1976	Bryan Trottier, NYI, C	32	63	95
1942	Knobby Warwick, NYR, RW	16	17	33	1977	Willi Plett, Atl., RW	33	23	56
1943	Gaye Stewart, Tor., LW	24	23	47	1978	Mike Bossy, NYI, RW	53	38	91
1944	Gus Bodnar, Tor., C	22	40	62	1979	Bobby Smith, Min., C	30	44	74
1945	Frank McCool, Tor., G	24-22-4;		3.22	1980	Ray Bourque, Bos., D	17	48	65
1946	Edgar Laprade, NYR, C	15	19	34	1981	Peter Stastny, Que., C	39	70	109
1947	Howie Meeker, Tor., RW	27	18	45	1982	Dale Hawerchuk, Win., C	45	58	103
1948	Jim McFadden, Det., C	24	24	48	1983	Steve Larmer, Chi., RW	43	47	90
1949	Penny Lund, NYR, RW	14	16	30	1984	Tom Barrasso, Buf., G	26-12-3;		2.84
1950	Jack Gelineau, Bos., G	22-30-15;		3.28	1985	Mario Lemieux, Pit., C	43	57	100
1951	Terry Sawchuk, Det., G	44-13-13;		1.99	1986	Gary Suter, Calg., D	18	50	68
1952	Bernie Geoffrion, Mon., RW	30	24	54	1987	Luc Robitaille, LA, LW	45	39	84
1953	Gump Worsley, NYR, G	13-29-8;		3.06	1988	Joe Nieuwendyk, Calg., C	51	41	92
1954	Camille Henry, NYR, LW	24	15	39	1989	Brian Leetch, NYR, D	23	48	71
1955	Ed Litzenberger, Mon-Chi., RW	23	28	51	1990	Sergei Makarov, Calg., RW	24	62	86
1956	Glenn Hall, Det., G	30-24-16;		2.11	1991	Ed Belfour, Chi., G	43-19-7;		2.47
1957	Larry Regan, Bos., RW	14	19	33	1992	Pavel Bure, Van., RW	34	26	60
1958	Frank Mahovlich, Tor., LW	20	16	36	1993	Teemu Selanne, Win., RW	76	56	132
1959	Ralph Backstrom, Mon., C	18	22	40	1994	Martin Brodeur, NJ, G	27-11-8;		2.40
1960	Billy Hay, Chi., C	18	37	55	1995	Peter Forsberg, Que., C	15	35	50
1961	Dave Keon, Tor., C	20	25	45	1996	Daniel Alfredsson, Ott., RW	26	35	61
1962	Bobby Rousseau, Mon., RW	21	24	45	1997	Bryan Berard, NYI, D	8	40	48
1963	Kent Douglas, Tor., D	7	15	22	1998	Sergei Samsonov, Bos., LW	22	25	47
1964	Jacques Laperriere, Mon., D	2	28	30	1999	Chris Drury, Col., C	20	24	44
1965	Roger Crozier, Det., G	40-23-7;		2.42	2000	Scott Gomez, NJ, C	19	51	70
1966	Brit Selby, Tor., LW	14	13	27	2001	Evgeni Nabokov, SJ, G	32-21-7;		2.19
1967	Bobby Orr, Bos., D	13	28	41	2002	Dany Heatley, Atl., RW	26	41	67

Vezina Trophy

From 1927-80, given to the principal goaltender(s) on the team allowing the fewest goals during the regular season. Trophy named after 1920's goalie Georges Vezina of the Montreal Canadiens, who died of tuberculosis in 1926. Since the 1980-81 season, the trophy has been awarded to the most outstanding goaltender of the year as selected by the league's general managers.

Multiple Winners: Jacques Plante (7, one of them shared); Bill Durnan and Dominik Hasek (6); Ken Dryden (5, three shared); Bunny Larocque (4, all shared); Terry Sawchuk (4, one shared); Tiny Thompson (4); Tony Esposito (3, one shared); George Hainsworth (3); Glenn Hall (3, two shared); Patrick Roy (2); Ed Belfour (2); Johnny Bower (2, one shared); Frankie Brimsek (2); Turk Broda (2); Chuck Gardiner (2); Charlie Hodge (2, one shared); Bernie Parent (2, one shared); Gump Worsley (2, both shared).

Year		Record	GAA	Year		Record	GAA
1927	George Hainsworth, Mon.	28-14-2	1.52	1931	Roy Worters, NYA	18-16-10	1.68
1928	George Hainsworth, Mon.	26-11-7	1.09	1932	Chuck Gardiner, Chi	18-19-11	1.92
1929	George Hainsworth, Mon.	22-7-15	0.98	1933	Tiny Thompson, Bos	25-15-8	1.83
1930	Tiny Thompson, Bos	38-5-1	2.23	1934	Chuck Gardiner, Chi	20-17-11	1.73

Annual Awards (Cont.)

Year	Record	GAA	Year	Record	GAA
1935 Lorne Chabot, Chi	26-17-5	1.83	1971 Ed Giacomin, NYR	27-10-7	2.16
1936 Tiny Thompson, Bos	22-20-6	1.71	& Gilles Villemure, NYR	22-8-4	2.30
1937 Norm Smith, Det	25-14-9	2.13	1972 Tony Esposito, Chi	31-10-6	1.77
1938 Tiny Thompson, Bos	30-11-7	1.85	& Gary Smith, Chi	14-5-6	2.42
1939 Frankie Brimsek, Bos	33-9-1	1.58	1973 Ken Dryden, Mon	33-7-13	2.26
			1974 (Tie) Bernie Parent, Phi	47-13-12	1.89
1940 Dave Kerr, NYR	27-11-10	1.60	Tony Esposito, Chi	34-14-21	2.04
1941 Turk Broda, Tor	28-14-6	2.06	1975 Bernie Parent, Phi	44-14-10	2.03
1942 Frankie Brimsek, Bos	24-17-6	2.45	1976 Ken Dryden, Mon	42-10-8	2.03
1943 John Mowers, Det	25-14-11	2.47	1977 Ken Dryden, Mon	41-6-8	2.14
1944 Bill Durnan, Mon	38-5-7	2.18	& Bunny Larocque, Mon	19-2-4	2.09
1945 Bill Durnan, Mon	38-8-4	2.42	1978 Ken Dryden, Mon	37-7-7	2.05
1946 Bill Durnan, Mon	24-11-5	2.60	& Bunny Larocque, Mon	22-3-4	2.67
1947 Bill Durnan, Mon	34-16-10	2.30	1979 Ken Dryden, Mon	30-10-7	2.30
1948 Turk Broda, Tor	32-15-13	2.38	& Bunny Larocque, Mon	22-7-4	2.84
1949 Bill Durnan, Mon	28-23-9	2.10			
1950 Bill Durnan, Mon	26-21-17	2.20	1980 Bob Sauve, Buf	20-8-4	2.36
1951 Al Rollins, Tor	27-5-8	1.77	& Don Edwards, Buf	27-9-12	2.57
1952 Terry Sawchuk, Det	44-14-12	1.90	1981 Richard Sevigny, Mon	20-4-3	2.40
1953 Terry Sawchuk, Det	32-15-16	1.90	Denis Herron, Mon	6-9-6	3.50
1954 Harry Lumley, Tor	32-24-13	1.86	& Bunny Larocque, Mon	16-9-3	3.03
1955 Terry Sawchuk, Det	40-17-11	1.96	1982 Billy Smith, NYI	32-9-4	2.97
1956 Jacques Plante, Mon	42-12-10	1.86	1983 Pete Peeters, Bos	40-11-9	2.36
1957 Jacques Plante, Mon	31-18-12	2.02	1984 Tom Barrasso, Buf	26-12-3	2.84
1958 Jacques Plante, Mon	34-14-8	2.11	1985 Pelle Lindbergh, Phi	40-17-7	3.02
1959 Jacques Plante, Mon	38-16-13	2.16	1986 John Vanbiesbrouck, NYR	31-21-5	3.32
			1987 Ron Hextall, Phi	37-21-6	3.00
1960 Jacques Plante, Mon	40-17-12	2.54	1988 Grant Fuhr, Edm	40-24-9	3.43
1961 Johnny Bower, Tor	33-15-10	2.50	1989 Patrick Roy, Mon	33-5-6	2.47
1962 Jacques Plante, Mon	42-14-14	2.37			
1963 Glenn Hall, Chi	30-20-16	2.55	1990 Patrick Roy, Mon	31-16-5	2.53
1964 Charlie Hodge, Mon	33-18-11	2.26	1991 Ed Belfour, Chi	43-19-7	2.47
1965 Johnny Bower, Tor	13-13-8	2.38	1992 Patrick Roy, Mon	36-22-8	2.36
& Terry Sawchuk, Tor	17-13-6	2.56	1993 Ed Belfour, Chi	41-18-11	2.59
1966 Gump Worsley, Mon	29-14-6	2.36	1994 Dominik Hasek, Buf	30-20-6	1.95
& Charlie Hodge, Mon	12-7-2	2.58	1995 Dominik Hasek, Buf	19-14-7	2.11
1967 Glenn Hall, Chi	19-5-5	2.38	1996 Jim Carey, Wash	35-24-9	2.26
& Denis Dejordy, Chi	22-12-7	2.46	1997 Dominik Hasek, Buf	37-20-10	2.27
1968 Gump Worsley, Mon	19-9-8	1.98	1998 Dominik Hasek, Buf	33-23-13	2.09
& Rogie Vachon, Mon	23-13-2	2.48	1999 Dominik Hasek, Buf	30-18-14	1.87
1969 Jacques Plante, St.L	18-12-6	1.96	2000 Olaf Kolzig, Wash	41-20-11	2.24
& Glenn Hall, St.L	19-12-8	2.17	2001 Dominik Hasek, Buf	37-24-4	2.11
1970 Tony Esposito, Chi	38-17-8	2.17	2002 Jose Theodore, Mon	30-24-10	2.11

Lady Byng Memorial Trophy

Awarded to the player "adjudged to have exhibited the best type of sportsmanship and gentlemanly conduct combined with a high standard of playing ability" and named after Lady Evelyn Byng, the wife of former Canadian Governor General (1921-26) Baron Byng of Vimy. Winners selected by PHWA.

Multiple winners: Frank Boucher (7); Wayne Gretzky (5); Red Kelly (4); Bobby Bauer, Mike Bossy, Alex Delvecchio and Ron Francis (3); Johnny Bucyk, Marcel Dionne, Paul Kariya, Dave Keon, Stan Mikita, Joey Mullen, Frank Nighbor, Jean Ratelle, Clint Smith and Sid Smith (2).

Year	Year	Year
1925 Frank Nighbor, Ott., C	1943 Max Bentley, Chi., C	1961 Red Kelly, Tor., D
1926 Frank Nighbor, Ott., C	1944 Clint Smith, Chi., C	1962 Dave Keon, Tor., C
1927 Billy Burch, NYA, C	1945 Bill Mosienko, Chi., RW	1963 Dave Keon, Tor., C
1928 Frank Boucher, NYR, C	1946 Toe Blake, Mon., LW	1964 Ken Wharram, Chi., RW
1929 Frank Boucher, NYR, C	1947 Bobby Bauer, Bos., RW	1965 Bobby Hull, Chi., LW
1930 Frank Boucher, NYR, C	1948 Buddy O'Connor, NYR, C	1966 Alex Delvecchio, Det., LW
1931 Frank Boucher, NYR, C	1949 Bill Quackenbush, Det., D	1967 Stan Mikita, Chi., C
1932 Joe Primeau, Tor., C		1968 Stan Mikita, Chi., C
1933 Frank Boucher, NYR, C	1950 Edgar Laprade, NYR, C	1969 Alex Delvecchio, Det., LW
1934 Frank Boucher, NYR, C	1951 Red Kelly, Det., D	
1935 Frank Boucher, NYR, C	1952 Sid Smith, Tor., LW	1970 Phil Goyette, St.L., C
1936 Doc Romnes, Chi., F	1953 Red Kelly, Det., D	1971 Johnny Bucyk, Bos., LW
1937 Marty Barry, Det., C	1954 Red Kelly, Det., D	1972 Jean Ratelle, NYR, C
1938 Gordie Drillon, Tor., RW	1955 Sid Smith, Tor., LW	1973 Gilbert Perreault, Buf., C
1939 Clint Smith, NYR, C	1956 Earl Reibel, Det., C	1974 Johnny Bucyk, Bos., LW
1940 Bobby Bauer, Bos., RW	1957 Andy Hebenton, NYR, RW	1975 Marcel Dionne, Det., C
1941 Bobby Bauer, Bos., RW	1958 Camille Henry, NYR, LW	1976 Jean Ratelle, NY-Bos., C
1942 Syl Apps, Tor., C	1959 Alex Delvecchio, Det., LW	1977 Marcel Dionne, LA, C
	1960 Don McKenney, Bos., C	1978 Butch Goring, LA, C

Year		Year		Year	
1979	Bob MacMillan, Atl., RW	1987	Joey Mullen, Calg., RW	1995	Ron Francis, Pit., C
1980	Wayne Gretzky, Edm., C	1988	Mats Naslund, Mon., LW	1996	Paul Kariya, Ana., LW
1981	Rick Kehoe, Pit., RW	1989	Joey Mullen, Calg., RW	1997	Paul Kariya, Ana., LW
1982	Rick Middleton, Bos., RW			1998	Ron Francis, Pit., C
1983	Mike Bossy, NYI, RW	1990	Brett Hull, St.L., RW	1999	Wayne Gretzky, NYR, C
1984	Mike Bossy, NYI, RW	1991	Wayne Gretzky, LA, C		
1985	Jari Kurri, Edm., RW	1992	Wayne Gretzky, LA, C	2000	Pavol Demitra, St.L, RW
1986	Mike Bossy, NYI, RW	1993	Pierre Turgeon, NYI, C	2001	Joe Sakic, Col., C
		1994	Wayne Gretzky, LA, C	2002	Ron Francis, Car., C

Note: Bill Quackenbush and Red Kelly are the only defensemen to win the Lady Byng.

James Norris Memorial Trophy

Awarded to the most outstanding defenseman of the year and named after James Norris, the late Detroit Red Wings owner-president. Winners selected by PHWA.

Multiple winners: Bobby Orr (8); Doug Harvey (7); Ray Bourque (5); Chris Chelios, Paul Coffey, Pierre Pilote and Denis Potvin (3); Rod Langway, Brian Leetch, Nicklas Lidstrom and Larry Robinson (2).

Year		Year		Year	
1954	Red Kelly, Detroit	1971	Bobby Orr, Boston	1988	Ray Bourque, Boston
1955	Doug Harvey, Montreal	1972	Bobby Orr, Boston	1989	Chris Chelios, Montreal
1956	Doug Harvey, Montreal	1973	Bobby Orr, Boston		
1957	Doug Harvey, Montreal	1974	Bobby Orr, Boston	1990	Ray Bourque, Boston
1958	Doug Harvey, Montreal	1975	Bobby Orr, Boston	1991	Ray Bourque, Boston
1959	Tom Johnson, Montreal	1976	Denis Potvin, NY Islanders	1992	Brian Leetch, NY Rangers
		1977	Larry Robinson, Montreal	1993	Chris Chelios, Chicago
1960	Doug Harvey, Montreal	1978	Denis Potvin, NY Islanders	1994	Ray Bourque, Boston
1961	Doug Harvey, Montreal	1979	Denis Potvin, NY Islanders	1995	Paul Coffey, Detroit
1962	Doug Harvey, NY Rangers			1996	Chris Chelios, Chicago
1963	Pierre Pilote, Chicago	1980	Larry Robinson, Montreal	1997	Brian Leetch, NY Rangers
1964	Pierre Pilote, Chicago	1981	Randy Carlyle, Pittsburgh	1998	Rob Blake, Los Angeles
1965	Pierre Pilote, Chicago	1982	Doug Wilson, Chicago	1999	Al MacInnis, St. Louis
1966	Jacques Laperriere, Montreal	1983	Rod Langway, Washington		
1967	Harry Howell, NY Rangers	1984	Rod Langway, Washington	2000	Chris Pronger, St. Louis
1968	Bobby Orr, Boston	1985	Paul Coffey, Edmonton	2001	Nicklas Lidstrom, Detroit
1969	Bobby Orr, Boston	1986	Paul Coffey, Edmonton	2002	Nicklas Lidstrom, Detroit
1970	Bobby Orr, Boston	1987	Ray Bourque, Boston		

Frank Selke Trophy

Awarded to the outstanding defensive forward of the year and named after the late Montreal Canadiens general manager. Winners selected by the PHWA.

Multiple winners: Bob Gainey (4); Guy Carbonneau (3); Sergei Fedorov, Jere Lehtinen and Michael Peca (2).

Year		Year		Year	
1978	Bob Gainey, Mon., LW	1987	Dave Poulin, Phi., C	1996	Sergei Fedorov, Det., C
1979	Bob Gainey, Mon., LW	1988	Guy Carbonneau, Mon., C	1997	Michael Peca, Buf., C
1980	Bob Gainey, Mon., LW	1989	Guy Carbonneau, Mon., C	1998	Jere Lehtinen, Dal., RW
1981	Bob Gainey, Mon., LW	1990	Rick Meagher, St.L., C	1999	Jere Lehtinen, Dal., RW
1982	Steve Kasper, Bos., C	1991	Dirk Graham, Chi., RW	2000	Steve Yzerman, Det., C
1983	Bobby Clarke, Phi., C	1992	Guy Carbonneau, Mon., C	2001	John Madden, NJ, LW
1984	Doug Jarvis, Wash., C	1993	Doug Gilmour, Tor., C	2002	Michael Peca, NYI, C
1985	Craig Ramsay, Buf., LW	1994	Sergei Fedorov, Det., C		
1986	Troy Murray, Chi., C	1995	Ron Francis, Pit., C		

Jack Adams Award

Awarded to the coach "adjudged to have contributed the most to his team's success" and named after the late Detroit Red Wings coach and general manager. Winners selected by NHL Broadcasters' Assn.; (*) indicates division champion.

Multiple winners: Pat Burns (3); Scotty Bowman, Jacques Demers and Pat Quinn (2).

Year			Improvement	Year			Improvement
1974	Fred Shero, Phi	37-30-11 to	50-16-12*	1989	Pat Burns, Mon	45-22-13 to	53-18-9*
1975	Bob Pulford, LA	41-14-23 to	37-35-8	1990	Bob Murdoch, Win	26-42-12 to	37-32-11
1976	Don Cherry, Bos	40-26-14 to	48-15-17*	1991	Brian Sutter, St.L	37-34-9 to	47-22-11
1977	Scotty Bowman, Mon	58-11-11* to	60-8-12*	1992	Pat Quinn, Van	28-43-9 to	42-26-12*
1978	Bobby Kromm, Det	6-55-9 to	32-34-14	1993	Pat Burns, Tor	30-43-7 to	44-29-11
1979	Al Arbour, NYI	48-17-15* to	51-15-14*	1994	Jacques Lemaire, NJ	40-37-7 to	47-25-12
1980	Pat Quinn, Phi	40-25-15 to	48-12-20*	1995	Marc Crawford, Que	34-42-8 to	30-13-5*
1981	Red Berenson, St.L	34-34-12 to	45-18-17*	1996	Scotty Bowman, Det	33-11-4* to	62-13-7*
1982	Tom Watt, Win	9-57-14 to	33-33-14	1997	Ted Nolan, Buf	33-42-7 to	40-30-12*
1983	Orval Tessier, Chi	30-38-12 to	47-23-10	1998	Pat Burns, Bos	26-47-9 to	39-30-13
1984	Bryan Murray, Wash	39-25-16 to	48-27-5	1999	Jacques Martin, Ott	34-33-15 to	44-23-15*
1985	Mike Keenan, Phi	44-26-10 to	53-20-7*	2000	Joel Quenneville, St.L	37-32-13 to	51-20-11*
1986	Glen Sather, Edm	49-20-11* to	56-17-7*	2001	Bill Barber, Phi	45-25-12 to	43-25-11-3
1987	Jacques Demers, Det	17-57-6 to	34-36-10	2002	Bob Francis, Pho	35-27-17-3 to	40-27-9-6
1988	Jacques Demers, Det	34-36-10 to	41-28-11*				

Annual Awards (Cont.)

Lester B. Pearson Award

Awarded to the season's most outstanding player and named after the former diplomat, Nobel Peace Prize winner and Canadian prime minister. Winners selected by the NHL Players Assn.

Multiple winners: Wayne Gretzky (5); Mario Lemieux (4); Guy Lafleur (3); Marcel Dionne, Phil Esposito, Dominik Hasek, Jaromir Jagr and Mark Messier (2).

Year	Year	Year
1971 Phil Esposito, Bos., C	1982 Wayne Gretzky, Edm., C	1993 Mario Lemieux, Pit., C
1972 Jean Ratelle, NYR, C	1983 Wayne Gretzky, Edm., C	1994 Sergei Fedorov, Det., C
1973 Bobby Clarke, Phi., C	1984 Wayne Gretzky, Edm., C	1995 Eric Lindros, Phi., C
1974 Phil Esposito, Bos., C	1985 Wayne Gretzky, Edm., C	1996 Mario Lemieux, Pit., C
1975 Bobby Orr, Bos., D	1986 Mario Lemieux, Pit., C	1997 Dominik Hasek, Buf., G
1976 Guy Lafleur, Mon., RW	1987 Wayne Gretzky, Edm., C	1998 Dominik Hasek, Buf., G
1977 Guy Lafleur, Mon., RW	1988 Mario Lemieux, Pit., C	1999 Jaromir Jagr, Pit., RW
1978 Guy Lafleur, Mon., RW	1989 Steve Yzerman, Det., C	2000 Jaromir Jagr, Pit., RW
1979 Marcel Dionne, LA, C	1990 Mark Messier, Edm., C	2001 Joe Sakic, Col., C
1980 Marcel Dionne, LA, C	1991 Brett Hull, St.L., RW	2002 Jarome Iginla, Calg., RW
1981 Mike Liut, St.L., G	1992 Mark Messier, NYR, C	

King Clancy Memorial Trophy

Awarded to the player who "best exemplifies leadership on and off the ice and who has made a noteworthy humanitarian contribution to his community" and named after former player, coach, official and executive Frank "King" Clancy. Presented by the NHL's Board of Governors.

Year	Year	Year
1988 Lanny McDonald, Calg., RW	1993 Dave Poulin, Bos., C	1998 Kelly Chase, St.L, RW
1989 Bryan Trottier, NYI, C	1994 Adam Graves, NYR, LW	1999 Rob Ray, Buf., RW
1990 Kevin Lowe, Edm., D	1995 Joe Nieuwendyk, Calg., C	2000 Curtis Joseph, Tor., G
1991 Dave Taylor, LA, RW	1996 Kris King, Win., LW	2001 Shjon Podein, Col., LW
1992 Ray Bourque, Bos., D	1997 Trevor Linden, Van., C	2002 Ron Francis, Car., C

Bill Masterton Trophy

Awarded to the player who "best exemplifies the qualities of perseverance, sportsmanship and dedication to hockey" and named after the 29-year-old rookie center of the Minnesota North Stars who died of a head injury sustained in a 1968 NHL game. Presented by the PHWA.

Year	Year	Year
1968 Claude Provost, Mon., RW	1980 Al MacAdam, Min., RW	1992 Mark Fitzpatrick, NYI, G
1969 Ted Hampson, Oak., C	1981 Blake Dunlop, St.L., C	1993 Mario Lemieux, Pit., C
1970 Pit Martin, Chi., C	1982 Chico Resch, Colo., G	1994 Cam Neely, Bos., RW
1971 Jean Ratelle, NYR, C	1983 Lanny McDonald, Calg., RW	1995 Pat LaFontaine, Buf., C
1972 Bobby Clarke, Phi., C	1984 Brad Park, Det., D	1996 Gary Roberts, Calg., LW
1973 Lowell MacDonald, Pit., RW	1985 Anders Hedberg, NYR, RW	1997 Tony Granato, SJ, LW
1974 Henri Richard, Mon., C	1986 Charlie Simmer, Bos., LW	1998 Jamie McLennan, St.L, G
1975 Don Luce, Buf., C	1987 Doug Jarvis, Hart., C	1999 John Cullen, TB, C
1976 Rod Gilbert, NYR, RW	1988 Bob Bourne, LA, C	2000 Ken Daneyko, NJ, D
1977 Ed Westfall, NYI, RW	1989 Tim Kerr, Phi., C	2001 Adam Graves, NYR, LW
1978 Butch Goring, LA, C	1990 Gord Kluzak, Bos., D	2002 Saku Koivu, Mon., C
1979 Serge Savard, Mon., D	1991 Dave Taylor, LA, RW	

Number One Draft Choices

Overall first choices in the NHL draft since the league staged its first universal amateur draft in 1969. Players are listed with team that selected them; those who became Rookie of the Year are in **bold** type.

Year	Year	Year
1969 Rejean Houle, Mon., LW	1981 **Dale Hawerchuk,** Win., C	1993 Alexandre Daigle, Ott., C
1970 **Gilbert Perreault,** Buf., C	1982 Gord Kluzak, Bos., D	1994 Ed Jovanovski, Fla., D
1971 Guy Lafleur, Mon., RW	1983 Brian Lawton, Min., C	1995 **Bryan Berard,** Ott., D
1972 Billy Harris, NYI, RW	1984 **Mario Lemieux,** Pit., C	1996 Chris Phillips, Ott., D
1973 **Denis Potvin,** NYI, D	1985 Wendel Clark, Tor., LW/D	1997 Joe Thornton, Bos., C
1974 Greg Joly, Wash., D	1986 Joe Murphy, Det., C	1998 Vincent Lecavalier, TB, C
1975 Mel Bridgman, Phi., C	1987 Pierre Turgeon, Buf., C	1999 Patrik Stefan, Atl., C
1976 Rick Green, Wash., D	1988 Mike Modano, Min., C	2000 Rick DiPietro, NYI, G
1977 Dale McCourt, Det., C	1989 Mats Sundin, Que., RW	2001 Ilya Kovalchuk, Atl., RW
1978 **Bobby Smith,** Min., C	1990 Owen Nolan, Que., RW	2002 Rick Nash, Clb., LW
1979 Rob Ramage, Colo., D	1991 Eric Lindros, Que., C	
1980 Doug Wickenheiser, Mon., C	1992 Roman Hamrlik, TB, D	

World Hockey Association
WHA Finals

The World Hockey Association began play in 1972-73 as a 12-team rival of the 56-year-old NHL. The WHA played for the AVCO World Trophy in its seven playoff finals (Avco Financial Services underwrote the playoffs).

Multiple winners: Winnipeg (3); Houston (2).

Year	Winner	Head Coach	Series	Loser	Head Coach
1973	New England Whalers	Jack Kelley	4-1 (WWLWW)	Winnipeg Jets	Bobby Hull
1974	Houston Aeros	Bill Dineen	4-0	Chicago Cougars	Pat Stapleton
1975	Houston Aeros	Bill Dineen	4-0	Quebec Nordiques	Jean-Guy Gendron
1976	Winnipeg Jets	Bobby Kromm	4-0	Houston Aeros	Bill Dineen
1977	Quebec Nordiques	Marc Boileau	4-3 (LWLWWLW)	Winnipeg Jets	Bobby Kromm
1978	Winnipeg Jets	Larry Hillman	4-0	NE Whalers	Harry Neale
1979	Winnipeg Jets	Larry Hillman	4-2 (WWLWLW)	Edmonton Oilers	Glen Sather

Playoff MVPs—1973—No award; **1974**—No award; **1975**—Ron Grahame, Houston, G; **1976**—Ulf Nilsson, Winnipeg, C; **1977**—Serg Bernier, Quebec, C; **1978**—Bobby Guindon, Winnipeg, C; **1979**—Rich Preston, Winnipeg, RW.

Most Valuable Player
(Gordie Howe Trophy, 1976-79)

Year		G	A	Pts
1973	Bobby Hull, Win., LW	51	52	103
1974	Gordie Howe, Hou., RW	31	69	100
1975	Bobby Hull, Win., LW	77	65	142
1976	Marc Tardif, Que., LW	71	77	148
1977	Robbie Ftorek, Pho., C	46	71	117
1978	Marc Tardif, Que., LW	65	89	154
1979	Dave Dryden, Edm., G	41-17-2;		2.89

Scoring Leaders

Year		Gm	G	A	Pts
1973	Andre Lacroix, Phi.	78	50	74	124
1974	Mike Walton, Min.	78	57	60	117
1975	Andre Lacroix, S. Diego	78	41	106	147
1976	Marc Tardif, Que	81	71	77	148
1977	Real Cloutier, Que	76	66	75	141
1978	Marc Tardif, Que	78	65	89	154
1979	Real Cloutier, Que	77	75	54	129

Note: In 1979, 18 year-old Rookie of the Year Wayne Gretzky finished third in scoring (46-64—110).

Rookie of the Year

Year		G	A	Pts
1973	Terry Caffery, N. Eng., C	39	61	100
1974	Mark Howe, Hou., LW	38	41	79
1975	Anders Hedberg, Win., RW	53	47	100
1976	Mark Napier, Tor., RW	43	50	93
1977	George Lyle, N. Eng., LW	39	33	72
1978	Kent Nilsson, Win., C	42	65	107
1979	Wayne Gretzky, Ind.-Edm., C	46	64	110

Best Goaltender

Year		Record	GAA
1973	Gerry Cheevers, Cleveland	32-20-0	2.84
1974	Don McLeod, Houston	33-13-3	2.56
1975	Ron Grahame, Houston	33-10-0	3.03
1976	Michel Dion, Indianapolis	14-15-1	2.74
1977	Ron Grahame, Houston	27-10-2	2.74
1978	Al Smith, New England	30-20-3	3.22
1979	Dave Dryden, Edmonton	41-17-2	2.89

Best Defenseman

Year	
1973	J.C. Tremblay, Quebec
1974	Pat Stapleton, Chicago
1975	J.C. Tremblay, Quebec
1976	Paul Shmyr, Cleveland
1977	Ron Plumb, Cincinnati
1978	Lars-Erik Sjoberg, Winnipeg
1979	Rick Ley, New England

Coach of the Year

Year		Improvement	
1973	Jack Kelley, N. Eng		46-30-2*
1974	Billy Harris, Tor	35-39-4	to 41-33-4
1975	Sandy Hucul, Pho	Expan.	to 39-31-8
1976	Bobby Kromm, Win	38-35-5	to 52-27-2*
1977	Bill Dineen, Hou	53-27-0*	to 50-24-6*
1978	Bill Dineen, Hou	50-24-6*	to 42-34-4
1979	John Brophy, Birm	36-41-3	to 32-42-6

*Won Division.

WHA All-Star Game

The WHA All-Star Game was an Eastern Division vs Western Division contest from 1973-75. In 1976, the league's five Canadian-based teams played the nine teams in the US. Over the final three seasons–East played West in 1977; AVCO Cup champion Quebec played a WHA All-Star team in 1978; and in 1979, a full WHA All-Star team played a three-game series with Moscow Dynamo of the Soviet Union.

Year	Result	Host	Coaches	Most Valuable Player
1973	East 6, West 2	Quebec	Jack Kelley, Bobby Hull	Wayne Carleton, Ottawa
1974	East 8, West 4	St. Paul, MN	Jack Kelley, Bobby Hull	Mike Walton, Minnesota
1975	West 6, East 4	Edmonton	Bill Dineen, Ron Ryan	Rejean Houle, Quebec
1976	Canada 6, USA 1	Cleveland	Jean-Guy Gendron, Bill Dineen	Can—Real Cloutier, Que. USA—Paul Shmyr, Cleve.
1977	East 4, West 2	Hartford	Jacques Demers, Bobby Kromm	East—L. Levasseur, Min. West—W. Lindstrom, Win.
1978	Quebec 5, WHA 4	Quebec	Marc Boileau, Bill Dineen	Quebec—Marc Tardif WHA—Mark Howe, NE
1979	WHA def. Moscow Dynamo 3 games to none (4-2, 4-2, 4-3)	Edmonton	Larry Hillman, P. Iburtovich	No awards

World Championship
Men

The World Hockey Championship tournament has been played regularly since 1930. The International Ice Hockey Federation (IIHF), which governs both the World and Winter Olympic tournaments, considers the Olympic champions from 1920-68 to also be the World champions. However the IIHF has not recognized an Olympic champion as World champion since 1968. The IIHF has sanctioned separate World Championships in Olympic years four times—in 1972, 1976, 1992 and 2002. The world championship is officially vacant for the three Olympic years from 1980-88.

Multiple winners: Soviet Union/Russia (23); Canada (21); Sweden (7); Czechoslovakia (6) Czech Republic (4), USA (2).

Year		Year		Year		Year	
1920	Canada	1951	Canada	1969	Soviet Union	1987	Sweden
1924	Canada	1952	Canada	1970	Soviet Union	1988	Not held
1928	Canada	1953	Sweden	1971	Soviet Union	1989	Soviet Union
1930	Canada	1954	Soviet Union	1972	Czechoslovakia	1990	Soviet Union
1931	Canada	1955	Canada	1973	Soviet Union	1991	Sweden
1932	Canada	1956	Soviet Union	1974	Soviet Union	1992	Sweden
1933	United States	1957	Sweden	1975	Soviet Union	1993	Russia
1934	Canada	1958	Canada	1976	Czechoslovakia	1994	Canada
1935	Canada	1959	Canada	1977	Czechoslovakia	1995	Finland
1936	Great Britain	1960	United States	1978	Soviet Union	1996	Czech Republic
1937	Canada	1961	Canada	1979	Soviet Union	1997	Canada
1938	Canada	1962	Sweden	1980	Not held	1998	Sweden
1939	Canada	1963	Soviet Union	1981	Soviet Union	1999	Czech Republic
1940-46	Not held	1964	Soviet Union	1982	Soviet Union	2000	Czech Republic
1947	Czechoslovakia	1965	Soviet Union	1983	Soviet Union	2001	Czech Republic
1948	Canada	1966	Soviet Union	1984	Not held	2002	Slovakia
1949	Czechoslovakia	1967	Soviet Union	1985	Czechoslovakia		
1950	Canada	1968	Soviet Union	1986	Soviet Union		

Women

The women's World Hockey Championship tournament is governed by the International Ice Hockey Federation (IIHF).

Multiple winners: Canada (7).

Year		Year		Year		Year	
1990	Canada	1994	Canada	1999	Canada	2001	Canada
1992	Canada	1997	Canada	2000	Canada		

Canada vs. USSR Summits

The first competition between the Soviet National Team and the NHL took place Sept. 2-28, 1972. A team of NHL All-Stars emerged as the winner of the heralded 8-game series, but just barely—winning with a record of 4-3-1 after trailing 1-3-1.

Two years later a WHA All-Star team played the Soviet Nationals and could win only one game and tie three others in eight contests. Two other Canada vs USSR series took place during NHL All-Star breaks: the three-game Challenge Cup at New York in 1979, and the two-game Rendez-Vous '87 in Quebec City in 1987.

The NHL All-Stars played the USSR in a three-game Challenge Cup series in 1979.

1972 Team Canada vs. USSR

NHL All-Stars vs Soviet National Team.

Date	City	Result	Goaltenders
9/2	Montreal	USSR, 7-3	Tretiak/Dryden
9/4	Toronto	Canada, 4-1	Esposito/Tretiak
9/6	Winnipeg	Tie, 4-4	Tretiak/Esposito
9/8	Vancouver	USSR, 5-3	Tretiak/Dryden
9/22	Moscow	USSR, 5-4	Tretiak/Esposito
9/24	Moscow	Canada, 3-2	Dryden/Tretiak
9/26	Moscow	Canada, 4-3	Esposito/Tretiak
9/28	Moscow	Canada, 6-5	Dryden/Tretiak

Standings

	W	L	T	Pts	GF	GA
Team Canada (NHL)	4	3	1	9	32	32
Soviet Union	3	4	1	7	32	32

Leading Scorers

1. Phil Esposito, Canada, (7-6—13); **2.** Aleksandr Yakushev, USSR (7-4—11); **3.** Paul Henderson, Canada (7-2—9); **4.** Boris Shadrin, USSR (3-5—8); **5.** Valeri Kharlamov, USSR (3-4—7) and Vladimir Petrov, USSR (3-4—7).

1974 Team Canada vs. USSR

WHA All-Stars vs Soviet National Team.

Date	City	Result	Goaltenders
9/17	Quebec City	Tie, 3-3	Tretiak/Cheevers
9/19	Toronto	Canada, 4-1	Cheevers/Tretiak
9/21	Winnipeg	USSR, 8-5	Tretiak/McLeod
9/23	Vancouver	Tie, 5-5	Tretiak/Cheevers
10/1	Moscow	USSR, 3-2	Tretiak/Cheevers
10/3	Moscow	USSR, 5-2	Tretiak/Cheevers
10/5	Moscow	Tie, 4-4	Cheevers/Tretiak
10/6	Moscow	USSR, 3-2	Sidelinkov/Cheevers

Standings

	W	L	T	Pts	GF	GA
Soviet Union	4	1	3	11	32	27
Team Canada (WHA)	1	4	3	5	27	32

Leading Scorers

1. Bobby Hull, Canada (7-2—9); **2.** Aleksandr Yakushev, USSR (6-2—8), Ralph Backstrom, Canada (4-4—8) and Valeri Kharlamov, USSR (2-6—8); **5.** Gordie Howe, Canada (3-4—7), Andre Lacroix, Canada (1-6—7) and Vladimir Petrov, USSR (1-6—7).

1979 Challenge Cup Series

NHL All-Stars vs Soviet National Team

Date	City	Result	Goaltenders
2/8	New York	NHL, 4-2	K. Dryden/Tretiak
2/10	New York	USSR, 5-4	Tretiak/K. Dryden
2/11	New York	USSR, 6-0	Myshkin/Cheevers

Rendez-Vous '87

NHL All-Stars vs Soviet National Team

Date	City	Result	Goaltenders
2/11	Quebec	NHL, 4-3	Fuhr/Belosheykhin
2/13	Quebec	USSR, 5-3	Belosheykhin/Fuhr

The Canada Cup

After organizing the historic 8-game Team Canada-Soviet Union series of 1972, NHL Players Association executive director Alan Eagleson and the NHL created the Canada Cup in 1976. For the first time, the best players from the world's six major hockey powers—Canada, Czechoslovakia, Finland, Russia, Sweden and the USA—competed together in one tournament.

1976
Round Robin Standings

	W	L	T	Pts	GF	GA
Canada	4	1	0	8	22	6
Czechoslovakia	3	1	1	7	19	9
Soviet Union	2	2	1	5	23	14
Sweden	2	2	1	5	16	18
United States	1	3	1	3	14	21
Finland	1	4	0	2	16	42

Finals (Best of 3)

Date	City	Score
9/13	Toronto	Canada 6, Czechoslovakia 0
9/15	Montreal	Canada 5, Czechoslovakia 4 (OT)

Note: Darryl Sittler scored the winning goal for Canada at 11:33 in overtime to clinch the Cup, 2 games to none.

Leading Scorers

1. Victor Hluktov, USSR (5-4—9), Bobby Orr, Canada (2-7—9) and Denis Potvin, Canada (1-8—9); **4.** Bobby Hull, Canada (5-3—8) and Milan Novy, Canada (5-3—8).

Team MVPs

Canada—Rogie Vachon
Czech.—Milan Novy
USSR—Alexandr Maltsev
Sweden—Borje Salming
USA—Robbie Ftorek
Finland—Matti Hagman

Tournament MVP—Bobby Orr, Canada

1981
Round Robin Standings

	W	L	T	Pts	GF	GA
Canada	4	0	1	9	32	13
Soviet Union	3	1	1	7	20	13
Czechoslovakia	2	1	2	6	21	13
United States	2	2	1	5	17	19
Sweden	1	4	0	2	13	20
Finland	0	4	1	1	6	31

Semifinals

Date	City	Score
9/11	Ottawa	USSR 4, Czechoslovakia 1
9/11	Montreal	Canada 4, United States 1

Finals

Date	City	Score
9/13	Montreal	USSR 8, Canada 1

Leading Scorers

1. Wayne Gretzky, Canada (5-7—12); **2.** Mike Bossy, Canada (8-3—11), Bryan Trottier, Canada (3-8—11), Guy Lafleur, Canada (2-9—11), Alexei Kasatonov, USSR (1-10—11).

All-Star Team

Goal—Vladislav Tretiak, Czech. and Alexei Kasatonov, USSR; **Defense**—Arnold Kadlec, Czech. and Alexei Kasatonov, USSR; **Forwards**—Mike Bossy, Canada, Gil Perreault, Canada, and Sergei Shepelev, USSR. **Tournament MVP**—Tretiak.

1984
Round Robin Standings

	W	L	T	Pts	GF	GA
Soviet Union	5	0	0	10	22	7
United States	3	1	1	7	21	13
Sweden	3	2	0	6	15	16
Canada	2	2	1	5	23	18
West Germany	0	4	1	1	13	29
Czechoslovakia	0	4	1	1	10	21

Semifinals

Date	City	Score
9/12	Edmonton	Sweden 9, United States 2
9/15	Montreal	Canada 3, USSR 2 (OT)

Note: Mike Bossy scored the winning goal for Canada at 12:29 in overtime.

Finals (Best of 3)

Date	City	Score
9/16	Calgary	Canada 5, Sweden 2
9/18	Edmonton	Canada 6, Sweden 5

Leading Scorers

1. Wayne Gretzky, Canada (5-7—12); **2.** Michel Goulet, Canada (5-6—11), Kent Nilsson, Sweden (3-8—11), Paul Coffey, Canada (3-8—11); **5.** Hakan Loob, Sweden (6-4—10).

All-Star Team

Goal—Vladimir Myshkin, USSR; **Defense**—Paul Coffey, Canada and Rod Langway, USA; **Forwards**—Wayne Gretzky, Canada, John Tonelli, Canada, and Sergei Makarov, USSR. **Tournament MVP**—Tonelli.

1987
Round Robin Standings

	W	L	T	Pts	GF	GA
Canada	3	0	2	8	19	13
Soviet Union	3	1	1	7	22	13
Sweden	3	2	0	6	17	14
Czechoslovakia	2	2	1	5	12	15
United States	2	3	0	4	13	14
Finland	0	5	0	0	9	23

Semifinals

Date	City	Score
9/8	Hamilton	USSR 4, Sweden 2
9/9	Montreal	Canada 5, Czechoslovakia 3

Finals (Best of 3)

Date	City	Score
9/11	Montreal	USSR 6, Canada 5 (OT)
9/13	Hamilton	Canada 6, USSR 5 (2 OT)
9/15	Hamilton	Canada 6, USSR 5

Note: In Game 1, Alexander Semak of USSR scored at 5:33 in overtime. In Game 2, Mario Lemieux of Canada scored at 10:01 in the second overtime period. Lemieux also won Game 3 on a goal with 1:26 left in regulation time.

Leading Scorers

1. Wayne Gretzky, Canada (3-18—21); **2.** Mario Lemieux, Canada (11-7—18); **3.** Sergei Makarov, USSR (7-8—15); **4.** Vladimir Krutov, USSR (7-7—14); **5.** Viacheslav Bykov, USSR (2-7—9); **6.** Ray Bourque, Canada (2-6—8).

All-Star Team

Goal—Grant Fuhr, Canada; **Defense**—Ray Bourque, Canada and Viacheslav Fetisov, USSR; **Forwards**—Wayne Gretzky, Canada, Mario Lemieux, Canada, and Vladimir Krutov, USSR. **Tournament MVP**—Gretzky.

1991

Round Robin Standings

	W	L	T	Pts	GF	GA
Canada	3	0	2	8	21	11
United States	4	1	0	8	19	15
Finland	2	2	1	5	10	13
Sweden	2	3	0	4	13	17
Soviet Union	1	3	1	3	14	14
Czechoslovakia	1	4	0	2	11	18

Semifinals

Date	City	Score
9/11	Hamilton	United States 7, Finland 3
9/12	Toronto	Canada 4, Sweden 0

Finals (Best of 3)

Date	City	Score
9/14	Montreal	Canada 4, United States 1
9/16	Hamilton	Canada 4, United States 2

Leading Scorers

1. Wayne Gretzky, Canada (4-8—12); **2.** Steve Larmer, Canada (6-5—11); **3.** Brett Hull, USA (2-7—9); **4.** Mike Modano, USA (2-7—9); **5.** Mark Messier, Canada (2-6—8).

All-Star Team

Goal—Bill Ranford, Canada; **Defense**—Al MacInnis, Canada and Chris Chelios, USA; **Forwards**—Wayne Gretzky, Canada, Jeremy Roenick, USA and Mats Sundin, Sweden. **Tournament MVP**—Bill Ranford.

The World Cup

Formed jointly by the NHL and the NHL Players Association in cooperation with the International Ice Hockey Federation. The inaugural World Cup held games in nine different cities throughout North America and Europe, the most ever by a single international hockey tournament.

1996

Round Robin Standings

European Pool	W	L	T	Pts	GF	GA
Sweden	3	0	0	6	14	3
Finland	2	1	0	4	17	11
Germany	1	2	0	2	11	15
Czech Republic	0	3	0	0	4	17

North American Pool	W	L	T	Pts	GF	GA
United States	3	0	0	6	19	8
Canada	2	1	0	4	11	10
Russia	1	2	0	2	12	14
Slovakia	0	3	0	0	10	18

Semifinals

Date	City	Score
9/7	Philadelphia	Canada 3, Sweden 2 (OT)
9/8	Ottawa	United States 5, Russia 2

Finals (Best of 3)

Date	City	Score
9/10	Philadelphia	Canada 4, United States 3 (OT)
9/12	Montreal	United States 5, Canada 2
9/14	Montreal	United States 5, Canada 2

Leading Scorers

1. Brett Hull, USA (7-4—11); **2.** John LeClair, USA (6-4—10); **3.** Mats Sundin, Sweden (4-3—7); Wayne Gretzky, Canada (3-4—7); Doug Weight, USA (3-4—7); Paul Coffey, Canada (0-7—7); Brian Leetch, USA (0-7—7).

All-Tournament Team

Goal—Mike Richter, USA; **Defense**—Calle Johansson, Sweden and Chris Chelios, USA; **Forwards**—Brett Hull, USA; John LeClair, USA and Mats Sundin, Sweden. **Tournament MVP**—Mike Richter, USA.

U.S. DIVISION I COLLEGE HOCKEY

NCAA Frozen Four

The NCAA Division I hockey tournament began in 1948 and was played at the Broadmoor Ice Palace in Colorado Springs from 1948-57. Since 1958, the tournament has moved around the country, stopping for consecutive years only at Boston Garden from 1972-74. Consolation games to determine third place were played from 1949-89 and discontinued in 1990.

Multiple Winners: Michigan (9); North Dakota (7); Denver and Wisconsin (5); Boston University and Minnesota (4); Lake Superior St. and Michigan Tech (3); Boston College, Colorado College, Cornell, Maine, Michigan St. and RPI (2).

Year	Champion	Head Coach	Score	Runner-up	Third Place		
1948	Michigan	Vic Heyliger	8-4	Dartmouth	Colorado College and Boston College		

Year	Champion	Head Coach	Score	Runner-up	Third Place	Score	Fourth Place
1949	Boston College	Snooks Kelley	4-3	Dartmouth	Michigan	10-4	Colorado Col.
1950	Colorado College	Cheddy Thompson	13-4	Boston Univ.	Michigan	10-6	Boston College
1951	Michigan	Vic Heyliger	7-1	Brown	Boston Univ.	7-4	Colorado College
1952	Michigan	Vic Heyliger	4-1	Colorado Col.	Yale	4-1	St. Lawrence
1953	Michigan	Vic Heyliger	7-3	Minnesota	RPI	6-3	Boston Univ.
1954	RPI	Ned Harkness	5-4*	Minnesota	Michigan	7-2	Boston College
1955	Michigan	Vic Heyliger	5-3	Colorado Col.	Harvard	6-3	St. Lawrence
1956	Michigan	Vic Heyliger	7-5	Michigan Tech	St. Lawrence	6-2	Boston College
1957	Colorado College	Tom Bedecki	13-6	Michigan	Clarkson	2-1†	Harvard
1958	Denver	Murray Armstrong	6-2	North Dakota	Clarkson	5-1	Harvard
1959	North Dakota	Bob May	4-3*	Michigan St.	Boston College	7-6†	St. Lawrence
1960	Denver	Murray Armstrong	5-3	Michigan Tech	Boston Univ.	7-6	St. Lawrence
1961	Denver	Murray Armstrong	12-2	St. Lawrence	Minnesota	4-3	RPI
1962	Michigan Tech	John MacInnes	7-1	Clarkson	Michigan	5-1	St. Lawrence
1963	North Dakota	Barry Thorndycraft	6-5	Denver	Clarkson	5-3	Boston College
1964	Michigan	Allen Renfrew	6-3	Denver	RPI	2-1	Providence
1965	Michigan Tech	John MacInnes	8-2	Boston College	North Dakota	9-5	Brown
1966	Michigan St.	Amo Bessone	6-1	Clarkson	Denver	4-3	Boston Univ.
1967	Cornell	Ned Harkness	4-1	Boston Univ.	Michigan St.	6-1	North Dakota
1968	Denver	Murray Armstrong	4-0	North Dakota	Cornell	6-1	Boston College
1969	Denver	Murray Armstrong	4-3	Cornell	Harvard	6-5†	Michigan Tech

Year	Champion	Head Coach	Score	Runner-up	Third Place	Score	Fourth Place
1970	Cornell	Ned Harkness	6-4	Clarkson	Wisconsin	6-5	Michigan Tech
1971	Boston Univ.	Jack Kelley	4-2	Minnesota	Denver	1-0	Harvard
1972	Boston Univ.	Jack Kelley	4-0	Cornell	Wisconsin	5-2	Denver
1973	Wisconsin	Bob Johnson	4-2	Denver	Boston College	3-1	Cornell
1974	Minnesota	Herb Brooks	4-2	Michigan Tech	Boston Univ.	7-5	Harvard
1975	Michigan Tech	John MacInnes	6-1	Minnesota	Boston Univ.	10-5	Harvard
1976	Minnesota	Herb Brooks	6-4	Michigan Tech	Brown	8-7	Boston Univ.
1977	Wisconsin	Bob Johnson	6-5*	Michigan	Boston Univ.	6-5	N. Hampshire
1978	Boston Univ.	Jack Parker	5-3	Boston College	Bowl. Green	4-3	Wisconsin
1979	Minnesota	Herb Brooks	4-3	North Dakota	Dartmouth	7-3	N. Hampshire
1980	North Dakota	Gino Gasparini	5-2	N. Michigan	Dartmouth	8-4	Cornell
1981	Wisconsin	Bob Johnson	6-3	Minnesota	Mich. Tech	5-2	N. Michigan
1982	North Dakota	Gino Gasparini	5-2	Wisconsin	Northeastern	10-4	N. Hampshire
1983	Wisconsin	Jeff Sauer	6-2	Harvard	Providence	4-3	Minnesota
1984	Bowling Green	Jerry York	5-4*	Minn-Duluth	North Dakota	6-5†	Michigan St.
1985	RPI	Mike Addesa	2-1	Providence	Minn-Duluth	7-6†	Boston College
1986	Michigan St.	Ron Mason	6-5	Harvard	Minnesota	6-4	Denver
1987	North Dakota	Gino Gasparini	5-3	Michigan St.	Minnesota	6-3	Harvard
1988	Lake Superior St.	Frank Anzalone	4-3*	St. Lawrence	Maine	5-2	Minnesota
1989	Harvard	Billy Cleary	4-3*	Minnesota	Michigan St.	7-4	Maine

Year	Champion	Head Coach	Score	Runner-up	Third Place
1990	Wisconsin	Jeff Sauer	7-3	Colgate	Boston College and Boston Univ.
1991	Northern Michigan	Rick Comley	8-7*	Boston Univ.	Maine and Clarkson
1992	Lake Superior St.	Jeff Jackson	5-3	Wisconsin	Michigan and Michigan St.
1993	Maine	Shawn Walsh	5-4	Lake Superior St.	Boston Univ. and Michigan
1994	Lake Superior St.	Jeff Jackson	9-1	Boston Univ.	Harvard and Minnesota
1995	Boston Univ.	Jack Parker	6-2	Maine	Michigan and Minnesota
1996	Michigan	Red Berenson	3-2*	Colorado Col.	Vermont and Boston Univ.
1997	North Dakota	Dean Blais	6-4	Boston Univ.	Colorado College and Michigan
1998	Michigan	Red Berenson	3-2*	Boston College	New Hampshire and Ohio St.
1999	Maine	Shawn Walsh	3-2*	New Hampshire	Boston College and Michigan St.
2000	North Dakota	Dean Blais	4-2	Boston College	St. Lawrence and Maine
2001	Boston College	Jerry York	3-2*	North Dakota	Michigan and Michigan St.
2002	Minnesota	Don Lucia	4-3*	Maine	Michigan and New Hampshire

*Championship game overtime goals: 1954—1:54; **1959**—4:22; **1977**—0: 23; **1984**—7:11 in 4th OT; **1988**—4:46; **1989**—4:16; **1991**—1:57 in 3rd OT; **1996**—3:35; **1998**—17:51; **1999**—10:50; **2001**—4:43; **2002**—16:58.

†Consolation game overtimes ended in 1st OT except in 1957, '59, and '69, which all ended in 2nd OT.

Note: Runners-up Denver (1973) and Wisconsin (1992) had participation voided by the NCAA for using ineligible players.

Most Outstanding Player

The Most Outstanding Players of each NCAA Div. I tournament since 1948. Winners of the award who did not play for the tournament champion are in **bold** type. In 1960, three players, none on the winning team, shared the award.

Multiple Winners: Lou Angotti and Marc Behrend (2).

Year
1948 **Joe Riley,** Dartmouth, F
1949 **Dick Desmond,** Dart., G

1950 **Ralph Bevins,** Boston U., G
1951 **Ed Whiston,** Brown, G
1952 **Ken Kinsley,** Colo. Col., G
1953 John Matchetts, Mich., F
1954 Abbie Moore, RPI, F
1955 **Phil Hilton,** Colo. Col., D
1956 Lorne Howes, Mich., G
1957 Bob McCusker, Colo. Col., F
1958 Murray Massier, Denver, F
1959 Reg Morelli, N. Dakota, F

1960 **Lou Angotti,** Mich. Tech, F;
   Bob Marquis, Boston U., F;
   & **Barry Urbanski,** BU, G
1961 Bill Masterton, Denver, F
1962 Lou Angotti, Mich. Tech, F
1963 Al McLean, N. Dakota, F
1964 Bob Gray, Michigan, G
1965 Gary Milroy, Mich. Tech, F

Year
1966 Gaye Cooley, Mich. St., G
1967 Walt Stanowski, Cornell, D
1968 Gerry Powers, Denver, G
1969 Keith Magnuson, Denver, D

1970 Dan Lodboa, Cornell, D
1971 Dan Brady, Boston U., G
1972 Tim Regan, Boston, U., G
1973 Dean Talafous, Wisc., F
1974 Brad Shelstad, Minn., G
1975 Jim Warden, Mich. Tech, G
1976 Tom Vanelli, Minn., F
1977 Julian Baretta, Wisc., G
1978 Jack O'Callahan, Boston U., D
1979 Steve Janaszak, Minn., G

1980 Doug Smail, N. Dakota, F
1981 Marc Behrend, Wisc., G
1982 Phil Sykes, N. Dakota, F
1983 Marc Behrend, Wisc., G
1984 Gary Kruzich, Bowl. Green, G
1985 **Chris Terreri,** Prov., G

Year
1986 Mike Donnelly, Mich. St., F
1987 Tony Hrkac, N. Dakota, F
1988 Bruce Hoffort, Lk. Superior, G
1989 Ted Donato, Harvard, F

1990 Chris Tancill, Wisconsin, F
1991 Scott Beattie, No. Mich., F
1992 Paul Constantin, Lk. Superior, F
1993 Jim Montgomery, Maine, F
1994 Sean Tallaire, Lk. Superior, F
1995 Chris O'Sullivan, Boston U., F
1996 Brendan Morrison, Michigan, F
1997 Matt Henderson, N. Dakota, F
1998 Marty Turco, Michigan, G
1999 Alfie Michaud, Maine, G

2000 Lee Goren, N. Dakota, F
2001 Chuck Kobasew, Boston College, F
2002 Grant Potulny, Minnesota, F

U.S. Division I College Hockey (Cont.)
Hobey Baker Award

College hockey's Player of the Year award; voted on by a national panel of sportswriters, broadcasters, college coaches and pro scouts. First presented in 1981 by the Decathlon Athletic Club of Bloomington, Minn., in the name of the Princeton collegiate hockey and football star who was killed in a plane crash.

Year	Year	Year
1981 Neal Broten, Minnesota, F	1989 Lane MacDonald, Harvard, F	1997 Brendan Morrison, Michigan, F
1982 George McPhee, Bowl. Green, F	1990 Kip Miller, Michigan St., F	1998 Chris Drury, Boston U., F
1983 Mark Fusco, Harvard, D	1991 Dave Emma, Boston College, F	1999 Jason Krog, UNH, F
1984 Tom Kurvers, Minn-Duluth, D	1992 Scott Pellerin, Maine, F	2000 Mike Mottau, Boston College, D
1985 Bill Watson, Minn-Duluth, F	1993 Paul Kariya, Maine, F	2001 Ryan Miller, Michigan St., G
1986 Scott Fusco, Harvard, F	1994 Chris Marinucci, Minn-Duluth, F	2002 Jordan Leopold, Minnesota, D
1987 Tony Hrkac, North Dakota, F	1995 Brian Holzinger, Bowl. Green, F	
1988 Robb Stauber, Minnesota, G	1996 Brian Bonin, Minnesota, F	

Coach of the Year

The Penrose Memorial Trophy, voted on by the American Hockey Coaches Association and first presented in 1951 in the name of Colorado gold and copper magnate Spencer T. Penrose. Penrose built the Broadmoor hotel and athletic complex in Colorado Springs that originally hosted the NCAA hockey championship from 1948-57.

Multiple winners: Len Ceglarski and Charlie Holt (3); Dean Blais, Rick Comley, Eddie Jeremiah, Snooks Kelly, John MacInnes, Joe Marsh, Jack Parker, Jack Riley and Cooney Weiland (2).

Year	Year	Year
1951 Eddie Jeremiah, Dartmouth	1969 Charlie Holt, New Hampshire	1988 Frank Anzalone, Lk. Superior
1952 Cheddy Thompson, Colo. Col.	1970 John MacInnes, Michigan Tech	1989 Joe Marsh, St. Lawrence
1953 John Mariucci, Minnesota	1971 Cooney Weiland, Harvard	1990 Terry Slater, Colgate
1954 Vic Heyliger, Michigan	1972 Snooks Kelly, BC	1991 Rick Comley, No. Michigan
1955 Cooney Weiland, Harvard	1973 Len Ceglarski, BC	1992 Ron Mason, Michigan St.
1956 Bill Harrison, Clarkson	1974 Charlie Holt, New Hampshire	1993 George Gwozdecky, Miami-OH
1957 Jack Riley, Army	1975 Jack Parker, BU	1994 Don Lucia, Colorado Col.
1958 Harry Cleverly, BU	1976 John MacInnes, Michigan Tech	1995 Shawn Walsh, Maine
1959 Snooks Kelly, BC	1977 Jerry York, Clarkson	1996 Bruce Crowder, UMass-Lowell
	1978 Jack Parker, BU	1997 Dean Blais, N. Dakota
1960 Jack Riley, Army	1979 Charlie Holt, New Hampshire	1998 Tim Taylor, Yale
1961 Murray Armstrong, Denver		1999 Dick Umile, UNH
1962 Jack Kelley, Colby	1980 Rick Comley, No. Michigan	
1963 Tony Frasca, Colorado Col.	1981 Bill O'Flarety, Clarkson	2000 Joe Marsh, St. Lawrence
1964 Tom Eccleston, Providence	1982 Fern Flaman, Northeastern	2001 Dean Blais, N. Dakota
1965 Jim Fulllerton, Brown	1983 Bill Cleary, Harvard	2002 Tim Whitehead, Maine
1966 Amo Bessone, Michigan St.	1984 Mike Sertich, Minn-Duluth	**Note:** 1960 winner Jack Riley won
& Len Ceglarski, Clarkson	1985 Len Ceglarski, BC	the award for coaching the USA to its
1967 Eddie Jeremiah, Dartmouth	1986 Ralph Backstrom, Denver	first hockey gold medal in the Winter
1968 Ned Harkness, Cornell	1987 Gino Gasparini, N. Dakota	Olympics at Squaw Valley.

NCAA Women's Frozen Four

Women's college hockey was officially introduced as an NCAA Division I sport in 2000-01.
Multiple Winner: Minnesota-Duluth (2).

Year	Champion	Head Coach	Score	Runner-up	Third Place	Score	Fourth Place
2001	Minnesota-Duluth	Shannon Miller	4-2	St. Lawrence	Harvard	3-2	Dartmouth
2002	Minnesota-Duluth	Shannon Miller	3-2	Brown	(tie) Niagara and Minnesota, 2-2		

Most Outstanding Player

The Most Outstanding Players of each NCAA Women's Division I tournament since 2001. Winner of the award who did not play for the tournament champion in **bold** type.

Year	Year
2001 Maria Rooth, Minn.-Duluth, F	2002 **Kristy Zamora**, Brown, F

Patty Kazmaier Award

Awarded annually to the women's Division I player who displays the highest standards of personal and team excellence during the season; voted on by a 12-member panel of national media, Division I college coaches, and one USA Hockey member. First presented in 1998, in the name of the Princeton collegiate hockey and lacrosse star who died in 1990 of a rare blood disease.

Year	Year	Year
1998 Brandy Fisher, New Hampshire, F	2000 Ali Brewer, Brown, G	2002 Brooke Whitney, Northeastern, F
1999 A.J. Mleczko, Harvard, F	2001 Jennifer Botterill, Harvard, F	

College Sports

NCAA top dog **Cedric Dempsey** announced
his retirement as of the end of 2002.

All Hail Cael

Iowa State's Cael Sanderson stakes his claim as the greatest collegiate wrestler in history.

Michael Morrison *is co-editor of the ESPN/Information Please Sports Almanac.*

His first official collegiate win was a 13–4 major decision over little-known Lucas Kluever in February 1998. His 159th win was a 12–4 major decision over Lehigh's Jon Trenge in March 2002. And in between were 157 more pins, decisions, takedowns and falls that all went in favor of Iowa State freestyle wrestling phenom Cael Sanderson.

Sanderson's dominating win over Trenge at the NCAA Division I Wrestling Championships was the perfect end to a perfect college career. He capped off a historic 159–0 run and became the only wrestler to win four national championships in an undefeated career.

"Perfection" is not a word that is thrown around lightly in the world of sports. The 1972 Dolphins were a perfect 17–0. John Wooden's UCLA men's basketball teams were pretty close to perfect in the late '60's and early '70's. Heavyweight Rocky Marciano was a perfect 49–0 when he retired in 1956.

But what makes Sanderson's and Marciano's accomplishments so special is the individual nature of their sports. As Louden Swain says in the 1985 wrestling cult classic, *Vision Quest*, "Wrestling is not a team sport! When you're out there on the mat with someone who is stronger and faster than you, there is not a whole hell of a lot your team can do for you."

If Bill Walton had an off day for UCLA, he could usually count on Keith Wilkes or Henry Bibby to pick up the slack. In wrestling, however, any letdown or loss of focus can have you pinned to the floor in a split second.

Whether he wants to or not, Sanderson seems to be carrying his sport on his broad shoulders. While relatively few Americans outside of the Midwest follow wrestling—at least the kind that doesn't involve silicone, metal cages and folding chairs—many have stopped to acknowledge Sanderson's

AP/Wide World Photos

*Iowa State's **Cael Sanderson** (top) works over Lehigh's Jon Trenge for the 197-pound title at the NCAA Division I Wrestling Championships in Albany on March 23.*

performance, as they did for Greco-Roman hero Rulon Gardner at the 2000 Sydney Olympics.

The 13,000-plus fans at the Pepsi Arena in Albany knew they had witnessed something special after Sanderson's 159th victory, rewarding him with a standing ovation that lasted nearly five minutes.

"This is a defining moment in wrestling," Iowa State coach Bobby Douglas said. "Wrestling has been like the invisible sport, and Cael has lit a fire with the media with his performance that will take wrestling into the 21st century and perhaps keep us alive."

Clearly more at home on the mat instead of behind a microphone, the introverted Utah native has shrugged off his newfound fame. He's getting used to it though. He has no choice.

"The toughest thing about going undefeated is winning all your matches," he joked at a recent press conference.

Aside from his numerous awards, Sanderson's picture has already appeared on a Wheaties box, and he's been asked to sing "Take Me Out to the Ballgame" at a Chicago Cubs game. And the national attention continues to pour in.

AP/Wide World Photos

*It was business as usual for Cal's **Natalie Coughlin** at the Division I Swimming and Diving Championships—three more titles, four meet records and another Swimmer of the Meet Award.*

Sports Illustrated recently ranked his perfect record as the second most impressive college sports feat ever, behind only Jesse Owens' four world-record day in 1935, and ahead of achievements by the likes of Barry Sanders, Jim Brown, Oscar Robertson and Walton.

He became the second amateur wrestler to win an ESPY Award (Best Male College Athlete), and was nominated for "Best Male Athlete" and "Best Record-Breaking Performance," both of which were won by Tiger Woods.

If anyone can appreciate what Sanderson has done it's legend Dan Gable, the former Iowa coach and Iowa State wrestler who went 117–0 before losing in a Buster Douglas-like upset to University of Washington underdog Larry Owings at the 1970 NCAA tournament.

"He doesn't just win," says Gable. "He dominates. Flat-out dominates."

After rolling through the best of the U.S., Sanderson now looks to make his mark on the international scene. He sat out the 2001 world championships because the Sept. 11 attacks not only

continued on page 442 ▶

The Ten Biggest Stories of the Year in College Sports

10 USC's Angela Williams and Tennessee's Justin Gatlin are victorious once again at the NCAA Division I Outdoor Track and Field Championships. Williams' win in the 100-meter dash makes her the third athlete in the championships' history to win the same event four times. Gatlin wins the 100- and 200-meter dashes for the second straight year.

9 Michigan booster Ed Martin pleads guilty to money laundering and admits to "lending" $280,000 to Chris Webber and various sums to other star hoopsters while they still played for the Wolverines. Webber is subsequently indicted for obstructing justice and lying to a grand jury.

8 California swimmer Natalie Coughlin wins three individual titles for the second consecutive year and sets four meet records at the NCAA Division I Women's Swimming and Diving Championships.

7 The Lords of Kenyon College (OH) win their remarkable 23rd consecutive title at the Division III Men's Swimming and Diving Championships. The streak is the longest of any sport in any division of the NCAA. The Kenyon Ladies grab their 18th title.

6 Stanford men's water polo coach Dante Dettamanti retires with 666 wins over 32 years in coaching and 25 years at the helm of the Cardinal. His team sends him out on top with his record-tying eighth NCAA championship.

5 Alan Webb, who became the most-anticipated college track and field athlete in recent memory after breaking Jim Ryun's 36-year-old prep mile record in 2001, decides to turn pro after competing for the University of Michigan for just one year. In his freshman year, Webb wins the Big Ten cross country title and the outdoor Big Ten 1500-meter championship.

4 NCAA President Cedric Dempsey announces his retirement at the end of 2002 after a nine-year tenure. He is just the third person to hold the top position at the NCAA since the birth of the position in 1951.

3 Stanford continues its NCAA dominance, winning its eighth consecutive Sears Directors' Cup as the best overall Division I college athletics program. The Cardinal record four national championships overall, and 17 top-10 finishes. UC–Davis (Division II), Williams (Division III) and Oklahoma City (NAIA) also win their respective divisions.

2 The George O'Leary résumé debacle at Notre Dame opens up a can of worms that causes the suspension and/or firing of numerous coaching and other athletic personnel throughout college sports.

1 Iowa State wrestler Cael Sanderson completes a perfect 159–0 college career and becomes just the second Division I wrestler in history to win four NCAA titles (Oklahoma State's Pat Smith is the other but he lost five matches over his career).

moved the event from New York to Bulgaria, but postponed the event, causing it to interfere with his Iowa State schedule. He was also shut out of the 2002 world championships in Iran because the U.S. team opted to stay home after terrorist threats were made.

At the 2004 Olympics in Athens, he should finally get his chance to show the world what he can do.

Picture Perfect

Listed below is Iowa State's Cael Sanderson's college wrestling record by season. You'll probably begin to notice a trend—he wins a lot.

	W-L	Pins
Freshman	39–0	10
Sophomore	40–0	10
Junior	40–0	18
Senior	40–0	23

No Repeat Performance

There hasn't been a back-to-back champion in Division I men's ice hockey in 30 years. The last to win in consecutive years was Boston University (1971–72). Below are the longest streaks without a back-to-back champ in NCAA history.

	Dates	Years
D. I Men's Hockey	1973–02	30
D. III Baseball	1980–01	22
D. I Baseball	1951–70	20
D. I Men's Basketball	1974–92	18

Source: *NCAA News*

Leading Leaders

Stanford water polo coach Dante Dettamanti won his eighth national title in 2002, but he's far from overall Division I all-time leader Al Scates.

A. Scates, UCLA Men's Volleyball	18
D. Gould, Stanford Men's Tennis	17
J. McDonnell, Arkansas Men's T&F	16
D. Williams, Houston Men's Golf	16

Source: *NCAA News*

Orange County

Syracuse has won seven Division I men's lacrosse titles (and had one vacated by the NCAA). Perhaps even more impressive is the fact that the Orangemen have been one of the top-four teams every year since 1980. Listed are the most consecutive appearances in Division I semifinals.

	Dates	Years
Syracuse M Lacrosse	1983–02	20
UNC W Soccer	1982–01	20
UCLA M Basketball	1967–76	10
Michigan M Hockey	1948–57	10

NCAA Schools & Champs

ESPN Information Please® SPORTS ALMANAC

NCAA Division I-A Football Schools

2002 Season

Conferences and coaches as of Sept. 1, 2002.

Joining Mid-American in 2002: CENTRAL FLORIDA from Independent.
Joining Conference USA in 2003: SOUTH FLORIDA from Independent.

	Nickname	Conference	Head Coach	Location	Colors
Air Force	Falcons	Mountain West	Fisher DeBerry	Colo. Springs, CO	Blue/Silver
Akron	Zips	Mid-American	Lee Owens	Akron, OH	Blue/Gold
Alabama	Crimson Tide	SEC-West	Dennis Franchione	Tuscaloosa, AL	Crimson/White
Arizona	Wildcats	Pac-10	John Mackovic	Tucson, AZ	Cardinal/Navy
Arizona St.	Sun Devils	Pac-10	Dirk Koetter	Tempe, AZ	Maroon/Gold
Arkansas	Razorbacks	SEC-West	Houston Nutt	Fayetteville, AR	Cardinal/White
Arkansas St.	Indians	Sun Belt	Steve Roberts	State Univ., AR	Scarlet/Black
Army	Cadets, Black Knights	USA	Todd Berry	West Point, NY	Black/Gold/Gray
Auburn	Tigers	SEC-West	Tommy Tuberville	Auburn, AL	Orange/Blue
Ball St.	Cardinals	Mid-American	Bill Lynch	Muncie, IN	Cardinal/White
Baylor	Bears	Big 12	Kevin Steele	Waco, TX	Green/Gold
Boise St.	Broncos	WAC	Dan Hawkins	Boise, ID	Orange/Blue
Boston College	Eagles	Big East	Tom O'Brien	Chestnut Hill, MA	Maroon/Gold
Bowling Green	Falcons	Mid-American	Urban Meyer	Bowling Green, OH	Orange/Brown
Brigham Young	Cougars	Mountain West	Gary Crowton	Provo, UT	Royal Blue/White
Buffalo	Bulls	Mid-American	Jim Hofher	Buffalo, NY	Royal Blue/White
California	Golden Bears	Pac-10	Jeff Tedford	Berkeley, CA	Blue/Gold
Central Florida	Golden Knights	Mid-American	Mike Kruczek	Orlando, FL	Black/Gold
Central Michigan	Chippewas	Mid-American	Mike DeBord	Mt. Pleasant, MI	Maroon/Gold
Cincinnati	Bearcats	USA	Rick Minter	Cincinnati, OH	Red/Black
Clemson	Tigers	ACC	Tommy Bowden	Clemson, SC	Purple/Orange
Colorado	Buffaloes	Big 12	Gary Barnett	Boulder, CO	Silver/Gold/Black
Colorado St.	Rams	Mountain West	Sonny Lubick	Ft. Collins, CO	Green/Gold
Connecticut	Huskies	Independent	Randy Edsall	Storrs, CT	Blue/White
Duke	Blue Devils	ACC	Carl Franks	Durham, NC	Royal Blue/White
East Carolina	Pirates	USA	Steve Logan	Greenville, NC	Purple/Gold
Eastern Michigan	Eagles	Mid-American	Jeff Woodruff	Ypsilanti, MI	Green/White
Florida	Gators	SEC-East	Ron Zook	Gainesville, FL	Orange/Blue
Florida St.	Seminoles	ACC	Bobby Bowden	Tallahassee, FL	Garnet/Gold
Fresno St.	Bulldogs	WAC	Pat Hill	Fresno, CA	Cardinal/Blue
Georgia	Bulldogs	SEC-East	Mark Richt	Athens, GA	Red/Black
Georgia Tech	Yellow Jackets	ACC	Chan Gailey	Atlanta, GA	Old Gold/White
Hawaii	Warriors	WAC	June Jones	Honolulu, HI	Green/White
Houston	Cougars	USA	Dana Dimel	Houston, TX	Scarlet/White
Idaho	Vandals	Sun Belt	Tom Cable	Moscow, ID	Silver/Gold
Illinois	Fighting Illini	Big Ten	Ron Turner	Champaign, IL	Orange/Blue
Indiana	Hoosiers	Big Ten	Gerry DiNardo	Bloomington, IN	Cream/Crimson
Iowa	Hawkeyes	Big Ten	Kirk Ferentz	Iowa City, IA	Old Gold/Black
Iowa St.	Cyclones	Big 12	Dan McCarney	Ames, IA	Cardinal/Gold
Kansas	Jayhawks	Big 12	Mark Mangino	Lawrence, KS	Crimson/Blue
Kansas St.	Wildcats	Big 12	Bill Snyder	Manhattan, KS	Purple/White
Kent St.	Golden Flashes	Mid-American	Dean Pees	Kent, OH	Navy Blue/Gold
Kentucky	Wildcats	SEC-East	Guy Morriss	Lexington, KY	Blue/White
LSU	Fighting Tigers	SEC-West	Nick Saban	Baton Rouge, LA	Purple/Gold
LA-Lafayette	Ragin' Cajuns	Sun Belt	Rickey Bustle	Lafayette, LA	Vermilion/White
LA-Monroe	Indians	Sun Belt	Bobby Keasler	Monroe, LA	Maroon/Gold
Louisiana Tech	Bulldogs	WAC	Jack Bicknell III	Ruston, LA	Red/Blue
Louisville	Cardinals	USA	John L. Smith	Louisville, KY	Red/Black/White
Marshall	Thundering Herd	Mid-American	Bob Pruett	Huntington, WV	Green/White
Maryland	Terrapins, Terps	ACC	Ralph Friedgen	College Park, MD	Red/White/Black/Gold

	Nickname	Conference	Head Coach	Location	Colors
Memphis	Tigers	USA	Tommy West	Memphis, TN	Blue/Gray
Miami-FL	Hurricanes	Big East	Larry Coker	Coral Gables, FL	Orange/Grn./Wt.
Miami-OH	RedHawks	Mid-American	Terry Hoeppner	Oxford, OH	Red/White
Michigan	Wolverines	Big Ten	Lloyd Carr	Ann Arbor, MI	Maize/Blue
Michigan St.	Spartans	Big Ten	Bobby Williams	E. Lansing, MI	Green/White
Middle Tenn. St.	Blue Raiders	Sun Belt	Andy McCollum	Murfreesboro, TN	Blue/White
Minnesota	Golden Gophers	Big Ten	Glen Mason	Minneapolis, MN	Maroon/Gold
Mississippi	Ole Miss, Rebels	SEC-West	David Cutcliffe	Oxford, MS	Cardinal/Navy Bl.
Mississippi St.	Bulldogs	SEC-West	Jackie Sherrill	Starkville, MS	Maroon/White
Missouri	Tigers	Big 12	Gary Pinkel	Columbia, MO	Old Gold/Black
Navy	Midshipmen	Independent	Paul Johnson	Annapolis, MD	Navy Blue/Gold
Nebraska	Cornhuskers	Big 12	Frank Solich	Lincoln, NE	Scarlet/Cream
Nevada	Wolf Pack	WAC	Chris Tormey	Reno, NV	Silver/Blue
New Mexico	Lobos	Mountain West	Rocky Long	Albuquerque, NM	Cherry/Silver
New Mexico St.	Aggies	Sun Belt	Tony Samuel	Las Cruces, NM	Crimson/White
North Carolina	Tar Heels	ACC	John Bunting	Chapel Hill, NC	Carolina Blue/Wt.
North Carolina St.	Wolfpack	ACC	Chuck Amato	Raleigh, NC	Red/White
North Texas	Mean Green	Sun Belt	Darrell Dickey	Denton, TX	Green/White
Northern Illinois	Huskies	Mid-American	Joe Novak	De Kalb, IL	Cardinal/Black
Northwestern	Wildcats	Big Ten	Randy Walker	Evanston, IL	Purple/White
Notre Dame	Fighting Irish	Independent	Tyrone Willingham	Notre Dame, IN	Gold/Blue
Ohio University	Bobcats	Mid-American	Brian Knorr	Athens, OH	Hunter Green/Wt.
Ohio St.	Buckeyes	Big Ten	Jim Tressel	Columbus, OH	Scarlet/Gray
Oklahoma	Sooners	Big 12	Bob Stoops	Norman, OK	Crimson/Cream
Oklahoma St.	Cowboys	Big 12	Les Miles	Stillwater, OK	Orange/Black
Oregon	Ducks	Pac-10	Mike Bellotti	Eugene, OR	Green/Yellow
Oregon St.	Beavers	Pac-10	Dennis Erickson	Corvallis, OR	Orange/Black
Penn St.	Nittany Lions	Big Ten	Joe Paterno	University Park, PA	Blue/White
Pittsburgh	Panthers	Big East	Walt Harris	Pittsburgh, PA	Blue/Gold
Purdue	Boilermakers	Big Ten	Joe Tiller	W. Lafayette, IN	Old Gold/Black
Rice	Owls	WAC	Ken Hatfield	Houston, TX	Blue/Gray
Rutgers	Scarlet Knights	Big East	Greg Schiano	New Brunswick, NJ	Scarlet
San Diego St.	Aztecs	Mountain West	Tom Craft	San Diego, CA	Scarlet/Black
San Jose St.	Spartans	WAC	Fitz Hill	San Jose, CA	Gold/White/Blue
South Carolina	Gamecocks	SEC-East	Lou Holtz	Columbia, SC	Garnet/Black
South Florida	Bulls	Independent	Jim Leavitt	Tampa, FL	Green/Gold
SMU	Mustangs	WAC	Phil Bennett	Dallas, TX	Red/Blue
Southern Miss.	Golden Eagles	USA	Jeff Bower	Hattiesburg, MS	Black/Gold
Stanford	Cardinal	Pac-10	Buddy Teevens	Stanford, CA	Cardinal/White
Syracuse	Orangemen	Big East	Paul Pasqualoni	Syracuse, NY	Orange
Temple	Owls	Big East	Bobby Wallace	Philadelphia, PA	Cherry/White
Tennessee	Volunteers	SEC-East	Phillip Fulmer	Knoxville, TN	Orange/White
Texas	Longhorns	Big 12	Mack Brown	Austin, TX	Burnt Orange/Wt.
Texas A&M	Aggies	Big 12	R.C. Slocum	College Station, TX	Maroon/White
TCU	Horned Frogs	USA	Gary Patterson	Ft. Worth, TX	Purple/White
Texas Tech	Red Raiders	Big 12	Mike Leach	Lubbock, TX	Scarlet/Black
Toledo	Rockets	Mid-American	Tom Amstutz	Toledo, OH	Blue/Gold
Troy State	Trojans	Independent	Larry Blakeney	Troy, AL	Cardinal/Slvr./Blk.
Tulane	Green Wave	USA	Chris Scelfo	New Orleans, LA	Olive Grn./Sky Bl.
Tulsa	Golden Hurricane	WAC	Keith Burns	Tulsa, OK	Blue/Gold
UAB	Blazers	USA	Watson Brown	Birmingham, AL	Green/Gold
UCLA	Bruins	Pac-10	Bob Toledo	Los Angeles, CA	Blue/Gold
UNLV	Rebels	Mountain West	John Robinson	Las Vegas, NV	Scarlet/Gray
USC	Trojans	Pac-10	Pete Carroll	Los Angeles, CA	Cardinal/Gold
Utah	Utes	Mountain West	Ron McBride	Salt Lake City, UT	Crimson/White
Utah St.	Aggies	Independent	Mick Dennehy	Logan, UT	Navy Blue/White
UTEP	Miners	WAC	Gary Nord	El Paso, TX	Orange/Blue/Wt.
Vanderbilt	Commodores	SEC-East	Bobby Johnson	Nashville, TN	Black/Gold
Virginia	Cavaliers	ACC	Al Groh	Charlottesville, VA	Orange/Blue
Virginia Tech	Hokies, Gobblers	Big East	Frank Beamer	Blacksburg, VA	Orange/Maroon
Wake Forest	Demon Deacons	ACC	Jim Grobe	Winston-Salem, NC	Old Gold/Black
Washington	Huskies	Pac-10	Rick Neuheisel	Seattle, WA	Purple/Gold
Washington St.	Cougars	Pac-10	Mike Price	Pullman, WA	Crimson/Gray
West Virginia	Mountaineers	Big East	Rich Rodriguez	Morgantown, WV	Old Gold/Blue
Western Michigan	Broncos	Mid-American	Gary Darnell	Kalamazoo, MI	Brown/Gold
Wisconsin	Badgers	Big Ten	Barry Alvarez	Madison, WI	Cardinal/White
Wyoming	Cowboys	Mountain West	Vic Koenning	Laramie, WY	Brown/Yellow

NCAA Division I-AA Football Schools
2002 Season
Conferences and coaches as of Sept. 1, 2002.

New Conference in 2002: Big South (4 teams)— CHARLESTON SOUTHERN, ELON, GARDNER-WEBB and LIBERTY.
Leaving I-AA Independent in 2002: CAL STATE-NORTHRIDGE (program discontinued).
Joining I-AA Independent in 2002: FLORIDA INTERNATIONAL (new program).
Joining Big South in 2003: VIRGINIA MILITARY INSTITUTE from Southern and COASTAL CAROLINA (new program).
Joining Southern in 2003: ELON from Big South.
Joining Ohio Valley in 2003: JACKSONVILLE ST. from Southland and SAMFORD from Independent.
To I-AA Independent in 2003: SOUTHEASTERN LOUISIANA (program reinstated).
To Atlantic 10 in 2004: TOWSON from Patriot.
To Southland in 2005: SOUTHEASTERN LOUISIANA from Independent.

	Nickname	Conference	Head Coach	Location	Colors
Alabama A&M	Bulldogs	SWAC	Anthony Jones	Huntsville, AL	Maroon/White
Alabama St.	Hornets	SWAC	L.C. Cole	Montgomery, AL	Black/Gold
Albany	Great Danes	Northeast	Bob Ford	Albany, NY	Purple/Gold
Alcorn St.	Braves	SWAC	Johnny Thomas	Lorman, MS	Purple/Gold
Appalachian St.	Mountaineers	Southern	Jerry Moore	Boone, NC	Black/Gold
Ark.-Pine Bluff	Golden Lions	SWAC	Lee Hardman	Pine Bluff, AR	Black/Gold
Austin Peay St.	Governors	Pioneer	Bill Schmitz	Clarksville, TN	Red/White
Bethune-Cookman	Wildcats	Mid-Eastern	Alvin Wyatt	Daytona Beach, FL	Maroon/Gold
Brown	Bears	Ivy	Phil Estes	Providence, RI	Brown/Red/White
Bucknell	Bison	Patriot	Tom Gadd	Lewisburg, PA	Orange/Blue
Butler	Bulldogs	Pioneer	Kit Cartwright	Indianapolis, IN	Blue/White
Cal Poly	Mustangs	Independent	Rich Ellerson	San Luis Obispo, CA	Green/Gold
Canisius	Golden Griffins	Metro Atlantic	Edward Argast	Buffalo, NY	Blue/Gold
Central Conn. St.	Blue Devils	Northeast	Paul Schudel	New Britain, CT	Blue/White
Charleston So.	Buccaneers	Big South	David Dowd	Charleston, SC	Blue/Gold
The Citadel	Bulldogs	Southern	Ellis Johnson	Charleston, SC	Blue/White
Colgate	Raiders	Patriot	Dick Biddle	Hamilton, NY	Maroon/White/Gray
Columbia	Lions	Ivy	Ray Tellier	New York, NY	Lt. Blue/White
Cornell	Big Red	Ivy	Tim Pendergast	Ithaca, NY	Carnelian/White
Dartmouth	Big Green	Ivy	John Lyons	Hanover, NH	Green/White
Davidson	Wildcats	Pioneer	Mike Toop	Davidson, NC	Red/Black
Dayton	Flyers	Pioneer	Mike Kelly	Dayton, OH	Red/Blue
Delaware	Blue Hens	Atlantic 10	K.C. Keeler	Newark, DE	Blue/Gold
Delaware St.	Hornets	Mid-Eastern	Ben Blacknall	Dover, DE	Red/Blue
Drake	Bulldogs	Pioneer	Rob Ash	Des Moines, IA	Blue/White
Duquesne	Dukes	Metro Atlantic	Greg Gattuso	Pittsburgh, PA	Red/Blue
East Tenn. St.	Buccaneers	Southern	Paul Hamilton	Johnson City, TN	Blue/Gold
Eastern Illinois	Panthers	Ohio Valley	Bob Spoo	Charleston, IL	Blue/Gray
Eastern Kentucky	Colonels	Ohio Valley	Roy Kidd	Richmond, KY	Maroon/White
Eastern Washington	Eagles	Big Sky	Paul Wulff	Cheney, WA	Red/White
Elon	Phoenix	Big South	Al Seagraves	Elon, NC	Maroon/Gold
Fairfield	Stags	Metro Atlantic	Joe Bernard	Fairfield, CT	Cardinal Red
Florida A&M	Rattlers	Mid-Eastern	Billy Joe	Tallahassee, FL	Orange/Green
Florida Atlantic	Owls	Independent	H. Schnellenberger	Boca Raton, FL	Blue/Red
Florida Int'l	Golden Panthers	Independent	Don Strock	Miami, FL	Blue/Gold
Fordham	Rams	Patriot	Dave Clawson	Bronx, NY	Maroon/White
Furman	Paladins	Southern	Bobby Lamb	Greenville, SC	Purple/White
Gardner-Webb	Bulldogs	Big South	Steve Patton	Boiling Springs, NC	Scarlet/Black
Georgetown	Hoyas	Patriot	Bob Benson	Washington, DC	Blue/Gray
Georgia Southern	Eagles	Southern	Mike Sewak	Statesboro, GA	Blue/White
Grambling St.	Tigers	SWAC	Doug Williams	Grambling, LA	Black/Gold
Hampton	Pirates	Mid-Eastern	Joe Taylor	Hampton, VA	Royal Blue/White
Harvard	Crimson	Ivy	Tim Murphy	Cambridge, MA	Crimson/Black/White
Hofstra	Flying Dutchmen	Atlantic 10	Joe Gardi	Hempstead, NY	Gray/White/Gold
Holy Cross	Crusaders	Patriot	Dan Allen	Worcester, MA	Royal Purple
Howard	Bison	Mid-Eastern	Rayford T. Petty	Washington, DC	Blue/Wt./Red
Idaho St.	Bengals	Big Sky	Larry Lewis	Pocatello, ID	Orange/Black
Illinois St.	Redbirds	Gateway	Denver Johnson	Normal, IL	Red/White
Indiana St.	Sycamores	Gateway	Tim McGuire	Terre Haute, IN	Royal Blue/White
Iona	Gaels	Metro Atlantic	Fred Mariani	New Rochelle, NY	Maroon/Gold
Jackson St.	Tigers	SWAC	Robert Hughes	Jackson, MS	Blue/White
Jacksonville	Dolphins	Pioneer	Steve Gilbert	Jacksonville, FL	Green/White
Jacksonville St.	Gamecocks	Southland	Jack Crowe	Jacksonville, AL	Red/White
James Madison	Dukes	Atlantic 10	Mickey Matthews	Harrisonburg, VA	Purple/Gold
Lafayette	Leopards	Patriot	Frank Tavani	Easton, PA	Maroon/White

	Nickname	Conference	Head Coach	Location	Colors
La Salle	Explorers	Metro Atlantic	Archie Stalcup	Philadelphia, PA	Blue/Gold
Lehigh	Engineers	Patriot	Pete Lembo	Bethlehem, PA	Brown/White
Liberty	Flames	Big South	Ken Karcher	Lynchburg, VA	Red/White/Blue
Maine	Black Bears	Atlantic 10	Jack Cosgrove	Orono, ME	Blue/White
Marist	Red Foxes	Metro Atlantic	Jim Parady	Poughkeepsie, NY	Red/White
Massachusetts	Minutemen	Atlantic 10	Mark Whipple	Amherst, MA	Maroon/White
McNeese St.	Cowboys	Southland	Tommy Tate	Lake Charles, LA	Blue/Gold
Miss. Valley St.	Delta Devils	SWAC	Willie Totten	Itta Bena, MS	Green/White
Monmouth	Hawks	Northeast	Kevin Callahan	W. Long Branch, NJ	Royal Blue/White
Montana	Grizzlies	Big Sky	Joe Glenn	Missoula, MT	Maroon/Gray
Montana St.	Bobcats	Big Sky	Mike Kramer	Bozeman, MT	Blue/Gold
Morehead St.	Eagles	Pioneer	Matt Ballard	Morehead, KY	Blue/Gold
Morgan St.	Bears	Mid-Eastern	Stanley Mitchell	Baltimore, MD	Blue/Orange
Morris Brown	Wolverines	Independent	Solomon Brannan	Atlanta, GA	Purple/Black
Murray St.	Racers	Ohio Valley	Joe Pannunzio	Murray, KY	Blue/Gold
New Hampshire	Wildcats	Atlantic 10	Sean McDonnell	Durham, NH	Blue/White
Nicholls St.	Colonels	Southland	Daryl Daye	Thibodaux, LA	Red/Gray
Norfolk State	Spartans	Mid-Eastern	Maurice Forte	Norfolk, VA	Green/Gold
North Carolina A&T	Aggies	Mid-Eastern	Bill Hayes	Greensboro, NC	Blue/Gold
Northeastern	Huskies	Atlantic 10	Don Brown	Boston, MA	Red/Black
Northern Arizona	Lumberjacks	Big Sky	Jerome Souers	Flagstaff, AZ	Blue/Gold
Northern Iowa	Panthers	Gateway	Mark Farley	Cedar Falls, IA	Purple/Old Gold
Northwestern St.	Demons	Southland	Scott Stoker	Natchitoches, LA	Purple/White
Pennsylvania	Quakers	Ivy	Al Bagnoli	Philadelphia, PA	Red/Blue
Portland St.	Vikings	Big Sky	Tim Walsh	Portland, OR	Green/Gray
Prairie View A&M	Panthers	SWAC	Larry Dorsey	Prairie View, TX	Purple/Gold
Princeton	Tigers	Ivy	Roger Hughes	Princeton, NJ	Orange/Black
Rhode Island	Rams	Atlantic 10	Tim Stowers	Kingston, RI	Light Blue/Navy/Wt.
Richmond	Spiders	Atlantic 10	Jim Reid	Richmond, VA	Red/Blue
Robert Morris	Colonials	Northeast	Joe Walton	Moon Township, PA	Blue/White
Sacramento St.	Hornets	Big Sky	John Volek	Sacramento, CA	Green/Gold
Sacred Heart	Pioneers	Northeast	Bill Lacey	Fairfield, CT	Scarlet/White
St. Francis-PA	Red Flash	Northeast	Dave Opfar	Loretto, PA	Red/White
St. John's-NY	Red Storm	Northeast	Bob Ricca	Jamaica, NY	Red/White
St. Mary's-CA	Gaels	Independent	Tim Landis	Moraga, CA	Red/Blue
St. Peter's	Peacocks	Metro Atlantic	Rob Stern	Jersey City, NJ	Blue/White
Sam Houston St.	Bearkats	Southland	Ron Randleman	Huntsville, TX	Orange/White
Samford	Bulldogs	Independent	Bill Gray	Birmingham, AL	Crimson/Blue
San Diego	Toreros	Pioneer	Kevin McGarry	San Diego, CA	Lt. Blue/Navy
Savannah St.	Tigers	Independent	Ken Pettiford	Savannah, GA	Orange/Blue
Siena	Saints	Metro Atlantic	Jay Bateman	Loudonville, NY	Green/Gold
South Carolina St.	Bulldogs	Mid-Eastern	Oliver Pough	Orangeburg, SC	Garnet/Blue
SE Missouri St.	Indians	Ohio Valley	Tim Billings	Cape Girardeau, MO	Red/Black
Southern-BR	Jaguars	SWAC	Pete Richardson	Baton Rouge, LA	Blue/Gold
Southern Illinois	Salukis	Gateway	Jerry Kill	Cardondale, IL	Maroon/White
Southern Utah	Thunderbirds	Independent	C. Ray Gregory	Cedar City, UT	Scarlet/White
SW Missouri St.	Bears	Gateway	Randy Ball	Springfield, MO	Maroon/White
SW Texas St.	Bobcats	Southland	Bob DeBesse	San Marcos, TX	Maroon/Gold
S.F. Austin St.	Lumberjacks	Southland	Mike Santiago	Nacogdoches, TX	Purple/White
Stony Brook	Seawolves	Northeast	Sam Kornhauser	Stony Brook, NY	Scarlet/Gray
Tenn-Chattanooga	Mocs	Southern	Donnie Kirkpatrick	Chattanooga, TN	Navy Blue/Old Gold
Tennessee-Martin	Skyhawks	Ohio Valley	Sam McCorkle	Martin, TN	Orange/White/Blue
Tennessee St.	Tigers	Ohio Valley	James Reese	Nashville, TN	Blue/White
Tennessee Tech	Golden Eagles	Ohio Valley	Mike Hennigan	Cookeville, TN	Purple/Gold
Texas Southern	Tigers	SWAC	Bill Thomas	Houston, TX	Maroon/Gray
Towson	Tigers	Patriot	Gordy Combs	Towson, MD	Gold/White
Valparaiso	Crusaders	Pioneer	Tom Horne	Valparaiso, IN	Brown/Gold
Villanova	Wildcats	Atlantic 10	Andy Talley	Villanova, PA	Blue/White
VMI	Keydets	Southern	Cal McCombs	Lexington, VA	Red/White/Yellow
Wagner	Seahawks	Northeast	Walt Hameline	Staten Island, NY	Green/White
Weber St.	Wildcats	Big Sky	Jerry Graybeal	Ogden, UT	Royal Purple/White
Western Carolina	Catamounts	Southern	Kent Briggs	Cullowhee, NC	Purple/Gold
Western Illinois	Leathernecks	Gateway	Don Patterson	Macomb, IL	Purple/Gold
Western Kentucky	Hilltoppers	Gateway	Jack Harbaugh	Bowling Green, KY	Red/White
William & Mary	Tribe	Atlantic 10	Jimmye Laycock	Williamsburg, VA	Green/Gold/Silver
Wofford	Terriers	Southern	Mike Ayers	Spartanburg, SC	Old Gold/Black
Yale	Bulldogs, Elis	Ivy	Jack Siedlecki	New Haven, CT	Yale Blue/White
Youngstown St.	Penguins	Gateway	Jon Heacock	Youngstown, OH	Red/White

NCAA Division I Basketball Schools

2002-2003 Season

Conferences and coaches as of Sept. 1, 2002.

Joining Atlantic Sun in 2002-2003: GARDNER-WEBB from Independent.
Joining Ohio Valley in 2003-2004: JACKSONVILLE ST., SAMFORD from Atlantic Sun.
Joining Atlantic Sun in 2003-2004: LIPSCOMB from Independent.
Joining Big South in 2003-2004: VIRGINIA MILITARY INSTITUTE from Southern.
Joining Southern in 2003-2004: ELON from Big South.

	Nickname	Conference	Head Coach	Location	Colors
Air Force	Falcons	Mountain West	Joe Scott	Colo. Springs, CO	Blue/Silver
Akron	Zips	Mid-American	Dan Hipsher	Akron, OH	Blue/Gold
Alabama	Crimson Tide	SEC-West	Mark Gottfried	Tuscaloosa, AL	Crimson/White
Alabama A&M	Bulldogs	SWAC	Vann Pettaway	Huntsville, AL	Maroon/White
Alabama St.	Hornets	SWAC	Rob Spivery	Montgomery, AL	Black/Gold
Albany	Great Danes	America East	Will Brown	Albany, NY	Purple/Gold
Alcorn St.	Braves	SWAC	Davey Whitney	Lorman, MS	Purple/Gold
American	Eagles	Patriot	Jeff Jones	Washington, DC	Red/Blue
Appalachian St.	Mountaineers	Southern	Houston Fancher	Boone, NC	Black/Gold
Arizona	Wildcats	Pac-10	Lute Olson	Tucson, AZ	Cardinal/Navy
Arizona St.	Sun Devils	Pac-10	Rob Evans	Tempe, AZ	Maroon/Gold
Arkansas	Razorbacks	SEC-West	Stan Heath	Fayetteville, AR	Cardinal/White
Ark.-Little Rock	Trojans	Sun Belt	Porter Moser	Little Rock, AR	Maroon/White
Ark.-Pine Bluff	Golden Lions	SWAC	Van Holt	Pine Bluff, AR	Black/Gold
Arkansas St.	Indians	Sun Belt	Dickey Nutt	State Univ., AR	Scarlet/Black
Army	Black Knights	Patriot	Jim Crews	West Point, NY	Black/Gold/Gray
Auburn	Tigers	SEC-West	Cliff Ellis	Auburn, AL	Orange/Blue
Austin Peay St.	Governors	Ohio Valley	Dave Loos	Clarksville, TN	Red/White
Ball St.	Cardinals	Mid-American	Tim Buckley	Muncie, IN	Cardinal/White
Baylor	Bears	Big 12	Dave Bliss	Waco, TX	Green/Gold
Belmont	Bruins	Atlantic Sun	Rick Byrd	Nashville, TN	Navy Blue/Red
Bethune-Cookman	Wildcats	Mid-Eastern	Clifford Reed	Daytona Beach, FL	Maroon/Gold
Binghamton	Bearcats	America East	Al Walker	Binghamton, NY	Green/Black/White
Birmingham Southern	Panthers	Big South	Duane Reboul	Birmingham, AL	Black/Gold
Boise St.	Broncos	WAC	Greg Graham	Boise, ID	Orange/Blue
Boston College	Eagles	Big East	Al Skinner	Chestnut Hill, MA	Maroon/Gold
Boston University	Terriers	America East	Dennis Wolff	Boston, MA	Scarlet/White
Bowling Green	Falcons	Mid-American	Dan Dakich	Bowling Green, OH	Orange/Brown
Bradley	Braves	Mo. Valley	Jim Les	Peoria, IL	Red/White
Brigham Young	Cougars	Mountain West	Steve Cleveland	Provo, UT	Royal Blue/White
Brown	Bears	Ivy	Glen Miller	Providence, RI	Brown/Cardinal/White
Bucknell	Bison	Patriot	Pat Flannery	Lewisburg, PA	Orange/Blue
Buffalo	Bulls	Mid-American	R. Witherspoon	Buffalo, NY	Royal Blue/White
Butler	Bulldogs	Horizon	Todd Lickliter	Indianapolis, IN	Blue/White
California	Golden Bears	Pac-10	Ben Braun	Berkeley, CA	Blue/Gold
Cal Poly	Mustangs	Big West	Kevin Bromley	San Luis Obispo, CA	Green/Gold
CS-Fullerton	Titans	Big West	Donny Daniels	Fullerton, CA	Blue/Orange/White
CS-Northridge	Matadors	Big West	Bobby Braswell	Northridge, CA	Red/White/Black
Campbell	Fighting Camels	Atlantic Sun	Billy Lee	Buies Creek, NC	Orange/Black
Canisius	Golden Griffins	Metro Atlantic	Mike MacDonald	Buffalo, NY	Blue/Gold
Centenary	Gentlemen	Independent	Kevin Johnson	Shreveport, LA	Maroon/White
Central Conn. St.	Blue Devils	Northeast	Howie Dickenman	New Britain, CT	Blue/White
Central Florida	Golden Knights	Atlantic Sun	Kirk Speraw	Orlando, FL	Black/Gold
Central Michigan	Chippewas	Mid-American	Jay Smith	Mt. Pleasant, MI	Maroon/Gold
Charleston So.	Buccaneers	Big South	Jim Platt	Charleston, SC	Blue/Gold
Charlotte	49ers	USA	Bobby Lutz	Charlotte, NC	Green/White
Chicago St.	Cougars	Mid-Continent	Bo Ellis	Chicago, IL	Green/White
Cincinnati	Bearcats	USA	Bob Huggins	Cincinnati, OH	Red/Black
The Citadel	Bulldogs	Southern	Pat Dennis	Charleston, SC	Blue/White
Clemson	Tigers	ACC	Larry Shyatt	Clemson, SC	Purple/Orange
Cleveland St.	Vikings	Horizon	Rollie Massimino	Cleveland, OH	Forest Green/White
Coastal Carolina	Chanticleers	Big South	Pete Strickland	Conway, SC	Green/Bronze/Black
Colgate	Raiders	Patriot	Emmett Davis	Hamilton, NY	Maroon/Gray/White
College of Charleston	Cougars	Southern	Tom Herrion	Charleston, SC	Maroon/White
Colorado	Buffaloes	Big 12	Ricardo Patton	Boulder, CO	Silver/Gold/Black
Colorado St.	Rams	Mountain West	Dale Layer	Ft. Collins, CO	Green/Gold
Columbia	Lions	Ivy	Armond Hill	New York, NY	Lt. Blue/White
Connecticut	Huskies	Big East	Jim Calhoun	Storrs, CT	Blue/White
Coppin St.	Eagles	Mid-Eastern	Ron Mitchell	Baltimore, MD	Royal Blue/Gold
Cornell	Big Red	Ivy	Steve Donahue	Ithaca, NY	Carnelian/White
Creighton	Bluejays	Mo. Valley	Dana Altman	Omaha, NE	Blue/White

NCAA Division I Basketball Schools (Cont.)

	Nickname	Conference	Head Coach	Location	Colors
Dartmouth	Big Green	Ivy	Dave Faucher	Hanover, NH	Green/White
Davidson	Wildcats	Southern	Bob McKillop	Davidson, NC	Red/Black
Dayton	Flyers	Atlantic 10	Oliver Purnell	Dayton, OH	Red/Blue
Delaware	Fightin' Blue Hens	Colonial	David Henderson	Newark, DE	Blue/Gold
Delaware St.	Hornets	Mid-Eastern	Greg Jackson	Dover, DE	Red/Columbia Blue
Denver	Pioneers	Sun Belt	Terry Carroll	Denver, CO	Crimson/Gold
DePaul	Blue Demons	USA	Dave Leitao	Chicago, IL	Scarlet/Blue
Detroit Mercy	Titans	Horizon	Perry Watson	Detroit, MI	Red/White/Blue
Drake	Bulldogs	Mo. Valley	Kurt Kanaskie	Des Moines, IA	Blue/White
Drexel	Dragons	Colonial	Bruiser Flint	Philadelphia, PA	Navy Blue/Gold
Duke	Blue Devils	ACC	Mike Krzyzewski	Durham, NC	Royal Blue/White
Duquesne	Dukes	Atlantic 10	Danny Nee	Pittsburgh, PA	Red/Blue
East Carolina	Pirates	USA	Bill Herrion	Greenville, NC	Purple/Gold
East Tenn. St.	Buccaneers	Southern	Ed DeChellis	Johnson City, TN	Blue/Gold
Eastern Illinois	Panthers	Ohio Valley	Rick Samuels	Charleston, IL	Blue/Gray
Eastern Kentucky	Colonels	Ohio Valley	Travis Ford	Richmond, KY	Maroon/White
Eastern Michigan	Eagles	Mid-American	Jim Boone	Ypsilanti, MI	Green/White
Eastern Washington	Eagles	Big Sky	Ray Giacoletti	Cheney, WA	Red/White
Elon	Phoenix	Big South	Mark Simons	Elon, NC	Maroon/Gold
Evansville	Aces	Mo. Valley	Steve Merfeld	Evansville, IN	Purple/White
Fairfield	Stags	Metro Atlantic	Tim O'Toole	Fairfield, CT	Cardinal Red
Fairleigh Dickinson	Knights	Northeast	Tom Green	Teaneck, NJ	Blue/Black
Florida	Gators	SEC-East	Billy Donovan	Gainesville, FL	Orange/Blue
Florida A&M	Rattlers	Mid-Eastern	Mike Gillespie	Tallahassee, FL	Orange/Green
Florida Atlantic	Owls	Atlantic Sun	Sidney Green	Boca Raton, FL	Blue/Red
Florida Int'l	Golden Panthers	Sun Belt	Donnie Marsh	Miami, FL	Blue/Gold
Florida St.	Seminoles	ACC	Leonard Hamilton	Tallahassee, FL	Garnet/Gold
Fordham	Rams	Atlantic 10	Bob Hill	Bronx, NY	Maroon/White
Fresno St.	Bulldogs	WAC	Ray Lopes	Fresno, CA	Cardinal/Blue
Furman	Paladins	Southern	Larry Davis	Greenville, SC	Purple/White
Gardner-Webb	Bulldogs	Atlantic Sun	Rick Scruggs	Boiling Springs, NC	Scarlet/Black
George Mason	Patriots	Colonial	Jim Larranaga	Fairfax, VA	Green/Gold
George Washington	Colonials	Atlantic 10	Karl Hobbs	Washington, DC	Buff/Blue
Georgetown	Hoyas	Big East	Craig Esherick	Washington, DC	Blue/Gray
Georgia	Bulldogs, 'Dawgs	SEC-East	Jim Harrick	Athens, GA	Red/Black
Georgia Southern	Eagles	Southern	Jeff Price	Statesboro, GA	Blue/White
Georgia St.	Panthers	Atlantic Sun	Lefty Driesell	Atlanta, GA	Roy. Blue/White
Georgia Tech	Yellow Jackets	ACC	Paul Hewitt	Atlanta, GA	Old Gold/White
Gonzaga	Bulldogs, Zags	West Coast	Mark Few	Spokane, WA	Blue/White/Red
Grambling St.	Tigers	SWAC	Larry Wright	Grambling, LA	Black/Gold
Hampton	Pirates	Mid-Eastern	Bobby Collins	Hampton, VA	Royal Blue/White
Hartford	Hawks	America East	Larry Harrison	W. Hartford, CT	Scarlet/White
Harvard	Crimson	Ivy	Frank Sullivan	Cambridge, MA	Crimson/Black/White
Hawaii	Rainbows	WAC	Riley Wallace	Honolulu, HI	Green/White
High Point	Panthers	Big South	Jerry Steele	High Point, NC	Purple/White
Hofstra	Flying Dutchmen	Colonial	Tom Pecora	Hempstead, NY	Blue/White/Gold
Holy Cross	Crusaders	Patriot	Ralph Willard	Worcester, MA	Royal Purple
Houston	Cougars	USA	Ray McCallum	Houston, TX	Scarlet/White
Howard	Bison	Mid-Eastern	Frankie Allen	Washington, DC	Blue/White/Red
Idaho	Vandals	Big West	Leonard Perry	Moscow, ID	Silver/Gold
Idaho St.	Bengals	Big Sky	Doug Oliver	Pocatello, ID	Orange/Black
Illinois	Fighting Illini	Big Ten	Bill Self	Champaign, IL	Orange/Blue
Illinois-Chicago	Flames	Horizon	Jim Collins	Chicago, IL	Navy Blue/Red
Illinois St.	Redbirds	Mo. Valley	Tom Richardson	Normal, IL	Red/White
Indiana	Hoosiers	Big Ten	Mike Davis	Bloomington, IN	Cream/Crimson
IPFW	Mastodons	Independent	Doug Noll	Fort Wayne, IN	Royal Blue/White
IU/PU-Indianapolis	Jaguars	Mid-Continent	Ron Hunter	Indianapolis, IN	Red/Gold
Indiana St.	Sycamores	Mo. Valley	Royce Waltman	Terre Haute, IN	Blue/White
Iona	Gaels	Metro Atlantic	Jeff Ruland	New Rochelle, NY	Maroon/Gold
Iowa	Hawkeyes	Big Ten	Steve Alford	Iowa City, IA	Old Gold/Black
Iowa St.	Cyclones	Big 12	Larry Eustachy	Ames, IA	Cardinal/Gold
Jackson St.	Tigers	SWAC	Andy Stoglin	Jackson, MS	Blue/White
Jacksonville	Dolphins	Atlantic Sun	Hugh Durham	Jacksonville, FL	Green/White
Jacksonville St.	Gamecocks	Atlantic Sun	Mike LaPlante	Jacksonville, AL	Red/White
James Madison	Dukes	Colonial	Sherman Dillard	Harrisonburg, VA	Purple/Gold
Kansas	Jayhawks	Big 12	Roy Williams	Lawrence, KS	Crimson/Blue

	Nickname	Conference	Head Coach	Location	Colors
Kansas St.	Wildcats	Big 12	Jim Wooldridge	Manhattan, KS	Purple/White
Kent St.	Golden Flashes	Mid-American	Jim Christian	Kent, OH	Navy Blue/Gold
Kentucky	Wildcats	SEC-East	Tubby Smith	Lexington, KY	Blue/White
La Salle	Explorers	Atlantic 10	Bill Hahn	Philadelphia, PA	Blue/Gold
Lafayette	Leopards	Patriot	Fran O'Hanlon	Easton, PA	Maroon/White
Lamar	Cardinals	Southland	Mike Deane	Beaumont, TX	Red/White
Lehigh	Mountain Hawks, Engineers	Patriot	Bill Taylor	Bethlehem, PA	Brown/White
Liberty	Flames	Big South	Randy Dunton	Lynchburg, VA	Red/White/Blue
Lipscomb	Bisons	Independent	Scott Sanderson	Nashville, TN	Purple/Gold
Long Beach St.	49ers	Big West	Larry Reynolds	Long Beach, CA	Black/Gold
LIU-Brooklyn	Blackbirds	Northeast	Jim Ferry	Brooklyn, NY	Blue/White
LSU	Fighting Tigers	SEC-West	John Brady	Baton Rouge, LA	Purple/Gold
LA-Lafayette	Ragin' Cajuns	Sun Belt	Jessie Evans	Lafayette, LA	Vermilion/White
LA-Monroe	Indians	Southland	Mike Vining	Monroe, LA	Maroon/Gold
Louisiana Tech	Bulldogs	WAC	Keith Richard	Ruston, LA	Red/Blue
Louisville	Cardinals	USA	Rick Pitino	Louisville, KY	Red/Black/White
Loyola Marymount	Lions	West Coast	Steve Aggers	Los Angeles, CA	Crimson/Blue
Loyola-IL	Ramblers	Horizon	Larry Farmer	Chicago, IL	Maroon/Gold
Loyola-MD	Greyhounds	Metro Atlantic	Scott Hicks	Baltimore, MD	Green/Gray
Maine	Black Bears	America East	John Giannini	Orono, ME	Blue/White
Manhattan	Jaspers	Metro Atlantic	Bobby Gonzalez	Riverdale, NY	Kelly Green/White
Marist	Red Foxes	Metro Atlantic	Dave Magarity	Poughkeepsie, NY	Red/White
Marquette	Golden Eagles	USA	Tom Crean	Milwaukee, WI	Blue/Gold
Marshall	Thundering Herd	Mid-American	Greg White	Huntington, WV	Green/White
Maryland	Terrapins, Terps	ACC	Gary Williams	College Park, MD	Red/Wt./Black/Gold
MD-Balt. County	Retrievers	Northeast	Tom Sullivan	Baltimore, MD	Black/Gold/Red
MD-Eastern Shore	Hawks	Mid-Eastern	Thomas Trotter	Princess Anne, MD	Maroon/Gray
Massachusetts	Minutemen	Atlantic 10	Steve Lappas	Amherst, MA	Maroon/White
McNeese St.	Cowboys	Southland	Tic Price	Lake Charles, LA	Blue/Gold
Memphis	Tigers	USA	John Calipari	Memphis, TN	Blue/Gray
Mercer	Bears	Atlantic Sun	Mark Slonaker	Macon, GA	Orange/Black
Miami-FL	Hurricanes	Big East	Perry Clark	Coral Gables, FL	Orange/Grn./White
Miami-OH	RedHawks	Mid-American	Charlie Coles	Oxford, OH	Red/White
Michigan	Wolverines	Big Ten	Tommy Amaker	Ann Arbor, MI	Maize/Blue
Michigan St.	Spartans	Big Ten	Tom Izzo	East Lansing, MI	Green/White
Middle Tenn. St.	Blue Raiders	Sun Belt	Kermit Davis Jr.	Murfreesboro, TN	Blue/White
Minnesota	Golden Gophers	Big Ten	Dan Monson	Minneapolis, MN	Maroon/Gold
Mississippi	Ole Miss, Rebels	SEC-West	Rod Barnes	Oxford, MS	Red/Blue
Mississippi St.	Bulldogs	SEC-West	Rick Stansbury	Starkville, MS	Maroon/White
Miss. Valley St.	Delta Devils	SWAC	Lafayette Stribling	Itta Bena, MS	Green/White
Missouri	Tigers	Big 12	Quin Snyder	Columbia, MO	Old Gold/Black
Missouri-KC	Kangaroos	Mid-Continent	Rich Zvosec	Kansas City, MO	Blue/Gold
Monmouth	Hawks	Northeast	Dave Calloway	W. Long Branch, NJ	Royal Blue/White
Montana	Grizzlies	Big Sky	Pat Kennedy	Missoula, MT	Copper/Silver/Gold
Montana St.	Bobcats	Big Sky	Mick Durham	Bozeman, MT	Blue/Gold
Morehead St.	Eagles	Ohio Valley	Kyle Macy	Morehead, KY	Blue/Gold
Morgan St.	Bears	Mid-Eastern	Butch Beard	Baltimore, MD	Blue/Orange
Morris Brown	Wolverines	Independent	Derek Thompson	Atlanta, GA	Purple/Black
Mt. St. Mary's	Mountaineers	Northeast	Jim Phelan	Emmitsburg, MD	Blue/White
Murray St.	Racers	Ohio Valley	Tevester Anderson	Murray, KY	Blue/Gold
Navy	Midshipmen	Patriot	Don DeVoe	Annapolis, MD	Navy Blue/Gold
Nebraska	Cornhuskers	Big 12	Barry Collier	Lincoln, NE	Scarlet/Cream
Nevada	Wolf Pack	WAC	Trent Johnson	Reno, NV	Silver/Blue
New Hampshire	Wildcats	America East	Phil Rowe	Durham, NH	Blue/White
New Mexico	Lobos	Mountain West	Ritchie McKay	Albuquerque, NM	Cherry/Silver
New Mexico St.	Aggies	Sun Belt	Lou Henson	Las Cruces, NM	Crimson/White
New Orleans	Privateers	Sun Belt	Monte Towe	New Orleans, LA	Royal Blue/Silver
Niagara	Purple Eagles	Metro Atlantic	Joe Mihalich	Lewiston, NY	Purple/White/Gold
Nicholls St.	Colonels	Southland	Ricky Blanton	Thibodaux, LA	Red/Gray
Norfolk State	Spartans	Mid-Eastern	Dwight Freeman	Norfolk, VA	Green/Gold
North Carolina	Tar Heels	ACC	Matt Doherty	Chapel Hill, NC	Carolina Blue/Wht.
North Carolina A&T	Aggies	Mid-Eastern	Curtis Hunter	Greensboro, NC	Blue/Gold
North Carolina St.	Wolfpack	ACC	Herb Sendek	Raleigh, NC	Red/White
NC-Asheville	Bulldogs	Big South	Eddie Biedenbach	Asheville, NC	Royal Blue/White
NC-Greensboro	Spartans	Southern	Fran McCaffrey	Greensboro, NC	Gold/White/Navy
NC-Wilmington	Seahawks	Colonial	Brad Brownell	Wilmington, NC	Green/Gold/Navy
North Texas	Mean Green	Sun Belt	Johnny Jones	Denton, TX	Green/White
Northeastern	Huskies	America East	Ron Everhart	Boston, MA	Red/Black
Northern Arizona	Lumberjacks	Big Sky	Mike Adras	Flagstaff, AZ	Blue/Gold
Northern Illinois	Huskies	Mid-American	Rob Judson	De Kalb, IL	Cardinal/Black

NCAA Division I Basketball Schools (Cont.)

	Nickname	Conference	Head Coach	Location	Colors
Northern Iowa	Panthers	Mo. Valley	Greg McDermott	Cedar Falls, IA	Purple/Old Gold
Northwestern	Wildcats	Big Ten	Bill Carmody	Evanston, IL	Purple/White
Northwestern St.	Demons	Southland	Mike McConathy	Natchitoches, LA	Purple/Orange/Wt.
Notre Dame	Fighting Irish	Big East	Mike Brey	Notre Dame, IN	Gold/Blue
Oakland-MI	Pioneers	Mid-Continent	Greg Kampe	Rochester, MI	Black/Gold
Ohio University	Bobcats	Mid-American	Tim O'Shea	Athens, OH	Hunter Green/White
Ohio St.	Buckeyes	Big Ten	Jim O'Brien	Columbus, OH	Scarlet/Gray
Oklahoma	Sooners	Big 12	Kelvin Sampson	Norman, OK	Crimson/Cream
Oklahoma St.	Cowboys	Big 12	Eddie Sutton	Stillwater, OK	Orange/Black
Old Dominion	Monarchs	Colonial	Blaine Taylor	Norfolk, VA	Slate Blue/Silver
Oral Roberts	Golden Eagles	Mid-Continent	Scott Sutton	Tulsa, OK	Navy Blue/White
Oregon	Ducks	Pac-10	Ernie Kent	Eugene, OR	Green/Yellow
Oregon St.	Beavers	Pac-10	Jay John	Corvallis, OR	Orange/Black
Pacific	Tigers	Big West	Bob Thomason	Stockton, CA	Orange/Black
Pennsylvania	Quakers	Ivy	Fran Dunphy	Philadelphia, PA	Red/Blue
Penn St.	Nittany Lions	Big Ten	Jerry Dunn	University Park, PA	Blue/White
Pepperdine	Waves	West Coast	Paul Westphal	Malibu, CA	Blue/Orange
Pittsburgh	Panthers	Big East	Ben Howland	Pittsburgh, PA	Gold/Blue
Portland	Pilots	West Coast	Mike Holton	Portland, OR	Purple/White
Portland St.	Vikings	Big Sky	Heath Schroyer	Portland, OR	Green/White
Prairie View A&M	Panthers	SWAC	Jerry Francis	Prairie View, TX	Purple/Gold
Princeton	Tigers	Ivy	J. Thompson III	Princeton, NJ	Orange/Black
Providence	Friars	Big East	Tim Welsh	Providence, RI	Black/White
Purdue	Boilermakers	Big Ten	Gene Keady	W. Lafayette, IN	Old Gold/Black
Quinnipiac	Bobcats	Northeast	Joe DeSantis	Hamden, CT	Blue/Gold
Radford	Highlanders	Big South	Byron Samuels	Radford, VA	Blue/Red/Green/Wt.
Rhode Island	Rams	Atlantic 10	Jim Baron	Kingston, RI	Lt. Blue/White/Navy
Rice	Owls	WAC	Willis Wilson	Houston, TX	Blue/Gray
Richmond	Spiders	Atlantic 10	Jerry Wainwright	Richmond, VA	Red/Blue
Rider	Broncs	Metro Atlantic	Don Harnum	Lawrenceville, NJ	Cranberry/White
Robert Morris	Colonials	Northeast	Mark Schmidt	Moon Township, PA	Blue/White
Rutgers	Scarlet Knights	Big East	Gary Waters	New Brunswick, NJ	Scarlet
Sacramento St.	Hornets	Big Sky	Jerome Jenkins	Sacramento, CA	Green/Gold
Sacred Heart	Pioneers	Northeast	Dave Bike	Fairfield, CT	Scarlet/White
St. Bonaventure	Bonnies	Atlantic 10	J. Van Breda Kolff	St. Bonaventure, NY	Brown/White
St. Francis-NY	Terriers	Northeast	Ron Ganulin	Brooklyn, NY	Red/Blue
St. Francis-PA	Red Flash	Northeast	Bobby Jones	Loretto, PA	Red/White
St. John's	Red Storm	Big East	Mike Jarvis	Jamaica, NY	Red/White
St. Joseph's-PA	Hawks	Atlantic 10	Phil Martelli	Philadelphia, PA	Crimson/Gray
Saint Louis	Billikens	USA	Brad Soderberg	St. Louis, MO	Blue/White
St. Mary's-CA	Gaels	West Coast	Randy Bennett	Moraga, CA	Red/Blue
St. Peter's	Peacocks	Metro Atlantic	Bob Leckie	Jersey City, NJ	Blue/White
Sam Houston St.	Bearkats	Southland	Bob Marlin	Huntsville, TX	Orange/White
Samford	Bulldogs	Atlantic Sun	Jimmy Tillette	Birmingham, AL	Red/Blue
San Diego	Toreros	West Coast	Brad Holland	San Diego, CA	Lt. Blue/Navy
San Diego St.	Aztecs	Mountain West	Steve Fisher	San Diego, CA	Scarlet/Black
San Francisco	Dons	West Coast	Phil Mathews	San Francisco, CA	Green/Gold
San Jose St.	Spartans	WAC	Phil Johnson	San Jose, CA	Gold/White/Blue
Santa Clara	Broncos	West Coast	Dick Davey	Santa Clara, CA	Bronco Red/White
Savannah St.	Tigers	Independent	Edward Daniels	Savannah, GA	Orange/Blue
Seton Hall	Pirates	Big East	Louis Orr	South Orange, NJ	Blue/White
Siena	Saints	Metro Atlantic	Rob Lanier	Loudonville, NY	Green/Gold
South Alabama	Jaguars	Sun Belt	John Pelphrey	Mobile, AL	Red/White/Blue
South Carolina	Gamecocks	SEC-East	Dave Odom	Columbia, SC	Garnet/Black
South Carolina St.	Bulldogs	Mid-Eastern	Cy Alexander	Orangeburg, SC	Garnet/Blue
South Florida	Bulls	USA	Seth Greenberg	Tampa, FL	Green/Gold
SE Missouri St.	Indians	Ohio Valley	Gary Garner	Cape Girardeau, MO	Red/Black
SE Louisiana	Lions	Southland	Billy Kennedy	Hammond, LA	Green/Gold
Southern Illinois	Salukis	Mo. Valley	Bruce Weber	Carbondale, IL	Maroon/White
SMU	Mustangs	WAC	Mike Dement	Dallas, TX	Red/Blue
Southern Miss	Golden Eagles	USA	James Green	Hattiesburg, MS	Black/Gold
Southern Utah	Thunderbirds	Mid-Continent	Bill Evans	Cedar City, UT	Scarlet/White
Southern-BR	Jaguars	SWAC	Ben Jobe	Baton Rouge, LA	Blue/Gold
SW Missouri St.	Bears	Mo. Valley	Barry Hinson	Springfield, MO	Maroon/White
SW Texas St.	Bobcats	Southland	Dennis Nutt	San Marcos, TX	Maroon/Gold
Stanford	Cardinal	Pac-10	Mike Montgomery	Stanford, CA	Cardinal/White
S.F. Austin St.	Lumberjacks	Southland	Danny Kaspar	Nacogdoches, TX	Purple/White

	Nickname	Conference	Head Coach	Location	Colors
Stetson	Hatters	Atlantic Sun	Derek Waugh	DeLand, FL	Green/White
Stony Brook	Seawolves	America East	Nick Macarchuk	Stony Brook, NY	Scarlet/Gray
Syracuse	Orangemen	Big East	Jim Boeheim	Syracuse, NY	Orange
Temple	Owls	Atlantic 10	John Chaney	Philadelphia, PA	Cherry/White
Tennessee	Volunteers	SEC-East	Buzz Peterson	Knoxville, TN	Orange/White
Tenn-Chattanooga	Mocs	Southern	Jeff Lebo	Chattanooga, TN	Navy Blue/Old Gold
Tenn-Martin	Skyhawks	Ohio Valley	Bret Campbell	Martin, TN	Orange/Wt./Royal Blue
Tennessee St.	Tigers	Ohio Valley	N. Richardson III	Nashville, TN	Blue/White
Tennessee Tech	Golden Eagles	Ohio Valley	Mike Sutton	Cookeville, TN	Purple/Gold
Texas	Longhorns	Big 12	Rick Barnes	Austin, TX	Burnt Orange/White
Texas A&M	Aggies	Big 12	Melvin Watkins	College Station, TX	Maroon/White
TX A&M Corpus-Christi	Islanders	Independent	Ronnie Arrow	Corpus Christi, TX	Blue/Green/Silver
TCU	Horned Frogs	USA	Neil Dougherty	Ft. Worth, TX	Purple/White
Texas Southern	Tigers	SWAC	Ronnie Courtney	Houston, TX	Maroon/Gray
Texas Tech	Red Raiders	Big 12	Bob Knight	Lubbock, TX	Scarlet/Black
TX-Arlington	Mavericks	Southland	Eddie McCarter	Arlington, TX	Royal Blue/White
TX-Pan American	Broncs	Independent	Bob Hoffman	Edinburg, TX	Green/White
TX-San Antonio	Roadrunners	Southland	Tim Carter	San Antonio, TX	Orange/Navy/White
Toledo	Rockets	Mid-American	Stan Joplin	Toledo, OH	Blue/Gold
Towson	Tigers	Colonial	Michael Hunt	Towson, MD	Gold/White/Black
Troy St.	Trojans	Atlantic Sun	Don Maestri	Troy, AL	Cardinal/Silver/Black
Tulane	Green Wave	USA	Shawn Finney	New Orleans, LA	Olive Grn./Sky Blue
Tulsa	Golden Hurricane	WAC	John Phillips	Tulsa, OK	Blue/Red/Gold
UAB	Blazers	USA	Mike Anderson	Birmingham, AL	Green/Gold
UC-Irvine	Anteaters	Big West	Pat Douglass	Irvine, CA	Blue/Gold
UCLA	Bruins	Pac-10	Steve Lavin	Los Angeles, CA	Blue/Gold
UC-Riverside	Highlanders	Big West	John Masi	Riverside, CA	Blue/Gold
UC-Santa Barbara	Gauchos	Big West	Bob Williams	Santa Barbara, CA	Blue/Gold
UNLV	Runnin' Rebels	Mountain West	Charlie Spoonhour	Las Vegas, NV	Scarlet/Gray
USC	Trojans	Pac-10	Henry Bibby	Los Angeles, CA	Cardinal/Gold
Utah	Utes	Mountain West	Rick Majerus	Salt Lake City, UT	Crimson/White
Utah St.	Aggies	Big West	Stew Morrill	Logan, UT	Navy Blue/White
UTEP	Miners	WAC	Jason Rabedeaux	El Paso, TX	Orange/Blue/Wt.
Valparaiso	Crusaders	Mid-Continent	Scott Drew	Valparaiso, IN	Brown/Gold
Vanderbilt	Commodores	SEC-East	Kevin Stallings	Nashville, TN	Black/Gold
Vermont	Catamounts	America East	Tom Brennan	Burlington, VT	Green/Gold
Villanova	Wildcats	Big East	Jay Wright	Villanova, PA	Blue/White
Virginia	Cavaliers	ACC	Pete Gillen	Charlottesville, VA	Orange/Blue
VCU	Rams	Colonial	Jeff Capel III	Richmond, VA	Black/Gold
VMI	Keydets	Southern	Bart Bellairs	Lexington, VA	Red/White/Yellow
Virginia Tech	Hokies, Gobblers	Big East	Ricky Stokes	Blacksburg, VA	Orange/Maroon
Wagner	Seahawks	Northeast	D. Whittenburg	Staten Island, NY	Green/White
Wake Forest	Demon Deacons	ACC	Skip Prosser	Winston-Salem, NC	Old Gold/Black
Washington	Huskies	Pac-10	Lorenzo Romar	Seattle, WA	Purple/Gold
Washington St.	Cougars	Pac-10	Paul Graham	Pullman, WA	Crimson/Gray
Weber St.	Wildcats	Big Sky	Joe Cravens	Ogden, UT	Purple/White
West Virginia	Mountaineers	Big East	John Beilein	Morgantown, WV	Old Gold/Blue
Western Carolina	Catamounts	Southern	Steve Shurina	Cullowhee, NC	Purple/Gold
Western Illinois	Leathernecks	Mid-Continent	Jim Kerwin	Macomb, IL	Purple/Gold
Western Kentucky	Hilltoppers	Sun Belt	Dennis Felton	Bowling Green, KY	Red/White
Western Michigan	Broncos	Mid-American	Robert McCullum	Kalamazoo, MI	Brown/Gold
Wichita St.	Shockers	Mo. Valley	Mark Turgeon	Wichita, KS	Yellow/Black
William & Mary	Tribe	Colonial	Rick Boyages	Williamsburg, VA	Green/Gold/Silver
Winthrop	Eagles	Big South	Gregg Marshall	Rock Hill, SC	Garnet/Gold
Wisconsin	Badgers	Big Ten	Bo Ryan	Madison, WI	Cardinal/White
WI-Green Bay	Phoenix	Horizon	Tod Kowalczyk	Green Bay, WI	Green/White/Red
WI-Milwaukee	Panthers	Horizon	Bruce Pearl	Milwaukee, WI	Black/Gold
Wofford	Terriers	Southern	Mike Young	Spartanburg, SC	Old Gold/Black
Wright St.	Raiders	Horizon	Ed Schilling	Dayton, OH	Green/Gold
Wyoming	Cowboys	Mountain West	Steve McClain	Laramie, WY	Brown/Yellow
Xavier	Musketeers	Atlantic 10	Thad Matta	Cincinnati, OH	Blue/White
Yale	Bulldogs, Elis	Ivy	James Jones	New Haven, CT	Yale Blue/White
Youngstown St.	Penguins	Horizon	John Robic	Youngstown, OH	Red/White

Notre Dame
Tyrone Willingham
Stanford to Notre Dame

Indiana
Gerry DiNardo
XFL to Indiana

Washington
Lorenzo Romar
Saint Louis to Washington

Tenn.-Chattanooga
Jeff Lebo
Tech to Chattanooga

Coaching Changes

New head coaches were named at 13 Division 1-A and 15 Division 1-AA football schools while 43 Division 1 basketball schools changed head coaches after the 2001-02 season. Coaching changes listed below are as of September 1, 2002.

Division I-A Football

	Old Coach	Record	Why Left?	New Coach	Old Job
Arkansas State	Joe Hollis	2-9	fired	Steve Roberts	Coach, Northwestern St.
California	Tom Holmoe	1-10	resigned	Jeff Tedford	Off. coord., Oregon
Florida	Steve Spurrier	10-2	to NFL Washington*	Ron Zook	Def. coord., NFL N. Orleans
Georgia Tech	George O'Leary	8-5&	to Notre Dame*	Chan Gailey	Off. coord., NFL Miami
Indiana	Cam Cameron	5-6	fired	Gerry DiNardo	Coach, XFL Birmingham
Kansas	Terry Allen	3-8†	fired	Mark Mangino	Off. coord., Oklahoma
LA-Lafayette	Jerry Baldwin	3-8	fired	Rickey Bustle	Off. coord., Va. Tech
Navy	Charlie Weatherbie	0-10@	fired	Paul Johnson	Coach, Georgia Southern
Notre Dame	Bob Davie	5-6	fired	George O'Leary	Coach, Georgia Tech
	George O'Leary	—	resigned%	Tyrone Willingham	Coach, Stanford
San Diego St.	Ted Tollner	3-8	fired	Tom Craft	Coach, Palomar JC
SMU	Mike Cavan	4-7	fired	Phil Bennett	Def. coord., Kansas St.
Stanford	Tyrone Willingham	9-3	to Notre Dame*	Buddy Teevens	Asst., Florida
Vanderbilt	Woody Widenhofer	2-9	resigned	Bobby Johnson	Coach, Furman

* as head coach
& O'Leary (7-5) resigned on Dec. 9, 2001 to take the head coaching job at Notre Dame. He was replaced by assistant head coach Mac McWhorter (1-0) for the final game of the season.
† Allen (2-6) was fired on Nov. 4, 2001 and replaced by defensive coordinator Tom Hayes (1-2) for the remainder of the season.
@ Weatherbie (0-7) was fired on Oct. 28, 2001 and replaced by defensive coordinator Rick Lantz (0-3) for the remainder of the season.
% O'Leary resigned on Dec. 14, 2001, just five days into his new position with Notre Dame after various inaccuracies on his resumé were uncovered. See box on following page.

Division I-AA Football

	Old Coach	Record	Why Left?	New Coach	Old Job
Alabama A&M	Ron Cooper	4-7	to Wisconsin**	Anthony Jones	Coach, Morehouse
Butler	Ken LaRose	5-5	resigned	Kit Cartwright	Off., coord., Butler
Delaware	Tubby Raymond	4-6	retired	K.C. Keeler	Coach, Rowan
Furman	Bobby Johnson	12-3	to Vanderbilt*	Bobby Lamb	Asst., Furman
Georgia Southern	Paul Johnson	12-2	to Navy*	Mike Sewak	Off. coord., Ga. Southern
Howard	Steve Wilson	2-9	fired	Rayford T. Petty	Def. coord., Norfolk. St.
La Salle	Bill Manlove	5-4	fired	Archie Stalcup	Def. coord., La Salle
Mississippi Valley St.	LaTraia Jones	0-11	fired	Willie Totten	Off. coord., Miss. Valley St.
Northwestern St.	Steve Roberts	8-4	to Arkansas St.*	Scott Stoker	Def. coord., McNeese St.
Sacred Heart	Jim Fleming	11-0	to North Carolina**	Bill Lacey	Off. coord., Sacred Heart
St. Francis-PA	Dave Jaumotte	0-10	resigned	Dave Opfar	Def. coord., Wash. & Jeff.
Samford	Pete Hurt	5-5†	fired	Bill Gray	Asst., Samford
Savannah St.	Bill Davis	2-7	died after season	Ken Pettiford	Coach, Maplewood (TN) HS
South Carolina St.	Willie Jeffries	6-5	retired	Oliver Pough	Asst., S.C. State
Western Carolina	Bill Bleil	7-4	fired	Kent Briggs	Def. coord., UConn

* as head coach
** as assistant coach
† Hurt (1-4) was fired on Oct. 16, 2001 and replaced by assistant Gray (4-1) for the remainder of the season. On Nov. 26 Gray was given the job on a permanent basis.
Note: Bucknell's head football coach Tom Gadd is taking the 2002 season off to "focus on regaining his health" after being diagnosed with cancer. Associate head coach Dave Kotulski will serve as the head coach for the season.

Division I Basketball

	Old Coach	Record	Why Left?	New Coach	Old Job
Albany	Scott Beeten	8-20†	fired	Will Brown	Asst., Albany
Arkansas	Nolan Richardson	14-15@	fired	Stan Heath	Coach, Kent St.
Arkansas-Pine Bluff	Harold Blevins	2-26	fired	Van Holt	Asst., Ark-Pine Bluff
Army	Pat Harris	12-16	fired	Jim Crews	Coach, Evansville
Bethune Cookman	Horace Broadnax	12-17#	resigned	Clifford Reed	Asst. Bethune Cookman
Boise St.	Rod Jensen	13-17	fired	Greg Graham	Asst., Oregon
Bradley	Jim Molinari	9-20	fired	Jim Les	Asst., WNBA Sacramento
College of Charleston	John Kresse	21-9	retired	Tom Herrion	Asst., Virginia
DePaul	Pat Kennedy	9-19	resigned	Dave Leitao	Asst., UConn
Evansville	Jim Crews	7-21	to Army*	Steve Merfeld	Coach, Hampton
Florida St.	Steve Robinson	12-17	fired	Leonard Hamilton	Fmr. coach, NBA Washington
Fresno St.	Jerry Tarkanian	19-15	retired	Ray Lopes	Asst., Oklahoma
Hampton	Steve Merfeld	26-7	to Evansville*	Bobby Collins	Asst. Hampton
Kent St.	Stan Heath	30-6	to Arkansas*	Jim Christian	Asst., Kent St.
Lehigh	Sal Mentesana	5-23	fired	Bill Taylor	Asst., NC-Greensboro
Liberty	Mel Hankinson	5-25	fired	Randy Dunton	Asst., Binghamton
Long Beach St.	Wayne Morgan	13-17	resigned	Larry Reynolds	Coach, CS-San Bern.
LIU-Brooklyn	Ray Martin	5-22&	resigned	Jim Ferry	Coach, Adelphi
Middle Tennessee St.	Randy Wiel	14-15	resigned	Kermit Davis Jr.	Asst., LSU
Montana	Don Holst	16-15	fired	Pat Kennedy	Coach, DePaul
New Mexico	Fran Fraschilla	16-14	resigned	Ritchie McKay	Coach, Oregon St.
Nicholls St.	Rickey Broussard	2-25	to LSU**	Ricky Blanton	Fmr. asst., Utah St.
NC-Wilmington	Jerry Wainwright	23-10	to Richmond*	Brad Brownell	Asst., NC-Wilmington
Norfolk St.	Wil Jones	10-19	fired	Dwight Freeman	Asst., Miami
Oregon St.	Ritchie McKay	12-17	to New Mexico*	Jay John	Asst. Arizona
Portland St.	Joel Sobotka	12-16	resigned	Heath Schroyer	Asst. Wyoming
Prairie View	Elwood Plummer	10-20	fired	Jerry Francis	Asst. Houston
Radford	Ron Bradley	15-16	to J. Madison**	Byron Samuels	Asst., Radford
Richmond	John Beilein	22-14	to West Virginia*	Jerry Wainwright	Coach, NC-Wilmington
Saint Louis	Lorenzo Romar	15-16	to Washington*	Brad Soderberg	Asst., Saint Louis
San Jose St.	Steve Barnes	10-22	to Iowa St.**	Phil Johnson	Asst., NBA Chicago
Savannah St.	Jack Grant	2-26	fired	Edward Daniels	Coach, Groves (GA) HS
South Alabama	Bob Weltlich	7-21	resigned	John Pelphrey	Asst. Florida
TCU	Billy Tubbs	16-15	resigned	Neil Dougherty	Asst., Kansas
Tenn.-Chattanooga	Henry Dickerson	16-14	fired	Jeff Lebo	Coach, Tennessee Tech
Tennessee Tech	Jeff Lebo	27-7	to Tenn.-Chattanooga*	Mike Sutton	Asst, Kentucky
UAB	Murry Bartow	13-17	resigned	Mike Anderson	Asst., Arkansas
Valparaiso	Homer Drew	25-8	retired	Scott Drew	Asst., Valparaiso
VCU	Mack McCarthy	21-11	resigned	Jeff Capel III	Asst., VCU
Washington	Bob Bender	11-18	resigned	Lorenzo Romar	Coach, Saint Louis
West Virginia	Gale Catlett	8-20$	retired	John Beilein	Coach, Richmond
Wisc.-Green Bay	Mike Heideman	9-21	fired	Tod Kowalczyk	Asst., Marquette
Wofford	Richard Johnson	11-18	promoted to AD	Mike Young	Asst., Wofford

* as head coach
** as assistant coach

† Beeten (1-7) was reassigned on Dec. 20, 2001 and replaced by assistant Brown (7-13) for the remainder of the season. On Mar. 13, 2002 Brown was given the job on a permanent basis.
@ Richardson (13-14) was fired on Mar. 1, 2002 and replaced by assistant Mike Anderson (1-1) for the remainder of the season.
# Broadnax (6-12) resigned on Jan. 31, 2002 and was replaced by assistant Reed (6-5) for the remainder of the season. On Apr. 8, 2002 Reed was given the job on a permanent basis.
& Martin (0-9) resigned on Jan. 3, 2002 and was replaced by assistant Ron Brown (5-13) for the remainder of the season.
$ Catlett (8-15) retired on Feb. 14, 2002 and was replaced by assistant Drew Catlett (0-5) for the remainder of the season.

Resumé Building

In December 2001, George O'Leary abruptly resigned from his new position as head football coach at Notre Dame after admitting he lied about his past academic and athletic achievements. O'Leary's resumé and the Georgia Tech media guide claimed he had a master's degree from New York University and was a three-time letter winner in football at the University of New Hampshire. In actuality, O'Leary took a couple of classes at NYU but never obtained a degree. And he never suited up for a game at UNH.

The increased scrutiny that followed uncovered inaccuracies in the resumés of several more NCAA coaches and athletic department personnel. Among others, Georgia basketball assistant coach Jim Harrick Jr., an assistant basketball coach at Richmond, the new athletic director at Dartmouth, two assistant football coaches at Georgia Tech, and even USOC president Sandra Baldwin were all either let go or reprimanded over resumé exaggerations. New Vanderbilt women's basketball coach Tom Collen was forced to resign in May because he listed two master's degrees from Miami of Ohio on his resumé, but records at the school showed him with only one. A month later it was proven that he really did have two, but it was too late to save Collen's job.

2001-02 Directors' Cup

Officially, the Sears Directors' Cup and sponsored by the National Association of Collegiate Directors of Athletics. Introduced in 1993-94 to honor the nation's best overall NCAA Division I athletic department (combining men's and women's sports), winners in NCAA Division II and III and NAIA were named for the first time following the 1995-96 season.

Standings are computed by NACDA with points awarded for each Div. I school's finish in 20 sports (top 10 scoring sports for both men and women). Div. II schools are awarded points in 14 sports (top 7 scoring sports for both men and women). Div III schools are awarded points in 18 sports (top 9 scoring sports for both men and women). NAIA schools are awarded points in 12 sports (top 6 scoring sports for both men and women). National champions in each sport earn 100 points, while 2nd through 64th-place finishers earn decreasing points depending on the size of the tournament field. Division I-A football points are based on the final ESPN/*USA Today* Coaches' Top 25 poll. Listed below are team conferences (for Div. I only), combined Final Four finishes (1st through 4th place) for men's and women's programs, overall points in **bold** type, and the previous year's ranking (for Div. I only).

Multiple winners: Stanford (8); Williams, MA (6); Simon Fraser, BC and UC-Davis (5).

Division I

		Conf	1-2-3-4	Pts	00-01 Rank			Conf	1-2-3-4	Pts	00-01 Rank
1	Stanford	Pac-10	4-2-2-1	**1499**	1	14	Ohio St.	Big Ten	0-1-0-1	**778.5**	6
2	Texas	Big 12	2-1-1-0	**1110.5**	19	15	Arizona St.	Pac-10	0-0-1-0	**767.5**	9
3	Florida	SEC	0-1-3-2	**1078**	7		USC	Pac-10	1-0-1-1	**767.5**	8
4	N. Carolina	ACC	1-1-1-0	**1065.5**	15	17	Oklahoma	Big 12	1-1-2-0	**760.5**	18
5	UCLA	Pac-10	0-4-2-0	**1026**	2	18	Colorado	Big 12	1-1-0-0	**751.5**	27
6	Michigan	Big Ten	1-0-1-2	**917**	4	19	Auburn	SEC	1-1-1-0	**738.5**	28
7	Minnesota	Big Ten	3-0-1-0	**886.5**	23	20	California	Pac-10	1-0-2-0	**738**	12
8	Georgia	SEC	0-3-1-0	**865**	3	21	Princeton	Ivy	1-1-1-0	**736**	24
9	Arizona	Pac-10	0-2-1-1	**852**	5	22	Nebraska	Big 12	0-0-1-0	**721.5**	13
10	LSU	SEC	2-0-1-1	**842.5**	22	23	BYU	Mountain West	1-0-0-0	**685**	17
11	S. Carolina	SEC	1-1-0-1	**828.5**	25	24	Penn St.	Big Ten	0-1-0-0	**676.5**	10
12	Tennessee	SEC	1-1-3-1	**821**	21	25	Washington	Pac-10	0-1-0-0	**639.5**	14
13	Notre Dame	Big East	0-0-1-0	**806.5**	11						

Division II

		1-2-3-4	Pts			1-2-3-4	Pts
1	UC-Davis	1-0-2-0	**743**	14	Abilene Christian, TX	2-1-1-1	**429.5**
2	Grand Valley St.	0-2-1-0	**687**	15	Central Missouri St.	0-0-1-0	**427.5**
3	UC-San Diego	1-0-1-1	**571.5**	16	North Florida	0-0-0-0	**421**
4	Truman St., MO	1-0-0-1	**541.5**	17	CS-Chico	0-1-1-0	**412**
5	Western St., CO	2-1-2-0	**535.5**		North Dakota St.	1-2-0-0	**412**
6	CS-Bakersfield	1-0-0-0	**530.5**	19	Nebraska-Kearney	0-0-0-0	**395**
7	North Dakota	1-1-0-1	**527**	20	Northern Kentucky	0-0-2-0	**392**
8	Northern Colorado	0-0-0-0	**507.5**	21	Tampa, FL	1-0-0-1	**374**
9	South Dakota St.	0-1-2-0	**465.5**	22	Nebraska-Omaha	0-0-0-0	**351**
10	Indiana, PA	0-0-1-0	**457**	23	Minnesota St.-Mankato	0-0-0-0	**344.5**
11	Barry, FL	1-1-1-1	**450**	24	Florida Southern	1-0-1-0	**344**
12	Adams St., CO	0-1-2-0	**445.5**	25	Lock Haven, PA	0-0-1-0	**343.5**
13	Ashland, OH	0-0-0-1	**437.5**				

Division III

		1-2-3-4	Pts			1-2-3-4	Pts
1	Williams, MA	3-1-1-2	**989**	14	De Pauw, IN	0-0-1-1	**433.5**
2	Ithaca, NY	1-0-3-0	**852**	15	Wartburg, IA	0-1-0-0	**432.5**
3	College of New Jersey	0-1-0-1	**751**	16	Claremont-Mudd-Scripps, CA	0-0-0-0	**422.5**
4	Middlebury, VT	3-0-1-0	**703.5**	17	Washington, MO	0-0-0-0	**421**
5	Emory, GA	0-2-1-0	**673**	18	Ohio Wesleyan	1-0-1-0	**409.5**
6	Wisconsin-Stevens Pt.	0-0-0-1	**656.5**	19	Trinity, TX	0-0-0-1	**399.5**
7	Amherst, MA	0-1-2-0	**623**	20	Wisconsin-Eau Claire	0-0-0-1	**388.5**
8	Wisconsin-Oshkosh	0-1-0-0	**552**	21	Nebraska Wesleyan	0-0-1-0	**385**
9	Wisconsin-La Crosse	3-0-1-3	**512**	22	Central, IA	0-0-0-0	**376**
10	Gustavus Adolphus, MN	0-0-2-0	**509**	23	Johns Hopkins, MD	0-1-1-0	**371.5**
11	Calvin, MI	0-2-0-0	**490**	24	Rowan, NJ	0-0-1-0	**352**
12	Cortland St., NY	1-0-0-0	**485**	25	Wheaton, MA	2-0-0-1	**350**
13	St. Thomas, MN	0-0-0-0	**446.5**				

NAIA

		1-2-3-4	Pts			1-2-3-4	Pts
1	Oklahoma City	3-3-1-0	771	14	California Baptist	0-1-2-0	393
2	Lindenwood, MO	1-0-2-0	704.5	15	Briar Cliff, IA	0-0-1-0	390.5
3	Simon Fraser, BC	1-0-2-1	654	16	Auburn-Montgomery, AL	1-2-0-0	390
4	Azusa Pacific, CA	2-2-2-0	578	17	Life, GA	1-1-1-0	368
5	Malone, OH	0-1-0-0	475	18	McKendree, IL	1-0-0-1	347
6	Cumberland, KY	0-0-0-0	457.5	19	Spring Hill, AL	0-0-0-0	344
7	Westmont, CA	1-0-0-0	451	20	Oklahoma Christian	0-0-1-0	335.5
8	Lewis-Clark, ID	1-0-0-0	449	21	Evangel, MO	1-0-0-0	334.5
9	Oklahoma Baptist	0-1-0-1	444	22	Southern Oregon	0-0-1-0	333
10	Hastings, NE	1-0-1-0	441.5	23	Black Hills St., SD	0-0-0-1	330
11	Mary, ND	0-0-1-0	433	24	Northwestern, IA	0-0-1-0	329
12	Pt. Loma Nazarene, CA	0-1-1-0	414.5	25	Concordia	0-1-0-0	324.5
13	Embry-Riddle, FL	0-0-0-1	414				

NCAA Division I Schools on Probation

As of Sept. 1, 2002, there were 25 Division I member institutions serving NCAA probations.

School	Sport	Yrs	Penalty To End	School	Sport	Yrs	Penalty To End
CS-Fullerton	M Basketball	4	11/13/02	Howard	Baseball	3	11/26/04
SMU	Football	2	12/13/02		M & W Swimming	3	11/26/04
Baylor	M Tennis	2	12/21/02		& M & W Basketball	3	11/26/04
Tennessee St.	Football	3	1/4/03	UNLV	M Basketball	4	12/11/04
	M Tennis	3	1/4/03	Jackson St.	M Track and XC	5	5/16/05
	& M Golf	3	1/4/03	New Mexico St.	M Basketball	4	6/19/05
Miss. Valley St.	No specific sport	2	1/23/03	Marshall	Football	4	12/20/05
Bucknell	M Wrestling	4	2/6/03		& M Basketball	4	12/20/05
Buffalo	M Basketball	2	3/21/03	Kentucky	Football	3	1/30/05
Dayton	M Basketball	3	4/18/03	California	Football	5	3/7/06
CS-Northridge	Football	3	6/1/03	Jacksonville	M Soccer	5	8/30/06
USC	Football	2	8/22/03	Wisconsin	M Basketball	5	10/1/06
	& W Swimming	2	8/22/03		& Football	5	10/1/06
South Alabama	M Basketball	2	12/18/03	Minnesota	W Basketball	4	10/22/06
Nebraska	M Swimming	2	1/22/04		& M Basketball	6	10/22/06
	& Wrestling	2	1/22/04	Alabama	Football	5	1/31/07
Northern Arizona	Football	3	4/17/04				
Stetson	M Basketball	2	5/8/04				

Remaining postseason and TV sanctions
2002-2003 postseason ban: Alabama football, California football, Howard baseball, Kentucky football.
2002-2003 television ban: None.

NCAA Graduation Rates

The following table compares graduation rates of NCAA Division I student athletes with the entire student body in those schools. Years given denote the year in which students entered college. Rates are based on students who enrolled as freshmen, received an athletics scholarship and graduated in six years or less. All figures are percentages.
Source: NCAA Graduation-Rate Report, 2001.

	1989	1990	1991	1992	1993	1994
All Student Athletes	58	58	57	58	58	58
Entire Student Body	57	56	56	56	56	56
Male Student Athletes	53	53	51	52	51	51
Male Student Body	55	54	53	54	54	54
Female Student Athletes	67	68	67	68	68	69
Female Student Body	59	58	58	59	59	59
Div. I-A Football Players	56	52	50	51	48	51
Male Basketball Players	44	45	41	41	42	40
Female Basketball Players	65	67	66	62	63	65

2001-02 NCAA Team Champions

Twelve schools won two or more national championships during the 2001-02 academic year, led by Division I Stanford with four.

Multiple winners: Four—STANFORD (National Div. men's and women's water polo, Div. I women's volleyball, Div. I women's tennis). **Three**—MIDDLEBURY, VT (Div. III men's and women's lacrosse, Div. III women's cross country); MINNESOTA (Div. I men's ice hockey, Div. I wrestling, Div. I men's golf); WISC.-LA CROSSE (Div. III men's cross country, indoor and outdoor track); WILLIAMS, MA (Div. III men's rowing, Div. III men's and women's tennis).

Two—ABILENE CHRISTIAN (Div. II men's indoor and outdoor track); BYU-HAWAII (Div. II men's and women's tennis); KENYON, OH (Div. III men's and women's swimming & diving); LSU (Div. I women's indoor track, Div. I men's outdoor track); TEXAS (Div. I men's swimming & diving, Div. I baseball); WESTERN ST., CO (Div. II men's and women's cross country); WHEATON, MA (Div. III women's indoor and outdoor track).

Overall titles in parentheses; (*) indicates defending champions.

FALL

Cross Country
Men

Div.	Winner		Runner-Up	Score
I	Colorado	(1)	Stanford	90-91
II	Western St., CO*	(4)	Abilene Christian	38-74
III	Wisc.-La Crosse	(2)	Calvin, MI*	80-140

Women

Div.	Winner		Runner-Up	Score
I	Brigham Young	(3)	North Carolina St.	62-148
II	Western St., CO*	(2)	Adams St., CO	46-55
III	Middlebury, VT*	(2)	Williams, MA	98-166

Field Hockey

Div.	Winner		Runner-Up	Score
I	Michigan	(1)	Maryland	2-0
II	Bentley, MA	(1)	E. Stroudsburg, PA	4-2
III	Cortland St., NY	(3)	Messiah, PA	1-0

Football

Div.	Winner		Runner-Up	Score
I-A	Miami-FL	(5)	Nebraska	37-14
I-AA	Montana	(2)	Furman	13-6
II	North Dakota	(1)	Grand Valley St., MI	17-14
III	Mt. Union, OH*	(6)	Bridgewater, MA	30-27

Note: There is no official Div. I-A playoff. Miami-FL defeated Nebraska in the BCS Championship Game (Rose Bowl).

Soccer
Men

Div.	Winner		Runner-Up	Score
I	North Carolina	(1)	Indiana	2-0
II	Tampa	(3)	CS-Dominguez Hills*	2-1
III	Richard Stockton, NJ	(1)	Redlands, CA	3-2

Women

Div.	Winner		Runner-Up	Score
I	Santa Clara	(1)	North Carolina*	1-0
II	UC San Diego*	(2)	Christian Brothers, TN	2-0
III	Ohio Wesleyan	(1)	Amherst, MA	1-0

Volleyball
Women

Div.	Winner		Runner-Up	Score
I	Stanford	(5)	Long Beach St.	3 games
II	Barry, FL	(2)	South Dakota St.	3 games
III	La Verne, CA	(2)	Wisc.-Whitewater	5 games

Water Polo
Men

Div.	Winner		Runner-Up	Score
National	Stanford	(9)	UCLA*	8-5

WINTER

Basketball
Men

Div.	Winner		Runner-Up	Score
I	Maryland	(1)	Indiana	64-52
II	Metropolitan St., CO	(2)	Kentucky Wesleyan*	80-72
III	Otterbein, OH	(1)	Elizabethtown, PA	102-83

Women

Div.	Winner		Runner-Up	Score
I	Connecticut	(3)	Oklahoma	82-70
II	Cal Poly Pomona*	(5)	SE Oklahoma St.	74-62
III	Wisc.-Stevens Point	(2)	St. Lawrence, NY	67-65

Fencing

Div.	Winner		Runner-Up	Score
Combined	Penn St.	(9)	St. John's, NY*	195-190

Gymnastics

Div.	Winner		Runner-Up	Margin
Men	Oklahoma	(4)	Ohio St.*	by .650
Women	Alabama	(4)	Georgia	by .325

Ice Hockey
Men

Div.	Winner		Runner-Up	Score
I	Minnesota	(4)	Maine	4-3 (OT)
III	Wisc.-Superior	(1)	Norwich, VT	3-2 (OT)

Women

Div.	Winner		Runner-Up	Score
National	Minn.-Duluth*	(2)	Brown	3-2
III	Elmira, NY	(1)	Manhattanville, NY	2-1

Note: In 2001-02, women's college hockey was inaugurated as an official NCAA sport at the Division III level. Championships were previously sponsored by the American Women's College Hockey Alliance (AWCHA).

Rifle

Div.	Winner		Runner-Up	Score
Combined	AK-Fairbanks*	(5)	Kentucky	6241-6209

Skiing

Div.	Winner		Runner-Up	Score
Combined	Denver*	(17)	Colorado	656-612

Swimming & Diving
Men

Div.	Winner		Runner-Up	Score
I	Texas*	(9)	Stanford	512-501
II	CS-Bakersfield*	(12)	North Dakota	529-507
III	Kenyon, OH*	(23)	Johns Hopkins	589-382

Women

Div.	Winner		Runner-Up	Score
I	Auburn	(1)	Georgia*	474-386
II	Truman, MO*	(2)	Drury, MO	733-548
III	Kenyon, OH	(18)	Denison, OH*	577-418

Indoor Track
Men

Div.	Winner		Runner-Up	Score
I	Tennessee	(1)	Alabama	62½-47
II	Abilene Christian	(9)	(tie) St. Augustine's, NC & Western St., CO	74-44
III	Wisc.-La Crosse*	(9)	Lincoln, PA	54-48

Women

Div.	Winner		Runner-Up	Score
I	LSU	(9)	UCLA*	57-43
II	North Dakota St.	(1)	St. Augustine's, NC*	67½-45
III	Wheaton, MA*	(4)	Wisc.-Oshkosh	65½-37

Wrestling

Div.	Winner		Runner-Up	Score
I	Minnesota*	(2)	Iowa St.	126½-104
II	Central Oklahoma	(5)	North Dakota St.*	128-116½
III	Augsburg, MN*	(8)	(tie) Upper Iowa & Wartburg, IA	87-81

SPRING
Baseball

Div.	Winner		Runner-Up	Score
I	Texas	(5)	South Carolina	12-6
II	Columbus St., GA	(1)	Cal State Chico	5-3
III	Eastern Conn. St.	(4)	Marietta, OH	8-0

Golf
Men

Div.	Winner		Runner-Up	Score
I	Minnesota	(1)	Georgia Tech	1134-1138
II	Rollins, FL	(2)	Cal St. Stanislaus	1194-1195
III	Guilford, NC	(1)	Greensboro, NC	1212-1218

Women

Div.	Winner		Runner-Up	Score
I	Duke	(2)	3-way tie	1164-1170
II	Fla. Southern*	(3)	Barry, FL	1234-1308
III	Methodist, NC*	(6)	Mary Hardin-Baylor	1310-1341

Lacrosse
Men

Div.	Winner		Runner-Up	Score
I	Syracuse	(7)	Princeton*	13-12
II	Limestone, SC	(2)	New York Tech	11-9
III	Middlebury, VT*	(3)	Gettysburg, PA	14-9

Women

Div.	Winner		Runner-Up	Score
I	Princeton	(2)	Georgetown	12-7
II	West Chester, PA	(1)	Stonehill, MA	11-6
III	Middlebury, VT	(4)	College of NJ	12-6

Rowing
Women

Div.	Winner		Runner-Up	Score
I	Brown	(3)	Washington*	67-63
II	UC Davis	(1)	Western Wash.	50-45
III	Williams, MA	(1)	Colby, ME	9-11

Note: In 2001-02, women's rowing was inaugurated as an official NCAA sport at the Division II and III levels. Since 1997, all three divisions had been grouped into one "National Collegiate Championship."

Softball

Div.	Winner		Runner-Up	Score
I	California	(1)	Arizona*	6-0
II	St. Mary's, TX	(1)	Grand Valley St., MI	6-0
III	Ithaca, NY	(1)	Lake Forest, IL	1-0

Tennis

Note that both Div. II tournaments were team-only.

Men

Div.	Winner		Runner-Up	Score
I	USC	(16)	Georgia*	4-1
II	BYU-Hawaii	(1)	Drury, MO	5-4
III	Williams, MA*	(3)	Emory, GA	4-3

Women

Div.	Winner		Runner-Up	Score
I	Stanford*	(12)	Florida	4-1
II	BYU-Hawaii	(3)	Armstrong Atlantic, GA	5-1
III	Williams, MA*	(2)	Emory, GA	6-3

Outdoor Track
Men

Div.	Winner		Runner-Up	Score
I	LSU	(4)	Tennessee*	64-57
II	Abilene Christian	(12)	St. Augustine's, NC*	91-88
III	Wisc.-La Crosse*	(7)	Calvin, MI	64-41

Women

Div.	Winner		Runner-Up	Score
I	South Carolina	(1)	UCLA	82-72
II	St. Augustine's, NC*	(4)	North Dakota St.	54-53
III	Wheaton, MA*	(2)	McMurry, TX	67-49

Volleyball
Men

Div.	Winner		Runner-Up	Score
National	Hawaii	(1)	Pepperdine	4 games

Water Polo
Women

Div.	Winner		Runner-Up	Score
National	Stanford	(1)	UCLA*	8-4

Real Gender Equity

Schools whose men's and women's teams won NCAA championships in the same sport, or its equivalent during the 2001-02 season.

School	Div.	Sports
BYU-Hawaii	II	Men's Tennis Women's Tennis
Kenyon, OH	III	Men's Swimming & Diving Women's Swimming & Diving
Middlebury, VT	III	Men's Lacrosse Women's Lacrosse
Stanford	Nat.	Men's Water Polo Women's Water Polo
Western St., CO	II	Men's Cross Country Women's Cross Country
Williams, MA	III	Men's Tennis Women's Tennis

St. John's
Ivan Lee
Fencing

AK-Fairbanks
Matthew Emmons
Rifle

UCLA
Jamie Dantzscher
Gymnastics

Denver
Ola Berger
Skiing

2001-02 Division I Individual Champions
Repeat champions in **bold** type.

FALL
Cross Country

Men (10,000 meters)	**Time**
1 Boaz Cheboiywo, Eastern Michigan	28:47
2 Jorge Torres, Colorado	29:06
3 Alistair Cragg, Arkansas	29:10

Women (6,000 meters)	**Time**
1 Tara Chaplin, Arizona	20:24
2 Renee Metvier, Georgia Tech	20:31
3 Lauren Fleshman, Stanford	20:35

WINTER
Fencing
Men

Event		Score
Foil	Nonpatat Panchan, Penn St.	15-13
Epee	Arpad Horvath, St. John's, NY	15-9
Sabre	**Ivan Lee**, St. John's, NY	15-9

Women

Event		Score
Foil	Alicja Kryczalo, Notre Dame	15-6
Epee	Kerry Walton, Notre Dame	15-12
Sabre	**Sada Jacobson**, Yale	15-9

Gymnastics
Men

Event		Points
All-Around	Raj Bhavsar, Ohio St.	55.875
Floor Exercise	**Clay Strother**, Minnesota	9.612
Pommel Horse	**Clay Strother**, Minnesota	9.775
Rings	Marshall Erwin, Stanford	9.825
Vault	Dan Gill, Stanford	9.487
Parallel Bars	Cody Moore, California	9.125
Horizontal Bar	Daniel Diaz-Luong, Michigan	9.612

Women

Event		Points
All-Around	Jamie Dantzscher, UCLA	39.675
Vault	Jamie Dantzscher, UCLA	9.9565
Uneven Bars	Andree' Pickens, Alabama	9.925
Balance Beam	Elise Ray, Michigan	9.925
Floor Exercise	Jamie Dantzscher, UCLA	9.950
	& Nicole Arnstad, LSU	9.950

Rifle
Combined
Number in parentheses denotes inner tens.
Smallbore

		Points
1 Matthew Emmons, AK-Fairbanks		1190 (96)
2 Hannah Kerr, Xavier		1179 (77)
3 Bradley Wheeldon, Kentucky		1175 (76)

Air Rifle

		Points
1 Ryan Tanoue, Nevada		392 (29)
2 Matthew Emmons, AK-Fairbanks		392 (26)
3 James Nash, Kentucky		391 (21)

Note: Tanoue won the event over Emmons due to more inner tens.

Skiing
Men

Event		Time
Slalom	Roger Brown, Dartmouth	1:43.60
Giant Slalom	Tommi Viirret, Nevada	2:14.42
10-k Classic	Ola Berger, Denver	27:33.5
20-k Freestyle	Ola Berger, Denver	51:28.8

Women

Event		Time
Slalom	Marte Dolve, New Mexico	1:31.24
Giant Slalom	Aurore De Maulmont, AK-Anchorage	1:55.90
5-k Classic	Mari Storeng, Colorado	15:27.0
15-k Freestyle	**Katerina Hanusova**, Nevada	42:57.9

Wrestling

Wgt	Champion	Runner-Up
125	**Stephen Abas**, Fresno St.	L. Eustice, Iowa
133	Johnny Thompson, Okla. St.	Ryan Lewis, Minnesota
141	Aaron Holker, Iowa St.	E. Larkin, Arizona St.
149	Jared Lawrence, Minnesota	Jared Frayer, Oklahoma
157	Luke Becker, Minnesota	B. Snyder, Nebraska
165	Joe Heskett, Iowa St.	M. Lackey, Illinois
174	Greg Jones, W. Virginia	G. Parker, Princeton
184	Rob Rohn, Lehigh	J. Lambrecht, Oklahoma
197	Cael Sanderson*, Iowa St.	J. Trenge, Lehigh
Hvy	Tommy Rowlands, Ohio St.	S. Mocco, Iowa

* Sanderson won titles the three previous years in the 184-lb class.

California
Natalie Coughlin
Swimming

Duke
V. Nirapathpongporn
Golf

Tennessee
Justin Gatlin
Track & Field

USC
Angela Williams
Track and Field

Swimming & Diving
(*) indicates meet record.

Men

Event (yards)		Time
50 free	Roland Schoeman, Arizona	19.08
100 free	**Anthony Ervin**, California	41.62*
200 free	Adam Sioui, Florida	1:34.67
500 free	**Klete Keller**, USC	4:12.83
1650 free	Erik Vendt, USC	14:37.48
100 back	Peter Marshall, Stanford	45.91
200 back	Markus Rogan, Stanford	1:41.52
100 breast	**Brendan Hansen**, Texas	52.47
200 breast	**Brendan Hansen**, Texas	1:52.88*
100 butterfly	**Ian Crocker**, USC	45.44*
200 butterfly	Ioan Gherghel, Alabama	1:42.68
200 IM	Markus Rogan, Stanford	1:44.03
400 IM	Erik Vendt, USC	3:40.65
200 free relay	**Stanford**	1:16.49*
400 free relay	California	2:50.01
800 free relay	USC	6:17.35*
200 medley relay	Stanford	1:25.47
400 medley relay	Stanford	3:06.81

Diving		Points
1-meter	**Troy Dumais**, Texas	390.35
3-meter	**Troy Dumais**, Texas	673.80
Platform	Imre Lengyel, Miami-FL	620.25

Women

Event (yards)		Time
50 free	Maritza Correia, Georgia	21.69*
100 free	Maritza Correia, Georgia	47.56*
200 free	**Sarah Tolar**, Arizona	1:44.66
500 free	Flavia Rigamonti, SMU	4:40.13
1650 free	Flavia Rigamonti, SMU	15:52.28
100 back	**Natalie Coughlin**, California	49.97*
200 back	**Natalie Coughlin**, California	1:49.52*
100 breast	**Tara Kirk**, Stanford	59.03
200 breast	Tara Kirk, Stanford	2:07.36*
100 butterfly	**Natalie Coughlin**, California	50.01*
200 butterfly	Shelly Ripple, Stanford	1:53.23*
200 IM	**Maggie Bowen**, Auburn	1:53.91*
400 IM	**Maggie Bowen**, Auburn	4:04.69
200 free relay	Georgia	1:28.74*
400 free relay	Georgia	3:13.71*
800 free relay	Arizona	7:05.10
200 medley relay	**Stanford**	1:37.79
400 medley relay	**Stanford**	3:31.74*

Diving		Points
1-meter	Blythe Hartley, USC	350.85
3-meter	**Yulia Pakhalina**, Houston	625.05
Platform	Blythe Hartley, USC	460.35

Indoor Track
(*) indicates meet record

Men

Event		Time
60 meters	Justin Gatlin, Tennessee	6.59
200 meters	Justin Gatlin, Tennessee	20.63
400 meters	Alleyene Francique, LSU	45.58*
800 meters	Otukile Lekote, South Carolina	1:46.88
Mile	Christian Goy, Illinois St.	4:00.06
3000 meters	Adrian Blincoe, Villanova	8:01.76
5000 meters	Alistair Cragg, Arkansas	13:49.80
60-m hurdles	Ron Bramlett, Alabama	7.59
4x400-m relay	Baylor	3:05.54
Distance medley relay	Villanova	9:31.00

Event		Hgt/Dist
High Jump	Tora Harris, Princeton	7-5
Pole Vault	Jeff Hansen, BYU	17-11¾
Long Jump	Miguel Pate, Alabama	27-4½
Triple Jump	**Walter Davis**, LSU	56-6½
Shot Put	Carl Meyerscough, Nebraska	69-9
35-lb Throw	Scott Russell, Kansas	80-11¼

Women

Event		Time
60 meters	Angela Williams, USC	7.13*
200 meters	Muna Lee, LSU	22.82*
400 meters	Allison Beckford, Rice	52.16
800 meters	Marian Burnett, LSU	2:05.33
Mile	Heather Sagan, Liberty	4:38.52
3000 meters	Lauren Fleshman, Stanford	9:07.45
5000 meters	Siri Alfheim, Oklahoma St.	16:12.28
60-m hurdles	Perdita Felicien, Illinois	7.90*
4x400-m relay	**South Carolina**	3:30.36
Distance medley relay	UCLA	10:58.19*

Event		Hgt/Dist
High Jump	Darnesha Griffith, UCLA	6-0¾
Pole Vault	Amy Linnen, Arizona	14-10¼*
Long Jump	Elva Goulbourne, Auburn	21-11
Triple Jump	Nicole Toney, LSU	45-0¼
Shot Put	Cleopatra Borel, UMBC	57-5
20-lb Throw	Candice Scott, Florida	75-7½#

#In a post-meet inspection it was determined the implement thrown by Scott did not meet proper specifications for record verification. However, second-place finisher Jamine Moton of Clemson was given credit for setting a new meet record with her throw of 73-10.

SPRING
Golf
Men

		Total
1	Troy Matteson, Georgia Tech	73-66-70-67—276
2	Adam Rubinson, TCU	69-67-72-69—277
3	Hunter Mahan, Oklahoma St.	68-71-67-72—278

Women

	Total
1 Virada Nirapathpongporn, Duke	.68-69-70-72—279*
2 Danielle Downey, Auburn	.73-69-70-72—284
Lorena Ochoa, Arizona	.71-69-71-73—284
Summer Sirmons, Georgia	.69-68-73-74—284
Lindsey Wright, Pepperdine	.70-71-71-72—284

* Score tied NCAA championship record.

Tennis

Men

Singles— Matias Boeker (Georgia) def. Jesse Witten (Kentucky), 7-5, 6-0.
Doubles— Andrew Colombo & Mark Kovacs (Auburn) def. Scott Lipsky & David Martin (Stanford), 6-2, 3-6, 6-2.

Women

Singles— Bea Bielik (Wake Forest) def. Jessica Lehnhoff (Florida), 6-2, 6-0.
Doubles— Lauren Kalvaria & Gabriela Lastra (Stanford) def. Megan Bradley & Lauren Fisher (UCLA), 6-2, 6-3.

Outdoor Track

(*) indicates meet record

Men

Event	Time
100 meters	**Justin Gatlin**, Tennessee	10.22
200 meters	**Justin Gatlin**, Tennessee	20.18
400 meters	Gary Kikaya, Tennessee	44.53
800 meters	**Otukile Lekote**, S. Carolina	1:45.17
1500 meters	Donald Sage, Stanford	3:42.65
5000 meters	David Kimani, Alabama	13:59.30
10,000 meters	Boaz Cheboiywo, Eastern Mich.	28:32.10
110-m hurdles	**Ron Bramlett**, Alabama	13.49
400-m hurdles	Rickey Harris, Florida	48.16
3000-m steeple	**Daniel Lincoln**, Arkansas	8:22.34
4x100-m relay	LSU	38.48
4x400-m relay	South Carolina	3:02.16

Event	Hgt/Dist
High Jump	Tora Harris, Princeton	7-4½
Pole Vault	Brian Hunter, Texas	18-8¼
Long Jump	Walter Davis, LSU	26-6¼
Triple Jump	**Walter Davis**, LSU	56-10¾
Shot Put	**Janus Robberts**, SMU	70-10½
Discus	Janus Robberts, SMU	204-7
Javelin	Scott Russell, Kansas	262-0
Hammer	**Andras Haklits**, Georgia	253-8
Decathlon	Claston Bernard, LSU	8094 pts

Women

Event	Time
100 meters	**Angela Williams**, USC	11.29
200 meters	Natasha Mayers, USC	22.93
400 meters	**Allison Beckford**, Rice	50.83
800 meters	Alice Schmidt, N. Carolina	2:04.73
1500 meters	Lena Nilsson, UCLA	4:12.60
3000 meters	Michaela Manova, BYU	9:45.94*
5000 meters	**Lauren Fleshman**, Stanford	15:53.91
10,000 meters	Kristin Price, N.C. State	34:26.63
100-m hurdles	Perdita Felicien, Illinois	12.91
400-m hurdles	Leshinda Demus, S. Carolina	54.85
4x100-m relay	South Carolina	43.12
4x400-m relay	South Carolina	3:26.46*

Event	Hgt/Dist
High Jump	Darnesha Griffith, UCLA	6-0
Pole Vault	Tracy O'Hara, UCLA	13-9¼
Long Jump	Elva Goulbourne, Auburn	22-4½
Triple Jump	Teresa Bundy, Florida St.	44-0
Shot Put	Jessica Cosby, UCLA	57-0¼
Discus	Chaniqua Ross, UCLA	182-0
Javelin	Serene Ross, Purdue	195-8
Hammer	Jamine Moton, Clemson	220-6*
Heptathlon	**Austra Skujyte**, Kansas St.	6061 pts*

2001-02 NAIA Team Champions

Total NAIA titles in parentheses.

FALL

Cross Country: MEN'S–Life, GA (4); WOMEN'S–Cedarville, OH (1). **Football:** MEN'S–Georgetown, KY (3). **Soccer:** MEN'S–Lindsey Wilson, KY (6); WOMEN'S–Westmont, CA (3). **Volleyball:** WOMEN'S–Columbia, MO (3).

WINTER

Basketball: MEN'S–Division I: Science and Arts, OK (1) and Division II: Evangel, MO (1); WOMEN'S–Division I: Oklahoma City (5) and Division II: Hastings, NE (1). **Swimming & Diving:** MEN'S–Seattle, WA (1); WOMEN'S–Simon Fraser, BC (9). **Indoor Track:** MEN'S–Azusa Pacific, CA (2); WOMEN'S–McKendree, IL (4). **Wrestling:** MEN'S–Lindenwood, MO (1).

SPRING

Baseball: MEN'S–Lewis-Clark St., ID (12). **Golf:** MEN'S–Oklahoma City (2); WOMEN'S–Southern Nazarene, OK (2). **Softball:** WOMEN'S–Oklahoma City (7). **Tennis:** MEN'S–Auburn-Montgomery, AL (4); WOMEN'S–Brenau, GA (2). **Outdoor Track:** MEN'S–Azusa Pacific, CA (13); WOMEN'S–Doane, NE (2).

Annual NCAA Division I Team Champions

Men's and women's NCAA Division I team champions from cross country to wrestling. Also see team champions for baseball, basketball, football, golf, ice hockey, soccer and tennis in the appropriate chapters throughout the almanac. See pages 458-460 for list of 2001-02 individual champions.

CROSS COUNTRY

Men

Colorado placed three finishers in the top 20 to win its first Division I cross country title, edging Stanford by just one point. Three-time defending champ Arkansas came in third. Jorge Torres paced the Buffaloes with a second place finish, while Dathan Ritzenheim and Ed Torres finished fourth and 15th, respectively. Eastern Michigan's Boaz Cheboiywo won the individual title, completing the 10,000-meter course in 28:47, breaking the course record by seven seconds. (*Greenville, SC; Nov. 19, 2001.*)

Multiple winners: Arkansas (11); Michigan St. (8); UTEP (7); Oregon and Villanova (4); Drake, Indiana, Penn St. and Wisconsin (3); Iowa St., San Jose St., Stanford and Western Michigan (2).

Year		Year		Year		Year		Year	
1938	Indiana	1950	Penn St.	1963	San Jose St.	1976	UTEP	1989	Iowa St.
1939	Michigan St.	1951	Syracuse	1964	Western Mich.	1977	Oregon	1990	Arkansas
1940	Indiana	1952	Michigan St.	1965	Western Mich.	1978	UTEP	1991	Arkansas
1941	Rhode Island	1953	Kansas	1966	Villanova	1979	UTEP	1992	Arkansas
1942	Indiana	1954	Oklahoma St.	1967	Villanova	1980	UTEP	1993	Arkansas
	& Penn St.	1955	Michigan St.	1968	Villanova	1981	UTEP	1994	Iowa St.
1943	Not held	1956	Michigan St.	1969	UTEP	1982	Wisconsin	1995	Arkansas
1944	Drake	1957	Notre Dame	1970	Villanova	1983	Vacated	1996	Stanford
1945	Drake	1958	Michigan St.	1971	Oregon	1984	Arkansas	1997	Stanford
1946	Drake	1959	Michigan St.	1972	Tennessee	1985	Wisconsin	1998	Arkansas
1947	Penn St.	1960	Houston	1973	Oregon	1986	Arkansas	1999	Arkansas
1948	Michigan St.	1961	Oregon St.	1974	Oregon	1987	Arkansas	2000	Arkansas
1949	Michigan St.	1962	San Jose St.	1975	UTEP	1988	Wisconsin	2001	Colorado

Women

Brigham Young won its third Division I cross country title in the past five years in a landslide, placing all five scorers in the top 25. Michaela Manova (fifth) was Brigham Young's top finisher while Jessie Kindschi (seventh) and Tara Northcutt (ninth) also grabbed spots in the top 10. They amassed a total of just 62 points to soundly beat runner-up N.C. State (148) and third-place Georgetown (180). Arizona's Tara Chaplin won the 6000-meter race in 20:24, seven seconds ahead of Georgia Tech's Renee Metvier. (*Greenville, SC; Nov. 29, 2001.*)

Multiple winners: Villanova (7); Brigham Young (3); Oregon, Virginia and Wisconsin (2).

Year		Year		Year		Year		Year	
1981	Virginia	1986	Texas	1991	Villanova	1996	Stanford	2001	Brigham Young
1982	Virginia	1987	Oregon	1992	Villanova	1997	Brigham Young		
1983	Oregon	1988	Kentucky	1993	Villanova	1998	Villanova		
1984	Wisconsin	1989	Villanova	1994	Villanova	1999	Brigham Young		
1985	Wisconsin	1990	Villanova	1995	Providence	2000	Colorado		

FENCING

Men & Women

After a runner-up finish to St. John's in 2001, Penn St. reclaimed its spot atop the college fencing world with its ninth title since 1990. With 195 points, the Nittany Lions finished ahead of St. John's (190) and Notre Dame (186). Penn State garnered just one individual victory — Nonpatat Panchan in the men's foil — while Stephanie Eim took second place to Notre Dame's Kerry Walton in the women's epée. St. John's Ivan Lee and Yale's Sada Jacobson successfully defended their 2001 titles in the sabre. (*Madison, NJ; Mar. 21-24, 2002.*)

Multiple winners: Penn St. (9); Columbia/Barnard (2). **Note:** Prior to 1990, men and women held separate championships. Men's multiple winners included: NYU (12); Columbia (11); Wayne St. (7); Navy, Notre Dame and Penn (3); Illinois (2). Women's multiple winners included: Wayne St. (3); Yale (2).

Year		Year		Year		Year	
1990	Penn St.	1994	Notre Dame	1998	Penn St.	2002	Penn St.
1991	Penn St.	1995	Penn St.	1999	Penn St.		
1992	Columbia/Barnard	1996	Penn St.	2000	Penn St.		
1993	Columbia/Barnard	1997	Penn St.	2001	St. John's		

FIELD HOCKEY

Women

Adrienne Hortillosa scored the game-winning goal with 2:13 remaining in the first half to lead Michigan to a 2-0 win over Maryland and its first NCAA field hockey title. Junior Jessica Rose added the insurance goal early in the second half and goaltender Maureen Tasch took care of the rest, turning away 20 Maryland shots for the shutout. Michigan ended the year with an 18-5 mark, while Maryland's loss put them at 20-4. (*Kent, OH; Nov. 18, 2001.*)

Multiple winners: Old Dominion (9); North Carolina (4); Maryland (3); Connecticut (2).

Year		Year		Year		Year		Year	
1981	Connecticut	1986	Iowa	1991	Old Dominion	1996	North Carolina	2001	Michigan
1982	Old Dominion	1987	Maryland	1992	Old Dominion	1997	North Carolina		
1983	Old Dominion	1988	Old Dominion	1993	Maryland	1998	Old Dominion		
1984	Old Dominion	1989	North Carolina	1994	J. Madison	1999	Maryland		
1985	Connecticut	1990	Old Dominion	1995	North Carolina	2000	Old Dominion		

Annual NCAA Division I Team Champions (Cont.)

GYMNASTICS
Men

Tournament host Oklahoma won its fourth overall men's gymnastics title by just .650 points over defending champ Ohio St. California placed third for the second consecutive year. Daniel Furney led the Sooners to their first title since 1991 and finished third in the individual all-around competition and third in the vault. Ohio State's Raj Bhavsar won the all-around individual title, and Minnesota's Clay Strother repeated as champion in the pommel horse and floor exercise. (*Norman, OK; Apr. 4-6, 2002.*)

Multiple winners: Penn St. (10); Illinois (9); Nebraska (8); California, Oklahoma and So. Illinois (4); Iowa St., Michigan, Ohio St. and Stanford (3); Florida St and UCLA (2).

Year	Year	Year	Year	Year
1938 Chicago	1956 Illinois	1969 Iowa	1980 Nebraska	1994 Nebraska
1939 Illinois	1957 Penn St.	& Michigan (T)	1981 Nebraska	1995 Stanford
1940 Illinois	1958 Michigan St.	1970 Michigan	1982 Nebraska	1996 Ohio St.
1941 Illinois	& Illinois	& Michigan (T)	1983 Nebraska	1997 California
1942 Illinois	1959 Penn St.	1971 Iowa St.	1984 UCLA	1998 California
1943-47 Not held	1960 Penn St.	1972 So. Illinois	1985 Ohio St.	1999 Michigan
1948 Penn St.	1961 Penn St.	1973 Iowa St.	1986 Arizona St.	2000 Penn St.
1949 Temple	1962 USC	1974 Iowa St.	1987 UCLA	2001 Ohio St.
1950 Illinois	1963 Michigan	1975 California	1988 Nebraska	2002 Oklahoma
1951 Florida St.	1964 So. Illinois	1976 Penn St.	1989 Illinois	(T) indicates won
1952 Florida St.	1965 Penn St.	1977 Indiana St.	1990 Nebraska	trampoline competi-
1953 Penn St.	1966 So. Illinois	& Oklahoma	1991 Oklahoma	tion (1969-70).
1954 Penn St.	1967 So. Illinois	1978 Oklahoma	1992 Stanford	
1955 Illinois	1968 California	1979 Nebraska	1993 Stanford	

Women

Alabama overcame the loss of star Raegan Tomasek (injured during the preliminaries) to win its fourth Division I women's gymnastics championship in front of its home crowd. The Crimson Tide was led by senior Andree' Pickens, who took second in the individual all-around competition and won the uneven bars. UCLA's Jamie Dantzscher won the all-around title, as well as the vault and the floor exercise, which she shared with LSU's Nicole Arnstad. Coach Suzanne Yoculan's Georgia squad placed second while UCLA took third. (*Tuscaloosa, AL; Apr. 18-20, 2002.*)

Multiple winners: Utah (9); Georgia (5); Alabama (4); UCLA (3).

Year	Year	Year	Year	Year
1982 Utah	1987 Georgia	1992 Utah	1997 UCLA	2002 Alabama
1983 Utah	1988 Alabama	1993 Georgia	1998 Georgia	
1984 Utah	1989 Georgia	1994 Utah	1999 Georgia	
1985 Utah	1990 Utah	1995 Utah	2000 UCLA	
1986 Utah	1991 Alabama	1996 Alabama	2001 UCLA	

LACROSSE
Men

For the third consecutive year it was Princeton battling Syracuse for the Division I men's lacrosse championship. In 2000, Syracuse took home the title with a 13-7 win. In 2001 it was Princeton's turn in a 10-9 overtime thriller. And in 2002, Syracuse reclaimed the crown as they upended the Tigers 13-12 for its record-tying seventh championship. The tournament's most outstanding player, Michael Powell, scored four goals for Syracuse and added two more in the team's semifinal victory over Virginia. (*New Brunswick, NJ; May 25-27, 2002.*)

Multiple winners: Johns Hopkins and Syracuse (7); Princeton (6); North Carolina (4); Cornell (3); Maryland and Virginia (2).

Year	Year	Year	Year	Year
1971 Cornell	1978 Johns Hopkins	1985 Johns Hopkins	1992 Princeton	1999 Virginia
1972 Virginia	1979 Johns Hopkins	1986 North Carolina	1993 Syracuse	2000 Syracuse
1973 Maryland	1980 Johns Hopkins	1987 Johns Hopkins	1994 Princeton	2001 Princeton
1974 Johns Hopkins	1981 North Carolina	1988 Syracuse	1995 Syracuse	2002 Syracuse
1975 Maryland	1982 North Carolina	1989 Syracuse	1996 Princeton	
1976 Cornell	1983 Syracuse	1990 Syracuse*	1997 Princeton	
1977 Cornell	1984 Johns Hopkins	1991 North Carolina	1998 Princeton	

*Title was later vacated due to action by the NCAA Committee on Infractions.

Women

Princeton took down Georgetown, 12-7, in the Division I women's lacrosse championship game for its first title since 1994 and second overall. The teams were all square, 4-4, heading into halftime, but Princeton exploded for eight goals in the second stanza, two off the stick of tournament most outstanding player Lauren Simone. It was the second consecutive runner-up finish for the Hoyas. Lindsey Biles also scored three times for Princeton while Wick Stanwick netted four for Georgetown. (*Baltimore, MD; May 17-19, 2002.*)

Multiple winners: Maryland (9); Penn St., Princeton, Temple and Virginia (2).

Year	Year	Year	Year	Year
1982 Massachusetts	1987 Penn St.	1992 Maryland	1997 Maryland	2002 Princeton
1983 Delaware	1988 Temple	1993 Virginia	1998 Maryland	
1984 Temple	1989 Penn St.	1994 Princeton	1999 Maryland	
1985 New Hampshire	1990 Harvard	1995 Maryland	2000 Maryland	
1986 Maryland	1991 Virginia	1996 Maryland	2001 Maryland	

RIFLE

Men & Women

Matthew Emmons successfully defended his title in the individual smallbore competition, took second in the air rifle discipline and led Alaska-Fairbanks to its fourth consecutive NCAA rifle championship. The Nanooks compiled 6,241 points to best runner-up Kentucky (6,209) and third-place Xavier (6,204). Nevada's Ryan Tanoue won the individual air rifle title in a squeaker over Emmons. (*Murray, KY; Mar. 14-16, 2002.*)

Multiple winners: West Virginia (13); Alaska-Fairbanks (5); Tennessee Tech (3); Murray St. (2).

Year		Year		Year		Year		Year	
1980	Tenn. Tech	1985	Murray St.	1990	West Virginia	1995	West Virginia	2000	AK-Fairbanks
1981	Tenn. Tech	1986	West Virginia	1991	West Virginia	1996	West Virginia	2001	AK-Fairbanks
1982	Tenn. Tech	1987	Murray St.	1992	West Virginia	1997	West Virginia	2002	AK-Fairbanks
1983	West Virginia	1988	West Virginia	1993	West Virginia	1998	West Virginia		
1984	West Virginia	1989	West Virginia	1994	AK-Fairbanks	1999	AK-Fairbanks		

ROWING

NCAA Championships
Women

One thing's for sure—there's no debating who the top two women's collegiate rowing teams are. For the sixth consecutive year, Brown and Washington fought tooth and nail for the championship and in 2002 Brown won its third title, tying Washington for the most all-time. Unlike the previous five years, the team that won the Varsity Eights did not win the overall competition. Washington won its fourth Varsity Eights, completing the 2,000-meter course in 6:36.41. Brown (6:39.87) outlasted California (6:40.96) for second place, which gave the Bears enough points for the title. Brown, whose only victory came in the Fours, finished with 67 points, while Washington came in second with 63 and California was third with 44. (*Indianapolis, IN; May 31-June 2, 2002*).

Multiple winners: Brown and Washington (3).

Year	Overall winner	Varsity Eights	Year	Overall winner	Varsity Eights
1997	Washington	Washington	2000	Brown	Brown
1998	Washington	Washington	2001	Washington	Washington
1999	Brown	Brown	2002	Brown	Washington

Intercollegiate Rowing Association Regatta
VARSITY EIGHTS
Men

California started strong, jumped out to a three-quarters of a length lead at the 1,000-meter mark and cruised to the Varsity Eights title at the 100th IRA Championships Regatta. It was the fourth consecutive win, and 14th overall, for the Bears. They crossed the finish line in 5:26.81, three seconds off the course record and well ahead of runner-up Wisconsin (5:28.32) and third-place Washington (5:30.25). (*Cooper River, Camden, NJ; May 30-June 1, 2002.*)

The IRA was formed in 1895 by several Northeastern colleges after Harvard and Yale quit the Rowing Association (established in 1871) to stage an annual race of their own. Since then the IRA Regatta has been contested over courses of varying lengths in Poughkeepsie, N.Y., Marietta, Ohio, Syracuse, N.Y. and Camden, N.J.

Distances: 4 miles (1895-97,1899-1916,1925-41); 3 miles (1898,1921-24,1947-49,1952-63,1965-67); 2 miles (1920,1950-51); 2000 meters (1964, since 1968).

Multiple winners: Cornell (24); California (14); Navy (13); Washington (11); Penn (9); Brown and Wisconsin (7); Syracuse (6); Columbia (4); Princeton (3); Northeastern (2).

Year		Year		Year		Year		Year	
1895	Columbia	1916	Syracuse	1939	California	1964	California	1985	Princeton
1896	Cornell	1917-19	Not held	1940	Washington	1965	Navy	1986	Brown
1897	Cornell	1920	Syracuse	1941	Washington	1966	Wisconsin	1987	Brown
1898	Penn	1921	Navy	1942-46	Not held	1967	Penn	1988	Northeastern
1899	Penn	1922	Navy	1947	Navy	1968	Penn	1989	Penn
1900	Penn	1923	Washington	1948	Washington	1969	Penn	1990	Wisconsin
1901	Cornell	1924	Washington	1949	California	1970	Washington	1991	Northeastern
1902	Cornell	1925	Navy	1950	Washington	1971	Cornell	1992	Dartmouth,
1903	Cornell	1926	Washington	1951	Wisconsin	1972	Penn		Navy & Penn†
1904	Syracuse	1927	Columbia	1952	Navy	1973	Wisconsin	1993	Brown
1905	Cornell	1928	California	1953	Navy	1974	Wisconsin	1994	Brown
1906	Cornell	1929	Columbia	1954	Navy*	1975	Wisconsin	1995	Brown
1907	Cornell	1930	Cornell	1955	Cornell	1976	California	1996	Princeton
1908	Syracuse	1931	Navy	1956	Cornell	1977	Cornell	1997	Washington
1909	Cornell	1932	California	1957	Cornell	1978	Syracuse	1998	Princeton
1910	Cornell	1933	Not held	1958	Cornell	1979	Brown	1999	California
1911	Cornell	1934	California	1959	Wisconsin	1980	Navy	2000	California
1912	Cornell	1935	California	1960	California	1981	Cornell	2001	California
1913	Syracuse	1936	Washington	1961	California	1982	Cornell	2002	California
1914	Columbia	1937	Washington	1962	Cornell	1983	Brown		
1915	Cornell	1938	Navy	1963	Cornell	1984	Navy		

*In 1954, Navy was disqualified because of an ineligible coxswain; no trophies were given.
†First dead heat in history of IRA Regatta.

Annual NCAA Division I Team Champions (Cont.)

National Rowing Championship
VARSITY EIGHTS
Men

National championship raced annually from 1982-96 in Bantam, Ohio over a 2,000-meter course on Lake Harsha. Winner received the Herschede Cup. Regatta discontinued in 1997.

Multiple winners: Harvard (6); Brown (3); Wisconsin (2).

Year	Champion	Time	Runner-up	Time	Year	Champion	Time	Runner-up	Time
1982	Yale	5:50.8	Cornell	5:54.15	1990	Wisconsin	5:52.5	Harvard	5:56.84
1983	Harvard	5:59.6	Washington	6:00.0	1991	Penn	5:58.21	Northeastern	5:58.48
1984	Washington	5:51.1	Yale	5:55.6	1992	Harvard	5:33.97	Dartmouth	5:34.28
1985	Harvard	5:44.4	Princeton	5:44.87	1993	Brown	5:54.15	Penn	5:56.98
1986	Wisconsin	5:57.8	Brown	5:59.9	1994	Brown	5:24.52	Harvard	5:25.83
1987	Harvard	5:35.17	Brown	5:35.63	1995	Brown	5:23.40	Princeton	5:25.83
1988	Harvard	5:35.98	Northeastern	5:37.07	1996	Princeton	5:57.47	Penn	6:03.28
1989	Harvard	5:36.6	Washington	5:38.93	1997	discontinued			

Women

National championship held over various distances at 10 different venues from 1979-96. Distances— 1000 meters (1979-81); 1500 meters (1982-83); 1000 meters (1984); 1750 meters (1985); 2000 meters (1986-88, 1991-96); 1852 meters (1989-90). Winner received the Ferguson Bowl. Regatta discontinued in 1997.

Multiple winners: Washington (7); Princeton (4); Boston University (2).

Year	Champion	Time	Runner-up	Time	Year	Champion	Time	Runner-up	Time
1979	Yale	3:06	California	3:08.6	1988	Washington	6:41.0	Yale	6:42.37
1980	California	3:05.4	Oregon St.	3:05.8	1989	Cornell	5:34.9	Wisconsin	5:37.5
1981	Washington	3:20.6	Yale	3:22.9	1991	Boston Univ.	7:03.2	Cornell	7:06.21
1982	Washington	4:56.4	Wisconsin	4:59.83	1992	Boston Univ.	6:28.79	Cornell	6:32.79
1983	Washington	4:57.5	Dartmouth	5:03.02	1993	Princeton	6:40.75	Washington	6:43.86
1984	Washington	3:29.48	Radcliffe	3:31.08	1994	Princeton	6:11.38	Yale	6:14.46
1985	Washington	5:28.4	Wisconsin	5:32.0	1995	Princeton	6:11.98	Washington	6:12.69
1986	Wisconsin	6:53.28	Radcliffe	6:53.34	1996	Brown	6:45.7	Princeton	6:49.3
1987	Washington	6:33.8	Yale	6:37.4	1997	discontinued			

The Harvard-Yale Regatta

Harvard made it three in a row and 16 of the last 18 by cruising to a sweep of Yale at the 137th running of the Harvard/Yale Regatta on June 8, 2002. Despite the blustery conditions, Harvard's Varsity Eights squad finished the four-mile course on the Thames River in New London, Conn. in 19:02.5, the eighth-fastest time in race history. Yale (19:43.8) came in 41.8 seconds later, the largest margin of victory in 27 years. Harvard's second varsity and freshman teams also won with ease. The Harvard/Yale Regatta is the nation's oldest intercollegiate sporting event. Harvard holds an 84-53 series edge.

SKIING

Men & Women

Denver won its third consecutive NCAA skiing championship and its 17th overall behind a double victory by cross country star Ola Berger. The freshman from Norway won both the 10-k classical and the 20-k freestyle races while teammates Pietro Broggini and Wolf Wallendorf took second and third, respectively in the 10-k to cement the win for the Pioneers. Denver accumulated 656 points to finish ahead of 15-time champ Colorado (612) and third-place Utah (609). Last year's only double winner, Katerina Hanusova of Nevada, successfully defended her title in the women's 15-k freestyle, but lost her 5-k classical crown to Colorado's Mari Storeng. Aurore De Maulmont of host Alaska-Anchorage won the women's giant slalom on her home course. (Anchorage, AK; March 6-9, 2002)

Multiple winners: Denver (17); Colorado (15); Utah (9); Vermont (5); Dartmouth and Wyoming (2).

Year		Year		Year		Year		Year	
1954	Denver	1965	Denver	1976	Colorado	1986	Utah	1997	Utah
1955	Denver	1966	Denver		& Dartmouth	1987	Utah	1998	Colorado
1956	Denver	1967	Denver	1977	Colorado	1988	Utah	1999	Colorado
1957	Denver	1968	Wyoming	1978	Colorado	1989	Vermont	2000	Denver
1958	Dartmouth	1969	Denver	1979	Colorado	1990	Vermont	2001	Denver
1959	Colorado	1970	Denver	1980	Vermont	1991	Colorado	2002	Denver
1960	Colorado	1971	Denver	1981	Utah	1992	Vermont		
1961	Denver	1972	Colorado	1982	Colorado	1993	Utah		
1962	Colorado	1973	Colorado	1983	Utah	1994	Vermont		
1963	Denver	1974	Colorado	1984	Utah	1995	Colorado		
1964	Denver	1975	Colorado	1985	Wyoming	1996	Utah		

SOFTBALL

Women

California won its first NCAA national championship in any women's sport with a 6-0 victory over Arizona in the Division I softball championship game. Locked in a scoreless tie through six innings, California did what few teams could — it finally got to Arizona pitching star Jennie Finch. The Golden Bears rallied for all six runs with two outs in the seventh, highlighted by a bases-loaded double by second baseman Jessica Pamanian. California hurler Jocelyn Forest stifled the Arizona bats, allowing just one hit through seven innings while whiffing eight. With four wins in the tournament, Forest earned most outstanding player honors. California ended the season at 56-19 while Arizona's loss put them at 55-12. (Oklahoma City, OK; May 23-27, 2002.)

Multiple winners: UCLA (8); Arizona (6); Texas A&M (2).

Year	Year	Year	Year	Year
1982 UCLA	1987 Texas A&M	1992 UCLA	1997 Arizona	2002 California
1983 Texas A&M	1988 UCLA	1993 Arizona	1998 Fresno St.	
1984 UCLA	1989 UCLA	1994 Arizona	1999 UCLA	
1985 UCLA	1990 UCLA	1995 UCLA*	2000 Oklahoma	
1986 CS-Fullerton	1991 Arizona	1996 Arizona	2001 Arizona	

*Title was later vacated due to action by the NCAA Committee on Infractions.

SWIMMING & DIVING

Men

Unlike last year when Texas cruised to an easy 140-point victory, this year's affair was a battle to the finish with Stanford. In the end it was the Longhorns emerging with their third consecutive championship, and their ninth overall. Texas finished with 512 points, while Stanford followed closely with 501 and Auburn placed third with 365½. The 11-point margin of victory was the closest since the current scoring system was put in place in 1985. Texas trailed coming into the meet's penultimate event, the platform dive, but brothers Justin and Troy Dumais placed second and fifth, respectively, to push their team into the lead. The Longhorns' third-place showing in the 400-yard freestyle relay was enough to clinch the title.

Troy Dumais won the one-meter dive for the third consecutive year and the three-meter dive the fourth straight time. Texas' Brendan Hansen successfully defended his titles in the 100- and 200-meter breaststrokes and Ian Crocker set an NCAA record in the 100-meter butterfly. Erik Vendt of USC won two individual titles, was runner-up in a third and was named swimmer of the meet. (Athens, GA; Mar. 28-30, 2002.)

Multiple winners: Michigan and Ohio St. (11); Texas and USC (9); Stanford (8); Indiana (6); Yale (4); Auburn, California and Florida (2).

Year	Year	Year	Year	Year
1937 Michigan	1951 Yale	1965 USC	1979 California	1993 Stanford
1938 Michigan	1952 Ohio St.	1966 USC	1980 California	1994 Stanford
1939 Michigan	1953 Yale	1967 Stanford	1981 Texas	1995 Michigan
1940 Michigan	1954 Ohio St.	1968 Indiana	1982 UCLA	1996 Texas
1941 Michigan	1955 Ohio St.	1969 Indiana	1983 Florida	1997 Auburn
1942 Yale	1956 Ohio St.	1970 Indiana	1984 Florida	1998 Stanford
1943 Ohio St.	1957 Michigan	1971 Indiana	1985 Stanford	1999 Auburn
1944 Yale	1958 Michigan	1972 Indiana	1986 Stanford	2000 Texas
1945 Ohio St.	1959 Michigan	1973 Indiana	1987 Stanford	2001 Texas
1946 Ohio St.	1960 USC	1974 USC	1988 Texas	2002 Texas
1947 Ohio St.	1961 Michigan	1975 USC	1989 Texas	
1948 Michigan	1962 Ohio St.	1976 USC	1990 Texas	
1949 Ohio St.	1963 USC	1977 USC	1991 Texas	
1950 Ohio St.	1964 USC	1978 Tennessee	1992 Stanford	

Women

Bolstered by ten top-three finishes and two individual titles by Maggie Bowen, Auburn unseated three-time defending champ Georgia to win its first Division I swimming and diving championship. The Tigers amassed 474 points to better runner-up Georgia (386) and third-place Stanford (301). Bowen won the 200- and 400-yard individual medleys and placed second in the 100-yard breaststroke.

For the second straight year, Swimmer of the Meet Natalie Coughlin of California won the 100-yard butterfly and the 100- and 200-yard backstrokes, setting meet records in each event. She also broke an NCAA record in her leg of the 400-meter freestyle relay. Other double winners were Georgia's Maritza Correia (50- and 100-yard freestyle), SMU's Flavia Rigamonti (500- and 1650-yard freestyles), Stanford's Tara Kirk (100- and 200-yard breaststrokes) and USC's Blythe Hartley (one-meter and platform dive). (Austin, TX; Mar. 21-23, 2002.)

Multiple winners: Stanford (8); Texas (7); Georgia (3).

Year	Year	Year	Year	Year
1982 Florida	1987 Texas	1992 Stanford	1997 USC	2002 Auburn
1983 Stanford	1988 Texas	1993 Stanford	1998 Stanford	
1984 Texas	1989 Stanford	1994 Stanford	1999 Georgia	
1985 Texas	1990 Texas	1995 Stanford	2000 Georgia	
1986 Texas	1991 Texas	1996 Stanford	2001 Georgia	

Annual NCAA Division I Team Champions (Cont.)

INDOOR TRACK

Men

Tennessee followed up its 2001 outdoor championship by winning its first-ever Division I indoor track & field title. Sprinter Justin Gatlin won both the 60- and 200-meter dashes and also ran a leg in the Volunteers' second-place finish in the 4x400-meter relay. Tennessee scored 62½ points for the title, and was followed by Alabama (47) and LSU (44). Leonard Scott placed second behind Gatlin in the 60-meter dash and took third in the 200 to add an additional 14 points to the Volunteers' total.

LSU's Walter Davis won his second consecutive indoor triple jump title with a leap of 56-6½, and LSU's Alleyene Francique set a championships record in the 400-meter dash with a time of 45.58. (Fayetteville, AR; Mar. 8-9, 2002.)

Multiple winners: Arkansas (16); UTEP (7); Kansas and Villanova (3); USC (2).

Year	Year	Year	Year	Year
1965 Missouri	1973 Manhattan	1981 UTEP	1989 Arkansas	1997 Arkansas
1966 Kansas	1974 UTEP	1982 UTEP	1990 Arkansas	1998 Arkansas
1967 USC	1975 UTEP	1983 SMU	1991 Arkansas	1999 Arkansas
1968 Villanova	1976 UTEP	1984 Arkansas	1992 Arkansas	2000 Arkansas
1969 Kansas	1977 Washington St.	1985 Arkansas	1993 Arkansas	2001 LSU
1970 Kansas	1978 UTEP	1986 Arkansas	1994 Arkansas	2002 Tennessee
1971 Villanova	1979 Villanova	1987 Arkansas	1995 Arkansas	
1972 USC	1980 UTEP	1988 Arkansas	1996 George Mason	

Women

After a four-year hiatus, LSU reclaimed its crown at the NCAA Division I Women's Track and Field Championships. It was the ninth overall title for the Tigers, who registered a total of 57 points and were followed by two-time defending champ UCLA (43) and Florida (35). Three individual winners paced LSU to victory — Marian Burnett in the 800-meter dash, Nicole Toney in the triple jump (45-0¼), and Muna Lee who ran a meet-record 22.82 in the 200-meter race.

There were a total of six meet records set, most notably USC's Angela Williams' 7.13 in the 60-meter dash. Runner-up UCLA received wins from Darnesha Griffith in the high jump and its distance medley relay team, which also broke the previous meet record. (Fayetteville, AR; Mar. 8-9, 2002.)

Multiple winners: LSU (9); Texas (5); Nebraska and UCLA (2).

Year	Year	Year	Year	Year
1983 Nebraska	1987 LSU	1991 LSU	1995 LSU	1999 Texas
1984 Nebraska	1988 Texas	1992 Florida	1996 LSU	2000 UCLA
1985 Florida St.	1989 LSU	1993 LSU	1997 LSU	2001 UCLA
1986 Texas	1990 Texas	1994 LSU	1998 Texas	2002 LSU

OUTDOOR TRACK

Men

Walter Davis won the long jump and the triple jump to lead LSU to its first outdoor track championship since 1990 and its fourth overall. Davis also ran a leg on LSU's victorious 4x100-meter relay. LSU, competing on its home track, recorded 64 points to outperform defending champ Tennessee (57) and third-place SMU (42). Claston Bernard came from behind to win the decathlon, the Tigers' only individual title.

Tennessee sprinter Justin Gatlin won the 100- and 200-meter dashes for the second straight year, the first person to win those two events in consecutive years since 1957. SMU's Janus Robberts joined Davis and Gatlin as the meet's only double winners with victories in the shot put and discus. (Baton Rouge, LA; May 29-June 1, 2002.)

Multiple winners: USC (26); Arkansas (9); UCLA (8); UTEP (6); Illinois and Oregon (5); LSU and Stanford (4); Kansas and Tennessee (3); SMU (2).

Year	Year	Year	Year	Year
1921 Illinois	1938 USC	1955 USC	1971 UCLA	1988 UCLA
1922 California	1939 USC	1956 UCLA	1972 UCLA	1989 LSU
1923 Michigan		1957 Villanova	1973 UCLA	
1924 Not held	1940 USC	1958 USC	1974 Tennessee	1990 LSU
1925 Stanford*	1941 USC	1959 Kansas	1975 UTEP	1991 Tennessee
1926 USC*	1942 USC		1976 USC	1992 Arkansas
1927 Illinois*	1943 USC	1960 Kansas	1977 Arizona St.	1993 Arkansas
1928 Stanford	1944 Illinois	1961 USC	1978 UCLA & UTEP	1994 Arkansas
1929 Ohio St.	1945 Navy	1962 Oregon	1979 UTEP	1995 Arkansas
	1946 Illinois	1963 USC		1996 Arkansas
1930 USC	1947 Illinois	1964 Oregon	1980 UTEP	1997 Arkansas
1931 USC	1948 Minnesota	1965 Oregon & USC	1981 UTEP	1998 Arkansas
1932 Indiana	1949 USC	1966 UCLA	1982 UTEP	1999 Arkansas
1933 LSU		1967 USC	1983 SMU	
1934 Stanford	1950 USC	1968 USC	1984 Oregon	2000 Stanford
1935 USC	1951 USC	1969 San Jose St.	1985 Arkansas	2001 Tennessee
1936 USC	1952 USC		1986 SMU	2002 LSU
1937 USC	1953 USC	1970 BYU, Kansas	1987 UCLA	
	1954 USC	& Oregon		

(*) indicates unofficial championship.

AP/Wide World Photos

*LSU's **Walter Davis** hits the pit during the long jump at the 2002 Outdoor Track and Field Championships. Davis won the event, as well as the triple jump, to boost the Tigers to their first NCAA Division I men's title since 1990.*

Women

The NCAA Women's Outdoor Track and Field Championships came down to the meet's final event, the 4x400-meter relay, and South Carolina emerged victorious to capture its first team title in any sport. The Gamecocks' relay win gave them a total of 82 points to finish ahead of UCLA (72) and USC (57). South Carolina was bolstered by wins in the 4x100-meter relay, Leshinda Demus's and Tiffany Ross's 1-2 finish in the 400-meter hurdles, and a 2-3-4 showing in the 400-meter dash.

USC's Angela Williams won the 100-meter dash for the fourth consecutive year, becoming only the third woman in history to win an event four times. UCLA tied a championships record by winning five individual events. (*Baton Rouge, LA; May 29-June 1, 2002.*)

Multiple winners: LSU (12); Texas (3); UCLA (2).

Year		Year		Year		Year		Year	
1982	UCLA	1987	LSU	1992	LSU	1997	LSU	2002	South Carolina
1983	UCLA	1988	LSU	1993	LSU	1998	Texas		
1984	Florida St.	1989	LSU	1994	LSU	1999	Texas		
1985	Oregon	1990	LSU	1995	LSU	2000	LSU		
1986	Texas	1991	LSU	1996	LSU	2001	USC		

VOLLEYBALL

Men

Hawaii had lost to Pepperdine three times during the 2002 season, but chose the best time to seek revenge, taking down its rival in four games to win its first men's volleyball championship. The Warriors, who finished the year at 24-8, lost the first game, 29-31, but roared back to take the next three, 31-29, 30-21, 30-24. Pepperdine ended the season 29-5 and saw its 17-match winning streak come to an end. Tournament Most Outstanding Player Costas Theocharidis recorded 19 kills and Tony Ching, 17, to lead Hawaii's offense. Sean Rooney led Pepperdine with 18. (*State College, PA; May 4, 2002.*)

Multiple winners: UCLA (18); Pepperdine and USC (4); Brigham Young (2).

Year		Year		Year		Year		Year	
1970	UCLA	1977	USC	1984	UCLA	1991	Long Beach St.	1998	UCLA
1971	UCLA	1978	Pepperdine	1985	Pepperdine	1992	Pepperdine	1999	Brigham Young
1972	UCLA	1979	UCLA	1986	Pepperdine	1993	UCLA	2000	UCLA
1973	San Diego St.	1980	USC	1987	UCLA	1994	Penn St.	2001	Brigham Young
1974	UCLA	1981	UCLA	1988	USC	1995	UCLA	2002	Hawaii
1975	UCLA	1982	UCLA	1989	UCLA	1996	UCLA		
1976	UCLA	1983	UCLA	1990	USC	1997	Stanford		

Annual NCAA Division I Team Champions (Cont.)
Women

Sydney Olympian and 2001 National Player of the Year Logan Tom slammed 25 kills to lead Stanford to a three-game victory over Long Beach State and its fifth overall NCAA Division I Women's Volleyball title. It was the first loss of the season for Long Beach (33-1), who went down 31-29, 30-28, 30-25. Stanford ended the season with a mark of 33-2, its only losses coming at the hands of Long Beach and USC.

Freshman Ogonna Nnamani added 19 kills for the Cardinal while setter Robyn Lewis dished out 56 assists. Six-foot-seven outside hitter Tayyiba Haneef led Long Beach with 18 kills. (*San Diego, CA; Dec. 15, 2001.*)

Multiple winners: Stanford (5); Hawaii, Long Beach St. and UCLA (3); Nebraska and Pacific (2).

Year		Year		Year		Year		Year	
1981	USC	1986	Pacific	1991	UCLA	1996	Stanford	2001	Stanford
1982	Hawaii	1987	Hawaii	1992	Stanford	1997	Stanford		
1983	Hawaii	1988	Texas	1993	Long Beach St.	1998	Long Beach St.		
1984	UCLA	1989	Long Beach St.	1994	Stanford	1999	Penn St.		
1985	Pacific	1990	UCLA	1995	Nebraska	2000	Nebraska		

WATER POLO
Men

Stanford sent head coach Dante Dettamanti into retirement on a winning note, defeating two-time defending champ UCLA, 8-5, for its ninth men's water polo championship. The title was Stanford's first since 1994 and Dettamanti's eighth overall, tying him for the all-time coaching lead. Freshman forward Tony Azevedo scored two goals, the last one putting a stop to a late Bruin rally, and was named the tournament's most outstanding player. Brian Darrow and Onno Koelman also chipped in two goals apiece for the Cardinal, while Alfonso Tucay and Brett Ormsby added two each for UCLA. (*Stanford, CA; Dec. 2, 2001.*)

Multiple winners: California (11); Stanford (9); UCLA (7); UC-Irvine (3).

Year		Year		Year		Year		Year	
1969	UCLA	1976	Stanford	1983	California	1990	California	1997	Pepperdine
1970	UC-Irvine	1977	California	1984	California	1991	California	1998	USC
1971	UCLA	1978	Stanford	1985	Stanford	1992	California	1999	UCLA
1972	UCLA	1979	UC-S. Barbara	1986	Stanford	1993	Stanford	2000	UCLA
1973	California	1980	Stanford	1987	Stanford	1994	Stanford	2001	Stanford
1974	California	1981	Stanford	1988	California	1995	UCLA		
1975	California	1982	UC-Irvine	1989	UC-Irvine	1996	UCLA		

Women

Stanford jumped out to an early 3-0 lead and hung on the defeat UCLA, 8-4 for its first NCAA women's water polo championship. The win put Stanford at 23-2 for the season and avenged UCLA's 5-4 victory over the Cardinal in last year's inaugural championship. A balanced scoring attack led by Ellen Estes and Julie Gardner, two goals each, and stellar goaltending by Jackie Franks (12 saves) carried Stanford to the title. Natalie Golda netted three goals for the Bruins who finished their season at 22-4. Loyola Marymount defeated Michigan, 6-4, in the third-place game. (*Los Angeles, CA; May 12, 2002.*)

Year		Year	
2001	UCLA	2002	Stanford

WRESTLING
Men

Iowa State standout Cael Sanderson won his fourth individual title, completing an incredible undefeated college career, but once again it wasn't enough to lift his team past Minnesota for the team title at the Division I NCAA Wrestling Championships. The Golden Gophers (126½ points) won their second consecutive championship over runner-up Iowa State (104) and Oklahoma (101½) on the strength of two individual titlists (Jared Lawrence at 149 pounds and Luke Becker at 157 pounds).

Sanderson won his previous three titles at the 184-pound class, but moved up to take the 197-pound title in 2002. The senior took down Lehigh sophomore Jon Trenge in the final match to run his college mark to a historic 159-0. (*Albany, NY; Mar. 21-23, 2002.*)

Multiple winners: Oklahoma St. (30); Iowa (20); Iowa St. (8); Oklahoma (7); Minnesota (2).

Year		Year		Year		Year		Year	
1928	Okla. A&M*	1942	Okla. A&M	1959	Okla. St.	1974	Oklahoma	1989	Okla. St.
1929	Okla. A&M	1943-45	Not held	1960	Oklahoma	1975	Iowa	1990	Okla. St.
1930	Okla. A&M	1946	Okla. A&M	1961	Oklahoma	1976	Iowa	1991	Iowa
1931	Okla. A&M*	1947	Cornell Col.	1962	Okla. St.	1977	Iowa St.	1992	Iowa
1932	Indiana*	1948	Okla. A&M	1963	Oklahoma	1978	Iowa	1993	Iowa
1933	Okla. A&M*	1949	Okla. A&M	1964	Okla. St.	1979	Iowa	1994	Okla. St.
	& Iowa St.*	1950	Northern Iowa	1965	Iowa St.	1980	Iowa	1995	Iowa
1934	Okla. A&M	1951	Oklahoma	1966	Okla. St.	1981	Iowa	1996	Iowa
1935	Okla. A&M	1952	Oklahoma	1967	Michigan St.	1982	Iowa	1997	Iowa
1936	Oklahoma	1953	Penn St.	1968	Okla. St.	1983	Iowa	1998	Iowa
1937	Okla. A&M	1954	Okla. A&M	1969	Iowa St.	1984	Iowa	1999	Iowa
1938	Okla. A&M	1955	Okla. A&M	1970	Iowa St.	1985	Iowa	2000	Iowa
1939	Okla. A&M	1956	Okla. A&M	1971	Okla. St.	1986	Iowa	2001	Minnesota
1940	Okla. A&M	1957	Oklahoma	1972	Iowa St.	1987	Iowa St.	2002	Minnesota
1941	Okla. A&M	1958	Okla. St.	1973	Iowa St.	1988	Arizona St.		

(*) indicates unofficial champions. **Note:** Oklahoma A&M became Oklahoma St. in 1958.

Halls of Fame & Awards

Ozzie Smith became the newest member of the Baseball Hall of Fame in 2002.

BASEBALL

National Baseball Hall of Fame & Museum

Established in 1935 by Major League Baseball to celebrate the game's 100th anniversary. **Address:** P.O. Box 590, Cooperstown, NY 13326. **Telephone:** (607) 547-7200.

Eligibility: In August 2001, the Hall of Fame announced changes in the way players are elected via the Veterans Committee. The voting done by Baseball Writers' Association of America remains unchanged. Nominated players must have played at least parts of 10 seasons in the major leagues and be retired for at least five. Certain nominated players not elected by the writers can become eligible via the Veterans Committee. The new Veterans Committee will be comprised of all living Hall of Famers (currently 58 people) as well as all living winners of the Ford Frick (13) and J.G. Taylor Spink (12) Awards and three members of the old 15-member Veterans Committee with unexpired terms. There was no Veterans Committee vote in 2002. Beginning in 2003 the new Veterans Committee will vote every two years on former players and every four years on managers, umpires and executives. Previously, the committee voted annually.

Also, the eligibility of all players that had been dropped from the ballots for not receiving five percent of the vote was restored and those players can now be immediately considered by the new Veterans Committee. The players on baseball's ineligible list are still excluded from consideration. Pete Rose is the only living ex-player on that list.

Class of 2002 (1): BBWAA vote—shortstop **Ozzie Smith**, San Diego (1978-81), St. Louis (1982-96).

2002 Top 10 vote-getters (472 BBWAA ballots cast, 354 needed to elect): 1. **Ozzie Smith** (433), 2. **Gary Carter** (343), 3. **Jim Rice** (260), 4. **Bruce Sutter** (238), 5. **Andre Dawson** (214), 6. **Rich Gossage** (203), 7. **Steve Garvey** (134), 8. **Tommy John** (127), 9. **Bert Blyleven** (124), 10. **Jim Kaat** (109).

Elected first year on ballot (37): Hank Aaron, Ernie Banks, Johnny Bench, George Brett, Lou Brock, Rod Carew, Steve Carlton, Ty Cobb, Bob Feller, Bob Gibson, Reggie Jackson, Walter Johnson, Al Kaline, Sandy Koufax, Mickey Mantle, Christy Mathewson, Willie Mays, Willie McCovey, Joe Morgan, Stan Musial, Jim Palmer, Kirby Puckett, Brooks Robinson, Frank Robinson, Jackie Robinson, Babe Ruth, Nolan Ryan, Mike Schmidt, Tom Seaver, Ozzie Smith, Warren Spahn, Willie Stargell, Honus Wagner, Ted Williams, Dave Winfield, Carl Yastrzemski and Robin Yount.

Members are listed with years of induction; (+) indicates deceased members.

Catchers

Bench, Johnny 1989	+ Cochrane, Mickey 1947	Fisk, Carlton...............2000
Berra, Yogi 1972	+ Dickey, Bill 1954	+ Hartnett, Gabby 1955
+ Bresnahan, Roger 1945	+ Ewing, Buck 1939	+ Lombardi, Ernie 1986
+ Campanella, Roy..........1969	+ Ferrell, Rick...............1984	+ Schalk, Ray 1955

1st Basemen

+ Anson, Cap 1939	+ Connor, Roger 1976	McCovey, Willie 1986
+ Beckley, Jake 1971	+ Foxx, Jimmie 1951	+ Mize, Johnny 1981
+ Bottomley, Jim............1974	+ Gehrig, Lou 1939	Perez, Tony................2000
+ Brouthers, Dan...........1945	+ Greenberg, Hank 1956	+ Sisler, George 1939
Cepeda, Orlando 1999	+ Kelly, George.............1973	+ Terry, Bill................1954
+ Chance, Frank 1946	Killebrew, Harmon 1984	

2nd Basemen

Carew, Rod 1991	+ Gehringer, Charlie 1949	+ McPhee, Bid..............2000
+ Collins, Eddie.............1939	+ Herman, Billy 1975	Morgan, Joe...............1990
Doerr, Bobby 1986	+ Hornsby, Rogers 1942	+ Robinson, Jackie 1962
+ Evers, Johnny 1946	+ Lajoie, Nap 1937	Schoendienst, Red 1989
+ Fox, Nellie 1997	+ Lazzeri, Tony 1991	
+ Frisch, Frankie 1947	Mazeroski, Bill............2001	

Shortstops

Aparicio, Luis..............1984	+ Jackson, Travis............1982	+ Tinker, Joe................1946
+ Appling, Luke.............1964	+ Jennings, Hugh 1945	+ Vaughan, Arky 1985
+ Bancroft, Dave...........1971	+ Maranville, Rabbit.........1954	+ Wagner, Honus 1936
Banks, Ernie...............1977	+ Reese, Pee Wee...........1984	+ Wallace, Bobby 1953
+ Boudreau, Lou 1970	Rizzuto, Phil..............1994	+ Ward, Monte 1964
+ Cronin, Joe................1956	+ Sewell, Joe...............1977	Yount, Robin 1999
+ Davis, George.............1998	Smith, Ozzie 2002	

3rd Basemen

+ Baker, Frank 1955	Kell, George...............1983	Robinson, Brooks...........1983
Brett, George 1999	+ Lindstrom, Fred 1976	Schmidt, Mike 1995
+ Collins, Jimmy 1945	+ Mathews, Eddie............1978	+ Traynor, Pie 1948

Center Fielders

+ Ashburn, Richie 1995	Doby, Larry................1998	+ Roush, Edd 1962
+ Averill, Earl...............1975	+ Duffy, Hugh 1945	Snider, Duke...............1980
+ Carey, Max 1961	+ Hamilton, Billy 1961	+ Speaker, Tris.............1937
+ Cobb, Ty 1936	+ Mantle, Mickey 1974	+ Waner, Lloyd 1967
+ Combs, Earle 1970	Mays, Willie 1979	+ Wilson, Hack 1979
+ DiMaggio, Joe.............1955	Puckett, Kirby 2001	

Left Fielders

Brock, Lou.................1985
+ Burkett, Jesse 1946
+ Clarke, Fred 1945
+ Delahanty, Ed............1945
+ Goslin, Goose 1968
+ Hafey, Chick 1971

+ Kelley, Joe................1971
Kiner, Ralph 1975
+ Manush, Heinie 1964
+ Medwick, Joe............1968
Musial, Stan..............1969
+ O'Rourke, Jim...........1945

+ Simmons, Al 1953
+ Stargell, Willie............1988
+ Wheat, Zack 1959
Williams, Billy 1987
+ Williams, Ted............1966
Yastrzemski, Carl.........1989

Right Fielders

Aaron, Hank 1982
+ Clemente, Roberto........1973
+ Crawford, Sam 1957
+ Cuyler, Kiki 1968
+ Flick, Elmer...............1963
+ Heilmann, Harry 1952
+ Hooper, Harry 1971
Jackson, Reggie 1993

Kaline, Al 1980
+ Keeler, Willie............1939
+ Kelly, King 1945
+ Klein, Chuck.............1980
+ McCarthy, Tommy 1946
+ Ott, Mel 1951
+ Rice, Sam 1963
Robinson, Frank...........1982

+ Ruth, Babe 1936
+ Slaughter, Enos 1985
+ Thompson, Sam 1974
+ Waner, Paul 1952
Winfield, Dave 2001
+ Youngs, Ross 1972

Pitchers

+ Alexander, Grover 1938
+ Bender, Chief.............1953
+ Brown, Mordecai 1949
Bunning, Jim.............1996
Carlton, Steve 1994
+ Chesbro, Jack 1946
+ Clarkson, John 1963

+ Coveleski, Stan 1969
+ Dean, Dizzy 1953
+ Drysdale, Don 1984
+ Faber, Red 1964
Feller, Bob 1962
Fingers, Rollie............1992
Ford, Whitey 1974

+ Galvin, Pud 1965
Gibson, Bob..............1981
+ Gomez, Lefty 1972
+ Grimes, Burleigh 1964
+ Grove, Lefty 1947
+ Haines, Jess 1970
+ Hoyt, Waite 1969

Major League Baseball's All-Time Team—Then and Now

The Baseball Writers' Association of America originally selected an all-time team as part of major league baseball's 100th anniversary, announcing the outcome of its vote on July 21, 1969. Vote totals were not released. Recently, another vote was released when a panel of 36 BWAA members picked an all-time team for the Classic Sports Network just before the 1997 All-Star Game. This time vote totals were given, the single outfield category was divided into three (left, center and right) and two recently popularized positions—the designated hitter and relief pitcher—were added. In the most recent vote two points were awarded for first-place votes and one point for second place. Point totals follow the names with the number of first-place votes in parentheses. All-time team members are listed in **bold** type.

1969 Vote

C	**Mickey Cochrane**, Bill Dickey, Roy Campanella	OF	**Babe Ruth**, **Ty Cobb**, **Joe DiMaggio**, Ted Williams, Tris Speaker, Willie Mays
1B	**Lou Gehrig**, George Sisler, Stan Musial		
2B	**Rogers Hornsby**, Charlie Gehringer, Eddie Collins	RHP	**Walter Johnson**, Christy Mathewson, Cy Young
SS	**Honus Wagner**, Joe Cronin, Ernie Banks	LHP	**Lefty Grove**, Sandy Koufax, Carl Hubbell
3B	**Pie Traynor**, Brooks Robinson, Jackie Robinson	Mgr.	**John McGraw**, Casey Stengel, Joe McCarthy

1969 Vote All-Time Outstanding Player: **Ruth**, Cobb, Wagner, DiMaggio

1997 Vote

C **Johnny Bench** (24) 52; Yogi Berra (4) 22; Roy Campanella (4) 17; Mickey Cochrane (1) 5; Bill Dickey (1) 4; Gabby Hartnett (1) 3; Carlton Fisk 2.

1B **Lou Gehrig** (31) 66½; Jimmie Foxx (3) 19; George Sisler (2) 8; Willie McCovey 6; Hank Greenberg 2½; Stan Musial, Eddie Murray, Mark McGwire and Frank Thomas 1.

2B **Rogers Hornsby** (17) 44; Joe Morgan (6) 23; Jackie Robinson (6) 15; Charley Gehringer (4) and Napolean Lajoie (3) 11; Eddie Collins (1) 3; Rod Carew 2; Ryne Sandberg 1.

SS **Honus Wagner** (23) 55; Cal Ripken Jr. (6) 24; Ozzie Smith (5) 16; Ernie Banks (1) 8; Lou Boudreau and Luke Appling 1.

3B **Mike Schmidt** (21) 50; Brooks Robinson (13) 37; Eddie Mathews 5; George Brett (1) 8; Pie Traynor 3; Pete Rose (1) 2; Frank Baker, Al Rosen and Wade Boggs 1.

LF **Ted Williams** (32) 68; Stan Musial (4) 36; Pete Rose, Ralph Kiner, Rickey Henderson and Barry Bonds 1.

CF **Willie Mays** (25) 57; Ty Cobb (7) 22; Joe DiMaggio (3) 17; Mickey Mantle (1) 10; Tris Speaker 2.

RF **Babe Ruth** (31) 67; Hank Aaron (5) 36; Frank Robinson 2; Al Kaline, Roberto Clemente and Tony Gwynn 1.

DH **Paul Molitor** (22) 48; Harold Baines (3) 12; Don Baylor (1) 10; Edgar Martinez (2) 9; Ty Cobb (2) 6; Hal McRae (1) 5; Mickey Mantle (1) and Dave Parker (1) 3; Joe DiMaggio (1) 2; Lee May, Frank Robinson and Tony Oliva 1.

RHP **Walter Johnson** (9) 30, Cy Young (12) 25; Christy Mathewson (5) 18; Bob Feller (4) 10; Bob Gibson (2) 9; Nolan Ryan (2) 7; Tom Seaver (1) 3; Greg Maddux (1), Grover Cleveland Alexander and Juan Marichal 2.

LHP **Sandy Koufax** (11) 32; Warren Spahn (11) 28; Lefty Grove (8) 25; Steve Carlton (4) 12; Carl Hubbell 6; Whitey Ford (1) 3; Eddie Plank (1) 3.

RP **Dennis Eckersley** (16) 40; Rollie Fingers (9) 29; Lee Smith (4) 13; Hoyt Wilhelm (3) 10; Rich Gossage (3) 9; Bruce Sutter (1) 6, Dan Quisenberry 1.

Mgr. **Casey Stengel** (6) 22; Joe McCarthy (6) 18; Connie Mack (7) 17; John McGraw (6) 14; Sparky Anderson (3) 11; Leo Durocher (2) 6; Dick Williams (1) 4; Billy Martin (1) 3; Al Lopez (1), Ned Hanlon (1), Whitey Herzog (1), Earl Weaver and Bobby Cox 2; Tony La Russa 1.

Baseball (Cont.)

+ Hubbell, Carl 1947
+ Hunter, Catfish 1987
  Jenkins, Ferguson 1991
+ Johnson, Walter 1936
+ Joss, Addie 1978
+ Keefe, Tim 1964
  Koufax, Sandy 1972
+ Lemon, Bob 1976
+ Lyons, Ted 1955
  Marichal, Juan 1983
+ Marquard, Rube 1971
+ Mathewson, Christy 1936
+ McGinnity, Joe 1946

  Niekro, Phil 1997
+ Newhouser, Hal 1992
+ Nichols, Kid 1949
  Palmer, Jim 1990
+ Pennock, Herb 1948
  Perry, Gaylord 1991
+ Plank, Eddie 1946
+ Radbourne, Old Hoss 1939
+ Rixey, Eppa 1963
  Roberts, Robin 1976
+ Ruffing, Red 1967
+ Rusie, Amos 1977
  Ryan, Nolan 1999

  Seaver, Tom 1992
  Spahn, Warren 1973
  Sutton, Don 1998
+ Vance, Dazzy 1955
+ Waddell, Rube 1946
+ Walsh, Ed 1946
+ Welch, Mickey 1973
+ Wilhelm, Hoyt 1985
+ Willis, Vic 1995
+ Wynn, Early 1972
+ Young, Cy 1937

Managers

+ Alston, Walter 1983
  Anderson, Sparky 2000
+ Durocher, Leo 1994
+ Hanlon, Ned 1996
+ Harris, Bucky 1975
+ Huggins, Miller 1964

  Lasorda, Tommy 1997
  Lopez, Al 1977
+ Mack, Connie 1937
+ McCarthy, Joe 1957
+ McGraw, John 1937
+ McKechnie, Bill 1962

+ Robinson, Wilbert 1945
+ Selee, Frank 1999
+ Stengel, Casey 1966
  Weaver, Earl 1996

Umpires

+ Barlick, Al 1989
+ Chylak, Nestor 1999
+ Conlan, Jocko 1974

+ Connolly, Tom 1953
+ Evans, Billy 1973

+ Hubbard, Cal 1976
+ Klem, Bill 1953
+ McGowan, Bill 1992

From Negro Leagues

+ Bell, Cool Papa (OF) 1974
+ Charleston, Oscar (1B-OF) . . .1976
+ Dandridge, Ray (3B) 1987
+ Day, Leon (P-OF-2B) 1995
+ Dihigo, Martin (P-OF) 1977
+ Foster, Rube (P-Mgr) 1981

+ Foster, Willie (P) 1996
+ Gibson, Josh (C) 1972
  Irvin, Monte (OF) 1973
+ Johnson, Judy (3B) 1975
+ Leonard, Buck (1B) 1972
+ Lloyd, Pop (SS) 1977

+ Paige, Satchel (P) 1971
+ Rogan, Wilber (P) 1998
+ Smith, Hilton 2001
+ Stearns, Turkey (OF) 2000
+ Wells, Willie (SS) 1997
+ Williams, Joe (P) 1999

Pioneers and Executives

+ Barrow, Ed 1953
+ Bulkeley, Morgan 1937
+ Cartwright, Alexander 1938
+ Chadwick, Henry 1938
+ Chandler, Happy 1982
+ Comiskey, Charles 1939
+ Cummings, Candy 1939
+ Frick, Ford 1970

+ Giles, Warren 1979
+ Griffith, Clark 1946
+ Harridge, Will 1972
+ Hulbert, William 1995
+ Johnson, Ban 1937
+ Landis, Kenesaw 1944
+ MacPhail, Larry 1978
  MacPhail, Lee 1998

+ Rickey, Branch 1967
+ Spalding, Al 1939
+ Veeck, Bill 1991
+ Weiss, George 1971
+ Wright, George 1937
+ Wright, Harry 1953
+ Yawkey, Tom 1980

Ford Frick Award

First presented in 1978 by the Hall of Fame for meritorious contributions by baseball broadcasters. Named in honor of the late newspaper reporter, broadcaster, National League president and commissioner, the Frick Award does not constitute induction into the Hall of Fame.

Year		Year		Year	
1978	Mel Allen & Red Barber	1987	Jack Buck	1996	Herb Carneal
1979	Bob Elson	1988	Lindsey Nelson	1997	Jimmy Dudley
1980	Russ Hodges	1989	Harry Caray	1998	Jaime Jarrin
1981	Ernie Harwell	1990	Byrum Saam	1999	Arch McDonald
1982	Vin Scully	1991	Joe Garagiola	2000	Marty Brennaman
1983	Jack Brickhouse	1992	Milo Hamilton	2001	Felo Ramirez
1984	Curt Gowdy	1993	Chuck Thompson	2002	Harry Kalas
1985	Buck Canel	1994	Bob Murphy		
1986	Bob Prince	1995	Bob Wolff		

J.G. Taylor Spink Award

First presented in 1962 by the Baseball Writers' Association of America for meritorious contributions by members of the BBWAA. Named in honor of the late publisher of *The Sporting News*, the Spink Award does not constitute induction into the Hall of Fame. Winners are honored in the year following their selection.

Year		Year		Year	
1962	J.G. Taylor Spink	1972	Dan Daniel, Fred Lieb & J. Roy Stockton	1978	Tim Murnane & Dick Young
1963	Ring Lardner			1979	Bob Broeg & Tommy Holmes
1964	Hugh Fullerton	1973	Warren Brown, John Drebinger & John F. Kieran	1980	Joe Reichler & Milt Richman
1965	Charley Dryden			1981	Bob Addie & Allen Lewis
1966	Grantland Rice	1974	John Carmichael & James Isaminger	1982	Si Burick
1967	Damon Runyon			1983	Ken Smith
1968	H.G. Salsinger	1975	Tom Meany & Shirley Povich	1984	Joe McGuff
1969	Sid Mercer	1976	Harold Kaese & Red Smith	1985	Earl Lawson
1970	Heywood C. Broun	1977	Gordon Cobbledick & Edgar Munzel	1986	Jack Lang
1971	Frank Graham			1987	Jim Murray

Year		Year		Year	
1988	Bob Hunter & Ray Kelly	1993	John Wendell Smith	1999	Hal Lebovitz
1989	Jerome Holtzman	1994	No award	2000	Ross Newhan
1990	Phil Collier	1995	Joseph Durso	2001	Joe Falls
1991	Ritter Collett	1996	Charley Feeney		
1992	Leonard Koppett	1997	Sam Lacy		
	& Buzz Saidt	1998	Bob Stevens		

BASKETBALL

Naismith Memorial Basketball Hall of Fame

Established in 1949 by the National Association of Basketball Coaches in memory of the sport's inventor, Dr. James Naismith. Original Hall opened in 1968 and a renovated version of the Hall opened in 1985. A completely new building opened Sept. 28, 2002. **Address:** 1000 West Columbus Avenue, Springfield, MA 01105. **Telephone:** (413) 781-6500.

Eligibility: Nominated players and referees must be retired for five years, coaches must have coached 25 years or be retired for five, and contributors must have already completed their noteworthy service to the game. Voting done by 24-member honors committee made up of media representatives, Hall of Fame members and trustees. Any nominee not elected after five years becomes eligible for consideration by the Veterans' Committee after a five-year wait.

Class of 2002 (6): PLAYERS—guard **Earvin "Magic" Johnson**, L.A. Lakers (1979-91, 1995-96); guard **Drazen Petrovic**, Yugoslavian and Croatian national teams, Portland (1989-91), New Jersey (1991-93); COACHES—**Larry Brown**, Carolina-ABA (1972-74), Denver-ABA/NBA (1974-79), UCLA-NCAA (1979-81), New Jersey-NBA (1981-83), Kansas-NCAA (1983-88), San Antonio-NBA (1988-92); L.A. Clippers (1992-93), Indiana (1993-97), Philadelphia (1997–); **Lute Olson**, Long Beach St. (1973-74), Iowa (1974-83), Arizona (1983–); **Kay Yow**, Elon College (1971-75), N.C. State (1975–).

2002 finalists (nominated but not elected): PLAYERS—Maurice Cheeks, Adrian Dantley, Bobby Jones, Earl Lloyd, Dino Meneghin, Chet Walker and James Worthy. COACHES—Forrest Anderson, Lefty Driesell, Harley Redin, Cathy Rush, Bill Sharman and Eddie Sutton. CONTRIBUTORS—Jerry Colangelo, Junius Kellogg, Grady Lewis and Tex Winter. TEAM—Harlem Globetrotters.

Note: John Wooden and **Lenny Wilkens**, who was rehonored by the Hall in 1998, are the only members to be inducted as both a player and a coach.

Members are listed with years of induction; (+) indicates deceased members.

Men

Abdul-Jabbar, Kareem	1995	Greer, Hal	1981	Mikkelsen, Vern	1995
Archibald, Nate	1991	+ Gruenig, Robert	1963	Monroe, Earl	1990
Arizin, Paul	1977	Hagan, Cliff	1977	Murphy, Calvin	1993
+ Barlow, Thomas (Babe)	1980	+ Hanson, Victor	1960	+ Murphy, Charles (Stretch)	1960
Barry, Rick	1987	Havlicek, John	1983	+ Page, Harlan (Pat)	1962
Baylor, Elgin	1976	Hawkins, Connie	1992	+ Petrovic, Drazen	2002
+ Beckman, John	1972	Hayes, Elvin	1990	Pettit, Bob	1970
Bellamy, Walt	1993	Haynes, Marques	1998	+ Phillip, Andy	1961
Belov, Sergei	1992	Heinsohn, Tom	1986	+ Pollard, Jim	1977
Bing, Dave	1990	+ Holman, Nat	1964	Ramsey, Frank	1981
Bird, Larry	1998	Houbregs, Bob	1987	Reed, Willis	1981
Borgmann, Bennie	1961	Howell, Bailey	1997	Risen, Arnie	1998
Bradley, Bill	1982	+ Hyatt, Chuck	1959	Robertson, Oscar	1979
+ Brennan, Joe	1974	Issel, Dan	1993	+ Roosma, John	1961
Cervi, Al	1984	+ Jeannette, Buddy	1994	Russell, Bill	1974
+ Chamberlain, Wilt	1978	+ Johnson, Bill (Skinny)	1976	+ Russell, John (Honey)	1964
+ Cooper, Charles (Tarzan)	1976	Johnson, Earvin (Magic)	2002	Schayes, Dolph	1972
+ Cosic, Kresimir	1996	+ Johnston, Neil	1990	+ Schmidt, Ernest J	1973
Cousy, Bob	1970	Jones, K. C.	1989	+ Schommer, John	1959
Cowens, Dave	1991	Jones, Sam	1983	+ Sedran, Barney	1962
Cunningham, Billy	1986	+ Krause, Edward (Moose)	1975	Sharman, Bill	1975
Davies, Bob	1969	Kurland, Bob	1961	+ Steinmetz, Christian	1961
+ DeBernardi, Forrest	1961	Lanier, Bob	1992	Thomas, Isiah	2000
DeBusschere, Dave	1982	+ Lapchick, Joe	1966	Thompson, David	1996
Dehnert, Dutch	1968	Lovellette, Clyde	1988	+ Thompson, John (Cat)	1962
+ Endacott, Paul	1971	Lucas, Jerry	1979	Thurmond, Nate	1984
English, Alex	1997	Luisetti, Hank	1959	· Twyman, Jack	1982
Erving, Julius (Dr. J)	1993	Macauley, Ed	1960	Unseld, Wes	1988
+ Foster, Bud	1964	Malone, Moses	2001	+ Vandivier, Robert (Fuzzy)	1974
Frazier, Walt	1987	+ Maravich, Pete	1987	+ Wachter, Ed	1961
+ Friedman, Marty	1971	Martin, Slater	1981	Walton, Bill	1993
+ Fulks, Joe	1977	McAdoo, Bob	2000	Wanzer, Bobby	1987
+ Gale, Laddie	1976	+ McCracken, Branch	1960	West, Jerry	1979
Gallatin, Harry	1991	+ McCracken, Jack	1962	Wilkens, Lenny	1989
+ Gates, William (Pop)	1989	+ McDermott, Bobby	1988	Wooden, John	1960
Gervin, George	1996	McGuire, Dick	1993	Yardley, George	1996
Gola, Tom	1975	McHale, Kevin	1999		
Goodrich, Gail	1996	Mikan, George	1959		

Women

Blazejowski, Carol	1994	Harris-Stewart, Lucia	1992	Semenova, Uljana	1993
Crawford, Joan	1997	Lieberman, Nancy	1996	White, Nera	1992
Curry, Denise	1997	Meyers, Ann	1993		
Donovan, Anne	1995	Miller, Cheryl	1995		

Basketball (Cont.)

Teams

Buffalo Germans 1961	Harlem Globetrotters. 2002	Original Celtics 1959
First Team 1959	New York Renaissance 1963	

Referees

+ Enright, Jim. 1978	+ Leith, Lloyd 1982	+ Shirley, J. Dallas 1979
+ Hepbron, George 1960	+ Mihalik, Red. 1986	+ Strom, Earl 1995
+ Hoyt, George. 1961	+ Nucatola, John. 1977	+ Tobey, Dave 1961
+ Kennedy, Pat 1959	+ Quigley, Ernest (Quig) 1961	+ Walsh, David 1961

Coaches

+ Allen, Forrest (Phog) 1959	Gomelsky, Aleksandr 1995	Meyer, Ray. 1978
+ Anderson, Harold (Andy) 1984	+ Hannum, Alex 1998	+ Miller, Ralph. 1988
Auerbach, Red. 1968	Harshman, Marv 1984	Moore, Billie. 1999
+ Barry, Sam 1978	Haskins, Don 1997	Newell, Pete. 1978
+ Blood, Ernest (Prof) 1960	+ Hickey, Eddie 1978	+ Nikolic, Aleksandar 1998
Brown, Larry. 2002	+ Hobson, Howard (Hobby) . . .1965	Olson, Lute 2002
+ Cann, Howard. 1967	+ Holzman, Red 1986	Ramsay, Jack 1992
+ Carlson, Henry (Doc) 1959	+ Iba, Hank 1968	Rubini, Cesare 1994
Carnesecca, Lou 1992	+ Julian, Alvin (Doggie) 1967	+ Rupp, Adolph. 1968
Carnevale, Ben 1969	+ Keaney, Frank 1960	+ Sachs, Leonard 1961
Carril, Pete 1997	+ Keogan, George 1961	+ Shelton, Everett 1979
+ Case, Everett 1981	Knight, Bob 1991	Smith, Dean 1982
Chaney, John 2001	Krzyzewski, Mike 2001	Summitt, Pat 2000
Conradt, Jody 1998	Kundla, John 1995	+ Taylor, Fred. 1986
Crum, Denny 1994	+ Lambert, Ward (Piggy) 1960	Thompson, John. 1999
Daly, Chuck 1994	+ Litwack, Harry 1975	+ Wade, Margaret 1984
+ Dean, Everett 1966	+ Loeffler, Ken 1964	Watts, Stan. 1985
+ Diaz-Miguel, Antonio 1997	+ Lonborg, Dutch 1972	Wilkens, Lenny. 1998
+ Diddle, Ed 1971	+ McCutchan, Arad 1980	Wooden, John 1972
+ Drake, Bruce 1972	+ McGuire, Al 1992	+ Woolpert, Phil 1992
Gaines, Clarence (Bighouse). .1981	+ McGuire, Frank 1976	Wooten, Morgan. 2000
+ Gardner, Jack 1983	+ McLendon, John. 1978	Yow, Kay. 2002
+ Gill, Amory (Slats). 1967	+ Meanwell, Walter (Doc) 1959	

Contributors

+ Abbott, Senda Berenson. 1984	+ Hinkle, Tony 1965	+ Ripley, Elmer. 1972
+ Bee, Clair 1967	+ Irish, Ned 1964	+ St. John, Lynn W 1962
+ Biasone, Danny 2000	+ Jones, R. William. 1964	+ Saperstein, Abe 1970
+ Brown, Walter A 1965	+ Kennedy, Walter 1980	+ Schabinger, Arthur 1961
+ Bunn, John 1964	+ Liston, Emil (Liz) 1974	+ Stagg, Amos Alonzo. 1959
+ Douglas, Bob 1971	+ Mokray, Bill 1965	Stankovic, Boris 1991
+ Duer, Al 1981	+ Morgan, Ralph. 1959	+ Steitz, Ed. 1983
Embry, Wayne. 1999	+ Morgenweck, Frank (Pop) . . .1962	+ Taylor, Chuck 1968
+ Fagan, Clifford B 1983	+ Naismith, James. 1959	+ Teague, Bertha. 1984
+ Fisher, Harry 1973	Newton, Charles M. 2000	+ Tower, Oswald. 1959
+ Fleisher, Larry. 1991	+ O'Brien, John J. (Jack). 1961	+ Trester, Arthur (A.L.) 1961
+ Gottlieb, Eddie. 1971	+ O'Brien, Larry 1991	+ Wells, Cliff 1971
+ Gulick, Luther 1959	+ Olsen, Harold G 1959	+ Wilke, Lou 1982
+ Harrison, Les 1979	+ Podoloff, Maurice 1973	+ Zollner, Fred. 1999
+ Hepp, Ferenc 1980	+ Porter, Henry (H.V.) 1960	
+ Hickox, Ed 1959	+ Reid, William A. 1963	

Curt Gowdy Award

First presented in 1990 by the Hall of Fame Board of Trustees for meritorious contributions by the media. Named in honor of the former NBC sportscaster, the Gowdy Award does not constitute induction into the Hall of Fame.

Year	**Year**	**Year**
1990 Curt Gowdy & Dick Herbert	1995 Dick Enberg & Bob Hammel	2000 Dave Kindred & Hubie Brown
1991 Dave Dorr & Marty Glickman	1996 Billy Packer & Bob Hentzen	2001 Dick Stockton
1992 Sam Goldaper & Chick Hearn	1997 Marv Albert & Bob Ryan	& Curry Kirkpatrick
1993 Leonard Lewin & Johnny Most	1998 Dick Vitale, Larry Donald	2002 Jim Nantz & Jim O'Connell
1994 Leonard Koppett	& Dick Weiss	
& Cawood Ledford	1999 Smith Barrier & Bob Costas	

BOWLING

International Bowling Hall of Fame & Museum

The National Bowling Hall is one museum with separate wings for honorees of the American Bowling Congress (ABC), Professional Bowlers' Association (PBA) and Women's International Bowling Congress (WIBC). The museum does not include the Pro Women Bowlers Hall of Fame, which is located in Las Vegas. **Address:** 111 Stadium Plaza, St. Louis, MO 63102. **Telephone:** (314) 231-6340.

Professional Bowlers Association

Established in 1975. **Eligibility:** Nominees must be PBA members and at least 35 years old. Voting done by 50-member panel that includes writers who have covered bowling for at least 12 years.

Note: The PBA is revamping their criteria and will wait until 2003 to induct their next class.

Members are listed with years of induction; (+) indicates deceased members.

Performance

+ Allen, Bill ...1983	+ Fazio, Buzz ...1976	Roth, Mark ...1987
+ Anthony, Earl ...1986	Ferraro, Dave ...1997	Salvino, Carmen ...1975
Aulby, Mike ...1996	+ Godman, Jim ...1987	Semiz, Teata ...1998
Berardi, Joe ...1990	Hardwick, Billy ...1977	Smith, Harry ...1975
Bluth, Ray ...1975	Holman, Marshall ...1990	Soutar, Dave ...1979
Bohn, Parker III ...2000	Hudson, Tommy ...1989	Stefanich, Jim ...1980
Buckley, Roy ...1992	Husted, Dave ...1996	Voss, Brian ...1994
Burton, Nelson Jr ...1979	Johnson, Don ...1977	Webb, Wayne ...1993
Carter, Don ...1975	Laub, Larry ...1985	Weber, Dick ...1975
Colwell, Paul ...1991	Monacelli, Amleto ...1997	Weber, Pete ...1998
Cook, Steve ...1993	Ozio, David ...1995	+ Welu, Billy ...1975
Davis, Dave ...1978	Pappas, George ...1986	Williams, Mark ...1999
Dickinson, Gary ...1988	Petraglia, John ...1982	Williams, Walter Ray Jr ...1995
Durbin, Mike ...1984	Ritger, Dick ...1978	Zahn, Wayne ...1981

Veterans

Allison, Glenn ...1984	+ Joseph, Joe ...1985	Schlegel, Ernie ...1997
Asher, Barry ...1988	Limongello, Mike ...1994	+ St. John, Jim ...1989
Baker, Tom ...1999	Marzich, Andy ...1990	Strampe, Bob ...1987
Foremsky, Skee ...1992	McCune, Don ...1991	
Guenther, Johnny ...1986	McGrath, Mike ...1988	

Meritorious Service

+ Antenora, Joe ...1993	+ Fitzgerald, Jim ...2000	Nakano, Keijiro ...1999
Archibald, John ...1989	+ Frantz, Lou ...1978	Pezzano, Chuck ...1975
Clemens, Chuck ...1994	Golden, Harry ...1983	Reichert, Jack ...1992
+ Elias, Eddie ...1976	Hoffman, Ted Jr ...1985	+ Richards, Joe ...1976
Esposito, Frank ...1975	Jowdy, John ...1988	Schenkel, Chris ...1976
Evans, Dick ...1986	Kelley, Joe ...1989	Stitzlein, Lorraine ...1980
Firestone, Raymond ...1987	Lichstein, Larry ...1996	Thompson, Al ...1991
Fisher, E.A. (Bud) ...1984	+ Nagy, Steve ...1977	Zeller, Roger ...1995

American Bowling Congress

Established in 1941 and open to professional and amateur bowlers. **Eligibility:** Nominated bowlers must have competed in at least 20 years of ABC tournaments. Voting done by 170-member panel made up of ABC officials, Hall of Fame members and media representatives.

Class of 2002 (4): PERFORMANCE—**Norm Duke** and **Pete Weber**; MERITORIOUS SERVICE—**Fred Borden, Mark Jensen** and **Max Skelton**.

Members are listed with years of induction; (+) indicates deceased members.

Performance

Allison, Glenn ...1979	+ Cassio, Marty ...1972	Hart, Bob ...1994
+ Anthony, Earl ...1986	+ Castellano, Graz ...1976	+ Hennessey, Tom ...1976
Asher, Barry ...1998	+ Clause, Frank ...1980	Hoover, Dick ...1974
+ Asplund, Harold ...1978	Cohn, Alfred ...1985	Horn, Bud ...1992
Aulby, Mike ...2001	Colwell, Paul ...1999	Howard, George ...1986
Baer, Gordy ...1987	+ Crimmins, Johnny ...1962	Jackson, Eddie ...1988
Beach, Bill ...1991	Davis, Dave ...1990	Johnson, Don ...1982
+ Benkovic, Frank ...1958	+ Daw, Charlie ...1941	Johnson, Earl ...1987
Berlin, Mike ...1994	+ Day, Ned ...1952	+ Joseph, Joe ...1969
+ Billick, George ...1982	Dickinson, Gary ...1992	+ Jouglard, Lee ...1979
+ Blouin, Jimmy ...1953	Duke, Norm ...2002	+ Kartheiser, Frank ...1967
Bluth, Ray ...1973	+ Easter, Sarge ...1963	+ Kawolics, Ed ...1968
+ Bodis, Joe ...1941	Ellis, Don ...1981	+ Kissoff, Joe ...1976
+ Bomar, Buddy ...1966	+ Falcaro, Joe ...1968	+ Klares, John ...1982
Bower, Gary ...2001	+ Faragalli, Lindy ...1968	+ Knox, Billy ...1954
+ Brandt, Allie ...1960	+ Fazio, Buzz ...1963	+ Koster, John ...1941
+ Brosius, Eddie ...1976	Fehr, Steve ...1993	+ Krems, Eddie ...1973
+ Bujack, Fred ...1967	+ Gersonde, Russ ...1968	Kristof, Joe ...1968
Bunetta, Bill ...1968	+ Gibson, Therm ...1965	+ Krumske, Paul ...1968
Burton, Nelson Jr ...1981	+ Godman, Jim ...1987	+ Lange, Herb ...1941
+ Burton, Nelson Sr ...1964	Goike, Robert ...1996	+ Lauman, Hank ...1976
+ Campi, Lou ...1968	+ Golembiewski, Billy ...1979	Lillard, Bill ...1972
+ Carlson, Adolph ...1941	Griffo, Greg ...1995	Lindemann, Tony ...1979
Carter, Don ...1970	Guenther, Johnny ...1988	+ Lindsey, Mort ...1941
+ Caruana, Frank ...1977	Hardwick, Billy ...1985	+ Lippe, Harry ...1989

Bowling (Cont.)

Lubanski, Ed 1971	Schlegel, Ernie 1997	Toft, Rod 1991
+ Lucci, Vince Sr 1978	Schroeder, Jim 1990	+ Totsky, Mike 1996
+ Marino, Hank 1941	+ Schwoegler, Connie 1968	Tountas, Pete 1989
+ Martino, John 1969	Scudder, Don 1999	Tucker, Bill 1988
Marzich, Andy 1993	Semiz, Teata 1991	Tuttle, Tommy 1995
McGrath, Mike 1993	+ Sielaff, Lou 1968	+ Varipapa, Andy 1957
+ McMahon, Junie 1967	+ Sinke, Joe 1977	+ Ward, Walter 1959
+ Meisel, Darold 1998	+ Sixty, Billy 1961	Weber, Dick 1970
+ Mercurio, Skang 1967	Smith, Harry 1978	Weber, Pete 2002
+ Meyers, Norm 1984	+ Smith, Jimmy 1941	+ Welu, Billy 1975
+ Nagy, Steve 1963	Soutar, Dave 1985	Wilcox, John 1999
+ Norris, Joe 1954	+ Sparando, Tony 1968	+ Wilman, Joe 1951
+ O'Donnell, Chuck 1968	Spigner, Bill 2001	+ Wolf, Phil 1961
Pappas, George 1989	+ Spinella, Barney 1968	Wonders, Rich 1990
+ Patterson, Pat 1974	+ Steers, Harry 1941	+ Young, George 1959
+ Powell, John (Junior) 2000	Stefanich, Jim 1983	Zahn, Wayne 1980
⸱ Ritger, Dick 1984	+ Stein, Otto Jr 1971	Zikes, Les 1983
+ Rogoznica, Andy 1993	Stoudt, Bud 1991	+ Zunker, Gil 1941
Salvino, Carmen 1979	Strampe, Bob 1977	
Schissler, Les 1991	+ Thoma, Sykes 1971	

Pioneers

+ Allen, Lafayette Jr 1994	+ Hall, William Sr 1994	+ Satow, Masao 1994
+ Briell, Frank 1996	Hirashima, Hirohito 1995	+ Schutte, Louis 1993
+ Carow, Rev. Charles 1995	+ Karpf, Samuel 1993	Shimada, Fuzzy 1997
+ Celestine, Sydney 1993	+ Moore, Henry 1996	+ Stein, Louis 1997
+ Curtis, Thomas 1993	+ Pasdeloup, Frank 1993	+ Thompson, William V. 1993
+ de Freitas, Eric 1994	+ Rhodman, Bill 1997	+ Timm, Dr. Henry 1993

Meritorious Service

+ Allen, Harold 1966	+ Franklin, Bill 1992	Pezzano, Chuck 1982
Archibald, John 1996	+ Hagerty, Jack 1963	Picchietti, Remo 1993
+ Baker, Frank 1975	+ Hattstrom, H.A. (Doc) 1980	Pluckhahn, Bruce 1989
+ Baumgarten, Elmer 1963	+ Hermann, Cornelius 1968	+ Raymer, Milt 1972
+ Bellisimo, Lou 1986	+ Howley, Pete 1941	+ Reed, Elmer 1978
+ Bensinger, Bob 1969	Jensen, Mark 2002	Reichert, Jack 1998
Borden, Fred 2002	Jowdy, John 2001	Rudo, Milt 1984
+ Chase, LeRoy 1972	+ Kennedy, Bob 1981	Schenkel, Chris 1988
+ Coker, John 1980	+ Langtry, Abe 1963	Skelton, Max 2002
+ Collier, Chuck 1963	+ Levine, Sam 1971	+ Sweeney, Dennis 1974
+ Cruchon, Steve 1983	+ Luby, David 1969	Tessman, Roger 1994
+ Ditzen, Walt 1973	Luby, Mort Jr 1988	+ Thum, Joe 1980
+ Dobs, Darold 1999	+ Luby, Mort Sr 1974	Weinstein, Sam 1970
+ Doehrman, Bill 1968	Matzelle, Al 1995	+ Whitney, Eli 1975
+ Elias, Eddie 1985	+ McCullough, Howard 1971	+ Wolf, Fred 1976
Esposito, Frank 1997	+ Patterson, Morehead 1985	
Evans, Dick 1992	+ Petersen, Louie 1963	

Women's International Bowling Congress

Established in 1953. **Eligibility:** Performance nominees must have won at least one WIBC Championship Tournament title, a WIBC Queens tournament title or an international competition title and have bowled in at least 15 national WIBC Championship Tournaments (unless injury or illness cut career short).
Class of 2002 (3): PERFORMANCE—**Cheryl Daniels** and **Tish Johnson**; MERITORIOUS SERVICE—**Nancy Chapman**. Members are listed with years of induction; (+) indicates deceased members.

Performance

Abel, Joy 1984	Dryer, Pat 1978	Havlish, Jean 1987
Adamek, Donna 1996	Duval, Helen 1970	+ Hoffman, Martha 1979
Ann, Patty 1995	+ Fellmeth, Catherine 1970	Holm, Joan 1974
Bolt, Mae 1978	Fothergill, Dotty 1980	+ Humphreys, Birdie 1979
Bouvia, Gloria 1987	+ Fulton, Louise 2001	Ignizio, Millie Martorella 1975
Boxberger, Loa 1984	+ Fritz, Deane 1966	Jacobson, D.D 1981
Buckner, Pam 1990	Garms, Shirley 1971	+ Jaeger, Emma 1953
+ Burling, Catherine 1958	Gianulias, Nikki 1997	Johnson, Tish 2002
+ Burns, Nina 1977	+ Gloor, Olga 1976	Kelly, Annese 1985
Cantaline, Anita 1979	Gonzalez, Ashie 1998	+ Knechtges, Doris 1983
Carter, LaVerne 1977	Graham, Linda 1992	Kuczynski, Betty 1981
Carter, Paula 1994	Graham, Mary Lou 1989	Ladewig, Marion 1964
Coburn, Doris 1976	+ Greenwald, Goldie 1953	+ Matthews, Merle 1974
Coburn-Carroll, Cindy 1998	Grinfelds, Vesma 1991	+ McCutcheon, Floretta 1956
Costello, Pat 1986	+ Harman, Janet 1985	Merrick, Marge 1980
Costello, Patty 1989	+ Hartrick, Stella 1972	+ Mikiel, Val 1979
Daniels, Cheryl 2002	+ Hatch, Grayce 1953	Miller-Mackey, Dana 2000

Miller, Carol 1997	Reichley, Susie 2000	+ Small, Tess 1971
+ Miller, Dorothy 1954	Rickard, Robbie 1994	+ Smith, Grace 1968
Mivelaz, Betty 1991	+ Robinson, Leona 1969	Soutar, Judy 1976
Mohacsi, Mary 1994	Romeo, Robin. 1995	+ Stockdale, Louise 1953
Morris, Betty 1983	+ Rump, Anita 1962	Toepfer, Elvira 1976
Naccarato, Jeanne 1999	+ Ruschmeyer, Addie 1961	+ Twyford, Sally 1964
Nichols, Lorrie Koch 1989	+ Ryan, Esther 1963	Wagner, Lisa 2000
Norman, Carol 2001	+ Sablatnik, Ethel 1979	+ Warmbier, Marie. 1953
Norman, Edie Jo 1993	Sandelin, Lucy 1999	Wene-Martin, Sylvia 1966
Norton, Virginia 1988	+ Schulte, Myrtle 1965	Wilkinson, Dorothy 1990
Notaro, Phyllis 1979	+ Shablis, Helen 1977	+ Winandy, Cecelia 1975
Ortner, Bev 1972	Sill, Aleta 1996	Zimmerman, Donna 1982
+ Powers, Connie 1973	+ Simon, Violet (Billy) 1960	

+ Baetz, Helen. 1977	+ Herold, Mitzi 1998	+ Phaler, Emma 1965
+ Baker, Helen. 1989	+ Higley, Margaret 1969	+ Porter, Cora 1986
+ Banker, Gladys 1994	+ Hochstadter, Bee 1967	+ Quin, Zoe. 1979
+ Bayley, Clover 1992	+ Kay, Nora. 1964	+ Rishling, Gertrude 1972
+ Berger, Winifred 1976	Keller, Pearl 1999	Robinson, Jeanette. 2000
+ Bohlen, Philena 1955	+ Kelly, Ellen 1979	Simone, Anne 1991
Borschuk, Lo. 1988	Kelone, Theresa 1978	Sloan, Catherine 1985
+ Botkin, Freda 1986	+ Knepprath, Jeannette 1963	+ Speck, Berdie. 1966
+ Chapman, Emily 1957	+ Lasher, Iolia 1967	Spitalnick, Mildred 1994
Chapman, Nancy 2002	+ Marrs, Mabel. 1979	+ Spring, Alma 1979
+ Crowe, Alberta 1982	+ McBride, Bertha. 1968	+ Switzer, Pearl. 1973
+ Dornblaser, Gertrude 1979	McLeary, Hazel 2000	+ Todd, Trudy. 1993
Duffy, Agnes. 1987	+ Menne, Catherine 1979	+ Veatch, Georgia 1974
Finke, Gertrude 1990	Mitchell, Flora 1996	+ White, Mildred 1975
+ Fisk, Rae. 1983	Morton, Clara 2001	+ Wood, Ann. 1970
+ Haas, Dorothy 1977	+ Mraz, Jo 1959	
Hagin, Elaine. 2000	O'Connor, Billie. 1992	

Meritorious Service

Professional Women Bowlers Hall of Fame

Established in 1995 by the Ladies Pro Bowlers Tour. The LPBT has since been renamed the Professional Women Bowlers Association. **Address:** Sam's Town Hotel, Gambling Hall and Bowling Center, 5111 Boulder Highway, Las Vegas, NV 89122. **Telephone:** (815) 332-5756.

Eligibility: Nominees in performance category must have at least five titles from organizations including All-Star, World Invitational, LPBT, WPBA, PWBA, TPA and LPBA. Voting done by 10-member committee of bowling writers appointed by PWBA president John Falzone.

Class of 2002 (2): PERFORMANCE—**Dana Miller-Mackie** and **Jeanne Naccarato**.

Members are listed with year of induction; (+) indicates deceased member.

Performance

Adamek, Donna 1995	Grinfelds, Vesma 1997	Naccarato, Jeanne 2002
Coburn-Carroll, Cindy 1997	Johnson, Tish 1998	Nichols, Lorrie 1996
Costello, Pat 1997	Ladewig, Marion 1995	Romeo, Robin. 1996
Costello, Patty 1995	Martorella, Millie. 1995	Sill, Aleta 1998
Fothergill, Dotty 1995	Miller-Mackie, Dana 2002	Wagner, Lisa 1996
Gianulias, Nikki 1996	Morris, Betty. 1995	

Pioneers

Able, Joy. 1998	Coburn, Doris 1996	Ortner, Bev. 1998
Boxberger, Loa. 1997	Duval, Helen 1995	Soutar, Judy 1997
Carter, LaVerne 1995	Garms, Shirley. 1995	Zimmerman, Donna 1996

Builders

+ Buehler, Janet. 1996	Robinson, Jeanette. 1996	+ Veatch, Georgia 1995
Keller, Pearl 1997	Sommer Jr., John 1997	

BOXING

International Boxing Hall of Fame

Established in 1984 and opened in 1989. **Address:** 1 Hall of Fame Drive, Canastota, NY 13032. **Tel.:** (315) 697-7095.

Eligibility: All nominees must be retired for five years. Voting done by 142-member panel made up of Boxing Writers' Association members and world-wide boxing historians.

Class of 2002 (17): MODERN ERA—**Pipino Cuevas**, **Jeff Fenech**, **Victor Galindez** and **Ingemar Johansson**. OLD TIMERS—**Benny Bass**, **Aaron "Dixie Kid" Brown**, **Sixto Escobar**, **Harry Harris**, **Charley Mitchell** and **Owen Moran**. PIONEER—**John C. Heenan**. NON-PARTICIPANTS—**Irving Cohen**, **Aileen Eaton** and **Sam Silverman**. OBSERVERS—**Jimmy Cannon**, **Reg Gutteridge** and **Damon Runyan**.

Members are listed with year of induction; (+) indicates deceased member.

Boxing (Cont.)
Modern Era

Ali, Muhammad	1990	
+ Angott, Sammy	1998	
Arguello, Alexis	1992	
+ Armstrong, Henry	1990	
Basilio, Carmen	1990	
Benitez, Wilfredo	1996	
Benvenuti, Nino	1992	
+ Berg, Jackie (Kid)	1994	
Bivins, Jimmy	1999	
+ Brown, Joe	1996	
Buchanan, Ken	2000	
+ Burley, Charley	1992	
Canto, Miguel	1998	
+ Carter, Jimmy	2000	
+ Cerdan, Marcel	1991	
Cervantes, Antonio	1998	
Chandler, Jeff	2000	
+ Charles, Ezzard	1990	
+ Conn, Billy	1990	
Cuevas, Pipino	2002	
+ Elorde, Gabriel (Flash)	1993	
Fenech, Jeff	2002	
Foster, Bob	1990	
Frazier, Joe	1990	
Fullmer, Gene	1991	
Galaxy, Khaosai	1999	
+ Galindez, Victor	2002	
Gavilan, Kid	1990	

Giardello, Joey	1993	
Gomez, Wilfredo	1995	
+ Graham, Billy	1992	
+ Graziano, Rocky	1991	
Griffith, Emile	1990	
Hagler, Marvelous Marvin	1993	
Harada, Masahiko (Fighting)	1995	
Jack, Beau	1991	
+ Jenkins, Lew	1999	
Jofre, Eder	1992	
Johansson, Ingemar	2002	
Johnson, Harold	1993	
Laguna, Ismael	2001	
LaMotta, Jake	1990	
Leonard, Sugar Ray	1997	
+ Liston, Sonny	1991	
+ Louis, Joe	1990	
+ Marciano, Rocky	1990	
+ Maxim, Joey	1994	
+ Montgomery, Bob	1995	
+ Monzon, Carlos	1990	
+ Moore, Archie	1990	
Muhammad, Matthew Saad	1998	
Napoles, Jose	1990	
Norton, Ken	1992	
Olivares, Ruben	1991	
+ Olson, Carl (Bobo)	2000	
Ortiz, Carlos	1991	

+ Ortiz, Manuel	1996	
Papp, Laszlo	2001	
+ Pastrano, Willie	2001	
Patterson, Floyd	1991	
Pedroza, Eusebio	1999	
Pep, Willie	1990	
+ Perez, Pascual	1995	
Pryor, Aaron	1996	
Ramos, Ultiminio	2001	
+ Robinson, Sugar Ray	1990	
+ Rodriguez, Luis	1997	
+ Saddler, Sandy	1990	
+ Saldivar, Vicente	1999	
+ Sanchez, Salvador	1991	
Schmeling, Max	1992	
Spinks, Michael	1994	
+ Tiger, Dick	1991	
Torres, Jose	1997	
+ Turpin, Randy	2001	
+ Walcott, Jersey Joe	1990	
+ Williams, Ike	1990	
+ Wright, Chalky	1997	
+ Zale, Tony	1991	
Zarate, Carlos	1994	
+ Zivic, Fritzie	1993	

Old-Timers

+ Ambers, Lou	1992	
+ Attell, Abe	1990	
+ Baer, Max	1995	
+ Barry, Jimmy	2000	
+ Bass, Benny	2002	
+ Berlenbach, Paul	2001	
+ Braddock, Jim	2001	
+ Britton, Jack	1990	
+ Brown, Aaron (Dixie Kid)	2002	
+ Brown, Panama Al	1992	
+ Burns, Tommy	1996	
+ Canzoneri, Tony	1990	
+ Carpentier, Georges	1991	
+ Chocolate, Kid	1991	
+ Choynski, Joe	1998	
+ Corbett, James J.	1990	
+ Coulon, Johnny	1999	
+ Darcy, Les	1993	
+ Delaney, Jack	1996	
+ Dempsey, Jack	1990	
+ Dempsey, Jack (Nonpareil)	1992	
+ Dillon, Jack	1995	
+ Dixon, George	1990	
+ Driscoll, Jim	1990	
+ Dundee, Johnny	1991	
+ Escobar, Sixto	2002	
+ Fitzsimmons, Bob	1990	
+ Flowers, Theodore (Tiger)	1993	

+ Gans, Joe	1990	
+ Genaro, Frankie	1998	
+ Gibbons, Mike	1992	
+ Gibbons, Tommy	1993	
+ Greb, Harry	1990	
+ Griffo, Young	1991	
+ Harris, Harry	2002	
+ Herman, Pete	1997	
+ Jackson, Peter	1990	
+ Jeanette, Joe	1997	
+ Jeffries, James J	1990	
+ Johnson, Jack	1990	
+ Ketchel, Stanley	1990	
+ Kilbane, Johnny	1995	
+ LaBarba, Fidel	1996	
+ Langford, Sam	1990	
+ Lavigne, George (Kid)	1998	
+ Leonard, Benny	1990	
+ Levinsky, Battling	2000	
+ Lewis, John Henry	1994	
+ Lewis, Ted (Kid)	1992	
+ Loughran, Tommy	1991	
+ Lynch, Benny	1998	
+ Mandell, Sammy	1998	
+ McAuliffe, Jack	1995	
+ McCoy, Charles (Kid)	1991	
+ McFarland, Packey	1992	
+ McGovern, Terry	1990	

McLarnin, Jimmy	1991	
+ McVey, Sam	1999	
+ Miller, Freddie	1997	
+ Mitchell, Charley	2002	
+ Moran, Owen	2002	
+ Nelson, Battling	1992	
+ O'Brien, Philadelphia Jack	1994	
+ Papke, Billy	2001	
+ Petrolle, Billy	2000	
+ Rosenbloom, Maxie	1993	
+ Ross, Barney	1990	
+ Ryan, Tommy	1991	
+ Sharkey, Jack	1994	
+ Steele, Freddie	1999	
+ Stribling, Young	1996	
+ Tendler, Lew	1999	
+ Tunney, Gene	1990	
+ Villa, Pancho	1994	
+ Walcott, Joe (Barbados)	1991	
+ Walker, Mickey	1990	
+ Welsh, Freddie	1997	
+ Wilde, Jimmy	1990	
+ Williams, Kid	1996	
+ Wills, Harry	1992	
+ Wolgast, Ad	2000	
+ Wolgast, Midget	2001	

Pioneers

+ Aaron, Barney	2001	
+ Belcher, Jem	1992	
+ Brain, Ben	1994	
+ Broughton, Jack	1990	
+ Burke, James (Deaf)	1992	
+ Chambers, Arthur	2000	
+ Cribb, Tom	1991	
+ Donovan, Prof. Mike	1998	
+ Duffy, Paddy	1994	
+ Figg, James	1992	

+ Heenan, John C.	2002	
+ Jackson, Gentleman John	1992	
+ Johnson, Tom	1995	
+ King, Tom	1992	
+ Langham, Nat	1992	
+ Mace, Jem	1990	
+ Mendoza, Daniel	1990	
+ Molineaux, Tom	1997	
+ Morrissey, John	1996	
+ Pearce, Henry	1993	

+ Richmond, Bill	1999	
+ Sam, Dutch	1997	
+ Sam, Young Dutch	2002	
+ Sayers, Tom	1990	
+ Spring, Tom	1992	
+ Sullivan, John L	1990	
+ Thompson, William	1991	
+ Ward, Jem	1995	

Non-Participants

+ Andrews, Thomas S 1992
+ Arcel, Ray.................1991
  Arum, Bob 1999
+ Ballarati, Giuseppe.......1999
  Benton, George...........2001
+ Blackburn, Jack 1992
+ Brady, William A. 1998
  Brenner, Teddy 1993
+ Chambers, John Graham ...1990
  Chargin, Don 2001
  Clancy, Gil 1993
+ Coffroth, James W. 1991
+ Cohen, Irving 2002
+ D'Amato, Cus. 1995
  Dickson, Jeff 2000
+ Donovan, Arthur 1993
  Duff, Mickey.............1999
  Dundee, Angelo..........1992
+ Dundee, Chris 1994

+ Dunphy, Don 1993
  Duva, Lou 1998
+ Eaton, Aileen 2002
+ Egan, Pierce 1991
+ Fleischer, Nat............1990
+ Fox, Richard K............1997
+ Futch, Eddie 1994
+ Goldman, Charley 1992
+ Goldstein, Ruby 1994
  Goodman, Murray 1999
+ Humphreys, Joe 1997
+ Ichinose, Sam............2001
+ Jacobs, Jimmy 1993
+ Jacobs, Mike 1990
+ Johnston, Jimmy 1999
+ Kearns, Jack (Doc)........1990
  King, Don 1997
  Lectoure, Tito 2000
+ Liebling, A.J 1992

+ Lonsdale, Lord 1990
+ Markson, Harry...........1992
  Mercante, Arthur 1995
+ Morgan, Dan 2000
+ Muldoon, William 1996
  Odd, Gilbert 1995
+ O'Rourke, Tom 1999
+ Parker, Dan 1996
+ Parnassus, George 1991
+ Queensberry, Marquis of ...1990
+ Rickard, Tex 1990
+ Rudd, Irving 1999
+ Siler, George 1995
+ Silverman, Sam 2002
+ Solomons, Jack 1995
  Steward, Emanuel 1996
+ Taub, Sam. 1994
+ Taylor, Herman 1998
+ Walker, James J. (Jimmy) ...1992

+ Bromberg, Lester 2001
+ Cannon, Jimmy 2002

Observers

Citro, Ralph 2001
Gallo, Bill 2001

Gutteridge, Reg...........2002
Runyon, Damon...........2002

Old *Ring* Hall Members Not in Int'l. Boxing Hall

Nat Fleischer, the late founder and editor-in-chief of *The Ring*, established his magazine's Boxing Hall of Fame in 1954, but it was abandoned after the 1987 inductions. One hundred and twenty-four members of the old *Ring* Hall have been elected to the International Hall since 1989. The 30 boxers and one sportswriter who have yet to be elected to the International Hall are listed below with their year of induction into the *Ring* Hall.

Modern Group

+ Apostoli, Fred..............1978
+ Garcia, Ceferino 1977

+ Lesnevich, Gus.............1973
+ Shirai, Yoshio..............1977

Old-Timers

+ Britt, Jimmy ...\..........1976
+ Chaney, George (K.O.) 1974
+ Corbett, Young II 1965
+ Fields, Jackie 1977
+ Houck, Leo 1969

+ Jeffra, Harry 1982
+ Klaus, Frank 1974
+ Maher, Peter..............1978
+ Ritchie, Willie 1962
+ Root, Jack 1961

+ Sharkey, Tom 1959
+ Smith, Jeff 1969
+ Taylor, Bud 1986
+ Willard, Jess..............1977

Pioneers

+ Chandler, Tom 1972
+ Clark, Nobby 1971
+ Collyer, Sam 1964
+ Donnelly, Dan 1960
+ Goss, Joe 1969

+ Gully, John 1959
+ Hyer, Jacob 1968
+ Hyer, Tom 1954
+ Jackling, Thomas..........1985
+ Kilrain, Jack 1965

+ Price, Ned 1962
+ Ryan, Paddy..............1973

Non-Participant

+ Daniel, Dan (sportswriter)....1977

FOOTBALL

College Football Hall of Fame

Established in 1955 by the National Football Foundation. **Address:** 111 South St. Joseph St., South Bend, IN 46601. **Telephone:** (574) 235-9999.

Eligibility: Nominated players must be out of college 10 years and a first team All-America pick by a major selector during their careers; coaches must be retired three years. Voting done by 12-member panel of athletic directors, conference and bowl officials and media representatives. The first year representatives from NCAA Div. I-AA, II, and III, and the NAIA were eligible for induction was 1996.

Class of 2002 (15): LARGE COLLEGE—SE **Terry Beasley**, Auburn (1969-71); TB **George "Sonny" Franck**, Minnesota (1938-40); RB **Cosmo Iacavazzi**, Princeton (1962-64); WR **John Jefferson**, Arizona St. (1974-77); S **Ronnie Lott**, USC (1977-80); QB **Dan Marino**, Pittsburgh (1979-82); TB **Napoleon McCallum**, Navy (1983-85); OG **Reggie McKenzie**, Michigan (1969-71); DB **Randy Rhino**, Georgia Tech (1972-74); OT **Jerry Sisemore**, Texas (1970-72); LB **Gary Spani**, Kansas St. (1974-77); DT **Reggie White**, Tennessee (1980-83); TE **Kellen Winslow**, Missouri (1976-78). COACHES—**Earle Bruce**, Tampa (1972), Iowa State (1973-78), Ohio State (1979-87), N. Iowa (1988), Colorado State (1989-92); **Carmen Cozza**, Yale (1965-96)

Note: **Bobby Dodd** and **Amos Alonzo Stagg** are the only members to be honored as both players and coaches.

Players are listed with final year they played in college and coaches are listed with year of induction; (+) indicates deceased members.

Players

+ Abell, Earl-Colgate 1915
  Agase, Alex-Purdue/III 1946
+ Agganis, Harry-Boston U 1952
  Albert, Frank-Stanford.......1941
+ Aldrich, Ki-TCU 1938

+ Aldrich, Malcolm-Yale.......1921
+ Alexander, Joe-Syracuse.....1920
  Allen, Marcus-USC 1981
  Alworth, Lance-Arkansas 1961
+ Ameche, Alan-Wisconsin 1954

+ Ames, Knowlton-Princeton ...1889
+ Amling, Warren-Ohio St......1946
  Anderson, Dick-Colorado....1967
  Anderson, Donny-Tex.Tech ..1966
+ Anderson, Hunk-N.Dame 1921

College Football Hall of Fame (Cont.)

Arnett, Jon-USC 1956
Atkins, Doug-Tennessee. 1952
Babich, Bob-Miami-OH 1968
+ Bacon, Everett-Wesleyan 1912
+ Bagnell, Reds-Penn 1950
+ Baker, Hobey-Princeton. 1913
+ Baker, John-USC 1931
+ Baker, Moon-N'western 1926
Baker, Terry-Oregon St 1962
+ Ballin, Harold-Princeton 1914
+ Banker, Bill-Tulane 1929
Banonis, Vince-Detroit. 1941
+ Barnes, Stan-California 1921
+ Barrett, Charles-Cornell. 1915
+ Baston, Bert-Minnesota. 1916
+ Battles, Cliff-WV Wesleyan . .1931
Baugh, Sammy-TCU 1936
Baughan, Maxie-Ga.Tech. 1959
+ Bausch, James-Kansas. 1930
Beagle, Ron-Navy 1955
Beasley, Terry-Auburn 1971
Beban, Gary-UCLA 1967
Bechtol, Hub-Texas 1946
Beck, Ray-Ga. Tech 1951
+ Beckett, John-Oregon 1916
Bednarik, Chuck-Penn 1948
Behm, Forrest-Nebraska 1940
Bell, Bobby-Minnesota 1962
Bellino, Joe-Navy. 1960
Below, Marty-Wisconsin 1923
+ Benbrook, Al-Michigan. 1910
+ Berry, Charlie-Lafayette. 1924
+ Bertelli, Angelo-N.Dame. 1943
+ Berwanger, Jay-Chicago 1935
+ Bettencourt, L.-St.Mary's. 1927
Biletnikoff, Fred-Fla.St. 1964
Blanchard, Doc-Army 1946
+ Blozis, Al-Georgetown 1942
Bock, Ed-Iowa St 1938
Bomar, Lynn-Vanderbilt 1924
+ Bomeisler, Bo-Yale 1913
+ Booth, Albie-Yale 1931
+ Borries, Fred-Navy 1934
+ Bosley, Bruce-West Va. 1955
Bosseler, Don-Miami,FL. 1956
Bottari, Vic-California 1938
+ Boynton, Ben-Williams 1920
+ Brewer, Charles-Harvard 1895
+ Bright, Johnny-Drake 1951
Brodie, John-Stanford 1956
+ Brooke, George-Penn 1895
Brosky, Al-Illinois 1952
Brown, Bob-Nebraska 1963
Brown, Geo-Navy/S.Diego St.1947
+ Brown, Gordon-Yale 1900
Brown, Jim-Syracuse 1956
+ Brown, John, Jr.-Navy 1913
+ Brown, Johnny Mack-Ala 1925
+ Brown, Tay-USC 1932
Browner, Ross-Notre Dame . .1977
Buddie, Brad-USC 1979
+ Bunker, Paul-Army 1902
Burford, Chris-Stanford 1959
+ Burris, Kurt-Oklahoma. 1954
Burton, Ron-N'western 1959
Butkus, Dick-Illinois 1964
Butler, Kevin-Georgia 1984
+ Butler, Robert-Wisconsin 1912
+ Cafego, George-Tenn 1939
+ Cagle, Red-SWLa/Army. 1929
+ Cain, John-Alabama 1932
Cameron, Ed-Wash.& Lee . . .1924
+ Campbell, David-Harvard 1901
Campbell, Earl-Texas. 1977

+ Cannon, Jack-N.Dame 1929
Cappelletti, John-Penn St 1973
+ Carideo, Frank-N.Dame. 1930
+ Carney, Charles-Illinois. 1921
Caroline, J.C.-Illinois 1954
Carpenter, Bill-Army 1959
+ Carpenter, Hunter-Va.Tech . . .1905
Carroll, Chas.-Washington . . .1928
Carter, Anthony-Michigan 1982
Casanova, Tommy-LSU 1971
+ Casey, Edward-Harvard. 1919
Cassady, Howard-Ohio St 1955
+ Chamberlin, Guy-Neb. 1915
Chapman, Sam-California 1938
Chappuis, Bob-Michigan 1947
+ Christman, Paul-Missouri 1940
+ Clark, Dutch-Colo. Col. 1929
Cleary, Paul-USC 1947
+ Clevenger, Zora-Indiana 1903
Cloud, Jack-Wm. & Mary 1948
+ Cochran, Gary-Princeton 1897
+ Cody, Josh-Vanderbilt 1919
Coleman, Don-Mich.St 1951
+ Conerly, Charlie-Miss 1947
Connor, George-HC/ND 1947
+ Corbin, William-Yale 1888
Corbus, William-Stanford. 1933
+ Cowan, Hector-Princeton 1889
+ Coy, Edward (Tad)-Yale 1909
+ Crawford, Fred-Duke 1933
Crow, John David-Tex.A&M. .1957
+ Crowley, Jim-Notre Dame 1924
Csonka, Larry-Syracuse 1967
Cutter, Slade-Navy 1934
+ Czarobski, Ziggie-N.Dame . .1947
Dale, Carroll-Va.Tech. 1959
+ Dalrymple, Gerald-Tulane 1931
+ Dalton, John-Navy. 1911
+ Daly, Chas.-Harvard/Army . . .1902
Daniell, Averell-Pitt. 1936
+ Daniell, James-Ohio St 1941
+ Davies, Tom-Pittsburgh 1921
+ Davis, Ernie-Syracuse 1961
Davis, Glenn-Army 1946
Davis, Robert-Ga.Tech 1947
Dawkins, Pete-Army 1958
DeLong, Steve-Tennessee 1964
+ DeRogatis, Al-Duke 1948
+ DesJardien, Paul-Chicago 1914
+ Devine, Aubrey-Iowa 1921
+ DeWitt, John-Princeton 1903
Dial, Buddy-Rice 1958
Dicus, Chuck-Arkansas 1970
Dierdorf, Dan-Michigan 1970
Ditka, Mike-Pittsburgh 1960
Dobbs, Glenn-Tulsa 1942
+ Dodd, Bobby-Tennessee 1930
Donan, Holland-Princeton. 1950
+ Donchess, Joseph-Pitt. 1929
Dorsett, Tony-Pitt. 1976
+ Dougherty, Nathan-Tenn. 1909
Dove, Bob-Notre Dame 1942
Drahos, Nick-Cornell. 1940
+ Driscoll, Paddy-N'western 1917
+ Drury, Morley-USC 1927
Duden, Dick-Navy 1945
Dudley, Bill-Virginia 1941
Duncan, Randy-Iowa 1958
Easley, Kenny-UCLA 1980
+ Eckersall, Walter-Chicago 1906
+ Edwards, Turk-Wash.St. 1931
+ Edwards, Wm.-Princeton 1899
+ Eichenlaub, Ray-N.Dame. 1914
Eisenhauer, Steve-Navy 1953

Elkins, Larry-Baylor 1964
Elliott, Bump-Mich/Purdue . . .1947
Elliott, Pete-Michigan. 1948
Elmendorf, Dave-Tex. A&M . .1970
Elway, John-Stanford 1982
+ Evans, Ray-Kansas. 1947
+ Exendine, Albert-Carlisle 1907
Falaschi, Nello-S.Clara. 1936
Fears, Tom-S.Clara/UCLA 1947
+ Feathers, Beattie-Tenn 1933
Fenimore, Bob-Okla.St 1946
+ Fenton, Doc-LSU. 1909
Ferguson, Bob-Ohio St. 1961
+ Ferraro, John-USC 1944
Fesler, Wes-Ohio St. 1930
+ Fincher, Bill-Ga.Tech 1920
Fischer, Bill-Notre Dame 1948
+ Fish, Hamilton-Harvard. 1909
+ Fisher, Robert-Harvard 1911
+ Flowers, Allen-Ga.Tech 1920
Flowers, Charlie-Ole Miss. 1959
+ Fortmann Danny-Colgate 1935
+ Fralic, Bill-Pittsburgh 1984
+ Francis, Sam-Nebraska 1936
Franck, George-Minnesota. . . .1940
Franco, Ed-Fordham 1937
+ Frank, Clint-Yale 1937
Franz, Rodney-California 1949
Frederickson, Tucker-Auburn . .1964
+ Friedman, Benny-Michigan . . .1926
Gabriel, Roman-N.C. State . . .1961
Gain, Bob-Kentucky 1950
+ Galiffa, Arnold-Army 1949
+ Gallarneau, Hugh-Stanford . . .1940
+ Garbisch, Edgar-W.& J./Army.1924
Garrett, Mike-USC 1965
+ Gelbert, Charles-Penn. 1896
+ Geyer, Forest-Oklahoma. 1915
Gibbs, Jake-Miss 1960
+ Giel, Paul-Minnesota 1953
Gifford, Frank-USC 1951
Gilbert, Chris-Texas 1968
+ Gilbert, Walter-Auburn 1936
Gilmer, Harry-Alabama 1947
+ Gipp, George-N.Dame 1920
+ Gladchuk, Chet-Boston Col . . .1940
Glass, Bill-Baylor 1956
Glover, Rich-Nebraska 1972
Goldberg, Marshall-Pitt. 1938
Goodreault, Gene-BC 1940
+ Gordon, Walter-Calif 1918
+ Governali, Paul-Columbia 1942
Grabowski, Jim-Illinois 1965
Gradishar, Randy-Ohio St. 1973
Graham, Otto-N'western 1943
+ Grange, Red-Illinois. 1925
+ Grayson, Bobby-Stanford 1935
Green, Hugh-Pitt 1980
+ Green, Jack-Tulane/Army. 1945
Green, Tim-Syracuse 1985
Greene, Joe-N.Texas St 1968
Griese, Bob-Purdue 1966
Griffin, Archie-Ohio St 1975
Groom, Jerry-Notre Dame 1950
+ Gulick, Merle-Toledo/Hobart.1929
Guglielmi, Ralph-N.Dame. 1954
+ Guyon, Joe-Ga.Tech 1918
Hadl, John-Kansas. 1961
+ Hale, Edwin-Miss.College 1921
Hall, Parker-Miss 1938
Ham, Jack-Penn St 1970
+ Hamilton, Bob-Stanford. 1935
+ Hamilton, Tom-Navy 1926
Hannah, John-Alabama 1972

College Football Hall of Fame (Cont.)

+ Wojciechowicz, Alex-Fordham . .1937
+ Wood, Barry-Harvard 1931
+ Wyant, Andy-Chicago 1894
+ Wyatt, Bowden-Tenn 1938
+ Wyckoff, Clint-Cornell 1895

+ Yarr, Tommy-N.Dame 1931
  Yary, Ron-USC 1967
+ Yoder, Lloyd-Carnegie 1926
+ Young, Claude-Illinois 1946
+ Young, Harry-Wash.& Lee . . .1916

  Young, Steve-Brigham Young .1983
+ Young, Waddy-Okla 1938
  Youngblood, Jack-Florida 1970
+ Younger, Paul-GRamblin 1948
  Zarnas, Gustave-Ohio St. 1937

Coaches

+ Aillet, Joe 1989
+ Alexander, Bill 1951
+ Anderson, Ed 1971
+ Armstrong, Ike 1957
+ Bachman, Charlie 1978
+ Banks, Earl 1992
+ Baujan, Harry 1990
+ Bell, Matty 1955
+ Bezdek, Hugo 1954
+ Bible, Dana X. 1951
+ Bierman, Bernie 1955
  Blackman, Bob. 1987
+ Blaik, Earl (Red) 1965
  Broyles, Frank 1983
  Bruce, Earle 2002
+ Bryant, Paul (Bear) 1986
+ Butts, Wally 1997
+ Caldwell, Charlie 1961
+ Camp, Walter 1951
  Casanova, Len. 1977
+ Cavanaugh, Frank. 1954
+ Claiborne, Jerry. 1999
+ Colman, Dick 1990
  Coryell, Don. 1999
  Cozza, Carmen. 2002
+ Crisler, Fritz 1954
+ Daugherty, Duffy 1984
+ Devaney, Bob. 1981
+ Devine, Dan 1985
+ Dobie, Gil. 1951
+ Dodd, Bobby 1993
  Donahue, Tom 2000
+ Donohue, Michael. 1951
  Dooley, Vince. 1994
+ Dorais, Gus 1954
+ Edwards, Bill 1986
+ Engle, Rip 1973
  Evashevski, Forest 2000
  Faurot, Don 1961
+ Gaither, Jake 1973
  Gillman, Sid 1989
+ Godfrey, Ernest 1972
  Graves, Ray 1990
+ Gustafson, Andy 1985
+ Hall, Edward 1951
+ Harding, Jack. 1980

+ Harlow, Richard. 1954
+ Harman, Harvey 1981
+ Harper, Jesse 1971
+ Haughton, Percy 1951
+ Hayes, Woody. 1983
+ Heisman, John W 1954
+ Higgins, Robert 1954
+ Hollingberry, Babe 1979
+ Howard, Frank. 1989
+ Ingram, Bill 1973
  James, Don. 1997
+ Jennings, Morley 1973
+ Jones, Biff 1954
+ Jones, Howard 1951
+ Jones, Tad 1958
+ Jordan, Lloyd 1978
+ Jordan, Ralph (Shug) 1982
+ Kerr, Andy 1951
  Kush, Frank. 1995
+ Leahy, Frank. 1970
+ Little, George 1955
+ Little, Lou 1960
+ Madigan, Slip 1974
  Maurer, Dave 1991
+ McClendon, Charley. 1986
+ McCracken, Herb 1973
+ McGugin, Dan 1951
+ McKay, John. 1988
+ McKeen, Allyn 1991
+ McLaughry, Tuss 1962
+ Merritt, John 1994
+ Meyer, Dutch 1956
+ Mollenkopf, Jack 1988
+ Moore, Bernie 1954
+ Moore, Scrappy 1980
+ Morrison, Ray 1954
+ Munger, George 1976
+ Munn, Clarence (Biggie) 1959
+ Murray, Bill. 1974
+ Murray, Frank 1983
+ Mylin, Ed (Hooks) 1974
+ Neale, Earle (Greasy). 1967
+ Neely, Jess 1971
+ Nelson, David 1987
+ Neyland, Robert 1956
+ Norton, Homer 1971

+ O'Neill, Frank (Buck) 1951
+ Osborne, Tom 1998
+ Owen, Bennie 1951
  Parseghian, Ara. 1980
+ Perry, Doyt 1988
+ Phelan, Jimmy 1973
+ Prothro, Tommy 1991
  Ralston, John 1992
+ Robinson, E.N. 1955
+ Rockne, Knute 1951
+ Romney, Dick 1954
+ Roper, Bill. 1951
  Royal,Darrell 1983
+ Sanders, Henry (Red) 1996
+ Sanford, George 1971
  Schembechler, Bo 1993
+ Schmidt, Francis 1971
+ Schwartzwalder, Ben 1982
+ Shaughnessy, Clark 1968
+ Shaw, Buck 1972
+ Smith, Andy 1951
+ Snavely, Carl 1965
+ Stagg, Amos Alonzo 1951
+ Sutherland, Jock. 1951
  Switzer, Barry 2001
+ Tatum, Jim 1984
  Teaff, Grant 2001
+ Thomas, Frank 1951
+ Vann, Thad. 1987
  Vaught, Johnny. 1979
+ Wade, Wallace 1955
+ Waldorf, Lynn (Pappy) 1966
+ Warner, Glenn (Pop). 1951
+ Wieman, E.E. (Tad) 1956
+ Wilce, John 1954
+ Wilkinson, Bud 1969
+ Williams, Henry. 1951
+ Woodruff, George. 1963
+ Woodson, Warren 1989
+ Wyatt, Bowden 1997
  Yeoman, Bill. 2001
  Young, Jim 1999
+ Yost, Fielding (Hurry Up) 1951
+ Zuppke, Bob. 1951

Pro Football Hall of Fame

Established in 1963 by National Football League to commemorate the sport's professional origins. **Address:** 2121 George Halas Drive NW, Canton, OH 44708. **Telephone:** (330) 456-8207.

Eligibility: Nominated players must be retired five years, coaches must be retired, and contributors can still be active. Voting done by 39-member panel made up of media representatives from all 31 NFL cities (two from New York), one PFWA representative and six selectors-at-large.

Class of 2002 (5): PLAYERS—TE **Dave Casper**, Oakland/L.A. Raiders (1974-80, 1984), Houston (1980-83), Minnesota (1983); DL **Dan Hampton**, Chicago (1979-90); QB **Jim Kelly**, Buffalo (1986-96); **John Stallworth**, Pittsburgh (1974-87); COACHES—**George Allen**, L.A. Rams (1966-70), Washington (1971-77).

Quarterbacks

  Baugh, Sammy. 1963
  Blanda, George (also PK) . . .1981
  Bradshaw, Terry. 1989
+ Clark, Dutch 1963
+ Conzelman, Jimmy 1964
  Dawson, Len. 1987
+ Driscoll, Paddy. 1965
  Fouts, Dan 1993
  Graham, Otto 1965

  Griese, Bob 1990
+ Herber, Arnie 1966
  Jurgensen, Sonny 1983
  Kelly, Jim . . . . :2002
+ Layne, Bobby 1967
+ Luckman, Sid 1965
  Montana, Joe. 2000
  Namath, Joe. 1985
  Parker, Clarence (Ace) 1972

  Starr, Bart 1977
  Staubach, Roger 1985
  Tarkenton, Fran 1986
  Tittle, Y.A. 1971
+ Unitas, Johnny 1979
+ Van Brocklin, Norm. 1971
+ Waterfield, Bob. 1965

Pro Football (Cont.)

Running Backs

+ Battles, Cliff 1968
  Brown, Jim 1971
  Campbell, Earl.............1991
  Canadeo, Tony 1974
  Csonka, Larry 1987
  Dickerson, Eric 1999
  Dorsett, Tony................1994
  Dudley, Bill 1966
  Gifford, Frank 1977
+ Grange, Red 1963
+ Guyon, Joe.................1966
  Harris, Franco 1990
+ Hinkle, Clarke 1964

  Hornung, Paul 1986
  Johnson, John Henry........1987
  Kelly, Leroy 1994
+ Leemans, Tuffy 1978
  Matson, Ollie 1972
  McAfee, George 1966
  McElhenny, Hugh 1970
+ McNally, Johnny (Blood) 1963
  Moore, Lenny 1975
+ Motley, Marion 1968
+ Nagurski, Bronko 1963
+ Nevers, Ernie 1963
+ Payton, Walter..............1993

  Perry, Joe 1969
  Riggins, John 1992
  Sayers, Gale 1977
  Simpson, O.J 1985
+ Strong, Ken 1967
  Taylor, Jim 1976
+ Thorpe, Jim 1963
  Trippi, Charley 1968
  Van Buren, Steve 1965
+ Walker, Doak...............1986

Ends & Wide Receivers

  Alworth, Lance..............1978
+ Badgro, Red................1981
  Berry, Raymond.............1973
  Biletnikoff, Fred 1988
  Casper, Dave...............2002
+ Chamberlin, Guy............1965
  Ditka, Mike 1988
+ Fears, Tom 1970
+ Hewitt, Bill 1971

  Hirsch, Elroy (Crazylegs) 1968
+ Hutson, Don 1963
  Joiner, Charlie 1996
  Largent, Steve 1995
  Lavelli, Dante 1975
  Mackey, John 1992
  Maynard, Don 1987
  McDonald, Tommy 1998
+ Millner, Wayne 1968

  Mitchell, Bobby 1983
  Newsome, Ozzie 1999
  Pihos, Pete 1970
  Smith, Jackie 1994
  Stallworth, John 2002
  Swann, Lynn................2001
  Taylor, Charley 1984
  Warfield, Paul 1983
  Winslow, Kellen 1995

Linemen (pre-World War II)

+ Edwards, Turk (T)...........1969
+ Fortmann, Dan (G) 1985
+ Healey, Ed (T)..............1964
+ Hein, Mel (C)...............1963
+ Henry, Pete (T) 1963

+ Hubbard, Cal (T) 1963
+ Kiesling, Walt (G) 1966
+ Kinard, Bruiser (T) 1971
+ Lyman, Link (T) 1964
+ Michalske, Mike (G) 1964

+ Musso, George (T-G).......1982
+ Stydahar, Joe (T)...........1967
+ Trafton, George (C).........1964
+ Turner, Bulldog (C).........1966
+ Wojciechowicz, Alex (C) 1968

Offensive Linemen

  Bednarik, Chuck (C-LB)......1967
  Brown, Roosevelt (T) 1975
  Dierdorf, Dan (T) 1996
  Gatski, Frank (C) 1985
  Gregg, Forrest (T-G) 1977
+ Groza, Lou (T-PK)...........1974
  Hannah, John (G) 1991
  Jones, Stan (T-G-DT)........1991
  Langer, Jim (C) 1987

  Little, Larry (G)..............1993
  Mack, Tom (G)..............1999
  McCormack, Mike (T)........1984
  Mix, Ron (T-G)...............1979
  Munchak, Mike (G).........2001
  Munoz, Anthony (T) 1998
+ Musso, George (T-G).........1982
  Otto, Jim (C)................1980
  Parker, Jim (G)..............1973

  Ringo, Jim (C)...............1981
  St. Clair, Bob (T) 1990
  Shaw, Billy (G)..............1999
  Shell, Art (T) 1989
  Slater, Jackie (T).............2001
  Stephenson, Dwight (C) 1998
  Upshaw, Gene (G) 1987
  Yary, Ron (T)................2001
+ Webster, Mike (C)...........1997

Defensive Linemen

  Atkins, Doug................1982
+ Buchanan, Buck............1990
  Creekmur, Lou 1996
  Davis, Willie.................1981
  Donovan, Art 1968
+ Ford, Len 1976
  Greene, Joe 1987
  Hampton, Dan 2002

  Jones, Deacon 1980
+ Jordan, Henry 1995
  Lilly, Bob 1980
  Long, Howie.................2000
  Marchetti, Gino 1972
+ Nomellini, Leo 1969
  Olsen, Merlin 1982
  Page, Alan 1988

  Robustelli, Andy.............1971
  Selmon, Lee Roy 1995
  Stautner, Ernie 1969
+ Weinmeister, Arnie 1984
  White, Randy................1994
  Willis, Bill 1977
  Youngblood, Jack 2001

Linebackers

  Bell, Bobby.................1983
  Buoniconti, Nick 2001
  Butkus, Dick 1979
  Connor, George (DT-OT) 1975
+ George, Bill 1974

  Ham, Jack 1988
  Hendricks, Ted 1990
  Huff, Sam 1982
  Lambert, Jack 1990
  Lanier, Willie 1986

+ Nitschke, Ray...............1978
  Schmidt, Joe................1973
  Singletary, Mike.............1998
  Taylor, Lawrence 1999
  Wilcox, Dave................2000

Defensive Backs

  Adderley, Herb 1980
  Barney, Lem 1992
  Blount, Mel 1989
  Brown, Willie................1984
+ Christiansen, Jack 1970
  Haynes, Michael 1997
  Houston, Ken 1986

  Johnson, Jimmy 1994
  Krause, Paul 1998
+ Lane, Dick (Night Train) 1974
  Lary, Yale 1979
  Lott, Ronnie.................2000
  Renfro, Mel.................1996
+ Tunnell, Emlen 1967

  Wilson, Larry 1978
  Wood, Willie 1989

Placekicker

  Stenerud, Jan 1991

Coaches

+ Allen, George 2002
+ Brown, Paul 1967
+ Ewbank, Weeb 1978
+ Flaherty, Ray 1976
  Gibbs, Joe 1996
  Gillman, Sid 1983

  Grant, Bud 1994
+ Halas, George 1963
+ Lambeau, Curly 1963
+ Landry, Tom 1990
  Levy, Marv 2001
+ Lombardi, Vince............1971

+ Neale, Earle (Greasy).......1969
  Noll, Chuck 1993
+ Owen, Steve 1966
  Shula, Don 1997
  Walsh, Bill 1993

Contributors

+ Bell, Bert 1963	Hunt, Lamar 1972	+ Rooney, Art. 1964
+ Bidwill, Charles 1967	+ Mara, Tim. 1963	Rooney, Dan. 2000
+ Carr, Joe. 1963	Mara, Wellington 1997	+ Rozelle, Pete. 1985
Davis, Al. 1992	+ Marshall, George 1963	Schramm, Tex. 1991
+ Finks, Jim 1995	+ Ray, Hugh (Shorty) 1966	
+ Halas, George. 1963	+ Reeves, Dan 1967	

Dick McCann Award

First presented in 1969 by the Pro Football Writers of America for long and distinguished reporting on pro football. Named in honor of the first director of the Hall, the McCann Award does not constitute induction into the Hall of Fame.

Year	Year	Year	Year
1969 George Strickler	1978 Murray Olderman	1987 Jerry Magee	1996 Paul Zimmerman
1970 Arthur Daley	1979 Pat Livingston	1988 Gordon Forbes	1997 Bob Roesler
1971 Joe King	1980 Chuck Heaton	1989 Vito Stellino	1998 Dave Anderson
1972 Lewis Atchison	1981 Norm Miller	1990 Will McDonough	1999 Art Spander
1973 Dave Brady	1982 Cameron Snyder	1991 Dick Connor	2000 Tom McEwen
1974 Bob Oates	1983 Hugh Brown	1992 Frank Luska	2001 Leonard Shapiro
1975 John Steadman	1984 Larry Felser	1993 Ira Miller	2002 Edwin Pope
1976 Jack Hand	1985 Cooper Rollow	1994 Don Pierson	
1977 Art Daley	1986 Bill Wallace	1995 Ray Didinger	

Pete Rozelle Award

First presented in 1989 by the Hall of Fame for exceptional longtime contributions to radio and TV in pro football. Named in honor of the former NFL commissioner, who was also a publicist and GM for the LA Rams, the Rozelle Award does not constitute induction into the Hall of Fame.

Year	Year	Year	Year
1989 Bill McPhail	1993 Curt Gowdy	1997 Charlie Jones	2001 Roone Arledge
1990 Lindsey Nelson	1994 Pat Summerall	1998 Val Pinchbeck Jr.	2002 John Madden
1991 Ed Sabol	1995 Frank Gifford	1999 Dick Enberg	
1992 Chris Schenkel	1996 Jack Buck	2000 Ray Scott	

NFL's All-Time Team

Selected by the Pro Football Hall of Fame voters and released Aug. 1, 2000 as part of the NFL Century celebration.

Offense

Wide Receivers: Don Hutson and Jerry Rice
Tight End: John Mackey
Tackles: Roosevelt Brown and Anthony Munoz
Guards: John Hannah and Jim Parker
Center: Mike Webster
Quarterback: Johnny Unitas
Running Backs: Jim Brown and Walter Payton

Defense

Ends: Deacon Jones and Reggie White
Tackles: Joe Greene and Bob Lilly
Linebackers: Dick Butkus, Jack Ham and Lawrence Taylor
Cornerbacks: Mel Blount and Dick (Night Train) Lane
Safeties: Ronnie Lott and Larry Wilson

Specialists

Placekicker: Jan Stenerud
Punter: Ray Guy
Kick Returner: Gale Sayers

Punt Returner: Deion Sanders
Special Teams: Steve Tasker

Canadian Football Hall of Fame

Established in 1963. Current Hall opened in 1972. **Address:** 58 Jackson Street West, Hamilton, Ontario, L8P 1L4. **Telephone:** (905) 528-7566.

Eligibility: Nominated players must be retired three years, but coaches and builders can still be active. Voting done by 15-member panel of Canadian pro and amateur football officials.

Class of 2002 (5): PLAYERS—OG **Roger Aldag**, Saskatchewan (1976-93); DB **Paul Bennett**, Toronto (1977-80), Winnipeg (1980-84), Hamilton (1985-87); DB **Less Browne**, Hamilton (1984-89), Winnipeg (1989-91), Ottawa (1992), British Columbia (1993-94); SB **Ray Elgaard**, Saskatchewan (1983-96); BUILDER—**Bob Ackles**.

Members are listed with year of induction; (+) indicates deceased members.

Players

Ah You, Junior 1997	+ Box, Ab. 1965	Clements, Tom 1994
Aldag, Roger 2002	+ Breen, Joe. 1963	Coffey, Tommy Joe. 1977
Atchison, Ron 1978	+ Bright, Johnny 1970	+ Conacher, Lionel 1963
+ Bailey, Byron 1975	Brown, Tom 1984	Copeland, Royal 1988
Baker, Bill 1994	Browne, Less 2002	Corrigall, Jim 1990
Barrow, John 1976	Brock, Dieter 1995	Covington, Grover 2000
Bass, Danny. 2000	Burden, Willie 2001	+ Cox, Ernest. 1963
+ Batstone, Harry 1963	Campbell, Jerry (Soupy) 1996	+ Craig, Ross. 1964
+ Beach, Ormond. 1963	Casey, Tom 1964	+ Cronin, Carl. 1967
Benecick, Al 1996	Charlton, Ken 1992	Cutler, Dave 1998
Bennett, Paul 2002	+ Clarke, Bill 1996	+ Cutler, Wes. 1968

Canadian Football (Cont.)

Dalla Riva, Peter	1993	
DiPietro, Rocky	1997	
+ Dixon, George	1974	
Elgaard, Ray	2002	
+ Eliowitz, Abe	1969	
+ Emerson, Eddie	1963	
Etcheverry, Sam	1969	
Evanshen, Terry	1984	
+ Faloney, Bernie	1974	
+ Fear, A.H. (Cap)	1967	
Fennell, Dave	1990	
+ Ferraro, John	1966	
Fieldgate, Norm	1979	
Fleming, Willie	1982	
Frank, Bill	2001	
Gabriel, Tony	1985	
Gaines, Gene	1994	
+ Gall, Hugh	1963	
Golab, Tony	1964	
Grant, Tom	1995	
Gray, Herbert	1983	
+ Griffing, Dean	1965	
Halloway, Condredge	1999	
+ Hanson, Fritz	1963	
Harris, Dickie	1999	
Harris, Wayne	1976	
Harrison, Herm	1993	
Helton, John	1986	
Henley, Garney	1979	
Hinton, Tom	1991	
+ Huffman, Dick	1987	
+ Isbister, Bob Sr	1965	
Jackson, Russ	1973	
+ Jacobs, Jack	1963	
+ James, Eddie (Dynamite)	1963	
James, Gerry	1981	
+ Kabat, Greg	1966	
Kapp, Joe	1984	
Keeling, Jerry	1989	
Kelly, Brian	1991	
Kelly, Ellison	1992	
Kepley, Dan	1996	
Krol, Joe	1963	
Kwong, Normie	1969	
Lancaster, Ron	1982	
+ Lawson, Smirle	1963	
+ Leadlay, Frank (Pep)	1963	
+ Lear, Les	1974	
Lewis, Leo	1973	
Lunsford, Earl	1983	
Luster, Marv	1990	
Luzzi, Don	1986	
+ McCance, Ches	1976	
+ McGill, Frank	1965	
McQuarters, Ed	1988	
Miles, Rollie	1980	
+ Molson, Percy	1963	
Moon, Warren	2001	
Morris, Frank	1983	
+ Morris, Ted	1964	
Mosca, Angelo	1987	
Murphy, James	2000	
+ Nelson, Roger	1986	
Neumann, Peter	1979	
+ O'Quinn, John (Red)	1981	
Pajaczkowski, Tony	1988	
Parker, Jackie	1971	
Parker, James	2001	
Patterson, Hal	1971	
Poplawski, Joe	1998	
Perry, Gordon	1970	
+ Perry, Norm	1963	
Ploen, Ken	1975	
+ Quilty, S.P. (Silver)	1966	
Raimey, Dave	2000	
+ Rebholz, Russ	1963	
Reed, George	1979	
+ Reeve, Ted	1963	
Rigney, Frank	1985	
Robinson, Larry	1998	
+ Rodden, Mike	1964	
+ Rowe, Paul	1964	
Ruby, Martin	1974	
+ Russel, Jeff	1963	
Scott, Tom	1998	
+ Scott, Vince	1982	
Shatto, Dick	1975	
+ Simpson, Ben	1963	
Simpson, Bob	1976	
+ Sprague, David	1963	
+ Stevenson, Art	1969	
Stewart, Ron	1977	
+ Stirling, Hugh (Bummer)	1966	
Sutherin, Don	1992	
Symons, Bill	1997	
Thelen, Dave	1989	
+ Timmis, Brian	1963	
Tinsley, Bud	1982	
+ Tommy, Andy	1989	
+ Trawick, Herb	1975	
+ Tubman, Joe	1968	
Tucker, Whit	1993	
Urness, Ted	1989	
Vaughan, Kaye	1978	
Wagner, Virgil	1980	
+ Welch, Hawley (Huck)	1964	
Wilkinson, Tom	1987	
Wilson, Al	1997	
Wylie, Harvey	1980	
Young, Jim	1991	
+ Zock, Bill	1985	

Builders

Ackles, Bob	2002	
+ Back, Leonard	1971	
+ Bailey, Harold	1965	
+ Ballard, Harold	1987	
Barker, Donald	1999	
+ Berger, Sam	1993	
+ Brook, Tom	1975	
+ Brown, D. Wes	1963	
Cambell, Hugh	2000	
+ Chipman, Arthur	1969	
Clair, Frank	1981	
+ Cooper, Ralph	1992	
Coulter, Bruce	1997	
+ Crighton, Hec	1986	
+ Currie, Andrew	1974	
Custis, Bernard	1998	
+ Davies, Dr. Andrew	1969	
+ DeGruchy, John	1963	
Dojack, Paul	1978	
+ Duggan, Eck	1981	
+ DuMoulin, Seppi	1963	
+ Forster, Sidney	2001	
+ Foulds, Willliam	1963	
Fulton, Greg	1995	
Gaudaur, J.G. (Jake)	1984	
Gibson, Frank	1996	
Grant, Bud	1983	
+ Grey, Lord Earl	1963	
+ Griffith, Dr. Harry	1963	
+ Halter, Sydney	1966	
+ Hannibal, Frank	1963	
+ Hayman, Lew	1975	
+ Hughes, W.P. (Billy)	1974	
Keys, Eagle	1990	
Kimball, Norman	1991	
+ Kramer, R.A. (Bob)	1987	
+ Lieberman, M.I. (Moe)	1973	
+ McBrien, Harry	1978	
+ McCaffrey, Jimmy	1967	
+ McCann, Dave	1966	
McNaughton, Don	1994	
+ McPherson, Don	1983	
+ Metras, Johnny	1980	
+ Montgomery, Ken	1970	
+ Newton, Jack	1964	
+ Preston, Ken	1990	
+ Ritchie, Alvin	1963	
+ Ryan, Joe B.	1968	
Sazio, Ralph	1988	
+ Shaughnessy, Frank (Shag)	1963	
+ Shouldice, W.T. (Hap)	1977	
+ Simpson, Jimmie	1986	
+ Slocomb, Karl	1989	
+ Spring, Harry	1976	
Stukus, Annis	1974	
+ Taylor, N.J. (Piffles)	1963	
+ Tindall, Frank	1985	
+ Warner, Clair	1965	
+ Warwick, Bert	1964	
+ Wilson, Seymour	1984	

GOLF

World Golf Hall of Fame

A new World Golf Hall of Fame opened its doors in 1998 at the World Golf Village outside of Jacksonville, Fla. **Address:** 21 World Golf Place, St. Augustine, FL 32092. **Telephone:** (904) 940-4000.

   Eligibility: Professionals have three avenues into the WGHF. A PGA Tour player qualifies for the ballot if he has at least 10 victories in approved tournaments, or at least two victories among The Players Championship, Masters, U.S. Open, British Open and PGA Championship, is at least 40 years old and has been a member of the Tour for 10 years. A senior PGA Tour player qualifies if he has been a Senior Tour member for five years and has 20 wins between the PGA Tour and Senior Tour or five wins among the PGA majors, the Players Championship and the senior majors (U.S. Senior Open, Tradition, PGA Seniors' Championship and Senior Players Championship).

   Any player qualifying for the LPGA Hall automatically qualifies for the WGHF. Until 1999, nominees must have had played 10 years on the LPGA tour and won 30 official events, including two major championships; 35 official events and one major;

or 40 official events and no majors. The eligibility requirements were loosened somewhat in 1999. The new guidelines are based on a system which awards two points for winning a major and one point for winning other tournaments, the Vare trophy (for lowest scoring average) and the player of the year award. Players must win at least one major, Vare trophy, or player of the year award and accumulate a total of 27 points to be inducted. For players not eligible for either the PGA Tour or the LPGA Hall of Fame, a body of over 300 international golf writers and historians will vote each year.

Members are listed with year of induction; (+) indicates deceased members.

Class of 2002 (6): MEN—**Tommy Bolt**, **Ben Crenshaw**, **Tony Jacklin** and **Bernhard Langer**; WOMEN—**Marlene Hagge**; CONTRIBUTORS—**Harvey Penick**.

Note: Annika Sorenstam (2003) and Karrie Webb (2005) already have enough points for entrance into the Hall but will be inducted after their 10th LPGA season.

Men

+	Anderson, Willie	1975
+	Armour, Tommy	1976
+	Ball, John, Jr.	1977
	Ballesteros, Seve	1999
+	Barnes, Jim	1989
	Beman, Deane	2000
	Bolt, Tommy	2002
	Bonallack, Sir Michael	2000
+	Boros, Julius	1982
+	Braid, James	1976
	Burke, Jack Jr.	2000
	Casper, Billy	1978
	Coles, Neil	2000
+	Cooper, Lighthorse Harry	1992
+	Cotton, Sir Henry	1980
	Crenshaw, Ben	2002
+	Demaret, Jimmy	1983
	De Vicenzo, Roberto	1989
+	Evans, Chick	1975

	Faldo, Nick	1997
	Floyd, Ray	1989
+	Guldahl, Ralph	1981
+	Hagen, Walter	1974
+	Hilton, Harold	1978
+	Hogan, Ben	1974
	Irwin, Hale	1992
	Jacklin, Tony	2002
	Jacobs, John	2000
+	Jones, Bobby	1974
	Langer, Bernhard	2002
+	Little, Lawson	1980
	Littler, Gene	1990
+	Locke, Bobby	1977
+	Mangrum, Lloyd	1998
+	Middlecoff, Cary	1986
	Miller, Johnny	1996
+	Morris, Tom Jr.	1975
+	Morris, Tom Sr	1976

	Nelson, Byron	1974
	Nicklaus, Jack	1974
	Norman, Greg	2001
+	Ouimet, Francis	1974
	Palmer, Arnold	1974
	Player, Gary	1974
+	Robertson, Allan	2001
+	Runyan, Paul	1990
+	Sarazen, Gene	1974
+	Smith, Horton	1990
+	Snead, Sam	1974
+	Stewart, Payne	2001
+	Taylor, John H	1975
	Thomson, Peter	1988
+	Travers, Jerry	1976
+	Travis, Walter	1979
	Trevino, Lee	1981
+	Vardon, Harry	1974
	Watson, Tom	1988

Women

	Alcott, Amy	1999
	Berg, Patty	1974
	Bradley, Pat	1986
	Carner, JoAnne	1985
	Caponi, Donna	2001
	Daniel, Beth	1999
	Hagge, Marlene	2002
	Haynie, Sandra	1977

+	Howe, Dorothy C.H	1978
	Inkster, Julie	2000
	Jameson, Betty	1951
	King, Betsy	1995
	Lopez, Nancy	1989
	Mann, Carol	1977
	Rankin, Judy	2000
	Rawls, Betsy	1987

	Sheehan, Patty	1993
	Suggs, Louise	1979
+	Vare, Glenna Collett	1975
+	Wethered, Joyce	1975
	Whitworth, Kathy	1982
	Wright, Mickey	1976
+	Zaharias, Babe Didrikson	1974

Contributors

	Bell, Judy	2001
	Campbell, William	1990
+	Corcoran, Fred	1975
+	Crosby, Bing	1978
+	Dey, Joe	1975
+	Graffis, Herb	1977

+	Harlow, Robert	1988
	Hope, Bob	1983
+	Jones, Robert Trent	1987
+	Penick, Harvey	2002
+	Roberts, Clifford	1978
	Rodriguez, Chi Chi	1992

+	Ross, Donald	1977
+	Solheim, Karsten	2001
+	Shore, Dinah	1994
+	Tufts, Richard	1992

Old PGA Hall Members Not in PGA/World Hall

The original PGA Hall of Fame was established in 1940 by the PGA of America, but abandoned after the 1982 inductions in favor of the PGA/World Hall of Fame. Twenty-nine members of the old PGA Hall have been elected to the PGA/World Hall since then. Players yet to make the cut are listed below with year of induction into old PGA Hall.

+	Brady, Mike	1960
+	Burke, Billy	1966
+	Cruickshank, Bobby	1967
+	Diegel, Leo	1955
+	Dudley, Ed	1964
+	Dutra, Olin	1962
+	Farroll, Johnny	1961

	Ford, Doug	1975
+	Ghezzi, Vic	1965
+	Harbert, Chick	1968
	Harper, Chandler	1969
+	Harrison, Dutch	1962
+	Hutchison, Jock Sr	1959
+	McDermott, John	1940

+	McLeod, Fred	1960
+	Picard, Henry	1961
+	Revolta, Johnny	1963
+	Shute, Denny	1957
+	Smith, Alex	1940
+	Smith, Macdonald	1954
+	Wood, Craig	1956

HOCKEY

Hockey Hall of Fame

Established in 1945 by the National Hockey League and opened in 1961. **Address:** BCE Place, 30 Yonge Street, Toronto, Ontario, M5E 1X8. **Telephone:** (416) 360-7735.

Eligibility: Nominated players and referees must be retired three years. However that waiting period has now been waived 10 times. Players that have had the waiting period waived are indicated with an asterisk. Voting done by 18-member panel made up of pro and amateur hockey personalities and media representatives. A 15-member Veterans Committee that selected older players was eliminated in 2000.

Class of 2002 (4): PLAYERS—C **Bernie Federko**, St. Louis (1976-89), Detroit (1989-90); LW **Clark Gillies**, N.Y. Islanders (1974-86), Buffalo (1986-88); D **Rod Langway**, Montreal (1978-82), Washington (1982-93). BUILDER—**Roger Neilson**, coach.

Members are listed with year of induction; (+) indicates deceased members.

Hockey (Cont.)
Forwards

+ Abel, Sid................1969
+ Adams, Jack..............1959
+ Apps, Syl 1961
  Armstrong, George........1975
+ Bailey, Ace..............1975
+ Bain, Dan...............1945
+ Baker, Hobey............1945
  Barber, Bill..............1990
+ Barry, Marty.............1965
  Bathgate, Andy..........1978
+ Bauer, Bobby............1996
  Beliveau, Jean*..........1972
+ Bentley, Doug...........1964
+ Bentley, Max............1966
+ Blake, Toe..............1966
  Bossy, Mike.............1991
+ Boucher, Frank..........1958
+ Bowie, Dubbie...........1945
+ Broadbent, Punch........1962
  Bucyk, John (Chief).......1981
+ Burch, Billy.............1974
  Clarke, Bobby...........1987
+ Colville, Neil...........1967
+ Conacher, Charlie.......1961
  Conacher, Roy..........1998
+ Cook, Bill..............1952
+ Cook, Bun..............1995
  Cournoyer, Yvan.........1982
+ Cowley, Bill............1968
+ Crawford, Rusty.........1962
+ Darragh, Jack...........1962
+ Davidson, Scotty........1950
+ Day, Hap...............1961
  Delvecchio, Alex.........1977
+ Denneny, Cy............1959
  Dionne, Marcel 1992
+ Drillon, Gordie.........1975
+ Drinkwater, Graham......1950
  Dumart, Woody..........1992
+ Dunderdale, Tommy......1974
+ Dye, Babe..............1970
  Esposito, Phil...........1984
+ Farrell, Arthur..........1965
  Federko, Bernie 2002
+ Foyston, Frank..........1958
+ Frederickson, Frank......1958
  Gainey, Bob............1992

+ Benedict, Clint..........1965
  Bower, Johnny..........1976
+ Brimsek, Frankie 1966
+ Broda, Turk............1967
  Cheevers, Gerry 1985
+ Connell, Alex...........1958
  Dryden, Ken...........1983
+ Durnan, Bill............1964
  Esposito, Tony..........1988
+ Gardiner, Chuck 1945

  Boivin, Leo 1986
+ Boon, Dickie............1952
  Bouchard, Butch........1966
+ Boucher, George........1960
+ Cameron, Harry.........1962
+ Clancy, King...........1958
+ Clapper, Dit*...........1947
+ Cleghorn, Sprague......1958
+ Conacher, Lionel........1994
  Coulter, Art............1974
+ Dutton, Red............1958
  Fetisov, Viacheslav 2001

+ Gardner, Jimmy 1962
  Gartner, Mike 2001
  Geoffrion, Bernie........1972
+ Gerard, Eddie 1945
  Gilbert, Rod 1982
  Gillies, Clark 2002
+ Gilmour, Billy 1962
  Goulet, Michel 1998
  Gretzky, Wayne*........1999
+ Griffis, Si..............1950
  Hawerchuk, Dale........2001
+ Hay, George 1958
+ Hextall, Bryan 1969
+ Hooper, Tom...........1962
+ Howe, Gordie*.........1972
+ Howe, Syd.............1965
  Hull, Bobby 1983
+ Hyland, Harry 1962
+ Irvin, Dick 1958
+ Jackson, Busher 1971
+ Joliat, Aurel 1947
+ Keats, Duke 1958
  Kennedy, Ted (Teeder).....1966
  Keon, Dave 1986
  Kurri, Jari 2001
+ Lach, Elmer 1966
  Lafleur, Guy 1988
+ Lalonde, Newsy.........1950
  Laprade, Edgar 1993
  Lemaire, Jacques 1984
  Lemieux, Mario*........1997
+ Lewis, Herbie 1989
  Lindsay, Ted*..........1966
+ MacKay, Mickey 1952
  Mahovlich, Frank........1981
+ Malone, Joe 1950
+ Marshall, Jack 1965
+ Maxwell, Fred 1962
  McDonald, Lanny 1992
+ McGee, Frank 1945
+ McGimsie, Billy 1962
  Mikita, Stan 1983
  Moore, Dickie 1974
+ Morenz, Howie 1945
+ Mosienko, Bill 1965
  Mullen, Joe 2000
+ Nighbor, Frank 1947

+ Noble, Reg.............1962
+ O'Connor, Buddy 1988
+ Oliver, Harry 1967
  Olmstead, Bert 1985
+ Patrick, Lynn 1980
  Perreault, Gilbert........1990
+ Phillips, Tom 1945
+ Primeau, Joe...........1963
  Pulford, Bob 1991
+ Rankin, Frank..........1961
  Ratelle, Jean 1985
  Richard, Henri 1979
+ Richard, Maurice (Rocket)* ..1961
+ Richardson, George 1950
+ Roberts, Gordie 1971
+ Russel, Blair 1965
+ Russell, Ernie 1965
+ Ruttan, Jack 1962
  Savard, Denis 2000
+ Scanlan, Fred...........1965
  Schmidt, Milt 1961
+ Schriner, Sweeney 1962
+ Seibert, Oliver 1961
  Shutt, Steve............1993
+ Siebert, Babe 1964
  Sittler, Darryl 1989
+ Smith, Alf 1962
  Smith, Clint............1991
+ Smith, Hooley...........1972
+ Smith, Tommy..........1973
+ Stanley, Barney 1962
  Stastny, Peter 1998
+ Stewart, Nels 1962
+ Stuart, Bruce...........1961
+ Taylor, Fred (Cyclone)....1947
+ Trihey, Harry 1950
  Trottier, Bryan..........1997
  Ullman, Norm 1982
+ Walker, Jack...........1960
+ Walsh, Marty 1962
  Watson, Harry 1994
+ Watson, Harry (Moose) 1962
+ Weiland, Cooney 1971
+ Westwick, Harry (Rat)......1962
+ Whitcroft, Fred..........1962

Goaltenders

  Giacomin, Eddie 1987
+ Hainsworth, George 1961
  Hall, Glenn.............1975
+ Hern, Riley 1962
+ Holmes, Hap 1972
+ Hutton, J.B. (Bouse) 1962
+ Lehman, Hughie.........1958
+ LeSueur, Percy 1961
+ Lumley, Harry 1980
+ Moran, Paddy 1958

  Parent, Bernie...........1984
+ Plante, Jacques 1978
  Rayner, Chuck 1973
+ Sawchuk, Terry*........1971
  Smith, Billy............1993
+ Thompson, Tiny 1959
  Tretiak, Vladislav 1989
+ Vezina, Georges 1945
  Worsley, Gump 1980
+ Worters, Roy 1969

Defensemen

  Flaman, Fernie..........1990
  Gadsby, Bill 1970
+ Gardiner, Herb 1958
+ Goheen, F.X. (Moose).....1952
+ Goodfellow, Ebbie 1963
+ Grant, Mike............1950
+ Green, Wilf (Shorty) 1962
+ Hall, Joe 1961
+ Harvey, Doug...........1973
  Horner, Red 1965
+ Horton, Tim............1977
  Howell, Harry 1979

+ Johnson, Ching 1958
+ Johnson, Ernie 1952
  Johnson, Tom 1970
  Kelly, Red*............1969
  Langway, Rod 2002
+ Laperriere, Jacques 1987
  Lapointe, Guy 1993
+ Laviolette, Jack 1962
+ Mantha, Sylvio..........1960
+ McNamara, George.......1958
  Orr, Bobby*............1979
  Park, Brad.............1988

+ Patrick, Lester 1947
  Pilote, Pierre 1975
+ Pitre, Didier 1962
  Potvin, Denis................1991
+ Pratt, Babe 1966
  Pronovost, Marcel 1978
+ Pulford, Harvey 1945

  Quackenbush, Bill 1976
  Reardon, Kenny............1966
  Robinson, Larry 1995
+ Ross, Art 1945
  Salming, Borje 1996
  Savard, Serge 1986
  Seibert, Earl 1963

+ Shore, Eddie 1947
+ Simpson, Joe 1962
  Stanley, Allan 1981
+ Stewart, Jack 1964
+ Stuart, Hod 1945
+ Wilson, Gordon (Phat) 1962

Referees & Linesmen

  Armstrong, Neil............1991
  Ashley, John 1981
  Chadwick, Bill 1964
  D'Amico, John 1993
+ Elliott, Chaucer 1961

+ Hayes, George 1988
+ Hewitson, Bobby 1963
+ Ion, Mickey.................1961
  Pavelich, Matt 1987
+ Rodden, Mike 1962

+ Smeaton, J. Cooper 1961
  Storey, Red 1967
  Udvari, Frank..............1973
  van Hellemond, Andy......1999

Builders

+ Adams, Charles............1960
+ Adams, Weston W. Sr 1972
+ Ahearn, Frank 1962
+ Ahearne, J.F. (Bunny) 1977
+ Allan, Sir Montagu 1945
  Allen, Keith 1992
  Arbour, Al..................1996
+ Ballard, Harold 1977
+ Bauer, Fr. David............1989
+ Bickell, J.P.................1978
  Bowman, Scotty 1991
+ Brown, George 1961
+ Brown, Walter 1962
+ Buckland, Frank 1975
  Bush, Walter...............2000
  Butterfield, Jack 1980
+ Calder, Frank 1945
+ Campbell, Angus 1964
+ Campbell, Clarence 1966
+ Cattarinich, Joseph 1977
+ Dandurand, Leo 1963
  Dilio, Frank................1964
+ Dudley, George 1958
+ Dunn, James 1968
  Francis, Emile..............1982
+ Gibson, Jack 1976
+ Gorman, Tommy 1963
+ Griffiths, Frank A. 1993
+ Hanley, Bill 1986
+ Hay, Charles 1984
+ Hendy, Jim 1968

+ Hewitt, Foster 1965
+ Hewitt, W.A................1945
+ Hume, Fred.................1962
+ Imlach, Punch 1984
+ Ivan, Tommy 1964
+ Jennings, Bill...............1975
+ Johnson, Bob 1992
+ Juckes, Gordon 1979
+ Kilpatrick, John 1960
+ Knox, Seymour III 1993
+ Leader, Al 1969
  LeBel, Bob.................1970
+ Lockhart, Tom 1965
+ Loicq, Paul 1961
+ Mariucci, John 1985
  Mathers, Frank.............1992
+ McLaughlin, Frederic 1963
+ Milford, Jake 1984
  Molson, Hartland 1973
  Morrison, Ian (Scotty) 1999
+ Murray, Athol (Pere) 1998
+ Nelson, Francis 1945
  Neilson, Roger.............2002
+ Norris, Bruce 1969
+ Norris, James D. 1962
+ Norris, James Sr 1958
+ Northey, William 1945
+ O'Brien, J.A...............1962
  O'Neill, Brian 1994
  Page, Fred 1993
  Patrick, Craig.............2001

+ Patrick, Frank 1958
+ Pickard, Allan 1958
+ Pilous, Rudy 1985
  Poile, Bud 1990
  Pollock, Sam...............1978
+ Raymond, Donat 1958
+ Robertson, John Ross 1945
+ Robinson, Claude 1945
+ Ross, Philip 1976
  Sather, Glen 1997
  Sebetzki, Gunther 1995
+ Selke, Frank 1960
  Sinden, Harry 1983
+ Smith, Frank 1962
+ Smythe, Conn..............1958
  Snider, Ed..................1988
+ Stanley, Lord of Preston ...1945
+ Sutherland, James 1945
+ Tarasov, Anatoli 1974
  Torrey, Bill.................1995
+ Turner, Lloyd...............1958
+ Tutt, William Thayer 1978
  Voss, Carl..................1974
+ Waghorne, Fred 1961
+ Wirtz, Arthur 1971
  Wirtz, Bill 1976
  Ziegler, John...............1987

Note: Alan Eagleson was inducted into the Hockey Hall of Fame in 1989 but resigned in 1998 after being found guilty of fraud.

Elmer Ferguson Award

First presented in 1984 by the Professional Hockey Writers' Association for meritorious contributions by members of the PHWA. Named in honor of the late Montreal newspaper reporter, the Ferguson Award does not constitute induction into the Hall of Fame and is not necessarily an annual presentation.

Year		Year		Year	
1984	Jacques Beauchamp, Jim Burchard, Red Burnett, Dink Carroll, Jim Coleman, Ted Damata, Marcel Desjardins, Jack Dulmage, Milt Dunnell, Elmer Ferguson, Tom Fitzgerald, Trent Frayne, Al Laney, Joe Nichols, Basil O'Meara, Jim Vipond & Lewis Walter	1986	Dick Johnston, Leo Monahan & Tim Moriarty	1995	Jake Gatecliff
		1987	Bill Brennan, Rex MacLeod, Ben Olan & Fran Rosa	1996	No award
		1988	Jim Proudfoot & Scott Young	1997	Ken McKenzie
		1989	Claude Larochelle & Frank Orr	1998	Yvon Pedneault
		1990	Bertrand Raymond	1999	Russ Conway
1985	Charlie Barton, Red Fisher, George Gross, Zotique L'Esperance, Charles Mayer & Andy O'Brien	1991	Hugh Delano	2000	Jim Matheson
		1992	No award	2001	Eric Duhatschek
		1993	Al Strachan	2002	Kevin Paul Dupont
		1994	No award		

Foster Hewitt Award

First presented in 1984 by the NHL Broadcasters' Association for meritorious contributions by members of the NHLBA. Named in honor of Canada's legendary "Voice of Hockey," the Hewitt Award does not constitute induction into the Hall of Fame and is not necessarily an annual presentation.

Year		Year		Year		Year		Year		Year	
1984	Fred Cusick, Foster Hewitt, Danny Gallivan & Rene Lecavelier	1985	Budd Lynch & Doug Smith	1988	Dick Irvin	1993	Al Shaver	1998	Howie Meeker
		1986	Wes McKnight & Lloyd Pettit	1989	Dan Kelly	1994	Ted Darling	1999	Richard Garneau
				1990	Jiggs McDonald	1995	Brian McFarlane	2000	Bob Miller
				1991	Bruce Martyn	1996	Bob Cole	2001	Mike Lange
		1987	Bob Wilson	1992	Jim Robson	1997	Gene Hart	2002	Gilles Tremblay

Hockey (Cont.)
U.S. Hockey Hall of Fame

Established in 1968 by the Eveleth (Minn.) Civic Association Project H Committee and opened in 1973. **Address:** 801 Hat Trick Ave., P.O. Box 657, Eveleth, MN 55734. **Telephone:** (218) 744-5167.

Eligibility: Nominated players and referees must be American-born and retired five years; coaches must be American-born and must have coached predominantly American teams. Voting done by 12-member panel made up of Hall of Fame members and U.S. hockey officials.

Class of 2002 (4): COACH—**Doug Woog**; PLAYERS—**Mark Fusco**, **Scott Fusco** and **Joe Riley**.

Members are listed with year of induction; (+) indicates deceased members.

Players

+ Abel, Clarence (Taffy) 1973	Fusco, Mark 2002	Moe, Bill 1974
+ Baker, Hobey 1973	Fusco, Scott 2002	Morrow, Ken 1995
Bartholome, Earl 1977	+ Garrison, John 1974	+ Moseley, Fred. 1975
+ Bessone, Peter 1978	Garrity, Jack 1986	Mullen, Joe 1998
Blake, Bob 1985	+ Goheen, Frank (Moose) 1973	+ Murray, Hugh (Muzz) Sr. ..1987
Boucha, Henry 1995	Grant, Wally 1994	+ Nelson, Hub. 1978
+ Brimsek, Frankie 1973	+ Harding, Austie 1975	+ Nyrop, William D. 1997
Broten, Neal. 2000	Iglehart, Stewart 1975	Olson, Eddie 1977
Cavanaugh, Joe 1994	Ikola, Willard 1990	+ Owen, George 1973
+ Chaisson, Ray 1974	Johnson, Paul 2001	+ Palmer, Winthrop 1973
Chase, John 1973	Johnson, Virgil 1974	Paradise, Bob 1989
Christian, Bill 1984	+ Karakas, Mike 1973	+ Purpur, Clifford (Fido) 1974
Christian, Dave 2001	Kirrane, Jack 1987	Ramsey, Mike. 2001
Christian, Roger. 1989	+ Lane, Myles 1973	Riley, Bill. 1977
Cleary, Bill 1976	Langevin, Dave 1993	Riley, Joe 2002
Cleary, Bob 1981	Langway, Rod 1999	+ Romnes, Elwin (Doc) 1973
+ Conroy, Tony 1975	Larson, Reed. 1996	+ Rondeau, Dick 1985
Curran, Mike 1998	+ Linder, Joe. 1975	Sheehy, Timothy. 1997
+ Dahlstrom, Carl (Cully) 1973	+ LoPresti, Sam 1973	Watson, Gordie. 1999
+ DesJardins, Vic. 1974	+ Mariucci, John 1973	+ Williams, Tom 1981
Desmond, Richard. 1988	Matchefts, John 1991	+ Winters, Frank (Coddy) 1973
+ Dill, Bob 1979	+ Mather, Bruce. 1998	+ Yackel, Ken. 1986
+ Everett, Doug 1974	Mayasich, John 1976	
Ftorek, Robbie 1991	McCartan, Jack 1983	

Coaches

+ Almquist, Oscar. 1983	+ Holt Jr., Charles E. 1997	Ramsay, Mike. 2001
Bessone, Amo 1992	Ikola, Willard 1990	Riley, Jack 1979
Brooks, Herb 1990	+ Jeremiah, Eddie 1973	+ Ross, Larry 1988
Ceglarski, Len 1992	+ Johnson, Bob 1991	+ Thompson, Cliff 1973
+ Fullerton, James 1992	Johnson, Paul 2001	+ Stewart, Bill 1982
Gambucci, Sergio 1996	Kelley, Jack 1993	Watson, Sid 1999
+ Gordon, Malcolm 1973	+ Kelly, John (Snooks). 1974	+ Winsor, Ralph 1973
Harkness, Ned. 1994	Nanne, Lou. 1998	Woog, Doug 2002
Heyliger, Vic. 1974	Pleban, Connie 1990	

Referee

Chadwick, Bill 1974

Contributor

+ Schulz, Charles M. 1993

Administrators

+ Brown, George 1973	+ Jennings, Bill. 1981	Pleau, Larry 2000
+ Brown, Walter 1973	+ Kahler, Nick 1980	Ridder, Bob 1976
Bush, Walter...............1980	+ Lockhart, Tom 1973	Trumble, Hal 1970
Clark, Don 1978	Marvin, Cal 1982	+ Tutt, Thayer 1973
Claypool, Jim..............1995	Palazzari, Doug. 2000	Wirtz, Bill. 1967
+ Gibson, J.L. (Doc) 1973	Patrick, Craig 1996	+ Wright, Lyle 1973

Members of Both Hockey and U.S. Hockey Halls of Fame

Players	Coach	Builders	
Hobey Baker	Bob Johnson	George Brown	Tom Lockhart
Frankie Brimsek		Walter Brown	Craig Patrick
Frank (Moose) Goheen	**Referee**	Walter Bush	Thayer Tutt
Rod Langway	Bill Chadwick	Doc Gibson	Bill Wirtz
John Mariucci		Bill Jennings	
Joe Mullen			

HORSE RACING

National Museum of Racing and Hall of Fame

Established in 1950 by the Saratoga Springs Racing Association and opened in 1955. **Address:** National Museum of Racing and Hall of Fame, 191 Union Ave., Saratoga Springs, NY 12866. **Telephone:** (518) 584-0400.

   Eligibility: Nominated horses must be retired five years; jockeys must be active at least 15 years; trainers must be active at least 25 years. Voting done by 100-member panel of horse racing media.

   Class of 2002 (5): JOCKEY—**Jack Westrope**. TRAINER—**Bud Delp**. HORSES—**Cigar**, **Noor** and **Serena's Song**. Members are listed with year of induction; (+) indicates deceased members.

Jockeys

+ Adams, Frank (Dooley)*.....1970	+ Garner, Andrew (Mack).....1969	+ Patrick, Gil.................1970
+ Adams, John 1965	+ Garrison, Snapper 1955	Pincay, Laffit Jr. 1975
+ Aitcheson, Joe Jr.*.........1978	+ Gomez, Avelino.............1982	+ Purdy, Sam.................1970
+ Arcaro, Eddie 1958	+ Griffin, Henry..............1956	+ Reiff, John.................1956
Atkinson, Ted 1957	+ Guerin, Eric 1972	+ Robertson, Alfred..........1971
Baeza, Braulio..............1976	Hartack, Bill 1959	Rotz, John L.................1983
Bailey, Jerry 1995	Hawley, Sandy 1992	+ Sande, Earl.................1955
+ Barbee, George............1996	+ Johnson, Albert 1971	+ Schilling, Carroll 1970
+ Bassett, Carroll* 1972	+ Knapp, Willie...............1969	Shoemaker, Bill 1958
Baze, Russell 1999	Krone, Julie.................2000	+ Simms, Willie...............1977
+ Blum, Walter 1987	+ Kummer, Clarence 1972	+ Sloan, Todhunter 1955
+ Bostwick, George H.* 1968	+ Kurtsinger, Charley 1967	+ Smithwick, A. Patrick* 1973
+ Boulmetis, Sam 1973	+ Loftus, Johnny..............1959	Stevens, Gary 1997
+ Brooks, Steve 1963	Longden, Johnny 1958	+ Stout, James 1968
Brumfield, Don..............1996	Maher, Danny 1955	+ Taral, Fred 1955
+ Burns, Tommy..............1983	+ McAtee, Linus..............1956	+ Tuckman, Bayard Jr.* 1973
+ Butwell, Jimmy 1984	McCarron, Chris 1989	Turcotte, Ron...............1979
+ Byers, J.D. (Dolly) 1967	+ McCreary, Conn 1975	+ Turner, Nash...............1955
Cauthen, Steve..............1994	+ McKinney, Rigan 1968	Ussery, Robert 1980
+ Coltiletti, Frank............1970	+ McLaughlin, James 1955	Vasquez, Jacinto 1998
Cordero, Angel Jr...........1988	+ Miller, Walter 1955	Velasquez, Jorge 1990
+ Crawford, Robert (Specs)*...1973	+ Murphy, Isaac 1955	+ Westrope, Jack 2002
Day, Pat 1991	+ Neves, Ralph 1960	+ Woolfe, George 1955
Delahoussaye, Eddie 1993	+ Notter, Joe 1963	+ Workman, Raymond 1956
+ Ensor, Lavelle (Buddy) 1962	+ O'Connor, Winnie 1956	Ycaza, Manuel 1977
+ Fator, Laverne 1955	+ Odom, George 1955	*Steeplechase jockey
Fires, Earlie................2001	+ O'Neill, Frank 1956	
Fishback, Jerry*...........1992	+ Parke, Ivan 1978	

Harness Racing Museum & Hall of Fame

Established by the U.S. Harness Writers Association (USHWA) in 1958. **Address:** Trotting Horse Museum, 240 Main Street, P.O. Box 590, Goshen, NY 10924; **Telephone:** (845) 294-6330.

   Eligibility: Open to all harness racing drivers, trainers and executives. Voting done by USHWA membership. There are 80 members of the Living Hall of Fame, but only the 46 drivers and trainer-drivers are listed below.

   Class of 2002 (3): DRIVER—**Catello Manzi**; TRAINER/DRIVER—**Jim Dennis** and **Harry Harvey**. Members are listed with years of induction; (+) indicates deceased members.

Trainer-Drivers

Abbatiello, Carmine 1986	Farrington, Bob 1980	+ O'Brien, Joe 1971
Abbatiello, Tony.........1995	Filion, Herve 1976	O'Donnell, Bill 1991
Ackerman, Doug 1995	+ Garnsey, Glen 1983	Patterson, John Sr.........1994
+ Avery, Earle 1975	Galbraith, Clint..........1990	+ Pownall, Harry..........1971
+ Baldwin, Ralph...........1972	Gilmour, Buddy 1990	Remmen, Ray...........1998
Beissinger, Howard 1975	Harner, Levi 1986	Riegle, Gene.............1992
Bostwick, Dunbar........1989	Harvey, Harry M........2002	+ Russell, Sanders 1971
+ Cameron, Del 1975	+ Haughton, Billy..........1969	+ Shively, Bion 1968
Campbell, John 1991	+ Hodgins, Clint...........1973	Sholty, George 1985
+ Chapman, John 1980	Insko, Del 1981	Simpson, John Sr 1972
Cruise, Jimmy 1987	Kopas, Jack..............1996	+ Smart, Curly.............1970
Dancer, Stanley 1970	Lachance, Mike 1996	Sylvester, Charles..........1998
Dancer, Vernon..........2001	Magee, Dave 2001	Waples, Keith............1987
Dennis, Jim 2002	Manzi, Catello 2002	Waples, Ron 1994
+ Ervin, Frank.............1969	Miller, Del 1969	

Horse Racing (Cont.)
Trainers

+ Barrera, Laz 1979
+ Bedwell, H. Guy 1971
+ Brown, Edward D. 1984
  Burch, Elliot 1980
+ Burch, Preston M. 1963
+ Burch, W.P. 1955
+ Burlew, Fred 1973
+ Childs, Frank E. 1968
+ Clark, Henry 1982
+ Cocks, W. Burling 1985
  Conway, James P. 1996
  Croll, Jimmy 1994
  Delp, Bud 2002
  Drysdale, Neil 2000
+ Duke, William 1956
+ Feustel, Louis 1964
+ Fitzsimmons, J. (Sunny Jim) . . .1958
  Frankel, Bobby. 1995
+ Gaver, John M. 1966
+ Healey, Thomas 1955
+ Hildreth, Samuel 1955
+ Hirsch, Max 1959
+ Hirsch, W.J. (Buddy) 1982
+ Hitchcock, Thomas Sr. 1973
+ Hughes, Hollie 1973

+ Hyland, John 1956
+ Jacobs, Hirsch 1958
+ Jerkens, H. Allen 1975
  Johnson, Philip 1997
+ Johnson, William R. 1986
+ Jolley, LeRoy 1987
+ Jones, Ben A. 1958
+ Jones, H.A. (Jimmy). 1959
+ Joyner, Andrew 1955
  Kelly, Tom 1993
+ Laurin, Lucien 1977
+ Lewis, J. Howard 1969
+ Lukas, D. Wayne 1999
+ Luro, Horatio 1980
  Mandella, Richard. 2001
+ Madden, John 1983
+ Maloney, Jim 1989
  Martin, Frank (Pancho) 1981
  McAnally, Ron 1990
+ McDaniel, Henry 1956
+ Miller, MacKenzie 1987
+ Molter, William, Jr. 1960
+ Mott, Bill 1998
+ Mulholland, Winbert. 1967
+ Neloy, Eddie 1983

  Nerud, John 1972
+ Parke, Burley 1986
+ Penna, Angel Sr. 1988
+ Pincus, Jacob 1988
+ Rogers, John. 1955
+ Rowe, James Sr.. 1955
  Schulhofer, Scotty 1992
  Sheppard, Jonathan 1990
+ Smith, Robert A. 1976
  Smith, Tom 2001
+ Smithwick, Mike 1976
+ Stephens, Woody 1976
  Tenny, Mesh 1991
+ Thompson, H.J. 1969
+ Trotsek, Harry 1984
  Van Berg, Jack 1985
+ Van Berg, Marion 1970
  Veitch, Sylvester 1977
+ Walden, Robert 1970
  Walsh, Michael 1997
+ Ward, Sherrill 1978
  Whiteley, Frank Jr.. 1978
+ Whittingham, Charlie 1974
+ Williamson, Ansel 1998
  Winfrey, W.C. (Bill). 1971

Horses
Year foaled in parentheses.

  A.P. Indy (1989) 2000
+ Ack Ack (1966). 1986
  Affectionately (1960) 1989
+ Affirmed (1975). 1980
  All-Along (1979) 1990
+ Alsab (1939) 1976
+ Alydar (1975) 1989
  Alysheba (1984) 1993
+ American Eclipse (1814) 1970
+ Armed (1941) 1963
+ Artful (1902) 1956
+ Arts and Letters (1966) 1994
+ Assault (1943). 1964
+ Battleship (1927). 1969
+ Bayakoa (1984) 1998
+ Bed O'Roses (1947) 1976
+ Beldame (1901) 1956
+ Ben Brush (1893) 1955
+ Bewitch (1945) 1977
+ Bimelech (1937) 1990
+ Black Gold (1919) 1989
+ Black Helen (1932). 1991
+ Blue Larkspur (1926). 1957
+ Bold 'n Determined (1977) . . .1997
+ Bold Ruler (1954) 1973
+ Bon Nouvel (1960) 1976
+ Boston (1833) 1955
+ Broomstick (1901). 1956
+ Buckpasser (1963) 1970
+ Busher (1942) 1964
+ Bushranger (1930) 1967
+ Cafe Prince (1970) 1985
+ Carry Back (1958) 1975
+ Cavalcade (1931). 1993
+ Challendon (1936) 1977
+ Chris Evert (1971) 1988
+ Cicada (1959). 1967
  Cigar (1990). 2002
+ Citation (1945) 1959
+ Coaltown (1945). 1983
+ Colin (1905) 1956
+ Commando (1898). 1956

+ Count Fleet (1940) 1961
+ Crusader (1923) 1995
+ Dahlia (1971) 1981
+ Damascus (1964) 1974
+ Dark Mirage (1965) 1974
+ Davona Dale (1976). 1985
+ Desert Vixen (1970) 1979
+ Devil Diver (1939) 1980
+ Discovery (1931) 1969
+ Domino (1891) 1955
+ Dr. Fager (1964) 1971
  Easy Goer (1986) 1997
+ Eight 30 (1936). 1994
+ Elkridge (1938). 1966
+ Emperor of Norfolk (1885) . . .1988
+ Equipoise (1928) 1957
+ Exceller (1973) 1999
+ Exterminator (1915) 1957
+ Fairmount (1921) 1985
+ Fair Play (1905) 1956
+ Firenze (1885). 1981
  Flatterer (1979) 1994
+ Foolish Pleasure (1972) 1995
+ Forego (1971) 1979
+ Fort Marcy (1964) 1998
+ Gallant Bloom (1966). 1977
+ Gallant Fox (1927) 1957
+ Gallant Man (1954) 1987
+ Gallorette (1942) 1962
+ Gamely (1964) 1980
  Genuine Risk (1977). 1986
+ Good and Plenty (1900) 1956
+ Go For Wand (1987) 1996
+ Granville (1933) 1997
+ Grey Lag (1918) 1957
+ Gun Bow (1960) 1999
+ Hamburg (1895) 1986
+ Hanover (1884) 1955
+ Henry of Navarre (1891) 1985
+ Hill Prince (1947) 1991
+ Hindoo (1878) 1955
  Holy Bull (1991) 2001

+ Imp (1894) 1965
+ Jay Trump (1957) 1971
  John Henry (1975) 1990
+ Johnstown (1936) 1992
+ Jolly Roger (1922). 1965
+ Kingston (1884) 1955
+ Kelso (1957) 1967
+ Kentucky (1861) 1983
  Lady's Secret (1982). 1992
+ La Prevoyante (1970) 1995
+ L'Escargot (1963) 1977
+ Lexington (1850) 1955
+ Longfellow (1867) 1971
+ Luke Blackburn (1877). 1956
+ Majestic Prince (1966) 1988
+ Man o' War (1917) 1957
  Maskette (1906) 2001
  Miesque (1984). 1999
+ Miss Woodford (1880) 1967
+ Myrtlewood (1933). 1979
+ Nashua (1952) 1965
+ Native Dancer (1950) 1963
+ Native Diver (1959) 1978
+ Needles (1953) 2000
+ Neji (1950) 1966
+ Noor (1945) 2002
+ Northern Dancer (1961) 1976
+ Oedipus (1941). 1978
+ Old Rosebud (1911). 1968
+ Omaha (1932) 1965
+ Pan Zareta (1910) 1972
+ Parole (1873) 1984
  Personal Ensign (1984) 1993
  Paseana (1987). 2001
+ Peter Pan (1904) 1956
  Princess Rooney (1980) 1991
+ Real Delight (1949). 1987
+ Regret (1912) 1957
+ Reigh Count (1925) 1978
  Riva Ridge (1969) 1998
+ Roamer (1911) 1981
+ Roseben (1901). 1956

+ Round Table (1954) 1972
+ Ruffian (1972) 1976
+ Ruthless (1864) 1975
+ Salvator (1886) 1955
+ Sarazen (1921)............1957
+ Seabiscuit (1933) 1958
+ Searching (1952) 1978
+ Seattle Slew (1974) 1981
+ Secretariat (1970).........1974
  Serena's Song (1992) 2002
+ Shuvee (1966) 1975
+ Silver Spoon (1956) 1978

+ Sir Archy (1805)...........1955
+ Sir Barton (1916) 1957
  Slew o'Gold (1980) 1992
+ Sun Beau (1925)............1996
+ Sunday Silence (1986).......1996
+ Stymie (1941) 1975
+ Susan's Girl (1969).........1976
+ Swaps (1952) 1966
+ Sword Dancer (1956)........1977
+ Sysonby (1902)............1956
+ Ta Wee (1966) 1994
+ Tim Tam (1955) 1985

+ Tom Fool (1949) 1960
+ Top Flight (1929)...........1966
+ Tosmah (1961)............1984
+ Twenty Grand (1928).......1957
+ Twilight Tear (1941) 1963
+ War Admiral (1934).........1958
+ Whirlaway (1938) 1959
+ Whisk Broom II (1907)......1979
  Winning Colors (1985) 2000
  Zaccio (1976) 1990
+ Zev (1920)................1983

Exemplars of Racing

+ Hanes, John W 1982
+ Jeffords, Walter M..........1973

+ Mellon, Paul...............1989

  Widener, George D 1971

MEDIA

National Sportscasters and Sportswriters Hall of Fame

Established in 1959 by the National Sportscasters and Sportswriters Association. A permanent museum for the NSSA Hall of Fame opened on May 1, 2000. **Address:** 322 East Innes St., Salisbury, NC 28144. **Telephone:** (704) 633-4275.

Eligibility: Nominees must be active for at least 25 years. Voting done by NSSA membership and other media representatives.
Class of 2002 (2): **Bud Collins** and **Bob Murphy**.

Members are listed with year of induction; (+) indicates deceased members.

Sportscasters

+ Allen, Mel..................1972
+ Barber, Walter (Red) 1973
+ Brickhouse, Jack 1983
+ Buck, Jack.................1990
+ Caray, Harry 1989
+ Cosell, Howard 1993
+ Dean, Dizzy 1976
+ Dunphy, Don 1986
+ Elson, Bob 1995
  Enberg, Dick 1996
+ Glickman, Marty 1992

  Gowdy, Curt 1981
  Harwell, Ernie 1989
+ Hearn, Chick 1997
+ Hodges, Russ 1975
+ Hoyt, Waite 1987
+ Husing, Ted 1963
  Jackson, Keith 1995
+ McCarthy, Clem 1970
  McKay, Jim................1987
+ McNamee, Graham 1964
  Michaels, Al 1998

  Miller, Jon..................1999
  Murphy, Bob 2002
+ Nelson, Lindsey 1979
+ Prince, Bob................1986
  Schenkel, Chris 1981
+ Scott, Ray 1982
  Scully, Vin 1991
  Simpson, Jim 2000
+ Stern, Bill 1974
  Summerall, Pat 1994
  Whitaker, Jack.............2001

Sportswriters

  Anderson, Dave............1990
  Bisher, Furman 1989
  Broeg, Bob 1997
+ Burick, Si.................1985
+ Cannon, Jimmy 1986
+ Carmichael, John P..........1994
  Collins, Bud 2002
+ Connor, Dick 1992
+ Considine, Bob 1980
+ Daley, Arthur 1976
  Deford, Frank..............1998
  Durslag, Mel...............1995

+ Gould, Alan 1990
+ Graham, Frank Sr...........1995
+ Grimsley, Will 1987
  Heinz, W.C................2001
  Izenberg, Jerry.............2000
  Jenkins, Dan 1996
+ Kieran, John 1971
+ Lardner, Ring 1967
+ Murphy, Jack 1988
+ Murray, Jim................1978
  Olderman, Murray 1993
+ Parker, Dan 1975

  Pope, Edwin...............1994
+ Povich, Shirley 1984
+ Rice, Grantland 1962
+ Runyon, Damon 1964
  Russell, Fred 1988
  Sherrod, Blackie 1991
+ Smith, Walter (Red) 1977
+ Spink, J.G. Taylor 1969
+ Stedman, John 1999
  Vecsey, George 2001
+ Ward, Arch 1973
+ Woodward, Stanley 1974

MOTORSPORTS

Motorsports Hall of Fame of America

Established in 1989. **Mailing Address:** P.O. Box 194, Novi, MI 48376. **Telephone:** (248) 349-7223.

Eligibility: Nominees must be retired at least three years or engaged in their area of motorsports for at least 20 years. Areas include: open wheel, stock car, dragster, sports car, motorcycle, off road, power boat, air racing, land speed records, historic and at-large.

Class of 2002 (8): DRIVERS—**Gaston Chevrolet** (Historic), **Dale Earnhardt** (Stock Cars), **Eddie Hill** (Drag Racing), **Gordon Johncock** (Open Wheel), **Eddie Lawson** (Motorcycles) and **Brian Redman** (Sports Cars). PILOT—**Paul Mantz.** CONTRIBUTOR—**Fred Offenhauser.**

Members are listed with year of induction; (+) indicates deceased members.

Drivers

  Allison, Bobby 1992
  Andretti, Mario 1990
  Arfons, Art 1991
+ Baker, Buck................1998
+ Baker, Cannonball 1989
+ Bettenhausen, Tony 1997

  Breedlove, Craig 1993
  Bryan, Jimmy 1999
+ Campbell, Sir Malcolm......1994
+ Cantrell, Bill 1992
+ Chenoweth, Dean 1991
+ Chevrolet, Gaston 2002

  Chrisman, Art..............1997
+ Clark, Jim 1990
+ Cook, Betty 1996
+ Cooper, Earl...............2001
  Cunningham, Briggs 1997
+ Davis, Jim 1997

Motorsports (Cont.)

D'Eath, Tom	2000	
DeCoster, Roger	1994	
+ DePalma, Ralph	1992	
+ DePaolo, Peter	1995	
+ Donahue, Mark	1990	
+ Earnhardt, Dale	2002	
Fittipaldi, Emerson	2001	
Flock, Tim	1999	
Follmer, George	1999	
Foyt, A.J.	1989	
Garlits, Don	1989	
Glidden, Bob	1994	
+ Gregg, Peter	2000	
Gurney, Dan.	1991	
Hanauer, Chip	1995	
Hannah, Bob	2000	
+ Hanks, Sam	2000	
+ Harroun, Ray	2000	
Hart, C.J.	1999	
Hill, Eddie	2002	
Hill, Phil	1989	
+ Holbert, Al	1993	
+ Horn, Ted	1993	
+ Hulme, Denis	1998	
Jarrett, Ned	1997	
Jenkins, Bill (Grumpy)	1996	

Johncock, Gordon	2002	
Johnson, Junior	1991	
Jones, Parnelli	1992	
Kalitta, Connie	1992	
+ Kurtis, Frank	1999	
Lawson, Eddie	2002	
Leonard, Joe	1991	
+ Lockhart, Frank	1999	
Lorenzen, Fred	2001	
+ McLaren, Bruce	1995	
Mann, Dick	1993	
Markle, Bart	1999	
+ Mays, Rex	1995	
McEwen, Tom	2001	
Mears, Rick	1998	
+ Meyer, Louis	1993	
+ Miles, Ken	2001	
+ Milton, Tommy	1998	
Muldowney, Shirley	1990	
Muncy, Bill	1989	
+ Murphy, Jimmy	1998	
+ Musson, Ron	1993	
Nickelson, Don	1998	
+ Nordskog, Bob	1997	
+ Oldfield, Barney	1989	
Ongais, Danny	2000	

Parks, Wally	1993	
Pearson, David	1993	
+ Petrali, Joe	1992	
+ Petty, Lee	1996	
Petty, Richard	1989	
Prudhomme, Don	1991	
Resweber, Carroll	1998	
Redman, Brian	2002	
+ Revson, Peter	1996	
+ Roberts, Fireball	1995	
Roberts, Kenny	1990	
Rutherford, Johnny	1996	
Seebold, Bill	1999	
+ Shaw, Wilbur	1991	
Slovak, Mira	2001	
Smith, Malcolm	1996	
Spencer, Freddie	2001	
+ Thompson, Mickey	1990	
Unser, Al	1991	
Unser, Bobby	1994	
+ Vukovich, Bill Sr.	1992	
Ward, Rodger	1995	
+ Wood, Gar.	1990	
Yarborough, Cale	1994	

Pilots

Cleland, Cook	2000	
+ Cochran, Jacqueline	1993	
+ Curtiss, Glenn	1990	
+. Doolittle, Jimmy	1989	

+ Earhart, Amelia	1992	
+ Falck, Bill	1994	
Greenmayer, Darryl	1997	
LeVier, Tony	2001	

+ Mantz, Paul	2002	
Shelton, Lyle	1999	
+ Turner, Roscoe	1991	
+ Steve Wittman	2002	

Contributors

+ Agajanian, J.C.	1992	
Bignotti, George	1993	
+ Black, Keith	1995	
+ Brawner, Clint	1998	
Chapman, Colin	1997	
+ Chevrolet, Louis	1995	
Duesenberg, Fred	1997	
Economaki, Chris	1994	
+ Ford, Henry	1996	

+ France, Bill Sr.	1990	
Granatelli, Andy	2001	
Hall, Jim	1994	
+ Hulman, Tony	1991	
+ Kiekhaefer, Carl	1998	
Little, Bernie	1994	
+ Miller, Harry	1999	
+ Offenhauser, Fred	2002	
Penske, Roger	1995	

+ Rickenbacker, Eddie	1994	
+ Rose, Mauri	1996	
Shelby, Carroll	1992	
Watson, A.J.	1996	
Wood, Glen	2000	
Wood, Leonard	2000	
+ Yunick, Smokey	2000	

International Motorsports Hall of Fame

Established in 1990 by the International Motorsports Hall of Fame Commission. **Mailing Address:** P.O. Box 1018, Talladega, AL 35160. **Telephone:** (256) 362-5002.

Eligibility: Nominees must be retired from their specialty in motorsports for five years. Voting done by 150-member panel made up of the world-wide auto racing media.

Class of 2002 (6): DRIVERS—**Denis Hulme, Jacky Ickx, Alan Kulwicki, Tim Richmond** and **Glen Wood**. CONTRIBUTOR—**Ettore Bugatti**.

Members are listed with year of induction; (+) indicates deceased members.

Drivers

Allison, Bobby	1993	
Andretti, Mario	2000	
+ Ascari, Alberto	1992	
+ Ascari, Alberto	1992	
+ Baker, Buck	1990	
Bonnett, Neil	2001	
+ Bettenhausen, Tony	1991	
Brabham, Jack	1990	
Bryan, Jimmy	2001	
+ Campbell, Sir Malcolm	1990	
+ Caracciola, Rudolph	1998	
+ Clark, Jim	1990	
+ DePalma, Ralph	1991	
+ Donahue, Mark	1990	
+ Evans, Richie	1996	
+ Fangio, Juan Manuel	1990	
+ Flock, Tim	1991	
Foyt, A.J.	2000	
+ Gregg, Peter	1992	

Gurney, Dan	1990	
Hailwood, Mike	2001	
+ Haley, Donald	1996	
+ Hill, Graham	1990	
Hill, Phil	1991	
+ Holbert, Al	1993	
+ Hulme, Denis	2002	
Ickx, Jacky	2002	
+ Isaac, Bobby	1996	
Jarrett, Ned	1991	
Johncock, Gordon	1999	
Johnson, Junior	1990	
Jones, Parnelli	1990	
+ Kulwicki, Alan	2002	
Lauda, Niki	1993	
Lorenzen, Fred	1991	
+ Lund, Tiny	1994	
+ Mays, Rex	1993	
+ McLaren, Bruce	1991	

+ Meyer, Louis	1992	
Moss, Stirling	1990	
+ Nuvolari, Tazio	1998	
+ Oldfield, Barney	1990	
Parsons, Benny	1994	
Pearson, David	1993	
+ Petty, Lee	1990	
Piquet, Nelson	2000	
Prodhomme, Don	2000	
Prost, Alain	1999	
+ Richmond, Tim	2002	
+ Roberts, Fireball	1990	
Roberts, Kenny	1992	
Rose, Mauri	1994	
Rutherford, Johnny	1996	
Scott, Wendell	1999	
+ Senna, Ayrton	2000	
+ Shaw, Wilbur	1991	
Smith, Louise	1999	

Stewart, Jackie............1990
Surtees, John 1996
+ Thomas, Herb.............1994
+ Turner, Curtis 1992

Unser, Al Sr..............1998
Unser, Bobby 1990
+ Vukovich, Bill 1991
Ward Rodger.............1992

+ Weatherly, Joe 1994
Wood, Glen.............2002
Yarborough, Cale 1993

Bignotti, George 1993
Breedlove, Craig.........2000
+ Bugatti, Ettore............2002
+ Chapman, Colin 1994
+ Chevrolet, Louis 1992
+ Ferrari, Enzo 1994
+ Ford, Henry 1993
+ France, Bill Sr............1990

Contributors

Granatelli, Andy 1992
+ Hulman, Tony............1990
Hyde, Harry..............1999
Marcum, John 1994
+ Matthews, Banjo 1998
Moody, Ralph 1994
+ Offenhauser, Fred 2001

Parks, Wally..............1992
Penske, Roger............1998
+ Porsche, Ferdinand 1996
+ Rickenbacker, Eddie 1992
Shelby, Carroll............1991
+ Thompson, Mickey 1990
+ Yunick, Smokey 1990

OLYMPICS

U.S. Olympic Hall of Fame

Established in 1983 by the United States Olympic Committee. **Mailing Address:** U.S. Olympic Committee, 1750 East Boulder Street, Colorado Springs, CO 80909. Plans for a permanent museum site have been suspended due to lack of funding. **Telephone:** (719) 866-4529.

Eligibility: Nominated athletes must be five years removed from active competition. Voting done by National Sportscasters and Sportswriters Association, Hall of Fame members and the USOC board members of directors.

Voting for membership in the Hall was suspended in 1993.

Members are listed with year of induction; (+) indicates deceased members.

Teams

1956 Basketball Dick Boushka, Carl Cain, Chuck Darling, Bill Evans, Gib Ford, Burdy Haldorson, Bill Hougland, Bob Jeangerard, K.C. Jones, Bill Russell, Ron Tomsic, +Jim Walsh and coach +Gerald Tucker.
1960 Basketball Jay Arnette, Walt Bellamy, Bob Boozer, Terry Dischinger, Burdy Haldorson, Darrall Imhoff, Allen Kelley, +Lester Lane, Jerry Lucas, Oscar Robertson, Adrian Smith, Jerry West and coach Pete Newell.
1964 Basketball Jim Barnes, Bill Bradley, Larry Brown, Joe Caldwell, Mel Counts, Richard Davies, Walt Hazzard, Luke Jackson, John McCaffrey, Jeff Mullins, Jerry Shipp, George Wilson and coach +Hank Iba.
1960 Ice Hockey Billy Christian, Roger Christian, Billy Cleary, Bob Cleary, Gene Grazia, Paul Johnson, Jack Kirrane, John Mayasich, Jack McCartan, Bob McKay, Dick Meredith, Weldon Olson, Ed Owen, Rod Paavola, Larry Palmer, Dick Rodenheiser, +Tom Williams and coach Jack Riley.
1980 Ice Hockey Bill Baker, Neal Broten, Dave Christian, Steve Christoff, Jim Craig, Mike Eruzione, John Harrington, Steve Janaszak, Mark Johnson, Ken Morrow, Rob McClanahan, Jack O'Callahan, Mark Pavelich, Mike Ramsey, Buzz Schneider, Dave Silk, Eric Strobel, Bob Suter, Phil Verchota, Mark Wells and coach Herb Brooks.

Alpine Skiing
Mahre, Phil...............1992

Bobsled
+ Eagan, Eddie (see Boxing)...1983

Boxing
Clay, Cassius*.............1983
+ Eagan, Eddie (see Bobsled)..1983
Foreman, George 1990
Frazier, Joe...............1989
Leonard, Sugar Ray 1985
Patterson, Floyd 1987
*Clay changed name to Muhammad Ali in 1964.

Cycling
Carpenter-Phinney, Connie...1992

Diving
King, Miki................1992
Lee, Sammy 1990
Louganis, Greg 1985
McCormick, Pat...........1985

Figure Skating
Albright, Tenley 1988
Button, Dick 1983
Fleming, Peggy 1983
Hamill, Dorothy 1991
Hamilton, Scott 1990

Gymnastics
Conner, Bart.............1991
Retton, Mary Lou 1985
Vidmar, Peter 1991

Rowing
+ Kelly, Jack Sr.............1990

Speed Skating
Heiden, Eric 1983

Swimming
Babashoff, Shirley 1987
Caulkins, Tracy 1990
+ Daniels, Charles 1988
de Varona, Donna.........1987
+ Kahanamoku, Duke 1984
+ Madison, Helene 1992
Meyer, Debbie 1986
Naber, John 1984
Schollander, Don 1983
Spitz, Mark..............1983
+ Weissmuller, Johnny 1983

Track & Field
Beamon, Bob 1983
Boston, Ralph 1985
+ Calhoun, Lee 1991
Campbell, Milt............1992
+ Davenport, Willie 1991
Davis, Glenn 1986
+ Didrikson, Babe 1983
Dillard, Harrison 1983
Evans, Lee...............1989
+ Ewry, Ray 1983
Fosbury, Dick 1992
Jenner, Bruce 1986
Johnson, Rafer 1983
+ Kraenzlein, Alvin 1985
Lewis, Carl 1985
Mathias, Bob 1983
Mills, Billy...............1984
Morrow, Bobby 1989

Moses, Edwin.............1985
O'Brien, Parry 1984
Oerter, Al 1983
+ Owens, Jesse 1983
+ Paddock, Charley 1991
Richards, Bob.............1983
+ Rudolph, Wilma...........1983
+ Sheppard, Mel.............1989
Shorter, Frank.............1984
+ Thorpe, Jim..............1983
Toomey, Bill 1984
Tyus, Wyomia 1985
Whitfield, Mal 1988
+ Wykoff, Frank 1984

Weight Lifting
+ Davis, John...............1989
Kono, Tommy 1990

Wrestling
Gable, Dan 1985

Contributors
Arledge, Roone 1989
+ Brundage, Avery 1983
+ Bushnell, Asa 1990
Hull, Col. Don 1992
+ Iba, Hank 1985
+ Kane, Robert 1986
+ Kelly, Jack Jr.............1992
McKay, Jim...............1988
Miller, Don 1984
+ Simon, William 1991
Walker, LeRoy 1987

SOCCER

International Soccer Hall of Champions

Established in 1998 by FIFA, soccer's international governing body. Located at Disneyland Paris.

Eligibility: Nominated players and coaches must be retired at least five years. Nominations made by a committee composed of FIFA members, the Hall of Champions management and three ad hoc members then submit a list to a panel of 32 soccer journalists from around the world who also have the chance to add nominees of their own as well as voting for a specific number of candidates in each category.

Class of 2001 (4): PLAYERS—**José Leandro Andrade** (Uruguay) and **Giuseppe Meazza** (Italy); MANAGER— **Vittorio Pozzo** (Italy); NATIONAL TEAM—**Argentina**.

Players

+ Andrade, José Leandro (URU)..................2001
  Beckenbauer, Franz (W. Ger)..1998
  Best, George (N. Ire)........2000
  Charlton, Sir Bobby (ENG)..1998
  Cruyff, Johan (NED)........1998
+ Didi (BRA)................2000
  Distefano, Alfredo (ARG/SPA)..1998
  Eusebio (POR)............1998
  Fontaine, Just (FRA)........1999
+ Garrincha (BRA)..........1999
+ Matthews, Sir Stanley (ENG)..1998
+ Meazza, Giuseppe (ITA)....2001
+ Moore, Bobby (ENG)......1999
  Müller, Gerd (W. Ger)......1999
  Pele (BRA)................1998
  Plantini, Michel (FRA)......1998

Puskas, Ferenc (HUN/SPA)..1998
Van Basten, Marko (HOL)..2000
+ Yashin, Lev (RUS)..........1998
Zico (BRA)................2000
Zoff, Dino (ITA)............1999

Managers

+ Busby, Sir Matt (SCO)......1998
Michels, Rinus (NED)......1998
+ Pozzo, Vittorio (ITA)........2001
+ Shankly, Bill (SCO)........1999

Referees

Taylor, Jack (ENG)..........1999
Vautrot, Michel (FRA)......1998

Pioneers

Havelange, Joao (BRA)......1999
+ Rimet, Jules (FRA)..........1998

Club Teams

Ajax Amsterdam (NED).....1999
FC Barcelona (SPA)........2000
Real Madrid (SPA)........1998

National Teams

Argentina 2001
Brazil....................1998
Germany.................1999
Italy.....................2000

Media

Ferran, Jacques (FRA)......1999
Goddett, Jacques (FRA)....1998

For the Good of the Game

+ Dassler, Horst (GER) 1998
+ Sastre, Fernard (FRA) 1999

National Soccer Hall of Fame

Established in 1950 by the Philadelphia Oldtimers Association. First exhibit unveiled in Oneonta, NY in 1982. Moved into new Hall of Fame building in the summer of 1999. **Address:** 18 Stadium Circle, Oneonta, NY 13820. **Telephone:** (607) 432-3351.

Eligibility: Nominated players must have represented the U.S. in international competition and be retired five years; other categories include Meritorious Service and Special Commendation.

Nominations made by state organizations and a veterans' committee. Voting done by nine-member committee made up of Hall of Famers, U.S. Soccer officials and members of the national media.

Class of 2002 (3): **Adolph Bachmeier, Vladislav Bogicevic** and **Shannon Higgins**.

Members are listed with home state and year of induction; (+) indicates deceased members.

Members

Abronzino, Umberto (CA) ...1971
Aimi, Milton (TX) 1991
+ Alonso, Julie (NY) 1972
+ Andersen, William (NY)....1956
Annis, Robert (CA)..........1976
+ Ardizzone, John (CA) 1971
+ Armstrong, James (NY)......1952
+ Auld, Andrew (RI) 1986
Bachmeier, Adolph (IL) 2002
Bahr, Walter (PA)..........1976
+ Barr, George (NY)..........1983
+ Barriskill, Joe (NY)..........1953
+ Beardsworth, Fred (MA)....1965
Beckenbauer, Franz (Ger) ..1998
Berling, Clay (CA)..........1995
Bernabei, Ray (PA) 1978
+ Best, John O. (CA)..........1982
Bogicevic, Vladislav (Yug)...2002
+ Bookie, Michael (PA).......1986
+ Booth, Joseph (CT)..........1952
Borghi, Frank (MO)........1976
+ Boulos, Frenchy (NY)......1980
+ Boxer, Matt (CA) 1961
Bradley, Gordon (Eng)......1996
+ Briggs, Lawrence E. (MA)...1978
+ Brittan, Harold (PA).........1951
+ Brock, John (MA)..........1950
+ Brown, Andrew M. (OH)....1950
+ Brown, David (NJ).........1951
Brown, George (NJ)........1995
+ Brown, James (NY).........1986
+ Cahill, Thomas W (NY) 1950

+ Carenza, Joe (MO) 1982
+ Caraffi, Ralph (OH).........1959
Chacurian, Chico (CT) 1992
+ Chesney, Stan (NY)........1966
Chinaglia, Giorgio (Italy)....2000
+ Chyzowych, Walter (PA)....1997
+ Coll, John (NY) 1986
+ Collins, George M. (MA)....1951
Collins, Peter (NY)..........1998
+ Colombo, Charlie (MO)....1976
+ Commander, Colin (OH) 1967
Coombes, Geoff (PA)......1976
+ Cordery, Ted (CA) 1975
+ Craddock, Robert (PA) 1959
Craddock Jr., Robert (PA)...1976
+ Craggs, Edmund (WA).....1969
Craggs, George (WA)......1981
+ Cummings, Wilfred R. (IL) ..1953
Danilo, Paul (PA) 1997
Davis, Rick (CA)..........2001
+ Delach, Joseph (PA).........1973
DeLuca, Enzo (NY).........1979
+ Dick, Walter (CA) 1989
Diorio, Nick (PA)..........1974
+ Donaghy, Edward J. (NY) ..1951
+ Donelli, Buff (PA)..........1954
+ Donnelly, George (NY)......1989
+ Douglas, Jimmy (NJ)........1953
+ Dresmich, John W. (PA) 1968
+ Duff, Duncan (CA) 1972
+ Duggan, Thomas (NJ).......1951
+ Dunn, James (MO) 1974

+ Edwards, Gene (WI)........1985
Ely, Alexander (PA) 1997
+ Epperlein, Rudy (NJ) 1951
+ Fairfield, Harry (PA) 1951
Feibusch, Ernst (CA)........1984
+ Ferguson, John (PA).........1950
+ Fernley, John A. (MA).......1951
+ Ferro, Charles (NY)..........1958
+ Fishwick, George E. (IL) 1974
+ Flamhaft, Jack (NY) 1964
+ Fleming, Harry G. (PA)......1967
+ Florie, Thomas (NJ) 1986
+ Foulds, Pal (MA)..........1953
+ Foulds, Sam (MA) 1969
+ Fowler, Dan (NY)..........1970
+ Fowler, Peg (NY) 1979
+ Fricker, Werner (PA) 1992
+ Fryer, William J. (NJ) 1951
Gabarra, Carin (CA) 2000
+ Gaetjens, Joe (NY) 1976
+ Gallagher, James (NY) 1986
+ Garcia, Pete (MO) 1964
Gard, Gino (IL) 1976
+ Gentle, James (PA).........1986
Getzinger, Rudy (IL).........1991
+ Giesler, Walter (MO) 1962
+ Glover, Teddy (NY) 1965
+ Gonsalves, Billy (MA) 1950
Gormley, Bob (PA).........1989
+ Gould, David L. (PA) 1953
+ Govier, Sheldon (IL)........1950
+ Greer, Don (CA) 1985

Gryzik, Joe (IL) 1973
+ Guelker, Bob (MO) 1980
Guennel, Joe (CO) 1980
Harker, Al (PA) 1979
+ Healey, George (MI) 1951
Heilpern, Herb (NY) 1988
Heinrichs, April (CO) 1998
+ Hemmings, William (IL). 1961
Hermann, Robert (MO). 2001
Higgins, Shannon (NC) 2002
+ Hudson, Maurice (CA) 1966
Hunt, Lamar (TX) 1982
Hynes, John (NY). 1977
+ Iglehart, Alfredda (MD) 1951
+ Japp, John (PA) 1953
+ Jeffrey, William (PA) 1951
+ Johnston, Jack (IL) 1952
+ Kabanica, Mike (WI) 1987
Kehoe, Bob (MO) 1990
+ Kelly, Frank (NJ). 1994
+ Kempton, George (WA) 1950
Keough, Harry (MO). 1976
+ Klein, Paul (NJ) 1953
Kleinaitis, Al (IN) 1995
+ Kozma, Oscar (CA) 1964
+ Kracher, Frank (IL) 1983
Kraft, Granny (MD) 1984
+ Kraus, Harry (NY) 1963
Kropfelder, Nicholas 1996
+ Kunter, Rudy (NY) 1963
+ Lamm, Karl (NY) 1979
Lang, Millard (MD) 1950
Larson, Bert (CT) 1988
+ Lewis, H. Edgar (PA) 1950
Lombardo, Joe (NY) 1984
Long, Denny (MO). 1993
+ Looby, Bill (MO). 2001
+ MacEwan, John J. (MI) 1953
+ Maca, Joe (NY) 1976
+ Magnozzi, Enzo (NY). 1977
+ Maher, Jack (IL) 1970
+ Manning, Dr. Randolf (NY) . .1950
+ Marre, John (MO) 1953
McBride, Pat (MO) 1994
+ McClay, Allan (MA) 1971

+ McGhee, Bart (NY) 1986
+ McGrath, Frank (MA) 1978
+ McGuire, Jimmy (NY) 1951
+ McGuire, John (NY) 1951
+ McIlveney, Eddie (PA) 1976
McLaughlin, Bennie (PA). 1977
+ McSkimming, Dent (MO) 1951
Merovich, Pete (PA). 1971
+ Mieth, Werner (NJ) 1974
+ Millar, Robert (NY) 1950
Miller, Al (OH) 1995
+ Miller, Milton (NY). 1971
+ Mills, Jimmy (PA) 1954
Monsen, Lloyd (NY) 1994
+ Moore, James F. (MO) 1971
Moore, Johnny (CA) 1997
+ Moorehouse, George (NY) . .1986
+ Morrison, Robert (PA) . . .1951
+ Morrissette, Bill (MA) 1967
Murphy, Edward (IL) 1998
Nanoski, Jukey (PA). 1993
+ Netto, Fred (IL) 1958
Newman, Ron (CA). 1992
+ Niotis, D.J. (IL) 1963
+ O'Brien, Shamus (NY) 1990
Olaff, Gene (NY) 1971
+ Oliver, Arnie (MA). 1968
Oliver, Len (PA) 1996
+ Palmer, William (PA) 1952
Pariani, Gino (MO). 1976
+ Patenaude, Bert (MA) 1971
+ Pearson, Eddie (GA) 1990
+ Peel, Peter (IL). 1951
Pelé (Brazil) 1993
+ Peters, Wally (NJ) 1967
Phillipson, Don (CO) 1987
+ Piscopo, Giorgio (NY) 1978
+ Pomeroy, Edgar (CA) 1955
+ Ramsden, Arnold (TX). 1957
+ Ratican, Harry (MO). 1950
+ Reese, Doc (MD) 1957
+ Renzulli, Pete (NY). 1951
Ringsdorf, Gene (MD). 1979
+ Roe, Jimmy (MO) 1997
Roth, Werner (NY). 1989

+ Rottenberg, Jack (NJ) 1971
Roy, Willy (IL) 1989
+ Ryan, Hun (PA). 1958
+ Sager, Tom (PA) 1968
Saunders, Harry (NY) 1981
Schaller, Willy (IL) 1995
Schellscheidt, Mannie (NJ). . . .1990
+ Schillinger, Emil (PA). 1960
+ Schroeder, Elmer (PA) 1951
+ Scwarcz, Erno (NY) 1951
+ Shields, Fred (PA) 1968
+ Single, Erwin (NY). 1981
Slone, Philip (NY) 1986
+ Smith, Alfred (PA) 1951
Smith, Patrick (OH) 1998
+ Souza, Ed (MA) 1976
Souza, Clarkie (MA) 1976
+ Spalding, Dick (PA) 1951
Spath, Reinhold (NY) 1997
+ Stark, Archie (NJ) 1950
+ Steelink, Nicolaas (CA) 1971
+ Steur, August (NY) 1969
+ Stewart, Douglas (PA) 1950
+ Stone, Robert T. (CO) 1971
+ Swords, Thomas (MA) 1951
+ Tintle, Joseph (NJ) 1952
+ Tracey, Ralph (MO). 1986
+ Triner, Joseph (IL) 1951
+ Vaughn, Frank (MO) 1986
+ Walder, Jimmy (PA). 1971
+ Wallace, Frank (MO) 1976
+ Washauer, Adolph (CA) 1977
+ Webb, Tom (WA). 1987
+ Weir, Alex (NY) 1975
+ Weston, Victor (WA) 1956
+ Wilson, Peter (NJ) 1950
Wolanin, Adam (IL) 1976
+ Wood, Alex (MI) 1986
+ Woods, John W. (IL) 1952
Woosnam, Phil (GA) 1997
Yeagley, Jerry (IN) 1989
+ Young, John (CA). 1958
+ Zampini, Dan (PA) 1963
Zerhusen, Al (CA) 1978

SWIMMING

International Swimming Hall of Fame

Established in 1965 by the U.S. College Coaches' Swim Forum. **Address:** One Hall of Fame Drive, Ft. Lauderdale, FL 33316. **Telephone:** (954) 462-6536.

Categories for induction are: swimming, diving, water polo, synchronized swimming, coaching, pioneers and contributors. Coaches and contributors are not included in the following list. Only U.S. men and women listed below.

Class of 2002 (7): U.S. WOMEN—**Patty Elsener, Peg Hogan, Summer Sanders** and **Jill Sterkel**; U.S. MEN—**Terry Schroeder** and **Melvin Stewart**.

Members are listed with year of induction; (+) indicates deceased members.

U.S. Men

+ Anderson, Miller 1967
Barrowman, Mike 1997
Biondi, Matt 1997
+ Boggs, Phil 1985
Breen, George 1975
+ Browning, Skippy 1975
Bruner, Mike. 1988
Burton, Mike. 1977
+ Cann, Tedford 1967
Carey, Rick 1993
Clark, Earl 1972
Clark, Steve 1966
+ Cleveland, Dick 1991
Clotworthy, Robert. 1980
+ Crabbe, Buster. 1965

+ Daniels, Charlie. 1965
Degener, Dick 1971
DeMont, Rick 1990
Dempsey, Frank 1996
+ Desjardins, Pete. 1966
Dysdale, Taylor 1994
Edgar, David 1996
+ Faricy, John 1990
+ Farrell, Jeff 1968
+ Fick, Peter. 1978
+ Flanagan, Ralph 1978
Ford, Alan 1966
Furniss, Bruce. 1987
Gaines, Rowdy 1995
Garton, Tim 1997

+ Glancy, Harrison 1990
Goodell, Brian 1986
+ Goodwin, Budd 1971
Graef, Jed. 1988
Haines, George 1977
Hall Sr., Gary 1981
+ Harlan, Bruce. 1973
Harper, Don 1998
+ Hebner, Harry 1968
+ Heidenreich, Jerry 1992
Hencken, John 1988
Hickcox, Charles 1976
Higgins, John 1971
+ Holiday, Harry 1991
Hough, Richard 1970

Irwin, Juno Stover 1980
Graham, Johnston 1998
Jager, Tom 2001
Jastremski, Chet 1977
+ Kahanamoku, Duke 1965
+ Kealoha, Warren 1968
Kiefer, Adolph 1965
Kinsella, John 1986
+ Kojac, George 1968
Konno, Ford 1972
+ Kruger, Stubby 1986
+ Kuehn, Louis 1988
+ Langer, Ludy 1988
+ Langner, G. Harold 1995
Larson, Lance 1980
Laufer, Walter 1973
Lee, Dr. Sammy 1968
Lemmon, Kelley 1999
+ LeMoyne, Harry 1988
Louganis, Greg 1993
Lundquist, Steve 1990
Mann, Thompson 1984
+ Martin, G. Harold 1999
McCormick, Pat 1965
+ McDermott, Turk 1969
+ McGillivray, Perry 1981
McKee, Tim 1998
McKenzie, Don 1989

McKinney, Frank 1975
McLane, Jimmy 1970
+ Medica, Jack 1966
Montgomery, Jim 1986
Morales, Pablo 1998
Mulliken, Bill 1984
Naber, John 1982
Nakama, Keo 1975
+ O'Connor, Wally 1966
Oyakawa, Yoshi 1973
+ Patnik, Al 1969
Prew, William 1998
+ Riley, Mickey 1977
+ Ris, Wally 1966
Robie, Carl 1976
Ross, Clarence 1988
+ Ross, Norman 1967
Roth, Dick 1987
Rouse, Jeff 2001
+ Ruddy Sr., Joe 1986
Russell, Doug 1985
Saari, Roy 1976
+ Schaeffer, E. Carroll 1968
Scholes, Clarke 1980
Schollander, Don 1965
Schroeder, Terry 2002
Shaw, Tim 1989
+ Sheldon, George 1989

Sitzberger, Ken 1994
+ Skelton, Robert 1988
Smith, Bill 1966
+ Smith, Dutch 1979
+ Smith, Jimmy 1992
Spitz, Mark 1977
+ Stack, Allen 1979
Stewart, Melvin 2002
Stickles, Ted 1995
Stock, Tom 1989
+ Swendsen, Clyde 1991
Taft, Ray 1996
Tobian, Gary 1978
Troy, Mike 1971
Vande Weghe, Albert 1990
Vassallo, Jesse 1997
+ Verdeur, Joe 1966
Vogel, Matt 1996
+ Vollmer, Hal 1990
+ Wayne, Marshall 1981
Webster, Bob 1970
+ Weissmuller, Johnny 1965
+ White, Al 1965
Wiggins, Al 1994
Wrightson, Bernie 1984
Yorzyk, Bill 1971

U.S. Women

Andersen, Teresa 1986
Atwood, Sue 1992
Babashoff, Shirley 1982
Babb-Sprague, Kristen 1999
Ball, Catie 1976
+ Bauer, Sybil 1967
Bean, Dawn Pawson 1996
Belote, Melissa 1983
Bleibtrey, Ethelda 1967
+ Boyle, Charlotte 1988
Bruner, Jayne Owen 1998
Burke, Lynn 1978
Bush, Lesley 1986
Callen, Gloria 1984
Caretto, Patty 1987
Carr, Cathy 1988
Caulkins, Tracy 1990
+ Chadwick, Florence 1970
Chandler, Jennifer 1987
Cohen, Tiffany 1996
+ Coleman, Georgia 1966
Cone, Carin 1984
Costie, Candy 1995
Cox, Lynne 2000
Crlenkovich, Helen 1981
Curtis, Ann 1966
Daniel, Ellie 1997
de Varona, Donna 1969
Dean, Penny 1996
+ Dorfner, Olga 1970
Draves, Vickie 1969
Duenkel, Ginny 1985
Dunbar, Barbara 2000
Ederle, Gertrude 1965
Ellis, Kathy 1991
Elsener, Patty 2002
Evans, Janet 2001
Fauntz, Jane 1991
Ferguson, Cathy 1978

Finneran, Sharon 1985
+ Fulton, Patty Robinson 2001
+ Galligan, Claire 1970
+ Garatti-Seville, Eleanor 1992
Gestring, Marjorie 1976
Gossick, Sue 1988
+ Guest, Irene 1990
Gundling, Buelah 1965
Hall, Kaye 1979
Henne, Jan 1979
Hogan, Peg 2002
Hogshead, Nancy 1994
Holm, Eleanor 1966
Hunt-Newman, Virginia 1993
Johnson, Gail 1983
Josephson, Karen 1997
Josephson, Sarah 1997
+ Kaufman, Beth 1967
+ Kight, Lenore 1981
King, Micki 1978
Kolb, Claudia 1975
+ Lackie, Ethel 1969
+ Landon, Alice Lord 1993
Linehan, Kim 1997
+ Madison, Helene 1966
Mann, Shelly 1966
McCormick, Kelly 1999
McGrath, Margo 1989
McKim, Josephine 1991
Meagher, Mary T. 1993
+ Meany, Helen 1971
Merlino, Maxine 1999
Meyer, Debbie 1977
Mitchell, Betsy 1998
Mitchell, Michele 1995
Moe, Karen 1992
Morris, Pam 1965
Mueller, Ardeth 1996
Neilson, Sandra 1986

Neyer, Megan 1997
+ Norelius, Martha 1967
Olsen, Zoe Ann 1989
O'Rourke, Heidi 1980
+ Osipowich, Albina 1986
Pedersen, Susan 1995
Pinkston, Betty Becker 1967
Pope, Paula Jean Meyers 1979
Potter, Cynthia 1987
+ Poynton, Dorothy 1968
+ Rawls, Katherine 1965
Redmond, Carol 1989
Riggin, Aileen 1967
Roper, Gail 1997
Ross, Anne 1984
Rothhammer, Keena 1991
Ruiz-Conforto, Tracie 1993
Ruuska, Sylvia 1976
Sanders, Summer 2002
Schuler, Carolyn 1989
Seller, Peg 1988
+ Smith, Caroline 1988
Steinseifer, Carrie 1999
Sterkel, Jill 2002
Stouder, Sharon 1972
+ Toner, Vee 1995
+ Vilen, Kay 1978
Von Saltza, Chris 1966
+ Wainwright, Helen 1972
Walker, Clara Lamore 1995
+ Watson, Lillian (Pokey) 1984
Wayte, Mary 2000
Wehselau, Mariechen 1989
Welshons, Kim 1988
Wichman, Sharon 1991
Williams, Esther 1966
+ Woodbridge, Margaret 1989
Woodhead, Cynthia 1994
Wyland, Wendy 2001

TENNIS

International Tennis Hall of Fame

Originally the National Tennis Hall of Fame. Established in 1953 by James Van Alen and sanctioned by the U.S. Tennis Association in 1954. Renamed the International Tennis Hall of Fame in 1976. **Address:** 194 Bellevue Ave., Newport, RI 02840. **Telephone:** (401) 849-3990.

Eligibility: Nominated players must be five years removed from being a "significant factor" in competitive tennis. Voting done by members of the international tennis media.

Class of 2002 (2): PLAYERS—**Pam Shriver** and **Mats Wilander**.

Members are listed with year of induction; (+) indicates deceased members.

Men

+ Adee, George 1964	+ Hackett, Harold 1961	Pietrangeli, Nicola 1986
+ Alexander, Fred...........1961	Hewitt, Bob 1992	+ Quist, Adrian 1984
+ Allison, Wilmer 1963	+ Hoad, Lew 1980	Ralston, Dennis 1987
+ Alonso, Manuel 1977	+ Hovey, Fred 1974	+ Renshaw, Ernest 1983
Anderson, Malcolm........2000	+ Hunt, Joe 1966	+ Renshaw, William 1983
+ Ashe, Arthur 1985	+ Hunter, Frank 1961	+ Richards, Vincent.........1961
+ Austin, Bunny 1997	+ Johnston, Bill............1958	+ Riggs, Bobby 1967
+ Behr, Karl 1969	+ Jones, Perry 1970	Roche, Tony 1986
Borg, Bjorn...............1987	Kelleher, Robert 2000	Rose, Mervyn 2001
+ Borotra, Jean 1976	Kodes, Jan 1990	Rosewall, Ken 1980
Bromwich, John 1984	Kramer, Jack 1968	Santana, Manuel 1984
+ Brookes, Norman 1977	+ Lacoste, Rene 1976	Savitt, Dick 1976
+ Brugnon, Jacques 1976	+ Larned, William 1956	Schroeder, Ted...........1966
+ Budge, Don 1964	Larsen, Art 1969	+ Sears, Richard 1955
+ Campbell, Oliver..........1955	Laver, Rod 1981	Sedgman, Frank 1979
+ Chace, Malcolm 1961	Lendl, Ivan 2001	Segura, Pancho 1984
+ Clark, Clarence 1983	+ Lott, George 1964	Seixas, Vic 1971
+ Clark, Joseph 1955	Mako, Gene 1973	+ Shields, Frank 1964
+ Clothier, William 1956	McEnroe, John............1999	+ Slocum, Henry 1955
+ Cochet, Henri 1976	McGregor, Ken 1999	Smith, Stan 1987
Connors, Jimmy 1998	+ McKinley, Chuck 1986	Stolle, Fred 1985
Cooper, Ashley 1991	+ McLoughlin, Maurice 1957	+ Talbert, Bill 1967
+ Crawford, Jack 1979	McMillan, Frew 1992	+ Tilden, Bill 1959
David, Herman 1998	+ McNeill, Don 1965	Trabert, Tony 1970
+ Doeg, John 1962	Mulloy, Gardnar 1972	Van Ryn, John............1963
+ Doherty, Lawrence 1980	Murray, Lindley 1958	Vilas, Guillermo 1991
+ Doherty, Reginald 1980	+ Myrick, Julian 1963	+ Vines, Ellsworth 1962
+ Drobny, Jaroslav 1983	Nastase, Ilie 1991	+ von Cramm, Gottfried.......1977
+ Dwight, James 1955	Newcombe, John...........1986	+ Ward, Holcombe...........1956
Emerson, Roy 1982	+ Nielsen, Arthur 1971	+ Washburn, Watson 1965
+ Etchebaster, Pierre........1978	Olmedo, Alex 1987	+ Whitman, Malcolm 1955
Falkenburg, Bob 1974	+ Osuna, Rafael 1979	Wilander, Mats 2002
Fraser, Neale 1984	+ Parker, Frank 1966	+ Wilding, Anthony 1978
+ Garland, Chuck 1969	+ Patterson, Gerald 1989	+ Williams, Richard 2nd 1957
+ Gonzalez, Pancho 1968	Patty, Budge 1977	Wood, Sidney 1964
+ Grant, Bryan (Bitsy).........1972	+ Perry, Fred 1975	+ Wrenn, Robert 1955
+ Griffin, Clarence 1970	+ Pettitt, Tom...............1982	+ Wright, Beals............1956

Women

+ Atkinson, Juliette 1974	Gibson, Althea 1971	Navratilova, Martina 2000
Austin, Tracy 1992	Goolagong Cawley, Evonne ..1988	+ Nuthall Shoemaker, Betty ...1977
+ Barger-Wallach, Maud 1958	+ Hansell, Ellen 1965	Osborne duPont, Margaret...1967
Betz Addie, Pauline 1965	Hard, Darlene 1973	+ Palfrey Danzig, Sarah 1963
+ Bjurstedt Mallory, Molla 1958	Hart, Doris 1969	+ Roosevelt, Ellen 1975
Bowrey, Lesley Turner 1997	Haydon Jones, Ann 1985	+ Round Little, Dorothy 1986
Brough Clapp, Louise 1967	Heldman, Gladys 1979	+ Ryan, Elizabeth 1972
+ Browne, Mary 1957	+ Hotchkiss Wightman, Hazel ...1957	+ Sears, Eleanora 1968
Bueno, Maria 1978	+ Jacobs, Helen Hull 1962	Shriver, Pam 2002
+ Cahill, Mabel.............1976	King, Billie Jean 1987	Smith Court, Margaret 1979
Casals, Rosie 1996	+ Lenglen, Suzanne 1978	+ Sutton Bundy, May 1956
+ Connolly Brinker, Maureen ..1968	Mandlikova, Hana 1994	+ Townsend Toulmin, Bertha....1974
+ Dod, Charlotte (Lottie).......1983	+ Marble, Alice.............1964	Wade, Virginia 1989
+ Douglass Chambers, Dorothy..1981	+ McKane Godfree, Kitty 1978	+ Wagner, Marie 1969
Evert, Chris 1995	+ Moore, Elisabeth 1971	+ Wills Moody Roark, Helen 1959
Fry Irvin, Shirley.............1970	Mortimer Barrett, Angela 1993	

Contributors

+ Baker, Lawrence Sr 1975	+ Gustaf, V (King of Sweden) ..1980	+ Maskell, Dan 1996
+ Chatrier, Philippe............1992	+ Hester, W.E. (Slew) 1981	+ Outerbridge, Mary 1981
Collins, Bud 1994	+ Hopman, Harry 1978	+ Pell, Theodore 1966
+ Cullman, Joseph F. 3rd 1990	Hunt, Lamar 1993	+ Tingay, Lance 1982
+ Danzig, Allison 1968	+ Laney, Al 1979	+ Tinling, Ted 1986
+ Davis, Dwight 1956	Martin, Alastair 1973	+ Van Alen, James 1965
+ Gray, David 1985	+ Martin, William M..........1982	+ Wingfield, Walter Clopton...1997

TRACK & FIELD

National Track & Field Hall of Fame

Established in 1974 by the The Athletics Congress (now USA Track & Field). Originally located in Charleston, WV, the Hall moved to Indianapolis in 1983 and reopened at the Hoosier Dome (now RCA Dome) in 1986. **Address:** One RCA Dome, Indianapolis, IN 46225. **Telephone:** (317) 261-0500.

Eligibility: Nominated athletes must be retired three years and coaches must have coached at least 20 years if retired or 35 years if still coaching. Voting done by 800-member panel made up of Hall of Fame and USA Track & Field officials, Hall of Fame members, current U.S. champions and members of the Track & Field Writers of America.

Class of 2001 (4): MEN—**Carl Lewis** (sprints/long jump), **Henry Marsh** (steeplechase), **Larry Myricks** (long jump), **Alberto Salazar** (distance running). Members are listed with year of induction; (+) indicates deceased members.

Men

+ Albritton, Dave............1980	Jenkins, Charlie............1992	Prinstein, Meyer............2000
Ashenfelter, Horace........1975	Jenner, Bruce 1980	+ Ray, Joie 1976
Banks, Willie 1999	+ Johnson, Cornelius 1994	+ Rice, Greg 1977
+ Bausch, James 1979	Johnson, Rafer 1974	Richards, Rev. Bob 1975
Beamon, Bob 1977	Jones, Hayes 1976	Robinson, Arnie 2000
Beatty, Jim................1990	Kelley, John 1980	Rodgers, Bill 1999
Bell, Greg................1988	+ Kiviat, Abel..............1985	+ Rose, Ralph 1976
+ Boeckmann, Dee 1976	+ Kraenzlein, Alvin 1974	Ryun, Jim................1980
Boston, Ralph 1974	Laird, Ron 1986	Salazar, Alberto 2001
+ Borican, Jonn 2000	+ Lash, Don 1995	+ Scholz, Jackson 1977
Bragg, Don................1996	+ Laskau, Henry 1997	Schul, Bob 1991
+ Calhoun, Lee 1974	Lewis, Carl..............2001	Seagren, Bob 1986
Campbell, Milt............1989	Liquori, Marty............1995	+ Sheppard, Mel............1976
Carr, Henry 1997	Long, Dr. Dallas..........1996	+ Sheridan, Martin..........1988
+ Clark, Ellery 1991	Marsh, Henry 2001	Shorter, Frank............1989
Connolly, Harold 1984	Mathias, Bob 1974	Silvester, Jay............1998
Courtney, Tom 1978	Matson, Randy............1984	Sime, Dave..............1981
+ Cunningham, Glenn 1974	McCluskey, Joe 1996	+ Simpson, Robert..........1974
+ Curtis, William..........1979	+ Meadows, Earle 1996	Smith, Tommie 1978
+ Davenport, Willie 1982	+ Meredith, Ted 1982	+ Stanfield, Andy 1977
Davis, Glenn 1974	Metcalfe, Ralph 1975	Steers, Les..............1974
Davis, Harold............1974	+ Milburn, Rod 1993	Stones, Dwight............1998
Dillard, Harrison 1974	Mills, Billy 1976	+ Taylor, Frederick Morgan ...2000
Dumas, Charles 1990	Moore, Charles 1999	+ Tewksbury, Dr. Walter......1996
Evans, Lee................1983	Moore, Tom 1988	Thomas, John 1985
+ Ewell, Barney 1986	Morrow, Bobby 1975	+ Thomson, Earl 1977
+ Ewry, Ray 1974	+ Mortensen, Jess 1992	+ Thorpe, Jim 1975
+ Flanagan, John 1975	Moses, Edwin..............1994	+ Tolan, Eddie 1982
Fosbury, Dick 1981	+ Myers, Lawrence 1974	Toomey, Bill 1975
Foster, Greg 1998	Myricks, Larry 2001	+ Towns, Forrest (Spec) 1976
+ Gordien, Fortune 1979	Nehemiah, Renaldo 1997	Warmerdam, Cornelius 1974
Greene, Charles 1992	O'Brien, Parry 1974	Whitfield, Mal 1974
+ Hahn, Archie 1983	Oerter, Al 1974	Wilkins, Mac 1993
+ Hardin, Glenn 1978	+ Osborn, Harold 1974	+ Williams, Archie 1992
+ Hayes, Bob..............1976	+ Owens, Jesse 1974	Wohlhuter, Rick 1990
Held, Bud 1987	+ Paddock, Charlie 1976	Woodruff, John 1978
Hines, Jim 1979	Patton, Mel 1985	Wottle, Dave 1982
+ Houser, Bud 1979	+ Peacock, Eulace..........1987	+ Wykoff, Frank 1977
+ Hubbard, DeHart 1979	+ Prefontaine, Steve 1976	Young, George 1981

Women

Ashford, Evelyn 1997	+ Hall Adams, Evelyne........1988	+ Rudolph, Wilma............1974
Brisco, Valerie 1995	Heritage, Doris Brown 1990	Schmidt, Kate............1994
Cheeseborough, Chandra ...2000	+ Jackson, Nell 1989	Seidler, Maren 2000
Coachman, Alice 1975	Larrieu Smith, Francie......1998	+ Shiley Newhouse, Jean 1993
+ Copeland, Lillian 1994	Manning-Mims, Madeline ...1984	+ Stephens, Helen..........1975
+ Didrikson, Babe............1974	McDaniel, Mildred 1983	Tyus, Wyomia 1980
+ Faggs, Mae 1976	McGuire, Edith 1979	+ Walsh, Stella 1975
Ferrell, Barbara 1988	Ritter, Louise 1995	Watson, Martha 1987
+ Griffith Joyner, Florence ...1995	+ Robinson, Betty 1977	White, Willye............1981

Coaches

+ Abbott, Cleve............1996	+ Easton, Bill 1975	+ Hurt, Edward 1975
+ Baskin, Weems 1982	+ Ellis, Larry 1999	+ Hutsell, Wilbur..........1975
+ Beard, Percy 1981	+ Elliott, Jumbo 1981	+ Jones, Thomas 1977
Bell, Sam................1992	+ Giegengack, Bob 1978	Jordan, Payton 1982
+ Botts, Tom 1983	+ Hamilton, Brutus 1974	+ Littlefield, Clyde 1981
+ Bowerman, Bill............1981	+ Haydon, Ted 1975	+ Moakley, Jack 1988
Bush, Jim 1987	+ Hayes, Billy 1976	+ Murphy, Michael 1974
+ Cromwell, Dean..........1974	+ Haylett, Ward 1979	Rosen, Mel 1995
Dellinger, Bill 2000	+ Higgins, Ralph 1982	+ Snyder, Larry 1978
+ Doherty, Ken 1976	+ Hillman, Harry 1976	Temple, Ed 1989

+ Templeton, Dink 1976
Walker, LeRoy 1983
+ Wilt, Fred 1981

+ Winter, Bud 1985
+ Wolfe, Vern 1996
Wright, Stan 1993

+ Yancy, Joseph 1984

Contributors

+ Abramson, Jesse 1981
Andersen, Roxanne 1991
+ Bakjian, Andy 1986
+ Brundage, Avery 1974

+ Ferris, Dan 1974
+ Griffith, John 1979
+ Lebow, Fred 1994
+ Nelson, Bert 1991

Nelson, Cordner 1988
+ Sullivan, James 1977

WOMEN

International Women's Sports Hall of Fame

Established in 1980 by the Women's Sports Foundation. **Address:** Women's Sports Foundation, Eisenhower Park, East Meadow, NY 11554. **Telephone:** (516) 542-4700.

Eligibility: Nominees' achievements and commitment to the development of women's sports must be internationally recognized. Athletes are elected in two categories—Pioneer (before 1960) and Contemporary (since 1960). Members are divided below by sport for the sake of easy reference; (*) indicates member inducted in Pioneer category. Coaching nominees must have coached at least 10 years. Members are listed with year of induction; (+) indicates deceased members.

Class of 2002 (4): CONTEMPORARY—**Jayne Torvill** (ice dancing) and **Valerie Brisco** (track and field); PIONEER—**Betty Cuthbert** (track & field); COACH—**Nikki Franke** (fencing).

Note: Charlotte Dod is inducted for tennis, as well as archery and golf; **Marie Marvingt** is inducted for aviation, as well as mountaineering; **Eleanora Sears** is inducted for golf, as well as polo and squash.

Alpine Skiing
Cranz, Christl* . . . . :1991
+ Golden Brosnihan, Diana 1997
Lawrence, Andrea Mead* . .1983
Moser-Pröll, Annemarie 1982

Auto Racing
Guthrie, Janet 1980

Aviation
+ Coleman, Bessie* 1992
+ Earhart, Amelia* 1980
+ Marvingt, Marie* 1987

Badminton
Hashman, Judy Devlin* 1995

Baseball
Stone, Toni* 1993

Basketball
Meyers, Ann 1985
Miller, Cheryl 1991

Bowling
Ladewig, Marion* 1984

Cycling
Carpenter Phinney, Connie . .1990

Diving
King, Micki 1983
McCormick, Pat* 1984
Riggin, Aileen* 1988

Equestrian
Hartel, Lis 1994

Fencing
Schacherer-Elek, Ilona* 1989

Figure Skating
Albright, Tenley* 1983
+ Blanchard, Theresa Weld* . .1989
Fleming, Peggy 1981
Heiss Jenkins, Carol* 1992
+ Henie, Sonja* 1982
Protopopov, Ludmila 1992
Rodnina, Irena 1988
Scott-King, Barbara Ann* 1997
Torvill, Jayne 2002

Golf
Berg, Patty* 1980
Carner, JoAnne 1987

Haynie, Sandra 1999
Hicks, Betty* 1995
Jameson, Betty* 1999
Mann, Carol 1982
Rawls, Betsy* 1986
+ Sears, Eleanora 1984
Suggs, Louise* 1987
+ Vare, Glenna Collett* 1981
Whitworth, Kathy 1984
Wright, Mickey 1981

Golf/Track & Field
+ Zaharias, Babe Didrikson* . .1980

Gymnastics
Caslavska, Vera 1991
Comaneci, Nadia 1990
Korbut, Olga 1982
Latynina, Larysa* 1985
Retton, Mary Lou 1993
Tourischeva, Lyudmila 1987

Orienteering
Kringstad, Annichen 1995

Shooting
Murdock, Margaret 1988

Softball
Joyce, Joan 1989

Speed Skating
+ Klein Outland, Kit* 1993
Young, Sheila 1981

Swimming
Caulkins, Tracy 1986
+ Chadwick, Florence* 1996
Curtis Cuneo, Ann* 1985
de Varona, Donna 1983
Ederle, Gertrude* 1980
Fraser, Dawn 1985
Holm, Eleanor* 1980
Meagher, Mary T. 1993
Meyer-Reyes, Debbie 1987
Ruiz-Confronto, Tracie 2001

Tennis
+ Connolly, Maureen* 1987
+ Dod, Charlotte (Lottie)* 1986
Evert, Chris 1981
Gibson, Althea* 1980
Goolagong Cawley, Evonne .1989

+ Hotchkiss Wightman, Hazel* .1986
King, Billie Jean 1980
+ Lenglen, Suzanne* 1984
Navratilova, Martina 1984
Osborne du Pont, Margaret* .1998
+ Sears, Eleanora* 1984
Smith Court, Margaret 1986

Track & Field
Ashford, Evelyn 1997
Blankers-Koen, Fanny* 1982
Brisco, Valerie 2002
Cheng, Chi 1994
Coachman Davis, Alice* 1991
Cuthbert, Betty* 2002
+ Faggs Star, Aeriwentha Mae* .1996
+ Griffith Joyner, Florence 1998
Manning Mims, Madeline . . .1987
Nelson, Marjorie Jackson* . .2001
+ Rudolph, Wilma 1980
Samuelson, Joan Benoit 1999
+ Stephens, Helen* 1983
Strickland de la Hunty, Shirley* .1998
Szewinska, Irena 1992
Tyus, Wyomia 1981
Waitz, Grete 1995
White, Willye 1988

Volleyball
+ Hyman, Flo 1986

Water Skiing
McGuire, Willa Worthington* . . .1990

Coaches
+ Applebee, Constance 1991
Backus, Sharron 1993
Carver, Chris 2001
Conradt, Judy 1995
Emery, Gail 1997
Franke, Nikki 2002
Green, Tina Sloan 1999
Grossfeld, Muriel 1991
Holum, Diana 1996
Jacket, Barbara 1995
+ Jackson, Nell 1990
Kanakogi, Rusty 1994
Summitt, Pat Head 1990
Van Derveer, Tara 1998
+ Wade, Margaret 1992

RETIRED NUMBERS

Major League Baseball

The New York Yankees have retired the most uniform numbers (14) in the major leagues; followed by the Brooklyn/Los Angeles Dodgers (10), the St. Louis Cardinals (9), the Chicago White Sox and the Pittsburgh Pirates (8) and the New York/San Francisco Giants (7). **Jackie Robinson** had his #42 retired by Major League Baseball in 1997. Players who were already wearing the number were allowed to continue to do so. Los Angeles had already retired Robinson's number so he's only listed with the Dodgers below. **Nolan Ryan** has had his number retired by three teams—#34 by Texas and Houston and #30 by California (now Anaheim). Five players and a manager have had their numbers retired by two teams: **Hank Aaron**—#44 by the Boston/Milwaukee/Atlanta Braves and the Milwaukee Brewers; **Rod Carew**—#29 by Minnesota and California (now Anaheim); **Rollie Fingers**—#34 by Milwaukee and Oakland; **Carlton Fisk**—#27 by Boston and #72 by the Chicago White Sox; **Frank Robinson**—#20 by Cincinnati and Baltimore; **Casey Stengel**—#37 by the New York Yankees and New York Mets.

Number retired in 2002 (1): HOUSTON—#49 worn by manager **Larry Dierker**.

American League

Two AL teams—the Seattle Mariners and the Toronto Blue Jays—have not retired any numbers. The Blue Jays have a "level of excellence" which includes Dave Steib (#11), George Bell (#37), and Cito Gaston (#43). All numbers have been used in recent years, however.

Anaheim Angels
11 Jim Fregosi
26 Gene Autry
29 Rod Carew
30 Nolan Ryan
50 Jimmie Reese

Baltimore Orioles
4 Earl Weaver
5 Brooks Robinson
8 Cal Ripken Jr.
20 Frank Robinson
22 Jim Palmer
33 Eddie Murray

Boston Red Sox
1 Bobby Doerr
4 Joe Cronin
8 Carl Yastrzemski
9 Ted Williams
27 Carlton Fisk

Chicago White Sox
2 Nellie Fox
3 Harold Baines
4 Luke Appling
9 Minnie Minoso
11 Luis Aparicio
16 Ted Lyons
19 Billy Pierce
72 Carlton Fisk

Cleveland Indians
3 Earl Averill
5 Lou Boudreau
14 Larry Doby
18 Mel Harder
19 Bob Feller
21 Bob Lemon
455 Fans (# of consecutive sellouts)

Detroit Tigers
2 Charlie Gehringer
5 Hank Greenberg
6 Al Kaline
16 Hal Newhouser
23 Willie Horton

Kansas City Royals
5 George Brett
10 Dick Howser
20 Frank White

Minnesota Twins
3 Harmon Killebrew
6 Tony Oliva
14 Kent Hrbek
29 Rod Carew
34 Kirby Puckett

Oakland Athletics
27 Catfish Hunter
34 Rollie Fingers

New York Yankees
1 Billy Martin
3 Babe Ruth
4 Lou Gehrig
5 Joe DiMaggio
7 Mickey Mantle
8 Yogi Berra & Bill Dickey
9 Roger Maris
10 Phil Rizzuto
15 Thurman Munson
16 Whitey Ford
23 Don Mattingly
32 Elston Howard
37 Casey Stengel
44 Reggie Jackson

Tampa Bay Devil Rays
12 Wade Boggs

Texas Rangers
34 Nolan Ryan

National League

Two NL teams—the Arizona Diamondbacks and Colorado Rockies—have not retired any numbers. San Francisco has honored former NY Giants Christy Mathewson and John McGraw even though they played before numbers were worn. As did the Philadelphia Phillies for Grover Cleveland Alexander and Chuck Klein.

Atlanta Braves
3 Dale Murphy
21 Warren Spahn
35 Phil Niekro
41 Eddie Mathews
44 Hank Aaron

Chicago Cubs
14 Ernie Banks
26 Billy Williams

Cincinnati Reds
1 Fred Hutchinson
5 Johnny Bench
8 Joe Morgan
18 Ted Kluszewski
20 Frank Robinson
24 Tony Perez

Florida Marlins
5 Carl Barger

Houston Astros
25 Jose Cruz
32 Jim Umbricht
33 Mike Scott
34 Nolan Ryan
40 Don Wilson
49 Larry Dierker

Los Angeles Dodgers
1 Pee Wee Reese
2 Tommy Lasorda
4 Duke Snider
19 Jim Gilliam
20 Don Sutton
24 Walter Alston
32 Sandy Koufax
39 Roy Campanella
42 Jackie Robinson
53 Don Drysdale

Milwaukee Brewers
4 Paul Molitor
19 Robin Yount
34 Rollie Fingers
44 Hank Aaron

Montreal Expos
8 Gary Carter
10 Rusty Staub & Andre Dawson

New York Mets
14 Gil Hodges
37 Casey Stengel
41 Tom Seaver

Philadelphia Phillies
1 Richie Ashburn
14 Jim Bunning
20 Mike Schmidt
32 Steve Carlton
36 Robin Roberts

Pittsburgh Pirates
1 Billy Meyer
4 Ralph Kiner
8 Willie Stargell
9 Bill Mazeroski
20 Pie Traynor
21 Roberto Clemente
33 Honus Wagner
40 Danny Murtaugh

St. Louis Cardinals
1 Ozzie Smith
2 Red Schoendienst
6 Stan Musial
9 Enos Slaughter
14 Ken Boyer
17 Dizzy Dean
20 Lou Brock
45 Bob Gibson
85 August (Gussie) Busch

San Diego Padres
6 Steve Garvey
31 Dave Winfield
35 Randy Jones

San Francisco Giants
3 Bill Terry
4 Mel Ott
11 Carl Hubbell
24 Willie Mays
27 Juan Marichal
30 Orlando Cepeda
44 Willie McCovey

National Basketball Association

Boston has retired the most numbers (20) in the NBA, followed by Portland (9); Syracuse Nats/Philadelphia 76ers (8); Detroit, Los Angeles Lakers, Milwaukee, New York Knicks, Phoenix Suns and the KC/Sacramento Kings have (7); Cleveland, New Jersey, the Rochester/Cincinnati Royals have (6). **Wilt Chamberlain** is the only player to have his number retired by three teams: #13 by the LA Lakers, Golden State and Philadelphia; Six players have had their numbers retired by two teams: **Kareem Abdul-Jabbar**—#33 by LA Lakers and Milwaukee; **Clyde Drexler**—#22 by Houston and Portland; **Julius Erving**—#6 by Philadelphia and #32 by New Jersey; **Bob Lanier**—#16 by Detroit and Milwaukee; **Oscar Robertson**—#1 by Milwaukee and #14 by Sacramento; **Nate Thurmond**—#42 by Cleveland and Golden State.

Numbers retired in 2002 (2): MINNESOTA—#2 worn by guard **Malik Sealy**; PHILADELPHIA—#2 worn by center **Moses Malone** (1984-92 with 76ers).

Eastern Conference

Two Eastern teams—the Miami Heat and Toronto Raptors—have not retired any numbers.

Boston Celtics

1 Walter A. Brown
2 Red Auerbach
3 Dennis Johnson
6 Bill Russell
10 Jo Jo White
14 Bob Cousy
15 Tom Heinsohn
16 Tom (Satch) Sanders
17 John Havlicek
18 Dave Cowens
19 Don Nelson
21 Bill Sharman
22 Ed Macauley
23 Frank Ramsey
24 Sam Jones
25 K.C. Jones
32 Kevin McHale
33 Larry Bird
35 Reggie Lewis
00 Robert Parish
Loscy Jim Loscutoff
Radio mic Johnny Most

Atlanta Hawks

9 Bob Pettit
21 Dominique Wilkins
23 Lou Hudson

Chicago Bulls

4 Jerry Sloan
10 Bob Love
23 Michael Jordan

Cleveland Cavaliers

7 Bingo Smith
22 Larry Nance
25 Mark Price
34 Austin Carr
42 Nate Thurmond
43 Brad Daugherty

Detroit Pistons

2 Chuck Daly
4 Joe Dumars
11 Isiah Thomas
15 Vinnie Johnson
16 Bob Lanier
21 Dave Bing
40 Bill Laimbeer

Indiana Pacers

30 George McGinnis
34 Mel Daniels
35 Roger Brown
529 Bob "Slick" Leonard

Milwaukee Bucks

1 Oscar Robertson
2 Junior Bridgeman
4 Sidney Moncrief
14 Jon McGlocklin
16 Bob Lanier
32 Brian Winters
33 Kareem Abdul-Jabbar

New York Knicks

10 Walt Frazier
12 Dick Barnett
15 Dick McGuire
   & Earl Monroe
19 Willis Reed
22 Dave DeBusschere
24 Bill Bradley
613 Red Holzman

New Jersey Nets

3 Drazen Petrovic
23 Wendell Ladner
23 John Williamson
25 Bill Melchionni
32 Julius Erving
52 Buck Williams

New Orleans Hornets

13 Bobby Phills

Orlando Magic

6 Fans ("Sixth Man")

Philadelphia 76ers

2 Moses Malone
6 Julius Erving
10 Maurice Cheeks
13 Wilt Chamberlain
15 Hal Greer
24 Bobby Jones
32 Billy Cunningham
34 Charles Barkley
P.A. mic Dave Zinkoff

Washington Wizards

11 Elvin Hayes
25 Gus Johnson
41 Wes Unseld

Western Conference

Two Western teams—the Los Angeles Clippers and Memphis Grizzlies—have not retired any numbers.

Dallas Mavericks

15 Brad Davis
22 Rolando Blackman

Denver Nuggets

2 Alex English
33 David Thompson
40 Byron Beck
44 Dan Issel

Golden St. Warriors

13 Wilt Chamberlain
14 Tom Meschery
16 Al Attles
24 Rick Barry
42 Nate Thurmond

Houston Rockets

22 Clyde Drexler
23 Calvin Murphy
24 Moses Malone
45 Rudy Tomjanovich

Los Angeles Lakers

13 Wilt Chamberlain
22 Elgin Baylor
25 Gail Goodrich
32 Magic Johnson
33 Kareem Abdul-Jabbar
42 James Worthy
44 Jerry West

Minnesota Timberwolves

2 Malik Sealy

Phoenix Suns

5 Dick Van Arsdale
6 Walter Davis
7 Kevin Johnson
24 Tom Chambers
33 Alvan Adams
42 Connie Hawkins
44 Paul Westphal

Portland Trail Blazers

1 Larry Weinberg
13 Dave Twardzik
15 Larry Steele
20 Maurice Lucas
22 Clyde Drexler
32 Bill Walton
36 Lloyd Neal
45 Geoff Petrie
77 Jack Ramsay

Sacramento Kings

1 Nate Archibald
6 Fans ("Sixth Man")
11 Bob Davies
12 Maurice Stokes
14 Oscar Robertson
27 Jack Twyman
44 Sam Lacey

San Antonio Spurs

13 James Silas
44 George Gervin
00 Johnny Moore

Seattle SuperSonics

10 Nate McMillan
19 Lenny Wilkens
32 Fred Brown
43 Jack Sikma
Radio mic Bob Blackburn

Utah Jazz

1 Frank Layden
7 Pete Maravich
35 Darrell Griffith
53 Mark Eaton

Retired Numbers (Cont.)
National Football League

The Chicago Bears have retired the most uniform numbers (13) in the NFL; followed by the New York Giants (11); the Dallas Texans/Kansas City Chiefs and San Francisco (8); the Baltimore-Indianapolis Colts (7); Detroit, Boston-New England Patriots and Philadelphia (6); Cleveland (5). No player has ever had his number retired by more than one NFL team. The NFL has recently discouraged (though not eliminated) the practice of retiring numbers. As a result, the Green Bay Packers retired the jersey (but not the #92) of defensive end Reggie White in 1999. Nonetheless, Packers GM Ron Wolf announced that there are no plans to reissue the number.

    Numbers retired in 2002 (1): MIAMI—#39 worn by **Larry Csonka** (1968-74, 1979 with Dolphins).

AFC

Four AFC teams—the Baltimore Ravens, Houston Texans, Jacksonville Jaguars and Oakland Raiders—have not retired any numbers.

Buffalo Bills
12 Jim Kelly

Cincinnati Bengals
54 Bob Johnson

Cleveland Browns
14 Otto Graham
32 Jim Brown
45 Ernie Davis
46 Don Fleming
76 Lou Groza

Denver Broncos
7 John Elway
18 Frank Tripucka
44 Floyd Little

Indianapolis Colts
19 Johnny Unitas
22 Buddy Young
24 Lenny Moore
70 Art Donovan
77 Jim Parker
82 Raymond Berry
89 Gino Marchetti

Kansas City Chiefs
3 Jan Stenerud
16 Len Dawson
28 Abner Haynes
33 Stone Johnson
36 Mack Lee Hill
63 Willie Lanier
78 Bobby Bell
86 Buck Buchanan

Miami Dolphins
12 Bob Griese
13 Dan Marino
39 Larry Csonka

New England Patriots
20 Gino Cappelletti
40 Mike Haynes
56 Andre Tippett
57 Steve Nelson
73 John Hannah
79 Jim Hunt
89 Bob Dee

New York Jets
12 Joe Namath
13 Don Maynard

Pittsburgh Steelers
70 Ernie Stautner

San Diego Chargers
14 Dan Fouts

Tennessee Titans
34 Earl Campbell
43 Jim Norton
63 Mike Munchak
65 Elvin Bethea

NFC

Dallas and the Carolina Panthers are the only NFC teams that haven't officially retired any numbers. The Falcons haven't issued uniform #10 (Steve Bartowski) and #78 (Mike Kenn) since those players retired. The Cowboys have a "Ring of Honor" at Texas Stadium that includes 10 players and one coach—Tony Dorsett, Bob Hayes, Chuck Howley, Lee Roy Jordan, Tom Landry, Bob Lilly, Don Meredith, Don Perkins, Mel Renfro, Roger Staubach and Randy White. The Panthers have a Hall of Honor that includes Mike McCormack and Sam Mills.

Arizona Cardinals
8 Larry Wilson
77 Stan Mauldin
88 J.V. Cain
99 Marshall Goldberg

Atlanta Falcons
31 William Andrews
57 Jeff Van Note
60 Tommy Nobis

Chicago Bears
3 Bronko Nagurski
5 George McAfee
7 George Halas
28 Willie Galimore
34 Walter Payton
40 Gale Sayers
41 Brian Piccolo
51 Dick Butkus
56 Bill Hewitt
61 Bill George
66 Bulldog Turner
77 Red Grange

Detroit Lions
7 Dutch Clark
22 Bobby Layne
37 Doak Walker
56 Joe Schmidt
85 Chuck Hughes
88 Charlie Sanders

Green Bay Packers
3 Tony Canadeo
14 Don Hutson
15 Bart Starr
66 Ray Nitschke

Minnesota Vikings
10 Fran Tarkenton
53 Mick Tingelhoff
70 Jim Marshall
77 Korey Stringer
88 Alan Page

New Orleans Saints
31 Jim Taylor
81 Doug Atkins

New York Giants
1 Ray Flaherty
4 Tuffy Leemans
7 Mel Hein
11 Phil Simms
14 Y.A. Tittle
16 Frank Gifford
32 Al Blozis
40 Joe Morrison
42 Charlie Conerly
50 Ken Strong
56 Lawrence Taylor

Philadelphia Eagles
15 Steve Van Buren
40 Tom Brookshier
44 Pete Retzlaff
60 Chuck Bednarik
70 Al Wistert
99 Jerome Brown

St. Louis Rams
7 Bob Waterfield
29 Eric Dickerson
74 Merlin Olsen
78 Jackie Slater
85 Jack Youngblood

San Francisco 49ers
12 John Brodie
16 Joe Montana
34 Joe Perry
37 Jimmy Johnson
39 Hugh McElhenny
70 Charlie Krueger
73 Leo Nomellini
79 Bob St. Clair
87 Dwight Clark

Seattle Seahawks
12 Fans ("12th Man")
80 Steve Largent

Tampa Bay Bucs
63 Lee Roy Selmon

Wash. Redskins
33 Sammy Baugh

National Hockey League

The Boston Bruins have retired the most uniform numbers (8) in the NHL; followed by Montreal (7); Detroit and N.Y. Islanders (6); Chicago (5); Buffalo, St. Louis and Philadelphia (4). Following his retirement in 1999, the NHL announced that the league would retire **Wayne Gretzky**'s #99. Three players have had their numbers retired by two teams: **Gordie Howe**—#9 by Detroit and Hartford; **Bobby Hull**—#9 by Chicago and Winnipeg (now Phoenix); and **Ray Bourque**—#77 by Boston and Colorado.

Numbers retired in 2002 (2): BOSTON—#24 worn by **Terry O'Reilly** (1971-1985 with Bruins); LOS ANGELES—#99 worn by **Wayne Gretzky** (1988-96 with Kings).

Eastern Conference

Five Eastern teams—the Atlanta Thrashers, Carolina Hurricanes, Florida Panthers, New Jersey Devils and Tampa Bay Lightning—have not retired any numbers. The Hartford Whalers had retired three numbers: #2 Rick Ley, #9 Gordie Howe and #19 John McKenzie. Mario Lemieux's retired #66 with Pittsburgh has been temporarily unretired during his recent comeback.

Boston Bruins
- 2 Eddie Shore
- 3 Lionel Hitchman
- 4 Bobby Orr
- 5 Dit Clapper
- 7 Phil Esposito
- 8 John Bucyk
- 15 Milt Schmidt
- 24 Terry O'Reilly
- 77 Ray Bourque

Buffalo Sabres
- 2 Tim Horton
- 7 Rick Martin
- 11 Gilbert Perreault
- 14 Rene Robert

Montreal Canadiens
- 1 Jacques Plante
- 2 Doug Harvey
- 4 Jean Beliveau
- 7 Howie Morenz
- 9 Maurice Richard
- 10 Guy Lafleur
- 16 Henri Richard

New York Islanders
- 5 Denis Potvin
- 9 Clark Gilles
- 19 Bryan Trottier
- 22 Mike Bossy
- 23 Bob Nystrom
- 31 Billy Smith

New York Rangers
- 1 Eddie Giacomin
- 7 Rod Gilbert

Ottawa Senators
- 8 Frank Finnigan

Philadelphia Flyers
- 1 Bernie Parent
- 4 Barry Ashbee
- 7 Bill Barber
- 16 Bobby Clarke

Pittsburgh Penguins
- 21 Michel Briere
- 66 Mario Lemieux

Toronto Maple Leafs
- 5 Bill Barilko
- 6 Ace Bailey

Washington Capitals
- 5 Rod Langway
- 7 Yvon Labre
- 32 Dale Hunter

Western Conference

Four Western teams—the Columbus Blue Jackets, Mighty Ducks of Anaheim, Nashville Predators and San Jose Sharks—have not retired any numbers. Note, the Quebec Nordiques retired the numbers of J.C. Tremblay (3), Marc Tardiff (8) and Michel Goulet (16) but these numbers have been worn since the team moved to Colorado.

Calgary Flames
- 9 Lanny McDonald

Chicago Blackhawks
- 1 Glenn Hall
- 9 Bobby Hull
- 18 Denis Savard
- 21 Stan Mikita
- 35 Tony Esposito

Colorado Avalanche
- 77 Ray Bourque

Dallas Stars
- 7 Neal Broten
- 8 Bill Goldsworthy
- 19 Bill Masterton

Detroit Red Wings
- 1 Terry Sawchuk
- 7 Ted Lindsay
- 9 Gordie Howe
- 10 Alex Delvecchio
- 12 Sid Abel

Edmonton Oilers
- 3 Al Hamilton
- 17 Jari Kurri
- 99 Wayne Gretzky

Los Angeles Kings
- 16 Marcel Dionne
- 18 Dave Taylor
- 30 Rogie Vachon
- 99 Wayne Gretzky

Minnesota Wild
- 1 Fans

Phoenix Coyotes
- 9 Bobby Hull
- 25 Thomas Steen

St. Louis Blues
- 3 Bob Gassoff
- 8 Barclay Plager
- 11 Brian Sutter
- 24 Bernie Federko

Vancouver Canucks
- 12 Stan Smyl

AWARDS

Associated Press Athletes of the Year

Selected annually by AP newspaper sports editors since 1931.

Male

Barry Bonds had one of the greatest seasons in baseball history in 2001. His record-breaking 73 home runs, .863 slugging percentage and unprecedented fourth MVP award added up to a year that more than earned him the 2001 AP Athlete of the Year award. Bonds broke Mark McGwire's three-year old home run record of 70, and also broke Babe Ruth's single-season slugging percentage and walks records.

The top 6 vote-getters (first place votes in parentheses): 1. **Barry Bonds**, baseball (33), 136 pts; 2. **Lance Armstrong**, cycling (26), 127 pts; 3. **Ichiro Suzuki**, baseball (7) and 4. **Tiger Woods**, golf (2), 43 pts; 5. **Randy Johnson**, baseball; 6. **Allen Iverson**, basketball.

Multiple winners: Michael Jordan and Tiger Woods (3); Don Budge, Sandy Koufax, Carl Lewis, Joe Montana and Byron Nelson (2).

Year		Year		Year	
1931	**Pepper Martin**, baseball	1941	**Joe DiMaggio**, baseball	1949	**Leon Hart**, college football
1932	**Gene Sarazen**, golf	1942	**Frank Sinkwich**, college football	1950	**Jim Konstanty**, baseball
1933	**Carl Hubbell**, baseball	1943	**Gunder Haegg**, track	1951	**Dick Kazmaier**, college football
1934	**Dizzy Dean**, baseball	1944	**Byron Nelson**, golf	1952	**Bob Mathias**, track
1935	**Joe Louis**, boxing	1945	**Byron Nelson**, golf	1953	**Ben Hogan**, golf
1936	**Jesse Owens**, track	1946	**Glenn Davis**, college football	1954	**Willie Mays**, baseball
1937	**Don Budge**, tennis	1947	**Johnny Lujack**, college football	1955	**Hopalong Cassady**, col. football
1938	**Don Budge**, tennis	1948	**Lou Boudreau**, baseball	1956	**Mickey Mantle**, baseball
1939	**Nile Kinnick**, college football				
1940	**Tom Harmon**, college football				

Awards (Cont.)

Year		Year		Year	
1957	**Ted Williams**, baseball	1972	**Mark Spitz**, swimming	1987	**Ben Johnson**, track
1958	**Herb Elliott**, track	1973	**O.J. Simpson**, pro football	1988	**Orel Hershiser**, baseball
1959	**Ingemar Johansson**, boxing	1974	**Muhammad Ali**, boxing	1989	**Joe Montana**, pro football
1960	**Rafer Johnson**, track	1975	**Fred Lynn**, baseball	1990	**Joe Montana**, pro football
1961	**Roger Maris**, baseball	1976	**Bruce Jenner**, track	1991	**Michael Jordan**, pro basketball
1962	**Maury Wills**, baseball	1977	**Steve Cauthen**, horse racing	1992	**Michael Jordan**, pro basketball
1963	**Sandy Koufax**, baseball	1978	**Ron Guidry**, baseball	1993	**Michael Jordan**, pro basketball
1964	**Don Schollander**, swimming	1979	**Willie Stargell**, baseball	1994	**George Foreman**, boxing
1965	**Sandy Koufax**, baseball	1980	**U.S. Olympic hockey team**	1995	**Cal Ripken Jr.**, baseball
1966	**Frank Robinson**, baseball	1981	**John McEnroe**, tennis	1996	**Michael Johnson**, track
1967	**Carl Yastrzemski**, baseball	1982	**Wayne Gretzky**, hockey	1997	**Tiger Woods**, golf
1968	**Denny McLain**, baseball	1983	**Carl Lewis**, track	1998	**Mark McGwire**, baseball
1969	**Tom Seaver**, baseball	1984	**Carl Lewis**, track	1999	**Tiger Woods**, golf
1970	**George Blanda**, pro football	1985	**Dwight Gooden**, baseball	2000	**Tiger Woods**, golf
1971	**Lee Trevino**, golf	1986	**Larry Bird**, pro basketball	2001	**Barry Bonds**, baseball

Female

Jennifer Capriati won her first major at the Australian Open and then followed it up with a victory at the French Open and captured the world number one ranking temporarily.

The top 5 vote-getters (first place votes in parentheses): 1. **Jennifer Capriati**, tennis (37), 157 pts; 2. **Venus Williams**, tennis (26), 120 pts; 3. **Annika Sorenstam**, golf, 94 pts; 4. **Stacy Dragila**, pole vault; 5. **Lisa Leslie**, basketball.

Multiple winners: Babe Didrikson Zaharias (6); Chris Evert (4); Patty Berg and Maureen Connolly (3); Tracy Austin, Althea Gibson, Billie Jean King, Nancy Lopez, Alice Marble, Martina Navratilova, Wilma Rudolph, Monica Seles, Kathy Whitworth and Mickey Wright (2).

Year		Year		Year	
1931	**Helene Madison**, swimming	1955	**Patty Berg**, golf	1979	**Tracy Austin**, tennis
1932	**Babe Didrikson**, track	1956	**Pat McCormick**, diving	1980	**Chris Evert Lloyd**, tennis
1933	**Helen Jacobs**, tennis	1957	**Althea Gibson**, tennis	1981	**Tracy Austin**, tennis
1934	**Virginia Van Wie**, golf	1958	**Althea Gibson**, tennis	1982	**Mary Decker Tabb**, track
1935	**Helen Wills Moody**, tennis	1959	**Maria Bueno**, tennis	1983	**Martina Navratilova**, tennis
1936	**Helen Stephens**, track	1960	**Wilma Rudolph**, track	1984	**Mary Lou Retton**, gymnastics
1937	**Katherine Rawls**, swimming	1961	**Wilma Rudolph**, track	1985	**Nancy Lopez**, golf
1938	**Patty Berg**, golf	1962	**Dawn Fraser**, swimming	1986	**Martina Navratilova**, tennis
1939	**Alice Marble**, tennis	1963	**Mickey Wright**, golf	1987	**Jackie Joyner-Kersee**, track
1940	**Alice Marble**, tennis	1964	**Mickey Wright**, golf	1988	**Florence Griffith Joyner**, track
1941	**Betty Hicks Newell**, golf	1965	**Kathy Whitworth**, golf	1989	**Steffi Graf**, tennis
1942	**Gloria Callen**, swimming	1966	**Kathy Whitworth**, golf	1990	**Beth Daniel**, golf
1943	**Patty Berg**, golf	1967	**Billie Jean King**, tennis	1991	**Monica Seles**, tennis
1944	**Ann Curtis**, swimming	1968	**Peggy Fleming**, skating	1992	**Monica Seles**, tennis
1945	**Babe Didrikson Zaharias**, golf	1969	**Debbie Meyer**, swimming	1993	**Sheryl Swoopes**, basketball
1946	**Babe Didrikson Zaharias**, golf	1970	**Chi Cheng**, track	1994	**Bonnie Blair**, speed skating
1947	**Babe Didrikson Zaharias**, golf	1971	**Evonne Goolagong**, tennis	1995	**Rebecca Lobo**, col. basketball
1948	**Fanny Blankers-Koen**, track	1972	**Olga Korbut**, gymnastics	1996	**Amy Van Dyken**, swimming
1949	**Marlene Bauer**, golf	1973	**Billie Jean King**, tennis	1997	**Martina Hingis**, tennis
1950	**Babe Didrikson Zaharias**, golf	1974	**Chris Evert**, tennis	1998	**Se Ri Pak**, golf
1951	**Maureen Connolly**, tennis	1975	**Chris Evert**, tennis	1999	**U.S. Soccer Team**
1952	**Maureen Connolly**, tennis	1976	**Nadia Comaneci**, gymnastics	2000	**Marion Jones**, track
1953	**Maureen Connolly**, tennis	1977	**Chris Evert**, tennis	2001	**Jennifer Capriati**, tennis
1954	**Babe Didrikson Zaharias**, golf	1978	**Nancy Lopez**, golf		

USOC Sportsman & Sportswoman of the Year

To the outstanding overall male and female athletes from within the U.S. Olympic Committee member organizations. Winners are chosen from nominees of the national governing bodies for Olympic and Pan American Games and affiliated organizations. Voting is done by members of the national media, USOC board of directors and Athletes' Advisory Council.

Sportsman

Multiple winners: Eric Heiden and Michael Johnson (3); Lance Armstrong, Matt Biondi and Greg Louganis (2).

Year		Year		Year	
1974	**Jim Bolding**, track	1984	**Edwin Moses**, track	1994	**Dan Jansen**, speed skating
1975	**Clint Jackson**, boxing	1985	**Willie Banks**, track	1995	**Michael Johnson**, track
1976	**John Naber**, swimming	1986	**Matt Biondi**, swimming	1996	**Michael Johnson**, track
1977	**Eric Heiden**, speed skating	1987	**Greg Louganis**, diving	1997	**Pete Sampras**, tennis
1978	**Bruce Davidson**, equestrian	1988	**Matt Biondi**, swimming	1998	**Jonny Moseley**, skiing
1979	**Eric Heiden**, speed skating	1989	**Roger Kingdom**, track	1999	**Lance Armstrong**, cycling
1980	**Eric Heiden**, speed skating	1990	**John Smith**, wrestling	2000	**Rulon Gardner**, wrestling
1981	**Scott Hamilton**, fig. skating	1991	**Carl Lewis**, track	2001	**Lance Armstrong**, cycling
1982	**Greg Louganis**, diving	1992	**Pablo Morales**, swimming		
1983	**Rick McKinney**, archery	1993	**Michael Johnson**, track		

Sportswoman

Multiple winners: Bonnie Blair, Tracy Caulkins, Jackie Joyner-Kersee, Picabo Street and Sheila Young Ochowicz (2).

Year		Year		Year	
1974	**Shirley Babashoff**, swimming	1983	**Tamara McKinney**, skiing	1993	**Gail Devers**, track
1975	**Kathy Heddy**, swimming	1984	**Tracy Caulkins**, swimming	1994	**Bonnie Blair**, speed skating
1976	**Sheila Young**, speedskating	1985	**Mary Decker Slaney**, track	1995	**Picabo Street**, skiing
1977	**Linda Fratianne**, fig. skating	1986	**Jackie Joyner-Kersee**, track	1996	**Amy Van Dyken**, swimming
1978	**Tracy Caulkins**, swimming	1987	**Jackie Joyner-Kersee**, track	1997	**Tara Lipinski**, figure skating
1979	**Sippy Woodhead**, swimming	1988	**Florence Griffith Joyner**, track	1998	**Picabo Street**, skiing
1980	**Beth Heiden**, speed skating	1989	**Janet Evans**, swimming	1999	**Jenny Thompson**, swimming
1981	**Sheila Ochowicz**, speed skating & cycling	1990	**Lynn Jennings**, track	2000	**Marion Jones**, track
1982	**Melanie Smith**, equestrian	1991	**Kim Zmeskal**, gymnastics	2001	**Jennifer Capriati**, tennis
		1992	**Bonnie Blair**, speed skating		

UPI International Athletes of the Year

Selected annually by United Press International's European newspaper sports editors from 1974-95.

Male

Multiple winners: Sebastian Coe, Alberto Juantorena and Carl Lewis (2).

Year		Year		Year	
1974	**Muhammad Ali**, boxing	1982	**Daley Thompson**, track	1990	**Stefan Edberg**, tennis
1975	**Joao Oliveira**, track	1983	**Carl Lewis**, track	1991	**Sergei Bubka**, track
1976	**Alberto Juantorena**, track	1984	**Carl Lewis**, track	1992	**Kevin Young**, track
1977	**Alberto Juantorena**, track	1985	**Steve Cram**, track	1993	**Miguel Indurain**, cycling
1978	**Henry Rono**, track	1986	**Diego Maradona**, soccer	1994	**Johan Olav Koss**, speed skating
1979	**Sebastian Coe**, track	1987	**Ben Johnson**, track	1995	**Jonathan Edwards**, track
1980	**Eric Heiden**, speed skating	1988	**Matt Biondi**, swimming	1996	discontinued
1981	**Sebastian Coe**, track	1989	**Boris Becker**, tennis		

Female

Multiple winners: Nadia Comaneci, Steffi Graf, Marita Koch and Monica Seles (2).

Year		Year		Year	
1974	**Irena Szewinska**, track	1983	**Jarmila Kratochvilova**, track	1992	**Monica Seles**, tennis
1975	**Nadia Comaneci**, gymnastics	1984	**Martina Navratilova**, tennis	1993	**Wang Junxia**, track
1976	**Nadia Comaneci**, gymnastics	1985	**Mary Decker Slaney**, track	1994	**Le Jingyi**, swimming
1977	**Rosie Ackermann**, track	1986	**Heike Drechsler**, track	1995	**Gwen Torrence**, track
1978	**Tracy Caulkins**, swimming	1987	**Steffi Graf**, tennis	1996	discontinued
1979	**Marita Koch**, track	1988	**Florence Griffith Joyner**, track		
1980	**Hanni Wenzel**, alpine skiing	1989	**Steffi Graf**, tennis		
1981	**Chris Evert Lloyd**, tennis	1990	**Merlene Ottey**, track		
1982	**Marita Koch**, track	1991	**Monica Seles**, tennis		

American-International Athlete Trophy

Formerly known as the Jesse Owens International Trophy, the trophy has been presented annually by the International Amateur Athletic Association since 1981 and selected by a worldwide panel of electors.

Multiple winners: Michael Johnson and Marion Jones (2).

Year		Year		Year	
1981	**Eric Heiden**, speed skating	1990	**Roger Kingdom**, track	1997	**Michael Johnson**, track
1982	**Sebastian Coe**, track	1991	**Greg LeMond**, cycling	1998	**Haile Gebrselassie**, track
1983	**Mary Decker**, track	1992	**Mike Powell**, track	1999	**Marion Jones**, track
1984	**Edwin Moses**, track	1993	**Vitaly Scherbo**, gymnastics	2000	**Lance Armstrong**, cycling
1985	**Carl Lewis**, track	1994	**Wang Junxia**, track	2001	**Marion Jones**, track
1986	**Said Aouita**, track	1995	**Johan Olva Koss**, speed skating	2002	**Ian Thorpe**, swimming
1987	**Greg Louganis**, diving	1996	**Michael Johnson**, track		
1988	**Ben Johnson**, track				

Honda Broderick Cup

To the outstanding collegiate woman athlete of the year in NCAA competition. Winner is chosen from nominees in each of the NCAA's 10 competitive sports. Final voting is done by member athletic directors. Award is named after founder and sportswear manufacturer Thomas Broderick.

Multiple winner: Tracy Caulkins (2).

Year		Year		
1977	**Lucy Harris**, Delta St ....basketball	1987	**Mary T. Meagher**, California..........swimming
1978	**Ann Meyers**, UCLA ....basketball	1988	**Teresa Weatherspoon**, La. Tech ....basketball
1979	**Nancy Lieberman**, Old Dominion .....basketball	1989	**Vicki Huber**, Villanova ....track
1980	**Julie Shea**, N.C. State ....track & field	1990	**Suzy Favor**, Wisconsin ....track
1981	**Jill Sterkel**, Texas ....swimming	1991	**Dawn Staley**, Virginia.................basketball
1982	**Tracy Caulkins**, Florida.............swimming	1992	**Missy Marlowe**, Utah ....gymnastics
1983	**Deitre Collins**, Hawaii ....volleyball	1993	**Lisa Fernandez**, UCLA ....softball
1984	**Tracy Caulkins**, Florida.............swimming & **Cheryl Miller**, USC.................basketball	1994	**Mia Hamm**, North Carolina ....soccer
1985	**Jackie Joyner**, UCLA ....track & field	1995	**Rebecca Lobo**, UConn..................basketball
1986	**Kamie Ethridge**, Texas ....basketball	1996	**Jennifer Rizzotti**, UConn................basketball
		1997	**Cindy Daws**, Notre Dame................soccer

Awards (Cont.)

Year		Year	
1998	**Chamique Holdsclaw**, Tennessee . . . . .basketball	2001	**Jackie Stiles**, SW Missouri St. . . . . .basketball
1999	**Misty May**, Long Beach St. . . . . .volleyball	2002	**Angela Williams**, USC . . . . .track
2000	**Cristina Teuscher**, Columbia . . . . .swimming		

Flo Hyman Award

Presented annually since 1987 by the Women's Sports Foundation for "exemplifying dignity, spirit and commitment to excellence" and named in honor of the late captain of the 1984 U.S. Women's Volleyball team. Voting by WSF members.

Year		Year		Year	
1987	**Martina Navratilova**, tennis	1993	**Lynette Woodward**, basketball	1999	**Bonnie Blair**, speed skating
1988	**Jackie Joyner-Kersee**, track	1994	**Patty Sheehan**, golf	2000	**Monica Seles**, tennis
1989	**Evelyn Ashford**, track	1995	**Mary Lou Retton**, gymnastics	2001	**Lisa Leslie**, basketball
1990	**Chris Evert**, tennis	1996	**Donna de Varona**, swimming	2002	**Dot Richardson**, softball
1991	**Diana Golden**, skiing	1997	**Billie Jean King**, tennis		
1992	**Nancy Lopez**, golf	1998	**Nadia Comaneci**, gymnastics		

James E. Sullivan Memorial Award

Presented annually by the Amateur Athletic Union since 1930. The Sullivan Award is named after the former AAU president and given to the athlete who, "by his or her performance, example and influence as an amateur, has done the most during the year to advance the cause of sportsmanship." An athlete cannot win the award more than once.

Olympic figure skater **Michelle Kwan** won the 2001 Sullivan Award. In 2001, Kwan won here fourth World Citle and fifth U.S. championship. Kwan joined 1949 Sullivan Award winner Dick Button as only the second figure skater to win the prestigious award. The four additional finalists are listed alphabetically: **Natalie Coughlin**, swimming; **Mark Prior**, baseball; **Sean Townsend**, gymnastics; **Alan Webb**, track. Vote totals were not released.

Year		Year		Year	
1930	**Bobby Jones**, golf	1955	**Harrison Dillard**, track	1980	**Eric Heiden**, speed skating
1931	**Barney Berlinger**, track	1956	**Pat McCormick**, diving	1981	**Carl Lewis**, track
1932	**Jim Bausch**, track	1957	**Bobby Morrow**, track	1982	**Mary Decker**, track
1933	**Glenn Cunningham**, track	1958	**Glenn Davis**, track	1983	**Edwin Moses**, track
1934	**Bill Bonthron**, track	1959	**Parry O'Brien**, track	1984	**Greg Louganis**, diving
1935	**Lawson Little**, golf	1960	**Rafer Johnson**, track	1985	**Joan B. Samuelson**, track
1936	**Glenn Morris**, track	1961	**Wilma Rudolph**, track	1986	**Jackie Joyner-Kersee**, track
1937	**Don Budge**, tennis	1962	**Jim Beatty**, track	1987	**Jim Abbott**, baseball
1938	**Don Lash**, track	1963	**John Pennel**, track	1988	**Florence Griffith Joyner**, track
1939	**Joe Burk**, rowing	1964	**Don Schollander**, swimming	1989	**Janet Evans**, swimming
1940	**Greg Rice**, track	1965	**Bill Bradley**, basketball	1990	**John Smith**, wrestling
1941	**Leslie MacMitchell**, track	1966	**Jim Ryun**, track	1991	**Mike Powell**, track
1942	**Cornelius Warmerdam**, track	1967	**Randy Matson**, track	1992	**Bonnie Blair**, speed skating
1943	**Gilbert Dodds**, track	1968	**Debbie Meyer**, swimming	1993	**Charlie Ward**, football
1944	**Ann Curtis**, swimming	1969	**Bill Toomey**, track	1994	**Dan Jansen**, speed skating
1945	**Doc Blanchard**, football	1970	**John Kinsella**, swimming	1995	**Bruce Baumgartner**, wrestling
1946	**Arnold Tucker**, football	1971	**Mark Spitz**, swimming	1996	**Michael Johnson**, track
1947	**John B. Kelly, Jr.**, rowing	1972	**Frank Shorter**, track	1997	**Peyton Manning**, football
1948	**Bob Mathias**, track	1973	**Bill Walton**, basketball	1998	**Chamique Holdsclaw**, basketball
1949	**Dick Button**, skating	1974	**Rich Wohlhuter**, track	1999	**Coco and Kelly Miller**, basketball
1950	**Fred Wilt**, track	1975	**Tim Shaw**, swimming		
1951	**Bob Richards**, track	1976	**Bruce Jenner**, track	2000	**Rulon Gardner**, wrestling
1952	**Horace Ashenfelter**, track	1977	**John Naber**, swimming	2001	**Michelle Kwan**, figure skating
1953	**Sammy Lee**, diving	1978	**Tracy Caulkins**, swimming		
1954	**Mal Whitfield**, track	1979	**Kurt Thomas**, gymnastics		

ESPY Awards

The ESPY Awards, which represent the convergence of the sports and entertainment communities, were created by ESPN in 1993 and are given for Excellence in Sports Performance in more than 30 categories. ESPYs are awarded by a panel of sports executives, journalists and retired athletes whose decisions are based on the performances of the nominees during the year preceding the awards ceremony. Note that not all categories are listed below.

Breakthrough Athlete

1993	Gary Sheffield, San Diego Padres	1999	Randy Moss, Minnesota Vikings
1994	Mike Piazza, Los Angeles Dodgers	2000	Kurt Warner, St. Louis Rams
1995	Jeff Bagwell, Houston Astros	2001	Daunte Culpepper, Minnesota Vikings
1996	Hideo Nomo, Los Angeles Dodgers	2002	Tom Brady, New England Patriots
1997	Tiger Woods, golf		
1998	Nomar Garciaparra, Boston Red Sox		

Best Coach/Manager

1993 Jimmy Johnson, Dallas Cowboys
1994 Jimmy Johnson, Dallas Cowboys
1995 George Siefert, San Francisco 49ers
1996 Gary Barnett, Northwestern
1997 Joe Torre, New York Yankees
1998 Jim Leyland, Florida Marlins
1999 Joe Torre, New York Yankees
2000 Joe Torre, New York Yankees
2001 Joe Torre, New York Yankees
2002 Phil Jackson, Los Angeles Lakers

Best Comeback Athlete

1993 Dave Winfield, Toronto Blue Jays
1994 Mario Lemieux, Pittsburgh Penguins
1995 Dan Marino, Miami Dolphins
1996 Michael Jordan, Chicago Bulls
1997 Evander Holyfield, boxer
1998 Roger Clemens, Toronto Blue Jays
1999 Eric Davis, Baltimore Orioles
2000 Lance Armstrong, cycling
2001 Andres Galarraga, baseball
2002 Jennifer Capriati, tennis

Best Female Athlete

1993 Monica Seles, tennis
1994 Julie Krone, jockey
1995 Bonnie Blair, speed skater
1996 Rebecca Lobo, basketball
1997 Amy Van Dyken, swimming
1998 Mia Hamm, soccer
1999 Chamique Holdsclaw, college basketball
2000 Mia Hamm, soccer
2001 Marion Jones, track
2002 Venus Williams, tennis

Best Male Athlete

1993 Michael Jordan, Chicago Bulls
1994 Barry Bonds, San Francisco Giants
1995 Steve Young, San Francisco 49ers
1996 Cal Ripken, Baltimore Orioles
1997 Michael Johnson, Olympic sprinter
1998 Tiger Woods, golf
1999 Mark McGwire, St. Louis Cardinals
2000 Tiger Woods, golf
2001 Tiger Woods, golf
2002 Tiger Woods, golf

Outstanding Performance Under Pressure

1993 Christian Laettner, Duke
1994 Joe Carter, Toronto Blue Jays
1995 Mark Messier, New York Rangers
1996 Martin Broduer, New Jersey Devils
1997 Kerri Strug, Olympic gymnast
1998 Terrell Davis, Denver Broncos
1999 Mark O'Meara, golf
2000 discontinued

Best Team

1993 Dallas Cowboys
1994 Toronto Blue Jays
1995 New York Rangers
1996 UConn women's hoops
1997 New York Yankees
1998 Denver Broncos
1999 New York Yankees
2000 U.S. Women's World Cup Soccer Team
2001 New York Yankees
2002 Los Angeles Lakers

Best Baseball Player

1993 Dennis Eckersley, Oakland A's
1994 Barry Bonds, San Francisco Giants
1995 Jeff Bagwell, Houston Astros
1996 Greg Maddux, Atlanta Braves
1997 Ken Caminiti, San Diego Padres
1998 Larry Walker, Colorado Rockies
1999 Mark McGwire, St. Louis Cardinals
2000 Pedro Martinez, Boston Red Sox
2001 Pedro Martinez, Boston Red Sox
2002 Barry Bonds, San Francisco Giants

Best NFL Player

1993 Emmitt Smith, Dallas Cowboys
1994 Emmitt Smith, Dallas Cowboys
1995 Barry Sanders, Detroit Lions
1996 Brett Favre, Green Bay Packers
1997 Brett Favre, Green Bay Packers
1998 Barry Sanders, Detroit Lions
1999 Terrell Davis, Denver Broncos
2000 Kurt Warner, St. Louis Rams
2001 Marshall Faulk, St. Louis Rams
2002 Marshall Faulk, St. Louis Rams

Best NBA Player

1993 Michael Jordan, Chicago Bulls
1994 Charles Barkley, Phoenix Suns
1995 Hakeem Olajuwon, Houston Rockets
1996 Hakeem Olajuwon, Houston Rockets
1997 Michael Jordan, Chicago Bulls
1998 Michael Jordan, Chicago Bulls
1999 Michael Jordan, Chicago Bulls
2000 Tim Duncan, San Antonio Spurs
2001 Shaquille O'Neal, Los Angeles Lakers
2002 Shaquille O'Neal, Los Angeles Lakers

Best WNBA Player

1998 Cynthia Cooper, Houston Comets
1999 Cynthia Cooper, Houston Comets
2000 Cynthia Cooper, Houston Comets
2001 Sheryl Swoopes, Houston Comets
2002 Lisa Leslie, Los Angeles Sparks

Best NHL Player

1993 Mario Lemieux, Pittsburgh Penguins
1994 Mario Lemieux, Pittsburgh Penguins
1995 Mark Messier, New York Rangers
1996 Eric Lindros, Philadelphia Flyers
1997 Joe Sakic, Colorado Avalanche
1998 Mario Lemieux, Pittsburgh Penguins
1999 Dominik Hasek, Buffalo Sabres
2000 Dominik Hasek, Buffalo Sabres
2001 Chris Pronger, St. Louis Blues
2002 Jarome Iginla, Calgary Flames

Outstanding College Football Performer of the Year

1993 Garrison Hearst, Georgia
1994 Charlie Ward, Florida State
1995 Rashaan Salaam, Colorado
1996 Eddie George, Ohio State
1997 Danny Wuerffel, Florida
1998 Peyton Manning, Tennessee
1999 Ricky Williams, Texas
2000 Michael Vick, Virginia Tech
2001 Chris Weinke, Florida State
2002 discontinued

Awards (Cont.)

Outstanding College Basketball Performer of the Year

1993	Christian Laettner, Duke
1994	Bobby Hurley, Duke
1995	Grant Hill, Duke
1996	Ed O'Bannon, UCLA
1997	Tim Duncan, Wake Forest
1998	Keith Van Horn, Utah
1999	Antawn Jamison, North Carolina
2000	Elton Brand, Duke
2001	Kenyon Martin, Cincinnati
2002	discontinued

Outstanding Women's College Hoops Performer of the Year

1993	Dawn Staley, Virginia
1994	Sheryl Swoopes, Texas Tech
1995	Charlotte Smith, North Carolina
1996	Rebecca Lobo, Connecticut
1997	Saudia Roundtree, Georgia
1998	Chamique Holdsclaw, Tennessee
1999	Chamique Holdsclaw, Tennessee
2000	Chamique Holdsclaw, Tennessee
2001	Tamika Catchings, Tennessee
2002	discontinued

Best Men's Tennis Player

1993	Jim Courier	1998	Pete Sampras
1994	Pete Sampras	1999	Pete Sampras
1995	Pete Sampras	2000	Andre Agassi
1996	Pete Sampras	2001	Pete Sampras
1997	Pete Sampras	2002	Lleyton Hewitt

Best Women's Tennis Player

1993	Monica Seles
1994	Steffi Graf
1995	Aranxta Sanchez Vicario
1996	Steffi Graf
1997	Steffi Graf
1998	Martina Hingis
1999	Lindsay Davenport
2000	Lindsay Davenport
2001	Venus Williams
2002	Venus Williams

Best Men's Golfer

1993	Fred Couples	1998	Tiger Woods
1994	Nick Price	1999	Mark O'Meara
1995	Nick Price	2000	Tiger Woods
1996	Corey Pavin	2001	Tiger Woods
1997	Tom Lehman	2002	Tiger Woods

Best Women's Golfer

1993	Dottie Mochrie	1998	Annika Sorenstam
1994	Betsy King	1999	Annika Sorenstam
1995	Laura Davies	2000	Julie Inkster
1996	Annika Sorenstam	2001	Karrie Webb
1997	Karrie Webb	2002	Annika Sorenstam

Best Jockey

1994	Mike Smith	1999	Kent Desormeaux
1995	Chris McCarron	2000	Chris Antley
1996	Jerry Bailey	2001	Kent Desormeaux
1997	Jerry Bailey	2002	Victor Espinoza
1998	Gary Stevens		

Best Bowler

1995	Norm Duke	2000	Parker Bohn III
1996	Mike Aulby	2001	Walter Ray Williams Jr.
1997	Bob Learn Jr.	2002	Pete Weber
1998	Walter Ray Williams Jr.		
1999	Walter Ray Williams Jr.		

Best Driver

1993	Nigel Mansell	1998	Jeff Gordon
1994	Nigel Mansell	1999	Jeff Gordon
1995	Al Unser Jr.	2000	Dale Jarrett
1996	Jeff Gordon	2001	Bobby Labonte
1997	Jimmy Vasser	2002	Michael Schumacher

Best Men's Track Athlete

1993	Kevin Young	1998	Wilson Kipketer
1994	Michael Johnson	1999	Maurice Greene
1995	Dennis Mitchell	2000	Michael Johnson
1996	Michael Johnson	2001	Maurice Greene
1997	Michael Johnson	2002	Maurice Greene

Best Women's Track Athlete

1993	Evelyn Ashford	1998	Marion Jones
1994	Gail Devers	1999	Marion Jones
1995	Gwen Torrence	2000	Marion Jones
1996	Kim Batten	2001	Marion Jones
1997	Marie-Jose Perec	2002	Marion Jones

Game of the Year

1996	AFC championship between Colts and Steelers
1997	Ohio State edges Arizona State in the Rose Bowl
1998	Super Bowl XXXII, Broncos over Packers
1999-	
2001	not awarded
2002	World Series, Diamondbacks-Yankees Game 7

Best Boxer

1993	Riddick Bowe	1998	Evander Holyfield
1994	Evander Holyfield	1999	Oscar De La Hoya
1995	George Foreman	2000	Roy Jones Jr.
1996	Roy Jones Jr.	2001	Felix Trinidad
1997	Evander Holyfield	2002	Lennox Lewis

Best Male College Athlete

2002	Cael Sanderson, wrestling

Best Female College Athlete

2002	Sue Bird, basketball

Best Male Soccer Player

2002	Landon Donovan

Best Female Soccer Player

2002	Tiffeny Milbrett

Best Outdoors Athlete

2002	Kevin VanDam, fishing

Best Action Sports Athlete

2002	Kelly Clark, snowboarding

AP/Wide World Photos

Hank Aaron, left, has his Presidential Medal of Freedom inspected by fellow award-winner Bill Cosby during a ceremony at the White House.

Presidential Medal of Freedom

Since President John F. Kennedy established the Medal of Freedom as America's highest civilian honor in 1963, only 10 sports figures have won the award. Note that (*) indicates the presentation was made posthumously.

Year		President	Year		President
1963	**Bob Kiphuth**, swimming	Kennedy	1986	**Earl (Red) Blaik**, football	Reagan
1976	**Jesse Owens**, track & field	Ford	1991	**Ted Williams**, baseball	Bush
1977	**Joe DiMaggio**, baseball	Ford	1992	**Richard Petty**, auto racing	Bush
1983	**Paul (Bear) Bryant***, football	Reagan	1993	**Arthur Ashe***, tennis	Clinton
1984	**Jackie Robinson***, baseball	Reagan	2002	**Hank Aaron**, baseball	Bush

Arthur Ashe Award for Courage

Presented since 1993 on the annual ESPN "ESPYs" telecast. Given to a member of the sports community who has exemplified the same courage, spirit and determination to help others despite personal hardship that characterized Arthur Ashe, the late tennis champion and humanitarian. Voting done by select 26-member committee of media and sports personalities.

Year		Year		Year	
1993	**Jim Valvano**, basketball	1997	**Muhammad Ali**, boxing	2001	**Cathy Freeman**, track
1994	**Steve Palermo**, baseball	1998	**Dean Smith**, college basketball	2002	**Todd Beamer, Mark Bingham, Tom Burnett** and **Jeremy Glick**, Flight 93
1995	**Howard Cosell**, TV & radio	1999	**Billie Jean King**, tennis		
1996	**Loretta Clairborne**, special olympics	2000	**Dave Sanders**, Columbine H.S. coach		

The Hickok Belt

Officially known as the S. Rae Hickok Professional Athlete of the Year Award and presented by the Kickik Manufacturing Co. of Arlington, Texas, from 1950-76. The trophy was a large belt of gold, diamonds and other jewels, reportedly worth $30,000 in 1976, the last year it was handed out. Voting was done by 270 newspaper sports editors from around the country.

Multiple winner: Sandy Koufax (2).

Year		Year		Year	
1950	**Phil Rizzuto**, baseball	1960	**Arnold Palmer**, golf	1970	**Brooks Robinson**, baseball
1951	**Allie Reynolds**, baseball	1961	**Roger Maris**, baseball	1971	**Lee Trevino**, golf
1952	**Rocky Marciano**, boxing	1962	**Maury Wills**, baseball	1972	**Steve Carlton**, baseball
1953	**Ben Hogan**, golf	1963	**Sandy Koufax**, baseball	1973	**O.J. Simpson**, football
1954	**Willie Mays**, baseball	1964	**Jim Brown**, football	1974	**Muhammad Ali**, boxing
1955	**Otto Graham**, football	1965	**Sandy Koufax**, baseball	1975	**Pete Rose**, baseball
1956	**Mickey Mantle**, baseball	1966	**Frank Robinson**, baseball	1976	**Ken Stabler**, football
1957	**Carmen Basilio**, boxing	1967	**Carl Yastrzemski**, baseball	1977	Discontinued
1958	**Bob Turley**, baseball	1968	**Joe Namath**, football		
1959	**Ingemar Johansson**, boxing	1969	**Tom Seaver**, baseball		

Awards (Cont.)
ABC's "Wide World of Sports" Athlete of the Year
Selected annually by the producers of ABC Sports since 1962.

Multiple winners: Greg LeMond and Tiger Woods (2).

Year	Year	Year
1962 **Jim Beatty**, track	1975 **Jack Nicklaus**, golf	1989 **Greg LeMond**, cycling
1963 **Valery Brumel**, track	1976 **Nadia Comaneci**, gymnastics	1990 **Greg LeMond**, cycling
1964 **Don Schollander**, swimming	1977 **Steve Cauthen**, horse racing	1991 **Carl Lewis**, track
1965 **Jim Clark**, auto racing	1978 **Ron Guidry**, baseball	**& Kim Zmeskal**, gymnastics
1966 **Jim Ryun**, track	1979 **Willie Stargell**, baseball	1992 **Bonnie Blair**, speed skating
1967 **Peggy Fleming**, figure skating	1980 **U.S. Olympic hockey team**	1993 **Evander Holyfield**, boxing
1968 **Bill Toomey**, track	1981 **Sugar Ray Leonard**, boxing	1994 **Al Unser Jr.**, auto racing
1969 **Mario Andretti**, auto racing	1982 **Wayne Gretzky**, hockey	1995 **Miguel Induráin**, cycling
1970 **Willis Reed**, basketball	1983 **Australia II**, yachting	1996 **Michael Johnson**, track
1971 **Lee Trevino**, golf	1984 **Edwin Moses**, track	1997 **Tiger Woods**, golf
1972 **Olga Korbut**, gymnastics	1985 **Pete Rose**, baseball	1998 **Mark McGwire**, baseball
1973 **O.J. Simpson**, football	1986 **Debi Thomas**, figure skating	1999 **Lance Armstrong**, cycling
& Jackie Stewart, auto racing	1987 **Dennis Conner**, yachting	2000 **Tiger Woods**, golf
1974 **Muhammad Ali**, boxing	1988 **Greg Louganis**, diving	2001 not awarded

The *Sporting News* Sportsman of the Year
Selected annually by the editors of The Sporting News since 1968. 'Man of the Year' changed to 'Sportsman' of the Year in 1993.

Multiple Winner: Mark McGwire (2).

Year	Year	Year
1968 **Denny McLain**, baseball	1982 **Whitey Herzog**, baseball	1995 **Cal Ripken Jr.**, baseball
1969 **Tom Seaver**, baseball	1983 **Bowie Kuhn**, baseball	1996 **Joe Torre**, baseball
1970 **John Wooden**, basketball	1984 **Peter Ueberroth**, LA Olympics	1997 **Mark McGwire**, baseball
1971 **Lee Trevino**, golf	1985 **Pete Rose**, baseball	1998 **Mark McGwire**
1972 **Charles O. Finley**, baseball	1986 **Larry Bird**, pro basketball	**& Sammy Sosa**, baseball
1973 **O.J. Simpson**, pro football	1987 No award	1999 **New York Yankees**, base-
1974 **Lou Brock**, baseball	1988 **Jackie Joyner-Kersee**, track	ball
1975 **Archie Griffin**, football	1989 **Joe Montana**, football	2000 **Kurt Warner**
1976 **Larry O'Brien**, basketball	1990 **Nolan Ryan**, baseball	**& Marshall Faulk**, football
1977 **Steve Cauthen**, horse racing	1991 **Michael Jordan**, basketball	2001 **Curt Schilling**, baseball
1978 **Ron Guidry**, baseball	1992 **Mike Krzyzewski**, col. bask.	
1979 **Willie Stargell**, baseball	1993 **Cito Gaston**	
1980 **George Brett**, baseball	**& Pat Gillick**, baseball	
1981 **Wayne Gretzky**, hockey	1994 **Emmitt Smith**, pro football	

Time Person of the Year
Since Charles Lindbergh was named *Time* magazine's first Man of the Year for 1927, two individuals with significant sports credentials have won the honor.

Year	
1984	**Peter Ueberroth**, president of the Los Angeles Olympic Organizing Committee.
1991	**Ted Turner**, owner-president of Turner Broadcasting System, founder of CNN cable news network, owner of the Atlanta Braves (NL) and Atlanta Hawks (NBA), and former winning America's Cup skipper.

TROPHY CASE

From the first organized track meet at Olympia in 776 B.C., to the Sydney Summer Olympics over 2,700 years later, championships have been officially recognized with prizes that are symbolically rich and eagerly pursued. Here are 15 of the most coveted trophies in America.

(Illustrations by Lynn Mercer Michaud)

America's Cup

First presented by England's Royal Yacht Squadron to the winner of an invitational race around the Isle of Wight on Aug. 22, 1851 . . . originally called the Hundred Guinea Cup . . . renamed after the U.S. boat America, winner of the first race . . . made of sterling silver and designed by London jewelers R. & G. Garrard . . . measures 2 feet, 3 inches high and weighs 16 lbs . . . originally cost 100 guineas ($500), now valued at $250,000 . . . bell-shaped base added in 1958 . . . challenged for every three to four years . . . trophy held by yacht club sponsoring winning boat . . . Cup was badly damaged when a Maori protester repeatedly smashed it with a sledgehammer on March 14, 1997. It was sent back to the original maker and fully restored.

Vince Lombardi Trophy

First presented at the AFL-NFL World Championship Game (now Super Bowl) on Jan. 15, 1967 . . . originally called the World Championship Game Trophy . . . renamed in 1971 in honor of former Green Bay Packers GM-coach and two-time Super Bowl winner Vince Lombardi, who died in 1970 as coach of Washington . . . made of sterling silver and designed by Tiffany & Co. of New York . . . measures 21 inches high and weighs 7 lbs (football depicted is regulation size) . . . valued at $12,500 . . . competed for annually . . . winning team keeps trophy.

Olympic Gold Medal

First presented by International Olympic Committee in 1908 (until then winners received silver medals) . . . second and third place finishers also got medals of silver and bronze for first time in 1908 . . . each medal must be at least 2.4 inches in diameter and 0.12 inches thick . . . the gold medal is actually made of silver, but must be gilded with at least 6 grams (0.21 ounces) of pure gold . . . the medals for the 1996 Atlanta Games were designed by Malcolm Grear Designers and produced by Reed & Barton of Taunton, Mass . . . 604 gold, 604 silver and 630 bronze medals were made . . . competed for every two years as Winter and Summer Games alternate . . . winners keep medals.

Awards (Cont.)

Stanley Cup

Donated by Lord Stanley of Preston, the Governor General of Canada and first presented in 1893 . . . original cup was made of sterling silver by an unknown London silversmith and measured 7 inches high with an 11½-inch diameter . . . in order to accommodate all the rosters of winning teams, the cup now measures 35½ inches high with a base 54 inches around and weighs 32 lbs . . . in order to add new names each year, bands on the trophy are often retired and displayed at the Hall of Fame . . . originally bought for 10 guineas ($48.67), it is now insured for $75,000 . . . actual cup retired to Hall of Fame and replaced in 1970 . . . presented to NHL playoff champion since 1918 . . . trophy loaned to winning team for one year.

World Cup

First presented by the Federation Internationale de Football Association (FIFA) . . . originally called the World Cup Trophy . . . renamed the Jules Rimet Cup (after the then FIFA president) in 1946, but retired by Brazil after that country's third title in 1970 . . . new World Cup trophy created in 1974 . . . designed by Italian sculptor Silvio Gazzaniga and made of solid 18 carat gold with two malachite rings inlaid at the base . . . measures 14.2 inches high and weighs 11 lbs . . . insured for $200,000 (U.S.) . . . competed for every four years . . . winning team gets gold-plated replica.

Commissioner's Trophy

First presented by the Commissioner of baseball to the winner of the 1967 World Series . . . also known as the World Championship Trophy . . . made of brass and gold plate with an ebony base and a baseball in the center made of pewter with a silver finish . . . designed by Balfour & Co. of Attleboro, Mass . . . 30 pennants represent 14 AL and 16 NL teams . . . measures 30 inches high and 36 inches around at the base and weighs 30 lbs . . . valued at $15,000 . . . competed for annually . . . winning team keeps trophy.

Larry O'Brien Trophy

First presented in 1978 to winner of NBA Finals . . . originally called the Walter A. Brown Trophy after the league pioneer and Boston Celtics owner (an earlier NBA championship bowl was also named after Brown) . . . renamed in 1984 in honor of outgoing commissioner O'Brien, who served from 1975-84 . . . made of sterling silver with 24 carat gold overlay and designed by Tiffany & Co. of New York . . . measures 2 feet high and weighs 14½ lbs (basketball depicted is regulation size) . . . valued at $13,500 . . . competed for annually . . . winning team keeps trophy.

Heisman Trophy

First presented in 1935 to the best college football player east of the Mississippi by the Downtown Athletic Club of New York . . . players across the entire country eligible since 1936 . . . originally called the DAC Trophy . . . renamed in 1936 following the death of DAC athletic director and former college coach John W. Heisman . . . made of bronze and designed by New York sculptor Frank Eliscu, it measures 13½ in. high, 6½ in. wide and 14 in. long at the base and weighs 25 lbs . . . valued at $2,000 . . . voting done by national media and former Heisman winners . . . trophy sponsor American Suzuki announced plans for limited fan voting starting in 1999 . . . awarded annually . . . winner keeps trophy.

James E. Sullivan Memorial Award

First presented by the Amateur Athletic Union (AAU) in 1930 as a gold medal and given to the nation's outstanding amateur athlete . . . trophy given since 1933 . . . named after the amateur sports movement pioneer, who was a founder and past president of AAU and the director of the 1904 Olympic Games in St. Louis . . . made of bronze with a marble base, it measures 17½ in. high and 11 in. wide at the base and weighs 13½ lbs . . . valued at $2,500 . . . voting done by AAU and USOC officials, former winners and selected media . . . awarded annually . . . winner keeps trophy.

Ryder Cup

Donated in 1927 by English seed merchant Samuel Ryder, who offered the gold cup for a biennial match between teams of golfing pros from Great Britain and the United States . . . the format changed in 1977 to include the best players on the European PGA Tour . . . made of 14 carat gold on a wood base and designed by Mappin and Webb of London . . . the golfer depicted on the top of the trophy is Ryder's friend and teaching pro Abe Mitchell . . . the cup measures 16 in. high and weighs 4 lbs . . . insured for $50,000 . . . competed for every two years at alternating European and U.S. sites . . . the cup is held by the PGA headquarters of the winning side.

Davis Cup

Donated by American college student and U.S. doubles champion Dwight F. Davis in 1900 and presented by the International Tennis Federation (ITF) to the winner of the annual 16-team men's competition . . . officially called the International Lawn Tennis Challenge Trophy . . . made of sterling silver and designed by Shreve, Crump and Low of Boston, the cup has a matching tray (added in 1921) and a very heavy two-tiered base containing rosters of past winning teams . . . it stands 34½ in. high and 108 in. around at the base and weighs 400 lbs . . . insured for $150,000 . . . competed for annually . . . trophy loaned to winning country for one year.

Borg-Warner Trophy

First presented by the Borg-Warner Automotive Co. of Chicago in 1936 to the winner of the Indianapolis 500 . . . replaced the Wheeler-Schebler Trophy which went to the 400-mile leader from 1911-32 . . . made of sterling silver with bas-relief sculptured heads of each winning driver and a gold bas-relief head of Tony Hulman, the owner of the Indy Speedway from 1945-77 . . . designed by Robert J. Hill and made by Gorham, Inc. of Rhode Island . . . measures 51½ in. high and weighs over 80 lbs . . . new base added in 1988 and the entire trophy restored in 1991 . . . competed for annually . . . insured for $1 million . . . trophy stays at Speedway Hall of Fame . . . winner gets a 14-in. high replica valued at $30,000.

NCAA Championship Trophy

First presented in 1952 by the NCAA to all 1st, 2nd and 3rd place teams in sports with sanctioned tournaments . . . 1st place teams receive gold-plated awards, 2nd place award is silver-plated and 3rd is bronze . . . replaced silver cup given to championship teams from 1939-51 . . . made of walnut, the trophy stands 24¾ in. high, 14⅛ in. wide and 4½ in. deep at the base and weighs 15 lbs . . . designed by Medallic Art Co. of Danbury, Conn. and made by House of Usher of Kansas City since 1990 . . . valued at $500 . . . competed for annually . . . winning teams keep trophies.

World Championship Belt

First presented in 1921 by the World Boxing Association, one of the three organizations (the World Boxing Council and International Boxing Federation are the others) generally accepted as sanctioning legitimate world championship fights . . . belt weighs 8 lbs. and is made of hand tanned leather . . . the outsized buckle measures 10½ in. high and 8 in. wide, is made of pewter with 24 carat gold plate and contains crystal and semi-precious stones . . . side panels of polished brass are for engraving title bout results . . . currently made by Champbelts by Ronn Scala in Pittsburgh . . . champions keep belts even if they lose their title.

World Championship Ring

Rings decorated with gems and engraving date back to ancient Egypt where the wealthy wore heavy gold and silver rings to indicate social status . . . championship rings in sports serve much the same purpose, indicating the wearer is a champion . . . As an example, the Dallas Cowboys' ring for winning Superbowl XXX on Jan. 28, 1996 was designed by Diamond Cutters International of Houston . . . each ring is made of 14 carat yellow gold, weighs 48-51 penny weights and features five trimmed marquis diamonds interlocking in the shape of the Cowboys' star logo as well as five more marquis diamonds (for the team's five Super Bowl wins) on a bed of 51 smaller diamonds . . . rings were appraised at over $30,000 each.

Who's Who

Sandy Koufax and **Don Drysdale**
were the original Randy Johnson and Curt
Schilling.

AP/Wide World Photos

Sports Personalities

Nine hundred twenty three entries dating back to the 19th century. Entries updated through September 25, 2002.

Hank Aaron (b. Feb. 5, 1934): Baseball OF; led NL in HRs and RBI 4 times each and batting twice with Milwaukee and Atlanta Braves; MVP in 1957; played in 24 All-Star Games, all-time leader in HRs (755), RBI (2,297), total bases (6,856), 3rd in hits (3,771); won 3 Gold Gloves; executive with Braves.

Kareem Abdul-Jabbar (b. Lew Alcindor, Apr. 16, 1947): Basketball C; led UCLA to 3 NCAA titles (1967-69); Final 4 MOP 3 times; Player of Year twice; led Milwaukee (1) and LA Lakers (5) to 6 NBA titles; playoff MVP twice (1971,85), regular season MVP 6 times (1971-72,74,76-77,80); retired in 1989 after 20 seasons as all-time leader in over 20 categories.

Andre Agassi (b. Apr. 29, 1970): Tennis; 53 career tournament wins including the career grand slam; Wimbledon (1992), U.S. Open (1994,99), Australian Open (1995,2000,01), French Open (1999); helped U.S. win 2 Davis Cup finals (1990,92); regained the world No. 1 ranking in 1999 for the first time since 1996.

Troy Aikman (b. Nov. 21, 1966): Football QB; consensus All-America at UCLA (1988); 1st overall pick in 1989 NFL Draft (by Dallas); led Cowboys to 3 Super Bowl titles (1992,93,95 seasons); MVP of Super Bowl XXVII.

Marv Albert (b. June 12, 1941): Radio-TV; NBC announcer and radio broadcaster for the New York Knicks, Rangers and Giants who pled guilty to a misdemeanor assault charge amid embarrassing allegations of his sex life. Rehired to MSG and Turner networks in 1998 and NBC in '99.

Tenley Albright (b. July 18, 1935): Figure skater; 2-time world champion (1953,55); won Olympic silver (1952) and gold (1956) medals; became a surgeon.

Amy Alcott (b. Feb. 22, 1956): Golfer; 29 career wins, including five majors; inducted into World Golf Hall of Fame in 1999.

Grover Cleveland (Pete) Alexander (b. Feb. 26, 1887, d. Nov. 4, 1950): Baseball RHP; won 20 or more games 9 times; 373 career wins and 90 shutouts.

Muhammad Ali (b. Cassius Clay, Jan. 17, 1942): Boxer; 1960 Olympic light heavyweight champion; 3-time world heavyweight champ (1964-67, 1974-78,1978-79); defeated Sonny Liston (1964), George Foreman (1974) and Leon Spinks (1978) for title; fought Joe Frazier in 3 memorable bouts (1971-75), winning twice; adopted Black Muslim faith in 1964 and changed name; stripped of title in 1967 after conviction for refusing induction into U.S. Army; verdict reversed by Supreme Court in 1971; career record of 56-5 with 37 KOs and 19 successful title defenses; lit the flaming cauldron to signal the beginning of the 1996 Summer Olympics in Atlanta.

Forrest (Phog) Allen (b. Nov. 18, 1885, d. Sept. 16, 1974): Basketball; college coach 48 years; directed Kansas to NCAA title (1952); 746 wins.

Bobby Allison (b. Dec. 3, 1937): Auto racer; 3-time winner of Daytona 500 (1978,82,88); NASCAR national champ in 1983; father of Davey.

Davey Allison (b. Feb. 25, 1961, d. July 13, 1993): Auto racer; stock car Rookie of Year (1987); winner of 19 NASCAR races, including 1992 Daytona 500; killed at age 32 in helicopter accident at Talladega Superspeedway; son of Bobby.

Roberto Alomar (b. Feb. 5, 1968): Baseball; perennial Gold Glove second baseman and All-Star; MVP of 1992 ALCS; became known well beyond baseball for spitting in the face of umpire John Hirschbeck during final weekend of 1996 season; named MVP of 1998 All-Star Game.

Walter Alston (b. Dec. 1, 1911, d. Oct. 1, 1984): Baseball; managed Brooklyn-LA Dodgers 23 years, won 7 pennants and 4 World Series (1955,59,63,65); retired after 1976 season with 2,063 wins (2,040 regular season and 23 postseason).

Gary Anderson (b. July 16, 1959): Football K; all-time leading scorer in NFL history; had perfect regular season in 1998 (59/59 PAT, 35/35 FG); holds NFL record for consecutive FG made (40); led AFC in scoring 3 times (1983-85 with Steelers) and NFC once (1998 with Vikings).

Sparky Anderson (b. Feb. 22, 1934): Baseball; only manager to win World Series in each league—Cincinnati in NL (1975-76) and Detroit in AL (1984); 3rd-ranked skipper on all-time career list with 2,228 wins (2,194 regular season and 34 postseason); inducted into the Baseball Hall of Fame in 2000.

Mario Andretti (b. Feb. 28, 1940): Auto racer; 4-time USAC-CART national champion (1965-66,69,84); only driver to win Daytona 500 (1967), Indy 500 (1969) and Formula One world title (1978); Indy 500 Rookie of Year (1965); retired after 1994 racing season ranked 1st in poles (67) and starts (407) and 2nd in wins (52) on all-time CART list; father of Michael and Jeff, uncle of John.

Michael Andretti (b. Oct. 5, 1962): Auto racer; 1991 CART national champion with single-season record 8 wins; Indy 500 Rookie of Year (1984); left IndyCar circuit for ill-fated Formula One try in 1993; returned to IndyCar (now CART) in '94; son of Mario.

Earl Anthony (b. Apr. 27, 1938, d. Aug. 14, 2001): Bowler; 6-time PBA Bowler of Year; 41 career titles; first to earn $100,000 in 1 season (1975); first to earn $1 million in career; came out of retirement in '96; ranked 11th on list of PBA career money leaders through 2001-02 season.

Saïd Aouita (b. Nov. 2, 1959): Moroccan runner; won gold (5000m) and bronze (800m) in 1984 Olympics; won 5000m at 1987 World Championships; formerly held 2 world records recognized by IAAF—2000m and 5000m.

Luis Aparicio (b. Apr. 29, 1934): Baseball SS; retired as all-time leader in most games, assists and double plays by shortstop; led AL in stolen bases 9 times (1956-64); 506 career steals.

Al Arbour (b. Nov. 1, 1932): Hockey; coached NY Islanders to 4 straight Stanley Cup titles (1980-83); retired after 1993-94 season; 2nd on all-time career list with 904 wins (781 regular season and 123 postseason); elected to Hockey Hall of Fame in 1996.

Eddie Arcaro (b. Feb. 19, 1916, d. Nov. 14, 1997): Jockey; 2-time Triple Crown winner (Whirlaway in 1941, Citation in '48); he won Kentucky Derby 5 times, Preakness and Belmont 6 times each.

Roone Arledge (b. July 8, 1931): Sports TV pioneer; innovator of live events, anthology shows, Olympic coverage, "Monday Night Football" and "Wide World of Sports"; ran ABC Sports from 1968-86; ran ABC News from 1977-98.

Henry Armstrong (b. Dec. 12, 1912, d. Oct. 22, 1988): Boxer; held feather-, light- and welterweight titles simultaneously in 1938; pro record 152-21-8 with 100 KOs.

Lance Armstrong (b. Sept. 18, 1971): Cyclist; First American 4-time winner of the Tour de France (1999-2002); member of the U.S. Postal Service team; returned from treatment for testicular cancer to become the world's top cyclist; only the second American winner in the race's history.

Arthur Ashe (b. July 10, 1943, d. Feb. 6, 1993): Tennis; first black man to win U.S. Championship (1968) and Wimbledon (1975); 1st U.S. player to earn $100,000 in 1 year (1970); won Davis Cup as player (1968-70) and captain (1981-82); wrote black sports history, *Hard Road to Glory*; announced in 1992 that he was infected with AIDS virus from a blood transfusion during 1983 heart surgery; in 1997, the new home for the U.S. Open was named Arthur Ashe Stadium.

Evelyn Ashford (b. Apr. 15, 1957): Track & Field; winner of 4 Olympic gold medals—100m in 1984, and 4x100m in 1984, '88 and '92; also won silver medal in 100m in '88; member of 5 U.S. Olympic teams (1976-92); Inducted into Track and Field and Women's Sports Halls of Fame in 1997.

Red Auerbach (b. Sept. 20, 1917): Basketball; 4th winningest coach (regular season and playoffs) in NBA history; won 1,037 times in 20 years; as coach-GM, led Boston to 9 NBA titles, including 8 in a row (1959-66); also coached defunct Washington Capitols (1946-49); NBA Coach of the Year award named after him; retired as Celtics coach in 1966 and as GM in '84; club president from 1970 to 1997 and then again beginning in 2001.

Tracy Austin (b. Dec. 12, 1962): Tennis; youngest player to win U.S. Open (age 16 in 1979); won 2nd U.S. Open in '81; named AP Female Athlete of Year twice before she was 20; recurring neck and back injuries shortened career after 1983; youngest player ever inducted into Tennis Hall of Fame (age 29 in 1992).

Paul Azinger (b. Jan. 6, 1960): Golf; PGA Player of Year (1987); 12 career wins, including '93 PGA Championship; missed most of '94 season overcoming lymphoma (a form of cancer) in right shoulder blade; member of 4 U.S. Ryder Cup teams (1989,91,93,2002).

Bob Baffert (b. Jan. 13, 1953): Horse racing; 3-time Eclipse Award winner as outstanding trainer (1997-99); trained 3 Kentucky Derby winners (1997,98,02), 4 Preakness winners (1997,98,01,02) and 1 Belmont Stakes winner (2001); 4-time leading annual money leader for trainers (1998-01).

Donovan Bailey (b. Dec. 16, 1967): Track; Jamaican-born Canadian sprinter who set world record in the 100m (9.84) in gold medal-winning performance at 1996 Olympics which stood until '99; set indoor record in 50m (5.56) in 1996; member of Canadian 4x100 relay that won gold in 1996 Olympics.

Oksana Baiul (b. Feb. 26, 1977): Ukrainian figure skater; 1993 world champion at age 15; edged Nancy Kerrigan by a 5-4 judges' vote for 1994 Olympic gold medal.

Hobey Baker (b. Jan. 15, 1892, d. Dec. 21, 1918): Football and hockey star at Princeton (1911-14); member of college football and pro hockey Halls of Fame; college hockey Player of Year award named after him; killed in plane crash.

Seve Ballesteros (b. Apr. 9, 1957): Spanish golfer; has won British Open 3 times (1979,84,88) and Masters twice (1980,83); 3-time European Golfer of Year (1986,88,91); has led Europe to 5 Ryder Cup titles (1985,87,89,95,97).

Ernie Banks (b. Jan. 31, 1931): Baseball SS-1B; led NL in home runs and RBI twice each; 2-time MVP (1958-59) with Chicago Cubs; 512 career HRs.

Roger Bannister (b. Mar. 23, 1929): British runner; first to run mile in less than 4 minutes (3:59.4 on May 6, 1954).

Walter (Red) Barber (b. Feb. 17, 1908, d. Oct. 22, 1992): Radio-TV; renowned baseball play-by-play broadcaster for Cincinnati, Brooklyn and N.Y. Yankees from 1934-66; won Peabody Award for radio commentary in 1991.

Charles Barkley (b. Feb. 20, 1963): Basketball F; 5-time All-NBA 1st team with Philadelphia and Phoenix; U.S. Olympic Dream Team member in '92; NBA regular season MVP in 1993; currently a basketball announcer for TNT.

Leon Barmore (b. June 3, 1944): college basketball coach; respected coach of Louisiana Tech Lady Techsters; retired in Aug., 2002; career win pct. of .869 (576-87, 20 yrs) is best all-time; won national championship with Louisiana Tech in 1988.

Rick Barry (b. Mar. 28, 1944): Basketball F; only player to lead both NBA and ABA in scoring; 5-time All-NBA 1st team; Finals MVP with Golden St. in 1975.

Sammy Baugh (b. Mar. 17, 1914): Football QB-DB-P; led Washington to NFL titles in 1937 (his rookie year) and '42; led league in passing 6 times, punting 4 times and interceptions once.

Elgin Baylor (b. Sept. 16, 1934): Basketball F; MOP of Final 4 in 1958; led Minneapolis-LA Lakers to 8 NBA Finals; 10-time All-NBA 1st team (1959-65,67-69); LA Clippers' vice president of basketball operations.

Bob Beamon (b. Aug. 29, 1946): Track & Field; won 1968 Olympic gold medal in long jump with world record (29-ft. 2½in.) that shattered old mark by nearly 2 feet; record finally broken by 2 inches in 1991 by Mike Powell.

Franz Beckenbauer (b. Sept. 11, 1945): Soccer; captain of West German World Cup champions in 1974 then coached West Germany to World Cup title in 1990; invented sweeper position; played in U.S. for NY Cosmos (1977-80,83); Member of International Soccer Hall of Champions.

Boris Becker (b. Nov. 22, 1967): German tennis player; 3-time Wimbledon champ (1985-86,89); youngest male (17) to win Wimbledon; led country to 1st Davis Cup win in 1988; has also won U.S. (1989) and Australian (1991,96) Opens.

Chuck Bednarik (b. May 1, 1925): Football C-LB; 2-time All-America at Penn and 7-time All-Pro with NFL Eagles as both center (1950) and linebacker (1951-56); missed only 3 games in 14 seasons; led Eagles to 1960 NFL title as a 35-year-old two-way player.

Clair Bee (b. Mar. 2, 1896, d. May 20, 1983): Basketball coach who led LIU to 2 undefeated seasons (1936,39) and 2 NIT titles (1939,41); his teams won 95 percent of their games between 1931-51, including 43 in a row from 1935-37; coached NBA Baltimore Bullets from 1952-54, but only won 34-116; contributions to game include 1-3-1 zone defense, 3-second rule and NBA 24-second clock.

Jean Beliveau (b. Aug. 31, 1931): Hockey C; led Montreal to 10 Stanley Cups in 17 playoffs; playoff MVP (1965); 2-time regular season MVP (1956,64).

Bert Bell (b. Feb. 25, 1895, d. Oct. 11, 1959): Football; team owner and 2nd NFL commissioner (1946-59); proposed college draft in 1935 and instituted TV blackout rule.

James (Cool Papa) Bell (b. May 17, 1903, d. Mar. 8, 1991): Baseball; member of the Negro Leagues; widely considered the fastest player ever to play baseball; also coached for the Kansas City Monarchs, teaching such players as Jackie Robinson; member of the National Baseball Hall of Fame.

Deane Beman (b. Apr. 22, 1938): Golf; 1st commissioner of PGA Tour (1974-94); introduced "stadium golf" and created The Players Championship; as player, won U.S. Amateur twice and British Amateur once; inducted into the World Golf Hall of Fame in 2000.

Johnny Bench (b. Dec. 7, 1947): Baseball C; led NL in HRs twice and RBI 3 times; 2-time regular season MVP (1970,72) with Cincinnati, World Series MVP in 1976; 389 career HRs.

Patty Berg (b. Feb. 13, 1918): Golfer; 57 career pro wins, including 15 majors; 3-time AP Female Athlete of Year (1938,43,55).

Chris Berman (b. May 10, 1955): Radio-TV; 6-time National Sportscaster of Year known for his nicknames and jovial studio anchoring on ESPN; narrated weekly highlights on "Monday Night Football" 1996-99.

Yogi Berra (b. May 12, 1925): Baseball C; played on 10 World Series winners with NY Yankees; holds WS records for games played (75), at bats (259) and hits (71); 3-time AL MVP (1951,54-55); managed both Yankees (1964) and NY Mets (1973) to pennants.

Jay Berwanger (b. Mar. 19, 1914, d. June 26, 2002): Football HB; Univ. of Chicago star; won 1st Heisman Trophy in 1935; top selection in the 1st-ever NFL Draft (1936).

Gary Bettman (b. June 2, 1952): Hockey; former NBA executive, who was named first commissioner of NHL on Dec. 11, 1992; took office on Feb. 1, 1993.

Abebe Bikila (b. Aug. 7, 1932, d. Oct. 25, 1973): Ethiopian runner; 1st to win consecutive Olympic marathons (1960,64).

Matt Biondi (b. Oct. 8, 1965): Swimmer; won 7 medals in 1988 Olympics, including 5 gold (2 individual, 3 relay); has won a total of 11 medals (8 gold, 2 silver and a bronze) in 3 Olympics (1984,88,92).

Larry Bird (b. Dec. 7, 1956): Basketball F; college Player of Year (1979) at Indiana St.; 1980 NBA Rookie of Year; 9-time All-NBA 1st team; 3-time regular season MVP (1984-86); led Boston to 3 NBA titles (1981,84, 86); 2-time Finals MVP (1984,86); U.S. Olympic Dream Team member in '92; inducted into Hall of Fame in 1998; in 1997, named coach of Indiana Pacers and won Coach of the Year honors in first season; led the Pacers to the NBA finals in 2000 but lost in 6 games to the Lakers; retired from coaching in 2000.

The Black Sox: Eight Chicago White Sox players who were banned from baseball for life in 1921 for allegedly throwing the 1919 World Series— RHP Eddie Cicotte (1884-1969), OF Happy Felsch (1891-1964), 1B Chick Gandil (1887-1970), OF Shoeless Joe Jackson (1889-1951), INF Fred McMullin (1891-1952), SS Swede Risberg (1894-1975), 3B-SS Buck Weaver (1890-1956), and LHP Lefty Williams (1893-1959).

Earl (Red) Blaik (b. Feb. 15, 1897, d. May 6, 1989): Football; coached Army to consecutive national titles in 1944-45; 166 career wins and 3 Heisman winners (Blanchard, Davis, Dawkins).

Bonnie Blair (b. Mar. 18, 1964): Speed skater; only American woman to win 5 Olympic gold medals in Winter Games; won 500-meters in 1988, then 500m and 1,000m in both 1992 and '94; added 1,000m bronze in 1988; Sullivan Award winner (1992); retired on 31st birthday as reigning world sprint champ.

Hector (Toe) Blake (b. Aug. 21, 1912, d. May 17, 1995): Hockey LW; led Montreal to 2 Stanley Cups as a player and 8 more as coach; regular season MVP in 1939.

Felix (Doc) Blanchard (b. Dec. 11, 1924): Football FB; 3-time All-America; led Army to national titles in 1944-45; Glenn Davis' running mate; won Heisman Trophy and Sullivan Award in 1945.

George Blanda (b. Sept. 17, 1927): Football QB-PK; was pro football's all-time leading scorer (2,002 points) until 2000 when he was finally passed by kicker Gary Anderson; led Houston to 2 AFL titles (1960-61); played 26 pro seasons; retired at 48.

Fanny Blankers-Koen (b. Apr. 26, 1918): Dutch sprinter; 30-year-old mother of two, who won 4 gold medals (100m, 200m, 800m hurdles and 4x100m relay) at 1948 Olympics.

Drew Bledsoe (b. Feb. 14, 1972): Football QB; 1st overall pick in 1993 NFL draft (by New England); holds NFL season record for most passes attempted (691) and game records for most passes completed (45) and attempted (70); traded to Buffalo before 2002 season.

Wade Boggs (b. June 15, 1958): Baseball 3B; 5 AL batting titles (1983,85-88) with Boston Red Sox; 11-time All-Star; two Gold Gloves; later played with NY Yankees and Tampa Bay; got 3000th career hit with a home run Aug. 7, 1999 against Cleveland.

Barry Bonds (b. July 24, 1964): Baseball OF; set major league single-season HR in 2001 with 73; set single-season walks record in 2001 with 177; 4-time NL MVP, twice with Pitt (1990,92) and twice with San Francisco (1993, 2002); one of only 3 players with 40 HRs and 40 SBs in same season (1996); became the 4th player to reach 600 career HRs in Aug., 2002; son of Bobby.

Bjorn Borg (b. June 6, 1956): Swedish tennis player; 2-time Player of Year (1979-80); won 6 French Opens and 5 straight Wimbledons (1976-80); led Sweden to 1st Davis Cup win in 1975; retired in 1983 at age 26; attempted unsuccessful comeback in 1991.

Mike Bossy (b. Jan. 22, 1957): Hockey RW; led NY Isles to 4 Stanley Cups; playoff MVP in 1982; 50 goals or more 9 straight years; 573 career goals.

Ralph Boston (b. May 9, 1939): Track & Field; medaled in 3 consecutive Olympic long jumps— gold (1960), silver (1964), bronze (1968).

Ray Bourque (b. Dec. 28, 1960): Hockey D; 12-time All-NHL 1st team; won Norris Trophy 5 times (1987-88,1990-91,94) with Boston; '96 All-Star Game MVP; all-time leader for points and assists by a defenseman; won Stanley Cup in 2001 with Colorado Avalanche; retired after 2000-01 season ranked 8th in scoring (1,579 points) and 3rd in games played (1,612).

Bobby Bowden (b. Nov. 8, 1929): Football; coached Florida St. to 2 national titles (1993,99); entered 2002 season with 323 wins including a 18-6-1 bowl record in 36 years as coach at Samford, West Va. and FSU; father of Clemson head coach Tommy and former Auburn coach Terry.

Riddick Bowe (b. Aug. 10, 1967): Boxer; won world heavyweight title with unanimous decision over champion Evander Holyfield on 11/13/92; lost title to Holyfield on maj. dec. 11/6/93; in 1996, was fined $250,000 because members of his entourage caused a riot at Madison Square Garden after opponent Andrew Golota was disqualified for repeated low blows.

Scotty Bowman (b. Sept. 18, 1933): Hockey coach; all-time winningest NHL coach in both regular season (1,244) and playoffs (223) over 30 seasons; coached a record nine Stanley Cup winners with Montreal (1973,76-79), Pittsburgh (1992) and Detroit (1997,98,2002); retired after 2001-02 season.

Jack Brabham (b. Apr. 2, 1926): Australian auto racer; 3-time Formula One champion (1959-60,66); 14 career wins; member of the Hall of Fame.

Bill Bradley (b. July 28, 1943): Basketball F; 2-time All-America at Princeton; Player of the Year and Final 4 MOP in 1965; captain of gold medal-winning 1964 U.S. Olympic team; Sullivan Award winner (1965); led NY Knicks to 2 NBA titles (1970,73); U.S. Senator (D, N.J.) 1979-95; ran for President in 2000.

Pat Bradley (b. Mar. 24, 1951): Golfer; 2-time LPGA Player of Year (1986,91); has won all four majors on LPGA tour, including 3 du Maurier Classics; inducted into the LPGA Hall of Fame on Jan. 18, 1992; among all-time LPGA money leaders and tournament winners (31); captained the 2000 U.S. Solheim Cup team.

Terry Bradshaw (b. Sept. 2, 1948): Football QB; led Pittsburgh to 4 Super Bowl titles (1975-76,79-80); 2-time Super Bowl MVP (1979-80) and regular season MVP in 1978; Fox TV studio analyst.

George Brett (b. May 15, 1953): Baseball 3B-1B; AL batting champion in 3 different decades (1976,80,90); MVP in 1980; led KC to World Series title in 1985; retired after 1993 season with 3,154 hits and .305 average; inducted into Hall of Fame in '99.

Valerie Brisco-Hooks (b. July 6, 1960): Track & Field; won three gold medals at the 1984 Olympics (200 meters, 400 meters and 4x100 relay); first athlete to ever win the 200 and 400 in the same Olympics.

Lou Brock (b. June 18, 1939): Baseball OF; former all-time stolen base leader (938); led NL in steals 8 times; led St. Louis to 2 World Series titles (1964,67); had 3,023 career hits.

Herb Brooks (b. Aug. 5, 1937): Hockey; former U.S. Olympic player (1964,68) who coached 1980 "Miracle on Ice" team to gold medal and 2002 U.S. team to silver medal; coached Minnesota to 3 NCAA titles (1974,76,78); also coached NY Rangers, Minnesota, New Jersey and Pittsburgh in NHL.

Jim Brown (b. Feb. 17, 1936): Football. FB; All-America at Syracuse (1956) and NFL Rookie of Year (1957); led NFL in rushing 8 times; 8-time All-Pro (1957-61,63-65); 3-time MVP (1958,63,65) with Cleveland; ran for 12,312 yards and scored 126 touchdowns in just 9 seasons; served 4 months of a 6-month jail sentence in 2002 after he was convicted of vandalizing his wife's car during a domestic dispute and refused court-ordered counseling.

Larry Brown (b. Sept. 14, 1940): Basketball; played in ACC, ABA, 1964 Olympics and ABA; 3-time assist leader (1968-70) and 3-time Coach of Year (1973,75-76) in ABA; coached ABA's Carolina and Denver and NBA's Denver, N. J., San Antonio, LA Clippers, Indiana and Phila.; also coached UCLA to NCAA Final (1980) and Kansas to NCAA title (1988).

Mordecai (Three-Finger) Brown (b. Oct. 18, 1876, d. Feb. 14, 1948): Baseball; nickname derived from injury in a childhood accident that left him with three digits on right hand; injury gave him a particularly nasty curve ball; won the decisive game of the the 1907 World Series as a Chicago Cub; in 1908, first pitcher to record 4 consecutive shutouts and finished at 29-9; career record of 239-130 with lifetime ERA of 2.06; member of Hall of Fame.

Paul Brown (b. Sept. 7, 1908, d. Aug. 5, 1991): Football innovator; coached Ohio St. to national title in 1942; in pros, directed Cleveland Browns to 4 straight AAFC titles (1946-49) and 3 NFL titles (1950,54-55); formed Cincinnati Bengals as head coach and part-owner in 1968 (reached playoffs in '70).

Valery Brumel (b. Apr. 14, 1942): Soviet high jumper; dominated event from 1961-64; broke world record 5 times; won silver medal in 1960 Olympics and gold in 1964; highest jump was 7-5 ¾.

Avery Brundage (b. Sept. 28, 1887, d. May 5, 1975): Amateur sports czar for over 40 years as president of AAU (1928-35), U.S. Olympic Committee (1929-53) and Int'l Olympic Committee (1952-72).

Kobe Bryant (b. Aug. 23, 1978): Basketball; guard/forward for the LA Lakers; graduated from Lower Merion (Penn.) HS and made the jump directly to the NBA; youngest player (18 yrs., 2 mos., 11 days) ever to appear in an NBA game; became the youngest all-star in NBA history in 1998 and scored a team-high 18 points; won 3 consecutive titles with the Lakers (2000,01,02).

Paul (Bear) Bryant (b. Sept. 11, 1913, d. Jan. 26, 1983): Football; coached at 4 colleges over 38 years; directed Alabama to 5 national titles (1961,64-65,78-79); retired as the winningest coach of all time (323-85-17 record); 15 bowl wins, including 8 Sugar Bowls.

Sergey Bubka (b. Dec. 4, 1963): Ukrainian pole vaulter; 1st man to clear 20 feet both indoors and out (1991); holder of indoor (20-2) and outdoor (20-1¾) world records on Sept. 1, 2002; 6-time world champion (1983,87,91,93,95,97); won Olympic gold medal in 1988, but failed to clear any height in 1992 Games.

Buck Buchanan (b. Sept. 10, 1940, d. July 16, 1992): Football; played both ways in college at Grambling; first player chosen in the first AFL draft by the Dallas Texans who later became the KC Chiefs; missed one game in a 13-year pro career; played in six AFL All-Star games and two Pro Bowls at def. tackle; defensive star of the Chiefs team that won Super Bowl IV; later coached for the New Orleans Saints and Cleveland Browns; member of Pro Football Hall of Fame.

Jack Buck (b. Aug. 21, 1924, d. June 18, 2002): Radio-TV; broadcast baseball games for St. Louis Cardinals from 1954-2001; CBS Radio voice for Monday Night Football (1978-96) and announcer for 1st televised AFL game in 1960; recipient of Baseball Hall of Fame's Ford Frick Award (1987) and Football Hall of Fame's Pete Rozelle Award (1996); received the Purple Heart in WWII; father of Fox baseball announcer, Joe.

Don Budge (b. June 13, 1915, d. Jan. 26, 2000): Tennis; in 1938 became 1st player to win the Grand Slam— the French, Wimbledon, U.S. and Australian titles in 1 year; led U.S. to 2 Davis Cups (1937-38); turned pro in late '38.

Maria Bueno (b. Oct. 11, 1939): Brazilian tennis player; won 4 U.S. Championships (1959,63-64,66) and 3 Wimbledons (1959-60,64).

Leroy Burrell (b. Feb. 21, 1967): Track & Field; set former world record of 9.85 in 100 meters, July 6, 1994; previously held record (9.90) in 1991; member of 4 world record-breaking 4x100m relay teams.

Susan Butcher (b. Dec. 26, 1956): Sled Dog racer; 4-time winner of Iditarod Trail race (1986-88,90).

Dick Butkus (b. Dec. 9, 1942): Football LB; 2-time All-America at Illinois (1963-64); All-Pro 7 of 9 NFL seasons with Chicago Bears; worked with XFL in 2001.

Dick Button (b. July 18, 1929): Figure skater; 5-time world champion (1948-52); 2-time Olympic champ (1948,52); Sullivan Award winner (1949); won Emmy Award as Best Analyst for 1980-81 TV season.

Walter Byers (b. Mar. 13, 1922): College athletics; 1st exec. director of NCAA, serving from 1951-88.

Frank Calder (b. Nov. 17, 1877, d. Feb. 4, 1943): Hockey; 1st NHL president (1917-43); guided league through its formative years; NHL's Rookie of the Year award named after him.

Lee Calhoun (b. Feb. 23, 1933, d. June 22, 1989): Track & Field; won consecutive Olympic gold medals in the 110m hurdles (1956,60).

Walter Camp (b. Apr. 7, 1859, d. Mar. 14, 1925): Football coach and innovator; established scrimmage line, center snap, downs, 11 players per side; elected 1st All-America team (1889).

Roy Campanella (b. Nov. 19, 1921, d. June 26, 1993): Baseball C; 3-time NL MVP (1951,53,55); led Brooklyn to 5 pennants and 1st World Series title (1955); career cut short when 1958 car accident left him paralyzed.

Clarence Campbell (b. July 9, 1905, d. June 24, 1984): Hockey; 3rd NHL president (1946-77), league tripled in size from 6 to 18 teams during his tenure.

Earl Campbell (b. Mar. 29, 1955): Football RB; won Heisman Trophy in 1977; led NFL in rushing 3 times; 3-time All-Pro; 2-time MVP (1978-79) at Houston.

John Campbell (b. Apr. 8, 1955): Harness racing; 5-time winner of Hambletonian (1987,88,90,95,98); 3-time Driver of Year; first driver to go over $100 million in career winnings.

Milt Campbell (b. Dec. 9, 1933): Track & Field; won silver medal in 1952 Olympic decathlon and gold medal in '56.

Jimmy Cannon (b. 1910, d. Dec. 5, 1973): Tough, opinionated New York sportswriter and essayist who viewed sports as an extension of show business; protégé of Damon Runyon; covered World War II for *Stars & Stripes*.

Jose Canseco (b. July 2, 1964): Baseball OF/DH; AL Rookie of the Year in 1986 and MVP in 1988 with the Oakland A's; in 1988 he became the first player in history with 40 HRs and 40 steals in a season; led AL in HRs in 1988 and tied for lead in 1991.

Tony Canzoneri (b. Nov. 6, 1908, d. Dec. 9, 1959): Boxer; 2-time world lightweight champion (1930-33,35-36); pro record 141-24-10 with 44 KOs.

Jennifer Capriati (b. Mar. 29, 1976): Tennis; youngest Grand Slam semifinalist ever (age 14 in 1990 French Open); surprise gold medal winner at 1992 Olympics; left tour from 1994 to '96 due to personal problems including an arrest for marijuana possession; French Open champ (2001) and 2-time Australian Open champ (2001,02).

Harry Caray (b. Mar. 1, 1917, d. Feb. 18, 1998): Radio-TV; baseball play-by-play broadcaster for St. Louis Cardinals, Oakland, Chicago White Sox and Cubs 1945-98; father of sportscaster Skip and grandfather of sportscaster Chip.

Rod Carew (b. Oct. 1, 1945): Baseball 2B-1B; led AL in batting 7 times (1969,72-75,77-78) with Minnesota; MVP in 1977; had 3,053 career hits.

Steve Carlton (b. Dec. 22, 1944): Baseball LHP; won 20 or more games 6 times; 4-time Cy Young winner (1972,77,80,82) with Philadelphia; 329-244 career record.

JoAnne Carner (b. Apr. 4, 1939): Golfer; 5-time U.S. Amateur champion; 2-time U.S. Open champ; 3-time LPGA Player of Year (1974,81-82); 7th in career wins (42).

Cris Carter (b. Nov. 25, 1965): Football; WR with Philadelphia (1987-89) and Minnesota (1990-2001); twice caught 122 passes in a season (1994, '95), the first time establishing an NFL record for catches in a season that was beaten a year later; 2nd player to reach 1000 career catches.

Don Carter (b. July 29, 1926): Bowler; 6-time Bowler of Year (1953-54,57-58,60-61); voted Greatest of All-Time in 1970.

Joe Carter (b. Mar. 7, 1960): Baseball OF; 3-time All-America at Wichita St. (1979-81); won 1993 World Series for Toronto with 3-run HR in bottom of the 9th of Game 6.

Alexander Cartwright (b. Apr. 17, 1820, d. July 12, 1892): Baseball; engineer and draftsman who spread gospel of baseball from New York City to California gold fields; widely regarded as the father of modern game; his guidelines included setting 3 strikes for an out and 3 outs for each half inning.

Billy Casper (b. June 24, 1931): Golfer; 2-time PGA Player of Year (1966,70); has won U.S. Open (1959,66), Masters (1970), U.S. Senior Open (1983); compiled 51 PGA Tour wins and 9 on Senior Tour.

Tracy Caulkins (b. Jan. 11, 1963): Swimmer; won 3 gold medals (2 individual) at 1984 Olympics; set 5 world records and won 48 U.S. national titles from 1978-84; Sullivan Award winner (1978); 2-time Honda Broderick Cup winner (1982,84).

Steve Cauthen (b. May 1, 1960): Jockey; became youngest jockey (18) to win the Triple Crown with Affirmed in 1978; won a record $6.1 million in 1977, winning the Eclipse Award as the nation's top rider and the award for AP male athlete of the year.

Evonne Goolagong Cawley (b. July 31, 1951): Australian tennis player; won Australian Open 4 times, Wimbledon twice (1971,80), French once (1971).

Florence Chadwick (b. Nov. 9, 1917, d. Mar. 15, 1995): Dominant distance swimmer of 1950s; set English Channel records from France to England (1950) and England to France (1951 and '55).

Wilt Chamberlain (b. Aug. 21, 1936, d. Oct. 12, 1999): Basketball C; consensus All-America in 1957 and '58 at Kansas; Final Four MOP in 1957; led NBA in scoring 7 times and rebounding 11 times; 7-time All-NBA first team; 4-time MVP (1960,66-68) in Philadelphia; scored 100 points vs. NY Knicks in Hershey, Pa., Mar. 2, 1962; led 76ers (1967) and LA Lakers (1972) to NBA titles; Finals MVP in 1972.

A.B. (Happy) Chandler (b. July 14, 1898, d. June 15, 1991): Baseball; former Kentucky governor and U.S. Senator who succeeded Judge Landis as commissioner in 1945; backed Branch Rickey's move in 1947 to make Jackie Robinson 1st black player in major leagues; deemed too pro-player and ousted by owners in 1951.

Michael Chang (b. Feb. 22, 1972): Tennis; won the 1989 French Open , becoming the youngest men's champion of a grand slam event (17 years, 3 months.); went 11 consecutive years (1988-98) with at least one title; finished in top 10 in the ATP year-end rankings from 1992-97 (career high no. 2 in 1996).

Julio Cesar Chavez (b. July 12, 1962): Mexican boxer; world jr. welterweight champ (1989-94); also held titles as jr. lightweight (1984-87) and lightweight (1987-89); won over 100 bouts; 90-bout unbeaten streak ended 1/29/94 when Frankie Randall won title on split decision; Chavez won title back 4 months later.

Linford Christie (b. Apr. 2, 1960): British sprinter; won 100-meter gold medals at both 1992 Olympics (9.96) and '93 World Championships (9.87).

Jim Clark (b. Mar. 14, 1936, d. Apr. 7, 1968): Scottish auto racer; 2-time Formula One world champion (1963,65); won Indy 500 in 1965; killed in car crash.

Bobby Clarke (b. Aug. 13, 1949): Hockey C; led Philadelphia Flyers to consecutive Stanley Cups in 1974-75; 3-time regular season MVP (1973,75-76); currently Flyers President/GM.

Ron Clarke (b. Feb. 21, 1937): Australian runner; from 1963-70 set 17 world records in races from 2 miles to 20,000m; never won Olympic gold medal.

Roger Clemens (b. Aug. 4, 1962): Baseball RHP; twice fanned MLB record 20 batters in 9-inning game (April 29, 1986 and Sept. 18, 1996); won a record 6 Cy Young Awards with Boston (1986-87,91), Toronto (1997,98) and N.Y. Yankees (2001); AL MVP in 1986; won pitching Triple Crown in 1997 and 98; won World Series rings with Yankees in 1999 and 2000.

Roberto Clemente (b. Aug. 18, 1934, d. Dec. 31, 1972): Baseball OF; hit over .300 13 times with Pittsburgh; led NL in batting 4 times; World Series MVP in 1971; regular season MVP in 1966; had 3,000 career hits; killed in plane crash; MLB Man of the Year award is named for him.

Alice Coachman (b. Nov. 9, 1923): Track & Field; became the first black woman to win an Olympic gold medal with her win in the high jump in 1948 (London); broke the high school and college high jump records despite not wearing any shoes; member of the National Track & Field Hall of Fame.

Ty Cobb (b. Dec. 18, 1886, d. July 17, 1961): Baseball OF; all-time highest career batting average (.367); hit over .400 3 times; led AL in batting 12 times and stolen bases 6 times with Detroit; MVP in 1911; had 4,191 career hits and 892 steals.

Mickey Cochrane (b. Apr. 6, 1903, d. June 28, 1962): Baseball C; led Philadelphia A's (1929-30) and Detroit (1935) to 3 World Series titles; 2-time AL MVP (1928,34).

Sebastian Coe (b. Sept. 29, 1956): British runner; won gold medal in 1500m and silver medal in 800m at both 1980 and '84 Olympics; long-time world record holder in 800m and 1000m; elected to Parliament as Conservative in 1992.

Paul Coffey (b. June 1, 1961): Hockey D; 3-time Norris Trophy winner; member of four Stanley Cup championship teams at Edmonton (1984-85,87) and Pittsburgh (1991); ranks 10th on NHL all-time scoring list.

Rocky Colavito (b. August 10, 1933): Baseball OF; six-time all-star who hit 374 HRs over his 14-year career; hugely popular in Cleveland where he played from 1955-59 and then 1965-67; led the league in HRs in 1959 with 42 and RBI in 1965 with 108; hit four consecutive HRs in one game.

Eddie Collins (b. May 2, 1887, d. Mar. 25, 1951): Baseball 2B; led Philadelphia A's (1910-11) and Chicago White Sox (1917) to 3 World Series titles; AL MVP in 1914; had 3,311 career hits and 743 stolen bases.

Nadia Comaneci (b. Nov. 12, 1961): Romanian gymnast; first to record perfect 10 in Olympics; won 3 individual golds at 1976 Olympics and 2 more in '80.

Lionel Conacher (b. May 24, 1901, d. May 26, 1954): Canada's greatest all-around athlete; NHL hockey (2 Stanley Cups), CFL football (1 Grey Cup), minor league baseball, soccer, lacrosse, track, amateur boxing champion; member of Parliament (1949-54).

Tony Conigliaro (b. Jan. 7, 1945, d. Feb. 24, 1990): Baseball OF; youngest (20 years old) to lead the AL in HRs (32 in 1965); hit in the face with a fastball in 1967; came back to hit 36 HRs in 1970 but was never the same.

Gene Conley (b. Nov. 10, 1930): Baseball and Basketball; played for World Series and NBA champions with Milwaukee Braves (1957) and Boston-Celtics (1959-61); winning pitcher in 1954 All-Star Game; 91-96 record in 11 seasons.

Billy Conn (b. Oct. 8, 1917, d. May 29, 1993): Boxer; Pittsburgh native and world light heavyweight champion from 1939-41; nearly upset heavyweight champ Joe Louis in 1941 title bout, but was knocked out in 13th round; pro record 63-11-1 with 14 KOs.

Dennis Conner (b. Sept. 16, 1942): Sailing; 3-time America's Cup-winning skipper aboard *Freedom* (1980), *Stars & Stripes* (1987) and the *Stars & Stripes* catamaran (1988); only American skipper to lose Cup, first in 1983 when *Australia II* beat *Liberty* and again in '95 when New Zealand's *Black* Magic swept Conner and his *Stars & Stripes* crew aboard the borrowed *Young America*.

Maureen Connolly (b. Sept. 17, 1934, d. June 21, 1969): Tennis; in 1953 1st woman to win Grand Slam (at age 18); riding accident ended her career in '54; won both Wimbledon and U.S. titles 3 times (1951-53); 3-time AP Female Athlete of Year (1951-53).

Jimmy Connors (b. Sept. 2, 1952): Tennis; No.1 player in world 5 times (1974-78); won 5 U.S. Opens, 2 Wimbledons and 1 Australian; rose from No. 936 at the close of 1990 to U.S. Open semifinals in 1991 at age 39; NCAA singles champ (1971); all-time leader in pro singles titles (109) and matches won at U.S. Open (98) and Wimbledon (84).

Jack Kent Cooke (b. Oct. 25, 1912, d. April 6, 1997): Football; sole owner of NFL Washington Redskins from 1985-97; teams won 2 Super Bowls (1988,92); also owned NBA Lakers and NHL Kings in LA; built LA Forum for $12 million in 1967.

Cynthia Cooper (b. April 14, 1963): Women's basketball G; won two NCAA basketball titles at USC (1983-84); won gold medal with U.S. team in 1988; 2-time WNBA MVP and 4-time league champion with Houston Comets; coach of WNBA's Phoenix Mercury 2001-02.

Angel Cordero Jr. (b. Nov. 8, 1942): Jockey; retired third on all-time list with 7,057 wins in 38,646 starts; won Kentucky Derby 3 times (1974,76,85), Preakness twice and Belmont once; 2-time Eclipse Award winner (1982-83).

Howard Cosell (b. Mar. 25, 1920, d. Apr. 23, 1995): Radio-TV; former ABC commentator on *Monday Night Football* and *Wide World of Sports*, who energized TV sports journalism with abrasive "tell it like it is" style.

Bob Costas (b. Mar. 22, 1952): Radio-TV; NBC broadcaster who has been anchor for NBA, NFL and Summer Olympics as well as baseball play-by-play man; 11-time Emmy winner as studio host/play-by-play and 8-time National Sportscaster of Year.

James (Doc) Counsilman (b. Dec. 28, 1920): Swimming; coached Indiana men's swim team to 6 NCAA championships (1968-73); coached the 1964 and '76 U.S. men's Olympic teams that won a combined 21 of 24 gold medals; in 1979 became oldest person (59) to swim English Channel; retired in 1990 with dual meet record of 287-36-1.

Fred Couples (b. Oct. 3, 1959): Golfer; 2-time PGA Tour Player of the Year (1991,92); 14 Tour victories, including 1992 Masters.

Jim Courier (b. Aug. 17, 1970): Tennis; No. 1 player in world in 1992, won 2 Australian Opens (1992-93) and 2 French Opens (1991-92); played on 1992 Davis Cup winner; Nick Bollettieri Academy classmate of Andre Agassi.

Margaret Smith Court (b. July 16, 1942): Australian tennis player; won Grand Slam in both singles (1970) and mixed doubles (1963 with Ken Fletcher); record 24 Grand Slam singles titles—11 Australian, 5 U.S., 5 French and 3 Wimbledon.

Bob Cousy (b. Aug. 9, 1928): Basketball G; led NBA in assists 8 times; 10-time All-NBA 1st team; 1957 MVP; led Boston to 6 NBA titles (1957,59-63); elected to Hall of Fame in 1970, one of NBA's 50 Greatest Players.

Buster Crabbe (b. Feb. 7, 1908, d. Apr. 23, 1983): Swimmer; 2-time Olympic freestyle medalist with bronze in 1928 (1500m) and gold in '32 (400m); became movie star and King of Serials as Flash Gordon and Buck Rogers.

Ben Crenshaw (b. Jan. 11, 1952): Golfer; co-NCAA champion with Tom Kite in 1972; battled Graves' disease in mid-1980s; 19 career Tour victories; won Masters for second time in 1995 and dedicated it to 90-year-old mentor Harvey Penick, who had died a week earlier; captain of 1999 Ryder Cup team.

Joe Cronin (b. Oct. 12, 1906, d. Sept. 7, 1984): Baseball SS; hit over .300 and drove in over 100 runs 8 times each; player-manager in Washington and Boston (1933-47); AL president (1959-73).

Larry Csonka (b. Dec. 25, 1946): Football RB; powerful runner and blocker who gained 8,081 yards in 11 seasons in the AFL and NFL; won two consecutive Super Bowls with the Miami Dolphins (1973-74) and was named MVP in the latter, rushing for 145 yards and two TDs; member of the College and Pro Football Halls of Fame.

Ann Curtis (b. Mar. 6, 1926): Swimming; won 2 gold medals and 1 silver in 1948 Olympics; set 4 world and 18 U.S. records during career; 1st woman and swimmer to win Sullivan Award (1944).

Betty Cuthbert (b. Apr. 20, 1938): Australian runner; won gold medals in 100 and 200 meters and 4x100m relay at 1956 Olympics; also won 400m gold at 1964 Olympics.

Bjørn Dæhlie (b. June 19, 1967): Norwegian cross-country skier; winner of a record eight gold and 12 overall Winter Olympic medals from 1992-98.

Chuck Daly (b. July 20, 1930): Basketball; coached Detroit to two NBA titles (1989-90) before leaving in 1992 to coach New Jersey; coached NBA "Dream Team" to gold medal in 1992 Olympics; retired in 1994 but returned in 1997 to coach Orlando Magic for two seasons.

John Daly (b. Apr. 28, 1966): Golfer; surprise winner of 1991 PGA Championship as unknown 25-year-old; battled through personal troubles in 1994 to return in '95 and win 2nd major at British Open, beating Italy's Costantino Rocca in 4-hole playoff.

Stanley Dancer (b. July 25, 1927): Harness racing; winner of 4 Hambletonians; trainer-driver of Triple Crown winners in trotting (Nevele Pride in 1968 and Super Bowl in '72) and pacing (Most Happy Fella in 1970).

Beth Daniel (b. Oct. 14, 1956): Golfer; 32 career wins, including 1 major; inducted into World Golf Hall of Fame in 1999.

Alvin Dark (b. Jan. 7, 1922): Baseball OF and MGR; hit .322 to win the NL Rookie of the Year award in 1948 with the Boston Braves; traded to the N.Y. Giants where he led the league in doubles (41) in 1951; won 994 games as a manager and led the Oakland A's to a World Series win in 1974.

Tamas Darnyi (b. June 3, 1967): Hungarian swimmer; 2-time double gold medal winner in 200m and 400m individual medley at 1988 and '92 Olympics; also won both events in 1986 and '91 world championships; set world records in both at '91 worlds; 1st swimmer to break 2 minutes in 200m IM (1:59:36).

Lindsay Davenport (b. June 8, 1976): Tennis player; first American female to be ranked No. 1 in the world (1998) since Chris Evert in 1985; won U.S. Open (1998), Wimbledon (1999) and Australian Open (2000); Olympic gold medalist at Atlanta in 1996.

Al Davis (b. July 4, 1929): Football; GM-coach of Oakland 1963-66; helped force AFL-NFL merger as AFL commissioner in 1966; returned to Oakland as managing general partner and directed club to 3 Super Bowl wins (1977,81,84); defied fellow NFL owners and moved Raiders to LA in 1982; turned down owners' 1995 offer to build him a new stadium in LA and moved back to Oakland instead.

Dwight Davis (b. July 5, 1879, d. Nov. 28, 1945): Tennis; donor of Davis Cup; played for winning U.S. team in 1st two Cup finals (1900,02); won U.S. and Wimbledon doubles titles in 1901; Secretary of War (1925-29) under President Coolidge.

Ernie Davis (b. Dec. 14, 1939, d. May 18, 1963): Football; star running back at Syracuse University; first black player to win the Heisman Trophy in 1961; drafted by the Washington Redskins and traded to Cleveland but died the following year of leukemia before playing a pro game.

Glenn Davis (b. Dec. 26, 1924): Football HB; 3-time All-America; led Army to national titles in 1944-45; Doc Blanchard's running mate; won Heisman Trophy in 1946.

John Davis (b. Jan. 12, 1921, d. July 13, 1984): Weightlifting; 6-time world champion; 2-time Olympic super-heavyweight champ (1948,52); undefeated from 1938-53.

Terrell Davis (b. Oct. 28, 1972): Football RB; 1998 NFL MVP, rushing for an league-leading 2,008 yards (3rd all-time); played for two Super Bowl winners in Denver (XXXII and XXXIII), earning MVP honors in the former with Super Bowl-record 3 rushing TDs; retired in Aug. 2002 after 3 injury-plagued seasons.

Pat Day (b. Oct. 13, 1953): Jockey; 4-time Eclipse award winner; ranked 3rd all-time in career wins through 2001; won Kentucky Derby (1992), 5 Preaknesses (1985,90,94-96) and 3 Belmonts (1989,94,2000); inducted into Hall of Fame in 1991.

Ron Dayne (b. Mar. 14, 1978): Football RB; NCAA Div. I-A all-time leading rusher, gaining 6,397 yards at Wisconsin (1996-99); 1999 Heisman Trophy winner; selected in 1st round (11th overall) of 2000 NFL draft by NY Giants.

Dizzy Dean (b. Jan. 16 1911, d. July 17, 1974): Baseball RHP; led NL in strikeouts and complete games 4 times; last NL pitcher to win 30 games (30-7 in 1934); MVP in 1934 with St. Louis; 150-83 record.

Dave DeBusschere (b. Oct. 16, 1940): Basketball F; youngest coach in NBA history (24 in 1964); player-coach of Detroit Pistons (1964-67); played in 8 All-Star games; won 2 NBA titles as player with NY Knicks; ABA commissioner (1975-76); also pitched 2 seasons for Chicago White Sox (1962-63) with 3-4 record.

Pierre de Coubertin (b. Jan. 1, 1863, d. Sept. 2, 1937): French educator; father of the Modern Olympic Games; IOC president from 1896-1925.

Anita DeFrantz (b. Oct. 4, 1952): Olympics; attorney who became the International Olympic Committee's first female vice president in 1997; first woman to represent U.S. on IOC (elected in 1986); member of USOC Executive Committee; member of bronze medal U.S. women's eight-oared shell at Montreal in 1976.

Oscar De La Hoya (b. Feb. 4, 1973): Boxer; won 1992 Olympic gold medal (lightweight); won the IBF lightweight title in 1995; won WBC Super Lightweight title over Julio Cesar Chavez in 1996 and WBC Welterweight title over Pernell Whitaker in 1997; lost WBC Welterweight belt to Felix Trinidad in a majority decision in 1999; lost to Sugar Shane Mosley in 2000 for his 2nd career defeat.

Cedric Dempsey (b. Apr. 14, 1932): College sports; succeeded Dick Schultz as NCAA executive director (title later changed to president) in 1993 and served until the end of 2002; former athletic director at Pacific (1967-79), San Diego St. (1979), Houston (1979-82) and Arizona (1983-93).

Jack Dempsey (b. June 24, 1895, d. May 31, 1983): Boxer; world heavyweight champion from 1919-26; lost title to Gene Tunney, then lost "Long Count" rematch in 1927 when he floored Tunney in 7th round but failed to retreat to neutral corner; pro record 64-6-9 with 49 KOs.

Bob Devaney (b. April 13, 1915, d. May 9, 1997): Football; head coach at Wyoming from 1957-1961; from 1962 to 1972 built Nebraska into a college football power; won two consecutive national championships in 1970-71; won eight Big Eight Conference titles; later served as Nebraska's athletic director.

Donna de Varona (b. Apr. 26, 1947): Swimming; won gold medals in 400 IM and 400 freestyle relay at 1964 Olympics; set 18 world records during career; co-founder of Women's Sports Foundation in 1974.

Gail Devers (b. Nov. 19, 1966): Track & Field; won Olympic gold medal in 100 meters in 1992 and '96; world champion in 100 meters (1993) and 100-meter hurdles (1993,95,99); overcame thyroid disorder (Graves' disease) that sidelined her in 1989-90 and nearly resulted in having both feet amputated.

Klaus Dibiasi (b. Oct. 6, 1947): Italian diver; won 3 consecutive Olympic gold medals in platform event (1968,72,76).

Eric Dickerson (b. Sept. 2, 1960): Football RB; led NFL in rushing 4 times (1983-84,86,88); ran for single-season record 2,105 yards in 1984; NFC Rookie of Year in 1983; All-Pro 5 times; traded from LA Rams to Indianapolis (Oct. 31, 1987) in 3-team, 10-player deal (including draft picks) that also involved Buffalo; 4th on all-time career rushing list with 13,259 yards in 11 seasons.

Harrison Dillard (b. July 8, 1923): Track & Field; only man to win Olympic gold medals in both sprints (100m in 1948) and hurdles (110m in 1952).

Joe DiMaggio (b. Nov. 25, 1914, d. Mar. 8, 1999): Baseball OF; hit safely in 56 straight games (1941); led AL in batting, HRs and RBI twice each; 3-time MVP (1939,41,47); hit .325 with 361 HRs over 13 seasons; led NY Yankees to 10 World Series titles.

Marcel Dionne (b. Aug. 3, 1951): Hockey C; fourth on NHL's all-time points list (1,771) and third on goals list (731) through 2002; tied Wayne Gretzky for the league lead in points (137) in 1980; scored 50 goals in a season 6 times; won the Lady Byng Award for gentlemanly play in 1975 and 1977; member of the Hockey Hall of Fame.

Mike Ditka (b. Oct. 18, 1939): Football; All-America at Pitt (1960); NFL Rookie of Year (1961); 5-time Pro Bowl tight end for Chicago Bears; returned to Chicago as head coach in 1982 and won Super Bowl XX in 1986; left Bears in 1992 and worked as a broadcaster at NBC for four years; coached the New Orleans Saints from 1997-99; compiled 127-101-0 record in 14 seasons.

Larry Doby (b. Dec. 13, 1924): Baseball OF; first black player in the AL; joined the Cleveland Indians in July 1947, three months after Jackie Robinson entered the Majors with the NL's Brooklyn Dodgers; an all-star centerfielder from 1949-55; managed the Chicago White Sox in 1978, becoming the second black major league manager; inducted into the Hall of Fame in 1998.

Charlotte (Lottie) Dod (b. Sept. 24, 1871, d. June 27, 1960): British athlete; was 5-time Wimbledon singles champion (1887-88,91-93); youngest player ever to win Wimbledon (15 in 1887); archery silver medalist at 1908 Olympics; member of national field hockey team in 1899; British Amateur golf champ in 1904.

Tony Dorsett (b. Apr. 7, 1954): Football RB; won Heisman Trophy leading Pitt to national title in 1976; 3rd all-time in NCAA Div. I-A rushing with 6,082 yards; led Dallas to Super Bowl title as NFC Rookie of Year (1977); NFC Player of Year (1981); ranks 5th on all-time NFL list with 12,739 yards gained in 12 years.

James (Buster) Douglas (b. Apr. 7, 1960): Boxer; 42-1 shot who knocked out undefeated Mike Tyson in 10th round on Feb. 10, 1990 to win heavyweight title in Tokyo; 8 1/2 months later, lost only title defense to Evander Holyfield by KO in 3rd round.

Vicki Manalo Draves (b. Dec. 31, 1924): Diver; First woman in olympic history to win gold medals in both platform diving and springboard diving; inducted into Int'l Swimming Hall of Fame in 1969.

The Dream Team Head coach Chuck Daly's "Best Ever" 12-man NBA All-Star squad that headlined the 1992 Summer Olympics in Barcelona and easily won the basketball gold medal; co-captained by Larry Bird and Magic Johnson, with veterans Charles Barkley, Clyde Drexler, Patrick Ewing, Michael Jordan, Karl Malone, Chris Mullin, Scottie Pippen, David Robinson, John Stockton and Duke's Christian Laettner.

Heike Drechsler (b. Dec. 16, 1964): German long jumper and sprinter; East German before reunification in 1991; set world long jump record (24-2 1/4) in 1988; won long jump gold medals at 1992 Olympics and 1983 and '93 World Championships; won silver medal in long jump and bronze medals in both 100- and 200-meter sprints at 1988 Olympics.

Ken Dryden (b. Aug. 8, 1947): Hockey G; led Montreal to 6 Stanley Cup titles; playoff MVP as rookie in 1971; won or shared 5 Vezina trophies; 2.24 career GAA; currently President of Toronto Maple Leafs.

Don Drysdale (b. July 23, 1936, d. July 3, 1993): Baseball RHP; led NL in strikeouts 3 times and games started 4 straight years; pitched record 6 shutouts in a row in 1968; won Cy Young (1962); had 209-166 record and hit 29 HRs in 14 years.

Charley Dumas (b. Feb. 12, 1937): U.S. high jumper; first man to clear 7 feet (7-0 1/2) on June 29, 1956; won gold medal at 1956 Olympics.

Tim Duncan (b. Apr. 25, 1976): Basketball; 1997 College Player of the Year at Wake Forest; #1 overall pick by the San Antonio Spurs (1997); 1998 NBA Rookie of the Year; 1999 NBA Finals MVP; 2002 NBA MVP.

Margaret Osborne du Pont (b. Mar. 4, 1918): Tennis; won 5 French, 7 Wimbledon and an unprecedented 25 U.S. national titles in singles, doubles and mixed doubles from 1941-62.

Roberto Duran (b. June 16, 1951): Panamanian boxer; one of only 4 fighters to hold 4 different world titles— lightweight (1972-79), welterweight (1980), junior middleweight (1983) and middleweight (1989-90); lost famous "No Mas" welterweight title bout when he quit in 8th round against Sugar Ray Leonard (1980); finally retired in 2002 at the age of 50 with a record of 104-16 (69 KOs).

Leo Durocher (b. July 27, 1905, d. Oct. 7, 1991): Baseball; managed in NL 24 years; won 2,015 games, including postseason; 3 pennants with Brooklyn (1941) and NY Giants (1951,54); won World Series in 1954.

Eddie Eagan (b. Apr. 26, 1898, d. June 14, 1967): Only athlete to win gold medals in both Summer and Winter Olympics (Boxing–1920, Bobsled–1932).

Alan Eagleson (b. Apr. 24, 1933): Hockey; Toronto lawyer, agent and 1st executive director of NHL Players Assn. (1967-90); midwived Team Canada vs. Soviet series (1972) and Canada Cup; charged with racketeering and defrauding NHLPA in indictment handed down by U.S. grand jury in 1994; was sentenced to 18 months in jail in Jan. 1998 after pleading guilty but only served 6 months; resigned from Hall of Fame in 1998.

Dale Earnhardt (b. Apr. 29, 1951, d. Feb. 18, 2001): Auto racer; 7-time NASCAR national champion (1980,86-87,90-91,93-94); Rookie of Year in 1979; was all-time NASCAR money leader (now 2nd) with over $34 million won and 6th on career wins list with 76 when he died; finally won Daytona 500 in 1998 on 20th attempt; died in last lap crash at the 2001 Daytona 500.

James Easton (b. July 26, 1935): Olympics; archer and sporting goods manufacturer (Easton softball bats); one of 4 American delegates to the International Olympic Committee; president of International Archery Federation (FITA); member of LA Olympic Organizing Committee in 1984.

Dennis Eckersley (b. Oct. 3, 1954): Baseball P; began his career as a starter in 1975 with Cleveland; no-hit Angels in 1977; won 20 games in 1978 with Boston; moved to the bullpen after 12 seasons as a starter and became one of the best closers of all-time with Oakland; won 1992 AL Cy Young and MVP.

Stefan Edberg (b. Jan. 19, 1966): Swedish tennis player; 2-time No.1 player (1990-91); 2-time winner of Australian Open (1985,87), Wimbledon (1988,90) and U.S. Open (1991-92).

Gertrude Ederle (b. Oct. 23, 1906): Swimmer; 1st woman to swim English Channel, breaking men's record by 2 hours in 1926; won 3 medals in 1924 Olympics.

Krisztina Egerszegi (b. Aug. 16, 1974): Hungarian swimmer; 3-time gold medal winner (100m and 200m backstroke and 400m IM) at 1992 Olympics; also won a gold (200m back) and silver (100m back) at 1988 Games; youngest (14) ever to win swimming gold. Won fifth gold medal (200m back) at '96 Games.

Lee Elder (b. July 14, 1934): Golf; in 1975, became the first black golfer to play in the Masters Tournament; also played in the 1977 Masters; member of the 1979 U.S. Ryder Cup team; played in South Africa's first integrated tournament in 1972.

Todd Eldredge (b. Aug. 28, 1971): Figure Skater; 6-time U.S. champion (1990,91,95,97,98,2002); 1996 World Champion; won U.S. titles at all three levels (novice, junior and senior); most decorated American figure skater without an Olympic medal.

Bill Elliott (b. Oct. 8, 1955): Auto racer; 2-time winner of Daytona 500 (1985,87); NASCAR national champ in 1988; 43 NASCAR wins as of Sept. 2002.

Herb Elliott (b. Feb. 25, 1938): Australian runner; undefeated from 1958-60; ran 17 sub-4:00 miles; 3 world records; won gold medal in 1500 meters at 1960 Olympics; retired at age 22.

Ernie Els (b. Oct. 17, 1969): Golfer; sweet swinging South African; 1994 PGA Tour Rookie of the Year and European Golfer of the Year; 2-time U.S. Open winner (1994,97); added 3rd major title in 2002 with British Open playoff win.

John Elway (b. June 28, 1960): Football QB; All-American at Stanford; #1 overall pick in the famous quarterback draft of 1983; known for his last-minute, game-winning scoring drives; led Broncos to 3 Super Bowl losses before back-to-back wins in Super Bowl XXXII and XXXIII; 1987 NFL MVP; 4-time Pro Bowler; one of only two quarterbacks (Marino) to throw for over 50,000 yards.

Roy Emerson (b. Nov. 3, 1936): Australian tennis player; won 12 majors in singles— 6 Australian, 2 French, 2 Wimbledon and 2 U.S. from 1961-67.

Kornelia Ender (b. Oct. 25, 1958): East German swimmer; 1st woman to win 4 gold medals at one Olympics (1976), all in world-record time.

Julius Erving (b. Feb. 22, 1950): Basketball F; "Dr. J"; in ABA (1971-76)— 3-time MVP, 2-time playoff MVP, led NY Nets to 2 titles (1974,76); in NBA (1976-87)— 5-time All-NBA 1st team, MVP in 1981, led Philadelphia 76ers to title in 1983.

Phil Esposito (b. Feb. 20, 1942): Hockey C; 1st NHL player to score 100 points in a season (126 in 1969); 6-time All-NHL 1st team with Boston (1969-74); 2-time MVP (1969,74); 5-time scoring champ; star of 1972 Canada-Soviet series; former president-GM of Tampa Bay Lightning.

Janet Evans (b. Aug. 28, 1971): Swimmer; won 3 individual gold medals (400m & 800m freestyle, 400m IM) at 1988 Olympics; 1989 Sullivan Award winner; won 1 gold (800m) and 1 silver (400m) at 1992 Olympics.

Lee Evans (b. Feb. 25, 1947): Track & Field; dominant quarter-miler in world from 1966-72; world record in 400m set at 1968 Olympics stood 20 years.

Chris Evert (b. Dec. 21, 1954): Tennis; No.1 player in world 5 times (1975-77,80-81); won at least 1 Grand Slam singles title every year from 1974-86; 18 majors in all— 7 French, 6 U.S., 3 Wimbledon and 2 Australian; retired after 1989 season with 154 singles titles and $8,896,195 in career earnings.

Weeb Ewbank (b. May 6, 1907, d. Nov. 18, 1998): Football; only coach to win NFL and AFL titles; led Baltimore to 2 NFL titles (1958-59) and NY Jets to Super Bowl III win.

Patrick Ewing (b. Aug. 5, 1962): Basketball C; 3-time All-America; led Georgetown to 3 NCAA Finals and 1984 title; Final 4 MOP in '84; 1986 NBA Rookie of Year with New York; All-NBA (1990); on U.S. Olympic gold medal-winning teams in 1984 and '92; named one of the NBA's 50 Greatest Players; retired after 2001-02 season.

Ray Ewry (b. Oct. 14, 1873, d. Sept. 29, 1937): Track & Field; won 10 gold medals (although 2 are not recognized by IOC) over 4 consecutive Olympics (1900,04,06,08); all events he won (Standing HJ, LJ and TJ) were discontinued in 1912.

Nick Faldo (b. July 18, 1957): British golfer; 3-time winner of British Open (1987,90,92) and Masters (1989, 90, 96); 3-time European Golfer of Year (1989-90,92); PGA Player of Year in 1990.

Juan Manuel Fangio (b. June 24, 1911, d. July 17, 1995): Argentine auto racer; 5-time Formula One world champion (1951,54-57); 24 career wins, retired in 1958.

Marshall Faulk (b. Feb. 26, 1973): Football RB; 3-time consensus All-America at San Diego. St.; 2-time NCAA Div. I-A rushing leader (1991-92); 2nd overall pick (Indianapolis) of the 1994 NFL draft; traded to St.L Rams in 1999; 3-time AP Offensive Player of the Year (1999-2001); NFL MVP in 2000 (AP/PFWA) and 2001 (Bell/PFWA); set NFL record with 26 TDs (18 rush, 8 rec.) in 2000.

Brett Favre (b. Oct. 10, 1969): Football QB; Selected in the second round (33rd overall) by the Atlanta Falcons in the 1991 NFL draft; traded to Green Bay Packers in 1992; league MVP in 1995, '96 and '97; 6-time Pro Bowl QB; 100th TD pass came in his 62nd game, third-fastest in league history; 39 TD passes in 1996 season broke his own NFC record of 38 set in 1995 (since broken by Kurt Warner – 41 in 1999); led Packers to Super Bowl victory in 1997.

Sergei Fedorov (b. Dec. 13, 1969): Hockey C; first Russian to win NHL Hart Trophy as 1993-94 regular season MVP; 5-time All-Star and 3-time Stanley Cup winner (1997,98,2002) with Detroit.

Donald Fehr (b. July 18, 1948): Baseball labor leader; protégé of Marvin Miller; executive director and general counsel of Major League Players Assn. since 1983; led players in 1994 "salary cap" strike that lasted eight months and resulted in first cancellation of World Series since 1904.

Bob Feller (b. Nov. 3, 1918): Baseball RHP; led AL in strikeouts 7 times and wins 6 times with Cleveland; threw 3 no-hitters and 12 one-hitters; 266-162 record.

Tom Ferguson (b. Dec. 20, 1950): Rodeo; 6-time All-Around champion (1974-79); 1st cowboy to win $100,000 in one season (1978); 1st to win $1 million in career (1986).

Herve Filion (b. Feb. 1, 1940): Harness racing; 10-time Driver of Year; all-time leader in races won with 14,783 in 35 years.

Rollie Fingers (b. Aug. 25, 1946): Baseball RHP; relief ace with 341 career saves; won AL MVP and Cy Young awards in 1981 with Milwaukee; World Series MVP in 1974 with Oakland.

Charles O. Finley (b. Feb. 22, 1918, d. Feb, 19, 1997): Baseball owner; moved KC A's to Oakland in 1968; won 3 straight World Series from 1972-74; also owned teams in NHL and ABA.

Bobby Fischer (b. Mar. 9, 1943): Chess; at 15, became youngest international grandmaster in chess history; only American to hold world championship (1972-75); was stripped of title in 1975 after refusing to defend against Anatoly Karpov and became recluse; re-emerged to defeat old foe and former world champion Boris Spassky in 1992.

Carlton Fisk (b. Dec. 26, 1947): Baseball C; holds all-time major league record for games caught (2,229); also all-time HR leader for catchers (376); AL Rookie of Year (1972) and 10-time All-Star; hit epic, 12th-inning Game 6 homer for Boston Red Sox in 1975 World Series; inducted into the Baseball Hall of Fame in 2000.

Emerson Fittipaldi (b. Dec. 12, 1946): Brazilian auto racer; 2-time Formula One world champion (1972,74); 2-time winner of Indy 500 (1989,93); won overall IndyCar title in 1989.

Bob Fitzsimmons (b. May 26, 1863, d. Oct. 22, 1917): British boxer; held three world titles— welterweight (1881-97), heavyweight (1897-99) and light heavyweight (1903-05); pro record 40-11 with 32 KOs.

James (Sunny Jim) Fitzsimmons (b. July 23, 1874, d. Mar. 11, 1966): Horse racing; trained horses that won over 2,275 races, including 2 Triple Crown winners— Gallant Fox in 1930 and Omaha in '35.

Jim Fixx (b. Apr. 23, 1932, d. July 20, 1984): Running; author who popularized the sport of running; his 1977 bestseller *The Complete Book of Running*, is credited with helping start America's fitness revolution; died of a heart attack while running.

Larry Fleisher (b. Sept. 26, 1930, d. May 4, 1989): Basketball; led NBA players union from 1961-89; increased average yearly salary from $9,400 in 1967 to $600,000 without a strike.

Peggy Fleming (b. July 27, 1948): Figure skating; 3-time world champion (1966-68); won Olympic gold medal in 1968.

Curt Flood (b. Jan. 18, 1938, d. Jan. 20, 1997): Baseball OF; played 15 years (1956-69,71) mainly with St. Louis; hit over .300 6 times with 7 Gold Gloves; refused trade to Phillies in 1969; lost challenge to baseball's reserve clause in Supreme Court in 1972.

Ray Floyd (b. Sept. 14, 1942): Golfer; has 22 PGA victories in 4 decades; joined Senior PGA Tour in 1992; has won Masters (1976), U.S. Open (1986), PGA twice (1969,82) and PGA Seniors Championship (1995); only player to ever win on PGA and Senior tours in same year (1992); member of 8 Ryder Cup teams and captain in 1989.

Doug Flutie (b. Oct. 23, 1962): Football QB; won Heisman Trophy with Boston College (1984); has played in USFL, NFL and CFL; 6-time CFL MVP with B.C. Lions (1991), Calgary (1992-94) and Toronto (1996-97); led Calgary (1992) and Toronto (1996-97) to Grey Cup titles; returned to NFL in 1998 with Buffalo and became part of QB controversy with Rob Johnson; signed by San Diego in 2001.

Whitey Ford (b. Oct. 21, 1928): Baseball LHP; all-time leader in World Series wins (10); led AL in wins 3 times; won Cy Young and World Series MVP in 1961 with NY Yankees; 236-106 record.

George Foreman (b. Jan. 10, 1949): Boxer; Olympic heavyweight champ (1968); world heavyweight champ (1973-74 and 94-95); lost title to Muhammad Ali (KO-8th) in '74; recaptured it on Nov. 5, 1994 at age 45 with a 10-round KO of WBA/IBF champ Michael Moorer, becoming the oldest man to win heavyweight crown; named AP Male Athlete of Year 20 years after losing title to Ali; stripped of WBA title in 1995 after declining to fight No. 1 contender; successfully defended title at age 46 against 26-year-old Axel Schulz in controversial maj. decision; gave up IBF title after refusing rematch with Schulz.

Dick Fosbury (b. Mar. 6, 1947): Track & Field; revolutionized high jump with back-first "Fosbury Flop"; won gold medal at 1968 Olympics.

Greg Foster (b. Aug. 4, 1958): Track & Field; 3-time winner of World Championship in 110-m hurdles (1983,87,91); won silver in 1984 Olympics; world indoor champion in 1991.

The Four Horsemen Senior backfield that led Notre Dame to national collegiate football championship in 1924; put together as sophomores by Irish coach Knute Rockne; immortalized by sportswriter Grantland Rice, whose report of the Oct. 19, 1924, Notre Dame-Army game began: "Outlined against a blue, gray October sky the Four Horsemen rode again . . ."; HB Jim Crowley (b. Sept. 10, 1902, d. Jan. 15, 1986), FB Elmer Layden (b. May 4, 1903, d. June 30, 1973), HB Don Miller (b. Mar. 30, 1902, d. July 28, 1979) and QB Harry Stuhldreher (b. Oct. 14, 1901, d. Jan. 26, 1965).

The Four Musketeers French quartet that dominated men's tennis in 1920s and '30s, winning 8 straight French singles titles (1925-32), 6 Wimbledons in a row (1924-29) and 6 consecutive Davis Cups (1927-32)— Jean Borotra (b. Aug. 13, 1898, d. July 17, 1994), Jacques Brugnon (b. May 11, 1895, d. Mar. 20, 1978), Henri Cochet (b. Dec. 14, 1901, d. Apr. 1, 1987), Rene Lacoste (b. July 2, 1905, d. Oct. 13, 1996).

Nellie Fox (b. Dec. 25, 1927, d. Dec. 1, 1975): Baseball 2B; batted .306 in 1959 to win the AL MVP award with the pennant-winning Chicago White Sox; led the league in fielding percentage nine times, hits four times and triples once; ended his 19-year career with 2,663 hits, 1,279 runs and .288 average.

Jimmie Foxx (b. Oct. 22, 1907, d. July 21, 1967): Baseball 1B; led AL in HRs 4 times and batting twice; won Triple Crown in 1933; 3-time MVP (1932-33,38) with Philadelphia and Boston; hit 30 HRs or more 12 years in a row; 534 career HRs.

A.J. Foyt (b. Jan. 16, 1935): Auto racer; 7-time USAC-CART national champion (1960-61,63-64,67,75,79); 4-time Indy 500 winner (1961,64,67,77); only driver in history to win Indy 500, Daytona 500 (1972) and 24 Hours of LeMans (1967 with Dan Gurney); retired in 1993 as all-time CART wins leader with 67.

Bill France Sr. (b. Sept. 26, 1909, d. June 7, 1992): Stock car pioneer and promoter; founded NASCAR in 1948; guided race circuit through formative years; built both Daytona (Fla.) Int'l Speedway and Talladega (Ala.) Superspeedway.

Dawn Fraser (b. Sept. 4, 1937): Australian swimmer; won gold medals in 100m freestyle at 3 consecutive Olympics (1956,60,64).

Joe Frazier (b. Jan. 12, 1944): Boxer; 1964 Olympic heavyweight champion; world heavyweight champ (1970-73); fought Muhammad Ali 3 times and won once; pro record 32-4-1 with 27 KOs.

Walt Frazier (b. March 29, 1945): Basketball G; won the NBA championship two times (1970 and 73) with the New York Knicks; 35 points and 19 assists in the 1970 championship game vs. the Lakers; averaged 18.9 PPG and 6.1 APG over his career; four-time all-NBA and a member of the Hall of Fame; nicknamed "Clyde" after well-dressed gangster Clyde Barrow.

Cathy Freeman (b. Feb. 16, 1973): Track & Field; Australian Aborigine who lit the cauldron at the start of the 2000 Olympic Games in Sydney and provided one of the games' most memorable moments by winning gold in the 400-meters on her home soil; 2-time world champion in the 400-meters (1997,99); won silver in the 400 at the 1996 Olympics in Atlanta.

Ford Frick (b. Dec. 19, 1894, d. Apr. 8, 1978): Baseball; sportswriter and radio announcer who served as NL president (1934-51) and commissioner (1951-65); convinced record-keepers to list Roger Maris' and Babe Ruth's season records separately; major leagues moved to West Coast and expanded from 16 to 20 teams during his tenure.

Frankie Frisch (b. Sept. 9, 1898, d. Mar. 12, 1973): Baseball 2B; played on 8 NL pennant winners in 19 years with NY and St. Louis; hit .300 or better 11 years in a row (1921-31); MVP in 1931; player-manager from 1933-37.

Dan Gable (b. Oct. 25, 1948): Wrestling; career wrestling record of 118-1 at Iowa St., where he was a 2-time NCAA champ (1968,69) and tourney MVP in 1969 (137 lbs); won gold medal (149 lbs) at 1972 Olympics; coached U.S. freestyle team in 1988; coached Iowa to 9 straight NCAA titles (1978-86) and 15 overall in 21 years.

Eddie Gaedel (b. June 8, 1925, d. June 18, 1961): Baseball PH; St. Louis Browns' 3-foot-7 player whose career lasted one at bat (he walked) on Aug 19, 1951; hired as a publicity stunt by eccentric owner Bill Veeck.

Clarence (Big House) Gaines (b. May 21, 1924): Basketball; retired as coach of Div. II Winston-Salem after 1992-93 season with 828-447 record in 47 years; ranks 3rd on all-time NCAA list behind Dean Smith (879) and Adolph Rupp (876).

Alonzo (Jake) Gaither (b. Apr. 11, 1903, d. Feb. 18, 1994): Football; head coach at Florida A&M for 25 years; led Rattlers to 6 national black college titles; retired after 1969 season with record of 203-36-4 and a winning percentage of .844; coined phrase, "I like my boys agile, mobile and hostile."

Cito Gaston (b. Mar. 17, 1944): Baseball; managed Toronto to consecutive World Series titles (1992-93); first black manager to win Series; shared The Sporting News 1993 Man of Year award with Blue Jays GM Pat Gillick.

Rulon Gardner (b. Aug. 16, 1971): Olympic wrestler; surprise winner of the super heavyweight Greco-Roman wrestling gold medal at the 2000 Sydney Games; beat unbeatable Russian legend Alexandre Kareline, 1-0; won 2000 Sullivan Award and USOC Sportsman of the Year Award.

Lou Gehrig (b. June 19, 1903, d. June 2, 1941): Baseball 1B; played in 2,130 consecutive games from 1925-39 a major league record until Cal Ripken Jr. surpassed it in 1995; led AL in RBI 5 times and HRs 3 times; drove in 100 runs or more 13 years in a row; 2-time MVP (1927,36); hit .340 with 493 HRs over 17 seasons; led NY Yankees to 6 World Series titles; died at age 37 of Amyotrophic Lateral Sclerosis (ALS), a rare and incurable disease of the nervous system now better known as Lou Gehrig's disease.

Bernie Geoffrion (b. Feb. 14, 1931): Hockey RW; credited with popularizing the slap shot, earning his nickname "Boom Boom"; scored 30 goals in 1952 to win the NHL's Calder Trophy (Rookie of the Year Award); won the MVP award (Hart) in 1955; became the second player in history to score 50 goals in one season; led the league in points in 1955 and 61; won 6 Stanley Cups with Montreal; member of the Hockey Hall of Fame.

George Gervin (b. April 27, 1952): Basketball G/F; joined the ABA in 1972 and came to the NBA with San Antonio in 1976; a five-time NBA all-star; led the league in scoring four times; scored 26,595 points with an average of 25.1 per game; known as the "Iceman" because of his cool style; elected to the Hall of Fame in 1996.

A. Bartlett Giamatti (b. Apr. 14, 1938, d. Sept. 1, 1989): Scholar and 7th commissioner of baseball; banned Pete Rose for life for betting on Major League games and associating with known gamblers; also served as president of Yale (1978-86) and National League (1986-89).

Joe Gibbs (b. Nov. 25, 1940): Football; coached Washington to 140 victories and 3 Super Bowl titles in 12 seasons before retiring in 1993; owner of NASCAR racing team that won 1993 Daytona 500 and 2000 Winston Cup title.

Althea Gibson (b. Aug. 25, 1927): Tennis; won both Wimbledon and U.S. championships in 1957 and '58; 1st black to play in either tourney and 1st to win each title.

Bob Gibson (b. Nov. 9, 1935): Baseball RHP; won 20 or more games 5 times; won 2 NL Cy Youngs (1968,70); MVP in 1968; led St. Louis to 2 World Series titles (1964,67); his ERA of 1.12 in 1968 is the lowest for a starter since 1914; 251-174 record.

Josh Gibson (b. Dec. 21, 1911, d. Jan. 20, 1947): Baseball C; the "Babe Ruth of the Negro Leagues"; Satchel Paige's battery mate with Pittsburgh Crawfords. The Negro Leagues did not keep accurate records but Gibson hit 84 home runs in one season and his Baseball Hall of Fame plaque says he hit "almost 800" home runs in his seventeen-year career.

Kirk Gibson (b. May 28, 1957): Baseball OF; All-America flanker at Mich. St. in 1978; chose baseball career and was AL playoff MVP with Detroit in 1984 and NL regular season MVP with Los Angeles in 1988; hit famous pinch-hit home run against Oakland's Dennis Eckersley in Game 1 of the 1988 World Series to vault the Dodgers to the title.

Frank Gifford (b. Aug. 16, 1930): Football HB; 4-time All-Pro (1955-57,59); NFL MVP in 1956; led NY Giants to 3 NFL title games; longtime TV sportscaster, beginning career in 1958 while still a player; scandal struck the married Gifford after he was videotaped in a compromising position with a former stewardess in 1997.

Sid Gillman (b. Oct. 26, 1911): Football innovator; coach elected to both College and Pro Football Halls of Fame; led college teams at Miami-OH and Cincinnati to combined 81-19-2 record from 1944-54; coached LA Rams (1955-59) in NFL, then led LA-San Diego Chargers to 5 Western titles and 1 league championship in first six years of AFL.

George Gipp (b. Feb. 18, 1895, d. Dec. 14, 1920): Football FB; died of throat infection 2 weeks before he made All-America; rushed for 2,341 yards, scored 156 points and averaged 38 yards a punt in 4 years (1917-20).

Marc Girardelli (b. July 18, 1963): Luxembourg Alpine skier; Austrian native who refused to join Austrian Ski Federation because he wanted to be coached by his father; won unprecedented 5th overall World Cup title in 1993; winless at Olympics, although he won 2 silver medals in 1992.

Tom Glavine (b. Mar. 26, 1966): Baseball LHP; Atlanta Braves' pitcher led the majors in wins from 1991-95 with 91; NL Cy Young winner in 1991 and '98; seven-time All-Star and was the NL starter twice; World Series MVP (1995).

Tom Gola (b. Jan. 13, 1933): Basketball F; 4-time All-America and 1955 Player of Year at La Salle; MOP in 1952 NIT and '54 NCAA Final 4, leading Pioneers to both titles; won NBA title as rookie with Philadelphia Warriors in 1956; 4-time NBA All-Star.

Marshall Goldberg (b. Oct. 24, 1917): Football HB; 2-time consensus All-America at Pittsburgh (1937-38); led Pitt to national championship in 1937; played with NFL champion Chicago Cardinals 10 years later.

Lefty Gomez (b. Nov. 26, 1908, d. Feb. 17, 1989): Baseball LHP; 4-time 20-game winner with NY Yankees; holds World Series record for most wins (6) without a defeat; pitched on 5 world championship clubs in 1930s.

Pancho Gonzales (b. May 9, 1928, d. July 3, 1995): Tennis; won consecutive U.S. Championships in 1947-48 before turning pro at 21; dominated pro tour from 1950-61; in 1969 at age 41, played longest Wimbledon match ever (5:12), beating Charlie Pasarell 22-24,1-6,16-14,6-3,11-9.

Bob Goodenow (b. Oct. 29, 1952): Hockey; succeeded Alan Eagleson as executive director of NHL Players Assn. in 1990; led players out on 10-day strike (Apr. 1-10) in 1992 and during 103-day owners' lockout in 1994-95.

Gail Goodrich (b. April 23, 1943): Basketball G; starred at UCLA and won two national championships in 1964 and 1965 under legendary coach John Wooden's tutelage; won the NBA championship with the L.A. Lakers in 1972 and led the team in scoring (25.9 ppg); averaged 18.6 ppg over his 14-year career.

Jeff Gordon (b. Aug. 4, 1971): Auto racer; NASCAR Rookie of Year (1993); 4-time Winston Cup champion (1995,97,98,2001); won inaugural Brickyard 400 in 1994; in 1997, at 25 became youngest winner of the Daytona 500; in 1998 he tied Richard Petty for the modern-era record for wins in a single season with 13; NASCAR's all-time leading money winner and currently 7th on the all-time victory list.

Goose Gossage (b. July 5, 1951): Baseball RHP; Nine-time All Star (1975-78, 80-82, 84-85); intimidating relief pitcher; Fireman of the Year in 1975 with White Sox and 1978 with Yankees; led AL in saves with 26 (1975), 27 (1978); 1,002 career appearances; 310 saves.

Shane Gould (b. Nov. 23, 1956): Australian swimmer; set world records in 5 different women's freestyle events between July 1971 and Jan. 1972; won 3 gold medals, a silver and bronze in 1972 Olympics then retired at age 16.

Alf Goullet (b. Apr. 5, 1891, d. Mar. 11, 1995): Cycling; Australian who gained fame and fortune early in century as premier performer on U.S. 6-day bike race circuit; won 8 annual races at Madison Square Garden with 6 different partners from 1913-23.

Curt Gowdy (b. July 31, 1919): Radio-TV; former radio voice of NY Yankees and then Boston Red Sox from 1949-66; TV play-by-play man for AFL, NFL and major league baseball; has broadcast World Series, All-Star Games, Rose Bowls, Super Bowls, Olympics and NCAA Final Fours for all 3 networks; hosted "The American Sportsman."

Steffi Graf (b. June 14, 1969): German tennis player; won Grand Slam and Olympic gold medal in 1988 at age 19; won three of four majors in 1993, '95 and '96; won 22 Grand Slam singles titles— 7 at Wimbledon, 6 French, 5 U.S. and 4 Australian Opens, retired in 1999 as 3rd all-time with 107 career singles titles and as all-time tour leader in career earnings with over $21 million in prize money; married to Andre Agassi.

Otto Graham (b. Dec. 6, 1921): Football QB and basketball All-America at Northwestern; in pro ball, led Cleveland Browns to 7 league titles in 10 years, winning 4 AAFC championships (1946-49) and 3 NFL (1950,54-55); 5-time All-Pro; 2-time NFL MVP (1953,55).

Cammi Granato (b. Mar. 25, 1971): Hockey; American women's hockey pioneer; captain of U.S. team that won gold at the inaugural olympic women's hockey competition in 1998 at Nagano; sister of NHL veteran Tony.

Red Grange (b. June 13, 1903, d. Jan. 28, 1991): Football HB; 3-time All-America at Illinois who brought 1st huge crowds to pro football when he signed with Chicago Bears in 1925; formed 1st AFL with manager-promoter C.C. Pyle in 1926, but league folded and he returned to Bears.

Bud Grant (b. May 20, 1927): Football and Basketball; only coach to win 100 games in both CFL and NFL and only member of both CFL and U.S. Pro Football Halls of Fame; led Winnipeg to 4 Grey Cup titles (1958-59,61-62) in 6 appearances, but his Minnesota Vikings lost all 4 Super Bowl attempts in 1970s; accumulated 122 CFL wins and 168 NFL wins; also All-Big Ten at Minnesota in both football and basketball in late 1940s; a 3-time CFL All-Star offensive end; also member of 1950 NBA champion Minneapolis Lakers.

Rocky Graziano (b. June 7, 1922, d. May 22, 1990): Boxer; world middleweight champion (1946-47); fought Tony Zale for title 3 times in 21 months, losing twice; pro record 67-10-6 with 52 KOs; movie "Somebody Up There Likes Me" based on his life.

Hank Greenberg (b. Jan. 1, 1911, d. Sept. 4, 1986): Baseball 1B; led AL in HRs and RBI 4 times each; 2-time MVP (1935,40) with Detroit; 331 career HRs, including 58 in 1938.

Joe Greene (b. Sept. 24, 1946): Football DT; 5-time All-Pro (1972-74,77,79); led Pittsburgh to 4 Super Bowl titles in 1970s; nicknamed "Mean Joe."

Maurice Greene (b. July 23, 1974): Track & Field; world 100m champion in 1997, 99 and 2001 and 200m champion in 1999; former world record holder (9.79) in the 100m; injury forced him out of the 1996 Olympics in Atlanta; won the gold medal in the 100m at the 2000 Olympics in Sydney; 100m WR broken by Tim Montgomery in Sept. 2002 (9.78).

Bud Greenspan (b. Sept. 18, 1926): Filmmaker specializing in the Olympic Games; has won Emmy awards for 22-part "The Olympiad" (1976-77) and historical vignettes for ABC-TV's coverage of 1980 Winter Games; won 1994 Emmy award for edited special on Lillehammer Winter Olympics; won The Peabody Award in 1996 for his outstanding service to chronicling the Olympic Games.

Wayne Gretzky (b. Jan. 26, 1961): Hockey C; 10-time NHL scoring champion; 9-time regular season MVP (1979-87,89) and 9-time All-NHL first team; scored 200 points or more in a season 4 times; led Edmonton to 4 Stanley Cups (1984-85,87-88); 2-time playoff MVP (1985,88); traded to LA Kings (Aug. 9, 1988); broke Gordie Howe's all-time NHL goal scoring record of 801 on Mar. 23, 1994; all-time NHL leader in points (2857), goals (894) and assists (1963); also all-time Stanley Cup leader in points, goals and assists; spent the end of the 1996 season with the St. Louis Blues and then signed a free agent contract with the New York Rangers; retired in 1999 at age 38 with 61 NHL scoring records in 20 seasons; became part-owner of NHL's Coyotes in 2000.

Bob Griese (b. Feb. 3, 1945): Football QB; 2-time All-Pro (1971,77); led Miami to undefeated season (17-0) in 1972 and consecutive Super Bowl titles (1973-74); father of Brian.

Ken Griffey Jr. (b. Nov. 21, 1969): Baseball OF; overall 1st pick of 1987 draft by Seattle; 10-time Gold Glove winner; 11-time All-Star; 1997 AL MVP; Mariners all-time leader in home runs and RBIs; MVP of 1992 All-Star game at age 23; hit home runs in 8 consecutive games in 1993; son of Ken Sr. and in 1990 they became the first father-son combination to appear in the same major league lineup; traded to the Cincinnati Reds before the 2000 season.

Archie Griffin (b. Aug. 21, 1954): Football RB; only college player to win two Heisman Trophies (1974-75); rushed for 5,177 yards in career at Ohio St.

Emile Griffith (b. Feb. 3, 1938): Boxer; world welterweight champion (1961,62-63,63-65); world middleweight champ (1966-67,67-68); pro record 85-24-2 with 23 KOs.

Dick Groat (b. Nov. 4, 1930): Basketball G and Baseball SS; 2-time basketball All-America at Duke and college Player of Year in 1951; won NL MVP award as shortstop with Pittsburgh in 1960; won World Series with Pirates (1960) and St. Louis (1964).

Lefty Grove (b. Mar. 6, 1900, d. May 23, 1975): Baseball LHP; won 20 or more games 8 times; led AL in ERA 9 times and strikeouts 7 times; 31-4 record and MVP in 1931 with Philadelphia; 300-141 record; real name: Robert Moses Grove

Lou Groza (b. Jan. 25, 1924, d. Nov. 29, 2000): Football T-PK; 6-time All-Pro; played in 13 championship games for Cleveland from 1946-67; kicked winning field goal in 1950 NFL title game; 1,608 career points (1,349 in NFL).

Janet Guthrie (b. Mar. 7, 1938): Auto racer; in 1977, became 1st woman to race in Indianapolis 500; placed 9th at Indy in 1978.

Tony Gwynn (b. May 9, 1960): Baseball OF; 8-time NL batting champion (1984,87-89,94-97) with San Diego, 15-time All-Star; got 3,000th career hit Aug. 6, 1999 at Montreal; played basketball at San Diego St. leaving as school's all-time assist leader; drafted in 10th round of 1981 NBA draft by San Diego Clippers.

Harvey Haddix (b. Sept. 18, 1925, d. Jan. 9, 1994): Baseball LHP; pitched 12 perfect innings for Pittsburgh, but lost to Milwaukee in the 13th, 1-0 (May 26, 1959); won Game 7 of 1960 World Series.

Walter Hagen (b. Dec. 21, 1892, d. Oct. 5, 1969): Pro golf pioneer; won 2 U.S. Opens (1914,19), 4 British Opens (1922,24,28-29), 5 PGA Championships (1921,24-27) and 5 Western Opens; retired with 40 PGA wins; 6-time U.S. Ryder Cup captain.

Marvin Hagler (b. May 23, 1954): Boxer; world middleweight champion 1980-87; enjoyed his nickname "Marvelous Marvin" so much he had his name legally changed; pro record of 62-3-2 with 52 KOs.

Mika Hakkinen (b. Sept. 28, 1968): Finnish auto racer; won two consecutive Formula One world drivers championships in 1998 and '99; recorded eight wins in '98 and five in '99; 20 career F1 wins.

George Halas (b. Feb. 2, 1895, d. Oct. 31, 1983): Football pioneer; MVP in 1919 Rose Bowl; player-coach-owner of Chicago Bears from 1920-83; signed Red Grange in 1925; coached Bears for 40 seasons and won 8 NFL titles (1921,32-33,40-41,43,46,63); 2nd on all-time career list with 324 wins; elected to NFL Hall of Fame in 1963.

Dorothy Hamill (b. July 26, 1956): Figure skater; won Olympic gold medal and world championship in 1976; Ice Capades headliner from 1977-84; bought the financially-strapped Ice Capades in 1993 and sold it several years later.

Scott Hamilton (b. Aug. 28, 1958): Figure skater; 4-time world champion (1981-84); won gold medal at 1984 Olympics.

Mia Hamm (b. Mar. 17, 1972): Soccer F; became all-time leading scorer in international soccer with her 108th goal on May 22, 1999; member of 1996 and 2000 U.S. Olympic teams, the 1991 and 1999 U.S. World Cup championship teams, and the 3rd-place 1995 World Cup team; made the U.S. National Team at 15; a three-time collegiate All-American; led UNC to 4 national titles (1989,90,92,93).

Tonya Harding (b. Nov. 12, 1970): Figure skater; 1991 U.S. women's champion; involved in bizarre plot hatched by ex-husband Jeff Gillooly to injure rival Nancy Kerrigan on Jan. 6, 1994 and keep her off Olympic team; won '94 U.S. women's title in Kerrigan's absence; denied any role in assault and sued USOC when her berth on Olympic team was threatened; finished 8th at Lillehammer (Kerrigan recovered and won silver medal); pled guilty on Mar. 16 to conspiracy to hinder investigation; stripped of 1994 title by U.S. Figure Skating Association.

Tom Harmon (b. Sept. 28, 1919, d. Mar. 17, 1990): Football HB; 2-time All-America at Michigan; won Heisman Trophy in 1940; played with AFL NY Americans in 1941 and NFL LA Rams (1946-47); World War II fighter pilot who won Silver Star and Purple Heart; became radio-TV commentator.

Franco Harris (b. Mar. 7, 1950): Football RB; ran for over 1,000 yards in a season 8 times; rushed for 12,120 yards in 13 years; led Pittsburgh to 4 Super Bowl titles.

Leon Hart (b. Nov. 2, 1928, d. Sept. 24, 2002): Football E; only player to win 3 national championships in college and 3 more in the NFL; won his titles at Notre Dame (1946-47,49) and with Detroit Lions (1952-53,57); 3-time All-America and last lineman to win Heisman Trophy (1949); All-Pro on both offense and defense in 1951.

Bill Hartack (b. Dec. 9, 1932): Jockey; won Kentucky Derby 5 times (1957,60,62,64,69), Preakness 3 times (1956,64,69), and the Belmont once (1960).

Doug Harvey (b. Dec. 19, 1924, d. Dec. 26, 1989): Hockey D; 10-time All-NHL 1st team; won Norris Trophy 7 times (1955-58,60-62); led Montreal to 6 Stanley Cups.

Dominik Hasek (b. Jan. 29, 1965): Czech hockey G; 2-time NHL MVP (1997,98) with Buffalo; 6-time Vezina Trophy winner (1994,95,97,98,99,2001); led Czech Republic to Olympic gold medal in 1998 at Nagano; won Stanley Cup with Detroit in 2002.

Billy Haughton (b. Nov. 2, 1923, d. July 15, 1986): Harness racing; 4-time winner of Hambletonian; trainer-driver of one Pacing Triple Crown winner (1968); 4,910 career wins.

João Havelange (b. May 8, 1916): Soccer; Brazilian-born president of Federation Internationale de Football Assoc. (FIFA) 1974-98; also member of International Olympic Committee.

John Havlicek (b. Apr. 8, 1940): Basketball F; played in 3 NCAA Finals at Ohio St. (1960-62); led Boston to 8 NBA titles (1963-66,68-69,74,76); Finals MVP in 1974; 4-time All-NBA 1st team.

Bob Hayes (b. Dec. 20, 1942, d. Sept. 18, 2002): Track & Field and Football; won gold medal in 100m at 1964 Olympics; all-pro SE for Dallas in 1966; won Super Bowl with Cowboys in 1972; convicted of drug trafficking in 1979 and served 18 months of a 5-year sentence.

Elvin Hayes (b. Nov. 17, 1945, d. Sept. 18, 2002): Basketball C; Known as "the Big E"; Overall number one pick of the 1968 NBA draft; three-time All-NBA first team (1975,77,79); 1978 Finals MVP; 12-time NBA all-star (1969-80); named to NBA's 50 Greatest Players; 6th leading scorer in NBA history with 27,313 points and 4th leading rebounder with 16,279; member of NBA Hall of Fame.

Woody Hayes (b. Feb. 14, 1913, d. Mar. 12, 1987): Football; coached Ohio St. to 6 national titles (1954,57,61,68,70) and 4 Rose Bowl victories; 238 career wins in 28 seasons at Denison, Miami-OH and OSU; his coaching career ended abruptly in 1978 after he attacked an opposing player on the sidelines.

Thomas Hearns (b. Oct. 18, 1958): Boxer; has held world titles as welterweight, junior middleweight, middleweight and light heavyweight; four career losses have come against Ray Leonard, Marvin Hagler and twice to Iran Barkley; pro record of 59-4-1, 46 KOs.

Eric Heiden (b. June 14, 1958): Speed skater; 3-time overall world champion (1977-79); won all 5 men's gold medals at 1980 Olympics, setting records in each; Sullivan Award winner (1980).

Mel Hein (b. Aug. 22, 1909, d. Jan. 31, 1992): Football C; NFL All-Pro 8 straight years (1933-40); MVP in 1938 with Giants; didn't miss a game in 15 years.

John W. Heisman (b. Oct. 23, 1869, d. Oct. 3, 1936): Football; coached at 9 colleges from 1892-1927; won 185 games; Director of Athletics at Downtown Athletic Club in NYC (1928-36); DAC named Heisman Trophy after him.

Carol Heiss (b. Jan. 20, 1940): Figure skater; 5-time world champion (1956-60); won Olympic silver medal in 1956 and gold in '60; married 1956 men's gold medalist Hayes Jenkins.

Rickey Henderson (b. Dec. 25, 1958): Baseball OF; AL playoff MVP (1989) and AL regular season MVP (1990); set single-season base stealing record of 130 in 1982; has led AL in steals a record 12 times; broke Lou Brock's all-time record of 938 on May 1, 1991; all-time leader in runs, steals, walks and HRs as leadoff batter.

Sonja Henie (b. Apr. 8, 1912, d. Oct. 12, 1969): Norwegian figure skater; 10-time world champion (1927-36); won 3 consecutive Olympic gold medals (1928,32,36); became movie star.

Foster Hewitt (b. Nov. 21, 1902, d. Apr. 21, 1985): Radio-TV; Canada's premier hockey play-by-play broadcaster from 1923-81; coined phrase, "He shoots, he scores!"

Damon Hill (b. Sept. 17, 1960): British auto racer; 1996 Formula One champion; 22 F1 wins places him 10th all-time.

Graham Hill (b. Feb. 15, 1929, d. Nov. 29, 1975): British auto racer; 2-time Formula One world champion (1962,68); won Indy 500 in 1966; killed in plane crash; father of Damon.

Phil Hill (b. Apr. 20, 1927): Auto racer; first U.S. driver to win Formula One championship (1961); 3 career wins (1958-64).

Martina Hingis (b. Sept. 30, 1980): Tennis player; in March 1997 at 16 years, 6 months, she became the youngest No. 1 ranked player since the ranking system began in 1975; has won Wimbledon (1997), U.S. Open (1997) and 3 Australian Opens (1997,98,99); first woman to surpass the $3 million mark in earnings for one season (1997).

Max Hirsch (b. July 30, 1880, d. Apr. 3, 1969): Horse racing; trained 1,933 winners from 1908-68; won Triple Crown with Assault in 1946.

Tommy Hitchcock (b. Feb. 11, 1900, d. Apr. 19, 1944): Polo; world class player at 20; achieved 10-goal rating 18 times from 1922-40.

Lew Hoad (b. Nov. 23, 1934, d. July 3, 1994): Australian tennis player; 2-time Wimbledon winner (1956-57); won Australian, French and Wimbledon titles in 1956, but missed capturing Grand Slam at Forest Hills when beaten by Ken Rosewall in 4-set final.

Gil Hodges (b. Apr. 4, 1924, d. Apr. 2, 1972): Baseball 1B-Manager; tied Major League record with four home runs in one game on Aug 31, 1950; won three Gold Gloves (1957-59); drove in 100 runs in seven consecutive seasons (1949-55); hit 370 home runs and 1,274 RBIs lifetime; won 660 games as manager (Senators and Mets).

Ben Hogan (b. Aug. 13, 1912, d. July 25, 1997): Golfer; 4-time PGA Player of Year; one of only five players to win all four Grand Slam titles (others are Nicklaus, Player, Sarazen and Woods); won 4 U.S. Opens, 2 Masters, 2 PGAs and 1 British Open between 1946-53; one of only two players (Woods) to win three of the four current majors in one year when he won Masters, U.S. Open and British Open in 1953; nearly killed in Feb. 2, 1949 car accident, but came back to win U.S. Open in '50; third on all-time list with 63 career wins.

Chamique Holdsclaw (b. Aug. 9, 1977): Basketball F; 2-time national player of the year, leading Tennessee to 3 straight national championships (1996,97,98); 1998 Sullivan Award winner; top selection by the Washington Mystics in the 1999 WNBA draft; 1999 Rookie of the Year.

Eleanor Holm (b. Dec. 6, 1913): Swimmer; won gold medal in 100m backstroke at 1932 Olympics; thrown off '36 U.S. team for drinking champagne in public and shooting craps on boat to Germany.

Nat Holman (b. Oct. 18, 1896, d. Feb. 12, 1995): Basketball pioneer; played with Original Celtics (1920-28); coached CCNY to both NCAA and NIT titles in 1950 (a year later, several of his players were caught up in a point-shaving scandal); 423 career wins.

Larry Holmes (b. Nov. 3, 1949): Boxer; heavyweight champion (WBC or IBF) from 1978-85; successfully defended title 20 times before losing to Michael Spinks; returned from first retirement in 1988 and was KO'd in 4th by champ Mike Tyson; launched second comeback in 1991; fought and lost title bids against Evander Holyfield in '92 and Oliver McCall in '95; beat Eric "Butterbean" Esch in a one-fight comeback in 2002; pro record of 69-6 and 44 KOs.

Lou Holtz (b. Jan. 6, 1937): Football; coached Notre Dame to national title in 1988; 2-time Coach of Year (1977,88); coached six schools in all — Wm. & Mary (3 years), N.C. State (4), Arkansas (7), Minnesota (2), ND (11) and S. Carolina (4+); also coached NFL N.Y. Jets for 13 games (3-10) in 1976.

Evander Holyfield (b. Oct. 19, 1962): Boxer; KO'd Buster Douglas in 3rd round to become world hvywt. champion in 1990; lost title to Riddick Bowe in 1992; beat Bowe to reclaim title in 1993; lost title again to Michael Moorer in 1994; defeated Mike Tyson in 1996 to win WBA belt; in 1997 rematch, Tyson was DQ'd for twice biting Holyfield's ear; escaped with controversial draw in 1999 unification bout with Lennox Lewis, then lost the rematch later that year; defeated John Ruiz in Aug. 2000 for vacant WBA belt then lost rematch and belt in March, 2001; the pair fought again in Dec. 2001, this time to a draw.

Red Holzman (b. Aug. 10, 1920, d. Nov. 13, 1998): Basketball; played for NBL and NBA champions at Rochester (1946,51); coached NY Knicks to 2 NBA titles (1970,73); Coach of Year (1970); ranks 13th on all-time NBA list with 754 wins.

Rogers Hornsby (b. Apr. 27, 1896, d. Jan. 5, 1963): Baseball 2B; hit .400 3 times, including .424 in 1924; led NL in batting 7 times; 2-time MVP (1925,29); career BA of .358 over 23 years is highest in NL.

Paul Hornung (b. Dec. 23, 1935): Football HB-PK; only Heisman Trophy winner to play for losing team (2-8 Notre Dame in 1956); 3-time NFL scoring leader (1959-61) at Green Bay; 176 points in 1960, an all-time record; MVP in 1961; suspended by NFL for 1963 season for betting on his own team.

Gordie Howe (b. Mar. 31, 1928): Hockey RW; played 32 seasons in NHL and WHA from 1946-80; led NHL in scoring 6 times; All-NHL 1st team 12 times; MVP 6 times in NHL (1952-53,57-58,60,63) with Detroit and once in WHA (1974) with Houston; ranks 2nd on all-time NHL list in goals (801) and points (1,850) to Wayne Gretzky; played with sons Mark and Marty at Houston (1973-77) and New England-Hartford (1977-80).

Cal Hubbard (b. Oct. 31, 1900, d. Oct. 17, 1977): Member of college football, pro football and baseball halls of fame; 9 years in NFL; 4-time All-Pro at end and tackle; AL umpire (1936-51).

William DeHart Hubbard (b. Nov. 25, 1903, d. June 23, 1976): Track & Field; won the long jump at the 1924 Olympics, becoming the first black athlete to win an Olympic gold medal in an individual event; set the long jump world record in 1925 (25-10¾) and tied the 100-yard dash record (9.6) in 1926.

Carl Hubbell (b. June 22, 1903, d. Nov. 21, 1988): Baseball LHP; led NL in wins and ERA 3 times each; 2-time MVP (1933,36) with NY Giants; fanned Ruth, Gehrig, Foxx, Simmons and Cronin in succession in 1934 All-Star Game; 253-154 career record.

Sam Huff (b. Oct. 4, 1934): Football LB; glamorized NFL's middle linebacker position with NY Giants from 1956-63; subject of "The Violent World of Sam Huff" TV special in 1961; helped club win 6 division titles and a world championship (1956).

Miller Huggins (b. Mar. 27, 1878, d. Sept. 25, 1929): Baseball; managed NY Yankees from 1918 until his death late in '29 season; led Yanks to 6 pennants and 3 World Series titles from 1921-28.

Bobby Hull (b. Jan. 3, 1939): Hockey LW; led NHL in scoring 3 times; 2-time MVP (1965-66) with Chicago; All-NHL first team 10 times; jumped to WHA in 1972, 2-time MVP there (1973,75) with Winnipeg; scored 913 goals in both leagues; father of Brett.

Brett Hull (b. Aug. 9, 1964): Hockey RW; NHL MVP in 1991 with St. Louis; holds single season RW scoring record with 86 goals; he and father Bobby have both won Hart (MVP), Lady Byng (sportsmanship) and All-Star Game MVP trophies; won Stanley Cup with Dallas in 1999 and Detroit in 2002.

Lamar Hunt (b. Aug. 2, 1932): Football/Soccer; Founder of the Kansas City Chiefs (formerly Dallas Texans); instrumental in forming the AFL in 1959 and merging the league with the NFL in 1966; elected to the Pro Football Hall of Fame in 1972; AFC Championship trophy is named for him; investor/operator of 2 Major League Soccer teams (Columbus, Kansas City).

Jim (Catfish) Hunter (b. Apr. 8, 1946, d. Sept. 9, 1999): Baseball RHP; won 20 games or more 5 times (1971-75); played on 5 World Series winners with Oakland and NY Yankees; threw perfect game in 1968; won AL Cy Young Award in 1974; 224-166 career record.

Ibrahim Hussein (b. June 3, 1958): Kenyan distance runner; 3-time winner of Boston Marathon (1988,91-92) and 1st African runner to win in Boston; won New York Marathon in 1987.

Don Hutson (b. Jan. 31, 1913, d. June 24, 1997): Football E-PK; led NFL in receptions 8 times and interceptions once; 9-time All-Pro (1936,38-45) for Green Bay; 99 career TD catches.

Flo Hyman (b. July 31, 1954, d. Jan. 24, 1986): Volleyball; 3-time All-America spiker at Houston and captain of 1984 U.S. Women's Olympic team; died of heart attack caused by Marfan Syndrome during a match in Japan in 1986; namesake of award given out annually by the Women's Sports Foundation.

Hank Iba (b. Aug. 6, 1904, d. Jan. 15, 1993): Basketball; coached Oklahoma A&M to 2 straight NCAA titles (1945-46); 767 career wins in 41 years; coached U.S. Olympic team to 2 gold medals (1964,68), but lost to Soviets in controversial '72 final.

Punch Imlach (b. Mar. 15, 1918, d. Dec. 1, 1987): Hockey; directed Toronto to 4 Stanley Cups (1962-64,67) in 11 seasons as GM-coach.

Miguel Induráin (b. July 16, 1964): Spanish cyclist; won a record 5th straight Tour de France in 1995, joining legends Jacques Anquetil and Bernard Hinault of France and Eddy Merckx of Belgium as the only 5-time winners; won gold in time trial at '96 Olympics; retired in 1997.

Juli Inkster (b. June 24, 1960): Golfer; 28 career LPGA victories as of Sept. 2002; winner of 7 major LPGA tournaments and 3 consecutive U.S. Women's Amateur tournaments (1980-82); inducted into the World Golf Hall of Fame in 2000; LPGA Rookie of the Year in 1984.

Hale Irwin (b. June 3, 1945): Golfer; oldest player ever to win U.S. Open (45 in 1990); NCAA champion in 1967; 20 PGA victories, including 3 U.S. Opens (1974,79,90); 5-time Ryder Cup team member; joined senior PGA tour in 1995 and has already won 35 titles through Sept. 2002.

Allen Iverson (b. June 7, 1975): Basketball G; former Georgetown Hoya chosen first overall by the Philadelphia 76ers in the 1996 NBA Draft; NBA Rookie of the Year (1997); 2-time NBA scoring leader (2001-02) and steals leader (2001-02); voted regular season MVP in 2001 and led 76ers to NBA Finals.

Bo Jackson (b. Nov. 30, 1962): Baseball OF and Football RB; won Heisman Trophy in 1985 and MVP of baseball All-Star Game in 1989; starter for both baseball's KC Royals and NFL's LA Raiders in 1988 and '89; severely injured left hip Jan. 13, 1991, in NFL playoffs; waived by Royals but signed by Chicago White Sox in 1991; missed entire 1992 season recovering from hip surgery; played for White Sox in 1993 and California in '94 before retiring.

Joe Jackson (b. July 16, 1889, d. Dec. 5, 1951): Baseball OF; hit .300 or better 11 times; nicknamed "Shoeless Joe;" career average of .356 (see Black Sox).

Phil Jackson (b. Sept. 17, 1945): Basketball; NBA champion as reserve forward with New York in 1973 (injured when Knicks won in '70); coached Chicago to six NBA titles in eight years (1991-93, 96-98); coach of the year in 1996 and '97; returned to coach the LA Lakers in 1999 and has won 3 more titles (2000,01,02); all-time leader in winning pct. for NBA coaches with 350 or more wins; all-time NBA leader in playoff wins (156).

Reggie Jackson (b. May 18, 1946): Baseball OF; led AL in HRs 4 times; MVP in 1973; played on 5 World Series winners with Oakland, NY Yankees; 1977 Series MVP with 5 HRs; 563 career HRs; all-time strikeout leader (2,597); member of the Hall of Fame.

Dr. Robert Jackson (b. Aug. 6, 1932): Surgeon; revolutionized sports medicine by popularizing the use of arthroscopic surgery to treat injuries; learned technique from Japanese physician that allowed athletes to return quickly from potentially career-ending injuries.

Helen Jacobs (b. Aug. 6, 1908, d. June 2, 1997): Tennis; 4-time winner of U.S. Championship (1932-35); Wimbledon winner in 1936; lost 4 Wimbledon finals to arch-rival Helen Wills Moody.

Jaromir Jagr (b. Feb. 15, 1972): Czech Hockey RW; fifth overall pick by Pittsburgh (1990); NHL All-Rookie team (1991); NHL MVP (1999); Won Art Ross Trophy (1995,98,99,00,01); 7-time NHL All-Star First Team; NHL single season record for most points by a right wing (149); NHL single season record for most assists by a RW (87); traded to Washington in 2001.

Dan Jansen (b. June 17, 1965): Speed skater; 1993 world record-holder in 500m; fell in 500m and 1,000m in 1988 Olympics at Calgary after learning of death of sister Jane; placed 4th in 500m and didn't attempt 1,000m 4 years later in Albertville; fell in 500m at '94 Games in Lillehammer, but finally won an Olympic medal with world record (1:12.43) effort in 1,000m, then took victory lap with baby daughter Jane in his arms; won 1994 Sullivan Award.

Dale Jarrett (b. Nov. 26, 1956): Auto racer; 1999 Winston Cup champion; 3-time Daytona 500 champion (1993,96,2000); son of driver Ned Jarrett.

James D. Jeffries (b. Apr. 15, 1875, d. Mar. 3, 1953): Boxer; world heavyweight champion (1899-1905); retired undefeated but came back to fight Jack Johnson in 1910 and lost (KO, 15th).

David Jenkins (b. June 29, 1936): Figure skater; brother of Hayes; 3-time world champion (1957-59); won gold medal at 1960 Olympics.

Hayes Jenkins (b. Mar. 23, 1933): Figure skater; 4-time world champion (1953-56); won gold medal at 1956 Olympics; married 1960 women's gold medalist Carol Heiss.

Bruce Jenner (b. Oct. 28, 1949): Track & Field; won gold medal in 1976 Olympic decathlon.

Jackie Jensen (b. Mar. 9, 1927, d. July 14, 1982): Football RB and Baseball OF; All-America at California in 1948; American League MVP with Boston Red Sox in 1958.

Ben Johnson (b. Dec. 30, 1961): Canadian sprinter; set 100m world record (9.83) at 1987 World Championships; won 100m at 1988 Olympics, but flunked drug test and forfeited gold medal; 1987 world record revoked in '89 for admitted steroid use; returned drug-free in 1991, but performed poorly; banned for life by IAAF in 1993 for testing positive again.

Bob Johnson (b. Mar. 4, 1931, d. Nov. 26, 1991): Hockey; coached Pittsburgh Penguins to 1st Stanley Cup title in 1991; led Wisconsin to 3 NCAA titles (1973,77,81); also coached 1976 U.S. Olympic team and NHL Calgary Flames (1982-87).

Earvin (Magic) Johnson (b. Aug. 14, 1959): Basketball G; led Michigan St. to NCAA title in 1979 and was Final 4 MOP; All-NBA 1st team 9 times; 3-time MVP (1987,89-90); led LA Lakers to 5 NBA titles; 3-time Finals MVP (1980, 82, 87); 2nd all-time in NBA assists with 10,141; retired on Nov. 7, 1991 after announcing he was HIV-positive; returned to score 25 points in 1992 NBA All-Star Game; U.S. Olympic Dream Team member in '92; announced NBA comeback then retired again before start of 1992-93 season; named head coach of Lakers on Mar. 23, 1994, but finished season at 5-11 and quit; later became minority owner of team; came back a final time and played 32 games during 1995-96 season before retiring for good.

Jack Johnson (b. Mar. 31, 1878, d. June 10, 1946): Boxer; controversial heavyweight champion (1908-15) and 1st black to hold title; defeated Tommy Burns for crown at age 30; fled to Europe in 1913 after Mann Act conviction; lost title to Jess Willard in Havana, but claimed to have taken a dive; pro record 78-8-12 with 45 KOs.

Jimmy Johnson (b. July 16, 1943): Football; All-SWC defensive lineman on Arkansas' 1964 national championship team; coached Miami-FL to national title in 1987; college record of 81-34-3 in 10 years; hired by old friend and new Dallas owner Jerry Jones to succeed Tom Landry in 1989; went 1-15 in '89, then led Cowboys to consecutive Super Bowl victories in 1992 and '93 seasons; quit in 1994 after feuding with Jones; became TV analyst; replaced Don Shula as Miami Dolphins head coach from 1996-99.

Judy Johnson (b. Oct. 26, 1899, d. June 13, 1989): Baseball IF; one of the great stars of the Negro Leagues; a terrific fielding third baseman who regularly batted over .300; when baseball integrated Johnson's playing days were over but he coached and scouted for the Philadelphia Athletics, Boston Braves and Philadelphia Phillies; member of Hall of Fame.

Junior Johnson (b. 1930): Auto Racing; won the second Daytona 500 in 1960; also won 13 NASCAR races in 1965, including the Rebel 300 at Darlington; retired from racing to become a highly successful car owner; his first driver was Bobby Allison.

Michael Johnson (b. Sep 13, 1967): Track & Field; Shattered world record in 200m (19.32) and set Olympic record in 400m (43.49) to become first man to win the gold in both races in the same Olympic Games at Atlanta in 1996; two-time world champion in 200 (1991,95) and four-time world champ in 400 (1993,95,97,99); set world record in 400m (43.18) at '99 world championships in Seville; won the 400 in Sydney in 2000 to become the only man to win the event in two consecutive Olympics; retired in 2001.

Rafer Johnson (b. Aug. 18, 1935): Track & Field; won silver medal in 1956 Olympic decathlon and gold medal in 1960.

Randy Johnson (b. Sept. 10, 1963): Baseball LHP; 6'10" flamethrower; threw no-hitter June 2, 1990 for Seattle; struck out over 300 batters 6 times (1993,98,99,00,01,02); led AL in Ks 4 times (1992-95) and NL 4 times (1999-2002); struck out 20 batters in a game (5/8/01); 4-time Cy Young Award winner (AL-1995, NL-1999,00,01); traded to Houston in 1998 and signed as a free agent with Arizona in 1999; won 3 games in 2001 World Series to earn first ring and co-MVP honors (Curt Schilling).

Walter Johnson (b. Nov. 6, 1887, d. Dec. 10, 1946): Baseball RHP; won 20 games or more 10 straight years; led AL in ERA 5 times, wins 6 times and strikeouts 12 times; twice MVP (1913, 24) with Washington; all-time leader in shutouts (110) and 2nd in wins (417); nicknamed "Big Train."

Ben A. Jones (b. Dec. 31, 1882, d. June 13, 1961): Horse racing; Calumet Farm trainer (1939-47); saddled 6 Kentucky Derby champions, including 2 Triple Crown winners—Whirlaway in 1941 and Citation in '48.

Bobby Jones (b. Mar. 17, 1902, d. Dec. 18, 1971): Won U.S. and British Opens plus U.S. and British Amateurs in 1930 to become golf's only Grand Slam winner ever; from 1922-30, won 4 U.S. Opens, 5 U.S. Amateurs, 3 British Opens, and played in 6 Walker Cups; founded Masters tournament in 1934.

Deacon Jones (b. Dec. 9, 1938): Football DE; 5-time All-Pro (1965-69) with LA Rams; unofficially 3rd all-time in NFL sacks with 173½ in 14 years.

Jerry Jones (b. Oct. 13, 1942): Football; owner-GM of Dallas Cowboys; maverick who bought declining team (3-13) and Texas Stadium for $140 million in 1989; hired old pal Jimmy Johnson to replace legendary Tom Landry as coach; their partnership led Cowboys to 2 Super Bowl titles (1993-94); when feud developed in 1994, he fired Johnson and hired Barry Switzer, who won Super Bowl in 1996; defied NFL Properties by signing separate sponsorship deals with Pepsi and Nike in 1995, causing NFL to file a $300 million lawsuit against him.

Marion Jones (b. Oct. 12, 1975): Track & Field; American sprinter who won 3 golds (100, 200, 4x100) at Sydney Games in 2000; 5-time world champion: 100m (1997,99), 200m (2001), 4x100m (1997,01); former college basketball star at North Carolina; voted Women's Athlete of the Year by *Track & Field News* in 1997,98 and 2000; 1999 Jesse Owens Award winner; 2000 AP and USOC Female Athlete of the Year.

Roy Jones Jr. (b. Jan. 16, 1969): Boxing; robbed of gold medal at 1988 Summer Olympics due to an error in scoring; still voted Outstanding Boxer of the Games; won IBF middleweight crown by beating Bernard Hopkins in 1993; moved up to super middleweight and won IBF title from James Toney in 1994; moved up to light heavyweight division winning WBC (in 1997), WBA (1998) and IBF titles (1999); suffered only pro loss in a disqualification to Montel Griffin which he avenged with a 1st round KO 5 months later.

Michael Jordan (b. Feb. 17, 1963): Basketball G; College Player of Year with North Carolina in 1984; NBA Rookie of the Year (1985); led NBA in scoring 7 years in a row (1987-93) and also 1996-98; 10-time All-NBA 1st team; 5-time regular season MVP (1988,91-92,96,98) and 6-time MVP of NBA Finals (1991-93,96-98); 3-time AP Male Athlete of Year; led U.S. Olympic team to gold medals in 1984 and '92; stunned sports world when he retired at age 30 on Oct. 6, 1993; signed as OF with Chi. White Sox and spent summer of '94 in AA with Birmingham; struggled with .204 average; made one of the most anticipated comebacks in sports history when he returned to the Bulls lineup on Mar. 19, 1995 but Bulls were eliminated by Orlando in second round of playoffs later that season; led Bulls to NBA titles for the next three years for 6 titles in all (1991-93,96-98); retired in 1999; became pres. of Wash. Wizards before unretiring again in 2001 and returning to play with Wizards.

Florence Griffith Joyner (b. Dec. 21, 1959, d. Sept. 21, 1998): Track & Field; set world records in 100 and 200 meters in 1988; won 3 gold medals at '88 Olympics (100m, 200m, 4x100m relay); Sullivan Award winner (1988); retired in 1989; named as co-chairperson of President's Council on Physical Fitness and Sports in 1993; sister-in-law of Jackie Joyner-Kersee; died of suffocation during an epileptic seizure in 1998.

Jackie Joyner-Kersee (b. Mar. 3, 1962): Track & Field; 2-time world champion in both long jump (1987,91) and heptathlon (1987,93); won heptathlon gold medals at 1988 and '92 Olympics and LJ gold at '88 Games; also won Olympic silver (1984) in heptathlon and bronze (1992,96) in LJ; Sullivan Award winner (1986); only woman to receive *The Sporting News* Man of Year award.

Alberto Juantorena (b. Nov. 21, 1950): Cuban runner; won both 400m and 800m gold medals at 1976 Olympics.

Sonny Jurgensen (b. Aug. 23, 1934): Football QB; played 18 seasons with Philadelphia and Washington; led NFL in passing twice (1967,69); All-Pro in 1961; 255 career TD passes.

Duke Kahanamoku (b. Aug. 24, 1890, d. Jan. 22, 1968): Swimmer; won 3 gold medals and 2 silver over 3 Olympics (1912,20,24); also surfing pioneer.

Al Kaline (b. Dec. 19, 1934): Baseball; youngest player (at age 20) to win batting title (led AL with .340 in 1955); had 3,007 hits, 399 HRs in 22 years with Detroit.

Paul Kariya (b. Oct. 16, 1974): Hockey LW; first-ever selection of Anaheim (4th overall in 1993); led Maine to an NCAA Div. I national title in 1993; won Hobey Baker Award in 1993 as a freshman.

Anatoly Karpov (b. May 23, 1951): Chess; Soviet world champion from 1975-85; regained International Chess Federation (FIDE) version of championship in 1993 when countryman Garry Kasparov was stripped of title after forming new Professional Chess Association; held FIDE title until 1999.

Garry Kasparov (b. Apr. 13, 1963): Chess; Azerbaijani who became youngest player (22 years, 210 days) ever to win world championship as Soviet in 1985; defeated countryman Anatoly Karpov for title; split with International Chess Federation (FIDE) to form Professional Chess Association (PCA) in 1993; stripped of FIDE title in '93 but successfully defended PCA title against Briton Nigel Short; beat IBM supercomputer "Deep Blue" 4 games to 2 in 1996 much-publicized match in New York; lost rematch to computer in 1997; finally lost world title to Vladimir Kramnik in 2000.

Mike Keenan (b. Oct. 21, 1949): Hockey; coach who finally led NY Rangers to Stanley Cup title in 1994 after 53 unsuccessful years; ranks 4th on list of all-time coaching wins through 2001-02.

Kipchoge (Kip) Keino (b. Jan. 17, 1940): Kenyan runner; policeman who beat USA's Jim Ryun to win 1,500m gold medal at 1968 Olympics; won again in steeplechase at 1972 Summer Games; his success spawned long line of distance champions from Kenya.

Johnny Kelley (b. Sept. 6, 1907): Distance runner; ran in his 61st and final Boston Marathon at age 84 in 1992, finishing in 5:58:36; won Boston twice (1935,45) and was 2nd seven times.

Jim Kelly (b. Feb. 14, 1960): Football QB; led Buffalo to four straight Super Bowls, and is only QB to lose four times; named to AFC Pro Bowl team 5 times; inducted into Pro Football Hall of Fame in 2002.

Leroy Kelly (b. May 20, 1942): Football; replaced Jim Brown in the Cleveland Browns backfield; in 1967, he led the NFL in rushing yards (1,205), rushing average (5.1 per carry) and rushing touchdowns (11).

Walter Kennedy (b. June 8, 1912, d. June 26, 1977): Basketball; 2nd NBA commissioner (1963-75), league doubled in size to 18 teams during his tenure.

Nancy Kerrigan (b. Oct. 13, 1969): Figure skating; 1993 U.S. women's champion and Olympic medalist in 1992 (bronze) and '94 (silver); victim of Jan. 6, 1994 assault at U.S. nationals in Detroit when Shane Stant clubbed her in right knee with metal baton after a practice session; conspiracy hatched by Jeff Gillooly, ex-husband of rival Tonya Harding; although unable to compete in nationals, she recovered and was granted berth on Olympic team; finished 2nd in Lillehammer to Oksana Baiul of Ukraine by a 5-4 judges' vote.

Billy Kidd (b. Apr. 13, 1943): Skiing; the first great American male Alpine skier; first American male to win an Olympic medal when he won a silver in the slalom and a bronze in the Alpine combined in 1964; competed respectably with the great Jean-Claude Killy; won the world Alpine combined event in 1970, which was the first world championship for an American male.

Harmon Killebrew (b. June 29, 1936): Baseball 3B-1B; led AL in HRs 6 times and RBI 3 times; MVP in 1969 with Minnesota; 573 career HRs ranks 7th.

Jean-Claude Killy (b. Aug. 30, 1943): French alpine skier; 2-time World Cup champion (1967-68); won 3 gold medals at 1968 Olympics in Grenoble; co-president of 1992 Winter Games in Albertville; president of coordination commission for 2006 Turin Games.

Ralph Kiner (b. Oct. 27, 1922): Baseball OF; led NL in home runs 7 straight years (1946-52) with Pittsburgh; 369 career HRs and 1,015 RBI in 10 seasons; long-time NY Mets announcer.

Betsy King (b. Aug. 13, 1955): Golfer; 2-time LPGA Player of Year (1984,89); 3-time winner of Dinah Shore (1987,90,97) and 2-time winner of U.S. Open (1989,90); 34 overall Tour wins; 1st player in LPGA history to break $5 million mark in career earnings; member of LPGA Hall of Fame.

Billie Jean King (b. Nov. 22, 1943): Tennis; women's rights pioneer; Wimbledon singles champ 6 times; U.S. champ 4 times; first woman athlete to earn $100,000 in one year (1971); beat 55-year-old Bobby Riggs 6-4,6-3,6-3, in "Battle of the Sexes" to win $100,000 at Astrodome in 1973; founded the Women's Sports Foundation in 1974; captained the U.S. Olympic team in 1996 and 2000.

Don King (b. Aug. 20, 1931): Boxing promoter; first major black promoter who has controlled heavyweight title off and on since 1978; first big promotion was Muhammad Ali's fight against George Foreman in 1974; former numbers operator who served 4 years for manslaughter (1967-70); acquitted of tax evasion and fraud in 1985; also promoted Larry Holmes, Mike Tyson, Evander Holyfield, Roberto Duran and Julio Cesar Chavez among others; also famous for his gravity-defying hairstyle and his catchphrase "Only in America!".

Karch Kiraly (b. Nov. 3, 1960): Volleyball; USA's preeminent volleyball player; led UCLA to three NCAA championships (1979,81,82); played on US national teams that won Olympic gold medals in 1984 and '88, world championships in '82 and '86; won the inaugural gold medal for Olympic beach volleyball with Kent Steffes in 1996.

Tom Kite (b. Dec. 9, 1949): Golfer; co-NCAA champion with Ben Crenshaw (1972); PGA Rookie of Year (1973); PGA Player of Year (1989); finally won 1st major with victory in 1992 U.S. Open at Pebble Beach; captain of 1997 US Ryder Cup team; 19 career PGA wins, played on the Senior tour since 2000, winning five times as of Sept. 1, 2002.

Gene Klein (b. Jan. 29, 1921, d. Mar. 12, 1990): Horseman; won 3 Eclipse awards as top owner (1985-87); his filly Winning Colors won 1988 Kentucky Derby; also owned San Diego Chargers football team (1966-84).

Bob Knight (b. Oct. 25, 1940): Basketball; coached Indiana to 3 NCAA titles (1976,81,87); 3-time Coach of Year (1975-76,89); coached 1984 U.S. Olympic team to gold medal; his volatile temper finally cost him when he was fired from Indiana in Sept. 2000 after a string of unacceptable incidents that included choking one of his players; returned to coaching with Texas Tech in 2001; 4th on all-time NCAA list with 787 wins in 36 years through 2002.

Phil Knight (b. Feb. 24, 1938): Founder and chairman of Nike, Inc., the multi-billion dollar shoe and fitness company founded in 1972 and based in Beaverton, Ore.; ; named "The Most Powerful Man in Sports" by *The Sporting News* in 1992.

Bill Koch (b. June 7, 1955): Cross country skiing; first highly accomplished American male in his sport; first American male to win a cross country Olympic medal when he took home a silver in the 30-kilometer race in 1976; in 1982, he was the first American male to win the Nordic World Cup.

Tommy Kono (b. June 27, 1930): weight lifter; won 2 olympic gold medals for U.S. (1952,56) and 1 silver (1960); all 3 medals were in different weight classes; set world records in four different classes; inducted into U.S. Olympic Hall of Fame in 1990.

Olga Korbut (b. May 16, 1955): Soviet gymnast; became the media darling of the 1972 Olympics in Munich by winning 3 gold medals (balance beam, floor exercise and team all-around); came back in the 1976 Olympics in Montreal as a part of the USSR's gold medal winning all-around team; first to perform back somersault on balance beam; was inducted into the International Women's Sports Hall of Fame in 1982, the first gymnast to be inducted.

Johann Olav Koss (b. Oct. 29, 1968): Norwegian speed skater; won three gold medals at 1994 Olympics in Lillehammer with world records in the 1,500m, 5,000m and 10,000m; also won 1,500m gold and 10,000m silver in 1992 Games; retired shortly after '94 Olympics.

Sandy Koufax (b. Dec. 30, 1935): Baseball LHP; led NL in strikeouts 4 times and ERA 5 straight years; won 3 Cy Young Awards (1963,65,66) with LA Dodgers; MVP in 1963; 2-time World Series MVP (1963, 65); threw perfect game against Chicago Cubs (1-0, Sept. 9, 1965) and had 3 other no-hitters in career.

Alvin Kraenzlein (b. Dec. 12, 1876, d. Jan. 6, 1928): Track & Field; won 4 individual gold medals in 1900 Olympics (60m, long jump and the 110m and 200m hurdles).

Jack Kramer (b. Aug. 1, 1921): Tennis; Wimbledon singles champ 1947; U.S. champ 1946-47; promoter and Open pioneer.

Lenny Krayzelburg (b. Sept. 28, 1975): Swimming; born in Ukraine but became an American citizen in 1995; won gold for U.S. in the 100m backstroke and 200m backstroke at the Sydney Games in 2000; was also part of U.S. team that set a world record in the 4x100m medley relay in Sydney; world record holder in the 50 and 100 meter backstrokes.

Ingrid Kristiansen (b. Mar. 21, 1956): Norwegian runner; 2-time Boston Marathon winner (1986,89); won New York City Marathon in 1989; former world record holder in the marathon.

Julie Krone (b. July 24, 1963): Jockey; only woman to ride winning horse in a Triple Crown race when she captured Belmont Stakes aboard Colonial Affair in 1993; retired in 1999 as all-time winningest female jockey with over 3,000 wins; in 2000 became the first female jockey elected to thoroughbred racing's hall of fame.

Mike Krzyzewski (b. Feb. 13, 1947): Basketball; has coached Duke to 9 Final Four appearances and 3 NCAA titles (1991-92,2001); has coached at Army (1976-80) and Duke (1981–); inducted into Hall of Fame in 2001.

Bowie Kuhn (b. Oct. 28, 1926): Baseball Commissioner; Elected commissioner on Feb. 4, 1969 and served until Sept. 30, 1984; kept Willie Mays and Mickey Mantle out of baseball for their employment with casinos; handed down one-year suspensions of several players for drug involvement; nixed Charlie Finley's sale of three players for $3.5 million; baseball enjoyed unprecedented attendance and television contracts during his reign.

Alan Kulwicki (b. Dec. 14, 1954, d. Apr. 1, 1993): Auto racer; 1992 NASCAR national champion; 1st college grad and Northerner to win title; NASCAR Rookie of Year in 1986; famous for driving car backwards on victory lap; killed at age 38 in plane crash near Bristol, Tenn.

Michelle Kwan (b. July 7, 1980): Figure Skater; 1998 Olympic silver medalist at Nagano and 2002 bronze medalist at Salt Lake City; 6-time U.S. Champion (1996,98-02) and 4-time World Champ (1996,98,00,01); set a U.S. record with 7 career overall medals at the World Championships (4 gold, 3 silver); was U.S. alternate to the Olympics in 1994 as a 13-year-old.

Marion Ladewig (b. Oct. 30, 1914): Bowler; named Woman Bowler of the Year 9 times (1950-54,57-59,63).

Guy Lafleur (b. Sept. 20, 1951): Hockey RW; led NHL in scoring 3 times (1976-78); 2-time MVP (1977-78), played for 5 Stanley Cup winners in Montreal; playoff MVP in 1977; returned to NHL as player in 1988 after election to Hall of Fame; retired again in 1991 with 560 goals and 1,353 points.

Napoleon (Nap) Lajoie (b. Sept. 5, 1874, d. Feb. 7, 1959): Baseball 2B; led AL in batting 3 times (1901,03-04); batted .422 in 1901; hit .339 for career with 3,251 hits.

Jack Lambert (b. July 8, 1952): Football LB; 6-time All-Pro (1975-76,79-82); led Pittsburgh to 4 Super Bowl titles.

Kenesaw Mountain Landis (b. Nov. 20, 1866, d. Nov. 25, 1944): U.S. District Court judge who became first baseball commissioner (1920-44); banned eight Chicago Black Sox from baseball for life.

Tom Landry (b. Sept. 11, 1924, d. Feb. 12, 2000): Football; All-Pro DB for NY Giants (1954); coached Dallas for 29 years (1960-88); won 2 Super Bowls (1972,78); 3rd on NFL all-time list with 270 wins.

Steve Largent (b. Sept. 28, 1954): Football WR; retired in 1989 after 14 years in Seattle with then NFL records in passes caught (819) and TD passes caught (100); elected to U.S. House of Representatives (R, Okla.) in 1994 and Pro Football Hall of Fame in '95; ran for governor of Oklahoma in 2002.

Don Larsen (b. Aug. 7, 1929): Baseball RHP; NY Yankees hurler who pitched the only perfect game in World Series history— a 2-0 victory over Brooklyn in Game 5 of the 1956 Series (Oct. 8); Series MVP that year; had career record of 81-91 in 14 seasons with 6 clubs.

Tommy Lasorda (b. Sept. 22, 1927): Baseball; managed LA Dodgers to 2 World Series titles (1981,88) in 4 appearances; retired as manager during 1996 season with 1,599 regular-season wins in 21 years; named interim GM of Dodgers in 1998; member of Baseball Hall of Fame; managed gold-medal winning U.S. Olympic team in 2000 at Sydney.

Larissa Latynina (b. Dec. 27, 1934): Soviet gymnast; won total of 18 medals, (9 gold) in 3 Olympics (1956,60,64).

Nikki Lauda (b. Feb. 22, 1949): Austrian auto racer; 3-time world Formula One champion (1975,77,84); 25 career wins from 1971-85.

Rod Laver (b. Aug. 9, 1938): Australian tennis player; only player to win Grand Slam twice (1962,69); Wimbledon champion 4 times; 1st to earn $1 million in prize money, won 11 Grand Slam singles titles.

Andrea Mead Lawrence (b. Apr. 19, 1932): Alpine skier; won 2 gold medals at 1952 Olympics.

Bobby Layne (b. Dec. 19, 1926, d. Dec. 1, 1986): Football QB; college star at Texas; master of 2-minute offense; led Detroit to 4 divisional titles and 3 NFL championships in 1950s.

Frank Leahy (b. Aug. 27, 1908, d. June 21, 1973): Football; coached Notre Dame to four national titles (1943,46-47,49); career record of 107-13-9 for a winning pct. of .864.

Jeanette Lee (b. July 9, 1971): Billiards; known as "The Black Widow"; won the 1994 Women's Professional Billiards Assoc. (WPBA) National Championship and vaulted to the No. 1 women's player in the world; voted 1994 WPBA Player of the Year and 1998 WPBA Sportsperson of the Year.

Sammy Lee (b. Aug. 1, 1920): Diving; won Olympic gold medals for U.S. in the platform diving event in 1948 and 1952, the first male diver in history to win 2 golds in that event; Sullivan Award winner (1953); former doctor in U.S. Army; trained Greg Louganis.

Brian Leetch (b. Mar. 3, 1968): Hockey D; NHL Rookie of Year in 1989; won Norris Trophy as top defenseman in 1992; Conn Smythe Trophy winner as playoffs' MVP in 1994 when he helped lead NY Rangers to 1st Stanley Cup title in 54 years.

Jacques Lemaire (b. Sept. 7, 1945): Hockey C; member of 8 Stanley Cup champions in Montreal; scored 366 goals in 12 seasons; coached Canadiens (1983-85) and NJ Devils (1993-98), won 1995 Stanley Cup with New Jersey; returned to coaching with the expansion Minnesota Wild in 2000.

Mario Lemieux (b. Oct. 5, 1965): Hockey C; 6-time NHL scoring leader (1988-89,92-93,96,97); Rookie of Year (1985); 4-time All-NHL 1st team (1988-89,93,96); 3-time regular season MVP (1988,93,96); 3-time All-Star Game MVP; led Pittsburgh to consecutive Stanley Cup titles (1991 and '92) and was playoff MVP both years; won 1993 scoring title despite missing 24 games to undergo radiation treatments for Hodgkin's disease; missed 62 games during 1993-94 season and entire 94-95 season due to back injuries and fatigue; returned in 1995-96 to lead NHL in scoring and win the MVP trophy; retired after 1996-97 season and inducted into the Hall of Fame; headed group of investors that bought bankrupt Penguins in 1999; made surprising return to the ice in 2001.

Greg LeMond (b. June 26, 1961): Cyclist; 3-time Tour de France winner (1986,89-90); only non-European to win the event until Lance Armstrong in 1999; retired in Dec. 1994 after being diagnosed with a rare muscular disease known as mitochondrial myopathy.

Ivan Lendl (b. Mar. 7, 1960): Czech tennis player; No. 1 player in world 4 times (1985-87,89); has won both French and U.S. Opens 3 times and Australian twice; owns 94 career tournament wins.

Suzanne Lenglen (b. May 24, 1899, d. July 4, 1938): French tennis player; dominated women's tennis from 1919-26; won both Wimbledon and French singles titles 6 times.

Sugar Ray Leonard (b. May 17, 1956): Boxer; light welterweight Olympic champ (1976); won world welterweight title 1979 and four more titles; retired after losing to Terry Norris on Feb. 9, 1991, with record of 36-2-1 and 25 KOs; misguided comeback in 1997 resulted in resounding defeat by Hector Camacho.

Walter (Buck) Leonard (b. Sept. 8, 1907, d. Nov. 27, 1997): Baseball 1B; won Negro League championship nine years in a row with the Homestead Grays; hit .391 in 1948 to lead the league; usually batted cleanup behind Josh Gibson; retired at the age of 48; member of the National Baseball Hall of Fame.

Lisa Leslie (b. Sept. 7, 1972): Basketball C; 2-time WNBA Finals MVP (2001-02) with the champion Los Angeles Sparks; 2001 regular season MVP; 3-time WNBA All-Star Game MVP (1999,2001-02); 2-time Olympic gold medalist (1996,2000); consensus National Player of the Year at USC (1994).

Marv Levy (b. Aug. 3, 1928): Football; coached Buffalo to four consecutive Super Bowls, but is one of two coaches who are 0-4 (Bud Grant is the other); won 50 games and two CFL Grey Cups with Montreal (1974,77).

Bill Lewis (b. Nov. 30, 1868, d. Jan. 1, 1949): Football; college star at Amherst College and then Harvard; first black player to be selected as an All-American (1892-93); also the first black admitted to the American Bar Association (1911); was U.S. Assistant Attorney General.

Carl Lewis (b. July 1, 1961): Track & Field; won 9 Olympic gold medals; 4 in 1984 (100m, 200m, 4x100m, LJ), 2 in '88 (100m, LJ), 2 in '92 (4x100m, LJ) and 1 in '96 (LJ); has record 8 World Championship titles and 9 medals in all; Sullivan Award winner (1981); two-time AP Athlete of the Year (1983-84).

Lennox Lewis (b. Sept. 2, 1965): British boxer; won 1988 Olympic super heavyweight gold medal for Canada; was awarded WBC heavyweight belt when Riddick Bowe tossed it in a London trash can in 1993; lost title in a 2nd round TKO loss to Oliver McCall; won rematch 3 years later when McCall suffered emotional breakdown in the ring; unified titles in his rematch with Evander Holyfield in Nov. 1999; lost belts in upset loss to Hasim Rahman in South Africa in April 2001 but regained them 7 months later; recorded 8th-round KO of Mike Tyson in June 2002.

Nancy Lieberman (b. July 1, 1958): Basketball; 3-time All-America and 2-time Player of Year (1979-80); led Old Dominion to consecutive AIAW titles in 1979 and '80; played in defunct WPBL and WABA and became 1st woman to play in men's pro league (USBL) in 1986; played in the inaugural season of the WNBA for the Phoenix Mercury and served as coach/GM of Detroit Shock (1998-2000).

Eric Lindros (b. Feb. 28, 1973): Hockey C; No. 1 pick in 1991 NHL draft by the Nordiques; sat out 1991-92 season rather than play in Quebec; traded to Philadelphia in 1992 for 6 players, 2 No. 1 picks and $15 million; elected Flyers captain at age 22; won Hart Trophy as league MVP in 1995; suffered series of concussions in 1999-00 but was traded to NY Rangers and inked big money deal with team in 2001.

Tara Lipinski (b. June 10, 1982): Figure Skater; won the 1998 women's figure skating gold medal at the Olympics in Nagano, becoming the youngest in history (15 yrs., 7 mos.) to do so; she and Michelle Kwan gave the U.S. its first 1-2 finish in that event since 1956; 1997 U.S. and World champion; turned pro in April 1998.

Sonny Liston (b. May 8, 1932, d. Dec. 30, 1970): Boxer; heavyweight champion (1962-64), who knocked out Floyd Patterson twice in the first round, then lost title to Muhammad Ali (then Cassius Clay) in 1964; pro record of 50-4 with 39 KOs.

Vince Lombardi (b. June 11, 1913, d. Sept. 3, 1970): Football; coached Green Bay to 5 NFL titles; won first 2 Super Bowls (1967-68); died as NFL's all-time winningest coach with percentage of .740 (105-35-6); Super Bowl trophy named in his honor.

Johnny Longden (b. Feb. 14, 1907): Jockey; first to win 6,000 races; rode Count Fleet to Triple Crown in 1943.

Jeannie Longo (b. Oct. 31, 1958): French cyclist; 12-time world cycling champion and 1996 olympic road race gold medallist.

Nancy Lopez (b. Jan. 6, 1957): Golfer; 4-time LPGA Player of the Year (1978-79,85,88); Rookie of Year (1977); 3-time winner of LPGA Championship; reached Hall of Fame by age 30 with 35 victories; 48 career wins.

Donna Lopiano (b. Sept. 11, 1946): Former basketball and softball star who was women's AD at Texas for 18 years before leaving to become executive director of Women's Sports Foundation in 1992.

Greg Louganis (b. Jan. 29, 1960): U.S. diver; widely considered the greatest diver in history; won platform and springboard gold medals at both 1984 and '88 Olympics; also won a silver medal at the 1976 Olympics at the age of 16; won five world championships and 47 U.S. National Diving titles; revealed on Feb. 22, 1995 that he has AIDS.

Joe Louis (b. May 13, 1914, d. Apr. 12, 1981): Boxer; world heavyweight champion from June 22, 1937 to Mar. 1, 1949; his reign of 11 years, 8 months longest in division history; successfully defended title 25 times; retired in 1949, but returned to lose title shot against successor Ezzard Charles in 1950 and then to Rocky Marciano in '51; pro record of 63-3 with 49 KOs.

Sid Luckman (b. Nov. 21, 1916, d. July 5, 1998): Football QB; 6-time All-Pro; led Chicago Bears to 4 NFL titles (1940-41,43,46); MVP in 1943.

Hank Luisetti (b. June 16, 1916): Basketball F; 3-time All-America at Stanford (1935-38); revolutionized game with one-handed shot.

Johnny Lujack (b. Jan. 4, 1925): Football QB; led Notre Dame to three national titles (1943,46-47); won Heisman Trophy in 1947.

Darrell Wayne Lukas (b. Sept. 2, 1935): Horse racing; 4-time Eclipse-winning trainer who saddled Horses of Year Lady's Secret in 1988 and Criminal Type in 1990; first trainer to earn over $100 million in purses; led nation in earnings 14 times since 1983; Grindstone's Kentucky Derby win in 1996 gave him six Triple Crown wins in a row; has won Preakness 5 times, Kentucky Derby 4 times and Belmont 4 times; his most recent Triple Crown victory came in the 2000 Belmont with Commendable; leads all Breeders' Cup trainers with 16 victories.

Gen. Douglas MacArthur (b. Jan. 26, 1880, d. Apr. 5, 1964): Controversial U.S. general of World War II and Korea; president of U.S. Olympic Committee (1927-28); college football devotee, National Football Foundation MacArthur Bowl named after him.

Connie Mack (b. Dec. 22, 1862, d. Feb. 8, 1956): Baseball owner; managed Philadelphia A's until he was 87 (1901-50); all-time major league wins leader with 3,755, including World Series; won 9 AL pennants and 5 World Series (1910-11,13,29-30); also finished last 17 times.

Andy MacPhail (b. Apr. 5, 1953): Baseball; Chicago Cubs president/CEO who was GM of 2 World Series champions in Minnesota (1987,91); won first title at age 34; son of Lee, grandson of Larry.

Larry MacPhail (b. Feb. 3, 1890, d. Oct. 1, 1975): Baseball executive and innovator; introduced major leagues to night games at Cincinnati (May 24, 1935); won pennant in Brooklyn (1941) and World Series with NY Yankees (1947); father of Lee.

Lee MacPhail (b. Oct. 25, 1917): Baseball; AL president (1974-83); president of owners' Player Relations Committee (1984-85); also GM of Baltimore (1959-65) and NY Yankees (1967-74); son of Larry and father of Andy.

Wendy Macpherson (b. Jan. 28, 1968): Bowling; voted Bowler of the Decade for the 1990s; Major titles include the 1986 BPAA U.S. Open, 1988 and 2000 WIBC Queens and 1999 Sam's Town Invitational; annual PWBA money winner 4 times (1996,97,99,2000).

John Madden (b. Apr. 10, 1936): Football and Radio-TV; won 112 games and a Super Bowl (1976 season) as coach of Oakland Raiders; has won 13 Emmy Awards since 1982 as NFL analyst; signed 4-year, $32 million deal with Fox in 1994— a richer contract than any NFL player at the time; joined Al Michaels in ABC's Monday Night Football booth in 2002 after 21 seasons alongside Pat Summerall.

Greg Maddux (b. Apr. 14, 1966): Baseball RHP; won unprecedented 4 straight NL Cy Young Awards with Cubs (1992) and Atlanta (1993-95); has led NL in ERA four times (1993-95,98); won 12th straight gold glove in 2001.

Larry Mahan (b. Nov. 21, 1943): Rodeo; 6-time All-Around world champion (1966-70,73).

Phil Mahre (b. May 10, 1957): Alpine skier; 3-time World Cup overall champ (1981-83); finished 1-2 with twin brother Steve in 1984 Olympic slalom.

Karl Malone (b. July 24, 1963): Basketball F; 11-time All-NBA 1st team (1989-99) with Utah; member of the 1992 and '96 Olympic Dream Teams; 2-time NBA MVP (1997,99); all-time NBA leader in free throws made (9,145), 2nd in career points (34,707) and 2nd in field goals made (12,737) entering the 2002-03 season; named one of the NBA's 50 greatest players.

Moses Malone (b. Mar. 23, 1955): Basketball C; signed with Utah of ABA at age 19; led NBA in rebounding 6 times; 4-time All-NBA 1st team; 3-time NBA MVP (1979,82-83); Finals MVP with Philadelphia in 1983; played in 21st pro season in 1994-95.

Nigel Mansell (b. Aug. 8, 1953): British auto racer; won 1992 Formula One driving championship with record 9 victories and 14 poles; quit Grand Prix circuit to race Indy cars in 1993; 1st rookie to win IndyCar title; 3rd driver to win IndyCar and F1 titles; returned to F1 after 1994 IndyCar season and won '94 Australian Grand Prix; left F1 again on May 23, 1995 with 31 wins and 32 poles in 15 years.

Mickey Mantle (b. Oct. 20, 1931, d. Aug. 13, 1995): Baseball OF; led AL in home runs 4 times; won Triple Crown in 1956; hit 52 HRs in 1956 and 54 in '61; 3-time MVP (1956-57,62); hit 536 career HRs; played in 12 World Series with NY Yankees and won 7 times; all-time Series leader in HRs (18), RBI (40), runs (42) and strikeouts (54).

Diego Maradona (b. Oct. 30, 1960): Soccer F; captain and MVP of 1986 World Cup champion Argentina; also led national team to 1990 World Cup final; consensus Player of Decade in 1980s; led Napoli to 2 Italian League titles (1987,90) and UEFA Cup (1989); tested positive for cocaine and suspended 15 months by FIFA in 1991; returned to World Cup as Argentine captain in 1994, but was kicked out of tournament after two games when doping test found 5 banned substances in his urine.

Pete Maravich (b. June 27, 1947, d. Jan. 5, 1988): Basketball; NCAA scoring leader 3 times at LSU (1968-70); averaged NCAA-record 44.2 points a game over career; Player of Year in 1970; NBA scoring champ in '77 with New Orleans.

Alice Marble (b. Sept. 28, 1913, d. Dec. 13, 1990): Tennis; 4-time U.S. champion (1936,38-40); won Wimbledon in 1939; swept U.S. singles, doubles and mixed doubles from 1938-40.

Gino Marchetti (b. Jan. 2, 1927): Football DE; 8-time NFL All-Pro (1957-64) with Baltimore Colts.

Rocky Marciano (b. Sept. 1, 1923, d. Aug. 31, 1969): Boxer; heavyweight champion (1952-56); retired undefeated; pro record of 49-0 with 43 KOs; killed in plane crash in Iowa.

Juan Marichal (b. Oct. 20, 1938): Baseball RHP; won 21 or more games 6 times for S.F. Giants from 1963-69; ended 16-year career at 243-142.

Dan Marino (b. Sept. 15, 1961): Football QB; 4-time leading passer in AFC (1983-84,86,89); set NFL single-season records for TD passes (48) and passing yards (5,084) in 1984; all-time leader in career TD passes, passing yards, attempts and completions.

Roger Maris (b. Sept. 10, 1934, d. Dec. 14, 1985): Baseball OF; broke Babe Ruth's season HR record with 61 in 1961 and held record until 1998; 2-time AL MVP (1960-61) with NY Yankees; 275 HRs in 12 years.

Jim Marshall (b. Dec. 30, 1937): Football; long-time Vikings DE and NFL ironman; played in an NFL-record 282 consecutive games (1960-1979); also famous for picking up a fumble and running 66 yards the wrong way into the opponent's (49ers) endzone.

Billy Martin (b. May 16, 1928, d. Dec. 25, 1989): Baseball; 5-time manager of NY Yankees; won 2 pennants and 1 World Series (1977); also managed Minnesota, Detroit, Texas and Oakland; played on 5 Yankee world champions in 1950s.

Casey Martin (b. June 2, 1972): Golfer; suffers from a birth defect in his right leg known as Klippel-Trenauney-Webber Syndrome; won lawsuit against the PGA Tour for the right to use a golf cart during competition under the Americans with Disabilities Act.

Pedro Martinez (b. Oct. 25, 1971): Baseball RHP; one of baseball's premier pitchers; won 1997 NL Cy Young award with Montreal; traded to Boston Red Sox in Nov. 1997; 2-time AL Cy Young Award winner with Boston (1999,2000).

Eddie Mathews (b. Oct. 13, 1931, d. Feb. 18, 2001): Baseball 3B; led NL in HRs twice (1953,59); hit 30 or more home runs 9 straight years; 512 career HRs.

Christy Mathewson (b. Aug. 12, 1880, d. Oct. 7, 1925): Baseball RHP; won 22 or more games 12 straight years (1903-14); 373 career wins; pitched 3 shutouts in 1905 World Series.

Bob Mathias (b. Nov. 17, 1930): Track & Field; youngest winner of decathlon with gold medal in 1948 Olympics at age 17; first to repeat as decathlon champ in 1952; Sullivan Award winner (1948); 4-term member of U.S. Congress (R, Calif.) from 1967-74.

Ollie Matson (b. May 1, 1930): Football HB; All-America at San Francisco (1951); bronze medal winner in 400m at 1952 Olympics; 4-time All-Pro for NFL Chicago Cardinals (1954-57); traded to LA Rams for 9 players in 1959; accounted for 12,884 all-purpose yards and scored 73 TDs in 14 seasons.

Don Mattingly (b. Apr. 20, 1961): Baseball 1B; American League MVP (1985); won AL batting title in 1984 (.343); led majors with 145 RBI in 1985; led AL with 238 hits (Yankee record) and 53 doubles in 1986; won 9 Gold Glove Awards at 1B (1985-89, 91-94); back injury shortened career.

Willie Mays (b. May 6, 1931): Baseball OF; nicknamed the "Say Hey Kid"; led NL in HRs and stolen bases 4 times each; 2-time MVP (1954,65) with NY-SF Giants; Hall of Famer who played in 24 All-Star Games, earning MVP honors twice (1963,68); 12-time Gold Glove winner; 660 HRs and 3,283 hits in career.

Bill Mazeroski (b. Sept. 5, 1936): Baseball 2B; career .260 hitter who won the 1960 World Series for Pittsburgh with a lead-off HR in the bottom of the 9th inning of Game 7; the pitcher was Ralph Terry of the NY Yankees, the count was 1-0 and the score was tied 9-9; also a sure-fielder, Maz won 8 Gold Gloves in 17 seasons.

Bob McAdoo (b. Sept. 25, 1951): Basketball F/C; 1972 Sporting News First Team All-American; NBA Rookie of the Year (1973); NBA MVP (1975); All-NBA First Team (1975); Led NBA in scoring three consecutive years (1974-76); 5-time All-Star (1974-78); two championships with LA Lakers (1982,85).

Joe McCarthy (b. Apr. 21, 1887, d. Jan. 13, 1978): Baseball; first manager to win pennants in both leagues (Chicago Cubs in 1929 and NY Yankees in 1932); greatest success came with Yankees when he won seven pennants and six World Series championships from 1936 to 1943; first manager to win four World Series in a row (1936-39); finished his career with the Boston Red Sox (1948-'50); lifetime record of 2125-1333; member of Baseball Hall of Fame.

Pat McCormick (b. May 12, 1930): U.S. diver; won women's platform and springboard gold medals in both 1952 and '56 Olympics.

Willie McCovey (b. Jan. 10, 1938): Baseball 1B; led NL in HRs 3 times and RBI twice; MVP in 1969 with SF; 521 career HRs; indicted for tax evasion in July 1995, pled guilty; "McCovey Cove," the bay outside the rightfield fence at San Francisco's Pacific Bell Park is named for him.

John McEnroe (b. Feb. 16, 1959): Tennis; No.1 player in the world 4 times (1981-84); 4-time U.S. Open champ (1979-81,84); 3-time Wimbledon champ (1981,83-84); played on 5 Davis Cup winners (1978,79,81,82,92); won NCAA singles title (1978); finished career with 77 singles championships, 77 more in men's doubles (including 9 Grand Slam titles), and U.S. Davis Cup records for years played (13) and singles matches won (41).

John McGraw (b. Apr. 7, 1873, d. Feb. 25, 1934): Baseball; managed NY Giants to 9 NL pennants between 1905-24; won 3 World Series (1905,21-22); 2nd on all-time career list with 2,866 wins in 33 seasons (2,840 regular season and 26 World Series).

Frank McGuire (b. Nov. 8, 1916, d. Oct. 11, 1994): Basketball; winner of 731 games as high school, college and pro coach; won at least 100 games at 3 colleges— St. John's (103), North Carolina (164) and South Carolina (283); won 550 games in 30 college seasons; 1957 UNC team went 32-0 and beat Kansas 54-53 in triple OT to win NCAA title; coached NBA Philadelphia Warriors to 49-31 record in 1961-62 season, but refused to move with team to San Francisco.

Mark McGwire (b. Oct. 1, 1963): Baseball 1B; Sporting News college player of the year (1984); Member of 1984 U.S. Olympic baseball team; won AL Rookie of the Year and hit rookie-record 49 HRs in 1987; shattered Roger Maris' season home run record (61) in 1998 with St. Louis (70); followed that magical season with 65 HRs and 147 RBI in 1999.

Jim McKay (b. Sept. 24, 1921): Radio-TV; host and commentator of ABC's Olympic coverage and "Wide World of Sports" show since 1961; 12-time Emmy winner; also given Peabody Award in 1988 and Life Achievement Emmy in 1990; became part owner of Baltimore Orioles in 1993.

Tamara McKinney (b. Oct. 16, 1962): Skiing; first American woman to win overall Alpine World Cup championship (1983); won World Cup slalom (1984) and giant slalom titles twice (1981,83).

Denny McLain (b. Mar. 29, 1944): Baseball RHP; last pitcher to win 30 games (1968); 2-time Cy Young winner (1968-69) with Detroit; convicted of racketeering, extortion and drug possession in 1985, served 29 months of 25-year jail term, sentence overturned when court ruled he had not received a fair trial; he has faced subsequent legal troubles.

Rick Mears (b. Dec. 3, 1951): Auto racer; 3-time CART national champ (1979,81-82); 4-time winner of Indy 500 (1979,84,88,91) and only driver to win 6 Indy 500 poles; Indy 500 Rookie of Year (1978); retired after 1992 season with 29 CART wins and 40 poles.

Mark Messier (b. Jan. 18, 1961): Hockey C; 2-time NHL MVP with Edmonton (1990) and NY Rangers (1992); captain of 1994 Rangers team that won 1st Stanley Cup since 1940; ranks 2nd in all-time playoff points, goals and assists; signed free agent contract with Vancouver Canucks in 1997 but returned to the Rangers in 2000; 3rd on all-time regular season points list entering 2002-03 season.

Anne Meyers (b. Mar. 26, 1955): Basketball G; In 1974, became first high school student to play for U.S. national team; 4-time All-American at UCLA (1976-79); member of 1976 U.S. Olympic team; Broderick Award and Cup winner (1978); Signed $50,000 no cut contract with NBA's Indiana Pacers (1980); married Dodger great Don Drysdale.

Debbie Meyer (b. Aug. 14, 1952): Swimmer; 1st swimmer to win 3 individual gold medals at one Olympics (1968).

George Mikan (b. June 18, 1924): Basketball C; 3-time All-America (1944-46); led DePaul to NIT title (1945); led Minneapolis Lakers to 5 NBA titles in 6 years (1949-54); first commissioner of ABA (1967-69).

Stan Mikita (b. May 20, 1940): Hockey C; led NHL in scoring 4 times; won both MVP and Lady Byng awards in 1967 and '68 with Chicago.

Cheryl Miller (b. Jan. 3, 1964): Basketball; 3-time College Player of Year (1984-86); led USC to NCAA title and U.S. to Olympic gold medal in 1984; coached USC to 44-14 record in 2 seasons before quitting to join Turner Sports as NBA reporter; coached WNBA's Phoenix Mercury for 4 seasons; sister of NBA star Reggie Miller.

Del Miller (b. July 5, 1913, d. Aug. 19, 1996): Harness racing; driver, trainer, owner, breeder, seller and track owner; drove to 2,441 wins from 1929-90.

Marvin Miller (b. Apr. 14, 1917): Baseball labor leader; executive director of Players' Assn. from 1966-82; increased average salary from $19,000 to over $240,000; led 13-day strike in 1972 and 50-day walk-out in '81.

Shannon Miller (b. Mar. 10, 1977): Gymnast; won 5 medals in 1992 Olympics and 2 golds in '96 Games; All-Around women's world champion in 1993 and '94.

Billy Mills (b. June 30, 1938): Track & Field; Native American who was upset winner of 10,000m gold medal at 1964 Olympics.

Bora Milutinovic (b. Sept. 7, 1944): Soccer; Serbian who coached United States national team from 1991-95; led Mexico (1986), Costa Rica ('90), USA ('94) and Nigeria ('98) into the 2nd round of the World Cup; coached China to its 1st World Cup in 2002 but went 0-3 in the 1st round.

Tommy Moe (b. Feb. 17, 1970): Alpine skier; won Downhill gold and Super-G silver at 1994 Winter Olympics; 1st U.S. man to win 2 Olympic alpine medals in one year.

Paul Molitor (b. Aug. 22, 1956): Baseball DH-1B; All-America SS at Minnesota in 1976; spent 15 years with Milwaukee, then 3 each with Toronto and Minnesota; led Blue Jays to 2nd straight World Series title as MVP (1993); hit .418 in 2 Series appearances (1982,93); holds World Series record with five hits in one game.

Joe Montana (b. June 11, 1956): Football QB; led Notre Dame to national title in 1977; led San Francisco to 4 Super Bowl titles in 1980s; only 3-time Super Bowl MVP; 2-time NFL MVP (1989-90); led NFL in passing 5 times; traded to Kansas City in 1993; ranks 2nd all-time in passing efficiency (92.3), 7th in TD passes (273) and 6th in yards passing (40,551); inducted into Pro Football Hall of Fame in 2000.

Helen Wills Moody (b. Oct. 6, 1905, d. Jan. 1, 1998): Tennis; won 8 Wimbledon singles titles, 7 U.S. and 4 French from 1923-38.

Warren Moon (b. Nov. 18, 1956): Football QB; MVP of 1978 Rose Bowl with Washington; MVP of CFL with Edmonton in 1983; led Eskimos to 5 consecutive Grey Cup titles (1978-82) and was playoff MVP twice (1980,82); entered NFL in 1984 and played for four different teams; picked for 9 Pro Bowls including a QB-record 8 straight (1988-95).

Archie Moore (b. Dec. 13, 1913, d. Dec. 9, 1998): Boxer; world light-heavyweight champion (1952-60); pro record 199-26-8 with a record 145 KOs.

Noureddine Morceli (b. Feb. 28, 1970): Algerian runner; 3-time world champion at 1,500 meters (1991,93,95) and 1996 Olympic gold medal winner; former holder of world records in several middle distance events.

Howie Morenz (b. June 21, 1902, d. Mar. 8, 1937): Hockey C; 3-time NHL MVP (1928,31,32); led Montreal Canadiens to 3 Stanley Cups; voted Outstanding Player of the Half-Century in 1950.

Joe Morgan (b. Sept. 19, 1943): Baseball 2B; led NL in walks 4 times; regular-season MVP both years he led Cincinnati to World Series titles (1975-76); 5th behind Rickey Henderson, Babe Ruth, Ted Williams and Barry Bonds in career walks with 1,865.

Bobby Morrow (b. Oct. 15, 1935): Track & Field; won 3 gold medals at 1956 Olympics (100m, 200m and 4x400m relay).

Willie Mosconi (b. June 27, 1913, d. Sept. 12, 1993): Pocket Billiards; 14-time world champion from 1941-57.

Annemarie Moser-Pröll (b. Mar. 27, 1953): Austrian alpine skier; won World Cup overall title 6 times (1971-75,79); all-time women's World Cup leader in career wins with 61; won Downhill in 1980 Olympics.

Edwin Moses (b. Aug. 31, 1955): Track & Field; won 400m hurdles at 1976 and '84 Olympics, bronze medal in '88; also winner of 122 consecutive races from 1977-87.

Stirling Moss (b. Sept. 17, 1929): Auto racer; won 194 of 466 career races and 16 Formula One events, but was never world champion.

Marion Motley (b. June 5, 1920, d. June 27, 1999): Football FB; all-time leading AAFC rusher; rushed for over 4,700 yards and 31 TDs for Cleveland Browns (1946-53).

Shirley Muldowney (b. June 19, 1940): Drag Racer; "Cha Cha"; women's racing pioneer; 3-time Winston drag racing Top Fuel champion (1977,80,82); recorded 18 career NHRA National Event Victories.

Anthony Munoz (b. Aug. 19, 1958): Football OT; drafted 3rd overall in 1980 out of USC; 11-time All Pro with Cincinnati; member of NFL 75th Anniv. All-Time Team; elected to Hall of Fame in 1998.

Calvin Murphy (b. May 9, 1948): Basketball G; NBA All-Rookie team (1971); holds NBA single season free throw percentage (.958); third all-time career free throw pct. (.892); elected to Basketball Hall of Fame in 1992; though only 5'9'' and 165 pounds, he is regarded as one of the best guards ever.

Dale Murphy (b. Mar. 12, 1956): Baseball OF; led NL in RBI 3 times and HRs twice; 2-time MVP (1982-83) with Atlanta; also played with Philadelphia and Colorado; retired in 1993 with 398 HRs.

Jack Murphy (b. Feb. 5, 1923, d. Sept. 24, 1980): Sports editor and columnist of *The San Diego Union* from 1951-80; instrumental in bringing AFL Chargers south from LA in 1961, landing Padres as NL expansion team in '69; and lobbying for 54,000-seat San Diego stadium that would later bear his name.

Eddie Murray (b. Feb. 24, 1956): Baseball 1B-DH; AL Rookie of Year in 1977; became 20th player in history, but only 2nd switch hitter (after Pete Rose) to get 3,000 hits; one of only 3 men (Aaron and Mays) with 500 HRs and 3,000 hits.

Jim Murray (b. Dec. 29, 1919, d. Aug. 16, 1998): Sports columnist for *LA Times* 1961-98; 14-time Sportswriter of the Year; won Pulitzer Prize for commentary in 1990.

Ty Murray (b. Oct. 11, 1969): Rodeo cowboy; 7-time All-Around world champion (1989-94,98); Rookie of Year in 1988; youngest (age 20) to win All-Around title; set single season earnings mark with $297,896 in 1993; career hampered by injury.

Stan Musial (b. Nov. 21, 1920): Baseball OF-1B; led NL in batting 7 times and RBI 2 times; 3-time MVP (1943,46,48) with St. Louis; played in 24 All-Star Games; had 3,630 career hits (4th all-time) and .331 average.

John Naber (b. Jan. 20, 1956): Swimmer; won 4 gold medals and a silver in 1976 Olympics.

Bronko Nagurski (b. Nov. 3, 1908, d. Jan. 7, 1990): Football FB-T; All-America at Minnesota (1929); All-Pro with Chicago Bears (1932-34); charter member of college and pro Halls of Fame.

James Naismith (b. Nov. 6, 1861, d. Nov. 28, 1939): Canadian physical education instructor who invented basketball in 1891 at the YMCA Training School (now Springfield College) in Springfield, Mass.

Joe Namath (b. May 31, 1943): Football QB; signed for unheard-of $400,000 as rookie with AFL's NY Jets in 1965; 2-time All-AFL (1968-69) and All-NFL (1972); led Jets to Super Bowl upset as MVP in '69 after making brash prediction of victory.

Ilie Nastase (b. July 19, 1946): Romanian tennis player; No.1 in the world twice (1972-73); won U.S. (1972) and French (1973) Opens; has since entered Romanian politics.

Martina Navratilova (b. Oct. 18, 1956): Tennis player; No.1 player in the world 7 times (1978-79,82-86); won her record 9th Wimbledon singles title in 1990; also won 4 U.S. Opens, 3 Australian and 2 French; in all, won 18 Grand Slam singles titles and 37 Grand Slam doubles titles; all-time leader among men and women in singles titles (167); 2nd all-time behind Graf on women's career money list ($20.5 million); still active in very limited competition; inducted into International Tennis Hall of Fame in 2000.

Cosmas Ndeti (b. Nov. 24, 1971): Kenyan distance runner; winner of three consecutive Boston Marathons (1993-95); set what is still the course record of 2:07:15 in 1994.

Earle (Greasy) Neale (b. Nov. 5, 1891, d. Nov. 2, 1973): Baseball and Football; hit .357 for Cincinnati in 1919 World Series; also played with pre-NFL Canton Bulldogs; later coached Philadelphia Eagles to 2 NFL titles (1948-49).

Primo Nebiolo (b. July 14, 1923, d. Nov. 7, 1999): Italian president of International Amateur Athletic Federation (IAAF) since 1981; also an at-large member of International Olympic Committee; regarded as dictatorial, but credited with elevating track & field to world class financial status.

Byron Nelson (b. Feb. 4, 1912): Golfer; 2-time winner of both Masters (1937,42) and PGA (1940,45); also U.S. Open champion in 1939; won 19 tournaments in 1945, including 11 in a row; also set all-time PGA stroke average with 68.33 strokes per round over 120 rounds in '45.

Lindsey Nelson (b. May 25, 1919, d. June 10, 1995): Radio-TV; all-purpose play-by-play broadcaster for CBS, NBC and others; 4-time Sportscaster of the Year (1959-62); voice of Cotton Bowl for 25 years and NY Mets from 1962-78; given Life Achievement Emmy Award in 1991.

Ernie Nevers (b. July 11, 1903, d. May 3, 1976): Football FB; earned 11 letters in four sports at Stanford; played pro football, baseball and basketball; scored 40 points for Chicago Cardinals in one NFL game (1929).

Paula Newby-Fraser (b. June 2, 1962): Zimbabwean triathlete; 8-time winner of Ironman Triathlon in Hawaii; established women's record of 8:55:28 in 1992.

John Newcombe (b. May 23, 1944): Australian tennis player; No.1 player in world 3 times (1967,70-71); won Wimbledon 3 times and U.S. and Australian championships twice each.

Pete Newell (b. Aug. 31, 1915): Basketball; coached at Univ. of San Francisco, Michigan St. and the Univ. of California; first coach to win NIT (San Francisco-1949), NCAA (California-1959) and Olympic gold medal (1960); later served as the general manager of the San Diego Rockets and LA Lakers in the NBA; member of Basketball Hall of Fame.

Jack Nicklaus (b. Jan. 21, 1940): Golfer; all-time leader in major tournament wins with 20— including 6 Masters, 5 PGAs, 4 U.S. Opens and 3 British Opens; oldest player to win Masters (46 in 1986); PGA Player of Year 5 times (1967,72-73,75-76); named Golfer of the Century by PGA in 1988; 6-time Ryder Cup player and 2-time captain (1983,87); won NCAA title (1961) and 2 U.S. Amateurs (1959,61); 70 PGA Tour wins (2nd to Sam Snead's 81); fourth win in Tradition in 1996 gave him 8 majors on Senior PGA Tour; nick-named "the Golden Bear."

Chuck Noll (b. Jan. 5, 1932): Football; coached Pittsburgh to 4 Super Bowl titles (1975-76,79-80); retired after 1991 season ranked 5th on all-time list with 209 wins (including playoffs) in 23 years.

Greg Norman (b. Feb. 10, 1955): Australian golfer; 73 tournament wins worldwide including 18 PGA Tour victories; 2-time British Open winner (1986,93); lost Masters by a stroke in both 1986 (to Jack Nicklaus) and '87 (to Larry Mize in sudden death); 1995 PGA Tour Player of the Year.

James D. Norris (b. Nov. 6, 1906, d. Feb. 25, 1966): Boxing promoter and NHL owner; president of International Boxing Club from 1949 until U.S. Supreme Court ordered its break-up (for anti-trust violations) in 1958; only NHL owner to win Stanley Cups in two cities: Detroit (1936-37,43) and Chicago (1961).

Paavo Nurmi (b. June 13, 1897, d. Oct. 2, 1973): Finnish runner; won 9 gold medals (6 individual) in 1920, '24 and '28 Olympics; from 1921-31 broke 23 world outdoor records in events ranging from 1,500 to 20,000 meters.

Dan O'Brien (b. July 18, 1966): Track & Field; Olympic decathlon gold medalist (1996); set former world record in decathlon (8,891 pts) in 1992, after shockingly failing to qualify for event at U.S. Olympic Trials; three-time gold medalist at World Championships (1991,93,95).

Larry O'Brien (b. July 7, 1917, d. Sept. 27, 1990): Basketball; former U.S. Postmaster General and 3rd NBA commissioner (1975-84); league absorbed 4 ABA teams and created salary cap during his term in office.

Parry O'Brien (b. Jan. 28, 1932): Track & Field; in 4 consecutive Olympics, won two gold medals, a silver and placed 4th in the shot put (1952-64).

Al Oerter (b. Sept. 19, 1936): Track & Field; his 4 discus gold medals in consecutive Olympics from 1956-68 is an unmatched Olympic record.

Sadaharu Oh (b. May 20, 1940): Baseball 1B; led Japan League in HRs 15 times; 9-time MVP for Tokyo Giants; hit 868 HRs in 22 years.

Hakeem Olajuwon (b. Jan. 21, 1963): Basketball C; Nigerian native who was All-America in 1984 and Final Four MOP in 1983 for Houston; overall 1st pick by Houston Rockets in 1984 NBA draft; led Rockets to back-to-back NBA titles (1994-95); regular season MVP (1994) and 2-time Finals MVP ('94-95); 6-time All-NBA 1st team (1987-89,93-95); all-time NBA blocks leader; traded to Toronto after 17 seasons with Houston.

Jose Maria Olazabal (b. Feb. 5, 1966): Spanish golfer; has 26 worldwide victories including 2 Masters (1994,99); played on 6 European Ryder Cup teams.

Barney Oldfield (b. Jan. 29, 1878, d. Oct. 4, 1946): Auto racing pioneer; drove cars built by Henry Ford; first man to drive car a mile per minute (1903).

Walter O'Malley (b. Oct. 9, 1903, d. Aug. 9, 1979): Baseball owner; moved Brooklyn Dodgers to Los Angeles after 1957 season; won 4 World Series (1955,59,63,65).

Shaquille O'Neal (b. Mar. 6, 1972): Basketball C; 2-time All-America at LSU (1991-92); overall 1st pick (as a junior) by Orlando in 1992 NBA draft; Rookie of Year in 1993; 2-time NBA scoring leader (1995,2000); regular season MVP (2000) and 3-time NBA Finals MVP (2000,01,02); named one of the NBA's 50 Greatest Players; has starred in several films and released several rap albums.

Bobby Orr (b. Mar. 20, 1948): Hockey D; league's only 8-time Norris Trophy winner as best defenseman (1968-75); credited with revolutionizing the position; 3-time Hart Trophy winner as NHL regular season MVP (1970-72); led NHL in scoring twice and assists 5 times; All-NHL 1st team 8 times; playoff MVP twice (1970,72) with Boston.

Tom Osborne (b. Feb. 23, 1937): Football; Nebraska head coach from 1973-97; career record of 255-49-3; his win pct. of .836 is fifth all-time; won national championships in 1994 and '95 and shared national title with Michigan in '97; elected to U.S. Congress (R., Neb.) in 2000.

Mel Ott (b. Mar. 2, 1909, d. Nov. 21, 1958): Baseball OF; joined NY Giants at age 16; led NL in HRs 6 times; had 511 HRs and 1,860 RBI in 22 years.

Kristin Otto (b. Feb. 7, 1966): East German swimmer; 1st woman to win 6 gold medals (4 individual) at one Olympics (1988).

Francis Ouimet (b. May 8, 1893, d. Sept. 3, 1967): Golfer; won 1913 U.S. Open as 20-year-old amateur playing on Brookline, Mass. course where he used to caddie; won U.S. Amateur twice; 8-time Walker Cup player.

Steve Owen (b. Apr. 21, 1898, d. May 17, 1964): Football; All-Pro guard (1927); coached NY Giants for 23 years (1931-53); won 153 career games and 2 NFL titles (1934,38).

Jesse Owens (b. Sept. 12, 1913, d. Mar. 31, 1980): Track & Field; broke 4 world records in one afternoon at Big Ten Championships (May 25, 1935); a year later, embarrassed Hitler by winning 4 golds (100m, 200m, 4x100m relay and long jump) at 1936 Olympics in Berlin.

Alan Page (b. Aug. 7, 1945): Football DE; All-America at Notre Dame in 1966 and member of two national championship teams; 6-time NFL All-Pro and 1971 Player of Year with Minnesota Vikings; later a lawyer who was elected to Minnesota Supreme Court in 1992.

Satchel Paige (b. July 7, 1906, d. June 6, 1982): Baseball RHP; pitched 55 career no-hitters over 20 seasons in Negro Leagues, entered major leagues with Cleveland in 1948 at age 42; had 28-31 record in 5 years; returned to AL at age 59 to start 1 game for Kansas City in 1965 (went 3 innings, gave up a hit and got a strikeout).

Se Ri Pak (b. Sept. 28, 1977): Golfer; won two Majors as an LPGA rookie in 1998 (LPGA Championship and U.S. Open; youngest player to win the U.S. Open (20); won British Open in 2001 and added her 2nd LPGA Championship in 2002.

Arnold Palmer (b. Sept. 10, 1929): Golfer; winner of 4 Masters, 2 British Opens and a U.S. Open; 2-time PGA Player of Year (1960,62); 1st player to earn over $1 million in career (1968); annual PGA Tour money leader award named after him; 60 wins on PGA Tour and 10 more on Senior Tour; made 48 consecutive Masters starts.

Jim Palmer (b. Oct. 15, 1945): Baseball RHP; 3-time Cy Young Award winner (1973,75-76); won 20 or more games 8 times with Baltimore; 1991 comeback attempt at age 45 scrubbed in spring training.

Bill Parcells (b. Aug. 22, 1941): Football; coached NY Giants to 2 Super Bowl titles (1987,91); retired after 1990 season then returned in '93 as coach of New England; led Patriots to Super Bowl loss against Green Bay in 1997; left Patriots in 1997 to coach the New York Jets; coached three seasons with the Jets (1997-99), turning them from 1-15 doormat to AFC East champ in two years; retired from coaching again in 2000 and became director of football operations with the club for one year; re-entered broadcasting in 2002.

Jack Pardee (b. Apr. 19, 1936): Football; All-America linebacker at Texas A&M; 2-time All-Pro with LA Rams (1963) and Washington (1971); 2-time NFL Coach of Year (1976,79) and winner of 87 games in 11 seasons; only man hired as head coach in NFL, WFL, USFL and CFL; also coached at University of Houston.

Bernie Parent (b. Apr. 3, 1945): Hockey G; led Philadelphia Flyers to 2 Stanley Cups as playoff MVP (1974,75); 2-time Vezina Trophy winner; posted 55 career shutouts and 2.55 GAA in 13 seasons.

Joe Paterno (b. Dec. 21, 1926): Football; has coached Penn St. to 2 national titles (1982,86) and 20-9-1 bowl record in 35 years; also had three unbeaten teams that didn't finish No. 1; 4-time Coach of Year (1968,78,82,86); entered 2002 season #1 on all-time wins list after passing Bear Bryant in 2001.

Craig Patrick (b. May 20, 1946): Hockey; 3rd generation Patrick to have name inscribed on Stanley Cup; GM of 2-time Cup champion Pittsburgh Penguins (1991-92); also captain of 1969 NCAA champion at Denver; assistant coach-GM of 1980 gold medal-winning U.S. Olympic team; grandson of Lester.

Lester Patrick (b. Dec. 30, 1883, d. June 1, 1960): Hockey; pro hockey pioneer as player, coach and general manager for 43 years; led NY Rangers to Stanley Cups as coach (1928,33) and GM (1940); grandfather of Craig.

Floyd Patterson (b. Jan. 4, 1935): Boxer; Olympic middleweight champ in 1952; world heavyweight champion (1956-59,60-62); 1st to regain heavyweight crown; fought Ingemar Johansson 3 times in 22 months from 1959-61 and won last two; pro record 55-8-1 with 40 KOs.

Walter Payton (b. July 25, 1954, d. Nov. 1, 1999): Football RB; nicknamed "Sweetness"; NFL's all-time leading rusher with 16,726 yards (entering 2002 season); scored 125 career TDs; All-Pro 7 times with Chicago; led NFC in rushing 5 times (1976-80); league MVP in 1977 (AP & PFWA) and 1985 (Bell); led Bears to Super Bowl title in Jan. 1986.

Calvin Peete (b. July 18, 1943): Golf; began playing golf at the age of 23; earned over $2 million in career earnings; selected to the U.S. Ryder Cup teams in 1983 and 1985.

Pelé (b. Oct. 23, 1940): Brazilian soccer F; given name— Edson Arantes do Nascimento; led Brazil to 3 World Cup titles (1958,62,70); came to U.S. in 1975 to play for NY Cosmos in NASL; scored 1,281 goals in 22 years including 12 goals in the World Cup; served as Brazil's minister of sport (1994-98).

Roger Penske (b. Feb. 20, 1937): Auto racing; national sports car driving champion (1964); established racing team in 1961; co-founder of Championship Auto Racing Teams (CART); Penske Racing has won 12 Indianapolis 500s and 9 CART points titles; announced surprising move to IRL for 2002 season.

Willie Pep (b. Sept. 19, 1922): Boxer; 2-time world featherweight champion (1942-48,49-50); pro record 230-11-1 with 65 KOs.

Marie-Jose Perec (b. 1968): Track & Field; French sprinter who became 2nd woman to win the 200m and 400m events in the same Olympics (1996); her time in the 400 (48.25) set an Olympic record; also won the 400 in 1992 Games.

Fred Perry (b. May 18, 1909, d. Feb. 2, 1995): British tennis player; 3-time Wimbledon champ (1934-36); first player to win all four Grand Slam singles titles, though not in same year; last native to win All-England men's title.

Gaylord Perry (b. Sept. 15, 1938): Baseball RHP; was only pitcher to win a Cy Young Award in both leagues until 1999 when Randy Johnson and Pedro Martinez joined him; retired in 1983 with 314-265 record and 3,534 strikeouts over 22 years and with 8 teams; brother Jim won 215 games for family total of 529.

Bob Pettit (b. Dec. 12, 1932): Basketball F; All-NBA 1st team 10 times (1955-64); 2-time MVP (1956,59) with St. Louis Hawks; first player to score 20,000 points.

Richard Petty (b. July 2, 1937): Auto racer; 7-time winner of Daytona 500; 7-time NASCAR national champ (1964,67,71-72,74-75,79); first stock car driver to win $1 million in career; all-time NASCAR leader in races won (200), poles (127) and wins in a single season (27 in 1967); retired after 1992 season; son of Lee (55 career wins) and father of Kyle (8 career wins).

Laffit Pincay Jr. (b. Dec. 29, 1946): Jockey; 5-time Eclipse Award winner (1971,73-74,79,85); winner of 3 Belmonts and 1 Kentucky Derby (aboard Swale in 1984); with his 8834th win in Dec., 1999 he passed Bill Shoemaker to become thoroughbred racing's all-time winningest jockey.

Scottie Pippen (b. Sept. 25, 1965): Basketball F; started on six NBA champions with Chicago (1991-93, 96-98); 3-time all-NBA first team (1994-96). Voted one of NBA's 50 Greatest Players.

Uta Pippig (b. Sept. 7, 1965): German marathoner; won three-straight Boston Marathons (1994,95,96); set a new course record in '94 (since broken in 2002).

Nelson Piquet (b. Aug. 17, 1952): Brazilian auto racer; 3-time Formula One world champion (1981,83,87); left circuit in 1991 with 23 career wins.

Rick Pitino (b. Sept. 18, 1952): Basketball; won 1996 NCAA title in his 7th year at Kentucky; previously coached the New York Knicks in the NBA (96-85 overall), Providence College (42-23) and Boston University (46-24); in 1997, became coach and president of Boston Celtics; resigned from Celtics in 2001 and returned to college coaching with Louisville.

Jacques Plante (b. Jan. 17, 1929, d. Feb. 27, 1986): Hockey G; led Montreal to 6 Stanley Cups (1953,56-60); won 7 Vezina Trophies; MVP in 1962; first goalie to regularly wear a mask; posted 82 shutouts with 2.38 GAA.

Gary Player (b. Nov. 1, 1936): South African golfer; 3-time winner of Masters and British Open; only player in 20th century to win British Open in three different decades (1959,68,74); one of only five players to win all four Grand Slam titles (others are Hogan, Nicklaus, Sarazen and Woods); has also won 2 PGAs, a U.S. Open and 2 U.S. Senior Opens; owner of 21 wins on PGA Tour and 19 more on Senior Tour.

Jim Plunkett (b. Dec. 5, 1947): Football QB; Heisman Trophy winner (Stanford) in 1970; AFL Rookie of the Year in 1971; led Oakland-LA Raiders to Super Bowl wins in 1981 and '84; MVP in '81.

Maurice Podoloff (b. Aug. 18, 1890, d. Nov. 24, 1985): Basketball; engineered merger of Basketball Assn. of America and National Basketball League into NBA in 1949; NBA commissioner (1949-63); league MVP trophy named after him.

Fritz Pollard (b. Jan. 27, 1894, d. May 11, 1986): Football; 1st black All-America RB (1916 at Brown); 1st black to play in Rose Bowl; 7-year NFL pro (1920-26); 1st black NFL coach, at Milwaukee and Hammond, Ind.

Sam Pollock (b. Dec. 15, 1925): Hockey GM; managed NHL Montreal Canadiens to 9 Stanley Cups in 14 years (1965-78).

Denis Potvin (b. Oct. 29, 1953): Hockey D; won Norris Trophy 3 times (1976,78-79); 5-time All-NHL 1st-team; led NY Islanders to 4 Stanley Cups.

Mike Powell (b. Nov. 10, 1963): Track & Field; broke Bob Beamon's 23-year-old long jump world record by 2 inches with leap of 29-ft., 4½ in. at the 1991 World Championships; Sullivan Award winner (1991); won long jump silver medals in 1988 and '92 Olympics; repeated as world champ in 1993.

Steve Prefontaine (b. Jan. 25, 1951, d. May 30, 1975): Track & Field; All-America distance runner at Oregon; first athlete to win same event at NCAA championships 4 straight years (5,000 meters from 1970-73); finished 4th in 5,000 at 1972 Munich Olympics; first athlete to endorse Nike running shoes; killed in a one-car accident.

Nick Price (b. Jan. 28, 1957): Zimbabwean golfer; PGA Tour Player of Year in 1993 and '94; became 1st since Nick Faldo in 1990 to win 2 Grand Slam titles in same year when he took British Open and PGA Championship in 1994; also won PGA in '92.

Alain Prost (b. Feb. 24, 1955): French auto racer; 4-time Formula One world champion (1985-86,89,93); sat out 1992 then returned to win title in 1993; retired after '93 season as all-time F1 wins leader with 51 (passed by Michael Schumacher in 2001).

Kirby Puckett (b. Mar. 14, 1961): Baseball OF; led Minnesota Twins to World Series titles in 1987 and '91; retired in 1996 due to an eye ailment with a batting title (1989), 2,304 hits and a .318 career average in 12 seasons; elected to Hall of Fame in 2001.

C.C. Pyle (b. 1882, d. Feb. 3, 1939): Promoter; known as "Cash and Carry"; hyped Red Grange's pro football debut by arranging 1925 barnstorming tour with Chicago Bears; had Grange bolt NFL for new AFL in 1926 (AFL folded in '27); also staged 2 Transcontinental Races (1928-29), known as "Bunion Derbies."

Bobby Rahal (b. Jan. 10, 1953): Auto racer; 3-time PPG Cup champ (1986,87,92); 24 career Indy-Car wins, including 1986 Indy 500; current CART team owner; acted as interim president-CEO of CART in 2000 but resigned to assume position with Jaguar Formula One team.

Jack Ramsay (b. Feb. 21, 1925): Basketball; coach who won 239 college games with St. Joseph's-PA in 11 seasons and 906 NBA games (including playoffs) with 4 teams over 21 years; placed 3rd in 1961 Final Four; led Portland to NBA title in 1977.

Bill Rassmussen (b. Oct. 15, 1932): Radio-TV; unemployed radio broadcaster who founded ESPN, the nation's first 24-hour all-sports cable-TV network, in 1978; bought out by Getty Oil in 1981.

Willis Reed (b. June 25, 1942): Basketball C; led NY Knicks to NBA titles in 1970 and '73, Finals MVP both years; regular season MVP 1970. Voted one of NBA's 50 Greatest Players.

Pee Wee Reese (b. July 23, 1918, d. Aug. 14, 1999): Baseball SS; member of Brooklyn/Los Angeles Dodgers from 1940-58; led NL in runs scored (132) in 1949 and stolen bases (30) in 1952; hit over .300 in a season once (.309 in 1954); led the NL in putouts four times; real name was Harold H. Reese.

Mary Lou Retton (b. Jan. 24, 1968): Gymnast; won gold medal in women's All-Around at the 1984 Olympics; also won 2 silvers and 2 bronzes.

Manon Rheaume (b. Feb. 24, 1972): Hockey; 2-time gold medallist (1992,94) at the Women's World Hockey Championships as goaltender for Canada; first woman to sign a professional hockey contract; started in goal in an exhibition game for the Tampa Bay Lightning on Sept. 23, 1992 to become the only woman to play in an NHL game.

Grantland Rice (b. Nov. 1, 1880, d. July 13, 1954): First celebrated American sportswriter; chronicled the Golden Age of Sport in 1920s; immortalized Notre Dame's "Four Horsemen."

Jerry Rice (b. Oct. 13, 1962): Football WR; 2-time Div. I-AA All-America at Mississippi Valley St. (1983-84); won 3 Super Bowls with San Francisco (1989,90,95); 10-time All-Pro; regular season MVP in 1987 and Super Bowl MVP in 1989; NFL all-time regular season and Super Bowl leader in touchdowns, receptions and receiving yards.

Henri Richard (b. Feb. 29, 1936): Hockey C; leap year baby who played on more Stanley Cup championship teams (11) than anybody else; at 5-foot-7, known as the "Pocket Rocket "; brother of Maurice.

Maurice Richard (b. Aug. 4, 1921, d. May 27, 2000): Hockey RW; the "Rocket"; 8-time NHL 1st team All-Star; MVP in 1947; 1st to score 50 goals in one season (1944-45); 544 career goals; played on 8 Stanley Cup winners in Montreal.

Bob Richards (b. Feb. 2, 1926): Track & Field; pole vaulter, ordained minister and original *Wheaties* pitchman, remains only 2-time Olympic pole vault champ (1952,56).

Nolan Richardson (b. Dec. 27, 1941): Basketball; coached Arkansas to consecutive NCAA finals, beating Duke in 1994 and losing to UCLA in '95; school bought out his contract in 2002, ending his 17-year reign.

Tex Rickard (b. Jan. 2, 1870, d. Jan. 6, 1929): Promoter who handled boxing's first $1 million gate (Dempsey vs. Carpentier in 1921); built Madison Square Garden in 1925; founded NY Rangers as Garden tenant in 1926 and named NHL team after himself (Tex's Rangers); also built Boston Garden in 1928.

Eddie Rickenbacker (b. Oct. 8, 1890, d. July 23, 1973): Mechanic and auto racer; became America's top flying ace (22 kills) in World War I; owned Indianapolis Speedway (1927-45) and ran Eastern Air Lines (1938-59).

Branch Rickey (b. Dec. 20, 1881, d. Dec. 9, 1965): Baseball innovator; revolutionized game with creation of modern farm system while GM of St. Louis Cardinals (1917-42); integrated major leagues in 1947 as president-GM of Brooklyn Dodgers when he brought up Jackie Robinson (whom he had signed on Oct. 23, 1945); later GM of Pittsburgh Pirates.

Leni Riefenstahl (b. Aug. 22, 1902): German filmmaker of 1930s; directed classic sports documentary "Olympia" on 1936 Berlin Summer Olympics; infamous, however, for also making 1934 Hitler propaganda film "Triumph of the Will."

Roy Riegels (b. Apr. 4, 1908, d. Mar. 26, 1993): Football; California center who picked up fumble in 2nd quarter of 1929 Rose Bowl and raced 70 yards in the wrong direction to set up a 2-point safety in 8-7 loss to Georgia Tech.

Bobby Riggs (b. Feb. 25, 1918, d. Oct. 25, 1995): Tennis; won Wimbledon once (1939) and U.S. title twice (1939,41); legendary hustler who made his biggest score in 1973 as 55-year-old male chauvinist challenging the best women players; beat No. 1 Margaret Smith Court 6-2,6-1, but was thrashed by No. 2 Billie Jean King, 6-4,6-3,6-3 in nationally televised "Battle of the Sexes" on Sept. 20, before 30,492 at the Astrodome.

Pat Riley (b. Mar. 20, 1945): Basketball; coached LA Lakers to 4 of their 5 NBA titles in 1980s (1982,85,87-88); coached New York Knicks from 1991-95, then signed with Miami Heat as coach, team president and part-owner; 3-time Coach of Year (1990,93,97); 2nd on list of all-time coaching victories behind Lenny Wilkens

Cal Ripken Jr. (b. Aug. 24, 1960): Baseball SS; broke Lou Gehrig's major league Iron Man record of 2,130 consecutive games played on Sept. 6, 1995; record streak began on May 30, 1982 and ended Sept. 19, 1998 after 2,632 games; 2-time AL MVP (1983,91) for Baltimore; AL Rookie of Year (1982); AL starter in All-Star Game from 1984-2001; 2-time All-Star Game MVP (1991,2001); holds record for career home runs by a shortstop.

Phil Rizzuto (b. Sept. 25, 1918): Baseball SS; nicknamed "the Scooter"; AL MVP with the Yankees in 1950; 5-time All-Star; retired in 1956 and became Yankees radio and television announcer; elected to the Hall of Fame in 1994.

Oscar Robertson (b. Nov. 24, 1938): Basketball G; 3-time College Player of Year (1958-60) at Cincinnati; led 1960 U.S. Olympic team to gold medal; NBA Rookie of Year (1961); 9-time All-NBA 1st team; MVP in 1964 with Cincinnati Royals; NBA champion in 1971 with Milwaukee Bucks; 6-time annual NBA assist leader; 3rd in career assists with 9,887; 8th in career points with 26,710.

Paul Robeson (b. Apr. 8, 1898, d. Jan. 23, 1976): Black 4-sport star and 2-time football All-America (1917-18) at Rutgers; 3-year NFL pro; also scholar, lawyer, singer, actor and political activist; long-tainted by Communist sympathies, he was finally inducted into College Football Hall of Fame in 1995.

Brooks Robinson (b. May 18, 1937): Baseball 3B; led AL in fielding 12 times from 1960-72 with Baltimore; AL MVP in 1964; World Series MVP in 1970; 16 Gold Gloves; entered Hall of Fame in 1983.

David Robinson (b. Aug. 6, 1965): Basketball C; College Player of Year at Navy in 1987; overall 1st pick by San Antonio in 1987 NBA draft; served in military from 1987-89; NBA Rookie of Year in 1990 and MVP in '95; 2-time All-NBA 1st team (1991,92); led NBA in scoring in 1994; member of 1988, '92 and '96 U.S. Olympic teams.

Eddie Robinson (b. Feb. 13, 1919): Football; head coach at Div. I-AA Grambling from 1941-97; winningest coach in college history (408-165-15); led Tigers to 8 national black college titles.

Frank Robinson (b. Aug. 31, 1935): Baseball OF; won MVP in NL (1961) and AL (1966); Triple Crown winner and World Series MVP in 1966 with Baltimore; 5th on all-time home run list with 586; 1st black manager in major leagues with Cleveland in 1975; also managed in SF, Baltimore and Montreal; served as the league's vice president of on-field operations (2000-01) before becoming manager of the Expos in 2002.

Jackie Robinson (b. Jan. 31, 1919, d. Oct. 24, 1972): Baseball 1B-2B-3B; 4-sport athlete at UCLA (baseball, basketball, football and track); hit .387 with K.C. Monarchs of Negro Leagues in 1945; signed by Brooklyn Dodgers on Oct. 23, 1945 and broke major league baseball's color line in 1947; Rookie of Year in 1947 and NL MVP in '49; hit .311 over 10 seasons. His #42 was retired by MLB in 1997.

Sugar Ray Robinson (b. May 3, 1921, d. Apr. 12, 1989): Boxer; arguably the greatest pound-for-pound prizefighter of all-time; world welterweight champion (1946-51); 5-time middleweight champ; retired at age 45 after 25 years in the ring; pro record 174-19-6 with 109 KOs.

Knute Rockne (b. Mar. 4, 1888, d. Mar. 31, 1931): Football; coached Notre Dame to 3 consensus national titles (1924,29,30); highest winning percentage in college history (.881) with record of 105-12-5 over 13 seasons; killed in plane crash.

Bill Rodgers (b. Dec. 23, 1947): Distance runner; won Boston and New York City marathons 4 times each from 1975-80.

Dennis Rodman (b. May 13, 1961): Basketball F; superb rebounder and defender; also known for dyeing his hair various colors and for getting suspended regularly; in 1997, he was suspended for 11 games for kicking a courtside cameraman; led NBA in rebounding 7 years in a row (1992-98); member of 5 NBA champion teams with Detroit (1989,90) and Chicago (1996-98); 2-time defensive player of the year (1990-91).

Irina Rodnina (b. Sept. 12, 1949): Soviet figure skater; won 10 world championships and 3 Olympic gold medals in pairs competition from 1971-80.

Alex Rodriguez (b. July 27, 1975): Baseball SS; one of baseball's best all-around players; led AL in his first full season in the majors (1996) with .358 batting average and 141 runs; in 1998 became third player ever with 40 HRs and 40 steals in one season; signed a 10-year, $252m deal (the biggest in U.S. sports history) with Texas in 2000; has hit at least 40 homers the last five years (1998-2002).

Juan (Chi Chi) Rodriguez (b. Oct. 23, 1935): Golfer; popular player with 8 PGA Tour victories and 22 Senior Tour wins; 1973 U.S. Ryder Cup Team member.

Ronaldo (b. Sept. 22, 1976): Soccer; Brazilian forward who has been compared to the great Pele; signed with a first division club in Brazil, Cruzeiro Belo Horizonte, before he was 18 and scored 58 goals in 60 games; named to the Brazilian National Team when he was 17; named FIFA Player of the Year in 1996 and '97; European Player of the Year in '97; named 1998 World Cup MVP; led Brazil to World Cup victory in 2002, scoring 8 times in the tournament including both of Brazil's goals in its 2-0 win over Germany in the final.

Art Rooney (b. Jan. 27, 1901, d. Aug. 25, 1988): Race track legend and pro football pioneer; bought Pittsburgh Steelers franchise in 1933 for $2,500; finally won NFL title with 1st of 4 Super Bowls in 1974 season.

Theodore Roosevelt (b. Oct. 27, 1858, d. Jan. 6, 1919): 26th President of the U.S.; physical fitness buff who boxed as undergraduate at Harvard; credited with presidential assist in forming of Intercollegiate Athletic Assn. (now NCAA) in 1905-06.

Mauri Rose (b. May 26, 1906, d. Jan. 1, 1981): Auto racer; 3-time winner of Indy 500 (1941,47-48).

Murray Rose (b. Jan. 6, 1939): Australian swimmer; won 3 gold medals at 1956 Olympics; added a gold, silver and bronze in 1960.

Pete Rose (b. Apr. 14, 1941): Baseball OF-IF; all-time hits leader with 4,256 and games leader with 3562; led NL in batting 3 times; regular-season MVP in 1973; World Series MVP in 1975; had 44-game hitting streak in '78; managed Cincinnati (1984-89); banned for life in 1989 for conduct detrimental to baseball; convicted of tax evasion in 1990 and sentenced to 5 months in prison; released Jan. 7, 1991.

Ken Rosewall (b. Nov. 2, 1934): Tennis; won French and Australian singles titles at age 18; U.S. champ twice, but never won Wimbledon.

Mark Roth (b. Apr. 10, 1951): Bowler; 4-time PBA Player of Year (1977-79,84); has 34 tournament wins and over $1.5 million in career earnings; U.S. Open champ in 1984.

Alan Rothenberg (b. Apr. 10, 1939): Soccer; president of U.S. Soccer 1990-98; surprised European skeptics by directing hugely successful 1994 World Cup tournament; successfully got oft-delayed outdoor Major League Soccer off ground in 1996.

Chad Rowan (Akebono) (b. May 8, 1969): Sumo Wrestling; 6-foot-9, 510-pound naturalized Japanese citizen born in Hawaii; first foreign grand champion in sumo wrestling's 2,000-year history; retired in Jan., 2001.

Patrick Roy (b. Oct. 5, 1965): Hockey G; led Montreal to 2 Stanley Cup titles (1986,93) and won 3rd and 4th Cups with Colorado (1996,2001); 3-time playoff MVP (as rookie in 1986,93,2001); won Vezina Trophy 3 times (1989-90,92); led NHL in goals against average 3 times (1989,92,2002); all-time leader in career regular season wins (516) and playoff wins (148).

Pete Rozelle (b. Mar. 1, 1926, d. December 6, 1996): Football; NFL Commissioner from 1960-89; presided over growth of league from 12 to 28 teams, merger with AFL, creation of Super Bowl and advent of huge TV rights fees.

Wilma Rudolph (b. June 23, 1940, d. Nov. 12, 1994): Track & Field; won 3 gold medals (100m, 200m and 4x100m relay) at 1960 Olympics; also won relay silver in '56 Games at age 16; 2-time AP Athlete of Year (1960-61) and Sullivan Award winner in 1961; suffered from polio and wore leg braces until she was 9.

John Ruiz (b. Jan. 4, 1972): Boxer; defeated Evander Holyfield by a decision in March, 2001 for the WBA heavyweight title; the first-ever Hispanic heavyweight champion of the world.

Damon Runyon (b. Oct. 4, 1884, d. Dec. 10, 1946): Kansas native who gained fame as New York journalist, sports columnist and short-story writer; best known for 1932 story collection, "Guys and Dolls."

Adolph Rupp (b. Sept. 2, 1901, d. Dec. 10, 1977): Basketball; 2nd in all-time college coaching wins with 876; led Kentucky to 4 NCAA championships (1948-49,51,58) and 1 NIT title (1946).

Bill Russell (b. Feb. 12, 1934): Basketball C; won titles in college (with San Francisco in 1995,56), Olympics (1956) and pros; 5-time NBA MVP (1958,61,62,63,65); led Boston to 11 titles from 1957-69; 4-time NBA rebound leader (1958-59,64-65); 2nd on all-time rebound list with 21,620; became first black NBA (and major pro sports) head coach in 1966.

Babe Ruth (b. Feb. 6, 1895, d. Aug. 16, 1948): Baseball LHP-OF; two-time 20-game winner with Boston Red Sox (1916-17); had a 94-46 record with a 2.28 ERA, while he was 3-0 in the World Series with an ERA of 0.87; sold to New York Yankees for $100,000 in 1920; AL MVP in 1923; led AL in slugging average 13 times, HRs 12 times, RBI 6 times and batting once (.378 in 1924); hit 60 HRs in 1927 and at least 54 3 other times; ended career with Boston Braves in 1935 with 714 HRs, 2,211 RBI, 2,062 walks and a batting average of .342; remains all-time leader in slugging percentage (.690); member of the Hall of Fame's inaugural class of 1936.

Johnny Rutherford (b. Mar. 12, 1938): Auto racer; 3-time winner of Indy 500 (1974,76,80); CART national champion in 1980.

Nolan Ryan (b. Jan. 31, 1947): Baseball RHP; recorded 7 no-hitters against Kansas City and Detroit (1973), Minnesota (1974), Baltimore (1975), LA Dodgers (1981), Oakland A's (1990) and Toronto (1991 at age 44); 2-time 20-game winner (1973-74); 2-time NL leader in ERA (1981,87); led AL in strikeouts 9 times and NL twice in 27 years; retired after 1993 season with 324 wins, 292 losses and all-time records for strike-outs (5,714) and walks (2,795); never won Cy Young Award; had his number retired by three teams (California, Houston, Texas).

Samuel Ryder (b. Mar. 24, 1858, d. Jan. 2, 1936): Golf; English seed merchant who donated the Ryder Cup in 1927 for competition between pro golfers from Great Britain and the U.S.; made his fortune by coming up with idea of selling seeds in small packages.

Toni Sailer (b. Nov. 17, 1935): Austrian skier; 1st to win 3 alpine gold medals in Winter Olympics — taking downhill, slalom and giant slalom events in 1956.

Alberto Salazar (b. Aug. 7, 1958): Track and Field; set one world and six U.S. records during his career; broke 12-year-old record at New York Marathon in 1981 and broke Boston Marathon record in 1982; won three straight NY Marathons (1980-82); qualified for the 1980 and 1984 U.S. Olympic teams.

Juan Antonio Samaranch (b. July 17, 1920): president of International Olympic Committee (1980-2001); the native of Barcelona was re-elected in 1996 after IOC's move in '95 to bump membership age limit to 80; replaced by Belgian Jacques Rogge.

Pete Sampras (b. Aug. 12, 1971): Tennis; No.1 player in world from 1993-98; youngest ever U.S. Open men's champion (19 years, 28 days) in 1990; his win at U.S. Open in 2002 gave him 14 grand slam singles titles for his career, more than any other male player; has won 2 Australian Opens (1994,97), 7 Wimbledons (1993,94,95,97,98,99,00) and 5 U.S. Opens (1990,93,95,96,2002); career money leader on ATP Tour.

Joan Benoit Samuelson (b. May 16, 1957): Distance runner; won Boston Marathon twice (1979,83); won first women's Olympic marathon in 1984 Games; Sullivan Award recipient in 1985.

Arantxa Sanchez Vicario (b. Dec. 18, 1971): Spanish tennis player; 29 tour singles victories through Sept., 2002 including 3 French Opens (1989,94,98) and 1 U.S. Open (1994); 6 doubles and 4 mixed doubles grand slam titles; finalist in three of four Grand Slam finals in '95; teamed with Conchita Martinez to win 5 Federation Cups from 1991-98.

Earl Sande (b. Nov. 13, 1898, d. Aug. 19, 1968): Jockey; rode Gallant Fox to Triple Crown in 1930; won 5 Belmonts and 3 Kentucky Derbies.

Barry Sanders (b. July 16, 1968): Football RB; won 1988 Heisman Trophy as junior at Oklahoma St.; all-time NCAA single season leader in rushing (2,628 yards), scoring (234 points) and TDs (39); 4-time NFL rushing leader with Detroit Lions (1990,94,96,97); NFC Rookie of Year (1988); 2-time NFL Player of Year (1991,97); NFC MVP (1994); rushed for 2,053 yards in 1997, second-best season total ever; No. 3 all-time rusher (15,269 yds); abruptly retired just prior to 1999 season.

Deion Sanders (b. Aug. 9, 1967): Baseball OF and Football DB-KR-WR; 2-time All-America at Florida St. in football (1987-88); 7-time NFL All-Pro CB with Atlanta, San Francisco and Dallas (1991-94,96-98); led majors in triples (14) with Atlanta in 1992 and hit .533 in World Series the same year; played on 2 Super Bowl winners (SF in XXIX, and Dallas in XXX); first 2-way starter in NFL since Chuck Bednarik in 1962; only athlete to play in both World Series and Super Bowl.

Cael Sanderson (b. June 20, 1979): Wrestling; first 4-time undefeated NCAA college wrestling champion (1999-2002); went 159-0 during 4-year career at Iowa State; 4-time NCAA Most Outstanding Wrestler.

Abe Saperstein (b. July 4, 1901, d. Mar. 15, 1966): Basketball; founded all-black, Harlem Globetrotters barnstorming team in 1927; coached sharpshooting comedians to 1940 world pro title in Chicago and established troupe as game's foremost goodwill ambassadors; also served as 1st commissioner of American Basketball League (1961-62).

Gene Sarazen (b. Feb. 27, 1902, d. May 13, 1999): Golfer; one of only five players to win all four Grand Slam titles (others are Hogan, Nicklaus, Player and Woods); won Masters, British Open, 2 U.S. Opens and 3 PGA titles between 1922-35; invented sand wedge in 1930.

Glen Sather (b. Sept. 2, 1943): Hockey; GM-coach of 4 Stanley Cup winners in Edmonton (1984-85,87-88) and GM-only for another in 1990; ranks 8th on all-time NHL coaching list with 553 wins (including playoffs); entered Hockey Hall of Fame in 1997; named pres-GM of NY Rangers in 2000.

Terry Sawchuk (b. Dec. 28, 1929, d. May 31, 1970): Hockey G; recorded 103 shutouts in 21 NHL seasons; 4-time Vezina Trophy winner; played on 4 Stanley Cup winners at Detroit and Toronto; posted career 2.52 GAA.

Gale Sayers (b. May 30, 1943): Football HB; 2-time All-America at Kansas; NFL Rookie of Year (1965) and 5-time All-Pro with Chicago; scored then-record 22 TDs in rookie year; led NFC in rushing twice (1966,69).

Chris Schenkel (b. Aug. 21, 1923): Radio-TV; 4-time Sportscaster of Year; easy-going baritone who covered basketball, bowling, football, golf and the Olympics for ABC and CBS; host of ABC's Pro Bowlers Tour for 33 years; received lifetime achievement Emmy Award in 1992.

Vitaly Scherbo (b. Jan. 13, 1972): Russian gymnast; winner of unprecedented 6 gold medals in gymnastics, including men's All-Around, for Unified Team in 1992 Olympics; won 3 bronze in '96 Games.

Curt Schilling (b. Nov. 14, 1966): Baseball RHP; led NL in strikeouts (1997-98); 2-time 20-game winner (2001-02); shared 2001 World Series MVP award with Diamondbacks teammate Randy Johnson.

Mike Schmidt (b. Sept. 27, 1949): Baseball 3B; led NL in HRs 8 times; 3-time MVP (1980,81,86) with Philadelphia; 548 career HRs and 10 Gold Gloves; inducted into Hall of Fame in 1995.

Don Schollander (b. Apr. 30, 1946): Swimming; won 4 gold medals at 1964 Olympics, plus one gold and one silver in 1968; won Sullivan Award in 1964.

Dick Schultz (b. Sept. 5, 1929): Reform-minded executive director of NCAA from 1988-93; announced resignation on May 11, 1993 in wake of special investigator's report citing Univ. of Virginia with improper student-athlete loan program during Schultz's tenure as athletic director (1981-87); executive director of the USOC 1995-2000.

Michael Schumacher (b. Jan. 3, 1969): German auto racer; became Formula One's all-time win leader with his 52nd grand prix victory on Sept. 2, 2001; 5-time world champion (1994,95,00,01,02); his 10th win in 2002 broke the all-time F1 single-season record; 63 career F1 wins.

Bob Seagren (b. Oct. 17, 1946): Track & Field; won gold medal in pole vault at 1968 Olympics; broke world outdoor record 5 times.

Tom Seaver (b. Nov. 17, 1944): Baseball RHP; won 3 Cy Young Awards (1969,73,75); led NL in K 5 times (1970,71,73,75,76); pitched no-hitter in 1978 for Cin.; had 311 wins, 3,640 strikeouts and 2.86 ERA over 20 years.

Peter Seitz (b. May 17, 1905, d. Oct. 17, 1983): Baseball arbitrator; ruled on Dec. 23, 1975 that players who perform for one season without a signed contract can become free agents; decision ushered in big money era for players.

Monica Seles (b. Dec. 2, 1973): Tennis; No. 1 in the world in 1991 and '92 after winning Australian, French and U.S. Opens both years; won 4 Australian, 3 French and 2 US Opens; winner of 30 singles titles in just 5 years before she was stabbed in the back by Steffi Graf fan Gunter Parche on Apr. 30, 1993 during match in Hamburg, Germany; spent remainder of 1993, all of '94 and most of '95 recovering; returned to tennis with win at the 1995 Canadian Open; won 1996 Australian Open; winner of 53 WTA tournaments.

Bud Selig (b. July 30, 1934): Baseball; Milwaukee car dealer who bought AL Seattle Pilots for $10.8 million in 1970 and moved team to Midwest; as de facto commissioner, he presided over 232-day players' strike that resulted in cancellation of World Series for first time since 1904; officially named baseball's ninth commissioner on July 2, 1998; made the controversial decision to end the 2002 All-Star Game after 11 inns., tied 7-7.

Frank Selke (b. May 7, 1893, d. July 3, 1985): Hockey; GM of 6 Stanley Cup champions in Montreal (1953,56-60); the annual NHL trophy for best defensive forward bears his name.

Ayrton Senna (b. Mar. 21, 1960, d. May 1, 1994): Brazilian auto racer; 3-time Formula One champion (1988,90-91); died as all-time F1 leader in poles (65) and 2nd in wins (41, currently in 3rd place); killed in crash at Imola, Italy during '94 San Marino Grand Prix.

Wilbur Shaw (b. Oct. 13, 1902, d. Oct. 30, 1954): Auto racer; 3-time winner and 3-time runner-up of Indy 500 from 1933-1940.

Patty Sheehan (b. Oct. 27, 1956): Golfer; LPGA Player of Year in 1983; clinched entry into LPGA Hall of Fame with her 30th career win in 1993; her 6 major titles include 3 LPGA Champ. (1983-84,93), 2 U.S. Opens (1992,94) 1 Dinah Shore (1996).

Bill Shoemaker (b. Aug. 19, 1931): Jockey; ranks second all-time in career wins with 8,833 (passed by Laffit Pincay Jr. in Dec. 1999); 3-time Eclipse Award winner as jockey (1981) and special award recipient (1976,81); won Belmont 5 times, Kentucky Derby 4 times and Preakness twice; oldest jockey to win Kentucky Derby (age 54, aboard Ferdinand in 1986); retired in 1990 to become trainer; paralyzed in 1991 auto accident but continued to train horses.

Eddie Shore (b. Nov. 25, 1902, d. Mar. 16, 1985): Hockey D; only NHL defenseman to win Hart Trophy as MVP 4 times (1933,35-36,38); led Boston Bruins to Stanley Cup titles in 1929 and '39; had 105 goals and 1,047 penalty minutes in 14 seasons.

Frank Shorter (b. Oct. 31, 1947): Track & Field; won gold medal in marathon at 1972 Olympics, 1st American to win in 64 years.

Don Shula (b. Jan. 4, 1930): Football; retired after 1995 season with an NFL-record 347 career wins (including playoffs) and a winning percentage of .665; took six teams to Super Bowl and won twice with Miami (VII, VIII); 4-time Coach of Year, twice with Baltimore (1964,68) and twice with Miami (1970-71); coached 1972 Dolphins to 17-0 record, the only undefeated team in NFL history.

Charlie Sifford (b. June 2, 1922): Golf; won the Hartford Open in 1967 with a final-round 64, becoming the first black player to win a PGA event; won the PGA Seniors Championship in 1975; amassed over $1 million in career earnings; published his autobiography "Just Let Me Play" in 1992.

Al Simmons (b. May 22, 1902, d. May 26, 1956): Baseball OF; led AL in batting twice (1930-31) with Philadelphia A's and knocked in 100 runs or more 11 straight years (1924-34).

O.J. Simpson (b. July 9, 1947): Football RB; won Heisman Trophy in 1968 at USC; ran for 2,003 yards in NFL in 1973; All-Pro 5 times; MVP in 1973; rushed for 11,236 career yards; TV analyst and actor after career ended; arrested June 17, 1994 as suspect in double murder of ex-wife Nicole Brown Simpson and her friend Ronald Goldman; acquitted on Oct. 3, 1995 by a Los Angeles jury in criminal trial but forced to make financial reparations after losing wrongful death suit.

George Sisler (b. Mar. 24, 1893, d. Mar. 26, 1973): Baseball 1B; hit over .400 twice (1920,22) and batted over .300 in 13 of his 15 seasons; his 257 hits in 1920 is still a major league record; played most of his career with the St. Louis Browns; inducted into Baseball Hall of Fame in 1939.

Mary Decker Slaney (b. Aug. 4, 1958): U.S. middle distance runner; has held 7 separate American track & field records from the 800 to 10,000 meters; won both 1,500 and 3,000 meters at 1983 World Championships in Helsinki, but no Olympic medals.

Raisa Smetanina (b. Feb. 29, 1952): Russian Nordic skier; all-time leading female Winter Olympics medalist with 10 cross country medals (4 gold, 5 silver and a bronze) in 5 appearances (1976,80,84,88,92) for USSR and Unified Team.

Billy Smith (b. Dec. 12, 1950): Hockey G; led NY Islanders to 4 consecutive Stanley Cups (1980-83); won Vezina Trophy in 1982; Stanley Cup MVP in 1983.

Dean Smith (b. Feb. 28, 1931): Basketball; No. 1 on all-time NCAA coaches victory list (879); led North Carolina to 25 NCAA tournaments in 34 years, reaching Final Four 10 times and winning championship twice (1982,93); coached U.S. Olympic team to gold medal in 1976.

Emmitt Smith (b. May 15, 1969): Football RB; consensus All-America (1989) at Florida; 4-time NFL rushing leader (1991-93,95); regular season and Super Bowl MVP in 1993; played on three Super Bowl champions (1993,94,96); entered the 2002 season with a record 148 rushing TDs and was poised to eclipse Walter Payton as NFL all-time leading rusher.

John Smith (b. Aug. 9, 1965): Wrestler; 2-time NCAA champion for Oklahoma St. at 134 lbs (1987-88) and Most Outstanding Wrestler of '88 championships; 3-time world champion; gold medal winner at 1988 and '92 Olympics at 137 lbs; won Sullivan Award (1990); coached Oklahoma St. to 1994 NCAA title and brother Pat was Most Outstanding Wrestler.

Lee Smith (b. Dec. 4, 1957): Baseball RHP; 3-time NL saves leader (1983,91-92); retired as all-time saves leader with 478 and an ERA of 3.03; 10 seasons with 30 or more saves and 3 times saved over 40.

Michelle Smith deBruin (b. Apr. 7, 1969): Irish swimmer; won three gold medals at the 1996 Olympics; accused of using performance-enhancing drugs but passed all tests until she was suspended for 4 years by FINA in 1998 for tampering with a urine sample.

Ozzie Smith (b. Dec. 26, 1954): Baseball SS; won 13 straight Gold Gloves (1980-92); played in 12 straight All-Star Games (1981-92); MVP of 1985 NL playoffs; all-time MLB assist leader (8,375); inducted into Baseball Hall of Fame in 2002.

Walter (Red) Smith (b. Sept. 25, 1905, d. Jan. 15, 1982): Sportswriter for newspapers in Philadelphia and New York from 1936-82; won Pulitzer Prize for commentary in 1976.

Conn Smythe (b. Feb. 1, 1895, d. Nov. 18, 1980): Hockey pioneer; built Maple Leaf Gardens in 1931; managed Toronto to 7 Stanley Cups.

Sam Snead (b. May 27, 1912, d. May 23, 2002): Golfer; won both Masters and PGA 3 times and British Open once; runner-up in U.S. Open 4 times; PGA Player of Year in 1949; oldest player (52 years, 10 months) to win PGA event with Greater Greensboro Open title in 1965; all-time PGA Tour career victory leader with 81.

Peter Snell (b. Dec. 17, 1938): Track & Field; New Zealander who won gold medal in 800m at 1960 Olympics, then won both the 800m and 1,500m at 1964 Games.

Duke Snider (b. Sept. 19, 1926): Baseball OF; hit 40 or more home runs five straight seasons (1953-57); led the league in runs scored 1953-55; played in six World Series with the Dodgers and batted .286 with 11 home runs; nicknamed "Duke of Flatbush"; in 18 seasons hit 407 home runs, scored 1,259 runs and had 1,333 RBI.

Annika Sorenstam (b. Oct. 9, 1970): Swedish golfer; College Player of the Year and NCAA champion in 1991; won more LPGA tournaments (18) than any other player in the 1990s, including 2 U.S. Opens (1995,96); also has 2 Nabisco Championship titles (2001-02); 4-time Rolex Player of the Year (1995,97-98,2001); shot an LPGA record 59 in round 2 of the 2001 Standard Register Ping; LPGA all-time leading money winner.

Sammy Sosa (b. Nov. 12, 1968): Baseball OF; slugging Chicago Cub who surpassed Roger Maris' season home run record (61), just after Mark McGwire did, in 1998 and finished the year with 66; followed that up with seasons of 63, 50 and 64 HR; NL MVP (1998); 6-time NL all-star (1995,98-2002).

Javier Sotomayor (b. Oct. 13, 1967): Cuban high jumper; first man to clear 8 feet (8-0) on July 29, 1989; won gold medal at 1992 Olympics with jump of only 7-ft, 8-in.; broke world record with leap of 8-0½ in 1993; had a controversial drug suspension reduced, which allowed him to participate in 2000 Olympics; won the silver medal in Sydney with a leap of 7-7¼.

Warren Spahn (b. Apr. 23, 1921): Baseball LHP; led NL in wins 8 times; won 20 or more games 13 times; Cy Young winner in 1957; most career wins (363) by a lefthander.

Tris Speaker (b. Apr. 4, 1888, d. Dec. 8, 1958): Baseball OF; all-time leader in outfield assists (449) and doubles (792); had .344 career BA and 3,515 hits.

J.G. Taylor Spink (b. Nov. 6, 1888, d. Dec. 7, 1962): Publisher of *The Sporting News* from 1914-62; BWAA annual meritorious service award named after him.

Leon Spinks (b. July 11, 1953): Boxing; won heavyweight crown in split decision over Muhammad Ali in Feb. 1978; Ali regained title seven months later; won gold medal in light heavyweight division at 1976 Olympics; brother Michael won the heavyweight title in 1983; were the only brothers to hold world titles; known more for frequent traffic violations and lavish lifestyle than bouts late in career; filed for bankruptcy in 1986.

Mark Spitz (b. Feb. 10, 1950): Swimmer; set 23 world and 35 U.S. records; won all-time record 7 gold medals (4 individual, 3 relay) in 1972 Olympics; also won 4 medals (2 gold, a silver and a bronze) in 1968 Games for a total of 11; comeback attempt at age 41 foundered in 1991.

Latrell Sprewell (b. Sept. 8, 1970): Basketball G; became an NBA All-Star in just his second pro season out of Alabama; led Golden State in scoring four years in a row; made headlines in 1997 after being suspended by the NBA for attacking Warriors head coach P.J. Carlesimo during a practice; currently a member of the N.Y. Knicks.

Lyn St. James (b. Mar. 13, 1947): Auto racer; one of just 3 women to qualify for the Indianapolis 500; best finish in the race came in 1992 when she came in 11th and won Indianapolis 500 Rookie of the Year.

Amos Alonzo Stagg (b. Aug. 16, 1862, d. Mar. 17, 1965): Football innovator; coached at U. of Chicago for 41 seasons and College of the Pacific for 14 more; 314-199-35 record; elected to both college football and baseball Halls of Fame.

Willie Stargell (b. Mar. 6, 1940, d. Apr. 9, 2001): Baseball OF-1B; "Pops"; led NL in home runs twice (1971,73); 475 career HRs; NL co-MVP and World Series MVP in 1979.

Bart Starr (b. Jan. 9, 1934): Football QB; led Green Bay to 5 NFL titles and 2 Super Bowl wins from 1961-67; regular season MVP in 1966; MVP of Super Bowls I and II.

Roger Staubach (b. Feb. 5, 1942): Football QB; Heisman Trophy winner as Navy junior in 1963; led Dallas to 2 Super Bowl titles (1972,78) and was Super Bowl MVP in 1972; 5-time leading passer in NFC (1971,73,77-79).

George Steinbrenner (b. July 4, 1930): Baseball; principal owner of NY Yankees since 1973; teams have won 9 pennants and 6 World Series (1977-78,96,98,99,00); has changed managers 21 times and GMs 11 times in 29 years; ordered by baseball commish Fay Vincent in 1990 to surrender control of club for dealings with small-time gambler; reinstated in 1993.

Casey Stengel (b. July 30, 1890, d. Sept. 29, 1975): Baseball; player for 14 years and manager for 25; outfielder and lifetime .284 hitter with 5 clubs (1912-25); guided NY Yankees to 10 AL pennants and 7 World Series titles from 1949-60; 1st NY Mets skipper from 1962-65.

Ingemar Stenmark (b. Mar. 18, 1956): Swedish alpine skier; 3-time World Cup overall champion (1976-78); posted 86 World Cup wins in 16 years; won 2 gold medals at 1980 Olympics.

Helen Stephens (b. Feb. 3, 1918, d. Jan. 17, 1994): Track & Field; set 3 world records in 100-yard dash and 4 more in 100 meters in 1935-36; won gold medals in 100 meters and 4x100-meter relay in 1936 Olympics; retired in 1937.

Woody Stephens (b. Sept. 1, 1913, d. Aug. 22, 1998): Horse racing; trainer who saddled an unprecedented 5 straight winners in Belmont Stakes (1982-86); also had two Kentucky Derby winners (1974,84) and one Preakness winner (1952); trained 1982 Horse of Year Conquistador Cielo; won Eclipse award as nation's top trainer in 1983.

David Stern (b. Sept. 22, 1942): Basketball; marketing expert and NBA commissioner since 1984; took office the year Michael Jordan turned pro; has presided over stunning artistic and financial success of NBA both nationally and internationally; league has grown from 23 teams to 29 during his watch and opened offices worldwide; oversaw launch of WNBA in 1997.

Teófilo Stevenson (b. Mar. 29, 1952): Cuban boxer; won 3 consecutive gold medals as Olympic heavyweight (1972,76,80); did not turn pro.

Jackie Stewart (b. June 11, 1939): Auto racer; won 27 Formula One races and 3 world driving titles from 1965-73.

John Stockton (b. Mar 26, 1962): Basketball G; all-time NBA leader in every major assist category, including most in a season (1,164), highest average in a season (14.5 per game) and most overall (15,177); also holds the NBA record for career steals (3,128); All-NBA team in '94 and '95; member of 1992 and '96 US Olympic basketball Dream Teams; 10-time All-Star.

Curtis Strange (b. Jan. 30, 1955): Golfer; won consecutive U.S. Open titles (1988-89); 3-time leading money winner on PGA Tour (1985,87-88); first PGA player to win $1 million in one year (1988); captain of the 2002 U.S. Ryder Cup team.

Picabo Street (b. Apr. 3, 1971): Skiing; 2-time Olympic medalist, gold (Super G in 1998) and silver (downhill in 1994); her 1995 World Cup downhill series title first-ever by U.S. woman, she repeated the feat in 1996.

Kerri Strug (b. Nov. 19, 1977): Gymnastics; delivered the most dramatic moment of the 1996 Summer Olympics when she completed a vault (9.712) after spraining her ankle; the second vault assured the first all-around gold medal for a US Women's gymnastics team; a poor performance by the Russian team on the beam had clinched the gold medal for the US but Strug was unaware when she made the second vault.

Louise Suggs (b. Sept. 7, 1923): Golfer; won 11 majors and 50 LPGA events overall from 1949-62.

James E. Sullivan (b. Nov. 18, 1862, d. Sept. 16, 1914): Track & Field; pioneer who founded Amateur Athletic Union (AAU) in 1888; director of St. Louis Olympic Games in 1904; AAU's annual Sullivan Award for performance and sportsmanship named after him.

John L. Sullivan (b. Oct. 15, 1858, d. Feb. 2, 1918): Boxer; world heavyweight champion (1882-92); last of bare-knuckle champions.

Pat Summitt (b. June 14, 1952): Basketball; women's basketball coach at Tennessee (1974—); entered 2002-03 season tied for the most all-time career victories (788) with Jody Conradt of Texas; coached 1984 US women's basketball team to its first Olympic gold medal; has coached Lady Vols to 6 national championships (1987,89,91,96,97,98).

Don Sutton (b. April 2, 1945): Baseball RHP; won 324 games and tossed 58 shutouts in his 23-year career; recorded NL record five career 1-hitters; played with Dodgers, Astros, Brewers, Athletics, Angels and was a 4-time All-Star; elected to Hall of Fame in 1998.

Ichiro Suzuki (b. Oct. 22, 1973): Baseball OF; speedy Seattle Mariners RF who in 2001 became the 2nd player (Fred Lynn) to win AL Rookie of the Year and MVP in same year; 1st Japanese-born position player to play in the majors; won 7 consecutive Japanese batting titles (1994-2000).

Lynn Swann (b. Mar. 7, 1952): Football WR; played nine seasons with Pittsburgh (1974-82); appeared in four Super Bowls and had 16 catches for 364 yards and three TDs; named MVP of Super Bowl X for 4 catch, 161 yard, 1 TD performance.

Barry Switzer (b. Oct. 5, 1937): Football; coached Oklahoma to 3 national titles (1974-75,85); 4th on all-time winning pct list at .837 (157-29-4); resigned in 1989 after OU was slapped with 3-year NCAA probation; hired as Dallas Cowboys head coach in 1994 and led team to victory in Super Bowl XXX in 1996.

Sheryl Swoopes (b. Mar. 25, 1971): Basketball; forward for WNBA's Houston Comets; 2-time WNBA regular season MVP (2000,02); Defensive Player of the Year in 2000, 2-time olympic gold medalist (1996,2000); led Texas Tech to Div. I NCAA championship in 1993; consensus National Player of the Year in 1993.

Paul Tagliabue (b. Nov. 24, 1940): Football; NFL attorney who was elected league's 4th commissioner in 1989; ushered in salary cap in 1994; the league has expanded from 28 teams to 32 in his tenure.

Anatoli Tarasov (b. 1918, d. June 23, 1995): Hockey; coached Soviet Union to 9 straight world championships and 3 Olympic gold medals (1964,68,72).

Jerry Tarkanian (b. Aug. 30, 1930): Basketball; amassed 778 wins in 31 years at Long Beach St., UNLV and Fresno St.; led UNLV to 4 Final Fours and 1 national title (1990); fought battle with NCAA over purity of UNLV program; quit as coach after going 26-2 in 1991-92; fired after 20 games (9-11) as coach of NBA San Antonio Spurs in 1992; unretired in 1995 to coach his alma mater, Fresno St.; retired again after 2001-02.

Fran Tarkenton (b. Feb. 3, 1940): Football QB; 2-time NFL All-Pro (1973,75); Player of Year (1975); threw for 47,003 yards and 342 TDs (both former NFL records) in 18 seasons with Vikings and Giants.

Chuck Taylor (b. June 24, 1901, d. June 23, 1969): Converse traveling salesman whose name came to grace the classic, high-top canvas basketball sneakers known as "Chucks"; over 500 million pairs have been sold since 1917; he also ran clinics worldwide and edited Converse Basketball Yearbook (1922-68).

Lawrence Taylor (b. Feb. 4, 1959): Football LB; All-America at North Carolina (1980); only defensive player in NFL history to be consensus Player of Year (1986); led NY Giants to Super Bowl titles in 1986 and '90 seasons; played in 10 Pro Bowls (1981-90); retired after 1993 season with 132½ sacks and has had several drug-related arrests since; inducted into Hall of Fame in 1999.

Marshall (Major) Taylor (b. Nov. 26, 1878, d. June 21, 1932): Cyclist; Considered one of the first African-American sports heroes; held seven world cycling records at the turn of the century, racing mostly in Europe, Australia and New Zealand after being barred from many events in the U.S. due to racial prejudices; won the world 1-mile championship in 1899.

Gustavo Thoeni (b. Feb. 28, 1951): Italian alpine skier; 4-time World Cup overall champion (1971-73,75); won giant slalom at 1972 Olympics.

Isiah Thomas (b. Apr. 30, 1961): Basketball; led Indiana to NCAA title as sophomore and Final 4 MOP in 1981; consensus All-America guard in '81; led Detroit to 2 NBA titles in 1989 and '90; NBA Finals MVP in 1990; 3-time All-NBA 1st team (1984-86); retired in 1994 at age 33 after tearing right Achilles tendon; returned to NBA in 2000 as coach of the Indiana Pacers after failed tenure as owner of the CBA; elected to Hall of Fame in 2000.

Thurman Thomas (b. May 16, 1966): Football RB; 3-time AFC rushing leader (1990-91,93); 2-time All-Pro (1990-91); NFL Player of Year (1991); led Buffalo to 4 straight Super Bowls (1991-94).

Daley Thompson (b. July 30, 1958): British Track & Field; won consecutive gold medals in decathlon at 1980 and '84 Olympics.

Jenny Thompson (b. Feb. 26, 1973): Swimmer; 8-time Olympic gold medalist (all in relays) and winner of 10 Olympic medals overall, more than any other American woman; won 3 gold (4x100 free, 4x200 free, 4x100 medley) and 1 bronze (100m freestyle) for the U.S. at the 2000 Olympics in Sydney.

John Thompson (b. Sept. 2, 1941): Basketball; coached centers Patrick Ewing, Alonzo Mourning and Dikembe Mutombo at Georgetown; reached NCAA tourney final 3 out of 4 years with Ewing, winning title in 1984; also led Hoyas to 6 Big East tourney titles; coached 1988 U.S. Olympic team to bronze medal; retired abruptly during 1999 season with 27-year mark of 596-239.

Bobby Thomson (b. Oct. 25, 1923): Baseball OF; career .270 hitter who won the 1951 NL pennant for the NY Giants with a 1-out, 3-run HR in the bottom of the 9th inning of Game 3 of a best-of-3 playoff with Brooklyn; the pitcher was Ralph Branca, the count was 0-1 and the Dodgers were ahead 4-2; the Giants had trailed Brooklyn by 13½ games on Aug. 11.

Ian Thorpe (b. Oct. 13, 1982): Swimming; Australian who won gold at Sydney Olympics in the 400m free (breaking his own world record) and silver in the 200m freestyle; was also part of relay team that won gold and broke the world record in the 4x100m and 4x200 freestyle relays; broke world records in the 200, 400 and 800m free at the 2001 world championships; 2002 Jesse Owens Award winner.

Jim Thorpe (b. May 28, 1888, d. May 28, 1953): 2-time All-America in football; won both pentathlon and decathlon at 1912 Olympics; stripped of medals a month later for playing semi-pro baseball prior to Games; medals restored in 1982; played major league baseball (1913-19) and pro football (1920-26,28); chosen "Athlete of the Half Century" by AP in 1950.

Bill Tilden (b. Feb. 10, 1893, d. June 5, 1953): Tennis; won 7 U.S. and 3 Wimbledon titles in 1920s; led U.S. to 7 straight Davis Cup victories (1920-26).

Tinker to Evers to Chance Chicago Cubs double play combination from 1903-10; immortalized in poem by New York sportswriter Franklin P. Adams— SS Joe Tinker (1880-1948), 2B Johnny Evers (1883-1947) and 1B Frank Chance (1877-1924); all 3 managed the Cubs and made the Hall of Fame.

Y.A. Tittle (b. Oct. 24, 1926): Football QB; Yelberton Abraham Tittle played 17 years in AAFC and NFL; All-Pro 4 times; league MVP with San Francisco (1957) and NY Giants (1962); passed for 28,339 career yards.

Alberto Tomba (b. Dec. 19, 1966): Italian alpine skier; winner of 5 Olympic medals (3 gold, 2 silver); became 1st alpine skier to win gold medals in 2 consecutive Winter Games when he won the slalom and giant slalom in 1988 then repeated in the GS in '92; also won silvers in slalom in 1992 and '94.

Dara Torres (b. April 15, 1967): Swimmer; her 9 career Olympic medals (4G, 1S, 4B) are the 2nd-most for an American woman; took a 7-year hiatus before returning to the pool to win 5 medals in Sydney 2000; participated in 4 olympic games overall (1984,88,92,2000).

Vladislav Tretiak (b. Apr. 25, 1952): Hockey G; led USSR to Olympic gold medals in 1972 and '76; starred for Soviets against Team Canada in 1972, and again in 2 Canada Cups (1976,81).

Lee Trevino (b. Dec. 1, 1939): Golfer; 2-time winner of 3 majors—U.S. Open (1968,71), British Open (1971-72) and PGA (1974,84); Player of Year once on PGA Tour (1971) and 3 times with Seniors (1990,92,94); 27 PGA Tour and 29 Senior Tour wins.

Felix Trinidad (b. Jan. 10, 1973): Puerto Rican boxer; former WBC/IBF welterweight champion; won WBC belt with a majority decision over Oscar De La Hoya in Sept., 1999; stepped up to junior middleweight and won the WBA title from David Reid in March, 2000; moved to middleweight and lost in a 12th-round TKO to Bernard Hopkins in Sept. 2001; announced retirement in 2002 with a record of 41-1 and 34 KOs.

Bryan Trottier (b. July 17, 1956): Hockey C; led NY Islanders to 4 straight Stanley Cups (1980-83); Rookie of Year (1976); scoring champion (134 points) and regular season MVP in 1979; playoff MVP (1980); added 5th and 6th Cups with Pittsburgh in 1991 and '92; entered Hockey Hall of Fame in 1997; hired as head coach of NY Rangers in 2002.

Gene Tunney (b. May 25, 1897, d. Nov. 7, 1978): Boxer; world heavyweight champion from 1926-28; beat 31-year-old champ Jack Dempsey in unanimous 10 round decision in 1926; beat him again in famous "long count" rematch in '27; quit while still champion in 1928 with 65-1-1 record and 47 KOs.

Ted Turner (b. Nov. 19, 1938): Sportsman and TV mogul; skippered Courageous to America's Cup win in 1977; owner of MLB Atlanta Braves, NBA Hawks and NHL Thrashers; owner of CNN, TNT and TBS; founder of Goodwill Games; 1991 Time Man of Year.

Mike Tyson (b. June 30, 1966): Boxer; youngest (age 19) to win heavyweight title (WBC in 1986); undisputed champ from 1987 until upset loss to 42-1 shot Buster Douglas on Feb. 10, 1990, in Tokyo; found guilty on Feb. 10, 1992, of raping 18-year-old Miss Black America contestant Desiree Washington in Indianapolis on July 19, 1991; sentenced to 6-year prison term; released May 9, 1995 after serving 3 years; reclaimed WBC and WBA belts with wins over Frank Bruno and Bruce Seldon in 1996; lost WBA title to Evander Holyfield in 1996; brought his career to a halt when he bit Holyfield twice in the ear during their WBA championship fight in 1997; suffered an 8th-round KO loss to Lennox Lewis in June 2002.

Wyomia Tyus (b. Aug. 29, 1945): Track & Field; 1st woman to win consecutive Olympic gold medals in 100m (1964-68).

Peter Ueberroth (b. Sept. 2, 1937): Organizer of 1984 Summer Olympics in LA; 1984 *Time* Man of Year; baseball commissioner from 1984-89; headed Rebuild Los Angeles for one year after 1992 riots.

Johnny Unitas (b. May 7, 1933, d. Sept. 11, 2002): Football QB; led Baltimore Colts to 2 NFL titles (1958-59) and a Super Bowl win (1971); All-Pro 5 times; 3-time MVP (1959,64,67); passed for 40,239 career yards and 290 TDs.

Al Unser Jr. (b. Apr. 19, 1962): Auto racer; 2-time CART-IndyCar national champion (1990,94); captured Indy 500 for 2nd time in 3 years in '94, giving Unser family 9 overall titles at the Brickyard; 31 CART wins in 18 years; left CART for Indy Racing League at the start of the 2000 season; son of Al and nephew of Bobby.

Al Unser Sr. (b. May 29, 1939): Auto racer; 3-time USAC-CART national champion (1970,83,85); 4-time winner of Indy 500 (1970-71,78,87); retired in 1994 ranked 3rd (now 4th) on all-time CART list with 39 wins; younger brother of Bobby and father of Al Jr.

Bobby Unser (b. Feb. 20, 1934): Auto racer; 2-time USAC-CART national champion (1968,74); 3-time winner of Indy 500 (1968,75,81); retired after 1981 season; ranks 5th on all-time CART list with 35 career wins.

Gene Upshaw (b. Aug. 15, 1945): Football G; 2-time All-AFL and 3-time All-NFL selection with Oakland; helped lead Raiders to 2 Super Bowl titles in 1976 and '80; executive director of NFL Players Assn. since 1987; agreed to application of salary cap in 1994.

Jim Valvano (b. Mar. 10, 1946, d. Apr. 28, 1993): Basketball; coach at N.C. State whose team upset Houston to win national title in 1983; in 19 seasons as a coach appeared in 8 NCAA tournaments; twice voted ACC Coach of the Year; career record 346-212; AD at N.C. State (1986-89) when a recruiting and admissions scandal forced him out of the job; worked as a broadcaster for ESPN and ABC; died after a year-long battle with cancer; The V Foundation for cancer research is named for him.

Norm Van Brocklin (b. Mar. 15, 1926, d. May 2, 1983): Football QB-P; led NFL in passing 3 times and punting twice; led LA Rams (1951) and Philadelphia (1960) to NFL titles; MVP in 1960.

Amy Van Dyken (b. Feb. 17, 1973): Swimming; first American woman to win four gold medals in one Olympics (1996); won the individual 50m freestyle, 100m butterfly, and was on the US team for the 4x100 freestyle and 4x50 medley; won gold at Sydney in 2000 as part of the US 4x100 freestyle relay.

Johnny Vander Meer (b. Nov. 2, 1914, d. Oct. 6, 1997): Baseball LHP; only major leaguer to pitch consecutive no-hitters (June 11 & 15, 1938).

Harold S. Vanderbilt (b. July 6, 1884, d. July 4, 1970): Sportsman; successfully defended America's Cup 3 times (1930, 34,37); also invented contract bridge in 1926.

Glenna Collett Vare (b. June 20, 1903, d. Feb. 10, 1989): Golfer; won record 6 U.S. Women's Amateur titles from 1922-35; "the female Bobby Jones."

Andy Varipapa (b. Mar. 31, 1891, d. Aug. 25, 1984): Bowler; trick-shot artist; won consecutive All-Star match game titles (1947-48) at age 55 and 56.

Bill Veeck (b. Feb. 9, 1914, d. Jan. 2, 1986): Maverick baseball executive; owned AL teams in Cleveland, St. Louis and Chicago from 1946-80; introduced ballpark giveaways, exploding scoreboards, Wrigley Field's ivy-covered walls and midget Eddie Gaedel; won World Series with Indians (1948) and pennant with White Sox (1959).

Jacques Villeneuve (b. Apr. 9, 1971): Canadian auto racer; Indianapolis 500 runner-up and IndyCar Rookie of Year in 1994; won 500 and IndyCar driving championship in 1995; jumped to Formula One racing in 1996 and won the F1 title in 1997.

Fay Vincent (b. May 29, 1938): Baseball; became 8th commissioner after death of A. Bartlett Giamatti in 1989; presided over World Series earthquake, owners' lockout and banishment of NY Yankees owner George Steinbrenner in his first year on the job; contentious relationship with owners resulted in his resignation on Sept. 7, 1992, four days after 18-9 "no confidence" vote.

Lasse Viren (b. July 22, 1949): Finnish runner; won gold medals at 5,000 and 10,000 meters in 1972 Munich Olympics; repeated 5,000/10,000 double in 1976 Games and added a fifth place finish in the marathon.

Dick Vitale (b. June 9, 1939): Broadcaster; Radio and television commentator for ESPN and ABC Sports known for his enthusiastic, almost spastic style; had successful college and pro basketball coaching career with the University of Detroit (1973-77) and the Detroit Pistons (1978-79).

Lanny Wadkins (b. Dec. 5, 1949): Golfer; member of 8 U.S. Ryder Cup teams and captain of 1995 team; 21 PGA Tour wins.

Honus Wagner (b. Feb. 24, 1874, d. Dec. 6, 1955): Baseball SS; hit .300 for 17 consecutive seasons (1897-1913) with Louisville and Pittsburgh; led NL in batting 8 times; ended career with 3,430 career hits, a .329 average and 722 stolen bases.

Lisa Wagner (b. May 19, 1961): Bowler; 4-time LPBT Player of Year (1983,86,88,93); 1980's Bowler of Decade; first woman to earn $100,000 in a season; winner of 32 pro titles.

Grete Waitz (b. Oct. 1, 1953): Norwegian runner; 9-time winner of New York City Marathon from 1978-88; won silver medal at 1984 Olympics.

Jersey Joe Walcott (b. Jan. 31, 1914, d. Feb. 27, 1994): Boxer; oldest heavyweight (37) to ever win the championship; lost four championship bouts before knocking out Ezzard Charles in the seventh round in 1951; lost the title the following year, losing to Rocky Marciano; won 50 bouts, 30 by knockout, lost 17 and fought one draw as a professional; later became sheriff of Camden County, NJ.

Doak Walker (b. Jan. 1, 1927, d. Sept. 27, 1998): Football HB; won Heisman Trophy as SMU junior in 1948; led Detroit to 2 NFL titles (1952-53); All-Pro 4 times in 6 years.

Herschel Walker (b. Mar. 3, 1962): Football RB; led Georgia to national title as freshman in 1980; won Heisman in 1982 then jumped to upstart USFL in '83; signed by Dallas Cowboys after USFL folded; led NFL in rushing in 1988; traded to Minnesota in 1989 for 5 players and 6 draft picks.

Rusty Wallace (b. Aug. 14, 1956): Auto racing; NASCAR Winston Cup champion in 1989 and runner-up in 1980, 1988 and 1993; recorded 54 victories and has won over $30 million in earnings in 23 years of racing as of Sept. 1, 2002.

Bill Walsh (b. Nov. 30, 1931): Football; Hall of Fame coach and GM of 3 Super Bowl winners with San Francisco (1982,85,89); retired after 1989 Super Bowl; returned to college coaching in 1992 for his second stint at Stanford; retired again after 1994 season; returned as 49er GM from 1999-2001.

Bill Walton (b. Nov. 5, 1952): Basketball C; 3-time College Player of Year (1972-74); led UCLA to 2 national titles (1972-73); led Portland to NBA title as MVP in 1977; regular season MVP in 1978; successful basketball analyst, hired for ESPN/ABC's coverage in 2002.

Darrell Waltrip (b. Feb. 5, 1947): Auto racing; 3-time NASCAR Winston Cup champion (1981,82,85); 84 career Winston Cup wins and 59 poles.

Arch Ward (b. Dec. 27, 1896, d. July 9, 1955): Promoter and sports editor of *Chicago Tribune* from 1930-55; founder of baseball All-Star Game (1933), Chicago College All-Star Football Game (1934) and the All-America Football Conference (1946-49).

Charlie Ward (b. Oct. 12, 1970): Football QB and Basketball G; first Heisman winner to play for national champs (Florida St. in 1993) since Tony Dorsett in 1976; won Sullivan Award (1993); 3-year starter for FSU basketball team; not taken in NFL draft; 1st round pick of NY Knicks in 1994 NBA draft.

Glenn (Pop) Warner (b. Apr. 5, 1871, d. Sept. 7, 1954): Football innovator; coached at 7 colleges over 49 years; 319 career wins 2nd only to Bear Bryant's 323 in Div. I-A; produced 47 All-Americas, including Jim Thorpe and Ernie Nevers.

Kurt Warner (b. June 22, 1971): Football QB; former Arena leaguer who led the St. Louis Rams to 2000 Super Bowl title over Tennessee; threw for a record 414 yards and was voted Super Bowl MVP; brought Rams back to the Super Bowl in 2002 and lost to the Patriots; 2-time NFL MVP (1999,2001).

Tom Watson (b. Sept. 4, 1949): Golfer; 6-time PGA Player of the Year (1977-80,82,84); has won 5 British Opens, 2 Masters and a U.S. Open; 4-time Ryder Cup member and captain of 1993 team; 34 PGA tour wins.

Earl Weaver (b. Aug. 14, 1930): Baseball; managed the Baltimore Orioles to 6 Eastern Division titles, four AL pennants and a World Series victory in 1970; was ejected 91 times and suspended four times for outbursts against umpires; record of 1,480-1,060 from 1968-82 and 1985-86.

Karrie Webb (b. Dec. 21, 1974): Golfer; youngest woman to win career Grand Slam; won 6 majors in all through 2002; her win in the 2002 British Open made her the first player to win the "Super Grand Slam" (5 different majors); has accumulated enough points to be eligible for induction to the LGPA Hall of Fame — needs only to meet the 10-year membership requirement.

Dick Weber (b. Dec. 23, 1929): Bowler; 3-time PBA Bowler of the Year (1961,63,65); won 30 PBA titles in 4 decades; father of Pete.

Pete Weber (b. Aug. 21, 1962): Bowler; 2nd on all-time PBA money list through 2001-02 season; 1990 PBA Rookie of the Year; inducted into PBA Hall of Fame (1998); son of Dick.

Johnny Weissmuller (b. June 2, 1904, d. Jan. 20 1984): Swimmer; won 3 gold medals at 1924 Olympics and 2 more at 1928 Games; became Hollywood's most famous Tarzan.

Jerry West (b. May 28, 1938): Basketball G; 2-time All-America and NCAA Final 4 MOP (1959) at West Virginia; led 1960 U.S. Olympic team to gold medal; 10-time All-NBA 1st-team; NBA finals MVP (1969); led LA Lakers to NBA title once as player (1972) and then 6 more times (1980,82,85,87,88,00) as an executive in various positions with the club; hired as President of Basketball Ops. by Memphis Grizzlies in 2002; his silhouette serves as the NBA's logo.

Pernell Whitaker (b. Jan. 2, 1964): Boxer; won Olympic gold medal as lightweight in 1984; won 4 world championships as lightweight, jr. welterweight, welterweight and jr. middleweight; outfought but failed to beat Julio Cesar Chavez when 1993 welterweight title defense ended in controversial draw; pro record of 41-3-1 (17 KOs).

Bill White (b. Jan. 28, 1934): Baseball; former NL president and highest ranking black executive in sports from 1989-94; as 1st baseman, won 7 Gold Gloves and hit .286 with 202 HRs in 13 seasons.

Byron (Whizzer) White (b. June 8, 1917, d. Apr. 15, 2002): Football; All-America HB at Colorado (1937); signed with Pittsburg in 1938 for the then largest contract in pro history ($15,800); took Rhodes Scholarship in 1939; returned to NFL in 1940 to lead league in rushing and retired in 1941; named to U.S. Supreme Court by President Kennedy in 1962 and stepped down in 1993.

Reggie White (b. Dec. 19, 1961): Football DE; consensus All-America in 1983 at Tennessee; 7-time All-NFL (1986-92) with Philadelphia; signed as free agent with Green Bay in 1993 for $17 million over 4 years; played key role in Packers 1997 Super Bowl victory; made headlines in 1998 after making controversial public comments about gays and minorities; retired in 1999 but returned with the Carolina Panthers in 2000; all-time NFL leader in sacks (198).

Kathy Whitworth (b. Sept. 27, 1939): Golf; 7-time LPGA Player of the Year (1966-69,71-73); won 6 majors; 88 tour wins, most on LPGA or PGA tour.

Hoyt Wilhelm (b. July 26, 1923, d. Aug. 23, 2002): Baseball RHP; Knuckleballer who is 3rd all-time in games pitched (1,070) and 1st in games finished (651) and games won in relief (123); career ERA of 2.52 and 227 saves; 1st reliever inducted into Hall of Fame (1985); threw no-hitter vs. NY Yankees (1958); also hit lone HR of career in first major league at bat (1952); won Purple Heart at the Battle of the Bulge.

Lenny Wilkens (b. Oct. 28, 1937): Basketball; NBA's all-time winningest coach; MVP of 1960 NIT as Providence guard; played 15 years in NBA, including 4 as player-coach; MVP of 1971 All-Star Game; coached Seattle to NBA title in 1979; Coach of Year in 1994 with Atlanta; one of only two men (John Wooden) to be honored by the Hall of Fame as player and coach; left Atlanta in 2000 to coach the Toronto Raptors; career record of 1268-1056 including playoffs.

Dominique Wilkins (b. Jan. 12, 1960): Basketball F; last player to lead NBA in scoring (1986) before Michael Jordan's 7-year reign; All-NBA 1st team in 1986; elder statesman of Dream Team II.

Bud Wilkinson (b. Apr. 23, 1916, d. Feb. 9, 1994): Football; played on 1936 national championship team at Minnesota; coached Oklahoma to 3 national titles (1950, 55, 56); won 4 Orange and 2 Sugar Bowls; teams had winning streaks of 47 (1953-57) and 31 (1948-50); retired after 1963 season with 145-29-4 record in 17 years; also coached St. Louis of NFL to 9-20 record from 1978-79.

Ricky Williams (b. May 21, 1977): Football RB; became all-time NCAA Div. I-A leader in rushing yards (6,279) and touchdowns (75) at Texas but has since been passed in both categories; 1998 Heisman Trophy winner; Mike Ditka and New Orleans Saints traded their entire draft to take him fifth overall in 1999 NFL draft; traded to Miami Dolphins in 2002.

Serena Williams (b. Sept. 26, 1981): Tennis; beat Martina Hingis for 1999 U.S. Open championship to become the first African-American woman to win a Grand Slam title since Althea Gibson in 1958; won Wimbledon, the French Open and U.S. Open in 2002, defeating sister Venus in the final of each; has won career doubles grand slam with Venus.

Ted Williams (b. Aug. 30, 1918, d. July 5, 2002): Baseball OF; led AL in batting 6 times, and HRs and RBI 4 times each; won Triple Crown twice (1942,47); 2-time MVP (1946,49); last player to bat .400 when he hit .406 in 1941; Marine Corps combat pilot who missed three full seasons during World War II (1943-45) and most of two others (1952-53) during Korean War; hit .344 lifetime with 521 HRs in 19 years with Boston Red Sox.

Venus Williams (b. June 17, 1980): Tennis; won career doubles grand slam with sister Serena; recorded fastest serve in WTA history with 127 mph blast; winner of 2 Wimbledon (2000,01) and 2 U.S. Open (2000,01) singles titles; 2000 Olympic singles and doubles (w/Serena) gold medalist.

Walter Ray Williams Jr. (b. Oct. 6, 1959): Bowling and Horseshoes; 5-time PBA Bowler of Year (1986,93,96,97,98); all-time leading money winner on the PBA Tour entering 2002-03 season; won 6 World Horseshoe Pitching titles.

Hack Wilson (b. Apr. 26, 1900, d. Nov. 23, 1948): Baseball; as a Chicago Cub, he produced one of baseball's most outstanding seasons in 1930 with 56 home runs, .356 batting average, 105 walks and, most amazingly, a major league record 191 RBIs that still stands; finished career with 1,461 hits, 244 homers, 1,062 RBIs; member of Baseball Hall of Fame.

Dave Winfield (b. Oct. 3, 1951): Baseball OF-DH; selected in 4 major sports league drafts in 1973— NFL, NBA, ABA, and MLB; chose baseball and played in 12 All-Star Games over 22-year career; at age 41, helped lead Toronto to World Series title in 1992; 3,110 hits and 465 HRs.

Katarina Witt (b. Dec. 3, 1965): East German figure skater; 4-time world champion (1984-85,87-88); won consecutive Olympic gold medals (1984,88).

John Wooden (b. Oct. 14, 1910): Basketball; College Player of Year at Purdue in 1932; coached UCLA to 10 national titles (1964-65,67-73,75); one of only two men (Lenny Wilkens) to be honored by the Hall of Fame as player and coach.

Tiger Woods (b. Dec. 30, 1975): Golfer; youngest (18) and first minority to win U.S. Amateur in 1994, won it again in '95 and '96; in first full year on the PGA tour, he won 6 of 25 events and broke the single season money record; won 1997 Masters by a record 18 under par and 13 stroke margin of victory; won second major at 1999 PGA Championship; in 2000 won the U.S. Open at Pebble Beach by a record 15 strokes, the British Open by 8 strokes and the PGA Championship in a playoff; one of only five players to win all four Grand Slam titles (others are Hogan, Nicklaus, Player and Sarazen); held all four Major titles simultaneously after his win at 2001 Masters; won 2 more majors in 2002 (Masters and U.S. Open); the all-time career money leader on the PGA Tour.

Mickey Wright (b. Feb. 14, 1935): Golfer; won 3 of 4 majors (LPGA, U.S. Open, Titleholders) in 1961; 4-time winner of both U.S. Open and LPGA titles; 82 career wins including 13 majors.

Early Wynn (b. Jan. 6, 1920, d. Mar. 4, 1999): Baseball RHP; won 20 games 5 times; Cy Young winner in 1959; 300-244 record in 23 years.

Kristi Yamaguchi (b. July 12, 1971): Figure Skating; finished second in the 1991 American nationals but won the world title that year; dominated the sport in 1992 by winning the national, world and Olympic titles and then turned professional.

Cale Yarborough (b. Mar. 27, 1940): Auto racer; 3-time NASCAR national champion (1976-78); 4-time winner of Daytona 500 (1968,77,83-84); ranks 5th on NASCAR all-time list with 83 wins.

Carl Yastrzemski (b. Aug. 22, 1939): Baseball OF; led AL in batting 3 times; won Triple Crown and MVP in 1967; had 3,419 hits and 452 HRs in 23 years with Boston; member of Hall of Fame.

Cy Young (b. Mar. 29, 1867, d. Nov. 4, 1955): Baseball RHP; all-time leader in wins (511), losses (313), complete games (751) and innings pitched (7,356); had career 2.63 ERA in 22 years (1890-1911); 30-game winner 5 times and 20-game winner 11 other times; threw three no-hitters and a perfect game (1904); annual AL and NL pitching awards named after him.

Sheila Young (b. Oct. 14, 1950): Speed skater and cyclist; 1st U.S. athlete to win 3 medals at Winter Olympics (1976); won speed skating overall and sprint cycling world titles in 1976.

Steve Young (b. Oct. 11, 1961): Football QB; All-America at BYU (1983); NFL Player of Year (1992) with SF 49ers; only QB to lead NFL in passer rating 4 straight years (1991-94); rating of 112.8 in 1994 was highest ever; threw record 6 TD passes in MVP performance in Super Bowl XXIX; retired with NFL records for highest passer rating (96.8) and completion percentage (64.4); 232 career TD passes and 33,124 yards.

Robin Yount (b. Sept. 16, 1955): Baseball SS-OF; AL MVP at 2 positions— as SS in 1982 and OF in '89; retired after 1993 season with 3,142 hits, 251 HRs and a major-league-record 123 sacrifice flies after 20 seasons with Milwaukee Brewers; inducted into Hall of Fame in 1999.

Steve Yzerman (b. May 9, 1965): Hockey C; Captained the Detroit Red Wings to Stanley Cup wins in 1997, 98 and 2002; won the Conn Smythe Trophy as the playoff MVP in 1998; one of only 13 NHL players to score 600 goals; entered the 2002-03 season 6th in career scoring (1,662 points).

Mario Zagalo (b. Aug. 9, 1931): Soccer; Brazilian forward who is one of only two men (Franz Beckenbauer is the other) to serve as both captain (1962) and coach (1970,94) of World Cup champion.

Babe Didrikson Zaharias (b. June 26, 1911, d. Sept. 27, 1956): All-around athlete who was chosen AP Female Athlete of Year 6 times from 1932-54; won 2 gold medals (javelin and 80-meter hurdles) and a silver (high jump) at 1932 Olympics; played baseball and acquired the nickname "Babe" for her tape measure home runs; real first name was Mildred; took up golf in 1935 and went on to win 55 pro and amateur events; won 10 majors, including 3 U.S. Opens (1948,50,54); helped found LPGA in 1949; chosen female "Athlete of the Half Century" by AP in 1950; when asked if there was anything she didn't play, she replied, "Yeah, dolls."

Tony Zale (b. May 29, 1913, d. March 20, 1997): Boxer; 2-time world middleweight champion (1941-47,48); fought Rocky Graziano for title 3 times in 21 months in 1947-48, winning twice; pro record 67-18-2 with 44 KOs.

Frank Zamboni (b. Jan. 16, 1901, d. July 27, 1988): Mechanic, ice salesman and skating rink owner in Paramount, Calif.; invented 1st ice-resurfacing machine in 1949; now there are very few skating rinks without one as thousands have been sold in more than 35 countries worldwide

Emil Zatopek (b. Sept. 19, 1922, d. Nov. 22, 2000): Czech distance runner; winner of 1948 Olympic gold medal in 10,000 meters; 4 years later, won unprecedented Olympic triple crown (5,000 meters, 10,000 meters and marathon) at 1952 Games in Helsinki.

John Ziegler (b. Feb. 9, 1934): Hockey; NHL president from 1977-92; negotiated settlement with rival WHA in 1979 that led to inviting four WHA teams (Edmonton, Hartford, Quebec and Winnipeg) to join NHL; stepped down June 12, 1992, 2 months after settling 10-day players' strike.

Kim Zmeskal (b. Feb 6, 1976): Gymnastics; Won three U.S. all-around championships in a row (1990-'92); first American gymnast to win the all-around competition in the world championships (1991).

Pirmin Zurbriggen (b. Feb. 4, 1963): Swiss alpine skier; 4-time World Cup overall champ (1984,87-88,90) and 3-time runner-up; 40 World Cup wins in 10 years; won gold and bronze medals at 1988 Olympics.

Ballparks & Arenas

The defending Super Bowl champion New England Patriots opened **Gillette Stadium** in 2002.

AP/Wide World Photos

ESPN
Information Please®
SPORTS ALMANAC

Coming Attractions

2002

NBA BASKETBALL

San Antonio (West): Groundbreaking for the SBC Center (SBC Communications Inc. is the title sponsor) took place on Aug. 23, 2000. The new arena seats 18,500 for basketball and 13,000 for minor league hockey, including 54 luxury suites, and serves as the home to the Spurs, the annual San Antonio Livestock Exposition and Rodeo and the AHL's San Antonio Rampage; estimated cost: $175 million; located adjacent to the Freeman Coliseum in East San Antonio. The Spurs opened the building with a preseason game against the New York Knicks on Oct. 18, 2002.

NFL FOOTBALL

Detroit (NFC): Groundbreaking of Ford Field (Ford Motor Co., is the title sponsor) took place Nov. 16, 1999. Stadium is located in downtown Detroit and incorporates the adjacent old Hudson's Warehouse which will house most of the stadium's suites and club level seating. Fans will have a view of the city skyline with natural light shining through the glass wall at the main entrance at Adams and Brush streets. The domed stadium will seat 65,000, including 125 luxury suites, for football; estimated cost: $300 million. The stadium opened Aug. 24, 2002 with a preseason game against the Pittsburgh Steelers.

New England (AFC): CMGI Field opened on May 11, 2002 with an MLS soccer game. The New England Revolution beat the Dallas Burn, 2-0, in front of a sell-out crowd of 22,006 (the stadium is downsized for Revolution games). CMGI Field was renamed Gillette Stadium when Boston-based Gillette Co. became the title sponsor on Aug. 5, 2002 after struggling internet company (and original title sponsor) CMGI bowed out. The new open-air, grass-field stadium seats 68,000 and includes 80 luxury suites and over 6,000 club seats; A light tower designed to evoke images of a New England lighthouse is the stadium's signature architectural feature; estimated cost of entire stadium: $325 million.

Houston (AFC): Reliant Stadium (Reliant Engergy is the title sponsor) opened Aug. 24, 2002 with a preseason NFL game between the Houston Texans and Miami Dolphins. The new home of the expansion Texans and annual Houston Livestock Show and Rodeo is the world's first retractable roof football stadium with a grass playing surface. The roof is able to open or close in 10 minutes. The stadium seats 69,500, including 147 luxury suites, but will be expandable up to 72,000 seats for events like the Super Bowl which it is set to host in 2004; estimated cost: $367 million.

Seattle (NFC): Seahawks Stadium and Exhibition Center opened on July 20, 2002 with an event called Public Fan Fare days which included self-guided tours, soccer, football and cheerleading clinics, etc. Stadium is located on old site of Kingdome, which was imploded on Mar. 26, 2000; open-air, grass-field stadium seats 67,000 (expanded capacity: 72,000) and includes 82 luxury suites and 7,000 club seats; approximately 70 percent of the seats are protected from the elements; stadium and exhibition center cost an estimated $430 million.

2003

BASEBALL

Cincinnati (NL): Construction of the Great American Ballpark (Great American Insurance is the title sponsor) began Aug. 1, 2000. The stadium site overlaps the current site of Cinergy Field (formerly known as Riverfront Stadium). Part of the left- and center-field stands at Cinergy were removed in January 2001 to clear space for the new construction to begin. The grass-field, baseball-only park is not expected to have any unusual angles in the outfield and will seat an estimated 42,060. Home plate of the new park will be set 568 feet from the Ohio River, probably a little too far for splash-down homers that have been made famous at San Francisco's Pacific Bell Park. Estimated cost of project: $297 million. Earliest opening would be spring 2003.

NBA BASKETBALL

Houston (West): Groundbreaking for the new Houston Arena (title sponsor pending) for the Rockets and WNBA Comets took place July 31, 2001. The multi-purpose complex will seat 18,500 for basketball and 17,800 for hockey, including 92 luxury suites and 2,800 club seats; estimated cost: $175 million; The arena will be located in downtown Houston on a four-block site bounded by LaBranch, Jackson, Bell and Polk streets. Earliest opening would be September 2003.

NFL FOOTBALL

Chicago (NFC): A total renovation of Soldier Field is underway. Part of a larger lakefront improvement project; estimated cost of entire project including the stadium, underground parking structure and additional infrastructure: $587 million. The improved stadium will seat an estimated 63,000 including 133 luxury suites and 8,600 club seats. Bears will play their home games of the 2002 season at the University of Illinois' Memorial Stadium and are scheduled to return to Soldier Field in 2003.

Green Bay (NFC): In September 2000, voters approved a plan to use a new 0.5 percent sales tax in Brown County to help fund a $295 million renovation of 43-year-old Lambeau Field. Unlike most stadium renovations, lack of luxury suites was not the issue here. The newly renovated stadium will actually have 32 fewer suites. Approximately 10,000 seats (including about 4,300 additional club seats) will be added bringing the total seating capacity to about 71,100, including 167 luxury suites. Plans also call for the team and the city of Green Bay to seek naming rights before the 2003 season. A minimum bid of $120 million would have to be considered; the team and city would split the proceeds; renovation is scheduled to be completed in September 2003.

Philadelphia (NFC): Three months after opening a $37 million corporate headquarters and training complex, the Eagles broke ground on the 66,000-seat, Lincoln Financial Field (Lincoln Financial Group is the title sponsor), located at 11th Street and Pattison Avenue in South Philadelphia. The city is responsible for site acquisition and preparation while the Eagles are covering construction and overrun costs. Estimated cost of $500 million includes $310 million contributed by the Eagles. Earliest Eagles' home opener could be August 2003.

NHL HOCKEY

Phoenix (West): Groundbreaking took place in 2002 on a 225-acre, three million square foot facility in Glendale, Ariz., featuring a new 17,500-seat, multi-purpose arena that will serve as a home to the Phoenix Coyotes. The complex, to be located at 101 Freeway and Glendale Avenue, features entertainment, retail, restaurants, office, hotel and residential venues and includes 70 luxury suites. The first phase of the project, expected to open in December 2003, will cost an estimated $550 million.

Seahawks Stadium was one of four new NFL stadiums opened in 2002.

2004

BASEBALL

Philadelphia (NL): Construction for the new as-yet-unnamed ballpark is underway. The baseball-only, grass-field park will be located adjacent to Veterans Stadium in South Philadelphia and offer scenic views of the Philadelphia skyline. Estimated cost of project is $346 million. Phillies home opener is set for April 2004.

St. Louis (NL): New ballpark for the Cardinals is in the planning stages. The proposed site is south of the existing Busch Stadium on the south stadium parking lot. The proposed open-air, baseball-only ballpark would offer a spectacular view of the Gateway Arch. Since the new site partially overlaps the current stadium site, for the first year the park would offer about 40,000 permanent and temporary seats, but by year two the stadium would be complete and the seating capacity would grow to 47,900. Estimated cost (including a new Cardinals Hall of Fame and Museum) is $370 million. Earliest opening would be April 2004.

San Diego (NL): Construction on the Padres new ballpark is well underway. The open-air, grass-field park will be located on a one-square-block downtown lot and be part of a larger redevelopment project that will include a new hotel, office space and retail space. The park will seat approximately 46,000, including 60 luxury suites, and cost an estimated $267.5 million. The adjacent historic Western Metal Supply Company building will be incorporated as a portion of the left field wall and foul pole. The earliest Padres' home opener would be April 2004.

2005

BASEBALL

Boston (AL): New Fenway Park is in the planning stages. The latest plans have the open-air, grass-field park located adjacent to the existing Fenway Park and emulating many of Fenway's features including the Green Monster and Pesky's Pole; part of the project includes preserving portions of the old ballpark as a public park; estimated cost of entire project: $627 million; would seat 44,130 and the earliest Red Sox home opener would be April 2005.

New York (NL): New ballpark for the Mets is in the early planning stages. To be located adjacent to Shea Stadium in Queens. The retractable-roof stadium would seat 45,000, including 78 luxury suites and 5,000 club seats. Estimated cost: $500 million. Earliest opening would be April 2005.

Florida (NL): The team is in discussions with the city of Miami involving financing for a new ballpark for the Marlins. Preliminary plans call for a $500 million ballpark to be built in downtown Miami. No realistic timetable has been set forth but the earliest home opener would likely be no earlier than April 2005.

NBA BASKETBALL

New Jersey (East): New arena for the Nets is in the planning stages. Funding from a new lease on Newark Airport will help pay for the project. Arena would be located in downtown Newark near Penn Station and would house the Nets and NHL's New Jersey Devils; estimated cost: $355 million. Earliest opening would be fall 2005.

NFL FOOTBALL

Arizona (NFC): New stadium for the Cardinals is in the planning stages. In August 2002, the Cardinals committed to a site in Glendale, Ariz. (the same community that will be home to a new arena for the NHL's Phoenix Coyotes). The 67,000-seat (expandable to 73,000) stadium would have a partially retractable roof and wall and feature a grass field that could be rolled out into the adjoining parking lot in order to help it grow. The stadium would include 88 luxury suites and 7,000 club seats; estimated cost: $350 million. Earliest Cardinals' home opener would be fall 2005.

San Francisco (NFC): New stadium for the 49ers is in the early planning stages. The stadium would likely be part of a retail and entertainment complex to be located at Candlestick Point. In 1997, area voters approved a $100 million bond measure to fund a new stadium/mall. Many aspects of the project are yet to be decided including estimated costs, further financing and the actual design. The Earliest 49ers' home opener would be in the fall of 2005.

NHL HOCKEY

New Jersey (East): New arena for the Devils is in the planning stages. Funding from a new lease on Newark Airport will help pay for the project. Arena would be located in downtown Newark near Penn Station and would house the Devils and NBA's New Jersey Nets; estimated cost: $355 million. Earliest opening would be fall 2005.

Home, Sweet Home

The home fields, home courts and home ice of the AL, NL, NBA, NFL, CFL, NHL, WNBA, NCAA Division I-A college football and Division I basketball. Also included are MLS stadiums, Formula One, CART, Indy Racing League and NASCAR auto racing tracks.

Attendance figures for the 2001 NFL regular season and the 2001-02 NBA and NHL regular seasons are provided. See Baseball chapter for 2002 AL and NL attendance figures.

MAJOR LEAGUE BASEBALL

American League

				Outfield Fences				
	Built	Capacity	LF	LCF	CF	RCF	RF	Field
Anaheim Angels . . . . **Edison International Field of Anaheim**	1966	**45,030**	365	387	400	370	365	Grass
Baltimore Orioles . . . . **Oriole Park at Camden Yards**	1992	**48,190**	337	376	406	391	320	Grass
Boston Red Sox . . . . **Fenway Park**	1912	**33,993**	310	379	390*	380	302	Grass
Chicago White Sox . . . . **Comiskey Park**	1991	**46,943**	330	377	400	372	335	Grass
Cleveland Indians . . . . **Jacobs Field**	1994	**43,068**	325	370	405	375	325	Grass
Detroit Tigers . . . . **Comerica Park**	2000	**40,120**	345	395	420	365	330	Grass
Kansas City Royals . . . . **Kauffman Stadium**	1973	**40,793**	330	375	400	375	330	Grass
Minnesota Twins . . . . **Hubert H. Humphrey Metrodome**	1982	**48,678**	343	385	408	367	327	Turf
New York Yankees . . . . **Yankee Stadium**	1923	**57,478**	318	399	408	385	314	Grass
Oakland Athletics . . . . . . **Network Associates Coliseum**	1966	**43,662**	330	367	400	367	330	Grass
Seattle Mariners . . . . **SAFECO Field**	1999	**47,116**	331	390	405	387	327	Grass
Tampa Bay Devil Rays . . . . **Tropicana Field**	1990	**43,761**	315	370	404	370	322	Turf
Texas Rangers . . . . **The Ballpark in Arlington**	1994	**49,115**	332	390	400	381	325	Grass
Toronto Blue Jays . . . . **SkyDome**	1989	**50,516**	328	375	400	375	328	Turf

*The straight-away center-field fence at Fenway Park is 390 feet from home plate but the deepest part of center-field, a.k.a. "the Triangle," is 420 feet away. The left-field fence, known as "the Green Monster," is 37 feet tall topped with a 23-foot screen.

National League

				Outfield Fences				
	Built	Capacity	LF	LCF	CF	RCF	RF	Field
Arizona Diamondbacks . . . . **Bank One Ballpark**	1998	**49,033**	330	376	407	376	334	Grass
Atlanta Braves . . . . **Turner Field**	1996	**50,091**	335	380	401	390	330	Grass
Chicago Cubs . . . . **Wrigley Field**	1914	**39,111**	355	368	400	368	353	Grass
Cincinnati Reds . . . . **Cinergy Field**	1970	**40,007**	325	370	393*	372	325	Turf
Colorado Rockies . . . . **Coors Field**	1995	**50,449**	347	390	415	375	350	Grass
Florida Marlins . . . . **Pro Player Stadium**	1987	**36,331**	330	385	434	385	345	Grass
Houston Astros . . . . **Minute Maid Park**	2000	**40,950**	315	362	436	373	326	Grass
Los Angeles Dodgers . . . . **Dodger Stadium**	1962	**56,000**	330	385	395	385	330	Grass
Milwaukee Brewers . . . . **Miller Park**	2001	**42,400**	340	374	400	378	345	Grass
Montreal Expos . . . . **Olympic Stadium**	1976	**46,500**	325	375	404	375	325	Turf
New York Mets . . . . **Shea Stadium**	1964	**56,749**	338	378	410	378	338	Grass
Philadelphia Phillies . . . . **Veterans Stadium**	1971	**62,418**	330	378	408	378	330	Turf
Pittsburgh Pirates . . . . **PNC Park**	2001	**37,898**	326	368	399*	375	324	Grass
St. Louis Cardinals . . . . **Busch Stadium**	1966	**49,814**	330	372	402	372	330	Grass
San Diego Padres . . . . **Qualcomm Stadium**	1967	**66,083**	334	367	396	382	322	Grass
San Francisco Giants . . . . **Pacific Bell Park**	2000	**41,467**	339	364	399	421	309	Grass

*The new dimensions of Cinergy field reflect the removal of the part of the left and center field stands to allow construction on the team's new stadium to continue. A 40-foot high wall was installed in center field. The deepest part of PNC Park is 410 feet between straight-away center and left-center.

Rank by Capacity

AL		NL	
New York	.57,478	San Diego	.66,083
Toronto	.50,516	Philadelphia	.62,418
Texas	.49,115	New York	.56,749
Minnesota	.48,678	Los Angeles	.56,000
Baltimore	.48,190	Colorado	.50,449
Seattle	.47,116	Atlanta	.50,091
Chicago	.46,943	St. Louis	.49,814
Anaheim	.45,030	Arizona	.49,033
Tampa Bay	.43,761	Montreal	.46,500
Oakland	.43,662	Milwaukee	.42,400
Cleveland	.43,068	San Francisco	.41,467
Kansas City	.40,793	Houston	.40,950
Detroit	.40,120	Cincinnati	.40,007
Boston	.33,993	Chicago	.39,111
		Pittsburgh	.37,898
		Florida	.36,331

Rank by Age

AL		NL	
Boston	.1912	Chicago	.1914
New York	.1923	Los Angeles	.1962
Anaheim	.1966	New York	.1964
Oakland	.1966	St. Louis	.1966
Kansas City	.1973	San Diego	.1967
Minnesota	.1982	Cincinnati	.1970
Toronto	.1989	Philadelphia	.1971
Tampa Bay	.1990	Montreal	.1976
Chicago	.1991	Florida	.1987
Baltimore	.1992	Atlanta	.1993
Cleveland	.1994	Colorado	.1995
Texas	.1994	Arizona	.1998
Seattle	.1999	Houston	.2000
Detroit	.2000	San Francisco	.2000
		Milwaukee	.2001
		Pittsburgh	.2001

Note: New York's Yankee Stadium (AL) was rebuilt in 1976.

Home Fields

Listed below are the principal home fields used through the years by current American and National League teams. The NL became a major league in 1876, the AL in 1901.

The capacity figures in the right-hand column indicate the largest seating capacity of the ballpark while the club played there. Capacity figures before 1915 (and the introduction of concrete grandstands) are sketchy at best and have been left blank.

American League

Anaheim Angels

1961	Wrigley Field (Los Angeles)	20,457
1962-65	Dodger Stadium	56,000
1966–	Edison International Field of Anaheim	45,030
	(1966 capacity—43,250)	

Baltimore Orioles

1901	Lloyd Street Grounds (Milwaukee)	—
1902-53	Sportsman's Park II (St. Louis)	30,500
1954-91	Memorial Stadium (Baltimore)	53,371
1992–	Oriole Park at Camden Yards	48,190

Boston Red Sox

1901-11	Huntington Ave. Grounds	—
1912–	Fenway Park	33,993
	(1934 capacity—27,000)	

Chicago White Sox

1901-10	Southside Park	—
1910-90	Comiskey Park I	43,931
1991–	Comiskey Park II	46,943

Cleveland Indians

1901-09	League Park I	—
1910-46	League Park II	21,414
1932-93	Cleveland Stadium	74,483
1994–	Jacobs Field	43,068

Detroit Tigers

1901-11	Bennett Park	—
1912-99	Tiger Stadium	46,945
2000–	Comerica Park	40,120
	(1912 capacity—23,000)	

Kansas City Royals

1969-72	Municipal Stadium	35,020
1973–	Kauffman Stadium	40,793
	(1973 capacity—40,762)	

Minnesota Twins

1901-02	American League Park (Washington, DC)	—
1903-60	Griffith Stadium	27,410
1960-81	Metropolitan Stadium (Bloomington, MN)	45,919
1982–	HHH Metrodome (Minneapolis)	48,678
	(1982 capacity—54,000)	

New York Yankees

1901-02	Oriole Park (Baltimore)	—
1903-12	Hilltop Park (New York)	—
1913-22	Polo Grounds II	38,000
1923-73	Yankee Stadium I	67,224
1974-75	Shea Stadium	55,101
1976–	Yankee Stadium II	57,478
	(1976 capacity—57,145)	

Oakland Athletics

1901-08	Columbia Park (Philadelphia)	—
1909-54	Shibe Park	33,608
1955-67	Municipal Stadium (Kansas City)	35,020
1968–	Network Associates Coliseum	43,662
	(1968 capacity—48,621)	

Seattle Mariners

1977-99	The Kingdome	59,166
1999–	SAFECO Field	47,116

Tampa Bay Devil Rays

1990–	Tropicana Field	43,761

Texas Rangers

1961	Griffith Stadium (Washington, DC)	27,410
1962-71	RFK Stadium	45,016
1972-93	Arlington Stadium (Texas)	43,521
1994–	The Ballpark in Arlington	49,115

Toronto Blue Jays

1977-89	Exhibition Stadium	43,737
1989–	SkyDome	50,516
	(1989 capacity—49,500)	

Ballpark Name Changes: ANAHEIM—**Edison International Field of Anaheim** originally Anaheim Stadium (1966-98); CHICAGO—**Comiskey Park I** originally White Sox Park (1910-12), then Comiskey Park in 1913, then White Sox Park again in 1962, then Comiskey Park again in 1976; CLEVELAND—**League Park** renamed Dunn Field in 1920, then League Park again in 1928; **Cleveland Stadium** originally Municipal Stadium (1932-74); DETROIT—**Tiger Stadium** originally Navin Field (1912-37), then Briggs Stadium (1938-60); KANSAS CITY—**Kauffman Stadium** originally Royals Stadium (1973-93); LOS ANGELES—**Dodger Stadium** referred to as Chavez Revine by AL while Angels played there (1962-65); OAKLAND—**Network Associates Coliseum** originally Oakland Alameda Coliseum (1968-98); PHILADELPHIA—**Shibe Park** renamed Connie Mack Stadium in 1953; ST. LOUIS—**Sportsman's Park** renamed Busch Stadium in 1953; WASHINGTON—**Griffith Stadium** originally National Park (1892-1920), **RFK Stadium** originally D.C. Stadium (1961-68).

National League

Arizona Diamondbacks

1998–	Bank One Ballpark	49,033

Atlanta Braves

1876-94	South End Grounds I (Boston)	—
1894-1914	South End Grounds II	—
1915-52	Braves Field	40,000
1953-65	County Stadium (Milwaukee)	43,394
1966-96	Atlanta-Fulton County Stadium	52,769
	(1966 capacity—50,000)	
1997–	Turner Field	50,091

Chicago Cubs

1876-77	State Street Grounds	—
1878-84	Lakefront Park	—
1885-91	West Side Park	—
1891-93	Brotherhood Park	—
1893-1915	West Side Grounds	—
1916–	Wrigley Field	39,111
	(1916 capacity—16,000)	

Cincinnati Reds

1876-79	Avenue Grounds	—
1880	Bank Street Grounds	—
1890-1901	Redland Field I	—
1902-11	Palace of the Fans	—
1912-70	Crosley Field	29,603
1970–	Cinergy Field	40,007
	(1970 capacity—52,000)	

Major League Baseball (Cont.)

Colorado Rockies

1993–94	Mile High Stadium (Denver)	76,100
1995–	Coors Field	50,449

Florida Marlins

1993–	Pro Player Stadium (Miami)	36,331
	(1993 capacity—47,662)	

Houston Astros

1962–64	Colt Stadium	32,601
1965–99	The Astrodome	54,370
	(1965 capacity—45,011)	
2000–	Minute Maid Park	40,950

Los Angeles Dodgers

1890	Washington Park I (Brooklyn)	—
1891–97	Eastern Park	—
1898–1912	Washington Park II	—
1913–56	Ebbets Field	31,497
1957	Ebbets Field	31,497
	& Roosevelt Stadium (Jersey City)	24,167
1958–61	Memorial Coliseum (Los Angeles)	93,600
1962–	Dodger Stadium	56,000

Milwaukee Brewers

1969	Sick's Stadium (Seattle)	59,166
1970–	County Stadium (Milwaukee)	53,192
2000	(1970 capacity—46,620)	
2001–	Miller Park	42,400

Montreal Expos

1969–76	Jarry Park	28,000
1977–	Olympic Stadium	46,500
	(1977 capacity—58,500)	

New York Mets

1962–63	Polo Grounds	55,987
1964–	Shea Stadium	56,749
	(1964 capacity—55,101)	

Philadelphia Phillies

1883–86	Recreation Park	—
1887–94	Huntingdon Ave. Grounds	—
1895–1938	Baker Bowl	18,800
1938–70	Shibe Park	33,608
1971–	Veterans Stadium	62,418
	(1971 capacity—56,371)	

Pittsburgh Pirates

1887–90	Recreation Park	—
1891–1909	Exposition Park	—
1909–70	Forbes Field	35,000
1970–2000	Three Rivers Stadium	47,687
	(1970 capacity—50,235)	
2001–	PNC Park	37,898

St. Louis Cardinals

1876–77	Sportsman's Park I	—
1885–86	Vandeventer Lot	—
1892–1920	Robison Field	18,000
1920–66	Sportsman's Park II	30,500
1966–	Busch Stadium	49,814
	(1966 capacity—50,126)	

San Diego Padres

1969–	Qualcomm Stadium	66,083
	(1969 capacity—47,634)	

San Francisco Giants

1876	Union Grounds (Brooklyn)	—
1883–88	Polo Grounds I (New York)	—
1889–90	Manhattan Field	—
1891–1957	Polo Grounds II	55,987
1958–59	Seals Stadium (San Francisco)	22,900
1960–99	3Com Park	63,000
	(1960 capacity—42,553)	
2000–	Pacific Bell Park	41,467

Ballpark Name Changes: ATLANTA—**Atlanta-Fulton County Stadium** originally Atlanta Stadium (1966-74), **Turner Field** originally Centennial Olympic Stadium (1996); CHICAGO—**Wrigley Field** originally Weeghman Park (1914-17), then Cubs Park (1918-25); CINCINNATI—**Redland Field** originally League Park (1890-93), **Crosley Field** originally Redland Field II (1912-33) and **Cinergy Field** originally Riverfront Stadium (1970-96); FLORIDA—**Pro Player Stadium** originally Joe Robbie Stadium (1987-96); HOUSTON—**Astrodome** originally Harris County Domed Stadium before it opened in 1965; **Enron Field** renamed Astros Field briefly and then Minute Maid Park in 2002; PHILADELPHIA—**Shibe Park** renamed Connie Mack Stadium in 1953; ST. LOUIS—**Robison Field** originally Vandeventer Lot, then League Park, then Cardinal Park all before becoming Robison Field in 1901, **Sportsman's Park** renamed Busch Stadium in 1953, and **Busch Stadium** originally Busch Memorial Stadium (1966-82); SAN DIEGO—**Qualcomm Stadium** originally San Diego Stadium (1967-81) and San Diego/Jack Murphy Stadium (1982-96); SAN FRANCISCO—**3Com Park** originally Candlestick Park (1960-95).

NATIONAL BASKETBALL ASSOCIATION

Western Conference

		Location	Built	Capacity
Dallas Mavericks	**American Airlines Center**	Dallas, Texas	2001	**19,200**
Denver Nuggets	**Pepsi Center**	Denver, Colo.	1999	**19,099**
Golden State Warriors	**The Arena in Oakland**	Oakland, Calif.	1997	**19,596**
Houston Rockets	**Compaq Center**	Houston, Texas	1975	**16,285**
Los Angeles Clippers	**Staples Center**	Los Angeles, Calif.	1999	**18,694**
Los Angeles Lakers	**Staples Center**	Los Angeles, Calif.	1999	**18,997**
Memphis Grizzlies	**The Pyramid**	Memphis, Tenn.	1990	**19,342**
Minnesota Timberwolves	**Target Center**	Minneapolis, Minn.	1990	**19,006**
Phoenix Suns	**America West Arena**	Phoenix, Ariz.	1992	**19,023**
Portland Trail Blazers	**Rose Garden**	Portland, Ore.	1995	**19,980**
Sacramento Kings	**ARCO Arena**	Sacramento, Calif.	1988	**17,317**
San Antonio Spurs	**SBC Center**	San Antonio, Texas	2002	**18,500**
Seattle SuperSonics	**KeyArena at Seattle Center**	Seattle, Wash.	1962	**17,072**
Utah Jazz	**Delta Center**	Salt Lake City, Utah	1991	**19,911**

Notes: Seattle's KeyArena was originally the Seattle Center Coliseum before being rebuilt in 1995; The Staples Center has different listed capacities for Clippers games and Lakers games because of different floor seating arrangements.

Eastern Conference

		Location	Built	Capacity
Atlanta Hawks	**Philips Arena**	Atlanta, Ga.	1999	**19,445**
Boston Celtics	**FleetCenter**	Boston, Mass.	1995	**18,624**
Chicago Bulls	**United Center**	Chicago, Ill.	1994	**21,711**
Cleveland Cavaliers	**Gund Arena**	Cleveland, Ohio	1994	**20,562**
Detroit Pistons	**The Palace of Auburn Hills**	Auburn Hills, Mich.	1988	**22,076**
Indiana Pacers	**Conseco Fieldhouse**	Indianapolis, Ind.	1999	**18,345**
Miami Heat	**AmericanAirlines Arena**	Miami, Fla.	1999	**16,500**
Milwaukee Bucks	**Bradley Center**	Milwaukee, Wisc.	1988	**18,717**
New Jersey Nets	**Continental Airlines Arena**	E. Rutherford, N.J.	1981	**20,049**
New Orleans Hornets	**New Orleans Arena**	New Orleans, La.	1999	**18,500**
New York Knicks	**Madison Square Garden**	New York, N.Y.	1968	**19,763**
Orlando Magic	**TD Waterhouse Centre**	Orlando, Fla.	1989	**17,248**
Philadelphia 76ers	**First Union Center**	Philadelphia, Penn.	1996	**20,444**
Toronto Raptors	**Air Canada Centre**	Toronto, Ont.	1999	**19,800**
Washington Wizards	**MCI Center**	Washington, D.C.	1997	**20,674**

Rank by Capacity

Western		Eastern	
Portland	19,980	Detroit	22,076
Utah	19,911	Chicago	21,711
Golden State	19,596	Washington	20,674
Memphis	19,342	Cleveland	20,562
Dallas	19,200	Philadelphia	20,444
Denver	19,099	New Jersey	20,049
Phoenix	19,023	Toronto	19,800
Minnesota	19,006	New York	19,763
LA Lakers	18,997	Atlanta	19,445
LA Clippers	18,694	Milwaukee	18,717
San Antonio	18,500	Boston	18,624
Sacramento	17,317	New Orleans	18,500
Seattle	17,072	Indiana	18,345
Houston	16,285	Orlando	17,248
		Miami	16,500

Rank by Age

Western		Eastern	
Seattle	1962	New York	1968
Houston	1975	New Jersey	1981
Sacramento	1988	Detroit	1988
Memphis	1990	Milwaukee	1988
Minnesota	1990	Orlando	1989
Utah	1991	Chicago	1994
Phoenix	1992	Cleveland	1994
Portland	1995	Boston	1995
Golden St.	1997	Philadelphia	1996
Denver	1999	Washington	1997
LA Clippers	1999	Toronto	1999
LA Lakers	1999	New Orleans	1999
Dallas	2001	Atlanta	1999
San Antonio	2002	Indiana	1999
		Miami	1999

Note: The Seattle Center Coliseum was rebuilt and renamed KeyArena in 1995.

2001-02 NBA Attendance

Official overall attendance in the NBA for the 2001-02 season was 20,172,998 for an average per game crowd of 16,966 over 1,189 games. Teams in each conference are ranked by attendance over 41 home games based on total tickets distributed. Rank column refers to rank in entire league. Numbers in parentheses indicate conference rank in 2000-01.

Western Conference

	Attendance	Rank	Average
1 San Antonio (1)	906,390	1	22,107
2 Dallas (8)	802,783	6	19,580
3 Portland (2)	797,821	7	19,459
4 LA Lakers (4)	778,777	8	18,994
5 Utah (3)	766,108	10	18,685
6 LA Clippers (11)	740,185	13	18,053
7 Minnesota (6)	731,673	14	17,845
8 Sacramento (7)	709,997	15	17,317
9 Phoenix (5)	668,939	27	16,315
10 Denver (10)	633,846	20	15,459
11 Seattle (9)	633,516	21	15,451
12 Golden St. (12)	593,182	24	14,467
13 Memphis (13)	591,030	25	14,415
14 Houston (14)	481,227	28	11,737
TOTAL	9,835,474	—	17,135

Eastern Conference

	Attendance	Rank	Average
1 Philadelphia (3)	842,976	2	20,560
2 Washington (9)	839,567	3	20,477
3 New York (2)	810,283	4	19,763
4 Toronto (4)	810,160	5	19,760
5 Chicago (1)	776,311	9	18,934
6 Detroit (12)	760,807	11	18,556
7 Milwaukee (6)	745,305	12	18,178
8 Indiana (5)	686,537	16	16,744
9 Boston (10)	659,751	18	16,091
10 Miami (7)	655,549	19	15,989
11 Orlando (13)	621,121	22	15,149
12 Cleveland (8)	596,115	23	14,539
13 New Jersey (14)	564,194	26	13,760
14 Atlanta (11)	506,110	27	12,344
15 Charlotte (11)	462,738	29	11,286
TOTAL	10,337,524	—	16,809

Note: The Charlotte Hornets moved to New Orleans following the 2001-02 season.

National Basketball Association (Cont.)
Home Courts

Listed below are the principal home courts used through the years by current NBA teams. The largest capacity of each arena is noted in the right-hand column. ABA arenas (1967-76) are included for Denver, Indiana, New Jersey and San Antonio.

Western Conference

Dallas Mavericks

| 1980–2000 | Reunion Arena | 18,187 |
| 2001– | American Airlines Center | 19,200 |

Denver Nuggets

1967–75	Auditorium Arena	6,841
1975–99	McNichols Sports Arena	17,171
	(1975 capacity—16,700)	
1999–	Pepsi Center	19,099

Golden State Warriors

1946–52	Philadelphia Arena	7,777
1952–62	Convention Hall (Philadelphia)	9,200
	& Philadelphia Arena	7,777
1962–64	Cow Palace (San Francisco)	13,862
1964–66	Civic Auditorium	7,500
	& (USF Memorial Gym)	6,000
1966–67	Cow Palace, Civic Auditorium	
	& Oakland Coliseum Arena	15,000
1967–71	Cow Palace	14,500
1971–96	Oakland Coliseum Arena	15,025
	(1971 capacity—12,905)	
1996–97	San Jose Arena	18,500
1997–	The Arena in Oakland	19,596

Houston Rockets

1967–71	San Diego Sports Arena	14,000
1971–72	Hofheinz Pavilion (Houston)	10,218
1972–73	Hofheinz Pavilion	10,218
	& HemisFair Arena (San Antonio)	10,446
1973–75	Hofheinz Pavilion	10,218
1975–	Compaq Center	16,285
	(1975 capacity—15,600)	

Los Angeles Clippers

1970–78	Memorial Auditorium (Buffalo)	17,300
1978–84	San Diego Sports Arena	12,167
1985–94	Los Angeles Sports Arena	16,005
1994–99	Los Angeles Sports Arena	16,021
	& Arrowhead Pond	18,211
1999–	Staples Center	18,694

Los Angeles Lakers

1948–60	Minneapolis Auditorium	10,000
1960–67	Los Angeles Sports Arena	14,781
1967–99	Great Western Forum (Inglewood, CA)	17,505
	(1967 capacity—17,086)	
1999–	Staples Center	18,997

Memphis Grizzlies

| 1995–2001 | General Motors Place (Vancouver) | 19,193 |
| 2001– | The Pyramid (Memphis, TN) | 19,342 |

Atlanta Hawks

1949–51	Wharton Field House (Moline, IL)	6,000
1951–55	Milwaukee Arena	11,000
1955–68	Kiel Auditorium (St. Louis)	10,000
1968–72	Alexander Mem. Coliseum (Atlanta)	7,166
1972–96	The Omni	16,378
1997–99	Georgia Dome	21,570
	& Alexander Mem. Coliseum	9,300
1999–	Philips Arena	19,445

Minnesota Timberwolves

| 1989–90 | Hubert H. Humphrey Metrodome | 23,000 |
| 1990– | Target Center | 19,006 |

Phoenix Suns

| 1968–92 | Arizona Veterans' Memorial Coliseum | 14,487 |
| 1992– | America West Arena | 19,023 |

Portland Trail Blazers

1970–95	Memorial Coliseum	12,888
1995–	Rose Garden	19,980
	(1995 capacity—21,538)	

Sacramento Kings

1948–55	Edgarton Park Arena (Rochester, NY)	5,000
1955–58	Rochester War Memorial	10,000
1958–72	Cincinnati Gardens	11,438
1972–74	Municipal Auditorium (Kansas City)	9,929
	& Omaha (NE) Civic Auditorium	9,136
1974–78	Kemper Arena (Kansas City)	16,785
	& Omaha Civic Auditorium	9,136
1978–85	Kemper Arena	16,785
1985–88	ARCO Arena I	10,333
1988–	ARCO Arena II	17,317
	(1988 capacity—16,517)	

San Antonio Spurs

1967–70	Memorial Auditorium (Dallas)	8,088
	& Moody Coliseum (Dallas)	8,500
1970–71	Moody Coliseum	8,500
	Tarrant Convention Center (Ft. Worth)	13,500
	& Municipal Coliseum (Lubbock)	10,400
1971–73	Moody Coliseum	9,500
	& Memorial Auditorium	8,088
1973–93	HemisFair Arena (San Antonio)	16,057
1993-2002	The Alamodome	20,557
2002–	SBC Center	18,500

Seattle SuperSonics

1967–78	Seattle Center Coliseum	14,098
1978–85	Kingdome	40,192
1985–94	Seattle Center Coliseum	14,252
1994–95	Tacoma Dome	19,000
1995–	KeyArena at Seattle Center	17,072

Utah Jazz

1974–75	Municipal Auditorium (New Orleans)	7,853
	& Louisiana Superdome	47,284
1975–79	Superdome	47,284
1979–83	Salt Palace (Salt Lake City)	12,519
1983–84	Salt Palace	12,519
	& Thomas & Mack Center (Las Vegas)	18,500
1984–91	Salt Palace	12,616
1991–	Delta Center	19,911

Eastern Conference

Boston Celtics

| 1946–95 | Boston Garden | 14,890 |
| 1995– | FleetCenter | 18,624 |

Note: From 1975-95 the Celtics played some regular season games at the Hartford Civic Center (15,418).

Chicago Bulls

1966–67	Chicago Amphitheater	11,002
1967–94	Chicago Stadium	18,676
1994–	United Center	21,711

Cleveland Cavaliers

1970–74	Cleveland Arena	11,000
1974–94	The Coliseum (Richfield, OH)	20,273
1994–	Gund Arena	20,562

Detroit Pistons

1948–52	North Side H.S. Gym (Ft. Wayne, IN)	3,800
1952–57	Memorial Coliseum (Ft. Wayne)	9,306
1957–61	Olympia Stadium (Detroit)	14,000
1961–78	Cobo Arena	11,147
1978–88	Silverdome (Pontiac, MI)	22,366
1988–	The Palace of Auburn Hills	22,076

Indiana Pacers

1967–74	State Fairgrounds (Indianapolis)	9,479
1974–99	Market Square Arena	16,530
	(1974 capacity—17,287)	
1999–	Conseco Fieldhouse	18,345

Miami Heat

1988–99	Miami Arena	15,200
2000–	AmericanAirlines Arena	16,500

Milwaukee Bucks

1968–88	Milwaukee Arena (The Mecca)	11,052
1988–	Bradley Center	18,717

New Jersey Nets

1967–68	Teaneck (NJ) Armory	3,500
1968–69	Long Island Arena (Commack, NY)	6,500
1969–71	Island Garden (W. Hempstead, NY)	5,250
1971–77	Nassau Coliseum (Uniondale, NY)	15,500
1977–81	Rutgers Ath. Center (Piscataway, NJ)	9,050
1981–	Continental Airlines Arena (E. Ruth., NJ)	20,049

New Orleans Hornets

1988–	Charlotte Coliseum	19,925
2002	(1988 capacity—23,500)	
2002–	New Orleans Arena	18,500

New York Knicks

1946–68	Madison Sq. Garden III (50th St.)	18,496
1968–	Madison Sq. Garden IV (33rd St.)	19,763
	(1968 capacity—19,694)	

Orlando Magic

1989–	TD Waterhouse Centre	17,248

Philadelphia 76ers

1949–51	State Fair Coliseum (Syracuse, NY)	7,500
1951–63	Onondaga County (NY) War Memorial	8,000
1963–67	Convention Hall (Philadelphia)	12,000
	& Philadelphia Arena	7,777
1967–96	CoreStates Spectrum	18,136
1996–	First Union Center	20,444

Toronto Raptors

1995–99	SkyDome	20,125
1999–	Air Canada Centre	19,800

Washington Wizards

1961–62	Chicago Amphitheater	11,000
1962–63	Chicago Coliseum	7,100
1963–73	Baltimore Civic Center	12,289
1973–97	USAir Arena (Landover, MD)	18,756
1997–	MCI Center	20,674

Note: From 1988-96 the Wizards (then Bullets) played four regular season games at Baltimore Arena (12,756).

Building Name Changes: HOUSTON—**Compaq Center** originally The Summit (1975-97); NEW JERSEY—**Continental Airlines Arena** originally Byrne Meadowlands Arena (1981-96); ORLANDO—**TD Waterhouse Centre** originally Orlando Arena (1989-99); PHILADELPHIA—**First Union Center** originally the CoreStates Center (1996-98) and **CoreStates Spectrum** originally The Spectrum (1967-94); WASHINGTON—**USAir Arena** originally Capital Centre (1973-93).

NATIONAL FOOTBALL LEAGUE

American Football Conference

		Location	Built	Capacity	Field
Baltimore Ravens	**Ravens Stadium**	Baltimore, Md.	1998	**69,084**	Grass
Buffalo Bills	**Ralph Wilson Stadium**	Orchard Park, N.Y.	1973	**73,967**	Turf
Cincinnati Bengals	**Paul Brown Stadium**	Cincinnati, Ohio	2000	**65,352**	Grass
Cleveland Browns	**Cleveland Browns Stadium**	Cleveland, Ohio	1999	**73,200**	Grass
Denver Broncos	**INVESCO Field at Mile High**	Denver, Colo.	2001	**76,125**	Grass
Houston Texans	**Reliant Stadium**	Houston, Tex.	2002	**69,500**	Grass
Indianapolis Colts	**RCA Dome**	Indianapolis, Ind.	1984	**56,127**	Turf
Jacksonville Jaguars	**ALLTEL Stadium**	Jacksonville, Fla.	1995	**73,000**	Grass
Kansas City Chiefs	**Arrowhead Stadium**	Kansas City, Mo.	1972	**79,451**	Grass
Miami Dolphins	**Pro Player Stadium**	Miami, Fla.	1987	**75,540**	Grass
New England Patriots	**Gillette Stadium**	Foxboro, Mass.	2002	**68,000**	Grass
New York Jets	**Giants Stadium**	E. Rutherford, N.J.	1976	**80,062**	Grass
Oakland Raiders	**Network Associates Coliseum**	Oakland, Calif.	1966	**63,132**	Grass
Pittsburgh Steelers	**Heinz Field**	Pittsburgh, Pa.	2001	**64,450**	Grass
San Diego Chargers	**Qualcomm Stadium**	San Diego, Calif.	1967	**71,000**	Grass
Tennessee Titans	**The Coliseum**	Nashville, Tenn.	1999	**68,798**	Grass

National Football Conference

		Location	Built	Capacity	Field
Arizona Cardinals	**Sun Devil Stadium**	Tempe, Ariz.	1958	**73,273**	Grass
Atlanta Falcons	**Georgia Dome**	Atlanta, Ga.	1992	**71,228**	Turf
Carolina Panthers	**Ericsson Stadium**	Charlotte, N.C.	1996	**73,500**	Grass
Chicago Bears	**Memorial Stadium***	Champaign, Ill.	1923	**69,249**	Turf
Dallas Cowboys	**Texas Stadium**	Irving, Texas	1971	**65,639**	Turf
Detroit Lions	**Ford Field**	Detroit, Mich.	2002	**65,000**	Turf
Green Bay Packers	**Lambeau Field**	Green Bay, Wis.	1957	**62,500**	Grass
Minnesota Vikings	**Hubert H. Humphrey Metrodome**	Minneapolis, Minn.	1982	**64,121**	Turf
New Orleans Saints	**Louisiana Superdome**	New Orleans, La.	1975	**68,395**	Turf
New York Giants	**Giants Stadium**	E. Rutherford, N.J.	1976	**80,062**	Grass
Philadelphia Eagles	**Veterans Stadium**	Philadelphia, Pa.	1971	**65,352**	Turf
St. Louis Rams	**Edward Jones Dome**	St. Louis, Mo.	1995	**66,000**	Turf

National Football League (Cont.)

	Location	Built	Capacity	Field
San Francisco 49ers.....................**Candlestick Park**	San Francisco, Calif.	1960	69,400	Grass
Seattle Seahawks.....................**Seahawks Stadium**	Seattle, Wash.	2002	67,000	Grass
Tampa Bay Buccaneers.............**Raymond James Stadium**	Tampa, Fla.	1998	65,657	Grass
Washington Redskins.....................**FedEx Field**	Raljon, Md.	1997	86,484	Grass

*The Chicago Bears will play their 2002 home games at Memorial Stadium on the campus of the University of Illinois while Soldier Field undergoes renovation. They will resume play at Soldier Field in 2003.

Rank by Capacity

AFC

NY Jets...........80,062	
Kansas City......79,451	
Denver...........76,125	
Miami............75,540	
Buffalo..........73,967	
Cleveland 73,200	
Jacksonville 73,000	
San Diego 71,000	
Houston 69,500	
Baltimore 69,084	
Tennessee........68,798	
New England 68,000	
Cincinnati 65,352	
Pittsburgh.......64,450	
Oakland 63,132	
Indianapolis 56,127	

NFC

Washington.......86,484	
NY Giants........80,062	
Arizona 73,273	
Carolina.........73,500	
Atlanta 71,228	
Chicago..........70,904	
San Francisco ...69,400	
New Orleans 68,395	
Seattle 67,000	
St. Louis 66,000	
Tampa Bay 65,657	
Dallas...........65,639	
Philadelphia 65,352	
Detroit 65,000	
Minnesota 64,121	
Green Bay 62,500	

Rank by Age

AFC

Oakland 1966	
San Diego 1967	
Kansas City.......1972	
Buffalo 1973	
NY Jets 1976	
Indianapolis 1984	
Miami 1987	
Jacksonville 1995	
Baltimore 1998	
Cleveland 1999	
Tennessee 1999	
Cincinnati 2000	
Denver 2001	
Pittsburgh.......2001	
New England 2002	
Houston 2002	

NFC

Chicago...........1923	
Green Bay 1957	
Arizona 1958	
San Francisco 1960	
Dallas............1971	
Philadelphia 1971	
New Orleans 1975	
NY Giants 1976	
Minnesota 1982	
Atlanta 1992	
St. Louis 1995	
Carolina 1996	
Washington........1997	
Tampa Bay 1998	
Seattle 2002	
Detroit 2002	

2001 NFL Attendance

Official overall paid attendance in the NFL for the 2001 season was 16,244,538 for an average per game crowd of 65,502 over 248 games. Teams in each conference are ranked by attendance over eight home games. Rank column indicates rank in entire league. Numbers in parentheses indicate conference rank in 2000.

AFC

		Attendance	Rank	Average
1	N.Y. Jets (2) 627,808		2	78,476
2	Kansas City (1)........617,488		4	77,186
3	Denver (3)............600,283		6	75,035
4	Miami (4) 588,067		7	73,508
5	Cleveland (5).........583,094		8	72,886
6	Baltimore (9).........485,526		11	69,360
7	Tennessee (7).........550,393		12	68,799
8	Buffalo (6)...........504,736		20	63,092
9	Pittsburgh (15).......499,191		21	62,398
10	Jacksonville (10)......483,542		22	60,442
11	Seattle (8)...........482,818		23	60,352
12	New England (11).......482,336		24	60,292
13	San Diego (16)........474,844		26	59,355
14	Oakland (13)..........472,091		27	59,011
15	Cincinnati (12)........453,449		28	56,681
16	Indianapolis (14) 450,746		29	56,343
	TOTAL 8,356,412		—	65,284

NFC

		Attendance	Rank	Average
1	NY Giants (3)..........627,985		1	78,498
2	Washington (1) 624,374		3	78,046
3	Detroit (2)...........601,815		5	75,226
4	Carolina (15) 579,080		9	72,385
5	New Orleans (10).......560,472		10	70,059
6	San Francisco (12).....539,756		13	67,469
7	Chicago (4) 535,552		14	66,944
8	St. Louis (5).........528,829		15	66,103
9	Philadelphia (7)......527,193		16	65,899
10	Tampa Bay (6) 524,468		17	65,558
11	Minnesota (8).........513,344		18	64,168
12	Dallas (9)............505,501		19	63,187
13	Green Bay (11) 478,433		25	59,804
14	Atlanta (13) 434,009		30	54,251
15	Arizona (14)..........307,315		31	38,414
	TOTAL 7,888,126		—	65,734

Home Fields

Listed below are the principal home fields used through the years by current NFL teams. The largest capacity of each stadium is noted in the right-hand column. All-America Football Conference stadiums (1946-49) are included for Cleveland and San Francisco.

AFC

Baltimore Ravens

1996–97	Memorial Stadium 65,000	
1998–	Ravens Stadium 69,084	

Buffalo Bills

1960–72	War Memorial Stadium 45,748	
1973–	Ralph Wilson Stadium (Orchard Park, NY)..........................73,967 (1973 capacity—80,020)	

Cincinnati Bengals

1968–69	Nippert Stadium (Univ. of Cincinnati) ...26,500	
1970–99	Cinergy Field ....60,389 (1970 capacity—56,200)	
2000–	Paul Brown Stadium 65,352	

Cleveland Browns

1946–95	Cleveland Stadium ....78,512 (1946 capacity—85,703)	
1999–	Cleveland Browns Stadium 73,200	

Denver Broncos

1960–	Mile High Stadium 76,123	
2000	(1960 capacity—34,000)	
2001–	INVESCO Field at Mile High..........76,125	

Houston Texans

2002–	Reliant Stadium 69,500	

Indianapolis Colts

1953–83	Memorial Stadium (Baltimore) 60,020	
1984–	RCA Dome (Indianapolis) ....56,127 (1984 capacity—60,127)	

Jacksonville Jaguars

1995–	ALLTEL Stadium	.73,000

Kansas City Chiefs

1960–62	Cotton Bowl (Dallas)	.72,000
1963–71	Municipal Stadium (Kansas City)	.47,000
1972–	Arrowhead Stadium	.79,451
	(1972 capacity—78,097)	

Miami Dolphins

1966–86	Orange Bowl	.75,206
1987–	Pro Player Stadium	.75,540

New England Patriots

1960–62	Nickerson Field (Boston Univ.)	.17,369
1963–68	Fenway Park	.33,379
1969	Alumni Stadium (Boston College)	.26,000
1970	Harvard Stadium	.37,300
1971-2001	Foxboro Stadium	.60,292
	(1971 capacity—61,114)	
2002–	Gillette Stadium	.68,000

New York Jets

1960–63	Polo Grounds	.55,987
1964–83	Shea Stadium	.60,372
1984–	Giants Stadium (E. Rutherford, NJ)	.80,062

Oakland Raiders

1960	Kesar Stadium (San Francisco)	.59,636
1961	Candlestick Park	.42,500
1962–65	Frank Youell Field (Oakland)	.20,000
1966–81	Oakland-Alameda County Coliseum	.54,587
1982–94	Memorial Coliseum (Los Angeles)	.67,800
1995–	Network Associates Coliseum	.63,132

Pittsburgh Steelers

1933–57	Forbes Field	.35,000
1958–63	Forbes Field	.35,000
	& Pitt Stadium	.54,500
1964–69	Pitt Stadium	.54,500
1970–	Three Rivers Stadium	.59,600
2000	(1970 capacity—49,000)	
2001–	Heinz Field	.64,450

San Diego Chargers

1960	Memorial Coliseum (Los Angeles)	.92,604
1961–66	Balboa Stadium (San Diego)	.34,000
1967–	Qualcomm Stadium	.71,000
	(1967 capacity—54,000)	

Tennessee Titans

1960–64	Jeppesen Stadium (Houston)	.23,500
1965–67	Rice Stadium (Rice Univ.)	.70,000
1968–96	Astrodome	.59,969
1997	Liberty Bowl (Memphis)	.62,380
1998	Vanderbilt Stadium (Nashville)	.41,600
1999–	The Coliseum (Nashville)	.68,798

Ballpark Name Changes: BALTIMORE—PSInet Stadium originally named Ravens Stadium (1998-99) and renamed **Ravens Stadium** in 2002; BUFFALO—**Ralph Wilson Stadium** originally Rich Stadium (1973-99); CINCINNATI—**Cinergy Field** originally Riverfront Stadium (1970-96); CLEVELAND—**Cleveland Stadium** originally Municipal Stadium (1932-74); DENVER—**Mile High Stadium** originally Bears Stadium (1948-66); INDIANAPOLIS—**RCA Dome** originally Hoosier Dome (1984-94); JACKSONVILLE—**ALLTEL Stadium** originally Jacksonville Municipal Stadium (1995-97); MIAMI—**Pro Player Stadium** originally Joe Robbie Stadium (1987-96); NEW ENGLAND—**Foxboro Stadium** originally Schaefer Stadium (1971-82), then Sullivan Stadium (1983-89); **Gillette Stadium** originally CMGI Field; OAKLAND—**Network Associates Coliseum** originally Oakland Alameda Coliseum (1995-99); SAN DIEGO—**Qualcomm Stadium** originally San Diego Stadium (1967-81) then San Diego/Jack Murphy Stadium (1981-96); TENNESSEE—**The Coliseum** originally Adelphia Coliseum (1999-2001).

NFC

Arizona Cardinals

1920–21	Normal Field (Chicago)	.7,500
1922–25	Comiskey Park	.28,000
1926–28	Normal Field	.7,500
1929–59	Comiskey Park	.52,000
1960–65	Busch Stadium (St. Louis)	.34,000
1966–87	Busch Memorial Stadium	.54,392
1988–	Sun Devil Stadium (Tempe, AZ)	.73,273

Atlanta Falcons

1966-91	Atlanta-Fulton County Stadium	.59,643
1992–	Georgia Dome	.71,228

Carolina Panthers

1995	Memorial Stadium (Clemson, SC)	.81,473
1996–	Ericsson Stadium	.73,500

Chicago Bears

1920	Staley Field (Decatur, IL)	—
1921–70	Wrigley Field (Chicago)	.37,741
1971-2001	Soldier Field	.66,944
	(1971 capacity—55,049)	
2002	Memorial Stadium (Champaign, IL)	.69,249

Dallas Cowboys

1960–70	Cotton Bowl	.72,132
1971–	Texas Stadium (Irving, TX)	.65,639
	(1971 capacity—65,101)	

Detroit Lions

1930–33	Spartan Stadium (Portsmouth, OH)	.8,200
1934–37	Univ. of Detroit Stadium	.25,000
1938–74	Tiger Stadium	.54,468
1975-2001	Pontiac Silverdome	.80,311
	(1975 capacity—80,638)	
2002–	Ford Field	.65,000

Green Bay Packers

1921–22	Hagemeister Brewery Park	—
1923–24	Bellevue Park	—
1925–56	City Stadium I	.24,800
1957–	Lambeau Field	.62,500
	(1957 capacity—32,150)	

Note: The Packers played games in Milwaukee from 1933-94: at Borchert Field, State Fair Park and Marquette Stadium (1933-52), and County Stadium (1953-94).

Minnesota Vikings

1961–81	Metropolitan Stadium (Bloomington)	.48,446
1982–	HHH Metrodome (Minneapolis)	.64,121
	(1982 capacity—62,220)	

New Orleans Saints

1967–74	Tulane Stadium	.80,997
1975–	Louisigna Superdome	.68,395
	(1975 capacity—74,472)	

New York Giants

1925–55	Polo Grounds II	.55,200
1956–73	Yankee Stadium I	.63,800
1973–74	Yale Bowl (New Haven, CT)	.70,896
1975	Shea Stadium	.60,372
1976–	Giants Stadium (E. Rutherford, NJ)	.80,062
	(1976 capacity—76,800)	

National Football League (Cont.)

Philadelphia Eagles

1933–35	Baker Bowl	18,800
1936–39	Municipal Stadium	73,702
1940	Shibe Park	33,608
1941	Municipal Stadium	73,702
1942	Shibe Park	33,608
1943	Forbes Field (Pittsburgh)	34,528
1944–57	Shibe Park	33,608
1958–70	Franklin Field (Univ. of Penn.)	60,546
1971–	Veterans Stadium	65,352
	(1971 capacity—65,000)	

St. Louis Rams

1937–42	Municipal Stadium (Cleveland)	85,703
1937	League Park (Cleveland)	—
1938	Shaw Stadium (Cleveland)	—
1937	League Park	—
1943	Suspended operations for one year.	
1944–45	Municipal Stadium	85,703
1946–79	Memorial Coliseum (Los Angeles)	92,604
1980–94	Anaheim Stadium	69,008
1995	Busch Stadium	60,000
1995–	Edward Jones Dome	66,000

San Francisco 49ers

1946–70	Kezar Stadium	59,636
1971–	Candlestick Park	69,400
	(1971 capacity—61,246)	

Seattle Seahawks

1976–94	Kingdome	66,000
1994	Kingdome	66,400
	& Husky Stadium	72,500
1995–99	Kingdome	66,400
2000-01	Husky Stadium	72,500
2002–	Seahawks Stadium	67,000

Tampa Bay Buccaneers

1976–97	Houlihan's Stadium	74,300
1998–	Raymond James Stadium	65,657

Washington Redskins

1932	Braves Field (Boston)	40,000
1933–36	Fenway Park	27,000
1937–60	Griffith Stadium (Washington, DC)	35,000
1961–97	RFK Stadium	56,454
1997–	FedEx Field (Raljon, MD)	86,484

Ballpark Name Changes: ATLANTA—**Atlanta-Fulton County Stadium** originally Atlanta Stadium (1966-74); CHICAGO—**Wrigley Field** originally Cubs Park (1916-25); DETROIT—**Tiger Stadium** originally Navin Field (1912-37), then Briggs Stadium (1938-60), also, **Pontiac Silverdome** originally Pontiac Metropolitan Stadium (1975); GREEN BAY—**Lambeau Field** originally City Stadium II (1957-64); PHILADELPHIA—**Shibe Park** renamed Connie Mack Stadium in 1953; ST. LOUIS—**Busch Memorial Stadium** renamed Busch Stadium in 1983, **Edward Jones Dome** originally Trans World Dome (1995-99), then The Dome at America's Center (2000-01); SAN FRANCISCO—**Candlestick Park** originally Candlestick Park (1960-94), then 3Com Park (1995-2001); TAMPA BAY—**Raymond James Stadium** originally Tampa Stadium (1976-96), then **Houlihan's Stadium** (1996-98); WASHINGTON—**RFK Stadium** originally D.C. Stadium (1961-68), also, **FedEx Field** originally Jack Kent Cooke Stadium (1997-99).

NATIONAL HOCKEY LEAGUE

Western Conference

Team	Arena	Location	Built	Capacity
Anaheim, Mighty Ducks of	**Arrowhead Pond**	Anaheim, Calif.	1993	**17,174**
Calgary Flames	**Pengrowth Saddledome**	Calgary, Alb.	1983	**17,135**
Chicago Blackhawks	**United Center**	Chicago, Ill.	1994	**20,500**
Colorado Avalanche	**Pepsi Center**	Denver, Colo.	1999	**18,007**
Columbus Blue Jackets	**Nationwide Arena**	Columbus, Ohio	2000	**18,136**
Dallas Stars	**American Airlines Center**	Dallas, Texas	2001	**18,532**
Detroit Red Wings	**Joe Louis Arena**	Detroit, Mich.	1979	**20,058**
Edmonton Oilers	**Skyreach Centre**	Edmonton, Alb.	1974	**16,839**
Los Angeles Kings	**Staples Center**	Los Angeles, Calif.	1999	**18,118**
Minnesota Wild	**Xcel Energy Center**	St. Paul, Minn.	2000	**18,064**
Nashville Predators	**Gaylord Entertainment Center**	Nashville, Tenn.	1994	**17,113**
Phoenix Coyotes	**America West Arena**	Phoenix, Ariz.	1992	**16,210**
St. Louis Blues	**Savvis Center**	St. Louis, Mo.	1994	**19,022**
San Jose Sharks	**Compaq Center at San Jose**	San Jose, Calif.	1993	**17,496**
Vancouver Canucks	**General Motors Place**	Vancouver, B.C.	1995	**18,422**

Eastern Conference

Team	Arena	Location	Built	Capacity
Atlanta Thrashers	**Philips Arena**	Atlanta, Ga.	1999	**18,545**
Boston Bruins	**FleetCenter**	Boston, Mass.	1995	**17,565**
Buffalo Sabres	**HSBC Arena**	Buffalo, N.Y.	1996	**18,690**
Carolina Hurricanes	**RBC Center**	Raleigh, N.C.	1999	**18,730**
Florida Panthers	**Office Depot Center**	Sunrise, Fla.	1998	**19,250**
Montreal Canadiens	**Bell Centre**	Montreal, Que.	1996	**21,273**
New Jersey Devils	**Continental Airlines Arena**	E. Rutherford, N.J.	1981	**19,040**
New York Islanders	**Nassau Veterans' Mem. Coliseum**	Uniondale, N.Y.	1972	**16,234**
New York Rangers	**Madison Square Garden**	New York, N.Y.	1968	**18,200**
Ottawa Senators	**Corel Centre**	Kanata, Ont.	1996	**18,500**
Philadelphia Flyers	**First Union Center**	Philadelphia, Penn.	1996	**18,523**
Pittsburgh Penguins	**Mellon Arena**	Pittsburgh, Penn.	1961	**16,958**
Tampa Bay Lightning	**St. Pete Times Forum**	Tampa Bay, Fla.	1996	**19,758**
Toronto Maple Leafs	**Air Canada Centre**	Toronto, Ont.	1999	**18,819**
Washington Capitals	**MCI Center**	Washington, D.C.	1997	**18,672**

Rank by Capacity

Western		Eastern	
Chicago	20,500	Montreal	21,273
Detroit	20,058	Tampa Bay	19,758
St. Louis	19,022	Florida	19,250
Dallas	18,532	New Jersey	19,040
Vancouver	18,422	Toronto	18,819
Columbus	18,136	Carolina	18,730
Los Angeles	18,118	Buffalo	18,690
Minnesota	18,064	Washington	18,672
Colorado	18,007	Atlanta	18,545
San Jose	17,496	Philadelphia	18,523
Anaheim	17,174	Ottawa	18,500
Calgary	17,135	NY Rangers	18,200
Nashville	17,113	Boston	17,565
Edmonton	16,839	Pittsburgh	16,958
Phoenix	16,210	NY Islanders	16,234

Rank by Age

Western		Eastern	
Edmonton	1974	Pittsburgh	1961
Detroit	1979	NY Rangers	1968
Calgary	1983	NY Islanders	1972
Phoenix	1992	New Jersey	1981
Anaheim	1993	Boston	1995
San Jose	1993	Montreal	1996
Chicago	1994	Ottawa	1996
St. Louis	1994	Buffalo	1996
Nashville	1994	Philadelphia	1996
Vancouver	1995	Tampa Bay	1996
Colorado	1999	Washington	1997
Los Angeles	1999	Florida	1998
Columbus	2000	Toronto	1999
Minnesota	2000	Carolina	1999
Dallas	2001	Atlanta	1999

2001-02 NHL Attendance

Official overall paid attendance for the 2001-02 season according to the NHL accounting office was 21,263,964 (paid tickets) for an average per game crowd of 17,288 over 1,230 games. Teams in each conference are ranked by attendance over 41 home games. Rank column refers to rank in entire league. Numbers in parentheses indicate conference rank in 2000-01.

Western Conference

		Attendance	Rank	Average
1	Detroit (1)	822,337	1	20,057
2	St. Louis (2)	777,688	5	18,968
3	Dallas (8)	759,607	6	18,527
4	Minnesota (3)	756,655	7	18,455
5	Columbus (6)	743,576	8	18,136
6	Colorado (4)	738,287	10	18,007
7	Vancouver (7)	726,192	11	17,712
8	San Jose (5)	714,220	12	17,420
9	Los Angeles (10)	686,996	16	16,756
10	Edmonton (11)	680,272	17	16,592
11	Calgary (9)	644,438	21	15,718
12	Chicago (13)	638,288	23	15,568
13	Nashville (12)	606,308	26	14,788
14	Phoenix (14)	539,765	29	13,165
15	Anaheim (15)	492,082	30	12,002
	TOTAL	10,326,711	—	16,791

Eastern Conference

		Attendance	Rank	Average
1	Montreal (1)	821,107	2	20,027
2	Philadelphia (2)	802,329	3	19,569
3	Toronto (3)	790,562	4	19,282
4	NY Rangers (4)	739,558	9	18,038
5	Washington (9)	710,981	13	17,341
6	Buffalo (5)	705,446	14	17,206
7	Ottawa (6)	693,679	15	16,919
8	Florida (13)	659,403	18	16,083
9	New Jersey (8)	652,925	19	15,925
10	Tampa Bay (12)	644,602	20	15,722
11	Pittsburgh (7)	640,051	22	15,611
12	Carolina (14)	635,828	24	15,508
13	Boston (10)	631,523	25	15,403
14	NY Islanders (15)	596,468	27	14,548
15	Atlanta (11)	560,388	28	13,668
	TOTAL	10,937,253	—	17,784

Home Ice

Listed below are the principal home buildings used through the years by current NHL teams. The largest capacity of each arena is noted in the right hand column. World Hockey Association arenas (1972-79) are included for Edmonton, Hartford (now Carolina), Quebec (now Colorado) and Winnipeg (now Phoenix).

Western Conference

Anaheim, Mighty Ducks of

1993–	Arrowhead Pond	17,174

Calgary Flames

1972–80	The Omni (Atlanta)	15,278
1980–83	Calgary Corral	7,424
1983–	Pengrowth Saddledome	17,135
	(1983 capacity—16,674)	

Chicago Blackhawks

1926–29	Chicago Coliseum	5,000
1929–94	Chicago Stadium	17,317
1994–	United Center	20,500

Colorado Avalanche

1972–95	Le Colisee de Quebec	15,399
1995–99	McNichols Arena (Denver)	16,061
1999–	Pepsi Center	18,007

Columbus Blue Jackets

2000–	Nationwide Arena	18,136

Dallas Stars

1967–93	Met Center (Bloomington, MN)	15,174
1993–2000	Reunion Arena (Dallas)	17,001
2001–	American Airlines Center	18,532

Detroit Red Wings

1926–27	Border Cities Arena (Windsor, Ont.)	3,200
1927–79	Olympia Stadium (Detroit)	16,700
1979–	Joe Louis Arena	20,058

Edmonton Oilers

1972–74	Edmonton Gardens	7,200
1974–	Skyreach Centre	16,839
	(1974 capacity—15,513)	

Los Angeles Kings

1967–99	Great Western Forum (Inglewood)	16,005
	(1967 capacity—15,651)	
1999–	Staples Center	18,118

Note: The Kings played 17 games at Long Beach Sports Arena and LA Sports Arena at the start of the 1967-68 season.

National Hockey League (Cont.)

Minnesota Wild

2000–	Xcel Energy Center (St. Paul)	18,064

Nashville Predators

1998–	Gaylord Entertainment Center	17,113

Phoenix Coyotes

1972–96	Winnipeg Arena	15,393
	(1972 capacity—10,177)	
1996–	America West (Phoenix)	16,210

St. Louis Blues

1967–94	St. Louis Arena	17,188
1994–	Savvis Center	19,022

San Jose Sharks

1991–93	Cow Palace (Daly City, CA)	11,100
1993–	Compaq Center at San Jose	17,496

Vancouver Canucks

1970–95	Pacific Coliseum	16,150
1995–	General Motors Place	18,422

Building Name Changes: CALGARY—**Pengrowth Saddledome** formerly named Canadian Airlines Saddledome (1996-2000) which was originally Olympic Saddledome (1983-95); DALLAS—**Met Center** in Minneapolis originally Metropolitan Sports Center (1967-82); EDMONTON—**Skyreach Centre** formerly named Edmonton Coliseum (1995-99) which was originally Northlands Coliseum (1974-94); LOS ANGELES—**Great Western Forum** originally The Forum (1967-88); NASHVILLE—**Gaylord Entertainment Center** originally Nashville Arena (1994-99); ST. LOUIS—**Savvis Center** originally Kiel Center (1994-2000), **St. Louis Arena** renamed The Checkerdome in 1977, then St. Louis Arena again in 1982; SAN JOSE—**Compaq Center at San Jose** originally San Jose Arena (1993-2000).

Eastern Conference

Atlanta Thrashers

1999–	Philips Arena	18,545

Boston Bruins

1924–28	Boston Arena	6,200
1928–95	Boston Garden	14,448
1995–	FleetCenter	17,565

Buffalo Sabres

1970–96	Memorial Auditorium (The Aud)	16,284
	(1970 capacity—10,429)	
1996–	HSBC Arena	18,690

Carolina Hurricanes

1972–73	Boston Garden	14,442
1973–74	Boston Garden (regular season)	14,442
	West Springfield (MA) Big E (playoffs)	5,513
1974–75	West Springfield Big E	5,513
	& Hartford (CT) Civic Center	10,507
1975–77	Hartford Civic Center	10,507
1977–78	Hartford Civic Center	10,507
	& Springfield (MA) Civic Center	7,725
1978–79	Springfield Civic Center	7,725
1979–80	Springfield Civic Center	7,725
	& Hartford Civic Center II	14,250
1980–97	Hartford Civic Center II	15,635
1997–99	Greensboro Coliseum	21,500
1999–	RBC Center	18,730

Note: The Hartford Civic Center roof caved in January 1978, forcing the Whalers to move their home games to Springfield, MA for two years.

Florida Panthers

1993–98	Miami Arena	14,703
1998–	Office Depot Center	19,250

Montreal Canadiens

1910–21	Jubilee Arena	3,200
1913–18	Montreal Arena (Westmount)	6,000
1918–26	Mount Royal Arena	6,750
1926–68	Montreal Forum I	15,500
1968–96	Montreal Forum II	17,959
1996–	Bell Centre	21,273

New Jersey Devils

1974–76	Kemper Arena (Kansas City)	16,300
1976–82	McNichols Arena (Denver)	15,900
1982–	Continental Airlines Arena	19,040
	(1982 capacity—19,023)	

New York Islanders

1972–	Nassau Veterans' Mem. Coliseum	16,234
	(1972 capacity—14,500)	

New York Rangers

1925–68	Madison Square Garden III	15,925
1968–	Madison Square Garden IV	18,200
	(1968 capacity—17,250)	

Ottawa Senators

1992–96	Ottawa Civic Center	10,755
1996–	Corel Centre (Kanata)	18,500

Philadelphia Flyers

1967–96	CoreStates Spectrum	17,380
	(1967 capacity—14,558)	
1996–	First Union Center	18,523

Pittsburgh Penguins

1967–	Mellon Arena	16,958
	(1967 capacity—12,508)	

Tampa Bay Lightning

1992–93	Expo Hall (Tampa)	10,500
1993–96	ThunderDome (St. Petersburg)	26,000
1996–	St. Pete Times Forum	19,758

Toronto Maple Leafs

1917–31	Mutual Street Arena	8,000
1931–99	Maple Leaf Gardens	15,746
	(1931 capacity—13,542)	
1999–	Air Canada Centre	18,819

Washington Capitals

1974–97	USAir Arena (Landover, MD)	18,130
1997–	MCI Center	18,672

Building Name Changes: BUFFALO—**HSBC Arena** originally Marine Midland Arena (1996-99); CALGARY—**Pengrowth Saddledome** originally Canadian Airlines Arena (1983-2000); CAROLINA—**RBC Center** originally Raleigh Entertainment and Sports Arena (1999-2002); DALLAS—**American Airlines Center** originally Reunion Arena (1993-2000); FLORIDA—**Office Depot Center** originally National Car Rental Center (1998-2002); MONTREAL—**Bell Centre** originally Molson Centre (1996-2002); NEW JERSEY—**Continental Airlines Arena** originally Meadowlands Arena (1982-96); PHILADELPHIA—**First Union Center** originally the CoreStates Center (1996-98) and **CoreStates Spectrum** originally The Spectrum (1967-94); PITTSBURGH—**Mellon Arena** originally Civic Center (1967-2000); TAMPA BAY—**St. Pete Times Forum** originally Ice Palace (1996-2002); WASHINGTON—**USAir Arena** originally Capital Centre (1974-93).

AUTO RACING

Formula One, NASCAR Winston Cup, CART and Indy Racing League (IRL) racing circuits. Qualifying records accurate as of Sept. 20, 2002. Capacity figures for NASCAR, CART and IRL tracks are approximate and pertain to grandstand seating only. Standing room and hillside terrain seating featured at most road courses are not included.

CART

	Location	Miles	Qual.mph record	Set by	Seats
Burke Lakefront Airport	Cleveland, Ohio	2.106**	134.385	Jimmy Vasser (1998)	36,000
California Speedway	Fontana, Calif.	2.029	241.428†	Gil de Ferran (2000)	122,000
Chicago Motor Speedway	Cicero, Ill.	1.029	167.567	Juan Montoya (2000)	40,000
Concord Pacific Place	Vancouver, B.C.	1.781**	106.144	Dario Franchitti (2000)	65,000
Exhibition Place	Toronto, Ont.	1.755**	110.565	Gil de Ferran (1999)	60,000
Fundidora Park	Monterrey, Mexico	2.1*	100.665	Kenny Brack (2001)	61,871
Circuit Gilles Villeneuve	Montreal, Quebec	2.75*	123.512	Christiano da Matta (2002)	
Grand Prix of the Americas	Miami, Fla.	1.54**	—	First race in 2002	
Grand Prix of Denver	Denver, Colo.	1.62**	96.093	Bruno Junqueira (2002)	
Laguna Seca Raceway	Monterey, Calif.	2.238*	118.969	Helio Castro-neves (2000)	8,000
Long Beach	Long Beach, Calif.	1.968**	104.969	Gil de Ferran (2000)	63,000
Mexico Gran Premio	Mexico City, Mexico	2.75*	—	First race in 2002	
Mid-Ohio Sports Car Course	Lexington, Ohio	2.258*	124.394	Dario Franchitti (1999) & Gil de Ferran (2000)	6,000
The Milwaukee Mile	West Allis, Wisc.	1.032	185.500	Patrick Carpentier (1998)	36,800
Portland International Raceway	Portland, Ore.	1.969*	122.768	Helio Castro-neves (2000)	50,000
Road America	Elkhart Lake, Wisc.	4.048*	145.924	Dario Franchitti (2000)	10,000
Rockingham Motor Speedway	Corby, England	1.5	210.859	Patrick Carpentier (2001)	27,500
Surfers Paradise	Queensland, Australia	2.795**	109.724	Dario Franchitti (1999)	55,000
Twin Ring Motegi	Motegi, Japan	1.549	219.000	Gil de Ferran (1999)	50,000

*Road courses (not ovals). **Temporary street circuits. †Indicates world closed-course record for auto racing.

Indy Racing League

Founded by Indianapolis Motor Speedway president Tony George, the Indy Racing League competes with CART and fielded 13 races, anchored by the Indianapolis 500, in 2002. Note that the track records listed are for normally-aspirated IRL cars unless otherwise noted by an asterisk.

	Location	Miles	Qual.mph Record	Set by	Seats
California Speedway	Fontana, Calif.	2.0	221.422	Eddie Cheever Jr. (2002)	92,109
Chicagoland Speedway	Joliet, Ill.	1.5	222.137	Robbie Buhl (2001)	75,000
Gateway International Raceway	Madison, Ill.	1.25	166.487	Robbie Buhl (2001)	60,000
Homestead-Miami Speedway	Homestead, Fla.	1.5	202.884	Sam Hornish (2002)	65,000
Indianapolis Motor Speedway	Indianapolis, Ind.	2.5	237.498	Arie Luyendyk (1996)*	250,000+
Kansas Speedway	Kansas City, Kan.	1.5	216.175	Scott Sharp (2001)	75,000
Kentucky Speedway	Sparta, Ky.	1.5	219.191	Scott Goodyear (2000)	70,000
Michigan Intl. Speedway	Brooklyn, Mich.	2.0	221.868	Tomas Scheckter (2002)	136,373
Nashville Superspeedway	Nashville, Tenn.	1.33	199.992	Greg Ray (2001)	50,000
Nazareth Speedway	Nazareth, Penn.	1.0	172.778	Gil de Ferran (2002)	44,044
Phoenix International Raceway	Phoenix, Ariz.	1.0	183.599	Arie Luyendyk (1996)*	78,450
Pikes Peak Int'l. Raceway	Fountain, Colo.	1.0	179.874	Greg Ray (2000)	42,787
Richmond International Raceway	Richmond, Va.	0.75	160.417	Jaques Lazier (2001)	95,920
Texas Motor Speedway	Fort Worth, Texas	1.5	225.979	Billy Boat (1998)	154,861

NASCAR Winston Cup

	Location	Miles	Qual.mph Record	Set by	Seats
Atlanta Motor Speedway	Hampton, Ga.	1.54	197.478	Geoff Bodine (1997)	124,000
Bristol Motor Speedway	Bristol, Tenn.	0.533	127.216	Jeff Gordon (2002)	147,000
California Speedway	Fontana, Calif.	2.0	187.432	Ryan Newman (2002)	92,000
Chicagoland Speedway	Joliet, Ill.	1.5	183.717	Todd Bodine (2001)	75,000
Darlington International Raceway	Darlington, S.C.	1.366	173.797	Ward Burton (1996)	65,000
Daytona International Speedway	Daytona Beach, Fla.	2.5	210.364	Bill Elliott (1987)	168,000
Dover Downs International Speedway	Dover, Del.	1.0	159.964	Rusty Wallace (1999)	140,000
Homestead-Miami Speedway	Homestead, Fla.	1.5	156.440	Steve Park (2000)	72,000
Indianapolis Motor Speedway	Indianapolis, Ind.	2.5	182.960	Tony Stewart (2002)	250,000+
Infineon Raceway	Sonoma, Calif.	1.949*	99.309	Rusty Wallace (2000)	42,500
Kansas Speedway	Kansas City, Kan.	1.5	176.499	Jason Leffler (2001)	75,000
Las Vegas Motor Speedway	Las Vegas, Nev.	1.5	172.850	Todd Bodine (2002)	126,000
Lowe's Motor Speedway	Concord, N.C.	1.5	186.464	Jimmie Johnson (2002)	167,000
Martinsville Speedway	Martinsville, Va.	0.526	95.371	Tony Stewart (2000)	91,000
Michigan Speedway	Brooklyn, Mich.	2.0	191.149	Dale Earnhardt Jr. (2000)	136,384
New Hampshire Int'l Speedway	Loudon, N.H.	1.058	132.089	Rusty Wallace (2000)	91,000
North Carolina Speedway	Rockingham, N.C.	1.017	158.035	Rusty Wallace (2000)	60,113
Phoenix International Raceway	Phoenix, Ariz.	1.0	134.178	Rusty Wallace (2000)	76,812
Pocono Raceway	Long Pond, Penn.	2.5	172.391	Tony Stewart (2000)	77,000

Auto Racing (Cont.)

	Location	Miles	Qual.mph Record	Set by	Seats
Richmond International Raceway	Richmond, Va.	0.75	127.389	Ward Burton (2002)	100,000+
Talladega Superspeedway	Talladega, Ala.	2.66	212.809	Bill Elliott (1987)	143,000
Texas Motor Speedway	Ft. Worth, Texas	1.5	194.224	Bill Elliott (2002)	154,861
Watkins Glen International	Watkins Glen, N.Y.	2.45*	122.698	Dale Jarret (2001)	40,000

*Road courses (not ovals).
Note: Richmond sells reserved seats only (no infield) for Winston Cup races.

Formula One

Race track capacity figures unavailable.

Grand Prix		Miles	Qual.mph Record	Set by
Australian	**Albert Park** (Melbourne)	3.274	137.883	Rubens Barrichello (2002)
Austrian	**A1-Ring** (Zeltwig, Austria)	2.684	141.595	Rubens Barrichello (2002)
Belgian	**Spa-Francorchamps**	4.333	143.418	Mika Hakkinen (1998)
Brazilian	**Interlagos** (Sao Paulo)	2.684	131.331	Juan Montoya (2002)
British	**Silverstone** (Towcester)	3.194	148.043	Nigel Mansell (1992)
Canadian	**Circuit Gilles Villeneuve** (Montreal)	2.747	133.941	Juan Montoya (2002)
European	**Nürburgring** (Nürburg, Germany)	2.822	135.959	Michael Schumacher (2001)
French	**Magny Cours** (Nevers)	2.641	159.792	Juan Montoya (2002)
German	**Hockenheim** (Germany)	2.796	204.450	Michael Schumacher (2002)
Hungarian	**Hungaroring** (Budapest)	2.468	120.984	Rubens Barrichello (2002)
Italian	**Autodromo Nazionale di Monza** (Milan)	3.585	159.951	Ayrton Senna (1991)
Japanese	**Suzuka** (Nagoya)	3.644	138.515	Gerhard Berger (1991)
Malaysian	**Sepang** (Kuala Lumpur)	3.444	130.218	Michael Schumacher (2001)
Monaco	**Monte Carlo** (Monaco)	2.082	141.595	Rubens Barrichello (2002)
San Marino	**Autodome Enzo di Ferrarit** (Imola, Italy)	3.063	138.265	Ayrton Senna (1994)
Spanish	**Catalunya** (Barcelona)	2.937	138.250	Michael Schumacher (2002)
United States	**Indianapolis Motor Speedway**	2.606	126.355	Michael Schumacher (2000)

SOCCER

World's Premier Soccer Stadiums

(Listed alphabetically by city)

Stadium	Location	Seats	Stadium	Location	Seats
Spiros Louis	Athens, Greece	74,443	Old Trafford	Manchester, England	67,650
Eden Park	Auckland, New Zealand	50,000	Azteca	Mexico City, Mexico	106,000
Camp Nou	Barcelona, Spain	98,000	Guiseppe Meazza	Milan, Italy	85,700
Workers'	Beijing, China	72,000	Centenario	Montevideo, Uruguay	73,609
Olympiastadion	Berlin, Germany	76,243	Luzhniki Stadion	Moscow, Russia	80,840
Népstadion	Budapest, Hungary	65,000	Olympiastadion	Munich, Germany	63,000
Antonio Liberti	Buenos Aires, Argentina	76,689	San Paolo	Naples, Italy	78,210
National	Cairo, Egypt	90,000	Stade de France	Paris, France	80,000
Salt Lake	Calcutta, India	120,000	Rungnado	Pyongyang, N. Korea	150,000
Millennium	Cardiff, Wales	72,500	Maracana	Rio de Janeiro, Brazil	122,268
Westfalenstadion	Dortmund, Germany	68,600	King Fahd II	Riyadh, Saudi Arabia	79,000
Lansdowne Road	Dublin, Ireland	48,000	Olimpico	Rome, Italy	82,307
Celtic Park	Glasgow, Scotland	60,506	Nacional	Santiago, Chile	77,000
Hampden Park	Glasgow, Scotland	52,670	Morumbi	Sao Paulo, Brazil	80,000
FNB Stadium	Johannesburg, S. Africa	90,000	Chasmil	Seoul, S. Korea	100,000
Olympic Stadium	Kiev, Ukraine	83,160	Stadium Australia	Sydney, Australia	80,000
Estadio da Luz	Lisbon, Portugal	77,844	Olympic Stadium	Tokyo, Japan	60,000
Wembley	London, England	78,000	Delle Alpi	Turin, Italy	69,041
Santiago Bernabeu	Madrid, Spain	87,000	Ernst Happel	Vienna, Austria	47,500

Major League Soccer

The 10-team MLS is the only U.S. Division I professional outdoor league sanctioned by FIFA and U.S. Soccer. Note that all capacity figures are approximate given the adjustments of football stadium seating to soccer.

Western Conference

	Stadium	Built	Seats	Field
Colorado Rapids	Invesco Field	2001	17,500	Grass
Dallas Burn	Cotton Bowl	1935	22,528	Grass
Kansas City Wizards	Arrowhead	1972	20,571	Grass
L.A. Galaxy	Rose Bowl	1922	30,000	Grass
San Jose Earthquakes	Spartan	1933	26,000	Grass

Eastern Conference

	Stadium	Built	Seats	Field
Chicago Fire	Cardinal*	1999	15,000	Turf
Columbus Crew	Columbus Crew	1999	22,555	Grass
D.C. United	RFK	1961	26,169	Grass
Metro Stars (N.Y./N.J.)	Giants	1976	25,576	Grass
N.E. Revolution	Gillette	2002	21,000	Grass

*Chicago will play temporarily at North Central College's Cardinal Stadium in Naperville, Ill. and will return to Soldier Field in 2003 following the current renovations.

MISCELLANEOUS

Minor League Baseball

AAA Ballparks
International League

North Division		Built	Seats	Field
Buffalo Bisons (Indians) ....**Dunn Tire Park**		1988	21,050	Grass
Ottawa Lynx (Expos) ....**JetForm Park**		1993	10,332	Grass
Pawtucket Red Sox (Red Sox) ....**McCoy Stadium**		1942	10,031	Grass
Rochester Red Wings (Orioles) ....**Frontier Field**		1997	10,840	Grass
Scranton/Wilkes-Barre Red Barons (Phillies) ....**Lackawanna County Stadium**		1989	11,232	Turf
Syracuse SkyChiefs (Blue Jays) ....**P&C Stadium**		1997	11,604	Turf
West Division		**Built**	**Seats**	**Field**
Columbus Clippers (Yankees) ....**Cooper Stadium**		1932	15,000	Grass
Indianapolis Indians (Brewers) ....**Victory Field**		1996	15,500	Grass
Louisville Bats (Reds) ....**Louisville Slugger Field**		2000	13,200	Grass
Toledo Mud Hens (Tigers) ....**Fifth Third Field**		2002	10,000	Grass
South Division		**Built**	**Seats**	**Field**
Charlotte Knights (White Sox) ....**Knights Stadium**		1990	10,002	Grass
Durham Bulls (Devil Rays) ....**Durham Bulls Athletic Park**		1995	10,000	Grass
Norfolk Tides (Mets) ....**Harbor Park**		1993	12,067	Grass
Richmond Braves (Braves) ....**The Diamond**		1985	12,134	Grass

Pacific Coast League

East Division		Built	Seats	Field
Oklahoma RedHawks (Rangers) ....**SBC Bricktown Ballpark**		1998	13,066	Grass
Memphis Redbirds (Cardinals) ....**AutoZone Park**		2000	14,300	Grass
Nashville Sounds (Pirates) ....**Herschel Greer Stadium**		1978	10,700	Grass
New Orleans Zephyrs (Astros) ....**Zephyr Field**		1997	11,000	Grass
North Division		**Built**	**Seats**	**Field**
Edmonton Trappers (Twins) ....**TELUS Field**		1995	9,200	Grass
Portland Beavers (Dodgers) ....**PGE Park**		1926*	23,000	Turf
Tacoma Rainiers (Mariners) ....**Cheney Stadium**		1960	9,600	Grass
Salt Lake Stingers (Angels) ....**Franklin Covey Field**		1993	15,500	Grass
Central Division		**Built**	**Seats**	**Field**
Albuquerque Isotopes (Marlins) ....**Albuquerque Sports Stadium**		1969*	11,095	Grass
Colorado Springs Sky Sox (Rockies) ....**Sky Sox Stadium**		1988	8,500	Grass
Iowa Cubs (Cubs) ....**Sec Taylor Stadium**		1992	10,888	Grass
Omaha Royals (Royals) ....**Johnny Rosenblatt Stadium**		1948	24,000	Turf
South Division		**Built**	**Seats**	**Field**
Las Vegas 51s (Padres) ....**Cashman Field**		1983	9,334	Grass
Fresno Grizzlies (Giants) ....**Fresno Stadium**		2002	12,500	Grass
Sacramento River Cats (Athletics) ....**Raley Field**		2000	14,111	Grass
Tucson Sidewinders (Diamondbacks) ....**Tucson Electric Park**		1998	11,000	Grass

*Portland's PGE Park, formerly known as Civic Stadium, underwent extensive renovations prior to the 2001 season. Albuquerque Sports Stadium underwent extensive renovations prior to the 2003 season.

Japanese Baseball League
Central League

		Location	Built	Seats	Field
Chunichi Dragons ....**Nagoya Dome**		Nagoya	1997	40,500	Turf
Hanshin Tigers.................................**Koshien Stadium**		Nisinomiya	1924	55,000	Grass
Hiroshima Carp ....**Hiroshima Municipal Stadium**		Hiroshima	1957	32,000	Grass
Yakult Swallows ....**Meiji Jingu Stadium**		Tokyo	1926	48,785	Turf
Yokohama BayStars ....**Yokohama Stadium**		Yokohama	1978	30,000	Turf
Yomiuri Giants ....**Tokyo Dome**		Tokyo	1988	48,000	Turf

Pacific League

		Location	Built	Seats	Field
Chiba Lotte Marines ....**Chiba Marine Stadium**		Chiba	1991	30,000	Turf
Fukuoka Daiei Hawks ....**Fukuoka Dome**		Fukuoka	1993	48,000	Turf
Kintetsu Buffaloes ....**Osaka Dome**		Osaka	1997	55,000	Turf
Nippon Ham Fighters ....**Tokyo Dome**		Tokyo	1988	48,000	Turf
Orix Blue Wave ....**Green Stadium Kobe**		Kobe	1988	35,000	Grass
Seibu Lions ....**Seibu Stadium**		Tokorozawa	1979	37,000	Turf

Canadian Football League
East Division

		Location	Built	Seats	Field
Hamilton Tiger-Cats.................................**Ivor Wynne Stadium**		Hamilton, Ont.	1932	28,830	Turf
Montreal Alouettes..............**Percival Molson Memorial Stadium**		Montreal, Que.	1976	19,461	Turf
Ottawa Renegades...........................**Frank Clair Stadium**		Ottawa, Ont.	1908	30,927	Turf
Toronto Argonauts ....**SkyDome**		Toronto, Ont.	1989	31,600*	Turf

*The regular season SkyDome capacity is 31,600 but it is expanded to 52,595 for postseason games.

Miscellaneous (Cont.)
West Division

		Location	Built	Seats	Field
British Columbia Lions	**B.C. Place Stadium**	Vancouver, B.C.	1983	40,800*	Turf
Calgary Stampeders	**McMahon Stadium**	Calgary, Alb.	1960	35,967	Turf
Edmonton Eskimos	**Commonwealth Stadium**	Edmonton, Alb.	1978	60,081	Grass
Saskatchewan Roughriders	**Taylor Field**	Regina, Sask.	1948	27,732	Turf
Winnipeg Blue Bombers	**Canad Inns Stadium**	Winnipeg, Man.	1953	29,544	Turf

*The regular season B.C. Place Stadium capacity is 40,800 but it is expanded to 59,478 for postseason games.

NFL Europe

		Location	Seats	Field
Amsterdam Admirals	**Amsterdam ArenA**	Amsterdam, Netherlands	51,328	Grass
F.C. Barcelona Dragons	**Olympic Stadium**	Barcelona, Spain	54,000	Grass
Berlin Thunder	**Jahn Stadium**	Berlin, Germany	20,000	Grass
Frankfurt Galaxy	**Waldstadion**	Frankfurt, Germany	54,000	Grass
Rhein Fire	**Rheinstadion**	Dusseldorf, Germany	57,000	Grass
Scottish Claymores	**Hampden Park**	Glasgow, Scotland	52,500	Grass

Arena Football League
American Conference

Western Division		Location	Built	Seats
Arizona Rattlers	**America West Arena**	Phoenix, Ariz.	1992	16,321
Colorado Crush	**Pepsi Center**	Denver, Colo.	1999	18,007
Dallas Desperados	**American Airlines Center**	Dallas, Texas	2001	16,971
Los Angeles Avengers	**Staples Center**	Los Angeles, Calif.	1999	16,096
San Jose SaberCats	**Compaq Center at San Jose**	San Jose, Calif.	1993	14,041
Central Division		Location	Built	Seats
Chicago Rush	**Allstate Arena**	Rosemont, Ill.	1979	18,500
Detroit Fury	**The Palace of Auburn Hills**	Auburn Hills, Mich.	1988	14,826
Grand Rapids Rampage	**Van Andel Arena**	Grand Rapids, Mich.	1996	10,424
Indiana Firebirds	**Conseco Fieldhouse**	Indianapolis, Ind.	1999	15,490

National Conference

Southern Division		Location	Built	Seats
Carolina Cobras	**Charlotte Coliseum**	Charlotte, N.C.	1988	22,375
Georgia Force	**The Arena at Gwinnett Center**	Gwinnett, Ga.	2003	11,200
Orlando Predators	**TD Waterhouse Centre**	Orlando, Fla.	1989	16,613
Tampa Bay Storm	**St. Pete Times Forum**	Tampa Bay, Fla.	1996	20,282
Eastern Division		Location	Built	Seats
Buffalo Destroyers	**HSBC Arena**	Buffalo, N.Y.	1996	18,457
New Jersey Gladiators	**Continental Airlines Arena**	E. Rutherford, N.J.	1981	17,500
New York Dragons	**Nassau Veterans' Mem. Coliseum**	Uniondale, N.Y.	1972	11,965
Toronto Phantoms	**Air Canada Centre**	Toronto, Ont.	1999	17,100

Women's Professional Basketball
Women's National Basketball Association

The WNBA teams play in the same arenas as the NBA teams in their respective cities. However, the capacities of some of the venues are "down-sized" for some games. The new, smaller capacity for WNBA games is listed where applicable.

Eastern		Location	Built	Seats
Charlotte Sting	**Charlotte Coliseum**	Charlotte, N.C.	1988	12,843
Cleveland Rockers	**Gund Arena**	Cleveland, Ohio	1994	11,751
Detroit Shock	**The Palace of Auburn Hills**	Auburn Hills, Mich.	1988	22,076
Indiana Fever	**Conseco Fieldhouse**	Indianapolis, Ind.	1999	18,345
Miami Sol	**AmericanAirlines Arena**	Miami, Fla.	1999	10,412
New York Liberty	**Madison Square Garden**	New York, N.Y.	1968	19,563
Orlando Miracle	**TD Waterhouse Centre**	Orlando, Fla.	1989	17,306
Washington Mystics	**MCI Center**	Washington, D.C.	1997	19,766
Western		Location	Built	Seats
Houston Comets	**Compaq Center**	Houston, Texas	1975	16,285
Los Angeles Sparks	**Staples Center**	Los Angeles, Calif.	1999	13,141
Minnesota Lynx	**Target Center**	Minneapolis, Minn.	1990	8,025
Phoenix Mercury	**America West Arena**	Phoenix, Ariz.	1992	10,746
Portland Fire	**Rose Garden**	Portland, Ore.	1995	10,816
Sacramento Monarchs	**ARCO Arena**	Sacramento, Calif.	1988	17,317
Seattle Storm	**KeyArena at Seattle Center**	Seattle, Wash.	1962	9,686
Utah Starzz	**Delta Center**	Salt Lake City, Utah	1991	8,915

Horse Racing
Triple Crown race tracks

Race	Racetrack	Seats	Infield
Kentucky Derby	Churchill Downs	48,500	65,000
Preakness Stakes	Pimlico Race Course	13,047	60,000
Belmont Stakes	Belmont Park	32,941	N/A

Record crowds: Kentucky Derby—163,628 (1974); Preakness—104,454 (2001); Belmont—103,222 (2002).
Note: Belmont Park does not open infield for Belmont Stakes.

Tennis
Grand Slam center courts

Event	Main Stadium	Seats
Australian Open	Melbourne Park	15,021
French Open	Stade Roland Garros	16,300
Wimbledon	Centre Court	13,813
U.S. Open	Arthur Ashe Stadium	22,547

COLLEGE BASKETBALL

The 50 Largest Arenas

The 50 largest arenas in Division I for the 2002-03 NCAA regular season. Note that (*) indicates part-time home court.

	Seats	Home Team		Seats	Home Team
1 Carrier Dome	33,000	Syracuse	26 Kohl Center	17,142	Wisconsin
2 Thompson-Boling Arena	24,535	Tennessee	27 Comcast Center	17,100	Maryland
3 Rupp Arena	23,000	Kentucky	28 Assembly Hall	16,450	Illinois
4 Marriott Center	22,700	BYU	29 Allen Fieldhouse	16,300	Kansas
5 Dean Smith Center	21,750	N. Carolina	30 Hartford Civic Center	16,294	UConn*
6 MCI Center	20,600	Georgetown*	31 Erwin Center	16,175	Texas
7 The Pyramid	20,142	Memphis	32 LA Sports Arena	16,161	USC
8 Continental Airlines Arena	20,049	Seton Hall	33 Carver-Hawkeye Arena	15,500	Iowa
9 Savvis Center	20,000	Saint Louis	Pepsi Arena	15,500	Siena
10 The Rose Garden	19,980	Portland St.*	35 Miami Arena	15,388	Miami*
11 RBC Center	19,722	N.C. State	36 Coleman Coliseum	15,316	Alabama
12 Bud Walton Arena	19,200	Arkansas	37 Bryce Jordan Center	15,261	Penn St.
Value City Arena	19,200	Ohio St.	38 United Spirit Arena	15,050	Texas Tech
14 First Union Center	19,010	Villanova*	39 Arena-Auditorium	15,028	Wyoming
15 Freedom Hall	18,865	Louisville	40 Huntsman Center	15,000	Utah
16 Bradley Center	18,717	Marquette	41 Breslin Events Center	14,759	Michigan St.
17 Thomas & Mack Center	18,500	UNLV	42 Joel Memorial Coliseum	14,665	Wake Forest
18 Madison Square Garden	18,470	St. John's*	43 Williams Arena	14,625	Minnesota
19 HSBC Arena	18,400	Canisius* & Niagara*	44 McKale Center	14,545	Arizona
20 University Arena (The Pit)	18,018	New Mexico	45 Wells Fargo Arena	14,198	Arizona St.
21 Alltel Arena	18,000	Arkansas-Little Rock	46 Memorial Gym	14,168	Vanderbilt
22 New Orleans Arena	17,832	Tulane*	47 Maravich Assembly Ctr.	14,164	LSU
23 Carolina Center	17,600	South Carolina	48 Mackey Arena	14,123	Purdue
24 Allstate Arena	17,500	DePaul	49 Hilton Coliseum	14,092	Iowa St.
25 Assembly Hall	17,257	Indiana	50 WVU Coliseum	14,000	West Virginia

Division I Conference Home Courts

NCAA Division I conferences for the 2002-03 season. Teams with home games in more than one arena are noted.

America East

	Home Floor	Seats
Albany	Rec & Convocation Ctr.	5,000
Binghamton	West Gym	2,275
Boston University	Case Gym	1,800
Hartford	Chase Family Arena	4,475
Maine	Alfond Arena	5,712
New Hampshire	Lundholm Gym	3,500
Northeastern	Solomon Court	1,500
Stony Brook	USB Sports Complex	4,103
Vermont	Patrick Gym	3,228

Atlantic Sun

	Home Floor	Seats
Belmont	Municipal Auditorium	5,000
Campbell	Carter Gym	1,050
Central Fla.	UCF Arena	5,100
Fla. Atlantic	FAU Gym	5,000
Gardner-Webb	Paul Porter Arena	5,000
Georgia St.	GSU Sports Arena	5,500
Jacksonville	Swisher Gym	1,500
Jacksonville St.	Mathews Coliseum	5,500
Mercer	Porter Gym	1,000
Samford	Seibert Hall	4,000
Stetson	Edmunds Center	5,000
Troy St.	Trojan Arena	3,000

Atlantic Coast

	Home Floor	Seats
Clemson	Littlejohn Coliseum	11,020
Duke	Cameron Indoor Stadium	9,314
Florida St.	Leon County Civic Center	12,200
Georgia Tech	Alexander Mem. Stadium	10,000
Maryland	Comcast Center	17,100
North Carolina	Dean Smith Center	21,750
N.C. State	RBC Center	19,722
Virginia	University Hall	8,864
Wake Forest	Joel Memorial Coliseum	14,665

Atlantic 10

	Home Floor	Seats
Dayton	U. of Dayton Arena	13,266
Duquesne	Palumbo Center	6,200
Fordham	Rose Hill Gym	3,470
George Washington	Smith Center	5,000
La Salle	Tom Gola Arena	4,000
Massachusetts	Mullins Center	9,493
Rhode Island	Ryan Center	7,800
Richmond	Robins Center	9,171
St. Bonaventure	Reilly Center	6,000
St. Joseph's-PA	Alumni Mem. Fieldhouse	3,200
Temple	Liacouras Center	10,206
Xavier-OH	Cintas Center	10,200

College Basketball (Cont.)

Big East

	Home Floor	Seats
Boston College	Conte Forum	8,606
Connecticut	Gampel Pavilion	10,027
	& Hartford Civic Center	16,294
Georgetown	MCI Center	20,600
	& McDonough Arena	2,500
Miami-FL	Miami Arena	15,388
	& Convocation Center	7,000
Notre Dame	Joyce Center	11,418
Pittsburgh	Petersen Event Center	12,500
Providence	Dunkin Donuts Center	12,993
Rutgers	Louis Brown Athletic Center	9,000
St. John's	Alumni Hall	6,008
	& Madison Square Garden	18,470
Seton Hall	Continental Airlines Arena	20,049
Syracuse	Carrier Dome	33,000
Villanova	The Pavilion	6,500
	& First Union Center	19,010
Virginia Tech	Cassell Coliseum	10,052
West Virginia	WVU Coliseum	14,000

Big Sky

	Home Floor	Seats
CS-Sacramento	Hornet Gym	1,500
Eastern Wash.	Reese Court	6,000
Idaho St.	Reed Gym	3,600
Montana	Adams Center	7,500
Montana St.	Worthington Arena	7,250
Northern Arizona	Walkup Skydome	7,000
Portland St.	Rose Garden	19,980
	& Stott Center	1,775
Weber St.	Dee Events Center	12,000

Big South

	Home Floor	Seats
Birmingham-Southern	Bill Battle Coliseum	2,000
Charleston Southern	CSU Fieldhouse	1,500
Coastal Carolina	Kimbel Gymnasium	1,037
Elon	Koury Center	2,000
High Point	Millis Center	3,000
Liberty	Vines Center	9,000
NC-Asheville	Justice Center	1,100
	& Asheville Civic Center	6,000
Radford	Dedmon Center	5,000
Winthrop	Winthrop Coliseum	6,100

Big Ten

	Home Floor	Seats
Illinois	Assembly Hall	16,450
Indiana	Assembly Hall	17,257
Iowa	Carver-Hawkeye Arena	15,500
Michigan	Crisler Arena	13,751
Michigan St.	Breslin Events Center	14,759
Minnesota	Williams Arena	14,625
Northwestern	Welsh-Ryan Arena	8,117
Ohio St.	Value City Arena	19,200
Penn St.	Bryce Jordan Center	15,261
Purdue	Mackey Arena	14,123
Wisconsin	Kohl Center	17,142

Big 12

	Home Floor	Seats
Colorado	Coors Events Conference Ctr.	11,076
Iowa St.	Hilton Coliseum	14,092
Kansas	Allen Fieldhouse	16,300
Kansas St.	Bramlage Coliseum	13,500
Missouri	Hearnes Center	13,545
Nebraska	Devaney Sports Center	13,500
Baylor	Ferrell Center	10,284
Oklahoma	Lloyd Noble Center	11,100
Oklahoma St.	Gallagher-Iba Arena	13,611
Texas	Erwin Center	16,175
Texas A&M	Reed Arena	12,700
Texas Tech	United Spirit Arena	15,050

Big West

	Home Floor	Seats
Cal Poly	Mott Gym	3,032
CS-Fullerton	Titan Gym	3,500
CS-Northridge	The Matadome	1,600
Idaho	Cowan Spectrum	7,000
Long Beach St.	The Pyramid	5,000
Pacific	Spanos Center	6,150
UC-Irvine	Bren Events Center	5,000
UC-Riverside	Student Rec. Center	3,168
UC-Santa Barbara	The Thunderdome	6,000
Utah St.	The Smith Spectrum	10,270

Colonial

	Home Floor	Seats
Delaware	Bob Carpenter Center	5,000
Drexel	Daskalis Athletic Center	2,300
George Mason	Patriot Center	10,000
Hofstra	Hofstra Arena	5,124
James Madison	JMU Convocation Center	7,156
NC-Wilmington	Trask Coliseum	6,100
Old Dominion	Ted Constant Convocation Ctr.	8,650
Towson	Towson Center	5,000
VCU	Siegel Center	7,500
Wm. & Mary	William & Mary Hall	8,600

Conference USA

	Home Floor	Seats
UAB	Bartow Arena	8,500
Cincinnati	Shoemaker Center	13,176
DePaul	Allstate Arena	17,500
East Carolina	Minges Coliseum	8,000
Houston	Hofheinz Pavilion	8,479
Louisville	Freedom Hall	18,865
Marquette	Bradley Center	18,717
Memphis	The Pyramid	20,142
UNC Charlotte	Halton Arena	9,105
Saint Louis	Savvis Center	20,000
South Florida	Sun Dome	10,411
Southern Miss.	Green Coliseum	8,095
TCU	Daniel-Meyer Coliseum	7,166
Tulane	New Orleans Arena	17,832
	& Fogelman Arena	3,600

Horizon League

	Home Floor	Seats
Butler	Hinkle Fieldhouse	11,043
Cleveland St.	CSU Convocation Center	13,610
Detroit Mercy	Calihan Hall	8,837
IL-Chicago	UIC Pavilion	8,000
Loyola-IL	Gentile Center	5,200
WI-Green Bay	Rush Center	10,400
WI-Milwaukee	Klotsche Center	5,000
Wright St.	Nutter Center	10,632
Youngstown St.	Beeghly Center	8,000

Ivy League

	Home Floor	Seats
Brown	Pizzitola Sports Center	2,800
Columbia	Levien Gymnasium	3,408
Cornell	Newman Arena	4,473
Dartmouth	Leede Arena	2,200
Harvard	Lavietes Pavilion	2,195
Penn	The Palestra	8,700
Princeton	Jadwin Gymnasium	6,854
Yale	Payne Whitney Gym	3,100

Metro Atlantic

	Home Floor	Seats
Canisius	HSBC Arena	18,400
	& Koessler Athletic Center	2,100
Fairfield	Bridgeport Arena	9,500
Iona	Mulcahy Center	3,200
Loyola-MD	Reitz Arena	3,000
Manhattan	Draddy Gymnasium	3,000
Marist	McCann Center	3,944
Niagara	HSBC Arena	18,400
	& Gallagher Center	2,400
Rider	Alumni Gymnasium	1,650
St. Peter's	Yanitelli Center	3,200
Siena	Pepsi Arena	15,500

Mid-American

	Home Floor	Seats
Akron	JAR Arena	5,942
Ball St.	John E. Wortham Arena	11,500
Bowling Green	Anderson Arena	5,000
Buffalo	Alumni Arena	8,500
Central Mich.	Rose Arena	5,200
Eastern Mich.	Convocation Center	8,824
Kent St	MAC Center	6,327
Marshall	Cam Henderson Center	9,043
Miami-OH	Millett Hall	9,200
Northern Illinois	Convocation Center	9,100
Ohio Univ.	Convocation Center	13,000
Toledo	Savage Hall	9,000
Western Mich.	University Arena	5,800

Mid-Continent

	Home Floor	Seats
Chicago St.	Dickens Athletic Center	2,500
IU-PUI	IU-PUI Gym	2,000
Missouri-K.C.	Municipal Auditorium	9,287
Oakland	Oakland Arena	3,000
Oral Roberts	Mabee Center	10,575
Southern Utah	Centrum	5,300
Valparaiso	Athletics-Recreation Center	4,500
Western Ill.	Western Hall	5,139

Mid-Eastern Athletic

	Home Floor	Seats
Bethune-Cookman	Moore Gym	3,000
Coppin St.	Coppin Center	3,000
Delaware St.	Memorial Hall	3,000
Florida A&M	Gaither Gym	3,365
Hampton	Hampton Convocation Center	7,500
Howard	Burr Gym	2,200
MD-East.Shore	W.P. Hytche Center	5,500
Morgan St.	Hill Fieldhouse	4,500
Norfolk St.	Echols Hall	7,600
N. Carolina A&T	Corbett Sports Center	6,700
S. Carolina St.	SHM Center	3,200

Missouri Valley

	Home Floor	Seats
Bradley	Carver Arena	11,300
Creighton	Omaha Civic Auditorium	9,377
Drake	Knapp Center	7,002
Evansville	Roberts Stadium	12,144
Illinois St.	Redbird Arena	10,200
Indiana St.	Hulman Center	10,200
Northern Iowa	UNI-Dome	10,000
Southern Ill.	SIU Arena	10,000
SW Missouri St.	Hammons Student Center	8,846
Wichita St.	Levitt Arena	10,556

Mountain West

	Home Floor	Seats
Air Force	Clune Arena	6,002
BYU	Marriott Center	22,700
Colorado St.	Moby Arena	8,745
San Diego St.	Cox Arena at the Aztec Bowl	12,414
UNLV	Thomas & Mack Center	18,500
New Mexico	The Pit	18,018
Utah	Huntsman Center	15,000
Wyoming	Arena-Auditorium	15,028

Northeast

	Home Floor	Seats
Central Conn. St.	Detrick Gym	3,200
Farleigh Dickinson	Rothman Center	5,000
LIU-Brooklyn	Schwartz Athletic Center	1,200
MD-Balt. County	Retriever Activity Center	4,024
Monmouth	Boylan Gym	2,500
Mt. St. Mary's	Knott Arena	3,196
Quinnipiac	Burt Kahn Court	1,500
Robert Morris	Sewall Center	3,056
Sacred Heart	Pitt Center	2,100
St. Francis-NY	Pope Center	1,200
St. Francis-PA	DeGol Arena	3,500
Wagner	Spiro Sports Center	2,100

Ohio Valley

	Home Floor	Seats
Austin Peay	Dunn Center	9,000
Eastern Illinois	Lantz Gym	5,300
Eastern Ky.	McBrayer Arena	6,500
Morehead St.	Johnson Arena	6,500
Murray St.	Regional Special Events Ctr.	8,600
SE Missouri St.	Show Me Center	7,000
Tennessee-Martin	Skyhawk Arena	6,700
Tennessee St.	Gentry Complex	10,500
Tennessee Tech	Eblen Center	10,152

Pacific-10

	Home Floor	Seats
Arizona	McKale Center	14,545
Arizona St.	Wells Fargo Arena	14,198
California	Haas Pavillion	12,172
Oregon	McArthur Court	9,087
Oregon St.	Gill Coliseum	10,400
Stanford	Maples Pavilion	7,500
UCLA	Pauley Pavilion	12,819
USC	LA Sports Arena	16,161
Washington	Bank of America Arena	10,000
Washington. St.	Friel Court	12,058

Patriot League

	Home Floor	Seats
American	Bender Arena	5,000
Army	Christl Arena	5,043
Bucknell	The Rack Pavilion	4,000
Colgate	Cotterell Court	3,000
Holy Cross	Hart Recreation Center	3,600
Lafayette	Kirby Field House	3,500
Lehigh	Stabler Arena	5,600
Navy	Alumni Hall	5,710

College Basketball (Cont.)

Southeastern

Eastern

	Home Floor	Seats
Florida	O'Connell Center	12,000
Georgia	Stegeman Coliseum	10,523
Kentucky	Rupp Arena	23,000
South Carolina	Carolina Center	17,600
Tennessee	Thompson-Boling Arena	24,535
Vanderbilt	Memorial Gymnasium	14,168

Western

	Home Floor	Seats
Alabama	Coleman Coliseum	15,316
Arkansas	Bud Walton Arena	19,200
Auburn	Eaves-Memorial Coliseum	10,500
LSU	Maravich Assembly Center	14,164
Mississippi	Tad Smith Coliseum	8,135
Mississippi St.	Humphrey Coliseum	10,500

Southern

	Home Floor	Seats
Appalachian St.	Seby Jones Arena	8,300
The Citadel	McAlister Field House	6,200
Coll. of Charleston	John Kresse Arena	3,500
Davidson	Belk Arena	5,700
E. Tenn. St.	Memorial Center	12,000
Furman	Timmons Arena	5,000
Ga. Southern	Hanner Fieldhouse	5,500
NC-Greensboro	Fleming Gymnasium	2,320
Tenn-Chatt.	McKenzie Arena	11,218
VMI	Cameron Hall	5,029
W. Carolina	Ramsey Center	7,286
Wofford	Johnson Arena	3,500

Southland

	Home Floor	Seats
Lamar	Montagne Center	10,080
Louisiana-Monroe	Fant-Ewing Coliseum	8,000
McNeese St.	Burton Coliseum	8,000
Nicholls St.	Stopher Gym	3,800
Northwestern St.	Prather Coliseum	4,300
Sam Houston St.	Johnson Coliseum	6,172
SE Louisiana	University Center	7,500
SW Texas St.	Strahan Coliseum	7,200
S.F. Austin St.	W.R. Johnson Coliseum	7,200
TX-Arlington	Texas Hall	4,200
TX-San Antonio	Convocation Center	5,100

Southwestern

	Home Floor	Seats
Alabama A&M	Elmore Healh/Science Building	6,000
Alabama St.	Joe Reed Acadome	8,000
Alcorn St.	Whitney Complex	7,000
Arkansas-Pine Bluff	HPER Complex	4,500
Grambling St.	Tiger Memorial Gym	4,500
Jackson St.	Williams Center	8,000
Miss.Valley St.	Harrison HPER Athletic Complex	6,000
Prairie View A&M	The Baby Dome	6,600
Southern-BR	Clark Activity Center	7,500
TX Southern	Health & P.E. Building	8,100

Sun Belt

	Home Floor	Seats
Arkansas-Little Rock	Alltel Arena	18,000
Arkansas St	Convocation Center	10,563
Denver	Magness Arena	7,200
Florida International	Golden Panther Arena	5,000
LA-Lafayette	The Cajundome	12,800
Middle Tenn. St.	Murphy Center	11,520
New Mexico St.	Pan American Center	13,071
New Orleans	Lakefront Arena	10,000
North Texas	The Super Pit	10,000
South Alabama	Mitchell Center	10,000
Western Ky.	E.A. Diddle Arena	11,300

West Coast

	Home Floor	Seats
Gonzaga	Martin Centre	4,000
Loyola Marymount	Gersten Pavilion	4,156
Pepperdine	Firestone Fieldhouse	3,104
Portland	Chiles Center	5,000
St. Mary's-CA	McKeon Pavilion	3,500
San Diego	Jenny Craig Pavilion	5,100
San Francisco	War Memorial Gym	5,300
Santa Clara	Leavy Center	5,000

Western Athletic

	Home Floor	Seats
Boise St.	BSU Pavilion	12,380
Fresno St.	Selland Arena	10,220
Hawaii	Stan Sherif Center	10,300
Louisiana Tech	Thomas Assembly Center	8,000
Nevada	Lawlor Events Center	11,200
Rice	Autry Court	5,000
San Jose St.	The Events Center	5,000
SMU	Moody Coliseum	8,998
Tulsa	Reynolds Center	8,355
UTEP	Haskins Center	12,000

Independents

	Home Floor	Seats
Centenary	Gold Dome	3,000
IPFW	Hilliard Gates Sports Center	2,700
Lipscomb	Lipscomb U. Arena	5,028
Morris Brown	John H. Lewis Gym	2,000
Savannah St.	Wiley Gym	2,100
Texas A&M-Corpus Christi	Memorial Coliseum	4,000
Texas-Pan Am	Health/PE Fieldhouse	3,500

Future NCAA Final Four Sites

Men

Year	Arena	Seats	Location
2003	Louisiana Superdome	53,500	New Orleans
2004	Alamodome	20,557*	San Antonio
2005	Edward Jones Dome	66,000	St. Louis
2006	RCA Dome	47,100	Indianapolis
2007	Georgia Dome	40,000	Atlanta

Women

Year	Arena	Seats	Location
2003	Georgia Dome	40,000	Atlanta
2004	New Orleans Sports Arena	17,832	New Orleans
2005	RCA Dome	56,127	Indianapolis
2006	FleetCenter	18,624	Boston
2007	Gund Arena	20,562	Cleveland

*This was the listed capacity for Spurs games at the Alamodome. It is likely that the seating will be reconfigured to fit more spectators for the Final Four.

COLLEGE FOOTBALL

The 40 Largest I-A Stadiums

The 40 largest stadiums in NCAA Division I-A college football heading into the 2002 season. Note that (*) indicates stadium not on campus.

		Location	Seats	Home Team	Conference	Built	Field
1	Michigan Stadium	Ann Arbor, Mich.	107,501	Michigan	Big Ten	1927	Grass
2	Beaver Stadium	University Park, Penn.	107,282	Penn St.	Big Ten	1960	Grass
3	Neyland Stadium	Knoxville, Tenn.	104,079	Tennessee	SEC-East	1921	Grass
4	Ohio Stadium	Columbus, Ohio	101,568	Ohio St.	Big Ten	1922	Grass
5	Rose Bowl*	Pasadena, Calif.	98,636	UCLA	Pac-10	1922	Grass
6	LA Memorial Coliseum*	Los Angeles, Calif.	92,000	USC	Pac-10	1923	Grass
7	Tiger Stadium	Baton Rouge, La.	91,600	LSU	SEC-West	1924	Grass
8	Sanford Stadium	Athens, Ga.	86,520	Georgia	SEC-East	1929	Grass
9	Jordan-Hare Stadium	Auburn, Ala.	86,063	Auburn	SEC-West	1939	Grass
10	Stanford Stadium	Stanford, Calif.	85,500	Stanford	Pac-10	1921	Grass
11	Bryant-Denny Stadium	Tuscaloosa, Ala.	83,818	Alabama	SEC-West	1929	Grass
12	Legion Field*	Birmingham, Ala.	83,091	Alabama/UAB	SEC-West/USA	1927	Grass
13	Florida Field	Gainesville, Fla.	83,000	Florida	SEC-East	1929	Grass
14	Memorial Stadium	Clemson, S.C.	81,474	Clemson	ACC	1942	Grass
15	Notre Dame Stadium	Notre Dame, Ind.	80,795	Notre Dame	Independent	1930	Grass
16	Kyle Field	College Station, Texas	80,650	Texas A&M	Big 12-South	1925	Grass
17	Williams-Brice Stadium	Columbia, S.C.	80,250	South Carolina	SEC-East	1934	Grass
18	Royal-Memorial Stadium	Austin, Texas	80,082	Texas	Big 12-South	1924	Grass
19	Doak Campbell Stadium	Tallahasse, Fla.	80,000	Florida St.	ACC	1950	Grass
20	Camp Randall Stadium	Madison, Wis.	76,634	Wisconsin	Big Ten	1917	Turf
21	Memorial Stadium	Berkeley, Calif.	75,028	California	Pac-10	1923	Grass
22	Memorial Stadium	Lincoln, Neb.	73,918	Nebraska	Big 12-North	1923	Turf
23	Sun Devil Stadium	Tempe, Ariz.	73,379	Arizona St.	Pac-10	1959	Grass
24	Gaylord Family-Okla. Memorial	Norman, Okla.	72,765	Oklahoma	Big 12-South	1924	Grass
25	Husky Stadium	Seattle, Wash.	72,500	Washington	Pac-10	1920	Turf
26	Orange Bowl*	Miami, Fla.	72,319	Miami-FL	Big East	1935	Grass
27	Spartan Stadium	East Lansing, Mich.	72,027	Michigan St.	Big Ten	1957	Turf
28	Donald W. Reynolds Razorback Stadium	Fayetteville, Ark.	72,000	Arkansas	SEC-West	1938	Grass
29	Kinnick Stadium	Iowa City, Iowa	70,397	Iowa	Big Ten	1929	Grass
30	Citrus Bowl*	Orlando, Fla.	70,188	Central Florida	Mid-American	1936	Grass
31	Rice Stadium	Houston, Texas	70,000	Rice	WAC	1950	Turf
32	Superdome*	New Orleans, La.	69,767	Tulane	USA	1975	Turf
33	Memorial Stadium	Champaign, Ill.	69,249	Illinois	Big Ten	1923	Turf
34	Commonwealth	Lexington, Ky.	67,530	Kentucky	SEC-East	1973	Grass
35	Veterans Stadium*	Philadelphia, Penn.	66,592	Temple	Big East	1971	Turf
36	Ross-Ade Stadium	W. Lafayette, Ind.	66,295	Purdue	Big Ten	1924	Grass
37	Lane Stadium	Blacksburg, Va.	65,115	Va. Tech	Big East	1965	Grass
38	LaVell Edwards Stadium	Provo, Utah	65,000	BYU	Mountain West	1964	Grass
39	Heinz Field*	Pittsburgh, Penn.	64,450	Pittsburgh	Big East	2001	Grass
40	HHH Metrodome*	Minneapolis, Minn.	64,172	Minnesota	Big Ten	1982	Turf

Note: The capacities for several stadiums including the Rose Bowl, Louisiana Superdome and Sun Devil Stadium are often listed differently for other events, such as bowl games, which they host.

2002 Conference Home Fields

NCAA Division I-A conference by conference listing includes member teams heading into the 2002 season. Note that (*) indicates stadium is not on campus.

Atlantic Coast

	Stadium	Built	Seats	Field
Clemson	Memorial	1942	81,474	Grass
Duke	Wallace Wade	1929	33,941	Grass
Florida St.	Doak Campbell	1950	80,000	Grass
Ga. Tech	Bobby Dodd	1913	46,000	Grass
Maryland	Byrd	1950	48,055	Grass
N. Carolina	Kenan Memorial	1927	60,000	Grass
N.C. State	Carter-Finley	1966	51,500	Grass
Virginia	Scott	1931	61,500	Grass
Wake Forest	Groves	1968	31,500	Grass

Big East

	Stadium	Built	Seats	Field
Boston Col.	Alumni	1957	44,500	Turf
Miami-FL	Orange Bowl*	1935	72,319	Grass
Pittsburgh	Heinz Field*	2001	64,450	Grass
Rutgers	Rutgers	1994	41,500	Grass
Syracuse	Carrier Dome	1980	49,550	Turf
Temple	Veterans*	1971	66,592	Turf
Va. Tech	Lane	1965	65,115	Grass
West Va.	Mountaineer Field	1980	63,500	Turf

College Football (Cont.)

Big Ten

	Stadium	Built	Seats	Field
Illinois	Memorial	1923	69,249	Turf
Indiana	Memorial	1960	52,354	Grass
Iowa	Kinnick	1929	70,397	Grass
Michigan	Michigan	1927	107,501	Grass
Michigan St.	Spartan	1957	72,027	Turf
Minnesota	HHH Metrodome*	1982	64,172	Turf
Northwestern	Ryan Field	1926	47,130	Grass
Ohio St.	Ohio	1922	101,568	Grass
Penn St.	Beaver	1960	107,282	Grass
Purdue	Ross-Ade	1924	66,295	Grass
Wisconsin	Camp Randall	1917	76,634	Turf

Big 12

NORTH	Stadium	Built	Seats	Field
Colorado	Folsom Field	1924	51,808	Turf
Iowa St.	Jack Trice Field	1975	43,000	Grass
Kansas	Memorial	1921	50,250	Turf
Kansas St.	Wagner Field	1968	50,000	Turf
Missouri	Faurot Field	1926	62,000	Grass
Nebraska	Memorial	1923	73,918	Grass

SOUTH	Stadium	Built	Seats	Field
Baylor	Floyd Casey	1950	50,000	Grass
Oklahoma	Gaylord Family-Oklahoma Memorial	1924	72,765	Grass
Oklahoma St.	Lewis Field	1920	48,000	Turf
Texas	Royal-Mem.	1924	80,082	Grass
Texas A&M.	Kyle Field	1925	80,650	Grass
Texas Tech	Jones-SBC	1947	50,500	Turf

Note: The annual Oklahoma-Texas game has been played at the Cotton Bowl (capacity 68,252) in Dallas since 1937.

Conference USA

	Stadium	Built	Seats	Field
UAB	Legion Field	1927	83,091	Grass
Army	Michie	1924	39,929	Grass
Cincinnati	Nippert	1924	35,000	Turf
E. Carolina	Dowdy-Ficklen	1963	43,000	Grass
Houston	Robertson	1942	32,000	Grass
Louisville	Papa John's Cardinal	1998	42,000	Turf
Memphis	Liberty Bowl*	1965	62,380	Grass
Southern Miss	M.M. Roberts	1976	33,000	Grass
TCU	Amon Carter	1929	44,008	Grass
Tulane	Superdome*	1975	69,767	Turf

Mid-American

	Stadium	Built	Seats	Field
Akron	Rubber Bowl*	1940	35,202	Turf
Ball St.	Ball State	1967	21,581	Grass
Bowling Green	Doyt Perry	1966	30,599	Grass
Buffalo	UB	1993	31,000	Grass
C. Florida	Citrus Bowl	1936	70,188	Grass
Central Mich.	Kelly/Shorts	1972	30,199	Turf
Eastern Mich.	Rynearson	1969	30,200	Turf
Kent	Dix	1969	30,520	Turf
Marshall	Marshall	1991	38,019	Turf
Miami-OH	Fred Yager	1983	30,012	Grass
Northern Ill.	Huskie	1965	31,000	Grass
Ohio Univ.	Peden	1929	24,000	Grass
Toledo	Glass Bowl	1937	26,248	Turf
Western Mich.	Waldo	1939	30,200	Grass

Mountain West

	Stadium	Built	Seats	Field
Air Force	Falcon	1962	52,480	Grass
BYU	LaVell Edwards	1964	65,000	Grass
Colorado St.	Hughes	1968	30,000	Grass
New Mexico	University	1960	37,370	Grass
San Diego St.	Qualcomm*	1967	54,000	Grass
UNLV	Sam Boyd*	1971	36,800	Grass
Utah	Rice-Eccles	1927†	45,634	Grass
Wyoming	War Memorial	1950	33,500	Grass

†Utah's Rice-Eccles Stadium was rebuilt in 1998.

Pacific-10

	Stadium	Built	Seats	Field
Arizona	Arizona	1928	56,002	Grass
Arizona St.	Sun Devil	1958	73,379	Grass
California	Memorial	1923	75,028	Grass
Oregon	Autzen	1967	41,698	Turf
Oregon St.	Reser's	1953	35,362	Turf
Stanford	Stanford	1921	85,500	Grass
UCLA	Rose Bowl*	1922	98,636	Grass
USC	LA Mem. Coliseum*	1923	92,000	Grass
Washington	Husky	1920	72,500	Turf
Washington St.	Martin	1972	37,600	Grass

Southeastern

EAST	Stadium	Built	Seats	Field
Florida	Florida Field	1929	83,000	Grass
Georgia	Sanford	1929	86,520	Grass
Kentucky	Commonwealth	1973	67,530	Grass
S. Carolina	Williams-Brice	1934	80,250	Grass
Tennessee	Neyland	1921	104,079	Grass
Vanderbilt	Vanderbilt	1981	41,600	Grass

WEST	Stadium	Built	Seats	Field
Alabama	Bryant-Denny	1929	83,818	Grass
	& Legion	1927	83,091	Grass
Arkansas	Donald W. Reynolds Razorback	1938	72,000	Grass
	& War Memorial*	1948	53,727	Grass
Auburn	Jordan-Hare	1939	86,063	Grass
LSU	Tiger	1924	91,600	Grass
Mississippi	Vaught-Hem'way	1915	60,580	Grass
Miss. St.	Davis-Wade	1915	52,884	Grass

Note: EAST–Vanderbilt Stadium was rebuilt in 1981.

Sun Belt

	Stadium	Built	Seats	Field
Arkansas St.	Indian	1974	33,410	Grass
Idaho	Kibbie Dome	1975	16,000	Turf
UL-Lafayette	Cajun Field	1971	31,000	Grass
UL-Monroe	Malone	1978	30,427	Turf
Middle Tennessee	Johnny Red Floyd	1933	30,788	Turf
New Mexico St.	Aggie Memorial	1978	30,343	Grass
North Texas	Fouts Field	1952	30,500	Turf

Western Athletic

	Stadium	Built	Seats	Field
Boise St.	Bronco	1970	30,000	Turf
Fresno St.	Bulldog	1980	41,031	Grass
Hawaii	Aloha*	1975	50,000	Turf
Louisiana Tech	Joe Aillet	1968	30,600	Grass
Nevada	Mackay	1967	31,545	Grass
Rice	Rice	1950	70,000	Grass
San Jose St.	Spartan	1933	30,456	Grass
SMU	Gerald J. Ford Stadium	2000	32,000	Grass
Tulsa	Skelly	1930	40,385	Turf
UTEP	Sun Bowl*	1963	51,500	Turf

I-A Independents

	Stadium	Built	Seats	Field
Connecticut	Memorial	1953	16,200	Grass
Navy	Navy-Marine Corps Memorial	1959	30,000	Grass
Notre Dame	Notre Dame	1930	80,795	Grass
S. Florida	Raymond James*	1988	41,444	Grass
Troy State	Memorial	1950	17,500	Grass
Utah St.	Romney	1968	30,257	Grass

Business

*It went down to the wire, but **Donald Fehr** and **Bud Selig** averted baseball's ninth work stoppage.*

AP/Wide World Photos

Brand Names for Less

In 2002, the names on the front of some stadiums took more hits than the teams playing in them.

Michael Morrison is co-editor of the ESPN/Information Please Sports Almanac.

Well it seemed like a good idea at the time. In 1999, the Houston Astros needed a sponsor for their brand new baseball venue, and when energy giant Enron came calling with an offer to pay $100 million over the next 30 years for the rights to slap its name on the stadium, how could the Astros refuse?

This would be the most lucrative naming-rights deal in baseball history. And it's not like Enron was in the tobacco industry or anything controversial like that. This was an energy company! And as one of the world's largest, it had cash coming out of the wazoo. Right?

In 2001–02, Enron became the symbol for corporate fraud in America. The collapse cost thousands of jobs and millions of dollars in retirement savings. It was the biggest company ever to file for Chapter 11 bankruptcy protection (until WorldCom took over the top spot seven months later).

As the Astros found out, the bigger they are, the harder they fall. In the end, the team had to fork over $2.1 million to terminate the contract (with 27 years left on the deal) and have the disgraced name removed from its stadium. After a brief period as Astros Field, the team signed another 30-year, $100 million deal in June, this time with orange juice makers Minute Maid.

Enron wasn't the only culprit, just the most famous. Thanks in part to the post-Sept. 11 economic fall-off and the bubble bursting on Internet stocks, six more sports venues recently had to find new sponsorship or rework their existing deals because their sponsoring companies fell on hard financial times.

Adelphia Coliseum (Tennessee Titans)—In 1999, Adelphia Business Solutions and the Titans agreed to a 15-year, $30 million deal. When the company filed for Chapter 11 protection in March 2002 and actually missed a

AP/Wide World Photos

Workers remove the red neon Adelphia sign from the Titans' home stadium in Nashville on Aug. 7. The company is one of several stadium sponsors to declare bankruptcy in 2001-02.

payment to the team, the Titans began looking for ways out of the deal. In June, the stadium became known simply as the Coliseum.

PSINet Stadium (Baltimore Ravens)—PSINet signed a 20-year, $105.5 million naming rights deal in January 1999. The company entered bankruptcy court in June 2001 and the Ravens paid a reported $5.9 million for the rights to remove PSINet's name. As of September 2002, the team changed its home's name to Ravens Stadium.

CMGI Field (New England Patriots/Revolution)—When CMGI inked a 15-year, $114 million deal with Patriots owner Bob Kraft in August 2000, its stock price was around $45. In mid-2002, it was down to 40 cents. Prior to the stadium's opening for football in August, CMGI stepped out of the deal, allowing Gillette to move in.

Trans World Dome (St. Louis Rams)—Trans World Airlines signed a 20-year, $36.7 million deal for naming rights in 1996. On Jan. 10, 2001, TWA filed for Chapter 11. In February 2002, the stadium signed a new deal with Edward Jones Financial Companies.

AP/Wide World Photos

Charlotte fans changed the "Go Hornets Go" sign to "Stay Hornets Stay," but it was too late to keep the owners from moving the team to New Orleans following the 2001-02 season.

Pro Player Stadium (Miami Dolphins/Florida Marlins)—In August 1996, Pro Player, a division of Fruit of the Loom, paid $20 million over 10 years for rights to the stadium in South Florida. Fruit of the Loom went Chapter 11 in December 1999. No new deal has been made as of yet.

Savvis Center (St. Louis Blues)— Savvis' stock price plummeted from about $8 at the time of its 20-year, $72 million deal in August 2000 to just 36 cents in September 2002, a drop of close to 96 percent. With the company in default on the agreement, a new deal was struck in August 2001.

The troubles of the aforementioned companies have obviously changed the way team executives conduct their business when seeking out sponsors. It's no longer a matter of selling to the highest bidder. Teams are doing much more research and even agreeing to take less cash for more financial security. Sadly, some teams found out the hard way.

Sources: Securities and Exchange Commission and *The Sports Business Journal.*

The Ten Biggest Stories of the Year in Business

10 ▪ The era of athletes selling body parts as advertising space truly arrives as Internet gambling site golden-palace.com turns numerous boxers into human billboards. And the fad isn't limited to body parts either. PWBA bowler Kim Adler puts an ad on eBay offering eight square inches of space on her shorts and skirts to hawk products.

9 ▪ Emmy Award-winning football analyst John Madden takes his tour bus from Fox Sports to ABC to pair up with *Monday Night Football* announcer Al Michaels. It is the first time Madden won't be working with longtime partner Pat Summerall in 21 years. His deal is worth an estimated $20 million over four years.

8 ▪ The Charlotte Hornets, who led the NBA in attendance for eight of the first nine years of their existence (1990–97), are forced to move to New Orleans after five years of declining attendance figures. Amidst all the move talk, the team still makes it into the second round of the 2002 playoffs.

7 ▪ The NBA signs a brand new six-year, $4.6 billion TV contract with ABC, ESPN, TNT and a new national cable network owned by the league and AOL/Time Warner. The deal is a 25 percent increase over the NBC/Turner Sports deal that expired after the 2001-02 season.

6 ▪ Major League Baseball buys the Montreal Expos from Jeffrey Loria for $120 million (taking out a $75 million loan in the process), but attempts to contract the team are unsuccessful. Recent reports show the cash-strapped Expos are costing the owners of the other 29 MLB teams about a half million dollars each in revenue losses for the year.

5 ▪ Leagues Owning Teams, Part Two—The NHL takes control of the Buffalo Sabres in June after team owner and former Adelphia Communications boss John Rigas is arrested for allegedly stealing millions from the bankrupt cable company.

4 ▪ After 70 years of Yawkey family ownership, the Boston Red Sox are sold at auction to Florida Marlins owner John Henry's group (which also includes Hollywood media mogul Tom Werner) for a record-shattering $660 million. The deal paves the way for the sale of the Marlins and Expos and turns into a 19-month soap opera when the losing (but apparently higher) bidders cry foul.

3 ▪ The sports world feels the bite of corporate misconduct and the country's post-Sept. 11 economic slowdown. The Astros pay $2.1 just to rid itself of any association with disgraced Enron. And the financial fall of CMGI, PSINet and many more causes sports executives to scramble for new sponsors.

2 • The Salt Lake City Olympics, which was recently mired in an embarrassing bribery scandal and projected to accumulate a record amount of financial losses, turns the corner under new Salt Lake Organizing Committee President Mitt Romney and reports $100 million in profits.

1 • On Aug. 30, the proposed strike date, the baseball players union and owners make nice and sign a new four-year collective bargaining agreement. While it still doesn't include a salary cap, it does contain an increased revenue sharing plan and a higher tax burden for teams with huge payrolls.

INSIDE the numbers

The Strike Zone

Baseball players were mere hours from their first labor strike since 1994. While many of the debated issues were the same back then, it's obvious by the table below that the league is very different.

	1994	2002
Highest Paid Player	B. Bonilla ($6.3M)	A. Rodriguez ($22.0M)
Avg. Salary	$1.168M	$2.385M
Avg. Ticket	$10.45	$18.30
Avg. Attend.	31,256	28,246

Note: 2002 avg attend. is through Sept. 16.

Nice Purse

The U.S. Open Tennis Championships dished out $16.1 million in prize money in 2002, making it the top purse for all sporting events.

	Prize Money
U.S. Open tennis	$16.1M
Wimbledon	13.0M
Daytona 500	12.3M
Indianapolis 500	10.0M

Source: USTA

Brands of Distinction

According to FutureBrand, a New York-based consulting firm and leader in brand research, The New York Yankees are the "most valuable brand" among all major U.S. pro teams based on performance, revenue and fan base.

(Figures are in millions.)

	League	Brand Value
New York Yankees	MLB	$334
Dallas Cowboys	NFL	300
Los Angeles Lakers	NBA	272
New York Knicks	NBA	236
Washington Redskins	NFL	191
New York Giants	NFL	167
Chicago Bulls	NBA	156
New York Rangers	NHL	155
Green Bay Packers	NFL	153
Detroit Red Wings	NHL	152
Boston Celtics	NBA	136
New York Mets	MLB	135
San Francisco 49ers	NFL	113
Detroit Pistons	NBA	112

Source: FutureBrand survey

2001-02 Top Rated TV Sports Events

Final 2001-02 network television ratings for nationally telecast sports events, according to Nielsen Media Research. Covers period from Sept. 1, 2001 through Aug. 31, 2002. Events are listed with ratings points and audience share; each ratings point represents 1,055,000 households and shares indicate percentage of TV sets in use.

Multiple entries: SPORTS—NFL Football (45); Winter Olympics (16); Major League Baseball (7); NBA Basketball (3); NCAA Football bowl games and NCAA Basketball (2). NETWORKS—FOX (25); NBC (20); ABC (16); CBS (15).

		Date	Net	Rtg/Sh
1	**Super Bowl XXXVI** (Patriots vs Rams)	2/3/02	FOX	40.4/61
2	**Winter Olympics** (Women's figure skating long program, men's GS)	2/21/02	NBC	26.8/41
3	**MLB World Series—Game 7** (Yankees at D'backs)	11/4/01	FOX	23.5/34
4	**NFC Championship Game** (Eagles at Rams)	1/27/02	FOX	22.7/40
5	**Winter Olympics** (Women's figure skating short program, women's b'sled final)	2/19/02	NBC	22.3/34
6	**AFC Championship Game** (Patriots at Steelers)	1/27/02	CBS	21.2/46
7	**Winter Olympics** (Pairs figure skating long program, men's singles luge final; men's halfpipe)	2/11/02	NBC	19.6/30
8	**NFC Playoff Game** (Packers at Rams)	1/20/02	FOX	19.5/36
	Winter Olympics (Women's slalom, men's/women's skeleton final; men's 1500 short track)	2/20/02	NBC	19.5/31
10	**Winter Olympics** (Men's figure skating short program, ski jumping)	2/12/02	NBC	18.5/29
11	**AFC Playoff Game** (Ravens at Steelers)	1/20/02	CBS	17.9/40
12	**Winter Olympics** (Figure skating champions gala, women's GS)	2/22/02	NBC	17.7/31
13	**Winter Olympics** (Men's downhill, ski jumping, women's halfpipe)	2/10/02	NBC	17.6/27
	Winter Olympics (Men's figure skating long program, men's snowboard par. GS)	2/14/02	NBC	17.6/29
15	**Winter Olympics** (Men's combined, women's luge & 1500 short track)	2/13/02	NBC	17.5/28
16	**AFC Playoff Game** (Raiders at Patriots)	1/19/02	CBS	17.4/29
17	**NFC Playoff Game** (Eagles at Bears)	1/19/02	FOX	17.1/32
	Winter Olympics (Pairs figure skating short program, women's moguls final)	2/9/02	NBC	17.1/30
	Winter Olympics (Ice dancing – original, women's super G)	2/17/02	NBC	17.1/26
	Winter Olympics (Ice dancing – free dance, team ski jumping)	2/18/02	NBC	17.1/26
21	**NFC Playoff Game** (49ers at Packers)	1/13/02	FOX	16.8/38
	AFC Playoff Game (Ravens at Dolphins)	1/13/02	CBS	16.8/32
23	**MLB World Series—Game 4** (D'backs at Yankees)	10/31/01	FOX	15.8/27
	Winter Olympics (Ice dancing, men's/women's snowboard parallel GS)	2/15/02	NBC	15.8/27
25	**Winter Olympics** (Men's/women's short track, men's slalom)	2/23/02	NBC	15.7/27

AP/Wide World Photos

*Over 28 million households watched **Sarah Hughes'** gold medal performance in the women's long program, making it the second-most watched sports event of the year.*

		Date	Net	Rtg/Sh
26	**MLB World Series—Game 3** (D'backs at Yankees)	10/30/01	FOX	15.4/24
27	**MLB World Series—Game 2** (Yankees at D'backs)	10/28/01	FOX	15.0/23
	NCAA Men's Basketball Championship Game (Maryland vs Indiana)	4/1/02	CBS	15.0/24
29	**MLB World Series—Game 5** (D'backs at Yankees)	11/1/01	FOX	14.4/24
	NFL Regular Season Late Game (Various teams)	1/6/02	CBS	14.4/26
	NBA Western Conf. Finals—Game 7 (Lakers at Kings)	6/2/02	NBC	14.4/24
32	**Winter Olympics** (Men's/women's short track finals, men's super G)	2/16/02	NBC	14.0/25
33	**AFC Playoff Game** (Jets at Raiders)	1/12/02	ABC	13.9/24
34	**MLB World Series—Game 6** (Yankees at D'backs)	11/3/01	FOX	13.8/24
	NFL Regular Season Late Game (Various teams)	12/2/01	FOX	13.8/27
	Rose Bowl (Miami-FL vs Nebraska)	1/3/02	ABC	13.8/22
37	**NFL Regular Season Late Game** (Various teams)	12/9/01	CBS	13.4/26
38	**NFL Monday Night Football** (Giants at Broncos)	9/10/01	ABC	13.2/23
	NFL Regular Season Early Game (Various teams)	12/9/01	FOX	13.2/30

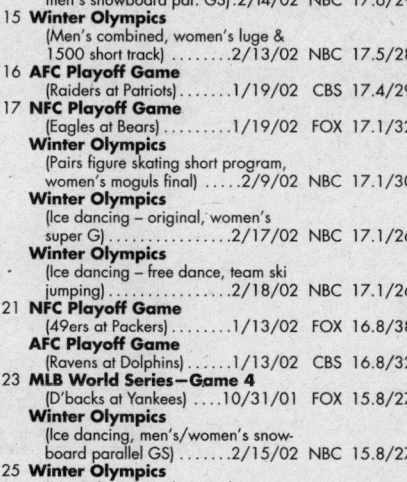

2001-02 Top Rated TV Sports Events (Cont.)

	Date	Net	Rtg/Sh
40 **NFL Regular Season Late Game**			
(Various teams) 12/16/01		FOX	13.1/26
NFC Playoff Game			
(Buccaneers at Eagles) 1/12/02		ABC	13.1/28
42 **NFL Monday Night Football**			
(Rams at Saints) 12/17/01		ABC	12.9/23
43 **NFL Regular Season Late Game**			
(Various teams) 11/18/01		FOX	12.7/24
44 **NFL Regular Season Late Game**			
(Various teams) 9/9/01		FOX	12.6/26
NFL Regular Season Late Game			
(Various teams) 12/30/01		CBS	12.6/25
46 **NFL Regular Season Early Game**			
(Various teams) 10/28/01		FOX	12.4/28
47 **MLB League Championship Series**			
(Gm 4: Mariners at Yankees			
Gm 5: D'backs at Braves) .10/21/01		FOX	12.3/19
NFL Monday Night Football			
(Buccaneers at Rams) 11/26/01		ABC	12.3/20
NFL Regular Season Early Game			
(Various teams) 12/30/01		FOX	12.3/28
NFL Monday Night Football			
(Vikings at Ravens).........1/7/02		ABC	12.3/20
51 **NFL Regular Season Late Game**			
(Various teams)...........11/4/01		CBS	12.1/24
52 **NFL Regular Season Late Game**			
(Various teams) 11/25/01		CBS	12.0/22
53 **NFL Monday Night Football**			
(Denver at Oakland) 11/5/01		ABC	11.9/20
NFL Regular Season Late Game			
(Various teams) 11/11/01		FOX	11.9/24
55 **NFL Monday Night Football**			
(Giants at Vikings).......11/19/01		ABC	11.8/20
56 **NFL Monday Night Football**			
(Redskins at Packers)......9/24/01		ABC	11.7/19
NFL Monday Night Football			
(Titans at Steelers)......10/29/01		ABC	11.7/20
NFL Thanksgiving Day Early Game			
(Packers at Lions)........11/22/01		FOX	11.7/31

	Date	Net	Rtg/Sh
59 **Fiesta Bowl**			
(Oregon vs Colorado)......1/1/02		ABC	11.3/20
NCAA Men's Basketball Semifinal Game			
(Maryland vs Kansas) 3/30/02		CBS	11.3/21
61 **NFL Monday Night Football**			
(49ers at Jets)...........10/1/01		ABC	11.2/18
62 **NFL Monday Night Football**			
(Rams at Lions)...........10/8/01		ABC	11.1/18
NFL Regular Season Late Game			
(Various teams) 10/28/01		CBS	11.1/21
NFL Regular Season Early Game			
(Various teams)...........1/6/02		FOX	11.1/23
NBA Western Conf. Finals—Game 6			
(Kings at Lakers)........5/31/02		NBC	11.1/22
66 **NFL Regular Season Early Game**			
(Various teams) 9/30/01		CBS	11.0/22
NFL Monday Night Football			
(Packers at Jaguars) 12/3/01		ABC	11.0/19
68 **NFL Regular Season Late Game**			
(Various teams)..........9/23/01		FOX	10.9/22
NFL Thanksgiving Day Late Game			
(Broncos at Cowboys) ...11/22/01		CBS	10.9/30
NFL Regular Season Late Game			
(Various teams) 12/23/01		CBS	10.9/25
Daytona 500			
(Ward Burton wins) 2/17/02		NBC	10.9/26
72 **NBA Finals—Game 4**			
(Lakers at Nets) 6/12/02		NBC	10.8/19
73 **Winter Olympics**			
(Men's hockey gold medal game:			
Canada vs USA) 2/24/02		NBC	10.7/24
74 **NFL Regular Season Late Game**			
(Various teams) 10/21/01		FOX	10.6/21
NFL Regular Season Early Game			
(Various teams)...........11/4/01		FOX	10.6/25
NFL Monday Night Football			
(Ravens at Titans) 11/12/01		ABC	10.6/19

AP/Wide World Photos

With a 60.2 Nielsen rating, the final episode of M*A*S*H in February 1983 still stands as the most-watched television program of all time.

All-Time Top-Rated TV Programs

NFL Football dominates television's All-Time Top-Rated 50 Programs with 22 Super Bowls and the 1981 NFC Championship Game making the list. Rankings based on surveys taken from January 1961 through August 31, 2002; include only sponsored programs seen on individual networks; and programs under 30 minutes scheduled duration are excluded. Programs are listed with ratings points, audience share and number of households watching, according to Nielsen Media Research.

Multiple entries: The Super Bowl (22); "Roots" (7); "The Beverly Hillbillies" and "The Thorn Birds" (3); "The Bob Hope Christmas Show," "The Ed Sullivan Show," "Gone With The Wind" and 1994 Winter Olympics (2).

	Program	Episode/Game	Net	Date	Rating	Share	Households
1	M*A*S*H (series)	Final episode	CBS	2/28/83	**60.2**	77	50,150,000
2	Dallas (series)	"Who Shot J.R.?"	CBS	11/21/80	**53.3**	76	41,470,000
3	Roots (mini-series)	Part 8	ABC	1/30/77	**51.1**	71	36,380,000
4	**Super Bowl XVI**	49ers 26, Bengals 21	CBS	1/24/82	**49.1**	73	40,020,000
5	**Super Bowl XVII**	Redskins 27, Dolphins 17	NBC	1/30/83	**48.6**	69	40,480,000
6	XVII Winter Olympics	Women's Figure Skating	CBS	2/23/94	**48.5**	64	45,690,000
7	**Super Bowl XX**	Bears 46, Patriots 10	NBC	1/26/86	**48.3**	70	41,490,000
8	Gone With the Wind (movie)	Part 1	NBC	11/7/76	**47.7**	65	33,960,000
9	Gone With the Wind (movie)	Part 2	NBC	11/8/76	**47.4**	64	33,750,000
10	**Super Bowl XII**	Cowboys 27, Broncos 10	CBS	1/15/78	**47.2**	67	34,410,000
11	**Super Bowl XIII**	Steelers 35, Cowboys 31	NBC	1/21/79	**47.1**	74	35,090,000
12	Bob Hope Special	Christmas Show	NBC	1/15/70	**46.6**	64	27,260,000
13	**Super Bowl XVIII**	Raiders 38, Redskins 9	CBS	1/22/84	**46.4**	71	38,800,000
	Super Bowl XIX	49ers 38, Dolphins 16	ABC	1/20/85	**46.4**	63	39,390,000
15	**Super Bowl XIV**	Steelers 31, Rams 19	NBC	1/20/80	**46.3**	67	35,330,000
16	**Super Bowl XXX**	Cowboys 27, Steelers 17	NBC	1/28/96	**46.0**	68	44,114,400
	ABC Theater (special)	"The Day After"	ABC	11/20/83	**46.0**	62	38,550,000
18	Roots (mini-series)	Part 6	ABC	1/28/77	**45.9**	66	32,680,000
	The Fugitive (series)	Final episode	ABC	8/29/67	**45.9**	72	25,700,000
20	**Super Bowl XXI**	Giants 39, Broncos 20	CBS	1/25/87	**45.8**	66	40,030,000
21	Roots (mini-series)	Part 5	ABC	1/27/77	**45.7**	71	32,540,000
22	**Super Bowl XXVIII**	Cowboys 30, Bills 13	NBC	1/30/94	**45.5**	66	42,860,000
	Cheers (series)	Final episode	NBC	5/20/93	**45.5**	64	42,360,500
24	The Ed Sullivan Show	Beatles' 1st appearance	CBS	2/9/64	**45.3**	60	23,240,000
25	**Super Bowl XXVII**	Cowboys 52, Bills 17	NBC	1/31/93	**45.1**	66	41,988,100
26	Bob Hope Special	Christmas Show	NBC	1/14/71	**45.0**	61	27,050,000
27	Roots (mini-series)	Part 3	ABC	1/25/77	**44.8**	68	31,900,000
28	**Super Bowl XXXII**	Broncos 31, Packers 24	NBC	1/25/98	**44.5**	67	43,630,000
29	**Super Bowl XI**	Raiders 32, Vikings 14	NBC	1/9/77	**44.4**	73	31,610,000
	Super Bowl XV	Raiders 27, Eagles 10	NBC	1/25/81	**44.4**	63	34,540,000
31	**Super Bowl VI**	Cowboys 24, Dolphins 3	CBS	1/16/72	**44.2**	74	27,450,000
32	XVII Winter Olympics	Women's Figure Skating	CBS	2/25/94	**44.1**	64	41,540,000
	Roots (mini-series)	Part 2	ABC	1/24/77	**44.1**	62	31,400,000
34	The Beverly Hillbillies (series)	Regular episode	CBS	1/8/64	**44.0**	65	22,570,000
35	Roots (mini-series)	Part 4	ABC	1/26/77	**43.8**	66	31,190,000
	The Ed Sullivan Show	Beatles' 2nd appearance	CBS	2/16/64	**43.8**	60	22,445,000
37	**Super Bowl XXIII**	49ers 20, Bengals 16	NBC	1/22/89	**43.5**	68	39,320,000
38	The Academy Awards	John Wayne wins Oscar	ABC	4/7/70	**43.4**	78	25,390,000
39	**Super Bowl XXXI**	Packers 35, Patriots 21	FOX	1/26/97	**43.3**	65	42,000,000
	Super Bowl XXXIV	Rams 23, Titans 16	ABC	1/30/00	**43.3**	63	43,618,000
41	The Thorn Birds (mini-series)	Part 3	ABC	3/29/83	**43.2**	62	35,990,000
42	The Thorn Birds (mini-series)	Part 4	ABC	3/30/83	**43.1**	62	35,900,000
43	**NFC Championship Game**	49ers 28, Cowboys 27	CBS	1/10/82	**42.9**	62	34,940,000
44	The Beverly Hillbillies (series)	Regular episode	CBS	1/15/64	**42.8**	62	21,960,000
45	**Super Bowl VII**	Dolphins 14, Redskins 7	NBC	1/14/73	**42.7**	72	27,670,000
46	The Thorn Birds (mini-series)	Part 2	ABC	3/28/83	**42.5**	59	35,400,000
47	**Super Bowl IX**	Steelers 16, Vikings 6	NBC	1/12/75	**42.4**	72	29,040,000
	The Beverly Hillbillies (series)	Regular episode	CBS	2/26/64	**42.4**	60	21,750,000
49	**Super Bowl X**	Steelers 21, Cowboys 17	CBS	1/18/76	**42.3**	78	29,440,000
	ABC Sunday Night Movie	"Airport"	ABC	11/11/73	**42.3**	63	28,000,000
	ABC Sunday Night Movie	"Love Story"	ABC	10/1/72	**42.3**	62	27,410,000
	Cinderella	Musical special	CBS	2/22/65	**42.3**	59	22,250,000
	Roots (mini-series)	Part 7	ABC	1/29/77	**42.3**	65	30,120,000

All-Time Top-Rated Cable TV Sports Events

All-time cable television for sports events, according to ESPN, Turner Sports research and *The Sports Business Daily*. Covers period from Sept. 1, 1980 through Aug. 31, 2002.

NFL Telecasts

		Date	Net	Rtg
1	Chicago at Minnesota	12/6/87	ESPN	17.6
2	Detroit at Miami	12/25/94	ESPN	15.1
3	Chicago at Minnesota	12/3/89	ESPN	14.7
4	Cleveland at San Fran	11/29/87	ESPN	14.2
5	Pittsburgh at Houston	12/30/90	ESPN	13.8

Non-NFL Telecasts

		Date	Net	Rtg
1	MLB: Chicago (NL)-St. Louis	9/7/98	ESPN	9.5
2	NBA: Detroit-Boston	6/1/88	TBS	8.8
3	NBA: Chicago-Detroit	5/31/89	TBS	8.2
4	NBA: Detroit-Boston	5/26/88	TBS	8.1
	MLB: Giants-Chicago (NL)	9/28/98	ESPN	8.1

Teams Bought in 2002

Five major league clubs acquired new majority owners from Sept. 1, 2001 through Sept. 20, 2002.

Major League Baseball

Boston Red Sox: The long-anticipated sale of the Red Sox to Florida Marlins owner John Henry and media mogul Tom Werner finally became official on Feb. 27, 2002. At $660 million, the deal shattered the previous mark for a baseball franchise ($323 million for the Cleveland Indians in 2000). It also ended the seven-decade long ownership reign of the Yawkey Trust. Also included in the deal was an 80 percent stake of New England Sports Network (NESN) and $40 million in assumed debt. The sale was originally agreed upon on Dec. 20, 2001 but controversy followed when it was discovered that higher bids were offered by groups led by Cablevision chairman Charles Dolan and lawyer Miles Prentice.

Florida Marlins: On Feb. 12, 2002 baseball owners approved the sale of the Marlins from owner John Henry to New York art dealer and Montreal Expos owner Jeffrey Loria for $158.5 million. The deal was approved by the owners before Henry and Loria even had a signed contract between them. It paved the way for Henry to officially take ownership of the Red Sox.

Montreal Expos: On Feb. 12, 2002 baseball owners approved the sale of the Expos from Jeffrey Loria to Baseball Expos LP, a partnership owned by the 29 other MLB teams. So in effect, the club was taken over by the commissioner's office. The cost of the deal was $120 million, $38.5 million less than Loria paid for the Marlins (the commissioner's office loaned him the difference).

NFL Football

Atlanta Falcons: On Feb. 2, 2002, NFL owners unanimously approved the sale of the Atlanta Falcons from the Smith family to Home Depot co-founder and retired co-chairman Arthur Blank. The sale was worth $545 million and gave Blank an 88 percent stake in the Falcons. He is just the second majority owner of the Falcons. The team was founded by Rankin Smith Sr. in 1965 and then placed in the trust of son Taylor and his four siblings after his death in 1997.

NHL Hockey

San Jose Sharks: On Feb. 26, 2002 original Sharks owner George Gund III announced the sale of the team to local investment group San Jose Sports and Entertainment Enterprises (SJSEE). Financial terms of the transaction were undisclosed but estimated to be between $120 million and $140 million. Also included in the deal were Gund's ownership of Silcon Valley Sports & Entertainment and the management company of the Compaq Center at San Jose. Lead investors of SJSEE include venture capitalist Kevin Compton and Brocade Systems CEO Greg Reyes. The ownership transfer was completed on May 3, 2002.

2001-02 Team Payrolls

Team payrolls for active players during the 2001-02 season for the NBA and NHL, the 2001 season for the NFL and the start of the 2002 season for Major League Baseball. Figures are in millions of dollars.

Note: The NFL and NBA use a salary cap to set payrolls. In 2001 the NFL's cap was $67.4 million. In 2001-02, the NBA's cap was $42.5. Teams can circumvent the cap, however, with bonuses and other exceptions. The NHL and MLB use no cap.

Sources: *Street & Smith's SportsBusiness Journal*, NHLPA, NFLPA, AP and *USA Today*.

NBA		MLB		NHL		NFL	
1 New York	$85.5	1 NY Yankees	$125.9	1 NY Rangers	$67.4	1 Denver	$94.0
2 Portland	83.8	2 Boston	108.4	2 Detroit	65.9	2 Green Bay	84.4
3 New Jersey	75.2	3 Texas	105.3	3 Colorado	59.6	3 Cleveland	83.3
4 Philadelphia	58.1	4 Arizona	102.8	4 St. Louis	57.5	4 Miami	78.3
5 Dallas	57.4	5 Los Angeles	94.9	5 Philadelphia	57.0	5 Pittsburgh	75.2
6 Milwaukee	56.2	6 NY Mets	94.6	6 Dallas	50.5	6 San Diego	74.6
7 Phoenix	56.2	7 Atlanta	93.5	7 Toronto	48.9	7 Tennessee	74.3
8 Sacramento	54.9	8 Seattle	80.3	8 San Jose	48.3	8 Chicago	72.2
9 Washington	54.8	9 Cleveland	78.9	9 Chicago	42.0	9 Oakland	71.2
10 Minnesota	54.6	10 San Francisco	78.3	10 Boston	41.3	10 Atlanta	71.0
11 Denver	54.4	11 Toronto	76.9	11 Los Angeles	41.0	11 Carolina	69.6
12 LA Lakers	53.5	12 Chicago-NL	75.7	12 Washington	40.6	12 Tampa Bay	69.4
13 Indiana	53.2	13 St. Louis	74.1	13 New Jersey	40.0	13 NY Jets	68.9
14 Utah	52.6	14 Houston	63.4	14 Montreal	39.1	14 Cincinnati	68.4
15 Miami	52.6	15 Anaheim	61.7	15 Anaheim	35.8	15 St. Louis	67.6
16 Toronto	52.3	16 Baltimore	60.5	16 NY Islanders	35.2	16 NY Giants	66.8
17 Atlanta	51.2	17 Philadelphia	58.0	17 Phoenix	32.9	17 Baltimore	64.5
18 Memphis	50.9	18 Chicago-AL	57.1	18 Pittsburgh	32.5	18 Arizona	64.2
19 Charlotte	50.0	19 Colorado	56.9	19 Buffalo	32.4	19 Seattle	62.9
20 Houston	49.2	20 Detroit	55.0	20 Carolina	32.4	20 Jacksonville	62.6
21 Golden St.	47.7	21 Milwaukee	50.3	21 Vancouver	30.6	21 New Orleans	62.0
22 Boston	47.5	22 Kansas City	47.3	22 Florida	30.6	22 Detroit	61.8
23 Orlando	45.8	23 Cincinnati	45.1	23 Ottawa	28.5	23 Kansas City	61.2
24 San Antonio	45.7	24 Pittsburgh	42.3	24 Calgary	26.3	24 Philadelphia	60.1
25 Cleveland	45.6	25 Florida	42.0	25 Edmonton	25.9	25 Minnesota	59.0
26 Seattle	45.4	26 San Diego	41.4	26 Tampa Bay	25.8	26 San Francisco	58.9
27 Chicago	42.6	27 Minnesota	40.2	27 Columbus	20.8	27 Buffalo	58.8
28 Detroit	42.4	28 Oakland	40.0	28 Atlanta	20.4	28 Indianapolis	58.7
29 LA Clippers	33.8	29 Montreal	38.7	29 Nashville	19.5	29 New England	55.5
		30 Tampa Bay	34.4	30 Minnesota	18.0	30 Washington	53.5
						31 Dallas	44.2

Top 10 Salaries In Each Sport

The top 10 highest paid athletes over the 2001-02 season for the NBA and NHL, 2002 for Major League Baseball and the 2001 season for the NFL. Figures are in millions of dollars.

Sources: *Street & Smith's SportsBusiness Journal*, NHLPA, AP and *USA Today*.

NFL

		Position	Team	Salary
1	Brian Griese	Quarterback	Denver	$15.154
2	Corey Dillon	Running Back	Cincinnati	15.000
3	Tim Couch	Quarterback	Cleveland	12.903
4	Leonard Davis	Off. Lineman	Arizona	11.615
5	Gerard Warren	Def. Lineman	Cleveland	11.582
6	Ray Buchanan	Cornerback	Atlanta	11.433
7	Marcellus Wiley	Def. Lineman	San Diego	11.001
8	John Mobley	Linebacker	Denver	9.955
9	Mark Brunell	Quarterback	Jacksonville	8.855
10	Bryan Robinson	Def. Lineman	Chicago	8.844
	League Avg			1.101

MLB

		Position	Team	Salary
1	Alex Rodriguez	Shortstop	Texas	$22.000
2	Carlos Delgado	First Base	Toronto	19.400
3	Kevin Brown	Pitcher	Los Angeles	15.714
4	Manny Ramirez	Left Field	Boston	15.463
5	Sammy Sosa	Right Field	Chicago-NL	15.000
	Barry Bonds	Right Field	San Fran.	15.000
7	Derek Jeter	Shortstop	NY Yankees	14.600
8	Pedro Martinez	Pitcher	Boston	14.000
9	Shawn Green	Right Field	Los Angeles	13.417
10	Randy Johnson	Pitcher	Arizona	13.350
	League Avg			2.385

NBA

		Position	Team	Salary
1	Kevin Garnett	Forward	Minnesota	$22.400
2	Shaquille O'Neal	Center	LA Lakers	21.429
3	Alonzo Mourning	Center	Miami	18.755
4	Juwan Howard	Forward	Dal/Den	18.750
5	Scottie Pippen	Forward	Portland	18.084
6	Karl Malone	Forward	Utah	17.500
7	Rasheed Wallace	Forward	Portland	14.400
8	Dikembe Mutombo	Center	Philadelphia	14.316
9	Gary Payton	Guard	Seattle	12.926
10	Allan Houston	Guard	New York	12.750
	Chris Webber	Forward	Sacramento	12.750
	League Avg			4.530

NHL

		Position	Team	Salary
1	Jaromir Jagr	Right Wing	Washington	$11.000
2	Pavel Bure	Right Wing	Fla-NYR	10.000
	Paul Kariya	Left Wing	Anaheim	10.000
4	Joe Sakic	Center	Colorado	9.833
5	Chris Pronger	Defense	St. Louis	9.500
	Teemu Selanne	Right Wing	San Jose	9.500
7	Rob Blake	Defense	Colorado	9.285
8	John LeClair	Left Wing	Philadelphia	9.000
	Doug Weight	Center	St. Louis	9.000
10	Brian Leetch	Defense	NY Rangers	8.680
	League Avg			1.430

Note: Colorado's Peter Forsberg was scheduled to make $11 million in 2001-02 but took the entire regular season off due to injuries.

Highest and Lowest Ticket Prices

The most expensive and least expensive average ticket prices for NFL and MLB franchises over the 2002 season, and NBA and NHL franchises for the 2001-02 season. Note that average ticket prices for each league are as follows: **NFL** $50.02, **MLB** $18.30, **NBA** $50.10 and **NHL** $49.86.

Source: *Team Marketing Report*

NFL

	Highest	Venue	Avg. Price
1	New England	Gillette Stadium	$76.19
2	Washington	FedEx Field	68.06
3	Jacksonville	ALLTEL Stadium	62.85
4	Oakland	Network Assoc. Col.	58.89
5	San Francisco	Candlestick Park	58.00

	Lowest	Venue	Avg. Price
1	Atlanta	Georgia Dome	$29.78
2	Arizona	Sun Devil Stadium	33.68
3	Buffalo	Ralph Wilson Stadium	37.61
4	Tennessee	The Coliseum	40.66
5	Carolina	Ericsson Stadium	42.27

MLB

	Highest	Venue	Avg. Price
1	Boston	Fenway Park	$39.68
2	Seattle	SAFECO Field	24.60
3	NY Yankees	Yankee Stadium	24.26
4	Chicago Cubs	Wrigley Field	24.05
5	NY Mets	Shea Stadium	22.53

	Lowest	Venue	Avg. Price
1	Montreal	Olympic Stadium	$9.00
2	Minnesota	HHH Metrodome	11.78
3	Anaheim	Edison Field	11.79
4	Kansas City	Kauffman Stadium	12.30
5	Florida	Pro Player Stadium	12.72

NBA

	Highest	Venue	Avg. Price
1	NY Knicks	Madison Sq. Garden	$89.80
2	LA Lakers	Staples Center	89.51
3	Houston	Compaq Center	65.45
4	Sacramento	ARCO Arena	61.99
5	Miami	AmericanAirlines Arena	59.98

		Venue	Avg. Price
1	Detroit	The Palace	$31.90
2	Charlotte	Charlotte Coliseum	34.80
3	Milwaukee	Bradley Center	36.32
4	Denver	Pepsi Center	38.11
5	Minnesota	Target Center	39.31

NHL

	Highest	Venue	Avg. Price
1	Dallas	American Airlines Center	$75.91
2	Toronto	Air Canada Centre	70.29
3	NY Rangers	Madison Sq. Garden	65.82
4	Colorado	Pepsi Center	65.35
5	Philadelphia	First Union Center	62.31

	Lowest	Venue	Avg. Price
1	Calgary	Pengrowth Saddledome	$32.79
2	Edmonton	Skyreach Centre	34.50
3	NY Islanders	Nassau Coliseum	34.68
4	Carolina	RBC Center	38.70
5	Montreal	Bell Centre	39.06

The Rights Stuff

Major sports and their television deals as of Sept. 1, 2002.

League	Network	Yrs (Ends)	Amount	League	Network	Yrs (Ends)	Amount
NFL	ESPN	8 (2006)	$4.8 billion	NCAA Women's Hoops			
	FOX	8 (2006)	4.4 billion	Tournament	ESPN	11 (2013)	$200 million@
	ABC	8 (2006)	4.4 billion	NCAA Football BCS	ABC	8 (2006)	$930 million
	CBS	8 (2006)	4.0 billion				
				NASCAR	NBC/Turner	6 (2006)	$1.2 billion
NBA	ABC/ESPN	6 (2008)	$2.4 billion		FOX	8 (2008)	1.6 billion
	TNT	6 (2008)	2.2 billion				
				Olympics	NBC	13 (2008)	$3.5 billion#
MLB	FOX	6 (2006)	$2.5 billion				
	ESPN	6 (2005)	undisclosed*	PGA Tour	ABC, CBS,		
				NBC, ESPN, USA			
NHL	ESPN/ABC	5 (2004)	$600 million	and The Golf Channel		4 (2006)	$850 million%
NCAA Men's Hoops				WNBA	ABC/ESPN	6 (2008)	undisclosed
Tournament	CBS	11 (2013)	$6.0 billion†				

* Terms of the deal are undisclosed but estimated to be valued at more than $850 million.
† This deal begins with the 2003 tournament.
@ This deal begins with the 2003 tournament. Also included are all rights to the College World Series and various other NCAA championships.
# NBC has a deal with the Olympics worth approximately $3.5 billion, which gave them exclusive rights to the 1996 Summer Games in Atlanta, the 2000 Summer Games in Sydney, the 2002 Winter Games in Salt Lake City, the 2004 Summer Games in Athens, the 2006 Winter Games in Turin (ITA), and the 2008 Summer Games (Beijing). The only Games it didn't have rights to since 1996 were the 1998 Winter Games in Nagano, which were owned by CBS.
% This deal begins with the 2003 season. USA will average 33 events per year, ABC 18, CBS 17, ESPN 14 and NBC 5. The Golf Channel will broadcast no PGA events but will have exclusive rights to the Buy.com Tour.

AWARDS

The Peabody Award

Presented annually since 1940 for outstanding achievement in radio and television broadcasting. Named after Georgia banker and philanthropist George Foster Peabody, the awards are administered by the Henry W. Grady College of Journalism and Mass Communication at the University of Georgia.

Television

Year
1960 **CBS** for coverage of 1960 Winter and Summer Olympic Games
1966 ABC's **"Wide World of Sports"** (for Outstanding Achievement in Promotion of International Understanding).
1968 **ABC Sports** coverage of both the 1968 Winter and Summer Olympic Games.
1972 **ABC Sports** coverage of the 1972 Summer Olympics in Munich.
1973 **Joe Garagiola** of NBC Sports (for "The Baseball World of Joe Garagiola").
1976 **ABC Sports** coverage of both the 1976 Winter and Summer Olympic Games.
1984 **Roone Arledge**, president of ABC News & Sports (for significant contributions to news and sports programming).
1986 **WFAA-TV**, Dallas for its investigation of the Southern Methodist University football program.
1988 **Jim McKay** of ABC Sports (for pioneering efforts and career accomplishments in the world of TV sports).
1991 **CBS Sports** coverage of the 1991 Masters golf tournament
     & **HBO Sports** and **Black Canyon Productions** for the baseball special "When It Was A Game."
1995 **Kartemquin Educational Films** and **KTCA-TV** in St. Paul, MN, presented on PBS for "Hoop Dreams"
     & **Turner Original Productions** for the baseball special "Hank Aaron: Chasing the Dream."
1996 **HBO Sports** for its documentary "The Journey of the African-American Athlete"
     & **Bud Greenspan**, a personal award for excellence in chronicling the Olympic Games.
1997 **HBO Pictures** and **The Thomas Carter Company** for the original movie "Don King: Only in America."
1998 **KTVX-TV**, Salt Lake City for its investigation into the policies and practices of the IOC during the Olympic bribery scandal & **HBO Sports** for its ongoing series of sports documentaries.
1999 **WCPO-TV**, Cincinnati for its investigation of fraud and misrepresentation in the construction of new sports stadiums, **HBO Sports** for its documentary "Dare to Compete: The Struggle of Women in Sports," and its documentary "Fists of Freedom: The Story of the '68 Summer Games" & **ESPN** for its "SportsCentury" series.
2000 **HBO Sports** for its documentary "Ali-Frazier 1: One Nation...Divisible."
2001 **The Ciesla Foundation** and **Cinemax** for the documentary "The Life and Times of Hank Greenberg."

Radio

Year
1974 **WSB** radio in Atlanta for "Henry Aaron: A Man with a Mission."
1991 **Red Barber** of National Public Radio (for his six decades as a broadcaster and his 10 years as a commentator on NPR's "Morning Edition").

National Emmy Awards
Sports Programming

Presented by the Academy of Television Arts and Sciences since 1948. Eligibility period covered the calendar year from 1948-57 and since 1988.

Multiple major award winners: ABC "Wide World of Sports" (20), NFL Films Football coverage (12); ABC Olympics coverage (9); ABC "Monday Night Football" (8); FOX MLB coverage (7); CBS NFL Football coverage, NBC Olympics coverage, ESPN "Outside the Lines" series and HBO "Real Sports with Bryant Gumbel" (6); CBS NCAA Basketball coverage and CBS "NFL Today" (5); ESPN "GameDay/Sunday NFL Countdown,"ESPN "SportsCenter" (4); ABC "The American Sportsman," ABC Indianapolis 500 coverage, ESPN "SportsCentury"series and FOX "NFL Sunday" (3); ABC Kentucky Derby coverage, ABC "Sportsbeat," Bud Greenspan Olympic specials, CBS Olympics coverage, CBS Golf coverage, ESPN "Speedworld," MTV Sports series and NBC World Series coverage (2).

1949
Coverage—"Wrestling" (KTLA, Los Angeles)

1950
Program—"Rams Football" (KNBH-TV, Los Angeles)

1954
Program—"Gillette Cavalcade of Sports" (NBC)

1965-66
Programs—"Wide World of Sports" (ABC), "Shell's Wonderful World of Golf" (NBC) and "CBS Golf Classic" (CBS)

1966-67
Program—"Wide World of Sports" (ABC)

1967-68
Program—"Wide World of Sports" (ABC)

1968-69
Program—"1968 Summer Olympics" (ABC)

1969-70
Programs—"NFL Football" (CBS) and "Wide World of Sports" (ABC)

1970-71
Program—"Wide World of Sports" (ABC)

1971-72
Program—"Wide World of Sports" (ABC)

1972-73
News Special—"Coverage of Munich Olympic Tragedy" (ABC)
Sports Programs—"1972 Summer Olympics" (ABC) and "Wide World of Sports" (ABC)

1973-74
Program—"Wide World of Sports" (ABC)

1974-75
Non-Edited Program—"Jimmy Connors vs. Rod Laver Tennis Challenge" (CBS)
Edited Program—"Wide World of Sports" (ABC)

1975-76
Live Special—"1975 World Series: Cincinnati vs. Boston" (NBC)
Live Series—"NFL Monday Night Football" (ABC)
Edited Specials—"1976 Winter Olympics" (ABC) and "Triumph and Tragedy: The Olympic Experience" (ABC)
Edited Series—"Wide World of Sports" (ABC)

1976-77
Live Special—"1976 Summer Olympics" (ABC)
Live Series—"The NFL Today/NFL Football" (CBS)
Edited Special—"1976 Summer Olympics Preview" (ABC)
Edited Series—"The Olympiad" (PBS)

1977-78
Live Special—"Muhammad Ali vs. Leon Spinks Heavyweight Championship Fight" (CBS)
Live Series—"The NFL Today/NFL Football" (CBS)
Edited Special—"The Impossible Dream: Ballooning Across the Atlantic" (CBS)
Edited Series—"The Way It Was" (PBS)

1978-79
Live Special—"Super Bowl XIII: Pittsburgh vs Dallas" (NBC)
Live Series—"NFL Monday Night Football" (ABC)
Edited Special—"Spirit of '78: The Flight of Double Eagle II" (ABC)
Edited Series—"The American Sportsman" (ABC)

1979-80
Live Special—"1980 Winter Olympics" (ABC)
Live Series—"NCAA College Football" (ABC)
Edited Special—"Gossamer Albatross: Flight of Imagination" (CBS)
Edited Series—"NFL Game of the Week" (NFL Films)

1980-81
Live Special—"1981 Kentucky Derby" (ABC)
Live Series—"PGA Golf Tour" (CBS)
Edited Special—"Wide World of Sports 20th Anniversary Show" (ABC)
Edited Series—"The American Sportsman" (ABC)

1981-82
Live Special—"1982 NCAA Basketball Final: North Carolina vs Georgetown" (CBS)
Live Series—"NFL Football" (CBS)
Edited Special—"1982 Indianapolis 500" (ABC)
Edited Series—"Wide World of Sports" (ABC)

1982-83
Live Special—"1982 World Series: St. Louis vs Milwaukee" (NBC)
Live Series—"NFL Football" (CBS)
Edited Special—"Wimbledon '83" (NBC)
Edited Series—"Wide World of Sports" (ABC)
Journalism—"ABC Sportsbeat" (ABC)

1983-84
No awards given—

1984-85
Live Special—"1984 Summer Olympics" (ABC)
Live Series—No award given
Edited Special—"Road to the Super Bowl '85" (NFL Films)
Edited Series—"The American Sportsman" (ABC)
Journalism—"ABC Sportsbeat" (ABC), "CBS Sports Sunday" (CBS), Dick Schaap features (ABC) and 1984 Summer Olympic features (ABC)

1985-86
No awards given—

1986-87
Live Special—"1987 Daytona 500" (CBS)
Live Series—"NFL Football" (CBS)
Edited Special—"Wide World of Sports 25th Anniversary Special" (ABC)
Edited Series—"Wide World of Sports" (ABC)

1987-88
Live Special—"1987 Kentucky Derby" (ABC)
Live Series—"NFL Monday Night Football" (ABC)
Edited Special—"Paris-Roubaix Bike Race" (CBS)
Edited Series—"Wide World of Sports" (ABC)

National Emmy Awards (Cont.)

1988
Live Special—"1988 Summer Olympics" (NBC)
Live Series—"1988 NCAA Basketball" (CBS)
Edited Special—"Road to the Super Bowl '88" (NFL Films)
Edited Series—"Wide World of Sports" (ABC)
Studio Show—"NFL GameDay" (ESPN)
Journalism—1988 Summer Olympic reporting (NBC)

1989
Live Special—"1989 Indianapolis 500" (ABC)
Live Series—"NFL Monday Night Football" (ABC)
Edited Special—"Trans-Antarctica! The International Expedition" (ABC)
Edited Series—"This is the NFL" (NFL Films)
Studio Show—"NFL Today" (CBS)
Journalism—1989 World Series Game 3 earthquake coverage (ABC)

1990
Live Special—"1990 Indianapolis 500" (ABC)
Live Series—"1990 NCAA Basketball Tournament" (CBS)
Edited Special—"Road to Super Bowl XXIV" (NFL Films)
Edited Series—"Wide World of Sports" (ABC)
Studio Show—"SportsCenter" (ESPN)
Journalism—"Outside the Lines: The Autograph Game" (ESPN)

1991
Live Special—"1991 NBA Finals: Chicago vs LA Lakers" (NBC)
Live Series—"1991 NCAA Basketball Tournament" (CBS)
Edited Special—"Wide World of Sports 30th Anniversary Special" (ABC)
Edited Series—"This is the NFL" (NFL Films)
Studio Show—"NFL GameDay" (ESPN) and "NFL Live" (NBC)
Journalism—"Outside the Lines: Steroids–Whatever It Takes" (ESPN)

1992
Live Special—"1992 Breeders' Cup" (NBC)
Live Series—"1992 NCAA Basketball Tournament" (CBS)
Edited Special—"1992 Summer Olympics" (NBC)
Edited Series—"MTV Sports" (MTV)
Studio Show—"The NFL Today" (CBS)
Journalism—"Outside the Lines: Portraits in Black and White" (ESPN)

1993
Live Special—"1993 World Series" (CBS)
Live Series—"Monday Night Football" (ABC)
Edited Special—"Road to the Super Bowl" (NFL Films)
Edited Series—"This is the NFL" (NFL Films)
Studio Show—"The NFL Today" (CBS)
Journalism (TIE)—"Outside the Lines: Mitch Ivey Feature" (ESPN) and "SportsCenter: University of Houston Football" (ESPN).
Feature—"Arthur Ashe: His Life, His Legacy" (NBC).

1994
Live Special—"NHL Stanley Cup Finals" (ESPN)
Live Series—"Monday Night Football" (ABC)
Edited Special—"Lillehammer '94: 16 Days of Glory" (Disney/Cappy Productions)
Edited Series—"MTV Sports" (MTV)
Studio Show—"NFL GameDay" (ESPN)
Journalism—"1994 Winter Olympic Games: Mossad feature" (CBS)
Feature (TIE)—"Heroes of Telemark" on Winter Olympic Games (CBS); and "SportsCenter: Vanderbilt running back Brad Gaines" (ESPN).

1995
Live Special—"Cal Ripken 2131" (ESPN)
Live Series—"ESPN Speedworld" (ESPN)
Edited Special (quick turn-around)—"Outside the Lines: Playball–Opening Day in America" (ESPN)
Edited Special (long turn-around)—"Lillehammer, an Olympic Diary" (CBS)
Edited Series—"NFL Films Presents" (NFL Films)
Studio Show (TIE)—"NFL GameDay" (ESPN) and "FOX NFL Sunday" (FOX)
Journalism—"Real Sports with Bryant Gumbel: Broken Promises" (HBO)
Feature (TIE)—"SportsCenter: Jerry Quarry" (ESPN) and "Real Sports with Bryant Gumbel: Coach" (HBO).

1996
Live Special—"1996 World Series" (FOX)
Live Series—"ESPN Speedworld" (ESPN)
Edited Special—"Football America" (TNT/NFL Films)
Edited Series—"NFL Films Presents" (NFL Films)
Live Event Turnaround—"The Centennial Olympic Games" (NBC)
Studio Show—"SportsCenter" (ESPN)
Journalism—"Outside the Lines: AIDS in Sports" (ESPN)
Feature—"Real Sports with Bryant Gumbel: 1966 Texas Western NCAA Champs" (HBO).

1997
Live Special—"The NBA Finals" (NBC)
Live Series—"NFL Monday Night Football" (ABC)
Edited Special—"Ironman Triathlon World Championship" (NBC/World Triathlon Corporation)
Edited Series—"NFL Films Presents" (NFL Films)
Live Event Turnaround—"Outside The Lines: Inside The Kentucky Derby" (ESPN)
Studio Show—"FOX NFL Sunday" (FOX)
Journalism—"Real Sports with Bryant Gumbel: Pros and Cons" (HBO)
Feature—"NFL Films Presents: Eddie George" (NFL Films).

1998
Live Special—"McGwire's 62nd Home Run Game" (FOX)
Live Series—"NBC Golf Tour" (NBC)
Edited Special—"A Cinderella Season: The Lady Vols Fight Back" (HBO)
Edited Series—"Real Sports with Bryant Gumbel" (HBO)
Live Event Turnaround—"Wimbledon '98" (NBC)
Studio Show—"FOX NFL Sunday" (FOX)
Journalism (TIE)—"Real Sports with Bryant Gumbel: Winning At All Costs" (HBO) and "Real Sports with Bryant Gumbel: Diamond Bucks" (HBO)
Feature—"NFL Films Presents: Steve Mariucci" (ESPN2 and NFL Films).

1999
Live Special—"2000 MLB All-Star Game" (FOX)
Live Series—"MLB Regular Season" (FOX)
Edited Special—"Ironman Triathlon World Championship" (NBC)
Edited Series—"SportsCentury: 50 Greatest Athletes" (ESPN)
Live Event Turnaround—"The World Track & Field Championships" (NBC)
Studio Show—"MLB Pre-Game Show" (FOX)
Journalism—"Real Sports with Bryant Gumbel: Fake Golf Clubs" (HBO)
Feature—"NFL Films Presents: Lt. Kalsu" (ESPN2)

"Baseball" Wins Prime Time Emmy

Ken Burns's miniseries "Baseball" won the 1994 Emmy Award for Outstanding Informational Series. The nine-part documentary aired from Sept. 18-28, 1994 and ran more than 18 hours, drawing the largest audience in PBS history.

2000

Live Special—"2000 World Series" (FOX)
Live Series—"NFL Sunday Night Football" (ESPN)
Edited Special—"Hoops and Hoosiers: The Story of the Final Four 2000" (CBS)
Edited Series—"SportsCentury: The Top 50 & Beyond" (ESPN)
Live Event Turnaround—"The Games of the XXVII Olympiad" (NBC)
Studio Show—"FOX NFL Sunday" (FOX)
Journalism—"Real Sports with Bryant Gumbel: Dominican Free-For-All" (HBO)
Feature—"The Games of the XXVII Olympiad" (NBC)

2001

Live Special—"2001 World Series" (FOX)
Live Series—"NASCAR on FOX" (FOX)
Edited Special—"ABC's Wide World of Sports 40th Anniversary Special" (ABC)
Edited Series—"SportsCentury" (ESPN Classic)
Live Event Turnaround—"Tour de France" (CBS)
Studio Show—Weekly—"Sunday NFL Countdown" (ESPN)
Studio Show—Daily—"Inside the NBA" (TNT/TBS)
Journalism—"Real Sports with Bryant Gumbel: Amare Stoudemire" (HBO)
Feature—"NFL Films Presents: Gerry Faust—The Golden Dream" (ESPN2)
Documentary—"Do You Believe in Miracles? The Story of the 1980 U.S. Hockey Team" (HBO)

Sportscasters of the Year
National Emmy Awards

An Emmy Award for Sportscasters was first introduced in 1968 and given for Outstanding Host/Commentator for the 1967-68 TV season. Two awards, one for Outstanding Host or Play-by-Play and the other for Outstanding Analyst, were first presented in 1981 for the 1980-81 season. Three awards, for Outstanding Studio Host, Play-by-Play and Studio Analyst, have been given since the 1993 season, and one more, Sports Event Analyst, was added in 1997.

Multiple winners: John Madden (13); Bob Costas (11); Jim McKay (9); Dick Enberg and Al Michaels (4); Keith Jackson (3); Terry Bradshaw, James Brown, Joe Buck, Cris Collinsworth and Tim McCarver (2). Note that Jim McKay has won a total of 12 Emmy awards: eight for Host/Commentator, one for Host/Play-by-Play, two for Sports Writing, and one for News Commentary.

Season	Host/Commentator	Season	Host/Play-by-Play	Season	Analyst
1967-68	Jim McKay, ABC	1980-81	Dick Enberg, NBC	1980-81	Dick Button, ABC
1968-69	No award	1981-82	Jim McKay, ABC	1981-82	John Madden, CBS
1969-70	No award	1982-83	Dick Enberg, NBC	1982-83	John Madden, CBS
1970-71	Jim McKay, ABC	1983-84	No award	1983-84	No award
	& Don Meredith, ABC	1984-85	George Michael, NBC	1984-85	No award
1971-72	No award	1985-86	No award	1985-86	No award
1972-73	Jim McKay, ABC	1986-87	Al Michaels, ABC	1986-87	John Madden, CBS
1973-74	Jim McKay, ABC	1987-88	Bob Costas, NBC	1987-88	John Madden, CBS
1974-75	Jim McKay, ABC	1988	Bob Costas, NBC	1988	John Madden, CBS
1975-76	Jim McKay, ABC	1989	Al Michaels, ABC	1989	John Madden, CBS
1976-77	Frank Gifford, ABC	1990	Dick Enberg, NBC	1990	John Madden, CBS
1977-78	Jack Whitaker, CBS	1991	Bob Costas, NBC	1991	John Madden, CBS
1978-79	Jim McKay, ABC	1992	Bob Costas, NBC	1992	John Madden, CBS
1979-80	Jim McKay, ABC				

Studio Host

Year		Year		Year	
1993	Bob Costas, NBC	1997	Dan Patrick, ESPN	2001	Bob Costas, HBO &
1994	Bob Costas, NBC	1998	James Brown, FOX		Ernie Johnson, TNT/TBS
1995	Bob Costas, NBC	1999	James Brown, FOX		
1996	Bob Costas, NBC	2000	Bob Costas, NBC		

Play-by-Play

Year		Year		Year	
1993	Dick Enberg, NBC	1996	Keith Jackson, ABC	1999	Joe Buck, FOX
1994	Keith Jackson, ABC	1997	Bob Costas, NBC	2000	Al Michaels, ABC
1995	Al Michaels, ABC	1998	Keith Jackson, ABC	2001	Joe Buck, FOX

Studio Analyst

Year		Year		Year	
1993	Billy Packer, CBS	1996	Howie Long, FOX	1999	Terry Bradshaw, FOX
1994	John Madden, FOX	1997	Cris Collinsworth, HBO/NBC	2000	Steve Lyons, FOX
1995	John Madden, FOX	1998	Cris Collinsworth, HBO/FOX	2001	Terry Bradshaw, FOX

Sports Events Analyst

Year		Year		Year	
1997	Joe Morgan, ESPN	1999	John Madden, FOX	2001	Tim McCarver, FOX
1998	John Madden, FOX	2000	Tim McCarver, FOX		

Lifetime Achievement Emmy Award

For outstanding work as an exemplary television sportscaster over many years.

Year	Year	Year	Year
1989 Jim McKay	1993 Pat Summerall	1997 Jim Simpson	2001 Herb Granath
1990 Lindsey Nelson	1994 Howard Cosell	1998 Keith Jackson	
1991 Curt Gowdy	1995 Vin Scully	1999 Jack Buck	
1992 Chris Schenkel	1996 Frank Gifford	2000 Dick Enberg	

National Sportscasters and Sportswriters Assn. Award

Sportscaster of the Year presented annually since 1959 by the National Sportscasters and Sportswriters Association, based in Salisbury, N.C. Voting is done by NSSA members and selected national media.

Multiple winners: Bob Costas (8); Chris Berman (6) Keith Jackson (5); Lindsey Nelson and Chris Schenkel (4); Dick Enberg, Al Michaels and Vin Scully (3); Curt Gowdy and Ray Scott (2).

Year	Year	Year	Year
1959 Lindsey Nelson	1971 Ray Scott	1982 Vin Scully	1994 Chris Berman
1960 Lindsey Nelson	1972 Keith Jackson	1983 Al Michaels	1995 Bob Costas
1961 Lindsey Nelson	1973 Keith Jackson	1984 John Madden	1996 Chris Berman
1962 Lindsey Nelson	1974 Keith Jackson	1985 Bob Costas	1997 Bob Costas
1963 Chris Schenkel	1975 Keith Jackson	1986 Al Michaels	1998 Jim Nantz
1964 Chris Schenkel	1976 Keith Jackson	1987 Bob Costas	1999 Dan Patrick
1965 Vin Scully	1977 Pat Summerall	1988 Bob Costas	2000 Bob Costas
1966 Curt Gowdy	1978 Vin Scully	1989 Chris Berman	2001 Chris Berman
1967 Chris Schenkel	1979 Dick Enberg	1990 Chris Berman	
1968 Ray Scott	1980 Dick Enberg	1991 Bob Costas	
1969 Curt Gowdy	& Al Michaels	1992 Bob Costas	
1970 Chris Schenkel	1981 Dick Enberg	1993 Chris Berman	

The Pulitzer Prize

The Pulitzer Prizes for journalism, letters and music have been presented annually since 1917 in the name of Joseph Pulitzer (1847-1911), the publisher of the *New York World*. Prizes are awarded by the president of Columbia University on the recommendation of a board of review. Sixteen Pulitzers have been awarded for newspaper sports reporting, sports commentary and sports photography.

News Coverage

1935 **Bill Taylor,** *NY Herald Tribune,* for his reporting on the 1934 America's Cup yacht races.

Special Citation

1952 **Max Kase**, *NY Journal-American,* for his reporting on the 1951 college basketball point-shaving scandal.

Meritorious Public Service

1954 **Newsday** (Garden City, N.Y.) for its expose of New York State's race track scandals and labor racketeering.

General Reporting

1956 **Arthur Daley,** *NY Times,* for his 1955 columns.

Investigative Reporting

1981 **Clark Hallas** & **Robert Lowe,** *(Tucson) Arizona Daily Star,* for their 1980 investigation of the University of Arizona athletic department.

1986 **Jeffrey Marx** & **Michael York,** Lexington (Ky.) *Herald-Leader,* for their 1985 investigation of the basketball program at the University of Kentucky and other major colleges.

Specialized Reporting

1985 **Randall Savage** & **Jackie Crosby,** Macon (Ga.) *Telegraph and News,* for their 1984 investigation of athletics and academics at the University of Georgia and Georgia Tech.

Beat Reporting

2000 **George Dohrmann**, St. Paul (Min.) *Pioneer Press,* for his investigation that revealed academic fraud in the men's basketball program at the University of Minnesota.

Feature Writing

1997 **Lisa Pollak**, *Baltimore Sun,* for her story about baseball umpire John Hirschbeck dealing with the death of one son and the illness of another from the same disease.

Commentary

1976 **Red Smith**, *NY Times,* for his 1975 columns.
1981 **Dave Anderson,** *NY Times,* for his 1980 columns.
1990 **Jim Murray**, *LA Times,* for his 1989 columns.

Red Smith Award

Presented annually by the Associated Press Sports Editors (APSE) to a person who has made "major contributions to sports journalism."

Year	Year	Year
1981 Red Smith, *NY Times*	1990 Dave Smith, *Dallas Morning News*	1997 Jerome Holtzman, *Chicago Tribune*
1982 Jim Murray, *LA Times*	1991 Dave Kindred, *National Sports Daily*	1998 Sam Lacy, *Baltimore Afro-American*
1983 Shirley Povich, *Washington Post*	1992 Ed Storin, *Miami Herald*	1999 Bud Collins, *Boston Globe*
1984 Fred Russell, *Nashville Banner*	1993 Tom McEwen, *Tampa Tribune*	2000 Jerry Izenberg, *Newark Star Ledger*
1985 Blackie Sherrod, *Dallas Morning News*	1994 Dave Anderson, *NY Times*	2001 John Steadman, *Baltimore Sun*
1986 Si Burick, *Dayton Daily News*	1995 Richard Sandler, *Newsday*	2002 Dick Schaap, *ESPN "The Sports Reporters"*
1987 Will Grimsley, AP	1996 Bill Dwyre, *LA Times*	
1988 Furman Bisher, *Atlanta Journal*		
1989 Edwin Pope, *Miami Herald*		

Photography

1949 **Nat Fein,** *NY Herald Tribune,* for his photo, "Babe Ruth Bows Out."

1952 **John Robinson** & **Don Ultang,** *Des Moines* (Iowa) *Register and Tribune,* for their sequence of six pictures of the 1951 Drake-Oklahoma A&M football game, in which Drake's Johnny Bright had his jaw broken.

1985 **The Photography Staff** of the *Orange County* (Calif.) *Register,* for their coverage of the 1984 Summer Olympics in Los Angeles.

1993 **William Snyder** & **Ken Geiger,** *The Dallas Morning News,* for their coverage of the 1992 Summer Olympics in Barcelona, Spain.

Sportswriter of the Year
NSSA Award

Presented annually since 1959 by the National Sportscasters and Sportswriters Association, based in Salisbury, N.C. Voting is done by NSSA members and selected national media.

Multiple winners: Jim Murray (14); Rick Reilly (7); Frank Deford (6); Red Smith (5); Will Grimsley (4); Peter Gammons (3).

Year		Year		Year	
1959	Red Smith, *NY Herald-Tribune*	1974	Jim Murray, *LA Times*	1989	Peter Gammons, *Sports Ill.*
1960	Red Smith, *NY Herald-Tribune*	1975	Jim Murray, *LA Times*	1990	Peter Gammons, *Boston Globe*
1961	Red Smith, *NY Herald-Tribune*	1976	Jim Murray, *LA Times*	1991	Rick Reilly, *Sports Ill.*
1962	Red Smith, *NY Herald-Tribune*	1977	Jim Murray, *LA Times*	1992	Rick Reilly, *Sports Ill.*
1963	Arthur Daley, *NY Times*	1978	Will Grimsley, *AP*	1993	Peter Gammons, *Boston Globe*
1964	Jim Murray, *LA Times*	1979	Jim Murray, *LA Times*	1994	Rick Reilly, *Sports Ill.*
1965	Red Smith, *NY Herald-Tribune*	1980	Will Grimsley, *AP*	1995	Rick Reilly, *Sports Ill.*
1966	Jim Murray, *LA Times*	1981	Will Grimsley, *AP*	1996	Rick Reilly, *Sports Ill.*
1967	Jim Murray, *LA Times*	1982	Frank Deford, *Sports Ill.*	1997	Dave Kindred, *The Sporting News*
1968	Jim Murray, *LA Times*	1983	Will Grimsley, *AP*		
1969	Jim Murray, *LA Times*	1984	Frank Deford, *Sports Ill.*	1998	Mitch Albom, *Detroit Free Press*
1970	Jim Murray, *LA Times*	1985	Frank Deford, *Sports Ill.*	1999	Rick Reilly, *Sports Ill.*
1971	Jim Murray, *LA Times*	1986	Frank Deford, *Sports Ill.*	2000	Bob Ryan, *Boston Globe*
1972	Jim Murray, *LA Times*	1987	Frank Deford, *Sports Ill.*	2001	Rick Reilly, *Sports Ill.*
1973	Jim Murray, *LA Times*	1988	Frank Deford, *Sports Ill.*		

Best Newspaper Sports Sections of 2001

Winners of the annual Associated Press Sports Editors contest for best daily and Sunday sports sections. Awards are divided into different categories, based on circulation figures. Selections are made by a committee of APSE members.

Circulation Over 250,000

Top 10 Daily		Top 10 Sunday	
Atlanta Journal-Constitution	Star-Ledger (Newark, NJ)	Atlanta Journal-Constitution	Los Angeles Times
Boston Globe	Daily News (NY)	Boston Globe	Minneapolis Star Tribune
Dallas Morning News	Newsday (NY)	Dallas Morning News	Daily News (NY)
Fort Worth Star-Telegram	St. Petersburg (FL) Times	Fort Worth Star-Telegram	New York Times
Los Angeles Times	USA Today	Kansas City Star	Orlando Sentinel

Circulation 100,000-250,000

Top 10 Daily		Top 10 Sunday	
Akron-Beacon Journal (OH)	Pittsburgh Post-Gazette	Charlotte Observer	St. Paul Pioneer Press
Contra Costa Times (Walnut Creek, CA)	The Record (Hackensack, NJ)	Colorado Springs Gazette	Seattle Times
Hartford Courant	St. Paul Pioneer Press	The State (Columbia, SC)	News Tribune (Tacoma, WA)
Daily News (Los Angeles)	Seattle Times	Des Moines Register	Tampa Tribune
Palm Beach Post	News Tribune (Tacoma, WA)	Hartford Courant	
		Palm Beach Post	

Best Sportswriting of 2001

Winners of the annual Associated Press Sports Editors Contest for best sportswriting in 2001. Eventual winners were chosen from five finalists in each writing division. Selections are made by a committee of APSE members. Note the investigative writing division included all circulation categories.

Circulation over 250,000

Column:	Sally Jenkins, *Washington Post*	**Game story:**	Mark Kiszla, *Denver Post*
Enterprise:	Michael Dobie and Arthur Staple, *Newsday (NY)*	**News story:**	Ed Hinton, Jim Leusner and Henry Pierson Curtis, *Orlando Sentinel*
Feature:	Jim O'Donnell, *Chicago Sun-Times*		

Circulation 100,000-250,000

Column:	Geoff Calkins, *The Commercial Appeal* (Memphis)	**Feature:**	Pat Forde, *Courier-Journal (Louisville)*
		Game story:	Les Carpenter, *Seattle Times*
Enterprise:	Peter St. Onge, *Charlotte Observer*	**News story:**	Craig Hill, *News Tribune (Tacoma)*

All Categories

Investigative: Russell Carollo, Doug Harris, Christine Vasconez and Mike Wagner, *Dayton Daily News*

Directory of Organizations

Listing of the major sports organizations, teams and media addresses and officials as of Sept. 25, 2002.

AUTO RACING

**CART
(Championship Auto Racing Teams, Inc.)**
5350 Lakeview Pkwy, Suite A, Indianapolis, IN 46268
(317) 715-4100 www.cart.com
President-CEO ....Christopher Pook
V.P. of Communications ....Adam Saal

**IRL
(Indy Racing League)**
4565 West 16th St., Indianapolis, IN 46222
(317) 484-6526 www.indyracing.com
Founder ....Tony George
Dir. of Racing Operations ....John Lewis
Director of Public Relations ....Ron Green

**FIA—Formula One
(Federation Internationale de L'Automobile)**
2 Chemin de Blandonnet, 1215 Geneva 15, Switzerland
TEL: 011-41-22544-4400 www.fia.com
President ....Max Mosley
Secretary General ....Pierre de Coninck
Director of Public Relations ...Francesco Longanesi-Cattani

**NASCAR
(National Assn. for Stock Car Auto Racing)**
P.O. Box 2875, Daytona Beach, FL 32120
(386) 253-0611 www.nascar.com
President ....Michael Helton
V.P. of Corporate Communications ....Jim Hunter

**NHRA
(National Hot Rod Association)**
2035 Financial Way, Glendora, CA 91741
(626) 914-4761 www.nhra.com
President ....Tom Compton
Sr. V.P. of Racing Operations ....Graham Light
V.P. of Communications ....Jerry Archambeault

MAJOR LEAGUE BASEBALL

Office of the Commissioner
245 Park Ave., 31st Floor, New York, NY 10167
(212) 931-7800 www.mlb.com
Commissioner ....Bud Selig
President-COO ....Robert DuPuy
General Counsel ....Thomas Ostertag
Senior Vice President ....Richard Levin
Sr. V.P. of Corporate Communications ......Jim Gallagher

Player Relations Committee
245 Park Ave.
New York, NY 10160
(212) 931-7800
Chief Labor Negotiator ....Frank Coonelly
Associate Counsels ....Jennifer Gefsky
                                        & Derek Jackson

Major League Baseball Players Association
12 East 49th St., 24th Floor
New York, NY 10017
(212) 826-0808
Exec. Director & General Counsel ....Donald Fehr
Associate General Counsel ....Gene Orza

AL

American League Office
245 Park Ave., 31st Floor, New York, NY 10167
(212) 931-7800

Anaheim Angels
2000 Gene Autry Way, Anaheim, CA 92806
(888) 796-4256 www.angelsbaseball.com
Chairman & CEO ....Michael Eisner
Owner ....Walt Disney Co.
Interim President ....Paul Pressler
V.P. & General Manager ....Bill Stoneman
V.P. of Communications ....Tim Mead

Baltimore Orioles
333 West Camden St., Baltimore, MD 21201
(410) 685-9800 www.theorioles.com
CEO ....Peter Angelos
Vice Chairman & COO ....Joseph Foss
V.P. of Baseball Operations ....Syd Thrift
Director of Public Relations ....Bill Stetka

Boston Red Sox
Fenway Park, 4 Yawkey Way, Boston, MA 02215
(617) 267-9440 www.redsox.com
Principal Owner ....John Henry
President-CEO ....Larry Lucchino
V.P. Baseball Ops./Interim GM ....Mike Port
Director of Communications ....Kevin Shea

Chicago White Sox
Comiskey Park, 333 W. 35th St., Chicago, IL 60616
(312) 674-1000 www.whitesox.com
Chairman ....Jerry Reinsdorf
Vice Chairman ....Eddie Einhorn
Senior V.P./General Manager ....Ken Williams
Director of Public Relations ....Scott Reifert

Cleveland Indians
Jacobs Field, 2401 Ontario St., Cleveland, OH 44115
(216) 420-4636 www.indians.com
Owner-Chairman-CEO ....Lawrence Dolan
General Manager ....Mark Shapiro
V.P., Public Relations ....Bob DiBiasio

Detroit Tigers
Comerica Park, 2100 Woodward Ave., Detroit, MI 48201
(313) 962-4000 www.detroittigers.com
Owner and Director ....Mike Ilitch
President/CEO/GM ....Dave Dombrowski
Sr. Dir. of Communications ....John Hahn

Kansas City Royals
One Royal Way, Kansas City, MO 64129
(816) 921-8000 www.kcroyals.com
Owner ....David Glass
Executive V.P./COO ....Herk Robinson
Senior V.P./General Manager ....Allard Baird
Sr. Director of Media Relations ....David Witty

Minnesota Twins
Hubert H. Humphrey Metrodome
34 Kirby Puckett Place, Minneapolis, MN 55415
(612) 375-1366 www.mntwins.com
Owner ....Carl Pohlad
President ....Jerry Bell
V.P./General Manager ....Terry Ryan
Director of Communications ....Brad Ruiter
Manager of Media Relations ....Sean Harlin

New York Yankees
Yankee Stadium, 161st St. and River Ave., Bronx, NY 10452
(718) 293-4300 www.yankees.com
Principal Owner ....George Steinbrenner
President ....Randy Levine
Sr. V.P./General Manager ....Brian Cashman
Dir. of Media Relations/Publicity ....Rick Cerrone

Oakland Athletics
7000 Coliseum Way
Oakland, CA 94621
(510) 638-4900 www.oaklandathletics.com
Co-Owners ....Steve Schott and Ken Hofmann
President ....Mike Crowley
V.P./General Manager ....Billy Beane
Baseball Information Manager ....Mike Selleck

Seattle Mariners
Safeco Field, 1250 1st Ave S, Seattle, WA 98134
(206) 346-4000 www.mariners.com
Chairman-CEO ....Howard Lincoln
President-COO ....Chuck Armstrong
Executive V.P./General Manager ....Pat Gillick
Director of Baseball Information ....Tim Hevly

Tampa Bay Devil Rays
Tropicana Field, One Tropicana Dr.
St. Petersburg, FL 33705
(727) 825-3137 www.devilrays.com
Managing General Partner/CEO ....Vincent J. Naimoli
Senior V.P., Baseball Ops./GM ....Chuck LaMar
V.P. of Public Relations ....Rick Vaughn

Texas Rangers
1000 Ballpark Way #400, Arlington, TX 76011
(817) 273-5222 www.texasrangers.com
Owner ....Thomas Hicks
Executive V.P., General Manager ....John Hart
Senior V.P. of Communications ....John Blake

Toronto Blue Jays
SkyDome, One Blue Jays Way, Suite 3200
Toronto, Ontario M5V 1J1
(416) 341-1000 www.bluejays.com
Majority Owner ....Rogers Communications
President & CEO ....Paul Godfrey
Sr. V.P. of Baseball Ops./GM .............J.P. Ricciardi
Director of Communications ....Jay Stenhouse

NL

National League Office
245 Park Ave., 31st Floor, New York, NY 10167
(212) 931-7800

Arizona Diamondbacks
P.O. Box 2095, Phoenix, AZ 85001
(602) 462-6500 www.azdiamondbacks.com
Chairman/CEO ....Jerry Colangelo
President ....Richard H. Dozer
V.P./General Manager ....Joe Garagiola Jr.
Director of Public Relations ....Mike Swanson

Atlanta Braves
P.O. Box 4064, Atlanta, GA 30302
(404) 522-7630 www.atlantabraves.com
President ....Stan Kasten
Exec. V.P./General Manager ....John Schuerholz
Director of Public Relations ....Jim Schultz

Chicago Cubs
1060 West Addison St., Chicago, IL 60613
(773) 404-2827 www.cubs.com
Owner ....The Tribune Company
President/CEO ....Andy MacPhail
General Manager ....Jim Hendry
Director of Media Relations ....Sharon Pannozzo

Cincinnati Reds
100 Cinergy Field, Cincinnati, OH 45202
(513) 421-4510 www.cincinnatireds.com
Majority Owner-CEO ....Carl Lindner
General Manager ....Jim Bowden
Director of Media Relations ....Rob Butcher

Colorado Rockies
Coors Field, 2001 Blake St., Denver, CO 80205
(303) 292-0200 www.coloradorockies.com
Chairman ....Jerry McMorris
President ....Keli McGregor
Executive V.P./General Manager ....Dan O'Dowd
Sr. Director Comm./PR ....Jay Alves

Florida Marlins
2267 Dan Marino Blvd., Miami, FL 33028
(305) 626-7400 www.flamarlins.com
Owner ....Jeffrey Loria
President ....David Samson
Senior V.P./General Manager ....Larry Beinfest
Director of Media Relations ....Steve Copses

Houston Astros
Minute Maid Park, P.O. Box 288, Houston, TX 77001
(713) 259-8000 www.astros.com
Chairman-CEO ....Drayton McLane Jr.
President of Baseball Ops. ....Tal Smith
General Manager ....Gerry Hunsicker
Director of Media Relations ....Warren Miller

Los Angeles Dodgers
1000 Elysian Park Ave., Los Angeles, CA 90012
(323) 224-1500 www.dodgers.com
Owner ....Bob Daly & Fox News Corp
President/COO ....Bob Graziano
Executive V.P./General Manager ....Dan Evans
Director of Public Relations ....John Olguin

Milwaukee Brewers
Miller Park, One Brewers Way, Milwaukee, WI 53214
(414) 902-4400 www.milwaukeebrewers.com
President ....Ulice Payne
General Manager ....Doug Melvin
Director of Media Relations ....Jon Greenberg

Montreal Expos
P.O. Box 500, Station M, Montreal, Quebec H1V 3P2
(514) 253-3434 www.montrealexpos.com
President ....Tony Tavares
V.P./General Manager ....Omar Minaya
Manager of Media Relations ....Matt Charbonneau

New York Mets
123-01 Roosevelt Ave., Flushing, NY 11368
(718) 507-6387 www.mets.com
President-CEO ....Fred Wilpon
Senior V.P./General Manager ....Steve Phillips
V.P. of Media Relations ....Jay Horwitz

Philadelphia Phillies
3501 South Broad St., Philadelphia, PA 19148
(215) 463-6000 www.phillies.com
General Partner/Pres./CEO ....David Montgomery
Partner/Chairman ....Bill Giles
General Manager & V.P. ....Ed Wade
V.P. of Public Relations ....Larry Shenk

Pittsburgh Pirates
115 Federal St., Pittsburgh, PA 15212
(412) 323-5000 www.pirateball.com
CEO/Managing General Partner ....Kevin McClatchy
COO ....Richard Freeman
Senior V.P. & General Manager ....Dave Littlefield
Director of Media Relations ....Jim Trdinich

St. Louis Cardinals
250 Stadium Plaza, St. Louis, MO 63102
(314) 421-3060   www.stlcardinals.com
Chairman ....Frederick O. Hanser
President ....Mark Lamping
V.P./General Manager ....Walt Jocketty
Director of Media Relations ....Brian Bartow

San Diego Padres
P.O. Box 122000, San Diego, CA 92112
(619) 881-6500   www.padres.com
Chairman ....John Moores
President-CEO ....Bob Vizas
Executive V.P./General Manager ....Kevin Towers
Exec. Director, Communications ....Glenn Geffner

San Francisco Giants
Pacific Bell Park, 24 Willie Mays Plaza
San Francisco, CA 94107
(415) 972-2000   www.sfgiants.com
President ....Peter Magowan
Executive V.P./COO ....Laurence Baer
Senior V.P./General Manager ....Brian Sabean
Manager of Media Relations ....Jim Moorehead

PRO BASKETBALL

NBA

League Office
Olympic Tower, 645 Fifth Ave., New York, NY 10022
(212) 407-8000   www.nba.com
Commissioner ....David Stern
Senior V.P. of Basketball Ops. ....Stuart Jackson
Deputy Commissioner ....Russell Granik
Sr. V.P. Sports Media Relations ....Brian McIntyre
Executive V.P. Global Media ....Heidi Ueberroth

NBA Players Association
1700 Broadway, Suite 1400, New York, NY 10019
(212) 655-0880
Exec. Director ....William Hunter
General Counsel ....Ron Klempner
President ....Michael Curry

Atlanta Hawks
One CNN Center, South Tower, Suite 405
Atlanta, GA 30303
(404) 827-3800   www.hawks.com
Owner ....AOL/Time-Warner
President ....Stan Kasten
General Manager ....Pete Babcock
V.P. of Communications ....Arthur Triche

Boston Celtics
151 Merrimac St., 4th Floor, Boston, MA 02114
(617) 523-6050   www.celtics.com
Chairman ....Paul Gaston
President ....Red Auerbach
General Manager ....Chris Wallace
V.P. of Media Relations ....Jeff Twiss

Chicago Bulls
United Center, 1901 West Madison St., Chicago, IL 60612
(312) 455-4000   www.bulls.com
Chairman ....Jerry Reinsdorf
Exec. V.P., Basketball Operations ....Jerry Krause
Sr. Director of Media Services ....Tim Hallam

Cleveland Cavaliers
Gund Arena, One Center Court, Cleveland, OH 44115
(216) 420-2000   www.cavs.com
Owner-Chairman ....Gordon Gund
Owner-Vice Chairman ....George Gund III
President & CEO ....Jim Boland
Senior V.P/General Manager ....Jim Paxson
Sr. Dir. of Communications and PR ....Bob Price

Dallas Mavericks
2500 Victory Avenue, Dallas, TX 75201
(214) 665-4660   www.dallasmavericks.com
Owner ....Mark Cuban
President/CEO ....Terdema Ussery
GM & Head Coach ....Don Nelson
V.P. Marketing and Communications ....Matt Fitzgerald

Denver Nuggets
1000 Chopper Cir., Denver, CO 80204
(303) 405-1100   www.nuggets.com
Owner ....Stan Kroenke
General Manager ....Kiki Vandeweghe
Manager of Media Relations ....Eric Sebastian

Detroit Pistons
The Palace of Auburn Hills
Two Championship Dr., Auburn Hills, MI 48326
(248) 377-0100   www.pistons.com
Managing Partner ....William Davidson
President ....Tom Wilson
President of Basketball Operations ....Joe Dumars
V.P. of Public Relations ....Matt Dobek

Golden State Warriors
1011 Broadway, Oakland, CA 94607
(510) 986-2200   www.warriors.com
Owner-CEO ....Chris Cohan
General Manager ....Garry St. Jean
Director of Public Relations ....Raymond Ridder

Houston Rockets
2 Greenway Plaza, Suite 400, Houston, TX 77046
(713) 627-3865   www.rockets.com
Owner-President ....Leslie L. Alexander
COO ....George Postolos
General Manager ....Carroll Dawson
Director of Media Relations ....Nelson Louis

Indiana Pacers
125 S. Pennsylvania Street, Indianapolis, IN 46204
(317) 917-2500   www.pacers.com
Owners ....Melvin Simon & Herb Simon
President ....Donnie Walsh
Director of Media Relations ....David Benner

Los Angeles Clippers
Staples Center
1111 S. Figueroa St., Suite 1100
Los Angeles, CA 90015
(213) 742-7500   www.clippers.com
Owner-Chairman ....Donald T. Sterling
Executive V.P. ....Andy Roeser
V.P., Basketball Operations ....Elgin Baylor
Director of Communications ....Rob Raichlen

Los Angeles Lakers
555 N. Nash St., El Segundo, CA 90245
(310) 426-6000   www.lakers.com
Owner ....Jerry Buss
General Manager ....Mitch Kupchak
Director of Public Relations ....John Black

Memphis Grizzlies
175 Toyota Plaza, Suite 150
Memphis, TN 38103
(901) 205-1234   www.grizzlies.com
Owner ....Michael Heisley
President of Basketball Ops. ....Jerry West
General Manager ....Dick Versace
Media Relations Director ....Kirk Clayborn

Miami Heat
American Airlines Arena, 601 Biscayne Blvd.
Miami, FL 33132
(786) 777-4328   www.heat.com
Managing General Partner ....Micky Arison
President & Head Coach ....Pat Riley
General Manager & President Basketball Ops. .Randy Pfund
V.P. of Sports Media Relations ....Tim Donovan

Milwaukee Bucks
Bradley Center, 1001 N. Fourth St., Milwaukee, WI 53203
(414) 227-0500   www.bucks.com
President ....Sen. Herb Kohl (D., Wisc.)
General Manager ....Ernie Grunfeld
Director of Public Relations ....Cheri Hanson

Minnesota Timberwolves
Target Center
600 First Ave. North, Minneapolis, MN 55403
(612) 673-1600   www.timberwolves.com
Owner ....Glen Taylor
President ....Rob Moor
V.P., Basketball Operations ....Kevin McHale
Dir. of Communications ....Kent Wipf

New Jersey Nets
390 Murray Hill Pkwy., East Rutherford, NJ 07073
(201) 935-8888   www.njnets.com
Co-Chair/Owner ....Lewis Katz
Co-Chairman/CEO ....Lou Lamoriello
President/GM ....Rod Thorn
Director of Public Relations ....Gary Sussman

New Orleans Hornets
1501 Girod St., New Orleans, LA 70113
(504) 301-4000   www.hornets.com
Owners ....George Shinn and Ray Wooldridge
Executive V.P., Basketball Operations ....Bob Bass
General Manager ....Jeff Bower
V.P. of Public Relations ....Harold Kaufman

New York Knickerbockers
Madison Square Garden
2 Penn Plaza, 14th Floor, New York, NY 10121
(212) 465-6000   www.knicks.com
Owner ....Cablevision Systems Inc.
President (Cablevision) ....James Dolan
President/General Manager ....Scott Layden
Director of Media Relations ....Jonathan Supranowitz

Orlando Magic
2 Magic Place
8701 Maitland Summit Blvd., Orlando, FL 32810
(407) 916-2400   www.orlandomagic.com
Owner ....Rich DeVos
President ....Bob Vander Weide
COO ....John Weisbrod
V.P., Basketball Ops. & GM ....John Gabriel
Director of Media Relations ....Joel Glass

Philadelphia 76ers
First Union Center
3601 S. Broad St., Philadelphia, PA 19148
(215) 339-7600   www.76ers.com
Owner ....Comcast-Spectacor
Chairman ....Ed Snider
General Manager ....Billy King
Sr. Director of Communications ....Karen Frascona

Phoenix Suns
201 E Jefferson St., Phoenix, AZ 85004
(602) 379-7900   www.suns.com
Chairman-CEO/Managing Gen. Partner .. Jerry Colangelo
President/General Manager ....Bryan Colangelo
Sr. V.P. of Player Personnel ....Dick Van Arsdale
V.P. of Basketball Communications ....Julie Fie

Portland Trail Blazers
One Center Court, Suite 200, Portland, OR 97227
(503) 234-9291   www.blazers.com
Owner-Chairman ....Paul Allen
President & General Manager ....Bob Whitsitt
Assistant General Manager ....Mark Warkentien
Executive Dir. of Communications ....Mike Hanson

Sacramento Kings
One Sports Parkway, Sacramento, CA 95834
(916) 928-0000   www.kings.com
Controlling Partners ....Joe and Gavin Maloof
President, Basketball Operations ....Geoff Petrie
V.P., Basketball Operations ....Wayne Cooper
Director of Media Relations ....Troy Hanson

San Antonio Spurs
One SBC Center
San Antonio, TX 78219
(210) 554-7700   www.spurs.com
Chairman ....Peter Holt
General Manager .........................R.C. Buford
Director of Player Personnel ....Sam Schuler
Director of Media Services ....Tom James

Seattle SuperSonics
351 Elliott Ave. West, Suite 500
Seattle, WA 98119
(206) 281-5800   www.supersonics.com
Chairman ....Howard Schultz
President & CEO ....Wally Walker
General Manager ....Rick Sund
Executive Vice President ....Billy McKinney
Director of Public Relations ....Marc Moquin

Toronto Raptors
40 Bay St., Suite 400
Toronto, Ontario M5J 2X2
(416) 815-5600   www.raptors.com
Chairman ....Steve Stavro
President ....Richard Peddie
Sr. V.P./General Manager ....Glen Grunwald
V.P. of Sports Comm. and Community Rel. ... John Lashway

Utah Jazz
Delta Center, 301 West South Temple
Salt Lake City, UT 84101
(801) 325-2500   www.utahjazz.com
Owner ....Larry Miller
President ....Dennis Haslam
V.P. of Basketball Operations ....Kevin O'Connor
Director of Media Relations ....Kim Turner

Washington Wizards
MCI Center, 601 F Street NW
Washington, D.C., 20004
(202) 661-5000   www.nba.com/wizards
Chairman ....Abe Pollin
President ....Susan O'Malley
General Manager ....Wes Unseld
Director of Public Relations ....Nicole Hawkins

Other Men's Pro Leagues

Continental Basketball Association
1412 W. Idaho St., Ste. 235
Boise, ID 83702
(208) 429-0101   www.cbahoopsonline.com
Commissioner ....Gary Hunter
Dir. of Public/Media Relations ....Bryant Kuechle
   Member teams (8): Dakota Wizards, Gary Steel-heads, Great Lakes Storm, Grand Rapids Hoops, Idaho Stampede, Rockford Lightning, Sioux Falls Skyforce and Yakima Sun Kings.

United States Basketball League
46 Quirk Road, Milford, CT 06460
(203) 877-9508
Commissioner ....Daniel T. Meisenheimer III
Dir. of Public Relations ....Dennis Truax
   Member teams (10): Adirondack (NY) Wildcats, Brevard (FL) Blue Ducks, Brooklyn Kings, Dodge City Legend, Florida Sea Dragons, Kansas Cagerz, Oklahoma Storm, Pennsylvania ValleyDawgs, St. Joseph (MO) Express, St. Louis SkyHawks.

National Basketball Development League
24 Vardry Street, Suite 201, Greenville, SC 29601
(864) 248-1100   www.nbdl.com
President ....Philip Evans
Executive Director ....Karl Hicks
Director of Communications ....Kent Partridge
   Member teams (8): Asheville (NC) Altitude; Columbus (GA) Riverdragons; Fayetteville (NC) Patriots; Greenville (SC) Groove; Huntsville (AL) Flight; Mobile (AL) Revelers; North Charleston (SC) Lowgators; Roanoke (VA) Dazzle.

WNBA

League Office
645 5th Ave., New York, NY 10022
(212) 826-7000   www.wnba.com
President ....Val Ackerman
V.P. of Player Personnel ....Renee Brown
Sr. Dir. of Sports Comm. ....Maureen Coyle

Charlotte Sting
3308 Oak Lace Blvd., Ste. B, Charlotte, NC 28208
(704) 357-0252   www.charlottesting.com
President ................................M.L. Carr
Head Coach ....Anne Donovan
Director of Public Relations ....John Maxwell

Cleveland Rockers
Gund Arena, One Center Court
Cleveland, OH 44115
(216) 420-2000   www.clevelandrockers.com
President ....Jim Boland
Head Coach ....Dan Hughes
General Manager ....Jim Paxson
Director of Media Relations ....Amanda Ludwig

Detroit Shock
The Palace of Auburn Hills
Two Championship Dr., Auburn Hills, MI 48326
(248) 377-0100   www.detroitshock.com
President ....Thomas S. Wilson
Head Coach ....Bill Laimbeer
Dir. of Public Relations & Business Ops. ....Dennis Sampier

Houston Comets
Two Greenway Plaza, Suite 400
Houston, TX 77046-3865
(713) 627-9622   www.houstoncomets.com
Owner/President ....Leslie L. Alexander
GM/Head Coach ....Van Chancellor
Director of Media Relations ....Bob Schranz

Indiana Fever
125 S. Pennsylvania St., Indianapolis, IN 46204
(317) 917-2500   www.wnba.com/fever
President ....Donnie Walsh
GM/Head Coach ....Nell Fortner
Director of Media Relations ....Tom Savage

Los Angeles Sparks
401 S. Prairie Avenue, Inglewood, CA 90301
(310) 330-2434   www.lasparks.com
General Manager ....Penny Toler
Head Coach ....Michael Cooper
Director of Media Relations ....Kristal Shipp

Miami Sol
601 Biscayne Blvd., Miami, FL 33132
(786) 777-1000   www.wnba.com/sol
Owner ....Micky Arison
President ....Pat Riley
GM/Head Coach ....Ron Rothstein
Media Relations Manager ....Alan Hancock

Minnesota Lynx
Target Center
600 First Ave. N., Minneapolis, MN 55403
(612) 673-1600   www.wnba.com/lynx
Owner ....Glen Taylor
GM/Head Coach ....Brain Agler
Manager of Media Relations ....Mike Cristaldi

New York Liberty
Madison Square Garden
Two Penn Plaza, New York, NY 10121
(212) 564-9622   www.nyliberty.com
Senior V.P./General Manager ....Carol Blazejowski
Head Coach ....Richie Adubato
Manager of Communications ....Brooke Lawer

Orlando Miracle
2 Magic Place
8701 Maitland Summit Blvd., Orlando, FL, 32810
(407) 916-2400   www.orlandomiracle.com
President ....Bob Vander Weide
Dir. of Player Personnel/Head Coach ....Dee Brown
Media Relations Manager ....Katherine Wu

Phoenix Mercury
America West Arena
201 E. Jefferson St.
Phoenix, AZ 85004
(602) 514-8333   www.phoenixmercury.com
President ....Bryan Colangelo
V.P., Operations ....Seth Sulka
Head Coach ....Cynthia Cooper
Director of Communications ....Tami Scott

Portland Fire
One Center Court, Suite 100
Portland, OR 97227
(503) 234-9291   www.firebasketball.com
Owner ....Paul Allen
GM/Head Coach ....Linda Hargrove
Director of Communications ....Jill Wiggins

Sacramento Monarchs
ARCO Arena, One Sports Pkwy.
Sacramento, CA 95834
(916) 928-0000   www.sacramentomonarchs.com
General Manager ....Jerry Reynolds
Head Coach ....Maura McHugh
Manager of Media Relations ....Kimberly Williams

Seattle Storm
351 Elliott Ave. W., Suite 500
Seattle, WA 98119
(206) 281-5800   www.wnba.com/storm
Chairman ....Howard Schultz
President & CEO ....Wally Walker
GM/Head Coach ....Lin Dunn
Director of Media Relations ....Valerie O'Neil

Utah Starzz
Delta Center, 301 West South Temple
Salt Lake City, UT 84101
(801) 325-2500   www.utahstarzz.com
V.P. of Basketball Operations ....Kevin O'Connor
Head Coach ....Candi Harvey
Director of Media/Comm. Relations ....Erin Bodily

Washington Mystics
MCI Center, 601 F St. NW
Washington D.C. 20004
(202) 661-5000 www.wnba.com/mystics
Sr. V.P. Business & Basketball Ops. . . . . Judy Holland-Burton
Head Coach . . . . Marianne Stanley
Dir. of Public Relations . . . . Dyani Gordon

BOWLING

ABC
(American Bowling Congress)
5301 South 76th St.
Greendale, WI 53129
(800) 514-2695 www.bowl.com/bowl/abc
Executive Director . . . . Roger Dalkin
President . . . . Jim Bevins

BPAA
(Bowling Proprietors' Assn. of America)
P.O. Box 5802
Arlington, TX 76011
(817) 649-5105 www.bpaa.com
Executive Director . . . . John F. Berglund
President . . . . Jack Moran
Director of Public Relations . . . . Cary Richmond

PWBA
(Professional Women's Bowling Association)
7171 Cherryvale Blvd.
Rockford, IL 61112
(815) 332-5756 www.pwba.com
President . . . . John Falzone
Media Director . . . . Gary Kohn

PBA
(Professional Bowlers Association)
719 Second Ave., Suite 701
Seattle, WA 98104
(206) 332-9688 www.pba.com
Commissioner . . . . Ian Hamilton
President . . . . Steve Miller
Dir. of Corporate Comm. . . . . Beth Marshall

WIBC
(Women's International Bowling Congress, Inc.)
5301 South 76th St., Greendale, WI 53129
(414) 421-9000 www.wibctournament.com
President . . . . Sylvia Broyles
Public Relations Director . . . . Darryl Nitsch

BOXING

IBF
(International Boxing Federation)
134 Evergreen Place, 9th Floor
East Orange, NJ 07018
(973) 414-0300 www.ibf-usba-boxing.com
President . . . . Marian Muhammad
Treasurer-Ratings Chairman . . . . Daryl Peoples

WBA
(World Boxing Association)
P.O. Box 377, Maracay 2101-A, Estado Aragua
Venezuela
TEL: 011-58-244-663-1584 www.wbaonline.com
President . . . . Gilberto Mendoza
General Counsel/U.S. Spokesman . . . . Jimmy Binns
300 Walnut St., Philadelphia, PA 19106
(215) 922-4000
Ratings Chairman . . . . Bolivar Icaza
P.O. Box 1833, Panama 1, Rep. de Panama
TEL: 011-507-63-5167

WBC
(World Boxing Council)
Genova 33-503, Col. Juarez,
MEXICO, 06600, D.F., Mexico
TEL: 011-525-208-2440 www.wbcboxing.com
President . . . . Jose Sulaiman
Ratings Chairman . . . . Frank Quill
Press Information/U.S. Spokesman . . . . John Brister
411 Ballentine St., Bay St. Louis, MS 39520
(209) 796-9766

WBO
(World Boxing Organization)
1st Federal Bldg.
1056 Ave Munoz Revera, Suite 711
San Juan, P.R. 00927
(787) 765-4444 www.wbo-int.com
President . . . . Francisco Paco Valcarcel
Past Pres./Attorney . . . . Luis Batista Salas
Ratings Chairman . . . . Luis Perez
Public Relations Dir. . . . . Mario Rivera-Martino

Don King Productions, Inc.
501 Fairway Dr.
Deerfield Beach, FL 33441
(954) 418-5800 www.donking.com
President . . . . Don King
V.P. of Boxing Ops. . . . . Bob Goodman
Director of Public Relations . . . . TBA

Top Rank
3980 Howard Hughes Pkwy. Ste. 580
Las Vegas, NV 89109
(702) 732-2717 www.toprank.com
Chairman . . . . Bob Arum
Director of Public Relations . . . . Lee Samuels

COLLEGE SPORTS

NAIA
(National Assn. of Intercollegiate Athletics)
23500 W. 105th Street, Olathe, KS 66051
(913) 791-0044 www.naia.org
President-CEO . . . . Steve Baker
Director of Sports Information . . . . Dawn Harmon

NCAA
(National Collegiate Athletic Association)
P.O. Box 6222, Indianapolis, IN 46206
(317) 917-6222 www.ncaa.com
President . . . . Cedric Dempsey (retiring end of 2002)
Senior Vice President . . . . Daniel Boggan Jr.
V.P. of Enforcement . . . . David Price
Director of Public Relations . . . . TBA

WSF
(Women's Sports Foundation)
Eisenhower Park, East Meadow, NY 11554
(516) 542-4700 www.womenssportsfoundation.org
Founder . . . . Billie Jean King
Executive Director . . . . Donna Lopiano
President . . . . Julie Foudy
Sr. Comm. Coordinator . . . . Ellie Seifert

Major NCAA Conferences
See pages 443-451 for football coaches, basketball coaches, nicknames and colors of all Division I-A and I-AA football schools and Division I basketball schools.

ATLANTIC COAST CONFERENCE
P.O. Drawer ACC
Greensboro, NC 27417-6724
(336) 854-8787 www.theacc.com
Founded: 1953
Commissioner . . . . John Swofford
Asst. Commis. of Media Relations . . . . Brian Morrison
2002-03 members: BASKETBALL & FOOTBALL (9)—
Clemson, Duke, Florida St., Georgia Tech, Maryland, North Carolina, N.C. State, Virginia and Wake Forest.

Clemson University
Clemson, SC 29633
SID: (864) 656-2114
Founded: 1889   www.clemsontigers.com
     Enrollment: 17,101
President ....James F. Barker
Athletic Director ....Terry Don Phillips
Sports Information Director ....Tim Bourret

Duke University
Durham, NC 27708
SID: (919) 684-2633   www.goduke.com
Founded: 1838   Enrollment: 6,246
President ....Nannerl Keohane
Athletic Director ....Joe Alleva
Sports Information Director ....Jon Jackson

Florida State University
Tallahassee, FL 32316
SID: (850) 644-1403   www.seminoles.com
Founded: 1857   Enrollment: 35,500
President ....Talbot (Sandy) D'Alemberte
Athletic Director ....Dave Hart Jr.
Sports Information Director ....Rob Wilson

Georgia Tech
Atlanta, GA 30332
SID: (404) 894-5445   www.ramblinwreck.com
Founded: 1885   Enrollment: 15,000
President ....Wayne Clough
Athletic Director ....Dave Braine
Sports Information Director ....Allison George

University of Maryland
College Park, MD 20741
SID: (301) 314-7064   www.umterps.com
Founded: 1807   Enrollment: 34,160
President ....Dr. Clayton D. Mote Jr.
Athletic Director ....Deborah Yow
Sports Information Director ....Dave Haglund

University of North Carolina
Chapel Hill, NC 27514
SID: (919) 962-2123   www.tarheelblue.com
Founded: 1789   Enrollment: 25,480
Chancellor ....James Moeser
Athletic Director ....Dick Baddour
Sports Information Director ....Steve Kirschner

North Carolina State University
Raleigh, NC 27695
SID: (919) 515-2102   www.gopack.com
Founded: 1887   Enrollment: 29,286
Chancellor ....Marye Anne Fox
Athletic Director ....Lee Fowler
Asst. AD for Media Relations ....Annabelle Vaughan

University of Virginia
Charlottesville, VA 22904
SID: (434) 982-5500   www.virginiasports.com
Founded: 1819   Enrollment: 18,848
President ....John T. Casteen III
Athletic Director ....Craig Littlepage
Sports Information Director ....Rich Murray

Wake Forest University
Winston-Salem, NC 27109
SID: (336) 758-5640   www.wakeforestsports.com
Founded: 1834   Enrollment: 4,080
President ....Thomas K. Hearn Jr.
Athletic Director ....Ron Wellman
Asst. Athletic Director/Media Relations ......Dean Buchan

BIG EAST CONFERENCE
222 Richmond Street, Suite 110, Providence, RI 02903
(401) 272-9108   www.bigeast.org
Founded: 1979
Commissioner ....Mike Tranghese
Assoc. Commissioner/Commun. ....John Paquette
     2002-03 members: BASKETBALL (14)—Boston College, Connecticut, Georgetown, Miami-FL, Notre Dame, Pittsburgh, Providence, Rutgers, St. John's, Seton Hall, Syracuse, Villanova, Virginia Tech and West Virginia; FOOTBALL (8)—Boston College, Miami-FL, Pittsburgh, Rutgers, Syracuse, Temple, Virginia Tech and West Virginia.

Boston College
Chestnut Hill, MA 02467
SID: (617) 552-3004   www.bceagles.com
Founded: 1863   Enrollment: 14,500
President ....Rev. William P. Leahy, S.J.
Athletic Director ....Gene DeFilippo
Sports Information Director ....Chris Cameron

University of Connecticut
Storrs, CT 06269
SID: (860) 486-3531   www.uconnhuskies.com
Founded: 1881   Enrollment: 23,419
President ....Philip Austin
Athletic Director ....Lew Perkins
Sports Information Director ....Michael Enright

Georgetown University
Washington, DC 20057
SID: (202) 687-2492   www.guhoyas.com
Founded: 1789   Enrollment: 6,418
President ....John J. DeGioia, Ph. D.
Athletic Director ....Joseph C. Lang
Sr. Sports Communication Director ....Bill Shapland

University of Miami
Coral Gables, FL 33146
SID: (305) 284-3244   www.hurricanesports.com
Founded: 1926   Enrollment: 13,963
President ....Dr. Donna E. Shalala
Athletic Director ....Paul Dee
Asst. Athletic Director/Communications ....Mark Pray

University of Notre Dame
Notre Dame, IN 46556
SID: (574) 631-7516   www.und.com
Founded: 1842   Enrollment: 10,310
President ....Rev. Edward (Monk) Malloy
Athletic Director ....Kevin White
Sports Information Director ....John Heisler

University of Pittsburgh
Pittsburgh, PA 15260
SID: (412) 648-8240   www.pittsburghpanthers.com
Founded: 1787   Enrollment: 33,554
Chancellor ....Mark A. Nordenberg
Athletic Director ....Steve Pederson
Sports Information Director .................E.J. Borghetti

Providence College
Providence, RI 02918
SID: (401) 865-2272   www.friars.com
Founded: 1917   Enrollment: 3,700
President ....Philip A. Smith, O.P.
Athletic Director ....Robert Driscoll
Sports Information Director ....Arthur Parks

Rutgers University
New Brunswick, NJ 08903
SID: (732) 445-4200   www.scarletknights.com
Founded: 1766   Enrollment: 33,500
Interim President ....Francis Lawrence
Athletic Director ....Robert E. Mulcahy III
Sports Information Director ....John Wooding

St. John's University
Jamaica, NY 11439
SID: (718) 990-1520 www.redstormsports.com
Founded: 1870 Enrollment: 18,300
President ....Rev. Donald J. Harrington, CM
Athletic Director ....David Wegrzyn
Sports Information Director ....Dominic Scianna

Seton Hall University
South Orange, NJ 07079
SID: (973) 761-9493 www.shupirates.com
Founded: 1856 Enrollment: 9,604
President ....Monsignor Robert Sheeran
Athletic Director ....Jeff Fogelson
Sports Information Director ....Marie Wozniak

Syracuse University
Syracuse, NY 13244
SID: (315) 443-2608 www.suathletics.com
Founded: 1870 Enrollment: 10,000
Chancellor ....Kenneth Shaw
Athletic Director ....Jake Crouthamel
Sports Information Director ....Sue Edson

Temple University
Philadelphia, PA 19122
SID: (215) 204-7445 www.owlsports.com
Founded: 1884 Enrollment: 30,000
President ....Dr. David Adamany
Athletic Director ....Bill Bradshaw
Sports Information Director ....Scott Cathcart

Villanova University
Villanova, PA 19085
SID: (610) 519-4120 www.villanova.edu
Founded: 1842 Enrollment: 6,295
President ....Rev. Edmund J. Dobbin, OSA
Athletic Director ....Vince Nicastro
Sports Information Director ....Dean Kenefick

Virginia Tech
Blacksburg, VA 24061
SID: (540) 231-6726 www.hokiesports.com
Founded: 1872 Enrollment: 25,000
President ....Charles Steger
Athletic Director ....Jim Weaver
Sports Information Director ....Dave Smith

West Virginia University
Morgantown, WV 26507
SID: (304) 293-2821 www.wvu.edu/~sports
Founded: 1867 Enrollment: 22,900
President ....David Hardesty
Athletic Director ....Ed Pastilong
Sports Information Director ....Shelly Poe

🐚   🐚   🐚

BIG 12 CONFERENCE
2201 Stemmons Fwy., Suite 2805
Dallas, TX 75207
(214) 742-1212 www.big12sports.com
Founded: 1996
Commissioner ....Kevin Weiberg
Assoc. Commis./Media Relations ....Bo Carter
2002-03 members: BASKETBALL & FOOTBALL (12)—
Baylor, Colorado, Iowa St., Kansas, Kansas St., Missouri,
Nebraska, Oklahoma, Oklahoma St., Texas, Texas A&M
and Texas Tech.

Baylor University
Waco, TX 76711
SID: (254) 710-2743 www.gobaylorbears.com
Founded: 1845 Enrollment: 14,118
President ....Robert B. Sloan
Athletic Director ....Tom Stanton
Sports Information Director ....Scott Stricklin

University of Colorado
Boulder, CO 80309
SID: (303) 492-5626 www.cubuffs.com
Founded: 1876 Enrollment: 26,035
President ....Dr. Elizabeth Hoffman
Athletic Director ....Dick Tharp
Sports Information Director ....Dave Plati

Iowa State University
Ames, IA 50011
SID: (515) 294-3372 www.cyclones.com
Founded: 1858 Enrollment: 27,815
President ....Gregory Geoffroy
Athletic Director ....Bruce Van De Velde
Sports Information Director ....Tom Kroeschell

University of Kansas
Lawrence, KS 66045
SID: (785) 864-3417 www.kuathletics.com
Founded: 1864 Enrollment: 26,894
Chancellor ....Robert Hemenway
Athletic Director ....Al Bohl
Asst. Athletic Director/Media Relations ....Doug Vance

Kansas State University
Manhattan, KS 66502
SID: (785) 532-6735 www.kstatesports.com
Founded: 1863 Enrollment: 21,500
President ....Jon Wefald
Athletic Director ....Tim Weiser
Sports Information Director ....Doug Dull

University of Missouri
Columbia, MO 65205
SID: (573) 882-0712 www.mutigers.com
Founded: 1839 Enrollment: 23,666
Chancellor ....Richard Wallace
Athletic Director ....Michael Alden
Media Relations Director ....Chad Moller

University of Nebraska
Lincoln, NE 68588
SID: (402) 472-2263 www.huskers.com
Founded: 1869 Enrollment: 25,000
Chancellor ....Harvey Perlman
Athletic Director ....Bill Byrne
Sports Information Director ....Chris Anderson

University of Oklahoma
Norman, OK 73019
SID: (405) 325-8231 www.soonersports.com
Founded: 1890 Enrollment: 28,954
President ....David Boren
Athletic Director ....Joe Castiglione
Dir. of Athletic Media Relations ....Kenny Mossman

Oklahoma State University
Stillwater, OK 74078
SID: (405) 744-7714 www.okstate.com
Founded: 1890 Enrollment: 21,000
President ....James Halligan
Athletic Director ....Harry Birdwell
Sports Information Director ....Steve Buzzard

University of Texas
Austin, TX 78713
SID: (512) 471-7437 www.texassports.com
Founded: 1883 Enrollment: 46,610
President ....Dr. Larry Faulkner
Athletic Director ....De Loss Dodds
Asst. AD for Media Relations ....John Bianco

Texas A&M University
College Station, TX 77843
SID: (979) 845-5725 — www.aggieathletics.com
Founded: 1876 — Enrollment: 44,081
President .... Dr. Robert Gates
Athletic Director .... Wally Groff
Asst. AD for Media Relations .... Alan Cannon

Texas Tech University
Lubbock, TX 79409
SID: (806) 742-3355 — www.texastech.com
Founded: 1923 — Enrollment: 24,101
Chancellor .... David R. Smith
Athletic Director .... Gerald Myers
Asst. Athletic Director/Media Relations .... Chris Cook

BIG TEN CONFERENCE
1500 West Higgins Road
Park Ridge, IL 60068-6300
(847) 696-1010 — www.bigten.org
Founded: 1896
Commissioner .... Jim Delany
Assoc. Commissioner of Media Relations .... Sue Lister
2002-03 members: BASKETBALL & FOOTBALL (11)—
Illinois, Indiana, Iowa, Michigan, Michigan St., Minnesota,
Northwestern, Ohio St., Penn St., Purdue and Wisconsin.

University of Illinois
Champaign, IL 61820
SID: (217) 333-1390 — www.fightingillini.com
Founded: 1867 — Enrollment: 36,000
President .... James J. Stukel
Athletic Director .... Ron Guenther
Dir. of Communications .... Kent Brown

Indiana University
Bloomington, IN 47408
SID: (812) 855-9399 — www.iuhoosiers.com
Founded: 1820 — Enrollment: 36,000
President .... Myles Brand
Athletic Director .... Michael McNeely
Sports Information Director .... Jeff Fanter

University of Iowa
Iowa City, IA 52242
SID: (319) 335-9411 — www.hawkeyesports.com
Founded: 1847 — Enrollment: 28,311
Interim President .... Willard Boyd
Athletic Director .... Bob Bowlsby
Sports Information Director .... Phil Haddy

University of Michigan
Ann Arbor, MI 48109
SID: (734) 763-1381 — www.mgoblue.com
Founded: 1817 — Enrollment: 38,248
President .... Mary Sue Coleman
Athletic Director .... William Martin
Sports Information Director .... Bruce Madej

Michigan State University
East Lansing, MI 48824
SID: (517) 355-2271 — www.msuspartans.com
Founded: 1855 — Enrollment: 44,227
President .... Peter McPherson
Athletic Director .... Ron Mason
Asst. AD for Media Relations .... John Lewandowski

University of Minnesota
Minneapolis, MN 55455
SID: (612) 625-4090 — www.gophersports.com
Founded: 1851 — Enrollment: 45,600
Interim President .... Robert Bruininks
Athletic Director .... Joel Maturi
Sports Information Director .... Shane Sandersfeld

Northwestern University
Evanston, IL 60208
SID: (847) 491-7503 — www.nusports.com
Founded: 1851 — Enrollment: 7,700
President .... Henry S. Bienen
Athletic Director .... Rick Taylor
Asst. Athletic Director/Media Services .... Mike Wolf

Ohio State University
Columbus, OH 43210
SID: (614) 292-6861 — www.ohiostatebuckeyes.com
Founded: 1870 — Enrollment: 47,952
President .... Karen A. Holbrook
Athletic Director .... Andy Geiger
Sports Information Director .... Steve Snapp

Penn State University
University Park, PA 16802
SID: (814) 865-1757 — www.gopsusports.com
Founded: 1855 — Enrollment: 41,050
President .... Graham Spanier
Athletic Director .... Tim Curley
Sports Information Director .... Jeff Nelson

Purdue University
West Lafayette, IN 47907
SID: (765) 494-3201 — www.purduesports.com
Founded: 1869 — Enrollment: 38,208
President .... Martin C. Jischke
Athletic Director .... Morgan Burke
Sports Information Director .... Tom Schott

University of Wisconsin
Madison, WI 53711
SID: (608) 262-1811 — www.uwbadgers.com
Founded: 1848 — Enrollment: 40,610
Chancellor .... John Wiley
Athletic Director .... Pat Richter
Sports Information Director .... Justin Doherty

CONFERENCE USA
35 East Wacker Drive, Suite 650, Chicago, IL 60601
(312) 553-0483 — www.c-usasports.com
Founded: 1995
Interim Commissioner .... Brenda Weare
Asst. Commissioner .... Brian Teter
2002-03 members: BASKETBALL (14)—UAB, Charlotte, Cincinnati, DePaul, East Carolina, Houston, Louisville,
Marquette, Memphis, Saint Louis, South Florida, Southern
Miss, TCU and Tulane; FOOTBALL (10)—UAB, Army, Cincinnati, East Carolina, Houston, Louisville, Memphis, Southern Miss, TCU and Tulane.

University of Alabama at Birmingham
Birmingham, AL 35294
SID: (205) 934-0722 — www.uabsports.com
Founded: 1969 — Enrollment: 16,081
President .... Carol Z. Garrison
Athletic Director .... Watson Brown
Asst. AD for Media Relations .... Norm Reilly

Army—U.S. Military Academy
West Point, NY 10996
SID: (845) 938-3303 — www.goarmysports.com
Founded: 1802 — Enrollment: 4,000
Superintendent .... Lt. Gen. William J. Lennox, Jr.
Athletic Director .... Rick Greenspan
Asst. AD for Media Relations .... Bob Beretta

University of Cincinnati
Cincinnati, OH 45221
SID: (513) 556-5191
Founded: 1819
President ....Dr. Joseph A. Steger
Athletic Director ....Bob Goin
Sports Information Director ....Tom Hathaway

www.ucbearcats.com
Enrollment: 34,000

DePaul University
Chicago, IL 60614
SID: (773) 325-7525
Founded: 1898
President ....Rev. John P. Minogue
Athletic Director ....Jean Ponsetto
Sports Information Director ....Scott Reed

www.depaulbluedemons.com
Enrollment: 20,548

East Carolina University
Greenville, NC 27858
SID: (252) 328-4522
Founded: 1907
Chancellor ....Dr. William V. Muse
Athletic Director ....Mike Hamrick
Sports Information Director ....Craig Wells

www.ecupirates.com
Enrollment: 19,700

University of Houston
Houston, TX 77204
SID: (713) 743-9404
Founded: 1927
President ....Arthur K. Smith
Athletic Director ....Dave Maggard
Sports Information Director ....Chris Burkhalter

www.uhcougars.com
Enrollment: 32,650

University of Louisville
Louisville, KY 40292
SID: (502) 852-6581
Founded: 1798
Acting President ....James Ramsey
Athletic Director ....Tom Jurich
Sports Information Director ....Kenny Klein

www.uoflsports.com
Enrollment: 22,000

Marquette University
Milwaukee, WI 53233
SID: (414) 288-7447
Founded: 1881
President ....Rev. Robert A. Wild S.J.
Athletic Director ....Bill Cords
Sports Information Director ....John Farina

www.gomarquette.com
Enrollment: 10,600

University of Memphis
Memphis, TN 38152
SID: (901) 678-2337
Founded: 1912
President ....Dr. Shirley Raines
Athletic Director ...........................R.C. Johnson
Sports Information Director ....Bob Winn

www.gotigersgo.com
Enrollment: 20,825

University of North Carolina at Charlotte
Charlotte, NC 28223
SID: (704) 687-6312
Founded: 1946
Chancellor ....J. H. Woodward
Athletic Director ....Judy Rose
Sports Information Director ....Tom Whitestone

www.charlotte49ers.com
Enrollment: 18,308

Saint Louis University
St. Louis, MO 63103
SID: (314) 977-2524
Founded: 1818
President ....Rev. Lawrence Biondi, S.J.
Athletic Director ....Doug Woolard
Sport Information Director ....Doug McIlhagga

www.slubillikens.com
Enrollment: 11,145

University of South Florida
Tampa, FL 33620
SID: (813) 974-4086
Founded: 1956
President ....Judy Genshaft
Athletic Director ....Lee Roy Selmon
Sports Information Director ....John Gerdes

www.gousfbulls.com
Enrollment: 36,000

University of Southern Mississippi
Hattiesburg, MS 39406
SID: (601) 266-4503
Founded: 1910
President ....Dr. Shelby Thames
Athletic Director ....Rich Giannini
Asst. AD for Media Relations ....Mike Montoro

www.southernmiss.com
Enrollment: 15,233

TCU—Texas Christian University
Fort Worth, TX 76129
SID: (817) 257-7969
Founded: 1873
Chancellor ....Dr. Michael Ferrari
Athletic Director ....Eric Hyman
Director of Media Relations ....Steve Fink

www.gofrogs.com
Enrollment: 8,066

Tulane University
New Orleans, LA 70118
SID: (504) 865-5506
Founded: 1834
President ....Dr. Scott S. Cowen
Athletic Director ....Rick Dickson
Asst. AD for Media Relations ....Donna Turner

www.tulanegreenwave.com
Enrollment: 12,381

❧   ❧   ❧

MID-AMERICAN CONFERENCE
24 Public Square, 15th Floor, Cleveland, OH 44113
(216) 566-4622
Founded: 1946
Commissioner ....Rick Chryst
Director of Communications ....Gary Richter
2002-03 members: FOOTBALL (14)—Akron, Ball St., Bowling Green, Buffalo, Central Florida, Central Michigan, Eastern Michigan, Kent St., Marshall, Miami-OH, Northern Illinois, Ohio University, Toledo and Western Michigan; BASKETBALL (13)—all except Central Florida.

www.mac-sports.com

University of Akron
Akron, OH 44325
SID: (330) 972-7468
Founded: 1870
President ....Luis Proenza
Athletic Director ....Michael J. Thomas
Director of Media Relations ....Shawn Nestor

www.gozips.com
Enrollment: 24,358

Ball State University
Muncie, IN 47306
SID: (765) 285-8242
Founded: 1918
President ....Dr. Blaine Brownell
Athletic Director ....Lawrence "Bubba" Cunningham
Sports Information Director ....Joe Hernandez

www.ballstatesports.com
Enrollment: 17,622

Bowling Green State University
Bowling Green, OH 43403
SID: (419) 372-7075
Founded: 1910
President ....Sidney Ribeau
Athletic Director ....Paul Krebs
Director of Athletic Communications .......J.D. Campbell

www.bgsufalcons.com
Enrollment: 20,650

University of Buffalo
Buffalo, NY 14260
SID: (716) 645-6311
Founded: 1846
President ....William R. Greiner
Athletic Director ....Bob Arkeilpane
Sports Information Director ....Paul Vecchio

www.ubathletics.buffalo.edu
Enrollment: 25,838

University of Central Florida
Orlando, FL 32816
SID: (407) 823-2729   www.ucfathletics.com
Founded: 1963   Enrollment: 38,000
President ....Dr. John C. Hitt
Athletic Director ....Steve Orsini
Sports Information Director ....John Marini

Central Michigan University
Mt. Pleasant, MI 48859
SID: (989) 774-3277   www.cmuchippewas.com
Founded: 1892   Enrollment: 28,015
President ....Michael Rao
Athletic Director ....Herb Deromedi
Sports Information Director ....Fred Stabley Jr.

Eastern Michigan University
Ypsilanti, MI 48197
SID: (734) 487-0317   www.emich.edu/goeagles
Founded: 1849   Enrollment: 24,000
President ....Dr. Samuel Kirkpatrick
Athletic Director ....Dr. David Diles
Sports Information Director ....Jim Streeter

Kent State University
Kent, OH 44242
SID: (330) 672-2110   www.kent.edu/athletics
Founded: 1910   Enrollment: 30,287
President ....Carol Cartwright
Athletic Director ....Laing Kennedy
Sports Information Director ....Will Roleson

Marshall University
Huntington, WV 25715
SID: (304) 696-4660   www.herdzone.com
Founded: 1837   Enrollment: 16,038
President ....Dan Angel
Athletic Director ....Bob Marcum
Sports Information Director ....Ricky Hazel

Miami University
Oxford, OH 45056
SID: (513) 529-4327   www.muredhawks.com
Founded: 1809   Enrollment: 16,000
President ....James C. Garland
Interim Athletic Director ....Steve Snyder
Athletics Media Relations Director ....Mike Harris

Northern Illinois University
DeKalb, IL 60115
SID: (815) 753-1706   www.niu.edu/athletics
Founded: 1895   Enrollment: 23,783
President ....John G. Peters
Athletic Director ....Cary Groth
Sports Information Director ....Michael Korcek

Ohio University
Athens, OH 45701
SID: (740) 593-1298   www.ohiobobcats.com
Founded: 1804   Enrollment: 26,404
President ....Robert Glidden
Athletic Director ....Tom Boeh
Dir. of Broadcasting and Media Relations ......Derek Scott

University of Toledo
Toledo, OH 43606
SID: (419) 530-4920   www.utrockets.com
Founded: 1872   Enrollment: 20,313
President ....Dr. Daniel Johnson
Athletic Director ....Mike O'Brien
Sports Information Director ....Paul Helgren

Western Michigan University
Kalamazoo, MI 49008
SID: (616) 387-4138   www.wmubroncos.com
Founded: 1903   Enrollment: 28,657
President ....Dr. Elson Floyd
Athletic Director ....Kathy Beauregard
Sports Information Director ....Dan Jankowski

     ❧   ❧   ❧

MOUNTAIN WEST CONFERENCE
15455 Gleneagle Drive, Suite 200
Colorado Springs, CO 80921
(719) 488-4040   www.themwc.com
Founded: 1999
Commissioner ....Craig Thompson
Associate Comm./Communications ....Bob Burda
     2002-03 members: BASKETBALL & FOOTBALL (8)—
Air Force, BYU, Colorado St., UNLV, New Mexico, San
Diego St., Utah and Wyoming.

U.S. Air Force Academy
US Academy, CO 80840
SID: (719) 333-2313   www.airforcesports.com
Founded: 1959   Enrollment: 4,000
Superintendent ....Lt. Gen. John R. Dallager
Athletic Director ....Col. Randall W. Spetman
Asst. AD for Media Relations ....Troy Garnhart

Brigham Young University
Provo, UT 84602
SID: (801) 378-4911   www.byucougars.com
Founded: 1875   Enrollment: 30,069
President ....Merrill J. Bateman
Athletic Director ....Val Hale
Sports Information Director ....Duff Tittle

Colorado State University
Fort Collins, CO 80523
SID: (970) 491-5067   www.csurams.com
Founded: 1870   Enrollment: 23,600
President ....Dr. Albert Yates
Athletic Director ....Jeff Hathaway
Sports Information Director ....Gary Ozzello

University of New Mexico
Albuquerque, NM 87131
SID: (505) 925-5520   www.golobos.com
Founded: 1889   Enrollment: 24,250
President ....F. Chris Garcia
Athletic Director ....Rudy Davalos
Sports Information Director ....Greg Remington

San Diego State University
San Diego, CA 92182
SID: (619) 594-5547   www.goaztecs.com
Founded: 1897   Enrollment: 34,171
President ....Dr. Stephen L. Weber
Athletic Director ....Rick Bay
Sports Information Director ....Kevin Klintworth

UNLV—University of Nevada, Las Vegas
Las Vegas, NV 89154
SID: (702) 895-3207   www.unlvrebels.com
Founded: 1957   Enrollment: 23,000
President ....Dr. Carol Harter
Athletic Director ....John Robinson
Sports Information Director ....Andy Grossman

University of Utah
Salt Lake City, UT 84112
SID: (801) 581-3510   www.utahutes.com
Founded: 1850   Enrollment: 25,391
President ....Dr. Bernard Machen
Athletic Director ....Dr. Chris Hill
Sports Information Director ....Liz Abel

University of Wyoming
Laramie, WY 82071
SID: (307) 766-2256 www.wyomingathletics.com
Founded: 1886 Enrollment: 12,402
President ....Philip Dubois
Athletic Director ....Lee Moon
Sports Information Director ....Kevin McKinney

         🍃   🍃   🍃

PACIFIC-10 CONFERENCE
800 South Broadway, Suite 400
Walnut Creek, CA 94596
(925) 932-4411 www.pac-10.org
Founded: 1915
Commissioner ....Thomas Hansen
Asst. Commissioner, Public Relations ....Jim Muldoon
2002-03 members: BASKETBALL & FOOTBALL (10)—
Arizona, Arizona St., California, Oregon, Oregon St.,
Stanford, UCLA, USC, Washington and Washington St.

University of Arizona
Tucson, AZ 85721
SID: (520) 621-4163 www.arizonaathletics.com
Founded: 1885 Enrollment: 35,000
President ....Peter Likins
Athletic Director ....Jim Livengood
Sports Information Director ....Tom Duddleston

Arizona State University
Tempe, AZ 85287
SID: (480) 965-6592 www.thesundevils.com
Founded: 1885 Enrollment: 45,693
President ....Michael Crow
Athletic Director ....Gene Smith
Sports Information Director ....Mark Brand

University of California
Berkeley, CA 94720
SID: (510) 642-5363 www.calbears.com
Founded: 1868 Enrollment: 32,000
Chancellor ....Robert Berdahl
Athletic Director ....Steve Gladstone
Exec. Assoc. AD for Communications ....Bob Rose

University of Oregon
Eugene, OR 97401
SID: (541) 346-5488 www.goducks.com
Founded: 1876 Enrollment: 19,091
President ....Dave Frohnmayer
Athletic Director ....Bill Moos
Sports Information Director ....Dave Williford

Oregon State University
Corvallis, OR 97331
SID: (541) 737-3720 www.osubeavers.com
Founded: 1868 Enrollment: 19,000
President ....Paul G. Risser
Athletic Director ....Bob De Carolis
Sports Information Director ....Hal Cowan

Stanford University
Stanford, CA 94305
SID: (650) 723-4418 www.gostanford.com
Founded: 1891 Enrollment: 13,075
President ....John Hennessy
Athletic Director ....Ted Leland
Sports Information Director ....Gary Migdol

UCLA—Univ. of California, Los Angeles
Los Angeles, CA 90024
SID: (310) 206-6831 www.uclabruins.com
Founded: 1919 Enrollment: 36,890
Chancellor ....Albert Carnesale
Athletic Director ....Dan Guerrero
Sports Information Director ....Marc Dellins

USC—Univ. of Southern California
Los Angeles, CA 90089
SID: (213) 740-8480 www.usctrojans.com
Founded: 1880 Enrollment: 28,600
President ....Steven Sample
Athletic Director ....Mike Garrett
Sports Information Director ....Tim Tessalone

University of Washington
Seattle, WA 98195
SID: (206) 543-2230 www.gohuskies.com
Founded: 1861 Enrollment: 26,800
President ....Richard McCormick
Athletic Director ....Barbara Hedges
Asst. AD for Media Relations ....Jim Daves

Washington State University
Pullman, WA 99164
SID: (509) 335-2684 www.wsucougars.com
Founded: 1890 Enrollment: 20,500
President ....V. Lane Rawlins
Athletic Director ....Jim Sterk
Sports Information Director ....Rod Commons

         🍃   🍃   🍃

SOUTHEASTERN CONFERENCE
2201 Richard Arrington Blvd. North
Birmingham, AL 35203
(205) 458-3000 www.secsports.com
Founded: 1933
Commissioner ....Mike Slive
Assoc. Commis. of Media Relations ....Charles Bloom
2002-03 members: BASKETBALL & FOOTBALL (12)—
Alabama, Arkansas, Auburn, Florida, Georgia, Kentucky,
LSU, Mississippi St., Ole Miss, South Carolina, Tennessee
and Vanderbilt.

University of Alabama
Tuscaloosa, AL 35487
SID: (205) 348-6084 www.rolltide.com
Founded: 1831 Enrollment: 19,400
Interim President ....Dr. J. Barry Mason
Athletic Director ....Mal Moore
Assoc. AD for Media Relations ....Larry White

University of Arkansas
Fayetteville, AR 72701
SID: (479) 575-2751 www.hogwired.com www.ladybacks.com
Founded: 1871 Enrollment: 15,795
Chancellor ....John White
Athletic Director ....Frank Broyles
Women's Athletic Director ....Bev Lewis
Sports Information Director ....Kevin Trainor

Auburn University
Auburn, AL 36831
SID: (334) 844-9800 www.auburn.edu/athletics
Founded: 1856 Enrollment: 21,775
President ....William Walker
Athletic Director ....David Housel
Sports Information Director ....Meredith Jenkins

University of Florida
Gainesville, FL 32604
SID: (352) 375-4683 ext. 6100 www.gatorzone.com
Founded: 1853 Enrollment: 45,937
President ....Charles E. Young
Athletic Director ....Jeremy Foley
Asst. AD for Sports Information ....Steve McClain

University of Georgia
Athens, GA 30603
SID: (706) 542-1621   www.georgiadogs.com
Founded: 1785   Enrollment: 32,400
President ....Michael F. Adams
Athletic Director ....Vince Dooley
Sports Information Director ....Claude Felton

University of Kentucky
Lexington, KY 40506
SID: (859) 257-3838   www.ukathletics.com
Founded: 1865   Enrollment: 32,500
President ....Dr. Lee Todd
Athletic Director ....Mitch Barnhart
Director of Media Relations ....Brooks Downing

LSU—Louisiana State University
Baton Rouge, LA 70894
SID: (225) 578-8226   www.lsusports.net
Founded: 1860   Enrollment: 29,022
Chancellor ....Dr. Mark Emmert
Athletic Director ....Skip Bertman
Sports Information Director ....Michael Bonnette

Mississippi State University
Starkville, MS 39762
SID: (662) 325-2703   www.mstateathletics.com
Founded: 1878   Enrollment: 16,878
Interim President ....Dr. J. Charles Lee
Athletic Director ....Larry Templeton
Sports Information Director ....Mike Nemeth

Ole Miss—University of Mississippi
University, MS 38677
SID: (662) 915-7522   www.olemisssports.com
Founded: 1848   Enrollment: 14,429
Chancellor ....Dr. Robert C. Khayat
Athletic Director ....Pete Boone
Sports Information Director ....Langston Rogers

University of South Carolina
Columbia, SC 29208
SID: (803) 777-5204   www.uscsports.com
Founded: 1801   Enrollment: 23,728
President ....Dr. Andrew Sorensen
Athletic Director ....Mike McGee
Sports Information Director ....Kerry Tharp

University of Tennessee
Knoxville, TN 37996
SID: (865) 974-1212   www.utsports.com   www.utladyvols.com
Founded: 1794   Enrollment: 25,587
President ....John W. Shumaker
Athletic Director ....Doug Dickey
Women's Athletic Director ....Joan Cronan
Sports Information Director ....Bud Ford

Vanderbilt University
Nashville, TN 37212
SID: (615) 322-4121   www.vucommodores.com
Founded: 1873   Enrollment: 6,037
Chancellor ....Gordon Gee
Athletic Director ....Todd Turner
Sports Information Director ....Rod Williamson

SUN BELT CONFERENCE
601 Poydras Street, Suite 2355
New Orleans, LA 70130
(504) 299-9066   www.sunbeltsports.org
Founded: 1976
Commissioner ....Wright Waters
Assoc. Commissioner/Media Relations ......Judy Wilson
   2002-03 members: BASKETBALL (11)—Arkansas-Little Rock, Arkansas St., Denver, Florida International, LA-Lafayette, Middle Tenn. St., New Mexico St., New Orleans, North Texas, South Alabama and Western Kentucky; FOOTBALL (7)—Arkansas St., Idaho, LA-Lafayette, LA-Monroe, Middle Tenn. State, New Mexico St. and North Texas.

Arkansas-Little Rock
Little Rock, AR 72204
SID: (501) 569-3449   www.ualr.edu/~athletics
Founded: 1927   Enrollment: 10,411
Chancellor ....Charles E. Hathaway
Athletic Director ....Chris Peterson
Sports Information Director ....Kevin Tankersley

Arkansas State
Jonesboro, AR 72467
SID: (870) 972-2541   www.asuindians.com
Founded: 1909   Enrollment: 10,568
President ....Dr. J. Leslie Wyatt
Athletic Director ....Dr. Dean Lee
Sports Information Director ....Gina Bowman

University of Denver
Denver, CO 80208
SID: (303) 871-4990   www.denverpioneers.com
Founded: 1864   Enrollment: 9,300
Chancellor ....Daniel L. Ritchie
Athletic Director ....Dr. M. Dianne Murphy
Director of Sports Media Relations ....Marla Rodriguez

Florida International University
Miami, FL 33199
SID: (305) 348-3164   www.fiu.edu/orgs/athletics
Founded: 1889   Enrollment: 33,000
President ....Modesto A. Maidique
Athletic Director ....Rick Mello
Asst. AD/Media Relations ....Rich Kelch

University of Idaho
Moscow, ID 83844
SID: (208) 885-0245   www.uiathletics.com
Founded: 1889   Enrollment: 12,067
President ....Bob Hoover
Athletic Director ....Mike Bohn
Asst. AD/Media Relations ....Becky Paull

University of Louisiana at Lafayette
Lafayette, LA 70506
SID: (337) 482-6331   www.ragincajuns.com
Founded: 1898   Enrollment: 14,869
President ....Ray Authement
Athletic Director ....Nelson Schexnayder
Sports Information Director ....Daryl Cetnar

University of Louisiana at Monroe
Monroe, LA 71209
SID: (318) 342-5460   www.ulmathletics.com
Founded: 1931   Enrollment: 8,760
President ....Dr. James E. Cofer
Athletic Director ....Bruce Hanks
Sports Information Director ....Hank Largin

Middle Tennessee State
Murfreesboro, TN 37132
SID: (615) 898-2450   www.goblueraiders.com
Founded: 1911   Enrollment: 20,073
President ....Dr. Sidney A. McPhee
Athletic Director ....Boots Donnelly
Sports Information Director ....Mark Owens

New Mexico State
Las Cruces, NM 88003
SID: (505) 646-3929   www.nmstatesports.com
Founded: 1888   Enrollment: 14,064
President ....Dr. Jay Gogue
Athletic Director ....Brian Faison
Asst. AD/Media Relations ....Sean Johnson

University of New Orleans
New Orleans, LA 70148
SID: (504) 280-6284   www.unoprivateers.com
Founded: 1958   Enrollment: 17,014
Chancellor ....Dr. Gregory O'Brien
Athletic Director ....Bob Brown
Sports Information Director ....Bob Boyle

University of North Texas
Denton, TX 76203
SID: (940) 565-2476   www.unt.edu/meangreen
Founded: 1890   Enrollment: 27,909
President ....Dr. Norval F. Pohl
Athletic Director ....Rick Villarreal
Asst. AD/Media Services ....Eric Capper

University of South Alabama
Mobile, AL 36688
SID: (251) 460-7035   www.usajaguars.com
Founded: 1963   Enrollment: 12,315
President ....V. Gordon Moulton
Athletic Director ....Joe Gottfried
Director of Athletic Media Relations ....Matt Smith

Western Kentucky University
Bowling Green, KY 42101
SID: (270) 745-4298   www.wkusports.com
Founded: 1906   Enrollment: 16,579
President ....Dr. Gary Ransdell
Athletic Director ....Dr. Camden Wood Selig
Sports Information Director ....Paul Just

ᔰ   ᔰ   ᔰ

WESTERN ATHLETIC CONFERENCE
9250 East Costilla Ave., Suite 300
Englewood, CO 80112
(303) 799-9221   www.wacsports.com
Founded: 1962
Commissioner ....Karl Benson
Asst. Commiss./Media Relations ....Dave Chaffin
   2002-03 members: BASKETBALL & FOOTBALL (10)—
Boise St., Fresno St., Hawaii, Louisiana Tech, Nevada,
Rice, San Jose St., SMU, Tulsa and UTEP.

Boise State
Boise, ID 83725
SID: (208) 426-1515   www.broncosports.com
Founded: 1932   Enrollment: 17,161
President ....Charles P. Ruch
Athletic Director ....Gene Bleymaier
Sports Information Director ....Max Corbet

Fresno State University
Fresno, CA 93740
SID: (559) 278-2509   www.gobulldogs.com
Founded: 1911   Enrollment: 20,013
President ....Dr. John D. Welty
Athletic Director ....Scott Johnson
Sports Information Director ....Steve Weakland

University of Hawaii
Honolulu, HI 96822
SID: (808) 956-7523   www.uhathletics.hawaii.edu
Founded: 1907   Enrollment: 17,828
President ....Dr. Evan Dobelle
Athletic Director ....Herman Frazier
Media Relations Director ....Lois Manin

Louisiana Tech University
Ruston, LA 71272
SID: (318) 257-3144   www.latechsports.com
Founded: 1894   Enrollment: 10,708
President ....Dan Reneau
Athletic Director ....Jim Oakes
Sports Information Director ....Malcolm Butler

University of Nevada
Reno, NV 89557
SID: (775) 784-6900   www.nevadawolfpack.com
Founded: 1874   Enrollment: 14,000
President ....Dr. John Lilley
Athletic Director ....Chris Ault
Media Services Director ....Jamie Klund

Rice University
Houston, TX 77005
SID: (713) 348-5775   www.riceowls.com
Founded: 1912   Enrollment: 4,320
President ....Dr. Malcolm Gillis
Athletic Director ....Bobby May
Sports Information Director ....Bill Cousins

San Jose State University
San Jose, CA 95192
SID: (408) 924-1217   www.sjsuspartans.com
Founded: 1857   Enrollment: 27,000
President ....Dr. Robert L. Caret
Athletic Director ....Chuck Bell
Sports Information Director ....Lawrence Fan

SMU—Southern Methodist University
Dallas, TX 75275
SID: (214) 768-2883   www.smumustangs.com
Founded: 1911   Enrollment: 10,038
President ....Dr. R. Gerald Turner
Athletic Director ....Jim Copeland
Sports Information Director ....Chris Walker

University of Tulsa
Tulsa, OK 74104
SID: (918) 631-2395   www.tulsahurricane.com
Founded: 1894   Enrollment: 4,100
President ....Dr. Bob Lawless
Athletic Director ....Judy MacLeod
Sports Information Director ....Don Tomkalski

UTEP—University of Texas at El Paso
El Paso, TX 79902
SID: (915) 747-6653   www.utepathletics.com
Founded: 1914   Enrollment: 16,220
President ....Dr. Diana Natalicio
Athletic Director ....Bob Stull
Sports Information Director ....Jeff Darby

ᔰ   ᔰ   ᔰ

Major Independents
Division I-A football independents in 2002.

University of Connecticut
Storrs, CT 06269
SID: (860) 486-3531   www.uconnhuskies.com
Founded: 1881   Enrollment: 23,419
President ....Philip Austin
Athletic Director ....Lew Perkins
Sports Information Director ....Michael Enright

Navy—U.S. Naval Academy
Annapolis, MD 21402
SID: (410) 293-2700   www.navysports.com
Founded: 1845   Enrollment: 4,000
Superintendent ....Vice Adm. Richard Naughton
Athletic Director ....Chet Gladchuk
Sports Information Director ....Scott Strasemeier

University of Notre Dame
Notre Dame, IN 46556
SID: (574) 631-7516   www.und.com
Founded: 1842   Enrollment: 10,310
President ....Rev. Edward (Monk) Malloy
Athletic Director ....Kevin White
Sports Information Director ....John Heisler

University of South Florida
Tampa, FL 33620
SID: (813) 974-4086   www.gousfbulls.com
Founded: 1956   Enrollment: 36,000
President ....Judy Genshaft
Athletic Director ....Lee Roy Selmon
Sports Information Director ....John Gerdes

Troy State University
Troy, AL 36082
SID: (334) 670-3229   www.troyst.edu/athletics
Founded: 1887   Enrollment: 6,630
Chancellor ....Dr. Jack Hawkins Jr.
Athletic Director ....Johnny Williams
Athletics Media Relations Dir. ....Tom Strother

Utah State University
Logan, UT 84322
SID: (435) 797-1361   www.utahstateaggies.com
Founded: 1888   Enrollment: 21,490
President ....Dr. Kermit L. Hall
Athletic Director ....Rance Pugmire
Asst. AD for Media Relations ....Mike Strauss

    🕸   🕸   🕸

Other Major Division I Conferences
Conferences that play either Division I basketball or Division I-AA football, or both.

America East
10 High St., Suite 860, Boston, MA 02110
(617) 695-6369   www.americaeast.com
Founded: 1979
Commissioner ....Chris Monasch
Director of Communications ....Matt Bourque
    2002-03 members: BASKETBALL (9)—Albany, Binghamton, Boston University, Hartford, Maine, New Hampshire, Northeastern, Stony Brook and Vermont.

Atlantic Sun Conference
3370 Vineville Ave., Suite 108-B
Macon, GA 31204
(478) 474-3394   www.atlanticsun.org
Founded: 1978
Commissioner ....Bill Bibb
Asst. Dir. of Media Relations ....Jo-Anne Gonzalez
    2002-03 members: BASKETBALL (12)—Belmont, Campbell, Central Florida, Florida Atlantic, Gardner-Webb, Georgia St., Jacksonville, Jacksonville St., Mercer, Samford, Stetson and Troy St.

Atlantic 10 Conference
230 S. Broad St., Suite 1700
Philadelphia, PA 19102
(215) 545-6678   www.atlantic10.org
Founded: 1976   A-10 Football founded: 1997
Commissioner ....Linda Bruno
Asst. Commissioner/P.R. ....Ray Cella
    2002-03 members: BASKETBALL (12)—Dayton, Duquesne, Fordham, George Washington, La Salle, Massachusetts, Rhode Island, Richmond, St. Bonaventure, St. Joseph's-PA, Temple and Xavier-OH. FOOTBALL (11)—Delaware, Hofstra, James Madison, Maine, Massachusetts, New Hampshire, Northeastern, Rhode Island, Richmond, Villanova and William & Mary.

Big Sky Conference
2491 Washington Blvd. Suite 201
Ogden, UT 84401
(801) 392-1978   www.bigskyconf.com
Founded: 1963
Commissioner ....Douglas Fullerton
Asst. Commissioner, Media Relations .....Dusty Clements
    2002-03 members: BASKETBALL & FOOTBALL (8)—CS-Sacramento, Eastern Washington, Idaho St., Montana, Montana St., Northern Arizona, Portland St. and Weber St.

Big South Conference
6428 Bannington Dr., Ste A
Charlotte, NC 28226
(704) 341-7990   www.bigsouthsports.com
Founded: 1983
Commissioner ....Kyle Kallander
Asst. Commissioner ....Drew Dickerson
    2002-03 members: BASKETBALL (9)—Birmingham Southern, Charleston Southern, Coastal Carolina, Elon, High Point, Liberty, NC-Asheville, Radford and Winthrop. FOOTBALL (4)—Charleston Southern, Elon, Gardner-Webb, Liberty.

Big West Conference
Two Corporate Park, Suite 206
Irvine, CA 92606
(949) 261-2525   www.bigwest.org
Founded: 1969
Commissioner ....Dennis Farrell
Director of Information ....Michael Daniels
    2002-03 members: BASKETBALL (10)—CS-Fullerton, CS-Northridge, Cal Poly, Idaho, Long Beach St., Pacific, UC-Irvine, UC-Riverside, UC-Santa Barbara and Utah St.

Colonial Athletic Association
8625 Patterson Ave., Richmond, VA 23229
(804) 754-1616   www.caasports.com
Founded: 1985
Commissioner ....Thomas E. Yeager
Asst. Commissioner/Commun. ....Rob Washburn
    2002-03 members: BASKETBALL (10)—Delaware, Drexel, George Mason, Hofstra, James Madison, NC-Wilmington, Old Dominion, Towson, Virginia Commonwealth and William & Mary.

Gateway Football Conference
1818 Chouteau Ave.
St. Louis, MO 63103
(314) 421-2268   www.gatewayfootball.org
Founded: 1985
Commissioner ....Patty Viverito
Asst. Commissioner ....Mike Kern
    2002 members: FOOTBALL (8)—Illinois St., Indiana St., Northern Iowa, Southern Illinois, SW Missouri St., Western Illinois, Western Kentucky and Youngstown St.

Horizon League
201 South Capitol Ave., Suite 500
Indianapolis, IN 46225
(317) 237-5622   www.horizonleague.org
Founded: 1979
Commissioner . . . . .Jon LeCrone
Associate Commissioner . . . . .Terry Powers
    2002-03 members: BASKETBALL (9)—Butler, Cleveland St., Detroit Mercy, Illinois-Chicago, Loyola-IL, Wisconsin-Green Bay, Wisconsin-Milwaukee, Wright St. and Youngstown St.

Ivy League
330 Alexander Street
Princeton, NJ 08544
(609) 258-6426   www.ivyleaguesports.com
Founded: 1954
Executive Director . . . . .Jeffrey Orleans
Director of Information .Brett Hoover
    2002-03 members: BASKETBALL & FOOTBALL (8)—Brown, Columbia, Cornell, Dartmouth, Harvard, Pennsylvania, Princeton and Yale.

Metro Atlantic Athletic Conference
712 Amboy Avenue
Edison, NJ 08837
(732) 738-5455   www.maacsports.com
Founded: 1980
Commissioner . . . . .Richard Ensor
Director of Media Relations . . . . Jill Skotarczak
    2002-03 members: BASKETBALL (10)—Canisius, Fairfield, Iona, Loyola-MD, Manhattan, Marist, Niagara, Rider, St. Peter's and Siena. FOOTBALL (8)—Canisius, Duquesne, Fairfield, Iona, La Salle, Marist, St. Peter's and Siena.

Mid-Continent Conference
340 West Butterfield Rd., Ste 3D
Elmhurst, IL 60126
(630) 516-0661   www.mid-con.com
Founded: 1982
Commissioner . . . . Jon Steinbrecher
Director of Media Relations . . . . .Tony Hamilton
    2002-03 members: BASKETBALL (8)—Chicago St., Indiana U-Purdue U Indianapolis, UMKC, Oakland, Oral Roberts, Southern Utah, Valparaiso and Western Illinois.

Mid-Eastern Athletic Conference
102 North Elm St.
SE Building, Suite 401
Greensboro, NC 27401
(336) 275-9961   www.meacsports.com
Founded: 1970
Commissioner . . . . .Dr. Dennis Thomas
Director of Media Relations . . . . .LeCounte Conaway
    2002-03 members: BASKETBALL (11)—Bethune-Cookman, Coppin St., Delaware St., Florida A&M, Hampton, Howard, MD-Eastern Shore, Morgan St., Norfolk St., North Carolina A&T and South Carolina St.; FOOTBALL (9)—all but Coppin St. and MD-Eastern Shore.

Missouri Valley Conference
1818 Chouteau Ave.
St. Louis, MO 63103
(314) 421-0339   www.mvc-sports.com
Founded: 1907
Commissioner . . . . .Doug Elgin
Asst. Commiss. Media Rel. . . . . Jack Watkins & Mike Kern
    2002-03 members: BASKETBALL (10)—Bradley, Creighton, Drake, Evansville, Illinois St., Indiana St., Northern Iowa, Southern Illinois, SW Missouri St. and Wichita St.

Northeast Conference
200 Cottontail Lane, Vantage Court North
Somerset, NJ 08873
(732) 469-0440   www.northeastconference.org
Founded: 1981
Commissioner . . . . John Iamarino
Asst. Commissioner, Public Relations . . . . .Ron Ratner
    2002-03 members: BASKETBALL (12)—Cent. Conn. St., Fairleigh Dickinson, LIU-Brooklyn, Maryland-Baltimore County, Monmouth, Mount St. Mary's, Quinnipiac, Robert Morris, Sacred Heart, St. Francis-NY, St. Francis-PA and Wagner. FOOTBALL (9)—Albany, Cent. Conn. St., Monmouth, Robert Morris, Sacred Heart, St. Francis-PA, St. John's, Stony Brook and Wagner.

Ohio Valley Conference
278 Franklin Road, Suite 103
Brentwood, TN 37027
(615) 371-1698   www.ovcsports.com
Founded: 1948
Commissioner . . . . .Dan Beebe
Director of Communications . . . . .Ryan Altizer
    2002-03 members: BASKETBALL (9)—Austin Peay St., Eastern Illinois, Eastern Kentucky, Morehead St., Murray St., SE Missouri St., Tennessee-Martin, Tennessee St. and Tennessee Tech; FOOTBALL (7)—Eastern Illinois, Eastern Kentucky, Murray St., SE Missouri St., Tennessee-Martin, Tennessee St. and Tennessee Tech.

Patriot League
3773 Corporate Pkwy, Suite 190
Center Valley, PA 18034
(610) 289-1950   www.patriotleague.com
Founded: 1984
Executive Director .Carolyn Femovich
Director of Media Relations . . . . .Tom Byrnes
    2002-03 members: BASKETBALL (8)—American, Army, Bucknell, Colgate, Holy Cross, Lafayette, Lehigh and Navy; FOOTBALL (8)—Bucknell, Colgate, Fordham, Georgetown, Holy Cross, Lafayette, Lehigh and Towson.

Pioneer Football League
1818 Chouteau Ave., St. Louis, MO 63103
(314) 421-2268   www.pioneer-football.org
Founded: 1993
Commissioner . . . . .Patty Viverito
Sports Information Director . . . . .Cody Bush
    2002 members: FOOTBALL (9): Austin Peay St., Butler, Davidson, Dayton, Drake, Jacksonville, Morehead St., San Diego and Valparaiso.

Southern Conference
905 East Main St.
Spartanburg, SC 29302
(864) 591-5100   www.soconsports.com
Founded: 1921
Commissioner . . . . .Dr. Daniel B. Morrison Jr.
Asst. Commissioner, Public Affairs . . . . .Steve Shutt
    2002-03 members: BASKETBALL (12)—Appalachian St., The Citadel, College of Charleston, Davidson, East Tennessee St., Furman, Georgia Southern, NC-Greensboro, Tennessee-Chattanooga, VMI, Western Carolina and Wofford; FOOTBALL (9)—all except College of Charleston, Davidson and NC-Greensboro.

Southland Conference
1700 Alma Drive, Suite 550
Plano, TX 75075
(972) 422-9500   www.southland.org
Founded: 1963
Commissioner . . . . .Greg Sankey
Asst. Commissioner for Media Relations . . . . .Bruce Ludlow
    2002-03 members: BASKETBALL (11)—Lamar,
LA-Monroe, McNeese St., Nicholls St., Northwestern St.,
Sam Houston St., SE Louisiana, Southwest Texas St.,
Stephen F. Austin St., Texas-Arlington and Texas-San Anto-
nio; FOOTBALL (7)—Jacksonville St., McNeese St., Nicholls
St., Northwestern St., Sam Houston St., Southwest Texas St.
and Stephen F. Austin St.

Southwestern Athletic Conference
1527 Fifth Ave. North
Birmingham, AL 35204
(205) 251-7573   www.swac.org
Founded: 1920
Commissioner . . . . .Robert C. Vowels Jr.
Asst. Comm. for Media Relations . . . . . .Wallace Dooley Jr.
    2002-03 members: BASKETBALL & FOOTBALL (10)—
Alabama A&M, Alabama St., Alcorn St., Arkansas-Pine
Bluff, Grambling St., Jackson St., Mississippi Valley St., Prai-
rie View A&M, Southern-Baton Rouge and Texas Southern.

West Coast Conference
1200 Bayhill Dr., Suite 302, San Bruno, CA 94066
(650) 873-8622   www.wccsports.com
Founded: 1952
Commissioner . . . . .Michael Gilleran
Asst. Comm. for Media Relations . . . . .Brad Walker
    2002-03 members: BASKETBALL (8)—Gonzaga,
Loyola Marymount, Pepperdine, Portland, St. Mary's-CA,
San Diego, San Francisco and Santa Clara.

PRO FOOTBALL

National Football League

League Office
280 Park Ave.
New York, NY 10017
(212) 450-2000   www.nfl.com
Commissioner . . . . .Paul Tagliabue
Exec. Vice President . . . . .Jeff Pash
AFC Info. Coordinator . . . . .Steve Alic
NFC Info. Coordinator .Mike Signora

NFL Management Council
280 Park Ave.
New York, NY 10017
(212) 450-2000
Chairman . . . . .Harold Henderson
Sr. V.P. of Broadcast/Network TV . . . . .Dennis Lewin

NFL Players Association
2021 L Street NW, Suite 600
Washington, DC 20036
(202) 463-2200   www.nflpa.org
Executive Director . . . . .Gene Upshaw
Asst. Exec. Director . . . . .Doug Allen
General Counsel . . . . .Richard Berthelsen
Asst. Director of Retired Players . . . . .Dee Becker

AFC

Baltimore Ravens
11001 Owings Mills Blvd.
Owings Mills, MD 21117
(410) 654-6200   www.baltimoreravens.com
Owner/CEO . . . . .Arthur B. Modell
President/COO . . . . .David Modell
V.P. of Public & Community Relations . . . . .Kevin Byrne

Buffalo Bills
One Bills Drive, Orchard Park, NY 14127
(716) 648-1800   www.buffalobills.com
Chairman & Owner . . . . .Ralph C. Wilson Jr.
President & GM . . . . .Tom Donahue
V.P. of Communications . . . . .Scott Berchtold

Cincinnati Bengals
One Paul Brown Stadium, Cincinnati, OH 45204
(513) 621-3550   www.bengals.com
President . . . . .Mike Brown
Sr. Vice President . . . . .Pete Brown
Public Relations Director . . . . .Jack Brennan

Cleveland Browns
76 Lou Groza Blvd., Berea, OH 44017
(440) 891-5000   www.clevelandbrowns.com
Owner/Chairman . . . . .Alfred Lerner
President/CEO . . . . .Carmen Policy
Exec. Dir. of Publicity/Media Relations . . . . . . .Todd Stewart

Denver Broncos
13655 Broncos Parkway, Englewood, CO 80112
(303) 649-9000   www.denverbroncos.com
Owner-President-CEO . . . . .Pat Bowlen
General Manager . . . . .Ted Sundquist
V.P. of Public Relations . . . . .Jim Saccomano

Houston Texans
Two Reliant Park
Houston, TX 77054
(832) 667-2000   www.houstontexans.com
Chairman & CEO .Robert C. McNair
Sr. V.P. & GM of Football Ops. . . . . .Charley Casserly
V.P. of Communications . . . . .Tony Wyllie

Indianapolis Colts
7001 W 56th St., Indianapolis, IN 46254
(317) 297-2658   www.colts.com
Owner-CEO . . . . .Jim Irsay
President . . . . .Bill Polian
Dir. of Football Operations . . . . .Dom Anile
V.P. of Public Relations . . . . .Craig Kelley

Jacksonville Jaguars
One ALLTEL Stadium Place
Jacksonville, FL 32202
(904) 633-6000   www.jaguars.com
Chairman & CEO . . . . .Wayne Weaver
Sr. V.P., Football Operations . . . . .Paul Vance
Exec. Dir. of Comm. & Broadcasting . . . . .Dan Edwards

Kansas City Chiefs
One Arrowhead Drive, Kansas City, MO 64129
(816) 920-9300   www.kcchiefs.com
Owner-Founder . . . . .Lamar Hunt
Chairman . . . . .Jack Steadman
President-CEO-General Manager . . . . .Carl Peterson
Director of Public Relations . . . . .Bob Moore

Miami Dolphins
7500 SW 30th St., Davie, FL 33314
(954) 452-7000   www.miamidolphins.com
Owner-Chairman . . . . .H. Wayne Huizenga
President . . . . .Eddie Jones
Sr. V.P. Football Ops & Player Personnel . . . . .Rick Spielman
Sr. V.P. of Media Relations . . . . .Harvey Greene

New England Patriots
One Patriot Place, Foxboro, MA 02035
(508) 543-8200   www.patriots.com
Owner & Chairman . . . . .Bob Kraft
Dir. of Player Personnel .Scott Pioli
Director of Media Relations . . . . .Stacey James

New York Jets
1000 Fulton Ave., Hempstead, NY 11550
(516) 560-8100 www.newyorkjets.com
Owner & Chairman ....Robert Wood Johnson IV
President ....Jay Cross
General Manager ....Terry Bradway
V.P. of Public Relations ....Ron Colangelo

Oakland Raiders
1220 Harbor Bay Parkway, Alameda, CA 94502
(510) 864-5000 www.raiders.com
Owner —Manager of General Partners ....Al Davis
Executive Assistant ....Al LoCasale
Director of Public Relations ....Mike Taylor

Pittsburgh Steelers
3400 South Water Street, Pittsburgh, PA 15203
(412) 432-7800 www.steelers.com
Owner-President...........................Dan Rooney
V.P.s .... John McGinley, Art Rooney Jr. & Art Rooney II
Communications Coordinator ....Ron Wahl

San Diego Chargers
4020 Murphy Canyon Rd.
San Diego, CA 92123
(858) 874-4500 www.chargers.com
Owner-Chairman ....Alex Spanos
President-Vice Chairman ....Dean Spanos
General Manager ....John Butler
Director of Public Relations ....Bill Johnston

Tennessee Titans
460 Great Circle Road, Nashville, TN 37228
(615) 565-4000 www.titansonline.com
Owner ..............................K.S. (Bud) Adams Jr.
President/COO ....Jeff Diamond
Exec. V.P./General Manager ....Floyd Reese
Director of Media Services ....Robbie Bohren

NFC

Arizona Cardinals
P.O. Box 888, Phoenix, AZ 85001
(602) 379-0101 www.azcardinals.com
Owner-President-General Counsel ....Bill Bidwill Sr.
Vice President ....Bill Bidwill Jr.
General Manager ....Bob Ferguson
Public Relations Director ....Paul Jensen

Atlanta Falcons
4400 Falcon Pkwy
Flowery Branch, GA 30542
(770) 965-3115 www.atlantafalcons.com
Chairman-President-CEO ....Arthur Blank
V.P. of Football Ops. ....Ron Hill
Director of Football Communications ....Aaron Salkin

Carolina Panthers
800 South Mint St.
Charlotte, NC 28202-1502
(704) 358-7000 www.panthers.com
Founder-Owner ....Jerry Richardson
President ....Mark Richardson
Dir. of Player Personnel ....Jack Bushofsky
Director of Communications ....Charlie Dayton

Chicago Bears
1000 Football Drive, Lake Forest, IL 60045
(847) 295-6600 www.chicagobears.com
Owner-Chairman Emeritus ....Edward McCaskey
Chairman of the Board ....Michael McCaskey
President-CEO ....Ted Phillips
General Manager ....Jerry Angelo
Director of Public Relations ....Scott Hagel

Dallas Cowboys
Cowboys Center
One Cowboys Parkway
Irving, TX 75063
(972) 556-9900 www.dallascowboys.com
Owner-President-GM ....Jerry Jones
Exec. V.P./Dir. of Player Personnel/COO ....Stephen Jones
Public Relations Director ....Rich Dalrymple

Detroit Lions
Detroit Lions Training & Practice Facility
222 Republic Drive, Allen Park, MI 48101
(313) 216-4000 www.detroitlions.com
Owner ....William Clay Ford
President & CEO ....Matt Millen
Exec. Dir. of Player Personnel ....Bill Tobin
Director of Media Relations ....Matt Barnhart

Green Bay Packers
1265 Lombardi Ave.
Green Bay, WI 54304
(920) 496-5700 www.packers.com
President & CEO ....Bob Harlan
General Manager & Head Coach ....Mike Sherman
Exec. Dir. of Public Relations ....Lee Remmel

Minnesota Vikings
9520 Viking Drive, Eden Prairie, MN 55344
(952) 828-6500 www.vikings.com
Owner ....Red McCombs
President ....Gary Woods
Executive Vice President ....:.............Michael Kelly
Director of Public Relations ....Bob Hagan

New Orleans Saints
5800 Airline Drive, Metairie, LA 70003
(504) 733-0255 www.neworleanssaints.com
Owner ....Tom Benson
General Manager ....Mickey Loomis
Dir. of Player Personnel ....Rick Mueller
Director of Media/Public Relations ....Greg Bensel

New York Giants
Giants Stadium
East Rutherford, NJ 07073
(201) 935-8111 www.giants.com
President/co-CEO ....Wellington Mara
Chairman/co-CEO ....Preston Robert Tisch
V.P. & General Manager ....Ernie Accorsi
V.P. of Communications ....Pat Hanlon

Philadelphia Eagles
NovaCare Complex
One NovaCare Way
Philadelphia, PA 19145
(215) 463-2500 www.philadelphiaeagles.com
Owner-Chairman-CEO ....Jeffrey Lurie
President ....Joe Banner
Head Coach/Exec. V.P. of Football Ops. ....Andy Reid
Dir. of Football Media Services ....Derek Boyko

St. Louis Rams
One Rams Way, St. Louis, MO 63045
(314) 982-7267 www.stlouisrams.com
Owner-Chairman ....Georgia Frontiere
Owner-Vice Chairman ....Stan Kroenke
President ....John Shaw
Pres. of Football Operations ....Jay Zygmunt
Director of Public Relations ....Rick Smith

San Francisco 49ers
4949 Centennial Blvd.
Santa Clara, CA 95054
(408) 562-4949   www.sf49ers.com
Owner ....Denise DeBartolo-York
President/CEO ....Peter Harris
General Manager ....Terry Donahue
Director of Public Relations ....Kirk Reynolds

Seattle Seahawks
11220 NE 53rd Street, Kirkland, WA 98033
(425) 827-9777   www.seahawks.com
Owner ....Paul Allen
President ....Bob Whitsitt
V.P./GM/Head Coach ....Mike Holmgren
Public Relations Director ....Dave Pearson

Tampa Bay Buccaneers
One Buccaneer Place, Tampa, FL 33607
(813) 870-2700   www.buccaneers.com
Owner-President ....Malcolm Glazer
General Manager ....Rich McKay
Communications Manager ....Jeff Kamis

Washington Redskins
Redskins Park
P.O. Box 17247, Washington D.C. 20041
(703) 726-7000   www.redskins.com
Owner ....Daniel M. Snyder
Asst. General Manager ....Bobby Mitchell
Director of Public Relations ....Michelle Tessier

Canadian Football League

League Office
50 Wellington St. East, 3rd Floor
Toronto, Ontario M5E 1C8
(416) 322-9650   www.cfl.ca
Acting Commissioner ....David Braley
V.P. of Football Operations ....Ed Chalupka
V.P. of Communications ....Shawn Lackie

CFL Players Association
603 Argus Rd., Suite 207
Oakville, Ontario L6J 6G6
(905) 844-7852   www.cfl.ca/cflpa
President ....Stu Laird
Legal Counsel ....Ed Molstad

British Columbia Lions
10605 135th St.
Surrey, B.C. V3T 4C8
(604) 930-5466   www.bclions.com
Owner ....David Braley
President & CEO ....Bob Ackles
General Manager ....Adam Rita
Dir. of Communications ....Debbie Butt

Calgary Stampeders
McMahon Stadium
1817 Crowchild Trail, NW
Calgary, Alberta T2M 4R6
(403) 289-0205   www.stampeders.com
Owner/Chairman/CEO ....Michael Feterik
President ....Stan Schwartz
General Manager & Head Coach ....Wally Buono
V.P. of Marketing & Communications ....Ron Rooke

Edmonton Eskimos
9023 111th Ave.
Edmonton, Alberta T5B 0C3
(780) 448-1525   www.esks.com
Owner ....Community-owned
President & CEO ....Hugh Campbell
Exec. Dir. Player Personnel/
Asst. Dir. Football Ops. ....Paul Jones
Dir. of Comm./Marketing ....Dave Jamieson

Hamilton Tiger-Cats
75 Balsam Ave. N
Hamilton, Ontario L8L 8C1
(905) 547-2418   www.tigercats.on.ca
Chairman/Owner ....David M. Macdonald
Vice Chairman/Owner/GM ....George Grant
Dir. Football Ops./Head Coach ....Ron Lancaster
Communications/Media Relations Manager ...Bob Hooper

Montreal Alouettes
1255 University St., Suite 120
Montreal, Quebec H3B 3A9
(514) 253-0008   www.alouettes.net
Owner ....Robert Wetenhall
President & CEO ....Ellis T. Prince
Dir. of Football Ops./GM ....Jim Popp
Dir. of Communications ....Louis-Philippe Dorais

Ottawa Renegades
1015 Bank St.
Ottawa, Ontario K1S 3W7
(613) 231-5608   www.ottawarenegades.net
Governor ....Randy Gillies
President ....Brad Watters
V.P. of Football Ops./GM ....Eric Tillman
Dir. of Public Relations ....Max Julien

Saskatchewan Roughriders
2940 —10th Avenue, P.O. Box 1277
Regina, Saskatchewan S4P 3B8
(306) 569-2323   www.saskriders.com
Owner ....Community-owned
President ....Tom Robinson
General Manager and Dir. of Football Ops. ...Roy Shivers
Media Coordinator ....Ryan Whippler

Toronto Argonauts
110 Eglinton Ave. W., Suite 303, Toronto, Ontario M4R 1A3
(416) 489-2746   www.argonauts.on.ca
Owner/Chairman ....Sherwood Schwarz
Dir. of Player Personnel ....Paul Masotti
Director of Public Relations ....Dave Haggith

Winnipeg Blue Bombers
1465 Maroons Road, Winnipeg, Manitoba R3G 0L6
(204) 784-2583   www.bluebombers.com
Owner ....Community-owned
President ....Lyle Bauer
V.P. of Football Ops./Head Coach ....Dave Ritchie
Dir. of Media/Public Relations ....Shawn Coates

NFL Europe

Vice President of Football Ops. ....John Beake
Director of Public Relations ....David Tossell
Public Relations Assistant ....Neil Reynolds

League Offices

Frankfurt
Westerbach Str. 47
Frankfurt, Germany 60489
011-49-69-978-2790

London
97/99 King Road
London, England SW3 4PA
011-44-207-225-3070

New York
280 Park Avenue
New York, NY 10017
(212) 450-2000   www.nfleurope.com
   Member teams (6): Amsterdam Admirals, Barcelona
Dragons, Berlin Thunder, Frankfurt Galaxy, Rhein Fire (Dusseldorf), Scottish Claymores (Edinburgh).

Arena Football League

20 North Wacker Dr., Suite 1231
Chicago, IL 60606
(312) 621-7000   www.arenafootball.com
Commissioner ....David C. Baker
V.P. of Football Operations ....Jerry Trice
V.P. of Communications ....Chris McCloskey

Member teams (16): American Conference—Arizona Rattlers, Chicago Rush, Dallas Desperados, Detroit Fury, Grand Rapids Rampage, Indiana Firebirds, Los Angeles Avengers and San Jose Sabercats. National Conference—Buffalo Destroyers, Carolina Cobras, Georgia Force, New Jersey Gladiators, New York Dragons, Orlando Predators, Tampa Bay Storm and Toronto Phantoms.

An additional seven teams are scheduled to begin play between 2003-05, including the Colorado Crush in 2003 and New Orleans Voodoo in 2004.

GOLF

LPGA Tour
(Ladies' Professional Golf Association)
100 International Golf Drive
Daytona Beach, FL 32124
(386) 274-6200   www.lpga.com
Commissioner ....Ty Votaw
Director of Media Relations ....Connie Wilson

PGA of America
100 Avenue of the Champions
Palm Beach Gardens, FL 33410
(561) 624-8400   www.pga.com
President................................Jack Connelly
CEO ....Jim Awtrey
Director of Public Relations ....Julius Mason

PGA European Tour
Wentworth Drive, Virginia Water
Surrey, England GU25 4LX
TEL: 011-44-1344-840400
Executive Director ....Ken Schofield
Director of P.R./Corporate Affairs ....Mitchell Platts
Director of Communications ....Gordon Simpson
                                         www.europeantour.com

PGA Tour
112 PGA Tour Blvd.
Ponte Vedra, FL 32082
(904) 285-3700   www.pgatour.com
Commissioner ....Tim Finchem
Senior V.P. of Communications ....Bob Combs

Royal & Ancient Golf Club of St. Andrews
St. Andrews, Fife
Scotland KY16 9JD
TEL: 011-44-1334-472112
Secretary ....Peter Dawson
Press Officer ....Stewart McDougall
                                         www.randa.org

USGA
(United States Golf Association)
P.O. Box 708, Liberty Corner Road
Far Hills, NJ 07931
(908) 234-2300   www.usga.org
President ....Reed McKenzie
Executive Director ....David Fay
Sr. Director of Communications ....Marty Parkes

PRO HOCKEY

NHL
National Hockey League
Commissioner ....Gary Bettman
Pres., NHL Enterprises ....Ed Horne
Exec. V.P., Dir. of Hockey Ops. ....Colin Campbell
V.P. of Media Relations ....Frank Brown

League Offices

Montreal
1800 McGill College Ave., Suite 2600
Montreal, Quebec H3A 3J6
(514) 841-9220

New York
1251 Avenue of the Americas, 47th Floor, New York, NY 10020
(212) 789-2000

Toronto
50 Bay St., 11th Floor
Toronto, Ontario M5J 2X8
(416) 981-2777   www.nhl.com

NHL Players' Association
777 Bay St., Suite 2400
P.O. Box 121
Toronto, Ontario M5G 2C8
(416) 408-4040   www.nhlpa.com
Executive Director ....Bob Goodenow
Media Relations ....Jonathan Weatherdon

Anaheim, Mighty Ducks of
Arrowhead Pond of Anaheim
2695 Katella Ave.
Anaheim, CA 92806
(714) 940-2900   www.mightyducks.com
Owner ....Walt Disney Co.
Governor ....Paul Pressler
Senior V.P./General Manager ....Bryan Murray
Dir., Communications and Team Services ....Alex Gilchrist

Atlanta Thrashers
1 CNN Center
12th Floor, South Tower
Atlanta, GA 30303
(404) 584-7825   www.atlantathrashers.com
Owner ....AOL-Time Warner
President/Governor ....Stan Kasten
V.P./General Manager ....Don Waddell
Director of Media Relations ....Tom Hughes

Boston Bruins
1 FleetCenter, Suite 250
Boston, MA 02114
(617) 624-1900   www.bostonbruins.com
Owner ....Jeremy Jacobs
President ....Harry Sinden
V.P & General Manager ....Mike O'Connell
Director of Media Relations ....Heidi Holland

Buffalo Sabres
HSBC Arena
One Seymour H. Knox III Plaza
Buffalo, NY 14203-3096
(716) 855-4100   www.sabres.com
Owner ....TBA
General Manager ....Darcy Regier
V.P. of Communications ....Michael Gilbert

Calgary Flames
Pengrowth Saddledome, P.O. Box 1540 Station M
Calgary, Alberta T2P 3B9
(403) 777-2177   www.calgaryflames.com
Owners .Harley Hotchkiss, Murray Edwards, Alvin G. Libin,
   Allan P. Markin, J.R. McCaig, Byron and Daryl Seamen
President & CEO ....Ken King
V.P./General Manager ....Craig Button
Director of Communications ....Peter Hanlon

Carolina Hurricanes
RBC Center
1400 Edward Mill Rd., Raleigh, NC 27607
(919) 467-7825   www.caneshockey.com
Owner ....Peter Karmanos Jr.
President & COO ....Jim Cain
CEO & General Manager ....Jim Rutherford
Dir., Media Relations ....Jerry Higgins

Chicago Blackhawks
United Center, 1901 West Madison St.
Chicago, IL 60612
(312) 455-7000   www.chicagoblackhawks.com
Owner-President ....William Wirtz
General Manager ....Mike Smith
Executive Director of Communications ....Jim DeMaria

Colorado Avalanche
1000 Chopper Cir., Denver, CO 80204
(303) 405-1100   www.coloradoavalanche.com
Owner ....Stan Kroenke
President/GM/Alt. Governor ....Pierre Lacroix
V.P. of Comm. & Team Services ....Jean Martineau

Columbus Blue Jackets
200 W. Nationwide Blvd., Suite Level, Columbus, OH 43215
(614) 246-4625   www.bluejackets.com
Owner ....John H. McConnell
President/General Manager ....Doug MacLean
Director of Communications ....Todd Sharrock

Dallas Stars
211 Cowboys Parkway, Irving, TX 75063
(972) 831-2453   www.dallasstars.com
Owner ....Thomas O. Hicks
General Manager ....Doug Armstrong
Sr. Director of Hockey Comm. ....Rob Scichili

Detroit Red Wings
Joe Louis Arena, 600 Civic Center Drive
Detroit, MI 48226
(313) 396-7544   www.detroitredwings.com
Owner/President ....Mike Ilitch
Owner/Secretary-Treasurer ....Marian Ilitch
General Manager ....Ken Holland
Sr. Director of Communications ....John Hahn

Edmonton Oilers
11230 110th St., Edmonton, Alberta, T5G 3H7
(780) 414-4000   www.edmontonoilers.com
Owners ....Edmonton Investors Group, Ltd.
President & CEO ....Patrick LaForge
Exec. V.P./General Manager ....Kevin Lowe
V.P./Media Relations ....Bill Tuele

Florida Panthers
Office Depot Center
1 Panther Parkway, Sunrise, FL 33323
(954) 835-7000   www.flpanthers.com
Chairman/CEO ....Alan Cohen
Governor ....Bill Torrey
General Manager ....Rick Dudley
Dir. of Media Relations ....Randy Sieminski

Los Angeles Kings
Staples Center
1111 S. Figueroa, Los Angeles, CA 90015
(310) 535-4543   www.lakings.com
Majority Owners ....Philip Anschutz and Ed Roski
President/Governor ....Tim Leiweke
Sr. V.P. & General Manager ....Dave Taylor
Director of Media Relations ....Mike Altieri

Minnesota Wild
317 Washington Street
St. Paul, MN 55102
(651) 222-9453   www.wild.com
Owner ....Bob Naegele Jr.
Exec. V.P. & General Manager ....Doug Risebrough
V.P. of Comm. & Broadcast ....Bill Robertson

Montreal Canadiens
Bell Centre, 1260 Gauchetière St. West
Montreal, Quebec H3B 5E8
(514) 932-2582   www.canadiens.com
Owner ....George N. Gillett Jr.
President ....Pierre Boivin
General Manager ....Andre Savard
V.P. of Communications ....Donald Beauchamp

Nashville Predators
501 Broadway, Nashville, TN 37203
(615) 770-2300   www.nashvillepredators.com
Chairman and Maj. Owner ....Craig Leipold
President ....Jack Diller
Exec. V.P. & General Manager ....David Poile
V.P. of Communications ....Gerry Helper

New Jersey Devils
Continental Airlines Arena, P.O. Box 504
East Rutherford, NJ 07073
(201) 935-6050   www.newjerseydevils.com
Owner ....YankeeNets
President-GM-CEO ....Lou Lamoriello
Director of Public Relations ....Jeff Altstadter

New York Islanders
1535 Old Country Road, Plainview, NY 11083
(516) 501-6700   www.newyorkislanders.com
Owner ....Charles Wang & Sanjay Kumar
General Manager ....Mike Milbury
V.P. of Communications ....Chris Botta

New York Rangers
2 Penn Plaza, 14th Floor
New York, NY 10121
(212) 465-6486   www.newyorkrangers.com
Owner ....'.....Cablevision Systems Inc.
President (MSG) ....James Dolan
President & General Manager ....Glen Sather
V.P. of Public Relations ....John Rosasco

Ottawa Senators
1000 Palladium Dr.
Kanata, Ontario, K2V 1A5
(613) 599-0250   www.ottawasenators.com
Chairman & Gov. ....Rod Bryden
President & CEO ....Roy Mlakar
General Manager ....John Muckler
Director of Communications ....Steve Keogh

Philadelphia Flyers
3601 S. Broad St., Philadelphia, PA 19148
(215) 465-4500   ·   www.philadelphiaflyers.com
Chairman ....Ed Snider
President & General Manager ....Bob Clarke
Director of Public Relations ....Zack Hill

Phoenix Coyotes
Alltel Ice Den, 9375 E. Bell Rd., Scottsdale, AZ 85260
(480) 473-5600 www.phoenixcoyotes.com
Chairman/CEO ....Steve Ellman
President/COO ....Jim Lites
Sr. Exec. V. P. of Hockey Ops. ....Cliff Fletcher
V.P. & General Manager ....Mike Barnett
V.P. of Media Relations ....Richard Nairn

Pittsburgh Penguins
Mellon Arena, 66 Mario Lemieux Place, Pittsburgh, PA 15219
(412) 642-1800 www.pittsburghpenguins.com
Owner/Chairman ....Mario Lemieux
Exec. V.P. & GM ....Craig Patrick
V.P. of Communications ....Tom McMillan

St. Louis Blues
Savvis Center, 1401 Clark Ave.
St. Louis, MO 63103
(314) 622-2500 www.stlouisblues.com
Owners ....Bill and Nancy Laurie
President/CEO ....Mark Sauer
Senior V.P./General Manager ....Larry Pleau
Director of Communications ....Frank Buonomo

San Jose Sharks
525 West Santa Clara St., San Jose, CA 95113
(408) 287-7070 www.sjsharks.com
Owner ......San Jose Sports and Entertainment Enterprises
President-CEO ....Greg Jamison
Exec. V.P.& GM ....Dean Lombardi
Director of Media Relations ....Ken Arnold

Tampa Bay Lightning
401 Channelside Drive, Tampa, FL 33602
(813) 301-6500 www.tampabaylightning.com
Owner ....Palace Sports & Ent.
CEO & Governor ....Tom Wilson
General Manager ....Jay Feaster
Director of Public Relations ....Jay Preble

Toronto Maple Leafs
Air Canada Centre
40 Bay Street, Toronto, Ontario M5J 2X2
(416) 815-5500 www.mapleleafs.com
Owner ....Steve Stavro
President ....Ken Dryden
Coach/G.M. ....Pat Quinn
Director of Media Relations ....Pat Park

Vancouver Canucks
General Motors Place, 800 Griffiths Way
Vancouver, B.C. V6B 6G1
(604) 899-4600 www.canucks.com
Owners ....John McCaw
COO ....David Cobb
President & General Manager ....Brian Burke
Manager of Media Relations ....Chris Brumwell

Washington Capitals
MCI Center, 401 9th St., Suite 7500
Washington, D.C. 20004
(202) 266-2200 www.washingtoncaps.com
Owners .Ted Leonsis, Dick Patrick, Raul Fernandez, George
Stamas, Jack Davies and Richard Kay
President ....Dick Patrick
V.P./General Manager ....George McPhee
Manager of Media Relations ....Brian Potter

AHL

American Hockey League
One Monarch Place, Springfield, MA 01144
(413) 781-2030 www.theahl.com
President/CEO ....David Andrews
V.P. of Hockey Ops. ....Jim Mill
Dir. of Media Relations/Communications .....Bret Stothart
  Member teams (28): Eastern Conference—Albany
River Rats, Binghamton Senators, Bridgeport Sound Tigers,
Hamilton Bulldogs, Hartford Wolf Pack, Lowell Lock Mon-
sters, Manchester Monarchs, Manitoba Moose, Portland
Pirates, Providence Bruins, Saint John Flames, Springfield
Falcons, St. John's Maple Leafs and Worcester IceCats.
  Western Conference—Chicago Wolves, Cincinnati
Mighty Ducks, Cleveland Barons, Grand Rapids Griffins,
Hershey Bears, Houston Aeros, Milwaukee Admirals, Nor-
folk Admirals, Philadelphia Phantoms, Rochester Americans,
San Antonio Rampage, Syracuse Crunch, Utah Grizzlies
and Wilkes-Barre/Scranton Penguins.

IIHF

International Ice Hockey Federation
Parkring 11
CH-8002 Zurich, Switzerland
TEL: 011-411-289-8600 www.iihf.com
President ....Rene Fasel
General Secretary ....Jan-Ake Edvinsson
Director of P.R./Marketing ....Kimmo Leinonen

HORSE RACING

Breeders' Cup Limited
PO Box 4230, Lexington, KY 40544–4230
(859) 223-5444 www.breederscup.com
President/NTRA Vice Chairman ........D.G. Van Clief, Jr.
V.P./Breeders' Cup & Event Mktg. ....Damon Thayer

National Museum of Racing and Hall of Fame
191 Union Ave.
Saratoga Springs, NY 12866
(518) 584-0400 www.racingmuseum.org
President ....John T. von Stade
Director ....Peter Hammell
Assistant Director ....Catherine Maguire
Communications Officer ....Richard Hamilton

NTRA
(National Thoroughbred Racing Association)
444 Madison Ave., Suite 5030
New York, NY 10022
(212) 907-9280 www.ntra.com
CEO-Commissioner ....Tim Smith
Deputy Commiss. & COO ....Greg Avioli
Sr. Director of Media Relations ....Eric Wing

TRA
(Thoroughbred Racing Associations of N. America, Inc.)
420 Fair Hill Drive, Suite 1
Elkton, MD 21921
(410) 392-9200 www.tra-online.com
President ....Bryan G. Krantz
Executive V.P. ....Christopher N. Scherf

USTA
(United States Trotting Association)
750 Michigan Ave., Columbus, OH 43215
(614) 224-2291 www.ustrotting.com
Executive V.P. ....Fred Noe
Director of Public Relations ....John Pawlak

MEDIA

PERIODICALS

ESPN, The Magazine
19 E 34th St., 7th Floor, New York, NY 10016
(212) 515-1000   www.espnmag.com
Editor in Chief . . . . .John Papanek
Executive Editors . . . . .Gary Hoenig, Steve Wulf
Senior V.P./GM . . . . John Skipper

Sports Illustrated
135 West 50th St., New York, NY 10020
(212) 522-9797   www.cnnsi.com
President/CEO . . . . .Bruce Hallett
Managing Editor . . . . .Terry McDonell
Executive Editors . . .B. Peter Carry, Rob Fleder and Charlie
                                  Leerhsen

The Sporting News
10176 Corporate Square Dr., Suite 200
St. Louis, MO 63132
(314) 997-7111   www.sportingnews.com
Senior V.P./Editorial Director . . . . .John D. Rawlings
President/CEO . . . . .James H. Nuckols

The Sports Business Daily
120 West Morehead St., Ste. 220
Charlotte, NC 28202
(704) 973-1500   www.sportsbizdaily.com
Editor-in-Chief . . . . .Abe Madkour
Editor-at-Large . . . . .Terry Lefton
Media Relations Mgr. . . . . .Bill Magrath

USA Today
1000 Wilson Blvd., Arlington, VA 22229
(703) 854-3400   www.usatoday.com
Owner . . . . .Gannett Co.
President-Publisher . . . . .Tom Curley
Managing Editor/Sports . . . . .Monte Lorell

WIRE SERVICES

Associated Press
50 Rockefeller Plaza 5th Floor, New York, NY 10020
(212) 621-1630   www.ap.org
Sports Editor . . . . .Terry Taylor
Deputy Sports Editor .Aaron Watson

United Press International
1510 H Street NW, Washington, DC 20005
(202) 898-8000   www.upi.com
Managing Editor, Sports . . . . .Ron Colbert

The Sports Network
2200 Byberry Rd., Suite 200
Hatboro, PA 19040
(215) 441-8444   www.sportsnetwork.com
CEO/President . . . . .Mickey Charles
Director of Operations . . . . .Phil Sokol

Sportsticker
800 Plaza Two, Harborside Financial Ctr., Jersey City, NJ 07311
(201) 309-1200   www.sportsticker.com
General Manager . . . . .Jim Morganthaler
Dir. of New Content .Lou Monaco

TV NETWORKS

ABC Sports
47 West 66th St., 13th Floor, New York, NY 10023
(212) 456-4867   www.abcsports.com
President . . . . .Howard Katz
Senior V.P., Production . . . . .Bob Toms
V.P. of Media Relations . . . . .Mark Mandel

CBC Sports
P.O. Box 500, Station A 5H 100
Toronto, Ontario M5W 1E6
(416) 205-6523   www.cbc.ca/sports
Executive Director-Sports .Nancy Lee
Sr. Executive Producer . . . . .Mike Brannagan
Publicist . . . . .Christian Hasse

CBS Sports
51 West 52nd St., 25th Floor
New York, NY 10019
(212) 975-5230   www.cbs.sportsline.com
President . . . . .Sean McManus
Executive Producer . . . . .Tony Petitti
Sr. V.P., Programming . . . . . . .Rob Correa and Mike Aresco
V.P., Communications . . . . .Leslie Ann Wade

ESPN
ESPN Plaza, Bristol, CT 06010
(860) 585-2000   www.espn.go.com
President . . . . .George Bodenheimer
Vice President . . . . .Chris LaPlaca
Sr. V.P. of Programming . . . . .John Wildhack
Sr. V.P. & Exec. Editor of Internet . . . . .John Walsh
Sr. V.P. and Managing Editor . . . . .Bob Eaton
Director of Communications . . . . .Mike Soltys

ESPN Classic
ESPN Plaza, Bristol, CT 06010
(860) 585-2000   www.espn.go.com/classic
Executive Producer . . . . .Vince Doria
Communications Coordinator . . . . .Amy Wildhack

FOX Sports
10201 W. Pico Blvd., Los Angeles, CA 90035
(310) 369-1000   www.foxsports.com
Chairman-CEO . . . . .David Hill
President . . . . .Ed Goren
Sr. V.P. of Media Relations (NYC) . . . . .Lou D'Ermilio

The Golf Channel
7580 Commerce Center Drive
Orlando, FL 32819
(407) 345-4653   www.thegolfchannel.com
President-CEO . . . . .David Manougian
V.P./Executive Producer . . . . .Tony Tortorici
Director of Public Relations . . . . .Dan Higgins

HBO Sports
1100 Ave. of the Americas
New York, NY 10036
(212) 512-1987   www.hbo.com/sports
President-CEO . . . . .Ross Greenburg
Sr. V.P./Exec. Producer . . . . .Rick Bernstein
Sr. V.P., Programming .Kery Davis
Director of Publicity .Ray Stallone

NBC Sports
30 Rockefeller Plaza, New York, NY 10112
(212) 664-2160   www.nbcsports.com
Chairman . . . . .Dick Ebersol
President . . . . .Ken Schanzer
Executive Producer . . . . .Tommy Roy
V.P. of Communications . . . . .Kevin Sullivan

TSN—The Sports Network
Nine Channel Nine Court
Scarborough, Ontario, M1S 4B5
(416) 332-7660   www.tsn.ca
President of CTV Inc. . . . . .Rick Brace
President . . . . .Keith Pelley
Communications Manager . . . . .Andrea Goldstein

Turner Sports
One CNN Center
13th Floor, Atlanta, GA 30303
(404) 827-1735   www.cnnsi.com/turnersports
President . . . . .Mark Lazarus
Executive Producer . . . . .Mike Pearl
Senior V.P. of Public Relations . . . . .Greg Hughes

Univision (Spanish)
9405 NW 41st St., Miami, FL 33178
(305) 471-3900   www.univision.com
President/COO . . . . .Ray Rodriguez
President/Sports . . . . .David Downs

USA Network
1230 Ave. of the Americas, New York, NY 10020
(212) 413-5000   www.usanetwork.com/sports
Sr. V.P., Production & Sports . . . . .Gordon Beck
V.P., Sports Programming . . . . .Kevin Landy
Sports Publicity . . . . .Tom Caraccioli

OLYMPICS

IOC
(International Olympic Committee)
Chateau de Vidy
CH-1007 Lausanne, Switzerland
TEL: 011-41-21-621-6111   www.olympic.org
President . . . . .Jacques Rogge
Director General . . . . .Francois Carrard

COC
(Canadian Olympic Committee)
2070 Peel St., Suite 300
Montreal, Quebec H3A 1W6
(514) 861-3371   www.coa.ca
Interim CEO . . . . .Lou Ragagnin
President . . . . .Michael Chambers
IOC members .Charmaine Crooks, Paul Henderson, Richard
                         Pound, James Worrall (Honourary)
Exec. Dir. of Marketing/Comm. . . . . .Nick Marrone

USOC
(United States Olympic Committee)
One Olympic Plaza
Colorado Springs, CO 80909
(719) 632-5551
                                                www.usoc.org
President . . . . .Marty Mankamyer
CEO . . . . .Lloyd Ward
IOC members . . Anita DeFrantz, James Easton & Bob Ctvrlik
Chief Communications Officer . . . . .Mike Moran

2004 SUMMER GAMES

Athens Olympic Organizing Committee
Iolkou & Filikis Etaireias, 142 34 Nea Ionia, Athens, Greece
TEL: 011-30-12004-000   www.athens.olympic.org
    Time difference: 7 hours ahead of New York (EDT)
Chairman . . . . .Gianna Angelopoulas-Daskalaki
Managing Director . . . . .Yannis Spanudakis
Chairman of Coord. Commission . . . . .Denis Oswald
    (XXVIIIth Olympic Summer Games, Aug. 13-29)

2006 WINTER GAMES

Turin Olympic Organizing Committee
Via Nizza 262/58–10126
Turin, Italy
TEL: 011-39-011-63-10-511 www.torino2006.it/eng/index.asp

President . . . . .Valentino Castellani
Deputy President . . . . .Evelina Christillin
Chairman of Coord. Commission . . . . . . .Jean Claude-Killy
Media Relations Manager . . . . .Giuseppe Gattino
    (XXth Olympic Winter Games, Feb. 10-26)

2008 SUMMER GAMES

Beijing Olympic Organizing Committee
Beijing Xin Qiao Hotel, 2, Dong Jiao Min Xiang
Beijing, China 100004
TEL: 86-10-65-28-20-09   www.beijing-2008.org

President . . . . .Liu Qi
Executive President . . . . .Yuan Weimin
Executive Vice President . . . . .Liu Jingmin
Secretary General . . . . : . . . . .Wang Wei

U.S. OLYMPICS TRAINING CENTERS

Colorado Springs Training Center
One Olympic Plaza, Colorado Springs, CO 80909
(719) 866-4500
Director . . . . .Lloyd Ward

Lake Placid Training Center
421 Old Military Road, Lake Placid, NY 12946
(518) 523-2600
Director . . . . .Jack Favro

Arco Olympic Training Center
2800 Olympic Parkway, Chula Vista, CA 91915
(619) 656-1500
Director . . . . .Patrice Milkovich

U.S. OLYMPIC ORGANIZATIONS

National Archery Association
One Olympic Plaza, Colorado Springs, CO 80909
(719) 866-4576   www.usarchery.org
President . . . . .Mark Miller
Executive Director . . . . .Brad Camp
Communications/Media Relations Mgr. . . .Desirae Freiherr

U.S. Badminton Association
One Olympic Plaza, Colorado Springs, CO 80909
(719) 866-4808   www.usabadminton.org
President . . . . .Don Chew
Executive Director . . . . .Dan Cloppas
Programs & Financial Services . . . . .Peggy Savosik

USA Baseball
3400 E Camino Camtestre, Tucson, AZ 85716
(520) 327-9700   www.usabaseball.com
Note: Offices are moving to Durham, NC in 2003.
Executive Director & CEO . . . . .Paul Seiler
Dir. of Communications . . . . .David Fannucchi

USA Basketball
5465 Mark Dabling Blvd.
Colorado Springs, CO 80918
(719) 590-4800   www.usabasketball.com
President . . . . .Tom Jernstedt
Executive Director . . . . .James Tooley
Asst. Exec. Director/Communications . . . . .Craig Miller

U.S. Biathlon Association
29 Ethan Allen Ave.
Colchester, VT 05446
(802) 654-7833   www.usbiathlon.org
President . . . . .Lyle Nelson
Exec. Director . . . . .Stephen Sands
Director of Summer Biathlon . . . . .Marc Sheppard
Public Relations Contact . . . . .Jerry Kokesh

U.S. Bobsled and Skeleton Federation
421 Old Military Road
Lake Placid, NY 12946
(518) 523-1842   www.usbsf.com
President . . . . .Jim Morris
Executive Director . . . . .Matt Roy
Media/P.R. Director . . . . .Julie Urbansky

USA Boxing
One Olympic Plaza, Colorado Springs, CO 80909
(719) 866-4506 www.usaboxing.org
President ....Dr. Robert Voy
Executive Director ....Eric Parthen
Media/Public Relations Contact ....Julie Goldsticker

U.S. Canoe and Kayak Team
15 Parkside Drive
Lake Placid, NY 12946
(518) 523-1855 www.usack.org
President ....Anne Blanchard
Executive Director ....Lisa Fish

USA Curling
1100 Center Point Drive, Box 866
Stevens Point, WI 54481
(715) 344-1199 www.usacurl.org
President ....Jack McNelly
Executive Director ....David Garber
Communications Director ....Rick Patzke

USA Cycling
One Olympic Plaza
Colorado Springs, CO 80909
(719) 866-4581 www.usacycling.org
President ....Jim Ochowicz
CEO ....Gerard Bisceglia
Director of Communications ....Deborah Engen

United States Diving, Inc.
201 South Capitol Avenue, Suite 430
Indianapolis, IN 46225
(317) 237-5252 www.usdiving.org
President ....William Walker
Executive Director ....Todd Smith
Director of Communications ....Kelli Servizzi

U.S. Equestrian Team
Pottersville Road, Gladstone, NJ 07934
(908) 234-1251 www.uset.com
President ....Armand Leone, Jr.
Executive Director ....Bonnie B. Jenkins
Director of Communications ....Marty Bauman
(508) 698-6810

U.S. Fencing Association
One Olympic Plaza, Colorado Springs, CO 80909
(719) 866-4511 www.usfencing.org
President ....Stacey Johnson
Executive Director ....Michael Massik
Media Relations Contact ....Cindy Bent

U.S. Field Hockey Association
One Olympic Plaza, Colorado Springs, CO 80909
(719) 866-4567 www.usfieldhockey.com
President ....Sharon Taylor
Executive Director ....Amy Frankenstein
Director of Sport/Public Info. ....Howard Thomas

U.S. Figure Skating Association
20 First Street, Colorado Springs, CO 80906
(719) 635-5200 www.usfsa.org
President ....Phyllis Howard
Executive Director ....John LeFevre
Director of Events ....Carrie Wolf
Director of Media Relations ....Bob Dunlop

USA Gymnastics (Artistic & Rhythmic)
Pan American Plaza, Suite 300
201 South Capitol Avenue, Indianapolis, IN 46225
(317) 237-5050 www.usa-gymnastics.org
President-Exec. Director ....Robert V. Colarossi
Communications Manager ....Courtney Caress

USA Hockey, Inc.
1775 Bob Johnson Dr., Colorado Springs, CO 80906
(719) 576-8724 www.usahockey.com
President ....Walter Bush Jr.
Executive Director ....Doug Palazzari
Dir. of Public and Media Relations ....Chuck Menke

United States Judo, Inc.
One Olympic Plaza, Suite 202
Colorado Springs, CO 80909
(719) 5866-4730 www.usjudo.org
President ....Dr. Ron Tripp
Exec. Director ....William Rosenberg
Public Relations Director ....John Miller

U.S. Luge Association
35 Church Street, Lake Placid, NY 12946
(518) 523-2071 www.usaluge.org
President ....Doug Bateman
Executive Director ....Ron Rossi
Public/Media Relations Manager ....John Lundin

USA Pentathlon
5407 Bandera Rd., Suite 512, San Antonio, TX 78238
(210) 229-2004 usmpa.home.texas.net
President ....Ralph Bender
Executive Director ....Robert Marbut

U.S. Rowing
201 South Capitol Avenue, Suite 400
Indianapolis, IN 46225
(317) 237-5656 www.usrowing.org
President ....Monk Terry
Executive Director ....John Dane
Director of Communications ....Brett Johnson

U.S. Sailing Association
P.O. Box 1260, 15 Maritime Drive, Portsmouth, RI 02871
(401) 683-0800 www.ussailing.org
President ....David Rosekrans
Executive Director ....Nick Craw
Communications Manager ....Penny Piva Rego

U.S. Shooting Team
One Olympic Plaza
Colorado Springs, CO 80909
(719) 866-4670 www.usashooting.com
Executive Director ....Robert Mitchell
Media/Public Relations ....Scott Engen

U.S. Ski & Snowboard Association
P.O. Box 100, 1500 Kearns Blvd.
Park City, UT 84060
(435) 649-9090 www.ussa.org
Chairman ....Jim McCarthy
CEO/President ....Bill Marolt
V.P. of Public Relations/Member Svcs. ....Tom Kelly
Public Relations Director ....Juliann Fritz

U.S. Soccer Federation
U.S. Soccer House
1801-1811 South Prairie Ave.
Chicago, IL 60616
(312) 808-1300 www.ussoccer.com
President ....Dr. S. Robert Contiguglia
Secretary General ....Dan Flynn
Director of Communications ....Jim Moorhouse

Amateur Softball Association
2801 N.E. 50th Street
Oklahoma City, OK 73111
(405) 424-5266 www.softball.org
President ....H. Franklin Taylor III
Executive Director ....Ron Radigonda
Director of Communications ....Brian McCall

U.S. Speed Skating
P.O. Box 450639, Westlake, OH 44145
(440) 899-0128 www.usspeedskating.org
President ....Andy Gabel
Executive Director ....Katie Marquard

USA Swimming
One Olympic Plaza, Colorado Springs, CO 80909
(719) 866-4578 www.usswim.org
President ....Dale Neuburger
Executive Director ....Chuck Wielgus
Dir. of Public and Media Relations ....Mary Wagner

U.S. Synchronized Swimming, Inc.
201 South Capitol Avenue, Suite 901
Indianapolis, IN 46225
(317) 237-5700 www.usasynchro.org
President ....Betty Hazle
Executive Director ....Terry Harper
Media Relations Director ....Brian Eaton

USA Table Tennis
One Olympic Plaza
Colorado Springs, CO 80909
(719) 866-4583 www.usatt.org
President ....Sherri Soderberg Pittman
Executive Director ....TBA
Director of Programs ....Debbie Moya

USA Team Handball
One Olympic Plaza
Colorado Springs, CO 80909
(719) 866-4036 www.usateamhandball.org
President ....Bob Djokovich
Executive Director ....Mike Cavanaugh
Program Directors ....Lindalisa Severo, Kim Miller

U.S. Tennis Association
70 West Red Oak Lane
White Plains, NY 10604
(914) 696-7000 www.usta.com
Chairman/President ....Mervin A. Heller
Executive Director ....Richard D. Fermin
Director of Communications/Marketing ....David Newman

USA Track and Field
One RCA Dome, Suite 140
Indianapolis, IN 46225
(317) 261-0500 www.usatf.org
President ....Bill Roe
CEO ....Craig Masback
Director of Communications ....Jill Geer

USA Triathlon
616 W. Monument St.
Colorado Springs, CO 80905
(719) 597-9090 www.usatriathlon.org
President ....Ray Plotecia
Executive Director ....Steven M. Locke
Communications/Media Relations Dir. .B.J. Hoeptner-Evans

USA Volleyball
715 S. Circle Dr., 2nd Floor
Colorado Springs, CO 80910
(719) 228-6800 www.usavolleyball.org
President ....Albert Monaco Jr.
Manager of Comm./Technology ....Brent Buzbee

United States Water Polo
1685 W. Uintah St., Colorado Springs, CO 80904
(719) 634-0699 www.usawaterpolo.com
President ....Rich Foster
Executive Director ....Bruce Wigo
Dir. of Media/Marketing ....Eric Velazquez

USA Weightlifting
One Olympic Plaza, Colorado Springs, CO 80909
(719) 866-4508 www.usaweightlifting.org
President ....Dennis Snethen
Exec. Director ....Wes Barnett

USA Wrestling
6155 Lehman Drive, Colorado Springs, CO 80918
(719) 598-8181 www.usawrestling.org
President ....Stan Dziedzic
Executive Director ....Rich Bender
Dir. of Comm./Special Projects ....Gary Abbott

PAN AMERICAN SPORT ORGANIZATIONS

USA Bowling
5301 South 76th St., Greendale, WI 53129
(800) 514-2695 www.usabowling.org
President ....Cathy Cooper
CEO/Executive Director ....Jerry Koenig

USA National Karate-Do Federation, Inc.
P.O. Box 77083, 8351 15th Ave. NW, Seattle, WA 98117-7083
(206) 440-8386 www.usankf.org
President ....Julius Thiry
Executive Director ....Brian Lynch
Public/Media Information ....Howard Nash

United States Racquetball Association
1685 West Uintah, Colorado Springs, CO 80904
(719) 635-5396 www.usra.org
President ....Otto Dietrich
Executive Director ....James L. Hiser
Associate Exec. Dir./Communications ....Linda Mojer

USA Roller Sports
4730 South Street, Lincoln, NE 68506
(402) 483-7551 www.usarollersports.com
President ....George Kolibaba
Executive Director ....Lou Marciani
Media/Public Relations Director ....Mary Beth Vorwerk

U.S. Squash Racquets Association
P.O. Box 1216 (23 Cynwyd Rd.)
Bala Cynwyd, PA 19004
(610) 667-4006 www.us-squash.org
President ....Kevin Jernigan
Executive Director ....Craig W. Brand

U.S. Taekwondo Union
One Olympic Plaza, Suite 104-C, Colorado Springs, CO 80909
(719) 866-4632 www.ustu.org
President ....Sang Chul Lee
Interim Executive Director ....Christine Simmons

USA Water Ski Association
1251 Holy Cow Road, Polk City, FL 33868
(863) 324-4341 www.usawaterski.org
President ....Sherm Schraft
Executive Director ....Steve McDermeit
Director of Communications ....Scott Atkinson

AFFILIATED ORGANIZATIONS

U.S. Orienteering Federation
P.O. Box 1444, Forest Park, GA 30298
(404) 363-2110 www.us.orienteering.org
President ....Charles Ferguson
Executive Director ....Robin Shannonhouse
Media Contact ....Jon Nash

USA Rugby
3595 East Fountain Blvd.
Colorado Springs, CO 80910
(719) 637-1022 www.usarugby.org
President ....Neal Brendel
Executive V.P. ....Bob Latham
Media/Public Relations Director ....Allison Swickard

SOCCER

FIFA

(Federation Internationale de Football Assn.)
P.O. Box 85, 8030 Zurich, Switzerland
TEL: 011-41-1-384-9595   www.fifa.com
President ....Joseph Blatter
Acting General Secretary ....Dr. Urs Linsi
Director of Communications ....Keith Cooper

MLS

Major League Soccer
110 E. 42nd Street, 10th Floor
New York, NY 10017
(212) 450-1200   www.mlsnet.com
Founder ....Alan I. Rothenberg
Commissioner ....Don Garber
Senior Dir. of Communications ....Trey Fitz-Gerald

Chicago Fire
980 N. Michigan Ave., Suite 1998
Chicago, IL 60611
(312) 705-7200   www.chicago-fire.com
Investor/Operator ....Philip F. Anschutz (AEG)
General Manager ....Peter Wilt
Director of Communications ....Diana Lopez

Colorado Rapids
555 17th Street, Suite 3350, Denver, CO 80202
(303) 299-1570   www.coloradorapids.com
Investor/Operator ....Philip F. Anschutz (AEG)
General Manager ....Dan Counce
Director of Public Relations ....Rich Schneider

Columbus Crew
Columbus Crew Stadium
One Black & Gold Blvd., Columbus, OH 43211
(614) 447-2739   www.thecrew.com
Investor/Operator ....Lamar Hunt and Family
President/GM ....Jim Smith
Director of Public Relations ....Jeff Wuerth

Dallas Burn
2602 McKinney Ave., Suite 200, Dallas, TX 75204
(214) 979-0303   www.dallasburn.com
Investor/Operator ....League-owned
President/GM ....Andy Swift
Sr. Director of Media Services ....Chris Ward

Kansas City Wizards
2 Arrowhead Drive
Kansas City, MO 64129
(816) 920-9300   www.kcwizards.com
Investor/Operator ....Lamar Hunt and Family
General Manager ....Curt Johnson
Assoc. Manager of Public Relations .. Justin Gorman, Staci Schottman

Los Angeles Galaxy
1010 Rose Bowl Dr., Pasadena, CA 91103
(626) 432-1540   www.lagalaxy.com
Investor/Operator ....Philip F. Anschutz (AEG)
V.P./General Manager ....Doug Hamilton
Manager of Media Relations ....Patrick Donnelly

New England Revolution
Gillette Stadium, One Patriot Place
Foxboro, MA 02035
(508) 543-5001   www.nerevolution.com
Investor/Operator ....Robert Kraft/Jonathan Kraft
General Manager ....TBA
Director of Media Relations ....Jurgen Mainka

New York/New Jersey MetroStars
One Harmon Plaza, 3rd Floor
Secaucus, NJ 07094
(201) 583-7000   www.metrostars.com
Investor/Operator ....Philip F. Anschutz (AEG)
President/GM ....Nick Sakiewicz
Director of Communications ....John Neves

San Jose Earthquakes
3550 Stevens Creek Blvd., Suite 200
San Jose, CA 95117
(408) 241-9922   www.sjearthquakes.com
Investor/Operator ......San Jose Sports and Entertainment Enterprises & AEG
General Manager ....Johnny Moore
Media Relations Manager ....Jed Mettee

Washington D.C. United
14120 Newbrook Drive, Suite 170, Chantilly, VA 20151
(703) 478-6600   www.dcunited.com
Investor/Operator ....Philip F. Anschutz (AEG)
Senior V.P./Managing Dir. of AEG Soccer ....Kevin Payne
Sr. Director of Communications ....Doug Hicks

Other Soccer

CONCACAF
(Confederation of North, Central American & Caribbean Association Football)
725 Fifth Ave., 17th Floor
New York, NY 10022
(212) 308-0044   www.concacaf.com
President ....Jack Austin Warner
General Secretary ....Chuck Blazer
Senior Consultant ....Clive Toye
Dir. of Communications ....Rick Lawes

U.S. Soccer
(United States Soccer Federation)
U.S. Soccer House, 1801-1811 South Prairie Ave.
Chicago, IL 60616
(312) 808-1300   www.ussoccer.com
President ....Dr. S. Robert Contiguglia
Secretary General ....Dan Flynn
Director of Communications ....Jim Moorhouse

MISL
(Major Indoor Soccer League)
1175 Post Road East
Westport, CT 06880
(203) 222-4900   www.misl.net
Commissioner ....Steve Ryan
V.P./Soccer Operations ....Brian Fleming
Public/Media Relations Director ....Greg Bibb
    Member teams (8): Baltimore Blast, Cleveland Crunch, Dallas Sidekicks, Harrisburg Heat, Kansas City Comets, Milwaukee Wave, Philadelphia Kixx and San Diego Sockers.

WUSA
(Women's United Soccer Association)
6205 Peachtree Dunwoody Rd., 15th Floor
Atlanta, GA 30328
(404) 269-8269   www.wusa.com
President/CEO ....Lynn Morgan
Commissioner ....Tony DiCicco
V.P. of Communications ....Dan Courtemanche
    Member teams (8): Atlanta Beat, Boston Breakers, Carolina Courage, New York Power, Philadelphia Charge, San Diego Spirit, San Jose CyberRays and Washington Freedom.

SWIMMING

FINA
(Federation Internationale de Natation Amateur)
4 ave de l'Avante Poste
1005 Lausanne, Switzerland
TEL: 011-4121-310-4710 www.fina.org
President ....Mustapha Larfaoui
Executive Director ....Cornel Marculescu
Honorary Secretary ....Bartolo Consolo

TENNIS

ATP Tour
(Association of Tennis Professionals)
201 ATP Boulevard
Ponte Vedra Beach, FL 32082
(904) 285-8000 www.atptennis.com
Chief Executive Officer ....Mark Miles
V.P. of Corporate Comm. ....David Higdon
Dir. of Public Relations .......................J.J. Carter

ITF
(International Tennis Federation)
Bank Lane, Roehampton
London, England SW15 5XZ
TEL: 011-44-208-878-6464 www.itftennis.com
President ....Francesco Ricci Bitti
Executive V.P. ....Juan Margets
Head of Communications ....Barbara Travers

World TeamTennis
712 Fifth Ave., 49th Floor
New York, NY 10019
(646) 282-8600 www.worldteamtennis.com
Director/Co-Founder ....Billie Jean King
Commissioner & CEO ....Ilana Kloss
Public Relations Spokesman .....Mickey Ryan—GEM Group
(303-237-0616)

Member teams (9): Delaware Smash, Hartford Fox-Force, Kansas City Explorers, New York Buzz, New York Hamptons, Philadelphia Freedoms, Sacramento Capitals, Springfield (Mo.) Lasers and St. Louis Aces.

USTA
(United States Tennis Association)
70 West Red Oak Lane, White Plains, NY 10604
(914) 696-7000 www.usta.com
President ....Mervin A. Heller
Executive Director ....Richard D. Fermin
Dir. of Communications/Marketing ......David Newman

Sanex WTA Tour
(Sanex Women's Tennis Association)
133 First Street, St. Petersburg, FL 33701
(727) 895-5000 www.wtatour.com
CEO ....Kevin Wulff
President/COO ....Josh Ripple
V.P. of Communications ....Chris De Maria

TRACK & FIELD

IAAF
(International Association of Athletics Federations)
Stade Louis II—Avenue Prince Hereditaire de Monaco
MC 98000 Monaco
TEL: 011-377-92-05-7068 www.iaaf.org
President ....Lamine Diack
Senior V.P. ....Dr. Arne Ljungquist
General Secretary ....Rober J. Fasulo

USA Track & Field
One RCA Dome, Suite 140
Indianapolis, IN 46225
(317) 261-0500 www.usatf.org
President ....Bill Roe
CEO ....Craig Masback
Director of Communications ....Jill Geer

MISCELLANEOUS

AAU
(Amateur Athletic Union)
P.O. Box 22409
Lake Buena Vista, FL 32830
(407) 934-7200 www.aausports.org
President/CEO ....Bobby Dodd
Media/Public Relations Director ....Melissa Wilson

All-American Soap Box Derby
P.O. Box 7225, Akron, OH 44306
(330) 733-8723 www.aasbd.org
Executive Director ....Tony DeLuca
General Manager ....Jeff Iula
Public Relations Director ....Bob Troyer

American Power Boat Association
17640 Nine Mile Road
Eastpointe, MI 48021
(586) 773-9700 www.apba.org
Chairman ....Charles D. Strang
Executive Administrator ....Gloria Urbin

Association of Surfing Professionals
P.O. Box 1095, Coolangatta
Queensland, Australia 4225
011-61-7-5599-1550 www.aspworldtour.com
President/CEO ....Wayne "Rabbit" Bartholomew
Tour Director ....Al Hunt
Media Relations ....Jesse Faen

BASS, Inc.
(Bass Anglers Sportsmen Society)
5845 Carmichael Road
Montgomery, AL 36141
(334) 272-9530 www.bassmaster.com
Owner ....ESPN
General Manager ....Dean Kessel
Director of Communications ....George McNeilly

Iditarod Trail Committee
P.O. Box 870800
Wasilla, AK 99687
(907) 376-5155 www.iditarod.com
Executive Director ....Stan Hooley
Race Director ....Joanne Potts

Little League Baseball, Incorporated
P.O. Box 3485
Williamsport, PA 17701
(570) 326-1921 www.littleleague.org
CEO-President ....Stephen Keener
Director of Comm. & Media Relations ....Lance Van Auken

Major League Lacrosse
One Harmon Plaza, 3rd Floor, Secaucus, NJ 07094
(201) 325-0800 www.majorleaguelacrosse.com
Executive Director ....Matthew Pace
Dir. of Communications ....Jaye Cavallo
Member teams (6): Baltimore Bayhawks, Boston Cannons, Bridgeport Barrage, Long Island Lizards, New Jersey Pride and Rochester Rattlers.

National Association for Girls and Women in Sport
1900 Association Drive, Reston, VA 20191
(703) 863-7549 www.nagws.org
Executive Director ....Athena Yiamouyiannis
President ....Sharon Shields
V.P. of Public Relations ....Shannon Tesdahl

National Lacrosse League
1212 Avenue of the Americas, 5th Floor, New York, NY 10036
(917) 510-9200　　　　　　　www.nationallacrosse.com
Commissioner .... Jim Jennings
Dir. of Public Relations ....Doug Fritts
　　Member teams (13): Albany Attack, Buffalo Bandits, Calgary Roughnecks, Columbus Landsharks, Montreal Express, New Jersey Storm, New York Saints, Ottawa Rebel, Philadelphia Wings, Rochester Knighthawks, Toronto Rock, Vancouver Ravens and Washington Power.

National Sports Foundation
P.O. Box 888886, Atlanta, GA 30356
(678) 417-0041　　　www.natlsportsfoundation.com
President ....Ed Harris

Professional Rodeo Cowboys Association
101 ProRodeo Drive
Colorado Springs, CO 80919
(719) 593-8840　　　　　　　www.prorodeo.com
Commissioner ....Steven J. Hatchell
Director of Communications ....Leslie King

Special Olympics
1325 G St. NW Suite 770
Washington, DC 20005
(202) 824-0328　　　　　www.specialolympics.org
Founder/Honorary Chairman .....Eunice Kennedy Shriver
Chairman ....Sargent Shriver
President/CEO ....Timothy P. Shriver
Sr. Media Relations Manager ....Betty Ann Hughes

U.S. Association of Blind Athletes
33 N. Institute St.
Colorado Springs, CO 80903
(719) 630-0422　　　　　　　www.usaba.org
Executive Director ....Mark Lucas
Communications Director ....Nicole Jomantas

U.S. Polo Association
771 Corporate Dr., Suite 505
Lexington, KY 40503
(859) 219-1000　　　　　　　www.us-polo.org
Chairman ....Orrin H. Ingram
Executive Director ....David Cummings

Wheelchair Sports USA
3595 East Fountain Blvd., Suite L-1
Colorado Springs, CO 80910
(719) 574-1150　　　　　　　www.wsusa.org
Chairman ....Paul DePace
Executive Director ....Patricia Shepherd

Women's Professional Billiard Association
6407 South Blvd.
Charlotte, NC 28217
(704) 556-1128　　　　　　　www.wpba.com
President .... Jan McWorter
Media Contact ....Andy Barton

Commissioners and Presidents

Chief Executives of Established Major Sports Organizations since 1876. (*) indicates died in office.

Major League Baseball

Commissioner	Tenure
Kenesaw Mountain Landis*	1920–44
Albert (Happy) Chandler	1945–51
Ford Frick	1951–65
William Eckert	1965–68
Bowie Kuhn	1969–84
Peter Ueberroth	1984–89
A. Bartlett Giamatti*	1989
Fay Vincent	1989–92
Bud Selig†	1998–

†Served as interim commissioner from 1992-98.

National League

President	Tenure
Morgan G. Bulkeley	1876
William A. Hulbert*	1877–82
A.G. Mills	1883–84
Nicholas Young	1885–1902
Henry Pulliam*	1903–09
Thomas J. Lynch	1910–13
John K. Tener	1914–18
John A. Heydler	1918–34
Ford Frick	1935–51
Warren Giles	1951–69
Charles (Chub) Feeney	1970–86
A. Bartlett Giamatti	1987–89
Bill White	1989–94
Leonard Coleman	1994–99

Note: League president jobs were eliminated after the 1999 season.

American League

President	Tenure
Bancroft (Ban) Johnson	1901–27
Ernest Barnard*	1927–31
William Harridge	1931–59
Joe Cronin	1959–73
Lee McPhail	1974–83
Bobby Brown	1984–94
Gene Budig	1994–99

Note: League president jobs were eliminated after the 1999 season.

NBA

Commissioner	Tenure
Maurice Podoloff	1949–63
Walter Kennedy	1963–75
Larry O'Brien	1975–84
David Stern	1984–

NFL

President	Tenure
Jim Thorpe	1920
Joe Carr	1921–39
Carl Storck	1939–41

Commissioner	Tenure
Elmer Layden	1941–46
Bert Bell*	1946–59
Austin Gunsel	1959–60
Pete Rozelle	1960–89
Paul Tagliabue	1989–

NHL

President	Tenure
Frank Calder*	1917–43
Red Dutton	1943–46
Clarence Campbell	1946–77
John Ziegler	1977–92
Gil Stein	1992–93

Commissioner	Tenure
Gary Bettman	1993–

NCAA

President	Tenure
Walter Byers	1951–88
Dick Schultz	1988–93
Cedric Dempsey	1993–2002
TBA	2003–

Note: Office was known as Executive Director until 1998.

IOC

President	Tenure
Demetrius Vikelas, Greece	1894–96
Baron Pierre de Coubertin, France	1896–1925
Count Henri de Baillet-Latour, Belgium	1925–42
Vacant	1942–46
J. Sigfried Edstrom, Sweden	1946–52
Avery Brundage, USA	1952–72
Lord Michael Killanin, Ireland	1972–80
Juan Antonio Samaranch, Spain	1980–2001
Jacques Rogge, Belgium	2001–

International Sports

Khalid Khannouchi, now an American citizen, broke the marathon world record in London.

AP/Wide World Photos

Tour de Lance

Lance Armstrong continued his amazing streak with a fourth dominating win at the Tour de France.

Gerry Brown *is co-editor of the ESPN/Information Please Sports Almanac.*

It's starting to get kind of scary. Who, exactly, does Lance Armstrong think he is? Actually, the answer is simple. He is the peloton's nightmare. He is the one and only Lance Armstrong.

Well, maybe make that Lance Legstrong, but either way put the emphasis on "strong." To the 188 other riders in the Tour de France, the skinny Texan is no less a strongman than the biggest, baddest musclehead.

What he did in 2002 for the fourth year in a row was beat the world's greatest cyclers in the world's greatest bicycle race.

As the three-time defending champion, Armstrong entered the race with the eyes of every competitor burning a hole in his back. Once again the man the other riders call "The Boss" played it cool before he entered the Pyrenees and pulled away from the proletariat in the peloton.

Armstrong was beaten in the first long-distance time trial by Colombian rider Santiago Botero. It was the first time he was beaten in a long-distance time-trial since his amazing streak began four years ago.

But his apparent vulnerability was just a mirage; he won the prologue and three more stages. And by the time he was cruising toward Paris with the leader's yellow on his familiar-looking back the only thing that could beat him was a thick stick in the spokes.

His total superiority continued to raise eyebrows, but the fact remains that he's never failed a drug test and every investigation has proved fruitless.

It appears that as a cyclist the only things negative about Armstrong are his drug tests. Physiology seems to be the explanation for his domination of the competition.

Doctors have told him that his body metabolizes oxygen at an unusually high rate, and that his famous muscles

AP/Wide World Photos

Lance Armstrong is far and away the leader of the pack in international cycling, winning the Tour de France for the fourth time in as many years in 2002.

produce unusually low amounts of lactic acid, the chemical that makes most riders legs ache.

There is not much reason to think that Armstrong will fall short in his bid for a fifth. All three riders that had previously won four straight Tour de France titles went on to win a fifth. In fact, some observers don't think he can be beat.

"There is no point trying for the Tour de France until Lance retires," up-and-coming British rider David Millar told the BBC.

Armstrong doesn't necessarily agree with Millar's assessment but seems patient, "If I want to win five," he said,

"I will have to ride six or seven because there are lots of other good riders and you can't win every year."

Now that Armstrong is one away from joining the legends as the fifth man with five Tour de France victories talk of an unprecedented sixth has begun.

None other than five-time Tour winner Bernard Hinault said, "It all depends on him, on whether he keeps the motivation to do it. He's just too good for the rest."

Fellow five-timer Miguel Indurain agrees, "It is true that he is still young and, therefore, in terms of age he could win two more. But staying at the top can

Tim Montgomery *took the most coveted title in track and field from fellow American Maurice Greene in 2002, becoming "the world's fastest man."*

be very exhausting," said Indurain.

But even with the proper motivation, Armstrong will need some help from his U.S. Postal Service teammates. Lance's underboss George Hincapie is the only one that has been there for all four Tour wins.

"I wanted to remember that cycling is a team sport. You need protection in the flats, and in the mountains. That security blanket makes a big difference. Some people talked about this team being the best in the history of cycling."

"The first (win) was the comeback, the second one confirmation, the third a really good time, and this year was the year of the team," said Armstrong.

No matter how good his team is, Armstrong still has to go out there and give everything he has to win every year.

Right?

His coach Chris Carmichael is not so sure. "The fact is, Lance is so strong that he doesn't have a real adversary. He doesn't have to give his maximum. And you've never seen the real Lance," said Carmichael.

For the peloton's sake, that is a scary thought.

The Ten Biggest Stories of the Year in International Sports

10 ▪ Italy is the surprise winner of the 2002 Women's World Volleyball Championships in Berlin. The Italians beat the United States, 3–2, in a thrilling five-set final for the gold medal. Neither team was among the pre-tournament favorites.

9 ▪ American Bode Miller, who won two silver medals in the Winter Games at Salt Lake City, finishes second in the slalom standings and fourth in the overall World Cup final standings. It is the best overall finish by an American since Phil Mahre finished first in 1983.

8 ▪ Nineteen-year-old Australian swimmer Ian Thorpe breaks his own world record in the 400-meter freestyle with a time of 3:40.08 to win the Commonwealth Games gold medal in Manchester, England.

7 ▪ Alexei Yagudin makes it a sweep with his win in the World Figure Skating Championships in Nagano, Japan just weeks after taking the Olympic gold medal in Salt Lake City. It gives Yagudin gold in the European championship, Olympics and world championship all in the same year. Michelle Kwan finishes second to Irina Slutskaya in the ladies final.

6 ▪ Moroccan-born American Khalid Khannouchi shaves four seconds off the world marathon record he already owned with his blistering 2:05:38 at the London Marathon pulling away from Haile Gebrselassie and then Paul Tergat late in the race. Khannouchi, who became an American citizen in 2000, also broke the American marathon record with the effort.

5 ▪ Ethiopian teenager Kenenisa Bekele dominates the competition and becomes the first person to win both the men's short and long course races at the IAAF World Cross Country Championships in Dublin, Ireland.

4 ▪ The World Anti-Doping Agency (WADA), whose motto is "think positive, test negative," sets a draft of the first set of universal anti-doping rules for international sports. The rules, which it calls the World Anti-Doping Code, establishes a single list of banned substances, mandates rigorous testing and sets standard penalties and suspensions. WADA, founded by the International Olympic Committee in 1999, plans to officially put the Code in place before the 2004 Olympic Games.

3 ▪ The USA Basketball team, stocked with NBA stars, suffers a serious flame-out in front of home crowds at the Men's Basketball World Championship in Indianapolis. Team USA loses three games and finishes in sixth place.

2 ▪ American sprinter. Tim Montgomery becomes "the world's fastest man," when he breaks Maurice Greene's world record in the 100-meter dash with his time of 9.78 seconds at September's IAAF Grand Prix final in Paris.

1 ▪ The apparently unbeatable Lance Armstrong extends his incredible streak with his fourth consecutive Tour de France victory. The wiry Texan now sits poised to join the sport's all-time greats with a fifth win in 2003.

INSIDE the numbers

Fastest Men Alive

Tim Montgomery added his name to the list of 100-meter dash world record holders in Sept. 2002. Here's a look at the men who have held that record.

Sprinter	Time
Donald Lippincott, USA, 1912	10.6
Charles Paddock, USA, 1921	10.4
Percy Williams, Canada, 1930	10.3
Jesse Owens, USA, 1936	10.2
Willie Williams, USA, 1956	10.1
Armin Hary, W. Germany, 1960	10.0
Jim Hines, USA, 1968	9.99
Jim Hines, USA, 1968	9.95
Calvin Smith, USA, 1983	9.93
Carl Lewis, USA, 1988	9.92
Leroy Burrell, USA, 1991	9.90
Carl Lewis, USA, 1991	9.86
Leroy Burrell, USA, 1994	9.85
Donovan Bailey, Canada, 1996	9.84
Maurice Greene, USA, 1999	9.79
Tim Montgomery, USA, 2002	9.78

Note: Before 1968 and the advent of automatic time, rather than hand timing, times were registered in tenths of a second.

American Perfection

Despite her less-than-perfect performances in the Olympics, Michelle Kwan has dominated at recent U.S. championships. In fact, she has been nearer to perfection than anyone else in U.S. history. Here is a look at the skaters that have received the most perfect scores at the U.S. Figure Skating Championships.

Skater(s)	6.0s
Michelle Kwan	25
Brian Boitano	9
Paul Wylie	7
Scott Hamilton	6
Jenni Meno & Todd Sand	6
Judy Blumberg & Michael Seibert	5

Note: The breakdown for Kwan's 6.0s is as follows: Presentation in a short program (7); Presentation in a free skate (2); Artistic in a short program (8); Artistic in a free skate (8).

2001-2002
Season in Review

ESPN
Information Please®
SPORTS ALMANAC

TRACK & FIELD

2002 IAAF Grand Prix Final

The 18th IAAF Grand Prix Final held in Paris, France, Sept. 14, 2002. Note that (WR) indicates world record and (MR) indicates meet record.

MEN

Event		Time	
100 meters	Tim Montgomery, USA	9.78	WR
400 meters	Michael Blackwood, JAM	44.72	
1500 meters	Hicham El Guerrouj, MOR	3:29.27	
3000 meters	Abraham Chebii, KEN	8:33.42	
400m hurdles	Felix Sanchez, DOM	47.62	MR

Event		Hgt/Dist
High Jump	Stefan Holm, SWE	7-7
Pole Vault	Jeff Hartwig, USA	18-10¼
Triple Jump	Christian Olsson, SWE	57-4¼
Shot Put	Adam Nelson, USA	70-0¼
Hammer Throw	Koji Murofushi, JPN	266-2

WOMEN

Event		Time	
100 meters	Marion Jones, USA	10.88	
400 meters	Ana Guevara, MEX	49.90	
1500 meters	Yelena Zadorozhnaya, RUS	4:00.63	
3000 meters	Gabriela Szabo, ROM	8:56.29	
100m hurdles	Gail Devers, USA	12.51	MR

Event		Hgt/Dist
Long Jump	Maurren Higa Maggi, BRA	23-0½
Discus	Natalya Sadova, RUS	215-10
Javelin	Osleidys Menendez, CUB	215-6

Grand Prix Season Standings

Final Top 10 standings from the 2002 IAAF Grand Prix season. Overall Men's and Women's winners receive $100,000 (US) each. All ties are broken by a complex Grand Prix scoring system.

MEN

1. Tim Montgomery, USA (116 points); 2. Hicham El Guerrouj, MOR (116); 3. Felix Sanchez, DOM (116); 4. Christian Olsson, SWE (102); 5. Jonathan Edwards, GBR (96); 6. Bernard Lagat, KEN (91); 7. Jeff Hartwig, USA (89); 8. Benjamin Limo, KEN (89); 9. Tim Lobinger, GER (84); 10. Stefan Holm, SWE (81.5).

WOMEN

1. Marion Jones, USA (116 points); 2. Gail Devers, USA (111); 3. Ana Guevara, MEX (108); 4. Osleidys Menendez, CUB (106); 5. Tatyana Shikolenko, RUS (101); 6. Berhane Adere, ETH (100); 7. Bridgette Foster, JAM (99); 8. Gabriela Szabo, ROM (98); 9. Lorraine Fenton, JAM (97); 10. Tayna Lawrence, JAM (93).

World Outdoor Records Set in 2002

World outdoor records set or equaled between Oct. 1, 2001 and Sept. 22, 2002; (p) indicates record is pending ratification by the IAAF.

MEN

Event	Name	Record	Old Mark	Former Holder
100 meters	**Tim Montgomery**, USA	9.78p	9.79	Maurice Greene, USA (1999)
Marathon†	**Khalid Khannouchi**, USA	2:05:38	2:05:42	Khalid Khannouchi, MOR* (1995)
3000m steeplechase	**Brahim Boulami**, MOR	7:53.17p	7:55.28	Brahim Boulami, MOR (2001)
20km walk	**Francisco Fernandez**, SPA	1:17:22p	1:17:26	Bernardo Seguro, MEX (1994)

†Marathon records are not officially recognized by the IAAF.
*When Khannouchi set the previous world record, he was a citizen of Morocco. He became a U.S. citizen on May 2, 2000.

WOMEN

Event	Name	Record	Old Mark	Former Holder
Marathon†	**Catherine Ndereba**, KEN	2:18:47	2:20:43	Tegla Loroupe, KEN (1999)
3000m steeplechase	**Alesya Turova**, BLR	9:16.51p	9:21.72	Alesya Turova, BLR (2002)

†The IAAF does not officially recognize world records for road races.
Note: The women's 3000-m steeplechase record was broken three times in 2002, first by Poland's Justyna Bak, then twice by Turova.

World, Olympic and American Records
As of Sept. 22, 2002

World outdoor records officially recognized by the International Amateur Athletics Federation (IAAF); (p) indicates record is pending ratification.

MEN
Running

Event	Time		Date Set	Location
100 meters:	**World** 9.78p	**Tim Montgomery**, USA	Sept. 14, 2002	Paris
	Olympic. 9.84	Donovan Bailey, Canada	July 27, 1996	Atlanta
	American. 9.78p	Montgomery (same as World)	—	—
200 meters:	**World** 19.32	**Michael Johnson**, USA	Aug. 1, 1996	Atlanta
	Olympic 19.32	Johnson (same as World)	—	—
	American 19.32	Johnson (same as World)	—	—
400 meters:	**World** 43.18	**Michael Johnson**, USA	Aug. 26, 1999	Seville
	Olympic 43.49	Michael Johnson, USA	July 29, 1996	Atlanta
	American 43.18	Johnson (same as World)	—	—
800 meters:	**World**. 1:41.11	**Wilson Kipketer**, Denmark	Aug. 24, 1997	Cologne
	Olympic. . . .1:42.58	Vebjoern Rodal, Norway	July 31, 1996	Atlanta
	American. . .1:42.60	Johnny Gray	Aug. 28, 1985	Koblenz, W. Ger.
1000 meters:	**World**. . . .2:11.96	**Noah Ngeny**, Kenya	Sept. 5, 1999	Rieti, ITA
	Olympic.	Not an event	—	—
	American . . .2:13.9	Rick Wohlhuter	July 30, 1974	Oslo
1500 meters:	**World**. . . .3:26.00	**Hicham El Guerrouj**, Morocco	July 14, 1998	Rome
	Olympic. . .3:32.07	Noah Ngeny, Kenya	Sept. 29, 2000	Sydney
	American . . .3:29.77	Sydney Maree	Aug. 25, 1985	Cologne
Mile:	**World**. . . .3:43.13	**Hicham El Guerrouj**, Morocco	July 7, 1999	Rome
	Olympic	Not an event	—	—
	American . . .3:47.69	Steve Scott	July 7, 1982	Oslo
2000 meters:	**World**. . . .4:44.79	**Hicham El Guerrouj**, Morocco	Sept. 7, 1999	Berlin
	Olympic	Not an event	—	—
	American . . .4:52.44	Jim Spivey	Sept. 15, 1987	Lausanne, SWI
3000 meters:	**World**. . . .7:20.67	**Daniel Komen**, Kenya	Sept. 1, 1996	Rieti, ITA
	Olympic	Not an event	—	—
	American . . .7:30.84	Bob Kennedy	Aug. 8, 1998	Monte Carlo
5000 meters:	**World** . . .12:39.36	**Haile Gebrselassie**, Ethiopia	June 13, 1998	Helsinki
	Olympic . .13:05.59	Said Aouita, Morocco	Aug. 11, 1984	Los Angeles
	American .12:58.21	Bob Kennedy	Aug. 14, 1996	Zurich
10,000 meters:	**World** . .26:22.75	**Haile Gebrselassie**, Ethiopia	June 1, 1998	Hengelo, NED
	Olympic . .27:07.34	Haile Gebrselassie, Ethiopia	July 29, 1996	Atlanta
	American .27:13.98	Meb Keflezighi	May 4, 2001	Stanford, Calif.
20,000 meters:	**World**. 56:55.6	**Arturo Barrios**, Mexico	Mar. 30, 1991	La Fleche, FRA
	Olympic	Not an event	—	—
	American . .58:15.0	Bill Rodgers	Aug. 9, 1977	Boston
Marathon:	**World**. . . . .2:05:38†	**Khalid Khannouchi**, USA	Apr. 14, 2002	London
	Olympic. . .2:09:21	Carlos Lopes, Portugal	Aug. 12, 1984	Los Angeles
	American. .2:05:38	Khannouchi (same as World)	—	—

Note: The Mile run is 1,609.344 meters and the Marathon is 42,194.988 meters (26 miles, 385 yards).
†Marathon records are not officially recognized by the IAAF.

Relays

Event	Time		Date Set	Location
4 x 100m:	**World** 37.40	**USA** (Marsh, Burrell, Mitchell, C. Lewis)	Aug. 8, 1992	Barcelona
	37.40	**USA** (Drummond, Cason, Mitchell, Burrell)	Aug. 21, 1993	Stuttgart
	Olympic 37.40	USA (same as World)	—	—
	American 37.40	USA (same as World)	—	—
4 x 200m:	**World** 1:18.68	**USA** (Marsh, Burrell, Heard, C. Lewis)	Apr. 17, 1994	Walnut, Calif.
	Olympic.	Not an event	—	—
	American . . .1:18.68	USA (same as World)	—	—
4 x 400m:	**World** 2:54.20	**USA** (Young, Pettigrew, Washington, Johnson)	July 22, 1998	Uniondale, N.Y.
	Olympic 2:55.74	USA (Valmon, Watts, Johnson, S. Lewis)	Aug. 8, 1992	Barcelona
	American 2:54.20	USA (same as World)	—	—
4 x 800m:	**World** 7:03.89	**Great Britain** (Elliott, Cook, Cram, Coe)	Aug. 30, 1982	London
	Olympic.	Not an event	—	—
	American 7:06.5	Santa Monica TC (J. Robinson, Mack, E. Jones, Gray)	Apr. 26, 1986	Walnut, Calif.
4 x 1500m:	**World** 14:38.8	**West Germany** (Wessinghage, Hudak, Lederer, Fleschen)	Aug. 17, 1977	Cologne
	Olympic.	Not an event	—	—
	American . . .14:46.3	USA (Aldredge, Clifford, Harbour, Duits)	June 24, 1979	Bourges, FRA

Hurdles

Event		Time		Date Set	Location
110 meters:	World	12.91	**Colin Jackson**, Great Britain	Aug. 20, 1993	Stuttgart
	Olympic	12.95	Allen Johnson, USA	July 29, 1996	Atlanta
	American	12.92	Roger Kingdom	Aug. 16, 1989	Zurich
		12.92	Allen Johnson	June 23, 1996	Atlanta
400 meters:	World	46.78	**Kevin Young**, USA	Aug. 6, 1992	Barcelona
	Olympic	46.78	Young (same as World)	—	—
	American	46.78	Young (same as World)	—	—

Note: The 10 hurdles at 110 meters are 3 feet, 6 inches high and those at 400 meters are 3 feet.

Walking

Event		Time		Date Set	Location
20 km:	World	1:17:22	**Francisco Fernandez**, Spain	Apr. 28, 2002	Turku, FIN
	Olympic	1:18:59	Robert Korzeniowski, Poland	Sept. 22, 2000	Sydney
	American	1:22:17	Tim Lewis	Sept. 24, 1989	Dearborn, Mich.
50 km:	World	3:40:58	**Thierry Toutain**, France	Sept. 29, 1996	Hericourt, FRA
	Olympic	3:38:29	Vyacheslav Ivanenko, USSR	Sept. 30, 1988	Seoul
	American	3:48:04	Curt Clausen	May. 2, 1999	Deauville, FRA

Steeplechase

Event		Time		Date Set	Location
3000 meters:	World	7:53.17p	**Brahim Boulami**, Morocco	Aug. 16, 2002	Zurich
	Olympic	8:05.51	Julius Kariuki, Kenya	Sept. 30, 1988	Seoul
	American	8:09.17	Henry Marsh	Aug. 28, 1985	Koblenz, W. Ger

Note: A men's steeplechase course consists of 28 hurdles (3 feet high) and seven water jumps (12 feet long).

Field Events

Event		Mark		Date Set	Location
High Jump:	World	8-0½	**Javier Sotomayor**, Cuba	July 27, 1993	Salamanca, SPA
	Olympic	7-10	Charles Austin, USA	July 28, 1996	Atlanta
	American	7-10½	Charles Austin	Aug. 7, 1991	Zurich
Pole Vault:	World	20-1¾	**Sergey Bubka**, Ukraine	July 31, 1994	Sestriere, ITA
	Olympic	19-5¼	Jean Galfione, France	Aug. 2, 1996	Atlanta
		19-5¼	Igor Trandenkov, Russia	Aug. 2, 1996	Atlanta
		19-5¼	Andrei Tiwontschik, Germany	Aug. 2, 1996	Atlanta
	American	19-9¼	Jeff Hartwig	June 14, 2000	Jonesboro, Ark.
Long Jump:	World	29-4¾*	**Ivan Pedroso**, Cuba	July 29, 1995	Sestriere, ITA
		29-4½	**Mike Powell**, USA	Aug. 30, 1991	Tokyo
	Olympic	29-2½	Bob Beamon, USA	Oct. 18, 1968	Mexico City
	American	29-4½	Powell (same as World)	—	—
Triple Jump:	World	60-0¼	**Jonathan Edwards**, GBR	Aug. 7, 1995	Göteborg, SWE
	Olympic	59-4¼	Kenny Harrison, USA	July 27, 1996	Atlanta
	American	59-4¼	Kenny Harrison (same as Olympic)	—	—
Shot Put:	World	75-10¼	**Randy Barnes**, USA	May 20, 1990	Los Angeles
	Olympic	73-8¾	Ulf Timmermann, East Germany	Sept. 23, 1988	Seoul
	American	75-10¼	Barnes (same as World)	—	—
Discus:	World	243-0	**Jurgen Schult**, East Germany	June 6, 1986	Neubrandenburg
	Olympic	227-8	Lars Riedel, Germany	July 31, 1996	Atlanta
	American	237-4	Ben Plucknett	July 7, 1981	Stockholm
Javelin:	World	323-1	**Jan Zelezny**, Czech Republic	May 25, 1996	Jena, GER
	Olympic	295-10	Jan Zelezny, Czech Republic	Sept. 23, 2000	Sydney
	American	285-10	Tom Pukstys	May 25, 1997	Jena, GER
Hammer:	World	284-7	**Yuriy Sedykh**, USSR	Aug. 30, 1986	Stuttgart
	Olympic	278-2	Sergey Litvinov, USSR	Sept. 26, 1988	Seoul
	American	270-9	Lance Deal	Sept. 7, 1996	Milan

Note: The international weights for men—**Shot** (16 lbs); **Discus** (4 lbs/6.55 oz); **Javelin** (minimum 1 lb/12¼ oz.); **Hammer** (16 lbs).

*Apparent world record disallowed because of interference with wind gauge at altitude.

Decathlon

Event		Points		Date Set	Location
Ten Events:	World	9026	**Roman Sebrle**, Czech Republic	May 26-27, 2001	Gotzis, AUT
	Olympic	8847	Daley Thompson, Great Britain	Aug. 8-9, 1984	Los Angeles
	American	8891	Dan O'Brien	Sept. 4-5, 1992	Talence, FRA

Note: Sebrle's WR times and distances, in order over two days—**100m** (10.64); **LJ** (26-7¼); **Shot** (50-3½); **HJ** (6-11½); **400m** (47.79); **110m H** (13.92); **Discus** (157-3); **PV** (15-9); **Jav** (230-2); **1500m** (4:21.98).

WOMEN
Running

Event		Time		Date Set	Location
100 meters:	World	10.49	**Florence Griffith Joyner**, USA	July 16, 1988	Indianapolis
	Olympic	10.62	Florence Griffith Joyner, USA	Sept. 24, 1988	Seoul
	American	10.49	Griffith Joyner (same as World)	—	—
200 meters:	World	21.34	**Florence Griffith Joyner**, USA	Sept. 29, 1988	Seoul
	Olympic	21.34	Griffith Joyner (same as World)	—	—
	American	21.34	Griffith Joyner (same as World)	—	—

Event		Time		Date Set	Location
400 meters:	**World**	.....47.60	**Marita Koch**, East Germany	Oct. 6, 1985	Canberra, AUS
	Olympic	.....48.25	Marie-Jose Perec, France	July 29, 1996	Atlanta
	American	...48.83	Valerie Brisco	Aug. 6, 1984	Los Angeles
800 meters:	**World**	.....1:53.28	**Jarmila Kratochvilova**, Czech.	July 26, 1983	Munich
	Olympic	...1:53.42	Nadezhda Olizarenko, USSR	July 27, 1980	Moscow
	American	...1:56.40	Jearl Miles-Clark	Aug. 11, 1999	Zurich
1000 meters:	**World**	....2:28.98	**Svetlana Masterkova**, Russia	Aug. 23, 1996	Brussels
	Olympic	....	Not an event	—	—
	American	...2:31.80	Regina Jacobs	July 3, 1999	Brunswick, Me.
1500 meters:	**World**	....3:50.46	**Qu Yunxia**, China	Sept. 11, 1993	Beijing
	Olympic	...3:53.96	Paula Ivan, Romania	Oct. 1, 1988	Seoul
	American	...3:57.12	Mary Slaney	July 26, 1983	Stockholm
Mile:	**World**	....4:12.56	**Svetlana Masterkova**, Russia	Aug. 14, 1996	Zurich
	Olympic	....	Not an event	—	—
	American	...4:16.71	Mary Slaney	Aug. 21, 1985	Zurich
2000 meters:	**World**	.....5:25.36	**Sonia O'Sullivan**, Ireland	July 8, 1994	Edinburgh
	Olympic	....	Not an event	—	—
	American	...5:32.7	Mary Slaney	Aug. 3, 1984	Eugene, Ore.
3000 meters:	**World**	.....8:06.11	**Wang Junxia**, China	Sept. 13, 1993	Beijing
	Olympic	...8:26.53	Tatyana Samolenko, USSR	Sept. 25, 1988	Seoul
	American	...8:25.83	Mary Slaney	Sept. 7, 1985	Rome
5000 meters:	**World**	.14:28.09	**Jiang Bo**, China	Oct. 23, 1997	Shanghai
	Olympic	.14:40.79	Gabriela Szabo, Romania	Sept. 25, 2000	Sydney
	American	.14:45.35	Regina Jacobs	July 27, 2000	Sacramento
10,000 meters:	**World**	.29:31.78	**Wang Junxia**, China	Sept. 8, 1993	Beijing
	Olympic	.30:17.49	Derartu Tulu, Ethiopia	Sept. 30, 2000	Sydney
	American	.30:50:32p	Deena Drossin	May 3, 2002	Stanford, Calif.
Marathon:	**World**	....2:18:47†	**Catherine Ndereba**, Kenya	Oct. 7, 2001	Chicago
	Olympic	...2:23:14	Naoko Takahashi, Japan	Sept. 24, 2000	Sydney
	American	..2:21:21	Joan Benoit Samuelson	Oct. 20, 1985	Chicago

Note: The Mile run is 1,609.344 meters and the Marathon is 42,194.988 meters (26 miles, 385 yards).
†Marathon records are not officially recognized by the IAAF.

Relays

Event		Time		Date Set	Location
4 x 100m:	**World**	.......41.37	**East Germany** (Gladisch, Rieger, Auerswald, Gohr)	Oct. 6, 1985	Canberra, AUS
	Olympic	......41.60	East Germany (Muller, Wockel, Auerswald, Gohr)	Aug. 1, 1980	Moscow
	American	.....41.47	USA (Gaines, Jones, Miller, Devers)	Aug. 9, 1997	Athens
4 x 200m:	**World**	.....1:27.46	**USA** (Jenkins, Colander-Richardson, Perry, Jones)	Apr. 29, 2000	Philadelphia
	Olympic	....	Not an event	—	—
	American	...1:27.46	USA (same as World)	—	—
4 x 400m:	**World**	.....3:15.17	**USSR** (Ledovskaya, Nazarova, Pinigina, Bryzgina)	Oct. 1, 1988	Seoul
	Olympic	...3:15.17	USSR (same as World)	—	—
	American	..3:15.51	USA (Howard, Dixon, Brisco, Griffith Joyner)	Oct. 1, 1988	Seoul
4 x 800m:	**World**	....7:50.17	**USSR** (Olizarenko, Gurina, Borisova, Podyalovskaya)	Aug. 5, 1984	Moscow
	Olympic	....	Not an event	—	—
	American	...8:17.09	Athletics West (Addison, Arbogast, Decker Slaney, Mullen)	Apr. 24, 1983	Walnut, Calif.

Hurdles

Event		Time		Date Set	Location
100 meters:	**World**	......12.21	**Yordanka Donkova**, Bulgaria	Aug. 20, 1988	Stara Zagora, BUL
	Olympic	.....12.38	Yordanka Donkova, Bulgaria	Sept. 30, 1988	Seoul
	American	...12.33	Gail Devers	July 23, 2000	Sacramento
400 meters:	**World**	......52.61	**Kim Batten**, USA	Aug. 11, 1995	Göteborg, SWE
	Olympic	.....52.82	Deon Hemmings, Jamaica	July 31, 1996	Atlanta
	American	...52.61	Batten (same as World)	—	—

Note: The 10 hurdles at 110 meters are 3 feet, 6 inches high and those at 400 meters are 3 feet.

Walking

Event		Time		Date Set	Location
20 km:	**World**	......1:26:52	**Olimpiada Ivanova**, Russia	Sept. 6, 2001	Brisbane
	Olympic	.....1:29:05	Wang Liping, China	Sept. 28, 2000	Sydney
	American	....1:31:51	Michelle Rohl	May 13, 2000	Kenosha, Wis.

Steeplechase

Event	Time		Date Set	Location
3000 meters:	**World**.....9:16:51p	**Alesya Turova**, Belarus	July 27, 2002	Gdansk, POL
	Olympic..........	Not an event	—	—
	American...9:41.94	Elizabeth Jackson	Sept. 4, 2001	Brisbane

Note: A women's steeplechase course consists of 28 hurdles (30 inches high) and seven water jumps (10 feet long).

Field Events

Event	Mark		Date Set	Location
High Jump:	**World**......6-10¼	**Stefka Kostadinova**, Bulgaria	Aug. 30, 1987	Rome
	Olympic......6-8¾	Stefka Kostadinova, Bulgaria	Aug. 3, 1996	Atlanta
	American.....6-8	Louise Ritter	July 8, 1988	Austin, Texas
Pole Vault:	**World**......15-9¼p	**Stacy Dragila**, USA	June 9, 2001	Palo Alto, Calif
	Olympic....15-1	Stacy Dragila, USA	Sept. 25, 2000	Sydney
	American...15-9¼p	Dragila (same as World)	—	—
Long Jump:	**World**.....24-8¼	**Galina Chistyakova**, USSR	June 11, 1988	Leningrad
	Olympic....24-3¼	Jackie Joyner-Kersee, USA	Sept. 29, 1988	Seoul
	American...24-7	Jackie Joyner-Kersee	May 22, 1994	New York
Triple Jump:	**World**.....50-10¼	**Inessa Kravets**, Ukraine	Aug. 8, 1995	Göteborg, SWE
	Olympic....50-3½	Inessa Kravets, Ukraine	July 31, 1996	Atlanta
	American...47-3½	Sheila Hudson	July 8, 1996	Stockholm
Shot Put:	**World**.....74-3	**Natalya Lisovskaya**, USSR	June 7, 1987	Moscow
	Olympic....73-6¼	Ilona Slupianek, E. Germany	July 24, 1980	Moscow
	American...66-2½	Ramona Pagel	June 25, 1988	San Diego
Discus:	**World**....252-0	**Gabriele Reinsch**, E. Germany	July 9, 1988	Neubrandenburg
	Olympic....237-2½	Martina Hellmann, E. Germany	Sept. 29, 1988	Seoul
	American .227-10p	Suzy Powell	Apr. 27, 2002	La Jolla, Calif.
Javelin:	**World**...234-8*p	**Osleidys Menendez**, Cuba	July 1, 2001	Rethymno, GRE
	Olympic...226-1*	Trine Hattestad, Norway	Sept. 30, 2000	Sydney
	American..199-1*p	Kim Kreiner	July 26, 2002	Rheinfelden, GER
Hammer:	**World**....249-7	**Mihaela Melinte**, Romania	Aug. 29, 1999	Rudlingen, SWI
	Olympic...233-5¾	Kamila Skolimowska, Poland	Sept. 29, 2000	Sydney
	American...236-3p	Anna Norgren-Mahon	July 28, 2002	Walnut, Calif.

*The IAAF changed the official design and weight for the women's javelin beginning April 1, 1999.
Note: The international weights for women—**Shot** (8 lbs/13 oz); **Discus** (2 lbs/3.27 oz); **Javelin** (minimum 1 lb/5.16 oz); **Hammer** (8 lbs/13 oz).

Heptathlon

Event	Points		Date Set	Location
Seven Events:	**World**.......7291	**Jackie Joyner-Kersee**, USA	Sept. 23-24, 1988	Seoul
	Olympic.......7291	Joyner-Kersee (same as World)	—	—
	American.....7291	Joyner-Kersee (same as World)	—	—

Note: Joyner-Kersee's WR times and distances, in order over two days—**100m H** (12.69); **HJ** (61¼); **Shot** (51-10); **200m** (22.56); **LJ** (2310¼); **Jav** (149-10); **800m** (2:08.51).

World Indoor Records Set in 2002

World indoor records set or equaled between Oct. 1, 2001 and Sept. 22, 2002.

WOMEN

Event	Name	Record	Old Mark	Former Holder
800 meters.........	**Jolanda Ceplak**, SLO	1:55.82p	1:56.40	Christine Wachtel, E. Ger (1988)
3000 meters.........	**Berhane Adere**, ETH	8:29.15	8:32.88	Gabriela Szabo, ROM (2001)
Pole Vault......	**Svetlana Feofanova**, RUS	15-7p	15-6¾	Svetlana Feofanova, RUS (2002)

Note: Feofanova broke the women's pole vault record five times in 2002. Her current mark was set on Mar. 3.

World and American Indoor Records

As of Sept. 22, 2002

World indoor records officially recognized by the International Amateur Athletics Federation (IAAF); (p) indicates record is pending ratification by the IAAF; (a) indicates record was set at an altitude over 1000 meters.

MEN
Running

Event	Time		Date Set	Location
50 meters:	**World**........5.56a	**Donovan Bailey**, Canada	Feb. 9, 1996	Reno, Nev.
	5.56	**Maurice Greene**, USA	Feb. 13, 1999	Los Angeles
	American......5.56	Greene (same as World)	Feb. 13, 1999	Los Angeles
60 meters:	**World**........6.39	**Maurice Greene**, USA	Feb. 3, 1998	Madrid
	6.39	**Maurice Greene**, USA	March 3, 2001	Atlanta
	American......6.39	Greene (same as World)	—	—
200 meters:	**World** 19.92	**Frankie Fredericks**, Namibia	Feb. 18, 1996	Lievin, FRA
	American 20.26	John Capel	Mar. 11, 2000	Fayetteville, Ark.
	20.26	Shawn Crawford	Mar. 11, 2000	Fayetteville, Ark.
400 meters:	**World** 44.63	**Michael Johnson**, USA	Mar. 4, 1995	Atlanta
	American 44.63	Johnson (same as World)	—	—
800 meters:	**World**.....1:42.67	**Wilson Kipketer**, Denmark	Mar. 9, 1997	Paris
	American...1:45.00	Johnny Gray	Mar. 8, 1992	Sindelfingen, GER

Event	Time		Date Set	Location
1000 meters:	**World**....2:14.96	**Wilson Kipketer**, Denmark	Feb. 20, 2000	Birmingham, ENG
	American..2:17.86p	David Krummenacker	Jan. 27, 2002	Boston
1500 meters:	**World**....3:31.18	**Hicham El Guerrouj**, Morocco	Feb. 2, 1997	Stuttgart
	American..3:38.12	Jeff Atkinson	Mar. 5, 1989	Budapest
Mile:	**World**....3:48.45	**Hicham El Guerrouj**, Morocco	Feb. 12, 1997	Ghent, BEL
	American...3:51.8	Steve Scott	Feb. 20, 1981	San Diego
3000 meters:	**World**....7:24.90	**Daniel Komen**, Kenya	Feb. 6, 1998	Budapest
	American..7:39.23p	Tim Broe	Jan. 27, 2002	Boston
5000 meters:	**World** ..12:50.38	**Haile Gebrselassie**, Ethiopia	Feb. 14, 1999	Birmingham, ENG
	American .13:20.55	Doug Padilla	Feb. 12, 1982	New York

Note: The Mile run is 1,609.344 meters.

Hurdles

Event	Time		Date Set	Location
50 meters:	**World**........6.25	**Mark McKoy**, Canada	Mar. 5, 1986	Kobe, JPN
	American......6.35	Greg Foster	Jan. 27, 1985	Rosemont, Ill.
	6.35	Greg Foster	Jan. 31, 1987	Ottawa
60 meters:	**World**........7.30	**Colin Jackson**, Great Britain	Mar. 6, 1994	Sindelfingen, GER
	American......7.36	Greg Foster	Jan. 16, 1987	Los Angeles

Note: The hurdles for both distances are 3 feet, 6 inches high. There are four hurdles in the 50 meters and five in the 60.

Walking

Event	Time		Date Set	Location
5000 meters:	**World** ...18:07.08	**Mikhail Shchennikov**, Russia	Feb. 14, 1995	Moscow
	American .19:18.40	Tim Lewis	Mar. 7, 1987	Indianapolis

Relays

Event	Time		Date Set	Location
4 x 200 meters:	**World**.....1:22.11	**Great Britain**	Mar. 3, 1991	Glasgow
	American..1:22.71	National Team	Mar. 3, 1991	Glasgow
4 x 400 meters:	**World**.....3:02.83	**United States**	Mar. 7, 1999	Maebashi, JPN
	American..3:02.83	National Team (same as World)	Mar. 7, 1999	Maebashi, JPN
4 x 800 meters:	**World**....7:13.94	**United States**	Feb. 6, 2000	Boston
	American..7:13.94	Global Athletics (same as World)	Feb. 6, 2000	Boston

Field Events

Event	Mark		Date Set	Location
High Jump:	**World** 7-11½	**Javier Sotomayor**, Cuba	Mar. 4, 1989	Budapest
	American 7-10½	Hollis Conway	Mar. 10, 1991	Seville
Pole Vault:	**World** 20-2	**Sergey Bubka**, Ukraine	Feb. 21, 1993	Donyetsk, UKR
	American ...19-9p	Jeff Hartwig	Mar. 10, 2002	Sindelfingen, GER
Long Jump:	**World**.....28-10¼	**Carl Lewis**, USA	Jan. 27, 1984	New York
	American ...28-10¼	Lewis (same as World)		
Triple Jump:	**World** 58-6	**Aliecer Urrutia**, Cuba	Mar. 1, 1997	Sindelfingen, GER
	American ...58-3¼	Mike Conley	Feb. 27, 1987	New York
Shot Put:	**World** 74-4¼	**Randy Barnes**, USA	Jan. 20, 1989	Los Angeles
	American ...74-4¼	Barnes (same as World)	—	—

Note: The international shot put weight for men is 16 lbs.

Heptathlon

	Points		Date Set	Location
Seven Events:	**World** 6476	**Dan O'Brien**, USA	Mar. 13-14, 1993	Toronto
	American 6476	O'Brien (same as World)	—	—

Note: O'Brien's WR times and distances, in order over two days—**60m** (6.67); **LJ** (25-8¾); **SP** (52-6¾); **HJ** (6-11¾); **60m H** (7.85); **PV** (17-0¾); **1000m** (2:57.96).

WOMEN
Running

Event	Time		Date Set	Location
50 meters:	**World**........5.96	**Irina Privalova**, Russia	Feb. 9, 1995	Madrid
	American......6.02	Gail Devers	Feb. 21, 1999	Lievin, FRA
60 meters:	**World**........6.92	**Irina Privalova**, Russia	Feb. 11, 1993	Madrid
	6.92	**Irina Privalova**, Russia	Feb. 9, 1995	Madrid
	American......6.95	Gail Devers	Mar. 12, 1993	Toronto
	6.95	Marion Jones	Mar. 7, 1998	Maebashi, JPN
200 meters:	**World** 21.87	**Merlene Ottey**, Jamaica	Feb. 13, 1993	Lievin, FRA
	American ...22.33	Gwen Torrence	Mar. 2, 1996	Atlanta
400 meters:	**World** 49.59	**Jarmila Kratochvilova**, Czech.	Mar. 7, 1982	Milan
	American ...50.64	Diane Dixon	Mar. 10, 1991	Seville
800 meters:	**World**....1:55.82p	**Jolanda Ceplak**, Slovenia	Mar. 3, 2002	Vienna
	American..1:58.71p	Nicole Teter	Mar. 2, 2002	New York
1000 meters:	**World**....2:30.94	**Maria Mutola**, Mozambique	Feb. 25, 1999	Stockholm
	American ...2:35.29	Regina Jacobs	Feb. 6, 2000	Boston
1500 meters:	**World**....4:00.27	**Doina Melinte**, Romania	Feb. 9, 1990	E. Rutherford, N.J.
	American ...4:00.8	Mary Slaney	Feb. 8, 1980	New York
Mile:	**World**....4:17.14	**Doina Melinte**, Romania	Feb. 9, 1990	E. Rutherford, N.J.
	American ...4:20.5	Mary Slaney	Feb. 19, 1982	San Diego

Event		Time		Date Set	Location
3000 meters:	**World**	8:29.15	**Berhane Adere**, Ethiopia	Feb. 3, 2002	Stuttgart
	American	8:39.14	Regina Jacobs	Mar. 7, 1999	Maebashi, JPN
5000 meters:	**World**	14:47.35	**Gabriela Szabo**, Romania	Feb. 13, 1999	Dortmund, GER
	American	15:07.33p	Marla Runyan	Feb. 18, 2001	New York City

Note: The Mile run is 1,609.344 meters.

Hurdles

Event		Time		Date Set	Location
50 meters:	**World**	6.58	**Cornelia Oschkenat**, E. Ger.	Feb. 20, 1988	East Berlin
	American	6.67a	Jackie Joyner-Kersee	Feb. 10, 1995	Reno, Nev.
60 meters:	**World**	7.69	**Ludmila Engquist**, USSR	Feb. 4, 1990	Chelyabinsk, USSR
	American	7.81	Jackie Joyner-Kersee	Feb. 5, 1989	Fairfax, Va.

Note: The hurdles for both distances are 2 feet, 9 inches high. There are four hurdles in the 50 meters and five in the 60.

Walking

Event		Time		Date Set	Location
3000 meters:	**World**	11:40.33	**Claudia Iovan**, Romania	Jan. 30, 1999	Bucharest
	American	12:20.79	Debbi Lawrence	Mar. 12, 1993	Toronto

Relays

Event		Time		Date Set	Location
4 x 200 meters:	**World**	1:32.55	**West Germany**	Feb. 20, 1988	Dortmund, W. Ger.
		1:32.55	Germany	Feb. 21, 1999	Karlsruhe, GER
	American	1:33.24	National Team	Feb. 12, 1994	Glasgow
4 x 400 meters:	**World**	3:24.25	**Russia**	Mar. 7, 1999	Maebashi, JPN
	American	3:27.59	National Team	Mar. 7, 1999	Maebashi, JPN
4 x 800 meters:	**World**	8:18.71	**Russia**	Feb. 4, 1994	Moscow
	American	8:25.5p	Villanova	Feb. 7, 1987	Gainesville, Fla.

Field Events

Event		Mark		Date Set	Location
High Jump:	**World**	6-9½	**Heike Henkel**, Germany	Feb. 9, 1992	Karlsruhe, GER
	American	6-7	Tisha Waller	Feb. 28, 1998	Atlanta
Pole Vault:	**World**	15-7p	**Svetlana Feofanova**, RUS	Mar. 3, 2002	Vienna
	American	15-5	Stacy Dragila	Feb. 17, 2001	Pocatello, Idaho
Long Jump:	**World**	24-2¼	**Heike Drechsler**, E. Germany	Feb. 13, 1988	Vienna
	American	23-4¾	Jackie Joyner-Kersee	Mar. 5, 1994	Atlanta
Triple Jump:	**World**	49-9	**Ashia Hansen**, Great Britain	Feb. 28, 1998	Valencia, SPA
	American	46-8¼	Sheila Hudson	Mar. 4, 1995	Atlanta
Shot Put:	**World**	73-10	**Helena Fibingerova**, Czech.	Feb. 19, 1977	Jablonec, CZE
	American	65-0¾	Ramona Pagel	Feb. 20, 1987	Inglewood, Calif.

Note: The international shotput weight for women is 8 lbs. and 13 oz.

Pentathlon

Event		Points		Date Set	Location
Five Events:	**World**	4991	**Irina Byelova**, Russia	Feb. 14-15, 1992	Berlin
	American	4753	DeDee Nathan	Mar. 4-5, 1999	Maebashi, JPN

Note: Byelova's WR times and distances, in order over two days—**60m H** (8.22); **HJ** (6-4); **SP** (43-5¾); **LJ** (21-1¾); **800m** (2:10.26).

SWIMMING

World, Olympic and American Records
As of September 22, 2002

World long course records officially recognized by the Federation Internationale de Natation Amateur (FINA). Note that (p) indicates preliminary heat; (r) relay lead-off split; and (s) indicates split time. Note that (*) denotes that a record is awaiting ratification.

MEN
Freestyle

Distance		Time		Date Set	Location
50 meters:	**World**	21.64	**Aleksandr Popov**, Russia	June 16, 2000	Moscow
	Olympic	21.91	Aleksandr Popov, Unified Team	July 30, 1992	Barcelona
	American	21.76	Gary Hall Jr.	Aug. 15, 2000	Indianapolis
100 meters:	**World**	47.84p	**P. van den Hoogenband**, Netherlands	Sept. 19, 2000	Sydney
	Olympic	47.84	P. van den Hoogenband, NED (same as World)	—	—
	American	48.33	Anthony Ervin	July 27, 2001	Fukuoka, JPN
200 meters:	**World**	1:44.06	**Ian Thorpe**, Australia	July 25, 2001	Fukuoka, JPN
	Olympic	1:45.35p	P. van den Hoogenband, NED	Sept. 18, 2000	Sydney
	American	1:46.73	Josh Davis	Sept. 18, 2000	Sydney
400 meters:	**World**	3:40.08*	**Ian Thorpe**, Australia	July 30, 2002	Manchester, GBR
	Olympic	3:40.59	Ian Thorpe, Australia	Sept. 16, 2000	Sydney
	American	3:47.00	Klete Keller	Sept. 16, 2000	Sydney
800 meters:	**World**	7:39.16*	**Ian Thorpe**, Australia	July 24, 2001	Fukuoka, JPN
	Olympic		Not an event	—	—
	American	7:52.05	Larsen Jensen	Aug. 25, 2002	Yokohama, JPN

Distance		Time		Date Set	Location
1500 meters:	**World**	...14:34.56	**Grant Hackett**, Australia	July 29, 2001	Fukuoka, JPN
	Olympic	..14:43.48	Kieren Perkins, Australia	July 31, 1992	Barcelona
	American	.14:56.81	Chris Thompson	Sept. 23, 2000	Sydney

Backstroke

Distance		Time		Date Set	Location
50 meters:	**World**	......24.99	**Lenny Krayzelburg**, USA	Aug. 28, 1999	Sydney
	Olympic	....	Not an event	—	—
	American	....24.99	Krayzelburg (same as World)	—	—
100 meters:	**World**	.....53.60	**Lenny Krayzelburg**, USA	Aug. 24, 1999	Sydney
	Olympic	.....53.72	Lenny Krayzelburg, USA	Sept. 18, 2000	Sydney
	American	....53.60	Krayzelburg (same as World)	—	—
200 meters:	**World**	....1:55.15	**Aaron Peirsol**, USA	Mar. 20, 2002	Minneapolis
	Olympic	....1:56.76	Lenny Krayzelburg, USA	Sept. 21, 2000	Sydney
	American	...1:55.15	Peirsol (same as World)	—	—

Breaststroke

Distance		Time		Date Set	Location
50 meters:	**World**	....27.18	**Oleg Lisogor**, UKR	Aug. 1, 2002	Berlin
	Olympic	....	Not an event	—	—
	American	...27.39	Ed Moses	Mar. 31, 2001	Austin, Texas
100 meters:	**World**	...59.94p	**Roman Sloudnov**, Russia	July 23, 2001	Fukuoka, JPN
	Olympic	...1:00.46	Domenico Fioravanti, Italy	Sept. 17, 2000	Sydney
	American	...1:00.29	Ed Moses	Mar. 28, 2001	Austin, Texas
200 meters:	**World**	....2:10.16	**Mike Barrowman**, USA	July 29, 1992	Barcelona
	Olympic	....2:10.16	Barrowman (same as World)	—	—
	American	..2:10.16	Barrowman (same as World)	—	—

Butterfly

Distance		Time		Date Set	Location
50 meters:	**World**	......23.44	**Geoff Huegill**, Australia	July 26, 2001	Fukuoka, JPN
	Olympic	....	Not an event	—	—
	American	...23.85	Ian Crocker	July 26, 2001	Fukuoka, JPN
100 meters:	**World**	......51.81	**Michael Klim**, Australia	Dec. 12, 1999	Canberra, AUS
	Olympic	...51.96p	Geoff Huegill, Australia	Sept. 21, 2000	Sydney
	American	...51.88	Michael Phelps	Aug. 16, 2002	Ft. Lauderdale, Fla.
200 meters:	**World**	.....1:54.58	**Michael Phelps**, USA	July 24, 2001	Fukuoka, JPN
	Olympic	....1:55.35	Tom Malchow, USA	Sept. 19, 2000	Sydney
	American	..1:54.58	Phelps (same as World)	July 24, 2001	Fukuoka, JPN

Individual Medley

Distance		Time		Date Set	Location
200 meters:	**World**	....1:58.16	**Jani Sievinen**, Finland	Sept. 11, 1994	Rome
	Olympic	....1:58.98	Massimiliano Rosolino, ITA	Sept. 21, 2000	Sydney
	American	..1:58.68	Michael Phelps	Aug. 12, 2002	Ft. Lauderdale, Fla.
400 meters:	**World**	.....4:11.09	**Michael Phelps**, USA	Aug. 15, 2002	Ft. Lauderdale, Fla.
	Olympic	....4:11.76	Tom Dolan, USA	Sept. 17, 2000	Sydney
	American	..4:11.09	Phelps (same as World)	—	—

Relays

Distance		Time		Date Set	Location
4x100m free:	**World**	.....3:13.67	**Australia** (Klim, Fydler, Callus, Thorpe)	Sept. 16, 2000	Sydney
	Olympic	...3:13.67	Australia (same as world)	—	—
	American	..3:13.86	USA (Ervin, Walker, Lezak, Hall Jr.)	Sept. 16, 2000	Sydney
4x200m free:	**World**	.....7:04.66	**Australia** (Hackett, Klim, Kirby, Thorpe)	July 27, 2001	Fukuoka, JPN
	Olympic	...7:07.05	**Australia** (Thorpe, Klim, Pearson, Kirby)	Sept. 19, 2000	Sydney
	American	..7:11.81	USA (Dusing, Keller, Phelps, Carvin)	Aug. 26, 2002	Yokohama, JPN
4x100m medley:	**World**	.....3:33.48	**USA** (Peirsol, Hansen, Phelps, Lezak)	Aug. 29, 2002	Yokohama, JPN
	Olympic	...3:33.73	USA (Krayzelburg, Moses, Crocker, Hall Jr.)	Sept. 23, 2000	Sydney
	American	..3:33.48	USA (same as World)	—	—

WOMEN
Freestyle

Distance		Time		Date Set	Location
50 meters:	**World**	......24.13p	**Inge de Bruijn**, Netherlands	Sept. 22, 2000	Sydney
	Olympic	...24.13	de Bruijn (same as World)	—	—
	American	...24.63	Dara Torres	Sept. 23, 2000	Sydney
100 meters:	**World**	......53.77p	**Inge de Bruijn**, Netherlands	Sept. 20, 2000	Sydney
	Olympic	...53.77	de Bruijn (same as World)	—	—
	American	...53.99	Natalie Coughlin	Aug. 29, 2002	Yokohama, JPN

Distance	Time		Date Set	Location
200 meters:	**World**.....1:56.64	**Franziska van Almsick**, Ger.	Aug. 3, 2002	Berlin
	Olympic....1:57.65	Heike Friedrich, E. Germany	Sept. 21, 1988	Seoul
	American...1:57.90	Nicole Haislett	July 27, 1992	Barcelona
400 meters:	**World**....4:03.85	**Janet Evans**, USA	Sept. 22, 1988	Seoul
	Olympic....4:03.85	Evans (same as World)	—	—
	American...4:03.85	Evans (same as World)	—	—
800 meters:	**World**....8:16.22	**Janet Evans**, USA	Aug. 20, 1989	Tokyo
	Olympic....8:19.67	Brooke Bennett, USA	Sept. 22, 2000	Sydney
	American...8:16.22	Evans (same as World)	—	—
1500 meters:	**World** ...15:52.10	**Janet Evans**, USA	Mar. 26, 1988	Orlando
	Olympic...........	Not an event	—	—
	American .15:52.10	Evans (same as World)	—	—

Backstroke

Distance	Time		Date Set	Location
50 meters:	**World** 28.25	**Sandra Völker**, Germany	June 17, 2000	Berlin
	Olympic..........	Not an event		
	American 28.49p	Natalie Coughlin	July 23, 2001	Fukuoka, JPN
100 meters:	**World** 59.58*	**Natalie Coughlin**, USA	Aug. 13, 2002	Ft. Lauderdale, Fla.
	Olympic....1:00.21	Diana Mocanu, Romania	Sept. 18, 2000	Sydney
	American 59.58	Coughlin (same as World)	—	—
200 meters:	**World**....2:06.62	**Krisztina Egerszegi**, Hungary	Aug. 25, 1991	Athens
	Olympic...2:07.06	Krisztina Egerszegi, Hungary	July 31, 1992	Barcelona
	American..2:08.53	Natalie Coughlin	Aug. 16, 2002	Ft. Lauderdale, Fla.

Breaststroke

Distance	Time		Date Set	Location
50 meters:	**World** 30.57*	**Zoe Baker**, Great Britain	July 30, 2002	Manchester, GBR
	Olympic..........	Not an event		
	American 31.34p	Megan Quann	Aug. 11, 2000	Indianapolis
100 meters:	**World**.....1:06.52p	**Penny Heyns**, South Africa	Aug. 23, 1999	Sydney
	Olympic...1:07.02	Penny Heyns, South Africa	July 21, 1996	Atlanta
	American...1:07.05	Megan Quann	Sept. 18, 2000	Sydney
200 meters:	**World**....2:22.99	**Hui Qi**, China	Apr. 13, 2001	Hangzhou, China
	Olympic...2:24.35	Agnes Kovacs, Hungary	Sept. 21, 2000	Sydney
	American..2:24.56	Kristy Kowal	Sept. 21, 2000	Sydney

Butterfly

Distance	Time		Date Set	Location
50 meters:	**World** 25.57	**Anna-Karin Kammerling**, SWE	July 30, 2002	Berlin
	Olympic..........	Not an event		
	American 26.50p	Dara Torres	Aug. 9, 2000	Indianapolis
100 meters:	**World** 56.61	**Inge de Bruijn**, Netherlands	Sept. 17, 2000	Sydney
	Olympic......56.61	de Bruijn (same as World)	—	—
	American 57.58p	Dara Torres	Aug. 9, 2000	Indianapolis
200 meters:	**World**....2:05.78	**Otylia Jedrzejczak**, Poland	Aug. 4, 2002	Berlin
	Olympic...2:05.88	Misty Hyman, USA	Sept. 20, 2000	Sydney
	American..2:05.88	Misty Hyman	Sept. 20, 2000	Sydney

Individual Medley

Distance	Time		Date Set	Location
200 meters:	**World**....2:09.72	**Wu Yanyan**, China	Oct. 17, 1997	Shanghai
	Olympic...2:10.68	Yana Klochkova, Ukraine	Sept. 19, 2000	Sydney
	American..2:11.91	Summer Sanders	July 30, 1992	Barcelona
400 meters:	**World**....4:33.59	**Yana Klochkova**, Ukraine	Sept. 16, 2000	Sydney
	Olympic...4:33.59	Klochkova, UKR (same as World)	—	—
	American..4:37.58	Summer Sanders	July 26, 1992	Barcelona

Relays

Distance	Time		Date Set	Location
4x100m free:	**World**....3:36.00	**Germany** (Meissner, Dallmann, Volker, van Almsick)	July 29, 2002	Berlin
	Olympic....3:36.61	USA (Van Dyken, Torres, Shealy, Thompson)	Sept. 16, 2000	Sydney
	American..3:36.61	USA (same as Olympic)	—	—
4x200m free:	**World**....7:55.47	**E. Germany** (Stellmach, Strauss, Mohring, Friedrich)	Aug. 18, 1987	Strasbourg, FRA
	Olympic ...7:57.80	USA (Arsenault, Munz, Benko, Thompson)	Sept. 20, 2000	Sydney
	American..7:56.53	USA (Coughlin, Teuscher, Hardt, Munz)	July 25, 2001	Fukuoka, JPN
4x100m medley:	**World**.....3:58.30	**USA** (Bedford, Quann, Thompson, Torres)	Sept. 23, 2000	Sydney
	Olympic....3:58.30	USA (same as World)	—	—
	American...3:58.30	USA (same as World)	—	—

World Swimming Records Set in 2002

World long course records set or equaled between Oct. 1, 2001 and Sept. 22, 2002; (*) indicates record is awaiting ratification.

MEN

Event	Name	Record	Old Mark	Former Holder
400m freestyle	**Ian Thorpe**, AUS	3:40.08*	3:40.17	Ian Thorpe, AUS (2001)
200m backstroke	**Aaron Peirsol**, USA	1:55.15	1:55.87	Lenny Krayzelburg, USA (1999)
50m breaststroke	**Oleg Lisogor**, UKR	27.18	27.39	Ed Moses, USA (2001)
400m IM	**Michael Phelps**, USA	4:11.09*	4:11.76	Tom Dolan, USA (2000)
4x100m medley	**USA**—Peirsol, Hansen, Phelps, Lezak	3:33.48	3:33.73	USA—Krayzelburg, Moses, Crocker, Hall Jr. (2000)

WOMEN

	Name	Record	Old Mark	Former Holder
200m freestyle	**Franziska van Almsick**, GER	1:56.64	1:56.78	Franziska van Almsick, GER (1994)
100m backstroke	**Natalie Coughlin**, USA	59.58*	1:00.16	He Cihong, CHN (1994)
50m breaststroke	**Zoe Baker**, GBR	30.57*	30.83	Penny Heyns, RSA (1999)
50m butterfly	**Anna-Karin Kammerling**, SWE	25.57	25.64	Inge de Bruijn, NED (2000)
200m butterfly	**Otylia Jedrejczak**, POL	2:05.78	2:05.81	Susan O'Neill, AUS (2000)
4x100m freestyle	**Germany**—Meissner, Dallmann, Volker, van Almsick	3:36.00	3:36.61	USA—Van Dyken, Torres, Shealy, Thompson (2000)

2002 FINA Short Course World Championships

The 6th FINA Short Course World Championships held in Moscow, Russia, April 3-7, 2002. Note that (WR) indicates world record and (CR) indicates championship meet record.

Final Medal Leaders—Top 10

		G	S	B	Total			G	S	B	Total
1	United States	8	9	9	26	7	Great Britain	1	2	3	6
2	Australia	10	7	1	18	8	Slovenia	1	2	1	4
3	China	3	4	5	12		Finland	1	1	2	4
4	Sweden	7	2	1	10	10	Slovakia	2	1	0	3
5	Ukraine	5	0	2	7		Argentina	1	1	1	3
	Russia	0	2	5	7		Canada	1	1	1	3

MEN

Event		Time	
50m free	Jose Martin Meolans, ARG	21.36	CR
100m free	Ashley Callus, AUS	46.99	
200m free	Klete Keller, USA	1:44.36	
400m free	Grant Hackett, AUS	3:38.29	
1500m free	Grant Hackett, AUS	14:33.94	
50m back	Matt Welsh, AUS	23.66	
100m back	Matt Welsh, AUS	51.26	
200m back	Aaron Peirsol, USA	1:51.17	WR
50m breast	Oleg Lisogor, UKR	26.42	CR
100m breast	Oleg Lisogor, UKR	58.33	CR
200m breast	Jim Piper, AUS	2:07.16	CR
50m fly	Geoff Huegill, AUS	22.89	CR
100m fly	Geoff Huegill, AUS	50.95	
200m fly	James Hickman, GBR	1:53.14	
100m I.M.	Peter Mankoc, SLO	52.90	
200m I.M.	Jani Sievinen, FIN	1:55.45	CR
400m I.M.	Thomas Wilkens, USA	4:04.82	CR
4x100m free	USA	3:10.64	
4x200m free	Australia	7:00.36	CR
4x100m medley	USA	3:29.00	WR

WOMEN

Event		Time	
50m free	Therese Alshammar, SWE	24.16	
100m free	Therese Alshammar, SWE	52.89	
200m free	Lindsay Benko, USA	1:54.04	WR
400m free	Yana Klochkova, UKR	4:01.26	
800m free	Chen Hua, CHN	8:16.34	CR
50m back	Jennifer Carroll, CAN	27.38	CR
100m back	Haley Cope, USA	59.07	
200m back	Lindsay Benko, USA	2:04.97	CR
50m breast	Emma Igelstrom, SWE	29.96	WR
100m breast	Emma Igelstrom, SWE	1:05.38	WR
200m breast	Qi Hui, CHN	2:20.91	
50m fly	Anna-Karin Kammerling, SWE	25.55	CR
100m fly	Martina Moravcova, SVK	57.04	
200m fly	Petria Thomas, AUS	2:05.76	CR
100m I.M.	Martina Moravcova, SVK	59.91	
200m I.M.	Yana Klochkova, UKR	2:08.82	
400m I.M.	Yana Klochkova, UKR	4:30.63	
4x100m free	Sweden	3:35.09	
4x200m free	China	7:46.30	WR
4x100m medley	Sweden	3:55.78	WR

WINTER SPORTS

Alpine Skiing
2002 World Cup Champions

MEN

Overall	Stephan Eberharter, Austria
Downhill	Stephan Eberharter, Austria
Slalom	Ivica Kostelic, Croatia
Giant Slalom	Frederic Covili, France
Super G	Stephan Eberharter, Austria
Combined	Kjetil Andre Aamodt, Norway

WOMEN

Overall	Michaela Dorfmeister, Austria
Downhill	Isolde Kostner, Italy
Slalom	Laure Pequegnot, France
Giant Slalom	Sonja Nef, Switzerland
Super G	Hilde Gerg, Germany
Combined	Renate Goetschl, Austria

Top Five Standings

Overall 1. Stephan Eberharter, AUT (1702 pts); 2. Kjetil Andre Aamodt, NOR (1096); 3. Didier Cuche, SWI (1064); 4. Bode Miller, USA (952); 5. Fritz Strobl, AUT (846).

Downhill 1. Stephan Eberharter, AUT (810 pts); 2. Fritz Strobl, AUT (520); 3. Kristian Ghedina, ITA (381); 4. Franco Cavegn, SWI (366); 5. Hannes Trinkl, AUT (350). *Best USA—Daron Rahlves (19th, 113 pts).*

Slalom 1. Ivica Kostelic, CRO (611 pts); 2. Bode Miller, USA (560); 3. Jean-Pierre Vidal, FRA (456); 4. Mitja Kunc, SLO (322); 5. Rainer Schoenfelder, AUT (318).

Giant Slalom 1. Frederic Covili, FRA (471 pts); 2. Benjamin Raich, AUT (429); 3. Stephan Eberharter, AUT (422); 4. Didier Cuche, SWI (420); 5. Fredrik Nyberg, SWE (405).

Super G 1. Stephan Eberharter, AUT (470 pts); 2. Didier Cuche, SWI (426); 3. Fritz Strobl, AUT (326); 4. Alessandro Fattori, ITA (294); 5. Andreas Schifferer, AUT (214). *Best USA—Daron Rahlves (12th, 118 pts).*

Combined 1. Kjetil Andre Aamodt, NOR (200 pts); 2. Lasse Kjus, NOR (140); 3. Andrej Jerman, SLO (82); 4. Bode Miller, USA (80); 5. Michael Walchhofer, AUT (60).

Top Five Standings

Overall 1. Michaela Dorfmeister, AUT (1271 pts); 2. Renate Goetschl, AUT (931); 3. Sonja Nef, SWI (904); 4. Hilde Gerg, GER (847); 5. Anja Paerson, SWE (840). *Best USA—Kristina Koznick (8th, 612 pts).*

Downhill 1. Isolde Kostner, ITA (568 pts); 2. Michaela Dorfmeister, AUT (469); 3. Corinne Rey Bellet, SWI (414); 4. Hilde Gerg, GER (412); 5. Renate Goetschl, AUT (408). *Best USA—Caroline Lalive (14th, 172 pts).*

Slalom 1. Laure Pequegnot, FRA (597 pts); 2. Kristina Koznick, USA (518); 3. Anja Paerson, SWE (480); 4. Sonja Nef, SWI (330); 5. Ylva Nowen, SWE (328).

Giant Slalom 1. Sonja Nef, SWI (574 pts); 2. Michaela Dorfmeister, AUT (494); 3. Anja Paerson, SWE (360); 4. Andrine Flemmen, NOR (335); 5. Stina Hofgard Nilsen, NOR (330). *Best USA—Sarah Schleper (20th, 114 pts).*

Super G 1. Hilde Gerg, GER (355 pts); 2. Alexandra Meissnitzer, AUT (248); 3. Michaela Dorfmeister, AUT (212); 4. Renate Goetschl, AUT (210); 5. Karen Putzer, ITA (192). *Best USA—Caroline Lalive (6th, 167 pts).*

Combined 1. Renate Goetschl, AUT (200 pts); 2. Michaela Dorfmeister, AUT (96); 3. Brigitte Obermoser, AUT (82); 4. (tie) Janette Hargin, SWE and Janica Kostelic, CRO (80).

2002 U.S. Championships
at Squaw Valley, Calif. (March 14-19)

MEN

Downhill	canceled (poor conditions)
Slalom	Bode Miller, Franconia, NH
Giant Slalom	Thomas Vonn, Newburgh, NY
Super G	Marco Sullivan, Squaw Valley, CA
Combined	Bode Miller, Franconia, NH

WOMEN

Downhill	canceled (poor conditions)
Slalom	Sarah Schleper, Vail, CO
Giant Slalom	Jonna Mendes, Heavenly, CA
Super G	Caroline Lalive, Steamboat Springs, CO
Combined	Caroline Lalive, Steamboat Springs, CO

Freestyle Skiing
World Cup Champions

MEN

Overall	Eric Bergoust, United States
Aerials	Eric Bergoust, United States
Moguls	Jeremy Bloom, United States
Dual Moguls	Richard Gay, France

WOMEN

Overall	Kari Traa, Norway
Aerials	Alla Tsuper, Belarus
Moguls	Kari Traa, Norway
Dual Moguls	Christine Gerg, Germany

2002 U.S. Championships
at Boise, Idaho (March 22-25)

MEN

Aerials	Ryan St. Onge, Winter Park, CO
Moguls	Travis Ramos, South Lake Tahoe, CA
Dual Moguls	Toby Dawson, Vail, CO

WOMEN

Aerials	Tracy Evans, Park City, UT
Moguls	Shannon Bahrke, Tahoe City, CA
Dual Moguls	Shannon Bahrke, Tahoe City, CA

Note: Jeremy Bloom was originally crowned the 2002 moguls champion, but over three weeks later an error in the points calculation was revealed and Ramos was awarded the title.

Cross Country
World Cup Champions

MEN

Overall

		Pts
1	Per Elofsson, Sweden	.780
2	Thomas Alsgaard, Norway	.777
3	Anders Aukland, Norway	.545
4	Kristen Skjeldal, Norway	.518
5	Frode Estil, Norway	.404

Sprint

		Pts
1	Trond Iversen, Norway	.328
2	Jens Arne Svartedal, Norway	.300
3	Cristian Zorzi, Italy	.264
4	Tobias Fredriksson, Sweden	.254
5	Haavard Bjerkeli, Norway	.249

WOMEN

Overall

		Pts
1	Bente Skari, Norway	.877
2	Katerina Neumannova, Czech Republic	.763
3	Stefania Belmondo, Italy	.760
4	Kristina Smigun, Estonia	.649
5	Julija Tchepalova, Russia	.612

Sprint

		Pts
1	Bente Skari, Norway	.319
2	Anita Moen, Norway	.307
3	Katerina Neumannova, Czech Republic	.293
4	Evi Sachenbacher, Germany	.237
5	Hilde G. Pedersen, Norway	.223

2002 U.S. Championships
at Bozeman, Mont. (Jan. 5-13)

MEN

10-k Classic	John Bauer, Duluth, MN
50-k Classic	John Bauer, Duluth, MN
30-k Freestyle	Carl Swenson, Boulder, CO
10-k Pursuit	John Bauer, Duluth, MN
Sprint	Lars Flora, Anchorage, AK

WOMEN

5-k Classic	Katerina Hanusova, Czech Republic*
30-k Classic	Nina Kemppel, Anchorage, AK
15-k Freestyle	Nina Kemppel, Anchorage, AK
5-k Pursuit	Katerina Hanusova, Czech Republic*
Sprint	Kikkan Randall, Anchorage, AK

*Since Hanusova is not from the U.S., the championships were awarded to runners-up Tara Hamilton, Anchorage, AK, in the 5-k Classic and Kemppel in the pursuit.

Nordic Combined
World Cup Champions
MEN

Overall

		Pts
1	Ronny Ackermann, Germany	.2110
2	Felix Gottwald, Austria	.1986
3	Samppa Lajunen, Finland	.1863
4	Jaakko Tallus, Finland	.1220
5	Daito Takahashi, Japan	.1101

Ski Jumping
World Cup Champions
MEN

Overall

		Pts
1	Adam Malysz, Poland	.1475
2	Sven Hannawald, Germany	.1259
3	Matti Hautamaeki, Finland	.1048
4	Andreas Widhoelzl, Austria	.874
5	Martin Schmitt, Germany	.795

2002 U.S. Ski Jumping/Nordic Combined Championships
at Steamboat Springs, Col. (March 27-28)

MEN

Nordic Combined

(90-m jump/10-k ski)	Bill Demong, Vermontville, NY
Normal Hill (90-m) jump	Alan Alborn, Anchorage, AK
Large Hill (114-m) jump	Alan Alborn, Anchorage, AK

WOMEN

Normal Hill (90-m) jump	Jessica Jerome, Park City, UT
Large Hill (114-m) jump	Jessica Jerome, Park City, UT

Snowboarding
World Cup Champions

MEN

Overall	Jasey Jay Anderson, Canada
Halfpipe	Jan Michaelis, Germany
Parallel Slalom	Mathieu Bozzetto, France
Giant Slalom	Dejan Kosir, Slovenia
Parallel Giant Slalom	Dejan Kosir, Slovenia
Snowboardcross	Jasey Jay Anderson, Canada
Big Air	Jukka Eratuli, Finland

WOMEN

Overall	Karine Ruby, France
Halfpipe	Nicola Pederzolli, Austria
Parallel Slalom	Karine Ruby, France
Giant Slalom	Steffi von Siebenthal, Switzerland
Parallel Giant Slalom	Isabelle Blanc, France
Snowboardcross	Doresia Krings, Austria

2002 U.S. Championships
at Northstar-at-Tahoe, Calif. (March 28-31)

MEN

Halfpipe	Wyatt Caldwell, Sun Valley, CA
Slalom	Chris Klug, Aspen, CO
Parallel Gaint Slalom	Ian Price, Manchester Center, VT
Snowboardcross	Seth Wescott, Kingfield, ME

WOMEN

Halfpipe	Gretchen Bleiler, Snowmass Village, CO
Slalom	Stacia Hookom, Edwards, CO
Parallel Giant Slalom	Stacia Hookom, Edwards, CO
Snowboardcross	Lindsey Jacobellis, Stratton Mt., VT

Speed Skating
World Cup Champions

MEN		WOMEN	
500 meters	Jeremy Wotherspoon, Canada	500 meters	Catriona Lemay-Doan, Canada
1000 meters	Jeremy Wotherspoon, Canada	1000 meters	Sabine Volker, Germany
1500 meters	Adne Sondral, Norway	1500 meters	Anni Friesinger, Germany
5000/10,000 meters	Gianni Romme, Netherlands	3000/5000 meters	Anni Friesinger, Germany

2002 World Championships
at Heerenveen, Netherlands (March 15-17)

MEN		WOMEN	
500 meters	Petter Andersen, Norway & Dmitri Shepel, Russia (tie)	500 meters	Jennifer Rodriguez, United States
1500 meters	Dmitri Shepel, Russia	1500 meters	Anni Friesinger, Germany
5000 meters	Jochem Uytdehaage, Netherlands	3000 meters	Anni Friesinger, Germany
10,000 meters	Jochem Uytdehaage, Netherlands	5000 meters	Claudia Pechstein, Germany
All-Around	Jochem Uytdehaage, Netherlands	All-Around	Anni Friesinger, Germany

2002 World Short Track Championships
at Montreal, Quebec, Canada (April 5-7)

MEN		WOMEN	
500 meters	Kim Dong-Sung, South Korea	500 meters	Yang Yang (A), China
1000 meters	Kim Dong-Sung, South Korea	1000 meters	Yang Yang (A), China
1500 meters	Kim Dong-Sung, South Korea	1500 meters	Yang Yang (A), China
3000 meters	Kim Dong-Sung, South Korea	3000 meters	Choi Eun-Kyung, South Korea
5000 meter relay	South Korea	3000 meter relay	South Korea
All-Around	Kim Dong-Sung, South Korea	All-Around	Yang Yang (A), China

Note: There are two Chinese skaters with the name Yang Yang. To differentiate, one goes by Yang Yang (A) and one by Yang Yang (S).

Figure Skating

World Championships
at Nagano, Japan (March 15-24)

Men's —1. Alexei Yagudin, Russia; 2. Tim Goebel, USA; 3. Honda Takeshi, Japan; 4. Alexander Abt, Russia; 5. Li Chengjiang, China.

Women's —1. Irina Slutskaya, Russia; 2. Michelle Kwan, USA; 3. Fumie Suguri, Japan; 4. Sasha Cohen, USA; 5. Yoshie Onda, Japan.

Pairs —1. Xue Shen & Hongbo Zhao, China; 2. Tatiana Totmianina & Maxim Marinin, Russia; 3. Kyoko Ina & John Zimmerman, USA; 4. Maria Petrova & Alexei Tikhonov, Russia; 5. Qing Pang & Jian Tong, China.

Ice Dance —1. Irina Lobacheva & Ilia Averbukh, Russia; 2. Shae-Lynn Bourne & Victor Kraatz, Canada; 3. Galit Chait & Sergei Sakhnovski, Israel; 4. Margarita Drobiazko & Povilas Vanagas, Lithuania; 5. Albena Denkova & Maxim Staviyski, Bulgaria.

U.S. Championships
at Los Angeles, Calif. (Jan. 6-13)

Men's	Todd Eldredge
Women's	Michelle Kwan
Pairs	Kyoko Ina & John Zimmerman
Ice Dance	Naomi Lang & Peter Tchernyshev

European Championships
at Lausanne, Switzerland (Jan. 14-20)

Men's	Alexei Yagudin, Russia
Women's	Maria Butyrskaya, Russia
Pairs	Tatiana Totmianina & Maxim Marinin, Russia
Ice Dance	Marina Anissina & Gwendal Peizerat, France

SUMMER SPORTS

Cross Country
IAAF World Championships
The 30th IAAF World Cross Country Championships held in Dublin, Ireland (March 23-24).

MEN	WOMEN
12 km ...... 1. Kenenisa Bekele, Ethiopia 34:52	8 km ...... 1. Paula Radcliffe, Great Britain 26:55
(7.46 mi) 2. John Yuda, Tanzania 34:58	(4.97 mi) 2. Deena Drossin, USA 27:04
3. Wilberforce Talel, Kenya 35:20	3. Colleen De Reuck, USA 27:17
Best USA—Abdihakem Abdirahman, 11th 36:03	

Cycling
Tour de France

The 89th Tour de France (July 6-28) ran 20 stages plus a prologue, covering 2,050 miles starting in Luxembourg, passing through the Alps and Pyrenees in France and finishing on the Avenue des Champs-Elysees in Paris.

For the fourth consecutive year, U.S. Postal Service rider Lance Armstrong sipped champagne and donned the yellow jersey as he rode down the Champs-Elysees to victory. He finished in 82 hours, 5 minutes and 12 seconds, defeating his closest competitor, Joseba Beloki of Spain , by 7 minutes and 17 seconds. He is one of five men in history, and the only American, to win at least four Tours.

Less than three years before Armstrong rode down the Champs-Elysees for his first Tour de France victory in 1999, he was diagnosed with testicular cancer. The cancer then spread to his lungs and his brain and doctors gave him less than a 40 percent chance of survival. He underwent two operations and extensive chemotherapy and began his comeback in early 1998. He is only the second American to win cycling's premier event.

		Team	Behind				Team	Behind
1	Lance Armstrong, USA	U.S. Postal	—	6	Jose Azevedo, POR	ONCE	15:44
2	Joseba Beloki, SPA.	ONCE	7:17	7	Francisco Mancebo, SPA	iBanesto.com	16:05
3	Raimondas Rumsas, LIT	Lampre	8:17	8	Levi Leipheimer, USA	Rabobank	17:11
4	Santiago Botero, COL	Kelme	13:10	9	Roberto Heras Hernandez, SPA	U.S. Postal	17:12
5	Igor Gonzalez Galdeano, SPA	ONCE	13:54	10	Carlos Sastre, Spain	CSC-Tiscali	19:05

Other Worldwide Champions

2002 Major UCI (Union Cycliste Internationale) Road results through Sept. 15. Note that in some instances, the date shown below is the final day of that particular race.

MEN

Race	Winner	Race	Winner
Jan. 20: Tour Down Under (AUS)	Michael Rogers, AUS	Mar. 31: Criterium Int'l (FRA)	Alberto Martinez, SPA
Feb. 7: Mallorca Challenge (SPA)	Francisco Cabello, SPA	Apr. 7: Tour de Flanders (BEL)	Andrea Tafi, ITA
Feb. 10: Tour de Langwaki (MAS)	H. Dario Munoz, COL	Apr. 10: Ghent-Wevelgem (BEL)	Mario Cipollini, ITA
Feb. 17: Mediterranean Tour (FRA)	Michele Bartoli, ITA	Apr. 14: Paris-Roubaix (FRA)	Johan Museeuw, BEL
Feb. 21: Ruta del Sol (SPA)	Antonio Colom, SPA	Apr. 21: Fleche Wallonne (BEL)	Mario Aerts, BEL
Mar. 2: Tour de Valencia (SPA)	Alex Zulle, SWI	May 5: Tour de Romandie (SWI)	Dario Frigo, ITA
Mar. 3: Omloop Het Volk (BEL)	Peter Van Petegem, BEL	May 12: Four Days of Dunkirk (FRA)	Sylvain Chavanel, FRA
Mar. 17: Paris-Nice (FRA)	Alexandre Vinokurov, KAZ	June 10: Giro d'Italia (ITA)	Paolo Savoldelli, ITA
Mar. 20: Tirreno-Adriatico (ITA)	Erik Dekker, NED	June 17: Dauphine Libere (FRA)	Lance Armstrong, USA
Mar. 23: Milan-San Remo (ITA)	Mario Cipollini, ITA	June 27: Tour of Switzerland (SWI)	Alex Zulle, SWI
Mar. 29: Semana Catalana (SPA)	Juan Miguel Mercado, SPA	Aug. 24: Tour of the Netherlands (NED)	Kim Kirchen, LUX

WOMEN

Race	Winner	Race	Winner
Mar. 6: Tour de Snowy (AUS)	Judith Arndt, GER	July 15: Giro d'Italia Femminile (ITA)	S. Boubnenkova, RUS
Mar. 23: Primavera Rosa (ITA)	Mirjam Melchers, NED	Aug. 18: Grande Boucle Feminine (FRA)	Z. Stahurskaia, BLR
Apr. 17: Fleche Wallonne (BEL)	Fabiana Luperini, ITA	Sept. 8: Grand Prix Suisse Feminin (SWI)	S. Boubnenkova, RUS
May 26: Tour de L'Aude (FRA)	Judith Arndt, GER	Sept. 15: Rotterdam Tour (NED)	Petra Rossner, GER
June 1: Montreal World Cup (CAN)	D. Demet-Barry, USA		
June 9: Liberty Classic (USA)	Petra Rossner, GER		
June 23: HP Women's Challenge (USA)	Judith Arndt, GER		

Softball
Women's World Championships
at Saskatoon, Saskatchewan, Canada
(July 26-Aug. 4)

Final Game

	1	2	3	4	5	6	7	R	H	E
Japan	0	0	0	0	0	0	0	—	0	3	0
USA	0	0	1	0	0	0	x	—	1	6	0

Win: Lisa Fernandez, USA (4-0). **Loss:** Juri Takayama, JPN (1-1).

2B: USA—Leah Amico. **RBI:** USA—Amico. **SB:** USA—Natasha Watley, Lovie Jung. **LOB:** JPN—2; USA—5.

Note: The United States (gold), Japan (silver), Taiwan (bronze) and China (4th place) all secured automatic bids for the 2004 Olympics.

Volleyball
Women's World Championships
at Berlin, Germany (Aug. 30-Sept. 15)

Semifinals
USA def. Russia—(5 sets) 21-25, 25-23, 25-20, 21-25, 15-8
Italy def. China—(4 sets) 25-21, 25-20, 21-25, 25-23

Bronze Medal Match
Russia def. China—(4 sets) 25-20, 21-25, 25-23, 25-16

Finals
Italy def. USA—(5 sets) 18-25, 25-18, 25-16, 22-25, 15-11

Marathons
2002 Boston Marathon

The 106th edition of the Boston Marathon was held Monday, April 15, 2002 and run, as always, from Hopkinton through Ashland, Framingham, Natick, Wellesley, Newton and Brookline to Boston, Mass. Kenyan policeman Rodgers Rop outdueled fellow countryman Christopher Cheboiboch to win the men's race in 2:09:02. It was sweet revenge for the Kenyans, whose string of ten consecutive Boston titles was broken in 2001 by South Korean Lee Bong-Ju.

In the women's division, Kenyan Margaret Okayo held off two-time defending champ Catherine Ndereba and broke the tape in a women's record, 2:20:43. The time shattered the previous mark (2:21:45) set in 1994 by German Uta Pippig.

In the men's wheelchair race, South Africa's Ernst VanDyk (1:23:19) successfully defended his 2001 crown, finishing a full two minutes and 45 seconds ahead of the rest of the field. In the women's division, 2001 runner-up Edith Hunkeler of Switzerland captured her first title with a time of 1:45:57. Winners in the men's and women's divisions earned $80,000. Winners of each wheelchair division earn $10,000.

Distance: 26.2 miles.

MEN

	Time
1 Rodgers Rop, Kenya	2:09:02
2 Christopher Cheboiboch, Kenya	2:09:05
3 Fred Kiprop, Kenya	2:09:45
4 Mbarak Hussein, Kenya	2:09:45
5 Lee Bong-Ju, South Korea	2:10:30

Best USA: 15th—Keith Dowling, Virginia, 2:13:28

WHEELCHAIR

	Time
1 Ernst VanDyk, South Africa	1:23:19
2 Krige Schabort, South Africa	1:26:04
3 Franz Nietlispach, Switzerland	1:30:08

WOMEN

	Time
1 Margaret Okayo, Kenya	2:20:43
2 Catherine Ndereba, Kenya	2:21:12
3 Elfenesh Alemu, Ethiopia	2:26:01
4 Sun Yingjie, China	2:27:26
5 Firaya Sultanova, Russia	2:27:58

Best USA: 13th—Jill Gaitenby, Massachusetts, 2:38:55

WHEELCHAIR

	Time
1 Edith Hunkeler, Switzerland	1:45:57
2 Christina Ripp, Illinois	1:49:32
3 Wakako Tsuchida, Japan	1:50:09

Other 2002 Winners

Tokyo

Feb. 10	Men	Eric Wainaina, ETH	2:08:43
	(No women's division)		

Los Angeles

Mar. 3	Men	Stephen Ndungu, KEN	2:10:27
	Women	Lyubov Denisova, RUS	2:28:49

Paris

Apr. 7	Men	Benoit Zwierzchlewski, FRA	2:08:18
	Women	Marleen Renders, BEL	2:23:04

London

Apr. 14	Men	Khalid Khannouchi, USA	2:05:38*
	Women	Paula Radcliffe, GBR	2:18:56

* world record

Turin

Apr. 21	Men	Alberico Di Cecco, ITA	2:10:27
	Women	Anatasha Ndereba, KEN	2:29:27

Rotterdam

Apr. 21	Men	Simon Biwott, KEN	2:08:39
	Women	Takami Ominami, JPN	2:23:43

Late 2001

Chicago

Oct. 7	Men	Ben Kimondiu, KEN	2:08:52
	Women	Catherine Ndereba, KEN	2:18:47*

* world record

New York City

Nov. 4	Men	Tesfaye Jifar, ETH	2:07:43
	Women	Margaret Okayo, KEN	2:24:21

Tokyo Women's

Nov. 18	Women	Derartu Tulu, ETH	2:25:08

Fukuoka

Dec. 2	Men	Gezahegne Abera, ETH	2:09:25
	(No women's division)		

Rowing
World Championships
at Seville, Spain (Sept. 15-22)

MEN

Eights	Canada, 5:26.92
Coxed Pairs	Germany, 6:47.93
Coxed Fours	Great Britain, 6:06.70
Coxless Pairs	Great Britain, 6:14.27
Coxless Fours	Germany, 5:41.35
Single Sculls	Marcel Hacker, GER, 6:36.33
Double Sculls	Hungary, 6:05.74
Quad Sculls	Germany, 5:39.57

WOMEN

Eights	United States, 6:04.25
Coxless Pairs	Romania, 6:53.80
Coxless Fours	Australia, 6:26.11
Single Sculls	Roumiana Neykova, BUL, 7:07.71
Double Sculls	New Zealand, 6:38.78
Quad Sculls	Germany, 6:15.66

TRACK & FIELD

IAAF World Championships

While the Summer Olympics have served as the unofficial world outdoor championships for track and field throughout the centuries, a separate World Championship meet was started in 1983 by the International Amateur Athletic Federation (IAAF). The meet was held every four years from 1983-91, but began an every-other-year cycle in 1993. World Championship sites include Helsinki (1983), Rome (1987), Tokyo (1991), Stuttgart (1993), Göteborg, Sweden (1995), Athens (1997), Seville, Spain (1999) and Edmonton (2001). Looking forward, the Championships will be held in Paris (2003) and Helsinki (2005). Note that (WR) indicates world record and (CR) indicates championship meet record.

MEN

Multiple gold medals (including relays): Michael Johnson (9); Carl Lewis (8); Sergey Bubka (6); Maurice Greene and Lars Riedel (5); Haile Gebrselassie, Ivan Pedroso, Antonio Pettigrew and Calvin Smith (4); Donovan Bailey, Tomas Dvorak, Hicham El Guerrouj, Greg Foster, John Godina, Werner Gunthor, Allen Johnson, Wilson Kipketer, Moses Kiptanui, Dennis Mitchell, Noureddine Morceli, Dan O'Brien, Butch Reynolds and Jan Zelezny (3); Andrey Abduvaliyev, Abel Anton, Leroy Burrell, Andre Cason, Maurizio Damilano, Jon Drummond, Jonathan Edwards, Colin Jackson, Ismael Kirui, Billy Konchellah, Robert Korzeniowski, Sergey Litvinov, Tim Montgomery, Edwin Moses, Mike Powell, Javier Sotomayor and Angelo Taylor (2).

100 Meters

Year		Time	
1983	Carl Lewis, USA	10.07	
1987	Carl Lewis, USA	9.93	
1991	Carl Lewis, USA	9.86	WR
1993	Linford Christie, GBR	9.87	
1995	Donovan Bailey, CAN	9.97	
1997	Maurice Greene, USA	9.86	
1999	Maurice Greene, USA	9.80	CR
2001	Maurice Greene, USA	9.82	

Note: Ben Johnson was the original winner in 1987, but was stripped of his title and world record time (9.83) following his 1989 admission of drug taking.

200 Meters

Year		Time	
1983	Calvin Smith, USA	20.14	
1987	Calvin Smith, USA	20.16	
1991	Michael Johnson, USA	20.01	
1993	Frank Fredericks, NAM	19.85	
1995	Michael Johnson, USA	19.79	CR
1997	Ato Boldon, USA	20.04	
1999	Maurice Greene, USA	19.90	
2001	Konstantinos Kenteris, GRE	20.04	

400 Meters

Year		Time	
1983	Bert Cameron, JAM	45.05	
1987	Thomas Schonlebe, E. Ger	44.33	
1991	Antonio Pettigrew, USA	44.57	
1993	Michael Johnson, USA	43.65	
1995	Michael Johnson, USA	43.39	
1997	Michael Johnson, USA	44.12	
1999	Michael Johnson, USA	43.18	WR
2001	Avard Moncur, BAH	44.64	

800 Meters

Year		Time	
1983	Willi Wülbeck, W. Ger	1:43.65	
1987	Billy Konchellah, KEN	1:43.06	CR
1991	Billy Konchellah, KEN	1:43.99	
1993	Paul Ruto, KEN	1:44.71	
1995	Wilson Kipketer, DEN	1:45.08	
1997	Wilson Kipketer, DEN	1:43.38	
1999	Wilson Kipketer, DEN	1:43.30	
2001	Andre Bucher, SWI	1:43.70	

1500 Meters

Year		Time	
1983	Steve Cram, GBR	3:41.59	
1987	Abdi Bile, SOM	3:36.80	
1991	Noureddine Morceli, ALG	3:32.84	
1993	Noureddine Morceli, ALG	3:34.24	
1995	Noureddine Morceli, ALG	3:33.73	
1997	Hicham El Guerrouj, MOR	3:35.83	
1999	Hicham El Guerrouj, MOR	3:27.65	CR
2001	Hicham El Guerrouj, MOR	3:30.68	

5000 Meters

Year		Time	
1983	Eamonn Coghlan, IRL	13:28.53	
1987	Said Aouita, MOR	13:26.44	
1991	Yobes Ondieki, KEN	13:14.45	
1993	Ismael Kirui, KEN	13:02.75	
1995	Ismael Kirui, KEN	13:16.77	
1997	Daniel Komen, KEN	13:07.38	
1999	Salah Hissou, MOR	12:58.13	CR
2001	Richard Limo, KEN	13:00.77	

10,000 Meters

Year		Time	
1983	Alberto Cova, ITA	28:01.04	
1987	Paul Kipkoech, KEN	27:38.63	
1991	Moses Tanui, KEN	27:38.74	
1993	Haile Gebrselassie, ETH	27:46.02	
1995	Haile Gebrselassie, ETH	27:12.95	CR
1997	Haile Gebrselassie, ETH	27:24.58	
1999	Haile Gebrselassie, ETH	27:57.27	
2001	Charles Kamathi, KEN	27:53.25	

Marathon

Year		Time	
1983	Rob de Castella, AUS	2:10:03	CR
1987	Douglas Wakiihuri, KEN	2:11:48	
1991	Hiromi Taniguchi, JPN	2:14:57	
1993	Mark Plaatjes, USA	2:13:57	
1995	Martin Fíz, SPA	2:11:41	
1997	Abel Anton, SPA	2:13:16	
1999	Abel Anton, SPA	2:13:36	
2001	Gezahegne Abera, ETH	2:12:42	

110-Meter Hurdles

Year		Time	
1983	Greg Foster, USA	13.42	
1987	Greg Foster, USA	13.21	
1991	Greg Foster, USA	13.06	
1993	Colin Jackson, GBR	12.91	WR
1995	Allen Johnson, USA	13.00	
1997	Allen Johnson, USA	12.93	
1999	Colin Jackson, GBR	13.04	
2001	Allen Johnson, USA	13.04	

400-Meter Hurdles

Year		Time	
1983	Edwin Moses, USA	47.50	
1987	Edwin Moses, USA	47.46	
1991	Samuel Matete, ZAM	47.64	
1993	Kevin Young, USA	47.18	CR
1995	Derrick Adkins, USA	47.98	
1997	Stephane Diagana, FRA	47.70	
1999	Fabrizio Mori, ITA	47.72	
2001	Felix Sanchez, DOM	47.49	

3000-Meter Steeplechase

Year		Time	
1983	Patriz Ilg, W. Ger	8:15.06	
1987	Francesco Panetta, ITA	8:08.57	
1991	Moses Kiptanui, KEN	8:12.59	
1993	Moses Kiptanui, KEN	8:06.36	
1995	Moses Kiptanui, KEN	8:04.16	CR
1997	Wilson B. Kipketer, KEN	8:05.84	
1999	Christopher Koskei, KEN	8:11.76	
2001	Reuben Kosgei, KEN	8:15.16	

4 x 100-Meter Relay

Year		Time	
1983	United States	37.86	WR
1987	United States	37.90	
1991	United States	37.50	WR
1993	United States	37.48	CR
1995	Canada	38.31	
1997	Canada	37.86	
1999	United States	37.59	
2001	United States	37.96	

4 x 400-Meter Relay

Year		Time	
1983	Soviet Union	3:00.79	
1987	United States	2:57.29	
1991	Great Britain	2:57.53	
1993	United States	2:54.29	WR
1995	United States	2:57.32	
1997	United States	2:56.47	
1999	United States	2:56.65	
2001	United States	2:57.54	

20-Kilometer Walk

Year		Time	
1983	Ernesto Canto, MEX	1:20.49	
1987	Maurizio Damilano, ITA	1:20.45	
1991	Maurizio Damilano, ITA	1:19.37	CR
1993	Valentin Massana, SPA	1:22.31	
1995	Michele Didoni, ITA	1:19.59	
1997	Daniel Garcia, MEX	1:21:43	
1999	Ilya Markov, RUS	1:23:34	
2001	Roman Rasskazov, RUS	1:20:31	

50-Kilometer Walk

Year		Time	
1983	Ronald Weigel, E. Ger	3:43:08	
1987	Hartwig Gauder, E. Ger	3:40:53	CR
1991	Aleksandr Potashov, USSR	3:53:09	
1993	Jesus Angel Garcia, SPA	3:41:41	
1995	Valentin Kononen, FIN	3:43.42	
1997	Robert Korzeniowski, POL	3:44:46	
1999	German Skurygin, RUS	3:44:23	
2001	Robert Korzeniowski, POL	3:42:08	

High Jump

Year		Height	
1983	Gennedy Avdeyenko, USSR	7- 7¼	
1987	Patrik Sjoberg, SWE	7- 9¾	
1991	Charles Austin, USA	7- 9¾	
1993	Javier Sotomayor, CUB	7-10½	CR
1995	Troy Kemp, BAH	7- 9¼	
1997	Javier Sotomayor, CUB	7- 9¼	
1999	Vyacheslav Voronin, RUS	7- 9¼	
2001	Martin Buss, GER	7- 8¾	

Pole Vault

Year		Height	
1983	Sergey Bubka, USSR	18- 8¼	
1987	Sergey Bubka, USSR	19- 2¼	
1991	Sergey Bubka, USSR	19- 6¼	CR
1993	Sergey Bubka, UKR	19- 8¼	
1995	Sergey Bubka, UKR	19- 5	
1997	Sergey Bubka, UKR	19- 8½	CR
1999	Maksim Tarasov, RUS	19- 9	CR
2001	Dmitri Markov, AUS	19-10¼	CR

Long Jump

Year		Distance	
1983	Carl Lewis, USA	28- 0¾	
1987	Carl Lewis, USA	28- 0¼	
1991	Mike Powell, USA	29- 4½	WR
1993	Mike Powell, USA	28- 2¼	
1995	Ivan Pedroso, CUB	28- 6½	
1997	Ivan Pedroso, CUB	27- 7½	
1999	Ivan Pedroso, CUB	28- 1	
2001	Ivan Pedroso, CUB	27- 6¾	

Triple Jump

Year		Distance	
1983	Zdzislaw Hoffmann, POL	57- 2	
1987	Khristo Markov, BUL	58- 9	
1991	Kenny Harrison, USA	58- 4	
1993	Mike Conley, USA	58- 7¼	
1995	Jonathan Edwards, GBR	60- 0¼	WR
1997	Yoelvis Quesada, CUB	58- 6¾	
1999	Charles Michael Friedek, GER	57- 8½	
2001	Jonathan Edwards, GBR	58- 9½	

Shot Put

Year		Distance	
1983	Edward Sarul, POL	70- 2¼	
1987	Werner Günthör, SWI	72-11¼	CR
1991	Werner Günthör, SWI	71- 1¼	
1993	Werner Günthör, SWI	72- 1	
1995	John Godina, USA	70- 5¼	
1997	John Godina, USA	70- 4¼	
1999	C.J. Hunter, USA	71- 6	
2001	John Godina, USA	71- 9	

Discus

Year		Distance	
1983	Imrich Bugar, CZE	222- 2	
1987	Jurgen Schult, E. Ger	225- 6	
1991	Lars Riedel, GER	217- 2	
1993	Lars Riedel, GER	222- 2	
1995	Lars Riedel, GER	225- 7	CR
1997	Lars Riedel, GER	224-10	
1999	Anthony Washington, USA	226- 7	CR
2001	Lars Riedel, GER	228- 9	CR

Hammer Throw

Year		Distance	
1983	Sergey Litvinov, USSR	271- 3	
1987	Sergey Litvinov, USSR	272- 6	
1991	Yuri Sedykh, USSR	268- 0	
1993	Andrey Abduvaliyev, TAJ	267-10	
1995	Andrey Abduvaliyev, TAJ	267- 7	
1997	Heinz Weis, GER	268- 4	
1999	Karsten Kobs, GER	263- 3	
2001	Szymon Ziolkowski, POL	273- 7	CR

Track & Field (Cont.)

Javelin

Year		Distance	
1983	Detlef Michel, E. Ger	293- 7	
1987	Seppo Raty, FIN	274- 1	
1991	Kimmo Kinnunen, FIN	297-11	CR
1993	Jan Zelezny, CZR	282- 1	
1995	Jan Zelezny, CZR	293-11	
1997	Marius Corbett, S. Afr.	290- 0	
1999	Aki Parviainen, FIN	293- 8	
2001	Jan Zelezny, CZR	304- 5	CR

Decathlon

Year		Points	
1983	Daley Thompson, GBR	8714	
1987	Torsten Voss, E. Ger	8680	
1991	Dan O'Brien, USA	8812	CR
1993	Dan O'Brien, USA	8817	CR
1995	Dan O'Brien, USA	8695	
1997	Tomas Dvorak, CZR	8837	CR
1999	Tomas Dvorak, CZR	8744	
2001	Tomas Dvorak, CZR	8902	CR

WOMEN

Multiple gold medals (including relays): Gail Devers and Marion Jones (5); Jackie Joyner-Kersee (4); Tatyana Samolenko Dorovskikh, Chryste Gaines, Silke Gladisch, Marita Koch, Astrid Kumbernuss, Jearl Miller, Inger Miller, Merlene Ottey, Gabriela Szabo and Gwen Torrence (3); Hassiba Boulmerka, Sabine Braun, Olga Bryzgina, Mary Decker, Stacy Dragila, Heike Daute Drechsler, Lyudmila Narozhilenko Enquist, Cathy Freeman, Trine Hattestad, Martina Optiz Hellmann, Stefka Kostadinova, Katrin Krabbe, Jarmila Kratochvilova, Fiona May, Maria Mutola, Marie-José Pérec, Zhanna Pintusevich-Block, Ana Quirot and Huang Zhihong (2).

100 Meters

Year		Time	
1983	Marlies Gohr, E. Ger	10.97	
1987	Silke Gladisch, E. Ger	10.90	
1991	Katrin Krabbe, GER	10.99	
1993	Gail Devers, USA	10.81	CR
1995	Gwen Torrence, USA	10.85	
1997	Marion Jones, USA	10.83	
1999	Marion Jones, USA	10.70	CR
2001	Zhanna Pintusevich-Block, UKR	10.82	

5000 Meters
Held as 3000-meter race from 1983-93

Year		Time	
1983	Mary Decker, USA	8:34.62	
1987	Tatyana Samolenko, USSR	8:38.73	
1991	T. Samolenko Dorovskikh, USSR	8:35.82	
1993	Qu Yunxia, CHN	8:28.71	CR
1995	Sonia O'Sullivan, IRL	14:46.47	CR
1997	Gabriela Szabo, ROM	14:57.68	
1999	Gabriela Szabo, ROM	14:41.82	CR
2001	Olga Yegorova, RUS	15:03.39	

200 Meters

Year		Time	
1983	Marita Koch, E. Ger	22.13	
1987	Silke Gladisch, E. Ger	21.74	CR
1991	Katrin Krabbe, GER	22.09	
1993	Merlene Ottey, JAM	21.98	
1995	Merlene Ottey, JAM	22.12	
1997	Zhanna Pintusevich, UKR	22.32	
1999	Inger Miller, USA	21.77	
2001	Marion Jones, USA	22.39	

10,000 Meters

Year		Time	
1983	Not held		
1987	Ingrid Kristiansen, NOR	31:05.85	
1991	Liz McColgan, GBR	31:14.31	
1993	Wang Junxia, CHN	30:49.30	CR
1995	Fernanda Ribeiro, POR	31:04.99	
1997	Sally Barsosio, KEN	31:32.92	
1999	Gete Wami, ETH	30:24.56	CR
2001	Derartu Tulu, ETH	31:48.81	

400 Meters

Year		Time	
1983	Jarmila Kratochvilova, CZE	47.99	WR
1987	Olga Bryzgina, USSR	49.38	
1991	Marie-José Pérec, FRA	49.13	
1993	Jearl Miles, USA	49.82	
1995	Marie-José Pérec, FRA	49.28	
1997	Cathy Freeman, AUS	49.77	
1999	Cathy Freeman, AUS	49.67	
2001	Amy Mbacke Thiam , SEN	49.86	

Marathon

Year		Time	
1983	Grete Waitz, NOR	2:28:09	
1987	Rose Mota, POR	2:25:17	CR
1991	Wanda Panfil, POL	2:29:53	
1993	Junko Asari, JPN	2:30:03	
1995	Manuela Machado, POR	2:25:39	
1997	Hiromi Suzuki, JPN	2:29:48	
1999	Jong Song-Ok, N. Kor	2:26:59	
2001	Lidia Simon, ROM	2:26:01	

800 Meters

Year		Time	
1983	Jarmila Kratochvilova, CZE	1:54.68	CR
1987	Sigrun Wodars, E. Ger	1:55.26	
1991	Lilia Nurutdinova, USSR	1:57.50	
1993	Maria Mutola, MOZ	1:55.43	
1995	Ana Quirot, CUB	1:56.11	
1997	Ana Quirot, CUB	1:57.14	
1999	Ludmila Formanova, CZR	1:56.68	
2001	Maria Mutola, MOZ	1:57.17	

100-Meter Hurdles

Year		Time	
1983	Bettine Jahn, E. Ger	12.35^w	
1987	Ginka Zagorcheva, BUL	12.34	CR
1991	Lyudmila Narozhilenko, USSR	12.59	
1993	Gail Devers, USA	12.46	
1995	Gail Devers, USA	12.68	
1997	Ludmila Enquist, SWE	12.50	
1999	Gail Devers, USA	12.37	
2001	Anjanette Kirkland, USA	12.42	

^{w} indicates wind-aided.

1500 Meters

Year		Time	
1983	Mary Decker, USA	4:00.90	
1987	Tatiana Samolenko, USSR	3:58.56	CR
1991	Hassiba Boulmerka, ALG	4:02.21	
1993	Liu Dong, CHN	4:00.50	
1995	Hassiba Boulmerka, ALG	4:02.42	
1997	Carla Sacramento, POR	4:04.24	
1999	Svetlana Masterkova, RUS	3:59.53	
2001	Gabriela Szabo, ROM	4:00.57	

400-Meter Hurdles

Year		Time	
1983	Yekaterina Fesenko, USSR	54.14	
1987	Sabine Busch, E. Ger	53.62	
1991	Tatiana Ledovskaya, USSR.	53.11	
1993	Sally Gunnell, GBR	52.74	WR
1995	Kim Batten, USA	52.61	WR
1997	Nezha Bidouane, MOR	52.97	
1999	Daima Pernia, CUB	52.89	
2001	Nezha Bidouane, MOR	53.34	

4 x 100-Meter Relay

Year		Time	
1983	East Germany	41.76	
1987	United States	41.58	
1991	Jamaica	41.94	
1993	Russia	41.49	CR
1995	United States	42.12	
1997	United States	41.47	CR
1999	Bahamas	41.92	
2001	United States	41.71	

4 x 400-Meter Relay

Year		Time	
1983	East Germany	3:19.73	
1987	East Germany	3:18.63	
1991	Soviet Union	3:18.43	
1993	United States	3:16.71	CR
1995	United States	3:22.39	
1997	Germany	3:20.92	
1999	Russia	3:21.98	
2001	Jamaica	3:20.65	

20-Kilometer Walk

Held as 10-Kilometer race from 1987-97

Year		Time	
1983	Not held		
1987	Irina Strakhova, USSR	44:12	
1991	Alina Ivanova, USSR	42:57	
1993	Sari Essayah, FIN	42:59	
1995	Irina Stankina, RUS	42:13	CR
1997	Anna Sidoti, ITA	42:55	
1999	Hongyu Liu, CHN	1:30:50	CR
2001	Olimpiada Ivanova, RUS	1:27:48	CR

High Jump

Year		Height	
1983	Tamara Bykova, USSR	6- 7	
1987	Stefka Kostadinova, BUL	6-10¼	WR
1991	Heike Henkel, GER	6- 8¾	
1993	Ioamnet Quintero, CUB	6- 6¼	
1995	Stefka Kostadinova, BUL	6- 7	
1997	Hanne Haugland, NOR	6- 6¼	
1999	Inga Babakova, UKR	6- 6¼	
2001	Hestrie Cloete, RSA	6- 6¾	

Pole Vault

Year		Height	
1999	Stacy Dragila, USA	15- 1	WR
2001	Stacy Dragila, USA	15- 7	CR

Long Jump

Year		Distance	
1983	Heike Daute, E. Ger	23-10¼ᵂ	
1987	Jackie Joyner-Kersee, USA	24- 1¾	CR
1991	Jackie Joyner-Kersee, USA	24- 0¼	
1993	Heike Drechsler, GER	23- 4	
1995	Fiona May, ITA	22-10¾ᵂ	
1997	Lyudmila Galkina, RUS	23- 1¾	
1999	Niurka Montalvo, SPA	23- 2	
2001	Fiona May, ITA	23- 0½	

ᵂ indicates wind-aided.

Triple Jump

Year		Distance	
1993	Ana Biryukova, RUS	46- 6¼	WR
1995	Inessa Kravets, UKR	50-10¾	WR
1997	Sarka Kasparkova, CZR	49-10½	
1999	Paraskevi Tsiamita, GRE	48- 10	
2001	Tatyana Lebedeva, RUS	50- 0½	

Shot Put

Year		Distance	
1983	Helena Fibingerova, CZE	69- 0	
1987	Natalia Lisovskaya, USSR	69- 8	CR
1991	Huang Zhihong, CHN	68- 4	
1993	Huang Zhihong, CHN	67- 6	
1995	Astrid Kumbernuss, GER	69- 7½	
1997	Astrid Kumbernuss, GER	67- 11½	
1999	Astrid Kumbernuss, GER	65- 1½	
2001	Yanina Korolchik, BLR	67- 7½	

Discus

Year		Distance	
1983	Martina Opitz, E. Ger	226- 2	
1987	Martina Opitz Hellmann, E. Ger	235- 0	CR
1991	Tsvetanka Khristova, BUL	233- 0	
1993	Olga Burova, RUS	221- 1	
1995	Ellina Zvereva, BLR	225- 2	
1997	Beatrice Faumuina, NZE	219- 3	
1999	Franka Dietzsch, GER	223- 6	
2001	Natalya Sadova, RUS	224- 11	

Hammer Throw

Year		Distance	
1999	Mihaela Melinte, ROM	246-8¾	
2001	Yipsi Moreno, CUB	231-9	

Javelin

Year		Distance	
1983	Tiina Lillak, FIN	232- 4	
1987	Fatima Whitbread, GBR	251- 5	CR
1991	Xu Demei, CHN	225- 8	
1993	Trine Hattestad, NOR	227- 0	
1995	Natalya Shikolenko, BLR	221- 8	
1997	Trine Hattestad, NOR	225- 8	
1999	Mirela Manjani-Tzelili, GRE	220- 1	
2001	Osleidys Menendez, CUB	228- 1	CR

Heptathlon

Year		Points	
1983	Ramona Neubert, E. Ger	6770	
1987	Jackie Joyner-Kersee, USA	7128	CR
1991	Sabine Braun, GER	6672	
1993	Jackie Joyner-Kersee, USA	6837	
1995	Ghada Shouaa, SYR	6651	
1997	Sabine Braun, GER	6739	
1999	Eunice Barber, FRA	6861	
2001	Yelena Prokhorova, RUS	6694	

World Cross Country Championships

MEN

Multiple winners: John Ngugi and Paul Tergat (5); Carlos Lopes (3); Mohammed Mourhit, Khalid Skah, William Sigei, John Treacy and Craig Virgin (2).

Year		Year		Year	
1973	Pekka Paivarinta, Finland	1983	Bekele Debele, Ethiopia	1993	William Sigei, Kenya
1974	Eric DeBeck, Belgium	1984	Carlos Lopes, Portugal	1994	William Sigei, Kenya
1975	Ian Stewart, Scotland	1985	Carlos Lopes, Portugal	1995	Paul Tergat, Kenya
1976	Carlos Lopes, Portugal	1986	John Ngugi, Kenya	1996	Paul Tergat, Kenya
1977	Leon Schots, Belgium	1987	John Ngugi, Kenya	1997	Paul Tergat, Kenya
1978	John Treacy, Ireland	1988	John Ngugi, Kenya	1998	Paul Tergat, Kenya
1979	John Treacy, Ireland	1989	John Ngugi, Kenya	1999	Paul Tergat, Kenya
1980	Craig Virgin, USA	1990	Khalid Skah, Morocco	2000	Mohammed Mourhit, Belgium
1981	Craig Virgin, USA	1991	Khalid Skah, Morocco	2001	Mohammed Mourhit, Belgium
1982	Mohammed Kedir, Ethiopia	1992	John Ngugi, Kenya	2002	Kenenisa Bekele, Ethiopia

Track & Field (Cont.)
WOMEN

Multiple winners: Grete Waitz (5); Lynn Jennings and Derartu Tulu (3); Zola Budd, Paola Cacchi, Maricica Puica, Paula Radcliffe, Annette Sergent, Carmen Valero and Gete Wami (2).

Year		Year		Year	
1973	Paola Cacchi, Italy	1983	Grete Waitz, Norway	1993	Albertina Dias, Portugal
1974	Paola Cacchi, Italy	1984	Maricica Puica, Romania	1994	Helen Chepngeno, Kenya
1975	Julie Brown, USA	1985	Zola Budd, England	1995	Derartu Tulu, Ethiopia
1976	Carmen Valero, Spain	1986	Zola Budd, England	1996	Gete Wami, Ethiopia
1977	Carmen Valero, Spain	1987	Annette Sergent, France	1997	Derartu Tulu, Ethiopia
1978	Grete Waitz, Norway	1988	Ingrid Kristiansen, Norway	1998	Sonia O'Sullivan, Ireland
1979	Grete Waitz, Norway	1989	Annette Sergent, France	1999	Gete Wami, Ethiopia
1980	Grete Waitz, Norway	1990	Lynn Jennings, USA	2000	Derartu Tulu, Ethiopia
1981	Grete Waitz, Norway	1991	Lynn Jennings, USA	2001	Paula Radcliffe, Gr. Britain
1982	Maricica Puica, Romania	1992	Lynn Jennings, USA	2002	Paula Radcliffe, Gr. Britain

Marathons
Boston

America's oldest regularly contested foot race, the Boston Marathon is held on Patriots' Day every April. It has been run at four different distances: 24 miles, 1232 yards (1897-1923); 26 miles, 209 yards (1924-26); 26 miles, 385 yards (1927-52, since 1957); 25 miles, 958 yards (1953-56).

MEN

Multiple winners: Clarence DeMar (7); Gerard Cote and Bill Rodgers (4); Ibrahim Hussein, Cosmas Ndeti, Eino Oksanen and Leslie Pawson (3); Tarzan Brown, Jim Caffrey, John A. Kelley, John Miles, Toshihiko Seko, Geoff Smith, Moses Tanui and Aurele Vandendriessche (2).

Year		Time	Year		Time
1897	John McDermott, New York	2:55:10	1940	Gerard Cote, Canada	2:28:28
1898	Ronald McDonald, Massachusetts	2:42:00	1941	Leslie Pawson, Rhode Island	2:30:38
1899	Lawrence Brignolia, Massachusetts	2:54:38	1942	Joe Smith, Massachusetts	2:26:51
			1943	Gerard Cote, Canada	2:28:25
1900	Jim Caffrey, Canada	2:39:44	1944	Gerard Cote, Canada	2:31:50
1901	Jim Caffrey, Canada	2:29:23	1945	John A. Kelley, Massachusetts	2:30:40
1902	Sam Mellor, New York	2:43:12	1946	Stylianos Kyriakides, Greece	2:29:27
1903	J.C. Lorden, Massachusetts	2:41:29	1947	Yun Bok Suh, Korea	2:25:39
1904	Mike Spring, New York	2:38:04	1948	Gerard Cote, Canada	2:31:02
1905	Fred Lorz, New York	2:38:25	1949	Karle Leandersson, Sweden	2:31:50
1906	Tim Ford, Massachusetts	2:45:45			
1907	Tom Longboat, Canada	2:24:24	1950	Kee Yonh Ham, Korea	2:32:39
1908	Tom Morrissey, New York	2:25:43	1951	Shigeki Tanaka, Japan	2:27:45
1909	Henri Renaud, New Hampshire	2:53:36	1952	Doroteo Flores, Guatemala	2:31:53
			1953	Keizo Yamada, Japan	2:18:51
1910	Fred Cameron, Nova Scotia	2:28:52	1954	Veiko Karvonen, Finland	2:20:39
1911	Clarence DeMar, Massachusetts	2:21:39	1955	Hideo Hamamura, Japan	2:18:22
1912	Mike Ryan, Illinois	2:21:18	1956	Antti Viskari, Finland	2:14:14
1913	Fritz Carlson, Minnesota	2:25:14	1957	John J. Kelley, Connecticut	2:20:05
1914	James Duffy, Canada	2:25:01	1958	Franjo Mihalic, Yugoslavia	2:25:54
1915	Edouard Fabre, Canada	2:31:41	1959	Eino Oksanen, Finland	2:22:42
1916	Arthur Roth, Massachusetts	2:27:16			
1917	Bill Kennedy, New York	2:28:37	1960	Paavo Kotila, Finland	2:20:54
1918	World War relay race		1961	Eino Oksanen, Finland	2:23:39
1919	Carl Linder, Massachusetts	2:29:13	1962	Eino Oksanen, Finland	2:23:48
			1963	Aurele Vandendriessche, Belgium	2:18:58
1920	Peter Trivoulidas, New York	2:29:31	1964	Aurele Vandendriessche, Belgium	2:19:59
1921	Frank Zuna, New Jersey	2:18:57	1965	Morio Shigematsu, Japan	2:16:33
1922	Clarence DeMar, Massachusetts	2:18:10	1966	Kenji Kimihara, Japan	2:17:11
1923	Clarence DeMar, Massachusetts	2:23:37	1967	David McKenzie, New Zealand	2:15:45
1924	Clarence DeMar, Massachusetts	2:29:40	1968	Amby Burfoot, Connecticut	2:22:17
1925	Charles Mellor, Illinois	2:33:00	1969	Yoshiaki Unetani, Japan	2:13:49
1926	John Miles, Nova Scotia	2:25:40			
1927	Clarence DeMar, Massachusetts	2:40:22	1970	Ron Hill, England	2:10:30
1928	Clarence DeMar, Massachusetts	2:37:07	1971	Alvaro Mejia, Colombia	2:18:45
1929	John Miles, Nova Scotia	2:33:08	1972	Olavi Suomalainen, Finland	2:15:39
			1973	Jon Anderson, Oregon	2:16:03
1930	Clarence DeMar, Massachusetts	2:34:48	1974	Neil Cusack, Ireland	2:13:39
1931	James Henigan, Massachusetts	2:46:45	1975	Bill Rodgers, Massachusetts	2:09:55
1932	Paul deBruyn, Germany	2:33:36	1976	Jack Fultz, Pennsylvania	2:20:19
1933	Leslie Pawson, Rhode Island	2:31:01	1977	Jerome Drayton, Canada	2:14:46
1934	Dave Komonen, Canada	2:32:53	1978	Bill Rodgers, Massachusetts	2:10:13
1935	John A. Kelley, Massachusetts	2:32:07	1979	Bill Rodgers, Massachusetts	2:09:27
1936	Ellison (Tarzan) Brown, Rhode Island	2:33:40			
1937	Walter Young, Canada	2:33:20	1980	Bill Rodgers, Massachusetts	2:12:11
1938	Leslie Pawson, Rhode Island	2:35:34	1981	Toshihiko Seko, Japan	2:09:26
1939	Ellison (Tarzan) Brown, Rhode Island	2:28:51	1982	Alberto Salazar, Oregon	2:08:52

Year	Time
1983 Greg Meyer, New Jersey	2:09:00
1984 Geoff Smith, England	2:10:34
1985 Geoff Smith, England	2:14:05
1986 Rob de Castella, Australia	2:07:51
1987 Toshihiko Seko, Japan	2:11:50
1988 Ibrahim Hussein, Kenya	2:08:43
1989 Abebe Mekonnen, Ethiopia	2:09:06
1990 Gelindo Bordin, Italy	2:08:19
1991 Ibrahim Hussein, Kenya	2:11:06
1992 Ibrahim Hussein, Kenya	2:08:14
1993 Cosmas Ndeti, Kenya	2:09:33

Year	Time
1994 Cosmas Ndeti, Kenya	2:07:15*
1995 Cosmas Ndeti, Kenya	2:09:22
1996 Moses Tanui, Kenya	2:09:16
1997 Lameck Aguta, Kenya	2:10:34
1998 Moses Tanui, Kenya	2:07:34
1999 Joseph Chebet, Kenya	2:09:52
2000 Elijah Lagat, Kenya	2:09:47
2001 Lee Bong-Ju, South Korea	2:09:43
2002 Rodgers Rop, Kenya	2:09:02

*Course record.

WOMEN

Multiple winners: Rosa Mota, Uta Pippig and Fatuma Roba (3); Joan Benoit, Miki Gorman, Ingrid Kristiansen, Olga Markova and Catherine Ndereba (2).

Year	Time
1972 Nina Kuscsik, New York	3:08:58
1973 Jacqueline Hansen, California	3:05:59
1974 Miki Gorman, California	2:47:11
1975 Liane Winter, West Germany	2:42:24
1976 Kim Merritt, Wisconsin	2:47:10
1977 Miki Gorman, California	2:48:33
1978 Gayle Barron, Georgia	2:44:52
1979 Joan Benoit, Maine	2:35:15
1980 Jacqueline Gareau, Canada	2:34:28
1981 Allison Roe, New Zealand	2:26:46
1982 Charlotte Teske, West Germany	2:29:33
1983 Joan Benoit, Maine	2:22:43
1984 Lorraine Moller, New Zealand	2:29:28
1985 Lisa Larsen Weidenbach, Mass	2:34:06
1986 Ingrid Kristiansen, Norway	2:24:55
1987 Rosa Mota, Portugal	2:25:21

Year	Time
1988 Rosa Mota, Portugal	2:24:30
1989 Ingrid Kristiansen, Norway	2:24:33
1990 Rosa Mota, Portugal	2:25:23
1991 Wanda Panfil, Poland	2:24:18
1992 Olga Markova, CIS	2:23:43
1993 Olga Markova, Russia	2:25:27
1994 Uta Pippig, Germany	2:21:45
1995 Uta Pippig, Germany	2:25:11
1996 Uta Pippig, Germany	2:27:12
1997 Fatuma Roba, Ethiopia	2:26:23
1998 Fatuma Roba, Ethiopia	2:23:21
1999 Fatuma Roba, Ethiopia	2:23:25
2000 Catherine Ndereba, Kenya	2:26:11
2001 Catherine Ndereba, Kenya	2:23:53
2002 Margaret Okayo, Kenya	2:20:43*

*Course record.

New York City

Started in 1970, the New York City Marathon is run in the fall, usually on the first Sunday in November. The route winds through all of the city's five boroughs and finishes in Central Park.

MEN

Multiple winners: Bill Rodgers (4); Alberto Salazar (3); Tom Fleming, John Kagwe, Orlando Pizzolato and German Silva (2).

Year	Time	Year	Time	Year	Time
1970 Gary Muhrcke, USA	2:31:38	1982 Alberto Salazar, USA	2:09:29	1994 German Silva, MEX	2:11:21
1971 Norman Higgins, USA	2:22:54	1983 Rod Dixon, NZE	2:08:59	1995 German Silva, MEX	2:11:00
1972 Sheldon Karlin, USA	2:27:52	1984 Orlando Pizzolato, ITA	2:14:53	1996 Giacomo Leone, ITA	2:09:54
1973 Tom Fleming, USA	2:21:54	1985 Orlando Pizzolato, ITA	2:11:34	1997 John Kagwe, KEN	2:08:12
1974 Norbert Sander, USA	2:26:30	1986 Gianni Poli, ITA	2:11:06	1998 John Kagwe, KEN	2:08:45
1975 Tom Fleming, USA	2:19:27	1987 Ibrahim Hussein, KEN	2:11:01	1999 Joseph Chebet, KEN	2:09:14
1976 Bill Rodgers, USA	2:10:09	1988 Steve Jones, WAL	2:08:20	2000 Abdelkhader El Mouaziz, MOR	2:10:08
1977 Bill Rodgers, USA	2:11:28	1989 Juma Ikangaa, TAN	2:08:01	2001 Tesfaye Jifar, ETH	2:07:43*
1978 Bill Rodgers, USA	2:12:12	1990 Douglas Wakiihuri, KEN	2:12:39	*Course record.	
1979 Bill Rodgers, USA	2:11:42	1991 Salvador Garcia, MEX	2:09:28		
1980 Alberto Salazar, USA	2:09:41	1992 Willie Mtolo, S. Afr.	2:09:29		
1981 Alberto Salazar, USA	2:08:13	1993 Andres Espinosa, MEX	2:10:04		

WOMEN

Multiple winners: Grete Waitz (9); Miki Gorman, Nina Kuscsik and Tegla Loroupe (2).

Year	Time	Year	Time	Year	Time
1970 No Finisher		1981 Allison Roe, NZE	2:25:29	1992 Lisa Ondieki, AUS	2:24:40
1971 Beth Bonner, USA	2:55:22	1982 Grete Waitz, NOR	2:27:14	1993 Uta Pippig, GER	2:26:24
1972 Nina Kuscsik, USA	3:08:41	1983 Grete Waitz, NOR	2:27:00	1994 Tegla Loroupe, KEN	2:27:37
1973 Nina Kuscsik, USA	2:57:07	1984 Grete Waitz, NOR	2:29:30	1995 Tegla Loroupe, KEN	2:28:06
1974 Katherine Switzer, USA	3:07:29	1985 Grete Waitz, NOR	2:28:34	1996 Anuta Catuna, ROM	2:28:18
1975 Kim Merritt, USA	2:46:14	1986 Grete Waitz, NOR	2:28:06	1997 F. Rochat-Moser, SWI	2:28:43
1976 Miki Gorman, USA	2:39:11	1987 Priscilla Welch, GBR	2:30:17	1998 Franca Fiacconi, ITA	2:25:17
1977 Miki Gorman, USA	2:43:10	1988 Grete Waitz, NOR	2:28:07	1999 Adriana Fernandez, MEX	2:25:06
1978 Grete Waitz, NOR	2:32:30	1989 Ingrid Kristiansen, NOR	2:25:30	2000 Ludmila Petrova, RUS	2:25:45
1979 Grete Waitz, NOR	2:27:33	1990 Wanda Panfil, POL	2:30:45	2001 Margaret Okayo, KEN	2:24:21*
1980 Grete Waitz, NOR	2:25:41	1991 Liz McColgan, GBR	2:27:23	*Course record.	

Track & Field (Cont.)
Annual Awards
Track & Field News Athletes of the Year

Voted on by an international panel of track and field experts and presented since 1959 for men and 1974 for women.

MEN

Multiple winners: Carl Lewis (3); Sergey Bubka, Sebastian Coe, Hicham El Guerrouj, Haile Gebrselassie, Michael Johnson, Alberto Juantorena, Noureddine Morceli, Jim Ryun and Peter Snell (2).

Year		Event	Year		Event
1959	Martin Lauer, W. Germany	110H/Decathlon	1981	Sebastian Coe, Great Britain	800/1500
1960	Rafer Johnson, USA	Decathlon	1982	Carl Lewis, USA	100/200/Long Jump
1961	Ralph Boston, USA	Long Jump/110 Hurdles	1983	Carl Lewis, USA	100/200/Long Jump
1962	Peter Snell, New Zealand	800/1500	1984	Carl Lewis, USA	100/200/Long Jump
1963	C.K. Yang, Taiwan	Decathlon/Pole Vault	1985	Said Aouita, Morocco	1500/5000
1964	Peter Snell, New Zealand	800/1500	1986	Yuri Sedykh, USSR	Hammer Throw
1965	Ron Clarke, Australia	5000/10,000	1987	Ben Johnson, Canada	100
1966	Jim Ryun, USA	800/1500	1988	Sergey Bubka, USSR	Pole Vault
1967	Jim Ryun, USA	1500	1989	Roger Kingdom, USA	110 Hurdles
1968	Bob Beamon, USA	Long Jump	1990	Michael Johnson, USA	200/400
1969	Bill Toomey, USA	Decathlon	1991	Sergey Bubka, USSR	Pole Vault
1970	Randy Matson, USA	Shot Put	1992	Kevin Young, USA	400 Hurdles
1971	Rod Milburn, USA	110 Hurdles	1993	Noureddine Morceli, Algeria	Mile/1500/3000
1972	Lasse Viren, Finland	5000/10,000	1994	Noureddine Morceli, Algeria	Mile/1500/3000
1973	Ben Jipcho, Kenya	1500/5000/Steeplechase	1995	Haile Gebrselassie, Ethiopia	5000/10,000
1974	Rick Wohlhuter, USA	800/1500	1996	Michael Johnson, USA	200/400
1975	John Walker, New Zealand	800/1500	1997	Wilson Kipketer, Denmark	800
1976	Alberto Juantorena, Cuba	400/800	1998	Haile Gebrselassie, Ethiopia	3000/5000/10,000
1977	Alberto Juantorena, Cuba	400/800	1999	Hicham El Guerrouj, Morocco	Mile/1500
1978	Henry Rono, Kenya	5000/10,000/Steeplechase	2000	Virgilijus Alekna, Lithuania	Discus
1979	Sebastian Coe, Great Britain	800/1500	2001	Hicham El Guerrouj, Morocco	Mile/1500
1980	Edwin Moses, USA	400 Hurdles			

WOMEN

Multiple winners: Marita Koch (4); Marion Jones and Jackie Joyner-Kersee (3); Evelyn Ashford (2).

Year		Event	Year		Event
1974	Irena Szewinska, Poland	100/200/400	1988	Florence Griffith Joyner, USA	100/200
1975	Faina Melnik, USSR	Shot Put/Discus	1989	Ana Quirot, Cuba	400/800
1976	Tatiana Kazankina, USSR	800/1500	1990	Merlene Ottey, Jamaica	100/200
1977	Rosemarie Ackermann, E. Germany	High Jump	1991	Heike Henkel, Germany	High Jump
1978	Marita Koch, E. Germany	100/200/400	1992	Heike Drechsler, Germany	Long Jump
1979	Marita Koch, E. Germany	100/200/400	1993	Wang Junxia, China	1500/3000/10,000
1980	Ilona Briesenick, E. Germany	Shot Put	1994	Jackie Joyner-Kersee, USA	100H/Heptathlon/LJ
1981	Evelyn Ashford, USA	100/200	1995	Sonia O'Sullivan, Ireland	1500/3000/5000
1982	Marita Koch, E. Germany	100/200/400	1996	Svetlana Masterkova, Russia	800/1500
1983	Jarmila Kratochvilova, Czech	200/400/800	1997	Marion Jones, USA	100/200
1984	Evelyn Ashford, USA	100	1998	Marion Jones, USA	100/200/LJ
1985	Marita Koch, E. Germany	100/200/400	1999	Gabriela Szabo, Romania	3000/5000
1986	Jackie Joyner-Kersee, USA	Heptathlon/Long Jump	2000	Marion Jones, USA	100/200/LJ
1987	Jackie Joyner-Kersee, USA	100H/Heptathlon/LJ	2001	Stacy Dragila, USA	Pole Vault

SWIMMING & DIVING

FINA World Championships

While the Summer Olympics have served as the unofficial world championships for swimming and diving throughout the centuries, a separate World Championship meet was started in 1973 by the Federation Internationale de Natation Amateur (FINA). The meet has varied between being held every two years, every three years or every four years. Currently it is held every two years. Sites have been Belgrade (1973); Cali, COL (1975); West Berlin (1978); Guayaquil, ECU (1982); Madrid (1986); Perth (1991 & 98), Rome (1994) and Fukuoka, JPN (2001). Looking forward, the Championships will be held in Barcelona (2003) and Montreal (2005).

MEN

Most gold medals (including relays): Ian Thorpe (8); Jim Montgomery (7); Matt Biondi and Michael Klim (6); Rowdy Gaines (5); Joe Bottom, Tamas Darnyi, Michael Gross, Grant Hackett, Tom Jager, David McCagg, Vladimir Salnikov and Tim Shaw (4); Billy Forrester, Andras Hargitay, Roland Matthes, John Murphy, Aleksandr Popov, Jeff Rouse, Norbert Rozsa, Matt Welsh and David Wilkie (3).

	50-Meter Freestyle				100-Meter Freestyle		
Year		Time		Year		Time	
1973-82	Not held			1973	Jim Montgomery, USA	51.70	
1986	Tom Jager, USA	22.49		1975	Tim Shaw, USA	51.25	
1991	Tom Jager, USA	22.16	CR	1978	David McCagg, USA	50.24	
1994	Aleksandr Popov, RUS	22.17		1982	Jorg Woithe, E. Ger	50.18	
1998	Bill Pilczuk, USA	22.29		1986	Matt Biondi, USA	48.94	
2001	Anthony Ervin, USA	22.09		1991	Matt Biondi, USA	49.18	
				1994	Aleksandr Popov, RUS	49.12	
				1998	Aleksandr Popov, RUS	48.93	CR
				2001	Anthony Ervin, USA	48.33	CR

200-Meter Freestyle

Year		Time
1973	Jim Montgomery, USA	1:53.02
1975	Tim Shaw, USA	1:52.04
1978	Billy Forrester, USA	1:51.02
1982	Michael Gross, W. Ger	1:49.84
1986	Michael Gross, W. Ger	1:47.92
1991	Giorgio Lamberti, ITA	1:47.27
1994	Antti Kasvio, FIN	1:47.32 **CR**
1998	Michael Klim, AUS	1:47.41
2001	Ian Thorpe, AUS	1:44.06 **WR**

400-Meter Freestyle

Year		Time
1973	Rick DeMont, USA	3:58.18
1975	Tim Shaw, USA	3:54.88
1978	Vladimir Salnikov, USSR	3:51.94
1982	Vladimir Salnikov, USSR	3:51.30
1986	Rainer Henkel, W. Ger	3:50.05
1991	Jorg Hoffman, GER	3:48.04
1994	Kieren Perkins, AUS	3:43.80 **WR**
1998	Ian Thorpe, AUS	3:46.29
2001	Ian Thorpe, AUS	3:40.17 **WR**

800-Meter Freestyle

Year		Time
1973-98 Not held		
2001	Ian Thorpe, AUS	7:39.16 **WR**

1500-Meter Freestyle

Year		Time
1973	Stephen Holland, AUS	15:31.85
1975	Tim Shaw, USA	15:28.92
1978	Vladimir Salnikov, USSR	15:03.99
1982	Vladimir Salnikov, USSR	15:01.77
1986	Rainer Henkel, W. Ger	15:05.31
1991	Jorg Hoffman, GER	14:50.36 **WR**
1994	Kieren Perkins, AUS	14:50.52
1998	Grant Hackett, AUS	14:51.70
2001	Grant Hackett, AUS	14:34.56 **WR**

50-Meter Backstroke

Year		Time
1973-98 Not held		
2001	Randall Bal, USA	25.34

100-Meter Backstroke

Year		Time
1973	Roland Matthes, E. Ger	57.47
1975	Roland Matthes, E. Ger	58.15
1978	Bob Jackson, USA	56.36
1982	Dirk Richter, E. Ger	55.95
1986	Igor Polianski, USSR	55.58
1991	Jeff Rouse, USA	55.23
1994	Martin Lopez-Zubero, SPA	55.17 **CR**
1998	Lenny Krayzelburg, USA	55.00
2001	Matt Welsh, AUS	54.31 **CR**

200-Meter Backstroke

Year		Time
1973	Roland Matthes, E. Ger	2:01.87
1975	Zoltan Varraszto, HUN	2:05.05
1978	Jesse Vassallo, USA	2:02.16
1982	Rick Carey, USA	2:00.82
1986	Igor Polianski, USSR	1:58.78 **CR**
1991	Martin Zubero, SPA	1:59.52
1994	Vladimir Selkov, RUS	1:57.42
1998	Lenny Krayzelburg, USA	1:58.84
2001	Aaron Peirsol, USA	1:57.13 **CR**

50-Meter Breaststroke

Year		Time
1973-98 Not held		
2001	Oleg Lisogor, UKR	27.52

100-Meter Breaststroke

Year		Time
1973	John Hencken, USA	1:04.02
1975	David Wilkie, GBR	1:04.26
1978	Walter Kusch, W. Ger	1:03.56
1982	Steve Lundquist, USA	1:02.75
1986	Victor Davis, CAN	1:02.71
1991	Norbert Rozsa, HUN	1:01.45 **WR**
1994	Norbert Rozsa, HUN	1:01.24
1998	Frederik deBurghgraeve, BEL	1:01.34
2001	Roman Sloudnov, RUS	1:00.16

200-Meter Breaststroke

Year		Time
1973	David Wilkie, GBR	2:19.28
1975	David Wilkie, GBR	2:18.23
1978	Nick Nevid, USA	2:18.37
1982	Victor Davis, CAN	2:14.77 **WR**
1986	Jozsef Szabo, HUN	2:14.27
1991	Mike Barrowman, USA	2:11.23 **WR**
1994	Norbert Rozsa, HUN	2:12.81
1998	Kurt Grote, USA	2:13.40
2001	Brendan Hansen, USA	2:10.69 **CR**

50-Meter Butterfly

Year		Time
1973-98 Not held		
2001	Geoff Huegill, AUS	23.50

100-Meter Butterfly

Year		Time
1973	Bruce Robertson, CAN	55.69
1975	Greg Jagenburg, USA	55.63
1978	Joe Bottom, USA	54.30
1982	Matt Gribble, USA	53.88
1986	Pablo Morales, USA	53.54
1991	Anthony Nesty, SUR	53.29
1994	Rafal Szukala, POL	53.51
1998	Michael Klim, AUS	52.25 **CR**
2001	Lars Frolander, SWE	52.10 **CR**

200-Meter Butterfly

Year		Time
1973	Robin Backhaus, USA	2:03.32
1975	Billy Forrester, USA	2:01.95
1978	Mike Bruner, USA	1:59.38
1982	Michael Gross, W. Ger	1:58.85
1986	Michael Gross, W. Ger	1:56.53
1991	Melvin Stewart, USA	1:55.69 **WR**
1994	Denis Pankratov, RUS	1:56.54
1998	Denys Sylantyev, UKR	1:56.61
2001	Michael Phelps, USA	1:54.58 **WR**

200-Meter Individual Medley

Year		Time
1973	Gunnar Larsson, SWE	2:08.36
1975	Andras Hargitay, HUN	2:07.72
1978	Graham Smith, CAN	2:03.65 **WR**
1982	Alexander Sidorenko, USSR	2:03.30
1986	Tamás Darnyi, HUN	2:01.57
1991	Tamás Darnyi, HUN	1:59.36 **WR**
1994	Janis Sievinen, FIN	1:58.16 **WR**
1998	Marcel Wouda, NET	2:01.18
2001	Massimiliano Rosolino, ITA	1:59.71

400-Meter Individual Medley

Year		Time
1973	Andras Hargitay, HUN	4:31.11
1975	Andras Hargitay, HUN	4:32.57
1978	Jesse Vassallo, USA	4:20.05 **WR**
1982	Ricardo Prado, BRA	4:19.78 **WR**
1986	Tamás Darnyi, HUN	4:18.98
1991	Tamás Darnyi, HUN	4:12.36 **WR**
1994	Tom Dolan, USA	4:12.30 **WR**
1998	Tom Dolan, USA	4:14.95
2001	Alessio Boggiatto, ITA	4:13.15

Swimming & Diving (Cont.)

4 x 100-Meter Freestyle Relay

Year		Time	
1973	United States	3:27.18	
1975	United States	3:24.85	
1978	United States	3:19.74	
1982	United States	3:19.26	WR
1986	United States	3:19.98	
1991	United States	3:17.15	
1994	United States	3:16.90	
1998	United States	3:16.69	CR
2001	Australia	3:14.10	CR

4 x 200-Meter Freestyle Relay

Year		Time	
1973	United States	7:33.22	WR
1975	West Germany	7:39.44	
1978	United States	7:20.82	
1982	United States	7:21.09	
1986	East Germany	7:15.91	
1991	Germany	7:13.50	CR
1994	Sweden	7:17.34	
1998	Australia	7:12.48	
2001	Australia	7:04.66	WR

4 x 100-Meter Medley Relay

Year		Time	
1973	United States	3:49.49	
1975	United States	3:49.00	
1978	United States	3:44.63	
1982	United States	3:40.84	WR
1986	United States	3:41.25	
1991	United States	3:39.66	
1994	United States	3:37.74	CR
1998	Australia	3:37.98	
2001	Australia	3:35.35	CR

WOMEN

Most gold medals (including relays): Kornelia Ender (8); Kristin Otto (7); Tracy Caulkins, Heike Friedrich, Le Jingyi, Rosemarie Kother, Ulrike Richter and Jenny Thompson (4); Hannalore Anke, Lu Bin, He Cihong, Inge De Bruijn, Janet Evans, Nicole Haislett, Lui Limin, Birgit Meineke, Joan Pennington, Manuela Stellmach, Petria Thomas, Amy Van Dyken, Renate Vogel and Cynthia Woodhead (3).

50-Meter Freestyle

Year		Time	
1973-82	Not held		
1986	Tamara Costache, ROM	25.28	WR
1991	Zhuang Yong, CHN	25.47	
1994	Le Jingyi, CHN	24.51	WR
1998	Amy Van Dyken, USA	25.15	
2001	Inge de Bruijn, NED	24.47	

100-Meter Freestyle

Year		Time	
1973	Kornelia Ender, E. Ger.	57.54	
1975	Kornelia Ender, E. Ger.	56.50	
1978	Barbara Krause, E. Ger.	55.68	
1982	Birgit Meineke, E. Ger.	55.79	
1986	Kristin Otto, E. Ger.	55.05	
1991	Nicole Haislett, USA	55.17	
1994	Le Jingyi, CHN	54.01	WR
1998	Jenny Thompson, USA	54.95	
2001	Inge de Bruijn, NED	54.18	

200-Meter Freestyle

Year		Time	
1973	Keena Rothhammer, USA	2:04.99	
1975	Shirley Babashoff, USA	2:02.50	
1978	Cynthia Woodhead, USA	1:58.53	WR
1982	Annemarie Verstappen, NED	1:59.53	
1986	Heike Friedrich, E. Ger.	1:58.26	
1991	Hayley Lewis, AUS	2:00.48	
1994	Franziska Van Almsick, GER	1:56.78	WR
1998	Claudia Poll, CRC.	1:58.90	
2001	Giaan Rooney, AUS	1:58.57	

400-Meter Freestyle

Year		Time	
1973	Heather Greenwood, USA	4:20.28	
1975	Shirley Babashoff, USA	4:22.70	
1978	Tracey Wickham, AUS	4:06.28	WR
1982	Carmela Schmidt, E. Ger.	4:08.98	
1986	Heike Friedrich, E. Ger.	4:07.45	
1991	Janet Evans, USA	4:08.63	
1994	Yang Aihua, CHN	4:09.64	
1998	Yan Chen, CHN	4:06.72	
2001	Yana Klochkova, UKR.	4:07.30	

800-Meter Freestyle

Year		Time	
1973	Novella Calligaris, ITA	8:52.97	
1975	Jenny Turrall, AUS	8:44.75	
1978	Tracey Wickham, AUS	8:25.94	
1982	Kim Linehan, USA	8:27.48	
1986	Astrid Strauss, E. Ger.	8:28.24	
1991	Janet Evans, USA	8:24.05	CR
1994	Janet Evans, USA	8:29.85	
1998	Brooke Bennett, USA	8:28.71	
2001	Hannah Stockbauer, GER	8:24.66	

1500-Meter Freestyle

Year		Time
1973-98	Not held	
2001	Hannah Stockbauer, GER	16:01.02

50-Meter Backstroke

Year		Time
1973-98	Not held	
2001	Haley Cope, USA.	28.51

100-Meter Backstroke

Year		Time	
1973	Ulrike Richter, E. Ger	1:05.42	
1975	Ulrike Richter, E. Ger	1:03.30	
1978	Linda Jezek, USA	1:02.55	
1982	Kristin Otto, E. Ger.	1:01.30	
1986	Betsy Mitchell, USA	1:01.74	
1991	Krisztina Egerszegi, HUN	1:01.78	
1994	He Cihong, CHN	1:00.57	WR
1998	Lea Maurer, USA	1:01.16	
2001	Natalie Coughlin, USA	1:00.37	

200-Meter Backstroke

Year		Time	
1973	Melissa Belote, USA.	2:20.52	
1975	Birgit Treiber, E. Ger.	2:15.46	WR
1978	Linda Jezek, USA	2:11.93	WR
1982	Cornelia Sirch, E. Ger.	2:09.91	WR
1986	Cornelia Sirch, E. Ger.	2:11.37	
1991	Krisztina Egerszegi, HUN	2:09.15	
1994	He Cihong, CHN	2:07.40	CR
1998	Roxanna Maracineanu, FRA	2:11.26	
2001	Diana Iuliana Mocanu, ROM	2:09.94	

50-Meter Breaststroke

Year		Time
1973-82	Not held	
2001	Xuejuan Luo, CHN	30.84

100-Meter Breaststroke

Year		Time	
1973	Renate Vogel, E. Ger	1:13.74	
1975	Hannalore Anke, E. Ger	1:12.72	
1978	Julia Bogdanova, USSR	1:10.31	WR
1982	Ute Geweniger, E. Ger	1:09.14	
1986	Sylvia Gerasch, E. Ger	1:08.11	WR
1991	Linley Frame, AUS	1:08.81	
1994	Samantha Riley, AUS	1:07.69	WR
1998	Kristy Kowal, USA	1:08.42	
2001	Xuejuan Luo, CHN	1:07.18	CR

200-Meter Breaststroke

Year		Time	
1973	Renate Vogel, E. Ger	2:40.01	
1975	Hannalore Anke, E. Ger	2:37.25	
1978	Lina Kachushite, USSR	2:31.42	WR
1982	Svetlana Varganova, USSR	2:28.82	
1986	Silke Hoerner, E. Ger	2:27.40	WR
1991	Elena Volkova, USSR	2:29.53	
1994	Samantha Riley, AUS	2:26.87	
1998	Agnes Kovacs, HUN	2:25.45	CR
2001	Agnes Kovacs, HUN	2:24.90	CR

50-Meter Butterfly

Year		Time
1973-98 Not held		
2001	Inge de Bruijn, NED	25.90

100-Meter Butterfly

Year		Time	
1973	Kornelia Ender, E. Ger	1:02.53	
1975	Kornelia Ender, E. Ger	1:01.24	WR
1978	Joan Pennington, USA	1:00.20	
1982	Mary T. Meagher, USA	59.41	
1986	Kornelia Gressler, E. Ger	59.51	
1991	Qian Hong, CHN	59.68	
1994	Liu Limin, CHN	58.98	
1998	Jenny Thompson, USA	58.46	CR
2001	Petria Thomas, AUS	58.27	CR

200-Meter Butterfly

Year		Time	
1973	Rosemarie Kother, E. Ger	2:13.76	
1975	Rosemarie Kother, E. Ger	2:15.92	
1978	Tracy Caulkins, USA	2:09.78	WR
1982	Ines Geissler, E. Ger	2:08.66	
1986	Mary T. Meagher, USA	2:08.41	
1991	Summer Sanders, USA	2:09.24	
1994	Liu Limin, CHN	2:07.25	CR
1998	Susie O'Neill, AUS	2:07.93	
2001	Petria Thomas, AUS	2:06.73	CR

200-Meter Individual Medley

Year		Time	
1973	Andre Huebner, E. Ger	2:20.51	
1975	Kathy Heddy, USA	2:19.80	
1978	Tracy Caulkins, USA	2:19.80	WR
1982	Petra Schneider, E. Ger	2:11.79	CR
1986	Kristin Otto, E. Ger	2:15.56	
1991	Lin Li, CHN	2:13.40	
1994	Lu Bin, CHN	2:12.34	
1998	Yanyan Wu, CHN	2:10.88	CR
2001	Maggie Bowen, USA	2:11.93	

400-Meter Individual Medley

Year		Time	
1973	Gudrun Wegner, E. Ger	4:57.71	
1975	Ulrike Tauber, E. Ger	4:52.76	
1978	Tracy Caulkins, USA	4:40.83	WR
1982	Petra Schneider, E. Ger	4:36.10	WR
1986	Kathleen Nord, E. Ger	4:43.75	
1991	Lin Li, CHN	4:41.45	
1994	Dai Guohong, CHN	4:39.14	
1998	Yan Chen, CHN	4:36.66	
2001	Yana Klochkova, UKR	4:36.98	

4 x 100-Meter Freestyle Relay

Year		Time	
1973	East Germany	3:52.45	
1975	East Germany	3:49.37	
1978	United States	3:43.43	WR
1982	East Germany	3:43.97	
1986	East Germany	3:40.57	
1991	United States	3:43.26	
1994	China	3:37.91	WR
1998	United States	3:42.11	
2001	Germany	3:39.58	

4 x 200-Meter Freestyle Relay

Year		Time	
1973-82 Not held			
1986	East Germany	7:59.33	WR
1991	Germany	8:02.56	
1994	China	7:57.96	CR
1998	Germany	8:01.46	
2001	Great Britain	7:58.69	

4 x 100-Meter Medley Relay

Year		Time	
1973	East Germany	4:16.84	
1975	East Germany	4:14.74	
1978	United States	4:08.21	
1982	East Germany	4:05.80	WR
1986	East Germany	4:04.82	
1991	United States	4:06.51	
1994	China	4:01.67	CR
1998	United States	4:01.93	
2001	Australia	4:01.50	CR

Diving

Multiple Gold Medals: MEN–Greg Louganis (5); Dmitri Sautin (4); Phil Boggs (3); Klaus Dibiasi, Tian Liang and Yu Zhuocheng (2). WOMEN–Irina Kalinina and Gao Min (3); Guo Jingjing and Fu Mingxia (2).

MEN

1-Meter Springboard

Year		Pts
1973-86 Not Held		
1991	Edwin Jongejans, NED	588.51
1994	Evan Stewart, ZIM	382.14
1998	Yu Zhuocheng, CHN	417.54
2001	Wang Feng, CHN	444.03

3-Meter Springboard

Year		Pts
1973	Phil Boggs, USA	618.57
1975	Phil Boggs, USA	597.12
1978	Phil Boggs, USA	913.95
1982	Greg Louganis, USA	752.67
1986	Greg Louganis, USA	750.06
1991	Kent Ferguson, USA	650.25

Year		Pts
1994	Yu Zhuocheng, CHN	655.44
1998	Dmitri Sautin, RUS	746.79
2001	Dmitri Sautin, RUS	725.82

Platform

Year		Pts
1973	Klaus Dibiasi, ITA	559.53
1975	Klaus Dibiasi, ITA	547.98
1978	Greg Louganis, USA	844.11
1982	Greg Louganis, USA	634.26
1986	Greg Louganis, USA	668.58
1991	Sun Shuwei, CHN	626.79
1994	Dmitri Sautin, RUS	634.71
1998	Dmitri Sautin, RUS	750.99
2001	Tian Liang, CHN	688.77

Swimming & Diving (Cont.)

3-Meter Synchronized

Year		Pts
1973-98	Not held	
2001	Peng Bo & Wang Kenan, CHN	342.63

10-Meter Synchronized

Year		Pts
1973-98	Not held	
2001	Tian Liang & Hu Jia, CHN	361.41

WOMEN

1-Meter Springboard

Year		Pts
1973-86	Not held	
1991	Gao Min, CHN	478.26
1994	Chen Lixia, CHN	279.30
1998	Irina Lashko, RUS	296.07
2001	Blythe Hartley, CAN	300.81

3-Meter Springboard

Year		Pts
1973	Christa Koehler, E. Ger	442.17
1975	Irina Kalinina, USSR	489.81
1978	Irina Kalinina, USSR	691.43
1982	Megan Neyer, USA	501.03
1986	Gao Min, CHN	582.90
1991	Gao Min, CHN	539.01
1994	Tan Shuping, CHN.	548.49
1998	Yulia Pakhalina, RUS	544.52
2001	Guo Jingjing, CHN	596.67

Platform

Year		Pts
1973	Ulrike Knape, SWE	406.77
1975	Janet Ely, USA	403.89
1978	Irina Kalinina, USSR	412.71
1982	Wendy Wyland, USA	438.79
1986	Chen Lin, CHN	449.67
1991	Fu Mingxia, CHN	426.51
1994	Fu Mingxia, CHN	434.04
1998	Olena Zhupyna	550.41
2001	Xu Mian, CHN	532.65

3-Meter Synchronized

Year		Pts
1973-98	Not held	
2001	Wu Minxia & Guo Jingjing, CHN	347.31

10-Meter Synchronized

Year		Pts
1973-98	Not held	
2001	Duan Qing & Sang Xue, CHN	329.94

ALPINE SKIING

World Cup Overall Champions

World Cup Overall Champions (downhill and slalom events combined) since the tour was organized in 1967.

MEN

Multiple winners: Marc Girardelli (5), Gustavo Thoeni and Pirmin Zurbriggen (4); Phil Mahre, Hermann Maier and Ingemar Stenmark (3); Jean-Claude Killy, Lasse Kjus and Karl Schranz (2).

Year		Year		Year	
1967	Jean-Claude Killy, France	1979	Peter Luescher, Switzerland	1991	Marc Girardelli, Luxembourg
1968	Jean-Claude Killy, France	1980	Andreas Wenzel, Liechtenstein	1992	Paul Accola, Switzerland
1969	Karl Schranz, Austria	1981	Phil Mahre, USA	1993	Marc Girardelli, Luxembourg
1970	Karl Schranz, Austria	1982	Phil Mahre, USA	1994	Kjetil Andre Aamodt, Norway
1971	Gustavo Thoeni, Italy	1983	Phil Mahre, USA	1995	Alberto Tomba, Italy
1972	Gustavo Thoeni, Italy	1984	Pirmin Zurbriggen, Switzerland	1996	Lasse Kjus, Norway
1973	Gustavo Thoeni, Italy	1985	Marc Girardelli, Luxembourg	1997	Luc Alphand, France
1974	Piero Gros, Italy	1986	Marc Girardelli, Luxembourg	1998	Hermann Maier, Austria
1975	Gustavo Thoeni, Italy	1987	Pirmin Zurbriggen, Switzerland	1999	Lasse Kjus, Norway
1976	Ingemar Stenmark, Sweden	1988	Pirmin Zurbriggen, Switzerland		
1977	Ingemar Stenmark, Sweden	1989	Marc Girardelli, Luxembourg	2000	Hermann Maier, Austria
1978	Ingemar Stenmark, Sweden	1990	Pirmin Zurbriggen, Switzerland	2001	Hermann Maier, Austria
				2002	Stephan Eberharter, Austria

WOMEN

Multiple winners: Annemarie Moser-Proell (6); Petra Kronberger and Vreni Schneider (3); Michela Figini, Nancy Greene, Erika Hess, Katja Seizinger, Maria Walliser and Hanni Wenzel (2).

Year		Year		Year	
1967	Nancy Greene, Canada	1980	Hanni Wenzel, Liechtenstein	1992	Petra Kronberger, Austria
1968	Nancy Greene, Canada	1981	Marie-Therese Nadig, Switzerland	1993	Anita Wachter, Austria
1969	Gertrud Gabi, Austria			1994	Vreni Schneider, Switzerland
1970	Michele Jacot, France	1982	Erika Hess, Switzerland	1995	Vreni Schneider, Switzerland
1971	Annemarie Pröll, Austria	1983	Tamara McKinney, USA	1996	Katja Seizinger, Germany
1972	Annemarie Pröll, Austria	1984	Erika Hess, Switzerland	1997	Pernilla Wiberg, Sweden
1973	Annemarie Pröll, Austria	1985	Michela Figini, Switzerland	1998	Katja Seizinger, Germany
1974	Annemarie Pröll, Austria	1986	Maria Walliser, Switzerland	1999	Alexandra Meissnitzer, Austria
1975	Annemarie Moser-Pröll, Austria	1987	Maria Walliser, Switzerland		
1976	Rosi Mittermaier, W. Germany	1988	Michela Figini, Switzerland	2000	Renate Goetschl, Austria
1977	Lise-Marie Morerod, Switzerland	1989	Vreni Schneider, Switzerland	2001	Janica Kostelic, Croatia
1978	Hanni Wenzel, Liechtenstein	1990	Petra Kronberger, Austria	2002	Michaela Dorfmeister, Austria
1979	Annemarie Moser-Pröll, Austria	1991	Petra Kronberger, Austria		

World Cup Event Champions

World Cup Champions in each individual event since the tour was organized in 1967.

MEN

Downhill

Multiple winners: Franz Klammer (5); Luc Alphand, Franz Heinzer and Peter Muller (3); Roland Collumbin, Marc Girardelli, Helmut Hoflehner, Hermann Maier, Bernard Russi, Karl Schranz and Pirmin Zurbriggen (2).

Year		Year		Year	
1967	Jean-Claude Killy, France	1979	Peter Muller, Switzerland	1991	Franz Heinzer, Switzerland
1968	Gerhard Nenning, Austria	1980	Peter Muller, Switzerland	1992	Franz Heinzer, Switzerland
1969	Karl Schranz, Austria	1981	Harti Weirather, Austria	1993	Franz Heinzer, Switzerland
1970	Karl Schranz, Austria	1982	Steve Podborski, Canada	1994	Marc Girardelli, Luxembourg
	Karl Cordin, Austria		Peter Muller, Switzerland	1995	Luc Alphand, France
1971	Bernard Russi, Switzerland	1983	Franz Klammer, Austria	1996	Luc Alphand, France
1972	Bernard Russi, Switzerland	1984	Urs Raber, Switzerland	1997	Luc Alphand, France
1973	Roland Collumbin, Switzerland	1985	Helmut Hoflehner, Austria	1998	Andreas Schifferer, Austria
1974	Roland Collumbin, Switzerland	1986	Peter Wirnsberger, Austria	1999	Lasse Kjus, Norway
1975	Franz Klammer, Austria	1987	Pirmin Zurbriggen, Switzerland	2000	Hermann Maier, Austria
1976	Franz Klammer, Austria	1988	Pirmin Zurbriggen, Switzerland	2001	Hermann Maier, Austria
1977	Franz Klammer, Austria	1989	Marc Girardelli, Luxembourg	2002	Stephan Eberharter, Austria
1978	Franz Klammer, Austria	1990	Helmut Hoflehner, Austria		

Slalom

Multiple winners: Ingemar Stenmark (8); Alberto Tomba (4); Jean-Noel Augert and Marc Girardelli (3); Armin Bittner, Thomas Sykora and Gustavo Thoeni (2).

Year		Year		Year	
1967	Jean-Claude Killy, France	1979	Ingemar Stenmark, Sweden	1992	Alberto Tomba, Italy
1968	Domeng Giovanoli, Switzerland	1980	Ingemar Stenmark, Sweden	1993	Tomas Fogdof, Sweden
1969	Jean-Noel Augert, France	1981	Ingemar Stenmark, Sweden	1994	Alberto Tomba, Italy
1970	Patrick Russel, France	1982	Phil Mahre, USA	1995	Alberto Tomba, Italy
	Alain Penz, France	1983	Ingemar Stenmark, Sweden	1996	Sebastien Amiez, France
1971	Jean-Noel Augert, France	1984	Marc Girardelli, Luxembourg	1997	Thomas Sykora, Austria
1972	Jean-Noel Augert, France	1985	Marc Girardelli, Luxembourg	1998	Thomas Sykora, Austria
1973	Gustavo Thoeni, Italy	1986	Rok Petrovic, Yugoslavia	1999	Thomas Stangassinger, Austria
1974	Gustavo Thoeni, Italy	1987	Bojan Krizaj, Yugoslavia	2000	Kjetil Andre Aamodt, Norway
1975	Ingemar Stenmark, Sweden	1988	Alberto Tomba, Italy	2001	Benjamin Raich, Austria
1976	Ingemar Stenmark, Sweden	1989	Armin Bittner, West Germany	2002	Ivica Kostelic, Croatia
1977	Ingemar Stenmark, Sweden	1990	Armin Bittner, West Germany		
1978	Ingemar Stenmark, Sweden	1991	Marc Girardelli, Luxembourg		

Giant Slalom

Multiple winners: Ingemar Stenmark (8); Alberto Tomba (4); Michael von Gruenigen, Hermann Maier and Pirmin Zurbriggen (3); Joel Gaspoz, Jean-Claude Killy, Phil Mahre and Gustavo Thoeni (2).

Year		Year		Year	
1967	Jean-Claude Killy, France	1981	Ingemar Stenmark, Sweden	1993	Kjetil Andre Aamodt, Norway
1968	Jean-Claude Killy, France	1982	Phil Mahre, USA	1994	Christian Mayer, Austria
1969	Karl Schranz, Austria	1983	Phil Mahre, USA	1995	Alberto Tomba, Italy
1970	Gustavo Thoeni, Italy	1984	Ingemar Stenmark, Sweden	1996	Michael von Gruenigen,
1971	Patrick Russel, France		Pirmin Zurbriggen, Switzerland		Switzerland
1972	Gustavo Thoeni, Italy	1985	Marc Girardelli, Luxembourg	1997	Michael von Gruenigen,
1973	Hans Hinterseer, Austria	1986	Joel Gaspoz, Switzerland		Switzerland
1974	Piero Gros, Italy	1987	Joel Gaspoz, Switzerland	1998	Hermann Maier, Austria
1975	Ingemar Stenmark, Sweden		Pirmin Zurbriggen, Switzerland	1999	Michael von Gruenigen,
1976	Ingemar Stenmark, Sweden	1988	Alberto Tomba, Italy		Switzerland
1977	Heini Hemmi, Switzerland	1989	Pirmin Zurbriggen, Switzerland	2000	Hermann Maier, Austria
	Ingemar Stenmark, Sweden	1990	Ole-Cristian Furuseth, Norway	2001	Hermann Maier, Austria
1978	Ingemar Stenmark, Sweden		Gunther Mader, Austria	2002	Frederic Covili, France
1979	Ingemar Stenmark, Sweden	1991	Alberto Tomba, Italy		
1980	Ingemar Stenmark, Sweden	1992	Alberto Tomba, Italy		

Super G

Multiple winners: Hermann Maier and Pirmin Zurbriggen (4).

Year		Year		Year	
1986	Markus Wasmeier,	1991	Franz Heinzer, Switzerland	1997	Luc Alphand, France
	West Germany	1992	Paul Accola, Switzerland	1998	Hermann Maier, Austria
1987	Pirmin Zurbriggen, Switzerland	1993	Kjetil Andre Aamodt, Norway	1999	Hermann Maier, Austria
1988	Pirmin Zurbriggen, Switzerland	1994	Jan Einar Thorsen, Norway	2000	Hermann Maier, Austria
1989	Pirmin Zurbriggen, Switzerland	1995	Peter Runggaldier, Italy	2001	Hermann Maier, Austria
1990	Pirmin Zurbriggen, Switzerland	1996	Atle Skaardal, Norway	2002	Stephan Eberharter, Austria

Alpine Skiing (Cont.)
Combined

Multiple winners: Marc Girardelli and Andreas Wenzel (4); Kjetil Andre Aamodt and Phil Mahre (3); Pirmin Zurbriggen (2).

Year	Year	Year
1979 Andreas Wenzel, Liechtenstein	1987 Pirmin Zurbriggen, Switzerland	1996 Gunther Mader, Austria
1980 Andreas Wenzel, Liechtenstein	1988 Hubert Strolz, Austria	1997-99 Not awarded
1981 Phil Mahre, USA	1989 Marc Girardelli, Luxembourg	2000 Kjetil Andre Aamodt, Norway
1982 Phil Mahre, USA	1990 Pirmin Zurbriggen, Switzerland	2001 Lasse Kjus, Norway
1983 Phil Mahre, USA	1991 Marc Girardelli, Luxembourg	2002 Kjetil Andre Aamodt, Norway
1984 Andreas Wenzel, Liechtenstein	1992 Paul Accola, Switzerland	
1985 Andreas Wenzel, Liechtenstein	1993 Marc Girardelli, Luxembourg	
1986 Markus Wasmeier, West Germany	1994 Kjetil Andre Aamodt, Norway	
	1995 Marc Girardelli, Luxembourg	

WOMEN
Downhill

Multiple winners: Annemarie Moser-Pröll (7), Michela Figini and Katja Seizinger (4); Renate Goetschl, Isolde Kostner, Isabelle Mir, Marie-Therese Nadig, Picabo Street, Bridgitte Totschnig-Habersatter and Maria Walliser (2).

Year	Year	Year
1967 Marielle Goitschel, France	1979 Annemarie Moser-Pröll, Austria	1990 Katrin Gutensohn-Knopf, Germany
1968 Isabelle Mir, France	1980 Marie-Therese Nadig, Switzerland	1991 Chantal Bournissen, Switzerland
Olga Pall, Austria	1981 Marie-Therese Nadig, Switzerland	1992 Katja Seizinger, Germany
1969 Wiltrud Drexel, Austria	1982 Marie-Cecile Gros-Gaudenier, France	1993 Katja Seizinger, Germany
1970 Isabelle Mir, France	1983 Doris De Agostini, Switzerland	1994 Katja Seizinger, Germany
1971 Annemarie Pröll, Austria	1984 Maria Walliser, Switzerland	1995 Picabo Street, USA
1972 Annemarie Pröll, Austria	1985 Michela Figini, Switzerland	1996 Picabo Street, USA
1973 Annemarie Pröll, Austria	1986 Maria Walliser, Switzerland	1997 Renate Goetschl, Austria
1974 Annemarie Pröll, Austria	1987 Michela Figini, Switzerland	1998 Katja Seizinger, Germany
1975 Annemarie Moser-Pröll, Austria	1988 Michela Figini, Switzerland	1999 Renate Goetschl, Austria
1976 Bridgitte Totschnig-Habersatter, Austria	1989 Michela Figini, Switzerland	2000 Regina Haeusl, Germany
1977 Bridgitte Totschnig-Habersatter, Austria		2001 Isolde Kostner, Italy
1978 Annemarie Moser-Pröll, Austria		2002 Isolde Kostner, Italy

Slalom

Multiple winners: Vreni Schneider (6); Erika Hess (5); Marielle Goitschel, Britt Lafforgue, Lisa-Marie Morerod and Roswitha Steiner (2).

Year	Year	Year
1967 Marielle Goitschel, France	1978 Hanni Wenzel, Liechtenstein	1991 Petra Kronberger, Austria
1968 Marielle Goitschel, France	1979 Regina Sackl, Austria	1992 Vreni Schneider, Switzerland
1969 Gertrud Gabl, Austria	1980 Perrine Pelene, France	1993 Vreni Schneider, Switzerland
1970 Ingrid Lafforgue, France	1981 Erika Hess, Switzerland	1994 Vreni Schneider, Switzerland
1971 Britt Lafforgue, France	1982 Erika Hess, Switzerland	1995 Vreni Schneider, Switzerland
1972 Britt Lafforgue, France	1983 Erika Hess, Switzerland	1996 Elfi Eder, Austria
1973 Patricia Emonet, France	1984 Tamara McKinney, USA	1997 Pernilla Wiberg, Sweden
1974 Christa Zechmeister, West Germany	1985 Erika Hess, Switzerland	1998 Ylva Nowen, Sweden
1975 Lisa-Marie Morerod, Switzerland	1986 Roswitha Steiner, Austria Erika Hess, Switzerland	1999 Sabine Egger, Austria
1976 Rosi Mittermaier, West Germany	1987 Corrine Schmidhauser, Switzerland	2000 Spela Pretnar, Slovenia
1977 Lisa-Marie Morerod, Switzerland	1988 Roswitha Steiner, Austria	2001 Janica Kostelic, Croatia
	1989 Vreni Schneider, Switzerland	2002 Laure Pequegnot, France
	1990 Vreni Schneider, Switzerland	

Giant Slalom

Multiple winners: Vreni Schneider (5); Lisa-Marie Morerod and Annemarie Moser-Pröll (3); Martina Ertl, Nancy Greene, Carole Merle, Sonja Nef, Anita Wachter and Hanni Wenzel (2).

Year	Year	Year
1967 Nancy Greene, Canada	1978 Lisa-Marie Morerod, Switzerland	1988 Mateja Svet, Yugoslavia
1968 Nancy Greene, Canada	1979 Christa Kinshofer, West Germany	1989 Vreni Schneider, Switzerland
1969 Marilyn Cochran, USA	1980 Hanni Wenzel, Liechtenstein	1990 Anita Wachter, Austria
1970 Michele Jacot, France Francoise Macchi, France	1981 Marie-Therese Nadig, Switzerland	1991 Vreni Schneider, Switzerland
1971 Annemarie Pröll, Austria	1982 Irene Epple, West Germany	1992 Carole Merle, France
1972 Annemarie Pröll, Austria	1983 Tamara McKinney, USA	1993 Carole Merle, France
1973 Monika Kaserer, Austria	1984 Erika Hess, Switzerland	1994 Anita Wachter, Austria
1974 Hanni Wenzel, Liechtenstein	1985 Maria Keihl, West Germany Michela Figini, Switzerland	1995 Vreni Schneider, Switzerland
1975 Annemarie Moser-Pröll, Austria	1986 Vreni Schneider, Switzerland	1996 Martina Ertl, Germany
1976 Lisa-Marie Morerod, Switzerland	1987 Vreni Schneider, Switzerland Maria Walliser, Switzerland	1997 Deborah Compagnoni, Italy
1977 Lisa-Marie Morerod, Switzerland		1998 Martina Ertl, Germany
		1999 Alexandra Meissnitzer, Austria
		2000 Michaela Dorfmeister, Austria
		2001 Sonja Nef, Switzerland
		2002 Sonja Nef, Switzerland

Super G

Multiple winners: Katja Seizinger (5); Carole Merle (4); Hilde Gerg (2).

Year	Year	Year
1986 Maria Kiehl, West Germany	1992 Carole Merle, France	1998 Katja Seizinger, Germany
1987 Maria Walliser, Switzerland	1993 Katja Seizinger, Germany	1999 Alexandra Meissnitzer, Austria
1988 Michela Figini, Switzerland	1994 Katja Seizinger, Germany	2000 Renate Goetschl, Austria
1989 Carole Merle, France	1995 Katja Seizinger, Germany	2001 Regine Cavagnoud, France
1990 Carole Merle, France	1996 Katja Seizinger, Germany	2002 Hilde Gerg, Germany
1991 Carole Merle, France	1997 Hilde Gerg, Germany	

Combined

Multiple winners: Brigitte Oertli (5); Anita Wachter and Hanni Wenzel (3); Sabine Ginther, Renate Goetschl and Pernilla Wiberg (2).

Year	Year	Year
1979 Annemarie Moser-Pröll, Austria	1986 Maria Walliser, Switzerland	1994 Pernilla Wiberg, Sweden
Hanni Wenzel, Liechtenstein	1987 Brigitte Oertli, Switzerland	1995 Pernilla Wiberg, Sweden
1980 Hanni Wenzel, Liechtenstein	1988 Brigitte Oertli, Switzerland	1996 Anita Wachter, Austria
1981 Maria-Therese Nadig, Switzerland	1989 Brigitte Oertli, Switzerland	1997–99 Not Awarded
1982 Irene Epple, West Germany	1989 Brigitte Oertli, Switzerland	2000 Renate Goetschl, Austria
1983 Hanni Wenzel, Liechtenstein	1990 Anita Wachter, Austria	2001 Janica Kostelic, Croatia
1984 Erika Hess, Switzerland	1991 Sabine Ginther, Austria	2002 Renate Goetschl, Austria
1985 Brigitte Oertli, Switzerland	1992 Sabine Ginther, Austria	
	1993 Anita Wachter, Austria	

TOUR DE FRANCE

The world's premier cycling event, the Tour de France is staged throughout the country (sometimes passing through neighboring countries) over four weeks. The 1946 Tour, however, the first after World War II, was only a five-day race.

Multiple winners: Jacques Anquetil, Bernard Hinault, Miguel Induráin and Eddy Merckx (5); Lance Armstrong (4); Louison Bobet, Greg LeMond and Philippe Thys (3); Gino Bartali Ottavio Bottecchia, Fausto Coppi, Laurent Fignon, Nicholas Frantz, Firmin Lambot, André Leducq, Sylvere Maes, Antonin Magne, Lucien Petit-Breton and Bernard Thevenet (2).

Year	Year	Year
1903 Maurice Garin, France	1938 Gino Bartali, Italy	1975 Bernard Thevenet, France
1904 Henri Cornet, France	1939 Sylvere Maes, Belgium	1976 Lucien van Impe, Belgium
1905 Louis Trousselier, France		1977 Bernard Thevenet, France
1906 René Pottier, France	1940-45 Not held	1978 Bernard Hinault, France
1907 Lucien Petit-Breton, France	1946 Jean Lazarides, France	1979 Bernard Hinault, France
1908 Lucien Petit-Breton, France	1947 Jean Robic, France	
1909 Francois Faber, Luxembourg	1948 Gino Bartali, Italy	1980 Joop Zoetemelk, Netherlands
	1949 Fausto Coppi, Italy	1981 Bernard Hinault, France
1910 Octave Lapize, France		1982 Bernard Hinault, France
1911 Gustave Garrigou, France	1950 Ferdinand Kubler, Switzerland	1983 Laurent Fignon, France
1912 Odile Defraye, Belgium	1951 Hugo Koblet, Switzerland	1984 Laurent Fignon, France
1913 Philippe Thys, Belgium	1952 Fausto Coppi, Italy	1985 Bernard Hinault, France
1914 Philippe Thys, Belgium	1953 Louison Bobet, France	1986 Greg LeMond, USA
1915-18 Not held	1954 Louison Bobet, France	1987 Stephen Roche, Ireland
1919 Firmin Lambot, Belgium	1955 Louison Bobet, France	1988 Pedro Delgado, Spain
	1956 Roger Walkowiak, France	1989 Greg LeMond, USA
1920 Philippe Thys, Belgium	1957 Jacques Anquetil, France	
1921 Léon Scieur, Belgium	1958 Charly Gaul, Luxembourg	1990 Greg LeMond, USA
1922 Firmin Lambot, Belgium	1959 Federico Bahamontes, Spain	1991 Miguel Induráin, Spain
1923 Henri Pelissier, France		1992 Miguel Induráin, Spain
1924 Ottavio Bottecchia, Italy	1960 Gastone Nencini, Italy	1993 Miguel Induráin, Spain
1925 Ottavio Bottecchia, Italy	1961 Jacques Anquetil, France	1994 Miguel Induráin, Spain
1926 Lucien Buysse, Belgium	1962 Jacques Anquetil, France	1995 Miguel Induráin, Spain
1927 Nicholas Frantz, Luxembourg	1963 Jacques Anquetil, France	1996 Bjarne Riis, Denmark
1928 Nicholas Frantz, Luxembourg	1964 Jacques Anquetil, France	1997 Jan Ullrich, Germany
1929 Maurice Dewaele, Belgium	1965 Felice Gimondi, Italy	1998 Marco Pantani, Italy
	1966 Lucien Aimar, France	1999 Lance Armstrong, USA
1930 André Leducq, France	1967 Roger Pingeon, France	
1931 Antonin Magne, France	1968 Jan Janssen, Netherlands	2000 Lance Armstrong, USA
1932 André Leducq, France	1969 Eddy Merckx, Belgium	2001 Lance Armstrong, USA
1933 Georges Speicher, France		2002 Lance Armstrong, USA
1934 Antonin Magne, France	1970 Eddy Merckx, Belgium	
1935 Romain Maes, Belgium	1971 Eddy Merckx, Belgium	
1936 Sylvere Maes, Belgium	1972 Eddy Merckx, Belgium	
1937 Roger Lapebie, France	1973 Luis Ocana, Spain	
	1974 Eddy Merckx, Belgium	

FIGURE SKATING

World Champions

Skaters who won World and Olympic championships in the same year are listed in **bold** type.

MEN

Multiple winners: Ulrich Salchow (10); Karl Schafer (7); Dick Button (5); Willy Bockl, Kurt Browning, Scott Hamilton and Hayes Jenkins and Alexei Yagudin (4); Emmerich Danzer, Gillis Grafstrom, Gustav Hugel, David Jenkins, Fritz Kachler, Ondrej Nepela and Elvis Stojko (3); Brian Boitano, Gilbert Fuchs, Jan Hoffmann, Felix Kaspar, Vladimir Kovalev and Tim Wood (2).

Year		Year		Year	
1896	Gilbert Fuchs, Germany	1934	Karl Schafer, Austria	1971	Ondrej Nepela, Czechoslovakia
1897	Gustav Hugel, Austria	1935	Karl Schafer, Austria	1972	**Ondrej Nepela**, Czechoslovakia
1898	Henning Grenander, Sweden	1936	**Karl Schafer**, Austria	1973	Ondrej Nepela, Czechoslovakia
1899	Gustav Hugel, Austria	1937	Felix Kaspar, Austria	1974	Jan Hoffmann, E. Germany
1900	Gustav Hugel, Austria	1938	Felix Kaspar, Austria	1975	Sergie Volkov, USSR
1901	Ulrich Salchow, Sweden	1939	Graham Sharp, Britain	1976	**John Curry**, Britain
1902	Ulrich Salchow, Sweden	1940-46	Not held	1977	Vladimir Kovalev, USSR
1903	Ulrich Salchow, Sweden	1947	Hans Gerschwiler, Switzerland	1978	Charles Tickner, USA
1904	Ulrich Salchow, Sweden	1948	**Dick Button**, USA	1979	Vladimir Kovalev, USSR
1905	Ulrich Salchow, Sweden	1949	Dick Button, USA	1980	Jan Hoffmann, E. Germany
1906	Gilbert Fuchs, Germany	1950	Dick Button, USA	1981	Scott Hamilton, USA
1907	Ulrich Salchow, Sweden	1951	Dick Button, USA	1982	Scott Hamilton, USA
1908	**Ulrich Salchow**, Sweden	1952	**Dick Button**, USA	1983	Scott Hamilton, USA
1909	Ulrich Salchow, Sweden	1953	Hayes Jenkins, USA	1984	**Scott Hamilton**, USA
1910	Ulrich Salchow, Sweden	1954	Hayes Jenkins, USA	1985	Alexander Fadeev, USSR
1911	Ulrich Salchow, Sweden	1955	Hayes Jenkins, USA	1986	Brian Boitano, USA
1912	Fritz Kachler, Austria	1956	**Hayes Jenkins**, USA	1987	Brian Orser, Canada
1913	Fritz Kachler, Austria	1957	David Jenkins, USA	1988	**Brian Boitano**, USA
1914	Gosta Sandhal, Sweden	1958	David Jenkins, USA	1989	Kurt Browning, Canada
1915-21	Not held	1959	David Jenkins, USA	1990	Kurt Browning, Canada
1922	Gillis Grafstrom, Sweden	1960	Alan Giletti, France	1991	Kurt Browning, Canada
1923	Fritz Kachler, Austria	1961	Not held	1992	**Viktor Petrenko**, CIS
1924	**Gillis Grafstrom,** Sweden	1962	Donald Jackson, Canada	1993	Kurt Browning, Canada
1925	Willy Bockl, Austria	1963	Donald McPherson, Canada	1994	Elvis Stojko, Canada
1926	Willy Bockl, Austria	1964	**Manfred Schnelldorfer**, W. Ger	1995	Elvis Stojko, Canada
1927	Willy Bockl, Austria			1996	Todd Eldredge, USA
1928	Willy Bockl, Austria	1965	Alain Calmat, France	1997	Elvis Stojko, Canada
1929	Gillis Grafstrom, Sweden	1966	Emmerich Danzer, Austria	1998	Alexei Yagudin, Russia
1930	Karl Schafer, Austria	1967	Emmerich Danzer, Austria	1999	Alexei Yagudin, Russia
1931	Karl Schafer, Austria	1968	Emmerich Danzer, Austria	2000	Alexei Yagudin, Russia
1932	**Karl Schafer**, Austria	1969	Tim Wood, USA	2001	Evgeni Plushenko, Russia
1933	Karl Schafer, Austria	1970	Tim Wood, USA	2002	**Alexei Yagudin**, Russia

WOMEN

Multiple winners: Sonja Henie (10); Carol Heiss and Herma Planck Szabo (5); Lily Kronberger, Michelle Kwan and Katarina Witt (4); Sjoukje Dijkstra, Peggy Fleming and Meray Horvath (3); Tenley Albright, Linda Fratianne, Anett Poetzsch, Beatrix Schuba, Barbara Ann Scott, Gabriele Seyfert, Megan Taylor, Alena Vrzanova and Kristi Yamaguchi (2).

Year		Year		Year	
1906	Madge Syers, Britain	1934	Sonja Henie, Norway	1962	Sjoukje Dijkstra, Netherlands
1907	Madge Syers, Britain	1935	Sonja Henie, Norway	1963	Sjoukje Dijkstra, Netherlands
1908	Lily Kronberger, Hungary	1936	**Sonja Henie**, Norway	1964	**Sjoukje Dijkstra**, Netherlands
1909	Lily Kronberger, Hungary	1937	Cecilia Colledge, Britain	1965	Petra Burka, Canada
1910	Lily Kronberger, Hungary	1938	Megan Taylor, Britain	1966	Peggy Fleming, USA
1911	Lily Kronberger, Hungary	1939	Megan Taylor, Britain	1967	Peggy Fleming, USA
1912	Meray Horvath, Hungary	1940-46	Not held	1968	**Peggy Fleming**, USA
1913	Meray Horvath, Hungary	1947	Barbara Ann Scott, Canada	1969	Gabriele Seyfert, E. Germany
1914	Meray Horvath, Hungary	1948	**Barbara Ann Scott**, Canada	1970	Gabriele Seyfert, E. Germany
1915-21	Not held			1971	Beatrix Schuba, Austria
1922	Herma Planck-Szabo, Austria	1949	Alena Vrzanova, Czechoslovakia	1972	**Beatrix Schuba**, Austria
1923	Herma Planck-Szabo, Austria	1950	Alena Vrzanova, Czechoslovakia	1973	Karen Magnussen, Canada
1924	**Herma Planck-Szabo**, Austria	1951	Jeannette Altwegg, Britain	1974	Christine Errath, E. Germany
		1952	Jacqueline Du Bief, France	1975	Dianne DeLeeuw, Netherlands
1925	Herma Planck-Szabo, Austria	1953	Tenley Albright, USA	1976	**Dorothy Hamill**, USA
1926	Herma Planck-Szabo, Austria	1954	Gundi Busch, W. Germany	1977	Linda Fratianne, USA
1927	Sonja Henie, Norway	1955	Tenley Albright, USA	1978	Anett Poetzsch, E. Germany
1928	**Sonja Henie**, Norway	1956	Carol Heiss, USA	1979	Linda Fratianne, USA
1929	Sonja Henie, Norway	1957	Carol Heiss, USA	1980	**Anett Poetzsch**, E. Germany
1930	Sonja Henie, Norway	1958	Carol Heiss, USA	1981	Denise Biellmann, Switzerland
1931	Sonja Henie, Norway	1959	Carol Heiss, USA	1982	Elaine Zayak, USA
1932	**Sonja Henie**, Norway	1960	**Carol Heiss**, USA	1983	Rosalyn Sumners, USA
1933	Sonja Henie, Norway	1961	Not held	1984	**Katarina Witt**, E. Germany

Year		Year		Year	
1985	Katarina Witt, E. Germany	1991	Kristi Yamaguchi, USA	1997	Tara Lipinski, USA
1986	Debi Thomas, USA	1992	**Kristi Yamaguchi**, USA	1998	Michelle Kwan, USA
1987	Katarina Witt, E. Germany	1993	Oksana Baiul, Ukraine	1999	Maria Butyrskaya, Russia
1988	**Katarina Witt**, E. Germany	1994	Yuka Sato, Japan	2000	Michelle Kwan, USA
1989	Midori Ito, Japan	1995	Lu Chen, China	2001	Michelle Kwan, USA
1990	Jill Trenary, USA	1996	Michelle Kwan, USA	2002	Irina Slutskaya, Russia

PAIRS

Year		Year		Year	
1908	**Anna Hubler & Heinrich Burger**, GER	1949	Andrea Kekessy & Ede Kiraly, HUN	1977	Irina Rodnina & Aleksandr Zaitsev, USSR
1909	Phyllis Johnson & James H. Johnson, GBR	1950	Karol Kennedy & Peter Kennedy, USA	1978	Irina Rodnina & Aleksandr Zaitsev, USSR
1910	Anna Hubler & Heinrich Burger, GER	1951	Ria Baran & Paul Falk, W. Ger	1979	Tai Babilonia & Randy Gardner, USA
1911	Ludowika Eilers, GER & Walter Jakobsson, FIN	1952	**Ria Falk-Baran & Paul Falk**, W. Ger	1980	Maria Cherkasova & Sergei Shakhrai, USSR
1912	Phyllis Johnson & James H. Johnson, GBR	1953	Jennifer Nicks & John Nicks, GBR	1981	Irina Vorobieva & Igor Lisovsky, USSR
1913	Helene Engelmann & Karl Majstrik, GER	1954	Frances Dafoe & Norris Bowden, CAN	1982	Sabine Baess & Tassilio Thierbach, E. Ger
1914	Ludowika Jakobsson-Eilers & Walter Jakobsson-Eilers, FIN	1955	Frances Dafoe & Norris Bowden, CAN	1983	Elena Valova & Oleg Vasiliev, USSR
1915-21	Not held	1956	**Elisabeth Schwarz & Kurt Oppelt**, AUT	1984	Barbara Underhill & Paul Martini, CAN
1922	**Helene Engelmann & Alfred Berger**, AUT	1957	Barbara Wagner & Robert Paul, CAN	1985	Elena Valova & Oleg Vasiliev, USSR
1923	Ludowika Jakobsson-Eilers & Walter Jakobsson-Eilers, FIN	1958	Barbara Wagner & Robert Paul, CAN	1986	Ekaterina Gordeeva & Sergei Grinkov, USSR
1924	Helene Engelmann & Alfred Berger, GER	1959	Barbara Wagner & Robert Paul, CAN	1987	Ekaterina Gordeeva & Sergei Grinkov, USSR
1925	Herma Jaross-Szabo & Ludwig Wrede, AUT	1960	**Barbara Wagner & Robert Paul**, CAN	1988	Elena Valova & Oleg Vasiliev, USSR
1926	Andree Joly & Pierre Brunet, FRA	1961	Not held	1989	Ekaterina Gordeeva & Sergei Grinkov, USSR
1927	Herma Jaross-Szabo & Ludwig Wrede, AUT	1962	Maria Jelinek & Otto Jelinek, CAN	1990	Ekaterina Gordeeva & Sergei Grinkov, USSR
1928	**Andree Joly & Pierre Brunet**, FRA	1963	Marika Kilius & H.J. Baumler, W. Ger	1991	Natalya Mishkutienok & Arhtur Dmitriev, USSR
1929	Lilly Scholz & Otto Kaiser, AUT	1964	Marika Kilius & H.J. Baumler, W. Ger	1992	**Natalya Mishkutienok & Arthur Dmitriev**, USSR
1930	Andree Brunet-Joly & Pierre Brunet-Joly, FRA	1965	Ludmila Protopopov & Oleg Protopopov, USSR	1993	Isabelle Brasseur & Lloyd Eisler, CAN
1931	Emilie Rotter & Laszlo Szollas, HUN	1966	Ludmila Protopopov & Oleg Protopopov, USSR	1994	Evgenia Shishkova & Vadim Naumov, RUS
1932	**Andree Brunet-Joly & Pierre Brunet-Joly**, FRA	1967	Ludmila Protopopov & Oleg Protopopov, USSR	1995	Radka Kovarikova & Rene Novotny, CZR
1933	Emilie Rotter & Laszlo Szollas, HUN	1968	**Ludmila Protopopov & Oleg Protopopov**, USSR	1996	Marina Eltsova & Andrey Buskhov, RUS
1934	Emilie Rotter & Laszlo Szollas, HUN	1969	Irina Rodnina & Alexsei Ulanov, USSR	1997	Mandy Wotzel & Ingo Steuer, GER
1935	Emilie Rotter & Laszlo Szollas, HUN	1970	Irina Rodnina & Aleksei Ulanov, USSR	1998	Jenni Meno & Todd Sand, USA
1936	**Maxi Herber & Ernst Baier**, GER	1971	Irina Rodnina & Aleksei Ulanov, USSR	1999	Elena Berezhnaya & Anton Sikharulidze, RUS
1937	Maxi Herber & Ernst Baier, GER	1972	**Irina Rodnina & Aleksei Ulanov**, USSR	2000	Maria Petrova & Alexei Tikhonov, RUS
1938	Maxi Herber & Ernst Baier, GER	1973	Irina Rodnina & Aleksandr Zaitsev, USSR	2001	Jamie Sale & David Pelletier, CAN
1939	Maxi Herber & Ernst Baier, GER	1974	Irina Rodnina & Aleksandr Zaitsev, USSR	2002	Xue Shen & Hongbo Zhao, CHN
1940-46	Not held	1975	Irina Rodnina & Aleksandr Zaitsev, USSR		
1947	Micheline Lannoy & Pierre Baugniet, BEL	1976	**Irina Rodnina & Aleksandr Zaitsev**, USSR		
1948	**Micheline Lannoy & Pierre Baugniet**, BEL				

Figure Skating (Cont.)
DANCE

Year		Year		Year	
1950	Lois Waring & Michael McGean, USA	1969	Diane Towler & Bernard Ford, GBR	1987	Natalia Bestemianova & Andrei Bukin, USSR
1951	Jean Westwood & Lawrence Demmy, GBR	1970	Lyudmila Pakhomova & Aleksandr Gorshkov, USSR	1988	**Natalia Bestemianova & Andrei Bukin**, USSR
1952	Jean Westwood & Lawrence Demmy, GBR	1971	Lyudmila Pakhomova & Aleksandr Gorshkov, USSR	1989	Marina Klimova & Sergei Ponomarenko, USSR
1953	Jean Westwood & Lawrence Demmy, GBR	1972	Lyudmila Pakhomova & Aleksandr Gorshkov, USSR	1990	Marina Klimova & Sergei Ponomarenko, USSR
1954	Jean Westwood & Lawrence Demmy, GBR	1973	Lyudmila Pakhomova & Aleksandr Gorshkov, USSR	1991	Isabelle Duchesnay & Paul Duchesnay, FRA
1955	Jean Westwood & Lawrence Demmy, GBR	1974	Lyudmila Pakhomova & Aleksandr Gorshkov, USSR	1992	**Marina Klimova & Sergei Ponomarenko**, USSR
1956	Pamela Wieght & Paul Thomas, GBR	1975	Irina Moiseeva & Andreij Minenkov, USSR	1993	Renee Roca & Gorsha Sur, USA
1957	June Markham & Courtney Jones, GBR	1976	**Lyudmila Pakhomova & Aleksandr Gorshkov**, USSR	1994	**Oksana Grishuk & Evgeny Platov**, RUS
1958	June Markham & Courtney Jones, GBR	1977	Irina Moiseeva & Andreij Minenkov, USSR	1995	Oksana Grishuk & Evgeny Platov, RUS
1959	Doreen D. Denny & Courtney Jones, GBR	1978	Natalia Linichuk & Gennadi Karponosov, USSR	1996	Oksana Grishuk & Evgeny Platov, RUS
1960	Doreen D. Denny & Courtney Jones, GBR	1979	Natalia Linichuk & Gennadi Karponosov, USSR	1997	Oksana Grishuk & Evgeny Platov, RUS
1961	Not held	1980	Krisztina Regoeczy & Andras Sallai, HUN	1998	Anjelika Krylova & Oleg Ovsyannikov, RUS
1962	Eva Romanova & Pavel Roman, CZE	1981	Jayne Torvill & Christopher Dean, GBR	1999	Anjelika Krylova & Oleg Ovsyannikov, RUS
1963	Eva Romanova & Pavel Roman, CZE	1982	Jayne Torvill & Christopher Dean, GBR	2000	Marina Anissina & Gwendal Peizerat, FRA
1964	Eva Romanova & Pavel Roman, CZE	1983	Jayne Torvill & Christopher Dean, GBR	2001	Barbara Fusar Poli & Maurizio Margaglio, ITA
1965	Eva Romanova & Pavel Roman, CZE	1984	**Jayne Torvill & Christopher Dean**, GBR	2002	Irina Lobacheva & Ilia Averbukh, RUS
1966	Diane Towler & Bernard Ford, GBR	1985	Natalia Bestemianova & Andrei Bukin, USSR		
1967	Diane Towler & Bernard Ford, GBR	1986	Natalia Bestemianova & Andrei Bukin, USSR		
1968	Diane Towler & Bernard Ford, GBR				

U.S. Champions

Skaters who won U.S., World and Olympic championships in same year are in **bold** type.

MEN

Multiple winners: Dick Button and Roger Turner (7); Todd Eldredge (6); Sherwin Badger and Robin Lee (5); Brian Boitano, Scott Hamilton, David Jenkins, Hayes Jenkins and Charles Tickner (4); Gordon McKellen, Nathaniel Niles and Tim Wood (3); Scott Allen, Christopher Bowman, Scott Davis, Eugene Turner, Gary Visconti and Michael Weiss (2).

Year		Year		Year		Year	
1914	Norman Scott	1938	Robin Lee	1961	Bradley Lord	1983	Scott Hamilton
1915-17	Not held	1939	Robin Lee	1962	Monty Hoyt	1984	**Scott Hamilton**
1918	Nathaniel Niles	1940	Eugene Turner	1963	Thomas Litz	1985	Brian Boitano
1919	Not held	1941	Eugene Turner	1964	Scott Allen	1986	Brian Boitano
1920	Sherwin Badger	1942	Robert Specht	1965	Gary Visconti	1987	Brian Boitano
1921	Sherwin Badger	1943	Arthur Vaughn	1966	Scott Allen	1988	**Brian Boitano**
1922	Sherwin Badger	1944-45	Not held	1967	Gary Visconti	1989	Christopher Bowman
1923	Sherwin Badger	1946	Dick Button	1968	Tim Wood	1990	Todd Eldredge
1924	Sherwin Badger	1947	Dick Button	1969	Tim Wood	1991	Todd Eldredge
1925	Nathaniel Niles	1948	**Dick Button**	1970	Tim Wood	1992	Christopher Bowman
1926	Chris Christenson	1949	Dick Button	1971	John (Misha) Petkevich	1993	Scott Davis
1927	Nathaniel Niles	1950	Dick Button	1972	Ken Shelley	1994	Scott Davis
1928	Roger Turner	1951	Dick Button	1973	Gordon McKellen	1995	Todd Eldredge
1929	Roger Turner	1952	**Dick Button**	1974	Gordon McKellen	1996	Rudy Galindo
1930	Roger Turner	1953	Hayes Jenkins	1975	Gordon McKellen	1997	Todd Eldredge
1931	Roger Turner	1954	Hayes Jenkins	1976	Terry Kubicka	1998	Todd Eldredge
1932	Roger Turner	1955	Hayes Jenkins	1977	Charles Tickner	1999	Michael Weiss
1933	Roger Turner	1956	**Hayes Jenkins**	1978	Charles Tickner	2000	Michael Weiss
1934	Roger Turner	1957	David Jenkins	1979	Charles Tickner	2001	Tim Goebel
1935	Robin Lee	1958	David Jenkins	1980	Charles Tickner	2002	Todd Eldredge
1936	Robin Lee	1959	David Jenkins	1981	Scott Hamilton		
1937	Robin Lee	1960	David Jenkins	1982	Scott Hamilton		

WOMEN

Multiple winners: Maribel Vinson (9); Theresa Weld Blanchard, Michelle Kwan and Gretchen Merrill (6); Tenley Albright, Peggy Fleming and Janet Lynn (5); Linda Fratianne and Carol Heiss (4); Dorothy Hamill, Beatrix Loughran, Rosalyn Summers, Joan Tozzer and Jill Trenary (3); Yvonne Sherman and Debi Thomas (2).

Year		Year		Year		Year	
1914	Theresa Weld	1938	Joan Tozzer	1960	**Carol Heiss**	1982	Rosalyn Sumners
1915-17	Not held	1939	Joan Tozzer	1961	Laurence Owen	1983	Rosalyn Sumners
1918	Rosemary Beresford	1940	Joan Tozzer	1962	Barbara Pursley	1984	Rosalyn Sumners
1919	Not held	1941	Jane Vaughn	1963	Lorraine Hanlon	1985	Tiffany Chin
1920	Theresa Weld	1942	Jane Sullivan	1964	Peggy Fleming	1986	Debi Thomas
1921	Theresa Blanchard	1943	Gretchen Merrill	1965	Peggy Fleming	1987	Jill Trenary
1922	Theresa Blanchard	1944	Gretchen Merrill	1966	Peggy Fleming	1988	Debi Thomas
1923	Theresa Blanchard	1945	Gretchen Merrill	1967	Peggy Fleming	1989	Jill Trenary
1924	Theresa Blanchard	1946	Gretchen Merrill	1968	**Peggy Fleming**	1990	Jill Trenary
1925	Beatrix Loughran	1947	Gretchen Merrill	1969	Janet Lynn	1991	Tonya Harding
1926	Beatrix Loughran	1948	Gretchen Merrill	1970	Janet Lynn	1992	**Kristi Yamaguchi**
1927	Beatrix Loughran	1949	Yvonne Sherman	1971	Janet Lynn	1993	Nancy Kerrigan
1928	Maribel Vinson	1950	Yvonne Sherman	1972	Janet Lynn	1994	vacated*
1929	Maribel Vinson	1951	Sonya Klopfer	1973	Janet Lynn	1995	Nicole Bobek
1930	Maribel Vinson	1952	Tenley Albright	1974	Dorothy Hamill	1996	Michelle Kwan
1931	Maribel Vinson	1953	Tenley Albright	1975	Dorothy Hamill	1997	Tara Lipinski
1932	Maribel Vinson	1954	Tenley Albright	1976	**Dorothy Hamill**	1998	Michelle Kwan
1933	Maribel Vinson	1955	Tenley Albright	1977	Linda Fratianne	1999	Michelle Kwan
1934	Suzanne Davis	1956	Tenley Albright	1978	Linda Fratianne	2000	Michelle Kwan
1935	Maribel Vinson	1957	Carol Heiss	1979	Linda Fratianne	2001	Michelle Kwan
1936	Maribel Vinson	1958	Carol Heiss	1980	Linda Fratianne	2002	Michelle Kwan
1937	Maribel Vinson	1959	Carol Heiss	1981	Elaine Zayak		

* Tonya Harding was stripped of the 1994 women's title and banned from membership in the U.S. Figure Skating Assn. for life on June 30, 1994 for violating the USFSA Code of Ethics after she pleaded guilty to a charge of conspiracy to hinder the prosecution related to the Jan. 6, 1994 attack on Nancy Kerrigan.

PAIRS

Year		Year		Year	
1914	Jeanne Chevalier & Norman M. Scott	1938	Joan Tozzer & M. Bernard Fox	1958	Nancy Rouillard Ludington & Ronald Ludington
1915-17	Not held	1939	Joan Tozzer & M. Bernard Fox	1959	Nancy Rouillard Ludington & Ronald Ludington
1918	Theresa Weld & Nathaniel W. Niles	1940	Joan Tozzer & M. Bernard Fox	1960	Nancy Rouillard Ludington & Ronald Ludington
1919	Not held	1941	Donna Atwood & Eugene Turner	1961	Maribel Y. Owen & Dudley S. Richards
1920	Theresa Weld & Nathaniel W. Niles	1942	Doris Schubach & Walter Noffke	1962	Dorothyann Nelson & Pieter Kollen
1921	Theresa Weld Blanchard & Nathaniel W. Niles	1943	Doris Schubach & Walter Noffke	1963	Judianne Fotheringill & Jerry J. Fotheringill
1922	Theresa Weld Blanchard & Nathaniel W. Niles	1944	Doris Schubach & Walter Noffke	1964	Judianne Fotheringill & Jerry J. Fotheringill
1923	Theresa Weld Blanchard & Nathaniel W. Niles	1945	Donna Jeanne Pospisil & Jean-Pierre Brunet	1965	Vivian Joseph & Ronald Joseph
1924	Theresa Weld Blanchard & Nathaniel W. Niles	1946	Donna Jeanne Pospisil & Jean-Pierre Brunet	1966	Cynthia Kauffman & Ronald Kauffman
1925	Theresa Weld Blanchard & Nathaniel W. Niles	1947	Yvonne Claire Sherman & Robert J. Swenning	1967	Cynthia Kauffman & Ronald Kauffman
1926	Theresa Weld Blanchard & Nathaniel W. Niles	1948	Karol Kennedy & Peter Kennedy	1968	Cynthia Kauffman & Ronald Kauffman
1927	Theresa Weld Blanchard & Nathaniel W. Niles	1949	Karol Kennedy & Peter Kennedy	1969	Cynthia Kauffman & Ronald Kauffman
1928	Maribel Vinson & Thornton L. Coolidge	1950	Karol Kennedy & Peter Kennedy	1970	Jo Jo Starbuck & Kenneth Shelley
1929	Maribel Vinson & Thornton L. Coolidge	1951	Karol Kennedy & Peter Kennedy	1971	Jo Jo Starbuck & Kenneth Shelley
1930	Beatrix Loughran & Sherwin C. Badger	1952	Karol Kennedy & Peter Kennedy	1972	Jo Jo Starbuck & Kenneth Shelley
1931	Beatrix Loughran & Sherwin C. Badger	1953	Carole Ann Ormaca & Robin Greiner	1973	Melissa Militano & Mark Militano
1932	Beatrix Loughran & Sherwin C. Badger	1954	Carole Ann Ormaca & Robin Greiner	1974	Melissa Militano & Johnny Johns
1933	Maribel Vinson & George E.B. Hill	1955	Carole Ann Ormaca & Robin Greiner	1975	Melissa Militano & Johnny Johns
1934	Grace E. Madden & James L. Madden	1956	Carole Ann Ormaca & Robin Greiner	1976	Tai Babilonia & Randy Gardner
1935	Maribel Vinson & George E.B. Hill	1957	Nancy Rouillard Ludington & Ronald Ludington	1977	Tai Babilonia & Randy Gardner
1936	Maribel Vinson & George E.B. Hill				
1937	Maribel Vinson & George E.B. Hill				

Figure Skating (Cont.)

Year		Year		Year	
1978	Tai Babilonia & Randy Gardner	1987	Jill Watson & Peter Oppegard	1996	Jenni Meno & Todd Sand
1979	Tai Babilonia & Randy Gardner	1988	Jill Watson & Peter Oppegard	1997	Kyoko Ina & Jason Dungjen
1980	Tai Babilonia & Randy Gardner	1989	Kristi Yamaguchi & Rudy Galindo	1998	Kyoko Ina & Jason Dungjen
1981	Caitlin Carruthers & Peter Carruthers	1990	Kristi Yamaguchi & Rudy Galindo	1999	Danielle Hartsell & Steve Hartsell
1982	Caitlin Carruthers & Peter Carruthers	1991	Natasha Kuchiki & Todd Sand	2000	Kyoko Ina & John Zimmerman
1983	Caitlin Carruthers & Peter Carruthers	1992	Calla Urbanski & Rocky Marval	2001	Kyoko Ina & John Zimmerman
1984	Caitlin Carruthers & Peter Carruthers	1993	Calla Urbanski & Rocky Marval	2002	Kyoko Ina & John Zimmerman
1985	Jill Watson & Peter Oppegard	1994	Jenni Meno & Todd Sand		
1986	Gillian Wachsman & Todd Waggoner	1995	Jenni Meno & Todd Sand		

RUGBY

World Cup

The inaugural Rugby World Cup was held in 1987. Like soccer's World Cup, it is held every four years. Sixteen national teams were assembled for the first three tournaments but beginning in 1999, 20 teams played for the William Webb Ellis Cup, named for the game's inventor. The Rugby World Cup is now billed as the world's third largest athletic event, behind the Olympics and the soccer World Cup. Australia will host the 2003 competition, to be held Oct. 10-Nov. 22.

Year	Winner	Score	Runner up	Host Country
1987	New Zealand	29-9	France	Australia & New Zealand
1991	Australia	12-6	England	United Kingdom & France
1995	South Africa	15-12	New Zealand	South Africa
1999	Australia	35-12	France	Wales

Six Nations Tournament

The annual Six Nations rugby tournament, a.k.a. the International Championship, was first contested in 1882 as a match between England and Wales. England, Ireland, Scotland and Wales competed in the early years. France made it five nations by joining the competition in 1910 and played until 1931 when they were expelled because of the sad state of French rugby. France rejoined the tournament in 1947. The Five Nations became the Six Nations in 2000 with the addition of Italy. Each team plays each other once (two points are earned for a win and one for a tie) and the team with the most points is declared the winner. (*) indicates Grand Slam, meaning the team won all of its games.

Multiple winners: England (35); Wales (33); Scotland (22); France (21); Ireland (18).

Year		Year		Year		Year	
1882	England	1911	Wales*	1940-46	Not held—WW II	1975	Wales
1883	England	1912	England & Ireland	1947	Wales & England	1976	Wales*
1884	England	1913	England*	1948	Ireland*	1977	France*
1885	Not completed	1914	England*	1949	Ireland	1978	Wales*
1886	England & Scotland	1915-19	Not held—WW I	1950	Wales*	1979	Wales
1887	Scotland	1920	England, Scotland & Wales	1951	Ireland	1980	England*
1888	Not completed			1952	Wales*	1981	France*
1889	Not completed	1921	England*	1953	England	1982	Ireland
1890	England & Scotland	1922	Wales	1954	England, France & Wales	1983	France & Ireland
1891	Scotland	1923	England*	1955	France & Wales	1984	Scotland*
1892	England	1924	England*	1956	Wales	1985	Ireland
1893	Wales	1925	Scotland*	1957	England*	1986	France & Scotland
1894	Ireland	1926	Scotland & Ireland	1958	England	1987	France*
1895	Scotland	1927	Scotland & Ireland	1959	France	1988	Wales & France
1896	Ireland	1928	England*	1960	France & England	1989	France
1897	Not completed	1929	Scotland	1961	France	1990	Scotland*
1898	Not completed	1930	England	1962	France	1991	England*
1899	Ireland	1931	Wales	1963	England	1992	England*
1900	Wales	1932	England, Wales & Ireland	1964	Scotland & Wales	1993	France
1901	Scotland			1965	Wales	1994	Wales
1902	Wales	1933	Scotland	1966	Wales	1995	England*
1903	Scotland	1934	England	1967	France	1996	England
1904	Scotland	1935	Ireland	1968	France*	1997	France*
1905	Wales	1936	Wales	1969	Wales	1998	France*
1906	Ireland & Wales	1937	England	1970	France & Wales	1999	Scotland
1907	Scotland	1938	Scotland	1971	Wales*	2000	England
1908	Wales*	1939	England, Wales & Ireland	1972	Not completed	2001	England
1909	Wales*			1973	Five way tie	2002	France*
1910	England			1974	Ireland		

Olympics

Long Island teenager **Sarah Hughes** won gold in women's figure skating with a flawless free skate.

AP/Wide World Photos

Gold Rush

A judging scandal erupted at a Winter Games that saw the USA take its biggest medal haul ever.

Anne Marie Cruz
is a senior reporter for ESPN The Magazine.

Salt Lake City was no stranger to scandal—hello, bribe-tainted bids—but no one could predict how quickly the 2002 Games would become embroiled in yet another web of international intrigue.

Everyone knows the story by now: Cutie-pie Canadian pairs skaters Jamie Sale and David Pelletier performed flawlessly, but finished second to wobbly-footed Russians Elena Berezhnaya and Anton Sikharulidze. Canada's ensuing fury was echoed by fans, conspiracy theorists and talk show hosts worldwide. Investigations were mounted while accusations flew. Turns out, the fix was in— and French judge Marie-Reine Le Gougne was the score-altering culprit.

Sale and Pelletier eventually got their co-golds, but the pall of collusion seeped into everything from biathlon to hockey. Le Gougne claimed she was just a cog in a multinational Olympic medal-swap. Protests became trendier than Roots berets. Press conferences seemed to be held every hour. The Russians even threatened to withdraw altogether. Suspicion became an Olympic event at the 2002 Games, and to that end, there were no winners.

Luckily, the scandal would not tarnish everything. The U.S. Olympians brought home an astounding 34 medals, nearly tripling its previous best one-Games haul (the old record was 13) and falling just one medal short of overall leader Germany.

Bode Miller brought swagger to U.S. alpine skiing, nabbing two silver medals with hard-to-believe come-from-behind attacks on both the combined and the giant slalom courses. Bobsledders Randy Jones and Garrett Hines, who took silver with driver Todd Hays in the four-man, joined fellow pusher Vonetta

AP/Wide World Photos

*Canada's **Jamie Sale** and **David Pelletier**, left, had their silver medals upgraded to gold in a special ceremony after a judging scandal erupted following their second-place finish to Russia's **Elena Berezhnaya** and **Anton Sikharulidze** in pairs figure skating.*

Flowers, the women's gold medalist, as African-Americans to win Winter Olympic medals, a group that until this year had one member (Debi Thomas).

Ross Powers, Danny Kass and Jarrett "J.J." Thomas ran the halfpipe table—only the second American threesome in Winter Games history to sweep—while Kelly Clark stomped the women's competition. Powered by patriotism and home soil advantage, the Olympic rings glowed red, white and blue.

Of course, the Americans weren't the only upstarts. Swiss ski jumper Simon Ammann—a dead ringer for Harry Potter—flew like a schoolboy wizard on a Nimbus 2000, soaring to lengths that left heavy favorites Adam Malysz of Poland and Martin Schmitt of Germany more than a bit stunned. Croatia's Janica Kostelic shot into the slopeside stratosphere occupied by Jean-Claude Killy and Toni Sailer: The trio are the only skiers to win three alpine golds (combined, slalom and giant slalom) at one Games. But Kostelic's super-G silver cleared an exclusive spot in the record books as the first skier with four

AP/Wide World Photos

*American skier **Bode Miller** was a fan favorite at the Winter Games with his aggressive style on the course. Miller took home silver medals in the men's giant slalom and combined.*

medals—all of them firsts for Croatia. Meanwhile, Norwegian biathlete Ole Einar Bjoerndalen earned an unprecedented four golds, not to mention the respect of King Harald.

Indeed, Utah had put on a show worthy of royalty. Yet even after Salt Lake's Olympic flame was extinguished, scandal reared its ugly head twice more.

First it was revealed that several atheletes, including Russian cross country skier Larissa Lazutina had failed post-race drug tests, then in late July, alleged Russian mob figure Alimzan Tokhtakhounov was arrested for conspiring to fix the ice dancing competition. Wiretaps implicated everyone from Olympic ice dancing champs, Marina Anissina and Gwendal Peizerat of France, to the president of the International Skating Union. The extent of the damage to the Olympic Games remains to be seen.

Anne Marie Cruz's Top Ten Scandal-Free Winter Olympic Memories

10 Though Michelle Kwan's dreams of Olympic glory in Salt Lake City turned into a nightmarish repeat of her shortfall at Nagano, she wears a plastic toy gold medal around her neck at the post-event press conference, a consolation prize given to her by Dorothy Hamill.

9 Todd Hays and Brian Shimer end 46 years of U.S. bobsledding futility, steering the Americans to silver and bronze medals. In his last run at his final Games, four-time Olympian Shimer nearly overtakes Hays, flying past World Cup champ Martin Annen of Switzerland.

8 Hermann Maier's longtime understudy, Stephan Eberharter of Austria collapses onto his back in the snow, overwhelmed with disbelief after rocketing down the icy steeps of Snowbird, Utah fast enough to escape the Herminator's shadow with giant slalom gold.

7 Before handwringing could supplant hockey as Canada's national pastime—Olympic gold had eluded them since 1952—our northern friends wrought pure gold from the rink ice, with decisive wins by both their men's and women's squads over the U.S.

6 Spills and thrills galore as short-track speedskater Apolo Anton Ohno staggers to silver after a final-lap pile-up in the 1,000, then nabs 1,500 gold when South Korean star Kim Dong-Sung is disqualified for blocking. Those novelty soul patches may have been fake, but the drama was real.

5 Teaming up with driver Jill Bakken, Vonetta Flowers becomes the first African-American to bring home Winter Olympic gold, slipping quietly past the drama swirling around the break-up of power team Jean Racine and Jen Davidson.

4 Mighty mite Derek Parra—the Mexican-American stands a mere 5-foot-4—slays the Dutch speedskating giants, stealing the 1,500-meter crown while shaving more than a second off the world record.

3 The day after National Donor Day, transplant recipient and snowboarder Chris Klug overcomes a liver ravaged by the same disease that killed football legend Walter Payton on the way to the bronze medal in the parallel giant slalom.

2 A distant fourth after the short program, 16-year-old Sarah

Hughes unleashes an exuberant long routine, nailing two unprecedented triple-triple combos while Michelle Kwan crumpled. Not even a roomful of French judges could take away Sarah's gold-medal moment.

1 ▪ Third-generation Olympian Jim Shea Jr. hurtles headfirst to skeleton glory, infused with the spirit of his late grandfather, Jack Shea, who died just a month before Opening Ceremonies. At the finish line, Shea's friends Martin Rettl of Austria and Gregor Staehli of Switzerland tackle him joyfully.

Afterward, Shea clutches his grandfather's photo, saying, "He can go up to heaven now."

Continental Divide

Although the U.S. men entered its gold medal hockey game with Canada unbeaten on home ice in 24 straight Olympic games, Canada's lineup had the edge based on NHL experience (and the numbers would have been even more lopsided had Patrick Roy decided to play for Team Canada). It's not clear that the advantage in NHL accolades is responsible for the Canadians' gold medal victory but it probably didn't hurt.

	CAN	USA
NHL All-Star Games	101	72
Stanley Cups	20	16
Conn Smythe Winners	6	1

Operation Gold

The USOC paid out a record sum in medal bonuses to American athletes following the U.S. team's surprising level of success in Salt Lake City. The USOC anted up a total of $1.27 million for their 34 American medals. The Operation Gold program awarded $25,000 for each gold, $15,000 for each silver and $10,000 for each bronze. Here is the breakdown of the payout:

	Total Bonus
11 individual golds	$275,000
14 individual silvers	$210,000
23 men's hockey silver	$345,000
20 women's hockey silver	$300,000
14 individual bronze	$140,000

2002 Salt Lake City
The Games in Review

ESPN
Information Please®
SPORTS ALMANAC

Final Medal Standings

Full results of the XIXth Olympic Winter Games at Salt Lake City, Utah in the United States of America from Feb. 8–24, 2002. National medal standings are not recognized by the IOC. The unofficial point totals are based on three points for every gold medal, two for each silver and one for each bronze. Seventy-eight nations competed, but only 25 medaled.

		G	S	B	Medals	Points			G	S	B	Medals	Points
1	Germany	12	16	7	35	75	14	South Korea	2	2	0	4	10
2	United States	10	13	11	34	67	15	Sweden	0	2	4	6	8
3	Norway	11	7	6	24	53	16	Estonia	1	1	1	3	6
4	Russia	6	6	4	16	34		Australia	2	0	0	2	6
5	Canada	6	3	8	17	32		Spain	2	0	0	2	6
6	Austria	2	4	11	17	25	19	Bulgaria	0	1	2	3	4
7	Italy	4	4	4	12	24		Czech Republic	1	0	1	2	4
	France	4	5	2	11	24		Great Britain	1	0	1	2	4
9	Switzerland	3	2	6	11	19	22	Japan	0	1	1	2	3
	Netherlands	3	5	0	8	19		Poland	0	1	1	2	3
11	Finland	4	2	1	7	17	24	Belarus	0	0	1	1	1
12	China	2	2	4	8	14		Slovenia	0	0	1	1	1
13	Croatia	3	1	0	4	11		TOTALS	79	78	77	234	470

1998 Nagano Top 10: 1. **Germany** (29 medals, 62 points); 2. **Norway** (25 medals, 55 pts.); 3. **Russia** (18 medals, 42 pts.); 4. **Canada** (15 medals, 32 pts.); 5. **Austria** (17 medals, 28 pts.) & **United States** (13 medals, 28 pts.); 7. **Netherlands** (11 medals, 25 pts.); 8. **Japan** (10 medals, 21 pts.); 9. **Finland** (12 medals, 20 pts.) & **Italy** (10 medals, 20 pts.).

Leading Medal Winners

Number of medals won on the left; gold, silver and bronze breakdown on right. USA medalists in **bold** type.

MEN

No		Sport	G-S-B
4	Ole Einar Bjoerndalen, NOR	Biathlon	4-0-0
3	Samppa Lajunen, FIN	Nordic Comb.	3-0-0
3	Jochem Uytdehaage, NED	Sp. Skating	2-1-0
3	Marc Gagnon, CAN	ST Sp. Skating	2-0-1
3	Frode Estil, NOR	Cross Country	1-2-0
3	Stephan Eberharter, AUT	Alpine	1-1-1
3	Felix Gottwald, AUT	Nordic Comb.	0-0-3
2	Simon Ammann, SWI	Ski Jumping	2-0-0
2	Kjetil Andre Aamodt, NOR	Alpine	2-0-0
2	Johann Muehlegg, SPA	Cross Country	2-0-0
2	Jaakko Tallus, FIN	Nordic Comb.	1-1-0
2	Sven Hannawald, GER	Ski Jumping	1-1-0
2	**Derek Parra**, USA	Sp. Skating	1-1-0
2	**Apolo Anton Ohno**, USA	ST Sp. Skating	1-1-0
2	Thomas Alsgaard, NOR	Cross Country	1-1-0
2	Jonathan Guilmette, CAN	ST Sp. Skating	1-1-0
2	Andrus Veerpalu, EST	Cross Country	1-1-0
2	Mathieu Turcotte, CAN	ST Sp. Skating	1-0-1
2	Sven Fischer, GER	Biathlon	0-2-0
2	Frank Luck, GER	Biathlon	0-2-0
2	Ronny Ackermann, GER	Nordic Comb.	0-2-0
2	**Bode Miller**, USA	Alpine	0-2-0
2	Adam Malysz, POL	Ski Jumping	0-1-1
2	Matti Hautamaeki, FIN	Ski Jumping	0-1-1
2	Cristian Zorzi, ITA	Cross Country	0-1-1
2	Raphael Poiree, FRA	Biathlon	0-1-1
2	Ricco Gross, GER	Biathlon	0-1-1
2	Lasse Kjus, NOR	Alpine	0-1-1
2	Li Jiajun, CHN	ST Sp. Skating	0-1-1
2	Benjamin Raich, AUT	Alpine	0-0-2

WOMEN

No		Sport	G-S-B
4	Janica Kostelic, CRO	Alpine	3-1-0
3	Kati Wilhelm, GER	Biathlon	2-1-0
3	Yang Yang (A), CHN	ST Sp. Skating	2-1-0
3	Bente Skari, NOR	Cross Country	1-1-1
3	Sabine Voelker, GER	Sp. Skating	0-2-1
2	Andrea Henkel, GER	Biathlon	2-0-0
2	Claudia Pechstein, GER	Sp. Skating	2-0-0
2	Olga Danilova, RUS	Cross Country	1-1-0
2	Uschi Disl, GER	Biathlon	1-1-0
2	Choi Eun-Kyung, S. Kor.	ST Sp. Skating	1-1-0
2	Evi Sachenbacher, GER	Cross Country	1-1-0
2	Ko Gi-Hyun, S. Kor.	ST Sp. Skating	1-1-0
2	Stefania Belmondo, ITA	Cross Country	1-1-0
2	Olga Pyleva, RUS	Biathlon	1-0-1
2	Julija Tchepalova, RUS	Cross Country	1-0-1
2	Liv Grete Poiree, NOR	Biathlon	0-2-0
2	Larissa Lazutina, RUS	Cross Country	0-2-0
2	Renate Goetschl, AUT	Alpine	0-1-1
2	Wang Chunlu, CHN	ST Sp. Skating	0-1-1
2	Anita Moen, NOR	Cross Country	0-1-1
2	Anja Paerson, SWE	Alpine	0-1-1
2	Evgenia Radanova, BUL	ST Sp. Skating	0-1-1
2	Yang Yang (S), CHN	ST Sp. Skating	0-1-1
2	Magdalena Forsberg, SWE	Biathlon	0-0-2
2	**Jennifer Rodriguez**, USA	Sp. Skating	0-0-2

Medal Sports

ALPINE SKIING

Medal breakdown (10 events): **Nine medals**—Austria (2-2-5); **Four**—Croatia (3-1-0); France (2-2-0); Norway (2-1-1); **Three**—Italy (1-1-1); **Two**—United States (0-2-0) and Sweden (0-1-1); **One**—Germany (0-0-1) and Switzerland (0-0-1).

MEN

Downhill

		Time
1	Fritz Strobl, AUT	1:39.13
2	Lasse Kjus, NOR	1:39.35
3	Stephan Eberharter, AUT	1:39.41

Top 10 USA: 9th, Marco Sullivan (1:40.37).

Slalom

		Time
1	Jean-Pierre Vidal, FRA	1:41.06
2	Sebastien Amiez, FRA	1:41.82
3	Benjamin Raich, AUT*	1:42.41

*Raich finished fourth but was awarded the bronze medal on March 21, 2002 after Great Britain's Alain Baxter (1:42.32) was disqualified for testing positive for methamphetamine—a stimulant banned by the IOC but found in over-the-counter decongestants like the one Baxter purportedly took to treat a stuffy nose.
Best USA: 12th, Chip Knight (1:44.86); 14th, Erik Schlopy (1:45.21); 25th, Bode Miller (1:52.79).

Giant Slalom

		Time
1	Stephan Eberharter, AUT	2:23.28
2	Bode Miller, USA	2:24.16
3	Lasse Kjus, NOR	2:24.32

Next best USA: 16th, Dane Spencer (2:25.68).

Super G

		Time
1	Kjetil Andre Aamodt, NOR	1:21.58
2	Stephan Eberharter, AUT	1:21.68
3	Andreas Schifferer, AUT	1:21.83

Top 10 USA: 8th, Daron Rahlves (1:22.48); 9th, Thomas Vonn (1:23.22).

Combined

		DH	SL	Time
1	Kjetil Andre Aamodt, NOR	1st	5th(t)	3:17.56
2	Bode Miller, USA	15th	5th(t)	3:17.84
3	Benjamin Raich, AUT	13th	3rd	3:18.26

Next best USA: 19th, Jakub Fiala (21st, 18th, 3:30.43).

WOMEN

Downhill

		Time
1	Carole Montillet, FRA	1:39.56
2	Isolde Kostner, ITA	1:40.01
3	Renate Goetschl, AUT	1:40.39

Best USA: 11th, Jonna Mendes (1:40.97); 12th, Kirsten L. Clark (1:41.03); 16th, Picabo Street (1:41.17).

Slalom

		Time
1	Janica Kostelic, CRO	1:46.10
2	Laure Pequegnot, FRA	1:46.17
3	Anja Paerson, SWE	1:47.09

Best USA: 32nd, Lindsey Kildow (2:00.73).

Giant Slalom

		Time
1	Janica Kostelic, CRO	2:30.01
2	Anja Paerson, SWE	2:31.33
3	Sonja Nef, SWI	2:31.67

Best USA: 17th, Kristina Koznick (2:34.22).

Super G

		Time
1	Daniela Ceccarelli, ITA	1:13.59
2	Janica Kostelic, CRO	1:13.64
3	Karen Putzer, ITA	1:13.86

Best USA: 14th, Kirsten L. Clark (1:15.13).

Combined

		DH	SL	Time
1	Janica Kostelic, CRO	1st	1st	2:43.28
2	Renate Goetschl, AUT	2nd	4th	2:44.77
3	Martina Ertl, GER	3rd	2nd	2:45.16

Top 10 USA: 6th, Lindsey Kildow (4th, 9th, 2:48.05).

BIATHLON

Cross country (any style) and rifle shooting (.22 caliber, small-bore, standing and prone). MT indicates missed targets.
Medal breakdown (8 events): **Nine medals**—Germany (3-5-1); **Six**—Norway (4-2-0); **Three**—Russia (1-0-2); **Two**—France (0-1-1) and Sweden (0-0-2); **One**—Austria (0-0-1) and Bulgaria (0-0-1).

MEN

10-km Sprint

		MT	Time
1	Ole Einar Bjoerndalen, NOR	0	24:51.3
2	Sven Fischer, GER	1	25:20.2
3	Wolfgang Perner, AUT	0	25:44.4

Best USA: 20th, Jeremy Teela (2 MT, 26:36.6).

12.5-km Pursuit

		MT	Time
1	Ole Einar Bjoerndalen, NOR	2	32:34.6
2	Raphael Poiree, FRA	1	33:17.6
3	Ricco Gross, GER	2	33:30.6

Best USA: 13th, Jay Hakkinen (1 MT, 34:11.8).

20-km Individual

		MT	Time
1	Ole Einar Bjoerndalen, NOR	2	51:03.3
2	Frank Luck, GER	0	51:39.4
3	Victor Maigourov, RUS	1	51:40.6

Best USA: 14th, Jeremy Teela (2 MT, 53:56.5).

4 x 7.5-km Relay

		MT	Time
1	Norway	0	1:23:42.3
2	Germany	1	1:24:27.6
3	France	0	1:24:36.6

NOR—Halvard Hanevold, Frode Andresen, Egil Gjelland, Ole Einar Bjoerndalen; **GER**—Ricco Gross, Peter Sendel, Sven Fischer, Frank Luck; **FRA**—Gilles Marguet, Vincent Defrasne, Julien Robert, Raphael Poiree.

USA entry: 15th, Jeremy Teela, Jay Hakkinen, Dan Campbell, Lawton Redman (2 MT, 1:30:27.1).

WOMEN

7.5-km Sprint

		MT	Time
1	Kati Wilhelm, GER	0	20:41.4
2	Uschi Disl, GER	1	20:57.0
3	Magdalena Forsberg, SWE	1	21:20.4

Best USA: 49th, Kara Salmela (3 MT, 23:44.1).

10–km Pursuit

		MT	Time
1	Olga Pyleva, RUS	1	31:07.7
2	Kati Wilhelm, GER	4	31:13.0
3	Irina Nikoultchina, BUL	2	31:15.8

Best USA: 45th, Kara Salmela (5 MT, 37:07.7).

15–km Individual

		MT	Time
1	Andrea Henkel, GER	1	47:29.1
2	Liv Grete Poiree, NOR	1	47:37.0
3	Magdalena Forsberg, SWE	2	48:08.3

Best USA: 31st, Rachel Steer (2 MT, 51:50.6).

4 x 7.5–km Relay

		MT	Time
1	Germany	1	1:27:55.0
2	Norway	0	1:28:25.6
3	Russia	2	1:29:19.7

GER—Katrin Apel, Uschi Disl, Andrea Henkel, Kati Wilhelm; **NOR**—Ann Elen Skjelbreid, Linda Tjoerhom, Gunn Margit Andreassen, Liv Grete Poiree; **RUS**—Olga Pyleva, Galina Koukleva, Svetlana Ishmouratova, Albina Akhatova.

USA entry: 15th, Andrea Nahrgang, Kara Salmela, Rachel Steer, Kristina Sabasteanski (3 MT, 1:41:16.0).

BOBSLED

Medal breakdown (3 events): **Four medals**—Germany (2-1-1); **Three**—United States (1-1-1); **Two**—Switzerland (0-1-1).

Two-Man

		Time
1	Germany I	3:10.11
2	Switzerland I	3:10.20
3	Switzerland II	3:10.62

GER I—Christoph Langen & Markus Zimmermann; **SWI I**—Christian Reich & Steve Anderhub; **SWI II**—Martin Annen & Beat Hefti.

Top 10 USA: 4th, USA I—Todd Hays & Garrett Hines (3:10.65).

Two-Woman

		Time
1	United States II	1:37.76
2	Germany I	1:38.06
3	Germany II	1:38.29

USA II—Jill Bakken & Vonetta Flowers; **GER I**—Sandra Prokoff & Ulrike Holzner; **GER II**—Susi-Lisa Erdmann & Nicole Herschmann.

Other top 10 USA: 5th, USA I— Jean Racine & Gea Johnson (1:38.73).

Four-Man

		Time
1	Germany II	3:07.51
2	United States I	3:07.81
3	United States II	3:07.86

GER II—Andre Lange, Enrico Kuehn, Kevin Kuske, Carsten Embach; **USA I**—Todd Hays, Randy Jones, Bill Schuffenhauer, Garrett Hines; **USA II**—Brian Shimer, Mike Kohn, Doug Sharp, Dan Steele.

AP/Wide World Photos

*Americans **Vonetta Flowers** and **Jill Bakken** weren't even considered the best women's bobsled team in the United States, let alone the world. Nevertheless, they held off both German sleds to capture the first women's Olympic bobsled gold medal.*

Salt Lake City Olympic Firsts

- Alpine skier Janica Kostelic of Croatia and cross country skiers Andrus Veerpalu and Jaak Mae of Estonia won the first Winter Games medals for their home countries.
- Short-track speed skaters Steven Bradbury and Yang Yang (A) captured the first Winter Games gold medals for Australia and China, respectively. Bradbury's gold was the first for any country in the Southern Hemisphere.
- Biathletes Raphael Poiree, of France, and Liv Grete Poiree, of Norway, became the first married couple to win medals (a pair of silvers for each) for two different countries.
- Luger **Georg Hackl**, of Germany, became the first Olympian, winter or summer, to win five medals in the same individual event—a feat he accomplished in five consecutive Games (1988–2002).

AP/Wide World Photos

CROSS COUNTRY SKIING

There are two techniques in cross country: classical (parallel skis) and freestyle (skating style). The Sprint features a qualification round with the fastest 16 skiers moving on to elimination heats. Top two finishers in each heat advance until there is a four-skier final. The Combined Pursuit is held on one day and consists of a classical race (10-km for men, 5-km for women) followed by a freestyle race (10-km for men, 5-km for women). The starting order in the freestyle portion of the Combined Pursuit is determined by the classical leg finish.

Medal breakdown (12 events): **10 medals**—Norway (3-4-3); **Seven**—Russia (3-3-1); **Five**—Italy (2-2-1); **Four**—Germany (1-2-1); **Three**—Estonia (1-1-1); **Two**—Spain (2-0-0) and Austria (0-1-1); **One**—Canada (0-0-1), Czech Republic (0-0-1) and Switzerland (0-0-1).

MEN
1.5-km Sprint

		Time
1	Tor Arne Hetland, NOR	2:56.9
2	Peter Schlickenrieder, GER	2:57.0
3	Cristian Zorzi, ITA	2:57.2

Best USA: No American skier qualified for the elimination heats.

15-km Classical

		Time
1	Andrus Veerpalu, EST	37:07.4
2	Frode Estil, NOR	37:43.4
3	Jaak Mae, EST	37:50.8

Best USA: 12th, John Bauer (38:55.7); 16th, Patrick Weaver (39:24.4).

Combined Pursuit

		Time
1	Johann Muehlegg, SPA	49:20.4
2	Frode Estil, NOR	49:48.9
2	Thomas Alsgaard, NOR	49:48.9

Best USA: 15th, Kris Freeman (50:32.0).

30-km Freestyle

		Time
1	Johann Muehlegg, SPA	1:09:28.9
2	Christian Hoffmann, AUT	1:11:31.0
3	Mikhail Botvinov, AUT	1:11:32.3

Best USA: 22nd, Andrew Johnson (1:14:26.9).

50-km Classical

		Time
1	Mikhail Ivanov, RUS*	2:06:20.8
2	Andrus Veerpalu, EST	2:06:44.5
3	Odd-Bjoern Hjelmeset, NOR	2:08:41.5

*Ivanov finished second to Spain's Johann Muehlegg, who was stripped of his gold medal after test results revealed he failed a pre-race drug test. Muehlegg tested positive for darbepoetin, a drug that can enhance performance in endurance sports by increasing oxygen capacity through greater red blood cell production. He was ordered to leave the Games but allowed to keep the two gold medals he won earlier.
Best USA: 34th, John Bauer (2:19:35.7).

4 x 10-km Mixed Relay

		Time
1	Norway	1:32:45.5
2	Italy	1:32:45.8
3	Germany	1:33:34.5

NOR—Anders Aukland, Frode Estil, Kristen Skjeldal, Thomas Alsgaard; **ITA**—Fabio Maj, Giorgio di Centa, Pietro Piller Cottrer, Cristian Zorzi; **GER**—Jens Filbrich, Andreas Schluetter, Tobias Angerer, Rene Sommerfeldt.
USA entry: 5th; John Bauer, Kris Freeman, Justin Wadsworth, Carl Swenson (1:34:05.5).

WOMEN
1.5-km Sprint

		Time
1	Julija Tchepalova, RUS	3:10.6
2	Evi Sachenbacher, GER	3:12.2
3	Anita Moen, NOR	3:12.7

Best USA: No American skier qualified for the elimination heats.

10-km Classical

		Time
1	Bente Skari, NOR	28:05.6
2	Olga Danilova, RUS	28:08.1
3	Julija Tchepalova, RUS	28:09.9

Best USA: 38th, Wendy Wagner (30:50.7); 40th, Nina Kemppel (30:51.9).

Combined Pursuit

		Time
1	Olga Danilova, RUS	24:52.1
2	Larissa Lazutina, RUS	24:59.0
3	Beckie Scott, CAN	25:09.9

Best USA: 32nd, Nina Kemppel (26:27.8).

15-km Freestyle

		Time
1	Stefania Belmondo, ITA	39:54.4
2	Larissa Lazutina, RUS	39:56.2
3	Katerina Neumannova, CZR	40:01.3

Best USA: 30th, Nina Kemppel (42:53.1).

30-km Classical

		Time
1	Gabriella Paruzzi, ITA*	1:30:57.1
2	Stefania Belmondo, ITA	1:31:01.6
3	Bente Skari, NOR	1:31:36.3

*Paruzzi finished second to Russia's Larissa Lazutina, who was stripped of her gold medal and ordered to leave the Games after failing a subsequent drug test. Lazutina tested positive for darbepoetin, a drug that can enhance performance in endurance sports by increasing oxygen capacity through greater red blood cell production. She was allowed to keep the two silver medals she won earlier but was barred from participating in the 20-km team relay.
Note: Russia's Olga Danilova, who finished eighth in this race, also tested positive for darbepoetin and was ordered to leave the Games. She was allowed to keep the gold and silver medals she won earlier.
Best USA: 15th, Nina Kemppel (1:37:08.7).

4 x 5-km Mixed Relay

		Time
1	Germany	49:30.6
2	Norway	49:31.9
3	Switzerland	50:03.6

GER—Manuela Henkel, Viola Bauer, Claudia Kuenzel, Evi Sachenbacher; **NOR**—Marit Bjoergen, Bente Skari, Hilde G. Pedersen, Anita Moen; **SWI**—Andrea Huber, Laurence Rochat, Brigitte Albrecht Loretan, Natascia Leonardi Cortesi.
USA entry: 13th; Wendy Wagner, Nina Kemppel, Barbara Jones, Aelin Peterson (53:23.4).

CURLING

Teams attempt to slide a 20-kg (42 lbs) stone into a three-circle target six feet in diameter called the "house." The team with the stone closest to the center circle, the "tee," gets a point. All stones of the winning team which are closer to the center than is the nearest stone of the opponent are also given one point each. After 10 rounds or "ends" the team with the most points wins.

Medal breakdown (2 events): **Two medals**—Canada (0-1-1) and Switzerland (0-1-1); **One**—Great Britain (1-0-0) and Norway (1-0-0).

MEN
Round Robin Standings

	W-L		W-L
*Canada	8-1	Germany	4-5
*Norway	7-2	United States	3-6
*Sweden	6-3	Denmark	3-6
*Switzerland	6-3	Great Britain	3-6
Finland	5-4	France	0-9

*Advanced to semifinal round.

Semifinals
Canada 6.............................Sweden 4
Norway 7 ....Switzerland 6

Bronze Medal
Switzerland 7...........................Sweden 6

Gold Medal
Norway 6 ....Canada 5

WOMEN
Round Robin Standings

	W-L		W-L
*Canada	8-1	Sweden	5-4
*Switzerland	7-2	Norway	4-5
*United States	6-3	Denmark	2-7
*Great Britain	5-4	Russia	2-7
Germany	5-4	Japan	1-8

*Advanced to semifinal round.

Semifinals
Switzerland 9 ....United States 4
Great Britain 6...........................Canada 5

Bronze Medal
Canada 9 ....United States 5

Gold Medal
Great Britain 4 ....Switzerland 3

FIGURE SKATING

All four events consist of a short program (two minutes and 40 seconds) and a free skate, sometimes called the "long program" (max. 4:40 for men and 4:10 for women). Skaters are ranked on technical merit and artistic impression in a consensus vote by nine judges. Factored placements (FP) in the men's, women's and pairs' competitions are determined by multiplying the final short program rank by 0.5 (0.2 for 1st and 2nd compulsory dance and 0.6 for the original dance in ice dancing) and then adding that number to the final free skate.

Medal breakdown (4 events): **Five medals**—Russia (2-3-0); **Three**—United States (1-0-2); **One**—Canada (1-0-0), France (1-0-0), China (0-0-1) and Italy (0-0-1).

MEN

		FP
1	Alexei Yagudin, RUS	1.5
2	Evgeni Plushenko, RUS	4.0
3	Timothy Goebel, USA	4.5

Other top 10 USA: 6th, Todd Eldredge (10.5); 7th, Michael Weiss (11.0).

Pairs

		FP
1	Elena Berezhnaya & Anton Sikharulidze, RUS	1.5
1	Jamie Sale & David Pelletier, CAN*	3.0
3	Xue Shen & Hongbo Zhao, CHN	4.5

*Canada's Sale & Pelletier placed second to Berezhnaya & Sikharulidze in the free skate, according to five of the event's nine judges, but were later awarded gold medals after French judge Marie-Reine Le Gougne admitted to officials that she had been pressured to put the Russians first.
Top 10 USA: 5th, Kyoko Ina & John Zimmerman (7.5).

WOMEN

		FP
1	Sarah Hughes, USA	3.0
2	Irina Slutskaya, RUS	3.0
3	Michelle Kwan, USA	3.5

Tiebreaker: The skater with the lower free-skate factored placement (Hughes 1.0, Slutskaya 2.0) wins the gold.
Other top 10 USA: 4th, Sasha Cohen (5.5).

Ice Dancing

		FP
1	Marina Anissina & Gwendal Peizerat, FRA	2.0
2	Irina Lobacheva & Ilia Averbukh, RUS	4.0
3	Barbara Fusar Poli & Maurizio Margaglio, ITA	6.0

Best USA: 11th, Naomi Lang & Peter Tchernyshev (22.2).

FREESTYLE SKIING

Aerials consist of two jumps with points awarded for execution and precision (50%), height and distance (20%) and landing (30%). Moguls consist of turns executed on a bumpy course (50%), two aerials (25%) and elapsed time (25%).

Medal breakdown (4 events): **Three medals**—United States (0-3-0); **Two**—Canada (0-1-1); **One**—Australia (1-0-0), Czech Republic (1-0-0), Finland (1-0-0), Norway (1-0-0), Belarus (0-0-1), France (0-0-1) and Japan (0-0-1).

MEN

Aerials

		Points
1	Ales Valenta, CZR	257.02
2	Joe Pack, USA	251.64
3	Alexei Grichin, BEL	251.19

Other top 10 USA: 6th, Brian Currutt (245.19); 9th, Jeret Peterson (238.05).

Moguls

		Points
1	Janne Lahtela, FIN	27.97
2	Travis Mayer, USA	27.59
3	Richard Gay, FRA	26.91

Other top 10 USA: 4th, Jonny Moseley (26.78); 9th, Jeremy Bloom (26.19).

WOMEN

Aerials

		Points
1	Alisa Camplin, AUS	193.47
2	Veronica Brenner, CAN	190.02
3	Deidre Dionne, CAN	189.26

Best USA: 14th, Tracy Evans (152.07).

Moguls

		Points
1	Kari Traa, NOR	25.94
2	Shannon Bahrke, USA	25.06
3	Tae Satoya, JPN	24.85

Other top 10 USA: 5th, Hannah Hardaway (24.77); 7th, Ann Battelle (24.62).

ICE HOCKEY

Medal breakdown (2 events): **Two medals**—Canada (2-0-0), United States (0-2-0); **One medal**—Russia (0-0-1) and Sweden (0-0-1).

MEN

Preliminary Round Standings

Group A	G	W-L-T	Pts	GF	GA
*Germany	3	3-0-0	6	10	3
Latvia	3	1-1-1	3	11	12
Austria	3	1-2-0	2	7	9
Slovakia	3	0-2-1	1	8	12

Group B	G	W-L-T	Pts	GF	GA
*Belarus	3	2-1-0	4	5	3
Ukraine	3	2-1-0	4	9	5
Switzerland	3	1-1-1	3	7	9
France	3	0-2-1	1	6	10

*Advanced to championship round competition.

Tiebreaker: Belarus beat Ukraine 1-0 in their only head-to-head action.

Placement round: 9th place—Latvia 9, Ukraine 2; **11th place**—Switzerland 4, Austria 1; **13th place**—Slovakia 7, France 1.

Championship Round Standings

Group C	G	W-L-T	Pts	GF	GA
Sweden	3	3-0-0	6	14	4
Czech Republic	3	1-1-1	3	12	7
Canada	3	1-1-1	3	8	10
Germany	3	0-3-0	0	5	18

Group D	G	W-L-T	Pts	GF	GA
United States	3	2-0-1	5	16	3
Finland	3	2-1-0	4	11	8
Russia	3	1-1-1	3	9	9
Belarus	3	0-3-0	0	6	22

Quarterfinals

Belarus 4	Sweden 3
Russia 1	Czech Republic 0
United States 5	Germany 0
Canada 2	Finland 1

Semifinals

Canada 7	Belarus 1
United States 3	Russia 2

Bronze Medal

Russia 7 ....Belarus 2

Note: Belarus forward Vasily Pankov was disqualified retroactively on March 21, 2002 by the IOC for testing positive after the bronze medal game for the banned substance 19-norandrosterone. The IOC also banned team doctor Evgeni Lositski from the 2004 Summer Olympics and the 2006 Winter Olympics for advising Pankov to take medication that contained the banned substance.

Gold Medal

Canada 5 ....United States 2

Gold Medal Game

	1	2	3	F
United States	1	1	0	2
Canada	2	1	2	5

Scoring: 1ST PERIOD—Tony Amonte, USA (Doug Weight, Tom Poti), 8:49; Paul Kariya, CAN (Chris Pronger, Mario Lemieux), 14:50; Jarome Iginla, CAN (Joe Sakic, Simon Gagne), 18:33. 2ND PERIOD—Brian Rafalski, USA (Mike Modano, Brett Hull), 15:30; Sakic, CAN (Ed Jovanovski, Rob Blake), 18:19 (pp). 3RD PERIOD—Iginla, CAN (Steve Yzerman, Sakic), 16:01; Sakic, CAN (Iginla), 18:40.

Goaltenders: UNITED STATES—Mike Richter (39 shots, 34 saves); CANADA—Martin Brodeur (33 shots, 31 saves).

AP/Wide World Photos

Team Sweden was plowing its way through the men's tournament until this 80-foot slap shot from Belarus defenseman Vladimir Kopat deflected off the helmet and glove of goalie **Tommy Salo** *and trickled into the net. Considered one of the biggest upsets in Olympic hockey history, the 4-3 loss eliminated Sweden and was dubbed the "Miracle of Minsk."*

Leading Scorers

	Gm	G	A	Pts	PM
Mats Sundin, SWE	4	5	4	9	10
Brett Hull, USA	6	3	5	8	6
John LeClair, USA	6	6	1	7	2
Joe Sakic, CAN	6	4	3	7	0
Marian Hossa, SVK	2	4	2	6	0
J.J. Aeschlimann, SWI	4	3	3	6	2
Philippe Bozon, FRA	4	3	3	6	2
Leonard Soccio, GER	7	3	3	6	8
Mario Lemieux, CAN	5	2	4	6	0
Steve Yzerman, CAN	6	2	4	6	2
Nicklas Lidstrom, SWE	4	1	5	6	0
Mike Modano, USA	6	0	6	6	4

Leading Goaltenders

(Minimum 150 min.)

	Gm	Min	SV%	GAA
Martin Gerber, SWI	4	157	.958	1.52
Martin Brodeur, CAN	6	300	.917	1.80
Dominik Hasek, CZR	4	239	.924	2.01
Mike Richter, USA	4	240	.932	2.25
Nikolai Khabibulin, RUS	6	359	.930	2.34
Tommy Salo, SWE	4	179	.924	2.35
Marc Seliger, GER	6	302	.911	2.98

WOMEN

Preliminary Round Standings

Group A	Gm	W-L-T	Pts	GF	GA
*Canada	3	3-0-0	6	25	0
*Sweden	3	2-1-0	4	10	13
Russia	3	1-2-0	2	6	11
Kazakhstan	3	0-3-0	0	1	18
Group B	**G**	**W-L-T**	**Pts**	**GF**	**GA**
*United States	3	3-0-0	6	27	1
*Finland	3	2-1-0	4	7	6
Germany	3	0-2-1	1	6	18
China	3	0-2-1	1	6	21

*Advanced to semifinals.

Placement round: 5th place—Russia 5, Germany 0;
7th place—China 2, Kazakhstan 1.

Semifinals

Canada 7 ....Finland 3
United States 4...........................Sweden 0

Bronze Medal

Sweden 2 ....Finland 1

Gold Medal

Canada 3 ....United States 2

Gold Medal Game

	1	2	3	F
Canada	1	2	0	3
United States	0	1	1	2

Scoring: 1ST PERIOD—Caroline Oullette, CAN (Cherie Piper), 1:45. 2ND PERIOD—Katie King, USA (Cammi Granato, Tara Mounsey), 1:59 (pp); Hayley Wickenheiser, CAN (Danielle Goyette), 4:10; Jayna Hefford, CAN (Becky Kellar, Therese Brisson), 19:59. 3RD PERIOD—Karyn Bye, USA (Mounsey, Jenny Potter), 16:27 (pp).
Goaltenders: CANADA—Kim St. Pierre (27 shots, 25 saves); UNITED STATES—Sara DeCosta (29 shots, 26 saves).

Leading Scorers

	Gm	G	A	Pts	PM
Hayley Wickenheiser, CAN	5	7	3	10	2
Cammi Granato, USA	5	6	4	10	0
Danielle Goyette, CAN	5	3	7	10	0
Natalie Darwitz, USA	5	7	1	8	2

Leading Goaltenders

(Minimum 150 min.)

	Gm	Min	SV%	GAA
Sara DeCosta, USA	5	180	.948	1.00
Kim St. Pierre, CAN	5	240	.936	1.25
Kim Martin, SWE	5	180	.939	1.67
Irina Gachennikova, RUS	5	300	.933	2.40

LUGE

Medal breakdown (3 events): **Five medals**—Germany (2-2-1); **Two**—United States (0-1-1); **One**—Italy (1-0-0) and Austria (0-0-1).

MEN

Singles

		Time
1	Armin Zoeggeler, ITA	2:57.941
2	Georg Hackl, GER	2:58.270
3	Markus Prock, AUT	2:58.283

Top 10 USA: 4th, Adam Heidt (2:58.606).

Doubles

		Time
1	Patric-Fritz Leitner & Alexander Resch, GER	1:26.082
2	Brian Martin & Mark Grimmette, USA	1:26.216
3	Chris Thorpe & Clay Ives, USA	1:26.220

WOMEN

Singles

		Time
1	Sylke Otto, GER	2:52.464
2	Barbara Niedernhuber, GER	2:52.785
3	Silke Kraushaar, GER	2:52.865

Top 10 USA: 5th, Becky Wilczak, USA (2:54.254); 8th, Ashley Hayden (2:54.658).

SKELETON

Held for the first time since 1948 Winter Games, the event's name is derived from the prototype of today's sleds, which resembled human skeletons. Women's event made its Olympic debut in 2002. Similar to luge except athletes lie stomach-down and head-first. Two runs held on one day, and medals are awarded for lowest aggregate times.

Medal breakdown (2 events): **Three medals**—United States (2-1-0); **One**—Austria (0-1-0), Great Britain (0-0-1) and Switzerland (0-0-1).

MEN

Singles

		Time
1	Jim Shea, USA	1:41.96
2	Martin Rettl, AUT	1:42.01
3	Gregor Staehli, SWI	1:42.15

Other top 10 USA: 5th, Lincoln Dewitt (1:42.83); 7th, Chris Soule (1:42.98).

WOMEN

Singles

		Time
1	Tristan Gale, USA	1:45.11
2	Lea Ann Parsley, USA	1:45.21
3	Alex Coomber, GBR	1:45.37

NORDIC COMBINED

Each event consists of a ski jump followed by a cross country race (freestyle). The cross country starting order in all events is determined by finish in ski jump. The Sprint event was added in 2002. The **Jump** column shows the athlete's final jump score, in points, with place in parentheses. Cross country times shown are adjusted to include the competitors' staggered start time.

Medal breakdown (3 events): **Four medals**—Finland (3-1-0); **Three**—Austria (0-0-3); **Two**—Germany (0-2-0).

Individual

Two jumps off normal hill followed the next day by a 15-km cross-country race.

		Jump	15-km
1	Samppa Lajunen, FIN.......	257.0 (3)	39:11.7
2	Jaakko Tallus, FIN.......	267.5 (1)	39:36.4
3	Felix Gottwald, AUT.......	235.0 (11)	40:06.5

Best USA: 7th, Todd Lodwick (240.5 (7), 41:39.4)

Sprint

One jump off large hill followed the next day by a 7.5-km cross-country race.

		Jump	7.5-km
1	Samppa Lajunen, FIN.......	123.8 (1)	16:40.1
2	Ronny Ackermann, GER......	119.9 (2)	16:49.1
3	Felix Gottwald, AUT.......	110.3 (11)	17:20.3

Best USA: 5th, Todd Lodwick (109.0 (12), 17:32.1)

Team

Two jumps off normal hill for each team's four skiers followed the next day by a 4 x 5-km cross-country relay race.

		Jump	4x5-km
1	Finland..............	967.5 (1)	48:42.2
2	Germany..............	893.5 (5)	48:49.7
3	Austria..............	938.5 (2)	48:53.2

FIN—Jari Mantila, Hannu Manninen, Jaakko Tallus, Samppa Lajunen; **GER**—Bjoern Kircheisen, Georg Hettich, Marcel Hoehlig, Ronny Ackermann; **AUT**—Christoph Bieler, Michael Gruber, Mario Stecher, Felix Gottwald.

USA entry: 4th, Todd Lodwick, Bill Demong, Johnny Spillane, Matt Dayton (905.0 (3), 49:54.1).

SKI JUMPING

Each competitor gets two jumps with points awarded for distance and style. The normal hill is 90 meters (295 feet) and the large hill is 120 meters (394 feet).

Medal breakdown (3 events): **Two medals**—Switzerland (2-0-0), Germany (1-1-0), Finland (0-1-1), Poland (0-1-1); **One**—Slovenia (0-0-1).

Normal Hill

		1st (ft)	2nd (ft)	Pts
1	Simon Ammann, SWI.......	321	323	269.0
2	Sven Hannawald, GER.......	318	324	267.5
3	Adam Malysz, POL..........	323	321	263.0

Best USA: 11th (TIE), Alan Alborn (298, 305, 240.0 pts).

Large Hill

		1st (ft)	2nd (ft)	Pts
1	Simon Ammann, SWI.......	434	436	281.4
2	Adam Malysz, POL..........	429	419	269.7
3	Matti Hautamaeki, FIN.......	416	411	256.0

Best USA: 34th, Alan Alborn (379, DNP, 105.4 pts).

Team (Large Hill)

		Pts
1	Germany..............	974.1
2	Finland..............	974.0
3	Slovenia..............	946.3

GER—Sven Hannawald, Stephan Hocke, Michael Uhrmann, Martin Schmitt; **FIN**—Matti Hautamaeki, Veli-Matti Lindstroem, Risto Jussilainen, Janne Ahonen; **SLO**—Damjan Fras, Primoz Peterka, Robert Kranjec, Peter Zonta.

USA entry: 11th; Brian Welch, Tommy Schwall, Clint Jones, Alan Alborn (728.4).

AP/Wide World Photos

*His likeness earned Switzerland's **Simon Ammann**, 20, the nickname, the Swiss Harry Potter, while his jumping earned him two gold medals. He joins Finland's Matti Nykänen as just the second Olympian to sweep both individual ski jumping events at a single Winter Games.*

Youngest and Oldest Gold Medalists in an Individual Event

Youngest:	MEN—Toni Nieminen, Finland, Large Hill Ski Jumping, 1992 (16 years, 261 days)
	WOMEN—Tara Lipinski, United States, Figure Skating, 1998 (15 years, 256 days)
Oldest:	MEN—Magnar Solberg, NOR, 20-km Biathlon, 1972 (35 years, 4 days)
	WOMEN—Christina Baas-Kaiser, Netherlands, 3,000m Speed Skating, 1972 (33 years, 268 days)

SNOWBOARDING

The halfpipe is a U-shaped course dug into a snow-covered hill. Each finalist makes two runs, with the higher score determining their final standing. The parallel giant slalom, introduced in 2002, is a bracketed tournament competition with snowboarders competing against each other in two-race heats on separate slalom courses.

Medal breakdown (4 events): **Five medals**—United States (2-1-2); **Three**—France (1-2-0); **Two**—Switzerland (1-0-1); **One**—Sweden (0-1-0) and Italy (0-0-1).

MEN

Halfpipe

Score refers to the boarders' highest after the two runs.

		Score
1	Ross Powers, USA	46.1
2	Danny Kass, USA	42.5
3	Jarret Thomas, USA	42.1

Other top 10 USA: 6th, Tommy Czeschin (40.6).

Parallel Giant Slalom

1 Philipp Schoch, SWI
2 Richard Richardsson, SWE
3 Chris Klug, USA

Note: BIG FINAL (gold medal)—Schoch def. Richardsson (+0.24, DSQ); SMALL FINAL (bronze medal)—Klug def. Nicolas Huet, FRA (-0.15, -1.21) -1.36.

Next best USA: No other American qualified for the elimination round.

WOMEN

Halfpipe

Score refers to the boarders' highest after the two runs.

		Score
1	Kelly Clark, USA	47.9
2	Doriane Vidal, FRA	43.0
3	Fabienne Reuteler, SWI	39.7

Other Top 10 USA: 5th, Shannon Dunn-Downing (37.2); 6th, Tricia Byrnes (36.4).

Parallel Giant Slalom

1 Isabelle Blanc, FRA
2 Karine Ruby, FRA
3 Lidia Trettel, ITA

Note: BIG FINAL (gold medal)—Blanc def. Ruby (-1.89, +0.15) -1.74; SMALL FINAL (bronze medal)—Trettel def. Jagna Marczulajtis, POL (+0.17, DSQ).

Best USA: Lisa Koglow def. Aasa Windahl, SWE, in the first elimination round and lost to Ruby, FRA, in the quarterfinal round.

SPEED SKATING

The long track oval measures 400 meters (1,312 feet). Distance laps: 500m (1¼ laps); 1,000m (2½ laps); 1,500m (3¾ laps); 3,000m (7½ laps); 5,000m (12½ laps); 10,000m (25 laps).

Medal breakdown (10 events): **Eight medals**—Netherlands (3-5-0), Germany (3-3-2) and United States (3-1-4); **Three**—Canada (1-0-2); **Two**—Norway (0-0-2); **One**—Japan (0-1-0).

MEN

500 meters

Times reflected are a combination of two heats with each skater racing once on the inside lane and once on the outside lane.

		Time	
1	Casey FitzRandolph, USA	69.23	OR
2	Hiroyasu Shimizu, JPN	69.26	
3	Kip Carpenter, USA	69.47	

Other top 10 USA: 6th, Joey Cheek (69.60).

Note: FitzRandolph's time of 34.42 in his first race established a new Olympic record.

1000 meters

		Time	
1	Gerard van Velde, NED	1:07.18	WR
2	Jan Bos, NED	1:07.53	
3	Joey Cheek, USA	1:07.61	

Other top 10 USA: 4th, Kip Carpenter (1:07.89); 6th, Nick Pearson (1:07.97); 7th, Casey FitzRandolph (1:08.15).

1500 meters

		Time	
1	Derek Parra, USA	1:43.95	WR
2	Jochem Uytdehaage, NED	1:44.57	
3	Adne Sondral, NOR	1:45.26	

Other top 10 USA: 4th, Joey Cheek (1:45.34); 6th, Nick Pearson (1:45.51).

5000 meters

		Time	
1	Jochem Uytdehaage, NED	6:14.66	WR
2	Derek Parra, USA	6:17.98	
3	Jens Boden, GER	6:21.73	

Other top 10 USA: 5th, KC Boutiette (6:22.97).

10,000 meters

		Time	
1	Jochem Uytdehaage, NED	12:58.92	WR
2	Gianni Romme, NED	13:10.03	
3	Lasse Saetre, NOR	13:16.92	

Best USA: 12th, Jason Hedstrand (13:32.99); 13th, Derek Parra (13:33.44).

WOMEN

500 meters

Times reflected are a combination of two heats with each skater racing once on the inside lane and once on the outside lane.

		Time	
1	Catriona Lemay-Doan, CAN	74.75	OR
2	Monique Garbrecht-Enfeldt, GER	74.94	
3	Sabine Voelker, GER	75.19	

Best USA: 14th, Christine Witty (76.73).

Note: Lemay-Doan's time of 37.30 in her first race established a new Olympic record.

1000 meters

		Time	
1	Chris Witty, USA	1:13.83	WR
2	Sabine Voelker, GER	1:13.96	
3	Jennifer Rodriguez, USA	1:14.24	

Next best USA: 14th, Amy Sannes (1:15.09); 16th, Becky Sundstrom (1:15.88).

1500 meters

		Time	
1	Anni Friesinger, GER	1:54.02	WR
2	Sabine Voelker, GER	1:54.97	
3	Jennifer Rodriguez, USA	1:55.32	

Other top 10 USA: 5th, Chris Witty (1:55.71); 8th, Amy Sannes (1:56.29).

3000 meters

		Time	
1	Claudia Pechstein, GER	3:57.70	**WR**
2	Renate Groenewold, NED	3:58.94	
3	Cindy Klassen, CAN	3:58.97	

Top 10 USA: 7th, Jennifer Rodriguez (4:04.99).

5000 meters

		Time	
1	Claudia Pechstein, GER	6:46.91	**WR**
2	Gretha Smit, NED	6:49.22	
3	Clara Hughes, CAN	6:53.53	

Top 10 USA: 9th, Catherine Raney (7:06.89).

SHORT TRACK SPEED SKATING

The short track oval is 111 meters (364 feet). Distance (laps): 500m (4½); 1,000m (9); 1,500m (13½); 3,000m (27); 5,000m (45).

Medal breakdown (8 events): **Seven medals**—China (2-2-3); **Six**—Canada (2-1-3); **Four**—South Korea (2-2-0); **Three**—United States (1-1-1); **Two**—Bulgaria (0-1-1); **One**—Australia (1-0-0) and Italy (0-1-0).

MEN

500 meters

		Time	
1	Marc Gagnon, CAN	41.802	**OR**
2	Jonathan Guilmette, CAN	41.994	
3	Rusty Smith, USA	42.027	

1000 meters

		Time
1	Steven Bradbury, AUS	1:29.109
2	Apolo Anton Ohno, USA	1:30.160
3	Mathieu Turcotte, CAN	1:30.563

Note: Turcotte's time of 1:27.185 in a quarterfinal heat established a new Olympic record.

1500 meters

		Time
1	Apolo Anton Ohno, USA*	2:18.541
2	Li Jiajun, CHN	2:18.731
3	Marc Gagnon, CAN	2:18.806

*Ohno finished second to Kim Dong-Sung, of South Korea, in the final, but was awarded the gold medal by chief referee James Hewish, who adjudged that Kim was guilty of cross-tracking, or interfering, with Ohno's path.

Note: Kim registered a time of 2:15.942 in a semifinal heat, establishing a new Olympic record.

5000-m Relay

		Time
1	Canada	6:51.579
2	Italy	6:56.327
3	China	6:59.633

Note: Canada's time of 6:45.455 in a semifinal heat established a new Olympic record.

Best USA: 4th, United States (7:03.926).

CAN—Marc Gagnon, Jonathan Guilmette, Francois-Louis Tremblay, Mathieu Turcotte; **ITA**—Maurizio Carnino, Fabio Carta, Nicola Franceschina, Nicola Rodigari; **CHN**—Feng Kai, Guo Wei, Li Jiajun, Li Ye.

WOMEN

500 meters

		Time
1	Yang Yang (A), CHN	44.187
2	Evgenia Radanova, BUL	44.252
3	Wang Chunlu, CHN	44.272

Note: Yang's time of 44.118 seconds in a semifinal heat established a new Olympic record.

Best USA: 5th, Caroline Hallisey (44.679).

1000 meters

		Time
1	Yang Yang (A), CHN	1:36.391
2	Ko Gi-Hyun, S. Kor.	1:36.427
3	Yang Yang (S), CHN	1:37.008

Note: Yang (A)'s time of 1:31.235 seconds in a quarterfinal heat established a new Olympic record.

Best USA: No American qualified for the final.

1500 meters

		Time
1	Ko Gi-Hyun, S. Kor.	2:31.581
2	Choi Eun-Kyung, S. Kor.	2:31.610
3	Evgenia Radanova, BUL	2:31.723

Note: Choi's time of 2:21.069 in a semifinal heat established a new world record.

Best USA: No Americans qualified for the final.

3000-m Relay

		Time	
1	South Korea	4:12.793	**WR**
2	China	4:13.236	
3	Canada	4:15.738	

Best USA: No American team qualified for the final.

S. Kor—Choi Eun-Kyung, Choi Min-Kyung, Joo Min-Jin, Park Hye-Won; **CHN**—Sun Dandan, Wang Chunlu, Yang Yang (A), Yang Yang (S); **CAN**—Isabelle Charest, Marie-Eve Drolet, Ameilie Goulet-Nadon, Alanna Kraus.

Steve Munday/Getty Images

In one of Salt Lake City's most memorable races, Australian speed skater **Steven Bradbury** *vaulted from last to first in the 1000-meter short-track race after a last-lap spill wiped out his competition and cleared the way for him to secure his country's first Winter Games gold medal.*

The Winter Olympics

The move toward a winter version of the Olympics began in 1908 when figure skating made an appearance at the Summer Games in London. Ten-time world champion Ulrich Salchow of Sweden, who originated the backwards, one revolution jump that bears his name, and Madge Syers of Britain were the first singles champions. Germans Anna Hubler and Heinrich Berger won the pairs competition.

Organizers of the 1916 Summer Games in Berlin planned to introduce a "Skiing Olympia," featuring nordic events in the Black Forest, but the Games were cancelled after the outbreak of World War I in 1914.

The Games resumed in 1920 at Antwerp, Belgium, where figure skating returned and ice hockey was added as a medal event. Sweden's Gillis Grafstrom and Magda Julin took individual honors, while Ludovika and Walter Jakobsson were the top pair. In hockey, Canada won the gold medal with the United States second and Czechoslovakia third.

Despite the objections of Modern Olympics' founder Baron Pierre de Coubertin and the resistance of the Scandinavian countries, which had staged their own Nordic championships every four or five years from 1901-26 in Sweden, the International Olympic Committee sanctioned an "International Winter Sports Week" at Chamonix, France, in 1924. The 11-day event, which included nordic skiing, speed skating, figure skating, ice hockey and bobsledding, was a huge success and was retroactively called the first Olympic Winter Games.

Seventy years after those first cold weather Games, the 17th edition of the Winter Olympics took place in Lillehammer, Norway, in 1994. The event ended the four-year Olympic cycle of staging both Winter and Summer Games in the same year and began a new schedule that calls for the two Games to alternate every two years.

Year	No	Location	Dates	Nations	Most medals	USA medals
1924	I	Chamonix, FRA	Jan. 25-Feb. 4	16	Norway (4-7-6—17)	1-2-1— 4 (3rd)
1928	II	St. Moritz, SWI	Feb. 11-19	25	Norway (6-4-5—15)	2-2-2— 6 (2nd)
1932	III	Lake Placid, USA	Feb. 4-15	17	USA (6-4-2—12)	6-4-2—12 (1st)
1936	IV	Garmisch-Partenkirchen, GER ..	Feb. 6-16	28	Norway (7-5-3—15)	1-0-3— 4 (T-5th)
1940-a	–	Sapporo, JPN	Cancelled (WWII)			
1944	–	Cortina d'Ampezzo, ITA	Cancelled (WWII)			
1948	V	St. Moritz, SWI	Jan. 30-Feb. 8	28	Norway (4-3-3—10), Sweden (4-3-3—10) & Switzerland (3-4-3—10)	3-4-2— 9 (4th)
1952-b	VI	Oslo, NOR	Feb. 14-25	30	Norway (7-3-6—16)	4-6-1—11 (2nd)
1956-c	VII	Cortina d'Ampezzo, ITA	Jan. 26-Feb. 5	32	USSR (7-3-6—16)	2-3-2— 7 (T-4th)
1960	VIII	Squaw Valley, USA	Feb. 18-28	30	USSR (7-5-9—21)	3-4-3—10 (2nd)
1964	IX	Innsbruck, AUT	Jan. 29-Feb. 9	36	USSR (11-8-6—25)	1-2-3— 6 (7th)
1968-d	X	Grenoble, FRA	Feb. 6-18	37	Norway (6-6-2—14)	1-5-1— 7 (T-7th)
1972	XI	Sapporo, JPN	Feb. 3-13	35	USSR (8-5-3—16)	3-2-3— 8 (6th)
1976-e	XII	Innsbruck, AUT	Feb. 4-15	37	USSR (13-6-8—27)	3-3-4—10 (T-3rd)
1980	XIII	Lake Placid, USA	Feb. 14-23	37	E. Germany (9-7-7—23)	6-4-2—12 (3rd)
1984	XIV	Sarajevo, YUG	Feb. 7-19	49	USSR (6-10-9—25)	4-4-0— 8 (T-5th)
1988	XV	Calgary, CAN	Feb. 13-28	57	USSR (11-9-9—29)	2-1-3— 6 (T-8th)
1992-f	XVI	Albertville, FRA	Feb. 8-23	63	Germany (10-10-6—26)	5-4-2—11 (6th)
1994-g	XVII	Lillehammer, NOR	Feb. 12-27	67	Norway (10-11-5—26)	6-5-2—13 (T-5th)
1998	XVIII	Nagano, JPN	Feb. 7-22	72	Germany (12-9-8—29)	6-3-4—13 (5th)
2002	XIX	Salt Lake City, USA	Feb. 8-24	78	Germany (12-16-7—35)	10-13-11—34 (2nd)
2006	XX	Turin, ITA	Feb. 4-19			

a—The 1940 Winter Games are originally scheduled for Sapporo, but Japan resigns as host in 1937 when the Sino-Japanese war breaks out. St. Moritz is the next choice, but the Swiss feel that ski instructors should not be considered professionals and the IOC withdraws its offer. Finally, Garmisch-Partenkirchen is asked to serve again as host, but the Germans invade Poland in 1939 and the Games are eventually cancelled.

b—Germany and Japan are allowed to rejoin the Olympic community for the first time since World War II. Though a divided country, the Germans send a joint East-West team through 1964.

c—The Soviet Union (USSR) participates in its first Winter Olympics and takes home the most medals, including the gold medal in ice hockey.

d—East Germany and West Germany officially send separate teams for the first time and will continue to do so through 1988.

e—The IOC grants the 1976 Winter Games to Denver in May 1970, but in 1972 Colorado voters reject a $5 million bond issue to finance the undertaking. Denver immediately withdraws as host and the IOC selects Innsbruck, the site of the 1964 Games, to take over.

f—Germany sends a single team after East and West German reunification in 1990 and the USSR competes as the Unified Team after the breakup of the Soviet Union in 1991.

g—The IOC moves the Winter Games' four-year cycle ahead two years in order to separate them from the Summer Games and alternate Olympics every two years.

Event-by-Event

Gold medal winners from 1924-2002 in the following events: Alpine Skiing, Biathlon, Bobsled, Cross Country Skiing, Curling, Figure Skating, Freestyle Skiing, Ice Hockey, Luge, Nordic Combined, Skeleton, Ski Jumping, Snowboarding and Speed Skating.

ALPINE SKIING

MEN

Multiple gold medals: Kjetil Andre Aamodt, Jean-Claude Killy, Toni Sailer and Alberto Tomba (3); Hermann Maier, Henri Oreiller, Ingemar Stenmark and Markus Wasmeier (2).

Downhill

Year	Time	Year	Time
1948 Henri Oreiller, FRA	2:55.0	1980 Leonhard Stock, AUS	1:45.50
1952 Zeno Colò, ITA	2:30.8	1984 Bill Johnson, USA	1:45.59
1956 Toni Sailer, AUT	2:52.2	1988 Pirmin Zurbriggen, SWI	1:59.63
1960 Jean Vuarnet, FRA	2:06.0	1992 Patrick Ortlieb, AUT	1:50.37
1964 Egon Zimmermann, AUT	2:18.16	1994 Tommy Moe, USA	1:45.75
1968 Jean-Claude Killy, FRA	1:59.85	1998 Jean-Luc Cretier, FRA	1:50.11
1972 Bernhard Russi, SWI	1:51.43	2002 Fritz Strobl, AUT	1:39.13
1976 Franz Klammer AUT	1:45.73		

Slalom

Year	Time	Year	Time
1948 Edi Reinalter, SWI	2:10.3	1980 Ingemar Stenmark, SWE	1:44.26
1952 Othmar Schneider, AUT	2:00.0	1984 Phil Mahre, USA	1:39.41
1956 Toni Sailer, AUT	3:14.7	1988 Alberto Tomba, ITA	1:39.47
1960 Ernst Hinterseer, AUT	2:08.9	1992 Finn Christian Jagge, NOR	1:44.39
1964 Pepi Stiegler, AUT	2:11.13	1994 Thomas Stangassinger, AUT	2:02.02
1968 Jean-Claude Killy, FRA	1:39.73	1998 Hans-Petter Buraas, NOR	1:49.31
1972 Francisco Ochoa, SPA	1:49.27	2002 Jean-Pierre Vidal, FRA:	1:41.06
1976 Piero Gros, ITA	2:03.29		

Giant Slalom

Year	Time	Year	Time
1952 Stein Eriksen, NOR	2:25.0	1980 Ingemar Stenmark, SWE	2:40.74
1956 Toni Sailer, AUS	3:00.1	1984 Max Julen, SWI	2:41.18
1960 Roger Staub, SWI	1:48.3	1988 Alberto Tomba, ITA	2:06.37
1964 Francois Bonlieu, FRA	1:46.71	1992 Alberto Tomba, ITA	2:06.98
1968 Jean-Claude Killy, FRA	3:29.28	1994 Markus Wasmeier, GER	2:52.46
1972 Gustav Thöni, ITA	3:09.62	1998 Hermann Maier, AUT	2:38.51
1976 Heini Hemmi, SWI	3:26.97	2002 Stephan Eberharter, AUT	2:23.28

Super G

Year	Time	Year	Time
1988 Frank Piccard, FRA	1:39.66	1998 Hermann Maier, AUT	1:34.82
1992 Kjetil Andre Aamodt, NOR	1:13.04	2002 Kjetil Andre Aamodt, NOR	1:21.58
1994 Markus Wasmeier, GER	1:32.53		

Alpine Combined

Year	Points	Year	Time
1936 Franz Pfnür, GER	99.25	1994 Lasse Kjus, NOR	3:17.53
1948 Henri Oreiller, FRA	3.27	1998 Mario Reiter, AUT	3:08.06
1952-84 Not held		2002 Kjetil Andre Aamodt, NOR	3:17.56
1988 Hubert Strolz, AUT	36.55		
1992 Josef Polig, ITA	14.58		

WOMEN

Multiple gold medals: Deborah Compagnoni, Janica Kostelic, Vreni Schneider and Katja Seizinger (3); Marielle Goitschel, Trude Jochum-Beiser, Petra Kronberger, Andrea Mead Lawrence, Rosi Mittermaier, Marie-Theres Nadig, Hanni Wenzel and Pernilla Wiberg (2).

Downhill

Year	Time	Year	Time
1948 Hedy Schlunegger, SWI	2:28.3	1980 Annemarie Moser-Pröll, AUT	1:37.52
1952 Trude Jochum-Beiser, AUT	1:47.1	1984 Michela Figini, SWI	1:13.36
1956 Madeleine Berthod, SWI	1:40.7	1988 Marina Kiehl, W. Ger	1:25.86
1960 Heidi Biebl, GER	1:37.6	1992 Kerrin Lee-Gartner, CAN	1:52.55
1964 Christl Haas, AUT	1:55.39	1994 Katja Seizinger, GER	1:35.93
1968 Olga Pall, AUT	1:40.87	1998 Katja Seizinger, GER	1:28.89
1972 Marie-Theres Nadig, SWI	1:36.68	2002 Carole Montillet, FRA	1:39.56
1976 Rosi Mittermaier, W. Ger	1:46.16		

Slalom

Year		Time	Year		Time
1948	Gretchen Fraser, USA	1:57.2	1980	Hanni Wenzel, LIE	1:25.09
1952	Andrea Mead Lawrence, USA	2:10.6	1984	Paoletta Magoni, ITA	1:36.47
1956	Renée Colliard, SWI	1:52.3	1988	Vreni Schneider, SWI	1:36.69
1960	Anne Heggtveit, CAN	1:49.6	1992	Petra Kronberger, AUT	1:32.68
1964	Christine Goitschel, FRA	1:29.86	1994	Vreni Schneider, SWI	1:56.01
1968	Marielle Goitschel, FRA	1:25.86	1998	Hilde Gerg, GER	1:32.40
1972	Barbara Cochran, USA	1:31.24	2002	Janica Kostelic, CRO	1:46.10
1976	Rosi Mittermaier, W. Ger	1:30.54			

Giant Slalom

Year		Time	Year		Time
1952	Andrea Mead Lawrence, USA	2:06.8	1980	Hanni Wenzel, LIE	2:41.66
1956	Ossi Reichert, GER	1:56.5	1984	Debbie Armstrong, USA	2:20.98
1960	Yvonne Rügg, SWI	1:39.9	1988	Vreni Schneider, SWI	2:06.49
1964	Marielle Goitschel, FRA	1:52.24	1992	Pernilla Wiberg, SWE	2:12.74
1968	Nancy Greene, CAN	1:51.97	1994	Deborah Compagnoni, ITA	2:30.97
1972	Marie-Theres Nadig, SWI	1:29.90	1998	Deborah Compagnoni, ITA	2:50.59
1976	Kathy Kreiner, CAN	1:29.13	2002	Janica Kostelic, CRO	2:30.01

Super G

Year		Time	Year		Time
1988	Sigrid Wolf, AUT	1:19.03	1998	Picabo Street, USA	1:18.02
1992	Deborah Compagnoni, ITA	1:21.22	2002	Daniela Ceccarelli, ITA	1:13.59
1994	Diann Roffe-Steinrotter, USA	1:22.15			

Alpine Combined

Year		Points	Year		Time
1936	Christl Cranz, GER	97.06	1994	Pernilla Wiberg, SWE	3:05.16
1948	Trude Beiser, AUT	6.58	1998	Katja Seizinger, GER	2:40.74
1952-84	Not held		2002	Janica Kostelic, CRO	2:43.28
1988	Anita Wachter, AUT	29.25			
1992	Petra Kronberger, AUT	2.55			

BIATHLON

MEN

Multiple gold medals (including relays): Ole Einar Bjoerndalen (5); Aleksandr Tikhonov (4); Mark Kirchner and Ricco Gross (3); Anatoly Alyabyev, Ivan Biakov, Sergei Chepikov, Sven Fischer, Halvard Hanevold, Frank Luck, Viktor Mamatov, Frank-Peter Roetsch, Magnar Solberg and Dmitri Vasilyev (2).

10 kilometers

Year		Time	Year		Time
1980	Frank Ulrich, E. Ger	32:10.69	1994	Sergei Chepikov, RUS	28:07.0
1984	Erik Kvalfoss, NOR	30:53.8	1998	Ole Einar Bjoerndalen, NOR	27:16.2
1988	Frank-Peter Roetsch, E. Ger	25:08.1	2002	Ole Einar Bjoerndalen, NOR	24:51.3
1992	Mark Kirchner, GER	26:02.3			

12.5 kilometers

Year		Time
2002	Ole Einar Bjoerndalen, NOR	32:34.6

20 kilometers

Year		Time	Year		Time
1960	Klas Lestander, SWE	1:33:21.6	1984	Peter Angerer, W. Ger	1:11:52.7
1964	Vladimir Melanin, USSR	1:20:26.8	1988	Frank-Peter Roetsch, E. Ger	56:33.3
1968	Magnar Solberg, NOR	1:13:45.9	1992	Yevgeny Redkine, UT	57:34.4
1972	Magnar Solberg, NOR	1:15:55.50	1994	Sergei Tarasov, RUS	57:25.3
1976	Nikolai Kruglov, USSR	1:14:12.26	1998	Halvard Hanevold, NOR	56:16.4
1980	Anatoly Alyabyev, USSR	1:08:16.31	2002	Ole Einar Bjoerndalen, NOR	51:03.3

4x7.5-kilometer Relay

Year		Time	Year		Time	Year		Time
1968	Soviet Union	2:13:02.4	1984	Soviet Union	1:38:51.7	1998	Germany	1:21:36.2
1972	Soviet Union	1:51:44.92	1988	Soviet Union	1:22:30.0	2002	Norway	1:23:42.3
1976	Soviet Union	1:57:55.64	1992	Germany	1:24:43.5			
1980	Soviet Union	1:34:03.27	1994	Germany	1:30:22.1			

BIATHLON (Cont.)
WOMEN

Multiple gold medals (including relays): Myriam Bedard, Andrea Henkel, Anfisa Reztsova and Kati Wilhelm (2). Note that Reztsova won a third gold medal in 1988 in the cross country 4x5-kilometer relay.

7.5 kilometers

Year		Time	Year		Time
1992	Anfisa Reztsova, UT	24:29.2	1998	Galina Koukleva, RUS	23:08.0
1994	Myriam Bedard, CAN	26:08.8	2002	Kati Wilhelm, GER	20:41.4

10 kilometers

Year		Time
2002	Olga Pyleva, RUS	31:07.7

15 kilometers

Year		Time	Year		Time
1992	Antje Misersky, GER	51:47.2	1998	Ekaterina Dafovska, BUL	54:52.0
1994	Myriam Bedard, CAN	52:06.6	2002	Andrea Henkel, GER	47:29.1

4x7.5-kilometer Relay

Year		Time	Year		Time
1992	France	1:15:55.6	1998	Germany	1:40:13.6
1994	Russia	1:47:19.5	2002	Germany	1:27:55.0

Note: Event featured three skiers per team in 1992.

BOBSLED

A two-woman bobsled event was added in 2002. Only drivers are listed in parentheses.

Multiple gold medals: DRIVERS—Meinhard Nehmer (3); Billy Fiske, Wolfgang Hoppe, Christoph Langen, Eugenio Monti, Andreas Ostler and Gustav Weder (2). CREW—Bernard Germeshausen (3); Donat Acklin, Luciano De Paolis, Cliff Gray, Lorenz Nieberl and Dietmar Schauerhammer (2).

Two-Man

Year		Time	Year		Time
1932	United States (Hubert Stevens)	8:14.74	1976	East Germany (Meinhard Nehmer)	3:44.42
1936	United States (Ivan Brown)	5:29.29	1980	Switzerland (Erich Schärer)	4:09.36
1948	Switzerland (Felix Endrich)	5:29.2	1984	East Germany (Wolfgang Hoppe)	3:25.56
1952	Germany (Andreas Ostler)	5:24.54	1988	Soviet Union (Janis Kipurs)	3:54.19
1956	Italy (Lamberto Dalla Costa)	5:30.14	1992	Switzerland I (Gustav Weder)	4:03.26
1960	Not held		1994	Switzerland I (Gustav Weder)	3:30.81
1964	Great Britain (Anthony Nash)	4:21.90	1998	(TIE) Italy I (Guenther Huber)	3:37.24
1968	Italy (Eugenio Monti)	4:41.54		& Canada I (Pierre Lueders)	3:37.24
1972	West Germany (Wolfgang Zimmerer)	4:57.07	2002	Germany I (Christoph Langen)	3:10.11

Two-Woman

Year		Time
2002	United States II (Jill Bakken)	1:37.76

Four-Man

Year		Time	Year		Time
1924	Switzerland (Eduard Scherrer)	5:45.54	1972	Switzerland (Jean Wicki)	4:43.07
1928	United States (Billy Fiske)	3:20.5	1976	East Germany (Meinhard Nehmer)	3:40.43
1932	United States (Billy Fiske)	7:53.68	1980	East Germany (Meinhard Nehmer)	3:59.92
1936	Switzerland (Pierre Musy)	5:19.85	1984	East Germany (Wolfgang Hoppe)	3:20.22
1948	United States (Francis Tyler)	5:20.1	1988	Switzerland (Ekkehard Fasser)	3:47.51
1952	Germany (Andreas Ostler)	5:07.84	1992	Austria I (Ingo Appelt)	3:53.90
1956	Switzerland (Franz Kapus)	5:10.44	1994	Germany II (Harald Czudaj)	3:27.78
1960	Not held		1998	Germany II (Christoph Langen)	2:39.41
1964	Canada (Vic Emery)	4:14.46	2002	Germany II (Andre Lange)	3:07.51
1968	Italy (Eugenio Monti)	2:17.39			

Note: Five-man sleds were used in 1928.

CROSS COUNTRY SKIING

Starting with the 1988 Winter Games in Calgary, the classical and freestyle (i.e., skating) techniques were designated for specific events. The Pursuit race was introduced in 1992 and revamped after the 1998 Nagano Games. The Sprint was added in 2002.

MEN

Multiple gold medals (including relays): Bjorn Dählie (8); Thomas Alsgaard, Sixten Jernberg, Gunde Svan, Thomas Wassberg and Nikolai Zimyatov (4); Veikko Hakulinen, Eero Mäntyranta and Vegard Ulvang (3); Hallgeir Brenden, Harald Grönningen, Thorleif Haug, Johann Muehlegg, Jan Ottoson, Kristen Skjeldal, Päl Tyldum and Vyacheslav Vedenine (2).

Multiple gold medals (including Nordic Combined): Johan Gröttumsbråten and Thorleif Haug (3).

1.5-kilometer Sprint
New event in 2002.

Year		Time
2002	Tor Arne Hetland, NOR	2:56.9

10 kilometers
Held as a classical event.

Year		Time	Year		Time
1992	Vegard Ulvang, NOR	27:36.0	1998	Bjorn Dählie, NOR	27:24.5
1994	Bjorn Dählie, NOR	24:20.1	2002	Not held	

Combined Pursuit (10km)
From 1992-98 the pursuit included a 10-km classical race and a 15-km freestyle race contested on separate days. Beginning in 2002, the pursuit was shortened to two 5-kilometer races held on the same day.

Year		Time	Year		Time
1992	Bjorn Dählie, NOR	1:05:37.9	1998	Thomas Alsgaard, NOR	1:07:01.7
1994	Bjorn Dählie, NOR	1:00:08.8	2002	Johann Muehlegg, SPA	49:20.4

15 kilometers
Held over 18 kilometers from 1924-52. Held as a classical event from 1956-88, and since 2002. Replaced by the 15-km combined pursuit (1992-98).

Year		Time	Year		Time
1924	Thorleif Haug, NOR	1:14:31.0	1968	Harald Grönningen, NOR	47:54.2
1928	Johan Gröttumsbråten, NOR	1:37:01.0	1972	Sven-Ake Lundback, SWE	45:28.24
1932	Sven Utterström, SWE	1:23:07.0	1976	Nikolai Bazhukov, USSR	43:58.47
1936	Erik-August Larsson, SWE	1:14:38.0	1980	Thomas Wassberg, SWE	41:57.63
1948	Martin Lundström, SWE	1:13:50.0	1984	Gunde Svan, SWE	41:25.6
1952	Hallgeir Brenden, NOR	1:01:34.0	1988	Mikhail Devyatyarov, USSR	41:18.9
1956	Hallgeir Brenden, NOR	49:39.0	1992-98	Not held	
1960	Hakon Brusveen, NOR	51:55.5	2002	Andrus Veerpalu, EST	37:07.4
1964	Eero Mäntyranta, FIN	50:54.1			

30 kilometers
Held as a freestyle event from 1956-94, and since 2002. Held as a classical event in 1998.

Year		Time	Year		Time
1956	Veikko Hakulinen, FIN	1:44:06.0	1984	Nikolai Zimyatov, USSR	1:28:56.3
1960	Sixten Jernberg, SWE	1:51:03.9	1988	Alexei Prokurorov, USSR	1:24:26.3
1964	Eero Mäntyranta, FIN	1:30:50.7	1992	Vegard Ulvang, NOR	1:22:27.8
1968	Franco Nones, ITA	1:35:39.2	1994	Thomas Alsgaard, NOR	1:12:26.4
1972	Vyacheslav Vedenine, USSR	1:36:31.15	1998	Mika Myllylae, FIN	1:33:55.8
1976	Sergei Saveliev, USSR	1:30:29.38	2002	Johann Muehlegg, SPA	1:09:28.9
1980	Nikolai Zimyatov, USSR	1:27:02.80			

50 kilometers
Held as a classical event from 1924-94, and since 2002. Held as a freestyle event in 1998.

Year		Time	Year		Time
1924	Thorleif Haug, NOR	3:44:32.0	1972	Päl Tyldum, NOR	2:43:14.75
1928	Per Erik Hedlund, SWE	4:52:03.0	1976	Ivar Formo, NOR	2:37:30.05
1932	Veli Saarinen, FIN	4:28:00.0	1980	Nikolai Zimyatov, USSR	2:27:24.60
1936	Elis Wiklund, SWE	3:30:11.0	1984	Thomas Wassberg, SWE	2:15:55.8
1948	Nils Karlsson, SWE	3:47:48.0	1988	Gunde Svan, SWE	2:04:30.9
1952	Veikko Hakulinen, FIN	3:33:33.0	1992	Bjorn Dählie, NOR	2:03:41.5
1956	Sixten Jernberg, SWE	2:50:27.0	1994	Vladimir Smirnov, KAZ	2:07:20.3
1960	Kalevi Hämäläinen, FIN	2:59:06.3	1998	Bjorn Dählie, NOR	2:05:08.2
1964	Sixten Jernberg, SWE	2:43:52.6	2002	Mikhail Ivanov, RUS*	2:06:20.8
1968	Ole Ellefsaeter, NOR	2:28:45.8			

*Ivanov finished second to Johann Muehlegg of Spain, who was disqualified for failing a drug test.

4x10-kilometer Mixed Relay
Two classical and two freestyle legs.

Year		Time	Year		Time	Year		Time
1936	Finland	2:41:33.0	1968	Norway	2:08:33.5	1992	Norway	1:39:26.0
1948	Sweden	2:32:08.0	1972	Soviet Union	2:04:47.94	1994	Italy	1:41:15.0
1952	Finland	2:20:16.0	1976	Finland	2:07:59.72	1998	Norway	1:40:55.7
1956	Soviet Union	2:15:30.0	1980	Soviet Union	1:57:03.46	2002	Norway	1:32:45.5
1960	Finland	2:18:45.6	1984	Sweden	1:55:06.3			
1964	Sweden	2:18:34.6	1988	Sweden	1:43:58.6			

CROSS COUNTRY SKIING (Cont.)
WOMEN

Multiple gold medals (including relays): Lyubov Egorova (6); Larissa Lazutina (5); Galina Kulakova and Raisa Smetanina (4); Claudia Boyarskikh, Olga Danilova and Marja-Liisa Hämäläinen and Elena Valbe (3); Stefania Belmondo, Manuela Di Centa, Nina Gavriluk, Toini Gustafsson, Barbara Petzold and Julija Tchepalova (2).

Multiple gold medals (including relays and Biathlon): Anfisa Reztsova (2).

1.5-kilometer Sprint
New event in 2002.

Year	Time
2002 Julija Tchepalova, RUS	3:10.6

5 kilometers
Held as a classical event from 1964-98. From 1992-98 it was half of the combined pursuit event. Discontinued after 1998.

Year	Time	Year	Time
1964 Claudia Boyarskikh, USSR	17:50.5	1984 Marja-Liisa Hämäläinen, FIN	17:04.0
1968 Toini Gustafsson, SWE	16:45.2	1988 Marjo Matikainen, FIN	15:04.0
1972 Galina Kulakova, USSR	17:00.50	1992 Marjut Lukkarinen, FIN	14:13.8
1976 Helena Takalo, FIN	15:48.69	1994 Lyubov Egorova, RUS	14:08.8
1980 Raisa Smetanina, USSR	15:06.92	1998 Larissa Lazutina, RUS	17:37.9

Combined Pursuit (10km)
From 1992-98 the pursuit consisted of a 10-km freestyle race in which the starting order was determined by order of finish in the 5-km classical race contested on separate days. Beginning in 2002, the pursuit was shortened to a 5-km classical race followed by a 5-km freestyle race contested on the same day. The 5-km classical is no longer a separate medal event.

Year	Time	Year	Time
1992 Lyubov Egorova, UT	40:07.7	1998 Larissa Lazutina, RUS	46:06.9
1994 Lyubov Egorova, RUS	41:38.1	2002 Olga Danilova, RUS	24:52.1

10 kilometers
Held as a classical event from 1952-88, and since 2002. Replaced by 10-km combined pursuit from 1992-98.

Year	Time	Year	Time
1952 Lydia Wideman, FIN	41:40.0	1976 Raisa Smetanina, USSR	30:13.41
1956 Lyubov Kosyreva, USSR	38:11.0	1980 Barbara Petzold, E. Ger.	30:31.54
1960 Maria Gusakova, USSR	39:46.6	1984 Marja-Liisa Hämäläinen, FIN	31:44.2
1964 Claudia Boyarskikh, USSR	40:24.3	1988 Vida Venciene, USSR	30:08.3
1968 Toini Gustafsson, SWE	36:46.5	1992-98 Not held	
1972 Galina Kulakova, USSR	34:17.82	2002 Bente Skari, NOR	28:05.6

15 kilometers
Held as a freestyle event from 1992-94, and since 2002. Held as a classical event in 1998.

Year	Time	Year	Time
1992 Lyubov Egorova, UT	42:20.8	1998 Olga Danilova, RUS	46:55.4
1994 Manuela Di Centa, ITA	39:44.5	2002 Stefania Belmondo, ITA	39:54.4

20 kilometers
Held as a classical event from 1984-88. Discontinued in 1992 and replaced by the 30-kilometer freestyle.

Year	Time	Year	Time
1984 Marja-Liisa Hämäläinen, FIN	1:01:45.0	1988 Tamara Tikhonova, USSR	55:53.6

30 kilometers
Replaced 20-km classical event in 1992. Held as a freestyle event 1992-98. Held as a classical event since 2002.

Year	Time	Year	Time
1992 Stefania Belmondo, ITA	1:22:30.1	1998 Julija Tchepalova, RUS	1:22:01.5
1994 Manuela Di Centa, ITA	1:25:41.6	2002 Gabriella Paruzzi, ITA*	1:30:57.1

*Paruzzi finished second to Larissa Lazutina of Russia, who was disqualified after failing a drug test.

4x5-kilometer Relay
Two classical and two freestyle legs since 1992. Event featured three skiers per team from 1956-72.

Year	Time	Year	Time	Year	Time
1956 Finland	1:09:01.0	1976 Soviet Union	1:07:49.75	1994 Russia	57:12.5
1960 Sweden	1:04:21.4	1980 East Germany	1:02:11.10	1998 Russia	55:13.5
1964 Soviet Union	59:20.2	1984 Norway	1:06:49.7	2002 Germany	49:30.6
1968 Norway	57:30.0	1988 Soviet Union	59:51.1		
1972 Soviet Union	48:46.15	1992 Unified Team	59:34.8		

CURLING

MEN

Year			
1998	**Switzerland**, Canada, Norway		
2002	**Norway**, Canada, Switzerland		

WOMEN

Year			
1998	**Canada**, Denmark, Sweden		
2002	**Great Britain**, Switzerland, Canada		

FIGURE SKATING

MEN

Multiple gold medals: Gillis Grafström (3); Dick Button and Karl Schäfer (2).

Year		Year		Year	
1908	Ulrich Salchow........SWE	1952	Dick Button.............USA	1984	Scott Hamilton........USA
1912	Not held	1956	Hayes Alan Jenkins......USA	1988	Brian Boitano...........USA
1920	Gillis Grafström.......SWE	1960	David Jenkins...........USA	1992	Victor Petrenko..........UT
1924	Gillis Grafström.......SWE	1964	Manfred Schnelldorfer,..GER	1994	Alexei Urmanov........RUS
1928	Gillis Grafström.......SWE	1968	Wolfgang Schwarz......AUT	1998	Ilia Kulik................RUS
1932	Karl Schäfer...........AUT	1972	Ondrej Nepela.........CZE	2002	Alexei Yagudin..........RUS
1936	Karl Schäfer...........AUT	1976	John Curry.............GBR		
1948	Dick Button............USA	1980	Robin Cousins..........GBR		

WOMEN

Multiple gold medals: Sonja Henie (3); Katarina Witt (2).

Year		Year		Year	
1908	Madge Syers..........GBR	1952	Jeanette Altwegg........GBR	1984	Katarina Witt........E. Ger
1912	Not held	1956	Tenley Albright..........USA	1988	Katarina Witt........E. Ger
1920	Magda Julin-Mauroy....SWE	1960	Carol Heiss..............USA	1992	Kristi Yamaguchi.......USA
1924	Herma Planck-Szabö....AUT	1964	Sjoukje Dijkstra.........NED	1994	Oksana Baiul...........UKR
1928	Sonja Henie...........NOR	1968	Peggy Fleming..........USA	1998	Tara Lipinski...........USA
1932	Sonja Henie...........NOR	1972	Beatrix Schuba..........AUT	2002	Sarah Hughes..........USA
1936	Sonja Henie...........NOR	1976	Dorothy Hamill..........USA		
1948	Barbara Ann Scott.....CAN	1980	Anett Pötzsch.........E. Ger		

Pairs

Multiple gold medals: MEN–Pierre Brunet, Artur Dmitriev, Sergei Grinkov, Oleg Protopopov and Aleksandr Zaitsev (2). WOMEN–Irina Rodnina (3); Ludmila Belousova, Ekaterina Gordeeva and Andree Joly Brunet (2).

Year		Year	
1908	Anna Hübler & Heinrich Burger...........Germany	1968	Ludmila Belousova & Oleg Protopopov.......USSR
1912	Not held	1972	Irina Rodnina & Aleksei Ulanov..............USSR
1920	Ludovika & Walter Jakobsson...............Finland	1976	Irina Rodnina & Aleksandr Zaitsev...........USSR
1924	Helene Engelmann & Alfred Berger.........Austria	1980	Irina Rodnina & Aleksandr Zaitsev...........USSR
1928	Andrée Joly & Pierre Brunet.................France	1984	Elena Valova & Oleg Vasiliev...............USSR
1932	Andrée & Pierre Brunet......................France	1988	Ekaterina Gordeeva & Sergei Grinkov.......USSR
1936	Maxi Herber & Ernst Baier................Germany	1992	Natalia Mishkutienok & Arthur Dmitriev..........UT
1948	Micheline Lannoy & Pierre Baugniet........Belgium	1994	Ekaterina Gordeeva & Sergei Grinkov........RUS
1952	Ria & Paul Falk........................Germany	1998	Oksana Kazakova & Artur Dmitriev.........RUS
1956	Elisabeth Schwartz & Kurt Oppelt..........Austria	2002	Elena Berezhnaya & Anton Sikharulidze........RUS
1960	Barbara Wagner & Robert Paul.............Canada		Jamie Sale & David Pelletier*.................CAN
1964	Ludmila Belousova & Oleg Protopopov.....USSR		

*Originally awarded silver medals, Sale & Pelletier later had them upgraded to gold after an investigation by the International Olympic Committee and the International Skating Union concluded that a judge was guilty of misconduct.

Ice Dancing

Multiple gold medals: Oksana Grishuk & Yevgeny Platov (2).

Year		Year	
1976	Lyudmila Pakhomova & Aleksandr Gorshkov...USSR	1992	Marina Klimova & Sergei Ponomarenko.........UT
1980	Natalia Linichuk & Gennady Karponosov......USSR	1994	Oksana Grishuk & Yevgeny Platov............RUS
1984	Jayne Torvill & Christopher Dean......Great Britain	1998	Oksana Grishuk & Yevgeny Platov............RUS
1988	Natalia Bestemianova & Andrei Bukin........USSR	2002	Marina Anissina & Gwendal Peizerat..........FRA

FREESTYLE SKIING

MEN

Aerials

Year		Points
1994	Andreas Schoebaechler, SWI..............234.67
1998	Eric Bergoust, USA.....................255.64
2002	Ales Valenta, CZR......................257.02

Moguls

Year		Points
1994	Jean-Luc Brassard, CAN...................27.24
1998	Jonny Moseley, USA.......................26.93
2002	Janne Lahtela, FIN.......................27.97

WOMEN

Aerials

Year		Points
1994	Lina Cherjazova, UZB.....................166.84
1998	Nikki Stone, USA........................193.00
2002	Alisa Camplin, AUS......................193.47

Moguls

Year		Points
1994	Stine Lise Hattestad, NOR.................25.97
1998	Tae Satoya, JPN.........................25.06
2002	Kari Traa, NOR..........................25.94

ICE HOCKEY

MEN

Multiple gold medals: Soviet Union/Unified Team (8); Canada (7); United States (2).

Year		Year	
1920	**Canada**, United States Czechoslovakia	1980	**United States**, Soviet Union, Sweden
1924	**Canada**, United States, Great Britain	1984	**Soviet Union**, Czechoslovakia, Sweden
1928	**Canada**, Sweden, Switzerland	1988	**Soviet Union**, Finland, Sweden
1932	**Canada**, United States, Germany	1992	**Unified Team**, Canada, Czechoslovakia
1936	**Great Britain**, Canada, United States	1994	**Sweden**, Canada, Finland
1948	**Canada**, Czechoslovakia, Switzerland	1998	**Czech Republic**, Russia, Finland
1952	**Canada**, United States, Sweden	2002	**Canada**, United States, Russia
1956	**Soviet Union**, United States, Canada		
1960	**United States**, Canada, Soviet Union		
1964	**Soviet Union**, Sweden, Czechoslovakia		**WOMEN**
1968	**Soviet Union**, Czechoslovakia, Canada	Year	
1972	**Soviet Union**, United States, Czechoslovakia	1998	**United States**, Canada, Finland
1976	**Soviet Union**, Czechoslovakia, West Germany	2002	**Canada**, United States, Sweden

---

U.S. Gold Medal Hockey Teams

1960

Forwards: Billy Christian, Roger Christian, Billy Cleary, Gene Grazia, Paul Johnson, Bob McVey, Dick Meredith, Weldy Olson, Dick Rodenheiser and Tom Williams. **Defensemen:** Bob Cleary, Jack Kirrane (captain), John Mayasich, Bob Owen and Rod Paavola. **Goaltenders:** Jack McCartan and Larry Palmer. **Coach:** Jack Riley.

1980

Forwards: Neal Broten, Steve Christoff, Mike Eruzione (captain), John Harrington, Mark Johnson, Rob McClanahan, Mark Pavelich, Buzz Schneider, Dave Silk, Eric Strobel, Phil Verchota and Mark Wells. **Defensemen:** Bill Baker, Dave Christian, Ken Morrow, Jack O'Callahan, Mike Ramsey and Bob Suter. **Goaltenders:** Jim Craig and Steve Janaszak. **Coach:** Herb Brooks.

1998

Forwards: Laurie Baker, Alana Blahoski, Lisa Brown-Miller, Karen Bye, Tricia Dunn, Cammi Granato, Katie King, Shelley Looney, A.J. Mleczko, Jenny Schmidgall, Gretchen Ulion, Sandra Whyte. **Defensemen:** Chris Bailey, Colleen Coyne, Sue Mertz, Tara Mounsey, Vicki Movessian, Angela Ruggiero. **Goaltenders:** Sarah DeCosta and Sarah Tueting. **Coach:** Ben Smith.

LUGE

MEN

Multiple gold medals: (including doubles): Georg Hackl (3); Jan Behrendt, Norbert Hahn, Paul Hildgartner, Thomas Köhler, Stefan Krausse and Hans Rinn (2).

Singles

Year		Time	Year		Time
1964	Thomas Köhler, GER	3:26.77	1988	Jens Müller, E. Ger	3:05.548
1968	Manfred Schmid, AUT	2:52.48	1992	Georg Hackl, GER	3:02.363
1972	Wolfgang Scheidel, E. Ger	3:27.58	1994	Georg Hackl, GER	3:21.571
1976	Dettlef Günther, E. Ger	3:27.688	1998	Georg Hackl, GER	3:18.436
1980	Bernhard Glass, E. Ger	2:54.796	2002	Armin Zoeggeler, ITA	2:57.941
1984	Paul Hildgartner, ITA	3:04.258			

Doubles

Year		Time	Year		Time
1964	Josef Feistmantl & Manfred Stengl, AUT	1:41.62	1988	Joerg Hoffmann & Jochen Pietzsch, E. Ger	1:31.940
1968	Klaus Bonsack & Thomas Köhler, E. Ger	1:35.85	1992	Jan Behrendt & Stefan Krausse, GER	1:32.053
1972	(TIE) Paul Hildgartner/Walter Plaikner, ITA. & Richard Bredow/Horst Hornlein, E. Ger.	1:28.35 1:28.35	1994	Kurt Brugger & Wilfred Huber, ITA.	1:36.720
1976	Norbert Hahn & Hans Rinn, E. Ger.	1:25.604	1998	Jan Behrendt & Stefan Krausse, GER	1:41.105
1980	Norbert Hahn & Hans Rinn, E. Ger.	1:19.331	2002	Patric-Fritz Leitner & Alexander Resch, GER.	1:26.082
1984	Hans Stangassinger & Franz Wembacher, W. Ger.	1:23.620			

WOMEN

Multiple gold medals: Steffi Martin Walter (2).

Singles

Year		Time	Year		Time
1964	Ortrun Enderlein, GER	3:24.67	1988	Steffi Martin Walter, E. Ger	3:03.973
1968	Erica Lechner, ITA	2:28.66	1992	Doris Neuner, AUT	3:06.696
1972	Anna-Maria Müller, E. Ger	2:59.18	1994	Gerda Weissensteiner, ITA.	3:15.517
1976	Margit Schumann, E. Ger	2:50.621	1998	Silke Kraushaar, GER	3:23.779
1980	Vera Zozulya, USSR	2:36.537	2002	Sylke Otto, GER	2:52.464
1984	Steffi Martin, E. Ger.	2:46.570			

NORDIC COMBINED

Ski jumping followed by a cross country race. Judges stopped converting cross country times into points after the 1994 Games. The times listed are final cross country times adjusted to include the competitors' staggered start time. The staggered start is determined by the Gundersen Method, which is a table that converts final ski jumping point differentials into time intervals.

Multiple gold medals: Samppa Lajunen and Ulrich Wehling (3); Bjarte Engen Vik, Johan Gröttumsbråten, Fred Boerre Lundberg, Takanori Kono and Kenji Ogiwara (2).

Individual

Year		Points	Year		Points
1924	Thorleif Haug, NOR	18.906	1972	Ulrich Wehling, E. Ger	413.340
1928	Johan Gröttumsbråten, NOR	17.833	1976	Ulrich Wehling, E. Ger	423.39
1932	Johan Gröttumsbråten, NOR	446.00	1980	Ulrich Wehling, E. Ger	432.200
1936	Oddbjörn Hagen, NOR	430.3	1984	Tom Sandberg, NOR	422.595
1948	Heikki Hasu, FIN	448.80	1988	Hippolyt Kempf, SWI	432.230
1952	Simon Slattvik, NOR	451.621	1992	Fabrice Guy, FRA	426.470
1956	Sverre Stenersen, NOR	455.000	1994	Fred Borre Lundberg, NOR	457.970
1960	Georg Thoma, GER	457.952			**Time**
1964	Tormod Knutsen, NOR	469.28	1998	Bjarte Engen Vik, NOR	41:21.1
1968	Franz Keller, W. Ger	449.04	2002	Samppa Lajunen, FIN	39:11.7

Sprint
New event in 2002.

Year		Time
2002	Samppa Lajunen, FIN	16:40.1

Team

Year		Points	Year		Time
1988	West Germany	792.08	1998	Norway	54:11.5
1992	Japan	1247.180	2002	Finland	48:42.2
1994	Japan	1368.860			

SKELETON

MEN
Singles

Year		Time
1928	Jennison Heaton, USA	3:01.8
1932-36	Not held	
1948	Nino Bibbia, ITA	5:23.2
1952-98	Not held	
2002	Jim Shea, USA	1:41.96

WOMEN
Singles

Year		Time
2002	Tristan Gale, USA	1:45.11

Note: This event was called Cresta when it was held in 1928 and 1948.

SKI JUMPING

Multiple gold medals (including team jumping): Matti Nykänen (4); Jens Weissflog (3); Simon Ammann, Birger Ruud and Toni Nieminen (2).

Normal Hill–90 Meters

Year		Points	Year		Points
1924-60	Not held		1984	Jens Weissflog, E. Ger	215.2
1964	Veikko Kankkonen, FIN	229.9	1988	Matti Nykänen, FIN	229.1
1968	Jiri Raska, CZE	216.5	1992	Ernst Vettori, AUT	222.8
1972	Yukio Kasaya, JPN	244.2	1994	Espen Bredesen, NOR	282.0
1976	Hans-Georg Aschenbach, E. Ger	252.0	1998	Jani Soininen, FIN	234.5
1980	Anton Innauer, AUT	266.3	2002	Simon Ammann, SWI	269.0

Note: Jump held at 70 meters from 1964-92.

Large Hill–120 Meters

Year		Points	Year		Points
1924	Jacob Tullin Thams, NOR	18.960	1972	Wojciech Fortuna, POL	219.9
1928	Alf Andersen, NOR	19.208	1976	Karl Schäabl, AUT	234.8
1932	Birger Ruud, NOR	228.1	1980	Jouko Törmänen, FIN	271.0
1936	Birger Ruud, NOR	232.0	1984	Matti Nykänen, FIN	231.2
1948	Petter Hugsted, NOR	228.1	1988	Matti Nykänen, FIN	224.0
1952	Arnfinn Bergmann, NOR	226.0	1992	Toni Nieminen, FIN	239.5
1956	Antti Hyvärinen, FIN	227.0	1994	Jens Weissflog, GER	274.5
1960	Helmut Recknagel, GER	227.2	1998	Kazuyoshi Funaki, JPN	272.3
1964	Toralf Engan, NOR	230.7	2002	Simon Ammann, SWI	281.4
1968	Vladimir Beloussov, USSR	231.3			

Note: Jump held at various lengths from 1924-56; at 80 meters from 1960-64; and at 90 meters from 1968-88.

SKI JUMPING (Cont.)
Team Large Hill

Year		Points	Year		Points
1988	Finland	634.4	1998	Japan	933.0
1992	Finland	644.4	2002	Germany	974.1
1994	Germany	970.1			

SNOWBOARDING

MEN
Halfpipe

Year		Points
1998	Gian Simmen, SWI	85.2
2002	Ross Powers, USA	46.1

Giant Slalom (Discont.)
Discontinued after 1998, replaced by Parallel Giant Slalom.

Year		Time
1998	Ross Rebagliati, CAN	2:03.96

Parallel Giant Slalom

Year		
2002	Philipp Schoch	SWI

WOMEN
Halfpipe

Year		Points
1998	Nicola Thost, GER	74.6
2002	Kelly Clark, USA	47.9

Giant Slalom (Discont.)
Discontinued after 1998, replaced by Parallel Giant Slalom.

Year		Time
1998	Karine Ruby, FRA	2:17.34

Parallel Giant Slalom

Year		
2002	Isabelle Blanc	FRA

SPEED SKATING

MEN

Multiple gold medals: Eric Heiden and Clas Thunberg (5); Ivar Ballangrud, Yevgeny Grishin and Johann Olav Koss (4); Hjalmar Andersen, Tomas Gustafson, Irving Jaffee and Ard Schenk (3); Gaétan Boucher, Knut Johannesen, Erhard Keller, Uwe-Jens Mey, Gianni Romme, Jack Shea and Jochem Uytdehaage (2). Note that Thunberg's total includes the All-Around, which was contested for the only time in 1924.

500 meters

Year		Time		Year		Time	
1924	Charles Jewtraw, USA	44.0		1968	Erhard Keller, W. Ger	40.3	
1928	(TIE) Bernt Evensen, NOR	43.4	OR	1972	Erhard Keller, W. Ger	39.44	OR
	& Clas Thunberg, FIN	43.4	OR	1976	Yevgeny Kulikov, USSR	39.17	OR
1932	Jack Shea, USA	43.4	=OR	1980	Eric Heiden, USA	38.03	OR
1936	Ivar Ballangrud, NOR	43.4	=OR	1984	Sergei Fokichev, USSR	38.19	
1948	Finn Helgesen, NOR	43.1	OR	1988	Uwe-Jens Mey, E. Ger	36.45	WR
1952	Ken Henry, USA	43.2		1992	Uwe-Jens Mey, GER	37.14	
1956	Yevgeny Grishin, USSR	40.2	=WR	1994	Aleksandr Golubev, RUS	36.33	OR
1960	Yevgeny Grishin, USSR	40.2	=WR	1998	Hiroyashu Shimizu, JPN	71.35*	OR
1964	Terry McDermott, USA	40.1	OR	2002	Casey FitzRandolph, USA	69.23	OR

*The two-race final was introduced; skater with the lowest combined time wins gold.

1000 meters

Year		Time		Year		Time	
1924-72	Not held			1992	Olaf Zinke, GER	1:14.85	
1976	Peter Mueller, USA	1:19.32		1994	Dan Jansen, USA	1:12.43	WR
1980	Eric Heiden, USA	1:15.18	OR	1998	Ids Postma, NED	1:10.64	OR
1984	Gaétan Boucher, CAN	1:15.80		2002	Gerard van Velde, NED	1:07.18	WR
1988	Nikolai Gulyaev, USSR	1:13.03	OR				

1500 meters

Year		Time		Year		Time	
1924	Clas Thunberg, FIN	2:20.8		1968	Kees Verkerk, NED	2:03.4	OR
1928	Clas Thunberg, FIN	2:21.1		1972	Ard Schenk, NED	2:02.96	OR
1932	Jack Shea, USA	2:57.5		1976	Jan Egil Storholt, NOR	1:59.38	OR
1936	Charles Mathisen, NOR	2:19.2	OR	1980	Eric Heiden, USA	1:55.44	OR
1948	Sverre Farstad, NOR	2:17.6	OR	1984	Gaétan Boucher, CAN	1:58.36	
1952	Hjalmar Andersen, NOR	2:20.4		1988	Andre Hoffman, E. Ger	1:52.06	WR
1956	(TIE) Yevgeny Grishin, USSR	2:08.6	WR	1992	Johann Olav Koss, NOR	1:54.81	
	& Yuri Mikhailov, USSR	2:08.6	WR	1994	Johann Olav Koss, NOR	1:51.29	WR
1960	(TIE) Roald Aas, NOR	2:10.4		1998	Aadne Sondral, NOR	1:47.87	WR
	& Yevgeny Grishin, USSR	2:10.4		2002	Derek Parra, USA	1:43.95	WR
1964	Ants Antson, USSR	2:10.3					

5000 meters

Year		Time		Year		Time	
1924	Clas Thunberg, FIN	8:39.0		1932	Irving Jaffee, USA	9:40.8	
1928	Ivar Ballangrud, NOR	8:50.5		1936	Ivar Ballangrud, NOR	8:19.6	OR

Year		Time		Year		Time	
1948	Reidar Liaklev, NOR	8:29.4		1980	Eric Heiden, USA	7:02.29	OR
1952	Hjalmar Andersen, NOR	8:10.6	OR	1984	Tomas Gustafson, SWE	7:12.28	
1956	Boris Shilkov, USSR	7:48.7	OR	1988	Tomas Gustafson, SWE	6:44.63	WR
1960	Viktor Kosichkin, USSR	7:51.3		1992	Geir Karlstad, NOR	6:59.97	
1964	Knut Johannesen, NOR	7:38.4	OR	1994	Johann Olav Koss, NOR	6:34.96	WR
1968	Fred Anton Maier, NOR	7:22.4	WR	1998	Gianni Romme, NED	6:22.20	WR
1972	Ard Schenk, NED	7:23.61		2002	Jochem Uytdehaage, NED	6:14.66	WR
1976	Sten Stensen, NOR	7:24.48					

10,000 meters

Year		Time		Year		Time	
1924	Julius Skutnabb, FIN	18:04.8		1972	Ard Schenk, NED	15:01.35	OR
1928	Irving Jaffee, USA*	18:36.5		1976	Piet Kleine, NED	14:50.59	OR
1932	Irving Jaffee, USA	19:13.6		1980	Eric Heiden, USA	14:28.13	WR
1936	Ivar Ballangrud, NOR	17:24.3	OR	1984	Igor Malkov, USSR	14:39.90	
1948	Ake Seyffarth, SWE	17:26.3		1988	Tomas Gustafson, SWE	13:48.20	WR
1952	Hjalmar Andersen, NOR	16:45.8	OR	1992	Bart Veldkamp, NED	14:12.12	
1956	Sigvard Ericsson, SWE	16:35.9	OR	1994	Johann Olav Koss, NOR	13:30.55	WR
1960	Knut Johannesen, NOR	15:46.6	WR	1998	Gianni Romme, NED	13:15.33	WR
1964	Jonny Nilsson, SWE	15:50.1		2002	Jochem Uytdehaage, NED	12:58.92	WR
1968	Johnny Höglin, SWE	15:23.6	OR				

*Unofficial, according to the IOC. Jaffee recorded the fastest time, but the event was called off in progress due to thawing ice.

WOMEN

Multiple gold medals: Lydia Skoblikova (6); Bonnie Blair (5); Claudia Pechstein (4); Karin Enke, Gunda Niemann-Stirnemann and Yvonne van Gennip (3); Tatiana Averina, Catriona Lemay-Doan, Christa Rothenburger and Marianne Timmer (2).

500 meters

Year		Time		Year		Time	
1960	Helga Haase, GER	45.9		1984	Christa Rothenburger, E. Ger	41.02	OR
1964	Lydia Skoblikova, USSR	45.0	OR	1988	Bonnie Blair, USA	39.10	WR
1968	Lyudmila Titova, USSR	46.1		1992	Bonnie Blair, USA	40.33	
1972	Anne Henning, USA	43.33	OR	1994	Bonnie Blair, USA	39.25	
1976	Sheila Young, USA	42.76	OR	1998	Catriona Lemay-Doan, CAN	76.60*	OR
1980	Karin Enke, E. Ger	41.78	OR	2002	Catriona Lemay-Doan, CAN	74.75	OR

*The two-race final was introduced; skater with the lowest combined time wins gold.

1000 meters

Year		Time		Year		Time	
1960	Klara Guseva, USSR	1:34.1		1984	Karin Enke, E. Ger	1:21.61	OR
1964	Lydia Skoblikova, USSR	1:33.2	OR	1988	Christa Rothenburger, E. Ger	1:17.65	WR
1968	Carolina Geijssen, NED	1:32.6	OR	1992	Bonnie Blair, USA	1:21.90	
1972	Monika Pflug, W. Ger	1:31.40	OR	1994	Bonnie Blair, USA	1:18.74	
1976	Tatiana Averina, USSR	1:28.43	OR	1998	Marianne Timmer, NED	1:16.51	OR
1980	Natalia Petruseva, USSR	1:24.10	OR	2002	Chris Witty, USA	1:13.83	WR

1500 meters

Year		Time		Year		Time	
1960	Lydia Skoblikova, USSR	2:25.2	WR	1984	Karin Enke, E. Ger	2:03.42	WR
1964	Lydia Skoblikova, USSR	2:22.6	OR	1988	Yvonne van Gennip, NED	2:00.68	OR
1968	Kaija Mustonen, FIN	2:22.4	OR	1992	Jacqueline Börner, GER	2:05.87	
1972	Dianne Holum, USA	2:20.85	OR	1994	Emese Hunyady, AUT	2:02.19	
1976	Galina Stepanskaya, USSR	2:16.58	OR	1998	Marianne Timmer, NED	1:57.58	WR
1980	Annie Borckink, NED	2:10.95	OR	2002	Anni Friesinger, GER	1:54.02	WR

3000 meters

Year		Time		Year		Time	
1960	Lydia Skoblikova, USSR	5:14.3		1984	Andrea Schöne, E. Ger	4:24.79	OR
1964	Lydia Skoblikova, USSR	5:14.9		1988	Yvonne van Gennip, NED	4:11.94	WR
1968	Johanna Schut, NED	4:56.2	OR	1992	Gunda Niemann, GER	4:19.90	
1972	Christina Baas-Kaiser, NED	4:52.14	OR	1994	Svetlana Bazhanova, RUS	4:17.43	
1976	Tatiana Averina, USSR	4:45.19	OR	1998	Gunda Niemann-Stirnemann, GER	4:07.29	OR
1980	Bjorg Eva Jensen, NOR	4:32.13	OR	2002	Claudia Pechstein, GER	3:57.70	WR

5000 meters

Year		Time		Year		Time	
1960-84 Not held				1994	Claudia Pechstein, GER	7:14.37	
1988	Yvonne van Gennip, NED	7:14.13	WR	1998	Claudia Pechstein, GER	6:59.61	WR
1992	Gunda Niemann, GER	7:31.57		2002	Claudia Pechstein, GER	6:46.91	WR

SHORT TRACK SPEED SKATING

MEN •

Multiple gold medals (including relays): Marc Gagnon and Kim Ki-Hoon (3).

500 meters

Year		Time
1994	Chae Ji-Hoon, S. Kor..............43.45	
1998	Takafumi Nishitani, JPN...........42.862	
2002	Marc Gagnon, CAN ....41.802 **OR**	

1000 meters

Year		Time
1992	Kim Ki-Hoon, S. Kor.............1:30.76 **WR**	
1994	Kim Ki-Hoon, S. Kor.............1:34.57	
1998	Kim Dong-Sung, S. Kor..........1:32.375	
2002	Steven Bradbury, AUS 1:29.109	

1500 meters

Year		Time
2002	Apolo Anton Ohno, USA* 2:18.541	

*Ohno finished second to South Korea's Kim Dong-Sung, who was disqualifed for cross-tracking.

5000-m Relay

Year		Time
1992	South Korea...................7:14.02 **WR**	
1994	Italy.........................7:11.74 **OR**	
1998	Canada 7:06.075	
2002	Canada 6:51.579	

WOMEN

Multiple gold medals (including relays): Chun Lee-Kyung (4); Kim Yun-Mi, Annie Perrault, Cathy Turner, Won Hye-Kyung and Yang Yang (A) (2).

500 meters

Year		Time
1992	Cathy Turner, USA 47.04	
1994	Cathy Turner, USA ....45.98 **OR**	
1998	Annie Perrault, CAN 46.568	
2002	Yang Yang (A), CHN 44.187	

1000 meters

Year		Time
1994	Chun Lee-Kyung, S. Kor...........1:36.87	
1998	Chun Lee-Kyung, S. Kor. 1:42.776	
2002	Yang Yang (A), CHN 1:36.391	

1500 meters

Year		Time
2002	Ko Gi-Hyun, S. Kor..............2:31.581	

3000-m Relay

Year		Time
1992	Canada 4:36.62	
1994	South Korea ....4:26.64 **WR**	
1998	South Korea ....4:16.260 **WR**	
2002	South Korea ....4:12.793 **WR**	

Athletes with Winter and Summer Medals

Only three athletes have won medals in both the Winter and Summer Olympics:

Eddie Eagan, USA–Light Heavyweight Boxing gold (1920) and Four-man Bobsled gold (1932).

Jacob Tullin Thams, Norway–Ski Jumping gold (1924) and 8-meter Yachting silver (1936).

Christa Luding-Rothenburger, East Germany–Speed Skating gold at 500 meters (1984) and 1,000-m (1988), silver at 500m (1988) and bronze at 500m (1992) and Match Sprint Cycling silver (1988). Luding-Rothenburger is the only athlete to ever win medals in both Winter and Summer Games in the same year.

All-Time Leading Medal Winners
MEN

No		Sport	G-S-B
12	Bjorn Dählie, NOR	Cross Country	8-4-0
9	Sixten Jernberg, SWE........	Cross Country	4-3-2
7	Clas Thunberg, FIN	Speed Skating	5-1-1
7	Ivar Ballangrud, NOR	Speed Skating	4-2-1
7	Ricco Gross, GER............	Biathlon	3-3-1
7	Veikko Hakulinen, FIN	Cross Country	3-3-1
7	Kjetil Andre Aamodt, NOR........	Alpine	3-2-2
7	Eero Mäntyranta, FIN	Cross Country	3-2-2
7	Bogdan Musiol, E. Ger/GER	Bobsled	1-5-1
6	Ole Einar Bjoerndalen, NOR......	Biathlon	5-1-0
6	Thomas Alsgaard, NOR......	Cross Country	4-2-0
6	Gunde Svan, SWE...........	Cross Country	4-1-1
6	Vegard Ulvang, NOR........	Cross Country	3-2-1
6	Johan Gröttumsbråten, NOR	Nordic	3-1-2
6	Wolfgang Hoppe, E. Ger/GER	Bobsled	2-3-1
6	Eugenio Monti, ITA.............	Bobsled	2-2-2
6	Vladimir Smirnov, USSR/UT/KAZ ..X-country		1-4-1
6	Mika Myllylae, FIN	Cross Country	1-1-4
6	Roald Larsen, NOR.........	Speed Skating	0-2-4
6	Harri Kirvesniemi, FIN	Cross Country	0-0-6
5	**Eric Heiden, USA**	Speed Skating	5-0-0
5	Yevgeny Grishin, USSR	Speed Skating	4-1-0
5	Johann Olav Koss, NOR	Speed Skating	4-1-0
5	Matti Nykänen, FIN	Ski Jumping	4-1-0
5	Aleksandr Tikhonov, USSR	Biathlon	4-1-0
5	Nikolai Zimyatov, USSR	Cross Country	4-1-0
5	Georg Hackl, GER.........	Luge	3-2-0
5	Samppa Lajunen, FIN........	Cross Country	3-2-0
5	Alberto Tomba, ITA..............	Alpine	3-2-0
5	Marc Gagnon, CAN	ST Sp. Skating	3-0-2
5	Harald Grönningen, NOR	Cross Country	2-3-0
5	Frank Luck, GER...............	Biathlon	2-3-0
5	Pål Tyldum, NOR..........	Cross Country	2-3-0
5	Sven Fischer, GER	Biathlon	2-2-1
5	Knut Johannesen, NOR	Speed Skating	2-2-1
5	Lasse Kjus, NOR............	Alpine	1-3-1
5	Peter Angerer, W. Ger/GER	Biathlon	1-2-2
5	Juha Mieto, FIN	Cross Country	1-2-2
5	Fritz Feierabend, SWI	Bobsled	0-3-2
5	Rintje Ritsma, NED	Speed Skating	0-2-3

WOMEN

No		Sport	G-S-B
10	Raisa Smetanina, USSR/UT...	Cross Country	4-5-1
9	Lyubov Egorova, UT/RUS......	Cross Country	6-3-0
9	Larissa Lazutina, UT/RUS.....	Cross Country	5-3-1
9	Stefania Belmondo, ITA	Cross Country	2-3-4
8	Galina Kulakova, USSR	Cross Country	4-2-2
8	Karin (Enke) Kania, E. Ger ...	Speed Skating	3-4-1
8	Gunda Neimann-Stirnemann, GER..........	Speed Skating	3-4-1
8	Ursula Disl, GER.................	Biathlon	2-4-2
7	Claudia Pechstein, GER	Speed Skating	4-1-2
7	Marja-Liisa (Hämäläinen) Kirvesniemi, FIN..........	Cross Country	3-0-4

No		Sport	G-S-B
7	Elena Valbe, UT/RUS	Cross Country	3-0-4
7	Andrea (Mitscherlich, Schöne) Ehrig, E. Ger	Speed Skating	1-5-1
6	Lydia Skoblikova, USSR	Speed Skating	6-0-0
6	**Bonnie Blair, USA**	Speed Skating	5-0-1
6	Manuela Di Centa, ITA	Cross Country	2-2-2
5	Lee-Kyung Chun, S. Kor	ST Sp. Skating	4-0-1
5	Olga Danilova, RUS	Cross Country	3-2-0

No		Sport	G-S-B
5	Anfisa Reztsova, USSR/UT	CC/Biathlon	3-1-1
5	Vreni Schneider, SWI	Alpine	3-1-1
5	Katja Seizinger, GER	Alpine	3-0-2
5	Helena Takalo, FIN	Cross Country	1-3-1
5	Bente (Martinsen) Skari, NOR	Cross Country	1-2-2
5	Alevtina Kolchina, USSR	Cross Country	1-1-3
5	Yang Yang (S), CHN	ST Sp. Skating	0-4-1
5	Anita Moen, NOR	Cross Country	0-3-2

Games Medaled In

MEN–**Aamodt** (1992,94,2002); **Alsgaard** (1994,98,2002); **Angerer** (1980,84,88); **Ballangrud** (1928,32,36); **Bjoerndalen** (1998,2002); **Dählie** (1992,94,98); **Feierabend** (1936,48,52); **Fischer** (1994,98,2002); **Gagnon** (1994,98,2002); **Grishin** (1956,60,64); **Gross** (1992,94,98,2002); **Gröttumsbråten** (1924,28,32); **Grönningen** (1960,64,68); **Hackl** (1988,92,94,98,2002) **Hakulinen** (1952,56,60); **Heiden** (1980); **Hoppe** (1984,88,92,94); **Jernberg** (1956,60,64); **Johannesen** (1956,60,64); **Kirvesniemi** (1980,84,92,94,98); **Kjus** (1994,98,2002); **Koss** (1992,94); **Lajunen** (1998,2002);**Larsen** (1924,28); **Luck** (1994,98,2002); **Mäntyranta** (1960,64,68); **Mieto** (1976,80,84); **Monti** (1956,60,64,68); **Musiol** (1980,84,88,92); **Myllylae** (1994,98); **Nykänen** (1984,88); **Ritsma** (1994,98); **Smirnov** (1988,92,94,98); **Svan** (1984,88); **Thunberg** (1924,28); **Tikhonov** (1968,72,76,80); **Tomba** (1988,92,94); **Tyldum** (1968,72,76); **Ulvang** (1988,92,94); **Zimyatov** (1980,84).

WOMEN–**Belmondo** (1992,94,98,2002); **Blair** (1988,92,94); **Chun** (1994,98); **Danilova** (1998,2002); **Di Centa** (1992,94); **Disl** (1992,94,98,2002); **Egorova** (1992,94); **Ehrig** (1976,80,84,88); **Kania** (1980,84,88); **Kirvesniemi** (1984,88,94); **Kolchina** (1956,64,68); **Kulakova** (1968,72,76,80); **Lazutina** (1992,94,98,2002); **Moen** (1994,98,2002); **Niemann-Stirnemann** (1992,94,98); **Pechstein** (1992,94,98,2002); **Reztsova** (1988,92,94); **Schneider** (1988,92,94); **Seizinger** (1992,94,98); **Skari** (1998,2002); **Skoblikova** (1960,64); **Smetanina** (1976,80,84,88,92); **Takalo** (1972,76,80); **Valbe** (1992,94,98); **Yang** (1998,2002).

Most Gold Medals

MEN

No		Sport	G-S-B
8	Bjorn Dählie, NOR	Cross Country	8-4-0
5	Clas Thunberg, FIN	Speed Skating	5-1-1
5	Ole Einar Bjoerndalen, NOR	Biathlon	5-1-0
5	**Eric Heiden, USA**	Speed Skating	5-0-0
4	Sixten Jernberg, SWE	Cross Country	4-3-2
4	Ivar Ballangrud, NOR	Speed Skating*	4-2-1
4	Thomas Alsgaard, NOR	Cross Country	4-2-0
4	Gunde Svan, SWE	Cross Country	4-1-1
4	Yevgeny Grishin, USSR	Speed Skating	4-1-0
4	Johann Olav Koss, NOR	Speed Skating	4-1-0
4	Matti Nykänen, FIN	Ski Jumping	4-1-0
4	Aleksandr Tikhonov, USSR	Biathlon	4-1-0
4	Nikolai Zimyatov, USSR	Cross Country	4-1-0

No		Sport	G-S-B
4	Thomas Wassberg, SWE	Cross Country	4-0-0

WOMEN

No		Sport	G-S-B
6	Lyubov Egorova, UT/RUS	Cross Country	6-3-0
6	Lydia Skoblikova, USSR	Speed Skating	6-0-0
5	Larissa Lazutina, UT/RUS	Cross Country	5-3-1
5	**Bonnie Blair, USA**	Speed Skating	5-0-1
4	Raisa Smetanina, USSR/UT	Cross Country	4-5-1
4	Galina Kulakova, USSR	Cross Country	4-2-2
4	Claudia Pechstein, GER	ST Sp. Skating	4-1-2
4	Lee-Kyung Chun, S. Kor	ST Sp. Skating	4-0-1

All-Time Leading USA Medalists

MEN

No		Sport	G-S-B
5	Eric Heiden	Speed Skating	5-0-0
3*	Irving Jaffee	Speed Skating	3-0-0
3	Pat Martin	Bobsled	1-2-0
3	John Heaton	Bobsled/Skeleton	0-2-1
2	Dick Button	Figure Skating	2-0-0
2†	Eddie Eagan	Boxing/Bobsled	2-0-0
2	Billy Fiske	Bobsled	2-0-0
2	Cliff Gray	Bobsled	2-0-0
2	Jack Shea	Speed Skating	2-0-0
2	Apolo Anton Ohno	ST Sp. Skating	1-1-0
2	Billy Cleary	Ice Hockey	1-1-0
2	Jennison Heaton	Bobsled/Skeleton	1-1-0
2	David Jenkins	Figure Skating	1-1-0
2	John Mayasich	Ice Hockey	1-1-0

No		Sport	G-S-B
2	Terry McDermott	Speed Skating	1-1-0
2	Dick Meredith	Ice Hockey	1-1-0
2	Tommy Moe	Alpine	1-1-0
2	Weldy Olson	Ice Hockey	1-1-0
2	Derek Parra	Speed Skating	1-1-0
2	Dick Rodenheiser	Ice Hockey	1-1-0
2	Ross Powers	Snowboarding	1-0-1
2	Stan Benham	Bobsled	0-2-0
2	Herb Drury	Ice Hockey	0-2-0
2	Eric Flaim	Sp. Skate/ST Sp. Skate	0-2-0
2	Bode Miller	Alpine	0-2-0
2	Frank Synott	Ice Hockey	0-2-0
2	John Garrison	Ice Hockey	0-1-1

*Jaffee is generally given credit for a third gold medal in the 10,000-meter Speed Skating race of 1928. He had the fastest time before the race was cancelled due to thawing ice. The IOC considers the race unofficial.
†Eagan won the light heavyweight boxing title at the 1920 Summer Games in Antwerp and the four-man Bobsled at the 1932 Winter Games in Lake Placid. He is the only athlete ever to win gold medals in both the Winter and Summer Olympics.

WOMEN

No		Sport	G-S-B	No		Sport	G-S-B
6	Bonnie Blair	Speed Skating	5-0-1	2	Carol Heiss	Figure Skating	1-1-0
4	Cathy Turner	ST Sp. Skating	2-1-1	2	Katie King	Ice Hockey	1-1-0
4	Dianne Holum	Speed Skating	1-2-1	2	Shelley Looney	Ice Hockey	1-1-0
3	Chris Witty	Speed Skating	1-1-1	2	Sue Merz	Ice Hockey	1-1-0
3	Sheila Young	Speed Skating	1-1-1	2	A.J. Mleczko	Ice Hockey	1-1-0
3	Leah Poulos Mueller	Speed Skating	0-3-0	2	Tara Mounsey	Ice Hockey	1-1-0
3	Beatrix Loughran	Figure Skating	0-2-1	2	Diann Roffe-Steinrotter	Alpine	1-1-0
3	Amy Peterson	ST Sp. Skating	0-2-1	2	Angela Ruggiero	Ice Hockey	1-1-0
2	Andrea Mead Lawrence	Alpine	2-0-0	2	Picabo Street	Alpine	1-1-0
2	Tenley Albright	Figure Skating	1-1-0	2	Sarah Teuting	Ice Hockey	1-1-0
2	Chris Bailey	Ice Hockey	1-1-0	2	Anne Henning	Speed Skating	1-0-1
2	Laurie Baker	Ice Hockey	1-1-0	2	Penny Pitou	Alpine	0-2-0
2	Karyn Bye	Ice Hockey	1-1-0	2	Nancy Kerrigan	Figure Skating	0-1-1
2	Sara DeCosta	Ice Hockey	1-1-0	2	Michelle Kwan	Figure Skating	0-1-1
2	Tricia Dunn	Ice Hockey	1-1-0	2	Jean Saubert	Alpine	0-1-1
2	Gretchen Fraser	Alpine	1-1-0	2	Nikki Ziegelmeyer	ST Sp. Skating	0-1-1
2	Cammi Granato	Ice Hockey	1-1-0	2	Jennifer Rodriguez	Speed Skating	0-0-2

Note: The term ST Sp. Skating refers to Short Track (or pack) Speed Skating.

All-Time Medal Standings, 1924-2002

All-time Winter Games medal standings, according to *The Golden Book of the Olympic Games*. Medal counts include figure skating medals (1908 and '20) and hockey medals (1920) awarded at the Summer Games. National medal standings for the Winter and Summer Games are not recognized by the IOC.

		G	S	B	Total			G	S	B	Total
1	Norway	94	94	75	263		Hungary	0	2	4	6
2	Soviet Union (1956-88)	78	57	59	194	25	Czech Republic (1998–)	2	1	2	5
3	**United States**	69	72	52	193		Kazakhstan (1994–)	1	2	2	5
4	Austria	41	57	64	162		Belgium	1	1	3	5
5	Finland	42	51	49	142		Bulgaria	1	1	3	5
6	Germany (1928-36, 52-64, 92–)	47	46	32	125		Belarus (1994–)	0	2	3	5
7	East Germany (1968-88)	43	39	36	118	30	Croatia	3	1	0	4
8	Sweden	39	30	39	108		Spain	3	0	1	4
9	Switzerland	32	33	38	103		Australia	2	0	2	4
10	Canada	31	28	37	96		Yugoslavia (1924-88)	0	3	1	4
11	Italy	31	31	27	89		Slovenia	0	0	4	4
12	France	22	22	28	72	35	Estonia	1	1	1	3
13	Netherlands	22	28	19	69		Ukraine (1994–)	1	1	1	3
14	Russia (1994–)	27	20	11	58		Slovenia (1992–)	0	0	3	3
15	West Germany (1968-88)	18	20	19	57	38	Luxembourg	0	2	0	2
16	Japan	8	10	13	31		North Korea	0	1	1	2
17	Great Britain	8	4	14	26	40	Uzbekistan (1994–)	1	0	0	1
	Czechoslovakia (1924-92)	2	8	16	26		Denmark	0	1	0	1
19	Unified Team (1992)	9	6	8	23		New Zealand	0	1	0	1
20	China	2	12	8	22		Romania	0	0	1	1
21	South Korea	11	5	4	20						
22	Liechtenstein	2	2	5	9						
23	Poland	1	2	3	6						

Combined totals	**G**	**S**	**B**	**Total**
Germany/E. Ger/W. Ger	108	105	87	300
USSR/UT/Russia	114	83	78	275

Notes: Athletes from the USSR participated in the Winter Games from 1956-88, returned as the Unified Team in 1992 after the breakup of the Soviet Union (in 1991) and then competed for the independent republics of Belarus, Kazakhstan, Russia, Ukraine, Uzbekistan and three others in 1994. Yugoslavia divided into Croatia and Bosnia-Herzegovina in 1992, while Czechoslovakia split into Slovakia and the Czech Republic in 1993.

Germany was barred from the Olympics in 1924 and 1948 as an aggressor nation in both World Wars I and II. Divided into East and West Germany after WWII, both countries competed under one flag from 1952-64, then as separate teams from 1968-88. Germany was reunified in 1990.

1896-2000
Through the Years

Information Please®
SPORTS ALMANAC

Modern Olympic Games

The original Olympic Games were celebrated as a religious festival from 776 B.C. until 393 A.D., when Roman emperor Theodosius I banned all pagan festivals (the Olympics celebrated the Greek god Zeus). On June 23, 1894, French educator Baron Pierre de Coubertin, speaking at the Sorbonne in Paris to a gathering of international sports leaders, proposed that the ancient games be revived on an international scale. The idea was enthusiastically received and the Modern Olympics were born. The first Olympics were held two years later in Athens, where 245 athletes from 14 nations competed in the ancient Panathenaic stadium to large and ardent crowds. Americans captured nine out of 12 track and field events, but Greece won the most medals with 47.

The Summer Olympics

Year	No	Location	Dates	Nations	Most medals	USA medals	
1896	I	Athens, GRE	Apr. 6-15	14	Greece (10-19-18—47)	11- 6- 2— 19	(2nd)
1900	II	Paris, FRA	May 20-Oct. 28	26	France (26-37-32—95)	18-14-15— 47	(2nd)
1904	III	St. Louis, USA.	July 1-Nov. 23	13	USA (78-84-82—244)	78-84-82—244	(1st)
1906-a	—	Athens, GRE	Apr. 22-May 2	20	France (15-9-16—40)	12- 6- 6— 24	(3rd)
1908	IV	London, GBR	Apr. 27-Oct. 31	22	Britain (54-46-38—138)	23-12-12— 47	(2nd)
1912	V	Stockholm, SWE	May 5-July 22	28	Sweden (23-24-17—64)	25-18-20— 63	(2nd)
1916	VI	Berlin, GER	Cancelled (WWI)				
1920	VII	Antwerp, BEL	Apr. 20-Sept. 12	29	USA (41-27-27—95)	41-27-27— 95	(1st)
1924	VIII	Paris, FRA	May 4-July 27	44	USA (45-27-27—99)	45-27-27— 99	(1st)
1928	IX	Amsterdam, NED	May 17-Aug. 12	46	USA (22-18-16—56)	22-18-16— 56	(1st)
1932	X	Los Angeles, USA.	July 30-Aug. 14	37	USA (41-32-30—103)	41-32-30—103	(1st)
1936	XI	Berlin, GER	Aug. 1-16	49	Germany (33-26-30—89)	24-20-12— 56	(2nd)
1940-b	XII	Tokyo, JPN	Cancelled (WWII)				
1944	XIII	London, GBR	Cancelled (WWII)				
1948	XIV	London, GBR	July 29-Aug. 14	59	USA (38-27-19—84)	38-27-19— 84	(1st)
1952-cd	XV	Helsinki, FIN	July 19-Aug. 3	69	USA (40-19-17—76)	40-19-17— 76	(1st)
1956-e	XVI	Melbourne, AUS	Nov. 22-Dec. 8	72	USSR (37-29-32—98)	32-25-17— 74	(2nd)
1960	XVII	Rome, ITA	Aug. 25-Sept. 11	83	USSR (43-29-31—103)	34-21-16— 71	(2nd)
1964	XVIII	Tokyo, JPN	Oct. 10-24	93	USSR (30-31-35—96)	36-26-28— 90	(2nd)
1968-f	XIX	Mexico City, MEX	Oct. 12-27	112	USA (45-28-34—107)	45-28-34—107	(1st)
1972	XX	Munich, W. GER	Aug. 26-Sept. 10	121	USSR (50-27-22—99)	33-31-30— 94	(2nd)
1976-g	XXI	Montreal, CAN	July 17-Aug. 1	92	USSR (49-41-35—125)	34-35-25— 94	(3rd)
1980-h	XXII	Moscow, USSR	July 19-Aug. 3	80	USSR (80-69-46—195)	Boycotted games	
1984-i	XXIII	Los Angeles, USA.	July 28-Aug. 12	140	USA (83-61-30—174)	83-61-30—174	(1st)
1988	XXIV	Seoul, S. KOR	Sept. 17-Oct. 2	159	USSR (55-31-46—132)	36-31-27— 94	(3rd)
1992-j	XXV	Barcelona, SPA	July 25-Aug. 9	169	UT (45-38-29—112)	37-34-37—108	(2nd)
1996	XXVI	Atlanta, USA	July 20-Aug. 4	197	USA (44-32-25—101)	44-32-25—101	(1st)
2000	XXVII	Sydney, AUS	Sept. 15-Oct. 1	199	USA (40-24-33—97)	40-24-33— 97	(1st)
2004	XXVIII	Athens, GRE	Aug. 13-29				
2008	XXIX	Beijing, CHN	July 25-Aug. 10				

a—The 1906 Intercalated Games in Athens are considered unofficial by the IOC because they did not take place in the four-year cycle established in 1896. However, most record books include these interim games with the others.

b—The 1940 Summer Games are originally scheduled for Tokyo, but Japan resigns as host after the outbreak of the Sino-Japanese War in 1937. Helsinki is the next choice, but the IOC cancels the Games after Soviet troops invade Finland in 1939.

c—Germany and Japan are allowed to rejoin the Olympic community for the first Summer Games since 1936. Though a divided country, the Germans send a joint East-West team until 1964.

d—The Soviet Union (USSR) participates in its first Olympics, Winter or Summer, since the Russian revolution in 1917 and takes home the second most medals (22-30-19—71).

e—Due to Australian quarantine laws, the equestrian events for the 1956 Games are held in Stockholm, June 10-17.

f—East Germany and West Germany send separate teams for the first time and will continue to do so through 1988.

g—The 1976 Games are boycotted by 32 nations, most of them from black Africa, because the IOC will not ban New Zealand. Earlier that year, a rugby team from New Zealand had toured racially segregated South Africa.

h—The 1980 Games are boycotted by 64 nations, led by the USA, to protest the Soviet invasion of Afghanistan on Dec. 27, 1979.

i—The 1984 Games are boycotted by 14 Eastern Bloc nations, led by the USSR, to protest America's overcommercialization of the Games, inadequate security and an anti-Soviet attitude by the U.S. government. Most believe, however, the communist walkout is simply revenge for 1980.

j—Germany sends a single team after East and West German reunification in 1990 and the USSR competes as the Unified Team after the breakup of the Soviet Union in 1991.

Event-by-Event

Gold medal winners from 1896-2000 in the following events: Baseball, Basketball, Boxing, Diving, Field Hockey, Gymnastics, Soccer, Softball, Swimming, Tennis and Track & Field.

BASEBALL

Multiple gold medals: Cuba (2).

Year		Year	
1992	**Cuba**, Taiwan, Japan	2000	**United States**, Cuba, South Korea
1996	**Cuba**, Japan, United States		

U.S. Medal-Winning Baseball Teams

1996 (bronze medal): P–Kris Benson, R.A. Dickey, Seth Greisinger, Billy Koch, Braden Looper, Jim Parque and Jeff Weaver; C–A.J. Hinch, Matt LeCroy and Brian Lloyd; INF–Troy Glaus, Kip Harkrider, Travis Lee, Warren Morris, Augie Ojeda and Jason Williams; OF–Chad Allen, Chad Green, Jacque Jones and Mark Kotsay; Manager–Skip Bertman. Final: Cuba over Japan, 13-9

2000 (gold medal): P–Kurt Ainsworth, Ryan Franklin, Chris George, Shane Heams, Rick Krivda, Roy Oswalt, Jon Rauch, Bobby Seay, Ben Sheets, Todd Williams and Tim Young; C–Pat Borders, Marcus Jensen and Mike Kinkade; INF–Brent Abernathy, Sean Burroughs, John Cotton, Gookie Dawkins, Adam Everett and Doug Mientkiewicz; OF–Mike Neill, Anthony Sanders, Brad Wilkerson and Ernie Young; Manager–Tommy Lasorda. Final: USA over Cuba, 4-0.

BASKETBALL

MEN

Multiple gold medals: USA (12), USSR (2).

Year		Year	
1936	**United States**, Canada, Mexico	1976	**United States**, Yugoslavia, Soviet Union
1948	**United States**, France, Brazil	1980	**Yugoslavia**, Italy, Soviet Union
1952	**United States**, Soviet Union, Uruguay	1984	**United States**, Spain, Yugoslavia
1956	**United States**, Soviet Union, Uruguay	1988	**Soviet Union**, Yugoslavia, United States
1960	**United States**, Soviet Union, Brazil	1992	**United States**, Croatia, Lithuania
1964	**United States**, Soviet Union, Brazil	1996	**United States**, Yugoslavia, Lithuania
1968	**United States**, Yugoslavia, Soviet Union	2000	**United States**, France, Lithuania
1972	**Soviet Union**, United States, Cuba		

U.S. Medal-Winning Men's Basketball Teams

1936 (gold medal): Sam Balter, Ralph Bishop, Joe Fortenberry, Tex Gibbons, Francis Johnson, Carl Knowles, Frank Lubin, Art Mollner, Don Piper, Jack Ragland, Carl Shy, Willard Schmidt, Duane Swanson and William Wheatley. Coach–Jim Needles; Assistant–Gene Johnson. Final: USA over Canada, 19-8.

1948 (gold medal): Cliff Barker, Don Barksdale, Ralph Beard, Louis Beck, Vince Boryla, Gordon Carpenter, Alex Groza, Wallace Jones, Bob Kurland, Ray Lumpp, R.C. Pitts, Jesse Renick, Robert (Jackie) Robinson and Ken Rollins. Coach–Omar Browning; Assistant–Adolph Rupp. Final: USA over France, 65-21.

1952 (gold medal): Ron Bontemps, Mark Freiberger, Wayne Glasgow, Charlie Hoag, Bill Hougland, John Keller, Dean Kelley, Bob Kenney, Bob Kurland, Bill Lienhard, Clyde Lovellette, Frank McCabe, Dan Pippin and Howie Williams. Coach–Warren Womble; Assistant–Forrest (Phog) Allen. Final: USA over USSR, 36-25.

1956 (gold medal): Dick Boushka, Carl Cain, Chuck Darling, Bill Evans, Gib Ford, Burdy Haldorson, Bill Hougland, Bob Jeangerard, K.C. Jones, Bill Russell, Ron Tomsic and Jim Walsh. Coach–Gerald Tucker; Assistant–Bruce Drake. Final: USA over USSR, 89-55.

1960 (gold medal): Jay Arnette, Walt Bellamy, Bob Boozer, Terry Dischinger, Jerry Lucas, Oscar Robertson, Adrian Smith, Burdy Haldorson, Darrall Imhoff, Allen Kelley, Lester Lane and Jerry West. Coach–Pete Newell; Assistant–Warren Womble. Final round: USA defeated USSR (81-57), Italy (112-81) and Brazil (90-63) in round robin.

1964 (gold medal): Jim (Bad News) Barnes, Bill Bradley, Larry Brown, Joe Caldwell, Mel Counts, Dick Davies, Walt Hazzard, Lucious Jackson, Pete McCaffrey, Jeff Mullins, Jerry Shipp and George Wilson. Coach–Hank Iba; Assistant–Henry Vaughn. Final: USA over USSR, 73-59.

1968 (gold medal): Mike Barrett, John Clawson, Don Dee, Cal Fowler, Spencer Haywood, Bill Hosket, Jim King, Glynn Saulters, Charlie Scott, Mike Silliman, Ken Spain, and Jo Jo White. Coach–Hank Iba; Assistant–Henry Vaughn. Final: USA over Yugoslavia, 65-50.

1972 (silver medal refused): Mike Bantom, Jim Brewer, Tom Burleson, Doug Collins, Kenny Davis, Jim Forbes, Tom Henderson, Bobby Jones, Dwight Jones, Kevin Joyce, Tom McMillen and Ed Ratleff. Coach–Hank Iba; Assistants– John Bach and Don Haskins. Final: USSR over USA, 51-50.

1976 (gold medal): Tate Armstrong, Quinn Buckner, Kenny Carr, Adrian Dantley, Walter Davis, Phil Ford, Ernie Grunfeld, Phil Hubbard, Mitch Kupchak, Tommy LaGarde, Scott May and Steve Sheppard. Coach–Dean Smith; Assistants–Bill Guthridge and John Thompson. Final: USA over Yugoslavia, 95-74.

1980 (no medal): USA boycotted Moscow Games. Final: Yugoslavia over Italy, 86-77.

1984 (gold medal): Steve Alford, Patrick Ewing, Vern Fleming, Michael Jordan, Joe Kleine, Jon Koncak, Chris Mullin, Sam Perkins, Alvin Robertson, Wayman Tisdale, Jeff Turner and Leon Wood. Coach–Bobby Knight; Assistants– Don Donoher and George Raveling. Final: USA over Spain, 96-65.

1988 (bronze medal): Stacey Augmon, Willie Anderson, Bimbo Coles, Jeff Grayer, Hersey Hawkins, Dan Majerle, Danny Manning, Mitch Richmond, J.R. Reid, David Robinson, Charles D. Smith and Charles E. Smith. Coach–John Thompson; Assistants–George Raveling and Mary Fenlon. Final: USSR over Yugoslavia, 76-63.

1992 (gold medal): Charles Barkley, Larry Bird, Clyde Drexler, Patrick Ewing, Magic Johnson, Michael Jordan, Christian Laettner, Karl Malone, Chris Mullin, Scottie Pippen, David Robinson and John Stockton. Coach–Chuck Daly; Assistants–Lenny Wilkens, Mike Krzyzewski and P.J. Carlesimo. Final: USA over Croatia, 117-85.

1996 (gold medal): Charles Barkley, Anfernee Hardaway, Grant Hill, Karl Malone, Reggie Miller, Hakeem Olajuwon, Shaquille O'Neal, Gary Payton, Scottie Pippen, David Robinson and John Stockton. Coach–Lenny Wilkens; Assistants–Bobby Cremins, Clem Haskins and Jerry Sloan. Final: USA over Yugoslavia, 95-69.

2000 (gold medal): Shareef Abdur-Rahim, Ray Allen, Vin Baker, Vince Carter, Kevin Garnett, Tim Hardaway, Allan Houston, Jason Kidd, Antonio McDyess, Alonzo Mourning, Gary Payton and Steve Smith. Coach–Rudy Tomjanovich; Assistants–Larry Brown, Gene Keady and Tubby Smith. Final: USA over France, 85-75.

WOMEN

Multiple gold medals: USA (4), USSR/UT (3).

Year		Year	
1976	**Soviet Union**, United States, Bulgaria	1992	**Unified Team**, China, United States
1980	**Soviet Union**, Bulgaria, Yugoslavia	1996	**United States**, Brazil, Australia
1984	**United States**, South Korea, China	2000	**United States**, Australia, Brazil
1988	**United States**, Yugoslavia, Soviet Union		

U.S. Gold Medal-Winning Women's Basketball Teams

1984 (gold medal): Cathy Boswell, Denise Curry, Anne Donovan, Teresa Edwards, Lea Henry, Janice Lawrence, Pamela McGee, Carol Menken-Schaudt, Cheryl Miller, Kim Mulkey, Cindy Noble and Lynette Woodard. Coach–Pat Summitt; Assistant–Kay Yow. Final: USA over South Korea, 85-55.

1988 (gold medal): Cindy Brown, Vicky Bullett, Cynthia Cooper, Anne Donovan, Teresa Edwards, Kamie Ethridge, Jennifer Gillom, Bridgette Gordon, Andrea Lloyd, Katrina McClain, Suzie McConnell and Teresa Weatherspoon. Coach–Kay Yow; Assistants–Sylvia Hatchell and Susan Yow. Final: USA over Yugoslavia, 77-70.

1996 (gold medal): Jennifer Azzi, Ruthie Bolton, Teresa Edwards, Venus Lacy, Lisa Leslie, Rebecca Lobo, Katrina McClain, Nikki McCray, Carla McGee, Dawn Staley, Katy Steding and Sheryl Swoopes. Coach—Tara VanDerveer; Assistants–Ceal Barry, Nancy Darsch and Marian Washington. Final: USA over Brazil, 111-87.

2000 (gold medal): Ruthie Bolton-Holyfield, Teresa Edwards, Yolanda Griffith, Chamique Holdsclaw, Lisa Leslie, Nikki McCray, Delisha Milton, Katie Smith, Dawn Staley, Sheryl Swoopes, Natalie Williams and Kara Wolters. Coach—Nell Fortner; Assistants–Geno Auriemma and Peggie Gillom. Final: USA over Australia, 76-54.

BOXING

Multiple gold medals: László Papp, Felix Savon and Teófilo Stevenson (3); Ariel Hernandez, Angel Herrera, Oliver Kirk, Jerzy Kulej, Boris Lagutin, Harry Mallin, Oleg Saitov and Hector Vinent (2). All fighters won titles in consecutive Olympics, except Kirk, who won both the bantamweight and featherweight titles in 1904 (he only had to fight once in each division).

Light Flyweight (106 lbs)

Year		Final Match	Year		Final Match
1968	Francisco Rodriguez, VEN	Decision, 3-2	1988	Ivailo Hristov, BUL	Decision, 5-0
1972	György Gedó, HUN	Decision, 5-0	1992	Rogelio Marcelo, CUB	Decision, 24-10
1976	Jorge Hernandez, CUB	Decision, 4-1	1996	Daniel Petrov Bojilov, BUL	Decision, 19-6
1980	Shamil Sabyrov, USSR	Decision, 3-2	2000	Brahim Asloum, FRA	Decision, 23-10
1984	Paul Gonzales, USA	Default			

Flyweight (112 lbs)

Year		Final Match	Year		Final Match
1904	George Finnegan, USA	Stopped, 1st	1964	Fernando Atzori, ITA	Decision, 4-1
1920	Frank Di Gennara, USA	Decision	1968	Ricardo Delgado, MEX	Decision, 5-0
1924	Fidel LaBarba, USA	Decision	1972	Georgi Kostadinov, BUL	Decision, 5-0
1928	Antal Kocsis, HUN	Decision	1976	Leo Randolph, USA	Decision, 3-2
1932	István Énekes, HUN	Decision	1980	Peter Lessov, BUL	Stopped, 2nd
1936	Willi Kaiser, GER	Decision	1984	Steve McCrory, USA	Decision, 4-1
1948	Pascual Perez, ARG	Decision	1988	Kim Kwang-Sun, S. Kor	Decision, 4-1
1952	Nate Brooks, USA	Decision, 3-0	1992	Su Choi-Chol, N. Kor	Decision, 12-2
1956	Terence Spinks, GBR	Decision	1996	Maikro Romero, CUB	Decision, 12-11
1960	Gyula Török, HUN	Decision, 3-2	2000	Wijan Ponlid, THA	Decision, 19-12

Bantamweight (119 lbs)

Year		Final Match	Year		Final Match
1904	Oliver Kirk, USA	Stopped, 3rd	1964	Takao Sakurai, JPN	Stopped, 2nd
1908	Henry Thomas, GBR	Decision	1968	Valery Sokolov, USSR	Stopped, 2nd
1920	Clarence Walker, RSA	Decision	1972	Orlando Martinez, CUB	Decision, 5-0
1924	William Smith, RSA	Decision	1976	Gu Yong-Ju, N. Kor	Decision, 5-0
1928	Vittorio Tamagnini, ITA	Decision	1980	Juan Hernandez, CUB	Decision, 5-0
1932	Horace Gwynne, CAN	Decision	1984	Maurizio Stecca, ITA	Decision, 4-1
1936	Ulderico Sergo, ITA	Decision	1988	Kennedy McKinney, USA	Decision, 5-0
1948	Tibor Csik, HUN	Decision	1992	Joel Casamayor, CUB	Decision, 14-8
1952	Pentti Hämäläinen, FIN	Decision, 2-1	1996	Istvan Kovacs, HUN	Decision, 14-7
1956	Wolfgang Behrendt, GER	Decision	2000	Guillermo Rigondeaux, CUB	Decision, 18-12
1960	Oleg Grigoryev, USSR	Decision			

Featherweight (125 lbs)

Year		Final Match	Year		Final Match
1904	Oliver Kirk, USA	Decision	1964	Stanislav Stepashkin, USSR	Decision, 3-2
1908	Richard Gunn, GBR	Decision	1968	Antonio Roldan, MEX	Won on Disq.
1920	Paul Fritsch, FRA	Decision	1972	Boris Kousnetsov, USSR	Decision, 3-2
1924	John Fields, USA	Decision	1976	Angel Herrera, CUB	KO, 2nd
1928	Lambertus van Klaveren, NED	Decision	1980	Rudi Fink, E. Ger	Decision, 4-1
1932	Carmelo Robledo, ARG	Decision	1984	Meldrick Taylor, USA	Decision, 5-0
1936	Oscar Casanovas, ARG	Decision	1988	Giovanni Parisi, ITA	Stopped, 1st
1948	Ernesto Formenti, ITA	Decision	1992	Andreas Tews, GER	Decision, 16-7
1952	Jan Zachara, CZE	Decision, 2-1	1996	Somluck Kamsing, THA	Decision, 8-5
1956	Vladimir Safronov, USSR	Decision	2000	Bekzat Sattarkhanov, KAZ	Decision, 22-14
1960	Francesco Musso, ITA	Decision, 4-1			

Boxing (Cont.)

Lightweight (132 lbs)

Year		Final Match	Year		Final Match
1904	Harry Spanger, USA	Decision	1964	József Grudzien, POL	Decision
1908	Frederick Grace, GBR	Decision	1968	Ronnie Harris, USA	Decision, 5-0
1920	Samuel Mosberg, USA	Decision	1972	Jan Szczepanski, POL	Decision, 5-0
1924	Hans Nielsen, DEN	Decision	1976	Howard Davis, USA	Decision, 5-0
1928	Carlo Orlandi, ITA	Decision	1980	Angel Herrera, CUB	Stopped, 3rd
1932	Lawrence Stevens, S. Afr	Decision	1984	Pernell Whitaker, USA	Foe quit, 2nd
1936	Imre Harangi, HUN	Decision	1988	Andreas Zuelow, E. Ger	Decision, 5-0
1948	Gerald Dreyer, S. Afr	Decision	1992	Oscar De La Hoya, USA	Decision, 7-2
1952	Aureliano Bolognesi, ITA	Decision, 2-1	1996	Hocine Soltani, ALG	Tiebreak, 3-3
1956	Richard McTaggart, GBR	Decision	2000	Mario Kindelan, CUB	Decision, 14-4
1960	Kazimierz Pazdzior, POL	Decision, 4-1			

Light Welterweight (139 lbs)

Year		Final Match	Year		Final Match
1952	Charles Adkins, USA	Decision, 2-1	1980	Patrizio Oliva, ITA	Decision, 4-1
1956	Vladimir Yengibaryan, USSR	Decision	1984	Jerry Page, USA	Decision, 5-0
1960	Bohumil Nemecek, CZE	Decision, 5-0	1988	Vyacheslav Yanovsky, USSR	Decision, 5-0
1964	Jerzy Kulej, POL	Decision, 5-0	1992	Hector Vinent, CUB	Decision, 11-1
1968	Jerzy Kulej, POL	Decision, 3-2	1996	Hector Vinent, CUB	Decision, 20-13
1972	Ray Seales, USA	Decision, 3-2	2000	Mahamadkadyz Abdullaev, UZB	Decision, 27-20
1976	Ray Leonard, USA	Decision, 5-0			

Welterweight (147 lbs)

Year		Final Match	Year		Final Match
1904	Albert Young, USA	Decision	1964	Marian Kasprzyk, POL	Decision, 4-1
1920	Bert Schneider, CAN	Decision	1968	Manfred Wolke, E. Ger	Decision, 4-1
1924	Jean Delarge, BEL	Decision	1972	Emilio Correa, CUB	Decision, 5-0
1928	Edward Morgan, NZE	Decision	1976	Jochen Bachfeld, E. Ger	Decision, 3-2
1932	Edward Flynn, USA	Decision	1980	Andrés Aldama, CUB	Decision, 4-1
1936	Sten Suvio, FIN	Decision	1984	Mark Breland, USA	Decision, 5-0
1948	Julius Torma, CZE	Decision	1988	Robert Wangila, KEN	KO, 2nd
1952	Zygmunt Chychla, POL	Decision, 3-0	1992	Michael Carruth, IRE	Decision, 13-10
1956	Nicolae Linca, ROM	Decision, 3-2	1996	Oleg Saitov, RUS	Decision, 14-9
1960	Nino Benvenuti, ITA	Decision, 4-1	2000	Oleg Saitov, RUS	Decision, 24-16

Light Middleweight (156 lbs)

Year		Final Match	Year		Final Match
1952	László Papp, HUN	Decision, 3-0	1980	Armando Martinez, CUB	Decision, 4-1
1956	László Papp, HUN	Decision	1984	Frank Tate, USA	Decision, 5-0
1960	Skeeter McClure, USA	Decision, 4-1	1988	Park Si-Hun, S. Kor	Decision, 3-2
1964	Boris Lagutin, USSR	Decision, 4-1	1992	Juan Lemus, CUB	Decision, 6-1
1968	Boris Lagutin, USSR	Decision, 5-0	1996	David Reid, USA	KO, 3rd
1972	Dieter Kottysch, W. Ger	Decision, 3-2	2000	Yermakhan Ibraimov, KAZ	Decision, 25-23
1976	Jerzy Rybicki, POL	Decision, 5-0			

Middleweight (165 lbs)

Year		Final Match	Year		Final Match
1904	Charles Mayer, USA	Stopped, 3rd	1964	Valery Popenchenko, USSR	Stopped, 1st
1908	John Douglas, GBR	Decision	1968	Christopher Finnegan, GBR	Decision, 3-2
1920	Harry Mallin, GBR	Decision	1972	Vyacheslav Lemechev, USSR	KO, 1st
1924	Harry Mallin, GBR	Decision	1976	Michael Spinks, USA	Stopped, 3rd
1928	Piero Toscani, ITA	Decision	1980	José Gomez, CUB	Decision, 4-1
1932	Carmen Barth, USA	Decision	1984	Shin Joon-Sup, S. Kor	Decision, 3-2
1936	Jean Despeaux, FRA	Decision	1988	Henry Maske, E. Ger	Decision, 5-0
1948	László Papp, HUN	Decision	1992	Ariel Hernandez, CUB	Decision, 12-7
1952	Floyd Patterson, USA	KO, 1st	1996	Ariel Hernandez, CUB	Decision, 11-3
1956	Gennady Schatkov, USSR	KO, 1st	2000	Jorge Gutierrez, CUB	Decision, 17-15
1960	Eddie Crook, USA	Decision, 3-2			

Light Heavyweight (178 lbs)

Year		Final Match	Year		Final Match
1920	Eddie Eagan, USA	Decision	1968	Dan Poznjak, USSR	Default
1924	Harry Mitchell, GBR	Decision	1972	Mate Parlov, YUG	Stopped, 2nd
1928	Victor Avendaño, ARG	Decision	1976	Leon Spinks, USA	Stopped, 3rd
1932	David Carstens, S. Afr.	Decision	1980	Slobodan Kacar, YUG	Decision, 4-1
1936	Roger Michelot, FRA	Decision	1984	Anton Josipovic, YUG	Default
1948	George Hunter, S. Afr	Decision	1988	Andrew Maynard, USA	Decision, 5-0
1952	Norvel Lee, USA	Decision, 3-0	1992	Torsten May, GER	Decision, 8-3
1956	Jim Boyd, USA	Decision	1996	Vasilii Jirov, KAZ	Decision, 17-4
1960	Cassius Clay, USA	Decision, 5-0	2000	Alexander Lebziak, RUS	Decision, 20-6
1964	Cosimo Pinto, ITA	Decision, 3-2			

Note: Cassius Clay changed his name to Muhammad Ali after winning the world heavyweight championship in 1964.

Heavyweight (201 lbs)

Year		Final Match	Year		Final Match
1984	Henry Tillman, USA	Decision, 5-0	1996	Felix Savon, CUB	Decision, 20-2
1988	Ray Mercer, USA	KO, 1st	2000	Felix Savon, CUB	Decision, 21-13
1992	Felix Savon, CUB	Decision, 14-1			

Super Heavyweight (Unlimited)

Year		Final Match	Year		Final Match
1904	Samuel Berger, USA	Decision	1964	Joe Frazier, USA	Decision, 3-2
1908	Albert Oldham, GBR	KO, 1st	1968	George Foreman, USA	Stopped, 2nd
1920	Ronald Rawson, GBR	Decision	1972	Teófilo Stevenson, CUB	Default
1924	Otto von Porat, NOR	Decision	1976	Teófilo Stevenson, CUB	KO, 3rd
1928	Arturo Rodriguez Jurado, ARG	Stopped, 1st	1980	Teófilo Stevenson, CUB	Decision, 4-1
1932	Santiago Lovell, ARG	Decision	1984	Tyrell Biggs, USA	Decision, 4-1
1936	Herbert Runge, GER	Decision	1988	Lennox Lewis, CAN	Stopped, 2nd
1948	Rafael Iglesias, ARG	KO, 2nd	1992	Roberto Balado, CUB	Decision, 13-2
1952	Ed Sanders, USA	Won on Disq.*	1996	Vladimir Klichko, UKR	Decision, 7-3
1956	Rademacher, USA	Stopped, 1st	2000	Audley Harrison, GBR	Decision, 30-16
1960	Franco De Piccoli, ITA	KO, 1st			

*Sanders' opponent, Ingemar Johansson, was disqualified in 2nd round for not trying.
Note: Called heavyweight through 1980.

DIVING

MEN

Multiple gold medals: Greg Louganis (4); Klaus Dibiasi (3); Pete Desjardins, Sammy Lee, Xiong Ni, Bob Webster and Albert White (2).

Springboard

Year		Points	Year		Points
1908	Albert Zürner, GER	85.5	1964	Ken Sitzberger, USA	159.90
1912	Paul Günther, GER	79.23	1968	Bernie Wrightson, USA	170.15
1920	Louis Kuehn, USA	675.4	1972	Vladimir Vasin, USSR	594.09
1924	Albert White, USA	696.4	1976	Phil Boggs, USA	619.05
1928	Pete Desjardins, USA	185.04	1980	Aleksandr Portnov, USSR	905.03
1932	Michael Galitzen, USA	161.38	1984	Greg Louganis, USA	754.41
1936	Richard Degener, USA	163.57	1988	Greg Louganis, USA	730.80
1948	Bruce Harlan, USA	163.64	1992	Mark Lenzi, USA	676.53
1952	David Browning, USA	205.29	1996	Xiong Ni, CHN	701.46
1956	Bob Clotworthy, USA	159.56	2000	Xiong Ni, CHN	708.72
1960	Gary Tobian, USA	170.00			

Platform

Year		Points	Year		Points
1904	George Sheldon, USA	12.66	1960	Bob Webster, USA	165.56
1906	Gottlob Walz, GER	156.0	1964	Bob Webster, USA	148.58
1908	Hjalmar Johansson, SWE	83.75	1968	Klaus Dibiasi, ITA	164.18
1912	Erik Adlerz, SWE	73.94	1972	Klaus Dibiasi, ITA	504.12
1920	Clarence Pinkston, USA	100.67	1976	Klaus Dibiasi, ITA	600.51
1924	Albert White, USA	97.46	1980	Falk Hoffmann, E. Ger	835.65
1928	Pete Desjardins, USA	98.74	1984	Greg Louganis, USA	710.91
1932	Harold Smith, USA	124.80	1988	Greg Louganis, USA	638.61
1936	Marshall Wayne, USA	113.58	1992	Sun Shuwei, CHN	677.31
1948	Sammy Lee, USA	130.05	1996	Dmitri Sautin, RUS	692.34
1952	Sammy Lee, USA	156.28	2000	Tian Liang, CHN	724.53
1956	Joaquin Capilla, MEX	152.44			

WOMEN

Multiple gold medals: Pat McCormick and Fu Mingxia (4); Ingrid Engel-Krämer (3); Vicki Draves, Dorothy Poynton Hill and Gao Min (2).

Springboard

Year		Points	Year		Points
1920	Aileen Riggin, USA	539.9	1968	Sue Gossick, USA	150.77
1924	Elizabeth Becker, USA	474.5	1972	Micki King, USA	450.03
1928	Helen Meany, USA	78.62	1976	Jennifer Chandler, USA	506.19
1932	Georgia Coleman, USA	87.52	1980	Irina Kalinina, USSR	725.91
1936	Marjorie Gestring, USA	89.27	1984	Sylvie Bernier, CAN	530.70
1948	Vicki Draves, USA	108.74	1988	Gao Min, CHN	580.23
1952	Pat McCormick, USA	147.30	1992	Gao Min, CHN	572.40
1956	Pat McCormick, USA	142.36	1996	Fu Mingxia, CHN	547.68
1960	Ingrid Krämer, GER	155.81	2000	Fu Mingxia, CHN	609.42
1964	Ingrid Engel-Kräamer, GER	145.00			

DIVING (Cont.)
Platform

Year		Points	Year		Points
1912	Greta Johansson, SWE	39.9	1964	Lesley Bush, USA	99.80
1920	Stefani Fryland-Clausen, DEN	34.6	1968	Milena Duchková, CZE	109.59
1924	Caroline Smith, USA	33.2	1972	Ulrika Knape, SWE	390.00
1928	Elizabeth Becker Pinkston, USA	31.6	1976	Elena Vaytsekhovskaya, USSR	406.59
1932	Dorothy Poynton, USA	40.26	1980	Martina Jäschke, E. Ger	596.25
1936	Dorothy Poynton Hill, USA	33.93	1984	Zhou Jihong, CHN	435.51
1948	Vicki Draves, USA	68.87	1988	Xu Yanmei, CHN	445.20
1952	Pat McCormick, USA	79.37	1992	Fu Mingxia, CHN	461.43
1956	Pat McCormick, USA	84.85	1996	Fu Mingxia, CHN	521.58
1960	Ingrid Krämer, GER	91.28	2000	Laura Wilkinson, USA	543.75

FIELD HOCKEY

MEN

Multiple gold medals: India (8); Great Britain and Pakistan (3); West Germany/Germany and Netherlands (2).

Year		Year	
1908	**Great Britain**, Ireland, Scotland	1968	**Pakistan**, Australia, India
1920	**Great Britain**, Denmark, Belgium	1972	**West Germany**, Pakistan, India
1928	**India**, Netherlands, Germany	1976	**New Zealand**, Australia, Pakistan
1932	**India**, Japan, United States	1980	**India**, Spain, Soviet Union
1936	**India**, Germany, Netherlands	1984	**Pakistan**, West Germany, Great Britain
1948	**India**, Great Britain, Netherlands	1988	**Great Britain**, West Germany, Netherlands
1952	**India**, Netherlands, Great Britain	1992	**Germany**, Australia, Pakistan
1956	**India**, Pakistan, Germany	1996	**Netherlands**, Spain, Australia
1960	**Pakistan**, India, Spain	2000	**Netherlands**, South Korea, Australia
1964	**India**, Pakistan, Australia		

WOMEN

Multiple gold medals: Australia (3).

Year		Year	
1980	**Zimbabwe**, Czechoslovakia, Soviet Union	1992	**Spain**, Germany, Great Britain
1984	**Netherlands**, West Germany, United States	1996	**Australia**, South Korea, Netherlands
1988	**Australia**, South Korea, Netherlands	2000	**Australia**, Argentina, Netherlands

GYMNASTICS

MEN

At least 4 gold medals (including team events): Sawao Kato (8); Nikolai Andrianov, Viktor Chukarin and Boris Shakhlin (7); Akinori Nakayama and Vitaly Scherbo (6); Yukio Endo, Anton Heida, Mitsuo Tsukahara and Takashi Ono (5); Vladimir Artemov, Georges Miez, Valentin Muratov and Alexei Nemov (4).

All-Around

Year		Points	Year		Points
1900	Gustave Sandras, FRA	.302	1956	Viktor Chukarin, USSR	.114.25
1904	Julius Lenhart, AUT	69.80	1960	Boris Shakhlin, USSR	.115.95
1906	Pierre Payssé, FRA	97.0	1964	Yukio Endo, JPN	.115.95
1908	Alberto Braglia, ITA	.317.0	1968	Sawao Kato, JPN	.115.9
1912	Alberto Braglia, ITA	.135.0	1972	Sawao Kato, JPN	.114.650
1920	Giorgio Zampori, ITA	88.35	1976	Nikolai Andrianov, USSR	.116.65
1924	Leon Stukelj, YUG	.110.340	1980	Aleksandr Dityatin, USSR	.118.65
1928	Georges Miez, SWI	.247.500	1984	Koji Gushiken, JPN	.118.7
1932	Romeo Neri, ITA	.140.625	1988	Vladimir Artemov, USSR	.119.125
1936	Alfred Schwarzmann, GER	.113.100	1992	Vitaly Scherbo, UT	59.025
1948	Veikko Huhtanen, FIN	.229.7	1996	Li Xiaosahuang, CHN	58.423
1952	Viktor Chukarin, USSR	.115.7	2000	Alexei Nemov, RUS	58.474

Horizontal Bar

Year		Points	Year		Points
1896	Hermann Weingärtner, GER	–	1968	(TIE) Akinori Nakayama, JPN	.19.55
1904	(TIE) Anton Heida, USA	.40		& Mikhail Voronin, USSR	.19.55
	& Edward Hennig, USA	.40	1972	Mitsuo Tsukahara, JPN	.19.725
1924	Leon Stukelj, YUG	.19.73	1976	Mitsuo Tsukahara, JPN	.19.675
1928	Georges Miez, SWI	.19.17	1980	Stoyan Deltchev, BUL	.19.825
1932	Dallas Bixler, USA	.18.33	1984	Shinji Morisue, JPN	.20.00
1936	Aleksanteri Saarvala, FIN	.19.367	1988	(TIE) Vladimir Artemov, USSR	.19.900
1948	Josef Stalder, SWI	.19.85		& Valeri Lyukin, USSR	.19.900
1952	Jack Günthard, SWI	.19.55	1992	Trent Dimas, USA	9.875
1956	Takashi Ono, JPN	.19.60	1996	Andreas Wecker, GER	9.850
1960	Takashi Ono, JPN	.19.60	2000	Alexei Nemov, RUS	9.787
1964	Boris Shakhlin, USSR	.19.625			

Parallel Bars

Year		Points	Year		Points
1896	Alfred Flatow, GER	–	1964	Yukio Endo, JPN	19.675
1904	George Eyser, USA	.44	1968	Akinori Nakayama, JPN	19.475
1924	August Güttinger, SWI	21.63	1972	Sawao Kato, JPN	19.475
1928	Ladislav Vácha, CZE	18.83	1976	Sawao Kato, JPN	19.675
1932	Romeo Neri, ITA	18.97	1980	Aleksandr Tkachyov, USSR	19.775
1936	Konrad Frey, GER	19.067	1984	Bart Conner, USA	19.95
1948	Michael Reusch, SWI	19.75	1988	Vladimir Artemov, USSR	19.925
1952	Hans Eugster, SWI	19.65	1992	Vitaly Scherbo, UT	9.900
1956	Viktor Chukarin, USSR	19.20	1996	Rustam Sharipov, UKR	9.837
1960	Boris Shakhlin, USSR	19.40	2000	Li Xiaopeng, CHN	9.825

Vault

Year		Points	Year		Points
1896	Karl Schumann, GER	–	1964	Haruhiro Yamashita, JPN	19.60
1904	(TIE) George Eyser, USA	.36	1968	Mikhail Voronin, USSR	19.00
	& Anton Heida, USA	.36	1972	Klaus Köste, E. Ger	18.85
1924	Frank Kriz, USA	9.98	1976	Nikolai Andrianov, USSR	19.45
1928	Eugen Mack, SWI	9.58	1980	Nikolai Andrianov, USSR	19.825
1932	Savino Guglielmetti, ITA	18.03	1984	Lou Yun, CHN	19.95
1936	Alfred Schwarzmann, GER	19.20	1988	Lou Yun, CHN	19.875
1948	Paavo Aaltonen, FIN	19.55	1992	Vitaly Scherbo, UT	9.856
1952	Viktor Chukarin, USSR	19.20	1996	Alexei Nemov, RUS	9.787
1956	(TIE) Helmut Bantz, GER	18.85	2000	Gervasio Deferr, SPA	9.712
	& Valentin Muratov, USSR	18.85			
1960	(TIE) Takashi Ono, JPN	19.35			
	& Boris Shakhlin, USSR	19.35			

Pommel Horse

Year		Points	Year		Points
1896	Louis Zutter, SWI	–	1968	Miroslav Cerar, YUG	19.325
1904	Anton Heida, USA	.42	1972	Viktor Klimenko, SOV	19.125
1924	Josef Wilhelm, SWI	21.23	1976	Zoltán Magyar, HUN	19.70
1928	Hermann Hänggi, SWI	19.75	1980	Zoltán Magyar, HUN	19.925
1932	Istvän Pelle, HUN	19.07	1984	(TIE) Li Ning, CHN	19.95
1936	Konrad Frey, GER	19.333		& Peter Vidmar, USA	19.95
1948	(TIE) Paavo Aaltonen, FIN	19.35	1988	(TIE) Dmitri Bilozerchev, USSR,	19.95
	Veikko Huhtanen, FIN	19.35		Zsolt Borkai, HUN	19.95
	& Heikki Savolainen, FIN	19.35		& Lyubomir Geraskov, BUL	19.95
1952	Viktor Chukarin, USSR	19.50	1992	(TIE) Pae Gil-Su, N. Kor	9.925
1956	Boris Shakhlin, USSR	19.25		& Vitaly Scherbo, UT	9.925
1960	(TIE) Eugen Ekman, FIN	19.375	1996	Li Donghua, SWI	9.875
	& Boris Shakhlin, USSR	19.375	2000	Marius Urzica, ROM	9.862
1964	Miroslav Cerar, YUG	19.525			

Rings

Year		Points	Year		Points
1896	Ioannis Mitropoulos, GRE	–	1968	Akinori Nakayama, JPN	19.45
1904	Hermann Glass, USA	.45	1972	Akinori Nakayama, JPN	19.35
1924	Francesco Martino, ITA	21.553	1976	Nikolai Andrianov, USSR	19.65
1928	Leon Stukelj, YUG	19.25	1980	Aleksandr Dityatin, USSR	19.875
1932	George Gulack, USA	18.97	1984	(TIE) Koji Gushiken, JPN	19.85
1936	Alois Hudec, CZE	19.433		& Li Ning, CHN	19.85
1948	Karl Frei, SWI	19.80	1988	(TIE) Holger Behrendt, E. Ger	19.925
1952	Grant Shaginyan, USSR	19.75		& Dmitri Bilozerchev, USSR	19.925
1956	Albert Azaryan, USSR	19.35	1992	Vitaly Scherbo, UT	9.937
1960	Albert Azaryan, USSR	19.725	1996	Yuri Chechi, ITA	9.887
1964	Takuji Haytta, JPN	19.475	2000	Szilveszter Csollany, HUN	9.850

Floor Exercise

Year		Points	Year		Points
1932	Istvan Pelle, HUN	9.60	1972	Nikolai Andrianov, USSR	19.175
1936	Georges Miez, SWI	18.666	1976	Nikolai Andrianov, USSR	19.45
1948	Ferenc Pataki, HUN	19.35	1980	Roland Brückner, E. Ger	19.75
1952	William Thoresson, SWE	19.25	1984	Li Ning, CHN	19.925
1956	Valentin Muratov, USSR	19.20	1988	Sergei Kharkov, USSR	19.925
1960	Nobuyuki Aihara, JPN	19.45	1992	Li Xiaosahuang, CHN	9.925
1964	Franco Menichelli, ITA	19.45	1996	Ioannis Melissanidis, GRE	9.850
1968	Sawao Kato, JPN	19.475	2000	Igors Vihrovs, LAT	9.812

Gymnastics (Cont.)
Team Combined Exercises

Year	Points	Year	Points
1904 United States	374.43	1960 Japan	575.20
1906 Norway	19.00	1964 Japan	577.95
1908 Sweden	438	1968 Japan	575.90
1912 Italy	265.75	1972 Japan	571.25
1920 Italy	359.855	1976 Japan	576.85
1924 Italy	839.058	1980 Soviet Union	598.60
1928 Switzerland	1718.625	1984 United States	591.40
1932 Italy	541.850	1988 Soviet Union	593.35
1936 Germany	657.430	1992 Unified Team	585.45
1948 Finland	1358.30	1996 Russia	576.778
1952 Soviet Union	574.40	2000 China	231.919
1956 Soviet Union	568.25		

WOMEN

At least 4 gold medals (including team events): Larissa Latynina (9); Vera Cáslavská (7); Polina Astakhova, Nadia Comaneci, Agnes Keleti and Nelli Kim (5); Olga Korbut, Ecaterina Szabó and Lyudmila Tourischeva (4).

All-Around

Year	Points	Year	Points
1952 Maria Gorokhovskaya, USSR	76.78	1980 Yelena Davydova, USSR	79.15
1956 Larissa Latynina, USSR	74.933	1984 Mary Lou Retton, USA	79.175
1960 Larissa Latynina, USSR	77.031	1988 Yelena Shushunova, USSR	79.662
1964 Vera Cáslavská, CZE	77.564	1992 Tatiana Gutsu, UT	39.737
1968 Vera Cáslavská, CZE	78.25	1996 Lilia Podkopayeva, UKR	39.255
1972 Lyudmila Tourischeva, USSR	77.025	2000 Simona Amanar, ROM*	38.642
1976 Nadia Comaneci, ROM	79.275		

*Amanar finished second to Andreea Raducan, Romania, who was disqualified for testing positive for pseudo-ephedrine, a drug banned by the IOC and found in Nurofen—an over-the-counter medicine she purportedly took to treat a cold.

Vault

Year	Points	Year	Points
1952 Yekaterina Kalinchuk, USSR	19.20	1980 Natalia Shaposhnikova, USSR	19.725
1956 Larissa Latynina, USSR	18.833	1984 Ecaterina Szabó, ROM	19.875
1960 Margarita Nikolayeva, USSR	19.316	1988 Svetlana Boginskaya, USSR	19.905
1964 Vera Cáslavská, CZE	19.483	1992 (TIE) Henrietta Onodi, HUN	9.925
1968 Vera Cáslavská, CZE	19.775	& Lavinia Milosovici, ROM	9.925
1972 Karin Janz, E. Ger	19.525	1996 Simona Amanar, ROM	9.775
1976 Nelli Kim, USSR	19.80	2000 Elena Zamolodtchikova, RUS	9.731

Uneven Bars

Year	Points	Year	Points
1952 Margit Korondi, HUN	19.40	1980 Maxi Gnauck, E. Ger	19.875
1956 Agnes Keleti, HUN	18.966	1984 (TIE) Julianne McNamora, USA	19.95
1960 Polina Astakhova, USSR	19.616	& Ma Yanhong, CHN	19.95
1964 Polina Astakhova, USSR	19.332	1988 Daniela Silivas, ROM	20.00
1968 Vera Cáslavská, CZE	19.65	1992 Lu Li, CHN	10.00
1972 Karin Janz, E. Ger	19.675	1996 Svetlana Khorkina, RUS	9.850
1976 Nadia Comaneci, ROM	20.00	2000 Svetlana Khorkina, RUS	9.862

Balance Beam

Year	Points	Year	Points
1952 Nina Bocharova, USSR	19.22	1980 Nadia Comaneci, ROM	19.80
1956 Agnes Keleti, HUN	18.80	1984 (TIE) Simona Pauca, ROM	19.80
1960 Eva Bosakova, CZE	19.283	& Ecaterina Szabó, ROM	19.80
1964 Vera Cáslavská, CZE	19.449	1988 Daniela Silivas, ROM	19.924
1968 Natalya Kuchinskaya, USSR	19.65	1992 Tatiana Lyssenko, UT	9.975
1972 Olga Korbut, USSR	19.40	1996 Shannon Miller, USA	9.862
1976 Nadia Comaneci, ROM	19.95	2000 Liu Xuan, CHN	9.825

Floor Exercise

Year	Points	Year	Points
1952 Agnes Keleti, HUN	19.36	1976 Nelli Kim, USSR	19.85
1956 (TIE) Agnes Keleti, HUN	18.733	1980 (TIE) Nadia Comaneci, ROM	19.875
& Larissa Latynina, USSR	18.733	& Nelli Kim, USSR	19.875
1960 Larissa Latynina, USSR	19.583	1984 Ecaterina Szabó, ROM	19.975
1964 Larissa Latynina, USSR	19.599	1988 Daniela Silivas, ROM	19.937
1968 (TIE) Vera Cáslavská, CZE	19.675	1992 Lavinia Milosovici, ROM	10.000
& Larissa Petrik, USSR	19.675	1996 Lilia Podkopayeva, UKR	9.887
1972 Olga Korbut, USSR	19.575	2000 Elena Zamolodtchikova, RUS	9.850

Team Combined Exercises

Year		Points	Year		Points
1928	Netherlands	316.75	1972	Soviet Union	380.50
1936	Germany	506.50	1976	Soviet Union	466.00
1948	Czechoslovakia	445.45	1980	Soviet Union	394.90
1952	Soviet Union	527.03	1984	Romania	392.02
1956	Soviet Union	444.800	1988	Soviet Union	395.475
1960	Soviet Union	382.320	1992	Unified Team	395.666
1964	Soviet Union	280.890	1996	United States	389.225
1968	Soviet Union	382.85	2000	Romania	154.608

SOCCER

MEN

Multiple gold medals: Great Britain and Hungary (3); Uruguay and USSR (2).

Year		Year	
1900	**Great Britain**, France, Belgium	1960	**Yugoslavia**, Denmark, Hungary
1904	**Canada**, USA I, USA II	1964	**Hungary**, Czechoslovakia, Germany
1906	**Denmark**, Smyrna (Int'l entry), Greece	1968	**Hungary**, Bulgaria, Japan
1908	**Great Britain**, Denmark, Netherlands	1972	**Poland**, Hungary, East Germany & Soviet Union
1912	**Great Britain**, Denmark, Netherlands	1976	**East Germany**, Poland, Soviet Union
1920	**Belgium**, Spain, Netherlands	1980	**Czechoslovakia**, East Germany, Soviet Union
1924	**Uruguay**, Switzerland, Sweden	1984	**France**, Brazil, Yugoslavia
1928	**Uruguay**, Argentina, Italy	1988	**Soviet Union**, Brazil, West Germany
1936	**Italy**, Austria, Norway	1992	**Spain**, Poland, Ghana
1948	**Sweden**, Yugoslavia, Denmark	1996	**Nigeria**, Argentina, Brazil
1952	**Hungary**, Yugoslavia, Sweden	2000	**Cameroon**, Spain, Chile
1956	**Soviet Union**, Yugoslavia, Bulgaria		

WOMEN

Year		Year	
1996	**United States**, China, Norway	2000	**Norway**, United States, Germany

SOFTBALL

Multiple gold medals: United States (2).

Year		Year	
1996	**United States**, China, Australia	2000	**United States**, Japan, Australia

U.S. Medal-Winning Softball Teams

1996 (gold medal): P–Lisa Fernandez, Michele Granger, Lori Harrigan and Michele Smith; C–Gillian Boxx and Shelly Stokes; INF–Sheila Cornell, Kim Maher, Leah O'Brien, Dot Richardson, Julie Smith and Dani Tyler; OF–Laura Berg, Dionna Harris; Manager–Ralph Raymond. Final: USA over China, 3-1.

2000 (gold medal): P–Lisa Fernandez, Lori Harrigan, Danielle Henderson, Michele Smith and Christa Williams; C–Stacey Nuveman and Michelle Venturella; INF–Jennifer Brundage, Crystl Bustos, Sheila Douty, Jennifer McFalls and Dot Richardson; OF–Christie Ambrosi, Laura Berg, Leah O'Brien-Amico; Manager–Ralph Raymond. Final: USA over Japan, 2-1.

SWIMMING

World and Olympic records below that appear to be broken or equaled by winning times in subsequent years, but are not so indicated, were all broken in preliminary heats leading up to the finals. Some events were not held at every Olympics.

MEN

At least 4 gold medals (including relays): Mark Spitz (9); Matt Biondi (8); Charles Daniels, Tom Jager, Don Schollander, and Johnny Weissmuller (5); Tamás Darnyi, Gary Hall Jr., Roland Matthes, John Naber, Aleksandr Popov, Murray Rose, Vladimir Salnikov and Henry Taylor (4).

50-meter Freestyle

Year		Time		Year		Time	
1904	Zoltán Halmay, HUN (50 yds)	28.0		1996	Aleksandr Popov, RUS	22.13	
1906-84	Not held			2000	(TIE) Anthony Ervin, USA	21.98	
1988	Matt Biondi, USA	22.14	**WR**		& Gary Hall Jr., USA	21.98	
1992	Aleksandr Popov, UT	21.91	**OR**				

100-meter Freestyle

Year		Time		Year		Time	
1896	Alfréd Hajós, HUN	1:22.2	**OR**	1936	Ferenc Csik, HUN	57.6	
1904	Zoltán Halmay, HUN (100 yds)	1:02.8		1948	Wally Ris, USA	57.3	**OR**
1906	Charles Daniels, USA	1:13.4		1952	Clarke Scholes, USA	57.4	
1908	Charles Daniels, USA	1:05.6	**WR**	1956	Jon Henricks, AUS	55.4	**OR**
1912	Duke Kahanamoku, USA	1:03.4		1960	John Devitt, AUS	55.2	**OR**
1920	Duke Kahanamoku, USA	1:00.4	**WR**	1964	Don Schollander, USA	53.4	**OR**
1924	Johnny Weissmuller, USA	59.0	**OR**	1968	Michael Wenden, AUS	52.2	**WR**
1928	Johnny Weissmuller, USA	58.6	**OR**	1972	Mark Spitz, USA	51.22	**WR**
1932	Yasuji Miyazaki, JPN	58.2		1976	Jim Montgomery, USA	49.99	**WR**

Swimming (Cont.)

Year		Time		Year		Time	
1980	Jorg Woithe, E. Ger	50.40		1992	Aleksandr Popov, UT	49.02	
1984	Rowdy Gaines, USA	49.80	OR	1996	Aleksandr Popov, RUS	48.74	
1988	Matt Biondi, USA	48.63	OR	2000	Pieter van den Hoogenband, NED	48.30	

200-meter Freestyle

Year		Time		Year		Time	
1900	Frederick Lane, AUS (220 yds)	2:25.2	OR	1984	Michael Gross, W. Ger	1:47.44	WR
1904	Charles Daniels, USA (220 yds)	2:44.2		1988	Duncan Armstrong, AUS	1:47.25	WR
1968	Michael Wenden, AUS	1:55.2		1992	Yevgeny Sadovyi, UT	1:46.70	OR
1972	Mark Spitz, USA	1:52.78	WR	1996	Danyon Loader, NZE	1:47.63	
1976	Bruce Furniss, USA	1:50.29	WR	2000	Pieter van den Hoogenband, NED	1:45.35	WR
1980	Sergei Kopliakov, USSR	1:49.81	OR				

400-meter Freestyle

Year		Time		Year		Time	
1896	Paul Neumann, AUT (550m)	8:12.6		1956	Murray Rose, AUS	4:27.3	OR
1904	Charles Daniels, USA (440 yds)	6:16.2		1960	Murray Rose, AUS	4:18.3	OR
1906	Otto Scheff, AUT	6:23.8		1964	Don Schollander, USA	4:12.2	WR
1908	Henry Taylor, GBR	5:36.8		1968	Mike Burton, USA	4:09.0	OR
1912	George Hodgson, CAN	5:24.4		1972	Bradford Cooper, AUS*	4:00.27	OR
1920	Norman Ross, USA	5:26.8		1976	Brian Goodell, USA	3:51.93	WR
1924	Johnny Weissmuller, USA	5:04.2	OR	1980	Vladimir Salnikov, USSR	3:51.31	OR
1928	Alberto Zorilla, ARG	5:01.6	OR	1984	George DiCarlo, USA	3:51.23	OR
1932	Buster Crabbe, USA	4:48.4	OR	1988	Uwe Dassler, E. Ger	3:46.95	WR
1936	Jack Medica, USA	4:44.5	OR	1992	Yevgeny Sadovyi, UT	3:45.00	WR
1948	Bill Smith, USA	4:41.0	OR	1996	Danyon Loader, NZE	3:47.97	
1952	Jean Boiteux, FRA	4:30.7	OR	2000	Ian Thorpe, AUS	3:40.59	WR

*Cooper finished second to Rick DeMont of the U.S., who was disqualified when he flunked the post-race drug test (his asthma medication was on the IOC's banned list).

1500-meter Freestyle

Year		Time		Year		Time	
1896	Alfréd Hajós, HUN (1200m)	18:22.2	OR	1956	Murray Rose, AUS	17:58.9	
1900	John Arthur Jarvis, GBR (1000m)	13:40.2		1960	Jon Konrads, AUS	17:19.6	OR
1904	Emil Rausch, GER (1 mile)	27:18.2		1964	Robert Windle, AUS	17:01.7	OR
1906	Henry Taylor, GBR (1 mile)	28:28.0		1968	Mike Burton, USA	16:38.9	OR
1908	Henry Taylor, GBR	22:48.4	WR	1972	Mike Burton, USA	15:52.58	WR
1912	George Hodgson, CAN	22:00.0	WR	1976	Brian Goodell, USA	15:02.40	WR
1920	Norman Ross, USA	22:23.2		1980	Vladimir Salnikov, USSR	14:58.27	WR
1924	Andrew (Boy) Charlton, AUS	20:06.6	WR	1984	Mike O'Brien, USA	15:05.20	
1928	Arne Borge, SWE	19:51.8	OR	1988	Vladimir Salnikov, USSR	15:00.40	
1932	Kusuo Kitamura, JPN	19:12.4	OR	1992	Kieren Perkins, AUS	14:43.48	WR
1936	Noboru Terada, JPN	19:13.7		1996	Kieren Perkins, AUS	14:56.40	
1948	James McLane, USA	19:18.5		2000	Grant Hackett, AUS	14:48.33	
1952	Ford Konno, USA	18:30.3	OR				

100-meter Backstroke

Year		Time		Year		Time	
1904	Walter Brack, GER (100 yds)	1:16.8		1960	David Theile, AUS	1:01.9	OR
1908	Arno Bieberstein, GER	1:24.6	WR	1968	Roland Matthes, E. Ger	58.7	OR
1912	Harry Hebner, USA	1:21.2		1972	Roland Matthes, E. Ger	56.58	OR
1920	Warren Kealoha, USA	1:15.2		1976	John Naber, USA	55.49	WR
1924	Warren Kealoha, USA	1:13.2	OR	1980	Bengt Baron, SWE	56.33	
1928	George Kojac, USA	1:08.2	WR	1984	Rick Carey, USA	55.79	
1932	Masaji Kiyokawa, JPN	1:08.6		1988	Daichi Suzuki, JPN	55.05	
1936	Adolf Kiefer, USA	1:05.9	OR	1992	Mark Tewksbury, CAN	53.98	OR
1948	Allen Stack, USA	1:06.4		1996	Jeff Rouse, USA	54.10	
1952	Yoshinobu Oyakawa, USA	1:05.4	OR	2000	Lenny Krayzelburg, USA	53.72	OR
1956	David Theile, AUS	1:02.2	OR				

200-meter Backstroke

Year		Time		Year		Time	
1900	Ernst Hoppenberg, GER	2:47.0		1984	Rick Carey, USA	2:00.23	
1964	Jed Graef, USA	2:10.3	WR	1988	Igor Poliansky, USSR	1:59.37	
1968	Roland Matthes, E. Ger	2:09.6	OR	1992	Martin Lopez-Zubero, SPA	1:58.47	OR
1972	Roland Matthes, E. Ger	2:02.82	=WR	1996	Brad Bridgewater, USA	1:58.54	
1976	John Naber, USA	1:59.19	WR	2000	Lenny Krayzelburg, USA	1:56.76	OR
1980	Sándor Wládar, HUN	2:01.93					

100-meter Breaststroke

Year		Time		Year		Time	
1968	Don McKenzie, USA	1:07.7	OR	1988	Adrian Moorhouse, GBR	1:02.04	
1972	Nobutaka Taguchi, JPN	1:04.94	WR	1992	Nelson Diebel, USA	1:01.50	OR
1976	John Hencken, USA	1:03.11	WR	1996	Fred deBurghgraeve, BEL	1:00.60	
1980	Duncan Goodhew, GBR	1:03.44		2000	Domenico Fioravanti, ITA	1:00.46	OR
1984	Steve Lundquist, USA	1:01.65	WR				

200-meter Breaststroke

Year		Time		Year		Time	
1908	Frederick Holman, GBR	3:09.2	WR	1964	Ian O'Brien, AUS	2:27.8	WR
1912	Walter Bathe, GER	3:01.8	OR	1968	Felipe Muñoz, MEX	2:28.7	
1920	Hakan Malmroth, SWE	3:04.4		1972	John Hencken, USA	2:21.55	WR
1924	Robert Skelton, USA	2:56.6		1976	David Wilkie, GBR	2:15.11	WR
1928	Yoshiyuki Tsuruta, JPN	2:48.8	OR	1980	Robertas Zhulpa, USSR	2:15.85	
1932	Yoshiyuki Tsuruta, JPN	2:45.4		1984	Victor Davis, CAN	2:13.34	WR
1936	Tetsuo Hamuro, JPN	2:41.5	OR	1988	József Szabó, HUN	2:13.52	
1948	Joseph Verdeur, USA	2:39.3	OR	1992	Mike Barrowman, USA	2:10.16	WR
1952	John Davies, AUS	2:34.4	OR	1996	Norbert Rozsa, HUN	2:12.57	
1956	Masaru Furukawa, JPN	2:34.7*	OR	2000	Domenico Fioravanti, ITA	2:10.87	
1960	Bill Mulliken, USA	2:37.4					

*In 1956, the butterfly stroke and breaststroke were separated into two different events.

100-meter Butterfly

Year		Time		Year		Time	
1968	Doug Russell, USA	55.9	OR	1988	Anthony Nesty, SUR	53.0	OR
1972	Mark Spitz, USA	54.27	WR	1992	Pablo Morales, USA	53.32	
1976	Matt Vogel, USA	54.35		1996	Dennis Pankratov, RUS	52.27	
1980	Pär Arvidsson, SWE	54.92		2000	Lars Frolander, SWE	52.00	
1984	Michael Gross, W. Ger	53.08	WR				

200-meter Butterfly

Year		Time		Year		Time	
1956	Bill Yorzyk, USA	2:19.3	OR	1980	Sergei Fesenko, USSR	1:59.76	
1960	Mike Troy, USA	2:12.8	WR	1984	Jon Sieben, AUS	1:57.04	WR
1964	Kevin Berry, AUS	2:06.6	WR	1988	Michael Gross, W. Ger	1:56.94	OR
1968	Carl Robie, USA	2:08.7		1992	Melvin Stewart, USA	1:56.26	OR
1972	Mark Spitz, USA	2:00.70	WR	1996	Dennis Pankratov, RUS	1:56.51	
1976	Mike Bruner, USA	1:59.23	WR	2000	Tom Malchow, USA	1:55.35	OR

200-meter Individual Medley

Year		Time		Year		Time	
1968	Charles Hickcox, USA	2:12.0	OR	1992	Tamás Darnyi, HUN	2:00.76	
1972	Gunnar Larsson, SWE	2:07.17	WR	1996	Attila Czene, HUN	1:59.91	
1984	Alex Baumann, CAN	2:01.42	WR	2000	Massimiliano Rosolino, ITA	1:58.98	OR
1988	Tamás Darnyi, HUN	2:00.17	WR				

400-meter Individual Medley

Year		Time		Year		Time	
1964	Richard Roth, USA	4:45.4	WR	1984	Alex Baumann, CAN	4:17.41	WR
1968	Charles Hickcox, USA	4:48.4		1988	Tamás Darnyi, HUN	4:14.75	WR
1972	Gunnar Larsson, SWE	4:31.98	OR	1992	Tamás Darnyi, HUN	4:14.23	OR
1976	Rod Strachan, USA	4:23.68	WR	1996	Tom Dolan, USA	4:14.90	
1980	Aleksandr Sidorenko, USSR	4:22.89	OR	2000	Tom Dolan, USA	4:11.76	WR

4x100-meter Freestyle Relay

Year		Time		Year		Time	
1964	United States	3:32.2	WR	1988	United States	3:16.53	WR
1968	United States	3:31.7	WR	1992	United States	3:16.74	
1972	United States	3:26.42	WR	1996	United States	3:15.41	
1976-80	Not held			2000	Australia	3:13.67	WR
1984	United States	3:19.03	WR				

4x200-meter Freestyle Relay

Year		Time		Year		Time	
1906	Hungary (x250m)	16:52.4		1948	United States	8:46.0	WR
1908	Great Britain	10:55.6	WR	1952	United States	8:31.1	OR
1912	Australia/New Zealand	10:11.6	WR	1956	Australia	8:23.6	WR
1920	United States	10:04.4	WR	1960	United States	8:10.2	WR
1924	United States	9:53.4	WR	1964	United States	7:52.1	WR
1928	United States	9:36.2	WR	1968	United States	7:52.33	
1932	Japan	8:58.4	WR	1972	United States	7:35.78	WR
1936	Japan	8:51.5	WR	1976	United States	7:23.22	WR

Swimming (Cont.)

Year		Time		Year		Time	
1980	Soviet Union	7:23.50		1992	Unified Team	7:11.95	**WR**
1984	United States	7:15.69	**WR**	1996	United States	7:14.84	
1988	United States	7:12.51	**WR**	2000	Australia	7:07.05	**WR**

4x100-meter Medley Relay

Year		Time		Year		Time	
1960	United States	4:05.4	**WR**	1984	United States	3:39.30	**WR**
1964	United States	3:58.4	**WR**	1988	United States	3:36.93	**WR**
1968	United States	3:54.9	**WR**	1992	United States	3:36.93	**=WR**
1972	United States	3:48.16	**WR**	1996	United States	3:34.84	
1976	United States	3:42.22	**WR**	2000	United States	3:33.73	**WR**
1980	Australia	3:45.70					

WOMEN

At least 4 gold medals (including relays): Jenny Thompson (8); Kristin Otto and Amy Van Dyken (6); Krisztina Egerszegi (5), Kornelia Ender, Janet Evans, Dawn Fraser and Dara Torres (4).

50-meter Freestyle

Year		Time		Year		Time	
1988	Kristin Otto, E. Ger	25.49	**OR**	1996	Amy Van Dyken, USA	24.87	
1992	Yang Wenyi, CHN	24.79	**WR**	2000	Inge de Bruijn, NED	24.32	

100-meter Freestyle

Year		Time		Year		Time	
1912	Fanny Durack, AUS	1:22.2		1968	Jan Henne, USA	1:00.0	
1920	Ethelda Bleibtrey, USA	1:13.6	**WR**	1972	Sandra Neilson, USA	58.59	**OR**
1924	Ethel Lackie, USA	1:12.4		1976	Kornelia Ender, E. Ger	55.65	**WR**
1928	Albina Osipowich, USA	1:11.0	**OR**	1980	Barbara Krause, E. Ger	54.79	**WR**
1932	Helene Madison, USA	1:06.8	**OR**	1984	(TIE) Nancy Hogshead, USA	55.92	
1936	Rie Mastenbroek, NED	1:05.9	**OR**		& Carrie Steinseifer, USA	55.92	
1948	Greta Andersen, DEN	1:06.3		1988	Kristin Otto, E. Ger	54.93	
1952	Katalin Szöke, HUN	1:06.8		1992	Zhuang Yong, CHN	54.65	**OR**
1956	Dawn Fraser, AUS	1:02.0	**WR**	1996	Le Jingyi, CHN	54.50	
1960	Dawn Fraser, AUS	1:01.2	**OR**	2000	Inge de Bruijn, NED	53.83	
1964	Dawn Fraser, AUS	59.5	**OR**				

200-meter Freestyle

Year		Time		Year		Time	
1968	Debbie Meyer, USA	2:10.5	**OR**	1988	Heike Friedrich, E. Ger	1:57:65	**OR**
1972	Shane Gould, AUS	2:03.56	**WR**	1992	Nicole Haislett, USA	1:57.90	
1976	Kornelia Ender, E. Ger	1:59.26	**WR**	1996	Claudia Poll, CRC	1:58.16	
1980	Barbara Krause, E. Ger	1:58.33	**OR**	2000	Susie O'Neill, AUS	1:58.24	
1984	Mary Wayte, USA	1:59.23					

400-meter Freestyle

Year		Time		Year		Time	
1920	Ethelda Bleibtrey, USA (300m)	4:34.0	**WR**	1968	Debbie Meyer, USA	4:31.8	**OR**
1924	Martha Norelius, USA	6:02.2	**OR**	1972	Shane Gould, AUS	4:19.44	**WR**
1928	Martha Norelius, USA	5:42.8	**OR**	1976	Petra Thümer, E. Ger	4:09.89	**WR**
1932	Helene Madison, USA	5:28.5	**WR**	1980	Ines Diers, E. Ger	4:08.76	**OR**
1936	Rie Mastenbroek, NED	5:26.4	**OR**	1984	Tiffany Cohen, USA	4:07.10	**OR**
1948	Ann Curtis, USA	5:17.8	**OR**	1988	Janet Evans, USA	4:03.85	**WR**
1952	Valéria Gyenge, HUN	5:12.1	**OR**	1992	Dagmar Hase, GER	4:07.18	
1956	Lorraine Crapp, AUS	4:54.6	**OR**	1996	Michelle Smith, IRE	4:07.25	
1960	Chris von Saltza, USA	4:50.6	**OR**	2000	Brooke Bennett, USA	4:05.80	
1964	Ginny Duenkel, USA	4:43.3	**OR**				

800-meter Freestyle

Year		Time		Year		Time	
1968	Debbie Meyer, USA	9:24.0	**OR**	1988	Janet Evans, USA	8:20.20	**OR**
1972	Keena Rothhammer, USA	8:53.68	**WR**	1992	Janet Evans, USA	8:25.52	
1976	Petra Thümer, E. Ger	8:37.14	**WR**	1996	Brooke Bennett, USA	8:27.89	
1980	Michelle Ford, AUS	8:28.90	**OR**	2000	Brooke Bennett, USA	8:19.67	**OR**
1984	Tiffany Cohen, USA	8:24.95	**OR**				

100-meter Backstroke

Year		Time		Year		Time	
1924	Sybil Bauer, USA	1:23.2	**OR**	1968	Kaye Hall, USA	1:06.2	**WR**
1928	Maria Braun, NED	1:22.0		1972	Melissa Belote, USA	1:05.78	**OR**
1932	Eleanor Holm, USA	1:19.4		1976	Ulrike Richter, E. Ger	1:01.83	**OR**
1936	Dina Senff, NED	1:18.9		1980	Rica Reinisch, E. Ger	1:00.86	**WR**
1948	Karen-Margrete Harup, DEN	1:14.4	**OR**	1984	Theresa Andrews, USA	1:02.55	
1952	Joan Harrison, S. Afr.	1:14.3		1988	Kristin Otto, E. Ger	1:00.89	
1956	Judy Grinham, GBR	1:12.9	**OR**	1992	Krisztina Egerszegi, HUN	1:00.68	**OR**
1960	Lynn Burke, USA	1:09.3	**OR**	1996	Beth Botsford, USA	1:01.19	
1964	Cathy Ferguson, USA	1:07.7	**WR**	2000	Diana Mocanu, ROM	1:00.21	**OR**

200-meter Backstroke

Year		Time		Year		Time	
1968	Pokey Watson, USA	2:24.8	OR	1988	Krisztina Egerszegi, HUN	2:09.29	OR
1972	Melissa Belote, USA	2:19.19	WR	1992	Krisztina Egerszegi, HUN	2:07.06	OR
1976	Ulrike Richter, E. Ger	2:13.43	OR	1996	Krisztina Egerszegi, HUN	2:07.83	
1980	Rica Reinisch, E. Ger	2:11.77	WR	2000	Diana Mocanu, ROM	2:08.16	
1984	Jolanda de Rover, NED	2:12.38					

100-meter Breaststroke

Year		Time		Year		Time	
1968	Djurdjica Bjedov, YUG	1:15.8	OR	1988	Tania Dangalakova, BUL	1:07.95	OR
1972	Cathy Carr, USA	1:13.58	WR	1992	Yelena Rudkovskaya, UT	1:08.00	
1976	Hannelore Anke, E. Ger	1:11.16		1996	Penny Heyns, RSA	1:07.73	
1980	Ute Geweniger, E. Ger	1:10.22		2000	Megan Quann, USA	1:07.05	
1984	Petra van Staveren, NED	1:09.88	OR				

200-meter Breaststroke

Year		Time		Year		Time	
1924	Lucy Morton, GBR	3:33.2	OR	1968	Sharon Wichman, USA	2:44.4	OR
1928	Hilde Schrader, GER	3:12.6		1972	Beverley Whitfield, AUS	2:41.71	OR
1932	Clare Dennis, AUS	3:06.3	OR	1976	Marina Koshevaya, USSR	2:33.35	WR
1936	Hideko Maehata, JPN	3:03.6		1980	Lina Kaciusyte, USSR	2:29.54	OR
1948	Petronella van Vliet, NED	2:57.2		1984	Anne Ottenbrite, CAN	2:30.38	
1952	Éva Székely, HUN	2:51.7		1988	Silke Hörner, E. Ger	2:26.71	WR
1956	Ursula Happe, GER	2:53.1	OR	1992	Kyoko Iwasaki, JPN	2:26.65	OR
1960	Anita Lonsbrough, GBR	2:49.5	WR	1996	Penny Heyns, RSA	2:25.41	
1964	Galina Prozumenshikova, USSR	2:46.4	OR	2000	Agnes Kovacs, HUN	2:24.35	

100-meter Butterfly

Year		Time		Year		Time	
1956	Shelly Mann, USA	1:11.0	OR	1980	Caren Metschuck, E. Ger	1:00.42	
1960	Carolyn Schuler, USA	1:09.5	OR	1984	Mary T. Meagher, USA	59.26	
1964	Sharon Stouder, USA	1:04.7	WR	1988	Kristin Otto, E. Ger	59.00	OR
1968	Lynn McClements, AUS	1:05.5		1992	Qian Hong, CHN	58.62	OR
1972	Mayumi Aoki, JPN	1:03.34	WR	1996	Amy Van Dyken, USA	59.13	
1976	Kornelia Ender, E. Ger	1:00.13	=WR	2000	Inge de Bruijn, NED	56.61	WR

200-meter Butterfly

Year		Time		Year		Time	
1968	Ada Kok, NED	2:24.7	OR	1988	Kathleen Nord, E. Ger	2:09.51	
1972	Karen Moe, USA	2:15.57	WR	1992	Summer Sanders, USA	2:08.67	
1976	Andrea Pollack, E. Ger	2:11.41	OR	1996	Susie O'Neill, AUS	2:07.76	
1980	Ines Geissler, E. Ger	2:10.44	OR	2000	Misty Hyman, USA	2:05.88	OR
1984	Mary T. Meagher, USA	2:06.90	OR				

200-meter Individual Medley

Year		Time		Year		Time	
1968	Claudia Kolb, USA	2:24.7	OR	1992	Lin Li, CHN	2:11.65	WR
1972	Shane Gould, AUS	2:23.07	WR	1996	Michelle Smith, IRE	2:13.93	
1984	Tracy Caulkins, USA	2:12.64	OR	2000	Yana Klochkova, UKR	2:10.68	OR
1988	Daniela Hunger, E. Ger	2:12.59	OR				

400-meter Individual Medley

Year		Time		Year		Time	
1964	Donna de Varona, USA	5:18.7	OR	1984	Tracy Caulkins, USA	4:39.24	
1968	Claudia Kolb, USA	5:08.5	OR	1988	Janet Evans, USA	4:37.76	
1972	Gail Neall, AUS	5:02.97	WR	1992	Krisztina Egerszegi, HUN	4:36.54	
1976	Ulrike Tauber, E. Ger	4:42.77	WR	1996	Michelle Smith, IRE	4:39.18	
1980	Petra Schneider, E. Ger	4:36.29	WR	2000	Yana Klochkova, UKR	4:33.59	WR

4x100-meter Freestyle Relay

Year		Time		Year		Time	
1912	Great Britain	5:52.8	WR	1964	United States	4:03.8	WR
1920	United States	5:11.6	WR	1968	United States	4:02.5	OR
1924	United States	4:58.8	WR	1972	United States	3:55.19	WR
1928	United States	4:47.6	WR	1976	United States	3:44.82	WR
1932	United States	4:38.0	WR	1980	East Germany	3:42.71	WR
1936	Netherlands	4:36.0	OR	1984	United States	3:43.43	
1948	United States	4:29.2	OR	1988	East Germany	3:40.63	OR
1952	Hungary	4:24.4		1992	United States	3:39.46	WR
1956	Australia	4:17.1	WR	1996	United States	3:39.29	
1960	United States	4:08.9	WR	2000	United States	3:36.61	WR

4x200-meter Freestyle Relay

Year		Time		Year		Time	
1996	United States	7:59.87		2000	United States	7:57.80	OR

Swimming (Cont.)
4x100-meter Medley Relay

Year		Time		Year		Time	
1960	United States	4:41.1	WR	1984	United States	4:08.34	
1964	United States	4:33.9	WR	1988	East Germany	4:03.74	OR
1968	United States	4:28.3	OR	1992	United States	4:02.54	WR
1972	United States	4:20.75	WR	1996	United States	4:02.88	
1976	East Germany	4:07.95	WR	2000	United States	3:58.30	WR
1980	East Germany	4:06.67	WR				

TENNIS

MEN

Multiple gold medals (including men's doubles): John Boland, Max Decugis, Laurie Doherty, Reggie Doherty, Arthur Gore, Andre Grobert, Vincent Richards, Charles Winslow and Beals Wright (2).

Singles

Year			Year		
1896	John Boland	Great Britain/Ireland	1920	Louis Raymond	South Africa
1900	Laurie Doherty,	Great Britain	1924	Vincent Richards	United States
1904	Beals Wright	United States	1928-84	Not held	
1906	Max Decugis	France	1988	Miloslav Mecir	Czechoslovakia
1908	Josiah Ritchie	Great Britain	1992	Marc Rosset	Switzerland
	(Indoor) Arthur Gore	Great Britain	1996	Andre Agassi	United States
1912	Charles Winslow	South Africa	2000	Yevgeny Kafelnikov	Russia
	(Indoor) André Gobert	France			

Doubles

Year		Year	
1896	John Boland, IRE & Fritz Traun, GER	1920	Noel Turnbull & Max Woosnam, GBR
1900	Laurie and Reggie Doherty	1924	Vincent Richards & Frank Hunter, USA
1904	Edgar Leonard & Beals Wright, USA	1928-84	Not held
1906	Max Decugis & Maurice Germot, FRA	1988	Ken Flach & Robert Seguso, USA
1908	George Hillyard & Reggie Doherty, GBR	1992	Boris Becker & Michael Stich, GER
	(Indoor) Arthur Gore & Herbert Barrett, GBR	1996	Todd Woodbridge & Mark Woodforde, AUS
1912	Charles Winslow & Harold Kitson, S. Afr.	2000	Sebastien Lareau & Daniel Nestor, CAN
	(Indoor) Andre Gobert & Maurice Germot, FRA		

WOMEN

Multiple gold medals (including women's doubles): Helen Wills, Gigi Fernandez, Mary Joe Fernandez and Venus Williams (2).

Singles

Year			Year		
1900	Charlotte Cooper	Great Britain	1924	Helen Wills	United States
1906	Esmee Simiriotou	Greece	1928-84	Not held	
1908	Dorothea Chambers	Great Britain	1988	Steffi Graf	West Germany
	(Indoor) Gwen Eastlake-Smith	Great Britain	1992	Jennifer Capriati	United States
1912	Marguerite Broquedis	France	1996	Lindsay Davenport	United States
	(Indoor) Edith Hannam	Great Britain	2000	Venus Williams	United States
1920	Suzanne Lenglen	France			

Doubles

Year		Year	
1920	Winifred McNair & Kitty McKane, GBR	1992	Gigi Fernandez & Mary Joe Fernandez, USA
1924	Hazel Wightman & Helen Wills, USA	1996	Gigi Fernandez & Mary Joe Fernandez, USA
1928-84	Not held	2000	Serena Williams & Venus Williams, USA
1988	Pam Shriver & Zina Garrison, USA		

TRACK & FIELD

World and Olympic records below that appear to be broken or equaled by winning times, heights and distances in subsequent years, but are not so indicated, were all broken in preliminary races and field events leading up to the finals.

MEN

At least 4 gold medals (including relays and discontinued events): Ray Ewry (10); Carl Lewis and Paavo Nurmi (9); Ville Ritola and Martin Sheridan (5); Harrison Dillard, Archie Hahn, Michael Johnson, Hannes Kolehmainen, Alvin Kraenzlein, Eric Lemming, Jim Lightbody, Al Oerter, Jesse Owens, Meyer Prinstein, Mel Sheppard, Lasse Viren and Emil Zátopek (4). Note that all of Ewry's gold medals came before 1912, in the Standing High Jump, Standing Long Jump and Standing Triple Jump.

100 meters

Year		Time		Year		Time	
1896	Tom Burke, USA	12.0		1920	Charley Paddock, USA	10.8	
1900	Frank Jarvis, USA	11.0		1924	Harold Abrahams, GBR	10.6	=OR
1904	Archie Hahn, USA	11.0		1928	Percy Williams, CAN	10.8	
1906	Archie Hahn, USA	11.2		1932	Eddie Tolan, USA	10.3	OR
1908	Reggie Walker, S. Afr.	10.8	=OR	1936	Jesse Owens, USA	10.3w	
1912	Ralph Craig, USA	10.8		1948	Harrison Dillard, USA	10.3	=OR

Year		Time		Year		Time	
1952	Lindy Remigino, USA	10.4		1980	Allan Wells, GBR	10.25	
1956	Bobby Morrow, USA	10.5		1984	Carl Lewis, USA	9.99	
1960	Armin Hary, GER	10.2	**OR**	1988	Carl Lewis, USA*	9.92	**WR**
1964	Bob Hayes, USA	10.0	**=WR**	1992	Linford Christie, GBR	9.96	
1968	Jim Hines, USA	9.95	**WR**	1996	Donovan Bailey, CAN	9.84	**WR**
1972	Valery Borzov, USSR	10.14		2000	Maurice Greene, USA	9.87	
1976	Hasely Crawford, TRI	10.06					

ʷindicates wind-aided.

*Lewis finished second to Ben Johnson of Canada, who set a world record of 9.79 seconds. Two days later, Johnson was stripped of his gold medal and his record when he tested positive for steroid use in a post-race drug test.

200 meters

Year		Time		Year		Time	
1900	Walter Tewksbury, USA	22.2		1960	Livio Berruti, ITA	20.5	**=WR**
1904	Archie Hahn, USA	21.6	**OR**	1964	Henry Carr, USA	20.3	**OR**
1908	Bobby Kerr, CAN	22.6		1968	Tommie Smith, USA	19.83	**WR**
1912	Ralph Craig, USA	21.7		1972	Valery Borzov, USSR	20.00	
1920	Allen Woodring, USA	22.0		1976	Donald Quarrie, JAM	20.23	
1924	Jackson Scholz, USA	21.6		1980	Pietro Mennea, ITA	20.19	
1928	Percy Williams, CAN	21.8		1984	Carl Lewis, USA	19.80	**OR**
1932	Eddie Tolan, USA	21.2	**OR**	1988	Joe DeLoach, USA	19.75	**OR**
1936	Jesse Owens, USA	20.7	**OR**	1992	Mike Marsh, USA	20.01	
1948	Mel Patton, USA	21.1		1996	Michael Johnson, USA	19.32	**WR**
1952	Andy Stanfield, USA	20.7		2000	Konstantinos Kenteris, GRE	20.09	
1956	Bobby Morrow, USA	20.6	**OR**				

400 meters

Year		Time		Year		Time	
1896	Tom Burke, USA	54.2		1956	Charley Jenkins, USA	46.7	
1900	Maxey Long, USA	49.4	**OR**	1960	Otis Davis, USA	44.9	**WR**
1904	Harry Hillman, USA	49.2	**OR**	1964	Mike Larrabee, USA	45.1	
1906	Paul Pilgrim, USA	53.2		1968	Lee Evans, USA	43.86	**WR**
1908	Wyndham Halswelle, GBR	50.0		1972	Vince Matthews, USA	44.66	
1912	Charlie Reidpath, USA	48.2	**OR**	1976	Alberto Juantorena, CUB	44.26	
1920	Bevil Rudd, S. Afr.	49.6		1980	Viktor Markin, USSR	44.60	
1924	Eric Liddell, GBR	47.6	**OR**	1984	Alonzo Babers, USA	44.27	
1928	Ray Barbuti, USA	47.8		1988	Steve Lewis, USA	43.87	
1932	Bill Carr, USA	46.2	**WR**	1992	Quincy Watts, USA	43.50	**OR**
1936	Archie Williams, USA	46.5		1996	Michael Johnson, USA	43.49	**OR**
1948	Arthur Wint, JAM	46.2		2000	Michael Johnson, USA	43.84	
1952	George Rhoden, JAM	45.9	**OR**				

800 meters

Year		Time		Year		Time	
1896	Teddy Flack, AUS	2:11.0		1956	Tom Courtney, USA	1:47.7	**OR**
1900	Alfred Tysoe, GBR	2:01.2		1960	Peter Snell, NZE	1:46.3	**OR**
1904	Jim Lightbody, USA	1:56.0	**OR**	1964	Peter Snell, NZE	1:45.1	**OR**
1906	Paul Pilgrim, USA	2:01.5		1968	Ralph Doubell, AUS	1:44.3	**=WR**
1908	Mel Sheppard, USA	1:52.8	**WR**	1972	Dave Wottle, USA	1:45.9	
1912	Ted Meredith, USA	1:51.9	**WR**	1976	Alberto Juantorena, CUB	1:43.50	**WR**
1920	Albert Hill, GBR	1:53.4		1980	Steve Ovett, GBR	1:45.4	
1924	Douglas Lowe, GBR	1:52.4		1984	Joaquim Cruz, BRA	1:43.00	**OR**
1928	Douglas Lowe, GBR	1:51.8	**OR**	1988	Paul Ereng, KEN	1:43.45	
1932	Tommy Hampson, GBR	1:49.7	**WR**	1992	William Tanui, KEN	1:43.66	
1936	John Woodruff, USA	1:52.9		1996	Vebjoern Rodal, NOR	1:42.58	**OR**
1948	Mal Whitfield, USA	1:49.2	**OR**	2000	Nils Schumann, GER	1:45.08	
1952	Mal Whitfield, USA	1:49.2	**=OR**				

1500 meters

Year		Time		Year		Time	
1896	Teddy Flack, AUS	4:33.2		1956	Ron Delany, IRE	3:41.2	**OR**
1900	Charles Bennett, GBR	4:06.2	**WR**	1960	Herb Elliott, AUS	3:35.6	**WR**
1904	Jim Lightbody, USA	4:05.4	**WR**	1964	Peter Snell, NZE	3:38.1	
1906	Jim Lightbody, USA	4:12.0		1968	Kip Keino, KEN	3:34.9	**OR**
1908	Mel Sheppard, USA	4:03.4	**OR**	1972	Pekka Vasala, FIN	3:36.3	
1912	Arnold Jackson, GBR	3:56.8	**OR**	1976	John Walker, NZE	3:39.17	
1920	Albert Hill, GBR	4:01.8		1980	Sebastian Coe, GBR	3:38.4	
1924	Paavo Nurmi, FIN	3:53.6	**OR**	1984	Sebastian Coe, GBR	3:32.53	**OR**
1928	Harry Larva, FIN	3:53.2	**OR**	1988	Peter Rono, KEN	3:35.96	
1932	Luigi Beccali, ITA	3:51.2	**OR**	1992	Fermin Cacho, SPA	3:40.12	
1936	John Lovelock, NZE	3:47.8	**WR**	1996	Noureddine Morceli, ALG	3:35.78	
1948	Henry Eriksson, SWE	3:49.8		2000	Noah Ngeny, KEN	3:32.07	**OR**
1952	Josy Barthel, LUX	3:45.1	**OR**				

Track & Field (Cont.)

5000 meters

Year		Time		Year		Time	
1912	Hannes Kolehmainen, FIN	14:36.6	WR	1964	Bob Schul, USA	13:48.8	
1920	Joseph Guillemot, FRA	14:55.6		1968	Mohamed Gammoudi, TUN	14:05.0	
1924	Paavo Nurmi, FIN	14:31.2	OR	1972	Lasse Viren, FIN	13:26.4	OR
1928	Ville Ritola, FIN	14:38.0		1976	Lasse Viren, FIN	13:24.76	
1932	Lauri Lehtinen, FIN	14:30.0	OR	1980	Miruts Yifter, ETH	13:21.0	
1936	Gunnar Höckert, FIN	14:22.2	OR	1984	Said Aouita, MOR	13:05.59	OR
1948	Gaston Reiff, BEL	14:17.6	OR	1988	John Ngugi, KEN	13:11.70	
1952	Emil Zátopek, CZE	14:06.6	OR	1992	Dieter Baumann, GER	13:12.52	
1956	Vladimir Kuts, USSR	13:39.6	OR	1996	Venuste Niyongabo, BUR	13:07.96	
1960	Murray Halberg, NZE	13:43.4		2000	Millon Wolde, ETH	13:35.49	

10,000 meters

Year		Time		Year		Time	
1912	Hannes Kolehmainen, FIN	31:20.8		1964	Billy Mills, USA	28:24.4	OR
1920	Paavo Nurmi, FIN	31:45.8		1968	Naftali Temu, KEN	29:27.4	
1924	Ville Ritola, FIN	30:23.2	WR	1972	Lasse Viren, FIN	27:38.4	WR
1928	Paavo Nurmi, FIN	30:18.8	OR	1976	Lasse Viren, FIN	27:40.38	
1932	Janusz Kusocinski, POL	30:11.4	OR	1980	Miruts Yifter, ETH	27:42.7	
1936	Ilmari Salminen, FIN	30:15.4		1984	Alberto Cova, ITA	27:47.54	
1948	Emil Zátopek, CZE	29:59.6	OR	1988	Brahim Boutaib, MOR	27:21.46	OR
1952	Emil Zátopek, CZE	29:17.0	OR	1992	Khalid Skah, MOR	27:46.70	
1956	Vladimir Kuts, USSR	28:45.6	OR	1996	Haile Gebrselassie, ETH	27:07.34	OR
1960	Pyotr Bolotnikov, USSR	28:32.2	OR	2000	Haile Gebrselassie, ETH	27:18.20	

Marathon

Year		Time		Year		Time	
1896	Spiridon Louis, GRE	2:58:50		1956	Alain Mimoun, FRA	2:25:00.0	
1900	Michel Théato, FRA	2:59:45		1960	Abebe Bikila, ETH	2:15:16.2	WB
1904	Thomas Hicks, USA	3:28:53		1964	Abebe Bikila, ETH	2:12:11.2	WB
1906	Billy Sherring, CAN	2:51:23.6		1968	Mamo Wolde, ETH	2:20:26.4	
1908	Johnny Hayes, USA*	2:55:18.4	OR	1972	Frank Shorter, USA	2:12:19.8	
1912	Kenneth McArthur, S. Afr.	2:36:54.8		1976	Waldemar Cierpinski, E. Ger	2:09:55.0	OR
1920	Hannes Kolehmainen, FIN	2:32:35.8	WB	1980	Waldemar Cierpinski, E. Ger	2:11:03.0	
1924	Albin Stenroos, FIN	2:41:22.6		1984	Carlos Lopes, POR	2:09:21.0	OR
1928	Boughèra El Ouafi, FRA	2:32:57.0		1988	Gelindo Bordin, ITA	2:10:32	
1932	Juan Carlos Zabala, ARG	2:31:36.0	OR	1992	Hwang Young-Cho, S. Kor	2:13:23	
1936	Sohn Kee-Chung, JPN†	2:29:19.2	OR	1996	Josia Thugwane, RSA	2:12:36	
1948	Delfo Cabrera, ARG	2:34:51.6		2000	Gezahenge Abera, ETH	2:10.11	
1952	Emil Zátopek, CZE	2:23:03.2	OR				

*Dorando Pietri of Italy placed first, but was disqualified for being helped across the finish line.

†Sohn was a Korean, but he was forced to compete under the name Kitei Son by Japan, which occupied Korea at the time.

Note: Marathon distances—40,000 meters (1896,1904); 40,260 meters (1900); 41,860 meters (1906); 42,195 meters (1908 and since 1924); 40,200 meters (1912); 42,750 meters (1920). Current distance of 42,195 meters measures 26 miles, 385 yards.

110-meter Hurdles

Year		Time		Year		Time	
1896	Tom Curtis, USA	17.6		1956	Lee Calhoun, USA	13.5	OR
1900	Alvin Kraenzlein, USA	15.4	OR	1960	Lee Calhoun, USA	13.8	
1904	Frederick Schule, USA	16.0		1964	Hayes Jones, USA	13.6	
1906	Robert Leavitt, USA	16.2		1968	Willie Davenport, USA	13.3	OR
1908	Forrest Smithson, USA	15.0	WR	1972	Rod Milburn, USA	13.24	=WR
1912	Frederick Kelly, USA	15.1		1976	Guy Drut, FRA	13.30	
1920	Earl Thomson, CAN	14.8	WR	1980	Thomas Munkelt, E. Ger	13.39	
1924	Daniel Kinsey, USA	15.0		1984	Roger Kingdom, USA	13.20	OR
1928	Syd Atkinson, S. Afr.	14.8		1988	Roger Kingdom, USA	12.98	OR
1932	George Saling, USA	14.6		1992	Mark McKoy, CAN	13.12	
1936	Forrest (Spec) Towns, USA	14.2		1996	Allen Johnson, USA	12.95	OR
1948	William Porter, USA	13.9	OR	2000	Anier Garcia, CUB	13.00	
1952	Harrison Dillard, USA	13.7	OR				

400-meter Hurdles

Year		Time		Year		Time	
1900	Walter Tewksbury, USA	57.6		1960	Glenn Davis, USA	49.3	OR
1904	Harry Hillman, USA	53.0		1964	Rex Cawley, USA	49.6	
1908	Charley Bacon, USA	55.0	WR	1968	David Hemery, GBR	48.12	WR
1920	Frank Loomis, USA	54.0	WR	1972	John Akii-Bua, UGA	47.82	WR
1924	Morgan Taylor, USA	52.6		1976	Edwin Moses, USA	47.64	WR
1928	David Burghley, GBR	53.4	OR	1980	Volker Beck, E. Ger	48.70	
1932	Bob Tisdall, IRE	51.7		1984	Edwin Moses, USA	47.75	
1936	Glenn Hardin, USA	52.4		1988	Andre Phillips, USA	47.19	OR
1948	Roy Cochran, USA	51.1	OR	1992	Kevin Young, USA	46.78	WR
1952	Charley Moore, USA	50.8	OR	1996	Derrick Adkins, USA	47.54	
1956	Glenn Davis, USA	50.1	=OR	2000	Angelo Taylor, USA	47.50	

3000-meter Steeplechase

Year		Time		Year		Time	
1900	George Orton, CAN	7:34.4		1960	Zdzislaw Krzyszkowiak, POL	8:34.2	OR
1904	Jim Lightbody, USA	7:39.6		1964	Gaston Roelants, BEL	8:30.8	OR
1908	Arthur Russell, GBR	10:47.8		1968	Amos Biwott, KEN	8:51.0	
1920	Percy Hodge, GBR	10:00.4	OR	1972	Kip Keino, KEN	8:23.6	OR
1924	Ville Ritola, FIN	9:33.6	OR	1976	Anders Gärderud, SWE	8:08.2	WR
1928	Toivo Loukola, FIN	9:21.8	WR	1980	Bronislaw Malinowski, POL	8:09.7	
1932	Volmari Iso-Hollo, FIN	10:33.4*		1984	Julius Korir, KEN	8:11.80	
1936	Volmari Iso-Hollo, FIN	9:03.8	WR	1988	Julius Kariuki, KEN	8:05.51	OR
1948	Thore Sjöstrand, SWE	9:04.6		1992	Matthew Birir, KEN	8:08.84	
1952	Horace Ashenfelter, USA	8:45.4	WR	1996	Joseph Keter, KEN	8:07.12	
1956	Chris Brasher, GBR	8:41.2	OR	2000	Reuben Kosgei, KEN	8:21.43	

*Iso-Hollo ran one extra lap due to lap counter's mistake.
Note: Other steeplechase distances– 2500 meters (1900); 2590 meters (1904); 3200 meters (1908) and 3460 meters (1932).

4x100-meter Relay

Year		Time		Year		Time	
1912	Great Britain	42.4		1964	United States	39.0	WR
1920	United States	42.2	WR	1968	United States	38.23	WR
1924	United States	41.0	=WR	1972	United States	38.19	WR
1928	United States	41.0	=WR	1976	United States	38.33	
1932	United States	40.0	WR	1980	Soviet Union	38.26	
1936	United States	39.8	WR	1984	United States	37.83	WR
1948	United States	40.6		1988	Soviet Union	38.19	
1952	United States	40.1		1992	United States	37.40	WR
1956	United States	39.5	WR	1996	Canada	37.69	
1960	Germany	39.5	=WR	2000	United States	37.61	

4x400-meter Relay

Year		Time		Year		Time	
1908	United States	3:29.4		1964	United States	3:00.7	WR
1912	United States	3:16.6	WR	1968	United States	2:56.16	WR
1920	Great Britain	3:22.2		1972	Kenya	2:59.8	
1924	United States	3:16.0	WR	1976	United States	2:58.65	
1928	United States	3:14.2	WR	1980	Soviet Union	3:01.1	
1932	United States	3:08.2	WR	1984	United States	2:57.91	
1936	Great Britain	3:09.0		1988	United States	2:56.16	=WR
1948	United States	3:10.4		1992	United States	2:55.74	WR
1952	Jamaica	3:03.9	WR	1996	United States	2:55.99	
1956	United States	3:04.8		2000	United States	2:56.35	
1960	United States	3:02.2	WR				

20-kilometer Walk

Year		Time		Year		Time	
1956	Leonid Spirin, USSR	1:31:27.4		1980	Maurizio Damilano, ITA	1:23:35.5	OR
1960	Vladimir Golubnichiy, USSR	1:34:07.2		1984	Ernesto Canto, MEX	1:23:13	OR
1964	Ken Matthews, GBR	1:29:34.0	OR	1988	Jozef Pribilinec, CZE	1:19:57	OR
1968	Vladimir Golubnichiy, USSR	1:33:58.4		1992	Daniel Plaza Montero, SPA	1:21:45	
1972	Peter Frenkel, E. Ger	1:26:42.4	OR	1996	Jefferson Perez, ECU	1:20:07	
1976	Daniel Bautista, MEX	1:24:40.6	OR	2000	Robert Korzeniowski, POL	1:18.59	OR

50-kilometer Walk

Year		Time		Year		Time	
1932	Thomas Green, GBR	4:50:10		1972	Bernd Kannenberg, W. Ger	3:56:11.6	OR
1936	Harold Whitlock, GBR	4:30:41.4	OR	1976	Not held		
1948	John Ljunggren, SWE	4:41:52		1980	Hartwig Gauder, E. Ger	3:49:24.0	OR
1952	Giuseppe Dordoni, ITA	4:28:07.8	OR	1984	Raul Gonzalez, MEX	3:47:26	OR
1956	Norman Read, NZE	4:30:42.8		1988	Vyacheslav Ivanenko, USSR	3:38:29	OR
1960	Don Thompson, GBR	4:25:30.0	OR	1992	Andrei Perlov, UT	3:50:13	
1964	Abdon Pamich, ITA	4:11:12.4	OR	1996	Robert Korzeniowski, POL	3:43:30	
1968	Christoph Höhne, E. Ger	4:20:13.6		2000	Robert Korzeniowski, POL	3:42.22	

High Jump

Year		Height		Year		Height	
1896	Ellery Clark, USA	5-11¼		1956	Charley Dumas, USA	6-11½	OR
1900	Irving Baxter, USA	6- 2¾	OR	1960	Robert Shavlakadze, USSR	7- 1	OR
1904	Sam Jones, USA	5-11		1964	Valery Brumel, USSR	7- 1¾	OR
1906	Cornelius Leahy, GBR/IRE	5-10		1968	Dick Fosbury, USA	7- 4¼	OR
1908	Harry Porter, USA	6- 3	OR	1972	Yuri Tarmak, USSR	7- 3¾	
1912	Alma Richards, USA	6- 4	OR	1976	Jacek Wszola, POL	7- 4½	OR
1920	Richmond Landon, USA	6- 4	=OR	1980	Gerd Wessig, E. Ger	7- 8¾	WR
1924	Harold Osborn, USA	6- 6	OR	1984	Dietmar Mögenburg, W. Ger	7- 8½	
1928	Bob King, USA	6- 4½		1988	Gennady Avdeyenko, USSR	7- 9¾	OR
1932	Duncan McNaughton, CAN	6- 5½		1992	Javier Sotomayor, CUB	7- 8	
1936	Cornelius Johnson, USA	6- 8	OR	1996	Charles Austin, USA	7- 10	OR
1948	John Winter, AUS	6- 6		2000	Sergey Klugin, RUS	7- 8½	
1952	Walt Davis, USA	6- 8½	OR				

Track & Field (Cont.)

Pole Vault

Year		Height		Year		Height	
1896	William Hoyt, USA	10-10		1952	Bob Richards, USA	14-11	OR
1900	Irving Baxter, USA	10-10		1956	Bob Richards, USA	14-11½	OR
1904	Charles Dvorak, USA	11- 5¾		1960	Don Bragg, USA	15- 5	OR
1906	Fernand Gonder, FRA	11- 5¾		1964	Fred Hansen, USA	16- 8¾	OR
1908	(TIE) Edward Cooke, USA	12- 2		1968	Bob Seagren, USA	17- 8½	OR
	& Alfred Gilbert, USA	12- 2	OR	1972	Wolfgang Nordwig, E. Ger	18- 0½	OR
1912	Harry Babcock, USA	12-11½	OR	1976	Tadeusz Slusarski, POL	18- 0½	=OR
1920	Frank Foss, USA	13- 5	WR	1980	Wladyslaw Kozakiewicz, POL	18-11½	WR
1924	Lee Barnes, USA	12-11½		1984	Pierre Quinon, FRA	18-10¼	
1928	Sabin Carr, USA	13- 9¼		1988	Sergey Bubka, USSR	19- 4¼	OR
1932	Bill Miller, USA	14- 1¾	OR	1992	Maksim Tarasov, UT	19- 0¼	
1936	Earle Meadows, USA	14- 3¼	OR	1996	Jean Galfione, FRA	19- 5¼	OR
1948	Guinn Smith, USA	14- 1¼		2000	Nick Hysong, USA	19- 4¼	

Long Jump

Year		Distance		Year		Distance	
1896	Ellery Clark, USA	20-10		1956	Greg Bell, USA	25- 8¼	
1900	Alvin Kraenzlein, USA	23- 6¾	OR	1960	Ralph Boston, USA	26- 7¾	OR
1904	Meyer Prinstein, USA	24- 1	OR	1964	Lynn Davies, GBR	26- 5¾	
1906	Meyer Prinstein, USA	23- 7½		1968	Bob Beamon, USA	29- 2½	WR
1908	Frank Irons, USA	24- 6½	OR	1972	Randy Williams, USA	27- 0½	
1912	Albert Gutterson, USA	24-11¼	OR	1976	Arnie Robinson, USA	27- 4¾	
1920	William Petersson, SWE	23- 5½		1980	Lutz Dombrowski, E. Ger	28- 0¼	
1924	De Hart Hubbard, USA	24- 5		1984	Carl Lewis, USA	28- 0¼	
1928	Ed Hamm, USA	25- 4½	OR	1988	Carl Lewis, USA	28- 7¼	
1932	Ed Gordon, USA	25- 0¾		1992	Carl Lewis, USA	28- 5½	
1936	Jesse Owens, USA	26- 5½	OR	1996	Carl Lewis, USA	27- 10¾	
1948	Willie Steele, USA	25- 8		2000	Ivan Pedroso, CUB	28- 0¾	
1952	Jerome Biffle, USA	24-10					

Triple Jump

Year		Distance		Year		Distance	
1896	James Connolly, USA	44-11¾		1956	Adhemar da Silva, BRA	53- 7¾	OR
1900	Meyer Prinstein, USA	47- 5¾	OR	1960	Józef Schmidt, POL	55- 2	
1904	Meyer Prinstein, USA	47- 1		1964	Józef Schmidt, POL	55- 3½	OR
1906	Peter O'Connor, GBR/IRE	46- 2¼		1968	Viktor Saneyev, USSR	57- 0¾	WR
1908	Timothy Ahearne, GBR/IRE	48-11¼	OR	1972	Viktor Saneyev, USSR	56-11¼	
1912	Gustaf Lindblom, SWE	48- 5¼		1976	Viktor Saneyev, USSR	56- 8¾	
1920	Vilho Tuulos, FIN	47- 7		1980	Jaak Uudmäe, USSR	56-11¼	
1924	Nick Winter, AUS	50-11¼	WR	1984	Al Joyner, USA	56- 7½	
1928	Mikio Oda, JPN	49-11		1988	Khristo Markov, BUL	57- 9¼	OR
1932	Chuhei Nambu, JPN	51- 7	WR	1992	Mike Conley, USA	59- 7½ ʷ	OR
1936	Naoto Tajima, JPN	52- 6	WR	1996	Kenny Harrison, USA	59- 4¼	OR
1948	Arne Ahman, SWE	50- 6¼		2000	Jonathan Edwards, GBR	58- 1¼	
1952	Adhemar da Silva, BRA	53- 2¾	WR		ʷindicates wind-aided.		

Shot Put

Year		Distance		Year		Distance	
1896	Bob Garrett, USA	36- 9¾		1956	Parry O'Brien, USA	60-11¼	OR
1900	Richard Sheldon, USA	46- 3¼	OR	1960	Bill Nieder, USA	64- 6¾	OR
1904	Ralph Rose, USA	48- 7	WR	1964	Dallas Long, USA	66- 8½	OR
1906	Martin Sheridan, USA	40- 5¼		1968	Randy Matson, USA	67- 4¾	
1908	Ralph Rose, USA	46- 7½		1972	Wladyslaw Komar, POL	69- 6	OR
1912	Patrick McDonald, USA	50- 4	OR	1976	Udo Beyer, E. Ger	69- 0¾	
1920	Ville Pörhölä, FIN	48- 7¼		1980	Vladimir Kiselyov, USSR	70- 0½	OR
1924	Bud Houser, USA	49- 2¼		1984	Alessandro Andrei, ITA	69- 9	
1928	John Kuck, USA	52- 0¾	WR	1988	Ulf Timmermann, E. Ger	73- 8¾	OR
1932	Leo Sexton, USA	52- 6	OR	1992	Mike Stulce, USA	71- 2½	
1936	Hans Woellke, GER	53- 1¾	OR	1996	Randy Barnes, USA	70- 11¼	
1948	Wilbur Thompson, USA	56- 2	OR	2000	Arsi Harju, FIN	69-10¼	
1952	Parry O'Brien, USA	57- 1½	OR				

Discus Throw

Year		Distance		Year		Distance	
1896	Bob Garrett, USA	95-7½		1956	Al Oerter, USA	184-11	OR
1900	Rudolf Bauer, HUN	118-3	OR	1960	Al Oerter, USA	194-2	OR
1904	Martin Sheridan, USA	128-10½	OR	1964	Al Oerter, USA	200-1	OR
1906	Martin Sheridan, USA	136-0		1968	Al Oerter, USA	212-6	OR
1908	Martin Sheridan, USA	134-2	OR	1972	Ludvik Danek, CZE	211-3	
1912	Armas Taipale, FIN	148-3	OR	1976	Mac Wilkins, USA	221-5	
1920	Elmer Niklander, FIN	146-7		1980	Viktor Rashchupkin, USSR	218-8	
1924	Bud Houser, USA	151-4	OR	1984	Rolf Danneberg, W. Ger	218-6	
1928	Bud Houser, USA	155-3	OR	1988	Jürgen Schult, E. Ger	225-9	OR
1932	John Anderson, USA	162-4	OR	1992	Romas Ubartas, LIT	213-8	
1936	Ken Carpenter, USA	165-7	OR	1996	Lars Riedel, GER	227-8	
1948	Adolfo Consolini, ITA	173-2	OR	2000	Virgilijus Alekna, LIT	227-4	
1952	Sim Iness, USA	180-6	OR				

Hammer Throw

Year		Distance		Year		Distance	
1900	John Flanagan, USA	163-1		1960	Vasily Rudenkov, USSR	220-2	OR
1904	John Flanagan, USA	168-1	OR	1964	Romuald Klim, USSR	228-10	OR
1908	John Flanagan, USA	170-4	OR	1968	Gyula Zsivótzky, HUN	240-8	OR
1912	Matt McGrath, USA	179-7	OR	1972	Anatoly Bondarchuk, USSR	247-8	OR
1920	Pat Ryan, USA	173-5		1976	Yuri Sedykh, USSR	254-4	OR
1924	Fred Tootell, USA	174-10		1980	Yuri Sedykh, USSR	268-4	WR
1928	Pat O'Callaghan, IRE	168-7		1984	Juha Tiainen, FIN	256-2	
1932	Pat O'Callaghan, IRE	176-11		1988	Sergey Litvinov, USSR	278-2	OR
1936	Karl Hein, GER	185-4	OR	1992	Andrei Abduvaliyev, UT	270-9	
1948	Imre Németh, HUN	183-11		1996	Balazs Kiss, HUN.	266-6	
1952	József Csérmák, HUN	197-11	WR	2000	Szymon Ziolkowski, POL.	262-6	
1956	Harold Connolly, USA	207-3	OR				

Javelin Throw

Year		Distance		Year		Distance	
1908	Eric Lemming, SWE	179-10	WR	1964	Pauli Nevala, FIN	271-2	
1912	Eric Lemming, SWE	198-11	WR	1968	Jänis Lüsis, USSR	295-7	OR
1920	Jonni Myyrä, FIN	215-10	OR	1972	Klaus Wolfermann, W. Ger	296-10	OR
1924	Jonni Myyrä, FIN	206-7		1976	Miklos Németh, HUN	310-4	WR
1928	Erik Lundkvist, SWE	218-6	OR	1980	Dainis Kula, USSR	299-2	
1932	Matti Järvinen, FIN	238-6	OR	1984	Arto Härkönen, FIN	284-8	
1936	Gerhard Stöck, GER	235-8		1988	Tapio Korjus, FIN	276-6	
1948	Kai Tapio Rautavaara, FIN	228-10		1992	Jan Zelezny, CZE	294-2*	OR
1952	Cy Young, USA	242-1	OR	1996	Jan Zelezny, CZE	289-3	
1956	Egil Danielson, NOR	281-2	WR	2000	Jan Zelezny, CZR	295-10	OR
1960	Viktor Tsibulenko, USSR	277-8					

*In 1986 the balance point of the javelin was modified and new records have been kept since.

Decathlon

Year		Points		Year		Points	
1904	Thomas Kiely, IRE	6036		1960	Rafer Johnson, USA	8392	OR
1906-08 Not held				1964	Willi Holdorf, GER	7887	
1912	Jim Thorpe, USA	8412	WR	1968	Bill Toomey, USA	8193	OR
1920	Helge Lövland, NOR	6803		1972	Nikolai Avilov, USSR	8454	WR
1924	Harold Osborn, USA	7711	WR	1976	Bruce Jenner, USA	8617	WR
1928	Paavo Yrjölä, FIN	8053	WR	1980	Daley Thompson, GBR	8495	
1932	Jim Bausch, USA	8462	WR	1984	Daley Thompson, GBR	8798	=WR
1936	Glenn Morris, USA	7900	WR	1988	Christian Schenk, E. Ger	8488	
1948	Bob Mathias, USA	7139		1992	Robert Zmelik, CZE	8611	
1952	Bob Mathias, USA	7887	WR	1996	Dan O'Brien, USA	8824	
1956	Milt Campbell, USA	7937	OR	2000	Erki Nool, EST	8641	

WOMEN

At least 4 gold medals (including relays): Evelyn Ashford, Fanny Blankers-Koen, Betty Cuthbert and Bärbel Eckert Wöckel (4).

100 meters

Year		Time		Year		Time	
1928	Betty Robinson, USA	12.2	=WR	1972	Renate Stecher, E. Ger	11.07	
1932	Stella Walsh, POL*	11.9	=WR	1976	Annegret Richter, W. Ger	11.08	
1936	Helen Stephens, USA	11.5ʷ		1980	Lyudmila Kondratyeva, USSR	11.06	
1948	Fanny Blankers-Koen, NED	11.9		1984	Evelyn Ashford, USA	10.97	OR
1952	Marjorie Jackson, AUS	11.5	=WR	1988	Florence Griffith Joyner, USA	10.54ʷ	
1956	Betty Cuthbert, AUS	11.5		1992	Gail Devers, USA	10.82	OR
1960	Wilma Rudolph, USA	11.0ʷ		1996	Gail Devers, USA.	10.94	
1964	Wyomia Tyus, USA	11.4		2000	Marion Jones, USA	10.75	
1968	Wyomia Tyus, USA	11.08	WR				

*An autopsy performed after Walsh's death in 1980 revealed that she was a man.
ʷindicates wind-aided.

Track & Field (Cont.)
200 meters

Year		Time		Year		Time	
1948	Fanny Blankers-Koen, NED	24.4		1976	Bärbel Eckert, E. Ger	22.37	OR
1952	Marjorie Jackson, AUS	23.7	OR	1980	Bärbel Eckert Wockel, E. Ger	22.03	OR
1956	Betty Cuthbert, AUS	23.4	=OR	1984	Valerie Brisco-Hooks, USA	21.81	OR
1960	Wilma Rudolph, USA	24.0		1988	Florence Griffith Joyner, USA	21.34	WR
1964	Edith McGuire, USA	23.0	OR	1992	Gwen Torrence, USA	21.81	
1968	Irena Szewinska, POL	22.5	WR	1996	Marie-Jose Perec, FRA	22.12	
1972	Renate Stecher, E. Ger	22.40	=WR	2000	Marion Jones, USA	21.84	

400 meters

Year		Time		Year		Time	
1964	Betty Cuthbert, AUS	52.0		1984	Valerie Brisco-Hooks, USA	48.83	OR
1968	Colette Besson, FRA	52.03	=OR	1988	Olga Bryzgina, USSR	48.65	OR
1972	Monika Zehrt, E. Ger	51.08	OR	1992	Marie-Jose Perec, FRA	48.83	
1976	Irena Szewinska, POL	49.29	WR	1996	Marie-Jose Perec, FRA	48.25	OR
1980	Marita Koch, E. Ger	48.88	OR	2000	Cathy Freeman, AUS	49.11	

800 meters

Year		Time		Year		Time	
1928	Lina Radke, GER	2:16.8	WR	1980	Nadezhda Olizarenko, USSR	1:53.42	WR
1932-56 Not held				1984	Doina Melinte, ROM	1:57.60	
1960	Lyudmila Shevtsova, USSR	2:04.3	=WR	1988	Sigrun Wodars, E. Ger	1:56.10	
1964	Ann Packer, GBR	2:01.1	OR	1992	Ellen van Langen, NED	1:55.54	
1968	Madeline Manning, USA	2:00.9	OR	1996	Svetlana Masterkova, RUS	1:57.73	
1972	Hildegard Falck, W. Ger	1:58.55	OR	2000	Maria Mutola, MOZ	1:56.15	
1976	Tatyana Kazankina, USSR	1:54.94	WR				

1500 meters

Year		Time		Year		Time	
1972	Lyudmila Bragina, USSR	4:01.4	WR	1988	Paula Ivan, ROM	3:53.96	OR
1976	Tatyana Kazankina, USSR	4:05.48		1992	Hassiba Boulmerka, ALG	3:55.30	
1980	Tatyana Kazankina, USSR	3:56.6	OR	1996	Svetlana Masterkova, RUS	4:00.83	
1984	Gabriella Dorio, ITA	4:03.25		2000	Nouria Merah-Benida, ALG	4:05.10	

5000 meters

Year		Time		Year		Time	
1984	Maricica Puica, ROM	8:35.96		1996	Wang Junxia, CHN	14:59.88	
1988	Tatyana Samolenko, USSR	8:26.53	OR	2000	Gabriela Szabo, ROM	14:40.79	OR
1992	Elena Romanova, UT	8:46.04			**Note:** Event held over 3000 meters from 1984-92.		

10,000 meters

Year		Time		Year		Time	
1988	Olga Bondarenko, USSR	31:05.21	OR	1996	Fernanda Ribeiro, POR	31:01.63	OR
1992	Derartu Tulu, ETH	31:06.02		2000	Derartu Tulu, ETH	30:17.49	OR

Marathon

Year		Time		Year		Time	
1984	Joan Benoit, USA	2:24:52		1996	Fatuma Roba, ETH	2:26:05	
1988	Rosa Mota, POR	2:25:40		2000	Naoko Takahashi, JPN	2:23:14	
1992	Valentina Yegorova, UT	2:32:41					

100-meter Hurdles

Year		Time		Year		Time	
1932	Babe Didrikson, USA	11.7	WR	1976	Johanna Schaller, E. Ger	12.77	
1936	Trebisonda Valla, ITA	11.7		1980	Vera Komisova, USSR	12.56	OR
1948	Fanny Blankers-Koen, NED	11.2	OR	1984	Benita Fitzgerald-Brown, USA	12.84	
1952	Shirley Strickland, AUS	10.9	WR	1988	Yordanka Donkova, BUL	12.38	OR
1956	Shirley Strickland, AUS	10.7	OR	1992	Paraskevi Patoulidou, GRE	12.64	
1960	Irina Press, USSR	10.8		1996	Ludmila Enquist, SWE	12.58	
1964	Karin Balzer, GER	10.5^w		2000	Olga Shishigina, KAZ	12.65	
1968	Maureen Caird, AUS	10.3	OR		^{w}indicates wind-aided.		
1972	Annelie Ehrhardt, E. Ger	12.59	WR		**Note:** Event held over 80 meters from 1932-68.		

400-meter Hurdles

Year		Time		Year		Time	
1984	Nawal El Moutawakel, MOR	54.61	OR	1996	Deon Hemmings, JAM	52.82	OR
1988	Debra Flintoff-King, AUS	53.17	OR	2000	Irina Privalova, RUS	53.02	
1992	Sally Gunnell, GBR	53.23					

4x100-meter Relay

Year		Time		Year		Time	
1928	Canada	48.4	WR	1972	West Germany	42.81	WR
1932	United States	46.9	WR	1976	East Germany	42.55	OR
1936	United States	46.9		1980	East Germany	41.60	WR
1948	Holland	47.5		1984	United States	41.65	
1952	United States	45.9	WR	1988	United States	41.98	
1956	Australia	44.5	WR	1992	United States	42.11	
1960	United States	44.5		1996	United States	41.95	
1964	Poland	43.6		2000	Bahamas	42.20	
1968	United States	42.87	WR				

4x400-meter Relay

Year		Time		Year		Time	
1972	East Germany	3:23.0	WR	1988	Soviet Union	3:15.18	WR
1976	East Germany	3:19.23	WR	1992	Unified Team	3:20.20	
1980	Soviet Union	3:20.2		1996	United States	3:20.91	
1984	United States	3:18.29	OR	2000	United States	3:22.62	

20-kilometer Walk

Year		Time	Year		Time
1992	Chen Yueling, CHN	44:32	2000	Wang Liping, CHN	1:29.05
1996	Yelena Ninikolayeva, RUS	41:49			

Note: Event was held over 10 kilometers from 1992-96.

High Jump

Year		Height		Year		Height	
1928	Ethel Catherwood, CAN	5- 2½		1972	Ulrike Meyfarth, W. Ger	6- 3½	=WR
1932	Jean Shiley, USA	5- 5¼	WR	1976	Rosemarie Ackermann, E. Ger	6- 4	OR
1936	Ibolya Csák, HUN	5- 3		1980	Sara Simeoni, ITA	6- 5½	OR
1948	Alice Coachman, USA	5- 6	OR	1984	Ulrike Meyfarth, W. Ger	6- 7½	OR
1952	Esther Brand, RSA	5- 5¾		1988	Louise Ritter, USA	6- 8	OR
1956	Mildred McDaniel, USA	5- 9¼	WR	1992	Heike Henkel, GER	6- 7½	
1960	Iolanda Balas, ROM	6- 0¾	OR	1996	Stefka Kostadinova, BUL	6- 8¾	
1964	Iolanda Balas, ROM	6- 2¾	OR	2000	Yelena Yelesina, RUS	6- 7	
1968	Miloslava Rezkova, CZE	5-11½					

Pole Vault

Year		Height	
2000	Stacy Draglia, USA	15- 1	OR

Long Jump

Year		Distance		Year		Distance	
1948	Olga Gyarmati, HUN	18- 8¼		1976	Angela Voigt, E. Ger	22- 0¾	
1952	Yvette Williams, NZE	20- 5¾	OR	1980	Tatyana Kolpakova, USSR	23- 2	OR
1956	Elzbieta Krzesinska, POL	20-10	=WR	1984	Anisoara Cusmir-Stanciu, ROM	22- 10	
1960	Vyera Krepkina, USSR	20-10¾	OR	1988	Jackie Joyner-Kersee, USA	24- 3¼	OR
1964	Mary Rand, GBR	22- 2¼	WR	1992	Heike Drechsler, GER	23- 5¼	
1968	Viorica Viscopoleanu, ROM	22- 4½	WR	1996	Chioma Ajunwa, NGR	23- 4½	
1972	Heidemarie Rosendahl, W. Ger	22- 3		2000	Heike Drechsler, GER	22- 11¼	

Triple Jump

Year		Distance	Year		Distance
1996	Inessa Kravets, UKR	50- 3½	2000	Tereza Marinova, BUL	49- 10½

Shot Put

Year		Distance		Year		Distance	
1948	Micheline Ostermeyer, FRA	45- 1½		1976	Ivanka Hristova, BUL	69- 5¼	OR
1952	Galina Zybina, USSR	50- 1¾	WR	1980	Ilona Slupianek, E. Ger	73- 6¼	OR
1956	Tamara Tyshkevich, USSR	54- 5	OR	1984	Claudia Losch, W. Ger	67- 2¼	
1960	Tamara Press, USSR	56- 10	OR	1988	Natalia Lisovskaya, USSR	72- 11¾	
1964	Tamara Press, USSR	59- 6¼	OR	1992	Svetlana Krivaleva, UT	69- 1¼	
1968	Margitta Gummel, E. Ger	64- 4	WR	1996	Astrid Kumbernuss, GER	67- 5½	
1972	Nadezhda Chizhova, USSR	69- 0	WR	2000	Yanina Korolchik, BLR	67- 5½	

Track & Field (Cont.)

Discus Throw

Year		Distance		Year		Distance	
1928	Halina Konopacka, POL	129-11¾	**WR**	1972	Faina Melnik, USSR	218- 7	**OR**
1932	Lillian Copeland, USA	133- 2	**OR**	1976	Evelin Schlaak, E. Ger	226- 4	**OR**
1936	Gisela Mauermayer, GER	156- 3	**OR**	1980	Evelin Schlaak Jahl, E. Ger	229- 6	**OR**
1948	Micheline Ostermeyer, FRA	137- 6		1984	Ria Stalman, NED	214- 5	
1952	Nina Romaschkova, USSR	168- 8	**OR**	1988	Martina Hellmann, E. Ger	237- 2½	**OR**
1956	Olga Fikotová, CZE	176- 1	**OR**	1992	Maritza Marten, CUB	229-10	
1960	Nina Ponomaryeva, USSR	180- 9	**OR**	1996	Ilke Wyludda, GER	228- 6	
1964	Tamara Press, USSR	187-10	**OR**	2000	Ellina Zvereva, BLR	224- 5	
1968	Lia Manoliu, ROM	191- 2	**OR**				

Hammer Throw

Year		Distance	
2000	Kamila Skolimowska, POL	233- 5¾	**OR**

Javelin Throw

Year		Distance		Year		Distance	
1932	Babe Didrikson, USA	143- 4		1972	Ruth Fuchs, E. Ger	209- 7	**OR**
1936	Tilly Fleischer, GER	148- 3	**OR**	1976	Ruth Fuchs, E. Ger	216- 4	**OR**
1948	Herma Bauma, AUT	149- 6	**OR**	1980	Maria Colon Rueñes, CUB	224- 5	**OR**
1952	Dana Zátopková, CZE	165- 7	**OR**	1984	Tessa Sanderson, GBR	228- 2	**OR**
1956	Ineze Jaunzeme, USSR	176- 8	**OR**	1988	Petra Felke, E. Ger	245- 0	**OR**
1960	Elvira Ozolina, USSR	183- 8	**OR**	1992	Silke Renk, GER	224- 2	
1964	Mihaela Penes, ROM	198- 7	**OR**	1996	Heli Rantanen, FIN	222- 11	
1968	Angéla Németh, HUN	198- 0		2000	Trine Hattestad, NOR	226- 1	**OR**

Heptathlon

Year		Points		Year		Points	
1964	Irina Press, USSR	5246	**WR**	1984	Glynis Nunn, AUS	6390	**OR**
1968	Ingrid Becker, W. Ger	5098		1988	Jackie Joyner-Kersee, USA	7291	**WR**
1972	Mary Peters, GBR	4801	**WR**	1992	Jackie Joyner-Kersee, USA	7044	
1976	Siegrun Siegl, E. Ger	4745		1996	Ghada Shouaa, SYR	6780	
1980	Nadezhda Tkachenko, USSR	5083	**WR**	2000	Denise Lewis, GBR	6584	

Note: Seven-event Heptathlon replaced five-event Pentathlon in 1984.

All-Time Leading Medal Winners – Single Games

Athletes who have won the most medals in a single Summer Olympics. Totals include individual, relay and team medals. U.S. athletes are in **bold** type.

MEN

No		Sport	G-S-B	No		Sport	G-S-B
8	Aleksandr Dityatin, USSR (1980)	Gym	3-4-1	6	Viktor Chukarin, USSR (1956)	Gym	4-2-0
7	**Mark Spitz**, USA (1972)	Swim	7-0-0	6	Konrad Frey, GER (1936)	Gym	3-1-2
7	**Willis Lee**, USA (1920)	Shoot	5-1-1	6	Ville Ritola, FIN (1924)	Track	4-2-0
7	**Matt Biondi**, USA (1988)	Swim	5-1-1	6	Hubert Van Innis, BEL (1920)	Arch	4-2-0
7	Boris Shakhlin, USSR (1960)	Gym	4-2-1	6	**Carl Osburn**, USA (1920)	Shoot	4-1-1
7	**Lloyd Spooner**, USA (1920)	Shoot	4-1-2	6	Louis Richardet, SWI (1906)	Shoot	3-3-0
7	Mikhail Voronin, USSR (1968)	Gym	2-4-1	6	**Anton Heida**, USA (1904)	Gym	5-1-0
7	Nikolai Andrianov, USSR (1976)	Gym	2-4-1	6	**George Eyser**, USA (1904)	Gym	3-2-1
6	Vitaly Scherbo, UT (1992)	Gym	6-0-0	6	**Burton Downing**, USA (1904)	Cycle	2-3-1
6	Li Ning, CHN (1984)	Gym	3-2-1	6	Alexei Nemov, RUS (1996)	Gym	2-1-3
6	Akinori Nakayama, JPN (1968)	Gym	4-1-1	6	Alexei Nemov, RUS (2000)	Gym	2-1-3
6	Takashi Ono, JPN (1960)	Gym	3-1-2				

WOMEN

No		Sport	G-S-B	No		Sport	G-S-B
7	Maria Gorokhovskaya, USSR (1952)	Gym	2-5-0	5	Ecaterina Szabó, ROM (1984)	Gym	4-1-0
6	Kristin Otto, E. Ger (1988)	Swim	6-0-0	5	Shane Gould, AUS (1972)	Swim	3-1-1
6	Agnes Keleti, HUN (1956)	Gym	4-2-0	5	Nadia Comaneci, ROM (1976)	Gym	3-1-1
6	Vera Cáslavská, CZE (1968)	Gym	4-2-0	5	Karin Janz, E. Ger (1972)	Gym	2-2-1
6	Larisa Latynina, USSR (1956)	Gym	4-1-1	5	Ines Diers, E. Ger (1980)	Swim	2-2-1
6	Larisa Latynina, USSR (1960)	Gym	3-2-1	5	**Shirley Babashoff**, USA (1976)	Swim	1-4-0
6	Daniela Silivas, ROM (1988)	Gym	3-2-1	5	**Mary Lou Retton**, USA (1984)	Gym	1-2-2
6	Larisa Latynina, USSR (1964)	Gym	2-2-2	5	**Shannon Miller**, USA (1992)	Gym	0-2-3
6	Margit Korondi, HUN (1956)	Gym	1-1-4	5	**Marion Jones**, USA (2000)	Track	3-0-2
5	Kornelia Ender, E. Ger (1976)	Swim	4-1-0	5	**Dara Torres**, USA (2000)	Swim	2-0-3

All-Time Leading Medal Winners – Career

MEN

No		Sport	G-S-B	No		Sport	G-S-B
15	Nikolai Andrianov, USSR	Gymnastics	7-5-3	10	**Carl Lewis**, USA	Track/Field	9-1-0
13	Boris Shakhlin, USSR	Gymnastics	7-4-2	10	Aladár Gerevich, HUN	Fencing	7-1-2
13	Edoardo Mangiarotti, ITA	Fencing	6-5-2	10	Akinori Nakayama, JPN	Gymnastics	6-2-2
13	Takashi Ono, JPN	Gymnastics	5-4-4	10	Aleksandr Dityatin, USSR	Gymnastics	3-6-1
12	Paavo Nurmi, FIN	Track/Field	9-3-0	9	Vitaly Scherbo, BLR	Gymnastics	6-0-3
12	Sawao Kato, JPN	Gymnastics	8-3-1	9*	**Martin Sheridan**, USA	Track/Field	5-3-1
12	Alexei Nemov, RUS	Gymnastics	4-2-6	9*	Zoltán Halmay, HUN	Swimming	3-5-1
11	**Mark Spitz**, USA	Swimming	9-1-1	9	Giulio Gaudini, ITA	Fencing	3-4-2
11†	**Matt Biondi**, USA	Swimming	8-2-1	9	Mikhail Voronin, USSR	Gymnastics	2-6-1
11	Viktor Chukarin, USSR	Gymnastics	7-3-1	9	Heikki Savolainen, FIN	Gymnastics	2-1-6
11	**Carl Osburn**, USA	Shooting	5-4-2	9	Yuri Titov, USSR	Gymnastics	1-5-3
10*	**Ray Ewry**, USA	Track/Field	10-0-0				

†Includes gold medal as preliminary member of 1st-place relay team.
*Medals won by Ewry (2-0-0), Sheridan (2-3-0) and Halmay (1-1-0) at the 1906 Intercalated games are not officially recognized by the IOC.

Games Participated In

Andrianov (1972,76,80); **Biondi** (1984,88,92); **Chukarin** (1952,56); **Dityatin** (1976,80); **Ewry** (1900,04,06,08); **Gerevich** (1932,36,48,52,56,60); **Gaudini** (1928,32,36); **Halmay** (1900,04,06,08); **Kato** (1968,72,76); **Lewis** (1984,88,92,96); **Mangiarotti** (1936,48,52,56,60); **Nakayama** (1968,72); **Nemov** (1996,2000) **Nurmi** (1920,24,28); **Ono** (1952,56,60,64); **Osburn** (1912,20, 24); **Savolainen** (1928,32,36,48,52); **Scherbo** (1992,96); **Shakhlin** (1956,60,64); **Sheridan** (1904,06,08); **Spitz** (1968,72); **Titov** (1956,60,64); **Voronin** (1968,72).

WOMEN

No		Sport	G-S-B
18	Larissa Latynina, USSR	Gymnastics	9-5-4
11	Vera Cáslavská, CZE	Gymnastics	7-4-0
10	Birgit Fischer, GER	Canoe/Kayak	7-3-0
10	**Jenny Thompson**, USA	Swimming	8-1-1
10	Agnes Keleti, HUN	Gymnastics	5-3-2
10	Polina Astakhova, USSR	Gymnastics	5-2-3
9	Nadia Comaneci, ROM	Gymnastics	5-3-1
9	Lyudmila Touristcheva, USSR	Gymnastics	4-3-2
9	**Dara Torres**, USA	Swimming	4-1-4
9	Kornelia Ender, E. Ger	Swimming	4-4-0
8	Dawn Fraser, AUS	Swimming	4-4-0
8	**Shirley Babashoff**, USA	Swimming	2-6-0
8	Sofia Muratova, USSR	Gymnastics	2-2-4
7	Krisztina Egerszegi, HUN	Swimming	5-1-1
7	Irena Kirszenstein Szewinska, POL	Track/Field	3-2-2
7	Shirley Strickland, AUS	Track/Field	3-1-3
7	Maria Gorokhovskaya, USSR	Gymnastics	2-5-0
7	Ildiko Sagine-Ujlaki-Rejto, HUN	Fencing	2-3-2
7	**Shannon Miller**, USA	Gymnastics	2-2-3
7	Susie O'Neill, AUS	Swimming	2-4-1
7	Merlene Ottey, JAM	Track/Field	0-2-5

Games Participated In

Astakhova (1956,60,64); **Babashoff** (1972,76); **Cáslavská** (1960,64,68); **Comaneci** (1976,80); **Egerszegi** (1988,92,96); **Ender** (1972,76); **Fischer** (1980,92,96,2000); **Fraser** (1956,60,64); **Gorokhovskaya** (1952); **Keleti** (1952,56); **Latynina** (1956,60,64); **Miller** (1992,96); **Muratova** (1956,60); **O'Neill** (1996,2000) **Ottey** (1980,84,88,92,96) **Sagine-Ujlaki-Rejto** (1960,64, 68,72,76); **Strickland** (1948,52,56); **Szewinska** (1964,68,72,76,80); **Thompson** (1992,96,2000); **Torres** (1984,88,92,2000) **Touristcheva** (1968, 72,76).

> ### Most Individual Medals
> Not including team competition.
>
> | | Sport | G-S-B |
> |---|-------|-------|
> | **Men:** 12-Nikolai Andrianov, USSR | Gym | 6-3-3 |
> | **Women:** 15-Larissa Latynina, USSR | Gym | 7-5-3 |

Most Gold Medals

MEN

No		Sport	G-S-B	No		Sport	G-S-B
10*	**Ray Ewry**, USA	Track/Field	10-0-0	7	Boris Shakhlin, USSR	Gymnastics	7-4-2
9	Paavo Nurmi, FIN	Track/Field	9-3-0	7	Viktor Chukarin, USSR	Gymnastics	7-3-1
9	**Mark Spitz**, USA	Swimming	9-1-1	7	Aladar Gerevich, HUN	Fencing	7-1-2
9	**Carl Lewis**, USA	Track/Field	9-1-0				
8	Sawao Kato, JPN	Gymnastics	8-3-1				
8†	**Matt Biondi**, USA	Swimming	8-2-1				
7	Nikolai Andrianov, USSR	Gymnastics	7-5-3				

*Medals won by Ewry (2-0-0) at the 1906 Intercalated games are not officially recognized by the IOC.
†Includes gold medal as preliminary member of 1st-place relay team.

WOMEN

No		Sport	G-S-B	No		Sport	G-S-B
9	Larissa Latynina, USSR	Gymnastics	9-5-4	4	Lyudmila Touristcheva, USSR	Gymnastics	4-3-2
8	**Jenny Thompson**, USA	Swimming	8-1-1	4	**Dara Torres**, USA	Swimming	4-1-4
7	Vera Cáslavská, CZE	Gymnastics	7-4-0	4	**Evelyn Ashford**, USA	Track/Field	4-1-0
7	Birgit Fischer, GER	Canoe/Kayak	7-3-0	4	**Janet Evans**, USA	Swimming	4-1-0
6	Kristin Otto, E. Ger	Swimming	6-0-0	4	Fu Mingxia, CHN	Diving	4-1-0
6†	**Amy Van Dyken**, USA	Swimming	6-0-0	4	Fanny Blankers-Koen, NED	Track/Field	4-0-0
5	Agnes Keleti, HUN	Gymnastics	5-3-2	4	Betty Cuthbert, AUS	Track/Field	4-0-0
5	Nadia Comaneci, ROM	Gymnastics	5-3-1	4	**Pat McCormick**, USA	Diving	4-0-0
5	Polina Astakhova, USSR	Gymnastics	5-2-3	4	Bärbel Eckert Wäckel, E. Ger	Track/Field	4-0-0
5	Krisztina Egerszegi, HUN	Swimming	5-1-1				
4	Kornelia Ender, E. Ger	Swimming	4-4-0				
4	Dawn Fraser, AUS	Swimming	4-4-0				

†Includes gold medal as preliminary member of 1st-place relay team.

All-Time Leading Medal Winners – Career (Cont.)
Most Silver Medals

MEN

No		Sport	G-S-B
6	Alexandr Dityatin, USSR	Gymnastics	3-6-1
6	Mikhail Voronin, USSR	Gymnastics	2-6-1
5	Nikolai Andrianov, USSR	Gymnastics	7-5-3
5	Edoardo Mangiarotti, ITA	Fencing	6-5-2
5	Zoltán Halmay, HUN	Swimming	3-5-1
5	Gustavo Marzi, ITA	Fencing	2-5-0
5	Yuri Titov, USSR	Gymnastics	1-5-3
5	Viktor Lisitsky, USSR	Gymnastics	0-5-0

WOMEN

No		Sport	G-S-B
6	**Shirley Babashoff**, USA	Swimming	2-6-0
5	Larissa Latynina, USSR	Gymnastics	9-5-4
5	Maria Gorokhovskaya, USSR	Gymnastics	2-5-0
4	Vera Cáslavská, CZE	Gymnastics	7-4-0
4	Kornelia Ender, E. Ger	Swimming	4-4-0
4	Dawn Fraser, AUS	Swimming	4-4-0
4	Erica Zuchold, E. Ger	Gymnastics	0-4-1

Most Bronze Medals

MEN

No		Sport	G-S-B
6	Alexei Nemov, RUS	Gymnastics	4-2-6
6	Heikki Savolainen, FIN	Gymnastics	2-1-6
5	Daniel Revenu, FRA	Fencing	1-0-5
5	Philip Edwards, CAN	Track/Field	0-0-5
5	Adrianus Jong, NED	Fencing	0-0-5

WOMEN

No		Sport	G-S-B
5	Merlene Ottey, JAM	Track/Field	0-2-5
4	Larissa Latynina, USSR	Gymnastics	9-5-4
4	**Dara Torres**, USA	Swimming	4-1-4
4	Sofia Muratova, USSR	Gymnastics	2-2-4

All-Time Leading USA Medal Winners
Most Overall Medals
MEN

No		Sport	G-S-B
11	Mark Spitz	Swimming	9-1-1
11†	Matt Biondi	Swimming	8-2-1
11	Carl Osburn	Shooting	5-4-2
10*	Ray Ewry	Track/Field	10-0-0
10	Carl Lewis	Track/Field	9-1-0
9*	Martin Sheridan	Track/Field	5-3-1
8	Charles Daniels	Swimming	5-1-2
8	Gary Hall Jr.	Swimming	4-3-1
7‡	Tom Jager	Swimming	5-1-1
7	Willis Lee	Shooting	5-1-1
7	Lloyd Spooner	Shooting	4-1-2

No		Sport	G-S-B
6	Anton Heida	Gymnastics	5-1-0
6	Don Schollander	Swimming	5-1-0
6	Johnny Weissmuller	Swim/Water Polo	5-0-1
6	Alfred Lane	Shooting	5-0-1
6	Jim Lightbody	Track/Field	4-2-0
6	George Eyser	Gymnastics	3-2-1
6	Ralph Rose	Track/Field	3-2-1
6	Michael Plumb	Equestrian	2-4-0
6	Burton Downing	Cycling	2-3-1
6	Bob Garrett	Track/Field	2-2-2

†Includes gold medal as prelim. member of 1st-place relay team.
*Medals won by Ewry (2-0-0) and Sheridan (2-3-0) at the 1906 Intercalated games are not officially recognized by the IOC.
‡Includes 3 gold medals as prelim. member of 1st-place relay teams.

Games Participated In
Biondi (1984,88,92); **Daniels** (1904,06,08); **Downing** (1904); **Ewry** (1900,04,06,08); **Eyser** (1904); **Garrett** (1896,1900); **Hall** (1996,2000) **Heida** (1904); **Jager** (1984,88,92); **Lane** (1912,20); **Lee** (1920); **Lewis** (1984,88,92,96); **Lightbody** (1904,06); **Osburn** (1912,20,24); **Plumb** (1960, 64,68,72,76,84); **Rose** (1904,08,12); **Schollander** (1964, 68); **Sheridan** (1904,06,08); **Spitz** (1968,72); **Spooner** (1920); **Weissmuller** (1924,28).

WOMEN

No		Sport	G-S-B
10	Jenny Thompson	Swimming	8-1-1
9	Dara Torres	Swimming	4-1-4
8	Shirley Babashoff	Swimming	2-6-0
7	Shannon Miller	Gymnastics	2-2-3
6†	Amy Van Dyken	Swimming	6-0-0
6	Jackie Joyner-Kersee	Track/Field	3-1-2
6	Angel Martino	Swimming	3-0-3
5	Evelyn Ashford	Track/Field	4-1-0
5	Janet Evans	Swimming	4-1-0
5	Florence Griffith Joyner	Track/Field	3-2-0
5†	Mary T. Meagher	Swimming	3-1-1
5	Gwen Torrence	Track/Field	3-2-0
5	Marion Jones	Track/Field	3-0-2
5	Mary Lou Retton	Gymnastics	1-2-2
4	Pat McCormick	Diving	4-0-0
4	Valerie Brisco-Hooks	Track/Field	3-1-0

No		Sport	G-S-B
4	Nancy Hogshead	Swimming	3-1-0
4	Sharon Stouder	Swimming	3-1-0
4	Wyomia Tyus	Track/Field	3-1-0
4	Wilma Rudolph	Track/Field	3-0-1
4	Chris von Saltza	Swimming	3-1-0
4	Sue Pedersen	Swimming	2-2-0
4	Eleanor Garatti Saville	Swimming	2-1-1
4	Jan Henne	Swimming	2-1-1
4	Mary Wayte	Swimming	2-1-1
4	Dorothy Poynton Hill	Diving	2-1-1
4†	Summer Sanders	Swimming	2-1-1
4	Kathy Ellis	Swimming	2-0-2
4	Jill Sterkel	Swimming	2-0-2
4	Amanda Beard	Swimming	1-2-1
4	Georgia Coleman	Diving	1-2-1
4	Ellie Daniel	Swimming	1-1-2

†Includes gold medal as prelim. member of 1st-place relay team.

Games Participated In
Ashford (1976,84,88,92); **Babashoff** (1972,76); **Beard** (1996,2000); **Brisco-Hooks** (1984,88); **Coleman** (1928,32); **Daniel** (1968,72); **Ellis** (1964); **Evans** (1988,92,96); **Garatti Saville** (1928,32); **Griffith Joyner** (1984,88); **Henne** (1968); **Hogshead** (1984); **Jones** (2000); **Joyner-Kersee** (1984,88,92,96); **Martino** (1992,96); **McCormick** (1952,56); **Meagher** (1984,88); **Miller** (1992, 96); **Pedersen** (1968); **Poynton Hill** (1928,32,36); **Retton** (1984); **Rudolph** (1956,60); **Sanders** (1992); **Sterkel** (1976,84,88); **Stouder** (1964); **Thompson** (1988,92,96,2000); **Torrence** (1988,92,96); **Torres** (1984,88,92,2000); **Tyus** (1964,68); **Van Dyken** (1996,2000); **von Saltza** (1960); **Wayte** (1984,88).

Most Gold Medals

MEN

No		Sport	G-S-B
10*	Raymond Ewry	Track/Field	10-0-0
9	Mark Spitz	Swimming	9-1-1
9	Carl Lewis	Track/Field	9-1-0
8†	Matt Biondi	Swimming	8-2-1
5	Carl Osburn	Shooting	5-4-2
5*	Martin Sheridan	Track/Field	5-3-1
5	Charles Daniels	Swimming	5-1-2
5†	Tom Jager	Swimming	5-1-1
5	Willis Lee	Shooting	5-1-1
5	Anton Heida	Gymnastics	5-1-0
5	Don Schollander	Swimming	5-1-0
5	Johnny Weissmuller	Swim/Water Polo	5-0-1
5	Alfred Lane	Shooting	5-0-1
5	Morris Fisher	Shooting	5-0-0
4	Gary Hall Jr.	Swimming	4-3-1
4	Jim Lightbody	Track/Field	4-2-0
4	Lloyd Spooner	Shooting	4-1-2
4	Greg Louganis	Diving	4-1-0
4	John Naber	Swimming	4-1-0
4	Meyer Prinstein	Track/Field	4-1-0
4	Mel Sheppard	Track/Field	4-1-0
4	Marcus Hurley	Cycling	4-0-1
4	Marcus Hurley	Cycling	4-0-1
4†	Jon Olsen	Swimming	4-0-1
4	Archie Hahn	Track/Field	4-0-0
4	Alvin Kraenzlein	Track/Field	4-0-0
4	Al Oerter	Track/Field	4-0-0
4	Jesse Owens	Track/Field	4-0-0

*Medals won by Ewry (2-0-0) and Sheridan (2-3-0) at the 1906 Intercalated games are not officially recognized by the IOC.

†Includes gold medal as prelim. member of 1st-place relay team.

‡ Includes 3 gold medals as prelim. member of 1st-place relay teams.

WOMEN

No		Sport	G-S-B
8	Jenny Thompson	Swimming	8-1-1
6†	Amy Van Dyken	Swimming	6-0-0
4	Dara Torres	Swimming	4-1-4
4	Evelyn Ashford	Track/Field	4-1-0
4	Janet Evans	Swimming	4-1-0
4	Pat McCormick	Diving	4-0-0
3	Florence Griffith Joyner	Track/Field	3-2-0
3	Jackie Joyner-Kersee	Track/Field	3-1-2
3†	Mary T. Meagher	Swimming	3-1-1
3	Gwen Torrence	Track/Field	3-1-1
3	Valerie Brisco-Hooks	Track/Field	3-1-0
3	Nancy Hogshead	Swimming	3-1-0
3	Sharon Stouder	Swimming	3-1-0
3	Wyomia Tyus	Track/Field	3-1-0
3	Chris von Saltza	Swimming	3-1-0
3	Wilma Rudolph	Track/Field	3-0-1
3	Melissa Belote	Swimming	3-0-0
3	Ethelda Bleibtrey	Swimming	3-0-0
3	Tracy Caulkins	Swimming	3-0-0
3†	Nicole Haislett	Swimming	3-0-0
3	Helen Madison	Swimming	3-0-0
3	Debbie Meyer	Swimming	3-0-0
3	Sandra Neilson	Swimming	3-0-0
3	Martha Norelius	Swimming	3-0-0
3†	Carrie Steinseifer	Swimming	3-0-0
3‡	Ashley Tappin	Swimming	3-0-0

†Includes gold medal as prelim. member of 1st-place relay team.

‡ Includes 3 gold medals as prelim. member of 1st-place relay teams.

Most Silver Medals

MEN

No		Sport	G-S-B
4	Carl Osburn	Shooting	5-4-2
4	Michael Plumb	Equestrian	2-4-0
3	Martin Sheridan	Track/Field	5-3-1
3	Burton Downing	Cycling	2-3-1
3	Irving Baxter	Track/Field	2-3-0

No		Sport	G-S-B
3	Earl Thomson	Equestrian	2-3-0
3	Alexander McKee	Swimming	0-3-0

WOMEN

No		Sport	G-S-B
6	Shirley Babashoff	Swimming	2-6-0

All-Time Medal Standings, 1896-2000

All-time Summer Games medal standings, based on *The Golden Book of the Olympic Games*. Medal counts include the 1906 Intercalated Games, which are not recognized by the IOC.

		G	S	B	Total
1	United States	872	658	586	2116
2	USSR (1952-88)	395	319	296	1010
3	Great Britain	180	233	225	638
4	France	188	193	217	598
5	Italy	179	143	157	479
6	Sweden	136	156	177	469
7	East Germany (1968-88)	159	150	136	445
8	Hungary	150	135	158	443
9	Germany (1896-64,92–)	137	138	160	435
10	Australia	102	110	138	350
11	West Germany (1968-88)	77	104	120	301
12	Finland	101	81	114	296
	Japan	97	97	102	296
14	Romania	74	83	108	265
15	Poland	56	72	113	241
16	Canada	51	81	98	230
17	China	80	79	64	223
18	Netherlands	61	67	85	213
19	Bulgaria	48	82	65	195
20	Switzerland	47	75	61	183
21	Denmark	40	63	58	161
22	Russia (1896-1912, 96–)	58	52	46	156
23	South Korea	46	52	56	154
24	Czechoslovakia (1924-92)	49	49	44	142
25	Belgium	37	51	52	140
26	Cuba	55	44	38	137
27	Norway	49	44	41	134
28	Greece	32	48	46	126
29	Unified Team (1992)	45	38	29	112
30	Yugoslavia (1924-88, 96–)	28	32	33	93
31	Austria	20	32	34	86
32	Spain	25	28	22	75
33	New Zealand	30	12	32	74
34	Brazil	12	19	35	66
35	Turkey	33	16	15	64
36	Rep. of S. Africa (1904-60, 92–)	19	20	24	63

All-Time Medal Standings, 1896-2000 (Cont.)

		G	S	B	Total
37	Argentina	13	23	18	54
	Kenya	16	20	18	54
39	Mexico	10	15	22	47
40	Iran	8	13	19	40
41	Jamaica	5	20	12	37
42	North Korea	8	7	15	30
43	Estonia	8	6	12	26
44	Ethiopia	12	2	10	24
45	Ukraine	3	10	10	23
46	Great Britain/Ireland	6	11	3	20
	Ireland	8	6	6	20
48	Czech Republic	6	6	7	19
49	Portugal	3	4	10	17
	Belarus	3	3	11	17
	Nigeria	2	8	7	17
52	India	8	3	5	16
	Egypt	6	5	5	16
	Indonesia	4	7	5	16
	Morocco	4	3	9	16
56	Mongolia	0	5	9	14
57	Algeria	4	1	7	12
58	Trinidad & Tobago	1	3	7	11
59	Pakistan	3	3	4	10
	Uruguay	2	2	6	10
	Latvia	1	6	3	10
	Chinese Taipei	0	4	6	10
63	Lithuania	3	0	6	9
	Thailand	2	1	6	9
	Chile	0	6	3	9
	Philippines	0	2	7	9
67	Slovakia	2	4	2	8
	Venezuela	1	2	5	8
	Georgia	0	0	8	8
70	Kazakhstan	3	4	0	7
	Croatia	2	2	3	7
	Colombia	1	2	4	7
73	Bahamas	2	2	2	6
	Slovenia	2	2	2	6
	Uganda	1	3	2	6
	Tunisia	1	2	3	6
	Uzbekistan	1	2	3	6
	Bohemia	0	1	5	6
	Puerto Rico	0	1	5	6
80	Azerbaijan	2	1	1	4
	Peru	1	3	0	4
	Costa Rica	1	1	2	4
	Namibia	0	4	0	4
	Lebanon	0	2	2	4
	Moldova	0	2	2	4
	Ghana	0	1	3	4
	Israel	0	1	3	4
88	Luxembourg	2	1	0	3
	Armenia	1	1	1	3
	Cameroon	1	1	1	3
	Iceland	0	1	2	3
	Malaysia	0	1	2	3
93	Syria	1	1	0	2
	Japan/Korea	1	0	1	2
	Mozambique	1	0	1	2
	Surinam	1	0	1	2
	Tanzania	0	2	0	2
	Great Britain/USA	0	1	1	2
	Haiti	0	1	1	2
	Russia/Estonia	0	1	1	2
	Saudi Arabia	0	1	1	2
	United Arab Republic	0	1	1	2
	Zambia	0	1	1	2
	The Antilles	0	0	2	2
	Panama	0	0	2	2
	Qatar	0	0	2	2
107	Australia/New Zealand	1	0	0	1
	Burkina Faso	1	0	0	1
	Cuba/USA	1	0	0	1
	Denmark/Sweden	1	0	0	1
	Ecuador	1	0	0	1
	Gr. Britain/Ireland/Germany	1	0	0	1
	Gr. Britain/Ireland/USA	1	0	0	1
	Hong Kong	1	0	0	1
	Ireland/USA	1	0	0	1
	Zimbabwe	1	0	0	1
	Belgium/Greece	0	1	0	1
	Ceylon	0	1	0	1
	France/USA	0	1	0	1
	France/Gr. Britain/Ireland	0	1	0	1
	Ivory Coast	0	1	0	1
	Netherlands Antilles	0	1	0	1
	Senegal	0	1	0	1
	Singapore	0	1	0	1
	Smyrna	0	1	0	1
	Tonga	0	1	0	1
	Vietnam	0	1	0	1
	Virgin Islands	0	1	0	1
	Australia/Great Britain	0	0	1	1
	Barbados	0	0	1	1
	Bermuda	0	0	1	1
	Bohemia/Great Britain	0	0	1	1
	Djibouti	0	0	1	1
	Dominican Republic	0	0	1	1
	France/Great Britain	0	0	1	1
	Guyana	0	0	1	1
	Iraq	0	0	1	1
	Kuwait	0	0	1	1
	Kyrgyzstan	0	0	1	1
	Macedonia	0	0	1	1
	Mexico/Spain	0	0	1	1
	Niger	0	0	1	1
	Scotland	0	0	1	1
	Sri Lanka	0	0	1	1
	Thessalonika	0	0	1	1
	Wales	0	0	1	1

Combined totals:	G	S	B	Total
USSR/UT/Russia	498	409	371	1278
Germany/E. Ger/W. Ger	374	392	416	1182

Notes: Athletes from the USSR participated in the Summer Games from 1952-88, returned as the Unified Team in 1992 after the breakup of the Soviet Union (in 1991) and have competed as independent republics since the 1994 Winter Games. Germany was barred from the Olympics in 1924 and 1948 following World Wars I and II. Divided into East and West Germany after WWII, both countries competed together from 1952-64, then separately from 1968-88. Germany was reunified in 1990. Czechoslovakia split into Slovakia and the Czech Republic in 1993. Croatia and Bosnia-Herzegovina gained independence from Yugoslavia in 1991. Yugoslavia was not invited to the 1992 games (though Serbian and Montenegrin athletes were allowed to compete as independent athletes) but returned in 1996. South Africa was banned from 1964-88 for using the apartheid policy in the selection of its teams. It returned in 1992 as the Republic of South Africa (RSA).

Soccer

Landon Donovan had the USA headed in the right direction at the 2002 World Cup.

Korean Score

Brazil wins the World Cup but co-host South Korea steals the show with a thrilling run to the semifinals.

Jack Edwards
has been ABC and ESPN's play-by-play voice of U.S. Soccer, MLS, and the World Cup since 2000.

Beyond Ronaldo's heroic comeback from years lost to injury to lead Brazil to a fifth World Cup, and the United States' sudden emergence as a final-eight team, the most compelling story of the 2002 World Cup was South Korea's fantasy-come-true.

The co-host nation had never won a World Cup game before 2002, and it somehow managed to go all the way to the semifinals.

Here is a personal timeline of the evening of Korea's round-of-16 match, a stunning 2–1 golden goal victory over Italy:

Ahn Jung-Hwan attempts a penalty kick in the fifth minute, hoping to give Korea an early lead, but the ball is stopped by Italian keeper Gianluigi Buffon and the game remains scoreless.

Christian Vieri heads in a corner by the near post to give Italy the lead in the 18th minute of the match. Vieri puts a finger to his lips to hush the Korean fans but they don't comply.

The later the game goes, the wilder the crowd gets. The indefatigable 41,000 chant and sing in unison, non-stop, trying to lift Korea's players.

Italy goes into a defensive shell in the second half. The incredibly fit Koreans seem to grow stronger as Italy fades. Seol Ki-Hyeon scores on a turnaround with two minutes left. The stadium rocks.

Five million Koreans are watching at public, giant screen viewing locations, one million in City Plaza in Seoul alone.

Overtime. Even under our broadcasting headsets in Daejeon, it's deafening.

The first overtime ends and we're just 15 minutes away from penalty kicks. The crowd is now hysterical. No one sits. Everyone is screaming.

Italy's catalyst, Francesco Totti, gets his second yellow card of the match for

Gary M. Prior/Getty Images

*South Korea's **Ahn Jung-Hwan** sends a ball past the goalkeeper and a nation into ecstasy with his overtime game-winning goal against Italy.*

taking an apparent dive in the penalty box. The Ecuadorian referee Byron Moreno was out of position to make the call but Italy will nonetheless continue with just ten men.

Ahn, who failed to convert his penalty kick early in the first half, earns eternal redemption when he out-jumps Italian captain Paolo Maldini on a long pass and scores the golden goal. Korea wins. Bliss.

We get back to Seoul two and a half hours after the game, at 1 a.m. There are approximately 300,000 people on the boulevard that leads to our hotel. About 200 policemen lock elbows and form a walking human wedge to get our van through the humanity.

People are singing, chanting *"Ko-re-a!"* We slide open the windows of our van. People are racing up to us and high-fiving us for no particular reason, just the joy of sharing a lifetime memory.

We hear thumping on the roof of the van. Two young men have commandeered it as a platform as we amble along behind the police. They attract a lot of bemused attention. Our Korean driver (who got into the stadium free,

Alex Livesey/Getty Images

Rivaldo and *Ronaldo* (center) kiss Brazil's fifth World Cup trophy after beating Germany, 2–0, in the championship match played at Yokohama, Japan.

on our passes, and wept for joy at game's end) asks them firmly but politely to get off. They jump, thank us, and disappear into the throbbing throng.

Shafts of bamboo have become hand-held missile silos to shoot off bottle rockets, Roman candles, and fire-crackers. The air is pungent with burnt gunpowder, thick with small explosions of green and red.

Amid the din of car horns, chanting, and cheering, we do not observe a single display of real misconduct. People are drunk, rowdy, and beyond

the fatigue (it was a work day) but no one is impinging on the rights of another.

It is well after 2 a.m. before I drift off to sleep, still hearing the bedlam eight floors below. At the moment, it is the happiest place on Earth, I am sure.

The next morning, analyst Ty Keough, producer Mitch Green and I take our morning constitutional to Starbucks. There are six people in business suits who are caved in, face-down at their cafe tables, sound asleep.

But how could their dreams possibly top the reality?

Jack Edwards' Ten Biggest Stories of the Year in Soccer

10 ▪ Major League Soccer folds two teams, the Miami Fusion and Tampa Bay Mutiny, and offers no promise of future expansion until at least 2004. The quality of play in the league generally improves, but fewer roster spots mean fewer places for young American players to develop.

9 ▪ High-powered Argentina collapses in the first round and exits the World Cup after pool play along with consensus co-favorite France.

8 ▪ France fails to score and becomes the first defending champion to depart a World Cup without putting at least one goal on the board in its three pool play matches.

7 ▪ Some European clubs teeter on the brink of insolvency after television rights holders suffer financial collapses. Lingering effects from the crisis mean there is none of the usual feeding frenzy for proven talent following the World Cup.

6 ▪ American Landon Donovan scores twice, forces an own-goal by Portugal, and has another one called back against Poland. His World Cup performance proves the 20-year-old can compete at any level.

5 ▪ The United States, which had never won either a World Cup match abroad or a World Cup elimination game anywhere, does both during a surprising World Cup run that ends with a 1–0 loss to eventual runners-up Germany in the round of eight.

4 ▪ Turkey puts up its best-ever World Cup showing, beating co-host Korea in a superbly played third-place game, which includes the fastest goal in World Cup history (Hakan Sukur scored after just 10.8 seconds).

3 ▪ The co-hosts are well-represented. Korea, which had never won a World Cup game, wins its group, shocks Italy and reaches the semifinals. Co-host Japan also makes noise, winning Group H before losing to Turkey in the round of 16.

2 ▪ Ronaldo returns from two years of knee injuries and surgeries and scores eight times to lead all the World Cup. He equals Pele's career record for most World Cup goals by a Brazilian (12) after scoring both his team's goals in the championship victory over Germany.

1 ▪ Brazil wins an unprecedented fifth World Cup with a convincing 2-0 victory over Germany and its tournament MVP, goalkeeper Oliver Kahn.

We Meet At Last

Brazil and Germany both competed in a record seventh World Cup Final in 2002, yet it was the first time the two countries met for the title. Here's a look at the countries with the most World Cup Final appearances.

	Finals	Titles
Brazil	7	5
Germany	7	3
Italy	5	3
Argentina	4	2

Cause-in Oliver

Germany recorded five shutouts in six games en route to its showdown with Brazil in the World Cup Final. The Germans outscored their opponents 14–1 in the process and became the first finalist in World Cup history with five shutouts on their record. Perhaps that's why German goalkeeper Oliver Kahn was named the tournament most valuable player.

	Shutouts
2002 Germany	5
1998 France*	4
1994 Brazil*	4
1974 West Germany*	4
1974 Netherlands	4
1966 England*	4
1958 Brazil*	4

*went on to win Final.

Continental Victory

Brazil's win in 2002 gave South America its ninth World Cup champion, more than any other continent. Actually, the only other continent to win one is Europe, which has eight. While North America, Africa, Asia and Australia certainly have some work to do, Antarctica doesn't even have a decent soccer field.

	World Cups
South America	9
Europe	8
Rest of world	0

American Goals

Brian McBride is the second leading men's World Cup scorer in American history but Landon Donovan is right on his heels and poised to break the all-time record in 2006. Here's a look at the American men with the most World Cup goals.

	Year(s)	Goals
Bert Patenaude	1930	4
Brian McBride	1998, 2002	3
Landon Donovan	2002	2
John Souza	1950	2
Bart McGhee	1930	2

2001-2002
Season in Review

ESPN
Information Please®
SPORTS ALMANAC

2002 World Cup Tournament

The FIFA World Cup is held every four years to determine the best national team in the world. In 2002 it was contested for the 17th time since its inception in 1930. Held May 31-June 30 in Japan and South Korea.

First Round

Round robin; each team played the other three teams in its group once. Note that three points were awarded for a win and one point for a tie. (*) indicates team advanced to second round.

Group A	W	L	T	Pts	GF	GA
*Denmark	2	0	1	7	5	2
*Senegal	1	0	2	5	5	4
Uruguay	0	1	2	2	4	5
France	0	2	1	1	0	3

Results

Date	Site (attendance)	Result
May 31	Seoul (62,561)	Senegal 1, France 0
June 1	Ulsan (30,157)	Denmark 1, Uruguay 1
June 6	Busan (38,289)	France 0, Uruguay 0
June 6	Daegu (43,500)	Denmark 1, Senegal 1
June 11	Incheon (48,100)	Denmark 2, France 0
June 11	Suwon (33,681)	Senegal 3, Uruguay 3

Group B	W	L	T	Pts	GF	GA
*Spain	3	0	0	9	9	4
*Paraguay	1	1	1	4	6	6
South Africa	1	1	1	4	5	5
Slovenia	0	3	0	0	2	7

Results

Date	Site (attendance)	Result
June 2	Busan (25,186)	Paraguay 2, South Africa 2
June 2	Gwangju (28,598)	Spain 3, Slovenia 1
June 7	Jeonju (24,000)	Spain 3, Paraguay 1
June 8	Daegu (47,226)	South Africa 1, Slovenia 0
June 12	Daejeon (31,024)	Spain 3, South Africa 2
June 12	Seogwipo (30,176)	Paraguay 3, Slovenia 1

Group C	W	L	T	Pts	GF	GA
*Brazil	3	0	0	9	11	3
*Turkey	1	1	1	4	5	3
Costa Rica	1	1	1	4	5	6
China	0	3	0	0	0	9

Results

Date	Site (attendance)	Result
June 3	Ulsan (33,842)	Brazil 2, Turkey 1
June 4	Gwangju (27,217)	Costa Rica 2, China 0
June 8	Seogwipo (36,750)	Brazil 4, China 0
June 9	Incheon (42,299)	Costa Rica 1, Turkey 1
June 13	Suwon (38,524)	Brazil 5, Costa Rica 2
June 13	Seoul (43,605)	Turkey 3, China 0

Group D	W	L	T	Pts	GF	GA
*South Korea	2	0	1	7	4	1
*United States	1	1	1	4	5	6
Portugal	1	2	0	3	6	4
Poland	1	2	0	3	3	7

Results

Date	Site (attendance)	Result
June 4	Busan (48,760)	South Korea 2, Poland 0
June 5	Suwon (37,306)	United States 3, Portugal 2
June 10	Daegu (60,778)	South Korea 1, United States 1
June 10	Jeonju (31,000)	Portugal 4, Poland 0
June 14	Incheon (50,239)	South Korea 1, Portugal 0
June 14	Daejeon (26,482)	Poland 3, United States 1

Group E	W	L	T	Pts	GF	GA
*Germany	2	0	1	7	11	1
*Ireland	1	0	2	5	5	2
Cameroon	1	1	1	4	2	3
Saudi Arabia	0	3	0	0	0	12

Results

Date	Site (attendance)	Result
June 1	Niigata (33,679)	Ireland 1, Cameroon 1
June 1	Sapporo (32,218)	Germany 8, Saudi Arabia 0
June 5	Ibaraki (35,854)	Germany 1, Ireland 1
June 6	Saitama (52,328)	Cameroon 1, Saudi Arabia 0
June 11	Shizuoka (47,085)	Germany 2, Cameroon 0
June 11	Yokohama (65,320)	Ireland 3, Saudi Arabia 0

Group F	W	L	T	Pts	GF	GA
*Sweden	1	0	2	5	4	3
*England	1	0	2	5	2	1
Argentina	1	1	1	4	2	2
Nigeria	0	2	1	1	1	3

Results

Date	Site (attendance)	Result
June 2	Saitama (52,721)	England 1, Sweden 1
June 2	Ibaraki (34,050)	Argentina 1, Nigeria 0
June 7	Kobe (36,194)	Sweden 2, Nigeria 1
June 7	Sapporo (35,927)	England 1, Argentina 0
June 12	Miyagi (45,777)	Argentina 1, Sweden 1
June 12	Osaka (44,864)	England 0, Nigeria 0

Group G	W	L	T	Pts	GF	GA
*Mexico	2	0	1	7	4	2
*Italy	1	1	1	4	4	3
Croatia	1	2	0	3	2	3
Ecuador	1	2	0	3	2	4

Results

Date	Site (attendance)	Result
June 3	Niigata (32,239)	Mexico 1, Croatia 0
June 3	Sapporo (31,081)	Italy 2, Ecuador 0
June 8	Ibaraki (36,472)	Croatia 2, Italy 1
June 9	Miyagi (45,610)	Mexico 2, Ecuador 1
June 13	Oita (39,291)	Mexico 1, Italy 1
June 13	Yokohama (65,862)	Ecuador 1, Croatia 0

Group H	W	L	T	Pts	GF	GA
*Japan	2	0	1	7	5	2
*Belgium	1	0	2	5	6	5
Russia	1	2	0	3	4	4
Tunisia	0	2	1	1	1	5

Results

Date	Site (attendance)	Result
June 4	Saitama (55,256)	Japan 2, Belgium 2
June 5	Kobe (30,957)	Russia 2, Tunisia 0
June 9	Yokohama (66,108)	Japan 1, Russia 0
June 10	Oita (39,700)	Tunisia 1, Belgium 1
June 14	Osaka (45,213)	Japan 2, Tunisia 0
June 14	Shizuoka (46,640)	Belgium 3, Russia 2

2002 World Cup

| ROUND OF 16 | QUARTERFINALS | SEMIFINALS | FINALS | SEMIFINALS | QUARTERFINALS | ROUND OF 16 |

Bracket:

Germany 1 / Paraguay 0 → Germany 1
USA 2 / Mexico 0 → USA 0
→ Germany 1
Ireland 1(2) / Spain 1(3) → Spain 0(3)
Italy 1 / South Korea 2 → South Korea 0(5)
→ South Korea 0

Brazil 2 / Germany 0 (Final)

THIRD PLACE GAME
Turkey 3 / South Korea 2

Brazil 1 → Brazil 2
Brazil 2 / Belgium 0 → Brazil 2
England 3 / Denmark 0 → England 1
England 1 →
Senegal 2 / Sweden 1 → Senegal 0
Turkey 1 / Japan 0 → Turkey 1
→ Turkey 0

Round of 16

Single elimination with a 30 minute "golden goal" overtime period. If still tied, games are decided by shoot-out.

Date	Site (attendance)	Result
June 15	Seogwipo (25,176)	Germany 1, Paraguay 0
June 15	Niigata (40,582)	England 3, Denmark 0
June 16	Oita (39,747)	Senegal 2, Sweden 1 (OT)
June 16	Suwon (38,926)	Spain 1, Ireland 1 (SO)*
June 17	Jeonju (36,380)	United States 2, Mexico 0
June 17	Kobe (40,440)	Brazil 2, Belgium 0
June 18	Miyagi (45,666)	Turkey 1, Japan 0
June 18	Daejeon (38,588)	S. Korea 2, Italy 1 (OT)

*Spain won shoot-out 3-2.

Quarterfinals

Date	Site (attendance)	Result
June 21	Shizuoka (47,436)	Brazil 2, England 1
June 21	Ulsan (37,337)	Germany 1, United States 0
June 22	Gwangju (42,114)	S. Korea 0, Spain 0 (SO)*
June 22	Osaka (44,233)	Turkey 1, Senegal 0 (OT)

*South Korea won shoot-out 5-3.

Semifinals

Date	Site (attendance)	Result
July 25	Seoul (65,256)	Germany 1, S. Korea 0
July 26	Saitama (61,058)	Brazil 1, Turkey 0

Third Place

| June 29 | Daegu (63,483) | Turkey 3, S. Korea 2 |

Final

| June 30 | Yokohama (69,029) | Brazil 2, Germany 0 |

2002 World Cup Scoring Leaders

Leading Goal Scorers   **Goals**

Leading Goal Scorers	Goals
Ronaldo, Brazil	8
Miroslav Klose, Germany	5
Rivaldo, Brazil	5

Most Valuable Player

Officially, the Golden Ball Award. Second and third place finishers win the Silver and Bronze Ball Awards, respectively.

	Votes
Oliver Kahn, Germany	147
Ronaldo, Brazil	126
Myung Bo Hong, S. Korea	108

Brazil 2, Germany 0

World Cup Final played June 30 at International Stadium in Yokohama, Japan. **Attendance:** 69,029; **Referee:** Pierluigi Collina (Italy); **Assistants:** Leif Lindberg (Sweden), Philip Sharp (England).

	1	2	–F
Germany	0	0	–0
Brazil	0	2	–2

Scoring
Second Half: Brazil—Ronaldo (67th and 79th minutes).

	Germany		Brazil
1	Oliver Kahn	1	Marcos
2	Thomas Linke	2	Cafu
5	Carsten Ramelow	3	Lucio
7	Oliver Neuville	4	Roque Junior
8	Dietmar Hamann	5	Edmilson
11	Miroslav Klose	6	Roberto Carlos
	20 Oliver Bierhoff (74')	8	Gilberto Silva
16	Jens Jeremies	9	Ronaldo
	14 Gerald Asamoah (77')		17 Denilson (90')
17	Marco Bode	10	Rivaldo
	6 Christian Ziege (84')	11	Ronaldinho
19	Bernd Schneider		19 J. Paulista (85')
21	Christoph Metzelder	15	Kleberson
22	Torsten Frings		**Yellow Cards**
	Yellow Cards		Roque Junior (6')
	Miroslav Klose (9')		**Red Cards**
	Red Cards		none
	none		

Germany	Match Statistics	Brazil
12	Shots	9
4	Shots on Goal	7
21	Fouls	19
13	Corner Kicks	3
2	Free Kicks	1
0	Penalty Kicks	0
1	Offsides	0
0	Own Goals	0
56%	Ball Possession	44%
28	Actual Playing Time	22

FIFA Top 50 World Rankings

FIFA announced a new monthly world ranking system on Aug. 13, 1993 designed to "provide a constant international comparison of national team performances." The rankings are based on a mathematical formula that weighs strength of schedule, importance of matches and goals scored for and against. Games considered include World Cup qualifying and final rounds, Continental championship qualifying and final rounds, and friendly matches.

The formula was altered slightly in January 1999. Now the rankings annually take into account a team's seven best matches of the last eight years, thereby favoring some teams that have been consistent over a long period of time but that may have stumbled just recently. At the end of the year, FIFA designates a Team of the Year. Teams of the Year so far have been Germany (1993), Brazil (1994-2000) and France (2001). The USA reached their highest ever ranking (eighth) in Sept. 2002.

2001

		Points	2000 Rank				Points	2000 Rank				Points	2000 Rank
1	France	812	2	19	Croatia		668	18	37	Ecuador		613	53
2	Argentina	802	3	20	Belgium		666	27	38	Cameroon		609	39
3	Brazil	793	1	21	Russia		665	21	39	Chile		604	19
4	Portugal	741	6	22	Uruguay		664	32		Nigeria		604	52
5	Colombia	739	15	23	Turkey		663	30	41	Egypt		602	33
6	Italy	734	4	24	**USA**		662	16	42	South Korea		599	40
7	Spain	730	7	25	Slovenia		650	35	43	Peru		598	45
8	Netherlands	722	8		Norway		650	14	44	Ivory Coast		596	51
9	Mexico	714	12		Honduras		650	46	45	Ukraine		593	34
10	England	712	17	28	Tunisia		648	26	46	Finland		588	59
11	Yugoslavia	710	9	29	Iran		642	36		Slovakia		588	24
12	Germany	707	11	30	Costa Rica		635	60	48	Australia		586	72
13	Paraguay	691	9	31	Saudi Arabia		632	36	49	Israel		583	41
14	Czech Republic	689	4	32	Trinidad and Tobago		630	29	50	Scotland		577	25
15	Romania	688	13	33	Poland		629	43					
16	Sweden	676	22	34	Japan		626	38					
17	Ireland	672	31		South Africa		626	20					
	Denmark	672	22	36	Morocco		623	28					

2002 (as of Sept. 18)

		Points	2001 Rank				Points	2001 Rank				Points	2001 Rank
1	Brazil	858	3	18	Colombia		675	5	35	Poland		626	33
2	France	774	1	19	Belgium		672	20	36	Morocco		620	36
	Spain	774	7		Yugoslavia		672	11	37	Saudi Arabia		618	31
4	Germany	770	12	21	South Korea		667	42	38	Norway		616	25
5	Argentina	760	2	22	Sweden		662	16	39	Tunisia		609	28
6	Mexico	730	9	23	Uruguay		655	22	40	Honduras		604	25
7	Turkey	721	23	24	Russia		652	21	41	Egypt		594	41
8	**USA**	720	24	25	Costa Rica		651	30	42	Trinidad and Tobago		580	32
9	England	718	10		Romania		651	15	43	Australia		579	48
10	Italy	717	6	27	Japan		648	34	44	Finland		572	46
11	Portugal	712	4	28	Slovenia		642	25	45	Slovakia		563	46
12	Netherlands	708	8	29	Croatia		641	19	46	Greece		562	57
13	Denmark	703	17		Nigeria		641	39	47	Ukraine		559	45
14	Ireland	701	17	31	Ecuador		639	37	48	New Zealand		558	83
15	Cameroon	682	38	32	Senegal		638	65	49	Ivory Coast		548	44
16	Paraguay	680	13	33	South Africa		635	34	50	Bulgaria		546	51
17	Czech Republic	676	14	34	Iran		633	29					

African Nations Cup

Contested for the 23rd time since its inception in 1957. Held Jan. 19-Feb. 10 in Ghana.

First Round

Round Robin; each team plays the other teams in its group once. Note that three points are awarded for a win and one for a tie. (*) indicates team advanced to quarterfinals.

Group A	W	L	T	GF	GA	Pts
*Nigeria	2	0	1	2	0	7
*Mali	1	0	2	3	1	5
Liberia	0	1	2	3	4	2
Algeria	0	2	1	2	5	1

RESULTS: **Jan. 19**–Mali 1, Liberia 1; **Jan. 21**–Nigeria 1, Algeria 0; **Jan. 24**–Mali 0, Nigeria 0; **Jan. 25**–Algeria 2, Liberia 2; **Jan. 28**–Mali 2, Algeria 0; Nigeria 1, Liberia 0.

Group B	W	L	T	GF	GA	Pts
*South Africa	1	0	2	3	1	5
*Ghana	1	0	2	2	1	5
Morocco	1	1	1	3	4	4
Burkina Faso	0	2	1	2	4	1

RESULTS: **Jan. 20**–Burkina Faso 0, South Africa 0; **Jan. 21**–Ghana 0, Morocco 0; **Jan 24**–Ghana 0, South Africa 0; **Jan. 26**–Morocco 2, Burkina Faso 1; **Jan. 30**–South Africa 3, Morocco 1; Ghana 2, Burkina Faso 1.

African Nations Cup (Cont.)

Group C	W	L	T	GF	GA	Pts
*Cameroon	3	0	0	5	0	9
*Congo (Zaire)	1	1	1	3	2	4
Togo	0	1	2	0	3	2
Ivory Coast	0	2	1	1	4	1

RESULTS: **Jan. 20**—Cameroon 1, Congo 0; **Jan. 21**—Ivory Coast 0, Togo 0; **Jan 25**—Cameroon 1, Ivory Coast 0; **Jan. 26**—Congo 0, Togo 0; **Jan. 29**—Cameroon 3, Togo 0; Congo 3, Ivory Coast 1.

Group D	W	L	T	GF	GA	Pts
*Senegal	2	0	1	2	0	7
*Egypt	2	1	0	3	2	6
Tunisia	0	1	2	0	1	2
Zambia	0	5	1	1	3	1

RESULTS: **Jan. 20**—Senegal 1, Egypt 0; **Jan. 21**—Tunisia 0, Zambia 0; **Jan. 25**—Egypt 1, Tunisia 0; **Jan. 26**—Senegal 1, Zambia 0; **Jan. 31**—Egypt 2, Zambia 1; Senegal 0, Tunisia 0.

Quarterfinals

Date	Result
Feb. 3	Mali 2, South Africa 0
Feb. 3	Nigeria 1, Ghana 0
Feb. 4	Cameroon 1, Egypt 0
Feb. 4	Senegal 2, Congo 0

Semifinals

Date	Result
Feb. 7	Senegal 2, Nigeria 1
Feb. 7	Cameroon 3, Mali 0

Third Place Match

Date	Site	Result
Feb. 9	Mopti, Mali	Nigeria 1, Mali 0

Final

Attendance: 50,000

Date	Site	Result
Feb. 10	Bamako, Mali	Cameroon 0, Senegal 0

Cameroon wins shoot-out, 3-2

Referee: Gamal Al Ghandour, Egypt

U.S. Men's National Team

2002 Schedule and Results

Through Sept. 15, 2002. Games in **bold** type are FIFA World Cup matches.

Date		Result	USA Goals	Site
Jan. 19	South Korea	W, 2-1	Donovan, Beasley	Pasadena, Calif.
Jan. 21	Cuba	W, 1-0	McBride	Pasadena, Calif.
Jan. 27	El Salvador	W, 4-0	McBride (3), Razov	Pasadena, Calif.
Jan. 30	Canada	T, 0-0	—	Pasadena, Calif.
Feb. 2	Costa Rica	W, 2-0	Wolff, Agoos	Pasadena, Calif.
Feb. 13	Italy	L, 0-1	—	Catania, Italy
Mar. 2	Honduras	W, 4-0	Donovan (2), Mathis (2)	Seattle, Wash.
Mar. 10	Ecuador	W, 1-0	Lewis	Birmingham, Ala.
Mar. 27	Germany	L, 2-4	Mathis (2)	Rostock, Germany
Apr. 3	Mexico	W, 1-0	Mathis	Denver, Colo.
Apr. 17	Ireland	L, 1-2	Pope	Dublin, Ireland
May 12	Uruguay	W, 2-1	Sanneh, Beasley	Washington, D.C.
May 16	Jamaica	W, 5-0	Wolff (2), Mathis, Donovan, Beasley	East Rutherford, N.J.
May 19	Netherlands	L, 0-2		Foxboro, MA
June 5	**Portugal**	W, 3-2	O'Brien, own goal, McBride	Suwon, S. Korea
June 10	**South Korea**	T, 1-1	Mathis	Daegu, S. Korea
June 14	**Poland**	L, 1-3	Donovan	Daejeon, S. Korea
June 17	**Mexico**	W, 2-0	McBride, Donovan	Jeonju, S. Korea
June 21	**Germany**	L, 0-1		Ulsan, S. Korea

Overall record: 11-6-2. **Team scoring:** Goals For–32; Goals Against–18.

2002 U.S. Men's National Team Statistics

Individual records for season through Sept. 15, 2002. Note that the column labeled "Career C/G" refers to career caps and goals.

Forwards	GP	GS	Mins	G	A	Pts	Career C/G
Jeff Cunningham	3	0	76	0	1	1	4/0
Landon Donovan	19	16	1473	6	2	14	28/7
Jovan Kirovski	2	1	70	0	0	0	54/7
Clint Mathis	14	9	809	7	2	16	25/10
Brian McBride	15	15	1177	6	3	15	65/20
Joe-Max Moore	8	2	328	0	2	2	100/24
Ante Razov	3	3	209	1	1	3	22/6
Josh Wolff	10	6	497	3	2	8	20/6

Defenders	GP	GS	Mins	G	A	Pts	Career C/G
Jeff Agoos	16	15	1256	1	1	3	133/4
Gregg Berhalter	8	6	519	0	0	0	29/0
Carlos Bocanegra	5	5	435	0	0	0	6/0
Danny Califf	1	1	90	0	0	0	1/0
Steve Cherundolo	5	5	435	0	0	0	10/0
Frankie Hejduk	14	11	1068	0	1	1	43/5
Carlos Llamosa	5	1	192	0	1	1	29/0
Pablo Mastroeni	11	10	985	0	0	0	13/0
Richard Mulrooney	3	2	270	0	0	0	3/0

Defenders	GP	GS	Mins	G	A	Pts	Career C/G
Eddie Pope	11	11	980	1	0	2	55/5
David Regis	4	4	350	0	0	0	27/0
Tony Sanneh	11	9	816	1	1	3	37/2
Greg Vanney	3	2	138	0	0	0	18/0

Midfielders	GP	GS	Mins	G	A	Pts	Career C/G
Chris Armas	11	11	924	0	1	1	46/2
DaMarcus Beasley	12	8	687	3	1	7	15/3
Bobby Convey	1	0	29	0	0	0	3/0
Cobi Jones	14	7	769	0	1	1	159/14
Manny Lagos	1	1	63	0	0	0	0/0
Eddie Lewis	14	9	826	1	1	3	3/0
Brian Maisonneuve	3	1	97	0	0	0	0/0
John O'Brien	9	9	720	1	2	4	0/0
Claudio Reyna	8	8	635	0	0	0	92/8
Earnie Stewart	10	9	542	0	0	0	84/15
Brian West	5	0	90	0	1	1	6/0
Richie Williams	3	0	78	0	0	0	19/0

Goalkeepers	GP	GS	Mins	W-L-T	SO	GAA	Career Caps
Brad Friedel	9	9	720	3-4-1	1	1.38	81
Tim Howard	1	1	90	1-0-0	1	0.00	1
Kasey Keller	10	8	802	6-2-1	5	0.79	60
Tony Meola	2	1	128	1-0-0	1	0.00	99

Yellow cards: Donovan (5), Berhalter, Hejduk, Mathis and Pope (3), Mastroeni and Wolff (2), Agoos, Armas, Beasley, Bocanegra, Califf, Friedel, Howard, Keller, Razov, Reyna and Sanneh. **Red cards:** Hejduk and Mathis.

Head coach: Bruce Arena; **Assistant coach:** Dave Sarachan; **Goal coach:** Milutin Soskic; **General manager:** Pam Perkins.

U.S. Women's National Team
2002 Schedule and Results
Through Sept. 15, 2002.

Date		Result	USA Goals	Site
Jan. 12	Mexico	W, 7-0	MacMillan (3), Lilly, Foudy, Fotopoulos, Wagner	Charleston, S.C.
Jan. 23	Norway	L, 0-1	—	Huadu, China
Jan. 25	Germany	T, 0-0	—	Panyu, China
Jan. 27	China	W, 2-0	MacMillan, Milbrett	Guangzhou, China
Mar. 1	Sweden	T, 1-1	MacMillan	Albufeira, Portugal
Mar. 3	England	W, 2-0	MacMillan, Wilson	Ferreiras, Portugal
Mar. 5	Norway	L, 2-3	MacMillan (2)	Lagos, Portugal
Mar. 7	Denmark	W, 3-2	MacMillan (3)	Albufeira, Portugal
Apr. 27	Finland	W, 3-0	Wambach, Fawcett, Kluegel	San Jose, Calif.
July 21	Norway	W, 3-0	Parlow (2), Milbrett, Hamm	Blaine, Minn.
Sept. 8	Scotland	W, 8-2	Hamm (3), Wambach (3), Parlow, MacMillan	Columbus, Ohio

Overall record: 7-2-2.
Team Scoring: Goals for–32; Goals against–9.

2002 U.S. Women's National Team Statistics
Individual records through Sept. 15, 2002. Note that the column labeled "Career C/G" refers to career caps and goals.

Forwards	GP	GS	Mins	G	A	Pts	Career C/G
Mandy Clemens	1	0	30	0	0	0	5/0
Danielle Fotopoulos	4	3	183	1	2	4	30/12
Mia Hamm	1	1	135	4	3	11	221/133
Shannon MacMillan	11	9	748	12	1	25	138/47
Tiffeny Milbrett	9	9	733	2	5	9	178/88
Heather O'Reilly	4	0	103	0	0	0	4/0
Cindy Parlow	7	7	497	3	2	8	108/49
Abby Wambach	3	2	157	4	2	10	4/4
Christie Welsh	1	0	15	0	0	0	21/12
Kelly Wilson	3	1	157	1	1	3	3/1

Defenders	GP	GS	Mins	G	A	Pts	Career C/G
Jenny Benson	2	1	119	0	1	1	3/0
Kylie Bivens	7	0	228	0	1	1	7/0
Thori Bryan	2	1	151	0	0	2	60/0
Brandi Chastain	7	6	406	0	0	0	150/25
Joy Fawcett	10	10	884	1	0	2	195/25
Kelly Lindsey	1	0	45	0	0	0	4/0
Heather Mitts	1	0	26	0	0	0	3/0
Catherine Reddick	9	6	652	0	0	0	18/1

Defenders	GP	GS	Mins	G	A	Pts	Career C/G
Danielle Slaton	8	8	690	0	0	0	32/1
Kate Sobrero	9	8	486	0	0	0	76/0

Midfielders	GP	GS	Mins	G	A	Pts	Career C/G
Aleisha Cramer	3	1	136	0	0	0	19/0
Lorrie Fair	11	7	632	0	1	1	100/7
Julie Foudy	10	10	769	1	0	2	212/39
Devvyn Hawkins	2	1	92	0	0	0	7/0
Angela Hucles	3	0	121	0	0	0	3/0
Jena Kluegel	7	2	327	1	0	2	20/1
Kristine Lilly	9	9	703	1	4	1	237/88
Tiffany Roberts	2	2	107	0	0	0	82/6
Aly Wagner	10	5	568	1	4	6	25/6

Goalkeepers	GP	GS	Mins	W-L-T	SO	GAA	Career Caps
LaKeysia Beene	8	8	655	4-1-2	3	0.54	12
Briana Scurry	2	0	90	1-0-0	0	0.00	105
Hope Solo	5	3	245	2-1-0	1	1.83	12

Yellow Cards: Bryan 2, Bivens, Fotopoulos, Lilly, Milbrett, Parlow. **Red Cards:** none.
Head coach: April Heinrichs; **General Manager:** Nils Krumins.

Club Team Competition
2001 European/South American Cup

Also known as the Toyota Cup and the Intercontinental Cup; a year-end match for the Club World Championship between the UEFA Champions League (formerly the European Cup) and Copa Liberatadores winners. Played on Nov. 27 at Tokyo's National Stadium. The 2002 edition was scheduled to be played Dec. 3 at Yokohama International Stadium, the site of the 2002 World Cup Final. Its winner is generally recognized as the Club World Champion but with the recent advent of FIFA's Club World Championship that could change. Note that the 2001 FIFA Club World Championship was postponed until 2003.

Final
Bayern Munich (Germany) 1 . . . . Boca Juniors (Argentina) 0
Scoring: Bayern Munich–Samuel Kuffour (110th).
Referee: Kim Milton Nielsen, Denmark

SOUTH AMERICA

2002 Liberatadores Cup

Contested by the league champions of South America's football union. Two-leg Semifinals and two-leg Final; home teams listed first. Winner Olimpia of Paraguay was to play UEFA Champions League winner Bayer Leverkusen in the 2002 Europe/South America Cup in Yokohama, Japan in December.

Final Four: America (Mexico), Gremio (Brazil), Olimpia (Paraguay) and Sao Caetano (Brazil)

Semifinals

Olimpia vs. Gremio

Olimpia 3.....................................Gremio 2
Gremio 1.....................................Olimpia 0
Aggregate tied 3-3, Olimpia won shoot-out, 5-4

Sao Caetano vs. America

Sao Caetano 2 ....America 0
America 1 ....Sao Caetano 1
Sao Caetano won 3-1 on aggregate

Final

Matches played July 24 in Asuncion, Paraguay and July 31 in Sao Paulo, Brazil.

Olimpia 0.................................Sao Caetano 1
Sao Caetano 1.............................Olimpia 2
Aggregate tied 2-2, Olimpia won shootout, 4-2

EUROPE

There are two major European club competitions sanctioned by the Union of European Football Associations (UEFA). The newly devised **Champions League** is a 72-team tournament made up from UEFA member countries. The teams are ranked 1-72 depending on how they finish in their own domestic leagues. UEFA ranks the quality of the 50 European national football associations (from number one Italy to number 50 Bosnia-Herzegovina) and assigns each association a number weighted by their respective ranking (UEFA calls this number a coefficient). Each team's domestic league finish is then multiplied by the coefficient and the teams are finally ranked (countries can enter a maximum of four teams).

The defending champions Real Madrid (from the UEFA Champions' Cup) and the other 15 highest-ranked teams form Group 1 and are given a direct entry into the League but the remaining 16 teams are determined by dividing teams 17-72 into three groups—Group 2 (teams 17-34), Group 3 (35-52) and Group 4 (53-72). The 22 teams in the lowest Group (Group 4) play two-leg, total goal elimination series. The 11 survivors advance to the Second Qualifying Phase and join the 17 teams from Group 3 to play 14 two-leg, total goal elimination series. The 14 clubs that survive this phase join the 18 teams from Group 2 to play in the Third Qualifying Phase. The winning clubs from the 16 two-leg, total goal elimination series advance to the Champions League for the right to play against the top-ranked 16 teams in Europe.

The 32 teams are separated into eight groups of four and play a round-robin series of home-and-home matches. The eight group winners and eight group runners-up advance to the next round where they are split up into four groups of four. The four group winners and runners-up then advance to the quarterfinals where home-and-home series are played through the semifinals until ultimately a single championship match for the European club championship is held. Winner Real Madrid plays Liberatadores Cup champion Olimpia of Argentina in the 2002 European/South American Cup in Tokyo.

The updated **UEFA Cup**, which is basically a combination of the what was known as the Cup Winners' Cup (played between national cup champions) and the old UEFA Cup (sort of a "best of the rest" tournament), is single-elimination throughout and features 121 additional teams plus 24 teams that have been already eliminated from the Champions League.

2001-02 Champions League

Following the first three qualifying phases, the first group phase starts with six-game double round-robin format in eight four-team groups (Sept. 11-Oct. 31); top two teams in each group advance to second group phase (Nov. 20-Mar. 20) where four, four-team groups compete in the same format. Group winners and runners-up advance to the quarterfinals. (*) indicates team advanced to the next round. Note that in results listing under each table the home team is listed first.

First Group Phase

Group A	W	L	T	GF	GA	Pts
*Real Madrid (Spain)	4	1	1	13	5	13
*Roma (Italy)	2	1	3	6	5	9
Lokomotiv Moscow (Russia)	2	3	1	9	9	7
Anderlecht (Belgium)	0	3	3	4	13	3

RESULTS: **Sept. 11**–Lokomotiv Moscow 1, Anderlecht 1; Roma 1, Real Madrid 2; **Sept. 19**–Anderlecht 0, Roma 0; Real Madrid 4, Lokomotiv Moscow 0; **Sept. 26**–Real Madrid 4, Anderlecht 1; Roma 2, Lokomotiv Moscow 1; **Oct. 16**–Roma 1, Lokomotiv Moscow 0; Anderlecht 0, Real Madrid 2; **Oct. 24**–Anderlecht 1, Lokomotiv Moscow 5; Real Madrid 1, Roma 1; **Oct. 30**–Lokomotiv Moscow 2, Real Madrid 0; Roma 1, Anderlecht 1.

Group B	W	L	T	GF	GA	Pts
*Liverpool (England)	3	0	3	7	3	12
*Boavista (Portugal)	2	2	2	8	7	8
Borussia Dortmund (Germany)	2	2	2	6	7	8
Dynamo Kiev (Ukraine)	1	4	1	5	9	4

RESULTS: **Sept. 11**–Dynamo Kiev 2, Borussia Dortmund 2; Liverpool 1, Boavista 1; **Sept. 19**–Boavista 3, Dynamo Kiev 1; Borussia Dortmund 0, Liverpool 0; **Sept. 26**–Boavista 2, Borussia Dortmund 1; Liverpool 1, Dynamo Kiev 0; **Oct. 16**–Borussia Dortmund 2, Boavista 1; Dynamo Kiev 1, Liverpool 2; **Oct. 24**–Boavista 1, Liverpool 1; Borussia Dortmund 1, Dynamo Kiev 0; **Oct. 30**–Dynamo Kiev 1, Boavista 0; Liverpool 2, Borussia Dortmund 0.

Group C	W	L	T	GF	GA	Pts
*Panathinaikos (Greece)......4	2	0	8	3	12
*Arsenal (England) 3	3	0	9	9	9
Mallorca (Spain) 3	3	0	9	9	9
Schalke 04 (Germany) 2	4	0	9	9	6

RESULTS: **Sept. 11**–Mallorca 1, Arsenal 0; Schalke 04 0, Panathinaikos 2; **Sept. 19**–Arsenal 3, Schalke 04 2; Panathinaikos 2, Mallorca 0; **Sept. 26**–Panathinaikos 1, Arsenal 0; Shalke 04 0, Mallorca 1; **Oct. 16**–Arsenal 2, Panathinaikos 1; Mallorca 0, Schalke 04 4; **Oct. 24**–Arsenal 3, Mallorca 1; Panathinaikos 2, Schalke 04 0; **Oct. 30**–Mallorca 1, Panathinaikos 0; Schalke 04 3, Arsenal 1.

Group D	W	L	T	GF	GA	Pts
*Nantes (France) 3	1	2	8	3	11
*Galatasaray (Turkey)........3	2	1	5	4	10
PSV Eindhoven (Netherlands) .2	3	1	6	9	7
Lazio (Italy) 2	4	0	4	7	6

RESULTS: **Sept. 11**–Galatasaray 1, Lazio 0; Nantes 4, PSV Eindhoven 1; **Sept. 19**–Lazio 1, Nantes 3; PSV Eindhoven 3, Galatasaray 1; **Sept. 26**–Nantes 0, Galatasaray 1; PSV Eindhoven 1, Lazio 0; **Oct. 16**–Galatasaray 0, Nantes 0; Lazio 2, PSV Eindhoven 1; **Oct. 24**–Lazio 1, Galatasaray 0; PSV Eindhoven 0, Nantes 0; **Oct. 30**–Galatasaray 2, PSV Eindhoven 0; Nantes 1, Lazio 0.

Group E	W	L	T	GF	GA	Pts
*Juventus (Italy).............3	1	2	11	8	11
*FC Porto (Portugal) 3	2	1	7	5	10
Celtic (Ireland) 1	3	0	8	11	9
Rosenborg (Norway) 1	4	1	4	6	4

RESULTS: **Sept. 18**–Juventus 3, Celtic 0; Rosenborg 1, FC Porto 2; **Sept. 25**–Celtic 1, FC Porto 0; Rosenborg 1, Juventus 1; **Oct. 10**–Celtic 1, Rosenborg 0; FC Porto 0, Juventus 0; **Oct. 17**–FC Porto 3, Celtic 0; Juventus 1, Rosenborg 0; **Oct. 23**–Juventus 3, FC Porto 1; Rosenborg 2, Celtic 0; **Oct. 31**–Celtic 4, Juventus 3; FC Porto 1, Rosenborg 0.

Group F	W	L	T	GF	GA	Pts
*Barcelona (Spain) 5	1	0	12	5	15
*Bayer Leverkusen (Germany) ..4	2	0	10	9	12
Lyon (France) 3	3	0	10	9	9
Fenerbahce (Turkey) 0	6	0	3	12	0

RESULTS: **Sept. 18**–Fenerbahce 0, Barcelona 3; Lyon 0, Bayer Leverkusen 1; **Sept. 25**–Bayer Leverkusen 2, Barcelona 1; Fenerbahce 0, Lyon 1; **Oct. 10**–Barcelona 2, Lyon 0; Bayer Leverkusen 2, Fenerbahce 1; **Oct. 17**–Barcelona 2, Bayer Leverkusen 1; Lyon 3, Fenerbahce 1; **Oct. 23**–Fenerbahce 1, Bayer Leverkusen 2; Lyon 2, Barcelona 3; **Oct. 31**–Barcelona 1, Fenerbahce 0; Bayer Leverkusen 2, Lyon 4.

Group G	W	L	T	GF	GA	Pts
*Deportivo La Coruna (Spain) ..2	0	4	10	8	10
*Manchester United (England) ..3	2	1	10	6	10
Lille (France) 1	2	3	7	6	5
Olympiakos (Greece) 1	3	2	6	12	5

RESULTS: **Sept. 18**–Deportivo La Coruna 2, Olympiakos 2; Manchester United 1, Lille 0; **Sept. 25**–Deportivo La Coruna 2, Manchester United 1; Lille 3, Olympiakos 1; **Oct. 10**–Lille 1, Deportivo La Coruna 1; Olympiakos 0, Manchester United 2; **Oct. 17**–Manchester United 2, Deportivo La Coruna 3; Olympiakos 2, Lille 1; **Oct. 23**–Deportivo La Coruna 1, Lille 1; Manchester United 3, Olympiakos 0; **Oct. 31**–Lille 1, Manchester United 1; Olympiakos 1, Deportivo La Coruna 1.

Group H	W	L	T	GF	GA	Pts
*Bayern Munich (Germany) 4	0	2	14	5	14
*Sparta Prague (Czech Rep.)..3	1	2	10	3	11
Feyenoord Rotterdam (NED) ..1	3	2	7	14	5
Spartak Moscow (Russia) 0	4	2	7	16	2

RESULTS: **Sept. 18**–Spartak Moscow 2, Feyenoord Rotterdam 2; Bayern Munich 0, Sparta Prague 0; **Sept. 25**–Spartak Moscow 1, Bayern Munich 3; Sparta Prague 4, Feyenoord Rotterdam 0; **Oct. 10**–Feyenoord Rotterdam 2, Bayern Munich 2; Sparta Prague 2, Spartak Moscow 0; **Oct. 17**–Bayern Munich 5, Spartak Moscow 1; Feyenoord Rotterdam 2, Sparta Prague 2; **Oct. 23**–Spartak Moscow 2, Sparta Prague 2; Bayern Munich 2, Feyenoord Rotterdam 1; **Oct. 31**–Feyenoord Rotterdam 2, Spartak Moscow 1; Sparta Prague 0, Bayern Munich 1.

Second Group Phase

Group A	W	L	T	GF	GA	Pts
*Manchester United...........3	0	3	13	3	12
*Bayern Munich..............3	0	3	5	2	12
Boavista....................1	3	2	2	8	5
Nantes.....................0	4	2	4	11	2

RESULTS: **Nov. 20**–Bayern Munich 1, Manchester United 1; Boavista 1, Nantes 0; **Dec. 5**–Manchester United 3, Boavista 0; Nantes 0, Bayern Munich 1; **Feb. 20**–Boavista 0, Bayern Munich 0; Nantes 1, Manchester United 1; **Feb. 26**–Bayern Munich 1, Boavista 0; Manchester United 5, Nantes 1; **Mar. 13**–Manchester United 0, Bayern Munich 0; Nantes 1, Boavista 1; **Mar 19**–Bayern Munich 2, Nantes 1; Boavista 0, Manchester United 3.

Group B	W	L	T	GF	GA	Pts
*Barcelona 2	1	3	7	7	9
*Liverpool 1	1	4	4	4	7
Roma 1	1	4	6	5	7
Galatasaray 0	1	5	5	6	5

RESULTS: **Nov. 20**–Galatasaray 1, Roma 1; Liverpool 1, Barcelona 3; **Dec. 5**–Barcelona 2, Galatasaray 2; Roma 0, Liverpool 0; **Feb. 20**–Barcelona 1, Roma 1; Liverpool 0, Galatasaray 0; **Feb. 26**–Galatasaray 1, Liverpool 1; Roma 3, Barcelona 0; **Mar. 13**–Barcelona 0, Liverpool 0; Roma 1, Galatasaray 1; **Mar. 19**–Galatasaray 1, Barcelona 1; Liverpool 2, Roma 0.

Group C	W	L	T	GF	GA	Pts
*Real Madrid 5	0	1	14	5	16
*Panathinaikos...............2	2	2	7	8	8
Sparta Prague 2	4	0	6	10	6
FC Porto 1	4	1	3	7	4

RESULTS: **Nov. 21**–Panathinaikos 0, FC Porto 0; Sparta Prague 2, Real Madrid 3; **Dec. 4**–FC Porto 0, Sparta Prague 1; Real Madrid 3, Panathinaikos 0; **Feb. 19**–Real Madrid 1, FC Porto 0; Sparta Prague 0, Panathinaikos 2; **Feb. 27**–FC Porto 1, Real Madrid 2; Panathinaikos 2, Sparta Prague 1; **Mar. 12**–FC Porto 2, Panathinaikos 1; Real Madrid 3, Sparta Prague 0; **Mar. 20**–Panathinaikos 2, Real Madrid 2; Sparta Prague 2, FC Porto 0.

Group D	W	L	T	GF	GA	Pts
*Bayer Leverkusen 3	2	1	11	11	10
*Deportivo La Coruna........3	2	1	7	6	10
Arsenal 2	3	1	8	8	7
Juventus 2	3	1	7	8	7

RESULTS: **Nov. 21**–Deportivo La Coruna 2, Arsenal 0; **Nov. 29**–Juventus 4, Bayer Leverkusen 0; **Dec. 4**–Arsenal 3, Juventus 1; Bayer Leverkusen 3, Deportivo La Coruna 0; **Feb. 19**–Bayer Leverkusen 1, Arsenal 1; Juventus 0, Deportivo La Coruna 0; **Feb. 27**–Arsenal 4, Bayer Leverkusen 1; Deportivo La Coruna 2, Juventus 0; **Mar. 12**–Arsenal 0, Deportivo La Coruna 2; Bayer Leverkusen 3, Juventus 1; **Mar. 20**–Deportivo La Coruna 1, Bayer Leverkusen 3; Juventus 1, Arsenal 0.

EUROPE (Cont.)
Quarterfinals
Two legs, total goals; home team listed first.

Real Madrid vs. Bayern Munich
Apr. 2	Bayern Munich 2 ....Real Madrid 1
Apr. 10	Real Madrid 2 ....Bayern Munich 0

Real Madrid wins 3-2 on aggregate

Liverpool vs. Bayer Leverkusen
Apr. 3	Liverpool 1.................Bayer Leverkusen 0
Apr. 9	Bayer Leverkusen 4................Liverpool 2

Bayer Leverkusen wins 4-3 on aggregate

Deportivo La Coruna vs. Manchester United
Apr. 2	Deportivo La Coruna 0....Manchester United 2
Apr. 10	Manchester United 3.....Deportivo La Coruna 2

Manchester United wins 5-2 on aggregate

Panathinaikos vs. Barcelona
Apr. 3	Panathinaikos 1 ....Barcelona 0
Apr. 9	Barcelona 3 ....Panathinaikos 1

Barcelona wins 3-2 on aggregate

Semifinals
Two legs, total goals; home team listed first.

Real Madrid vs. Barcelona
Apr. 23	Barcelona 0..................Real Madrid 2
May 1	Real Madrid 1...................Barcelona 1

Real Madrid wins 3-1 on aggregate

Manchester United vs. Bayer Leverkusen
Apr. 24	Manchester United 2 ....Bayer Leverkusen 2
Apr. 30	Bayer Leverkusen 1 ....Manchester United 1

Bayer Leverkusen wins on away goals

Final
May 15 at Hampden Park, Glasgow, Scotland
Attendance: 52,000

Bayer Leverkusen 1......................Real Madrid 2

Scoring: Real Madrid–Gonzalez Blanco Raul (8th min), Zinedine Zidane (45th); Bayer Leverkusen–Ferreira Lucio (14th).

2002 UEFA Cup
Two-leg Quarterfinals and Semifinals, one-game Final; home team listed first.
Final Eight: Borussia Dortmund (Germany), Feyenoord Rotterdam (Netherlands), Hapoel Tel-Aviv (Israel), Internazionale (Italy), Milan (Italy), PSV Eindhoven (Netherlands), Slovan Liberec (Czech Republic) and Valencia (Spain).

Quarterfinals
Feyenoord Rotterdam vs. PSV Eindhoven
PSV Eindhoven 1.......Feyenoord Rotterdam 1
Feyenoord Rotterdam 6........PSV Eindhoven 5
Feyenoord Rotterdam wins 7-6 on aggregate

Hapoel Tel-Aviv vs. Milan
Hapoel Tel-Aviv 1.....................Milan 0
Milan 2......................Hapoel Tel-Aviv 0
Milan wins 2-1 on aggregate

Slovan Liberec vs. Borussia Dortmund
Slovan Liberec 0 ....Borussia Dortmund 0
Borussia Dortmund 4 ....Slovan Liberec 0
Borussia Dortmund wins 4-0 on aggregate

Internazionale vs. Valencia
Valencia 1 ....Internazionale 1
Internazionale 1 ....:......Valencia 0
Internazionale wins 2-1 on aggregate

Semifinals
Borussia Dortmund vs. Milan
Borussia Dortmund 4 ....Milan 0
Milan 3 ....Borussia Dortmund 1
Borussia Dortmund wins 5-3 on aggregate

Internazionale vs. Feyenoord Rotterdam
Internazionale 0 ....Feyenoord Rotterdam 1
Feyenoord Rotterdam 2 ....Internazionale 2
Feyenoord Rotterdam wins 3-2 on aggregate

Final
May 8 in Rotterdam, Netherlands. **Attendance:** 45,000

Feyenoord Rotterdam 3............................... Borussia Dortmund 2

Scoring: Feyenoord Rotterdam–Pierre van Hooijdonk (pen. 33rd) and (40th), Jon Dahl Tomasson (50th); Borussia Dortmund–Marcio Amoroso (pen 47th) and Jan Koller (58th).

2002 U.S. Open Cup
Dating back to 1914, the U.S. Open Cup is the oldest soccer competition in the United States and is among the oldest in the world. The U.S. Open Cup is a single-elimination tournament open to all amateur and professional teams in the United States. Thirty-two teams competed for the 88-year-old Dewar Cup trophy in the 2002 U.S. Open Cup.

Quarterfinals
Columbus Crew (MLS) def. MetroStars (MLS), 2-1
Kansas City Wizards (MLS) def. Milwaukee Rampage (A-League), 2-0
Dallas Burn (MLS) def. Colorado Rapids (MLS), 1-0 (OT)
Los Angeles Galaxy (MLS) def. San Jose Earthquakes (MLS), 1-0 (OT)

Semifinals
Columbus Crew def. Kansas City Wizards, 3-2 (OT)
Los Angeles Galaxy def. Dallas Burn, 4-1

Final
Oct. 24, 2002
Columbus Crew vs. Los Angeles Galaxy
See Updates chapter.

Major League Soccer
2002 Final Regular Season Standings

Conference champions (*) and playoff qualifiers (†) are noted. Teams receive three points for a win and one for a tie. The GF and GA columns refer to Goals For and Goals Against in regulation play. Number of seasons listed after each head coach refers to current tenure with club through the 2002 season.

Eastern Conference

Team	W	L	T	Pts	GF	GA
*N.E. Revolution	12	14	2	38	49	49
†Columbus Crew	11	12	5	38	44	43
†Chicago Fire	11	13	4	37	43	38
MetroStars	11	15	2	35	41	47
D.C. United	9	14	5	32	31	40

Head Coaches: NE—Fernando Clavijo (3rd season, 2-4-1) was fired on May 23, 2002 and replaced on an interim basis by Steve Nicol (10-10-1); **Clb**—Greg Andrulis (2nd); **Chi**—Bob Bradley (5th); **Met**—Octavio Zambrano (3rd); **DC**—Ray Hudson (1st).

Western Conference

Team	W	L	T	Pts	GF	GA
*Los Angeles Galaxy	16	9	3	51	44	33
†San Jose Earthquakes	14	11	3	45	45	35
†Colorado Rapids	13	11	4	43	43	48
†Dallas Burn	12	9	7	43	44	43
†Kansas City Wizards	9	10	9	36	37	45

Head Coaches: LA—Sigi Schmid (4th season); **SJ**—Frank Yallop (2nd); **Colo**—Tim Hankinson (2nd); **Dal**—Mike Jeffries (2nd); **KC**—Bob Gansler (4th).

Leading Scorers

Points

	Gm	G	A	Pts
Taylor Twellman, NE	28	23	6	52
Carlos Ruiz, LA	26	24	1	49
Jeff Cunningham, Clb	27	16	5	37
Ante Razov, Chi	25	14	8	36
Ariel Graziani, SJ	28	14	5	33
Mark Chung, Col	27	11	10	32
Jason Kreis, Dal	27	13	4	30
Mamadou Diallo, Met	24	12	5	29
Steve Ralston, NE	28	12	5	29
Chris Henderson, Col	28	11	7	29
Rodrigo Faria, Met	28	12	5	29

Assists

	Gm	No
Steve Ralston, NE	27	19
Carlos Valderrama, Col	27	16
Andy Williams, Met	24	15
Cobi Jones, LA	19	13
Preki, KC	25	10
Simon Elliott, LA	26	10
Antonio Martinez, Dal	26	10
Mark Chung, Col	27	10
Joselito Vaca, Dal	25	9
Ramiro Corrales, SJ	28	9

Goals

	Gm	No
Carlos Ruiz, LA	26	24
Taylor Twellman, NE	28	23
Jeff Cunningham, Clb	27	16
Ante Razov, Chi	24	14
Ariel Graziani, SJ	24	14
Jason Kreis, Dal	27	13
Mamadou Diallo, Met	24	12
Rodrigo Faria, Met	28	12
Chris Carrieri, Col	25	11
Mark Chung, Col	27	11
Chris Henderson, Col	28	11

Shots

	Gm	No
Ante Razov, Chi	25	115
Carlos Ruiz, LA	26	100
Taylor Twellman, NE	28	92
Rodrigo Faria, Met	28	90
Preki, KC	25	84
Mark Chung, Col	27	83
Mamadou Diallo, Met	24	81
Jason Kreis, Dal	27	81
Jeff Cunningham, Clb	27	78
Ariel Graziani, SJ	28	69

Shots on Goal

	Gm	No
Taylor Twellman, NE	28	58
Ante Razov, Chi	25	56
Carlos Ruiz, LA	26	56
Mamadou Diallo, Met	24	51
Rodrigo Faria, Met	28	49
Preki, KC	25	44
Ariel Graziani, SJ	28	39
Jason Kreis, Dal	27	38
Jeff Cunningham, Clb	27	37
Mark Chung, Col	27	33

Game-Winning Goals

	Gm	GWG
Carlos Ruiz, LA	26	9
Ariel Graziani, SJ	28	6
Chris Carrieri, Col	25	5
Jason Kreis, Dal	27	5
Taylor Twellman, NE	28	5
Mamadou Diallo, Met	24	4

Seven tied with 3 each.

MLS All-Star Game

East 6, West 6

Played Saturday, August 3, 2002 at RFK Stadium in Washington, D.C. between the U.S. National Team and an MLS All-Star team; **Attendance:** 31,096; **Coaches:** Frank Yallop, MLS All-Stars and Bruce Arena, U.S. National Team; **MVP:** Marco Etcheverry, MLS All-Stars.

	1	2	Final
USA	0	2	—2
MLS	0	3	—3

Scoring

2nd Half: USA—Landon Donovan (Chris Henderson, DaMarcus Beasley) 58; MLS—Jason Kreis (Chris Klein) 59; MLS—Marco Etcheverry (Joselito Vaca, Wade Barrett) 72; USA—Cobi Jones (Brian McBride, Brian Maisonneuve) 76; MLS—Steve Ralston (Kreis, Klein) 81.

Goaltenders

Saves: USA—Tony Meola 2, Juergen Sommer 2; MLS—Joe Cannon 8. Tim Howard 1.

Major League Soccer (Cont.)

Hat Tricks

	Gm	Hats
Mamadou Diallo, Met	24	1
Chris Carrieri, Col	25	1
Ante Razov, Chi	25	1
Carlos Ruiz, LA	26	1
Bobby Rhine, Dal	27	1
Taylor Twellman, NE	28	1

Fouls Committed

	Gm	No
Carlos Ruiz, LA	26	71
Oscar Pareja, Dal	24	64
Ramiro Corrales, SJ	28	59
Richie Williams, DC	26	57
Brian Maisonneuve, Clb	26	57
Jesse Marsch, Chi	28	57
Alexi Lalas, LA	26	56
Ariel Graziani, SJ	28	56
Taylor Twellman, NE	28	55
Wes Hart, Col	27	54
Jason Kreis, Dal	27	54

Fouls Suffered

	Gm	No
Taylor Twellman, NE	28	87
Andy Williams, Met	24	86
DaMarcus Beasley, Chi	19	83
Richard Mulrooney, SJ	26	73
Carlos Ruiz, LA	26	71
Mamadou Diallo, Met	24	62
Mark Chung, Col	27	61
Oscar Pareja, Dal	24	58
Jesse Marsch, Chi	28	56
Marco Etcheverry, DC	24	54
Kerry Zavagnin, KC	27	54

2002 MLS Attendance
Number in parentheses indicates last year's rank.

	Gm	Total	Avg
Colorado (5)	14	289,663	20,690
Los Angeles (4)	14	266,664	19,047
MetroStars (2)	14	254,174	18,155
Columbus (3)	14	243,999	17,429
New England (7)	14	236,973	16,927
D.C. United (1)	14	231,264	16,519
Dallas (8)	14	183,702	13,122
Chicago (6)	14	180,908	12,922
Kansas City (10)	14	171,568	12,255
San Jose (12)	14	156,104	11,150
TOTAL	140	2,215,019	15,822

Offsides

	Gm	Offs
Mamadou Diallo, TB	24	54
Jeff Cunningham, Clb	27	40
Carlos Ruiz, LA	26	38
Ante Razov, Chi	25	35
Dwayne DeRosario, SJ	27	34
Chris Henderson, Col	28	33
Rodrigo Faria, Met	28	30
Chris Garreri, Col	25	26
Ariel Graziani, SJ	28	25
Ronald Cerritos, Dal	23	23

Cautions

	Gm	No
Joe Franchino, NE	23	9
Marco Etcheverry, DC	24	9
Rick Titus, Col	25	9
Jimmy Conrad, SJ	25	9
Carlos Ruiz, LA	26	9
Chad McGarty, Clb	18	8
Richie Williams, DC	26	8
Ten tied with seven each.		

Ejections

	Gm	No
Tony Meola, KC	17	2
Chad McCarty, Clb	18	2
Forty tied with one each.		

Corner Kicks

	Gm	CKs
Marco Etcheverry, DC	24	139
Richard Mulrooney, SJ	26	129
Simon Elliott, LA	26	82
Steve Ralston, NE	27	69
Cobi Jones, LA	19	68
Antonio Martinez, Dal	26	62
Preki, KC	25	60
Chad Deering, Dal	27	60
Chris Henderson, Col	28	59
Ante Razov, Chi	25	56

Minutes Played

	Mins
Nick Rimando, DC	2588
Jesse Marsch, Chi	2557
Wade Barrett, SJ	2555
Matt Jordan, Dal	2511
Nick Garcia, KC	2499
Kerry Zavagnin, KC	2484
Zach Thornton, Chi	2483
Carlos Valderrama, Col	2479
Tim Howard, Met	2463
Steve Ralston, NE	2460

Leading Goaltenders
Goals Against Average

	Gm	Min	Shts	Svs	GAA	W-L-T
Kevin Hartman, LA	18	1648	108	83	**1.09**	11-6-1
Jon Busch, Clb	14	1236	80	63	**1.09**	8-3-2
Joe Cannon, SJ	26	2375	136	100	**1.10**	13-10-3
Zach Thornton, Chi	27	2483	164	124	**1.23**	10-13-4
Adin Brown, NE	16	1460	102	72	**1.23**	9-6-1
Tony Meola, KC	17	1519	88	65	**1.24**	6-5-5
Nick Rimando, DC	28	2588	183	131	**1.39**	9-14-5
Matt Jordan, Dal	27	2511	158	109	**1.51**	12-9-6
Scott Garlick, Col	15	1374	92	61	**1.57**	6-7-2
Tim Howard, Met	27	2463	195	140	**1.61**	11-14-2

Saves

	Gm	No
Tim Howard, Met	27	140
Nick Rimando, DC	28	131
Zach Thornton, Chi	27	124
Matt Jordan, Dal	27	109
Joe Cannon, SJ	26	100
Kevin Hartman, LA	18	83

Shutouts

	Gm	No
Joe Cannon, SJ	26	8
Zach Thornton, Chi	27	7
Nick Rimando, DC	28	7
Jon Busch, Clb	14	5
Adin Brown, NE	16	5
Kevin Hartman, LA	18	5

Save Percentage

	Svs	SOG	SV Pct
Jon Busch, Clb	63	80	.788
Kevin Hartman, LA	83	108	.769
Zach Thornton, Chi	124	164	.756
Tony Meola, KC	65	88	.739
Joe Cannon, SJ	100	136	.735
Tim Howard, Met	140	195	.718

Save Average

	Svs	Min	Avg
Tim Howard, Met	140	2463	5.12
Tom Presthus, Clb	73	1365	4.81
Jon Busch, Clb	63	1236	4.59
Nick Rimando, DC	131	2588	4.56
Kevin Hartman, LA	83	1648	4.53
Bo Oshoniyi, KC	55	1096	4.52

Team-by-Team Statistics

Players who played with more than one club during the season are listed with final team.

Eastern Conference

Chicago Fire

	Pos	Gm	Min	G	A	Pts
Ante Razov	F	25	2120	14	8	36
Josh Wolff	F	14	1223	5	5	15
Dema Kovalenko	M	23	2034	1	8	10
DaMarcus Beasley	M	19	1719	3	4	10
Peter Nowak	M	16	1377	3	4	10
Jesse Marsch	M	28	2557	1	7	9
Kelly Gray	M/D	25	1780	2	5	9
Hristo Stoitchkov	F	16	693	2	3	7
Carlos Bocanegra	D	26	2291	2	3	7
Jim Curtin	D	24	2121	2	0	4
Amos Magee	F	5	197	2	0	4
C.J. Brown	D	24	2153	0	3	3
David Vaudreuil	M/D	17	1280	1	1	3
Sergi Daniv	M	8	480	1	0	2
Jason Moore	M	10	314	1	0	2
John Wolyniec	F	2	180	1	0	2
Billy Walsh	M	13	776	0	1	1
Billy Sleeth	D	13	799	0	1	1
Chris Armas	M	4	347	0	1	1
Orlando Perez	D	11	808	0	0	0
Mike Nugent	F	4	54	0	0	0
Craig Capano	M	4	92	0	0	0
Johnny Torres	F	2	73	0	0	0
Evan Whitfield	D	2	138	0	0	0
Aleksey Korol	F	1	22	0	0	0
Dipsy Selolwane	F	1	1	0	0	0

Goalkeepers	Gm	Min	W-L-T	Shts	Svs	GAA
Zach Thornton	27	2483	10-13-4	164	124	1.23
Henry Ring	1	90	1-0-0	7	3	4.00

Columbus Crew

	Pos	Gm	Min	G	A	Pts
Jeff Cunningham	F	27	1962	16	5	37
Edson Buddle	F	21	1304	9	5	23
Brian McBride	F	14	1239	5	5	15
Dante Washington	F	21	1122	6	2	14
Brian West	M/F	24	1944	1	8	10
Kyle Martino	M	22	1455	2	5	9
Brian Maisonneuve	M	26	2238	1	6	8
John Wilmar Perez	M	20	1256	1	4	6
Eric Denton	M/D	23	1875	1	4	6
Duncan Oughton	D	20	1608	0	4	4
Chad McCarty	D	18	1176	1	2	4
Mike Clark	D	21	1599	1	0	2
Freddy Garcia	M	5	215	0	2	2
Robert Warzycha	M	15	495	0	2	2
John Harkes	M	11	739	0	2	2
Brian Dunseth	D	27	2436	0	1	1
Daniel Torres	D	25	2085	0	1	1
Todd Yeagley	M/D	3	74	0	1	1
Chris Leitch	D	13	989	0	0	0
Mike Lapper	D	4	141	0	0	0
Jeff Mateo		1	14	0	0	0

Goalkeepers	Gm	Min	W-L-T	Shts	Svs	GAA
Jon Busch	14	1236	8-3-2	80	63	1.09
Tom Presthus	15	1365	3-9-3	103	73	1.85

D.C. United

	Pos	Gm	Min	G	A	Pts
Marco Etcheverry	M	24	2146	3	8	14
Bobby Convey	M	26	2248	5	3	13
Ali Curtis	F	20	806	5	1	11
Ryan Nelson	M	20	1596	4	3	11
Jaime Moreno	F	16	1157	3	4	10
Santino Quaranta	F	11	949	3	4	10
Petter Villegas	M	25	1953	2	8	12
Eliseo Quintanilla	F	9	726	2	2	6
Ivan McKinley	D	23	1786	1	2	4
Eddie Pope	D	17	1471	1	1	3
Richie Williams	M	26	2307	0	3	3
Henry Zambrano	M	5	240	1	0	2
Milton Reyes	D	24	2204	0	2	2
Abdul Thompson Conteh	F	5	286	1	0	2
Jose Alegria	M	14	900	0	1	1
Ben Olsen	M	10	718	0	1	1
Lazo Alavanja	M	17	1001	0	0	0
Roy Lassiter	F	14	501	0	0	0
Orlando Perez	D	10	366	0	0	0
Brandon Prideaux	D	27	2389	0	0	0
Dennis Ludwig	F	2	30	0	0	0
Bryan Namoff	M	11	442	0	0	0
Justin Mapp	M	3	28	0	0	0

Goalkeepers	Gm	Min	W-L-T	Shts	Svs	GAA
Nick Rimando	28	2588	9-14-5	183	131	1.39

Major League Soccer (Cont.)

MetroStars

	Pos	Gm	Min	G	A	Pts
Rodrigo Faria	F	28	2285	12	5	29
Mamadou Diallo	F	24	1623	12	5	29
Andy Williams	F	24	1814	2	15	19
Brad Davis	M	24	1246	4	3	11
Clint Mathis	M/F	14	1106	4	2	10
Ross Paule	M	26	2207	2	2	6
Ted Chronopoulos	D	23	1877	0	6	6
Mark Lisi	M	23	874	2	1	5
Tab Ramos	M	14	926	0	3	3
Steve Jolley	D	27	2327	1	1	3
Jeff Moore	M	18	1482	0	3	3
Joe Addo	D	15	918	0	1	1
Mike Petke	D	27	2398	0	0	0
Byron Alvarez	M/F	8	119	0	0	0
Craig Ziadie	D	21	1637	0	0	0
Nelson Akwari	D	7	325	0	0	0
Sam Forko	D	9	356	0	0	0
Birahim Diop	D	4	228	0	0	0
Dustin Sheppard	M	2	64	0	0	0
Darin Lewis	F	3	48	0	0	0
Marcelo Balboa	D	1	5	0	0	0
Brian Piesner	M	1	1	0	0	0

Goalkeepers	Gm	Min	W-L-T	Shts	Svs	GAA
Tim Howard	27	2463	11-14-2	195	140	1.61
Paul Grafer	2	91	0-1-0	7	3	2.97

New England Revolution

	Pos	Gm	Min	G	A	Pts
Taylor Twellman	F	28	2418	23	6	52
Steve Ralston	M	27	2460	5	19	29
Brian Kamler	M	24	1680	3	6	12
Jay Heaps	M/D	27	2389	2	6	10
Daniel Hernandez	D	28	2301	3	3	9
Wolde Harris	F	22	1117	4	0	8
Diego Serna	F	13	944	2	4	8
Joe Franchino	M	23	2015	1	5	7
Leo Cullen	D	28	2444	2	2	4
Jim Rooney	M	20	1715	1	2	4
Winston Griffiths	F	17	755	1	2	4
Ian Fuller	F	11	446	0	3	3
Daouda Kante	D	8	729	1	0	2
John Wilson	D	1	16	1	0	2
Braeden Cloutier	M	11	608	0	1	1
Carlos Llamosa	D	14	1056	0	1	1
Carlos Semedo	D	9	631	0	1	1
Rusty Pierce	D	14	1161	0	1	1
Shaker Asad	M	6	140	0	0	0
Nick Downing	D	12	667	0	0	0

Goalkeepers	Gm	Min	W-L-T	Shts	Svs	GAA
Adin Brown	16	1460	9-6-1	102	72	1.23
Juergen Sommer	12	1090	3-8-1	87	53	2.39

Western Conference

Colorado Rapids

	Pos	Gm	Min	G	A	Pts
Mark Chung	M	27	2401	11	10	32
Chris Henderson	M	28	2414	11	7	29
Chris Carrieri	F	25	1830	11	5	27
Carlos Valderrama	M	27	2479	1	16	18
John Spencer	M/F	16	1149	5	4	14
Zach Kingsley	M	15	997	4	2	10
Raul Palacios	M	16	836	0	5	5
Jeff Stewart	D	23	1723	0	3	3
Pablo Mastroeni	M	15	1329	0	3	3
Wes Hart	M	27	2063	0	2	2
Ritchie Kotschau	D	23	1757	0	2	2
Kyle Beckerman	M	14	477	0	1	1
Rick Titus	D	25	2202	0	1	1
Robin Fraser	D	28	2453	0	1	1
Marvin Quijano	M/F	6	77	0	1	1
Imad Baba	M	10	443	0	0	0
Steve Herdsman	D	13	858	0	0	0
Seth Trembly	M/D	4	43	0	0	0
Musa Shannon	M/F	1	30	0	0	0
Danny Jackson	D	1	15	0	0	0
Steve Shak	D	1	1	0	0	0

Goalkeepers	Gm	Min	W-L-T	Shts	Svs	GAA
Scott Garlick	15	1374	6-7-2	92	61	1.57
David Kramer	13	1195	7-4-2	75	49	1.81

Dallas Burn

	Pos	Gm	Min	G	A	Pts
Jason Kreis	F	27	2303	13	4	30
Bobby Rhine	F	27	1686	7	6	20
Antonio Martinez	M	26	1774	4	10	18
Ronald Cerritos	F	23	1209	4	6	14
Joselito Vaca	M	25	2005	1	9	11
Jorge Rodriguez	M/D	22	1693	4	2	10
Oscar Pareja	M	24	2000	1	6	8
Chad Deering	M	27	2168	1	4	6
Ronnie O'Brien	M	11	506	2	2	6
Steve Morrow	D	24	2199	3	0	6
Edward Johnson	F	11	326	2	1	5
Ryan Suarez	M	24	2061	1	2	4
Paul Broome	M	25	2315	0	4	4
Hamisi Amani-Dove	F	6	101	0	1	1
Carl Bussey	M	9	184	0	1	1
Tenywa Bonseu	F	27	2370	0	0	0
Richard Farrer	D	8	508	0	0	0
Percy Olivares	M	6	251	0	0	0
Matt Behncke	M/D	3	190	0	0	0
Lee Morrison	D	3	103	0	0	0
Jordan Stone	M	4	91	0	0	0

Goalkeepers	Gm	Min	W-L-T	Shts	Svs	GAA
D.J. Countess	1	100	0-0-1	7	6	0.90
Matt Jordan	27	2511	12-9-6	158	109	1.51

Kansas City Wizards

	Pos	Gm	Min	G	A	Pts
Preki	M	25	2141	7	10	24
Chris Klein	M	25	2171	7	5	19
Dario Fabbro	F	16	1116	6	3	15
Igor Simutenkov	F	19	1480	4	5	13
Stephen Armstrong	M	26	1791	3	6	12
Chris Brown	M/F	28	1512	4	3	11
Carey Talley	D	24	1902	3	1	7
Diego Gutierrez	M	22	1914	1	3	5
Francisco Gomez	M	20	1249	0	4	4
Kerry Zavagnin	M	27	2484	1	2	4
Matt McKeon	M	23	1146	1	2	4
Nick Garcia	D	27	2499	0	2	2
Eric Quill	F	16	992	0	1	1
Mike Burns	D	24	1966	0	1	1
Tony Meola	GK	17	1519	0	1	1
Chris Brunt	D	5	158	0	0	0
Davy Arnaud	M	3	43	0	0	0
Gary Glasgow	M/F	3	174	0	0	0
Peter Vermes	D	3	1181	0	0	0

Goalkeepers	Gm	Min	W-L-T	Shts	Svs	GAA
Tony Meola	17	1519	6-5-5	88	65	1.24
Bo Oshoniyi	13	1096	3-5-4	80	55	1.97

Los Angeles Galaxy

	Pos	Gm	Min	G	A	Pts
Carlos Ruiz	F	26	2376	24	1	49
Cobi Jones	M/F	19	1638	3	13	19
Simon Elliott	M	26	2347	1	10	12
Mauricio Cienfuegos	M	23	1879	2	8	12
Alexi Lalas	D	26	2364	4	4	12
Ezra Hendrickson	D	23	2048	2	8	12
Sasha Victorine	M	25	1985	2	5	9
Brian Mullan	F	21	1019	3	2	8
Gavin Glinton	F	22	790	1	4	6
Tyrone Marshall	M/D	24	1838	0	5	5
Peter Vagenas	M	17	1390	0	3	3
Danny Califf	D	25	2118	1	0	2
Alejandro Moreno	F	12	561	0	2	2
Chris Albright	F	15	814	0	1	1
Craig Waibel	D	12	860	0	1	1
Jesus Ochoa	M	9	352	0	1	1
Adam Frye	D	20	956	0	0	0
Alex Bengard	M	4	26	0	0	0

Goalkeepers	Gm	Min	W-L-T	Shts	Svs	GAA
Kevin Hartman	18	1648	11-6-1	108	83	1.09
Matt Reis	11	929	5-3-2	47	33	1.26

San Jose Earthquakes

	Pos	Gm	Min	G	A	Pts
Ariel Graziani	F	28	2289	14	5	33
Ronnie Ekelund	M	27	2347	6	8	20
Landon Donovan	F	20	1681	7	3	17
Dwayne DeRosario	F	27	1637	4	8	16
Ramiro Corrales	D	28	2354	3	9	15
Manny Lagos	M	26	1683	3	4	10
Richard Mulrooney	M	26	2312	1	8	10
Wade Barrett	D	28	2555	1	6	8
Jimmy Conrad	D	25	2248	1	3	5
Eddie Robinson	M/D	19	1427	2	1	5
Ian Russell	M	24	1348	0	2	2
Troy Dayak	D	15	1235	0	1	1
Zak Ibsen	D	17	1077	0	1	1
Jeff Agoos	D	12	839	0	0	0
Devin Barclay	F	12	321	0	0	0
Luchi Gonzalez	F	8	47	0	0	0
Chris Roner	M	4	29	0	0	0

Goalkeepers	Gm	Min	W-L-T	Shts	Svs	GAA
Joe Cannon	26	2375	13-10-3	136	100	1.10
Jon Conway	3	181	1-1-0	17	11	2.98

MLS Playoffs

See Updates Chapter.

Women's United Soccer Association

The WUSA (Women's United Soccer Association) is the top women's outdoor professional league. The league was formed in 2000 and began play in 2001.

2002 WUSA Final Standings

Three points awarded for a win, one point for a tie; (*) indicates team advanced to semifinals.

	W	L	T	Pts	GF	GA
*Carolina	12	5	4	40	40	30
*Philadelphia	11	4	6	39	36	22
*Washington	11	5	5	38	40	29
*Atlanta	11	9	1	34	34	29
San Jose	8	8	5	29	34	30
Boston	6	8	7	25	36	35
San Diego	5	11	5	20	28	42
New York	3	17	1	10	31	62

Goals

	Goals
Katia, SJ	15
Marinette Pichon, Phi	14
Birgit Prinz, Car.	12
Danielle Fotopoulos, Car	11
Charmaine Hooper, Atl	11
Dagny Mellgren, Bos	11
Abby Wambach, Was	10
Tiffeny Milbrett, NY	10
Kristine Lilly, Bos	8
Mia Hamm, Was	8
Emily Janss, NY	8

League Leaders
Points

	G	A	Pts
Katia, SJ	15	5	35
Danielle Fotopoulos, Car	11	10	32
Birgit Prinz, Car.	12	8	32
Maren Meinert, Bos	7	16	30
Abby Wambach, Was	10	9	29
Marinette Pichon, Phi	14	1	29
Kristine Lilly, Bos	8	13	29
Tiffeny Milbrett, NY	10	8	28
Hege Riise, Car	6	13	19
Charmaine Hooper, Atl	11	3	25

Assists

	Assists
Maren Meinert, Bos	16
Hege Riise, Car	13
Kristine Lilly, Bos	13
Danielle Fotopoulos, Car	10
Abby Wambach, Was	9
Bettina Wiegmann, Bos	9
Sissi, SJ	9

Five tied with eight each.

Goal Against Average

	GAA
Melissa Moore, Phi	1.00
Siri Mullinix, Was	1.19
Briana Scurry, Atl	1.33
LaKeysia Beene, SJ	1.35
Kristin Luckenbill, Car	1.43

	GAA
Karina LeBlanc, Bos	1.59
Erin Fahey, Was	1.65
Melanie Wilson, Atl	1.67
Dawn Greathouse, Was	1.70
Carly Smolak, SD	1.75

Women's United Soccer Association (Cont.)
Playoffs

Semifinals

Games played Aug. 17, 2002.

Carolina 2 .... Atlanta 1
Washington 1 .... Philadelphia 0

Final

Founders Cup II was held Aug. 24, 2002 at Herndon Stadium, Atlanta, Ga; **Attendance:** 15,321

Carolina 3 .... Washington 2

Scoring

First Half: CAR—Hege Riise (Danielle Fotopoulos, Staci Burt) 20th min.; WASH—own goal 31st.
Second Half: CAR—Fotopoulos (Birgit Prinz, Venus James) 53rd; CAR—Prinz (unassisted) 58th; WASH—Mia Hamm (Abby Wambach) 64th.

Team-by-Team Statistics

Atlanta Beat

	Pos	Gm	Min	G	A	Pts
Charmaine Hooper	F	19	1561	11	3	25
Homare Sawa	F	21	1829	7	6	20
Cindy Parlow	F	10	1431	5	4	14
Nikki Serlenga	M	21	1847	3	6	12
Sun Wen	F/M	18	853	4	0	8
Kylie Bivens	D/M	18	1443	1	4	6
Liping Wang	D/M	14	835	1	2	4
Emily Burt	F	14	451	0	4	4
Kelly Cagle	F	18	636	1	1	3
Nancy Augustyniak	D	19	1525	0	3	3
Lisa Krzykowski	D	13	814	0	2	2
Julie Augustyniak	D	20	1628	0	1	1
Marci Miller	M	18	997	0	1	1
Sharolta Nonen	D	21	1876	0	1	1
Amanda Cromwell	D	12	740	0	0	0
Dayna Smith	D	5	425	0	0	0

Goalkeepers	Gm	Min	W-L-T	Shts	Svs	GAA
Briana Scurry	18	1620	9-8-1	115	80	1.33
Melanie Wilson	3	270	2-1-0	18	13	1.67

Carolina Courage

	Pos	Gm	Min	G	A	Pts
Birgit Prinz	F	15	1350	12	8	32
Danielle Fotopoulos	F	21	1836	11	10	32
Hege Riise	M	19	1701	6	13	25
Danielle Slaton	D	18	1381	4	0	8
Venus James	M	20	624	2	2	6
Unni Lehn	F/M	18	1511	2	2	6
Tiffany Roberts	D/M	19	1710	1	4	6
Staci Burt	D	20	1800	0	4	4
Nel Fettig	D/M	21	1785	0	3	3
Katie Barnes	F	15	571	0	1	1
Meghan Anderson	M	16	489	0	0	0
Erin Baxter	D/M	16	1148	0	0	0
Brooke O'Hanley	D	18	1094	0	0	0
Carla Overbeck	D	9	424	0	0	0
Staci Wilson	D	14	882	0	0	0
Kim Yankowski	F	11	495	0	0	0

Goalkeepers	Gm	Min	W-L-T	Shts	Svs	GAA
Kristin Luckenbill	21	1890	12-5-4	156	114	1.43

Boston Breakers

	Pos	Gm	Min	G	A	Pts
Maren Meinert	F/M	21	1783	7	16	30
Kristine Lilly	F/M	19	1699	8	13	29
Dagny Mellgren	F/M	20	1616	11	2	24
Bettina Wiegmann	M	20	1664	2	9	13
Angela Hucles	M	19	1496	3	4	10
Sarah Yohe	M	13	469	1	4	6
Allie Kemp	F/M	14	219	2	0	4
Alexa Borisjuk	M	13	363	1	1	3
Jena Kluegel	D	19	1677	0	2	2
Heather Aldama	D	17	1354	0	1-	1
Sarah Dacey	M	16	955	0	1	1
Monica Gonzalez	D	12	750	0	1	1
Ragnhild Gulbrandsen	F	6	77	0	1	1
Christine McCann	D	21	1879	0	1	1
Kate Sobrero	D	16	1369	0	1	1
Kalli Kamholz	D/M	2	173	0	0	0
Keri Sanchez	D/M	16	1145	0	0	0

Goalkeepers	Gm	Min	W-L-T	Shts	Svs	GAA
Karina LeBlanc	17	1530	5-6-6	101	64	1.59
Tracy Ducar	4	360	1-2-1	21	13	2.00

New York Power

	Pos	Gm	Min	G	A	Pts
Tiffeny Milbrett	F	19	1605	10	8	28
Emily Janss	M	21	1336	8	1	17
Tammy Pearman	F/D	20	1569	4	1	9
Linda Ormen	F	14	1032	2	3	7
Krista Davey	D/M	20	727	2	1	5
Anita Rapp	M	19	1364	2	1	5
Minna Mustonen	F	12	505	1	2	4
Ronnie Fair	M	21	1751	0	4	4
Wynne McIntosh	D/M	14	827	1	1	3
J. Baumgardt-Yamada	M	10	548	0	3	3
Jaclyn Raveia	D	10	876	1	0	2
Jennifer Lalor	F/M	20	1457	0	1	1
Christie Pearce	D	19	1699	0	1	1
Emily Stauffer	F	15	538	0	1	1
Katie Tracy	D/M	8	368	0	1	1
Sara Whalen	D/M	10	872	0	1	1
Kristy Whelchel	D	20	1701	0	1	1
Rachel Hoffman	F	7	123	0	0	0

Goalkeepers	Gm	Min	W-L-T	Shts	Svs	GAA
Nicole Williams	4	272	0-4-0	23	15	2.65
Saskia Webber	14	1258	3-9-1	132	91	2.86
Gao Hong	4	360	0-4-0	37	21	3.50

Philadelphia Charge

	Pos	Gm	Min	G	A	Pts
Marinette Pichon	F/M	18	1394	14	1	29
Zhao Lihong	M	17	1362	2	8	12
Kelly Smith	M	7	603	4	3	11
Mandy Clemens	F	18	1046	2	2	6
Liu Ailing	M	20	1235	2	2	6
Kerry Connors	M	18	1212	2	1	5
Jennifer Tietjen	D	20	1800	1	3	5
Lorrie Fair	M	19	1638	0	5	5
Erica Iverson	D	19	1691	2	0	4
Erin Martin	F	11	482	2	0	4
Stacey Tullock	D/M	14	1012	2	0	4
Mary-Frances Monroe	M	15	830	1	2	4
Heather Mitts	D	16	1386	0	4	4
Jenny Benson	M	19	1582	0	3	3
Tara Koleski	F	6	201	0	1	1
Andrea Alfiler	D	5	339	0	0	0
Michelle Demko	M	5	132	0	0	0
Karyn Hall	D	4	263	0	0	0
Rebekah McDowell	M	12	673	0	0	0

Goalkeepers	Gm	Min	W-L-T	Shts	Svs	GAA
Melissa Moore	20	1800	11-3-6	110	86	1.00
Maite Zabala	1	90	0-1-0	5	3	2.00

San Diego Spirit

	Pos	Gm	Min	G	A	Pts
Shannon MacMillan	F	17	1424	5	8	18
Julie Foudy	M	19	1645	5	4	14
Zhang Ouying	M	17	1352	5	2	12
Lori Lindsey	M	20	1231	2	5	9
Julie Fleeting	F	8	641	3	1	7
Shannon Boxx	M	20	1349	2	2	6
Jen Mascaro	M	11	665	1	4	6
Shauna Rohbock	F	12	481	2	0	4
Sherrill Kester	M	21	1342	1	2	4
Joy Fawcett	D	19	1627	1	1	3
Mercy Akide	F	10	470	0	1	1
Fan Yunjie	D	17	1387	0	1	1
Kim Pickup	D	15	576	0	1	1
Amy Sauer	D	20	1489	0	1	1
Anna Kraus	D	9	746	0	0	0
Flo Omagbemi	M	6	241	0	0	0
Rhiannon Tanaka	M	18	1438	0	0	0
Margaret Tietjen	D	13	585	0	0	0

Goalkeepers	Gm	Min	W-L-T	Shts	Svs	GAA
Carly Smolak	10	721	3-4-2	40	25	1.75
Jaime Pagliarulo	15	1168	2-7-3	86	54	2.16

San Jose CyberRays

	Pos	Gm	Min	G	A	Pts
Katia	F	21	1847	15	5	35
Tisha Venturini-Hoch	M	21	1734	6	1	13
Brandi Chastain	F/D	18	1561	4	3	11
Pretinha	F	21	1749	4	3	11
Sissi	M	21	1754	1	9	11
Michelle French	D/M	20	1600	1	5	7
Kim Clark	F	15	643	1	4	6
M. Hendershot-Brown	F	9	159	1	0	2
Lisa Nanez	D/M	10	444	1	0	2
Theresa Wagner	M	14	354	0	2	2
Christina Bell	D	10	371	0	1	1
Dianne Alagich	D/M	17	1438	0	0	0
Danielle Borgman	D	14	862	0	0	0
Thori Bryan	D	21	1890	0	0	0
Carey Dorn	M	13	755	0	0	0
Kelly Lindsey	D	19	1649	0	0	0

Goalkeepers	Gm	Min	W-L-T	Shts	Svs	GAA
LaKeysia Beene	20	1800	8-7-5	104	72	1.35
Dawn Greathouse	1	90	0-1-0	4	2	3.00

Washington Freedom

	Pos	Gm	Min	G	A	Pts
Abby Wambach	F	19	1689	10	9	29
Mia Hamm	M	11	506	8	6	22
Bai Jie	M	16	887	6	5	17
Jacqui Little	F	20	1019	3	4	10
Pu Wei	M	20	1667	1	8	10
Monica Gerardo	M	19	985	3	1	7
Emmy Barr	D	21	1863	2	3	7
Anne Makinen	M	14	824	2	2	6
Jennifer Grubb	D	21	1890	2	0	4
Skylar Little	D	20	1751	1	1	3
Meredith Beard	F	5	84	1	0	2
Steffi Jones	M	13	1170	0	2	2
Ann Cook	M	18	747	0	1	1
Tracey Milburn	F	11	448	0	1	1
Sarah Kate Noftsinger	M	5	289	0	1	1
Carrie Moore	D	18	1491	0	0	0
Stephanie Rigamat	F	6	92	0	0	0
Lindsay Stoecker	D/M	11	928	0	0	0
Casey Zimny	D	15	570	0	0	0

Goalkeepers	Gm	Min	W-L-T	Shts	Svs	GAA
Siri Mullinix	14	1139	7-3-4	104	84	1.19
Erin Fahey	6	327	2-0-1	35	27	1.65

Colleges

MEN

2001 Final *Soccer America* Top 20

Final 2001 regular season poll including games through Nov. 11. Conducted by the national weekly *Soccer America* and released in the Nov. 26 issue. Listing includes records through conference playoffs as well as NCAA tournament record and team lost to. Teams in **bold** type went on to reach NCAA Final Four. All tournament games decided by penalty kicks are considered ties.

		Nov. 11 Record	NCAA Recap			Nov. 11 Record	NCAA Recap
1	SMU	17-0-0	2-1 (St. John's)	12	Rutgers	13-5-3	1-1 (Indiana)
2	Virginia	16-0-1	0-1 (Virginia)	13	South Carolina	11-4-2	0-2 (UAB)
3	Saint Louis	15-1-0	2-1 (Stanford)	14	Loyola (Md.)	15-1-2	1-1 (St. Louis)
4	Stanford	14-1-1	3-1 (N. Carolina)	15	Princeton	10-2-5	0-1 (Fairleigh Dickinson)
5	Connecticut	14-3-2	0-1 (Rutgers)				
6	North Carolina	15-3-0	5-0	16	Washington	12-4-0	0-1 (Portland)
7	Indiana	14-3-1	4-1 (N. Carolina)	17	Notre Dame	10-5-0	0-1 (Maryland)
8	Clemson	14-4-0	2-1 (Indiana)	18	Furman	14-4-0	0-1 (UAB)
9	Wake Forest	13-4-1	0-1 (American)	19	Portland	11-5-1	2-1 (Stanford)
10	St. John's	12-2-3	3-1 (Indiana)	20	UCLA	10-6-4	2-1 (SMU)
11	Penn St.	11-4-1	1-1 (St. John's)				

Colleges (Cont.)

NCAA Division I Tournament

First Round (Nov. 23)

First and second round games played at regional locations. Host sites: Bloomington, Ind.; Chapel Hill, N.C.; Charlottesville, Va.; College Park, Md.; Columbia, S.C.; Dallas, Texas; Garden City, N.J.; Princeton, N.J.; St. Louis, Mo.; San Diego, Calif.; Seattle, Wash.; Stanford, Calif.; State College, Penn.; Storrs, Conn.; Winston-Salem, N.C.

New Mexico 1	Fla. International 0	Kentucky 1	Mercer 0
Santa Clara 1 ....3 OT	California 0	Towson 4	James Madison 1
UCLA 3 ....2 OT	Loyola Marymount 0	Alabama-Birmingham 1 ...OT	Furman 0
Portland 1	Gonzaga 0	American 2	Ohio St. 1
South Florida 2	Akron 1	Rutgers 1	Harvard 0
Maryland 1	Notre Dame 0	Fairleigh Dickinson ....3 OT	Boston College 0
Massachusetts 1	Creighton 0	Michigan St. 2	Butler 1
Missouri-KC 2 ....OT	WI-Milwaukee 1	Seton Hall 2	Coastal Carolina 0

Second Round (Nov. 25)

SMU 2	New Mexico 0	Clemson ....3 OT	Kentucky 0
Stanford 3	Santa Clara 1	North Carolina 3	Towson 0
UCLA 4	San Diego 0	Alabama-Birmingham 3 ...OT	South Carolina 2
Portland 1	Washington 0	American 3	Wake Forest 0
Penn St. 1 ....3 OT	South Florida 0	Rutgers 2 ....3 OT	Connecticut 1
Loyola (Md.) 1 ....2 OT	Maryland 0	Fairleigh Dickinson 2	Princeton 1
St. John's 1	Massachusetts 0	Indiana 1	Michigan St. 0
Saint Louis 2	Missouri-KC 1	Seton Hall 1	Virginia 0

Third Round (Nov. 30–Dec. 2)

at Stanford 3	Portland 1
at St. John's 2 ....3 OT	Penn St. 1
at Saint Louis 3	Loyola 0
at SMU 1	UCLA 0
Fairleigh Dickinson 1	at Seton Hall 0
at North Carolina 1 ......OT	American 0
at Clemson 3 ....2 OT	Alabama-Birmingham 2
at Indiana 3	Rutgers 0

Quarterfinals (Dec. 7–9)

at Stanford 1	Saint Louis 0
at North Carolina 3 ......3 OT	Fairleigh Dickinson 2
St. John's 2	at SMU 0
at Indiana 2	Clemson 0

2001 College Cup

at Columbus, Ohio (Dec. 14 & 16)

Semifinals

Indiana 2 ....2 OT	St. John's 1
North Carolina 3 ......4 OT	Stanford 2

Championship

North Carolina 2 .... Indiana 0

Scoring:
First Half: UNC—Ryan Kneipper (Matt Crawford, Grant Porter), 11:37.
Second Half: UNC—Danny Jackson, 74:50.
Attendance: 7,113

Final records: North Carolina (21-4-0); Indiana (18-4-1).
Most Outstanding Offensive Player: Ryan Kneipper, N. Carolina. **Most Outstanding Defensive Player:** David Stokes, N. Carolina.
All-Tournament Team: Kneipper, Stokes, Matt Crawford, Michael Ueltschey and Danny Jackson from North Carolina; Pat Noonan and Mike Ambersley from Indiana; Shalrie Joseph and Jeff Mateo from St. John's; Todd Dunivant and Matt Moses from Stanford.

WOMEN

2001 Final *Soccer America* Top 20

Final 2001 regular season poll including games through Nov. 11. Conducted by the national weekly *Soccer America* and released in the Nov. 26 issue. Listing includes records through conference playoffs as well as NCAA tournament record and team lost to. Teams in **bold** type went on to reach NCAA Final Four. All tournament games decided by penalty kicks are considered ties.

		Nov. 11 Record	NCAA Recap			Nov. 11 Record	NCAA Recap
1	North Carolina	19-0-0	5-1 (Santa Clara)	11	Virginia	14-3-2	3-1 (Santa Clara)
2	Santa Clara	17-2-0	6-0	12	Nebraska	15-4-1	2-1 (Portland)
3	Portland	16-3-0	4-1 (North Carolina)	13	St. Mary's	14-2-2	1-1 (Stanford)
4	UCLA	17-2-0	3-1 (Florida)	14	West Virginia	16-4-1	0-1 (Miami-OH)
5	Texas A&M	13-3-1	3-1 (Portland)	15	Clemson	13-4-1	2-1 (Florida)
6	Florida	17-3-1	4-1 (Santa Clara)	16	Connecticut	17-5-0	2-1 (Penn St.)
7	Notre Dame	17-2-1	1-1 (Cincinnati)	17	Washington	12-4-2	1-1 (Portland)
8	Penn St.	18-3-1	3-1 (North Carolina)	18	Florida St.	14-7-1	1-1 (Clemson)
9	Stanford	13-3-2	2-1 (Texas A&M)	19	Auburn	11-7-1	0-1 (Florida St.)
10	Texas	14-5-0	0-1 (SMU)	20	Illinois	12-7-1	0-1 (Syracuse)

NCAA Division I Tournament
First Round (Nov. 15-16)

Connecticut 3 ....Sacred Heart 0	Miami-OH 1 ....West Virginia 0
Harvard 1 ....4 OT ....Hartford 0	Florida St. 1 ....Auburn 0
BYU 1 ....Kansas 0	Clemson 1 ....OT.............Kentucky 0
Nebraska 5 ....Boston College 0	Florida 4 ....C. Florida 0
North Carolina 3 ....NC-Greensboro 0	Cincinnati 3 ....Oakland 2
Duke 1 ....4 OT ....Tennessee 1	Notre Dame 2 ....E. Illinois 0
Duke won shoot-out, 4-2	Virginia 1 ....Liberty 0
Rutgers 4 ....Boston Univ. 1	William & Mary 2........2 OT..........Wake Forest 1
Princeton 3 ....Loyola (Md.) 1	Dartmouth 1 ....WI-Milwaukee 0
Penn St. 3 ....Bucknell 1	Michigan 1 ....Marquette 0
Villanova 2...........................Pennsylvania 0	Santa Clara 3 ....Evansville 0
Pepperdine 1 ....USC 0	Syracuse 1 ....Illinois 0
UCLA 3 ....CS-Fullerton 0	Portland 5 ....Idaho St. 0
Dayton 1 ....Maryland 0	Washington 2.............................San Diego 0

Second Round (Nov. 17-18)

Connecticut 1 ....Harvard 0	Florida 3 ....Georgia 0
Nebraska 3 ....BYU 0	Stanford 3 ....St. Mary's 1
North Carolina 2............................Duke 0	Cincinnati 3 ....Notre Dame 2
UCLA 2 ....Pepperdine 1	Texas A&M 2 ....OT.................SMU 1
Rutgers 1 ....Princeton 0	Portland 2 ....Washington 0
Dayton 2 ....Miami-OH 1	Santa Clara 4 ....Syracuse 1
Penn St. 3 ....Villanova 0	Dartmouth 1 ....Michigan 0
Clemson 1 ....Florida St. 0	Virginia 4 ....William & Mary 1

Third Round (Nov. 23-25)

Texas A&M 1 ....Stanford 0	
Portland 4 ....Nebraska 0	
Penn St. 2 ....Connecticut 0	
North Carolina 2............................Rutgers 0	
Virginia 4...................................Cincinnati 0	
Santa Clara 2 ....Dartmouth 0	
UCLA 3 ....Dayton 1	
Florida 3...................................Clemson 1	

Quarterfinals (Nov. 30-Dec. 2)

North Carolina 2 ....Penn St. 1	
Santa Clara 3 ....Virginia 2	
Florida 2................2 OT................UCLA 0	
Portland 4 ....Texas A&M 1	

2001 College Cup
at Dallas, Texas (Dec. 7 and 9)

Semifinals	Championship
North Carolina 2........................Portland 1	Santa Clara 1.......................North Carolina 0
Santa Clara 3.............................Florida 2	**Scoring:** SC—Aly Wagner (Leslie Osborne, Jessica Ballweg), 40:44.
	Attendance: 7,090

Final records: Santa Clara (23-2), North Carolina (24-1).
Most Outstanding Offensive Player: Aly Wagner, Santa Clara; **Most Outstanding Defensive Player:** Danielle Slaton, Santa Clara.
All Tournament Team: Wagner, Slaton, Veronica Zepeda, Anna Kraus, Leslie Osborne and Jessica Ballweg from Santa Clara; Jena Kluegel, Sara Randolph, Anne Remy, Catherine Reddick and Jordan Kellgren from North Carolina.

2001 Annual Awards
Men's Players of the Year

Hermann Trophy ....Luchi Gonzalez, SMU
MAC Award/NSCAA.............Luchi Gonzalez, SMU
Soccer America ....Luchi Gonzalez, SMU

Women's Player of the Year

Hermann Trophy.................Christie Welsh, Penn St.
MAC Award/NSCAA ....Christie Welsh, Penn St.
Soccer America ....Aly Wagner, Santa Clara

NSCAA Coaches of the Year

Division I: Women's..............Jerry Smith, Santa Clara
Men's..........Elmar Bolowich, North Carolina

Colleges (Cont.)
Division I All-America Teams

MEN

The 2001 first team All-America selections of the National Soccer Coaches Association of America (NSCAA). Holdovers from the 2000 NSCAA All-America team are in **bold** type.

GOALKEEPER—Byron Foss, SMU, Sr.

DEFENDERS—**Chris Gbandi**, Connecticut, Sr.; Daniel Jackson, North Carolina, Sr.; Lee Morrison, Stanford, Sr.

MIDFIELDERS—Luchi Gonzalez, SMU, Sr.; Kyle Martino, Virignia, Jr.; Diego Walsh, SMU, Sr.

FORWARDS—Nicholas McCreath, Rhode Island, Sr.; Pat Noonan, Indiana, Jr..; Dipsy Selolwane, Saint Louis, Sr.; **John Barry Nusum**, Furman, Sr.

WOMEN

The 2001 first team All-America selections of the National Soccer Coaches Association of America (NSCAA). Holdovers from the combined 2000 All-America team are in **bold** type.

GOALKEEPER—**Emily Oleksiuk**, Penn St., Sr.

DEFENDERS—**Danielle Slaton**, Santa Clara, Sr.; Danielle Borgman, North Carolina, Sr.; Casey Zimny, Connecticut, Sr.

MIDFIELDERS—Joanna Lohman, Penn St., So.; Mary-Frances Monroe, UCLA, Sr.; Aly Wagner, Santa Clara, Jr.

FORWARDS—**Christie Welch**, Penn State, Jr.; Katie Barnes, West Va., Sr.; Christine Sinclair, Portland, Fr.; Abby Wambach, Florida, Sr.

Small College Final Fours

MEN
NCAA Division II
at Tampa, Fla. (Nov. 30-Dec. 2)

Semifinals: Cal. St. Domingo Hills def. Dowling (N.Y.), 1-0 (OT); Tampa def. SIU-Edwardsville, 2-1 (OT).

Championship: Tampa def. Cal. St. Domingo Hills, 2-1. Final records: Cal. St. Domingo Hills (20-3-2), Tampa (19-0-2).

NCAA Division III
at Messiah College, Grantham, Penn. (Nov. 24-25)

Semifinals: Redlands (Calif.) def. Messiah (Penn.), 2-1 (OT); Richard Stockton (N.J.) def. Ohio Wesleyan, 0-0 (3-1 on PKs).

Championship: Richard Stockton def. Redlands, 3-2; Final records: Richard Stockton (26-1-0); Redlands (20-4-0).

NAIA
at Bowling Green, Ky. (Nov. 19-20)

Semifinals: Lindsey Wilson (Ky.) def. Rio Grande (Ohio), 2-1; Auburn-Montgomery (Ala.) def. William Carey (Miss.), 2-2 (5-3 on PKs).

Championship: Lindsey Wilson def. Auburn-Montgomery, 4-0; Final records: Lindsey Wilson (24-2-0), Auburn-Montgomery (20-3-3).

WOMEN
NCAA Division II
at San Diego (Nov. 29-Dec. 1)

Semifinals: UC-San Diego def. Northern Kentucky, 3-2; Christian Brothers (Tenn.) def. Franklin Pierce (N.H.), 4-1.

Championship: UC-San Diego def. Christian Brothers, 2-0. Final records: UC-San Diego (21-2-0), Christian Brothers. (22-1-0).

NCAA Division III
at Delaware, Ohio (Nov. 16-17)

Semifinals: Ohio Wesleyan def. Willamette, 2-1 (OT); Amherst (Mass.) def. Wheaton (Ill.), 1-0.

Championship: Ohio Wesleyan def. Amherst, 1-0. Final records: Ohio Wesleyan (22-1-0), Amherst (16-5-1).

NAIA
at St. Charles, Mo. (Nov. 19-20)

Semifinals: Westmont (Calif.) def. Lindsey Wilson (Ky.), 2-1 (2 OT); Oklahoma City def. Azusa Pacific (Calif.), 2-2 (3-0 on PKs).

Championship: Westmont def. Oklahoma City, 1-0; Final records: Westmont (19-4-0), Oklahoma City (23-2-1).

1930-2002
Through the Years

**ESPN
Information Please®
SPORTS ALMANAC**

The World Cup

The Federation Internationale de Football Association (FIFA) began the World Cup championship tournament in 1930 with a 13-team field in Uruguay. Sixty-four years later, 138 countries competed in qualifying rounds to fill 24 berths in the 1994 World Cup finals. FIFA increased the World Cup '98 tournament field from 24 to 32 teams, and it remained at 32 in 2002 including automatic berths for defending champion France and co-hosts Japan and South Korea. The other 29 slots were allotted by region: Europe (13), Africa (5), South America (4), CONCACAF (3), Asia (2), the two remaining positions were determined via two home-and-away playoff series. One was between the #14 European team (Ireland) and the #3 Asian team (Iran) and the other was between the #5 South American team (Uruguay) and the champion of Oceania (Australia).

Tournaments have been played once in Asia (Japan/South Korea), three times in North America (Mexico 2 and U.S.), four times in South America (Argentina, Chile, Brazil and Uruguay) and nine times in Europe (France 2, Italy 2, England, Spain, Sweden, Switzerland and West Germany). Following an outcry when Germany was awarded the 2006 World Cup over South Africa, FIFA announced that, starting in 2010, the World Cup will be rotated among six continents.

Brazil retired the first World Cup (called the Jules Rimet Trophy after FIFA's first president) in 1970 after winning it for the third time. The new trophy, first presented in 1974, is known as simply the World Cup.

Multiple winners: Brazil (5); Italy and West Germany (3); Argentina and Uruguay (2).

Year	Champion	Manager	Score	Runner-up	Host Country	Third Place
1930	Uruguay	Alberto Suppici	4-2	Argentina	Uruguay	No game
1934	Italy	Vittório Pozzo	2-1*	Czechoslovakia	Italy	Germany 3, Austria 2
1938	Italy	Vittório Pozzo	4-2	Hungary	France	Brazil 4, Sweden 2
1942-46	Not held					
1950	Uruguay	Juan Lopez	2-1	Brazil	Brazil	No game
1954	West Germany	Sepp Herberger	3-2	Hungary	Switzerland	Austria 3, Uruguay 1
1958	Brazil	Vicente Feola	5-2	Sweden	Sweden	France 6, W. Ger. 3
1962	Brazil	Aimoré Moreira	3-1	Czechoslovakia	Chile	Chile 1, Yugoslavia 0
1966	England	Alf Ramsey	4-2*	W. Germany	England	Portugal 2, USSR 1
1970	Brazil	Mario Zagalo	4-1	Italy	Mexico	W. Ger. 1, Uruguay 0
1974	West Germany	Helmut Schoen	2-1	Netherlands	W. Germany	Poland 1, Brazil 0
1978	Argentina	Cesar Menotti	3-1*	Netherlands	Argentina	Brazil 2, Italy 1
1982	Italy	Enzo Bearzot	3-1	W. Germany	Spain	Poland 3, France 2
1986	Argentina	Carlos Bilardo	3-2	W. Germany	Mexico	France 4, Belgium 2*
1990	West Germany	Franz Beckenbauer	1-0	Argentina	Italy	Italy 2, England 1
1994	Brazil	Carlos Parreira	0-0†	Italy	USA	Sweden 4, Bulgaria 0
1998	France	Aimé Jacquet	3-0	Brazil	France	Croatia 2, Netherlands 1
2002	Brazil	Luiz Felipe Scolari	2-0	Germany	Japan/S. Korea	Turkey 3, S. Korea 2
2006	at Germany (June 9-July 9)					

*Winning goals scored in overtime (no sudden death); †Brazil defeated Italy in shootout (3-2) after scoreless overtime period.

All-Time World Cup Leaders

Career Goals

World Cup scoring leaders through 2002. Years listed are years played in World Cup.

	No
Gerd Müller, West Germany (1970, 74)	14
Just Fontaine, France (1958)	13
Pelé, Brazil (1958, 62, 66, 70)	12
Ronaldo, Brazil (1994, 98, 2002)	12
Sandor Kocsis, Hungary (1954)	11
Juergen Klinsmann, Germany (1990, 94, 98)	11
Helmut Rahn, West Germany (1954, 58)	10
Teofilo Cubillas, Peru (1970, 78)	10
Gregorz Lato, Poland (1974, 78, 82)	10
Gary Lineker, England (1986, 90)	10

Single Tournament Goals

World Cup tournament scoring leaders through 2002.

Year		Gm	No
1930	Guillermo Stabile, Argentina	4	8
1934	Angelo Schiavio, Italy	3	4
	Oldrich Nejedly, Czechoslovakia	4	4
	Edmund Conen, Germany	4	4
1938	Leônidas, Brazil	3	8
1950	Ademir, Brazil	6	7
1954	Sandor Kocsis, Hungary	5	11
1958	Just Fontaine, France	6	13
1962	Drazen Jerkovic, Yugoslavia	6	4
1966	Eusébio, Portugal	6	9
1970	Gerd Müller, West Germany	6	10
1974	Grzegorz Lato, Poland	7	7
1978	Mario Kempes, Argentina	7	6
1982	Paolo Rossi, Italy	7	6
1986	Gary Lineker, England	5	6
1990	Toto Schillaci, Italy	7	6
1994	Oleg Salenko, Russia	3	6
	Hristo Stoitchkov, Bulgaria	7	6
1998	Davor Suker, Croatia	7	6
2002	Ronaldo, Brazil	7	8

Most Valuable Player

Officially, the Golden Ball Award, the Most Valuable Player of the World Cup tournament has been selected since 1982 by a panel of international soccer journalists.

Year		Year	
1982	Paolo Rossi, Italy	1994	Romario, Brazil
1986	Diego Maradona, Arg.	1998	Ronaldo, Brazil
1990	Toto Schillaci, Italy	2002	Oliver Kahn, Germany

All-Time World Cup Ranking Table

Since the first World Cup in 1930, Brazil is the only country to play in all 17 final tournaments. The FIFA all-time table below ranks all nations that have ever qualified for a World Cup final tournament by points earned through 2002. Victories, which earned two points from 1930-90, were awarded three points starting in 1994. Note that Germany's appearances include 10 made by West Germany from 1954-90. Participants in the 2002 World Cup final are in **bold** type.

		App	Gm	W	L	T	Pts	GF	GA
1	**Brazil**	17	87	60	13	14	141	191	82
2	**Germany**	15	85	50	17	18	123	176	106
3	**Italy**	15	70	39	14	17	96	110	67
4	**Argentina**	13	60	30	19	11	72	102	71
5	**England**	11	50	26	13	15	61	68	45
6	**Spain**	11	45	20	15	10	54	71	53
7	**France**	11	44	21	16	7	49	86	61
8	**Sweden**	10	42	15	16	10	42	71	65
9	**Russia**	9	37	17	14	6	41	64	44
10	Yugoslavia	9	37	16	13	8	40	60	46
	Uruguay	10	40	15	15	10	40	65	57
12	Netherlands	7	31	14	9	9	37	56	36
13	**Poland**	6	28	14	9	5	34	42	36
14	Hungary	9	32	15	14	3	33	87	57
	Mexico	12	41	10	20	11	33	43	80
16	**Belgium**	11	36	10	17	9	30	46	63
17	Austria	7	29	12	13	4	28	43	47
18	Czech Republic	8	30	11	14	5	27	44	45
19	Romania	7	21	8	8	5	21	30	32
20	Chile	7	25	7	12	6	20	31	40
21	**Paraguay**	6	19	5	8	6	18	25	34
	Denmark	3	13	7	4	2	18	24	18
23	**South Korea**	6	21	4	12	5	17	19	49
24	**Cameroon**	5	17	4	6	7	16	15	29
	USA	7	22	6	14	2	16	25	45
26	**Portugal**	3	12	7	5	0	15	25	16
	Scotland	8	23	4	12	7	15	25	41
	Switzerland	7	22	6	13	3	15	33	51
	Turkey	2	10	4	4	1	15	20	17
30	Bulgaria	7	26	3	15	8	14	22	53
31	**Croatia**	2	10	6	4	0	13	13	8
32	**Ireland**	4	13	2	4	7	12	10	10
33	Peru	4	15	4	8	3	11	19	31
	No. Ireland	3	13	3	5	5	11	13	23
35	**Nigeria**	3	11	4	6	1	9	14	16
36	Morocco	4	13	2	7	4	8	12	18
	Colombia	4	13	3	8	2	8	14	23
	Costa Rica	2	7	3	3	1	8	9	12
	Senegal	1	5	2	1	2	8	7	6
40	Norway	2	8	2	3	3	7	7	8
	Japan	2	7	2	4	1	7	6	7
42	East Germany	1	6	2	2	2	6	5	5
	South Africa	2	6	1	2	3	6	8	11
44	**Saudi Arabia**	3	10	2	7	1	5	7	25
	Algeria	2	6	2	3	1	5	6	10
	Wales	1	5	1	1	3	5	4	4
	Tunisia	3	9	1	5	3	5	5	11
48	Iran	2	6	1	4	1	3	4	12
	North Korea	1	4	1	2	1	3	5	9
	Cuba	1	3	1	1	1	3	5	12
	Jamaica	1	3	1	2	0	3	3	9
52	**Ecuador**	1	3	1	2	0	2	2	4
	Egypt	2	4	0	2	2	2	3	6
	Honduras	1	3	0	1	2	2	2	3
	Israel	1	3	0	1	2	2	1	3
56	Bolivia	3	6	0	5	1	1	1	20
	Australia	1	3	0	2	1	1	0	5
	Kuwait	1	3	0	2	1	1	2	6
59	El Salvador	2	6	0	6	0	0	1	22
	Canada	1	3	0	3	0	0	0	5
	East Indies	1	1	0	1	0	0	0	6
	Greece	1	3	0	3	0	0	0	10
	Haiti	1	3	0	3	0	0	2	14
	Iraq	1	3	0	3	0	0	1	4
	Slovenia	1	3	0	3	0	0	2	7
	New Zealand	1	3	0	3	0	0	2	12
	UAE	1	3	0	3	0	0	2	11
	China	1	3	0	3	0	0	0	9
	Zaire	1	3	0	3	0	0	0	14

The United States in the World Cup

While the United States has fielded a national team every year of the World Cup, only seven of those teams have been able to make it past the preliminary competition and qualify for the final World Cup tournament. The 1994 national team automatically qualified because the U.S. served as host of the event for the first time. The U.S. played in three of the first four World Cups (1930, '34 and '50) and each of the last four (1990, '94, '98 and 2002). The Americans have a record of 6-14-2 in 22 World Cup matches.

1930

1st Round Matches

United States 3 . . . . Belgium 0
United States 3 . . . . Paraguay 0

Semifinals

Argentina 6 . . . . United States 1
U.S. Scoring—Bert Patenaude (3), Bart McGhee (2), James Brown and Thomas Florie.

1934

1st Round Match

Italy 7 . . . . United States 1
U.S. Scoring—Buff Donelli (who later became a noted college and NFL football coach).

1950

1st Round Matches

Spain 3 . . . . United States 1
United States 1 . . . . England 0
Chile 5 . . . . United States 2
U.S. Scoring—Joe Gaetjens, Joe Maca, John Souza and Frank Wallace.

1990

1st Round Matches

Czechoslovakia 5 . . . . United States 1
Italy 1 . . . . United States 0
Austria 2 . . . . United States 1
U.S. Scoring—Paul Caligiuri and Bruce Murray.

1994

1st Round Matches

United States 1 . . . . Switzerland 1
United States 2 . . . . Colombia 1
Romania 1 . . . . United States 0

Round of 16

Brazil 1 . . . . United States 0
U.S. Scoring—Eric Wynalda, Earnie Stewart and own goal (Colombia defender Andres Escobar).

1998
1st Round Matches
Germany 2 . . . . .United States 0
Iran 2. . . . . .United States 1
Yugoslavia 1 . . . . .United States 0
U.S. Scoring–Brian McBride.

2002
1st Round Matches
United States 3 . . . . .Portugal 2
United States 1 . . . . .So. Korea 1
Poland 3 . . . . .United States 1
Round of 16
United States 2 . . . . .Mexico 0
Round of 8
Germany 1 . . . . .United States 0
U.S. Scoring– Landon Donovan (2), Brian McBride (2), John O'Brien, own goal (Portugal defender Jorge Costa) and Clint Mathis.

World Cup Finals
Brazil and Germany (formerly West Germany) have played in the most Cup finals with seven but faced each other for the first time in a final in 2002. Note that a four-team round robin determined the 1950 championship–the deciding game turned out to be the last one of the tournament between Uruguay and Brazil.

1930
Uruguay 4, Argentina 2
(at Montevideo, Uruguay)

		1	2–T
July 30	Uruguay (4-0)	1	3–4
	Argentina (4-1)	2	0–2

Goals: Uruguay–Pablo Dorado (12th minute), Pedro Cea (54th), Santos Iriarte (68th), Castro (89th); Argentina–Carlos Peucelle (20th), Guillermo Stabile (37th).
Uruguay–Ballesteros, Nasazzi, Mascheroni, Andrade, Fernandez, Gestido, Dorado, Scarone, Castro, Cea, Iriarte.
Argentina–Botasso, Della Torre, Paternoster, J. Evaristo, Monti, Suarez, Peucelle, Varallo, Stabile, Ferreira, M. Evaristo.
Attendance: 90,000. **Referee:** Langenus (Belgium).

1934
Italy 2, Czechoslovakia 1 (OT)
(at Rome)

		1	2	OT–T
June 10	Italy (4-0-1)	0	1	1–2
	Czechoslovakia (3-1)	0	1	0–1

Goals: Italy–Raimondo Orsi (80th minute), Angelo Schiavio (95th); Czechoslovakia–Puc (70th).
Italy–Combi, Monzeglio, Allemandi, Ferraris IV, Monti, Bertolini, Guaita, Meazza, Schiavio, Ferrari, Orsi.
Czechoslovakia–Planicka, Zenisek, Ctyroky, Kostalek, Cambal, Krcil, Junek, Svoboda, Sobotka, Nejedly, Puc.
Attendance: 55,000. **Referee:** Eklind (Sweden).

1938
Italy 4, Hungary 2
(at Paris)

		1	2–T
June 19	Italy (4-0)	3	4–1
	Hungary (3-1)	1	1–2

Goals: Italy–Gino Colaussi (5th minute), Silvio Piola (16th), Colaussi (35th), Piola (82nd); Hungary–Titkos (7th), Georges Sarosi (70th).
Italy–Olivieri, Foni, Rava, Serantoni, Andreolo, Locatelli, Biavati, Meazza, Piola, Ferrari, Colaussi.
Hungary–Szabo, Polgar, Biro, Szalay, Szucs, Lazar, Sas, Vincze, G. Sarosi, Szengeller, Titkos.
Attendance: 65,000. **Referee:** Capdeville (France).

1950
Uruguay 2, Brazil 1
(at Rio de Janeiro)

		1	2–T
July 16	Uruguay (3-0-1)	0	2–2
	Brazil (4-1-1)	0	1–1

Goals: Uruguay–Juan Schiaffino (66th minute), Chico Ghiggia (79th); Brazil–Friaca (47th).
Uruguay–Maspoli, M. Gonzales, Tejera, Gambetta, Varela, Andrade, Ghiggia, Perez, Miguez, Schiaffino, Moran.
Brazil–Barbosa, Augusto, Juvenal, Bauer, Danilo, Bigode, Friaça, Zizinho, Ademir, Jair, Chico.
Attendance: 199,854. **Referee:** Reader (England).

1954
West Germany 3, Hungary 2
(at Berne, Switzerland)

		1	2–T
July 4	West Germany (4-1)	2	1–3
	Hungary (4-1)	2	0–2

Goals: West Germany–Max Morlock (10th minute), Helmut Rahn (18th), Rahn (84th); Hungary–Ferenc Puskas (4th), Zoltan Czibor (9th).
West Germany–Turek, Posipal, Liebrich, Kohlmeyer, Eckel, Mai, Rahn, Morlock, O. Walter, F. Walter, Schaefer.
Hungary–Grosics, Buzansky, Lorant, Lantos, Bozsik, Zakarias, Czibor, Kocsis, Hidegkuti, Puskas, J. Toth.
Attendance: 60,000. **Referee:** Ling (England).

1958
Brazil 5, Sweden 2
(at Stockholm)

		1	2–T
June 29	Brazil (5-0-1)	2	3–5
	Sweden (4-1-1)	1	1–2

Goals: Brazil–Vava (9th minute), Vava (32nd), Pelé (55th), Mario Zagalo (68th), Pelé (90th); Sweden–Nils Liedholm (3rd), Agne Simonsson (80th).
Brazil–Gilmar, D. Santos, N. Santos, Zito, Bellini, Orlando, Garrincha, Didi, Vava, Pelé, Zagalo.
Sweden–Svensson, Bergmark, Axbom, Boerjesson, Gustavsson, Parling, Hamrin, Gren, Simonsson, Liedholm, Skoglund.
Attendance: 49,737. **Referee:** Guigue (France).

World Cup Finals (Cont.)

1962

Brazil 3, Czechoslovakia 1
(at Santiago, Chile)

	1	2-T
June 17 Brazil (5-0-1)	1	2-3
Czechoslovakia (3-2-1)	1	0-1

Goals: Brazil–Amarildo (17th minute), Zito (68th), Vava (77th); Czechoslovakia–Josef Masopust (15th).
Brazil–Gilmar, D. Santos, N. Santos, Zito, Mauro, Zozimo, Garrincha, Didi, Vava, Amarildo, Zagalo.
Czechoslovakia–Schroiff, Tichy, Novak, Pluskal, Popluhar, Masopust, Pospichal, Scherer, Kvasniak, Kadraba, Jelinek.
Attendance: 68,679. **Referee:** Latishev (USSR).

1966

England 4, West Germany 2 (OT)
(at London)

	1	2	OT-T
July 30 England (5-0-1)	1	1	2-4
West Germany (4-1-1)	1	1	0-2

Goals: England–Geoff Hurst (18th minute), Martin Peters (78th), Hurst (101st), Hurst (120th); West Germany–Helmut Haller (12th), Wolfgang Weber (90th).
England–Banks, Cohen, Wilson, Stiles, J. Charlton, Moore, Ball, Hurst, B. Charlton, Hunt, Peters.
West Germany–Tilkowski, Hottges, Schnellinger, Beckenbauer, Schulz, Weber, Haller, Seeler, Held, Overath, Emmerich.
Attendance: 93,802. **Referee:** Dienst (Switzerland).

1970

Brazil 4, Italy 1
(at Mexico City)

	1	2-T
June 21 Brazil (6-0)	1	3-4
Italy (3-1-2)	1	0-1

Goals: Brazil–Pelé (18th minute), Gerson (65th), Jairzinho (70th), Carlos Alberto (86th); Italy–Roberto Boninsegna (37th).
Brazil–Felix, C. Alberto, Everaldo, Clodoaldo, Brito, Piazza, Jairzinho, Gerson, Tostão, Pelé, Rivelino.
Italy–Albertosi, Burgnich, Facchetti, Bertini (Juliano, 73rd), Rosato, Cera, Domenghini, Mazzola, Boninsegna (Rivera, 84th), De Sisti, Riva.
Attendance: 107,412. **Referee:** Glockner (E. Germany).

1974

West Germany 2, Netherlands 1
(at Munich)

	1	2-T
July 7 West Germany (6-1)	2	0-2
Netherlands (5-1-1)	1	0-1

Goals: West Germany–Paul Breitner (25th minute, penalty kick), Gerd Müller (43rd); Netherlands–Johan Neeskens (1st, penalty kick).
West Germany–Maier, Beckenbauer, Vogts, Breitner, Schwarzenbeck, Overath, Bonhof, Hoeness, Grabowski, Muller, Holzenbein.
Netherlands–Jongbloed, Suurbier, Rijsbergen (De Jong, 58th), Krol, Haan, Jansen, Van Hanegem, Neeskens, Rep, Cruyff, Rensenbrink (R. Van de Kerkhof, 46th).
Attendance: 77,833. **Referee:** Taylor (England).

1978

Argentina 3, Netherlands 1 (OT)
(at Buenos Aires)

	1	2	OT-T
June 25 Argentina (5-1-1)	1	0	2-3
Netherlands (3-2-2)	0	1	0-1

Goals: Argentina–Mario Kempes (37th minute), Kempes (104th), Daniel Bertoni (114th); Netherlands–Dirk Nanninga (81st).
Argentina–Fillol, Olguin, L. Galvan, Passarella, Tarantini, Ardiles (Larrosa, 65th), Gallego, Kempes, Luque, Bertoni, Ortiz (Houseman, 77th).
Netherlands–Jongbloed, Jansen (Suurbier, 72nd), Brandts, Krol, Poortvliet, Haan, Neeskens, W. Van de Kerkhof, R. Van de Kerkhof, Rep (Nanninga, 58th), Rensenbrink.
Attendance: 77,260. **Referee:** Gonella (Italy).

1982

Italy 3, West Germany 1
(at Madrid)

	1	2-T
July 11 Italy (4-0-3)	0	3-3
West Germany (4-2-1)	0	1-1

Goals: Italy–Paolo Rossi (57th minute), Marco Tardelli (68th), Alessandro Altobelli (81st); West Germany–Paul Breitner (83rd).
Italy–Zoff, Scirea, Gentile, Cabrini, Collovati, Bergomi, Tardelli, Oriali, Conti, Rossi, Graziani (Altobelli, 8th, and Causio, 89th).
West Germany–Schumacher, Stielike, Kaltz, Briegel, K.H. Forster, B. Forster, Breitner, Dremmler (Hrubesch, 61st), Littbarski, Fischer, Rummenigge (Muller, 69th).
Attendance: 90,080. **Referee:** Coelho (Brazil).

1986

Argentina 3, West Germany 2
(at Mexico City)

	1	2-T
June 29 Argentina (6-0-1)	1	2-3
West Germany (4-2-1)	0	2-2

Goals: Argentina–Jose Brown (22nd minute), Jorge Valdano (55th), Jorge Burruchaga (83rd); West Germany–Karl-Heinz Rummenigge (73rd), Rudi Voller (81st).
Argentina–Pumpido, Cuciuffo, Olarticoechea, Ruggeri, Brown, Batista, Burruchaga (Trobbiani, 89th), Giusti, Enrique, Maradona, Valdano.
West Germany–Schumacher, Jakobs, B. Forster, Berthold, Briegel, Eder, Brehme, Matthaus, Rummenigge, Magath (Hoeness, 61st), Allofs (Voller, 46th).
Attendance: 114,590. **Referee:** Filho (Brazil).

1990

West Germany 1, Argentina 0
(at Rome)

	1	2-T
July 8 West Germany (6-0-1)	0	1-1
Argentina (4-2-1)	0	0-0

Goals: West Germany–Andreas Brehme (85th minute, penalty kick).
West Germany–Illgner, Berthold (Reuter, 73rd), Kohler, Augenthaler, Buchwald, Brehme, Haessler, Matthaus, Littbarski, Klinsmann, Voller.
Argentina–Goycoechea, Ruggeri (Monzon, 46th), Simon, Serrizuela, Lorenzo, Basualdo, Troglio, Burruchaga (Calderon, 53rd), Sensini, Dezotti, Maradona.
Attendance: 73,603. **Referee:** Codesal (Mexico).

1994

Brazil 0, Italy 0 (Shootout)
(at Pasadena, Calif.)

	1	2	OT–T
July 17 Brazil (6-0-1) ....:.............	0	0	0–0*
Italy (4-2-1)	0	0	0–0

*Brazil wins shootout, 3-2.

Shootout (five shots each, alternating): ITA–Baresi (miss, 0-0); BRA–Santos (blocked, 0-0); ITA– Albertini (goal, 1-0); BRA–Romario (goal, 1-1); ITA–Evani (goal, 2-1); BRA–Branco (goal, 2-2); ITA–Massaro (blocked, 2-2); BRA–Dunga (goal, 2-3); ITA–R. Baggio (miss, 2-3).

Brazil–Taffarel, Jorginho (Cafu, 21st minute), Branco, Aldair, Santos, Mazinho, Silva, Dunga, Zinho (Viola, 106th), Bebeto, Romario.

Italy–Pagliuca, Mussi (Apolloni, 35th minute), Baresi, Benarrivo, Maldini, Albertini, D. Baggio (Evani, 95th), Berti, Donadoni, R. Baggio, Massaro.

Attendance: 94,194. **Referee:** Puhl (Hungary).

1998

France 3, Brazil 0
(at Paris)

	1	2–T
July 12 Brazil (6-1)	0	0–0
France (7-0)	2	1–3

Goals: France–Zinedine Zidane (27th and 46th minutes), Petit (92).

Brazil–Taffarel, Cafu, Aldair, Baiano, Carlos, Sampaio (Edmundo, 74th minute), Dunga, Rivaldo, Leonardo (Denilson, 46th minute), Bebeto, Ronaldo.

France–Barthez, Lizarazu, Desailly, Thuram, Leboeuf, Djorkaeff (Viera, 75th minute), Deschamps, Zidane, Petit, Karembeu (Boghossian, 57th minute), Guivarc'h, Dugarry.

Attendance: 75,000. **Referee:** Belqola (Morocco).

2002

Brazil 2, Germany 0
(at Yokohama, Japan)

	1	2–T
June 30 Germany (5-2)	0	0–0
Brazil (7-0)	0	2–2

Goals: Brazil–Ronaldo (67th and 79th minutes).

Germany–Kahn, Linke, Ramelow, Neuville, Hamann, Klose (Bierhoff, 74th minute), Jeremies (Asamoah, 77th minute), Bode (Ziege, 84th minute), Schneider, Metzelder, Frings.

Brazil–Marcos, Cafu, Lucio, Junior, Edmilson, Carlos, Silva, Ronaldo (Denilson, 90th minute), Rivaldo, Ronaldinho (Paulista, 85th minute), Kleberson.

Attendance: 69,029. **Referee:** Collina (Italy).

Year-by-Year Comparisons

How the 17 World Cup tournaments have compared in nations qualifying, matches played, players participating, goals scored, average goals per game, overall attendance and attendance per game.

Year	Host	Continent	Nations	Matches	Players	Scored	Goals Per Game	Attendance Overall	Per Game
1930	Uruguay	So. America	13	18	189	70	3.8	589,300	32,739
1934	Italy	Europe	16	17	208	70	4.1	361,000	21,235
1938	France	Europe	15	18	210	84	4.7	376,000	20,889
1942-46	Not held								
1950	Brazil	So. America	13	22	192	88	4.0	1,044,763	47,489
1954	Switzerland	Europe	16	26	233	140	5.3	872,000	33,538
1958	Sweden	Europe	16	35	241	126	3.6	819,402	23,411
1962	Chile	So. America	16	32	252	89	2.8	892,812	27,900
1966	England	Europe	16	32	254	89	2.8	1,464,944	45,780
1970	Mexico	No. America	16	32	270	95	3.0	1,690,890	52,840
1974	West Germany	Europe	16	38	264	97	2.6	1,809,953	47,630
1978	Argentina	So. America	16	38	277	102	2.7	1,685,602	44,358
1982	Spain	Europe	24	52	396	146	2.8	2,108,723	40,552
1986	Mexico	No. America	24	52	414	132	2.5	2,393,031	46,020
1990	Italy	Europe	24	52	413	115	2.2	2,516,354	48,391
1994	United States	No. America	24	52	437	140	2.7	3,587,088	68,982
1998	France	Europe	32	64	704	171	2.7	2,775,400	43,366
2002	Japan/So. Korea	Asia	32	64	736	161	2.5	2,705,197	42,269

World Cup Shootouts

Introduced in 1982; winning sides in **bold** type.

Year	Round		Final	SO
1982	Semi	**W. Germany** vs. France	3-3	(5-4)
1986	Quarter	**Belgium** vs. Spain	1-1	(5-4)
	Quarter	**France** vs. Brazil	1-1	(4-3)
	Quarter	**W. Germany** vs. Mexico	0-0	(4-1)
1990	Second	**Ireland** vs. Romania	0-0	(5-4)
	Quarter	**Argentina** vs.Yugoslavia	0-0	(3-2)
	Semi	**Argentina** vs. Italy	1-1	(4-3)
	Semi	**W. Germany** vs. England	1-1	(4-3)

Year	Round		Final	SO
1994	Second	**Bulgaria** vs. Mexico	1-1	(3-1)
	Quarter	**Sweden** vs. Romania	2-2	(5-4)
	Final	**Brazil** vs. Italy	0-0	(3-2)
1998	Second	**Argentina** vs. England	2-2	(4-3)
	Quarter	**France** vs. Italy	0-0	(4-3)
2002	Second	**Spain** vs. Ireland	1-1	(3-2)
	Quarter	**So. Korea** vs. Spain	0-0	(5-3)

World Team of the 20th Century

The team, comprised of the century's best players, was voted on by a panel that included 250 international soccer journalists and released on June 10, 1998 in conjunction with the opening of the 1998 World Cup. The panel first selected the European and South American Teams of the Century and then chose the World Team from those two lists.

World Team

Pos		Pos	
GK	Lev Yashin, Soviet Union	MF	Alfredo Di Stefano, Argentina
D	Carlos Alberto, Brazil	MF	Michel Platini, France
D	Franz Beckenini, West Germany	F	Pele, Brazil
D	Bobby Moore, England	F	Garrincha, Brazil
D	Nilton Santos, Brazil	F	Diego Maradona, Argentina
MF	Johan Cruyff, Netherlands		

European Team		South American Team	
Pos		**Pos**	
GK	Lev Yashin, Soviet Union	GK	Ubaldo Fillol, Argentina
D	Paolo Maldini, Italy	D	Carlos Alberto, Brazil
D	Franz Beckenbauer, West Germany	D	Elias Figueroa, Chile
D	Bobby Moore, England	D	Daniel Passarella, Argentina
D	Franco Baresi, Italy	D	Nilton Santos, Brazil
MF	Johan Cruyff, Netherlands	MF	Didi, Brazil
MF	Eusebio, Portugal	MF	Alfredo Di Stefano, Argentina
MF	Michel Platini, France	MF	Rivelino, Brazil
F	Ferenc Puskas, Hungary	F	Pele, Brazil
F	Bobby Charlton, England	F	Garrincha, Brazil
F	Marco Van Basten, Netherlands	F	Diego Maradona, Argentina

OTHER WORLDWIDE COMPETITION

The Olympic Games

Held every four years since 1896, except during World War I (1916) and World War II (1940-44). Soccer was not a medal sport in 1896 at Athens or in 1932 at Los Angeles. By agreement between FIFA and the IOC, Olympic soccer competition is currently limited to players 23 years old and under with a few exceptions.

Multiple winners: England and Hungary (3); Soviet Union and Uruguay (2).

MEN

Year		Year	
1900	**England**, France, Belgium	1960	**Yugoslavia**, Denmark, Hungary
1904	**Canada**, USA I, USA II	1964	**Hungary**, Czechoslovakia, Germany
1906	**Denmark**, Smyrna (Int'l entry), Greece	1968	**Hungary**, Bulgaria, Japan
1908	**England**, Denmark, Netherlands	1972	**Poland**, Hungary, East Germany & Soviet Union
1912	**England**, Denmark, Netherlands	1976	**East Germany**, Poland, Soviet Union
1920	**Belgium**, Spain, Netherlands	1980	**Czechoslovakia**, East Germany, Soviet Union
1924	**Uruguay**, Switzerland, Sweden	1984	**France**, Brazil, Yugoslavia
1928	**Uruguay**, Argentina, Italy	1988	**Soviet Union**, Brazil, West Germany
1936	**Italy**, Austria, Norway	1992	**Spain**, Poland, Ghana
1948	**Sweden**, Yugoslavia, Denmark	1996	**Nigeria**, Argentina, Brazil
1952	**Hungary**, Yugoslavia, Sweden	2000	**Cameroon**, Spain, Chile
1956	**Soviet Union**, Yugoslavia, Bulgaria		

WOMEN

Year		Year	
1996	**USA**, China, Norway	2000	**Norway**, USA, Germany

The Under-20 World Cup

Held every two years since 1977. Officially, the World Youth Championship for the FIFA/Coca-Cola Cup.

Multiple winners: Argentina (4); Brazil (3); Portugal (2).

Year		Year	
1977	Soviet Union	1991	Portugal
1979	Argentina	1993	Brazil
1981	West Germany	1995	Argentina
1983	Brazil	1997	Argentina
1985	Brazil	1999	Spain
1987	Yugoslavia	2001	Argentina
1989	Portugal		

The Under-17 World Cup

Held every two years since 1985. Officially, the U-17 World Championship for the FIFA/JVC Cup.

Multiple winners: Brazil, Ghana and Nigeria (2).

Year		Year	
1985	Nigeria	1995	Ghana
1987	Soviet Union	1997	Brazil
1989	Saudi Arabia	1999	Brazil
1991	Ghana	2001	France
1993	Nigeria		

Indoor World Championship

First held in 1989. FIFA's only Five-a-Side tournament.

Multiple winner: Brazil (3).

Year		Year	
1989	Brazil	1996	Brazil
1992	Brazil	2000	Spain

Women's World Cup

First held in 1991. Officially, the FIFA Women's World Championship.

Multiple winner: United States (2).

Year		Year	
1991	United States	1999	United States
1995	Norway	2003	(at China)

Confederations Cup

First held in 1992. Contested by the Continental champions of Africa, Asia, Europe, North America and South America and originally called the Intercontinental Championship for the King Fahd Cup until it was redubbed the FIFA/Confederations Cup for the King Fahd Trophy in 1997.

Year		Year	
1992	Argentina	1999	Mexico
1995	Denmark	2001	France
1997	Brazil		

CONTINENTAL COMPETITION

European Championship

Held every four years since 1960. Officially, the European Football Championship. Winners receive the Henri Delaunay trophy, named for the Frenchman who first proposed the idea of a European Soccer Championship in 1927. The first one would not be played until five years after his death in 1955.

Multiple winners: Germany/West Germany (3); France (2).

Year		Year		Year		Year	
1960	Soviet Union	1972	West Germany	1984	France	1996	Germany
1964	Spain	1976	Czechoslovakia	1988	Netherlands	2000	France
1968	Italy	1980	West Germany	1992	Denmark	2004	(at Portugal)

Copa America

Held irregularly since 1916. Unofficially, the Championship of South America.

Multiple winners: Argentina and Uruguay (14); Brazil (6); Paraguay and Peru (2).

Year		Year		Year		Year		Year	
1916	Uruguay	1925	Argentina	1942	Uruguay	1957	Argentina	1987	Uruguay
1917	Uruguay	1926	Uruguay	1945	Argentina	1958	Argentina	1989	Brazil
1919	Brazil	1927	Argentina	1946	Argentina	1959	Uruguay	1991	Argentina
1920	Uruguay	1929	Argentina	1947	Argentina	1963	Bolivia	1993	Argentina
1921	Argentina	1935	Uruguay	1949	Brazil	1967	Uruguay	1995	Uruguay
1922	Brazil	1937	Argentina	1953	Paraguay	1975	Peru	1997	Brazil
1923	Uruguay	1939	Peru	1955	Argentina	1979	Paraguay	1999	Brazil
1924	Uruguay	1941	Argentina	1956	Uruguay	1983	Uruguay	2001	Colombia
								2004	(at Peru)

African Nations Cup

Contested since 1957 and held every two years since 1968.

Multiple winners: Cameroon, Egypt and Ghana (4); Congo/Zaire (3); Nigeria (2).

Year		Year		Year		Year		Year	
1957	Egypt	1968	Zaire	1978	Ghana	1988	Cameroon	1998	Egypt
1959	Egypt	1970	Sudan	1980	Nigeria	1990	Algeria	2000	Cameroon
1962	Ethiopia	1972	Congo	1982	Ghana	1992	Ivory Coast	2002	Cameroon
1963	Ghana	1974	Zaire	1984	Cameroon	1994	Nigeria	2004	(at Tunisia)
1965	Ghana	1976	Morocco	1986	Egypt	1996	South Africa		

CONCACAF Gold Cup

The Confederation of North, Central American and Caribbean Football Championship. Contested irregularly from 1963-81 and revived as CONCACAF Gold Cup in 1991.

Multiple winners: Mexico (6); Costa Rica (2).

Year		Year		Year		Year		Year	
1963	Costa Rica	1969	Costa Rica	1977	Mexico	1993	Mexico	2000	Canada
1965	Mexico	1971	Mexico	1981	Honduras	1996	Mexico	2004	(at USA)
1967	Guatemala	1973	Haiti	1991	United States	1998	Mexico		

CLUB COMPETITION
European/South American Cup

Also known as the Toyota Cup and Intercontinental Cup. Contested annually in December between the winners of the European Champions League (formerly European Cup) and South America's Copa Libertadores for the unofficial World Club Championship. Four European Cup winners refused to participate in the championship match in the 1970s and were replaced each time by the European Cup runner-up: Panathinaikos (Greece) for Ajax Amsterdam (Netherlands) in 1971; Juventus (Italy) for Ajax in 1973; Atlético Madrid (Spain) for Bayern Munich (West Germany) in 1974; and Malmo (Sweden) for Nottingham Forest (England) in 1979. Another European Cup winner, Marseille of France, was prohibited by the Union of European Football Associations (UEFA) from playing for the 1993 Toyota Cup because of its involvement in a match-rigging scandal.

Best-of-three game format from 1960-68, then a two-game/total goals format from 1969-79. Toyota became Cup sponsor in 1980, changed the format to a one-game championship and moved it to Toyko.

Multiple winners: AC Milan, Nacional and Penarol (3); Ajax Amsterdam, Bayern Munich, Boca Juniors, Independiente, Inter Milan, Juventus, Real Madrid, Santos and Sao Paulo (2).

Year	Year	Year
1960 Real Madrid (Spain)	1974 Atlético Madrid (Spain)	1988 Nacional (Uruguay)
1961 Penarol (Uruguay)	1975 Not held	1989 AC Milan (Italy)
1962 Santos (Brazil)	1976 Bayern Munich (W. Germany)	1990 AC Milan (Italy)
1963 Santos (Brazil)	1977 Boca Juniors (Argentina)	1991 Red Star (Yugoslavia)
1964 Inter Milan (Italy)	1978 Not held	1992 Sao Paulo (Brazil)
1965 Inter Milan (Italy)	1979 Olimpia (Paraguay)	1993 Sao Paulo (Brazil)
1966 Penarol (Uruguay)	1980 Nacional (Uruguay)	1994 Velez Sarsfield (Argentina)
1967 Racing Club (Argentina)	1981 Flamengo (Brazil)	1995 Ajax Amsterdam (Netherlands)
1968 Estudiantes (Argentina)	1982 Penarol (Uruguay)	1996 Juventus (Italy)
1969 AC Milan (Italy)	1983 Gremio (Brazil)	1997 Borussia Dortmund (Germany)
1970 Feyenoord (Netherlands)	1984 Independiente (Argentina)	1998 Real Madrid (Spain)
1971 Nacional (Uruguay)	1985 Juventus (Italy)	1999 Manchester United (England)
1972 Ajax Amsterdam (Netherlands)	1986 River Plate (Argentina)	2000 Boca Juniors (Argentina)
1973 Independiente (Argentina)	1987 FC Porto (Portugal)	2001 Bayern Munich (Germany)

European Cup/Champions League

Contested annually since the 1955-56 season by the league champions of the member countries of the Union of European Football Associations (UEFA). In 1999, UEFA announced the formation of a new competition called the UEFA Champions League to take the place of the Cup competition.

Multiple winners: Real Madrid (9); AC Milan (5); Ajax Amsterdam, Bayern Munich and Liverpool (4); Benfica, Inter-Milan, Juventus and Nottingham Forest (2).

Year	Year	Year
1956 Real Madrid (Spain)	1972 Ajax Amsterdam (Netherlands)	1988 PSV Eindhoven (Netherlands)
1957 Real Madrid (Spain)	1973 Ajax Amsterdam (Netherlands)	1989 AC Milan (Italy)
1958 Real Madrid (Spain)	1974 Bayern Munich (W. Germany)	
1959 Real Madrid (Spain)	1975 Bayern Munich (W. Germany)	1990 AC Milan (Italy)
	1976 Bayern Munich (W. Germany)	1991 Red Star Belgrade (Yugo.)
1960 Real Madrid (Spain)	1977 Liverpool (England)	1992 Barcelona (Spain)
1961 Benfica (Portugal)	1978 Liverpool (England)	1993 Marseille (France)*
1962 Benfica (Portugal)	1979 Nottingham Forest (England)	1994 AC Milan (Italy)
1963 AC Milan (Italy)		1995 Ajax Amsterdam (Netherlands)
1964 Inter Milan (Italy)	1980 Nottingham Forest (England)	1996 Juventus (Italy)
1965 Inter Milan (Italy)	1981 Liverpool (England)	1997 Borussia Dortmund (Germany)
1966 Real Madrid (Spain)	1982 Aston Villa (England)	1998 Real Madrid (Spain)
1967 Glasgow Celtic (Scotland)	1983 SV Hamburg (W. Germany)	1999 Manchester United (England)
1968 Manchester United (England)	1984 Liverpool (England)	
1969 AC Milan (Italy)	1985 Juventus (Italy)	2000 Real Madrid (Spain)
	1986 Steaua Bucharest (Romania)	2001 Bayern Munich (Germany)
1970 Feyenoord (Netherlands)	1987 FC Porto (Portugal)	2002 Real Madrid (Spain)
1971 Ajax Amsterdam (Netherlands)		*title vacated

European Cup Winner's Cup

Contested annually from the 1960-61 season through the 1999-2000 season by the cup winners of the member countries of the Union of European Football Associations (UEFA). The Cup Winner's Cup was absorbed by the UEFA Cup in 2000.

Multiple winners: Barcelona (4); AC Milan, RSC Anderlecht, Chelsea and Dinamo Kiev (2).

Year	Year	Year
1961 Fiorentina (Italy)	1972 Glasgow Rangers (Scotland)	1983 Aberdeen (Scotland)
1962 Atletico Madrid (Spain)	1973 AC Milan (Italy)	1984 Juventus (Italy)
1963 Tottenham Hotspur (England)	1974 FC Magdeburg (E. Germany)	1985 Everton (England)
1964 Sporting Lisbon (Portugal)	1975 Dinamo Kiev (USSR)	1986 Dinamo Kiev (USSR)
1965 West Ham United (England)	1976 RSC Anderlecht (Belgium)	1987 Ajax Amsterdam (Netherlands)
1966 Borussia Dortmund (W.Germany)	1977 SV Hamburg (W. Germany)	1988 Mechelen (Belgium)
1967 Bayern Munich (W. Germany)	1978 RSC Anderlecht (Belgium)	1989 Barcelona (Spain)
1968 AC Milan (Italy)	1979 Barcelona (Spain)	
1969 Slovan Bratislava (Czech.)	1980 Valencia (Spain)	1990 Sampdoria (Italy)
	1981 Dinamo Tbilisi (USSR)	1991 Manchester United (England)
1970 Manchester City (England)	1982 Barcelona (Spain)	1992 Werder Bremen (Germany)
1971 Chelsea (England)		1993 Parma (Italy)

Year	Year	Year
1994 Arsenal (England)	1997 Barcelona (Spain)	2000 discontinued
1995 Real Zaragoza (Spain)	1998 Chelsea (England)	
1996 Paris St. Germain (France)	1999 Lazio (Italy)	

UEFA Cup

Contested annually since the 1957-58 season by teams other than league champions and cup winners of the Union of European Football Associations (UEFA). Teams selected by UEFA based on each country's previous performance in the tournament. Teams from England were banned from UEFA Cup play from 1985-90 for the criminal behavior of their supporters. In 1999, with the formation of the new Champions League, UEFA announced that the UEFA Cup would be expanded and include any teams that would have normally played in the Cup Winner's Cup.

Multiple winners: Barcelona, Inter Milan, Juventus and Liverpool (3); Borussia Mönchengladbach, Feyenoord, IFK Göteborg, Leeds United, Parma, Real Madrid, Tottenham Hotspur and Valencia (2).

Year	Year	Year
1958 Barcelona (Spain)	1974 Feyenoord (Netherlands)	1988 Bayer Leverkusen (W. Germany)
1959 Not held	1975 Borussia Mönchengladbach (W. Germany)	1989 Napoli (Italy)
1960 Barcelona (Spain)	1976 Liverpool (England)	1990 Juventus (Italy)
1961 AS Roma (Italy)	1977 Juventus (Italy)	1991 Inter Milan (Italy)
1962 Valencia (Spain)	1978 PSV Eindhoven (Netherlands)	1992 Ajax Amsterdam (Netherlands)
1963 Valencia (Spain)	1979 Borussia Mönchengladbach (W. Germany)	1993 Juventus (Italy)
1964 Real Zaragoza (Spain)		1994 Inter Milan (Italy)
1965 Ferencvaros (Hungary)		1995 Parma (Italy)
1966 Barcelona (Spain)	1980 Eintracht Frankfurt (W. Germany)	1996 Bayern Munich (Germany)
1967 Dinamo Zagreb (Yugoslavia)	1981 Ipswich Town (England)	1997 Schalke 04 (Germany)
1968 Leeds United (England)	1982 IFK Göteborg (Sweden)	1998 Inter Milan (Italy)
1969 Newcastle United (England)	1983 RSC Anderlecht (Belgium)	1999 Parma (Italy)
1970 Arsenal (England)	1984 Tottenham Hotspur (England)	
1971 Leeds United (England)	1985 Real Madrid (Spain)	2000 Galatasaray (Turkey)
1972 Tottenham Hotspur (England)	1986 Real Madrid (Spain)	2001 Liverpool (England)
1973 Liverpool (England)	1987 IFK Göteborg (Sweden)	2002 Feyenoord (Netherlands)

Copa Libertadores

Contested annually since the 1955-56 season by the league champions of South America's football union.

Multiple winners: Independiente (7); Peñarol (5); Boca Juniors (4); Estudiantes, Nacional-Uruguay and Olimpia (3); Cruzeiro, Gremio, River Plate, Santos and São Paulo (2).

Year	Year	Year
1960 Peñarol (Uruguay)	1975 Independiente (Argentina)	1990 Olimpia (Paraguay)
1961 Peñarol (Uruguay)	1976 Cruzeiro (Brazil)	1991 Colo Colo (Chile)
1962 Santos (Brazil)	1977 Boca Juniors (Argentina)	1992 São Paulo (Brazil)
1963 Santos (Brazil)	1978 Boca Juniors (Argentina)	1993 São Paulo (Brazil)
1964 Independiente (Argentina)	1979 Olimpia (Paraguay)	1994 Velez Sarsfield (Argentina)
1965 Independiente (Argentina)		1995 Gremio (Brazil)
1966 Peñarol (Uruguay)	1980 Nacional (Uruguay)	1996 River Plate (Argentina)
1967 Racing Club (Argentina)	1981 Flamengo (Brazil)	1997 Cruzeiro (Brazil)
1968 Estudiantes de la Plata (Argentina)	1982 Peñarol (Uruguay)	1998 Vasco da Gama (Brazil)
1969 Estudiantes de la Plata (Argentina)	1983 Gremio (Brazil)	1999 Palmeiras (Brazil)
1970 Estudiantes de la Plata (Argentina)	1984 Independiente (Argentina)	
1971 Nacional (Uruguay)	1985 Argentinos Jrs. (Argentina)	2000 Boca Juniors (Argentina)
1972 Independiente (Argentina)	1986 River Plate (Argentina)	2001 Boca Juniors (Argentina)
1973 Independiente (Argentina)	1987 Peñarol (Uruguay)	2002 Olimpia (Paraguay)
1974 Independiente (Argentina)	1988 Nacional (Uruguay)	
	1989 Nacional Medellin (Colombia)	

Annual Awards
World Player of the Year

Presented by FIFA, the European Sports Magazine Association (ESM) and Adidas, the sports equipment manufacturer, since 1991. Winners are selected by national team coaches from around the world.

Multiple winners: Ronaldo and Zinedine Zidane (2).

Year		Nat'l Team	Year		Nat'l Team
1991	Lothar Matthäus, Inter Milan	Germany	1997	Ronaldo, Inter Milan	Brazil
1992	Marco Van Basten, AC Milan	Netherlands	1998	Zinedine Zidane, Juventus	France
1993	Roberto Baggio, Juventus	Italy	1999	Rivaldo, Barcelona	Brazil
1994	Romario, Barcelona	Brazil	2000	Zinedine Zidane, Juventus	France
1995	George Weah, AC Milan	Liberia	2001	Luis Figo, Real Madrid	Portugal
1996	Ronaldo, Barcelona	Brazil			

Women's World Player of the Year

Presented by FIFA since 2001. Winners are selected by national team coaches from around the world.

Year		Nat'l Team
2001	Mia Hamm, Washington Freedom	USA

European Player of the Year

Officially, the "Ballon d'Or," or "Golden Ball," and presented by *France Football* magazine since 1956. Candidates are limited to European players in European leagues and winners are selected by a poll of European soccer journalists.

Multiple winners: Johan Cruyff, Michel Platini and Marco Van Basten (3); Franz Beckenbauer, Alfredo di Stéfano, Kevin Keegan and Karl-Heinz Rummenigge (2).

Year		Nat'l Team	Year		Nat'l Team
1956	Stanley Matthews, Blackpool	England	1979	Kevin Keegan, SV Hamburg	England
1957	Alfredo di Stéfano, Real Madrid	Arg./Spain	1980	K.H. Rummenigge, Bayern Munich	W. Ger.
1958	Raymond Kopa, Real Madrid	France	1981	K.H. Rummenigge, Bayern Munich	W. Ger.
1959	Alfredo di Stéfano, Real Madrid	Arg./Spain	1982	Paolo Rossi, Juventus	Italy
1960	Luis Suarez, Barcelona	Spain	1983	Michel Platini, Juventus	France
1961	Enrique Sivori, Juventus	Arg./Italy	1984	Michel Platini, Juventus	France
1962	Josef Masopust, Dukla Prague	Czech.	1985	Michel Platini, Juventus	France
1963	Lev Yashin, Dinamo Moscow	Soviet Union	1986	Igor Belanov, Dinamo Kiev	Soviet Union
1964	Denis Law, Manchester United	Scotland	1987	Ruud Gullit, AC Milan	Netherlands
1965	Eusébio, Benfica	Portugal	1988	Marco Van Basten, AC Milan	Netherlands
1966	Bobby Charlton, Manchester United	England	1989	Marco Van Basten, AC Milan	Netherlands
1967	Florian Albert, Ferencvaros	Hungary	1990	Lothar Matthäus, Inter Milan	W. Ger.
1968	George Best, Manchester United	No. Ireland	1991	Jean-Pierre Papin, Marseille	France
1969	Gianni Rivera, AC Milan	Italy	1992	Marco Van Basten, AC Milan	Netherlands
1970	Gerd Müller, Bayern Munich	W. Ger.	1993	Roberto Baggio, Juventus	Italy
1971	Johan Cruyff, Ajax Amsterdam	Netherlands	1994	Hristo Stoitchkov, Barcelona	Bulgaria
1972	Franz Beckenbauer, Bayern Munich	W. Ger.	1995	George Weah, AC Milan	Liberia
1973	Johan Cruyff, Barcelona	Netherlands	1996	Matthias Sammer, Bor. Dortmund	Germany
1974	Johan Cruyff, Barcelona	Netherlands	1997	Ronaldo, Inter Milan	Brazil
1975	Oleg Blokhin, Dinamo Kiev	Soviet Union	1998	Zinedine Zidane, Juventus	France
1976	Franz Beckenbauer, Bayern Munich	W. Ger.	1999	Rivaldo, Barcelona	Brazil
1977	Allan Simonsen, B. Mönchengladbach	Denmark	2000	Luis Figo, Real Madrid	Portugal
1978	Kevin Keegan, SV Hamburg	England	2001	Michael Owen, Liverpool	England

South American Player of the Year

Presented by El Pais of Uruguay since 1971. Candidates are limited to South American players in South American leagues and winners are selected by a poll of South American sports editors.

Multiple winners: Elias Figueroa and Zico (3); Enzo Francescoli, Diego Maradona and Carlos Valderrama (2).

Year		Nat'l Team	Year		Nat'l Team
1971	Tostao, Cruzeiro	Brazil	1987	Carlos Valderrama, Deportivo Cali	Colombia
1972	Teofilo Cubillas, Alianza Lima	Peru	1988	Ruben Paz, Racing Buenos Aires	Uruguay
1973	Pelé, Santos	Brazil	1989	Bebeto, Vasco da Gama	Brazil
1974	Elias Figueroa, Internacional	Chile	1990	Raul Amarilla, Olimpia	Paraguay
1975	Elias Figueroa, Internacional	Chile	1991	Oscar Ruggeri, Velez Sarsfield	Argentina
1976	Elias Figueroa, Internacional	Chile	1992	Rai, Sao Paulo	Brazil
1977	Zico, Flamengo	Brazil	1993	Carlos Valderrama, Atl. Junior	Colombia
1978	Mario Kempes, Valencia	Argentina	1994	Cafu, Sao Paulo	Brazil
1979	Diego Maradona, Argentinos Juniors	Argentina	1995	Enzo Francescoli, River Plate	Uruguay
1980	Diego Maradona, Boca Juniors	Argentina	1996	Jose Luis Chilavert, Velez Sarsfield	Paraguay
1981	Zico, Flamengo	Brazil	1997	Marcelo Salas, River Plate	Chile
1982	Zico, Flamengo	Brazil	1998	Martin Palermo, Boca Juniors	Argentina
1983	Socrates, Corinthians	Brazil	1999	Javier Saviola, River Plate	Argentina
1984	Enzo Francescoli, River Plate	Uruguay	2000	Romario, Vasco da Gama	Brazil
1985	Julio Cesar Romero, Fluminense	Paraguay	2001	Juan Roman Riquelme, Boca Juniors	Argentina
1986	Antonio Alzamendi, River Plate	Uruguay			

African Player of the Year

Officially, the African "Ballon d'Or" and presented by *France Football* magazine from 1970-96. The Arican Player of the Year award has been presented by the CAF (African Football Confederation) since 1997. All African players are eligible for the award.

Multiple winners: George Weah and Abedi Pelé (3); Nwankwo Kanu, Roger Milla and Thomas N'Kono (2).

Year	Year	Year
1970 Salif Keita, Mali	1981 Lakhdar Belloumi, Algeria	1992 Abedi Pelé, Ghana
1971 Ibrahim Sunday, Ghana	1982 Thomas N'Kono, Cameroon	1993 Abedi Pelé, Ghana
1972 Cherif Souleymane, Guinea	1983 Mahmoud Al-Khatib, Egypt	1994 George Weah, Liberia
1973 Tshimimu Bwanga, Zaire	1984 Theophile Abega, Cameroon	1995 George Weah, Liberia
1974 Paul Moukila, Congo	1985 Mohamed Timoumi, Morocco	1996 Nwankwo Kanu, Nigeria
1975 Ahmed Faras, Morocco	1986 Badou Zaki, Morocco	1997 Victor Ikpeba, Nigeria
1976 Roger Milla, Cameroon	1987 Rabah Madjer, Algeria	1998 Mustapha Hadji, Morocco
1977 Dhiab Tarak, Tunisia	1988 Kalusha Bwalya, Zambia	1999 Nwankwo Kanu, Nigeria
1978 Abdul Razak, Ghana	1989 George Weah, Liberia	2000 Patrick Mboma, Cameroon
1979 Thomas N'Kono, Cameroon	1990 Roger Milla, Cameroon	2001 El Hadji Diouf, Senegal
1980 Jean Manga Onguene, Cameroon	1991 Abedi Pelé, Ghana	

U.S. Player of the Year

Presented by Honda and the Spanish-speaking radio show "Futbol de Primera" since 1991. Candidates are limited to American players who have played with the U.S. National Team and winners are selected by a panel of U.S. soccer journalists.

Multiple winner: Eric Wynalda (2).

Year		Year		Year		Year	
1991	Hugo Perez	1994	Marcelo Balboa	1997	Eddie Pope	2000	Claudio Reyna
1992	Eric Wynalda	1995	Alexi Lalas	1998	Cobi Jones	2001	Earnie Stewart
1993	Thomas Dooley	1996	Eric Wynalda	1999	Kasey Keller		

U.S. PRO LEAGUES

OUTDOOR
Major League Soccer

Sanctioned by U.S. Soccer and FIFA, the international soccer federation. MLS was founded on the heels of the successful 1994 World Cup tournament hosted by the United States and it remains the only FIFA-sanctioned division I outdoor league in the United States. The annual MLS title game is known as the MLS Cup.

Multiple winner: D.C. United (3).

MLS Cup

Year	Winner	Head Coach	Score	Loser	Head Coach	Site
1996	D.C. United	Bruce Arena	3-2	Los Angeles Galaxy	Lothar Osiander	Foxboro, Mass.
1997	D.C. United	Bruce Arena	2-1	Colorado Rapids	Glen Myernick	Washington, D.C.
1998	Chicago Fire	Bob Bradley	2-0	D.C. United	Bruce Arena	Pasadena, Calif.
1999	D.C. United	Thomas Rongen	2-0	Los Angeles Galaxy	Sigi Schmid	Foxboro, Mass.
2000	K.C. Wizards	Bob Gansler	1-0	Chicago Fire	Bob Bradley	Washington, D.C.
2001	San Jose Earthquakes	Frank Yallop	2-1	Los Angeles Galaxy	Sigi Schmid	Columbus, Ohio
2002	See Updates chapter.					

MLS Cup '96
D.C. United, 3-2 (OT)
Oct. 20 at Foxboro Stadium, Foxboro, Mass.
Attendance: 34,643

	1	2	OT	
Los Angeles Galaxy	1	1	0	—2
D.C. United	0	2	1	—3

First Half: LA–Eduardo Hurtado (Mauricio Cienfuegos), 5th minute.
Second Half: LA–Chris Armas (unassisted), 56th; DC–Tony Sanneh (Marco Etcheverry), 73rd; DC–Shawn Medved (unassisted), 82nd.
Overtime: DC–Eddie Pope (Etcheverry), 94th.
MVP: Marco Etcheverry, D.C. United, Midfielder

MLS Cup '97
D.C. United, 2-1
Oct. 26 at RFK Stadium, Washington, D.C.
Attendance: 57,431

	1	2	
Colorado Rapids	0	1	—1
D.C. United	1	1	—2

First Half: DC–Jaime Moreno (Tony Sanneh, David Vaudreuil), 37th minute.
Second Half: DC–Sanneh (John Harkes, Richie Williams), 68th; COL–Adrian Paz (David Patino, Matt Kmosko), 75th.
MVP: Jaime Moreno, D.C. United, Forward

MLS Cup '98
Chicago Fire, 2-0
Oct. 25 at the Rose Bowl, Pasadena, Calif.
Attendance: 51,350

	1	2	
D.C. United	0	0	—0
Chicago	2	0	—2

First Half: CHI–Jerzy Podbrozny (Peter Nowak, Ante Razov), 29th minute; CHI–Diego Gutierrez (Nowak), 45th.
MVP: Nowak, Chicago, Midfielder

MLS Cup '99
D.C. United, 2-0
Nov. 21 at Foxboro Stadium, Foxboro, Mass.
Attendance: 44,910

	1	2	
D.C. United	2	0	—2
Los Angeles	0	0	—0

First Half: DC–Jaime Moreno (Roy Lassiter), 19th minute; DC–Ben Olsen (unassisted), 48th
MVP: Olsen, D.C. United, Midfielder

MLS Cup 2000
Kansas City Wizards, 1-0
Oct. 15 at RFK Stadium, Washington, D.C.
Attendance: 39,159

	1	2	
Chicago	0	0	—0
Kansas City	1	0	—1

First Half: DC– Miklos Molnar (Chris Klein), 11th minute.
MVP: Tony Meola, Kansas City, Goalkeeper

MLS Cup 2001
San Jose Earthquakes, 2-1
Oct. 21 at Crew Stadium, Columbus, Ohio
Attendance: 21,626

	1	2	OT	
San Jose	1	0	1	—2
Los Angeles	1	0	0	—1

First Half: LA–Luis Hernandez (Greg Vanney, Kevin Hartman), 21st minute; SJ-Landon Donovan (Ian Russell, Richard Mulrooney), 43rd.
Overtime: SJ-Dwayne DeRosario (Ronnie Ekelund, Zak Ibsen), 96th.
MVP: Dwayne DeRosario, San Jose, Forward

U.S. Pro Leagues (Cont.)
Regular Season

Most Valuable Player		Leading Scorer	G	A	Pts
1996	Carlos Valderrama, Tampa Bay	1996 Roy Lassiter, Tampa Bay	27	4	58
1997	Preki, Kansas City	1997 Preki, Kansas City	12	17	41
1998	Marco Etcheverry, D.C.	1998 Stern John, Columbus	26	5	57
1999	Jason Kreis, Dallas	1999 Jason Kreis, Dallas	18	15	51
2000	Tony Meola, Kansas City	2000 Mamadou Diallo, Tampa Bay	26	4	56
2001	Alex Pineda Chacón, Miami	2001 Alex Pineda Chacón	19	9	47
2002	See Updates chapter	2002 Taylor Twellman, New England	23	6	52

Women's United Soccer Association

The eight-team WUSA was formed in 2000 as the top women's outdoor professional league and play began in 2001. The league championship game is known as the Founders Cup.

Founders Cup

Year	Winner	Score	Loser
2001	Bay Area CyberRays	3-3*	Atlanta Beat
2002	Carolina Courage	3-2	Washington Freedom

*Bay Area won shoot-out, 4-2.

National Professional Soccer League (1967)

Not sanctioned by FIFA, the international soccer federation. The NPSL recruited individual players to fill the rosters of its 10 teams. The league lasted only one season.

		Playoff Final			Regular Season			
Year	Winner	Scores	Loser	Leading Scorer		G	A	Pts
1967	Oakland Clippers	0-1, 4-1	Baltimore Bays	Yanko Daucik, Toronto		20	8	48

United Soccer Association (1967)

Sanctioned by FIFA. Originally called the North American Soccer League, it became the USA to avoid being confused with the National Professional Soccer League (see above). Instead of recruiting individual players, the USA imported 12 entire teams from Europe to represent its 12 franchises. It, too, only lasted a season. The league champion Los Angeles Wolves were actually Wolverhampton of England and the runner-up Washington Whips were Aberdeen of Scotland.

		Playoff Final			Regular Season			
Year	Winner	Score	Loser	Leading Scorer		G	A	Pts
1967	Los Angeles Wolves	6-5 (OT)	Washington Whips	Roberto Boninsegna, Chicago		10	1	21

North American Soccer League (1968-84)

The NPSL and USA merged to form the NASL in 1968 and the new league lasted through 1984. The NASL championship was known as the Soccer Bowl from 1975-84. One game decided the NASL title every year but five. There were no playoffs in 1969; a two-game/aggregate goals format was used in 1968 and '70; and a best-of-three games format was used in 1971 and '84; (*) indicates overtime and (†) indicates game decided by shootout.

Multiple winners: NY Cosmos (5); Chicago (2).

		Playoff Final		Regular Season			
Year	Winner	Score(s)	Loser	Leading Scorer	G	A	Pts
1968	Atlanta Chiefs	0-0,3-0	San Diego Toros	John Kowalik, Chicago	30	9	69
1969	Kansas City Spurs	No game	Atlanta Chiefs	Kaiser Motaung, Atlanta	16	4	36
1970	Rochester Lancers	3-0,1-3	Washington Darts	Kirk Apostolidis, Dallas	16	3	35
1971	Dallas Tornado	1-2*,4-1,2-0	Atlanta Chiefs	Carlos Metidieri, Rochester	19	8	46
1972	New York Cosmos	2-1	St. Louis Stars	Randy Horton, New York	9	4	22
1973	Philadelphia Atoms	2-0	Dallas Tornado	Kyle Rote Jr., Dallas	10	10	30
1974	Los Angeles Aztecs	3-3†	Miami Toros	Paul Child, San Jose	15	6	36
1975	Tampa Bay Rowdies	2-0	Portland Timbers	Steve David, Miami	23	6	52
1976	Toronto Metros	3-0	Minnesota Kicks	Giorgio Chinaglia, New York	19	11	49
1977	New York Cosmos	2-1	Seattle Sounders	Steve David, Los Angeles	26	6	58
1978	New York Cosmos	3-1	Tampa Bay Rowdies	Giorgio Chinaglia, New York	34	11	79
1979	Vancouver Whitecaps	2-1	Tampa Bay Rowdies	Oscar Fabbiani, Tampa Bay	25	8	58
1980	New York Cosmos	3-0	Ft. Laud. Strikers	Giorgio Chinaglia, New York	32	13	77
1981	Chicago Sting	0-0†	New York Cosmos	Giorgio Chinaglia, New York	29	16	74
1982	New York Cosmos	1-0	Seattle Sounders	Giorgio Chinaglia, New York	20	15	55
1983	Tulsa Roughnecks	2-0	Toronto Blizzard	Roberto Cabanas, New York	25	16	66
1984	Chicago Sting	2-1,3-2	Toronto Blizzard	Steve Zungul, Golden Bay	20	10	50

Note: In 1969, Kansas City won the NASL regular season championship with 110 points to 109 for Atlanta. There were no playoffs.

Regular Season MVP

Regular season Most Valuable Player as designated by the NASL.

Multiple winner: Carlos Metidieri (2).

Year		Year		Year	
1967	Rueben Navarro, Phila (NPSL)	1973	Warren Archibald, Miami	1979	Johan Cruyff, Los Angeles
1968	John Kowalik, Chicago	1974	Peter Silvester, Baltimore	1980	Roger Davies, Seattle
1969	Cirilio Fernandez, KC	1975	Steve David, Miami	1981	Giorgio Chinaglia, New York
1970	Carlos Metidieri, Rochester	1976	Pelé, New York	1982	Peter Ward, Seattle
1971	Carlos Metidieri, Rochester	1977	Franz Beckenbauer, New York	1983	Roberto Cabanas, New York
1972	Randy Horton, New York	1978	Mike Flanagan, New England	1984	Steve Zungul, Golden Bay

A-League (American Professional Soccer League)

The American Professional Soccer League was formed in 1990 with the merger of the Western Soccer League and the New American Soccer League. The APSL was officially sanctioned as an outdoor pro league in 1992 and changed its name to the A-League in 1995.

Multiple winners: Rochester (3); Colorado and Seattle (2).

Year		Year		Year	
1990	Maryland Bays	1994	Montreal Impact	1998	Rochester Rhinos
1991	SF Bay Blackhawks	1995	Seattle Sounders	1999	Minnesota Thunder
1992	Colorado Foxes	1996	Seattle Sounders	2000	Rochester Rhinos
1993	Colorado Foxes	1997	Milwaukee Rampage	2001	Rochester Rhinos

INDOOR

Major Soccer League (1978-92)

Originally the Major Indoor Soccer League from 1978-79 season through 1989-90. The MISL championship was decided by one game in 1980 and 1981; a best-of-three games series in 1979, best-of-five games in 1982 and 1983; and best-of-seven games since 1984. The MSL folded after the 1991-92 season.

Multiple winners: San Diego (8); New York (4).

Playoff Final / Regular Season

Year	Winner	Series	Loser	Leading Scorer	G	A	Pts
1979	New York Arrows	2-0	Philadelphia	Fred Grgurev, Philadelphia	46	28	74
1980	New York Arrows	7-4 (1 game)	Houston	Steve Zungul, New York.	90	46	136
1981	New York Arrows	6-5 (1 game)	St. Louis	Steve Zungul, New York.	108	44	152
1982	New York Arrows	3-2 (LWWLW)	St. Louis	Steve Zungul, New York	103	60	163
1983	San Diego Sockers	3-2 (WWLLW)	Baltimore	Steve Zungul, NY/Golden Bay	75	47	122
1984	Baltimore Blast	4-1 (LWWWW)	St. Louis	Stan Stamenkovic, Baltimore	34	63	97
1985	San Diego Sockers	4-1 (WWLWW)	Baltimore	Steve Zungul, San Diego	68	68	136
1986	San Diego Sockers	4-3 (WLLLWWW)	Minnesota	Steve Zungul, Tacoma	55	60	115
1987	Dallas Sidekicks	4-3 (LLWWLWW)	Tacoma	Tatu, Dallas	73	38	111
1988	San Diego Sockers	4-0	Cleveland	Eric Rasmussen, Wichita	55	57	112
1989	San Diego Sockers	4-3 (LWWWLLW)	Baltimore	Preki, Tacoma	51	53	104
1990	San Diego Sockers	4-2 (LWWWLW)	Baltimore	Tatu, Dallas	64	49	113
1991	San Diego Sockers	4-2 (WLWLWW)	Cleveland	Tatu, Dallas	78	66	144
1992	San Diego Sockers	4-2 (WWWLLW)	Dallas	Zoran Karic, Cleveland	39	63	102

Playoff MVPs

MSL playoff Most Valuable Players, selected by a panel of soccer media covering the playoffs.

Multiple winners: Steve Zungul (4); Brian Quinn (2).

Year		Year	
1979	Shep Messing, NY	1986	Brian Quinn, SD
1980	Steve Zungul, NY	1987	Tatu, Dallas
1981	Steve Zungul, NY	1988	Hugo Perez, SD
1982	Steve Zungul, NY	1989	Victor Nogueira, SD
1983	Juli Veee, SD	1990	Brian Quinn, SD
1984	Scott Manning, Bal.	1991	Ben Collins, SD
1985	Steve Zungul, SD	1992	Thompson Usiyan, SD

Regular Season MVPs

MSL regular season Most Valuable Players, selected by a panel of soccer media from every city in the league.

Multiple winners: Steve Zungul (6); Victor Nogueira and Tatu (2).

Year		Year	
1979	Steve Zungul, NY	1986	Steve Zungul, SD/Tac.
1980	Steve Zungul, NY	1987	Tatu, Dallas
1981	Steve Zungul, NY	1988	Erik Rasmussen, Wich.
1982	Steve Zungul, NY & Stan Terlecki, Pit.	1989	Preki, Tacoma
1983	Alan Mayer, SD	1990	Tatu, Dallas
1984	Stan Stamenkovic, Bal.	1991	Victor Nogueira, SD
1985	Steve Zungul, SD	1992	Victor Nogueira, SD

NASL Indoor Champions (1980-84)

The North American Soccer League started an indoor league in the fall of 1979. The indoor NASL, which featured many of the same teams and players who played in the outdoor NASL, crowned champions from 1980-82 before suspending play. It was revived for the 1983-84 indoor season but folded for good in 1984. The NASL held indoor tournaments in 1975 (San Jose Earthquakes won) and 1976 (Tampa Bay Rowdies won) before the indoor league was started.

Multiple winner: San Diego (2).

Year		Year		Year		Year	
1980	Tampa Bay Rowdies	1982	San Diego Sockers	1983	Play suspended	1984	San Diego Sockers
1981	Edmonton Drillers						

U.S. Pro Leagues (Cont.)
Major Indoor Soccer League

The winter indoor MISL began as the American Indoor Soccer Association in 1984-85, then changed its name to the National Professional Soccer League in 1989-90 and was known as the NPSL until 2001 when the name was changed again and the league was relaunched as the MISL.

Multiple winners: Canton (5); Cleveland and Milwaukee (3); Kansas City (2).

Year		Year		Year		Year	
1985	Canton (OH) Invaders	1990	Canton Invaders	1995	St. Louis Ambush	2000	Milwaukee Wave
1986	Canton Invaders	1991	Chicago Power	1996	Cleveland Crunch	2001	Milwaukee Wave
1987	Louisville Thunder	1992	Detroit Rockers	1997	Kansas City Attack	2002	Philadelphia Kixx
1988	Canton Invaders	1993	Kansas City Attack	1998	Milwaukee Wave		
1989	Canton Invaders	1994	Cleveland Crunch	1999	Cleveland Crunch		

Continental Indoor Soccer League (1993-97)

The summer indoor CISL played its first season in 1993 and folded following the 1997 season.

Multiple winner: Monterrey (2).

Year		Year		Year	
1993	Dallas Sidekicks	1995	Monterrey La Raza	1997	Seattle Seadogs
1994	Las Vegas Dustdevils	1996	Monterrey La Raza		

U.S. COLLEGES

NCAA Men's Division I Champions

NCAA Division I champions since the first title was contested in 1959. The championship has been shared three times—in 1967, 1968 and 1989. There was a playoff for third place from 1974-81.

Multiple winners: Saint Louis (10); Indiana, San Francisco and Virginia (5); UCLA (3); Clemson, Connecticut, Howard and Michigan St. (2).

Year	Winner	Head Coach	Score	Runner-up	Host/Site	Semifinalists
1959	Saint Louis	Bob Guelker	5-2	Bridgeport	Connecticut	West Chester, CCNY
1960	Saint Louis	Bob Guelker	3-2	Maryland	Brooklyn	West Chester, Connecticut
1961	West Chester	Mel Lorback	2-0	Saint Louis	Saint Louis	Bridgeport, Rutgers
1962	Saint Louis	Bob Guelker	4-3	Maryland	Saint Louis	Mich. St., Springfield
1963	Saint Louis	Bob Guelker	3-0	Navy	Rutgers	Army, Maryland
1964	Navy	F.H. Warner	1-0	Michigan St.	Brown	Army, Saint Louis
1965	Saint Louis	Bob Guelker	1-0	Michigan St.	Saint Louis	Army, Navy
1966	San Francisco	Steve Negoesco	5-2	LIU-Brooklyn	California	Army, Mich. St.
1967-a	Michigan St. & Saint Louis	Gene Kenney Harry Keough	0-0	–	Saint Louis	LIU-Bklyn, Navy
1968-b	Michigan St. & Maryland	Gene Kenney Doyle Royal	2-2 (2 OT)	–	Ga. Tech	Brown, San Jose St.
1969	Saint Louis	Harry Keough	4-0	San Francisco	San Jose St.	Harvard, Maryland
1970	Saint Louis	Harry Keough	1-0	UCLA	SIU-Ed'sville	Hartwick, Howard
1971-c	Howard	Lincoln Phillips	3-2	Saint Louis	Miami	Harvard, San Fran.
1972	Saint Louis	Harry Keough	4-2	UCLA	Miami	Cornell, Howard
1973	Saint Louis	Harry Keough	2-1 (OT)	UCLA	Miami	Brown, Clemson

Year	Winner	Head Coach	Score	Runner-up	Host/Site	Third Place
1974	Howard	Lincoln Phillips	2-1 (4OT)	Saint Louis	Saint Louis	Hartwick 3, UCLA 1
1975	San Francisco	Steve Negoesco	4-0	SIU-Ed'sville	SIU-Ed'sville	Brown 2, Howard 0
1976	San Francisco	Steve Negoesco	1-0	Indiana	Penn	Hartwick 4, Clemson 3
1977	Hartwick	Jim Lennox	2-1	San Francisco	California	SIU-Ed'sville 3, Brown 2
1978-d	San Francisco	Steve Negoesco	4-3 (OT)	Indiana	Tampa	Clemson 6, Phi. Textile 2
1979	SIU-Ed'sville	Bob Guelker	3-2	Clemson	Tampa	Penn St. 2, Columbia 1
1980	San Francisco	Steve Negoesco	4-3 (OT)	Indiana	Tampa	Ala. A&M 2, Hartwick 0
1981	Connecticut	Joe Morrone	2-1 (OT)	Alabama A&M	Stanford	East. Ill. 4, Phi. Textile 2

Year	Winner	Head Coach	Score	Runner-up	Host/Site	Semifinalists
1982	Indiana	Jerry Yeagley	2-1 (8 OT)	Duke	Ft. Lauderdale	Connecticut, SIU-Ed'sville
1983	Indiana	Jerry Yeagley	1-0 (2 OT)	Columbia	Ft. Lauderdale	Connecticut, Virginia
1984	Clemson	I.M. Ibrahim	2-1	Indiana	Seattle	Hartwick, UCLA
1985	UCLA	Sigi Schmid	1-0 (8 OT)	American	Seattle	Evansville, Hartwick
1986	Duke	John Rennie	1-0	Akron	Tacoma	Fresno St., Harvard
1987	Clemson	I.M. Ibrahim	2-0	San Diego St.	Clemson	Harvard, N. Carolina
1988	Indiana	Jerry Yeagley	1-0	Howard	Indiana	Portland, S. Carolina
1989-e	Santa Clara & Virginia	Steve Sampson Bruce Arena	1-1 (2 OT)	–	Rutgers	Indiana, Rutgers
1990-f	UCLA	Sigi Schmid	0-0 (PKs)	Rutgers	South Fla.	Evansville, N.C. State
1991-g	Virginia	Bruce Arena	0-0 (PKs)	Santa Clara	Tampa	Indiana, Saint Louis

Year	Winner	Head Coach	Score	Runner-up	Host/Site	Semifinalists
1992	Virginia	Bruce Arena	2-0	San Diego	Davidson	Davidson, Duke
1993	Virginia	Bruce Arena	2-0	South Carolina	Davidson	CS-Fullerton, Princeton
1994	Virginia	Bruce Arena	1-0	Indiana	Davidson	Rutgers, UCLA
1995	Wisconsin	Jim Launder	2-0	Duke	Richmond	Portland, Virginia
1996	St. John's	Dave Masur	4-1	Fla. International	Richmond	Creighton, NC-Charlotte
1997	UCLA	Sigi Schmid	2-0	Virginia	Richmond	Indiana, Saint Louis
1998	Indiana	Jerry Yeagley	3-1	Stanford	Richmond	Maryland, Santa Clara
1999	Indiana	Jerry Yeagley	1-0	Santa Clara	Charlotte	Connecticut, UCLA
2000	Connecticut	Ray Reid	2-0	Creighton	Charlotte	Indiana, Southern Methodist
2001	North Carolina	Elmar Bolowich	2-0	Indiana	Columbus	St. John's, Stanford

a–game declared a draw due to inclement weather after regulation time; **b**–game declared a draw after two overtimes; **c**–Howard vacated title for using ineligible player; **d**–San Francisco vacated title for using ineligible player; **e**–game declared a draw due to inclement weather after two overtimes. **f**–UCLA wins on penalty kicks (4-3) after four overtimes; **g**–Virginia wins on penalty kicks (3-1) after four overtimes.

Women's NCAA Division I Champions

NCAA Division I women's champions since the first tournament was contested in 1982.

Multiple winner: North Carolina (16).

Year	Winner	Coach	Score	Runner-up	Host/Site
1982	North Carolina	Anson Dorrance	2-0	Central Florida	Central Florida
1983	North Carolina	Anson Dorrance	4-0	George Mason	Central Florida
1984	North Carolina	Anson Dorrance	2-0	Connecticut	North Carolina
1985	George Mason	Hank Leung	2-0	North Carolina	George Mason
1986	North Carolina	Anson Dorrance	2-0	Colorado College	George Mason
1987	North Carolina	Anson Dorrance	1-0	Massachusetts	Massachusetts
1988	North Carolina	Anson Dorrance	4-1	N.C. State	North Carolina
1989	North Carolina	Anson Dorrance	2-0	Colorado College	N.C. State
1990	North Carolina	Anson Dorrance	6-0	Connecticut	North Carolina
1991	North Carolina	Anson Dorrance	3-1	Wisconsin	North Carolina
1992	North Carolina	Anson Dorrance	9-1	Duke	North Carolina
1993	North Carolina	Anson Dorrance	6-0	George Mason	North Carolina
1994	North Carolina	Anson Dorrance	5-0	Notre Dame	Portland
1995	Notre Dame	Chris Petrucelli	1-0 (3OT)	Portland	North Carolina
1996	North Carolina	Anson Dorrance	1-0 (2OT)	Notre Dame	Santa Clara
1997	North Carolina	Anson Dorrance	2-0	Connecticut	NC-Greensboro
1998	Florida	Becky Burleigh	1-0	North Carolina	NC-Greensboro
1999	North Carolina	Anson Dorrance	2-0	Notre Dame	San Jose, Calif.
2000	North Carolina	Anson Dorrance	2-1	UCLA	San Jose, Calif.
2001	Santa Clara	Jerry Smith	1-0	North Carolina	Dallas

Annual Awards
MEN
Hermann Trophy

College Player of the Year. Voted on by Division I college coaches and selected sportswriters and first presented in 1967 in the name of Robert Hermann, one of the founders of the North American Soccer League.

Multiple winners: Mike Fisher, Mike Seerey, Ken Snow and Al Trost (2).

Year	Year	Year
1967 Dov Markus, LIU	1979 Jim Stamatis, Penn St.	1991 Alexi Lalas, Rutgers
1968 Manuel Hernandez, San Jose St.	1980 Joe Morrone, Jr. Connecticut	1992 Brad Friedel, UCLA
1969 Al Trost, Saint Louis	1981 Armando Betancourt, Indiana	1993 Claudio Reyna, Virginia
1970 Al Trost, Saint Louis	1982 Joe Ulrich, Duke	1994 Brian Maisonneuve, Indiana
1971 Mike Seerey, Saint Louis	1983 Mike Jeffries, Duke	1995 Mike Fisher, Virginia
1972 Mike Seerey, Saint Louis	1984 Amr Aly, Columbia	1996 Mike Fisher, Virginia
1973 Dan Counce, Saint Louis	1985 Tom Kain, Duke	1997 Johnny Torres, Creighton
1974 Farrukh Quraishi, Oneonta St.	1986 John Kerr, Duke	1998 Wojtek Krakowiak, Clemson
1975 Steve Ralbovsky, Brown	1987 Bruce Murray, Clemson	1999 Ali Curtis, Duke
1976 Glenn Myernick, Hartwick	1988 Ken Snow, Indiana	2000 Chris Gbandi, Connecticut
1977 Billy Gazonas, Hartwick	1989 Tony Meola, Virginia	2001 Luchi Gonzalez, SMU
1978 Angelo DiBernardo, Indiana	1990 Ken Snow, Indiana	

Missouri Athletic Club Award

College Player of the Year. Voted on by men's team coaches around the country from Division I to junior college level and first presented in 1986 by the Missouri Athletic Club of St. Louis.

Multiple winners: Claudio Reyna and Ken Snow (2).

Year	Year	Year
1986 John Kerr, Duke	1992 Claudio Reyna, Virginia	1998 Jay Heaps, Duke
1987 John Harkes, Virginia	1993 Claudio Reyna, Virginia	1999 Sasha Victorine, UCLA
1988 Ken Snow, Indiana	1994 Todd Yeagley, Indiana	2000 Ali Curtis, Duke
1989 Tony Meola, Virginia	1995 Matt McKeon, St. Louis	2001 Luchi Gonzalez, SMU
1990 Ken Snow, Indiana	1996 Mike Fisher, Virginia	
1991 Alexi Lalas, Rutgers	1997 Johnny Torres, Creighton	

U.S. Colleges (Cont.)
Coach of the Year

Men's Coach of the Year. Voted on by the National Soccer Coaches Association of America. From 1973-81 all Senior College coaches were eligible. In 1982, the award was split into several divisions. The Division I Coach of the Year is listed since 1982.

Multiple winner: Jerry Yeagley (5).

Year	Year	Year
1973 Robert Guelker, SIU-Edwardsville	1983 Dieter Ficken, Columbia	1993 Bob Bradley, Princeton
1974 Jack MacKenzie, Quincy College	1984 James Lennox, Hartwick	1994 Jerry Yeagley, Indiana
1975 Paul Reinhardt, Vermont	1985 Peter Mehleft, American	1995 Jim Launder, Wisconsin
1976 Jerry Yeagley, Indiana	1986 Steve Parker, Akron	1996 Dave Masur, St. John's
1977 Klass Deboer, Cleveland St.	1987 Anson Dorrance, N. Carolina	1997 Sigi Schmid, UCLA
1978 Cliff McCrath, Seattle Pacific	1988 Keith Tucker, Howard	1998 Jerry Yeagley, Indiana
1979 Walter Bahr, Penn St.	1989 Steve Sampson, Santa Clara	1999 Jerry Yeagley, Indiana
1980 Jerry Yeagley, Indiana	1990 Bob Reasso, Rutgers	2000 Ray Reid, Connecticut
1981 Schellas Hyndman, E. Illinois	1991 Mitch Murray, Santa Clara	2001 Elmar Bolowich, North Carolina
1982 John Rennie, Duke	1992 Charles Slagle, Davidson	

WOMEN
Hermann Trophy

Women's College Player of the year. Voted on by Division I college coaches and selected sportswriters and first presented in 1988 in the name of Robert Hermann, one of the founders of the North American Soccer League.

Multiple winners: Mia Hamm and Cindy Parlow (2).

Year	Year	Year
1988 Michelle Akers, Central Fla.	1993 Mia Hamm, N. Carolina	1998 Cindy Parlow, N. Carolina
1989 Shannon Higgins, N. Carolina	1994 Tisha Venturini, N. Carolina	1999 Mandy Clemens, Santa Clara
1990 April Kater, Massachusetts	1995 Shannon McMillan, Portland	2000 Anne Makinen, Notre Dame
1991 Kristine Lilly, N. Carolina	1996 Cindy Daws, Notre Dame	2001 Christie Welsh, Penn St.
1992 Mia Hamm, N. Carolina	1997 Cindy Parlow, N. Carolina	

Missouri Athletic Club Award

Women's College Player of the Year. Voted on by women's team coaches around the country from Division I to junior college level and first presented in 1991 by the Missouri Athletic Club of St. Louis.

Multiple winners: Mia Hamm and Cindy Parlow (2).

Year	Year	Year
1991 Kristine Lilly, N. Carolina	1995 Shannon McMillan, Portland	1999 Mandy Clemens, Santa Clara
1992 Mia Hamm, N. Carolina	1996 Cindy Daws, Notre Dame	2000 Anne Makinen, Notre Dame
1993 Mia Hamm, N. Carolina	1997 Cindy Parlow, N. Carolina	2001 Christie Welsh, Penn St.
1994 Tisha Venturini, N. Carolina	1998 Cindy Parlow, N. Carolina	

Coach of the Year

Women's Coach of the Year. Voted on by the National Soccer Coaches Association of America. From 1982-87 all Senior College coaches were eligible. In 1988, the award was split into several divisions. The Division I Coach of the Year is listed since 1988.

Multiple winners: Kalenkeni M. Banda, Anson Dorrance and Chris Petrucelli (2).

Year	Year	Year
1982 Anson Dorrance, N. Carolina	1989 Austin Daniels, Hartford	1996 John Walker, Nebraska
1983 David Lombardo, Keene St.	1990 Lauren Gregg, Virginia	1997 Len Tsantiris, Connecticut
1984 Phillip Picince, Brown	1991 Greg Ryan, Wisc-Madison	1998 Becky Burleigh, Florida
1985 Kalenkeni M. Banda, UMass	1992 Bell Hempen, Duke	1999 Patrick Farmer, Penn St.
1986 Anson Dorrance, N. Carolina	1993 Jac Cicala, George Mason	2000 Jillian Ellis, UCLA
1987 Kalenkeni M. Banda, UMass	1994 Chris Petrucelli, Norte Dame	2001 Jerry Smith, Santa Clara
1988 Larry Gross, N.C. State	1995 Chris Petrucelli, Norte Dame	

All-Century Teams

Soccer America named their Men's and Women's Collegiate All-Century Teams as well as their Men's Player of the Century (Claudio Reyna) and Women's Player of the Century (Mia Hamm) in their Jan. 17, 2000 issue.

Men

Pos	Player	Years Played
GK	Brad Friedel, UCLA	1990-95
D	Erik Imler, Virginia	1989-92
D	Paul Caligiuri, UCLA	1982-83, 85-86
D	Adubarie Otorubio, Clemson	1981-84
M	Andy Atuegbu, San Francisco	1974-77
M	Claudio Reyna, Virginia	1991-93
M	Mike Fisher, Virginia	1993-96
M	Bruce Murray, Clemson	1984-87
F	Angelo DiBernardo, Indiana	1976-78
F	Ken Snow, Indiana	1987-89
F	Armando Betancourt, Indiana	1979-81

Women

Pos	Player	Years Played
GK	Kim Maslin, George Mason	1983-86
D	Carla Werden, North Carolina	1986-89
D	Debbie Belkin, Massachusetts	1984-87
D	Sara Whalen, Connecticut	1994-97
M	Kristine Lilly, North Carolina	1989-92
M	Shannon Higgins, North Carolina	1986-89
M	Michelle Akers, Central Florida	1984-89
M	Julie Foudy, Stanford	1989-92
F	April Heinrichs, North Carolina	1983-86
F	Carin Jennings, UC-Santa Barbara	1983-86
F	Mia Hamm, North Carolina	1989-90, 92-93

Bowling

Perennial bridesmaid **Carolyn Dorin-Ballard**
won a record-tying seven titles in 2002.

PWBA Tour

Changing Lanes

Dick Evans writes for the Miami Herald and the Daytona Beach News-Journal and is a member of the PBA Hall of Fame.

Bowling seeks more recognition even as its major governing bodies face a time of transition and uncertainty.

The sport of bowling mirrored the mood of most American citizens as the 2001–02 season produced its share of high points, low points and points of discussion.

The low points came on the heels of the Sept. 11 disasters in New York, Washington, D.C. and Pennsylvania. One pro tournament, the Professional Women's Bowling Association's Paula Carter Classic in Davie, Fla., was in progress and a second, the Professional Bowlers Association's Columbia 300 Open in Wichita, Kan., was about to launch the much anticipated new PBA season when the four American planes were hijacked.

John Falzone, president of the PWBA, agonized about whether to continue the tournament after a day of mourning or to crown a winner following just two days of competition.

Among the many people he consulted was a priest at Ground Zero in Manhattan, who urged him to continue the event in order to help demonstrate to the world that the hijackers were not going to hold Americans hostage with their cowardly act.

So after much discussion, Falzone decided the tournament would continue. As you might expect, critics rushed to attack his decision. Liz Johnson said after winning the title that she was not sure if they should have continued until she saw the happy faces of the spectators at the finals.

But the PBA was not so fortunate with the Columbia 300 Open, scheduled for Sept. 13–18. With the nation's airlines grounded, the PBA was forced to juggle its schedule by moving the tournament to the spring and instead launching its new tour with a tournament in Peoria, Ill. the following week.

Both tours had two bowlers jump into the spotlight—seven-time champion

PBA Tour

*The energetic **Pete Weber** won three PBA titles in 2001–02, electrifying crowds and annoying some of his competitors with his over-the-top, attention-grabbing antics.*

Carolyn Dorin-Ballard and U.S. Open and WIBC Queens champion Kim Terrell for the women, and Player of the Year Parker Bohn III and television sensation Pete Weber on the men's tour.

While the pros were fighting for titles, the amateur bowlers were fighting over the future of the two governing organizations—the American Bowling Congress (established in 1895) and the Women's International Bowling Congress (formed in 1916).

Under the single membership proposal, the ABC, WIBC, Young American Bowling Alliance (YABA) and USA Bowling would be abolished, and all of their members would join a new United States Bowling Association (USBA).

The delegates to the ABC Convention in Billings, Mont., in March, approved a proposal that would put the single membership vote on the ballot at the 2003 ABC Convention in Knoxville, Tenn.

Everyone thought the WIBC delegates would follow suit during their April convention in Milwaukee. Everyone was wrong—the women were not about to give up their beloved home turf without a fight.

PWBA Tour

Kim Terrell recorded two wins in 2001-02 but made them count, cashing in for a $55,000 jackpot at the U.S. Open and then another $18,000 at the WIBC Queens.

Under new business, two delegates caught their leaders by surprise, proposing that the controversial single membership vote by the WIBC be delayed from the 2003 convention to the 2004 convention. With a thundering "yes" vote, the dissenters approved the motion to delay the vote, even though the board of directors did not support the delay.

Many believe the USBA would be an important stepping stone towards bowling's recognition by the International Olympic Committee.

Also playing a role in the quest for Olympic recognition was the news that Florida joined the growing list of states with approved high school bowling programs, and word that Fairleigh Dickinson University became the 40th school to field a women's bowling team, which would qualify the sport for official recognition from the NCAA.

Leaders from all of these organizations recognize that bowling needs strong high school and collegiate programs if it hopes to regain some of its lost luster from the 1980's.

Dick Evans' Ten Biggest Stories of the Year in Bowling

10 ▪ Bowling leaders make a big pitch during the Winter Olympics in Salt Lake City but worry that bowling's hopes of ever gaining recognition from the International Olympic Committee will disappear if the IOC votes not to add any additional sports in the future.

9 ▪ The bowling world stops to celebrate the 20th anniversary of bowling's first 300-300-300—900 series by "Mr. 900," Glenn Allison. Unfortunately the ABC still doesn't recognize the achievement because it was allegedly bowled on illegally doctored lanes.

8 ▪ ESPN carries a record 180 minutes of live bowling competition on Dec. 9, starting with the men's U.S. Open in the Los Angeles area and then picking up the women's U.S. Open from Laughlin, Nev. The network also announces it will feature 20 Sunday afternoon telecasts from the PBA's 2002–03 schedule, running from October through March.

7 ▪ Brett Wolfe, an amateur using an antiquated 1993 model, Blue Hammer bowling ball that the PBA did not want to approve, beats the world's top professional stars to win $100,000 in the prestigious ABC Masters. And in the ABC Senior Masters, Walter Roy of Redding, Calif., becomes the first wheelchair bowler to compete in the tournament, averaging a 151.

6 ▪ AMF, which operates more than 450 bowling centers world wide, escapes from Chapter 11 in just eight months.

5 ▪ Popular PWBA Tour veteran Kim Terrell of Daly City, Calif., becomes the first black bowler in history to win back-to-back major events—the 2001 women's U.S. Open and the 2002 Women's International Bowling Congress Queens Tournament. The U.S. Open victory nets her $55,000, the largest prize ever in a professional women's bowling tournament.

4 ▪ Fairleigh Dickinson University announces it will become the 40th school to field a women's bowling team, which means that women's bowling will earn official recognition from the NCAA for the first time. Also, the high school bandwagon picks up steam as Florida joins the growing list of states approving high school bowling as a letter sport.

3 ▪ Parker Bohn III is named PBA player of the year for the combined 2001–2002 tour seasons, but the controversial Pete Weber grabs most of the headlines with his sizzling television performances. On the women's side, Carolyn Dorin-Ballard, a bridesmaid in the four previous bowler of the year ballots, wins a record seven titles on the Professional Women's Bowling Association tour.

2 ■ Delegates to the Women's International Bowling Congress surprise the nation's bowling leaders by voting to delay their upcoming vote on the controversial single membership issue from the 2003 to 2004 convention. The initiative would establish the all-encompassing U.S. Bowling Association as bowling's national governing body.

1 ■ Despite the Sept. 11 disaster and the falling U.S. economy, the PBA bounces back and reports a 35 percent increase in tournament entries, a 20 percent hike in membership and an 18 percent jump in television ratings. Many bowling centers report a big increase in business after Sept. 11 as Americans choose to stay close to home.

Runner-Up No More

After four straight runner-up finishes, Carolyn Dorin-Ballard finally captured her first PWBA player of the year honors following the 2001 season. And she did it with authority, breaking or tying 11 PWBA season records, including:

Records

1. Pro titles won in a season (7, tied)
2. PWBA titles won in a season (7)
3. Consecutive titles won (3, tied)
4. Competition points in a season (17,415)
5. Consecutive 200+ games during TV finals (9, tied)
6. TV appearances in a season (18)
7. Consecutive TV appearances in a season (6, tied)
8. Consecutive 200+ games (9, tie)
9. Games on TV in a season (25)
10. TV match-play wins in a season (16)
11. Games bowled in a season (985)

Where the Bowlers Are

According to the ABC, WIBC and YABA, here are the U.S. states and cities where the largest amount of their almost 3.4 million combined members reside.

States	Members	Pct.
Michigan	303,233	9.0
New York	239,951	7.1
Ohio	239,010	7.1
Cities	**Members**	**Pct.**
Detroit	107,064	3.2
Chicago	43,791	1.3
Washington, DC	38,017	1.1

Money Milestone

Player of the Year Parker Bohn III was one of 15 bowlers to earn more than $100,000 last season, establishing a new PBA Tour record.

Season	Events	Bowlers $100K+
2001-02	30	15
1994	30	12
1993	36	12

Three seasons tied with 11 over $100K.

2001-2002
Season in Review

Information Please®
SPORTS ALMANAC

Tournament Results

Winners of stepladder finals in all PBA, Seniors and PWBA tournaments from Sept. 9, 2001 through Sept. 26, 2002; major tournaments in **bold** type. Note (a) indicates amateur.

PBA
2001-02 Season

Final	Event	Winner	Earnings	Score	Runner-up
Sept. 9	Oronamin C Japan Cup	Bob Learn Jr.	$50,000	176-172	Ryan Shafer
Sept. 25	Peoria Open	Kurt Pilon	40,000	202-182	Paul Koehler
Oct. 2	Greater Nashville Open	Chris Barnes	40,000	234-195	Mike Scroggins
Oct. 9	Miller High Life Open	Dave Arnold	40,000	222-160	Roger Bowker
Oct. 16	Great Lakes Classic	Pete Weber	40,000	235-201	Parker Bohn III
Oct. 23	Greater Detroit Open	Patrick Allen	40,000	236-204	Robert Smith
Oct. 30	Johnny Petraglia Open	Danny Wiseman	40,000	255-226	Steve Jaros
Nov. 11	Greater Cincinnati Open	Walter Ray Williams Jr.	40,000	247-194	Mike Machuga
Nov. 18	Long Island Open	Tommy Delutz Jr.	40,000	215-213	Chris Barnes
Nov. 25	Greater Louisville Open	Pete Weber	40,000	289-279	Michael Haugen Jr.
Dec. 9	**BPAA U.S. Open**	Mika Koivuniemi	100,000	247-182	Patrick Healy Jr.
Jan. 6	Earl Anthony Memorial Classic	Parker Bohn III	40,000	235-215	Patrick Healy Jr.
Jan. 13	Medford Open	Ricky Ward	40,000	215-214	Ryan Shafer
Jan. 20	**ABC Masters**	a-Brett Wolfe	100,000	269-172	Dennis Horan
Jan. 24	Orleans Casino Open	Brian Voss	40,000	194-185	Ricky Ward
Feb. 3	Dallas Open	Ritchie Allen	40,000	245-237	Rick Steelsmith
Feb. 10	Columbia 300 Tar Heel Open	Pete Weber	40,000	218-214	Roger Bowker
Feb. 17	Empire State Open	Robert Smith	40,000	243-226	Jason Couch
Feb. 24	Flagship Open	Steve Wilson	40,000	267-257	Jason Queen
Mar. 3	**PBA World Championship***	Doug Kent	120,000	215-160	Lonnie Waliczek
Mar. 17	Battle at Litte Creek	Parker Bohn III	40,000	279-212	Patrick Healy Jr.

*Formerly known as the PBA National Championship.

Note: The Columbia 300 Tar Heel Open, originally scheduled for Sept. 18, 2001, was postponed due to the attack on America. Instead, it was held on Feb. 10, 2002, replacing the Florida Open, which was cancelled.

Note: The ABC Masters is not an official PBA Tour event.

2002-03 PBA Tour Schedule

Major tournaments are in **bold** type. See Updates chapter for results through mid-October.

August—Dream Bowl 2002, Yokohama, JPN (Aug. 30-Sept. 2).

September—Oronamin C Japan Cup, Tokyo, JPN (Sept. 3-8).

October—Wichita Open, Wichita, Kan. (Oct. 9-13); Greater Kansas City Classic, Blue Springs, Mo. (Oct. 16-20); Memphis Open, Memphis, Tenn. (Oct. 23-27); Miller High Life Open, Vernon Hills, Ill. (Oct. 30-Nov. 3).

November—Greater Detroit Open, Taylor, Mich. (Nov. 6-10); Banquet Classic, Grand Rapids, Mich. (Nov. 13-17); Greater Philadelphia Open, Springfield, Penn. (Nov. 20-24); Long Island Open, Syosset, N.Y. (Nov. 27-Dec. 1).

December—Empire State Open, Latham, N.Y. (Dec. 4-8); **Tournament of Champions at Mohegan Sun,** Uncasville, Conn. (Dec. 12-15).

January—Earl Anthony Classic, Tacoma, Wash. (Jan. 1-5); Medford Open, Medford, Ore. (Jan. 8-12); **ABC Masters,** Reno, Nev. (Jan. 14-19); Las Vegas Open, Las Vegas, Nev. (Jan. 19-23); **BPAA U.S. Open,** Fountain Valley, Calif. (Jan. 27-Feb. 2).

February—Dallas Open, Dallas, Texas (Feb. 5-9); Orlando Open, Orlando, Fla. (Feb. 12-16); Tar Heel Open, Burlington, N.C. (Feb. 19-23); Odor-Eaters Open, Louisville, Ky. (Feb. 26-Mar. 2).

March—PBA World Championship, Toledo, Ohio (Mar. 3-9).

SENIOR PBA
2002 Spring/Summer Tour

Final	Event	Winner	Earnings	Score	Runner-up
April 30	Chillicothe Open	Steve Neff	$8,000	214-193	Bob Glass
May 7	Pennsylvanian Open	Bob Chamberlain	8,000	248-173	Bob Glass
May 14	Greater Detroit Open	Dave Davis	8,000	217-171	Norb Wetzel
May 31	**ABC Senior Masters**	Pete Couture	20,000	2-0	Darrell Storkson
June 7	**Suncoast Senior World Championship**†	Mark Roth	20,000	3-1	Mel Wolf
June 12	Northern California Classic	Gene Stus	8,000	279-213	Bob Chamberlain
June 19	Epicenter Classic	Ron Winger	8,000	278-247	John Shreve
June 26	Northwest Classic	John Bennett	8,000	243-216	Bob Glass
Aug. 21	Lake County Open	Dave Soutar	8,000	236-211	Mark Roth
Aug. 28	Jackson Open	Pete Couture	8,000	2-1	Vince Mazzanti Jr.

†formerly known as the PBA Senior National Championship (1981-2001).
Note: In 2002, major tournaments on the Senior PBA Tour followed a different final-round format than non-majors. Final round results are as follows: **ABC Masters**—Best-of-three match final, (Couture def. Storkson, 633-492, 629-609); **Suncoast World Championship**—Best-of-five match final, Roth def. Wolf (209-187, 203-234, 256-169, 203-167). The season-ending **Jackson Open** also followed a best-of-three match final, Couture def. Mazzanti Jr. (223-232, 205-194, 232-214).

PWBA
Late 2001 Fall Tour

Final	Event	Winner	Earnings	Score	Runner-up
Nov. 1	Las Cruces New Mexico Open	Dede Davidson	$9,000	194-186	Carolyn Dorin-Ballard
Nov. 10	Brunswick World Open	Carolyn Dorin-Ballard	15,000	280-258	Michelle Feldman
Nov. 11	**BPAA U.S. Open**	Kim Terrell	55,000	234-220	Wendy Macpherson

2002 Spring/Summer Tour

Final	Event	Winner	Earnings	Score	Runner-up
May 10	**WIBC Queens**	Kim Terrell	$18,000	227-214	Kim Adler
May 16	St. Clair Shores Classic	Michelle Feldman	10,000	211-206	Kim Adler
May 23	St. Clair Classic	Kim Adler	10,500	226-216	Cara Honeychurch
June 2	Collegiate/Pro Doubles Challenge	Kendra Gaines/ Melissa Brownie	10,500*	214-196	Michelle Feldman/ April Ellis
June 9	Greater Terre Haute Open	Brenda Norman	10,500	195-148	Tiffany Stanbrough
June 16	Greater Harrisburg Open	Cara Honeychurch	10,500	195-148	Kim Terrell
June 23	Empire State Classic	Leanne Barrette	10,000	237-236	Wendy Macpherson
June 30	Greater Syracuse Classic	Leanne Barrette	10,000	248-245	Kendra Gaines
July 19	Dallas Open	Carolyn Dorin-Ballard	10,000	223-184	Tiffany Stanbrough
July 25	Miller High Life National Players Championship	Marianne DiRupo	13,000	180-158	Leanne Barrette
Aug. 1	Louisville Open	Michelle Feldman	10,000	255-180	Kim Terrell

*PWBA member Gaines earned $10,500, while her collegiate teammate, Brownie, won $5,000 in scholarship funds.
Note: The Women's International Bowling Congress Queens tournament is not an official PWBA Tour event.

2002 Fall Tour

Final	Event	Winner	Earnings	Score	Runner-up
Sept. 19	Three Rivers Open	Leanne Barrette	$9,000	225-166	Marianne DiRupo
Sept. 26	Burlington Open	Carolyn Dorin-Ballard	9,000	255-184	Kendra Gaines

Remaining 2002 PWBA Tour Fall Schedule
Major tournaments are in **bold** type. See Updates chapter for results through mid-October.
September—Lady Ebonite Classic, Columbia, Tenn. (Sept. 29-Oct. 3).
October—Greater Pasadena Open, Pasadena, Texas (Oct. 6-10); Rollers and Pro Bowlers, Mesa, Ariz. (Oct. 14-18); Wheelchair Awareness Classic, Mesa, Ariz. (Oct. 20-24); Greater San Diego Open, San Diego, Calif. (Oct. 27-Nov. 1).
November—Storm Las Vegas PWBA Challenge, Las Vegas, Nev. (Nov. 3-8); Storm Las Vegas Shootout (Nov. 8).
December—**BPAA U.S. Open**, TBD.

Tour Leaders

Official standings for 2001 and 2002 (with the exception of the PWBA, which are through Aug. 1). Note that (TB) indicates Tournaments Bowled; (CR) Championship Rounds as Stepladder Finalist; and (1st) Titles Won.

FINAL 2001
SENIOR PBA

Top 5 Money Winners

		TB	CR	1st	Earnings
1	Bob Glass	13	10	4	$78,900
2	Bob Chamberlain	14	7	2	50,100
3	Steve Neff	12	4	1	44,780
4	Dale Eagle	14	4	1	39,305
5	Rohn Morton	14	3	1	37,438

Note: Earnings include ABC Senior Masters.

Top 5 Averages

		TB	Games	Avg
1	Bob Glass	13	561	223.19
2	Larry Laub	7	274	222.69
3	Steve Neff	12	441	221.79
4	Mark Roth	10	417	220.11
5	John Bennett	11	393	220.04

PWBA

Top 10 Money Winners

		TB	CR	1st	Earnings
1	Carolyn Dorin-Ballard	23	18	7	$135,045
2	Kim Terrell	22	5	1	96,500
3	Wendy Macpherson	23	10	1	92,940
4	Cara Honeychurch	23	13	6	92,565
5	Michelle Feldman	23	4	2	90,285
6	Leanne Barrette	23	10	2	88,655
7	Liz Johnson	20	10	4	85,827
8	Kelly Kulick	23	9	0	65,057
9	Anne Marie Duggan	23	4	0	47,342
10	Dede Davidson	22	4	1	40,615

Note: Earnings include WIBC Queens and BPAA U.S. Open.

Top 10 Averages

		TB	Games	Avg
1	Carolyn Dorin-Ballard	23	985	214.73
2	Liz Johnson	20	795	212.41
3	Cara Honeychurch	23	929	212.36
4	Wendy Macpherson	23	946	212.36
5	Leanne Barrette	23	926	210.42
6	Michelle Feldman	23	903	209.17
7	Kim Adler	23	901	208.79
8	Kendra Gaines	19	704	208.30
9	Kelly Kulick	23	860	208.02
10	Kim Terrell	22	855	208.00

2002
PBA

Top 10 Money Winners

		TB	CR	1st	Earnings
1	Parker Bohn III	30	9	5	$245,200
2	Doug Kent	29	4	1	185,010
3	Pete Weber	26	4	3	170,125
4	Walter Ray Williams Jr.	30	8	2	164,450
5	Mika Koivuniemi	27	3	1	158,550
6	Jason Couch	29	9	1	157,475
7	Chris Barnes	30	5	1	143,165
8	Patrick Healey Jr.	27	4	0	139,708
9	Ricky Ward	23	5	2	133,150
10	Ryan Shafer	30	5	1	132,200

Note: Earnings include ABC Masters and BPAA U.S. Open.

Top 10 Averages

		TB	Games	Avg
1	Parker Bohn III	30	829	221.54
2	Jason Couch	29	753	220.93
3	Chris Barnes	30	729	219.03
4	Pete Weber	26	645	217.99
5	Ryan Shafer	30	750	217.83
6	Patrick Healey Jr.	27	644	217.40
7	Walter Ray Williams Jr.	30	743	217.20
8	Brian Voss	28	675	217.00
9	Norm Duke	30	752	216.35
10	Tommy Delutz Jr.	30	728	215.91

SENIOR PBA

Top 5 Money Winners

		TB	CR	1st	Earnings
1	Mark Roth	7	3	1	$34,375
2	Pete Couture	10	2	2	32,725
3	Bob Glass	10	6	0	27,780
4	Bob Chamberlain	10	4	1	25,575
5	Gene Stus	10	3	1	25,200

Note: Earnings include ABC Senior Masters.

Top 5 Averages

		TB	Games	Avg
1	Bob Glass	10	302	221.56
2	Ron Winger	10	298	219.86
3	Gene Stus	10	322	219.62
4	Steve Neff	8	278	219.37
5	Dale Eagle	10	280	218.40

PWBA (through Sept. 26)

Top 10 Money Winners

		TB	CR	1st	Earnings
1	Leanne Barrette	13	6	3	$57,835
2	Michelle Feldman	13	7	2	55,955
3	Kim Terrell	13	6	1	52,027
4	Carolyn Dorin-Ballard	13	7	2	47,710
5	Kim Adler	13	3	1	44,395
6	Kendra Gaines	13	7	1	42,420
7	Cara Honeychurch	11	5	1	38,342
8	Marianne DiRupo	13	3	1	32,860
9	Wendy Macpherson	13	4	0	30,300
10	Brenda Norman	13	1	1	23,875

Note: Earnings include WIBC Queens.

Top 10 Averages

		TB	Games	Avg
1	Carolyn Dorin-Ballard	13	491	217.71
2	Leanne Barrette	13	491	215.95
3	Michelle Feldman	13	493	215.52
4	Cara Honeychurch	11	342	213.89
5	Kendra Gaines	13	624	213.51
6	Wendy Macpherson	13	491	212.44
7	Liz Johnson	13	415	211.04
8	Tammy Turner	13	419	210.87
9	Kim Terrell	13	496	210.73
10	Marianne DiRupo	13	467	210.32

Major Championships
MEN
BPAA U.S. Open

Started in 1941 by the Bowling Proprietors' Association of America, 18 years before the founding of the Professional Bowlers Association. Originally the BPAA All-Star Tournament, it became the U.S. Open in 1971.

Multiple winners: Don Carter and Dick Weber (4); Dave Husted (3); Del Ballard Jr., Marshall Holman, Junie McMahon, Connie Schwoegler, Andy Varipapa and Pete Weber (2).

Year		Year		Year		Year	
1942	John Crimmins	1957	Don Carter	1972	Don Johnson	1987	Del Ballard Jr.
1943	Connie Schwoegler	1958	Don Carter	1973	Mike McGrath	1988	Pete Weber
1944	Ned Day	1959	Billy Welu	1974	Larry Laub	1989	Mike Aulby
1945	Buddy Bomar			1975	Steve Neff		
1946	Joe Wilman	1960	Harry Smith	1976	Paul Moser	1990	Ron Palombi Jr.
1947	Andy Varipapa	1961	Bill Tucker	1977	Johnny Petraglia	1991	Pete Weber
1948	Andy Varipapa	1962	Dick Weber	1978	Nelson Burton Jr.	1992	Robert Lawrence
1949	Connie Schwoegler	1963	Dick Weber	1979	Joe Berardi	1993	Del Ballard Jr.
		1964	Bob Strampe			1994	Justin Hromek
1950	Junie McMahon	1965	Dick Weber	1980	Steve Martin	1995	Dave Husted
1951	Dick Hoover	1966	Dick Weber	1981	Marshall Holman	1996	Dave Husted
1952	Junie McMahon	1967	Les Schissler	1982	Dave Husted	1997	Not held
1953	Don Carter	1968	Jim Stefanich	1983	Gary Dickinson	1998	Walter Ray Williams Jr
1954	Don Carter	1969	Billy Hardwick	1984	Mark Roth	1999	Bob Learn Jr.
1955	Steve Nagy	1970	Bobby Cooper	1985	Marshall Holman	2000	Robert Smith
1956	Bill Lillard	1971	Mike Limongello	1986	Steve Cook	2001	Miko Koivuniemi

PBA World Championship

The Professional Bowlers Association was formed in 1958 and its first national championship tournament was held in Memphis in 1960. Formerly known as the PBA National Championship, the name was changed in 2002. The tournament has been held in Toledo, Ohio, since 1981.

Multiple winners: Earl Anthony (6); Mike Aulby, Dave Davis, Mike McGrath, Pete Weber and Wayne Zahn (2).

Year		Year		Year		Year	
1960	Don Carter	1971	Mike Limongello	1982	Earl Anthony	1993	Ron Palombi Jr.
1961	Dave Soutar	1972	Johnny Guenther	1983	Earl Anthony	1994	David Traber
1962	Carmen Salvino	1973	Earl Anthony	1984	Bob Chamberlain	1995	Scott Alexander
1963	Billy Hardwick	1974	Earl Anthony	1985	Mike Aulby	1996	Butch Soper
1964	Bob Strampe	1975	Earl Anthony	1986	Tom Crites	1997	Rick Steelsmith
1965	Dave Davis	1976	Paul Colwell	1987	Randy Pedersen	1998	Pete Weber
1966	Wayne Zahn	1977	Tommy Hudson	1988	Brian Voss	1999	Tim Criss
1967	Dave Davis	1978	Warren Nelson	1989	Pete Weber		
1968	Wayne Zahn	1979	Mike Aulby			2000	Norm Duke
1969	Mike McGrath			1990	Jim Pencak	2001	Walter Ray Williams Jr
1970	Mike McGrath	1980	Johnny Petraglia	1991	Mike Miller	2002	Doug Kent
		1981	Earl Anthony	1992	Eric Forkel		

Brunswick World Tournament of Champions

Originally the Firestone Tournament of Champions (1965-93), the tournament has also been sponsored by General Tire (1994) and Brunswick Corp. (since 1995). Held in Akron, Ohio in 1965, then Fairlawn, Ohio (1966-94), Lake Zurich, Ill. (1995-96), Reno, N.V. (1997) and Overland Park, Kan. (since 1998).

Multiple winners: Mike Durbin (3); Earl Anthony, Jason Couch, Dave Davis, Jim Godman, Marshall Holman and Mark Williams (2).

Year		Year		Year		Year	
1965	Billy Hardwick	1975	Dave Davis	1985	Mark Williams	1995	Mike Aulby
1966	Wayne Zahn	1976	Marshall Holman	1986	Marshall Holman	1996	Dave D'Entremont
1967	Jim Stefanich	1977	Mike Berlin	1987	Pete Weber	1997	John Gant
1968	Dave Davis	1978	Earl Anthony	1988	Mark Williams	1998	Bryan Goebel
1969	Jim Godman	1979	George Pappas	1989	Del Ballard Jr.	1999	Jason Couch
1970	Don Johnson	1980	Wayne Webb	1990	Dave Ferraro	2000	Jason Couch
1971	Johnny Petraglia	1981	Steve Cook	1991	David Ozio	2001	Not held
1972	Mike Durbin	1982	Mike Durbin	1992	Marc McDowell		
1973	Jim Godman	1983	Joe Berardi	1993	George Branham III		
1974	Earl Anthony	1984	Mike Durbin	1994	Norm Duke		

ABC Masters Tournament

Sponsored by the American Bowling Congress, the Masters is not a PBA event, but is considered one of the four major tournaments on the men's tour and is open to qualified pros and amateurs.

Multiple winners: Mike Aulby (3); Earl Anthony, Billy Golembiewski, Dick Hoover and Billy Welu (2).

Year	Year	Year	Year
1951 Lee Jouglard	1964 Billy Welu	1977 Earl Anthony	1990 Chris Warren
1952 Willard Taylor	1965 Billy Welu	1978 Frank Ellenburg	1991 Doug Kent
1953 Rudy Habetler	1966 Bob Strampe	1979 Doug Myers	1992 Ken Johnson
1954 Red Elkins	1967 Lou Scalia	1980 Neil Burton	1993 Norm Duke
1955 Buzz Fazio	1968 Pete Tountas	1981 Randy Lightfoot	1994 Steve Fehr
1956 Dick Hoover	1969 Jim Chestney	1982 Joe Berardi	1995 Mike Aulby
1957 Dick Hoover	1970 Don Glover	1983 Mike Lastowski	1996 Ernie Schlegel
1958 Tom Hennessey	1971 Jim Godman	1984 Earl Anthony	1997 Jason Queen
1959 Ray Bluth	1972 Bill Beach	1985 Steve Wunderlich	1998 Mike Aulby
1960 Billy Golembiewski	1973 Dave Soutar	1986 Mark Fahy	1999 Brian Boghosian
1961 Don Carter	1974 Paul Colwell	1987 Rick Steelsmith	2000 Mika Koivuniemi
1962 Billy Golembiewski	1975 Eddie Ressler Jr.	1988 Del Ballard Jr.	2001 Parker Bohn III
1963 Harry Smith	1976 Nelson Burton Jr.	1989 Mike Aulby	2002 Brett Wolfe

WOMEN

BPAA U.S. Open

Started by the Bowling Proprietors' Association of America in 1949. Originally the BPAA Women's All-Star Tournament (1949-70); and U.S. Open since 1971. There were two BPAA All-Star tournaments in 1955, in January and December.

Multiple winners: Marion Ladewig (8); Donna Adamek, Paula Sperber Carter, Pat Costello, Dotty Fothergill, Dana Miller-Mackie, Aleta Sill and Sylvia Wene (2).

Year	Year	Year	Year
1949 Marion Ladewig	1962 Shirley Garms	1976 Patty Costello	1990 Dana Miller-Mackie
1950 Marion Ladewig	1963 Marion Ladewig	1977 Betty Morris	1991 Anne Marie Duggan
1951 Marion Ladewig	1964 LaVerne Carter	1978 Donna Adamek	1992 Tish Johnson
1952 Marion Ladewig	1965 Ann Slattery	1979 Diana Silva	1993 Dede Davidson
1953 Not held	1966 Joy Abel	1980 Patty Costello	1994 Aleta Sill
1954 Marion Ladewig	1967 Gloria Simon	1981 Donna Adamek	1995 Cheryl Daniels
1955 Sylvia Wene	1968 Dotty Fothergill	1982 Shinobu Saitoh	1996 Liz Johnson
1955 Anita Cantaline	1969 Dotty Fothergill	1983 Dana Miller	1997 Not held
1956 Marion Ladewig	1970 Mary Baker	1984 Karen Ellingsworth	1998 Aleta Sill
1957 Not held	1971 Paula Sperber	1985 Pat Mercatanti	1999 Kim Adler
1958 Merle Matthews	1972 Lorrie Koch	1986 Wendy Macpherson	2000 Tennelle Grijalva
1959 Marion Ladewig	1973 Millie Martorella	1987 Carol Norman	2001 Kim Terrell
1960 Sylvia Wene	1974 Patty Costello	1988 Lisa Wagner	
1961 Phyllis Notaro	1975 Paula Sperber Carter	1989 Robin Romeo	

WIBC Queens

Sponsored by the Women's International Bowling Congress, the Queens is not a PWBA event, but is open to qualified pros and amateurs.

Multiple winners: Millie Martorella (3); Donna Adamek, Dotty Fothergill, Wendy Macpherson, Aleta Sill and Katsuko Sugimoto (2).

Year	Year	Year	Year
1961 Janet Harman	1972 Dotty Fothergill	1983 Aleta Sill	1994 Anne Marie Duggan
1962 Dorothy Wilkinson	1973 Dotty Fothergill	1984 Kazue Inahashi	1995 Sandra Postma
1963 Irene Monterosso	1974 Judy Soutar	1985 Aleta Sill	1996 Lisa Wagner
1964 D.D. Jacobson	1975 Cindy Powell	1986 Cora Fiebig	1997 Sandra Jo Odom
1965 Betty Kuczynski	1976 Pam Rutherford	1987 Cathy Almeida	1998 Lynda Norry
1966 Judy Lee	1977 Dana Stewart	1988 Wendy Macpherson	1999 Leanne Barrette
1967 Millie Martorella	1978 Loa Boxberger	1989 Carol Gianotti	2000 Wendy Macpherson
1968 Phyllis Massey	1979 Donna Adamek	1990 Patty Ann	2001 Carolyn Dorin-Ballard
1969 Ann Feigel	1980 Donna Adamek	1991 Dede Davidson	2002 Kim Terrell
1970 Millie Martorella	1981 Katsuko Sugimoto	1992 Cindy Coburn-Carroll	
1971 Millie Martorella	1982 Katsuko Sugimoto	1993 Jan Schmidt	

WPBA National Championship (1960-1980)

The Women's Professional Bowling Association National Championship tournament was discontinued when the WPBA broke up in 1981. The WPBA changed its name from the Professional Women Bowlers Association (PWBA) in 1978.

Multiple winners: Patty Costello (3); Dotty Fothergill (2).

Year	Year	Year	Year
1960 Marion Ladewig	1966 Judy Lee	1972 Patty Costello	1978 Toni Gillard
1961 Shirley Garms	1967 Betty Mivelaz	1973 Betty Morris	1979 Cindy Coburn
1962 Stephanie Balogh	1968 Dotty Fothergill	1974 Pat Costello	1980 Donna Adamek
1963 Janet Harman	1969 Dotty Fothergill	1975 Pam Buckner	
1964 Betty Kuczynski	1970 Bobbe North	1976 Patty Costello	
1965 Helen Duval	1971 Patty Costello	1977 Vesma Grinfelds	

Annual Leaders
Average

PBA Tour

The George Young Memorial Award, named after the late ABC Hall of Fame bowler. Based on at least 16 national PBA tournaments from 1959-78, and at least 400 games of tour competition since 1979.

Multiple winners: Mark Roth (6); Earl Anthony (5); Walter Ray Williams Jr. (4); Marshall Holman (3); Parker Bohn III, Norm Duke, Billy Hardwick, Don Johnson and Wayne Zahn (2).

Year		Avg	Year		Avg	Year		Avg
1962	Don Carter	212.84	1976	Mark Roth	215.97	1990	Amleto Monacelli	218.16
1963	Billy Hardwick	210.35	1977	Mark Roth	218.17	1991	Norm Duke	218.21
1964	Ray Bluth	210.51	1978	Mark Roth	219.83	1992	Dave Ferraro	219.70
1965	Dick Weber	211.90	1979	Mark Roth	221.66	1993	Walter Ray Williams Jr.	222.98
1966	Wayne Zahn	208.63	1980	Earl Anthony	218.54	1994	Norm Duke	222.83
1967	Wayne Zahn	212.14	1981	Mark Roth	216.70	1995	Mike Aulby	225.49
1968	Jim Stefanich	211.90	1982	Marshall Holman	216.15	1996	Walter Ray Williams Jr.	225.37
1969	Billy Hardwick	212.96	1983	Earl Anthony	216.65	1997	Walter Ray Williams Jr.	222.00
1970	Nelson Burton Jr.	214.91	1984	Marshall Holman	213.91	1998	Walter Ray Williams Jr.	226.13
1971	Don Johnson	213.98	1985	Mark Baker	213.72	1999	Parker Bohn III	228.04
1972	Don Johnson	215.29	1986	John Gant	214.38	2000	Chris Barnes	220.93
1973	Earl Anthony	215.80	1987	Marshall Holman	216.80	2002	Parker Bohn III	221.54
1974	Earl Anthony	219.34	1988	Mark Roth	218.04			
1975	Earl Anthony	219.06	1989	Pete Weber	215.43			

Note: After its first nine events of 2001, the PBA instituted a new September-to-March schedule with the statistics for those first nine tournaments rolled over into players' final 2001-02 statistics.

PWBA Tour

The Professional Women's Bowling Association (PWBA) went by the name Ladies Professional Bowling Tour (LPBT) from 1981-97 and the Women's Professional Bowling Association prior to that. This table is based on at least 282 games of tour competition.

Multiple winners: Leanne Barrette, Nikki Gianulias, Wendy Macpherson and Lisa Rathgeber Wagner (3); Anne Marie Duggan and Aleta Sill (2).

Year		Avg	Year		Avg	Year		Avg
1981	Nikki Gianulias	213.71	1988	Lisa Wagner	213.02	1995	Anne Marie Duggan	215.79
1982	Nikki Gianulias	210.63	1989	Lisa Wagner	211.87	1996	Tammy Turner	215.23
1983	Lisa Rathgeber	208.50	1990	Leanne Barrette	211.53	1997	Wendy Macpherson	214.68
1984	Aleta Sill	210.68	1991	Leanne Barrette	211.48	1998	Dede Davidson	217.25
1985	Aleta Sill	211.10	1992	Leanne Barrette	211.36	1999	Wendy Macpherson	218.85
1986	Nikki Gianulias	213.89	1993	Tish Johnson	215.39	2000	Cara Honeychurch	215.18
1987	Wendy Macpherson	211.11	1994	Anne Marie Duggan	213.47	2001	Carolyn Dorin-Ballard	214.73

Money Won
PBA Tour

Since 1998 annual totals have included two non-PBA Tour events: BPAA U.S. Open and ABC Masters.

Multiple winners: Earl Anthony (6); Walter Ray Williams Jr. (5); Mark Roth and Dick Weber (4); Mike Aulby (3); Parker Bohn III, Don Carter and Norm Duke (2).

Year		Earnings	Year		Earnings	Year		Earnings
1959	Dick Weber	$7,672	1974	Earl Anthony	$99,585	1989	Mike Aulby	$298,237
1960	Don Carter	22,525	1975	Earl Anthony	107,585	1990	Amleto Monacelli	204,775
1961	Dick Weber	26,280	1976	Earl Anthony	110,833	1991	David Ozio	225,585
1962	Don Carter	49,972	1977	Mark Roth	105,583	1992	Marc McDowell	176,215
1963	Dick Weber	46,333	1978	Mark Roth	134,500	1993	Walter Ray Williams Jr.	296,370
1964	Bob Strampe	33,592	1979	Mark Roth	124,517	1994	Norm Duke	273,752
1965	Dick Weber	47,675	1980	Wayne Webb	116,700	1995	Mike Aulby	219,792
1966	Wayne Zahn	54,720	1981	Earl Anthony	164,735	1996	Walter Ray Williams Jr.	244,630
1967	Dave Davis	54,165	1982	Earl Anthony	134,760	1997	Walter Ray Williams Jr.	240,544
1968	Jim Stefanich	67,375	1983	Earl Anthony	135,605	1998	Walter Ray Williams Jr.	238,225
1969	Billy Hardwick	64,160	1984	Mark Roth	158,712	1999	Parker Bohn III	232,595
1970	Mike McGrath	52,049	1985	Mike Aulby	201,200	2000	Norm Duke	136,900
1971	Johnny Petraglia	85,065	1986	Walter Ray Williams Jr.	145,550	2002	Parker Bohn III	245,200
1972	Don Johnson	56,648	1987	Pete Weber	179,516			
1973	Don McCune	69,000	1988	Brian Voss	225,485			

Note: After its first nine events of 2001, the PBA instituted a new September-to-March schedule with the statistics for those first nine tournaments rolled over into players' final 2001-02 statistics.

WPBA and PWBA Tours

WPBA leaders through 1980; PWBA leaders since 1981. Totals include the WIBC Queens, but do not include TV incentives.
Multiple winners: Aleta Sill (6); Donna Adamek and Wendy Macpherson (4); Patty Costello, Tish Johnson and Betty Morris (3); Dotty Fothergill (2).

Year	Earnings	Year	Earnings	Year	Earnings
1965 Betty Kuczynski	$ 3,792	1978 Donna Adamek	$31,000	1990 Tish Johnson	$94,420
1966 Joy Abel	5,795	1979 Donna Adamek	26,280	1991 Leanne Barrette	87,618
1967 Shirley Garms	4,920			1992 Tish Johnson	96,872
1968 Dotty Fothergill	16,170	1980 Donna Adamek	31,907	1993 Aleta Sill	57,995
1969 Dotty Fothergill	9,220	1981 Donna Adamek	41,270	1994 Aleta Sill	126,325
		1982 Nikki Gianulias	45,875	1995 Tish Johnson	123,440
1970 Patty Costello	9,317	1983 Aleta Sill	42,525	1996 Wendy Macpherson	107,230
1971 Vesma Grinfelds	4,925	1984 Aleta Sill	81,452	1997 Wendy Macpherson	165,425
1972 Patty Costello	11,350	1985 Aleta Sill	52,655	1998 Carol Gianotti-Block	150,350
1973 Judy Cook	11,200	1986 Aleta Sill	36,212	1999 Wendy Macpherson	86,265
1974 Betty Morris	30,037	1987 Betty Morris	55,095	2000 Wendy Macpherson	108,525
1975 Judy Soutar	20,395	1988 Lisa Wagner	105,500	2001 Carolyn Dorin-Ballard	135,045
1976 Patty Costello	39,585	1989 Robin Romeo	113,750		
1977 Betty Morris	23,802				

All-Time Leaders

All-time leading money winners on the PBA and PWBA tours, through 2001. PBA figures date back to 1959, while PWBA figures include Women's Pro Bowlers Association (WPBA) earnings through 1980. National tour titles are also listed.

Money Won

PBA Top 20

		Titles	Earnings
1	Walter Ray Williams Jr.	33	$2,559,951
2	Pete Weber	25	2,237,548
3	Parker Bohn III	27	2,042,276
4	Mike Aulby	27	2,038,540
5	Brian Voss	20	1,776,204
6	Amleto Monacelli	18	1,767,209
7	Marshall Holman	22	1,694,595
8	Norm Duke	19	1,635,331
9	Dave Husted	14	1,579,013
10	Mark Roth	34	1,564,357
11	Earl Anthony	41	1,441,061
12	Wayne Webb	20	1,363,366
13	David Ozio	11	1,363,366
14	Gary Dickinson	8	1,333,299
15	Tom Baker	9	1,139,190
16	Mark Williams	7	1,137,427
17	Del Ballard Jr.	12	1,120,627
18	Dave Soutar	17	1,084,103
19	Johnny Petraglia	14	1,062,343
20	Bob Learn Jr.	4	1,048,538

Note: PBA career earnings do not include winnings from the 2001-02 season, which began in September of 2001.

WPBA-PWBA Top 10

		Titles	Earnings
1	Wendy Macpherson	19	$1,139,735
2	Aleta Sill	31	1,070,894
3	Tish Johnson	24	1,023,655
4	Leanne Barrette	23	937,383
5	Anne Marie Duggan	15	909,001
6	Carol Gianotti-Block	16	875,172
7	Lisa (Rathgeber) Wagner	32	853,796
8	Carolyn Dorin-Ballard	17	797,054
9	Kim Adler	14	748,322
10	Cheryl Daniels	10	723,607

Senior PBA Top 5

		Titles	Earnings
1	Gene Stus	10	$450,080
2	John Handegard	14	447,066
3	Dave Soutar	5	435,165
4	John Hricsina	7	415,965
5	Gary Dickinson	10	412,945

Annual Awards

MEN

BWAA Bowler of the Year

Winners selected by Bowling Writers Association of America.

Multiple winners: Earl Anthony and Don Carter (6); Walter Ray Williams Jr. (5); Mark Roth (4); Mike Aulby and Dick Weber (3); Parker Bohn III, Buddy Bomar, Ned Day, Norm Duke, Billy Hardwick, Don Johnson and Steve Nagy (2).

Year		Year		Year		Year	
1942	John Crimmins	1958	Don Carter	1973	Don McCune	1989	Mike Aulby
1943	Ned Day	1959	Ed Lubanski	1974	Earl Anthony	1990	Amleto Monacelli
1944	Ned Day	1960	Don Carter	1975	Earl Anthony	1991	David Ozio
1945	Buddy Bomar	1961	Dick Weber	1976	Earl Anthony	1992	Marc McDowell
1946	Joe Wilman	1962	Don Carter	1977	Mark Roth	1993	Walter Ray Williams Jr.
1947	Buddy Bomar	1963	Dick Weber	1978	Mark Roth	1994	Norm Duke
1948	Andy Varipapa	1964	Billy Hardwick	1979	Mark Roth	1995	Mike Aulby
1949	Connie Schwoegler	1965	Dick Weber			1996	Walter Ray Williams Jr.
1950	Junie McMahon	1966	Wayne Zahn	1980	Wayne Webb	1997	Walter Ray Williams Jr.
1951	Lee Jouglard	1967	Dave Davis	1981	Earl Anthony	1998	Walter Ray Williams Jr.
1952	Steve Nagy	1968	Jim Stefanich	1982	Earl Anthony	1999	Parker Bohn III
1953	Don Carter	1969	Billy Hardwick	1983	Earl Anthony		
1954	Don Carter			1984	Mark Roth	2000	Norm Duke
1955	Steve Nagy	1970	Nelson Burton Jr.	1985	Mike Aulby	2001	Parker Bohn III
1956	Bill Lillard	1971	Don Johnson	1986	Walter Ray Williams Jr.		
1957	Don Carter	1972	Don Johnson	1987	Marshall Holman		
				1988	Brian Voss		

Annual Awards (Cont.)
PBA Player of the Year

Named after longtime broadcaster Chris Schenkel, winners are selected by members of Professional Bowlers Association. The PBA Player of the Year has differed from the BWAA Bowler of the Year four times–in 1963, '64, '89 and '92.

Multiple winners: Earl Anthony (6); Walter Ray Williams Jr. (5); Mark Roth (4); Mike Aulby, Parker Bohn III, Norm Duke, Billy Hardwick, Don Johnson and Amleto Monacelli (2).

Year		Year		Year		Year	
1963	Billy Hardwick	1973	Don McCune	1983	Earl Anthony	1993	Walter Ray Williams Jr.
1964	Bob Strampe	1974	Earl Anthony	1984	Mark Roth	1994	Norm Duke
1965	Dick Weber	1975	Earl Anthony	1985	Mike Aulby	1995	Mike Aulby
1966	Wayne Zahn	1976	Earl Anthony	1986	Walter Ray Williams Jr.	1996	Walter Ray Williams Jr.
1967	Dave Davis	1977	Mark Roth	1987	Marshall Holman	1997	Walter Ray Williams Jr.
1968	Jim Stefanich	1978	Mark Roth	1988	Brian Voss	1998	Walter Ray Williams Jr.
1969	Billy Hardwick	1979	Mark Roth	1989	Amleto Monacelli	1999	Parker Bohn III
1970	Nelson Burton Jr.	1980	Wayne Webb	1990	Amleto Monacelli	2000	Norm Duke
1971	Don Johnson	1981	Earl Anthony	1991	David Ozio	2002	Parker Bohn III
1972	Don Johnson	1982	Earl Anthony	1992	Dave Ferraro		

Note: After its first nine events of 2001, the PBA instituted a new September-to-March schedule with the statistics for those first nine tournaments rolled over into players' final 2001-02 statistics. Individual awards were handed out in 2002.

PBA Rookie of the Year

Named after PBA Hall of Famer Harry Golden, who was the PBA's national tournament director for 30 years. Winners selected by members of Professional Bowlers Association.

Year		Year		Year		Year	
1964	Jerry McCoy	1974	Cliff McNealy	1984	John Gant	1994	Tony Ament
1965	Jim Godman	1975	Guy Rowbury	1985	Tom Crites	1995	Billy Myers Jr.
1966	Bobby Cooper	1976	Mike Berlin	1986	Marc McDowell	1996	C.K. Moore
1967	Mike Durbin	1977	Steve Martin	1987	Ryan Shafer	1997	Anthony Lombardo
1968	Bob McGregor	1978	Joseph Groskind	1988	Rick Steelsmith	1998	Chris Barnes
1969	Larry Lichstein	1979	Mike Aulby	1989	Steve Hoskins	1999	Paul Fleming
1970	Denny Krick	1980	Pete Weber	1990	Brad Kiszewski	2000	Joe Ciccone
1971	Tye Critchlow	1981	Mark Fahy	1991	Ricky Ward	2002	Tommy Jones
1972	Tommy Hudson	1982	Mike Steinbach	1992	Jason Couch		
1973	Steve Neff	1983	Toby Contreras	1993	Mark Scroggins		

Note: After its first nine events of 2001, the PBA instituted a new September-to-March schedule with the statistics for those first nine tournaments rolled over into players' final 2001-02 statistics. Individual awards were handed out in 2002.

WOMEN
BWAA Bowler of the Year

Winners selected by Bowling Writers Association of America.

Multiple winners: Marion Ladewig (9); Donna Adamek, Lisa Rathgeber Wagner and Wendy Macpherson (4); Tish Johnson and Betty Morris (3); Patty Costello, Dotty Fothergill, Shirley Garms, Val Mikiel, Aleta Sill, Judy Soutar and Sylvia Wene (2).

Year		Year		Year		Year	
1948	Val Mikiel	1962	Shirley Garms	1976	Patty Costello	1990	Tish Johnson
1949	Val Mikiel	1963	Marion Ladewig	1977	Betty Morris	1991	Leanne Barrette
1950	Marion Ladewig	1964	LaVerne Carter	1978	Donna Adamek	1992	Tish Johnson
1951	Marion Ladewig	1965	Betty Kuczynski	1979	Donna Adamek	1993	Lisa Wagner
1952	Marion Ladewig	1966	Joy Abel	1980	Donna Adamek	1994	Anne Marie Duggan
1953	Marion Ladewig	1967	Millie Martorella	1981	Donna Adamek	1995	Tish Johnson
1954	Marion Ladewig	1968	Dotty Fothergill	1982	Nikki Gianulias	1996	Wendy Macpherson
1955	Sylvia Wene	1969	Dotty Fothergill	1983	Lisa Rathgeber	1997	Wendy Macpherson
1956	Anita Cantaline	1970	Mary Baker	1984	Aleta Sill	1998	Carol Gianotti-Block
1957	Marion Ladewig	1971	Paula Sperber	1985	Aleta Sill	1999	Wendy Macpherson
1958	Marion Ladewig	1972	Patty Costello	1986	Lisa Wagner	2000	Wendy Macpherson
1959	Marion Ladewig	1973	Judy Soutar	1987	Betty Morris	2001	Carolyn Dorin-Ballard
1960	Sylvia Wene	1974	Betty Morris	1988	Lisa Wagner		
1961	Shirley Garms	1975	Judy Soutar	1989	Robin Romeo		

PWBA Player of the Year

Winners selected by members of Professional Women's Bowling Association. The PWBA Player of the Year has differed from the BWAA Bowler of the Year three times–in 1985, '86 and '90.

Multiple winners: Wendy Macpherson (4); Lisa Rathgeber Wagner (3); Leanne Barrette and Tish Johnson (2).

Year		Year		Year		Year	
1983	Lisa Rathgeber	1988	Lisa Wagner	1993	Lisa Wagner	1998	Carol Gianotti-Block
1984	Aleta Sill	1989	Robin Romeo	1994	Anne Marie Duggan	1999	Wendy Macpherson
1985	Patty Costello	1990	Leanne Barrette	1995	Tish Johnson	2000	Wendy Macpherson
1986	Jeanne Maiden	1991	Leanne Barrette	1996	Wendy Macpherson	2001	Carolyn Dorin-Ballard
1987	Betty Morris	1992	Tish Johnson	1997	Wendy Macpherson		

Note: This award was known as the LPBT Player of the Year Award from 1983-97.

Horse Racing

*Jockey **Chris McCarron** announced his retirement in June and claimed career victory 7,141 in his final race aboard Came Home at Hollywood Park.*

AP/Wide World Photos

Sign of the Times

War Emblem becomes the fourth horse in five years to fall one race short of the Triple Crown.

John Gettings *is associate editor of the ESPN/Information Please Sports Almanac.*

Considering that 2003 will mark 25 years since thoroughbred horse racing fans last extolled a Triple Crown champion, it's understandable if they're getting pessimistic about crowning another anytime soon.

Fear not, this drought does have precedent and a reason to be optimistic.

In 1948, Citation won horse racing's eighth Triple Crown after cruising to victories in the Kentucky Derby, Preakness Stakes and Belmont Stakes.

Over the next quarter-century 15 horses won two of the three jewels in the same year, including seven who won the first two races before failing at Belmont.

When the 1972 horse racing season came to a close, fans were lamenting that the next year would mark 25 years with no Triple Crown champ. And despite three near-misses in the last five years (Forward Pass in 1968; Majestic Prince in 1969; Canonero II in 1971), fans felt, understandably, downtrodden.

All that changed the following spring with the arrival of a giant chestnut colt named Secretariat. He claimed all three of the Triple Crown races—each victory more extraordinary than the last. His performance elevated horse racing and made him one of the most popular sports figures of the 20th century.

Thirty years after Citation's triple, Affirmed became the 11th Triple Crown winner in 1978.

Since then 14 horses have won two of the three races in the same year, including eight that took Derby and Preakness titles to Belmont.

Over the last five years fans have been teased by four near-misses (Silver Charm in 1997, Real Quiet in 1998, Charismatic in 1999 and Point Given in 2001).

AP/Wide World Photos

*Kentucky Derby and Preakness Stakes winner **War Emblem**, third from left, stumbles out of Gate 10 at the 134th Belmont Stakes. The poor start results in an eighth-place finish and means everyone will have to wait at least one more year for a Triple Crown champion.*

That being said, one can't assume we'll see another Secretariat in 2003, but fans confident in history repeating itself do have a reason to be optimistic about 2003.

Nobody seems more determined to end the current streak than trainer Bob Baffert. The three-time Eclipse Award winner has saddled three of the four recent Triple Crown near-misses, including War Emblem in 2002.

War Emblem first got the attention of Baffert and gifted Saudi horse owner Prince Ahmed bin Salman in April. The black 3-year-old colt lit up an otherwise murky day at Sportsman's Park,

outside Chicago, by scorching heavily favored Repent at the Illinois Derby.

With the Kentucky Derby less than a month away and no clear-cut Derby hopeful in their stable, Baffert and bin Salman hoped they had just found their champion.

Five days later, April 11, Baffert agreed to buy a 90 percent stake in War Emblem for nearly $1 million on behalf of bin Salman's *The Thoroughbred Corp.*, which owned the famed 2001 Horse of the Year Point Given.

War Emblem was a 20–1 longshot when he left the gate at Churchill Downs at the 128th Kentucky Derby.

AP/Wide World Photos

*Trainer **Bob Baffert**, left, and owner **Prince Ahmed bin Salman** teamed up to lead War Emblem to two Triple Crown victories in 2002. But triumph turned to tragedy in July when bin Salman died of a heart attack at age 43.*

Less than two minutes later, jockey Victor Espinoza was celebrating atop the Derby's first wire-to-wire champion since 1988.

Baffert became the sixth trainer in history to win three Kentucky Derbys and found himself in the hunt for another Crown.

Two weeks later at Pimlico, War Emblem held off a late charge from 45–1 surprise Magic Weisner to win the Preakness Stakes by three-quarters of a length. War Emblem, like 15 other horses before him, was headed to Elmont, N.Y. with two Triple Crown wins.

A record crowd packed Belmont Park expecting to see history. But War Emblem's bid ended abruptly. A graceless stumble out of the gate practically dropped him to his knees, and Espinoza said later he was lucky to stay in the saddle.

After the stumble, War Emblem got caught in heavy traffic before recomposing and making a last run at history.

continued on page 776 ▶

The Top Ten Biggest Stories of the Year in Horse Racing

10 • It happened too late in the year to make last year's list, so we'll start with it this year: A chilly October afternoon at Belmont Park is warmed by thrilling performances at the Breeders' Cup World Thoroughbred Championships. Tiznow noses out an unprecedented defense of his $4 million Classic title, and Hall of Fame trainer Bobby Frankel ends an 0-for-38 Breeders' Cup losing streak.

9 • Two-time Horse of the Year Cigar and former champion filly Serena's Song are inducted into the National Museum of Racing and Hall of Fame in their first year of eligibility. It's the proper kudos for two of the 1990's best horses.

8 • Ogden Phipps dies at age 93. The Eclipse Award-winning breeder and owner was active in thoroughbred racing for close to 70 years, campaigning some of racing's finest champions, including Buckpasser, Easy Goer and Personal Ensign.

7 • Hall of Fame jockey Chris McCarron, 47, retires in June, taking with him more than 7,100 career victories and $260 million in rider earnings. His final race is a victory aboard Came Home at Hollywood Park.

6 • Harness racing drivers John Campbell & Dave Magee become the fifth and sixth drivers to surpass 9,000 career victories.

5 • Two legendary horses pass away. Seattle Slew, the last living Triple Crown winner and one of racing's greatest sires, dies on the 25th anniversary of his Kentucky Derby victory. And Sunday Silence, horse of the year in 1989, dies in Japan at age 16.

4 • *Seabiscuit: An American Legend*, the Laura Hillenbrand book that tells the story of the 1938 horse of the year, becomes hot, pop culture fare. The hardcover spends eight weeks at #1 on *The New York Times* bestseller list. And a major motion picture based on the book—starring Tobey Maguire—is set for release in late 2003.

3 • Sarava, who put the "long" in "longshot" at 70–1, steals the show at the Belmont Stakes. It's a bit of redemption for trainer Ken McPeek, whose top Derby prospects—Repent and Harlan's Holiday—were big disappointments

2 • Just three months after becoming the first Arab owner to win a Kentucky Derby, Saudi Prince Ahmed bin Salman dies of a heart attack at age 43. The racing community is shocked by the loss of one of the sport's brightest rising stars.

1 • War Emblem fights valiantly for a chance to wear the Triple Crown but falls short at Belmont. The 25 years with no Triple Crown champion ties the longest span in the sport's history.

He moved into second briefly at the mile before giving in, struggling to an eighth-place finish.

If not for War Emblem, eventual Belmont Stakes winner Sarava may have been the story of the year. The colt left the gate at 70–1 and held on for a shocking half-length victory to become the longest-priced winner in the race's 134-year history.

Sarava's upset means horse racing fans' wait for the 12th Triple Crown champion will last at least one more year. But remember, there is reason to be optimistic.

Long$hot Luck

Sarava's upset victory in the Belmont Stakes was sure to make some folks happy. Specifically, those jokers who thought it would be funny to drop a two-spot on an unheralded 70–1 longshot. Sarava's half-length victory paid $142.50 on a $2 wager, breaking the race record of $132.10 set by Sherluck in 1961. Although impressive, that payout is not the highest of the three Triple Crown races.

Race	Horse	Payout on $2 bet
Ky. Derby	Donerail	$184.90
Preakness	Master Derby	48.80
Belmont	Sarava	142.50

Note: Donerail won the Kentucky Derby in 1913, Master Derby won the Preakness Stakes in 1975 and Sarava won the Belmont in 2002.

Crown Class

Trainer Bob Baffert won the seventh and eighth Triple Crown races of his career with War Emblem in 2002. Baffert is among an impressive list of trainers with the most wins in Triple Crown races but still has quite a way to go before taking over the top.

Trainer	Wins
James "Sunny Jim" Fitzsimmons	13
D. Wayne Lukas	13
Robert Walden	12
James Rowe	10
Ben Jones	9
Max Hirsch	9
Bob Baffert	8

Note: Fitzsimmons, Jones and Hirsch won at least one Triple Crown.

2001-2002
Season in Review

ESPN
Information Please®
SPORTS ALMANAC

Thoroughbred Racing
Major Stakes Races

Winners of major stakes races from Nov. 17, 2001 through Sept. 28, 2002; (T) indicates turf race course; F indicates furlongs.

LATE 2001

Date	Race	Track	Miles	Winner	Jockey	Purse
Nov. 17	Frank J. DeFrancis Mem.	Laurel Park	6 F	Delaware Township	Jerry Bailey	$300,000
Nov. 25	Matriarch Stakes	Hollywood	1¼ (T)	Starine	John Velazquez	500,000
Nov. 26	Hollywood Derby	Hollywood	1⅛ (T)	Denon	Chris McCarron	500,000
Nov. 26	Japan Cup	Tokyo Racecourse	1½	Agnes Digital	Hirofumi Shii	4,284,000
Dec. 15	Hollywood Futurity	Hollywood	1¹⁄₁₆	Siphonic	Jerry Bailey	460,750
Dec. 16	Hollywood Turf Cup	Hollywood	1½ (T)	Super Quercus	Alex Solis	250,000

2002 (through Sept. 28)

Date	Race	Track	Miles	Winner	Jockey	Purse
Jan. 3	Spectacular Bid Stakes	Gulfstream	6 F	Maybry's Boy	John Velazquez	$100,000
Jan. 12	Golden Gate Derby	Golden Gate	1¹⁄₁₆	Danthebluegrassman	Joe Steiner	125,000
Jan. 13	San Miguel Stakes	Santa Anita	6 F	Popular	Victor Espinoza	100,000
Jan. 19	Holy Bull Stakes	Gulfstream	1¹⁄₁₆	Booklet	Eibar Coa	100,000
Jan. 19	Santa Catalina Stakes	Santa Anita	1¹⁄₁₆	Labamta Babe	Kent Desormeaux	150,000
Feb. 2	Hutcheson Stakes	Gulfstream	7 F	Showmeitall	Jorge Chavez	150,000
Feb. 2	Charles H. Strub Stakes	Santa Anita	1⅛	Mizzen Mast	Kent Desormeaux	400,000
Feb. 2	San Vicente Stakes	Santa Anita	7 F	Came Home	Chris McCarron	150,000
Feb. 9	Donn Handicap	Gulfstream	1⅛	Mongoose	Edgar Prado	500,000
Feb. 16	Gulfstream Park BC H.	Gulfstream	1¼	Cetewayo	Cornelio Velasquez	200,000
Feb. 16	Fountain of Youth Stakes	Gulfstream	1¹⁄₁₆	Booklet	Jorge Chavez	200,000
Mar. 2	San Rafael Stakes	Santa Anita	1	Came Home	Chris McCarron	200,000
Mar. 2	The Southwest	Oaklawn	1	Private Emblem	Donnie Meche	75,000
Mar. 2	Rampart Handicap	Gulfstream	1¹⁄₁₆	Forest Secrets	Pat Day	200,000
Mar. 9	El Camino Real Derby	Golden Gate	1¹⁄₁₆	Yougottawanna	Jason Lumpkins	200,000
Mar. 9	Santa Anita Oaks	Santa Anita	1¹⁄₁₆	You	Jerry Bailey	300,000
Mar. 10	Santa Margarita Invit'l H.	Santa Anita	1⅛	Azeri	Mike Smith	300,000
Mar. 10	Louisiana Derby	Fairgrounds	1¹⁄₁₆	Repent	Jerry Bailey	750,000
Mar. 16	Florida Derby	Gulfstream	1⅛	Harlan's Holiday	Edgar Prado	1,000,000
Mar. 16	Swale Stakes	Gulfstream	7 F	Ethan Man	Pat Day	150,000
Mar. 17	San Felipe Stakes	Santa Anita	1¹⁄₁₆	Medaglia d'Oro	Laffit Pincay Jr.	250,000
Mar. 17	Gotham Stakes	Aqueduct	1	Mayakovsky	Edgar Prado	200,000
Mar. 17	Tampa Bay Derby	Tampa Bay	1¹⁄₁₆	Equality	Ramon Dominguez	200,000
Mar. 23	Santa Anita Handicap	Santa Anita	1¼	Golden Apples	Garrett Gomez	150,000
Mar. 23	Rebel Stakes	Oaklawn	1¹⁄₁₆	Windward Passage	Donnie Meche	100,000
Mar. 23	Spiral Stakes	Turfway	1¹⁄₁₆	Perfect Drift	Eddie Delahoussaye	500,000
Mar. 23	UAE Derby	Nad al-Sheba	1¼	Essence of Dubai	Frankie Dettori	2,000,000
Mar. 23	Dubai World Cup*	Nad al-Sheba	1¼	Street Cry	Jerry Bailey	6,000,000
Apr. 6	Santa Anita Derby	Santa Anita	1⅛	Came Home	Chris McCarron	750,000
Apr. 6	Ashland Stakes	Keeneland	1¹⁄₁₆	Take Charge Lady	Anthony D'Amico	557,750
Apr. 6	The Oaklawn Handicap	Oaklawn	1⅛	Kudos	Eddie Delahoussaye	500,000
Apr. 6	Illinois Derby	Sportsman's Park	1⅛	War Emblem	Larry Sterling Jr.	500,000
Apr. 6	Apple Blossom Handicap	Oaklawn	1¹⁄₁₆	Azeri	Mike Smith	500,000
Apr. 7	Lafayette Stakes	Keeneland	7 F	Cashel Castle	Pat Day	111,300
Apr. 13	Wood Memorial	Aqueduct	1⅛	Buddha	Pat Day	750,000
Apr. 13	Blue Grass Stakes	Keeneland	1⅛	Harlan's Holiday	Edgar Prado	750,000
Apr. 13	Bay Shore Stakes	Aqueduct	7 F	Roman Dancer	Kent Desormeaux	150,000
Apr. 20	Federico Tesio Stakes	Pimlico	1⅛	Smoked Em	Richard Migliore	107,250
Apr. 20	Lexington Stakes	Keeneland	1¹⁄₁₆	Proud Citizen	Mike Smith	364,650
Apr. 21	San Juan Capistrano H.	Santa Anita	1¾	Ringaskiddy	Eddie Delahoussaye	400,000
Apr. 21	Queen Elizabeth Cup II*	Sha Tin	1¼	Eishin Preston	Yuichi Fukunaga	1,780,000
Apr. 27	Derby Trial	Churchill Downs	1	Sky Terrace	Craig Perret	112,800
Apr. 28	Snow Chief Stakes	Hollywood	1⅛	Calkins Road	Laffit Pincay Jr.	250,000
May 3	Kentucky Oaks	Churchill Downs	1⅛	Farda Amiga	Chris McCarron	562,100
May 4	**Kentucky Derby**	Churchill Downs	1¼	War Emblem	Victor Espinoza	2,175,000#
May 4	Withers Stakes	Aqueduct	1	Fast Decision	Jose Santos	150,000

Major Stakes Races (Cont.)

Date	Race	Track	Miles	Winner	Jockey	Purse
May 11	Lone Star Derby	Lone Star	1 1/8	Wiseman's Ferry	Jorge Chavez	$500,000
May 11	Singapore Airlines Int'l Cup*	Singapore TC	1 1/8	Grandera	Frankie Dettori	3,000,000
May 17	Black-Eyed Susan Stakes	Pimlico	1 1/8	Chamrousse	Jerry Bailey	200,000
May 18	**Preakness Stakes**	Pimlico	1 3/16	War Emblem	Victor Espinoza	1,000,000
May 25	Peter Pan Stakes	Belmont	1 1/8	Sunday Break	Gary Stevens	200,000
May 27	Shoemaker BC Mile	Hollywood	1 (T)	Ladies Din	Pat Valenzuela	408,000
May 27	Metropolitan Mile	Belmont	1	Swept Overboard	Jorge Chavez	750,000
June 1	Massachusetts Handicap	Suffolk Downs	1 1/8	Macho Uno	Gary Stevens	500,000
June 7	Acorn Stakes	Belmont	1	You	Jerry Bailey	250,000
June 8	**Belmont Stakes**	Belmont	1 1/2	Sarava	Edgar Prado	1,000,000
June 8	Riva Ridge Stakes	Belmont	7 F	Gygistar	Pat Day	190,000
June 8	Leonard Richards Stakes	Delaware	1 1/16	Running Tide	Ramon Dominguez	250,900
June 8	Vodafone English Derby	Epsom Downs	1 1/2 (T)	High Chaparral	Johnny Murtagh	1,100,000
June 15	Charles Whittingham Handicap	Hollywood Park	1 1/4 (T)	Denon	Garrett Gomez	350,000
June 15	The Californian	Hollywood Park	1 1/8	Milwaukee Brew	Kent Desormeaux	500,000
June 15	Hollywood Oaks†	Hollywood Park	1 1/16	Adoration	Garrett Gomez	266,800
June 15	Stephen Foster Handicap	Churchill Downs	1 1/8	Street Cry	Jerry Bailey	833,250
June 22	Vanity Handicap	Hollywood Park	1 1/8	Azeri	Mike Smith	250,000
June 23	Affirmed Handicap	Hollywood Park	1 1/16	Came Home	Chris McCarron	107,500
June 23	Queen's Plate	Woodbine	1 1/4	T J's Lucky Moon	Steven Bahen	1,000,000
June 29	Beverly Hills Handicap	Hollywood Park	1 1/4 (T)	Astra	Kent Desormeaux	250,000
June 29	Mother Goose Stakes	Belmont	1 1/8	Nonsuch Bay	Jerry Bailey	242,500
June 30	Irish Derby	Curragh	1 1/2 (T)	High Chaparral	Mick Kinane	1,143,028
July 4	Jersey Shore BC	Monmouth	6 F	Boston Common	Eddie Martin	100,000
July 6	Suburban Handicap	Belmont	1 1/4	E Dubai	John Velazquez	500,000
July 6	American Oaks	Hollywood Park	1 1/4 (T)	Megahertz	Alex Solis	500,000
July 7	Dwyer Stakes	Belmont	1 1/16	Gygistar	John Velazquez	150,000
July 13	Carry Back Stakes	Calder	6 F	Royal Lad	Jerry Bailey	250,000
July 14	Hollywood Gold Cup	Hollywood Park	1 1/4	Sky Jack	Laffit Pincay Jr.	750,000
July 14	Swaps Stakes	Hollywood Park	1 1/8	Came Home	Mike Smith	500,000
July 20	Ohio Derby	Thistledown	1 1/8	Magic Weisner	Richard Migliore	300,000
July 20	Coaching Club Am. Oaks	Belmont	1 1/2	Jilbab	Mike Luzzi	350,000
July 27	Round Table Stakes	Arlington	1 1/8	Cowboy Stuff	Patrick Valenzuela	100,000
July 27	K. George VI and Q. Elizabeth Diamond Stakes*	Ascot	1 1/2 (T)	Golan	Kieren Fallon	1,172,531
July 28	Eddie Read Handicap	Del Mar	1 1/8 (T)	Sarafan	Corey Nakatani	400,000
July 28	Go for Wand Handicap	Saratoga	1 1/8	Dancethruthedawn	Jerry Bailey	250,000
Aug. 3	Amsterdam Stakes	Saratoga	6 F	Listen Here	Pat Day	150,000
Aug. 3	Whitney Handicap	Saratoga	1 1/8	Left Bank	John Velazquez	750,000
Aug. 4	Jim Dandy Stakes	Saratoga	1 1/8	Medaglia d'Oro	Jerry Bailey	500,000
Aug. 4	Haskell Invitational	Monmouth	1 1/8	War Emblem	Victor Espinoza	990,000
Aug. 17	Arlington Million*	Arlington	1 1/4 (T)	Beat Hollow	Jerry Bailey	1,000,000
Aug. 17	Alabama Stakes	Saratoga	1 1/4	Farda Amiga	Pat Day	750,000
Aug. 17	Saratoga BC Handicap	Saratoga	1 1/4	Evening Attire	Shaun Bridgmohan	300,000
Aug. 18	Philip H. Iselin Handicap	Monmouth	1 1/8	Cat's At Home	Jose Velez Jr.	350,000
Aug. 23	Personal Ensign Handicap	Saratoga	1 1/4	Summer Colony	John Velazquez	400,000
Aug. 24	Travers Stakes	Saratoga	1 1/4	Medaglia d'Oro	Jerry Bailey	1,000,000
Aug. 24	King's Bishop Stakes	Saratoga	7 F	Gygistar	John Velazquez	200,000
Aug. 25	Oklahoma Derby	Remington	1 1/16	The Judge Sez Who	Cornelio Velasquez	295,000
Aug. 25	Pacific Classic	Del Mar	1 1/4	Came Home	Mike Smith	1,000,000
Sept. 1	UAE Grosser Preis von Baden*	Baden-Baden	1 1/2 (T)	Marienbard	Frankie Dettori	845,420
Sept. 7	Man o' War Stakes	Belmont	1 3/8 (T)	With Anticipation	Pat Day	500,000
Sept. 7	The Woodward Stakes	Belmont	1 1/8	Lido Palace	Jorge Chavez	500,000
Sept. 7	Irish Champion Stakes*	Leopardstown	1 1/4	Grandera	Frankie Dettori	1,068,798
Sept. 8	Atto Mile	Woodbine	1 (T)	Good Journey	Pat Day	1,000,000
Sept. 14	Jerome Handicap	Belmont	1	Boston Common	Jorge Chavez	150,000
Sept. 14	Kentucky Cup Classic	Turfway	1 1/8	Pure Prize	Mike Smith	400,000
Sept. 15	Matron Stakes	Belmont	1 1/8	Storm Flag Flying	John Velazquez	200,000
Sept. 15	Futurity Stakes	Belmont	1	Whywhywhy	Edgar Prado	200,000
Sept. 21	Vosburgh Stakes	Belmont	7 F	Bonapaw	Gerard Melancon	300,000
Sept. 21	Mazarine B.C. Stakes	Woodbine	1 1/16	Brusque	Emile Ramsammy	272,000
Sept. 21	Kentucky Cup Mile	Kentucky Downs	1	Jake the Flake	Calvin Borel	200,000
Sept. 21	Kentucky Cup Turf	Kentucky Downs	1 1/2 (T)	Rochester	Eddie Martin Jr.	300,000
Sept. 28	Jockey Club Gold Cup	Belmont	1 1/4	Evening Attire	Shaun Bridgmohan	1,000,000
Sept. 28	Queen Elizabeth II Stakes	Ascot	1 (T)	Where or When	Kevin Darley	500,000

*World Series Racing Championship series race (see standings on page 780).

#Includes $1,000,000 bonus offered by Sportsman's Park to Illinois Derby winner for winning a Triple Crown race.

†The Hollywood Oaks was run a month earlier (June 15) and shortened from 1 1/8 miles to make way for Hollywood Park's new American Oaks race for 3-year-old fillies, run on July 6.

Notes: The Flamingo Stakes was cancelled due to the closing of Florida's Hialeah Park after the 2001 season. The Pimlico Special was suspended but will return in 2003 per an agreement between the track and the Maryland Jockey Club.

The 2002 Triple Crown

128th KENTUCKY DERBY

Grade I for three-year-olds; 9th race at Churchill Downs in Louisville. **Date**—May 4, 2002; **Distance**—1¼ miles; **Stakes Purse**—$1,175,000 ($875,000 to winner; $170,000 for 2nd; $85,000 for 3rd; $45,000 for 4th); **Track**—Fast; **Off**—6:12 p.m. EDT; **Favorite**—Harlan's Holiday (6-1 odds). **Winner**—War Emblem; **Field**—18 horses; **Time**—2:01.13; **Start**—Good for all; **Won**—Driving; **Sire**—Our Emblem; **Dam**—Sweetest Lady; **Record** (going into race)—7 starts, 4 wins, 0 second, 0 third; **Last start**—1st in Illinois Derby (Apr. 6); **Breeder**—Charles Nuckols Jr. & Sons (Ky.).

Order of Finish	Jockey	PP	1/4	1/2	3/4	Mile	Stretch	Finish	To $1
War Emblem	Victor Espinoza	5	1-½	1-1½	1-1½	1-1½	1-1½	1-4	20.50
Proud Citizen	Mike Smith	12	2-1	2-½	2-½	3-1	2-hd	2-¾	23.30
Perfect Drift	Eddie Delahoussaye	3	4-hd	3-1	3-½	2-hd	3-3½	3-3¼	7.90
Medaglia d'Oro	Laffit Pincay Jr.	9	10-1	9-1	7-½	8-3	6-1	4-1½	6.90
Request for Parole	Robby Albarado	7	6-hd	5-½	5-hd	5-hd	5-½	5-¾	29.80
Came Home	Chris McCarron	14	3-½	4-½	4-½	4-2	4-½	6-2	8.20
Harlan's Holiday	Edgar Prado	13	9-½	11-1	8-hd	6-hd	7-1	7-¾	6.00
Johannesburg	Gary Stevens	1	11-½	10-1	10-½	9-½	8-1	8-no	8.10
Essence of Dubai	David Flores	8	13-2	12-hd	12-hd	7-½	9-3	9-1	10.00
Saarland	John Velazquez	15	17-2	17-2	14-½	16-hd	13-½	10-2½	6.90
Blue Burner	Pat Day	18	5-hd	8-½	9-1½	10-½	11-hd	11-½	24.20
Castle Gandolfo	Jerry Bailey	11	15-hd	15-1	15-½	14-1	12-2½	12-4¼	14.50
Easy Grades	Jorge Chavez	17	12-1	14-hd	16-hd	11-hd	14-2	13-nk	43.80
Private Emblem	Donnie Meche	10	7-1	7-hd	11-1½	12-hd	10-1	14-4½	22.40
Lusty Latin	Glenn Corbett	4	18	18	18	18	18	15-2¼	22.10
It'sallinthechase	Eddie Martin Jr.	16	16-2½	16-hd	17-2	13-1½	15-3	16-2¾	94.50
Ocean Sound	Alex Solis	6	14-hd	13-1	13-1½	17-2	17-2	17-2¼	48.70
Wild Horses	Rene Douglas	2	8-½	6-1	6-hd	15-hd	16-½	18	58.50

Times—23.25; 47.04; 1:11.75; 1:36.70; 2:01.13

$2 Mutual Prices—#5 War Emblem ($43.00, $22.80, $13.60); #13 Proud Citizen ($24.60, 13.40); #3 Perfect Drift ($6.40). **Exacta**—(5-13) for $1,300.80; **Trifecta**—(5-13-3) for $18,373.20; **Superfecta**—(5-13-3-9) for $91,764.50; **Pick Six**—(7-10-4-12-3-5) for $1,583.70; **Scratched**—Buddah and Danthebluegrassman; **Overweights**—none; **Attendance**—145,033; **TV Rating**—8.3/21 share (NBC).

Trainers & Owners (by finish): **1**—Bob Baffert & The Thoroughbred Corp.; **2**—D. Wayne Lukas & Robert Baker/David Cornstein/William Mack; **3**—Murray Johnson & Stonecrest Farm; **4**—Bobby Frankel & Edmund Gann; **5**—Stephen Margolis & Jeri/Sam Knighton; **6**—Paco Gonzalez & William Farish/John Toffan/Trudy McCaffery; **7**—Ken McPeek & Starlight Stable; **8**—Aidan O'Brien & Michael Tabor/Mrs. John Magnier; **9**—Saeed bin Suroor & Godolphin Racing Inc.; **10**—Shug McGaughey & Cynthia Phipps; **11**—Bill Mott & Kinsman Stable; **12**—Aidan O'Brien & Mrs. John Magnier; **13**—Ted West & Desperado Stables; **14**—Steven Asmussen & James Cassels/Bob Zollars; **15**—Jeff Mullins & Joey/Wendy Platts; **16**—Wilson Brown & Darwin Olson; **17**—James Cassidy & K.M. Stable/Jim Ford/Deron Pearson; **18**—Todd Pletcher & Peachtree Stable.

127th PREAKNESS STAKES

Grade I for three-year-olds; 12th race at Pimlico in Baltimore. **Date**—May 18, 2002; **Distance**—1$^{3}/_{16}$ miles; **Stakes Purse**—$1,000,000 ($650,000 to winner; $200,000 for 2nd; $100,000 for 3rd; $50,000 for 4th); **Track**—Fast; **Off**—6:12 p.m. EDT; **Favorite**—War Emblem (5-2 odds). **Winner**—War Emblem; **Field**—13 horses; **Time**—1:56.36; **Start**—Good for all; **Won**—Driving; **Sire**—Our Emblem; **Dam**—Sweetest Lady; **Record** (going into race)—8 starts, 5 wins; **Last start**—1st in Kentucky Derby (May 4); **Breeder**—Charles Nuckols Jr. & Sons (Ky.).

Order of Finish	Jockey	PP	1/4	1/2	3/4	Stretch	Finish	To $1
War Emblem	Victor Espinoza	8	2-1	2-1	2-½	1-1½	1-¾	2.80
Magic Weisner	Richard Migliore	2	11-2	1-1½	7-1½	4-1½	2-¾	45.70
Proud Citizen	Mike Smith	12	6-½	5-1½	3-½	2-4½	3-1½	7.40
Harlan's Holiday	Edgar Prado	6	10-hd	9-hd	6-1½	3-½	4-nk	5.20
Easyfromthegitgo	Donnie Meche	7	7-½	7-1½	9-½	5-5	5-7	23.40
U S S Tinosa	Kent Desormeaux	1	5-hd	6-2	4-hd	6-1½	6-6½	10.20
Crimson Hero	Chris McCarron	4	13	13	13	10-3	7-½	14.80
Medaglia d'Oro	Jerry Bailey	5	3-hd	3-hd	5-1	7-3	8-¾	3.00
Straight Gin	Robby Albarado	3	12-7	11-hd	11-3	8-1½	9-3	28.00
Menacing Dennis	Mario Pino	11	1-hd	1-hd	1-hd	9-½	10-6¾	51.20
Table Limit	Gary Stevens	9	8-1	8-hd	10-hd	11-4	11-hd	23.10
Booklet	Pat Day	10	4-1	4-hd	8-hd	12-½	12-½	9.90
Equality	Ramon Dominguez	13	9-1	12-6	12-2	13	13	27.50

Times—22.87; 46.10; 1:10.60; 1:36.22; 1:56.36

$2 Mutual Prices—#8 War Emblem ($7.60, $6.00, $4.40); #2 Magic Weisner ($33.00, $14.00); #12 Proud Citizen ($5.00).

Exacta—(8-2) for $327.00; **Trifecta**—(8-2-12) for $2,311.00; **Pick Six**—none; **Scratched**—none; **Overweights**—none; **Attendance**—101,138; **TV Rating**—6.5/16 share (NBC).

Trainers & Owners (by finish): **1**—Bob Baffert & The Thoroughbred Corp.; **2**—Nancy Alberts & Nancy Alberts; **3**—D. Wayne Lukas & Robert Baker/David Cornstein/William Mack; **4**—Ken McPeek & Starlight Stable; **5**—Steven Asmussen & James Cassels/Bob Zollars; **6**—Jerry Hollendorfer & Peter Abruzzo/Barry Thiriot; **7**—Nick Zito & Tracy Farmer; **8**—Bobby Frankel & Edmund Gann; **9**—Nick Zito & Marylou Whitney Stable; **10**—Jeff Bonde & JMJ Racing Stables LLC; **11**—D. Wayne Lukas & Overbrook Farm; **12**—John Ward & John Oxley; **13**—Graham Motion & Pin Oak Stable.

The 2002 Triple Crown (Cont.)

134th BELMONT STAKES

Grade I for three-year-olds; 10th race at Belmont Park in Elmont, N.Y. **Date**—June 8, 2002; **Distance**—1½ miles; **Stakes Purse**—$1,000,000 ($600,000 to winner; $200,000 for 2nd; $110,000 for 3rd; $60,000 for 4th; $30,000 for 5th); **Track**—Fast; **Off**—6:15 p.m. EDT; **Favorite**—War Emblem (6-5 odds). **Winner**—Sarava; **Field**—11 horses; **Time**—2:29.71; **Start**—Good for all but #1, #10; **Won**—Driving; **Sire**—Wild Again; **Dam**—Rhythm of Life; **Record** (going into race)—8 starts, 2 wins, 3 seconds; **Last Start**—1st in Sir Barton Stakes (May 18); **Breeder**—Timber Bay Farm.

Order of Finish	Jockey	PP	1/4	1/2	Mile	1-1/4	Stretch	Finish	To $1
Sarava	Edgar Prado	11	5-hd	5-3½	4-hd	3-hd	1-½	1-½	70.25
Medaglia d'Oro	Kent Desormeaux	7	2-½	2-½	1-hd	1-½	2-5½	2-9½	16.00
Sunday Break	Gary Stevens	5	7-½	7-½	6-4½	4-1½	3-3½	3-1	8.10
Magic Weisner	Richard Migliore	10	6-2½	6-½	7-½	6-2½	5-½	4-1¼	7.30
Proud Citizen	Mike Smith	8	4-1½	3-½	3-1	2-hd	4-2	5-1¼	7.00
Essence of Dubai	Jerry Bailey	4	10-2½	10-½	10-8	8-5	6-½	6-4¼	20.60
Like a Hero	Pat Day	2	11	11	9-½	7-3½	8-22	7-1¾	25.50
War Emblem	Victor Espinoza	9	3-hd	4-2½	2-½	5-2½	7-5	8-30¾	1.25
Wiseman's Ferry	Jorge Chavez	3	1-1½	1-½	5-½	10-12	9-hd	9-1	18.80
Perfect Drift	Eddie Delahoussaye	6	9-2	9-6	8-6	9-hd	10-24	10-24¾	5.60
Artax Too	Jose Santos	1	8-hd	8-½	11	11	11	11	71.75

Times—24.11; 48.09; 1:12.38; 1:37.01; 2:03.50; 2:29.71.

$2 Mutual Prices—#12 Sarava ($142.50, $50.00, $22.40); #8 Medaglia d'Oro ($16.00, $10.60); #5 Sunday Break ($7.10). **Exacta**—(12-8) for $2,454.00; **Trifecta**—(12-8-5) for $25,209.00; **Pick Three**—None; **Scratched**—Puzzlement (#7); **Overweights**—None; **Attendance**—103,222; **TV Rating**—7.6/21 share (NBC).

Trainers & Owners (by finish): **1**—Ken McPeek & New Phoenix Stable/Mrs. Susan Roy; **2**—Bobby Frankel & Edmund Gann; **3**—Neil Drysdale & Koji Maeda; **4**—Nancy Alberts & Nancy Alberts; **5**—D. Wayne Lukas & Robert Baker/David Cornstein/William Mack; **6**—Saeed bin Suroor & Godolphin Racing Inc.; **7**—Beau Greely & Columbine Stable; **8**—Bob Baffert & The Thoroughbred Corp.; **9**—Niall O'Callaghan & Lee Sacks/Morton Fink/Swifty Farms; **10**—Murray Johnson & Stonecrest Farm; **11**—Jennifer Pedersen & Paraneck Stable.

NTRA National Thoroughbred Poll

The NTRA Thoroughbred Poll conducted by National Thoroughbred Racing Association, covering races through Sept. 29, 2002. Rankings are based on the votes of sports and thoroughbred media representatives on a 10-9-8-7-6-5-4-3-2-1 basis. First place votes are in parentheses.

		Pts	Age	Sex	'02 Record Sts—1-2-3	Owner	Trainer
1	Came Home (8)	160	3	Colt	7—6-0-0	Bill Farish, John Goodman, Trudy McCaffery & John Toffan	Paco Gonzalez
2	Medaglia D'Oro (5)	152	3	Colt	8—4-2-0	Edmund Gann	Bobby Frankel
3	Azeri (5)	145	4	Filly	7—6-1-0	Allen Paulson Living Trust	Laura de Seroux
4	Beat Hollow	114	5	Horse	6—4-2-0	Juddmonte Farm	Bobby Frankel
5	War Emblem (2)	101	3	Colt	9—5-0-0	The Thoroughbred Corp.	Bob Baffert
6	Xtra Heat (1)	93	4	Filly	8—6-1-1	Kenneth Taylor, Harry Deitchman & John Salzman	John Salzman
7	Summer Colony	74	4	Filly	6—4-2-0	Edward P. Evans	Mark Hennig
8	Farda Amiga	67	3	Filly	5—3-0-0	Marcos Simon, Julio Camargo & Jose DeCamargo	Paulo Lobo
9	Evening Attire	53	4	Gelding	7—4-1-0	Mary/Joseph Grant & Thomas Kelly	Patrick Kelly
10	With Anticipation	46	7	Gelding	7—3-2-0	Augustin Stable	Jonathan Sheppard

Others receiving votes: 11. Orientate (40 points); **12.** Denon (20); **13.** Lido Palace (17); **14.** Vindication (10); **15.** Harlan's Holiday (9); **16.** Bonapaw and Milwaukee Brew (8); **18.** Golden Apples (7); **19.** Repent (6); **20.** Ballingarry & Kazzia (5); **22.** Gygistar (2); **23.** Sarafan, Sky Mess & Tenpins (1).

2002 World Series Racing Championship

The World Series Racing Championship includes 14 prestigious thoroughbred races in 11 countries on four continents. Points are awarded to the top six finishers in each race as follows: 12–6–4–3–2–1. The current standings for the top horses, jockeys and trainers are listed below. Through Sept. 29, 2002 and eight series races.

Horses

		Pts
1	Grandera (IRE)	28
2	Street Cry (IRE)	12
	Eishin Preston (USA)	12
	Golan (IRE)	12
	Beat Hollow (GBR)	12
	Marienbard (IRE)	12
	Ballingarry (IRE)	12
8	Paolini (GER)	8
	Falcon Flight (FRA)	8
	Indigenous (IRE)	8

Jockeys

		Pts
1	Frankie Dettori	44
2	Jerry Bailey	24
3	Mick Kinane	18
4	Kieren Fallon	13
5	Yuichi Fukunaga	12
6	Andreas Suborics	10
7	Hirofumi Shii	7

Six tied with 6 each.

Trainers

		Pts
1	Saeed bin Suroor	60
2	Aidan O'Brien	21
3	Sir Michael Stoute	14
4	Shuji Kitahashi	12
	Ivan Allen	12
	Bobby Frankel	12
7	Mark Johnston	10
8	Jerry Barton	9
9	Andreas Schutz	8
	Andreas Wohler	8
	Don Burke III	8

Remaining 2002 World Series races: Prix de l'Arc de Triomphe (France), Oct. 6; Carlton Draught Cox Plate (Australia), Oct. 26; Breeders' Cup Turf (United States), Oct. 26; Breeders' Cup Classic (United States), Oct. 26; Japan Cup (Japan), Nov. 24; Hong Kong Cup (China), Dec. 15.

2001-02 Money Leaders

Official Top 10 standings for 2001 and unofficial Top 10 standings for 2002, through Sept. 29, 2002.

FINAL 2001 — 2002 (Through Sept. 29)

HORSES	Age	Sts	1-2-3	Earnings	HORSES	Age	Sts	1-2-3	Earnings
Captain Steve	4	6	2-1-1	$4,201,200	Street Cry	4	3	2-1-0	$4,266,615
Point Given	3	7	6-0-0	3,350,000	War Emblem	3	9	5-0-0	3,455,000
Tiznow	4	6	3-1-2	2,981,880	Came Home	3	7	6-0-0	1,624,500
Fantastic Light	5	3	2-1-0	2,896,615	Harlan's Holiday	3	8	3-2-1	1,585,000
Jungle Pocket	3	1	1-0-0	2,036,423	Medaglia d'Oro	3	8	4-2-0	1,460,600
Albert the Great	4	9	3-4-1	1,740,000	Beat Hollow	5	6	4-2-0	1,377,150
Monarchos	3	7	4-1-1	1,711,600	Sei Mi	6	1	0-1-0	1,200,000
Unbridled Elaine	3	8	4-1-1	1,663,175	Milwaukee Brew	5	6	2-0-2	1,110,000
Sakhee	4	2	1-1-0	1,640,000	Grandera	4	3	1-0-0	1,077,004
Include	4	9	5-1-2	1,435,400	Eishin Preston	5	1	1-0-0	1,025,600
JOCKEYS		**Mts**	**1st**	**Earnings**	**JOCKEYS**		**Mts**	**1st**	**Earnings**
Jerry Bailey		912	227	$22,597,720	Jerry Bailey		717	184	$17,805,063
John Velazquez		1411	305	15,073,790	Edgar Prado		1249	239	13,685,062
Pat Day		1197	249	14,497,859	John Velazquez		1120	231	11,654,448
Edgar Prado		1569	259	14,133,395	Pat Day		850	183	11,515,163
Jorge Chavez		1344	247	13,856,699	Jorge Chavez		964	186	10,827,738
Chris McCarron		607	123	12,933,932	Victor Espinoza		842	138	9,927,225
Gary Stevens		535	99	12,000,331	Kent Desormeaux		784	135	9,713,046
Alex Solis		1200	222	11,531,521	Alex Solis		846	167	8,915,549
Robby Albarado		1401	272	10,631,669	Patrick Angel Valenzuela		983	166	8,306,026
Ramon Dominguez		1864	431	10,514,207	Jose Santos		904	138	7,513,951
TRAINERS		**Sts**	**1st**	**Earnings**	**TRAINERS**		**Sts**	**1st**	**Earnings**
Bob Baffert		660	138	$16,354,996	Bobby Frankel		368	90	$13,113,476
Bobby Frankel		392	101	14,727,446	Bob Baffert		503	106	8,882,476
Bill Mott		744	152	9,418,657	Saeed bin Suroor		63	15	8,342,108
Steve Asmussen		1459	294	8,068,409	Steve Asmussen		1362	296	8,024,997
Scott Lake		1566	407	7,817,856	Todd Pletcher		543	112	6,654,350
Todd Pletcher		583	128	7,731,203	Bill Mott		525	118	6,281,317
D. Wayne Lukas		646	96	5,947,971	Scott Lake		1291	284	5,719,029
Saeed bin Suroor		43	8	5,751,828	Ken McPeek		324	56	5,217,320
Christophe Clement		356	75	5,557,669	Mark Hennig		370	72	5,125,705
Jerry Hollendorfer		1133	263	5,497,046	D. Wayne Lukas		359	64	4,821,990

Harness Racing

2001-02 Major Stakes Races

Winners of major stakes races from Nov. 9, 2001 through Sept. 28, 2002; all paces and trots cover one mile; (BC) indicates year-end Breeders' Crown series.

LATE 2001

Date	Race	Raceway	Winner	Time	Driver	Purse
Nov. 9	Windy City Pace	Maywood	Rattle And Rock	1:51⅘	Ryan Anderson	$325,000
Nov. 24	Three Diamonds Pace	Meadowlands	Worldly Beauty	1:52⅖	Luc Ouellette	350,000
Nov. 24	Valley Victory	Meadowlands	Chip Chip Hooray	1:57	Eric Ledford	360,000
Nov. 24	Governor's Cup	Meadowlands	Western Shooter	1:50	John Campbell	500,000

2002 (through Sept. 28)

Date	Race	Raceway	Winner	Time	Driver	Purse
May 11	Berry's Creek	Meadowlands	Mach Three	1:51	John Campbell	$300,000
June 1	New Jersey Classic	Meadowlands	McArdle	1:50⅕	Cat Manzi	500,000
June 22	North America Cup	Woodbine	Red River Hanover	1:48⅘	Luc Ouellette	1,500,000
July 12	Del Miller Memorial	Meadowlands	Cameron Hall	1:54⅖	Mike Lachance	400,000
July 12	Stanley Dancer Trot*	Meadowlands	Kadabra	1:54⅕	David Miller	400,000
July 13	Meadowlands Pace	Meadowlands	Mach Three	1:49	John Campbell	1,000,000
July 27	BC Open Pace	Meadowlands	Real Desire	1:48⅗	John Campbell	500,000
July 27	BC Open Trot	Meadowlands	Fool's Goal	1:51⅗	Jack Moiseyev	1,000,000
July 27	BC Mare Pace	Meadowlands	Molly Can Do It	1:49⅘	Jack Moiseyev	350,000
Aug. 1	Peter Haughton Memorial	Meadowlands	CC's Chuckie T	1:57⅗	David Miller	460,000
Aug. 1	Merrie Annabelle Final	Meadowlands	Southwind Maywood	1:57⅕	David Miller	460,000
Aug. 3	Sweetheart Pace	Meadowlands	Must See	1:53⅖	George Brennan	450,000
Aug. 3	Woodrow Wilson Pace	Meadowlands	Allamerican Native	1:51⅕	George Brennan	700,000
Aug. 3	**Hambletonian**	Meadowlands	Chip Chip Hooray	1:53⅗	Eric Ledford	1,000,000
Aug. 3	Hambletonian Oaks	Meadowlands	Windylane Hanover	1:53	Ron Pierce	500,000
Aug. 3	Nat Ray	Meadowlands	Victory Tilly	1:50⅘	Stig Johansson	500,000
Aug. 10	Adios Final	Ladbroke	Million Dollar Cam	1:50⅘	John Campbell	300,000
Aug. 10	Hoosier Cup	Hoosier Park	Art Major	1:50⅘	John Campbell	450,000
Aug. 18	Confederation Cup XXV	Flamboro	Art Major	1:51⅕	Steve Condren	519,000
Aug. 24	**Yonkers Trot**	Yonkers	Bubba Dunn	1:58⅕	Jeff Gregory	338,623
Aug. 31	Metro Pace	Woodbine	Sir Luck	1:59⅘	Mike Saftic	1,100,000
Aug. 31	World Trotting Derby	Du Quoin	American Pie	1:59⅘	Rod Allen	110,000

Harness Racing (Cont.)

Date	Race	Raceway	Winner	Time	Driver	Purse
Sept. 2	**Cane Pace**	Freehold	Art Major	1:53⅕	John Campbell	$369,188
Sept. 14	Maple Leaf Trot	Woodbine	Fools Goal	1:53⅕	Jack Moiseyev	851,000
Sept. 19	**Little Brown Jug**	Delaware	Million Dollar Cam	1:50⅖	Luc Ouellette	334,057

*Formerly known as the Budweiser Beacon Course, renamed in 2002.

2001-02 Money Leaders

Official Top 10 standings for 2001 and unofficial Top 10 standings for 2002 through Sept. 29, 2002.

FINAL 2001 / 2002 (through Sept. 29)

HORSES	Age	Sts	1-2-3	Earnings	HORSES	Age	Sts	1-2-3	Earnings
Bettor's Delight	3pc	16	9-5-0	$1,776,800	Fool's Goal	7tg	14	7-3-0	$1,258,940
Real Desire	3pc	17	7-7-2	1,646,036	Mach Three	3pc	16	11-1-2	1,169,297
S J's Caviar	3tc	20	15-1-0	1,198,490	McArdle	3pc	17	11-3-1	1,017,526
Bunny Lake	3pf	21	19-2-0	1,146,219	Real Desire	4ph	12	9-1-1	1,014,790
Gallo Blue Chip	4pg	19	10-4-1	1,123,940	Like A Prayer	3tc	15	6-5-2	857,629
Cathedra Dot Com	3pf	25	11-8-2	1,082,619	Kadabra	3tc	10	7-2-0	799,468
Syrinx Hanover	3tf	12	12-0-0	1,018,629	Red River Hanover	3pc	17	9-1-1	788,446
Magician	6tg	19	10-3-1	979,375	Art Major	3pc	20	11-2-1	788,289
Mach Three	2pc	9	7-2-0	954,708	Plesac	5th	20	6-5-6	762,082
Western Shooter	2pc	14	9-1-1	904,462	Million Dollar Cam	3pc	23	12-2-2	729,701

DRIVERS	Mts	1st	Earnings	DRIVERS	Mts	1st	Earnings
John Campbell	1803	340	$14,184,863	John Campbell	1483	278	$9,064,130
Mike Lachance	2093	237	10,696,993	David Miller	2041	306	8,136,716
Randy Waples	2759	550	10,636,348	Luc Ouellette	1800	308	7,109,525
David Miller	2786	457	10,551,102	Mike Lachance	1693	196	7,037,095
Luc Ouellette	2211	378	10,006,054	Ron Pierce	1515	217	5,590,753
Chris Christoforou	3060	622	9,570,998	Chris Christoforou	2113	378	4,860,579
Mario Baillageon	2270	304	7,461,680	Eric Ledford	1040	147	4,178,084
Mike Saftic	2050	216	6,120,014	Tony Morgan	2654	552	4,112,389
Sylvain Filion	2106	463	5,830,873	Cat Manzi	2024	312	3,992,634
Eric Ledford	1563	181	5,417,365	George Brennan	1424	165	3,770,386

Hambletonian Society/Breeders Crown Standardbred Poll

Final Poll conducted by Harness Racing Communications as of Sept. 30, 2002 and based on the votes of 35 harness racing media representatives. First place votes are in parentheses. (p-pacer, t-trotter, h-horse, f-filly, m-mare, c-colt, g-gelding).

		Pts	Age/Gait/Sex	'02 Sts—1-2-3	Earnings
1	Real Desire (30)	340	4ph	12—9-1-1	$1,014,790
2	Fool's Goal (2)	272	7tg	14—7-3-0	1,258,940
3	Kadabra (1)	246	3tc	10—7-2-0	799,468
4	Worldly Beauty (1)	216	3pf	10—8-2-0	566,517
5	Mach Three	172	3pc	16—11-1-2	1,169,297
6	Eternal Camnation	134	5pm	21—7-3-3	521,741
7	Art Major	102	3pc	20—11-2-1	788,289
8	Million Dollar Cam (1)	76	3pc	23—12-2-2	729,701
9	Sir Luck	64	2pc	13—8-3-1	600,431
10	Victory Tilly	46	7tg	14—10-0-2	831,306

Others receiving votes: 11. Chip Chip Hooray (43 points); **12.** Cameron Hall (38); **13.** Like A Prayer (35); **14.** McArdle (24); **15.** Broadway Hall (18); **16.** Fan Idole & Andover Hall (15); **18.** Lyell Creek N (13); **19.** Precious Delight (10); **20.** Varenne (7); **21.** Pizza Dolce & Plesac (6); **23.** Striking Memory (4); **24.** Always Cam, Art's Tribute & CC's Chuckie T (3); **27.** Check And Raise, Yankee Cruiser & Make A Success (1).

Steeplechase Racing
2001-02 Major Stakes Races

Winners of major steeplechase races from Nov. 17, 2001 through Aug. 29, 2002.

LATE 2001

Date	Race	Location	Miles	Winner	Jockey	Purse
Nov. 17	Colonial Cup	Camden, S.C.	2¾	Lord Zada	Gus Brown	$100,000

2002 (through Aug. 29)

Date	Race	Location	Miles	Winner	Jockey	Purse
Apr. 13	Atlanta Cup	Kingston, Ga.	2	Pinkie Swear	J.W. Delozier	$75,000
Apr. 20	Grand National	Butler, Md.	3	Sam Sullivan	Blair Waterman	30,000
Apr. 27	Maryland Hunt Cup	Glyndon, Md.	4	Young Dubliner	Brian Moran	65,000
May 4	Virginia Gold Cup	The Plains, Va.	4	Make Me A Champ	Blythe Miller	50,000
May 11	Iroquois	Nashville, Tenn.	3	All Gong	Blythe Miller	100,000
Aug. 29	N.Y. Turf Writers Cup	Saratoga, N.Y.	2⅜	Zabenz	Craig Thornton	100,000

1867-2002
Through the Years

Thoroughbred Racing
The Triple Crown

The term "Triple Crown" was coined by sportswriter Charles Hatton while covering the 1930 victories of Gallant Fox in the Kentucky Derby, Preakness Stakes and Belmont Stakes. Before then, only Sir Barton (1919) had won all three races in the same year. Since then, nine horses have won the Triple Crown. Two trainers, James (Sunny Jim) Fitzsimmons and Ben A. Jones, have saddled two Triple Crown champions, while Eddie Arcaro is the only jockey to ride two champions.

Year		Jockey	Trainer	Owner	Sire/Dam
1919	**Sir Barton**	Johnny Loftus	H. Guy Bedwell	J.K.L. Ross	Star Shoot/Lady Sterling
1930	**Gallant Fox**	Earl Sande	J.E. Fitzsimmons	Belair Stud	Sir Gallahad III/Marguerite
1935	**Omaha**	Willie Saunders	J.E. Fitzsimmons	Belair Stud	Gallant Fox/Flambino
1937	**War Admiral**	Charley Kurtsinger	George Conway	Samuel Riddle	Man o' War/Brushup
1941	**Whirlaway**	Eddie Arcaro	Ben A. Jones	Calumet Farm	Blenheim II/Dustwhirl
1943	**Count Fleet**	Johnny Longden	Don Cameron	Mrs. J.D. Hertz	Reigh Count/Quickly
1946	**Assault**	Warren Mehrtens	Max Hirsch	King Ranch	Bold Venture/Igual
1948	**Citation**	Eddie Arcaro	Ben A. Jones	Calumet Farm	Bull Lea/Hydroplane II
1973	**Secretariat**	Ron Turcotte	Lucien Laurin	Meadow Stable	Bold Ruler/Somethingroyal
1977	**Seattle Slew**	Jean Cruguet	Billy Turner	Karen Taylor	Bold Reasoning/My Charmer
1978	**Affirmed**	Steve Cauthen	Laz Barrera	Harbor View Farm	Exclusive Native/Won't Tell You

Note: Gallant Fox (1930) is the only Triple Crown winner to sire another Triple Crown winner, Omaha (1935). Wm. Woodward Sr., owner of Belair Stud, was breeder-owner of both horses and both were trained by Sunny Jim Fitzsimmons.

Triple Crown Near Misses

Forty-six horses have won two legs of the Triple Crown. Of those, sixteen won the Kentucky Derby (KD) and Preakness Stakes (PS) only to be beaten in the Belmont Stakes (BS). Two others, Burgoo King (1932) and Bold Venture (1936), won the Derby and Preakness, but were forced out of the Belmont with the same injury—a bowed tendon—that effectively ended their racing careers. In 1978, Alydar finished second to Affirmed in all three races, the only time that has happened. Note that the Preakness preceded the Kentucky Derby in 1922, '23 and '31; (*) indicates won on disqualification.

Year		KD	PS	BS
1877	**Cloverbrook**	DNS	won	won
1878	**Duke of Magenta**	DNS	won	won
1880	**Grenada**	DNS	won	won
1881	**Saunterer**	DNS	won	won
1895	**Belmar**	DNS	won	won
1920	**Man o' War**	DNS	won	won
1922	**Pillory**	DNS	won	won
1923	**Zev**	won	12th	won
1931	**Twenty Grand**	won	2nd	won
1932	**Burgoo King**	won	won	DNS
1936	**Bold Venture**	won	won	DNS
1939	**Johnstown**	won	5th	won
1940	**Bimelech**	2nd	won	won
1942	**Shut Out**	won	5th	won
1944	**Pensive**	won	won	2nd
1949	**Capot**	2nd	won	won
1950	**Middleground**	won	2nd	won
1953	**Native Dancer**	2nd	won	won
1955	**Nashua**	2nd	won	won
1956	**Needles**	won	2nd	won
1958	**Tim Tam**	won	won	2nd
1961	**Carry Back**	won	won	7th
1963	**Chateaugay**	won	2nd	won
1964	**Northern Dancer**	won	won	3rd
1966	**Kauai King**	won	won	4th
1967	**Damascus**	3rd	won	won
1968	**Forward Pass**	won*	won	2nd
1969	**Majestic Prince**	won	won	2nd
1971	**Canonero II**	won	won	4th
1972	**Riva Ridge**	won	4th	won
1974	**Little Current**	5th	won	won
1976	**Bold Forbes**	won	3rd	won
1979	**Spectacular Bid**	won	won	3rd
1981	**Pleasant Colony**	won	won	3rd
1984	**Swale**	won	7th	won
1987	**Alysheba**	won	won	4th
1988	**Risen Star**	3rd	won	won
1989	**Sunday Silence**	won	won	2nd
1991	**Hansel**	10th	won	won
1994	**Tabasco Cat**	6th	won	won
1995	**Thunder Gulch**	won	3rd	won
1997	**Silver Charm**	won	won	2nd
1998	**Real Quiet**	won	won	2nd
1999	**Charismatic**	won	won	3rd
2001	**Point Given**	5th	won	won
2002	**War Emblem**	won	won	8th

The Triple Crown Challenge (1987-93)

Seeking to make the Triple Crown more than just a media event and to insure that owners would not be attracted to more lucrative races, officials at Churchill Downs, the Maryland Jockey Club and the New York Racing Association created Triple Crown Productions in 1985 and announced that a $1 million bonus would be given to the horse that performs best in the Kentucky Derby, Preakness Stakes and Belmont Stakes. Furthermore, a bonus of $5 million would be presented to any horse winning all three races.

Revised in 1991, the rules stated that the winning horse must: 1. finish all three races; 2. earn points by finishing first, second, third or fourth in at least one of the three races; and 3. earn the highest number of points based on the following system—10 points to win, five to place, three to show and one to finish fourth. In the event of a tie, the $1 million is distributed equally among the top point-getters. From 1987-90, the system was five points to win, three to place and one to show. The Triple Crown Challenge was discontinued in 1994.

Year	Winner	KD	PS	BS	Pts	Year	Winner	KD	PS	BS	Pts
1987	1 **Bet Twice**	2nd	2nd	1st—	11	1991	1 **Hansel**	10th	1st	1st—	20
	2 Alysheba	1st	1st	4th—	10		2 Strike the Gold	1st	6th	2nd—	15
	3 Cryptoclearance	4th	3rd	2nd—	4		3 Mane Minister	3rd	3rd	3rd—	9
1988	1 **Risen Star**	3rd	1st	1st—	11	1992	1 **Pine Bluff**	5th	1st	3rd—	13
	2 Winning Colors	1st	3rd	6th—	6		2 Casual Lies	2nd	3rd	5th—	8
	3 Brian's Time	6th	2nd	3rd—	4		(No other horses ran all three races.)				
1989	1 **Sunday Silence**	1st	1st	2nd—	13	1993	1 **Sea Hero**	1st	5th	7th—	10
	2 Easy Goer	2nd	2nd	1st—	11		2 Wild Gale	3rd	8th	3rd—	6
	3 Hawkster	5th	5th	5th—	0		(No other horses ran all three races.)				
1990	1 **Unbridled**	1st	2nd	4th—	8						
	2 Summer Squall	2nd	1st	DNR—	6						
	3 Go and Go	DNR	DNR	1st—	5						
	(Unbridled was only horse to run all three races.)										

Kentucky Derby

For three-year-olds. Held the first Saturday in May at Churchill Downs in Louisville, Ky. Inaugurated in 1875.
Originally run at 1½ miles (1875-95), shortened to present 1¼ miles in 1896.

Trainers with most wins: Ben Jones (6); D. Wayne Lukas and Dick Thompson (4); Bob Baffert, Sunny Jim Fitzsimmons and Max Hirsch (3).

Jockeys with most wins: Eddie Arcaro and Bill Hartack (5); Bill Shoemaker (4); Angel Cordero Jr., Issac Murphy, Earl Sande and Gary Stevens (3).

Winning fillies: Regret (1915), Genuine Risk (1980) and Winning Colors (1988).

Year	Winner (Margin)	Time	Jockey	Trainer	2nd place	3rd place
1875	**Aristides** (1)	2:37¾	Oliver Lewis	Ansel Anderson	Volcano	Verdigris
1876	**Vagrant** (2)	2:38¼	Bobby Swim	James Williams	Creedmore	Harry Hill
1877	**Baden-Baden** (2)	2:38	Billy Walker	Ed Brown	Leonard	King William
1878	**Day Star** (2)	2:37¼	Jimmy Carter	Lee Paul	Himyar	Leveler
1879	**Lord Murphy** (1)	2:37	Charlie Shauer	George Rice	Falsetto	Strathmore
1880	**Fonso** (1)	2:37½	George Lewis	Tice Hutsell	Kimball	Bancroft
1881	**Hindoo** (4)	2:40	Jim McLaughlin	James Rowe Sr.	Lelex	Alfambra
1882	**Apollo** (½)	2:40¼	Babe Hurd	Green Morris	Runnymede	Bengal
1883	**Leonatus** (3)	2:43	Billy Donohue	John McGinty	Drake Carter	Lord Raglan
1884	**Buchanan** (2)	2:40¼	Isaac Murphy	William Bird	Loftin	Audrain
1885	**Joe Cotton** (nk)	2:37¼	Babe Henderson	Alex Perry	Bersan	Ten Booker
1886	**Ben Ali** (½)	2:36½	Paul Duffy	Jim Murphy	Blue Wing	Free Knight
1887	**Montrose** (2)	2:39¼	Isaac Lewis	John McGinty	Jim Gore	Jacobin
1888	**MacBeth II** (1)	2:38¼	George Covington	John Campbell	Gallifet	White
1889	**Spokane** (ns)	2:34½	Thomas Kiley	John Rodegap	Proctor Knott	Once Again
1890	**Riley** (2)	2:45	Isaac Murphy	Edward Corrigan	Bill Letcher	Robespierre
1891	**Kingman** (1)	2:52¼	Isaac Murphy	Dud Allen	Balgowan	High Tariff
1892	**Azra** (ns)	2:41½	Lonnie Clayton	John Morris	Huron	Phil Dwyer
1893	**Lookout** (5)	2:39¼	Eddie Kunze	Wm. McDaniel	Plutus	Boundless
1894	**Chant** (2)	2:41	Frank Goodale	Eugene Leigh	Pearl Song	Sigurd
1895	**Halma** (3)	2:37½	Soup Perkins	Byron McClelland	Basso	Laureate
1896	**Ben Brush** (ns)	2:07¾	Willie Simms	Hardy Campbell	Ben Eder	Semper Ego
1897	**Typhoon II** (hd)	2:12½	Buttons Garner	J.C. Cahn	Ornament	Dr. Catlett
1898	**Plaudit** (nk)	2:09	Willie Simms	John E. Madden	Lieber Karl	Isabey
1899	**Manuel** (2)	2:12	Fred Taral	Robert Walden	Corsini	Mazo
1900	**Lieut. Gibson** (4)	2:06¼	Jimmy Boland	Charles Hughes	Florizar	Thrive
1901	**His Eminence** (2)	2:07¾	Jimmy Winkfield	F.B. Van Meter	Sannazarro	Driscoll
1902	**Alan-a-Dale** (ns)	2:08¾	Jimmy Winkfield	T.C. McDowell	Inventor	The Rival
1903	**Judge Himes** (¾)	2:09	Hal Booker	J.P. Mayberry	Early	Bourbon
1904	**Elwood** (½)	2:08½	Shorty Prior	C.E. Durnell	Ed Tierney	Brancas
1905	**Agile** (3)	2:10¾	Jack Martin	Robert Tucker	Ram's Horn	Layson
1906	**Sir Huon** (2)	2:08⅘	Roscoe Troxler	Pete Coyne	Lady Navarre	James Reddick
1907	**Pink Star** (2)	2:12⅗	Andy Minder	W.H. Fizer	Zal	Ovelando
1908	**Stone Street** (1)	2:15⅕	Arthur Pickens	J.W. Hall	Sir Cleges	Dunvegan
1909	**Wintergreen** (4)	2:08⅕	Vincent Powers	Charles Mack	Miami	Dr. Barkley

Year	Winner (Margin)	Time	Jockey	Trainer	2nd place	3rd place
1910	Donau (½)	2:06⅖	Fred Herbert	George Ham	Joe Morris	Fighting Bob
1911	Meridian (¾)	2:05	George Archibald	Albert Ewing	Governor Gray	Colston
1912	Worth (nk)	2:09⅖	C.H. Shilling	Frank Taylor	Duval	Flamma
1913	Donerail (½)	2:04⅘	Roscoe Goose	Thomas Hayes	Ten Point	Gowell
1914	Old Rosebud (8)	2:03⅖	John McCabe	F.D. Weir	Hodge	Bronzewing
1915	Regret (2)	2:05⅖	Joe Notter	James Rowe Sr.	Pebbles	Sharpshooter
1916	George Smith (nk)	2:04	Johnny Loftus	Hollie Hughes	Star Hawk	Franklin
1917	Omar Khayyam (2)	2:04⅗	Charles Borel	C.T. Patterson	Ticket	Midway
1918	Exterminator (1)	2:10⅘	William Knapp	Henry McDaniel	Escoba	Viva America
1919	SIR BARTON (5)	2:09⅘	Johnny Loftus	H. Guy Bedwell	Billy Kelly	Under Fire
1920	Paul Jones (hd)	2:09	Ted Rice	Billy Garth	Upset	On Watch
1921	Behave Yourself (hd)	2:04⅕	Charles Thompson	Dick Thompson	Black Servant	Prudery
1922	Morvich (1½)	2:04⅗	Albert Johnson	Fred Burlew	Bet Mosie	John Finn
1923	Zev (1½)	2:05⅖	Earl Sande	David Leary	Martingale	Vigil
1924	Black Gold (½)	2:05⅕	John Mooney	Hanly Webb	Chilhowee	Beau Butler
1925	Flying Ebony (1½)	2:07⅗	Earl Sande	William Duke	Captain Hal	Son of John
1926	Bubbling Over (5)	2:03⅘	Albert Johnson	Dick Thompson	Bagenbaggage	Rock Man
1927	Whiskery (hd)	2:06	Linus McAtee	Fred Hopkins	Osmand	Jock
1928	Reigh Count (3)	2:10⅖	Chick Lang	Bert Michell	Misstep	Toro
1929	Clyde Van Dusen (2)	2:10⅘	Linus McAtee	Clyde Van Dusen	Naishapur	Panchio
1930	GALLANT FOX (2)	2:07⅗	Earl Sande	Jim Fitzsimmons	Gallant Knight	Ned O.
1931	Twenty Grand (4)	2:01⅘	Charley Kurtsinger	James Rowe Jr.	Sweep All	Mate
1932	Burgoo King (5)	2:05⅕	Eugene James	Dick Thompson	Economic	Stepenfetchit
1933	Brokers Tip (ns)	2:06⅘	Don Meade	Dick Thompson	Head Play	Charley O.
1934	Cavalcade (2½)	2:04	Mack Garner	Bob Smith	Discovery	Agrarian
1935	OMAHA (1½)	2:05	Willie Saunders	Jim Fitzsimmons	Roman Soldier	Whiskolo
1936	Bold Venture (hd)	2:03⅗	Ira Hanford	Max Hirsch	Brevity	Indian Broom
1937	WAR ADMIRAL (1¾)	2:03⅕	Charley Kurtsinger	George Conway	Pompoon	Reaping Reward
1938	Lawrin (1)	2:04⅘	Eddie Arcaro	Ben Jones	Dauber	Can't Wait
1939	Johnstown (8)	2:03⅖	James Stout	Jim Fitzsimmons	Challedon	Heather Broom
1940	Gallahadion (1½)	2:05	Carroll Bierman	Roy Waldron	Bimelech	Dit
1941	WHIRLAWAY (8)	2:01⅖	Eddie Arcaro	Ben Jones	Staretor	Market Wise
1942	Shut Out (2½)	2:04⅖	Wayne Wright	John Gaver	Alsab	Valdina Orphan
1943	COUNT FLEET (3)	2:04	Johnny Longden	Don Cameron	Blue Swords	Slide Rule
1944	Pensive (4½)	2:04⅕	Conn McCreary	Ben Jones	Broadcloth	Stir Up
1945	Hoop Jr (6)	2:07	Eddie Arcaro	Ivan Parke	Pot O'Luck	Darby Dieppe
1946	ASSAULT (8)	2:06⅗	Warren Mehrtens	Max Hirsch	Spy Song	Hampden
1947	Jet Pilot (hd)	2:06⅘	Eric Guerin	Tom Smith	Phalanx	Faultless
1948	CITATION (3½)	2:05⅖	Eddie Arcaro	Ben Jones	Coaltown	My Request
1949	Ponder (3)	2:04⅕	Steve Brooks	Ben Jones	Capot	Palestinian
1950	Middleground (1¼)	2:01⅗	William Boland	Max Hirsch	Hill Prince	Mr. Trouble
1951	Count Turf (4)	2:02⅗	Conn McCreary	Sol Rutchick	Royal Mustang	Ruhe
1952	Hill Gail (2)	2:01⅗	Eddie Arcaro	Ben Jones	Sub Fleet	Blue Man
1953	Dark Star (hd)	2:02	Hank Moreno	Eddie Hayward	Native Dancer	Invigorator
1954	Determine (1½)	2:03	Raymond York	Willie Molter	Hasty Road	Hasseyampa
1955	Swaps (1½)	2:01⅘	Bill Shoemaker	Mesh Tenney	Nashua	Summer Tan
1956	Needles (¾)	2:03⅖	David Erb	Hugh Fontaine	Fabius	Come On Red
1957	Iron Liege (nk)	2:02⅕	Bill Hartack	Jimmy Jones	Gallant Man	Round Table
1958	Tim Tam (½)	2:05	Ismael Valenzuela	Jimmy Jones	Lincoln Road	Noureddin
1959	Tomy Lee (ns)	2:02⅕	Bill Shoemaker	Frank Childs	Sword Dancer	First Landing
1960	Venetian Way (3½)	2:02⅖	Bill Hartack	Victor Sovinski	Bally Ache	Victoria Park
1961	Carry Back (¾)	2:04	John Sellers	Jack Price	Crozier	Bass Clef
1962	Decidedly (2¼)	2:00⅖	Bill Hartack	Horatio Luro	Roman Line	Ridan
1963	Chateaugay (1¼)	2:01⅘	Braulio Baeza	James Conway	Never Bend	Candy Spots
1964	Northern Dancer (nk)	2:00	Bill Hartack	Horatio Luro	Hill Rise	The Scoundrel
1965	Lucky Debonair (nk)	2:01⅕	Bill Shoemaker	Frank Catrone	Dapper Dan	Tom Rolfe
1966	Kauai King (½)	2:02	Don Brumfield	Henry Forrest	Advocator	Blue Skyer
1967	Proud Clarion (1)	2:00⅗	Bobby Ussery	Loyd Gentry	Barbs Delight	Damascus
1968	Forward Pass* (nk)	—	Ismael Valenzuela	Henry Forrest	Francie's Hat	T.V. Commercial
1969	Majestic Prince (nk)	2:01⅘	Bill Hartack	Johnny Longden	Arts and Letters	Dike
1970	Dust Commander (5)	2:03⅖	Mike Manganello	Don Combs	My Dad George	High Echelon
1971	Canonero II (3¼)	2:03⅕	Gustavo Avila	Juan Arias	Jim French	Bold Reason
1972	Riva Ridge (3¼)	2:01⅘	Ron Turcotte	Lucien Laurin	No Le Hace	Hold Your Peace
1973	SECRETARIAT (2½)	1:59⅖	Ron Turcotte	Lucien Laurin	Sham	Our Native
1974	Cannonade (2¼)	2:04	Angel Cordero Jr.	Woody Stephens	Hudson County	Agitate
1975	Foolish Pleasure (1¾)	2:02	Jacinto Vasquez	LeRoy Jolley	Avatar	Diabolo
1976	Bold Forbes (1)	2:01⅗	Angel Cordero Jr.	Laz Barrera	Honest Pleasure	Elocutionist
1977	SEATTLE SLEW (1¾)	2:02⅕	Jean Cruguet	Billy Turner	Run Dusty Run	Sanhedrin
1978	AFFIRMED (1½)	2:01⅕	Steve Cauthen	Laz Barrera	Alydar	Believe It

Kentucky Derby (Cont.)

Year	Winner (Margin)	Time	Jockey	Trainer	2nd place	3rd place
1979	**Spectacular Bid** (2 3/4)	2:02 2/5	Ron Franklin	Bud Delp	General Assembly	Golden Act
1980	**Genuine Risk** (1)	2:02	Jacinto Vasquez	LeRoy Jolley	Rumbo	Jaklin Klugman
1981	**Pleasant Colony** (3/4)	2:02	Jorge Velasquez	John Campo	Woodchopper	Partez
1982	**Gato Del Sol** (2 1/2)	2:02 2/5	E. Delahoussaye	Eddie Gregson	Laser Light	Reinvested
1983	**Sunny's Halo** (2)	2:02 1/5	E. Delahoussaye	David Cross Jr.	Desert Wine	Caveat
1984	**Swale** (3 1/4)	2:02 2/5	Laffit Pincay Jr.	Woody Stephens	Coax Me Chad	At The Threshold
1985	**Spend A Buck** (5 1/4)	2:00 1/5	Angel Cordero Jr.	Cam Gambolati	Stephan's Odyssey	Chief's Crown
1986	**Ferdinand** (2 1/4)	2:02 4/5	Bill Shoemaker	Chas. Whittingham	Bold Arrangement	Broad Brush
1987	**Alysheba** (3/4)	2:03 2/5	Chris McCarron	Jack Van Berg	Bet Twice	Avies Copy
1988	**Winning Colors** (nk)	2:02 1/5	Gary Stevens	D. Wayne Lukas	Forty Niner	Risen Star
1989	**Sunday Silence** (2 1/2)	2:05	Pat Valenzuela	Chas. Whittingham	Easy Goer	Awe Inspiring
1990	**Unbridled** (3 1/2)	2:02	Craig Perret	Carl Nafzger	Summer Squall	Pleasant Tap
1991	**Strike the Gold** (1 3/4)	2:03	Chris Antley	Nick Zito	Best Pal	Mane Minister
1992	**Lil E. Tee** (1)	2:03	Pat Day	Lynn Whiting	Casual Lies	Dance Floor
1993	**Sea Hero** (2 1/2)	2:02 2/5	Jerry Bailey	Mack Miller	Prairie Bayou	Wild Gale
1994	**Go For Gin** (2)	2:03 3/5	Chris McCarron	Nick Zito	Strodes Creek	Blumin Affair
1995	**Thunder Gulch** (2 1/4)	2:01 1/5	Gary Stevens	D. Wayne Lukas	Tejano Run	Timber Country
1996	**Grindstone** (ns)	2:01	Jerry Bailey	D. Wayne Lukas	Cavonnier	Prince of Thieves
1997	**Silver Charm** (hd)	2:02 2/5	Gary Stevens	Bob Baffert	Captain Bodgit	Free House
1998	**Real Quiet** (1/2)	2:02 1/5	Kent Desormeaux	Bob Baffert	Victory Gallop	Indian Charlie
1999	**Charismatic** (nk)	2:03 1/5	Chris Antley	D. Wayne Lukas	Menifee	Cat Thief
2000	**Fusaichi Pegasus** (1 1/2)	2:01 1/5	Kent Desormeaux	Neil Drysdale	Aptitude	Impeachment
2001	**Monarchos** (4 3/4)	1:59 4/5	Jorge Chavez	John Ward Jr.	Invisible Ink	Congaree
2002	**War Emblem** (4)	2:01	Victor Espinoza	Bob Baffert	Proud Citizen	Perfect Drift

*Dancer's Image finished first (in 2:02 1/5), but was disqualified after traces of prohibited medication were found in his system.

Preakness Stakes

For three-year-olds. Held two weeks after the Kentucky Derby at Pimlico Race Course in Baltimore. Inaugurated 1873. Note that the 1918 race was held over two divisions. Originally run at 1 1/2 miles (1873-88), then at 1 1/4 miles (1889), 1 1/2 miles (1890), 1 1/16 miles (1894-1900), 1 mile & 70 yards (1901-07), 1 1/16 miles (1908), 1 mile (1909-1910), 1 1/8 miles (1911-24), and the present 1 3/16 miles since 1925.

Trainers with most wins: Robert W. Walden (7); T.J. Healey and D. Wayne Lukas (5); Bob Baffert, Sunny Jim Fitzsimmons and Jimmy Jones (4); J. Whalen (3).

Jockeys with most wins: Eddie Arcaro (6); Pat Day (5); G. Barbee, Bill Hartack and Lloyd Hughes (3).

Winning fillies: Flocarline (1903), Whimsical (1906), Rhine Maiden (1915) and Nellie Morse (1924).

Year	Winner (Margin)	Time	Jockey	Trainer	2nd place	3rd place
1873	**Survivor** (10)	2:43	G. Barbee	A.D. Pryor	John Boulger	Artist
1874	**Culpepper** (3/4)	2:56 1/2	W. Donohue	H. Gaffney	King Amadeus	Scratch
1875	**Tom Ochiltree** (2)	2:43 1/2	L. Hughes	R.W. Walden	Viator	Bay Final
1876	**Shirley** (4)	2:44 3/4	G. Barbee	W. Brown	Rappahannock	Compliment
1877	**Cloverbrook** (2)	2:45 1/2	C. Holloway	J. Walden	Bombast	Lucifer
1878	**Duke of Magenta** (2)	2:41 3/4	C. Holloway	R.W. Walden	Bayard	Albert
1879	**Harold** (1)	2:40 1/2	L. Hughes	R.W. Walden	Jericho	Rochester
1880	**Grenada** (3/4)	2:40 1/2	L. Hughes	R.W. Walden	Oden	Emily F.
1881	**Saunterer** (1/2)	2:40 1/2	T. Costello	R.W. Walden	Compensation	Baltic
1882	**Vanguard** (nk)	2:44 1/2	T. Costello	R.W. Walden	Heck	Col. Watson
1883	**Jacobus** (4)	2:42 1/2	G. Barbee	R. Dwyer	Parnell	(2-horse race)
1884	**Knight of Ellerslie** (2)	2:39 1/2	S. Fisher	T.B. Doswell	Welcher	(2-horse race)
1885	**Tecumseh** (2)	2:49	Jim McLaughlin	C. Littlefield	Wickham	John C.
1886	**The Bard** (3)	2:45	S. Fisher	J. Huggins	Eurus	Elkwood
1887	**Dunboyne** (1)	2:39 1/2	W. Donohue	W. Jennings	Mahoney	Raymond
1888	**Refund** (3)	2:49	F. Littlefield	R.W. Walden	Bertha B.*	Glendale
1889	**Buddhist** (8)	2:17 1/2	W. Anderson	J. Rogers	Japhet	(2-horse race)
1890	**Montague** (3)	2:36 3/4	W. Martin	E. Feakes	Philosophy	Barrister
1891-93	Not held					
1894	**Assignee** (3)	1:49 1/4	F. Taral	W. Lakeland	Potentate	Ed Kearney
1895	**Belmar** (1)	1:50 1/2	F. Taral	E. Feakes	April Fool	Sue Kittie
1896	**Margrave** (1)	1:51	H. Griffin	Byron McClelland	Hamilton II	Intermission
1897	**Paul Kauvar** (1 1/2)	1:51 1/4	T. Thorpe	T.P. Hayes	Elkins	On Deck
1898	**Sly Fox** (2)	1:49 3/4	W. Simms	H. Campbell	The Huguenot	Nuto
1899	**Half Time** (1)	1:47	R. Clawson	F. McCabe	Filigrane	Lackland
1900	**Hindus** (hd)	1:48 2/5	H. Spencer	J.H. Morris	Sarmatian	Ten Candles
1901	**The Parader** (2)	1:47 1/5	F. Landry	T.J. Healey	Sadie S.	Dr. Barlow
1902	**Old England** (ns)	1:45 4/5	L. Jackson	G.B. Morris	Maj. Daingerfield	Namtor
1903	**Flocarline** (1/2)	1:44 4/5	W. Gannon	H.C. Riddle	Mackey Dwyer	Rightful
1904	**Bryn Mawr** (1)	1:44 1/5	E. Hildebrand	W.F. Presgrave	Wotan	Dolly Spanker
1905	**Cairngorm** (hd)	1:45 4/5	W. Davis	A.J. Joyner	Kiamesha	Coy Maid

Year	Winner (Margin)	Time	Jockey	Trainer	2nd place	3rd place
1906	**Whimsical** (4)	1:45	Walter Miller	T.J. Gaynor	Content	Larabie
1907	**Don Enrique** (1)	1:45⅖	G. Mountain	J. Whalen	Ethon	Zambesi
1908	**Royal Tourist** (4)	1:46⅖	Eddie Dugan	A.J. Joyner	Live Wire	Robert Cooper
1909	**Effendi** (1)	1:39⅘	Willie Doyle	F.C. Frisbie	Fashion Plate	Hill Top
1910	**Layminster** (½)	1:40⅗	R. Estep	J.S. Healy	Dalhousie	Sager
1911	**Watervale** (1)	1:51	Eddie Dugan	J. Whalen	Zeus	The Nigger
1912	**Colonel Holloway** (5)	1:56⅗	C. Turner	D. Woodford	Bwana Tumbo	Tipsand
1913	**Buskin** (nk)	1:53⅖	James Butwell	J. Whalen	Kleburne	Barnegat
1914	**Holiday** (¾)	1:53⅘	A. Schuttinger	J.S. Healy	Brave Cunarder	Defendum
1915	**Rhine Maiden** (1½)	1:58	Douglas Hoffman	F. Devers	Half Rock	Runes
1916	**Damrosch** (1½)	1:54⅘	Linus McAtee	A.G. Weston	Greenwood	Achievement
1917	**Kalitan** (2)	1:54⅖	E. Haynes	Bill Hurley	Al M. Dick	Kentucky Boy
1918	**War Cloud** (¾)	1:53⅗	Johnny Loftus	W.B. Jennings	Sunny Slope	Lanius
1918	**Jack Hare Jr** (2)	1:53⅖	Charles Peak	F.D. Weir	The Porter	Kate Bright
1919	**SIR BARTON** (4)	1:53	Johnny Loftus	H. Guy Bedwell	Eternal	Sweep On
1920	**Man o' War** (1½)	1:51⅗	Clarence Kummer	L. Feustel	Upset	Wildair
1921	**Broomspun** (¾)	1:54⅕	F. Coltiletti	James Rowe Sr.	Polly Ann	Jeg
1922	**Pillory** (hd)	1:51⅗	L. Morris	Thomas Healey	Hea	June Grass
1923	**Vigil** (1¼)	1:53⅗	B. Marinelli	Thomas Healey	General Thatcher	Rialto
1924	**Nellie Morse** (1½)	1:57⅕	John Merimee	A.B. Gordon	Transmute	Mad Play
1925	**Coventry** (4)	1:59	Clarence Kummer	William Duke	Backbone	Almadel
1926	**Display** (hd)	1:59⅘	John Maiben	Thomas Healey	Blondin	Mars
1927	**Bostonian** (½)	2:01⅗	Whitey Abel	Fred Hopkins	Sir Harry	Whiskery
1928	**Victorian** (ns)	2:00⅕	Sonny Workman	James Rowe Jr.	Toro	Solace
1929	**Dr. Freeland** (1)	2:01⅗	Louis Schaefer	Thomas Healey	Minotaur	African
1930	**GALLANT FOX** (¾)	2:00⅗	Earl Sande	Jim Fitzsimmons	Crack Brigade	Snowflake
1931	**Mate** (1½)	1:59	George Ellis	J.W. Healy	Twenty Grand	Ladder
1932	**Burgoo King** (hd)	1:59⅘	Eugene James	Dick Thompson	Tick On	Boatswain
1933	**Head Play** (4)	2:02	Charley Kurtsinger	Thomas Hayes	Ladysman	Utopian
1934	**High Quest** (ns)	1:58⅕	Robert Jones	Bob Smith	Cavalcade	Discovery
1935	**OMAHA** (6)	1:58⅖	Willie Saunders	Jim Fitzsimmons	Firethorn	Psychic Bid
1936	**Bold Venture** (ns)	1:59	George Woolf	Max Hirsch	Granville	Jean Bart
1937	**WAR ADMIRAL** (hd)	1:58⅖	Charley Kurtsinger	George Conway	Pompoon	Flying Scot
1938	**Dauber** (7)	1:59⅘	Maurice Peters	Dick Handlen	Cravat	Menow
1939	**Challedon** (1¼)	1:59⅘	George Seabo	Louis Schaefer	Gilded Knight	Volitant
1940	**Bimelech** (3)	1:58⅗	F.A. Smith	Bill Hurley	Mioland	Gallahadion
1941	**WHIRLAWAY** (5½)	1:58⅘	Eddie Arcaro	Ben Jones	King Cole	Our Boots
1942	**Alsab** (1)	1:57	Basil James	Sarge Swenke	Requested & Sun Again (dead heat)	
1943	**COUNT FLEET** (8)	1:57⅖	Johnny Longden	Don Cameron	Blue Swords	Vincentive
1944	**Pensive** (¾)	1:59⅕	Conn McCreary	Ben Jones	Platter	Stir Up
1945	**Polynesian** (2½)	1:58⅘	W.D. Wright	Morris Dixon	Hoop Jr.	Darby Dieppe
1946	**ASSAULT** (nk)	2:01⅖	Warren Mehrtens	Max Hirsch	Lord Boswell	Hampden
1947	**Faultless** (1¼)	1:59	Doug Dodson	Jimmy Jones	On Trust	Phalanx
1948	**CITATION** (5½)	2:02⅖	Eddie Arcaro	Jimmy Jones	Vulcan's Forge	Bovard
1949	**Capot** (hd)	1:56	Ted Atkinson	J.M. Gaver	Palestinian	Noble Impulse
1950	**Hill Prince** (5)	1:59⅕	Eddie Arcaro	Casey Hayes	Middleground	Dooly
1951	**Bold** (7)	1:56⅖	Eddie Arcaro	Preston Burch	Counterpoint	Alerted
1952	**Blue Man** (3½)	1:57⅖	Conn McCreary	Woody Stephens	Jampol	One Count
1953	**Native Dancer** (nk)	1:57⅘	Eric Guerin	Bill Winfrey	Jamie K.	Royal Bay Gem
1954	**Hasty Road** (nk)	1:57⅖	Johnny Adams	Harry Trotsek	Correlation	Hasseyampa
1955	**Nashua** (1)	1:54⅗	Eddie Arcaro	Jim Fitzsimmons	Saratoga	Traffic Judge
1956	**Fabius** (¾)	1:58⅖	Bill Hartack	Jimmy Jones	Needles	No Regrets
1957	**Bold Ruler** (2)	1:56⅕	Eddie Arcaro	Jim Fitzsimmons	Iron Liege	Inside Tract
1958	**Tim Tam** (1½)	1:57⅕	Ismael Valenzuela	Jimmy Jones	Lincoln Road	Gone Fishin'
1959	**Royal Orbit** (4)	1:57	William Harmatz	R. Cornell	Sword Dancer	Dunce
1960	**Bally Ache** (4)	1:57⅗	Bobby Ussery	Jimmy Pitt	Victoria Park	Celtic Ash
1961	**Carry Back** (¾)	1:57⅗	Johnny Sellers	Jack Price	Globemaster	Crozier
1962	**Greek Money** (ns)	1:56⅕	John Rotz	V.W. Raines	Ridan	Roman Line
1963	**Candy Spots** (3½)	1:56⅕	Bill Shoemaker	Mesh Tenney	Chateaugay	Never Bend
1964	**Northern Dancer** (2¼)	1:56⅘	Bill Hartack	Horatio Luro	The Scoundrel	Hill Rise
1965	**Tom Rolfe** (nk)	1:56⅕	Ron Turcotte	Frank Whiteley	Dapper Dan	Hail To All
1966	**Kauai King** (1¾)	1:55⅖	Don Brumfield	Henry Forrest	Stupendous	Amberoid
1967	**Damascus** (2¼)	1:55⅕	Bill Shoemaker	Frank Whiteley	In Reality	Proud Clarion
1968	**Forward Pass** (6)	1:56⅘	Ismael Valenzuela	Henry Forrest	Out Of the Way	Nodouble
1969	**Majestic Prince** (hd)	1:55⅗	Bill Hartack	Johnny Longden	Arts and Letters	Jay Ray
1970	**Personality** (nk)	1:56⅕	Eddie Belmonte	John Jacobs	My Dad George	Silent Screen
1971	**Canonero II** (1½)	1:54	Gustavo Avila	Juan Arias	Eastern Fleet	Jim French
1972	**Bee Bee Bee** (1¼)	1:55⅗	Eldon Nelson	Red Carroll	No Le Hace	Key To The Mint
1973	**SECRETARIAT** (2½)	1:54⅖	Ron Turcotte	Lucien Laurin	Sham	Our Native

Preakness Stakes (Cont.)

Year	Winner (Margin)	Time	Jockey	Trainer	2nd place	3rd place
1974	**Little Current** (7)	1:54⅗	Miguel Rivera	Lou Rondinello	Neapolitan Way	Cannonade
1975	**Master Derby** (1)	1:56⅖	Darrel McHargue	Smiley Adams	Foolish Pleasure	Diabolo
1976	**Elocutionist** (3½)	1:55	John Lively	Paul Adwell	Play The Red	Bold Forbes
1977	**SEATTLE SLEW** (1½)	1:54⅖	Jean Cruguet	Billy Turner	Iron Constitution	Run Dusty Run
1978	**AFFIRMED** (nk)	1:54⅖	Steve Cauthen	Laz Barrera	Alydar	Believe It
1979	**Spectacular Bid** (3½)	1:54⅕	Ron Franklin	Bud Delp	Golden Act	Screen King
1980	**Codex** (4¾)	1:54⅕	Angel Cordero Jr.	D. Wayne Lukas	Genuine Risk	Colonel Moran
1981	**Pleasant Colony** (1)	1:54⅗	Jorge Velasquez	John Campo	Bold Ego	Paristo
1982	**Aloma's Ruler** (½)	1:55⅖	Jack Kaenel	John Lenzini Jr.	Linkage	Cut Away
1983	**Deputed Testamony** (2¾)	1:55⅖	Donald Miller Jr.	Bill Boniface	Desert Wine	High Honors
1984	**Gate Dancer** (1½)	1:53⅗	Angel Cordero Jr.	Jack Van Berg	Play On	Fight Over
1985	**Tank's Prospect** (hd)	1:53⅖	Pat Day	D. Wayne Lukas	Chief's Crown	Eternal Prince
1986	**Snow Chief** (4)	1:54⅘	Alex Solis	Melvin Stute	Ferdinand	Broad Brush
1987	**Alysheba** (½)	1:55⅘	Chris McCarron	Jack Van Berg	Bet Twice	Cryptoclearance
1988	**Risen Star** (1¼)	1:56⅕	E. Delahoussaye	Louie Roussel III	Brian's Time	Winning Colors
1989	**Sunday Silence** (ns)	1:53⅘	Pat Valenzuela	Chas. Whittingham	Easy Goer	Rock Point
1990	**Summer Squall** (2¼)	1:53⅗	Pat Day	Neil Howard	Unbridled	Mister Frisky
1991	**Hansel** (7)	1:54	Jerry Bailey	Frank Brothers	Corporate Report	Mane Minister
1992	**Pine Bluff** (¾)	1:55⅗	Chris McCarron	Tom Bohannan	Alydeed	Casual Lies
1993	**Prairie Bayou** (½)	1:56⅗	Mike Smith	Tom Bohannan	Cherokee Run	El Bakan
1994	**Tabasco Cat** (¾)	1:56⅖	Pat Day	D. Wayne Lukas	Go For Gin	Concern
1995	**Timber Country** (½	1:54⅖	Pat Day	D. Wayne Lukas	Oliver's Twist	Thunder Gulch
1996	**Louis Quatorze** (3¼)	1:53⅖	Pat Day	Nick Zito	Skip Away	Editor's Note
1997	**Silver Charm** (hd)	1:54⅖	Gary Stevens	Bob Baffert	Free House	Captain Bodgit
1998	**Real Quiet** (2¼)	1:54⅘	Kent Desormeaux	Bob Baffert	Victory Gallop	Classic Cat
1999	**Charismatic** (1½)	1:55⅕	Chris Antley	D. Wayne Lukas	Menifee	Badge
2000	**Red Bullet** (3¾)	1:56	Jerry Bailey	Joe Orseno	Fusaichi Pegasus	Impeachment
2001	**Point Given** (2¼)	1:55⅖	Gary Stevens	Bob Baffert	A P Valentine	Congaree
2002	**War Emblem** (¾)	1:56⅕	Victor Espinoza	Bob Baffert	Magic Weisner	Proud Citizen

* Later named Judge Murray.

Belmont Stakes

For three-year-olds. Held three weeks after Preakness Stakes at Belmont Park in Elmont, N.Y. Inaugurated in 1867 at Jerome Park, moved to Morris Park in 1890 and then to Belmont Park in 1905.

Originally run at 1 mile and 5 furlongs (1867-89), then 1¼ miles (1890-1905), 1⅜ miles (1906-25), and the present 1½ miles since 1926.

Trainers with most wins: James Rowe Sr. (8); Sam Hildreth (7); Sunny Jim Fitzsimmons (6); Woody Stephens (5); Max Hirsch, D. Wayne Lukas and Robert W. Walden (4); Elliott Burch, Lucien Laurin, F. McCabe and D. McDaniel (3).

Jockeys with most wins: Eddie Arcaro and Jim McLaughlin (6); Earl Sande and Bill Shoemaker (5); Braulio Baeza, Pat Day, Laffit Pincay Jr., Gary Stevens and James Stout (3).

Winning fillies: Ruthless (1867) and Tanya (1905).

Year	Winner (Margin)	Time	Jockey	Trainer	2nd place	3rd place
1867	**Ruthless** (½)	3:05	J. Gilpatrick	A.J. Minor	DeCourcey	Rivoli
1868	**General Duke** (2)	3:02	Bobby Swim	A. Thompson	Northumberland	Fanny Ludlow
1869	**Fenian** (6)	3:04¼	C. Miller	J. Pincus	Glenelg	Invercauld
1870	**Kingfisher** (nk)	2:59½	W. Dick	R. Colston	Foster	Midday
1871	**Harry Bassett** (3)	2:56	W. Miller	D. McDaniel	Stockwood	By the Sea
1872	**Joe Daniels** (¾)	2:58¼	James Roe	D. McDaniel	Meteor	Shylock
1873	**Springbok** (¾)	3:01¾	James Roe	D. McDaniel	Count d'Orsay	Strachino
1874	**Saxon** (nk)	2:39½	G. Barbee	W. Prior	Grinstead	Aaron Pennington
1875	**Calvin** (2)	2:42¼	Bobby Swim	A. Williams	Aristides	Milner
1876	**Algerine** (½)	2:40½	Billy Donohue	Major Doswell	Fiddlesticks	Barricade
1877	**Cloverbrook** (1)	2:46	C. Holloway	J. Walden	Loiterer	Baden-Baden
1878	**Duke of Magenta** (2)	2:43½	L. Hughes	R.W. Walden	Bramble	Sparta
1879	**Spendthrift** (6)	2:42¾	George Evans	T. Puryear	Monitor	Jericho
1880	**Grenada** (nk)	2:47	L. Hughes	R.W. Walden	Ferncliffe	Turenne
1881	**Saunterer** (nk)	2:47	T. Costello	R.W. Walden	Eole	Baltic
1882	**Forester** (5)	2:43	Jim McLaughlin	L. Stuart	Babcock	Wyoming
1883	**George Kinney** (3)	2:42½	Jim McLaughlin	James Rowe Sr.	Trombone	Renegade
1884	**Panique** (nk)	2:42	Jim McLaughlin	James Rowe Sr.	Knight of Ellerslie	Himalaya
1885	**Tyrant** (3)	2:43	Paul Duffy	W. Claypool	St. Augustine	Tecumseh
1886	**Inspector B** (1)	2:41	Jim McLaughlin	F. McCabe	The Bard	Linden
1887	**Hanover** (15)	2:43½	Jim McLaughlin	F. McCabe	Oneko	(2-horse race)
1888	**Sir Dixon** (15)	2:40¼	Jim McLaughlin	F. McCabe	Prince Royal	(2-horse race)
1889	**Eric** (½)	2:47¼	W. Hayward	J. Huggins	Diablo	Zephyrus
1890	**Burlington** (2)	2:07¾	Pike Barnes	A. Cooper	Devotee	Padishah
1891	**Foxford** (nk)	2:08¾	Ed Garrison	M. Donavan	Montana	Laurestan

Year	Winner (Margin)	Time	Jockey	Trainer	2nd place	3rd place
1892	**Patron** (6)	2:12	W. Hayward	L. Stuart	Shellbark	(2-horse race)
1893	**Commanche** (hd)	1:53¼	Willie Simms	G. Hannon	Dr. Rice	Rainbow
1894	**Henry of Navarre** (1½)	1:56½	Willie Simms	B. McClelland	Prig	Assignee
1895	**Belmar** (hd)	2:11½	Fred Taral	E. Feakes	Counter Tenor	Nanki Poo
1896	**Hastings** (hd)	2:24½	H. Griffin	J.J. Hyland	Handspring	Hamilton II
1897	**Scottish Chieftain** (1)	2:23¼	J. Scherrer	M. Byrnes	On Deck	Octagon
1898	**Bowling Brook** (6)	2:32	F. Littlefield	R.W. Walden	Previous	Hamburg
1899	**Jean Beraud** (hd)	2:23	R. Clawson	Sam Hildreth	Half Time	Glengar
1900	**Ildrim** (ns)	2:21¼	Nash Turner	H.E. Leigh	Petruchio	Missionary
1901	**Commando** (2)	2:21	H. Spencer	James Rowe Sr.	The Parader	All Green
1902	**Masterman** (2)	2:22⅗	John Bullman	J.J. Hyland	Renald	King Hanover
1903	**Africander** (2)	2:21¾	John Bullman	R. Miller	Whorler	Red Knight
1904	**Delhi** (4)	2:06⅗	George Odom	James Rowe Sr.	Graziallo	Rapid Water
1905	**Tanya** (½)	2:08	E. Hildebrand	J.W. Rogers	Blandy	Hot Shot
1906	**Burgomaster** (4)	2:20	Lucien Lyne	J.W. Rogers	The Quail	Accountant
1907	**Peter Pan** (1)	N/A	G. Mountain	James Rowe Sr.	Superman	Frank Gill
1908	**Colin** (hd)	N/A	Joe Notter	James Rowe Sr.	Fair Play	King James
1909	**Joe Madden** (8)	2:21⅗	E. Dugan	Sam Hildreth	Wise Mason	Donald MacDonald
1910	**Sweep** (6)	2:22	James Butwell	James Rowe Sr.	Duke of Ormonde	(2-horse race)
1911-12	Not held					
1913	**Prince Eugene** (½)	2:18	Roscoe Troxler	James Rowe Sr.	Rock View	Flying Fairy
1914	**Luke McLuke** (8)	2:20	Merritt Buxton	J.F. Schorr	Gainer	Charlestonian
1915	**The Finn** (4)	2:18⅖	George Byrne	E.W. Heffner	Half Rock	Pebbles
1916	**Friar Rock** (3)	2:22	E. Haynes	Sam Hildreth	Spur	Churchill
1917	**Hourless** (10)	2:17⅘	James Butwell	Sam Hildreth	Skeptic	Wonderful
1918	**Johren** (2)	2:20⅖	Frank Robinson	A. Simons	War Cloud	Cum Sah
1919	**SIR BARTON** (5)	2:17⅖	John Loftus	H. Guy Bedwell	Sweep On	Natural Bridge
1920	**Man o' War** (20)	2:14⅕	Clarence Kummer	L. Feustel	Donnacona	(2-horse race)
1921	**Grey Lag** (3)	2:16⅘	Earl Sande	Sam Hildreth	Sporting Blood	Leonardo II
1922	**Pillory** (2)	2:18⅘	C.H. Miller	T.J. Healey	Snob II	Hea
1923	**Zev** (1½)	2:19	Earl Sande	Sam Hildreth	Chickvale	Rialto
1924	**Mad Play** (2)	2:18⅘	Earl Sande	Sam Hildreth	Mr. Mutt	Modest
1925	**American Flag** (8)	2:16⅘	Albert Johnson	G.R. Tompkins	Dangerous	Swope
1926	**Crusader** (1)	2:32⅕	Albert Johnson	George Conway	Espino	Haste
1927	**Chance Shot** (1½)	2:32⅖	Earl Sande	Pete Coyne	Bois de Rose	Flambino
1928	**Vito** (3)	2:33⅕	Clarence Kummer	Max Hirsch	Genie	Diavolo
1929	**Blue Larkspur** (¾)	2:32⅘	Mack Garner	C. Hastings	African	Jack High
1930	**GALLANT FOX** (3)	2:31⅗	Earl Sande	Jim Fitzsimmons	Whichone	Questionnaire
1931	**Twenty Grand** (10)	2:29⅗	Charley Kurtsinger	James Rowe Jr.	Sun Meadow	Jamestown
1932	**Faireno** (1½)	2:32⅘	Tom Malley	Jim Fitzsimmons	Osculator	Flag Pole
1933	**Hurryoff** (1½)	2:32⅗	Mack Garner	H. McDaniel	Nimbus	Union
1934	**Peace Chance** (6)	2:29⅕	W.D. Wright	Pete Coyne	High Quest	Good Goods
1935	**OMAHA** (1½)	2:30⅗	Willie Saunders	Jim Fitzsimmons	Firethorn	Rosemont
1936	**Granville** (ns)	2:30	James Stout	Jim Fitzsimmons	Mr. Bones	Hollyrood
1937	**WAR ADMIRAL** (3)	2:28⅗	Charley Kurtsinger	George Conway	Sceneshifter	Vamoose
1938	**Pasteurized** (nk)	2:29⅖	James Stout	George Odom	Dauber	Cravat
1939	**Johnstown** (5)	2:29⅗	James Stout	Jim Fitzsimmons	Belay	Gilded Knight
1940	**Bimelech** (¾)	2:29⅗	Fred Smith	Bill Hurley	Your Chance	Andy K.
1941	**WHIRLAWAY** (2½)	2:31	Eddie Arcaro	Ben Jones	Robert Morris	Yankee Chance
1942	**Shut Out** (2)	2:29⅕	Eddie Arcaro	John Gaver	Alsab	Lochinvar
1943	**COUNT FLEET** (25)	2:28⅕	Johnny Longden	Don Cameron	Fairy Manhurst	Deseronto
1944	**Bounding Home** (½)	2:32⅕	G.L. Smith	Matt Brady	Pensive	Bull Dandy
1945	**Pavot** (5)	2:30⅕	Eddie Arcaro	Oscar White	Wildlife	Jeep
1946	**ASSAULT** (3)	2:30⅘	Warren Mehrtens	Max Hirsch	Natchez	Cable
1947	**Phalanx** (5)	2:29⅖	R. Donoso	Syl Veitch	Tide Rips	Tailspin
1948	**CITATION** (8)	2:28⅕	Eddie Arcaro	Jimmy Jones	Better Self	Escadru
1949	**Capot** (½)	2:30⅕	Ted Atkinson	John Gaver	Ponder	Palestinian
1950	**Middleground** (1)	2:28⅗	William Boland	Max Hirsch	Lights Up	Mr. Trouble
1951	**Counterpoint** (4)	2:29	David Gorman	Syl Veitch	Battlefield	Battle Morn
1952	**One Count** (2½)	2:30⅕	Eddie Arcaro	Oscar White	Blue Man	Armageddon
1953	**Native Dancer** (nk)	2:28⅗	Eric Guerin	Bill Winfrey	Jamie K.	Royal Bay Gem
1954	**High Gun** (nk)	2:30⅘	Eric Guerin	Max Hirsch	Fisherman	Limelight
1955	**Nashua** (9)	2:29	Eddie Arcaro	Jim Fitzsimmons	Blazing Count	Portersville
1956	**Needles** (nk)	2:29⅘	David Erb	Hugh Fontaine	Career Boy	Fabius
1957	**Gallant Man** (8)	2:26⅗	Bill Shoemaker	John Nerud	Inside Tract	Bold Ruler
1958	**Cavan** (6)	2:30⅕	Pete Anderson	Tom Barry	Tim Tam	Flamingo
1959	**Sword Dancer** (¾)	2:28⅖	Bill Shoemaker	Elliott Burch	Bagdad	Royal Orbit
1960	**Celtic Ash** (5½)	2:29⅕	Bill Hartack	Tom Barry	Venetian Way	Disperse
1961	**Sherluck** (2¼)	2:29⅕	Braulio Baeza	Harold Young	Globemaster	Guadalcanal

Belmont Stakes (Cont.)

Year	Winner (Margin)	Time	Jockey	Trainer	2nd place	3rd place
1962	**Jaipur** (ns)	2:28⅘	Bill Shoemaker	B. Mulholland	Admiral's Voyage	Crimson Satan
1963	**Chateaugay** (2½)	2:30⅕	Braulio Baeza	James Conway	Candy Spots	Choker
1964	**Quadrangle** (2)	2:28⅖	Manuel Ycaza	Elliott Burch	Roman Brother	Northern Dancer
1965	**Hail to All** (nk)	2:28⅖	John Sellers	Eddie Yowell	Tom Rolfe	First Family
1966	**Amberoid** (2½)	2:29⅗	William Boland	Lucien Laurin	Buffle	Advocator
1967	**Damascus** (2½)	2:28⅘	Bill Shoemaker	F.Y. Whiteley Jr.	Cool Reception	Gentleman James
1968	**Stage Door Johnny** (1¼)	2:27⅕	Gus Gustines	John Gaver	Forward Pass	Call Me Prince
1969	**Arts and Letters** (5½)	2:28⅘	Braulio Baeza	Elliott Burch	Majestic Prince	Dike
1970	**High Echelon** (¾)	2:34	John Rotz	John Jacobs	Needles N Pens	Naskra
1971	**Pass Catcher** (¾)	2:30⅖	Walter Blum	Eddie Yowell	Jim French	Bold Reason
1972	**Riva Ridge** (7)	2:28	Ron Turcotte	Lucien Laurin	Ruritania	Cloudy Dawn
1973	**SECRETARIAT** (31)	2:24	Ron Turcotte	Lucien Laurin	Twice A Prince	My Gallant
1974	**Little Current** (7)	2:29⅕	Miguel Rivera	Lou Rondinello	Jolly Johu	Cannonade
1975	**Avatar** (nk)	2:28⅕	Bill Shoemaker	Tommy Doyle	Foolish Pleasure	Master Derby
1976	**Bold Forbes** (nk)	2:29	Angel Cordero Jr.	Laz Barrera	McKenzie Bridge	Great Contractor
1977	**SEATTLE SLEW** (4)	2:29⅗	Jean Cruguet	Billy Turner	Run Dusty Run	Sanhedrin
1978	**AFFIRMED** (hd)	2:26⅘	Steve Cauthen	Laz Barrera	Alydar	Darby Creek Road
1979	**Coastal** (3¼)	2:28⅗	Ruben Hernandez	David Whiteley	Golden Act	Spectacular Bid
1980	**Temperence Hill** (2)	2:29⅘	Eddie Maple	Joseph Cantey	Genuine Risk	Rockhill Native
1981	**Summing** (nk)	2:29	George Martens	Luis Barerra	Highland Blade	Pleasant Colony
1982	**Conquistador Cielo** (14)	2:28⅕	Laffit Pincay Jr.	Woody Stephens	Gato Del Sol	Illuminate
1983	**Caveat** (3½)	2:27⅘	Laffit Pincay Jr.	Woody Stephens	Slew o' Gold	Barberstown
1984	**Swale** (4)	2:27⅕	Laffit Pincay Jr.	Woody Stephens	Pine Circle	Morning Bob
1985	**Creme Fraiche** (½)	2:27	Eddie Maple	Woody Stephens	Stephan's Odyssey	Chief's Crown
1986	**Danzig Connection** (1¼)	2:29⅘	Chris McCarron	Woody Stephens	Johns Treasure	Ferdinand
1987	**Bet Twice** (14)	2:28⅕	Craig Perret	Jimmy Croll	Cryptoclearance	Gulch
1988	**Risen Star** (14¾)	2:26⅖	E. Delahoussaye	Louie Roussel III	Kingpost	Brian's Time
1989	**Easy Goer** (8)	2:26	Pat Day	Shug McGaughey	Sunday Silence	Le Voyageur
1990	**Go And Go** (8¼)	2:27⅕	Michael Kinane	Dermot Weld	Thirty Six Red	Baron de Vaux
1991	**Hansel** (hd)	2:28	Jerry Bailey	Frank Brothers	Strike the Gold	Mane Minister
1992	**A.P. Indy** (¾)	2:26	E. Delahoussaye	Neil Drysdale	My Memoirs	Pine Bluff
1993	**Colonial Affair** (2)	2:29⅘	Julie Krone	Scotty Schulhofer	Kissin Kris	Wild Gale
1994	**Tabasco Cat** (2)	2:26⅘	Pat Day	D. Wayne Lukas	Go For Gin	Strodes Creek
1995	**Thunder Gulch** (2)	2:32	Gary Stevens	D. Wayne Lukas	Star Standard	Citadeed
1996	**Editor's Note** (1)	2:28⅘	Rene Douglas	D. Wayne Lukas	Skip Away	My Flag
1997	**Touch Gold** (¾)	2:28⅘	Chris McCarron	David Hofmans	Silver Charm	Free House
1998	**Victory Gallop** (ns)	2:29	Gary Stevens	Elliott Walden	Real Quiet	Thomas Jo
1999	**Lemon Drop Kid** (hd)	2:27⅘	Jose Santos	Scotty Schulhofer	Vision and Verse	Charismatic
2000	**Commendable** (1½)	2:31⅕	Pat Day	D. Wayne Lukas	Aptitude	Unshaded
2001	**Point Given** (12¼)	2:26⅖	Gary Stevens	Bob Baffert	A P Valentine	Monarchos
2002	**Sarava** (½)	2:29⅗	Edgar Prado	Ken McPeek	Medaglia d'Oro	Sunday Break

Breeders' Cup Championship

Inaugurated on Nov. 10, 1984, the Breeders' Cup World Thoroughbred Championships consists of eight races on one track on one day late in the year to determine thoroughbred racing's principle champions.

The Breeders' Cup has been (will be) held at the following tracks (in alphabetical order): Aqueduct Racetrack (N.Y.) in 1985; Arlington Park (Ill.) in 2002; Belmont Park (N.Y.) in 1990, '95 and 2001; Churchill Downs (Ky.) in 1988, '91, '94, '98 and 2000; Gulfstream Park (Fla.) in 1989, '92 and '99; Hollywood Park (Calif.) in 1984, '87 and '97; Santa Anita Park (Calif.) in 1986 and '93 and Woodbine (Toronto) in 1996.

Horses with most wins: Bayakoa, Da Hoss, Lure, Miesque and Tiznow (2).

Trainers with most wins: D. Wayne Lukas (16); Shug McGaughey (7); Neil Drysdale (6); Bill Mott (5); Ron McAnally (4); Francois Boutin, Patrick Byrne and Andre Fabre (3).

Jockeys with most wins: Jerry Bailey and Pat Day (12); Chris McCarron (9); Mike Smith and Gary Stevens (8); Eddie Delahoussaye and Laffit Pincay Jr. (7); Jose Santos and Pat Valenzuela (6); Corey Nakatani (5); Angel Cordero Jr. and Craig Perret (4); Frankie Dettori and Randy Romero (3).

Juvenile

Distances: one mile (1984-85, 87); 1 1/16 miles (1986 and since 1988).

Year	Winner (Margin)	Time	Jockey	Trainer	2nd place	3rd place
1984	**Chief's Crown** (¾)	1:36⅕	Don MacBeth	Roger Laurin	Tank's Prospect	Spend A Buck
1985	**Tasso** (ns)	1:36⅕	Laffit Pincay Jr.	Neil Drysdale	Storm Cat	Scat Dancer
1986	**Capote** (1¼)	1:43⅘	Laffit Pincay Jr.	D. Wayne Lukas	Qualify	Alysheba
1987	**Success Express** (1¾)	1:35⅕	Jose Santos	D. Wayne Lukas	Regal Classic	Tejano
1988	**Is It True** (1¼)	1:46⅗	Laffit Pincay Jr.	D. Wayne Lukas	Easy Goer	Tagel
1989	**Rhythm** (2)	1:43⅗	Craig Perret	Shug McGaughey	Grand Canyon	Slavic
1990	**Fly So Free** (3)	1:43⅖	Jose Santos	Scotty Schulhofer	Take Me Out	Lost Mountain
1991	**Arazi** (4¾)	1:44⅗	Pat Valenzuela	Francois Boutin	Bertrando	Snappy Landing
1992	**Gilded Time** (¾)	1:43⅖	Chris McCarron	Darrell Vienna	It'sali'lknownfact	River Special
1993	**Brocco** (5)	1:42⅘	Gary Stevens	Randy Winick	Blumin Affair	Tabasco Cat
1994	**Timber Country** (½)	1:44⅖	Pat Day	D. Wayne Lukas	Eltish	Tejano Run

Year	Winner (Margin)	Time	Jockey	Trainer	2nd place	3rd place
1995	Unbridled's Song (nk)	1:41³/₅	Mike Smith	James Ryerson	Hennessy	Editor's Note
1996	Boston Harbor (nk)	1:43²/₅	Jerry Bailey	D. Wayne Lukas	Acceptable	Ordway
1997	Favorite Trick (5½)	1:41²/₅	Pat Day	Patrick Byrne	Dawson's Legacy	Nationalore
1998	Answer Lively (hd)	1:44	Jerry Bailey	Bobby Barnett	Aly's Alley	Cat Thief
1999	Anees (2½)	1:42¹/₅	Gary Stevens	Alex Hassinger Jr.	Chief Seattle	High Yield
2000	Macho Uno (ns)	1:42	Jerry Bailey	Joe Orseno	Point Given	Street Cry
2001	Johannesburg (2¼)	1:42¹/₅	Michael Kinane	Aidan O'Brien	Repent	Siphonic

Juvenile Fillies

Distances: one mile (1984-85, 87); 1¹/₁₆ miles (1986 and since 1988).

Year	Winner (Margin)	Time	Jockey	Trainer	2nd place	3rd place
1984	Outstandingly*	1:37⁴/₅	Walter Guerra	Pancho Martin	Dusty Heart	Fine Spirit
1985	Twilight Ridge (1)	1:35⁴/₅	Jorge Velasquez	D. Wayne Lukas	Family Style	Steal A Kiss
1986	Brave Raj (5½)	1:43¹/₅	Pat Valenzuela	Melvin Stute	Tappiano	Saros Brig
1987	Epitome (ns)	1:36²/₅	Pat Day	Phil Hauswald	Jeanne Jones	Dream Team
1988	Open Mind (1¾)	1:46³/₅	Angel Cordero Jr.	D. Wayne Lukas	Darby Shuffle	Lea Lucinda
1989	Go for Wand (2¾)	1:44¹/₅	Randy Romero	Wm. Badgett Jr.	Sweet Roberta	Stella Madrid
1990	Meadow Star (5)	1:44	Jose Santos	LeRoy Jolley	Private Treasure	Dance Smartly
1991	Pleasant Stage (nk)	1:46²/₅	Eddie Delahoussaye	Chris Speckert	La Spia	Cadillac Women
1992	Eliza (nk)	1:42⁴/₅	Pat Valenzuela	Alex Hassinger	Educated Risk	Boots 'n Jackie
1993	Phone Chatter (hd)	1:43	Laffit Pincay Jr.	Richard Mandella	Sardula	Heavenly Prize
1994	Flanders (hd)	1:45¹/₅	Pat Day	D. Wayne Lukas	Serena's Song	Stormy Blues
1995	My Flag (½)	1:42²/₅	Jerry Bailey	Shug McGaughey	Cara Rafaela	Golden Attraction
1996	Storm Song (4½)	1:43³/₅	Craig Perret	Nick Zito	Love That Jazz	Critical Factor
1997	Countess Diana (8½)	1:42¹/₅	Shane Sellers	Patrick Byrne	Career Collection	Primaly
1998	Silverbulletday (½)	1:43³/₅	Gary Stevens	Bob Baffert	Excellent Meeting	Three Ring
1999	Cash Run (1¼)	1:43¹/₅	Jerry Bailey	D. Wayne Lukas	Chilukki	Surfside
2000	Caressing (½)	1:42³/₅	John Velazquez	David Vance	Platinum Tiara	She's a Devil Due
2001	Tempera (1½)	1:41²/₅	David Flores	Eoin Harty	Imperial Gesture	Bella Bellucci

*In 1984, winner Fran's Valentine was disqualified for interference in the stretch and placed 10th.

Sprint

Distance: six furlongs (since 1984).

Year	Winner (Margin)	Time	Jockey	Trainer	2nd place	3rd place
1984	Eillo (ns)	1:10¹/₅	Craig Perret	Budd Lepman	Commemorate	Fighting Fit
1985	Precisionist (¾)	1:08²/₅	Chris McCarron	L.R. Fenstermaker	Smile	Mt. Livermore
1986	Smile (1¼)	1:08²/₅	Jacinto Vasquez	Scotty Schulhofer	Pine Tree Lane	Bedside Promise
1987	Very Subtle (4)	1:08⁴/₅	Pat Valenzuela	Melvin Stute	Groovy	Exclusive Enough
1988	Gulch (¾)	1:10²/₅	Angel Cordero Jr.	D. Wayne Lukas	Play The King	Afleet
1989	Dancing Spree (nk)	1:09	Angel Cordero Jr.	Shug McGaughey	Safely Kept	Dispersal
1990	Safely Kept (nk)	1:09³/₅	Craig Perret	Alan Goldberg	Dayjur	Black Tie Affair
1991	Sheikh Albadou (nk)	1:09¹/₅	Pat Eddery	Alexander Scott	Pleasant Tap	Robyn Dancer
1992	Thirty Slews (nk)	1:08¹/₅	Eddie Delahoussaye	Bob Baffert	Meafara	Rubiano
1993	Cardmania (nk)	1:08³/₅	Eddie Delahoussaye	Derek Meredith	Meafara	Gilded Time
1994	Cherokee Run (nk)	1:09²/₅	Mike Smith	Frank Alexander	Soviet Problem	Cardmania
1995	Desert Stormer (nk)	1:09	Kent Desormeaux	Frank Lyons	Mr. Greeley	Lit de Justice
1996	Lit de Justice 1¼)	1:08³/₅	Corey Nakatani	Jenine Sahadi	Paying Dues	Honour and Glory
1997	Elmhurst ½)	1:08¹/₅	Corey Nakatani	Jenine Sahadi	Hesabull.	Bet On Sunshine
1998	Reraise (2).	1:09	Corey Nakatani	Craig Dollase	Grand Slam	Kona Gold
1999	Artax (½)	1:07⁴/₅	Jorge Chavez	Louis Albertrani	Kona Gold	Big Jag
2000	Kona Gold (½)	1:07³/₅	Alex Solis	Bruce Headley	Honest Lady	Bet On Sunshine
2001	Squirtle Squirt (½)	1:08²/₅	Jerry Bailey	Bobby Frankel	Xtra Heat	Caller One

Mile

Year	Winner (Margin)	Time	Jockey	Trainer	2nd place	3rd place
1984	Royal Heroine (1½)	1:32³/₅	Fernando Toro	John Gosden	Star Choice	Cozzene
1985	Cozzene (2¼)	1:35	Walter Guerra	Jan Nerud	Al Mamoon*	Shadeed
1986	Last Tycoon (hd)	1:35¹/₅	Yves St.-Martin	Robert Collet	Palace Music	Fred Astaire
1987	Miesque (3½)	1:32⁴/₅	Freddie Head	Francois Boutin	Show Dancer	Sonic Lady
1988	Miesque (4).	1:38³/₅	Freddie Head	Francois Boutin	Steinlen	Simply Majestic
1989	Steinlen (¾)	1:37¹/₅	Jose Santos	D. Wayne Lukas	Sabona	Most Welcome
1990	Royal Academy (nk)	1:35¹/₅	Lester Piggott	M.V. O'Brien	Itsallgreektome	Priolo
1991	Opening Verse (2¼)	1:37²/₅	Pat Valenzuela	Dick Lundy	Val des Bois	Star of Cozzene
1992	Lure (3)	1:32⁴/₅	Mike Smith	Shug McGaughey	Paradise Creek	Brief Truce
1993	Lure (2¼)	1:33²/₅	Mike Smith	Shug McGaughey	Ski Paradise	Fourstars Allstar
1994	Barathea (hd)	1:34²/₅	Frankie Dettori	Luca Cumani	Johann Quatz	Unfinished Symph
1995	Ridgewood Pearl (2)	1:43³/₅	John Murtagh	John Oxx	Fastness	Sayyedati
1996	Da Hoss (1½)	1:34⁴/₅	Gary Stevens	Michael Dickinson	Spinning World	Same Old Wish
1997	Spinning World (2)	1:32³/₅	Cash Asmussen	Jonathan Pease	Geri	Decorated Hero
1998	Da Hoss (hd)	1:35¹/₅	John Velazquez	Michael Dickinson	Hawksley Hill	Labeeb
1999	Silic (nk)	1:34¹/₅	Corey Nakatani	Julio Canani	Tuzla	Docksider
2000	War Chant (nk)	1:34³/₅	Gary Stevens	Neil Drysdale	North East Bound	Dansili
2001	Val Royal (1¾)	1:32	Jose Valdivia	Julio Canani	Forbidden Apple	Bach

*In 1985, 2nd place finisher Palace Music was disqualified for interference and placed 9th.

Breeders' Cup Championship (Cont.)

Distaff

Distances: 1¼ miles (1984-87); 1⅛ miles (since 1988).

Year	Winner (Margin)	Time	Jockey	Trainer	2nd place	3rd place
1984	**Princess Rooney** (7)	2:02⅖	Eddie Delahoussaye	Neil Drysdale	Life's Magic	Adored
1985	**Life's Magic** (6¼)	2:02	Angel Cordero Jr.	D. Wayne Lukas	Lady's Secret	DontstopThemusic
1986	**Lady's Secret** (2½)	2:01⅕	Pat Day	D. Wayne Lukas	Fran's Valentine	Outstandingly
1987	**Sacahuista** (2¼)	2:02⅘	Randy Romero	D. Wayne Lukas	Clabber Girl	Oueee Bebe
1988	**Personal Ensign** (ns)	1:52	Randy Romero	Shug McGaughey	Winning Colors	Goodbye Halo
1989	**Bayakoa** (1½)	1:47⅖	Laffit Pincay Jr.	Ron McAnally	Gorgeous	Open Mind
1990	**Bayakoa** (6¾)	1:49⅕	Laffit Pincay Jr.	Ron McAnally	Colonial Waters	Valay Maid
1991	**Dance Smartly** (½)	1:50⅘	Pat Day	Jim Day	Versailles Treaty	Brought to Mind
1992	**Paseana** (4)	1:48	Chris McCarron	Ron McAnally	Versailles Treaty	Magical Maiden
1993	**Hollywood Wildcat** (ns)	1:48⅕	Eddie Delahoussaye	Neil Drysdale	Paseana	Re Toss
1994	**One Dreamer** (nk)	1:50⅗	Gary Stevens	Thomas Proctor	Heavenly Prize	Miss Dominique
1995	**Inside Information** (13½)	1:46	Mike Smith	Shug McGaughey	Heavenly Prize	Lakeway
1996	**Jewel Princess** (1½)	1:48⅕	Corey Nakatani	Wallace Dollase	Serena's Song	Different
1997	**Ajina** (2)	1:47⅕	Mike Smith	Bill Mott	Sharp Cat	Escena
1998	**Escena** (ns)	1:49⅘	Gary Stevens	Bill Mott	Banshee Breeze	Keeper Hill
1999	**Beautiful Pleasure** (¾)	1:47⅖	Jorge Chavez	John Ward Jr.	Banshee Breeze	Heritage of Gold
2000	**Spain** (1½)	1:47⅗	Victor Espinoza	D. Wayne Lukas	Surfside	Heritage of Gold
2001	**Unbridled Elaine** (hd)	1:49⅕	Pat Day	Dallas Stewart	Spain	Two Item Limit

Turf

Distance: 1½ miles (since 1984).

Year	Winner (Margin)	Time	Jockey	Trainer	2nd place	3rd place
1984	**Lashkari** (nk)	2:25⅕	Yves St.-Martin	de Royer-Dupre	All Along	Raami
1985	**Pebbles** (nk)	2:27	Pat Eddery	Clive Brittain	StrawberryRoad II	Mourjane
1986	**Manila** (nk)	2:25⅖	Jose Santos	Leroy Jolley	Theatrical	Estrapade
1987	**Theatrical** (½)	2:24⅖	Pat Day	Bill Mott	Trempolino	Village Star II
1988	**Gt. Communicator** (½)	2:35⅕	Ray Sibille	Thad Ackel	Sunshine Forever	Indian Skimmer
1989	**Prized** (hd)	2:28	Eddie Delahoussaye	Neil Drysdale	Sierra Roberta	Star Lift
1990	**In The Wings** (½)	2:29⅗	Gary Stevens	Andre Fabre	With Approval	El Senor
1991	**Miss Alleged** (2)	2:30⅘	Eric Legrix	Pascal Bary	Itsallgreektome	Quest for Fame
1992	**Fraise** (ns)	2:24	Pat Valenzuela	Bill Mott	Sky Classic	Quest for Fame
1993	**Kotashaan** (½)	2:25	Kent Desormeaux	Richard Mandella	Bien Bien	Luazur
1994	**Tikkanen** (1½)	2:26⅖	Mike Smith	Jonathan Pease	Hatoof	Paradise Creek
1995	**Northern Spur** (nk)	2:42	Chris McCarron	Ron McAnally	Freedom Cry	Carnegie
1996	**Pilsudski** (1¼)	2:30⅕	Walter Swinburn	Michael Stoute	Singspiel	Swain
1997	**Chief Bearhart** (¾)	2:24	Jose Santos	Mark Frostad	Borgia	Flag Down
1998	**Buck's Boy** (1¼)	2:28⅗	Shane Sellers	Noel Hickey	Yagli	Dushyantor
1999	**Daylami** (2½)	2:24⅗	Frankie Dettori	Saeed bin Suroor	Royal Anthem	Buck's Boy
2000	**Kalanisi** (½)	2:26⅘	John Murtagh	Sir Michael Stoute	Quiet Resolve	John's Call
2001	**Fantastic Light** (¾)	2:24⅕	Frankie Dettori	Saeed bin Suroor	Milan	Timboroa

Filly & Mare Turf

Distance: 1⅜ miles (1999-2000); 1¼ miles (since 2001).

Year	Winner (Margin)	Time	Jockey	Trainer	2nd place	3rd place
1999	**Soaring Softly** (¾)	2:13⅘	Jerry Bailey	James J. Toner	Coretta	Zomarradah
2000	**Perfect Sting** (¾)	2:13	Jerry Bailey	Joe Orseno	Tout Charmant	Catella
2001	**Banks Hill** (5½)	2:00⅕	Olivier Peslier	Andre Fabre	Spook Express	Spring Oak

Classic

Distance: 1¼ miles (since 1984).

Year	Winner (Margin)	Time	Jockey	Trainer	2nd place	3rd place
1984	**Wild Again** (hd)	2:03⅖	Pat Day	Vincent Timphony	Slew o' Gold	Gate Dancer*
1985	**Proud Truth** (hd)	2:00⅘	Jorge Velasquez	John Veitch	Gate Dancer	Turkoman
1986	**Skywalker** (1¼)	2:00⅖	Laffit Pincay Jr.	M. Whittingham	Turkoman	Precisionist
1987	**Ferdinand** (ns)	2:01⅖	Bill Shoemaker	C. Whittingham	Alysheba	Judge Angelucci
1988	**Alysheba** (ns)	2:04⅘	Chris McCarron	Jack Van Berg	Seeking the Gold	Waquoit
1989	**Sunday Silence** (½)	2:00⅕	Chris McCarron	C. Whittingham	Easy Goer	Blushing John
1990	**Unbridled** (1)	2:02⅕	Pat Day	Carl Nafzger	Ibn Bey	Thirty Six Red
1991	**Black Tie Affair** (1¼)	2:02⅘	Jerry Bailey	Ernie Poulos	Twilight Agenda	Unbridled
1992	**A.P. Indy** (2)	2:00⅕	Eddie Delahoussaye	Neil Drysdale	Pleasant Tap	Jolypha
1993	**Arcangues** (2)	2:00⅘	Jerry Bailey	Andre Fabre	Bertrando	Kissin Kris
1994	**Concern** (nk)	2:02⅖	Jerry Bailey	Richard Small	Tabasco Cat	Dramatic Gold
1995	**Cigar** (2½)	1:59⅖	Jerry Bailey	Bill Mott	L'Carriere	Unaccounted For
1996	**Alphabet Soup** (ns)	2:01	Chris McCarron	David Hofmans	Louis Quatorze	Cigar
1997	**Skip Away** (6)	1:59⅕	Mike Smith	Hubert Hine	Deputy Commander	Dowty
1998	**Awesome Again** (¾)	2:02	Pat Day	Patrick Byrne	Silver Charm	Swain
1999	**Cat Thief** (1¼)	1:59⅖	Pat Day	D. Wayne Lukas	Budroyale	Golden Missile
2000	**Tiznow** (nk)	2:00⅗	Chris McCarron	Jay Robbins	Giant's Causeway	Captain Steve
2001	**Tiznow** (ns)	2:00⅗	Chris McCarron	Jay Robbins	Sakhee	Albert the Great

*In 1984, 2nd place finisher Gate Dancer was disqualified for interference and placed 3rd.

Breeders' Cup Leaders

The all-time money-winning horses and jockeys in the history of the Breeders' Cup through 2001.

Top 10 Horses

		Sts	1-2-3	Earnings
1	Tiznow	2	2-0-0	$4,560,400
2	Awesome Again	1	1-0-0	2,662,400
3	Skip Away	2	1-0-0	2,288,000
4	Cat Thief	3	1-0-1	1,200,000
5	Alysheba	3	1-1-1	2,133,000
6	Alphabet Soup	1	1-0-0	2,080,000
7	Cigar	2	1-0-1	2,040,000
8	Spain	3	1-1-0	1,755,200
9	Unbridled	2	1-0-1	1,710,000
10	Black Tie Affair (IRE)	3	1-0-1	1,668,000

Top 10 Jockeys

		Sts	1-2-3	Earnings
1	Pat Day	101	12-15-10	$21,718,200
2	Chris McCarron	101	9-12-7	17,669,600
3	Jerry Bailey	75	12-5-7	13,699,400
4	Gary Stevens	86	8-15-10	13,361,160
5	Mike Smith	42	8-3-4	8,194,200
6	Eddie Delahoussaye	68	7-3-6	7,775,000
7	Laffit Pincay Jr.	61	7-4-9	6,811,000
8	Corey Nakatani	43	5-6-6	6,440,360
9	Angel Cordero Jr.	48	4-7-7	6,020,000
10	Jose Santos	53	6-2-4	5,828,200

Annual Money Leaders
Horses

Annual money-leading horses since 1910, according to *The American Racing Manual*.

Multiple leaders: Round Table, Buckpasser, Alysheba and Cigar (2).

Year		Age	Sts	1-2-3	Earnings
1910	Novelty	2	16	11—	$72,630
1911	Worth	2	13	10—	16,645
1912	Star Charter	4	17	6—	14,655
1913	Old Rosebud	2	14	12—	19,057
1914	Roamer	3	16	12—	29,105
1915	Borrow	7	9	4—	20,195
1916	Campfire	2	9	6—	49,735
1917	Sun Briar	2	9	5—	59,505
1918	Eternal	2	8	6—	56,173
1919	Sir Barton	3	13	8-3-2	88,250
1920	Man o' War	3	11	11-0-0	166,140
1921	Morvich	2	11	11-0-0	115,234
1922	Pillory	3	7	4-1-1	95,654
1923	Zev	3	14	12-1-0	272,008
1924	Sarzen	2	12	8-1-1	95,640
1925	Pompey	2	10	7-2-0	121,630
1926	Crusader	3	15	9-4-0	166,033
1927	Anita Peabody	2	7	6-0-1	111,905
1928	High Strung	2	6	5-0-0	153,590
1929	Blue Larkspur	3	6	4-1-0	153,450
1930	Gallant Fox	3	10	9-1-0	308,275
1931	Gallant Flight	2	7	7-0-0	219,000
1932	Gusto	3	16	4-3-2	145,940
1933	Singing Wood	2	9	3-2-2	88,050
1934	Cavalcade	3	7	6-1-0	111,235
1935	Omaha	3	9	6-1-2	142,255
1936	Granville	3	11	7-3-0	110,295
1937	Seabiscuit	4	15	11-2-2	168,580
1938	Stagehand	3	15	8-2-3	189,710
1939	Challedon	3	15	9-2-3	184,535
1940	Bimelech	3	7	4-2-1	110,005
1941	Whirlaway	3	20	13-5-2	272,386
1942	Shut Out	3	12	8-2-0	238,872
1943	Count Fleet	3	6	6-0-0	174,055
1944	Pavot	2	8	8-0-0	179,040
1945	Busher	3	13	10-2-1	273,735
1946	Assault	3	15	8-2-3	424,195
1947	Armed	6	17	11-4-1	376,325
1948	Citation	3	20	19-1-0	709,470
1949	Ponder	3	21	9-5-2	321,825
1950	Noor	5	12	7-4-1	346,940
1951	Counterpoint	3	15	7-2-1	250,525
1952	Crafty Admiral	4	16	9-4-1	277,225
1953	Native Dancer	3	10	9-1-0	513,425
1954	Determine	3	15	10-3-2	328,700
1955	Nashua	3	12	10-1-1	752,550
1956	Needles	3	8	4-2-0	$440,850
1957	Round Table	3	22	15-1-3	600,383
1958	Round Table	4	20	14-4-0	662,780
1959	Sword Dancer	3	13	8-4-0	537,004
1960	Bally Ache	3	15	10-3-1	445,045
1961	Carry Back	3	16	9-1-3	565,349
1962	Never Bend	2	10	7-1-2	402,969
1963	Candy Spots	3	12	7-2-1	604,481
1964	Gun Bow	4	16	8-4-2	580,100
1965	Buckpasser	2	11	9-1-0	568,096
1966	Buckpasser	3	14	13-1-0	669,078
1967	Damascus	3	16	12-3-1	817,941
1968	Forward Pass	3	13	7-2-0	546,674
1969	Arts and Letters	3	14	8-5-1	555,604
1970	Personality	3	18	8-2-1	444,049
1971	Riva Ridge	2	9	7-0-0	503,263
1972	Droll Role	4	19	7-3-4	471,633
1973	Secretariat	3	12	9-2-1	860,404
1974	Chris Evert	3	8	5-1-2	551,063
1975	Foolish Pleasure	3	11	5-4-1	716,278
1976	Forego	6	8	6-1-1	401,701
1977	Seattle Slew	3	7	6-1-1	641,370
1978	Affirmed	3	11	8-2-0	901,541
1979	Spectacular Bid	3	12	10-1-1	1,279,334
1980	Temperence Hill	3	17	8-3-1	1,130,452
1981	John Henry	6	10	8-0-0	1,798,030
1982	Perrault (GBR)	5	8	4-1-2	1,197,400
1983	All Along (FRA)	4	7	4-1-1	2,138,963
1984	Slew o' Gold	4	6	5-0-1	2,627,944
1985	Spend A Buck	3	7	5-1-1	3,552,704
1986	Snow Chief	3	9	6-1-1	1,875,200
1987	Alysheba	3	10	3-3-1	2,511,156
1988	Alysheba	4	9	7-1-0	3,808,600
1989	Sunday Silence	3	9	7-2-0	4,578,454
1990	Unbridled	3	11	4-3-2	3,718,149
1991	Dance Smartly	3	8	8-0-0	2,876,821
1992	A.P. Indy	3	7	5-0-1	2,622,560
1993	Kotashaan (FRA)	5	10	6-3-0	2,619,014
1994	Paradise Creek	5	11	8-2-1	2,610,187
1995	Cigar	5	10	10-0-0	4,819,800
1996	Cigar	6	8	5-2-1	4,910,000
1997	Skip Away	4	11	4-5-2	4,089,000
1998	Silver Charm	4	9	6-2-0	4,696,506
1999	Almutawakel	4	4	1-1-1	3,290,000
2000	Dubai Millennium (GBR)	4	1	1-0-0	3,600,000
2001	Captain Steve	4	6	2-1-1	4,201,200

Annual Money Leaders (Cont.)
Jockeys

Annual money-leading jockeys since 1910, according to *The American Racing Manual.*

Multiple leaders: Bill Shoemaker (10); Laffit Pincay Jr. (7); Eddie Arcaro (6); Braulio Baeza (5); Jerry Bailey, Chris McCarron and Jose Santos (4); Angel Cordero Jr. and Earl Sande (3); Ted Atkinson, Pat Day, Laverne Fator, Mack Garner, Bill Hartack, Charley Kurtsinger, Johnny Longden, Mike Smith, Gary Stevens, Sonny Workman and Wayne Wright (2).

Year		Mts	Wins	Earnings	Year		Mts	Wins	Earnings
1910	Carroll Shilling	.506	172	$176,030	1956	Bill Hartack	.1387	347	$2,343,955
1911	Ted Koerner	.813	162	88,308	1957	Bill Hartack	.1238	341	3,060,501
1912	Jimmy Butwell	.684	144	79,843	1958	Bill Shoemaker	.1133	300	2,961,693
1913	Merritt Buxton	.887	146	82,552	1959	Bill Shoemaker	.1285	347	2,843,133
1914	J. McCahey	.824	155	121,845					
1915	Mack Garner	.775	151	96,628	1960	Bill Shoemaker	.1227	274	2,123,961
1916	John McTaggart	.832	150	155,055	1961	Bill Shoemaker	.1256	304	2,690,819
1917	Frank Robinson	.731	147	148,057	1962	Bill Shoemaker	.1126	311	2,916,844
1918	Lucien Luke	.756	178	201,864	1963	Bill Shoemaker	.1203	271	2,526,925
1919	John Loftus	.177	65	252,707	1964	Bill Shoemaker	.1056	246	2,649,553
					1965	Braulio Baeza	.1245	270	2,582,702
1920	Clarence Kummer	.353	87	292,376	1966	Braulio Baeza	.1341	298	2,951,022
1921	Earl Sande	.340	112	263,043	1967	Braulio Baeza	.1064	256	3,088,888
1922	Albert Johnson	.297	43	345,054	1968	Braulio Baeza	.1089	201	2,835,108
1923	Earl Sande	.430	122	569,394	1969	Jorge Velasquez	.1442	258	2,542,315
1924	Ivan Parke	.844	205	290,395					
1925	Laverne Fator	.315	81	305,775	1970	Laffit Pincay Jr.	.1328	269	2,626,526
1926	Laverne Fator	.511	143	361,435	1971	Laffit Pincay Jr.	.1627	380	3,784,377
1927	Earl Sande	.179	49	277,877	1972	Laffit Pincay Jr.	.1388	289	3,225,827
1928	Linus McAtee	.235	55	301,295	1973	Laffit Pincay Jr.	.1444	350	4,093,492
1929	Mack Garner	.274	57	314,975	1974	Laffit Pincay Jr.	.1278	341	4,251,060
					1975	Braulio Baeza	.1190	196	3,674,398
1930	Sonny Workman	.571	152	420,438	1976	Angel Cordero Jr.	.1534	274	4,709,500
1931	Charley Kurtsinger	.519	93	392,095	1977	Steve Cauthen	.2075	487	6,151,750
1932	Sonny Workman	.378	87	385,070	1978	Darrel McHargue	.1762	375	6,188,353
1933	Robert Jones	.471	63	226,285	1979	Laffit Pincay Jr.	.1708	420	8,183,535
1934	Wayne Wright	.919	174	287,185					
1935	Silvio Coucci	.749	141	319,760	1980	Chris McCarron	.1964	405	7,666,100
1936	Wayne Wright	.670	100	264,000	1981	Chris McCarron	.1494	326	8,397,604
1937	Charley Kurtsinger	.765	120	384,202	1982	Angel Cordero Jr.	.1838	397	9,702,520
1938	Nick Wall	.658	97	385,161	1983	Angel Cordero Jr.	.1792	362	10,116,807
1939	Basil James	.904	191	353,333	1984	Chris McCarron	.1565	356	12,038,213
					1985	Laffit Pincay Jr.	.1409	289	13,415,049
1940	Eddie Arcaro	.783	132	343,661	1986	Jose Santos	.1636	329	11,329,297
1941	Don Meade	.1164	210	398,627	1987	Jose Santos	.1639	305	12,407,355
1942	Eddie Arcaro	.687	123	481,949	1988	Jose Santos	.1867	370	14,877,298
1943	Johnny Longden	.871	173	573,276	1989	Jose Santos	.1459	285	13,847,003
1944	Ted Atkinson	.1539	287	899,101					
1945	Johnny Longden	.778	180	981,977	1990	Gary Stevens	.1504	283	13,881,198
1946	Ted Atkinson	.1377	233	1,036,825	1991	Chris McCarron	.1440	265	14,456,073
1947	Douglas Dodson	.646	141	1,429,949	1992	Kent Desormeaux	.1568	361	14,193,006
1948	Eddie Arcaro	.726	188	1,686,230	1993	Mike Smith	.1510	343	14,024,815
1949	Steve Brooks	.906	209	1,316,817	1994	Mike Smith	.1484	317	15,979,820
					1995	Jerry Bailey	.1367	287	16,311,876
1950	Eddie Arcaro	.888	195	1,410,160	1996	Jerry Bailey	.1187	298	19,465,376
1951	Bill Shoemaker	.1161	257	1,329,890	1997	Jerry Bailey	.1136	269	18,206,013
1952	Eddie Arcaro	.807	188	1,859,591	1998	Gary Stevens	.869	178	19,358,840
1953	Bill Shoemaker	.1683	485	1,784,187	1999	Pat Day	.1265	254	18,092,845
1954	Bill Shoemaker	.1251	380	1,876,760	2000	Pat Day	.1219	267	17,479,838
1955	Eddie Arcaro	.820	158	1,864,796	2001	Jerry Bailey	.912	227	22,597,720

Trainers

Annual money-leading trainers since 1908, according to *The American Racing Manual.*

Multiple Leaders: D. Wayne Lukas (14); Sam Hildreth (9); Charlie Whittingham (7); Sunny Jim Fitzsimmons and Jimmy Jones (5); Bob Baffert, Laz Barrera, Ben Jones and Willie Molter (4); Hirsch Jacobs, Eddie Neloy and James Rowe Sr. (3); H. Guy Bedwell, Jack Gaver, John Schorr, Humming Bob Smith, Silent Tom Smith and Mesh Tenney (2).

Year		Wins	Earnings	Year		Wins	Earnings
1908	James Rowe Sr.	.50	$284,335	1916	Sam Hildreth	.39	$70,950
1909	Sam Hildreth	.73	123,942	1917	Sam Hildreth	.23	61,698
1910	Sam Hildreth	.84	148,010	1918	H. Guy Bedwell	.53	80,296
1911	Sam Hildreth	.67	49,418	1919	H. Guy Bedwell	.63	208,728
1912	John Schorr	.63	58,110	1920	Louis Feustel	.22	186,087
1913	James Rowe Sr.	.18	45,936	1921	Sam Hildreth	.85	262,768
1914	R.C. Benson	.45	59,315	1922	Sam Hildreth	.74	247,014
1915	James Rowe Sr.	.19	75,596	1923	Sam Hildreth	.75	392,124

Year		Wins	Earnings
1924	Sam Hildreth	77	$255,608
1925	G.R. Tompkins	30	199,245
1926	Scott Harlan	21	205,681
1927	W.H. Bringloe	63	216,563
1928	John Schorr	65	258,425
1929	James Rowe Jr.	25	314,881
1930	Sunny Jim Fitzsimmons	47	397,355
1931	Big Jim Healy	33	297,300
1932	Sunny Jim Fitzsimmons	68	266,650
1933	Humming Bob Smith	53	135,720
1934	Humming Bob Smith	43	249,938
1935	Bud Stotler	87	303,005
1936	Sunny Jim Fitzsimmons	42	193,415
1937	Robert McGarvey	46	209,925
1938	Earl Sande	15	226,495
1939	Sunny Jim Fitzsimmons	45	266,205
1940	Silent Tom Smith	14	269,200
1941	Ben Jones	70	475,318
1942	Jack Gaver	48	406,547
1943	Ben Jones	73	267,915
1944	Ben Jones	60	601,660
1945	Silent Tom Smith	52	510,655
1946	Hirsch Jacobs	99	560,077
1947	Jimmy Jones	85	1,334,805
1948	Jimmy Jones	81	1,118,670
1949	Jimmy Jones	76	978,587
1950	Preston Burch	96	637,754
1951	Jack Gaver	42	616,392
1952	Ben Jones	29	662,137
1953	Harry Trotsek	54	1,028,873
1954	Willie Molter	136	1,107,860
1955	Sunny Jim Fitzsimmons	66	1,270,055
1956	Willie Molter	142	1,227,402
1957	Jimmy Jones	70	1,150,910
1958	Willie Molter	69	1,116,544
1959	Willie Molter	71	847,290
1960	Hirsch Jacobs	97	748,349
1961	Jimmy Jones	62	759,856
1962	Mesh Tenney	58	1,099,474

Year		Sts	Wins	Earnings
1963	Mesh Tenney	192	40	$860,703
1964	Bill Winfrey	287	61	1,350,534
1965	Hirsch Jacobs	610	91	1,331,628
1966	Eddie Neloy	282	93	2,456,250
1967	Eddie Neloy	262	72	1,776,089
1968	Eddie Neloy	212	52	1,233,101
1969	Elliott Burch	156	26	1,067,936
1970	Charlie Whittingham	551	82	1,302,354
1971	Charlie Whittingham	393	77	1,737,115
1972	Charlie Whittingham	429	79	1,734,020
1973	Charlie Whittingham	423	85	1,865,385
1974	Pancho Martin	846	166	2,408,419
1975	Charlie Whittingham	487	3	2,437,244
1976	Jack Van Berg	2362	496	2,976,196
1977	Laz Barrera	781	127	2,715,848
1978	Laz Barrera	592	100	3,307,164
1979	Laz Barrera	492	98	3,608,517
1980	Laz Barrera	559	99	2,969,151
1981	Charlie Whittingham	376	74	3,993,302
1982	Charlie Whittingham	410	63	4,587,457
1983	D. Wayne Lukas	595	78	4,267,261
1984	D. Wayne Lukas	805	131	5,835,921
1985	D. Wayne Lukas	1140	218	11,155,188
1986	D. Wayne Lukas	1510	259	12,345,180
1987	D. Wayne Lukas	1735	343	17,502,110
1988	D. Wayne Lukas	1500	318	17,842,358
1989	D. Wayne Lukas	1398	305	16,103,998
1990	D. Wayne Lukas	1396	267	14,508,871
1991	D. Wayne Lukas	1497	289	15,942,223
1992	D. Wayne Lukas	1349	230	9,806,436
1993	Bobby Frankel	345	79	8,933,252
1994	D. Wayne Lukas	693	147	9,247,457
1995	D. Wayne Lukas	837	194	12,834,485
1996	D. Wayne Lukas	1006	192	15,966,344
1997	D. Wayne Lukas	824	169	9,993,569
1998	Bob Baffert	538	139	15,000,870
1999	Bob Baffert	735	169	16,934,607
2000	Bob Baffert	678	146	11,831,605
2001	Bob Baffert	660	138	16,354,996

All-Time Leaders

The all-time money-winning horses and race-winning jockeys of North America through 2001, according to the *The American Racing Manual*. Records include all available information on races in foreign countries.

Top 30 Horses—Money Won

Note that horses who raced in 2001 are in **bold** type.

		Sts	1st	2nd	3rd	Earnings
1	Cigar	33	19	4	5	$9,999,815
2	Skip Away	38	18	10	6	9,616,360
3	**Fantastic Light**	25	12	5	3	8,486,957
4	Silver Charm	24	12	7	2	6,944,369
5	**Captain Steve**	25	9	3	7	6,828,356
6	Alysheba	26	11	8	2	6,679,242
7	John Henry	83	39	15	9	6,591,860
8	**Tiznow**	15	8	4	2	6,427,830
9	Singspiel	20	9	8	0	5,952,825
10	Best Pal	47	18	11	4	5,668,245
11	Taiki Blizzard	23	6	8	2	5,523,549
12	Sunday Silence	14	9	5	0	4,968,554
13	**Jim and Tonic**	36	13	12	4	4,959,719
14	Easy Goer	20	14	5	1	4,873,770
15	Daylami	21	11	3	4	4,614,762
16	Behrens	27	9	8	3	$4,563,500
17	Unbridled	24	8	6	6	4,489,475
18	Awesome Again	12	9	0	2	4,374,590
19	Spend A Buck	15	10	3	2	4,220,689
20	Pilsudski	22	10	6	2	4,080,297
21	Broad Appeal	34	12	5	5	4,032,632
22	Creme Fraiche	64	17	12	13	4,024,727
23	Seeking the Pearl	21	8	2	3	4,021,716
24	**Point Given**	13	9	3	0	3,968,500
25	Cat Thief	30	4	9	8	3,951,012
26	Devil His Due	41	11	12	3	3,920,405
27	Sandpit	40	14	11	6	3,812,591
28	Swain	22	10	4	6	3,797,566
29	Ferdinand	29	8	9	6	3,777,978
30	Almutawakel	19	4	4	1	3,643,021

Top 30 Jockeys—Races Won

Note that jockeys active in 2001 are in **bold** type.

		Yrs	Wins	Earnings			Yrs	Wins	Earnings
1	**Laffit Pincay Jr.**	36	9277	$225,612,657	16	**Ron Ardoin**	29	5132	$57,284,881
2	Bill Shoemaker	42	8833	123,375,524	17	Jacinto Vasquez	37	5231	80,764,853
3	**Pat Day**	29	8132	255,997,761	18	Rudy Baez	25	4875	30,474,225
4	**Russell Baze**	28	7643	110,861,293	19	Eddie Arcaro	31	4779	30,039,543
5	David Gall	43	7396	24,972,821	20	**Mario Pino**	24	4778	71,223,751
6	**Chris McCarron**	28	7084	259,889,889	21	**Rick Wilson**	29	4777	73,335,913
7	Angel Cordero Jr.	35	7057	164,561,227	22	**Gary Stevens**	23	4646	202,116,805
8	Jorge Velasquez	33	6795	125,544,379	23	Don Brumfield	37	4573	43,567,861
9	Sandy Hawley	31	6449	88,681,292	24	Steve Brooks	34	4451	18,239,817
10	Larry Snyder	35	6388	47,207,289	25	**Edgar Prado**	18	4402	94,087,589
11	Carl Gambardella	39	6349	29,389,041	26	Eddie Maple	34	4398	105,338,573
12	**E. Delahoussaye**	34	6317	190,193,124	27	Walter Blum	22	4382	26,497,189
13	**Earlie Fires**	37	6177	78,038,404	28	**Anthony Black**	31	4374	44,433,928
14	John Longden	41	6032	24,665,800	29	**Craig Perret**	35	4304	107,134,501
15	**Jerry Bailey**	27	5149	218,341,153	30	Randy Romero	26	4294	75,264,198

Eclipse Awards

The Eclipse Awards, honoring the Horse of the Year and other champions of the sport, are sponsored by the National Thoroughbred Racing Association (NTRA), *Daily Racing Form* and the National Turf Writers Assn. In 1998, the NTRA replaced the Thoroughbred Racing Associations of North America as co-sponsor.

The awards are named after the 18th century racehorse and sire, Eclipse, who began racing at age five and was unbeaten in 18 starts (eight wins were walkovers). As a stallion, Eclipse sired winners of 344 races, including three Epsom Derby champions.

Horses listed in CAPITAL letters won the Triple Crown that year. Age of horse in parentheses where necessary.

Multiple winners: (horses): Forego (8); John Henry (7); Affirmed, Lonesome Glory and Secretariat (5); Cigar, Flatterer, Seattle Slew, Skip Away and Spectacular Bid (4); Ack Ack, Susan's Girl, Tiznow and Zaccio (3); All Along, Alysheba, Bayakoa, Black Tie Affair, Cafe Prince, Charismatic, Conquistador Cielo, Desert Vixen, Favorite Trick, Ferdinand, Flawlessly, Go for Wand, Holy Bull, Housebuster, Kotashaan, Lady's Secret, Life's Magic, Miesque, Morley Street, Open Mind, Paseana, Point Given, Riva Ridge, Silverbulletday, Slew o' Gold and Spend A Buck (2).

Multiple winners: (people): Laffit Pincay Jr. (6); Jerry Bailey (5); Laz Barrera, Pat Day, John Franks, D. Wayne Lukas, Allen Paulson and Frank Stronach (4); Bob Baffert, Steve Cauthen, Bobby Frankel, Harbor View Farm, Fred W. Hooper, Nelson Bunker Hunt, Juddmonte Farms, Mr. & Mrs. Gene Klein, Dan Lasater, John & Betty Mabee, Paul Mellon, Ogden Phipps, Bill Shoemaker, Edward Taylor and Charlie Whittingham (3); Braulio Baeza, C.T. Chenery, Claiborne Farm, Angel Cordero Jr., Kent Desormeaux, William S. Farish, John W. Galbreath, Chris McCarron, Bill Mott and Mike Smith (2).

Horse of the Year

Year		Year		Year		Year	
1971	Ack Ack (5)	1979	Affirmed (4)	1987	Ferdinand (4)	1995	Cigar (5)
1972	Secretariat (2)	1980	Spectacular Bid (4)	1988	Alysheba (4)	1996	Cigar (6)
1973	SECRETARIAT (3)	1981	John Henry (6)	1989	Sunday Silence (3)	1997	Favorite Trick (2)
1974	Forego (4)	1982	Conquistador Cielo (3)	1990	Criminal Type (5)	1998	Skip Away (5)
1975	Forego (5)	1983	All Along (4)	1991	Black Tie Affair (5)	1999	Charismatic (3)
1976	Forego (6)	1984	John Henry (9)	1992	A.P. Indy (3)	2000	Tiznow (3)
1977	SEATTLE SLEW (3)	1985	Spend A Buck (3)	1993	Kotashaan (5)	2001	Point Given (3)
1978	AFFIRMED (3)	1986	Lady's Secret (4)	1994	Holy Bull (3)		

Horse of the Year (1936-70)

In 1971, the *Daily Racing Form*, the Thoroughbred Racing Associations, and the National Turf Writers Assn. joined forces to create the Eclipse Awards. Before then, however, the *Racing Form* (1936-70) and the TRA (1950-70) issued separate selections for Horse of the Year. Their picks differed only four times from 1950-70 and are so noted. Horses listed in CAPITAL letters are Triple Crown winners; (f) indicates female.

Multiple winners: Kelso (5); Challedon, Native Dancer and Whirlaway (2).

Year		Year		Year		Year	
1936	Granville	1946	ASSAULT	1955	Nashua	1964	Kelso
1937	WAR ADMIRAL	1947	Armed	1956	Swaps	1965	Roman Brother (DRF)
1938	Seabiscuit	1948	CITATION	1957	Bold Ruler (DRF)		Moccasin (TRA)
1939	Challedon	1949	Capot		Dedicate (TRA)	1966	Buckpasser
1940	Challedon	1950	Hill Prince	1958	Round Table	1967	Damascus
1941	WHIRLAWAY	1951	Counterpoint	1959	Sword Dancer	1968	Dr. Fager
1942	Whirlaway	1952	One Count (DRF)	1960	Kelso	1969	Arts and Letters
1943	COUNT FLEET		Native Dancer (TRA)	1961	Kelso	1970	Fort Marcy (DRF)
1944	Twilight Tear (f)	1953	Tom Fool	1962	Kelso		Personality (TRA)
1945	Busher (f)	1954	Native Dancer	1963	Kelso		

Older Male

Year		Year		Year		Year	
1971	Ack Ack (5)	1979	Affirmed (4)	1987	Ferdinand (4)	1995	Cigar (5)
1972	Autobiography (4)	1980	Spectacular Bid (4)	1988	Alysheba (4)	1996	Cigar (6)
1973	Riva Ridge (4)	1981	John Henry (6)	1989	Blushing John (4)	1997	Skip Away (4)
1974	Forego (4)	1982	Lemhi Gold (4)	1990	Criminal Type (5)	1998	Skip Away (5)
1975	Forego (5)	1983	Bates Motel (4)	1991	Black Tie Affair (5)	1999	Victory Gallop (4)
1976	Forego (6)	1984	Slew o' Gold (4)	1992	Pleasant Tap (5)	2000	Lemon Drop Kid (4)
1977	Forego (7)	1985	Vanlandingham (4)	1993	Bertrando (4)	2001	Tiznow (4)
1978	Seattle Slew (4)	1986	Turkoman (4)	1994	The Wicked North (4)		

Older Filly or Mare

Year		Year		Year		Year	
1971	Shuvee (5)	1979	Waya (5)	1987	North Sider (5)	1995	Inside Information (4)
1972	Typecast (6)	1980	Glorious Song (4)	1988	Personal Ensign (4)	1996	Jewel Princess (4)
1973	Susan's Girl (4)	1981	Relaxing (5)	1989	Bayakoa (5)	1997	Hidden Lake (4)
1974	Desert Vixen (4)	1982	Track Robbery (6)	1990	Bayakoa (6)	1998	Escena (5)
1975	Susan's Girl (6)	1983	Amb. of Luck (4)	1991	Queena (5)	1999	Beautiful Pleasure (4)
1976	Proud Delta (4)	1984	Princess Rooney (4)	1992	Paseana (5)	2000	Riboletta (5)
1977	Cascapedia (4)	1985	Life's Magic (4)	1993	Paseana (6)	2001	Gourmet Girl (6)
1978	Late Bloomer (4)	1986	Lady's Secret (4)	1994	Sky Beauty (4)		

3-Year-Old Colt or Gelding

Year		Year		Year		Year	
1971	Canonero II	1979	Spectacular Bid	1987	Alysheba	1995	Thunder Gulch
1972	Key to the Mint	1980	Temperence Hill	1988	Risen Star	1996	Skip Away
1973	SECRETARIAT	1981	Pleasant Colony	1989	Sunday Silence	1997	Silver Charm
1974	Little Current	1982	Conquistador Cielo	1990	Unbridled	1998	Real Quiet
1975	Wajima	1983	Slew o' Gold	1991	Hansel	1999	Charismatic
1976	Bold Forbes	1984	Swale	1992	A.P. Indy	2000	Tiznow
1977	SEATTLE SLEW	1985	Spend A Buck	1993	Prairie Bayou	2001	Point Given
1978	AFFIRMED	1986	Snow Chief	1994	Holy Bull		

3-Year-Old Filly

Year		Year		Year		Year	
1971	Turkish Trousers	1979	Davona Dale	1987	Sacahuista	1995	Serena's Song
1972	Susan's Girl	1980	Genuine Risk	1988	Winning Colors	1996	Yanks Music
1973	Desert Vixen	1981	Wayward Lass	1989	Open Mind	1997	Ajina
1974	Chris Evert	1982	Christmas Past	1990	Go for Wand	1998	Banshee Breeze
1975	Ruffian	1983	Heartlight No. One	1991	Dance Smartly	1999	Silverbulletday
1976	Revidere	1984	Life's Magic	1992	Saratoga Dew	2000	Surfside
1977	Our Mims	1985	Mom's Command	1993	Hollywood Wildcat	2001	Xtra Heat
1978	Tempest Queen	1986	Tiffany Lass	1994	Heavenly Prize		

2-Year-Old Colt or Gelding

Year		Year		Year		Year	
1971	Riva Ridge	1979	Rockhill Native	1987	Forty Niner	1995	Maria's Mon
1972	Secretariat	1980	Lord Avie	1988	Easy Goer	1996	Boston Harbor
1973	Protagonist	1981	Deputy Minister	1989	Rhythm	1997	Favorite Trick
1974	Foolish Pleasure	1982	Roving Boy	1990	Fly So Free	1998	Answer Lively
1975	Honest Pleasure	1983	Devil's Bag	1991	Arazi	1999	Anees
1976	Seattle Slew	1984	Chief's Crown	1992	Gilded Time	2000	Macho Uno
1977	Affirmed	1985	Tasso	1993	Dehere	2001	Johannesburg
1978	Spectacular Bid	1986	Capote	1994	Timber Country		

2-Year-Old Filly

Year		Year		Year		Year	
1971	Numbered Account	1979	Smart Angle	1988	Open Mind	1997	Countess Diana
1972	La Prevoyante	1980	Heavenly Cause	1989	Go for Wand	1998	Silverbulletday
1973	Talking Picture	1981	Before Dawn	1990	Meadow Star	1999	Chilukki
1974	Ruffian	1982	Landaluce	1991	Pleasant Stage	2000	Caressing
1975	Dearly Precious	1983	Althea	1992	Eliza	2001	Tempera
1976	Sensational	1984	Outstandingly	1993	Phone Chatter		
1977	Lakeville Miss	1985	Family Style	1994	Flanders		
1978	(TIE) Candy Eclair	1986	Brave Raj	1995	Golden Attraction		
	& It's in the Air	1987	Epitome	1996	Storm Song		

Champion Turf Horse

Year		Year		Year		Year	
1971	Run the Gantlet (3)	1973	SECRETARIAT (3)	1975	Snow Knight (4)	1977	Johnny D (3)
1972	Cougar II (6)	1974	Dahlia (4)	1976	Youth (3)	1978	Mac Diarmida (3)

Eclipse Awards (Cont.)

Champion Male Turf Horse

Year		Year		Year		Year	
1979	Bowl Game (5)	1985	Cozzene (4)	1991	Tight Spot (4)	1997	Chief Bearhart (4)
1980	John Henry (5)	1986	Manila (3)	1992	Sky Classic (5)	1998	Buck's Boy (5)
1981	John Henry (6)	1987	Theatrical (5)	1993	Kotashaan (5)	1999	Daylami (5)
1982	Perrault (5)	1988	Sunshine Forever (3)	1994	Paradise Creek (5)	2000	Kalanisi (4)
1983	John Henry (8)	1989	Steinlen (6)	1995	Northern Spur (4)	2001	Fantastic Light (5)
1984	John Henry (9)	1990	Itsallgreektome (3)	1996	Singspiel (4)		

Champion Female Turf Horse

Year		Year		Year		Year	
1979	Trillion (5)	1985	Pebbles (4)	1991	Miss Alleged (4)	1997	Ryafan (3)
1980	Just A Game II (4)	1986	Estrapade (6)	1992	Flawlessly (4)	1998	Fiji (4)
1981	De La Rose (3)	1987	Miesque (3)	1993	Flawlessly (5)	1999	Soaring Softly (4)
1982	April Run (4)	1988	Miesque (4)	1994	Hatoof (5)	2000	Perfect Sting (4)
1983	All Along (4)	1989	Brown Bess (7)	1995	Possibly Perfect (5)	2001	Banks Hill (3)
1984	Royal Heroine (4)	1990	Laugh and Be Merry (5)	1996	Wandesta (5)		

Sprinter

Year		Year		Year		Year	
1971	Ack Ack (5)	1979	Star de Naskra (4)	1988	Gulch (4)	1997	Smoke Glacken (3)
1972	Chou Croute (4)	1980	Plugged Nickle (3)	1989	Safely Kept (3)	1998	Reraise (3)
1973	Shecky Greene (3)	1981	Guilty Conscience (5)	1990	Housebuster (3)	1999	Artax (4)
1974	Forego (4)	1982	Gold Beauty (4)	1991	Housebuster (4)	2000	Kona Gold (6)
1975	Gallant Bob (3)	1983	Chinook Pass (4)	1992	Rubiano (5)	2001	Squirtle Squirt (3)
1976	My Juliet (4)	1984	Eillo (4)	1993	Cardmania (7)		
1977	What a Summer (4)	1985	Precisionist (4)	1994	Cherokee Run (4)		
1978	(TIE) Dr. Patches (4)	1986	Smile (4)	1995	Not Surprising (4)		
	& J.O. Tobin (4)	1987	Groovy (4)	1996	Lit de Justice (6)		

Steeplechase or Hurdle Horse

Year		Year		Year		Year	
1971	Shadow Brook (7)	1979	Martie's Anger (4)	1987	Inlander (5)	1995	Lonesome Glory (7)
1972	Soothsayer (5)	1980	Zaccio (4)	1988	Jimmy Lorenzo (6)	1996	Correggio (5)
1973	Athenian Idol (5)	1981	Zaccio (5)	1989	Highland Bud (4)	1997	Lonesome Glory (9)
1974	Gran Kan (8)	1982	Zaccio (6)	1990	Morley Street (6)	1998	Flat Top (5)
1975	Life's Illusion (4)	1983	Flatterer (4)	1991	Morley Street (7)	1999	Lonesome Glory (11)
1976	Straight and True (6)	1984	Flatterer (5)	1992	Lonesome Glory (4)	2000	All Gong (6)
1977	Cafe Prince (7)	1985	Flatterer (6)	1993	Lonesome Glory (5)	2001	Pompeyo (8)
1978	Cafe Prince (8)	1986	Flatterer (7)	1994	Warm Spell (6)		

Outstanding Jockey

Year		Year		Year		Year	
1971	Laffit Pincay Jr.	1979	Laffit Pincay Jr.	1987	Pat Day	1995	Jerry Bailey
1972	Braulio Baeza	1980	Chris McCarron	1988	Jose Santos	1996	Jerry Bailey
1973	Laffit Pincay Jr.	1981	Bill Shoemaker	1989	Kent Desormeaux	1997	Jerry Bailey
1974	Laffit Pincay Jr.	1982	Angel Cordero Jr.	1990	Craig Perret	1998	Gary Stevens
1975	Braulio Baeza	1983	Angel Cordero Jr.	1991	Pat Day	1999	Jorge Chavez
1976	Sandy Hawley	1984	Pat Day	1992	Kent Desormeaux	2000	Jerry Bailey
1977	Steve Cauthen	1985	Laffit Pincay Jr.	1993	Mike Smith	2001	Jerry Bailey
1978	Darrel McHargue	1986	Pat Day	1994	Mike Smith		

Outstanding Apprentice Jockey

Year		Year		Year		Year	
1971	Gene St. Leon	1979	Cash Asmussen	1987	Kent Desormeaux	1995	Ramon B. Perez
1972	Thomas Wallis	1980	Frank Lovato Jr.	1988	Steve Capanas	1996	Neil Poznansky
1973	Steve Valdez	1981	Richard Migliore	1989	Michael Luzzi	1997	Roberto Rosado
1974	Chris McCarron	1982	Alberto Delgado	1990	Mark Johnston		& Philip Teator
1975	Jimmy Edwards	1983	Declan Murphy	1991	Mickey Walls	1998	Shaun Bridgmohan
1976	George Martens	1984	Wesley Ward	1992	Rosemary Homeister	1999	Ariel Smith
1977	Steve Cauthen	1985	Art Madrid Jr.	1993	Juan Umana	2000	Tyler Baze
1978	Ron Franklin	1986	Allen Stacy	1994	Dale Beckner	2001	Jeremy Rose

Outstanding Trainer

Year		Year		Year		Year	
1971	Charlie Whittingham	1979	Laz Barrera	1987	D. Wayne Lukas	1995	Bill Mott
1972	Lucien Laurin	1980	Bud Delp	1988	Shug McGaughey	1996	Bill Mott
1973	H. Allen Jerkens	1981	Ron McAnally	1989	Charlie Whittingham	1997	Bob Baffert
1974	Sherill Ward	1982	Charlie Whittingham	1990	Carl Nafzger	1998	Bob Baffert
1975	Steve DiMauro	1983	Woody Stephens	1991	Ron McAnally	1999	Bob Baffert
1976	Laz Barrera	1984	Jack Van Berg	1992	Ron McAnally	2000	Bobby Frankel
1977	Laz Barrera	1985	D. Wayne Lukas	1993	Bobby Frankel	2001	Bobby Frankel
1978	Laz Barrera	1986	D. Wayne Lukas	1994	D. Wayne Lukas		

Outstanding Owner

Year		Year		Year		Year	
1971	Mr. & Mrs. E.E. Fogleson	1979	Harbor View Farm	1986	Mr. & Mrs. Gene Klein	1994	John Franks
1972-73	No award	1980	Mr. & Mrs. Bertram Firestone	1987	Mr. & Mrs. Gene Klein	1995	Allen Paulson
1974	Dan Lasater	1981	Dotsam Stable	1988	Ogden Phipps	1996	Allen Paulson
1975	Dan Lasater	1982	Viola Sommer	1989	Ogden Phipps	1997	Carolyn Hine
1976	Dan Lasater	1983	John Franks	1990	Frances Genter	1998	Frank Stronach
1977	Maxwell Gluck	1984	John Franks	1991	Sam-Son Farms	1999	Frank Stronach
1978	Harbor View Farm	1985	Mr. & Mrs. Gene Klein	1992	Juddmonte Farms	2000	Frank Stronach
				1993	John Franks	2001	Richard Englander

Outstanding Breeder

Year		Year		Year		Year	
1971	Paul Mellon	1979	Claiborne Farm	1987	Nelson Bunker Hunt	1995	Juddmonte Farms
1972	C.T. Chenery	1980	Mrs. Henry Paxson	1988	Ogden Phipps	1996	Farnsworth Farms
1973	C.T. Chenery	1981	Golden Chance Farm	1989	North Ridge Farm	1997	John & Betty Mabee
1974	John W. Galbreath	1982	Fred W. Hooper	1990	Calumet Farm	1998	John & Betty Mabee
1975	Fred W. Hooper	1983	Edward P. Taylor	1991	John & Betty Mabee	1999	William S. Farish
1976	Nelson Bunker Hunt	1984	Claiborne Farm	1992	William S. Farish	2000	Frank Stronach
1977	Edward P. Taylor	1985	Nelson Bunker Hunt	1993	Allan Paulson	2001	Juddmonte Farms
1978	Harbor View Farm	1986	Paul Mellon	1994	William T. Young		

Award of Merit

Year		Year		Year		Year	
1976	Jack J. Dreyfus	1985	Keene Daingerfield	1992	Joe Hirsch & Robert P. Strub	1997	Robert & Beverly Lewis
1977	Steve Cauthen	1986	Herman Cohen	1993	Paul Mellon	1998	D.G. Van Clief Jr.
1978	Dinny Phipps	1987	J.B. Faulconer	1994	Alfred G. Vanderbilt	2000	Jim McKay
1979	Jimmy Kilroe	1988	John Forsythe	1995	Ted Bassett III	2001	Pete Pederson & Harry T. Mangurian
1980	John D. Shapiro	1989	Michael Sandler	1996	Allen Paulson		
1981	Bill Shoemaker	1990	Warner L. Jones				
1984	John Gaines	1991	Fred W. Hooper				

Special Award

Year		Year		Year		Year	
1971	Robert J. Kleberg	1985	Arlington Park	1995	Russell Baze	2001	Sheikh Mohammed al-Maktoum
1974	Charles Hatton	1987	Anheuser-Busch	1998	Oak Tree Racing Assoc.		
1976	Bill Shoemaker	1988	Edward J. DeBartolo Sr.	1999	Laffit Pincay Jr.		
1980	John T. Landry & Pierre E. Bellocq	1989	Richard Duchossois	2000	John Hettinger		
1984	C.V. Whitney	1994	Eddie Arcaro & John Longden				

HARNESS RACING

Triple Crown Winners

PACERS

Nine three-year-olds have won the Cane Pace, Little Brown Jug and Messenger Stakes in the same year since the Pacing Triple Crown was established in 1956. No trainer or driver has won it more than once.

Year		Driver	Trainer	Owner
1959	**Adios Butler**	Clint Hodgins	Paige West	Paige West & Angelo Pellillo
1965	**Bret Hanover**	Frank Ervin	Frank Ervin	Richard Downing
1966	**Romeo Hanover**	Bill Myer & George Sholty*	Jerry Silverman	Lucky Star Stables & Morton Finder
1968	**Rum Customer**	Billy Haughton	Billy Haughton	Kennilworth Farms & L.C. Mancuso
1970	**Most Happy Fella**	Stanley Dancer	Stanley Dancer	Egyptian Acres Stable
1980	**Niatross**	Clint Galbraith	Clint Galbraith	Niagara Acres, Niatross Stables & Clint Galbraith
1983	**Ralph Hanover**	Ron Waples	Stew Firlotte	Waples Stable, Pointsetta Stable, Grant's Direct Stable & P.J. Baugh
1997	**Western Dreamer**	Mike Lachance	Bill Robinson Stable	Matthew, Daniel and Patrick Daly
1999	**Blissful Hall**	Ron Pierce	Benn Wallace	Daniel Plouffe

*Myer drove Romeo Hanover in the Cane, Sholty in the other two races.

TROTTERS

Six three-year-olds have won the Yonkers Trot, Hambletonian and Kentucky Futurity in the same year since the Trotting Triple Crown was established in 1955. Stanley Dancer is the only driver/trainer to win it twice.

Year		Driver/Trainer	Owner
1955	**Scott Frost**	Joe O'Brien	S.A. Camp Farms
1963	**Speedy Scot**	Ralph Baldwin	Castleton Farms
1964	**Ayres**	John Simpson Sr.	Charlotte Sheppard
1968	**Nevele Pride**	Stanley Dancer	Nevele Acres & Lou Resnick
1969	**Lindy's Pride**	Howard Beissinger	Lindy Farms
1972	**Super Bowl**	Stanley Dancer	Rachel Dancer & Rose Hild Breeding Farm

Harness Racing (Cont.)
Triple Crown Near Misses

PACERS

Nine horses have won the first two legs of the Triple Crown, but not the third. The Cane Pace (CP), Little Brown Jug (LBJ), and Messenger Stakes (MS) have not always been run in the same order so numbers after races won indicate sequence for that year.

Year		CP	LBJ	MS
1957	**Torpid**	won, 1	won, 2	DNF*
1960	**Countess Adios**	won, 2	NE	won, 1
1971	**Albatross**	won, 2	2nd*	won, 1
1976	**Keystone Ore**	won, 1	won, 2	2nd*
1986	**Barberry Spur**	won, 1	won, 2	2nd*
1990	**Jake and Elwood**	won, 1	NE	won, 2
1992	**Western Hanover**	won, 1	2nd*	won, 2
1993	**Rijadh**	won, 1	2nd*	won, 2
1998	**Shady Character**	won, 1	won, 2	6th*

*Winning horses: Meadow Lands (1957), Nansemond (1971), Windshield Wiper (1976), Amity Chef (1986), Fake Left (1992), Life Sign (1993), Fit for Life (1998).

Note: Torpid (1957) scratched before the final heat; Countess Adios (1960) and Jake and Elwood (1990) not eligible for Little Brown Jug.

TROTTERS

Eight horses have won the first two legs of the Triple Crown—the Yonkers Trot (YT) and the Hambletonian (Ham)—but not the third. The winner of the Ky. Futurity (KF) is listed.

Year		YT	Ham	KF
1962	**A.C.'s Viking**	won	won	Safe Mission
1976	**Steve Lobell**	won	won	Quick Pay
1977	**Green Speed**	won	won	Texas
1978	**Speedy Somolli**	won	won	Doublemint
1987	**Mack Lobell**	won	won	Napoletano
1993	**American Winner**	won	won	Pine Chip
1996	**Continentalvictory**	won	won	Running Sea
1998	**Muscles Yankee**	won	won	Trade Balance

Note: Green Speed (1977) not eligible for Ky. Futurity; Continentalvictory (1996) was withdrawn from the Ky. Futurity due to a leg injury.

The Hambletonian

For three-year-old trotters. Inaugurated in 1926 and has been held in Syracuse, N.Y.; Lexington, Ky.; Goshen, N.Y.; Yonkers, N.Y.; Du Quoin, Ill.; and since 1981 at The Meadowlands in East Rutherford, N.J.

Run at one mile since 1947. Winning horse must win two heats.

Drivers with most wins: John Campbell (5); Stanley Dancer, Billy Haughton and Ben White (4); Howard Beissinger, Del Cameron, Mike Lachance and Henry Thomas (3).

Year		Driver	Fastest Heat	Year		Driver	Fastest Heat
1926	**Guy McKinney**	Nat Ray	2:04¾	1965	**Egyptian Candor**	Del Cameron	2:03⅘
1927	**Iosola's Worthy**	Marvin Childs	2:03¾	1966	**Kerry Way**	Frank Ervin	1:58⅘
1928	**Spencer**	W.H. Lessee	2:02½	1967	**Speedy Streak**	Del Cameron	2:00
1929	**Walter Dear**	Walter Cox	2:02¾	1968	**Nevele Pride**	Stanley Dancer	1:59⅖
1930	**Hanover's Bertha**	Tom Berry	2:03	1969	**Lindy's Pride**	Howard Beissinger	1:57¾
1931	**Calumet Butler**	R.D. McMahon	2:03¼	1970	**Timothy T**	John Simpson Jr.	1:58⅗
1932	**The Marchioness**	Will Caton	2:01¼	1971	**Speedy Crown**	Howard Beissinger	1:57⅖
1933	**Mary Reynolds**	Ben White	2:03¾	1972	**Super Bowl**	Stanley Dancer	1:56⅖
1934	**Lord Jim**	Doc Parshall	2:02¾	1973	**Flirth**	Ralph Baldwin	1:57⅕
1935	**Greyhound**	Sep Palin	2:02¼	1974	**Christopher T**	Billy Haughton	1:58⅗
1936	**Rosalind**	Ben White	2:01¾	1975	**Bonefish**	Stanley Dancer	1:59
1937	**Shirley Hanover**	Henry Thomas	2:01½	1976	**Steve Lobell**	Billy Haughton	1:56⅖
1938	**McLin Hanover**	Henry Tomas	2:02¼	1977	**Green Speed**	Billy Haughton	1:55⅗
1939	**Peter Astra**	Doc Parshall	2:04¼	1978	**Speedy Somolli**	Howard Beissinger	1:55
1940	**Spencer Scott**	Fred Egan	2:02	1979	**Legend Hanover**	George Sholty	1:56⅕
1941	**Bill Gallon**	Lee Smith	2:05	1980	**Burgomeister**	Billy Haughton	1:56⅗
1942	**The Ambassador**	Ben White	2:04	1981	**Shiavay St. Pat**	Ray Remmen	2:01⅕
1943	**Volo Song**	Ben White	2:02½	1982	**Speed Bowl**	Tommy Haughton	1:56⅘
1944	**Yankee Maid**	Henry Thomas	2:04	1983	**Duenna**	Stanley Dancer	1:57⅖
1945	**Titan Hanover**	Harry Pownall Sr.	2:04	1984	**Historic Freight**	Ben Webster	1:56⅖
1946	**Chestertown**	Thomas Berry	2:02½	1985	**Prakas**	Bill O'Donnell	1:54⅘
1947	**Hoot Mon**	Sep Palin	2:00	1986	**Nuclear Kosmos**	Ulf Thoresen	1:55⅖
1948	**Demon Hanover**	Harrison Hoyt	2:02	1987	**Mack Lobell**	John Campbell	1:53⅖
1949	**Miss Tilly**	Fred Egan	2:01⅖	1988	**Armbro Goal**	John Campbell	1:54⅖
1950	**Lusty Song**	Del Miller	2:02	1989	**Park Avenue Joe**	Ron Waples	1:54⅗
1951	**Mainliner**	Guy Crippen	2:02⅗		**& Probe ***	Bill Fahy	
1952	**Sharp Note**	Bion Shively	2:02⅗	1990	**Harmonious**	John Campbell	1:54⅕
1953	**Helicopter**	Harry Harvey	2:01⅗	1991	**Giant Victory**	Jack Moiseyev	1:54⅘
1954	**Newport Dream**	Del Cameron	2:02⅖	1992	**Alf Palema**	Mickey McNichol	1:56⅖
1955	**Scott Frost**	Joe O'Brien	2:00⅗	1993	**American Winner**	Ron Pierce	1:53⅕
1956	**The Intruder**	Ned Bower	2:01⅖	1994	**Victory Dream**	Mike Lachance	1:54⅕
1957	**Hickory Smoke**	John Simpson Sr.	2:00⅕	1995	**Tagliabue**	John Campbell	1:54⅘
1958	**Emily's Pride**	Flave Nipe	1:59⅘	1996	**Continentalvictory**	Mike Lachance	1:52⅘
1959	**Diller Hanover**	Frank Ervin	2:01⅕	1997	**Malabar Man**	Mal Burroughs	1:55
1960	**Blaze Hanover**	Joe O'Brien	1:59⅗	1998	**Muscles Yankee**	John Campbell	1:52⅘
1961	**Harlan Dean**	James Arthur	1:58⅖	1999	**Self Possessed**	Mike Lachance	1:51⅗
1962	**A.C.'s Viking**	Sanders Russell	1:59⅗	2000	**Yankee Paco**	Trevor Ritchie	1:53⅖
1963	**Speedy Scot**	Ralph Baldwin	1:57⅗	2001	**Scarlet Knight**	Stefan Melander	1:53⅘
1964	**Ayres**	John Simpson Sr.	1:56⅘	2002	**Chip Chip Hooray**	Eric Ledford	1:53⅗

*In 1989, Park Avenue Joe and Probe finished in a dead heat in the race-off. They were later declared co-winners, but Park Avenue Joe was awarded 1st place money because his three-race summary (2-1-1) was better than Probe's (1-9-1).

The Little Brown Jug

Harness racing's most prestigious race for three-year-old pacers. Inaugurated in 1946 and held annually at the Delaware, Ohio County Fairgrounds. Winning horse must win two heats.

Drivers with most wins: Billy Haughton and Mike Lachance (5); Stanley Dancer (4); John Campbell, Frank Ervin and John Simpson Sr. (3); Adelbert Cameron, Herve Filion, Jack Moiseyev, Joe O'Brien, Bill O'Donnell, Ron Pierce, "Curly" Smart and Ron Waples (2).

Year		Driver	Fastest Heat	Year		Driver	Fastest Heat
1946	Ensign Hanover	"Curly" Smart	2:02	1975	Seatrain	Ben Webster	1:56⅘
1947	Forbes Chief	Adelbert Cameron	2:05	1976	Keystone Ore	Stanley Dancer	1:56⅘
1948	Knight Dream	Frank Safford	2:07	1977	Governor Skipper	John Chapman	1:56⅕
1949	Good Time	Frank Ervin	2:03⅖	1978	Happy Escort	Bill Popfinger	1:55⅖
				1979	Hot Hitter	Herve Filion	1:55⅗
1950	Dudley Hanover	Delvin Miller	2:02⅗				
1951	Tar Heel	Adelbert Cameron	2:00	1980	Niatross	Clint Galbraith	1:54⅘
1952	Meadow Rice	"Curly" Smart	2:01⅗	1981	Fan Hanover (f)	Glen Garnsey	1:56
1953	Keystoner	Frank Ervin	2:02⅕	1982	Merger	John Campbell	1:54⅗
1954	Adios Harry	Morris MacDonald	2:02⅖	1983	Ralph Hanover	Ron Waples	1:55⅗
1955	Quick Chief	Billy Haughton	2:00	1984	Colt Fortysix	Chris Boring	1:53⅗
1956	Noble Adios	John Simpson Sr.	2:00⅘	1985	Nihilator	Bill O'Donnell	1:52⅕
1957	Torpid	John Simpson Sr.	2:00⅘	1986	Barberry Spur	Bill O'Donnell	1:52⅘
1958	Shadow Wave	Joe O'Brien	2:01	1987	Jaguar Spur	Dick Stillings	1:54
1959	Adios Butler	Clint Hodgkins	1:59⅖	1988	B.J. Scoot	Mike Lachance	1:52⅗
				1989	Goalie Jeff	Mike Lachance	1:54⅕
1960	Bullet Hanover	John Simpson Sr.	1:58⅗				
1961	Henry T. Adios	Stanley Dancer	1:58⅘	1990	Beach Towel	Ray Remmen	1:53⅗
1962	Lehigh Hanover	Stanley Dancer	1:58⅘	1991	Precious Bunny	Jack Moiseyev	1:53⅘
1963	Overtrick	John Patterson Sr.	1:57⅕	1992	Fake Left	Ron Waples	1:53⅗
1964	Vicar Hanover	Billy Haughton	2:00⅘	1993	Life Sign	John Campbell	1:52
1965	Bret Hanover	Frank Ervin	1:57	1994	Magical Mike	Mike Lachance	1:52⅗
1966	Romeo Hanover	George Sholty	1:59⅗	1995	Nick's Fantasy	John Campbell	1:51⅖
1967	Best Of All	Jim Hackett	1:59	1996	Armbro Operative	Jack Moiseyev	1:52⅗
1968	Rum Customer	Billy Haughton	1:59⅗	1997	Western Dreamer	Mike Lachance	1:51⅕
1969	Laverne Hanover	Billy Haughton	2:00⅖	1998	Shady Character	Ron Pierce	1:52⅗
				1999	Blissfull Hall	Ron Pierce	1:55⅗
1970	Most Happy Fella	Stanley Dancer	1:57⅕				
1971	Nansemond	Herve Filion	1:57⅖	2000	Astreos	Chris Christoforou	1:55⅗
1972	Strike Out	Keith Waples	1:56⅗	2001	Bettor's Delight	Mike Lachance	1:51⅘
1973	Melvin's Woe	Joe O'Brien	1:57⅗	2002	Million Dollar Cam	Luc Ouellette	1:50⅖
1974	Armbro Omaha	Billy Haughton	1:57				

All-Time Leaders

The all-time winning trotters, pacers and drivers through 2001, according to *The Trotting and Pacing Guide*. Purses for horses include races in foreign countries. Earnings and wins for drivers include only races held in North America.

Top 10 Horses—Money Won

		T/P	Sts	1st	Earnings
1	Moni Maker	T	91	60	$5,589,256
2	Varenne	T	N/A	47	4,245,141
3	Peace Corps	T	42	35	4,137,737
4	Ourasi (FRA)	T	N/A	32	4,010,105
5	Mack Lobell	T	86	65	3,917,594
6	Gallo Blue Chip	P	56	37	3,704,111
7	Reve d'Udon	T	23	18	3,611,351
8	Zoogin	T	N/A	N/A	3,513,324
9	Nihilator	P	38	35	3,225,653
10	Sea Cove	T	N/A	N/A	3,138,986

Top 10 Drivers—Races Won

		Yrs	1st	Earnings
1	Herve Filion	35	14,783	$85,044,653
2	Walter Case Jr.	24	10,119	40,372,205
3	Cat Manzi	34	9,235	83,785,547
4	Mike Lachance	34	9,042	139,391,026
5	Dave Magee	29	8,940	68,708,010
6	John Campbell	30	8,824	201,811,667
7	Dave Palone	20	8,233	33,831,394
8	Jack Moiseyev	26	8,090	84,861,238
9	Eddie Davis	38	7,836	42,619,078
10	Bill (Zeke) Parker Jr.	31	7,697	18,431,822

Annual Awards

Harness Horse of the Year

Selected since 1947 by U.S. Trotting Association and the U.S. Harness Writers Association; age of winning horse is noted; (t) indicates trotter and (p) indicates pacer.

Multiple winners: Bret Hanover and Nevele Pride (3); Adios Butler, Albatross, Cam Fella, Good Time, Mack Lobell, Moni Maker, Niatross and Scott Frost (2).

Year		Year		Year		Year	
1947	Victory Song (4t)	1952	Good Time (6p)	1958	Emily's Pride (3t)	1963	Speedy Scot (3t)
1948	Rodney (4t)	1953	Hi Lo's Forbes (5p)	1959	Bye Bye Byrd (4p)	1964	Bret Hanover (2p)
1949	Good Time (3p)	1954	Stenographer (3t)			1965	Bret Hanover (3p)
		1955	Scott Frost (3t)	1960	Adios Butler (4p)	1966	Bret Hanover (4p)
1950	Proximity (8t)	1956	Scott Frost (4t)	1961	Adios Butler (5p)	1967	Nevele Pride (2t)
1951	Pronto Don (6t)	1957	Torpid (3p)	1962	Su Mac Lad (8t)	1968	Nevele Pride (3t)

Annual Awards (Cont.)

Year		Year		Year		Year	
1969	Nevele Pride (4t)	1978	Abercrombie (3p)	1987	Mack Lobell (3t)	1996	Continentalvictory (3t)
1970	Fresh Yankee (7t)	1979	Niatross (2p)	1988	Mack Lobell (4t)	1997	Malabar Man (3t)
1971	Albatross (3p)	1980	Niatross (3p)	1989	Matt's Scooter (4p)	1998	Moni Maker (5t)
1972	Albatross (4p)	1981	Fan Hanover (3p)	1990	Beach Towel (3p)	1999	Moni Maker (6t)
1973	Sir Dalrae (4p)	1982	Cam Fella (3p)	1991	Precious Bunny (3p)		
1974	Delmonica Hanover (5t)	1983	Cam Fella (4p)	1992	Artsplace (4p)	2000	Gallo Blue Chip (3p)
1975	Savoir (7t)	1984	Fancy Crown (3t)	1993	Staying Together (4p)	2001	Bunny Lake (3p)
1976	Keystone Ore (3p)	1985	Nihilator (3p)	1994	Cam's Card Shark (3p)		
1977	Green Speed (3t)	1986	Forrest Skipper (4p)	1995	CR Kay Suzie (3t)		

Driver of the Year

Determined by Universal Driving Rating System (UDR) and presented by the Harness Tracks of America since 1968. Eligible drivers must have at least 1,000 starts for the season.

Multiple winners: Herve Filion (10); John Campbell, Walter Case Jr. and Mike Lachance (3); Tony Morgan, Bill O'Donnell, Luc Ouellette, Dave Palone and Ron Waples (2).

Year		Year		Year		Year	
1968	Stanley Dancer	1977	Donald Dancer	1985	Mike Lachance	1994	Dave Magee
1969	Herve Filion	1978	Carmine Abbatiello	1986	Mike Lachance	1995	Luc Ouellette
1970	Herve Filion		& Herve Filion	1987	Mike Lachance	1996	Tony Morgan
1971	Herve Filion	1979	Ron Waples	1988	John Campbell		& Luc Ouellette
1972	Herve Filion	1980	Ron Waples	1989	Herve Filion	1997	Tony Morgan
1973	Herve Filion	1981	Herve Filion			1998	Walter Case Jr.
1974	Herve Filion	1982	Bill O'Donnell	1990	John Campbell	1999	Dave Palone
1975	Joe O'Brien	1983	John Campbell	1991	Walter Case Jr.		
1976	Herve Filion	1984	Bill O'Donnell	1992	Walter Case Jr.	2000	Dave Palone
				1993	Jack Moiseyev	2001	Stephane Bouchard

STEEPLECHASE RACING

Champion Horses

Annual horse of the year since 1956 based on vote of the National Turf Writers Association and other selected media.

Multiple winners: Lonesome Glory (5); Flatterer (4); Bon Nouvel and Zaccio (3); Café Prince, Morley Street and Neji (2).

Year		Year		Year		Year	
1956	Shipboard	1968	Bon Nouvel	1979	Martie's Anger	1990	Morley Street
1957	Neji	1969	L'Escargot	1980	Zaccio	1991	Morley Street
1958	Neji	1970	Top Bid	1981	Zaccio	1992	Lonesome Glory
1959	Ancestor	1971	Shadow Brok	1982	Zaccio	1993	Lonesome Glory
1960	Benguala	1972	Soothsayer	1983	Flatterer	1994	Warm Spell
1961	Peal	1973	Athenian Idol	1984	Flatterer	1995	Lonesome Glory
1962	Barnaby's Bluff	1974	Gran Kan	1985	Flatterer	1996	Correggio
1963	Amber Diver	1975	Life's Illusion	1986	Flatterer	1997	Lonesome Glory
1964	Bon Nouvel	1976	Fire Control	1987	Inlander	1998	Flat Top
1965	Bon Nouvel		& Straight and True	1988	Jimmy Lorenzo	1999	Lonesome Glory
1966	Tuscalee & Mako	1977	Café Prince	1989	Highland Bud		
1967	Quick Pitch	1978	Café Prince			2000	All Gong
						2001	Pompeyo

Champion Jockeys

Annual leading jockeys by races won since 1956, according to the National Steeplechase Association.

Multiple winners: Joe Aitcheson Jr. (7); Jerry Fishback (5); John Cushman and Alfred P. Smithwick (4); Tom Skiffington and Jeff Teter (3); Gus Brown, Ricky Hendriks, Jonathan Kiser, James Lawrence, Blythe Miller, Chip Miller and Thomas Walsh (2).

Year		Year		Year		Year	
1956	Alfred P. Smithwick	1968	Joe Aitcheson Jr.	1980	John Cushman	1992	Craig Thornton
1957	Alfred P. Smithwick	1969	Joe Aitcheson Jr.	1981	John Cushman	1993	James Lawrence
1958	Alfred P. Smithwick	1970	Joe Aitcheson Jr.	1982	John Cushman	1994	Blythe Miller
1959	James Murphy	1971	Jerry Fishback	1983	John Cushman	1995	Blythe Miller
1960	Thomas Walsh	1972	Michael O'Brien	1984	Jeff Teter	1996	Chip Miller
1961	Joe Aitcheson Jr.	1973	Jerry Fishback	1985	Bernie Houghton	1997	Arch Kingsley Jr.
1962	Alfred P. Smithwick	1974	Jerry Fishback	1986	Ricky Hendriks		& Jonathan Kiser
1963	Joe Aitcheson Jr.	1975	Jerry Fishback	1987	Ricky Hendriks	1998	Chip Miller
1964	Joe Aitcheson Jr.	1976	Tom Skiffington	1988	Jonathan Smart		& Sean Clancy
1965	Doug Small Jr.	1977	Jerry Fishback	1989	James Lawrence	1999	Jonathan Kiser
1966	Thomas Walsh	1978	Tom Skiffington				
1967	Joe Aitcheson Jr.	1979	Tom Skiffington	1990	Jeff Teter	2000	Gus Brown
				1991	Jeff Teter	2001	Gus Brown

Tennis

*Pete **Sampras*** *and **Andre Agassi*** *gave the crowd a charge at the 2002 U.S. Open.*

AP/Wide World Photos

All in the Family

Both Williams sisters ruled the courts in 2002, but younger Serena truly stole the show.

Michael Morrison is co-editor of the ESPN/Information Please Sports Almanac.

Several years ago, Richard Williams predicted his then teenage daughters Serena and Venus would eventually face each other in the finals at Wimbledon. He also predicted they'd be ranked Nos. 1 and 2 in the world. Some agreed. More than a few thought he was a little crazy.

While plenty of people still believe he might just be a little crazy, claiming among other things that he orchestrates which one of his daughters will win when the two square off, no one can deny his knack for prognostication. And no one can deny the overwhelming confidence he shows in his daughters, or the amount of love and respect his daughters have for him.

In 2001 it was Venus' time to shine with singles titles at Wimbledon and the U.S. Open, the latter a 6–2, 6–4 whipping of Serena. But if 2001 was to Richard's liking, 2002 must have made him euphoric.

As he had predicted, Serena and Venus ended the year head and shoulders above every other female tennis player in the world. And the icing on the cake? The dynamic duo faced off in the Wimbledon finals. In fact, three of the four Grand Slam singles finals featured Serena versus Venus, and in each one of them, younger Serena came out on top.

She is the first person, male or female, to win three consecutive Grand Slam singles titles since Martina Hingis in 1997–98. Had she not sprained her ankle and withdrawn mere hours before her first match at the Australian Open, she may have become the first Grand Slam winner (four majors in one season) since Steffi Graf in 1988. A 2003 Australian Open title would make her the champion of all four Grand Slam events simultaneously, something the cocky 20-year-old has dubbed the "Serena Slam."

AP/Wide World Photos

Serena Williams' game in 2002 was as tight as her some of her outfits. She won three consecutive Grand Slam titles in the same year for the first time since Steffi Graf in 1996.

In addition to surpassing her sister in competition, Serena also seemed to overtake Venus as the fashion queen of the Tour. At the 2001 Australian Open it was Venus who made heads turn with her low-cut, revealing, blue and black bra-shirt combo thingy. At the 2002 U.S. Open, it was blonde-haired Serena who had the tabloids talking with her clingy, black Lycra cat suit.

But in the end it wasn't her clothes that boosted Serena over her sister and the rest of the WTA Tour, it was her phenomenal athleticism and her amazingly accurate 100-plus mph serve.

As you might expect, not everyone shares Richard's joy that it's seemingly become the Williams sisters in one tier and everyone else in another. Amelie Mauresmo said of the Williams domination, "I think people are getting to be bored of always seeing the same final."

Former champ Gabriela Sabatini recently summed it up, telling *The Mail* newspaper, "Perhaps they hit the ball too hard for the good of the game. Unless other players are motivated to fight, the game could start to be boring."

Speaking of boring, the 2002 men's tour was slogging along as it had the past couple of years, trailing behind the

AP/Wide World Photos

Lleyton Hewitt, *the world's top-ranked men's player, did a whole lot of fist pumping in 2002. He defeated David Nalbandian in the Wimbledon finals for his second career Grand Slam title.*

women in terms of popularity. While the women's tour featured several recognizable stars, the men's tour had to make do with relative unknowns. Thomas Johansson, Albert Costa and Lleyton Hewitt won the first three major tournaments of the year. Taking nothing away from their achievements and their immense talents, they just don't have the star power of the women's tour—in the U.S. anyway.

Blame it on the brand of tennis. Blame it on player parity. Blame it on the lack of cat suits. Whatever you like. The fact remains, at Wimbledon in 2002, NBC's rating for the women's doubles final (won by the Williams sisters) easily outdistanced the rating for the men's singles final (Hewitt over David Nalbandian).

What the men's tour needed was a jumpstart. And they got it at the 2002 U.S. Open. American tennis icons Pete Sampras, 31, and Andre Agassi, 32, each supposedly in the twilights of their career, faced off in the finals of a Grand Slam event for what could be the final time.

continued on page 808 ▶

The Ten Biggest Stories
of the Year in Tennis

10 ▪ Australian Ryan Henry and Clement Morel of France wage an epic battle in the second round of the Wimbledon junior tournament, with the final set reaching a Wimbledon singles record 50 games. With the crowd shouting, "Stop the agony," Henry finally emerges victorious, 7–5, 6–7, 26–24.

9 ▪ On the heels of their first-ever Davis Cup win in 2000, Juan Carlos Ferrero, Carlos Moya and Albert Costa spearhead a Spanish invasion into the top ten of the ATP points race. Costa and Ferrero make it an all-Spanish French Open final in 2002.

8 ▪ Corina Morariu makes an emotional comeback to the WTA Tour after missing a year and a half due to leukemia. She has the misfortune of drawing Serena Williams in the first round of the U.S. Open, but her valiant return to the court is still a victory.

7 ▪ Jennifer Capriati successfully defends her Australian Open title with a stirring finals win over Martina Hingis. She battles back from a Grand Slam finals record four match points.

6 ▪ Controversy hits the U.S. Fed Cup team when captain Billie Jean King kicks ace Jennifer Capriati off the team for violating team policy by scheduling a private practice session. The top-seeded U.S. team is subsequently ousted from the tournament in the first round.

5 ▪ Politics takes a back seat as the doubles team of Israeli Amir Hadad and Pakistani Muslim Aisam-ul-Haq Qureshi advances to the third round of Wimbledon and second round of the U.S. Open. The government of Pakistan threatens to bar Qureshi from returning to the country, but later rescinds.

4 ▪ Australian Lleyton Hewitt becomes the youngest player in the history of the ATP Tour to finish the season (2001) ranked No. 1. He follows that up with a straight-set win at Wimbledon in 2002 for his second major victory.

3 ▪ It seems the only player that can beat Venus Williams in 2002 is her sister, Serena. The elder Venus advances to the finals of three Grand Slam events and wins seven events through September.

2 ▪ Friendly rivals Pete Sampras and Andre Agassi give the ATP a much-needed shot in the arm, advancing to the finals of the U.S. Open. After losing in the finals the prior two years, Sampras finally breaks through with his 14th Grand Slam victory.

1 ▪ Serena Williams grabs the world's top ranking from sister, Venus, and wins the last three Grand Slam events of the year, defeating Venus in the finals of each. The unstoppable Williams sisters have now won eight of the last 13 Grand Slam tournaments.

Agassi was ranked No. 6 entering the match. Sampras was ranked No. 17 and hadn't won a tournament since his Wimbledon title in 2000. But there's something about Flushing Meadows that brings out Sampras' "A" game. When he put the finishing touches on his 6–3, 6–4, 5–7, 6–4 masterpiece, Sampras had his fourteenth major win and had become the oldest U.S. Open champ since Ken Rosewall (35) in 1970.

The match also drew the highest TV ratings since Sampras and Agassi battled for the 1990 U.S. Open title. For the ATP Tour, it may have been just what the doctor ordered.

Young Guns

In 2001, Australian phenom Lleyton Hewitt became the youngest player in the history of the ATP rankings to end the year ranked No. 1 in the world. Listed are the top-five youngest of all-time.

	Year	Age
Lleyton Hewitt	2001	20 yrs, 10 mos
Jimmy Connors	1974	22 yrs, 3 mos
Jim Courier	1992	22 yrs, 4 mos
Pete Sampras	1993	22 yrs, 4 mos
John McEnroe	1981	22 yrs, 10 mos

Sibling Rivalry

As the list below indicates, two sisters have met in the finals of a Grand Slam singles event just five times since 1884.

Year	Tourn.	
1884	Wim.	M. Watson def. L. Watson
2001	U.S.	V. Williams def. S. Williams
2002	French	S. Williams def. V. Williams
2002	Wim.	S. Williams def. V. Williams
2002	U.S.	S. Williams def. V. Williams

Bombs Away

Great Britain's Greg Rusedski still holds the record for fastest serve ever recorded on the ATP Tour. Listed below are the top-five fastest.

	MPH	Year
Greg Rusedski, GBR	149	1998
Taylor Dent, USA	144	2001
Andy Roddick, USA	144	2002
Mark Philippoussis, AUS	142	1997
Andy Roddick, USA	141	2001

The Battle Rages On

When Pete Sampras and Andre Agassi met in the finals of the 2002 U.S. Open, it marked the 34th time the two have faced each other in competition. In most categories, Sampras has the edge.

Overall Record	Sampras, 20-14
Clay	Agassi, 3-2
Grass	Sampras, 2-0
Hardcourt	Sampras, 11-9
Carpet	Sampras, 5-2
Tournament Finals	Sampras, 8-7

2001-2002
Season in Review

ESPN Information Please®
SPORTS ALMANAC

Tournament Results

Winners of men's and women's pro singles championships from Nov. 4, 2001 through Sept. 29, 2002.

Men's ATP Tour

LATE 2001

Finals	Tournament	Winner	Earnings	Runner-Up	Score
Nov. 4	TMS—Paris	Sebastien Grosjean	$434,000	Y. Kafelnikov	76 61 67 64
Nov. 11	ATP World Doubles Champs (Bangalore)	cancelled			
Nov. 18	Tennis Masters Cup (Sydney)	Lleyton Hewitt	1,520,000	S. Grosjean	63 63 64
Dec. 2	Davis Cup Final (Melbourne)	France	—	Australia	3-2

Note: The ATP Tour cancelled the World Doubles Championships, which were to be held in Bangalore, India, citing security concerns.

2002

Finals	Tournament	Winner	Earnings	Runner-Up	Score
Jan. 6	AAPT Championships (Adelaide)	Tim Henman	$45,500	M. Philippoussis	64 67 63
Jan. 6	Qatar Open (Doha)	Younes El Aynaoui	133,000	F. Mantilla	46 62 62
Jan. 6	Tata Open (Chennai)	Guillermo Canas	51,500	P. Srichaphan	64 76
Jan. 12	adidas International (Sydney)	Roger Federer	45,500	J.I. Chela	63 63
Jan. 12	Heineken Open (Auckland)	Greg Rusedski	45,500	J. Golmard	67 64 75
Jan. 27	**Australian Open** (Melbourne)	Thomas Johansson	520,000	M. Safin	36 64 64 76
Feb. 3	Milan Indoors	Davide Sanguinetti	48,850	R. Federer	76 46 61
Feb. 17	Marseille Open	Thomas Enqvist	61,500	N. Escude	67 63 61
Feb. 17	Copenhagen Open	Lars Burgsmuller	48,850	O. Rochus	63 63
Feb. 17	BellSouth Open (Vina Del Mar)	Fernando Gonzalez	48,850	N. Lapentti	63 67 76
Feb. 24	Kroger St. Jude (Memphis)	Andy Roddick	130,000	J. Blake	64 36 75
Feb. 24	ABN/AMRO World Tennis Tournament (Rotterdam)	Nicolas Escude	128,400	T. Henman	36 76 64
Feb. 24	AT&T Cup (Buenos Aires)	Nicolas Massu	55,000	A. Calleri	26 76 62
Mar. 3	Mexican Open (Acapulco)	Carlos Moya	126,000	F. Meligeni	76 76
Mar. 3	Dubai Open	Fabrice Santoro	162,100	Y. El Aynaoui	64 36 63
Mar. 10	Franklin Templeton Classic (Scottsdale)	Andre Agassi	51,500	J. Balcells	62 76
Mar. 17	TMS—Indian Wells	Lleyton Hewitt	392,000	T. Henman	61 62
Mar. 31	TMS—Miami	Andre Agassi	456,000	R. Federer	63 63 36 64
Apr. 14	Estoril Open	David Nalbandian	68,300	J. Nieminen	64 76
Apr. 14	Grand Prix Hassan II (Casablanca)	Younes El Aynaoui	48,850	G. Canas	36 63 62
Apr. 21	TMS—Monte Carlo	Juan Carlos Ferrero	372,000	C. Moya	75 63 64
Apr. 28	Open Seat Godo (Barcelona)	Gaston Gaudio	136,000	A. Costa	64 60 62
Apr. 28	U.S. Claycourt Championships (Houston)	Andy Roddick	51,000	P. Sampras	76 63
May 5	BMW Open (Munich)	Younes El Aynaoui	48,850	R. Schuettler	64 64
May 5	Mallorca Open	Gaston Gaudio	48,850	J. Nieminen	62 63
May 12	TMS—Rome	Andre Agassi	372,000	T. Haas	63 63 60
May 19	TMS—Hamburg	Roger Federer	372,000	M. Safin	61 63 64
May 25	ATP World Team Championship (Dusseldorf)	Argentina	500,000	Russia	3-0
May 25	International Raiffeisen Grand Prix (St. Poelten)	Nicolas Lapentti	48,850	F. Vicente	75 64
June 9	**French Open** (Paris)	Albert Costa	737,216	J.C. Ferrero	61 60 46 63
June 16	Gerry Weber Open (Halle)	Yevgeny Kafelnikov	100,500	N. Kiefer	26 64 64
June 16	Stella Artois Championships (London)	Lleyton Hewitt	84,200	T. Henman	46 61 64
June 23	Ordina Open (s'Hertogenbosch)	Sjeng Schalken	48,850	A. Clement	36, 63, 62
June 23	Nottingham Open	Jonas Bjorkman	48,850	W. Arthurs	62 67 62
July 7	**Wimbledon** (London)	Lleyton Hewitt	798,000	D. Nalbandian	61 63 62
July 14	Swedish Open (Bastad)	Carlos Moya	48,850	Y. El Aynaoui	63 26 75
July 14	Gstaad Open	Alex Corretja	78,450	G. Gaudio	63 76(3) 76(3)
July 14	Hall of Fame Championships (Newport)	Taylor Dent	51,500	J. Blake	61 46 64
July 21	Mercedes Cup (Stuttgart)	Mikhail Youzhny	64,850	G. Canas	63 36 36 64 64
July 21	Energis Open (Amersfoort)	Juan Ignacio Chela	48,850	A. Costa	61 76(4)
July 21	Croatian Open (Umag)	Carlos Moya	48,850	D. Ferrer	62 63
July 28	Generali Open (Kitzbuhel)	Alex Corretja	141,700	J.C. Ferrero	64 61 63

Tournament Results (Cont.)

Finals	Tournament	Winner	Earnings	Runner-Up	Score
July 28	Idea Prokom Open (Sopot)	Jose Acasuso	$48,850	F. Squillari	26 61 63
July 28	Mercedes-Benz Cup (Los Angeles)	Andre Agassi	51,500	J. Gambill	62 64
Aug. 4	TMS—Toronto	Guillermo Canas	392,000	A. Roddick	64 75
Aug. 11	TMS—Cincinnati	Carlos Moya	392,000	L. Hewitt	75 76
Aug. 18	RCA Championships (Indianapolis)	Greg Rusedski	111,600	F. Mantilla	67 64 64
Aug. 18	Legg Mason Classic (Washington D.C.)	James Blake	111,600	P. Srichaphan	16 76 64
Aug. 25	TD Waterhouse Cup (Commack)	Paradorn Srichapan	51,500	J.I. Chella	57 62 62
Sept. 8	**U.S. Open** (Flushing)	Pete Sampras	900,000	A. Agassi	63 64 57 64
Sept. 14	President's Cup (Tashkent)	Yevgeny Kafelnikov	42,000	V. Voltchkov	76 75
Sept. 15	Romanian Open (Bucharest)	David Ferrer	356,000	J. Acasuso	63 62
Sept. 15	Brazil Open (Salvador)	Gustavo Kuerten	74,500	G. Coria	67 75 76
Sept. 29	Salem Open (Hong Kong)	Juan Carlos Ferrero	51,500	C. Moya	63 16 76
Sept. 29	International Championship of Sicily (Palermo)	Fernando Gonzalez	48,850	J. Acasuso	57 63 61

Note: In 2000, the ATP Tour replaced the prestigious Mercedes Super 9 and the ATP Championship tournaments with the Tennis Masters Series and the Tennis Masters Cup. Tennis Masters Series tournaments are identified by TMS.

Women's WTA Tour

LATE 2001

Finals	Tournament	Winner	Earnings	Runner-Up	Score
Nov. 4	Tour Championship (Munich)	Serena Williams	$750,000	L. Davenport	walkover*
Nov. 11	Volvo Open (Pattaya City)	Patty Schnyder	16,000	H. Nagova	60 64
Nov. 11	Fed Cup Final	Belgium	—	Russia	2-1

*The final match of the Sanex Tour Championship on Nov. 4 was cancelled after Lindsay Davenport withdrew due to a knee injury.

2002

Finals	Tournament	Winner	Earnings	Runner-Up	Score
Jan. 6	Australian Hardcourt Champs (Gold Coast)	Venus Williams	$27,000	J. Henin	75 62
Jan. 6	ASB Bank Classic (Auckland)	Anna Smashnova	22,000	T. Panova	62 62
Jan. 12	adidas International (Sydney)	Martina Hingis	93,000	M. Shaughnessy	62 63
Jan. 12	ANZ Tasmanian Int'l (Hobart)	Martina Sucha	16,000	A. Garrigues	76 61
Jan. 12	Canberra International	Anna Smashnova	16,000	T. Tanasugarn	75 62
Jan. 27	**Australian Open** (Melbourne)	Jennifer Capriati	516,000	M. Hingis	46 76 62
Feb. 3	Pan Pacific Open (Tokyo)	Martina Hingis	182,000	M. Seles	76 46 63
Feb. 10	Open Gaz de France (Paris)	Venus Williams	93,000	J. Dokic	walkover*
Feb. 17	Proximus Diamond Games (Antwerp)	Venus Williams	93,000	J. Henin	63 57 63
Feb. 17	Qatar Open (Doha)	Monica Seles	27,000	T. Tanasugarn	76 63
Feb. 23	Dubai Open	Amelie Mauresmo	93,000	S. Testud	64 76
Feb. 24	Kroger St. Jude (Memphis)	Lisa Raymond	27,000	A. Stevenson	46 63 76
Feb. 24	Copa Colsanitas (Bogota)	Fabiola Zuluaga	27,000	K. Srebotnik	61 64
Mar. 3	State Farm Tennis Classic (Scottsdale)	Serena Williams	93,000	J. Capriati	62 46 64
Mar. 16	TMS—Indian Wells	Daniela Hantuchova	332,000	M. Hingis	63 64
Mar. 30	Nasdaq 100 Open (Miami)	Serena Williams	385,000	J. Capriati	75 76
Apr. 7	Porto Ladies Open	Angeles Montolio	22,000	M. Serna	61 26 75
Apr. 7	Sarasota Open	Jelena Dokic	22,000	T. Panova	62 62
Apr. 14	Bausch & Lomb Championships (Amelia Island)	Venus Williams	93,000	J. Henin	26 75 76
Apr. 14	Estoril Open	Magui Serna	68,300	A. Barna	64 62
Apr. 22	Family Circle Cup (Charleston)	Iva Majoli	182,000	P. Schnyder	76 64
Apr. 22	Budapest Open	Martina Muller	16,000	M. Casanova	62 36 64
May 5	Betty Barclay Cup (Hamburg)	Kim Clijsters	93,000	V. Williams	16 63 64
May 5	Croatian Bol Open	Asa Svensson	27,000	I. Majoli	63 46 61
May 12	German Open (Berlin)	Justine Henin	182,000	S. Williams	62 16 76
May 12	J&S Cup (Warsaw)	Elena Bovina	170,000	H. Nagyova	63 61
May 19	Italian Open (Rome)	Serena Williams	182,000	J. Henin	76 64
May 26	Strasbourg International	Silvia Farina Elia	27,000	J. Dokic	64 36 63
May 26	Madrid Open	Monica Seles	27,000	C. Rubin	64 62
June 9	**French Open** (Paris)	Serena Williams	586,618	V. Williams	75 63
June 16	DFS Classic (Birmingham)	Jelena Dokic	27,000	A. Myskina	62 63
June 16	UNIQA Grand Prix (Vienna)	Anna Smashnova	27,000	I. Tulyaganova	64 61
June 16	Tashkent Open	Marie-Gaianeh Mikaelian	22,000	T. Poutchek	64 64
June 23	Ordina Open ('s-Hertogenbosch)	Eleni Daniilidou	27,000	E. Dementieva	36 62 63
June 23	Britannic Asset Management (Eastbourne)	Chanda Rubin	93,000	A. Myskina	61 63
July 7	**Wimbledon** (London)	Serena Williams	728,783	V. Williams	76 63
July 14	French Community Championships (Brussels)	Myriam Casanova	22,000	A. S. Vicario	46 62 61

Finals	Tournament	Winner	Earnings	Runner-Up	Score
July 14	Palermo International	Mariana Diaz-Oliva	$16,000	V. Zvonareva	67(6) 61 63
July 14	Grand Prix De S.A.R. (Casablanca)	Patricia Wartusch	22,000	K. Koukalova	57 63 63
July 28	Bank of the West Classic (Stanford)	Venus Williams	93,000	K. Clijsters	63 63
July 28	Prokom Polish Open (Sopot)	Dinara Safina	50,000	H. Nagyova	63 40 ret.
Aug. 4	Acura Classic (San Diego)	Venus Williams	115,000	J. Dokic	62 62
Aug. 11	JP Morgan Chase Open (Los Angeles)	Chanda Rubin	93,000	L. Davenport	57 76 63
Aug. 11	Nordea Nordic Light Open (Helsinki)	Svetlana Kuznetsova	22,000	D. Chladkova	06 63 76
Aug. 18	Rogers AT&T Cup (Montreal)	Amelie Mauresmo	182,000	J. Capriati	64 61
Aug. 25	Pilot Pen Tennis (New Haven)	Venus Williams	93,000	L. Davenport	75 60
Sept. 7	**U.S. Open** (Flushing)	Serena Williams	900,000	V. Williams	64 63
Sept. 15	Brazil Open (Bahia)	Anastasia Myskina	99,200	E. Daniilidou	63 06 62
Sept. 15	Big Island Championships (Waikoloa)	Cara Black	22,000	L. Raymond	76 64
Sept. 15	SVW Polo Open (Shanghai)	Anna Smashnova	22,000	A. Kournikova	63 62
Sept. 22	Princess Cup (Tokyo)	Serena Williams	93,000	K. Clijsters	26 63 63
Sept. 22	Bell Challenge (Quebec)	Elena Bovina	27,000	M. Mikaelian	63 64
Sept. 29	Sparkassen Cup (Leipzig)	Serena Williams	93,000	A. Myskina	63 62
Sept. 29	Wismilak International (Bali)	Svetlana Kuznetsova	35,000	C. Martinez	36 76 75

*The final match of the Open Gaz de France on Feb. 10 was cancelled after Jelena Dokic withdrew due to a thigh injury.

2002 Grand Slam Tournaments
Australian Open

MEN'S SINGLES

FINAL EIGHT—#7 Tommy Haas; #9 Marat Safin; #16 Thomas Johansson; #26 Jiri Novak; plus unseeded Jonas Bjorkman, Wayne Ferreira, Stefan Koubek and Marcelo Rios.

Quarterfinals

Haas def. Rios	76(2) 64 67(2) 76(5)
Safin def. Ferreira	52 ret.
Novak def. Koubek	62 63 62
Johansson def. Bjorkman	60 26 63 64

Semifinals

Safin def. Haas	67(5) 76(4) 36 60 62
Johansson def. Novak	76(5) 06 46 63 64

Final

Johansson def. Safin	36 64 64 76(4)

WOMEN'S SINGLES

FINAL EIGHT—#1 Jennifer Capriati; #2 Venus Williams; #3 Martina Hingis; #4 Kim Clijsters; #6 Justine Henin; #7 Amelie Mauresmo; #8 Monica Seles; plus unseeded Adriana Serra Zanetti.

Quarterfinals

Capriati def. Mauresmo	62 62
Clijsters def. Henin	62 63
Hingis def. Serra Zanetti	62 63
Seles def. V. Williams	67(4) 62 63

Semifinals

Capriati def. Clijsters	75 36 61
Hingis def. Seles	46 61 64

Final

Capriati def. Hingis	46 76(7) 62

DOUBLES FINALS

Men—#9 Mark Knowles & Daniel Nestor def. Michael Liodra & Fabrice Santoro, 7-6 (7-4), 6-3.

Women—#8 Martina Hingis & Anna Kournikova def. #13 Daniela Hantuchova & Arantxa Sanchez Vicario, 6-2, 6-7 (4-7), 6-1.

Mixed—Kevin Ullyett & Daniela Hantuchova def. Gaston Etlis & Paola Suarez, 6-3, 6-2.

French Open

MEN'S SINGLES

FINAL EIGHT—#2 Marat Safin; #4 Andre Agassi; # 10 Sebastien Grosjean; #11 Juan Carlos Ferrero; #15 Guillermo Canas; #18 Alex Corretja; #20 Albert Costa; and #22 Andrei Pavel.

Quarterfinals

Costa def. Canas	75 36 67(3) 64 60
Corretja def. Pavel	76(5) 75 75
Ferrero def. Agassi	63 57 75 63
Safin def. Grosjean	63 62 62

Semifinals

Costa def. Corretja	63 64 36 63
Ferrero def. Safin	63 62 64

Final

Costa def. Ferrero	61 60 46 63

WOMEN'S SINGLES

FINAL EIGHT—#1 Jennifer Capriati; #2 Venus Williams; #3 Serena Williams; #6 Monica Seles; #7 Jelena Dokic; plus unseeded Clarisa Fernandez, Mary Pierce, and Paola Suarez.

Quarterfinals

Capriati def. Dokic	64 46 61
S. Williams def. Pierce	61 61
Fernandez def. Suarez	26 76(5) 61
V. Williams def. Seles	64 63

Semifinals

S. Williams def. Capriati	36 76(2) 62
V. Williams def. Fernandez	61 64

Final

S. Williams def. V. Williams	75 63

DOUBLES FINALS

Men—Paul Haarhuis & Yevgeny Kafelnikov def. #2 Mark Knowles & Daniel Nestor, 7-5, 6-4.

Women—#2 Virginia Ruano-Pascual & Paola Suarez def. #1 Lisa Raymond & Rennae Stubbs, 6-4, 6-2.

Mixed—#5 Cara Black & Wayne Black def. Elena Bovina & Mark Knowles, 6-3, 6-3.

Wimbledon

MEN'S SINGLES

FINAL EIGHT—#1 Lleyton Hewitt, #4 Tim Henman, #18 Sjeng Schalken, #22 Nicolas Lapentti, #27 Xavier Malisse, #28 David Nalbandian; plus unseeded Richard Krajicek and Andre Sa.

Quarterfinals

Hewitt def. Schalken	62 62 67(5) 16 75
Henman def. Sa	63 57 64 63
Malisse def. Krajicek	61 46 62 36 97
Nalbandian def. Lapentti	64 64 46 46 64

Semifinals

Hewitt def. Henman	75 61 75
Nalbandian def. Malisse	76(2) 64 16 26 62

Final

Hewitt def. Nalbandian	61 63 62

WOMEN'S SINGLES

FINAL EIGHT—#1 Venus Williams, #2 Serena Williams, #3 Jennifer Capriati, #4 Monica Seles, #6 Justine Henin, #9 Amelie Mauresmo, #11 Daniela Hantuchova; plus unseeded Elena Likhovtseva.

Quarterfinals

V. Williams def. Likhovtseva	62 60
Henin def. Seles	75 76(4)
Mauresmo def. Capriati	63 62
S. Williams def. Hantuchova	63 62

Semifinals

V. Williams def. Henin	63 62
S. Williams def. Mauresmo	62 61

Final

S. Williams def. V. Williams	76(4) 63

DOUBLES FINALS

Men—#5 Jonas Bjorkman & Todd Woodbridge def. #2 Mark Knowles & Daniel Nestor, 6-1, 6-2, 6-7(9-7), 7-5.

Women—#3 Venus Williams & Serena Williams def. #2 Virginia Ruano Pascual & Paola Suarez, 6-2, 7-5.

Mixed—#3 Mahesh Bhupathi & Elena Likhovtseva def. #4 Kevin Ullyett & Daniela Hantuchova, 2-6, 6-1, 1-6.

U.S. Open

MEN'S SINGLES

FINAL EIGHT—#1 Lleyton Hewitt, #6 Andre Agassi, #11 Andy Roddick, #17 Pete Sampras, #20 Younes El Aynaoui, #24 Sjeng Schalken, #28 Fernando Gonzalez and #32 Max Mirnyi.

Quarterfinals

Hewitt def. El Aynaoui	61 76(6) 46 62
Agassi def. Mirnyi	67(5) 63 75 63
Sampras def. Roddick	63 62 64
Schalken def. Gonzalez	67(5) 63 63 67(5) 76(2)

Semifinals

Agassi def. Hewitt	64 76(5) 67(1) 62
Sampras def. Schalken	76(6) 76(4) 62

Final

Sampras def. Agassi	63 64 57 64

WOMEN'S SINGLES

FINAL EIGHT—#1 Serena Williams, #2 Venus Williams, #3 Jennifer Capriati, #4 Linday Davenport, #6 Monica Seles, #10 Amelie Mauresmo, #11 Daniela Hantuchova; plus unseeded Elena Bovina.

Quarterfinals

S. Williams def. Hantuchova	62 62
Davenport def. Bovina	63 60 62
Mauresmo def. Capriati	46 76(5) 63
V. Williams def. Seles	62 63

Semifinals

S. Williams def. Davenport	63 75
V. Williams def. Mauresmo	63 57 64

Final

S. Williams def. V. Williams	64 63

DOUBLES FINALS

Men—#3 Mahesh Bhupathi & Max Mirnyi def. #11 Jiri Novak & Radek Stepanek 6-3, 3-6, 6-4.

Women—#2 Virginia Ruano Pascual & Paola Suarez def. #6 Elena Dementieva & Janette Husarova 6-2, 6-1.

Mixed—#2 Lisa Raymond & Mike Bryan def. Katarina Srebotnik & Bob Bryan 7-6 (11-9), 7-6 (7-1).

Fed Cup

Originally the Federation Cup and started in 1963 by the International Tennis Federation as the Davis Cup of women's tennis.

2001 FINAL

Belgium 2, Russia 1

at Madrid, Spain (Nov. 11)

Singles—Justine Henin (BEL) def. Nadia Petrova (RUS) 6-0, 6-3; Kim Clijsters (BEL) def. Elena Dementieva (RUS) 6-0, 6-4.

Doubles—Petrova & Elena Likhovtseva (RUS) def. Els Callens & Laurence Courtois (BEL) 7-5, 7-6 (7-2).

2002 Early Rounds

FIRST ROUND

(April 27-28)

Winner	Loser
Austria 3	at United States 2
at Slovakia 3	Switzerland 2
at Croatia 3	Czech Republic 2
France 3	at Argentina 2
at Spain 4	Hungary 1
at Italy 5	Sweden 0

Winner	Loser
at Germany 3	Russia 2
at Belgium 3	Australia 1

Quarterfinals

(July 20-21)

Winner	Loser
at Austria 4	Croatia 1
at Slovakia 4	France 1
at Spain 5	Germany 0
at Italy 4	Belgium 1

SEMIFINALS & FINAL

The 2002 Fed Cup semifinals and final was to be held in Maspalomas, a city on the island of Gran Canaria, in Spain's Canary Islands the week starting Oct. 28. Spain was to face Austria and Slovakia was to play Italy in the semifinals. Austria and Spain have only met once before in Fed Cup competition, with Austria taking the honors in 1984. This was to be the first meeting of Slovakia and Italy.

Singles Leaders

Official Top 20 rankings and money leaders of men's and women's tours for 2001 and unofficial rankings for 2002 (through Sept. 29), as compiled by the ATP Tour (Association of Tennis Professionals) and WTA (Women's Tennis Association). Note that money lists include doubles earnings.

Final 2001 Rankings and Money Won

Listed are events won and times a finalist and semifinalist (Finish, 1-2-SF), match record (W-L), and earnings for the year.

MEN

		Finish 1-2-SF	W-L	Earnings
1	Lleyton Hewitt	6-0-6	79-17	$4,045,618
2	Gustavo Kuerten	6-2-1	60-18	4,091,004
3	Andre Agassi	4-1-2	45-15	2,341,766
4	Yevgeny Kafelnikov	2-2-7	69-28	3,238,889
5	Juan Carlos Ferrero	4-2-2	57-21	2,179,671
6	Sebastien Grosjean	1-2-5	51-24	1,918,584
7	Patrick Rafter	1-3-3	47-18	1,670,592
8	Tommy Haas	4-0-4	57-21	1,544,640
9	Tim Henman	2-1-3	51-20	1,118,699
10	Pete Sampras	0-4-1	35-16	994,331
11	Marat Safin	2-2-3	45-27	2,027,702
12	Roger Federer	1-2-2	49-21	865,425
13	Goran Ivanisevic	1-1-1	29-22	1,245,040
14	Guillermo Canas	1-3-3	45-21	636,341
15	Alex Corretja	1-1-1	34-20	897,819
16	Andy Roddick	3-0-1	42-16	766,504
17	Arnaud Clement	0-1-1	37-28	848,999
18	Thomas Johansson	2-0-2	46-25	742,792
19	Carlos Moya	1-1-3	35-24	597,862
20	Albert Portas	1-1-4	32-28	841,804

WOMEN

		Finish 1-2-SF	W-L	Earnings
1	Lindsay Davenport	7-3-3	62-9	$2,102,242
2	Jennifer Capriati	3-4-5	56-14	2,268,624
3	Venus Williams	6-0-3	46-5	2,662,610
4	Martina Hingis	3-3-9	60-15	1,765,116
5	Kim Clijsters	3-3-5	54-18	1,335,659
6	Serena Williams	3-1-0	38-7	2,136,263
7	Justine Henin	3-2-3	56-18	998,704
8	Jelena Dokic	3-3-3	53-23	1,169,716
9	Amelie Mauresmo	4-1-1	42-11	867,702
10	Monica Seles	4-2-3	40-10	627,211
11	Sandrine Testud	1-2-3	53-27	815,601
12	Meghann Shaughnessy	0-2-2	45-24	593,776
13	Nathalie Tauziat	1-1-4	34-21	925,785
14	Silvia Farina Elia	1-1-1	45-27	471,426
15	Elena Dementieva	0-2-2	33-21	567,964
16	Magdalena Maleeva	1-1-2	35-24	481,784
17	Arantxa Sanchez Vicario	2-1-2	34-21	725,342
18	Anke Huber	0-2-2	35-20	516,522
19	Amanda Coetzer	1-1-2	32-21	560,857
20	Iroda Tulyaganova	2-0-1	31-24	285,740

2002 Tour Rankings (through Sept. 29)

Listed are tournaments won and times a finalist and semifinalist (Finish, 1-2-SF), match record (W-L), and points earned (Pts). The **ATP Champions Race** replaced the men's pro tennis tour's 27-year-old computer ranking system in 2000. Under the new system players start from zero on Jan. 1 and accumulate points during the calendar year with the player accumulating the most points becoming the World No. 1. Points are awarded in 18 tournaments: nine Tennis Masters Series events, four Grand Slams and five other International Series events.

MEN

Final ATP Tour singles rankings will be based on points earned from 18 tournaments played in 2002. Tournaments, titles and match won-lost records are for 2002 only.

Rank 02	(01)		Finish 1-2-SF	W-L	Pts
1	1	Lleyton Hewitt	4-1-3	51-11	690
2	3	Andre Agassi	4-2-2	46-8	554
3	11	Marat Safin	0-2-1	43-19	441
4	5	Juan Carlos Ferrero	2-2-1	39-18	425
5	9	Tim Henman	1-3-2	47-16	420
6	19	Carlos Moya	4-2-2	49-16	402
7	37	Albert Costa	1-2-0	34-16	393
8	8	Tommy Haas	0-1-4	43-18	388
9	16	Andy Roddick	2-3-4	52-19	383
10	12	Roger Federer	2-2-1	41-17	356
11	32	Jiri Novak	0-1-6	43-21	349
12	10	Pete Sampras	1-1-1	27-17	347
13	14	Guillermo Canas	2-2-2	43-20	329
14	18	Thomas Johansson	1-0-1	26-18	312
15	15	Alex Corretja	2-0-2	37-16	296
16	40	Younes El Aynaoui	3-2-0	45-21	285
	135	Fernando Gonzalez	2-0-1	40-15	285
18	70	David Nalbandian	1-1-0	28-20	284
19	47	Gaston Gaudio	2-1-2	40-15	279
20	26	Sjeng Schalken	1-0-2	32-25	259

WOMEN

Sanex WTA Tour singles ranking system based on total Round and Quality Points for each tournament played during the last 12 months. Tournaments, titles and match won-lost records, however, are for 2002 only.

Rank 02	(01)		Finish 1-2-SF	W-L	Pts
1	6	Serena Williams	8-1-1	53-4	6099
2	3	Venus Williams	7-4-2	60-7	4843
3	2	Jennifer Capriati	1-3-4	45-12	3759
4	10	Monica Seles	2-1-6	46-13	3152
5	8	Jelena Dokic	2-3-6	50-21	3074
6	7	Justine Henin	1-4-3	45-18	2994
7	9	Amelie Mauresmo	2-0-4	43-13	2908
8	1	Lindsay Davenport	0-2-3	17-5	2680
9	5	Kim Clijsters	1-2-4	36-16	2618
10	4	Martina Hingis	2-2-2	33-8	2514
11	38	Daniela Hantuchova	1-0-3	46-21	2423
12	59	Anastasia Myskina	1-3-1	48-24	2003
13	54	Chanda Rubin	2-1-0	27-9	1733
14	14	Silvia Farina Elia	1-0-2	42-23	1722
15	11	Sandrine Testud	0-1-1	17-15	1573
16	15	Elena Dementieva	0-1-1	31-22	1503
17	37	Patty Schnyder	0-1-1	30-23	1353
18	87	Anna Smashnova	4-0-1	42-20	1348
19	30	Ai Sugiyama	0-0-3	36-24	1254
20	40	Tatiana Panova	0-2-0	26-26	1222

2002 Money Winners

Amounts include singles and doubles earnings through Sept. 29, 2002.

MEN

		Earnings			Earnings			Earnings
1	Lleyton Hewitt	$2,113,989	11	Andy Roddick	$922,145	21	Jonas Bjorkman	$693,664
2	Andre Agassi	1,639,486	12	Jiri Novak	898,210	22	James Blake	599,296
3	Pete Sampras	1,222,999	13	Yevgeny Kafelnikov	854,190	23	Daniel Nestor	592,596
4	Juan Carlos Ferrero	1,176,998	14	Thomas Johansson	852,999	24	Fernando Gonzalez	561,557
5	Albert Costa	1,162,839	15	Max Mirnyi	820,377	25	Gaston Gaudio	543,934
6	Guillermo Canas	1,124,417	16	Tommy Haas	805,619	26	Fabrice Santoro	542,035
7	Carlos Moya	1,087,964	17	Alex Corretja	736,286	27	Juan Ignacio Chela	515,880
8	Roger Federer	1,084,062	18	Sjeng Schalken	722,356	28	Xavier Malisse	504,302
9	Marat Safin	1,029,291	19	Younes El Aynaoui	721,757	29	Rainer Schuettler	504,184
10	Tim Henman	970,899	20	David Nalbandian	713,382	30	Sebastien Grosjean	504,007

WOMEN

		Earnings			Earnings			Earnings
1	Serena Williams	$3,275,826	11	Kim Clijsters	$664,302	21	Lindsay Davenport	$382,733
2	Venus Williams	2,043,761	12	Jelena Dokic	642,265	22	Arantxa Sanchez Vicario	371,498
3	Jennifer Capriati	1,400,679	13	Virginia Ruano Pascual	605,992	23	Patty Schnyder	355,712
4	Martina Hingis	1,046,024	14	Elena Dementieva	494,251	24	Ai Sugiyama	354,590
5	Daniela Hantuchova	1,027,379	15	Elena Likhovtseva	475,874	25	Iva Majoli	349,556
6	Amelie Mauresmo	911,165	16	Anastasia Myskina	458,476	26	Cara Black	343,145
7	Monica Seles	856,913	17	Silvia Farina Elia	454,454	27	Rennae Stubbs	338,421
8	Justine Henin	834,119	18	Chanda Rubin	416,666	28	Meghann Shaughnessy	335,286
9	Paola Suarez	741,953	19	Anna Kournikova	414,344	29	Elena Bovina	314,887
10	Lisa Raymond	672,707	20	Janette Husarova	404,171	30	Katarina Srebotnik	312,861

Davis Cup

France won its ninth Davis Cup title in 2001 with a 3-2 upset of host Australia. France was sparked by the play of Nicolas Escude. The 27th-ranked player in the world defeated the world's number one, Lleyton Hewitt, on the first day and then secured the game-winning point with a victory over Wayne Arthurs on the final day.

2001 FINAL

France 3, Australia 2
at Melbourne, Australia (Nov. 30–Dec. 2)

Day One—Nicolas Escude (FRA) def. Lleyton Hewitt (AUS) 4-6, 6-3, 3-6, 6-4; Patrick Rafter (AUS) def. Sebastian Grosjean (FRA) 6-3, 7-6, 7-5.

Day Two—Fabrice Santoro & Cedric Pioline (FRA) def. Hewitt & Rafter (AUS) 2-6, 6-3, 7-6 (7-5), 6-1.

Day Three—Hewitt (AUS) def. Grosjean (FRA) 6-3, 6-2, 6-3; Escude (FRA) def. Wayne Arthurs (AUS) 7-6 (7-3), 6-7 (5-7), 6-3, 6-3.

2002 Early Rounds
FIRST ROUND
(Feb. 8-10)

Winner	Loser
at France 3	Netherlands 2
at Czech Republic 4	Brazil 1
at Spain 3	Morocco 2
at United States 5	Slovakia 0
at Russia 3	Switzerland 2
Sweden 3	at Great Britain 2
at Croatia 4	Germany 1
at Argentina 5	Australia 0

QUARTERFINALS
(Apr. 5-7)

Winner	Loser
at France 3	Czech Republic 2
at United States 3	Spain 1
at Russia 4	Sweden 1
at Argentina 3	Croatia 2

SEMIFINALS
France 3, United States 2
at Paris, France (Sept. 20-22)

Day One—Arnaud Clement (FRA) def. Andy Roddick (USA) 4-6, 7-6 (8-6), 7-6 (7-5), 6-1; Sebastien Grosjean (FRA) def. James Blake (USA) 6-4, 6-1, 6-7 (7-9), 7-5.

Day Two—Blake & Todd Martin (USA) def. Michael Llodra & Fabrice Santoro (FRA) 2-6, 7-6 (7-2), 2-6, 6-4, 6-4.

Day Three—Grosjean (FRA) def. Roddick (USA) 6-4, 3-6, 6-3, 6-4; Blake (USA) def. Clement (FRA) 6-4, 6-3.

Russia 3, Argentina 2
at Moscow, Russia (Sept. 20-22)

Day One—Marat Safin (RUS) def. Juan Ignacio Chela (ARG) 6-7 (1-7), 7-5, 7-5, 6-1; Yevgeny Kafelnikov (RUS) def. Gaston Gaudio (ARG) 3-6, 7-5, 6-3, 2-6, 8-6.

Day Two—Lucas Arnold & David Nalbandian (ARG) def. Kafelnikov & Safin (RUS) 6-4, 6-4, 5-7, 6-6, 19-17.

Day Three—Safin (RUS) def. Nalbandian (ARG) 7-6 (7-3), 6-7 (5-7), 6-0, 6-3; Ignacio Chela (ARG) def. Mikhail Youzhny (RUS) 7-6 (7-5), 6-7 (3-7), 6-4.

2002 FINAL

The 2002 Davis Cup final between France and Russia was to be held from Nov. 29 through Dec. 1 in Paris, France. Defending champion France is 2-1 lifetime against Russia, but the teams had not faced each other since 1983, when France claimed a 4-1 victory.

1877-2002
Through the Years

Grand Slam Championships
Australian Open
MEN

Became an Open Championship in 1969. Two tournaments were held in 1977; the first in January, the second in December. Tournament moved back to January in 1987, so no championship was decided in 1986. **Surface:** Synpave Rebound Ace (hardcourt surface composed of polyurethane and synthetic rubber).

Multiple winners: Roy Emerson (6); Jack Crawford and Ken Rosewall (4); Andre Agassi, James Anderson, Rod Laver, Adrian Quist, Mats Wilander and Pat Wood (3); Boris Becker, Jack Bromwich, Ashley Cooper, Jim Courier, Stefan Edberg, Rodney Heath, Johan Kriek, Ivan Lendl, John Newcombe, Pete Sampras, Frank Sedgman, Guillermo Vilas and Tony Wilding (2).

Year	Winner	Loser	Score	Year	Winner	Loser	Score
1905	Rodney Heath	A. Curtis	46 63 64 64	1958	Ashley Cooper	M. Anderson	75 63 64
1906	Tony Wilding	H. Parker	60 64 64	1959	Alex Olmedo	N. Fraser	61 62 36 63
1907	Horace Rice	H. Parker	63 64 64				
1908	Fred Alexander	A. Dunlop	36 36 60 62 63	1960	Rod Laver	N. Fraser	57 36 63 86 86
1909	Tony Wilding	E. Parker	61 75 62	1961	Roy Emerson	R. Laver	16 63 75 64
				1962	Rod Laver	R. Emerson	86 06 64 64
1910	Rodney Heath	H. Rice	64 63 62	1963	Roy Emerson	K. Fletcher	63 63 61
1911	Norman Brookes	H. Rice	61 62 63	1964	Roy Emerson	F. Stolle	63 64 62
1912	J. Cecil Parke	A. Beamish	36 63 16 61 75	1965	Roy Emerson	F. Stolle	79 26 64 75 61
1913	Ernie Parker	H. Parker	26 61 62 63	1966	Roy Emerson	A. Ashe	64 68 62 63
1914	Pat Wood	G. Patterson	64 63 57 61	1967	Roy Emerson	A. Ashe	64 61 61
1915	Francis Lowe	H. Rice	46 61 61 64	1968	Bill Bowrey	J. Gisbert	75 26 97 64
1916-18 Not held World War I				1969	Rod Laver	A. Gimeno	63 64 75
1919	A.R.F. Kingscote	E. Pockley	64 60 63				
				1970	Arthur Ashe	D. Crealy	64 97 62
1920	Pat Wood	R. Thomas	63 46 68 61 63	1971	Ken Rosewall	A. Ashe	61 75 63
1921	Rhys Gemmell	A. Hedeman	75 61 64	1972	Ken Rosewall	M. Anderson	76 63 75
1922	James Anderson	G. Patterson	60 36 36 63 62	1973	John Newcombe	O. Parun	63 67 75 61
1923	Pat Wood	C.B. St. John	61 61 63	1974	Jimmy Connors	P. Dent	76 64 46 63
1924	James Anderson	R. Schlesinger	63 64 36 57 63	1975	John Newcombe	J. Connors	75 36 64 75
1925	James Anderson	G. Patterson	11-9 26 62 63	1976	Mark Edmondson	J. Newcombe	67 63 76 61
1926	John Hawkes	J. Willard	61 63 61	1977	Roscoe Tanner	G. Vilas	63 63 63
1927	Gerald Patterson	J. Hawkes	36 64 36 18-16 63		Vitas Gerulaitis	J. Lloyd	63 76 57 36 62
1928	Jean Borotra	R.O. Cummings	64 61 46 57 63	1978	Guillermo Vilas	J. Marks	64 64 36 63
1929	John Gregory	R. Schlesinger	62 62 57 75	1979	Guillermo Vilas	J. Sadri	76 63 62
1930	Gar Moon	H. Hopman	63 61 63	1980	Brian Teacher	K. Warwick	75 76 63
1931	Jack Crawford	H. Hopman	64 62 26 61	1981	Johan Kriek	S. Denton	62 76 67 64
1932	Jack Crawford	H. Hopman	46 63 36 63 61	1982	Johan Kriek	S. Denton	63 63 62
1933	Jack Crawford	K. Gledhill	26 75 63 62	1983	Mats Wilander	I. Lendl	61 64 64
1934	Fred Perry	J. Crawford	63 75 61	1984	Mats Wilander	K. Curren	67 64 76 62
1935	Jack Crawford	F. Perry	26 64 64 64	1985	Stefan Edberg	M. Wilander	64 63 63
1936	Adrian Quist	J. Crawford	62 63 46 36 97	1986 Not held			
1937	Viv McGrath	J. Bromwich	63 16 60 26 61	1987	Stefan Edberg	P. Cash	63 64 36 57 63
1938	Don Budge	J. Bromwich	64 62 61	1988	Mats Wilander	P. Cash	63 67 36 61 86
1939	Jack Bromwich	A. Quist	64 61 63	1989	Ivan Lendl	M. Mecir	62 62 62
1940	Adrian Quist	J. Crawford	63 61 62	1990	Ivan Lendl	S. Edberg	46 76 52 (ret.)
1941-45 Not held World War II				1991	Boris Becker	I. Lendl	16 64 64 64
1946	Jack Bromwich	D. Pails	57 63 75 36 62	1992	Jim Courier	S. Edberg	63 36 64 62
1947	Dinny Pails	J. Bromwich	46 64 36 75 86	1993	Jim Courier	S. Edberg	62 61 26 75
1948	Adrian Quist	J. Bromwich	64 36 63 26 63	1994	Pete Sampras	T. Martin	76 64 64
1949	Frank Sedgman	J. Bromwich	63 63 62	1995	Andre Agassi	P. Sampras	46 61 76 64
1950	Frank Sedgman	K. McGregor	63 64 46 61	1996	Boris Becker	M. Chang	62 64 26 62
1951	Dick Savitt	K. McGregor	63 26 63 61	1997	Pete Sampras	C. Moya	62 63 63
1952	Ken McGregor	F. Sedgman	75 12-10 26 62	1998	Petr Korda	M. Rios	62 62 62
1953	Ken Rosewall	M. Rose	60 63 64	1999	Yevgeny Kafelnikov	T. Enqvist	46 60 63 76
1954	Mervyn Rose	R. Hartwig	62 06 64 62				
1955	Ken Rosewall	L. Hoad	97 64 64	2000	Andre Agassi	Y. Kafelnikov	36 63 62 64
1956	Lew Hoad	K. Rosewall	64 36 64 75	2001	Andre Agassi	A. Clement	64 62 62
1957	Ashley Cooper	N. Fraser	63 9-11 64 62	2002	Thomas Johansson	M. Safin	36 64 64 76

WOMEN

Became an Open Championship in 1969. Two tournaments were held in 1977, the first in January, the second in December. Tournament moved back to January in 1987, so no championship was decided in 1986.

Multiple winners: Margaret Smith Court (11); Nancye Wynne Bolton (6); Daphne Akhurst (5); Evonne Goolagong Cawley, Steffi Graf and Monica Seles (4); Joan Hartigan, Martina Hingis and Martina Navratilova (3); Coral Buttsworth, Jennifer Capriati, Chris Evert Lloyd, Thelma Long, Hana Mandlikova, Mall Molesworth and Mary Carter Reitano (2).

Year	Winner	Loser	Score	Year	Winner	Loser	Score
1922	Mall Molesworth	E. Boyd	63 10-8	1965	Margaret Smith	M. Bueno	57 64 52 (ret)
1923	Mall Molesworth	E. Boyd	61 75	1966	Margaret Smith	N. Richey	walkover
1924	Sylvia Lance	E. Boyd	63 36 64	1967	Nancy Richey	L. Turner	61 64
1925	Daphne Akhurst	E. Boyd	16 86 64	1968	Billie Jean King	M. Smith	61 62
1926	Daphne Akhurst	E. Boyd	61 63	1969	Margaret Court	B.J. King	64 61
1927	Esna Boyd	S. Harper	57 61 62				
1928	Daphne Akhurst	E. Boyd	75 62	1970	Margaret Court	K. Melville	61 63
1929	Daphne Akhurst	L. Bickerton	61 57 62	1971	Margaret Court	E. Goolagong	26 76 75
				1972	Virginia Wade	E. Goolagong	64 64
1930	Daphne Akhurst	S. Harper	10-8 26 75	1973	Margaret Court	E. Goolagong	64 75
1931	Coral Buttsworth	M. Crawford	16 63 64	1974	Evonne Goolagong	C. Evert	76 46 60
1932	Coral Buttsworth	K. Le Messurier	97 64	1975	Evonne Goolagong	M. Navratilova	63 62
1933	Joan Hartigan	C. Buttsworth	64 63	1976	Evonne Cawley	R. Tomanova	62 62
1934	Joan Hartigan	M. Molesworth	61 64	1977	Kerry Reid	D. Balestrat	75 62
1935	Dorothy Round	N. Lyle	16 61 63		Evonne Cawley	H. Gourlay	63 60
1936	Joan Hartigan	N. Bolton	64 64	1978	Chris O'Neil	B. Nagelsen	63 76
1937	Nancye Wynne	E. Westacott	63 57 64	1979	Barbara Jordan	S. Walsh	63 63
1938	Dorothy Bundy	D. Stevenson	63 62				
1939	Emily Westacott	N. Hopman	61 62	1980	Hana Mandlikova	W. Turnbull	60 75
				1981	Martina Navratilova	C. Evert Lloyd	67 64 75
1940	Nancye Wynne	T. Coyne	57 64 60	1982	Chris Evert Lloyd	M. Navratilova	63 26 63
1941-45	Not held World War II			1983	Martina Navratilova	K. Jordan	62 76
1946	Nancye Bolton	J. Fitch	64 64	1984	Chris Evert Lloyd	H. Sukova	67 61 63
1947	Nancye Bolton	N. Hopman	63 62	1985	Martina Navratilova	C. Evert Lloyd	62 46 62
1948	Nancye Bolton	M. Toomey	63 61	1986	Not held		
1949	Doris Hart	N. Bolton	63 64	1987	Hana Mandlikova	M. Navratilova	75 76
				1988	Steffi Graf	C. Evert	61 76
1950	Louise Brough	D. Hart	64 36 64	1989	Steffi Graf	H. Sukova	64 64
1951	Nancye Bolton	T. Long	61 75	1990	Steffi Graf	M.J. Fernandez	63 64
1952	Thelma Long	H. Angwin	62 63	1991	Monica Seles	J. Novotna	57 63 61
1953	Maureen Connolly	J. Sampson	63 62	1992	Monica Seles	M.J. Fernandez	62 63
1954	Thelma Long	J. Staley	63 64	1993	Monica Seles	S. Graf	46 63 62
1955	Beryl Penrose	T. Long	64 63	1994	Steffi Graf	A.S. Vicario	60 62
1956	Mary Carter	T. Long	36 62 97	1995	Mary Pierce	A.S. Vicario	63 62
1957	Shirley Fry	A. Gibson	63 64	1996	Monica Seles	A. Huber	64 61
1958	Angela Mortimer	L. Coghlan	63 64	1997	Martina Hingis	M. Pierce	62 62
1959	Mary Reitano	T. Schuurman	62 63	1998	Martina Hingis	C. Martinez	63 63
				1999	Martina Hingis	A. Mauresmo	62 63
1960	Margaret Smith	J. Lehane	75 62				
1961	Margaret Smith	J. Lehane	61 64	2000	Lindsay Davenport	M. Hingis	61 75
1962	Margaret Smith	J. Lehane	60 62	2001	Jennifer Capriati	M. Hingis	64 63
1963	Margaret Smith	J. Lehane	62 62	2002	Jennifer Capriati	M. Hingis	46 76 62
1964	Margaret Smith	L. Turner	63 62				

French Open
MEN

From 1891 to 1925, entry was restricted to members of French clubs. Became an Open Championship in 1968, but closed to contract pros in 1972. Note that Max Decugis won eight tournaments before 1925 (1903-04, 1907-09, 1912-14) to lead all men. **Surface:** Red clay.

Multiple winners (since 1925): Bjorn Borg (6); Henri Cochet (4); Gustavo Kuerten, Rene Lacoste, Ivan Lendl and Mats Wilander (3); Sergi Bruguera, Jim Courier, Jaroslav Drobny, Roy Emerson, Jan Kodes, Rod Laver, Frank Parker, Nicola Pietrangeli, Ken Rosewall, Manuel Santana, Tony Trabert and Gottfried von Cramm (2).

Year	Winner	Loser	Score	Year	Winner	Loser	Score
1925	Rene Lacoste	J. Borotra	75 61 64	1938	Don Budge	R. Menzel	63 62 64
1926	Henri Cochet	R. Lacoste	62 64 63	1939	Don McNeill	B. Riggs	75 60 63
1927	Rene Lacoste	B. Tilden	64 46 57 63 11-9				
1928	Henri Cochet	R. Lacoste	57 63 61 63	1941-45	Not held World War II		
1929	Rene Lacoste	J. Borotra	63 26 60 26 86	1946	Marcel Bernard	J. Drobny	36 26 61 64 63
				1947	Joseph Asboth	E. Sturgess	86 75 64
1930	Henri Cochet	B. Tilden	36 86 63 61	1948	Frank Parker	J. Drobny	64 75 57 86
1931	Jean Borotra	C. Boussus	26 64 75 64	1949	Frank Parker	B. Patty	63 16 61 64
1932	Henri Cochet	G. de Stefani	60 64 46 63	1950	Budge Patty	J. Drobny	61 62 36 57 75
1933	Jack Crawford	H. Cochet	86 61 63	1951	Jaroslav Drobny	E. Sturgess	63 63 63
1934	Gottfried von Cramm	J. Crawford	64 79 36 75 63	1952	Jaroslav Drobny	F. Sedgman	62 60 36 64
1935	Fred Perry	G. von Cramm	63 36 61 63	1953	Ken Rosewall	V. Seixas	63 64 16 62
1936	Gottfried von Cramm	F. Perry	60 26 62 26 60	1954	Tony Trabert	A. Larsen	64 75 61
1937	Henner Henkel	H. Austin	61 64 63	1955	Tony Trabert	S. Davidson	26 61 64 62

Year	Winner	Loser	Score
1956	Lew Hoad	S. Davidson	64 86 63
1957	Sven Davidson	H. Flam	63 64 64
1958	Mervyn Rose	L. Ayala	63 64 64
1959	Nicola Pietrangeli	I. Vermaak	36 63 64 61
1960	Nicola Pietrangeli	L. Ayala	36 63 64 46 63
1961	Manuel Santana	N. Pietrangeli	46 61 36 60 62
1962	Rod Laver	R. Emerson	36 26 63 97 62
1963	Roy Emerson	P. Darmon	36 61 64 64
1964	Manuel Santana	N. Pietrangeli	63 61 46 75
1965	Fred Stolle	T. Roche	36 60 62 63
1966	Tony Roche	I. Gulyas	61 64 75
1967	Roy Emerson	T. Roche	61 64 26 62
1968	Ken Rosewall	R. Laver	63 61 26 62
1969	Rod Laver	K. Rosewall	64 63 64
1970	Jan Kodes	Z. Franulovic	62 64 60
1971	Jan Kodes	I. Nastase	86 62 26 75
1972	Andres Gimeno	P. Proisy	46 63 61 61
1973	Ilie Nastase	N. Pilic	63 63 60
1974	Bjorn Borg	M. Orantes	26 67 60 61 61
1975	Bjorn Borg	G. Vilas	62 63 64
1976	Adriano Panatta	H. Solomon	61 64 46 76
1977	Guillermo Vilas	B. Gottfried	60 63 60
1978	Bjorn Borg	G. Vilas	61 61 63
1979	Bjorn Borg	V. Pecci	63 61 67 64
1980	Bjorn Borg	V. Gerulaitis	64 61 62
1981	Bjorn Borg	I. Lendl	61 46 62 36 61
1982	Mats Wilander	G. Vilas	16 76 60 64
1983	Yannick Noah	M. Wilander	62 75 76
1984	Ivan Lendl	J. McEnroe	36 26 64 75 75
1985	Mats Wilander	I. Lendl	36 64 62 62
1986	Ivan Lendl	M. Pernfors	63 62 64
1987	Ivan Lendl	M. Wilander	75 62 36 76
1988	Mats Wilander	H. Leconte	75 62 61
1989	Michael Chang	S. Edberg	61 36 46 64 62
1990	Andres Gomez	A. Agassi	63 26 64 64
1991	Jim Courier	A. Agassi	36 64 26 61 64
1992	Jim Courier	P. Korda	75 62 61
1993	Sergi Bruguera	J. Courier	64 26 62 36 63
1994	Sergi Bruguera	A. Berasategui	63 75 26 61
1995	Thomas Muster	M. Chang	75 62 64
1996	Yevgeny Kafelnikov	M. Stich	76 75 76
1997	Gustavo Kuerten	S. Bruguera	63 64 62
1998	Carlos Moya	A. Corretja	63 75 63
1999	Andre Agassi	A. Medvedev	16 26 64 63 64
2000	Gustavo Kuerten	M. Norman	62 63 26 76
2001	Gustavo Kuerten	A. Corretja	67 75 62 60
2002	Albert Costa	J.C. Ferrero	61 60 46 63

WOMEN

From 1897 to 1925, entry was restricted to members of French clubs. Became an Open Championship in 1968, but closed to contract pros in 1972. Note that Suzanne Lenglen won two titles prior to 1925, giving her six total.

Multiple winners (since 1925): Chris Evert Lloyd (7); Steffi Graf (6); Margaret Smith Court (5); Helen Wills Moody (4); Arantxa Sanchez Vicario, Monica Seles and Hilde Sperling (3); Maureen Connolly, Margaret Osborne duPont, Doris Hart, Ann Haydon Jones, Suzanne Lenglen, Simone Mathieu, Margaret Scriven, Martina Navratilova and Lesley Turner (2).

Year	Winner	Loser	Score
1925	Suzanne Lenglen	K. McKane	61 62
1926	Suzanne Lenglen	M. Browne	61 60
1927	Kea Bouman	I. Peacock	62 64
1928	Helen Wills	E. Bennett	61 62
1929	Helen Wills	S. Mathieu	63 64
1930	Helen Moody	H. Jacobs	62 61
1931	Cilly Aussem	B. Nuthall	86 61
1932	Helen Moody	S. Mathieu	75 61
1933	Margaret Scriven	S. Mathieu	62 46 64
1934	Margaret Scriven	H. Jacobs	75 46 61
1935	Hilde Sperling	S. Mathieu	62 61
1936	Hilde Sperling	S. Mathieu	63 64
1937	Hilde Sperling	S. Mathieu	62 64
1938	Simone Mathieu	N. Landry	60 63
1939	Simone Mathieu	J. Jedrzejowska	63 86
1940-45	Not held World War II		
1946	Margaret Osborne	P. Betz	16 86 75
1947	Patricia Todd	D. Hart	63 36 64
1948	Nelly Landry	S. Fry	62 06 60
1949	Margaret duPont	N. Adamson	75 62
1950	Doris Hart	P. Todd	64 46 62
1951	Shirley Fry	D. Hart	63 36 63
1952	Doris Hart	S. Fry	64 64
1953	Maureen Connolly	D. Hart	62 64
1954	Maureen Connolly	G. Bucaille	64 61
1955	Angela Mortimer	D. Knode	26 75 10-8
1956	Althea Gibson	A. Mortimer	60 12-10
1957	Shirley Bloomer	D. Knode	61 63
1958	Susi Kormoczi	S. Bloomer	64 16 62
1959	Christine Truman	S. Kormoczi	64 75
1960	Darlene Hard	Y. Ramirez	63 64
1961	Ann Haydon	Y. Ramirez	62 61
1962	Margaret Smith	L. Turner	63 36 75
1963	Lesley Turner	A. Jones	26 63 75
1964	Margaret Smith	M. Bueno	57 61 62
1965	Lesley Turner	M. Smith	63 64
1966	Ann Jones	N. Richey	63 61
1967	Francoise Durr	L. Turner	46 63 64
1968	Nancy Richey	A. Jones	57 64 61
1969	Margaret Court	A. Jones	61 46 63
1970	Margaret Court	H. Niessen	62 64
1971	Evonne Goolagong	H. Gourlay	63 75
1972	Billie Jean King	E. Goolagong	63 63
1973	Margaret Court	C. Evert	67 76 64
1974	Chris Evert	O. Morozova	61 62
1975	Chris Evert	M. Navratilova	26 62 61
1976	Sue Barker	R. Tomanova	62 06 62
1977	Mima Jausovec	F. Mihai	62 67 61
1978	Virginia Ruzici	M. Jausovec	62 62
1979	Chris Evert Lloyd	W. Turnbull	62 60
1980	Chris Evert Lloyd	V. Ruzici	60 63
1981	Hana Mandlikova	S. Hanika	62 64
1982	Martina Navratilova	A. Jaeger	76 61
1983	Chris Evert Lloyd	M. Jausovec	61 62
1984	Martina Navratilova	C. Evert Lloyd	63 61
1985	Chris Evert Lloyd	M. Navratilova	63 67 75
1986	Chris Evert Lloyd	M. Navratilova	26 63 63
1987	Steffi Graf	M. Navratilova	64 46 86
1988	Steffi Graf	N. Zvereva	60 60
1989	A. Sanchez Vicario	S. Graf	76 36 75
1990	Monica Seles	S. Graf	76 64
1991	Monica Seles	A.S. Vicario	63 64
1992	Monica Seles	S. Graf	62 36 10-8
1993	Steffi Graf	M.J. Fernandez	46 62 64
1994	A. Sanchez Vicario	M. Pierce	64 64
1995	Steffi Graf	A.S. Vicario	76 46 60
1996	Steffi Graf	A.S. Vicario	63 61
1997	Iva Majoli	M. Hingis	64 62
1998	A. Sanchez Vicario	M. Seles	76 06 62
1999	Steffi Graf	M. Hingis	46 75 62
2000	Mary Pierce	C. Martinez	62 75
2001	Jennifer Capriati	K. Clijsters	16 64 1210
2002	Serena Williams	V. Williams	75 63

Wimbledon

MEN

Officially called "The Lawn Tennis Championships" at the All England Club, Wimbledon. Challenge round system (defending champion qualified for following year's final) used from 1877-1921. Became an Open Championship in 1968, but closed to contract pros in 1972. **Surface:** Grass.

Multiple winners: Willie Renshaw and Pete Sampras (7); Bjorn Borg and Laurie Doherty (5); Reggie Doherty, Rod Laver and Tony Wilding (4); Wilfred Baddeley, Boris Becker, Arthur Gore, John McEnroe, John Newcombe, Fred Perry and Bill Tilden (3); Jean Borotra, Norman Brookes, Don Budge, Henri Cochet, Jimmy Connors, Stefan Edberg, Roy Emerson, Roy Emerson, John Hartley, Lew Hoad, Rene Lacoste, Gerald Patterson and Joshua Pim (2).

Year	Winner	Loser	Score
1877	Spencer Gore	W. Marshall	61 62 64
1878	Frank Hadow	S. Gore	75 61 97
1879	John Hartley	V. St. L. Gould	62 64 62
1880	John Hartley	H. Lawford	60 62 26 63
1881	Willie Renshaw	J. Hartley	60 62 61
1882	Willie Renshaw	E. Renshaw	61 26 46 62 62
1883	Willie Renshaw	E. Renshaw	26 63 63 46 63
1884	Willie Renshaw	H. Lawford	60 64 97
1885	Willie Renshaw	H. Lawford	75 62 46 75
1886	Willie Renshaw	H. Lawford	60 57 63 64
1887	Herbert Lawford	E. Renshaw	16 63 36 64 64
1888	Ernest Renshaw	H. Lawford	63 75 60
1889	Willie Renshaw	E. Renshaw	64 61 36 60
1890	William Hamilton	W. Renshaw	68 62 36 61 61
1891	Wilfred Baddeley	J. Pim	64 16 75 60
1892	Wilfred Baddeley	J. Pim	46 63 63 62
1893	Joshua Pim	W. Baddeley	36 61 63 62
1894	Joshua Pim	W. Baddeley	10-8 62 86
1895	Wilfred Baddeley	W. Eaves	46 26 86 62 63
1896	Harold Mahony	W. Baddeley	62 68 57 86 63
1897	Reggie Doherty	H. Mahony	64 64 63
1898	Reggie Doherty	L. Doherty	63 63 26 57 61
1899	Reggie Doherty	A. Gore	16 46 62 63 63
1900	Reggie Doherty	S. Smith	68 63 61 62
1901	Arthur Gore	R. Doherty	46 75 64 64
1902	Laurie Doherty	A. Gore	64 63 36 60
1903	Laurie Doherty	F. Riseley	75 63 60
1904	Laurie Doherty	F. Riseley	61 75 86
1905	Laurie Doherty	N. Brookes	86 62 64
1906	Laurie Doherty	F. Riseley	64 46 62 63
1907	Norman Brookes	A. Gore	64 62 62
1908	Arthur Gore	R. Barrett	63 62 46 36 64
1909	Arthur Gore	M. Ritchie	68 16 62 62 62
1910	Tony Wilding	A. Gore	64 75 46 62
1911	Tony Wilding	R. Barrett	64 46 26 62 (ret)
1912	Tony Wilding	A. Gore	64 64 46 64
1913	Tony Wilding	M. McLoughlin	86 63 10-8
1914	Norman Brookes	T. Wilding	64 64 75
1915-18	Not held World War I		
1919	Gerald Patterson	N. Brookes	63 75 62
1920	Bill Tilden	G. Patterson	26 63 62 64
1921	Bill Tilden	B. Norton	46 26 61 60 75
1922	Gerald Patterson	R. Lycett	63 64 62
1923	Bill Johnston	F. Hunter	60 63 61
1924	Jean Borotra	R. Lacoste	61 36 61 36 64
1925	Rene Lacoste	J. Borotra	63 63 46 86
1926	Jean Borotra	H. Kinsey	86 61 63
1927	Henri Cochet	J. Borotra	46 46 63 64 75
1928	Rene Lacoste	H. Cochet	61 46 64 62
1929	Henri Cochet	J. Borotra	64 63 64
1930	Bill Tilden	W. Allison	63 97 64
1931	Sidney Wood	F. Shields	walkover
1932	Ellsworth Vines	H. Austin	64 62 60
1933	Jack Crawford	E. Vines	46 11-9 62 26 64
1934	Fred Perry	J. Crawford	63 60 75
1935	Fred Perry	G. von Cramm	62 64 64
1936	Fred Perry	G. von Cramm	61 61 60
1937	Don Budge	G. von Cramm	63 64 62
1938	Don Budge	H. Austin	61 60 63
1939	Bobby Riggs	E. Cooke	26 86 36 63 62

Year	Winner	Loser	Score
1940-45	Not held World War II		
1946	Yvon Petra	G. Brown	62 64 79 57 64
1947	Jack Kramer	T. Brown	61 63 62
1948	Bob Falkenburg	J. Bromwich	75 06 62 36 75
1949	Ted Schroeder	J. Drobny	36 60 63 46 64
1950	Budge Patty	F. Sedgman	61 8-10 62 63
1951	Dick Savitt	K. McGregor	64 64 64
1952	Frank Sedgman	J. Drobny	46 62 63 62
1953	Vic Seixas	K. Nielsen	97 63 64
1954	Jaroslav Drobny	K. Rosewall	13-11 46 62 97
1955	Tony Trabert	K. Nielsen	63 75 61
1956	Lew Hoad	K. Rosewall	62 46 75 64
1957	Lew Hoad	A. Cooper	62 61 62
1958	Ashley Cooper	N. Fraser	36 63 64 13-11
1959	Alex Olmedo	R. Laver	64 63 64
1960	Neale Fraser	R. Laver	64 36 97 75
1961	Rod Laver	C. McKinley	63 61 64
1962	Rod Laver	M. Mulligan	62 62 61
1963	Chuck McKinley	F. Stolle	97 61 64
1964	Roy Emerson	F. Stolle	64 12-10 46 63
1965	Roy Emerson	F. Stolle	62 64 64
1966	Manuel Santana	D. Ralston	64 11-9 64
1967	John Newcombe	W. Bungert	63 61 61
1968	Rod Laver	T. Roche	63 64 62
1969	Rod Laver	J. Newcombe	64 57 64 64
1970	John Newcombe	K. Rosewall	57 63 62 36 61
1971	John Newcombe	S. Smith	63 57 26 64 64
1972	Stan Smith	I. Nastase	46 63 63 46 75
1973	Jan Kodes	A. Metreveli	61 98 63
1974	Jimmy Connors	K. Rosewall	61 61 64
1975	Arthur Ashe	J. Connors	61 61 57 64
1976	Bjorn Borg	I. Nastase	64 62 97
1977	Bjorn Borg	J. Connors	36 62 61 57 64
1978	Bjorn Borg	J. Connors	62 62 63
1979	Bjorn Borg	R. Tanner	67 61 36 63 64
1980	Bjorn Borg	J. McEnroe	16 75 63 67 86
1981	John McEnroe	B. Borg	46 76 76 64
1982	Jimmy Connors	J. McEnroe	36 63 67 76 64
1983	John McEnroe	C. Lewis	62 62 62
1984	John McEnroe	J. Connors	61 61 62
1985	Boris Becker	K. Curren	63 67 76 64
1986	Boris Becker	I. Lendl	64 63 75
1987	Pat Cash	I. Lendl	76 62 75
1988	Stefan Edberg	B. Becker	46 76 64 62
1989	Boris Becker	S. Edberg	60 76 64
1990	Stefan Edberg	B. Becker	62 62 36 36 64
1991	Michael Stich	B. Becker	64 76 64
1992	Andre Agassi	G. Ivanisevic	67 64 64 16 64
1993	Pete Sampras	J. Courier	76 76 36 63
1994	Pete Sampras	G. Ivanisevic	76 76 60
1995	Pete Sampras	B. Becker	67 62 64 62
1996	Richard Krajicek	M. Washington	63 64 63
1997	Pete Sampras	C. Pioline	64 62 64
1998	Pete Sampras	G. Ivanisevic	67 76 64 36 62
1999	Pete Sampras	A. Agassi	63 64 75
2000	Pete Sampras	P. Rafter	67 76 64 62
2001	Goran Ivanisevic	P. Rafter	63 36 63 26 97
2002	Lleyton Hewitt	D. Nalbandian	61 63 62

WOMEN

Officially called "The Lawn Tennis Championships" at the All England Club, Wimbledon. Challenge round system (defending champion qualified for following year's final) used from 1877-1921. Became an Open Championship in 1968, but closed to contract pros in 1972.

Multiple winners: Martina Navratilova (9); Helen Wills Moody (8); Dorothea Douglass Chambers and Steffi Graf (7); Blanche Bingley Hillyard, Billie Jean King and Suzanne Lenglen (6); Lottie Dod and Charlotte Cooper Sterry (5); Louise Brough (4); Maria Bueno, Maureen Connolly, Margaret Smith Court and Chris Evert Lloyd (3); Evonne Goolagong Cawley, Althea Gibson, Kathleen McKane Godfrey, Dorothy Round, May Sutton, Maud Watson and Venus Williams (2).

Year	Winner	Loser	Score	Year	Winner	Loser	Score
1884	Maud Watson	L. Watson	68 63 63	1949	Louise Brough	M. duPont	10-8 16 10-8
1885	Maud Watson	B. Bingley	61 75	1950	Louise Brough	M. duPont	61 36 61
1886	Blanche Bingley	M. Watson	63 63	1951	Doris Hart	S. Fry	61 60
1887	Lottie Dod	B. Bingley	62 60	1952	Maureen Connolly	L. Brough	75 63
1888	Lottie Dod	B. Hillyard	63 63	1953	Maureen Connolly	D. Hart	86 75
1889	Blanche Hillyard	L. Rice	46 86 64	1954	Maureen Connolly	L. Brough	62 75
1890	Lena Rice	M. Jacks	64 61	1955	Louise Brough	B. Fleitz	75 86
1891	Lottie Dod	B. Hillyard	62 61	1956	Shirley Fry	A. Buxton	63 61
1892	Lottie Dod	B. Hillyard	61 61	1957	Althea Gibson	D. Hard	63 62
1893	Lottie Dod	B. Hillyard	68 61 64	1958	Althea Gibson	A. Mortimer	86 62
1894	Blanche Hillyard	E. Austin	61 61	1959	Maria Bueno	D. Hard	64 63
1895	Charlotte Cooper	H. Jackson	75 86	1960	Maria Bueno	S. Reynolds	86 60
1896	Charlotte Cooper	W. Pickering	62 63	1961	Angela Mortimer	C. Truman	46 64 75
1897	Blanche Hillyard	C. Cooper	57 75 62	1962	Karen Susman	V. Sukova	64 64
1898	Charlotte Cooper	L. Martin	64 64	1963	Margaret Smith	B.J. Moffitt	63 64
1899	Blanche Hillyard	C. Cooper	62 63	1964	Maria Bueno	M. Smith	64 79 63
1900	Blanche Hillyard	C. Cooper	46 64 64	1965	Margaret Smith	M. Bueno	64 75
1901	Charlotte Sterry	B. Hillyard	62 62	1966	Billie Jean King	M. Bueno	63 36 61
1902	Muriel Robb	C. Sterry	75 61	1967	Billie Jean King	A. Jones	63 64
1903	Dorothea Douglass	E. Thomson	46 64 62	1968	Billie Jean King	J. Tegart	97 75
1904	Dorothea Douglass	C. Sterry	60 63	1969	Ann Jones	B.J. King	36 63 62
1905	May Sutton	D. Douglass	63 64	1970	Margaret Court	B.J. King	14-12 11-9
1906	Dorothea Douglass	M. Sutton	63 97	1971	Evonne Goolagong	M. Court	64 61
1907	May Sutton	D. Chambers	61 64	1972	Billie Jean King	E. Goolagong	63 63
1908	Charlotte Sterry	A. Morton	64 64	1973	Billie Jean King	C. Evert	60 75
1909	Dora Boothby	A. Morton	64 46 86	1974	Chris Evert	O. Morozova	60 64
1910	Dorothea Chambers	D. Boothby	62 62	1975	Billie Jean King	E. Cawley	60 61
1911	Dorothea Chambers	D. Boothby	60 60	1976	Chris Evert	E. Cawley	63 46 86
1912	Ethel Larcombe	C. Sterry	63 61	1977	Virginia Wade	B. Stove	46 63 61
1913	Dorothea Chambers	R. McNair	60 64	1978	Martina Navratilova	C. Evert	26 64 75
1914	Dorothea Chambers	E. Larcombe	75 64	1979	Martina Navratilova	C. Evert Lloyd	64 64
1915-18	Not held World War I			1980	Evonne Cawley	C. Evert Lloyd	61 76
1919	Suzanne Lenglen	D. Chambers	10-8 46 97	1981	Chris Evert Lloyd	H. Mandlikova	62 62
1920	Suzanne Lenglen	D. Chambers	63 60	1982	Martina Navratilova	C. Evert Lloyd	61 36 62
1921	Suzanne Lenglen	E. Ryan	62 60	1983	Martina Navratilova	A. Jaeger	60 63
1922	Suzanne Lenglen	M. Mallory	62 60	1984	Martina Navratilova	C. Evert Lloyd	76 62
1923	Suzanne Lenglen	K. McKane	62 62	1985	Martina Navratilova	C. Evert Lloyd	46 63 62
1924	Kathleen McKane	H. Wills	46 64 64	1986	Martina Navratilova	H. Mandlikova	76 63
1925	Suzanne Lenglen	J. Fry	62 60	1987	Martina Navratilova	S. Graf	75 63
1926	Kathleen Godfrey	L. de Alvarez	62 46 63	1988	Steffi Graf	M. Navratilova	57 62 61
1927	Helen Wills	L. de Alvarez	62 64	1989	Steffi Graf	M. Navratilova	62 67 61
1928	Helen Wills	L. de Alvarez	62 63	1990	Martina Navratilova	Z. Garrison	64 61
1929	Helen Wills	H. Jacobs	61 62	1991	Steffi Graf	G. Sabatini	64 36 86
1930	Helen Moody	E. Ryan	62 62	1992	Steffi Graf	M. Seles	62 61
1931	Cilly Aussem	H. Kranwinkel	62 75	1993	Steffi Graf	J. Novotna	76 16 64
1932	Helen Moody	H. Jacobs	63 61	1994	Conchita Martinez	M. Navratilova	64 36 63
1933	Helen Moody	D. Round	64 68 63	1995	Steffi Graf	A.S. Vicario	46 61 75
1934	Dorothy Round	H. Jacobs	62 57 63	1996	Steffi Graf	A.S. Vicario	63 75
1935	Helen Moody	H. Jacobs	63 36 75	1997	Martina Hingis	J. Novotna	26 63 63
1936	Helen Jacobs	H.K. Sperling	62 46 75	1998	Jana Novotna	N. Tauziat	64 76
1937	Dorothy Round	J. Jedrzejowska	62 26 75	1999	Lindsay Davenport	S. Graf	64 75
1938	Helen Moody	H. Jacobs	64 60	2000	Venus Williams	L. Davenport	63 76
1939	Alice Marble	K. Stammers	62 60	2001	Venus Williams	J. Henin	61 36 60
1940-45	Not held World War II			2002	Serena Williams	V. Williams	76 63
1946	Pauline Betz	L. Brough	62 64				
1947	Margaret Osborne	D. Hart	62 64				
1948	Louise Brough	D. Hart	63 86				

U.S. Open
MEN

Challenge round system (defending champion qualified for following year's final) used from 1884 to 1911. Known as the Patriotic Tournament in 1917 during World War I. Amateur and Open Championships held in 1968 and '69. Became an exclusively Open Championship in 1970.

Surface: Decoturf II (acrylic cement).

Multiple winners: Bill Larned, Richard Sears and Bill Tilden (7); Jimmy Connors and Pete Sampras (5); John McEnroe and Robert Wrenn (4); Oliver Campbell, Ivan Lendl, Fred Perry and Malcolm Whitman (3); Andre Agassi, Don Budge, Stefan Edberg, Roy Emerson, Neale Fraser, Pancho Gonzales, Bill Johnston, Jack Kramer, Rene Lacoste, Rod Laver, Maurice McLoughlin, Lindley Murray, John Newcombe, Frank Parker, Patrick Rafter, Bobby Riggs, Ken Rosewall, Frank Sedgman, Henry Slocum Jr., Tony Trabert, Ellsworth Vines and Dick Williams (2).

Year	Winner	Loser	Score	Year	Winner	Loser	Score
1881	Richard Sears	W. Glyn	60 63 62	1943	Joe Hunt	J. Kramer	63 68 10-8 60
1882	Richard Sears	C. Clark	61 64 60	1944	Frank Parker	B. Talbert	64 36 63 63
1883	Richard Sears	J. Dwight	62 60 97	1945	Frank Parker	B. Talbert	14-12 61 62
1884	Richard Sears	H. Taylor	60 16 60 62	1946	Jack Kramer	T. Brown, Jr.	97 63 60
1885	Richard Sears	G. Brinley	63 46 60 63	1947	Jack Kramer	F. Parker	46 26 61 60 63
1886	Richard Sears	R. Beeckman	46 61 63 64	1948	Pancho Gonzales	E. Sturgess	62 63 14-12
1887	Richard Sears	H. Slocum Jr.	61 63 62	1949	Pancho Gonzales	F. Schroeder	16-18 26 61 62 64
1888	Henry Slocum Jr.	H. Taylor	64 61 60	1950	Arthur Larsen	H. Flam	63 46 57 64 63
1889	Henry Slocum Jr.	Q. Shaw	63 61 46 62	1951	Frank Sedgman	V. Seixas	64 61 61
1890	Oliver Campbell	H. Slocum Jr.	62 46 63 61	1952	Frank Sedgman	G. Mulloy	61 62 63
1891	Oliver Campbell	C. Hobart	26 75 79 61 62	1953	Tony Trabert	V. Seixas	63 62 63
1892	Oliver Campbell	F. Hovey	75 36 63 75	1954	Vic Seixas	R. Hartwig	36 62 64 64
1893	Robert Wrenn	F. Hovey	64 36 64 64	1955	Tony Trabert	K. Rosewall	97 63 63
1894	Robert Wrenn	M. Goodbody	68 61 64 64	1956	Ken Rosewall	L. Hoad	46 62 63 63
1895	Fred Hovey	R. Wrenn	63 62 64	1957	Mal Anderson	A. Cooper	10-8 75 64
1896	Robert Wrenn	F. Hovey	75 36 60 16 61	1958	Ashley Cooper	M. Anderson	62 36 46 10-8 86
1897	Robert Wrenn	W. Eaves	46 86 63 26 62	1959	Neale Fraser	A. Olmedo	63 57 62 64
1898	Malcolm Whitman	D. Davis	36 62 62 61	1960	Neale Fraser	R. Laver	64 64 97
1899	Malcolm Whitman	P. Paret	61 62 36 75	1961	Roy Emerson	R. Laver	75 63 62
1900	Malcolm Whitman	B. Larned	64 16 62 62	1962	Rod Laver	R. Emerson	62 64 57 64
1901	Bill Larned	B. Wright	62 68 64 64	1963	Rafael Osuna	F. Froehling	75 64 62
1902	Bill Larned	R. Doherty	46 62 64 86	1964	Roy Emerson	F. Stolle	64 64 62
1903	Laurie Doherty	B. Larned	60 63 10-8	1965	Manuel Santana	C. Drysdale	62 79 75 61
1904	Holcombe Ward	B. Clothier	10-8 64 97	1966	Fred Stolle	J. Newcombe	46 12-10 63 64
1905	Beals Wright	H. Ward	62 61 11-9	1967	John Newcombe	C. Graebner	64 64 86
1906	Bill Clothier	B. Wright	63 60 64	1968	Am-Arthur Ashe	B. Lutz	46 63 8-10 60 64
1907	Bill Larned	R. LeRoy	62 62 64		Op-Arthur Ashe	T. Okker	14-12 57 63 36 63
1908	Bill Larned	B. Wright	61 62 86	1969	Am-Stan Smith	B. Lutz	97 63 61
1909	Bill Larned	B. Clothier	61 62 57 16 61		Op-Rod Laver	T. Roche	79 61 63 62
1910	Bill Larned	T. Bundy	61 57 60 68 61	1970	Ken Rosewall	T. Roche	26 64 76 63
1911	Bill Larned	M. McLoughlin	64 64 62	1971	Stan Smith	J. Kodes	36 63 62 76
1912	Maurice McLoughlin	W.F. Johnson	36 26 62 64 62	1972	Ilie Nastase	A. Ashe	36 63 67 64 63
1913	Maurice McLoughlin	R. Williams	64 57 63 61	1973	John Newcombe	J. Kodes	64 16 46 62 63
1914	Dick Williams	M. McLoughlin	63 86 10-8	1974	Jimmy Connors	K. Rosewall	61 60 61
1915	Bill Johnston	M. McLoughlin	16 60 75 10-8	1975	Manuel Orantes	J. Connors	64 63 63
1916	Dick Williams	J. Johnston	46 64 06 62 64	1976	Jimmy Connors	B. Borg	64 36 76 64
1917	Lindley Murray	N. Niles	57 86 63 63	1977	Guillermo Vilas	J. Connors	26 63 76 60
1918	Lindley Murray	B. Tilden	63 61 75	1978	Jimmy Connors	B. Borg	64 62 62
1919	Bill Johnston	B. Tilden	64 64 63	1979	John McEnroe	V. Gerulaitis	75 63 63
1920	Bill Tilden	B. Johnston	61 16 75 57 63	1980	John McEnroe	B. Borg	76 61 67 57 64
1921	Bill Tilden	W. Johnson	61 63 61	1981	John McEnroe	B. Borg	46 62 64 63
1922	Bill Tilden	B. Johnston	46 36 62 63 64	1982	Jimmy Connors	I. Lendl	63 62 46 64
1923	Bill Tilden	B. Johnston	64 61 64	1983	Jimmy Connors	I. Lendl	63 67 75 60
1924	Bill Tilden	B. Johnston	61 97 62	1984	John McEnroe	I. Lendl	63 64 61
1925	Bill Tilden	B. Johnston	46 11-9 63 46 63	1985	Ivan Lendl	J. McEnroe	76 63 64
1926	Rene Lacoste	J. Borotra	64 60 64	1986	Ivan Lendl	M. Mecir	64 62 60
1927	Rene Lacoste	B. Tilden	11-9 63 11-9	1987	Ivan Lendl	M. Wilander	67 60 76 64
1928	Henri Cochet	F. Hunter	46 64 36 75 63	1988	Mats Wilander	I. Lendl	64 46 63 57 64
1929	Bill Tilden	F. Hunter	36 63 46 62 64	1989	Boris Becker	I. Lendl	76 16 63 76
1930	John Doeg	F. Shields	10-8 16 64 16 14	1990	Pete Sampras	A. Agassi	64 63 62
1931	Ellsworth Vines	G. Lott Jr.	79 63 97 75	1991	Stefan Edberg	J. Courier	62 64 60
1932	Ellsworth Vines	H. Cochet	64 64 64	1992	Stefan Edberg	P. Sampras	36 64 76 62
1933	Fred Perry	J. Crawford	63 11-13 46 60 61	1993	Pete Sampras	C. Pioline	64 64 63
1934	Fred Perry	W. Allison	64 63 16 86	1994	Andre Agassi	M. Stich	61 76 75
1935	Wilmer Allison	S. Wood	62 62 63	1995	Pete Sampras	A. Agassi	64 63 46 75
1936	Fred Perry	D. Budge	26 62 86 16 10-8	1996	Pete Sampras	M. Chang	61 64 76
1937	Don Budge	G. von Cramm	61 79 61 36 61	1997	Patrick Rafter	G. Rusedski	63 62 46 75
1938	Don Budge	G. Mako	63 68 62 61	1998	Patrick Rafter	M. Philippoussis	63 36 62 60
1939	Bobby Riggs	S.W. van Horn	64 62 64	1999	Andre Agassi	T. Martin	64 67 67 63 62
1940	Don McNeill	B. Riggs	46 68 63 63 75	2000	Marat Safin	P. Sampras	64 63 63
1941	Bobby Riggs	F. Kovacs	57 61 63 63	2001	Lleyton Hewitt	P. Sampras	76 61 61
1942	Fred Schroeder	F. Parker	86 75 36 46 62	2002	Pete Sampras	A. Agassi	63 64 57 64

WOMEN

Challenge round system used from 1887-1918. Five set final played from 1887 to 1901. Amateur and Open Championships held in 1968 and '69. Became an exclusively Open Championship in 1970.

Multiple winners: Molla Bjurstedt Mallory (8); Helen Wills Moody (7); Chris Evert Lloyd (6); Margaret Smith Court and Steffi Graf (5); Pauline Betz, Maria Bueno, Helen Jacobs, Billie Jean King, Alice Marble, Elizabeth Moore, Martina Navratilova and Hazel Hotchkiss Wightman (4); Juliette Atkinson, Mary Browne, Maureen Connolly and Margaret Osborne duPont (3); Tracy Austin, Mabel Cahill, Sarah Palfrey Cooke, Althea Gibson, Darlene Hard, Doris Hart, Marion Jones, Monica Seles, Bertha Townsend, Serena Williams and Venus Williams (2).

Year	Winner	Loser	Score	Year	Winner	Loser	Score
1887	Ellen Hansell	L. Knight	61 60	1947	Louise Brough	M. Osborne	86 46 61
1888	Bertha Townsend	E. Hansell	63 65	1948	Margaret duPont	L. Brough	46 64 15-13
1889	Bertha Townsend	L. Voorhes	75 62	1949	Margaret duPont	D. Hart	64 61
1890	Ellen Roosevelt	B. Townsend	62 62	1950	Margaret duPont	D. Hart	64 63
1891	Mabel Cahill	E. Roosevelt	64 61 46 63	1951	Maureen Connolly	S. Fry	63 16 64
1892	Mabel Cahill	E. Moore	57 63 64 46 62	1952	Maureen Connolly	D. Hart	63 75
1893	Aline Terry	A. Schultz	61 63	1953	Maureen Connolly	D. Hart	62 64
1894	Helen Hellwig	A. Terry	75 36 60 36 63	1954	Doris Hart	L. Brough	68 61 86
1895	Juliette Atkinson	H. Hellwig	64 62 61	1955	Doris Hart	P. Ward	64 62
1896	Elisabeth Moore	J. Atkinson	64 46 62 62	1956	Shirley Fry	A. Gibson	63 64
1897	Juliette Atkinson	E. Moore	63 63 46 36 63	1957	Althea Gibson	L. Brough	63 62
1898	Juliette Atkinson	M. Jones	63 57 64 26 75	1958	Althea Gibson	D. Hard	36 61 62
1899	Marion Jones	M. Banks	61 61 75	1959	Maria Bueno	C. Truman	61 64
1900	Myrtle McAteer	E. Parker	62 62 60	1960	Darlene Hard	M. Bueno	64 10-12 64
1901	Elizabeth Moore	M. McAteer	64 36 75 26 62	1961	Darlene Hard	A. Haydon	63 64
1902	Marion Jones	E. Moore	61 10(ret)	1962	Margaret Smith	D. Hard	97 64
1903	Elizabeth Moore	M. Jones	75 86	1963	Maria Bueno	M. Smith	75 64
1904	May Sutton	E. Moore	61 62	1964	Maria Bueno	C. Graebner	61 60
1905	Elizabeth Moore	H. Homans	64 57 61	1965	Margaret Smith	B.J. Moffitt	86 75
1906	Helen Homans	M. Barger-Wallach	64 63	1966	Maria Bueno	N. Richey	63 61
1907	Evelyn Sears	C. Neely	63 62	1967	Billie Jean King	A. Jones	11-9 64
1908	Maud B. Wallach	Ev. Sears	63 16 63	1968	Am-Margaret Court	M. Bueno	62 62
1909	Hazel Hotchkiss	M. Wallach	60 61		Op-Virginia Wade	B.J. King	64 62
1910	Hazel Hotchkiss	L. Hammond	64 62	1969	Am-Margaret Court	V. Wade	46 63 60
1911	Hazel Hotchkiss	F. Sutton	8-10 61 97		Op-Margaret Court	N. Richey	62 62
1912	Mary Browne	E. Sears	64 62	1970	Margaret Court	R. Casals	62 26 61
1913	Mary Browne	D. Green	62 75	1971	Billie Jean King	R. Casals	64 76
1914	Mary Browne	M. Wagner	62 16 61	1972	Billie Jean King	K. Melville	63 75
1915	Molla Bjurstedt	H. Wightman	46 62 60	1973	Margaret Court	E. Goolagong	76 57 62
1916	Molla Bjurstedt	L. Raymond	60 61	1974	Billie Jean King	E. Goolagong	36 63 75
1917	Molla Bjurstedt	M. Vanderhoef	46 60 62	1975	Chris Evert	E. Cawley	57 64 62
1918	Molla Bjurstedt	E. Goss	64 63	1976	Chris Evert	E. Cawley	63 60
1919	Hazel Wightman	M. Zinderstein	61 62	1977	Chris Evert	W. Turnbull	76 62
1920	Molla Mallory	M. Zinderstein	63 61	1978	Chris Evert	P. Shriver	75 64
1921	Molla Mallory	M. Browne	46 64 62	1979	Tracy Austin	C. Evert Lloyd	64 63
1922	Molla Mallory	H. Wills	63 61	1980	Chris Evert Lloyd	H. Mandlikova	57 61 61
1923	Helen Wills	M. Mallory	62 61	1981	Tracy Austin	M. Navratilova	16 76 76
1924	Helen Wills	M. Mallory	61 63	1982	Chris Evert Lloyd	H. Mandlikova	63 61
1925	Helen Wills	K. McKane	36 60 62	1983	Martina Navratilova	C. Evert Lloyd	61 63
1926	Molla Mallory	E. Ryan	46 64 97	1984	Martina Navratilova	C. Evert Lloyd	46 64 64
1927	Helen Wills	B. Nuthall	61 64	1985	Hana Mandlikova	M. Navratilova	76 16 76
1928	Helen Wills	H. Jacobs	62 61	1986	Martina Navratilova	H. Sukova	63 62
1929	Helen Wills	P. Watson	64 62	1987	Martina Navratilova	S. Graf	76 61
1930	Betty Nuthall	A. Harper	61 64	1988	Steffi Graf	G. Sabatini	63 36 61
1931	Helen Moody	E. Whitingstall	64 61	1989	Steffi Graf	M. Navratilova	36 75 61
1932	Helen Jacobs	C. Babcock	62 62	1990	Gabriela Sabatini	S. Graf	62 76
1933	Helen Jacobs	H. Moody	86 36 30(ret)	1991	Monica Seles	M. Navratilova	76 61
1934	Helen Jacobs	S. Palfrey	61 64	1992	Monica Seles	A.S. Vicario	63 63
1935	Helen Jacobs	S. Fabyan	62 64	1993	Steffi Graf	H. Sukova	63 63
1936	Alice Marble	H. Jacobs	46 63 62	1994	A. Sanchez Vicario	S. Graf	16 76 64
1937	Anita Lizana	J. Jedrzejowska	64 62	1995	Steffi Graf	M. Seles	76 06 63
1938	Alice Marble	N. Wynne	60 63	1996	Steffi Graf	M. Seles	75 64
1939	Alice Marble	H. Jacobs	60 8-10 64	1997	Martina Hingis	V. Williams	60 64
1940	Alice Marble	H. Jacobs	62 63	1998	Lindsay Davenport	M. Hingis	63 75
1941	Sarah Cooke	P. Betz	75 62	1999	Serena Williams	M. Hingis	63 76
1942	Pauline Betz	L. Brough	46 61 64	2000	Venus Williams	L. Davenport	64 75
1943	Pauline Betz	L. Brough	63 57 63	2001	Venus Williams	S. Williams	62 64
1944	Pauline Betz	M. Osborne	63 86	2002	Serena Williams	V. Williams	64 63
1945	Sarah Cooke	P. Betz	36 86 64				
1946	Pauline Betz	P. Canning	11-9 63				

Grand Slam Summary

Singles winners of the four Grand Slam tournaments–Australian, French, Wimbledon and United States–since the French was opened to all comers in 1925. Note that there were two Australian Opens in 1977 and none in 1986.

MEN

Three wins in one year: Jack Crawford (1933); Fred Perry (1934); Tony Trabert (1955); Lew Hoad (1956); Ashley Cooper (1958); Roy Emerson (1964); Jimmy Connors (1974); Mats Wilander (1988).

Two wins in one year: Roy Emerson and Pete Sampras (4 times); Bjorn Borg (3 times); Rene Lacoste, Ivan Lendl, John Newcombe and Fred Perry (twice); Andre Agassi, Boris Becker, Don Budge, Henri Cochet, Jimmy Connors, Jim Courier, Neale Fraser, Jack Kramer, John McEnroe, Alex Olmedo, Budge Patty, Bobby Riggs, Ken Rosewall, Dick Savitt, Frank Sedgman and Guillermo Vilas (once).

Year	Australian	French	Wimbledon	U.S.
1925	Anderson	Lacoste	Lacoste	Tilden
1926	Hawkes	Cochet	Borotra	Lacoste
1927	Patterson	Lacoste	Cochet	Lacoste
1928	Borotra	Cochet	Lacoste	Cochet
1929	Gregory	Lacoste	Cochet	Tilden
1930	Moon	Cochet	Tilden	Doeg
1931	Crawford	Borotra	Wood	Vines
1932	Crawford	Cochet	Vines	Vines
1933	Crawford	Crawford	Crawford	Perry
1934	Perry	von Cramm	Perry	Perry
1935	Crawford	Perry	Perry	Allison
1936	Quist	von Cramm	Perry	Perry
1937	McGrath	Henkel	Budge	Budge
1938	**Budge**	**Budge**	**Budge**	**Budge**
1939	Bromwich	McNeill	Riggs	Riggs
1940	Quist	—	—	McNeill
1941	—	—	—	Riggs
1942	—	—	—	Schroeder
1943	—	—	—	Hunt
1944	—	—	—	Parker
1945	—	—	-	Parker
1946	Bromwich	Bernard	Petra	Kramer
1947	Pails	Asboth	Kramer	Kramer
1948	Quist	Parker	Falkenburg	Gonzales
1949	Sedgman	Parker	Schroeder	Gonzales
1950	Sedgman	Patty	Patty	Larsen
1951	Savitt	Drobny	Savitt	Sedgman
1952	McGregor	Drobny	Sedgman	Sedgman
1953	Rosewall	Rosewall	Seixas	Trabert
1954	Rose	Trabert	Drobny	Seixas
1955	Rosewall	Trabert	Trabert	Trabert
1956	Hoad	Hoad	Hoad	Rosewall
1957	Cooper	Davidson	Hoad	Anderson
1958	Cooper	Rose	Cooper	Cooper
1959	Olmedo	Pietrangeli	Olmedo	Fraser
1960	Laver	Pietrangeli	Fraser	Fraser
1961	Emerson	Santana	Laver	Emerson
1962	**Laver**	**Laver**	**Laver**	**Laver**
1963	Emerson	Emerson	McKinley	Osuna
1964	Emerson	Santana	Emerson	Emerson

Year	Australian	French	Wimbledon	U.S.
1965	Emerson	Stolle	Emerson	Santana
1966	Emerson	Roche	Santana	Stolle
1967	Emerson	Emerson	Newcombe	Newcombe
1968	Bowrey	Rosewall	Laver	Ashe
1969	**Laver**	**Laver**	**Laver**	**Laver**
1970	Ashe	Kodes	Newcombe	Rosewall
1971	Rosewall	Kodes	Newcombe	Smith
1972	Rosewall	Gimeno	Smith	Nastase
1973	Newcombe	Nastase	Kodes	Newcombe
1974	Connors	Borg	Connors	Connors
1975	Newcombe	Borg	Ashe	Orantes
1976	Edmondson	Panatta	Borg	Connors
1977	Tanner & Gerulaitis	Vilas	Borg	Vilas
1978	Vilas	Borg	Borg	Connors
1979	Vilas	Borg	Borg	McEnroe
1980	Teacher	Borg	Borg	McEnroe
1981	Kriek	Borg	McEnroe	McEnroe
1982	Kriek	Wilander	Connors	Connors
1983	Wilander	Noah	McEnroe	Connors
1984	Wilander	Lendl	McEnroe	McEnroe
1985	Edberg	Wilander	Becker	Lendl
1986	—	Lendl	Becker	Lendl
1987	Edberg	Lendl	Cash	Lendl
1988	Wilander	Wilander	Edberg	Wilander
1989	Lendl	Chang	Becker	Becker
1990	Lendl	Gomez	Edberg	Sampras
1991	Becker	Courier	Stich	Edberg
1992	Courier	Courier	Agassi	Edberg
1993	Courier	Bruguera	Sampras	Sampras
1994	Sampras	Bruguera	Sampras	Agassi
1995	Agassi	Muster	Sampras	Sampras
1996	Becker	Kafelnikov	Krajicek	Sampras
1997	Sampras	Kuerten	Sampras	Rafter
1998	Korda	Moya	Sampras	Rafter
1999	Kafelnikov	Agassi	Sampras	Agassi
2000	Agassi	Kuerten	Sampras	Safin
2001	Agassi	Kuerten	Ivanisevic	Hewitt
2002	Johansson	Costa	Hewitt	Sampras

Men's, Women's & Mixed Doubles Grand Slam

The tennis Grand Slam has only been accomplished in doubles competition six times in the same calendar year. Here are the doubles teams to accomplish the feat. The two men and three women to win the singles Grand Slam are noted in the Grand Slam Summary tables beginning on page 824.

Men's Doubles

1951 . . . . Frank Sedgman, Australia
        & Ken McGregor, Australia

Mixed Doubles

1963 . . . . Ken Fletcher, Australia
        & Margaret Smith, Australia

1967 . . . . Owen Davidson and two partners*

*Davidson's partners: AUS–Lesley Turner; FR, WIM, U.S.–Billie Jean King.

Women's Doubles

1960 . . . . Maria Bueno, Brazil & two partners†

1984 . . . . Martina Navratilova, USA
        & Pam Shriver, USA

1998 . . . . . Martina Hingis, Switzerland & two partners#

†Bueno's partners: AUS–Christine Truman; FR, WIM, U.S.–Darlene Hard.

#Hingis' partners: AUS–Mirjana Lucic; FR, WIM, U.S.–Jana Novotna.

WOMEN

Three in one year: Helen Wills Moody (1928 and '29); Margaret Smith Court (1962, '65, '69 and '73); Billie Jean King (1972); Martina Navratilova (1983 and '84); Steffi Graf (1989, '93, '95 and '96); Monica Seles (1991 and '92); Martina Hingis (1997) and Serena Williams (2002).

Two in one year: Chris Evert Lloyd (5 times); Helen Wills Moody and Martina Navratilova (3 times); Maria Bueno, Maureen Connolly, Margaret Smith Court, Althea Gibson, Billie Jean King and Venus Williams (twice); Cilly Aussem, Pauleen Betz, Louise Brough, Jennifer Capriati, Evonne Goolagong Cawley, Shirley Fry, Darlene Hard, Margaret Osborne duPont, Suzanne Lenglen, Alice Marble, Arantxa Sanchez Vicario and Serena Williams (once).

Year	Australian	French	Wimbledon	U.S.	Year	Australian	French	Wimbledon	U.S.
1925	Akhurst	Lenglen	Lenglen	Wills	1965	Smith	Turner	Smith	Smith
1926	Akhurst	Lenglen	Godfree	Mallory	1966	Smith	Jones	King	Bueno
1927	Boyd	Bouman	Wills	Wills	1967	Richey	Durr	King	King
1928	Akhurst	Wills	Wills	Wills	1968	King	Richey	King	Wade
1929	Akhurst	Wills	Wills	Wills	1969	Court	Court	Jones	Court
1930	Akhurst	Moody	Moody	Nuthall	1970	**Court**	**Court**	**Court**	**Court**
1931	Buttsworth	Aussem	Aussem	Moody	1971	Court	Goolagong	Goolagong	King
1932	Buttsworth	Moody	Moody	Jacobs	1972	Wade	King	King	King
1933	Hartigan	Scriven	Moody	Jacobs	1973	Court	Court	King	Court
1934	Hartigan	Scriven	Round	Jacobs	1974	Goolagong	Evert	Evert	King
1935	Round	Sperling	Moody	Jacobs	1975	Goolagong	Evert	King	Evert
1936	Hartigan	Sperling	Jacobs	Marble	1976	Cawley	Barker	Evert	Evert
1937	Bolton	Sperling	Round	Lizana	1977	Reid	Jausovec	Wade	Evert
1938	Bundy	Mathieu	Moody	Marble		& Cawley			
1939	Westacott	Mathieu	Marble	Marble	1978	O'Neil	Ruzici	Navratilova	Evert
1940	Bolton	—	—	Marble	1979	Jordan	Evert Lloyd	Navratilova	Austin
1941	—	—	—	Cooke	1980	Mandlikova	Evert Lloyd	Cawley	Evert Lloyd
1942	—	—	—	Betz	1981	Navratilova	Mandlikova	Evert Lloyd	Austin
1943	—	—	—	Betz	1982	Evert Lloyd	Navratilova	Navratilova	Evert Lloyd
1944	—	—	—	Betz	1983	Navratilova	Evert Lloyd	Navratilova	Navratilova
1945	—	—	—	Cooke	1984	Evert Lloyd	Navratilova	Navratilova	Navratilova
1946	Bolton	Osborne	Betz	Betz	1985	Navratilova	Evert Lloyd	Navratilova	Mandlikova
1947	Bolton	Todd	Osborne	Brough	1986	–	Evert Lloyd	Navratilova	Navratilova
1948	Bolton	Landry	Brough	du Pont	1987	Mandlikova	Graf	Navratilova	Navratilova
1949	Hart	du Pont	Brough	du Pont	1988	**Graf**	**Graf**	**Graf**	**Graf**
1950	Brough	Hart	Brough	du Pont	1989	Graf	Vicario	Graf	Graf
1951	Bolton	Fry	Hart	Connolly	1990	Graf	Seles	Navratilova	Sabatini
1952	Long	Hart	Connolly	Connolly	1991	Seles	Seles	Graf	Seles
1953	**Connolly**	**Connolly**	**Connolly**	**Connolly**	1992	Seles	Seles	Graf	Seles
1954	Long	Connolly	Connolly	Hart	1993	Seles	Graf	Graf	Graf
1955	Penrose	Mortimer	Brough	Hart	1994	Graf	Vicario	Martinez	Vicario
1956	Carter	Gibson	Fry	Fry	1995	Pierce	Graf	Graf	Graf
1957	Fry	Bloomer	Gibson	Gibson	1996	Seles	Graf	Graf	Graf
1958	Mortimer	Kormoczi	Gibson	Gibson	1997	Hingis	Majoli	Hingis	Hingis
1959	Reitano	Truman	Bueno	Bueno	1998	Hingis	Vicario	Novotna	Davenport
1960	Smith	Hard	Bueno	Hard	1999	Hingis	Graf	Davenport	S. Williams
1961	Smith	Haydon	Mortimer	Hard	2000	Davenport	Pierce	V. Williams	V. Williams
1962	Smith	Smith	Susman	Smith	2001	Capriati	Capriati	V. Williams	V. Williams
1963	Smith	Turner	Smith	Bueno	2002	Capriati	S. Williams	S. Williams	S. Williams
1964	Smith	Smith	Bueno	Bueno					

Overall Leaders

All-Time Grand Slam titleists including all singles and doubles championships at the four major tournaments. Titles listed under each heading are singles, doubles and mixed doubles. Players active in 2002 are in **bold** type.

MEN

		Career	Australian	French	Wimbledon	U.S.	S-D-M	Total Titles
1	Roy Emerson	1959-71	6-3-0	2-6-0	2-3-0	2-4-0	12-16-0	28
2	John Newcombe	1965-76	2-5-0	0-3-0	3-6-0	2-3-1	7-17-1	25
3	Frank Sedgman	1949-52	2-2-2	0-2-2	1-3-2	2-2-2	5-9-8	22
4	Bill Tilden	1913-30	*	0-0-1	3-1-0	7-5-4	10-6-5	21
5	Rod Laver	1959-71	3-4-0	2-1-1	4-1-2	2-0-0	11-6-3	20
6	Jack Bromwich	1938-50	2-8-1	0-0-0	0-2-2	0-3-1	2-13-4	19
	Neale Fraser	1957-62	0-3-1	0-3-0	1-2-1	2-3-3	3-11-5	19
	Todd Woodbridge	1988—	0-3-1	0-1-1	0-7-1	0-2-3	0-13-6	19
9	Ken Rosewall	1953-72	4-3-0	2-2-0	0-2-0	2-2-1	8-9-1	18
	Jean Borotra	1925-36	1-1-1	1-5-2	2-3-1	0-0-1	4-9-5	18
	Fred Stolle	1962-69	0-3-1	1-2-0	0-2-3	1-3-2	2-10-6	18
12	John McEnroe	1977-93	0-0-0	0-0-1	3-5-0	4-4-0	7-9-1	17
	Jack Crawford	1929-35	4-4-3	1-1-1	1-1-1	0-0-0	6-6-5	17
	Mark Woodforde	1985-2000	0-2-2	0-1-1	0-6-1	0-3-1	0-12-5	17
	Adrian Quist	1936-50	3-10-0	0-1-0	0-2-0	0-1-0	3-14-0	17

WOMEN

	Career	Australian	French	Wimbledon	U.S.	S-D-M	Total Titles
1 Margaret Smith Court	1960-75	11-8-2	5-4-4	3-2-5	5-5-8	24-19-19	62
2 **Martina Navratilova**	1974-95, 2000—	3-8-0	2-7-2	9-7-3	4-9-2	18-31-7	56
3 Billie Jean King	1961-81	1-0-1	1-1-2	6-10-4	4-5-4	12-16-11	39
4 Margaret du Pont	1941-60	*	2-3-0	1-5-1	3-13-9	6-21-10	37
5 Louise Brough	1942-57	1-1-0	0-3-0	4-5-4	1-12-4	6-21-8	35
Doris Hart	1948-55	1-1-2	2-5-3	1-4-5	2-4-5	6-14-15	35
7 Helen Wills Moody	1923-38	*	4-2-0	8-3-1	7-4-2	19-9-3	31
8 Elizabeth Ryan	1914-34	*	0-4-0	0-12-7	0-1-2	0-17-9	26
9 Suzanne Lenglen	1919-26	*	6-2-2	6-6-3	0-0-0	12-8-5	25
10 Steffi Graf	1982-99	4-0-0	6-0-0	7-1-0	5-0-0	22-1-0	23
11 Pam Shriver	1981-97	0-7-0	0-4-1	0-5-0	0-5-0	0-21-1	22
12 Chris Evert	1974-89	2-0-0	7-2-0	3-1-0	6-0-0	18-3-0	21
Darlene Hard	1958-69	*	1-3-2	0-4-3	2-6-0	3-13-5	21
14 **Natasha Zvereva**	1989—	0-3-2	0-6-0	0-5-0	0-4-0	0-18-2	20
Nancye Wynne Bolton	1935-52	6-10-4	0-0-0	0-0-0	0-0-0	6-10-4	20
Maria Bueno	1958-68	0-1-0	0-1-1	3-5-0	4-5-0	7-12-1	20

All-Time Grand Slam Singles Titles

Men and women with the most singles championships in the Australian, French, Wimbledon and U.S. championships, through 2002. Note that (*) indicates player never played in that particular Grand Slam event; and players active in singles play in 2002 are in **bold** type.

Top 10 Men

	Aus	Fre	Wim	US	Total
1 **Pete Sampras**	2	0	7	5	14
2 Roy Emerson	6	2	2	2	12
3 Bjorn Borg	0	6	5	0	11
Rod Laver	3	2	4	2	11
5 Bill Tilden	*	0	3	7	10
6 Jimmy Connors	1	0	2	5	8
Ivan Lendl	2	3	0	3	8
Fred Perry	1	1	3	3	8
Ken Rosewall	4	2	0	2	8
10 **Andre Agassi**	3	1	1	2	7
Henri Cochet	*	4	2	1	7
Rene Lacoste	*	3	2	2	7
Bill Larned	*	*	0	7	7
John McEnroe	0	0	3	4	7
John Newcombe	2	0	3	2	7
Willie Renshaw	*	*	7	*	7
Dick Sears	*	*	0	7	7
Mats Wilander	3	3	*	1	7

Top 15 Women

	Aus	Fre	Wim	US	Total
1 Margaret Smith Court	11	5	3	5	24
2 Steffi Graf	4	6	7	5	22
3 Helen Wills Moody	*	4	8	7	19
4 Chris Evert	2	7	3	6	18
Martina Navratilova	3	2	9	4	18
6 Billie Jean King	1	1	6	4	12
Suzanne Lenglen	*	6	6	0	12
8 Maureen Connolly	1	2	3	3	9
Monica Seles	4	3	0	2	9
10 Molla Bjurstedt Mallory	*	*	0	8	8
11 Maria Bueno	0	0	3	4	7
Evonne Goolagong	4	1	2	0	7
Dorothea D. Chambers	*	*	7	0	7
14 Nancy Bolton	6	0	0	0	6
Louise Brough	1	0	4	1	6
Margaret du Pont	*	2	1	3	6
Doris Hart	1	2	1	2	6
Blanche Bingley Hillyard	*	*	6	*	6

Annual Number One Players

Unofficial world rankings for men and women determined by the *London Daily Telegraph* from 1914-72. Since then, official world rankings computed by men's and women's tours. Rankings included only amateur players from 1914 until the arrival of open (professional) tennis in 1968. No rankings were released during World Wars I and II.

MEN

Multiple winners: Pete Sampras and Bill Tilden (6); Jimmy Connors (5); Henri Cochet, Rod Laver, Ivan Lendl and John McEnroe (4); John Newcombe and Fred Perry (3); Bjorn Borg, Don Budge, Ashley Cooper, Stefan Edberg, Roy Emerson, Neale Fraser, Jack Kramer, Rene Lacoste, Ilie Nastase, Frank Sedgman and Tony Trabert (2).

Year		Year		Year		Year	
1914	Maurice McLoughlin	1937	Don Budge	1962	Rod Laver	1982	John McEnroe
1915-18	No rankings	1938	Don Budge	1963	Rafael Osuna	1983	John McEnroe
1919	Gerald Patterson	1939	Bobby Riggs	1964	Roy Emerson	1984	John McEnroe
1920	Bill Tilden	1940-45	No rankings	1965	Roy Emerson	1985	Ivan Lendl
1921	Bill Tilden	1946	Jack Kramer	1966	Manuel Santana	1986	Ivan Lendl
1922	Bill Tilden	1947	Jack Kramer	1967	John Newcombe	1987	Ivan Lendl
1923	Bill Tilden	1948	Frank Parker	1968	Rod Laver	1988	Mats Wilander
1924	Bill Tilden	1949	Pancho Gonzales	1969	Rod Laver	1989	Ivan Lendl
1925	Bill Tilden	1950	Budge Patty	1970	John Newcombe	1990	Stefan Edberg
1926	Rene Lacoste	1951	Frank Sedgman	1971	John Newcombe	1991	Stefan Edberg
1927	Rene Lacoste	1952	Frank Sedgman	1972	Ilie Nastase	1992	Jim Courier
1928	Henri Cochet	1953	Tony Trabert	1973	Ilie Nastase	1993	Pete Sampras
1929	Henri Cochet	1954	Jaroslav Drobny	1974	Jimmy Connors	1994	Pete Sampras
1930	Henri Cochet	1955	Tony Trabert	1975	Jimmy Connors	1995	Pete Sampras
1931	Henri Cochet	1956	Lew Hoad	1976	Jimmy Connors	1996	Pete Sampras
1932	Ellsworth Vines	1957	Ashley Cooper	1977	Jimmy Connors	1997	Pete Sampras
1933	Jack Crawford	1958	Ashley Cooper	1978	Jimmy Connors	1998	Pete Sampras
1934	Fred Perry	1959	Neale Fraser	1979	Bjorn Borg	1999	Andre Agassi
1935	Fred Perry	1960	Neale Fraser	1980	Bjorn Borg	2000	Gustavo Kuerten
1936	Fred Perry	1961	Rod Laver	1981	John McEnroe	2001	Lleyton Hewitt

WOMEN

Multiple winners: Helen Wills Moody (9); Steffi Graf (8); Margaret Smith Court and Martina Navratilova (7); Chris Evert Lloyd and Billie Jean King (5); Margaret Osborne duPont (4); Maureen Connolly, Martina Hingis and Monica Seles (3); Maria Bueno, Lindsay Davenport, Althea Gibson and Suzanne Lenglen (2).

Year		Year		Year		Year	
1925	Suzanne Lenglen	1949	Margaret duPont	1968	Billie Jean King	1987	Steffi Graf
1926	Suzanne Lenglen	1950	Margaret duPont	1969	Margaret Court	1988	Steffi Graf
1927	Helen Wills	1951	Doris Hart	1970	Margaret Court	1989	Steffi Graf
1928	Helen Wills	1952	Maureen Connolly	1971	Evonne Goolagong	1990	Steffi Graf
1929	Helen Wills Moody	1953	Maureen Connolly	1972	Billie Jean King	1991	Monica Seles
1930	Helen Wills Moody	1954	Maureen Connolly	1973	Margaret Court	1992	Monica Seles
1931	Helen Wills Moody	1955	Louise Brough	1974	Billie Jean King	1993	Steffi Graf
1932	Helen Wills Moody	1956	Shirley Fry	1975	Chris Evert	1994	Steffi Graf
1933	Helen Wills Moody	1957	Althea Gibson	1976	Chris Evert	1995	Steffi Graf
1934	Dorothy Round	1958	Althea Gibson	1977	Chris Evert		& Monica Seles*
1935	Helen Wills Moody	1959	Maria Bueno	1978	Martina Navratilova	1996	Steffi Graf
1936	Helen Jacobs	1960	Maria Bueno	1979	Martina Navratilova	1997	Martina Hingis
1937	Anita Lizana	1961	Angela Mortimer	1980	Chris Evert Lloyd	1998	Lindsay Davenport
1938	Helen Wills Moody	1962	Margaret Smith	1981	Chris Evert Lloyd	1999	Martina Hingis
1939	Alice Marble	1963	Margaret Smith	1982	Martina Navratilova		
1940-45	No rankings	1964	Margaret Smith	1983	Martina Navratilova	2000	Martina Hingis
1946	Pauline Betz	1965	Margaret Smith	1984	Martina Navratilova	2001	Lindsay Davenport
1947	Margaret Osborne	1966	Billie Jean King	1985	Martina Navratilova		
1948	Margaret duPont	1967	Billie Jean King	1986	Martina Navratilova		

*Upon her return to the WTA Tour on Aug. 15, 1995, Seles retained her #1 ranking and was co-ranked at #1 through her first six tournaments (August '95-May '96). Seles was on leave since April 1993 when she was stabbed by a fan during a match.

Annual Top 10 World Rankings (since 1968)

Year by year Top 10 world computer rankings for men (ATP Tour) and women (WTA Tour) since the arrival of open tennis in 1968. Rankings from 1968-72 made by Lance Tingay of the *London Daily Telegraph*. Since 1973 the WTA Tour and ATP tour had compiled its own computer rankings. Since 2000, the men's rankings reflect the final standings of the ATP Champions Race.

MEN

1968	**1971**	**1974**	**1977**	**1980**
1 Rod Laver	1 John Newcombe	1 Jimmy Connors	1 Jimmy Connors	1 Bjorn Borg
2 Arthur Ashe	2 Stan Smith	2 John Newcombe	2 Guillermo Vilas	2 John McEnroe
3 Ken Rosewall	3 Rod Laver	3 Bjorn Borg	3 Bjorn Borg	3 Jimmy Connors
4 Tom Okker	4 Ken Rosewall	4 Rod Laver	4 Vitas Gerulaitis	4 Gene Mayer
5 Tony Roche	5 Jan Kodes	5 Guillermo Vilas	5 Brian Gottfried	5 Guillermo Vilas
6 John Newcombe	6 Arthur Ashe	6 Tom Okker	6 Eddie Dibbs	6 Ivan Lendl
7 Clark Graebner	7 Tom Okker	7 Arthur Ashe	7 Manuel Orantes	7 Harold Solomon
8 Dennis Ralston	8 Marty Riessen	8 Ken Rosewall	8 Raul Ramirez	8 Jose-Luis Clerc
9 Cliff Drysdale	9 Cliff Drysdale	9 Stan Smith	9 Ilie Nastase ·	9 Vitas Gerulaitis
10 Pancho Gonzales	10 Ilie Nastase	10 Ilie Nastase	10 Dick Stockton	10 Eliot Teltscher

1969	**1972**	**1975**	**1978**	**1981**
1 Rod Laver	1 Stan Smith	1 Jimmy Connors	1 Jimmy Connors	1 John McEnroe
2 Tony Roche	2 Ken Rosewall	2 Guillermo Vilas	2 Bjorn Borg	2 Ivan Lendl
3 John Newcombe	3 Ilie Nastase	3 Bjorn Borg	3 Guillermo Vilas	3 Jimmy Connors
4 Tom Okker	4 Rod Laver	4 Arthur Ashe	4 John McEnroe	4 Bjorn Borg
5 Ken Rosewall	5 Arthur Ashe	5 Manuel Orantes	5 Vitas Gerulaitis	5 Jose-Luis Clerc
6 Arthur Ashe	6 John Newcombe	6 Ken Rosewall	6 Eddie Dibbs	6 Guillermo Vilas
7 Cliff Drysdale	7 Bob Lutz	7 Ilie Nastase	7 Brian Gottfried	7 Gene Mayer
8 Pancho Gonzales	8 Tom Okker	8 John Alexander	8 Raul Ramirez	8 Eliot Teltscher
9 Andres Gimeno	9 Marty Riessen	9 Roscoe Tanner	9 Harold Solomon	9 Vitas Gerulaitis
10 Fred Stolle	10 Andres Gimeno	10 Rod Laver	10 Corrado Barazzutti	10 Peter McNamara

1970	**1973**	**1976**	**1979**	**1982**
1 John Newcombe	1 Ilie Nastase	1 Jimmy Connors	1 Bjorn Borg	1 John McEnroe
2 Ken Rosewall	2 John Newcombe	2 Bjorn Borg	2 Jimmy Connors	2 Jimmy Connors
3 Tony Roche	3 Jimmy Connors	3 Ilie Nastase	3 John McEnroe	3 Ivan Lendl
4 Rod Laver	4 Tom Okker	4 Manuel Orantes	4 Vitas Gerulaitis	4 Guillermo Vilas
5 Arthur Ashe	5 Stan Smith	5 Raul Ramirez	5 Roscoe Tanner	5 Vitas Gerulaitis
6 Ilie Nastase	6 Ken Rosewall	6 Guillermo Vilas	6 Guillermo Vilas	6 Jose-Luis Clerc
7 Tom Okker	7 Manuel Orantes	7 Adriano Panatta	7 Arthur Ashe	7 Mats Wilander
8 Roger Taylor	8 Rod Laver	8 Harold Solomon	8 Harold Solomon	8 Gene Mayer
9 Jan Kodes	9 Jan Kodes	9 Eddie Dibbs	9 Jose Higueras	9 Yannick Noah
10 Cliff Richey	10 Arthur Ashe	10 Brian Gottfried	10 Eddie Dibbs	10 Peter McNamara

Annual Top 10 World Rankings (since 1968) (Cont.)
MEN

1983
1 John McEnroe
2 Ivan Lendl
3 Jimmy Connors
4 Mats Wilander
5 Yannick Noah
6 Jimmy Arias
7 Jose Higueras
8 Jose-Luis Clerc
9 Kevin Curren
10 Gene Mayer

1984
1 John McEnroe
2 Jimmy Connors
3 Ivan Lendl
4 Mats Wilander
5 Andres Gomez
6 Anders Jarryd
7 Henrik Sundstrom
8 Pat Cash
9 Eliot Teltscher
10 Yannick Noah

1985
1 Ivan Lendl
2 John McEnroe
3 Mats Wilander
4 Jimmy Connors
5 Stefan Edberg
6 Boris Becker
7 Yannick Noah
8 Anders Jarryd
9 Miloslav Mecir
10 Kevin Curren

1986
1 Ivan Lendl
2 Boris Becker
3 Mats Wilander
4 Yannick Noah
5 Stefan Edberg
6 Henri Leconte
7 Joakim Nystrom
8 Jimmy Connors
9 Miloslav Mecir
10 Andres Gomez

1987
1 Ivan Lendl
2 Stefan Edberg
3 Mats Wilander
4 Jimmy Connors
5 Boris Becker
6 Miloslav Mecir
7 Pat Cash
8 Yannick Noah
9 Tim Mayotte
10 John McEnroe

1988
1 Mats Wilander
2 Ivan Lendl
3 Andre Agassi
4 Boris Becker
5 Stefan Edberg
6 Kent Carlsson
7 Jimmy Connors
8 Jakob Hlasek
9 Henri Leconte
10 Tim Mayotte

1989
1 Ivan Lendl
2 Boris Becker
3 Stefan Edberg
4 John McEnroe
5 Michael Chang
6 Brad Gilbert
7 Andre Agassi
8 Aaron Krickstein
9 Alberto Mancini
10 Jay Berger

1990
1 Stefan Edberg
2 Boris Becker
3 Ivan Lendl
4 Andre Agassi
5 Pete Sampras
6 Andres Gomez
7 Thomas Muster
8 Emilio Sanchez
9 Goran Ivanisevic
10 Brad Gilbert

1991
1 Stefan Edberg
2 Jim Courier
3 Boris Becker
4 Michael Stich
5 Ivan Lendl
6 Pete Sampras
7 Guy Forget
8 Karel Novacek
9 Petr Korda
10 Andre Agassi

1992
1 Jim Courier
2 Stefan Edberg
3 Pete Sampras
4 Goran Ivanisevic
5 Boris Becker
6 Michael Chang
7 Petr Korda
8 Ivan Lendl
9 Andre Agassi
10 Richard Krajicek

1993
1 Pete Sampras
2 Michael Stich
3 Jim Courier
4 Sergi Bruguera
5 Stefan Edberg
6 Andrei Medvedev
7 Goran Ivanisevic
8 Michael Chang
9 Thomas Muster
10 Cedric Pioline

1994
1 Pete Sampras
2 Andre Agassi
3 Boris Becker
4 Sergi Bruguera
5 Goran Ivanisevic
6 Michael Chang
7 Stefan Edberg
8 Alberto Berasategui
9 Michael Stich
10 Todd Martin

1995
1 Pete Sampras
2 Andre Agassi
3 Thomas Muster
4 Boris Becker
5 Michael Chang
6 Yevgeny Kafelnikov
7 Thomas Enqvist
8 Jim Courier
9 Wayne Ferreira
10 Goran Ivanisevic

1996
1 Pete Sampras
2 Michael Chang
3 Yevgeny Kafelnikov
4 Goran Ivanisevic
5 Thomas Muster
6 Boris Becker
7 Richard Krajicek
8 Andre Agassi
9 Thomas Enqvist
10 Wayne Ferreira

1997
1 Pete Sampras
2 Patrick Rafter
3 Michael Chang
4 Jonas Bjorkman
5 Yevgeny Kafelnikov
6 Greg Rusedski
7 Carlos Moya
8 Sergi Bruguera
9 Thomas Muster
10 Marcelo Rios

1998
1 Pete Sampras
2 Marcelo Rios
3 Alex Corretja
4 Patrick Rafter
5 Carlos Moya
6 Andre Agassi
7 Tim Henman
8 Karol Kucera
9 Greg Rusedski
10 Richard Krajicek

1999
1 Andre Agassi
2 Yevgeny Kafelnikov
3 Pete Sampras
4 Thomas Enqvist
5 Gustavo Kuerten
6 Nicolas Kiefer
7 Todd Martin
8 Nicolas Lapentti
9 Marcelo Rios
10 Richard Krajicek

2000
1 Gustavo Kuerten
2 Marat Safin
3 Pete Sampras
4 Magnus Norman
5 Yevgeny Kafelnikov
6 Andre Agassi
7 Lleyton Hewitt
8 Alex Corretja
9 Thomas Enqvist
10 Tim Henman

2001
1 Lleyton Hewitt
2 Gustavo Kuerten
3 Andre Agassi
4 Yevgeny Kafelnikov
5 Juan Carlos Ferrero
6 Sebastien Grosjean
7 Patrick Rafter
8 Tommy Haas
9 Tim Henman
10 Pete Sampras

Maiden and Married Names of Women's Champions

Maiden Name	Married Name	Maiden Name	Married Name
Blanche Bingley	Blanche Hillyard	Hazel Hotchkiss	Hazel Wightman
Molla Bjurstedt	Molla Mallory	Hilde Krahwinkel	Hilde Sperling
Patricia Canning	Patricia Todd	Kerry Melville	Kerry Reid
Mary Carter	Mary Raitano	Kathleen McKane	Kathleen Godfrey
Charlotte Cooper	Charlotte Sterry	Billie Jean Moffitt	Billie Jean King
Thelma Coyne	Thelma Long	Margaret Osborne	Margaret duPont
Dorothea Douglass	Dorothea Lambert Chambers	Sarah Palfrey	Sarah Fabyan Cooke
Chris Evert	Chris Evert Lloyd*	Margaret Smith	Margaret Smith Court
Evonne Goolagong	Evonne Cawley	Helen Wills	Helen Wills Moody
Louise Hammond	Louise Raymond	Nancye Wynne	Nancye Bolton
Ann Haydon	Ann Haydon Jones		

*Chris Evert Lloyd divorced husband John Lloyd in 1987, and has since gone by the name Chris Evert.

WOMEN

1968
1 Billie Jean King
2 Virginia Wade
3 Nancy Richey
4 Maria Bueno
5 Margaret Court
6 Ann Jones
7 Judy Tegart
8 Annette du Plooy
9 Leslie Bowrey
10 Rosie Casals

1969
1 Margaret Court
2 Ann Jones
3 Billie Jean King
4 Nancy Richey
5 Julie Heldman
6 Rosie Casals
7 Kerry Melville
8 Peaches Bartkowicz
9 Virginia Wade
10 Leslie Bowrey

1970
1 Margaret Court
2 Billie Jean King
3 Rosie Casals
4 Virginia Wade
5 Helga Niessen
6 Kerry Melville
7 Julie Heldman
8 Karen Krantzcke
9 Francoise Durr
10 Nancy R. Gunter

1971
1 Evonne Goolagong
2 Billie Jean King
3 Margaret Court
4 Rosie Casals
5 Kerry Melville
6 Virginia Wade
7 Judy Tegart
8 Francoise Durr
9 Helga N. Masthoff
10 Chris Evert

1972
1 Billie Jean King
2 Evonne Goolagong
3 Chris Evert
4 Margaret Court
5 Kerry Melville
6 Virginia Wade
7 Rosie Casals
8 Nancy R. Gunter
9 Francoise Durr
10 Linda Tuero

1973
1 Margaret S. Court
2 Billie Jean King
3 Evonne G. Cawley
4 Chris Evert
5 Rosie Casals
6 Virginia Wade
7 Kerry Reid
8 Nancy Richey
9 Julie Heldman
10 Helga Masthoff

1974
1 Billie Jean King
2 Evonne G. Cawley
3 Chris Evert
4 Virginia Wade
5 Julie Heldman
6 Rosie Casals
7 Kerry Reid
8 Olga Morozova
9 Lesley Hunt
10 Francoise Durr

1975
1 Chris Evert
2 Billie Jean King
3 Evonne G. Cawley
4 Martina Navratilova
5 Virginia Wade
6 Margaret S. Court
7 Olga Morozova
8 Nancy Richey
9 Francoise Durr
10 Rosie Casals

1976
1 Chris Evert
2 Evonne G. Cawley
3 Virginia Wade
4 Martina Navratilova
5 Sue Barker
6 Betty Stove
7 Dianne Balestrat
8 Mima Jausovec
9 Rosie Casals
10 Francoise Durr

1977
1 Chris Evert
2 Billie Jean King
3 Martina Navratilova
4 Virginia Wade
5 Sue Barker
6 Rosie Casals
7 Betty Stove
8 Dianne Balestrat
9 Wendy Turnbull
10 Kerry Reid

1978
1 Martina Navratilova
2 Chris Evert Lloyd
3 Evonne G. Cawley
4 Virginia Wade
5 Billie Jean King
6 Tracy Austin
7 Wendy Turnbull
8 Kerry Reid
9 Betty Stove
10 Dianne Balestrat

1979
1 Martina Navratilova
2 Chris Evert Lloyd
3 Tracy Austin
4 Evonne G. Cawley
5 Billie Jean King
6 Dianne Balestrat
7 Wendy Turnbull
8 Virginia Wade
9 Kerry Reid
10 Sue Barker

1980
1 Chris Evert Lloyd
2 Tracy Austin
3 Martina Navratilova
4 Hana Mandlikova
5 Evonne G. Cawley
6 Billie Jean King
7 Andrea Jaeger
8 Wendy Turnbull
9 Pam Shriver
10 Greer Stevens

1981
1 Chris Evert Lloyd
2 Tracy Austin
3 Martina Navratilova
4 Andrea Jaeger
5 Hana Mandlikova
6 Sylvia Hanika
7 Pam Shriver
8 Wendy Turnbull
9 Bettina Bunge
10 Barbara Potter

1982
1 Martina Navratilova
2 Chris Evert Lloyd
3 Andrea Jaeger
4 Tracy Austin
5 Wendy Turnbull
6 Pam Shriver
7 Hana Mandlikova
8 Barbara Potter
9 Bettina Bunge
10 Sylvia Hanika

1983
1 Martina Navratilova
2 Chris Evert Lloyd
3 Andrea Jaeger
4 Pam Shriver
5 Sylvia Hanika
6 Jo Durie
7 Bettina Bunge
8 Wendy Turnbull
9 Tracy Austin
10 Zina Garrison

1984
1 Martina Navratilova
2 Chris Evert Lloyd
3 Hana Mandlikova
4 Pam Shriver
5 Wendy Turnbull
6 Manuela Maleeva
7 Helena Sukova
8 Claudia Kohde-Kilsch
9 Zina Garrison
10 Kathy Jordan

1985
1 Martina Navratilova
2 Chris Evert Lloyd
3 Hana Mandlikova
4 Pam Shriver
5 Claudia Kohde-Kilsch
6 Steffi Graf
7 Manuela Maleeva
8 Zina Garrison
9 Helena Sukova
10 Bonnie Gadusek

1986
1 Martina Navratilova
2 Chris Evert Lloyd
3 Steffi Graf
4 Hana Mandlikova
5 Helena Sukova
6 Pam Shriver
7 Claudia Kohde-Kilsch
8 M. Maleeva-Fragniere
9 Zina Garrison
10 Gabriela Sabatini

1987
1 Steffi Graf
2 Martina Navratilova
3 Chris Evert
4 Pam Shriver
5 Hana Mandlikova
6 Gabriela Sabatini
7 Helena Sukova
8 M. Maleeva-Fragniere
9 Zina Garrison
10 Claudia Kohde-Kilsch

1988
1 Steffi Graf
2 Martina Navratilova
3 Chris Evert
4 Gabriela Sabatini
5 Pam Shriver
6 M. Maleeva-Fragniere
7 Natalia Zvereva
8 Helena Sukova
9 Zina Garrison
10 Barbara Potter

1989
1 Steffi Graf
2 Martina Navratilova
3 Gabriela Sabatini
4 Z. Garrison-Jackson
5 A. Sanchez Vicario
6 Monica Seles
7 Conchita Martinez
8 Helena Sukova
9 M. Maleeva-Fragniere
10 Chris Evert

1990
1 Steffi Graf
2 Monica Seles
3 Martina Navratilova
4 Mary Joe Fernandez
5 Gabriela Sabatini
6 Katerina Maleeva
7 A. Sanchez Vicario
8 Jennifer Capriati
9 M. Maleeva-Fragniere
10 Z. Garrison-Jackson

1991
1 Monica Seles
2 Steffi Graf
3 Gabriela Sabatini
4 Martina Navratilova
5 A. Sanchez Vicario
6 Jennifer Capriati
7 Jana Novotna
8 Mary Joe Fernandez
9 Conchita Martinez
10 M. Maleeva-Fragniere

1992
1 Monica Seles
2 Steffi Graf
3 Gabriela Sabatini
4 A. Sanchez Vicario
5 Martina Navratilova
6 Mary Joe Fernandez
7 Jennifer Capriati
8 Conchita Martinez
9 M. Maleeva-Fragniere
10 Jana Novotna

1993
1 Steffi Graf
2 A. Sanchez Vicario
3 Martina Navratilova
4 Conchita Martinez
5 Gabriela Sabatini
6 Jana Novotna
7 Mary Joe Fernandez
8 Monica Seles
9 Jennifer Capriati
10 Anke Huber

1994
1 Steffi Graf
2 A. Sanchez Vicario
3 Conchita Martinez
4 Jana Novotna
5 Mary Pierce
6 Lindsay Davenport
7 Gabriela Sabatini
8 Martina Navratilova
9 Kimiko Date
10 Natasha Zvereva

1995
1 Steffi Graf
  Monica Seles*
2 Conchita Martinez
3 A. Sanchez Vicario
4 Kimiko Date
5 Mary Pierce
6 Magdalena
  Maleeva
7 Gabriela
  Sabatini
8 Mary Joe Fernandez
9 Iva Majoli
10 Anke Huber

1996
1 Steffi Graf
2 Monica Seles†
  A. Sanchez Vicario
3 Jana Novotna
4 Martina Hingis
5 Conchita Martinez
6 Anke Huber
7 Iva Majoli
8 Kimiko Date
9 Lindsay Davenport
10 Barbara Paulus

Annual Top 10 World Rankings (since 1968) (Cont.)
WOMEN

1997	1998	1999	2000	2001
1 Martina Hingis	1 Lindsay Davenport	1 Martina Hingis	1 Martina Hingis	1 Lindsay Davenport
2 Jana Novotna	2 Martina Hingis	2 Lindsay Davenport	2 Lindsay Davenport	2 Jennifer Capriati
3 Lindsay Davenport	3 Jana Novotna	3 Venus Williams	3 Venus Williams	3 Venus Williams
4 Amanda Coetzer	4 A. Sanchez Vicario	4 Serena Williams	4 Monica Seles	4 Martina Hingis
5 Monica Seles	5 Venus Williams	5 Mary Pierce	5 Conchita Martinez	5 Kim Clijsters
6 Iva Majoli	6 Monica Seles	6 Monica Seles	6 Serena Williams	6 Serena Williams
7 Mary Pierce	7 Mary Pierce	7 Nathalie Tauziat	7 Mary Pierce	7 Justine Henin
8 Irina Spirlea	8 Conchita Martinez	8 Barbara Schett	8 Anna Kournikova	8 Jelena Dokic
9 A. Sanchez Vicario	9 Steffi Graf	9 Julie Halard-Decugis	9 A. Sanchez Vicario	9 Amelie Mauresmo
10 Mary Joe Fernandez	10 Nathalie Tauziat	10 Amelie Mauresmo	10 Nathalie Tauziat	10 Monica Seles

*Returning to the WTA Tour on Aug. 15, 1995, Seles was co-ranked #1 for her first six tournaments. Seles had been absent from the Tour since April 1993 when she was stabbed by a fan during a match. She was ranked #1 at the time of the stabbing.

†Seles' ranking was revised in May 1996. The revision stipulated that her new modified ranking would be calculated using a divisor of the actual number of tournaments she had played (13), and she would be co-ranked with the player whose average is immediately below her average (Sanchez Vicario).

All-Time Singles Leaders
Tournaments Won

All-time tournament wins from the arrival of open tennis in 1968 through 2001. Men's totals include ATP Tour, Grand Prix and WCT tournaments. Players active in singles play in 2002 are in **bold** type.

MEN

		Total			Total			Total
1	Jimmy Connors	109	11	Thomas Muster	44	21	Vitas Gerulaitis	27
2	Ivan Lendl	94	12	Stefan Edberg	41	22	Jose-Luis Clerc	25
3	John McEnroe	77	13	Stan Smith	39		Brian Gottfried	25
4	**Pete Sampras**	63	14	**Michael Chang**	34	24	**Yevgeny Kafelnikov**	24
5	Bjorn Borg	62	15	Arthur Ashe	33	25	Jim Courier	23
	Guillermo Vilas	62		Mats Wilander	33		Yannick Noah	23
7	Ilie Nastase	57	17	John Newcombe	32	27	Eddie Dibbs	22
8	**Andre Agassi**	49		Manuel Orantes	32		**Goran Ivanisevic**	22
	Boris Becker	49		Ken Rosewall	32		Harold Solomon	22
10	Rod Laver	47	20	Tom Okker	31	30	Andres Gomez	21

WOMEN

		Total			Total			Total
1	Martina Navratilova	167	11	**Conchita Martinez**	32	20	Pam Shriver	21
2	Chris Evert	154	12	Olga Morozova	31		**Venus Williams**	21
3	Steffi Graf	107	13	Tracy Austin	29	22	Julie Heldman	20
4	Margaret Smith Court.	92		**A. Sanchez Vicario**	29	23	M. Maleeva-Fragniere	19
5	Billie Jean King	67	15	Hana Mandlikova	27	24	Virginia Ruzici	17
6	E. Goolagong Cawley	65		Gabriela Sabatini	27		Regina Marsikova	17
7	Virginia Wade	55	17	Nancy Richey	25	26	Sue Barker	15
8	**Monica Seles**	51	18	Jana Novotna	24		**Mary Pierce**	15
9	**Martina Hingis**	38	19	Kerry Melville Reid	22			
10	**Lindsay Davenport**	37						

Money Won

All-time money winners from the arrival of open tennis in 1968 through 2001. Totals include doubles earnings.

MEN

		Earnings			Earnings			Earnings
1	Pete Sampras	$42,057,490	11	Michael Stich	$12,590,152	21	Wayne Ferreira	$8,818,867
2	Boris Becker	25,080,956	12	John McEnroe	12,539,622	22	Jimmy Connors	8,641,040
3	Andre Agassi	23,482,490	13	Thomas Muster	12,224,410	23	Mark Woodforde	8,324,401
4	Yevgeny Kafelnikov	21,423,535	14	Sergi Bruguera	11,610,759	24	Jonas Bjorkman	8,316,076
5	Ivan Lendl	21,262,417	15	Patrick Rafter	11,103,311	25	Todd Woodbridge	8,241,522
6	Stefan Edberg	20,630,941	16	Petr Korda	10,448,450	26	Mats Wilander	7,976,256
7	Goran Ivanisevic	19,682,620	17	Richard Krajicek	9,816,081	27	Greg Rusedski	7,396,370
8	Michael Chang	18,904,768	18	Thomas Enqvist	9,366,741	28	Todd Martin	7,384,751
9	Jim Courier	14,033,132	19	Alex Corretja	9,047,953	29	Paul Haarhuis	7,375,149
10	Gustavo Kuerten	13,014,325	20	Marcelo Rios	8,898,021	30	Tim Henman	6,988,179

WOMEN

		Earnings			Earnings			Earnings
1	Steffi Graf	$21,895,277	11	Gabriela Sabatini	$8,785,850	21	Jennifer Capriati	$4,756,624
2	Mart. Navratilova	20,475,735	12	Natasha Zvereva	7,714,430	22	Gigi Fernandez	4,681,906
3	Martina Hingis	16,845,441	13	Nathalie Tauziat	6,633,727	23	Z. Garrison Jackson	4,590,816
4	A. Sanchez Vicario	16,472,594	14	Helena Sukova	6,391,245	24	Larisa Neiland	4,083,936
5	Lindsay Davenport	14,036,870	15	Mary Pierce	6,259,366	25	Iva Majoli	3,876,807
6	Monica Seles	13,518,919	16	Serena Williams	6,106,324	26	Lisa Raymond	3,747,341
7	Jana Novotna	11,249,134	17	Pam Shriver	5,460,566	27	Lori McNeil	3,555,494
8	Conchita Martinez	9,779,780	18	Mary Joe Fernandez	5,258,471	28	Sandrine Testud	3,375,821
9	Venus Williams	9,319,337	19	Amanda Coetzer	4,813,285	29	Hana Mandlikova	3,340,959
10	Chris Evert	8,896,195	20	Anke Huber	4,768,292	30	M. Maleeva-Fragniere	3,244,811

Year-end Tournaments

MEN

Tennis Masters Cup

The year-end championship featuring the top eight players in the Tennis Masters Series rankings. Two groups of four players square off in a round-robin tournament followed by a single-elimination semifinals and finals. Originally called the Masters in 1970, the tournament followed a round-robin format, but was revised in 1972 to include a round-robin to decide the four semi-finalists then a single elimination format after that. Replaced by ATP Tour World Championship in 1990 through 1999.

Multiple Winners: Ivan Lendl and Pete Sampras (5); Ilie Nastase (4); Boris Becker and John McEnroe (3); Bjorn Borg (2).

Year	Winner	Runner-Up
1970	Stan Smith (4-1) *	Rod Laver (4-1)
1971	Ilie Nastase (6-0)	Stan Smith (4-2)

Year	Winner	Loser	Score
1972	Ilie Nastase	S. Smith	63 62 36 26 63
1973	Ilie Nastase	T. Okker	63 75 46 63
1974	Guillermo Vilas	I. Nastase	76 62 36 36 64
1975	Ilie Nastase	B. Borg	62 62 61
1976	Manuel Orantes	W. Fibak	57 62 06 76 61
1978	Jimmy Connors	B. Borg	64 16 64
1979	John McEnroe	A. Ashe	67 63 75
1980	Bjorn Borg	V. Gerulaitis	62 62
1981	Bjorn Borg	I. Lendl	64 62 62
1982	Ivan Lendl	V. Gerulaitis	67 26 76 62 64
1983	Ivan Lendl	J. McEnroe	64 64 62
1984	John McEnroe	I. Lendl	63 64 64
1985	John McEnroe	I. Lendl	75 60 64
1986	Ivan Lendl	B. Becker	62 76 63

Year	Winner	Loser	Score
1986	Ivan Lendl	B. Becker	64 64 64
1987	Ivan Lendl	M. Wilander	62 62 63
1988	Boris Becker	I. Lendl	57 76 36 62 76
1989	Stefan Edberg	B. Becker	46 76 63 61
1990	Andre Agassi	S. Edberg	57 76 75 62
1991	Pete Sampras	J. Courier	36 76 63 64
1992	Boris Becker	J. Courier	64 63 75
1993	Michael Stich	P. Sampras	76 26 76 63
1994	Pete Sampras	B. Becker	46 63 75 64
1995	Boris Becker	M. Chang	76 60 76
1996	Pete Sampras	B. Becker	36 76 76 67 64
1997	Pete Sampras	Y. Kafelnikov	63 62 62
1998	Alex Corretja	C. Moya	36 36 75 63 75
1999	Pete Sampras	A. Agassi	61 75 64
2000	Gustavo Kuerten	A. Agassi	64 64 64
2001	Lleyton Hewitt	S. Grosjean	63 63 64

*Smith was declared the winner because he beat Laver in their round-robin match (4-6, 6-3, 6-4).
Note: The tournament switched from December to January in 1977-78, then back to December in 1986.

Playing Sites

1970—Tokyo; **1971**—Paris; **1972**—Barcelona; **1973**—Boston; **1974**—Melbourne; **1975**—Stockholm; **1976**—Houston; **1977-89**—New York City; **1990-95**—Frankfurt, GER; **1996-99**—Hannover, GER; **2000**—Lisbon, POR; **2001**—Sydney, AUS; **2002**—Shanghai, CHN.

WCT Championship (1971-89)

World Championship Tennis was established in 1967 to promote professional tennis and led the way into the open era. Its major singles and doubles championships were held every May among the top eight regular season finishers on the circuit from 1971 until the WCT folded in 1989.

Multiple winners: John McEnroe (5); Jimmy Connors, Ivan Lendl and Ken Rosewall (2).

Year	Winner	Loser	Score	Year	Winner	Loser	Score
1971	Ken Rosewall	R. Laver	64 16 76 76	1973	Stan Smith	A. Ashe	63 63 46 64
1972	Ken Rosewall	R. Laver	46 60 63 67 76	1974	John Newcombe	B. Borg	46 63 63 62

Year-end Tournaments (Cont.)

Year	Winner	Loser	Score	Year	Winner	Loser	Score
1975	Arthur Ashe	B. Borg	36 64 64 60	1983	John McEnroe	I. Lendl	62 46 63 67 76
1976	Bjorn Borg	G. Vilas	16 61 75 61	1984	John McEnroe	J. Connors	61 62 63
1977	Jimmy Connors	D. Stockton	67 61 64 63	1985	Ivan Lendl	T. Mayotte	76 64 61
1978	Vitas Gerulaitis	E. Dibbs	63 62 61	1986	Anders Jarryd	B. Becker	67 61 61 64
1979	John McEnroe	B. Borg	75 46 62 76	1987	Miloslav Mecir	J. McEnroe	60 36 62 62
1980	Jimmy Connors	J. McEnroe	26 76 61 62	1988	Boris Becker	S. Edberg	64 16 75 62
1981	John McEnroe	J. Kriek	61 62 64	1989	John McEnroe	B. Gilbert	63 63 76
1982	Ivan Lendl	J. McEnroe	62 36 63 63				

WOMEN
Sanex Championships

Originally the Virginia Slims Championships from 1971-94. The WTA Tour's year-end tournament took place in March from 1972 until 1986 when the WTA decided to adopt a January-to-November playing season. Given the changeover, two championships were held in 1986. Held every year since 1979 at Madison Square Garden in New York.

Multiple winners: Martina Navratilova (8); Steffi Graf (5); Chris Evert (4); Monica Seles (3); Evonne Goolagong, Martina Hingis and Gabriela Sabatini (2).

Year	Winner	Loser	Score	Year	Winner	Loser	Score
1972	Chris Evert	K. Reid	75 64	1989	Steffi Graf	M. Navratilova	64 75 26 62
1973	Chris Evert	N. Richey	63 63				
1974	Evonne Goolagong	C. Evert	63 64	1990	Monica Seles	G. Sabatini	64 57 36 64 62
1975	Chris Evert	M. Navratilova	64 62	1991	Monica Seles	M. Navratilova	64 36 75 60
1976	Evonne Goolagong	C. Evert	63 57 63	1992	Monica Seles	M. Navratilova	75 63 61
1977	Chris Evert	S. Barker	26 61 61	1993	Steffi Graf	A. S. Vicario	61 64 36 61
1978	M. Navratilova	E. Goolagong	76 64	1994	Gabriela Sabatini	L. Davenport	63 62 64
1979	M. Navratilova	T. Austin	63 36 62	1995	Steffi Graf	A. Huber	61 26 61 46 63
				1996	Steffi Graf	M. Hingis	63 46 60 46 60
1980	Tracy Austin	M. Navratilova	62 26 62	1997	Jana Novotna	M. Pierce	76 62 63
1981	M. Navratilova	A. Jaeger	63 76	1998	Martina Hingis	L. Davenport	75 64 46 62
1982	Sylvia Hanika	M. Navratilova	16 63 64	1999	Lindsay Davenport	M. Hingis	64 62
1983	M. Navratilova	C. Evert	62 60				
1984	M. Navratilova	C. Evert	63 75 61	2000	Martina Hingis	M. Seles	67 64 64
1985	M. Navratilova	H. Sukova	63 75 64	2001	Serena Williams	L. Davenport	walkover
1986	M. Navratilova	H. Mandlikova	62 60 36 61				
1986	M. Navratilova	S. Graf	76 63 62	**Notes:** Two tournaments were held in 1986 due to change			
1987	Steffi Graf	G. Sabatini	46 64 60 64	in playing season. The final was best-of-five sets from			
1988	Gabriela Sabatini	P. Shriver	75 62 62	1984-98 and best-of-three sets from 1972-83 and since 1999.			

Davis Cup

Established in 1900 as an annual international tournament by American player Dwight Davis. Originally called the International Lawn Tennis Challenge Trophy. Challenge round system until 1972. Since 1981, the top 16 nations in the world have played a straight knockout tournament over the course of a year. The format is a best-of-five match of two singles, one doubles and two singles over three days. Note that from 1900-24 Australia and New Zealand competed together as Australasia.

Multiple winners: USA (31); Australia (21); France (9); Sweden (7); Australasia (6); British Isles (5); Britain (4); Germany (3).

Challenge Rounds

Year	Winner	Loser	Score	Site	Year	Winner	Loser	Score	Site
1900	USA	British Isles	3-0	Boston	1927	France	USA	3-2	Philadelphia
1901	Not held				1928	France	USA	4-1	Paris
1902	USA	British Isles	3-2	New York	1929	France	USA	3-2	Paris
1903	British Isles	USA	4-1	Boston					
1904	British Isles	Belgium	5-0	Wimbledon	1930	France	USA	4-1	Paris
1905	British Isles	USA	5-0	Wimbledon	1931	France	Britain	3-2	Paris
1906	British Isles	USA	5-0	Wimbledon	1932	France	USA	3-2	Paris
1907	Australasia	British Isles	3-2	Wimbledon	1933	Britain	France	3-2	Paris
1908	Australasia	USA	3-2	Melbourne	1934	Britain	USA	4-1	Wimbledon
1909	Australasia	USA	5-0	Sydney	1935	Britain	USA	5-0	Wimbledon
1910	Not held				1936	Britain	Australia	3-2	Wimbledon
					1937	USA	Britain	4-1	Wimbledon
1911	Australasia	USA	5-0	Christchurch, NZ	1938	USA	Australia	3-2	Philadelphia
1912	British Isles	Australasia	3-2	Melbourne	1939	Australia	USA	3-2	Philadelphia
1913	USA	British Isles	3-2	Wimbledon					
1914	Australasia	USA	3-2	New York	1940-45	Not held World War II			
1915-18	Not held World War I				1946	USA	Australia	5-0	Melbourne
1919	Australasia	British Isles	4-1	Sydney	1947	USA	Australia	4-1	New York
					1948	USA	Australia	5-0	New York
1920	USA	Australasia	5-0	Auckland, NZ	1949	USA	Australia	4-1	New York
1921	USA	Japan	5-0	New York					
1922	USA	Australasia	4-1	New York	1950	Australia	USA	4-1	New York
1923	USA	Australasia	4-1	New York	1951	Australia	USA	3-2	Sydney
1924	USA	Australia	5-0	Philadelphia	1952	Australia	USA	4-1	Adelaide
1925	USA	France	5-0	Philadelphia	1953	Australia	USA	3-2	Melbourne
1926	USA	France	4-1	Philadelphia	1954	USA	Australia	3-2	Sydney
					1955	Australia	USA	5-0	New York

Year	Winner	Loser	Score	Site	Year	Winner	Loser	Score	Site
1956	Australia	USA	5-0	Adelaide	1962	Australia	Mexico	5-0	Brisbane
1957	Australia	USA	3-2	Melbourne	1963	USA	Australia	3-2	Adelaide
1958	USA	Australia	3-2	Brisbane	1964	Australia	USA	3-2	Cleveland
1959	Australia	USA	3-2	New York	1965	Australia	Spain	4-1	Sydney
1960	Australia	Italy	4-1	Sydney	1966	Australia	India	4-1	Melbourne
1961	Australia	Italy	5-0	Melbourne	1967	Australia	Spain	4-1	Brisbane

Final Rounds

Year	Winner	Loser	Score	Site	Year	Winner	Loser	Score	Site
1968	USA	Australia	4-1	Adelaide	1985	Sweden	W. Germany	3-2	Munich
1969	USA	Romania	5-0	Cleveland	1986	Australia	Sweden	3-2	Melbourne
1970	USA	W. Germany	5-0	Cleveland	1987	Sweden	India	5-0	Göteborg
1971	USA	Romania	3-2	Charlotte	1988	W. Germany	Sweden	4-1	Göteborg
1972	USA	Romania	3-2	Bucharest	1989	W. Germany	Sweden	3-2	Stuttgart
1973	Australia	USA	5-0	Cleveland	1990	USA	Australia	3-2	St. Petersburg
1974	So. Africa	India	walkover	Not held	1991	France	USA	3-1	Lyon
1975	Sweden	Czech.	3-2	Stockholm	1992	USA	Switzerland	3-1	Ft. Worth
1976	Italy	Chile	4-1	Santiago	1993	Germany	Australia	4-1	Dusseldorf
1977	Australia	Italy	3-1	Sydney	1994	Sweden	Russia	4-1	Moscow
1978	USA	Britain	4-1	Palm Springs	1995	USA	Russia	3-2	Moscow
1979	USA	Italy	5-0	San Francisco	1996	France	Sweden	3-2	Malmo
1980	Czech.	Italy	4-1	Prague	1997	Sweden	USA	5-0	Göteborg
1981	USA	Argentina	3-1	Cincinnati	1998	Sweden	Italy	4-1	Milan
1982	USA	France	4-1	Grenoble	1999	Australia	France	3-2	Nice
1983	Australia	Sweden	3-2	Melbourne	2000	Spain	Australia	3-1	Barcelona
1984	Sweden	USA	4-1	Göteborg	2001	France	Australia	3-2	Melbourne

Note: In 1974, India refused to play the final as a protest against the South African government's policies of apartheid.

Fed Cup

Originally the Federation Cup started by the International Tennis Federation as the Davis Cup of women's tennis. Played by 32 teams over one week at one site from 1963-94. Tournament changed to Davis Cup-style format of four rounds and home site from 1995-99. In 2000, a 12-nation, round-robin tournament was played over two weeks, with the previous year's winner hosting the semifinals and finals.
Multiple winners: USA (17); Australia (7); Czechoslovakia and Spain (5); Germany (2).

Year	Winner	Loser	Score	Site	Year	Winner	Loser	Score	Site
1963	USA	Australia	2-1	London	1983	Czech.	W. Germany	2-1	Zurich
1964	Australia	USA	2-1	Philadelphia	1984	Czech.	Australia	2-1	Brazil
1965	Australia	USA	2-1	Melbourne	1985	Czech.	USA	2-1	Japan
1966	USA	W. Germany	2-0	Italy	1986	USA	Czech.	3-0	Prague
1967	USA	Britain	2-0	W. Germany	1987	W. Germany	USA	2-1	Vancouver
1968	Australia	Holland	3-0	Paris	1988	Czech.	USSR	2-1	Melbourne
1969	USA	Australia	2-1	Athens	1989	USA	Spain	3-0	Tokyo
1970	Australia	Britain	3-0	W. Germany	1990	USA	USSR	2-1	Atlanta
1971	Australia	Britain	3-0	Perth	1991	Spain	USA	2-1	Nottingham
1972	So. Africa	Britain	2-1	Africa	1992	Germany	Spain	2-1	Frankfurt
1973	Australia	So. Africa	3-0	W. Germany	1993	Spain	Australia	3-0	Frankfurt
1974	Australia	USA	2-1	Italy	1994	Spain	USA	3-0	Frankfurt
1975	Czech.	Australia	3-0	France	1995	Spain	USA	3-2	Valencia
1976	USA	Australia	2-1	Philadelphia	1996	USA	Spain	5-0	Atlantic City
1977	USA	Australia	2-1	Eastbourne	1997	France	Netherlands	4-1	Nice, France
1978	USA	Australia	2-1	Melbourne	1998	Spain	Switzerland	3-2	Geneva
1979	USA	Australia	3-0	Spain	1999	USA	Russia	4-1	Palo Alto
1980	USA	Australia	3-0	W. Germany	2000	USA	Spain	5-0	Las Vegas
1981	USA	Britain	3-0	Tokyo	2001	Belgium	Russia	2-1	Madrid
1982	USA	W. Germany	3-0	Santa Clara					

COLLEGES

NCAA team titles were not sanctioned until 1946. NCAA women's individual and team championships started in 1982.

Men's NCAA Individual Champions (1883-1945)

Multiple winners: Malcolm Chace and Pancho Segura (3); Edward Chandler, George Church, E.B. Dewhurst, Fred Hovey, Frank Guernsey, W.P. Knapp, Robert LeRoy, P.S. Sears, Cliff Sutter, Ernest Sutter and Richard Williams (2).

Year		Year		Year	
1883	J. Clark, Harvard (spring)	1887	P.S. Sears, Harvard	1891	Fred Hovey, Harvard
	H. Taylor, Harvard (fall)	1888	P.S. Sears, Harvard	1892	William Larned, Cornell
1884	W.P. Knapp, Yale	1889	R.P. Huntington Jr., Yale	1893	Malcolm Chace, Brown
1885	W.P. Knapp, Yale	1890	Fred Hovey, Harvard	1894	Malcolm Chace, Yale
1886	G.M. Brinley, Trinity, CT			1895	Malcolm Chace, Yale

Colleges (Cont.)

Year		Year		Year	
1896	Malcolm Whitman, Harvard	1913	Richard Williams, Harv.	1931	Keith Gledhill, Stanford
1897	S.G. Thompson, Princeton	1914	George Church, Princeton	1932	Cliff Sutter, Tulane
1898	Leo Ware, Harvard	1915	Richard Williams, Harv.	1933	Jack Tidball, UCLA
1899	Dwight Davis, Harvard	1916	G.C. Caner, Harvard	1934	Gene Mako, USC
1900	Ray Little, Princeton	1917-1918	Not held	1935	Wilbur Hess, Rice
1901	Fred Alexander, Princeton	1919	Charles Garland, Yale	1936	Ernest Sutter, Tulane
1902	William Clothier, Harvard			1937	Ernest Sutter, Tulane
1903	E.B. Dewhurst, Penn	1920	Lascelles Banks, Yale	1938	Frank Guernsey, Rice
1904	Robert LeRoy, Columbia	1921	Philip Neer, Stanford	1939	Frank Guernsey, Rice
1905	E.B. Dewhurst, Penn	1922	Lucien Williams, Yale		
1906	Robert LeRoy, Columbia	1923	Carl Fischer, Phi. Osteo.	1940	Don McNeill, Kenyon
1907	G.P. Gardner Jr., Harvard	1924	Wallace Scott, Wash.	1941	Joseph Hunt, Navy
1908	Nat Niles, Harvard	1925	Edward Chandler, Calif.	1942	Fred Schroeder, Stanford
1909	Wallace Johnson, Penn	1926	Edward Chandler, Calif.	1943	Pancho Segura, Miami-FL
		1927	Wilmer Allison, Texas	1944	Pancho Segura, Miami-FL
1910	R.A. Holden Jr., Yale	1928	Julius Seligson, Lehigh	1945	Pancho Segura, Miami-FL
1911	E.H. Whitney, Harvard	1929	Berkeley Bell, Texas		
1912	George Church, Princeton	1930	Cliff Sutter, Tulane		

NCAA Men's Division I Champions

Multiple winners (Teams): Stanford (17); USC (16); UCLA (15); Georgia (4); William & Mary (2). (Players): Matias Boeker, Alex Olmedo, Mikael Pernfors, Dennis Ralston and Ham Richardson (2).

Year	Team winner	Individual Champion	Year	Team winner	Individual Champion
1946	USC	Bob Falkenburg, USC	1975	UCLA	Bill Martin, UCLA
1947	Wm. & Mary	Garner Larned, Wm.& Mary	1976	USC & UCLA	Bill Scanlon, Trinity-TX
1948	Wm. & Mary	Harry Likas, San Francisco	1977	Stanford	Matt Mitchell, Stanford
1949	San Francisco	Jack Tuero, Tulane	1978	Stanford	John McEnroe, Stanford
			1979	UCLA	Kevin Curren, Texas
1950	UCLA	Herbert Flam, UCLA			
1951	USC	Tony Trabert, Cincinnati	1980	Stanford	Robert Van't Hof, USC
1952	UCLA	Hugh Stewart, USC	1981	Stanford	Tim Mayotte, Stanford
1953	UCLA	Ham Richardson, Tulane	1982	UCLA	Mike Leach, Michigan
1954	UCLA	Ham Richardson, Tulane	1983	Stanford	Greg Holmes, Utah
1955	USC	Jose Aguero, Tulane	1984	UCLA	Mikael Pernfors, Georgia
1956	UCLA	Alex Olmedo, USC	1985	Georgia	Mikael Pernfors, Georgia
1957	Michigan	Barry MacKay, Michigan	1986	Stanford	Dan Goldie, Stanford
1958	USC	Alex Olmedo, USC	1987	Georgia	Andrew Burrow, Miami-FL
1959	Tulane & Notre Dame	Whitney Reed, San Jose St.	1988	Stanford	Robby Weiss, Pepperdine
			1989	Stanford	Donni Leaycraft, LSU
1960	UCLA	Larry Nagler, UCLA			
1961	UCLA	Allen Fox, UCLA	1990	Stanford	Steve Bryan, Texas
1962	USC	Rafael Osuna, USC	1991	USC	Jared Palmer, Stanford
1963	USC	Dennis Ralston, USC	1992	Stanford	Alex O'Brien Stanford
1964	USC	Dennis Ralston, USC	1993	USC	Chris Woodruff, Tennessee
1965	UCLA	Arthur Ashe, UCLA	1994	USC	Mark Merklein, Florida
1966	USC	Charlie Pasarell, UCLA	1995	Stanford	Sargis Sargisian, Ariz. St.
1967	USC	Bob Lutz, USC	1996	Stanford	Cecil Mamiit, USC
1968	USC	Stan Smith, USC	1997	Stanford	Luke Smith, UNLV
1969	USC	Joaquin Loyo-Mayo, USC	1998	Stanford	Bob Bryan, Stanford
			1999	Georgia	Jeff Morrison, Florida
1970	UCLA	Jeff Borowiak, UCLA			
1971	UCLA	Jimmy Connors, UCLA	2000	Stanford	Alex Kim, Stanford
1972	Trinity-TX	Dick Stockton, Trinity-TX	2001	Georgia	Matias Boeker, Georgia
1973	Stanford	Alex Mayer, Stanford	2002	USC	Matias Boeker, Georgia
1974	Stanford	John Whitlinger, Stanford			

NCAA Women's Division I Champions

Multiple winners (Teams): Stanford (12); Florida (3); Georgia, Texas and USC (2). (Players): Sandra Birch, Patty Fendick, Laura Granville and Lisa Raymond (2).

Year	Team winner	Individual Champion	Year	Team winner	Individual Champion
1982	Stanford	Alycia Moulton, Stanford	1993	Texas	Lisa Raymond, Florida
1983	USC	Beth Herr, USC	1994	Georgia	Angela Lettiere, Georgia
1984	Stanford	Lisa Spain, Georgia	1995	Texas	Keri Phoebus, UCLA
1985	USC	Linda Gates, Stanford	1996	Florida	Jill Craybas, Florida
1986	Stanford	Patty Fendick, Stanford	1997	Stanford	Lilia Osterloh, Stanford
1987	Stanford	Patty Fendick, Stanford	1998	Florida	Vanessa Webb, Duke
1988	Stanford	Shaun Stafford, Florida	1999	Stanford	Zuzana Lesenarova, S. Diego
1989	Stanford	Sandra Birch, Stanford	2000	Georgia	Laura Granville, Stanford
1990	Stanford	Debbie Graham, Stanford	2001	Stanford	Laura Granville, Stanford
1991	Stanford	Sandra Birch, Stanford	2002	Stanford	Bea Bielik, Wake Forest
1992	Florida	Lisa Raymond, Florida			

Golf

*A joyous European team surrounds captain **Sam Torrance** after reclaiming the Ryder Cup.*

AP/Wide World Photos

Rich and Famous

Unheralded Rich Beem wins his first major title while Tiger continues his assault on the PGA record book.

Karl Ravech
is an analyst for ESPN's golf coverage.

In 2002, parity struck the golf world. How else can you explain that the most exciting major of the year, the PGA Championship, was won by a guy who used to sell electronics for a living?

In one of his other lives Rich Beem was also an assistant golf pro at the El Paso Country Club. Routinely he screwed up members' tee times, as juggling menial tasks proved difficult. So how in the world could he withstand a charging Tiger Woods and win by a shot? He shouldn't have been able to, but he did. Such was life on the PGA Tour this year.

The first 15 events were won by 15 different players. In that group were guys named Gogel, Mattiace, Leggatt, Perks and of course, Woods. Woods  was also the first to win twice. His second win also happened to be his third Masters.

Considering every superlative has already been used to describe the man who already is being called by many "the greatest golfer to ever live," not too many were shocked when Woods broke out of the gate at Augusta and cruised during the final round. His lead was never fewer than two strokes on Sunday, and as Phil Mickelson (a.k.a. Tiger's bridesmaid) pointed out, "When other guys are up there, there's a good chance they might come back two or three shots, but Tiger doesn't ever seem to do that." Very prophetic words.

Those same words would echo down the fairways of the world-class Bethpage Black Course two months later for the playing of the 2002 United States Open.

Since the U.S. Open is played on the country's most famous golf courses, the selection of a state-owned public facility for the first time in the tourna-

AP/Wide World Photos

Tiger Woods watches his shot on the 13th hole at Bethpage Black during the final round of the 2002 U.S. Open. He would be the only player to finish the tournament under par.

ment's history garnered most of the pre-tournament publicity, and rightfully so. Bethpage Black has a magnificent layout in Farmingdale on Long Island. It's a course that does not allow carts and has a first-come, first-serve policy that requires those who want to play on it to sleep in their cars the night before. During tournament week, sleeping was all but impossible as passionate, boisterous crowds filled the grounds for six straight days.

The masses came to see the world's No. 1 player. And he didn't disappoint. Tiger's game was so polished

over the first three rounds that he could afford to shoot a 2-over-par 72 on Sunday and still win by three strokes. Once again, the praise rained down on Woods.

"Nothing is out of his reach," said fellow pro Brad Faxon.

Now he was reaching for a Grand Slam, and he was halfway there.

The dream died across The Pond. The British Open was played at Muirfield and Saturday brought some of the worst weather conditions imaginable. High winds and low temperatures brought scores way up. Tiger

*The scoreboard and the smile tell the story as unlikely winner **Rich Beem** celebrates his title at the PGA Championship in Minnesota.*

shot a third-round 81. He finished tied for 28th, six shots behind Ernie Els. Els emerged victorious in the first-ever four-man playoff at a British Open.

The final major chapter would be written two months later at Hazeltine National Golf Club in Chaska, Minnesota, which brings us back to the electronics salesman.

Rich Beem still carries his ID card from the Seattle electronics store in his wallet. He's a good player, groomed by a father who demanded his son understand the mechanics of a golf swing. While his father never believed his son was listening, Beem proved him and every other doubting Thomas wrong. He didn't exactly stare Woods down, like many contend (they didn't play in the final group together), but he was aware of the four straight birdies Tiger put on the board to finish, and even then he was unmoved. Beem's swashbuckling, go-for-broke approach proved the perfect elixir to put his demons to bed and subdue a charging Tiger at the same time.

The Ten Biggest Stories of the Year in Golf

10 ▪ Augusta National Golf Club sets a new Masters policy regarding the playing eligibility of former champions. Beginning in 2004, past winners age 65 or under can play only if they compete in ten official tournaments in the previous year. In the past, champions received a lifetime exemption.

9 ▪ Hall of Famer Juli Inkster overcomes a final round two-stroke deficit to defeat Annika Sorenstam and win the U.S. Women's Open, her seventh major title. The win earns her $535,000 of the LPGA-record $3 million purse.

8 ▪ Martha Burk, chairwoman of the National Council of Women's Organizations, organizes an effort to have women allowed membership to Augusta National, but club chairman Hootie Johnson refuses to give in to her demands. When NCWO reportedly puts pressure on the Masters sponsors, Johnson counters by removing them, creating a commercial-free broadcast.

7 ▪ Behind two points heading into the final day, the U.S. women defeat Europe 8½–3½ in singles matches to recapture the Solheim Cup.

6 ▪ Tiger Woods wins his third Masters in the last six years with a 12-under-par, three-stroke victory over Retief Goosen. He joins Jack Nicklaus and Nick Faldo as the only golfers to win back-to-back Masters titles.

5 ▪ Easy Ernie Els squanders a three-shot lead on the back-nine on Sunday at the British Open, then defeats Thomas Levet on the first sudden death hole after a four-way, four-hole playoff for the win. Tiger Woods shoots a third-round 81 in rainy, blustery conditions, dashing his hopes of a Grand Slam.

4 ▪ Annika Sorenstam wins nine LPGA titles through early October, including her fourth major at the Nabisco Championship. She breaks her own LPGA single season earnings mark. Perhaps the truly amazing story is that she actually missed the cut at the British Open, her first miss in 75 tournaments.

3 ▪ At The Belfry in England, Irishman Paul McGinley sinks an eight-foot putt to seal the victory as the jubilant Europeans reclaim the Ryder Cup with a 15½–12½ victory over the U.S.

2 ▪ Tiger tames Bethpage Black— In front of a boisterous crowd on the longest (and the first truly public) course in U.S. Open history, Tiger Woods finishes 3-under-par and three shots ahead of Phil Mickelson for his eighth major championship.

1 ▪ "Regular guy" Rich Beem fends off a ferocious final-round charge from Tiger Woods to win the PGA Championship. Woods birdies the last four holes but Beem holds on for the one-stroke victory.

American Express Charge

Tiger Woods' 25-under-par at the American Express Championship in September 2002 is the lowest score (in relation to par) of his PGA career for a four-round event.

	To Par	Place
2002 AmEx Champ.	–25	1st
2000 NCR Classic	–23	3rd
2000 Canadian Open	–22	1st
1999 Buick Invitational	–22	1st

Note: Woods' rounds at the 2002 American Express Championship were 65-65-67-66.

Slammin' Sammy

Legend Sam Snead died on May 23, leaving behind a formidable list of PGA records and accomplishments. His most notable mark is his career record 81 Tour wins, but Snead also holds the single-season win mark (since 1950).

	Year	Wins
Sam Snead	1950	11
Tiger Woods	2000	9
Tiger Woods	1999	8
Johnny Miller	1974	8
Arnold Palmer	1960	8

Note: The record for wins in a single season before 1950 is 18, by Byron Nelson in 1945. Ben Hogan had 13 in 1946.

High Beem

The 2002 PGA Championship was just the fourth major event Rich Beem competed in. Below are the fewest majors played in before a win (since 1980).

	Event Won	Major Played
John Daly	1991 PGA	3rd
Rich Beem	2002 PGA	4th
Bob Tway	1986 PGA	4th

Green with Envy

In 2002 Tiger Woods won his third Masters title in just his eighth Masters start, tying him with Jack Nicklaus and Arnold Palmer as the quickest to win three green jackets.

	Starts to 3 Wins	Masters Titles
Tiger Woods	8	3
Jack Nicklaus	8	6
Arnold Palmer	8	4
Jimmy Demaret	9	3
Nick Faldo	13	3

Empty Cup

As the table below shows, Tiger Woods' performance at the Ryder Cup has been less than spectacular thus far. (W-L-T)

	Foursomes	Singles	Total
2002	2-2-0	0-0-1	2-2-1
1999	1-3-0	1-0-0	2-3-0
1997	1-2-1	0-1-0	1-3-1
Totals	4-7-1	1-1-1	5-8-2

2001-2002
Season in Review

ESPN
Information Please®
SPORTS ALMANAC

Tournament Results

Schedules and results of PGA, European PGA, PGA Seniors and LPGA tournaments from Nov. 4, 2001 through Oct. 13, 2002.

PGA Tour

LATE 2001

Last Rd	Tournament	Winner	Earnings	Runner-Up
Nov. 4	Southern Farm Bureau Classic	Cameron Beckham (269)	$432,000	C. Campbell (270)
Nov. 4	The Tour Championship	Mike Weir (270)*	900,000	3-way tie (270)
Nov. 11	Franklin Templeton Shootout	Brad Faxon/ Scott McCarron (183)	225,000 (each)	J. Daly/ F. Lickliter II (185)
Nov. 18@	WGC: EMC World Cup	South Africa (264)*	1,000,000	3-way tie (264)
Nov. 26@	Skins Game	Greg Norman (18 skins)	1,000,000	3-way tie (0 skins)
Dec. 9@	Hyundai Team Matches	Mark Calcavecchia/ Fred Couples (1-up)	100,000 (each)	T. Lehman/D. Waldorf
Dec. 16@	Williams World Challenge	Tiger Woods (273)	1,000,000	V. Singh (276)

@ Unofficial PGA Tour money event.

*Playoffs: Tour Championship—Weir won on 1st hole; **WGC: EMC World Cup**—South Africa (E. Els, R. Goosen) won on 2nd hole.

Second place ties (3 players or more): 3-WAY—**Tour Championship** (D. Toms, S. Garcia, E. Els); **EMC World Cup** (Denmark, United States, New Zealand); **Skins Game** (C. Montgomerie, J. Parnevik, T. Woods).

2002

Last Rd	Tournament	Winner	Earnings	Runner-Up
Jan. 6	Mercedes Championships	Sergio Garcia (274)*	$720,000	D. Toms (274)
Jan. 13	Sony Open	Jerry Kelly (266)	720,000	J. Cook (267)
Jan. 20	Bob Hope Chrysler Classic	Phil Mickelson (330)+*	720,000	D. Berganio (330)
Jan. 27	Phoenix Open	Chris DiMarco (267)	720,000	K. Yokoo & K. Perry (268)
Feb. 3	AT&T Pebble Beach Pro-Am	Matt Gogel (274)	720,000	P. Perez (277)
Feb. 10	Buick Invitational	Jose Maria Olazabal (275)	648,000	M. O'Meara & J.L. Lewis (276)
Feb. 17	Nissan Open	Len Mattiace (269)	666,000	3-way tie (270)
Feb. 24	WGC: Accenture Match Play Championship	Kevin Sutherland (1-up)	1,000,000	S. McCarron
Feb. 24	Tucson Open	Ian Leggatt (268)	540,000	L. Roberts & D. Peoples (270)
Mar. 3	Genuity Championship	Ernie Els (271)	846,000	T. Woods (273)
Mar. 10	Honda Classic	Matt Kuchar (269)	630,000	B. Faxon & J. Sindelar (271)
Mar. 17	Bay Hill Invitational	Tiger Woods (275)	720,000	M. Campbell (279)
Mar. 24	The Players Championship	Craig Perks (280)	1,080,000	S. Ames (282)
Mar. 31	Shell Houston Open	Vijay Singh (266)	720,000	D. Clarke (272)
Apr. 7	BellSouth Classic	Retief Goosen (272)	684,000	J. Parnevik (276)
Apr. 14	**The Masters** (Augusta, Ga.)	Tiger Woods (276)	1,008,000	R. Goosen (279)
Apr. 21	WorldCom Classic	Justin Leonard (270)	720,000	H. Slocum (271)
Apr. 28	Greater Greensboro Chrysler Classic	Rocco Mediate (272)	684,000	M. Calcavecchia (275)
May 5	Compaq Classic of New Orleans	K.J. Choi (271)	810,000	G. Ogilvy & D. Hart (275)
May 12	Verizon Byron Nelson Classic	Shigeki Maruyama (266)	864,000	B. Crane (268)
May 19	MasterCard Colonial	Nick Price (267)	774,000	D. Toms & K. Perry (272)
May 26	Memorial Tournament	Jim Furyk (274)	810,000	D. Peoples & J. Cook (276)
June 2	Kemper Insurance Open	Bob Estes (273)	648,000	R. Beem (274)
June 9	Buick Classic	Chris Smith (272)	630,000	3-way tie (274)
June 16	**U.S. Open** (Farmingdale, N.Y.)	Tiger Woods (277)	1,000,000	P. Mickelson (280)
June 23	Cannon Greater Hartford Open	Phil Mickelson (266)	720,000	D. Love III & J. Kaye (267)
June 30	FedEx St. Jude Classic	Len Mattiace (266)	684,000	T. Petrovic (267)
July 7	Advil Western Open	Jerry Kelly (269)	720,000	D. Love III (271)
July 14	Greater Milwaukee Open	Jeff Sluman (261)	558,000	T. Herron & S. Lowery (265)
July 21	**British Open** (Guiland, Scot.)	Ernie Els (278)*	1,106,140	3-way tie (278)
July 21	B.C. Open	Spike McRoy (269)	378,000	F. Funk (270)
July 28	John Deere Classic	J.P. Hayes (262)	540,000	R. Gamez (266)
Aug. 4	The International†	Rich Beem (44)	810,000	S. Lowery (43)
Aug. 11	Buick Open	Tiger Woods (271)	594,000	4-way tie (275)
Aug. 18	**PGA Championship** (Chaska, Minn.)	Rich Beem (278)	990,000	T. Woods (279)
Aug. 25	WGC: NEC Invitational	Craig Parry (268)	1,000,000	R. Allenby & F. Funk (272)

Tournament Results (Cont.)

Last Rd	Tournament	Winner	Earnings	Runner-Up
Aug. 25	Reno-Tahoe Open	Chris Riley (271)*	$540,000	J. Kaye (271)
Sept. 1	Air Canada Championship	Gene Sauers (269)	630,000	S. Lowery (270)
Sept. 8	Bell Canadian Open	John Rollins (272)*	720,000	J. Leonard & N. Lancaster (272)
Sept. 15	SEI Pennsylvania Classic	Dan Forsman (270)	594,000	R. Allenby & B. Andrade (271)
Sept. 22	WGC: American Express Championship	Tiger Woods (263)	1,000,000	R. Goosen (264)
Sept. 22	Tampa Bay Classic	K.J. Choi (267)	468,000	G. Day (274)
Sept. 29	Valero Texas Open	Loren Roberts (261)	630,000	3-way tie (264)
Sept. 29	The Ryder Cup (Sutton, ENG)	Europe (15½)	—	United States (12½)
Oct. 6	Michelob Championship at Kingsmill	Charles Howell III (270)	666,000	S. Hoch & B. Jobe (272)
Oct. 13	Invensys Classic at Las Vegas	Phil Tataurangi (330)+	900,000	S. Appleby & J. Sluman (331)

+This is a five-round, 90-hole event played over five days.

†The scoring for The International is based on a modified Stableford system (8 points for a double eagle, 5 for an eagle, 2 for a birdie, 0 for a par, –1 for a bogey, –3 for double bogey or worse).

*Playoffs: Mercedes—Garcia won on 1st hole; Bob Hope—Mickelson won on 1st hole; British Open—Els won on 1st hole of sudden death after four-hole playoff; Reno-Tahoe—Riley won on 1st hole; Canadian Open—Rollins won on 1st hole.

Second place ties (3 players or more): 4-WAY—Buick Open (M. O'Meara, B. Gay, F. Funk, E. Toledo); 3-WAY—Nissan (R. Sabbatini, B. Faxon, S. McCarron); Buick Classic (D. Gossett, P. Perez, L. Roberts); British Open (T. Levet, S. Appleby, S. Elkington); Texas Open (F. Couples, F. Funk, G. Willis).

PGA Majors

The Masters

Edition: 66th **Dates:** April 11–14
Site: Augusta National GC, Augusta, Ga.
Par: 36-36—72 (7270 yards) **Purse:** $5,600,000

		1 2 3 4 Tot	Earnings
1	Tiger Woods	70-69-66-71—276	$1,008,000
2	Retief Goosen	69-67-69-74—279	604,800
3	Phil Mickelson	69-72-68-71—280	380,800
4	Jose Maria Olazabal	70-69-71-71—281	268,800
5	Ernie Els	70-67-72-72—282	212,800
	Padraig Harrington	69-70-72-71—282	212,800
7	Vijay Singh	70-65-72-76—283	187,600
8	Sergio Garcia	68-71-70-75—284	173,600
9	Miguel A. Jimenez	70-71-74-70—285	151,200
	Adam Scott	71-72-72-70—285	151,200
	Angel Cabrera	68-71-73-73—285	151,200

Early round leaders: 1st—Davis Love III (67); 2nd—Singh (135); 3rd—Woods (205).
Top amateur: none.

U.S. Open

Edition: 102nd **Dates:** June 13–16
Site: Black Course, Bethpage State Park, Farmingdale, N.Y.
Par: 35-35—70 (7214 yards) **Purse:** $5,500,000

		1 2 3 4 Tot	Earnings
1	Tiger Woods	67-68-70-72—277	$1,000,000
2	Phil Mickelson	70-73-67-70—280	585,000
3	Jeff Maggert	69-73-68-72—282	362,356
4	Sergio Garcia	68-74-67-74—283	252,546
5	Nick Faldo	70-76-66-73—285	182,882
	Scott Hoch	71-75-70-69—285	182,882
	Billy Mayfair	69-74-68-74—285	182,882
8	Tom Byrum	72-72-70-72—286	138,669
	Padraig Harrington	70-68-73-75—286	138,669
	Nick Price	72-75-69-70—286	138,669

Early round leaders: 1st—Woods (67); 2nd—Woods (135); 3rd—Woods (205).
Top amateur: Kevin Warrick (307).

British Open

Edition: 131st **Dates:** July 18–21
Site: Muirfield Golf Links, Guilland, Scotland
Par: 36-35—71 (7034 yards) **Purse:** $4,720,650

		1 2 3 4 Tot	Earnings
1	Ernie Els*	70-66-72-70—278	$1,106,140
	Thomas Levet	72-66-74-66—278	452,991
	Stuart Appleby	73-70-70-65—278	452,991
	Steve Elkington	71-73-68-66—278	452,991
5	Gary Evans	72-68-74-65—279	221,228
	Padraig Harrington	69-67-76-67—279	221,228
	Shigeki Maruyama	68-68-75-68—279	221,228
8	Peter O'Malley	72-68-75-65—280	122,466
	Scott Hoch	74-69-71-66—280	122,466
	Retief Goosen	71-68-74-67—280	122,466
	Thomas Bjorn	68-70-73-69—280	122,466
	Sergio Garcia	71-69-71-69—280	122,466
	Soren Hansen	68-69-73-70—280	122,466

*Els defeated Levet on the first hole of sudden death after a four-hole playoff with two other golfers. Appleby and Elkington were were eliminated after the playoff.

Note: Tiger Woods (70-68-81-65—284) finished tied for 28th.

Early round leaders: 1st—Duffy Waldorf, David Toms and Carl Pettersson (67); 2nd—Els, Maruyama, Harrington, Waldorf and Bob Tway (136); 3rd—Els (208).
Top amateur: none.

PGA Championship

Edition: 84th **Dates:** Aug. 15–18
Site: Hazeltine National GC, Chaska, Minn.
Par: 36-36—72 (7360 yards) **Purse:** $5,500,000

		1 2 3 4 Tot	Earnings
1	Rich Beem	72-66-72-68—278	$990,000
2	Tiger Woods	71-69-72-67—279	594,000
3	Chris Riley	71-70-72-70—283	374,000
4	Fred Funk	68-70-73-73—284	235,000
	Justin Leonard	72-66-69-77—284	235,000
6	Rocco Mediate	72-73-70-70—285	185,000
7	Mark Calcavecchia	70-68-74-74—286	172,000
8	Vijay Singh	71-74-74-68—287	159,000
9	Jim Furyk	68-73-76-71—288	149,000
10	Jose Coceres	72-71-72-74—289	110,714
	Steve Lowery	71-71-73-74—289	110,714
	Pierre Fulke	72-68-78-71—289	110,714
	Ricardo Gonzalez	74-73-71-71—289	110,714
	Sergio Garcia	75-73-73-68—289	110,714
	Stewart Cink	74-74-72-69—289	110,714
	Robert Allenby	76-66-77-70—289	110,714

Early round leaders: 1st—Funk and Furyk (68); 2nd—Retief Goosen, Beem, Calcavecchia, Funk and Leonard (138); 3rd—Leonard (207).
Top amateur: none.

The Official World Golf Ranking

Begun in 1986, the Official World Golf Ranking (formerly the Sony World Ranking) combines the best golfers on the world's leading professional tours—Asian, PGA Tour of Australia, European, European Challenge, Japan Golf Tour, Southern African and U.S. (PGA Tour, Buy.com). Rankings are based on a rolling two-year period and weighted in favor of more recent results. Points are awarded after each worldwide tournament according to finish. Final points-per-tournament averages are determined by dividing a player's total points by the number of tournaments played over that two-year period (through Oct. 13, 2002).

	Avg			Avg			Avg
1 Tiger Woods, USA	17.54	6 Padraig Harrington, IRE	6.11	11 Nick Price, ZIM	4.76
2 Phil Mickelson, USA	8.96	7 David Toms, USA	5.60	12 David Duval, USA	4.50
3 Ernie Els, RSA	7.80	8 Vijay Singh, FIJ	5.39	13 Chris DiMarco, USA	4.10
4 Retief Goosen, RSA	6.92	9 Davis Love III, USA	5.37	14 Colin Montgomerie, GBR	4.08
5 Sergio Garcia, SPA	6.59	10 Jim Furyk, USA	4.97	15 Justin Leonard, USA	4.03

European PGA Tour

Official money won on the European Tour is presented in euros (€).

LATE 2001

Last Rd	Tournament	Winner	Earnings	Runner-Up
Nov. 4	Italian Open	Gregory Havret (268)	€166,660	B. Dredge (269)
Nov. 11	Volvo Masters	Padraig Harrington (204)#	539,074	P. McGinley (205)
Nov. 18	WGC: EMC World Cup	South Africa (264)*	1,119,190	3-way tie (264)
Nov. 25	Asian Open	Jarmo Sandelin (278)	273,702	J.M. Olazabal & T. Jaidee (279)
Dec. 2	Hong Kong Open	Jose Maria Olazabal (262)	128,848	H. Bjornstad (263)

#Weather-shortened

*Playoffs: WGC: EMC World Cup—South Africa (E. Els, R. Goosen) won on 2nd hole.
Second place ties (3 players or more): 3-WAY—**EMC World Cup** (Denmark, United States, New Zealand).

2002

Last Rd	Tournament	Winner	Earnings	Runner-Up
Jan. 13	South African Open	Tim Clark (269)	€128,052	S. Webster (271)
Jan. 20	Alfred Dunhill Championship	Justin Rose (268)	128,173	3-way tie (270)
Jan. 27	Johnnie Walker Classic	Retief Goosen (274)	243,640	P. Fulke (282)
Feb. 3	Heineken Classic	Ernie Els (271)	221,385	3-way tie (276)
Feb. 10	ANZ Championship†	Richard S. Johnson (46)	195,079	C. Parry & S. Laycock (44)
Feb. 24	WGC: Accenture Match Play Championship	Kevin Sutherland (1-up)	1,145,476	S. McCarron
Feb. 24	Singapore Masters	Arjun Atwal (274)	171,855	R. Green (279)
Mar. 3	Malaysian Open	Alastair Forsyth (267)*	184,366	S. Leaney (267)
Mar. 10	Dubai Desert Classic	Ernie Els (272)	273,335	N. Fasth (276)
Mar. 17	Qatar Masters	Adam Scott (269)	285,650	N. Dougherty & J.F. Remesy (275)
Mar. 24	Madeira Island Open	Diego Borrego (281)	91,660	I. Giner & M. Lafeber (282)
Apr. 7	Portugal Open	Carl Pettersson (142)*#	125,000	D. Gilford (142)
Apr. 14	The Masters Tournament	Tiger Woods (276)	1,144,807	R. Goosen (279)
Apr. 21	The Seve Trophy	Great Britain & Ireland (14½)	150,000 (each)	Europe (11½)
Apr. 28	Canarias Open	Sergio Garcia (275)	287,000	E. Canonica (279)
May 5	French Open	Malcolm Mackenzie (274)	333,330	T. Immelman (275)
May 12	Benson & Hedges International	Angel Cabrera (278)	294,356	B. Lane (279)
May 19	Deutsche Bank-SAP Open	Tiger Woods (268)*	450,000	C. Montgomerie (268)
May 26	Volvo PGA Championship	Anders Hansen (269)	528,708	C. Montgomerie & E. Romero (274)
June 2	British Masters	Justin Rose (269)	329,373	I. Poulter (270)
June 9	English Open	Darren Clarke (271)	208,797	S. Hansen (274)
June 16	U.S. Open	Tiger Woods (277)	1,058,313	P. Mickelson (280)
June 23	The Great North Open	Miles Tunnicliff (279)	155,960	S. Struver (283)
June 30	Murphy's Irish Open	Soren Hansen (270)*	266,660	3-way tie (270)
July 7	Smurfit European Open	Michael Campbell (282)	515,584	4-way tie (283)
July 14	The Barclay's Scottish Open	Eduardo Romero (273)*	573,016	F. Jacobson (273)
July 21	British Open	Ernie Els (278)*	1,095,514	3-way tie (278)
July 28	The TNT Open	Tobias Dier (263)	300,000	J. Spence (264)
Aug. 4	Scandinavian Masters	Graeme McDowell (270)	316,660	T. Immelman (271)
Aug. 11	Wales Open	Paul Lawrie (272)	291,432	J. Bickerton (277)
Aug. 18	PGA Championship	Rich Beem (278)	1,019,144	T. Woods (279)
Aug. 18	North West of Ireland Open	Adam Mednick (281)	58,330	A. Coltart & C. Rocca (286)
Aug. 25	WGC: NEC Invitational	Craig Parry (268)	1,000,000	R. Allenby & F. Funk (272)
Aug. 25	Scottish PGA Championship	Adam Scott (262)	260,461	R. Russell (272)

Tournament Results (Cont.)

Last Rd	Tournament	Winner	Earnings	Runner-Up
Sept. 1	BMW International Open	Thomas Bjorn (264)	€300,000	J. Bickerton & B. Langer (268)
Sept. 8	European Masters	Robert Karlsson (270)	250,000	P. Lawrie & T. Immelman (274)
Sept. 15	German Masters	Stephen Leaney (266)	500,000	A. Cejka (267)
Sept. 22	WGC: American Express Championship	Tiger Woods (263)	1,026,378	R. Goosen (264)
Sept. 29	The Ryder Cup	Europe (15½)	—	United States (12½)
Oct. 6	Dunhill Links Championship	Padraig Harrington (269)*	818,662	E. Romero (269)
Oct. 13	Trophee Lancome	Alex Cejka (272)	239,640	C. Rodiles (274)

†The scoring for the ANZ Championship is based on a modified Stableford system (8 points for a double eagle, 5 for an eagle, 2 for a birdie, 0 for a par, −1 for a bogey, −3 for double bogey or worse).

*Playoffs: **Malaysian**—Forsyth won on 2nd hole; **Portugal**—Pettersson won on 1st hole; **SAP Open**—Woods won on the 3rd hole; **Irish Open**—Hansen won on 4th hole; **Scottish Open**—Romero won on 1st hole; **British Open**—Els won on 1st hole of sudden death; **Dunhill Links**—Harrington won on 2nd hole.

Second place ties (3 players or more): 4-WAY—**European Open** (R. Goosen, P. Lawrie, B. Dredge, P. Harrington). 3-WAY—**Alfred Dunhill Championship** (M. Foster, R. Goosen, M. Maritz); **Heineken** (P. O'Malley, P. Fowler, D. Howell); **Irish Open** (R. Bland, N. Fasth, D. Fichardt); **British Open** (S. Elkington, S. Appleby, T. Levet).

Senior PGA Tour

LATE 2001

Last Rd	Tournament	Winner	Earnings	Runner-Up
Nov. 11@	Senior Slam	Allen Doyle (134)	$300,000	T. Watson (136)
Dec. 2@	Office Depot Father/Son Challenge	Raymond/Robert Floyd (124)	100,000 (each)	Hale/Steve Irwin (125)
Dec. 9@	Hyundai Team Matches	Allen Doyle/Dana Quigley (1-up)	100,000 (each)	A. North/T. Watson

2002

Last Rd	Tournament	Winner	Earnings	Runner-Up
Jan. 21	MasterCard Championship	Tom Kite (199)#	$258,000	J. Jacobs (105)
Jan. 27@	Senior Skins Game	Hale Irwin (11 skins)	450,000	J. Nicklaus (7)
Feb. 3	Royal Caribbean Classic	John Jacobs (133)#	217,500	3-way tie (134)
Feb. 10	Ace Group Classic	Hale Irwin (200)	225,000	T. Watson (201)
Feb. 17	Verizon Classic	Doug Tewell (203)	225,000	H. Irwin (204)
Feb. 24	Audi Senior Classic	Bruce Lietzke (208)	255,000	H. Irwin & G. McCord (209)
Mar. 3	SBC Classic	Tom Kite (212)*	217,500	T. Watson (212)
Mar. 10	Toshiba Classic	Hale Irwin (196)	225,000	A. Doyle (201)
Mar. 17	Siebel Classic in Silicon Valley	Dana Quigley (212)	210,000	B. Gilder & F. Zoeller (213)
Mar. 31	Emerald Coast Classic	Dave Eichelberger (130)#	217,500	D. Tewell (132)
Apr. 7@	Liberty Mutual Legends of Golf	Doug Tewell (205)	308,000	B. Wadkins (206)
Apr. 28	**Countrywide Tradition** (Superstition Mt., Ariz.)	Jim Thorpe (277)*	300,000	J. Jacobs (277)
May 5	Bruno's Memorial Classic	Sammy Rachels (201)*	210,000	D. Quigley (201)
May 12	TD Waterhouse Championship	Bruce Lietzke (133)#	240,000	L. Nelson (135)
May 19	The Instinet Classic	Isao Aoki (201)	225,000	J. Jacobs (205)
May 26	Farmers Charity Classic	Jay Sigel (203)	225,000	M. Hatalsky (205)
June 2	NFL Golf Classic	James Mason (207)	195,000	3-way tie (209)
June 9	**Senior PGA Championship** (South Akron, Ohio)	Fuzzy Zoeller (278)	360,000	H. Irwin & B. Wadkins (280)
June 16	BellSouth Senior Classic at Opryland	Gil Morgan (202)	240,000	3-way tie (205)
June 23	Greater Baltimore Classic	J. C. Snead (203)	217,500	3-way tie (204)
June 30	**U.S. Senior Open** (Owings Mills, Md.)	Don Pooley (274)*	450,000	T. Watson (274)
July 7	AT&T Canada Senior Open	Tom Jenkins (195)	240,000	3-way tie (198)
July 14	**Ford Senior Players Championship** (Dearborn, Mich.)	Stewart Ginn (274)	375,000	3-way tie (275)
July 21	SBC Senior Open	Bob Gilder (204)*	217,500	H. Irwin (204)
July 2	FleetBoston Classic	Bob Gilder (203)*	225,000	J. Mahaffey (203)
Aug. 4	Lightpath Long Island Classic	Hubert Green (199)*	255,000	H. Irwin (199)
Aug. 11	3M Championship	Hale Irwin (204)	262,500	H. Green (207)
Aug. 25	Uniting Fore Care Classic†	Morris Hatalsky (42)	225,000	J. Sigel (30)
Sept. 1	Allianz Championship	Bob Gilder (200)	277,500	J. Bland (201)
Sept. 8	Kroger Senior Classic	Bob Gilder (200)*	225,000	T. Jenkins (200)
Sept. 15	RJR Championship	Bruce Fleisher (191)	240,000	H. Irwin (196)
Sept. 22	SAS Championship	Bruce Lietzke (202)	255,000	3-way tie (206)

Last Rd	Tournament	Winner	Earnings	Runner-Up
Oct. 6	Turtle Bay Championship	Hale Irwin (208)*	$225,000	G. McCord (208)
Oct. 13	Napa Valley Championship	Tom Kite (204)	195,000	F. Gibson & B. Fleisher (205)

#Weather-shortened.

@ Unofficial Senior PGA Tour money event.

†The scoring for the Uniting Fore Care Classic is based on a modified Stableford system (8 points for a double eagle, 5 for an eagle, 2 for a birdie, 0 for a par, –1 for a bogey, –3 for double bogey or worse).

*Playoffs: SBC Classic—Kite won on 2nd hole; **Tradition**—Thorpe won on 1st hole; **Bruno's**—Rachels won on 2nd hole; **U.S. Open**—Pooley won on 5th hole; **SBC Open**—Gilder won on 1st hole; **FleetBoston**—Gilder won on 3rd hole; **Long Island**—Green won on 7th hole; **Kroger**—Gilder won on 2nd hole; **Turtle Bay**—Irwin on on 1st hole.

Second place ties (3 players or more): 3-WAY—**Royal Caribbean Classic** (I. Aoki, T. Watson, B. Fleisher); **NFL Classic** (M. Hatalsky, B. Fleisher, D. Eichelberger); **BellSouth** (M. McCullough, B. Fleisher, D. Quigley); **Greater Baltimore** (J. Mahaffey, D. Tewell, B. Wadkins); **Canada Open** (W. Morgan, M. Hatalsky, B. Lietzke); **Players Championship** (J. Thorpe, M. McCullogh, H. Green); **SAS Championship** (S. Rachels, G. Morgan, T. Watson).

Senior PGA Majors

The Tradition

Edition: 14th **Dates:** April 25–28
Site: The Prospector Course, Superstition Mountain, Ariz.
Par: 36-36—72 (7225 yards) **Purse:** $2,000,000

		1	2	3	4	Tot	Earnings
1	Jim Thorpe*	67	70	70	70	277	$300,000
	John Jacobs	68	72	66	71	277	176,000
3	Bruce Summerhays	70	70	70	68	278	132,000
	Bob Gilder	69	68	71	70	278	132,000
5	Tom Watson	72	70	70	68	280	96,000
6	Hale Irwin	71	72	68	70	281	80,000
7	Tom Kite	71	72	71	68	282	68,000
	Tom Purtzer	72	72	68	70	282	68,000
9	Bruce Fleisher	68	73	74	68	283	50,000
	John Mahaffey	70	72	72	69	283	50,000
	Don Pooley	67	73	73	70	283	50,000
	Dick Mast	67	73	71	72	283	50,000

*Thorpe won on the 1st playoff hole.
Early round leaders: 1st—Allen Doyle (66); 2nd—Thorpe, Bob Eastwood and Gilder (137); 3rd—Jacobs (206).
Top amateur: none.

Senior PGA Championship

Edition: 65th **Dates:** June 6–9
Site: Firestone Country Club, South Akron, Ohio
Par: 35-35—70 (6927 yards) **Purse:** $1,800,000

		1	2	3	4	Tot	Earnings
1	Fuzzy Zoeller	69	71	70	68	278	$360,000
2	Hale Irwin	71	70	71	68	280	176,000
	Bobby Wadkins	70	70	69	71	280	176,000
4	Jim Thorpe	69	71	72	69	281	86,000
	Roy Vucinich	70	72	68	71	281	86,000
6	Gil Morgan	76	70	69	68	283	60,000
	Bruce Fleisher	70	72	71	70	283	60,000
	Wayne Levi	69	68	75	71	283	60,000
	Larry Nelson	70	68	72	73	283	60,000
10	Morris Hatalsky	72	72	74	67	285	42,600
	Dana Quigley	72	71	70	72	285	42,600
	Bob Gilder	71	69	72	73	285	42,600
	Walter Hall	70	68	73	74	285	42,600
	Jay Overton	70	70	71	74	285	42,600

Early round leaders: 1st—Kite, Ted Goin, and Mike Smith (68); 2nd—Levi (137); 3rd—Wadkins (209).
Top amateur: none.

U.S. Senior Open

Edition: 23rd **Dates:** June 27–30
Site: Caves Valley GC, Owings Mill, Md.
Par: 36-35—71 (7005 yards) **Purse:** $2,500,000

		1	2	3	4	Tot	Earnings
1	Don Pooley*	71	70	63	70	274	$450,000
	Tom Watson	67	71	69	67	274	265,000
3	Tom Kite	69	67	73	68	277	171,182
4	Ed Dougherty	71	69	68	70	278	119,609
5	Morris Hatalsky	73	68	69	70	280	91,597
	Fred Gibson	69	69	73	69	280	91,597
7	Larry Nelson	71	71	72	67	281	71,689
	Jose Maria Canizares	68	68	76	69	281	71,689
	Allen Doyle	70	69	71	71	281	71,689
10	Bob Gilder	71	71	70	71	283	60,792

*Pooley (4-4-4-3-3) def. Watson (4-4-4-3-x) on the fifth hole of a playoff.
Early round leaders: 1st—R.W. Eaks (64); 2nd—Walter Hall (135); 3rd—Pooley (204).
Top amateur: Bob Clark (299).

PGA Sr. Players Championship

Edition: 20th **Dates:** July 11–14
Site: TPC of Michigan, Dearborn, Mich.
Par: 36-36—72 (6986 yards) **Purse:** $2,500,000

		1	2	3	4	Tot	Earnings
1	Stewart Ginn	66	72	70	66	274	$375,000
2	Jim Thorpe	74	69	67	65	275	183,333
	Mike McCullough	68	69	67	71	275	183,333
	Hubert Green	71	63	71	70	275	183,333
5	Doug Tewell	73	68	68	69	278	120,000
6	Ed Dougherty	70	72	70	67	279	95,000
	Hale Irwin	64	63	72	70	279	95,000
8	Dave Stockton	72	68	71	69	280	75,000
	Larry Nelson	71	69	69	71	280	75,000
10	Tom Kite	71	72	70	68	281	62,500
	Fuzzy Zoeller	70	73	69	69	281	62,500

Early round leaders: 1st—Irwin (64); 2nd—Green (134); 3rd—McCullough (204).
Top amateur: none.

LPGA Tour

LATE 2001

Last Rd	Tournament	Winner	Earnings	Runner-Up
Nov. 4	Mizuno Classic	Annika Sorenstam (203)	$162,000	L. Davies (206)
Nov. 11	Tyco/ADT Tour Championship	Karrie Webb (279)	215,000	A. Sorenstam (281)

2002

Last Rd	Tournament	Winner	Earnings	Runner-Up
Mar. 2	Takefuji Classic	Annika Sorenstam (196)*	$135,000	L. Kane (196)
Mar. 17	Ping Banner Health	Rachel Teske (281)*	150,000	A. Sorenstam (281)
Mar. 24	Welch's/Circle K Championship	Laura Diaz (270)	120,000	J. Inkster (271)
Mar. 31	**Nabisco Championship** (Rancho Mirage, Calif.)	Annika Sorenstam (280)	225,000	L. Neumann (281)
Apr. 21	Longs Drugs Challenge	Cristie Kerr (280)	135,000	H. Han (281)
May 5	Chick-fil-A Charity Championship	Juli Inkster (132)	187,500	K. Robbins (134)
May 12	Aerus Electrolux USA Championship	Annika Sorenstam (271)	120,000	P. Hurst (272)
May 19	Asahi Ryokuken International	Janice Moodie (273)	187,500	L. Davies (280)
May 26	Corning Classic	Laura Diaz (274)	150,000	R. Jones (276)
June 2	Kellogg-Keebler Classic	Annika Sorenstam (195)	180,000	3-way tie (206)
June 9	**McDonald's LPGA Championship** (Wilmington, Del.)	Se Ri Pak (279)	225,000	B. Daniel (282)
June 15	Evian Masters	Annika Sorenstam (269)	315,000	M. Hjorth & M. Hyun Kim (273)
June 23	Wegmen's Rochester	Karrie Webb (276)	180,000	M. Hyun Kim (277)
June 30	ShopRite Classic	Annika Sorenstam (201)	180,000	3-way-tie (204)
July 7	**U.S. Women's Open** (Hutchinson, Kan.)	Juli Inkster (276)	535,000	A. Sorenstam (278)
July 14	Jamie Farr Kroger Classic	Rachel Teske (270)	150,000	B. Bauer (272)
July 21	Giant Eagle Classic	Mi Hyun Kim (202)	150,000	K. Robbins (203)
July 28	Big Apple Classic	Gloria Park (270)*	142,500	H. Han
Aug. 4	Wendy's Championship for Children	Mi Hyun Kim (208)	150,000	H. Han
Aug. 11	**Weetabix Women's British Open** (Turnberry, Wales)	Karrie Webb (273)	236,383	M. Ellis & P. Marti (275)
Aug. 18	Bank of Montreal Canadian Open	Meg Mallon (284)	180,000	3-way tie (287)
Aug. 25	First Union Betsy King Classic	Se Ri Pak (267)	180,000	A. Stanford (270)
Sept. 1	State Farm Classic	Patricia Meunier-Lebouc (270)	165,000	S. Ri Pak & M. Hyun Kim (272)
Sept. 8	Williams Championship	Annika Sorenstam (199)	150,000	L. Kane (203)
Sept. 15	Safeway Classic	Annika Sorenstam (199)	150,000	K. Golden (200)
Sept. 22	Solheim Cup	United States (15½)	—	Europe (12½)
Oct. 6	Samsung World Championship	Annika Sorenstam (266)	162,000	C. Kerr (272)
Oct. 13	Mobile Tournament of Champions	Se Ri Pak (268)	122,000	C. Matthew & C. Koch (272)

*Playoffs: Takefuji—Sorenstam won on 1st hole; **Ping Banner**—Teske won on 2nd hole; **Big Apple**—Park won on 1st hole.

Second place ties (3 players or more): 3-WAY—**Kellogg-Keebler** (M. Redman, M. McKay, D. Ammaccapane; **Shop-Rite Classic** (C. Koch, K. Golden, J. Inkster); **Canadian Open** (M. Redman, M. Ellis, C. Matthew).

LPGA Majors

Nabisco Championship

Edition: 31st   **Dates:** March 21–24
Site: Mission Hills CC, Rancho Mirage, Calif.
Par: 36-36—72 (6520 yards)   **Purse:** $1,500,000

		1 2 3 4	Tot	Earnings
1	Annika Sorenstam	70-71-71-68	280	$225,000
2	Liselotte Neumann	69-70-73-69	281	136,987
3	Cristie Kerr	74-70-70-68	282	88,125
	Rosie Jones	72-69-72-69	282	88,125
5	Akiko Fukushima	73-76-68-66	283	56,250
	Carin Koch	73-73-71-66	283	56,250
7	Karrie Webb	75-70-67-72	284	42,375
8	a-Lorena Ochoa	75-69-71-70	285	—
9	Grace Park	75-73-70-68	286	31,050
	Se Ri Pak	74-71-71-70	286	31,050
	Leta Lindley	72-72-72-70	286	31,050
	Lorie Kane	73-72-70-71	286	31,050
	Becky Iverson	71-74-68-73	286	31,050

Early round leaders: 1st—Neumann (69); 2nd—Neumann (139); 3rd—Webb, Sorenstam and Neumann (212).

LPGA Championship

Edition: 48th   **Dates:** June 6–9
Site: DuPont CC, Wilmington, Del.
Par: 35-36-71 (6408 yards)   **Purse:** $1,500,000

		1 2 3 4	Tot	Earnings
1	Se Ri Pak	71-70-68-70	279	$225,000
2	Beth Daniel	67-70-68-77	282	136,987
3	Annika Sorenstam	70-76-73-65	284	99,375
4	Juli Inkster	69-75-70-71	285	69,375
	Karrie Webb	68-71-72-74	285	69,375
6	Carin Koch	68-73-73-72	286	46,500
	Michele Redman	74-69-70-73	286	46,500
8	Catriona Matthew	70-73-75-70	288	37,125
9	Kristi Albers	74-73-73-70	290	30,625
	Karen Stupples	75-70-70-75	290	30,625
	Michelle McGann	71-72-72-75	290	30,625

Early round leaders: 1st—Daniel (67); 2nd—Daniel (137); 3rd—Daniel (205).
Top amateur: none.

U.S. Women's Open

Edition: 57th **Dates:** July 4–7
Site: Prairie Dunes CC, Hutchinson, Kan.
Par: 35-35–70 (6267 yds Thu. & Fri;
6293 yds Sat. & Sun.) **Purse:** $3,000,000

		1 2 3 4	Tot	Earnings
1	Juli Inkster	67-72-71-66	276	$535,000
2	Annika Sorenstam	70-69-69-70	278	315,000
3	Shani Waugh	67-73-71-72	283	202,568
4	Raquel Carriedo	75-71-72-66	284	141,219
5	Se Ri Pak	74-75-68-68	285	114,370
6	Mhairi McKay	70-75-71-70	286	101,421
7	Jennifer Rosales	73-72-74-68	287	78,016
	Kelli Kuehne	70-76-72-69	287	78,016
	Beth Daniel	71-76-71-69	287	78,016
	Laura Diaz	67-72-77-71	287	78,016
	Janice Moodie	71-72-71-73	287	78,016

Early round leaders: 1st—Diaz, Waugh and Inkster (67); 2nd—Diaz, Sorenstam and Inkster (139); 3rd—Sorenstam (208).

Top amateurs: Aree Song Wongluekiet and Angela Jerman (294).

Women's British Open

Edition: 9th **Dates:** Aug. 8–11
Site: Turnberry GC, Turnberry, Wales
Par: 36-36—72 (6479 yards) **Purse:** $1,500,000

		1 2 3 4	Tot	Earnings
1	Karrie Webb	66-71-70-66	273	$263,383
2	Michelle Ellis	69-70-68-68	275	129,629
	Paula Marti	69-68-69-69	275	129,629
4	Jeong Jang	73-69-66-69	277	64,528
	Catrin Nilsmark	70-69-69-69	277	64,528
	Candie Kung	65-71-71-70	277	64,528
	Jennifer Rosales	69-70-65-73	277	64,528
8	Meg Mallon	69-71-68-70	278	38,380
	Beth Bauer	70-67-70-71	278	38,380
	Carin Koch	68-68-68-74	278	38,380

Early round leaders: 1st—Kung (65); 2nd—Kung and Koch (136); 3rd—Koch and Rosales (204).
Top amateur: none.

2002 Tour Statistics (through Oct. 13)

Statistical leaders on the PGA, European PGA, Senior PGA and LPGA tours.

PGA

	Scoring	Avg.		Putting	Putts		Driving Distance	Avg.
1	Tiger Woods	68.49	1	Bob Heintz	1.688	1	John Daly	306.8
2	Ernie Els	69.46	2	David Toms	1.712	2	Mike Heinen	299.4
3	Vijay Singh	69.47	3	Chris Riley	1.713	3	Boo Weekley	297.7
4	Nick Price	69.53	4	Phil Mickelson	1.714	4	Matthew Goggin	296.1
5	Phil Mickelson	69.62	5	Ben Crane	1.718	5	Dennis Paulson	295.8

European PGA

	Scoring	Avg.		Putting	Putts		Driving Distance	Avg.
1	Padraig Harrington	69.70	1	Michael Campbell	1.704	1	Emanuele Canonica	304.4
2	Ernie Els	70.07	2	Paul Casey	1.718	2	Des Terblanche	301.7
3	Retief Goosen	70.10		Marcel Siem	1.718	3	Ricardo Gonzalez	300.5
4	Eduardo Romero	70.16	4	Colin Montgomerie	1.719	4	Angel Cabrera	298.9
5	Vijay Singh	70.27	5	Sam Torrance	1.724	5	Ernie Els	297.4

Senior PGA

	Scoring	Avg.		Putting	Putts		Driving Distance	Avg.
1	Hale Irwin	68.80	1	Hale Irwin	1.711	1	R.W. Eaks	295.1
2	Tom Kite	69.48	2	Morris Hatalsky	1.730	2	John Jacobs	285.0
3	Bruce Fleisher	69.58	3	Ben Crenshaw	1.750	3	Clyde Hughey	284.6
4	Doug Tewell	69.66	4	Larry Nelson	1.753	4	Rodger Davis	282.1
5	Morris Hatalsky	69.72	5	Bruce Fleisher	1.755	5	Sammy Rachels	281.2
				Dana Quigley	1.755			

LPGA

	Scoring	Avg.		Putting	Putts		Driving Distance	Avg.
1	Annika Sorenstam	68.55	1	Nancy Lopez	28.32	1	Akiko Fukushima	269.3
2	Se Ri Pak	69.96	2	Rosie Jones	28.66	2	Wendy Doolan	268.0
3	Karrie Webb	70.34	3	Juli Inkster	28.84	3	Sherri Turner	267.3
4	Juli Inkster	70.63	4	Liselotte Neumann	28.88	4	Maria Hjorth	266.1
5	Mi Hyun Kim	70.69	5	Laura Davies	28.94	5	Annika Sorenstam	265.7
				Pat Hurst	28.94			

Note: Putts per round.

Key: Scoring—average strokes per round adjusted to the average score of the field each week. If the field is under par, each player's score is adjusted upward a corresponding amount and vice-versa if the field is over par. This keeps a player from receiving an advantage for playing easier-than-average courses; **Putting**—average number of putts taken on greens hit in regulation; **Driving Distance**—average computed by charting exact distances of two tee shots on the most open par four or five holes on both front and back nine.

2002 Ryder Cup

The 34th Ryder Cup tournament, Sept. 27-29, at The Belfry, Sutton Coldfield, England.

ROSTERS

The 2001 U.S. Team (the 2001 event was postponed one year due to safety concerns after the September attacks on America) players were chosen on the basis of points awarded for wins and top-10 finishes at official PGA events from Jan. 9, 2000 through Aug. 19, 2001. The top 10 finishers on the points list automatically qualified for the 12-member team, and U.S. Captain Curtis Strange selected the final two players.

The 2001 European Team players were chosen on the basis of points awarded from September 2000 to September 2001. Each player received one point for each euro won during this period in Ryder Cup ranking events. The top-10 in the standings after the final event automatically qualified for the 12-member team, and European Team captain Sam Torrance selected the final two players.

United States: Qualifiers—Mark Calcavecchia, Stewart Cink, David Duval, Jim Furyk, Scott Hoch, Davis Love III, Phil Mickelson, Hal Sutton, David Toms and Tiger Woods; Captain's selections—Paul Azinger and Scott Verplank.

Europe: Qualifiers—Thomas Bjorn (Denmark), Darren Clarke (Northern Ireland), Niclas Fasth (Sweden), Pierre Fulke (Sweden), Padraig Harrington (Ireland), Bernhard Langer (Germany), Paul McGinley (Ireland), Colin Montgomerie (Scotland), Phillip Price (Wales) and Lee Westwood (England); Captain's selections—Sergio Garcia (Spain) and Jesper Parnevik (Sweden).

First Day

Four-Ball Match Results			Foursome Match Results		
Winner	Score	Loser	Winner	Score	Loser
Clarke/Bjorn	1-up	Woods/Azinger	Sutton/Verplank	2&1	Clarke/Bjorn
Garcia/Westwood	4&3	Duval/Love III	Garcia/Westwood	2&1	Woods/Calcavecchia
Montgomerie/Langer	4&3	Hoch/Furyk	Montgomerie/Langer	halved	Mickelson/Toms
Mickelson/Toms	1-up	Harrington/Fasth	Cink/Furyk	3&2	Harrington/McGinley
Europe wins morning, 3-1			USA wins afternoon, 2½-1½; (Europe leads, 4½-3½)		

Second Day

Foursome Match Results			Four-Ball Match Results		
Winner	Score	Loser	Winner	Score	Loser
Mickelson/Toms	2&1	Fulke/Price	Calcavecchia/Duval	1-up	Fasth/Parnevik
Garcia/Westwood	2&1	Cink/Furyk	Montgomerie/Harrington	2&1	Mickelson/Toms
Woods/Love III	4&3	Clarke/Bjorn	Woods/Love III	1-up	Garcia/Westwood
Montgomerie/Langer	1-up	Verplank/Hoch	Hoch/Furyk	halved	Clarke/McGinley
Teams tie morning, 2-2; (Europe leads, 6½-5½)			USA wins afternoon, 2½-1½; (Teams tied, 8-8)		

Third Day

Singles Match Results

Winner	Score	Loser
Montgomerie	5&4	Hoch
Toms	1-up	Garcia
Clarke	halved	Duval
Langer	4&3	Sutton
Harrington	5&4	Calcavecchia
Bjorn	2&1	Cink
Verplank	2&1	Westwood
Fasth	halved	Azinger
McGinley	halved	Furyk
Fulke	halved	Love III
Price	3&2	Mickelson
Parnevik	halved	Woods

Europe wins day, 7½-4½

Europe wins Ryder Cup, 15½-12½

Overall Records

Team and Individual match play combined

United States	W-L-H	Pts	Europe	W-L-H	Pts
David Toms	3-1-1	3½	Colin Montgomerie	4-0-1	4½
Davis Love III	2-1-1	2½	Bernhard Langer	3-0-1	3½
Phil Mickelson	2-2-1	2½	Sergio Garcia	3-2-0	3
Tiger Woods	2-2-1	2½	Lee Westwood	3-2-0	3
Scott Verplank	2-1-0	2	Thomas Bjorn	2-2-0	2
Jim Furyk	1-2-2	2	Padraig Harrington	2-2-0	2
David Duval	1-1-1	1½	Darren Clarke	1-2-2	2
Hal Sutton	1-1-0	1	Phillip Price	1-1-0	1
Mark Calcavecchia	1-2-0	1	Paul McGinley	0-1-2	1
Stewart Cink	1-2-0	1	Pierre Fulke	0-1-1	½
Paul Azinger	0-1-1	½	Jesper Parnevik	0-1-1	½
Scott Hoch	0-3-1	½	Niclas Fasth	0-2-1	½

2002 Solheim Cup

The 7th Solheim Cup tournament, Sept. 20-22, at Interlachen Country Club, Edina, Minn.

ROSTERS

The 2002 U.S. Team players were chosen on the basis of points awarded for wins and top-10 finishes at official LPGA events. The top 10 finishers on the points list automatically qualified for the 12-member team, and U.S. Captain Patty Sheehan selected the final two players.

The 2002 European Team players were chosen on the basis of points awarded weekly to the top 20 finishers at official Ladies European Tour (LET) events. The top seven players in the LET points standings automatically qualify for the 12-member team, and team captain Dale Reid selected the final four players. Ordinarily the European Team captain would pick five players, but because there was a tie for seventh in the point standings, eight players automatically qualified.

United States: Qualifiers—Beth Daniel, Laura Diaz, Juli Inkster, Rosie Jones, Cristie Kerr, Emilee Klein, Kelly Kuehne, Meg Mallon, Michele Redman and Wendy Ward; Captain's selections—Pat Hurst and Kelly Robbins.

Europe: Qualifiers—Raquel Carriedo (Spain), Sophie Gustafson (Sweden), Maria Hjorth (Sweden), Karine Icher (France), Paula Marti (Spain), Suzann Pettersen (Norway), Annika Sorenstam (Sweden) and Iben Tinning (Denmark); Captain's selections—Helen Alfredsson (Sweden), Laura Davies (England), Carin Koch (Sweden) and Mhairi McKay (Scotland).

First Day

Foursome Match Results

Winner	Score	Loser
Davies/Marti	2-up	Inkster/Diaz
Daniel/Ward	1-up	Tinning/Carriedo
Alfredsson/Pettersen	4&2	Robbins/Hurst
Sorenstam/Koch	3&2	Mallon/Kuehne

Europe wins morning, 3-1

Four-Ball Match Results

Winner	Score	Loser
Jones/Kerr	1-up	Davies/Marti
Diaz/Klein	4&3	Gustafson/Icher
Redman/Mallon	2&1	Sorenstam/Hjorth
McKay/Koch	3&2	Inkster/Kuehne

USA wins afternoon, 3-1; (Teams tied, 4-4)

Second Day

Foursome Match Results

Winner	Score	Loser
Sorenstam/Koch	4&3	Kerr/Redman
Klein/Ward	3&2	Tinning/McKay
Mallon/Inkster	2&1	Marti/Davies
Diaz/Robbins	3&1	Alfredsson/Pettersen

USA wins morning, 3-1; (USA leads, 7-5)

Four-Ball Match Results

Winner	Score	Loser
Sorenstam/Koch	4&3	Daniel/Ward
Hjorth/Tinning	1-up	Hurst/Kuehne
Icher/Carriedo	1-up	Jones/Kerr
Davies/Gustafson	1-up	Robbins/Klein

Europe wins afternoon, 4-0; (Europe leads, 9-7)

Third Day

Singles Match Results

Winner	Score	Loser
Inkster	4&3	Carriedo
Diaz	5&3	Marti
Klein	2&1	Alfredsson
Tinning	3&2	Kuehne
Redman	halved	Pettersen
Ward	halved	Sorenstam
Robbins	5&3	Hjorth
Gustafson	3&2	Kerr
Mallon	3&2	Davies
Hurst	3&2	McKay
Daniel	halved	Koch
Jones	3&2	Icher

USA wins day, 8½-3½

USA wins Solheim Cup, 15½-12½

Overall Records

Team and Individual match play combined

United States

	W-L-H	Pts
Laura Diaz	3-1-0	3
Emilee Klein	3-1-0	3
Meg Mallon	3-1-0	3
Wendy Ward	2-1-1	2½
Rosie Jones	2-1-0	2
Juli Inkster	2-2-0	2
Kelly Robbins	2-2-0	2
Beth Daniel	1-1-1	1½
Michele Redman	1-1-1	1½
Pat Hurst	1-2-0	1
Cristie Kerr	1-3-0	1
Kelly Kuehne	0-4-0	0

Europe

	W-L-H	Pts
Carin Koch	4-0-1	4½
Annika Sorenstam	3-1-1	3½
Sophie Gustafson	2-1-0	2
Iben Tinning	2-2-0	2
Laura Davies	2-3-0	2
Suzann Pettersen	1-1-1	1½
Helen Alfredsson	1-2-0	1
Raquel Carriedo	1-2-0	1
Karine Icher	1-2-0	1
Maria Hjorth	1-2-0	1
Mhairi McKay	1-2-0	1
Paula Marti	1-3-0	1

Money Leaders

Official money leaders of PGA, European PGA, Senior PGA and LPGA tours for 2001 and unofficial money leaders for 2002, as compiled by the PGA, European PGA and LPGA. All European amounts are in euros (€).

PGA

Arnold Palmer Award standings: listed are tournaments played (TP); cuts made (CM); 1st, 2nd and 3rd place finishes; and earnings for the year.

FINAL 2001

		TP	CM	Finish 1-2-3	Earnings
1	Tiger Woods	19	19	5-0-1	$5,687,777
2	Phil Mickelson	23	20	2-4-4	4,403,883
3	David Toms	28	23	3-1-0	3,791,595
4	Vijay Singh	26	24	0-2-4	3,440,829
5	Davis Love III	20	17	1-3-0	3,169,463
6	Sergio Garcia	18	14	2-2-0	2,898,635
7	Scott Hoch	24	17	2-1-0	2,875,319
8	David Duval	20	18	1-2-1	2,801,760
9	Bob Estes	26	20	2-1-1	2,795,477
10	Scott Verplank	26	24	1-1-1	2,783,401

2002 (through Oct. 13)

		TP	CM	Finish 1-2-3	Earnings
1	Tiger Woods	16	16	5-2-1	$6,496,025
2	Phil Mickelson	24	21	2-1-4	3,870,371
3	Ernie Els	17	16	2-0-0	3,180,695
4	Rich Beem	28	17	2-1-0	2,845,362
5	Vijay Singh	26	22	1-0-2	2,842,873
6	Jerry Kelly	26	19	2-0-0	2,698,749
7	Justin Leonard	25	22	1-1-0	2,641,235
8	David Toms	24	22	0-2-0	2,597,406
9	Retief Goosen	14	13	1-2-0	2,471,004
10	Sergio Garcia	20	18	1-2-0	2,319,993

EUROPEAN PGA

Volvo Order of Merit standings: listed are tournaments played (TP); cuts made (CM); 1st, 2nd and 3rd place finishes; and earnings for the year.

FINAL 2001

		TP	CM	Finish 1-2-3	Earnings
1	Retief Goosen	23	21	3-1-0	€2,862,806
2	Padraig Harrington	22	22	1-6-0	2,090,165
3	Darren Clarke	23	22	1-1-2	1,988,055
4	Ernie Els	12	12	0-1-1	1,716,287
5	Colin Montgomerie	23	20	2-0-1	1,578,676
6	Bernard Langer	16	15	2-0-1	1,577,129
7	Thomas Bjorn	22	21	1-2-1	1,474,802
8	Paul McGinley	25	24	1-2-1	1,464,433
9	Paul Lawrie	25	22	1-1-0	1,428,830
10	Niclas Fasth	23	19	0-2-1	1,224,587

2002 (through Oct. 13)

		TP	CM	Finish 1-2-3	Earnings
1	Retief Goosen	20	20	1-4-0	€2,299,070
2	Ernie Els	16	16	3-0-0	2,251,708
3	Padraig Harrington	19	19	1-1-2	2,245,041
4	Eduardo Romero	19	19	1-2-0	1,784,015
5	Colin Montgomerie	22	22	0-2-2	1,545,071
6	Sergio Garcia	10	10	1-0-1	1,402,469
7	Michael Campbell	21	21	1-0-1	1,325,403
8	Justin Rose	23	23	2-0-1	1,282,438
9	Vijay Singh	9	9	0-0-2	1,230,315
10	Adam Scott	22	22	2-0-1	1,171,119

SENIOR PGA

FINAL 2001

		TP	CM	Finish 1-2-3	Earnings
1	Allen Doyle	34	34	2-5-3	$2,553,582
2	Bruce Fleisher	31	31	3-3-4	2,411,543
3	Hale Irwin	26	26	3-2-4	2,147,422
4	Larry Nelson	28	27	5-1-2	2,109,936
5	Gil Morgan	24	24	2-4-1	1,885,871
6	Jim Thorpe	35	35	2-2-2	1,827,223
7	Doug Tewell	28	27	1-5-0	1,721,339
8	Bob Gilder	30	30	2-1-1	1,684,986
9	Dana Quigley	37	37	1-2-2	1,537,931
10	Tom Kite	23	23	1-0-4	1,398,802

2002 (through Oct. 13)

		TP	CM	Finish 1-2-3	Earnings
1	Hale Irwin	25	25	4-6-4	$2,829,041
2	Bob Gilder	32	32	4-1-2	2,027,037
3	Bruce Fleisher	29	28	1-4-2	1,810,445
4	Tom Kite	21	21	3-0-1	1,570,147
5	Doug Tewell	25	25	2-2-1	1,541,695
6	Bruce Lietzke	20	20	3-1-1	1,438,581
7	Jim Thorpe	30	30	1-1-2	1,430,641
8	Dana Quigley	33	33	1-2-0	1,321,139
9	Morris Hatalsky	22	22	1-3-1	1,278,569
10	Allen Doyle	30	30	0-1-2	1,259,531

LPGA

FINAL 2001

		TP	CM	Finish 1-2-3	Earnings
1	Annika Sorenstam	26	26	8-6-1	$2,105,868
2	Se Ri Pak	21	19	5-5-2	1,623,009
3	Karrie Webb	22	22	3-4-0	1,535,404
4	Lorie Kane	27	26	1-2-2	947,489
5	Maria Hjorth	29	24	0-4-2	848,195
6	Rosie Jones	23	23	2-0-1	785,010
7	Dottie Pepper	23	21	0-2-4	776,482
8	Mi Hyun Kim	29	28	0-3-0	762,363
9	Laura Diaz	27	26	0-4-1	751,466
10	Catriona Matthew	29	26	1-1-2	747,970

2002 (through Oct. 13)

		TP	CM	Finish 1-2-3	Earnings
1	Annika Sorenstam	19	18	9-3-3	$2,408,907
2	Se Ri Pak	20	20	4-1-1	1,375,518
3	Juli Inkster	19	17	2-2-0	1,140,349
4	Mi Hyun Kim	24	24	2-3-1	989,436
5	Karrie Webb	19	18	2-0-2	900,760
6	Laura Diaz	23	18	2-0-3	809,790
7	Cristie Kerr	23	19	1-1-3	643,336
8	Rosie Jones	21	19	0-1-3	602,482
9	Michele Redman	22	22	0-2-1	599,071
10	Rachel Teske	23	19	2-0-0	589,649

1860-2002
Through the Years

ESPN
Information Please®
SPORTS ALMANAC

Major Golf Championships
MEN
The Masters

The Masters has been played every year (except during World War II) since 1934 at the Augusta National Golf Club in Augusta, Ga. Both the course and the tournament were created by Bobby Jones; (*) indicates playoff winner.

Multiple winners: Jack Nicklaus (6); Arnold Palmer (4); Jimmy Demaret, Nick Faldo, Gary Player, Sam Snead and Tiger Woods (3); Seve Ballesteros, Ben Crenshaw, Ben Hogan, Bernhard Langer, Byron Nelson, Jose Maria Olazabal, Horton Smith and Tom Watson (2).

Year	Winner	Score	Runner-up
1934	Horton Smith	284	Craig Wood (285)
1935	Gene Sarazen*	282	Craig Wood (282)
1936	Horton Smith	285	Harry Cooper (286)
1937	Byron Nelson	283	Ralph Guldahl (285)
1938	Henry Picard	285	Ralph Guldahl & Harry Cooper (287)
1939	Ralph Guldahl	279	Sam Snead (280)
1940	Jimmy Demaret	280	Lloyd Mangrum (284)
1941	Craig Wood	280	Byron Nelson (283)
1942	Byron Nelson*	280	Ben Hogan (280)
1943-45	Not held		World War II
1946	Herman Keiser	282	Ben Hogan (283)
1947	Jimmy Demaret	281	Frank Stranahan & Byron Nelson (283)
1948	Claude Harmon	279	Cary Middlecoff (284)
1949	Sam Snead	282	Lloyd Mangrum & Johnny Bulla (285)
1950	Jimmy Demaret	283	Jim Ferrier (285)
1951	Ben Hogan	280	Skee Riegel (282)
1952	Sam Snead	286	Jack Burke Jr. (290)
1953	Ben Hogan	274	Porky Oliver (279)
1954	Sam Snead*	289	Ben Hogan (289)
1955	Cary Middlecoff	279	Ben Hogan (286)
1956	Jack Burke Jr.	289	Ken Venturi (290)
1957	Doug Ford	283	Sam Snead (286)
1958	Arnold Palmer	284	Doug Ford & Fred Hawkins (285)
1959	Art Wall Jr.	284	Cary Middlecoff (285)
1960	Arnold Palmer	282	Ken Venturi (283)
1961	Gary Player	280	Arnold Palmer & Charles R. Coe (281)
1962	Arnold Palmer*	280	Dow Finsterwald & Gary Player (280)
1963	Jack Nicklaus	286	Tony Lema (287)
1964	Arnold Palmer	276	Jack Nicklaus & Dave Marr (282)
1965	Jack Nicklaus	271	Arnold Palmer & Gary Player (280)
1966	Jack Nicklaus*	288	Gay Brewer Jr. & Tommy Jacobs (288)
1967	Gay Brewer Jr.	280	Bobby Nichols (281)
1968	Bob Goalby	277	Roberto DeVicenzo (278)
1969	George Archer	281	Billy Casper, George Knudson & Tom Weiskopf (282)
1970	Billy Casper*	279	Gene Littler (279)
1971	Charles Coody	279	Jack Nicklaus & Johnny Miller (281)
1972	Jack Nicklaus	286	Bruce Crampton, Bobby Mitchell & Tom Weiskopf (289)
1973	Tommy Aaron	283	J.C. Snead (284)
1974	Gary Player	278	Tom Weiskopf, & Dave Stockton (280)
1975	Jack Nicklaus	276	Johnny Miller & Tom Weiskopf (277)
1976	Ray Floyd	271	Ben Crenshaw (279)
1977	Tom Watson	276	Jack Nicklaus (278)
1978	Gary Player	277	Hubert Green, Rod Funseth & Tom Watson (278)
1979	Fuzzy Zoeller*	280	Ed Sneed & Tom Watson (280)
1980	Seve Ballesteros	275	Gibby Gilbert & Jack Newton (279)
1981	Tom Watson	280	Jack Nicklaus & Johnny Miller (282)
1982	Craig Stadler*	284	Dan Pohl (284)
1983	Seve Ballesteros	280	Ben Crenshaw & Tom Kite (284)
1984	Ben Crenshaw	277	Tom Watson (279)
1985	Bernhard Langer	282	Curtis Strange, Seve Ballesteros & Ray Floyd (284)
1986	Jack Nicklaus	279	Greg Norman & Tom Kite (280)
1987	Larry Mize*	285	Seve Ballesteros & Greg Norman (285)
1988	Sandy Lyle	281	Mark Calcavecchia (282)
1989	Nick Faldo*	283	Scott Hoch (283)
1990	Nick Faldo*	278	Ray Floyd (278)
1991	Ian Woosnam	277	J.M. Olazabal (278)
1992	Fred Couples	275	Ray Floyd (277)
1993	Bernhard Langer	277	Chip Beck (281)
1994	J.M. Olazabal	279	Tom Lehman (281)
1995	Ben Crenshaw	274	Davis Love III (275)
1996	Nick Faldo	276	Greg Norman (281)
1997	Tiger Woods	270	Tom Kite (282)
1998	Mark O'Meara	279	Fred Couples & David Duval (280)
1999	J.M. Olazabal	280	Davis Love III (282)
2000	Vijay Singh	278	Ernie Els (281)
2001	Tiger Woods	272	David Duval (274)
2002	Tiger Woods	276	Retief Goosen (279)

The Masters (Cont.)
*PLAYOFFS:

1935: Gene Sarazen (144) def. Craig Wood (149) in 36 holes. **1942:** Byron Nelson (69) def. Ben Hogan (70) in 18 holes. **1954:** Sam Snead (70) def. Ben Hogan (71) in 18 holes. **1962:** Arnold Palmer (68) def. Gary Player (71) and Dow Finsterwald (77) in 18 holes. **1966:** Jack Nicklaus (70) def. Tommy Jacobs (72) and Gay Brewer Jr. (78) in 18 holes. **1970:** Billy Casper (69) def. Gene Littler (74) in 18 holes. **1979:** Fuzzy Zoeller (4-3) def. Ed Sneed (4-4) and Tom Watson (4-4) on 2nd hole of sudden death. **1982:** Craig Stadler (4) def. Dan Pohl (5) on 1st hole of sudden death. **1987:** Larry Mize (4-3) def. Greg Norman (4-4) and Seve Ballesteros (5) on 2nd hole of sudden death. **1989:** Nick Faldo (5-3) def. Scott Hoch (5-4) on 2nd hole of sudden death. **1990:** Nick Faldo (4-4) def. Raymond Floyd (4) on second hole of sudden death.

U.S. Open

Played at a different course each year, the U.S. Open was launched by the new U.S. Golf Association in 1895. The Open was a 36-hole event from 1895-97 and has been 72 holes since then. It switched from a 3-day, 36-hole Saturday finish to 4 days of play in 1965. Note that (*) indicates playoff winner and (a) indicates amateur.

Multiple winners: Willie Anderson, Ben Hogan, Bobby Jones and Jack Nicklaus (4); Hale Irwin (3); Julius Boros, Billy Casper, Ernie Els, Ralph Guldahl, Walter Hagen, Lee Janzen, John McDermott, Cary Middlecoff, Andy North, Gene Sarazen, Alex Smith, Payne Stewart, Curtis Strange, Lee Trevino and Tiger Woods (2).

Year	Winner	Score	Runner-up	Course	Location
1895	Horace Rawlins	173	Willie Dunn (175)	Newport GC	Newport, R.I.
1896	James Foulis	152	Horace Rawlins (155)	Shinnecock Hills GC	Southampton, N.Y.
1897	Joe Lloyd	162	Willie Anderson (163)	Chicago GC	Wheaton, Ill.
1898	Fred Herd	328	Alex Smith (335)	Myopia Hunt Club	Hamilton, Mass.
1899	Willie Smith	315	George Low, W.H. Way & Val Fitzjohn (326)	Baltimore CC	Baltimore
1900	Harry Vardon	313	J.H. Taylor (315)	Chicago GC	Wheaton, Ill.
1901	Willie Anderson*	331	Alex Smith (331)	Myopia Hunt Club	Hamilton, Mass.
1902	Laurie Auchterlonie	307	Stewart Gardner (313)	Garden City GC	Garden City, N.Y.
1903	Willie Anderson*	307	David Brown (307)	Baltusrol GC	Springfield, N.J.
1904	Willie Anderson	303	Gil Nicholls (308)	Glen View Club	Golf, Ill.
1905	Willie Anderson	314	Alex Smith (316)	Myopia Hunt Club	Hamilton, Mass.
1906	Alex Smith	295	Willie Smith (302)	Onwentsia Club	Lake Forest, Ill.
1907	Alec Ross	302	Gil Nicholls (304)	Phila. Cricket Club	Chestnut Hill, Pa.
1908	Fred McLeod*	322	Willie Smith (322)	Myopia Hunt Club	Hamilton, Mass.
1909	George Sargent	290	Tom McNamara (294)	Englewood GC	Englewood, N.J.
1910	Alex Smith*	298	Macdonald Smith & John McDermott (298)	Phila. Cricket Club	Chestnut Hill, Pa.
1911	John McDermott*	307	George Simpson & Mike Brady (307)	Chicago GC	Wheaton, Ill.
1912	John McDermott	294	Tom McNamara (296)	CC of Buffalo	Buffalo
1913	a-Francis Ouimet*	304	Harry Vardon & Ted Ray (304)	The Country Club	Brookline, Mass.
1914	Walter Hagen	290	a-Chick Evans (291)	Midlothian CC	Blue Island, Ill.
1915	a-John Travers	297	Tom McNamara (298)	Baltusrol GC	Springfield, N.J.
1916	a-Chick Evans	286	Jock Hutchinson (288)	Minikahda Club	Minneapolis
1917-18	Not held		World War I		
1919	Walter Hagen*	301	Mike Brady (301)	Brae Burn CC	West Newton, Mass.
1920	Ted Ray	295	Jock Hutchinson, Jack Burke, Leo Diegel & Harry Vardon (296)	Inverness Club	Toledo, Ohio
1921	Jim Barnes	289	Walter Hagen & Fred McLeod (298)	Columbia CC	Chevy Chase, Md.
1922	Gene Sarazen	288	a-Bobby Jones & John Black (289)	Skokie CC	Glencoe, Ill.
1923	a-Bobby Jones*	296	Bobby Cruickshank (296)	Inwood CC	Inwood, N.Y.
1924	Cyril Walker	297	a-Bobby Jones (300)	Oakland Hills CC	Birmingham, Mich.
1925	Willie Macfarlane*	291	a-Bobby Jones (291)	Worcester CC	Worcester, Mass.
1926	a-Bobby Jones	293	Joe Turnesa (294)	Scioto CC	Columbus, Ohio
1927	Tommy Armour*	301	Harry Cooper (301)	Oakmont CC	Oakmont, Pa.
1928	Johnny Farrell*	294	a-Bobby Jones (294)	Olympia Fields CC	Matteson, Ill.
1929	a-Bobby Jones*	294	Al Espinosa (294)	Winged Foot CC	Mamaroneck, N.Y.
1930	a-Bobby Jones	287	Macdonald Smith (289)	Interlachen CC	Hopkins, Minn.
1931	Billy Burke*	292	George Von Elm (292)	Inverness Club	Toledo, Ohio
1932	Gene Sarazen	286	Bobby Cruickshank & Phil Perkins (289)	Fresh Meadow CC	Flushing, N.Y.
1933	a-Johnny Goodman	287	Ralph Guldahl (288)	North Shore GC	Glenview, Ill.
1934	Olin Dutra	293	Gene Sarazen (294)	Merion Cricket Club	Ardmore, Pa.
1935	Sam Parks Jr.	299	Jimmy Thomson (301)	Oakmont CC	Oakmont, Pa.
1936	Tony Manero	282	Harry E. Cooper (284)	Baltusrol GC	Springfield, N.J.
1937	Ralph Guldahl	281	Sam Snead (283)	Oakland Hills CC	Birmingham, Mich.
1938	Ralph Guldahl	284	Dick Metz (290)	Cherry Hills CC	Denver
1939	Byron Nelson*	284	Craig Wood & Denny Shute (284)	Philadelphia CC	Philadelphia

Year	Winner	Score	Runner-up	Course	Location
1940	Lawson Little*	287	Gene Sarazen (287)	Canterbury GC	Cleveland
1941	Craig Wood	284	Denny Shute (287)	Colonial Club	Ft. Worth
1942-45	Not held		World War II		
1946	Lloyd Mangrum*	284	Byron Nelson & Vic Ghezzi (284)	Canterbury GC	Cleveland
1947	Lew Worsham*	282	Sam Snead (282)	St. Louis CC	Clayton, Mo.
1948	Ben Hogan	276	Jimmy Demaret (278)	Riviera CC	Los Angeles
1949	Cary Middlecoff	286	Clayton Heafner & Sam Snead (287)	Medinah CC	Medinah, Ill.
1950	Ben Hogan*	287	Lloyd Mangrum & George Fazio (287)	Merion Golf Club	Ardmore, Pa.
1951	Ben Hogan	287	Clayton Heafner (289)	Oakland Hills CC	Birmingham, Mich.
1952	Julius Boros	281	Porky Oliver (285)	Northwood Club	Dallas
1953	Ben Hogan	283	Sam Snead (289)	Oakmont CC	Oakmont, Pa.
1954	Ed Furgol	284	Gene Littler (285)	Baltusrol GC	Springfield, N.J.
1955	Jack Fleck*	287	Ben Hogan (287)	Olympic CC	San Francisco
1956	Cary Middlecoff	281	Ben Hogan & Julius Boros (282)	Oak Hill CC	Rochester, N.Y.
1957	Dick Mayer*	282	Cary Middlecoff (282)	Inverness Club	Toledo, Ohio
1958	Tommy Bolt	283	Gary Player (287)	Southern Hills CC	Tulsa
1959	Billy Casper	282	Bob Rosburg (283)	Winged Foot GC	Mamaroneck, N.Y.
1960	Arnold Palmer	280	Jack Nicklaus (282)	Cherry Hills CC	Denver
1961	Gene Littler	281	Doug Sanders & Bob Goalby (282)	Oakland Hills CC	Birmingham, Mich.
1962	Jack Nicklaus*	283	Arnold Palmer (283)	Oakmont CC	Oakmont, Pa.
1963	Julius Boros*	293	Arnold Palmer & Jacky Cupit (293)	The Country Club	Brookline, Mass.
1964	Ken Venturi	278	Tommy Jacobs (282)	Congressional CC	Bethesda, Md.
1965	Gary Player*	282	Kel Nagle (282)	Bellerive CC	St. Louis
1966	Billy Casper*	278	Arnold Palmer (278)	Olympic CC	San Francisco
1967	Jack Nicklaus	275	Arnold Palmer (279)	Baltusrol GC	Springfield, N.J.
1968	Lee Trevino	275	Jack Nicklaus (279)	Oak Hill CC	Rochester, N.Y.
1969	Orville Moody	281	Al Geiberger, Deane Beman & Bob Rosburg (282)	Champions GC	Houston
1970	Tony Jacklin	281	Dave Hill (288)	Hazeltine National GC	Chaska, Minn.
1971	Lee Trevino*	280	Jack Nicklaus (280)	Merion GC	Ardmore, Pa.
1972	Jack Nicklaus	290	Bruce Crampton (293)	Pebble Beach GL	Pebble Beach, Calif.
1973	Johnny Miller	279	John Schlee (280)	Oakmont CC	Oakmont, Pa.
1974	Hale Irwin	287	Forest Fezler (289)	Winged Foot GC	Mamaroneck, N.Y.
1975	Lou Graham*	287	John Mahaffey (287)	Medinah CC	Medinah, Ill.
1976	Jerry Pate	277	Al Geiberger & Tom Weiskopf (279)	Atlanta AC	Duluth, Ga.
1977	Hubert Green	278	Lou Graham (279)	Southern Hills CC	Tulsa
1978	Andy North	285	Dave Stockton & J.C. Snead (286)	Cherry Hills CC	Denver
1979	Hale Irwin	284	Gary Player & Jerry Pate (286)	Inverness Club	Toledo, Ohio
1980	Jack Nicklaus	272	Isao Aoki (274)	Baltusrol GC	Springfield, N.J.
1981	David Graham	273	George Burns & Bill Rogers (276)	Merion GC	Ardmore, Pa.
1982	Tom Watson	282	Jack Nicklaus (284)	Pebble Beach GL	Pebble Beach, Calif.
1983	Larry Nelson	280	Tom Watson (281)	Oakmont CC	Oakmont, Pa.
1984	Fuzzy Zoeller*	276	Greg Norman (276)	Winged Foot GC	Mamaroneck, N.Y.
1985	Andy North	279	Dave Barr, T.C. Chen & Denis Watson (280)	Oakland Hills CC	Birmingham, Mich.
1986	Ray Floyd	279	Lanny Wadkins & Chip Beck (281)	Shinnecock Hills GC	Southampton, N.Y.
1987	Scott Simpson	277	Tom Watson (278)	Olympic Club	San Francisco
1988	Curtis Strange*	278	Nick Faldo (278)	The Country Club	Brookline, Mass.
1989	Curtis Strange	278	Chip Beck, Ian Woosnam & Mark McCumber (279)	Oak Hill CC	Rochester, N.Y.
1990	Hale Irwin*	280	Mike Donald (280)	Medinah CC	Medinah, Ill.
1991	Payne Stewart*	282	Scott Simpson (282)	Hazeltine National GC	Chaska, Minn.
1992	Tom Kite	285	Jeff Sluman (287)	Pebble Beach GL	Pebble Beach, Calif.
1993	Lee Janzen	272	Payne Stewart (274)	Baltusrol GC	Springfield, N.J.
1994	Ernie Els*	279	Colin Montgomerie (279) & Loren Roberts (279)	Oakmont CC	Oakmont, Pa.
1995	Corey Pavin	280	Greg Norman (282)	Shinnecock Hills GC	Southampton, N.Y.
1996	Steve Jones	278	Davis Love III & Tom Lehman (279)	Oakland Hills CC	Bloomfield Hills, Mich.

U.S. Open (Cont.)

Year	Winner	Score	Runner-up	Course	Location
1997	Ernie Els	276	Colin Montgomerie (277)	Congressional CC	Bethesda, Md.
1998	Lee Janzen	280	Payne Stewart (281)	Olympic Club	San Francisco
1999	Payne Stewart	279	Phil Mickelson (280)	Pinehurst CC	Pinehurst, N.C.
2000	Tiger Woods	272	Miguel Angel Jimenez & Ernie Els (287)	Pebble Beach GL	Pebble Beach, Calif.
2001	Retief Goosen*	276	Mark Brooks (276)	Southern Hills CC	Tulsa
2002	Tiger Woods	277	Phil Mickelson (280)	Bethpage State Park (Black Course)	Farmingdale, N.Y.

*PLAYOFFS:

1901: Willie Anderson (85) def. Alex Smith (86) in 18 holes. **1903:** Willie Anderson (82) def. David Brown (84) in 18 holes. **1908:** Fred McLeod (77) def. Willie Smith (83) in 18 holes. **1910:** Alex Smith (71) def. John McDermott (75) & Macdonald Smith (77) in 18 holes. **1911:** John McDermott (80) def. Mike Brady (82) & George Simpson (85) in 18 holes. **1913:** Francis Ouimet (72) def. Harry Vardon (77) & Edward Ray (78) in 18 holes. **1919:** Walter Hagen (77) def. Mike Brady (78) in 18 holes. **1923:** Bobby Jones (76) def. Bobby Cruickshank (78) in 18 holes. **1925:** Willie Macfarlane (75-72—147) def. Bobby Jones (75-73—148) in 36 holes. **1927:** Tommy Armour (76) def. Harry Cooper (79) in 18 holes. **1928:** Johnny Farrell (70-73—143) def. Bobby Jones (73-71—144) in 36 holes. **1929:** Bobby Jones (141) def. Al Espinosa (164) in 36 holes. **1931:** Billy Burke (149-148) def. George Von Elm (149-149) in 72 holes. **1939:** Byron Nelson (68-70) def. Craig Wood (68-73) and Denny Shute (76) in 36 holes. **1940:** Lawson Little (70) def. Gene Sarazen (73) in 18 holes. **1946:** Lloyd Mangrum (72-72—144) def. Byron Nelson (72-73—145) and Vic Ghezzi (72-73—145) in 36 holes. **1947:** Lew Worsham (69) def. Sam Snead (70) in 18 holes. **1950:** Ben Hogan (69) def. Lloyd Mangrum (73) & George Fazio (75) in 18 holes. **1955:** Jack Fleck (69) def. Ben Hogan (72) in 18 holes. **1957:** Dick Mayer (72) def. Cary Middlecoff (79) in 18 holes. **1962:** Jack Nicklaus (71) def. Arnold Palmer (74) in 18 holes. **1963:** Julius Boros (70) def. Jacky Cupit (73) & Arnold Palmer (76) in 18 holes. **1965:** Gary Player (71) def. Kel Nagle (74) in 18 holes. **1966:** Billy Casper (69) def. Arnold Palmer (73) in 18 holes. **1971:** Lee Trevino (68) def. Jack Nicklaus (71) in 18 holes. **1975:** Lou Graham (71) def. John Mahaffey (73) in 18 holes. **1984:** Fuzzy Zoeller (67) def. Greg Norman (75) in 18 holes. **1988:** Curtis Strange (71) def. Nick Faldo (75) in 18 holes. **1990:** Hale Irwin (74-3) def. Mike Donald (74-4) on 1st hole of sudden death after 18 holes. **1991:** Payne Stewart (75) def. Scott Simpson (77) in 18 holes. **1994:** Ernie Els (74-4-4) def. Loren Roberts (74-4-5) and Colin Montgomerie (78) on 2nd hole of sudden death after 18 holes; **2001:** Goosen (70) def. Brooks (72) in 18 holes.

British Open

The oldest of the Majors, the Open began in 1860 to determine "the champion golfer of the world." While only professional golfers participated in the first year of the tournament, amateurs have been invited ever since. Competition was extended from 36 to 72 holes in 1892. Conducted by the Royal and Ancient Golf Club of St. Andrews, the Open is rotated among select golf courses in England and Scotland. Note that (*) indicates playoff winner and (a) indicates amateur winner.

Multiple winners: Harry Vardon (6); James Braid, J.H. Taylor, Peter Thomson and Tom Watson (5); Walter Hagen, Bobby Locke, Tom Morris Sr., Tom Morris Jr. and Willie Park (4); Jamie Anderson, Seve Ballesteros, Henry Cotton, Nick Faldo, Bob Ferguson, Bobby Jones, Jack Nicklaus and Gary Player (3); Harold Hilton, Bob Martin, Greg Norman, Arnold Palmer, Willie Park Jr. and Lee Trevino (2).

Year	Winner	Score	Runner-up	Course	Location
1860	Willie Park	174	Tom Morris Sr. (176)	Prestwick Club	Ayrshire, Scotland
1861	Tom Morris Sr.	163	Willie Park (167)	Prestwick Club	Ayrshire, Scotland
1862	Tom Morris Sr.	163	Willie Park (176)	Prestwick Club	Ayrshire, Scotland
1863	Willie Park	168	Tom Morris Sr. (170)	Prestwick Club	Ayrshire, Scotland
1864	Tom Morris Sr.	167	Andrew Strath (169)	Prestwick Club	Ayrshire, Scotland
1865	Andrew Strath	162	Willie Park (164)	Prestwick Club	Ayrshire, Scotland
1866	Willie Park	169	David Park (171)	Prestwick Club	Ayrshire, Scotland
1867	Tom Morris Sr.	170	Willie Park (172)	Prestwick Club	Ayrshire, Scotland
1868	Tom Morris Jr.	157	Robert Andrew (159)	Prestwick Club	Ayrshire, Scotland
1869	Tom Morris Jr.	154	Tom Morris Sr. (157)	Prestwick Club	Ayrshire, Scotland
1870	Tom Morris Jr.	149	Bob Kirk (161)	Prestwick Club	Ayrshire, Scotland
1871	Not held				
1872	Tom Morris Jr.	166	David Strath (169)	Prestwick Club	Ayrshire, Scotland
1873	Tom Kidd	179	Jamie Anderson (180)	St. Andrews	St. Andrews, Scotland
1874	Mungo Park	159	Tom Morris Jr. (161)	Musselburgh	Musselburgh, Scotland
1875	Willie Park	166	Bob Martin (168)	Prestwick Club	Ayrshire, Scotland
1876	Bob Martin*	176	David Strath (176)	St. Andrews	St. Andrews, Scotland
1877	Jamie Anderson	160	Bob Pringle (162)	Musselburgh	Musselburgh, Scotland
1878	Jamie Anderson	157	Bob Kirk (159)	Prestwick Club	Ayrshire, Scotland
1879	Jamie Anderson	169	Andrew Kirkaldy & James Allan (172)	St. Andrews	St. Andrews, Scotland
1880	Bob Ferguson	162	Peter Paxton (167)	Musselburgh	Musselburgh, Scotland
1881	Bob Ferguson	170	Jamie Anderson (173)	Prestwick Club	Ayrshire, Scotland
1882	Bob Ferguson	171	Willie Fernie (174)	St. Andrews	St. Andrews, Scotland
1883	Willie Fernie*	159	Bob Ferguson (159)	Musselburgh	Musselburgh, Scotland
1884	Jack Simpson	160	Douglas Rolland & Willie Fernie (164)	Prestwick Club	Ayrshire, Scotland
1885	Bob Martin	171	Archie Simpson (172)	St. Andrews	St. Andrews, Scotland
1886	David Brown	157	Willie Campbell (159)	Musselburgh	Musselburgh, Scotland
1887	Willie Park Jr.	161	Bob Martin (162)	Prestwick Club	Ayrshire, Scotland
1888	Jack Burns	171	David Anderson & Ben Sayers (172)	St. Andrews	St. Andrews, Scotland
1889	Willie Park Jr.*	155	Andrew Kirkaldy (155)	Musselburgh	Musselburgh, Scotland

Year	Winner	Score	Runner-up	Course	Location
1890	a-John Ball	164	Willie Fernie (167) & A. Simpson (167)	Prestwick Club	Ayrshire, Scotland
1891	Hugh Kirkaldy	166	Andrew Kirkaldy & Willie Fernie (168)	St. Andrews	St. Andrews, Scotland
1892	a-Harold Hilton	305	John Ball, Sandy Herd & Hugh Kirkaldy (308)	Muirfield	Gullane, Scotland
1893	Willie Auchterlonie	322	Johnny Laidley (324)	Prestwick Club	Ayrshire, Scotland
1894	J.H. Taylor	326	Douglas Rolland (331)	Royal St. George's	Sandwich, England
1895	J.H. Taylor	322	Sandy Herd (326)	St. Andrews	St. Andrews, Scotland
1896	Harry Vardon*	316	J.H. Taylor (316)	Muirfield	Gullane, Scotland
1897	a-Harold Hilton	314	James Braid (315)	Hoylake	Hoylake, England
1898	Harry Vardon	307	Willie Park Jr. (308)	Prestwick Club	Ayrshire, Scotland
1899	Harry Vardon	310	Jack White (315)	Royal St. George's	Sandwich, England
1900	J.H. Taylor	309	Harry Vardon (317)	St. Andrews	St. Andrews, Scotland
1901	James Braid	309	Harry Vardon (312)	Muirfield	Gullane, Scotland
1902	Sandy Herd	307	Harry Vardon (308)	Hoylake	Hoylake, England
1903	Harry Vardon	300	Tom Vardon (306)	Prestwick Club	Ayrshire, Scotland
1904	Jack White	296	James Braid (297)	Royal St. George's	Sandwich, England
1905	James Braid	318	J.H. Taylor (323) & Rowland Jones (323)	St. Andrews	St. Andrews, Scotland
1906	James Braid	300	J.H. Taylor (304)	Muirfield	Gullane, Scotland
1907	Arnaud Massy	312	J.H. Taylor (314)	Hoylake	Hoylake, England
1908	James Braid	291	Tom Ball (299)	Prestwick Club	Ayrshire, Scotland
1909	J.H. Taylor	295	James Braid (299)	Deal	Deal, England
1910	James Braid	299	Sandy Herd (303)	St. Andrews	St. Andrews, Scotland
1911	Harry Vardon*	303	Arnaud Massy (303)	Royal St. George's	Sandwich, England
1912	Ted Ray	295	Harry Vardon (299)	Muirfield	Gullane, Scotland
1913	J.H. Taylor	304	Ted Ray (312)	Hoylake	Hoylake, England
1914	Harry Vardon	306	J.H. Taylor (309)	Prestwick Club	Ayrshire, Scotland
1915-19 Not held			World War I		
1920	George Duncan	303	Sandy Herd (305)	Deal	Deal, England
1921	Jock Hutchison*	296	Roger Wethered (296)	St. Andrews	St. Andrews, Scotland
1922	Walter Hagen	300	George Duncan & Jim Barnes (301)	Royal St. George's	Sandwich, England
1923	Arthur Havers	295	Walter Hagen (296)	Royal Troon	Troon, Scotland
1924	Walter Hagen	301	Ernest Whitcombe (302)	Hoylake	Hoylake, England
1925	Jim Barnes	300	Archie Compston & Ted Ray (301)	Prestwick Club	Ayrshire, Scotland
1926	a-Bobby Jones	291	Al Watrous (293)	Royal Lytham	Lytham, England
1927	a-Bobby Jones	285	Aubrey Boomer (291)	St. Andrews	St. Andrews, Scotland
1928	Walter Hagen	292	Gene Sarazen (294)	Royal St. George's	Sandwich, England
1929	Walter Hagen	292	Johnny Farrell (298)	Muirfield	Gullane, Scotland
1930	a-Bobby Jones	291	Macdonald Smith & Leo Diegel (293)	Hoylake	Hoylake, England
1931	Tommy Armour	296	Jose Jurado (297)	Carnoustie	Carnoustie, Scotland
1932	Gene Sarazen*	283	Macdonald Smith (288)	Prince's	Prince's, England
1933	Denny Shute*	292	Craig Wood (292)	St. Andrews	St. Andrews, Scotland
1934	Henry Cotton	283	Sid Brews (288)	Royal St. George's	Sandwich, England
1935	Alf Perry	283	Alf Padgham (287)	Muirfield	Gullane, Scotland
1936	Alf Padgham	287	Jimmy Adams (288)	Hoylake	Hoylake, England
1937	Henry Cotton	290	Reg Whitcombe (292)	Carnoustie	Carnoustie, Scotland
1938	Reg Whitcombe	295	Jimmy Adams (297)	Royal St. George's	Sandwich, England
1939	Dick Burton	290	Johnny Bulla (292)	St. Andrews	St. Andrews, Scotland
1940-45 Not held			World War II		
1946	Sam Snead	290	Bobby Locke (294) & Johnny Bulla (294)	St. Andrews	St. Andrews, Scotland
1947	Fred Daly	293	Frank Stranahan & Reg Horne (294)	Hoylake	Hoylake, England
1948	Henry Cotton	284	Fred Daly (289)	Muirfield	Gullane, Scotland
1949	Bobby Locke*	283	Harry Bradshaw (283)	Royal St. George's	Sandwich, England
1950	Bobby Locke	279	Roberto de Vicenzo (281)	Royal Troon	Troon, Scotland
1951	Max Faulkner	285	Tony Cerda (287)	Royal Portrush	Portrush, Ireland
1952	Bobby Locke	287	Peter Thomson (288)	Royal Lytham	Lytham, England
1953	Ben Hogan	282	Frank Stranahan, Dai Rees, Tony Cerda & Peter Thomson (286)	Carnoustie	Carnoustie, Scotland
1954	Peter Thomson	283	Sid Scott, Dai Rees & Bobby Locke (284)	Royal Birkdale	Southport, England
1955	Peter Thomson	281	Johny Fallon (283)	St. Andrews	St. Andrews, Scotland
1956	Peter Thomson	286	Flory Van Donck (289)	Hoylake	Hoylake, England
1957	Bobby Locke	279	Peter Thomson (282)	St. Andrews	St. Andrews, Scotland

British Open (Cont.)

Year	Winner	Score	Runner-up	Course	Location
1958	Peter Thomson*	278	Dave Thomas (278)	Royal Lytham	Lytham, England
1959	Gary Player	284	Flory Van Donck & Fred Bullock (286)	Muirfield	Gullane, Scotland
1960	Kel Nagle	278	Arnold Palmer (279)	St. Andrews	St. Andrews, Scotland
1961	Arnold Palmer	284	Dai Rees (285)	Royal Birkdale	Southport, England
1962	Arnold Palmer	276	Kel Nagle (282)	Royal Troon	Troon, Scotland
1963	Bob Charles*	277	Phil Rodgers (277)	Royal Lytham	Lytham, England
1964	Tony Lema	279	Jack Nicklaus (284)	St. Andrews	St. Andrews, Scotland
1965	Peter Thomson	285	Christy O'Connor & Brian Huggett (287)	Royal Birkdale	Southport, England
1966	Jack Nicklaus	282	Doug Sanders & Dave Thomas (283)	Muirfield	Gullane, Scotland
1967	Roberto de Vicenzo	278	Jack Nicklaus (280)	Hoylake	Hoylake, England
1968	Gary Player	289	Jack Nicklaus & Bob Charles (291)	Carnoustie	Carnoustie, Scotland
1969	Tony Jacklin	280	Bob Charles (282)	Royal Lytham	Lytham, England
1970	Jack Nicklaus*	283	Doug Sanders (283)	St. Andrews	St. Andrews, Scotland
1971	Lee Trevino	278	Lu Liang Huan (279)	Royal Birkdale	Southport, England
1972	Lee Trevino	278	Jack Nicklaus (279)	Muirfield	Gullane, Scotland
1973	Tom Weiskopf	276	Johnny Miller & Neil Coles (279)	Royal Troon	Troon, Scotland
1974	Gary Player	282	Peter Oosterhuis (286)	Royal Lytham	Lytham, England
1975	Tom Watson*	279	Jack Newton (279)	Carnoustie	Carnoustie, Scotland
1976	Johnny Miller	279	Seve Ballesteros & Jack Nicklaus (285)	Royal Birkdale	Southport, England
1977	Tom Watson	268	Jack Nicklaus (269)	Turnberry	Turnberry, Scotland
1978	Jack Nicklaus	281	Tom Kite, Ray Floyd, Ben Crenshaw & Simon Owen (283)	St. Andrews	St. Andrews, Scotland
1979	Seve Ballesteros	283	Jack Nicklaus & Ben Crenshaw (286)	Royal Lytham	Lytham, England
1980	Tom Watson	271	Lee Trevino (275)	Muirfield	Gullane, Scotland
1981	Bill Rogers	276	Bernhard Langer (280)	Royal St. George's	Sandwich, England
1982	Tom Watson	284	Peter Oosterhuis & Nick Price (285)	Royal Troon	Troon, Scotland
1983	Tom Watson	275	Hale Irwin & Andy Bean (276)	Royal Birkdale	Southport, England
1984	Seve Ballesteros	276	Bernhard Langer & Tom Watson (278)	St. Andrews	St. Andrews, Scotland
1985	Sandy Lyle	282	Payne Stewart (283)	Royal St. George's	Sandwich, England
1986	Greg Norman	280	Gordon J. Brand (285)	Turnberry	Turnberry, Scotland
1987	Nick Faldo	279	Paul Azinger & Rodger Davis (280)	Muirfield	Gullane, Scotland
1988	Seve Ballesteros	273	Nick Price (275)	Royal Lytham	Lytham, England
1989	Mark Calcavecchia*	275	Greg Norman & Wayne Grady (275)	Royal Troon	Troon, Scotland
1990	Nick Faldo	270	Payne Stewart & Mark McNulty (275)	St. Andrews	St. Andrews, Scotland
1991	Ian Baker-Finch	272	Mike Harwood (274)	Royal Birkdale	Southport, England
1992	Nick Faldo	272	John Cook (273)	Muirfield	Gullane, Scotland
1993	Greg Norman	267	Nick Faldo (269)	Royal St. George's	Sandwich, England
1994	Nick Price	268	Jesper Parnevik (269)	Turnberry	Turnberry, Scotland
1995	John Daly*	282	Costantino Rocca (282)	St. Andrews	St. Andrews, Scotland
1996	Tom Lehman	271	Mark McCumber & Ernie Els (273)	Royal Lytham	Lytham, England
1997	Justin Leonard	272	Jesper Parnevik & Darren Clarke (275)	Royal Troon	Troon, Scotland
1998	Mark O'Meara*	280	Brian Watts (280)	Royal Birkdale	Southport, England
1999	Paul Lawrie*	290	Justin Leonard & Jean Van de Velde (290)	Carnoustie	Carnoustie, Scotland
2000	Tiger Woods	269	Thomas Bjorn & Ernie Els (277)	St. Andrews	St. Andrews, Scotland
2001	David Duval	274	Niclas Fasth (277)	Royal Lytham	Lytham, England
2002	Ernie Els*	278	Thomas Levet, Stuart Appleby & Steve Elkington (278)	Muirfield	Gullane, Scotland

*PLAYOFFS:

1876: Bob Martin awarded title when David Strath refused playoff. **1883:** Willie Fernie (158) def. Robert Ferguson (159) in 36 holes. **1889:** Willie Park Jr. (158) def. Andrew Kirkaldy (163) in 36 holes. **1896:** Harry Vardon (157) def. John H. Taylor (161) in 36 holes. **1911:** Harry Vardon won when Arnaud Massy conceded at 35th hole. **1921:** Jock Hutchison (150) def. Roger Wethered (159) in 36 holes. **1933:** Denny Shute (149) def. Craig Wood (154) in 36 holes. **1949:** Bobby Locke

(135) def. Harry Bradshaw (147) in 36 holes. **1958:** Peter Thomson (139) def. Dave Thomas (143) in 36 holes. **1963:** Bob Charles (140) def. Phil Rogers (148) in 36 holes. **1970:** Jack Nicklaus (72) def. Doug Sanders (73) in 18 holes. **1975:** Tom Watson (71) def. Jack Newton (72) in 18 holes. **1989:** Mark Calcavecchia (4-3-3-3 — 13) def. Wayne Grady (4-4-4-4 — 16) and Greg Norman (3-3-4) in 4 holes. **1995:** John Daly (3-4-4-4 — 15) def. Costantino Rocca (4-5-7-3 — 19) in 4 holes. **1998:** Mark O'Meara (4-4-5-4 — 17) def. Brian Watts (5-4-5-5 — 19) in 4 holes. **1999:** Paul Lawrie (5-4-3-3 — 15) def. Justin Leonard (5-4-4-5 — 18) and Jean Van de Velde (6-4-3-5 — 18) in 4 holes. **2002:** Els (4-3-5-4 — 16) and Levet (4-2-5-5 — 16) remained tied after a four-hole playoff that also included Appleby (4-4-4-5 — 17) and Elkington (5-3-4-5 — 17). The pair moved on to sudden death, where Els (4) def. Levet (5) on the 1st hole.

PGA Championship

The PGA Championship began in 1916 as a professional golfers match play tournament, but switched to stroke play in 1958. Conducted by the PGA of America, the tournament is played on a different course each year.

Multiple winners: Walter Hagen and Jack Nicklaus (5); Gene Sarazen and Sam Snead (3); Jim Barnes, Leo Diegel, Ray Floyd, Ben Hogan, Byron Nelson, Larry Nelson, Gary Player, Nick Price, Paul Runyan, Denny Shute, Dave Stockton, Lee Trevino and Tiger Woods (2).

Year	Winner	Score	Runner-up	Course	Location
1916	Jim Barnes	1-up	Jock Hutchison	Siwanoy CC	Bronxville, N.Y.
1917-18	Not held		World War I		
1919	Jim Barnes	6 & 5	Fred McLeod	Engineers CC	Roslyn, N.Y.
1920	Jock Hutchison	1-up	J. Douglas Edgar	Flossmoor CC	Flossmoor, Ill.
1921	Walter Hagen	3 & 2	Jim Barnes	Inwood CC	Inwood, N.Y.
1922	Gene Sarazen	4 & 3	Emmet French	Oakmont CC	Oakmont, Pa.
1923	Gene Sarazen*	1-up/38	Walter Hagen	Pelham CC	Pelham, N.Y.
1924	Walter Hagen	2-up	Jim Barnes	French Lick CC	French Lick, Ind.
1925	Walter Hagen	6 & 5	Bill Mehlhorn	Olympia Fields CC	Matteson, Ill.
1926	Walter Hagen	5 & 3	Leo Diegel	Salisbury GC	Westbury, N.Y.
1927	Walter Hagen	1-up	Joe Turnesa	Cedar Crest CC	Dallas
1928	Leo Diegel	6 & 5	Al Espinosa	Five Farms CC	Baltimore
1929	Leo Diegel	6 & 4	John Farrell	Hillcrest CC	Los Angeles
1930	Tommy Armour	1-up	Gene Sarazen	Fresh Meadow CC	Flushing, N.Y.
1931	Tom Creavy	2 & 1	Denny Shute	Wannamoisett CC	Rumford, R.I.
1932	Olin Dutra	4 & 3	Frank Walsh	Keller GC	St. Paul, Minn.
1933	Gene Sarazen	5 & 4	Willie Goggin	Blue Mound CC	Milwaukee
1934	Paul Runyan*	1-up/38	Craig Wood	Park CC	Williamsville, N.Y.
1935	Johnny Revolta	5 & 4	Tommy Armour	Twin Hills CC	Oklahoma City
1936	Denny Shute	3 & 2	Jimmy Thomson	Pinehurst CC	Pinehurst, N.C.
1937	Denny Shute*	1-up/37	Harold McSpaden	Pittsburgh FC	Aspinwall, Pa.
1938	Paul Runyan	8 & 7	Sam Snead	Shawnee CC	Shawnee-on-Del, Pa.
1939	Henry Picard*	1-up/37	Byron Nelson	Pomonok CC	Flushing, N.Y.
1940	Byron Nelson	1-up	Sam Snead	Hershey CC	Hershey, Pa.
1941	Vic Ghezzi*	1-up/38	Byron Nelson	Cherry Hills CC	Denver
1942	Sam Snead	2 & 1	Jim Turnesa	Seaview CC	Atlantic City, N.J.
1943	Not held		World War II		
1944	Bob Hamilton	1-up	Byron Nelson	Manito G & CC	Spokane, Wash.
1945	Byron Nelson	4 & 3	Sam Byrd	Morraine CC	Dayton, Ohio
1946	Ben Hogan	6 & 4	Porky Oliver	Portland GC	Portland, Ore.
1947	Jim Ferrier	2 & 1	Chick Harbert	Plum Hollow CC	Detroit
1948	Ben Hogan	7 & 6	Mike Turnesa	Norwood Hills CC	St. Louis
1949	Sam Snead	3 & 2	John Palmer	Hermitage CC	Richmond, Va.
1950	Chandler Harper	4 & 3	Henry Williams Jr.	Scioto CC	Columbus, Ohio
1951	Sam Snead	7 & 6	Walter Burkemo	Oakmont CC	Oakmont, Pa.

Major Championship Leaders
Through 2002; active PGA players in **bold** type.

	US Open	British Open	PGA	Masters	US Am	British Am	Total
Jack Nicklaus	4	3	5	6	2	0	20
Bobby Jones	4	3	0	0	5	1	13
Walter Hagen	2	4	5	0	0	0	11
Tiger Woods	2	1	2	3	3	0	11
Ben Hogan	4	1	2	2	0	0	9
Gary Player	1	3	2	3	0	0	9
John Ball	0	1	0	0	0	8	9
Arnold Palmer	1	2	0	4	1	0	8
Tom Watson	1	5	0	2	0	0	8
Harold Hilton	0	2	0	0	1	4	7
Gene Sarazen	2	1	3	1	0	0	7
Sam Snead	0	1	3	3	0	0	7
Harry Vardon	1	6	0	0	0	0	7
Nick Faldo	0	3	0	3	0	0	6
Lee Trevino	2	2	2	0	0	0	6

Tournaments: U.S. Open, British Open, PGA Championship, Masters, U.S. Amateur and British Amateur.

PGA Championship (Cont.)

Year	Winner	Score	Runner-up	Course	Location
1952	Jim Turnesa	1-up	Chick Harbert	Big Spring CC	Louisville
1953	Walter Burkemo	2 & 1	Felice Torza	Birmingham CC	Birmingham, Mich.
1954	Chick Harbert	4 & 3	Walter Burkemo	Keller GC	St. Paul, Minn.
1955	Doug Ford	4 & 3	Cary Middlecoff	Meadowbrook CC	Detroit
1956	Jack Burke	3 & 2	Ted Kroll	Blue Hill CC	Boston
1957	Lionel Hebert	2 & 1	Dow Finsterwald	Miami Valley GC	Dayton, Ohio
1958	Dow Finsterwald	276	Billy Casper (278)	Llanerch CC	Havertown, Pa.
1959	Bob Rosburg	277	Jerry Barber & Doug Sanders (278)	Minneapolis GC	St. Louis Park, Minn.
1960	Jay Hebert	281	Jim Ferrier (282)	Firestone CC	Akron, Ohio
1961	Jerry Barber**	277	Don January (277)	Olympia Fields CC	Matteson, Ill.
1962	Gary Player	278	Bob Goalby (279)	Aronimink GC	Newtown Square, Pa.
1963	Jack Nicklaus	279	Dave Ragan (281)	Dallas AC	Dallas
1964	Bobby Nichols	271	Jack Nicklaus & Arnold Palmer (274)	Columbus CC	Columbus, Ohio
1965	Dave Marr	280	Jack Nicklaus & Billy Casper (282)	Laurel Valley GC	Ligonier, Pa.
1966	Al Geiberger	280	Dudley Wysong (284)	Firestone CC	Akron, Ohio
1967	Don January**	281	Don Massengale (281)	Columbine CC	Littleton, Colo.
1968	Julius Boros	281	Arnold Palmer & Bob Charles (282)	Pecan Valley CC	San Antonio
1969	Ray Floyd	276	Gary Player (277)	NCR GC	Dayton, Ohio
1970	Dave Stockton	279	Arnold Palmer & Bob Murphy (281)	Southern Hills CC	Tulsa
1971	Jack Nicklaus	281	Billy Casper (283)	PGA National GC	Palm Beach Gardens, Fla.
1972	Gary Player	281	Jim Jamieson & Tommy Aaron (283)	Oakland Hills GC	Birmingham, Mich.
1973	Jack Nicklaus	277	Bruce Crampton (281)	Canterbury GC	Cleveland
1974	Lee Trevino	276	Jack Nicklaus (277)	Tanglewood GC	Winston-Salem, N.C.
1975	Jack Nicklaus	276	Bruce Crampton (278)	Firestone CC	Akron, Ohio
1976	Dave Stockton	281	Don January & Ray Floyd (282)	Congressional CC	Bethesda, Md.
1977	Lanny Wadkins**	282	Gene Littler (282)	Pebble Beach GL	Pebble Beach, Calif.
1978	John Mahaffey**	276	Jerry Pate & Tom Watson (276)	Oakmont CC	Oakmont, Pa.
1979	David Graham**	272	Ben Crenshaw (272)	Oakland Hills CC	Birmingham, Mich.
1980	Jack Nicklaus	274	Andy Bean (281)	Oak Hill CC	Rochester, N.Y.
1981	Larry Nelson	273	Fuzzy Zoeller (277)	Atlanta AC	Duluth, Ga.
1982	Ray Floyd	272	Lanny Wadkins (275)	Southern Hills CC	Tulsa
1983	Hal Sutton	274	Jack Nicklaus (275)	Riviera CC	Los Angeles
1984	Lee Trevino	273	Lanny Wadkins & Gary Player (277)	Shoal Creek	Birmingham, Ala.
1985	Hubert Green	278	Lee Trevino (280)	Cherry Hills CC	Denver
1986	Bob Tway	276	Greg Norman (278)	Inverness Club	Toledo, Ohio
1987	Larry Nelson**	287	Lanny Wadkins (287)	PGA National	Palm Beach Gardens, Fla.
1988	Jeff Sluman	272	Paul Azinger 275)	Oak Tree GC	Edmond, Okla.
1989	Payne Stewart	276	Andy Bean, Mike Reid & Curtis Strange (277)	Kemper Lakes GC	Hawthorn Woods, Ill.
1990	Wayne Grady	282	Fred Couples (285)	Shoal Creek	Birmingham, Ala.
1991	John Daly	276	Bruce Lietzke (279)	Crooked Stick GC	Carmel, Ind.
1992	Nick Price	278	Nick Faldo, John Cook, Jim Gallagher & Gene Sauers (281)	Bellerive CC	St. Louis
1993	Paul Azinger**	272	Greg Norman (272)	Inverness Club	Toledo, Ohio
1994	Nick Price	269	Corey Pavin (275)	Southern Hills CC	Tulsa
1995	Steve Elkington**	267	Colin Montgomerie (267)	Riviera CC	Pacific Palisades, Calif.
1996	Mark Brooks**	277	Kenny Perry (277)	Valhalla GC	Louisville, Ky.
1997	Davis Love III	269	Justin Leonard (274)	Winged Foot GC	Mamaroneck, N.Y.
1998	Vijay Singh	271	Steve Stricker (273)	Sahalee CC	Redmond, Wash.
1999	Tiger Woods	277	Sergio Garcia (278)	Medinah CC	Medinah, Ill.
2000	Tiger Woods**	270	Bob May (270)	Valhalla GC	Louisville, Ky.
2001	David Toms	265	Phil Mickelson (266)	Atlanta AC	Duluth, Ga.
2002	Rich Beem	278	Tiger Woods (279)	Hazeltine National GC	Chaska, Minn.

*While the PGA Championship was a match play tournament from 1916-57, the two finalists played 36 holes for the title. In the five years that a playoff was necessary, the match was decided on the 37th or 38th hole.

**PLAYOFFS:

1961: Jerry Barber (67) def. Don January (68) in 18 holes. **1967:** Don January (69) def. Don Massengale (71) in 18 holes. **1977:** Lanny Wadkins (4-4-4) def. Gene Littler (4-4-5) on 3rd hole of sudden death. **1978:** John Mahaffey (4-3) def. Jerry Pate (4-4) and Tom Watson (4-5) on 2nd hole of sudden death. **1979:** David Graham (4-4-2) def. Ben Crenshaw (4-4-4) on 3rd hole of sudden death. **1987:** Larry Nelson (4) def. Lanny Wadkins (5) on 1st hole of sudden death. **1993:** Paul Azinger

(4-4) def. Greg Norman (4-5) on 2nd hole of sudden death. **1995:** Steve Elkington (3) def. Colin Montgomerie (4) on 1st hole of sudden death. **1996:** Mark Brooks (4) def. Kenny Perry (5) on 1st hole of sudden death. **2000:** Tiger Woods (3-4-5–12) won a three-hole playoff over Bob May (4-4-5–13).

Grand Slam Summary

The only golfer ever to win a recognized Grand Slam—four major championships in a single season—was Bobby Jones in 1930. That year, Jones won the U.S. and British Opens as well as the U.S. and British Amateurs.

The men's professional Grand Slam—the Masters, U.S. Open, British Open and PGA Championship—did not gain acceptance until 30 years later when Arnold Palmer won the 1960 Masters and U.S. Open. The media wrote that the popular Palmer was chasing the "new" Grand Slam and would have to win the British Open and the PGA to claim it. He did not, but then nobody has before or since.

Three wins in one year (2): Ben Hogan (1953) and Tiger Woods (2000). **Two wins in one year** (20): Jack Nicklaus (5 times); Ben Hogan, Arnold Palmer, Tom Watson and Tiger Woods (twice); Nick Faldo, Mark O'Meara, Gary Player, Nick Price, Sam Snead, Lee Trevino and Craig Wood (once).

Year	Masters	US Open	Brit. Open	PGA	Year	Masters	US Open	Brit. Open	PGA
1934	H. Smith	Dutra	Cotton	Runyan	1964	Palmer	Venturi	Lema	Nichols
1935	Sarazen	Parks	Perry	Revolta	1965	Nicklaus	Player	Thomson	Marr
1936	H. Smith	Manero	Padgham	Shute	1966	Nicklaus	Casper	Nicklaus	Geiberger
1937	B. Nelson	Guldahl	Cotton	Shute	1967	Brewer Jr.	Nicklaus	De Vicenzo	January
1938	Picard	Guldahl	Whitcombe	Runyan	1968	Goalby	Trevino	Player	Boros
1939	Guldahl	B. Nelson	Burton	Picard	1969	Archer	Moody	Jacklin	Floyd
1940	Demaret	Little	—	B. Nelson	1970	Casper	Jacklin	Nicklaus	Stockton
1941	Wood	Wood	—	Ghezzi	1971	Coody	Trevino	Trevino	Nicklaus
1942	B. Nelson	—	—	Snead	1972	Nicklaus	Nicklaus	Trevino	Player
1943	—	—	—	—	1973	Aaron	J. Miller	Weiskopf	Nicklaus
1944	—	—	—	Hamilton	1974	Player	Irwin	Player	Trevino
1945	—	—	—	B. Nelson	1975	Nicklaus	L. Graham	T. Watson	Nicklaus
1946	Keiser	Mangrum	Snead	Hogan	1976	Floyd	J. Pate	Miller	Stockton
1947	Demaret	Worsham	F. Daly	Ferrier	1977	T. Watson	H. Green	T. Watson	L. Wadkins
1948	Harmon	Hogan	Cotton	Hogan	1978	Player	North	Nicklaus	Mahaffey
1949	Snead	Middlecoff	Locke	Snead	1979	Zoeller	Irwin	Ballesteros	D. Graham
1950	Demaret	Hogan	Locke	Harper	1980	Ballesteros	Nicklaus	T. Watson	Nicklaus
1951	Hogan	Hogan	Faulkner	Snead	1981	T. Watson	D. Graham	Rogers	L. Nelson
1952	Snead	Boros	Locke	Turnesa	1982	Stadler	T. Watson	T. Watson	Floyd
1953	Hogan	Hogan	Hogan	Burkemo	1983	Ballesteros	L. Nelson	T. Watson	Sutton
1954	Snead	Furgol	Thomson	Harbert	1984	Crenshaw	Zoeller	Ballesteros	Trevino
1955	Middlecoff	Fleck	Thomson	Ford	1985	Langer	North	Lyle	H. Green
1956	Burke	Middlecoff	Thomson	Burke	1986	Nicklaus	Floyd	Norman	Tway
1957	Ford	Mayer	Locke	L. Hebert	1987	Mize	S. Simpson	Faldo	L. Nelson
1958	Palmer	Bolt	Thomson	Finsterwald	1988	Lyle	Strange	Ballesteros	Sluman
1959	Wall	Casper	Player	Rosburg	1989	Faldo	Strange	Calcavecchia	Stewart
1960	Palmer	Palmer	Nagle	J. Hebert	1990	Faldo	Irwin	Faldo	Grady
1961	Player	Littler	Palmer	J. Barber	1991	Woosnam	Stewart	Baker-Finch	J. Daly
1962	Palmer	Nicklaus	Palmer	Player	1992	Couples	Kite	Faldo	Price
1963	Nicklaus	Boros	Charles	Nicklaus	1993	Langer	Janzen	Norman	Azinger

Vardon Trophy

Awarded since 1937 by the PGA of America to the PGA Tour regular with the lowest adjusted scoring average. The award is named after Harry Vardon, the six-time British Open champion who also won the U.S. Open in 1900. A point system was used from 1937-41.

Multiple winners: Billy Casper and Lee Trevino (5); Arnold Palmer and Sam Snead (4); Ben Hogan, Greg Norman, Tom Watson and Tiger Woods (3); Fred Couples, Bruce Crampton, Tom Kite, Lloyd Mangrum and Nick Price (2).

Year		Pts	Year		Avg	Year		Avg
1937	Harry Cooper	500	1961	Arnold Palmer	69.85	1982	Tom Kite	70.21
1938	Sam Snead	520	1962	Arnold Palmer	70.27	1983	Ray Floyd	70.61
1939	Byron Nelson	473	1963	Billy Casper	70.58	1984	Calvin Peete	70.56
1940	Ben Hogan	423	1964	Arnold Palmer	70.01	1985	Don Pooley	70.36
1941	Ben Hogan	494	1965	Billy Casper	70.85	1986	Scott Hoch	70.08
1942-46	No award		1966	Billy Casper	70.27	1987	Dan Pohl	70.25
			1967	Arnold Palmer	70.18	1988	Chip Beck	69.46
Year		**Avg**	1968	Billy Casper	69.82	1989	Greg Norman	69.49
1947	Jimmy Demaret	69.90	1969	Dave Hill	70.34	1990	Greg Norman	69.10
1948	Ben Hogan	69.30	1970	Lee Trevino	70.64	1991	Fred Couples	69.59
1949	Sam Snead	69.37	1971	Lee Trevino	70.27	1992	Fred Couples	69.38
1950	Sam Snead	69.23	1972	Lee Trevino	70.89	1993	Nick Price	69.11
1951	Lloyd Mangrum	70.05	1973	Bruce Crampton	70.57	1994	Greg Norman	68.81
1952	Jack Burke	70.54	1974	Lee Trevino	70.53	1995	Steve Elkington	69.62
1953	Lloyd Mangrum	70.22	1975	Bruce Crampton	70.51	1996	Tom Lehman	69.32
1954	E.J. Harrison	70.41	1976	Don January	70.56	1997	Nick Price	68.98
1955	Sam Snead	69.86	1977	Tom Watson	70.32	1998	David Duval	69.13
1956	Cary Middlecoff	70.35	1978	Tom Watson	70.16	1999	Tiger Woods	68.43
1957	Dow Finsterwald	70.30	1979	Tom Watson	70.27	2000	Tiger Woods	67.79
1958	Bob Rosburg	70.11	1980	Lee Trevino	69.73	2001	Tiger Woods	68.81
1959	Art Wall	70.35	1981	Tom Kite	69.80			
1960	Billy Casper	69.95						

Grand Slam Summary (Cont.)

Year	Masters	US Open	Brit. Open	PGA	Year	Masters	US Open	Brit. Open	PGA
1994	Olazabal	Els	Price	Price	1999	Olazabal	Stewart	Lawrie	Woods
1995	Crenshaw	Pavin	Daly	Elkington	2000	Singh	Woods	Woods	Woods
1996	Faldo	S. Jones	Lehman	Brooks	2001	Woods	Goosen	Duval	Toms
1997	Woods	Els	Leonard	Love	2002	Woods	Woods	Els	Beem
1998	O'Meara	Janzen	O'Meara	Singh					

U.S. Amateur

Match play from 1895-64, stroke play from 1965-72, match play 1973-79, 36-hole stroke-play qualifying before match play since 1979.

Multiple winners: Bobby Jones (5); Jerry Travers (4); Walter Travis and Tiger Woods (3); Deane Beman, Charles Coe, Gary Cowan, H. Chandler Egan, Chick Evans, Lawson Little, Jack Nicklaus, Francis Ouimet, Jay Sigel, William Turnesa, Bud Ward, Harvie Ward, and H.J. Whigham (2).

Year		Year		Year		Year	
1895	Charles Macdonald	1922	Jess Sweetser	1951	Billy Maxwell	1977	John Fought
1896	H.J. Whigham	1923	Max Marston	1952	Jack Westland	1978	John Cook
1897	H.J. Whigham	1924	Bobby Jones	1953	Gene Littler	1979	Mark O'Meara
1898	Findlay Douglas	1925	Bobby Jones	1954	Arnold Palmer		
1899	H.M. Harriman	1926	George Von Elm	1955	Harvie Ward	1980	Hal Sutton
		1927	Bobby Jones	1956	Harvie Ward	1981	Nathaniel Crosby
1900	Walter Travis	1928	Bobby Jones	1957	Hillman Robbins	1982	Jay Sigel
1901	Walter Travis	1929	Harrison Johnston	1958	Charles Coe	1983	Jay Sigel
1902	Louis James			1959	Jack Nicklaus	1984	Scott Verplank
1903	Walter Travis	1930	Bobby Jones			1985	Sam Randolph
1904	H. Chandler Egan	1931	Francis Ouimet	1960	Deane Beman	1986	Buddy Alexander
1905	H. Chandler Egan	1932	Ross Somerville	1961	Jack Nicklaus	1987	Billy Mayfair
1906	Eben Byers	1933	George Dunlap	1962	Labron Harris	1988	Eric Meeks
1907	Jerry Travers	1934	Lawson Little	1963	Deane Beman	1989	Chris Patton
1908	Jerry Travers	1935	Lawson Little	1964	Bill Campbell		
1909	Robert Gardner	1936	John Fischer	1965	Bob Murphy	1990	Phil Mickelson
		1937	John Goodman	1966	Gary Cowan	1991	Mitch Voges
1910	W.C. Fownes Jr.	1938	William Turnesa	1967	Bob Dickson	1992	Justin Leonard
1911	Harold Hilton	1939	Bud Ward	1968	Bruce Fleisher	1993	John Harris
1912	Jerry Travers			1969	Steve Melnyk	1994	Tiger Woods
1913	Jerry Travers	1940	Richard Chapman			1995	Tiger Woods
1914	Francis Ouimet	1941	Bud Ward	1970	Lanny Wadkins	1996	Tiger Woods
1915	Robert Gardner	1942-45	Not held	1971	Gary Cowan	1997	Matt Kuchar
1916	Chick Evans	1946	Ted Bishop	1972	Vinny Giles	1998	Hank Kuehne
1917-18	Not held	1947	Skee Riegel	1973	Craig Stadler	1999	David Gossett
1919	Davidson Herron	1948	William Turnesa	1974	Jerry Pate		
		1949	Charles Coe	1975	Fred Ridley	2000	Jeff Quinney
1920	Chick Evans			1976	Bill Sander	2001	Bubba Dickerson
1921	Jesse Guilford	1950	Sam Urzetta			2002	Ricky Barnes

British Amateur

Match play since 1885.

Multiple winners: John Ball (8); Michael Bonallack (5); Harold Hilton (4); Joe Carr (3); Horace Hutchinson, Ernest Holderness, Trevor Homer, Johnny Laidley, Lawson Little, Peter McEvoy, Dick Siderowf, Frank Stranahan, Freddie Tait and Cyril Tolley (2).

Year		Year		Year		Year	
1885	Allen MacFie	1907	John Ball	1933	Michael Scott	1960	Joe Carr
1886	Horace Hutchinson	1908	E.A. Lassen	1934	Lawson Little	1961	Michael Bonallack
1887	Horace Hutchinson	1909	Robert Maxwell	1935	Lawson Little	1962	Richard Davies
1888	John Ball			1936	Hector Thomson	1963	Michael Lunt
1889	Johnny Laidley	1910	John Ball	1937	Robert Sweeny Jr.	1964	Gordon Clark
		1911	Harold Hilton	1938	Charles Yates	1965	Michael Bonallack
1890	John Ball	1912	John Ball	1939	Alexander Kyle	1966	Bobby Cole
1891	Johnny Laidley	1913	Harold Hilton			1967	Bob Dickson
1892	John Ball	1914	J.L.C. Jenkins	1940-45	Not held	1968	Michael Bonallack
1893	Peter Anderson	1915-19	Not held	1946	James Bruen	1969	Michael Bonallack
1894	John Ball			1947	William Turnesa		
1895	Leslie Balfour-Melville	1920	Cyril Tolley	1948	Frank Stranahan	1970	Michael Bonallack
1896	Freddie Tait	1921	William Hunter	1949	Samuel McCready	1971	Steve Melnyk
1897	Jack Allan	1922	Ernest Holderness			1972	Trevor Homer
1898	Freddie Tait	1923	Roger Wethered	1950	Frank Stranahan	1973	Dick Siderowf
1899	John Ball	1924	Ernest Holderness	1951	Richard Chapman	1974	Trevor Homer
		1925	Robert Harris	1952	Harvie Ward	1975	Vinny Giles
1900	Harold Hilton	1926	Jess Sweetser	1953	Joe Carr	1976	Dick Siderowf
1901	Harold Hilton	1927	William Tweddell	1954	Douglas Bachli	1977	Peter McEvoy
1902	Charles Hutchings	1928	Thomas Perkins	1955	Joe Conrad	1978	Peter McEvoy
1903	Robert Maxwell	1929	Cyril Tolley	1956	John Beharrell	1979	Jay Sigel
1904	Walter Travis			1957	Reid Jack		
1905	Arthur Barry	1930	Bobby Jones	1958	Joe Carr	1980	Duncan Evans
1906	James Robb	1931	Eric Smith	1959	Deane Beman	1981	Phillipe Ploujoux
		1932	John deForest				

Year		Year		Year		Year	
1982	Martin Thompson	1988	Christian Hardin	1994	Lee James	2000	Mikko Ilonen
1983	Philip Parkin	1989	Stephen Dodd	1995	Gordon Sherry	2001	Michael Hoey
1984	Jose-Maria Olazabal	1990	Rolf Muntz	1996	Warren Bledon	2002	Alejandro Larrazabal
1985	Garth McGimpsey	1991	Gary Wolstenholme	1997	Craig Watson		
1986	David Curry	1992	Stephen Dundas	1998	Sergio Garcia		
1987	Paul Mayo	1993	Ian Pyman	1999	Graeme Storm		

WOMEN
Nabisco Championship

Formerly known as the Colgate Dinah Shore (1972-81) and the Nabisco Dinah Shore (1982-99), the tournament became the LPGA's fourth designated major championship in 1983. Shore's name, which was dropped from the tournament in 2000, is preserved with the Nabisco Dinah Shore Trophy, which is awarded to the winner. The tourney has been played at Mission Hills CC in Rancho Mirage, Calif., since it began; (*) indicates playoff winner.

Multiple winners: (as a major): Amy Alcott and Betsy King (3); Juli Inkster, Dottie Pepper and Annika Sorenstam (2).

Year	Winner	Score	Runner-up	Year	Winner	Score	Runner-up
1972	Jane Blalock	.213	Carol Mann & Judy Rankin (216)	1990	Betsy King	.283	Kathy Postlewait & Shirley Furlong (285)
1973	Mickey Wright	.284	Joyce Kazmierski (286)	1991	Amy Alcott	.273	Dottie Pepper (281)
1974	Jo Anne Prentice*	.289	Jane Blalock & Sandra Haynie (289)	1992	Dottie Pepper*	.279	Juli Inkster (279)
				1993	Helen Alfredsson	.284	Amy Benz & Tina Barrett (286)
1975	Sandra Palmer	.283	Kathy McMullen (284)				
1976	Judy Rankin	.285	Betty Burfeindt (288)				
1977	Kathy Whitworth	.289	JoAnne Carner & Sally Little (290)	1994	Donna Andrews	.276	Laura Davies (277)
1978	Sandra Post*	.283	Penny Pulz (283)	1995	Nanci Bowen	.285	Susie Redman (286)
1979	Sandra Post	.276	Nancy Lopez (277)	1996	Patty Sheehan	.281	Kelly Robbins, Meg Mallon & Annika Sorenstam (276)
1980	Donna Caponi	.275	Amy Alcott (277)				
1981	Nancy Lopez	.277	Carolyn Hill (279)				
1982	Sally Little	.278	Hollis Stacy & Sandra Haynie (281)	1997	Betsy King	.276	Kris Tschetter (278)
1983	Amy Alcott	.282	Beth Daniel & Kathy Whitworth (284)	1998	Pat Hurst	.281	Helen Dobson (282)
				1999	Dottie Pepper	.269	Meg Mallon (275)
1984	Juli Inkster*	.280	Pat Bradley (280)	2000	Karrie Webb	.274	Dottie Pepper (284)
1985	Alice Miller	.275	Jan Stephenson (278)	2001	Annika Sorenstam	.281	Akiko Fukushima, Janice Moodie, Dottie Pepper, Rachel Teske & Karrie Webb (284)
1986	Pat Bradley	.280	Val Skinner (282)				
1987	Betsy King*	.283	Patty Sheehan (283)				
1988	Amy Alcott	.274	Colleen Walker (276)	2002	Annika Sorenstam	.280	Liselotte Neumann (281)
1989	Juli Inkster	.279	Tammie Green & JoAnne Carner (284)				

*PLAYOFFS:

1974: Jo Ann Prentice def. Jane Blalock in sudden death. **1978:** Sandra Post def. Penny Pulz in sudden death. **1984:** Juli Inkster def. Pat Bradley in sudden death. **1987:** Betsy King def. Patty Sheehan in sudden death. **1992:** Dottie Pepper def. Juli Inkster in sudden death.

U.S. Women's Open

The U.S. Women's Open began under the direction of the defunct Women's Professional Golfers Assn. in 1946, passed to the LPGA in 1949 and to the USGA in 1953. The tournament used a match play format its first year then switched to stroke play; (*) indicates playoff winner and (a) indicates amateur.

Multiple winners: Betsy Rawls and Mickey Wright (4); Susie Maxwell Berning, Hollis Stacy and Babe Zaharias (3); JoAnne Carner, Donna Caponi, Juli Inkster, Betsy King, Patty Sheehan, Annika Sorenstam, Louise Suggs and Karrie Webb (2).

Year	Winner	Score	Runner-up	Course	Location
1946	Patty Berg	.5&4	Betty Jameson	Spokane CC	Spokane, Wash.
1947	Betty Jameson	.295	a-Sally Sessions & a-Polly Riley (301)	Starmount Forest CC	Greensboro, N.C.
1948	Babe Zaharias	.300	Betty Hicks (308)	Atlantic City CC	Northfield, N.J.
1949	Louise Suggs	.291	Babe Zaharias (305)	Prince Georges CC	Landover, Md.
1950	Babe Zaharias	.291	a-Betsy Rawls (300)	Rolling Hills CC	Wichita, Kan.
1951	Betsy Rawls	.293	Louise Suggs (298)	Druid Hills GC	Atlanta, Ga.
1952	Louise Suggs	.284	Marlene Hagge (291)	Bala GC	Philadelphia, Penn.
1953	Betsy Rawls*	.302	Jackie Pung (302)	CC of Rochester	Rochester, N.Y.
1954	Babe Zaharias	.291	Betty Hicks (303)	Salem CC	Peabody, Mass.
1955	Fay Crocker	.299	Mary Lena Faulk (303)	Wichita CC	Wichita, Kan.
1956	Kathy Cornelius*	.302	Barbara McIntire (302)	Northland CC	Duluth, Minn.
1957	Betsy Rawls	.299	Patty Berg (305)	Winged Foot GC	Mamaroneck, N.Y.
1958	Mickey Wright	.290	Louise Suggs (295)	Forest Lake CC	Detroit, Mich.
1959	Mickey Wright	.287	Louise Suggs (289)	Churchill Valley CC	Pittsburgh, Penn.
1960	Betsy Rawls	.292	Joyce Ziske (293)	Worcester CC	Worcester, Mass.
1961	Mickey Wright	.293	Betsy Rawls (299)	Baltusrol GC	Springfield, N.J.

U.S. Women's Open (Cont.)

Year	Winner	Score	Runner-up	Course	Location
1962	Murle Breer	301	Jo Anne Prentice & Ruth Jessen (303)	Dunes GC	Myrtle Beach, S.C.
1963	Mary Mills	289	Sandra Haynie & Louise Suggs (292)	Kenwood CC	Cincinnati, Ohio
1964	Mickey Wright*	290	Ruth Jessen (290)	San Diego CC	Chula Vista, Calif.
1965	Carol Mann	290	Kathy Cornelius (292)	Atlantic City CC	Northfield, N.J.
1966	Sandra Spuzich	297	Carol Mann (298)	Hazeltine National GC	Chaska, Minn.
1967	a-Catherine LaCoste	294	Susie Berning & Beth Stone (296)	Hot Springs GC	Hot Springs, Va.
1968	Susie Berning	289	Mickey Wright (292)	Moselem Springs GC	Fleetwood, Penn.
1969	Donna Caponi	294	Peggy Wilson (295)	Scenic Hills CC	Pensacola, Fla.
1970	Donna Caponi	287	Sandra Haynie (288)	Muskogee CC	Muskogee, Okla.
1971	JoAnne Carner	288	Kathy Whitworth (295)	Kahkwa CC	Erie, Penn.
1972	Susie Berning	299	Kathy Ahern, Pam Barnett & Judy Rankin (300)	Winged Foot GC	Mamaroneck, N.Y.
1973	Susie Berning	290	Gloria Ehret (295)	CC of Rochester	Rochester, N.Y.
1974	Sandra Haynie	295	Carol Mann & Beth Stone (296)	La Grange CC	La Grange, Ill.
1975	Sandra Palmer	295	JoAnne Carner, a-Nancy Lopez & Sandra Post (299)	Atlantic City CC	Northfield, N.J.
1976	JoAnne Carner*	292	Sandra Palmer (292)	Rolling Green CC	Springfield, Penn.
1977	Hollis Stacy	292	Nancy Lopez (294)	Hazeltine National GC	Chaska, Minn.
1978	Hollis Stacy	289	JoAnne Carner & Sally Little (290)	CC of Indianapolis	Indianapolis, Ind.
1979	Jerilyn Britz	284	Debbie Massey & Sandra Palmer (286)	Brooklawn CC	Fairfield, Conn.
1980	Amy Alcott	280	Hollis Stacy (289)	Richland CC	Nashville, Tenn.
1981	Pat Bradley	279	Beth Daniel (280)	La Grange CC	La Grange, Ill.
1982	Janet Anderson	283	Beth Daniel, Sandra Haynie & Donna White (289)	Del Paso CC	Sacramento, Calif.
1983	Jan Stephenson	290	JoAnne Carner (291)	Cedar Ridge CC	Tulsa, Okla.
1984	Hollis Stacy	290	Rosie Jones (291)	Salem CC	Peabody, Mass.
1985	Kathy Baker	280	Judy Dickenson (283)	Baltusrol GC	Springfield, N.J.
1986	Jane Geddes*	287	Sally Little (287)	NCR CC	Dayton, Ohio
1987	Laura Davies*	285	Ayako Okamoto & JoAnne Carner (285)	Plainfield CC	Plainfield, N.J.
1988	Liselotte Neumann	277	Patty Sheehan (280)	Baltimore CC	Baltimore, Md.
1989	Betsy King	278	Nancy Lopez (282)	Indianwood GC	Lake Orion, Mich.
1990	Betsy King	284	Patty Sheehan (285)	Atlanta Athletic Club	Duluth, Ga.
1991	Meg Mallon	283	Pat Bradley (285)	Colonial CC	Ft. Worth, Texas
1992	Patty Sheehan*	280	Juli Inkster (280)	Oakmont CC	Oakmont, Penn.
1993	Lauri Merten	280	Donna Andrews & Helen Alfredsson (281)	Crooked Stick GC	Carmel, Ind.
1994	Patty Sheehan	277	Tammie Green (278)	Indianwood CC	Lake Orion, Mich.
1995	Annika Sorenstam	278	Meg Mallon (279)	The Broadmoor	Colorado Springs, Colo.
1996	Annika Sorenstam	272	Kris Tschetter (278)	Pine Needles Lodge & GC	Southern Pines, N.C.
1997	Alison Nicholas	274	Nancy Lopez (275)	Pumpkin Ridge GC	Cornelius, Ore.
1998	Se Ri Pak*	290	a-Jenny Chuasiriporn (290)	Blackwolf Run GC	Kohler, Wis.
1999	Juli Inkster	272	Sherri Turner (277)	Old Waverly GC	West Point, Miss.
2000	Karrie Webb	282	Cristie Kerr & Meg Mallon (287)	Merit Club	Libertyville, Ill.
2001	Karrie Webb	273	Se Ri Pak (281)	Pine Needles Lodge & GC	Southern Pines, N.C.
2002	Juli Inkster	276	Annika Sorenstam (278)	Prairie Dunes CC	Hutchinson, Kan.

*PLAYOFFS:

1953: Betsy Rawls (70) def. Jackie Pung (77) in 18 holes. **1956:** Kathy Cornelius (75) def. Barbara McIntire (82) in 18 holes. **1964:** Mickey Wright (70) def. Ruth Jessen (72) in 18 holes. **1976:** JoAnne Carner (76) def. Sandra Palmer (78) in 18 holes. **1986:** Jane Geddes (71) def. Sally Little (73) in 18 holes. **1987:** Laura Davies (71) def. Ayako Okamoto (73) and JoAnne Carner (74) in 18 holes. **1992:** Patty Sheehan (72) def. Juli Inkster (74) in 18 holes. **1998:** Se Ri Pak def. Jenny Chuasiriporn on the second sudden death hole after both players were tied after an 18-hole playoff.

LPGA Championship

Officially the McDonald's LPGA Championship since 1994 (Mazda was the title sponsor from 1987-93), the tournament began in 1955 and has had extended stays at the Stardust CC in Las Vegas (1961-66), Pleasant Valley CC in Sutton, Mass. (1967-68, 70-74), the Jack Nicklaus Sports Center at Kings Island, Ohio (1978-89), Bethesda CC in Maryland (1990-93) and DuPont CC in Wilmington, Del. (since 1994); (*) indicates playoff winner and (#) weather-shortened.

    Multiple winners: Mickey Wright (4); Nancy Lopez, Patty Sheehan and Kathy Whitworth (3); Donna Caponi, Laura Davies, Sandra Haynie, Juli Inkster, Mary Mills, Se Ri Pak and Betsy Rawls (2).

Year	Winner	Score	Runner-up
1955	Beverly Hanson	220	Louise Suggs (223)
1956	Marlene Hagge*	291	Patty Berg (291)
1957	Louise Suggs	285	Wiffi Smith (288)
1958	Mickey Wright	288	Fay Crocker (294)
1959	Betsy Rawls	288	Patty Berg (289)
1960	Mickey Wright	292	Louise Suggs (295)
1961	Mickey Wright	287	Louise Suggs (296)
1962	Judy Kimball	282	Shirley Spork (286)
1963	Mickey Wright	294	Mary Lena Faulk & Mary Mills (296)
1964	Mary Mills	278	Mickey Wright (280)
1965	Sandra Haynie	279	Clifford A. Creed (280)
1966	Gloria Ehret	282	Mickey Wright (285)
1967	Kathy Whitworth	284	Shirley Englehorn (285)
1968	Sandra Post	294	Kathy Whitworth (294)
1969	Betsy Rawls	293	Susie Berning & Carol Mann (297)
1970	Shirley Englehorn	285	Kathy Whitworth (285)
1971	Kathy Whitworth	288	Kathy Ahern (292)
1972	Kathy Ahern	293	Jane Blalock (299)
1973	Mary Mills	288	Betty Burfeindt (289)
1974	Sandra Haynie	288	JoAnne Carner (290)
1975	Kathy Whitworth	288	Sandra Haynie (289)
1976	Betty Burfeindt	287	Judy Rankin (288)
1977	Chako Higuchi	279	Pat Bradley, Sandra Post & Judy Rankin (282)
1978	Nancy Lopez	275	Amy Alcott (281)
1979	Donna Caponi	279	Jerilyn Britz (282)
1980	Sally Little	285	Jane Blalock (288)

Year	Winner	Score	Runner-up
1981	Donna Caponi	280	Jerilyn Britz & Pat Meyers (281)
1982	Jan Stephenson	279	JoAnne Carner (281)
1983	Patty Sheehan	279	Sandra Haynie (281)
1984	Patty Sheehan	272	Beth Daniel & Pat Bradley (282)
1985	Nancy Lopez	273	Alice Miller (281)
1986	Pat Bradley	277	Patty Sheehan (278)
1987	Jane Geddes	275	Betsy King (275)
1988	Sherri Turner	281	Amy Alcott (282)
1989	Nancy Lopez	274	Ayako Okamoto (277)
1990	Beth Daniel	280	Rosie Jones (281)
1991	Meg Mallon	274	Pat Bradley & Ayako Okamoto (275)
1992	Betsy King	267	JoAnne Carner, Karen Noble & Liselotte Neumann (278)
1993	Patty Sheehan	275	Lauri Merten (276)
1994	Laura Davies	279	Alice Ritzman (280)
1995	Kelly Robbins	274	Laura Davies (275)
1996	Laura Davies#	213	Julie Piers (214)
1997	Chris Johnson*	281	Leta Lindley (281)
1998	Se Ri Pak	273	Donna Andrews & Lisa Hackney (276)
1999	Juli Inkster	268	Liselotte Neumann (272)
2000	Juli Inkster*	281	Stefania Croce (281)
2001	Karrie Webb	270	Laura Diaz (272)
2002	Se Ri Pak	279	Beth Daniel (282)

*PLAYOFFS:

1956: Marlene Hagge def. Patti Berg in sudden death. **1968:** Sandra Post (68) def. Kathy Whitworth (75) in 18 holes. **1970:** Shirley Englehorn def. Kathy Whitworth in sudden death. **1997:** Chris Johnson def. Leta Lindley in sudden death. **2000:** Juli Inkster def. Stefania Croce in sudden death.

Women's British Open

Sponsored by Weetabix, this has been an official stop on the LPGA Tour since 1994, and it became the fourth designated major championship in 2001 when it replaced the du Maurier Classic.

Multiple winners Karrie Webb (3); and Sherri Steinhauer (2); (as a major): none.

Year	Winner	Score	Runner-up	Course	Location
1994	Liselotte Neumann	280	Dottie Mochrie & Annika Sorenstam (283)	Woburn G&CC	Milton Keynes, England
1995	Karrie Webb	278	Annika Sorenstam & Jill McGill (284)	Woburn G&CC	Milton Keynes, England
1996	Emilee Klein	277	Penny Hammel & Amy Alcott (284)	Woburn G&CC	Milton Keynes, England
1997	Karrie Webb	269	Rosie Jones (277)	Sunningdale GC	Berkshire, England
1998	Sherri Steinhauer	292	Sophie Gustafson & Brandie Burton (293)	Royal Lytham	Lytham, England
1999	Sherri Steinhauer	283	Annika Sorenstam (284)	Woburn G&CC	Milton Keynes, England
2000	Sophie Gustafson	282	Kirsty Taylor, Liselotte Neumann, Becky Iverson & Meg Mallon (284)	Royal Birkdale	Southport, England
2001	Se Ri Pak	277	Mi Hyun Kim (279)	Sunningdale GC	Berkshire, England
2002	Karrie Webb	273	Michelle Ellis & Paula Marti (275)	Turnberry GC	Turnberry, Scotland

du Maurier Classic (1979–2000)

The du Maurier Classic was considered a major title on the women's tour from 1979-2000; (*) indicates playoff winner.

Multiple winners (as a major): Pat Bradley (3); Brandie Burton (2).

Year		Year		Year		Year	
1973	Jocelyne Bourassa	1980	Pat Bradley	1987	Jody Rosenthal	1994	Martha Nause
1974	Carole Jo Skala	1981	Jan Stephenson	1988	Sally Little	1995	Jenny Lidback
1975	JoAnne Carner	1982	Sandra Haynie	1989	Tammie Green	1996	Laura Davies
1976	Donna Caponi	1983	Hollis Stacy	1990	Cathy Johnston	1997	Colleen Walker
1977	Judy Rankin	1984	Juli Inkster	1991	Nancy Scranton	1998	Brandie Burton
1978	JoAnne Carner	1985	Pat Bradley	1992	Sherri Steinhauer	1999	Karrie Webb
1979	Amy Alcott	1986	Pat Bradley*	1993	Brandie Burton*	2000	Meg Mallon

Titleholders Championship (1937–72)

The Titleholders was considered a major title on the women's tour until it was discontinued after the 1972 tournament.
Multiple winners: Patty Berg (7); Louise Suggs (4); Babe Zaharias (3); Dorothy Kirby, Marilynn Smith, Kathy Whitworth and Mickey Wright (2).

Year		Year		Year		Year	
1937	Patty Berg	1947	Babe Zaharias	1955	Patty Berg	1963	Marilynn Smith
1938	Patty Berg	1948	Patty Berg	1956	Louise Suggs	1964	Marilynn Smith
1939	Patty Berg	1949	Peggy Kirk	1957	Patty Berg	1965	Kathy Whitworth
1940	Betty Hicks	1950	Babe Zaharias	1958	Beverly Hanson	1966	Kathy Whitworth
1941	Dorothy Kirby	1951	Pat O'Sullivan	1959	Louise Suggs	1967-71	Not held
1942	Dorothy Kirby	1952	Babe Zaharias	1960	Fay Crocker	1972	Sandra Palmer
1943-45	Not held	1953	Patty Berg	1961	Mickey Wright		
1946	Louise Suggs	1954	Louise Suggs	1962	Mickey Wright		

Western Open (1930–67)

The Western Open was considered a major title on the women's tour until it was discontinued after the 1967 tournament.
Multiple winners: Patty Berg (7); Louise Suggs and Babe Zaharias (4); Mickey Wright (3); June Beebe, Opal Hill, Betty Jameson and Betsy Rawls (2).

Year		Year		Year		Year	
1930	Mrs. Lee Mida	1940	Babe Zaharias	1950	Babe Zaharias	1960	Joyce Ziske
1931	June Beebe	1941	Patty Berg	1951	Patty Berg	1961	Mary Lena Faulk
1932	Jane Weiller	1942	Betty Jameson	1952	Betsy Rawls	1962	Mickey Wright
1933	June Beebe	1943	Patty Berg	1953	Louise Suggs	1963	Mickey Wright
1934	Marian McDougall	1944	Babe Zaharias	1954	Betty Jameson	1964	Carol Mann
1935	Opal Hill	1945	Babe Zaharias	1955	Patty Berg	1965	Susie Maxwell
1936	Opal Hill	1946	Louise Suggs	1956	Beverly Hanson	1966	Mickey Wright
1937	Betty Hicks	1947	Louise Suggs	1957	Patty Berg	1967	Kathy Whitworth
1938	Bea Barrett	1948	Patty Berg	1958	Patty Berg		
1939	Helen Dettweiler	1949	Louise Suggs	1959	Betsy Rawls		

Grand Slam Summary

From 1955-66, the U.S. Open, LPGA Championship, Western Open and Titleholders tournaments served as the Women's Grand Slam. From 1983-2000, however, the U.S. Open, LPGA, du Maurier Classic and Nabisco Championship were the major events. In 2001, the Weetabix Women's British Open replaced the du Maurier Classic as the tour's fourth major. No one has won a four-event Grand Slam on the women's tour.
Three wins in one year (3): Babe Zaharias (1950), Mickey Wright (1961) and Pat Bradley (1986).
Two wins in one year (19): Patty Berg and Mickey Wright (3 times); Juli Inkster, Louise Suggs and Karrie Webb (twice); Laura Davies, Sandra Haynie, Betsy King, Meg Mallon, Se Ri Pak, Betsy Rawls and Kathy Whitworth (once).

Year	LPGA	US Open	T'holders	Western	Year	LPGA	US Open	T'holders	Western
1937	—	—	Berg	Hicks	1948	—	Zaharias	Berg	Berg
1938	—	—	Berg	Barrett	1949	—	Suggs	Kirk	Suggs
1939	—	—	Berg	Dettweiler	1950	—	Zaharias	Zaharias	Zaharias
1940	—	—	Hicks	Zaharias	1951	—	Rawls	O'Sullivan	Berg
1941	—	—	Kirby	Berg	1952	—	Suggs	Zaharias	Rawls
1942	—	—	Kirby	Jameson	1953	—	Rawls	Berg	Suggs
1943	—	—	—	Berg	1954	—	Zaharias	Suggs	Jameson
1944	—	—	—	Zaharias	1955	Hanson	Crocker	Berg	Berg
1945	—	—	—	Zaharias	1956	Hagge	Cornelius	Suggs	Hanson
1946	—	Berg	Suggs	Suggs	1957	Suggs	Rawls	Berg	Berg
1947	—	Jameson	Zaharias	Suggs	1958	Wright	Wright	Hanson	Berg

Major Championship Leaders

Through 2002; active LPGA players in **bold** type.

	US Open	LPGA	Nabisco	British Open	duM	Title	Western	US Am	Brit Am	Total
Patty Berg	1	0	0	0	0	7	7	1	0	**16**
Mickey Wright	4	4	0	0	0	2	3	0	0	**13**
Louise Suggs	2	1	0	0	0	4	4	1	1	**13**
Babe Didrikson Zaharias	3	0	0	0	0	3	4	1	1	**12**
Juli Inkster	2	2	2	0	1	0	0	3	0	**10**
Betsy Rawls	4	2	0	0	0	0	2	0	0	**8**
JoAnne Carner	2	0	0	0	0	0	0	5	0	**7**
Kathy Whitworth	0	3	0	0	0	2	1	0	0	**6**
Pat Bradley	1	1	1	0	3	0	0	0	0	**6**
Betsy King	2	1	3	0	0	0	0	0	0	**6**
Patty Sheehan	2	3	1	0	0	0	0	0	0	**6**
Glenna C. Vare	0	0	0	0	0	0	0	6	0	**6**
Karrie Webb	2	1	1	1	1	0	0	0	0	**6**

Tournaments: U.S. Open, LPGA Championship, Nabisco Championship, British Open, du Maurier Classic (1979-2000), Titleholders (1930-72), Western Open (1937-67), U.S. Amateur and British Amateur.

Year	LPGA	US Open	T'holders	Western
1959	Rawls	Wright	Suggs	Rawls
1960	Wright	Rawls	Crocker	Ziske
1961	Wright	Wright	Wright	Faulk
1962	Kimball	Lindstrom	Wright	Wright
1963	Wright	Mills	M. Smith	Wright
1964	Mills	Wright	M. Smith	Mann
1965	Haynie	Mann	Whitworth	Maxwell
1966	Ehret	Spuzich	Whitworth	Wright
1967	Whitworth	a-LaCoste	—	Whitworth
1968	Post	Berning	—	—
1969	Rawls	Caponi	—	—
1970	Englehorn	Caponi	—	—
1971	Whitworth	Carner	—	—
1972	Ahern	Berning	Palmer	—
1973	Mills	Berning	—	—
1974	Haynie	Haynie	—	—
1975	Whitworth	Palmer	—	—
1976	Burfeindt	Carner	—	—
1977	Higuchi	Stacy	—	—
1978	Lopez	Stacy	—	—

Year	LPGA	US Open	duMaurier	Nabisco
1979	Caponi	Britz	Alcott	—
1980	Little	Alcott	Bradley	—
1981	Caponi	Bradley	Stephenson	—

Year	LPGA	US Open	duMaurier	Nabisco
1982	Stephenson	Anderson	Haynie	—
1983	Sheehan	Stephenson	Stacy	Alcott
1984	Sheehan	Stacy	Inkster	Inkster
1985	Lopez	Baker	Bradley	Miller
1986	Bradley	Geddes	Bradley	Bradley
1987	Geddes	Davies	Rosenthal	King
1988	Turner	Neumann	Little	Alcott
1989	Lopez	King	Green	Inkster
1990	Daniel	King	Johnston	King
1991	Mallon	Mallon	Scranton	Alcott
1992	King	Sheehan	Steinhauer	Pepper
1993	Davies	Merten	Burton	Alfredsson
1994	Davies	Sheehan	Nause	Andrews
1995	Robbins	Sorenstam	Lidback	Bowen
1996	Davies	Sorenstam	Davies	Sheehan
1997	Johnson	Nicholas	Walker	King
1998	Pak	Pak	Burton	Hurst
1999	Inkster	Inkster	Webb	Pepper
2000	Inkster	Webb	Mallon	Webb

Year	LPGA	US Open	Brit. Open	Nabisco
2001	Webb	Webb	Pak	Sorenstam
2002	Pak	Inkster	Webb	Sorenstam

U.S. Women's Amateur

Stroke play in 1895, match play since 1896.

Multiple winners: Glenna Collett Vare (6); JoAnne Gunderson Carner (5); Margaret Curtis, Beatrix Hoyt, Dorothy Campbell Hurd, Juli Inkster, Alexa Stirling, Virginia Van Wie, Anne Quast Decker Welts (3); Kay Cockerill, Beth Daniel, Vicki Goetze, Katherine Harley, Genevieve Hecker, Betty Jameson, Kelli Kuehne and Barbara McIntire (2).

Year		Year		Year		Year	
1895	Mrs. C.S. Brown	1904	Georgianna Bishop	1913	Gladys Ravenscroft	1923	Edith Cummings
1896	Beatrix Hoyt	1905	Pauline Mackay	1914	Katherine Harley	1924	Dorothy C. Hurd
1897	Beatrix Hoyt	1906	Harriot Curtis	1915	Florence Vanderbeck	1925	Glenna Collett
1898	Beatrix Hoyt	1907	Margaret Curtis	1916	Alexa Stirling	1926	Helen Stetson
1899	Ruth Underhill	1908	Katherine Harley	1917-18	Not held	1927	Miriam Burns Horn
		1909	Dorothy Campbell	1919	Alexa Stirling	1928	Glenna Collett
1900	Frances Griscom					1929	Glenna Collett
1901	Genevieve Hecker	1910	Dorothy Campbell	1920	Alexa Stirling		
1902	Genevieve Hecker	1911	Margaret Curtis	1921	Marion Hollins	1930	Glenna Collett
1903	Bessie Anthony	1912	Margaret Curtis	1922	Glenna Collett	1931	Helen Hicks

Vare Trophy

The Vare Trophy for best scoring average by a player on the LPGA Tour has been awarded since 1937 by the LPGA. The award is named after Glenna Collett Vare, winner of six U.S. women's amateur titles from 1922-35.

Multiple winners: Kathy Whitworth (7); JoAnne Carner and Mickey Wright (5); Annika Sorenstam (4); Patty Berg, Beth Daniel, Nancy Lopez, Judy Rankin and Karrie Webb (3); Pat Bradley and Betsy King (2).

Year		Avg	Year		Avg	Year		Avg
1953	Patty Berg	75.00	1970	Kathy Whitworth	72.26	1987	Betsy King	71.14
1954	Babe Zaharias	75.48	1971	Kathy Whitworth	72.88	1988	Colleen Walker	71.26
1955	Patty Berg	74.47	1972	Kathy Whitworth	72.38	1989	Beth Daniel	70.38
1956	Patty Berg	74.57	1973	Judy Rankin	73.08	1990	Beth Daniel	70.54
1957	Louise Suggs	74.64	1974	JoAnne Carner	72.87	1991	Pat Bradley	70.66
1958	Beverly Hanson	74.92	1975	JoAnne Carner	72.40	1992	Dottie Pepper	70.80
1959	Betsy Rawls	74.03	1976	Judy Rankin	72.25	1993	Betsy King	70.85
1960	Mickey Wright	73.25	1977	Judy Rankin	72.16	1994	Beth Daniel	70.90
1961	Mickey Wright	73.55	1978	Nancy Lopez	71.76	1995	Annika Sorenstam	71.00
1962	Mickey Wright	73.67	1979	Nancy Lopez	71.20	1996	Annika Sorenstam	70.47
1963	Mickey Wright	72.81	1980	Amy Alcott	71.51	1997	Karrie Webb	70.00
1964	Mickey Wright	72.46	1981	JoAnne Carner	71.75	1998	Annika Sorenstam	69.99
1965	Kathy Whitworth	72.61	1982	JoAnne Carner	71.49	1999	Karrie Webb	69.43
1966	Kathy Whitworth	72.60	1983	JoAnne Carner	71.41	2000	Karrie Webb	70.05
1967	Kathy Whitworth	72.74	1984	Patty Sheehan	71.40	2001	Annika Sorenstam	69.42
1968	Carol Mann	72.04	1985	Nancy Lopez	70.73			
1969	Kathy Whitworth	72.38	1986	Pat Bradley	71.10			

U.S. Women's Amateur (Cont.)

Year		Year		Year		Year	
1932	Virginia Van Wie	1952	Jacqueline Pung	1969	Catherine Lacoste	1986	Kay Cockerill
1933	Virginia Van Wie	1953	Mary Lena Faulk	1970	Martha Wilkinson	1987	Kay Cockerill
1934	Virginia Van Wie	1954	Barbara Romack	1971	Laura Baugh	1988	Pearl Sinn
1935	Glenna Collett Vare	1955	Patricia Lesser	1972	Mary Budke	1989	Vicki Goetze
1936	Pamela Barton	1956	Marlene Stewart	1973	Carol Semple		
1937	Estelle Lawson	1957	JoAnne Gunderson	1974	Cynthia Hill	1990	Pat Hurst
1938	Patty Berg	1958	Anne Quast	1975	Beth Daniel	1991	Amy Fruhwirth
1939	Betty Jameson	1959	Barbara McIntire	1976	Donna Horton	1992	Vicki Goetze
				1977	Beth Daniel	1993	Jill McGill
1940	Betty Jameson	1960	JoAnne Gunderson	1978	Cathy Sherk	1994	Wendy Ward
1941	Elizabeth Hicks	1961	Anne Quast Decker	1979	Carolyn Hill	1995	Kelli Kuehne
1942-45	Not held	1962	JoAnne Gunderson			1996	Kelli Kuehne
1946	Babe D. Zaharias	1963	Anne Quast Welts	1980	Juli Inkster	1997	Silvia Cavalleri
1947	Louise Suggs	1964	Barbara McIntire	1981	Juli Inkster	1998	Grace Park
1948	Grace Lenczyk	1965	Jean Ashley	1982	Juli Inkster	1999	Dorothy Delasin
1949	Dorothy Porter	1966	JoAnne G. Carner	1983	Joanne Pacillo		
1950	Beverly Hanson	1967	Mary Lou Dill	1984	Deb Richard	2000	Marcy Newton
1951	Dorothy Kirby	1968	JoAnne G. Carner	1985	Michiko Hattori	2001	Meredith Duncan
						2002	Becky Lucidi

British Women's Amateur

Match play since 1893.

Multiple winners: Cecil Leitch and Joyce Wethered (4); May Hezlet, Lady Margaret Scott, Jessie Anderson Valentine, Brigitte Varangot and Enid Wilson (3); Rhona Adair, Pam Barton, Dorothy Campbell, Elizabeth Chadwick, Helen Holm, Rebecca Hudson, Marley Spearman, Frances Stephens and Michelle Walker (2).

Year		Year		Year		Year	
1893	Lady Margaret Scott	1922	Joyce Wethered	1952	Moira Paterson	1977	Angela Uzielli
1894	Lady Margaret Scott	1923	Doris Chambers	1953	Marlene Stewart	1978	Edwina Kennedy
1895	Lady Margaret Scott	1924	Joyce Wethered	1954	Frances Stephens	1979	Maureen Madill
1896	Amy Pascoe	1925	Joyce Wethered	1955	Jessie Valentine		
1897	Edith Orr	1926	Cecil Leitch	1956	Wiffi Smith	1980	Anne Quast Sander
1898	Lena Thomson	1927	Simone de la Chaume	1957	Philomena Garvey	1981	Belle Robertson
1899	May Hezlet	1928	Nanette le Blan	1958	Jessie Valentine	1982	Kitrina Douglas
		1929	Joyce Wethered	1959	Elizabeth Price	1983	Jill Thornhill
1900	Rhona Adair					1984	Jody Rosenthal
1901	Mary Graham	1930	Diana Fishwick	1960	Barbara McIntire	1985	Lillian Behan
1902	May Hezlet	1931	Enid Wilson	1961	Marley Spearman	1986	Marnie McGuire
1903	Rhona Adair	1932	Enid Wilson	1962	Marley Spearman	1987	Janet Collingham
1904	Lottie Dod	1933	Enid Wilson	1963	Brigitte Varangot	1988	Joanne Furby
1905	Bertha Thompson	1934	Helen Holm	1964	Carol Sorenson	1989	Helen Dobson
1906	Mrs. W. Kennion	1935	Wanda Morgan	1965	Brigitte Varangot		
1907	May Hezlet	1936	Pam Barton	1966	Elizabeth Chadwick	1990	Julie Wade Hall
1908	Maud Titterton	1937	Jessie Anderson	1967	Elizabeth Chadwick	1991	Valerie Michaud
1909	Dorothy Campbell	1938	Helen Holm	1968	Brigitte Varangot	1992	Bernille Pedersen
1910	Elsie Grant-Suttie	1939	Pam Barton	1969	Catherine Lacoste	1993	Catriona Lambert
1911	Dorothy Campbell	1940-45	Not held			1994	Emma Duggleby
1912	Gladys Ravenscroft	1946	Jean Hetherington	1970	Dinah Oxley	1995	Julie Wade Hall
1913	Muriel Dodd	1947	Babe Zaharias	1971	Michelle Walker	1996	Kelli Kuehne
1914	Cecil Leitch	1948	Louise Suggs	1972	Michelle Walker	1997	Alison Rose
1915-19	Not held	1949	Frances Stephens	1973	Ann Irvin	1998	Kim Rostron
				1974	Carol Semple	1999	Marine Monnet
1920	Cecil Leitch	1950	Lally de St. Sauveur	1975	Nancy Roth Syms		
1921	Cecil Leitch	1951	Catherine MacCann	1976	Cathy Panton	2000	Rebecca Hudson
						2001	Marta Prieto
						2002	Rebecca Hudson

Senior PGA
The Tradition

Sponsored by mortgage lender Countrywide Credit Industries, Inc. since 2000, it was originally called The Tradition at Desert Mountain and then simply The Tradition since 1992. Held at Golf Club at Desert Mountain (Cochise) in Scottsdale, Ariz. (1989–2001) and The Prospector Course in Superstition Mountain, Ariz. (since 2002).

Multiple winners: Jack Nicklaus (4); Gil Morgan (2).

Year		Year		Year		Year	
1989	Don Bies	1993	Tom Shaw	1997	Gil Morgan	2001	Doug Tewell
1990	Jack Nicklaus	1994	Ray Floyd*	1998	Gil Morgan	2002	Jim Thorpe*
1991	Jack Nicklaus	1995	Jack Nicklaus*	1999	Graham Marsh		
1992	Lee Trevino	1996	Jack Nicklaus	2000	Tom Kite		

*PLAYOFFS:

1994: Ray Floyd def. Dale Douglas on 1st extra hole. **1995:** Jack Nicklaus def. Isao Aoki on 3rd extra hole; **2002:** Jim Thorpe def. John Jacobs on 1st extra hole.

Senior PGA Championship

First played in 1937. Two championships played in 1979 and 1984.

Multiple winners: Sam Snead (6); Hale Irwin, Gary Player, Al Watrous and Eddie Williams (3); Julius Boros, Jock Hutchison, Don January, Arnold Palmer, Paul Runyan, Gene Sarazen and Lee Trevino (2).

Year		Year		Year		Year	
1937	Jock Hutchison	1955	Mortie Dutra	1972	Sam Snead	1987	Chi Chi Rodriguez
1938	Fred McLeod*	1956	Pete Burke	1973	Sam Snead	1988	Gary Player
1939	Not held	1957	Al Watrous	1974	Roberto De Vicenzo	1989	Larry Mowry
1940	Otto Hackbarth*	1958	Gene Sarazen	1975	Charlie Sifford*	1990	Gary Player
1941	Jack Burke	1959	Willie Goggin	1976	Pete Cooper	1991	Jack Nicklaus
1942	Eddie Williams	1960	Dick Metz	1977	Julius Boros	1992	Lee Trevino
1943-44	Not held	1961	Paul Runyan	1978	Joe Jiminez*	1993	Tom Wargo*
1945	Eddie Williams	1962	Paul Runyan	1979	Jack Fleck*	1994	Lee Trevino
1946	Eddie Williams*	1963	Herman Barron	1979	Don January	1995	Ray Floyd
1947	Jock Hutchison	1964	Sam Snead	1980	Arnold Palmer*	1996	Hale Irwin
1948	Charles McKenna	1965	Sam Snead	1981	Miller Barber	1997	Hale Irwin
1949	Marshall Crichton	1966	Fred Haas	1982	Don January	1998	Hale Irwin
1950	Al Watrous	1967	Sam Snead	1983	Not held	1999	Allen Doyle
1951	Al Watrous*	1968	Chandler Harper	1984	Arnold Palmer	2000	Doug Tewell
1952	Ernest Newnham	1969	Tommy Bolt	1984	Peter Thomson	2001	Tom Watson
1953	Harry Schwab	1970	Sam Snead	1985	Not held	2002	Fuzzy Zoeller
1954	Gene Sarazen	1971	Julius Boros	1986	Gary Player		

*PLAYOFFS

1938: Fred McLeod def. Otto Hackbarth in 18 holes. **1940:** Otto Hackbarth def. Jock Hutchison in 36 holes. **1946:** Eddie Williams def. Jock Hutchison in 18 holes. **1951:** Al Watrous def. Jock Hutchison in 18 holes. **1975:** Charlie Sifford def. Fred Wampler on 1st extra hole **1978:** Joe Jiminez def. Paul Harney on 1st extra hole. **1979:** Jack Fleck def. Bill Johnston on 1st extra hole. **1980:** Arnold Palmer def. Paul Harney on 1st extra hole. **1993:** Tom Wargo def. Bruce Crampton on 2nd extra hole.

U.S. Senior Open

Established in 1980 for senior players 55 years old and over, the minimum age was dropped to 50 (the PGA Seniors Tour entry age) in 1981. Arnold Palmer, Billy Casper, Hale Irwin, Orville Moody, Jack Nicklaus and Lee Trevino are the only golfers who have won both the U.S. Open and U.S. Senior Open.

Multiple winners: Miller Barber (3); Hale Irwin, Jack Nicklaus and Gary Player (2).

Year		Year		Year		Year	
1980	Roberto De Vicenzo	1986	Dale Douglass	1992	Larry Laoretti	1998	Hale Irwin
1981	Arnold Palmer*	1987	Gary Player	1993	Jack Nicklaus	1999	Dave Eichelberger
1982	Miller Barber	1988	Gary Player*	1994	Simon Hobday	2000	Hale Irwin
1983	Bill Casper*	1989	Orville Moody	1995	Tom Weiskopf	2001	Bruce Fleisher
1984	Miller Barber	1990	Lee Trevino	1996	Dave Stockton	2002	Don Pooley*
1985	Miller Barber	1991	Jack Nicklaus*	1997	Graham Marsh		

*PLAYOFFS

1981: Arnold Palmer (70) def. Bob Stone (74) and Billy Casper (77) in 18 holes. **1983:** Tied at 75 after 18-hole playoff, Casper def. Rod Funseth with a birdie on the 1st extra hole. **1988:** Gary Player (68) def. Bob Charles (70) in 18 holes. **1991:** Jack Nicklaus (65) def. Chi Chi Rodriguez (69) in 18 holes. **2002:** Don Pooley and Tom Watson remained tied after a three hole playoff and Pooley won on the second hole of sudden death.

Senior Players Championship

First played in 1983 and contested in Cleveland (1983-86), Ponte Vedra, Fla. (1987-89) and Dearborn, Mich. (since 1990).

Multiple winners: Ray Floyd, Arnold Palmer and Dave Stockton (2).

Year		Year		Year		Year	
1983	Miller Barber	1988	Billy Casper	1993	Jim Colbert	1998	Gil Morgan
1984	Arnold Palmer	1989	Orville Moody	1994	Dave Stockton	1999	Hale Irwin
1985	Arnold Palmer	1990	Jack Nicklaus	1995	J.C. Snead*	2000	Ray Floyd
1986	Chi Chi Rodriguez	1991	Jim Albus	1996	Ray Floyd	2001	Allen Doyle*
1987	Gary Player	1992	Dave Stockton	1997	Larry Gilbert	2002	Stewart Ginn

*PLAYOFF

1995: J.C. Snead def. Jack Nicklaus on 1st extra hole. **2001:** Allen Doyle def. Doug Tewell on 1st extra hole.

Major Senior Championship Leaders

Through 2002. All players are still active.

		Senior PGA	US Open	Senior Players	Trad	Total			Senior PGA	US Open	Senior Players	Trad	Total
1	Jack Nicklaus	1	2	1	4	8	6	Miller Barber	0	2	1	0	3
2	Hale Irwin	3	2	1	0	6		Gil Morgan	0	0	1	2	3
	Gary Player	3	2	1	0	6		Arnold Palmer	1	0	2	0	3
4	Ray Floyd	1	0	2	1	4		Dave Stockton	0	1	2	0	3
	Lee Trevino	2	1	0	1	4							

Grand Slam Summary

The Senior Grand Slam has officially consisted of The Tradition, the Senior PGA Championship, the Senior Players Championship and the U.S. Senior Open since 1990. Jack Nicklaus won three of the four events in 1991, but no one has won all four in one season.

Three wins in one year: Jack Nicklaus (1991). **Two wins in one year** (8): Gary Player (twice); Hale Irwin, Gil Morgan, Orville Moody, Jack Nicklaus, Arnold Palmer and Lee Trevino (once).

Year	Tradition	Sr. PGA	Players	US Open	Year	Tradition	Sr. PGA	Players	US Open
1983	—	—	M. Barber	Casper	1993	Shaw	Wargo	Colbert	Nicklaus
1984	—	Palmer	Palmer	M. Barber	1994	Floyd	Trevino	Stockton	Hobday
1985	—	Thomson	Palmer	M. Barber	1995	Nicklaus	Floyd	Snead	Weiskopf
1986	—	Player	Rodriguez	Douglass	1996	Nicklaus	Irwin	Floyd	Stockton
1987	—	Rodriguez	Player	Player	1997	Morgan	Irwin	Gilbert	Marsh
1988	—	Player	Casper	Player	1998	Morgan	Irwin	Morgan	Irwin
1989	Bies	Mowry	Moody	Moody	1999	Marsh	Irwin	Doyle	Eichelberger
1990	Nicklaus	Player	Nicklaus	Trevino	2000	Kite	Tewell	Floyd	Irwin
1991	Nicklaus	Nicklaus	Albus	Nicklaus	2001	Tewell	Watson	Doyle	Fleisher
1992	Trevino	Trevino	Stockton	Laoretti	2002	Thorpe	Zoeller	Ginn	Pooley

Annual Money Leaders

Official annual money leaders on the PGA, European PGA, Senior PGA and LPGA tours.

PGA

Multiple leaders: Jack Nicklaus (8); Ben Hogan and Tom Watson (5); Arnold Palmer and Tiger Woods (4); Greg Norman, Sam Snead and Curtis Strange (3); Julius Boros, Billy Casper, Tom Kite, Byron Nelson and Nick Price (2).

Year		Earnings	Year		Earnings	Year		Earnings
1934	Paul Runyan	$6,767	1957	Dick Mayer	$65,835	1980	Tom Watson	$530,808
1935	Johnny Revolta	9,543	1958	Arnold Palmer	42,608	1981	Tom Kite	375,699
1936	Horton Smith	7,682	1959	Art Wall	53,168	1982	Craig Stadler	446,462
1937	Harry Cooper	14,139	1960	Arnold Palmer	75,263	1983	Hal Sutton	426,668
1938	Sam Snead	19,534	1961	Gary Player	64,540	1984	Tom Watson	476,260
1939	Henry Picard	10,303	1962	Arnold Palmer	81,448	1985	Curtis Strange	542,321
1940	Ben Hogan	10,655	1963	Arnold Palmer	128,230	1986	Greg Norman	653,296
1941	Ben Hogan	18,358	1964	Jack Nicklaus	113,285	1987	Curtis Strange	925,941
1942	Ben Hogan	13,143	1965	Jack Nicklaus	140,752	1988	Curtis Strange	1,147,644
1943	No records kept		1966	Billy Casper	121,945	1989	Tom Kite	1,395,278
1944	Byron Nelson	37,968	1967	Jack Nicklaus	188,998	1990	Greg Norman	1,165,477
1945	Byron Nelson	63,336	1968	Billy Casper	205,169	1991	Corey Pavin	979,430
1946	Ben Hogan	42,556	1969	Frank Beard	164,707	1992	Fred Couples	1,344,188
1947	Jimmy Demaret	27,937	1970	Lee Trevino	157,037	1993	Nick Price	1,478,557
1948	Ben Hogan	32,112	1971	Jack Nicklaus	244,491	1994	Nick Price	1,499,927
1949	Sam Snead	31,594	1972	Jack Nicklaus	320,542	1995	Greg Norman	1,654,959
1950	Sam Snead	35,759	1973	Jack Nicklaus	308,362	1996	Tom Lehman	1,780,159
1951	Lloyd Mangrum	26,089	1974	Johnny Miller	353,022	1997	Tiger Woods	2,066,833
1952	Julius Boros	37,033	1975	Jack Nicklaus	298,149	1998	David Duval	2,591,031
1953	Lew Worsham	34,002	1976	Jack Nicklaus	266,439	1999	Tiger Woods	6,616,585
1954	Bob Toski	65,820	1977	Tom Watson	310,653	2000	Tiger Woods	9,188,321
1955	Julius Boros	63,122	1978	Tom Watson	362,429	2001	Tiger Woods	5,687,777
1956	Ted Kroll	72,836	1979	Tom Watson	462,636			

Note: In 1944-45, Nelson's winnings were in War Bonds.

Senior PGA

Multiple leaders: Don January (3); Miller Barber, Bob Charles, Jim Colbert, Hale Irwin, Dave Stockton and Lee Trevino (2).

Year		Earnings	Year		Earnings	Year		Earnings
1980	Don January	$44,100	1988	Bob Charles	$533,929	1996	Jim Colbert	$1,627,890
1981	Miller Barber	83,136	1989	Bob Charles	725,887	1997	Hale Irwin	2,343,364
1982	Miller Barber	106,890	1990	Lee Trevino	1,190,518	1998	Hale Irwin	2,861,945
1983	Don January	237,571	1991	Mike Hill	1,065,657	1999	Bruce Fleisher	2,515,705
1984	Don January	328,597	1992	Lee Trevino	1,027,002	2000	Larry Nelson	2,708,005
1985	Peter Thomson	386,724	1993	Dave Stockton	1,175,944	2001	Allen Doyle	2,553,582
1986	Bruce Crampton	454,299	1994	Dave Stockton	1,402,519			
1987	Chi Chi Rodriguez	509,145	1995	Jim Colbert	1,444,386			

European PGA

Official money in the Volvo Order of Merit was awarded in British pounds from 1961-98 and euros since 1999.

Multiple leaders: Colin Montgomerie (7); Seve Ballesteros (6); Sandy Lyle (3); Gay Brewer Jr., Nick Faldo, Bernard Hunt, Bernhard Langer, Peter Thomson and Ian Woosnam (2).

Year		Earnings	Year		Earnings	Year		Earnings
1961	Bernard Hunt	£4,492	1966	Bruce Devlin	£13,205	1971	Gary Player	£11,281
1962	Peter Thomson	5,764	1967	Gay Brewer Jr.	20,235	1972	Bob Charles	18,538
1963	Bernard Hunt	7,209	1968	Gay Brewer Jr.	23,107	1973	Tony Jacklin	24,839
1964	Neil Coles	7,890	1969	Billy Casper	23,483	1974	Peter Oosterhuis	32,127
1965	Peter Thomson	7,011	1970	Christy O'Connor	31,532	1975	Dale Hayes	20,507

Year	Earnings	Year	Earnings	Year	Earnings
1976	Seve Ballesteros £39,504	1985	Sandy Lyle £254,711	1994	Colin Montgomerie . . . £920,647
1977	Seve Ballesteros 46,436	1986	Seve Ballesteros 259,275	1995	Colin Montgomerie . .1,038,718
1978	Seve Ballesteros 54,348	1987	Ian Woosnam 439,075	1996	Colin Montgomerie . .1,034,752
1979	Sandy Lyle 49,233	1988	Seve Ballesteros 502,000	1997	Colin Montgomerie . .1,583,904
1980	Greg Norman 74,829	1989	Ronan Rafferty 465,981	1998	Colin Montgomerie . .1,082,833
1981	Bernhard Langer 95,991	1990	Ian Woosnam 737,977	1999	C. Montgomerie . . €2,066,885
1982	Sandy Lyle 86,141	1991	Seve Ballesteros 790,811	2000	Lee Westwood 3,125,147
1983	Nick Faldo 140,761	1992	Nick Faldo 1,220,540	2001	Retief Goosen 2,862,806
1984	Bernhard Langer 160,883	1993	Colin Montgomerie . . .798,145		

LPGA

Multiple leaders: Kathy Whitworth (8); Annika Sorenstam and Mickey Wright (4); Patty Berg, JoAnne Carner, Beth Daniel, Betsy King, Nancy Lopez and Karrie Webb (3); Pat Bradley, Judy Rankin, Betsy Rawls, Louise Suggs and Babe Zaharias (2).

Year	Earnings	Year	Earnings	Year	Earnings
1950	Babe Zaharias $14,800	1968	Kathy Whitworth $48,379	1986	Pat Bradley $492,021
1951	Babe Zaharias 15,087	1969	Carol Mann 49,152	1987	Ayako Okamoto 466,034
1952	Betsy Rawls 14,505	1970	Kathy Whitworth 30,235	1988	Sherri Turner 350,851
1953	Louise Suggs 19,816	1971	Kathy Whitworth 41,181	1989	Betsy King 654,132
1954	Patty Berg 16,011	1972	Kathy Whitworth 65,063	1990	Beth Daniel 863,578
1955	Patty Berg 16,492	1973	Kathy Whitworth 82,864	1991	Pat Bradley 763,118
1956	Marlene Hagge 20,235	1974	JoAnne Carner 87,094	1992	Dottie Pepper 693,335
1957	Patty Berg 16,272	1975	Sandra Palmer 76,374	1993	Betsy King 595,992
1958	Beverly Hanson 12,639	1976	Judy Rankin 150,734	1994	Laura Davies 687,201
1959	Betsy Rawls 26,774	1977	Judy Rankin 122,890	1995	Annika Sorenstam 666,533
1960	Louise Suggs 16,892	1978	Nancy Lopez 189,814	1996	Karrie Webb 1,002,000
1961	Mickey Wright 22,236	1979	Nancy Lopez 197,489	1997	Annika Sorenstam . .1,236,789
1962	Mickey Wright 21,641	1980	Beth Daniel 231,000	1998	Annika Sorenstam . .1,092,748
1963	Mickey Wright 31,269	1981	Beth Daniel 206,998	1999	Karrie Webb 1,591,959
1964	Mickey Wright 29,800	1982	JoAnne Carner 310,400	2000	Karrie Webb 1,876,853
1965	Kathy Whitworth 28,658	1983	JoAnne Carner 291,404	2001	Annika Sorenstam . .2,105,868
1966	Kathy Whitworth 33,517	1984	Betsy King 266,771		
1967	Kathy Whitworth 32,937	1985	Nancy Lopez 416,472		

All-Time Leaders

PGA, Senior PGA and LPGA leaders through 2001.

Tournaments Won

PGA

		No
1	Sam Snead	.81
2	Jack Nicklaus	.70
3	Ben Hogan	.63
4	Arnold Palmer	.60
5	Byron Nelson	.52
6	Billy Casper	.51
7	Walter Hagan	.40
	Cary Middlecoff	.40
9	Gene Sarazen	.38
10	Lloyd Mangrum	.36
11	Tom Watson	.34
12	Horton Smith	.32
13	Harry Cooper	.31
	Jimmy Demaret	.31
15	Leo Diegel	.30
16	Gene Littler	.29
	Paul Runyan	.29
	Tiger Woods	.29
19	Lee Trevino	.27
20	Henry Picard	.26

Senior PGA

		No
1	Hale Irwin	.32
2	Lee Trevino	.29
3	Miller Barber	.24
4	Bob Charles	.23
5	Don January	.22
	Chi Chi Rodriguez	.22
7	Bruce Crampton	.20
	Jim Colbert	.20
	Gil Morgan	.20
10	George Archer	.19
	Gary Player	.19
12	Mike Hill	.18
13	Larry Nelson	.16
14	Dave Stockton	.14
	Raymond Floyd	.14
	Bruce Fleisher	.14
17	Jim Dent	.12
18	Dale Douglass	.11
	Orville Moody	.11
	Bob Murphy	.11
	Peter Thomson	.11

LPGA

		No
1	Kathy Whitworth	.88
2	Mickey Wright	.82
3	Patty Berg	.60
4	Louise Suggs	.58
5	Betsy Rawls	.55
6	Nancy Lopez	.48
7	JoAnne Carner	.43
8	Sandra Haynie	.42
9	Babe Zaharias	.41
10	Carol Mann	.38
11	Patty Sheehan	.35
12	Betsy King	.34
13	Beth Daniel	.32
14	Pat Bradley	.31
	Annika Sorenstam	.31
16	Amy Alcott	.29
17	Jane Blalock	.27
18	Judy Rankin	.26
	Juli Inkster	.26
	Karrie Webb	.26

All-Time Leaders (Cont.)
Money Won
PGA
All-time earnings through 2001.

#	Player	Earnings	#	Player	Earnings	#	Player	Earnings
1	Tiger Woods	$26,191,227	10	Greg Norman	$13,344,142	19	Tom Kite	$10,865,959
2	Davis Love III	17,994,690	11	Fred Couples	12,681,268	20	Jeff Sluman	10,634,572
3	Phil Mickelson	17,837,998	12	Tom Lehman	12,088,396	21	Loren Roberts	9,866,485
4	David Duval	15,312,553	13	Mark O'Meara	12,025,198	22	Brad Faxon	9,777,678
5	Scott Hoch	14,553,202	14	Ernie Els	12,016,635	23	Tom Watson	9,593,631
6	Vijay Singh	14,524,452	15	Payne Stewart	11,737,008	24	Corey Pavin	9,536,170
7	Nick Price	14,477,425	16	Paul Azinger	11,687,965	25	David Toms	9,412,686
8	Hal Sutton	13,885,946	17	Jim Furyk	11,493,593			
9	Mark Calcavecchia	13,409,349	18	Justin Leonard	10,919,999			

European PGA
All-time earnings through 2001.

#	Player	Earnings	#	Player	Earnings	#	Player	Earnings
1	C. Montgomerie	€16,804,817	10	Retief Goosen	€7,886,587	19	Costantino Rocca	€4,914,681
2	Tiger Woods	12,574,703	11	M. A. Jimenez	7,152,295	20	Mark James	4,863,845
3	Bernhard Langer	11,968,873	12	Seve Ballesteros	6,762,223	21	Barry Lane	4,786,892
4	Ian Woosnam	10,418,158	13	Sam Torrance	6,732,771	22	Paul McGinley	4,705,328
5	Ernie Els	10,048,787	14	Padraig Harrington	6,521,151	23	Michael Campbell	4,423,820
6	Darren Clarke	9,884,138	15	Vijay Singh	6,444,373	24	Paul Lawrie	4,205,075
7	Lee Westwood	8,690,009	16	Thomas Björn	6,014,744	25	Fred Couples	4,179,315
8	Nick Faldo	8,675,721	17	Mark McNulty	5,629,132			
9	Jose Maria Olazabal	8,321,974	18	Eduardo Romero	5,036,977			

Senior PGA
All-time earnings through 2001.

#	Player	Earnings	#	Player	Earnings	#	Player	Earnings
1	Hale Irwin	$13,921,874	10	Jim Dent	$7,832,042	19	J.C. Snead	$6,292,146
2	Jim Colbert	10,553,940	11	Isao Aoki	7,557,949	20	Dana Quigley	6,199,307
3	Gil Morgan	9,749,317	12	Mike Hill	7,379,796	21	Allen Doyle	6,135,610
4	Lee Trevino	9,426,642	13	Bruce Fleisher	7,301,226	22	Bruce Summerhays	6,012,684
5	Dave Stockton	9,140,870	14	Bob Murphy	6,559,963	23	Tom Wargo	5,940,650
6	Bob Charles	8,564,577	15	Chi Chi Rodriguez	6,558,025	24	Jim Albus	5,666,339
7	Ray Floyd	8,229,505	16	Dale Douglass	6,444,470	25	Gary Player	5,624,585
8	Larry Nelson	8,086,397	17	Graham Marsh	6,426,654			
9	George Archer	8,000,911	18	Jay Sigel	6,422,862			

LPGA
All-time earnings through 2001.

#	Player	Earnings	#	Player	Earnings	#	Player	Earnings
1	Annika Sorenstam	$8,306,464	8	Pat Bradley	$5,743,605	15	Se Ri Pak	$4,002,481
2	Karrie Webb	7,698,299	9	Laura Davies	5,695,525	16	Sherri Steinhauer	3,802,527
3	Betsy King	7,187,444	10	Rosie Jones	5,683,934	17	Jane Geddes	3,736,152
4	Dottie Pepper	6,658,613	11	Patty Sheehan	5,504,005	18	Lorie Kane	3,597,320
5	Juli Inkster	6,512,487	12	Nancy Lopez	5,310,391	19	Tammie Green	3,590,042
6	Beth Daniel	6,433,001	13	Kelly Robbins	4,440,314	20	Brandie Burton	3,442,242
7	Meg Mallon	5,954,573	14	Liselotte Neumann	4,208,348			

Official World Ranking

Begun in 1986, the Official World Golf Ranking (formerly the Sony World Ranking) combines the best golfers on the six pro men's tours which make up the International Federation of PGA Tours. Rankings are based on a rolling two-year period and weighed in favor of more recent results. While annual winners are not announced, certain players reaching No. 1 have dominated each year.

Multiple winners (at year's end): Greg Norman (6); Tiger Woods (5); Nick Faldo (3); Seve Ballesteros (2).

Year		Year		Year		Year	
1986	Seve Ballesteros	1990	Nick Faldo	1993	Nick Faldo	1998	Tiger Woods
1987	Greg Norman		& Greg Norman	1994	Nick Price	1999	Tiger Woods
1988	Greg Norman	1991	Ian Woosnam	1995	Greg Norman	2000	Tiger Woods
1989	Seve Ballesteros	1992	Fred Couples	1996	Greg Norman	2001	Tiger Woods
	& Greg Norman		& Nick Faldo	1997	Tiger Woods		

Annual Awards
PGA of America Player of the Year

Awarded by the PGA of America; based on points scale that weighs performance in major tournaments, regular events, money earned and scoring average.

Multiple winners: Tom Watson (6); Jack Nicklaus (5); Ben Hogan and Tiger Woods (4); Julius Boros, Billy Casper, Arnold Palmer and Nick Price.

Year		Year		Year		Year	
1948	Ben Hogan	1962	Arnold Palmer	1976	Jack Nicklaus	1990	Nick Faldo
1949	Sam Snead	1963	Julius Boros	1977	Tom Watson	1991	Corey Pavin
1950	Ben Hogan	1964	Ken Venturi	1978	Tom Watson	1992	Fred Couples
1951	Ben Hogan	1965	Dave Marr	1979	Tom Watson	1993	Nick Price
1952	Julius Boros	1966	Billy Casper	1980	Tom Watson	1994	Nick Price
1953	Ben Hogan	1967	Jack Nicklaus	1981	Bill Rogers	1995	Greg Norman
1954	Ed Furgol	1968	No award	1982	Tom Watson	1996	Tom Lehman
1955	Doug Ford	1969	Orville Moody	1983	Hal Sutton	1997	Tiger Woods
1956	Jack Burke	1970	Billy Casper	1984	Tom Watson	1998	Mark O'Meara
1957	Dick Mayer	1971	Lee Trevino	1985	Lanny Wadkins	1999	Tiger Woods
1958	Dow Finsterwald	1972	Jack Nicklaus	1986	Bob Tway	2000	Tiger Woods
1959	Art Wall Jr.	1973	Jack Nicklaus	1987	Paul Azinger	2001	Tiger Woods
1960	Arnold Palmer	1974	Johnny Miller	1988	Curtis Strange		
1961	Jerry Barber	1975	Jack Nicklaus	1989	Tom Kite		

PGA Tour Player of the Year

Award by the PGA Tour starting in 1990. Winner voted on by tour members from list of nominees. Winner receives the Jack Nicklaus Trophy, which originated in 1997.

Multiple winners: Tiger Woods (4); Fred Couples and Nick Price (2).

Year		Year		Year		Year	
1990	Wayne Levi	1993	Nick Price	1996	Tom Lehman	1999	Tiger Woods
1991	Fred Couples	1994	Nick Price	1997	Tiger Woods	2000	Tiger Woods
1992	Fred Couples	1995	Greg Norman	1998	Mark O'Meara	2001	Tiger Woods

PGA Tour Rookie of the Year

Awarded by the PGA Tour in 1990. Winner voted on by tour members from list of first-year nominees.

Year		Year		Year		Year	
1990	Robert Gamez	1993	Vijay Singh	1996	Tiger Woods	1999	Carlos Franco
1991	John Daly	1994	Ernie Els	1997	Stewart Cink	2000	Michael Clark II
1992	Mark Carnevale	1995	Woody Austin	1998	Steve Flesch	2001	Charles Howell III

PGA Senior Player of the Year

Awarded by th PGA Seniors Tour starting in 1990. Winner voted on by tour members from list of nominees.
Multiple winner: Lee Trevino (3); Jim Colbert and Hale Irwin (2).

Year		Year		Year		Year	
1990	Lee Trevino	1993	Dave Stockton	1997	Hale Irwin	2001	Allen Doyle
1991	George Archer	1994	Lee Trevino	1998	Hale Irwin		
	& Mike Hill	1995	Jim Colbert	1999	Bruce Fleisher		
1992	Lee Trevino	1996	Jim Colbert	2000	Larry Nelson		

European Golfer of the Year

Officially, the Ritz Club Trophy (1985-92), Johnnie Walker Trophy (1993-97) and Asprey and Garrard Golfer of the Year (1998-present); voting done by panel of European golf writers and tour members.

Multiple winners: Colin Montgomerie (4); Seve Ballesteros and Nick Faldo (3); Bernhard Langer and Lee Westwood (2).

Year		Year		Year		Year	
1985	Bernhard Langer	1990	Nick Faldo	1995	Colin Montgomerie	2000	Lee Westwood
1986	Seve Ballesteros	1991	Seve Ballesteros	1996	Colin Montgomerie	2001	Retief Goosen
1987	Ian Woosnam	1992	Nick Faldo	1997	Colin Montgomerie		
1988	Seve Ballesteros	1993	Bernhard Langer	1998	Lee Westwood		
1989	Nick Faldo	1994	Ernie Els	1999	Colin Montgomerie		

Annual Awards (Cont.)
LPGA Player of the Year
Sponsored by Rolex and awarded by the LPGA; based on performance points accumulated during the year.
Multiple winners: Kathy Whitworth (7); Nancy Lopez and Annika Sorenstam (4); JoAnne Carner, Beth Daniel and Betsy King (3); Pat Bradley, Judy Rankin and Karrie Webb (2).

Year		Year		Year		Year	
1966	Kathy Whitworth	1975	Sandra Palmer	1984	Betsy King	1993	Betsy King
1967	Kathy Whitworth	1976	Judy Rankin	1985	Nancy Lopez	1994	Beth Daniel
1968	Kathy Whitworth	1977	Judy Rankin	1986	Pat Bradley	1995	Annika Sorenstam
1969	Kathy Whitworth	1978	Nancy Lopez	1987	Ayako Okamoto	1996	Laura Davies
1970	Sandra Haynie	1979	Nancy Lopez	1988	Nancy Lopez	1997	Annika Sorenstam
1971	Kathy Whitworth	1980	Beth Daniel	1989	Betsy King	1998	Annika Sorenstam
1972	Kathy Whitworth	1981	JoAnne Carner	1990	Beth Daniel	1999	Karrie Webb
1973	Kathy Whitworth	1982	JoAnne Carner	1991	Pat Bradley	2000	Karrie Webb
1974	JoAnne Carner	1983	Patty Sheehan	1992	Dottie Mochrie	2001	Annika Sorenstam

LPGA Rookie of the Year
Sponsored by Rolex and awarded by the LPGA; based on performance points accumulated during the year. Winner receives Louise Suggs Trophy, which originated in 2000.

Year		Year		Year		Year	
1962	Mary Mills	1972	Jocelyne Bourassa	1982	Patti Rizzo	1992	Helen Alfredsson
1963	Clifford Ann Creed	1973	Laura Baugh	1983	Stephanie Farwig	1993	Suzanne Strudwick
1964	Susie Berning	1974	Jan Stephenson	1984	Juli Inkster	1994	Annika Sorenstam
1965	Margie Masters	1975	Amy Alcott	1985	Penny Hammel	1995	Pat Hurst
1966	Jan Ferraris	1976	Bonnie Lauer	1986	Jody Rosenthal	1996	Karrie Webb
1967	Sharron Moran	1977	Debbie Massey	1987	Tammie Green	1997	Lisa Hackney
1968	Sandra Post	1978	Nancy Lopez	1988	Liselotte Neumann	1998	Se Ri Pak
1969	Jane Blalock	1979	Beth Daniel	1989	Pamela Wright	1999	Mi Hyun Kim
1970	JoAnne Carner	1980	Myra Van Hoose	1990	Hiromi Kobayashi	2000	Dorothy Delasin
1971	Sally Little	1981	Patty Sheehan	1991	Brandie Burton	2001	Hee-Wan Han

National Team Competition
MEN
Ryder Cup
The Ryder Cup was presented by British seed merchant and businessman Samuel Ryder in 1927 for competition between professional golfers from Great Britain and the United States. The British team was expanded to include Irish players in 1973 and the rest of Europe in 1979. The 2001 event was postponed due to the attacks on America, causing the event to switch from an odd- to even-year schedule. The United States leads the series 24-8-2 after 34 matches.

Year		Year		Year		Year	
1927	USA, 9½-2½	1951	USA, 9½-2½	1969	Draw, 16-16	1987	Europe, 15-13
1929	Britain-Ireland, 7-5	1953	USA, 6½-5½	1971	USA, 18½-13½	1989	Draw, 14-14
1931	USA, 9-3	1955	USA, 8-4	1973	USA, 19-13	1991	USA, 14½-13½
1933	Great Britain, 6½-5½	1957	Britain-Ireland, 7½-4½	1975	USA, 21-11	1993	USA, 15-13
1935	USA, 9-3	1959	USA, 8½-3½	1977	USA, 12½-13½	1995	Europe, 14½-13½
1937	USA, 8-4	1961	USA, 14½-9½	1979	USA, 17-11	1997	Europe, 14½-13½
1939-45	Not held	1963	USA, 23-9	1981	USA, 18½-9½	1999	USA, 14½-13½
1947	USA, 11-1	1965	USA, 19½-12½	1983	USA, 14½-13½	2002	Europe, 15½-12½
1949	USA, 7-5	1967	USA, 23½-8½	1985	Europe, 16½-11½		

Playing Sites
1927—Worcester CC (Mass.); **1929**—Moortown, England; **1931**—Scioto CC (Ohio); **1933**—Southport & Ainsdale, England; **1935**—Ridgewood CC (N.J.); **1937**—Southport & Ainsdale, England; **1939-45**—Not held. **1947**—Portland CC (Ore.); **1949**—Ganton GC, England; **1951**—Pinehurst CC (N.C.); **1953**—Wentworth, England; **1955**—Thunderbird Ranch & CC (Calif.); **1957**—Lindrick GC, England; **1959**—Eldorado CC (Calif.); **1961**—Royal Lytham & St. Annes, England; **1963**—East Lake CC (Ga.); **1965**—Royal Birkdale, England; **1967**—Champions GC (Tex.); **1969**—Royal Birkdale, England; **1971**—Old Warson CC (Mo.); **1973**—Muirfield, Scotland; **1975**—Laurel Valley GC (Pa.); **1977**—Royal Lytham & St. Annes, England; **1979**—The Greenbrier (W.Va.); **1981**—Walton Heath GC, England; **1983**—PGA National GC (Fla.); **1985**—The Belfry, England; **1987**—Muirfield Village GC (Ohio); **1989**—The Belfry, England; **1991**—Ocean Course (S.C.); **1993**—The Belfry, England; **1995**—Oak Hill CC (N.Y.); **1997**—Valderrama, Costa del Sol, Spain; **1999**—The Country Club (Mass.); **2002**—The Belfry, England; **2004**—Oakland Hills CC (Mich.); **2006**—Kildare Hotel & CC, Ireland; **2008**—Medinah CC (Ill.).

Walker Cup
The Walker Cup was presented by American businessman George Herbert Walker in 1922 for competition between amateur golfers from Great Britain, Ireland and the United States. The U.S. leads the series against the combined Great Britain-Ireland team, 31-6-1, after 38 matches.

Year		Year		Year		Year	
1922	USA, 8-4	1926	USA, 6½-5½	1932	USA, 9½-2½	1938	Britain-Ireland, 7½-4½
1923	USA, 6½-5½	1928	USA, 11-1	1934	USA, 9½-2½	1940-46	Not held
1924	USA, 9-3	1930	USA, 10-2	1936	USA, 10½-1½	1947	USA, 8-4

Year		Year		Year		Year	
1949	USA, 10-2	1965	Draw, 12-12	1981	USA, 15-9	1995	Britain-Ireland, 14-10
1951	USA, 7½-4½	1967	USA, 15-9	1983	USA, 13½-10½	1997	USA, 18-6
1953	USA, 9-3	1969	USA, 13-11	1985	USA, 13-11	1999	Britain-Ireland, 15-9
1955	USA, 10-2	1971	Britain-Ireland, 13-11	1987	USA, 16½-7½	2001	Britain-Ireland, 15-9
1957	USA, 8½-3½	1973	USA, 14-10	1989	Britain-Ireland,		
1959	USA, 9-3	1975	USA, 15½-8½		12½-11½		
1961	USA, 11-1	1977	USA, 16-8	1991	USA, 14-10		
1963	USA, 14-10	1979	USA, 15½-8½	1993	USA, 19-5		

Presidents Cup

The Presidents Cup is a biennial event played in non-Ryder Cup years in which the world's best non-European players compete against players from the United States. The U.S. leads the series, 3-1.

Year		Year	
1994	USA, 20-12	1998	International, 20½-11½
1996	USA, 16½-15½	2000	USA, 21½-10½

WOMEN
Solheim Cup

The Solheim Cup was presented by the Karsten Manufacturing Co. in 1990 for competition between women professional golfers from Europe and the United States. The event was switched from even- to odd-numbered years after 2002 so it would not conflict with the men's Ryder Cup event. The U.S. leads the series, 5-2.

Year		Year		Year	
1990	USA, 11½-4½	1996	USA, 17-11	2002	USA, 15½-12½
1992	Europe, 11½-6½	1998	USA, 16-12		
1994	USA, 13-7	2000	Europe, 14½-11½		

Playing Sites

1990—Lake Nona CC (Fla.); **1992**—Dalmahoy CC, Scotland; **1994**—The Greenbrier (W. Va.); **1996**—Marriott St. Pierre Hotel G&CC, Wales; **1998**—Muirfield Village GC (Ohio); **2000**—Loch Lomond GC, Scotland; **2002**—Interlachen CC (Minn.); **2003**—Barseback G&CC, Sweden; **2005**—Crooked Stick CC (Ind.).

Curtis Cup

Named after British golfing sisters Harriot and Margaret Curtis, the Curtis Cup was first contested in 1932 between teams of women amateurs from the United States and the British Isles.

Competed for every other year since 1932 (except during WWII). The U.S. leads the series, 23-6-3, after 32 matches.

Year		Year		Year		Year	
1932	USA, 5½-3½	1956	British Isles, 5-4	1974	USA, 13-5	1992	British Isles, 10-8
1934	USA, 6½-2½	1958	Draw, 4½-4½	1976	USA, 11½-6½	1994	Draw, 9-9
1936	Draw, 4½-4½	1960	USA, 6½-2½	1978	USA, 12-6	1996	British Isles, 11½-6½
1938	USA, 5½-3½	1962	USA, 8-1	1980	USA, 13-5	1998	USA, 10-8
1940-46	Not held	1964	USA, 10½-7½	1982	USA, 14½-3½	2000	USA, 10-8
1948	USA, 6½-2½	1966	USA, 13-5	1984	USA, 9½-8½	2002	USA, 11-7
1950	USA, 7½-1½	1968	USA, 10½-7½	1986	British Isles, 13-5		
1952	British Isles, 5-4	1970	USA, 11½-6½	1988	British Isles, 11-7		
1954	USA, 6-3	1972	USA, 10-8	1990	USA, 14-4		

COLLEGES

Men's NCAA Division I Champions

College championships decided by match play from 1897-1964 and stroke play since 1965.

Multiple winners (Teams): Yale (21); Houston (16); Oklahoma St. (9); Stanford (7); Harvard (6); Florida, LSU and North Texas (4); Wake Forest (3); Arizona St., Michigan, Ohio St. and Texas (2).

Multiple winners (Individuals): Ben Crenshaw and Phil Mickelson (3); Dick Crawford, Dexter Cummings, G.T. Dunlop, Fred Lamprecht and Scott Simpson (2).

Year	Team winner	Individual champion	Year	Team winner	Individual champion
1897	Yale	Louis Bayard, Princeton	1905	Yale	Robert Abbott, Yale
1898	Harvard (spring)	John Reid, Yale	1906	Yale	W.E. Clow Jr., Yale
1898	Yale (fall)	James Curtis, Harvard	1907	Yale	Ellis Knowles, Yale
1899	Harvard	Percy Pyne, Princeton	1908	Yale	H.H. Wilder, Harvard
			1909	Yale	Albert Seckel, Princeton
1900	Not held				
1901	Harvard	H. Lindsley, Harvard	1910	Yale	Robert Hunter, Yale
1902	Yale (spring)	Chas. Hitchcock Jr., Yale	1911	Yale	George Stanley, Yale
1902	Harvard (fall)	Chandler Egan, Harvard	1912	Yale	F.C. Davison, Harvard
1903	Harvard	F.O. Reinhart, Princeton	1913	Yale	Nathaniel Wheeler, Yale
1904	Harvard	A.L. White, Harvard	1914	Princeton	Edward Allis, Harvard

Colleges (Cont.)

Year	Team winner	Individual champion	Year	Team winner	Individual champion
1915	Yale	Francis Blossom, Yale	1961	Purdue	Jack Nicklaus, Ohio St.
1916	Princeton	J.W. Hubbell, Harvard	1962	Houston	Kermit Zarley, Houston
1917-18	Not held		1963	Oklahoma St.	R.H. Sikes, Arkansas
1919	Princeton	A.L. Walker Jr., Columbia	1964	Houston	Terry Small, San Jose St.
			1965	Houston	Marty Fleckman, Houston
1920	Princeton	Jess Sweetser, Yale	1966	Houston	Bob Murphy, Florida
1921	Dartmouth	Simpson Dean, Princeton	1967	Houston	Hale Irwin, Colorado
1922	Princeton	Pollack Boyd, Dartmouth	1968	Florida	Grier Jones, Oklahoma St.
1923	Princeton	Dexter Cummings, Yale	1969	Houston	Bob Clark, Cal St.-LA
1924	Yale	Dexter Cummings, Yale			
1925	Yale	Fred Lamprecht, Tulane	1970	Houston	John Mahaffey, Houston
1926	Yale	Fred Lamprecht, Tulane	1971	Texas	Ben Crenshaw, Texas
1927	Princeton	Watts Gunn, Georgia Tech	1972	Texas	Ben Crenshaw, Texas
1928	Princeton	Maurice McCarthy, G'town			& Tom Kite, Texas
1929	Princeton	Tom Aycock, Yale	1973	Florida	Ben Crenshaw, Texas
			1974	Wake Forest	Curtis Strange, W.Forest
1930	Princeton	G.T. Dunlap Jr., Princeton	1975	Wake Forest	Jay Haas, Wake Forest
1931	Yale	G.T. Dunlap Jr., Princeton	1976	Oklahoma St.	Scott Simpson, USC
1932	Yale	J.W. Fischer, Michigan	1977	Houston	Scott Simpson, USC
1933	Yale	Walter Emery, Oklahoma	1978	Oklahoma St.	David Edwards, Okla. St.
1934	Michigan	Charles Yates, Ga.Tech	1979	Ohio St.	Gary Hallberg, Wake Forest
1935	Michigan	Ed White, Texas			
1936	Yale	Charles Kocsis, Michigan	1980	Oklahoma St.	Jay Don Blake, Utah St.
1937	Princeton	Fred Haas Jr., LSU	1981	Brigham Young	Ron Commans, USC
1938	Stanford	John Burke, Georgetown	1982	Houston	Billy Ray Brown, Houston
1939	Stanford	Vincent D'Antoni, Tulane	1983	Oklahoma St.	Jim Carter, Arizona St.
			1984	Houston	John Inman, N.Carolina
1940	Princeton & LSU	Dixon Brooke, Virginia	1985	Houston	Clark Burroughs, Ohio St.
1941	Stanford	Earl Stewart, LSU	1986	Wake Forest	Scott Verplank, Okla. St.
1942	LSU & Stanford	Frank Tatum Jr., Stanford	1987	Oklahoma St.	Brian Watts, Oklahoma St.
1943	Yale	Wallace Ulrich, Carleton	1988	UCLA	E.J. Pfister, Oklahoma St.
1944	Notre Dame	Louis Lick, Minnesota	1989	Oklahoma	Phil Mickelson, Ariz. St.
1945	Ohio State	John Lorms, Ohio St.			
1946	Stanford	George Hamer, Georgia	1990	Arizona St.	Phil Mickelson, Ariz. St.
1947	LSU	Dave Barclay, Michigan	1991	Oklahoma St.	Warren Schuette, UNLV
1948	San Jose St.	Bob Harris, San Jose St.	1992	Arizona	Phil Mickelson, Ariz. St.
1949	North Texas	Harvie Ward, N.Carolina	1993	Florida	Todd Demsey, Ariz. St.
			1994	Stanford	Justin Leonard, Texas
1950	North Texas	Fred Wampler, Purdue	1995	Oklahoma St.	Chip Spratlin, Auburn
1951	North Texas	Tom Nieporte, Ohio St.	1996	Arizona St.	Tiger Woods, Stanford
1952	North Texas	Jim Vickers, Oklahoma	1997	Pepperdine	Charles Warren, Clemson
1953	Stanford	Earl Moeller, Oklahoma St.	1998	UNLV	James McLean, Minnesota
1954	SMU	Hillman Robbins, Memphis St.	1999	Georgia	Luke Donald, Northwestern
1955	LSU	Joe Campbell, Purdue			
1956	Houston	Rick Jones, Ohio St.	2000	Oklahoma St.	Charles Howell, Oklahoma St.
1957	Houston	Rex Baxter Jr., Houston	2001	Florida	Nick Gilliam, Florida
1958	Houston	Phil Rodgers, Houston	2002	Minnesota	Troy Matteson, Georgia Tech
1959	Houston	Dick Crawford, Houston			
1960	Houston	Dick Crawford, Houston			

Women's NCAA Division I Champions

College championships decided by stroke play since 1982.

Multiple winners (teams): Arizona St. (6); Arizona, Duke, Florida, San Jose St. and Tulsa (2).

Year	Team winner	Individual champion	Year	Team winner	Individual champion
1982	Tulsa	Kathy Baker, Tulsa	1994	Arizona St.	Emilee Klein, Ariz. St.
1983	TCU	Penny Hammel, Miami	1995	Arizona St.	K. Mourgue d'Algue, Ariz. St.
1984	Miami-FL	Cindy Schreyer, Georgia	1996	Arizona	Marisa Baena, Arizona
1985	Florida	Danielle Ammaccapane, Ariz.St.	1997	Arizona St.	Heather Bowie, Texas
1986	Florida	Page Dunlap, Florida	1998	Arizona St.	Jennifer Rosales, USC
1987	San Jose St.	Caroline Keggi, New Mexico	1999	Duke	Grace Park, Arizona St.
1988	Tulsa	Melissa McNamara, Tulsa	2000	Arizona	Jenna Daniels, Arizona
1989	San Jose St.	Pat Hurst, San Jose St.	2001	Georgia	Candy Hannemann, Duke
1990	Arizona St.	Susan Slaughter, Arizona	2002	Duke	Virada Nirapathpongporn, Duke
1991	UCLA	Annika Sorenstam, Arizona			
1992	San Jose St.	Vicki Goetze, Georgia			
1993	Arizona St.	Charlotta Sorenstam, Ariz. St.			

Auto Racing

Rubens Barrichello, left, takes the trophy handoff from Ferrari teammate **Michael Schumacher** at the Austrian Grand Prix.

AP/Wide World Photos

Shifting Gears

The success of NASCAR's young guns may signal a power shift on the Winston Cup circuit.

John Gettings *is associate editor of the ESPN/Information Please Sports Almanac.*

It had been a while since NASCAR's Winston Cup series had seen a good old-fashioned points race like the one it saw in 2002.

Seasons marked by Jeff Gordon-Ray Evernham dominance and a year shrouded in the tragic death of Dale Earnhardt have given way to the circuit's most entertaining race in years.

With four races to go in the season, five drivers were still in the thick of the championship hunt. And while it wasn't that surprising to find names like Tony Stewart, Mark Martin and Rusty Wallace in the top five, it's downright shocking to see two rookies there this late in the season.

Twenty-seven-year-old Jimmie Johnson and 24-year-old Ryan Newman clearly are no ordinary rookies. Johnson has driven the Gordon-owned #48 Chevrolet to unprecedented success, becoming the first rookie to win three races and lead the overall drivers point standings.

Newman was spectacular as well, especially in the second half of the season. His 14 top-five finishes through late October may be enough to fend off Johnson in the rookie of the year race.

And their history-making exploits don't end there. The duo also became the first rookies in the modern-era to sweep a Winston Cup front row, which they did at the Monte Carlo 400 at Richmond, Va.

Johnson and Newman were chasing points leader Stewart, who also happens to hold the previous best showing by a Winston Cup rookie in the drivers point standings—fourth place in 1999. While displaying an unusual level of maturity on the track, their youth occasionally shines through. When asked recently about the thought of winning the 2002 points championship, Johnson replied, "Right now, all I can say is that it would be cool."

AP/Wide World Photos

*Winston Cup rookie **Jimmie Johnson**, left, appears to be getting some good advice this year from owner **Jeff Gordon**. Johnson has three victories (through October), which is already more than Dale Earnhardt, Bill Elliott or Gordon had in their first season.*

CART

Even as driver Cristiano da Matta was in the midst of his impressive run through the competition on the CART circuit, rumors regarding a possible move to Formula One dogged him. The Brazilian da Matta clinched the points title with a win in his adopted hometown of Miami at the Grand Prix of the Americas on Oct. 6.

But observers wondered whether his stay atop the CART charts would be short-lived and if he would follow the path that so many recent CART champions have taken in changing lanes and going on to other circuits. Jacques Villeneuve went to F1 after winning the 1995 CART title, then Alex Zanardi, who won back-to-back Vanderbilt Cups in 1997 and 1998, joined Villeneuve on the international scene. Juan Montoya pulled a Zanardi a year after winning the drivers championship in 1999. Then Gil de Ferran, who won the series titles in 2000 and 2001, jumped to the Indy Racing League with Team Penske this year.

As it is, CART mainstays Michael Andretti and Christian Fittipaldi both have announced plans to defect for other opportunities, Fittipaldi to NASCAR and Andretti to the IRL.

*Don't be surprised if **Helio Castroneves** has the healthiest skin in auto racing right now. For the second straight year he captured the checkered flag at the Indianapolis 500, which comes with its own do-it-yourself milk bath.*

IRL

Sam Hornish Jr. took the IRL title for the second year in a row, beating runner-up Helio Castroneves in a thrilling finish at the season-ending Chevy 500. The two raced side-by-side down the stretch before Hornish bested the two-time Indy 500-winner by mere inches. It was Hornish's fifth win of the season, setting a new IRL record. Castroneves' victory at the Brickyard in 2002 was a controversial one in which second-place finisher Paul Tracy took the lead late in the race but was ruled to have passed Castroneves just after a caution flag had been issued on the 199th lap. After reviewing the incident for five and half hours following the race, officials finally determined Castroneves the winner.

Formula One

The story of the Formula One season is easy to tell. German star Michael Schumacher won an incredible single-season record 11 races this year. In fact, the big-budget Ferrari team dominated so thoroughly this season, they won 15 of 17 races. Schumacher and his teammate Rubens Barrichello took the top

continued on page 878 ▶

The Ten Biggest Stories of the Year in Auto Racing

10 ▪ The prestigious Indianapolis 500 is often referred to as "The Greatest Spectacle in Racing," but the 2002 event on May 26 isn't even the most-watched race of the day. NASCAR's Coca-Cola Racing Family 600 on Fox draws a rating of 5.1, edging ABC's Indy 500, which draws a 4.8.

9 ▪ IRL's Sarah Fisher makes history by becoming the first woman to win a pole position at a major series event. The 21-year-old sets a track record, 221.290 mph, in qualifying for the Belterra Casino 300 in August. She finishes the actual race in eighth.

8 ▪ Jeff Gordon, possibly distracted by a messy divorce battle with wife Brooke, goes 31 consecutive NASCAR races without a win. He finally ends his nightmarish streak at the Sharpie 500 in August after bumping leader Rusty Wallace, also mired in a long drought.

7 ▪ A restart after a late crash at the Daytona 500 causes a three-lap mad dash to the checkered flag. Dodge driver Ward Burton emerges victorious after front-runner Sterling Marlin is penalized for illegally jumping out of his car during the stoppage to fix his damaged front fender.

6 ▪ Brazilian Newman/Haas driver Cristiano da Matta wins a CART record-tying four consecutive races en route to his first FedEx Series title.

5 ▪ In a disputed finish, Helio Castroneves wins his second straight Indy 500. The outcome is appealed by the team of Paul Tracy, who claim Tracy passed Castroneves on the penultimate lap just before a yellow caution period began. The appeal was denied by IRL president Tony George.

4 ▪ Ferrari creates a stir by instructing driver Rubens Barrichello to allow teammate Michael Schumacher to pass him in the final stages of the Austrian Grand Prix. The team is fined by FIA when Schumacher hands the race trophy to Barrichello and has him stand on the top step of the podium. Schumacher seemingly returns the favor on Sept. 29, letting Barrichello win at Indianapolis.

3 ▪ CART is dealt a serious blow when its co-founder Roger Penske takes his team, including defending champ Gil de Ferran, to the rival IRL. Michael Andretti (to IRL) and Christian Fittipaldi (to NASCAR) later join the exodus.

2 ▪ With three wins and five starts from the pole through mid-October, NASCAR's Jimmie Johnson has the most successful rookie season in Winston Cup history.

1 ▪ German Michael Schumacher rewrites the Formula One record books, winning an astounding 11 races and seven poles in capturing his fifth World Drivers' Championship.

two spots in more than half of the races this year and finished 1-2 by a mile in the final Formula One drivers' standings. Schumacher also became the first driver in F1 history to finish in the top three of every grand prix as he won his record-tying (Juan Manuel Fangio) fifth career series title.

The dominance was too much for F1 organizers, however, as television ratings responded negatively to the predictable outcomes. Plans for slowing down the Ferraris could be in the works for 2003 and may include adding weights to the fastest cars and having drivers rotate among teams.

Horse Power

With 11 wins by Michael Schumacher and four more by teammate Rubens Barrichello, Ferrari equalled the all-time record for wins by a constructor, set by McLaren in 1988.

Constructor	Year	Wins
McLaren	1988	15
Ferrari	2002	15
Williams	1996	12
McLaren	1984	12
Bennetton	1995	11

Photo Finishes

The final two races of the 2002 IRL season (both won by Sam Hornish Jr.) had the closest finishes in league history. (Margins are in seconds.)

Track	Winner	Margin
Chicagoland (9/8/02)	Hornish Jr.	.0024
Texas (9/15/02)	Hornish Jr.	.0096
Texas (6/8/02)	Ward	.0111
Texas (10/6/01)	Hornish Jr.	.0188
California (3/24/02)	Hornish Jr.	.0281

Quick Learner

With his Sept. 1 win at the Mountain Dew Southern 500 at Darlington, four-time series champion Jeff Gordon became the seventh Winston Cup driver to win 60 career races. As the table to the right shows, it took him fewer races to accomplish the feat than any other driver in NASCAR history.

Driver	Starts to 60 wins	Career Wins
Jeff Gordon	318	61*
Darrell Waltrip	321	84
David Pearson	356	105
Richard Petty	358	200
Cale Yarborough	379	83
Dale Earnhardt	454	76
Bobby Allison	492	84
*through Oct. 20, 2002		

2001-2002
Season in Review

NASCAR RESULTS

Winston Cup Series

Winners of NASCAR Winston Cup races from Oct. 28, 2001 through Oct. 13, 2002. Note that earnings include bonus money. See Updates chapter for later results.

LATE 2001

Date	Event	Location	Winner (Pos.)	Avg.mph	Earnings	Pole	Qual.mph
Oct. 28	Checker Auto Parts 500	Phoenix	Jeff Burton (3)	102.613	$213,491	C. Atwood	131.295
Nov. 4	Pop Secret 400	Rockingham	Joe Nemechek (13)	128.941	157,535	K. Wallace	154.689
Nov. 11	Pennzoil 400	Homestead	Bill Elliott (1)	117.449	319,273	B. Elliott	155.226
Nov. 18	NAPA 500	Atlanta	Bobby Labonte (39)	151.746	233,227	D. Earnhardt Jr.	192.047
Nov. 23	New Hampshire 300	Loudon	Robby Gordon (31)	103.594	203,924	J. Gordon	—**

**Qualification cancelled. Pole awarded to current Winston Cup points leader.

Winning cars (2001 season): CHEVY MONTE CARLO (16)—J. Gordon (6), Earnhardt Jr. (3), Harvick (2), R. Gordon, Hamilton, Nemechek, Park, Waltrip; FORD TAURUS (11)—Jarrett (4), J. Burton (2), Rudd (2), Craven, Sadler, R.Wallace. PONTIAC GRAND PRIX (5)—Stewart (3), B. Labonte (2); DODGE INTREPID (4)—Marlin (2), W. Burton, Elliott.

2002 SEASON

Date	Event	Location	Winner (Pos.)	Avg.mph	Earnings	Pole	Qual.mph
Feb. 17	**Daytona 500**	Daytona	Ward Burton (19)	142.971	$1,383,017	J. Johnson	185.831
Feb. 24	Subway 400	Rockingham	Matt Kenseth (25)	115.478	157,400	R. Craven	156.008
Mar. 3	UAW-DaimlerChrysler 400	Las Vegas	Sterling Marlin (24)	136.754	412,842	T. Bodine	172.850
Mar. 10	MBNA America 500	Atlanta	Tony Stewart (9)	148.443	174,978	B. Elliott	191.542
Mar. 17	Dodge Dealers 400	Darlington	Sterling Marlin (11)	126.070	190,642	R. Craven	170.089
Mar. 24	Food City 500	Bristol	Kurt Busch (27)	82.281	143,840	J. Gordon	127.216
Apr. 7	Samsung/Radio Shack 500	Ft. Worth	Matt Kenseth (31)	142.453	418,275	B. Elliott	194.224
Apr. 14	Virginia 500	Martinsville	Bobby Labonte (15)	73.951	168,078	J. Gordon	94.180
Apr. 21	Aaron's 499	Talladega	Dale Earnhardt Jr. (4)	159.022	184,830	J. Johnson	186.532
Apr. 28	NAPA Auto Parts 500	Fontana	Jimmie Johnson (4)	150.088	176,750	R. Newman	187.432
May 5	Pontiac Excitement 400	Richmond	Tony Stewart (3)	86.824	185,653	W. Burton	127.388
May 18@	The Winston	Charlotte	Ryan Newman (27)	110.005	750,000	M. Kenseth	143.442
May 26	**Coca-Cola Racing Family 600**	Charlotte	Mark Martin (25)	137.729	1,280,033*	J. Johnson	186.464
June 2	MBNA Platinum 400	Dover	Jimmie Johnson (10)	117.551	152,400	M. Kenseth	154.938
June 9	Pocono 500	Long Pond	Dale Jarrett (13)	143.426	206,298	S. Marlin	—**
June 16	Sirius Satellite Radio 400	Brooklyn	Matt Kenseth (20)	154.822	154,100	D. Jarrett	189.070
June 23	Dodge/Save Mart 350	Sonoma	Ricky Rudd (7)	81.007	184,992	T. Stewart	93.475
July 6	Pepsi 400	Daytona	Michael Waltrip (7)	135.952	172,975	K. Harvick	185.040
July 14	Tropicana 400	Joliet	Kevin Harvick (32)	136.832	200,028	R. Newman	183.051
July 21	New England 300	Loudon	Ward Burton (31)	92.342	231,850	B. Elliott	131.469
July 28	Pennsylvania 500	Long Pond	Bill Elliott (1)	125.809	193,401	B. Elliott	170.567
Aug. 4	**Brickyard 400**	Indianapolis	Bill Elliott (2)	125.014	449,056	T. Stewart	182.960
Aug. 11	Sirius Satellite Radio at The Glen	Watkins Glen	Tony Stewart (3)	82.208	165,303	R. Rudd	122.695
Aug. 18	Pepsi 400	Brooklyn	Dale Jarrett (8)	140.556	179,530	D. Earnhardt Jr.	189.668
Aug. 22	Sharpie 500	Bristol	Jeff Gordon (1)	77.097	245,543	J. Gordon	124.034
Sept. 1	**Southern 500**	Darlington	Jeff Gordon (3)	118.617	217,183	S. Marlin	—**
Sept. 7	Chevy Monte Carlo 400	Richmond	Matt Kenseth (25)	94.787	163,595	J. Johnson	126.144
Sept. 15	New Hampshire 300†	Loudon	Ryan Newman (1)	105.081	202,550	R. Newman	132.241
Sept. 22	MBNA All-American Heroes 400	Dover	Jimmie Johnson (19)	120.805	152,735	R. Wallace	156.822
Sept. 29	Protection One 400	Kansas City	Jeff Gordon (10)	119.394	217,928	D. Earnhardt Jr.	177.924
Oct. 6	**EA Sports 500**	Talladega	Dale Earnhardt Jr. (13)	183.671	166,040	J. Johnson	—**
Oct. 13	UAW-GM Quality 500	Charlotte	Jamie McMurray (5)	141.481	215,717	T. Stewart	—**

*Includes $1 million Winston "No Bull 5" bonus.

@ Non-points exhibition event.

**Qualifying was cancelled due to inclement weather and the pole was awarded to the current Winston Cup points leader.

†Due to rain and darkness the New Hampshire 300 was shortened to 207 laps instead of the scheduled 300.

Winning Cars: FORD TAURUS (11)—Kenseth (4), Jarrett (2), Newman (2), Busch, Martin, Rudd; CHEVY MONTE CARLO (10)—J. Gordon (3), Johnson (3), Earnhardt Jr. (2), Harvick, Waltrip; DODGE INTREPID (7)—W. Burton (2), Elliott (2), Marlin (2), McMurray; PONTIAC GRAND AM (4)—Stewart (3), B. Labonte.

2002 NASCAR Winston Cup Race Locations

February—DAYTONA 500 at Daytona International Speedway in Daytona Beach, Fla.; SUBWAY 400 at North Carolina Motor Speedway in Rockingham, N.C.

March—UAW-DAIMLERCHRYSLER 400 at Las Vegas (Nev.) Motor Speedway; MBNA AMERICA 500 at Atlanta (Ga.) Motor Speedway; CAROLINA DODGE DEALERS 400 at Darlington (S.C.) International Raceway; FOOD CITY 500 at Bristol (Tenn.) Motor Speedway.

April—SAMSUNG/RADIO SHACK 500 at Texas Motor Speedway in Ft. Worth, Texas; VIRGINIA 500 at Martinsville (Va.) Speedway; AARON'S 499 at Talladega (Ala.) Superspeedway; NAPA AUTO PARTS 500 at California Speedway in Fontana, Calif.

May—PONTIAC EXCITEMENT 400 at Richmond (Va.) International Speedway; THE WINSTON at Lowe's Motor Speedway in Charlotte, N.C.; COCA-COLA RACING FAMILY 600 at Lowe's.

June—MBNA PLATINUM 400 at Dover (Del.) Downs International Speedway; POCONO 500 at Pocono International Raceway in Long Pond, Penn.; SIRIUS SATELLITE RADIO 400 at Michigan Speedway in Brooklyn, Mich.; DODGE/SAVE MART 350 at Infineon Raceway in Sonoma, Calif.

July—PEPSI 400 at Daytona; TROPICANA 400 at Chicagoland Speedway in Joliet, Ill.; NEW ENGLAND 300 at New Hampshire International Speedway in Loudon, N.H.; PENNSYLVANIA 500 at Pocono.

August—BRICKYARD 400 at Indianapolis (Ind.) Motor Speedway; SIRIUS SATELLITE RADIO AT THE GLEN at Watkins Glen (N.Y.) International; PEPSI 400 at Michigan; SHARPIE 500 at Bristol.

September—MOUNTAIN DEW SOUTHERN 500 at Darlington; CHEVROLET MONTE CARLO 400 at Richmond; NEW HAMPSHIRE 300 at New Hampshire; MBNA ALL-AMERICAN HEROES 400 at Dover Downs; PROTECTION ONE 400 at Kansas Speedway in Kansas City, Mo.

October—EA SPORTS 500 at Talladega; UAW-GM QUALITY 500 at Lowe's; OLD DOMINION 500 at Martinsville; NAPA 500 at Atlanta.

November—POP SECRET MICROWAVE POPCORN 400 at North Carolina; CHECKER AUTO PARTS 500 at Phoenix (Ariz.) International Raceway; FORD 400 at Miami-Dade Homestead Motorsports Complex in Homestead, Fla.

2002 Daytona 500

Date—Sunday, Feb. 17, 2002, at Daytona International Speedway. **Distance**—500 miles; **Course**—2.5 miles; **Field**—43 cars; **Average speed**—142.971 mph; **Margin of victory**—0.193 seconds; **Time of race**—3 hours, 29 minutes, 50 seconds; **Caution flags**—9 for 38 laps; **Lead changes**—20 among 12 drivers; **Lap leaders**—Marlin (78), Schrader (46), Waltrip (20), Gordon (19), Busch (15), W. Burton (5), Kenseth (4), Harvick, B. Labonte and Nadeau (3), J. Burton (2) and Andretti (1). **Pole sitter**—Jimmie Johnson at 185.831 mph; **Attendance**—150,000 (estimated). **Rating**—10.9/26 share (NBC). (r) indicates rookie driver.

Driver (start pos.)	Team	Car	Laps	Ended	Earnings
1 Ward Burton (19)	Caterpillar	Dodge Intrepid	200	Running	$1,362,430
2 Elliott Sadler (41)	Motorcraft	Ford Taurus	200	Running	957,037
3 Geoffrey Bodine (35)	Miccosukee Indian Gaming	Ford Taurus	200	Running	644,187
4 Kurt Busch (15)	Rubbermaid	Ford Taurus	200	Running	499,462
5 Michael Waltrip (4)	NAPA Auto Parts	Chevrolet Monte Carlo	200	Running	409,159
6 Mark Martin (39)	Pfizer/Viagra	Ford Taurus	200	Running	300,995
7 r-Ryan Newman (23)	ALLTEL	Ford Taurus	200	Running	246,587
8 Sterling Marlin (13)	Coors Light	Dodge Intrepid	200	Running	248,779
9 Jeff Gordon (3)	DuPont	Chevrolet Monte Carlo	200	Running	289,674
10 Johnny Benson (38)	Valvoline	Pontiac Grand Prix	200	Running	198,612
11 Bill Elliott (29)	Dodge Dealers/UAW	Dodge Intrepid	200	Running	189,968
12 Jeff Burton (33)	CITGO Racing	Ford Taurus	200	Running	201,026
13 Robby Gordon (12)	Cingular Wireless	Chevrolet Monte Carlo	200	Running	183,965
14 Dale Jarrett (21)	UPS	Ford Taurus	200	Running	179,787
15 r-Jimmie Johnson (1)	Lowe's	Chevrolet Monte Carlo	199	Running	159,463
16 Brett Bodine (27)	Wells Fargo /Timberland	Ford Taurus	199	Running	158,001
17 Ricky Craven (43)	Tide	Ford Taurus	199	Running	156,762
18 Rusty Wallace (37)	Miller Lite	Ford Taurus	198	Running	189,909
19 Jeff Green (30)	America Online	Chevrolet Monte Carlo	197	Running	145,334
20 Terry Labonte (11)	Kellogg's	Chevrolet Monte Carlo	194	Accident	184,170
21 Mike Wallace (17)	Autoliv	Chevrolet Monte Carlo	193	Running	175,707
22 Robert Pressley (31)	BrandSource.com	Dodge Intrepid	190	Engine	147,709
23 Mike Skinner (20)	Kodak	Chevrolet Monte Carlo	190	Running	147,034
24 Shawna Robinson (36)	BAM Racing	Dodge Intrepid	187	Running	142,559
25 Dave Blaney (42)	Jesper Engines & Transmissions	Ford Taurus	186	Running	152,925
26 Ken Schrader (7)	M&M's	Pontiac Grand Prix	179	Running	163,937
27 Stacy Compton (24)	Conseco	Pontiac Grand Prix	178	Running	143,859
28 Jerry Nadeau (8)	UAW/Delphi	Chevrolet Monte Carlo	174	Accident	162,359
29 Dale Earnhardt Jr. (5)	Budweiser	Chevrolet Monte Carlo	171	Running	175,137
30 Kenny Wallace (18)	Pennzoil	Chevrolet Monte Carlo	161	Running	169,709
31 Todd Bodine (22)	Kmart	Ford Taurus	158	Running	138,834
32 Bobby Hamilton (32)	Schneider Electric	Chevrolet Monte Carlo	156	Running	145,337
33 Matt Kenseth (40)	DeWalt Power Tools	Ford Taurus	154	Accident	145,062
34 Bobby Labonte (10)	Interstate Batteries	Pontiac Grand Prix	153	Engine	187,837
35 Casey Atwood (26)	Sirius Satellite Radio	Dodge Intrepid	153	Accident	136,984
36 Kevin Harvick (2)	GM Goodwrench	Chevrolet Monte Carlo	148	Accident	190,437
37 John Andretti (16)	Cheerios	Dodge Intrepid	148	Accident	163,292
38 Ricky Rudd (9)	Havoline	Ford Taurus	148	Accident	185,904
39 Jeremy Mayfield (28)	Dodge Dealers/UAW	Dodge Intrepid	148	Accident	143,159
40 Joe Nemechek (25)	Kmart School Spirit	Ford Taurus	148	Accident	159,174
41 Kyle Petty (34)	Sprint	Dodge Intrepid	146	Engine	133,912
42 Dave Marcis (14)	Realtree Camouflage	Chevrolet Monte Carlo	79	Engine	112,575
43 Tony Stewart (6)	Home Depot	Pontiac Grand Prix	2	Engine	197,848

Top 5 Finishing Order + Pole
2002 SEASON

No.	Event	Winner	2nd	3rd	4th	5th	Pole
1	Daytona 500	W. Burton	E. Sadler	G. Bodine	K. Busch	M. Waltrip	J. Johnson
2	Subway 400	M. Kenseth	S. Marlin	B. Labonte	T. Stewart	R. Craven	R. Craven
3	UAW-DaimlerChrysler 400	S. Marlin	J. Mayfield	M. Martin	R. Newman	T. Stewart	T. Bodine
4	MBNA America 500	T. Stewart	D. Earnhardt Jr.	J. Johnson	M. Kenseth	R. Craven	B. Elliott
5	Dodge Dealers 400	S. Marlin	E. Sadler	K. Harvick	D. Earnhardt Jr.	R. Newman	R. Craven
6	Food City 500	K. Busch	J. Spencer	R. Rudd	D. Earnhardt Jr.	B. Labonte	J. Gordon
7	Samsung/Radio Shack 500	M. Kenseth	J. Gordon	M. Martin	R. Rudd	T. Stewart	B. Elliott
8	Virginia 500	B. Labonte	M. Kenseth	T. Stewart	D. Jarrett	D. Earnhardt Jr.	J. Gordon
9	Aaron's 499	D. Earnhardt Jr.	M. Waltrip	K. Busch	J. Gordon	S. Marlin	J. Johnson
10	NAPA Auto Parts 500	J. Johnson	K. Busch	R. Rudd	B. Elliott	M. Martin	R. Newman
11	Pontiac Excitement 400	T. Stewart	R. Newman	J. Burton	M. Martin	J. Mayfield	W. Burton
12	Coca-Cola Racing Family 600	M. Martin	M. Kenseth	R. Craven	R. Rudd	J. Gordon	J. Johnson
13	MBNA Platinum 400	J. Johnson	B. Elliott	J. Burton	R. Newman	D. Jarrett	M. Kenseth
14	Pocono 500	D. Jarrett	M. Martin	J. Johnson	S. Marlin	J. Gordon	S. Marlin
15	Sirius Satellite Radio 400	M. Kenseth	D. Jarrett	R. Newman	M. Waltrip	J. Gordon	D. Jarrett
16	Dodge/Save Mart 350	R. Rudd	T. Stewart	T. Labonte	K. Busch	J. Green	T. Stewart
17	Pepsi 400	M. Waltrip	R. Wallace	S. Marlin	J. Spencer	M. Martin	K. Harvick
18	Tropicana 400	K. Harvick	J. Gordon	T. Stewart	J. Johnson	R. Newman	R. Newman
19	New England 300	W. Burton	J. Green	D. Jarrett	R. Wallace	R. Newman	B. Elliott
20	Pennsylvania 500	B. Elliott	K. Busch	S. Marlin	D. Jarrett	R. Newman	B. Elliott
21	Brickyard 400	B. Elliott	R. Wallace	M. Kenseth	R. Newman	K. Harvick	T. Stewart
22	Sirius Satellite Radio at The Glen	T. Stewart	R. Newman	R. Gordon	P. Jones	R. Rudd	R. Rudd
23	Pepsi 400	D. Jarrett	T. Stewart	K. Harvick	J. Burton	M. Martin	D. Earnhardt Jr.
24	Sharpie 500	J. Gordon	R. Wallace	D. Earnhardt Jr.	K. Harvick	M. Kenseth	J. Gordon
25	Southern 500	J. Gordon	R. Newman	B. Elliott	S. Marlin	D. Jarrett	S. Marlin
26	Chevy Monte Carlo 400	M. Kenseth	R. Newman	J. Green	D. Earnhardt Jr.	T. Bodine	J. Johnson
27	New Hampshire 300	R. Newman	K. Busch	T. Stewart	J. Benson	B. Labonte	R. Newman
28	MBNA Heroes 400	J. Johnson	M. Martin	D. Jarrett	M. Kenseth	T. Stewart	R. Wallace
29	Protection One 400	J. Gordon	R. Newman	R. Wallace	J. Nemechek	B. Elliott	D. Earnhardt Jr.
30	EA Sports 500	D. Earnhardt Jr.	T. Stewart	R. Rudd	K. Busch	J. Green	J. Johnson
31	UAW-GM Quality 500	J. McMurray	B. Labonte	T. Stewart	J. Gordon	R. Wallace	T. Stewart

Winston Cup Point Standings

Official Top 10 NASCAR Winston Cup point leaders and top-10 money leaders for 2001 and unofficial leaders for 2002. Points awarded for all qualifying drivers (winner receives 175) and lap leaders. Earnings include in-season bonuses. Listed are starts (Sts), top-5 finishes (1-2-3-4-5), poles won (PW) and points (Pts).

FINAL 2001

		Sts	Finishes 1-2-3-4-5	PW	Pts
1	Jeff Gordon	36	6-6-3-2-1	6	5112
2	Tony Stewart	36	3-3-2-3-4	0	4763
3	Sterling Marlin	36	2-3-2-1-4	3	4741
4	Ricky Rudd	36	2-2-5-4-1	1	4706
5	Dale Jarrett	36	4-2-1-4-1	4	4612
6	Bobby Labonte	36	2-1-1-1-2	1	4561
7	Rusty Wallace	36	1-0-2-2-3	0	4481
8	Dale Earnhardt Jr.	36	3-2-3-1-0	2	4460
9	Kevin Harvick	35	2-3-1-0-0	0	4406
10	Jeff Burton	36	2-1-2-1-3	0	4394

Other wins (9): Ward Burton, Ricky Craven, Bill Elliott, Robby Gordon, Bobby Hamilton, Joe Nemechek, Steve Park, Elliott Sadler and Michael Waltrip.

2002 (through Oct. 13)

		Sts	Finishes 1-2-3-4-5	PW	Pts
1	Tony Stewart	31	3-3-4-1-3	2*	4128
2	Jimmie Johnson	31	3-0-2-1-0	4*	4031
3	Mark Martin	31	1-2-2-1-3	0	4006
4	Ryan Newman	31	1-5-1-3-4	3	3963
5	Rusty Wallace	31	0-3-1-1-1	1	3946
6	Jeff Gordon	31	3-2-0-2-3	1	3917
7	Matt Kenseth	31	4-2-1-2-1	1	3823
8	Bill Elliott	31	2-1-1-1-1	4	3787
9	Kurt Busch	31	1-3-1-3-0	0	3766
10	Ricky Rudd	31	1-0-3-2-1	1	3758

*Does not include pole awarded for being points leader when qualification was cancelled.
Other wins (12): Ward Burton, Dale Earnhardt Jr., Dale Jarrett, Sterling Marlin (2 each); Kevin Harvick, Bobby Labonte, Jamie McMurray and Michael Waltrip.

Money Leaders

FINAL 2001

		Earnings
1	Jeff Gordon	$6,649,076
2	Dale Earnhardt Jr.	5,384,627
3	Dale Jarrett	4,608,366
4	Rusty Wallace	4,272,406
5	Bobby Labonte	4,139,851
6	Ricky Rudd	3,976,203
7	Jeff Burton	3,866,333
8	Kevin Harvick	3,716,633
9	Tony Stewart	3,493,043
10	Mark Martin	3,487,719

2002 (through Oct. 13)

		Earnings
1	Mark Martin	$4,668,390
2	Ward Burton	4,386,390
3	Jeff Gordon	4,354,118
4	Tony Stewart	4,179,429
5	Dale Earnhardt Jr.	4,173,381
6	Ryan Newman	3,978,201
7	Sterling Marlin	3,711,150
8	Rusty Wallace	3,565,690
9	Ricky Rudd	3,528,253
10	Dale Jarrett	3,459,293

CART RESULTS

Schedule and results of CART races from Oct. 28, 2001 through Oct. 13, 2002. Note that CART does not release per-race winnings. See Updates chapter for later results.

FedEx Championship Series

LATE 2001

Date	Event	Location	Winner (Pos.)	Time	Avg.mph	Pole	Qual.mph
Oct. 28	Honda Indy 300	Queensland	Cristiano da Matta (3)	1:51:47.260	97.511	R. Moreno	109.257
Nov. 4	Marlboro 500	Fontana	Cristiano da Matta (2)	2:59:39.716	149.073	A. Tagliani	228.727

Winning cars (entire 2001 season): REYNARD/HONDA (7)—Castroneves (3), de Ferran (2), Andretti, Franchitti; LOLA/FORD (6)—Brack (4), Papis (2); LOLA/TOYOTA (4)—da Matta (3), Junqueira; REYNARD/TOYOTA (2)—Dixon, Moreno; REYNARD/FORD (1)—Carpentier.

2002 SEASON

Date	Event	Location	Winner (Pos.)	Time	Avg.mph	Pole	Qual.mph
Mar. 10	Monterrey GP	Monterrey	Cristiano da Matta (5)	1:58:30.642	90.544	A. Fernandez	95.965
Apr. 14	Toyota GP	Long Beach	Michael Andretti (15)	2:02:14.542	86.935	J. Vasser	104.585
Apr. 27	Potenza 500	Montegi	Bruno Junqueira (1)	2:00:05.882	155.447	B. Junqueira	215.108
June 2	Miller Lite 250	Milwaukee	Paul Tracy (2)	1:59:27.602	129.583	A. Fernandez	167.532
June 9	GP of Monterey featuring the Shell 300	Monterey	Cristiano da Matta (1)	1:55:28.745	101.164	C. da Matta	115.970
June 16	G.I. Joe's 200	Portland	Cristiano da Matta (1)	2:03:19.113	105.381	C. da Matta	120.800
June 30	GP of Chicago	Cicero	Cristiano da Matta (3)	2:07:00.698	121.524	D. Franchitti	158.118
July 7	Molson Indy	Toronto	Cristiano da Matta (2)	2:06:19.372	93.361	C. da Matta	108.678
July 14	Marconi GP	Cleveland	Patrick Carpentier (2)	2:00:05.785	120.998	C. da Matta	132.917
July 28	Molson Indy	Vancouver	Dario Franchitti (3)	1:59:25.063	89.484	C. da Matta	106.260
Aug. 11	GP of Mid-Ohio	Lexington	Patrick Carpentier (1)	1:56:17.573	106.680	P. Carpentier	122.925
Aug. 18	Motorola 220	Elkhart Lake	Cristiano da Matta (2)	1:56:43.030	124.856	B. Junqueira	142.659
Aug. 25	Molson Indy	Montreal	Dario Franchitti (2)	1:59:40.938	108.648	C. da Matta	123.512
Sept. 1	GP of Denver	Denver	Bruno Junqueira (1)	1:49:22.547	90.349	B. Junqueira	96.093
Sept. 14	Rockingham 500	Corby	Dario Franchitti (5)	1:58:44.754	157.682	K. Brack	213.763
Oct. 6	GP of the Americas	Miami	Cristiano da Matta (6)	2:07:09.003	68.723	T. Kanaan	81.503

Note: The German 500, scheduled for Sept. 21, was cancelled. EuroSpeedway in Lausitz, Germany, which hosted last year's inaugural race, filed for bankruptcy in July and race officials said the track would not be ready to host the event.

Winning cars: LOLA/TOYOTA (9)—da Matta (7), Junqueira (2); LOLA/HONDA (4)—Franchitti (3), Tracy; FORD-COSWORTH/REYNARD (2)—Carpentier (2); REYNARD/HONDA (1)—Andretti.

2002 Race Locations

March—TECATE TELMEX MONTERREY GRAND PRIX at Fundidora Park in Monterrey, Mexico.

April—TOYOTA GP OF LONG BEACH in Long Beach, Calif.; BRIDGESTONE POTENZA 500 at Twin Ring Motegi in Motegi, Japan.

June—MILLER LITE 250 at The Milwaukee Mile in West Allis, Wis.; GRAND PRIX OF MONTEREY FEATURING THE SHELL 300 at Mazda Raceway Laguna Seca in Monterey, Calif.; GI JOE's 200 at Portland (Ore.) International Raceway; GRAND PRIX OF CHICAGO at Chicago Motor Speedway in Cicero, Ill.

July—MOLSON INDY TORONTO at Canadian National Exhibition Place in Toronto, Ontario, Canada; THE MARCONI GRAND PRIX OF CLEVELAND Presented by U.S. Bank at Burke Lakefront Airport in Cleveland, Ohio; MOLSON INDY VANCOUVER at Concord Pacific Place in Vancouver, B.C., Canada.

August—GRAND PRIX OF MID-OHIO at Mid-Ohio Sports Car Course in Lexington, Ohio; THE GRAND PRIX AT ROAD AMERICA Featuring the Motorola 220 at Road America in Elkhart Lake, Wis.; MOLSON INDY MONTREAL at Circuit Gilles Villeneuve in Montreal, Quebec, Canada.

September—SHELL GRAND PRIX OF DENVER in Denver, Colo.; THE SURE FOR MEN ROCKINGHAM 500 at Rockingham Motor Speedway, Corby, England.

October—GRAND PRIX AMERICAS at Bayfront Park, Miami, Fla.; HONDA INDY 300 at Surfer's Paradise, Queensland, Australia.

November—THE 500 Presented by Toyota at California Speedway in Fontana, Calif.; MEXICO GRAN PREMIO 2002 at Autodromo Hermanos Rodriguez in Mexico City, Mexico.

Top 5 Finishing Order + Pole

2002 Season

No.	Event	Winner	2nd	3rd	4th	5th	Pole
1	Monterrey GP	C. da Matta	D. Franchitti	C. Fittipaldi	M. Jourdain	A. Tagliani	A. Fernandez
2	Toyota GP	M. Andretti	J. Vasser	M. Papis	K. Brack	M. Jourdain	J. Vasser
3	Potenza 500	B. Junqueira	A. Tagliani	D. Franchitti	P. Carpenter	M. Jourdain	B. Junqueira
4	Miller Lite 250	P. Tracy	A. Fernandez	M. Papis	C. Fittipaldi	M. Jourdain	A. Fernandez
5	Bridgestone GP of Monterey	C. da Matta	C. Fittipaldi	K. Brack	B. Junqueira	P. Carpenter	C. da Matta
6	G.I. Joe's 200	C. da Matta	B. Junqueira	D. Franchitti	T. Bell	P. Carpenter	C. da Matta
7	GP of Chicago	C. da Matta	B. Junqueira	D. Franchitti	T. Takagi	S. Nakano	D. Franchitti
8	Molson Indy	C. da Matta	K. Brack	C. Fittipaldi	S. Nakano	S. Dixon	C. da Matta
9	Marconi GP	P. Carpenter	M. Andretti	P. Tracy	K. Brack	A. Tagliani	C. da Matta
10	Molson Indy	D. Franchitti	P. Tracy	T. Kanaan	M. Jourdain Jr.	P. Carpenter	C. da Matta
11	GP of Mid-Ohio	P. Carpenter	C. Fittipaldi	M. Andretti	B. Junqueira	S. Dixon	P. Carpenter
12	Motorola 220	C. da Matta	A. Tagliani	B. Junqueira	T. Kanaan	J. Vasser	B. Junqueira
13	Molson Indy	D. Franchitti	C. da Matta	T. Kanaan	P. Tracy	J. Vasser	A. Tagliani
14	GP of Denver	B. Junqueira	S. Dixon	C. da Matta	A. Fernandez	C. Fittipaldi	B. Junqueira
15	Rockingham 500	D. Franchitti	C. da Matta	P. Carpenter	O. Servia	B. Junqueira	K. Brack
16	GP of the Americas	C. da Matta	C. Fittipaldi	J. Vasser	A. Tagliani	B. Junqueira	T. Kanaan

CART Point Standings & Money Leaders (through Oct. 6)

Unofficial top-10 FedEx Championship Series point leaders and money leaders for 2002. Points awarded for places 1 to 12, pole winner at oval events, fastest driver on each day of qualifying at road/street events and overall lap leader. Listed are starts (Sts), top-5 finishes, poles won (PW) and points (Pts).

Points

		Sts	Finishes 1-2-3-4-5	PW	Pts
1	Cristiano da Matta	16	7-2-1-0-0	6	212
2	Bruno Junqueira	16	2-2-1-2-2	3	143
3	Dario Franchitti	16	3-2-3-0-0	1	129
4	Patrick Carpenter	16	2-0-1-1-3	1	115
5	Christian Fittipaldi	16	0-2-2-1-1	0	114
6	Michel Jourdain	16	0-0-0-2-3	0	102
7	Alex Tagliani	16	0-2-0-1-2	0	95
8	Michael Andretti	16	1-1-1-0-0	0	90
	Jimmy Vasser	16	0-1-1-0-2	1	90
10	Paul Tracy	16	1-1-1-1-0	0	87

Other poles (4): Adrian Fernandez (2), Kenny Brack and Tony Kanaan.

Earnings

		Earnings
1	Cristiano da Matta	$957,750
2	Dario Franchitti	632,000
3	Bruno Junqueira	599,750
4	Patrick Carpenter	506,500
5	Christian Fittipaldi	484,750
6	Michael Andretti	429,750
7	Paul Tracy	420,500
8	Alex Tagliani	399,250
9	Jimmy Vasser	372,750
10	Michel Jourdain	366,250

INDY RACING LEAGUE RESULTS

Schedule and results of Indy Racing League events during the 2002 season.

2002 SEASON

Date	Event	Location	Winner (Pos.)	Time	Avg.mph	Pole	Qual.mph
Mar. 2	GP of Miami	Miami	Sam Hornish Jr. (1)	2:08:16.4427	140.325	S. Hornish Jr.	202.884
Mar. 17	Copper World 200	Phoenix	Helio Castroneves (1)	1:43:00.0278	116.504	H. Castroneves	179.888
Mar. 24	Yamaha 400	Fontana	Sam Hornish Jr. (4)	2:13:49.2106	179.345	E. Cheever Jr.	221.422
Apr. 21	Firestone 225	Nazareth	Scott Sharp (11)	2:14:35.0016	93.789	G. de Ferran	172.778
May 26	**Indianapolis 500**	Indianapolis	Helio Castroneves (13)	3:00:10.8714	166.499	B. Junqueira	231.342
June 8	Boomtown 500	Ft. Worth	Jeff Ward (7)	1:45:49.7079	164.984	T. Scheckter	220.146
June 16	Radisson 225	Pikes Peak	Gil de Ferran (1)	1:51:08.6092	121.465	G. de Ferran	177.998
June 29	SunTrust Challenge	Richmond	Sam Hornish Jr. (3)	1:53:29.6359	99.124	G. de Ferran	168.705
July 7	Ameristar Casino 200	Kansas City	Airton Dare (6)	1:42:10.1790	178.527	T. Scheckter	218.547
July 20	Firestone 200	Nashville	Alex Barron (5)	2:01:52.6791	127.997	B. Boat	203.774
July 28	Michigan 400	Brooklyn	Tomas Scheckter (1)	2:14:02.7124	179.044	T. Scheckter	221.868
Aug. 11	Belterra Casino 300	Sparta	Felipe Giaffone (3)	1:59:10.5244	149.024	S. Fisher	221.390
Aug. 25	Gateway 250	St. Louis	Gil de Ferran (1)	1:44:22.5736	143.711	G. de Ferran	175.120
Sept. 8	Delphi 300	Joliet	Sam Hornish Jr. (3)	2:04:39.5354	146.319	M. Hornish Jr.	222.867
Sept. 15	Chevy 500	Ft. Worth	Sam Hornish Jr. (3)	1:46:28.5609	163.981	V. Meira	221.594

Winning cars: DALLARA/CHEVROLET (12)—Hornish Jr. (5), Castroneves (2), de Ferran (2), Barron, Dare and Sharp; G FORCE/CHEVROLET (2)—Giaffone, Ward; DALLARA/INFINITI (1)—Scheckter.

INDY RACING LEAGUE RESULTS (Cont.)

IRL Race Locations

March—20TH ANNIVERSARY GRAND PRIX OF MIAMI at Homestead-Miami (Fla.) Speedway; BOMBARDIER ATV COPPER WORLD INDY 200 at Phoenix (Ari.) International Raceway; YAMAHA 400 at California Speedway in Fontana, Calif. **April**—FIRESTONE INDY 225 at Nazareth (Pa.) Speedway. **May**—INDIANAPOLIS 500 at Indianapolis (Ind.) Motor Speedway. **June**—BOOMTOWN 500 at Texas Motor Speedway in Fort Worth, Texas; RADISSON INDY 225 at Pikes Peak International Raceway in Colorado Springs, Colo.; SUNTRUST INDY CHALLENGE at Richmond (Va.) International Raceway. **July**—AMERISTAR CASINO INDY 200 at Kansas Speedway in Kansas City, Mo.; FIRESTONE INDY 200 at Nashville (Tenn.) Superspeedway; MICHIGAN INDY 400 at Michigan International Speedway in Brooklyn, Mich. **August**—BELTERRA CASINO INDY 300 at Kentucky Speedway in Sparta, Ky.; GATEWAY INDY 250 at Gateway International Speedway in St. Louis, Mo. **September**—DELPHI INDY 300 at Chicagoland Speedway in Joliet, Ill.; CHEVY 500 at Texas Motor Speedway.

86th Indianapolis 500

Date—Sunday, May 26, 2002, at Indianapolis Motor Speedway. **Distance**—500 miles; **Course**—2.5 mile oval; **Field**—33 cars; **Winner's average speed**—166.499 mph; **Margin of victory**—under caution; **Time of race**—3 hours, 10.8714 seconds; **Caution flags**—5 for 35 laps; **Lead changes**—19 by 9 drivers; **Lap leaders**—Scheckter (85), Junqueira (32), Castroneves (24), Kanaan (23), de Ferran (13), Giaffone (12), Barron (7), Sharp (3), Unser Jr. (1); **Pole Sitter**—Bruno Junqueira at 231.342; **Attendance**—400,000 (est.); **TV Rating**—4.8/15 share (ABC). Note that (r) indicates rookie driver.

	Driver (start pos.)	Country	Car	Laps	Ended	Earnings
1	Helio Castroneves (13)	Brazil	D/C/F	200	Running	$1,606,215
2	Paul Tracy (29)	Canada	D/C/F	200	Running	489,315
3	Felipe Giaffone (4)	Brazil	G/C/F	200	Running	475,315
4	r-Alex Barron (26)	United States	D/C/F	200	Running	412,115
5	Eddie Cheever Jr. (6)	United States	D/I/F	200	Running	348,515
6	Richie Hearn (22)	United States	D/C/F	200	Running	330,815
7	Michael Andretti (25)	United States	D/C/F	200	Running	218,715
8	Robby Gordon (11)	United States	D/C/F	200	Running	204,000
9	Jeff Ward (15)	United States	G/C/F	200	Running	308,815
10	Gil de Ferran (14)	Brazil	D/C/F	200	Running	293,165
11	Kenny Brack (21)	Sweden	G/C/F	200	Running	188,315
12	Al Unser Jr. (12)	United States	D/C/F	199	Running	288,765
13	Airton Dare (30)	Brazil	D/C/F	199	Running	281,815
14	Arie Luyendyk (24)	Netherlands	G/C/F	199	Running	313,815
15	Buddy Lazier (20)	United States	D/C/F	198	Accident	277,615
16	Robbie Buhl (2)	United States	G/I/F	198	Running	288,315
17	r-George Mack (32)	United States	G/C/F	198	Running	283,565
18	Billy Boat (23)	United States	D/C/F	198	Running	283,315
19	r-Dario Franchitti (28)	Scotland	D/C/F	197	Running	153,565
20	r-Shigeaki Hattori (27)	Japan	D/I/F	197	Running	161,565
21	Raul Boesel (3)	Brazil	D/C/F	197	Running	268,315
22	r-Laurent Redon (16)	France	D/I/F	196	Accident	256,565
23	r-Max Papis (18)	Italy	D/I/F	196	Running	153,565
24	Sarah Fisher (9)	United States	G/I/F	196	Running	163,315
25	Sam Hornish Jr. (7)	United States	D/C/F	186	Running	253,815
26	r-Tomas Scheckter (10)	South Africa	D/I/F	172	Accident	294,815
27	Scott Sharp (8)	United States	D/C/F	137	Engine	255,655
28	r-Tony Kanaan (5)	Brazil	G/C/F	89	Accident	167,665
29	r-Rick Treadway (17)	United States	D/C/F	88	Accident	147,565
30	Jimmy Vasser (19)	United States	D/C/F	87	Gearbox	151,315
31	Bruno Junqueira (1)	Brazil	G/C/F	87	Gearbox	282,715
32	Mark Dismore (33)	United States	D/C/F	58	Handling	145,315
33	Greg Ray (31)	United States	D/C/F	28	Accident	245,315

Car Legend: Chassis/Engine/Tires. D—Dallara; G—G Force (chassis); C—Chevrolet Indy V-8; I—Nissan Infiniti V-8 (engine); F—Firestone (tires).

"The Double"

In 1994, John Andretti became the first driver to attempt "The Double," an auto racing double-header that involves racing in the Indianapolis 500 and NASCAR Winston Cup Series' Coca-Cola 600 on the same day. In addition to the 1,100 miles of racing (600 possible laps) and nearly seven hours of drive time, the feat requires the driver to travel from Indianapolis to Charlotte, N.C. (430 miles) between races.

Three different drivers in four years have completed "The Double." Here is a look at their results. Laps refers to laps completed.

		Indy 500		Coca-Cola 600	
Date	Driver	Finish	Laps	Finish	Laps
5/29/1994	John Andretti	10th	196	36th*	220
5/30/1999	Tony Stewart	9th	196	4th	400
5/27/2001	Tony Stewart	6th	200	3rd	400
5/26/2002	Robby Gordon	8th	200	16th	399

*Andretti's car had engine trouble and he did not finish the race.
Note: Robby Gordon attempted "The Double" in 1997 but rain postponed the Indianapolis 500 until the following Monday. He tried again in 2000 but a three hour rain delay at Indianapolis caused him to miss the start of the Coca-Cola 600.

Top 5 Finishing Order + Pole
2002 Season

No.	Event	Winner	2nd	3rd	4th	5th	Pole
1	GP of Miami	S. Hornish Jr.	G. de Ferran	H. Castroneves	J. Ward	E. Salazar	S. Hornish Jr.
2	Copper World 200	H. Castroneves	G. de Ferran	S. Hornish Jr.	E. Salazar	A. Unser Jr.	H. Castroneves
3	Yamaha 400	S. Hornish Jr.	J. Lazier	L. Redon	G. de Ferran	H. Castroneves	E. Cheever Jr.
4	Firestone 225	S. Sharp	F. Giaffone	G. de Ferran	S. Fisher	H. Castroneves	G. de Ferran
5	Indy 500	H. Castroneves	P. Tracy	F. Giaffone	A. Barron	E. Cheever Jr.	B. Junqueira
6	Boomtown 500	J. Ward	A. Unser Jr.	A. Dare	H. Castroneves	F. Giaffone	T. Scheckter
7	Radisson 225	G. de Ferran	H. Castroneves	S. Hornish Jr.	F. Giaffone	S. Sharp	G. de Ferran
8	SunTrust Challenge	S. Hornish Jr.	G. de Ferran	F. Giaffone	T. Scheckter	A. Unser Jr.	G. de Ferran
9	Ameristar Casino 200	A. Dare	S. Hornish Jr.	H. Castroneves	F. Giaffone	G. de Ferran	T. Scheckter
10	Firestone 200	A. Barron	G. de Ferran	S. Hornish Jr.	R. Hearn	R. Boesel	B. Boat
11	Michgan 400	T. Scheckter	B. Rice	F. Giaffone	T. Renna	G. de Ferran	T. Scheckter
12	Belterra Casino 300	F. Giaffone	S. Hornish Jr.	B. Lazier	S. Sharp	H. Castroneves	S. Fisher
13	Gateway 250	G. de Ferran	H. Castroneves	A. Barron	B. Rice	S. Hornish Jr.	G. de Ferran
14	Delphi 300	S. Hornish Jr.	A. Unser Jr.	B. Lazier	H. Castroneves	E. Cheever Jr.	S. Hornish Jr.
15	Chevy 500	S. Hornish Jr.	H. Castroneves	V. Meira	S. Sharp	A. Barron	V. Meira

Indy Racing League Point Standings & Money Leaders

Official top-10 Indy Racing League driver points leaders and money leaders for 2002. Points awarded for places 1 to 33 (winner receives 50) and overall lap leader. Listed are starts (Sts), top-5 finishes, poles won (PW) and points (Pts).

Points

		Sts	Finishes 1-2-3-4-5	PW	Pts
1	Sam Hornish Jr.	15	5-2-3-0-1	2	531
2	Helio Castroneves	15	2-3-2-2-3	1	511
3	Gil de Ferran	14	2-4-1-1-2	4	443
4	Felipe Giaffone	15	1-1-3-2-1	0	432
5	Alex Barron	15	1-0-1-1-1	0	366
6	Scott Sharp	15	1-0-0-2-1	0	332
7	Al Unser Jr.	13	0-2-0-0-2	0	311
8	Buddy Lazier	15	0-0-2-0-0	0	305
9	Airton Dare	15	1-0-1-0-0	0	304
10	Eddie Cheever Jr.	15	0-0-0-0-2	1	280

Earnings

		Earnings
1	Helio Castroneves	$2,512,965
2	Sam Hornish Jr.	1,435,615
3	Felipe Giaffone	1,306,315
4	Gil de Ferran	1,267,715
5	Alex Barron	1,119,765
6	Jeff Ward	944,015
7	Scott Sharp	933,215
8	Al Unser Jr.	931,015
9	Airton Dare	923,015
10	Buddy Lazier	900,265

Other wins (2): Jeff Ward and Tomas Scheckter.

Other poles (7): Tomas Scheckter (3), Billy Boat, Sarah Fisher, Bruno Junqueira and Vitor Meira.

FORMULA ONE RESULTS

Results of Formula One Grand Prix races in 2002.

2002 SEASON

Date	Grand Prix	Location	Winner (Pos.)	Time	Avg.mph	Pole	Qual.mph
Mar. 3	Australian	Melbourne	Michael Schumacher (2)	1:35:36.792	193.011	R. Barrichello	138.188
Mar. 17	Malaysian	Kuala Lumpur	Ralf Schumacher (4)	1:34:12.912	122.833	M. Schumacher	130.155
Mar. 31	Brazilian	Sao Paulo	Michael Schumacher (2)	1:31:43.663	124.335	J. Montoya	131.834
Apr. 14	San Marino	Imola	Michael Schumacher (1)	1:29:10.789	127.762	M. Schumacher	136.079
Apr. 28	Spanish	Barcelona	Michael Schumacher (1)	1:30:29.981	126.606	M. Schumacher	138.556
May 12	Austrian	Spielberg	Michael Schumacher (3)	1:33:51.562	122.002	R. Barrichello	142.137
May 26	Monaco	Monaco	David Coulthard (2)	1:45:39.055	92.758	J. Montoya	98.316
June 9	Canadian	Montreal	Michael Schumacher (2)	1:33:36.111	121.591	J. Montoya	135.778
June 23	European	Nürburgring	Rubens Barrichello (4)	1:35:07.426	121.006	J. Montoya	113.357
July 7	Great Britain	Silverstone	Michael Schumacher (3)	1:31:45.015	125.299	J. Montoya	120.345
July 21	French	Magny-Cours	Michael Schumacher (2)	1:32:09.837	123.737	J. Montoya	159.757
July 28	German	Hockenheim	Michael Schumacher (2)	1:27:52.078	130.029	M. Schumacher	205.233
Aug. 18	Hungarian	Budapest	Rubens Barrichello (1)	1:41:49.001	112.073	R. Barrichello	121.253
Sept. 1	Belgian	Spa	Michael Schumacher (1)	1:21:20.634	140.411	M. Schumacher	150.271
Sept. 15	Italian	Monza	Rubens Barrichello (4)	1:16:19.982	149.806	J. Montoya	161.450
Sept. 29	U.S.	Indianapolis	Rubens Barrichello (2)	1:31:07.934	125.191	M. Schumacher	132.466
Oct. 13	Japan	Suzuka	Michael Schumacher (1)	1:26:59.698	132.131	M. Schumacher	142.594

Winning Constructors: FERRARI (15)—M. Schumacher (11), Barrichello (4); MCLAREN/MERCEDES (1)—Coulthard (1); WILLIAMS/BMW (1)—R. Schumacher.

FORMULA ONE RESULTS (Cont.)
Top 5 + Pole Finishing Order

No.	Event	Winner	2nd	3rd	4th	5th	Pole
1	Australian	M. Schumacher	J. Montoya	K. Raikkonen	E. Irvine	M. Webber	R. Barrichello
2	Malaysian	R. Schumacher	J. Montoya	M. Schumacher	J. Button	N. Heidfeld	M. Schumacher
3	Brazilian	M. Schumacher	R. Schumacher	D. Coulthard	J. Button	J. Montoya	J. Montoya
4	San Marino	M. Schumacher	R. Barrichello	R. Schumacher	J. Montoya	J. Button	M. Schumacher
5	Spanish	M. Schumacher	J. Montoya	D. Coulthard	N. Heidfeld	F. Massa	M. Schumacher
6	Austrian	M. Schumacher	R. Barrichello	J. Montoya	R. Schumacher	G. Fisichella	R. Barrichello
7	Monaco	D. Coulthard	M. Schumacher	R. Schumacher	J. Trulli	G. Fisichella	J. Montoya
8	Canadian	M. Schumacher	D. Coulthard	R. Barrichello	K. Raikkonen	G. Fisichella	J. Montoya
9	European	R. Barrichello	M. Schumacher	K. Raikkonen	R. Schumacher	J. Button	J. Montoya
10	British	M. Schumacher	R. Barrichello	J. Montoya	J. Villeneuve	O. Panis	J. Montoya
11	French	M. Schumacher	K. Raikkonen	D. Coulthard	J. Montoya	R. Schumacher	J. Montoya
12	German	M. Schumacher	J. Montoya	R. Barrichello	D. Coulthard	M. Schumacher	J. Montoya
13	Hungarian	R. Barrichello	M. Schumacher	R. Schumacher	K. Raikkonen	D. Coulthard	R. Barrichello
14	Belgian	M. Schumacher	R. Barrichello	J. Montoya	D. Coulthard	R. Schumacher	M. Schumacher
15	Italian	R. Barrichello	M. Schumacher	E. Irvine	J. Trulli	J. Button	J. Montoya
16	U.S.	R. Barrichello	M. Schumacher	D. Coulthard	J. Montoya	J. Trulli	M. Schumacher
17	Japan	M. Schumacher	R. Barrichello	K. Raikkonen	J. Montoya	T. Sato	M. Schumacher

Formula One Point Standings

Official top-10 Formula One World Drivers and Constructors Championship point leaders for 2002. Points awarded for places 1 through 6 only (i.e., 10-6-4-3-2-1). Listed are starts (Sts), top-6 finishes, poles won (PW) and points (Pts). **Note:** Formula One does not keep money leader standings.

FINAL 2002 (Drivers)

		Sts	Finishes 1-2-3-4-5-6	PW	Pts
1	Michael Schumacher	17	11-5-1-0-0-0	7	144
2	Rubens Barrichello	15	4-5-1-1-0-0	3	77
3	Juan Montoya	17	0-4-3-4-1-0	7	50
4	Ralf Schumacher	17	1-1-4-3-2-0	0	42
5	David Coulthard	17	1-1-4-1-2-2	0	41
6	Kimi Raikkonen	17	0-1-3-1-0-0	0	24
7	Jenson Button	17	0-0-0-2-3-1	0	14
8	Jarno Trulli	17	0-0-0-0-2-1	0	9
9	Eddie Irvine	17	0-0-1-1-0-1	0	8
10	Nick Heidfeld	12	0-0-0-1-1-1	0	7
	Giancarlo Fisichella	16	0-0-0-0-3-1	0	7

FINAL 2002 (Constructors)

		Pts
1	Ferrari	221
2	Williams BMW	92
3	McLaren Mercedes	65
4	Renault	23
5	Sauber Petronas	11
6	Jordan Honda	9
7	Jaguar	8
8	BAR Honda	7
9	Minardi	2
	Toyota	2
	Arrows Cosworth	2

Major 2002 Endurance Races

24 Hours of Daytona
Feb. 2-3, at Daytona Beach, Fla.

Officially the Rolex 24 at Daytona and first held in 1962 (as a 3-hour race). An IMSA Camel GT race for exotic prototype sports cars and contested over a 3.56-mile road course at Daytona International Speedway. Listed are qualifying position, drivers, chassis, class and laps completed.
1 (1) Didier Theys, Fredy Lienhard, Max Papis and Mauro Baldi; JUDD DALLARA; 716 laps (2,548.96 miles) at 106.143 mph; margin of victory six laps.
2 (4) Guy Smith, Jim Matthews, Scott Sharp and Robby Gordon; ELAN R&S, 710 laps.
3 (17) Anthony Lazzaro, Bill Rand, Terry Borcheller and Ralf Kelleners; NISSAN LOLA, 695 laps.
4 (8) Andy Wallace, Hurley Haywood, Sascha Maassen, and Lucas Luhr; PORSCHE LOLA; 681 laps.
5 (15) Paul Gentilozzi, Brian Simo, Scott Pruett and Michael Lauer; JAGUAR; 575 laps.
Top qualifier: Didier Theys, JUDD DALLARA, 125.576 mph (1:42.058).
Weather: Clear. **Attendance:** 40,000 (est.).

24 Hours of Le Mans
June 15-16, at Le Mans, France

Officially the Le Mans Grand Prix d'Endurance and first held in 1923. Contested over the 8.62-mile Circuit de la Sarthe in Le Mans, France. Listed are qualifying position, drivers, car, and laps completed.
1 (2) Tom Kristensen, Frank Biela and Emanuele Pirro; AUDI R8; 375 laps (3,232.50 miles).
2 (1) Johnny Herbert, Rinaldo Capello and Christian Pescatori; AUDI R8; 374 laps.
3 (3) Michael Krumm, Philipp Peter and Marco Werner; AUDI R8; 372 laps.
4 (11) Andy Wallace, Eric van de Poele and Butch Leitzinger; BENTLEY EXP SPEED 8; 362 laps.
5 (7) Olivier Beretta, Erik Comas and Pedro Lamy; DALLARA JUDD LMP; 359 laps.
Top qualifier: Johnny Herbert, AUDI R8, 145.466 mph (3:29.905).
Weather: Clear. **Attendance:** 220,000 (est.).

NHRA RESULTS

Winners of National Hot Rod Association Drag Racing events in the Top Fuel, Funny Car and Pro Stock divisions through Oct. 13, 2002. All times are based on two cars racing head-to-head from a standing start over a straight line, quarter-mile course. Differences in reaction time account for apparently faster losing times.

2002 Season

Date	Event	Event	Winner	Time	MPH	2nd Place	Time	MPH
Feb. 10	K&N Filters Winternationals...	Top Fuel	Larry Dixon	4.535	324.75	K. Bernstein	4.612	324.67
		Funny Car	John Force	6.260	219.76	D. Worsham	6.642	243.68
		Pro Stock	George Marnell	6.880	200.89	J. Yates	6.812	202.61
Feb. 24	Kragen Nationals	Top Fuel	Tony Schumacher	4.946	299.40	L. Dixon	5.044	296.89
		Funny Car	Del Worsham	4.940	312.86	J. Force	7.749	114.25
		Pro Stock	Bruce Allen	6.904	199.02	W. Johnson	7.470	148.76
Mar. 17	Mac Tools Gatornationals	Top Fuel	Larry Dixon	4.629	319.75	K. Bernstein	4.677	319.29
		Funny Car	Tony Pedregon	5.090	281.25	G. Scelzi	5.750	197.13
		Pro Stock	Darrell Alderman	6.927	200.77	J. Coughlin	6.940	200.14
Apr. 7	SummitRacing.com Nationals...	Top Fuel	Larry Dixon	4.639	319.29	C. McClenathan	4.728	319.29
		Funny Car	Gary Densham	5.409	205.13	T. Johnson Jr.	5.447	272.61
		Pro Stock	Ron Krisher	7.016	197.83	D. Alderman	7.026	197.54
Apr. 14	O'Reilly Spring Nationals	Top Fuel	Kenny Bernstein	4.695	319.37	T. Schumacher	4.900	304.94
		Funny Car	John Force	4.991	310.20	T. Johnson Jr.	5.170	288.77
		Pro Stock	Mike Edwards	6.892	199.70	K. Johnson	6.910	200.77
Apr. 28	Thunder Valley Nationals	Top Fuel	Larry Dixon	4.644	317.87	D. Russell	4.977	268.01
		Funny Car	Whit Bazemore	4.936	310.27	G. Densham	6.400	141.67
		Pro Stock	Warren Johnson	6.986	198.41	R. Krisher	6.975	198.15
May 5	Southern Nationals	Top Fuel	Larry Dixon	4.637	318.09	D. Hebert	5.039	231.87
		Funny Car	Whit Bazemore	4.963	310.41	J. Force	5.559	195.51
		Pro Stock	Allen Johnson	6.907	200.92	G. Anderson	7.676	138.41
May 19	Matco Tools SuperNationals .	Top Fuel	Kenny Bernstein	4.600	321.96	L. Dixon	4.818	319.90
		Funny Car	Gary Densham	5.046	316.38	B. Sarver	7.310	115.29
		Pro Stock	Greg Anderson	6.808	201.91	J. Coughlin	6.812	202.33
May 26	O'Reilly Summer Nationals ...	Top Fuel	Darrell Russell	4.638	314.90	L. Dixon	4.670	316.38
		Funny Car	Tony Pedregon	4.910	320.58	T. Wilkerson	4.999	302.69
		Pro Stock	Troy Coughlin	6.924	198.44	M. Whisnant	6.991	197.59
June 2	Chicagoland Dodge Dealers Nationals.................	Top Fuel	Larry Dixon	4.580	319.37	K. Bernstein	4.620	317.72
		Funny Car	Del Worsham	4.878	312.21	S. Cannon	11.208	78.21
		Pro Stock	Bruce Allen	6.888	199.55	T. Hammonds	6.869	199.61
June 16	Pontiac Excitement Nationals...	Top Fuel	Larry Dixon	4.619	319.14	D. Herbert	6.278	163.61
		Funny Car	Ron Capps	6.027	235.60	B. Sarver	6.942	257.97
		Pro Stock	Greg Anderson	6.924	199.05	D. Alderman	11.094	79.81
June 30	Sears Craftsman Nationals ...	Top Fuel	Kenny Bernstein	5.065	293.22	A. Cowin	5.291	263.87
		Funny Car	John Force	8.837	87.98	S. Cannon	5.053	295.85*
		Pro Stock	Jeg Coughlin	6.928	199.52	G. Anderson	6.930	199.91
July 21	Mile-High Nationals	Top Fuel	Darrell Russell	4.898	295.53	C. McClenathan	4.877	301.07
		Funny Car	Del Worsham	5.160	293.15	T. Pedregon	5.193	291.13
		Pro Stock	Mike Edwards	7.339	188.41	A. Johnson	7.347	189.07
July 28	Northwest Nationals........	Top Fuel	Darrell Russell	4.657	308.00	K. Bernstein	5.788	159.12
		Funny Car	Tony Pedregon	5.049	293.22	B. Sarver	6.827	130.15
		Pro Stock	Jeg Coughlin	6.864	200.14	M. Whisnant	9.309	96.20
Aug. 4	Autolite Nationals	Top Fuel	Doug Herbert	4.727	308.85	D. Kalitta	4.766	305.36
		Funny Car	John Force	4.953	303.09	R. Capps	4.956	300.46
		Pro Stock	Larry Morgan	6.845	201.58	G. Anderson	6.799	202.45
Aug. 18	Rugged Liner Nationals	Top Fuel	Kenny Bernstein	4.830	303.16	L. Dixon	5.410	218.12
		Funny Car	John Force	5.405	216.62	G. Densham	6.929	130.27
		Pro Stock	Jeg Coughlin	6.918	199.11	G. Anderson	6.984	199.82
Sept. 2	Mac Tools U.S. Nationals	Top Fuel	Tony Schumacher	4.663	315.93	L. Dixon	5.161	240.29
		Funny Car	John Force	5.028	280.02	T. Johnson Jr.	4.996	308.43
		Pro Stock	Jeg Coughlin	6.953	199.08	J. Yates	6.934	200.08
Sept. 16	Lucas Oil Nationals	Top Fuel	Doug Kalitta	4.560	320.51	K. Bernstein	4.581	322.11
		Funny Car	Tony Pedregon	4.829	318.62	W. Bazemore	4.814	319.98
		Pro Stock	Jim Yates	6.870	199.67	M. Edwards	6.911	199.43
Sept. 22	O'Reilly Mid-South Nationals.................	Top Fuel	Larry Dixon	4.600	318.69	T. Schumacher	4.798	286.44
		Funny Car	Tony Pedregon	4.909	315.12	D. Worsham	5.144	263.15
		Pro Stock	Jeg Coughlin	6.849	200.80	G. Wilson	6.877	200.20
Sept. 29	Craftsman 75th Anniversary Nationals.................	Top Fuel	Doug Kalitta	4.594	323.27	D. Russell	7.331	120.74
		Funny Car	Tony Pedregon	4.924	310.84	R. Capps	6.403	145.85
		Pro Stock	Jeg Coughlin	6.875	200.89	R. Krisher	6.896	200.02
Oct. 13	O'Reilly Fall Nationals	Top Fuel	Doug Kalitta	4.582	322.58	C. McClenathan	6.565	130.62
		Funny Car	Del Worsham	4.862	319.48	B. Sarver	broke	—
		Pro Stock	Jeg Coughlin	6.826	202.33	G. Wilson	6.833	202.33

*Scotty Cannon was disqualified for a false start and John Force coasted to victory.

NASCAR CIRCUIT
The Crown Jewels

The five biggest races on the NASCAR (National Association for Stock Car Auto Racing) circuit are the Daytona 500, the EA Sports 500, the Coca-Cola 600, the Mountain Dew Southern 500, and the Brickyard 400. They are the Winston Cup Series' biggest (Daytona), fastest (EA Sports), longest (Coca-Cola), oldest (Southern) and richest (Brickyard) races. The only drivers to win three of the races in a year are Lee Roy Yarbrough (1969), David Pearson (1976), Bill Elliott (1985) Dale Jarrett (1996) and Jeff Gordon (1997-98).

Daytona 500

Held over 200 laps on 2.5-mile oval at Daytona International Speedway in Daytona Beach, Fla. First race in 1959, although stock car racing at Daytona dates back to 1936. Winners who started from pole position are in **bold** type.

Multiple winners: Richard Petty (7); Cale Yarborough (4); Bobby Allison and Dale Jarrett (3); Bill Elliott, Jeff Gordon and Sterling Marlin (2). **Multiple poles:** Buddy Baker and Cale Yarborough (4); Bill Elliott, Dale Jarrett, Fireball Roberts and Ken Schrader (3); Donnie Allison (2).

Year	Winner	Car	Owner	MPH	Pole Sitter	MPH
1959	Lee Petty	Oldsmobile	Petty Enterprises	135.521	Bob Welborn	140.121
1960	Junior Johnson	Chevrolet	Ray Fox	124.740	Cotton Owens	149.892
1961	Marvin Panch	Pontiac	Smokey Yunick	149.601	Fireball Roberts	155.709
1962	**Fireball Roberts**	Pontiac	Smokey Yunick	152.529	Fireball Roberts	156.999
1963	Tiny Lund	Ford	Wood Brothers	151.566	Fireball Roberts	160.943
1964	Richard Petty	Plymouth	Petty Enterprises	154.334	Paul Goldsmith	174.910
1965-a	Fred Lorenzen	Ford	Holman-Moody	141.539	Darel Dieringer	171.151
1966-b	**Richard Petty**	Plymouth	Petty Enterprises	160.627	Richard Petty	175.165
1967	Mario Andretti	Ford	Holman-Moody	149.926	Curtis Turner	180.831
1968	**Cale Yarborough**	Mercury	Wood Brothers	143.251	Cale Yarborough	189.222
1969	Lee Roy Yarbrough	Ford	Junior Johnson	157.950	Buddy Baker	188.901
1970	Pete Hamilton	Plymouth	Petty Enterprises	149.601	Cale Yarborough	194.015
1971	Richard Petty	Plymouth	Petty Enterprises	144.462	A.J. Foyt	182.744
1972	A.J. Foyt	Mercury	Wood Brothers	161.550	Bobby Isaac	186.632
1973	Richard Petty	Dodge	Petty Enterprises	157.205	Buddy Baker	185.662
1974-c	Richard Petty	Dodge	Petty Enterprises	140.894	David Pearson	185.017
1975	Benny Parsons	Chevrolet	L.G. DeWitt	153.649	Donnie Allison	185.827
1976	David Pearson	Mercury	Wood Brothers	152.181	Ramo Stott	183.456
1977	Cale Yarborough	Chevrolet	Junior Johnson	153.218	Donnie Allison	188.048
1978	Bobby Allison	Ford	Bud Moore	159.730	Cale Yarborough	187.536
1979	Richard Petty	Oldsmobile	Petty Enterprises	143.977	Buddy Baker	196.049
1980	**Buddy Baker**	Oldsmobile	Ranier Racing	177.602*	Buddy Baker	194.099
1981	Richard Petty	Buick	Petty Enterprises	169.651	Bobby Allison	194.624
1982	Bobby Allison	Buick	DiGard Racing	153.991	Benny Parsons	196.317
1983	Cale Yarborough	Pontiac	Ranier Racing	155.979	Ricky Rudd	198.864
1984	**Cale Yarborough**	Chevrolet	Ranier Racing	150.994	Cale Yarborough	201.848
1985	**Bill Elliott**	Ford	Melling Racing	172.265	Bill Elliott	205.114
1986	Geoff Bodine	Chevrolet	Hendrick Motorsports	148.124	Bill Elliott	205.039
1987	**Bill Elliott**	Ford	Melling Racing	176.263	Bill Elliott	210.364†
1988	Bobby Allison	Buick	Stavola Brothers	137.531	Ken Schrader	198.823
1989	Darrell Waltrip	Chevrolet	Hendrick Motorsports	148.466	Ken Schrader	196.996
1990	Derrike Cope	Chevrolet	Bob Whitcomb	165.761	Ken Schrader	196.515
1991	Ernie Irvan	Chevrolet	Morgan-McClure	148.148	Davey Allison	195.955
1992	Davey Allison	Ford	Robert Yates	160.256	Sterling Martin	192.213
1993	Dale Jarrett	Chevrolet	Joe Gibbs Racing	154.972	Kyle Petty	189.426
1994	Sterling Marlin	Chevrolet	Morgan-McClure	156.931	Loy Allen	190.158
1995	Sterling Marlin	Chevrolet	Morgan-McClure	141.710	Dale Jarrett	193.498
1996	Dale Jarrett	Ford	Robert Yates	154.308	Dale Earnhardt	189.510
1997	Jeff Gordon	Chevrolet	Rick Hendrick	148.295	Mike Skinner	189.813
1998	Dale Earnhardt	Chevrolet	Richard Childress	172.712	Bobby Labonte	192.415
1999	**Jeff Gordon**	Chevrolet	Rick Hendrick	161.551	Jeff Gordon	195.067
2000	**Dale Jarrett**	Ford	Robert Yates	155.669	Dale Jarrett	191.091
2001	Michael Waltrip	Chevrolet	Dale Earnhardt, Inc.	161.783	Bill Elliott	183.565
2002	Ward Burton	Dodge	Bill Davis	142.971	Jimmie Johnson	185.831

*Track and race record for winning speed. †Track and race record for qualifying speed.
Notes: a—rain shortened 1965 to 332+ miles; **b**—rain shortened 1966 race to 495 miles; **c**—in 1974, race shortened 50 miles due to energy crisis. **Also:** Pole sitters determined by pole qualifying race (1959-65); by two-lap average (1966-68); by fastest single lap (since 1969).

EA Sports 500

Held over 188 laps on 2.66-mile tri-oval at Talladega Superspeedway in Talladega, Ala.

Previously known as Winston 500 (1970-93, 1997-2000) and Winston Select 500 (1994-96). It's been EA Sports 500 since 2001. Winners who started from pole position are in **bold** type.

Multiple winners: Dale Earnhardt (4); Bobby Allison, Davey Allison, Buddy Baker and David Pearson (3); Dale Earnhardt Jr., Mark Martin, Darrell Waltrip and Cale Yarborough (2).

Year		Year		Year		Year	
1970	Pete Hamilton	1979	Bobby Allison	1987	Davey Allison	1995	**Mark Martin**
1971	**Donnie Allison**	1980	Buddy Baker	1988	Phil Parsons	1996	Sterling Marlin
1972	David Pearson	1981	**Bobby Allison**	1989	Davey Allison	1997	Mark Martin
1973	David Pearson	1982	Darrell Waltrip			1998	Dale Jarrett
1974	**David Pearson**	1983	Richard Petty	1990	**Dale Earnhardt**	1999	Dale Earnhardt
1975	**Buddy Baker**	1984	**Cale Yarborough**	1991	Harry Gant		
1976	Buddy Baker	1985	**Bill Elliott**	1992	Davey Allison	2000	Dale Earnhardt
1977	Darrell Waltrip	1986	Bobby Allison	1993	Ernie Irvan	2001	Dale Earnhardt Jr.
1978	**Cale Yarborough**			1994	Dale Earnhardt	2002	Dale Earnhardt Jr.

Coca-Cola 600

Held over 400 laps on 1.5-mile oval at Lowe's Motor Speedway in Concord, N.C.

Previously known as World 600 (1960-85). It has been Coca-Cola 600 since 1986 (in 2002, sponsors announced a one-time-only name change to The Coca-Cola Racing Family 600). Winners who started from pole position are in **bold** type.

Multiple winners: Darrell Waltrip (5); Bobby Allison, Buddy Baker, Dale Earnhardt, Jeff Gordon and David Pearson (3); Neil Bonnett, Jeff Burton, Fred Lorenzen, Jim Paschal and Richard Petty (2).

Year		Year		Year		Year	
1960	Joe Lee Johnson	1971	Bobby Allison	1982	Neil Bonnett	1993	Dale Earnhardt
1961	David Pearson	1972	Buddy Baker	1983	Neil Bonnett	1994	**Jeff Gordon**
1962	Nelson Stacy	1973	**Buddy Baker**	1984	Bobby Allison	1995	Bobby Labonte
1963	Fred Lorenzen	1974	**David Pearson**	1985	Darrell Waltrip	1996	Dale Jarrett
1964	Jim Paschal	1975	Richard Petty	1986	Dale Earnhardt	1997	**Jeff Gordon**
1965	**Fred Lorenzen**	1976	**David Pearson**	1987	Kyle Petty	1998	**Jeff Gordon**
1966	Marvin Panch	1977	Richard Petty	1988	Darrell Waltrip	1999	Jeff Burton
1967	Jim Paschal	1978	Darrell Waltrip	1989	Darrell Waltrip		
1968	Buddy Baker	1979	Darrell Waltrip	1990	Rusty Wallace	2000	Matt Kenseth
1969	Lee Roy Yarbrough			1991	Davey Allison	2001	Jeff Burton
1970	Donnie Allison	1980	Benny Parsons	1992	Dale Earnhardt	2002	Mark Martin
		1981	Bobby Allison				

Mountain Dew Southern 500

Held over 367 laps on 1.366-mile oval at Darlington International Raceway in Darlington, S.C.

Previously known as Southern 500 (1950-88); Heinz 500 (1989-91); and Pepsi Southern 500 (1998-2000). It was the Mountain Dew Southern 500 from 1992-97, and since 2001. Winners who started from pole position are in **bold** type.

Multiple winners: Jeff Gordon and Cale Yarborough (5); Bobby Allison (4); Buck Baker, Dale Earnhardt, Bill Elliott, David Pearson and Herb Thomas (3); Harry Gant and Fireball Roberts (2).

Year		Year		Year		Year	
1950	Johnny Mantz	1964	Buck Baker	1978	Cale Yarborough	1991	Harry Gant
1951	Herb Thomas	1965	Ned Jarrett	1979	David Pearson	1992	Darrell Waltrip
1952	**Fonty Flock**	1966	Darel Dieringer			1993	Mark Martin
1953	Buck Baker	1967	**Richard Petty**	1980	Terry Labonte	1994	Bill Elliott
1954	Herb Thomas	1968	Cale Yarborough	1981	Neil Bonnett	1995	Jeff Gordon
1955	Herb Thomas	1969	Lee Roy Yarbrough	1982	Cale Yarborough	1996	Jeff Gordon
1956	Curtis Turner			1983	Bobby Allison	1997	Jeff Gordon
1957	Speedy Thompson	1970	Buddy Baker	1984	**Harry Gant**	1998	Jeff Gordon
1958	Fireball Roberts	1971	**Bobby Allison**	1985	**Bill Elliott**	1999	Jeff Burton
1959	Jim Reed	1972	**Bobby Allison**	1986	**Tim Richmond**		
		1973	Cale Yarborough	1987	Dale Earnhardt	2000	Bobby Labonte
1960	Buck Baker	1974	Cale Yarborough	1988	**Bill Elliott**	2001	Ward Burton
1961	Nelson Stacy	1975	Bobby Allison	1989	Dale Earnhardt	2002	Jeff Gordon
1962	Larry Frank	1976	**David Pearson**				
1963	Fireball Roberts	1977	David Pearson	1990	**Dale Earnhardt**		

Brickyard 400

Held over 160 laps at 2.5-mile Indianapolis Motor Speedway in Indianapolis, Ind.

Winners who started from pole position are in **bold** type.

Multiple winners: Jeff Gordon (3); Dale Jarrett (2).

Year		Year		Year		Year		Year	
1994	Jeff Gordon	1996	Dale Jarrett	1998	Jeff Gordon	2000	Bobby Labonte	2002	Bill Elliott
1995	Dale Earnhardt	1997	Ricky Rudd	1999	Dale Jarrett	2001	Jeff Gordon		

NASCAR Circuit (Cont.)
Winston Cup Series Champions

Originally the Grand National Championship, 1949-70, and based on official NASCAR records. Note that earnings totals include bonus awards.

Multiple winners: (drivers) Dale Earnhardt and Richard Petty (7); Jeff Gordon (4); David Pearson, Lee Petty, Darrell Waltrip and Cale Yarborough (3); Buck Baker, Tim Flock, Ned Jarrett, Terry Labonte, Herb Thomas and Joe Weatherly (2).

Multiple winners: (cars) Chevrolet (22); Ford (6); Plymouth (5); Dodge and Oldsmobile (4); Buick, Hudson and Pontiac (3); and Chrysler (2).

Year	Car #	Driver	Car	Owner	Sts	Wins	Poles	Earnings
1949	22	**Red Byron**	Oldsmobile	Raymond Parks	5	2	1	$5,800
1950	60	**Bill Rexford**	Oldsmobile	Julian Buesink	17	1	0	6,175
1951	92	**Herb Thomas**	Hudson	Herb Thomas	34	7	4	18,200
1952	91	**Tim Flock**	Hudson	Ted Chester	33	8	4	20,210
1953	92	**Herb Thomas**	Hudson	Herb Thomas	37	11	10	27,300
1954	42	**Lee Petty**	Chrysler	Herb Thomas	34	7	3	26,706
1955	300	**Tim Flock**	Chrysler	Carl Kiekhaefer	38	18	19	33,750
1956	300B	**Buck Baker**	Chevrolet	Carl Kiekhaefer	48	14	12	29,790
1957	87	**Buck Baker**	Chevrolet	Buck Baker	40	10	5	24,712
1958	42	**Lee Petty**	Oldsmobile	Petty Enterprises	49	7	4	20,600
1959	42	**Lee Petty**	Plymouth	Petty Enterprises	42	10	2	45,570
1960	4	**Rex White**	Chevrolet	White-Clements	40	6	3	45,260
1961	11	**Ned Jarrett**	Chevrolet	W.G. Holloway Jr.	46	1	4	27,285
1962	8	**Joe Weatherly**	Pontiac	Bud Moore	52	9	6	56,110
1963	8	**Joe Weatherly**	Mercury	Wood Brothers	53	3	6	58,110
1964	43	**Richard Petty**	Plymouth	Petty Enterprises	61	9	8	98,810
1965	11	**Ned Jarrett**	Ford	Bondy Long	54	13	9	77,960
1966	6	**David Pearson**	Dodge	Cotton Owens	42	14	7	59,205
1967	43	**Richard Petty**	Plymouth	Petty Enterprises	48	27	18	130,275
1968	17	**David Pearson**	Ford	Holman-Moody	48	16	12	118,842
1969	17	**David Pearson**	Ford	Holman-Moody	51	11	14	183,700
1970	71	**Bobby Isaac**	Dodge	Nord Krauskopf	47	11	13	121,470
1971	43	**Richard Petty**	Plymouth	Petty Enterprises	46	21	9	309,225
1972	43	**Richard Petty**	Plymouth	Petty Enterprises	31	8	3	227,015
1973	72	**Benny Parsons**	Chevrolet	L.G. DeWitt	28	1	0	114,345
1974	43	**Richard Petty**	Dodge	Petty Enterprises	30	10	7	299,175
1975	43	**Richard Petty**	Dodge	Petty Enterprises	30	13	3	378,865
1976	11	**Cale Yarborough**	Chevrolet	Junior Johnson	30	9	2	387,173
1977	11	**Cale Yarborough**	Chevrolet	Junior Johnson	30	9	3	477,499
1978	11	**Cale Yarborough**	Oldsmobile	Junior Johnson	30	10	8	530,751
1979	43	**Richard Petty**	Chevrolet	Petty Enterprises	31	5	1	531,292
1980	2	**Dale Earnhardt**	Chevrolet	Rod Osterlund	31	5	0	588,926
1981	11	**Darrell Waltrip**	Buick	Junior Johnson	31	12	11	693,342
1982	11	**Darrell Waltrip**	Buick	Junior Johnson	30	12	7	873,118
1983	22	**Bobby Allison**	Buick	Bill Gardner	30	6	0	828,355
1984	44	**Terry Labonte**	Chevrolet	Billy Hagan	30	2	2	713,010
1985	11	**Darrell Waltrip**	Chevrolet	Junior Johnson	28	3	4	1,318,735
1986	3	**Dale Earnhardt**	Chevrolet	Richard Childress	29	5	1	1,783,880
1987	3	**Dale Earnhardt**	Chevrolet	Richard Childress	29	11	1	2,099,243
1988	9	**Bill Elliott**	Ford	Harry Meling	29	6	6	1,574,639
1989	27	**Rusty Wallace**	Pontiac	Raymond Beadle	29	6	4	2,247,950
1990	3	**Dale Earnhardt**	Chevrolet	Richard Childress	29	9	4	3,083,056
1991	3	**Dale Earnhardt**	Chevrolet	Richard Childress	29	4	0	2,396,685
1992	7	**Alan Kulwicki**	Ford	Alan Kulwicki	29	2	6	2,322,561
1993	3	**Dale Earnhardt**	Chevrolet	Richard Childress	30	6	2	3,353,789
1994	3	**Dale Earnhardt**	Chevrolet	Richard Childress	31	4	2	3,400,733
1995	24	**Jeff Gordon**	Chevrolet	Rick Hendrick	31	7	8	4,347,343
1996	5	**Terry Labonte**	Chevrolet	Rick Hendrick	31	2	4	4,030,648
1997	24	**Jeff Gordon**	Chevrolet	Rick Hendrick	32	10	1	6,375,658
1998	24	**Jeff Gordon**	Chevrolet	Rick Hendrick	33	13	7	9,306,584
1999	88	**Dale Jarrett**	Ford	Robert Yates	34	4	0	6,649,596
2000	18	**Bobby Labonte**	Pontiac	Joe Gibbs	34	4	2	7,361,387
2001	24	**Jeff Gordon**	Chevrolet	Rick Hendrick	36	6	6	10,879,757

NASCAR Rookie of the Year

Sponsored by Raybestos, the official brake of NASCAR, and presented to rookie driver who accumulates the most Winston Cup Series Raybestos Robkie of the Year points based on their best 17 finishes.

Year		Year		Year		Year	
1958	Shorty Rollins	1960	David Pearson	1962	Tom Cox	1964	Doug Cooper
1959	Richard Petty	1961	Woodie Wilson	1963	Billy Wade	1965	Sam McQuagg

Year		Year		Year		Year	
1966	James Hylton	1975	Bruce Hill	1984	Rusty Wallace	1993	Jeff Gordon
1967	Donnie Allison	1976	Skip Manning	1985	Ken Schrader	1994	Jeff Burton
1968	Pete Hamilton	1977	Ricky Rudd	1986	Alan Kulwicki	1995	Ricky Craven
1969	Dick Brooks	1978	Ronnie Thomas	1987	Davey Allison	1996	Johnny Benson
1970	Bill Dennis	1979	Dale Earnhardt	1988	Ken Bouchard	1997	Mike Skinner
1971	Walter Ballard	1980	Jody Ridley	1989	Dick Trickle	1998	Kenny Irwin
1972	Larry Smith	1981	Ron Bouchard	1990	Rob Moroso	1999	Tony Stewart
1973	Lennie Pond	1982	Geoff Bodine	1991	Bobby Hamilton	2000	Matt Kenseth
1974	Earl Ross	1983	Sterling Marlin	1992	Jimmy Hensley	2001	Kevin Harvick

All-Time Leaders

NASCAR's all-time Top 20 drivers in victories, pole positions and earnings based on records through 2001. Drivers active in 2002 are in **bold** type.

Victories

1	Richard Petty 200	7	**Jeff Gordon**......58	13	Buck Baker 46	19	**Dale Jarrett**......28
2	David Pearson....105	8	Lee Petty...........55	14	**Bill Elliott**........41	20	Fred Lorenzen......26
3	Bobby Allison 84	9	**Rusty Wallace** ...54	15	Tim Flock...........40		Rex White.........26
	Darrell Waltrip....84	10	Ned Jarrett........50	16	Bobby Isaac.......37		
5	Cale Yarborough...83		Junior Johnson......50	17	Fireball Roberts.....32		
6	Dale Earnhardt 76	12	Herb Thomas.......48		**Mark Martin**.....32		

Pole Positions

1	Richard Petty 126	8	Junior Johnson 47	15	**Geoff Bodine** 37
2	David Pearson.............113	9	Buck Baker..............44	16	Ned Jarrett 35
3	Cale Yarborough...........70	10	**Mark Martin**.............41		Fireball Roberts 35
4	Darrell Waltrip............59	11	Buddy Baker.............40		**Rusty Wallace** 35
5	Bobby Allison 57	12	Tim Flock.................39		Rex White.................35
6	Bobby Isaac..............51		Herb Thomas 39	20	Fonty Flock 34
	Bill Elliott 51		**Jeff Gordon** 39		

Earnings

1	**Jeff Gordon** ...$45,748,580	8	**Bobby Labonte** .$25,953,024	15	**Michael Waltrip** .$14,828,476
2	Dale Earnhardt....41,708,384	9	**Ricky Rudd** 24,530,223	16	**Kyle Petty** 13,331,568
3	**Dale Jarrett**.....33,274,832	10	**Jeff Burton** 22,958,499	17	**Ward Burton**....12,993,310
4	**Rusty Wallace** ..29,647,184	11	**Sterling Marlin** ..19,899,539	18	**Bobby Hamilton** .12,990,059
5	**Mark Martin**...29,165,322	12	Darrell Waltrip 19,412,618	19	**Jimmy Spencer** ..12,747,382
6	**Bill Elliott** 27,306,174	13	**Ken Schrader** 18,124,281	20	**Tony Stewart** 11,773,950
7	**Terry Labonte**...26,536,692	14	**Geoff Bodine** 14,829,269		

CART CIRCUIT

FedEx Series Champions

Officially the FedEx Championship Series since 1997. Formerly, AAA (American Automobile Assn., 1909-55), USAC (U.S. Auto Club, 1956-78), CART (Championship Auto Racing Teams, 1979-91). CART was renamed IndyCar in 1992 and then lost use of the name in 1997.

Multiple titles: A.J. Foyt (7); Mario Andretti (4); Jimmy Bryan, Earl Cooper, Ted Horn, Rick Mears, Louie Meyer, Bobby Rahal, Al Unser (3); Tony Bettenhausen, Gil de Ferran, Ralph DePalma, Peter DePaolo, Joe Leonard, Rex Mays, Tommy Milton, Ralph Mulford, Jimmy Murphy, Wilbur Shaw, Al Unser Jr., Bobby Unser, Rodger Ward and Alex Zanardi (2).

AAA

Year		Year		Year		Year	
1909	George Robertson	1920	Tommy Milton	1931	Louis Schneider	1942-45	No racing
1910	Ray Harroun	1921	Tommy Milton	1932	Bob Carey	1946	Ted Horn
1911	Ralph Mulford	1922	Jimmy Murphy	1933	Louie Meyer	1947	Ted Horn
1912	Ralph DePalma	1923	Eddie Hearne	1934	Bill Cummings	1948	Ted Horn
1913	Earl Cooper	1924	Jimmy Murphy	1935	Kelly Petillo	1949	Johnnie Parsons
1914	Ralph DePalma	1925	Peter DePaolo	1936	Mauri Rose	1950	Henry Banks
1915	Earl Cooper	1926	Harry Hartz	1937	Wilbur Shaw	1951	Tony Bettenhausen
1916	Dario Resta	1927	Peter DePaolo	1938	Floyd Roberts	1952	Chuck Stevenson
1917	Earl Cooper	1928	Louie Meyer	1939	Wilbur Shaw	1953	Sam Hanks
1918	Ralph Mulford	1929	Louie Meyer	1940	Rex Mays	1954	Jimmy Bryan
1919	Howard Wilcox	1930	Billy Arnold	1941	Rex Mays	1955	Bob Sweikert

USAC

Year		Year		Year		Year	
1956	Jimmy Bryan	1962	Rodger Ward	1968	Bobby Unser	1974	Bobby Unser
1957	Jimmy Bryan	1963	A.J. Foyt	1969	Mario Andretti	1975	A.J. Foyt
1958	Tony Bettenhausen	1964	A.J. Foyt	1970	Al Unser	1976	Gordon Johncock
1959	Rodger Ward	1965	Mario Andretti	1971	Joe Leonard	1977	Tom Sneva
1960	A.J. Foyt	1966	Mario Andretti	1972	Joe Leonard	1978	A.J. Foyt
1961	A.J. Foyt	1967	A.J. Foyt	1973	Roger McCluskey		

CART Circuit (Cont.)
CART

Year	Driver	Car	Team	Sts	Wins	Poles	Earnings
1979	**Rick Mears**	Penske Ford	Penske	14	3	2	$408,078
1980	**Johnny Rutherford**	Chaparral Ford	Chaparral	12	5	3	503,595
1981	**Rick Mears**	Penske Ford	Penske	11	6	2	323,670
1982	**Rick Mears**	Penske Ford	Penske	11	4	8	306,454
1983	**Al Unser**	Penske Ford	Penske	13	1	0	500,109
1984	**Mario Andretti**	Lola Ford	Newman/Haas	16	6	8	931,929
1985	**Al Unser**	March Ford	Penske	14	1	1	843,885
1986	**Bobby Rahal**	March Ford	TrueSports	17	6	2	1,488,049
1987	**Bobby Rahal**	Lola Ford	TrueSports	15	3	1	1,261,098
1988	**Danny Sullivan**	Penske Chevrolet	Penske	15	4	9	1,222,791
1989	**Emerson Fittipaldi**	Penske Chevrolet	Patrick	15	5	4	2,166,078
1990	**Al Unser Jr.**	Lola Chevrolet	Galles-Kraco	16	6	1	1,946,833
1991	**Michael Andretti**	Lola Chevrolet	Newman/Haas	17	8	8	2,461,734
1992	**Bobby Rahal**	Lola Chevrolet	Rahal-Hogan	16	4	3	2,235,298
1993	**Nigel Mansell**	Lola Ford	Newman/Haas	15	5	7	2,526,953
1994	**Al Unser Jr.**	Penske Ilmor	Marlboro Team Penske	16	8	4	3,535,813
1995	**Jacques Villeneuve**	Reynard Ford	Team Green	17	4	6	2,996,269
1996	**Jimmy Vasser**	Reynard Honda	Target Chip Ganassi	16	4	4	3,071,500
1997	**Alex Zanardi**	Reynard Honda	Target Chip Ganassi	16	5	4	2,096,250
1998	**Alex Zanardi**	Reynard Honda	Target Chip Ganassi	19	7	0	2,229,250
1999	**Juan Montoya**	Reynard Honda	Target Chip Ganassi	20	7	7	1,973,000
2000	**Gil de Ferran**	Reynard Honda	Marlboro Team Penske	20	2	5	1,677,000
2001	**Gil de Ferran**	Reynard Honda	Marlboro Team Penske	20	2	5	1,761,500

CART Rookie of the Year

Officially, Jim Trueman Rookie of the Year Award. Named after the late founder of the two-time champion TrueSports Racing Team, it's presented to the rookie who accumulates the most FedEx Championship Series points among first year drivers.

Year		Year		Year		Year	
1979	Bill Alsup	1985	Arie Luyendyk	1991	Jeff Andretti	1997	Patrick Carpentier
1980	Dennis Firestone	1986	Dominic Dobson	1992	Stefan Johansson	1998	Tony Kanaan
1981	Bob Lazier	1987	Fabrizio Barbazza	1993	Nigel Mansell	1999	Juan Montoya
1982	Bobby Rahal	1988	John Jones	1994	Jacques Villeneuve	2000	Kenny Brack
1983	Teo Fabi	1989	Bernard Jourdain	1995	Gil de Ferran	2001	Scott Dixon
1984	Roberto Guerrero	1990	Eddie Cheever	1996	Alex Zanardi		

All-Time CART Leaders

CART's all-time Top 20 drivers in victories, pole positions and earnings, based on records through 2001. Drivers active in 2002 are in **bold** type. Totals include victories, poles and earnings before CART was established in 1979. Earnings totals include year-end performance awards. (*) Denotes driver is active, but in Indy Racing League not CART; (†) denotes driver is active, but in Formula One not CART.

Victories

1	A.J. Foyt	67	8	Johnny Rutherford	27	
2	Mario Andretti	52	9	Roger Ward	26	Emerson Fittipaldi ... 22
3	**Michael Andretti**	41	10	Gordon Johncock	25	16 Earl Cooper ... 20
4	Al Unser	39	11	Ralph DePalma	24	17 Jimmy Bryan ... 19
5	Bobby Unser	35		Bobby Rahal	24	Jimmy Murphy ... 19
6	Al Unser Jr.*	31	13	Tommy Milton	23	19 **Paul Tracy** ... 18
7	Rick Mears	29	14	Tony Bettenhausen	22	20 Ralph Mulford ... 17
						Danny Sullivan ... 17

Pole Positions

1	Mario Andretti	67	8	Gordon Johncock	20	Don Branson ... 14
2	A.J. Foyt	53	9	Rex Mays	19	Tom Sneva ... 14
3	Bobby Unser	49		Danny Sullivan	19	Juan Montoya† ... 14
4	Rick Mears	40	11	Bobby Rahal	18	18 **Paul Tracy** ... 13
5	**Michael Andretti**	32	12	Emerson Fittipaldi	17	19 Parnelli Jones ... 12
6	Al Unser	27	13	Gil de Ferran*	16	20 Danny Ongais ... 11
7	Johnny Rutherford	23	14	Tony Bettenhausen	14	Rodger Ward ... 11

Earnings

1	Al Unser Jr.*	$18,828,406	8	Danny Sullivan	$8,884,126	15 Alex Zanardi ... $5,893,750
2	**Michael Andretti**	17,709,369	9	**Paul Tracy**	8,331,520	16 Scott Pruett ... 5,440,144
3	Bobby Rahal	16,344,008	10	Arie Luyendyk	7,732,188	17 A.J. Foyt ... 5,357,589
4	Emerson Fittipaldi	14,293,625	11	Gil de Ferran*	7,390,703	18 Teo Fabi ... 5,045,881
5	Mario Andretti	11,552,154	12	Raul Boesel	6,971,887	19 **Christian Fittipaldi** ... 4,991,668
6	Rick Mears	11,050,807	13	Al Unser	6,740,843	20 Scott Brayton ... 4,807,274
7	**Jimmy Vasser**	10,125,494	14	**Adrian Fernandez**	6,305,265	

INDY RACING LEAGUE CIRCUIT

Indianapolis 500

Held every Memorial Day weekend; 200 laps around a 2.5-mile oval at Indianapolis Motor Speedway. First race was held in 1911. The Indy Racing League began in 1996 and made the Indianapolis 500 its cornerstone event. Winning drivers are listed with starting positions. Winners who started from pole position are in **bold** type.

Multiple wins: A.J. Foyt, Rick Mears and Al Unser (4); Louis Meyer, Mauri Rose, Johnny Rutherford, Wilbur Shaw and Bobby Unser (3); Helio Castroneves, Emerson Fittipaldi, Gordon Johncock, Arie Luyendyk, Tommy Milton, Al Unser Jr., Bill Vukovich and Rodger Ward (2).

Multiple poles: Rick Mears (6); A.J. Foyt and Rex Mays (4); Mario Andretti, Arie Luyendyk, Johnny Rutherford and Tom Sneva (3); Scott Brayton, Bill Cummings, Ralph DePalma, Leon Duray, Parnelli Jones, Jimmy Murphy, Duke Nalon, Eddie Sachs and Bobby Unser (2).

Year	Winner (Pos.)	Car	MPH	Pole Sitter	MPH
1911	Ray Harroun (28)	Marmon Wasp	74.602	Lewis Strang	–
1912	Joe Dawson (7)	National	78.719	Gil Anderson	–
1913	Jules Goux (7)	Peugeot	75.933	Caleb Bragg	–
1914	Rene Thomas (15)	Delage	82.474	Jean Chassagne	–
1915	Ralph DePalma (2)	Mercedes	89.840	Howard Wilcox	98.90
1916-a	Dario Resta (4)	Peugeot	84.001	John Aitken	96.69
1917-18	Not held	World War I			
1919	Howdy Wilcox (2)	Peugeot	88.050	Rene Thomas	104.78
1920	Gaston Chevrolet (6)	Monroe	88.618	Ralph DePalma	99.15
1921	Tommy Milton (20)	Frontenac	89.621	Ralph DePalma	100.75
1922	**Jimmy Murphy** (1)	Murphy Special	94.484	Jimmy Murphy	100.50
1923	**Tommy Milton** (1)	H.C.S. Special	90.954	Tommy Milton	108.17
1924	L.L. Corum & Joe Boyer (21)	Duesenberg Special	98.234	Jimmy Murphy	108.037
1925	Peter DePaolo (2)	Duesenberg Special	101.127	Leon Duray	113.196
1926-b	Frank Lockhart (20)	Miller Special	95.904	Earl Cooper	111.735
1927	George Souders (22)	Duesenberg	97.545	Frank Lockhart	120.100
1928	Louie Meyer (13)	Miller Special	99.482	Leon Duray	122.391
1929	Ray Keech (6)	Simplex Piston Ring Special	97.585	Cliff Woodbury	120.599
1930	**Billy Arnold** (1)	Miller-Hartz Special	100.448	Billy Arnold	113.268
1931	Louis Schneider (13)	Bowes Seal Fast Special	96.629	Russ Snowberger	112.796
1932	Fred Frame (27)	Miller-Hartz Special	104.144	Lou Moore	117.363
1933	Louie Meyer (6)	Tydol Special	104.162	Bill Cummings	118.530
1934	Bill Cummings (10)	Boyle Products Special	104.863	Kelly Petillo	119.329
1935	Kelly Petillo (22)	Gilmore Speedway Special	106.240	Rex Mays	120.736
1936	Louie Meyer (28)	Ring Free Special	109.069	Rex Mays	119.644
1937	Wilbur Shaw (2)	Shaw-Gilmore Special	113.580	Bill Cummings	123.343
1938	**Floyd Roberts** (1)	Burd Piston Ring Special	117.200	Floyd Roberts	125.681
1939	Wilbur Shaw (3)	Boyle Special	115.035	Jimmy Snyder	130.138
1940	Wilbur Shaw (2)	Boyle Special	114.277	Rex Mays	127.850
1941	Floyd Davis & Mauri Rose (17)	Noc-Out Hose Clamp Special	115.117	Mauri Rose	128.691
1942-45	Not held	World War II			
1946	George Robson (15)	Thorne Engineering Special	114.820	Cliff Bergere	126.471
1947	Mauri Rose (3)	Blue Crown Spark Plug Special	116.338	Ted Horn	126.564
1948	Mauri Rose (3)	Blue Crown Spark Plug Special	119.814	Rex Mays	130.577
1949	Bill Holland (4)	Blue Crown Spark Plug Special	121.327	Duke Nalon	132.939
1950-c	Johnnie Parsons (5)	Wynn's Friction Proofing	124.002	Walt Faulkner	134.343
1951	Lee Wallard (2)	Belanger Special	126.244	Duke Nalon	136.498
1952	Troy Ruttman (7)	Agajanian Special	128.922	Fred Agabashian	138.010
1953	**Bill Vukovich** (1)	Fuel Injection Special	128.740	Bill Vukovich	138.392
1954	Bill Vukovich (19)	Fuel Injection Special	130.840	Jack McGrath	141.033
1955	Bob Sweikert (14)	John Zink Special	128.213	Jerry Hoyt	140.045
1956	**Pat Flaherty** (1)	John Zink Special	128.490	Pat Flaherty	145.596
1957	Sam Hanks (13)	Belond Exhaust Special	135.601	Pat O'Connor	143.948
1958	Jimmy Bryan (7)	Belond AP Parts Special	133.791	Dick Rathmann	145.974
1959	Rodger Ward (2)	Leader Card 500 Roadster	135.857	Johnny Thomson	145.908
1960	Jim Rathmann (2)	Ken-Paul Special	138.767	Eddie Sachs	146.592
1961	A.J. Foyt (7)	Bowes Seal Fast Special	139.130	Eddie Sachs	147.481
1962	Rodger Ward (2)	Leader Card 500 Roadster	140.293	Parnelli Jones	150.370
1963	**Parnelli Jones** (1)	Agajanian-Willard Special	143.137	Parnelli Jones	151.153
1964	A.J. Foyt (5)	Sheraton-Thompson Special	147.350	Jim Clark	158.828
1965	Jim Clark (2)	Lotus Ford	150.686	A.J. Foyt	161.233
1966	Graham Hill (15)	American Red Ball Special	144.317	Mario Andretti	165.899
1967-d	A.J. Foyt (4)	Sheraton-Thompson Special	151.207	Mario Andretti	168.982
1968	Bobby Unser (3)	Rislone Special	152.882	Joe Leonard	171.559
1969	Mario Andretti (2)	STP Oil Treatment Special	156.867	A.J. Foyt	170.568
1970	**Al Unser** (1)	Johnny Lightning Special	155.749	Al Unser	170.221

Indy Racing League Circuit (Cont.)

Year	Winner (Pos.)	Car	MPH	Pole Sitter	MPH
1971	Al Unser (5)	Johnny Lightning Special	157.735	Peter Revson	178.696
1972	Mark Donohue (3)	Sunoco McLaren	162.962	Bobby Unser	195.940
1973-e	Gordon Johncock (11)	STP Double Oil Filters	159.036	Johnny Rutherford	198.413
1974	Johnny Rutherford (25)	McLaren	158.589	A.J. Foyt	191.632
1975-f	Bobby Unser (3)	Jorgensen Eagle	149.213	A.J. Foyt	193.976
1976-g	**Johnny Rutherford** (1)	Hy-Gain McLaren/Goodyear	148.725	Johnny Rutherford	188.957
1977	A.J. Foyt (4)	Gilmore Racing Team	161.331	Tom Sneva	198.884
1978	Al Unser (5)	FNCTC Chaparral Lola	161.363	Tom Sneva	202.156
1979	**Rick Mears** (1)	The Gould Charge	158.899	Rick Mears	193.736
1980	**Johnny Rutherford** (1)	Pennzoil Chaparral	142.862	Johnny Rutherford	192.256
1981-h	**Bobby Unser** (1)	Norton Spirit Penske PC-9B	139.084	Bobby Unser	200.546
1982	Gordon Johncock (5)	STP Oil Treatment	162.029	Rick Mears	207.004
1983	Tom Sneva (4)	Texaco Star	162.117	Teo Fabi	207.395
1984	Rick Mears (3)	Pennzoil Z-7	163.612	Tom Sneva	210.029
1985	Danny Sullivan (8)	Miller American Special	152.982	Pancho Carter	212.583
1986	Bobby Rahal (4)	Budweiser/Truesports/March	170.722	Rick Mears	216.828
1987	Al Unser (20)	Cummins Holset Turbo	162.175	Mario Andretti	215.390
1988	**Rick Mears** (1)	Pennzoil Z-7/Penske Chevy V-8	144.809	Rick Mears	219.198
1989	Emerson Fittipaldi (3)	Marlboro/Penske Chevy V-8	167.581	Rick Mears	223.885
1990	Arie Luyendyk (3)	Domino's Pizza Chevrolet	185.981*	Emerson Fittipaldi	225.301
1991	**Rick Mears** (1)	Marlboro Penske Chevy	176.457	Rick Mears	224.113
1992	Al Unser Jr. (12)	Valvoline Galmer '92	134.477	Roberto Guerrero	232.482
1993	Emerson Fittipaldi (9)	Marlboro Penske Chevy	157.207	Arie Luyendyk	223.967
1994	**Al Unser Jr.** (1)	Marlboro Penske Mercedes	160.872	Al Unser Jr.	228.011
1995	Jacques Villeneuve (5)	Player's Ltd. Reynard Ford	153.616	Scott Brayton	231.604
1996	Buddy Lazier (5)	Reynard Ford	147.956	Tony Stewart	233.100&
1997	**Arie Luyendyk** (1)	G-Force Olds Aurora	145.827	Arie Luyendyk	218.263
1998	Eddie Cheever Jr. (17)	Dallara Olds Aurora	145.155	Billy Boat	223.503
1999	Kenny Brack (8)	Dallara Olds Aurora	153.176	Arie Luyendyk	225.179
2000	Juan Montoya (2)	G-Force Olds Aurora	167.607	Greg Ray	223.471
2001	Helio Castroneves (11)	Dallara Olds Aurora	153.601	Scott Sharp	226.037
2002-i	Helio Castroneves (13)	Dallara Chevrolet	166.499	Bruno Junqueira	231.342

*Track record for winning time.

& Scott Brayton won the pole position with an avg. mph of 233.718 but was killed in a practice run. Stewart was given pole position with the next fastest speed.

Notes: a—1916 race scheduled for 300 miles; **b**—rain shortened 1926 race to 400 miles; **c**—rain shortened 1950 race to 345 miles; **d**—1967 race postponed due to rain after 18 laps (May 30), resumed next day (May 31); **e**—rain shortened 1973 race to 332.5 miles; **f**—rain shortened 1975 race to 435 miles; **g**—rain shortened 1976 race to 255 miles; **h**—in 1981, runner-up Mario Andretti was awarded 1st place when winner Bobby Unser was penalized a lap after the race was completed for passing cars illegally under the caution flag. Unser and car-owner Roger Penske appealed the race stewards' decision to the U.S. Auto Club. Four months later, USAC overturned the ruling, saying that the penalty was too harsh and Unser should be fined $40,000 rather than stripped of his championship; **i**—Team Green, runner-up Paul Tracy's team, appealed Castroneves' victory, citing video evidence and driver testimonials that proved Tracy passed Castroneves moments before the caution flag on lap 199. The IRL denied the appeal the following day.

Indy 500 Rookie of the Year

Voted on by a panel of auto racing media. Award does not necessarily go to highest-finishing first-year driver. Graham Hill won the race on his first try in 1966, but the rookie award went to Jackie Stewart, who led with 10 laps to go only to lose oil pressure and finish 6th.

Father and son winners: Mario and Michael Andretti (1965 and 1984); Bill and Billy Vukovich III (1968 and 1988).

Year		Year		Year		Year	
1952	Art Cross	1966	Jackie Stewart	1980	Tim Richmond	1993	Nigel Mansell
1953	Jimmy Daywalt	1967	Denis Hulme	1981	Josele Garza	1994	Jacques Villeneuve
1954	Larry Crockett	1968	Bill Vukovich	1982	Jim Hickman	1995	Christian Fittipaldi
1955	Al Herman	1969	Mark Donohue	1983	Teo Fabi	1996	Tony Stewart
1956	Bob Veith	1970	Donnie Allison	1984	Michael Andretti	1997	Jeff Ward
1957	Don Edmunds	1971	Denny Zimmerman		& Roberto Guerrero	1998	Steve Knapp
1958	George Amick	1972	Mike Hiss	1985	Arie Luyendyk	1999	Robby McGehee
1959	Bobby Grim	1973	Graham McRae	1986	Randy Lanier	2000	Juan Montoya
1960	Jim Hurtubise	1974	Pancho Carter	1987	Fabrizio Barbazza	2001	Helio Castroneves
1961	Parnelli Jones	1975	Bill Puterbaugh	1988	Billy Vukovich III	2002	Alex Barron
	& Bobby Marshman	1976	Vern Schuppan	1989	Bernard Jourdain		& Tomas Scheckter
1962	Jimmy McElreath	1977	Jerry Sneva		& Scott Pruett		
1963	Jim Clark	1978	Rick Mears	1990	Eddie Cheever		
1964	Johnny White		& Larry Rice	1991	Jeff Andretti		
1965	Mario Andretti	1979	Howdy Holmes	1992	Lyn St. James		

IRL Champions

The Indy Racing League (IRL) announced its split from the open-wheel CART series in 1994. Led by Indianapolis Motor Speedway President Tony George, the league's inaugural three-race series began in January 1996 and ended with the league's keystone event—the Indianapolis 500. Past series' sponsors include Pep Boys (1998-99) and Northern Light Technology, Inc., an Internet search engine (2000-01).

Multiple winner: Sam Hornish Jr. (2).

Year	Driver	Car	Team	Sts	Wins	Poles	Earnings
1996	**Buzz Calkins**	Reynard Ford	A.J. Foyt Enterprises	3	1	0	$345,553
	Scott Sharp	Lola Ford	A.J. Foyt Enterprises	3	0	0	330,303
1997	**Tony Stewart**	Dallara Oldsmobile	Team Menard	10	1	4	1,142,450
1998	**Kenny Brack**	Dallara Oldsmobile	A.J. Foyt Enterprises	11	3	0	2,106,700
1999	**Greg Ray**	Dallara Oldsmobile	Team Menard	10	3	4	2,061,800
2000	**Buddy Lazier**	Dallara Oldsmobile	Hemelgarn Racing	9	2	1	2,176,200
2001	**Sam Hornish Jr.**	Dallara Oldsmobile	Panther Racing	13	3	0	2,477,025
2002	**Sam Hornish Jr.**	Dallara Oldsmobile	Panther Racing	15	5	2	1,435,615

Note: In 1996, Calkins and Sharp were named co-champions after finishing the series tied in drivers' points (246).

IRL Rookie of the Year

Officially the Chevy Rookie of the Year Award, presented to rookie driver who accumulates the most points in the IRL standings.

Year		Year		Year		Year	
1996	None	1998	Robby Unser	2000	Airton Dare	2002	Laurent Redon
1997	Jim Guthrie	1999	Scott Harrington	2001	Felipe Giaffone		

All-Time IRL Leaders

IRL's all-time Top 10 drivers in victories and earnings, and Top 5 in pole positions, based on records through 2001. Earnings totals include season-ending contingency awards. Drivers active in 2002 are in **bold** type. (*) Denotes driver is active, but in NASCAR Winston Cup Series not IRL; (†) Denotes driver is active, but in CART not IRL.

Victories

1. **Buddy Lazier** 8
2. **Scott Sharp** 6
3. **Eddie Cheever Jr.** 5
   Greg Ray 5
5. Kenny Brack† 4
   Arie Luyendyk 4
7. **Scott Goodyear** 3
   Sam Hornish Jr. 3
   Tony Stewart* 3
10. **Robbie Buhl** 2
   Al Unser Jr. 2

Pole Positions

1. **Greg Ray** 13
2. **Billy Boat** 8
3. Tony Stewart* 7
4. **Scott Sharp** 5
5. **Mark Dismore** 4
   Arie Luyendyk 4

Earnings

1. **Buddy Lazier** $7,273,429
2. **Eddie Cheever Jr.** . .5,387,428
3. Kenny Brack† 4,494,440
4. **Greg Ray** 4,419,325
5. **Scott Sharp** 4,195,828
6. **Billy Boat** 3,963,275
7. **Arie Luyendyk** 3,778,378
8. **Jeff Ward** 3,642,125
9. **Scott Goodyear** 3,554,775
10. **Mark Dismore** 3,463,128

FORMULA ONE CIRCUIT

United States Grand Prix

Federation Internationale Sportive Automobile (FISA) sanctioned two annual U.S. Grand Prix–USA/East and USA/West–from 1976-80 and 1983-84. Phoenix was the site of the U.S. Grand Prix from 1989-91. Indianapolis Motor Speedway has hosted the U.S. Grand Prix since 2000.

Indianapolis 500

Officially sanctioned as Grand Prix race from 1950-60 only.

U.S. Grand Prix—East

Held from 1959-80 and 1981-88 at the following locations: Sebring, Fla. (1959); Riverside, Calif. (1960); Watkins Glen, N.Y. (1961-80); and Detroit (1982-88). There was no race in 1981. Race discontinued in 1989.

Multiple winners: Jim Clark, Graham Hill and Ayrton Senna (3); James Hunt, Carlos Reutemann and Jackie Stewart (2).

Year		Car	Year		Car
1959	Bruce McLaren, NZE	Cooper Climax	1974	Carlos Reutemann, ARG	Brabham Ford
1960	Stirling Moss, GBR	Lotus Climax	1975	Niki Lauda, AUT	Ferrari
1961	Innes Ireland, GBR	Lotus Climax	1976	James Hunt, GBR	McLaren Ford
1962	Jim Clark, GBR	Lotus Climax	1977	James Hunt, GBR	McLaren Ford
1963	Graham Hill, GBR	BRM	1978	Carlos Reutemann, ARG	Ferrari
1964	Graham Hill, GBR	BRM	1979	Gilles Villeneuve, CAN	Ferrari
1965	Graham Hill, GBR	BRM	1980	Alan Jones, AUS	Williams Ford
1966	Jim Clark, GBR	Lotus BRM	1981	Not held	
1967	Jim Clark, GBR	Lotus Ford	1982	John Watson, GBR	McLaren Ford
1968	Jackie Stewart, GBR	Matra Ford	1983	Michele Alboreto, ITA	Tyrrell Ford
1969	Jochen Rindt, AUT	Lotus Ford	1984	Nelson Piquet, BRA	Brabham BMW Turbo
1970	Emerson Fittipaldi, BRA	Lotus Ford	1985	Keke Rosberg, FIN	Williams Honda Turbo
1971	Francois Cevert, FRA	Tyrrell Ford	1986	Ayrton Senna, BRA	Lotus Renault Turbo
1972	Jackie Stewart, GBR	Tyrrell Ford	1987	Ayrton Senna, BRA	Lotus Honda Turbo
1973	Ronnie Peterson, SWE	Lotus Ford	1988	Ayrton Senna, BRA	McLaren Honda Turbo

Formula One Circuit (Cont.)
U.S. Grand Prix—West

Held from 1976-83 at Long Beach, Calif. Races also held in Las Vegas (1981-82), Dallas (1984) and Phoenix (1989-91). Race discontinued in 1992.

Multiple winners: Alan Jones and Ayrton Senna (2).

Year	Car	Year	Car
1976 Clay Regazzoni, SWI	Ferrari	1983 John Watson, GBR	McLaren Ford
1977 Mario Andretti, USA	Lotus Ford	1984 Keke Rosberg, FIN	Williams Honda Turbo
1978 Carlos Reutemann, ARG	Ferrari	1985-88 Not held	
1979 Gilles Villeneuve, CAN	Ferrari	1989 Alain Prost, FRA	McLaren Honda
1980 Nelson Piquet, BRA	Brabham Ford	1990 Ayrton Senna, BRA	McLaren Honda
1981 Alan Jones, AUS	Williams Ford	1991 Ayrton Senna, BRA	McLaren Honda
1982 Niki Lauda, AUT	McLaren Ford		

U.S. Grand Prix
Held since 2000 at Indianapolis Motor Speedway.

Year	Car	Year	Car
2000 Michael Schumacher, GER	Ferrari	2002 Rubens Barrichello, BRA	Ferrari
2001 Mika Hakkinen, FIN	McLaren Mercedes		

World Champions

Officially called the World Championship of Drivers and based on Formula One (Grand Prix) records through the 2002 racing season.

Multiple winners: Juan-Manuel Fangio and Michael Schumacher (5); Alain Prost (4); Jack Brabham, Niki Lauda, Nelson Piquet, Ayrton Senna and Jackie Stewart (3); Alberto Ascari, Jim Clark, Emerson Fittipaldi, Mika Hakkinen and Graham Hill (2).

Year	Driver	Country	Car	Sts	Wins	Poles	Runner(s)-up
1950	Guiseppe Farina	Italy	Alfa Romeo	7	3	2	J.M. Fangio, ARG
1951	Juan-Manuel Fangio	Argentina	Alfa Romeo	8	3	4	A. Ascari, ITA
1952	Alberto Ascari	Italy	Ferrari	8	6	5	G. Farina, ITA
1953	Alberto Ascari	Italy	Ferrari	9	5	6	J.M. Fangio, ARG
1954	Juan-Manuel Fangio	Argentina	Maserati/Mercedes	9	6	5	F. Gonzalez, ARG
1955	Juan-Manuel Fangio	Argentina	Mercedes	7	4	3	S. Moss, GBR
1956	Juan-Manuel Fangio	Argentina	Lancia/Ferrari	8	3	5	S. Moss, GBR
1957	Juan-Manuel Fangio	Argentina	Maserati	8	4	4	S. Moss, GBR
1958	Mike Hawthorn	Great Britain	Ferrari	11	1	4	S. Moss, GBR
1959	Jack Brabham	Australia	Cooper Climax	9	2	1	T. Brooks, GBR
1960	Jack Brabham	Australia	Cooper Climax	10	5	3	B. McLaren, NZE
1961	Phil Hill	United States	Ferrari	8	2	5	W. von Trips, GER
1962	Graham Hill	Great Britain	BRM	9	4	1	J. Clark, GBR
1963	Jim Clark	Great Britain	Lotus Climax	10	7	7	G. Hill, GBR & R. Ginther, USA
1964	John Surtees	Great Britain	Ferrari	10	2	2	G. Hill, GBR
1965	Jim Clark	Great Britain	Lotus Climax	10	6	6	G. Hill, GBR
1966	Jack Brabham	Australia	Brabham Repco	9	4	3	J. Surtees, GBR
1967	Denis Hulme	New Zealand	Brabham Repco	11	2	0	J. Brabham, AUS
1968	Graham Hill	Great Britain	Lotus Ford	12	3	2	J. Stewart, GBR
1969	Jackie Stewart	Great Britain	Matra Ford	11	6	2	J. Ickx, BEL
1970	Jochen Rindt	Austria	Lotus Ford	13	5	3	J. Ickx, BEL
1971	Jackie Stewart	Great Britain	Tyrrell Ford	11	6	6	R. Peterson, SWE
1972	Emerson Fittipaldi	Brazil	Lotus Ford	12	5	3	J. Stewart, GBR
1973	Jackie Stewart	Great Britain	Tyrrell Ford	15	5	3	E. Fittipaldi, BRA
1974	Emerson Fittipaldi	Brazil	McLaren Ford	15	3	2	C. Regazzoni, SWI
1975	Niki Lauda	Austria	Ferrari	14	5	9	E. Fittipaldi, BRA
1976	James Hunt	Great Britain	McLaren Ford	16	6	8	N. Lauda, AUT
1977	Niki Lauda	Austria	Ferrari	17	3	2	J. Scheckter, RSA
1978	Mario Andretti	United States	Lotus Ford	16	6	8	R. Peterson, SWE
1979	Jody Scheckter	South Africa	Ferrari	15	3	1	G. Villeneuve, CAN
1980	Alan Jones	Australia	Williams Ford	14	5	3	N. Piquet, BRA
1981	Nelson Piquet	Brazil	Brabham Ford	15	3	4	C. Reutemann, ARG
1982	Keke Rosberg	Finland	Williams Ford	16	1	1	D. Pironi, FRA & J. Watson, GBR
1983	Nelson Piquet	Brazil	Brabham BMW Turbo	15	3	1	A. Prost, FRA
1984	Niki Lauda	Austria	McL. TAG Turbo	16	5	0	A. Prost, FRA
1985	Alain Prost	France	McL. TAG Turbo	16	5	2	M. Alboreto, ITA
1986	Alain Prost	France	McL. TAG Turbo	16	4	1	N. Mansell, GBR
1987	Nelson Piquet	Brazil	Williams Honda Turbo	16	3	4	N. Mansell, GBR
1988	Ayrton Senna	Brazil	McLaren Honda Turbo	16	8	13	A. Prost, FRA
1989	Alain Prost	France	McLaren Honda	16	4	2	A. Senna, BRA
1990	Ayrton Senna	Brazil	McLaren Honda	16	6	10	A. Prost, FRA
1991	Ayrton Senna	Brazil	McLaren Honda	16	7	8	N. Mansell, GBR
1992	Nigel Mansell	Great Britain	Williams Renault	16	9	14	R. Patrese, ITA
1993	Alain Prost	France	Williams Renault	16	7	13	A. Senna, BRA

Year	Driver	Country	Car	Sts	Wins	Poles	Runner(s)-up
1994	**Michael Schumacher**	Germany	Benetton Ford	14	8	6	D. Hill, GBR
1995	**Michael Schumacher**	Germany	Benetton Renault	17	9	4	D. Hill, GBR
1996	**Damon Hill**	Great Britain	Williams Renault	16	8	9	J. Villeneuve, CAN
1997	**Jacques Villeneuve**	Canada	Williams Renault	17	7	10	H.H. Frentzen, GER
1998	**Mika Hakkinen**	Finland	McLaren Mercedes	16	8	9	M. Schumacher, GER
1999	**Mika Hakkinen**	Finland	McLaren Mercedes	16	5	11	E. Irvine, GBR
2000	**Michael Schumacher**	Germany	Ferrari	17	9	9	M. Hakkinen, FIN
2001	**Michael Schumacher**	Germany	Ferrari	17	9	11	D. Coulthard, GBR
2002	**Michael Schumacher**	Germany	Ferrari	17	11	7	R. Barrichello, BRA

All-Time Leaders

The all-time Top 15 Grand Prix winning drivers, based on records through 2001. Listed are starts (Sts), poles won (Pole), wins (1st), second place finishes (2nd), and third (3rd). Drivers active in 2002 and career victories in **bold** type.

		Sts	Pole	1st	2nd	3rd			Sts	Pole	1st	2nd	3rd
1	M. Schumacher	151	41	**53**	25	16	9	Nelson Piquet	207	24	**23**	20	17
2	Alain Prost	199	33	**51**	35	20	10	Damon Hill	99	20	**22**	15	5
3	Ayrton Senna	161	65	**41**	23	16	11	Mika Hakkinen	163	27	**20**	14	17
4	Nigel Mansell	187	32	**31**	17	11	12	Stirling Moss	66	16	**16**	5	3
5	Jackie Stewart	99	17	**27**	11	5	13	Jack Brabham	126	13	**14**	10	7
6	Jim Clark	72	33	**25**	1	6		Emerson Fittipaldi	144	6	**14**	13	8
	Niki Lauda	171	24	**25**	20	9		Graham Hill	176	13	**14**	15	7
8	Juan-Manuel Fangio	51	28	**24**	10	1							

ENDURANCE RACES

The 24 Hours of Le Mans

Officially, the Le Mans Grand Prix. First run May 22-23, 1923. All subsequent races have been held in June, except in 1956 (July) and 1968 (September). Originally contested on a 10.73-mile track, the circuit was shortened to 8.383 miles in 1932 and has fluxuated around 8.5 miles ever since. The original start of Le Mans, where drivers raced across the track to their unstarted cars, was discontinued in 1970.

Multiple winners: Jacky Ickx (6); Derek Bell (5); Yannick Dalmas, Oliver Gendebien, Tom Kristensen and Henri Pescarolo (4); Woolf Barnato, Frank Biela, Luigi Chinetti, Hurley Haywood, Phil Hill, Al Holbert, Klaus Ludwig and Emanuele Pirro (3); Sir Henry Birkin, Ivoe Bueb, Ron Flockhart, Jean-Pierre Jaussaud, Gerard Larrousse, Andre Rossignol, Raymond Sommer, Hans Stuck, Gijs van Lennep and Jean-Pierre Wimille (2).

Year	Drivers	Car	MPH
1923	Andre Lagache & Rene Leonard	Chenard & Walcker	57.21
1924	John Duff & Francis Clement	Bentley	53.78
1925	Gerard de Courcelles & Andre Rossignol	La Lorraine	57.84
1926	Robert Bloch & Andre Rossignol	La Lorraine	66.08
1927	J.D. Benjafield & Sammy Davis	Bentley	61.35
1928	Woolf Barnato & Bernard Rubin	Bentley	69.11
1929	Woolf Barnato & Sir Henry Birkin	Bentley Speed 6	73.63
1930	Woolf Barnato & Glen Kidston	Bentley Speed 6	75.88
1931	Earl Howe & Sir Henry Birkin	Alfa Romeo	78.13
1932	Raymond Sommer & Luigi Chinetti	Alfa Romeo	76.48
1933	Raymond Sommer & Tazio Nuvolari	Alfa Romeo	81.40
1934	Luigi Chinetti & Philippe Etancelin	Alfa Romeo	74.74
1935	John Hindmarsh & Louis Fontes	Lagonda	77.85
1936	Not held		
1937	Jean-Pierre Wimille & Robert Benoist	Bugatti 57G	85.13
1938	Eugene Chaboud & Jean Tremoulet	Delahaye	82.36
1939	Jean-Pierre Wimille & Pierre Veyron	Bugatti 57G	86.86
1940-48	Not held		

Year	Drivers	Car	MPH
1949	Luigi Chinetti & Lord Selsdon	Ferrari	82.28
1950	Louis Rosier & Jean-Louis Rosier	Talbot-Lago	89.71
1951	Peter Walker & Peter Whitehead	Jaguar C	93.50
1952	Hermann Lang & Fritz Reiss	Mercedes-Benz	96.67
1953	Tony Rolt & Duncan Hamilton	Jaguar C	98.65
1954	Froilan Gonzalez & Maurice Trintignant	Ferrari 375	105.13
1955	Mike Hawthorn & Ivor Bueb	Jaguar D	107.05
1956	Ron Flockhart & Ninian Sanderson	Jaguar D	104.47
1957	Ron Flockhart & Ivor Bueb	Jaguar D	113.83
1958	Oliver Gendebien & Phil Hill	Ferrari 250	106.18
1959	Roy Salvadori & Carroll Shelby	Aston Martin	112.55
1960	Oliver Gendebien & Paul Fräre	Ferrari 250	109.17
1961	Oliver Gendebien & Phil Hill	Ferrari 250	115.88
1962	Oliver Gendebien & Phil Hill	Ferrari 250	115.22
1963	Lodovico Scarfiotti & Lorenzo Bandini	Ferrari 250	118.08
1964	Jean Guichel & Nino Vaccarella	Ferrari 275	121.54
1965	Masten Gregory & Jochen Rindt	Ferrari 250	121.07

ENDURANCE RACES (Cont.)

Year	Drivers	Car	MPH
1966	Bruce McLaren & Chris Amon	Ford Mk. II	125.37
1967	A.J. Foyt & Dan Gurney	Ford Mk. IV	135.46
1968	Pedro Rodriguez & Lucien Bianchi	Ford GT40	115.27
1969	Jacky Ickx & Jackie Oliver	Ford GT40	129.38
1970	Hans Herrmann & Richard Attwood	Porsche 917	119.28
1971	Gijs van Lennep & Helmut Marko	Porsche 917	138.13
1972	Graham Hill & Henri Pescarolo	Matra-Simca	121.45
1973	Henri Pescarolo & Gerard Larrousse	Matra-Simca	125.67
1974	Henri Pescarolo & Gerard Larrousse	Matra-Simca	119.27
1975	Derek Bell & Jacky Ickx	Mirage-Ford	118.98
1976	Jacky Ickx & Gijs van Lennep	Porsche 936	123.49
1977	Jacky Ickx, Jurgen Barth & Hurley Haywood	Porsche 936	120.95
1978	Jean-Pierre Jaussaud & Didier Pironi	Renault-Alpine	130.60
1979	Klaus Ludwig, Bill Wittington & Don Whittington	Porsche 935	108.10
1980	Jean-Pierre Jaussaud & Jean Rondeau	Rondeau-Cosworth	119.23
1981	Jacky Ickx & Derek Bell	Porsche 936	124.94
1982	Jacky Ickx & Derek Bell	Porsche 956	126.85
1983	Vern Schuppan, Hurley Haywood & Al Holbert	Porsche 956	130.70
1984	Klaus Ludwig & Henri Pescarolo	Porsche 956	126.88
1985	Klaus Ludwig, Paolo Barilla & John Winter	Porsche 956	131.75
1986	Derek Bell, Hans Stuck & Al Holbert	Porsche 962	128.75
1987	Derek Bell, Hans Stuck & Al Holbert	Porsche 962	124.06
1988	Jan Lammers, Johnny Dumfries & Andy Wallace	Jaguar XJR	137.75
1989	Jochen Mass, Manuel Reuter & Stanley Dickens	Sauber-Mercedes	136.39
1990	John Nielsen, Price Cobb & Martin Brundle	Jaguar XJR-12	126.71
1991	Volker Weider, Johnny Herbert & Bertrand Gachof	Mazda 787B	127.31
1992	Derek Warwick, Yannick Dalmas & Mark Blundell	Peugeot 905B	123.89
1993	Geoff Brabham, Christophe Bouchut & Eric Helary	Peugeot 905	132.58
1994	Yannick Dalmas, Hurley Haywood & Mauro Baldi	Porsche 962LM	129.82
1995	Yannick Dalmas, J.J. Lehto & Masanori Sekiya	McLaren BMW	105.00
1996	Davy Jones, Manuel Reuter & Alexander Wurz	TWR Porsche	124.65
1997	Michele Alberto, Stefan Johansson & Tom Kristensen	TWR Porsche	126.88
1998	Laurent Aiello, Allan McNish & Stephane Ortelli	Porsche 911 GT1	123.86
1999	Yannick Dalmas, Joachim Winkelhock & Pierluigi Martini	BMW V-12 LMR	129.38
2000	Frank Biela, Tom Kristensen & Emanuele Pirro	Audi R8	128.34
2001	Frank Biela, Tom Kristensen & Emanuele Pirro	Audi R8	129.66
2002	Frank Biela, Tom Kristensen & Emanuele Pirro	Audi R8	131.89

Mark Thompson/Allsport

*Audi drivers **Emanuele Pirro**, **Tom Kristensen** and **Frank Biela** became the first team in the race's 79-year history to win three straight 24 Hours of Le Mans titles in 2002.*

The 24 Hours of Daytona

Officially, the Rolex 24 at Daytona. First run in 1962 as a three-hour race and won by Dan Gurney in a Lotus 19 Ford. Contested over a 3.56-mile course at Daytona (Fla.) International Speedway. There have been several distance changes since 1962: the event was a three-hour race (1962-63); a 2,000-kilometer race (1964-65); a 24-hour race (1966-71); a six-hour race (1972) and a 24-hour race again since 1973. The race was canceled in 1974 due to a national energy crisis.

Multiple winners: Hurley Haywood (5); Peter Gregg, Pedro Rodriguez and Bob Wollek (4); Derek Bell, Butch Leitzinger, Rolf Stommelen and Andy Wallace (3); Mauro Baldi, A.J. Foyt, Al Holbert, Ken Miles, John Paul Jr., Brian Redman, Elliott Forbes-Robinson, Lloyd Ruby, Didier Theys and Al Unser Jr. (2).

Year	Drivers	Car	MPH
1962	Dan Gurney	Lotus 19 Ford	104.101
1963	Pedro Rodriguez	Ferrari GTO	102.074
1964	Pedro Rodriguez & Phil Hill	Ferrari GTO	98.230
1965	Ken Miles & Lloyd Ruby	Ford GT	99.944
1966	Ken Miles & Lloyd Ruby	Ford Mk. II	108.020
1967	Lorenzo Bandini & Chris Amon	Ferrari 330	105.688
1968	Vic Elford & Jochen Neerpasch	Porsche 907	106.697
1969	Mark Donohue & Chuck Parsons	Lola Chevrolet	99.268
1970	Pedro Rodriguez & Leo Kinnunen	Porsche 917	114.866
1971	Pedro Rodriguez & Jackie Oliver	Porsche 917K	109.203
1972	Mario Andretti & Jacky Ickx	Ferrari 312P	122.573
1973	Peter Gregg & Hurley Haywood	Porsche Carrera	106.225
1974	Not held		
1975	Peter Gregg & Hurley Haywood	Porsche Carrera	108.531
1976	Peter Gregg, Brian Redman & John Fitzpatrick	BMW CSL	104.040
1977	Hurley Haywood, John Graves & Dave Helmick	Porsche Carrera	108.801
1978	Peter Gregg, Rolf Stommelen & Antoine Hezemans	Porsche Turbo	108.743
1979	Hurley Haywood, Ted Field & Danny Ongais	Porsche Turbo	109.249
1980	Rolf Stommelen, Volkert Merl & Reinhold Joest	Porsche Turbo	114.303
1981	Bobby Rahal, Brian Redman & Bob Garretson	Porsche Turbo	113.153
1982	John Paul Sr., John Paul Jr. & Rolf Stommelen	Porsche Turbo	114.794
1983	A.J. Foyt, Preston Henn, Bob Wollek & Claude Ballot-Lena	Porsche Turbo	98.781
1984	Sarel van der Merwe, Tony Martin & Graham Duxbury	March Porsche	103.119
1985	A.J. Foyt, Bob Wollek, Al Unser Sr. & Thierry Boutsen	Porsche 962	104.162
1986	Al Holbert, Derek Bell & Al Unser Jr	Porsche 962	105.484
1987	Al Holbert, Derek Bell, Chip Robinson & Al Unser Jr	Porsche 962	111.599
1988	Raul Boesel, Martin Brundle & John Nielsen	Jaguar XJR-9	107.943
1989	John Andretti, Derek Bell & Bob Wollek	Porsche 962	92.009
1990	Davy Jones, Jan Lammers & Andy Wallace	Jaguar XJR-12	112.857
1991	Hurley Haywood, John Winter, Frank Jelinski, Henri Pescarolo & Bob Wollek	Porsche 962-C	106.633
1992	Masahiro Hasemi, Kazuyoshi Hoshino & Toshio Suzuki	Nissan R-91	112.897
1993	P.J. Jones, Mark Dismore & Rocky Moran	Toyota Eagle	103.537
1994	Paul Gentilozzi, Scott Pruett, Butch Leitzinger & Steve Millen	Nissan 300 ZXT	104.80
1995	Jurgen Lassig, Christophe Bouchut, Giovanni Lavaggi & Marco Werner	Porsche Spyder	102.280
1996	Wayne Taylor, Scott Sharp & Jim Pace	Oldsmobile Arness MK-III	103.32
1997	Rob Dyson, James Weaver, Butch Leitzinger, Andy Wallace, John Paul Jr., Eliot Forbes-Robinson & John Schneider	Ford R&S MK-III	102.29
1998	Mauro Baldi, Arie Luyendyk, Gianpiero Moretti & Didier Theys	Ferrari 333	105.40
1999	Elliot Forbes-Robinson, Butch Leitzinger & Andy Wallace	Riley & Scott Ford	104.957
2000	Olivier Beretta, Dominique Dupuy & Karl Wendlinger	Dodge Viper	107.207
2001	Ron Fellows, Franck Freon, Chris Kneifel & Johnny O'Connell	Chevy Corvette	97.293
2002	Mauro Baldi, Fredy Lienhard, Max Papis & Didier Theys	Dallara LMP900	106.143

NHRA DRAG RACING

NHRA Champions

Based on points earned during the NHRA POWERade Drag Racing series. The series, originally sponsored by the R.J. Reynolds Tobacco Company's Winston brand, began for Top Fuel, Funny Car and Pro Stock in 1975. The Coca-Cola Company's POWERade brand soft drink began a five-year sponsorship deal with the series in 2002.

Top Fuel

Multiple winners: Joe Amato (5); Don Garlits, Shirley Muldowney and Gary Scelzi (3); Kenny Bernstein and Scott Kalitta (2).

Year		Year		Year		Year	
1975	Don Garlits	1982	Shirley Muldowney	1989	Gary Ormsby	1996	Kenny Bernstein
1976	Richard Tharp	1983	Gary Beck	1990	Joe Amato	1997	Gary Scelzi
1977	Shirley Muldowney	1984	Joe Amato	1991	Joe Amato	1998	Gary Scelzi
1978	Kelly Brown	1985	Don Garlits	1992	Joe Amato	1999	Tony Schumacher
1979	Rob Bruins	1986	Don Garlits	1993	Eddie Hill	2000	Gary Scelzi
1980	Shirley Muldowney	1987	Dick LaHaie	1994	Scott Kalitta	2001	Kenny Bernstein
1981	Jeb Allen	1988	Joe Amato	1995	Scott Kalitta		

Funny Car

Multiple winners: John Force (11); Don Prudhomme, Kenny Bernstein (4); Raymond Beadle (3); Frank Hawley (2).

Year		Year		Year		Year	
1975	Don Prudhomme	1982	Frank Hawley	1989	Bruce Larson	1996	John Force
1976	Don Prudhomme	1983	Frank Hawley	1990	John Force	1997	John Force
1977	Don Prudhomme	1984	Mark Oswald	1991	John Force	1998	John Force
1978	Don Prudhomme	1985	Kenny Bernstein	1992	Cruz Pedregon	1999	John Force
1979	Raymond Beadle	1986	Kenny Bernstein	1993	John Force	2000	John Force
1980	Raymond Beadle	1987	Kenny Bernstein	1994	John Force	2001	John Force
1981	Raymond Beadle	1988	Kenny Bernstein	1995	John Force		

Pro Stock

Multiple winners: Bob Glidden (9); Warren Johnson (6); Lee Shepherd (4); Darrell Alderman and Jim Yates (2).

Year		Year		Year		Year	
1975	Bob Glidden	1982	Lee Shepherd	1989	Bob Glidden	1996	Jim Yates
1976	Larry Lombardo	1983	Lee Shepherd	1990	John Myers	1997	Jim Yates
1977	Don Nicholson	1984	Lee Shepherd	1991	Darrell Alderman	1998	Warren Johnson
1978	Bob Glidden	1985	Bob Glidden	1992	Warren Johnson	1999	Warren Johnson
1979	Bob Glidden	1986	Bob Glidden	1993	Warren Johnson	2000	Jeg Coughlin Jr.
1980	Bob Glidden	1987	Bob Glidden	1994	Darrell Alderman	2001	Warren Johnson
1981	Lee Shepherd	1988	Bob Glidden	1995	Warren Johnson		

All-Time Leaders

Career Victories

All-time leaders through 2001. Drivers active in 2002 are in **bold**.

	Top Fuel			Funny Car			Pro Stock	
1	Joe Amato	52	1	**John Force**	98	1	**Warren Johnson**	87
2	**Don Garlits**	35	2	Don Prudhomme	35	2	Bob Glidden	85
3	**Kenny Bernstein**	31	3	**Kenny Bernstein**	30	3	**Darrell Alderman**	27
4	**Cory McClenathan**	26	4	**Cruz Pedregon**	22	4	Lee Shepherd	26
5	**Gary Scelzi**	25	5	Ed McCulloch	18	5	**Jim Yates**	23
				Mark Oswald	18		**Jeg Coughlin**	23

National-Event Victories (pro categories)

1	**John Force**	98	9	John Myers	33	16	**Jim Yates**	23
2	**Warren Johnson**	87	10	**Matt Hines**	28		**Jeg Coughlin**	23
3	Bob Glidden	85	11	**Darrell Alderman**	27	18	Ed McCulloch	22
4	**Kenny Bernstein**	61	12	Lee Shepherd	26		**Cruz Pedregon**	22
5	Joe Amato	52		**Cory McClenathan**	26		**Kurt Johnson**	22
6	Don Prudhomme	49	14	**Gary Scelzi**	25		**Mike Dunn**	22
7	Dave Schultz	45	15	Terry Vance	24		**Angelle Savoie**	22
8	**Don Garlits**	35						

Fastest Mile-Per-Hour Speeds

Fastest performances in NHRA major event history through 2001.

Top Fuel	Funny Car	Pro Stock
MPH	**MPH**	**MPH**
333.08 Tony Schumacher, 10/6/2001	325.69 Whit Bazemore, 9/1/2001	204.35 Mark Osborne, 10/7/2001
332.18 Kenny Bernstein, 10/6/2001	325.45 Whit Bazemore, 9/30/2001	203.83 Troy Coughlin, 10/7/2001
331.61 Mike Dunn, 3/23/2001	325.37 W. Bazemore, 10/19/2001	203.74 Kurt Johnson, 10/6/2001
331.53 Mike Dunn, 5/25/2001	325.14 John Force, 10/6/2001	203.74 Mark Osborne, 10/7/2001
330.88 Kenny Bernstein, 6/2/2001	324.98 Gary Densham, 11/11/2001	203.40 Troy Coughlin, 10/7/2001

Boxing

Welterweight **Vernon Forrest** was sky high after shocking unbeaten Shane Mosley for the WBC belt.

AP/Wide World Photos

Defining Moments

Oscar De La Hoya and Lennox Lewis both made bold moves in 2002 to solidify their status as all-time greats.

Gerry Brown *is co-editor of the ESPN/Information Please Sports Almanac.*

Quien es mas macho? Oscar De La Hoya answered that question and may have defined his career with his gut-check win over bitter rival Fernando Vargas Sept. 14 in Las Vegas.

Vargas had publicly berated De La Hoya and claimed he was "more Mexican" than De La Hoya. The lead up to the fight got nasty, prompting the usually coolly detached De La Hoya to admit that he hated Vargas and would enjoy beating him.

On fight night, Vargas lived up to his "Ferocious" nickname and, as expected, came out slugging from the start. Hoping to capitalize on his natural power advantage, Vargas pursued De La Hoya and seemed to be on the right track early in the fight, getting in some good shots with De La Hoya on the ropes.

De La Hoya survived the avalanche of fists and took over, as his superior fitness and boxing skills became an advantage later in the bout. "The Golden Boy," steadily landing more and more shots, got to Vargas late in the 10th and again in the 11th, dropping him with a big left to the jaw.

Vargas got up but soon crumbled again under the weight of De La Hoya's rapid-fire punches. Referee Joe Cortez jumped in and ended the fight at 1:48 with Vargas slumped in a corner. After the fight, De La Hoya was all smiles, while Vargas was taken to a local hospital as a precaution.

The marquee match-up of the year in the heavyweight division was certainly the long-time-coming meeting of Lennox Lewis and Mike Tyson. Although Tyson is not the world's baddest man any longer, many thought he might have a shot against the larger Lewis following the big heavyweight's surprising knockout loss to

AP/Wide World Photos

***Oscar De La Hoya**, right, saw to it that he beat fellow Angelino **Fernando Vargas** with an 11th-round technical knockout in their heavily hyped junior middleweight title fight.*

lightly regarded Hasim Rahman last November. Suspicions regarding Lewis's chin were floated and observers wondered if Tyson might be able to get lucky with one of his trademark short, hard punches.

That the fight came off at all was somewhat of a surprise to some who were convinced that Tyson would do anything to avoid having to answer the opening bell. At a pre-fight press conference a full-scale brawl exploded when Tyson crossed the stage and shoved a member of Lewis's entourage.

After allegations of another Tyson bite (this time on a ballroom stage instead of inside a boxing ring) were settled, the fight was finally on for June 8 at The Pyramid in Memphis, Tenn.

In order to avoid another fracas that might jeopardize the payday for all involved, a phalanx of yellow-clad security guards separated the ring in half to keep the two men at bay.

Following an even opening round, Tyson was outclassed over the remainder of the fight. In the end the man who once shouted his desire to eat Lewis's children was knocked out for the third time in his career, left bat-

*World champion **Lennox Lewis** cemented his heavyweight legacy with a commanding eighth-round knockout of fallen former champion **Mike Tyson**.*

tered and bloody after failing to answer referee Eddie Cotton's count in the eighth round.

The win was an important one for Lewis. It helped strengthen his image as the dominant heavyweight of his era. It's a reputation that seems to have been given to him reluctantly and is one that he is anxious to protect.

Perhaps the most entertaining point of the evening was a rambling postfight interview given by Tyson in which in answering a question about what was next for him, said, "I don't know. I might just fade into Bolivian."

Whatever Tyson's future is, a rematch with Lennox Lewis (while maybe inevitable) is unnecessary. That issue was settled in Memphis and it is painfully apparent that the fighter who became the youngest heavyweight champion in history and then returned from a three-year jail sentence to regain his title is not with us any more. Tyson, once the king of professional boxing, has now lost three straight title fights.

The man who was also considered the dominant heavyweight of his era and was a fearsome Elvis-sized presence has left the building and this time he's not coming back.

The Ten Biggest Stories of the Year in Boxing

10 ▪ Former heavyweight contender David Tua bounces back from the brink of irrelevancy and makes a statement by destroying former linear heavyweight champion Michael Moorer, knocking him out just 30 seconds into round one.

9 ▪ Felix "Tito" Trinidad unexpectedly announces his retirement. The former world champion was dethroned by Bernard Hopkins in September 2001 but TKO'd Hacine Cherifi in the fourth round of their non-title bout in May 2002. Despite the fact that Trinidad has no shortage of big money fights waiting for him, including potential blockbuster rematches with Hopkins and Oscar De La Hoya, he maintains that he has made his decision to end his fighting career.

8 ▪ Undisputed light heavyweight champion Roy Jones Jr., whose legacy seemingly suffers from his lack of quality opposition, announces a plan to move up to heavyweight and face WBA champion John Ruiz. Ruiz accepts the challenge and Jones's list of demands and a March 1 date for the bout at the Thomas and Mack Center in Las Vegas was set. Jones has said he would bulk up to about 190 pounds before facing the 233-pound Ruiz.

7 ▪ The supremely confident young junior welterweight Zab Judah is knocked silly with two straight rights from veteran underdog Kostya Tszyu in the second round of their Nov. 3, 2001 world title unification bout in Las Vegas. Judah throws a stool across the ring and shoves a glove into referee Jay Nady's face to protest what he thought was a premature stoppage.

6 ▪ With more than 10 sanctioning bodies handing out belts to so-called world champions in 17 weight divisions, figuring out who's the best of the best has gotten confusing. In April 2002 *The Ring* magazine stepped in to help. There are only four ways to become a Ring champion: **1.** Defeat a reigning Ring champion. **2.** Unify the WBC, IBF and WBA titles in a division that doesn't already have a *Ring* champion. **3.** Under certain conditions, *The Ring* will recognize a fighter as champion if a dominant alphabet titlist (IBF, WBA, WBC) beats another champion in the same division. **4.** If Ring's top two contenders in a division fight and the magazine's title is vacant, the winner earns the title.

5 ▪ Micky Ward and Arturo Gatti hook up in a bloody ten-round war on May 22. The two tough junior welterweights slug it out in what many consider the fight of the year. Ward wins the hard-fought majority decision.

4 ▪ Marco Antonio Barrera beats Erik Morales by unanimous decision in their long-awaited rematch. Morales won their legendary first meeting in a controversial split decision but this time there is no doubting that Barrera is the better man.

3 ■ Heavy underdog Vernon Forrest upsets previously unbeaten welterweight "Sugar" Shane Mosley for the WBC title in January and then proves to everyone that it was no fluke in the July 20 rematch, earning a second 12-round unanimous decision over Mosley, a man many had crowned as their pound-for-pound champion.

2 ■ Lennox Lewis exposes Hasim Rahman as a one-hit wonder and reclaims the heavyweight title in November 2001, then knocks out for-mer champion Mike Tyson in the eighth round of their highly publicized title bout.

1 ■ Oscar De La Hoya stops an angry Fernando Vargas in the 11th round of their roller coaster junior middleweight world title fight. Vargas' unexplained hatred of De La Hoya turns this meeting of the world's top 154-pound fighters into a barrio grudge match between two Los Angeles-area Mexican-Americans. Vargas seems to have De La Hoya where he wants him in the fifth round but his assault soon falters and De La Hoya asserts himself as the fight draws on, ending the feud with a TKO in the 11th.

Defensive Position

Bernard Hopkins has made 15 consecutive successful middleweight title defenses—a division record. He passed Carlos Monzon for the record with a TKO of Carl Daniels in February 2002. Here is the list of the most consecutive successful title defenses in the middleweight division.

Fighter, Years	Bouts	Lost to
Bernard Hopkins, 96—	15	—
Carlos Monzon, 71-77	14	retired
Marvin Hagler, 81-87	13	Leonard

Lennox the Late Bloomer

With his dismantling of Mike Tyson in June 2002, Lennox Lewis improved to 6-1 in title bouts since turning 34 years old. No other heavyweight in history has a higher career win percentage in title bouts after turning 34.

Fighter	W-L-D	Pct
Lennox Lewis	6-1-0	.857
Muhammad Ali	7-2-0	.778
Evander Holyfield	5-2-2	.667
George Foreman	2-1-0	.667
Jack Johnson	2-1-1	.625

2001-2002
Season in Review

Information Please®
SPORTS ALMANAC

Current Champions
WBA, WBC and IBF Titleholders (through Oct. 31, 2002)

The champions of professional boxing's 17 principal weight divisions, as recognized by the Word Boxing Association (WBA), World Boxing Council (WBC) and International Boxing Federation (IBF). Where applicable, records listed below fighters' names indicate wins-losses-draws-no contest.

	Weight Limit	WBA Champion	WBC Champion	IBF Champion
Heavyweight	—	John Ruiz 38-4-0, 27 KOs	Lennox Lewis 40-2-1, 31 KOs	vacant
Cruiserweight	190 lbs	Jean-Marc Mormeck 28-2-0, 20 KOs	Wayne Braithwaite 18-0-0, 15 KOs	Vassiliy Jirov 31-0-0, 27 KOs
Light Heavyweight	175 lbs	Roy Jones Jr.* 47-1-0, 38 KOs	Roy Jones Jr. 47-1-0, 38 KOs	Roy Jones Jr. 47-1-0, 38 KOs
Super Middleweight	168 lbs	Byron Mitchell 25-1-1, 18 KOs	Eric Lucas 36-4-3, 13 KOs	Sven Ottke 28-0-0, 6 KOs
Middleweight	160 lbs	Bernard Hopkins* 41-2-1-1, 30 KOs	Bernard Hopkins 41-2-1-1, 30 KOs	Bernard Hopkins 41-2-1-1, 30 KOs
Jr. Middleweight	154 lbs	Oscar De La Hoya* 35-2-0, 28 KOs	Oscar De La Hoya 35-2-0, 28 KOs	Ronald Wright 44-3-0, 25 KOs
Welterweight	147 lbs	Richard Mayorga 23-1-1-1, 21 KOs	Vernon Forrest 35-0-0, 26 KOs	Michele Piccirillo 37-1-0-1, 23 KOs
Jr. Welterweight	140 lbs	Kostya Tszyu* 29-1-1, 23 KOs	Kostya Tszyu 29-1-1, 23 KOs	Kostya Tszyu 29-1-1, 23 KOs
Lightweight	135 lbs	Leonard Dorin 20-0-0, 7 KOs	Floyd Mayweather Jr. 28-0-0, 20 KOs	Paul Spadafora 35-0-0, 14 KOs
Jr. Lightweight	130 lbs	Acelino Freitas* 32-0-0, 29 KOs	Sirimongkol Singmanassak 40-1-0, 22 KOs	vacant
Featherweight	126 lbs	Derrick Gainer 38-5-1, 24 KOs	vacant	vacant
Jr. Featherweight	122 lbs	Salim Medjkoune 40-3-1, 21 KOs	Willie Jorrin* 28-0-1, 12 KOs	Manny Pacquiao 35-2-1, 25 KOs
Bantamweight	118 lbs	Johnny Bredahl 52-2-0, 26 KOs	Veerapol Saphrom 39-1-1, 26 KOs	Tim Austin 25-0-1, 22 KOs
Jr. Bantamweight	115 lbs	Alexander Munoz 23-0-0, 23 KOs	Masamori Tokuyama 27-2-1, 8 KOs	Felix Machado 22-3-1, 11 KOs
Flyweight	112 lbs	Eric Morel 32-0-0, 18 KOs	Pongsaklek Wonjongkam 45-2-0, 26 KOs	Irene Pacheco 26-0-0, 20 KOs
Jr. Flyweight	108 lbs	Rosendo Alvarez 31-2-1, 20 KOs	Jorge Arce 30-3-1, 22 KOs	Ricardo Lopez 50-0-1, 37 KOs
Minimumweight	105 lbs	Noel Arambulent 18-2-1-1, 10 KOs	Jose Antonio Aguirre 29-1-1, 19 KOs	Miguel Barrera 19-0-2, 11 KOs

Note: The following weight divisions are also known by these names—**Cruiserweight** as Jr. Heavyweight; **Jr. Middleweight** as Super Welterweight; **Jr. Welterweight** as Super Lightweight; **Jr. Lightweight** as Super Featherweight; **Jr. Featherweight** as Super Bantamweight; **Jr. Bantamweight** as Super Flyweight; **Jr. Flyweight** as Light Flyweight; and **Minimumweight** as Strawweight or Mini-Flyweights.

*Roy Jones Jr. is the WBA light heavyweight "super world champion;" Bernard Hopkins is the WBA middleweight "super world champion;" Santiago Samaniego (36-6-1, 29 KOs) is the interim WBA junior middleweight champion; Kostya Tszyu is the WBA super lightweight "super world champion;" Acelino Freitas is the WBA super featherweight "super world champion;" Oscar Larios (45-3-1, 32 KOs) is currently the interim WBC junior featherweight champion.

Major Bouts, 2001–02

Division by division, from Nov. 1, 2001 through Oct. 31, 2002.

WBA, WBC and IBF champions are listed in **bold** type. Note the following Result columm abbreviations (in alphabetical order): **Disq.** (won by disqualification); **KO** (knockout); **MDraw** (majority draw); **NC** (no contest); **SDraw** (split draw); **TDraw** (technical draw); **TKO** (technical knockout); **TWm** (won by technical majority decision); **TWs** (won by technical split decision); **TWu** (won by technical unanimous decision); **Wm** (won by majority decision); **Ws** (won by split decision) and **Wu** (won by unanimous decision).

Heavyweights

Date	Winner	Loser	Result	Title	Site
Nov. 17	Lennox Lewis	**Hasim Rahman**	KO 4	**IBF/WBC**	Las Vegas
Dec. 1	Fres Oquendo	David Izon	TKO 3	—	New York City
Dec. 1	Jameel McCline	Goofi Whitaker	Wu 12	—	New York City
Dec. 8	Vitali Klitschko	Ross Puritty	TKO 11	—	Oberhausen, Germany
Dec. 8	Clifford Etienne	Dan Ward	TKO 2	—	Biloxi, Miss.
Dec. 9	Michael Moorer	Terry Porter	TKO 4	—	Tulsa, Okla.
Dec. 15	**John Ruiz**	Evander Holyfield	Draw 12	**WBA**	Mashantucket, Conn.
Dec. 19	David Tua	Garing Lane	TKO 8	—	Oroville, Calif.
Feb. 2	Goofi Whitaker	Willie Chapman	TKO 4	—	Phoenix
Feb. 2	Clifford Etienne	Gabe Brown	TKO 7	—	Miami
Feb. 8	Vitali Klitschko	Vaughn Bean	TKO 11	—	Braunschweig, Germany
Feb. 16	Michael Moorer	Robert Davis	Wu 10	—	Uncasville, Conn.
Mar. 9	Michael Grant	Reynaldo Minus	TKO 4	—	Pittsburgh
Mar. 16	Wladimir Klitschko	Frans Botha	TKO 8	—	Stuttgart, Germany
Mar. 17	Corey Sanders	Oleg Maskaev	TKO 8	—	Oroville, Calif.
Apr. 13	David Tua	Fres Oquendo	TKO 9	—	Chester, W.V.
Apr. 13	Michael Grant	Joe Lenart	TKO 5	—	Chester, W.V.
Apr. 27	Clifford Etienne	Terrance Lewis	Wu 10	—	Uncasville, Conn.
Apr. 27	Jameel McCline	Shannon Briggs	Wu 10	—	New York City
June 1	Michael Grant	Anthony Willis	TKO 2	—	Las Vegas
June 1	Evander Holyfield	Hasim Rahman	TWs 8*	—	Las Vegas
June 8	**Lennox Lewis**	Mike Tyson	KO 8	**IBF/WBC**	Memphis, Tenn.
June 8	Chris Byrd	Jeff Pegues	TKO 3	—	Mt. Pleasant, Mich.
June 29	Wladimir Klitschko	Ray Mercer	TKO 6	—	Atlantic City
July 27	**John Ruiz**	Kirk Johnson	Disq. 10†	**WBA**	Las Vegas
July 27	Clifford Etienne	Frans Botha	MDraw 10	—	New Orleans
Aug. 3	Michael Grant	Robert Davis	TKO 3	—	Mashantucket, Conn.
Aug. 17	David Tua	Michael Moorer	KO 1	—	Atlantic City
Aug. 17	Juan Carlos Gomez	Daniel Frank	TKO 3	—	Berlin
Sept. 22	Lou Savarese	Tim Witherspoon	TKO 5	—	Friant, Calif.
Oct. 18	Joe Mesi	David Izon	TKO 9	—	Buffalo, N.Y.
Oct. 19	Marcelo Domínguez	Fabio Moli	Wu 12	—	Buenos Aires

*Evander Holyfield was awarded the technical decision after the bout was halted in the eighth round when an expanded hematoma developed on the head of Hasim Rahman due to an earlier unintentional headbutt.

†John Ruiz retained his title when Kirk Johnson was disqualified in the 10th round for repeated low blows.

Cruiserweights (190 lbs)

(Jr. Heavyweights)

Date	Winner	Loser	Result	Title	Site
Nov. 3	**Juan Carlos Gomez**	Pietro Aurino	TKO 6	**WBC**	Lubeck, Germany
Dec. 22	Fabrice Tiozzo	Tiwon Taylor	TKO 3	—	Orleans, France
Feb. 1	**Vassiliy Jirov**	Jorge Castro	Wu 12	**IBF**	Phoenix
Feb. 23	Jean-Marc Mormeck	**Virgil Hill**	TKO 9	**WBA**	Marseille, France
Mar. 22	James Toney	Sione Asipeli	Wu 10	—	Phoenix
Apr. 6	Johnny Nelson	Ezra Sellers	KO 8	—	Copenhagen
Apr. 9	O'Neil Bell	Ka-Dy King	TKO 3	—	Rosemont, Ill.
May 31	James Toney	Michael Rush	TKO 10	—	Lincoln City, Ore.
June 29	O'Neil Bell	Eric Davis	TKO 5	—	Atlanta
Aug. 10	**Jean-Marc Mormeck**	Dale Brown	TKO 8	**WBA**	Marseille, France
Aug. 18	James Toney	Jason Robinson	KO 7	—	Tecmecula, Calif.
Oct. 12	Wayne Braithwaite	Vincenzo Cantatore	TKO 10	**WBC***	Campione d'Italia, Italy

*Wayne Braithwaite won the WBC cruiserweight title that was vacated by Juan Carlos Gomez when he moved up to heavyweight.

Light Heavyweights (175 lbs)

Date	Winner	Loser	Result	Title	Site
Dec. 14	Eric Harding	George Jones	KO 7	—	Uncasville, Conn.
Dec. 15	Dariusz Michalczewski	Richard Hall	TKO 11	—	Berlin, Germany
Dec. 22	Bruno Girard	Robert Koon	TKO 11	WBA*	Orleans, France
Jan. 25	Antonio Tarver	Reggie Johnson	Ws 12	—	Chicago
Feb. 2	**Roy Jones Jr.**	Glen Kelly	KO 10	**WBA/WBC/IBF**	Miami
Apr. 20	Dariusz Michalczewski	Joey DeGrandis	KO 2	—	Danzig, Poland
May 23	Bruno Girard	Thomas Hansvoll	Wu 12	WBA*	Levallois, France
July 13	Bruno Girard	Lou del Valle	Ws 12	WBA*	Palavas-Les Flots, France
July 20	Antonio Tarver	Eric Harding	TKO 5	—	Indianapolis
July 20	Montell Griffin	Derrick Harmon	Wu 12	—	Friant, Calif.
Sept. 7	**Roy Jones Jr.**	Clinton Woods	TKO 6	**WBA/WBC/IBF**	Portland, Ore.
Sept. 14	Dariusz Michalczewski	Richard Hall	TKO 10	—	Braunschweig, Germany

*Roy Jones Jr. is the WBA light heavyweight "super world champion."

Super Middleweights (168 lbs)

Date	Winner	Loser	Result	Title	Site
Nov. 30	**Eric Lucas**	Dingaan Thobela	TKO 8	**WBC**	Montreal
Dec. 1	**Sven Ottke**	Anthony Mundine	KO 10	**IBF**	Dortmund, Germany
Mar. 1	**Eric Lucas**	Vinny Pazienza	Wu 12	**WBC**	Mashantucket, Conn.
Mar. 16	**Sven Ottke**	Rick Thornberry	Wu 12	**IBF**	Magdeburg, Germany
Apr. 9	Antwun Echols	Kabary Salem	Wu 12	—	Chicago
Apr. 20	Joe Calzaghe	Charles Brewer	Wu 12	—	Cardiff, Wales
June 1	**Sven Ottke**	Thomas Tate	Wu 12	**IBF**	Magdeburg, Germany
June 27	Antwun Echols	Oscar Bravo	KO 1	—	Bernalillo, N.M.
June 28	Dana Rosenblatt	Juan Carlos Viloria	TDraw 3	—	Boston
July 27	**Byron Mitchell**	Julio Cesar Green	TKO 4	**WBA**	Las Vegas
Aug. 17	Joe Calzaghe	Miguel Jimenez	Wu 12	—	Cardiff, Wales
Aug. 24	**Sven Ottke**	Joe Gatti	KO 9	**IBF**	Leipzig, Germany
Sept. 6	**Eric Lucas**	Omar Sheika	Wu 12	**WBC**	Montreal

Middleweights (160 lbs)

Date	Winner	Loser	Result	Title	Site
Nov. 17	William Joppy	Howard Eastman	Wm 12	WBA*	Las Vegas
Dec. 27	Erland Betare	Joseph Sarkody	TKO 4	—	Orleans, France
Feb. 2	**Bernard Hopkins**	Carl Daniels	TKO 10	**WBA/WBC/IBF**	Reading, Penn.
Apr. 6	Harry Simon	Armand Kranjc	Wu 12	—	Copenhagen, Denmark
May 11	Felix Trinidad	Hacine Cherifi	TKO 4	—	San Juan, Puerto Rico
Oct. 10	William Joppy	Naotaka Hozumi	TKO 10	WBA*	Tokyo
Oct. 16	Hacine Cherifi	Christophe Tendil	Wu 10	—	Andrezieux-Bouthéon, France

*William Joppy won the vacant WBA title. Note that Bernard Hopkins is the WBA middleweight "super world champion."

Junior Middleweights (154 lbs)

(Super Welterweights)

Date	Winner	Loser	Result	Title	Site
Nov. 24	Julio Cesar Chavez	Terry Thomas	TKO 2	—	Juarez, Mexico
Feb. 2	**Ronald Wright**	Jason Papillion	TKO 5	**IBF**	Miami
Mar. 16	Daniel Santos	Yory Boy Campos	TKO 11	—	Las Vegas
Apr. 26	Javier Castillejo	Pierre Moreno	KO 7	—	Barcelona
July 12	Javier Castillejo	Roman Karmazin	Wu 12	WBC*	Parla, Spain
Aug. 10	Santiago Samaniego	Mamadou Thiam	TKO 12	WBA*	Marseille, France
Aug. 17	Daniel Santos	Mehrdud Takaloobighashi	Wu 12	—	Cardiff, Wales
Sept. 7	**Ronald Wright**	Bronco McKart	Disq. 8†	**IBF**	Portland, Ore.
Sept. 14	**Oscar de la Hoya**	**Fernando Vargas**	TKO 11	**WBA/WBC**	Las Vegas
Oct. 13	Epifanio Mendoza	Tokunbo Olajide	TKO 1	—	New York City

*interim title.

†Ronald "Winky" Wright retained his title when Bronco McKart was disqualified in the eighth round for repeated low blows.

Major Bouts, 2001–02 (Cont.)

Welterweights (147 lbs)

Date	Winner	Loser	Result	Title	Site
Jan. 26	Vernon Forrest	**Shane Mosley**	Wu 12	**WBC**	New York City
Mar. 16	Antonio Margarito	Antonio Diaz	TKO 10	—	Las Vegas
Mar. 30	Richard Mayorga	**Andrew Lewis**	TKO 5	**WBA**	Reading, Penn.
Apr. 13	Michele Piccirillo	Cory Spinks	Wu 12	**IBF***	Campione d'Italia, Italy
June 14	Thomas Damgaard	Peter Malinga	KO 9	—	Copenhagen
July 20	**Vernon Forrest**	Shane Mosley	Wu 12	**WBC**	Indianapolis
Aug. 23	Cory Spinks	Rafael Pineda	TWs 7†	—	Miami
Oct. 12	Antonio Margarito	Danny Perez	Wu 12	—	Anaheim, Calif.

*Michele Piccirillo won the vacant IBF welterweight title.

†Cory Spinks won the technical split decision after an accidental clash of heads at the end of the seventh round forced the fight to go to the scorecards.

Junior Welterweights (140 lbs)

(Super Lightweights)

Date	Winner	Loser	Result	Title	Site
Nov. 3	**Kostya Tszyu**	**Zab Judah**	TKO 2	**WBA/WBC/IBF**	Las Vegas
Jan. 4	Diobelys Hurtado	Ricky Quiles	Wu 12	—	Miami
Jan. 5	Jesse James Leija	Micky Ward	TWs 5*	—	San Antonio, Texas
Jan. 19	DeMarcus Corley	Ener Julio	Wu 12	—	Miami
Feb. 2	Randall Bailey	Demetrio Ceballos	TKO 5	WBA†	Reading, Penn.
Mar. 21	Omar Weis	Hector Camacho Jr.	Wu 10	—	Phoenix
Mar. 28	Sharmba Mitchell	Bernard Harris	Wu 12	—	Washington, D.C.
May 11	Diobelys Hurtado	Randall Bailey	KO 7	WBA†	San Juan, Puerto Rico
May 18	**Kostya Tszyu**	Ben Tackie	Wu 12	**WBA/WBC/IBF**	Las Vegas
July 2	Sharmba Mitchell	Frank Houghtaling	Wu 10	—	Washington, D.C.
July 13	Zab Judah	Omar Weis	Wu 10	—	Tunica, Miss.
Oct. 19	Vivian Harris	Diobelys Hurtado	TKO 2	WBA†	Houston

*Jesse James Leija was cut over the right eye in the first round on what was ruled an accidental headbutt. After the fifth round Leija was awarded the split technical decision when the fight was stopped because of the cut.

†Randall Bailey won the vacant WBA title on Feb. 2 then lost it to Diobelys Hurtado on May 11 who in turn lost it to Vivian Harris on Oct. 19. Note that Kostya Tszyu is the WBA junior welterweight "super world champion."

Lightweights (135 lbs)

Date	Winner	Loser	Result	Title	Site
Jan. 5	Leonard Dorin	**Raul Balbi**	Ws 12	**WBA**	San Antonio, Texas
Jan. 5	Artur Grigorian	Rocky Martinez	TKO 8	—	Magdeburg, Germany
Jan. 25	Jose Luis Castillo*	Juan Angel Macias	TKO 8	—	Laughlin, Nev.
Mar. 8	Juan Lazcano	Julio Cesar Sanchez	TKO 8	—	Oroville, Calif.
Mar. 9	**Paul Spadafora**	Angel Manfredy	Wu 12	**IBF**	Pittsburgh
Apr. 20	Floyd Mayweather Jr.	**Jose Luis Castillo**	Wu 12	**WBC**	Las Vegas
Apr. 20	Stevie Johnston	Alejandro Gonzalez	Wm 12	—	Las Vegas
May 31	**Leonard Dorin**	Raul Balbi	Wu 12	**WBA**	Bucharest, Romania
July 14	Kevin Kelley	Humberto Soto	Wm 12	—	Las Vegas
Sept. 14	Artur Grigorian	Stefano Zoff	Wu 12	—	Braunschweig, Germany
Sept. 20	Juan Lazcano	David Armstrong	KO 6	—	El Paso, Texas
Oct. 19	Juan Diaz	Roy Delgado	TKO 6	—	Houston
Oct. 25	Leavander Johnson	Julian Wheeler	Wm 12	—	Mashantucket, Conn.

*Jose Luis Castillo's WBC lightweight title was not at risk in his Jan. 25 bout with Juan Macias.

Junior Lightweights (130 lbs)

(Super Featherweights)

Date	Winner	Loser	Result	Title	Site
Nov. 10	**Floyd Mayweather Jr.** . . .	Jesus Chavez	TKO 9	**WBC**	San Francisco
Jan. 12	Acelino Freitas	**Joel Casamayor**	Wu 12	**WBA**	Las Vegas
Jan. 26	Arturo Gatti	Terronn Millett	KO 4	—	New York
Jan. 28	Lakva Sim	Hidenobu Matsunobu	TKO 6	—	Yokohama, Japan
Mar. 22	Jesus Chavez	Gerardo Zayas	TKO 3	—	Austin, Texas
Mar. 27	Kevin Kelley	Raul Martin Franco	TKO 2	—	Las Vegas
Apr. 13	Yodsanan Nanthachai	Lakva Sim	Wu 12	WBA*	Nakornratchasima, Thailand
May 18	Micky Ward	Arturo Gatti	Wm 10	—	Uncasville, Conn.
June 8	Joel Casamayor	Juan Arias	TKO 8	—	Memphis, Tenn.
Aug. 3	**Acelino Freitas**	Daniel Attah	Wu 12	**WBA**	Phoenix
Aug. 18	Steve Forbes	David Santos	Ws 12	**IBF†**	Tecmecula, Calif.

Date	Winner	Loser	Result	Title	Site
Aug. 24	Sirimongkol Singmanassak	Kengo Nagashima	KO 2	**WBC‡**	Tokyo
Oct. 25	Sirimongkol Singmanassak**	Richard Cabillo	KO 2	—	Nonthaburi, Thailand

Yodsanan Nanthachai won the vacant WBA super featherweight title. Note that Acelino Freitas is the WBA super featherweight "super world champion."

Steve Forbes was stripped of the IBF belt when he failed to make weight.

Sirimongkol Singmanassak won the vacant WBC super featherweight title. Floyd Mayweather Jr. relinquished the belt when he moved up to lightweight.

**Sirimongkol Singmanassak's WBC title was not at risk for his Oct. 25 bout against Richard Cabillo.

Featherweights (126 lbs)

Date	Winner	Loser	Result	Title	Site
Nov. 16	Manuel Medina	**Frankie Toledo**	TKO 6	IBF	Las Vegas
Jan. 19	Johnny Tapia	Eduardo Alvarez	TKO 1	—	London
Mar. 9	Juan Manuel Marquez	Robbie Peden	TKO 10	—	Pittsburgh
Mar. 30	Injin Chi	Samuel Duran	KO 3	—	South Korea
Apr. 27	Johnny Tapia	**Manuel Medina**	Wu 12	IBF	New York City
May 18	Naseem Hamed	Manuel Calvo	Wu 12	—	London
June 21	Juan Manuel Marquez	Hector Marquez	KO 10	—	Las Vegas
June 22	Marco Antonio Barrera	**Erik Morales**	Wu 12	WBC*	Las Vegas
Aug. 24	Derrick Gainer	Daniel Seda	TDraw 2†	WBA	Carolina, Puerto Rico
Aug. 31	Julio Chacon	Victor Hugo Paz	Wu 10	—	Mendoza, Argentina
Oct. 19	Rocky Juarez	Hector Acero-Sanchez	Wu 10	—	Houston
Oct. 19	Scott Harrison	Juan Pablo Chacon	Wu 12	—	Glasgow, Scotland

*Marco Antonio Barrera declined to accept the WBC featherweight belt that he earned by beating Morales.

†Derrick Gainer retained his WBA belt when the bout was ruled a technical draw due to an accidental clash of heads in the second round.

Junior Featherweights (122 lbs)

(Super Bantamweights)

Date	Winner	Loser	Result	Title	Site
Nov. 10	**Manny Pacquiao**	Agapito Sanchez	TDraw 6*	IBF	San Francisco
Nov. 17	Yober Ortega	Jose Rojas	KO 4	WBA†	Las Vegas
Feb. 5	**Willie Jorrin**	Osamu Sato	MDraw 12	WBC	Toyko
Feb. 21	Yoddamrong Sithyodthong	**Yober Ortega**	Wu 12	WBA	Bangkok
Feb. 23	Paulie Ayala	Clarence Adams	Wu 12	—	Las Vegas
May 17	Oscar Larios	Israel Vazquez	TKO 12	WBC‡	Sacramento
May 18	Osamu Sato	**Yoddamrong Sithyodthong**	KO 8	WBA	Saitama, Japan
June 8	**Manny Pacquiao**	Jorge Julio	TKO 2	IBF	Memphis, Tenn.
July 26	Yoddamrong Sithyodthong	Edward Escriber	KO 2	—	Bangkok
Aug. 24	Oscar Larios	Manabu Fukushima	TKO 8	WBC‡	Tokyo
Oct. 9	Salim Medjkoune	**Osamu Sato**	Wu 12	WBA	Tokyo
Oct. 26	**Manny Pacquiao**	Fabbrakob Rakkiatgym	TKO 1	IBF	Davao, Philippines

*MAnny Pacquiao retained the title when the bout was ruled a technical draw due to an accidental headbutt.

†Yober Ortega won the vacant WBA title.

‡Oscar Larios won the interim WBC super bantamweight title.

Bantamweights (118 lbs)

Date	Winner	Loser	Result	Title	Site
Dec. 15	**Tim Austin**	Ratanachai Vorapin	Wu 12	IBF	Mashantucket, Conn.
Jan. 11	**Veerapol Saphrom**	Sergio Perez	Wu 12	WBC	Bangkok
Feb. 23	Rafael Marquez	Mark Johnson	TKO 8	—	Las Vegas
Mar. 9	Alexander Munoz	Celes Kobayashi	TKO 8	—	Tokyo
Mar. 15	Cruz Carbajal	Mauricio Martinez	KO 9	—	Veracruz, Mexico
Mar. 30	Veerapol Saphrom*	Joel Sungahed	KO 4	—	Nonthaburi, Thailand
Apr. 19	Johnny Bredahl	**Eidy Moya**	KO 9	WBA	Copenhagen, Denmark
May 1	**Veerapol Saphrom**	Julio Coronell	Wu 12	WBC	Nonthaburi, Thailand
July 27	**Tim Austin**	Adan Vargas	TKO 10	IBF	Las Vegas
July 12	Rafael Marquez	Jorge Otero	TKO 6	—	McAllen, Texas
Aug. 24	Veerapol Saphrom*	Daven Bermudez	TKO 3	—	Bangkok
Sept. 27	Cruz Carbajal	Danny Romero	TKO 4	—	Albuquerque, N.M.
Oct. 25	Veerapol Saphrom*	Alex Escaner	TKO 6	—	Nonthaburi, Thailand

*Veerapol Saphrom's WBC bantamweight title was not at risk for his Mar. 30 bout against Joel Sungahed, his Aug. 24 bout against Daven Bermudez or his Oct. 25 bout against Alex Escaner.

Junior Bantamweights (115 lbs)

(Super Flyweights)

Date	Winner	Loser	Result	Title	Site
Mar. 8	Alexander Munoz	Celes Kobayashi	TKO 8	WBA	Tokyo
Mar. 23	Masamori Tokuyama	Ryuko Kazuhiro	KO 9	WBC	Yokohama, Japan
Mar. 30	Felix Machado	Martin Castillo	TWu 6*	IBF	Reading, Penn.
July 31	Alexander Munoz	Eiji Kojima	KO 2	WBA	Osaka, Japan
Aug. 26	Masamori Tokuyama	Erick Lopez	TKO 7	WBC	Tokyo

*Felix Machado retained the belt on a unanimous technical decision when Martin Castillo was unable to continue due to an accidental headbutt in the sixth round.

Flyweights (112 lbs)

Date	Winner	Loser	Result	Title	Site
Nov. 9	Irene Pacheco	Mike Trejo	TKO 4	IBF	San Antonio
Dec. 6	Pongsaklek Wonjongkam	Luis Lazarte	TKO 2	WBC	Pattaya, Thailand
Jan. 11	Eric Morel*	Alex Ali Baba	Wu 10	—	Caguas, Puerto Rico
Mar. 2	Jake Matlala	Juan Herrera	TKO 7	—	Carnival City, S. Africa
Apr. 19	Pongsaklek Wonjongkam	Daisuke Naito	KO 1	WBC	Khonkaen, Thailand
July 13	Omar Narvaez	Adonis Rivas	Wu 12	—	Buenos Aires
Sept. 6	Pongsaklek Wonjongkam	Jesus Martinez	Wu 12	WBC	Bangkok, Thailand
Sept. 13	Omar Narvaez	Luis Lazarte	Disq. 10†	—	Trelew, Argentina
Oct. 12	Eric Morel	Denkaosaen Kaowichit	TKO 11	WBA	Anaheim, Calif.

*Eric Morel's WBA flyweight title was not at risk in his bout with Alex Ali Baba.
†Omar Narvaez won by disqualification after an intentional headbutt from Lazarte opened a deep cut on his forehead.

Junior Flyweights (108 lbs)

(Light Flyweights)

Date	Winner	Loser	Result	Title	Site
Jan. 19	Rosendo Alvarez	Pitchit Siriwat	TKO 12	WBA	Miami
Feb. 23	Choi Yo-Sam	Shingo Yamaguchi	TKO 10	WBC	Chiba, Japan
July 6	Jorge Arce	Choi Yo-Sam	TKO 6	WBC	Seoul, S. Korea
Aug. 24	Nelson Dieppa	John Molina	TDraw 2*	—	Carolina, Puerto Rico

*The bout was ruled a technical draw after an accidental headbutt gave Nelson Dieppa a deep cut on his forehead and rendered him unable to continue.

Minimumweights (105 lbs)

(Strawweights or Mini-Flyweights)

Date	Winner	Loser	Result	Title	Site
Nov. 11	Jose Antonio Aguirre	Wolf Yasuo	TKO 3	WBC	Okayama, Japan
Jan. 4	Roberto Leyva	Frankie Soto	TKO 5	IBF	Ensenada, Mexico
Jan. 29	Keitaro Hoshino	Joma Gamboa	Wu 12	WBA*	Yokohama, Japan
Mar. 9	Roberto Leyva†	Manny Melchor	Wu 10	—	Aguascalientes, Mexico
July 28	Noel Arambulent	Keitaro Hoshino	Wm 12	WBA	Yokohama, Japan
Aug. 9	Miguel Barrera	Roberto Leyva	Wu 12	IBF	Las Vegas
Oct. 19	Jose Antonio Aguirre	Juan Palacios	Ws 12	WBC	Villahermosa, Mexico

*Keitaro Hoshino won the WBA minimumweight title that was left vacant following the unexpected retirement of Yutaka Niida.
†Roberto Leyva's IBF title was not at risk for his Mar. 9 bout with Manny Melchor.

ESPN Information Please® SPORTS ALMANAC

1884-2002
Through the Years

World Heavyweight Championship Fights

Widely accepted world champions in **bold** type. Note following result abbreviations: KO (knockout), TKO (technical knockout), Wu (unanimous decision), Wm (majority decision), Ws (split decision), Ref (referee's decision), ND (no decision), Disq. (won on disqualification).

Year	Date	Winner	Age	Wgt	Loser	Wgt	Result	Location
1892	Sept. 7	James J. Corbett	26	178	John L. Sullivan	212	KO 21	New Orleans
1894	Jan. 25	**James J. Corbett**	27	184	Charley Mitchell	158	KO 3	Jacksonville, Fla.
1897	Mar. 17	Bob Fitzsimmons	34	167	**James J. Corbett**	183	KO 14	Carson City, Nev.
1899	June 9	James J. Jeffries	24	206	**Bob Fitzsimmons**	167	KO 11	Coney Island, N.Y.
1899	Nov. 3	**James J. Jeffries**	24	215	Tom Sharkey	183	Ref 25	Coney Island, N.Y.
1900	Apr. 6	James J. Jeffries	24	NA	Jack Finnegan	NA	KO 1	Detroit
1900	May 11	James J. Jeffries	25	218	James J. Corbett	188	KO 23	Coney Island, N.Y.
1901	Nov. 15	James J. Jeffries	26	211	Gus Ruhlin	194	TKO 6	San Francisco
1902	July 25	James J. Jeffries	27	219	Bob Fitzsimmons	172	KO 8	San Francisco
1903	Aug. 14	James J. Jeffries	28	220	James J. Corbett	190	KO 10	San Francisco
1904	Aug. 25	**James J. Jeffries***	29	219	Jack Munroe	186	TKO 2	San Francisco
1905	July 3	Marvin Hart	28	190	Jack Root	171	KO 12	Reno, Nev.
1906	Feb. 23	Tommy Burns	24	180	**Marvin Hart**	188	Ref 20	Los Angeles
1906	Oct. 2	**Tommy Burns**	25	NA	Jim Flynn	NA	KO 15	Los Angeles
1906	Nov. 28	**Tommy Burns**	25	172	Phila. Jack O'Brien	163½	Draw 20	Los Angeles
1907	May 8	**Tommy Burns**	25	180	Phila. Jack O'Brien	167	Ref 20	Los Angeles
1907	July 4	**Tommy Burns**	26	181	Bill Squires	180	KO 1	Colma, Calif.
1907	Dec. 2	**Tommy Burns**	26	177	Gunner Moir	204	KO 10	London
1908	Feb. 10	**Tommy Burns**	26	NA	Jack Palmer	NA	KO 4	London
1908	Mar. 17	**Tommy Burns**	26	NA	Jem Roche	NA	KO 1	Dublin
1908	Apr. 18	**Tommy Burns**	26	NA	Jewey Smith	NA	KO 5	Paris
1908	June 13	**Tommy Burns**	26	184	Bill Squires	183	KO 8	Paris
1908	Aug. 24	**Tommy Burns**	27	181	Bill Squires	184	KO 13	Sydney
1908	Sept. 2	**Tommy Burns**	27	183	Bill Lang	187	KO 6	Melbourne
1908	Dec. 26	Jack Johnson	30	192	**Tommy Burns**	168	TKO 14	Sydney
1909	Mar. 10	**Jack Johnson**	30	NA	Victor McLaglen	NA	ND 6	Vancouver
1909	May 19	**Jack Johnson**	31	205	Phila. Jack O'Brien	161	ND 6	Philadelphia
1909	June 30	**Jack Johnson**	31	207	Tony Ross	214	ND 6	Pittsburgh
1909	Sept. 9	**Jack Johnson**	31	209	Al Kaufman	191	ND 10	San Francisco
1909	Oct. 16	**Jack Johnson**	31	205½	Stanley Ketchel	170¼	KO 12	Colma, Calif.
1910	July 4	**Jack Johnson**	32	208	James J. Jeffries	227	KO 15	Reno, Nev.
1912	July 4	**Jack Johnson**	34	195½	Jim Flynn	175	TKO 9	Las Vegas, Nev.
1913	Dec. 19	**Jack Johnson**	35	NA	Jim Johnson	NA	Draw 10	Paris
1914	June 27	**Jack Johnson**	36	221	Frank Moran	203	Ref 20	Paris
1915	Apr. 5	Jess Willard	33	230	**Jack Johnson**	205½	KO 26	Havana
1916	Mar. 25	**Jess Willard**	34	225	Frank Moran	203	ND 10	NYC (Mad.Sq. Garden)
1919	July 4	Jack Dempsey	24	187	**Jess Willard**	245	TKO 4	Toledo, Ohio
1920	Sept. 6	**Jack Dempsey**	25	185	Billy Miske	187	KO 3	Benton Harbor, Mich.
1920	Dec. 14	**Jack Dempsey**	25	188¼	Bill Brennan	197	KO 12	NYC (Mad. Sq. Garden)
1921	July 2	**Jack Dempsey**	26	188	Georges Carpentier	172	KO 4	Jersey City, N.J.
1923	July 4	**Jack Dempsey**	28	188	Tommy Gibbons	175½	Ref 15	Shelby, Mont.
1923	Sept. 14	**Jack Dempsey**	28	192½	Luis Firpo	216½	KO 2	NYC (Polo Grounds)
1926	Sept. 23	Gene Tunney	29	189½	**Jack Dempsey**	190	Wu 10	Philadelphia
1927	Sept. 22	**Gene Tunney**	30	189½	Jack Dempsey	192½	Wu 10	Chicago
1928	July 26	**Gene Tunney***	31	192	Tom Heeney	203	TKO 11	NYC (Yankee Stadium)

*James J. Jeffries retired as champion on May 13, 1905, then came out of retirement to fight Jack Johnson for the title in 1910.
**Gene Tunney retired as champion in 1928.

World Heavyweight Championship Fights (Cont.)

Year	Date	Winner	Age	Wgt	Loser	Wgt	Result	Location
1930	June 12	Max Schmeling	24	188	Jack Sharkey	197	Disq. 4	NYC (Yankee Stadium)
1931	July 3	**Max Schmeling**	25	189	Young Stribling	186½	TKO 15	Cleveland
1932	June 21	Jack Sharkey	29	205	**Max Schmeling**	188	Ws 15	Long Island City, N.Y.
1933	June 29	Primo Carnera	26	260½	**Jack Sharkey**	201	KO 6	Long Island City, N.Y.
1933	Oct. 22	**Primo Carnera**	26	259½	Paulino Uzcudun	229¼	Wu 15	Rome
1934	Mar. 1	**Primo Carnera**	27	270	Tommy Loughran	184	Wu 15	Miami
1934	June 14	Max Baer	25	209½	**Primo Carnera**	263¼	TKO 11	Long Island City, N.Y.
1935	June 13	James J. Braddock	29	193¾	**Max Baer**	209	Wu 15	Long Island City, N.Y.
1937	June 22	Joe Louis	23	197¼	**James J. Braddock**	197	KO 8	Chicago
1937	Aug. 30	**Joe Louis**	23	197	Tommy Farr	204¼	Wu 15	NYC (Yankee Stadium)
1938	Feb. 23	**Joe Louis**	23	200	Nathan Mann	193½	KO 3	NYC (Mad. Sq. Garden)
1938	Apr. 1	**Joe Louis**	23	202½	Harry Thomas	196	KO 5	Chicago
1938	June 22	**Joe Louis**	24	198¾	Max Schmeling	193	KO 1	NYC (Yankee Stadium)
1939	Jan. 25	**Joe Louis**	24	200¼	John Henry Lewis	180¾	KO 1	NYC (Mad. Sq. Garden)
1939	Apr. 17	**Joe Louis**	24	201¼	Jack Roper	204¾	KO 1	Los Angeles
1939	June 28	**Joe Louis**	25	200¾	Tony Galento	233¾	TKO 4	NYC (Yankee Stadium)
1939	Sept. 20	Bob Pastor	25	200	Bob Pastor	183	KO 11	Detroit
1940	Feb. 9	**Joe Louis**	25	203	Arturo Godoy	202	Ws 15	NYC (Mad. Sq. Garden)
1940	Mar. 29	**Joe Louis**	25	201½	Johnny Paychek	187½	KO 2	NYC (Mad. Sq. Garden)
1940	June 20	**Joe Louis**	26	199	Arturo Godoy	201¼	TKO 8	NYC (Yankee Stadium)
1940	Dec. 16	**Joe Louis**	26	202¼	Al McCoy	180¾	TKO 6	Boston
1941	Jan. 31	**Joe Louis**	26	202½	Red Burman	188	KO 5	NYC (Mad. Sq. Garden)
1941	Feb. 17	**Joe Louis**	26	203½	Gus Dorazio	193½	KO 2	Philadelphia
1941	Mar. 21	**Joe Louis**	26	202	Abe Simon	254½	TKO 13	Detroit
1941	Apr. 8	**Joe Louis**	26	203½	Tony Musto	199½	TKO 9	St. Louis
1941	May 23	**Joe Louis**	27	201½	Buddy Baer	237½	Disq. 7	Washington, D.C.
1941	June 18	**Joe Louis**	27	199½	Billy Conn	174	KO 13	NYC (Polo Grounds)
1941	Sept. 29	**Joe Louis**	27	202¼	Lou Nova	202½	TKO 6	NYC (Polo Grounds)
1942	Jan. 9	**Joe Louis**	27	206¾	Buddy Baer	250	KO 1	NYC (Mad. Sq. Garden)
1942	Mar. 27	**Joe Louis**	27	207½	Abe Simon	255½	KO 6	NYC (Mad. Sq. Garden)
1942-45 World War II								
1946	June 9	**Joe Louis**	32	207	Billy Conn	187	KO 8	NYC (Yankee Stadium)
1946	Sept. 18	**Joe Louis**	32	211	Tami Mauriello	198½	KO 1	NYC (Yankee Stadium)
1947	Dec. 5	**Joe Louis**	33	211½	Jersey Joe Walcott	194½	Ws 15	NYC (Mad. Sq. Garden)
1948	June 25	Joe Louis*	34	213½	Jersey Joe Walcott	194¾	KO 11	NYC (Yankee Stadium)
1949	June 22	**Ezzard Charles**	28	181¾	Jersey Joe Walcott	195½	Wu 15	Chicago
1949	Aug. 10	**Ezzard Charles**	28	180	Gus Lesnevich	182	TKO 8	NYC (Yankee Stadium)
1949	Oct. 14	**Ezzard Charles**	28	182	Pat Valentino	188½	KO 8	San Francisco
1950	Aug. 15	**Ezzard Charles**	29	183¼	Freddie Beshore	184½	TKO 14	Buffalo
1950	Sept. 27	**Ezzard Charles**	29	184½	Joe Louis	218	Wu 15	NYC (Yankee Stadium)
1950	Dec. 5	**Ezzard Charles**	29	185	Nick Barone	178½	KO 11	Cincinnati
1951	Jan. 12	**Ezzard Charles**	29	185	Lee Oma	193	TKO 10	NYC (Mad. Sq. Garden)
1951	Mar. 7	**Ezzard Charles**	29	186	Jersey Joe Walcott	193	Wu 15	Detroit
1951	May 30	**Ezzard Charles**	29	182	Joey Maxim	181½	Wu 15	Chicago
1951	July 18	Jersey Joe Walcott	37	194	**Ezzard Charles**	182	KO 7	Pittsburgh
1952	June 5	**Jersey Joe Walcott**	38	196	Ezzard Charles	191½	Wu 15	Philadelphia
1952	Sept. 23	Rocky Marciano	29	184	**Jersey Joe Walcott**	196	KO 13	Philadelphia
1953	May 15	**Rocky Marciano**	29	184½	Jersey Joe Walcott	197¾	KO 1	Chicago
1953	Sept. 24	**Rocky Marciano**	30	185	Roland LaStarza	184¾	TKO 11	NYC (Polo Grounds)
1954	June 17	**Rocky Marciano**	30	187½	Ezzard Charles	185½	Wu 15	NYC (Yankee Stadium)
1954	Sept. 17	**Rocky Marciano**	31	187	Ezzard Charles	192½	KO 8	NYC (Yankee Stadium)
1955	May 16	**Rocky Marciano**	31	189	Don Cockell	205	TKO 9	San Francisco
1955	Sept. 21	**Rocky Marciano****	32	188¼	Archie Moore	188	KO 9	NYC (Yankee Stadium)
1956	Nov. 30	Floyd Patterson	21	182¼	Archie Moore	187¾	KO 5	Chicago
1957	July 29	**Floyd Patterson**	22	184	Tommy Jackson	192½	TKO 10	NYC (Polo Grounds)
1957	Aug. 22	**Floyd Patterson**	22	187¼	Pete Rademacher	202	KO 6	Seattle
1958	Aug. 18	**Floyd Patterson**	23	184½	Roy Harris	194	TKO 13	Los Angeles
1959	May 1	**Floyd Patterson**	24	182½	Brian London	206	KO 11	Indianapolis
1959	June 26	Ingemar Johansson	26	196	**Floyd Patterson**	182	TKO 3	NYC (Yankee Stadium)
1960	June 20	Floyd Patterson	25	190	**Ingemar Johansson**	194¾	KO 5	NYC (Polo Grounds)

*Joe Louis retired as champion on Mar. 1, 1949, then came out of retirement to fight Ezzard Charles for the title in 1950.
**Rocky Marciano retired as undefeated champion on Apr. 27, 1956.

Year	Date	Winner	Age	Wgt	Loser	Wgt	Result	Location
1961	Mar. 13	**Floyd Patterson**	26	194¾	Ingemar Johansson	206½	KO 6	Miami Beach
1961	Dec. 4	**Floyd Patterson**	26	188½	Tom McNeeley	197	KO 4	Toronto
1962	Sept. 25	Sonny Liston	30	214	**Floyd Patterson**	189	KO 1	Chicago
1963	July 22	**Sonny Liston**	31	215	Floyd Patterson	194½	KO 1	Las Vegas
1964	Feb. 25	Cassius Clay**	22	210½	**Sonny Liston**	218	TKO 7	Miami Beach
1965	Mar. 5	Ernie Terrell WBA	25	199	Eddie Machen	192	Wu 15	Chicago
1965	May 25	**Muhammad Ali**	23	206	Sonny Liston	215¼	KO 1	Lewiston, Maine
1965	Nov. 1	Ernie Terrell WBA	26	206	George Chuvalo	209	Wu 15	Toronto
1965	Nov. 22	**Muhammad Ali**	23	210	Floyd Patterson	196¾	TKO 12	Las Vegas
1966	Mar. 29	**Muhammad Ali**	24	214½	George Chuvalo	216	Wu 15	Toronto
1966	May 21	**Muhammad Ali**	24	201½	Henry Cooper	188	TKO 6	London
1966	June 28	Ernie Terrell WBA	27	209½	Doug Jones	187½	Wu 15	Houston
1966	Aug. 6	**Muhammad Ali**	24	209½	Brian London	201½	KO 3	London
1966	Sept. 10	**Muhammad Ali**	24	203½	Karl Mildenberger	194¼	TKO 12	Frankfurt, W. Ger.
1966	Nov. 14	**Muhammad Ali**	24	212¾	Cleveland Williams	210½	TKO 3	Houston
1967	Feb. 6	**Muhammad Ali**	25	212¼	Ernie Terrell WBA	212¼	Wu 15	Houston
1967	Mar. 22	**Muhammad Ali**	25	211½	Zora Folley	202½	KO 7	NYC (Mad. Sq. Garden)
1968	Mar. 4	Joe Frazier	24	204½	Buster Mathis	243½	TKO 11	NYC (Mad. Sq. Garden)
1968	Apr. 27	Jimmy Ellis	28	197	Jerry Quarry	195	Wm 15	Oakland
1968	June 24	Joe Frazier NY	24	203½	Manuel Ramos	208	TKO 2	NYC (Mad. Sq. Garden)
1968	Aug. 14	Jimmy Ellis WBA	28	198	Floyd Patterson	188	Ref 15	Stockholm
1968	Dec. 10	Joe Frazier NY	24	203	Oscar Bonavena	207	Wu 15	Philadelphia
1969	Apr. 22	Joe Frazier NY	25	204½	Dave Zyglewicz	190½	KO 1	Houston
1969	June 23	Joe Frazier NY	25	203½	Jerry Quarry	198½	TKO 8	NYC (Mad. Sq. Garden)
1970	Feb. 16	Joe Frazier NY	26	205	Jimmy Ellis WBA	201	TKO 5	NYC (Mad. Sq. Garden)
1970	Nov. 18	**Joe Frazier**	26	209	Bob Foster	188	KO 2	Detroit
1971	Mar. 8	**Joe Frazier**	27	205½	Muhammad Ali	215	Wu 15	NYC (Mad. Sq. Garden)
1972	Jan. 15	**Joe Frazier**	28	215½	Terry Daniels	195	TKO 4	New Orleans
1972	May 26	**Joe Frazier**	28	217½	Ron Stander	218	TKO 5	Omaha, Neb.
1973	Jan. 22	George Foreman	24	217½	**Joe Frazier**	214	TKO 2	Kingston, Jamaica
1973	Sept. 1	**George Foreman**	24	219½	Jose (King) Roman	196½	KO 1	Tokyo
1974	Mar. 26	**George Foreman**	25	224¾	Ken Norton	212¾	TKO 2	Caracas, Venezuela
1974	Oct. 30	Muhammad Ali	32	216½	**George Foreman**	220	KO 8	Kinshasa, Zaire
1975	Mar. 24	**Muhammad Ali**	33	223½	Chuck Wepner	225	TKO 15	Cleveland
1975	May 16	**Muhammad Ali**	33	224½	Ron Lyle	219	TKO 11	Las Vegas
1975	June 30	**Muhammad Ali**	33	224½	Joe Bugner	230	Wu 15	Kuala Lumpur, Malaysia
1975	Oct. 1	**Muhammad Ali**	33	224½	Joe Frazier	215	TKO 14	Manila, Philippines
1976	Feb. 20	**Muhammad Ali**	34	226	Jean Pierre Coopman	206	KO 5	San Juan, P.R.
1976	Apr. 30	**Muhammad Ali**	34	230	Jimmy Young	209	Wu 15	Landover, Md.
1976	May 24	**Muhammad Ali**	34	220	Richard Dunn	206½	TKO 5	Munich, W. Ger.
1976	Sept. 28	**Muhammad Ali**	34	221	Ken Norton	217½	Wu 15	NYC (Yankee Stadium)
1977	May 16	**Muhammad Ali**	35	221¼	Alfredo Evangelista	209¼	Wu 15	Landover, Md.
1977	Sept. 29	**Muhammad Ali**	35	225	Earnie Shavers	211¼	Wu 15	NYC (Mad. Sq. Garden)
1978	Feb. 15	Leon Spinks	24	197¼	**Muhammad Ali**	224¼	Ws 15	Las Vegas
1978	June 9	Larry Holmes	28	209	Ken Norton WBC††	220	Ws 15	Las Vegas
1978	Sept. 15	Muhammad Ali†	36	221	**Leon Spinks**	201	Wu 15	New Orleans
1978	Nov. 10	Larry Holmes WBC	29	214	Alfredo Evangelista	208¼	KO 7	Las Vegas
1979	Mar. 23	Larry Holmes WBC	29	214	Osvaldo Ocasio	207	TKO 7	Las Vegas
1979	June 22	Larry Holmes WBC	29	215	Mike Weaver	202	TKO 12	NYC (Mad. Sq. Garden)
1979	Sept. 28	Larry Holmes WBC	29	210	Earnie Shavers	211	TKO 11	Las Vegas
1979	Oct. 20	John Tate	24	240	Gerrie Coetzee	222	Wu 15	Pretoria, S. Africa
1980	Feb. 3	Larry Holmes WBC	30	213½	Lorenzo Zanon	215	TKO 6	Las Vegas
1980	Mar. 31	Mike Weaver	27	232	John Tate WBA	232	KO 15	Knoxville, Tenn.
1980	Mar. 31	Larry Holmes WBC	30	211	Leroy Jones	254½	TKO 8	Las Vegas
1980	July 7	Larry Holmes WBC	30	214¼	Scott LeDoux	226	TKO 7	Minneapolis
1980	Oct. 2	Larry Holmes WBC	30	211½	Muhammad Ali	217½	TKO 11	Las Vegas
1980	Oct. 25	Mike Weaver WBA	28	210	Gerrie Coetzee	226½	KO 13	Sun City, S. Africa
1981	Apr. 11	**Larry Holmes**	31	215	Trevor Berbick	215½	Wu 15	Las Vegas
1981	June 12	**Larry Holmes**	31	212½	Leon Spinks	200¼	TKO 3	Detroit
1981	Oct. 3	Mike Weaver WBA	29	215	James (Quick) Tillis	209	Wu 15	Rosemont, Ill.

**After defeating Liston, Cassius Clay announced that he had changed his name to Muhammad Ali. He was later stripped of his title by the WBA and most state boxing commissions after refusing induction into the U.S. Army on Apr. 28, 1967.
† Muhammad Ali retired as champion on June 27, 1979, then came out of retirement to fight Larry Holmes for the title in 1980.
†† WBC recognized Ken Norton as world champion when Leon Spinks refused to meet Norton before Spinks' rematch with Muhammad Ali. Norton had scored a 15-round split decision over Jimmy Young on Nov. 5, 1977 in Las Vegas.

World Heavyweight Championship Fights (Cont.)

Year	Date	Winner	Age	Wgt	Loser	Wgt	Result	Location
1981	Nov. 6	**Larry Holmes**	32	213¼	Renaldo Snipes	215¾	TKO 11	Pittsburgh
1982	June 11	**Larry Holmes**	32	212½	Gerry Cooney	225½	TKO 13	Las Vegas
1982	Nov. 26	**Larry Holmes**	33	217½	Randall (Tex) Cobb	234¼	Wu 15	Houston
1982	Dec. 10	Michael Dokes	24	216	Mike Weaver WBA	209¾	TKO 1	Las Vegas
1983	Mar. 27	**Larry Holmes**	33	221	Lucien Rodriguez	209	Wu 12	Scranton, Pa.
1983	May 20	Michael Dokes WBA	24	223	Mike Weaver	218½	Draw 15	Las Vegas
1983	May 20	**Larry Holmes**	33	213	Tim Witherspoon	219½	Ws 12	Las Vegas
1983	Sept. 10	**Larry Holmes**	33	223	Scott Frank	211¼	TKO 5	Atlantic City
1983	Sept. 23	Gerrie Coetzee	28	215	Michael Dokes WBA	217	KO 10	Richfield, Ohio
1983	Nov. 25	**Larry Holmes**	34	219	Marvis Frazier	200	TKO 1	Las Vegas
1984	Mar. 9	Tim Witherspoon*	26	220¼	Greg Page	239½	Wm 12	Las Vegas
1984	Aug. 31	Pinklon Thomas	26	216	Tim Witherspoon	217	Wm 12	Las Vegas
1984	Nov. 9	**Larry Holmes** IBF	35	221½	Bonecrusher Smith	227	TKO 12	Las Vegas
1984	Dec. 1	Greg Page	26	236½	Gerrie Coetzee WBA	218	KO 8	Sun City, S. Africa
1985	Mar. 15	**Larry Holmes** IBF	35	223½	David Bey	233¼	TKO 10	Las Vegas
1985	Apr. 29	Tony Tubbs	26	229	Greg Page WBA	239½	Wu 15	Buffalo
1985	May 20	**Larry Holmes** IBF	35	224¼	Carl Williams	215	Wu 15	Las Vegas
1985	June 15	Pinklon Thomas WBC	27	220¼	Mike Weaver	221¼	KO 8	Las Vegas
1985	Sept. 21	Michael Spinks	29	200	**Larry Holmes** IBF	221½	Wu 15	Las Vegas
1986	Jan. 17	Tim Witherspoon	28	227	Tony Tubbs WBA	229	Wm 15	Atlanta
1986	Mar. 22	Trevor Berbick	33	218½	Pinklon Thomas WBC	222¾	Wu 15	Las Vegas
1986	Apr. 19	**Michael Spinks** IBF	29	205	Larry Holmes	223	Ws 15	Las Vegas
1986	July 19	Tim Witherspoon WBA	28	234¾	Frank Bruno	228	TKO 11	Wembley, England
1986	Sept. 6	**Michael Spinks** IBF	30	201	Steffen Tangstad	214¾	TKO 4	Las Vegas
1986	Nov. 22	Mike Tyson	20	221¼	Trevor Berbick WBC	218½	TKO 2	Las Vegas
1986	Dec. 12	Bonecrusher Smith	33	228½	Tim Witherspoon WBA	233½	TKO 1	NYC (Mad. Sq. Garden)
1987	Mar. 7	Mike Tyson WBC	20	219	Bonecrusher Smith WBA	233	Wu 12	Las Vegas
1987	May 30	Mike Tyson	20	218¾	Pinklon Thomas	217¾	TKO 6	Las Vegas
1987	May 30	Tony Tucker**	28	222¼	Buster Douglas	227¼	TKO 10	Las Vegas
1987	June 15	**Michael Spinks**†	30	208¾	Gerry Cooney	238	TKO 5	Atlantic City
1987	Aug. 1	Mike Tyson	21	221	Tony Tucker IBF	221	Wu 12	Las Vegas
1987	Oct. 16	Mike Tyson	21	216	Tyrell Biggs	228¾	TKO 7	Atlantic City
1988	Jan. 22	Mike Tyson	21	215¾	Larry Holmes	225¾	TKO 4	Atlantic City
1988	Mar. 20	Mike Tyson	21	216¼	Tony Tubbs	238¼	KO 2	Tokyo
1988	June 27	Mike Tyson	21	218¼	**Michael Spinks**	212¼	KO 1	Atlantic City
1989	Feb. 25	**Mike Tyson**	22	218	Frank Bruno	228	TKO 5	Las Vegas
1989	July 21	**Mike Tyson**	23	219¼	Carl Williams	218	TKO 1	Atlantic City
1990	Feb. 10	Buster Douglas	29	231½	**Mike Tyson**	220½	KO 10	Tokyo
1990	Oct. 25	Evander Holyfield	28	208	**Buster Douglas**	246	KO 3	Las Vegas
1991	Apr. 19	**Evander Holyfield**	28	208	George Foreman	257	Wu 12	Atlantic City
1991	Nov. 23	**Evander Holyfield**	29	210	Bert Cooper	215	TKO 7	Atlanta
1992	June 19	**Evander Holyfield**	29	210	Larry Holmes	233	Wu 12	Las Vegas
1992	Nov. 13	Riddick Bowe	25	235	**Evander Holyfield**	205	Wu 12	Las Vegas
1993	Feb. 6	Riddick Bowe	25	243	Michael Dokes	244	TKO 1	NYC (Mad. Sq. Garden)
1993	May 8	Lennox Lewis WBC‡	27	235	Tony Tucker	235	Wu 12	Las Vegas
1993	May 22	**Riddick Bowe**	25	244	Jesse Ferguson	224	TKO 2	Washington, D.C.
1993	Oct. 1	Lennox Lewis WBC	28	233	Frank Bruno	238	TKO 7	Cardiff, Wales
1993	Nov. 6	Evander Holyfield	31	217	**Riddick Bowe** WBA/IBF	246	Wm 12	Las Vegas
1994	Apr. 22	Michael Moorer	26	214	**Evander Holyfield**	214	Wm 12	Las Vegas
1994	May 6	Lennox Lewis WBC	28	235	Phil Jackson	218	TKO 8	Atlantic City
1994	Sept. 25	Oliver McCall	29	231¼	**Lennox Lewis** WBC	238	TKO 2	London
1994	Nov. 5	George Foreman!	45	250	**Michael Moorer**	222	KO 10	Las Vegas
1995	Apr. 8	Oliver McCall WBC	29	231	Larry Holmes	236	Wu 12	Las Vegas
1995	Apr. 8	Bruce Seldon!	28	236	Tony Tucker	240	TKO 7	Las Vegas
1995	Apr. 22	**George Foreman!**	46	256	Axel Schulz	221	Ws 12	Las Vegas

*WBC recognized winner of Mar. 9, 1984 fight between Tim Witherspoon and Greg Page as world champion after Larry Holmes relinquished title in dispute. IBF then recognized Holmes.

**IBF recognized winner of May 30, 1987 fight between Tony Tucker and James (Buster) Douglas as world champion after Michael Spinks relinquished title in dispute.

†The July 15, 1987 Spinks-Cooney fight was not an official championship bout because it was not sanctioned by any boxing associations, councils or federations.

‡WBC recognized Lennox Lewis as world champion when Riddick Bowe gave up that portion of his title on Dec. 14, 1992, rather than fight Lewis, the WBC's mandatory challenger.

!George Foreman won WBA and IBF championships when he beat Michael Moorer on Nov. 5, 1994. He was stripped of WBA title on Mar. 4, 1995, when he refused to fight No. 1 contender Tony Tucker, and he relinquished IBF title on June 29, 1995, rather than give Axel Schulz a rematch. Tucker lost to Bruce Seldon in their April 8, 2001 fight for vacant WBA title.

Year	Date	Winner	Age	Wgt	Loser	Wgt	Result	Location
1995	Aug. 19	Bruce Seldon WBA	28	234	Joe Hipp	223	TKO 10	Las Vegas
1995	Sept. 2	Frank Bruno	33	248	Oliver McCall WBC	235	Wu 12	London
1995	Dec. 9	Frans Botha*	27	237	Axel Schulz	222	Wu 12	Stuttgart, GER
1996	Mar. 16	Mike Tyson	29	220	Frank Bruno WBC	247	TKO 3	Las Vegas
1996	June 22	Michael Moorer*	28	222	Axel Schulz	223	Ws 12	Dortmund, GER
1996	Sept. 7	Mike Tyson WBC†	30	219	Bruce Seldon WBA	229	TKO 1	Las Vegas
1996	Nov. 9	Evander Holyfield	34	215	**Mike Tyson** WBA	222	TKO 11	Las Vegas
1997	Feb. 7	Lennox Lewis†	31	251	Oliver McCall	237	TKO 5	Las Vegas
1997	Mar. 29	Michael Moorer IBF	29	212	Vaughn Bean	212	Wm 12	Las Vegas
1997	June 28	**Evander Holyfield** WBA‡	34	218	Mike Tyson	218	Disq. 3	Las Vegas
1997	July 12	Lennox Lewis WBC	31	242	Henry Akinwande	237½	Disq. 5	Stateline, Nev.
1997	Oct. 4	Lennox Lewis WBC	32	244	Andrew Golota	244	TKO 1	Atlantic City
1997	Nov. 8	Evander Holyfield WBA	35	214	Michael Moorer IBF	223	TKO 8	Las Vegas
1998	Mar. 28	Lennox Lewis WBC	32	243	Shannon Briggs	228	TKO 5	Atlantic City
1998	Sept. 19	**Evander Holyfield** WBA/IBF	35	217	Vaughn Bean	231	Wu 12	Atlanta
1998	Sept. 26	Lennox Lewis WBC	33	250	Zeljko Mavrovic	220	Wu 12	Uncasville, Conn.
1999	Mar. 13	Lennox Lewis WBC	33	246	**Evander Holyfield** WBA/IBF	215	Draw 12	NYC (Mad. Sq. Garden)
1999	Nov. 13	Lennox Lewis WBC	34	240	**Evander Holyfield** WBA/IBF	218	Wu 12	Las Vegas
2000	Apr. 29	**L. Lewis** WBC/IBFI	34	247	Michael Grant	250	KO 2	NYC (Mad. Sq. Garden)
2000	July 15	**L. Lewis** WBC/IBF	34	250	Frans Botha	237	TKO 2	London
2000	Aug. 12	Evander Holyfield	37	221	John Ruiz	224	Wu 12	Las Vegas
2000	Nov. 11	**L. Lewis** WBC/IBF	35	249	David Tua	245	Wu 12	Las Vegas
2001	Mar. 3	John Ruiz	29	227	Evander Holyfield	217	Wu 12	Las Vegas
2001	Apr. 22	Hasim Rahman	28	237	**L. Lewis** WBC/IBF	253	KO 5	Johannesburg, S. Africa
2001	Nov. 17	Lennox Lewis	36	247	**H. Rahman** WBC/IBF	236	KO 4	Las Vegas
2001	Dec. 15	**John Ruiz** WBA	29	232	Evander Holyfield	219	Draw 12	Mashantucket, Conn.
2002	June 8	**L. Lewis** WBC/IBF	36	249	Mike Tyson	235	KO 8	Memphis, Tenn.
2002	July 27	**John Ruiz** WBA	30	233	Kirk Johnson	238	Disq. 10	Las Vegas

*Frans Botha won the vacant IBF title with a controversial 12-round decision over Axel Schulz on Dec. 9, 1995, but after legal sparring, was eventually stripped of the IBF belt for using anabolic steroids. Moorer then claimed the revacated title with his June 22, 1996 win over Schulz.

†Mike Tyson won the WBC belt from Frank Bruno on Mar. 16, 1996 and still held it at the time of his Sept. 7, 1996 win over Bruce Seldon (although it was not at risk for that fight) but was forced to relinquish the title after the bout for not fighting mandatory challenge Lennox Lewis. Tyson also paid Lewis $4 million to step aside and allow the Tyson-Seldon bout to take place. Lewis then fought Oliver McCall for the vacant WBC belt. The fight was stopped 55 seconds into round 5 because, inexplicably, McCall was visibly distraught and stopped throwing punches.

‡Holyfield won the bout by disqualification and retained the WBA belt after Tyson spit out his mouthpiece and bit off a piece of Holyfield's ear. Tyson had received a two-point deduction from referee Mills Lane and after a stern warning and a short delay the fight was allowed to continue. Later in round 3, he bit Holyfield's other ear and Tyson was disqualified.

ILewis was stripped of the WBA title for choosing to fight Michael Grant instead of John Ruiz, the WBA's #1 challenger. The WBA sanctioned the Evander Holyfield-John Ruiz August 12 bout for its vacant heavyweight belt.

All-Time Heavyweight Upsets

Buster Douglas was a 42-1 underdog when he defeated previously-unbeaten heavyweight champion Mike Tyson on Feb. 10, 1990. That 10th-round knockout ranks as the biggest upset in boxing history. By comparison, 45-year-old George Foreman was only a 3-1 underdog before he unexpectedly won the title from Michael Moorer on Nov. 5, 1994.

Here are the best-known upsets in the annals of the heavyweight division. All fights were for the world championship except the Max Schmeling-Joe Louis bout.

Date	Winner	Loser	Result	KO Time	Location
9/7/1892	James J. Corbett	John L. Sullivan	KO 21	1:30	Olympic Club, New Orleans
4/5/1915	Jess Willard	Jack Johnson	KO 26	1:26	Mariano Race Track, Havana
9/23/26	Gene Tunney	Jack Dempsey	Wu 10	–	Sesquicentennial Stadium, Phila.
6/13/35	James J. Braddock	Max Baer	Wu 15	–	Mad. Sq.Garden Bowl, L.I. City
6/19/36	Max Schmeling	Joe Louis	KO 12	2:29	Yankee Stadium, New York
7/18/51	Jersey Joe Walcott	Ezzard Charles	KO 7	0:55	Forbes Field, Pittsburgh
6/26/59	Ingemar Johansson	Floyd Patterson	TKO 3	2:03	Yankee Stadium, New York
2/25/64	Cassius Clay	Sonny Liston	TKO 7	*	Convention Hall, Miami Beach
10/30/74	Muhammad Ali	George Foreman	KO 8	2:58	20th of May Stadium, Zaire
2/15/78	Leon Spinks	Muhammad Ali	Ws 15	–	Hilton Pavilion, Las Vegas
9/21/85	Michael Spinks	Larry Holmes	Wu 15	–	Riviera Hotel, Las Vegas
2/10/90	Buster Douglas	Mike Tyson	KO 10	1:23	Tokyo Dome, Tokyo
11/5/94	George Foreman	Michael Moorer	KO 10	2:03	MGM Grand, Las Vegas
11/9/96	Evander Holyfield	Mike Tyson	TKO 11	0:37	MGM Grand, Las Vegas
4/22/01	Hasim Rahman	Lennox Lewis	KO 5	2:32	Johannesburg, South Africa

*Liston failed to answer bell for Round 7.

Muhammad Ali's Career Pro Record

Born Cassius Marcellus Clay, Jr. on Jan. 17, 1942, in Louisville; Amateur record of 100-5; won light-heavyweight gold medal at 1960 Olympic Games; Pro record of 56-5 with 37 KOs in 61 fights.

1960

Date	Opponent (location)	Result
Oct. 29	Tunney Hunsaker, Louisville	Wu 6
Dec. 27	Herb Siler, Miami Beach	TKO 4

1961

Date	Opponent (location)	Result
Jan. 17	Tony Esperti, Miami Beach	TKO 3
Feb. 7	Jim Robinson, Miami Beach	TKO 1
Feb. 21	Donnie Fleeman, Miami Beach	TKO 7
Apr. 19	Lamar Clark, Louisville	KO 2
June 26	Duke Sabedong, Las Vegas	Wu 10
July 22	Alonzo Johnson, Louisville	Wu 10
Oct. 7	Alex Miteff, Louisville	TKO 6
Nov. 29	Willi Besmanoff, Louisville	TKO 7

1962

Date	Opponent (location)	Result
Feb. 10	Sonny Banks, New York	TKO 4
Feb. 28	Don Warner, Miami Beach	TKO 4
Apr. 23	George Logan, Los Angeles	TKO 4
May 19	Billy Daniels, Los Angeles	TKO 7
July 20	Alejandro Lavorante, Los Angeles	KO 5
Nov. 15	Archie Moore, Los Angeles	KO 4

1963

Date	Opponent (location)	Result
Jan. 24	Charlie Powell, Pittsburgh	KO 3
Mar. 13	Doug Jones, New York	Wu 10
June 18	Henry Cooper, London	TKO 5

1964

Date	Opponent (location)	Result
Feb. 25	Sonny Liston, Miami Beach	TKO 7

(won World Heavyweight title)

After the fight, Clay announces he is a member of the Black Muslim religious sect and has changed his name to Muhammad Ali.

1965

Date	Opponent (location)	Result
May 25	Sonny Liston, Lewiston, Me	KO 1
Nov. 22	Floyd Patterson, Las Vegas	TKO 12

1966

Date	Opponent (location)	Result
Mar. 29	George Chuvalo, Toronto	Wu 15
May 21	Henry Cooper, London	TKO 6
Aug. 6	Brian London, London	KO 3
Sept. 10	Karl Mildenberger, Frankfurt	TKO 12
Nov. 14	Cleveland Williams, Houston	TKO 3

1967

Date	Opponent (location)	Result
Feb. 6	Ernie Terrell, Houston	Wu 15
Mar. 22	Zora Folley, New York	KO 7
Apr. 28	Refuses induction into U.S. Army and is stripped of world title by WBA and most state commissions the next day.	
June 20	Found guilty of draft evasion in Houston; fined $10,000 and sentenced to 5 years; remains free pending appeals, but is barred from the ring.	

1968-69 (Inactive)

1970

Date	Opponent (location)	Result
Feb. 3	Announces retirement.	
Oct. 26	Jerry Quarry, Atlanta	TKO 3
Dec. 7	Oscar Bonavena, New York	TKO 15

1971

Date	Opponent (location)	Result
Mar. 8	Joe Frazier, New York	Lu 15

(for World Heavyweight title)

June 28	U.S. Supreme Court reverses Ali's 1967 conviction saying he had been drafted improperly.	
July 26	Jimmy Ellis, Houston	TKO 12

(won vacant NABF Heavyweight title)

Nov. 17	Buster Mathis, Houston	Wu 12
Dec. 26	Jurgen Blin, Zurich	KO 7

1972

Date	Opponent (location)	Result
Apr. 1	Mac Foster, Tokyo	Wu 15
May 1	George Chuvalo, Vancouver	Wu 12
June 27	Jerry Quarry, Las Vegas	TKO 7
July 19	Al (Blue) Lewis, Dublin, Ire	TKO 11
Sept. 20	Floyd Patterson, New York	TKO 7
Nov. 21	Bob Foster, Stateline, Nev.	TKO 8

1973

Date	Opponent (location)	Result
Feb. 14	Joe Bugner, Las Vegas	Wu 12
Mar. 31	Ken Norton, San Diego	Ls 12

(lost NABF Heavyweight title)

Sept. 10	Ken Norton, Inglewood, Calif	Ws 12

(regained NABF Heavyweight title)

Oct. 20	Rudi Lubbers, Jakarta, Indonesia	Wu 12

1974

Date	Opponent (location)	Result
Jan. 28	Joe Frazier, New York	Wu 12
Oct. 30	George Foreman, Kinshasa, Zaire	KO 8

(regained World Heavyweight title)

1975

Date	Opponent (location)	Result
Mar. 24	Chuck Wepner, Cleveland	TKO 15
May 16	Ron Lyle, Las Vegas	TKO 11
June 30	Joe Bugner, Kuala Lumpur, Malaysia	Wu 15
Oct. 1	Joe Frazier, Manila, Philippines	TKO 14

1976

Date	Opponent (location)	Result
Feb. 20	Jean Pierre Coopman, San Juan	KO 5
Apr. 30	Jimmy Young, Landover, Md	Wu 15
May 24	Richard Dunn, Munich	TKO 5
Sept. 28	Ken Norton, New York	Wu 15

1977

Date	Opponent (location)	Result
May 16	Alfredo Evangelista, Landover	Wu 15
Sept. 29	Earnie Shavers, New York	Wu 15

1978

Date	Opponent (location)	Result
Feb. 15	Leon Spinks, Las Vegas	Ls 15

(lost World Heavyweight title)

Sept. 15	Leon Spinks, New Orleans	Wu 15

(regained World Heavyweight title)

1979

Date		
June 27	Announces retirement.	

1980

Date	Opponent (location)	Result
Oct. 2	Larry Holmes, Las Vegas	TKO by 11

1981

Date	Opponent (location)	Result
Dec. 11	Trevor Berbick, Nassau	Lu 10

(retires after fight)

Major Titleholders

Note the following sanctioning body abbreviations: NBA (National Boxing Association), WBA (World Boxing Association), WBC (World Boxing Council), GBR (Great Britain), IBF (International Boxing Federation), plus other national and state commissions. Fighters who retired as champion are indicated by (*) and champions who abandoned or relinquished their titles are indicated by (†).

Heavyweights

Widely accepted champions in CAPITAL letters. Current champions in **bold** type (as of Oct. 23, 2001).

Note: Muhammad Ali was stripped of his world title in 1967 after refusing induction into the Army (see Muhammad Ali's Career Pro Record). George Foreman was stripped of his WBA and IBF titles in 1995, but remained active as linear champion.

Champion	Held Title
JOHN L. SULLIVAN	1885–92
JAMES J. CORBETT	1892–97
BOB FITZSIMMONS	1897–99
JAMES J. JEFFRIES	1899–1905*
MARVIN HART	1905–06
TOMMY BURNS	1906–08
JACK JOHNSON	1908–15
JESS WILLARD	1915–19
JACK DEMPSEY	1919–26
GENE TUNNEY	1926–28*
MAX SCHMELING	1930–32
JACK SHARKEY	1932–33
PRIMO CARNERA	1933–34
MAX BAER	1934–35
JAMES J. BRADDOCK	1935–37
JOE LOUIS	1937–49*
EZZARD CHARLES	1949–51
JERSEY JOE WALCOTT	1951–52
ROCKY MARCIANO	1952–56*
FLOYD PATTERSON	1956–59
INGEMAR JOHANSSON	1959–60
FLOYD PATTERSON	1960–62
SONNY LISTON	1962–64
CASSIUS CLAY (MUHAMMAD ALI)	1964–67
Ernie Terrell (WBA)	1965–67
Joe Frazier (NY)	1968–70
Jimmy Ellis (WBA)	1968–70
JOE FRAZIER	1970–73
GEORGE FOREMAN	1973–74
MUHAMMAD ALI	1974–78
LEON SPINKS	1978
Ken Norton (WBC)	1978
Larry Holmes (WBC)	1978–80
MUHAMMAD ALI	1978–79*
John Tate (WBA)	1979–80
Mike Weaver (WBA)	1980–82
LARRY HOLMES	1980–85
Michael Dokes (WBA)	1982–83
Gerrie Coetzee (WBA)	1983–84
Tim Witherspoon (WBC)	1984
Pinklon Thomas (WBC)	1984–86
Greg Page (WBA)	1984–85
MICHAEL SPINKS	1985–87
Tim Witherspoon (WBA)	1986
Trevor Berbick (WBC)	1986
Mike Tyson (WBC)	1986–87
James (Bonecrusher) Smith (WBA)	1986–87
Tony Tucker (IBF)	1987
MIKE TYSON (WBC, WBA, IBF)	1987–90
BUSTER DOUGLAS (WBC, WBA, IBF)	1990
EVANDER HOLYFIELD (WBC, WBA, IBF)	1990–92
RIDDICK BOWE (WBA, IBF)	1992–93
Lennox Lewis (WBC)	1992–94
EVANDER HOLYFIELD (WBA, IBF)	1993–94
MICHAEL MOORER (WBA, IBF)	1994
Oliver McCall (WBC)	1994–95
GEORGE FOREMAN (WBA, IBF)	1994–95
Bruce Seldon (WBA)	1995–96
GEORGE FOREMAN	1995–96
Frank Bruno (WBC)	1995–96
Mike Tyson (WBC)	1996†
Mike Tyson (WBA)	1996
Michael Moorer (IBF)	1996–1997
Evander Holyfield (WBA, IBF)	1996–2000
Lennox Lewis (WBC)	1997–2000
LENNOX LEWIS (WBA, WBC, IBF)	2000
Evander Holyfield (WBA)	2000–01
LENNOX LEWIS (WBC, IBF)	2000–01
John Ruiz (WBA)	2001–
Hasim Rahman (WBC, IBF)	2001
LENNOX LEWIS (WBC, IBF)	2001–02†
LENNOX LEWIS (WBC)	2001–

Note: John L. Sullivan held the Bare Knuckle championship from 1882-85.

Cruiserweights

Current champions in **bold** type.

Champion	Held Title
Marvin Camel (WBC)	1980
Carlos De Leon (WBC)	1980–82
Ossie Ocasio (WBA)	1982–84
S.T. Gordon (WBC)	1982–83
Carlos De Leon (WBC)	1983–85
Marvin Camel (IBF)	1983–84
Lee Roy Murphy (IBF)	1984–86
Piet Crous (WBA)	1984–85
Alfonso Ratliff (WBC)	1985
Dwight Braxton (WBA)	1985–86
Bernard Benton (WBC)	1985–86
Carlos De Leon (WBC)	1986–88
Evander Holyfield (WBA)	1986–88
Ricky Parkey (IBF)	1986–87
Evander Holyfield (WBA/IBF)	1987–88
Evander Holyfield	1988†
Toufik Belbouli (WBA)	1989
Robert Daniels (WBA)	1989–91
Carlos De Leon (WBC)	1989–90
Glenn McCrory (IBF)	1989–90
Jeff Lampkin (IBF)	1990
Massimiliano Duran (WBC)	1990–91
Bobby Czyz (WBA)	1991–92†
Anaclet Wamba (WBC)	1991–95
James Pritchard (IBF)	1991
James Warring (IBF)	1991–92
Alfred Cole (IBF)	1992–96
Orlin Norris (WBA)	1993–95
Nate Miller (WBA)	1995–97
Marcelo Dominguez (WBC)	1996–98
Adolpho Washington (IBF)	1996–97
Uriah Grant (IBF)	1997
Imamu Mayfield (IBF)	1997–98
Arthur Williams (IBF)	1998–99
Fabrice Tiozzo (WBA)	1997–2000
Juan Carlos Gomez (WBC)	1998–2002†
Vassiliy Jirov (IBF)	1999–
Virgil Hill (WBA)	2000–02
Jean-Marc Mormeck (WBA)	2002–
Wayne Braithwaite (WBC)	2002–

Major Titleholders (Cont.)
Light Heavyweights
Widely accepted champions in CAPITAL letters. Current champions in **bold** type.

Champion	Held Title	Champion	Held Title
JACK ROOT	1903	Mike Rossman (WBA)	1978–79
GEORGE GARDNER	1903	Marvin Johnson (WBC)	1978–79
BOB FITZSIMMONS	1903–05	Matthew (Franklin) Saad Muhammad (WBC)	1979–81
PHILADELPHIA JACK O'BRIEN	1905–12*	Marvin Johnson (WBA)	1979–80
JACK DILLON	1914–16	Eddie (Gregory)	
BATTLING LEVINSKY	1916–20	Mustapha Muhammad (WBA)	1980–81
GEORGES CARPENTIER	1920–22	Michael Spinks (WBA)	1981–83
BATTLING SIKI	1922–23	Dwight (Braxton) Muhammad Qawi (WBC)	1981–83
MIKE McTIGUE	1923–25	MICHAEL SPINKS	1983–85†
PAUL BERLENBACH	1925–26	J.B.Williamson (WBC)	1985–86
JACK DELANEY	1926–27†	Slobodan Kacar (IBF)	1985–86
Jimmy Slattery (NBA)	1927	Marvin Johnson (WBA)	1986–87
TOMMY LOUGHRAN	1927-29	Dennis Andries (WBC)	1986–87
JIMMY SLATTERY	1930	Bobby Czyz (IBF)	1986–87
MAXIE ROSENBLOOM	1930–34	Leslie Stewart (WBA)	1987
George Nichols (NBA)	1932	Virgil Hill (WBA)	1987–91
Bob Godwin (NBA)	1933	Prince Charles Williams (IBF)	1987–93
BOB OLIN	1934–35	Thomas Hearns (WBC)	1987
JOHN HENRY LEWIS	1935–38	Donny Lalonde (WBC)	1987–88
MELIO BETTINA (NY)	1939	Sugar Ray Leonard (WBC)	1988
Len Harvey (GBR)	1939–42	Dennis Andries (WBC)	1989
BILLY CONN	1939–40†	Jeff Harding (WBC)	1989–90
ANTON CHRISTOFORIDIS (NBA)	1941	Dennis Andries (WBC)	1990–91
GUS LESNEVICH	1941–48	Jeff Harding (WBC)	1991–94
Freddie Mills (GBR)	1942–46	Thomas Hearns (WBA)	1991–92
FREDDIE MILLS	1948–50	Iran Barkley (WBA)	1992†
JOEY MAXIM	1950–52	Virgil Hill (WBA)	1992–97
ARCHIE MOORE	1952–62	Henry Maske (IBF)	1993–96
Harold Johnson (NBA)	1961	Virgil Hill (WBA/IBF)	1996–97
HAROLD JOHNSON	1962–63	Mike McCallum (WBC)	1994–95
WILLIE PASTRANO	1963–65	Fabrice Tiozzo (WBC)	1995–96
Eddie Cotton (Mich.)	1963–64	Roy Jones Jr. (WBC)	1996
JOSE TORRES	1965–66	Montell Griffin (WBC)	1996
DICK TIGER	1966–68	D. Michaelczewski (WBA/IBF)	1997†
BOB FOSTER	1968–74*	William Guthrie (IBF)	1997–98
Vicente Rondon (WBA)	1971–72	Lou Del Valle (WBA)	1997–98
John Conteh (WBC)	1974–77	**ROY JONES JR.** (WBA/WBC)	1997–
Victor Galindez (WBA)	1974–78	Reggie Johnson (IBF)	1998–99
Miguel A. Cuello (WBC)	1977–78	**ROY JONES JR.** (WBA/WBC/IBF)	1999–
Mate Parlov (WBC)	1978		

Super Middleweights
Current champions in **bold** type.

Champion	Held Title	Champion	Held Title
Murray Sutherland (IBF)	1984	Frank Liles (WBA)	1994–99
Chong-Pal Park (IBF)	1984–87	Roy Jones (IBF)	1994–96
Chong-Pal Park (WBA)	1987–88	Thulane Malinga (WBC)	1996
Graziano Rocchigiani (IBF)	1988–89	Vincenzo Nardiello (WBC)	1996
Fugencio Obelmejias (WBA)	1988–89	Robin Reid (WBC)	1996–97
Ray Leonard (WBC)	1988–90†	Charles Brewer (IBF)	1997–98
In-Chut Baek (WBA)	1989–90	**Sven Ottke** (IBF)	1998–
Lindell Holmes (IBF)	1990–91	Thulane Malinga (WBC)	1997–98
Christophe Tiozzo (WBA)	1990–91	Richie Woodhall (WBC)	1998–99
Mauro Galvano (WBC)	1990–92	Byron Mitchell (WBA)	1999–2000
Victor Cordova (WBA)	1991	Markus Beyer (WBC)	1999–2000
Darrin Van Horn (IBF)	1991–92	Glenn Gatley (WBC)	2000
Iran Barkley (WBA)	1992	Dingaan Thobela (WBC)	2000
Nigel Benn (WBC)	1992–96	Bruno Girard (WBA)	2000–01†
James Toney (WBC)	1992–94	Dave Hilton (WBC)	2000†
Michael Nunn (WBA)	1992–94	**Byron Mitchell** (WBA)	2001–
Steve Little (WBA)	1994	**Eric Lucas** (WBC)	2001–

Middleweights
Widely accepted champions in CAPITAL letters. Current champions in **bold** type.

Champion	Held Title	Champion	Held Title
JACK (NONPAREIL) DEMPSEY	1884–91	TOMMY RYAN	1898–1907
BOB FITZSIMMONS	1891–97	STANLEY KETCHEL	1908
CHARLES (KID) McCOY	1897–98	BILLY PAPKE	1908

Champion	Held Title
STANLEY KETCHEL	1908–10
FRANK KLAUS	1913
GEORGE CHIP	1913–14
AL McCOY	1914–17
Jeff Smith (AUS)	1914
Mick King (AUS)	1914
Jeff Smith (AUS)	1914–15
Lee Darcy (AUS)	1915–17
MIKE O'DOWD	1917–20
JOHNNY WILSON	1920–23
Wm. Bryan Downey (Ohio)	1921–22
Dave Rosenberg (NY)	1922
Jock Malone (Ohio)	1922–23
Mike O'Dowd (NY)	1922
Lou Bogash (NY),	1923
HARRY GREB	1923–26
TIGER FLOWERS	1926
MICKEY WALKER	1926–31†
GORILLA JONES	1931–32
MARCEL THIL	1932–37
Ben Jeby (NY)	1932–33
Lou Brouillard (NBA, NY)	1933
Vince Dundee (NBA, NY)	1933–34
Teddy Yarosz (NBA, NY)	1934–35
Babe Risko (NBA, NY)	1935–36
Freddie Steele (NBA, NY)	1936–38
FRED APOSTOLI	1937–39
Al Hostak (NBA)	1938
Solly Krieger (NBA)	1938–39
Al Hostak (NBA)	1939–40
CEFERINO GARCIA	1939–40
KEN OVERLIN	1940–41
Tony Zale (NBA)	1940–41
BILLY SOOSE	1941
TONY ZALE	1941–47
ROCKY GRAZIANO	1947–48
TONY ZALE	1948
MARCEL CERDAN	1948–49
JAKE La MOTTA	1949–51
SUGAR RAY ROBINSON	1951
RANDY TURPIN	1951
SUGAR RAY ROBINSON	1951–52*
CARL (BOBO) OLSON	1953–55
SUGAR RAY ROBINSON	1955–57
GENE FULLMER	1957
SUGAR RAY ROBINSON	1957
CARMEN BASILIO	1957–58
SUGAR RAY ROBINSON	1958–60
Gene Fullmer (NBA)	1959–62
PAUL PENDER	1960–61
TERRY DOWNES	1961–62
PAUL PENDER	1962–63
Dick Tiger (WBA)	1962–63
DICK TIGER	1963
JOEY GIARDELLO	1963–65
DICK TIGER	1965–66
EMILE GRIFFITH	1966–67
NINO BENVENUTI	1967
EMILE GRIFFITH	1967–68
NINO BENVENUTI	1968–70
CARLOS MONZON	1970–77*
Rodrigo Valdez (WBC)	1974–76
RODRIGO VALDEZ	1977–78
HUGO CORRO	1978–79
VITO ANTUOFERMO	1979–80
ALAN MINTER	1980
MARVELOUS MARVIN HAGLER	1980–87
SUGAR RAY LEONARD	1987
Frank Tate (IBF)	1987–88
Sumbu Kalambay (WBA)	1987–89
Thomas Hearns (WBC)	1987–88
Iran Barkley (WBC)	1988–89
Michael Nunn (IBF)	1988–91
Roberto Duran (WBC)	1989–90*
Mike McCallum (WBA)	1989–91
Julian Jackson (WBC)	1990–93
James Toney (IBF)	1991–93†
Reggie Johnson (WBA)	1992–93
Roy Jones Jr. (IBF)	1993–94†
Gerald McClellan (WBC)	1993–95†
John David Jackson (WBA)	1993–94
Jorge Castro (WBA)	1994–97
Julian Jackson (WBC)	1995
Bernard Hopkins (IBF)	1995–
Quincy Taylor (WBC)	1995–96
Shinji Takehara (WBA)	1995–96
William Joppy (WBA)	1996–97
Keith Holmes (WBC)	1996–98
Julio Cesar Green (WBA)	1997–98
William Joppy (WBA)	1998–2001
Hassine Cherifi (WBC)	1998–99
Keith Holmes (WBC)	1999–2001
Bernard Hopkins (IBF/WBC)	2001–
Felix Trinidad (WBA)	2001
BERNARD HOPKINS (IBF/WBA/WBC)	2001–

Junior Middleweights

Widely accepted champions in CAPITAL letters. Current champions in **bold** type.

Champion	Held Title
ERNILE GRIFFITH (EBU)	1962–63
DENNIS MOYER	1962–63
RALPH DUPAS	1963
SANDRO MAZZINGHI	1963–65
NINO BENVENUTI	1965–66
KI-SOO KIM	1966–68
SANDRO MAZZINGHI	1968
FREDDLIE LITTLE	1969–70
CARMELO BOSSI	1970–71
KOICHI WAJIMA	1971–74
OSCAR ALBARADO	1974–75
KOICHI WAJIMA	1975
Miguel de Oliveira (WBC)	1975–76
JAE-DO YUH	1975–76
Elisha Obed (WBC)	1975–76
KOICHI WAJIMA	1976
JOSE DURAN	1976
Eckhard Dagge (WBC)	1976–77
MIGUEL ANGEL CASTELLINI	1976–77
EDDIE GAZO	1977–78
Rocky Mattioli (WBC)	1977–79
MASASHI KUDO	1978–79
Maurice Hope (WBC)	1979–81
AYUB KALULE	1979–81
Wilfred Benitez (WBC)	1981–82
SUGAR RAY LEONARD	1981–82
Tadashi Mihara (WBA)	1981–82
Davey Moore (WBA)	1982–83
Thomas Hearns (WBC)	1982–84
Roberto Duran (WBA)	1983–84
Mark Medal (IBF)	1984
THOMAS HEARNS	1984–86
Mike McCallum (WBA)	1984–87
Carlos Santos (IBF)	1984–86
Buster Drayton (IBF)	1986–87
Duane Thomas (WBC)	1986–87
Matthew Hilton (IBF)	1987–88
Lupe Aquino (WBC)	1987
Gianfranco Rosi (WBC)	1987–88
Julian Jackson (WBA)	1987–90
Donald Curry (WBC)	1988–89
Robert Hines (IBF)	1988–89

Major Titleholders (Cont.)

Champion	Held Title
Darrin Van Horn (IBF)	1989
Rene Jacquote (WBC)	1989
John Mugabi (WBC)	1989–90
Gianfranco Rosi (IBF)	1989–94
Terry Norris (WBC)	1990–94
Gilbert Dele (WBA)	1991
Vinny Pazienza (WBA)	1991–92
Julio Cesar Vasquez (WBA)	1992–95
Simon Brown (WBC)	1994
Terry Norris (WBC)	1994–
Vincent Pettway (IBF)	1994–95
Paul Vaden (IBF)	1995
Carl Daniels (WBA)	1995
Terry Norris (WBC)	1995–97

Champion	Held Title
Terry Norris (IBF)	1995–96
Laurent Boudouani (WBA)	1996–99
Raul Marquez (IBF)	1997
Keith Mullings (WBC)	1997–99
Yori Boy Campas (IBF)	1997–98
Fernando Vargas (IBF)	1998–2000
Javier Castillejo (WBC)	1999–2001
David Reid (WBA)	1999–00
Felix Trinidad (WBA/IBF)	2000–01†
Oscar De La Hoya (WBC)	2001–
Fernando Vargas (WBA)	2001–02
Ronald Wright (IBF)	2001–
Oscar De La Hoya (WBA/WBC)	2002–

Welterweights

Widely accepted champions in CAPITAL letters. Current champions in **bold** type.

Champion	Held Title
PADDY DUFFY	1888–90
MYSTERIOUS BILLY SMITH	1892–94
TOMMY RYAN	1894–98
MYSTERIOUS BILLY SMITH	1898–1900
MATTY MATTHEWS	1900
EDDIE CONNOLLY	1900
JAMES (RUBE) FERNS	1900
MATTY MATHEWS	1900–01
JAMES (RUBE) FERNS	1901
JOE WALCOTT	1901–04
THE DIXIE KID	1904–05
HONEY MELLODY	1906–07
Mike (Twin) Sullivan	1907–08†
Harry Lewis	1908–11
Jimmy Gardner	1908
Jimmy Clabby	1910–11
WALDEMAR HOLBERG	1914
TOM McCORMICK	1914
MATT WELLS	1914–15
MIKE GLOVER	1915
JACK BRITTON	1915
TED (KID) LEWIS	1915–16
JACK BRITTON	1916–17
TED (KID) LEWIS	1917–19
JACK BRITTON	1919–22
MICKEY WALKER	1922–26
PETE LATZO	1926–27
JOE DUNDEE	1927–29
JACKIE FIELDS	1929–30
YOUNG JACK THOMPSON	1930
TOMMY FREEMAN	1930–31
YOUNG JACK THOMPSON	1931
LOU BROUILLARD	1931–32
JACKIE FIELDS	1932–33
YOUNG CORBETT III	1933
JIMMY McLARNIN	1933–34
BARNEY ROSS	1934
JIMMY McLARNIN	1934–35
BARNEY ROSS	1935–38
HENRY ARMSTRONG	1938–40
FRITZIE ZIVIC	1940–41
Izzy Jannazzo (Md.)	1940–41
Freddie (Red) Cochrane	1941–46
MARTY SERVO	1946*
SUGAR RAY ROBINSON	1946–51†
Johnny Bratton	1951
KID GAVILAN	1951–54
JOHNNY SAXTON	1954–55
TONY DeMARCO	1955
CARMEN BASILIO	1955–56
JOHNNY SAXTON	1956
CARMEN BASILIO	1956–57†
VIRGIL AKINS	1958

Champion	Held Title
DON JORDAN	1958–60
BENNY (KID) PARET	1960–61
EMILE GRIFFITH	1961
BENNY (KID) PARET	1961–62
EMILE GRIFFITH	1962–63
LUIS RODRIGUEZ	1963
EMILE GRIFFITH	1963–66†
Charlie Shipes (Calif.)	1966–67
CURTIS COKES	1966–69
JOSE NAPOLES	1969–70
BILLY BACKUS	1970–71
JOSE NAPOLES	1971–75
Hedgemon Lewis (NY)	1972–73
Angel Espada (WBA)	1975–76
JOHN H. STRACEY	1975–76
CARLOS PALOMINO	1976–79
Pipino Cuevas (WBA)	1976–80
WILFREDO BENITEZ	1979
SUGAR RAY LEONARD	1979–80
ROBERTO DURAN	1980
Thomas Hearns (WBA)	1980–81
SUGAR RAY LEONARD	1980–82
Donald Curry (WBA)	1983–85
Milton McCrory (WBC)	1983–85
DONALD CURRY	1985–86
LLOYD HONEYGHAN	1986–87
JORGE VACA (WBC)	1987–88
LLOYD HONEYGHAN (WBC)	1988–89
Mark Breland (WBA)	1987
Marlon Starling (WBA)	1987–88
Tomas Molinares (WBA)	1988–89
Simon Brown (IBF)	1988–91
Mark Breland (WBA)	1989–90
MARLON STARLING (WBC)	1989–90
Aaron Davis (WBA)	1990–91
Maurice Blocker (WBC)	1990–91
Meldrick Taylor (WBA)	1991–92
Simon Brown (WBC)	1991
Maurice Blocker (IBF)	1991–93
Buddy McGirt (WBC)	1991–93
Crisanto Espana (WBA)	1992–94
Pernell Whitaker (WBC)	1993–97
Felix Trinidad (IBF)	1993–99
Ike Quartey (WBA)	1994–98†
James Page (WBA)	1998–2000†
Oscar De La Hoya (WBC)	1997–99
Felix Trinidad (WBC/IBF)	1999–2000†
Oscar De La Hoya (WBC)	2000
Shane Mosley (WBC)	2000–
Andrew Lewis (WBA)	2001–02
Vernon Forrest (IBF)	2001–02†
Vernon Forrest (WBC)	2002–
Richard Mayorga (WBA)	2002–

Junior Welterweights
Widely accepted champions in CAPITAL letters. Current champions in **bold** type.

Champion	Held Title	Champion	Held Title
PINKEY MITCHELL	1922–25	Ubaldo Sacco (WBA)	1985–86
RED HERRING	1925	Lonnie Smith (WBC)	1985–86
MUSHY CALLAHAN	1926–30	Patrizio Oliva (WBA)	1986–87
JACK (KID) BERG	1930–31	Gary Hinton (IBF)	1986
TONY CANZONERI	1931–32	Rene Arredondo (WBC)	1986
JOHNNY JADICK	1932–33	Tsuyoshi Hamada (WBC)	1986–87
Sammy Fuller	1932–33	Joe Louis Manley (IBF)	1986–87
BATTLING SHAW	1933	Terry Marsh (IBF)	1987
TONY CANZONERI	1933	Juan Coggi (WBA)	1987–90
BARNEY ROSS	1933–35	Rene Arredondo (WBC)	1987
TIPPY LARKIN	1946	Roger Mayweather (WBC)	1987–89
CARLOS ORTIZ	1959–60	James McGirt (IBF)	1988
DUILIO LOI	1960–62	Meldrick Taylor (IBF)	1988–90
EDDIE PERKINS	1962	Julio Cesar Chavez (WBC)	1989–94
DUILIO LOI	1962–63	Julio Cesar Chavez (IBF)	1990–91
Roberto Cruz	1963	Loreto Garza (WBA)	1990–91
EDDIE PERKINS	1963–65	Juan Coggi (WBA)	1991
CARLOS HERNANDEZ	1965–66	Edwin Rosario (WBA)	1991–92
SANDRO LOPOPOLO	1966–67	Rafael Pineda (IBF)	1991–92
PAUL FUJII	1967–68	Akinobu Hiranaka (WBA)	1992
NICOLINO LOCHE	1968–72	Pernell Whitaker (IBF)	1992–93†
Pedro Adigue (WBC)	1968–70	Charles Murray (IBF)	1993–94
Bruno Arcari (WBC)	1970–74	Jake Rodriguez (IBF)	1994–95
ALFONSO FRAZER	1972	Juan Coggi (WBA)	1993–94
ANTONIO CERVANTES	1972–76	Frankie Randall (WBC)	1994
Perico Fernandez (WBC)	1974–75	Frankie Randall (WBA)	1994–96
Saensak Muangsurin (WBC)	1975–76	Juan Coggi (WBA)	1996
WILFRED BENITEZ	1976–79	Julio Cesar Chavez (WBC)	1994–96
Miguel Velasquez (WBC)	1976	Kostya Tszyu (IBF)	1995–97
Saensak Muangsurin (WBC)	1976–78	Frankie Randall (WBA)	1996–97
Antonio Cervantes (WBA)	1977–80	Oscar De La Hoya (WBC)	1996–97†
Sang-Hyun Kim (WBC)	1978–80	Khalid Rahilou (WBA)	1997–98
Saoul Mamby (WBC)	1980–82	Sharmba Mitchell (WBA)	1998–2001
Aaron Pryor (WBA)	1980–83	Vincent Phillips (IBF)	1997–99
Leroy Haley (WBC)	1982–83	Terronn Millet (IBF)	1999–00†
Aaron Pryor (IBF)	1983–85	**Kostya Tszyu** (WBC)	1999–
Bruce Curry (WBC)	1983–84	Zab Judah (IBF)	2000–01
Johnny Bumphus (WBA)	1984	**Kostya Tszyu** (WBA/WBC)	2001–
Bill Costello (WBC)	1984–85	**KOSTYA TSZYU** (IBF/WBA/WBC)	2001–
Gene Hatcher (WBA)	1984–85		

Lightweights
Widely accepted champions in CAPITAL letters. Current champions in **bold** type.

Champion	Held Title	Champion	Held Title
JACK McAULIFFE	1886–94	Beau Jack (NY)	1942–43
GEORGE (KID) LAVIGNE	1896–99	Slugger White (Md.)	1943
FRANK ERNE	1899–02	Bob Montgomery (NY)	1943
JOE GANS	1902–04	Sammy Angott (NBA)	1943–44
JIMMY BRITT	1904–05	Beau Jack (NY)	1943–44
BATTLING NELSON	1905–06	Bob Montgomery (NY)	1944–47
JOE GANS	1906–08	Juan Zurita (NBA)	1944–45
BATTLING NELSON	1908–10	IKE WILLIAMS	1947–51
AD WOLGAST	1910–12	JAMES CARTER	1951–52
WILLIE RITCHIE	1912–14	LAURO SALAS	1952
FREDDIE WELSH	1915–17	JAMES CARTER	1952–54
BENNY LEONARD	1917–25*	PADDY DeMARCO	1954
JIMMY GOODRICH	1925	JAMES CARTER	1954–55
ROCKY KANSAS	1925–26	WALLACE (BUD) SMITH	1955–56
SAMMY MANDELL	1926–30	JOE BROWN	1956–62
AL SINGER	1930	CARLOS ORTIZ	1962–65
TONY CANZONERI	1930–33	Kenny Lane (Mich.)	1963–64
BARNEY ROSS	1933–35†	ISMAEL LAGUNA	1965
TONY CANZONERI	1935–36	CARLOS ORTIZ	1965–68
LOU AMBERS	1936–38	CARLOS TEO CRUZ	1968–69
HENRY ARMSTRONG	1938–39	MANDO RAMOS	1969–70
LOU AMBERS	1939–40	ISMAEL LAGUNA	1970
Sammy Angott (NBA)	1940–41	KEN BUCHANAN	1970–72
LEW JENKINS	1940–41	Pedro Carrasco (WBC)	1971–72
SAMMY ANGOTT	1941–42	Mando Ramos (WBC)	1972

Major Titleholders (Cont.)

Champion	Held Title
ROBERTO DURAN	1972–79†
Chango Carmona (WBC)	1972
Rodolfo Gonzalez (WBC)	1972–74
Ishimatsu Suzuki (WBC)	1974–76
Esteban De Jesus (WBC)	1976–78
Jim Watt (WBC)	1979–81
Ernesto Espana (WBA)	1979–80
Hilmer Kenty (WBA)	1980–81
Sean O'Grady (WBA,WAA)	1981
Alexis Arguello (WBC)	1981–82
Claude Noel (WBA)	1981
Andrew Ganigan (WAA)	1981–82
Arturo Frias (WBA)	1981–82
Ray Mancini (WBA)	1982–84
ALEXIS ARGUELLO	1982–83
Edwin Rosario (WBC)	1983–84
Choo Choo Brown (IBF)	1984
Livingstone Bramble (WBA)	1984–86
Harry Arroyo (IBF)	1984–85
Jose Luis Ramirez (WBC)	1984–85
Jimmy Paul (IBF)	1985–86
Hector Camacho (WBC)	1985–86
Edwin Rosario (WBA)	1986–87
Greg Haugen (IBF)	1986–87
Julio Cesar Chavez (WBA)	1987–88
Jose Luis Ramirez (WBC)	1987–88
JULIO CESAR CHAVEZ (WBC,WBA)	1988–89
Vinny Pazienza (IBF)	1987–88
Greg Haugen (IBF)	1988–89
Pernell Whitaker (IBF,WBC)	1989–90

Champion	Held Title
Edwin Rosario (WBA)	1989–90
Juan Nazario (WBA)	1990
PERNELL WHITAKER (IBF, WBC, WBA)	1990–92†
Joey Gamache (WBA)	1992
Miguel A. Gonzalez (WBC)	1992–96
Tony Lopez (WBA)	1992–93
Dingaan Thobela (WBA)	1993
Fred Pendleton (IBF)	1993–94
Orzubek Nazarov (WBA)	1993–98
Rafael Ruelas (IBF)	1994–95
Oscar De La Hoya (IBF)	1995†
Phillip Holiday (IBF)	1995–97
Jean-Baptiste Mendy (WBC)	1996–97
Stevie Johnston (WBC)	1997–98
Shane Mosley (IBF)	1997–99†
Cesar Bazan (WBC)	1998–99
Jean-Baptiste Mendy (WBA)	1998–99
Julien Lorcy (WBA)	1999
Stevie Johnston (WBC)	1999–00
Stefano Zoff (WBA)	1999
Israel Cardona (IBF)	1999
Paul Spadafora (IBF)	1999–
Gilberto Serrano (WBA)	1999–00
Takanori Hatekayama (WBA)	2000–01
Jose Luis Castillo (WBC)	2000–02
Julien Lorcy (WBA)	2001
Raul Balbi (WBA)	2001–02
Leonard Dorin (WBA)	2002–
Floyd Mayweather (WBC)	2002–

Junior Lightweights

Widely accepted champions in CAPITAL letters. Current champions in **bold** type.

Champion	Held Title
JOHNNY DUNDEE	1921–23
JACK BERNSTEIN	1923
JOHNNY DUNDEE	1923–24
STEVE (KID) SULLIVAN	1924–25
MIKE BALLERINO	1925
TOD MORGAN	1925–29
BENNY BASS	1929–31
KID CHOCOLATE	1931–33
FRANKIE KLICK	1933–34
SANDY SADDLER	1949–50
HAROLD GOMES	1959–60
GABRIEL (FLASH) ELORDE	1960–67
YOSHIAKI NUMATA	1967
HIROSHI KOBAYASHI	1967–71
Rene Barrientos (WBC)	1969–70
Yoshiaki Numata (WBC)	1970–71
ALFREDO MARCANO	1971–72
Ricardo Arredondo (WBC)	1971–74
BEN VILLAFLOR	1972–73
KUNIAKI SHIBATA	1973
BEN VILLAFLOR	1973–76
Kuniaki Shibata (WBC)	1974–75
Alfredo Escalera (WBC)	1975–78
SAMUEL SERRANO	1976–80
Alexis Arguello (WBC)	1978–80
YASUTSUNE UEHARA	1980–81
Rafael Limon (WBC)	1980–81
Cornelius Boza-Edwards (WBC)	1981
SAMUEL SERRANO	1981–83
Rolando Navarrete (WBC)	1981–82
Rafael Limon (WBC)	1982
Bobby Chacon (WBC)	1982–83
ROGER MAYWEATHER	1983–84
Hector Camacho (WBC)	1983–84
ROCKY LOCKRIDGE	1984–85

Champion	Held Title
Hwan-Kil Yuh (IBF)	1984–85
Julio Cesar Chavez (WBC)	1984–87
Lester Ellis (IBF)	1985
WILFREDO GOMEZ	1985–86
Barry Michael (IBF)	1985–87
ALFREDO LAYNE	1986
BRIAN MITCHELL	1986–91
Rocky Lockridge (IBF)	1987–88
Azumah Nelson (WBC)	1988–94
Tony Lopez (IBF)	1988–89
Juan Molina (IBF)	1989–90
Tony Lopez (IBF)	1990–91
Joey Gamache (WBA)	1991
Brian Mitchell (IBF)	1991
Genaro Hernandez (WBA)	1991–95
James Leija (WBC)	1994
Juan Molina (IBF)	1991–95
Gabriel Ruelas (WBC)	1994–95
Eddie Hopson (IBF)	1995
Tracy Patterson (IBF)	1995
Azumah Nelson (WBC)	1995–97
Choi Yong-Soo (WBA)	1995–98
Arturo Gatti (IBF)	1995–98†
Genaro Hernandez (WBC)	1997–98
Floyd Mayweather Jr. (WBC)	1998–2002†
Takanori Hatekayama (WBA)	1998–99
Roberto Garcia (IBF)	1998–99
Lavka Sim (WBA)	1999
Diego Corrales (IBF)	1999–2001
Baek Jong-Kwon (WBA)	1999–2000
Joel Casamayor (WBA)	2000–02
Steve Forbes (IBF)	2001-02†
Acelino Freitas (WBA)	2002–
Sirimongkol Singmanassak (WBC)	2002–

Featherweights

Widely accepted champions in CAPITAL letters. Current champions in **bold** type.

Champion	Held Title
TORPEDO BILLY MURPHY	1890
YOUNG GRIFFO	1890–92
GEORGE DIXON	1892–97
SOLLY SMITH	1897–98
Ben Jordan (GBR)	1898–99
Eddie Santry (GBR)	1899–1900
DAVE SULLIVAN	1898
GEORGE DIXON	1898–1900
TERRY McGOVERN	1900–01
YOUNG CORBETT II	1901–04
JIMMY BRITT	1904
ABE ATTELL	1904
BROOKLYN TOMMY SULLIVAN	1904–05
ABE ATTELL	1906–12
JOHNNY KILBANE	1912–23
Jem Driscoll (GBR)	1912–13
EUGENE CRIQUI	1923
JOHNNY DUNDEE	1923–24†
LOUIS (KID) KAPLAN	1925–26†
Dick Finnegan (Mass.)	1926–27
BENNY BASS	1927–28
TONY CANZONERI	1928
ANDRE ROUTIS	1928–29
BATTLING BATTALINO	1929–32†
Tommy Paul (NBA)	1932–33
Kid Chocolate (NY)	1932–33
Freddie Miller (NBA)	1933–36
Baby Arizmendi (MEX)	1935–36
Mike Belloise (NY)	1936–37
Petey Sarron (NBA)	1936–37
HENRY ARMSTRONG	1937–38†
Joey Archibald (NY)	1938–39
Leo Rodak (NBA)	1938–39
JOEY ARCHIBALD	1939–40
Petey Scalzo (NBA)	1940–41
Jimmy Perrin (La.)	1940–41
HARRY JEFFRA	1940–41
JOEY ARCHIBALD	1941
Richie Lemos (NBA)	1941
CHALKY WRIGHT	1941–42
Jackie Wilson (NBA)	1941–43
WILLIE PEP	1942–48
Jackie Callura (NBA)	1943
Phil Terranova (NBA)	1943–44
Sal Bartolo (NBA)	1944–46
SANDY SADDLER	1948–49
WILLIE PEP	1949–50
SANDY SADDLER	1950–57*
HOGAN (KID) BASSEY	1957–59
DAVEY MOORE	1959–63
ULTIMINIO (SUGAR) RAMOS	1963–64
VICENTE SALDIVAR	1964–67*
Howard Winstone (GBR)	1968
Raul Rojas (WBA)	1968
Jose Legra (WBC)	1968–69
Shozo Saijyo (WBA)	1968–71
JOHNNY FAMECHON (WBC)	1969–70

Champion	Held Title
VICENTE SALDIVAR (WBC)	1970
KUNIAKI SHIBATA (WBC)	1970–72
Antonio Gomez (WBA)	1971–72
CLEMENTE SANCHEZ (WBC)	1972
Ernesto Marcel (WBA)	1972–74
JOSE LEGRA (WBC)	1972–73
EDER JOFRE (WBC)	1973–74
Ruben Olivares (WBA)	1974
Bobby Chacon (WBC)	1974–75
ALEXIS ARGUELLO (WBA)	1974–76†
Ruben Olivares (WBC)	1975
David (Poison) Kotey (WBC)	1975–76
DANNY (LITTLE RED) LOPEZ (WBC)	1976–80
Rafael Ortega (WBA)	1977
Cecilio Lastra (WBA)	1977–78
Eusebio Pedroza (WBA)	1978–85
SALVADOR SANCHEZ (WBC)	1980–82
Juan LaPorte (WBC)	1982–84
Wilfredo Gomez (WBC)	1984
Min-Keun Oh (IBF)	1984–85
Azumah Nelson (WBC)	1984–88
Barry McGuigan (WBA)	1985–86
Ki-Young Chung (IBF)	1985–86
Steve Cruz (WBA)	1986–87
Antonio Rivera (IBF)	1986–88
Antonio Esparragoza (WBA)	1987–91
Calvin Grove (IBF)	1988
Jorge Paez (IBF)	1988–91†
Jeff Fenech (WBC)	1988–90†
Marcos Villasana (WBC)	1990–91
Yung-Kyun Park (WBA)	1991–93
Troy Dorsey (IBF)	1991
Manuel Medina (IBF)	1991–93
Paul Hodkinson (WBC)	1991–93
Tom Johnson (IBF)	1993–97
Goyo Vargas (WBC)	1993
Kevin Kelley (WBC)	1993–95
Eloy Rojas (WBA)	1993–96
Alejandro Gonzalez (WBC)	1995
Manuel Medina (WBC)	1995–96
Wilfredo Vasquez (WBA)	1996–98†
Luisito Espinosa (WBC)	1995–99
Naseem Hamed (IBF)	1997†
Hector Lizarraga (IBF)	1997–98
Freddie Norwood (WBA)	1998
Manuel Medina (IBF)	1998–99
Antonio Cermeno (WBA)	1998–99
Cesar Soto (WBC)	1999–00
Paul Ingle (IBF)	1999–2000
Mbuelo Botile (IBF)	2000–01
Guty Espadas (WBC)	2000–01
Freddie Norwood (WBA)	1999–00
Derrick Gainer (WBA)	2000–
Erik Morales (WBC)	2001–02
Frankie Toledo (IBF)	2001
Manuel Medina (IBF)	2001–02
Johnny Tapia (IBF)	2002†

Junior Featherweights

Current champions in **bold** type.

Champion	Held Title
Jack (Kid) Wolfe	1922–23
Carl Duane	1923–24
Rigoberto Riasco (WBC)	1976
Royal Kobayashi (WBC)	1976
Dong-Kyun Yum (WBC)	1976–77
Wilfredo Gomez (WBC)	1977–83
Soo-Hwan Hong (WBA)	1977–78
Ricardo Cardona (WBA)	1978–80
Leo Randolph (WBA)	1980
Sergio Palma (WBA)	1980–82

Champion	Held Title
Leonardo Cruz (WBA)	1982–84
Jaime Garza (WBC)	1983
Bobby Berna (IBF)	1983–84
Loris Stecca (WBA)	1984
Seung-Il Suh (IBF)	1984–85
Victor Callejas (WBA)	1984–85
Juan (Kid) Meza (WBC)	1984–85
Ji-Woo Kim (IBF)	1985–86
Lupe Pintor (WBC)	1985–86
Samart Payakaroon (WBC)	1986–87

Major Titleholders (Cont.)

Champion	Held Title	Champion	Held Title
Seung-Hoon Lee (IBF)	1987–88	Kennedy McKinney (IBF)	1993–94
Louie Espinoza (WBA)	1987	Wilfredo Vasquez (WBA)	1992–95
Jeff French (WBC)	1987	Vuyani Bungu (IBF)	1994–99†
Julio Gervacio (WBA)	1987–88	Hector Acero Sanchez (WBC)	1994–95
Daniel Zaragoza (WBC)	1988–90	Antonio Cermeno (WBA)	1995–98†
Jose Sanabria (IBF)	1988–90	Daniel Zaragoza (WBC)	1995–97
Bernardo Pinango (WBA)	1988	Erik Morales (WBC)	1997–00†
Juan Jose Estrada (WBA)	1988–89	Enrique Sanchez (WBA)	1998
Fabrice Benichou (IBF)	1989–90	Nestor Garza (WBA)	1998–00
Jesus Salud (WBA)	1989–90	Lehlohonolo Ledwaba (IBF)	1999–2001
Welcome Ncita (IBF)	1990–92	Clarence Adams (WBA)	2000–01†
Paul Banke (WBC)	1990	**Willie Jorrin** (WBC)	2000–
Luis Mendoza (WBA)	1990–91	**Manny Pacquiao** (IBF)	2001–
Raul Perez (WBA)	1992	Yorber Ortega (WBA)	2001–02
Pedro Decima (WBC)	1990–91	Yoddamrong Sithyodthong (WBA)	2002
Kiyoshi Hatanaka (WBC)	1991	Osamu Sato (WBA)	2002
Daniel Zaragoza (WBC)	1991–92	**Salim Medjkoune** (WBA)	2002–
Tracy Patterson (WBC)	1992–94		

Bantamweights

Widely accepted champions in CAPITAL letters. Current champions in **bold** type.

Champion	Held Title	Champion	Held Title
TOMMY (SPIDER) KELLY	1887	HAROLD DADE	1947
HUGHEY BOYLE	1887–88	MANUEL ORTIZ	1947–50
TOMMY (SPIDER) KELLY	1889	VIC TOWEEL	1950–52
CHAPPIE MORAN	1889–90	JIMMY CARRUTHERS	1952–54*
Tommy (Spider) Kelly	1890–92	ROBERT COHEN	1954–56
GEORGE DIXON	1890–91	Raul Macias (NBA)	1955–57
Billy Plummer	1892–95	MARIO D'AGATA	1956–57
JIMMY BARRY	1894–99	ALPHONSE HALIMI	1957–59
Pedlar Palmer	1895–99	JOE BECERRA	1959–60*
TERRY McGOVERN	1899–1900	Johnny Caldwell (EBU)	1961–62
HARRY HARRIS	1901–02	EDER JOFRE	1961–65
DANNY DOUGHERTY	1900–01	MASAHIKO FIGHTING HARADA	1965–68
HARRY FORBES	1901–03	LIONEL ROSE	1968–69
FRANKIE NEIL	1903–04	RUBEN OLIVARES	1969–70
JOE BOWKER	1904–05	CHUCHO CASTILLO	1970–71
JIMMY WALSH	1905–06†	RUBEN OLIVARES	1971–72
OWEN MORAN	1907–08	RAFAEL HERRERA	1972
MONTE ATTELL	1909–10	ENRIQUE PINDER	1972–73
FRANKIE CONLEY	1910–11	ROMEO ANAYA	1973
JOHNNY COULON	1911–14	Rafael Herrera (WBC)	1973–74
Digger Stanley (GBR)	1910–12	ARNOLD TAYLOR	1973–74
Charles Ledoux (GBR)	1912–13	SOO-HWAN HONG	1974–75
Eddie Campi (GBR)	1913–14	Rodolfo Martinez (WBC)	1974–76
KID WILLIAMS	1914–17	ALFONSO ZAMORA	1975–77
Johnny Ertle	1915–18	Carlos Zarate (WBC)	1976–79
PETE HERMAN	1917–20	JORGE LUJAN	1977–80
Memphis Pal Moore	1918–19	Lupe Pintor (WBC)	1979–83
JOE LYNCH	1920–21	JULIAN SOLIS	1980
PETE HERMAN	1921	JEFF CHANDLER	1980–84
JOHNNY BUFF	1921–22	Albert Davila (WBC)	1983–85
JOE LYNCH	1922–24	RICHARD SANDOVAL	1984–86
ABE GOLDSTEIN	1924	Satoshi Shingaki (IBF)	1984–85
CANNONBALL EDDIE MARTIN	1924–25	Jeff Fenech (IBF)	1985
PHIL ROSENBERG	1925–27	Daniel Zaragoza (WBC)	1985
Teddy Baldock (GBR)	1927	Miguel (Happy) Lora (WBC)	1985–88
BUD TAYLOR (NBA)	1927–28†	GABY CANIZALES	1986
Willie Smith (GBR)	1927–28	BERNARDO PINANGO	1986–87
Bushy Graham (NY)	1928–29	Wilfredo Vasquez (WBA)	1987–88
PANAMA AL BROWN	1929–35	Kevin Seabrooks (IBF)	1987–88
Sixto Escobar (NBA)	1934–35	Kaokor Galaxy (WBA)	1988
BALTAZAR SANGCHILLI	1935–36	Moon Sung-Kil (WBA)	1988–89
Lou Salica (NBA)	1935	Kaokor Galaxy (WBA)	1989
Sixto Escobar (NBA)	1935–36	Raul Perez (WBA)	1988–91
TONY MARINO	1936	Orlando Canizales (IBF)	1988–94†
SIXTO ESCOBAR	1936–37	Luisito Espinosa (WBA)	1989–91
HARRY JEFFRA	1937–38	Greg Richardson	1991
SIXTO ESCOBAR	1938–39*	Joichiro Tatsuyoshi (WBC)	1991–92
Georgie Pace (NBA)	1939–40	Israel Contreras (WBA)	1991–92
LOU SALICA	1940–42	Eddie Cook (WBA)	1992
MANUEL ORTIZ	1942–47	Victor Rabanales (WBC)	1992–93

Champion	Held Title
Jorge Julio (WBA)	1992–93
Jung-Il Byun (WBC)	1993
Junior Jones (WBA)	1993–94
Yasuei Yakushiji (WBC)	1993–95
John M. Johnson (WBA)	1994
Daorung Chuvatana (WBA)	1994–95
Harold Mestre (IBF)	1995
Mbuelo Botile (IBF)	1995–97
Wayne McCullough (WBC)	1995–96
Veeraphol Sahaprom (WBA)	1995–96
Nana Yaw Konadu (WBA)	1996

Champion	Held Title
Daorung Chuvatana (WBA)	1996–97
Nana Yaw Konadu (WBA)	1997–98
Sirimongkol Singmanassak (WBC)	1996–97
Tim Austin (IBF)	1997–
Joichiro Tatsuyoshi (WBC)	1997–98
Johnny Tapia (WBA)	1998–99
Veerapol Sahaprom (WBC)	1998–
Paulie Ayala (WBA)	1999–2001
Eidy Moya (WBA)	2001–02
Johnny Bredahl (WBA)	2002–

Junior Bantamweights

Widely accepted champions in CAPITAL letters. Current champions in **bold** type.

Champion	Held Title
Rafael Orono (WBC)	1980–81
Chul-Ho Kim (WBC)	1981–82
Gustavo Ballas (WBA)	1981
Rafael Pedroza (WBA)	1981–82
Jiro Watanabe (WBA)	1982–84
Rafael Orono (WBC)	1982–83
Payao Poontarat (WBC)	1983–84
Joo-Do Chun (IBF)	1983–85
JIRO WATANABE	1984–86
Kaosai Galaxy (WBA)	1984
Ellyas Pical (IBF)	1985–86
Cesar Polanco (IBF)	1986
GILBERTO ROMAN	1986–87
Ellyas Pical (IBF)	1986
Santos Laciar (WBC)	1987
Tae-Il Chang (IBF)	1987
Sugar Rojas (WBC)	1987–88
Ellyas Pical (IBF)	1987–89
Gilberto Roman (WBC)	1988–89
Juan Polo Perez (IBF)	1989–90
Nana Konadu (WBC)	1989–90
Sung-Kil Moon (WBC)	1990–93
Robert Quiroga (IBF)	1990–93

Champion	Held Title
Julio Borboa (IBF)	1993–94
Katsuya Onizuka (WBA)	1993–94
Lee Hyung-Chul (WBA)	1994–95
Jose Luis Bueno (WBC)	1993–94
Hiroshi Kawashima (WBC)	1994–97
Harold Grey (IBF)	1994–95
Alimi Goitia (WBA)	1995–96
Yokthai Sith-Oar (WBA)	1996–97
Carlos Salazar (IBF)	1995–96
Harold Grey (IBF)	1996
Danny Romero (IBF)	1996–97
Gerry Penalosa (WBC)	1997–98
Johnny Tapia (IBF)	1997–98†
Satoshi Lida (WBA)	1997–98
Cho In-Joo (WBC)	1998–00
Jesus Rojas (WBA)	1998–99
Mark Johnson (IBF)	1999–00†
Hideki Todaka (WBA)	1999–2000
Masanori Tokuyama (WBC)	2000–
Felix Machado (IBF)	2000–
Leo Gamez (WBA)	2000–01
Celes Kobayashi (WBA)	2001–02
Alexander Munoz (WBA)	2002–

Flyweights

Widely accepted champions in CAPITAL letters. Current champions in **bold** type.

Champion	Held Title
Sid Smith (GBR)	1913
Bill Ladbury (GBR)	1913–14
Percy Jones (GBR)	1914
Joe Symonds (GBR)	1914–16
JIMMY WILDE	1916–23
PANCHO VILLA	1923–25
FIDEL LaBARBA	1925–27*
FRENCHY BELANGER (NBA,IBU)	1927–28
Izzy Schwartz (NY)	1927–29
Johnny McCoy (Calif.)	1927–28
Newsboy Brown (Calif.)	1928
FRANKIE GENARO (NBA,IBU)	1928–29
Johnny Hill (GBR)	1928–29
SPIDER PLADNER (NBA,IBU)	1929
FRANKIE GENARO (NBA,IBU)	1929–31
Willie LaMorte (NY)	1929–30
Midget Wolgast (NY)	1930–35
YOUNG PEREZ (NBA,IBU)	1931–32
JACKIE BROWN (NBA,IBU)	1932–35
BENNY LYNCH	1935–38†
Small Montana (NY,Calif.)	1935–37
PETER KANE	1938–43
Little Dado (NBA,Calif.)	1938–40
JACKIE PATERSON	1943–48
RINTY MONAGHAN	1948–50*
TERRY ALLEN	1950
SALVADOR (DADO) MARINO	1950–52
YOSHIO SHIRAI	1953–54
PASCUAL PEREZ	1954–60
PONE KINGPETCH	1960–62
MASAHIKO (FIGHTING) HARADA	1962–63

Champion	Held Title
PONE KINGPETCH	1963
HIROYUKI EBIHARA	1963–64
PONE KINGPETCH	1964–65
SALVATORE BURRINI	1965–66
Horacio Accavallo (WBA)	1966–68
WALTER McGOWAN	1966
CHARTCHAI CHIONOI	1966–69
EFREN TORRES	1969–70
Hiroyuki Ebihara (WBA)	1969
Bernabe Villacampo (WBA)	1969–70
CHARTCHAI CHIONOI	1970
Berkrerk Chartvanchai (WBA)	1970
Masao Ohba (WBA)	1970–73
ERBITO SALAVARRIA (WBC)	1970–73
Betulio Gonzalez (WBC)	1972
Venice Borkorsor (WBC)	1972–73
VENICE BORKORSOR	1973
Chartchai Chionoi (WBA)	1973–74
Betulio Gonzalez (WBA)	1973–74
Shoji Oguma (WBC)	1974–75
Susumu Hanagata (WBA)	1974–75
Miguel Canto (WBC)	1975–79
Erbito Salavarria (WBA)	1975–76
Alfonso Lopez (WBA)	1976
Guty Espadas (WBA)	1976–78
Betulio Gonzalez (WBA)	1978–79
Chan-Hee Park (WBC)	1979–80
Luis Ibarra (WBA)	1979–80
Tae-Shik Kim (WBA)	1980
Shoji Oguma (WBC)	1980–81
Peter Mathebula (WBA)	1980–81

Major Titleholders (Cont.)

Champion	Held Title
Santos Laciar (WBA)	1981
Antonio Avelar (WBC)	1981–82
Luis Ibarra (WBA)	1981
Juan Herrera (WBA)	1981–82
Prudencio Cardona (WBC)	1982
Santos Laciar (WBA)	1982–85
Freddie Castillo (WBC)	1982
Eleoncio Mercedes (WBC)	1982–83
Charlie Magri (WBC)	1983
Frank Cedeno (WBC)	1983–84
Soon-Chun Kwon (IBF)	1983–85
Koji Kobayashi (WBC)	1984
Gabriel Bernal (WBC)	1984
Sot Chitalada (WBC)	1984–88
Hilario Zapate (WBA)	1985–87
Chong-Kwan Chung (IBF)	1985–86
Bi-Won Chung (IBF)	1986
Hi-Sup Shin (IBF)	1986–87
Dodie Penalosa (IBF)	1987
Fidel Bassa (WBA)	1987–89
Choi Chang-Ho (IBF)	1987–88
Rolando Bohol (IBF)	1988
Yong-Kang Kim (WBC)	1988–89
Duke McKenzie (IBF)	1988–89
Dave McAuley (IBF)	1989–92
Sot Chitalada (WBC)	1989–91

Champion	Held Title
Jesus Rojas (WBA)	1989–90
Yul-Woo Lee (WBA)	1990
Leopard Tamakuma (WBA)	1990–91
Muangchai Kittikasem (WBC)	1991–92
Yong-Kang Kim (WBA)	1991–92
Rodolfo Blanco (IBF)	1992
Yuri Arbachakov (WBC)	1992–97
Aquiles Guzman (WBA)	1992
Phichit Sithbangprachan (IBF)	1992–94†
David Griman (WBA)	1992–94
Saen Sor Ploenchit (WBA)	1994–96
Francisco Tejedor (IBF)	1995
Danny Romero (IBF)	1995–96
Mark Johnson (IBF)	1996–99†
Jose Bonilla (WBA)	1996–97
Chatchai Sasakul (WBC)	1997–98
Hugo Soto (WBA)	1998–99
Manny Pacquiao (WBC)	1998–99
Irene Pacheco (IBF)	1999–
Leo Gamez (WBA)	1999
Medgoen Lukchaopormasak (WBC)	1999–00
Sornpichai Kratindaenggym (WBA)	1999–00
Eric Morel (WBA)	2000–
Malcolm Tunacao (WBC)	2000–01
Pongsaklek Wonjongkam (WBC)	2001–

Junior Flyweights
Current champions in **bold** type.

Champion	Held Title
Franco Udella (WBC)	1975
Jaime Rios (WBA)	1975–76
Luis Estaba (WBC)	1975–78
Juan Guzman (WBA)	1976
Yoko Gushiken (WBA)	1976–81
Freddy Castillo (WBC)	1978
Netrnoi Vorasingh (WBC)	1978
Sung-Jun Kim (WBC)	1978–80
Shigeo Nakajima (WBC)	1980
Hilario Zapata (WBC)	1980–82
Pedro Flores (WBA)	1981
Hwan-Jin Kim (WBA)	1981
Katsuo Tokashiki (WBA)	1981–83
Amado Urzua (WBC)	1982
Tadashi Tomori (WBC)	1982
Hilario Zapata (WBA)	1982–83
Jung-Koo Chang (WBC)	1983–88
Lupe Madera (WBA)	1983–84
Dodie Penalosa (IBF)	1983–86
Francisco Quiroz (WBA)	1984–85
Joey Olivo (WBA)	1985
Myung-Woo Yuh (WBA)	1985–91
Jum-Hwan Choi (IBF)	1986–88
Tacy Macalos (IBF)	1988–89
German Torres (WBC)	1988–89
Yul-Woo Lee (WBC)	1989

Champion	Held Title
Muangchai Kittikasem (IBF)	1989–90
Humberto Gonzalez (WBC)	1989–90
Michael Carbajal (IBF)	1990–94
Rolando Pascua (WBC)	1990
Melchor Cob Castro (WBC)	1991
Humberto Gonzalez (WBC)	1991–93
Hirokia Ioka (WBA)	1991–92
Michael Carbajal (WBC)	1993–94
Myung-Woo Yuh (WBA)	1993
Leo Gamez (WBA)	1993–95
Humberto Gonzalez (WBC/IBF)	1994–95
Choi Hi-Yong (WBA)	1995–96
Saman Sor Jaturong (WBC/IBF)	1995–96
Carlos Murillo (WBA)	1996
Keiji Yamaguchi (WBA)	1996
Michael Carbajal (IBF)	1996–97
Saman Sor Jaturong (WBC)	1995–99
Phichit Chor Siriwat (WBA)	1996–00†
Mauricio Pastrana (IBF)	1997–98†
Will Grigsby (IBF)	1999
Choi Yo-Sam (WBC)	1999–2002
Ricardo Lopez (IBF)	1999–
Beibis Mendoza (WBA)	2000–01
Rosendo Alvarez (WBA)	2001–
Jorge Arce (WBC)	2002–

Strawweights
Current champions in **bold** type.

Champion	Held Title
Franco Udella (WBC)	1975
Jaime Rios (WBA)	1975–76
Luis Estaba (WBC)	1975–78
Juan Guzman (WBA)	1976
Yoko Gushiken (WBA)	1976–81
Freddy Castillo (WBC)	1978
Netrnoi Vorasingh (WBC)	1978
Sung-Jun Kim (WBC)	1978–80
Shigeo Nakajima (WBC)	1980
Hilario Zapata (WBC)	1980–82
Pedro Flores (WBA)	1981

Champion	Held Title
Hwan-Jin Kim (WBA)	1981
Katsuo Tokashiki (WBA)	1981–83
Amado Urzua (WBC)	1982
Tadashi Tomori (WBC)	1982
Hilario Zapata (WBC)	1982–83
Jung-Koo Chang (WBC)	1983–88
Lupe Madera (WBA)	1983–84
Dodie Penalosa (IBF)	1983–86
Francisco Quiroz (WBA)	1984–85
Joey Olivo (WBA)	1985
Myung-Woo Yuh (WBA)	1985–93

Champion	Held Title	Champion	Held Title
Jum-Hwan Choi (IBF)	1986–88	Ricardo Lopez (WBA/WBC)	1998–99†
Tacy Macalos (IBF)	1988–89	Zolani Petelo (IBF)	1997–2001†
German Torres (WBC)	1988–89	Wandee Chor Chareon (WBC)	1999–00
Yul-Woo Lee (WBC)	1989	Noel Arambulet (WBA)	1999–00†
Muangchai Kittikasem (IBF)	1989–90	Joma Gamboa (WBA)	2000
Humberto Gonzalez (WBC)	1989–90	Keitaro Hoshino (WBA)	2000–01
Michael Carbajal (IBF)	1990	**Jose Antonio Aguirre** (WBC)	2000–
Rolando Pascua (WBC)	1990	Chana Porpaoin (WBA)	2001
Melchor Cob Castro (WBC)	1991	Robert Leyva (IBF)	2001–02
Ricardo Lopez (WBC)	1990–98	Yutaka Niida (WBA)	2001*
Ratanapol Voraphin (IBF)	1992–97	Keitaro Hoshino (WBA)	2002
Chana Porpaoin (WBA)	1993–95	**Noel Arambulent** (WBA)	2002–
Rosendo Alvarez (WBA)	1995–98	**Miguel Barrera** (IBF)	2002–

Annual Awards
Ring Magazine Fight of the Year

First presented in 1945 by Nat Fleischer, who started *The Ring* magazine in 1922.

Multiple matchups: Muhammad Ali vs. Joe Frazier, Carmen Basilio vs. Sugar Ray Robinson and Rocky Graziano vs. Tony Zale (2).

Multiple fights: Muhammad Ali (6); Carmen Basilio (5); George Foreman and Joe Frazier (4); Rocky Graziano, Rocky Marciano and Tony Zale (3); Nino Benvenuti, Bobby Chacon, Ezzard Charles, Arturo Gatti, Marvin Hagler, Thomas Hearns, Evander Holyfield, Sugar Ray Leonard, Floyd Patterson, Sugar Ray Robinson and Jersey Joe Walcott (2).

Year	Winner	Loser	Result		Year	Winner	Loser	Result	
1945	Rocky Graziano	Red Cochrane	KO	10	1974	Muhammad Ali	George Foreman	KO	8
1946	Tony Zale	Rocky Graziano	KO	6	1975	Muhammad Ali	Joe Frazier	KO	14
1947	Rocky Graziano	Tony Zale	KO	6	1976	George Foreman	Ron Lyle	KO	4
1948	Marcel Cerdan	Tony Zale	KO	12	1977	Jimmy Young	George Foreman	W	12
1949	Willie Pep	Sandy Saddler	W	15	1978	Leon Spinks	Muhammad Ali	W	15
					1979	Danny Lopez	Mike Ayala	KO	15
1950	Jake LaMotta	Laurent Dauthuille	KO	15	1980	Saad Muhammad	Yaqui Lopez	KO	14
1951	Jersey Joe Walcott	Ezzard Charles	KO	7	1981	Sugar Ray Leonard	Thomas Hearns	KO	14
1952	Rocky Marciano	Jersey Joe Walcott	KO	13	1982	Bobby Chacon	Rafael Limon	W	15
1953	Rocky Marciano	Roland LaStarza	KO	11	1983	Bobby Chacon	C. Boza-Edwards	W	12
1954	Rocky Marciano	Ezzard Charles	KO	8	1984	Jose Luis Ramirez	Edwin Rosario	KO	4
1955	Carmen Basilio	Tony DeMarco	KO	12	1985	Marvin Hagler	Thomas Hearns	KO	3
1956	Carmen Basilio	Johnny Saxton	KO	9	1986	Stevie Cruz	Barry McGuigan	W	15
1957	Carmen Basilio	Sugar Ray Robinson	W	15	1987	Sugar Ray Leonard	Marvin Hagler	W	12
1958	Sugar Ray Robinson	Carmen Basilio	W	15	1988	Tony Lopez	Rocky Lockridge	W	12
1959	Gene Fullmer	Carmen Basilio	KO	14	1989	Roberto Duran	Iran Barkley	W	12
1960	Floyd Patterson	Ingemar Johansson	KO	5	1990	Julio Cesar Chavez	Meldrick Taylor	KO	12
1961	Joe Brown	Dave Charnley	W	15	1991	Robert Quiroga	Akeem Anifowoshe	W	12
1962	Joey Giardello	Henry Hank	W	10	1992	Riddick Bowe	Evander Holyfield	W	12
1963	Cassius Clay	Doug Jones	W	10	1993	Michael Carbajal	Humberto Gonzalez	KO	7
1964	Cassius Clay	Sonny Liston	KO	7	1994	Jorge Castro	John David Jackson	TKO	9
1965	Floyd Patterson	George Chuvalo	W	12	1995	Saman Sorjaturong	Chiquita Gonzalez	KO	7
1966	Jose Torres	Eddie Cotton	W	15	1996	Evander Holyfield	Mike Tyson	TKO	11
1967	Nino Benvenuti	Emile Griffith	W	15	1997	Arturo Gatti	Gabriel Ruelas	KO	5
1968	Dick Tiger	Frank DePaula	W	10	1998	Ivan Robinson	Arturo Gatti	W	10
1969	Joe Frazier	Jerry Quarry	KO	7	1999	Paulie Ayala	Johnny Tapia	W	12
1970	Carlos Monzon	Nino Benvenuti	KO	12	2000	Erik Morales	Marco Antonio Barrera	W	12
1971	Joe Frazier	Muhammad Ali	W	15					
1972	Bob Foster	Chris Finnegan	KO	14	2001	Micky Ward	Emanuel Burton	W	10
1973	George Foreman	Joe Frazier	KO	2					

Ring Magazine Fighter of the Year

First presented in 1928 by Nat Fleischer, who started *The Ring* magazine in 1922.

Multiple winners: Muhammad Ali (5); Joe Louis (4); Joe Frazier, Evander Holyfield and Rocky Marciano (3); Ezzard Charles, George Foreman, Marvin Hagler, Thomas Hearns, Ingemar Johansson, Sugar Ray Leonard, Tommy Loughran, Floyd Patterson, Sugar Ray Robinson, Barney Ross, Dick Tiger and Mike Tyson (2).

Year		Year		Year		Year	
1928	Gene Tunney	1935	Barney Ross	1943	Fred Apostoli	1951	Sugar Ray Robinson
1929	Tommy Loughran	1936	Joe Louis	1944	Beau Jack	1952	Rocky Marciano
1930	Max Schmeling	1937	Henry Armstrong	1945	Willie Pep	1953	Carl (Bobo) Olson
1931	Tommy Loughran	1938	Joe Louis	1946	Tony Zale	1954	Rocky Marciano
1932	Jack Sharkey	1939	Joe Louis	1947	Gus Lesnevich	1955	Rocky Marciano
1933	No award	1940	Billy Conn	1948	Ike Williams	1956	Floyd Patterson
1934	Tony Canzoneri & Barney Ross	1941	Joe Louis	1949	Ezzard Charles	1957	Carmen Basilio
		1942	Sugar Ray Robinson	1950	Ezzard Charles	1958	Ingemar Johansson
						1959	Ingemar Johansson

Year		Year		Year		Year	
1960	Floyd Patterson	1972	Muhammad Ali	1982	Larry Holmes	1993	Michael Carbajal
1961	Joe Brown		& Carlos Monzon	1983	Marvin Hagler	1994	Roy Jones Jr.
1962	Dick Tiger	1973	George Foreman	1984	Thomas Hearns	1995	Oscar De La Hoya
1963	Cassius Clay	1974	Muhammad Ali	1985	Donald Curry	1996	Evander Holyfield
1964	Emile Griffith	1975	Muhammad Ali		& Marvin Hagler	1997	Evander Holyfield
1965	Dick Tiger	1976	George Foreman	1986	Mike Tyson	1998	Floyd Mayweather Jr.
1966	No award	1977	Carlos Zarate	1987	Evander Holyfield	1999	Paulie Ayala
1967	Joe Frazier	1978	Muhammad Ali	1988	Mike Tyson		
1968	Nino Benvenuti	1979	Sugar Ray Leonard	1989	Pernell Whitaker	2000	Felix Trinidad
1969	Jose Napoles					2001	Bernard Hopkins
		1980	Thomas Hearns	1990	Julio Cesar Chavez		
1970	Joe Frazier	1981	Sugar Ray Leonard	1991	James Toney		
1971	Joe Frazier		& Salvador Sanchez	1992	Riddick Bowe		

Note: Cassius Clay changed his name to Muhammad Ali after winning the heavyweight title in 1964.

All-Time Leaders

As compiled by *The Ring Record Book and Encyclopedia.*

Knockouts

	Division	Career	No
1	Archie Moore............Lt. Heavy	1936–63	130
2	Young Stribling..............Heavy	1921–33	126
3	Billy Bird...................Welter	1920–48	125
4	George Odwel ....Welter	1930–45	114
5	Sugar Ray Robinson ....Middle	1940–65	110
6	Sandy Saddler.............Feather	1944–56	103
7	Sam Langford............Middle	1902–26	102
8	Henry Armstrong ....Welter	1931–45	100
9	Jimmy Wilde ....Fly	1911–23	98
10	Len Wickwar............Lt. Heavy	1928–47	93

Total Bouts

	Division	Career	No
1	Len Wickwar..............Lt. Heavy	1928–47	463
2	Jack Britton ....Welter	1905–30	350
3	Johnny Dundee ....Feather	1910–32	333
4	Billy Bird....................Welter	1920–48	318
5	George Marsden..............n/a	1928–46	311
6	Maxie Rosenbloom ....Lt. Heavy	1923–39	299
7	Harry Greb.................Middle	1913–26	298
8	Young Stribling...........Lt. Heavy	1921–33	286
9	Battling Levinsky...........Lt. Heavy	1910–29	282
10	Ted (Kid) Lewis ....Welter	1909–29	279

Triple Champions

Fighters who have won widely-accepted world titles in more than two divisions. Henry Armstrong is the only fighter listed to hold three titles simultaneously. Note that (*) indicates title claimant.

Sugar Ray Leonard (5) WBC Welterweight (1979-80,80-82); WBA Jr. Middleweight (1981); WBC Middleweight (1987); WBC Super Middleweight (1988-90); WBC Light Heavyweight (1988).

Oscar De La Hoya (4) IBF Lightweight (1995-96); WBC Super Lightweight (1996-97); WBC Welterweight (1997-99); WBC Jr. Middleweight (2001–); WBA Jr. Middleweight (2002–).

Roberto Duran (4) Lightweight (1972-79); WBC Welterweight (1980); WBA Jr. Middleweight (1983-84); WBC Middleweight (1989-90).

Leo Gamez (4) WBA Strawweight (1988-90); WBA Jr. Flyweight (1993-95); WBA Flyweight (1999); WBA Junior Bantamweight (2000-01).

Thomas Hearns (4) WBA Welterweight (1980-81); WBC Jr. Middleweight (1982-84); WBC Light Heavyweight (1987); WBA Light Heavyweight (1991); WBC Middleweight (1987-88).

Pernell Whitaker (4) IBF/WBC/WBA Lightweight (1989-92); IBF Jr. Welterweight (1992-93); WBC Welterweight (1993-97); WBC Jr. Middleweight (1995).

Alexis Arguello (3) WBA Featherweight (1974-77); WBC Jr. Lightweight (1978-80); WBC Lightweight (1981-83).

Henry Armstrong (3) Featherweight (1937-38); Welterweight (1938-40); Lightweight (1938-39).

Iran Barkley (3) WBC Middleweight (1988-89); IBF Super Middleweight (1992-93); WBA Light Heavyweight (1992).

Wilfredo Benitez (3) Jr. Welterweight (1976-79); Welterweight (1979); WBC Jr. Middleweight (1981-82).

Tony Canzoneri (3) Featherweight (1928); Lightweight (1930-33); Jr. Welterweight (1931-32,33).

Julio Cesar Chavez (3) WBC Jr. Lightweight (1984-87); WBA/WBC Lightweight (1987-89); WBC/IBF Jr. Welterweight (1989-91); WBC Jr. Welterweight (1991-94, 1994).

Jeff Fenech (3) IBF Bantamweight (1985); WBC Jr. Featherweight (1986-88); WBC Featherweight (1988-90).

Bob Fitzsimmons (3) Middleweight (1891-97); Light Heavyweight (1903-05); Heavyweight (1897-99).

Wilfredo Gomez (3) WBC Super Bantamweight (1977-83); WBC Featherweight (1984); WBA Jr. Lightweight (1985-86).

Emile Griffith (3) Welterweight (1961,62-63,63-66); Jr. Middleweight (1962-63); Middleweight (1966-67,67-68).

Roy Jones Jr. (3) IBF Middleweight (1993-94); IBF Super Middleweight (1994-96); WBC Light Heavyweight (1996, 1997–); WBA Light Heavyweight (1998–); IBF Light Heavyweight (1999–).

Mike McCallum (3) WBA Jr. Middleweight (1984-88); WBA Middleweight (1989-91); WBC Light Heavyweight (1994-95).

Terry McGovern (3) Bantamweight (1889-1900); Featherweight (1900-01); Lightweight* (1900-01).

Barney Ross (3) Lightweight (1933-35); Jr. Welterweight (1933-35); Welterweight (1934, 35-38).

Johnny Tapia (3) IBF Jr. Bantamweight (1997-98); WBA Bantamweight (1998-99); IBF Featherweight (2002).

Felix Trinidad (3) IBF/WBC Welterweight (1993-2000); WBA/IBF Jr. Middleweight (2000-01); WBA Middleweight (2001).

Wilfredo Vazquez (3) WBA Bantamweight (1987-88); WBA Jr. Featherweight (1992-95); WBA Featherweight (1996-98).

Miscellaneous Sports

*Louisville's **Aaron Alvey** threw his way into the record books at the 2002 Little League World Series.*

AP/Wide World Photos

CHESS

World Champions

Garry Kasparov became the youngest man to win the world chess championship when he beat fellow Russian Anatoly Karpov in 1985 at age 22. In 1993, Kasparov and then-#1 challenger Nigel Short of England broke away from the established International Chess Federation (FIDE) to form the Professional Chess Association (the PCA was disbanded in 1998). FIDE retaliated by stripping Kasparov of the world title and arranging a playoff that was won by Karpov, the former title-holder. Karpov successfully defended the FIDE title several times before failing to show up for the 1999 FIDE World Championship Tournament that was won by Alexander Khalifman. Indian Viswanathan Anand won the 2000 FIDE World Championship. Ruslan Ponomariov won the 2001 FIDE World Championship in Moscow and is the current FIDE World Champion.

In his first title defense in five years, Kasparov faced world #2 Vladimir Kramnik for 16 matches in the unofficial (though more widely recognized) world championship from Oct. 8-Nov. 4, 2000 in London. The 25-year-old Kramnik defeated the longtime world champion 8½-6½ in a stunning result. Kasparov failed to win a single game, but despite the loss is still the top-ranked player in the world.

A plan to unify the world chess championship has been hatched and is scheduled to culminate in a tournament including the world's top players in late 2003. The semifinals have been tenatively set: World No. 1 Kasparov will play reigning FIDE champion Ponomariov and Kramnik, who took Kasparov's title, will face Peter Leko of Hungary, winner of the 2002 World Championship Candidates' tournament held in Dortmund, Germany.

Years		Years		Years	
1866-94	Wilhelm Steinitz, Austria	1957-58	Vassily Smyslov, USSR	1975-85	Anatoly Karpov, USSR
1894-1921	Emanuel Lasker, Germany	1958-59	Mikhail Botvinnik, USSR	1985-2000	Garry Kasparov, RUS
1921-27	Jose Capablanca, Cuba	1960-61	Mikhail Tal, USSR	2000–	Vladimir Kramnik, RUS
1927-35	Alexander Alekhine, France	1961-63	Mikhail Botvinnik, USSR		
1935-37	Max Euwe, Holland	1963-69	Tigran Petrosian, USSR	*Fischer defaulted the championship in 1975.	
1937-46	Alexander Alekhine, France	1969-72	Boris Spassky, USSR		
1948-57	Mikhail Botvinnik, USSR	1972-75	Bobby Fischer, USA*		

U.S. Champions

Years		Years		Years	
1857-71	Paul Morphy	1957-61	Bobby Fischer	1987	Joel Benjamin
1871-76	George Mackenzie	1961-62	Larry Evans		& Nick DeFirmian
1876-80	James Mason	1962-68	Bobby Fischer	1988	Michael Wilder
1880-89	George Mackenzie	1968-69	Larry Evans	1989	Roman Dzindzichashvili,
1889-90	Samuel Lipschutz	1969-72	Samuel Reshevsky		Stuart Rachels
1890	Jackson Showalter	1972-73	Robert Byrne		& Yasser Seirawan
1890-91	Max Judd	1973-74	Lubomir Kavalek	1990	Lev Alburt
1891-92	Jackson Showalter		& John Grefe	1991	Gata Kamsky
1892-94	Samuel Lipschutz	1974-77	Walter Browne	1992	Patrick Wolff
1894	Jackson Showalter	1978-80	Lubomir Kabalek	1993	Alexander Shabalov
1894-95	Albert Hodges	1980-81	Larry Evans,		& Alex Yermolinsky
1895-97	Jackson Showalter		Larry Christiansen	1994	Boris Gulko
1897-1906	Harry Pillsbury		& Walter Browne	1995	Alexander Ivanov
1906-09	Vacant	1981-83	Walter Browne	1996	Alexander Yermolinsky
1909-36	Frank Marshall		& Yasser Seirawan	1997	Joel Benjamin
1936-44	Samuel Reshevsky	1983	Roman Dzindzichashvili,	1998	Nick de Firmian
1944-46	Arnold Denker		Larry Christiansen	1999	Boris Gulko
1946-48	Samuel Reshevsky		& Walter Browne	2000	Joel Benjamin, Yasser Seirawan & Alex Shabalov
1948-51	Herman Steiner	1984-85	Lev Alburt		
1951-54	Larry Evans	1986	Yasser Seirawan	2001	Not held
1954-57	Arthur Bisguier			2002	Larry Christiansen

DOGS

Iditarod Trail Sled Dog Race

In 2002, Martin Buser won his fourth Iditarod race and his first since in 1997, setting a new race record of eight days, 22 hours, 46 minutes and two seconds. When Buser crossed the burled arch marking the finish line on Front Street in Nome, Alaska he became the first musher to do so in less than nine days. Besting runner-up Ramy Brooks by just over two hours, Buser earned $62,800 and the keys to a new pick-up truck. The Swiss-born Buser became an American citizen the day after he finished the race, taking the oath of allegiance at the race's famous finish line. Celebrants that had gathered for the ceremony were forced to scatter when the dog team of Al Hardman came down Front Street to finish in 21st place.

Buser, who finished in 24th place in 2001 (his worst ever) credited his renewed focus on training with his team as the reason for his success. Sixty-four teams began the race on March 4 in Anchorage, 55 would finish.

In even-numbered years the trail follows the 1,151-mile Northern Route, while in odd-numbered years, it takes a slightly different 1,161-mile Southern Route.

Multiple winners: Rick Swenson (5); Martin Buser, Susan Butcher and Doug Swingley (4); Jeff King (3).

Year		Elapsed Time	Year		Elapsed Time
1973	Dick Wilmarth	20 days, 00:49:41	1979	Rick Swenson	15 days, 10:37:47
1974	Carl Huntington	20 days, 15:02:07	1980	Joe May	14 days, 07:11:51
1975	Emmitt Peters	14 days, 14:43:45	1981	Rick Swenson	12 days, 08:45:02
1976	Gerald Riley	18 days, 22:58:17	1982	Rick Swenson	16 days, 04:40:10
1977	Rick Swenson	16 days, 16:27:13	1983	Rick Mackey	12 days, 14:10:44
1978	Dick Mackey	14 days, 18:52:24	1984	Dean Osmar	12 days, 15:07:33

Year		Elapsed Time	Year		Elapsed Time
1985	Libby Riddles	18 days, 00:20:17	1995	Doug Swingley	9 days, 02:42:19
1986	Susan Butcher	11 days, 15:06:00	1996	Jeff King	9 days, 05:43:13
1987	Susan Butcher	11 days, 02:05:13	1997	Martin Buser	9 days, 08:31:45
1988	Susan Butcher	11 days, 11:41:40	1998	Jeff King	9 days, 05:52:26
1989	Joe Runyan	11 days, 05:24:34	1999	Doug Swingley	9 days, 14:31:07
1990	Susan Butcher	11 days, 01:53:23	2000	Doug Swingley	9 days, 00:58:06
1991	Rick Swenson	12 days, 16:34:39	2001	Doug Swingley	9 days, 19:55:50
1992	Martin Buser	10 days, 19:17:00	2002	Martin Buser	8 days, 22:46:02*
1993	Jeff King	10 days, 15:38:15		*Race record.	
1994	Martin Buser	10 days, 13:02:39			

Westminster Kennel Club

Best in Show

Best in Show at the 126th annual All-Breed Dog Show of the Westminster Kennel Club held February 11-12, 2002, was the Miniature Poodle Ch Surrey Spice Girl. The 3-year-old, ornately groomed bitch was the winner of the non-sporting group and is owned by Ron L. and Barbara Scott. Spice, who was selected among 2,500 dogs in 159 breeds, was bred by Anne Clark, Barbara Furbush and Kaz Hosaka. It was a bit of an upset as many observers thought Mick, the heavily favored Kerry blue terrier, would earn the title of top dog.

The Westminster show is the most prestigious dog show in the country, and one of America's oldest annual sporting events.

Multiple winners: Ch. Warren Remedy (3); Ch. Chinoe's Adamant James, Ch. Comejo Wycollar Boy, Ch. Flornell Spicy Piece of Halleston; Ch. Matford Vic, Ch. My Own Brucie, Ch. Pendley Calling of Blarney, Ch. Rancho Dobe's Storm (2).

Year		Breed	Year		Breed
1907	Warren Remedy	Fox Terrier	1955	Kippax Fearnought	Bulldog
1908	Warren Remedy	Fox Terrier	1956	Wilber White Swan	Toy Poodle
1909	Warren Remedy	Fox Terrier	1957	Shirkhan of Grandeur	Afghan Hound
			1958	Puttencove Promise	Standard Poodle
1910	Sabine Rarebit	Fox Terrier	1959	Fontclair Festoon	Miniature Poodle
1911	Tickle Em Jock	Scottish Terrier			
1912	Kenmore Sorceress	Airedale	1960	Chick T'Sun of Caversham	Pekingese
1913	Strathway Prince Albert	Bulldog	1961	Cappoquin Little Sister	Toy Poodle
1914	Brentwood Hero	Old English Sheepdog	1962	Elfinbrook Simon	W. Highland Terrier
1915	Matford Vic	Old English Sheepdog	1963	Wakefield's Black Knight	English Springer Spaniel
1916	Matford Vic	Old English Sheepdog	1964	Courtenay Fleetfoot of Pennyworth	Whippet
1917	Comejo Wycollar Boy	Fox Terrier	1965	Carmichaels Fanfare	Scottish Terrier
1918	Haymarket Faultless	Bull Terrier	1966	Zeloy Mooremaides Magic	Fox Terrier
1919	Briergate Bright Beauty	Airedale	1967	Bardene Bingo	Scottish Terrier
			1968	Stingray of Derryabah	Lakeland Terrier
1920	Comejo Wycollar Boy	Fox Terrier	1969	Glamoor Good News	Skye Terrier
1921	Midkiff Seductive	Cocker Spaniel			
1922	Boxwood Barkentine	Airedale	1970	Arriba's Prima Donna	Boxer
1923	No best-in-show award		1971	Chinoe's Adamant James	E.S. Spaniel
1924	Barberryhill Bootlegger	Sealyham	1972	Chinoe's Adamant James	E.S. Spaniel
1925	Governor Moscow	Pointer	1973	Acadia Command Performance	Standard Poodle
1926	Signal Circuit	Fox Terrier	1974	Gretchenhof Columbia River	German SH Pointer
1927	Pinegrade Perfection	Sealyham	1975	Sir Lancelot of Barvan	Old Eng. Sheepdog
1928	Talavera Margaret	Fox Terrier	1976	Jo Ni's Red Baron of Crofton	Lakeland Terrier
1929	Land Loyalty of Bellhaven	Collie	1977	Dersade Bobby's Girl	Sealyham
			1978	Cede Higgens	Yorkshire Terrier
1930	Pendley Calling of Blarney	Fox Terrier	1979	Oak Tree's Irishtocrat	Irish Water Spaniel
1931	Pendley Calling of Blarney	Fox Terrier			
1932	Nancolleth Markable	Pointer	1980	Sierra Cinnar	Siberian Husky
1933	Warland Protector of Shelterock	Airedale	1981	Dhandy Favorite Woodchuck	Pug
1934	Flornell Spicy Bit of Halleston	Fox Terrier	1982	St. Aubrey Dragonora of Elsdon	Pekingese
1935	Nunsoe Duc de la Terrace of Blakeen	Stan. Poodle	1983	Kabik's The Challenger	Afghan Hound
1936	St. Margaret Magnificent of Clairedale	Sealyham	1984	Seaward's Blackbeard	Newfoundland
1937	Flornell Spicy Bit of Halleston	Fox Terrier	1985	Braeburn's Close Encounter	Scottish Terrier
1938	Daro of Maridor	English Setter	1986	Marjetta National Acclaim	Pointer
1939	Ferry v.Rauhfelsen of Giralda	Doberman	1987	Covy Tucker Hill's Manhattan	German Shepherd
			1988	Great Elms Prince Charming II	Pomeranian
1940	My Own Brucie	Cocker Spaniel	1989	Royal Tudor's Wild As The Wind	Doberman
1941	My Own Brucie	Cocker Spaniel			
1942	Wolvey Pattern of Edgerstoune	W. Highland Terrier	1990	Wendessa Crown Prince	Pekingese
1943	Pitter Patter of Piperscroft	Miniature Poodle	1991	Whisperwind on a Carousel	Stan. Poodle
1944	Flornell Rarebit of Twin Ponds	Welsh Terrier	1992	Lonesome Dove	Fox Terrier
1945	Shieling's Signature	Scottish Terrier	1993	Salilyn's Condor	E.S. Spaniel
1946	Hetherington Model Rhythm	Fox Terrier	1994	Chidley Willum	Norwich Terrier
1947	Warlord of Mazelaine	Boxer	1995	Gaelforce Post Script	Scottish Terrier
1948	Rock Ridge Night Rocket	Bedling. Terrier	1996	Clussex Country Sunrise	Clumber Spaniel
1949	Mazelaine's Zazarac Brandy	Boxer	1997	Parsifal di Casa Netzer	Standard Schnauzer
			1998	Fairewood Frolic	Norwich Terrier
1950	Walsing Winning Trick of Edgerstoune	Scot. Terrier	1999	Loteki's Supernatural Being	Papillon
1951	Bang Away of Sirrah Crest	Boxer			
1952	Rancho Dobe's Storm	Doberman	2000	Salilyn 'N Erin's Shameless	E.S. Spaniel
1953	Rancho Dobe's Storm	Doberman	2001	Special Times Just Right	Bichon Frise
1954	Carmor's Rise and Shine	Cocker Spaniel	2002	Surrey Spice Girl	Miniature Poodle

FISHING

IGFA All-Tackle World Records

All-tackle records are maintained for the heaviest fish of any species caught on any line up to 130-lb (60 kg) class and certified by the International Game Fish Association. Records logged through Oct. 1, 2002. **Address:** 300 Gulf Stream Way, Dania Beach, Fla. 33004. **Telephone:** (954) 927-2628.

FRESHWATER FISH

Species	Lbs-Oz	Where Caught	Date	Angler
Barramundi	83-7	N. Queensland, Australia	Sept. 23, 1999	David Powell
Bass, Guadalupe	3-11	Lake Travis, TX	Sept. 25, 1983	Allen Christenson Jr.
Bass, largemouth	22-4	Montgomery Lake, GA	June 2, 1932	George W. Perry
Bass, Roanoke	1-5	Nottoway River, VA	Nov. 11, 1991	Tom Elkins
Bass, rock	3-0	York River, Ontario	Aug. 1, 1974	Peter Gulgin
	3-0	Lake Erie, PA	June 18, 1998	Herbert G. Ratner Jr.
Bass, shoal	8-12	Apalachicola River, FL	Jan. 28, 1995	Carl W. Davis
Bass, smallmouth	10-14	Dale Hollow, TN	Apr. 24, 1969	John T. Gorman
Bass, spotted	10-4	Pine Flat Lake, CA	Apr. 21, 2001	Bryan Shishido
Bass, striped (landlocked)	67-8	O'Neill Forebay, San Luis, CA	May 7, 1992	Hank Ferguson
Bass, Suwannee	3-14	Suwannee River, FL	Mar. 2, 1985	Ronnie Everett
Bass, white	6-13	Lake Orange, VA	July 31, 1989	Ronald L. Sprouse
Bass, whiterock	27-5	Greers Ferry Lake, AR	Apr. 24, 1997	Jerald C. Shaum
Bass, yellow	2-9	Duck River, TN	Feb. 27, 1998	John T. Chappell
Bass, yellow (hybrid)	3-5	Big Cypress Bayou, TX	Mar. 27, 1991	Patrick Collin Myers
Bluegill	4-12	Ketona Lake, AL	Apr. 9, 1950	T.S. Hudson
Bowfin	21-8	Florence, SC	Jan. 29, 1980	Robert L. Harmon
Buffalo, bigmouth	70-5	Bussey Brake, Bastrop, LA	Apr. 21, 1980	Delbert Sisk
Buffalo, black	63-6	Mississippi River, IA	Aug. 14, 1999	Jim Winters
Buffalo, smallmouth	82-3	Athens Lake, AL	June 6, 1993	Randy Collins
Bullhead, black	7-7	Mill Pond, NY	Aug. 25, 1993	Kevin Kelly
Bullhead, brown	6-1	Waterford, NY	Apr. 26, 1998	Bobby Triplett
Bullhead, yellow	4-4	Mormon Lake, AZ	May 11, 1984	Emily Williams
Burbot	18-11	Angenmanelren, Sweden	Oct. 22, 1996	Margit Agren
Carp, bighead	61-15	Old Hickory Lake, TN	Mar. 27, 2002	Rick Richard
Carp, black	40-12	Chiba, Japan	Apr. 1, 2000	Kenichi Hosoi
Carp, common	75-11	St. Cassien, France	May 21, 1987	Leo van der Gugten
Carp, crucian	5-1	Kaltersee, Italy	July 16, 1991	Jorg Marquard
Catfish, blue	116-12	Mississippi River, AR	Aug. 3, 2001	Charles Ashley Jr.
Catfish, channel	58-0	Santee-Cooper Res., SC	July 7, 1964	W.B. Whaley
Catfish, flathead	123-0	Elk City Reservoir, KS	Mar. 14, 1998	Ken Paulie
Catfish, flatwhiskered	16-15	Xingu River, Brazil	Aug. 7, 2001	Ian-Arthur de Sulocki
Catfish, gilded	85-8	Amazon River, Brazil	Nov. 15, 1986	Gilberto Fernandes
Catfish, redtail	97-7	Amazon River, Brazil	July 16, 1988	Gilberto Fernandes
Catfish, sharptoothed	79-5	Orange River, South Africa	Dec. 5, 1992	Hennie Moller
Catfish, white	21-8	East Lyme, CT	Apr. 22, 2001	Thomas Urquahart
Char, Arctic	32-9	Tree River, Canada	July 30, 1981	Jeffery Ward
Crappie, black	4-8	Kerr Lake, VA	Mar. 1, 1981	L. Carl Herring Jr.
Crappie, white	5-3	Enid Dam, MS	July 31, 1957	Fred L. Bright
Dolly Varden	20-14	Wulik River, AK	July 7, 2001	Raz Reid
Dorado	51-5	Corrientes, Argentina	Sept. 27, 1984	Armando Giudice
Drum, freshwater	54-8	Nickajack Lake, TN	Apr. 20, 1972	Benny E. Hull
Gar, alligator	279-0	Rio Grande, TX	Dec. 2, 1951	Bill Valverde
Gar, Florida	10-0	The Everglades, FL	Jan. 28, 2002	Herbert G. Ratner Jr.
Gar, longnose	50-5	Trinity River, TX	July 30, 1954	Townsend Miller
Gar, shortnose	5-12	Rend Lake, IL	July 16, 1995	Donna K. Willmart
Gar, spotted	9-12	Lake Mexia, TX	Apr. 7, 1994	Rick Rivard
Goldfish	6-10	Lake Hodges, CA	Apr. 17, 1996	Florentino M. Abena
Grayling, Arctic	5-15	Katseyedie River, N.W.T.	Aug. 16, 1967	Jeanne P. Branson
Inconnu	53-0	Pah River, AK	Aug. 20, 1986	Lawrence E. Hudnall
Kokanee	9-6	Okanagan Lake, Brit. Columbia	June 18, 1988	Norm Kuhn
Muskellunge	67-8	Hayward, WI	July 24, 1949	Cal Johnson
Muskellunge, tiger	51-3	Lac Vieux-Desert, WI-MI	July 16, 1919	John A. Knobla
Peacock, butterfly	12-9	Chiguao River, Venezuela	Jan. 6, 2000	Antonio Campa G.
Peacock, speckled	27-0	Rio Negro, Brazil	Dec. 4, 1994	Gerald (Doc) Lawson
Perch, Nile	230-0	Lake Nasser, Egypt	Dec. 20, 2000	William Toth
Perch, white	3-1	Forest Hill Park, NJ	May 6, 1989	Edward Tango
Perch, yellow	4-3	Bordentown, NJ	May, 1865	Dr. C.C. Abbot
Pickerel, chain	9-6	Homerville, GA	Feb. 17, 1961	Baxley McQuaig Jr.
Pickerel, grass	1-0	Dewart Lake, IN	June 9, 1990	Mike Berg
Pickerel, redfin	2-4	Gall Berry Swamp, NC	June 27, 1997	Edward C. Davis
Pike, northern	55-1	Lake of Grefeern, Germany	Oct. 16, 1986	Lothar Louis
Redhorse, greater	9-3	Salmon River, Pulaski, NY	May 11, 1985	Jason Wilson

Species	Lbs-Oz	Where Caught	Date	Angler
Redhorse, silver	11-7	Plum Creek, WI	May 29, 1985	Neal D.G. Long
Salmon, Atlantic	79-2	Tana River, Norway	1928	Henrik Henriksen
Salmon, chinook	97-4	Kenai River, AK	May 17, 1985	Les Anderson
Salmon, chum	35-0	Edye Pass, Brit. Columbia	July 11, 1995	Todd Johansson
Salmon, coho	33-4	Salmon River, Pulaski, NY	Sept. 27, 1989	Jerry Lifton
Salmon, pink	14-13	Monroe, WA	Sept. 30, 2001	Alexander Minerich
Salmon, sockeye	15-3	Kenai River, AK	Aug. 9, 1987	Stan Roach
Sauger	8-12	Lake Sakakawea, ND	Oct. 6, 1971	Mike Fischer
Shad, American	11-4	Conn. River, S. Hadley, MA	May 19, 1986	Bob Thibodo
Shad, gizzard	4-6	Lake Michigan, IN	Mar. 2, 1996	Mike Berg
Sturgeon, lake	168-0	Georgian Bay, Canada	May 29, 1982	Edward Paszkowski
Sturgeon, white	468-0	Benicia, CA	July 9, 1983	Joey Pallotta 3rd
Tigerfish, giant	97-0	Zaire River, Kinshasa, Zaire	July 9, 1988	Raymond Houtmans
Tilapia, spotted	3-0	Pembroke Pines, FL	Mar. 20, 1999	Jay Wright Jr.
Trout, Apache	5-3	White Mountain, AZ	May 29, 1991	John Baldwin
Trout, brook	14-8	Nipigon River, Ontario	July, 1916	Dr. W.J. Cook
Trout, brown	40-4	Little Red River, AR	May 9, 1992	Rip Collins
Trout, bull	32-0	Lake Pend Orielle, ID	Oct. 27, 1949	N.L. Higgins
Trout, cutthroat	41-0	Pyramid Lake, NV	Dec., 1925	John Skimmerhorn
Trout, golden	11-0	Cooks Lake, WY	Aug. 5, 1948	Charles S. Reed
Trout, lake	72-0	Great Bear Lake, N.W.T.	Aug. 19, 1995	Lloyd E. Bull
Trout, rainbow	42-2	Bell Island, AK	June 22, 1970	David Robert White
Trout, tiger	20-13	Lake Michigan, WI	Aug. 12, 1978	Peter M. Friedland
Walleye	25-0	Old Hickory Lake, TN	Aug. 2, 1960	Mabry Harper
Warmouth	2-7	Guess Lake, Holt, FL	Oct. 19, 1985	Tony D. Dempsey
Whitefish, lake	14-6	Meaford, Ontario	May 21, 1984	Dennis M. Laycock
Whitefish, mountain	5-8	Elbow River, Manitoba	Aug. 1, 1995	Randy G. Woo
Whitefish, round	6-0	Putahow River, Manitoba	June 14, 1984	Allan J. Ristori
Zander	25-2	Trosa, Sweden	June 12, 1986	Harry Lee Tennison

SALTWATER FISH

Species	Lbs-Oz	Where Caught	Date	Angler
Albacore	88-2	Gran Canaria, Canary Islands	Nov. 19, 1977	Siegfried Dickemann
Amberjack, greater	155-12	Challenger Bank, Bermuda	Aug. 16, 1992	Larry Trott
Angelfish, gray	4-0	S.Beach Jetty, Miami, FL	July 12, 1999	Rene G. de Dios
Barracuda, great	85-0	Christmas Is., Rep. of Kiribati	Apr. 11, 1992	John W. Helfrich
Barracuda, Mexican	21-0	Phantom Island, Costa Rica	Mar. 27, 1987	E. Greg Kent
Barracuda, pickhandle	25-5	Scottburgh, South Africa	July 3, 1996	Demetrios Stamatis
Bass, barred sand	13-3	Huntington Beach, CA	Aug. 29, 1988	Robert Halal
Bass, black sea	10-4	Virginia Beach, VA	Jan. 1, 2000	Allan P. Paschall
Bass, European	20-14	Cap d'Agde, France	Sept. 8, 1999	Robert Mari
Bass, giant sea	563-8	Anacapa Island, CA	Aug. 20, 1968	J.D. McAdam Jr.
Bass, striped	78-8	Atlantic City, NJ	Sept. 21, 1982	Albert R. McReynolds
Bluefish	31-12	Hatteras, NC	Jan. 30, 1972	James M. Hussey
Bonefish	19-0	Zululand, South Africa	May 26, 1962	Brian W. Batchelor
Bonito, Atlantic	18-4	Faial Island, Azores	July 8, 1953	D. Gama Higgs
Bonito, Pacific	21-3	Malibu, CA	July 30, 1978	Gino M. Picciolo
Cabezon	23-0	Juan de Fuca Strait, WA	Aug. 4, 1990	Wesley Hunter
Cobia	135-9	Shark Bay, W. Australia	July 9, 1985	Peter W. Goulding
Cod, Atlantic	98-12	Isle of Shoals, NH	June 8, 1969	Alphonse Bielevich
Cod, Pacific	35-0	Unalaska Bay, AK	June 16, 1999	Jim Johnson
Conger	133-4	South Devon, England	June 5, 1995	Vic Evans
Dolphinfish	88-0	Highbourne Cay, Bahamas	May 5, 1998	Richard D. Evans
Drum, black	113-1	Lewes, DE	Sept. 15, 1975	Gerald M. Townsend
Drum, red	94-2	Avon, NC	Nov. 7, 1984	David G. Deuel
Eel, American	9-4	Cape May, NJ	Nov. 9, 1995	Jeff Pennick
Eel, marbled	36-1	Durban, South Africa	June 10, 1984	Ferdie van Nooten
Flounder, southern	20-9	Nassau Sound, FL	Dec. 23, 1983	Larenza Mungin
Flounder, summer	22-7	Montauk, NY	Sept. 15, 1975	Charles Nappi
Grouper, goliath	680-0	Fernandina Beach, FL	May 20, 1961	Lynn Joyner
Grouper, Warsaw	436-12	Gulf of Mexico, Destin, FL	Dec. 22, 1985	Steve Haeusler
Haddock	14-15	Saltraumen, Germany	Aug. 15, 1997	Heike Neblinger
Halibut, Atlantic	355-6	Valevag, Norway	Oct. 20, 1997	Odd Arve Gunderstad
Halibut, California	58-9	Santa Rosa Island, CA	June 26, 1999	Roger W. Borrell
Halibut, Pacific	459-0	Dutch Harbor, AK	June 11, 1996	Jack Tragis
Jack, almaco (Pacific)	132-0	La Paz, Baja Calif., Mexico	July 21, 1964	Howard H. Hahn
Jack, crevalle	58-6	Barra do Kwanza, Angola	Dec. 10, 2000	Nuno A.P. da Silva
Jack, horse-eye	29-8	Ascencion Island, South Atlantic	May 28, 1993	Mike Hanson
Kawakawa	29-0	Clarion Island, Mexico	Dec. 17, 1986	Ronald Nakamura
Lingcod	76-9	Gulf of Alaska	Aug. 11, 2001	Antwan D. Tinsley
Mackerel, cero	17-2	Islamorada, FL	Apr. 5, 1986	G. Michael Mills

FISHING (Cont.)

Species	Lbs-Oz	Where Caught	Date	Angler
Mackerel, king	93-0	San Juan, Puerto Rico	Apr. 18, 1999	Steve Perez Graulau
Mackerel, Spanish	13-0	Ocracoke Inlet, NC	Nov. 4, 1987	Robert Cranton
Marlin, Atlantic blue	1402-2	Vitoria, Brazil	Feb. 29, 1992	Paulo R.A. Amorim
Marlin, black	1560-0	Cabo Blanco, Peru	Aug. 4, 1953	A.C. Glassell Jr.
Marlin, Pacific blue	1376-0	Kaaiwi Point, Kona, HI	May 31, 1982	Jay W. deBeaubien
Marlin, striped	494-0	Tutakaka, New Zealand	Jan. 16, 1986	Bill Boniface
Marlin, white	181-14	Vitoria, Brazil	Dec. 8, 1979	Evandro Luiz Coser
Permit	56-2	Ft. Lauderdale, FL	June 30, 1997	Thomas Sebestyen
Pollack, European	27-6	Salcombe, Devon, England	Jan. 16, 1986	Robert S. Milkins
Pollock	50-0	Salstraumen, Norway	Nov. 30, 1996	Thor-Magnus Lekang
Pompano, African	50-8	Daytona Beach, FL	Apr. 21, 1990	Tom Sargent
Roosterfish	114-0	La Paz, Baja Calif., Mexico	June 1, 1960	Abe Sackheim
Runner, blue	11-2	Dauphin Island, AL	June 28, 1997	Stacey M. Moiren
Runner, rainbow	37-9	Clarion Island, Mexico	Nov. 21, 1991	Tom Pfleger
Sailfish, Atlantic	141-1	Luanda, Angola	Feb. 19, 1994	Alfredo de Sousa Neves
Sailfish, Pacific	221-0	Santa Cruz Is., Ecuador	Feb. 12, 1947	C.W. Stewart
Seabass, white	83-12	San Felipe, Mexico	Mar. 31, 1953	L.C. Baumgardner
Seatrout, spotted	17-7	Ft. Pierce, FL	May 11, 1995	Craig F. Carson
Shark, blue	528-0	Montauk Point, NY	Aug. 9, 2001	Joe Seidel
Shark, great white	2664-0	Ceduna, S. Australia	Apr. 21, 1959	Alfred Dean
Shark, Greenland	1708-9	Trondheimsfjord, Norway	Oct. 18, 1987	Terje Nordtvedt
Shark, hammerhead	991-0	Sarasota, FL	May 30, 1982	Allen Ogle
Shark, shortfin mako	1221-0	Chatham, MA	July 21, 2001	Luke Sweeney
Shark, porbeagle	507-0	Pentland Firth, Scotland	Mar. 9, 1993	Christopher Bennet
Shark, bigeye thresher	802-0	Tutukaka, New Zealand	Feb. 8, 1981	Dianne North
Shark, tiger	1780-0	Cherry Grove, SC	June 14, 1964	Walter Maxwell
Snapper, cubera	121-8	Cameron, LA	July 5, 1982	Mike Hebert
Snapper, red	50-4	Gulf of Mexico, LA	June 23, 1996	Capt. Doc Kennedy
Snook, Pacific black	57-12	Rio Naranjo, Quepos, Costa Rica	Aug. 23, 1991	George Beck
Spearfish, Mediterranean	90-13	Madeira Island, Portugal	June 2, 1980	Joseph Larkin
Swordfish	1182-0	Iquique, Chile	May 7, 1953	Louis Marron
Tarpon	283-4	Sherbro Is., Sierra Leone	Apr. 16, 1991	Yvon Victor Sebag
Tautog	25-0	Ocean City, NJ	Jan. 20, 1998	Anthony R. Monica
Tuna, Atlantic bigeye	392-6	Gran Canaria, Puerto Rico	July 25, 1996	Dieter Vogel
Tuna, blackfin	45-8	Key West, FL	May 4, 1996	Sam J. Burnett
Tuna, bluefin	1496-0	Aulds Cove, Nova Scotia	Oct. 26, 1979	Ken Fraser
Tuna, longtail	79-2	Montague Is., NSW, Australia	Apr. 12, 1982	Tim Simpson
Tuna, Pacific bigeye	435-0	Cabo Blanco, Peru	Apr. 17, 1957	Dr. Russell Lee
Tuna, skipjack	45-4	Flathead Bank, Mexico	Nov. 16, 1996	Brian Evans
Tuna, southern bluefin	348-5	Whakatane, New Zealand	Jan. 16, 1981	Rex Wood
Tuna, yellowfin	388-12	San Benedicto Island, Mexico	Apr. 1, 1977	Curt Wiesenhutter
Tunny, little	35-2	Cap de Garde, Algeria	Dec. 14, 1988	Jean Yves Chatard
Wahoo	158-8	Loreto, Baja Calif., Mexico	June 10, 1996	Keith Winter
Weakfish	19-2	Jones Beach, Long Island, NY	Oct. 11, 1984	Dennis R. Rooney
	19-2	Delaware Bay, DE	May 20, 1989	William E. Thomas

BASSMASTERS Classic

Jay Yelas of Tyler, Texas, became the 32nd annual CITGO BASSMASTERS Classic champion on the waters of Birmingham, Alabama's Lay Lake. Yelas won the 2002 title, landing a total of 45 pounds, 13 ounces, posting a 6-pound-plus margin of victory over California pro Aaron Martens and becoming only the fourth wire-to-wire winner in Classic history. The others to win all three days' competition were Bo Dowden (1980), Stanley Mitchell (1981) and Rick Clunn (1984). All of Yelas' best bass were caught on a ⅝-ounce prototype "Berkley Jay Yelas Power Jig" trimmed with a black, brown and pumpkinseed skirt and a green-pumpkinseed Power Frog chunk-type trailer, both on a 25-pound test. Yelas earned cash and prizes worth $203,000, the largest purse in Classic history.

The CITGO BASSMASTERS Classic, hosted by B.A.S.S. (Bass Anglers Sportsman Society), is professional bass fishing's world championship. Qualifiers for the three-day event include the 40 top pros on the CITGO BASSMASTER Tour and the five top-ranked anglers from each of three CITGO BASSMASTER Open circuits. Anglers may weigh only five bass per day and each bass must be at least 12 inches long. Only artificial lures are permitted. The first Classic, held at Lake Mead, Nev. in 1971, was a $10,000 winner-take-all event.

Multiple winners: Rick Clunn (4); George Cochran, Bobby Murray and Hank Parker (2).

Year		Weight	Year		Weight
1971	Bobby Murray, Hot Springs, Ark.	43-11	1979	Hank Parker, Clover, S.C	31-0
1972	Don Butler, Tulsa, Okla.	38-11	1980	Bo Dowden, Natchitoches, La	54-10
1973	Rayo Breckenridge, Paragould, Ark	52-8	1981	Stanley Mitchell, Fitzgerald, Ga	35-2
1974	Tommy Martin, Hemphill, Tex.	33-7	1982	Paul Elias, Laurel, Miss	32-8
1975	Jack Hains, Rayne, La	45-4	1983	Larry Nixon, Hemphill, Tex.	18-1
1976	Rick Clunn, Montgomery, Tex	59-15	1984	Rick Clunn, Montgomery, Tex.	75-9
1977	Rick Clunn, Montgomery, Tex.	27-7	1985	Jack Chancellor, Phenix City, Ala	45-0
1978	Bobby Murray, Nashville, Tenn	37-9	1986	Charlie Reed, Broken Bow, Okla	23-9

Year		Weight	Year		Weight
1987	George Cochran, N. Little Rock, Ark	15-5	1995	Mark Davis, Mount Ida, Ark	47-14
1988	Guido Hibdon, Gravois Mills, Mo	28-8	1996	George Cochran, Hot Springs, Ark	31-14
1989	Hank Parker, Denver, N.C.	31-6	1997	Dion Hibdon, Stover, Mo.	34-13
1990	Rick Clunn, Montgomery, Tex.	34-5	1998	Denny Brauer, Camdenton, Mo.	46-3
1991	Ken Cook, Meers, Okla	33-2	1999	Davy Hite, Prosperity, S.C.	55-10
1992	Robert Hamilton Jr., Brandon, Miss	59-6	2000	Woo Daves, Spring Grove, Va.	27-13
1993	David Fritts, Lexington, N.C.	48-6	2001	Kevin Van Dam, Kalamazoo, Mich.	32-5
1994	Bryan Kerchal, Newtown, Conn	36-7	2002	Jay Yelas, Tyler, Texas	45-13

LITTLE LEAGUE BASEBALL

World Series

Twelve-year-old Aaron Alvey, who pitched a record 22 scoreless innings in the tournament, led the way as Louisville, Ky., became the first American team to win the Little League World Series since 1998 beating Sendai, Japan, 1-0 in the championship game on Aug. 25, 2002. In the first inning, Alvey, Louisville's ace, slugged a 250-foot home run to centerfield, scoring the game's only run. He struck out 11 in the game to set a LLWS record for most strikeouts in a tournament with 44. Alvey, who threw a nine-inning no-hitter against Forth Worth in the U.S. semifinals, also tied the record for consecutive no-hit innings (12) when he retired the first six batters in the title game.

In the third-place game, Willemstad, Curacao, Netherlands Antilles beat Worcester, Mass., 9-1.

Played annually in late August in Williamsport, Penn. at Original Field in Williamsport, Penn. from 1947-1958 and at Howard J. Lamade Stadium since 1959 and also at newly constructed Volunteer Stadium starting in 2001.

In order to be invited to the World Series, teams must first win their regional tournaments. There are eight regions from the U.S. (Great Lakes, Midwest, Mid-Atlantic, New England, Northwest, Southeast, Southwest and West) and eight outside of the U.S. (Asia, Canada, Caribbean, European, Latin America, Mexico, Pacific and Trans-Atlantic). The eight U.S. regions then play each other and the the eight international regions play each other and the two winners from each meet in the championship game. This insures that a team from the U.S. will always participate in the final game.

Multiple winners: Taiwan (16); California and Japan (5); Connecticut, New Jersey and Pennsylvania (4); Mexico (3); New York, South Korea, Texas and Venezuela (2).

Year	Winner	Score Loser	Year	Winner	Score Loser
1947	Williamsport, PA	16-7 Lock Haven, PA	1976	Tokyo, Japan	10-3 Campbell, CA
1948	Lock Haven, PA	6-5 St. Petersburg, FL	1977	Li-Teh, Taiwan	7-2 El Cajon, CA
1949	Hammonton, NJ	5-0 Pensacola, FL	1978	Pin-Tung, Taiwan	11-1 Danville, CA
			1979	Hsien, Taiwan	2-1 Campbell, CA
1950	Houston, TX	2-1 Bridgeport, CT			
1951	Stamford, CT	3-0 Austin, TX	1980	Hua Lian, Taiwan	4-3 Tampa, FL
1952	Norwalk, CT	4-3 Monongahela, PA	1981	Tai-Chung, Taiwan	4-2 Tampa, FL
1953	Birmingham, AL	1-0 Schenectady, NY	1982	Kirkland, WA	6-0 Hsien, Taiwan
1954	Schenectady, NY	7-5 Colton, CA	1983	Marietta, GA	3-1 Barahona, D. Rep.
1955	Morrisville, PA	4-3 Merchantville, NJ	1984	Seoul, S. Korea	6-2 Altamonte, FL
1956	Roswell, NM	3-1 Merchantville, NJ	1985	Seoul, S. Korea	7-1 Mexicali, Mex.
1957	Monterrey, Mexico	4-0 La Mesa, CA	1986	Tainan Park, Taiwan	12-0 Tucson, AZ
1958	Monterrey, Mexico	10-1 Kankakee, IL	1987	Hua Lian, Taiwan	21-1 Irvine, CA
1959	Hamtramck, MI	12-0 Auburn, CA	1988	Tai Ping, Taiwan	10-0 Pearl City, HI
			1989	Trumbull, CT	5-2 Kaohsiung, Taiwan
1960	Levittown, PA	5-0 Ft. Worth, TX			
1961	El Cajon, CA	4-2 El Campo, TX	1990	Taipei, Taiwan	9-0 Shippensburg, PA
1962	San Jose, CA	3-0 Kankakee, IL	1991	Taichung, Taiwan	11-0 Danville, CA
1963	Granada Hills, CA	2-1 Stratford, CT	1992	Long Beach, CA	6-0 Zamboanga, Phil.
1964	Staten Island, NY	4-0 Monterrey, Mex.	1993	Long Beach, CA	3-2 Panama
1965	Windsor Locks, CT	3-1 Stoney Creek, Can.	1994	Maracaibo, Venezuela	4-3 Northridge, CA
1966	Houston, TX	8-2 W. New York, NJ	1995	Tainan, Taiwan	17-3 Spring, TX
1967	West Tokyo, Japan	4-1 Chicago, IL	1996	Taipei, Taiwan	13-3 Cranston, RI
1968	Osaka, Japan	1-0 Richmond, VA			(called after 5th inn.)
1969	Taipei, Taiwan	5-0 Santa Clara,CA	1997	Guadalupe, Mexico	5-4 Mission Viejo, CA
			1998	Toms River, NJ	12-9 Kashima, Japan
1970	Wayne, NJ	2-0 Campbell, CA	1999	Osaka, Japan	5-0 Phenix City, AL
1971	Tainan, Taiwan	12-3 Gary, IN			
1972	Taipei, Taiwan	6-0 Hammond, IN	2000	Maracaibo, Venezuela	3-2 Bellaire, TX
1973	Tainan City, Taiwan	12-0 Tucson, AZ	2001	Tokyo, Japan	2-1 Apopka, FL
1974	Kao Hsiung, Taiwan	12-1 Red Bluff, CA	2002	Louisville, KY	1-0 Sendai, Japan
1975	Lakewood, NJ	4-3 *Tampa, FL			

*Foreign teams were banned from the tournament in 1975, but allowed back in the following year.

Note: In 1992, Zamboanga City of the Philippines beat Long Beach, 15-4, but was stripped of the title a month later when it was discovered that the team had used several players from outside the city limits. Long Beach was then awarded the title by forfeit, 6-0 (one run for each inning of the game).

AP/Wide World Photos

Dave Villwock piloted Miss Budweiser to victory at over 140 miles per hour in the 99th APBA Gold Cup on the Detroit River.

POWER BOAT RACING

APBA Gold Cup

At the event's 99th edition, Dave Villwock won his fifth APBA Gold Cup, piloting *Miss Budweiser* to victory July 14, 2002 on the Detroit River. It was the 38th career Unlimited victory for the 47-year-old Villwock and the 133rd for team owner Bernie Little, who was hospitalized and couldn't attend the race. It was Little's 14th Gold Cup win as an owner. Villwock got off to a terrific start in lane one, took the lead and never relinquished it.

"The Detroit River is always very challenging and this year it showed its teeth again," said Villwock. "The River owed me for last year's rough ride and we are ecstatic to bring the Miss Budweiser team another Gold Cup victory. We definitely missed Bernie being here in Detroit and we really wanted to win this one for him."

The American Power Boat Association Gold Cup for unlimited hydroplane racing is the oldest active motorsports trophy in North America. The first Gold Cup was competed for on the Hudson River in New York in June and September 1904. Since then several cities have hosted the race, led by Detroit (33 times) and Seattle (14). Note that (*) indicates driver was also owner of the winning boat.

Drivers with multiple wins: Chip Hanauer (11); Bill Muncey (8); Dave Villwock and Gar Wood (5); Dean Chenoweth (4); Caleb Bragg, Tom D'Eath, Lou Fageol, Ron Musson, George Reis and J.M. Wainwright (3); Danny Foster, George Henley, Vic Kliesrath, E.J. Schroeder, Bill Schumacher, Zalmon G. Simmons Jr., Joe Taggart, Mark Tate and George Townsend (2).

Year	Boat	Driver	Avg. MPH	Year	Boat	Driver	Avg. MPH
1904	*Standard* (June)	Carl Riotte*	23.160	1920	*Miss America I*	Gar Wood*	62.022
1904	*Vingt-Et-Un II* (Sept.)	W. Sharpe Kilmer*	24.900	1921	*Miss America I*	Gar Wood*	52.825
				1922	*Packard Chriscraft*	J.G. Vincent*	40.253
1905	*Chip I*	J.M. Wainwright*	15.000	1923	*Packard Chriscraft*	Caleb Bragg	43.867
1906	*Chip II*	J.M. Wainwright*	25.000	1924	*Baby Bootlegger*	Caleb Bragg*	45.302
1907	*Chip II*	J.M. Wainwright*	23.903	1925	*Baby Bootlegger*	Caleb Bragg*	47.240
1908	*Dixie II*	E.J. Schroeder*	29.938	1926	*Greenwich Folly*	George Townsend*	47.984
1909	*Dixie II*	E.J. Schroeder*	29.590				
1910	*Dixie III*	F.K. Burnham*	32.473	1927	*Greenwich Folly*	George Townsend*	47.662
1911	*MIT II*	J.H. Hayden*	37.000				
1912	*P.D.Q. II*	A.G. Miles*	39.462	1928	Not held		
1913	*Ankle Deep*	C.S. Mankowski*	42.779	1929	*Imp*	Richard Hoyt*	48.662
1914	*Baby Speed Demon II*	Jim Blackton & Bob Edgren	48.458	1930	*Hotsy Totsy*	Vic Kliesrath*	52.673
				1931	*Hotsy Totsy*	Vic Kliesrath*	53.602
1915	*Miss Detroit*	Johnny Milot & Jack Beebe	37.656	1932	*Delphine IV*	Bill Horn	57.775
				1933	*El Lagarto*	George Reis*	56.260
1916	*Miss Minneapolis*	Bernard Smith	48.860	1934	*El Lagarto*	George Reis*	55.000
1917	*Miss Detroit II*	Gar Wood*	54.410	1935	*El Lagarto*	George Reis*	55.056
1918	*Miss Detroit II*	Gar Wood	51.619	1936	*Impshi*	Kaye Don	45.735
1919	*Miss Detroit III*	Gar Wood*	42.748	1937	*Notre Dame*	Clell Perry	63.675

Year	Boat	Driver	Avg. MPH
1938	Alagi	Theo Rossi*	64.340
1939	My Sin	Z.G. Simmons Jr.*	66.133
1940	Hotsy Totsy III	Sidney Allen*	48.295
1941	My Sin	Z.G. Simmons Jr.*	52.509
1942-45	Not held		
1946	Tempo VI	Guy Lombardo*	68.132
1947	Miss Peps V	Danny Foster	57.000
1948	Miss Great Lakes	Danny Foster	46.845
1949	My Sweetie	Bill Cantrell	73.612
1950	Slo-Mo-Shun IV	Ted Jones	78.216
1951	Slo-Mo-Shun V	Lou Fageol	90.871
1952	Slo-Mo-Shun IV	Stan Dollar	79.923
1953	Slo-Mo-Shun IV	Joe Taggart & Lou Fageol	99.108
1954	Slo-Mo-Shun V	Lou Fageol	92.613
1955	Gale V	Lee Schoenith	99.552
1956	Miss Thriftway	Bill Muncey	96.552
1957	Miss Thriftway	Bill Muncey	101.787
1958	Hawaii Kai III	Jack Regas	103.000
1959	Maverick	Bill Stead	104.481
1960	Not held		
1961	Miss Century 21	Bill Muncey	99.678
1962	Miss Century 21	Bill Muncey	100.710
1963	Miss Bardahl	Ron Musson	105.124
1964	Miss Bardahl	Ron Musson	103.433
1965	Miss Bardahl	Ron Musson	103.132
1966	Tahoe Miss	Mira Slovak	93.019
1967	Miss Bardahl	Bill Shumacher	101.484
1968	Miss Bardahl	Bill Shumacher	108.173
1969	Miss Budweiser	Bill Sterett	98.504
1970	Miss Budweiser	Dean Chenoweth	99.562
1971	Miss Madison	Jim McCormick	98.043
1972	Atlas Van Lines	Bill Muncey	104.277

Year	Boat	Driver	Avg. MPH
1973	Miss Budweiser	Dean Chenoweth	99.043
1974	Pay 'n Pak	George Henley	104.428
1975	Pay 'n Pak	George Henley	108.921
1976	Miss U.S.	Tom D'Eath	100.412
1977	Atlas Van Lines	Bill Muncey*	111.822
1978	Atlas Van Lines	Bill Muncey*	100.412
1979	Atlas Van Lines	Bill Muncey*	100.765
1980	Miss Budweiser	Dean Chenoweth	106.932
1981	Miss Budweiser	Dean Chenoweth	116.387
1982	Atlas Van Lines	Chip Hanauer	120.050
1983	Atlas Van Lines	Chip Hanauer	118.507
1984	Atlas Van Lines	Chip Hanauer	130.175
1985	Miller American	Chip Hanauer	120.643
1986	Miller American	Chip Hanauer	116.523
1987	Miller American	Chip Hanauer	127.620
1988	Miss Circus Circus	Chip Hanauer & Jim Prevost	123.756
1989	Miss Budweiser	Tom D'Eath	131.209
1990	Miss Budweiser	Tom D'Eath	143.176
1991	Winston Eagle	Mark Tate	137.771
1992	Miss Budweiser	Chip Hanauer	136.282
1993	Miss Budweiser	Chip Hanauer	141.296
1994	Smokin' Joe's	Mark Tate	145.532
1995	Miss Budweiser	Chip Hanauer	149.160
1996	Pico/American Dream	Dave Villwock	149.328
1997	Miss Budweiser	Dave Villwock	129.366
1998	Miss Budweiser	Dave Villwock	140.704
1999	Miss Pico	Chip Hanauer	152.591
2000	Miss Budweiser	Dave Villwock	139.416
2001	Tubby's Subs	Mike Hanson	140.519
2002	Miss Budweiser	Dave Villwock	143.093

PRO RODEO

All-Around Champion Cowboy

Cody Ohl of Stephenville, Texas, won the coveted all-around cowboy title at the 2001 National Finals Rodeo, finishing with a total of $296,419. Ohl, a calf-roping specialist, was just short of Ty Murray's all-time earnings record set in 1993. He would have almost certainly surpassed the record had he not torn the ACL and MCL in his right knee while roping a calf on the second to last day of competition at the NFR, with the all-around cowboy title already secured.

The Professional Rodeo Cowboys Association (PRCA) title of all-around world champion cowboy goes to the rodeo athlete who wins the most prize money in a single year in two or more events, earning a minimum of $3,000 in each event. Only prize money earned in sanctioned PRCA rodeos is counted. From 1929-44, all-around champions were named by the Rodeo Association of America (earnings for those years are not available).

Multiple winners: Ty Murray (7); Tom Ferguson and Larry Mahan (6); Jim Shoulders (5); Joe Beaver, Lewis Feild and Dean Oliver (3); Everett Bowman, Louis Brooks, Clay Carr, Bill Linderman, Phil Lyne, Gerald Roberts, Casey Tibbs and Harry Tompkins (2).

Year		Year		Year		Year	
1929	Earl Thode	1934	Leonard Ward	1939	Paul Carney	1944	Louis Brooks
1930	Clay Carr	1935	Everett Bowman	1940	Fritz Truan	1945-46	No award
1931	John Schneider	1936	John Bowman	1941	Homer Pettigrew		
1932	Donald Nesbit	1937	Everett Bowman	1942	Gerald Roberts		
1933	Clay Carr	1938	Burel Mulkey	1943	Louis Brooks		

Year		Earnings	Year		Earnings	Year		Earnings
1947	Todd Whatley	$18,642	1960	Harry Tompkins	$32,522	1973	Larry Mahan	$64,447
1948	Gerald Roberts	21,766	1961	Benny Reynolds	31,309	1974	Tom Ferguson	66,929
1949	Jim Shoulders	21,495	1962	Tom Nesmith	32,611	1975	Tom Ferguson	50,300
1950	Bill Linderman	30,715	1963	Dean Oliver	31,329	1976	Tom Ferguson	87,908
1951	Casey Tibbs	29,104	1964	Dean Oliver	31,150	1977	Tom Ferguson	65,981
1952	Harry Tompkins	30,934	1965	Dean Oliver	33,163	1978	Tom Ferguson	83,734
1953	Bill Linderman	33,674	1966	Larry Mahan	40,358	1979	Tom Ferguson	96,272
1954	Buck Rutherford	40,404	1967	Larry Mahan	51,996	1980	Paul Tierney	105,568
1955	Casey Tibbs	42,065	1968	Larry Mahan	49,129	1981	Jimmie Cooper	105,861
1956	Jim Shoulders	43,381	1969	Larry Mahan	57,726	1982	Chris Lybbert	123,709
1957	Jim Shoulders	33,299	1970	Larry Mahan	41,493	1983	Roy Cooper	153,391
1958	Jim Shoulders	32,212	1971	Phil Lyne	49,245	1984	Dee Pickett	122,618
1959	Jim Shoulders	32,905	1972	Phil Lyne	60,852	1985	Lewis Feild	130,347

AP/Wide World Photos

Calf-roper **Cody Ohl** *lassooed this calf and the title of PRCA all-around champion cowboy at the 2001 National Finals Rodeo, finishing the season with earnings of nearly $300,000.*

Year		Earnings	Year		Earnings	Year		Earnings
1986	Lewis Feild	$166,042	1992	Ty Murray	$225,992	1998	Ty Murray	$264,673
1987	Lewis Feild	144,335	1993	Ty Murray	297,896	1999	Fred Whitfield	217,819
1988	Dave Appleton	121,546	1994	Ty Murray	246,170	2000	Joe Beaver	225,396
1989	Ty Murray	134,806	1995	Joe Beaver	141,753	2001	Cody Ohl	296,419
1990	Ty Murray	213,772	1996	Joe Beaver	166,103			
1991	Ty Murray	244,231	1997	Dan Mortensen	184,559			

SOAP BOX DERBY

All-American Soap Box Derby

At the 65th annual Soap Box Derby, Evan Griffin, age 15, rolled to the Masters title in 28.26 seconds in his tiger-striped car. Roger Youmans Jr., 13, raced to a win in the Super Stock division in 28.57 and Anderson, Ind. native, Cameron Vannatta won with a time of 28.67 in a photo finish over Ashley Porter and Lavera Allen in the Stock division.

The All-America Soap Box Derby is a coasting race for small gravity-powered cars built by their drivers and assembled within strict guidelines on size, weight and cost. The Derby was started by Dayton, Ohio newsman Myron Scott after he witnessed several boys racing handmade carts down a hill while on a photographic assignment in 1933. Scott decided to start an organized race for kids and the first All-American Soap Box Derby was held in Dayton in 1934. The race got its name because early on most cars were built from wooden soap boxes. The following year, the race was moved to Akron because of its central location and hilly terrain. In 1936, town leaders saw the need for a permanent site for the growing event and with the help of the Works Progress Administration, Derby Downs was constructed.

Held every summer on the second Saturday in August at Derby Downs in Akron, the Soap Box Derby is open to all boys and girls from 9 to 16 years old who qualify. There are three competitive divisions: 1. Stock (ages 9-16) — made up of generic, pre-fab racers that come from Derby-approved kits, can be assembled in four hours and don't exceed 200 pounds when driver, car and wheels are weighed together; 2. Super Stock (ages 10-16) — the same as Stock only with a weight limit of 220 pounds; 3. Masters (ages 11-16) — made up of racers designed by the drivers, but constructed with Derby-approved hardware. The racing ramp at Derby Downs is 989 feet, four inches with an 11 percent grade.

One champion reigned at the All-American Soap Box Derby each year from 1934-75; Junior and Senior division champions from 1976-87; Kit and Masters champions from 1988-91; Stock, Kit and Masters champions from 1992-94; Stock, Super Stock and Masters champions starting in 1995.

Year		Hometown	Age	Year		Hometown	Age
1934	Robert Turner	Muncie, IN	11	1938	Robert Berger	Omaha, NE	14
1935	Maurice Bale Jr.	Anderson, IN	13	1939	Clifton Hardesty	White Plains, NY	11
1936	Herbert Muench Jr.	St. Louis	14	1940	Thomas Fisher	Detroit	12
1937	Robert Ballard	White Plains, NY	12	1941	Claude Smith	Akron, OH	14

Year	Hometown	Age
1942-45 Not held		
1946 Gilbert Klecan	San Diego	14
1947 Kenneth Holmboe	Charleston, WV	14
1948 Donald Strub	Akron, OH	13
1949 Fred Derks	Akron, OH	15
1950 Harold Williamson	Charleston, WV	15
1951 Darwin Cooper	Williamsport, PA	15
1952 Joe Lunn	Columbus, GA	11
1953 Fred Mohler	Muncie, IN	14
1954 Richard Kemp	Los Angeles	14
1955 Richard Rohrer	Rochester, NY	14
1956 Norman Westfall	Rochester, NY	14
1957 Terry Townsend	Anderson, IN	14
1958 James Miley	Muncie, IN	15
1959 Barney Townsend	Anderson, IN	13
1960 Fredric Lake	South Bend, IN	11
1961 Dick Dawson	Wichita, KS	13
1962 David Mann	Gary, IN	14
1963 Harold Conrad	Duluth, MN	12
1964 Gregory Schumacher	Tacoma, WA	14
1965 Robert Logan	Santa Ana, CA	12
1966 David Krussow	Tacoma, WA	12
1967 Kenneth Cline	Lincoln, NE	13
1968 Branch Lew	Muncie, IN	11
1969 Steve Souter	Midland, TX	12
1970 Samuel Gupton	Durham, NC	13
1971 Larry Blair	Oroville, CA	13
1972 Robert Lange Jr.	Boulder, CO	14
1973 Bret Yarborough	Elk Grove, CA	11
1974 Curt Yarborough	Elk Grove, CA	11
1975 Karren Stead	Lower Bucks, PA	11
1976 JR: Phil Raber	Sugarcreek, OH	11
SR: Joan Ferdinand	Canton, OH	14
1977 JR: Mark Ferdinand	Canton, OH	10
SR: Steve Washburn	Bristol, CT	15
1978 JR: Darren Hart	Salem, OR	11
SR: Greg Cardinal	Flint, MI	13
1979 JR: Russell Yurk	Flint, MI	10
SR: Craig Kitchen	Akron, OH	14
1980 JR: Chris Fulton	Indianapolis	11
SR: Dan Porul	Sherman Oaks, CA	12
1981 JR: Howie Fraley	Portsmouth, OH	11
SR: Tonia Schlegel	Hamilton, OH	13
1982 JR: Carol A. Sullivan	Rochester, NH	10
SR: Matt Wolfgang	Lehigh Val., PA	12
1983 JR: Tony Carlini	Del Mar, CA	10
SR: Mike Burdgick	Flint, MI	14
1984 JR: Chris Hess	Hamilton, OH	11
SR: Anita Jackson	St. Louis	15

Year	Hometown	Age
1985 JR: Michael Gallo	Danbury, CT	12
SR: Matt Sheffer	York, PA	14
1986 JR: Marc Behan	Dover, NH	9
SR: Tami Jo Sullivan	Lancaster, OH	13
1987 JR: Matt Margules	Danbury, CT	11
SR: Brian Drinkwater	Bristol, CT	14
1988 KIT: Jason Lamb	Des Moines, IA	10
MAS: David Duffield	Kansas City	13
1989 KIT: David Schiller	Dayton, OH	12
MAS: Faith Chavarria	Ventura, CA	12
1990 MAS: Sami Jones	Salem, OR	13
KIT: Mark Mihal	Valparaiso, IN	12
1991 MAS: Danny Garland	San Diego, CA	14
KIT: Paul Greenwald	Saginaw, MI	13
1992 MAS: Bonnie Thornton	Redding, CA	12
KIT: Carolyn Fox	Sublimity, OR	11
STK: Loren Hurst	Hudson, OH	10
1993 MAS: Dean Lutton	Delta, OH	14
KIT: D.M. Del Ferraro	Stow, OH	12
STK: Owen Yuda	Boiling Springs, PA	10
1994 MAS: D.M. Del Ferraro	Akron, OH	13
KIT: Joel Endres	Akron, OH	14
STK: Kristina Damond	Jamestown, NY	13
1995 MAS: J. Fensterbush	Kingman, AZ	11
SS: Darcie Davisson	Kingman, AZ	11
STK: Karen Thomas	Jamestown, NY	11
1996 MAS: Tim Scrofano	Conneaut, OH	12
SS: Jeremy Phillips	Charlestown, WV	14
STK: Matt Perez	No. Canton, OH	12
1997 MAS: Wade Wallace	Elk Hart, IN	11
SS: Dolline Vance	Salem, OR	13
STK: Mark Stephens	Waynesboro, VA	13
1998 MAS: James Marsh	Cleveland, OH	12
SS: Stacy Sharp	Kingman, AZ	14
STK: Hailey Simpson	Salem, OR	10
1999 MAS: Allan Endres	Barberton, OH	14
SS: Alisha Ebner	Salem, OR	15
STK: Justin Pillow	Deland, FL	12
2000 MAS: Cody Butler	Anderson, IN	12
SS: Derek Etherington	Anderson, IN	11
STK: Rachel Curran	Medina, OH	13
2001 MAS: Michael Flynn	Harrison Township, MI	12
SS: James Rogers	Hilton, NY	15
STK: Chad Eyerly	Altaloma, CA	11
2002 MAS: Evan Griffin	Winter Park, FL	15
SS: Roger Youmans Jr.	Spencerport, NY	13
STK: C. Vannatta	Anderson, IN	12

SOFTBALL

Men's and women's national champions since 1933 in Major Fast Pitch, Major Slow Pitch and Super Slow Pitch (men only). Sanctioned by the Amateur Softball Association of America.

MEN
Major Fast Pitch

Multiple winners: Clearwater Bombers (10); Raybestos Cardinals (5); Sealmasters (4); Briggs Beautyware, Decatur Pride, Pay'n Pak and Zollner Pistons (3); Billard Barbell, Frontier Players Casino, Hammer Air Field, Kodak Park, Meierhoffer, National Health Care, Penn Corp and Peterbilt Western (2).

Year	Year	Year
1933 J.L. Gill Boosters, Chicago	1943 Hammer Air Field, Fresno, CA	1953 Briggs Beautyware
1934 Ke-Nash-A, Kenosha, WI	1944 Hammer Air Field	1954 Clearwater Bombers
1935 Crimson Coaches, Toledo, OH	1945 Zollner Pistons, Ft. Wayne, IN	1955 Raybestos Cardinals,
1936 Kodak Park, Rochester, NY	1946 Zollner Pistons	1956 Clearwater Bombers
1937 Briggs Body Team, Detroit	1947 Zollner Pistons	1957 Clearwater Bombers
1938 The Pohlers, Cincinnati	1948 Briggs Beautyware, Detroit	1958 Raybestos Cardinals
1939 Carr's Boosters, Covington, KY	1949 Tip Top Tailors, Toronto	1959 Sealmasters, Aurora, IL
1940 Kodak Park	1950 Clearwater (FL) Bombers	1960 Clearwater Bombers
1941 Bendix Brakes, South Bend, IN	1951 Dow Chemical, Midland, MI	1961 Sealmasters
1942 Deep Rock Oilers, Tulsa, OK	1952 Briggs Beautyware	1962 Clearwater Bombers

Softball (Cont.)

Year		
1963 Clearwater Bombers	1979 McArdle Pontiac/Cadillac, Midland, MI	1991 Gianella Bros., Rohnert Park, CA
1964 Burch Tool, Detroit		1992 National Health Care, Sioux City, IA
1965 Sealmasters	1980 Peterbilt Western, Seattle	1993 National Health Care
1966 Clearwater Bombers	1981 Archer Daniels Midland, Decatur, IL	1994 Decatur (IL) Pride
1967 Sealmasters		1995 Decatur Pride
1968 Clearwater Bombers	1982 Peterbilt Western	1996 Green Bay All-Car, Green Bay, WI
1969 Raybestos Cardinals	1983 Franklin Cardinals, Stratford, CA	1997 Tampa Bay Smokers, Tampa Bay, FL
1970 Raybestos Cardinals	1984 California Kings, Merced, CA	1998 Meierhoffer-Fleeman, St. Joseph, MO
1971 Welty Way, Cedar Rapids, IA	1985 Pay'n Pak, Seattle	
1972 Raybestos Cardinals	1986 Pay'n Pak	1999 Decatur Pride
1973 Clearwater Bombers	1987 Pay'n Pak	
1974 Gianella Bros., Santa Rosa, CA	1988 TransAire, Elkhart, IN	2000 Meierhoffer
1975 Rising Sun Hotel, Reading, PA	1989 Penn Corp, Sioux City, IA	2001 Frontier Players Casino, St. Joseph, MO
1976 Raybestos Cardinals		2002 Frontier Players Casino
1977 Billard Barbell, Reading, PA	1990 Penn Corp	
1978 Billard Barbell		

Super Slow Pitch

Multiple winners: Ritch's/Superior (4); Howard's/Western Steer and Steele's Sports (3); Lighthouse/Worth and Long Haul (2).

Year		
1981 Howard's/Western Steer, Denver, NC	1988 Starpath, Monticello, KY	1995 Lighthouse/Worth, Stone Mt., GA
1982 Jerry's Catering, Miami	1989 Ritch's Salvage, Harrisburg, NC	1996 Ritch's/Superior
1983 Howard's/Western Steer	1990 Steele's Silver Bullets	1997 Ritch's/Superior
1984 Howard's/Western Steer	1991 Sun Belt/Worth, Atlanta	1998 Lighthouse/Worth
1985 Steele's Sports, Grafton, OH	1992 Ritch's/Superior, Windsor Locks, CT	1999 Team Easton, California
1986 Steele's Sports	1993 Ritch's/Superior	2000 Team TPS, Louisville, KY
1987 Steele's Sports	1994 Bellcorp., Tampa	2001 Long Haul, Albertville, MN
		2002 Long Haul

Major Slow Pitch

Multiple winners: Gatliff Auto Sales, Riverside Paving and Skip Hogan A.C. (3); Campbell Carpets, Hamilton Tailoring, Howard's Furniture, Long Haul TPS and New Construction (2).

Year		
1953 Shields Construction, Newport, KY	1971 Pile Drivers, Va. Beach, VA	1988 Bell Corp/FAF, Tampa, FL
1954 Waldneck's Tavern, Cincinnati	1972 Jiffy Club, Louisville, KY	1989 Ritch's Salvage, Harrisburg, NC
1955 Lang Pet Shop, Covington, KY	1973 Howard's Furniture, Denver, NC	1990 New Construction, Shelbyville, IN
1956 Gatliff Auto Sales, Newport, KY	1974 Howard's Furniture	1991 Riverside Paving, Louisville
1957 Gatliff Auto Sales	1975 Pyramid Cafe, Lakewood, OH	1992 Vernon's, Jacksonville, FL
1958 East Side Sports, Detroit	1976 Warren Motors, J'ville, FL	1993 Back Porch/Destin (FL) Roofing
1959 Yorkshire Restaurant, Newport, KY	1977 Nelson Painting, Okla. City	1994 Riverside Paving, Louisville
1960 Hamilton Tailoring, Cincinnati	1978 Campbell Carpets, Concord, CA	1995 Riverside Paving
1961 Hamilton Tailoring	1979 Nelco Mfg. Co., Okla. City	1996 Bell II, Orlando, FL
1962 Skip Hogan A.C., Pittsburgh	1980 Campbell Carpets	1997 Long Haul TPS, Albertville, MN
1963 Gatliff Auto Sales	1981 Elite Coating, Gordon, CA	1998 Chase Mortgage/Easton, Wilmington, NC
1964 Skip Hogan A.C.	1982 Triangle Sports, Minneapolis	
1965 Skip Hogan A.C.	1983 No. 1 Electric & Heating, Gastonia, NC	1999 Gasoline Heaven/Worth, Commack, NY
1966 Michael's Lounge, Detroit	1984 Lilly Air Systems, Chicago	2000 Long Haul TPS
1967 Jim's Sport Shop, Pittsburgh	1985 Blanton's Fayetteville, NC	2001 New Construction
1968 County Sports, Levittown, NY	1986 Non-Ferrous Metals, Cleveland	2002 Twin States/Worth, Montgomery, AL
1969 Copper Hearth, Milwaukee	1987 Stapath, Monticello, KY	
1970 Little Caesar's, Southgate, MI		

WOMEN
Major Fast Pitch

Multiple winners: Raybestos/Stratford Brakettes (22); Orange Lionettes (9); Jax Maids (5); California Commotion (4); Arizona Ramblers and Redding Rebels (3); Hi-Ho Brakettes, J.J. Krieg's, National Screw & Manufacturing and Phoenix Storm (2).

Year		
1933 Great Northerns, Chicago	1943 Jax Maids	1953 Betsy Ross Rockets, Fresno, CA
1934 Hart Motors, Chicago	1944 Lind & Pomeroy, Portland, OR	1954 Leach Motor Rockets, Fresno, CA
1935 Bloomer Girls, Cleveland	1945 Jax Maids	1955 Orange Lionettes
1936 Nat'l Screw & Mfg., Cleveland	1946 Jax Maids	1956 Orange Lionettes
1937 Nat'l Screw & Mfg.	1947 Jax Maids	1957 Hacienda Rockets, Fresno, CA
1938 J.J. Krieg's, Alameda, CA	1948 Arizona Ramblers	1958 Raybestos Brakettes, Stratford, CT
1939 J.J. Krieg's	1949 Arizona Ramblers	1959 Raybestos Brakettes
1940 Arizona Ramblers, Phoenix	1950 Orange (CA) Lionettes	1960 Raybestos Brakettes
1941 Higgins Midgets, Tulsa, OK	1951 Orange Lionettes	1961 Gold Sox, Whittier, CA
1942 Jax Maids, New Orleans	1952 Orange Lionettes	

Year		Year		Year	
1962	Orange Lionettes	1977	Raybestos Brakettes	1991	Raybestos Brakettes
1963	Raybestos Brakettes	1978	Raybestos Brakettes	1992	Raybestos Brakettes
1964	Erv Lind Florists, Portland, OR	1979	Sun City (AZ) Saints	1993	Redding (CA) Rebels
1965	Orange Lionettes	1980	Raybestos Brakettes	1994	Redding Rebels
1966	Raybestos Brakettes	1981	Orlando (FL) Rebels	1995	Redding Rebels
1967	Raybestos Brakettes	1982	Raybestos Brakettes	1996	California Commotion,
1968	Raybestos Brakettes	1983	Raybestos Brakettes		Woodland Hills
1969	Orange Lionettes	1984	Los Angeles Diamonds	1997	California Commotion
1970	Orange Lionettes	1985	Hi-Ho Brakettes, Stratford, CT	1998	California Commotion
1971	Raybestos Brakettes	1986	So. California Invasion	1999	California Commotion
1972	Raybestos Brakettes	1987	Orange County Majestics,	2000	Phoenix Storm, Phoenix, AZ
1973	Raybestos Brakettes		Anaheim, CA	2001	Phoenix Storm
1974	Raybestos Brakettes	1988	Hi-Ho Brakettes	2002	Stratford Brakettes, Stratford, CT
1975	Raybestos Brakettes	1989	Whittier (CA) Raiders		
1976	Raybestos Brakettes	1990	Raybestos Brakettes		

Major Slow Pitch

Multiple winners: Spooks (5); Dana Gardens (4); Universal Plastics (3); Cannan's Illusions, Bob Hoffman's Dots, Key Ford Mustangs and Marks Brothers Dots (2).

Year		Year		Year	
1959	Pearl Laundry, Richmond, VA	1975	Marks Brothers Dots	1988	Spooks
1960	Carolina Rockets, High Pt., NC	1976	Sorrento's Pizza, Cincinnati	1989	Cannan's Illusions, Houston
1961	Dairy Cottage, Covington, KY	1977	Fox Valley Lassies,	1990	Spooks
1962	Dana Gardens, Cincinnati		St. Charles, IL	1991	Cannan's Illusions, San Antonio
1963	Dana Gardens	1978	Bob Hoffman's Dots, Miami	1992	Universal Plastics, Cookeville, TN
1964	Dana Gardens	1979	Bob Hoffman's Dots	1993	Universal Plastics
1965	Art's Acres, Omaha, NE	1980	Howard's Rubi-Otts,	1994	Universal Plastics
1966	Dana Gardens		Graham, NC	1995	Armed Forces, Sacramento
1967	Ridge Maintenance, Cleveland	1981	Tifton (GA) Tomboys	1996	Spooks
1968	Escue Pontiac, Cincinnati	1982	Richmond (VA) Stompers	1997	Taylor's, Glendale, MD
1969	Converse Dots, Hialeah, FL	1983	Spooks, Anoka, MN	1998	Not held
1970	Rutenschruder Floral, Cincinnati	1984	Spooks	1999	Lakerettes, Conneaut Lake, PA
1971	Gators, Ft. Lauderdale, FL	1985	Key Ford Mustangs,		
1972	Riverside Ford, Cincinnati		Pensacola, FL	2000	Premier Sports, Pittsboro, NC
1973	Sweeney Chevrolet, Cincinnati	1986	Sur-Way Tomboys, Tifton, GA	2001	Shooters/Nike, Orlando, FL
1974	Marks Brothers Dots, Miami	1987	Key Ford Mustangs	2002	Diamond Queens, Nashville, TN

Other 2002 Champions

Slow Pitch

MEN

East Class A—W.W. Gay Aubrey/TPS, Gainesville, FL
West Class A—Advanced/Mountain Top/USA Cash/
    TPS, Texarkana, TX
Major Industrial—Sikorsky Aircraft, Stratford, CT
Class A Industrial—Elite Softball Club, Inc., Suwanee, GA
35-Over—Warthen Fuel/Eagle Group/TPS, Dover, DE
40-Over—X-treme Impact, Woodbridge, VA
45-Over—Maroadi Transfer, Jeannette, PA
50-Over Major—Florida Crush, Boca Raton, FL
55-Over Major—Faith Electric, Cartersville, GA
60-Over—Florida Legends, Fort Myers, FL
Church—CIA/Everlasting Life, Gadsden, AL

WOMEN

Class A—Armed Forces, Jacksonville, FL
Industrial—Walt Disney World, Orlando, FL
35-Over—Lakerettes, Conneaut, PA

COED

Major—Jonny's Saloon, Rochester, MN
Class A—Advance Door, Parma, OH

Fast Pitch

MEN

Class A—Lyons, Fresno, CA
Class B—Ohio Drillers, Orrville, OH
Class C—Taylor Farms, Salinas, CA
40-Over—Harold Super Market, Warrensburg, MO
45-Over—California Savala Painters, Stockton, CA
23-Under— Salt Lake City Teamsters, Salt Lake City, UT

WOMEN

Class A—Storm USA, Lake Forrest, CA
Class B—Lady Explorers, Midland, MI
Class C—Hi-5, Ventura, CA

Modified Pitch

Women's Major—Vyper Sportswear, Spokane, WA
Men's (10) Class A—Dillingers, Fon du Lac, WI
Men's (9) Class A—L & P/Kaytes/LPP, Staten Island, NY

TRIATHLON

World Championship

Contested since 1989, the Triathlon World Championship consists of a 1.5-kilometer swim, a 40-kilometer bike ride and a 10-kilometer run. The 2002 championship was scheduled for Nov. 9-10 in Cancun, Mexico.

Multiple winners: MEN—Simon Lessing (4); Spencer Smith (2). WOMEN—Emma Carney, Michellie Jones and Karen Smyers (2).

MEN			WOMEN		
Year	Winner	Time	Year	Winner	Time
1989	Mark Allen, United States	1:58:46	1989	Erin Baker, New Zealand	2:10:01
1990	Greg Welch, Australia	1:51:37	1990	Karen Smyers, United States	2:03:33
1991	Miles Stewart, Australia	1:48:20	1991	Joanne Ritchie, Canada	2:02:04
1992	Simon Lessing, Great Britain	1:49:04	1992	Michellie Jones, Australia	2:02:08
1993	Spencer Smith, Great Britain	1:51:20	1993	Michellie Jones, Australia	2:07:41
1994	Spencer Smith, Great Britain	1:51:04	1994	Emma Carney, Australia	2:03:19
1995	Simon Lessing, Great Britain	1:48:29	1995	Karen Smyers, USA	2:04:58
1996	Simon Lessing, Great Britain	1:39:50	1996	Jackie Gallagher, Australia	1:50:52
1997	Chris McCormack, Australia	1:48:29	1997	Emma Carney, Australia	1:59:22
1998	Simon Lessing, Great Britain	1:55:31	1998	Joanne King, Australia	2:07:25
1999	Dimitry Gaag, Kazakhstan	1:45:25	1999	Loretta Harrop, Australia	1:55:28
2000	Oliver Marceau, France	1:51:41	2000	Nicole Hackett, Australia	1:54:43
2001	Peter Robertson, Australia	1:48:01	2001	Siri Lindley, United States	1:58:51

Ironman Championship

Contested in Hawaii since 1978, the Ironman Triathlon Championship consists of a 2.4-mile swim, a 112-mile bike ride and 26.2-mile run. The race begins at 7 a.m. and continues all day until the course is closed at midnight.

MEN

Multiple winners: Mark Allen and Dave Scott (6); Tim DeBoom, Luc Van Lierde, Peter Reid and Scott Tinley (2).

Year	Date	Winner	Time	Runner-up	Margin	Start	Finish	Location
I	2/18/78	Gordon Haller	11:46	John Dunbar	34:00	15	12	Waikiki Beach
II	1/14/79	Tom Warren	11:15:56	John Dunbar	48:00	15	12	Waikiki Beach
III	1/10/80	Dave Scott	9:24:33	Chuck Neumann	1:08	108	95	Ala Moana Park
IV	2/14/81	John Howard	9:38:29	Tom Warren	26:00	326	299	Kailua-Kona
V	2/6/82	Scott Tinley	9:19:41	Dave Scott	17:16	580	541	Kailua-Kona
VI	10/9/82	Dave Scott	9:08:23	Scott Tinley	20:05	850	775	Kailua-Kona
VII	10/22/83	Dave Scott	9:05:57	Scott Tinley	0:33	964	835	Kailua-Kona
VIII	10/6/84	Dave Scott	8:54:20	Scott Tinley	24:25	1036	903	Kailua-Kona
IX	10/25/85	Scott Tinley	8:50:54	Chris Hinshaw	25:46	1018	965	Kailua-Kona
X	10/18/86	Dave Scott	8:28:37	Mark Allen	9:47	1039	951	Kailua-Kona
XI	10/10/87	Dave Scott	8:34:13	Mark Allen	11:06	1380	1284	Kailua-Kona
XII	10/22/88	Scott Molina	8:31:00	Mike Pigg	2:11	1277	1189	Kailua-Kona
XIII	10/15/89	Mark Allen	8:09:15	Dave Scott	0:58	1285	1231	Kailua-Kona
XIV	10/6/90	Mark Allen	8:28:17	Scott Tinley	9:23	1386	1255	Kailua-Kona
XV	10/19/91	Mark Allen	8:18:32	Greg Welch	6:01	1386	1235	Kailua-Kona
XVI	10/10/92	Mark Allen	8:09:08	Cristian Bustos	7:21	1364	1298	Kailua-Kona
XVII	10/30/93	Mark Allen	8:07:45	Paulli Kiuru	6:37	1438	1353	Kailua-Kona
XVIII	10/15/94	Greg Welch	8:20:27	Dave Scott	4:05	1405	1290	Kailua-Kona
XIX	10/7/95	Mark Allen	8:20:34	Thomas Hellriegel	2:25	1487	1323	Kailua-Kona
XX	10/26/96	Luc Van Lierde	8:04:08	Thomas Hellriegel	1:59	1420	1288	Kailua-Kona
XXI	10/18/97	Thomas Hellriegel	8:33:01	Jurgen Zack	6:17	1534	1365	Kailua-Kona
XXII	10/3/98	Peter Reid	8:24:20	Luc Van Lierde	7:37	1487	1379	Kailua-Kona
XXIII	10/23/99	Luc Van Lierde	8:17:17	Peter Reid	5:37	1471	1419	Kailua-Kona
XXIV	10/14/00	Peter Reid	8:21:01	Tim DeBoom	2:09	1525	1426	Kailua-Kona
XXV	10/6/01	Tim DeBoom	8:31:18	Cameron Brown	14:52	1558	1364	Kailua-Kona
XXVI	10/19/02	Tim DeBoom	8:29:56	Peter Reid	3:10	1540	1457	Kailua-Kona

WOMEN

Multiple winners: Paula Newby-Fraser (8); Natascha Badmann (4); Erin Baker and Sylviane Puntous (2).

Year	Winner	Time	Runner-up	Year	Winner	Time	Runner-up
1978	No finishers			1990	Erin Baker	9:13:42	P. Newby-Fraser
1979	Lyn Lemaire	12:55.00	None	1991	Paula Newby-Fraser	9:07:52	Erin Baker
1980	Robin Beck	11:21:24	Eve Anderson	1992	Paula Newby-Fraser	8:55:28	Julie Anne White
1981	Linda Sweeney	12:00:32	Sally Edwards	1993	Paula Newby-Fraser	8:58:23	Erin Baker
1982	Kathleen McCartney	11:09:40	Julie Moss	1994	Paula Newby-Fraser	9:20:14	Karen Smyers
1982	Julie Leach	10:54:08	Joann Dahlkoetter	1995	Karen Smyers	9:16:46	Isabelle Mouthon
1983	Sylviane Puntous	10:43:36	Patricia Puntous	1996	Paula Newby-Fraser	9:06:49	Natascha Badmann
1984	Sylviane Puntous	10:25:13	Patricia Puntous	1997	Heather Fuhr	9:31:43	Lori Bowden
1985	Joanne Ernst	10:25:22	Liz Bulman	1998	Natascha Badmann	9:24:16	Lori Bowden
1986	Paula Newby-Fraser	9:49:14	Sylviane Puntous	1999	Lori Bowden	9:13:02	Karen Smyers
1987	Erin Baker	9:35:25	Sylviane Puntous	2000	Natascha Badmann	9:26:17	Lori Bowden
1988	Paula Newby-Fraser	9:01:01	Erin Baker	2001	Natascha Badmann	9:28:37	Lori Bowden
1989	Paula Newby-Fraser	9:00:56	Sylviane Puntous	2002	Natascha Badmann	9:07:54	Nina Kraft

X GAMES

The ESPN Extreme Games, originally envisioned as a biannual showcase for "alternative" sports, were first held June 24-July 1, 1995 in Newport and Providence, R.I. and Mt. Snow, Vt. The success of the inaugural event prompted organizers to make it an annual competition. Newport would again serve as host for the redubbed X Games in 1996 before they moved to San Diego for 1997 and 1998. The X Games has evolved rapidly since its inception. New sports and events have been added while others have been dropped.

In 1997, the first Winter X Games were held at Snow Summit Mountain Resort in Big Bear Lake, Calif. before moving to Crested Butte, Colo. in 1998.

The 1999 and 2000 Summer X Games were held in San Francisco. The 1999 Winter X Games were again held in Crested Butte, Colo., Jan. 14-17. The Winter X Games took place at Mt. Snow, Vt. in 2000 and 2001. The Summer X Games were held in Philadelphia in 2001 and 2002. The 2002 Winter X Games were held in Aspen, Colorado and will return there for 2003.

Summer X Games
Bicycle Stunt

Year	Vert	Year	Dirt	Year	Street/Stunt Park	Year	Flatland
1995	Matt Hoffman	1995	Jay Miron	1996	Dave Mirra	1997	Trevor Meyer
1996	Matt Hoffman	1996	Joey Garcia	1997	Dave Mirra	1998	Trevor Meyer
1997	Dave Mirra	1997	T.J. Lavin	1998	Dave Mirra	1999	Trevor Meyer
1998	Dave Mirra	1998	Brian Foster	1999	Dave Mirra	2000	Martti Kuoppa
1999	Dave Mirra	1999	T.J. Lavin	2000	Dave Mirra	2001	Martti Kuoppa
2000	Jamie Bestwick	2000	Ryan Nyquist	2001	Bruce Crisman	2002	Martti Kuoppa
2001	Dave Mirra	2001	Stephen Murray	2002	Ryan Nyquist		
2002	Dave Mirra	2002	Allan Cooke				

Year	Downhill
2001	Brandon Meadows
2002	Robbie Miranda

Big-Air Snowboarding

Year	Men
1997	Peter Line
1998	Kevin Jones
1999	Peter Line
2000	Event discontinued

Year	Women
1997	Tina Dixon
1998	Janet Matthews
1999	Barrett Christy
2000	Event discontinued

Moto X

Year	Freestyle
1999	Travis Pastrana
2000	Travis Pastrana
2001	Travis Pastrana
2002	Mike Metzger

Year	Step Up
2001	Tommy Clowers
2002	Tommy Clowers

Year	Big Air
2001	Kenny Bartman
2002	Mike Metzger

Bungee Jumping

Year	
1995	Doug Anderson
1996	Peter Bihun
1997	Event discontinued

Skysurfing

Year	
1995	Fradet/Zipser
1996	Furrer/Scmid
1997	Hartman/Pappadato
1998	Rozov/Burch
1999	Fradet/Iodice
2000	Klaus/Rogers
2001	Event discontinued

Street Luge

Year	Dual
1995	Bob Pereyra
1996	Shawn Goular
1997	Biker Sherlock
1998	Biker Sherlock
1999	Dennis Derammelaere
2000	Bob Ozman
2001	Event discontinued

Year	Mass
1995	Shawn Gilbert
1996	Biker Sherlock
1997	Biker Sherlock
1998	Rat Sult
1999	Event discontinued

Year	Super Mass
1997	Biker Sherlock
1998	Rat Sult
1999	David Rogers
2000	Bob Pereyra
2001	Brent DeKeyser
2002	Event discontinued

Year	King of the Hill
2001	Dennis Derammelaere
2002	Event discontinued

Skateboard

Year	Vert Singles
1995	Tony Hawk
1996	Andy Macdonald
1997	Tony Hawk
1998	Andy Macdonald
1999	Bucky Lasek
2000	Bucky Lasek
2001	Bob Burnquist
2002	Pierre-Luc Gagnon

Year	Vert Doubles
1997	Hawk/Macdonald
1998	Hawk/Macdonald
1999	Hawk/Macdonald
2000	Hawk/Macdonald
2001	Hawk/Macdonald
2002	Hawk/Macdonald

Year	Street/Park
1995	Chris Senn
1996	Rodil de Araujo Jr.
1997	Chris Senn
1998	Rodil de Araujo Jr.
1999	Chris Senn
2000	Eric Koston
2001	Kerry Getz
2002	Rodil de Araujo Jr.

Year	Vert Best Trick
2000	Bob Burnquist
2001	Matt Dove
2002	Pierre-Luc Gagnon

Year	Street Best Trick
2001	Kerry Getz
2002	Rodil de Araujo Jr.

X Games (Cont.)

Sportclimbing

Year	Men's Difficulty
1995	Ian Vickers
1996	Arnaud Petit
1997	Francois Legrand
1998	Christian Core
1999	Chris Sharma
2000	Event discontinued

Year	Women's Difficulty
1995	Robyn Erbersfield
1996	Katie Brown
1997	Katie Brown
1998	Katie Brown
1999	Stephanie Bodet
2000	Event discontinued

Year	Men's Speed
1995	Hans Florine
1996	Hans Florine
1997	Hans Florine
1998	Vladimir Netsvetaev
1999	Aaron Shamy
2000	Vladimir Zakharov
2001	Maxim Stenkovoy
2002	Maxim Stenkovoy

Year	Women's Speed
1995	Elena Ovtchinnikova
1996	Cecile Le Flem
1997	Elena Ovtchinnikova
1998	Elena Ovtchinnikova
1999	Renata Piszczek
2000	Etti Hendrawati
2001	Elena Repko
2002	Tori Allen

X-Venture Race

Year	
1995	Team Threadbo*
1996	Team Kobeer
1997	Team Presidio
1998	Event discontinued

*In 1995, Team Threadbo won the Eco-Challenge which was held in conjunction with the ESPN Extreme Games.

In-Line Skating

Year	Men's Vert
1995	Tom Fry
1996	Rene Hulgreen
1997	Tim Ward
1998	Cesar Mora
1999	Eito Yasutoko
2000	Eito Yasutoko
2001	Taig Khris
2002	Not held

Year	Women's Vert
1995	Tash Hodgevan
1996	Fabiola da Silva
1997	Fabiola da Silva
1998	Fabiola da Silva
1999	Ayumi Kawasaki
2000	Fabiola da Silva
2001	Fabiola da Silva
2002	Not held

Year	Combined Vert
2002	Takeshi Yasutoko

Note: In 2002 the men's and women's vert events were combined.

Year	Men's Street/Park
1995	Matt Salerno
1996	Arlo Eisenberg
1997	Arron Feinberg
1998	Jonathan Bergeron
1999	Nicky Adams
2000	Sven Boekhorst
2001	Jaren Grob
2002	Jaren Grob

Year	Women's Street/Park
1997	Sayaka Yabe
1998	Jenny Curry
1999	Sayaka Yabe
2000	Fabiola da Silva
2001	Martina Svobodova
2002	Martina Svobodova

Year	Vert Triples
1998	Malina/Fogarty/Popa
1999	Khris/Bujanda/Boekhorst
2000	Event discontinued

Year	Men's Downhill
1995	Derek Downing
1996	Dante Muse
1997	Derek Downing
1998	Patrick Naylor
1999	Event discontinued

Year	Women's Downhill
1995	Julie Brandt
1996	Gypsy Tidwell
1997	Gypsy Tidwell
1998	Julie Brandt
1999	Event discontinued

Watersports

Year	Barefoot Waterski Jumping
1995	Justin Seers
1996	Ron Scarpa
1997	Peter Fleck
1998	Peter Fleck
1999	Event discontinued

Year	Men's Wakeboarding
1996	Parks Bonifay
1997	Jeremy Kovak
1998	Darin Shapiro
1999	Parks Bonifay
2000	Darin Shapiro
2001	Danny Harf
2002	Danny Harf

Year	Women's Wakeboarding
1997	Tara Hamilton
1998	Andrea Gaytan
1999	Meaghan Major
2000	Tara Hamilton
2001	Dallas Friday
2002	Emily Copeland

Winter X Games

CrossOver

Year	
1997	Brian Patch
1998	Event discontinued

Skiboarding

Year	
1998	Mike Nick
1999	Chris Hawks
2000	Neal Lyons
2001	Event discontinued

Ice Climbing

Year	Men's Difficulty
1997	Jaren Ogden
1998	Will Gadd
1999	Will Gadd
2000	Event discontinued

Year	Women's Difficulty
1997	Bird Lew
1998	Kim Csizmazia
1999	Kim Csizmazia
2000	Event discontinued

Year	Men's Speed
1997	Jared Ogden
1998	Will Gadd
1999	Event discontinued

Year	Women's Speed
1997	Bird Lew
1998	Kim Csizmazia
1999	Event discontinued

Skiing

Year	Men's Big Air
1999	J.F. Cusson
2000	Candide Thovex
2001	Tanner Hall
2002	Not held

Year	Men's Skier X
1998	Dennis Rey
1999	Enak Gavaggio
2000	Shaun Palmer
2001	Zach Crist
2002	Reggie Crist

Year	Women's Skier X
1999	Aleisha Cline
2000	Anik Demers
2001	Aleisha Cline
2002	Aleisha Cline

Year	SuperPipe
2002	Jon Olsson

Year	Men's Slopestyle
2002	Tanner Hall

Snowboarding

Year	Men's Big Air
1997	Jimmy Halopoff
1998	Jason Borgstede
1999	Kevin Sansalone
2000	Peter Line
2001	Jussi Oksanen
2002	Not held

Year	Women's Big Air
1997	Barrett Christy
1998	Tina Basich
1999	Barrett Christy
2000	Tara Dakides
2001	Tara Dakides

Year Women's Big Air
2002 Not held

Year Men's Boarder X
1997 Shaun Palmer
1998 Shaun Palmer
1999 Shaun Palmer
2000 Drew Neilson
2001 Scott Gaffney
2002 Philippe Conte

Year Women's Boarder X
1997 Jennie Waara
1998 Tina Dixon
1999 Maelle Ricker
2000 Leslee Olson
2001 Line Oestvold
2002 Ine Poetzl

Year Men's Halfpipe
1997 Todd Richards
1998 Ross Powers
1999 Jimi Scott
2000 Todd Richards
2001 Event discontinued

Year Women's Halfpipe
1997 Shannon Dunn
1998 Cara-Beth Burnside
1999 Michele Taggart
2000 S. Brun Kjeldaas
2001 Event discontinued

Year Men's Superpipe
2001 Dan Kass
2002 J.J. Thomas

Year Women's Superpipe
2001 Shannon Dunn
2002 Kelly Clark

Year Men's Slopestyle
1997 Daniel Franck
1998 Ross Powers
1999 Peter Line
2000 Kevin Jones
2001 Kevin Jones
2002 Travis Rice

Year Women's Slopestyle
1997 Barrett Christy
1998 Jennie Waara
1999 Tara Dakides
2000 Tara Dakides
2001 Jaime MacLeod
2002 Tara Dakides

Super-modified Shovel Racing

Year
1997 Don Adkins
1998 Event discontinued

Snow Mountain Bike Racing

Year Men's Downhill
1997 Shaun Palmer
1998 Andrew Shandro
1999 Event discontinued

Year Women's Downhill
1997 Missy Giove
1998 Marla Streb
1999 Event discontinued

Year Men's Speed
1997 Phil Tintsman
1998 Jurgen Beneke
1999 Event discontinued

Year Women's Speed
1997 Cheri Elliott
1998 Elke Brutsaert
1999 Event discontinued

Year Men's Biker X
1999 Steve Peat
2000 Myles Rockwell
2001 Not held

Year Women's Biker X
1999 Tara Llanes
2000 Katrina Miller
2001 Not held

Snomobiling

Year Snocross
1998 Toni Haikonen
1999 Chris Vincent
2000 Tucker Hibbert
2001 Blair Morgan
2002 Blair Morgan

Year Hillcross
2001 Carl Kuster
2002 Carl Kuster

Ultracross

Year
2000 McLain/Lind
2001 Palmer/Takizawa
2002 Wescott/Lind

Moto X

Year Big Air
2001 Mike Jones
2002 Brian Deegan

2002 Great Outdoors Games

Held July 11-14 in Lake Placid, N.Y. Winners of each event listed below.

Fishing

Flyfishing, Fish Length: Peter Erickson, Boise, Idaho
Flyfishing, Flycasting: Carter Andrews, Crooked Island, Bahamas
Bass Fishing: Shaw Grigsby, Gainesville, Fla.

Sporting Dogs
(owners listed first)

Retriever Trials: Alexandra Washburn & Ticket, The Plains, Va.
Big Air: Michael Jackson & Little Morgan, Shakopee, Minn.
Superweave (large dogs)**:** Olga Chaiko & Luz, N. Hollywood, Calif.
Superweave (small dogs)**:** Erin Schaefer & Jag, Phoenixville, Penn.
Agility (large dogs)**:** Olga Chaiko & Luz, N. Hollywood, Calif.
Agility (small dogs)**:** Erin Schaefer & Jag, Phoenixville, Penn.

Target Sports

Rifle: Jerry Miculek, Princeton, La.
Shotgun: Robbie Purser, Macon, Ga.
Archery: Randy Hendrix, Clemons, N.C.

Timber Events

Women's Endurance: Sheree Taylor, Te Aroha, NZE
Men's Endurance: Matt Bush, Croghan, N.Y.
Hot Saw: Mike Sullivan, Winstead, Conn.
Springboard: Mitch Hewitt, Wamuran, Queensland, AUS
Men's Boom Run: Jamie Fischer, Stillwater, Minn.
Women's Boom Run: Mandy Erdmann, LaCrosse, Wis.

Mixed Doubles Boom Run: Taylor Duffy, Hayward, Wis., & Jamie Fischer, Stillwater, Minn.
Men's Log Rolling: Darren Hudson, Barrington, Nova Scotia
Women's Log Rolling: Tina Bosworth, Lake Geneva, Wis.
Speed Climbing: Brian Bartow, Grants Pass, Ore.
Tree Topping: Wade Stewart, Parksville, B.C.
Team Relay: Team Clarke (Andy Colle, Syracuse, N.Y., Ray Gleason, Randale, Wash., Dion Lane, Auckland, New Zealand, Alyson Clarke, Dargaville, New Zealand, and Arden Cogar Jr., Charleston, W.V.)

YACHTING

The America's Cup

International yacht racing was launched in 1851 when England's Royal Yacht Squadron staged a 60-mile regatta around the Isle of Wight and offered a silver trophy to the winner. The 101-foot schooner *America*, sent over by the New York Yacht Club, won the race and the prize. Originally called the Hundred-Guinea Cup, the trophy was renamed The America's Cup after the winning boat's owners deeded it to the NYYC with instructions to defend it whenever challenged.

From 1870-1980, the NYYC successfully defended the Cup 25 straight times; first in large schooners and J-class boats that measured up to 140 feet in overall length, then in 12-meter boats. A foreign yacht finally won the Cup in 1983 when *Australia II* beat defender *Liberty* in the seventh and deciding race off Newport, R.I. Four years later, the San Diego Yacht Club's *Stars & Stripes* won the Cup back, sweeping the four races of the final series off Fremantle, Australia.

Then in 1988, New Zealand's Mercury Bay Boating Club, unwilling to wait the usual three- to four-year period between Cup defenses, challenged the SDYC to a match race, citing the Cup's 102-year-old Deed of Gift, which clearly stated that every challenge had to be honored. Mercury Bay announced it would race a 133-foot monohull. San Diego countered with a 60-foot catamaran. The resulting best-of-three series (Sept. 7-8) was a mismatch as the SDYC's catamaran *Stars & Stripes* won two straight by margins of better than 18 and 21 minutes. Mercury Bay syndicate leader Michael Fay protested the outcome and took the SDYC to court in New York State (where the Deed of Gift was first filed) claiming San Diego had violated the spirit of the deed by racing a catamaran instead of a monohull. N.Y. State Supreme Court judge Carmen Ciparick agreed and on March 28, 1989, ordered the SDYC to hand the Cup over to Mercury Bay. The SDYC refused, but did consent to the court's appointment of the New York Yacht Club as custodian of the Cup until an appeal was ruled on.

On Sept. 19, 1989, the Appellate Division of the N.Y. Supreme Court overturned Ciparick's decision and awarded the Cup back to the SDYC. An appeal by Mercury Bay was denied by the N.Y. Court of Appeals on April 26, 1990, ending three years of legal wrangling. To avoid the chaos of 1988-90, a new class of boat—75-foot monohulls with 110-foot masts—has been used by all competing countries since 1992. Note that (*) indicates skipper was also owner of the boat.

Challenger Series races began in October 2002 and were scheduled to finish by Jan. 21, 2003 for the next America's Cup races scheduled for Feb. 15-Mar. 3, 2003.

Schooners And J-Class Boats

Year	Winner	Skipper	Series	Loser	Skipper
1851	*America*	Richard Brown	—	—	—
1870	*Magic*	Andrew Comstock	1-0	*Cambria*, GBR	J. Tannock
1871	*Columbia* (2-1) & *Sappho* (2-0)	Nelson Comstock Sam Greenwood	4-0	*Livonia*, GBR	J.R. Woods
1876	*Madeleine*	Josephus Williams	2-0	*Countess of Dufferin*, CAN	J.E. Ellsworth
1881	*Mischief*	Nathanael Clock	2-0	*Atalanta*, CAN	Alexander Cuthbert*
1885	*Puritan*	Aubrey Crocker	2-0	*Genesta*, GBR	John Carter
1886	*Mayflower*	Martin Stone	2-0	*Galatea*, GBR	Dan Bradford
1887	*Volunteer*	Henry Haff	2-0	*Thistle*, GBR	John Barr
1893	*Vigilant*	William Hansen	3-0	*Valkyrie II*, GBR	Wm. Granfield
1895	*Defender*	Henry Haff	3-0	*Valkyrie III*, GBR	Wm. Granfield
1899	*Columbia*	Charles Barr	3-0	*Shamrock I*, GBR	Archie Hogarth
1901	*Columbia*	Charles Barr	3-0	*Shamrock II*, GBR	E.A. Sycamore
1903	*Reliance*	Charles Barr	3-0	*Shamrock III*, GBR	Bob Wringe
1920	*Resolute*	Charles F. Adams	3-2	*Shamrock IV*, GBR	William Burton
1930	*Enterprise*	Harold Vanderbilt*	4-0	*Shamrock V*, GBR	Ned Heard
1934	*Rainbow*	Harold Vanderbilt*	4-2	*Endeavour*, GBR	T.O.M. Sopwith
1937	*Ranger*	Harold Vanderbilt*	4-0	*Endeavour II*, GBR	T.O.M. Sopwith

12-Meter Boats

Year	Winner	Skipper	Series	Loser	Skipper
1958	*Columbia*	Briggs Cunningham	4-0	*Sceptre*, GBR	Graham Mann
1962	*Weatherly*	Bus Mosbacher	4-1	*Gretel*, AUS	Jock Sturrock
1964	*Constellation*	Bob Bavier & Eric Ridder	4-0	*Sovereign*, AUS	Peter Scott
1967	*Intrepid*	Bus Mosbacher	4-0	*Dame Pattie*, AUS	Jock Sturrock
1970	*Intrepid*	Bill Ficker	4-1	*Gretel II*, AUS	Jim Hardy
1974	*Courageous*	Ted Hood	4-0	*Southern Cross*, AUS	John Cuneo
1977	*Courageous*	Ted Turner	4-0	*Australia*	Noel Robins
1980	*Freedom*	Dennis Conner	4-1	*Australia*	Jim Hardy
1983	*Australia II*	John Bertrand	4-3	*Liberty*, USA	Dennis Conner
1987	*Stars & Stripes*	Dennis Conner	4-0	*Kookaburra III*, AUS	Iain Murray

60-ft Catamaran vs 133-ft Monohull

Year	Winner	Skipper	Series	Loser	Skipper
1988	*Stars & Stripes*	Dennis Conner	2-0	*New Zealand*, NZE	David Barnes

75-ft International America's Cup Class

Year	Winner	Skipper	Series	Loser	Skipper
1992	*America*[3]	Bill Koch* & Buddy Melges	4-1	*Il Moro di Venezia*, ITA	Paul Cayard
1995	*Black Magic*, NZE	Russell Coutts	5-0	*Young America*, USA	Dennis Conner & Paul Cayard
2000	*Black Magic*, NZE	Russell Coutts & Dean Barker	5-0	*Luna Rossa*, ITA	Francesco de Angelis

Deaths

Baseball fans, and all of America, mourned the death of "The Kid," **Ted Williams**, who died on July 5 at age 83.

AP/Wide World Photos

Bob Akin, 66; endurance race car driver; two-time 12 Hours of Sebring winner; raced in six 24 Hours of Le Mans races, finishing fourth in 1984; of injuries sustained in a crash during a test run; in Atlanta, April 29.

Mary Carew Armstrong, 88; won a gold medal as a member of the United States' world record-setting 4x100-meter relay team at the 1932 Los Angeles Olympics; cause of death was not given; in Framingham, Mass., July 12.

Buck Baker, 83; stock car racing pioneer and the Winston Cup series' first back-to-back champion (1956-57); born Elzie Wylie Baker; won 46 Winston Cup races, placing him 13th all-time; started 631 races, 44 from the pole; two-time Southern 500 winner; retired in 1976; operated Buck Baker Racing School since early 1980s; his son, Buddy, was a 34-year Winston Cup veteran; member of the National Motorsports Press Association and International Motorsports halls of fame; following surgery involving a pacemaker; in Charlotte, N.C., April 14.

Alice Bauer, 74; one of the 13 founding members of the Ladies Professional Golf Association; colorful and outgoing, she began her career by touring the country in the 1940s with her sister, Marlene, a future hall of famer; first woman to attempt to qualify for a men's tournament (1949), missing out by nine strokes; received LPGA's Commissioner's Award in 2000 (along with her co-founders) for her contributions to women's golf; of cancer; in Palm Desert, Calif., March 6.

Bo Belinsky, 64; highly touted rookie pitcher in 1962, whose rapid decline will forever be associated with his rise to Hollywood playboy status; pitched a no-hitter as a rookie with the then L.A. Angels; posted a record of 28-51 and a 4.10 ERA over an eight-year career with L.A., Philadelphia, Houston, Pittsburgh and Cincinnati; gained more notoriety in the 1960s for driving flashy cars and dating starlets like Ann-Margret and Mamie Van Doren, to whom he was engaged briefly; of a heart attack; in Las Vegas, Nov. 23, 2001.

Jay Berwanger, 88; star halfback at the University of Chicago and first winner of the Heisman Trophy in 1935; first pick at the first National Football League draft in 1936; unsure of what to do with his Downtown Athletic Club Award (renamed Heisman in 1936), he gave it to his aunt, who reportedly used it as a doorstop for years (it's now kept by his alma mater); sculpture on Heisman Trophy is based on a photo of him; drafted by the Philadelphia Eagles, but Bears coach George Halas bought his rights; his asking price of $25,000 over two seasons was too much and he never signed a contract, instead taking a job as a foam-rubber salesman; inducted into College Football Hall of Fame in 1954; of lung cancer; in Oak Brook, Ill., June 26.

Prince Ahmed bin Salman, 43; Saudi Arabian businessman and owner of War Emblem, winner of the 2002 Kentucky Derby and Preakness Stakes; purchased 90 percent of the colt for nearly $1 million less than three weeks before the Derby; headed The Thoroughbred Corp., the California-based stable that also produced 2001 Horse of the Year Point Given; chairman of Saudi Research and Marketing, which owns some 30 publications; of a heart attack; in Riyadh, Saudi Arabia, July 22.

Joe Black, 78; Brooklyn Dodgers pitcher, who won rookie of the year honors and became the first African-American pitcher to win a World Series game in 1952; helped Brooklyn win National League pennant his rookie year, going 15-4 with 15 saves and a 2.15 ERA; earned a complete-game, 4-2 victory in Game 1 of 1952 Series; arm injuries restricted him to 34 appearances and a 6-4 record in 1953; played for Cincinnati and Washington before retiring in 1957; longtime executive with Greyhound and consultant for Major League Baseball; of prostate cancer; in Scottsdale, Ariz., May 17.

Sir Peter Blake, 53; two-time America's Cup winner, who was shot dead by pirates in the Amazon; led Team New Zealand to the Cup in 1995 and 2000; won prestigious Whitbread Round the World Race in 1989 and was the only man to compete in the event's first five races; named New Zealand's sportsman of the year twice and yachtsman of the year four times; knighted in 1995; a national hero in his home country, 30,000 people gathered for a memorial service in Auckland; of gun shot wounds; in Macapa, Brazil, Dec. 6, 2001.

Jack Buck, 77; radio voice of the St. Louis Cardinals for almost 50 years; considered one of the game's best storytellers, his body of work includes almost every sport; recognized in 11 halls of fame around the country, including the Pro Football and National Baseball halls of fame; a WWII veteran and Purple Heart recipient; began broadcasting in college at Ohio State in late 1940s; got his first break was calling Cardinals games alongside Harry Caray in 1954; retired as Cardinals announcer in 2001; called Monday Night Football games and 17 Super Bowls for CBS radio from 1978-96; Cardinals added a pennant with "That's a winner." on it—a call he made famous after the team's victories—to their roster of retired players' numbers in 2002; after a long battle with lung cancer; in St. Louis, June 18.

Chris Campbell, 21; University of Miami Hurricanes senior linebacker killed in a car accident; three-year starter who appeared in 41 games and had 221 tackles and six sacks; of injuries sustained in the car crash; in Coral Gables, Fla., Feb. 16.

Regine Cavagnoud, 31; reigning World Cup Super G champion from France; persevered through injury-plagued career to become a star on the Alpine World Cup circuit; earned first World Cup victory in 10th season (downhill, 1998-99); appeared in two Olympic Winter Games (1992, 1998); of serious injuries suffered in a collision with a German ski coach; in Innsbruck, Austria, Oct. 31, 2001.

Brittanie Cecil, 13; eighth-grader struck in the head by a errant puck while watching a Columbus Blue Jackets NHL game at Nationwide Arena; honor student and cheerleader at Twin Valley South Middle School near Dayton; of head and neck injuries sustained in the incident; in Columbus, March 18.

Tom Cheney, 67; Washington Senators pitcher, who set the current Major League Baseball record with 21 strikeouts in a 16-inning 2-1 win over Baltimore on Sept. 12, 1962; cause of death not given; in Rome, Ga., Nov. 1, 2001.

Mike Clark, 61; kicker for the Dallas Cowboys' 1971 Super Bowl team; played for Dallas, Philadelphia and Pittsburgh during 11-year NFL career; finished with 724 career points; of a heart attack; in Dallas, July 24.

Richard Cleveland, 72; three-time All-American swimmer at Ohio State (1952-54); won three NCAA titles: two in the 50-meter freestyle and one in the 100-meter freestyle; established four world records and 13 American records; one of the fastest swimmers of his day, he revolutionized the sport by incorporating heavy weights into his training, a practice once thought harmful to a swimmer's development; won three gold medals at the 1951 Pan American Games; inducted into International Swimming Hall of Fame in 1991; of cancer; in Kailua-Kona, Hawaii, July 27.

Al Cowens, 50; journeyman major league outfielder, won a Gold Glove and finished second in MVP voting in 1977, hitting .312 with 23 HR, 112 RBI and 14 triples; played 13 major league seasons with the Royals, Angels, Tigers and Mariners; of a heart attack; in Downey, Calif., March 11.

University of Chicago
Jay Berwanger

St. Louis Cardinals
Jack Buck

St. Louis Cardinals
Darryl Kile

Hansie Cronje, 32; beloved South African cricket captain, who was the unlikely conspirator in a match-fixing scandal that rocked international cricket in 2000; admitted to accepting bribes in exchange for playing badly and asking teammates to do the same in matches, but denied ever "fixing" a match; banned for life by the country's United Cricket Board in October 2000; of injuries suffered in a plane crash; in George, South Africa, June 1.

Frank Crosetti, 91; shortstop on eight N.Y. Yankees world championship teams from 1932-48; played for 17 seasons and coached third-base for 20 more, taking part in 15 more World Series as a coach; led league in stolen bases in 1938; of complications from a fall; in Stockton, Calif., Feb. 11.

John Cuniff, 57; member of the N.J. Devils organization for 13 years and longtime assistant to the U.S. men's international hockey team; served as assistant coach to the U.S. squad at three Winter Olympics, including Salt Lake City; two-time All-American at Boston College; played on 1967 U.S. men's national team and 1968 U.S. Olympic team; coached Hartford Whalers for 13 games (1982-83 season) and was assistant in Boston for three seasons before joining the Devils in 1989 as head coach; most recently a special assignment scout for the Devils; of cancer; in Albany, N.Y., May 9.

Faye Dancer, 77; free-spirited outfielder in the women's professional baseball league of the 1940s, and the inspiration for "All the Way Mae," the character portrayed by Madonna in the 1992 film "A League of Their Own"; her all-out hustle and rebelliousness earned her the nickname "All the Way Faye"; first woman in the All-American Girls Professional Baseball League to hit two home runs in a game; stole 108 bases in 1948; her spikes and gloves are on display at the National Baseball Hall of Fame; of complications from cancer surgery; in Los Angeles, May 22.

Kevin Dare, 19; Penn State sophomore pole vaulter killed after landing on his head during an attempt at the Big Ten Indoor Track and Field Championships; won pole vault (16-6¾) at the U.S. Track & Field Junior National Championships in June 2001; former high school (Penn.) state champion; of head injuries sustained in the fall; in State College, Penn., Feb. 23.

Mike Darr, 25; San Diego Padres utility outfielder killed in a car accident hours before spring training was set to begin; first full season in the majors was 2001; batted .277 with 34 RBI and six stolen bases; of injuries sustained in the car crash; in Phoenix, Feb. 15.

Willie Davenport, 59; four-time Olympic hurdler, who in 1980 reached his fifth Olympics as a member of the U.S. bobsled team, becoming one of eight athletes to participate in both the Summer and Winter Games; won gold medal in 110-meter hurdles at the 1968 Mexico City Olympics and a bronze in the same event in Montreal in 1976; inducted into U.S. Olympic Hall of Fame in 1991; of a heart attack; in Singapore, June 17.

Leonard Robert (Bob) Davids, 75; founder of the Society for American Baseball Research (SABR) in 1971; cause of death not given; in Washington D.C., Feb. 10.

Mildred (Millie) Deegan, 82; played second base and pitcher for the Rockford Peaches of the All-American Girls Professional Baseball League from 1943-52; of cancer; in New Port Richey, Fla., July 21.

Bertalan de Nemethy, 90; Hungarian-born riding instructor, who coached the U.S. Equestrian show jumping team from 1955-80; won Olympic silver medals in 1960 and 1972; his book "The de Nemethy Method" and the instructional videos have become standards for training world-class, show-jumping horses and riders; charter member of the Show Jumping Hall of Fame; of pneumonia; in Sarasota, Fla., Jan. 16.

Dan Devine, 77; longtime major college football coach; capped his career by leading Notre Dame to a national title in 1977; compiled 172-57-9 record in 26 seasons at Arizona State, Missouri and Notre Dame; inducted into College Football Hall of Fame in 1985; after a long illness; in Tempe, Ariz., May 9.

Michael Downing, 65; New England Patriots fan, who suffered a heart attack and died minutes after the team's overtime playoff victory over Oakland and the final game played at Foxboro Stadium; of a heart attack; in Foxboro, Mass., Jan. 19.

Ferris Fain, 80; American League batting champion in 1951 and 1952 and four-time all-star; played with four teams in nine major league seasons, batting .290 with 48 HRs and 570 RBI; of leukemia; in Georgetown, Calif., Nov. 12, 2001.

Pat Flaherty, 76; winner of the 1956 Indianapolis 500; raced at Indy six times (once as a relief driver), earning three top-10 finishes; cause of death not given; in Oxnard, Calif., April 9.

Sam Francis, 88; University of Nebraska fullback; earned All-America honors and finished second in Heisman Trophy voting in 1936; placed fourth in the shot put at the 1936 Berlin Olympics; elected to College Football Hall of Fame in 1977; cause of death not given; in Springfield, Mo., April 23.

Paul Giel, 70; record-setting, multi-sport star at the University of Minnesota in the early 1950s; two-time All-American halfback; Heisman Trophy runner-up in 1953; received offers from the Chicago Bears and the Canadian Football League, but chose a baseball career instead; signed to pitch for the New York Giants baseball team; appeared in 102 games with four major-league teams over six seasons; retired with an 11-9 record and 5.39 ERA; served as Minnesota's athletic director from 1972-88; inducted into College Football Hall of Fame in 1975; of a heart attack; in Minneapolis, Minn., May 22.

Harrison Smith Glancy, 98; lead swimmer on the United States' 800-meter freestyle team that set a world record at the 1924 Paris Olympics; also won a gold at the 1928 Games for swimming a preliminary heat for the 800; served as an Olympic swimming judge; inducted into International Swimming Hall of Fame in 1990; cause of death not given; in New Orleans, Sept. 22.

Alfredo Goyeneche, 63; president of the Spanish Olympic Committee; member of the International Olympic Committee since 2000; vice president of the SOC from 1987-98; of injuries sustained in one-car crash; in Madrid, Spain, March 16.

Leon Gray, 49; former New England Patriots offensive tackle, who teamed with Hall of Famer John Hannah in a formidable blocking duo in the 1970s; waiver-wire selection in 1973; played six seasons and appeared in two Pro Bowls (1976 and 1978); played for Houston and New Orleans before retiring in 1983; cause of death not given; in Boston, Nov. 11, 2001.

Pete Gray, 87; disabled baseball player, who played one season (77 games) with the St. Louis Browns in 1945; lost right arm in childhood accident; batted .218 with 51 hits, had 13 RBI and just 11 strikeouts; his glove is on display at the National Baseball Hall of Fame; cause of death not given; in Nanticoke, Penn., June 30.

Steve Gromek, 82; Cleveland Indians pitcher captured in a joyful embrace with black teammate Larry Doby in a 1948 World Series' photo recognized as a groundbreaker in the struggle to integrate baseball; played 17 seasons with Cleveland and Detroit, winning 123 games; won World Series with Cleveland in 1948; of pneumonia and complications from a stroke; in Clinton Township, Mich., March 12.

Alex Hannum, 78; hall of fame basketball coach, who was the first to lead two different teams to NBA titles; won titles with the St. Louis Hawks in 1958 and Philadelphia 76ers in 1967; his teams won the only two NBA titles not won by the Boston Celtics between 1957-69; Philadelphia 76ers team in 1967-68 started 46-4 and ended the season with a NBA-record .840 (68-13) winning percentage; guided Oakland Oaks to ABA title in 1978; first coach to win titles in both the NBA and the ABA; won 471 NBA games and 178 in the ABA; elected to Basketball Hall of Fame in 1998; cause of death not given; in San Diego, Calif., Jan. 18.

Leon Hart, 73; two-way lineman at Notre Dame, who helped lead the Irish to a 36-0-2 record and three national titles during his four years there in the late 1940s; also led the NFL's Detroit Lions to four conference titles and three league titles in eight pro seasons; played end, defensive end and fullback with the Lions; earned NFL All-Pro honors for offense and defense in 1951; one of two linemen (and the last) to win a Heisman Trophy (1949); AP athlete of the year in 1949; inducted into College Football Hall of Fame in 1973; cause of death not given; in South Bend, Ind., Sept. 24.

Bob Hayes, 59; big-play wide receiver and world-class sprinter, who was a star with the Dallas Cowboys in the late 1960's and remains the only person to win an Olympic gold medal and a Super Bowl ring; nicknamed "Bullet"; once considered "the fastest man alive," he won a gold medal in the 100-meter dash at the 1964 Tokyo Olympics, tying the then world record of 10.05 seconds; also anchored the gold-medal winning U.S. 4x100 relay team; seventh round pick of the Cowboys in 1965; his blazing speed altered NFL defenses forever, forcing them from man-to-man coverage into new zone schemes; played receiver and returned punts and kicks for 11 seasons; caught 371 passes for 7,414 yards (a career average of 20 yards per catch) and 71 touchdowns; won Super Bowl title with Dallas in 1972; three-time Pro Bowler; battled drug and alcohol addiction after his retirement in 1975 and served 10 months in federal prison for selling narcotics in 1979; became the 11th member of the Cowboys "Ring of Fame" in 2001; of complications from liver and kidney ailments as well as prostate cancer; in Jacksonville, Fla., Sept. 18.

Chick Hearn, 85; Los Angeles Lakers broadcaster, whose play-by-play announcing told the story of nine NBA championships; revered by generations of Southern California sports fans; introduced words like "slam dunk," "air ball" and "finger roll" to the basketball lexicon; called 3,362 Lakers games over 42 seasons, including 3,338 consecutive games from Nov. 21, 1965 to Dec. 16, 2002; underwent heart surgery in December 2002; born Francis Dayle Hearn, two-time National Sportscaster of the Year; member of the Naismith Memorial Basketball and American Sportscasters halls of fame; of a brain injury suffered after a fall at his home; in Northridge, Calif., Aug. 5.

Jerry Heidenreich, 52; former U.S. Olympic swimmer; won four medals, including two gold, at the 1972 Munich Olympics; four-time All-American at Southern Methodist University; won 18 conference titles and one NCAA title; longtime swimming instructor in his native Texas; elected to International Swimming Hall of Fame in 1992; suffered a debilitating stroke in summer 2001; a suicide; in Paris, Texas, Aug. 5.

Wayne Hightower, 62; Philadelphia high school legend and Warriors first-round selection, whose move to the American Basketball Association helped give the new NBA-rival league credibility; appeared in the NBA Finals with the Warriors in 1964; played five seasons in the ABA for five teams; retired after the 1971-72 season; of a heart attack; in Philadelphia, April 18.

Willis Hudlin, 96; Cleveland Indians pitcher, who gave up Babe Ruth's 500th home run during a 6-5 victory on Aug. 11, 1929; played 15 of his 16 pro seasons with the Tribe; ranks third in team history in games pitched and fourth in innings pitched; the cause of his death was not given; in Little Rock, Ark., Aug. 5.

Kira Ivanova, 38; figure skating bronze medalist at the 1984 Olympics, who was found dead in her apartment; Soviet team member 1976-88; first Soviet woman to win an Olympic medal in women's singles; of stab wounds; in Moscow, Dec. 21, 2001.

Ed Jucker, 85; former University of Cincinnati men's basketball coach; led the Bearcats to NCAA titles in 1961 and 1962; compiled 11-1 career record in NCAA tournament games; missed out on third straight title in 1963 when his team lost to Loyola of Chicago, 60-58 in overtime; compiled 113-28 record at UC and school-record .801 winning percentage; coached NBA's Cincinnati Royals for two seasons; past athletic director at Rollins College in Winter Park, Fla.; cause of death not given; in Callawassie Island, S.C., Feb. 2.

Darryl Kile, 33; St. Louis Cardinals pitcher, who died in his sleep three days after pitching his team into first place in the National League's Central Division and less than 24 hours after the funeral for longtime Cardinals announcer Jack Buck; won 133 games and had a 4.12 ERA in 12 major league seasons with Houston, Colorado and St. Louis; was 5-4 in 14 starts with a 3.72 ERA in 2002; drafted by Houston in 1987; made major league debut in 1991 with the Astros; signed with Colorado before 1998 season; won 20 games in 2000, his first season with St. Louis; had four seasons with 15+ wins and five seasons where he pitched 200+ innings; recorded ninth no-hitter in Astros' history on Sept. 8, 1993, beating the Mets, 7-1; three-time NL All-Star; of hardening of the coronary artery; in Chicago, June 22.

Andy Kirby, 40; NASCAR Busch Series driver; started 12 races in 2002, finishing a season-high sixth at Talladega Superspeedway in April; made 28 career Busch Series starts; raced for eight seasons at Fairgrounds Speedway in Nashville where he was a track champion three times; of injuries sustained in a motorcycle accident; in White House, Tenn., July 18.

Ted Kroll, 82; eight-time PGA Tour winner and year-end money leader in 1956; member of three Ryder Cup teams in the 1950s; played on Senior PGA Tour from 1980-90; suffered from Parkinson's disease; cause of death not given; in Boca Raton, Fla., April 23.

Bob Lackey, 53; Marquette forward, who joined coach Al McGuire's team as a diamond in the rough and left as his smooth-playing captain; Casper Junior College (Wyo.) transfer, who was a two-time letterwinner at Marquette; averaged 15.2 points and 8.1 rebounds a game as a senior captain in 1971-72, earning All-America honors as well; drafted by the NBA's Hawks and ABA's Nets in 1972; played for the Nets for one season before playing abroad in the Netherlands and France; of cancer; in Evanston, Ill., June 4.

Dick (Night Train) Lane, 73; undrafted junior college player and former Army soldier, who left his job at an airplane plant to try out with the L.A. Rams in 1952, launching a career that would eventually make him one of the best defensive backs in NFL history; his record 14 interceptions in 1952 has stood for 50 years and occurred during a 12-game season; his 68 career interceptions is third all-time; nickname borrowed from a Buddy Morrow Orchestra recording and given to him by his Rams teammates Tom Fears and Ben Sheets; played 14 NFL seasons with the Rams, Chicago Cardinals and Detroit Lions; six-time Pro Bowl selection; selected all-time cornerback by the Pro Football Hall of Fame in 1969; member of the NFL's 75th anniversary team; inducted into Pro Football Hall of Fame in 1974; of a heart attack; in Austin, Texas, Jan. 29.

Al Lerner, 69; billionaire owner of the Cleveland Browns; bought Browns expansion team for $530 million in 1998, at the time the highest price paid for a sports team; chairman/CEO of MBNA, the world's largest credit-card issuer; ranked 36th on Forbes magazine's 2002 list of richest Americans; reportedly had surgery to remove a brain tumor in 2001; cause of death not given; in Cleveland, Oct. 23.

John Mabee, 80; three-time Eclipse Award winning breeder, who with his wife, Betty, were major figures in California, and American, thoroughbred racing for 45 years; founded Golden Eagle Farm in Ramona, Calif.; most famous horse was Best Pal, who is 10th all-time in career earnings; original board member of the Del Mar Thoroughbred Club, serving as the track's president and then as its chairman for a total of nearly 25 years; owned approximately 400 horses at the time of his death; of complications from a stroke; in Del Mar, Calif., April 24.

Harold (Mush) March, 93; Chicago Blackhawks right winger for 17 seasons, beginning in 1928; won two Stanley Cups (1934, 1948); scored overtime goal that earned the franchise its first Stanley Cup in 1934; appeared in 759 NHL games, collecting 153 goals and 230 assists for 383 career points; cause of death not given; in Chicago, Jan 9.

Harvey Martin, 51; four-time Pro Bowl defensive end with the Dallas Cowboys and the first Super Bowl MVP to die; won co-MVP honors with Randy White at Super Bowl XII in 1978; one of the most popular Cowboys of the 1970s and early 80s, he led Dallas in sacks seven times; holds team's sack record for a career (113) and a season (20); won defensive player of the year honors in 1977; struggled with substance abuse, domestic violence and bankruptcy issues after retiring in 1984; of pancreatic cancer; in Grapevine, Texas, Dec. 24, 2001.

Ned Martin, 78; baseball broadcaster, who was the radio and television voice of the Boston Red Sox for 32 years; cause of death not given; in Raleigh-Durham, N.C., July 23.

Lee Maye, 67; Milwaukee Braves teammate of Hank Aaron, who will be remembered for juggling his duties in the outfield with a successful singing career in the 1960s; batted .274 with 94 HR and 419 RBI over 13 major league seasons, his first six with the Braves; performed with the doo-wop group Arthur Lee Maye and the Crowns and sometimes sang with The Platters; of pancreatic cancer; in Riverside, Calif., July 17.

Kim McDonald, 45; English-born distance runner, whose scouting, coaching and managerial work with Kenya's most talented athletes over the last 20 years had earned him the nickname "Father of Athletics" in that African nation; most recently managed defending 1500 meters Olympic champion Noah Ngeny; served as special advisor to IAAF president Lamine Diack; of a heart attack; in Brisbane, Australia, Nov. 7, 2001.

Creighton Miller, 79; All-American halfback at Notre Dame and Cleveland lawyer, who organized pro football's first players' union in 1957; won a national title at Notre Dame and led the country in rushing in 1943; as manager of the Cleveland Browns he hired Paul Brown and turned a loose group of griping players into an organization that evolved into today's NFL Players' Association, obtaining the players' first pension agreements through collective bargaining; inducted into College Football Hall of Fame in 1976; cause of death not given; in Shaker Heights, Ohio, May 24.

Carl (Bobo) Olson, 73; Hawaiian-born boxer, who was named *Ring* magazine's Fighter of the Year in 1953 for defeating Randy Turpin for the middleweight championship; lost the title two years later to Sugar Ray Robinson, who would beat him three more times in his career; compiled 99-16-2 record with 49 knockouts in 117 career fights; inducted into World Boxing Hall of Fame in 1958 and International Boxing Hall of Fame in 2000; after a long battle with Alzheimer's disease; in Honolulu, Jan 16.

Micheline Ostermeyer, 78; French track and field star, who won two gold medals (discus, shot put) and one bronze (high jump) at the 1948 London Olympics; retired in 1950 and later toured Europe as a renowned classical pianist. The cause of her death was not given.; in Rouen, France, Oct. 17.

Ogden Phipps, 93; New York financier and pre-eminent thoroughbred race horse owner for nearly 70 years; his champions include Buckpasser, Personal Ensign, Easy Goer and Bold Ruler, the sire of Secretariat; past chairman of The Jockey Club; won three Eclipse Awards: best owner (1988-89) and best breeder (1988); seven-time U.S. court tennis champion and British amateur champ in 1949; inducted into International Court Tennis Hall of Fame in 2001; cause of death not given; in West Palm Beach, Fla., April 22.

AP/Wide World Photos
Sam Snead

Indianapolis Colts
Johnny Unitas

University of Colorado
Byron "Whizzer" White

Wally Pontiff, 21; LSU junior third baseman and team captain; ranks in school's top-10 in three categories: hits, doubles and batting average; drafted in the 21st round of the 2002 MLB draft by the Oakland A's; of natural causes, but an autopsy revealed a heart abnormality; in Baton Rouge, La., July 24.

Darrell Porter, 50; three-time all-star catcher and MVP of the 1982 World Series; first-round draft pick of the Brewers in 1971; played six seasons in Milwaukee; traded to Kansas City and made two All-Star Game appearances and won three AL pennants with the Royals; signed by St. Louis after the 1980 season; batted .286 and had 8 RBI for St. Louis in the 1982 World Series; played final two seasons in Texas; sought drug rehab in 1980; his fight with drug addiction and recovery was chronicled in a 1984 book "Snap Me Perfect!: The Darrell Porter Story"; of a condition called excited delirium, which caused his body to overheat and heart to stop (an autopsy revealed he had cocaine in his system); in Sugar Creek, Mo., Aug. 5.

Tony Razzano, 77; longtime NFL scout credited with helping put together teams that won San Francisco's first four Super Bowl titles; head of the 49ers scouting department from 1979-91; area scout for New England, San Diego and Washington in the 1960s and 1970s; son, David, is a scout for St. Louis; cause of death not given; in Palo Alto, Calif., July 2.

Polly Riley, 75; renowned amateur golfer, who won the Ladies Professional Golf Association Tour's first sanctioned event in 1950 (Tampa Open); finished tied for second at the 1947 U.S. Open, at age 21; six-time Curtis Cup team member and captain of the U.S. squad in 1962; of cancer; in Ft. Worth, Texas, March 13.

Franziska Rochat-Moser, 35; Swiss distance runner, who became household name in her home country after winning the 1997 New York City marathon; appeared in two Olympics (1992, 1996); retired in July 2001 following a hip operation; of injuries sustained in an avalanche; in Lausanne, Switzerland, March 7.

Kyle Rote, 73; All-American back at SMU, who became a popular captain of the N.Y. Giants; won four conference titles and one NFL title (1956); played 11 seasons with the Giants and retired as the teams' all-time leader in receptions, receiving yardage and touchdown receptions; co-starred in the SMU backfield with Doak Walker in 1948-49; runner up in Heisman Trophy voting in 1950; elected to College Football Hall of Fame in 1964; cousin of former NFL quarterback, Tobin; of pneumonia following hernia surgery earlier in the month; in St. Michaels, Md., Aug. 15.

Ed Runge, 87; American League umpire from 1954-70 and the father and grandfather of major league umpires; worked three World Series (he was in right field during Don Larsen's perfect game in 1956) and five All-Star Games; his son, Paul, was a National League umpire from 1974-97; when Paul's son, Brian, became a National League umpire in 1999, the Runges became the only three-generation family of major league umpires; cause of death not given; in San Diego, July 26.

Paul Runyan, 93; a 29-time winner on the PGA Tour and World Golf Hall of Fame member; though just 5-7, 125 pounds and lacking the size and power of other golfers of his day, his deadly short game earned him the nickname "Little Poison"; won two PGA Championship titles in 1934 and 1938, the latter an upset of Sam Snead; won a tour-high nine tournaments in 1933; member of two Ryder Cup teams in the 1930s; won consecutive Senior PGA Championships in 1961-62; tutored several pros, including 1961 U.S. Open champ Gene Littler; won PGA of America's Distinguished Service Award in 1998; cause of death not given; in Palm Springs, Calif., March 17.

Dick Schaap, 67; author and Emmy award-winning sports broadcaster; wrote more than 30 books, including bestsellers "Instant Replay" with Jerry Kramer of the Green Bay Packers in 1968 and "Bo Knows Bo" with 1980s two-sport star Bo Jackson; collaborated on autobiographies with Hank Aaron, Joe Montana, Tom Seaver and others; won two sports Emmys for his work on ESPN and three for features on ABC's "20/20" and "World News Tonight"; editor at Newsweek and editor/columnist at the New York Herald Tribune in the 1960s; edited Sport magazine and broadcast sports and features for NBC and ABC in the 1970s and 80s; he joined ESPN in 1989, hosting "The Sports Reporters"; he was also a fixture on ESPN Classic broadcasts and ESPN radio where he was host of "The Sporting Life With Dick Schaap," often working with his son, Jeremy; of complications following hip surgery; in New York, N.Y., Dec. 21, 2001.

Seattle Slew, 28; big, black thoroughbred, who captured 1977 Triple Crown and became one of horse racing's greatest sires; last surviving Triple Crown champion; won 14 of 17 career races; earned $1,208,726 for his career despite retiring at age 4, in 1978; sired 102 stakes winners, including Swale, A.P. Indy, Capote and Slew o' Gold; died on the 25th anniversary of his Kentucky Derby victory; of complications after a second operation on his spine; in Lexington, Ky., May 7.

Frank (Spec) Shea, 81; New York Yankees pitcher, who capped his remarkable rookie season in 1947 by notching two World Series victories over the Brooklyn Dodgers; first rookie to win an All-Star Game; posted 14-5 record and 3.07 ERA, but lost NL rookie of the year honors to Jackie Robinson; earned his nickname as a freckle-faced kid; helped Robert Redford with his throwing techniques during filming of the baseball classic, "The Natural"; of complications from heart-valve surgery; in New Haven, Conn., July 19.

Jack Shea, 91; patriarch of America's first family with three generations of Olympians and was oldest living Winter Games gold medallist; won 500- and 1500-meter speed skating events at 1932 Games in his hometown of Lake Placid; son, Jim, competed at 1964 Innsbruck Games and grandson, Jim Jr., won gold in the skeleton at the 2002 Salt Lake City Games; of injuries sustained in a car crash; in Lake Placid, N.Y., Jan. 22.

Wayne Simmons, 32; NFL linebacker, who won a Super Bowl title with Green Bay in 1996; first-round pick of the Packers in 1993; traded to Kansas City in 1997 and released in 1998; of injuries sustained in a one-car accident; in Independence, Mo., Aug. 23.

Enos Slaughter, 86; St. Louis Cardinals outfielder best remembered for his "mad dash" from first base to score the winning run over Boston in Game 7 of the 1946 World Series; tied 3-3, Slaughter led off the ninth with a single to center; after two outs, he was off with the pitch when teammate Harry Walker lined a hit into center field; his stunning and memorable 270-foot dash to the plate proved to be the championship-winning run, upsetting the favored Red Sox; played 13 seasons in St. Louis and appeared in 10 straight All-Star Games (1942-53); won four World Series titles: two with St. Louis and two with the Yankees; led the NL with 130 RBI in 1946; hit .300 over 19 seasons, had 2,348 hits and scored 1,247 runs; nickname "Country" originates from his youth where he grew up the son of a tobacco farmer in rural North Carolina; selected for enshrinement in the Baseball Hall of Fame in 1985, 26 years after he retired; delay attributed to stories of his fervent opposition to the integration of major league baseball and his attempt to organize a strike when Jackie Robinson joined the Dodgers; of complications of colon and stomach surgery; in Durham, N.C., Aug. 12.

Phil Smith, 50; All-American guard at the University of San Francisco and a member of the Golden State Warriors' 1975 NBA championship squad; all-NBA 2nd-team selection in 1976; Achilles injury in 1979 ended his career; of cancer; in Escondido, Calif., July 29.

Sam Snead, 89; golf's seven-time Grand Slam champion, whose effortless swing, unmatched golf success, and down-home sense of humor made him one of the most loved and admired athletes of the 20th century; only golfer to win sanctioned tournaments in six decades, won a PGA Tour record 81 tournaments, 17 of them after his 40th birthday; he made a career out of setting new standards for golfers of advancing age: became oldest player (52 years, 10 months) to win on PGA Tour (1965); youngest player to shoot his age (67 at Quad Cities Open in 1979); shot a 78 on his 85th birthday in 1997; won three Masters, three PGA Championships, and one British Open; never won a U.S. Open, finishing runner-up four times; won 11 tournaments in 1950; member of seven Ryder Cup teams and captain three times; helped launch the PGA Senior Tour in 1978 by winning its inaugural Legends of Golf event with Gardner Dickinson; won PGA Tour Lifetime Achievement Award in 1998; elected to World Golf Hall of Fame in 1974; suffered a series of small strokes in the months leading to his death; cause of his death was not given; in Hot Springs, Va., May 23.

Hank Soar, 87; two-way back with the N.Y. Giants in the late 1930s and longtime baseball umpire; caught game-winning touchdown in 1938 NFL title game; retired from football in 1946 and briefly coached the Providence Steamrollers of the Basketball Association of America; American League umpire from 1950-75; worked five World Series and was at first base when Don Larsen pitched his perfect game in 1956; cause of death not given; in Pawtucket, R.I., Dec. 24, 2001.

Jim Spencer, 54; first baseman on the N.Y. Yankees team that won the 1978 World Series; played for five teams in 15-year career; appeared in 1973 All-Star Game and won two Gold Gloves; a heart attack; in Ft. Lauderdale, Fla., Feb. 10.

Fred Taylor, 77; legendary Ohio State basketball coach, who led teams in the 1960s that included John Havlicek, Jerry Lucas and Bobby Knight to three straight NCAA championship games; won 1960 NCAA title and returned to title game in 1961 and 1962; his .778 winning percentage (14-4) in the NCAA tournament was eighth highest at the time of his death; won 297 games in 18 seasons at Ohio State and seven Big Ten titles, including five in a row (1960-64); played baseball and basketball at Ohio State, winning All-America honors as a first baseman in 1950; two-time national coach of the year; elected to Basketball Hall of Fame in 1986; after a long illness; in Columbus, Ohio, Jan. 6.

Jim Thompson, 60; CEO of the Canadian Olympic Committee, who came out of retirement in January to fill the post left vacant by Carol Anne Letheren, who died in February 2001; accomplished sports broadcasting executive in Canada for more than three decades; of a heart attack; in Vancouver, B.C., Canada, Aug. 14.

Willie Thrower, 71; became NFL's first African-American quarterback when he appeared in a game for the Chicago Bears on Oct. 18, 1953; never appeared in another game and it would be 15 years before another black quarterback would take a snap in a pro game; cut by the Bears the next year and played in the Canadian Football League until a separated shoulder forced him to retire at age 27; led Michigan State to national championship in 1952; of a heart attack; in New Kensington, Penn., Feb. 20.

Mickey Trotman, 26; Trinidad and Tobago soccer star; scored game-winning goal over Costa Rica in CONCACAF Gold Cup quarterfinals in 2001; played for MLS teams in Dallas and Miami from 1998-99; forward on Rochester Rhinos of U.S. A-league; of injuries sustained in a car crash; in Port-of-Spain, Trinidad, Oct. 3.

Johnny Unitas, 69; record-setting quarterback of the Baltimore Colts, whose black, high-top cleats and dark crew cut will forever be symbols of the franchise's success in the late 1950s and 1960s; revered by teammates for his instinctive play-calling and fearless leadership; led Colts to NFL titles in 1958 and 1959, the former a 23-17 overtime victory over the Giants often called the greatest NFL game ever; threw at least one touchdown pass in 47 consecutive games, still a league record; first quarterback to pass for 40,000 in a career; his 290 TD passes are sixth-most in NFL history; selected in the ninth round in 1955 by his hometown Pittsburgh Steelers; he was dropped before playing a single down and was relegated to playing semi-pro football for $6 a game before being signed by the Colts in 1956; completed 2,830 of 5,186 passes for 40,239 yards during his 18-year career; three-time league MVP; 10-time Pro Bowl selection; retired in 1973 after one season in San Diego; voted the league's best quarterback as part of the NFL's 50th anniversary festivities in 1969 and maintained the same distinction when a new team was assembled in 2000; inducted into Pro Football Hall of Fame in 1979; sustained injuries during his career that would later claim both his knees and partially debilitate his right arm; had triple bypass surgery in 1993; of a heart attack while working out in a physical therapy center; in Towson, Md., Sept. 11.

Billy Vessels, 70; All-American halfback at Oklahoma, who became the school's first Heisman Trophy winner in 1952; won national title with the Sooners in 1950; two-time all-conference selection; member of the College Football Hall of Fame; after a long illness; in Coral Gables, Fla., Nov. 17, 2001.

Art Wall Jr., 77; golfer best remembered for his comeback to win 1959 Masters; birdied five of his last six holes to close with a 66, passing Cary Middlecoff and defending champ Arnold Palmer to capture his only Green Jacket; won 14 career titles, including four in 1959, which earned him that year's player of the year award; member of three U.S. Ryder Cup teams; of respiratory failure; in Scranton, Penn., Oct. 31, 2001.

Jimmy Warfield, 60; trainer with the Cleveland Indians the last 26 seasons; a well-respected, player favorite, the team honored him by wearing a patch with his initials on their caps the remainder of the 2002 season; of complications from a brain hemorrhage; in Cleveland, July 16.

Mike Webster, 50; nine-time Pro Bowl center, who helped the Pittsburgh Steelers win four Super Bowl titles in his first six NFL seasons; an undersized (225 pounds), but tough center when he was selected by the Steelers in the fifth round of the 1974 draft—one of four future hall of famers drafted by the team that day; played from 1974-88 with Pittsburgh and his final two seasons with Kansas City; sustained serious head injuries during his career that led to brain damage that wasn't diagnosed until 1999; tragically, his condition led to bouts with drug addiction and homelessness after he retired; member of the All-Time NFL team selected in 2000; inducted into Pro Football Hall of Fame in 1997; cause of death not given; in Pittsburgh, Sept. 24.

Wes Westrum, 79; two-time all-star catcher with the New York Giants; managed the New York Mets after Casey Stengel broke his hip during the 1964 season through 1967; also managed the San Francisco Giants (1974-75); caught every World Series game for the Giants in 1951 and 1954; of cancer; in Clearbrook, Minn., May 28.

Nancy Chaffee Whitaker, 73; leading tennis player in the 1950s, who won three consecutive national indoor championships from 1950-52; married sportscaster Jack Whitaker in 1991; former sports commentator for ABC; of complications from cancer; in Coronado, Calif., Aug. 11.

Byron (Whizzer) White, 84; college football star at the University of Colorado in the 1930s, who after a brief pro career, exchanged his playbooks for law books, becoming a successful lawyer before serving more than three decades as a U.S. Supreme Court justice; senior class valedictorian and Rhodes scholar, he earned seven varsity letters at Colorado in basketball, baseball, and football; a star halfback, he was the first in school history (in any sport) to earn All-America honors; led the Buffaloes to an 8-0 record in 1937 and was MVP of the 1938 Cotton Bowl; Denver sports writer Leonard Kahn gave him his nickname (which White detested) because, "he seemed to whiz by people"; said to have held four dozen of Colorado's football records; finished second in Heisman Trophy voting in 1937; first pick of the Pittsburgh Pilots (now Steelers) in 1938; signed the then largest contract in pro sports history ($15,800 for one season); his three seasons in the NFL were briefly interrupted by post-graduate work at Oxford University, but he returned to lead the league in rushing and earn All-Pro honors with the Detroit Lions in 1940 and 1941; served as an officer in naval intelligence during World War II, where he formed a friendship with future President John F. Kennedy; graduated first in his class at Yale Law School in 1946; a successful run as a corporate lawyer and political organizer culminated with his appointment to the U.S. Supreme Court, by Kennedy, in 1962; stepped down in 1993; of complications from pneumonia; in Denver, April 15.

Hoyt Wilhelm, 79; knuckleball pitcher, who in 1985 became the first relief pitcher elected to the Baseball Hall of Fame; held the record for games pitched (1,070) when he retired in 1972 (since passed by Jesse Orosco and Dennis Eckersley); won 143 games and saved 227 with a 2.52 ERA over 21 seasons and nine teams; last pitcher to no-hit the New York Yankees, doing so on Sept. 2, 1958 at Memorial Stadium as a member of the Baltimore Orioles; the cause of his death was not given; in Sarasota, Fla., Aug. 23.

Curtis Williams, 24; University of Washington safety, who was paralyzed during a football game against Stanford in October 2000; started 24 games and recorded 142 tackles and one interception; the Huskies' Rose Bowl victory in 2001 was dedicated to him and his initials appear on their winner's rings; of complications associated with his paralysis; in Fresno, Calif., May 6.

Ted Williams, 83; left-handed hitting outfielder for the Boston Red Sox, whose passion for hitting was unrivaled, as were his results; a hero to a generation of fans in the 1940s-50s, he was both a booming giant of patriotic, John Wayne-like bravado and a kindhearted philanthropist devoted to the Jimmy Fund—a Red Sox charity for children with cancer; nicknamed, "The Kid," "The Splendid Splinter," "Teddy Ballgame"; his career .344 batting average is sixth-highest since 1900, and he remains the last player to average .400 in a season; compiled .406 average (185 for 456) in 1941; won AL Triple Crowns in 1942 (.356-36-137) and 1947 (.343-32-114); two-time AL MVP; his 521 career home runs place him 12th on the all-time list (fourth among left-handed batters); first in on-base-percentage (a stunning .483) and third all-time in walks (2,019); played in 18 All-Star Games; won six American League batting titles, including one at age 39 (1957) and another at age 40 (1958); hitting success attributed to his painstaking research and practice, plus superior eyesight; missed all or part of five seasons due to military service as a Marine fighter pilot in WWII and the Korean War; wrote best-selling "The Science of Hitting" with John Underwood in 1971; hit home run in final at bat in 1960, immortalized in John Updike article, "Hub Fans Bid Kid Adieu," in the *New Yorker*; briefly managed Washington Senators/Texas Rangers (1969-72); after retiring he became a renowned fisherman; inducted into National Baseball Hall of Fame in 1966; suffered several strokes in the 1990s; underwent open heart surgery in 2001; of cardiac arrest; in Inverness, Fla., July 5.

Mamo Wolde, 70; Ethiopian sports hero and 1968 Olympic marathon gold medallist; second Ethiopian (Abebe Bikila) to win an Olympic gold medal; added a silver medal in the 10,000-meter race in 1968 and a bronze in the marathon at the 1972 Games; imprisoned in the early 1990s, along with hundreds of others, on charges of murder and other war crimes, stemming from his service as head of the imperial guard for Emperor Haile Selassie, who was deposed in 1974; released in January 2001; buried next to his idol, Bikila, who died in 1973; cause of death was not given; in Addis Ababa, Ethiopia, May 26.

Walter Wright, 89; pitcher and outfielder in the Negro Leagues during the 1930s; organized the Old Timers Baseball Club in 1957, which was composed of former Negro Leagues players; cause of death not given; in New Orleans, March 4.

John Zimmerman, 74; groundbreaking sports photojournalist; known as a technical wizard and credited with inventing techniques for first capturing unique action shots during games which are commonplace today; hired by *Sports Illustrated* and shot 107 of their covers before leaving in the early 1960s for a freelance career; shot 10 Olympics for *SI*, *Time* and *Life* magazines; of complications of lymphoma; in Pebble Beach, Calif., Aug. 3.

RESEARCH MATERIAL

Many sources were used in the gathering of information for this almanac. Day-to-day material was almost always found in copies of *USA Today*, *The Boston Globe*, and *The New York Times* or online at various World Wide Web addresses (see below).

Several weekly and bi-weekly periodicals were also used in the past year's pursuit of facts and figures, among them— *Baseball America*, *Boxing Digest*, *ESPN the Magazine*, *FIFA News* (Soccer), *The Hockey News*, *The NCAA News*, *Soccer America*, *Sports Illustrated*, *The Sporting News*, *Street & Smith's Sports Business Journal*, *Track & Field News* and *USA Today Baseball Weekly*.

In addition, the following books provided background material for one or more chapters of the almanac.

Arenas & Ballparks

The Ballparks, by Bill Shannon and George Kalinsky; Hawthorn Books, Inc. (1975); New York.

Diamonds, by Michael Gershman; Houghton Mifflin Co. (1993); Boston.

Green Cathedrals (Revised Edition), by Philip Lowry; Addison-Wesley Publishing Co. (1992); Reading, Mass.

The NFL's Encyclopedic History of Professional Football, Macmillan Publishing Co. (1977); New York.

Take Me Out to the Ballpark, by Lowell Reidenbaugh; The Sporting News Publishing Co. (1983); St. Louis.

24 Seconds to Shoot (An Informal History of the NBA), by Leonard Koppett; Macmillan Publishing Co. (1968); New York.

Auto Racing

Indy: 75 Years of Racing's Greatest Spectacle, by Rich Taylor; St. Martin's Press (1991); New York.

2002 CART FedEx Championship Series Media Guide; Championship Auto Racing Teams; Troy, Mich.

2002 Indy Racing League Media Guide, by IMS Publications; Indianapolis.

2002 NASCAR Winston Cup Series Media Guide, compiled and edited by Sports Marketing Enterprises; NASCAR Winston Cup Series; Winston-Salem, N.C.

Marlboro Grand Prix Guide, 1950-1998 (1999 Edition), compiled by Jacques Deschenaux and Claude Michele Deschenaux; Charles Stewart & Company Ltd; Brentford, England.

NASCAR Online, produced by Turner Sports Interactive, http://www.nascar.com

CART Online, maintained by CART and VFX Digital Solutions, http://www.cart.com

Indy Racing Online, maintained by IRL, http://www.indyracingleague.com

NHRA Online, maintained by NHRA, http://www.nhra.com

Baseball

The All-Star Game (A Pictorial History, 1933 to Present), by Donald Honig; The Sporting News Publishing Co. (1987); St. Louis.

The Baseball Chronology, edited by James Charlton; Macmillian Publishing Co. (1991); New York.

The Baseball Encyclopedia (Ninth Edition), editorial director, Rick Wolff; Macmillan Publishing Co. (1993); New York.

The Complete 2001 Baseball Record Book, edited by Craig Carter; The Sporting News Publishing Co.; St. Louis.

The Scrapbook History of Baseball by Jordan Deutsch, Richard Cohen, Roland Johnson and David Neft; Bobbs-Merrill Company, Inc. (1975); Indianapolis/New York.

2001 Sporting News Official Baseball Guide, edited by Craig Carter and Dave Sloan; The Sporting News Publishing Co.; St. Louis.

2001 Sporting News Official Baseball Register, edited by Jeff Paur, David Walton, John Duxbury; The Sporting News Publishing Co.; St. Louis.

The Sports Encyclopedia: Baseball (1996 Edition), edited by David Neft and Richard Cohen; St. Martin's Press; New York.

Total Baseball (Seventh Edition), edited by John Thorn, Pete Palmer and Michael Gershman; Total Sports Publishing (2001); Kingston, N.Y.

The Official Site of Major League Baseball, produced by Major League Baseball Properties, Inc., http://www.mlb.com

College Basketball

All the Moves (A History of College Basketball), by Neil D. Issacs; J.B. Lippincott Company (1975); New York.

College Basketball, U.S.A. (Since 1892), by John D. McCallum; Stein and Day (1978); New York.

Collegiate Basketball: Facts and Figures on the Cage Sport, by Edwin C. Caudle; The Paragon Press (1960); Montgomery, Ala.

The Encyclopedia of the NCAA Basketball Tournament, written and compiled by Jim Savage; Dell Publishing (1990); New York.

The Final Four (Reliving America's Basketball Classic), compiled by Billy Reed; Host Communications, Inc. (1988); Lexington, Ky.

2000 NCAA Final Four Records Book, compiled by Gary Johnson; edited by Marty Benson; NCAA Books; Indianapolis.

The Modern Encyclopedia of Basketball (Second Revised Edition), edited by Zander Hollander; Dolphins Books (1979); Doubleday & Company, Inc.; Garden City, N.Y.

2000 NCAA Men's Records Book, compiled by Gary Johnson and Sean Straziscar; edited by Marty Benson; NCAA Books; Indianapolis.

2000 NCAA Women's Records Book, compiled by Richard M. Campbell and Jenifer L. Scheibler; edited by Vanessa L. Abell; NCAA Books; Indianapolis.

NCAA Online, produced by National Collegiate Athletic Association, http://www.ncaa.org

Plus many 2001-2002 NCAA Division I conference guides from America East to the WAC.

Pro Basketball

The Official NBA Basketball Encyclopedia (Third Edition), edited by Jan Hubbard; Doubleday (2000); New York.

2001-02 Sporting News Official NBA Guide; edited by Craig Carter and John Hareas; The Sporting News Publishing Co.; St. Louis.

2001-02 Sporting News Official NBA Register, edited by Jeff Paur, David Walton, John Gardella and John Hareas; The Sporting News Publishing Co.; St. Louis.

NBA Online, produced by NBA Media Ventures, LLC, ESPN Internet Ventures and/or Starwave Corporation, http://www.nba.com

Bowling

1995 Bowlers Journal Annual & Almanac; Luby Publishing; Chicago.

2001 PWBA Guide, Professional Women's Bowling Association; Rockford, Ill.

2001-02 PBA Tour Media Guide; Professional Bowlers Association; Seattle, Wash.

PBA Online, produced by the Pro Bowlers Association, http://www.pba.com

PWBA Online, produced by Professional Women's Bowling Association, http://www.pwba.com

Boxing

The Boxing Record Book (1996 Edition), edited by Phill Marder; Fight Fax Inc.; Sicklerville, N.J.

The Ring 1985 Record Book & Boxing Encyclopedia, edited by Herbert G. Goldman; The Ring Publishing Corp.; New York.

The Ring: Boxing, The 20th Century, Steven Farhood, editor-in-chief; BDD Illustrated Books (1993); New York.

College Sports

1994-95 National Collegiate Championships, edited by Ted Breidenthal; NCAA Books; Overland Park, Kan.

1999-2000 National Directory of College Athletics, edited by Kevin Cleary; Collegiate Directories, Inc.; Cleveland.

NCAA Online, produced by National Collegiate Athletic Association, http://www.ncaa.org

NAIA.org, produced by National Association of Intercollegiate Athletics, http://www.naia.org

College Football

Football: A College History, by Tom Perrin; McFarland & Company, Inc. (1987); Jefferson, N.C.

Football: Facts & Figures, by Dr. L.H. Baker; Farrar & Rinehart, Inc. (1945); New York.

Great College Football Coaches of the Twenties and Thirties, by Tim Cohane; Arlington House (1973); New Rochelle, N.Y.

2000 NCAA College Football Records Book, compiled by Richard M. Campbell, John Painter and Sean Straziscar; edited by Scott Deitch; NCAA Books; Indianapolis.

Saturday Afternoon, by Richard Whittingham; Workman Publishing Co., Inc. (1985); New York.

Saturday's America, by Dan Jenkins; Sports Illustrated Books; Little, Brown & Company (1970); Boston.

Tournament of Roses, The First 100 Years, by Joe Hendrickson; Knapp Press (1989); Los Angeles.

NCAA Online, produced by National Collegiate Athletic Association, http://www.ncaa.org

Plus numerous college football team and conference guides, especially the 2001 guides compiled by the Atlantic Coast Conference, Big Ten, Big 12 and Southeastern Conference.

Pro Football

2000 Canadian Football League Guide, compiled by the CFL Communications Dept.; Toronto.

The Football Encyclopedia (The Complete History of NFL Football from 1892 to the Present), compiled by David Neft and Richard Cohen; St. Martin's Press (1994); New York.

The Official NFL Encyclopedia, by Beau Riffenburgh; New American Library (1986); New York.

Official NFL 1999 Record and Fact Book, compiled by the NFL Communications Dept. and Seymour Siwoff, Elias Sports Bureau; edited by Chris McCloskey and Matt Marini; produced by NFL Properties, Inc.; Los Angeles.

The Scrapbook History of Pro Football, by Richard Cohen, Jordan Deutsch, Roland Johnson and David Neft; Bobbs-Merrill Company, Inc. (1976); Indianapolis/New York.

2001 Sporting News Football Guide, edited by Craig Carter, Terry Shea and Christen Sager; The Sporting News Publishing Co.; St. Louis.

2001 Sporting News Football Register, edited Brendan Roberts; The Sporting News Publishing Co.; St. Louis.

1995 Sporting News Super Bowl Book, edited by Tom Dienhart, Joe Hoppel and Dave Sloan; The Sporting News Publishing Co.; St. Louis.

Total Football II, edited by Bob Carroll, Michael Gershman, David Neft and John Thorn; HarperCollins; New York.

NFL Online, produced by Starwave Corp., http://www.nfl.com

CFL Online, produced by SLAM! Sports, http://www.cfl.ca

Golf

The Encyclopedia of Golf (Revised Edition), compiled by Nevin H. Gibson; A.S. Barnes and Company (1964); New York.

Guinness Golf Records: Facts and Champions, by Donald Steel; Guinness Superlatives Ltd. (1987); Middlesex, England.

The History of the PGA Tour, by Al Barkow; Doubleday (1989); New York.

The Illustrated History of Women's Golf, by Rhonda Glenn, Taylor Publishing Co. (1991); Dallas.

2002 LPGA Player Guide, produced by LPGA Communications Dept.; Ladies Professional Golf Assn. Tour; Daytona Beach, Fla.

2001 PGA Tour Guide, written and edited by Chuck Adams, James Cramer, Nelson Luis and Lee Patterson; Professional Golfers Assn. Tour; Ponte Vedra, Fla.

Official Guide of the PGA Championships; Triumph Books (1994); Chicago.

The PGA World Golf Hall of Fame Book, by Gerald Astor, Prentice Hall Press (1991); New York.

2001 Senior PGA Tour Guide, written and edited by Dave Senko, Phil Stambaugh and Joan Von Thron-Alexander; Professional Golfers Assn. Tour; Ponte Vedra, Fla.

Pro-Golf 2001, PGA European Tour Media Guide, Virginia Water, Surrey, England.

The Random House International Encyclopedia of Golf, by Malcolm Campbell; Random House (1991); New York.

USGA Record Books (1895-1959, 1960-80 and 1981-90); U.S. Golf Association; Far Hills, N.J.

LPGA Online, produced by the LPGA and Ignite Sports Media LLC., http://www.lpga.com

PGA Online, produced by the PGA of America, http://www.pgaonline.com

PGATour Online, produced by PGA Tour Inc., http://www.pgatour.com

Hockey

Canada Cup '87: The Official History, No.1 Publications Ltd.; Toronto.

The Complete Encyclopedia of Hockey; edited by Zander Hollander; Visible Ink Press (1993); Detroit.

The Hockey Encyclopedia, by Stan Fischler and Shirley Walton Fischler; research editor, Bob Duff; Macmillan Publishing Co. (1983); New York.

Hockey Hall of Fame (The Official History of the Game and Its Greatest Stars), by Dan Diamond and Joseph Romain; Doubleday (1988); New York.

The National Hockey League, by Edward F. Dolan Jr.; W H Smith Publishers Inc. (1986); New York.

The Official National Hockey League 75th Anniversary Commemorative Book, edited by Dan Diamond; McClelland & Stewart, Inc. (1991); Toronto.

2000-01 Official NHL Guide & Record Book, compiled by the NHL Public Relations Dept.; New York/Montreal/Toronto.

2001-02 Sporting News Hockey Guide, edited by Craig Carter; The Sporting News Publishing Co.; St. Louis.

2001-02 Sporting News Hockey Register, edited by David Walton; The Sporting News Publishing Co.; St. Louis.

The Stanley Cup, by Joseph Romain and James Duplacey; Gallery Books (1989); New York.

The Trail of the Stanley Cup (Volumes I-III), by Charles L. Coleman; Progressive Publications Inc. (1969); Sherbrooke, Quebec.

Total Hockey (Second Edition), edited by Dan Diamond, et al.; Total Sports Publishing; Kingston, N.Y.

NHL Online, produced by the NHL Interactive Cyber Enterprises, http://www.nhl.com

Horse Racing

1999 NTRA Media Guide, compiled by the National Thoroughbred Racing Association; New York.

1997 American Racing Manual, compiled by the Daily Racing Form; Hightstown, N.J.

1997 Breeders' Cup Statistics; Breeders' Cup Limited; Lexington, Ky.

1996 Directory and Record Book, Thoroughbred Racing Associations of North America Inc.; Elkton, Md.

2001 Trotting and Pacing Guide, compiled and edited by John Pawlak; United States Trotting Association; Columbus, Ohio.

USTA Online, produced by the USTA, http://www.ustrotting.com

NTRA Online, hosted by Equibase Company LLC, http://www.ntra.com

Equibase.com, hosted by Equibase Company LLC, http://www.equibase.com

International Sports

Athletics: A History of Modern Track and Field (1860-1990, Men and Women), by Roberto Quercetani; Vallardi & Associati (1990); Milan, Italy.

1999 International Track & Field Annual, Association of Track & Field Statisticians; edited by Peter Matthews; SportsBooks Ltd.; Surrey, England.

Track & Field News' Little Blue Book; Metric conversion tables; From the editors of Track & Field News (1989); Los Altos, Calif.

US Ski Team Online, produced by US Ski Team and SportsLine USA, http://www.usskiteam.com

Miscellaneous

The America's Cup 1851-1987 (Sailing for Supremacy), by Gary Lester and Richard Sleeman; Lester-Townsend Publishing (1986); Sydney, Australia.

The Encyclopedia of Sports (Fifth Revised Edition), by Frank G. Menke; revisions by Suzanne Treat; A.S. Barnes and Co., Inc. (1975); Cranbury, N.J.

ESPN SportsCentury, edited by Michael McCambridge; Hyperion (1999); New York.

The Great American Sports Book, by George Gipe; Doubleday & Company, Inc. (1978); Garden City, N.Y.

The 2002 Time/Information Please Almanac, edited by Borgna Brunner; Family Education Network; Boston.

1999 Official PRCA Media Guide, edited by Steve Fleming; Professional Rodeo Cowboys Association; Colorado Springs.

The Sail Magazine Book of Sailing, by Peter Johnson; Alfred A. Knopf (1989); New York.

Ten Years of the Ironman, Triathlete magazine; October, 1988; Santa Monica, Calif.

The Ultimate Book of Sports Lists, by Mike Meserole; DK Publishing (1999); New York.

Iditarod Online, produced by the Iditarod Trail Committee and GCI, http://www.iditarod.com

PRCA Online, produced by the Pro Rodeo Cowboys Association, http://www.prorodeo.com

Olympics

All That Glitters Is Not Gold (An Irreverent Look at the Olympic Games); by William O. Johnson, Jr.; G.P. Putnam's Sons (1972); New York.

Barcelona/Albertville 1992; edited by Lisa H. Albertson; for U.S. Olympic Committee by Commemorative Publications; Salt Lake City.

Chamonix to Lillehammer (The Glory of the Olympic Winter Games); edited by Lisa H. Albertson; for U.S. Olympic Committee by Commemorative Publication (1994); Salt Lake City.

The Complete Book of the Olympics (1992 Edition); by David Wallechinsky; Little, Brown and Co.; Boston.

The Games Must Go On (Avery Brundage and the Olympic Movement), by Allen Guttmann; Columbia University Press (1984); New York.

The Golden Book of the Olympic Games, edited by Erich Kamper and Bill Mallon; Vallardi & Associati (1992); Milan, Italy.

Hitler's Games (The 1936 Olympics), by Duff Hart-Davis; Harper & Row (1986); New York/London.

An Illustrated History of the Olympics (Third Edition); by Dick Schaap; Alfred A. Knopf (1975); New York.

The Nazi Olympics, by Richard D. Mandell; Souvenir Press (1972); London.

The Official USOC Book of the 1984 Olympic Games (1984), by Dick Schaap; Random House/ABC Sports; New York.

The Olympics: A History of the Games, by William Oscar Johnson; Oxmoor House (1992); Birmingham, Ala.

Pursuit of Excellence (The Olympic Story), by The Associated Press and Grolier; Grolier Enterprises Inc. (1979); Danbury, Conn.

The Story of the Olympic Games (776 B.C. to 1948 A.D.), by John Kieran and Arthur Daley; J.B. Lippincott Company (1948); Philadelphia/New York.

United States Olympic Books (Seven Editions): 1936 and 1948-88; U.S. Olympic Association; New York.

The USA and the Olympic Movement, produced by the USOC Information Dept.; edited by Gayle Plant; U.S. Olympic Committee (1988); Colorado Springs.

Soccer

The American Encyclopedia of Soccer, edited by Zander Hollander; Everest House Publishers (1980); New York.

The European Football Yearbook (1994-95 Edition), edited by Mike Hammond; Sports Projects Ltd; West Midlands, England.

The Guinness Book of Soccer Facts & Feats, by Jack Rollin; Guinness Superlatives Ltd. (1978); Middlesex, England.

History of Soccer's World Cup, by Michael Archer; Chartwell Books, Inc. (1978); Secaucus, N.J.

The Simplest Game, by Paul Gardner; Collier Books (1994); New York.

The Story of the World Cup, by Brian Glanville; Faber and Faber Limited (1993); London/Boston.

2001 MLS Official Media Guide, edited by the MLS Communications staff; Los Angeles.

1991-92 MSL Official Guide, Major (Indoor) Soccer League; Overland Park, Kan.

FIFA Online, produced by FIFA, http://www.fifa.com

MLSnet, produced by Major League Soccer, http://mlsnet.com

Tennis

Bud Collins' Modern Encyclopedia of Tennis, edited by Bud Collins and Zander Hollander; Visible Ink Press (1994); Detroit.

The Illustrated Encyclopedia of World Tennis, by John Haylett and Richard Evans; Exeter Books (1989); New York.

Official Encyclopedia of Tennis, edited by the staff of the U.S. Lawn Tennis Assn.; Harper & Row (1972); New York.

2002 ATP Tour Player Guide, edited by Greg Sharko; Association of Tennis Professionals Tour Publications; Ponte Vedra Beach, Fla.

2002 Sanex WTA Tour Media Guide, compiled by Sanex WTA Public Relations staff; St. Petersburg, Fla.

ATP TourOnline, produced by ATP Tour, Inc., http://www.atptour.com

WTA Tour Online, produced by the WTA Tour, http://www.wtatour.com

Who's Who

The Guinness International Who's Who of Sport, edited by Peter Mathews, Ian Buchanan and Bill Mallon; Guinness Publishing (1993); Middlesex, England.

101 Greatest Athletes of the Century, by Will Grimsley and the Associated Press Sports Staff; Bonanza Books (1987); Crown Publishers, Inc.; New York.

The New York Times Book of Sports Legends, edited by Joseph Vecchione; Simon & Schuster (1991); New York.

Superstars, by Frank Litsky; Vineyard Books, Inc. (1975); Secaucus, N.J.

A Who's Who of Sports Champions (Their Stories and Records), by Ralph Hickok, Houghton Mifflin Co. (1995); Boston.

Other Reference Books/Sites

Facts & Dates of American Sports, by Gorton Carruth & Eugene Ehrlich; Harper & Row, Publishers, Inc. (1988); New York.

Sports Market Place 1997 (January Edition), edited by Kevin J. Myers; Franklin Quest Sports; Phoenix, Ariz.

The World Book Encyclopedia (1988 Edition); World Book, Inc.; Chicago.

The World Book Yearbook (Annual Supplements, 1954-95); World Book, Inc.; Chicago.

ESPN.com, produced by ESPN Internet Ventures., http://espn.com

CBS SportsLine, produced by CBS and SportsLine USA, http://cbs.sportsline.com

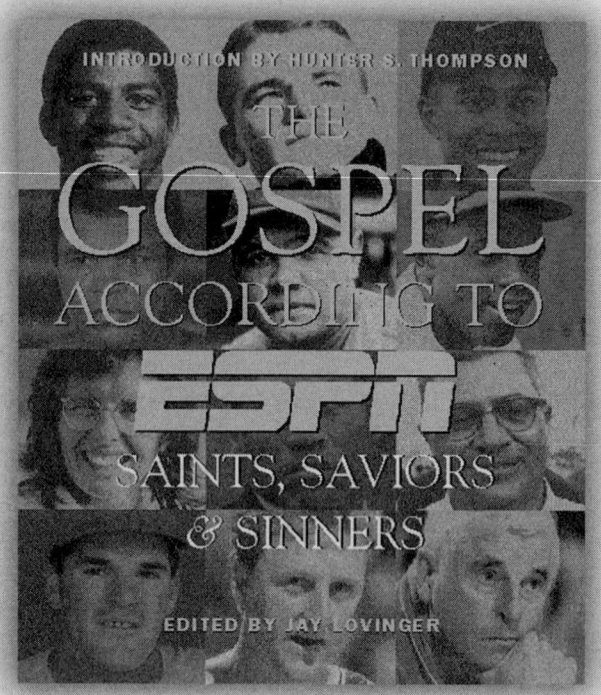